EASTERN THEATER

JAN	FEB	MAR	APR	MAY	JUN	JUL	AUG	SEP	OCT	NOV	DEC

1861

FIRST BULL RUN

1862

PENINSULAR CAMPAIGN

ANTIETAM CAMPAIGN

FREDERICKSBURG CAMPAIGN

SIEGE OF YORKTOWN — SEVEN PINES — SEVEN DAYS' BATTLES

ANTIETAM

FREDERICKSBURG

JACKSON'S VALLEY CAMPAIGN

SECOND BULL RUN CAMPAIGN

KERNSTOWN

FRONT ROYAL — PORT REPUBLIC

WINCHESTER — CROSS KEYS

CEDAR MT. — SECOND BULL RUN

1863

CHANCELLORS-VILLE CAMPAIGN

GETTYSBURG CAMPAIGN

OPERATIONS ALONG ORANGE AND RAPIDAN RY

CHANCELLORSVILLE

GETTYSBURG

BRISTOE STATION — MINE RUN

1864

ARMY OF THE JAMES

DREWRY'S BLUFF — ATTACK ON PETERSBURG

ARMY OF THE POTOMAC

WILDERNESS

SIEGE OF PETERSBURG

SHENANDOAH VALLEY

CEDAR CREEK

FISHERS HILL

1865

ARMY OF THE POTOMAC

SIEGE OF PETERSBURG

LEE'S ASSAULT

LEE SURRENDERS AT APPOMATOX 9 APRIL 1865

FIVE FORKS

SHERIDAN JOINS GRANT

NEW JERSEY

DELAWARE

ATLANTIC OCEAN

D0952069

THE CIVIL WAR DICTIONARY

By the same author

MILITARY CUSTOMS AND TRADITIONS

The CIVIL WAR *Dictionary*

By MARK MAYO BOATNER III

LIEUTENANT COLONEL, INFANTRY, UNITED STATES ARMY

Maps and Diagrams

By MAJOR ALLEN C. NORTHROP

and

LOWELL I. MILLER

DAVID McKAY COMPANY, INC.

New York

Library of Congress Catalogue Card Number: 59-12267

MANUFACTURED IN THE UNITED STATES OF AMERICA

12 13 14 15 16 17 18 19 20

ISBN: 0-679-50013-8

For my collaborator

PATRICIA DILWORTH BOATNER

ACKNOWLEDGMENTS

To my wife, Patricia Dilworth Boatner, I am indebted not only in all those ways that only another author's wife would understand but also for her literary collaboration. She researched and wrote most of the biographical entries, which is another way of saying that over half the book is hers. It is only on her insistence, and for other reasons that defy masculine logic, that her name does not appear as co-author.

A work of this nature is, of course, a synthesis of the scholarship of uncounted writers, living and dead. These have been acknowledged throughout the book, and the principal sources are listed under Authorities Cited.

I am particularly indebted to the following for assistance in various ways: James I. Robertson, Jr., of Emory University; T. Harry Williams, of Louisiana State University; the United States Military Academy's Department of Military Art and Engineering, its libraries and its museum —particularly Frederick P. Todd; Stanley F. Horn; Albert Castel; E. B. Potter and Richard S. West, Jr., of the United States Naval Academy; V. C. Jones; and Bruce Catton. For assistance in research I am indebted to Marjorie H. Kutchinski and Rex D. Minckler.

For reading the book in proof form I would like to acknowledge the valuable assistance of Charles A. Collier, Willis G. Ryckman, Ralph Righton, Palmer Bradley, T. Harry Williams, and Bell I. Wiley, all of whom suggested corrections and additions. Lieutenant Colonel John R. Elting was of great help in last-minute checking and research.

I must include a special word of thanks and appreciation to E. B. Long, who took time out from his own work to make many valuable suggestions and corrections.

However, I should add that the final result is mine, and I alone am accountable for any errors that have crept in.

The map work was done by Major A. C. Northrop with the assistance of Lowell I. Miller. These two translated my rough sketches and suggestions into finished maps with speed, professionalism, and a high regard for quality. The principal sources used in the preparation of the maps are: *Campaign Summaries* (United States Military Academy); National

Park Service, Historical Handbook Series; *Atlas to Accompany Steele's American Campaigns* (edited by Colonel V. J. Esposito, United States Military Academy); *The War of the Rebellion: A Compilation of the Official Records of the Union and Confederate Armies; Battles and Leaders of the Civil War; Campaigns of the American Civil War,* atlas (G. J. Fiebeger, United States Military Academy).

The Misses Wendy Young, Judy Amick, and Diane Barrett put in many hundreds of hours as research assistants and materially contributed to the production of the book. The final typing was done by Miss Marion Spangenberg and Mrs. Helen I. Rose.

CONTENTS

INTRODUCTION

As a reference work on so vast and thoroughly documented a subject as the American Civil War this book cannot be all things to all readers. An inspection of the following pages will indicate their value to you personally. With a certain amount of use the general concept and the organization of the book will be apparent. Some explanatory comments are, however, necessary.

First, this book is more for the researcher and the serious student of the Civil War period of American history than it is for the casual reader; it presupposes some familiarity with the subject. Second, the emphasis is on inclusiveness rather than comprehensiveness—in other words, on briefly covering the maximum number of important subjects rather than attempting a more detailed treatment of a smaller number of selected high spots. Third, the book is designed more to point the way to further research than to attempt to be the ultimate source book of Civil War history.

If you want a biographical sketch of a major Civil War personality, for example, the place to look is in a general encyclopedia or biographical dictionary. This book does not, therefore, attempt to duplicate the material that can be readily found in such sources. Major personalities and events will be treated very briefly, and will emphasize basic facts, dates, and figures. On the other hand, in this book you will find characters, battles, and events that you would have to spend many hours searching for in other reference works—if, indeed, you could find the reference works.

In line with Carlyle's assertion that "history is the essence of innumerable biographies," over half of *The Civil War Dictionary* is devoted to people. All of the full generals on both sides are covered, as well as the outstanding officers of lower rank. Prominent civilian leaders, personalities, and famous women are also included. Many of these biographical entries are extremely brief, but they contain the fundamental facts of the subject's career and provide "leads" to the appropriate state and unit histories where fuller information (if this exists), may be found. A rather cryptic style had to be adopted for the shorter biographical entries, and this will be explained below.

Military operations comprise the second largest category of entries. The twenty or so major campaigns and an equal number of lesser ones are described in separate articles. Their purpose is to tie together the separate battles and engagements as well as to cover the organization and strategy common to these individual military actions. Cross references (shown in small

CAPITAL LETTERS) are made to the individual battles and engagements, which, in most instances, will be found in their proper alphabetical sequence. This practice—pulling the individual battles out of the narrative of the campaign—was adopted to facilitate reference, since a given battle will usually be cross-referenced from many other articles.

The special maps prepared by Major Northrop and Mr. Miller are designed not only to supplement but also, in many instances, to take the place of explanatory text. Note, for example, that the battle of Antietam is covered almost exclusively by the maps.

Other major categories of entries include military organizations, weapons, tactics and strategy, military terms, naval matters, and political issues.

"Covering" or summary articles are provided where appropriate. The brief entry on WEAPONS, for example, will direct your attention to the three major classifications of CANNON, SMALL ARMS, and EDGED WEAPONS. Each of the latter gives a general survey of the topic and refers you to such entries as NAPOLEON GUN and JOE BROWN'S PIKES. Other examples of summary articles are BROTHER AGAINST BROTHER; HORSES, Famous; and STRATEGY.

As mentioned above, the biographical entries require special explanation. The book contains a disproportionately higher percentage of Union officers than Confederate officers. One reason is because the Union Army was larger and had more officers. A second reason is that Northern writers and statisticians did a much more thorough job after the war, and there is more data available on Union officers than on their opposite numbers. The Confederates did not have a Cullum, Dyer, Heitman, or Phisterer (see List of Authorities Cited, page 970). Finally, the Confederates did not have anything comparable to the brevet system, which I was able to use to select outstanding officers who did not attain the grade of full-rank general. Almost all of the more than one thousand persons identified in this book as "Union officer" are those whose highest Civil War rank was brevet general. Providing the Confederates equitable representation could have been accomplished only by leaving out Union officers who deserved to be mentioned.

A man is identified as "Union gen." or "CSA gen." only if he attained the full rank of B.G. or higher.

Birth and death dates are given if known. If the abbreviation c. appears before the date of birth, it has in most instances been arrived at from knowing the year of death and age at that time. Thus, this date is usually within one year of being correct.

State (or occasionally country) of birth will follow birth and death dates. If he was appointed to the army from a different state this will be shown with the abbreviation "Appt.-" *unless* this is apparent from the state units in which he is shown as serving. (An officer serving in an Ohio regiment, for example, would have had to be appointed from Ohio.)

R.A., if shown at the beginning of a military biography, means the officer was in the regular army before the war and, therefore, had had some military experience.

USMA indicates graduate of the United States Military Academy at West Point. The year of graduation is shown, his class standing, the arm into which he was commissioned, and subsequent arms or services in which he served. Thus, "USMA 1848 (22/38); Inf.-Cav." means that the subject graduated from West Point in 1848, standing No. 22 out of a class of 38 men, was commissioned in the infantry, and subsequently transferred into the cavalry.

Commands of brigade and larger units are shown by a series of numbers and abbreviations followed by dates in parentheses. Union commands are indicated in the following sequence: brigade, division, corps (in Roman numerals), and army, department, or other territorial organization. Hence, "3, 2, IV Potomac (3 July '63; 4 May '64–9 Apr. '65)" means that he commanded the 3d Brigade of the 2d Division, IV Corps in the Army of the Potomac on 3 July 1863 and then from 4 May 1864 until 9 April 1865. For Union officers this information was taken from Heitman, Cullum, and Dyer. For the Confederates it was compiled for the most part by the laborious process of tracing each officer through the Order of Battle sections of *Battles and Leaders,* and from the individual volume tables of contents of the *Official Records.* Again, nobody has compiled the dates of command for the Confederates as Dyer has done for the Union officers.

Brevet citations are mentioned for Union officers since the battles or other actions for which they were breveted can be considered high lights of their military careers. An officer was frequently breveted several times for the same engagement; this will be indicated by a number in parentheses: e.g., "Antietam (2)." Cross reference to a battle or other event within a biography is made only when some additional information is to be found about the individual in that cross reference.

Authorities are cited (usually in parentheses) for facts, figures, or opinions that might be subject to conflicting views, or if the source is otherwise of interest. A List of Authorities Cited will be found on page 970. Citations within this book will generally show only the author and the page number, e.g. ("Dyer, 1043.)" If a book is adequately indexed, or if it is important only to show the source (author or book) so that the reader familiar with Civil War authorities can apply his own standard of credibility to the statement, page numbers will not be given.

If more than one of a certain author's works are cited throughout this book, references will be made to shortened titles, e.g. "(Wiley, *Reb.,* 62)." The List of Authorities Cited will identify these sources fully.

MARK M. BOATNER III

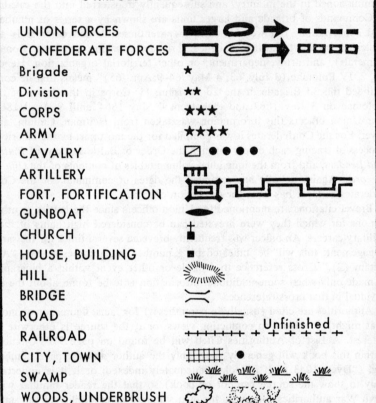

SYMBOLS USED ON BATTLE MAPS

UNION FORCES	
CONFEDERATE FORCES	
Brigade	★
Division	★★
CORPS	★★★
ARMY	★★★★
CAVALRY	
ARTILLERY	
FORT, FORTIFICATION	
GUNBOAT	
CHURCH	
HOUSE, BUILDING	
HILL	
BRIDGE	
ROAD	
RAILROAD	Unfinished
CITY, TOWN	
SWAMP	
WOODS, UNDERBRUSH	

LIST OF ABBREVIATIONS

(Also used but not listed are months, directions of the compass, states, universities, etc
Roman numerals are used for corps, arabic numerals for brigades and divisions.)

A.D.C. . . .	Aide de Camp
A.N.V. . . .	Army of Northern Virginia
Add.	Additional—e.g., Add. A.D.C.
	—Additional Aide de Camp
Adj.	Adjutant
Adm.	Admiral
Appt.- . .	Appointed from
Arty. . . .	Artillery
Asst. . . .	Assistant—e.g., Asst. Adj. Gen.
	—Assistant Adjutant General
Atty. . . .	Attorney
B.G.	Brigadier General
Bn. . . .	Battalion
Brig. . . .	Brigade
Btry. . . .	Battery
Bvt. . . .	Brevet(ed)
c.	Circa
C. d'A. . .	Corps d'Afrique
C. in C. .	Commander in Chief
C. of S. .	Chief of Staff
C.G. . . .	Commanding General
C.H. . . .	Court House
C.R. . . .	Cross Roads
C.S.A. . .	Confederate States Army; Con-federate States of America
CSN . . .	Confederate States Navy
Cal. . . .	Caliber (NOTE: Calif. for California)
Capt. . .	Captain
Cav. . . .	Cavalry
Chap. . .	Chaplain
Co. . . .	Company
Col. . . .	Colonel; Colored (NOTE: Colo. for Colorado)
Comdg. .	Commanding—e.g., Comdg. Gen.—Commanding General (see also C.G.)
Comdr. .	Commander—e.g., Comdr. in Chief (see also C. in C.)
Comsy. .	Commissary—e.g., Comsy. of Subsist.—Commissary of Subsistence
Confed. .	Confederate
Cpl. . . .	Corporal

D.O.W. .	Died of Wounds
Def. . . .	Defense(s)
Dept. . .	Department
Dist. . . .	District
Div. . . .	Division
Engr(s). .	Engineer, Engineers
Exp. . . .	Expedition
Fed. . . .	Federal
Ft. . . .	Fort
G.A.R. . .	Grand Army of the Republic
Gen., gen.	General
Gov. . .	Governor
Hv. . . .	Heavy
I.G. . . .	Inspector General (see also Insp.)
Inf. . . .	Infantry
Indpt. . .	Independent
Insp. . . .	Inspector—e.g., Med. Insp.—Medical Inspector
J.A.G. . .	Judge Advocate General
Jct. . . .	Junction
K.I.A. . .	Killed in Action
Lgt. . . .	Light—e.g., Lgt. Arty.—Light Artillery
Lt.	Lieutenant
M.I.A. . .	Missing in Action
Maj. . . .	Major
Med. . . .	Medical
Mid. . . .	Middle
Mil. . . .	Military; Militia
Mtd. . . .	Mounted—e.g., Mtd. Rifles
Mtn. . . .	Mountain—e.g., Mtn. Dept.—Mountain Department
N.G. . . .	National Guards
Natl. . . .	National

O.Q.M.G.   Office of the Quartermaster General

Off. . . . Officer

Opns. . . Operations

Ord. . . . Ordnance

P.M. . . . Provost Marshal

P.M.G. . Provost Marshal General

P.O.W. . Prisoner of War

Paymr. . . Paymaster

Prov. . . Provisional—e.g., Prov. Dist.— Provisional District

Pt. . . . . Port

Pvt. . . . Private

Q.M. . . Quartermaster

Q.M.G. . Quartermaster General

R. . . . . River

R.A. . . . Regular Army

R.R. . . . Railroad

Regt. . . Regiment

Rep. . . . Republic

Res. . . . Reserve(s)

S.M. . . . State Militia—e.g., N.Y.S.M.— New York State Militia

Sec. . . . Secretary—e.g., Sec. of the Int. —Secretary of the Interior; Sec. of the Treas.—Secretary of the Treasury

Sep. . . . Separate (NOTE: Sept. for September)

Sgt. . . . Sergeant

Sig. . . . Signal

Sta. . . . Station

Subsist. . Subsistence—e.g., Comsy. of Subsist.—Commissary of Subsistence

Surg. . . Surgeon—e.g., Surg. Gen.— Surgeon General

Sv. . . . Service

Ter. . . . Territory

Topo. . . Topographical—e.g., Topo. Engr.—Topographical Engineer

US . . . United States

USA . . . United States Army; United States of America

USCT . . United States Colored Troops

USMA . . United States Military Academy

USN . . . United States Navy

USNA . . United States Naval Academy

USS . . . United States Ship

USV . . United States Volunteers (see also Vol[s])

V . . . . Volunteers (see also Vol[s])

Vet. . . . Veterans—e.g., Veterans Reserve

Vol(s). . Volunteer(s)

W.I.A. . . Wounded in Action

THE CIVIL WAR DICTIONARY

A

A.A.G. Assistant Adjutant General. In the Civil War there was only one adjutant general in the US Army. All other officers who performed A.G. duties to commanders other than the General in Chief of the Army were assistant adjutant generals (Wilhelm).

ABATIS (ah'bah tee). An obstacle formed of trees felled toward the enemy.

ABBOT, Henry Larcom. Union officer. 1831–1927. Mass. USMA 1854 (2/46); Topo. Engr.–Arty. 1st Lt. Topo. Engrs. (1st Bull Run & Peninsula); Capt. 18 June '62; aide to Gen. Barnard; Chief Topo. Engr. of Banks's expedition to the Gulf; Col. 1st Conn. Hv. Arty. 19 Jan. '63; Defenses of Washington 28 Feb. '63–10 Mar. '64; in charge of siege arty., including "DICTATOR" in Grant's Virginia campaign. Breveted B.G. USV and USA; Bvt. Maj. Gen. USV. Bvts. for 1st Bull Run, Yorktown, Petersburg siege (2), war service (2), Richmond. As consulting engineer for the Panama Canal, he was influential in the adoption of the lock plan. Note: Sometimes confused with Henry Livermore ABBOTT, also of Mass.

ABBOTT, Henry Livermore. Union officer. Mass. 2d Lt. 20th Mass. 28 Aug. '61; 1st Lt. 8 Nov. '61; Capt. 28 Dec. '62; Maj. 10 Oct. '63; killed in action in the Wilderness 6 May '64 and breveted B.G. USV posthumously as of that date. This officer is sometimes confused with Henry Larcom ABBOT.

ABBOTT, Ira Coray. Union officer. Mich. Capt. 1st Mich. 1 May '61; mustered out 7 Aug. '61; Capt. 1st Mich. 12 Sept. '61; Maj. 28 Apr. '62; Lt. Col. 30 Aug. '62; Col. 18 Mar. '63; resigned 22 Dec. '64; Bvt. B.G. USV (war service). W.I.A. Fredericksburg (2), Gettysburg.

ABBOTT, Joseph Carter. Union officer. 1825–81. N.H. Lt. Col. 7th N.H. 13 Dec. '61; Col. 17 Nov. '63; Bvt. B.G. USV 15 Jan. '65 (Ft. Fisher). Commanded 2, 1, X; 2, 1, XXIV; Abbott's Brig., Terry's Prov. Dist., Dept. of N.C.; 2, 1, X; Abbott's Detached Brig., X. A New England editor before the war, he settled in North Carolina to become an infamous editor and politician during Reconstruction.

ABERCROMBIE, John Joseph. Union gen. 1798–1877. Tenn. USMA 1822 (37/40); Inf. Fighting in the Black Hawk War, the Seminole War (1 bvt.), and the Mexican War (1 wound, 1 bvt.), he was Patterson's A.D.C. 1846–47. Commissioned Col. 7th US Inf. 25 Feb. '61, he was in command at Falling Waters (Va.) 2 Jul. '61 when he led 6th Brig., 2d Div., Pa. He also commanded 2d Brig., Shenandoah (25 Jul.–17 Aug. '61); 2d Brig., Banks's Division, Potomac (17 Aug. '61–13 Mar. '62) and 2, 1, Banks's V (13 Mar.–4 Apr. '62). In Apr. '62 he led 2d Brig., 1st Div., Shenandoah, and in May he led 2, 2, II, Potomac. In the Peninsular campaign, he also led 2, 1, IV (24 May–5 July '62) at Fair Oaks (wounded) and Malvern Hill. Promoted B.G. USV 31 Aug. '61, he commanded 1st Div., IV, Potomac (12 July–12 Aug. '62) and Abercrombie's division in the Defenses of Washington (Oct. '62–26 June '63). After serving on military boards and commissions, he was in charge of depots at Fredericksburg in May '64 and took part in their defense against Hampton's Legion in June. Breveted B.G. USA for long and faithful service in the army, he was mustered out of USV 24 June '64 and retired 12 June '65.

ABERT, William Stretch. Union officer. 1836-67. D.C. R.A. Capt. 3d US Cav., then 6th US Cav. With regiment to July '62 (Williamsburg & Hanover C.H.); then aide to McClellan until Sept. '62. Lt. Col. Asst. I.G. Dept. of Gulf 17 Nov. '62-6 Oct. '64; injured by fall from horse while reconnoitering Port Hudson. Col. 3d Mass. Hv. Arty. 3 Dec. '64-Sept. '65. Commanded 2d. Brig., Def. North of Potomac, XXII. Breveted B.G. USV (Hanover C.H., Antietam, war service). Maj. 7th Cav. until death of yellow fever at Galveston.

ABOLITION OF SLAVERY. Adopted in 1865, the 13th Amendment to the Constitution provides that neither slavery nor involuntary servitude, except as punishment for a crime, can exist in the US or any area under its jurisdiction. See also EMANCIPATION PROCLAMATION.

ABOLITIONISTS. Group favoring the abolishment of slavery, characterized just prior to the Civil War by Harriet Beecher Stowe's *Uncle Tom's Cabin,* the UNDERGROUND RAILROAD and the Abolitionist congressmen. The initial outcry against slavery came as early as 1624 in the colonies, and this feeling gained enough adherents to bring about abolition in most of the northern states before the Revolution. Spurred by Great Britain's abolishing the slave trade in 1807 and slavery in the colonies in 1833 and Wilberforce's efforts toward this end, the movement took the form of the AMERICAN ANTI-SLAVERY SOCIETY (1833). This unification of regional organizations was largely the result of work done by William Lloyd GARRISON. At this period in the South such men as James G. BIRNEY, Cassius M. Clay, John G. Fee, Hinton Helper, and John

Rankin agitated for a modified form of abolition, as opposed to the immediate, uncompensated emancipation demanded by Garrison, Benjamin Lundy, Elijah Lovejoy, and the New England group composed of Theodore Parker, Henry Ward BEECHER, William Ellery Channing, Wendell PHILLIPS and John G. Whittier. Although rent by schisms and sectional differences, their abolitionist fervor was strong enough to influence the formation of the LIBERTY and FREE-SOIL PARTIES, and politics thereafter became their strongest weapon.

ACCOUTERMENTS. Items of equipment, other than weapons and clothing, carried by a soldier (e.g., cartridge box, canteen).

ACKER, George Sigourney. Union officer. N.Y. Capt. 1st Mich. Cav. 26 Aug. '61; Maj. 2 Sept. '62; Lt. Col. 9th Mich. Cav. 22 Jan. '63; Col. 2 July '64; Bvt. B.G. USV. (Brevets for Morristown, Bean's Station, Tenn.; Cynthiana, Ky.) W.I.A. Bean's Station 14 Dec. '63. Died 1879.

ACOUSTIC SHADOW ("silent battles"). A phenomenon that results in sound being inaudible to persons a short distance from the source while the same sound may be heard over a hundred miles away in another direction. Prominent instances are mentioned in connection with the battles of Seven Pines, Gaines's Mill, Perryville, and Chancellorsville. In some instances the sounds of battle appear to have been blocked by dense woods (e.g., Peninsula and Chancellorsville), by folds in the ground (e.g., Perryville), wind, or by "acoustic opacity" due to varying air densities. (See "The Cause of a Silent Battle," B.&L., II, 365.)

ADAMS, Alonzo W. Union officer. N.Y. Maj. 1st N.Y. Cav. 13 Sept. '61; Lt. Col. 1 Aug. '63; Col. 27 July '64; Bvt. B.G. USV (war service). Died 1887.

ADAMS, Charles Francis. Statesman. 1807–86. Mass. US Minister to Great Britain during the Civil War (1861–68) and one of the five arbitrators at Geneva Tribunal which settled the ALABAMA CLAIMS (1871–72). Son of John Quincy Adams (6th President of the US) and father of Charles Francis Adams (Jr.), he was in Congress 1858–61.

ADAMS, Charles Francis, Jr. Union officer, economist, and historian. 1835–1915. Mass. 1st Lt. 1st Mass. Cav. 28 Dec. '61; Capt. 1 Dec. '62; mustered out 1 Sept. '64; Lt. Col. 5th Mass. Cav. 8 Sept. '64; Col. 14 Mar. '65; Bvt. B.G. USV (Secessionville, South Mountain, Antietam, war service). Son of Charles F. Adams and grandson of John Quincy Adams. President of the Union Pacific R.R. and author of many works, including *Autobiography*.

ADAMS, Charles Powell. Union officer. Pa. Capt. 1st Minn. 29 Apr. '61; Maj. 14 Nov. '62; Lt. Col. 11 June '63; mustered out 5 May '64; Maj. in Hatch's Bn. Minn. Cav. 15 July '64; Lt. Col. 5 Sept. '64; Bvt. B.G. USV (war service). Died 1893.

ADAMS, Charles W. Union officer. N.Y. Col. 12th Kans. 30 Sept. '62; Bvt. B.G. USV. Commanded 2d Brig., Frontier Div., VII; 1st Brig., Frontier Div., VII.

ADAMS, Daniel Weisiger. C.S.A. gen. 1820–72. Ky. He practiced law and was acquitted of killing a man in a duel. In 1861 he was a member of the three-man board appointed by the Louisiana governor to prepare the state for war. Named Lt. Col. of Infantry and Col. 30 Oct. '61, he was on duty at Pensacola. He commanded 1st La. at Shiloh, taking over the 1st Brig., 2d Div., II Corps, and was blinded in one eye. B.G. C.S.A. 23 May '62, he led the 2d (La.) Brig., 2d Div., Army of the Miss. at Perryville

under Hardee and the 1st Brig., 1st Div., Hardee's Corps at Stones River where he was again wounded. He commanded Adams's brigade, Breckinridge's division, Hill's corps until wounded a third time at Chickamauga. He recovered to lead a cavalry brigade in northern Alabama and Mississippi and took command on 24 Sept. '64 of the Dist. of Central Alabama. After 11 Mar. '65 he commanded all forces in Alabama north of the District of the Gulf, seeing action at Selma 2 Apr. and Montgomery 16 Apr. '65. Paroled at Meridian 9 May, he resumed law practice. Brother of Wirt ADAMS.

ADAMS, John. C.S.A. gen. 1825–64. Tenn. USMA 1846 (25/59); Dragoons. After serving in the Mexican War (1 bvt.), on the frontier, and in Indian fighting and scouting, he resigned 27 May '61 as Capt. to become Capt. of Cavalry C.S.A. He commanded the post of Memphis, then served in western Kentucky and at Jackson (Miss.). Promoted Col. in early 1862 and B.G. C.S.A. 29 Dec. '62 (Wright says this was not confirmed, that he was reappointed, but gives no other date), he fought at Vicksburg and Jackson and then under Polk in Miss. and Ala. During the Atlanta campaign and Hood's Tennessee campaign, he commanded Adams's Brig., Loring's Div., Polk's Corps. He was killed 30 Nov. '64 leading an assault at Franklin, Tenn.

ADAMS, Robert Newton. Union officer. 1835–?. Ohio. Pvt. Co. B ("University Rifles" from Miami University, Oxford), 20th Ohio 18 Apr.–18 Aug. '61; Capt. 81st Ohio 30 Aug. '61; Lt. Col. 19 May '62; Col. 12 Aug. '64; Bvt. B.G. USV (war service). Commanded 2, 2, XVI (led regiment and brigade with distinction at Atlanta 22 July '64 [B.&L.]); 2, 4, XV. W.I.A. Jonesboro.

ADAMS, Will A. Union officer. Tenn.
2d Lt. 22d Ind. 11 July '61; 1st Lt. Adj.
3 Dec. '61; mustered out 9 Nov. '64;
Lt. Col. 145th Ind. 18 Feb. '65; Col.
22 Feb. '65; Bvt. B.G. USV (war service). Died 1874.

ADAMS, Wirt. C.S.A. gen. 1819–88.
Born in Ky., but appointed from Miss.
Active in bringing his state into the Confederacy, he raised the 1st Miss. Cav.
and was commissioned its Col. 15 Oct.
'61. Engaged in scouting and picket duty,
he was named Van Dorn's Chief of Arty.
at Corinth in spring '62 and fought at
Shiloh, Iuka, and Corinth. In 1863 he
unsuccessfully opposed Grierson's Raid.
Appointed B.G. C.S.A. 25 Sept. '63 for
Vicksburg siege. During 1864 he operated in northern Alabama, Mississippi,
western Tennessee. Joining Forrest in
1865, he unsuccessfully opposed Wilson's raid to Selma. He was killed in
1888 at Jackson, Miss., in a private feud.
Brother of Daniel W. ADAMS.

ADDITIONAL AIDE DE CAMP.
An unlimited number of these positions
was authorized in the regular army by
an act of Congress 5 Aug. '61. Just before this, when the authorized number
of general officers in the army was 14,
only 33 aides and 46 additional aides
were specified in regulations. The abbreviation is Add. A.D.C. (Heitman)

AGNEW. Name of attire worn by
SANITARY COMMISSION nurses in the
Peninsular campaign. This consisted of
a man's army shirt, the original one having been borrowed from a Dr. Agnew,
with the collar open, sleeves rolled up,
and shirttails out, worn over a full skirt
less the hoops.

AGNUS, Félix. Union officer. 1839–
1925. France. Sgt. Co. H 5th N.Y.
9 May '61; 2d Lt. 6 Sept. '61; 1st Lt.
8 July '62; Capt. 165th N.Y. 6 Nov. '62;
Maj. 2 Sept. '63; Bvt. B.G. USV. Brevets
for Gaines's Mill, Port Hudson, war

service. As a member of the 3d Zouaves,
he fought under Garibaldi and at Monte-
bello in May 1859. He was employed by
Tiffany & Co. when Lincoln's call for
troops came, and enlisted wearing his old
Zouave uniform. He was a wealthy
newspaper publisher in Baltimore after
the war and served on the USMA Board
of Visitors.

ALABAMA. The third state to secede
from the Union (11 Jan. '61). Its capital, Montgomery, saw the establishment
of the Confederacy in Feb. '61 and was
the seat of that government until July.
Alabama was readmitted to the Union
on 13 July '68.

ALABAMA, THE. Launched in England on 15 May '62, the vessel was one
of those contracted for by Capt. J. D.
BULLOCH and built by private shipyards,
for the Confederacy. Although the Union
ambassador, Charles F. ADAMS, protested vigorously, the British through a
series of delays failed to keep the ship
from leaving on what was called a trial
voyage. She was provisioned with guns,
ammunition, and coal in the Azores,
and Capt. Raphael SEMMES took command. Sailing all over the Atlantic, she
menaced US vessels and ran the blockade at Galveston. She was defeated and
sunk by the USS KEARSARGE 19 June
'64 off Cherbourg. In her career she had
sunk, burned, or captured 69 ships.

ALABAMA CLAIMS. General term
for US grievances against England during and just after the Civil War. These
included the proclamation of neutrality,
the Confederate vessels built or armed
in England, and the tremendous sums
of money raised for the Confederacy
there. Seward had directed the Ambassador, Charles F. ADAMS, early in the
war to demand payment for the damage
inflicted by the ALABAMA, and this
brought to some extent a halt in Confederate shipbuilding and outfitting

there. The US demanded payment of $19,021,000 for the damage done by 11 ships. This was broken down to total $6,547,609 for the *Alabama,* $6,488,320 for the *Shenandoah,* and $3,698,609 for the *Florida.* These claims, repeated several times, drew no response until 1868, when a convention was signed to cover all Anglo-American claims since 1853 but ignoring those of the *Alabama.* This was overwhelmingly voted down by Congress, but in 1871 the Treaty of Washington proposed, among other things, that the claims be submitted to arbitration. The next year a board of five from America, England, Italy, Switzerland, and Brazil decided that Great Britain had failed in her responsibilities as a neutral and awarded the US $15,500,000 in gold. The claims were paid in 1873.

ALABAMA, MISSISSIPPI, AND FAST LOUISIANA, Confed. Dept. of. Successor to the Dept. of MISS. AND E. LA., this was created 9 May '64 and S. D. Lee assigned temporary command (O.R., I, XXXIX, 3) when Polk left with his troops to join Johnston for the Atlanta campaign. Maury was assigned to command on 26 July. On 15 Aug. Richard Taylor was assigned, and on 6 Sept. he took command with headquarters at Meridian. Principal operations included FORREST'S OPERATIONS DURING THE ATLANTA CAMPAIGN; Federal operations against FORTS GAINES, etc., in Mobile Bay; the MOBILE CAMPAIGN; WILSON'S RAID TO SELMA, Ala. Taylor was briefly in command of Hood's shattered Army of Tennessee between the time that unit returned from the Franklin and Nashville campaign and before it left for the Carolinas campaign. Taylor had a strength of 12,000 troops when he surrendered his department to E. R. S. Canby 2 May '65. This is the date Taylor accepted Canby's

terms; the two met on the 4th to make the surrender official; and on the 8th the paroles of Taylor's men were accepted by Canby's commissioners. All three dates have been given for the surrender. The actual surrender was 2 May; the official surrender was 4 May; and 8 May is the date Taylor regarded as the date of surrender. (Taylor, 363)

ALABAMA AND WEST FLORIDA, Confed. Dept. of. Constituted 14 Oct. '61 under Bragg and its area extended 12 Dec. to include Pascagoula Bay and Mississippi east of the Pascagoula River. The department included Pensacola and Bragg's Army of PENSACOLA. Samuel Jones assumed command 28 Feb. '62. Bragg announced his resumption of command 4 Mar. '62; "it does not appear, however, that effect was ever given to his order...." (O.R., I, VII, 2.) J. H. Forney took command 28 Apr., and on 29 June '62 the department was discontinued.

ALBEMARLE, THE. Confederate ram built on the Roanoke River and commanded by James W. Cooke. On 19 Apr. '64 she sank the gunboat *Southfield,* put the *Miami* to flight, and assisted in the capture of PLYMOUTH, N.C. On 5 May she fought to a draw against Capt. Melancton Smith's seven blockaders in the mouth of the Roanoke. On 27 Oct. '64 Lt. William B. CUSHING with 15 men in a small launch sank her with a torpedo attached to a spar.

ALBEMARLE COUNTY, Va. 28 Feb.–1 Mar. '64. Diversion by Custer's 3d Cav. Div. to Charlottesville, Va., in support of the KILPATRICK-DAHLGREN RAID TO RICHMOND. There were skirmishes at Stanardsville, near Charlottesville, and at Burton's Ford. Custer reported the capture of over 50 prisoners and about 500 horses, and the liberation of "over 100 contrabands" without the loss of a single Federal. (O.R.)

ALBRIGHT, Charles. Union officer. Pa. Maj. 132d Pa. 21 Aug. '62; Lt. Col. 18 Sept. '62; Col. 24 Jan. '63; mustered out 24 May '63; Col. 34th Pa. Mil. 3 July '63; mustered out 10 Aug. '63; Col. 202d Pa. 4 Sept. '64; Bvt. B.G. USV 7 Mar. '65. Commanded 3, 3, II. Died 1880.

ALCOTT, Louisa May. Author. 1832–88. Pa. While best known as the author of *Little Women* (1868), she contributed to the vast store of Civil War literature by publishing *Hospital Sketches* (1863), a collection of letters to her family written while a nurse in a Union hospital in Georgetown.

ALDEN, Alonzo. Union officer. N.Y. 2d Lt. 30th N.Y. 1 June '61; 1st Lt. and Regt. Adj. 15 June '62; Maj. 169th N.Y. 6 Oct. '62; Lt. Col. 12 Apr. '64; Col. 9 Nov. '64; Bvt. B.G. USV 15 Jan. '65. Commanded 3, 2, X. Died 1900.

ALDIE, Va. 17 June '63. (GETTYS-BURG CAMPAIGN) Fitzhugh Lee, W. H. F. Lee, and Robertson's brigades were screening Longstreet's right flank as he moved from Culpeper to the Blue Ridge. Fitz Lee's brigade (under Munford) had been sent to occupy a gap in the Bull Run Mountains at Aldie. W. H. F. Lee's brigade (under Chambliss) scouted toward Thoroughfare Gap, and Robertson was at Rectorville (or Rectortown). Pleasonton reached Aldie at 4:30 P.M. with Kilpatrick's brigade of Gregg's division. The Confederate pickets were being driven back when Rosser's 5th Va. charged with sabers and pushed back the Federal scouts. The Confederates then built up a defensive position, supported by artillery, against which the Federals launched a spirited series of mounted and dismounted attacks that lasted until about dark, when Munford was ordered to withdraw. Union casualties: 305 (Fox); Confederate: between 100 and 119. The 1st R.I. Cav., attached

to Kilpatrick's brigade, was annihilated this same day at MIDDLEBURG.

ALEXANDER, Andrew Jonathan. Union officer. Ky. R.A. 1st Lt. US Mtd. Rifles 26 July '61; Banks's staff in Washington and McClellan's on the Peninsula; Lt. Col. Asst. Adj. Gen. 1 Jan–10 Aug. '63; 23 Apr. '64–24 Apr. '65; in Stoneman's raid; staff officer XVII Corps during Atlanta, and Franklin and Nashville campaigns; chief of staff to J. H. Wilson; Bvt. B.G. USV 5 Jan. '65; bvt. B.G. USA 16 Apr. '65. Brevets for Peninsula, Gettysburg, Atlanta, Selma, Ebenezer Church, Columbus (Ga.), war service. Commanded 2, 4, Wilson's cavalry corps. Continued in R.A. until retired as Lt. Col. Died 1887.

ALEXANDER, Barton S. Union officer. 1819–78. Ky. USMA 1842 (7/56); Engrs. He was engaged in various engineer construction projects, including several buildings at West Point, 1848–52. During the Civil War he was Div. Engr. for Tyler at Blackburn's Ford and 1st Bull Run and was detailed to instruct engineering troops for the Army of the Potomac until 1 Apr. '62. After fighting in the Peninsular campaign at Yorktown, West Point, Mechanicsville, Fair Oaks, Gaines's Mill, Golding's Farm, and Harrison's Landing, he was Asst. Engr. in the defenses of Washington until 7 Apr. '63, having been promoted Maj. 3 Mar. '63. He then served in the East and on boards and commissions until becoming Sheridan's consulting engineer in the Shenandoah Valley, participating in Cedar Creek. He continued in the R.A. until his death on active duty as Lt. Col. and was breveted B.G. USA.

ALEXANDER, Edmund Brooke. Union officer. c.1803–88. Va. Appt.-Ky. USMA 1823 (33/35); Inf. He served on the frontier and fought in the Mexican War (2 brevets) before going on the Utah Expedition in 1858. During the Civil War he was stationed in Dakota and Nebraska until 1863, when he became a recruiting officer in Missouri as Col. 10th US Inf. (since 1855). He was retired in 1868 after having been breveted B.G. USA, 18 Oct. '65.

ALEXANDER, Edward Porter. C.S.A. gen. 1835-1910. Ga. USMA 1857 (3/38); Engrs. He taught at West Point, went on the Utah Expedition, and returned to West Point as an instructor in 1859. That same year he worked with Myer in the development of the "wigwag" system. (See SIGNAL COMMUNICATIONS.) After then serving on the frontier, he resigned when his state seceded and became Capt. of Engrs., C.S.A., 3 June '61. As Beauregard's Engineer and Chief of Signal Service he was at 1st Bull Run, where he sent Evans the historic "wigwag" message that his flank was being turned. He was later Beauregard's Chief of Ordnance. During the Peninsular, 2d Bull Run, and Antietam campaigns he was a Maj. and in Nov. '62 was given command of an artillery battalion under Longstreet. Promoted Col. in Dec. '62, he commanded the guns on Marye's Heights (Fredericksburg) and marched with Jackson at Chancellorsville. At Gettysburg he also commanded Longstreet's reserve artillery and went with him to Georgia in Sept. '63 but arrived too late for the battle of Chickamauga. He fought at Knoxville and returned to the A. N.V. in early '64, being commissioned B.G. and Chief of Arty. in Longstreet's corps, 26 Feb. '64. He fought at Spotsylvania, Cold Harbor, and Petersburg where he foresaw the mine attempt and warned Lee. Wounded and out of action for a time, he next fought at Drewry's and Chafin's Bluffs, the defense of the James River, and surrendered at Appomattox. After the war he taught engineering at S.C. University and engaged in the oil and rail-

road business, planting, and held several public offices. Besides several books on railroading, he published the classic *Military Memoirs of a Confederate* in 1907.

ALEXANDRIA, La. 1-8 May '64. (RED RIVER CAMPAIGN) While Joseph BAILEY was constructing the dams to save Porter's fleet, Banks's forces had to delay their retreat to protect the operation. Taylor deployed his forces as described in the account of the campaign, and a series of encounters took place around Alexandria. On 30 Apr. a Federal cavalry brigade (of XIX Corps) moved from Pineville to attack Liddell and was surprised and defeated with a loss of 30 men at Hudnot's Plantation (O.R., Liddell's report). The next day Wm. Steele attacked on the Rapides road and drove the Federals to within three miles of Alexandria. On the evening of the 3d the Confederates attacked on the Bayou Robert road and drove the enemy to within three miles of the Governor Moore plantation, where the day before a foraging party of the 83d Ohio and the 3d R.I. Cav. had lost 12 men. At Ashwood Landing the 64th U.S.C.T. had lost seven men during the period 1-4 May.

Meanwhile the cavalry under J. P. Major had successfully attacked Federal boats at Davide's Ferry (Snaggy Point). On 1 May he captured and destroyed the transport *Emma* "after an exciting chase of 2 miles" (O.R.). On the 3d he captured the transport *City Belle,* taking about 250 men and all the officers of the 120th Ohio. On the 5th he attacked and destroyed the Federal tinclads *Signal* and *Covington* as they attempted to convoy the transport *Warner* (carrying the 56th Ohio, and some of McClernand's captured cotton) past his position. After a five hour fire fight the *Covington* had to be blown up to prevent capture and the other two surrendered. Major sank the *Signal* so as to obstruct the channel thereby cutting off Alexandria from Federal forces on the Mississippi. Banks reported 250 casualties in this last action, which he calls Dunn's Bayou. (Col. G. W. Baylor, 2d Ariz. Cav., commanding one of Major's two brigades, led most of the above actions.)

ALGER, Russell Alexander. Union officer. 1836–1907. Ohio. A lawyer and lumberman, he was commissioned Capt. 2d Mich. Cav. 2 Oct. '61 and Maj. 2 Apr. '62. He was captured near Booneville (Miss.) 1 June '62 but escaped on the same day and was made Lt. Col. 6th Mich. Cav. 30 Oct. '62. Promoted Col. 5th Mich. Cav. 11 June '63, he fought at Gettysburg and was severely wounded at Boonsboro, Md., 8 July. He fought under Sheridan in the Valley in 1864 and around Petersburg. Breveted B.G. USV and Maj. Gen. USV 11 June '65 for war service, he had resigned 20 Sept. '64. He was Governor of Michigan and Secretary of War (1897–99).

ALLAIRE, Anthony Johnson. Union officer. Ohio. Capt. 133d N.Y. 29 Aug. '62; Maj. 4 Aug. '64; Lt. Col. 24 Dec. '64; Bvt. B.G. USV (war service).

ALLATOONA, Ga., 5 Oct. '64. (FRANKLIN AND NASHVILLE CAMPAIGN) This important Federal supply depot, containing a million rations of bread for Sherman's army in Atlanta, was successfully defended against French's division. Although there was severe fighting, the action is best known for a number of dramatic incidents associated with it. The garrison was composed of 860 men under the command of Lt. Col. John F. Tourtelotte, 4th Minn. When it looked as if the place might be raided, Sherman sent a signal to Corse (4, XIV) in Rome to reinforce Allatoona. French made a night march from Ackworth and made contact with Federal pickets around the town at 3 A.M. He did not know that two hours previously Corse had arrived with Rowett's (3d) brigade. By 8:30 A.M. the Confederates had cut the main routes by which the place could be reinforced. There followed an interchange of notes in which French called on the Federals to surrender "to avoid a needless effusion of blood," and Corse answered "we are prepared for the 'needless effusion of blood' whenever it is agreeable to you." (See B.&L., IV, 323.)

Sherman, meanwhile, had reached Kenesaw Mountain and could see that Allatoona (13 miles northwest) was surrounded. He could also see the campfires of Hood's main body to the west near Dallas. Since the telegraph wires north of Marietta had been cut, and his order to Corse in Rome had been sent by signal flag "over the heads of the enemy," Sherman did not know whether Corse had actually reinforced Allatoona. Messages had been signaled the afternoon of the 4th by Vandever on Kenesaw Mountain to the "Commanding Officer, Allatoona." At 2 P.M. this message was sent: "Sherman is coming. Hold out." At 6:30 P.M. this additional one went out: "General Sherman says hold fast. We are coming." (O.R. Series I, Vol. XXXIX, Part III, p. 78.) Additional messages were sent the morning of the 5th, but there had been no answer. Finally, while Sherman was with him, the signal officer "caught a faint glimpse of the telltale flag through an embrasure, and, after much time he made out these letters: "C," "R," "S," "E," "H," "E," "R," and translated this message, "Corse is here." (Sherman's *Memoirs*, II, 147.) This interchange of messages was "freely translated by current journalism into: 'Hold the fort; I am coming.' . . . The episode inspired the revival hymn *Hold the Fort*—and so the pages of history were embellished with another indelible myth." (Horn, *The Army of Tennessee*, 377.)

Meanwhile, there had been heavy fighting. Sears's brigade and W. H. Young's Texans made repeated attacks against the key ridge. For two and a half hours the 7th and 93d Ill. and the 39th Iowa, under the command of Col. R. Rowett, fought off attacks from three sides. When they were finally driven back at about 11 A.M., Redfield's detachment of the 39th Iowa delayed the enemy long enough for the main body to reach and secure the main fort on the northwest shoulder of Allatoona Pass. Redfield fell dead of four wounds, and Rowett was wounded; but this delaying action proved decisive. Although there was no Federal infantry within supporting distance until the morning of 6 Oct. (Sherman's official report notwithstanding; see Horn, 377), French broke off the engagement early in the afternoon and withdrew.

Corse had been creased by a Minié bullet at about 1 P.M. and was unconscious for over 30 minutes. The next day at 2 P.M. he signaled Sherman's aide this much-publicized message: "I am short a cheek-bone and an ear, but am able to whip all h—l yet."

The Federals lost 707 out of 1,944 present for duty. French reported a loss of 799 out of "a little over 2,000" engaged in the assaulting force. W. H. Young was wounded and captured.

ALLATOONA HILLS, Ga. See DALLAS, Georgia.

ALLCOCK, Thomas R. Union officer. England. Maj. 4th N.Y. Hv. Arty. 14 Nov. '61; Lt. Col. 23 May '63; Bvt. B.G. USV. Brevets for Reams's Station, Richmond campaign 1864, Petersburg siege. Commanded 4th Brig., Defenses South of Potomac; 1st Brig., Defenses North of Potomac (XXII). Died 1891.

ALLEGHENY, Confed. Army of the. See NORTHWEST, Confed. Army of the.

ALLEN, E. J. See Allan PINKERTON.

ALLEN, Harrison. Union officer. Pa Maj. 10th Pa. Res. 11 Aug. '61; resigned 11 Feb. '62; Capt. 151st Pa. 30 Oct. '62; Col. 11 Nov. '62; Bvt. B.G. USV (war service). Note: Not to be confused with Union army doctor of same name.

ALLEN, Henry Watkins. C.S.A. Gen. 1820–66. Va. After college and law study he joined the Texas army during their revolution. Eloping shortly after that, he fought a duel with his father-in-law, who then forgave and presented the couple with a Mississippi plantation. His wife soon died. Allen served in the legislature, studied law at Harvard, and then sailed for Italy to join Garibaldi, but the war ending before he arrived. he traveled throughout Europe instead. Coming back for the Civil War, he was commissioned Lt. Col. 4th La. and in Mar. '62 became Col. Commanding his regiment, he fought at Shiloh and was wounded. For a time he was in the defenses of Vicksburg, and went with Breckinridge to Baton Rouge as commander of the La. Brig. During the battle of Baton Rouge, 5 Aug. '62, he was severely wounded in both legs and refused to have the right one amputated. After a slow convalescence he was commissioned B.G. C.S.A. 19 Aug. '63, ordered to the Trans-Mississippi Dept., and elected Governor of Louisiana in 1864. Called by D.A.B. "the single great administrator developed by the Confederacy," he rescued the region from chaos and starvation by selling cotton and bringing supplies in through the blockade, leaving it in 1865 actually stronger than it had been during the war. He counseled Kirby Smith to surrender, thus sparing the area much devastation. Going to Mexico, he ran an English-language newspaper for a year or so before his death. Wright gives his death date as 1894; however, D.A.B., Appleton's, and C.M.H. all agree on its being

1866. He wrote *Travels of a Sugar Planter*, about his European experiences.

ALLEN, Robert. Union Q.M. Gen. 1811–86. Ohio. Appt.-Ind. USMA 1836 (33/49); Arty.-Q.M. Q.M. Maj.; Col. and Add. A.D.C.; full B.G. USV 23 May '63; Bvt. Maj. Gen. USV 13 Mar. '65; mustered out 1 Sept. '66. Serving in the Seminole and Mexican wars (1 brevet), he was Maj. Q.M. 17 May '61 and Chief Q.M., Dept. of Mo., at the start of the Civil War. He was promoted Col. A.D.C. 19 Feb. '62 and B.G. USV 23 May '62. From Nov. '63–'66, he was Chief Q.M. of Miss. Valley. He was mustered out in '66, with brevets for Maj. Gen. USV and USA. He continued in the R.A. until retired in 1878 as Col. He was an outstanding logistician.

ALLEN, Thomas Scott. Union officer. N.Y. Capt. 2d Wis. 11 June '61; Maj. 22 Aug. '62; Lt. Col. 1 Sept. '62; Col. 5th Wis. 26 Jan. '63; Bvt. B.G. USV (war service). Led regiment with distinction at Marye's Heights 3 May '63 (B.&L.). Commanded 3d Brig., 1st Div., VI Corps (Potomac, Shenandoah).

ALLEN, William Wirt. C.S.A. gen. 1835–94. Ala. After graduating from Princeton, he studied law and ran his plantation. He was commissioned Maj. 1st Ala. Cav. 18 Mar. '62 shortly after entering the Confederate Army as 1st Lt. of Cav. Elected Col. in the latter part of 1862, he fought at Shiloh and was wounded at Perryville. After leading a brigade at Stones River and being seriously wounded, he was appointed B.G. C.S.A. 26 Feb. '64 and led a mounted brigade under Wheeler in the Atlanta campaign. He then opposed Sherman in the March to the Sea and was promoted Maj. Gen. 4 Mar. '65. After the war, he returned to his plantation and later held several public offices.

ALLEN'S FARM, Va., 29 June '62. Savage's Station.

ALLIGATOR, THE. Union Submarine.

"ALL QUIET ALONG THE POTOMAC." Poem, first called "The Picket Guard," by Mrs. Ethelind Eliot Beers, published in *Harper's Weekly* 30 Nov. '61. It was inspired by McClellan's telegrams to the Sec. of War that reported "all is quiet tonight."

ALSOP'S FARM, Va., 8 May '64, Spotsylvania.

ALVORD, Benjamin. Union gen. 1813–84. Vt. USMA 1833 (22/43); Inf. Serving in the Seminole and Mexican wars (2 brevets), he was Maj. paymaster (1854) when the war began and was promoted B.G. USV 12 Apr. '62. He commanded the Dist. of Oregon throughout the war where he performed important, if not spectacular, administrative and military governmental functions for which he received 3 brevets, one being Bvt. B.G. USA. Continuing in the R.A., he was Paymaster Gen. of the Army (1872–80) when he retired. He wrote a number of significant mathematical and botanical papers.

AMELIA SPRINGS (JETERSVILLE), Va., 5 Apr. '65. (Appomattox Campaign) In the morning Sheridan sent H. E. Davies' brigade (Crook) from Jetersville northwest to determine whether Lee was retreating in this direction from Amelia C.H. At Paineville, about five miles from Jetersville, the 1st Pa. Cav. found and attacked a wagon train that was being escorted westward by Martin W. Gary's cavalry brigade. Davies' troopers charged through a swamp, captured a gun that was just going into position, and routed the train guard of about 400 men. Davies reported that he set fire to 200 vehicles and captured 5 guns, 11 flags, 320 white prisoners and about as many Negro teamsters, and over 400 animals. R. E. Lee's headquarters records may have been destroyed in this action. Fitz Lee and Gary pursued to Amelia Springs, where Davies was able to hold until reinforced by the cavalry brigade of J. I. Gregg. Sheridan reported 20 Federals killed and 96 wounded. The action is also known as Jetersville.

AMERICA, THE. Famous American yacht which in 1851 won the "America's Cup" from the Royal Yacht Squadron. In the first part of the Civil War she was a Confederate despatch boat and was found sunk in a tributary of the St. John's River (S.C.) in 1862. Recovered by the South Atlantic Squadron (Union), she was sent to Annapolis as a practice boat and successfully defended her Cup in 1870. Three years later she was sold to B. F. Butler. In 1921 she was permanently docked at the Naval Academy.

AMERICAN ANTI-SLAVERY SOCIETY. Demanding the immediate and uncompensated emancipation of the slaves, it was formed in 1833 by a coalition of the New England Anti-Slavery Society, organized by GARRISON, and other abolitionist groups. The Society engaged in issuing pamphlets and books, publishing periodicals, and deluging Congress with abolitionist petitions. Among its leaders were Garrison, Theodore D. Weld, Arthur and Lewis Tappan, and George G. Finney. Other similar organizations were the New England (later Massachusetts) Anti-Slavery Society, the National Anti-Slavery Society, and the New York Anti-Slavery Society.

AMERICAN COLONIZATION SOCIETY. Founded in 1816 by anti-slave supporters including Henry Clay and John Randolph of Roanoke, its purpose was to return Negroes to Africa. It also had some encouragement from slaveholders in Virginia, Maryland, and Kentucky who feared the effect of free Negroes in the US. Purchasing part of

Liberia, the society failed to obtain a congressional appropriation in 1827 and by 1831 had returned to Liberia only 1,420 Negroes, a number equal to one third those born annually into slavery in the US. From this meager start Liberia has grown to become one of the first independent Negro states in the world and is governed by descendants of the original slaves.

AMERICAN FLAG DISPATCH. When John A. Dix, recently appointed Secretary of the Treasury, was informed on 29 Jan. '61 by his agent, W. Hemphill Jones, that the captain of the revenue cutter *McClelland* refused to obey Dix's order to surrender command of the vessel to the Federal government in New Orleans, Dix sent these instructions: "Tell Lieutenant Caldwell to arrest Captain Breshwood, assume command of the cutter, and obey the order I gave through you. If Captain Breshwood, after arrest, undertakes to interfere with the command of the cutter, tell Lieutenant Caldwell to consider him as a mutineer, and treat him accordingly. If anyone attempts to haul down the American flag, shoot him on the spot." (B.&L., I, 149n)

AMERICAN RED CROSS. See Clara BARTON.

AMES, Adelbert. Union gen. Reconstruction Gov. Miss. 1835-1933. USMA May '61 (5/45); Arty.-Inf. Ten weeks after graduation he was at 1st Bull Run (with 21 of his 44 classmates) where, commanding a section of Griffin's battery, he refused evacuation despite a serious thigh wound and continued to give orders until "too weak to sit upon the caisson where he had been placed by the men of his command" (Heitman). For this he was awarded the Medal of Honor (1 Sept. '93). After six weeks' sick leave he took part in the Peninsular campaign as commander of Battery A,

5th US Arty. (Yorktown, Gaines's Mill, Malvern Hill). Appointed Col. 20th Me. 20 Aug. '62, he was in Antietam campaign (not engaged) and at Fredericksburg (in 3d Brig., 1st Div., V Corps). He was Meade's aide 2–4 May '63 at Chancellorsville. Promoted B.G. USV 20 May '63, he commanded 2, 1, XI (24 May–6 Aug. '63), seeing action at Beverly Ford, and taking command of the division for the second and third days at Gettysburg (retained command until 14 July). He was in operations of X Corps (South) (Aug. '63–19 Apr. '64); and commanded a brigade and division of XVIII Corps in operations around Petersburg (25 Apr.–17 Sept. '64) at Port Walthall Jct. and Cold Harbor. He also commanded 1st Div., X Corps. Va. and N.C. (10 Oct.–2 Dec. '64) at Darbytown Road, and led the corps 4–18 Nov. He then took command of 2d Div., XXIV Corps, 2 Dec. '64—which was designated Ames's Division, Terry's provisional corps, 6 Jan. '65—and led it until 27 Mar. '65 in First and Second Expeditions to Fort Fisher and operations in N.C. He later took over 2d Div., X Corps, 27 Mar., and commanded the corps 13 May–1 Aug. '65. He commanded Dist. of Western S.C. 5 Sept. '65–30 Apr. '66 and was named Lt. Col. USA 28 July '66. Resigning in 1870, he had been made temporary governor of Mississippi 15 July '68 and US senator from Miss. in '70. He was elected governor in '73. Unable to cope with reconstruction politics, he resigned in '76 to avoid impeachment by Democrats who had regained state control. In 1870 he had married Blanche, the daughter of B. F. Butler. Named B.G. USV 20 June '90, he served through the Spanish-American War (Santiago campaign) and died in 1933 at age of 97.

AMES, John Worthington. Union officer. Mass. R.A. 1st Lt. 16th US Inf.; Capt. 11th US Inf. 14 May '61; Col.

6th US Col. Inf. 28 Sept. '63; Bvt. B.G. USV 15 Jan. '65. Commanded 2d and 3d Brig., XVIII; 2d Brig., 1st Div. and 2d Brig., Dist. of Wilmington, XXV. Brevets for Gaines's Mill, Gettysburg. Resigned in '66. Died 1878. Wrote article in B.&L. "In Front of the Stone Wall at Fredericksburg."

AMES, William. Union officer. 1842–1914. R.I. 2d Lt. 2d R.I. 5 June '61; 1st Lt. 25 Oct. '61; Capt. 24 July '62; Maj. 3d R.I. Hv. Arty. 10 Feb. '63; Lt. Col. 1 Apr. '64; Bvt. B.G. USV (war service). Later prominent in industry, commerce, and finance.

AMMEN, Jacob. Union gen. 1808–94. Va. Appt.-Ohio. USMA 1831 (12/33); Arty. After teaching mathematics, infantry tactics, and philosophy at USMA and serving in garrison in South Carolina, he resigned in 1837 to teach mathematics in Kentucky, Mississippi, and Indiana colleges. A civil engineer when the war began, he was commissioned Capt. 12th Ohio 18 Apr. and Lt. Col. 2 May '61. As Col. 24th Ohio (22 June '61), he led his regiment at Cheat Mountain and Greenbriar and commanded, in the Army of the Ohio, 10th Brig. (Nov.–Dec. '61) and 10th Brig., 4th Div. (2 Dec. '61–16 Aug. '62) at Shiloh and Corinth. As B.G. USV 16 July '62, he also commanded the 4th Div. (16–23 Aug. '62) and 4th Div., XXIII, Ohio (10 Apr. '62–4 Jan. '65), as well as Covington (Ky.), Camp Dennison, Camp Douglas, Dist. of Illinois, and of Middle Tenn. and Ky. He resigned 4 Jan. '65 and went back to engineering, later serving on the Board of Visitors of USMA and on the commission to investigate proposed isthmian canal routes in Central America (1874).

AMORY, Thomas Jonathan Coffin. Union officer. c. 1830–64. Mass. USMA 1851 (30/42); Inf. Capt. 7th US Inf. 7 May '61; Maj. 8th US Inf. 19 Sept. '64;

Col. 17th Mass. 2 Sept. '61; Bvt. B.G. USV 1 Oct. '64; died of yellow fever at New Bern, N.C. 8 Oct. '64. Brigade and division commander in XVIII Corps (N.C.); finally commanded New Bern defenses.

ANACONDA PLAN. Scott's strategic plan for the defeat of the Confederacy by: occupying the line of the Mississippi with an army of 60,000 under McClellan, from Cairo to the Gulf; and blockading Confederate ports. The Union would then wait for Unionist sentiment in the South to convince the rebel government that they should sue for peace. The war as finally fought had certain features of Scott's plan. When proposed, however, it was derided as "Scott's Anaconda."

ANDERSON, Allen Latham. Union officer. 1837–1910. Ohio. USMA 1859 (16/22); Inf. 1st Lt. 2d US Inf. 14 May '61; Adj. 31 Dec. '61–3 Dec. '62; Capt. 3 Dec. '62; Col. 8th Cal. 7 Mar. '65; mustered out USV 10 Nov. '65; Bvt. B.G. USV. Brevets for Valverde, N. Mex. (war service). Resigned USA 1867.

ANDERSON, Charles D. C.S.A. gen. S.C. Appt.-Texas. Failing to graduate from West Point (ex-1850), he entered the R.A. in 1856 as 2d Lt. 4th US Arty. He served until 1 Apr. '61 when he resigned as 1st Lt. to join the Confederacy. Heitman lists him as Col. 21st Ala. and B.G. CSA, and Wood gives the date of his appointment as May '64. However, Wright does not include him in his list of general officers and he is not listed in C.M.H. He is credited with leading his regiment and the 3d Brig. of 1st Div., Polk's Corps, in the Atlanta campaign. (B.&L.)

ANDERSON, George Burgwyn. C.S.A. gen. 1831–62. N.C. After graduating first in his class at Chapel Hill, he entered West Point at 17 and graduated in 1852 (10/43). He went into the

Dragoons. After frontier service he resigned 25 Apr. '61 as 1st Lt. to become Col. 4th N.C. He was post commandant of Manassas Junction after 1st Bull Run. Staying there until March '62, he commanded his regiment at Williamsburg in a dashing charge witnessed by Jefferson Davis who thereupon named him B.G. C.S.A. (9 June '62). He led the N.C. brigade (formerly Featherston's) during the Seven Days' Battles and was severely wounded at Malvern Hill. Commanding Anderson's brigade, in Hill's division, he fought at South Mountain and was seriously wounded in the ankle at Antietam. Taken first to Richmond and then to Raleigh, he died 16 Oct. '62 after an amputation. C.M.H. describes him as standing "full six feet, broad-shouldered, round-limbed, with a deep, musical voice."

ANDERSON, George Thomas. C.S.A. gen. 1824–1901. Ga. In the Mexican War and served in the R.A. 1855–58. Commissioned Col. 11th Ga., he fought in the Seven Days' Battles, 2d Bull Run (wounded), and Antietam. He was named B.G. C.S.A. 1 Nov. '62 after leading his brigade in Jones's division at the last battle. Commanding his brigade in Hood's division of Longstreet's Corps, at Fredericksburg and Gettysburg, he was seriously wounded in Devil's Den. He led his brigade at Chickamauga, Knoxville, Wilderness (now in Field's division), Spotsylvania, Cold Harbor, Petersburg, and at Appomattox. After the war he held a number of public offices and was Chief of Police in Atlanta.

ANDERSON, James Patton. C.S.A. gen. 1822–72. Tenn. Appt.-Fla. A doctor, he fought in the Mexican War and was a Mississippi legislator and territorial delegate from Washington. Commissioned Col. 1st Fla., he served under Bragg at Pensacola and was appointed B.G. C.S.A. 10 Feb. '62. He led a brigade under Bragg at Shiloh and a division in the invasion of Kentucky and at Perryville. At Stones River he led Walthall's brigade. Here he captured the Union artillery in a desperate charge and then succeeded Hindman in command of his division at Chickamauga, leading it at Missionary Ridge as well. Promoted Maj. Gen. 17 Feb. '64, he was sent to command the Dist. of Florida and its defenses, and after Hood took over the Army of Tennessee, Anderson was sent to Atlanta to command Hindman's division. He fought at Ezra Church and Utoy Creek before being seriously wounded at Jonesboro. In the Carolinas, he commanded Taliaferro's division against his doctor's orders. After the war he edited an agricultural newspaper in Memphis.

ANDERSON, John Fromen. Union officer. Me. 1st Lt. and Adj. 24th Mass. 2 Sept. '61; Maj. and A.D.C. 9 June '63; Bvt. B.G. USV (war service).

ANDERSON, Joseph Reid. C.S.A. gen. and president of Tredegar Iron Works. 1813–92. Va. USMA 1836 (4/49); Arty.-Engrs. Resigning a year after graduation, he was a civil engineer in Virginia, building the Valley Turnpike from Staunton to Winchester. He also served in the legislature, and in 1858 became owner of the Tredegar Iron Works. He entered the C.S. Army as Maj. of artillery (Aug. '61) and remained in charge of the works. Appointed B.G. C.S.A. 3 Sept. '61, he was given a field command, with the understanding that he would return to Tredegar if needed. First commanding the Dist. of Cape Fear, he temporarily headed the Dept. of N.C. (15–24 Mar. '62). He then led the 3d N.C. Brig. on the Peninsula and was wounded at Frayser's Farm. Incapacitated for further field service, he resigned 19 July '62 and returned to run the ironworks. D.A.B. says he "displayed unperturbable resourcefulness and ... never suspended operations until April 1865."

ANDERSON, Nicholas Longworth. Union officer. Ohio. c. 1830–92. Commissioned 1st Lt. and Regt. Adj. 6th Ohio 12 May '61, he was promoted Lt. Col. 21 June of that year and Col. 9 Nov. '62. Mustered out 23 June '64, he was breveted for B.G. USV (Stones River) and Maj. Gen. USV (Chickamauga).

ANDERSON, Richard Heron. ("Dick") C.S.A. gen. 1821–79. S.C. USMA 1842 (40/56); Dragoons. He served in the Mexican War (1 brevet) and in the Kansas border disturbances before resigning 3 Mar. '61 as Capt. Commissioned Col. 1st S.C., he served during the bombardment of Ft. Sumter and succeeded Beauregard in command at Charleston in July, being appointed B.G. C.S.A. on the 19th. In Aug. he joined Bragg in Pensacola and then commanded a brigade under Longstreet in early '62. He fought at Williamsburg, Seven Pines, and the Seven Days' Battles and was left on the Peninsula to watch McClellan. Promoted Maj. Gen. 14 July '62, he took over Huger's division to join Lee for 2d Bull Run. In the Maryland campaign he fought at Crampton's Gap and was wounded at Antietam, recovering in time to command his division at Fredericksburg. Conspicuous at Chancellorsville, he was in A. P. Hill's corps at Gettysburg and at the Wilderness succeeded Longstreet in command of the corps, leading it at Spotsylvania, Cold Harbor, and the battles around Richmond and Petersburg before Longstreet returned in Oct. '64. He was promoted Lt. Gen. 31 May '64 and led Bushrod Johnson's division at Sayler's Creek. After the war he lived in distressed financial circumstances that reduced him at one period virtually to the status of a day laborer.

ANDERSON, Robert. Union general. 1805–71. Ky. USMA 1825 (15/37); Arty. The "hero of Fort Sumter" served in Indian fighting, taught artillery tactics at West Point, and fought in the Seminole War (1 brevet) before being severely wounded in the Mexican War (1 brevet). He then served on a number of boards and commissions until taking command of the defenses of Charleston harbor in 1860. On 26 Dec. '60 he transferred the garrison from Fort Moultrie to FORT SUMTER and sustained the opening bombardment of the Civil War. Anderson was promoted B.G. USA 15 May '61 and took command of the Dept. of Ky. (28 May–15 Aug. '61) and Dept. of the Cumberland (15 Aug.–8 Oct. '61). Retired for disabilities on 27 Oct. '63, he was breveted Maj. Gen. USA 3 Feb. '65. He had translated several French field manuals for the US Army. On 14 Apr. '65 he was at Sumter when the original flag was reraised.

ANDERSON, Robert Houston. C.S.A. gen. 1835–88. Ga. USMA 1857 (35/38); Inf. He served in garrison and on the frontier before resigning in 1861 to become 1st Lt. C.S.A. Arty. on 6 Mar. of that year. Promoted Maj. in Sept. '61 and named Acting Adj. Gen. of troops on the Georgia coast, he served at Ft. McAllister from Feb. to Mar. '63 against the Federal monitors. On 20 Jan. '63 he was named Col. 5th Ga. Cav. and fought in the Atlanta campaign in Allen's Ga. Cav. brigade, Wheeler's division. He took command of the brigade and was later appointed B.G. C.S.A. 26 July '64. During the March to the Sea and through the Carolinas he continued to oppose Sherman and surrendered with Johnston in N.C. After the war, he was chief of police in Savannah and a member of the USMA Board of Visitors.

ANDERSON, Samuel R. C.S.A. gen. 1804–83. Appointed from Tenn. as Maj. Gen. of state troops 9 May '61, he was commissioned B.G. C.S.A. 9 July '61. He commanded a brigade under Loring in West Va. in the summer and fall of '61; fought in the Valley under Jackson, and on the Peninsula under Magruder. After resigning 10 May '62 he was reappointed B.G. C.S.A., 19 Nov. '64 to rank from 7 Nov. '64. He had been active in war work in the interim.

ANDERSON, William B. Union officer. Ill. Lt. Col. 60th Ill. 17 Feb. '62; Col. 4 Apr. '63; Bvt. B.G. USV (war service).

ANDERSON'S CORPS. See IV CORPS (R. H. Anderson's), Confed. A.N.V.

ANDERSONVILLE PRISON. In existence from Feb. '64 to Apr. '65, it was a military PRISON in Georgia, hastily built when it became apparent that such large numbers of prisoners were a military hazard in Richmond and were also a drain on the local food supply. Properly named Camp Sumter and situated northeast of Americus, the prison consisted of a log stockade of 16½ acres (later enlarged to 26 acres) with a stream of water running through it. Rations were the same as those of the Confed. soldier in the field: corn meal, beans, and rarely meat. The disease and death rates were fantastic, with poor sanitation, crowding, exposure, and inadequate diet contributing to the unhealthful conditions. Only enlisted men were confined there, and in the summer of 1864 the number totaled 32,899. There are 12,912 graves in the National Cemetery there, and estimates place the number of deaths at a much higher figure. When Sherman approached in Sept. '64, all well prisoners were sent to Charleston. Capt. Henry WIRZ was commandant of the prison, and Gen. J. H. WINDER was in charge of all Confederate prisons east of the Mississippi.

ANDREW, John Albion. Governor of Mass. 1818–67. Maine. After graduating from Bowdoin, he practiced law and was one of the organizers of the Free-Soil party, entering politics to further his anti-slavery ideals. He later joined the Republican party and sat in the legislature before being elected Governor in 1860. Re-elected in 1862 and 1864, he brought the state militia to a high state of preparedness, and a Massachusetts regiment, the 6th, was the first body of troops to reach Washington after Lincoln called for volunteers. This same spirit characterized all his actions throughout the war.

ANDREWS, Christopher Columbus. Union gen. 1829-1922. N.H. After Harvard Law School, he practiced in New England, Kansas, and Minnesota, where he was state senator (1859). Enlisting as Pvt. 3d Minn., he was commissioned Capt. 4 Nov. '61 and was surrendered to Forrest in July '62 near Murfreesboro, being a P.O.W. until Oct. He was named Lt. Col. 1 Dec. '62, fought at Vicksburg, and promoted Col. 9 Aug. '63, participating in the capture of Little Rock. Promoted B.G. USV 5 Jan. '64, he commanded 2, 2, VII, Ark. (19 May–16 June '64) and moved to division until 28 Dec. '64. He then commanded 3d Brig., Reserve Corps, Gulf, until 13 Feb. '65, when he took over 2d Div., Reserve Corps, and then 2, XIII, 18 Feb.–20 July '65. Breveted Maj. Gen. USV, 9 Mar. '65, he was mustered out in 1866. After the war he was minister to Sweden and Norway (1869–78) and consul general to Brazil (1882–85). His military works include *My Experience in Rebel Prisons* and *History of the Campaign of Mobile.*

ANDREWS, George Leonard. Union gen. 1828–99. Mass. USMA 1851 (1/42); Engrs. Resigning in 1855, he was a civil engineer when commissioned Lt. Col. 2d Mass. 24 May '61, fighting at Winchester under Banks and being promoted Col. 13 June '62. He led his regiment at Cedar Mountain and Antie-

tam and, as B.G. USV, 10 Nov. '62, commanded 2, 2, V, Potomac (Nov.- 14 Dec. '62 and Jan.–Feb. '63). In the Dept. of the Gulf he commanded the defenses of New Orleans (22 Sept.–16 Dec. '62); 1, 3, XIX (3–29 Jan. and 12 Feb.–5 Mar. '63); and 2d Div., XIX (27–28 May '63). He was Banks's Chief of Staff 6 Mar.–9 July '63 and fought at Ft. Bisland (13–14 Apr.) and Pt. Hudson. In command of the Corps d'Afrique (10 July '63–13 Feb. '65), he also commanded the Dist. of Baton Rouge and Pt. Hudson. He was Provost Marshal General of the Army of the Gulf (27 Feb.–6 June '65) and was present at Mobile (26 Mar.–12 Apr. '65) and was Canby's Chief of Staff 6 June–24 Aug. '65 when he was mustered out. Breveted Maj. Gen. USV 26 Mar. '65 for Mobile, he was later a planter in Mississippi and professor at USMA (1871–92).

ANDREWS' RAID. Culminating in what is often called "The Great Locomotive Chase," this raid on the night of 12 Apr. '62 was perpetrated by 22 Union volunteers who went deep into Confederate territory to cut the rail line that served as a vital supply link between Marietta (Ga.) and Chattanooga. Taking a north-bound train to Big Shanty (now Kenesaw, Ga.), they piled off the side opposite the station when the breakfast stop was announced, climbed into the engine General, and took off. Stopping after a few miles to cut the telegraph lines and pile crossties on the track, they continued toward Chattanooga while the Confederates pursued in the engine Texas. The pirated locomotive ran out of fuel near Graysville after nearly 90 miles, and the Federals took to the woods. All were shortly captured, and Andrews and seven others were tried and executed in Atlanta. The other 14 remained in prison until Oct. '62 when eight overwhelmed their guards and escaped. About a year later the remaining six were paroled and became the first to receive the MEDAL OF HONOR.

"ANGEL OF CAIRO." See Mary J. SAFFORD.

ANGLE. See "BLOODY ANGLE."

ANNAPOLIS, Union Department of. Constituted 27 Apr. '61, to include the counties for 20 miles on each side of the railroad from Annapolis to Washington, as far as Bladensburg, Maryland. Changed to the Department of Maryland 19 July and merged into the Department of Pennsylvania 25 July '61. Commanders: Brig. Gen. B. F. Butler until 15 May '61; Maj. Gen. George Cadwalader to 11 June; Maj. Gen. N. P. Banks to 19 July; Maj. Gen. John A. Dix to 25 July '61.

ANTHONY, DeWitt Clinton. Union officer. Ind. Lt. Col. 23d Ind. 29 July '61; Col. 66th Ind. 22 Sept. '62; Bvt. B.G. USV (war service). Commanded 1, 2, XVI. Died 1891.

ANTHONY, Susan Brownell. Reformer. 1820–1906. A woman suffrage leader, teacher, and lecturer on temperance, abolition and women's rights, she was one of the organizers of the Women's Loyal League in support of Lincoln in 1863.

ANTHONY'S BRIDGE, Ga., 31 Sept. '64. See JONESBORO, same date.

ANTIETAM (Sharpsburg) CAMPAIGN. Sept. '62. After defeating Pope at the 2d Bull Run, Lee undertook his first invasion of the North. Although not strong enough to attack the Army of the Potomac directly, he was determined to retain the initiative. By moving into Maryland he hoped to swing the people of that border state to the side of the Confederacy, to strengthen the anti-war movement in the North, to draw Federal troops from areas from which they were menacing the Confederacy, and to relieve Virginia for a time of the ravages of war. When he reached Frederick, Md.,

Federal armies—now back under the command of McClellan—started cautiously in pursuit. To secure his line of communications for further advance to the north, Lee decided to capture Harpers Ferry, after which he could shift his supply lines from the east of the Blue Ridge into the more protected Shenandoah Valley. So on 9 Sept. he issued his famous Special Order No. 191, splitting his forces into two wings: Jackson and six divisions were to converge on Harpers Ferry; Longstreet and three divisions were to move toward Hagerstown. Four days later McClellan found a copy of this order when he arrived at Frederick, thereby gaining a rare opportunity to take advantage of Lee's hazardous division of strength. However, McClellan moved slowly, partly because the cautious Halleck warned him that this might be a trap and that Confederate forces might be planning an attack

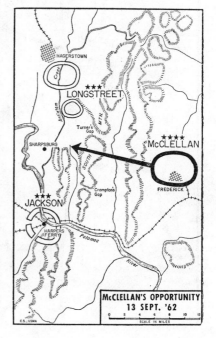

McCLELLAN'S OPPORTUNITY
13 SEPT. '62

SCALE IN MILES

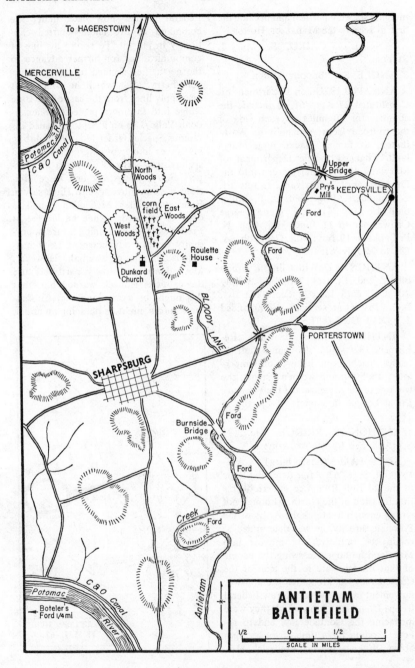

To HAGERSTOWN

MERCERVILLE

Potomac R.

C & O Canal

North Woods

corn field

East Woods

West Woods

Dunkard Church

Roulette House

Upper Bridge

Prys Mill

KEEDYSVILLE

Ford

Ford

BLOODY LANE

PORTERSTOWN

SHARPSBURG

Ford

Burnside Bridge

Ford

Ford

Creek   Ford

Antietam

Potomac

C & O Canal

Boteler's Ford 1/4 ml

River

ANTIETAM BATTLEFIELD

1/2   0   1/2   1
SCALE IN MILES

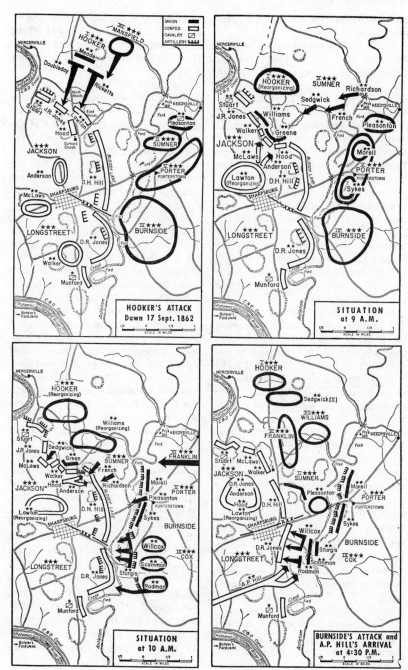

HOOKER'S ATTACK
Dawn 17 Sept. 1862

SITUATION
at 9 A.M.

SITUATION
at 10 A.M.

BURNSIDE'S ATTACK and
A.P. HILL'S ARRIVAL
at 4:30 P.M.

on Washington from south of the Potomac.

Battle of Crampton's Gap—14 Sept. '62. Franklin's US VI Corps reached Crampton's Gap about noon on the 14th with the mission of pushing through to relieve Harpers Ferry. The Confederate McLaws, commanding his own division and that of Anderson, was working his troops and his artillery up onto rugged Maryland Heights to attack Harpers Ferry from the northeast. Menaced from the rear, McLaws reluctantly turned to meet the new threat. By nightfall Franklin, with a total loss of 533 men, had carried the pass and forced the enemy back into a vulnerable defensive position in the low ground of Pleasant Valley; but overestimating the enemy's strength caused him to delay until it was too late to save Harpers Ferry or to destroy McLaws' force.

Battle of South Mountain—14 Sept. '62. Federal cavalry under Pleasanton found D. H. Hill's division defending Turner's Gap on the morning of the 14th. By nine o'clock J. D. Cox attacked with his division and by noon the rest of the IX Corps under Reno arrived to press the attack through Fox's Gap. Hooker's I Corps arrived later and attacked about a mile to the north. Burnside, commanding the right wing of McClellan's army (I and IX corps), soon appeared on the field to coordinate the operations. By 10 P.M. the Federals had succeeded by dint of vigorous fighting in seizing the high ground commanding Turner's Gap, and the Confederates started withdrawing about midnight. Reno was killed. The Confederate Brig. Gen. Samuel Garland, Jr., was killed. Numbers and losses at South Mountain were:

	Effectives	Killed	Wounded	Missing	Total
US (I and IX Corps)	28,480	325	1,403	85	1,813
Confederates	17,852	325	1,560	800	2,685

Confederate figures are estimates arrived at by Livermore on the basis of official reports amplified by "experience factors." He states that their losses were probably higher.

The night of 13 Sept., when Lee learned that McClellan knew his plan, he immediately ordered Longstreet's withdrawal to support D. H. Hill. On the morning of the 15th Lee was withdrawing the 19,000 men he had north of the Potomac to join Jackson, who had not yet captured Harpers Ferry. McLaws was still in his precarious position in Pleasant Valley.

Capture of Harpers Ferry—15 Sept. '62. The Federal position at Harpers Ferry was tactically untenable. In ordering it to be held, Halleck committed a serious strategic blunder; however, in so doing he unwittingly came near to providing the bait for trapping Lee, who had miscalculated the time required for capturing this place. The Federal force at Martinsburg had fallen back before Jackson's enveloping wing of three divisions which had come from Fredericksburg (leaving 10 Sept.) through Williamsport, across the Potomac, and thence down the B. & O. Railroad. By 13 Sept. Jackson was a mile and a half west of Harpers Ferry; Walker's division, which had crossed the Potomac below the town, was in position on Loudoun Heights, a little over a mile to the southeast; and the next day McLaws was in position on Maryland Heights to the northeast. D. S. Miles was bottled up with 12,000 men. That night a body of 1,300 Federal cavalry fought their way out. (See DAVIS AND DAVIS ESCAPE. . . .) Early on the 15th the Confederates started shelling the Federal positions from all sides and Miles, considering his position hopeless, surrendered at 9 A.M. He was accidentally killed after the white flags were up.

Battle of Antietam (Sharpsburg)— 17 Sept. '62. About noon of the 15th

Lee was moving with the rear guard through Sharpsburg when he got word of Jackson's success. This news, supplemented by his knowledge of McClellan's cautious nature, led him to make the audacious decision to stand and fight at Sharpsburg. With only 19,000 men immediately available, and 40,000 total strength when the rest of his forces could arrive from Harpers Ferry, Lee was standing with his back to a river against an enemy almost twice his size.

It is difficult to determine what McClellan's plan was supposed to be. Apparently he intended to attack both flanks simultaneously, his main effort being against Lee's left, and then strike with his reserves in the center as soon as one of the other attacks was successful. Instead of moving rapidly, he took until the evening of the 16th to close up to the battlefield, get his forces into position, and make final arrangements.

In "the bloodiest single day of the war" the Federals launched a series of uncoordinated, piecemeal attacks first at the Confederate left (north flank), then the center, and finally the right. While Burnside delayed his attack on the Confederate right, Lee was able to shift forces from that area to oppose the assaults of Hooker, Mansfield, and Sumner. There was desperate fighting at places whose names have become part of the national legend: the Corn Field, the West Woods, the East Woods, Dunkard Church, the Roulette house, and Bloody Lane. By midafternoon Burnside had finally forced the crossing of the stone bridge that has since borne his name. Although the Confederate left and center had been secured, their right was now being driven back. At this moment A. P. Hill's division arrived at the end of a forced march from Harpers Ferry and delivered a crushing counterattack which saved Lee's right.

According to Livermore, the Federals had 75,316 effectives and lost 12,410 (2,108 killed, 9,549 wounded, and 753 missing). He disagrees sharply with the reported Confederate effective strength, estimating that they had 51,844 effectives. He puts Confederate losses at 13,724 (2,700 killed, 9,024 wounded, and about 2,000 missing). (Livermore, 92–93.)

Despite his heavy casualties, Lee did not withdraw immediately. It was not until around noon of the 18th that Jackson and Longstreet could convince him that a counterattack was impossible. McClellan, on the other hand, felt that he also was too badly crippled to renew the attack, even though 24,000 of his troops had not been engaged the first day (Porter's and Franklin's corps) and over 12,000 fresh troops arrived the morning of the 18th (Couch's and Humphreys' divisions).

The night of the 18th Lee withdrew into Virginia.

Antietam is considered by some historians to be the turning point of the war. Although it was not a tactical victory, it was the improvement in the North's military fortunes for which Lincoln had been waiting to announce the EMANCIPATION PROCLAMATION. This changed the entire aspect of the war from a political affair to preserve the Union to a crusade to free the slaves. Popular sentiment in Europe swung to the side of the North and destroyed the South's last hope of foreign assistance.

APPLETON, John Francis. Union officer. 1839–70. Me. Capt. 12th Me. 15 Nov. '61; Col. 81st US Col. Inf. 25 June '63; Bvt. B.G. USV (war service); resigned 29 July '64. Commanded Ullman's brigade, USCT, at Port Hudson; 2d Brig., 1st Corps d'Afrique (Gulf). Prominent lawyer and son of famous Me. judge.

APPOMATTOX CAMPAIGN, Va. 29 Mar.–9 Apr. '65. Although the dividing line is somewhat arbitrary, the PETERSBURG CAMPAIGN is generally considered to have ended with the Confederate failure at FT. STEDMAN, 25 Mar., and the Appomattox campaign to have started 29 Mar.

The arrival of Sheridan's cavalry on the Petersburg front and the unsuccessful assault of Ft. Stedman convinced Lee that Petersburg and Richmond could no longer be held. He planned to move south to link up with J. E. Johnston's forces that were retreating from Sherman in N.C. To do this it was essential that he hold the line of the Southside R.R. On 29 Mar. Grant ordered the II and V Corps to attack the right of the Petersburg defenses, and he ordered Sheridan to advance to cut the railroad. The decisive action was Sheridan's victory at FIVE FORKS, 1 Apr. Subsidiary engagements were QUAKER ROAD, WHITE OAK ROAD, DINWIDDIE COURTHOUSE, the PETERSBURG FINAL ASSAULT, and the RICHMOND SURRENDER.

The next phase of the campaign was the pursuit to Appomattox. Although ultimate Federal triumph was inevitable, the war could have been considerably prolonged if Grant had not acted vigorously and effectively to prevent the linkup of Lee's forces with J. E. Johnston. Confederate forces from Petersburg, Bermuda Hundred, and Richmond headed for a junction at Amelia Courthouse. Here they expected to find supplies and to use the Danville and Richmond R.R. to join Johnston. Sheridan's cavalry led the pursuit south of the Appomattox, in which area Anderson's corps and Fitz Lee's cavalry were retreating.

Rear-guard cavalry actions took place at NAMOZINE CHURCH, 3 Apr., and AMELIA SPRINGS, 5 Apr. The rest of Lee's forces retreated north of the James. Arrival of Sheridan at Jetersville cut the Confederate line of retreat south along the railroad, so when Lee's forces converged at Amelia Courthouse they proceeded west. A running fight took place. At SAYLER'S CREEK, 6 Apr., Ewell's rear guard was cut off and destroyed. Rearguard actions took place at HIGH BRIDGE the same day and FARMVILLE on the 7th. Sheridan, meanwhile, led the encircling force and got across the Confederate line of retreat. The final actions took place at APPOMATTOX STATION, 8 Apr., and APPOMATTOX COURTHOUSE the next day. This made inevitable Lee's surrender on 9 Apr. '65.

Effective strengths in this campaign, according to Livermore (p. 141), were 112,892 Federals and 49,496 Confederates. Federal casualties were 1,316 killed, 7,750 wounded, 1,714 missing, or a total of 10,780. An estimated 26,765 Confederates were surrendered at Appomattox, an additional 13,769 were captured during the campaign, 6,266 were killed and wounded, approximately 3,800 deserted. In addition, an estimated 1,000 cavalry "left the ranks" during the campaign and 2,400 cavalry escaped at Appomattox.

APPOMATTOX COURTHOUSE (CLOVER HILL), Va., 9 Apr. '65. (APPOMATTOX CAMPAIGN) At 5 A.M. Gordon's 1,600 infantry and Fitz Lee's 2,400 cavalry successfully attacked the earthworks the Federal cavalry had hastily constructed along Bent Creek Road. Within an hour, however, Federal infantry started an envelopment of the Confederate right and their cavalry demonstrated against the opposite flank. About 8 A.M. the II and VI Corps started an attack on Longstreet's rear guard. With his last supplies destroyed at Appomattox Station and Gordon unable to open the route of withdrawal to the south, Lee realized that surrender was inevitable. See SURRENDER DATES.

APPOMATTOX STATION, Va. 8 Apr. '65. (APPOMATTOX CAMPAIGN) Approaching this point during the morning Sheridan was notified by his scouts that Confederate supply trains had recently arrived. Custer's division moved swiftly forward, drove off two Confederate divisions under Walker, captured the train, and 30 artillery pieces. Custer pursued toward Appomattox Courthouse, approximately two and a half miles northeast, and discovered the enemy defenses southwest of that place. Sheridan soon arrived with the rest of his command and prepared to attack. See APPOMATTOX COURTHOUSE, 9 Apr. '65.

AQUIA, Confed. Dist. of. One of three districts established within the Dept. of NORTHERN VIRGINIA when the latter was created 22 Oct. '61. Under command of T. H. Holmes, the Aquia District included the area between Powell's River and the mouth of the Potomac, including the Northern Neck and embracing the counties on either side of the Rappahannock River from its mouth to Fredericksburg. Holmes's command had previously been known as the Dept. of Fredericksburg. When he went to N.C., in compliance with a letter order dated 22 Mar. '62, he was temporarily succeeded by G. W. Smith (*Lee's Lts.*, I, 145).

ARCHER, James Jay. C.S.A. gen. 1817–64. Md. After attending Princeton and the Univ. of Md., he was a lawyer and fought in the Mexican War (1 brevet). Re-entering the regular army as Capt. 9th U.S. Inf. in 1855, he resigned 14 May '61 to join the Confederacy. He was commissioned Col. of the 5th Tex. in Hood's brigade in the fall of 1861 and was appointed B.G. C.S.A. 3 June '62 to succeed Robert Hatton as C.G. of the Texas Brig. In the ensuing campaigns of the Army of Northern Virginia he commanded his brigade at the Seven Days' Battles, Cedar Mtn., 2d Bull Run, Antietam, Fredericksburg, Chancellorsville, and Gettysburg. Captured at the last-named battle, he was held for over a year.

After being released, he was assigned to the Army of Tenn. 9 Aug. '64 and ten days later to the A.N.V. He died 24 Oct. '64.

ARKANSAS. The eighth state to secede from the Union (6 May '61). Admitted as a state in 1836, Ark. was one of the four of the eight border states to join the Confederacy. The state was readmitted to the Union on 22 June '68.

ARKANSAS, THE. Confederate ironclad that, after passing through the Federal fleet in front of Vicksburg, was five miles away from Baton Rouge when she became disabled 5 Aug. '62. On her way to help Breckinridge retake the La. city she was then run ashore and blown up to avoid capture by the Federals.

ARKANSAS CAMPAIGN IN 1864. As part of the RED RIVER CAMPAIGN Steele was supposed to move against Confederate forces in southwest Arkansas to prevent their opposing Banks's advance on Shreveport. Steele planned to mass the infantry divisions of Frederick Salomon and E. M. Thayer (Dept. of the Frontier) and the cavalry division of E. A. Carr (12,000 total) at Arkadelphia and draw toward him the two infantry divisions of Sterling Price (under Churchill and Parsons) that were at Spring Hill. Confederate cavalry divisions (under Fagan, Marmaduke, and Maxey) in the vicinity of Camden and Princeton could then be driven off and these places occupied.

Although Sherman had asked Steele to begin his movement on 1 Mar., it did not get started until the 23d. This was three days after the divisions of Churchill and Parsons had left to reinforce Taylor in Louisiana. Steele's delay was a major factor, if not the decisive one, in preventing the Federal capture of Shreveport (Fiebeger, 394).

On 29 Mar. Steele's column from Little Rock reached Arkadelphia, having skirmished heavily with Confederate cavalry the entire way. A few days later Thayer's Frontier Division joined him from Fort Smith. Confederate cavalry continued to be aggressive, and there were skirmishes at Mt. Elba, 30 Mar.; Spoonville (Terre Noire Creek) and Antoine, 2 Apr.; Okolona, 3 Apr.; and Elkin's Ford (Little Missouri River), 4–6 Apr.

Steele had no word from Thayer's column until the evening of the 6th. He waited in the vicinity of Elkin's Ford, where Thayer joined him the night of 9–10 Apr. (At this time Banks had decided to abandon his operation against Shreveport.) Steele now moved with his combined force in the direction of Spring Hill to draw the Confederate cavalry in that direction and permit his capture of Camden. He was engaged at Prairie d'Ann 10–13 Apr. (This place is about halfway on a direct line between Arkadelphia and Spring Hill. O. R. Atlas CLIX.) Steele then turned eastward and occupied Camden 15 Apr.; here he learned of Banks's failure.

Kirby Smith knew of Banks's withdrawal on 10 Apr., the day after Pleasant Hill, and decided to move with his main infantry force against Steele in Arkansas. He reached Camden 20 Apr. with the divisions of Churchill and Parsons and with J. G. Walker's division from Louisiana. To turn Steele's position he sent a force across the Washita below the city to cut his line of communications. At Marks's Mills, 25 Apr., this column captured a train of 211 wagons that was moving from Camden to Pine Bluff under heavy escort. Steele withdrew via Princeton. At Jenkins' Ferry, 29–30 Apr., he was attacked while astride the Saline River and forced to abandon his ponton train. He entered Little Rock on 3 May. (This campaign is also known as the Expedition to Camden.)

ARKANSAS, Confed. District of. On 22 July '61 Hardee assumed command

in northwestern Arkansas. On 2 Aug. the state and military operations in Missouri were placed under Polk, who commanded Dist. No. 2. On 11 May '62 J. S. Roane was assigned to command in Ark. On 18 Mar. '63 T. H. Holmes assumed command of the Dist. of Ark. Price superseded Holmes on 24 July, and Holmes resumed command on 25 Sept. '63. On 16 Mar. '64 Price again superseded Holmes as district commander. On 1 Feb. '65 Magruder assumed command, and on the 15th Mosby Parsons was assigned to temporary command.

On 7 Mar. '65 Price was assigned command of the Mo. Div. of Inf., and Parsons assigned command of Parsons' Missouri brigade. Price assumed command on the 8th and was superseded on the 12th by Parsons. On 19 Apr. '65 the districts of Ark. and Western La. were consolidated into the (single) Dist. of Ark. and Western La. under Buckner.

ARKANSAS POST (Ft. Hindman) Expedition, 4–12 Jan. '63. In Oct. '62 Maj. Gen. John A. McClernand had gotten Lincoln's approval of an operation against Vicksburg. Neither Halleck in Washington, nor Grant, in whose department the operation would take place, was consulted. Troops raised in the midwest by McClernand and sent to Memphis for his independent operation ended up being diverted initially to make up the force led by Sherman in the unsuccessful Chickasaw Bluffs operation (VICKSBURG CAMPAIGN). Before Sherman could withdraw, McClernand arrived and assumed command by virtue of his seniority. (See MISSISSIPPI, MC-CLERNAND'S UNION ARMY OF THE.) Instead of attacking Vicksburg he decided to capture Arkansas Post, a place 50 miles up the Arkansas River from which the Confederates could send gunboats into the Mississippi.

Ft. Hindman was a bastioned fort surrounded by an 18-foot ditch and manned by about 4,500 men under Brig. Gen. T. J. Churchill. McClernand's army of about 30,000 men, 50 transports, and 13 gunboats (under command of David Porter) tied up three miles below their objective on the night of 9 Jan. Lindsey's brigade (Osterhaus) with supporting cavalry and artillery was landed on the west bank of the river to block the enemy's retreat across the river. The other forces landed on the east bank, and by 11 o'clock on the morning of 10 Jan. started to envelop the fort from the land side. Steele's division took a wrong turn and got lost in the swamps, not rejoining the main body until the next day. The other forces drove in the Confederate defenders from the outlying earthworks and maneuvered into position for their assault. McClernand at about 3 P.M. told Porter the land assault was ready to start. The naval forces moved to within range and engaged the guns of Ft. Hindman. The Federal gunboats silenced the Confederate artillery but dropped back out of range when the land attack failed to materialize. Churchill got orders during the night to hold at all cost. It was not until the morning of the 11th that a coordinated attack of land and naval forces could be launched. By 3 P.M. Porter's gunboats had silenced the Confederate guns, and the admiral had entered the fort from the *Black Hawk,* met by white flags. The Confederates opposing the land attack started showing white flags shortly thereafter.

When Grant learned of McClernand's operation, he ordered the latter to withdraw immediately so that his forces would be in position to support Grant's next moves against Vicksburg.

Union losses were 1,061 out of 28,944 engaged (Livermore). Confederate strength was about 5,000, according to most accounts; Livermore estimates it at 4,564. Marcus Wright puts Confederate losses at 4,900, of whom 4,791 were "missing" (mostly captured) (Miller, X, 142).

ARKANSAS, Union Department of. Created 6 Jan. '64 to consist of Arkansas except Fort Smith, which was added 17 Apr. '64. It was included in the Military Division of West Mississippi 7 May '64 to 17 May '65. Its troops were in the VII Corps, which was commanded by Maj. Gen. Frederick Steele until 22 Dec. '64, and then by Maj. Gen. J. J. Reynolds until 1 Aug. '65, when the department was discontinued. Headquarters: Little Rock.

ARLINGTON, Va. The family estate of Robert E. Lee which was seized by the Federal government upon his resignation from the Union army. Arlington House was built by Washington's stepson, John Parke Custis, and passed to Lee through his father-in-law, George Washington Custis. Restitution was made to the Lee family and the estate is now the site of the National Cemetery.

"ARME BLANCHE." Romantic term for the sword, and often applied to other types of EDGED WEAPONS, particularly the bayonet.

ARMIES. There were at least 16 Union and 23 Confederate "operational organizations" that were known officially or unofficially as an army. As mentioned in the article on ORGANIZATION, an army usually took its name from the department or other territorial organization in which it operated. Furthermore, it was usually headed by the same general who commanded the territorial organization. Although each army is covered separately in this book, the following partial list may also be useful:

Federal Armies

Army of the Cumberland; the Frontier; Georgia; the Gulf; the James; Kansas; the Mississippi (there were several); the Mountain Department; the Ohio; the Potomac; the Shenandoah; the Southwest; the Tennessee; Virginia; West Tennessee; and the Army of West Virginia.

Confederate Armies

Army of Central Kentucky; East Tennessee; Eastern Kentucky; the Kanawha; Kentucky; Louisiana; Middle Tennessee; the Mississippi; Missouri; Mobile; New Mexico; Northern Virginia; the Northwest; the Peninsula; Pensacola; the Potomac; the Shenandoah; the Southwestern Army; Army of Tennessee; the Trans-Mississippi Dept.; Vicksburg; the West; and West Tennessee. See also DEPARTMENTS.

ARMISTEAD, Lewis Addison. C.S.A. gen. 1817–63. N.C. An ex-cadet at West Point (x-1837), he served in the 2d US Inf., winning two brevets in the Mexican War, and resigned 26 May '61. Commissioned Maj. C.S.A. from Va. to date from 16 Mar. '61, he was promoted Col. in that year and given command of the 57th Va. He was named B.G. C.S.A. 1 Apr. '62 and commanded his brigade from the Peninsula to Gettysburg, first in Huger's and then Pickett's Division. He led his brigade in "Pickett's Charge," cheering his men with his cap on his upraised sword. A monument stands where he fell 3 July '63, marking "the high tide of the Confederacy." (See also Alonzo CUSHING.)

ARMORY. See ARSENAL.

ARMSTRONG, Frank C. C.S.A. gen. 1835–1909. Indian Territory. Appt.-Ark. After college he joined the R.A., participating in Indian fighting and the Utah expedition. He resigned 13 Aug. '61 and was McCulloch's volunteer A.D.C. at Wilson's Creek and with Col. James McIntosh at Chustenahlah (Cherokee Nation) 26 Dec. '61. At Pea Ridge he was Lt. and Asst. Adj. Gen. Promoted Col. 3d La., he went with Price to Tupelo. On 7 July '62 he was named

Acting B.G. C.S.A. to command Price's cavalry at Courtland (Ala.) and in west Tenn. about a month later. During the battles of Iuka and Corinth he commanded the cavalry. After being appointed B.G. C.S.A. 23 Apr. '63 to date from 20 Jan. '63 he fought at Tullahoma, Stones River, Chickamauga, Knoxville, in the Atlanta campaign, at Franklin, Nashville, and Selma (2 Apr. '65). After the war he was with the Overland Mail Service and the Bureau of Indian Affairs.

ARMSTRONG, Samuel Chapman. Union officer. 1839–92. Hawaii. Capt. 125th N.Y. 27 Aug. '62; Maj. 1 Nov. '63; Lt. Col. 9th US Col. Inf. 23 Nov. '63; Col. 8th US Col. Inf. 3 Nov. '64; Bvt. B.G. USV (war service). Commanded 2, 3, X (Va. and N.C.); 2, 2, XXV (Texas). The son of New England missionaries to the Sandwich Isles, he was in college in this country when the war started. His troop experience started him on his life's work as a Negro educator, and he is famous chiefly for founding Hampton Institute.

ARMSTRONG GUN. An English rifled gun first produced in 1855 and subsequently manufactured in various calibers up to 600-pounders (13.3-inch) (Benton, 543). Both breech-loaders and muzzle-loaders were made. In the 3-inch, field-artillery, class the muzzle-loader took a studded projectile weighing about 10 pounds and having three rows of small brass studs. The 3-inch breech-loader fired a 10-pound projectile that had lead driving bands around its middle. A 4-inch and a 16-pounder Armstrong were also imported (Weller, 66-67). The field pieces had a range of 2,100 and 2,200 yards at five degrees elevation (*ibid.*). The Confederates used a few Armstrongs.

ARMSTRONG'S MILL, Va., 5–7 Feb. '65. DABNEY'S MILLS, same dates.

ARMY, CONFEDERATE. See Confederate Army.

ARMY, UNION. See Union Army.

ARNOLD, Lewis Golding. Union gen.
1817–71. N.J. USMA 1837 (10/50);
Arty. After serving in the Florida war,
on the Canadian frontier, and in the
Mexican War (2 brevets and 2 wounds),
he was Maj. 1st US Arty. (15 May '61)
in command of Ft. Pickens (Fla.) during its bombardment (2 Aug. '61–May
'62). Promoted B.G. USV 24 Jan. '62,
he was commanding general of the Dept.
of Fla. (25 Feb.–1 Oct. '62) and of the
forces at New Orleans (1 Oct.–10 Nov.
'62). He suffered a stroke on the latter
date and was on sick leave until 8 Feb.
'64 when he was retired as Lt. Col., his
B.G. commission having expired the
same day.

ARNOLD, Richard. Union gen. 1828–
82. R.I. USMA 1850 (13/44); Arty. He
served in Florida and in the West and
was Gen. Wool's A.D.C. 1855–61. As
Capt. 5th US Arty. (14 May '61), he
commanded a battery at 1st Bull Run
and was Chief of Arty. for Franklin's
Div. (Mar.–7 May '62) in the Peninsular campaign. As Acting I.G. VI Corps,
he was at Savage's Station, Glendale,
Malvern Hill, and Harrison's Landing.
He served as Chief of Arty. (Nov. '62–
Sept. '64) and of Cav. (June–Aug. '64)
in the Dept. of the Gulf, seeing service
at Port Hudson, on the Red River Expedition of '64 where he commanded
the Cav. Div., and at the siege of Ft.
Morgan on Mobile Bay. He was breveted
for Savage's Station, Port Hudson siege,
Port Hudson, and Ft. Morgan as Maj.
Gen. USV, war service as B.G. and
Maj. Gen. USA. He continued in the
R.A., dying on active duty as Lt. Col.

ARNOLD, Samuel. See Lincoln's
Assassination and Dr. Samuel Mudd.

ARSENAL. The terms arsenal,
armory, depot, and laboratory need

definition. An arsenal is "a place of
deposit for ordnance and ordnance
stores," says Scott's Military Dictionary
of 1861, "but there are also arsenals of
construction and repairs." An armory,
likewise, can be a place of manufacture or deposit, according to the same
source. Subsequent military dictionaries,
Wilhelm (1881), Garber and Bond
(1936), bear out the synonymity of the
words arsenal and armory. The official
army dictionary of today (S.R. 320-5-1,
1950) says that an arsenal has the primary mission of manufacture but may
also store and issue. The reader can
therefore expect to find these terms
used in various senses.

An arsenal in the strictest sense was
a depository which had under its supervision an armory (which did the manufacturing of arms), a laboratory (which
made ammunition as well as setting
standards and construction procedures),
and a depot (which was located at some
detached place and could have the missions of collection, repair, and issue of
arms). "Some depots became arsenals
and vice versa," say Albaugh and Simmons in their Confederate Arms, p. 76,
which should be consulted for organization of the Confederate ordnance operations.

ARTILLERY. See Cannon of the
Civil War.

ARTILLERY SUPPORTS. See Supports.

ASBOTH, Alexander Sandor. Union
gen. 1811–68. Hungary. A cuirassier in
the Austrian Army, he later studied law
and practiced engineering in Banat. An
adherent of Kossuth in the Hungarian
Revolt of 1848–49, he followed him to
Turkey and then to the US in '51. A
naturalized citizen, he went to Missouri
in July '61 with Frémont and served as
his chief of staff. Frémont appointed
him B.G. 3 Sept. and gave him com-

mand of the 4th Div., but the appointment was not recognized by the government and ceased in Mar. '62. This same month (21 Mar.) the government appointed him full B.G. USV. During the Pea Ridge campaign he commanded the 2d Div., Army Southwest Mo., and was severely wounded. He commanded Dist. of Columbus (Ohio) in Jan. '61 and, when this became the 6th Div., XVI Corps, on 31 Mar., he kept command until 4 Aug. '63. In August he was transferred to command the Dist. of W. Fla. At the battle of Marianna he was severely wounded in the face and left arm. He also led the 2d Brig., 3d Div., XIX Corps (Feb.–June '64). He was breveted Maj. Gen. USV 13 Mar. and mustered out 24 Aug. '65. He was US Minister to Argentina and Uruguay 1866–68. He went to Paris to have the bullet removed from his face by the surgeon who had performed a similar operation on Garibaldi. He later died in Buenos Aires from this wound.

ASHBY, Turner. C.S.A. cavalry gen. 1828–62. Va. A grain dealer, planter, and local politician of wealth and influence in the Shenandoah Valley, he had raised a volunteer cavalry company in 1859 and led it to Harpers Ferry when John Brown invaded the state that year. Jackson named him commander of the Point of Rocks area in the Harpers Ferry Dist., and he was promoted Lt. Col. 25 June '61. As Col., he joined with Stuart in masking Johnston's link-up with Beauregard before 1st Bull Run. Named Jackson's cavalry commander in Oct. '61 as Col. 7th Va. Cav., he commanded a brigade during the Valley campaign and was appointed B.G. C.S.A. 23 May '62. He had already become a legend when he was killed 6 June '62 in a rear-guard action near Harrisonburg. D. S. Freeman describes him as "dark, almost swarthy . . . the popular conception of an Arab."

ASHLEY, James Mitchell. Legislator. 1824–96. Pa. As congressman from Ohio (1859–69), he prepared and helped pass the bill that abolished slavery in the District of Columbia in 1862. He also introduced the bill to amend the Constitution to prohibit slavery and saw it passed as the 13th Amendment (see ABOLITION OF SLAVERY) in 1865. One of the RADICAL REPUBLICANS, he initiated the move to impeach President Johnson. He was a delegate to the first national Republican convention and served as Governor of the Montana Territory in 1869–70.

ASKEW, Frank. Union officer. 1837–1902. Ohio. 2d Lt. 17th Ohio 17 Apr. '61; 1st Lt. 17 May '61; mustered out 15 Aug. '61; Capt. 15th Ohio 13 Sept. '61; Lt. Col. 28 Nov. '62; Col. 28 July '64; Bvt. B.G. USV 14 July '65. W.I.A. Stones River and Nashville.

ASSASSINATION. See LINCOLN'S ASSASSINATION.

ASTOR, John Jacob, Jr. Union officer and philanthropist. 1822–90. N.Y. He served as Col., Volunteer A.D.C. to McClellan, 30 Nov. '61–11 July '62. On 13 Mar. '65 he was breveted B.G. USV, for the Peninsular campaign. Grandson of the financier, he inherited and expanded the family fortune.

ATHENS, Ala. 23–24 Sept. '64. 600 Federals captured. See FORREST'S OPERATIONS DURING ATLANTA CAMPAIGN.

ATKINS, Smith Dykins. Union officer. N.Y. Commissioned Capt. 11th Ill. 20 Apr. '61, he was promoted Maj. 21 Mar. '62 and resigned 17 Apr. of that year. On 4 Sept. '62, he was commissioned Col. 92d Ill. and served with them for the rest of the war, being mustered out in June '65 and breveted B.G. USV (12 Jan. '65) and Maj. Gen. USV.

ATLANTA, Battle of ("Hood's Second Sortie"). 22 July '64. (ATLANTA

CAMPAIGN) After his failure at PEACH TREE CREEK, 20 July, the aggressive Hood fell back on the prepared defenses of Atlanta. Thinking Hood was evacuating the city, Sherman ordered McPherson to pursue south and east while the other two armies closed in on Atlanta from the north and east. Actually, Hood had planned an attack against McPherson's exposed southern flank. While Cheatham's and Stewart's corps, reinforced by 5,000 Georgia militia under G. W. Smith, held the Atlanta intrenchments, Hardee was ordered to make a night march, get behind McPherson's army and attack it from the south and rear. Wheeler's cavalry corps was to strike Decatur.

ATLANTA
22 JULY 1864

After a 15-mile march Hardee was not ready to attack until about noon. Meanwhile, Dodge's XVI Corps was moving up to extend the Federal left. Although Hardee's sudden attack achieved surprise, Dodge was able to deploy the divisions of Sweeny and Fuller to block it.

General Dodge rode to Sweeny's (2d) division and took personal charge of moving Mersy's brigade (2, 2, XVI) into position. Fuller's (4th) division formed on his right. Bate and W.H.T.

Walker attacked from the woods to the south and advanced down a hill, across a branch of Sugar Creek, and northwest toward the Federal positions. Two attacks were repulsed, and Walker was killed. McPherson rode to the scene of action just in time to witness a successful counterattack by the 81st, 39th, and 27th Ohio.

McPherson noticed a gap between the XVI and XVII Corps and ordered a brigade from XV Corps to fill it. Logan sent Wangelin (3, 1). Satisfied that Dodge would be able to hold his position, McPherson was riding toward Blair's positions when he was killed by skirmishers of Cleburne's division advancing into this gap. Fuller, whose right was vulnerable to this new Confederate threat, sent forward the 64th Ill., armed with Henry repeating rifles, and the Confederates were driven back.

Cleburne and Maney then launched a coordinated attack, supported by heavy artillery fire, against the flank and rear of the XVII Corps. This hit G. A. Smith's 4th Division, and particularly heavy fighting took place in the 3d Brigade: the 16th Iowa (245 men) was cut off and captured. W. W. Belknap of the 15th Iowa (and later Secretary of War) distinguished himself in this action. The attackers swept over Bald Hill and drove back the Federal left flank until stopped by the arrival of Wangelin's brigade. Blair was then able to form a new line between Dodge on his left and Logan.

Hood had been observing the battle from the Atlanta intrenchments and was bitterly disappointed by Hardee's delay and his failure to hit *behind* the Federal flank. About 3 P.M., just as Hardee's attacks were being brought to a halt, he ordered Cheatham and G. W. Smith to attack Logan's XV Corps frontally. Manigault's brigade spearheaded this attack down the railroad.

He enveloped two infantry regiments and a section of artillery under the command of Col. W. S. Jones of the 53d Ohio that held an outpost about a half mile forward of the main line. DeGress's nearby battery of four 20-pounder Parrott guns (Btry. "H," 1st Ill.) was captured at about 4 o'clock. Lightburn's (formerly M. L. Smith's) 2d Division was then routed and the flank units of C. R. Woods's 1st Division to his right driven back. Mersy's brigade, brought up from XVI Corps, recaptured DeGress's battery. Woods's division also counterattacked and stopped Cheatham's advance. Under the direction of Sherman, massed artillery and Lightburn's counterattack restored the main battle line. The Confederates made several more costly but unsuccessful assaults.

The absence of Garrard's cavalry (on a raid to Covington) had not only permitted Hardee to gain surprise, but it also enabled Wheeler to reach Decatur. Federal trains at this place were being guarded by Sprague's brigade (2, 4, XVI). Although the latter had 225 men captured, he managed to protect the supplies and hold off two Confederate regiments until reinforcements arrived to help drive the enemy off.

Livermore estimates Federal losses at 3,722 out of 30,477 engaged. He figures there were about 8,000 Confederate casualties out of 36,934 engaged. Most writers accept Hardee's opinion that this battle was "one of the most desperate and bloody of the war."

ATLANTA CAMPAIGN. 1 May–8 Sept. '64. After the CHATTANOOGA CAMPAIGN Bragg retreated 25 miles south to Dalton, Ga., and intrenched. Grant had not pursued, since he was concerned with going to Burnside's relief at KNOXVILLE. As a result of public clamor Bragg asked to be relieved and was succeeded in Dec. by Joseph E.

Johnston. The Confederate authorities planned a new offensive into Tenn. and, during the winter of 1863-64, reinforced Johnston to a strength of about 62,000, including 2,000 cavalry under Joseph Wheeler. His corps commanders were Hardee, Hood, and (soon after the campaign started) Polk.

Sherman had 100,000 men in seven infantry corps and a cavalry corps. Thomas's Army of the Cumberland consisted of the following corps: O. O. Howard's IV, J. M. Palmer's XIV, Hooker's XX, and W. L. Elliott's Cavalry Corps. McPherson's Army of the Tenn. consisted of John A. Logan's XV, G. M. Dodge's XVI, F. P. Blair's XVII. Schofield's Army of the Ohio consisted of his XXIII Corps and Stoneman's cavalry. J. E. Smith's (3d) division of XV Corps, XVII Corps, and three cavalry brigades were designated to guard the lines of communications.

Sherman's orders from Grant were "to move against Johnston's army, to break it up, and to get into the interior of the enemy's country as far as you can, inflicting all the damage you can against their war resources. . . ." Since Atlanta was a vital supply, manufacturing, and communications center, Sherman advanced toward that point while Johnston was pressed back toward it.

Sherman's advance started 7 May, about the same time as Grant, with Meade's Army of the Potomac, started the offensive in the east. Since Johnston's position at Dalton was too strong to attack, Sherman sent McPherson, preceded by Kilpatrick's cavalry division, to turn (see TURNING MOVEMENT) it from the west while Thomas advanced frontally along the railroad. Schofield threatened the Confederate right. This resulted in the actions around ROCKY FACE RIDGE, 5–9 May '64. Johnston withdrew without becoming decisively engaged.

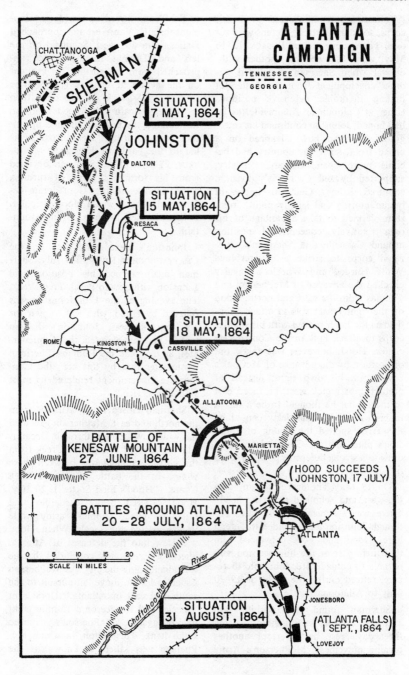

ATLANTA CAMPAIGN

TENNESSEE
GEORGIA

SHERMAN

SITUATION
7 MAY, 1864

JOHNSTON

DALTON

SITUATION
15 MAY, 1864

RESACA

SITUATION
18 MAY, 1864

ROME   KINGSTON   CASSVILLE

ALLATOONA

BATTLE OF
KENESAW MOUNTAIN
27 JUNE, 1864

MARIETTA

(HOOD SUCCEEDS
JOHNSTON, 17 JULY)

BATTLES AROUND ATLANTA
20—28 JULY, 1864

0   5   10   15   20
SCALE IN MILES

Chattahoochee River

ATLANTA

JONESBORO

(ATLANTA FALLS
1 SEPT., 1864)

SITUATION
31 AUGUST, 1864

LOVEJOY

Johnston, now reinforced by Polk's corps, took up a strong defensive position. The actions around RESACA, 13–16 May, were followed by another withdrawal when Sherman threatened another envelopment from the west. Not finding favorable defensive positions either at Calhoun or Adairsville, as he had hoped, Johnston continued his retrograde. Sherman now advanced on a broad front, since the country had become more open. Garrard's cavalry, supported by Jeff C. Davis's division, captured Rome, Ga., an important manufacturing and supply point. Johnston planned to take advantage of his own relatively concentrated position around Cassville and Sherman's separated corps to strike a counterblow. While Hardee and Wheeler's cavalry checked the advance of McPherson and Thomas from the west and north, Hood on the right (east) was to attack Schofield as the latter moved with his smaller corps to attack Polk in the Confederate center. Hood, however, was faked out of position by the advance of McCook's cavalry on his own right; instead of preparing to attack west, he faced east to meet what he thought to be a threat to his own right. The delay caused by this error spoiled the timing of Johnston's plan, and the Confederates withdrew to a strong defensive position south of Cassville.

On 19 May Thomas closed in from the west, and Schofield from the north. There was skirmishing until dark. Although Johnston had intended to defend here, Hood and Polk convinced him that their part of the line was too vulnerable to enfilade fire. Johnston, therefore, retired during the night of 19–20 May to Allatoona Pass.

Sherman found this position too strong to assault. After giving his army three days' rest, he undertook another turning movement. McPherson's Army

of the Tenn. moved on a wide envelopment through Van Wert and approached Dallas from due west. Schofield on the left and Thomas in the center approached from the north. This brought on the action at DALLAS (New Hope Church), 25–27 May. Sherman then moved east again and forced Johnston to abandon his position to take up another one to protect the railroad. This led to the battle of KENESAW MOUNTAIN, 27 June. Here Sherman deviated from his former strategy of turning, rather than assaulting, Confederate defenses; the result was a bloody repulse. Polk was killed 14 June at Pine Mountain.

Johnston's next stand was on the CHATTAHOOCHEE RIVER, 4–9 July. Sherman again turned his position and Johnston withdrew to Peach Tree Creek. The evening of the 17th Johnston was relieved by Hood, who was known for his aggressiveness. Johnston's Fabian tactics had exasperated the Confederates, as they had the Romans. Sherman wrote later that by this act "the Confederate Government rendered us most valuable service."

Sherman closed in on Atlanta from the north and east. McPherson executed the wide envelopment through Decatur. Thomas crossed Peach Tree Creek from the north. Schofield was between these wings. In the battle of PEACH TREE CREEK ("Hood's First Sortie"), 20 July, Hood suffered heavy casualties and failed to defeat Thomas's army while it was astride the creek. When Hood withdrew into the defenses of Atlanta, Sherman erroneously concluded that he was abandoning the city. As McPherson issued orders to move "in pursuit to the south and east of Atlanta," Hood sent Wheeler and Hardee on a 15-mile night march against McPherson's exposed south flank. This action, in which McPherson was killed, is known as the battle of ATLANTA ("Hood's Second Sortie"), 22 July. The Confederates, however, were finally checked with a loss of about 8,500 as compared with a Union loss of 3,700.

McPherson's death precipitated a reorganization of command. Howard became C.G., Army of the Tenn. Hooker, who ranked Howard and felt himself entitled to McPherson's post, resigned command of XX Corps and was succeeded by Slocum. Palmer, a little later, resigned command of XIV Corps because he did not want to serve under Schofield, whom he claimed was junior. Jeff C. Davis became C.G., XIV Corps.

By 25 July Sherman had invested Atlanta on the north and east. Hood's line of communications via the railroad to the south was still open, and Sherman now directed operations to cut it. This resulted in two failures: STONEMAN'S AND McCOOK'S RAIDS, 26–31 July, and the battle of EZRA CHURCH, 28 July.

July ended with Hood's holding Atlanta with 37,000 infantry reinforced by 5,000 Georgia State Militia under G. W. Smith. Sherman had 85,000 infantry. The only cavalry he had fit for field service was Garrard's division and a brigade that had joined Schofield after Stoneman's departure. Stoneman's division had been all but wiped out. "McCook's division had been dispersed and its fractions were seeking safety at various points on the Chattahoochee below the railroad" (Fiebeger, 353). Kilpatrick's cavalry division, which had been guarding communications to the rear, was ordered to relieve McCook's division in protecting Sherman's right flank.

In another effort to extend his lines west and cut Hood's rail lines to the south, the XXIII Corps was moved from Sherman's left to the right and reinforced two days later by the XIV Corps. Positions thus evacuated were filled by Garrard's dismounted troopers in the former XXIII Corps sector, and by thinning the lines of the XX and IV Corps. This movement led to frustration on UTOY CREEK.

Before Sherman could carry out his next plan, to move his entire force west of the Atlanta-Marietta R.R. and turn Hood's position by an advance south, he was diverted by WHEELER'S RAID, 10 Aug.–10 Sept. '64. On 16 August Sherman learned that the bulk of Hood's cavalry was near Dalton. He decided to take advantage of this situation to raid Hood's line of communications and force him to retreat. KILPATRICK'S RAID TO JONESBORO, 18–22 Aug., was a failure.

Sherman then prepared to employ his infantry. The night of 25 Aug. he started regrouping his forces to turn Hood's west flank. On 27 Aug. his forces were on line along the Sandtown Road with Howard, Thomas, and Schofield from right to left. The next day Howard and Thomas reached the Montgomery and Atlanta R.R. at Fairburn and Redoak Station, respectively. By midnight of 31 Aug. Schofield had cut the railroad at Rough and Ready; Thomas had cut it about halfway between that place and Jonesboro. Howard had closed up to the latter place from the west.

The night of 30 Aug. Hood, knowing of Howard's location but not that of the other two commanders, had sent the corps of Hardee and S. D. Lee to defend Jonesboro. The next day they made an unsuccessful attack. S. D. Lee was then ordered back toward Atlanta. Sherman then failed to destroy Hardee's isolated force. These actions are known as the battle of JONESBORO, GA., 31 Aug.–1 Sept. '64.

Hood evacuated Atlanta at 5 P.M., 1 Sept., and the XX Corps took possession the next morning. Sherman pursued Hood to Lovejoy but found him concentrated with his entire command in a position that was too strong to be assaulted. Union forces returned to Atlanta 4–8 Sept. Thomas's command occupied the town, Howard's was located at East Point, and Schofield's was at Decatur. Unable to advance farther, but determined to hold his gains, Sherman evacuated the Southern civilians from the city and converted it into an armed camp that could be held with the smallest possible force. In Sept. Hood moved north to attack Sherman's 140-mile line of communications to Chattanooga, with the hope that this would force him to abandon Atlanta. This operation is known as the FRANKLIN AND NASHVILLE CAMPAIGN. After frustrating Hood's threat to his line of communications and then leaving Thomas to take care of Hood's subsequent invasion of Tenn., Sherman in Nov. cut loose from his base in Atlanta and undertook his MARCH TO THE SEA.

ATTACKS may be classified as penetrations, ENVELOPMENTS, TURNING MOVEMENTS, and FRONTAL ATTACKS. A commander normally groups his forces so as to provide a main attack, secondary attack, and reserve. The former, as its name indicates, contains the greatest possible concentration of combat power (troops, artillery support, etc.) and is given the decisive mission. The secondary attack is allocated minimum essential combat power and gives maximum assistance to the main attack by deceiving the enemy as to the location of the main attack, forcing him to commit his reserves prematurely and at the wrong place, and fixing certain enemy troops in position so they cannot be shifted to oppose the main attack. Failure to provide for a secondary attack, or failure of the secondary attack to perform its role properly, accounted for McClellan's failure at Antietam and contributed to Lee's failure in the sec-

ond day's fighting at Gettysburg. The reserve is a force held out of the battle initially. Its mission in the attack is to clinch the victory or exploit success. A good general avoids committing it PIECEMEAL or prematurely. He constitutes a new reserve as soon as the original one is employed.

ATZERODT, George. See LINCOLN'S ASSASSINATION.

AUBURN, Va. 14 Oct. '63. See CATLETT'S STATION, same date.

AUGUR, Christopher Colon. Union gen. 1821–98. N.Y. Appt.-Mich. USMA 1843 (16/39); Inf. In the Mexican War as A.D.C. to Gen. Hopping, then to Gen. Cushing. As Capt. 4th US Inf., he fought Indians on the frontier and was promoted Maj. 14 May '61 while serving as Commandant of Cadets at West Point. Appointed B.G. USV 12 Nov. '61, he served in Washington until 10 Mar. '62. As a brigade commander he was engaged in operations on the Rappahannock Mar.–July '62, commanding the force that captured Fredericksburg 21 Apr. Leading a division of Banks's II Corps, he was severely wounded at Cedar Mountain, was promoted Maj. Gen. USV to rank from 9 Aug. '62 (Cedar Mountain), and served on the military court that investigated Miles's surrender of Harpers Ferry. He joined Banks in the Dept. of the Gulf in Nov. and commanded the Dist. of Baton Rouge 20 Jan.–20 May '63. Taking part in the operations against Port Hudson, he commanded the action of 21 May and commanded the left wing of the army 22 May– 8 July '63. This was the end of his field service. Returning to the East, he served on various boards and commanded the XXII Corps and Dept. of Washington 13 Oct. '63–13 Aug. '66. Breveted B.G. and Maj. Gen. USA (Port Hudson and war service), he continued in the R.A.

and retired in 1885 as B.G. USA (since 1869).

AUKENY, Rollin V. Union officer. Col. 142d Ill., and Bvt. B.G. USV 13 Mar. '65 (Phisterer). He at one time commanded the 3d Brig., Dist. of Memphis. He is not listed as an officer by Heitman.

AVERASBORO, N.C. 16 Mar. '65. (CAROLINAS CAMPAIGN) As Slocum's column approached Averasboro the Federals found Hardee's corps defending a narrow ridge between the river and a swamp. Jackson's and Ward's divisions of XX Corps were deployed to attack, and Sherman, who was present, ordered an infantry brigade to envelop the Confederate right. In the latter operation Case's brigade drove back Taliaferro's division to a second line where McLaws' division was intrenched. Darkness ended the Federal attack on this line, Hardee withdrew during the night, and Sherman continued his advance. Losses were 678 Federals and 865 Confederates (Fox).

AVERELL, William Woods. Union gen. 1832–1900. N.Y. USMA 1855 (26/34); Mtd. Inf.-Cav. Wounded in the Indian wars, he served on the frontier and on garrison duty. Named 1st Lt. 3d US Cav. 14 May '61, he was promoted Capt. 17 July '62 and named Col. 3d Pa. Cav. 23 Aug. '61. He commanded cavalry brigade protecting Defenses of Washington, Oct. '61–Mar. '62. He was promoted B.G. USV 26 Sept. '62 and commanded 2d Cav. Div. (22 Feb.–4 May '63); 4th Separate Brig. VIII Corps (16 May '63–26 Apr. '64); and 2d Cav. Div. (26 Apr. '64–18 May '65). On 3 May '63 Hooker relieved him of command when he returned from a reconnaissance to report the country on the army's right flank impracticable for cavalry work (Steele, 347). In late Sept. '64 he was relieved of command

by Sheridan for lack of aggressiveness in pursuing Early (SHENANDOAH VALLEY CAMPAIGN OF SHERIDAN). He was breveted for Kelly's Ford, Droop Mountain, Salem Expedition, Moorefield, and war service (Maj. Gen. USV). On 18 May '65 he resigned. Appointed US Consul General of Canada (1866–69), he then became president of a large manufacturing company. A prominent inventor in several industrial fields (steel, asphalt, paving, electrical power), he acquired considerable wealth.

AVERELL'S RAID TO LEWISBURG, W. Va. 1–8 Nov. '63. On 1 Nov. a mixed brigade under Averell left Beverly and on the 3d another under Duffié left Charleston, W. Va., to unite at Lewisburg and then cut the East Tenn. & Va. R.R. At Droop Mountain, about 20 miles north of Lewisburg, Averell's brigade met and defeated a mixed brigade under John Echols on the 6th. The next day the two Federal columns joined in Lewisburg, but were in no condition to continue on to accomplish their mission. They returned to their stations. During this time the main Confederate force in the area was engaged in the operations against Knoxville in E. Tenn.

AVERILL, John Thomas. Union officer. 1825–89. Me. Lt. Col. 6th Minn. 22 Aug. '62; Col. 22 Nov. '64; Bvt. B.G. USV 18 Oct. '65 (for recruitment of army). A leading manufacturer and, later, Congressman from Minnesota.

AVERY, Matthew Henry. Union officer. Maj. 10th N.Y. Cav. 25 Nov. '61; Col. 28 Dec. '64; 1st Prov. N.Y. Cav. 17 June '65; Bvt. B.G. USV Sayler's Creek, war service.

AVERY, Robert. Union officer. Pa. Commissioned Capt. 12th N.Y. Sept. '61, he transferred to the 102d N.Y. in Feb. '62 and fought as Lt. Col. (1 Jan. '63) at Chancellorsville and Lookout

Mountain. Wounded at both battles and losing his right leg at the latter, he was mustered out 27 June '64 and commissioned Maj. Vet. Res. Corps 27 Apr. '65. He retired in 1870 as Lt. Col., having been breveted for Chancellorsville, Lookout Mountain (B.G. USV) and war service (Maj. Gen. USV).

AVOYELLES PRAIRIE, La. Alternate name of skirmish at Marksville Prairie 15 May '64 during RED RIVER CAMPAIGN.

AYRES, Romeyn Beck. Union gen. 1825–88. N.Y. USMA 1847 (22/38); Arty. He served in the Mexican War, on the frontier, and in Eastern garrisons and was promoted Capt. 5th US Arty. 14 May '61. He fought at 1st Bull Run and served as Chief of Arty. for W. F. Smith's division (1 Oct. '61–Nov. '62) and of VI Corps (Potomac) to 4 Apr. '63. In these positions he was at the siege of Yorktown, Lee's Mill, Williamsburg, Gaines's Mill, Golding's Farm, Glendale, Harrison's Landing, South Moun-

tain, Antietam, and Fredericksburg. Promoted B.G. USV 29 Nov. '62, he took command of 1, 2, V, Potomac 21 Apr. '63 and led it at Chancellorsville; he commanded the division at Gettysburg and during the New York Draft Riots. He fought in subsequent actions of the V Corps, commanding 4th Brig., 1st Div. (Mar. '64), 1st Brig., 1st Div. from the Wilderness through Cold Harbor (Apr.–5 June '64), and commanded 2d Div. (6 June '64–Jan. '65) at Petersburg where he was wounded. He also commanded 3d Div., Prov. Corps, Potomac 28 June '65 and Dist. Shenandoah 23 Aug. '65–30 Apr. '66. He was breveted for Gettysburg, the Wilderness; as Maj. Gen. USV for the Wilderness, Spotsylvania, Jericho Ford, Totopotomoy, Bethesda Church, Petersburg, Globe Tavern, Weldon R.R.; Five Forks as B.G. USA; war service as Maj. Gen. USA. D.A.B. describes him as tall, distinguished, meticulous in dress, and a hard fighter. He continued in the R.A. until his death on active duty as Col.

B

BABBITT, Edwin Burr. Union officer. c. 1803–81. Conn. Appt.-Ind. USMA 1826 (28/41); Inf.-Q.M. After serving in Indian fighting, the Seminole War, and the Mexican War (1 brevet), he was Chief Q.M. of the Dept. of Oregon until 13 Sept. '61 and then of the Dept. of the Pacific until 5 Sept. '65. He was promoted Maj. 10 May '61 and Lt. Col. 3 Aug. '61 and breveted Col. and B.G. USA 13 Mar. '65.

BABCOCK, Orville E. Union officer. c. 1836–84. Vt. USMA May '61 (3/45); Engrs. He served as Banks's A.D.C. until Aug. '61 in constructing defenses

around Washington, fought in the Peninsular campaign attached to an engineer battalion, and was Chief Engineer of the Left Grand Div. 16 Nov.–18 Dec. '62, having been promoted 1st Lt. 17 Nov. '61. Named Lt. Col. USV 1 Jan. '63, he served as Asst. I.G. of the VI Corps 1 Jan.–6 Feb. '63 and as Asst. I.G. and Chief Engr. of the IX Corps 6 Feb.–10 Apr. '63 and as Chief Engr. of the Central Dist. of Ky. 10 Apr.–9 June '63. He was with the IX Corps at Vicksburg and in the East Tenn. campaign at Blue Lick Springs, Hough Ferry, and Campbell's Station. After fighting at Knoxville, he was Chief Engr. for the Dept. of the Ohio 23 Jan.–20 Mar. '64 and Grant's A.D.C. (Lt. Col. 29 Mar. '64) at the Wilderness, Spotsylvania, Cold Harbor, and the Petersburg siege. He took dispatches from Grant to Sherman in Dec. '64 and to Schofield at Wilmington, N.C., in Feb. '65. Breveted B.G. USA for war service, he continued to be Grant's A.D.C. until 1877 and served on various engineering projects until he drowned in Florida in 1884.

BACHE, Hartman. Union officer. 1798–1872. Pa. USMA 1818 (19/23); Engrs. After serving on surveying duty on the East Coast, he participated in the construction of harbors, defenses, lighthouses, railroads, and canals before being named head of the Bureau of Topographical Engineers 11 Apr.–11 Dec. '61 as Lt. Col. (6 Aug. '61). He was promoted Col. 3 Mar. '63 and served throughout the Civil War in engineering and lighthouse duty in the East. Retired in 1867, he was breveted B.G. USA.

BADEAU, Adam. Union officer. 1831–95. N.Y. Capt. A.D.C. Vols. staff of Gen. Sherman 29 Apr. '62; Lt. Col. mil. sec. to Gen Grant 29 Mar. '64–24 July '66; Bvt. B.G. USV 9 Apr. 65 (war service). In R.A. from '66 to '69 as Col. A.D.C. to Grant; retired as Capt.; 5 brevets 2 Mar. '67 for war service. He served in various legations and consulates during Grant's term of office and later traveled through Europe with him. Author of *Military History of Ulysses S. Grant* and *Grant in Peace,* he helped Grant write his *Memoirs* and was in a controversy with Col. Frederick Grant (and Grant, himself) over his payment.

BADGES, Corps. The first use of a distinctive device to identify an organization is believed to have been when Philip Kearny had his men of the 3d Div., III Corps, wear a red diamond.

(An earlier origin may be credited to the WASHINGTON ARTILLERY. W. M. Owen's *In Camp and Field with the Washington Artillery* speaks (page 43) of red flannel strips worn by his unit as identification at 1st Bull Run.) When Joe Hooker took command of the Army of the Potomac he prescribed that all his corps be identified, and Dan BUTTERFIELD is credited with having designed the patches. These appeared in the Army of the Potomac in the spring of 1863, but not in the West until the next year. When a veteran western soldier of the badgeless XV Corps first saw the easterners of the XII Corps with a star on each cap, he asked disapprovingly: "You boys all generals?" When asked about his own corps insignia, he slapped his cartridge box and said it was "Forty rounds in the cartridge box and twenty in the pocket." Unwittingly, he had created the design for the XV Corps patch.

Badges were stamped out of flannel cloth, were about 1½ inches across, and were fastened conspicuously on the men's caps. Some time after the corps badges were prescribed, it became the practice to designate divisions by a corps badge in red, white, or blue, for the 1st, 2d, 3d Div. of the corps. Green was used if a 4th Div. existed. Each corps and division had a corresponding flag bearing the same device. The following is a list of US corps badges.

Note: Confederate corps had no badges.

I	Disk
II	Trefoil
III	Lozenge
IV	Triangle
V	Maltese Cross
VI	St. Andrew's Cross
VII	Crescent and Star
VIII	Six-pointed Star
IX	Shield, crossed by Anchor and Cannon

X	Square Bastion
XI	Crescent
XII	Five-pointed Star
XIII	None
XIV	Acorn
XV	Cartridge Box (forty rounds)
XVI	Crossed Cannon
XVII	Arrow
XVIII	Trefoil Cross
XIX	Maltese Cross-like figure
XX	Star
XXI	None
XXII	Pentagon Cross
XXIII	Shield
XXIV	Heart
XXV	Lozenge on a Square

BAGBY, Arthur Pendleton. C.S.A. gen. 1832–1921. Ala. Appt.-At Large. USMA 1852 (36/43); Inf. Serving in garrison and on the frontier, he resigned the next year to practice law and then moved to Texas. In 1861 he was commissioned Maj. 7th Tex. and the next year was promoted Col. He marched with Sibley in N.Mex., fought at Galveston 1 Jan. '63 and then served under Taylor in western La. Wounded at Berwick Bay and promoted B.G. C.S.A. in Mar. '64 on Kirby Smith's recommendation, he led a brigade in the Red River campaign at Mansfield and Pleasant Hill. Kirby Smith promoted him Maj. Gen. C.S.A. 16 May '65. He is not listed as a general officer by Wright, but both Heitman and Cullum give his highest rank as B.G. C.S.A. C.M.H. supplies the data about his last promotion. After the war he was a lawyer in Texas. He was the last surviving member of his West Point class.

BAILEY, Joseph. Union gen. 1827–67. Ohio. Commissioned Capt. 4th Wis. Cav. 2 July '61, he was acting Engineer of Defense in New Orleans in Dec. '62 and was promoted Maj. 30 May '63. He was one of 15 Army officers during the entire war to receive the Thanks of Congress (for his engineering feat that saved Banks's fleet in the RED RIVER CAMPAIGN in 1864). Promoted Col. 1 June '64 and B.G. USV 10 Nov. '64, he commanded the Engr. Brig., XIX, Gulf (11 June–10 Aug. '64); Dist. West Fla. (20 Oct.–25 Nov. '64); Dist. Baton Rouge (3–28 Dec. '64); Cavalry Div., Gulf (28 Dec. '64–9 Feb. '65); Eng. Brig., Mil. Div. W. Miss. (11 Mar.–2 May '65) and 2, 2d Cav. Div., Gulf. His appointment expired 4 Mar. '65 and he was reappointed 16 Apr. '65 to date from the original commission. Breveted for the Red River Campaign (B.G. USV 7 June '64) and Mobile (Maj. Gen. USV), he resigned 7 July '65 and was killed two years later while sheriff of Newton County, Mo.

BAILEY, Silas Milton. Union officer. Pa. Capt. 8th Pa. Res. 13 June '61; Maj. 4 June '62; Col. 1 Mar. '63. Bvt. B.G. USV (Wilderness, Spotsylvania Court House). Died 1900.

BAILEY, Theodorus. Union naval officer. 1805–77. N.Y. Appointed in the Navy in 1818, he became naval commander 2 May '61 in the blockade of Pensacola and second in command to Farragut in the attack on New Orleans, where he led the fleet in the gunboat *Cayuga*. In Nov. '62 he assumed command of the East Gulf blockade squadron, and during the next 18 months his force captured some 150 blockade runners. In 1866 he was promoted to Rear Admiral and retired because of ill health.

BAIRD, Absalom. Union gen. 1824–1905. Pa. USMA 1849 (9/43); Arty.-Adj. Gen.-I.G. After fighting in the Seminole War and teaching mathematics at West Point, he was Bvt. Capt. Asst. Adj. Gen. 11 May '61 and served as Adj. Gen. at 1st Bull Run. He was I.G. and Chief of Staff of the IV Corps at Yorktown and Williamsburg. He was named B.G. USV 28 Apr. '62 and commanded 27th Brig., 7th Div., Ohio (12 Apr.–10 Oct. '62) at Cumberland Gap. He also led 4th Brig., Cumberland Div., Ohio; Baird's Division, Army Ky.; 1st Div., Res. Corps, Cumberland (8 June–11 Aug. '63); 1st Div., XIV, Cumberland (23 Aug.–21 Sept. '63) at Dug Gap, Chickamauga, and Rossville; and 3d Div., XIV, Cumberland (10–25 Oct. and 25 Nov. '63–20 July '65) at Missionary Ridge, Resaca, Kenesaw Mountain, Vining's Station, Peach Tree Creek, Atlanta, Utoy Creek, Jonesboro, Savannah, and Bentonville. Breveted for Chickamauga, Chattanooga, Atlanta (B.G. USA), war service (Maj. Gen. USA) and Resaca-Jonesboro-Savannah (Maj. Gen. USV 1 Sept. '64), he was awarded the Medal of Honor in 1896 for Jonesboro. He continued in the R.A., retiring in 1888 as B.G. I.G.

BAKER, Alpheus. C.S.A. gen. 1828–91. S.C. At first a schoolteacher, he practiced law in Alabama and was a delegate to that state's secession convention. As Capt. of a militia company, he went to Pensacola and in Nov. '61 marched to Ft. Pillow. Elected Col. 54th Ala., he fought at New Madrid, was captured at Island No. 10, and was exchanged in Sept. '62. He led his regiment at Ft. Pemberton on the Yazoo and Baker's Creek where he was wounded in the foot during the Vicksburg campaign. Appointed B.G. C.S.A. 5 Mar. '64, he commanded Baker's brigade, Stewart's division, under Hood in the Atlanta campaign, having his horse shot from under him at Resaca and being slightly wounded at Ezra Church. He was sent to Mobile and in Jan. '65 went to the Carolinas, fighting at Bentonville. After the war he resumed his law practice.

BAKER, Benjamin Franklin. Union officer. N.Y. Commissioned Maj. 43d N.Y. 21 Sept. '61, he was promoted Lt. Col. about a year later and Col. the next day (25 Sept.). He resigned 1 Feb. '64 and was breveted B.G. USV for war service.

BAKER, Edward Dickinson. Union gen. 1811–61. England. A Whig state Representative and Senator and US Congressman, he resigned in 1846 to command Shields's brigade from the battle of Cerro Gordo until the end of the war. He was a friend of Lincoln, who had named his second son for Baker. Going to the West Coast, he was US senator from Oregon and a leading lawyer in San Francisco when named B.G. USV 17 May '61. He declined this and was then commissioned Col. 71st Pa. 22 June (called the "First California" in his honor). He commanded 3, Stones's division, Potomac (3 Oct.–21 Oct. '61) when he was killed on the latter date at BALLS BLUFF. Offered Maj. Gen. USV 21 Sept. '61, he had not accepted.

BAKER, James Heaton. Union officer. 1829–1913. Ohio. Col. 10th Minn. 17 Nov. '62; Bvt. B.G. USV (war service). Commanded 1st Brig., 2d Div. (Tenn.). An early adherent of the Republican party, he was prominent as a politician, journalist, and historian.

BAKER, Lafayette Curry. Union gen. and special agent. 1826–68. N.Y. A member of the vigilance committee of San Francisco in 1856, he was later a detective in the State Dept. and when war came was used as a special agent. Sent by Gen. Scott to gather information about the enemy, he went to Richmond in July and was so successful that the Confederates sent him back North in the belief that he was their spy. Another famous exploit was his 100-mile ride through enemy lines after 2d Bull Run as a courier between Sec. Stanton and Banks. Commissioned Col. 1st D.C. Cav. 5 May '63, he led this regiment, which was under direct control of the War Dept., in security missions in the vicinity of the capital. Named B.G. USV 26 Apr. '65, he organized the pursuit of Booth after Lincoln's assassination and was present at his capture and death. Author of *History of the United States Secret Service.*

BAKER, Laurence Simmons. C.S.A. gen. 1830–1907. N.C. USMA 1851 42/42); Mtd. Rifles. Serving in garrison and on the frontier in Indian scouting and fighting, he resigned as a 1st Lt. 10 May '61 to go with his state although personally opposed to secession. Appointed Lt. Col. 1st N.C. Cav. in 1861, he was promoted Col. in the spring of 1862 and fought under Lee from the Peninsula to Appomattox. He led his regiment at Antietam, Fredericksburg, and Gettysburg, succeeding Hampton in command of his brigade at the last. Promoted B.G. C.S.A. 23 July '63, he was wounded in a skirmish later that month. On 9 June '64 he was ordered to the territorial command of N.C., with his headquarters in Goldsboro. During this time he was again wounded but later that year he took a brigade of reserves to meet Sherman in S.C. He led a division for a few days but was relieved 26 Dec. '64 when his old wound broke out. He commanded a brigade at Bentonville and tried to join Johnston but was prevented by Federal troops in the area. He was paroled at Raleigh 8 May '65 and after the war worked as railroad agent at Suffolk. His first name is usually spelled "Lawrence," the result of a clerical error made when he entered West Point.

BAKER'S CREEK, Miss. Another name for battle of Champion's Hill during VICKSBURG CAMPAIGN.

BALCH, Joseph Pope. Union officer. R.I. Maj. 1st R.I. 2 May '62; Bvt. B.G. USV (war service). Died 1872.

BALDEY, George. Union officer. Pa. R.A. Pvt. in 1847–48; Pvt. and Sgt.

2d Colo., Cav. 14 Sept. '62; 1st Lt. and Adj. 20 Nov. '62; served in N.Mex., Mo., Ark., and on the Plains; Maj. 2d Mo. (later 65th USCT) 28 Jan. '64; Lt. Col. 21 June '65; Bvt. B.G. USV (war service). Continued R.A. after the war; discharged as Capt. 1870.

"BALD HILL." See maps of the Battle of ATLANTA, 22 July '64, and 1st BULL RUN, 21 July '61, in both of which actions there figured a "Bald Hill."

BALDWIN, Charles Pierce. Union officer. Me. Capt. 11th Me. 8 Sept. '62; Maj. 3 July '64; Lt. Col. 1 May '65; Bvt. B.G. USV 1 Apr. '65 (Deep Bottom, Hatcher's Run).

BALDWIN, William E. C.S.A. gen. 1827–64. Appointed from Miss. Commissioned Col. 14th Miss. in early '61, he served in central Kentucky and commanded the 2d Brig. under Buckner at Ft. Donelson. After being exchanged, he was assigned to the Army of West Tenn. and fought at Coffeyville 6 Dec. '62. He was appointed B.G. C.S.A. 19 Sept. '62. During the Vicksburg campaign he commanded the 1st Brig. under Smith at Pt. Gibson, Champion's Hill, Big Black River, and the Vicksburg siege and assaults. Captured again, he was exchanged and led a brigade in the Dist. of Mobile until his death 19 Feb. '64.

BALDWIN, William Henry. Union officer. 1832–98. Me. Lt. Col. 83d Ohio 13 Sept. '62; Bvt. B.G. USV 22 Aug. '65 (Mobile and defenses; Blakely, Ala.). Graduating from Harvard Law School in 1858, he practiced for a year, then joined Garibaldi's army in 1860 and hurried home for the Civil War. He was a member of Banks's Red River expedition.

BALDY. Gen. Meade bought the bright bay horse from the Q.M. after his owner had been seriously wounded at 1st Bull Run and the horse himself had been hurt. Meade's staff complained that the animal's gait, faster than a walk and slower than a trot, caused them extreme discomfort, but the general rode him until the spring of 1864. Baldy was wounded twice at 1st Bull Run and left on the field for dead at Antietam. In the next Federal advance at this battle he was found calmly grazing on the battlefield with a deep neck wound. He carried Meade at Fredericksburg, Chancellorsville, and Gettysburg, where he was wounded again. Retired before the Wilderness, he rejoined Meade after the surrender and remained with him until Meade's death in 1872, when Baldy followed the hearse.

BALL, William H. Union officer. Va. Col. 122d Ohio 8 Oct. '62; Bvt. B.G. USV 19 Oct. '64 (Richmond, Shenandoah Valley). Commanded 2, 3, VI. Was with Butler at Bermuda Hundred, in N.Y. for the riots and with Sheridan in the Valley.

BALLIER, John Frederick. Union officer. Germany. 1st Lt. 1846–48; Col. 21st Pa. 29 Apr. '61; mustered out 9 Aug. '61; Col. 98th Pa. 30 Sept. '61; Bvt. B.G. USV 13 July '64 (Richmond campaign). Commanded 1, 2, VI (Wheaton's Brig.); 3, 3, VI. Died 1893.

BALLOCH, George Williamson. Union officer. N.H. 1st Lt. 5th N.H. 23 Oct. '61; Capt. 21 July '62 and Lt. Col. 13 May '63–9 May '67 Comsy. of Subsist.; Bvt. B.G. USV (merit).

BALLS BLUFF, Va. 21 Oct. '61. Col. Edward D. BAKER, ex-Congressman and close personal friend of Lincoln's, was authorized to make "a slight demonstration" against Confederate forces opposite the Potomac fords near Poolesville. In a brave but tactically inept operation Baker got his command ambushed by the Confederate Evans (of 1st Bull Run fame); total Federal losses were 921, of whom Baker and 48 others were killed, 158 were wounded, and 714

captured or missing. The Confederates lost 149 (33 K.I.A.; 115 W.I.A.; 1 missing). See also Charles P. STONE.

BALLS BLUFF AFFAIR. See STONE, Charles P.

BALL'S FERRY, Ga. 23–25 Nov. '64 (MARCH TO THE SEA). Howard's Right Wing had difficulty trying to cross the Oconee near Ball's Bluff. The 1st (US) Ala. Cav., as advance guard, skirmished with pickets that were reinforced by the command of Maj. A. L. Hartridge and some of Wheeler's cavalry. Unable to dislodge Hartridge by frontal assault, Blair (C.G., XVII) ordered his engineers to construct a flying bridge two miles above the ferry. During the night of 24–25 Nov. about 200 men crossed, turning Hartridge's position. The Confederates withdrew, a ponton bridge was put across, and the Federal advance resumed. Losses in killed and wounded were 21 Federals and nine Confederates.

BALTIMORE CROSS ROADS (Crump's C.R.), 1–2 July '63. To support Getty's advance to the SOUTH ANNA RIVER and threaten Richmond during the Gettysburg campaign, Keyes led 6,000 men of his IV Corps up the Peninsula toward Bottom's Bridge on the Chickahominy. After a tiring all-day march over muddy roads the Federals made contact and bivouacked the night of 1–2 July near Bottom's Bridge. The morning of 2 July Keyes decided to withdraw along the New Kent road to Baltimore Cross Roads (5 mi. east of Bottom's Bridge) to guard against attack from the flank or rear. Col. R. M. West's brigade of three regiments, which had led the advance the preceding day, was ordered to cover this withdrawal of H. D. Terry's and B. Porter's brigades. At sunset West was attacked and fought a delaying action to the crossroads; he was supported in this operation by Porter's brigade. The Confederates broke off the action before making contact with Keyes's main force.

Failure of troops in Dix's department to accomplish anything useful resulted in 20,000 of its troops being ordered to Washington for employment elsewhere.

BALTIMORE RIOT. On 19 Apr. '61, when Pennsylvania and Massachusetts militia were en route to Washington, they were attacked by secessionist sympathizers in Baltimore. As the railroad was not continuous through the city, the cars were drawn by horses from one terminal to the other, and after a few cars got through, the tracks were blocked and obstructed. The militia was forced to march while the crowd pursued, throwing bricks and firing a few pistol shots. The militia fired indiscriminately at the people blocking their path. Finally near the terminal police were able to hold the crowd back, while the troops boarded their trains. Four militiamen and 12 civilians were killed. The number wounded is not known.

BANGS, Isaac Sparrow. Union officer. Me. Capt. 20th Me. 29 Aug. '62; Col. 81st US Col. Inf. 2 Mar. '63; Bvt. B.G. USV (Port Hudson).

BANKHEAD, Henry Cary. Union officer. 1828–94. Md. Appt.-N.Y. USMA 1850 (35/44); Inf. Capt. 5th U.S. Inf. 25 June '61; Lt. Col. Asst. I.G. 1 Jan. '63–1 Aug. '65; W.I.A. Dabney's Mill; Bvt. B.G. USV 1 Apr. '65. Brevets for Gettysburg, Spotsylvania, Petersburg, Five Forks.

BANKS, Nathaniel Prentiss. Politician, Union gen. 1816–94. Mass. Maj. Gen. USV 16 May '61; mustered out 24 Aug. '65. Prominent member of Congress 1853–57; Governor of Massachusetts 1858–61; president Illinois Central R.R. He headed Dept. of Annapolis, then Dept. of the Shenandoah. In March '62 he took command of V Corps, which was detached from McClellan's Army of the Potomac in April for service in the Shenandoah Valley. After defeating Stonewall Jackson at Kernstown, detachments from Banks's force and ill-advised reorganizations ordered from Washington helped make Banks a victim of Jackson's brilliant strategic diversion. Subsequent reorganization put him at the head of II Corps in Pope's Army of Va.; at Cedar Mountain he was outgeneraled and defeated again by Jackson. When Pope's army was abolished 12 Sept. '62 Banks commanded the Mil. Dist. cf Washington from that date until 27 Oct. '62. He then succeeded Butler in command of the Dept. of the Gulf. Leading the RED RIVER CAMPAIGN OF 1863 he met several bloody repulses at Port Hudson, capturing that place only after the fall of Vicksburg had rendered it untenable. For this he was given the Thanks of Congress "for the skill, courage, and endurance which compelled the surrender of Port Hudson and thus removed the last obstruction to the free navigation of the Mississippi River." After the unsuccessful RED RIVER CAMPAIGN OF 1864 he was superseded by Canby and resigned. An honest and forthright soldier, he proved consistently unsuccessful as a tactician. He returned to Congress where he served, with the exception of one term, until 1877. He was re-elected in 1888. (Starting in 1853, he served in ten Congresses, although not continuously.) "Owing to an increasing mental disorder" (Miller), he was forced in 1890 to retire from public life. The next year Congress voted him an annual pension of $1,200; three years later he died at his home in Waltham, Mass.

BANKS'S FORD, Va., 4 May '63 (CHANCELLORSVILLE CAMPAIGN). Rivercrossing operation by which Sedgwick withdrew his VI Corps in final stage of Chancellorsville campaign. Benham constructed two ponton bridges near Scott's dam (ford) about a mile below Banks's Ford.

BANNING, Henry B. Union officer. Ohio. Commissioned Capt. 4th Ohio 5 June '61, he was named Col. 87th Ohio 25 June '62 and mustered out the next Oct. On 1 Jan. '63 he was named Lt. Col. 125th Ohio and transferred to the 121st Ohio 5 Apr. '63. He was promoted Col. 10 Nov. '63 and resigned 21 Jan. '65, having been breveted B.G. and Maj. Gen. USV for war service. He died in 1881.

BARBEE'S CROSSROADS (Southeast Manassas Gap), Va. Scene of three separate cavalry actions. The most significant one was 5 Nov. '62, when Pleasonton with about 1,500 attacked about 3,000 Confederate cavalry under Wade Hampton. Col. Gregg led his 8th Pa. Cav. and the 6th US Cav. around the enemy's right, while Col. Davis with the 8th N.Y. attacked the left, and Col. Farnsworth with the 8th Ill. Cav. attacked the center. The Confederates withdrew, and there was no pursuit. Official records give 15 Union and 36 Confederate casualties. This action also called Chester Gap and Markham. (See H. B. McClellan, 180–84.) The minor affair of 25 July '63 involved Maj. Brewer with a portion of the 1st Mich. Cav. On 1 Sept. '63 a detachment of about 50 men of the 6th Ohio Cav. under Maj. Cryer was ambushed by 150 men under Lt. Col. White of the 35th Va. Cav.; the Federals fought their way out with a loss of 30 (Reid, II, 791).

BARBER, Gershom Morse. Union officer. 1822–92. N.Y. 2d Lt. 5th Co. Ohio Sharpshooters 7 Oct. '62; Capt. 1 Nov. '62; Lt. Col. 197th Ohio 15 Apr. '65; Bvt. B.G. USV (war service). He later served as a lawyer and jurist in Cleveland.

BARBETTE. A platform from which a gun can fire over a parapet without an embrasure. A "barbette gun" is one mounted to fire in this manner.

BARDSTOWN, Ky. 5 July '63. A 25-man detachment from the 4th US Cav., under Lt. Sullivan, was surrounded in this place by over 300 men under Col. R. C. Morgan. The Federals fortified and defended a livery stable. The Confederates strung ropes across the streets to prevent their fighting their way out. After refusing several ultimatums, Sullivan surrendered, after fighting off Morgan's men 24 hours, when Confederate artillery was brought into position. (Bardstown was also important in Bragg's campaign in fall of '62 and scene of skirmishes 3, 4, 19 Oct. '62 and 1 Aug. '64.)

BARKER, Mrs. Stephen. SANITARY COMMISSION hospital superintendent. The wife of the 13th Mass. chaplain, she went to Washington with her husband in July '61 and became a nurse. She continued until '64 when she became a "hospital visitor" or superintendent for a number of Washington infirmaries. In the latter part of the year she and her husband were sent on a tour through New York State to lecture and raise money for the Commission. After Appomattox they returned to the capital to aid the homecoming veterans.

BARKSDALE, William. C.S.A. gen. 1821–63. Tenn. After attending the University of Nashville, he studied law and ran a pro-slavery newspaper before fighting in the Mexican War. He resigned his congressional seat as a Democrat from Miss. 12 Jan. '61 when his state seceded, and was named Q.M. Gen. of the Miss. Army from March of that year until he entered the C.S.A. as Col. 13th Miss. He led his regiment at 1st Bull Run and during the Peninsular campaign until 29 June at Savage's Station, when he was given a brigade in McLaws' division, Longstreet's corps. Appointed B.G. C.S.A. 12 Aug. '62, he commanded this brigade at Antietam, Fredericksburg, Chancellorsville, and Gettysburg. Mortally wounded and captured in the Peach Orchard, he died the next day, 3 July.

BARKSDALE'S MISSISSIPPI BRIGADE. In McLaws' division of Longstreet's corps the brigade of William Barksdale was composed of the 13th, 17th, 18th and 21st Miss. regiments. They saw particularly heavy fighting in the defense of Marye's Heights in the first and second battles of Fredericksburg. In the former, on 13 Dec. '62, they lost 29 killed, 151 wounded, and 62 missing, in the successful defense of the position. In the latter, during the Chancellorsville campaign, they held off repeated attacks by Sedgwick's VI Corps until, during a truce to collect the wounded, the Federals saw that the Mississippians had been reduced to a skeleton force. The Federals then attacked again, broke through the Mississippians, and captured several guns of the famous WASHINGTON ARTILLERY. In this action Barksdale's brigade lost 43 killed, 208 wounded, and 341 missing, or a total of 592.

BARLOW, Francis Channing. Union gen. 1834–96. N.Y. Standing first in his Harvard class, he studied law and was a member of the New York *Tribune's* editorial staff. He enlisted as Pvt. 12th N.Y. Mil. 19 Apr. '61 and was married the next day. Named 1st Lt. 1 May, he was mustered out 1 Aug. and commissioned Lt. Col. 61st N.Y. 9 Nov. '61. As Col. (14 Apr. '62), he was at the siege of Yorktown and Fair Oaks and was promoted B.G. USV 19 Sept. '62 after Antietam, where he was severely wounded. He commanded 2, 2, XI (17 Apr.–24 May '63) at Chancellorsville.

Leading the 1st Div. of that corps (24 May–1 July '63), he was severely wounded in the first day's fighting at Gettysburg and left on the field for dead. There is a story that Confederate General John B. Gordon found him, gave him water, and put him in a building for safety. After being exchanged, and after 10 months in the hospital, he commanded 1st Div., II Corps (25 Mar.–29 July '64) at the Wilderness, Spotsylvania, Cold Harbor, and Petersburg. His health then broke, and he went to Europe on an extended leave of absence, returning to command 2d Div., II (6 Apr.–28 May '65) at Sayler's Creek (in reserve) and Farmville. Promoted Maj. Gen. 25 May '65, he commanded the II Corps 22 Apr.–5 May and resigned 16 Nov. '65. He was breveted Maj. Gen. USV 1 Aug. '64 for Spotsylvania. After the war he practiced law and was one of the founders of the American Bar Association. Active in Republican politics, he investigated the Hayes-Tilden election irregularities and held several public offices. As Attorney General for New York he conducted the prosecution of "Boss" Tweed and his ring. Described by D.A.B. as of "medium size, slender, with smooth [clean shaven] face, temperamentally enthusiastic and energetic," he carried "a huge saber, which he says he likes, because when he hits a straggler he wants to hurt him" (Lyman). A monument was erected to him at Gettysburg.

BARNARD, John Gross. Union gen. 1815–82. Mass. USMA 1833 (2/43); Engrs. After serving with engineering projects on the East Coast and on the Gulf, he was in the Mexican War (1 brevet), served on the Pacific coast, and taught engineering at West Point. He was also the Military Academy's Superintendent and when war came was Chief Engineer of Washington (Apr.–July '61) as Maj. (since 1858). Named

B.G. USV 23 Sept. '61, he had participated in the 1st Bull Run campaign and had directed the reconnaissance upon which it was based. As Chief Engineer of the Army of the Potomac (2 July '61–16 Aug. '62), he directed the siege works at Yorktown, and was present at Williamsburg. He reconnoitered and selected the position at which Gaines's Mill was fought and was also at White Oak Swamp and Malvern Hill. Again named Chief Engineer of Washington, he held this post until 5 June '64 when he became Chief Engineer of the Armies in the field on Grant's staff. Breveted for the Peninsula, Lee's surrender (B.G. USA), and war service (Maj. Gen. USA and USV 4 July '64), he continued in the R.A., retiring in 1881 as Col. He wrote many scientific and engineering papers and reports and *The CSA and the Battle of Bull Run* (1862).

BARNES, Charles. Union officer. Ohio. Capt. 9th Pa. Res. 1 May '61; Maj. 1 Apr. '63; mustered out 12 May '64; Capt. 6th Pa. Hv. Arty. 8 Sept. '64; Col. 13 Sept. '64; Bvt. B.G. USV 28 Sept. '65 (war service). Commanded 2d Brig., Defenses South of Potomac, XXII. Died 1896.

BARNES, James. Union gen. 1801–69. Mass. USMA 1829 (5/46); Arty. He taught French and tactics at West Point and served on garrison duty before resigning in 1836 to go into railroad building. Commissioned Col. 18th Mass. 26 July '61, he led his regiment in the Peninsular campaign. He commanded 1, 1, V, Potomac, 10 July–26 Dec. '62 (Antietam and Fredericksburg), 1 Feb.–5 May '63 (Chancellorsville), and 18 Aug.–21 Sept. '63. Promoted B.G. USV 29 Nov. '62, he led the 1st Div., V, 26 Dec. '62–1 Feb. '63 and 5 May–21 July '63 (Aldie, Upperville, and Gettysburg where wounded). He also commanded Norfolk and Portsmouth Dist. 1 Oct. '63–8 Jan. '64 and

Dist. St. Mary's 2–7 July '64 and served on court-martial duty until mustered out in 1866. He never fully recovered from wounds and exposure. He was breveted B.G. USV 29 Nov. '62 and Maj. Gen. USV (war service).

BARNES, Joseph. Union gen. Pa. Entering the R.A. in 1840, as Asst. Surg., he served at West Point, in the Seminole War, and the Mexican War, and on the frontier. He was promoted Lt. Col. Med. Insp. 9 Feb. '63 (Maj. since 1856) and Col. Med. I.G. 10 Aug. of that same year. On 22 Aug. '64 he was named B.G. USA Surg. Gen., and continued in the R.A., retiring in 1882. He died in 1883. He was breveted Maj. Gen. USA for war service.

BARNETT, James. Union officer. 1821–1911. Ohio. Col. 1st Ohio Arty. 16 Oct. '61; Bvt. B.G. USV. Whitelaw Reid in *Ohio in the War* claims that one of Barnett's guns fired the first shot in the war in the West (at Philippi, W.Va.). He was A.D.C. to Thomas and Chief of Arty. for both Rosecrans and Thomas. He later became a prominent banker and businessman.

BARNETT'S FORD, Va. 6–7 Feb. '64. The morning of the 6th Merritt's 1st Cav. Div. (Potomac) drove the Confederate pickets from the Robertson River to the Rapidan. Here, at about 4 P.M., Col. Chapman with parts of the 1st and 2d Brig. was opposed by three Confederate cavalry regiments of Lomax's brigade. On the morning of the 7th Merritt's attempt to cross was blocked by an infantry brigade that had reinforced Lomax. A fire fight lasted until noon. Two Confederate batteries were brought into action. Merritt continued his demonstration until ordered to withdraw. Union losses were 20 killed and wounded (S.G.O.); 5 Confederates were captured (T.U.A.).

BARNEY, Albert Milton. Union officer. N.Y. 1st Lt. 16th N.Y. 15 May '61; Capt. 25 June '62; Lt. Col. 142d N.Y. 12 Feb. '63; Col. 16 Feb. '65; Bvt. B.G. USV 11 Mar. '65 (gallantry in the field). Commanded 1, 2, X (Va. and N.C.; N.C.) Died 1886.

BARNEY, Benjamin Griffin. Union officer. N.Y. Capt. 2d Pa. Hv. Arty. 28 Nov. '62; Lt. Col. 2d Pa. Prov. Hv. Arty. 20 Apr. '64; Bvt. B.G. USV (Petersburg trenches and assault). Died 1886.

BARNEY, Lewis Tappan. Union officer. N.Y. Commissioned 1st Lt. 68th N.Y. 20 Nov. '62, he was promoted Capt. Asst. Adj. Gen. 29 Feb. '64 and resigned 21 June of that year. He was then commissioned Col. 106th N.Y. but not mustered in and was breveted B.G. and Maj. Gen. USV for war service.

BARNUM, Henry A. Union gen. 1833-92. N.Y. A teacher and lawyer, he enlisted as Pvt. 12th N.Y. and was commissioned Capt. on the same day, 13 May '61. He fought at Blackburn's Ford and 1st Bull Run and was promoted Maj. 1 Nov. '61. Gravely wounded at Malvern Hill, he was captured and held in Libby until June. A body believed to be his was buried and a funeral oration delivered at his home. He was named Col. 149th N.Y. 17 Sept. '62 and led his regiment at Gettysburg and Lookout Mountain where he was again wounded. He commanded 3, 2, XX (9 Sept. '64-1 June '65) and was the first officer to enter Savannah. Breveted Maj. Gen. USV for war service, he was given the Medal of Honor in 1889 for Lookout Mountain. He resigned in 1866 and was N.Y. Inspector of Prisons.

BARRETT, Theodore Harvey. Union officer. N.Y. 2d Lt. 9th Minn. 15 Aug. '62; Capt. 29 Aug. '62; Col. 62d Col. Inf. 29 Dec. '63; Bvt. B.G. USV (war service). Commanded Prov. Brig. 1, USCT Dist. Morganza, Dept. of the

Gulf; 2, 2, XV; 3, 1, XV; 2, 2, XV. Died 1900.

BARRETT, Wallace W. Union officer. N.Y.; Mich. R.A. Capt. 44th Ill. 13 Sept. '61; Col. 1 Jan. '63; Bvt. B.G. USV. Brevets for war service, Stones River, Chickamauga, Peach Tree Creek. Commanded 2, 3, XX. Died 1879.

BARRIGER, John Walker. Union officer. c.1832-1906. Ky. USMA 1856 (13/49); Arty.-Comsy. of Subsist. He served in garrison and on the frontier before being promoted 1st Lt. 2d U.S. Arty. 2 May '61. After fighting at 1st Bull Run, he was Chief of Commissariat for Indiana 20 Aug.-20 Nov. '61 and for West Va. until July '62 and 12 Dec. '62-Apr. '63. He was promoted Capt. Com. of Subsis. 3 Aug. '61 and Lt. Col. USV 17 Nov. '63. After serving as Insp. Commissary Dept. of the Ohio Apr.-Nov. '63, he became Chief Commissary of the Army of the Ohio 17 Nov. '63 until Aug. '65 and received four brevets for war service, including Bvt. B.G. USA. He continued in the R.A., retiring in 1896 as Col.

BARRINGER, Rufus. C.S.A. gen. 1821-95. N.C. Graduating from the U. of N.C., he was a lawyer and legislator in the Whig party. Although opposed to secession, he followed his state and was commissioned Capt. 1st N.C. 16 May '61. He fought on the Peninsula and at 2d Bull Run, Antietam, Fredericksburg, Chancellorsville, and Brandy Station, where he was severely wounded. Promoted Maj. 26 Aug. '63 and Lt. Col. Nov. '63, he was appointed B.G. C.S.A. in June '64 and led his brigade under W. H. F. Lee until Sayler's Creek where he was captured 3 Apr. '65. He was held prisoner until July '65. During the war he was wounded three times and lost two horses shot from under him. After the war he espoused the Republican party, practicing law and running his plantation. He was brother-in-law of Stonewall Jackson and D. H. Hill.

BARRY, Henry W. Union officer. Ky. ?–1875. A schoolteacher and lawyer, he was commissioned 1st Lt. 10th Ky. 21 Nov. '61 and resigned 17 Nov. '62. As Col. 8th US Col. Arty. (28 Apr. '64), he raised the first Negro regiment in Ky. As Bvt. B.G. and Maj. Gen. USV, he was mustered out in 1866 and moved to Mississippi, where he was active in Reconstruction politics. He sat in Congress from 1868 until his death.

BARRY, John Decatur. C.S.A. gen. 1839–67. N.C. After enlisting in what became the 18th N.C., he was elected captain in Apr. '62, and fought in Branch's (later Lane's) Brig. through the Seven Days' Battles, and the campaigns of 2d Bull Run and Antietam. A major at Chancellorsville, he is apparently the one who gave the fateful order to fire that resulted in the death of Stonewall Jackson (see Alexander, 341). Appointed colonel, he led the regiment in "Pickett's Charge" at Gettysburg. When Lane was wounded at Cold Harbor, Barry assumed command of the brigade and on 11 Aug. '64 was announced as B.G. to date from the 3d. He was himself wounded a few days later by a sharpshooter, Lane returned to duty, and Barry's B.G. appointment was canceled. While Ezra Warner says he was disabled and assigned to departmental duty in N.C., returns for 31 Jan. '65 show him back in command of the 18th N.C. and those for 28 Feb. show him again commanding the brigade, as a colonel (A.P. Wade). He edited a newspaper in Wilmington after the war, and died there at the age of 27.

BARRY, William Farquhar. Union gen. 1818–79. N.Y. USMA 1838 (17/45); Arty. Serving on the frontier and in the Mexican War, he also fought in the Seminole War and was stationed at Leavenworth during the "Bleeding Kansas" years. Shortly after graduation he had assisted Maj. Ringgold in organizing the first battery of light arty. in the US Army. As Maj. 5th US Arty. 14 May '61, he was in the defense of Ft. Pickens (Fla.) and then fought at 1st Bull Run as McDowell's Chief of Arty. Named B.G. USV 20 Aug. '61, he was Chief of Arty. during the Peninsular campaign and fought at Yorktown, Gaines's Mill, Mechanicsville, Charles City Crossroads, Malvern Hill, and Harrison's Landing. From 20 Sept. '62 to 1 Mar. '64, he was Chief of Arty of the defenses of Washington. In Mar. '64 he became Sherman's Chief of Arty. Breveted for Atlanta (Col. and Mai Gen. USA 1 Sept. '64), J. E. Johnston's surrender (B.G. USA), and war service (Maj. Gen. USA), he continued in the R.A., dying on active duty as Col. 2d US Arty. after heading the Arty. School at Fort Monroe for ten years.

BAR SHOT. See CHAIN SHOT.

BARSTOW, Simon Forrester. Union officer. Mass. R.A. Capt. Asst. A.G. Vols. 6 Mar. '62; Capt. Add. A.D.C 18 Mar. '62; Maj. Asst. A.G. Vols. 15 July '62; Bvt. B.G. USV. Brevets for Richmond, Gettysburg, Petersburg, war service. Died 1882.

BARSTOW, Wilson. Union officer. 1830–69. N.Y. 2d Lt. 37th N.Y. 28 Sept. '61; Capt. Add. A.D.C. 20 June '62; Bvt. B.G. USV (war service); on staffs of Dix and Hooker.

BARTHOLOMEW, Orion A. Union officer. Ind. Sgt. Co. A 7th Ind. 26 Apr. '61; mustered out 2 Aug. '61; 2d Lt. 70th Ind. 1 Aug. '62; 1st Lt. 25 Apr. '63; Lt. Col. 15th US Col. Inf. 1 Jan. '64; Col. 109th US Col. Inf. 25 June '64; Bvt. B.G. USV (war service). Commanded 1, 2, XV.

BARTLETT, Charles Gratiot. Union officer. N.Y. R.A. Sgt. Co. F 7th N.Y. State Mil. 17 Apr. '61; Capt. 5th N.Y. 9 May '61; mustered out 8 Sept. '61; Capt. 12th US Inf. 5 Aug. '61; Lt. Col.

BARTLETT, J. J. **48**

150th N.Y. 29 Sept. '62; mustered out USV 31 Dec. '64; Col. 119th US Col. Inf. 10 May '65; Bvt. B.G. USV. Brevets for Resaca, war service. Retired USA 1896. Drowned 1901.

BARTLETT, Joseph Jackson. Union gen. c. 1834–93. N.Y. Commissioned Maj. 27th N.Y. 21 May and Col. 21 Sept. '61, he commanded 2, 1, VI, Potomac (18 May–Nov.; Dec. '62–1 July '63; 2–4 July '63; 5 Aug.–6 Nov. '63). He was promoted B.G. USV 4 Oct. '62, and his commission expired 4 Mar. '63. Reappointed 30 Mar. '63, he commanded the 3d Div., VI, Potomac (4 July–4 Aug. '63) and 3, 1, V, Potomac (3 Apr.–20 July; 9–17 Aug.; 1 Oct.–23 Dec. '64; 6–27 Jan. '65 and 7 Mar.–1 Apr.). Succeeding to Division (6 Nov.–31 Dec. '63; 3 Feb.–3 Apr. '64; 21 July–9 Aug. '64; 23 Dec. '64–4 Jan. '65), he also commanded 2d Div., IX Corps, Potomac 22 Apr.–3 May '65. Breveted Maj. Gen. USV 1 Aug. '64 for the campaign before Richmond, he was mustered out in 1866 and was US minister to Norway and Sweden 1867–69.

BARTLETT, William Chambers. Union officer. 1839–1908. N.Y. Appt.-At Large. USMA 1862 (20/28); Arty.-Inf. 2d Lt. 3d US Arty. 17 June '62; Capt. A.D.C. Vols. 19 Mar.–16 Nov. '64; Lt. Col. 2d N.C. Mounted Inf. 17 Nov. '64; Bvt. B.G. USV; 1st Lt. 3d Arty. 14 Oct. '64; retired 1892 as Capt. Brevets for Antietam, Campbell's Station, Atlanta, war service. Commanded 1, 4, XXIII; 1, 4th Div. Dist. of East. Tenn.

BARTLETT, William Francis. Union gen. 1840–76. Mass. A student at Harvard, he enlisted as Pvt. 4th Bn. Mass. Vols. 14 Apr. '61, returned to school for a while, and was commissioned Capt. 20th Mass. 8 Aug. '61. Losing a leg at Yorktown, he was mustered out 12 Nov. '62 and then organized and was elected Col. of the 49th Mass. 19 Nov. '62. Twice wounded at Pt. Hudson, he organized the 57th Mass. (Col.) 9 Apr. '64 and was wounded leading it in the Wilderness. As B.G. USV 20 June '64, he commanded 1, 1, IX, Potomac (23–30 July '64) in the Petersburg mine assault where he was wounded and captured. He also commanded the division (17 June–15 July '65) and was mustered out in 1866 after being breveted Maj. Gen. USV for war service. He was later in business in Richmond (Va.) and Pittsfield (Mass.).

BARTON, Clara. Philanthropist. 1821–1912. Mass. A clerk in the Washington Patent Office when the Civil War broke out, she organized an agency for getting medical supplies, aid, and care to the soldiers. Lincoln in 1865 appointed her to attend to correspondence with relatives of missing prisoners, and she compiled from burial and hospital records a list of these men. In 1869 she went to Geneva as a member of the International Red Cross and succeeded in 1882 in having the US sign the Geneva agreement. She organized the American National Committee in 1877, which three years later became the American Red Cross, and was its first president (1882–1904). She also served in Cuba during the Spanish-American war and published in 1882 the *History of the Red Cross*.

BARTON, Seth Maxwell. C.S.A. gen. 1829–1900. Va. USMA 1849 (28/43); Inf. Serving in garrison and on the frontier in Indian fighting, he resigned 11 June '61 as Capt. to become Capt. of C.S.A. Inf. In July '61 he joined the 3d Ark. at Cheat Mountain and Greenbrier River and was Jackson's Chief Engr. that winter. He was appointed B.G. C.S.A. to rank from 11 Mar. '62 and led a brigade under Kirby Smith in east Tenn. until Dec. when he went to Vicksburg. Leading the 1st Brig. under Stevenson at Chickasaw Bayou, Chickasaw Bluffs (while O.R. lists such an engagement and Union Army called it that, there are no Chickasaw Bluffs), Champion's Hill, and the Vicksburg siege, he was paroled and exchanged and took Armistead's brigade to N.C. for recruiting and reorganization. He commanded his brigade at New Bern in Jan. '64 and under Ransom at the Wilderness and was criticized both times for lack of cooperation. He asked for a Court of Inquiry that was never granted, and the regimental commanders in the brigade sent a petition to Richmond stating their confidence in him. He was finally given a brigade that fall in the defenses of Richmond. He was captured at Sayler's Creek and released from Ft. Warren in July '65.

BARTON, William Brainerd. Union officer. N.J. Lt. Col. 48th N.Y. 21 Aug. '61; Col. 18 June '62; Bvt. B.G. USV (Ft. Wagner, S.C.; war service). Commanded Barton's brigade, Dist. Hilton Head (S.C.), X Corps, and Fla. Expedition, X Corps; Ames's div., Dist. of Fla.; 2, 2, Dept. of Va. and N.C. Died 1891.

BARTOW, Francis S. C.S.A. officer. Ga. A lawyer and legislator, he was a C.S.A. Congressman and Capt. of the Oglethorpe Rifles, an infantry company in Savannah. A detail from this volunteer organization seized Ft. Pulaski and the company became part of the 8th Ga. Bartow was elected the regiment's colonel and joined Johnston's Army of the Shenandoah. He was killed leading the 2d Brigade at 1st Bull Run (21 July '61). He is not listed as a general officer by Wright but is carried on Heitman's list, and Wood gives the date of B.G. commission as 21 July '61. Freeman, who has many references to the "chivalrous" Bartow in *Lee's Lieutenants,* says that he was indeed only a colonel, but

"popularly he was counted as a general officer."

BASSETT, Isaac C. Union officer. Pa. Capt. 82d Pa. 21 Sept. '61; Maj. 7 Feb. '63; Col. 3 May '63; Bvt. B.G. USV 12 Dec. '64 (Richmond campaign). Commanded 3, 1, VI (Potomac; Shenandoah). Died 1869.

BATCHELDER, Richard Napoleon. Union officer. N.H. R.A. 1st Lt. Rgt. Q.M. 1st N.H. 2 May '61; mustered out 9 Aug. '61; Capt. Asst. Q.M. Vols. 3 Aug. '61–8 June '65; Lt. Col. Q.M. assigned 1 Jan. '63–1 Aug. '64; Col. Q.M. assigned 2 Aug. '64–5 Sept. '65; Capt. assigned Q.M. USA 16 Feb. '65; Bvt. B.G. USV (war service). Medal of Honor 20 May '95 for gallantry against Mosby's guerrillas between Catlett's and Fairfax Stations 13–15 Oct. '63. B.G. Q.M. Gen. 26 June '90; retired 27 July '96. Died 1901.

BATE, William Brimage. C.S.A. gen. 1826–1905. Tenn. After working on a Miss. river boat, he fought in the Mexican War and ran a Democratic newspaper before sitting in the state legislature. He then went to the law school at Lebanon (Tenn.) and held various public offices as a strong advocate of secession and states rights. Commissioned Col. 2d Tenn., he was wounded at Shiloh and was appointed B.G. C.S.A. 3 Oct. '62. He fought at Stones River, Chattanooga, Missionary Ridge, in the Atlanta campaign, and at Franklin and Nashville, having been promoted Maj. Gen. 23 Feb. '64. Wounded three times during the war, he had six horses shot from under him. He was offered the governorship of Tennessee in 1863 and refused it, saying that so long as the enemy was in his state, his duty was to fight, not to reap civil honors. In 1882 he was elected Governor for the first of two terms and was Senator

1886-1905 as well as a Democratic power in his state.

BATES, Delevan. Union officer. N.Y. 2d Lt. 121st N.Y. 23 Aug. '62; 1st Lt. 4 July '63; mustered out 19 Mar. '64; Col. 30th US Col. Inf. 23 Mar. '64; Bvt. B.G. USV 30 July '64 for Cemetery Hill (Va.); mustered out 10 Dec. '65; awarded Medal of Honor 22 June '91 for gallantry at Cemetery Hill (Va.) 30 July '64. Commanded 1, 3, IX; 1, 1, XXV; 1, 3, XXV; 1, Paine's division, Terry's Prov. Corps; 1, 3, X; 3d Div., X Corps.

BATES, Edward. Union Attorney General. 1793-1869. Va. A lawyer in Missouri, he held numerous minor political offices and sat in the state legislature and US Congress. He was a leader in the Whig party before joining the Republicans and was the subject of a strong movement for the presidency in 1860. Lincoln appointed him Attorney General, and he served until 24 Nov. '64, when he resigned to return to Missouri. There he defeated the RADICAL REPUBLICANS who had seized control of the state government.

BATES, Erastus Newton. Union officer. Mass. Maj. 80th Ill. 25 Aug. '62; Lt. Col. 25 Jan. '65; Bvt. B.G. USV (war service).

BATON ROUGE, La. 5 Aug. '62. The Federals had occupied Baton Rouge 12 May '62, been frustrated in their attempts to capture Vicksburg by naval action, and had finally dropped back to Baton Rouge 26 July. Van Dorn then ordered an attack by 5,000 picked men of Breckinridge's command, which were to be reinforced by another 1,000 troops under Ruggles. Breckinridge organized his force into two divisions: the first, under Charles Clark, included the brigades of B. H. Helm and T. B. Smith; the second, under Ruggles, comprised the brigades of A. P. Thompson and

H. W. Allen. Three artillery batteries and two mounted companies of Partisan Rangers (about 250 men) were also attached. The Confederate ram *Arkansas* was to attack Federal gunboats while land forces attacked Baton Rouge from the east. Brig. Gen. Thomas Williams defended the town with approximately 2,500 effectives in seven regiments of XIX Corps (see below). (B.&L., III, 585, gives details of opposing forces.) With Clark on the right (north), Breckinridge attacked in a dense fog between the Clinton and Clay Cut roads. The 14th Me., 21st Ind., and 6th Mich. were forced back; reinforcement by the 4th Wis. and 9th Conn. (from the Federal left) and the 30th Mass. (from the right flank) could not stop the Confederates until they had overrun and destroyed the Federal camps and come under the fire of the gunboats *Essex, Kineo,* and *Katahdin.* The Confederate *Arkansas* had developed engine trouble two days previously but had pressed on. It arrived during the land battle and was preparing to attack the *Essex* when failure of the starboard engine drove her hard aground. Deprived of this vital naval support, the Confederates were driven back. Williams was killed and Union losses were 383. The Confederates lost 453 out of 2,600 engaged, 250 of whom the Federals buried on the field.

BATTLE, Cullen Andrews. C.S.A. gen. 1829-1905. Ga. A lawyer, he was an ardent secessionist and spoke throughout the South in favor of secession. When John Brown attacked Harpers Ferry in 1859, Battle organized a volunteer company in Alabama and offered it to Gov. Wise of Virginia for the state's defense. This was not accepted, but the company was expanded and organized as a militia regiment with Battle as Lt. Col. His state commission was terminated so that he could become Maj. 3d Ala. in 1861. He was promoted Lt. Col. at the outset of the Peninsular campaign and as Col. led the regiment at Seven Pines, Antietam (in Rodes's brigade), and Fredericksburg. Hurt a few days before Chancellorsville by a fall from his horse, he led the 3d Ala. briefly but wrenched his back and was out of action for seven weeks. At Gettysburg his regiment fought in O'Neal's brigade and he was promoted B.G. C.S.A. 20 Aug. '63 for his actions in that battle. At the Wilderness and Spotsylvania he led a brigade in Rodes's division, Ewell's corps. During the battle of Cedar Creek he was severely wounded leading his brigade in Ramseur's division and saw no more field service. D.A.B. incorrectly says he was promoted Maj. Gen. C.S.A. Wright does not list him as such. After the war he was active as a lawyer and elected to Congress but was not admitted because he would not take the IRONCLAD OATH.

BATTLE ABOVE THE CLOUDS. Another name for action at Lookout Mountain during CHATTANOOGA CAMPAIGN.

"BATTLE HYMN OF THE REPUBLIC." Lyrics written in 1861 by Mrs. Julia Ward Howe for the Union Army because she disliked the words sung by a regiment to the music written by William Steffe in 1852. The song had been known as "John Brown's Body Lies A-moulderin' in the Grave" and "We'll Hang Old Jeff Davis from a Sour Apple Tree." Mrs. Howe's "Battle Hymn" was first printed in Feb. '62, in the *Atlantic Monthly,* and almost immediately became popular.

BATTLE MOUNTAIN, Va., 24 July '63. Advance guard, 5th Mich. Cav. of Custer's brigade, moving from Amissville toward Newby's C.R. to strike the flank of the retreating Confederate forces, made contact with forces from A. P. Hill's corps and Benning's brigade of Longstreet's corps. Custer attacked with the rest of his brigade and forced the Confederate column to halt and fight. In withdrawing in the face of superior forces, the 5th and 6th were cut off and had to fight their way out.

BAXTER, DeWitt Clinton. Union officer. Mass. Lt. Col. 19th Pa. 27 Apr. '61; mustered out 9 Aug. '61; Col. 72d Pa. 10 Aug. '61; Bvt. B.G. USV (Gettysburg, Wilderness). Commanded 2, 2, II; 1, 2, II; 2, II. Died 1881.

BAXTER, Henry. Union gen. 1821–73. N.Y. Commissioned Capt. 7th Mich. 22 Aug. '61 and Lt. Col. 1 July '62, he led the regiment in an assault crossing at Fredericksburg 13 Dec. '62 to drive out enemy sharpshooters who were preventing the crossing of the main force. He was shot in the lung during this. Promoted B.G. USV 12 Mar. '63, he commanded 2, 2, V, Potomac (Apr.–6 May '63); 2, 2, I (21 Apr.–31 Dec. '63); and 2d Div., V, Potomac (24 Mar.–Apr. '64). Breveted for the Wilderness-Dabney's Mills-Five Forks (Maj. Gen. USV 1 Apr. '65), he was mustered out 24 Aug. '65 after having been wounded three times in the course of the war. He was US Minister to Honduras 1866–69.

BAXTER SPRINGS, Kans., 6 Oct. '63. Quantrill's raiders surprised and routed a Federal escort of 100 men accompanying the movement of Gen. James G. Blunt's headquarters (Army of the Frontier) from Ft. Scott to Ft. Smith. Maj. H. S. Curtis, son of Gen. S. R. Curtis, was among approximately 65 Federals killed. The raiders, who wore Federal uniforms, are alleged to have given no quarter and to have mutilated corpses. As part of this action a nearby camp of 100 Federals was surprised during dinner; the defenders, two thirds of whom were colored troops, had to run a gauntlet of enemy fire to get to their weapons. (See Monaghan, 293ff.)

BAYARD, George Dashiell. Union gen. 1835–62. N.Y. Appt.-At Large. USMA 1856 (11/49); Cav. Fighting in the Indian Wars and wounded in the face by a poisoned arrow, he was cavalry instructor at West Point (Capt. 4th US Cav. 20 Aug. '61) when given leave of absence to command 1st Pa. Cav. (Col. 14 Sept. '61). He fought at Dranesville and against Jackson in the Valley at Harrisonburg and Pt. Republic. He was named B.G. USV 28 Apr. '62 and commanded Cav. Brig., III, Army Va. (26 June–12 Sept. '62). Led advance to Cedar Mountain (9 Aug.). Leading the Cav. Brig., Left Grand Div., Potomac (Sept.–13 Dec. '62), he was mortally wounded at Fredericksburg and died 14 Dec.

BAYLOR, John R. C.S.A. officer and Governor of the Arizona Territory. As Capt. in the Texas militia, he organized in Dec. '60 a "buffalo hunt" that turned into the nucleus of the state Confederate forces. Named Lt. Col. C.S.A., he was in the command that took Twiggs's surrender in May in San Antonio and then led a body of 300 troops up the Rio Grande into the New Mex. Territory in June '61. Occupying Messilla, he captured Ft. Fillmore on 27 July and was then joined briefly by A. S. Johnston's party on their way from California to Richmond. On 1 Aug. '61 he took possession of the Arizona Territory. Baylor was Governor of Confed. States Terr. of Arizona in '61 and '62 until removed by Davis and his commission revoked. He served as a private in Galveston Campaign of '63 and remained a private. Heitman lists him, however, as a general officer.

BAYONET ATTACKS were rare in the Civil War. Among the few recorded instances are the charge of the 17th Wisc. at Corinth, Miss., 3 Oct. '62, routing a Mississippi brigade; and the night bayonet attack of the 6th Me. and 5th Wisc. at RAPPAHANNOCK BRIDGE AND KELLY'S FORD, Va., 7 Nov. '63. See also EDGED WEAPONS for casualty figures showing ineffectiveness of the bayonet.

BAYOU RAPIDES, La. Alternate name for action at Henderson's Hill, 21 Mar. '64 in RED RIVER CAMPAIGN.

BAYOU TECHE, La., 3 Nov. '62; 14 Jan. '63; and 12–14 Apr. '63. Three actions are associated with Bayou Teche, La. The first, 3 Nov. '62, was an affair involving the 21st Ind. Vol. Regt. and the Union gunboats *Kinsman, Estrella, St. Mary, Calhoun,* and *Diana.*

The second, 14 Jan. '63, was fought by all of the above gunboats except *St. Mary* and troops of the recently-created XIX Corps.

For the action of 12–14 Apr. '63 see IRISH BEND AND FORT BISLAND, LA.

BEADLE, William Henry Harrison. Union officer. 1838–1915. Ind. 1st Lt. 31st Ind. 5 Sept. '61; Capt. 9 Nov. '61; resigned 9 Feb. '62; Lt. Col. 1st Mich. Sharpshooters 1 Jan. '63; resigned 15 June '64; Maj. Vet. Res. Corps 30 May '64; Bvt. B.G. USV (war service). Commanded 3, Defenses S. of Potomac, XXII. W.I.A. Bridge Creek (Miss.) in left leg. Prominent in Dakota public education, he is credited with saving the public lands for the school system.

BEAL, George Lafayette. Union gen. 1825–96. Me. Commissioned Capt. 1st Me. 3 May and mustered out 5 Aug. '61, he was named Col. 10th Me. 26 Oct. '61, mustered out 8 May '63 and commissioned Col. 29th Me. 17 Dec. '63. As B.G. USV 30 Nov. '64, he commanded, in the Gulf, 2, 1, XIX (15 Feb.–24 Mar. '64) and 1, 1, XIX (18

ۡpr.–5 July '64). He also led the brigade ۡn the Army of the Shenandoah (6 Aug.– 14 Oct. and 13 Dec. '64–20 Mar. '65) and led 1st Brig., 1st Prov. Div., Army Shenandoah, and 1, Dwight's Div., XXII, Washington. Breveted for war service (B.G. USV 22 Aug. '64 and Maj. Gen. USV), he was mustered out in 1866.

BEALE, Richard Lee Turberville. C.S.A. gen. 1819–93. Va. After Dickinson College and the University of Virginia he studied law and served in the state legislature and US Congress. In May '61 he was commissioned 1st Lt. in "Lee's Legion" or "Lee's Light Horse" on patrol duty along the Potomac. He was promoted Capt. in July and Maj. in October. In the spring of '62 this company was merged with the 9th Va. Cav. and Beale was promoted Lt. Col. in Apr. He fought in the Peninsula, at 2d Bull Run and in Maryland, certainly to the satisfaction of his superiors but not happily, for he submitted his resignation three times and in the last letter begged to be allowed to form a company of independent rangers or to enlist as a private. He was promoted Col. of the 9th Va. Cav. in Oct. and led it at Fredericksburg and Gettysburg. He was severely wounded in a skirmish in Sept. '63. His troops killed Dahlgren and forwarded the controversial DAHLGREN PAPERS to Richmond. Late in '64 he was given a brigade and finally appointed B.G. C.S.A. 6 Feb. '65 (D.A.B.). His commission was late because his papers were misplaced when the War Office clerks were drafted. Wright gives the date of his B.G. commission as 6 Jan. '65. After the war he returned to the law and to Congress.

BEALETON STATION, Va., 28 Mar. '62. Reconnaissance in force by elements of Howard's and Meagher's brigades (5th N.H., 61st N.Y., 8th Ill., plus attachments). Enemy withdrew,

burned bridge across Rappahannock. Two brigades of Ewell's corps were driven by Federal artillery from opposite shore.

BEALL, William N.R. C.S.A. gen. 1825–83. Ky. Appt.-Ark. USMA 1848 (30/38); Inf.-Cav. He served on the frontier in Indian fighting and scouting, exploration, and in Kansas during the border disturbances before resigning as Capt. 20 Aug. '61 to be commissioned Capt. C.S.A. At first in Arkansas under Van Dorn, he was appointed B.G. C.S.A. 11 Apr. '62 and on the 23d of that month assigned by Beauregard to command the cavalry at Corinth. He commanded the post of Pt. Hudson starting 25 Sept. '62 and then commanded a brigade there until surrendered 8 July '63. Released on parole '64 to act as Confed. agent in exchange of prisoners with office in N.Y., he was finally released 2 Aug. '65. He became a general commission merchant in St. Louis.

BEAN'S STATION, Tenn., 15 Dec. '63. (KNOXVILLE CAMPAIGN) Having learned that three Federal cavalry brigades were at this place, Longstreet undertook to capture them. His plan was to move his infantry directly on the station from his bivouac at Rogersville. W. T. Martin with four cavalry brigades was to go down the south side of the Holston River and cross at or below the station, while "Grumble" Jones with two cavalry brigades was to go down the north side of the Clinch Mountains and cut off the Federal retreat at Bean's Station gap. Although Jones and the infantry performed their part of the operation well, Martin mishandled his part, and Shackelford's cavalry escaped to Blain's C.R. without more serious loss than a few wagons. "Pursuit was attempted but was futile, Longstreet maintained, because Evander Law was slow and Lafayette McLaws was loath to move before bread was issued the hungry men" (*Lee's Lts.*, III, 299). The failure was one of the frustrations of the campaign that led Longstreet to relieve Law, McLaws, and Jerome Robertson of command.

BEARDSLEE TELEGRAPH. A portable military telegraph developed by George W. Beardslee and adopted by A. J. MYER to provide a mobile field telegraph system. The instrument was operated by hand-turned magnetos and did not require the heavy batteries needed in the civilian telegraphs. Instead of using the usual key for transmission, it had an alphabet dial and pointer. When the index was set at a letter on the sending set, a similar index indicated the same letter on a receiving set. The instrument was protected by a rugged wooden box and was transported in a "Flying Telegraph Train." The latter consisted of two Beardslees in two wagons along with five hand reels, five miles of gutta-percha insulated wire, 200 lance poles, and miscellaneous tools. About 70 sets were produced and some 30 Flying Trains organized.

Limitations of the instrument were its short range of about ten miles due to insufficient power, slow transmission, frequent lack of synchronization between sending and receiving sets, and vulnerability of the field wire to curious soldiers.

It was first used 24 May '62 in the Peninsular campaign. Its first major triumph was during the battle of Fredericksburg when it provided Burnside with communications across the river when fog and smoke had rendered the usual visual signal communication impossible. After this its popularity declined since it was often competing with the faster and more powerful commercial telegraph facilities.

When the Signal Corps lost the battle with the Military Telegraph Service, and was required by Stanton on 10 Nov. '63 to turn over all its telegraph equipment to the latter, the Beardslee system was discarded. Only its insulated field wire was kept in use.

BEATTY, John. Union gen. 1828–1914. Ohio. A bank clerk, he was commissioned Lt. Col. 3d Ohio 27 Apr. '61 and Col. 12 Feb. '62. As B.G. USV (29 Nov. '62) at Stones River, he commanded 2, 1st Div. Center, XIV, Cumberland (26 Dec. '62–9 Jan. '63) and then led 2, 1, XIV (19 Jan.–17 Apr. '63). He then led the 1st Brig. (17 Apr.–10 Oct. '63) and 2d Brig. (10 Nov. '63–1 Feb. '64) in the 2d Div., XIV. He resigned 28 Jan. '64. He was later in Congress.

BEATTY, Samuel. Union gen. 1820–85. Pa. After the Mexican War he was sheriff and then commissioned Capt. 19th Ohio 27 Apr. '61 and Col. 29 May '61. He commanded in the Army Ohio, 11th Brig., 5th Div. (27 May–29 Sept. '62) and 11th Brig., 5th Div., II (Sept.–Nov. '62). At Stones River he led 1, 3d Div. Left Wing, XIV (5 Nov.–31 Dec. '62) and succeeded to command of the division (31 Dec. '62–9 Jan. '63). Promoted B.G. USV 29 Nov. '62, he commanded 1, 3, XXI (11 Apr.–9 Oct. '63) and the division (9 Jan.–13 Mar. '63). He also commanded 3, 3, IV (10 Oct. '63–7 Feb. '64; 16 Apr.–23 May '64; 6 Nov.–2 Dec. '64 and 20 Mar.–7 June '65) and 2, 3, IV (7 June–1 Aug. '65). At Franklin and Nashville he led the 3d Div., IV (2 Dec. '64–31 Jan. '65 and 7 Feb.–20 Mar. '65). One of the outstanding commanders in the West, he was breveted Maj. Gen. USV for war service and mustered out in 1866.

BEAUFORT, N.C. 11–26 Apr. '62. Besieged and captured by Federals in BURNSIDE'S EXPEDITION TO N.C.

BEAUREGARD, Pierre Gustave Toutant. C.S.A. gen. 1818–93. La. USMA 1838 (2/45); Engrs. He served in the Mexican War as Engr. on Scott's staff (2 brevets, 2 wounds). With the title of Chief Engr. in charge of draining New Orleans 1858–61, he did not actually do any work on this project. He did improve navigation of the mouths of the Miss. R. and direct construction of the customhouse. Then Superintendent of West Point 23–28 Jan. '61, he was transferred after telling a La. cadet he would go with his state if it seceded. Resigning 20 Feb. '61 as Bvt. Maj., he was at once appointed B.G. C.S.A. (1 Mar. '61) and sent to Charleston where he commanded the attack on FT. SUMTER. The "Hero of Sumter," he returned to Richmond as the conqueror who could lead the Confederacy to victory. On 1 June '61 he was given command of the Confederate forces near Manassas Junction. At 1ST BULL RUN, he commanded the line while J. E. Johnston, in over-all command, hurried reinforcements forward. Promoted Gen. in the regular C.S.A. on 31 Aug. '61 to rank from 21 July, he was transferred in early '62 to the West where he was second-in-command to A. S. Johnston at SHILOH. He turned over his command temporarily, he thought, to Bragg in June '62 when he went on sick leave. Jeff Davis, however, relieved him on the charge of leaving his post without authority. Upon his recovery he returned to Charleston in command of the defenses of the Carolina and Georgia coasts and early in '64 he defeated Butler at DREWRY'S BLUFF and bottled him up in Bermuda Hundred. He fought off the PETERSBURG ASSAULTS of 15–18 June '64 and then his command was merged with the A.N.V. After commanding the DIVISION OF THE WEST, he returned as second-in-command to J. E. Johnston in the CAROLINAS CAMPAIGN. After the war he was a railroad president, refusing offers to command the Rumanian and Egyptian armies. He later was supervisor of

drawings for the La. Lottery, for which he was criticized. Writing on military subjects, he published, among others, *Report on the Defenses of Charleston* (1864) and *A Commentary on the Campaign and Battle of Manassas* (1891).

BEAUREGARD'S CORPS. See CORPS, Confed., I, A.N.V.

BEAVER, James Addams. Union officer. 1837–1914. Pa. 1st Lt. 2d Pa. 21 Apr. '61; mustered out 22 July '61; Lt. Col. 45th Pa. 21 Oct. '61; resigned 4 Sept. '62; Col. 148th Pa. 8 Sept. '62; Bvt. B.G. USV (Cold Harbor). Commanded 1, 1, II (Potomac); 3, 1, II (Potomac). Discharged 22 Dec. '64. W.I.A. Chancellorsville 3 May '63 and Reams's Station 25 Aug. '64. Elected Governor of Pa. in 1887; also prominent as judge and conservationist.

BEAVER DAM STATION, Va., 9–10 May '64. (SHERIDAN'S RICHMOND RAID) On 9 May the 1st Mich. Cav. entered this place at the head of Custer's brigade and destroyed two locomotives, more than 100 railroad cars, 10 miles of track, reserve medical stores, 504,000 bread rations, and 915,000 meat rations. (*Lee's Lts.,* III, 414.) The transportation loss was the most serious, since the Virginia Central R.R. had only eight engines in running order and 108 cars. (*R. E. Lee,* III, 314.) Custer also recaptured 378 Union prisoners who had been taken in the Wilderness.

BECKWITH, Amos. Union officer. 1825–94. Vt. USMA 1850 (21/44); Arty. Capt. Comsy. of Subsist. 10 May '61; Maj. Comsy. of Subsist. 29 Sept. '61; Col. Add. A.D.C. 1 Jan. '62; mustered out as Add. A.D.C. 31 May '66; Lt. Col. Asst. Comsy. Gen. of Subsist. 1874; Col. 28 Aug. '88; retired 1889; Bvt. B.G. USV; Bvt. Maj. Gen. USA. Brevets for Atlanta, war service. He served as chief of the commissary depot in Washington, chief of commissariat (Mil. Div. Miss.), on Sherman's staff during Atlanta campaign, and as chief of commissary, Dept. of the Gulf.

BECKWITH, Edward G. Union officer. c. 1818–81. N.Y. USMA 1842 (13/56); Arty. He fought in the Mexican War, and served in western explorations and Indian fighting before becoming chief of commissariat for the Dept. of Pa. (29 Apr.–25 July '61), of the Shenandoah (25 July '61–Feb. '62), of the V Corps (8 Mar.–27 June '62) and of the Army of Va. (27 June–2 Sept. '62). Named Col. Add. A.D.C. (5 July '62–31 May '66), he continued to be chief of commissariat, outfitting Banks's New Orleans expedition and of the Dept. of the Gulf (17 Dec. '62–July '65). He was promoted Maj. 2d U.S. Arty. 8 Feb. '64 and breveted B.G. USA for war service. He continued in the R.A., retiring in 1879 because of ill health.

BEDEL, John. Union officer. 1822–75. N.H. Maj. 3d N.H. 26 Aug. '61; Lt. Col. 27 June '62; Col. 6 Apr. '64; Bvt. B.G. USV (war service). Captured 18 July '63 at Ft. Wagner; paroled 9 Dec. '64. Also served as Sgt. and 2d Lt. in 1847–48. Later a lawyer and politician.

BEE, Barnard Elliott. C.S.A. gen. 1824–61. S.C. USMA 1845 (33/41); Inf. He served on the frontier and in the Mexican War (2 brevets, 1 wound) and resigned 3 Mar. '61 as Capt. to become Maj. of C.S.A. Inf. Appointed B.G. C.S.A. 17 June '61, he commanded a brigade under Johnston at 1st Bull Run and immortalized Jackson and his brigade by his famous "stonewall" allusion. (See STONEWALL BRIGADE for circumstances and exact wording.) Mortally wounded, he died the next day, 22 July. D.A.B. says that he had "a capacity for command that was not usual in the early days of the war." His father was Secretary of State in the Republic of Texas.

BEE, Hamilton Prioleau. C.S.A. gen. 1822–97. S.C. Appt.-Tex. The brother of Barnard E. Bee, he had held various public offices before fighting in the Mexican War with the Texas Rangers. A legislator and B.G. in the Tex. militia, he was appointed B.G. C.S.A. 6 Mar. '62 to rank from the 4th and given the command at Brownsville. An excellent administrator, he had no field experience until the spring of 1864 when he was given a cav. brig. in the Red River Expedition. He was criticized for his actions at Sabine Crossroads and Monett's Ferry. In Feb. '65 he led his division in Wharton's cavalry corps and then took over a brig. in Maxey's infantry division. Although he was paroled as Maj. Gen., no record of appointment or confirmation has been found.

BEECHER, Henry Ward. Preacher. 1813–87. Conn. Pastor of the Plymouth Congregational Church in Brooklyn and an impressive speaker, he had a nationwide influence as an advocate of abolition and women suffrage. His sister was Harriet Beecher STOWE, author of *Uncle Tom's Cabin.* See also "BEECHER'S BIBLES."

BEECHER, James Chaplin. Union officer. 1828–86. Mass. Chap. 67th N.Y. 31 Aug. '61; resigned 8 Sept. '62; Lt. Col. 141st N.Y. 14 Oct. '62; resigned 6 Mar. '63; Lt. Col. 35th US Col. Inf. 18 May '63; Col. 9 June '63; Bvt. B.G. USV (war service). Commanded 3d African Brig., Forces N. End Folly Island, X; 3, Vodges's Div., X. Son of Lyman Beecher, the Congregationalist preacher, and brother of Henry Ward Beecher. He was a missionary to China at the outbreak of the war and went back to the ministry afterward. He committed suicide in 1886.

"BEECHER'S BIBLES" were SHARPS CARBINES (Shields, 88) and/or rifles, so called because many of them were shipped into BLEEDING KANSAS in crates labeled "Bibles" and/or because Henry Ward BEECHER had professed to see "more moral power in one of those instruments so far as the slaveholders were concerned than in a hundred Bibles." (Bruce, 112.)

BEECH GROVE, Tenn. See TULLAHOMA CAMPAIGN.

BELKNAP, William Worth. Union gen. and Secretary of War. 1829–90. N.Y. After Princeton, he practiced law and was a Democratic state legislator when commissioned Maj. 15th Iowa, 7 Dec. '61. He fought at Shiloh, was promoted Lt. Col. 20 Aug. '62 and fought at Corinth. As Col. 3 June '63, he fought in the Vicksburg campaign. He was named B.G. USV 30 July '64 and commanded, in the Atlanta campaign, 3, 4, XVII, Tenn. (31 July–21 Sept. and 31 Oct. '64–29 May '65). He also led the 4th Div. (20 Sept.–31 Oct. 64; 1–26 June '65 and 9–27 July '65) and the XVII Corps (19 July–1 Aug. '65). Breveted Maj. Gen. USV for war service, he was mustered out 24 Aug. '65. Serving as Grant's Secretary of War 1869–76, he was impeached for accepting bribes, but as his resignation came before the trial began, the charges were dropped for lack of jurisdiction.

BELL, George. Union officer. c. 1828–1907. Md. USMA 1853 (14/52); Arty.-Comsy. He fought in the Seminole war and served on the frontier before being named Capt. Staff Comsy. of Subsist. 3 Aug. '61 (1st Lt. since 1855). During the Civil War he was with the Alexandria Subsistence Depot and the Army of the Potomac, being breveted B.G. USA 9 Apr. '65 for war service.

BELL, John Hann. Union officer. c. 1836–75. Mich. 1st Lt. 5th N.Y. 12 Nov. '61; Capt. 14 June '62; Maj. 12 Jan. '63; Maj. Vet. Res. Corps 9 June '63; Lt. Col. 29 Sept. '63; Bvt. B.G.

USV 30 Nov. '65 (war service). W.I.A. Yorktown in left shoulder and head.

BELL, Joseph Warren. Union officer. N.C. Col. 13th Ill. Cav. 31 Dec. '61; Bvt. B.G. USV (war service); mustered out 25 May '63. Died 1879.

BELL, Tyree H. C.S.A. gen. 1815–1902. Tenn. Commissioned Capt. 12th Tenn. 4 June '61 he was shortly elected Lt. Col. and led the regiment at Belmont and Shiloh, where he had two horses shot from under him. In July '62 he was promoted Col. and fought at Richmond (Ky.) and then had a cavalry command in Tenn. and Ky. During the battle of Perryville he was raiding in the Union rear and during Stones River he was menacing their flank and rear. On 25 Jan. '64 he was given a cavalry brigade by Forrest and fought at Ft. Pillow, Tishomingo Creek, Harrisburg in the Tupelo campaign, and in other of Forrest's raids during the remainder of the war. He was commissioned B.G. C.S.A. 28 Feb. '65.

BELLE GROVE, Va. 19 Oct. '64. CEDAR CREEK, same date.

BELLE ISLE. Confederate prison in the James River at Richmond. Used only for enlisted men, it was occupied continuously after 1st Bull Run and by the end of 1863 held about 10,000 men. Since it was the objective of a number of cavalry forays, notably the KILPATRICK-DAHLGREN RAID, and was also a drain on the city's food supply, the prisoners were moved to ANDERSONVILLE, Ga.

BELMONT, Mo. 7 Nov. '61. On 1 Nov. '61 Grant had been directed to make demonstrations down both sides of the Mississippi from his base at Cairo, while C. F. Smith was to conduct similar operations from Paducah to keep the Confederate force of Polk at Columbus, Ky., off balance. A short time later Grant was ordered to undertake diversions that would assist a movement being made from Pilot Knob, Mo., to drive the forces of M. Jeff Thompson from southeast Missouri into Arkansas. Grant had started moving the brigades of Oglesby and Wallace and the 10th Ia. along the west side of the Mississippi in the general direction of New Madrid, and was moving Cook's brigade toward Columbus on the east bank, while he himself led another demonstration down the Mississippi toward Belmont to menace that place. In cooperation with these movements C. F. Smith ordered Paine's brigade with a reinforcing regiment from Paducah to advance in the direction of Columbus.

Grant personally led a force of 3,114 troops down the river in transports, under the protection of the gunboats *Tyler* and *Lexington,* to a point on the Kentucky shore nine miles below Cairo. Having made these dispositions to worry Polk about a possible attack, Grant got a report (which turned out to be incorrect) on the night of 6–7 Nov. that the Confederates were moving troops into Missouri from Columbus to reinforce Sterling Price. Since this would endanger Oglesby, Grant decided to turn his demonstration into an actual attack on Belmont.

Grant's column landed three miles above Belmont at about 8:30 A.M. Leaving five companies to guard the four transports, Grant moved with the rest of his force forward. With four and a half infantry regiments, two companies of cavalry, and a six-gun battery, Grant drove through thick woods against six Confederate regiments. He occupied the enemy camp and drove the defenders to the shelter of the riverbank, where they were protected by the guns from Columbus across the river. While the Federals were looting and burning the abandoned camp, Polk put 10,000 troops across the river below Belmont and attempted to cut Grant off from his

transports. The latter was able to withdraw with six captured guns, some horses, and a few prisoners.

In a fight that had ranged from 10:30 A.M. to sunset, the Confederates lost 642 out of about 4,000 engaged, and Grant lost 607 out of 3,114 engaged (B.&L., I, 353 and 355).

While Belmont is cited often as an example of how much Grant had to learn about generalship, considering that he acted on erroneous intelligence, and considering that there was no reason for him to hold Belmont, his performance was not uncreditable. (See K. P. Williams, III, 75–100.) For concurrent operations in Missouri, see WILSON'S CREEK CAMPAIGN, Aug.–Nov. '61.

BENDIX, John E. Union officer. 1818–77. N.Y. Col. 7th N.Y. 23 Apr. '61; resigned 6 Aug. '61; Col. 10th N.Y. 2 Sept. '61; Bvt. B.G. USV (war service); mustered out 7 May '63.

BENEDICT, Lewis. Union officer. 1817–64, N.Y. Col. 162d N.Y. 12 Sept. '62; Bvt. B.G. USV (Port Hudson); K.I.A. 9 Apr. '64 at Pleasant Hill (La.). Attorney and politician before the war. Captured at Williamsburg, he spent several months in Libby and Salisbury prisons before being exchanged. Commanded 1, 3, XIX; 3, 1, XIX.

BENHAM, Henry Washington. Union gen. 1813–84. Conn. USMA 1837 (1/50); Engrs. After being engaged in improving and building harbors and coastal defenses, he then fought in the Mexican War (1 brevet) and was Chief Engr., Dept. of the Ohio, 14 May–22 July '61. Promoted Maj. 6 Aug. '61 and B.G. USV 13 Aug. '61, he commanded Benham's brigade, Army of Occupation. W. Va. (Sept.–Oct. '61). He took part in the capture of Ft. Pulaski and James Island. After his failure at SECESSIONVILLE, 16 June '62, he was relieved of command and arrested for disobedience of orders. On Halleck's recommendation his appointment as B.G. was revoked by Lincoln on 7 Aug.; this revocation was canceled on 6 Feb. '63. (O.R., I, XIV, 979 and 991.) Meanwhile he was put in charge of superintending the fortifications of Boston and Plymouth. During Hooker's advance and retreat across the Rappahannock in the Chancellorsville campaign and at FRANKLIN'S CROSSING (5 June '63), and in crossing the Potomac at Edward's Ferry (21 June '63), he distinguished himself in the construction of ponton bridges. He commanded the Ponton Depot in Washington (July '63–May '64) and superintended the JAMES RIVER BRIDGE. Breveted for Carrick's Ford, Lee's surrender (B.G. USA), and war service (Maj. Gen. USA and USV), he continued in the R.A. until 1882, when he retired as a Col.

BENJAMIN, Judah Philip. C.S.A. cabinet officer. 1811–84. West Indies. Born in St. Croix, he was raised in S.C. where his English-Jewish parents settled, and entered Yale at fourteen. He moved to New Orleans and practiced law, taking a prominent part in the legal profession as well as holding a number of minor political offices. A US Senator and law partner of John SLIDELL, he resigned 4 Feb. '61 to become Attorney General in the provisional Confederate government, serving from 25 Feb. '61 until 17 Sept. of that year. He then succeeded Leroy P. Walker as Secretary of War. It was during his tenure in this office that the LORING-JACKSON INCIDENT occurred. On 18 Mar. '62, with the establishment of the permanent government, he took over from R. M. T. Hunter as Secretary of State and held this post until the surrender. He fled through Florida to the Bahamas and from there to England. He took up the practice of law there and became Queen's Counsel in 1872,

building up a successful and remunerative practice and writing a treatise on the sale of personal property that, like his digest of Supreme Court decisions written earlier in New Orleans, became a classic in law.

BENJAMIN, William Henry. Union officer. Conn. Maj. 8th N.Y. Cav. 28 Nov. '61; Lt. Col. 1 Mar. '64; Bvt. B.G. USV (war service).

BENNETT, John E. Union officer. 1833–93. N.Y. Lt. Col. 75th Ill. 2 Sept. '62; Col. 23 Apr. '63; Bvt. B.G. USV 6 Apr. '65; transferred to R.A. and resigned 1868 as 1st Lt. Brevets for war service, Lookout Mt., Franklin (Tenn.), Nashville. Commanded 3, 1, IV. He was Judge Advocate of the Ark.–Miss. district during reconstruction. A Republican leader, he was appointed to the Supreme Courts of Ark. and S. D.

BENNETT, Thomas Warren. Union officer. 1831–93. Ind. Capt. 15th Ind. 14 June '61; Maj. 36th Ind. 23 Oct. '61; Col. 69th Ind. 1 Nov. '62; Bvt. B.G. USV 5 Mar. '65. Commanded 3, 1, XIII; 2, 3, XIX. A lawyer and state senator, he returned to politics after the war and was appointed Governor of the Idaho Territory 1871–75.

BENNETT, William True. Union officer. Mich. Capt. 1st US Col. Inf. 11 June '63; Lt. Col. 102d US Col. Inf. 14 Apr. '64; Col. 33d US Col. Inf. 18 Dec. '64; Bvt. B.G. USV 25 May '65 (Honey Hill, Fla.).

BENNING, Henry Lewis ("Rock"). C.S.A. gen. 1814–75. Ga. After graduating from the University of Georgia, he practiced law and sat in the legislature where he was totally against emancipation (on economic grounds). However, he believed that abolition was inevitable if the South remained in the Union and so was a secessionist but in favor of the South forming a republic with strong, centralized powers. As Associate Justice of the Ga. Supreme Court, he handed down the decision that the court was not bound by the U.S. Supreme Court on constitutional questions, but rather that both bodies are "coordinate and co-equal." He participated in the state secession convention and was commissioned Col. of the 17th Ga. in Aug. '61, leading them at Malvern Hill and 2d Bull Run. He commanded Toombs's brigade at Antietam and Fredericksburg. Promoted B.G. C.S.A. 23 Apr. '63 to rank from 17 Jan. '63, he commanded his brigade under Hood at Gettysburg, Knoxville, and Chickamauga (where he had two horses shot from under him) and at the Wilderness under Field where he was severely wounded. He also commanded this brigade at Petersburg and Appomattox. He was a lawyer after the war. Fort Benning, Ga., one of the country's largest posts and "The Infantry Center," was named for him.

BENSON, Eugene. WAR CORRESPONDENT and painter. 1837-1908. N.Y. He was sent to Charleston just before the bombardment of Ft. Sumter by *Frank Leslie's Illustrated Newspaper* to make sketches of the city, harbor, and forts. Later he lived mainly on the Continent and achieved a fair amount of fame for his impressionistic style of painting.

BENTLEY, Richard Charles. Union officer. N.Y. 1st Lt. and Adj. 30th N.Y. 1 June '61; Maj. 63d N.Y. 14 Feb. '62; Lt. Col. 1 Nov. '62; Bvt. B.G. USV (war service); mustered out 18 Sept. '64. Died 1871.

BENTLEY, Robert Henry. Union officer. 1835-1900. Ohio. Sgt. 1st Ohio 17 Apr. '61; mustered out 2 Aug. '61; 1st Lt. Regt. Q.M. 32d Ohio 31 Aug. '61; Lt. Col. 25 Dec. '61; Lt. Col. 12th Ohio Cav. 24 Nov. '63; Bvt. B.G. USV (war service). He participated in the

Virginia salt works raid and Stoneman's raid.

BENTON, Samuel. C.S.A. gen. 1820-64. Appt.-Miss. Commissioned Col. 37th Miss. early in 1862, he fought at Shiloh and spent the rest of the year and most of 1863 in northern Mississippi. At the beginning of the Atlanta campaign he was commanding both the 24th and 27th Miss. regiments but gave them up on 11 May '64 to take back his old regiment, now designated the 34th Miss. He led it until 26 July '64 when he was appointed B.G. C.S.A. and took command of Walthall's brigade in Hindman's division. He was mortally wounded 28 July at Atlanta.

BENTON, Thomas Hart, Jr. Union officer. Tenn. Col. 29th Iowa 1 Dec. '62; Bvt. B.G. USV 15 Dec. '64. Commanded 2, 3d Ark. Exp.; 2, 2, VII. Nephew of Thomas Hart Benton, and cousin of Mrs. J. C. Frémont.

BENTON, William Plummer. Union gen. 1828-67. Md. In the Mexican War he was a judge and lawyer when commissioned Col. 8th Ind. 27 Apr. '61. Mustered out 6 Aug. '61 after Rich Mountain, he re-enlisted in the regiment 5 Sept. '61, fought under Frémont in Missouri and Kansas, and led his regiment at Pea Ridge. Promoted B.G. USV 28 Apr. '62, he commanded 1st Div. Army Southeast Mo.; 1, 14, XIII, Tenn. (28 Mar.–July '63) at Vicksburg; 1, 1, XIII, Tenn. (28 July–7 Aug. '63); 1st Div., XIII, Gulf (7 Aug.–15 Sept.; 25 Nov. '63–8 Feb. '64); 2, 2, XIII, Gulf (17 Apr.–9 Mar. '64); XIII, Gulf (4 May–11 June '64); Dist. Baton Rouge, (25–31 May and 13 June–3 Dec. '64); 3d Div., Res. Corps, Gulf; 3d Div., XIII, Gulf (18 Feb.–28 May and 3 June–20 July '65). Breveted Maj. Gen. USV 26 Mar. '65, he was mustered out 24 Aug. '65.

BENTONVILLE, N.C., 19 Mar. '65.
After Slocum's two corps (XIV and XX) had encountered Hardee's (C) troops near Averasboro, 16 Mar. Slocum advanced toward Bentonville. Howard's two corps moved along parallel routes to the right, while Kilpatrick's cavalry (in pursuit of Hardee) advanced on Slocum's left flank. Sherman was moving toward Goldsboro to link up with the forces of Schofield and Terry, who were coming in from the coast. Johnston, with a total effective force of about 21,000 Confederates, massed to defeat Slocum's wing. The morning of the 19th the leading division (Carlin's) of XIV Corps encountered and pushed back Hampton's cavalry. Johnston then counterattacked and forced the Federals back. Slocum massed his forces and successfully withstood several desperate attacks. Johnston withdrew to a position in front of Mill Creek, with his left protected by a swamp. Little fighting was done on the 20th, but by 4 P.M. Sherman's entire force was in position to attack Johnston. On the morning of the 21st Mower's division made an attempt to move through the swamp and take Mill Creek bridge to cut off Johnston's retreat; the rest of the Federal army attacked frontally. Johnston detected Mower's maneuver, blocked it with his reserves, and held his main position. That night the Confederates retreated toward Smithfield. Of 16,127 Federals and 16,895 Confederates engaged (Livermore, 141), the losses were 1,646 and 2,606, respectively (Fox).

BERDAN, Hiram. Union officer. c. 1823–93. N.Y. Col. 1st US SHARPSHOOTERS 30 Nov. '61; Bvt. B.G. USV (Chancellorsville); Bvt. Maj. Gen. USV (Gettysburg). Commanded 2, 3, III; 3, 3, III; 2, 1, III. Resigned 2 Jan. '64. A mechanical engineer in N.Y.C. when the war started, he had been the top rifle shot in the country for fifteen years prior to the Civil War. He is identified with the two regiments of US SHARPSHOOTERS, and with the "breech-loader question" (see SMALL ARMS). Although the crusty Winfield Scott was "very favorably impressed" with this aggressive man, "an associate of Berdan called him 'most unscrupulous' and 'totally unfit for a command.' Major Dyer of the Springfield Armory considered Berdan 'thoroughly unscrupulous and unreliable.'" (Bruce, 109.) He had invented a repeating rifle and a patented musket ball before the war. Later he developed a twin-screw submarine gunboat, a torpedo boat for evading torpedo nets, a long-distance range finder, and a distance fuze for shrapnel.

BERMUDA HUNDRED, Va. See BERMUDA LINE.

BERMUDA LINE, Va. 17 May–14 June '64. After his failure at DREWRY'S BLUFF, 12–16 May, Butler withdrew his X and XVIII Corps into "the historic bottle [Bermuda Hundred], which was at once carefully corked by a Confederate earth-work." (W. F. Smith in B.&L., IV, 211.) An action took place at WARE BOTTOM CHURCH, 20 May. There was also action along the line during the first part of the PETERSBURG CAMPAIGN.

BERRY, Hiram Gregory. Union gen. 1824–63. Me. Col. 4th Me. 15 June '61; Brig. Gen. USV 17 Mar. '62; Maj. Gen. USV 29 Nov. '62; K.I.A. 3 May '63. Carpenter, navigator, businessman, state legislator, Mayor of Rockland, militia captain. As Col. 4th Me. was engaged in 1st Bull Run and Yorktown siege. As brigade commander in Kearny's division was at Fair Oaks, Williamsburg, Seven Days. On sick leave until returning for Fredericksburg, where he led his brigade with distinction. As Maj. Gen. commanded 2d Div., III

Corps (vice Sickles); killed leading bayonet attack at Chancellorsville.

BERRY, Nathaniel Springer. Governor of New Hampshire. 1796–? Me. Apprenticed as a boy to a tanner and currier, he was later a leather manufacturer and active in the militia. He was then elected judge and later legislator as a Democrat until 1840 when he helped organize the Free-Soil party in his state. In Mar. '61 he was elected governor by the Republicans and served until June '63. He was also active in the Methodist Church.

BERRYVILLE, Va. 13 June '63. (Gettysburg campaign) Rodes's division with A. G. Jenkins's cavalry brigade attached moved via Millwood on 12 June to capture the Federal brigade under Col. A. T. McReynolds at Berryville. The Confederate infantry took an unfrequented road from Cedarville toward Millwood; the main part of the cavalry went via Nineveh Church and White Post, with a detachment sent to occupy Millwood. As a result of Jenkins's failure to screen Millwood, Federal cavalry detected the arrival of Rodes's force there early 13 June and alerted McReynolds. Jenkins was sent to the left to cut the road between Berryville and Winchester, while infantry moved around both sides of the town to cut it off from the rear. McReynolds, however, skillfully extricated his force and the bulk of his supplies. Sending his supply train to Bunker Hill with a company of infantry and one of cavalry for protection, McReynolds led the rest of his force south and then via Summit Point to Winchester. He reached the latter place about 9 P.M. and moved into the Star Fort. The Confederates were too disorganized for an effective pursuit, but Jenkins found and attacked the two companies at Bunker Hill, capturing 75 to 100 and driving the rest toward Martinsburg. The Federals reported 300 missing for the entire operation; Confederate losses were negligible.

BERTRAM, Henry. Union officer. Germany. Pvt., Cpl., Sgt. Co. D 2d US Arty. 21 Aug. '46–20 Jan. '51 when, Heitman says (Vol. I, p. 214), "he deserted—his proper name was Henry Beeger." Civil War record is as follows: 1st Lt. 3d Wis. 29 June '61; Regt. Adj. 26 Aug. '61; Capt. 1 Oct. '61; Lt. Col. 20th Wis. 31 July '62; Col. 10 Dec. '62; Bvt. B.G. USV (war service). Commanded 1st Brig., 3d Div. Army Frontier, Dept. of Mo.; 2, 2, XIII; Bertram's Brig., US Forces Mobile Bay; US Forces Mobile Bay; 1, 2, XIII. Had horse shot from under him at Prairie Grove (Ark.) 7 Dec. '62. Died 1878.

BETHESDA CHURCH, Va., 30 May '64. See TOTOPOTOMOY CREEK.

BETHESDA CHURCH, Va., 31 May–1 June '64. See COLD HARBOR.

BEVERIDGE, John Lourie. 1824–? Union officer. N.Y. Maj. 8th Ill. Cav. 18 Sept. '61; discharged 2 Nov. '63; Col. 17th Ill. Cav. 28 Jan. '64; Bvt. B.G. USV 7 Mar. '65. Commanded the St. Louis and Central Mo. districts, Dept. of Mo. A lawyer, he was Governor of Illinois 1873–77.

BICKERDYKE, Mary Ann Ball ("Mother Bickerdyke"). SANITARY COMMISSION worker. 1817–1901. Assigned in 1861 to a field hospital at Ft. Donelson, she served throughout the war in the West, working later on warships in the Mississippi and with Grant's army at Vicksburg. Sherman requested her for the XV Corps and she served with that unit throughout the Atlanta campaign as the Sanitary Commission field agent. She rode a horse at the head of the corps in the Grand Review.

BIDDLE, Charles John. Union gen. 1819–73. Pa. After Princeton he practiced law and served in the Mexican

War (1 brevet). Commissioned Col. 13th Pa. Res. 21 June '61, he was appointed B.G. USV 31 Aug. '61. Declining this, he was elected to Congress in Oct. '61 and resigned from the Army 11 Dec. After the war, he was editor in chief and a proprietor of *The Philadelphia Age.* Son of Nicholas Biddle (US Bank).

BIDDLE, James. Union officer. Pa. 1st Lt. 10th N.Y. 2 May '61; mustered out 31 Aug. '61; Capt. 15th US 5 Aug. '61; Col. 6th Ind. Cav. 11 Nov. '62; mustered out USV 27 June '65; in R.A. until retirement in 1896 as Col. 9th US Cav.; Bvt. B.G. USV; brevets for Richmond (Ky.), Nashville, war service. Commanded 2d Div., Cav. Corps, Dept. Ohio; 1st Brig., Cav. Div., XIII Corps; 2d Brig., 6th Div. Cav. Corps, Mil. Div. Miss.

BIDWELL, Daniel Davidson. Union gen. 1819-64. N.Y. Prominent in military organizations for 20 years, he was a police justice when commissioned Col. 49th N.Y. 21 Oct. '61. He led his regiment in the Peninsular campaign and at South Mountain, Antietam, Fredericksburg, Chancellorsville, and Gettysburg. He commanded 3, 2, VI, Potomac (28 May–10 June '63; Feb.–25 Mar. '64; 6 May–8 July '64) and was named B.G. USV 11 Aug. '64. Leading the same brigade in the Army of the Shenandoah (6 Aug.–19 Oct. '64), he was killed at Cedar Creek.

BIG BETHEL, Va. 10 June '61. First land battle of the war. In May B. F. Butler was sent with a division to reinforce the garrison of Fort Monroe. He ordered E. W. Pierce to lead an attack against an outpost at Big Bethel Church, eight miles above Hampton. At 1 A.M. on the 10th the 7th N.Y. (Duryea's Zouaves) moved out to occupy New Market Bridge on the road from Hampton to Big Bethel. An hour later six other regiments advanced in two different columns to rendezvous at a road junction about a mile and a half south of Little Bethel for a surprise attack on Big Bethel, three miles farther in the direction of Yorktown. This resulted in an accidental exchange of fire between the two columns, with a loss of two killed and 21 wounded.

Meanwhile, the Confederate force— principally Col. D. H. Hill's 1st N.C.— had learned of the Federal advance and deployed to meet it. In a poorly-managed attack the Federals were repulsed and forced to withdraw in disorder.

Federal troops engaged were 4,400 men of the 1st, 2d, 3d, 5th, and 7th N.Y., 1st Vermont, 4th Massachusetts, and the 2d U. S. Artillery. They sustained a loss of 76, including Maj. Theodore Winthrop of Butler's staff "shot while standing on the fence flourishing his sword" (O.R. Atlas, LXI, 4) and Lt. J. T. Greble, the artillery commander, both killed. The Confederates lost 11 of their 1,408 engaged.

Although a minor skirmish, it was reported by Col. J. B. ("Prince John") Magruder, newly-appointed Confederate commander of the defenses of the Peninsula, as a significant victory.

BIG BLACK RIVER, Miss., 17 May '63. Engagement of VICKSBURG CAMPAIGN.

BIG BLACK RIVER, Miss., 4 Feb. '64. Skirmishes in MERIDIAN CAMPAIGN.

BIGGS, Herman. Union officer. c. 1832-87. N.Y. USMA 1856 (35/49); Inf.-Q.M. 1st Lt. 1st US Inf. 1 May '61; Capt. Asst. Q.M. 3 Aug. '61; Lt. Col. Q.M. Assigned 22 July '62–2 Aug. '64; Col. Q.M. Assigned 2 Aug. '64–9 Oct. '65; Bvt. B.G. USV (war service) 8 Mar. '65; resigned 9 Oct. '65; Capt. on retired list 5 Feb. '83 (reinstated by Act of Congress 18 Jan. '83).

BIGGS, Jonathan. Union officer. Lt. Col. 123d Ill. Bvt. B.G. USV 13 Mar. '65. (Phisterer.) Not in Heitman.

BIG HILL (Richmond), Ky. 23 Aug. '62. See Kirby SMITH'S INVASION OF KENTUCKY.

BILES, Edwin Ruthwin. Union officer. Pa. 1st Lt. and Adj. 99th Pa. 25 Feb. '62; Lt. Col. 1 July '62; Col. 23 Aug. '64; Bvt. B.G. USV (war service, Deep Bottom). Died 1883.

BILLY. George H. Thomas's war horse, a bay, was named after his friend Sherman. About 16 hands high and stout in build, Billy is described in Miller as "like his owner, sedate in all his movements and was not easily disturbed from his habitual calm by bursting shells. . . . Even in retreat, the horse did not hurry his footsteps unduly, and provoked the staff by his deliberate pace."

BINGHAM, Henry Harrison. Union officer. 1841–? Pa. 1st Lt. 140th Pa. 22 Aug. '62; Capt. 9 Sept. '62; Maj. Judge Advocate Vols. 20 Sept. '64; Bvt. B.G. USV 9 Apr. '65; brevets for Wilderness, Spotsylvania, Gettysburg, war service. Medal of Honor 26 Aug. '93 for Wilderness 6 May '64. He was active for many years in the Republican party, holding several public offices.

BINGHAM, Judson David. Union officer. 1831–1909 N.Y. Appt.-Ind. USMA 1854 (9/46); Arty.-QM. He served in garrison and in the suppression of John Brown's Harpers Ferry raid before being promoted Capt. Asst. Q.M. for Banks Aug. '61–12 Feb. '62. Going to the West, he was Chief Q.M. of the XVII Corps 1 Jan. '63–23 Apr. '64 and of the Army of the Tenn. until 25 Aug. '64, participating in Lake Providence, Milliken's Bend, Vicksburg, and the Atlanta campaign. He was then Insp. for the Q.M. Dept. until 1866 and was breveted B.G. USA 9 Apr. '65 for

war service. He continued in the R.A. and retired in 1895 as Col.

BINTLIFF, James. Union officer. England. Capt. 22d Wis. 1 Sept. '62; resigned 27 Dec. '63; Col. 38th Wis. 27 Apr. '64; Bvt. B.G. USV 2 Apr. '65 (Petersburg assault). Commanded 1, 1, IX; 3, 1, IX.

BIRGE, Henry Warner. Union gen. 1825–88. Conn. On the governor's staff at the beginning of the war, he organized Connecticut's first regiment. Commissioned Maj. 4th Conn. 23 May '61, he resigned 13 Nov. '61 and was named Col. 13th Conn. 18 Feb. '62. He was named B.G. USV 19 Sept. '63 and commanded in the Gulf: 3, 4, XIX (3 Jan.–10 July '63); 1, 4, XIX (10 Aug. '63–25 Jan. '64); Dist. LaFourche, XIX (Sept. '63–4 May '64); Dist. Baton Rouge, XIX (2–25 May '64); 2, 2, XIX (15 Feb.–30 Apr. and 7 May–27 June '64); and 1, 2, XIX (2–5 July '64). He then led 1, 2, XIX, Army Shenandoah (6 Aug.–19 Oct.; 10 Nov.–8 Dec. '64; 28 Dec. '64–6 Jan. '65); 1, Grover's division, South (6 Jan.–12 Feb. '65); Grover's division, South (12 Feb.–26 Mar. '65); 1st Div., X, N.C. (27 Mar.–4 July '65); and Dist. Savannah, South (5–26 June '65). Breveted Maj. Gen. USV 25 Feb. '65, he resigned 18 Oct. '65 and was awarded a Vote of Thanks by the state legislature.

BIRNEY, David Bell. Union gen. 1825–64. Alabama. Lt. Col. 23d Pa. 21 Apr. '61; mustered out 31 July '61; Col. 23d Pa. 31 Aug. '61; full B.G. USV 17 Feb. '62; full Maj. Gen. USV 20 May '63. Born in Huntsville, Ala., son of the Abolitionist leader JAMES G. BIRNEY. Educated at Andover; studied law in Cincinnati, where his father published a paper; then moved with his parents to Michigan and finally to Philadelphia, where he practiced law. He recruited the 23d Pa. largely at his own expense, and led it at Falling Waters and the occupation of Winchester. As B.G. he commanded a brigade in Kearny's division, III Corps. He was court-martialed and acquitted of charge of "halting his command a mile from the enemy" at Fair Oaks. After the Peninsular campaign he continued to lead his brigade through the 2d Bull Run campaign, taking temporary command of the division after Kearny was killed at Chantilly. As Maj. Gen. he commanded a division at Fredericksburg and Chancellorsville. At Gettysburg he took command of III Corps after Sickles was W.I.A.; although he himself received two slight wounds here, he continued to command the corps until February. When the army was reorganized he was given command of X Corps. While serving in this capacity he contracted malaria and died 18 Oct. '64. He was a brother of William BIRNEY.

BIRNEY, James Gillespie. Antislavery leader. 1792–1857. Ky. A lawyer in Kentucky and Alabama, he secured laws there helping the slaves. An agent of the American Colonization Society and executive secretary of the American Anti-Slavery Society, he proposed political action only, in contrast to William Lloyd Garrison. A founder of the Liberal party (1840), he was their presidential nominee in 1840 and 1844 and polled enough votes the latter time to assure Polk rather than Clay as president. Sons William and David B. were generals in the Union army.

BIRNEY, William. Union gen. 1819–?. Ala. Son of James G. Birney and sharing his strong anti-slavery sentiments, he was educated at Centre College and Yale and spent five years in Europe. In France he took an active part in the revolution of 1848 and was appointed professor of English literature at Bourges. Commissioned Capt. 1st N.J. 22 May '61, he was at 1st Bull Run and promoted Maj. 4th N.J. 27 Sept. '61. Fighting at 2d Bull Run, Chantilly, and Fredericksburg, he was promoted Col. 13 Jan. '63 and Col. USCT (22 May–22 Dec. '63) and B.G. USV 22 May '63. He raised and sent to the field seven colored regiments. After the Union defeat at Olustee (20 Feb. '64), he was given command of the Dist. Fla. (25 Apr.–13 May and 2 June–29 July '64) and regained important portions of the state. He also commanded Dist. Hilton Head (13 May–2 June '64); 1, 3, X (1 Sept.–5 Oct. '64); 3d Div., X (27 Aug.–1 Sept. '64; 5–20 Oct. '64; 29 Oct.–3 Dec. '64); 2d Div., XXV (3 Dec. '64–21 Feb. '65 and 27 Mar.–10 Apr. '65). Breveted Maj. Gen. USV for war service, he was mustered out 24 Aug. '65 and was later Attorney for the District of Columbia.

BISHOP, Judson Wade. Union officer. 1831–? N.Y. Capt. 2d Minn. 26 June '61; Maj. 15 May '62; Lt. Col. 15 Oct. '62; Col. 26 Mar. '65; Bvt. B.G. USV 7 June '65 (meritorious service). He was well known after the war as a civil engineer and railroad promoter in the Middle West.

BLACK, John Charles. Union officer. 1839–1915. Miss. Pvt. and Sgt. Maj. 11th Ind. 25 Apr.–4 Aug. '61; Maj. 37th Ill. 5 Sept. '61; Lt. Col. 12 July '62; Col. 31 Dec. '62; Bvt. B.G. USV 9 Apr. '65 (Ft. Blakely, Ala.). Medal of Honor 31 Oct. '93 for Prairie Grove (Ark.) 7 Dec. '62. In Dept. of Gulf he commanded 1, 2, XIII; 2, 2, Res. Corps; 3, 2, XIII. W.I.A. Prairie Grove (Ark.). Commander in Chief of G.A.R. 1903–04.

BLACKBURN'S FORD, Va. 18 July '61. Engagement of 1st Bull Run campaign, this is the action the Confederates called "First Bull Run." See MANASSAS.

BLACK CODES. Laws passed by Southern state governments under the Johnson Reconstruction Plan to control and regulate the conduct of the Negro freedmen. These laws, which represented the Southern definition of the status of the emancipated Negro, imposed such restrictions as forbidding them to sit on juries, limiting their right to testify against white men, requiring them to have steady work and subjecting them to special penalties for labor contract violations. They also included vagrancy and apprenticeship laws, penal codes, and punishment recommendations. These were superseded by the governments imposed by the Radical Reconstructionists but were followed by most Southern whites, and not until the 1954 Supreme Court decision on integrated education was any concrete action taken to change this.

BLACKFORD'S FORD, Va., 19–20 Sept. '62. (Boteler's or Shepherdstown Ford) (ANTIETAM CAMPAIGN) After Lee had withdrawn his army across the Potomac following the battle of Antietam, he was awakened at about midnight of 19–20 Sept. by his chief of artillery, Pendleton, with the news that the entire reserve artillery had been captured. This turned out to be an exaggeration, but during the afternoon parts of the 1st and 2d divisions, V Corps, had pushed aggressively across the Potomac and had taken four guns. A. P. Hill's division counterattacked and drove the Federals back over the river with a heavy loss of 92 killed, 131 wounded, and 103 missing. Almost all the casualties were sustained by the newly raised 118th Pa. ("Corn Exchange Regiment"). It had advanced too far without support and had borne the brunt of Hill's counterattack. Out of 800 taken into this action it lost 63 killed, 101 wounded, and 105 missing. Five officers were killed, and the regimental commander, C. M. PREVOST, wounded "while waving the colors to encourage the men" (Fox, 293). A. P.

Hill reported his own loss at 30 killed and 231 wounded. Pendleton, who was much criticized for his performance in this operation, had lost seven men.

BLACK HAT BRIGADE. Earlier name of John Gibbon's IRON BRIGADE.

BLACKMAN, Albert Milton. Union officer. Ohio. Capt. 21st Ohio 23 Apr. '61; Lt. Col. 49th Ohio 20 Aug. '61; resigned 30 Sept. '62; Lt. Col. 27th US Col. Inf. 24 Mar. '64; Col. 1 Sept. '64; Bvt. B.G. USV 27 Oct. '64 (Hatcher's Run, Va.). Died 1881.

BLACK REPUBLICANS. Although the expression had been used earlier, it gained its greatest currency as a contemptuous Southern epithet for Republicans who aided the Negro FREEDMAN during the RECONSTRUCTION.

BLACK RIVER, Miss. See BIG BLACK RIVER.

BLACKWELL, Elizabeth. Physician. 1821–1910. England. After a poor childhood, she entered medical school after several attempts and graduated as an M.D. in 1849, the first woman to do so. She then studied in Europe and returned to organize with her sister Emily, also a doctor, the N.Y. Infirmary for Women and Children. At the beginning of the Civil War she held the first meeting in N.Y. that organized the centralization of women's relief activities which became in a few months the SANITARY COMMISSION. After the war she was active both in America and England in gynecology and obstetrics.

BLAIR, Austin. Gov. of Michigan. 1818–1894. N.Y. After graduating from college he studied law and entered politics in Michigan. A Republican, he sat in the legislature and was Governor from 1861 to 1865. He was elected to Congress the next year, serving until 1873, when he resumed his law practice.

BLAIR, Charles White. Union officer. Ohio. Capt. 2d Kans. 14 May '61; Lt. Col. 22 May '61; resigned 9 Oct. '61; Maj. 2d Kans. Cav. 28 Feb. '62; Lt. Col. 26 Sept. '63; Col. 20 Nov. '63; Bvt. B.G. USV 13 Feb. '65. Died 1899. Phisterer lists this officer as Col. of the 14th Kans. Cav., but Heitman gives his regiment as the 2d Kans. Cav.

BLAIR, Francis Preston (Jr.). Union statesman and gen. 1821-75. Ky.; Appt.-Mo. Private in Mexican War. Col. 1st Mo. 26 Apr. '61; Col. 1st Mo. Arty. 12 June '61; B.G. USV 7 Aug. '62; Maj. Gen. USV 29 Nov. '62; resigned 7 June '65 (Phisterer) or 1 Nov. '65 (Heitman). Son of Francis P. Blair. Graduated 1841 from Princeton, studied law at Transylvania University. Practiced law in St. Louis two years and then spent two years in Rocky Mountains for his health. A strong Unionist, he acted to counter secessionist trends in Missouri. In 1848 he founded and led the Free-Soil party in Missouri, and established and edited the *Barnburner,* a free-soil paper. Was US Representative '56–'58 and '60–'62. In the confused situation preceding the outbreak of war he organized the WIDE-AWAKES and was instrumental in saving Missouri and Kentucky for the Union by directing, without authority, the capture of the St. Louis arsenal (see CAMP JACKSON, 10 May '61), and subsequent armed moves of Union forces under NATHANIEL LYON. Involved in controversies with FRÉMONT. Later he raised seven regiments and entered military service as a Colonel; was soon a Major General (see above for dates). In the Yazoo expedition he commanded a brigade and was later a division commander of XV Corps. At Chattanooga he commanded the corps. He led XVII Corps in the Atlanta campaign and subsequent operations of Sherman. As a result of private means spent in support of the Union he was financially ruined at the end of the war. His opposition to reconstruction policies led to the Senate's rejection of his nomination by President Johnson as revenue collector in St. Louis and as US Minister to Austria. Returning to the Democratic fold, he organized the party in Missouri and was its candidate for vice-president in 1868. In 1871 he was elected to the Senate to fill an unexpired term, but failed at reelection in 1873. At his death he was, nominally, State Superintendent of Insurance.

BLAIR, Louis Jackson. Union officer. Ohio. Capt. 88th Ind. 29 Aug. '62; Maj. 29 Oct. '63; Bvt. B.G. USV (war service). Phisterer lists this officer as Col. in the 88th Ind., while Heitman gives his highest full rank as Maj., although he was breveted a Col.

BLAIR, Montgomery. Union Postmaster General. 1813-83. Ky. USMA 1835 (18/56); Arty. Resigning the next year after serving in the Seminole War, he studied law at Transylvania University and settled in Missouri, where he entered Democratic politics. He moved to Silver Spring, Md., in 1853 to be near his father, Francis P. Blair, and continued to practice law. His free-soil views made him change to the Republican party and he was Scott's counsel in the Dred Scott Case. Appointed Postmaster General by Lincoln, he resigned after four years at Lincoln's request, to keep peace in the cabinet. After the war he opposed the Radical Republicans in their persecution of Johnson and eventually rejoined the Democratic party. Brother of Francis P. Blair (Jr.).

BLAIR, William H. Union officer. Pa. 1st Lt. 4th Pa. 19 Apr. '61; mustered out 27 July '61; 1st Lt. 51st Pa. 4 Oct. '61; Capt. 12 Feb. '62; Col. 179th Pa. 8 Dec. '62; Bvt. B.G. USV (Antietam Bridge); mustered out 27 July '63. Died 1888.

BLAIR'S LANDING (Pleasant Hill), La. 12 Apr. '64. Attacks on Federal gunboats *Osage* and *Lexington* and elements of Kilby Smith's division of XVII Corps by Thomas Green's cavalry during RED RIVER CAMPAIGN, in which Green was killed.

BLAISDELL, William. Union officer. N.H. Enlisted man in 1841–53; Lt. Col. 11th Mass. 13 June '61; Col. 11 Oct. '61; Bvt. B.G. USV 23 June '64 (gallantry); K.I.A. 23 June '64 at Petersburg. Commanded 1, 2, III; 4, 2, II. At the time of his death he was temporarily in command of the CORCORAN LEGION.

BLAKE, George Alexander Hamilton. Union officer. Pa. Joining the R.A. in 1836, he fought in the Seminole War and the Mexican War (1 brevet) and served on the frontier in Indian fighting. He was promoted Lt. Col. 1st U.S. Cav. 13 May '61 (Maj. since 1850) and Col. 15 Feb. '62. After the Seven Days' Battles, he was slightly wounded at Gaines's Mill and served until 1863 as Chief Commissary of Musters in the Dept. of Va. and the Cav. Corps of the Army of the Potomac. For the remainder of the war he was on special duty with the Cavalry Bureau. Continuing in the R.A., he retired in 1870 as Bvt. B.G. USA (Gettysburg). He died in 1884.

BLAKELY, Ala. 1–9 Apr. '65. Last infantry battle of the war. (MOBILE CAMPAIGN) On 1 Apr. Spurling's (2d) cavalry brigade of XIII Corps, leading the advance of Steele's column, encountered Confederate outposts five miles from Blakely. In a dismounted action by the 2d Me. Cav. later supported by the 2d Ill. Cav., the 46th Miss. and other troops were driven back to within a mile of their works at Blakely. The Confederates lost 74 men and the colors

of the 46th Miss. whereas the attackers lost only two. Confederate prisoners were forced to remove land mines ("torpedoes") they had placed and that had accounted for one of the Federal casualties.

Steele's entire force, 10,000 infantry and 2,000 cavalry, now laid siege to Blakely. From left to right the lines of attack were held by the divisions of Garrard (2, XVI), Veatch, and C. C. Andrews (1, 2, XIII), Hawkins's colored troops (4, XVI). The Confederate defenders consisted initially of F. M. Cockrell's (formerly French's) division on the left and Wm. T. Thomas's brigade of "boy reserves" on the right.

After the fall of SPANISH FORT on 8 Apr., Canby massed his entire force of 45,000 along a four-mile line opposite Blakely. A general assault started with 16,000 men at 5:30 the afternoon of the 9th, and in twenty minutes the works had been captured. With a loss of 629 Federals (113 killed, 516 wounded; Fox), 3,423 Confederate prisoners and more than 40 guns were captured. (B.&L., IV, 411).

Maury destroyed the small works at Forts Huger and Tracy the night of the 11th, and moved his remaining 4,500 troops, 27 guns, and his wagon train toward Montgomery, Ala. On 4 May his command was surrendered by Dick Taylor.

BLAKELY GUN. An English rifled gun of radically new design which the Confederates used in small numbers. South Carolina imported a battery of large ones for coastal defense (see Miller, V, 120–1). Caleb Huse bought six 3.1-inch and three 8-inch field pieces during the winter of 1862–63, and Wade Hampton imported a field battery at his own expense. "The short and light Blakely guns kicked like a mule, and for this and other reasons they gradually disappeared," according to one report, but they were "especially favored by the horse batteries" says another. (*Lee's Lts.*, I, 310n; and Wise, 243.) "The Gallant Pelham" used one in his remarkable exploit at Fredericksburg (see *Lee's Lts.*, II, 349). The gun fired several types of ammunition, including flanged and studded projectiles. According to Weller (p. 66), Blakely breechloaders saw little service and "None survive either here or abroad."

BLAKESLEE, Erastus. Union officer. 1838–1908. Conn. 1st Lt. and Adj. 1st Conn. Cav. 26 Oct. '61; Capt. 28 Mar. '62; Maj. 18 Dec. '63; Lt. Col. 31 May '64; Col. 6 June '64; Bvt. B.G. USV (Ashland, Va., 1 June '64); mustered out 26 Oct. '64. Said to be the only B.G. from Conn. to serve in every grade from 2d Lt. up (D.A.B.). A businessman and inventor, he also served as a Congregationalist minister and was prominent in religious education.

BLANCHARD, Albert Gallatin. C.S.A. gen. 1810–91. Mass. USMA 1829 (26/46); Inf. He served mainly on the frontier until his resignation in 1840 to be a merchant and director of public schools in Louisiana. After fighting in the Mexican War he went back in the R.A. as Maj. 12th US Inf. and resigned in 1847 to be a schoolteacher, surveyor, and railroad employee. He was commissioned Col. 1st La. and sent to Norfolk, where he commanded a division in May '61 under Huger. Appointed B.G. C.S.A. 21 Sept. '61, he led a brigade at Portsmouth, South Mills, and Seven Pines. He saw no more field service after June '62 due to his advanced age, but commanded at Drewry's Bluff and North Carolina for the rest of the war. Afterward he was a surveyor and held several public offices.

BLANCHARD, Justus Wardwell. Union officer. 1811–77. N.H. Capt. 3d N.Y. 14 May '61; Lt. Col. 162d N.Y.

18 Oct. '62; Col. 18 June '64; Bvt. B.G. USV (war service). Commanded 3, 1, XIX, Gulf. Participated in Banks's Red River expedition and Sheridan's Valley campaign.

BLANDEN, Leander. Union officer. N.Y. Maj. 95th Ill. 4 Sept. '62; Lt. Col. 21 May '63; Col. 1 Sept. '64; Bvt. B.G. USV 26 Mar. '65 (Mobile). Commanded 2d Brig., 3d Div. Detachment Army Tenn.

"BLEEDING KANSAS." Term applied to violence-torn territory of Kansas, where a five-year border war followed enactment of the Kansas-Nebraska Bill in 1854. This ruled that the slavery question would be left up to popular sovereignty and opened the territory to organized migrations of proslave and anti-slave groups as well as squatters, speculators, and adventurers from both the North and South. The civil warfare that followed included the plundering of Lawrence and John Brown's massacre at Pottawatamie in 1856, the massacre in 1858 at Marais des Cygnes, and battles at Black Jack, Franklin, Fort Saunders, Hickory Point, and Slough Creek. The major fighting ended early in 1859, but disorder continued until the Civil War.

BLENKER, Louis. Union gen. 1812–63. Germany. First in the Bavarian Legion, he was a leading member of the 1848 revolutionary government and came to the US in Sept. '49 after being forced to leave first Germany and then Switzerland. He was a farmer and then a N.Y.C. businessman and was commissioned Col. 8th N.Y. 23 Apr. '61. At 1st Bull Run his regiment, initially in reserve, effectively helped cover the Union retreat. He was named B.G. USV 9 Aug. '61 and commanded 1st Brig., 5th Div. Army Northeast Va., Potomac; and Blenker's brigade, Div. Potomac (3 Oct.–Dec. '61). Given a division of three German brigades from the East and Midwest (Blenker's division Dec. '61–Mar. '62), he was ordered in March to leave McClellan's command and join Frémont in W. Va. The six-week march became famous; due to neglect by the War Dept., the 10,000-man command was lacking basic military necessities, including maps. They suffered great hardships and were reduced to looting and thievery. He commanded this division in the Mtn. Dept. from 1 Apr. until 26 June '62, fighting at Cross Keys. Ordered to Washington after that, he saw no further service, was discharged 31 Mar. '63, and died 31 Oct. '63 of injuries received in a fall from his horse earlier in the war.

BLOCKADE. Lincoln forbade trade with the seceded states on 16 Apr. '61 and proclaimed the blockade of Southern ports on 19 and 27 Apr. '61. Although the Federal navy was handicapped by the loss of the Norfolk Navy Yard, the Union fleet of small and obsolete ships was expanded, and by July '61 the blockade began to take effect. Burnside's capture of Roanoke Island and New Bern, Gillmore's capture of Ft. Pulaski at the entrance to the Savannah approaches, and Farragut's capture of New Orleans substantially increased the effectiveness of the blockade. Chances of capture were estimated as 1 in 10 in 1861, but by 1864 they were 1 in 3. Some 600 Federal vessels were engaged in the blockade of 3,550 miles of coast. See also BLOCKADE RUNNING.

BLOCKADE RUNNING. This was a profitable though risky violation by ships of neutral nations, mainly British, and Confederate vessels of the Federal blockade of Southern ports. (See BLOCKADE.) In the first year around 800 ships evaded the Federals. However, in the peacetime year of 1860 around 6,000 ships had entered and cleared Southern ports. Using the Bahamas as a stop, the blockade runners were believed to have brought in goods valued at over $200,000,000, including more than 600,000 small arms. Successfully avoiding the 600 blockading ships, the Confederacy exported some 1,250,000 bales of cotton. There were an estimated 8,250 successful blockade runners, and the risk of failure averaged 16 per cent. Confederate law required all English vessels entering Southern ports to bring arms and supplies. Certainly the Confederacy would have starved without these violations, and might have won its independence but for the Union navy. However, the blockade was highly successful: Southern cotton exports shrank from $191,000,000 in 1860 to $4,000,000 in 1862.

"BLOODY ANGLE." Landmarks in the battles of GETTYSBURG (third day) and SPOTSYLVANIA.

"BLOODY LANE." Landmark in the fighting at ANTIETAM.

BLOOMFIELD, Ira Jackson. Union officer. Ohio. Capt. 26th Ill. 28 Jan. '62; Lt. Col. 24 Jan. '65; Col. 11 May '65; Bvt. B.G. USV (war service).

BLOUNTSVILLE, Tenn. 13 Oct. '63. Skirmish between S. P. Carter's Federal cavalry brigade and retreating forces under J. S. Williams, following the action at BLUE SPRINGS, 10 Oct.

"BLUE AND GRAY." Nicknames for the Federal and Confederate armies respectively, derived from the color of their uniforms.

BLUE SPRINGS, Tenn. 10 Oct. '63. In late Sept. '63 J. S. Williams took command of C.S.A. forces in East Tenn. and advanced to Blue Springs with about 1,700 effectives and two artillery batteries. Part of Burnside's command was at Bull Gap, nine miles away. On 10 Oct. Shackelford's cavalry attacked Williams. About 5 P.M. the

Confederates were driven back by infantry of the IX Corps that had reinforced the cavalry. That night Williams withdrew toward Virginia with a loss of 66 killed and wounded and 150 missing; the Federals lost 100 total. Col. J. W. Foster's 2d Brig. lost 25 men in a skirmish at Rheatown the next day. At daylight of this same day (11 Oct.), at Henderson's Mill, Williams fought his way through an encircling force (5th Ind. Cav. of Foster's brigade) that had gotten astride his line of retreat the preceding day. There was another action at Blountsville, Tenn., 13 Oct., in which S. P. Carter's cavalry brigade inflicted 44 casualties on Williams's retreating forces, while suffering only six himself. On 4 Nov. J. S. Williams was relieved at his own request and succeeded by H. L. Giltner. These were part of the operations that preceded the KNOXVILLE CAMPAIGN.

BLUNT, Asa Peabody. Union officer. Vt. 1st Lt. Adj. 3d Vt. 20 June '61; mustered out 31 Aug. '61; Lt. Col. 6th Vt. 15 Oct. '61; mustered out 18 Sept. '62; Col. 12th Vt. 4 Oct. '62; mustered out 14 July '63; Capt. Asst. Q.M. Vols. 29 Feb. '64–9 Apr. '67; Bvt. B.G. USV. Brevets for war service, Lee's Mill, Savage's Station (Va.). Commanded 2d Brig. Casey's division Mil. Dist. Wash.; 2d Brig., Casey's division, XII Corps. Died 1889.

BLUNT, James Gilpatrick. Union gen. 1826–81. Me. A seaman in his teens, he then graduated from an Ohio medical school, practiced there and later engaged in Kansas politics. An ardent abolitionist, he was associated with John Brown in helping escaped slaves reach Canada. He was named Lt. Col. 3d Kansas in July 1861, commanded the cavalry of Lane's brigade and, promoted B.G. USV 8 Apr. '62, took command of the Dept. of Kans. (15 May–19 Sept. '62). At Old Ft. Wayne in Oct. he de-feated a large force of Indians under Col. D. H. Cooper. He commanded 1st Div., Army of the Frontier (12 Oct.–31 Dec. '62), defeating Marmaduke at Cane Hill (28 Nov. '62) and, joining forces with Herron, defeated Hindman at Prairie Grove (7 Dec. '62). Promoted Maj. Gen. USV 29 Nov. '62, he then captured Ft. Van Buren. Taking command of the Dist. of the Frontier (9 June '63–6 Jan. '64), he suffered a humiliating defeat at BAXTER SPRINGS. At Honey Springs he again defeated Cooper. He commanded the Dist. of Upper Ark. (25 July–22 Dec. '64) and the Dist. of South Kans. (10 Oct. '64–28 June '65). He successfully opposed PRICE'S RAID IN MISSOURI thereby ending the last Confederate threat in the West. Mustered out 29 July '65, he settled in Leavenworth, Kans.

BODINE, Robert Lewis. Union officer. Pa. Comsy. Sgt. 26th Pa. 5 May '61; Capt. 14 Jan. '62; Maj. 15 July '62; Lt. Col. 28 Oct. '63; Bvt. B.G. USV (war service); mustered out 18 June '64. Died 1874.

BOGGS, William Robertson. C.S.A. gen. 1829–1911. Ga. USMA 1853 (4/52); Topo. Engrs.-Ord. He taught artillery at West Point and then served on railroad survey expeditions and on the frontier before resigning 1 Feb. '61 as a 1st Lt. to become Capt. C.S.A. Engrs. He served at Charleston, Pensacola, and Santa Rosa and on 21 Dec. '61 resigned his C.S.A. commission to be Georgia's Chief Engineer. After serving under Pemberton's orders in Georgia and Florida, he was commissioned B.G. C.S.A. 4 Nov. '62. He then went with Kirby Smith to the Trans-Miss. Dept. where he was Chief of Staff until the end of the war. Afterwards he was variously an architect, a railroad, civil, and mining engineer, and taught drawing and mechanics at V.P.I.

BOHEMIAN BRIGADE. See WAR CORRESPONDENTS.

BOHLEN, Henry. Union gen. 1810–62. Germany. Coming to Philadelphia as a boy, he acquired a fortune in the liquor business and was commissioned Col. 75th Pa. 30 Sept. '61. He commanded 3, Blenker's division, Potomac (Dec. '61–Mar. '62); 3d Brig., Blenker's division, II, Potomac; 3d Brig., Blenker's division, Mountain (Apr.–25 June '62) and 1, 3, I, Army of Va. (26 June–22 Aug. '62). Named B.G. USV 28 Apr. '62, he was killed on 22 Aug. '62 at Freemans Ford (Va.) when outnumbered in a rear-guard action on the Rappahannock while covering the retreat of the army.

BOLINGER, Henry Clay. Union officer. Pa. Capt. 7th Pa. Res. 1 June '61; Lt. Col. 5 May '62; Col. 1 Aug. '62; Bvt. B.G. USV (Wilderness); resigned 19 Aug. '64. Commanded 2, Pa. Res., XXII.

BOLLES, John Augustus. Union officer. 1809–78. Conn. Appt.-Mass. Capt. Add. A.D.C. 30 Jan. '62; Maj. Judge Advocate Vols. 3 Sept. '62–18 July '63; Maj. Add. A.D.C. 20 June '62; Bvt. B.G. USV 17 July '65 (war service). A prominent lawyer and Mass. Sec. of State (1843), he was Judge Advocate (1862–65) on the staff of Gen. John A. Dix, his brother-in-law.

BOLTON, William Jordan. Union officer. Pa. Capt. 4th Pa. 20 Apr. '61; mustered out 25 July '61; Capt. 51st Pa. 12 Sept. '61; Maj. 17 Sept. '62; Col. 26 June '64; Bvt. B.G. USV (war service).

BOMFORD, James Voty. Union officer. c. 1812–92. N.Y. Appt.-D.C. USMA 1832 (34/45); Inf. He served on the frontier and in the Mexican War (2 brevets) before being captured 9 May '61 when Twiggs surrendered Texas to the Confederacy. Promoted Lt. Col. 16th US Inf. 10 Jan. '62 and released

9 Apr. '62, he served under Buell in Alabama and Kentucky and was Maj. Gen. McCook's Chief of Staff at Perryville. From 1 Jan. '63 until the end of the war he saw no more field service and was promoted Col. 8th US Inf. 18 May '64 while in command of Ft. Columbus, N.Y. He was breveted for Perryville and war service (B.G. USA).

BOND, John Randolph. Union officer. N.Y. 1st Lt. and Adj. 20th Ohio 11 Sept. '61; Maj. 16 Oct. '61; Lt. Col. 67th Ohio 27 July '62; Col. 111th Ohio 28 Aug. '62; Bvt. B.G. USV (war service); discharged 18 Oct. '64. Commanded 2, 2, XIII. Died 1877.

BONHAM, Edward. Union officer. Ill. Pvt. and 1st Sgt. Co. G 47th Ill. 16 Aug. '61; 2d Lt. 27 Nov. '62; 1st Lt. 26 Sept. '63; Maj. 10 Feb. '65; Lt. Col. 2 May '62; Bvt. B.G. USV (war service).

BONHAM, Milledge Luke. C.S.A. gen. and Gov. of S. C. 1813–90. S.C. After South Carolina College he studied law, fought in the Seminole War, where he commanded the S.C. brigade, and served in the state militia as Maj. Gen. He was also in the legislature and in the Mexican War where his adjutant was Winfield S. Hancock and his brigade commander was Franklin Pierce. Named to Congress for the unexpired term of his cousin Preston Brooks (see Charles SUMNER), he was a states-rights Democrat. When the state seceded, he was appointed commander in chief of S.C. troops around Charleston by the Governor and waived his rank to serve under Beauregard during the bombardment of Sumter. Appointed B.G. C.S.A. 23 Apr. '61, he led his brigade at Fairfax, Centreville, Vienna, and 1st Bull Run and resigned 29 Jan. '62. Then in the C.S.A. Congress, he was also Governor of S.C. from Dec. '62 to Dec. '64. He was reappointed B.G. C.S.A. 20 Feb. '65 and served under Johnston until his surrender. He was later a legislator, railroad commissioner, and Democratic politician.

BONNEVILLE, Benjamin L. E. Union officer and noted explorer. 1793–1878. France. Appt.-N.Y. USMA 1815* (35/40); Lgt. Arty.-Inf. Remembered for his western explorations in 1831–36, he fought in the Mexican War (1 wound, 1 brevet). He was retired from active service for disabilities on 9 Sept. '61 and during the war commanded recruiting and mustering activities in Mo. as Col. Breveted B.G. USA for his war services, he continued serving until 1866. Washington Irving used his journal as the basis for *The Adventures of Captain Bonneville* (1843).

"BONNIE BLUE FLAG, THE." Confederate song first performed in Richmond and New Orleans theaters in 1861. Experts disagree as to the author and exact date of composition. It has been said that the bonnie blue flag was the blue field of the United States flag bearing first a single star for South Carolina (which seceded first), joined later, according to the song, by the other ten, and was used before the adoption of the now-familiar Confederate flags.

BOONEVILLE, Miss. 1 July '62. Shortly after he had taken command of the 2d Cav. Brig. (2d Mich. and 2d Iowa Cav.), Sheridan was attacked at Booneville, a station on the Mobile & Ohio R.R. about 22 miles south of Corinth. An estimated 5,000 Confederate cavalry under J. R. Chalmers drove in the Federal pickets and threatened to annihilate the smaller force. Although authorized to withdraw, Sheridan launched a surprise attack against Chalmers's rear and routed his much larger force. Sheridan

* There was no class standing prior to 1818, and the cadets are listed in the order they were commissioned.

reported his effective strength at 827, and estimated the enemy's at "not less than five thousand men." B.&L. puts Chalmers's strength at 1,200 to 1,500, and T.U.A. says it was between 4,000 and 5,000. Sheridan was promoted B.G. to date from this battle, and his superiors reported to Halleck, "He is worth his weight in gold."

BOOTH, John Wilkes. Actor and Lincoln's assassin. 1838–65. After success in Shakespearean roles in 1859, he joined the Virginia militia regiment that assisted in the capture and execution of John BROWN that same year. For six months he planned with several others to abduct Lincoln to Richmond at the outbreak of war, but this plot failed when the President did not appear where the conspirators lay in wait. On 14 Apr. '65 he learned that the President would attend the performance that evening of *Our American Cousin* starring Laura Keene at Ford's Theatre. After arranging plans with his co-plotters that afternoon, he leaped into Lincoln's box shortly after 10 P.M., shot the President, and jumped on the stage shouting, "*Sic semper tyrannis!* The South is avenged!" His spur caught in the folds of the American flag draped over the box, and he fell, breaking his leg. He escaped backstage to a waiting horse and was not found until 26 Apr., in a barn near Bowling Green (Va.). The barn was set on fire, and Booth was shot to death as he made his escape. Although the original plot had called for killing several high Union officials, all escaped harm except Seward, who was severely stabbed. Booth was the brother of Edwin Booth, the great Shakespearean actor, and son of Junius Brutus Booth, the English tragedian. See also LINCOLN'S ASSASSINATION.

BORDER SLAVE STATE CONVENTION. See WASHINGTON PEACE CONFERENCE.

BORDER STATES. Those slave states in which considerable anti-slavery sentiment was evident. The appearance of Federal troops kept Delaware, Kentucky, Maryland, and Missouri within the Union, although these states were well represented on both sides of the battles. Virginia seceded, and the manufacturing and mining interests in the western part of the state seceded from Virginia and were recognized in 1861 by Congress as the state of West Virginia.

BORDER STATE WAR GOVERNORS. *Kentucky:* Beriah Magoffin (1859–62), James F. Robinson (1862–63), Thomas E. Bramlette (1863–67); *Maryland:* Thomas H. Hicks (1857–61), A. W. Bradford (1861–65); *Missouri:* H. R. Gamble (1861–64), T. C. Fletcher (1864–68).

BORDER WAR. See BLEEDING KANSAS.

BOREMAN, Arthur Ingram. Gov. of West Virginia. 1823–96. Pa. A lawyer and member of the Virginia legislature, he vigorously opposed secession and in 1861 joined the Wheeling Convention that granted statehood to the mountain counties. Elected the first Governor of West Virginia in 1863, he was twice re-elected and then sent to the U.S. Senate.

BORMANN FUZE. Developed by a Belgian officer, this was a punch-type powder-train time fuze used with field and siege guns. "Accurate and reliable, especially for spherical-case shot," according to the West Point text (Benton), it was found by Civil War gunners to be extremely erratic.

BOUGHTON, Horace. Union officer. N.Y. 1st Lt. 13th N.Y. 14 May '61; Capt. 9 Jan. '62; Lt. Col. 143d N.Y. 23 Oct. '62; Col. 1 May '63; Bvt. B.G. USV (war service). Commanded 1, 3, XI; 3, 1, XX; 3d Brig., 1st Dist. Beaufort (N.C.). Died 1891.

BOUNTIES. To stimulate Northern enlistments, military bounties were given by Federal, state, and local authorities. In the militia draft of 1862 the Federal government gave $25.00 to nine months' volunteers and $50.00 to twelve months' volunteers. For three-year men Congress voted $100 in July '61, and this was offered to draftees during the conscription who would volunteer for a longer time. After the Enrollment Act of 3 Mar. '63, $100 was given to conscripts and substitutes; $300 to three-year volunteers; and $400 to five-year volunteers. The bounties were paid over a period of time rather than as one lump sum. The state bounties were raised to fill the ranks without CONSCRIPTION, which was considered a disgrace to the congressional district that had to resort to it. This resulted in wealthy districts luring soldiers away from the poorer areas with a high bounty. Shannon estimates that the Federal government paid over $300,000,000 in bounties, and in the last two years of the war state and local agencies paid about the same amount. Total bounty payments for the war came to around $750,000,000. See also BOUNTY BROKER and BOUNTY JUMPER.

The Confederate government authorized a $10 enlistment bounty on 16 May '61 and on 22 Jan. '62 increased this to $50. There were various provisions for deferring payment of the total amount, but an act of 17 Feb. '62 prescribed "That the bounty of fifty dollars, allowed by existing laws to soldiers enlisting for the war, or re-enlisting for two years, or recruited, shall be payable as soon as the volunteer entitled thereto shall have been sworn into the Confederate service, and shall have been pronounced by any surgeon, or assistant surgeon of the Confederate States after inspection, as being fit and able to do military service" (C.S.A. *Statutes at Large,* 1864, 278).

BOUNTY BROKER. Agents who recruited men and robbed them of much of their BOUNTIES. They also enlisted men unfit for service who would have to be discharged after their bounties had been paid. See BOUNTY JUMPER.

BOUNTY JUMPER. Such men, aided by BOUNTY BROKERS, would enlist, collect BOUNTIES, desert, and then repeat the cycle until apprehended. One man confessed to deserting 32 times and was sentenced to four years in prison. The large bounty payment, rather than having the amount spread over the period of enlistment, was partly responsible for the high desertion rate of the Union Army, totaling 268,000 men.

BOUTON, Edward. Union officer. 1834-1921. N.Y. Capt. 1st Ill. Arty. 10 Feb. '62; Col. 59th US Col. Inf. 28 June '63; Bvt. B.G. USV 28 Feb. '65. He was Provost Marshal of Memphis after its capture. Turned to sheep raising in California after war.

BOUTWELL, George Sewall. Lawyer and politician. 1818-1905. Mass. An organizer of the Republican party, he was for a time chairman of the Committee on Reconstruction while serving as US Representative (1863-69). He was also one of the managers chosen to conduct the impeachment proceedings against Johnson, and delivered one of the final arguments for the prosecution. Before that he had served in the Massachusetts legislature and was elected Governor of that state by a coalition of the Free-soilers and Democrats in 1851. Serving as Grant's Secretary of the Treasury, he substantially reduced the national debt and was the person responsible for the release of the government gold that defeated the attempt to corner that market on "Black Friday" in 1869 by Gould and Fisk.

BOWEN, James. Union gen. 1808-86. N.Y. A wealthy New Yorker, he was the first president of the Erie R.R., a state legislator, holder of various civic offices, and the first police commissioner of N.Y.C. After raising several regiments, he was named B.G. USV 11 Oct. '62 and was Provost Marshal of the Dept. of the Gulf. Breveted Maj. Gen. USV for war service, he resigned 27 July '64.

BOWEN, John S. C.S.A. gen. 1830-63. Ga. USMA 1853 (13/51); Mtd. Rifles. He served on the frontier and in garrison before resigning in 1856 to become an architect in Savannah and St. Louis. Active in the Mo. militia, he was acting Chief of Staff to Frost when Camp Jackson was searched by Lyon and was commissioned Col. 1st Mo. 11 June '61. Serving under Polk at Columbus (Ky.), he commanded a brigade for a month before being appointed B.G. C.S.A. 14 Mar. '62. He was leading his unit at Shiloh when wounded on the first day. Recovering in time for the Vicksburg campaign, he was promoted Maj. Gen. 25 May '63 after fighting at Port Gibson. He was captured in command of his division at Vicksburg and after his parole was sent to Raymond (Miss.), where he died 13 July '63 of a disease contracted during the siege.

BOWEN, Thomas Meed. Union officer. 1835-1906. Iowa. Capt. 1st Nebr. Cav. 11 June '61; resigned 5 Feb. '62; 1st Lt. 9th Kans. Cav. 11 July '62; Capt. 30 July '62; Col. 13th Kans. 20 Sept. '62; Bvt. B.G. USV 13 Feb. '65. Commanded 3, Dist. Frontier; 3, Dist. Frontier, VII; 1, 1 (VII). He was prominent in Ark. reconstruction politics, serving as Chief Justice of the state Supreme Court. In 1871 he was appointed Governor of Idaho Territory, a position which he shortly resigned. He also served as Judge and US Senator from Colorado. He made and lost several fortunes in mining.

BOWERMAN, Richard Neville. Union officer. Md. Cpl. Co. G 7th N.Y. State Militia 26 Apr. '61; mustered out 3 June '61; 1st Lt. 11th N.Y. 11 July '61; Capt. 4 Oct. '61; mustered out 19 Apr. '62; Lt. Col. 4th Md. 1 Aug. '62; Col. 4 Apr. '63; Bvt. B.G. USV 1 Apr. '65 (Five Forks, Va.). Commanded 3, 2, V; 2, 2, V.

BOWERS, Theodore S. Union officer. Pa. Enlisting as Pvt. 48th Ill. Oct. '61, he was named 1st Lt. in Mar. '62 and became Grant's A.D.C. the next month. He was promoted Capt. and A.D.C. USV in Nov. '62 and Maj. and Judge Advocate of the Dept. of the Tenn. Feb. '63. Commissioned Capt. and Asst. Q.M. USA in July '64, he continued in the R.A. as Maj. and Asst. Adj. Gen. Jan. '65. Breveted for war service (B.G. USA), he died in 1866 after serving under Grant in Washington.

BOWIE, George Washington. Union officer. Md. Col. 5th Cal. 8 Nov. '61; Bvt. B.G. USV (war service); mustered out 14 Dec. '64. As 1st Lt. and Capt. ('47–'48); he won a brevet in the Mexican War.

BOWIE KNIFE. Popularized by the Mexican and Indian fighter Col. James Bowie (rhymes with Louis), this was the name given to all sheath knives which most Confederate soldiers carried until they learned to discard them as excess baggage. Officially known as "side knives," they had no set pattern.

BOWLES, Pinckney Downie. C.S.A. gen. 1838–? S.C. After graduating from a Charleston military academy and the University of Virginia, he practiced law in Alabama and was commissioned Capt. 4th Ala. 2 May '61. Sent to Harpers

Ferry, he fought under Bee at 1st Bull Run and then was stationed in the vicinity of Norfolk. He participated in Seven Pines, went to the Valley for part of Jackson's campaign, and then returned to the Peninsula for the Seven Days' Battles under Jackson. Promoted Maj. 22 Aug. '62, he fought at 2d Bull Run and Antietam and on 30 Sept. '62 was named Lt. Col. As Col. 4th Ala. (3 Oct. '62), he led his regiment at Fredericksburg, Chancellorsville, Gettysburg, the Wilderness, Spotsylvania, Cold Harbor, Petersburg, and battles around Richmond. He was appointed B.G. C.S.A. 2 Apr. '65 and surrendered at Appomattox. Later he practiced law.

BOWMAN, Samuel M. Union officer. Pa. Maj. 4th Ill. Cav. 5 Sept. '61; Col. 84th Pa. 21 June '62; Bvt. B.G. USV (war service). Commanded 2, 3, III; Dist. Del. VIII. Died 1885.

BOWYER, Eli. Union officer. Ohio. Maj. 11th Mo. 6 Aug. '61; Lt. Col. 16 Nov. '64; Col. 22 May '65; Bvt. B.G. USV (war service). Died 1886.

BOYD, Belle. Confederate spy. 1843–1900. Va. As a 17-year-old girl, she took information on Yankee troop movements to Stonewall Jackson during his Valley campaign. Having lived in W. Va. and FRONT ROYAL, she was familiar with the countryside and performed valuable services for the Confederacy. She was twice arrested and each time released, escaping in 1863 to England, where she went on the stage. She returned to the U.S. and died at Kibourne, Wis., while on tour.

BOYD, Joseph Fulton. Union officer. Ohio. Appt.-Ky. Capt. Asst. Q.M. Vols. 7 Oct. '61; appointment expired 4 Mar. '63; Capt. Asst. Q.M. Vols. 4 Mar. '63; Lt. Col. Q.M. Assigned 17 Mar.–10 Nov. '63; Lt. Col. Q.M. Assigned 25 Feb. '64; Col. Q.M. Assigned 21 June '65–13 Mar. '66; Bvt. B.G. USV (war service).

BOYDTON PLANK ROAD, Va., 27 Oct. '64. HATCHER'S RUN, same date. —— 5–7 Feb. '65. DABNEY'S MILLS, same dates.

BOYLE, Jeremiah Tilford. Union gen. 1818–71. Ky. After Princeton he practiced law and was commissioned B.G. USV 9 Nov. '61. He helped organize the defense of Kentucky and was Military Governor 1862–64. In the Army of the Ohio he commanded the 11th Brig. when it was in the 1st Div. (5 Dec. '61–9 Mar. '62) and in the 5th Div. (9 Mar.–27 May '62). He also commanded the Dist. Louisville and Dist. West Ky. (17 Nov. '62–4 Apr. '63). Resigned 26 Jan. '64. He was president of several railroads until his death.

BOYNTON, Henry. Union officer. Me. Capt. 8th Me. 7 Sept. '61; Maj. 21 Dec. '63; Lt. Col. 11 Apr. '64; Col. 13 Sept. '64; Bvt. B.G. USV (war service).

BOYNTON, Henry Van Ness. Union officer. 1835–? Mass. Maj. 35th Ohio 29 July '61; Lt. Col. 13 July '63; Bvt. B.G. USV (Chickamauga, Missionary Ridge); discharged 8 Sept. '64. Medal of Honor 15 Nov. '93 for Missionary Ridge 25 Nov. '63, where he was also wounded. An instructor at Kentucky Military Institute prior to the war, he was a journalist and author later; particularly known for his criticism of Sherman's Atlanta campaign.

BRADFORD, Augustus W. Gov. of Maryland. 1805–81. Md. A lawyer, he entered politics as a Whig and was an ardent worker for the preservation of the Union. He was a delegate to the Washington peace conference during secession winter and succeeded Hicks as Governor in 1862, elected by the Unionist element in the state. Serving until 1866, he continued Hicks's Federal policies and held the state in the Union. His house was burned in July '64 by Confederate raiders and also that year

he was influential in the passage of a new state constitution abolishing slavery.

BRADLEY, Amy M. Union nurse. Me. Serving as nurse for the 3d Me., she was at 1st Bull Run and in Sept. '61 transferred to the 5th Me. Later that fall she took over the brigade hospital in Washington and in May '62 went to the Peninsula as a SANITARY COMMISSION worker. There she worked on the *Elm City* and took charge of the *Knickerbocker*, both hospital ships. In Sept. '62 she took charge of the Commission's Soldiers' Home in Washington and went also to Camp Distribution, a gathering place of the army's derelicts, as special relief agent. This place, known as "Camp Misery" by the soldiers, was changed within days from a dirty, filth-ridden backwater to a clean and cheerful camp with an appreciable increase in administrative efficiency processes at the same time. She also set the idle soldiers to publishing the *Soldier's Journal*, which explained the processes and rules and methods of obtaining pay, clothing, furloughs and other privileges about which the average soldier was ignorant.

BRADLEY, Luther Prentice. Union gen. 1822–? Conn. Named Lt. Col. 51st Ill. 6 Nov. '61, he fought at Island No. 10, New Madrid, Farmington, and Nashville. As Col. 15 Oct. '62, he fought at Stones River, commanding 3, 3d Div. Rgt. Wing, XIV, Cumberland 31 Dec. '62–9 Jan. '63. He led 3, 3, XX, Cumberland (9 Jan.–28 Sept. '63) at Chickamauga, where he was wounded. As B.G. USV 30 July '64, he led 3, 2, IV, Cumberland (27 June–16 Dec. '64 and 25 May–5 June '65) during the Atlanta campaign and at Franklin where he was wounded. Breveted for Chickamauga and Resaca (B.G. USA), he continued in the R.A. until 1886, when he retired as Col. 13th US Inf.

BRADSHAW, Robert Charles. Union officer. Mo. Pvt. Co. A 13th Mo. 14 June '61; 2d Lt. 20 June '61; 1st Lt. 25th Mo. 1 Aug. '61; Capt. 16 May '62; resigned 1 Jan. '64; Maj. 87th Mo. Enrolled Mil. 13 July '64; Lt. Col. 15 July '64; Col. 44th Mo. 29 Sept. '64; Bvt. B.G. USV (war service).

BRADY, Mathew B. Pioneer photographer. 1823–96. He accompanied the Union armies throughout the war and compiled an elaborate collection of battle scenes and military and civilian leaders. A famous portrait photographer in New York and the winner of international prizes in the infant medium, he used the bulky and imperfect wet-plate process to record many scenes actually under fire as well as to compile portraits of the leaders on both sides, thus making an invaluable record of the war.

BRADY, Thomas Jefferson. Union officer. Ind. Capt. 8th Ind. 21 Apr. '61; mustered out 6 Aug. '61; Capt. 8th Ind. 5 Sept. '61; Maj. 10 May '62; resigned 28 Sept. '63; Col. 117th Ind. 4 Oct. '63; mustered out 29 Feb. '64; Col. 140th Ind. 24 Oct. '64; Bvt. B.G. USV (war service).

BRAGG, Braxton. C.S.A. gen. 1817–76. N.C. USMA 1837 (5/50); Arty. He fought in the Seminole War, served on the frontier, and won three brevets in the Mexican War before resigning in 1856. (See DOUBLE SHOTTING.) While running his Louisiana plantation, he designed a drainage and levee system for the state. He was commissioned Col. and then Maj. Gen. in the militia early in 1861. Appointed B.G. C.S.A. 7 Mar. '61, he commanded the coast between Pensacola and Mobile and was promoted Maj. Gen. 12 Sept. of that year. Foreseeing important events in Kentucky, he asked to be sent there and served under A. S. Johnston in the re-organization of the army at Corinth. He commanded the II CORPS and was Johnston's Chief of Staff during this time, and led the Confederate right at SHILOH. On 12 Apr. '62 he was appointed full General in the regular Confederate army and on 27 June relieved Beauregard as commander of the ARMY OF TENNESSEE. He then led BRAGG'S INVASION OF KENTUCKY and fought at PERRYVILLE and STONES RIVER. After further demonstrating his ineptitude for high command in the TULLAHOMA CAMPAIGN, at CHICKAMAUGA and CHATTANOOGA, he was relieved by J. E. Johnston and returned to Richmond as military advisor to Davis (24 Feb. '64–31 Jan. '65). He then held several minor commands and went with Davis to Georgia where he was captured 9 May '65. After his parole, he was a civil engineer in Texas. D.A.B. describes him as "Tall, bearded and ungainly... intelligent and energetic...[with] a a stern sense of duty.... Irritable and quarrelsome, he made many enemies." "Indeed, Braxton Bragg was a strange and unfortunate mixture," writes Horn, in summing up his character. "Nearly all observers, on both sides, give him credit for the highest moral character and for skill in planning and carrying out some military maneuvers, but his execution of his own plans was hampered by an innate vagueness of purpose, and his unpopularity with practically everyone he encountered greatly diminished his effectiveness. In his defense it should be said that he was the victim of a painful and distressing chronic ailment—migraine, or sick headache—and he was often ill from other causes during his campaigning. 'He was frequently in the saddle when the more appropriate place for him would have been in bed,' wrote an officer in his army who was no great admirer.... Recognition of Bragg's genuine patriotism and unselfish devotion to the Southern cause is general." Brother of Thomas Bragg.

BRAGG, Edward Stuyvesant. Union gen. 1827–? N.Y. A public officeholder, he was commissioned Capt. 6th Wis. (part of the IRON BRIGADE) 16 July '61 and promoted Maj. 17 Sept. '61. He was named Lt. Col. 21 June '62, Col. 24 Mar. '63 and B.G. USV 25 June '64. With his regiment he saw action in all the campaigns of the Army of the Potomac except the Peninsular. In the V Corps he led 3, 3d Div. (24 Aug.–13 Sept. '64); 1, 3d Div. (13 Sept.–22 Dec. '64 and 18 Jan.–14 Feb. '65); 1, 4th Div. (7 June–24 Aug. '64); and 3, 4th Div. (6 May–6 June '64). He was mustered out 9 Oct. '65 and became a prominent Democrat, attending many national conventions. He was famous for the phrase he used in seconding Cleveland's nomination in 1884: "We love him for the enemies he has made." A Congressman, he was also Minister to Mexico 1888–89 and Consul General to Havana in 1902 and to Hong Kong 1902–06.

BRAGG, Thomas. C.S.A. Attorney General. 1810–72. N.C. Brother of Gen. Braxton Bragg, he attended a New England military academy and then practiced law in his state. First sitting in the legislature, he was Democatic Governor 1854–58 and Senator 1858–61. Resigning, he followed his state and was Attorney General from 21 Nov. '61, following Benjamin, until 18 Mar. '62 when Thomas H. Watts took over his portfolio. He returned to his law practice and carried it on until his death.

"BRAGG'S A GOOD DOG, BUT HOLD FAST'S A BETTER." Statement attributed to Rosecrans, referring to himself as "Hold Fast," after successfully withstanding Bragg's attacks at Stones River (Murfreesboro), 31 Dec. '62 (B.&L., III, 634).

BRAGG'S CORPS. See II CORPS, Confed., A. of Miss. and of Tenn.

BRAGG'S INVASION OF KENTUCKY, Aug.–Sept. '62. After the ill-defined strategy agreed to between Bragg and Kirby Smith and leading to Kirby SMITH'S INVASION OF KENTUCKY, Bragg launched his invasion of Kentucky. On 28 Aug. the corps of Polk and Hardee crossed the Tennessee above Chattanooga and reached Glasgow, Ky., on 13 Sept. Bragg then captured MUNFORDVILLE, Ky., 14–17 Sept. Although this put him astride Buell's line of communications where he would have forced a decisive battle, Bragg continued north. He felt he should avoid battle at this place and move into the Blue Grass region where he expected to get recruits as well as supplies. Bragg disposed his army in the vicinity of Bardstown during the period 23 Sept.–3 Oct. Meanwhile, he turned over command to Polk on 28 Sept. and went first to Harrodsburg to establish a supply depot, and then to Lexington to confer with Kirby Smith. He then went to Frankfort where he established Richard Hawes as provisional Confederate governor of Kentucky on 4 Oct. He then ordered all his remaining troops up from Chattanooga and Knoxville.

When Buell learned that Bragg had undertaken the offensive, he first believed its purpose was merely to turn his position at Bridgeport (25 miles west of Chattanooga). He had to abandon an attempt to concentrate at Altamont. On 5 Sept. he was at Murfreesboro. Learning that Bragg was due east at Sparta on this same date, and continuing north, Buell retreated toward Nashville. He reached Munfordville on 21 Sept., the day after the Confederates left. On the 29th his leading troops reached Louisville. Here he found 39,-721 raw troops under William ("Bull") Nelson. After integrating these into his veteran divisions, Buell left Louisville on 1 Oct. to attack Bragg. This resulted in the battle of PERRYVILLE, 8 Oct. '62.

BRAILEY, Moses Randolph. Union officer. N.Y. Maj. 38th Ohio 28 Jan. '62; resigned 9 Feb. '62; Capt. 85th Ohio 10 June '62; Maj. 111th Ohio 28 Aug. '62; Lt. Col. 13 Feb. '63; Bvt. B.G. USV (Mill Spring, Ky.); discharged 29 Dec. '63. Died 1888.

BRAMLETTE, Thomas E. Union Gov. of Kentucky. 1817–75. Ky. A lawyer, he served as judge until 1861, when he resigned to raise the 3d Ky. and become its Colonel. He was elected Governor in 1863 after having been appointed B.G. USV (24 Apr. '63) and declining it. Re-elected, he served until 1867 and then practiced law.

BRANCH, Lawrence O'Bryan. C.S.A. gen. 1820–62. N.C. From a prominent and wealthy family, he was reared by his uncle, a Governor of the state, and tutored by William J. Brigham and Salmon P. Chase. He attended the U. of N.C. and graduated from Princeton, worked on a newspaper, practiced law in Florida, and fought in the Seminole War. He was also a Democratic congressman who cautioned the South about "immoderation," but when the Southern states were "coerced" he resigned and advocated secession. Named Q.M. and Paymaster General of state troops, he was commissioned Col. 33d N.C. and on 16 Nov. '61 was appointed B.G. C.S.A. and commanding general of the forces around New Bern. In June he joined Jackson to fight at Hanover Courthouse, Seven Days' Battles, Cedar Run, 2d Bull Run, Fairfax Courthouse, Ox Hill, Harpers Ferry, and Antietam, where he was killed (17 Sept. '62).

BRANDON, William L. C.S.A. gen. c. 1801–90. Appt.-Miss. Educated at Princeton, he became a Miss. legislator and Lt. Col. of 21st Miss. Wright says

that he was appointed Gen. 18 June '64. After losing a leg at Malvern Hill, he commanded the Conscription Bureau in Miss. '64–'65. He was paroled at Meridian (Miss.) 10 May '65. Miller incorrectly says that he commanded a cavalry brigade. He is not listed by C.M.H.

BRANDY STATION, Va. 9 June '63 (Gettysburg Campaign). Known also as Fleetwood (Hill) or Beverly Ford, this was "the first true cavalry combat of the war" (Steele) and the largest (Commager).

After the action at FRANKLIN'S CROSSING Hooker ordered further reconnaissance to determine the extent and significance of Lee's movements from Fredericksburg toward the west. Pleasonton's cavalry corps, supported by the infantry brigades of Ames (2, 1, XI) and Russell (3, 1, VI), plus six light batteries—a strength of about 11,000— left Falmouth 8 June and moved toward Culpeper. Stuart's cavalry was screening along the Rappahannock; with the exception of A. P. Hill, at Fredericksburg, Lee's army was at Culpeper.

Pleasonton's plan was to attack across the river at dawn with two columns. Buford's cavalry division with Ames's brigade assembled secretly near Beverly Ford; opposite them was the Confederate cavalry brigade of W. E. ("Grumble") Jones. Six miles downstream, at Kelly's Ford, the cavalry divisions of Gregg and Duffié, with Russell in support, were to attack at the same time; this crossing was outposted by Robertson's Confederate cavalry brigade, with Wade Hampton's cavalry nearby.

Under cover of a morning haze the two columns attacked at about 4 o'clock and achieved surprise. Buford drove Jones toward Brandy Station and, in fierce fighting, Fleetwood Hill changed hands several times. Gregg pushed Robertson's pickets back from Kelly's Ford but, fortunately for the Confederates, Duffié was late.

Although Federal infantry was on the field and Confederate infantry (Rodes's division) was hurrying up, Brandy Station was predominately a cavalry engagement. "During the day the First New Jersey Cavalry, alone, made six regimental charges, besides a number of smaller ones; the fighting and charging of the regular and Sixth Pennsylvania Cavalry was kept up for over twelve hours...." (Charles D. Rhodes in Miller, IV, 228.)

Just as Buford withdrew to the east, Gregg attacked from the south. A counterattack by Wade Hampton resecured Fleetwood Hill. Gregg moved to Brandy Station but was finally driven out. Stuart retained possession of the battlefield.

At Stevensburg, five and a half miles south, Duffié's division was drawn into a fight with 500 Confederate cavalrymen of the 2d S.C. and 4th Va. In a confused, far-spreading fight about half of the 4th Va. was captured. However, the action kept Duffié from arriving at Brandy Station in time to participate.

The Confederates lost 523, and Union losses were 936, including 486 captured (*Lee's Lts.;* in his earlier *R. E. Lee,* III, 32, Freeman puts Confederate losses at around 485 and Federal losses at approximately 930, citing O.R.) Pleasonton had accomplished his mission, and Hooker now knew that Lee was leaving Fredericksburg and heading north. Stuart was humiliated by the battle and strongly criticized by the Southern press; his Gettysburg raid was prompted largely by a desire to re-establish his reputation.

"One result of incalculable importance certainly did follow this battle," says H. B. McClellan in an opinion seconded by other Civil War historians, "... it *made* the Federal cavalry. Up to that time confessedly inferior to the Southern horsemen, they gained on this day that confidence in themselves and in their commanders which enabled them to contest so fiercely the subsequent battlefields of June, July, and October."

Much currency has been given to the unfounded stories: 1) that this battle spoiled plans Stuart had for a raid starting 10 June; 2) that documents were captured from Stuart's headquarters (or those of his chief of artillery) that told of Lee's plans for the coming invasion; 3) that Rodes's infantrymen arrived at Brandy Station by train in time to take part in repulsing the Federals. The official reports of neither side support these misconceptions.

Lee's son, "Rooney," was seriously wounded; Wade Hampton's brother, Frank, and Stuart's chief scout, Will Farley, were mortally wounded. The Mississippian, "Grimes" Davis, was killed leading a Federal charge.

BRANNAN, John Milton. Union gen. 1819–92. D.C. Appt.-Ind. USMA 1841 (23/52); Arty. He served on the frontier, in garrison, and fought in the Mexican War (1 brevet, 1 wound) and the Seminole War. As Capt. 1st US Arty. (1854), he was named B.G. USV 28 Sept. '61 and commanded the Dist. of Key West (Mar.–June '62). He then commanded the Dist. Beaufort (June–22 Aug. '62) and US Forces Beaufort X, South (17 Sept.–1 Oct. '62). Between commanding the X Corps and Dept. of the South (13–17 Sept. and 27 Oct.–20 Jan. '63), he led the St. John's River (Fla.) expedition and fought at Pocotaligo 24 Oct. '62. He then commanded in the Army of the Cumberland, 1st Div., XXI (13 Apr.–20 May '63) and 3d Div., XIV (10 May–10 Oct. '63) at Hoover's Gap and Chickamauga. From 10 Oct. '63–25 June '65 he was Chief of Arty. for the Army of the Cumberland and was present at Missionary

Ridge, Dalton, Resaca, Dallas, Kenesaw Mountain, Chattahoochee, Peach Tree Creek, Atlanta, and Jonesboro. He was breveted for Jacksonville (Fla.), Chickamauga, Atlanta (B.G. USV), and war service (Maj. Gen. USV 23 Jan. '65 and Maj. Gen. USA). He continued in the R.A. until retired in 1888 as Col.

BRANTLY, William F. C.S.A. gen. 1830-70. Col. 29th Miss. Wright says that he was appointed temporary B.G. C.S.A. 26 July '64 to rank from the same date, and that this was confirmed 21 Feb. '65. His parole was dated 1 May '65 at Greensboro (N.C.). Miller adds that he commanded a brigade in Tennessee for a time, but Wood and C.M.H. do not list him as a general officer. He was assassinated 2 Nov. 1870.

BRATTON, John. C.S.A. gen. 1831-98. S.C. After graduating from South Carolina College and medical school, he was a doctor until named Capt. 6th S.C. in 1861. Promoted Col. in 1862, he led the regiment on the Peninsula and was wounded and captured at Seven Pines. Upon exchange he fought at the Wilderness and was named temporary B.G. C.S.A. 6 May '64. He continued to fight with the Army of Northern Virginia until Appomattox and then became a farmer, Congressman, legislator, and Democratic politician. Nicknamed "Old Reliable."

BRAYMAN, Mason. Union gen. 1813-95. N.Y. A printer, editor, and lawyer, he was the Government Commissioner on the withdrawal of the Mormons from Ill. in 1843. Later lawyer for the Ill. Central R.R., he was commissioned Maj. 29th Ill. 19 Aug. '61 and fought at Belmont, Ft. Donelson, and Shiloh. He was promoted Col. 19 Apr. '62 and commanded 1, 3, XVI, Tenn. (18 Mar.-28 May '63) after having been named B.G. USV 24 Sept. '62. He also commanded at Natchez (9 July '64-26 Feb. '65) and Dist. Cairo (9

Mar.-24 Apr. '64). Breveted Maj. Gen. USV, he was mustered out 24 Aug. '65. He was Governor of Idaho 1877-80.

BRAYTON, Charles Ray. Union officer. 1840-1910. R.I. 1st Lt. 3d R.I. Hv. Arty. 27 Aug. '61; Capt. 28 Nov. '62; Lt. Col. 17 Nov. '63; Col. 1 Apr. '64; Bvt. B.G. USV (war service); mustered out 5 Oct. '64. An early Republican, he was that party's political boss of Rhode Island for more than 30 years.

BRECK, Samuel. Union officer. c. 1834-1918. Mass. USMA 1855 (7/34); Arty.-Adj. Gen. He fought in the Seminole War, taught at West Point, and served in garrison before being promoted 1st Lt. 1st U.S. Arty. 11 Apr. '61. Named Capt. Asst. Adj. Gen. 29 Nov. '62, he served with McDowell (Dec. '61-24 Mar. '62), I Corps (24 Mar.-4 Apr. '62), Dept. of the Rappahannock (4 Apr.-20 June '62) and in the Adj. Gen. office in Washington for the remainder of the war. He received three brevets for war service, including Bvt. B.G. USA, and continued in the R.A. Retired in 1898 as B.G. Adj. Gen.

BRECKINRIDGE, John Cabell. C.S.A. gen. and Sec. of War. 1821-75. Ky. After graduating from Centre College, he studied law at Transylvania University and fought in the Mexican War where he sided with Pillow in the dispute with Scott. Active in Democratic politics, he served in the legislature and US Congress and was Buchanan's vice-president. He ran for president against Lincoln and then served as US Senator. Fleeing his native state on 2 Oct. '61 to escape arrest by the military government, he was declared a traitor to the United States and was appointed B.G. C.S.A. 2 Nov. '61. He served under A. S. Johnston and commanded the RESERVE CORPS at Shiloh. Promoted Maj. Gen. 14 Apr. '62, he attacked Baton Rouge in an unsuccessful foray and then fortified Port Hudson. At

Stones River he commanded the II Div. under Hardee and in May '63 served with J. E. Johnston in the Vicksburg campaign. He led a division of D. H. Hill's corps at Chickamauga and Missionary Ridge and succeeded Morgan in command of the Dept. of southwest Tenn. Going to the Shenandoah Valley, he later commanded his division at Cold Harbor and fought with Early at Monocacy, the Washington raid, and Martinsburg. He then returned to the Dept. of Southwest Va. until Davis made him Sec. of War on 4 Feb. '65. After Appomattox he continued to travel south with the rest of the cabinet and was J. E. Johnston's advisor during the surrender negotiations. He went to Cuba, Europe, and Canada before returning to Kentucky, where he practiced law and worked on railroad developments. See also BROTHER AGAINST BROTHER.

BRECKINRIDGE, Margaret E. SANITARY COMMISSION worker. c. 1832–64. N.J. Cousin of the Confederate leader John Breckinridge, she served as a nurse and Sanitary Commission agent under Grant in the West beginning in the spring of 1862. She ran a relief boat that plied between St. Louis and Vicksburg. Weakened by overwork and typhoid fever, she died 27 July '64 just as she was preparing to return to the field, this time in Virginia. See also BROTHER AGAINST BROTHER.

BRECKINRIDGE'S CORPS. See CORPS, Confed.

BRENT, Joseph Lancaster. C.S.A. gen. 1826–? Md. La. After college in Georgetown (D.C.), he was in California when the war began. Starting for the South, he was arrested with others by E. V. Sumner and held prisoner, finally being paroled and then released. He was commissioned Capt. and assigned to Magruder's staff during the winter of 1861–62 and was Maj. of Arty. and Magruder's Chief of Ordnance during

the Peninsular campaign. After that action he was assigned to Dick Taylor's staff in the Dist. of Western La. and was named Col. and Chief of Arty. and Ordnance (July '62). In the early spring of 1863 he led the force that captured the Federal ironclad *Indianola*, and then took over the 1st La. brigade of cavalry. He was appointed B.G. of Cav. in Oct. '64 (although never officially commissioned as such) and served in this position until the surrender, when he was in command of the forces in the front line of the West from Arkansas to the Gulf. After the war he practiced law in Baltimore before returning to Louisiana as a planter and legislator.

BRENTWOOD, Tenn. 25 Mar. '63. Forrest surprised, surrounded, and captured a post held by Lt. Col. Edward Bloodgood of the 22d Wis. Rosecrans sent G. C. Smith's cavalry brigade to their support. Smith reported overtaking the Confederates six miles from Brentwood (an action listed in E.&B. as Franklin and Little Harpeth). He had recaptured the wagons, ambulances, and arms when Forrest brought up reinforcements and drove him back to Brentwood. Although Rosecrans reported that Bloodgood's detachment numbered only 300, the Confederates claimed capture of 759 (Drake); Fiebeger accepts the latter figure (*op. cit.,* 208). Federal losses in Smith's action were 63 (E.&B.), and Forrest's were 30 (Drake). "Smith reports 350 to 400 of the enemy killed. Brought in 40 prisoners," according to Rosecrans's report (T.U.A.).

BREVARD, Theodore W. C.S.A. gen. 1835–82. Appt.-Fla. Commissioned Maj., he served in the Dept. of Fla. in 1862–63, leading a regiment called Brevard's Partisan Rangers. They skirmished at Jacksonville 11 Mar. '63 and he was promoted Lt. Col. in Dec. His regiment was then called 1st Fla. and fought at Olustee before being sent to Cold Harbor. In Aug. '64 he commanded the

11th Fla. at Petersburg. The last general officer appointed by Davis, he was appointed B.G. C.S.A. 22 Mar. '65.

BREVET RANK. For practical purposes brevet rank can be regarded as an honorary title, awarded for gallant or meritorious action in time of war, and having none of the authority, precedence, or pay of real or full rank. There were occasions, however, when an officer could claim that his brevet rank be recognized as real rank. The regulations were so vague that controversies arose throughout the war. An article of war of 1806 prescribed that although brevet rank had no real significance while an officer continued to serve within his own organization (regiment, troop, or company), or within his own "corps" (here used in the sense of Infantry, Artillery, Engineers, etc.), his brevet rank could have the recognition of real rank when he served "in courts-martial and on detachments, when composed of different corps." His brevet rank could also be claimed when he served with provisional formations made up of different regiments or companies, or "on other occasions." Garfield is quoted as saying during the war "it is now impossible to judge from an officer's title or uniform what his actual position and command may be.... Captains command majors and colonels, and a colonel not infrequently finds two or three brevet colonels among the company and field officers of his regiment." Not until 1869 was the A.W. of 1806 repealed. "The provisions in [this act]," writes R. N. Scott, "render valueless a long series of decisions and opinions, from the second comptrollers and the attorney generals, as to the condition under which pay and command, according to brevet rank, obtained under current legislation." (p. 252) The new act prescribed that "brevet rank shall not entitle an officer to precedence or command except by special assignment of the President; but such assignment shall not entitle any officer to additional pay or allowances."

An act of 3 Mar. '63 authorized the award of brevet rank to officers of the USV. Approximately 1,700 officers were breveted Maj. Gen. or B.G. of the R.A. or USV. (This abuse led to abandonment of the brevet system in the US Army.) Biographical sketches in this book will classify an officer as "Union officer" if his only claim to general officer rank was by brevet. The actions for which an officer was breveted can be considered highlights of his military career. Since the vast majority of the brevets were awarded 13 Mar. '65, this date is to be assumed when no other is given.

BREWERTON, Henry. Union officer. 1801–79. N.Y. USMA 1819 (5/29): Engrs. He taught engineering at West Point and served on river and harbor construction and fortifications before returning to the Military Academy as Superintendent in 1845. Promoted Lt. Col. 6 Aug. '61 (Maj. since 1856), he worked on the defenses of Baltimore Harbor, Pt. Lookout, Md., and Hampton Roads. He was retired in 1867 after having been made Bvt. B.G. USA.

BREWSTER, William R. Union officer. Conn. Maj. 28th N.Y. State Mil. 10 May '61; Col. 73d N.Y. 13 Sept. '61; Bvt. B.G. USV 2 Dec. '64 (Richmond); mustered out 25 Oct. '64. Commanded 2, 2, III; 2, 4, II; 4, 3, II. Died 1869.

BRIAR CREEK, Ga. See WAYNESBORO, 26–29 Nov. '64.

BRICE, Benjamin W. Union officer. c. 1806–92. Va. Appt.-Ohio. USMA 1829 (40/46); Inf. He served on the frontier in Indian fighting before resigning in 1832 to practice law in Ohio.

There he was active in the militia and sat on the bench for a time. He returned to the army during the Mexican War and in 1852 was commissioned Maj. Staff Paymaster in 1852. During the Civil War he was Col. Paymaster General (29 Nov. '64) and breveted Maj. Gen. USA. He retired in 1872 as B.G. USA Paymaster General.

BRICE'S CROSS ROADS (Guntown; Tishomingo Creek), Miss., 10 June '64. (FORREST'S OPERATIONS DURING THE ATLANTA CAMPAIGN) At the head of S. D. Sturgis' force of 4,800 infantry, 3,000 cavalry, and 18 guns sent from Memphis to destroy Forrest's cavalry, the Federal cavalry made contact at about 9:30 A.M. at Brice's Cross Roads. Waring's brigade had approached on a road that led due south. This road crossed a swampy area about a mile and a half north of the crossroads, and was elevated here to form a sort of causeway, about three quarters of a mile in length. This "defile" played an important role in the coming action. Grierson halted Waring's brigade and sent out reconnaissance. A squadron moving southeast toward Guntown, six miles away on the Mobile & Ohio R.R., encountered enemy pickets after going about a mile. Grierson then dismounted his command and deployed to hold the crossroads until the infantry arrived. The area around the crossroads was wooded within a radius of about a mile, and beyond these woods there were open fields to the east and south. Waring's brigade formed a line to the east and Winslow to the north, about a mile away from the crossroads, and so located as to cover these open fields.

Forrest had been on his way to raid the railroads in middle Tennessee when a dispatch from S. D. Lee called him back to meet A. J. Smith's advance. The night of the 9th he learned that the enemy was advancing toward Brice's Cross Roads, and he moved out at 4 the next morning to attempt to beat Smith to this point. Lyon's brigade made contact with Grierson's men and probed their defenses while Forrest brought up his artillery and additional troops. At 1 P.M., when these reinforcements arrived, Forrest started attacking.

Grierson's brigades were driven back to a second line at 2 P.M. At this time the Federal infantry started arriving (in poor condition after a five-mile forced march in intense heat) and were under musket fire as they moved into position. Fighting was in dense underbrush. Forrest brought heavy pressure to bear on both flanks of Sturgis' line. About 5 P.M. the Federal flanks began to give way, and confusion soon gave way to panic. "Before reaching Tishomingo Creek [about 400 yards north of the crossroads]," reported Forrest, "the road was so blockaded with abandoned vehicles of every description that it was difficult to move the artillery forward." The pursuit continued until dark, and resumed at 1 o'clock the next morning. Sturgis was unable to restore order until he had reached Stubb's plantation, 10 miles to the north.

A Federal force of 7,800 had been defeated by less than half that number. Sturgis lost 223 killed, 394 wounded, and 1,623 captured. Forrest captured 16 of his 18 guns, and the entire train of 250 vehicles, complete with 184 horses, rations, and ammunition. He reported having 3,500 engaged, and puts his own loss at 492.

A board was appointed on 25 June to investigate the "disaster to the late expedition under Brigadier-General Sturgis." It submitted a report that takes up 73 pages of the *Official Records*. Although no "findings" are included, Sturgis finished the war "awaiting orders."

BRIDGET, IRISH. See Bridget DIVERS.

BRIER, William N. Misspelling by Phisterer for William N. GRIER.

BRIGADE. See ORGANIZATION. Many of the Confederate brigades, which were designated by the name of a commander, rather than by number as in the Union Army, will be found immediately following the officer whose name is primarily associated with it. Brigade organizations were not permanent during the war, except for a few units such as the VERMONT BRIGADE. Many, however, contained a few regiments that remained with it throughout the war. The most famous brigades are covered separately. For example, IRISH BRIGADE, IRON BRIGADE, STONEWALL BRIGADE.

BRIGGS, Henry Shaw. Union gen. 1824–87. Mass. A graduate of Williams College, he practiced law until commissioned Capt. 8th Mass. Mil. 30 Apr. '61. He was promoted Col. 10th Mass. 21 July '61 and assumed command of 1, 1, IV, Potomac, 13 Mar.–30 Apr. '62. He distinguished himself at Fair Oaks and was promoted B.G. USV 17 July '62. He also led 3d Sep. Brig., VIII, Potomac (14 Feb.–July '63) and 1st Div., I Corps, Potomac (13–22 Aug.). He was serving as a member of a general court-martial at the end of the war and was mustered out 4 Dec. '65.

BRINKERHOF, Roeliff. Union officer. 1828–1911. N.Y. Appt.-Ohio. Capt. Asst. Q.M. Vols. 4 Nov. '61; Col. Q.M. Assigned 24 June '65–30 Sept. '66; Bvt. B.G. USV 30 Sept. '66 (war service). Engaged as a young man in teaching, he left his upstate N.Y. home to conduct a planter's private school near Nashville. In time he became the family tutor for Andrew Jackson, Jr., at the Hermitage. This position afforded him the time and opportunity to read extensively in Gen. Jackson's library. In 1849 he went into law and became also the editor-owner of a Mansfield (Ohio)

newspaper. He published *The Volunteer Quartermaster,* a handbook, in 1865. At first a Democrat, he became a Republican over the slavery question. That party's protective tariff drew his ire, however, and in 1869–70 he went on a speaking tour through the Midwest raising the question of tariff reforms. He then joined the Liberal Republican movement and when they were defeated returned to the Democratic party. He established the Mansfield Savings Bank and went into philanthropy and penology. He succeeded former President Hayes as president of the National Prison Association and was vice-president of the International Prison Congress.

BRISBIN, James Sanks. Union gen. c. 1838–92. Pa. Well known as an anti-slavery orator, he enlisted as a private and was shortly commissioned 2d Lt. 1st US Drag. 26 Apr. '61. He was wounded twice at 1st Bull Run, transferred to 1st US Cav. 3 Aug. '61 and was promoted Capt. 6th US Cav. 5 Aug. He fought in the Peninsular campaign and with Pleasonton in the '63 Blue Ridge Mountain Expedition. Named Col. 5th US Col. Cav. 1 Mar. '64, he was in the Red River Expedition of '64 and then served on recruiting duty in Kentucky and as Burbridge's chief of staff. Promoted B.G. USV 1 May '65, he was mustered out of USV in '66, later went in the R.A. as Maj. and died on active duty as Col. 1st US Cav. He was breveted for Beverly Ford (Va.), Marion (Tenn.), and war service (B.G. USV 12 Dec. '64 and Maj. Gen. USV).

BRISCOE, James C. Union officer. Ireland. Pvt. and Sgt. Co. E 1st N.Y. 7 May '61; 2d Lt. 15 May '62; 1st Lt. 14 Oct. '62; Capt. 40th N.Y. 31 Oct. '63; Maj. A.D.C. Vols. 3 Sept. '64; Col. 199th Pa. 3 Oct. '64; transferred to 188th Pa. 28 June '65; Bvt. B.G. USV (Ft. Gregg, Va.). Commanded 1, 1, X;

1, 1, XXIV; 2d Indpt. Brig. XXIV. Died 1869.

BRISTOE CAMPAIGN, Va. 9 Oct.–9 Nov. '63. After GETTYSBURG the two opposing armies maneuvered south. On 24 July Lee started concentrating around Culpeper. Two days later Meade, who had moved along the east side of the Blue Ridge, started concentrating opposite Lee along the Rappahannock. Both armies were then reduced in strength. From the Army of the Potomac a detachment went to S.C. and another went to N.Y. for the DRAFT RIOTS. From the Army of Northern Va. Longstreet went with two divisions to CHICKAMAUGA. When Meade learned of the latter detachment, which gave him a two-to-one numerical superiority, he advanced to Culpeper, and Lee withdrew behind the Rapidan.

In Oct. Lee learned that Meade had lost the XI and XII Corps, which Hooker had taken west to participate in the CHATTANOOGA CAMPAIGN. Lee then took the offensive with the objective of turning the Federal position from the west, in somewhat the same maneuver he had used in 2d Bull Run campaign. There followed an indecisive one-month period of maneuver in which Lee forced Meade's retreat but failed to cut him off before he could reach a strong defensive position behind Bull Run.

The only significant infantry action was at BRISTOE STATION, 14 Oct., where A. P. Hill's corps was repulsed with heavy losses. A minor skirmish took place at CATLETT'S STATION (Auburn), 14 Oct. There was a spirited cavalry clash at BUCKLAND MILLS, 19 Oct., in which Stuart routed Kilpatrick's 3d Cav. Div. ("The Buckland Races"). At RAPPAHANNOCK BRIDGE, 7 Nov., Russell led one of the most brilliant small actions of the war.

Lee failed to cut off Meade's withdrawal, and the campaign had no significant strategic result, but the Bristoe campaign illustrates the principle of the offensive that made Lee one of history's great commanders. "Although [Meade] had a numerical superiority of eight to five, he retreated about forty miles and permitted his adversary to destroy the railroad which it took a month to repair" (Fiebeger).

Meade then attempted an offensive, the MINE RUN CAMPAIGN.

BRISTOE STATION, Va. 14 Oct. '63. Attempting to cut off Meade's withdrawal during the BRISTOE CAMPAIGN, Lee's leading corps under A. P. Hill reached Greenwich about 10 A.M. on the 14th. In his haste to attack what he believed to be only the Federal III Corps near Bristoe Station and destroy them while they were astride Broad Run, Hill overlooked the presence of the II Corps. The latter, temporarily under Caldwell in the absence of Warren, had taken up strong positions behind the railroad embankment.

When Heth's brigades of Cooke and Kirkland advanced east to cut off the crossings of Broad Run they were surprised by a devastating fire from three divisions and the artillery of II Corps to their southeast. Instead of turning north across the stream to get away from this fire, the two Confederate brigades wheeled south and charged the strong enemy position. Here the Federal divisions were deployed with the 1st, 3d, and 2d divisions from left to right, and with their artillery located so as to fire over the heads of the friendly infantry.

Both Cooke and Kirkland were seriously wounded. The former lost 700 men including 33 officers and 290 of the 416 men in the 27th N.C. Kirkland lost 602, of whom nearly half were captured. Lee's total loss was about 1,900. Carnot Posey was mortally wounded.

Federal losses were 548 in II Corps. Units most heavily engaged were the 1st and 3d brigades of Webb's 2d Div., and the 3d Brig. of Hays's 3d Div. "These were the splendid veterans who had repulsed Pickett at Gettysburg." (*Lee's Lts.*, III, 246n.)

BRODHEAD, Thornton F. Union officer. 1822–62. N.H. Col. 1st Mich. Cav. 22 Aug. '61; Bvt. B.G. USV 30 Aug. '62 (2d Bull Run). W.I.A. 30 Aug. '62 at 2d Bull Run; died from wounds 2 Sept. '62. A lawyer and politician, he had served as 1st Lt. and Capt. in 1847–48, and was breveted for Contreras and Churubusco.

BRONSON, Stephen. Union officer. N.Y. Capt. 12th Ill. Cav. 28 Feb. '62; Maj. 1 Jan. '63; resigned 3 Mar. '64; Col. 141st Ill. 21 June '64; mustered out 10 Oct. '64; Col. 153d Ill. 27 Feb. '65; Bvt. B.G. USV 28 Sept. '65 (war service). Died 1896.

BROOKE, John Mercer. C.S.N. Chief of (Naval) Ordnance and Hydrography. 1826–1904. Fla. An Annapolis graduate (1847) who accompanied Perry on the first visit to Japan, he invented the BROOKE GUN, designed and built the ordnance and armor of the *Merrimac* (*Virginia*), and was in charge of experiments with submarine boats, torpedoes, and deep-sea sounding apparatus. He was a professor at V.M.I. after the war.

BROOKE, John Rutter. Union gen. 1838–1926. Pa. He was commissioned Capt. (20 Apr. '61) in the 4th Pa., which claimed its discharge just before 1st Bull Run and marched back to Pa. on the same morning the rest of the army marched forward to Va. Apparently more disposed to soldiering than his erstwhile comrades, he was named Col. 53d Pa. 7 Nov. '61 and led his regiment in the Peninsula. He commanded 3, 1, II (20 July–10 Aug. '62 and 6 Sept.–6 Oct. '62) at Antietam,

led his regiment at Fredericksburg, and then took over 3, 2, II (29 Dec. '62–20 Mar. '63). He led 4, 1, II (13 Apr.–20 May '63) at Chancellorsville; Gettysburg (12 June –29 Aug. '63) where he was wounded in the Wheat Field. He later described his condition as "severely bruised." He also commanded this brigade 20 Sept.–29 Dec. '63 and 25 Mar.–3 June '64 at the Wilderness, Spotsylvania, and Cold Harbor, where he was severely wounded and taken unconscious from the field. He also commanded 2d Prov. Div., Cav. Corps, Army Shenandoah. He was promoted B.G. USV 12 May '64 and breveted for Gettysburg, Totopotomoy, and Cold Harbor (Maj. Gen. USV, 1 Aug. '64), and Spotsylvania (B.G. USA). Resigning his USV commission in '66, he went into the R.A. During the Spanish-American War he was held partly responsible for the lack of sanitary conditions at the training camp in Chickamauga Park (Ga.). He landed with his troops in Puerto Rico where, after a skirmish at Guayama, he was preparing to attack at Cayey when the armistice was declared. He was then Military Governor of Puerto Rico and of Cuba and also commanded Dept. of the East, retiring in 1902 as Maj. Gen. USA.

BROOKE GUN. Invented by J. M. BROOKE of the Confederate Navy, this was a rifled gun that resembled the PARROTT in shape and construction with the variation that the reinforcing band was made up of iron rings not welded together. The rifling was similar to that of the Blakely (i.e., one-sided grooves). It was made in various calibers, including a 3-inch fieldpiece that weighed 900 pounds and fired a 10-pound projectile a maximum range of 3,500 yards (Miller, V, 157).

BROOKS, Horace. Union officer. c. 1815–94. Mass. USMA 1835 (9/56); Arty. He fought in the Seminole War

(1 brevet), taught mathematics at West Point, and served in the Mexican War (2 brevets) before serving on the Utah Expedition and fighting Indians in the West. As Maj. 2d U.S. Arty. 28 Apr. '61 (Capt. since 1846), he served at Ft. Pickens, Fla., and was promoted Lt. Col. (26 Oct. '61) and sent to Ft. Jefferson, Fla., Nov. '61–Mar. '62. He then commanded at Philadelphia until May '62 and served on boards and commissions for the rest of the war. He was promoted Col. 4th U.S. Arty. 1 Aug. '63 and breveted B.G. USA for war service. He retired in 1877 from the R.A.

BROOKS, William Thomas Harbaugh. Union gen. 1821–70. Ohio USMA 1841 (46/52); Inf. He fought in the Seminole War, served on the frontier, and participated in the Mexican War (2 brevets), where he served under Lee during the reconnaissance of Contreras. He was A.D.C. to Gen. Twiggs and active in Indian fighting, where the arduous field service undermined his health. He was Capt. 3d US Inf. (1851) when he was promoted B.G. USV 28 Sept. '61 and took over command of 1st, W. F. Smith's div., Potomac (3 Oct. '61–13 Mar. '62). He led 2, 2, IV, 13 Mar.–18 May '62 (Yorktown and Lee's Mill) and 2, 2, VI, 18 May–18 Oct. '62 (Golding's Farm, Savage's Station, where he was wounded, Glendale, Crampton's Pass, and Antietam where he was wounded again). He led 1st Div., VI, Potomac, 18 Oct. '62–23 May '63, during the Rappahannock campaign, commanded Dist. of Monongahela June '63–Apr. '64, and led 1st Div., XVIII, Va. and N.C., 28 Apr.–18 June '64, at Swift's Creek, Drewry's Bluff, Bermuda Hundred, and Cold Harbor. He was commanding X Corps, Va. and N.C. (21 June–18 July '64 at Petersburg) when his health brought about his resignation. He farmed in Huntsville (Ala.) until his death, a favored Yankee

in that Southern community for his "amiable disposition, simplicity of character, and sound common sense." (D.A.B.)

BROOKS-SUMNER AFFAIR. 22 May '56. See Charles SUMNER.

BROTHER AGAINST BROTHER. The crisis that split the Union split many families as well, particularly in the divided border states. At Gettysburg, the 7th W. Va. (Union), commanded by Lt. Col. Jonathan Lockwood, drove back the Confederate 7th Va. A Lt. Lockwood, C.S.A., and nephew of the regimental commander, was wounded and captured by his uncle's troops. (Fox.) The Crittendens of Kentucky were another case. Maj. Gen. George B. CRITTENDEN went with the South, while Maj. Gen. Thomas L. CRITTENDEN and Col. Eugene W. Crittenden fought with the Union army. Their father, John J. CRITTENDEN, was a US Senator. Maj. Gen. John C. BRECKINRIDGE, the former vice-president, and his three sons fought with the Confederacy, while their two cousins, Presbyterian ministers, stayed in the Union. One of these had two sons in the Confederacy and two in the Union army. A Yankee Breckinridge captured his Confederate brother in the battle before Atlanta. (B.&L., III). A daughter, Margaret E. BRECKINRIDGE, was a Sanitary Commission worker. In the *Monitor-Merrimac* battle the latter was commanded by Franklin BUCHANAN, C. S. Navy, while his brother McKean, who had remained with the Union Navy, was killed in the sinking of the *Congress*. William R. TERRILL, B.G. USV, was killed at the battle of Perryville 8 Oct. '62, and his brother, James B. TERRILL, B.G. C.S.A., was killed near Bethesda Church in May '64. Chester Hardy, Bvt. B.G. USV and son of the noted portrait painter, had one brother in the Union Army and two in the Confederacy. Mrs. Lincoln, a native of Kentucky, had one full brother, three half-brothers, and three brothers-in-law in the Confederate Army. Her half-sister Emilie, widow of the Confederate general Ben Hardin HELM, visited her in the White House in the winter of 1863-64.

Confederate commissioner John SLIDELL was the paternal uncle of Union Gen. Ranald Slidell MACKENZIE and Union naval officer Alexander Slidell Mackenzie. Va.-born Philip St. George COOKE chose to stay with the Union, while his son John R. COOKE and his son-in-law J. E. B. STUART went with the South. All three became generals. Philip St. George's nephew, John Esten COOKE, also chose the Confederacy. Edwin V. SUMNER's son-in-law, Armistead LONG, resigned from the US Army while serving as Sumner's aide and rose to be a Confederate Gen.

BROUGH, John. Gov. of Ohio. 1811-65. Ohio. As publisher of the Lancaster *Eagle* and joint owner and editor of the Cincinnati *Enquirer,* he was the leading Democratic newspaperman in the West. He was a stanch supporter of the Union and in 1863 vigorously attacked VALLANDIGHAM and his Southern sympathizers. This won him the Republican nomination for governor, and he defeated Vallandigham in the election. He died in office 29 Aug. '65.

BROWN, Charles Elwood. Union officer. 1834-? Ohio. Pvt. Co. B 63d Ohio 2 Sept. '61; Capt. 23 Oct. '61; Maj. 10 Mar. '63; Lt. Col. 17 May '65; Col. 6 June '65; Bvt. B.G. USV (war service). Whitelaw Reid in *Ohio in the War* says that at Corinth 3-4 Oct. '62 Brown was the only officer in the left wing of the regiment unhurt. W.I.A. 22 July '63 at Atlanta and lost left leg. Served as Provost Marshal of the XVIII Corps, Ohio Dist.

BROWN, Egbert Benson. Union gen. 1816-1902. N.Y. As a young man he sailed on a long whaling voyage in the Pacific and later settled in Toledo where he became mayor at 33 and was also a railroad manager. Commissioned Lt. Col. 7th Mo. 21 Aug. '61, he resigned 1 May '62 and was named B.G. Mo. State Militia 10 May '62. He commanded Dist. Southwest Mo., XIX, 5 June-24 Sept. '62 and 10 Nov. '62-30 Mar. '63, having been named B.G. USV 29 Nov. '62. He was severely wounded at Springfield 8 Jan. '63 and later commanded Dist. Central Mo. 9 June '63-24 July '64 and 3 Sept.-3 Nov. '64 and Dist. Rolla 31 Dec. '64-6 Mar. '65. He resigned 10 Nov. '65 with one shoulder totally disabled and a bullet in the hip. Later he farmed and held numerous public offices.

BROWN, Harvey. Union officer. 1796-1874. N.J. USMA 1818 (6/23); Lgt. Arty.-Arty. He served in garrison, fought in the Seminole wars (1 brevet), and was twice breveted for the Mexican War. Promoted Lt. Col. 4th US Arty. 28 Apr. '61 and Col. 5th U.S. Arty. 14 May '61, he commanded Ft. Pickens (Fla.) 16 Apr. '61-25 Feb. '62 during the fight at Santa Rosa Island and the bombardments of the fort. (Breveted B.G. USA 23 Nov. '61.) (See PENSACOLA BAY.) He declined the appointment of B.G. USV 28 Sept. '61 and took command of the defenses of N.Y. Harbor and the city itself from 5 Apr. '62 to 16 July '63. After the DRAFT RIOTS on the latter date he commanded Ft. Schuyler until 29 June '64 and was breveted Maj. Gen. USA in 1866 for suppressing the riots. He retired 1 Aug. '63 from active service.

BROWN, Hiram Loomis. Union officer. Pa. Capt. Erie Reg. Pa. Vols. 21 Apr.-25 July '61; Capt. 83d Pa. 13 Sept. '61; resigned 26 Oct. '62; Col. 145th Pa. 5 Sept. '64; Bvt. B.G. USV

3 Sept. '64. Commanded 3, 1, II; 1, II; 4, 1, II. Died 1880.

BROWN, John. Fanatic ABOLITIONIST. 1800–59. Conn. His incendiary actions on the eve of the Civil War led to his death. He kept a station of the UNDERGROUND RAILROAD in Richmond (Ohio), but in 1855, when his sons went to Kansas to help win the state for the anti-slave forces, he followed with a large supply of weapons to aid in the struggle. He became a surveyor and militia captain at Osawatomie, and the success of the pro-slave raid on Lawrence in 1856 roused him to a fury. Asserting that he was an instrument of God, he, four of his sons, and two other men deliberately murdered five pro-slavery men on the banks of the Pottawatamie. Gathering a group of men, he led many attacks in the guerrilla warfare of the border and became nationally known in the abolitionist press. Late in 1857 he began to lay his plans for a massed invasion of the South to free the slaves. In 1859 he seized the US Armory at Harpers Ferry with a band of 21 men, captured the inhabitants, and took possession of the town. Local militia blocked his escape, and the next morning a company of US Marines commanded by Robert E. Lee assaulted the group, killed 10 of the men, and captured Brown. He was convicted of treason and on 2 Dec. '59 was hanged at Charlestown. Regarded by Northern sympathizers as a martyr, he became the hero of a marching song, "John Brown's Body." See "BATTLE HYMN OF THE REPUBLIC."

BROWN, John Calvin. C.S.A. gen. 1827–89. Tenn. A lawyer, he had taken an extended trip in Europe just before the war, returning to enlist as private. Soon made Col. 3d Tenn. (16 May '61), he was captured at Fort Donelson and exchanged in Aug. '62. Appointed B.G. C.S.A. on the 30th of that month, he fought in Ky. and Tenn. under Bragg and was wounded at Perryville. He fought under Johnston and Hood in Ga. and Tenn., was promoted Maj. Gen. 4 Aug. '64, and again wounded at Franklin. After the war he was a legislator and Democratic Gov. of Tenn. (1870–74), as his older brother had been before the war. He was president of the Texas and Pacific R.R.

BROWN, John Marshall. Union officer. Me. 1st Lt. and Adj. 20th Me. 29 Aug. '62–27 July '63; Capt. Asst. Adj. Gen. Vols. 23 June '63; resigned 10 May '64; Lt. Col. 32d Me. 5 May '64; Bvt. B.G. USV; resigned 12 Sept. '64. Brevets for Gettysburg, war service.

BROWN, Joseph Emerson. C.S.A. governor of Ga. 1821–95. S.C. After graduating from Yale and studying law, he entered the Georgia legislature and was named Superior Court Judge before being elected Governor in 1857. Re-elected in 1859, 1861, and 1863, he ordered the seizure of the Federal forts Pulaski and Jackson in Jan. '61, put two regiments in the field before the Confederacy was organized, and personally seized the government arsenal at Augusta. Along with Robert TOOMBS and Alexander STEPHENS, he opposed Davis's administration of the government and his conduct of the war, and after the surrender advised acquiescence to the Reconstruction program. He had a unique political career, ranging from precipitate secessionism to RADICAL REPUBLICANISM back to the established Democratic party of the South. In 1868 he was named Chief Justice of the state Supreme Court. Resigning two years later, he engaged in railroading and in 1880 went to the US Senate. S.B.N. says that "by soft words and substantial favors skillfully bestowed, he habitually turned political enemies into enthusiastic friends, and without any sacrifice of dignity . . . [also] though his tone was nasal, his pronunciation provincial, and his manner on the stump awkward, yet with audiences justly appreciating Toombs, Stephens . . . [etc.] he was one of the most effective speakers of his day."

BROWN, Lewis Gove. Union officer. N.Y. 1st Lt. 11th Ohio 2 Aug. '62; Capt. 3 Oct. '62; Col. 117th US Col. Inf. 22 July '64; Bvt. B.G. USV (war service). Commanded 2, 2, XXV.

BROWN, Nathan Williams. Union officer. N.Y. Entering the R.A. in 1849, he served mainly on the frontier and was in the evacuation of Ft. Smith (Ark.) in 1861. During the Civil War he was in the West and was promoted Lt. Col. Deputy Paymaster Gen. 4 Apr. '64 (Maj. since 1849). He retired in 1882 as B.G. USA Paymaster Gen., having been breveted B.G. USA in 1866.

BROWN, Orlando. Union officer. Conn. Asst. Surg. 18th Mass. 24 Aug. '61; Surg. 29th Mass. 1 Jan. '62; mustered out 22 July '62; Capt. Asst. Q.M. Vols. 13 Oct. '63; Col. 24th US Col. Inf. 19 June '65; Bvt. B.G. USV 6 Jan. '66 (war service).

BROWN, Samuel B. Union officer erroneously listed by Phisterer. See BROWN, Simeon Batcheldor.

BROWN, Simeon Batcheldor. Union officer. N.H. Maj. 6th Mich. Cav. 16 Oct. '62; resigned 17 July '63; Col. 11th Mich. Cav. 10 Dec. '63; Bvt. B.G. USV (Marion, Va.). Commanded 1, 1st Dist. Ky., XXIII (Ohio); 2d Brig., Cav. Dist. East Tenn. (Cumberland). Died 1893. Phisterer lists him as Brown, Samuel B.

BROWN, S. Lockwood. Union officer. Ohio. Appt.-Ill. Capt. Asst. Q.M. Vols. 31 Oct. '61; Col. Q.M. Assigned 2 Aug. '64-1 Jan. '67; Bvt. B.G. USV (war service).

BROWN, Theodore Frelinghuysen. Union officer. Ill. 2d Lt. 51st Ill. 20

Sept. '61; 1st Lt. 1 Jan. '62; Capt. 7 Nov. '62; Bvt. B.G. USV. Brevets for Kenesaw Mountain (war service).

BROWN, William Rufus. Union officer. N.Y. Capt. 4th W. Va. 22 July '61; discharged 31 Aug. '62; Lt. Col. 13th W. Va. 10 Oct. '62; Col. 18 Jan. '64; Bvt. B.G. USV (war service). Died 1878.

BROWNE, P. P., Jr. Union officer. Col. 7th US Vet. Vol. Inf. Bvt. B.G. USV 13 Mar. '65 (Phisterer). He is not listed by Heitman as an officer.

BROWNE, Thomas McLellan. Union officer. Ohio. Capt. 7th Ind. Cav. 28 Aug. '63; Lt. Col. 1 Oct. '63; Col. 10 Oct. '65; Bvt. B.G. USV (war service). Died 1891.

BROWNE, William Henry. Union officer. c. 1826–1900. N.Y. Lt. Col. 31st N.Y. 13 June '61; Col. 36th N.Y. 2 Aug. '62; mustered out 15 July '63; Col. Vet. Res. Corps 19 Dec. '64; Bvt. B.G. USV (war service). Commanded 2, 3, VI (Potomac); 2, Vet. Res. Corps Div., XXII. W.I.A. in leg at Salem Heights. He served in the Mexican War. Ex-cadet USMA, 1861.

BROWNE, William M. C.S.A. gen. ?–1884. England. Appt.-Ga. A daily newspaper editor in Washington, he was Jefferson Davis's A.D.C. as Col. of C.S.A. Cav. On 11 Nov. '64 Davis appointed him B.G. C.S.A. and sent him to Savannah to command a brigade in Mercer's division during Sherman's siege. The Senate on 18 Feb. '65 refused to confirm the appointment, but he was paroled as B.G. After the war he was a planter and publisher, engaging in Democratic politics as well as teaching history at the University of Georgia. He wrote a biography of Alexander H. Stephens.

BROWNELL, Francis Edwin. Union soldier who killed James T. JACKSON on

24 May '61 after the latter had killed ELLSWORTH. A Pvt. in Co. A, 11th N.Y. ("Fire Zouaves") 20 Apr.–4 July '61, he became a 2d Lt. 14 May and a 1st Lt. 24 Oct. '61. He retired 4 Nov. '63 and died in 1894. In 1877 he was awarded the Medal of Honor for his exploit (Heitman).

BROWNELL, Kady. VIVANDIÈRE. 1842–? Africa. Daughter of a British soldier and born while he was on campaign, she followed her American husband, Robert S., to war when he joined the 1st R.I. Carrying a rifle and sword as well as the colors, she became proficient in the use of both weapons. She participated in 1st Bull Run, and when her husband re-enlisted in the 5th R.I. when his three months were up, she went with him to New Bern in Jan. '62. Her husband was wounded there in March and after a convalescence of 18 months he was invalided out of the army. Kady then returned to being a housewife, with her discharge signed by Burnside and with her sword and her colors.

BROWNING, Orville Hickman. Union statesman. 1806–81. An organizer of the Republican party, he helped secure that party's nomination of Lincoln in 1860 and was appointed US Senator to fill Douglas's seat after his death in 1861. He broke with Lincoln over the latter's plans for reconstruction, lost his chance for re-election and, remaining in Washington, championed Johnson in his reconstruction plans. He was appointed to the Cabinet and was one of Johnson's close friends and advisers during the impeachment proceedings.

BROWNLOW, James P. Union officer. Tenn. Capt. 1st Tenn. Cav. 1 Apr. '62; Lt. Col. 1 Aug. '62; Col. 15 June '64; Bvt. B.G. USV (war service). Commanded 1, 1, Cav. Corps (Cumberland). Died 1879.

BROWNLOW, William Gannaway. 1805–77. A leading Tennessee Unionist during the Civil War. Originally a Methodist minister (thus earning the lifelong nickname of "Parson"), he became editor of the *Knoxville Whig* in 1849. Although a strong pro-slavery man, he violently opposed secession in 1861 and soon became a leader of Unionist elements in east Tennessee. Confederate authorities suppressed his newspaper and later imprisoned him for several months during the winter of '61–'62 on suspicion of complicity in the bridge burnings that so incensed Jeff Davis. Later released, he became a firm advocate of a "hard war" against the South. He was elected governor of Tennessee on the Republican ticket in 1865 and again in 1867. In 1869 he became a US senator.

BROWNSVILLE, Tex. 6 Nov. '63. Occupied during TEXAS COAST OPERATIONS and garrisoned by McClernand's XIII Corps. On 18 Feb. '64 it was opened to commerce.

BRUCE, John. Union officer. Scotland. Capt. 19th Iowa 17 Aug. '62; Maj. 8 Dec. '62; Lt. Col. 10 Mar. '64; Bvt. B.G. USV. Brevets for Spanish Ft. (Ala.) war service.

BRUMBACK, Jefferson. Union officer. Ohio. Maj. 95th Ohio 19 Aug. '62; Lt. Col. 19 Aug. '63; Bvt. B.G. USV (war service).

BRUSH, Daniel Harmon. Union officer. 1813–90. Vt. Capt. 18th Ill. 28 May '61; Maj. 27 July '62; Lt. Col. 27 Sept. '62; Col. 25 May '63; Bvt. B.G. USV (Ft. Donelson, Shiloh); resigned 8 Sept. '63; W.I.A. Ft. Donelson and Shiloh. In later years a successful lawyer, merchant, and banker.

BRYAN, Goode. C.S.A. gen. c. 1812–85. Ga. USMA 1834 (25/36); Inf. He served in garrison before resigning the next year to engage in engineering, planting, and politics. He fought in the

Mexican War and maintained his interest in the militia until being commissioned Capt. 16th Ga. in 1861. Elected Col. in Feb. '62, he fought in the Seven Days' Battles and led the regiment at Antietam, Fredericksburg, Chancellorsville, and Gettysburg. He succeeded Semmes as brigade commander at the last-named battle and also led it at Chickamauga, having been appointed B.G. C.S.A. 29 Aug. '63. Despite failing health, he led these troops at Knoxville, the Wilderness, Spotsylvania, Cold Harbor, and Petersburg. He resigned 20 Sept. '64 because of health.

BUCHANAN, Franklin. C.S.A. admiral. 1800–74. Md. Entering the navy as midshipman in 1815, he was Bancroft's chief advisor in planning the Naval Academy and was its first Superintendent 1845–47. He fought in the Mexican War and commanded the flagship in Perry's expedition to China and Japan 1852–55. Named to command the Washington Navy Yard as Capt. in 1859, he resigned 22 Apr. '61 and had second thoughts when Maryland did not secede. Commissioned Capt. in the C.S. Navy 5 Sept. '61, he was named Chief of Orders and Details and took command of the Chesapeake Bay Squadron early in 1862. He commanded the MERRIMAC in its initial appearance in Hampton Roads, 8 Mar. '62. He himself was wounded and his brother, Paymaster McKean Buchanan, was lost when the *Congress* was sunk. (See MONITOR-MERRIMAC.) He was appointed Admiral 21 Aug. '62. Later that year he was defeated by Farragut at MOBILE BAY. After the war he was president of Maryland State Agricultural College.

BUCHANAN, James. Fifteenth president of the United States. 1791–1868. Pa. After serving in the War of 1812 and being admitted to the bar, he became a US Representative (1821–31), chairman of the Judiciary Committee, and a Democrat. After being US Minister to Russia (1832–34) and US Senator (1834–45) he was Secretary of State during Polk's administration (1845–49) and was responsible for the treaty that followed the Mexican War. He was US Minister to Great Britain (1853–56) and helped draw up the Ostend Manifesto. Elected president in 1857, he tried to maintain the balance and peace between the North and South and failed to take any action on South Carolina's secession in 1860. In his retirement he supported the Union in its struggles. His niece, Harriet LANE, was his official hostess.

BUCHANAN, Robert Christie. Union gen. 1811–78. Md. Appt.–D.C. USMA 1830 (31/42); Inf. He fought in the Black Hawk, Seminole, and Mexican wars, receiving two brevets in the last. Promoted Lt. Col. 4th US Inf. 9 Sept. '61, he commanded 1, 2, V, Potomac (18 May '62–27 Jan. '63) at Malvern Hill where his brigade captured some colors and marched to Harrison's Landing where they covered McClellan's withdrawal. They fought on the left at 2d Bull Run, at Antietam, and in front of the "stone wall" at Fredericksburg. His appointment expired 4 Mar. '63 and he then served on several investigative commissions and with the Freedman's Bureau and commanded the Dept. of Louisiana. D.A.B. cites his "wide experience, fine attainments and high sense of duty and discipline." He was called "Old Buck" by his Civil War soldiers. He continued in the R.A. until retiring as a Col. in 1870. His brevets were for Gaines's Mill, Malvern Hill (B.G. USV), and 2d Bull Run, and Fredericksburg (Maj. Gen. USV).

"BUCK AND BALL." Three buckshot behind a regular-size musket ball, a common load used by Confederate soldiers in cal. .69 muskets.

BUCK AND GAG. A form of punishment. The soldier was gagged and seated with his hands and feet tied. His knees were drawn up, the arms passed around them, and a rod inserted, horizontal to the ground, between the arms and the backs of the knees. Thus immobilized in a highly uncomfortable position, he was left for a period of time varying with the seriousness of the offense.

BUCKHEAD CREEK, Ga. See WAYNESBORO, 26–29 Nov. '64.

BUCKINGHAM, Catharinus Putnam. Union gen. 1808–88. Ohio. USMA 1829 (6/46); Arty. After topographical duty and teaching at West Point, he resigned in 1831 to become professor of mathematics and natural philosophy at Kenyon College. After that he was principal of a private school and manufacturer and proprietor of the Kokosing Iron Works. Commissioned Asst. Adj. Gen. of Ohio 3–8 May '61, he was then named Comsy. Gen. 8 May–1 July '61 and Adj. Gen. 1 July '61–2 Apr. '62. Named B.G. USV 16 July '62, he was on special duty in the War Dept. until he resigned 11 Feb. '63. A merchant in N.Y.C. for a short while, he rebuilt the I.C. grain elevators in 1868–73, after the Chicago fire, having built them originally in 1858. He wrote several books on mathematics.

BUCKINGHAM, William Alfred. Gov. of Connecticut. 1804–75. Conn. A successful merchant and manufacturer, he was the Republican Governor from 1858 to 1866 when he refused nomination. During the war he worked closely with Lincoln and raised more troops than were required from the state. He served in the Senate until his death and contributed generously to philanthropies, including the Yale theological school. There is a statue of him in the statehouse in Hartford.

BUCKLAND, Ralph Pomeroy. Union gen. 1812–92. Mass. A lawyer and state Senator, he was commissioned Col. 72d Ohio 10 Jan. '62 and at Shiloh commanded 4th Brig., 5th Div., Army Tenn. (1 Mar.–15 May '62). Named B.G. USV 29 Nov. '62, he commanded 5th Brig., Dist. Memphis, XIII (26 Oct.–12 Nov. '62); 3d Brig., 1st Div. Dist. Memphis, XIII (12 Nov.–18 Dec. '62); 3, 8, XVI (18 Dec. '62–12 Feb. '63); 1, 3, XV (3 Apr.–22 June '63; 10 Sept.–15 Oct. '63; 15 Nov.–20 Dec. '63); 3d Div., XV (9 Aug.–11 Sept. '63); 1, 1, XVI (20 Dec. '63–22 Jan. '64); and Dist. Memphis XVI (25 Jan.–31 Mar. '63 and 25 Jan.–June '64). Resigning 6 Jan. '65 to enter Congress, he was breveted Maj. Gen. USV for war service. After the war he was active in politics, business, and veterans' affairs.

BUCKLAND MILLS., Va. 19 Oct. '63. Cavalry skirmish during BRISTOE CAMPAIGN in which Stuart's cavalry routed Kilpatrick's 3d Cav. Div. (and other troops). Stuart's men called their pursuit the "Buckland Races," claiming 250 prisoners, although Kilpatrick reported a total loss of only 150. (*Lee's Lts.,* III, 262.)

BUCKNER, Simon Bolivar. C.S.A. gen. 1823–1914. Ky. USMA 1844 (11/25); Inf. He served in garrison, taught philosophy at West Point, fought in the Mexican War (two brevets, 1 wound), returned to the Military Academy as a tactical officer, and was stationed on the frontier before resigning in 1855. A construction superintendent, he was active in Chicago real estate and drew up Kentucky's militia bill in 1860. Named I.G. and Maj. Gen. in that organization, he worked for Kentucky's neutrality and dealt with McClellan in this. Offered general officer commissions by both the North and the South, he refused all until Ky. was invaded by the Federals from Cairo and by Polk at Columbus. He then went to A. S. Johnston in Bowling Green and was appointed B.G. C.S.A. 14 Sept. '61. Sent to relieve Ft. Donelson, he was left in command when Floyd and Pillow escaped and had no alternative but UNCONDITIONAL SURRENDER to Grant. Exchanged in Aug. '62, he was promoted Maj. Gen. on the 16th and served under Bragg in Chattanooga before leading the 3d Div. under Hardee at Perryville. In Dec. he was ordered by Davis to fortify Mobile and was at the port four months before taking over East Tenn. In Sept. '63 he joined Bragg in northern Ga. and at Chickamauga led his corps in the left wing. In 1864 he was given command of the Dist. of La. and was promoted Lt. Gen. on 20 Sept. This was not confirmed until 17 Jan. '65. After Appomattox, he and Price negotiated with Canby for surrender. At first he was unable to return to Ky. and worked in New Orleans on a newspaper and in the insurance business. In 1868 he became editor of the Louisville *Courier* and, recovering his Chicago property he had wisely turned over to his brother-in-law just before the war, sold his real estate holdings for $500,000. He was Democratic Gov. of Ky. 1887–92 and bolted the party in 1896 when they embraced the free-silver platform to run as vice-president on the National Democratic ticket. His lifelong friendship with Grant stemmed from their West Point days, and Buckner lent him money to get home after Grant resigned in 1854, offered him financial assistance in his last days (which Grant refused), and was pallbearer at his funeral. He was the father of the World War II general of the same name who was killed while commanding the 10th US Army on Okinawa in 1945.

BUCKNER'S CORPS. See CORPS, Confed.

"BUCKTAILS." See 13th PENNSYLVANIA RESERVES.

BUELL, Don Carlos. Union gen. 1818–98. Ohio; Appt.-Ind. USMA 1841 (32/52); Inf. Lt. Col. A.A.G. 11 May '61; B.G. USV 17 May '61; Maj. Gen. USV 21 Mar. '62; mustered out 23 May '64. Mexican War (W.I.A.; three brevets). After initial duty of organizing troops around Washington, in August '61 he was given command of a division of the Army of the Potomac. In Nov. he succeeded Sherman and became C.G. Dept. of the Ohio. Aided by Grant's advance on Forts Henry and Donelson, he occupied Bowling Green 14 Feb. '62 and during the next two weeks occupied Gallatin (Tenn.) and Nashville. He arrived at Shiloh to contribute to the Union victory. On 12 July '62 he headed the reconstituted Dept. of the Ohio and undertook the Stones River campaign. Bragg's invasion of Kentucky forced Buell to evacuate central Tennessee and retreat in haste to save Louisville and Cincinnati. On 30 Sept. Buell was ordered to turn over his command to Thomas, but was reinstated the next day. Buell then started a pursuit that ended in the drawn battle at Perryville. Public opinion led to Buell's being replaced by Rosecrans. Ropes calls Buell "as able a general as any in the service." During the period 24 Nov. '62–10 May '63 he was before a military commission to investigate his campaign in Tenn. and Ky. The report was never published, but from 10 May '63 to 1 June '64 he was in the status of "waiting orders" at Indianapolis. He was mustered out of volunteer service 23 May '64; resigned from the regular service 1 June '64. Grant made several attempts to have the government restore him to military service. He was president of the Green River Iron Co. and pension agent in Louisville 1885–89. Although Buell's prewar reputation indicated a brilliant future, he proved unequal to the task of leading volunteer troops in the Civil War. He lacked the personality; he showed a pedantic approach to campaigning; and, although personally courageous, was too deliberate and cautious.

BUELL, George Pearson. Union officer. Ind. Lt. Col. 58th Ind. 17 Dec. '61; Col. 24 June '62; Bvt. B.G. USV 12 Jan. '65. Brevets for war service, Missionary Ridge. Commanded 1, 1st Div. Left Wing, XIV; Pioneer Brig. (Army of the Cumberland); 1, 1, XXI; 2, 1, XIV; 1st Div., XIV. Died 1883.

BUFFINGTON ISLAND (St. George Creek), Ohio. 19 July '63. Decisive action in MORGAN'S OHIO RAID.

BUFORD, Abraham. C.S.A. gen. 1820–84. Ky. USMA 1841 (51/52); Dragoons. He attended Centre College before going to the Military Academy and after graduation served on the frontier and in the Mexican War (1 brevet). Resigning in 1854, he raised thoroughbred cattle and horses in Kentucky until being commissioned B.G. C.S.A. 2 Sept. '62. He commanded the Ky. troops covering Bragg's retreat to Knoxville, led his brigade at Stones River, and was then under Loring until the spring of 1864. Taking over a cavalry brigade under Forrest, he was wounded at Lindville 24 Dec. '64 and out of action until the next spring. Returning to his plantation, he became one of the state's foremost turfmen. The death of his wife and only son and financial reverses led him to suicide in 1884. He was kin to JOHN BUFORD.

BUFORD, Lt. Harry. See Loreta Janeta VELAQUES.

BUFORD, John. Union gen. 1826–63. Ky. Appt.-Ill. USMA 1848 (16/38); Dragoons-Cav. Serving in the frontier in Indian fighting and on the Utah Expedition, he was promoted Maj. Staff Asst. I.G. 12 Nov. '61. He served on Pope's staff in 1862 before taking command of the cavalry brigade in the 2d Bull Run campaign. Appointed B.G. USV 27 July '62, he immediately showed the traits of a truly outstanding cavalry leader. At Thoroughfare Gap (27 Aug. '62) his brigade alone opposed the advance of Longstreet's corps. After recovering from a wound received at 2d Bull Run, he was McClellan's Chief of Cav. in the Maryland campaign. In command of cavalry units he fought at Fredericksburg, on Stoneman's raid, and at Beverly Ford, Aldie, Middleburg, and Upperville. He was promoted Maj. Gen. USV 1 June '63. Reconnoitering ahead of the army in Pa., Buford encountered the enemy advancing on Gettysburg from the northwest. Grasping the importance of the strategic road junction at Gettysburg, Buford immediately dismounted his troopers to hold McPherson Ridge at all costs until Federal infantry could reinforce them. Without Buford's action it is unlikely that Gettysburg would have become one of the decisive battles of history. He went on sick leave in Nov. and died 16 Dec. '63 of exposure and exhaustion at the age of 37. Half-brother of NAPOLEON B. BUFORD.

BUFORD, Napoleon Bonaparte. Union gen. 1807–83. Ky. USMA 1827 (6/38); Arty. Col. 27th Ill. 10 Aug. '61; full B.G. USV 15 Apr. '62; full Maj. Gen. USV 29 Nov. '62–4 Mar. '63; Bvt. Maj. Gen. USV 13 Mar. '65; mustered out 24 Aug. '65 as full B.G. USV. Resigned from R.A. in 1835 after studying at Harvard and serving as assistant professor natural and experimental philosophy at West Point. Engineer in Kentucky; then in iron business, banker, railroad president in Illinois. In command of Cairo, Ill., '61–'62; fought at Belmont, Columbus (Ky.), Island No. 10, Union City, Ft. Pillow. As B.G.

was in the Miss. campaigns of '62–'63. Commanded Dist. of East Arkansas (XVI Corps) 19 Sept. '63–6 Jan. '64, and the same district of VII Corps to 9 Mar. '65. He was on leave of absence to 24 Aug. '65. Special US Indian Commissioner; govt. inspector of the Union Pacific R.R. until 1869. Half-brother of John Buford.

BUILT-UP GUN. Cannon in which the principal parts are formed separately and then united by welding, shrinking, forcing, or screwing. Examples of this type were the ARMSTRONG, BLAKELY, BROOKE, PARROTT, and the large WHITWORTH. The older construction method was the "cast metal homogeneous," the best known of which were the COLUMBIAD, DAHLGREN, RODMAN, and NAPOLEON.

BUKEY, Van Hartness. Union officer. Ohio. Pvt. 11th W. Va. 28 Oct. '61; 1st Lt. 15 Jan. '62; Capt. 2 July '62; Maj. 28 Feb. '63; Lt. Col. 3 Aug. '63; Col. 3 Nov. '64; Bvt. B.G. USV (war service); mustered out 26 Dec. '64.

BULLOCH, James D. Comdr. in C.S.N. and foreign agent. 1823–1901, Ga. In 1839 he became a midshipman, U.S.N., and in 1854 resigned to work in a commercial mail service. When Ga. seceded he was commissioned Comdr. and sent to England as a naval agent. He outfitted many important ships, among them the *Alabama, Florida, Shenandoah,* and *Stonewall.* Abroad throughout the war, he settled in Liverpool. Wrote *The Secret Service of the Confederate States in Europe.*

BULLOCK, Robert. C.S.A. gen. 1828–? Appt.-Fla. As Lt. Col. 7th Fla., he served in eastern Tenn. in 1862 and fought at Stones River. He was promoted Col. in '63 and led his regiment at Chickamauga, Missionary Ridge, and in the Atlanta campaign. Named B.G.

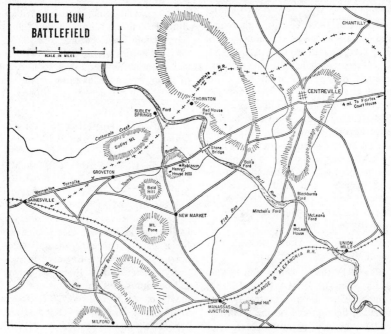

BULL RUN BATTLEFIELD

SCALE IN MILES

C.S.A. 29 Nov. '64, he was severely wounded at Franklin leading a brigade.

BULL RUN CAMPAIGN, Va. 1st. July '61.

Although the army protested that officers and men were still too green for offensive operations, the authorities in Washington directed that they be undertaken. One reason was that the field armies at that time consisted largely of three months' militia whose term of service was about to expire. McDowell was ordered to attack Beauregard and drive him from the vital railroad junction at Manassas. Patterson, whose advance from Harrisburg, Pa., had caused Johnston to fall back from the Potomac, was directed to keep pressure on the Confederates in the Shenandoah so they could not get away to reinforce Beauregard.

On 15 July Patterson moved forward to Bunker Hill and stopped. The next day McDowell began his advance. On 16 July Patterson withdrew to Charlestown so as to base himself on Harpers Ferry.

McDowell reached Centreville on the afternoon of 18 July with about 30,600 men (T.L.L.). An attack the next morning against Beauregard's 20,000 would probably have succeeded (Fiebeger); however, his logistical situation was so poor, due to the inexperience of his officers and the indiscipline of the men, that McDowell felt he could not attack.

Blackburn's Ford, 18 July '61, was the scene of a RECONNAISSANCE IN FORCE by Tyler's division against the brigades of Bonham (at Mitchell's Ford) and Longstreet (at Blackburn's Ford). Tyler was repulsed with a loss of 83 casualties. Confederate losses were 68. (Alexander.) Although Union reports refer to "the affair at Blackburn's Ford," the Confederates, feeling it was a significant victory, called this "the 1st Battle of Bull Run."

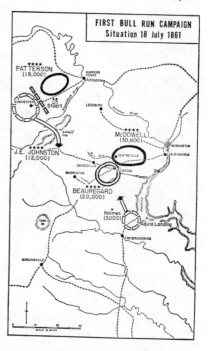

FIRST BULL RUN CAMPAIGN
Situation 18 July 1861

When the authorities in Richmond learned of McDowell's advance they immediately ordered Johnston and Holmes to reinforce Beauregard. Johnston received his orders at midnight of the 17th. Since Patterson had withdrawn on this day toward Harpers Ferry, Johnston was able to start immediately via Ashby Gap, Piedmont, and thence by rail. Jackson's brigade arrived at Manassas about noon 20 July and all but 2,500 of the 12,000 who had been opposing Patterson were there about 24 hours later. This movement is significant in military history as the first use of a railroad to achieve strategic mobility.

1st Bull Run. Sunday 21 July '61.

The sketch shows McDowell's attack.

Allowing for the fact that McDowell had no way of knowing of Johnston's arrival, the Federal plan was good.

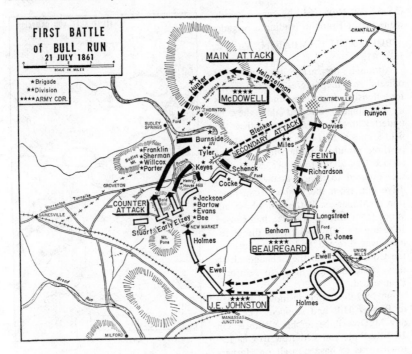

FIRST BATTLE
of BULL RUN
21 JULY 1861
SCALE IN MILES

★Brigade
★★Division
★★★★ARMY CDR.

However, it was too much for green troops to execute, and the fourteen-mile daylight envelopment precluded surprise. At 8:45 A.M. E. P. ALEXANDER, detected the Federal movement from his position on Signal Hill and flashed the message to N. G. Evans at Stone Bridge eight miles away: "Look out for your left; you are turned."

On his own initiative Evans moved part of his half-brigade from the Stone Bridge to oppose the envelopment. He was joined on the enemy side of Young's Branch by the brigades of Bee and Bartow (from Johnston's army). Although Johnston and Beauregard reacted slowly, they finally did shift troops in time from the unthreatened right to Henry House Hill. Beauregard, being more familiar with the terrain, took personal command of the line of battle, while his superior, Johnston, took over the task

of directing reinforcements toward the threatened flank.

Despite slow execution of the envelopment, the Federal attack was initially successful and Confederate forces were driven back onto Henry House Hill. Here Jackson's brigade formed the nucleus of a new defensive line and, in the process, earned the nickname "STONEWALL."

Movement of additional Confederate troops from the unthreatened right flank, plus the arrival at about 3:30 P.M. of the last brigade (Kirby Smith's) from the Valley, enabled the Confederates to hold and then to counterattack the exposed Federal right. The regular army batteries of Griffin and Ricketts, supported by the FIRE ZOUAVES, were attacked and driven back by Jeb Stuart's cavalry regiment.

Covered by Sykes's Regulars and a

few other units, the Federal force started an orderly withdrawal at 4 P.M. The retreat soon turned into a rout. Unable to re-form his troops at Centreville, McDowell retreated into the defenses of Washington. The Confederate troops in contact were too exhausted to pursue, and their officers were too inexperienced to organize a pursuit by the fresh units available. As a consequence the Confederates were not able to reap fully the strategic rewards of their tactical victory.

The statistics show that the Federal soldiers actually fought more effectively than the Confederates: although they had 5.2 per cent killed and wounded, they killed or wounded approximately seven of the enemy for each 100 Federals engaged, while on the same basis the Confederates, although sustaining 6.1 per cent casualties, inflicted 4.6 per cent casualties. (Reference is to the system used by T. L. Livermore in his *Numbers and Losses in the Civil War* for comparing the "courage and efficiency" of opposing forces.) The basic reason for Southern success at 1st Bull Run is that when both sides are green the defender has the advantage, as J. E. Johnston pointed out.

According to Livermore, 28,452 Union troops were actually engaged and there were 2,645 casualties (418 killed, 1,011 wounded, 1,216 missing). Phisterer puts total casualties at 2,952, and Fox gives a figure of 3,334. Livermore gives Confederate strength as 32,232 effective, and puts their total loss at 1,981 (387 killed, 1,582 wounded, and 12 missing). Phisterer puts Confederate losses at 1,752, and Fox estimates 1,982.

BULL RUN CAMPAIGN, Va., 2d. June–Sept. '62.

After the failure of Frémont, Banks, and McDowell to destroy Stonewall Jackson's greatly outnumbered force in

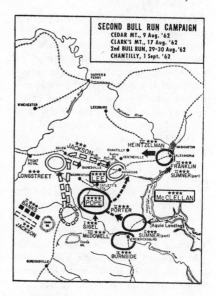

SECOND BULL RUN CAMPAIGN
CEDAR MT., 9 Aug. '62
CLARK'S MT., 17 Aug. '62
2nd BULL RUN, 29-30 Aug. '62
CHANTILLY, 1 Sept. '62

the Shenandoah Valley, the top Federal leaders realized the necessity for UNITY OF COMMAND. The short-lived US Army of Va. was formed 26 June '62, under the command of John Pope, to be composed initially of the three separate commands just mentioned. When Frémont refused to serve under Pope, Franz Sigel succeeded him. The new army numbered about 47,000.

Pope's mission was threefold: to cover Washington; to protect the Valley; and to move east of the Blue Ridge Mountains toward Charlottesville so as to present a threat that would assist McClellan by drawing Lee's strength away from the defense of the Southern capital. The day the Army of Va. was ordered into existence Lee started the Seven Days' Battles, which caused the failure of McClellan's Peninsular campaign.

Lincoln's unilateral selection of Pope has been singled out as one of the President's errors of the war. As a "western man," Pope was not accepted warmly by the Federal forces of the Eastern theater. He got off to a bad start by the publication of a bombastic address. (See Pope's address.) He antagonized the South by prescribing harsh treatment of Confederate sympathizers. The mild-mannered Lee developed a personal animosity toward his new opponent, referring to him as "the miscreant Pope" and saying that he must be "suppressed."

On 14 July Pope started an advance toward Gordonsville. With about 80,000 troops around Richmond, Lee had McClellan's army of 90,000 in front of him and Pope's 50,000 converging from the north. Alert to the certainty of eventual defeat unless he seized the initiative, Lee took advantage of McClellan's inactivity and sent Jackson north toward Gordonsville with 12,000 men. On Jackson's request, Lee next sent A. P. Hill to reinforce Jackson, raising the latter's strength to 24,000.

Cedar Mountain, 9 Aug. '62.

Federal forces were advancing slowly toward Culpeper, and Jackson saw the opportunity of striking rapidly toward that place to destroy the first enemy corps to arrive. Having done this, he thought he would then be able to operate from a central position and defeat the other two corps, one at a time, as he had done at Cross Keys and Port Republic. However, Jackson's movement was slow because in his mania for secrecy he did not keep his division commanders—Winder, Ewell, and A. P. Hill—informed of his plans and the subsequent modifications.

A meeting engagement took place at Cedar Mountain 9 Aug. Banks attacked furiously and was driving Winder and Ewell back when A. P. Hill finally came up to save the day with a crushing counterattack against the Federal east flank. Banks had made the mistake of attacking without reserves and without sending back a request for reinforcements.

	Banks (US)	Jackson
Engaged	8,030	16,868
Killed	314	231
Wounded	1,445	1,107
Missing	594	0
Total losses	2,353	1,338

By now Lee knew that McClellan's army was being withdrawn by water to reinforce Pope. Seeing the opportunity of striking the latter before this reinforcement could take place, Lee moved with Longstreet's corps to join Jackson. Pope's army was in position with its center opposite Cedar Mountain and its left opposite Clark's Mountain. Both forces numbered 55,000. Lee saw the opportunity of using Clark's Mountain to shield the concentration of his army and then deliver a crushing attack against Pope's eastern flank; such an operation would not only cut the line along which McClellan's forces were moving to reinforce the Federal army of Virginia, but it would also cut Pope's line of retreat to Washington and might well-destroy his entire force. However, poor staff work again delayed the attack. Then Pope captured J. E. B. Stuart's adjutant general (Major Norman R. Fitz Hugh, on the night of 17–18 Aug.) with a copy of Lee's plan and was able to withdraw in time to avoid the threat. Stuart was surprised and almost captured with his entire command group the morning of the 18th.

While the two armies faced each other across the Rappahannock, Lee probed the enemy lines in a vain effort to find a vulnerable point. In one of the daring Confederate cavalry raids Fitzhugh Lee captured Pope's headquarters near Catlett's Station (22 Aug.) and brought back information that within five days Federal reinforcements from the Peninsula would swell Pope's ranks to 130,000

Lee's Strategic Envelopment

Refusing to abandon the hope of a decisive blow against the enemy, Lee adopted a bold plan that is still controversial among military historians. Against an enemy that now outnumbered him 75,000 to 55,000, he intended to split his forces, send one half on a wide strategic envelopment to get astride the Federal line of communications and to follow a day later with the rest of his army. Success depended on speed, deception, and the skill of his subordinate commanders. Failure would have meant the destruction of most, if not all, of his army. On the other hand, a defensive role would have led to inevitable defeat. As always, Lee was taking advantage of the mediocre Federal generalship and the panic he knew would result from any maneuver that put him between the Federal army and Washington.

On the morning of 25 Aug. Jackson and Stuart's cavalry left the line of the Rappahannock with three days' rations and a small wagon train. That night they bivouacked at Salem, 26 miles away. The next night Jackson was destroying the Federal supply depot at Manassas, after having marched an additional 36 miles.

Lee's Turning Movement

Pope had observed Jackson's movement on 25 Aug., but assumed he was going to the Valley, perhaps to precede Lee's entire army to Front Royal. He had ordered no pursuit. Longstreet kept up a show of activity the 25th, but the next day started off to join Jackson. On the 26th Pope had also been content to maintain his original position. Early that evening, however, he learned that enemy forces were on the railroad to his rear. Subsequent reports convinced him that this was more than a raid and he started withdrawing. Pope ordered the concentration of Sigel and McDowell at Gainesville, Porter and Banks at Warrenton Junction, and Reno and Heintzelman in between, at Greenwich and Bristoe Station. This put a Federal force of 75,000 between Jackson's 24,000 (at Manassas) and Longstreet's 30,000, which were still west of the Bull Run mountains, about 20 miles away. Pope had a rare opportunity to block Longstreet while annihilating Jackson with overwhelming superiority of force. However, Jackson's next moves so thoroughly confused Pope that he completely lost his head and threw away his chance for victory.

Jackson's problem was to take up a position on the enemy's flank which had enough natural strength to enable him to hold until Lee could come up with Longstreet's corps. He also wanted to be able to strike the Federals if feasible and to retreat if Longstreet were blocked. Stony Ridge (Sudley Mountain) satisfied his requirements admirably. But further to gain time and to observe his maxim of "always mystify, mislead, and surprise the enemy if possible," A. P. Hill was ordered to march on Centreville, Ewell was to cross Bull Run and move along the north side of that stream, Taliaferro was to move direct; all were to join up on Stony Ridge. This maneuver, starting during the night of 27–28 Aug., was completed by midafternoon.

Lacking accurate information, and drawing inept conclusions, Pope ordered successive movements in vain efforts to capture Jackson, while ignoring Longstreet's advance until too late to prevent junction. He reached Manassas the morning of the 28th to find the Confederates gone. Getting reports of enemy in Centreville, Pope assumed this was Jackson's whole force and issued orders at 4:15 P.M. for his entire force to proceed there. At about 5:30 King's division was moving east along the Warrenton pike when it was fired on near Groveton.

Battle of Groveton—28 Aug. '62.

By disclosing his position Jackson accepted the risk of being overwhelmed before the rest of the army could reinforce him. However, the Confederate commander realized that the entire campaign would be futile if Pope were permitted to move to the strong defensive positions around Centreville. In one of the fiercest little skirmishes of the war both Confederate division commanders were wounded and the casualties were high on both sides. This was the "baptism of fire" for John Gibbon's "Black Hat" (later "Iron") brigade: it suffered 33 per cent casualties. The Federals did not withdraw until around midnight.

When Pope learned of this fight he drew the erroneous conclusion that King had hit the head of Jackson's troops withdrawing toward the Valley. He ordered his forces to assemble in the vicinity of Groveton to destroy Jackson. The stage was set for the main battle.

2d Battle of Bull Run—29–30 Aug. '62.

Pope had 62,000 with which to destroy Jackson's 20,000 before Longstreet's corps could arrive. Pope conducted a series of piecemeal, uncoordinated frontal attacks, all of which failed to drive Jackson from his strong position behind a railroad cut.

Longstreet came up alongside Jackson's right flank about 11 A.M. By failing to attack on the first day of the battle (29 Aug.), Longstreet deprived Lee of a victory that would have destroyed the bulk of the Federal army. Although neither side was aware of it at the time, there was a two-mile gap between the corps of Fitz-John Porter (on the south) and the rest of the Federal forces which were attacking Jack-

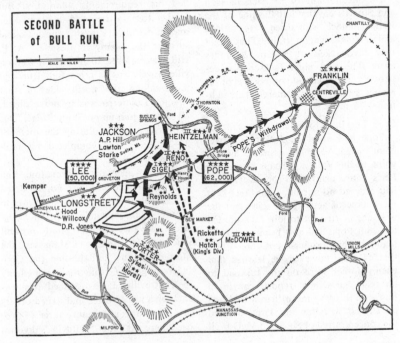

son. (See also PORTER, Fitz-John, and PORTER CASE.) At'the end of the first day Jackson withdrew from positions he had reached in following up the repulse of Pope's attacks. The Federal commander interpreted this movement as a retreat and ordered a vigorous pursuit for the next day.

On the second day (30 Aug.) the Federal attack was repulsed with heavy losses. Pope still did not realize that Longstreet had arrived. Lee permitted Pope to commit his forces against the Confederate left, then he enveloped the weakened Federal left flank with Longstreet's corps. Pope suffered a decisive tactical defeat, although the retention of Henry House Hill by Federal forces permitted the bulk of his troops to retreat across Bull Run via the Stone Bridge and the neighboring fords.

Battle of Chantilly (or Ox Hill)—1 Sept. '62

Maintaining the offensive, Lee executed another wide envelopment, moving around the west flank of the Federal position at Centreville. Striking toward Fairfax Courthouse, Jackson's corps hit Federal forces under Stevens and Kearny near Chantilly. A hot encounter followed and lasted until nightfall, when the Union force withdrew. This skirmish was costly for the Union, however, because Stevens and Kearny—two of the most promising commanders of the army —were both killed. Losses were 1,300 Federals and 800 Confederates (E.&B.). Although reinforcements were near, Pope withdrew into the defenses of Washington.

Summary and Evaluation

Tactical failures of Jackson and Longstreet at Cedar Mountain, Clark's Mountain, and Bull Run had deprived Lee of the opportunity of destroying Pope's army in the 2d Bull Run campaign. However, his over-all strategic accom-

plishment during the first three months of his command of the Army of Northern Virginia was remarkable. Starting in an apparently hopeless situation, with McClellan moving on Richmond from the Peninsula and other Federal forces advancing from the north, Lee had succeeded not only in eliminating the immediate threat, but had driven the Federals back into Washington. While the Peninsula campaign, Jackson's Valley campaign, and the 2d Bull Run campaign are usually considered separately, the three actually comprise a single strategic operation. The outcome represented a remarkable Confederate accomplishment and pointed up the marked superiority of Southern generalship at this stage of the war in the East.

Livermore estimates the following numbers and losses:

	Union	Confederate
Engaged	75,696	48,527
Killed	1,724	1,481
Wounded	8,372	7,627
Missing	5,958	89
Total losses	16,054 (21%)	9,197 (19%)

The Federals lost 13 per cent killed and wounded, as compared to 19 per cent for their opponents. Using Livermore's "hit by 1,000" method of comparing effectiveness of the two sides, the Federals killed and wounded 120 of the enemy for every 1,000 of their own troops engaged, whereas the Confederates hit 208 Federals.

BULLY SOUP. See PANADA.

BUMMERS. Nickname of Sherman's foragers during the March to the Sea and through the Carolinas.

BURBANK, Sidney. Union officer. c. 1807–82. Mass. USMA 1829 (17/46); Inf. He served in Indian fighting, taught infantry tactics at West Point, and fought in the Seminole War before being promoted Lt. Col. 13th U.S. Inf. 14 May '61. As Col. 2d U.S. Inf. 16 Sept. '62, he commanded an R.A. brigade (Apr.–May and 2 July '63–Jan. '64) at Chancellorsville and Gettysburg. He was breveted B.G. USA for Gettysburg and commanded the draft rendezvous at Columbus (Ohio) and the 2d U.S. Inf., headquartered in Kentucky. After the war he was on several boards and commissions before retiring in 1870.

BURBRIDGE, Stephen Gano. Union gen. 1831–94. Ky. A businessman in Georgetown (D.C.) and plantation owner in Ky., he was commissioned Col. 26th Ky. 27 Aug. '61 and distinguished himself at Shiloh. Named B.G. USV 9 June '62, he commanded 1, 1st Div. Army Ky., Ohio (Oct.–13 Nov. '62); 1st Div. Army Ky., Ohio (Aug.–Oct. '62) 1, 1st Div., Yazoo Exp., Tenn.; 1, 10, XIII, Tenn. at Pt. Gibson, Arkansas Post, and Vicksburg; 1, 3, XIII, Gulf (17 Aug.–20 Sept. '63); 4th Div., XIII, Gulf (20 Sept.–5 Dec. '63); Dist. Ky. 5th Div., XXIII, Ohio (10 Apr. '64–22 Feb. '65). Breveted Maj. Gen. USV 4 July '64 for repulsing MORGAN'S OHIO RAID. He resigned 1 Dec. '65.

BURGESS FARM, Va., 27 Oct. '64. HATCHER'S RUN, same date.

BURKE, Joseph Walter. Union officer. Ireland. Maj. 10th Ohio 8 May '61; Lt. Col. 9 Jan. '62; Col. 20 Jan. '63; Bvt. B.G. USV (war service); mustered out 17 June '64. Commanded Reserve Brigade, Army of the Cumberland. Born in County Mayo, he was so opposed to British policy that he joined in the 1848 revolt despite his four high-ranking brothers in the British Army. He himself had been educated for the army. Coming to America, he practiced law. Died 1900.

BURKE, Martin. Union officer. Md. Appt.–D.C. Entering the R.A. in 1820,

he fought in the Seminole War and in the Mexican War (2 brevets). He was promoted Lt. Col. 3d U.S. Arty. 28 Aug. '61 and was retired 11 Aug. '63 after commanding the Narrows of New York Harbor during the Civil War. Breveted B.G. USA, he died in 1882.

BURLING, George Childs. Union officer. N.J. Capt. 6th N.Y. 26 Aug. '61; Maj. 18 Mar. '62; Lt. Col. 7 May '62; Col. 10 Sept. '62; Bvt. B.G. USV (Gettysburg); resigned 4 Mar. '64. Commanded 3, 2, III. Died 1885.

BURNED HICKORY. DALLAS, GA.

BURNETT, Henry Lawrence. Union officer. 1838–1916. Ohio. Capt. 2d Ohio Cav. 23 Aug. '61; Maj. Judge Adv. Vols. 10 Aug. '63; Bvt. B.G. USV (Bureau of Military Justice). Served as Judge Advocate for the Dept. of the Ohio. In 1864 Gov. Morton requested that he be sent to Indiana to prosecute members of the Knights of the Golden Circle (see VALLANDIGHAM, Clement, L.) He also took part in the conspiracy cases to take over Chicago and liberate the Camp Douglas prisoners (see also SWEET, Benjamin Jeffery). D.A.B. says that in the trials of Lincoln's assassins he seems to have prepared the major portion of the evidence. Burnett joined the army at the outbreak of the war when, while making a speech on the necessity of preserving the Union, a man challenged him: "Why don't you enlist?" "I will," he promptly replied. (D.A.B.) After the war he was prominent as a lawyer, serving as counsel for the Erie R.R. and as federal District Attorney. He was active in Republican party organization and behind-the-scenes planning. McKinley called him "Lightning Eyes Burnett."

BURNHAM, Hiram. Union gen. ?–1864. Me. Commissioned Lt. Col. 6th Me. 15 July '61 and Col. 12 Dec. '61, he led the regiment through the Peninsula, at Antietam, at Fredericksburg, and at Gettysburg. Commanding Light Division, VI, Potomac (3–11 May '63) at Chancellorsville, he also led 3, 1, VI (Feb.–5 Apr. '64); 1st Div., XVIII, Va. and N.C. (31 July–3 Aug. '64) and 2, 1, XVIII, Va. and N.C. (28 Apr.–31 July and 27–29 Sept. '64) when he was killed at CHAFIN'S FARM (Ft. Harrison).

BURNS, John. "The Old Hero of Gettysburg." An old regular soldier who had fought in the War of 1812, the Seminole wars, and the Mexican War, according to various sources, he walked into the area of the 7th Wis. around noon on the first day of Gettysburg and joined the fight. He also fought with the 150th Pa. and the Iron Brigade during the three days and was wounded three times. Over 70 years old at the time, he was captured and nearly hanged as a combatant out of uniform. He lived until 1872.

BURNS, William Wallace. Union gen. 1825–92. Ohio. USMA 1847 (28/38); Inf.-Comsy. In the Mexican War, Seminole wars, on the frontier, and in garrison, he was Chief Comsy. of Subsist. Dept. of Ohio (24 Mar.–30 Oct. '61) as Maj. 3 Aug. '61. Named B.G. USV 28 Sept. '61, he served on boards and courts-martial until Mar. '62 when he was in the Peninsular campaign. He commanded 3d Brig., Stone's Division, Potomac (22 Oct. '61–13 Mar. '62), he then led 2, 2, II, Potomac (13 Mar.–10 July '62) at Yorktown, Lee's Mill, West Point, Fair Oaks, Peach Orchard, Savage's Station where he was wounded, Glendale, and Malvern Hill. He also commanded this brigade (10 Oct.–12 Nov. '62) at Snicker's Gap. At Fredericksburg he commanded 1st Div., IX (2 Nov. '62–7 Feb. '63). From Sept. '63 until Oct. '65, he was Chief Comsy. of Subsist. of the Dept. of the Northwest. Breveted for Savage's Station,

Glendale, and war service (B.G. USA), he continued in the R.A. until 1889, when he retired as Col.

BURNS. See MCCLELLAN'S HORSES.

BURNSIDE, Ambrose Everett. Union gen. 1824–81, Ind. USMA 1847 (18/38); Arty. After service in Mexican and Indian wars, he resigned in 1853 to manufacture firearms in Bristol, R.I.; invented breech-loading rifle (1856); Maj. Gen. R. I. Mil. ('55–'57); treasurer of Illinois Central R.R. in 1861. Entered Civil War as Col. of 1st R.I. Volunteers; commanded brigade at 1st Bull Run and promoted B.G.; led successful expedition against coastal installations in N.C., gaining promotion to Maj. Gen. and reputation for independent command. Twice refused offer to command Army of Potomac. His undistinguished leadership of McClellan's left wing at Antietam was main reason for Lee's escaping annihilation. Again offered command of Army of Potomac, he accepted only on the urging of other generals who did not want Hooker to have the position. Relieved of command after FREDERICKSBURG, for which failure Burnside publicly admitted blame, he consented to remain in the army in subordinate positions. As commander of the Army of the Ohio (25 Mar.–12 Dec. '63) he succeeded in the capture of Morgan's Raiders and the siege of Knoxville. Returning to the East as commander of the IX Corps, he fought in the Battle of the Wilderness, Spotsylvania, North Anna, Totopotomoy, Bethesda Church. He was again relieved of command for mishandling troops in the Petersburg mine assault. After the war he was successful in engineering and managerial work with several railroads; Governor of R.I. in 1866 and twice re-elected; then served as US Senator from that state until his death. A six-foot, handsome man of impressive mien, he was described by Grant in his memoirs as "an officer who was generally liked and respected. He was not, however, fitted to command an army. No one knew this better than himself." Famous for his mutton-chop whiskers, his name is still associated with that barber's specialty.

BURNSIDE CARBINE. After making a few experimental carbines, a second model was invented and patented by A. E. BURNSIDE 25 Mar. '56. A third model was soon developed and about 1,000 ordered in 1860. The fourth and final type, and the most popular, was then developed. During the Civil War the government bought 55,567 of these and almost 22,000,000 cartridges.

The Burnside breech-loading percussion carbine fired a cal. .54 metallic cartridge. Weighing about seven pounds, the arm was 39¼ inches in total length and had a 21-inch round barrel rifled with five grooves.

Burnside's original Bristol Fire Arms Company was organized in 1855 and failed in May '60. Reorganized as the Burnside Arms Company it manufactured the carbines under patents Burnside had assigned to his creditors. (Gluckman, 375.)

BURNSIDE'S EXPEDITION TO NORTH CAROLINA, Feb.–July '62. In Oct. '61 Burnside got approval of a plan to organize a special division for operations along the coast. His brigade commanders were J. G. Foster, Jesse L. Reno, and J. G. Parke. While troops assembled at Annapolis for training, Burnside went to New York to assemble a heterogeneous collection of light draught vessels for his proposed amphibious operations. With a supporting naval force under Admiral Goldsborough (19 warships and the flag steamer), Burnside's armada of 65 vessels (B.&L., I, 666) entered Pamlico Sound and on 7 Feb. '62 approached Roanoke Island on the west. At 10:30 A.M. an enemy signal gun was fired, and at 11:30 the naval action started against the Confederate forts and gunboats. During the afternoon and night Burnside landed his troops near Ashby's Harbor. The next day (8 Feb.) he defeated a force under the command of Henry Wise and took 2,500 prisoners. Federal losses were 14 in the naval force and 264 in Burnside's division. The Confederates lost six wounded on their gunboats and 143 killed, wounded, and missing among their land force.

Leaving a garrison on Roanoke Island, Burnside pursued to New Bern and captured that place on 14 Mar. In this operation he had 471 casualties and inflicted a loss of 578. He laid siege to Beaufort on 11 Apr. and captured it on the 26th. Expeditions were sent from New Bern to operate against Washington, Plymouth, and Edenton, N.C., and to threaten Norfolk and Suffolk, Va.

On 3 July Burnside was ordered to Fortress Monroe with 7,500 men to reinforce McClellan. The same number of troops was left, under J. G. Foster, to hold the department. The latter became the XVIII Corps.

After the fall of Roanoke Island and New Bern, T. H. Holmes was sent from the Aquia District to command the Confederate Dept. of N.C.

BURNT HICKORY, Ga., 24 May '64. DALLAS.

BURTON, Henry S. Union officer. c. 1818–69. N.Y. Appt. Vt. USMA 1839 (9/31); Arty. He fought in the Seminole wars, taught infantry and artillery tactics at West Point, and fought in the Mexican War before being promoted Maj. 3d U.S. Arty. 14 May '61 (Capt. since 1847). During the Civil War he commanded the prison at Ft. Delaware from June '62 to Sept. '63 and was promoted Lt. Col. 4th U.S. Arty. 25 July and Col. 5th U.S. Arty. 11 Aug. '63. After several months on detached service he commanded the Arty. Reserve of the Army of the Potomac Jan.–May '64, and was Insp. of Arty. May–June '64. He commanded the Arty. of the XVIII Corps until July of that year and took command of the 5th US Arty. and Ft. Richmond, N.Y., until 2 Dec. '64. For the rest of his life he served on various boards and commissions and was breveted B.G. USA for Petersburg.

BUSEY, Samuel Thompson. Union officer. Ind. Capt. 76th Ill. 22 June '62; Lt. Col. 22 Aug. '62; Col. 7 Jan. '63; Bvt. B.G. USV (Ft. Blakely).

BUSHWHACKER. Usually a term for a backwoodsman in American folklore, it was applied to Confederate guerrillas, implying private plunder as well. See William C. QUANTRILL.

BUSSEY, Cyrus. Union gen. 1833–98. Ohio. A state legislator, he was delegate to the Democratic convention that nominated Douglas and was commissioned Col. 3d. Iowa Cav. 5 Sept. '61 after commanding the militia in the southern part of the state. He commanded 2, 2d Div. Cav. Eastern Ark., Mo. (Dec. '62–Jan. '63) and in the Army of the Tenn.: 2, 2d Cav. Div., XIII (Feb.–Apr. '63); 2, Cav. Div. Eastern Ark., XVI (May–June '63) and the division (Apr.–May '63); Cav. Brig., Herron's Div.; 1, 1st Div. Cav. Ark. Exp. (Dec. '63–6 Jan. '64); 1st Cav. Div. Ark. Exp. (3 Nov.–Dec. '63). In the Dept. of Arkansas he led 3, 1, VII (25 May–25 July '64); 1st Div., VII (25 July–9 Sept. '64) and 3d Div., VII (6 Feb.–1 Aug. '65). Breveted Maj. Gen. USV for war service, he was mustered out 24 Aug. '65. After the war he was a commission merchant in St. Louis and New Orleans, and president of the Chamber of Commerce in the latter city. He was also Asst. Secretary of the Interior, 1889–93.

BUTLER, Benjamin Franklin. Union gen. and politician. 1818–93. N.H. B.G.

Mass. militia 17 Apr. '61; Maj. Gen. USV 16 May '61; resigned 30 Nov. '65. Before the war an astute criminal lawyer and active politician. Took command of the Dist. of Annapolis in early 1861, and on 13 May occupied Baltimore without opposition. In Aug. he captured Forts Hatteras and Clark in N.C., acquiring a reputation as a strategist, and then returned to Mass. to recruit an expedition to operate in the Gulf. On 1 May '62 he occupied New Orleans after Farragut's fleet had reduced its defenses. A capable military governor, he exhibited a genius for arousing adverse criticism at home and embarrassing his government in Europe. The most famous incidents were his hanging William Mumford, who had pulled down the Union flag from the mint; his "WOMAN ORDER" and his confiscation of $800,000 which he claimed had been entrusted to the Dutch consul for purchasing war supplies. Nicknamed "Spoons" for allegedly stealing silverware from Southerners. He was recalled 16 Dec. '62 and replaced by Banks. Late in 1863 he took command of the Dept. of Va. and N.C., later known as the Dept. (and Army) of the James. In Oct. '64 he was sent to N.Y.C. to handle anticipated election riots. Although an incompetent general, Butler was so influential that Lincoln could not relieve him until after the 1864 elections. After Butler had failed to act decisively with the Army of the Potomac against Petersburg, and after his blundering failure against Ft. Fisher, Grant was able to get Lincoln's consent to relieve Butler of command. In 1866 he was elected to Congress on a Republican ticket; he remained—except for one term—until 1879, and was prominent in the impeachment of Johnson. After several defeats he became Governor of Massachusetts in 1883; the next year he was an unsuccessful candidate for President.

BUTLER, Matthew Calbraith. C.S.A. gen. 1836–1909. S.C. After graduating from S.C. College and studying law, he married the daughter of S.C. Governor Pickens. A legislator, he resigned his seat to be commissioned Capt. in the Hampton Legion and fought at 1st Bull Run. Promoted Maj., he fought in the Peninsular campaign and was promoted Col. 2d S.C. in Aug. '62. At Antietam and Fredericksburg he commanded his regiment and lost his right foot at Brandy Station in June '63. When he returned to active duty, he was appointed B.G. C.S.A. 1 Sept. '63 (at 27 years of age) and commanded his brigade in the fighting around Richmond. He was promoted Maj. Gen. 17 Sept. '64 and joined Johnston in opposing Sherman in the Carolinas. After the war he was a lawyer, legislator, and Democratic Senator. McKinley appointed him Maj. Gen. USV in 1898 during the Spanish-American War. He also engaged in mining in New Mexico and was active in the Southern Historical Society. D.A.B. describes him as "Handsome, graceful, cool, he personally led his soldiers to battle, with only a silver-mounted riding whip in his hand."

BUTLER, Thomas Harvey. Union officer. Ind. Capt. 76th Ind. 20 July '62; mustered out 20 Aug. '62; Capt. 5th Ind. 17 Sept. '62; Lt. Col. 10 Dec. '62; Col. 1 Mar. '64; Bvt. B.G. USV (campaigns of 1863 and 1864). Commanded 2, 2, Cav. Corps, Army of Ohio; 1, Cav. Div., XXIII; 2, Cav. Div., XXIII; 1, 6, Cav. Corps, Mil. Div. Miss.

BUTLER MEDAL. Ben Butler had 200 medals made by Tiffany's and presented to Negro soldiers of the XXV Corps for their performance in the storming of New Market Heights and Chafin's Farm in Sept. '64. The first 46 of these were presented in May '65. Suspended by a red, white, and blue ribbon, "The obverse ... shows a bastion fort charged upon by negro soldiers, and bears the inscription 'Ferro iis libertas prevenient.' The reverse bears the words, 'Campaign before Richmond,' encircling the words, 'Distinguished for Courage' " (Butler's autobiography). See also DECORATIONS.

BUTTERFIELD, Daniel. Union gen. 1831–1901. N.Y. Son of the famous expressman, he graduated from Union College in 1849 and was a merchant in New York City when the war started. He had been 1st Sgt., Clay Guards, D.C. Vols. (12 Apr. '61) and became Col. 12th N.Y. Mil. 2 May. He led the latter unit to Washington in July and then joined Patterson in the Shenandoah Valley where he commanded the 8th Brig. 3d Div., during the 1st Bull Run campaign. Commissioned Lt. Col. in the R.A. 14 May '61, he was made B.G. USV 7 Sept. '61. He led the 3d Brig., 1st Div. (Morell), V Corps (Porter) in the Peninsular campaign (wounded at Gaines's Mill), and in the 2d Bull Run and Antietam campaigns. He succeeded Morell in temporary command of the division (1–16 Nov. '62) and took command of the corps 16 Nov. He led V Corps in the desperate assaults against Marye's Heights in the Battle of Fredericksburg. He became Maj. Gen. USV 29 Nov. '62. During the Chancellorsville and Gettysburg campaigns he was Chief of Staff, Army of the Potomac. Wounded at Gettysburg. Moving to the West, he was Hooker's Chief of Staff in the battles around Chattanooga and the beginning of the Atlanta campaign. Commanding the 3d Div., XX Corps (Cumberland) during the period 14 Apr.–29 June '64, he took part in the battles of Buzzard Roost, Resaca, Dallas, New

Hope Church, Kenesaw, and Lost Mountain. He was breveted B.G. and Maj. Gen. USA for gallant and meritorious field service during the war. In 1892 he was awarded the Medal of Honor for his gallantry at Gaines's Mill, where he had seized the colors of the 3d Pa. and rallied that regiment at a critical moment. Staying in the army after the war, he was in New York City until 1869, where he was superintendent of the US Army recruiting service and commander of troops in New York harbor. He resigned 14 Mar. '70, headed the US Subtreasury in New York City, and then was connected with the American Express Co. He married in 1886. He was in charge of several notable public ceremonies: Sherman's funeral, the Washington Centennial celebration (1889), and Dewey's triumphal return after the Battle of Manila (1899). Dan Butterfield, whose tomb is the most ornate in the West Point cemetery, is remembered in the US Army for having written the bugle call "Taps" (composed while at Harrison's Landing) and for designing the system of corps badges.

He is the author of *Camp and Outpost Duty* (1862).

BUTTERNUT GUERRILLAS. Small volunteer force of nine men from 7th Ill. Cav. organized during GRIERSON'S RAID for reconnaissance missions and led by Sgt. Richard Surby.

BUTTERNUTS. Nickname for Confederate soldiers whose uniforms were commonly dyed butternut brown (walnut hulls or copperas solution).

BUZZARD ROOST, Ga. See DALTON, Ga., 22–27 Feb. '64 and ROCKY FACE RIDGE, Ga., 5–11 May '64.

BY-LINES. For origin of in the Civil War, see Joseph HOOKER.

BYRNE, James J. Union officer. Ireland. Commissioned 1st Lt. and Adj. 163d N.Y. 24 July '62, he was mustered out 11 Dec. of that year and named Col. 18th N.Y. Cav. 24 Feb. '64. He was mustered out again in 1866, having been breveted for Pleasant Hill and Campti (B.G. USV) and Moore's Plantation and Yellow Bayou (Maj. Gen. USV). Heitman says that he was killed by Indians in 1880.

C

CABELL, William Lewis. C.S.A. gen. 1827–1911. Va. USMA 1850 (33/44); Inf. Serving in garrison and on the frontier, he resigned as Capt. in 1861 to become a Maj. in the C.S.A. and was sent by Davis, then in Montgomery, to Richmond to organize the commissary and quartermaster departments. He was Chief Q.M. on Beauregard's staff during 1st Bull Run and then served under J. E. Johnston. In Jan. '62 he became A. S. Johnston's Chief Q.M. and later served under Van Dorn in the Trans-Miss.

Dept. He handled the logistics of Van Dorn's movement from the Pea Ridge battlefield to Miss. He was then W.I.A. at Corinth and at Hatcher's Ridge. Reporting back for duty Feb. '63, he was given command of all troops in northwest Arkansas and was appointed (from Arkansas) B.G. 23 Apr. '63 to date from 20 Jan. He was captured leading his cavalry brigade at MARAIS DES CYGNES, Kans. 25 Oct. '64. Released from Ft. Warren in Aug. '65, he moved to Ft. Smith, Ark., to practice law and then went to Dallas. Four times Mayor, he was active in Democratic politics, railroading, and veterans' organizations.

CABINET. See UNION CABINET and CONFEDERATE CABINET.

CADWALADER, George. Union gen. 1803–79. Pa. A lawyer, he fought in the Mexican War with the rank of B.G. USV and was breveted Maj. Gen. USA for Chapultepec. Appointed Maj. Gen. Pa. Vols. 19 Apr. '61, he took command of Baltimore in May, when that place was in revolt. In June he went with Patterson, as second in command, in the advance into the Shenandoah Valley. He was promoted Maj. Gen. USV 25 Apr. '62, after having been mustered out of the Pa. troops 19 July '61. In Dec. '62 he became a member of a board appointed to revise military laws and regulations and he resigned 5 July '65.

CADY, Albemarle. Union officer. c. 1807–88. N.H. USMA 1829 (24/46); Inf. He served in the Seminole War, on the frontier, in the Mexican War (1 wound, 1 brevet), and in the West in Indian fighting before being promoted Lt. Col. 7th U.S. Inf. 6 June '61. Then he commanded the Dist. of Oregon 23 Oct. '61–7 Apr. '62 and served in the Dept. of the Pacific and in New England before being retired 18 May '64 for ill health as Col. 8th U.S. Inf. (20 Oct. '63). He was breveted B.G. USA 13 Mar. '65.

CAHABA (ALA.) PRISON. Used by the Confederates, it was an old cotton shed, only partly covered, that started being used in early 1864. Although this PRISON had bunks for 500 men, by Oct. '64 more than 2,000 were held in the stockade around it. Prisoners cooked their own food, and the water, while plentiful, was at one time polluted.

CALDWELL, John Curtis. Union gen. 1833–? Vt. Commissioned Col.

11th Me. 12 Nov. '61, he fought in every action of the Army of the Potomac from its organization until Grant took command in 1864. He was promoted B.G. USV 28 Apr. '62 and commanded 1, 1, II (4 June–13 Dec. '62 and 14 Feb.–22 May '63); 1st Div., II (17 Sept. '62; 22 May–9 Dec. '63 and 15 Jan.–24 Mar. '64); and II Corps (26 Aug.–2 Sept. '63; 16–29 Dec. '63; and 9–15 Jan. '64). Spending the last year of the war on a War Dept. board, he was breveted Maj. Gen. USV 19 Aug. '65 for war service and mustered out in 1866. After the war he held many public offices, among them Senator from Maine, Minister to Uruguay and Paraguay, and Consul at Valparaiso.

CALFKILLER CREEK (Sparta), Tenn., 17 Aug. '63. Cavalry skirmish between Minty (Fed.) and Dibrell. No casualties reported. The 5th Tenn. Cav. (US) had two skirmishes here: on 22 Feb. '64 two companies were attacked and fought their way back to Sparta; on 11 Mar. another skirmish took place. (T.U.A.)

CALHOUN, John Caldwell. Southern statesman. 1782–1850. S.C. After graduating from Yale he studied law in Litchfield (Conn.), sat in the S.C. Legislature, and went to the US Congress in 1811. He was Monroe's Secretary of War in 1817 and Vice-President of the US 1824–32. During the protective tariff dispute in the latter year he resigned his office to be elected to the Senate and defend his theory of nullification, i.e., that a state has the right to declare null and void and to set aside any Federal law that violates the compact of Union which was voluntarily accepted by the state. This was the first hint of secession, but upon adoption of a compromise tariff the matter subsided. Calhoun sat in the Senate until 1843, when he returned to S.C. to write and run his plantation. In 1844–45 he was

CALENDARS OF DAYS, 1860–65.

1860

S	M	T	W	T	F	S
JANUARY						
1	2	3	4	5	6	7
8	9	10	11	12	13	14
15	16	17	18	19	20	21
22	23	24	25	26	27	28
29	30	31	--	--	--	--
--	--	--	--	--	--	--
FEBRUARY						
--	--	--	1	2	3	4
5	6	7	8	9	10	11
12	13	14	15	16	17	18
19	20	21	22	23	24	25
26	27	28	29	--	--	--
--	--	--	--	--	--	--
MARCH						
--	--	--	--	1	2	3
4	5	6	7	8	9	10
11	12	13	14	15	16	17
18	19	20	21	22	23	24
25	26	27	28	29	30	31
--	--	--	--	--	--	--
APRIL						
1	2	3	4	5	6	7
8	9	10	11	12	13	14
15	16	17	18	19	20	21
22	23	24	25	26	27	28
29	30	--	--	--	--	--
--	--	--	--	--	--	--
MAY						
--	--	1	2	3	4	5
6	7	8	9	10	11	12
13	14	15	16	17	18	19
20	21	22	23	24	25	26
27	28	29	30	31	--	--
--	--	--	--	--	--	--
JUNE						
--	--	--	--	--	1	2
3	4	5	6	7	8	9
10	11	12	13	14	15	16
17	18	19	20	21	22	23
24	25	26	27	28	29	30
--	--	--	--	--	--	--
JULY						
1	2	3	4	5	6	7
8	9	10	11	12	13	14
15	16	17	18	19	20	21
22	23	24	25	26	27	28
29	30	31	--	--	--	--
--	--	--	--	--	--	--
AUGUST						
--	--	--	1	2	3	4
5	6	7	8	9	10	11
12	13	14	15	16	17	18
19	20	21	22	23	24	25
26	27	28	29	30	31	--
--	--	--	--	--	--	--
SEPTEMBER						
--	--	--	--	--	--	1
2	3	4	5	6	7	8
9	10	11	12	13	14	15
16	17	18	19	20	21	22
23	24	25	26	27	28	29
30	--	--	--	--	--	--
OCTOBER						
--	1	2	3	4	5	6
7	8	9	10	11	12	13
14	15	16	17	18	19	20
21	22	23	24	25	26	27
28	29	30	31	--	--	--
--	--	--	--	--	--	--
NOVEMBER						
--	--	--	--	1	2	3
4	5	6	7	8	9	10
11	12	13	14	15	16	17
18	19	20	21	22	23	24
25	26	27	28	29	30	--
--	--	--	--	--	--	--
DECEMBER						
--	--	--	--	--	--	1
2	3	4	5	6	7	8
9	10	11	12	13	14	15
16	17	18	19	20	21	22
23	24	25	26	27	28	29
30	31	--	--	--	--	--

1861

S	M	T	W	T	F	S
JANUARY						
--	--	1	2	3	4	5
6	7	8	9	10	11	12
13	14	15	16	17	18	19
20	21	22	23	24	25	26
27	28	29	30	31	--	--
--	--	--	--	--	--	--
FEBRUARY						
--	--	--	--	--	1	2
3	4	5	6	7	8	9
10	11	12	13	14	15	16
17	18	19	20	21	22	23
24	25	26	27	28	--	--
--	--	--	--	--	--	--
MARCH						
--	--	--	--	--	1	2
3	4	5	6	7	8	9
10	11	12	13	14	15	16
17	18	19	20	21	22	23
24	25	26	27	28	29	30
31	--	--	--	--	--	--
APRIL						
--	1	2	3	4	5	6
7	8	9	10	11	12	13
14	15	16	17	18	19	20
21	22	23	24	25	26	27
28	29	30	--	--	--	--
--	--	--	--	--	--	--
MAY						
--	--	--	1	2	3	4
5	6	7	8	9	10	11
12	13	14	15	16	17	18
19	20	21	22	23	24	25
26	27	28	29	30	31	--
--	--	--	--	--	--	--
JUNE						
--	--	--	--	--	--	1
2	3	4	5	6	7	8
9	10	11	12	13	14	15
16	17	18	19	20	21	22
23	24	25	26	27	28	29
30	--	--	--	--	--	--
JULY						
--	1	2	3	4	5	6
7	8	9	10	11	12	13
14	15	16	17	18	19	20
21	22	23	24	25	26	27
28	29	30	31	--	--	--
--	--	--	--	--	--	--
AUGUST						
--	--	--	--	1	2	3
4	5	6	7	8	9	10
11	12	13	14	15	16	17
18	19	20	21	22	23	24
25	26	27	28	29	30	31
--	--	--	--	--	--	--
SEPTEMBER						
1	2	3	4	5	6	7
8	9	10	11	12	13	14
15	16	17	18	19	20	21
22	23	24	25	26	27	28
29	30	--	--	--	--	--
--	--	--	--	--	--	--
OCTOBER						
--	--	1	2	3	4	5
6	7	8	9	10	11	12
13	14	15	16	17	18	19
20	21	22	23	24	25	26
27	28	29	30	31	--	--
--	--	--	--	--	--	--
NOVEMBER						
--	--	--	--	--	1	2
3	4	5	6	7	8	9
10	11	12	13	14	15	16
17	18	19	20	21	22	23
24	25	26	27	28	29	30
--	--	--	--	--	--	--
DECEMBER						
1	2	3	4	5	6	7
8	9	10	11	12	13	14
15	16	17	18	19	20	21
22	23	24	25	26	27	28
29	30	31	--	--	--	--
--	--	--	--	--	--	--

1862

S	M	T	W	T	F	S
JANUARY						
--	--	--	1	2	3	4
5	6	7	8	9	10	11
12	13	14	15	16	17	18
19	20	21	22	23	24	25
26	27	28	29	30	31	--
--	--	--	--	--	--	--
FEBRUARY						
--	--	--	--	--	--	1
2	3	4	5	6	7	8
9	10	11	12	13	14	15
16	17	18	19	20	21	22
23	24	25	26	27	28	--
--	--	--	--	--	--	--
MARCH						
--	--	--	--	--	--	1
2	3	4	5	6	7	8
9	10	11	12	13	14	15
16	17	18	19	20	21	22
23	24	25	26	27	28	29
30	31	--	--	--	--	--
APRIL						
--	--	1	2	3	4	5
6	7	8	9	10	11	12
13	14	15	16	17	18	19
20	21	22	23	24	25	26
27	28	29	30	--	--	--
--	--	--	--	--	--	--
MAY						
--	--	--	--	1	2	3
4	5	6	7	8	9	10
11	12	13	14	15	16	17
18	19	20	21	22	23	24
25	26	27	28	29	30	31
--	--	--	--	--	--	--
JUNE						
1	2	3	4	5	6	7
8	9	10	11	12	13	14
15	16	17	18	19	20	21
22	23	24	25	26	27	28
29	30	--	--	--	--	--
--	--	--	--	--	--	--
JULY						
--	--	1	2	3	4	5
6	7	8	9	10	11	12
13	14	15	16	17	18	19
20	21	22	23	24	25	26
27	28	29	30	31	--	--
--	--	--	--	--	--	--
AUGUST						
--	--	--	--	--	1	2
3	4	5	6	7	8	9
10	11	12	13	14	15	16
17	18	19	20	21	22	23
24	25	26	27	28	29	30
31	--	--	--	--	--	--
SEPTEMBER						
--	1	2	3	4	5	6
7	8	9	10	11	12	13
14	15	16	17	18	19	20
21	22	23	24	25	26	27
28	29	30	--	--	--	--
--	--	--	--	--	--	--
OCTOBER						
--	--	--	1	2	3	4
5	6	7	8	9	10	11
12	13	14	15	16	17	18
19	20	21	22	23	24	25
26	27	28	29	30	31	--
--	--	--	--	--	--	--
NOVEMBER						
--	--	--	--	--	--	1
2	3	4	5	6	7	8
9	10	11	12	13	14	15
16	17	18	19	20	21	22
23	24	25	26	27	28	29
30	--	--	--	--	--	--
DECEMBER						
--	1	2	3	4	5	6
7	8	9	10	11	12	13
14	15	16	17	18	19	20
21	22	23	24	25	26	27
28	29	30	31	--	--	--
--	--	--	--	--	--	--

1863

S	M	T	W	T	F	S
JANUARY						
--	--	--	--	1	2	3
4	5	6	7	8	9	10
11	12	13	14	15	16	17
18	19	20	21	22	23	24
25	26	27	28	29	30	31
--	--	--	--	--	--	--
FEBRUARY						
1	2	3	4	5	6	7
8	9	10	11	12	13	14
15	16	17	18	19	20	21
22	23	24	25	26	27	28
--	--	--	--	--	--	--
MARCH						
1	2	3	4	5	6	7
8	9	10	11	12	13	14
15	16	17	18	19	20	21
22	23	24	25	26	27	28
29	30	31	--	--	--	--
--	--	--	--	--	--	--
APRIL						
--	--	--	1	2	3	4
5	6	7	8	9	10	11
12	13	14	15	16	17	18
19	20	21	22	23	24	25
26	27	28	29	30	--	--
--	--	--	--	--	--	--
MAY						
--	--	--	--	--	1	2
3	4	5	6	7	8	9
10	11	12	13	14	15	16
17	18	19	20	21	22	23
24	25	26	27	28	29	30
31	--	--	--	--	--	--
JUNE						
--	1	2	3	4	5	6
7	8	9	10	11	12	13
14	15	16	17	18	19	20
21	22	23	24	25	26	27
28	29	30	--	--	--	--
--	--	--	--	--	--	--
JULY						
--	--	--	1	2	3	4
5	6	7	8	9	10	11
12	13	14	15	16	17	18
19	20	21	22	23	24	25
26	27	28	29	30	31	--
--	--	--	--	--	--	--
AUGUST						
--	--	--	--	--	--	1
2	3	4	5	6	7	8
9	10	11	12	13	14	15
16	17	18	19	20	21	22
23	24	25	26	27	28	29
30	31	--	--	--	--	--
SEPTEMBER						
--	--	1	2	3	4	5
6	7	8	9	10	11	12
13	14	15	16	17	18	19
20	21	22	23	24	25	26
27	28	29	30	--	--	--
--	--	--	--	--	--	--
OCTOBER						
--	--	--	--	1	2	3
4	5	6	7	8	9	10
11	12	13	14	15	16	17
18	19	20	21	22	23	24
25	26	27	28	29	30	31
--	--	--	--	--	--	--
NOVEMBER						
1	2	3	4	5	6	7
8	9	10	11	12	13	14
15	16	17	18	19	20	21
22	23	24	25	26	27	28
29	30	--	--	--	--	--
--	--	--	--	--	--	--
DECEMBER						
--	--	1	2	3	4	5
6	7	8	9	10	11	12
13	14	15	16	17	18	19
20	21	22	23	24	25	26
27	28	29	30	31	--	--
--	--	--	--	--	--	--

1864

S	M	T	W	T	F	S
JANUARY						
--	--	--	--	--	1	2
3	4	5	6	7	8	9
10	11	12	13	14	15	16
17	18	19	20	21	22	23
24	25	26	27	28	29	30
31	--	--	--	--	--	--
FEBRUARY						
--	1	2	3	4	5	6
7	8	9	10	11	12	13
14	15	16	17	18	19	20
21	22	23	24	25	26	27
28	29	--	--	--	--	--
--	--	--	--	--	--	--
MARCH						
--	--	1	2	3	4	5
6	7	8	9	10	11	12
13	14	15	16	17	18	19
20	21	22	23	24	25	26
27	28	29	30	31	--	--
--	--	--	--	--	--	--
APRIL						
--	--	--	--	--	1	2
3	4	5	6	7	8	9
10	11	12	13	14	15	16
17	18	19	20	21	22	23
24	25	26	27	28	29	30
MAY						
1	2	3	4	5	6	7
8	9	10	11	12	13	14
15	16	17	18	19	20	21
22	23	24	25	26	27	28
29	30	31	--	--	--	--
--	--	--	--	--	--	--
JUNE						
--	--	--	1	2	3	4
5	6	7	8	9	10	11
12	13	14	15	16	17	18
19	20	21	22	23	24	25
26	27	28	29	30	--	--
--	--	--	--	--	--	--
JULY						
--	--	--	--	--	1	2
3	4	5	6	7	8	9
10	11	12	13	14	15	16
17	18	19	20	21	22	23
24	25	26	27	28	29	30
31	--	--	--	--	--	--
AUGUST						
--	1	2	3	4	5	6
7	8	9	10	11	12	13
14	15	16	17	18	19	20
21	22	23	24	25	26	27
28	29	30	31	--	--	--
--	--	--	--	--	--	--
SEPTEMBER						
--	--	--	--	1	2	3
4	5	6	7	8	9	10
11	12	13	14	15	16	17
18	19	20	21	22	23	24
25	26	27	28	29	30	--
--	--	--	--	--	--	--
OCTOBER						
--	--	--	--	--	--	1
2	3	4	5	6	7	8
9	10	11	12	13	14	15
16	17	18	19	20	21	22
23	24	25	26	27	28	29
30	31	--	--	--	--	--
NOVEMBER						
--	--	1	2	3	4	5
6	7	8	9	10	11	12
13	14	15	16	17	18	19
20	21	22	23	24	25	26
27	28	29	30	--	--	--
--	--	--	--	--	--	--
DECEMBER						
--	--	--	--	1	2	3
4	5	6	7	8	9	10
11	12	13	14	15	16	17
18	19	20	21	22	23	24
25	26	27	28	29	30	31

1865

S	M	T	W	T	F	S
JANUARY						
1	2	3	4	5	6	7
8	9	10	11	12	13	14
15	16	17	18	19	20	21
22	23	24	25	26	27	28
29	30	31	--	--	--	--
--	--	--	--	--	--	--
FEBRUARY						
--	--	--	1	2	3	4
5	6	7	8	9	10	11
12	13	14	15	16	17	18
19	20	21	22	23	24	25
26	27	28	--	--	--	--
--	--	--	--	--	--	--
MARCH						
--	--	--	1	2	3	4
5	6	7	8	9	10	11
12	13	14	15	16	17	18
19	20	21	22	23	24	25
26	27	28	29	30	31	--
--	--	--	--	--	--	--
APRIL						
--	--	--	--	--	--	1
2	3	4	5	6	7	8
9	10	11	12	13	14	15
16	17	18	19	20	21	22
23	24	25	26	27	28	29
30	--	--	--	--	--	--
MAY						
--	1	2	3	4	5	6
7	8	9	10	11	12	13
14	15	16	17	18	19	20
21	22	23	24	25	26	27
28	29	30	31	--	--	--
--	--	--	--	--	--	--
JUNE						
--	--	--	--	1	2	3
4	5	6	7	8	9	10
11	12	13	14	15	16	17
18	19	20	21	22	23	24
25	26	27	28	29	30	--
--	--	--	--	--	--	--
JULY						
--	--	--	--	--	--	1
2	3	4	5	6	7	8
9	10	11	12	13	14	15
16	17	18	19	20	21	22
23	24	25	26	27	28	29
30	31	--	--	--	--	--
AUGUST						
--	--	1	2	3	4	5
6	7	8	9	10	11	12
13	14	15	16	17	18	19
20	21	22	23	24	25	26
27	28	29	30	31	--	--
--	--	--	--	--	--	--
SEPTEMBER						
--	--	--	--	--	1	2
3	4	5	6	7	8	9
10	11	12	13	14	15	16
17	18	19	20	21	22	23
24	25	26	27	28	29	30
--	--	--	--	--	--	--
OCTOBER						
1	2	3	4	5	6	7
8	9	10	11	12	13	14
15	16	17	18	19	20	21
22	23	24	25	26	27	28
29	30	31	--	--	--	--
--	--	--	--	--	--	--
NOVEMBER						
--	--	--	1	2	3	4
5	6	7	8	9	10	11
12	13	14	15	16	17	18
19	20	21	22	23	24	25
26	27	28	29	30	--	--
--	--	--	--	--	--	--
DECEMBER						
--	--	--	--	--	1	2
3	4	5	6	7	8	9
10	11	12	13	14	15	16
17	18	19	20	21	22	23
24	25	26	27	28	29	30
31	--	--	--	--	--	--

Tyler's Secretary of State and re-entered the Senate in the latter year. His last appearance and speech, read by Mason of Virginia, was on 4 Mar. '50, and he died in the latter part of that month.

CALIBER. The diameter of the bore of a firearm or the weight of its projectile. It may also be the diameter of the projectile.

The caliber of small arms was originally determined by the number of bullets required to weigh a pound. By the time of the Civil War it was commonly expressed in inches or millimeters (mm.). The Springfield musket, for example, was known as a caliber .58 (inch) weapon, while the Confederate Minié rifle was an 18.04 mm. (.71 inch) weapon. It is easy to correlate the two systems of measurement on the basis of one inch being equal to 25.4 mm.

With cannon (artillery) the matter is more complicated. First, it was conventional to designate the caliber of field guns and field howitzers in pounds, and siege and seacoast howitzers, Columbiads, and mortars in inches. Rifled fieldpieces, however, were commonly designated in inches. It is not possible to make precise correlations between the two systems in the case of all guns, since odd-shaped projectiles were used. The 12-pounder Napoleon, for example, had a larger caliber (4.62 inches) than the 30-pounder Parrott (4.2 inches), since the latter was a rifled piece and threw an oblong rather than a spherical projectile. Armstrong (rifle) shells for the 3-inch gun varied between less than 10 and more than 16 pounds (Wise, 66). Cannon are, therefore, usually designated both as to weight of projectile and diameter of bore and/or projectile.

The following table of conversions is given by Benton as the "calibers in American service":

6-pounder	3.67 inches
9-pounder	4.2 inches
12-pounder	4.62 inches
18-pounder	5.2 inches
24-pounder	5.82 inches
32-pounder	6.4 inches
42-pounder	7.0 inches

CALIFORNIA, UNION DEPARTMENT OF. In existence at the start of the war, it comprised Calif., the area now known as Ariz., that portion of the present state of Nev. west of the 117 degree of longitude, and the southwest corner of the present state of Ore. Headquarters were at San Francisco. After 1 Jan. '61 this department no longer existed and its territories were included in the Dept. of the Pacific.

CALIFORNIA COLUMN. A force of 11 companies of infantry, two of cavalry, and two artillery batteries, was ordered by George Wright, C. G. Dept. of the Pacific, to join Canby in N. Mex. The column, under Col. J. H. CARLETON left southern California on 13 Apr. '62, marched through hostile Indian country, and reached Santa Fe 20 Sept. (B.&L., II, 698n.). Although Sibley's invasion of N. Mex. had been repulsed, Carleton's arrival caused the Confederates to withdraw all the way to San Antonio. (See also NEW MEXICO AND ARIZONA OPERATIONS IN 1861–62.)

CALLENDER, Franklin D. Union officer. c. 1816–82. N.Y. He fought in the Seminole War and the Mexican War (2 wounds, 1 brevet) before taking command of the St. Louis Arsenal in 1861 and serving as Chief of Ord. of the Dept. of the Mo. 19 Nov. '61–11 Mar. '62. Holding the same post in the Dept. of the Miss. 11 Mar.–11 July '62, he returned to Mo., where he was on the Governor's staff and then served in the advance upon and siege of Corinth. He then returned to the Dept. of the Mo. and the St. Louis Arsenal 11 July '62 and commanded it throughout the war. Promoted Maj. 3 Mar. '63, he was breveted for Corinth, St. Louis, and war service (B.G. USA 9 Apr. '65). He continued in the R.A. until his retirement in 1879.

CALLIS, John Benton. Union officer. 1828–98. N.C. Capt. 7th Wis. 30 Aug. '61; Maj. 5 Jan. '63; discharged 29 Nov. '63; Maj. Vet. Res. Corps 24 May '64; Lt. Col. 11 Feb. '65; Bvt. B.G. USV. Bvts. for war service, Gettysburg. W.I.A. Gettysburg. Transferring to the R.A., he served for a time on the Freedman's Bureau Commission. Later a Reconstruction politician in Alabama.

CAMDEN, Ark. Steele's Expedition to. See ARKANSAS CAMPAIGN IN 1864.

CAMERON, Daniel. Union officer. Scotland. Lt. Col. 65th Ill. 1 Mar. '62; Col. 1 May '62; Bvt. B.G. USV (war service); resigned 31 July '64. Commanded 2, 3, XXIII; 1, 4, XXIII. Died 1879.

CAMERON, Hugh. Union officer. N.Y. 1st Sgt. Co. F 2d Kans. Cav. July '61; 1st Lt. 7 Nov. '61; Capt. 27 Dec. '61; Lt. Col. 2d Ark. Cav. 20 Feb. '64; Bvt. B.G. USV (war service).

CAMERON, Robert Alexander. Union gen. 1828–94. N.Y. A newspaper editor and Republican legislator, he was commissioned Capt. 9th Ind. 23 Apr. '61, Lt. Col. 29 July, and, transferring to 34th Ind. 3 Feb. '62, he had fought at New Madrid, Island No. 10, and Memphis when promoted Col. 15 June '62. He led his regiment at Vicksburg and was named B.G. USV 11 Aug. '63. During the Red River Expedition of 1864 he commanded 1, 3, XIII, 5 Feb.– 3 Mar. '64 and 24 May–11 June '64 (as well as 8 Oct.–6 Dec. '63) and 3d Div., XIII, Gulf, 3 Mar.–8 Apr. '64 and 27 Apr.–24 May '64. He also commanded Dist. LaFourche from 9 June '64 until July '65 when he resigned, being brev-

eted Maj. Gen. USV for war service. Settling in the West, he organized Union Colony, which became Greeley (Colo.), and Fountain Colony, which became Colorado Springs.

CAMERON, Simon. Union Secretary of War. 1799–1889. Pa. A lawyer, he entered politics, served in the Senate, and joined the new Republican party. While in the Senate in 1857 he built up the party machine in Pa. that he controlled the rest of his life. In 1860 Lincoln received his powerful support only after Lincoln's managers had promised him a cabinet post, and the President, reluctantly recognizing the bargain made without his knowledge, appointed him Secretary of War. Taking an independent course, he repeatedly embarrassed Lincoln, and the scandals and corruption emanating from army contracts and military appointments brought a censure from the House of Representatives. Lincoln, meanwhile, appointed him Minister to Russia in Jan. '62. Re-elected to the Senate in 1867, he served for 10 more years, and his political machine survived until 1921.

CAMOUFLET. A land mine whose explosion does not rupture the surface of the ground.

CAMPBELL, Alexander William. C.S.A. gen. 1828–93. Tenn. Commissioned Col. 33d Tenn. in 1861, he commanded his regiment in reserve at Belmont and fought at Shiloh, where he was wounded. Just before the battle of Stones River he was named Polk's Adj. and I.G. He then joined Pillow's volunteer and conscript bureau and was captured in July '63 at Lexington, Tenn. "Apparently not exchanged until February 1865" (Warner), he then led a cavalry brigade in W. H. Jackson's division of Forrest's Corps. His commission as B.G. was dated 1 Mar. '65 (Wright; Warner).

CAMPBELL, Charles Thomas. Union gen. 1823–95. Pa. He served in the R.A. during the Mexican War and then in politics. Commissioned Capt. Btry. A Pa. Light Arty. 29 May '61, Lt. Col. 1st Pa. Arty. 5 Aug. '61 and Col. 13 Sept. '61, he was wounded three times at Fair Oaks and twice at Fredericksburg, his horse shot from under him at each place. At Fredericksburg he and his regiment were captured, but released themselves, taking 200 rebels back as prisoners. A total of seven wounds at this point kept him from further field service. He was promoted B.G. USV 29 Nov. '62 (this appointment expired 4 Mar. '63) and reappointed 13 Mar. '63, continuing to serve with this rank until mustered out in 1866.

CAMPBELL, Cleaveland J. Union officer. 1836–65. N.Y. 2d Lt. 1st N.Y. Cav. 28 Oct. '61; 1st Lt. and Adj. 152d N.Y. 15 Oct. '62; Capt. 121st N.Y. 22 Apr. '63; Lt. Col. 23d US Col. Inf. 21 Mar. '64; Col. 15 July '64; Bvt. B.G. USV (war service). Died 13 June '65 from injuries received 30 July '64 during the Petersburg mine assault.

CAMPBELL, Edward Livingston. Union officer. N.J. Capt. 3d N.Y. 28 May '61; Lt. Col. 15th N.Y. 29 Sept. '62; Col. 4th N.Y. 2 June '65; Bvt. B.G. USV 9 Apr. '65. Brevets for Cedar Creek, Richmond, Lee's surrender. Commanded 1, 1, VI (Potomac; Shenandoah).

CAMPBELL, Jacob Miller. Union officer. Pa. 1st Lt. Regt. Q.M. 3d Pa. 20 Apr. '61; mustered out 30 July '61; Col. 54th Pa. 27 Feb. '62; Bvt. B.G. USV (Piedmont, Va.); discharged 3 Sept. '64. Commanded 4, 1, VIII; in Army of W. Va. commanded Campbell's brigade, then 3d Brig. (1st Div.) and 1st Brig. (2d Div.); then commanded 3d Brig., 2d Inf. Div., Dept. N. Mex. Died 1888.

CAMPBELL, John Allen. Union officer. 1835–80. Ohio. 1st Lt. 1st Ohio, 31 Oct. '61; Maj. Asst. Adj. Gen. Vols. 27 Oct. '62; Lt. Col. Asst. Adj. Gen. Assigned 31 Jan.–1 Aug. '65; Bvt. B.G. USV. Brevets for war service (2), Shiloh, Stones River, Resaca, Franklin (Tenn.). In '62 he was Gen. McCook's ordnance officer and in March '63 on the staff of Gen. Schofield. Trained as a printer, he went into the R.A. for a time and later was appointed the first Governor of the Wyoming Territory. He was also 3d Asst. Sec. of State.

CAMPBELL, John Archibald. Jurist and Confederate statesman. 1811–1889. Ga. Appointed an Associate Justice of the Supreme Court in 1853, he followed the Jeffersonian theory of democracy and tended to a strict interpretation of the Constitution. He opposed the policy of secession as impractical, although he believed in it as the right of the states and ardently worked to prevent the war. When Seward would not receive the Confederate commissioners, he became the intermediary and understood Seward to assure him that Ft. Sumter would be evacuated. Thus the provisioning of the garrison there was considered a breach of faith in the South. Campbell resigned from the Supreme Court and in 1862 became Asst. Sec. of War for the Confederacy. He was one of the Southern commissioners at the futile Hampton Roads Peace Conference and after the war spent four months in prison. Renewing his reputation as an able lawyer in New Orleans, he appeared in the famous Slaughter House Cases where he sought unsuccessfully to invoke the newly passed 14th Amendment against a monopoly.

CAMPBELL, William Bowen. Union gen. 1807–67. Tenn. He had practiced law, fought in the Seminole War, and in the Mexican War and served as US Congressman before becoming Whig

Governor of Tenn. in 1851. A proponent of the Compromise of 1850 and a stanch enemy of secession in the divided border state, Campbell refused a high rank from the C.S.A. to become B.G. USV 30 Jun '62. He resigned 26 Jan. '63, was elected to the House of Representatives in 1865, and became one of Johnson's supporters.

CAMPBELL'S STATION, Tenn. 16 Nov. '63. Delaying action by the IX Corps; 2d Div., XXIII Corps; and Sanders's cavalry covering Burnside's withdrawal into KNOXVILLE. Initial contact resulted when Hartranft's division beat McLaws' division in a race to secure the vital crossroad. Col. Wm. Humphrey's brigade, meanwhile, delayed Jenkins's advance. This enabled Burnside's trains to get by safely, while other troops formed a line to which Hartranft then withdrew. In the ensuing skirmish the Federals lost 318 and the Confederates 174.

CAMP CHASE. First used as a training camp, the place, located west of Columbus, Ohio, was later more important as a Federal prison camp. In 1863 there were about 8,000 Confederate prisoners there.

CAMP DISTRIBUTION. See Amy M. BRADLEY.

CAMP DOUGLAS. Established originally for the training of Ill. volunteers, the sixty-acre area served also as a prison camp after the fall of Ft. Donelson. Its total number of Confederate prisoners was 30,000. Located to the south of Chicago, it was dismantled in Nov. '65.

CAMP FORD AND CAMP GROCE. These Confederate PRISONS, near Tyler and Hempstead, Texas, respectively, held both officers and men from 1863 until the end of the war. At Camp Ford the prisoners built log cabins, and the food, water, and sanitary conditions

were more than adequate. There was so little sickness that the camps had no hospitals. However, after Banks's RED RIVER CAMPAIGN OF 1864, severe overcrowding took place, and disease resulted from this influx of prisoners. Camp Groce was a camp in an open field enclosed by guard lines, and little is known about it.

CAMP GROCE. See CAMP FORD AND CAMP GROCE.

CAMP JACKSON, Mo., 10 May '61. While F. P. BLAIR, JR., organized the pro-Union forces in Missouri during the early part of 1861, pro-secession Gov. C. F. JACKSON bent every effort toward turning the state over to the Confederacy. Failing in an attempt to have a pro-secession state convention elected, Jackson then worked out a plan with B.G. D. M. Frost to seize the Federal arsenal in St. Louis. Frustrated by Nathaniel LYON and Blair, Frost's small brigade of volunteer militia went into camp (6 May '61) in the western outskirts of St. Louis (Lindell Grove) and named it Camp Jackson. The night of the 8th a shipment of arms from Jeff Davis arrived from Baton Rouge.

Determined to break up this Confederate threat, Lyon decided on the 7th to attack Camp Jackson. "Tradition says that Lyon drove next day to the rebel camp, heavily veiled and in a woman's dress, a pistol under a basket of eggs ostensibly for sale—unlikely, surely, for Lyon's spies knew all that was necessary about Lindell Grove, and his rough red beard could not be disguised by any veil" (Monaghan, 130–31). On the 10th Lyon moved in with four volunteer regiments and a battalion of regulars and captured Frost with between 635 and 1000 prisoners (B.&L., I, 265; Monaghan, 132). The only casualties so far were Lyon, kicked in the stomach by an aide's horse, and Franz Sigel, whose leg had been injured when his horse slipped on the paved street and fell. A large crowd had gathered, and among the spectators were W. T. Sherman, who was at that time a businessman in St. Louis, and U. S. Grant, then a mustering officer for the Governor of Illinois and on leave.

As the prisoners were marched back to the St. Louis arsenal a hostile crowd pelted the Federal volunteers and, after a drunk wounded an officer with a pistol, Col. Boernstein ordered his regiment to open fire. In this incident and others along the route a total of 28 people were killed.

CAMP LAWTON. Confederate PRISON at Millen (Ga.) built in the summer of 1864 to take care of the excess prisoners at ANDERSONVILLE. Much like that prison, it was a square stockade enclosing about 42 acres with the interior divided by streets into divisions. Prisoners made their own huts from branches of the trees used in the stockade. By Nov. '64 it held around 10,000 men.

"CAMP MISERY." See Amy M. BRADLEY.

CAMP MORTON. At Indianapolis, this Federal PRISON was originally the fair grounds and consisted of barracks without floors or sturdy walls in an enclosure. In the winter the barracks were impossible to keep clean, and fuel was scarce despite a large number of trees within the enclosure.

CAMP SUMTER at Anderson (Ga.). Original name for ANDERSONVILLE.

CANBY, Edward Richard Sprigg. Union gen. 1817–73. Ky. Appt.-Ind. USMA 1839 (30/31); Inf. He fought in the Seminole War and Mexican War (2 brevets) and served in garrison and on the frontier. Named Col. 19th US Inf. 14 May '61, in New Mexico, he commanded the Dept. of N. Mex. holding that territory for the Union and

preventing a Confederate invasion of California by Sibley. Going to the east, he was Asst. Adj. Gen. in Washington. Named B.G. USV 31 Mar. '62, he commanded troops in N.Y.C. after the draft riots. Promoted Maj. Gen. USV 7 May '64, he commanded the Mil. Div. Western Miss. (11 May '64–May '65) and was severely wounded by guerrillas. He led the assault on Mobile and received the surrender of Taylor and Kirby Smith. Succeeding to the command of the Army and Dept. of the Gulf (3–27 June '65), he was breveted B.G. USA for Valverde (N. Mex.) and Maj. Gen. USA for Mobile. As B.G. USA (1866) he commanded the Dept. of the Columbia and was murdered by the Modoc Indians while arranging a peace treaty with them.

CANDY, Charles. Union officer. Ky. R.A. Pvt. Gen. Sv. and 1st US Inf. 1856–1 Jan. '61; Capt. Asst. Adj. Gen. Vols. 21 Sept. '61; resigned 3 Dec. '61; Col. 66th Ohio 17 Dec. '61; Bvt. B.G. USV (war service). Commanded 1, 2, XII (Potomac; Cumberland); 2d Div., XII Corps.

CANE AND RED RIVER, La., 26–27 Apr. '64. J. H. Caudle's attack against Porter's flagship, *Cricket,* the *Fort Hindman, Juliet,* and two pump boats during the RED RIVER CAMPAIGN.

CANE HILL, Ark., 28 Nov. '62. Gen. James G. Blunt with his 1st Div., Army of the Frontier, was in bivouac at Lindsay's Prairie after his defeat of Cooper at OLD FORT WAYNE, when he learned that Marmaduke was located north of the Boston Mountains with a force of 8,000 Confederate cavalry. Suspecting that this was the vanguard of Hindman's army moving up for another invasion of Missouri, Blunt marched south with 5,000 men to attempt to destroy Marmaduke's force before it could be joined by Hindman's main body. After a 35-mile march he made contact at Cane Hill. Surprised, the Confederates retreated into the Boston Mountains, Blunt pursued a short distance but then withdrew because of the danger of ambush in the mountain defiles. Gen. J. O. Shelby conducted the rear guard and led one unsuccessful counterattack. Under a flag of truce both sides collected their dead and wounded. The Federals reported their own loss at 40 and the Confederate loss at 435.

CANISTER. Artillery projectile consisting of a tin can (canister) filled with small cast-iron or lead balls (bullets) or long slugs, set in dry sawdust, that scattered immediately on leaving the muzzle. With much the same effect as the later-day machine gun, canister was most effectively fired from a smooth-bore cannon at ranges of between 100 and 200 yards. Maximum effective range was 400 yards. (Roberts, 114.) It was used primarily in the defense. Canister is sometimes confused with other forms of CASE SHOT.

CANNON, William. Gov. of Delaware. 1809–65. Del. Active in the Methodist Church from the time he was a young man, he entered politics as a Democrat, serving in the legislature. In 1861 he was a member of the peace conference in Washington and advocated the Crittenden Compromise but when Ft. Sumter was fired upon he changed to favor war. He was elected Governor in 1864 by the Unionists in the state and faced an unsympathetic legislature, to which he proposed continued support of the Federal government and emancipation of slaves.

CANNON, famous names. See DICTATOR (Petersburg Express), OLD SACRAMENTO, WHISTLING DICK, SWAMP ANGEL.

CANNON OF THE CIVIL WAR. The basic artillery piece of the war, on both sides, was the NAPOLEON, a smooth-bore, muzzle-loading, 12-pounder-gun howitzer. Rifled cannon played a secondary role in field artillery operations, and their use diminished further as the war progressed; the principal piece, however, was the ORDNANCE GUN (3-inch). There were eight other standard types of field artillery (see below) and a dozen additional types of field rifles. There was a tremendous variety of ammunition, other than the projectiles for the standard cannon. And there were a great many more types of cannon and projectile in the category of siege and seacoast artillery. All of these will be mentioned below and most are to be found in their alphabetical place throughout this book, but it should be kept in mind that the Napoleon probably inflicted more casualties than all the others combined. Second in importance were the 3-inch rifles, the Ordnance and PARROTT.

"Cannon" is the best generic term for all firearms larger than SMALL ARMS. Strictly speaking, it is a metal tube; put on a mount, it becomes "artillery." Cannon are classified in many different ways. They are guns, mortars, or howitzers in accordance with their trajectories—or the path followed by their projectile: a gun has a relatively flat trajectory; a mortar has a high, arching one; a howitzer has a trajectory that is in between the other two. (Also, to be technical, a gun has no chamber. Benton, 182.) Civil War artillery was also classified according to its tactical employment; the main categories were field, seacoast, and siege artillery, but there also was prairie and mountain artillery. The brass 24-pounder COEHORN mortar was also classed as artillery, as was the PETARD.

Within the above categories there are smoothbores and rifled cannon; breech- and muzzle-loaders; and iron, bronze (brass), and steel cannon. With regard to their method of construction cannon were "cast metal homogeneous" (COLUMBIAD, DAHLGREN, NAPOLEON, and RODMAN) or BUILT-UP GUN (ARMSTRONG, BLAKELY, BROOKE, PARROTT, WHITWORTH).

Cannon are also classified as to CALIBER, or size of the bore or projectile expressed in terms of its diameter or weight.

As for ammunition, the nine common calibers in the Union army came as solid SHOT, GRAPE, CANISTER (or CASE SHOT), SHELL, and CHAIN or bar shot. Principal types of projectile were the Armstrong, Blakely, Dimmick, DYER, HOTCHKISS, JAMES, Parrott, REED, SCHENKLE (or Shenkl) and Whitworth. There was a type of incendiary shell known as CARCASS. FUZES came in three general types.

To add to the complexity of the problem, a name such as Dahlgren, James, Parrott, etc., does not necessarily indicate a *specific* artillery piece or even projectile. Each type of cannon existed in different calibers, and many could be either rifled or smoothbore (e.g., Columbiads), breech-, or muzzle-loaders (e.g., Armstrongs, Blakelys, and Whitworths) and could even be brass or iron (e.g., Napoleons). Projectiles of a certain name could be of entirely different design (e.g., Blakelys and Armstrongs).

The standard field artillery pieces of the Civil War, used on both sides, were: the 6- and 12-pounder guns; the 12-, 24- and 32-pounder howitzers; the 12-pounder mountain howitzer; the 12-pounder Napoleon gun howitzer; the 10- and 20-pounder Parrott rifles; and the 3-inch Ordnance gun. All of these were muzzle-loaders, and all but the last three were bronze smoothbores. The last three, the rifled guns, were iron or steel. These ten types of cannon, according to Weller, "accounted for far more than 90 per cent of the battlefield rounds fired during the war" (p. 65).

What Weller calls "miscellaneous nonstandard field rifles" used by both sides were: the cast bronze 12- and 24-pounder James; the cast-steel 6- and 10-pounder Wiard; the 3.67-inch Small Sawyer; three Whitworths: the 6- and 12-pounder breech-loaders, and a 12-pounder muzzle-loader; the 12-pounder Blakely; two types of 3-inch Armstrong, one a breech-loader and another a muzzle-loader; and the Confederate bronze 2.25-inch Mountain Rifle. Additional Confederate types were the Brooke, some Austrian cannon, and the remarkable WILLIAMS rapid-fire cannon. The GATLING gun was employed in small numbers by the Federals as artillery.

As for the ratio of smoothbores to rifled guns, at Chancellorsville the Federals had about seven rifles to three smoothbores, and the Confederate ratio was about two to three (Bigelow). "At Gettysburg the proportion of guns in both armies was 50 per cent smoothbores, mostly Napoleons, and 50 per cent rifles, mostly 3-inch," writes Downey in *The Guns at Gettysburg,* 178. The 20-pounder Parrott was the largest field rifle regularly used, but after Gettysburg it lost popularity with both Federal and Confederate gunners (Weller, 34).

Maximum effective field artillery ranges were about 1,500 yards for smoothbores and 2,500 yards for rifles.

Rate of fire for the fieldpieces was between two and three rounds a minute, depending on the proficiency of the crew.

Artillery SUPPORTS were the infantry troops detailed for close-in security of the pieces. With the advent of rifled small arms on the Civil War battlefield, artillery was frequently outranged by enemy riflemen and, needless to say, very vulnerable.

Siege artillery included 8- and 10-inch

howitzers, which were smoothbore muzzle-loaders with ranges of over 2,000 yards. They fired 45- and 90-pound shells. There were 8- and 10-inch siege mortars. These heavy guns lacked the mobility to keep up with a field army, but they did play a role in the battles of Malvern Hill, Shiloh, Fredericksburg, and the affair at Belmont.

Seacoast artillery of the heavy ordnance class included: the 32- and 42-pounder seacoast guns; the 8- and 10-inch seacoast howitzers (on barbette carriages); the 8-, 10-, and 12-inch Columbiads; and the 13-inch seacoast mortar (like the DICTATOR). Heavy ordnance included cannon of the Armstrong, Blakely, Parrott, Rodman, Dahlgren, and Whitworth type.

See also: CANNON, famous names; DOUBLE SHOTTING; EPROUVETTE; HOT SHOT; SPIKING AND UNSPIKING CANNON.

When the war started, the Union had on hand 4,167 pieces of artillery, of which only 163 were field guns and howitzers (K. P. Williams, I, 64). When the Confederates took over Federal arsenals they acquired a considerable number of heavy guns but only 35 fieldpieces (Wise, 37). Some militia companies, such as the Richmond Howitzers and the Washington Artillery of New Orleans, had their own fieldpieces, as did some of the states; but many of these were pre-1812 models. Furthermore, the South had practically no facilities for manufacturing and lacked the skilled labor. "The only foundry at which a cannon had ever been cast was the Richmond Tredegar Works, and copper, so necessary for field artillery purposes, was just being obtained in East Tennessee," writes Wise.

Supply of artillery in the North was never an acute problem. "There were only 7,892 cannon issued to the army during the period of over five years, from 1861 to 1866, whereas during the same period over 4,000,000 small arms were issued." (Shannon, I, 126.) The Cold Spring Foundry is credited with production of more than 1,700 cannon as well as 3,000,000 projectiles.

The Tredegar Works made most of the field artillery used by the Southern armies, only a few pieces being cast in New Orleans, Nashville, and Rome, Ga. (Wise, 41–2). During the first two years of the war Caleb Huse had purchased only 129 pieces in England, nearly half of these being 6-pounder smoothbores. "Gradually we captured Federal guns to supply most of our needs," writes Alexander, "but we were handicapped by our own ammunition until the close of the war." (Alexander, 54.)

CANTEY, James. C.S.A. gen. 1818–74. S.C. After S.C. College he became a lawyer and fought in the Mexican War (1 wound). He then moved to Alabama to run his plantation and was commissioned Col. 15th Ala. in 1861. In the Valley with Jackson, he fought also in the Seven Days' Battles and was sent to Mobile. He was appointed B.G. C.S.A. 8 Jan. '63 and given a brigade, leading a division for a time. However, in the Atlanta campaign and in Tennessee under Hood he commanded his brigade, fighting through the Carolinas and at Bentonville. He resumed running his plantation after the war.

CAPEHART, Henry. Union officer. Pa. Commissioned Surgeon 1st W. Va. Cav. 6 Sept. '61, he was named Col. 22 Feb. '64 and mustered out in July '65. Breveted B.G. USV and Maj. Gen. USV 17 June '65 for war service, he won the Medal of Honor in 1895 for saving a drowning soldier under fire at Greenbrier River, 22 May '64. He died in 1895.

CAPERS, Ellison. C.S.A. gen. 1837–1908. S.C. The son of a Methodist bishop, he attended S.C. Military Academy and taught mathematics there until commissioned Maj. during the bombardment of Ft. Sumter. Named Lt. Col. 24th S.C., he spent two years on the Carolina coast before being ordered to join Johnston in May '63 for the relief of Vicksburg. He was wounded at Jackson and led his regiment as Col. at Chickamauga. He fought at Franklin and was appointed B.G. C.S.A. 1 Mar. '65, succeeding Gist as brigade commander. He surrendered at Bentonville. After the war he became an Episcopal minister, later serving as Bishop of S.C. and Chancellor of the University of the South (Sewanee) in 1904.

CAPRON, Horace. Union officer. 1804–85. Mass. Lt. Col. 14th Ill. Cav. 3 Dec. '62; Col. 6 Feb. '63; Bvt. B.G. USV (war service). Commanded in the Army of the Ohio: 2, 2, Cav. Corps; 1, Cav., XXIII; 3, Cav., XXIII; Dismounted Brig., Cav. Div., XXIII; Cav. Div., XXIII; 3, Cav. Dist. Ky. XXIII; 5th Div., XXIII. He also commanded 1, 6, Cav. Corps (Mil. Dist. Miss.). He prepared for USMA but failed to receive an appointment. First in cotton manufacturing, he later engaged in progressive and scientific farming in Maryland. Pres. Fillmore appointed him Special Indian Agent over the Tex. tribes. He was an Ill. cattle breeder for a time and in 1867 was Commissioner of Agriculture. The Japanese government engaged him as advisor in the development and settlement of Hokkaido (Island of Yemo). He was well known for his writings on Japan, agriculture, and soil renewal.

CARCASS. A hollow cast-iron projectile filled with burning composition, the flame of which issues through four fuze holes to set fire to combustible objects. (Benton, 371.)

CARD, Benjamin Cozzens. Union officer. R.I. Appt.-Kans. He was commissioned 1st Lt. 12th U.S. Inf. and Capt. and Asst. Q.M. USA in Sept. '61 and served on the Q.M. staff of the Army of the Potomac until 1862, when he went to the Q.M. Gen. office in Washington. Continuing in the R.A., he retired in 1889 as Lt. Col. and Bvt. B.G. USA for war service.

CARLE, James. Union officer. N.Y. 1st Lt. 6th Pa. Res. 30 May '61; Capt. 1 Nov. '61; Col. 191st Pa. 6 June '64; Bvt. B.G. USV (war service). Commanded 3, 3, V.

CARLETON, Charles Ames. Union officer. 1836–97. N.Y. Pvt. 12th N.Y. State Mil. 2 May–2 Aug. '61; 2d Lt. 4th N.H. 18 Sept. '61; 1st Lt. and Adj. 1 Jan. '63; Capt. Asst. Adj. Gen. Vols. 15 July '64; Maj. Asst. Adj. Gen. Vols. 15 Jan. '65; Lt. Col. Asst. Adj. Gen. Assigned 8 July–1 Aug. '65; Bvt. B.G. USV. Brevets for Ft. Fisher, war service. Although he studied law, he never practiced. After the war was connected with a N.Y. publishing house.

CARLETON, James Henry. Union gen. 1814–73. Me. He joined the R.A. in 1839 after the so-called "Aroostook War" in his state. With Kearny on the Rocky Mountain Expedition of 1846, he was on Wool's staff in the Mexican War where he earned a brevet and subsequently served on exploration and Indian fighting expeditions. He transferred to the 1st US Cav. 3 Aug. '61 as a Capt. and was promoted Maj. 6th US Cav. 7 Sept. He became Col. 1st Cal. Inf. 19 Aug. '61 and in the spring of '62 raised the "CALIFORNIA COLUMN," marching them across the Yuma and Gila deserts to Mesilla on the Rio Grande. Promoted B.G. USV 28 Apr. '62, he relieved Canby in the Dept. of N. Mex. and headed it from 18 Sept. '62 until 27 June '65. He was breveted for service in N. Mex. (B.G. USV) and war service (Maj. Gen. USA). He continued in the R.A., dying on active duty. He wrote "The Battle of Buena Vista Etc." in 1848 and articles for military periodicals.

CARLIN, William Passmore. Union gen. 1829–1903. Ill. USMA 1850 (20/44); Inf. He had served on garrison duty, the Utah Expedition, and Indian fighting when named Capt. 6th US Inf. 2 Mar. '61. Named Col. 38th Ill. 15 Aug. '61, he defeated Jefferson Thompson at Fredericktown (Mo.) 21 Oct. and pursued Beauregard from Corinth. He then commanded 2d Brig., 4th Div., Army Miss. (1 June–26 Sept. '62); 31st Brig., 9th Div., Army Ohio, and 31, 9, III, Army Ohio at Perryville. Promoted B.G. USV 29 Nov. '62, he led 2, 1 Right Wing, XIV, Cumberland, at Knob Gap and Stones River (5 Nov. '62–9 Jan. '63) and 2, 1, XX, Cumberland (9 Jan.–15 Feb. '63 and 16 Mar.–10 Oct. '63), at Liberty Gap and Chickamauga. He also commanded, in the Cumberland, 1, 1, XIV at Lookout Mountain, Missionary Ridge, and Ringgold Gap (19 Oct.–5 Dec. '63); at Buzzard Roost, Resaca, and Kenesaw Mountain (5 Jan.–2 July '64) and during the siege of Atlanta (3–17 Aug. '64). He went up to division (17 Aug.–21 Nov. '64) for Jonesboro and later (8 Nov. '64–28 Mar. '65); and led the 2d Inf. Div., W. Va., in May '65. Breveted for Chattanooga, Jonesboro, Bentonville (B.G. USA) and war service (Maj. Gen. USA and Maj. Gen. USV 19 Mar. '65), he continued in the R.A. until retired in 1893 as B.G. USA.

CARLISLE, PA., 1 July '63. (Stuart's Gettysburg raid) Stuart reached this place late in the afternoon of 1 July looking for Ewell's corps. His troops were too exhausted for an immediate attack and, on learning that the place was held only by militia troops, he had Fitz Lee send in a white flag demanding surrender of the place or evacuation of women and children. W. F. ("Baldy") Smith, who was in command, sent back word that he had evacuated the noncombatants and was ready to fight. Stuart took up a desultory shelling of the town with one battery, during the course of which he received a message informing him of Lee's location. After ordering the burning of the cavalry barracks at Carlisle Barracks, Stuart moved toward Gettysburg.

CARMAN, Ezra Ayers. Union officer. N.J. Lt. Col. 7th N.Y. 19 Sept. '61; Col. 13th N.J. 8 July '62; Bvt. B.G. USV (war service). Commanded 3, 1, XII; 2, 1, XX.

CARNAHAN, Robert Huston. Union officer. Pa. Capt. 3d Ill. Cav. 24 Aug. '61; Lt. Col. 20 Sept. '64; Col. 9 Apr. '65; Bvt. B.G. USV 28 Oct. '65 (war service).

CARNEGIE, Andrew. 1835–1919. Scotland. The steel magnate and public benefactor who, as a young man, served with the Union War Department in the transportation division during the Civil War.

CARNIFEX FERRY, W. Va., 10 Sept. '61. (WEST VIRGINIA OPERATIONS IN 1861) At about 3 P.M. Benham's brigade attacked a well-organized position of J. B. Floyd. Rosecrans' forces made several unsuccessful assaults in the heavily wooded area. After dark the Confederates withdrew toward Dogwood Gap. Although Rosecrans had 7,000 troops at Sutton, only five regiments were engaged. He lost about 150. Floyd reported 20 wounded out of the 5,800 engaged. He himself was slightly wounded.

CAROLINAS CAMPAIGN (including Schofield's operations from New Bern and Fort Fisher to Goldsboro). 1865. After Sherman's March to the Sea, Grant planned to have the combined armies of Sherman, Meade, and

Butler converge to destroy Lee's Army of Northern Va. To ease Sherman's logistical problem, and to give him an alternate base in case he should encounter serious enemy resistance in his advance through the Carolinas, Grant ordered the capture of Fort Fisher and Wilmington. Federal forces would then advance from Wilmington and New Bern to Goldsboro, giving Sherman access to a shorter line of communications when he reached the latter place.

In Jan. '65 Grover's 2d Div., XIX Corps, reached Savannah from the Valley to relieve the division of the XX Corps that had been occupying the city. This made Sherman's entire command available for the advance north. Although he had intended to start his operation the middle of Jan., he was delayed until 1 Feb. by bad weather.

Along the N.C. coast, meanwhile, the subsidiary operations were under way.

FORT FISHER was captured by Terry (15 Jan. '65) after Butler's failure in Dec. '64. The latter part of Jan. troops of Schofield's XXIII Corps started arriving from the West. He was given command of the re-created Dept. of N.C. and assigned the mission of capturing Wilmington and Goldsboro. Schofield captured Fort Anderson, 19 Jan., and forced Hoke to abandon Wilmington, 22 Feb. Garrison troops in the area, Terry's Provisional Corps, the two divisions of the XXIII Corps, a division of green troops under Ruger, and a collection of convalescents (Meagher's Provisional Division) were reorganized into a field force of 30,000 for Schofield's operations.

Since New Bern would for several reasons make a better supply base for Sherman than Wilmington (better harbor, closer to northern supply points, repairable railroad), Schofield now

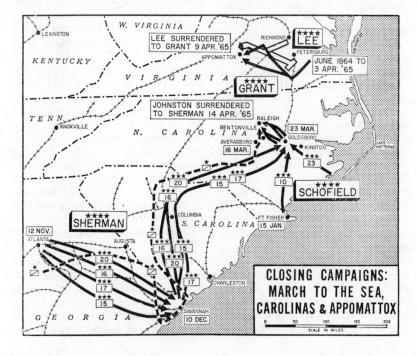

shifted his main effort to that area. Cox was sent to New Bern 26 Feb. with the mission of opening up this line of communications. (New Bern had been in Federal hands since Burnside's N.C. Expedition of 1862.) Reorganizing the various troops sent to the area for the operation, Cox formed the divisions of I. N. Palmer and S. P. Carter. Ruger's new division was also assigned to his command. (These three divisions later constituted "Cox's Provisional Corps," 1–21 Mar.) Cox bivouacked 10 miles from New Bern to cover the construction of the railroad to his rear. This new threat caused Bragg to order Hoke's division from the railroad between Wilmington and Goldsboro to Kinston, and to reinforce him later with elements of the Army of Tenn. (see below). After a series of actions at Kinston, 7–10 Mar., in which Hoke was unable to defeat Cox, the Confederates withdrew in the face of rapidly mounting Federal strength. Schofield was now in a position to push on to a linkup with Sherman at Goldsboro.

Sherman, meanwhile, had started his advance from Savannah. In concentrating his forces (for composition, see MARCH TO THE SEA) he moved in such a manner as to feint toward Charleston and Augusta. Howard's two corps (XV and XVII) went by water to the head of Port Royal Sound. As for Slocum's army, the XX Corps crossed the Savannah near the railroad bridge, while the XIV Corps moved 30 miles up the river and crossed there. Exceptionally heavy rains delayed farther advance until 1 Feb., on which date Sherman moved out with 60,000 troops, 2,500 wagons, and 600 ambulances.

The following Confederate forces were available to oppose him. Hardee with the divisions of McLaws and A. R. Wright (8,000 total) near the head of Port Royal Sound; Taliaferro's division

of S.C. Mil. (3,000) at Charleston; and M. C. Butler's cavalry division (1,500) from the Army of Northern Va.

At Augusta were located G. W. Smith's Ga. Mil. (1,500) and Wheeler's cavalry (6,700) with D. H. Hill in overall command. Stevenson's corps (4,000) of the Army of Tenn. reached Augusta 30–31 Jan. from Tupelo, Miss. When Beauregard arrived on 3 Feb. to confer with Hardee, D. H. Hill, and G. W. Smith he found he had 22,500 troops with which to oppose Sherman. Before the Confederates could dispose their forces to block him Sherman had reached the Augusta–Charleston R.R. (7 Feb.) between Bamberg and Windsor. This forced Hardee to withdraw across the Edisto to points northwest of Charleston and for Stevenson to withdraw to Orangeburg. Howard then moved through Orangeburg on Columbia, and Slocum from Windsor to Lexington. Kilpatrick continued to operate on the flank of Slocum's left wing. This advance resulted in a strategic penetration of the Confederates.

At this time Beauregard was put in command of all Confederate forces in S.C., and Wade Hampton was made a Lt. Gen. and given command of all the cavalry in the state. Beauregard immediately ordered Hardee to evacuate Charleston and to move all his forces to Cheraw, S.C. He also directed D. H. Hill to send the corps of Stewart and Cheatham from Augusta to Chester.

Sherman remained near Columbia a few days destroying the railroads and then started for Cheraw. (See COLUMBIA, S.C., BURNED, 17 Feb.) Heavy rains delayed his arrival at Cheraw until 3 Mar.

Lee had been given over-all command of the Confederate armies in Jan. At Lee's request J. E. Johnston was brought back from retirement to command operations in S.C.; Beauregard became second-in-command. At this time Sherman's forces were crossing the Wateree River and heading for Cheraw. Schofield's forces had taken Wilmington. D. H. Hill was in command of the Army of Tenn. (pending Stewart's arrival) while this army assembled at Chester. Hardee was hurrying his forces toward Cheraw. Bragg had withdrawn Hoke's division to a point between Wilmington and Goldsboro. In view of Sherman's advance on Cheraw, it became apparent to the Confederates that they would have to attempt a concentration of forces at Fayetteville, N.C. Johnston therefore directed that the Army of Tenn. troops be moved by rail from Chester north through Greensboro and Raleigh to Smithfield (northeast of Fayetteville). This movement was delayed not only by the fact that the troops had not yet reached Chester, but also because the railroad was already severely strained supplying the Army of Northern Va.

Although Sherman had encountered no significant enemy resistance his advance had been slowed by heavy rains. Consequently he did not reach Cheraw until 3 Mar. Hardee, who had just gotten his troops to that place, was forced to drop back to Fayetteville. Sherman left Cheraw 6 Mar. and reached Fayetteville on the 12th.

Schofield, meanwhile, had started advancing on Kinston from New Bern. This caused Bragg to move Hoke's division to Kinston from the railroad between Wilmington and Goldsboro. By this time Johnston had established headquarters at Raleigh and he took command of Bragg's forces also. When the first corps of the Army of Tenn. reached Smithfield, 7 Mar., Cox's leading division had gotten almost to Kinston. At Bragg's request, Johnston agreed to send troops of the Army of Tenn. on to Kinston as they arrived at Smithfield.

This led to the action of Kinston, 7–10 Mar., which resulted in Confederate withdrawal in the face of rapidly mounting Federal strength after Bragg had failed to defeat Cox in detail.

Johnston's plans had been disrupted by the delay in getting the Army of Tenn. from Chester to Smithfield, and also by the failure at Kinston. Hardee retreated from Fayetteville to Smithfield; Bragg dropped back to Goldsboro, reaching there the 16th. Johnston's "estimate of the situation" was that Sherman would move from Fayetteville against Raleigh or Goldsboro. Capture of Raleigh would virtually sever the main line of supply to Lee's Army of Northern Va. Sherman's advance on Goldsboro, on the other hand, would accomplish the link up of his forces with those of Schofield. On the 15th, therefore, Lee suggested to Johnston that he attack one of Sherman's columns before the two could unite.

Sherman started his advance from Fayetteville the morning of the 15th in three columns. Slocum moved on the left (north) with five divisions toward Smithfield and then east toward Bentonville. His other division moved with the trains of his two corps. Of Howard's right wing, the XVII Corps moved on Sherman's extreme right (south) and the XV Corps marched by a middle route.

After an engagement between the XX Corps and Hardee's troops near Averasboro, 16 Mar., Hardee retreated during the night toward Smithfield. On the 17th the XIV Corps led Slocum's advance toward Bentonville.

Johnston started preparations for a counterblow. At Smithfield he could muster 21,000 effectives: Bragg's 6,500; the Army of Tenn.'s 4,000; Hardee's 7,500; and Hampton's 3,000 cavalry. In the largest engagement of the campaign, Bentonville, 19 Mar., Slocum's forces fought off Johnston's attacks while Sherman rushed the rest of his troops to the scene. Johnston fell back a short distance and dug in. On the 21st Sherman's entire force was in position to attack Johnston, and the latter withdrew toward Smithfield.

On the 22d Sherman marched toward Goldsboro, arriving the next day. Cox's corps reached there the same day. Terry's command had left Wilmington the 15th, had joined Sherman west of Goldsboro on the 22d, and had accompanied him to Goldsboro. Sherman had now massed his entire force of 80,000. He went to Petersburg to confer with Grant, and returned to begin his movement on Raleigh the day Lee surrendered.

While Johnston's army was at Smithfield he was joined by S. D. Lee. Johnston reorganized all his troops as the Army of Tenn., consisting of the corps of Hardee, A. P. Stewart, and S. D. Lee. By 13 Apr., however, he realized that the situation was hopeless and the next day requested an armistice. Without renewal of hostilities, he surrendered on 26 Apr. '65.

Some historians consider that Sherman was the greatest Federal general to emerge from the Civil War. This reputation is based primarily on his Savannah and Carolinas campaigns.

From Savannah to Goldsboro the Grand Army of the West had marched 425 miles in fifty days, of which ten were allocated to rest. Though but little interfered with by the enemy's forces and attended by but little loss (at Averasboro, 554; at Bentonville, 1,646), yet the march through the Carolinas had been one continuous battle with the elements, and must be reckoned a much greater achievement than the more famous march through Georgia, which by camparison was a mere pleasure trip. As a triumph of physical endurance and mechanical skill on the part of the army and of inflexible resolution in the general, it stands unrivalled in the history of modern war; and it has as direct an influence upon the final issue of the campaign round Richmond as if it had been conducted within sound of Lee's guns. (Wood and Edmonds, *The Civil War in the United States,* 465–66.)

CARONDELET. Union boat that ran the batteries at Island No. 10 in Apr. '62 to protect troops crossing below there and forced the evacuation of the Confederates. A Mississippi River steamer, she was equipped with a sloping iron casemate and 13 guns. She also fought at Fts. Henry and Donelson.

CARPETBAGGERS. Northerners who swarmed to the South during the Reconstruction era and came into control of many Southern state and municipal governments strictly for financial gain. So called because they packed their belongings in the then-popular luggage called "carpetbags." (See SCALAWAGS.)

CARR, Eugene Asa. Union gen. 1820–1910. N.Y. USMA 1850 (19/44); Mtd. Rifles-Cav. He served on the frontier in Indian fighting where he was severely wounded. A Capt. in the 1st US Cav. (1858), he transferred to the 4th US Cav. 3 Aug. '61, fought with his regiment at Wilson's Creek 10 Aug., and was named Col. 3d Ill. Cav. 16 Aug. '61. In the Dept. of the Mo., he commanded 3d Brig., Army Southwest Mo. 12 Oct.–28 Dec. '61 and the 4th Div., Army Southwest Mo. at Pea Ridge where he was wounded three times but, refusing to leave the field, was bandaged on his horse. He won the Medal of Honor and a promotion (B.G. USV) for this. He also led 2d Div., Dist. East Ark.; Army Southwest Mo., Dist. East Ark. (7 Oct.–13 Nov. '62); Dist. St. Louis (13 Nov. '62–23 Feb. '63); and 2d Div. Army

Southeast Mo. (Feb.–Mar. '63). At Port Gibson, Champion's Hill, Big Black River, and during the siege and assault of Vicksburg, he commanded 14th Div., XIII, Tenn. (28 Mar.–28 July '63). He also commanded 2d Div. Ark. Expedition (30 Nov. '63–6 Jan. '64) and left wing, XVI, Tenn. (3 Sept.–15 Oct. '63) as well as 2d Div., VII, Ark. (6 Jan.–13 Feb. '64). In the VII Corps, Dept. of Ark., he also led the 1st Cav. Div. (13 Feb.–11 May '64) at the crossing of the Little Missouri and Poison Spring and commanded the Dist. of Little Rock during the fighting at Clarendon (20 June '64) and Camden (21 Jan.–4 Feb. '65). He commanded the 3d Div., XVI, Gulf, 14 Mar.–20 July '65 during the battle of Mobile and Spanish Fort. He was breveted for Wilson's Creek, Black River Bridge, Little Rock (B.G. USA), and war service (Maj. Gen. USV 11 Mar. '65 and Maj. Gen. USA). Continuing in the R.A., he fought in the 5th and 6th US Cav. from '68 till '91, with such success against the Cheyennes, Sioux, and Apaches that he is chiefly remembered today as one of the great Indian fighters. His Indian opponents called him "War Eagle."

CARR, Joseph Bradford. Union gen. 1828–95. N.Y. In the tobacco business in N.Y.C., he was a Col. in the N.Y. State Militia and commissioned Col. 2d N.Y. 14 May '61. His description of green troops training at Ft. Monroe and Big Bethel appears in B.&L., II, 144–52. Leading his regiment in the Peninsula and at 2d Bull Run, he commanded 3, 2, III, 1–6 June '62 and was promoted B.G. USV 7 Sept. '62. He commanded 1, 2, III, 16 Sept. '62–12 Jan. '63; 8 Feb.–3 May '63, and 23 May–5 Oct. '63 when they bore the brunt of the second day's fighting at Gettysburg. His appointment expired 4 Mar. '63, but he was reappointed on the 30th. Still in the III Corps, he led the 2d Div.

12 Jan.–8 Feb. '63 and, succeeding Barry at Chancellorsville, 3–23 May '63 and 9–10 July '63. He also commanded the 3d Div., III Corps, 5 Oct. '63–24 Mar. '64. From 25 Mar. to 2 May '64 he led the 4th Div., II Corps, taking over the 3d Div., XVIII, Va. and N.C. 29 July and the 1st Div., XVIII on 3 Aug. until 3 Sept. '64. He was breveted Maj. Gen. USV for war service and mustered out 24 Aug. '65. A Maj. Gen. in the N.Y. State Militia after the war, he was in manufacturing and Republican politics.

CARRICK'S FORD (Cheat River), W. Va., 13 July '61. (WEST VIRGINIA OPERATIONS IN 1861) When Garnett at Laurel Hill learned the night of the 11th that Pegram had been defeated at RICH MOUNTAIN, he retreated the next morning to Kaler's Ford on the Cheat River. Garnett's movement was slowed by rain and by his desire to save his trains. After a delaying action at Carrick's Ford, Garnett was killed at another ford, a short distance away, while commanding a small rear guard of 10 men. His troops continued their retreat to Monterey. The Federals reported a loss of 53, and estimated the enemy's loss at 20 killed, 10 wounded, and 50 prisoners. About 40 wagons and "a fine piece of rifled artillery" were reported captured.

CARRINGTON, Henry Beebe. Union gen. 1824–1912. Conn. Appt.-Ohio. R.A. As a young man he heard John Brown and became an abolitionist. He went to Yale, taught, and was practicing law in Ohio when he assisted in organizing the Republican party there. A friend of Gov. Chase, he organized the state militia in 1857, a task done so well that Ohio could send nine militia companies across the river to keep W. Va. in the Union before the volunteers could be organized. He was named Col. 18th US Inf. 14 May '61 and in charge of an R.A. camp in Ohio, when Gov. Morton of

Indiana requested he set up levies there for service. He was promoted B.G. USV 29 Nov. '62 and was active in exposing and trying the SONS OF LIBERTY and other disloyal groups. His conduct of the military court was criticized and later overruled by the Supreme Court, but at the time he was upheld by Lincoln and by popular sentiment. He was mustered out of USV 24 Aug. '65 and rejoined his regiment in the Army of the Cumberland, becoming head of the commission that tried the Louisville guerrillas in 1865. He was then sent to the west where he built Ft. Phil Kearny, fought in the Red Cloud War, and was severely wounded. He later established friendly relations with the important Indian chiefs and taught military science at Wabash College before retiring in 1870. Encouraged by Washington Irving toward a literary career in his youth, he later wrote *The Battles of the American Revolution* (1876) as well as many other books on international, military, and Indian affairs.

CARROLL, Samuel Sprigg. Union gen. 1832–93. D.C. USMA 1856 (44/49); Inf. A descendant of Charles Carroll of Carrollton, he was on the frontier. Q.M. of West Point, and promoted 1st Lt. 10th US Inf. 25 Apr. and Capt. 1 Nov. '61. He was named Col. 18th Ohio 7 Dec. '61 and joined his regiment at Romney. During the Valley campaign he commanded 4th Brig., Shields's division (10 May–26 June '62) at Kernstown and Pt. Republic and 4, 2, III, Army of Va. (26 June–24 Aug. '62) at Cedar Mountain and a skirmish on the Rapidan where W.I.A. He then led 2d Brig., Whipple's division Mil. Dist. Washington and 2, 3, III (8 Nov. '62– 12 Jan. '63) at Fredericksburg. At the Wilderness and Spotsylvania, where he was twice wounded, he commanded 3, 2, II (25 Mar.–13 May '64). Promoted B.G. USV 12 May '64, he also com-

manded 1, 3, II, Apr.–July '63 and 7 Sept. '63–24 Mar. '64 at Chancellorsville, Gettysburg, Bristoe Station, and Mine Run. He then commanded the 4th Prov. Div., W. Va., 2 Apr.–8 May '65 and the Dept. of W. Va. 27 Feb.– 7 Mar. '65. He was breveted for Chancellorsville, Gettysburg, the Wilderness, Spotsylvania (B.G. USA), and war service (Maj. Gen. USA and USV). Continuing in the R.A., he retired in 1869 as Maj. Gen.

CARROLL, William H. C.S.A. gen. 1820–? Appt.–Tenn. When his state seceded, he was a militia B.G. and organized the Tenn. troops. Appointed B.G. C.S.A. 26 Oct. '61, he was stationed at Memphis under Johnston and then sent to eastern Tenn. In command of the post of Knoxville, he fought at Mill Spring. He resigned 1 Feb. '63.

CARRUTH, Sumner. Union officer. Mass. Capt. 1st Mass. 23 May '61; Maj. 35th Mass. 21 Aug. '62; Lt. Col. 21 Sept. '62; Col. 1 May '63; Bvt. B.G. USV 2 Apr. '65 (Petersburg). Commanded 2, 2, IX (Ohio and Potomac); 1, 1, IX; 1, 2, IX. W.I.A. Fair Oaks in arm and Antietam in neck. Captured at White Sulphur Springs 14 Nov. '62. Died 1892.

CARRUTHERS, Robert Looney. C.S.A. Gov. of Tenn. 1800–82. Tenn. A lawyer, he held various minor public offices before becoming legislator, Congressman, and associate justice of the state Supreme Court. In 1861 he was a member of the provisional C.S.A. Congress and in 1863 was elected Governor, succeeding Harris. Never inaugurated, he was named B.G. in the state militia in 1864 as well as serving as Governor, and after the war he was active in law and in education.

CARSON, Christopher ("Kit"). Union officer and famed Indian fighter. 1809–68. Ky. Appt.–Mo. Lt. Col. 1st N. Mex. Cav. 25 July '61; Col. 20 Sept.

'61; Bvt. B.G. USV (Valverde, N. Mex.). Best known as guide, Indian agent, and frontiersman in the West. He served with Frémont and Kearny during the Mexican War. See also INDIAN TROUBLES.

CARTER, John Carpenter. C.S.A. gen. 1837–64. Ga. Appt.-Tenn. Commissioned Capt. 38th Tenn. in 1861, he fought at Shiloh before being promoted Maj., Lt. Col., and Col. in rapid succession. He commanded the regiment at Perryville, Stones River, and Chickamauga and Chattanooga, and led Wright's brigade of Cheatham's division in the Atlanta campaign. Appointed B.G. C.S.A. 7 July '64, he was given temporary command 1 Sept. '64 of Cheatham's division at Jonesboro. He was mortally wounded 30 Nov. '64 leading a brigade in the battle of Franklin, Tenn.

CARTER, Samuel Powhatan. Union gen. 1819–91. Tenn. After Princeton he became a midshipman, serving in the Pacific and on the Great Lakes and graduating from USNA in 1846. In the Mexican War he was also at the naval observatory, in the Mediterranean, a USNA mathematics instructor, and with the East Indian Squadron. When the war began, he was detached from the navy to organize and drill Tenn. volunteers for the Union. Named a Lt. Comdr. 16 July '62 and a B.G. USV 1 May '62, he led the first important Union cavalry raid at Holston, Carter's Station, and Jonesville, relieving Rosecrans at Murfreesboro. His other commands were 12th Brig., Army Ohio; 12th Brig., 1st Div., Army Ohio; 24th Brig., 7th Div., Army Ohio (26 Mar.–10 Oct. '62); 1st Brig., Dist. Central Ky., Ohio (18 Mar.–24 June '63); 1, 1, XXIII, Ohio (24 June–10 July '63 and 15 July–6 Aug. '63); 1st Div., XXIII, Ohio (10–15 July '63); 4th Div., XXIII, Ohio (6 Aug.–10 Sept. '63); 2d Div., Dist. Beaufort, N.C. (1–18 Mar. '65); Div. Dist. Beaufort, N.C. (18 Mar.–2 Apr. '65); 3d Div., XXIII, N.C. (7 Apr.–27 June '65); XXIII Corps, N.C. (27 June–1 Aug. '65). He was breveted Maj. Gen. USV for war service, mustered out of USV and continued in the navy, retiring as Commodore in 1881. He was named Rear Admiral on the Retired List of 1882 and is the only American officer to have been both a Rear Admiral and a Maj. Gen. (D.A.B.). He was described as being ". . . tall, handsome and dignified, graceful in carriage, and very affable . . . [a] soldierly Christian of sincere piety and undoubted courage." (D.A.B.)

CARTER'S RAID INTO E. TENN. Dec. '62. The day Rosecrans advanced from Nashville (26 Dec.) in the movement that brought on the battle of Stones River, S. P. Carter's small Federal cavalry brigade (7th Ohio and 9th Pa. Cav.) left Manchester, Ky., crossed the mountains east of Cumberland Gap, and entered the upper Tennessee Valley. Southeast of Blountsville, at Wautauga Bridge and Carter's Station, he destroyed two important railroad bridges, inflicting 295 casualties with a loss of only three Federals. He returned safely to Manchester. "Though unimportant in its results, it was the first successful Union cavalry operation in the West" (Fiebeger, 137).

CASCABLE. Sometimes considered to be merely the *knob* on the end of the breech of a cannon (C.O.M.), but more properly the entire portion of the gun in rear of the base of the breach, composed generally of the knob, the neck, and the fillet (Benton).

CASE, Henry. Union officer. Conn. 1st Lt. 14th Ill. 25 May '61; Capt. 25 Nov. '61; Maj. 7th Ill. Cav. 1 Feb. '62; resigned 24 Apr. '62; Capt. 129th Ill. 9 Aug. '62; Lt. Col. 8 Sept. '62; Col. 15 May '63; Bvt. B.G. USV (Ga. and

Carolinas campaigns; Smith's Farm, N.C.). Commanded 1, 3, XX. Died 1884.

CASEMENT, John Stephen. Union officer. N.Y. Maj. 7th Ohio 25 Apr. '61; resigned 25 May '62; Col. 103d Ohio 8 Sept. '62; Bvt. B.G. USV 25 Jan. '65. Commanded 2, 3, XXIII (Ohio; Potomac).

CASE SHOT. The three principal kinds of case shot were GRAPE, CANISTER, and SHRAPNEL (or spherical case shot), according to Benton's West Point textbook of the period. "Case shot" is sometimes used synonymously with "canister," however, and may even refer to "shrapnel." Roberts, the other standard reference, uses the terms "case shot" and "shrapnel" synonymously. The reader must therefore be on guard and interpret the meaning of "case shot" in terms of context and the accuracy of his source.

CASEY, Silas. Union gen. 1807–82. R.I. USMA 1826 (39/41); Inf. He was best known as author of the two-volume *System of Infantry Tactics* (1861), which was adopted by the US Army in 1862 and also widely used by the Confederates (who generally favored *Hardee's Tactics,* however). In 1863 he published *Infantry Tactics for Colored Troops.* A veteran of Indian fighting and of the Mexican War (2 brevets, 1 wound), he was made B.G. USV 31 Aug. '61. After a period of training troops in the Washington area he took part in the Peninsular campaign as commander of the 3d (later the 2d) Div., IV Corps (13 Mar.–24 June '62). He was severely engaged at Fair Oaks, 31 May '62, and his promotion to Maj. Gen. USV was dated from that action. He returned to the Washington area to train troops, commanding the Provisional Brigade and, later, the Dist. of Washington, XXII Corps. From May

'63 until July '65 he was president of the board for the examination of candidates for officers of colored troops. His son, Silas, was born in 1841 and graduated from the USNA in 1860. He took part in the first attack on Fort Sumter and in the naval actions in Charleston Harbor.

CASSIDY, Ambrose Spencer. Union officer. N.Y. 1st Lt. Regt. Q.M. 84th N.Y. 23 May '61; Maj. 93d N.Y. 16 Jan. '62; Bvt. B.G. USV (war service); mustered out 19 Nov. '63. Died 1889.

CASSVILLE, Ga., 19–22 May '64. (ATLANTA CAMPAIGN) Skirmishes during Confederate retreat to Atlanta. See ATLANTA CAMPAIGN for account of how Hood's error spoiled Johnston's opportunity for a counterblow.

CASTLE PINCKNEY. Confederate PRISON at Charleston. Originally a fort, it usually held soldiers, although some officers, among them Michael CORCORAN, were held there.

CASTLE THUNDER. Name of Confederate prisons in Richmond and Petersburg. Although both were converted tobacco warehouses, the one in the capital was used for political prisoners, much in the same manner as the Federals used the OLD CAPITOL PRISON in Washington. Occasionally holding spies and criminals charged with treason, it had an unsavory reputation, and its officers were charged with unnecessary brutality and cruelty. When Richmond fell, the Federals used it to hold Confederates charged with war crimes. The Petersburg Castle Thunder was for Union prisoners of war and was named by them for the sound of artillery fire during the long siege.

CAST METAL HOMOGENEOUS. See BUILT-UP GUN.

CASUALTY, definition of. Loss in numerical strength as a result of death wounds, capture, desertion, sickness, or discharge. In modern practice a distinction is made between battle and non-battle casualties; however, in Civil War literature the word "casualty" is not used within this precise definition. Casualty figures may be given within the restricted sense of "battle casualties," or they may include stragglers, sick and administrative losses (discharged personnel). In this book "casualty" will be used in the former sense, unless otherwise specified. The abbreviations K.I.A. (killed in action), D.O.W. (died of wounds), M.I.A. (missing in action), P.O.W. (prisoner of war), as used here, are post-Civil War administrative abbreviations; they are used for brevity.

CATLETT'S STATION, Va., 22–23 Aug. '62. Pope's headquarters captured. See STUART'S CATLETT'S STATION RAID.

CATLETT'S STATION (Auburn), Va., 14 Oct. '63. Skirmish of BRISTOE CAMPAIGN, in which Owen's Brig. (3, 3, II) and the 12th N.J. of Smyth's (2, 3, II) brigade repulsed an attack by part of Stuart's cavalry. Federal loss was 24, and they claimed 28 prisoners. Col. Ruffin, 1st N.C. Cav., was mortally wounded.

CATLIN, Isaac S. Union officer. N.Y. During the Civil War he served as Col. 109th N.Y. and was breveted for the Wilderness, Petersburg, and war service (B.G. USV and Maj. Gen. USV). Continuing in the R.A., he retired in 1870 as Col.

CATTERSON, Robert Francis. Union gen. Ind. Enlisting as 1st Sgt. 14th Ind. 7 June '61, he was named 2d Lt. 5 July '61, 1st Lt. 15 Mar. '62, Capt. 4 May '62, Lt. Col. 97th Ind. 18 Oct. '62, and Col. 25 Nov. '62. He commanded 2, 1, XV, Tenn. (22 Nov. '64–28 Mar. '65 and 4 Apr.–26 July '65), having been promoted B.G. USV 31 May '65. He was mustered out in 1866.

CAVALRY BATTLES were rare during the Civil War. See BRANDY STATION, Va., 9 June '63, and EDGED WEAPONS.

CAVENDER, John Smith. Union officer. N.H. Capt. 1st Mo. Arty. 23 Apr. '61; Maj. 21 Nov. '61; resigned 26 Aug. '62; Col. 29th Mo. 18 Oct. '62; Bvt. B.G. USV (Ft. Donelson, Shiloh); resigned 19 Feb. '63. Died 1886.

CEDAR CREEK, Va., 19 Oct. '64. (SHENANDOAH VALLEY CAMPAIGN OF SHERIDAN) On 6 Oct. Sheridan began to withdraw down the Valley in accordance with the new Federal strategy, and on the 16th he had left his army for a conference in Washington. Early followed the retiring Federals and on 13 Oct. was at Fishers Hill. Although outnumbered two to one, he still had confidence in his ability to beat Sheridan.

From the Confederate signal station at Three Top Mountain the entire Federal line along Cedar Creek could be seen with a strong glass. On 17 Oct. Gordon and Jed Hotchkiss carefully examined the ground and formed a plan of attack which Early later approved. Gordon proposed to construct a foot-bridge across the Shenandoah at Fishers Hill and cross three divisions. These would make a night march south of the river and recross at Bowman's Ford. Wharton's division was to move along the Valley Pike and Kershaw's about a mile to his right. By this excellent plan Early could bring overwhelming combat superiority against a flank the Federals believed to be unassailable. Furthermore, Wright believed a report of Crook's that on the 18th the Confederates had retired up the Valley for lack of food and forage.

Early's move was made skillfully the night of the 18th, and long before daylight the three divisions of his corps (Ramseur, Pegram, and Gordon) were in position south of the river ready to attack Crook's rear at dawn. With them

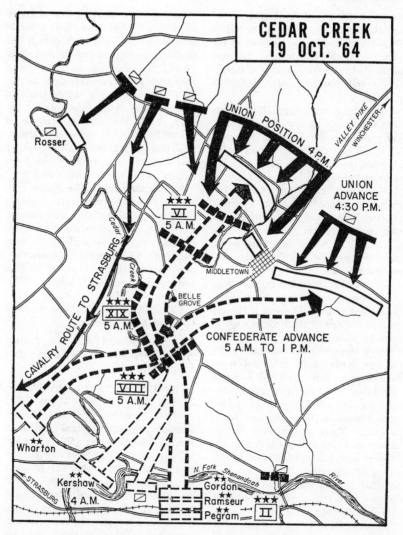

CEDAR CREEK
19 OCT. '64

Rosser

UNION POSITION 4 P.M.

VALLEY PIKE

WINCHESTER

UNION ADVANCE 4:30 P.M.

VI 5 A.M.

CEDAR CREEK

CAVALRY ROUTE TO STRASBURG

MIDDLETOWN

BELLE GROVE

XIX 5 A.M.

CONFEDERATE ADVANCE 5 A.M. TO 1 P.M.

VIII 5 A.M.

Wharton

STRASBURG

Kershaw 4 A.M.

N. Fork Shenandoah   River

Gordon

Ramseur

Pegram

II

was a small cavalry force with the mission of capturing Sheridan. Kershaw and Wharton were also in position to support the attack.

Crook's corps was surprised and driven in confusion to the rear. Wright failed in his attempt to form the VI and XIX Corps for a stand along the Pike. The VI Corps made a short stand and then withdrew to a position in the fields west of Middletown, while the XIX Corps was pushed back in disorder and rallied behind them. Then, although attacked in front and flank, the VI Corps held its second position for about an hour (8–9 A.M.) before withdrawing again. Getty's division (2, VI) became separated from the rest of the corps and fell back to a ridge a mile north of Middletown and just west of the Valley Pike. On the same ridge and east of the Pike the cavalry had formed. The rest of the Federal units withdrew to a position a mile farther north of Getty's position.

Although Gordon urged him to exploit his success by a continued attack, Early believed the Federals, who had lost 1,300 prisoners and 18 guns, would abandon the battlefield. After 10 A.M., as he waited for the Federals to retreat, Early learned that his troops had broken formation to loot the enemy's camps. He later gave this as one of the reasons why he had lost the victory by failing to continue his attack late in the morning. Consequently, Getty's position was not threatened.

Sheridan had spent the night at Winchester on his return from Washington. He arrived on the field about 10:30 and ordered the rest of the Federal units to form on the ridge to the west of Getty. Crook's corps was left in reserve. By the time Early finally ordered Gordon to make a probing attack the Federals' "third line" was able to repulse it without difficulty. Early's attitude turned from triumph to perplexity and finally to alarm. There was another lull of about two hours during which time the Federal line was strengthened by the return of stragglers. During this time Sheridan learned that the Confederates had not been reinforced by Longstreet, as a fake message had said.

Shortly before 4 P.M. Sheridan counterattacked and drove Early back with heavy losses to Fishers Hill. From this place the Confederate infantry divisions withdrew early the next day to New Market.

Sheridan's return to the field was dramatized by the poem of T. Buchanan Read, "Sheridan's Ride." ("Up from the South at break of day,/ Bringing to Winchester fresh dismay,/ The affrighted air with a shudder bore,/ Like a herald in haste to the chieftain's door,/ The terrible grumble, and rumble, and roar,/ Telling the battle was on once more,/ And Sheridan twenty [14] miles away," etc.) Although Wright had the situation under control by the time Sheridan got back, it was the inspiring presence of "Little Phil" and his subsequent leadership that turned this Federal disaster into a victory that virtually ended the fighting in the Shenandoah Valley.

Numbers engaged were 30,829 Federals and 18,410 Confederates. Sheridan lost 5,665, of whom 1,591 were missing. Early lost 2,910 (of whom 1,050 were missing), most of his artillery (25 guns captured), all his ambulances, ammunition wagons, and most of his baggage and forage wagons (O'Connor, 231). Ramseur was killed.

This battle is known also as Belle Grove or Middletown.

CEDAR MOUNTAIN, Va., 9 Aug. '62. Engagement of 2d BULL RUN CAMPAIGN.

CENTRALIA (MO.) MASSACRE, 27 Sept. '64. William ("Bloody Bill") Anderson led his Confederate bushwhackers (including Frank and Jesse James) into this place (50 miles north of Jefferson City) and captured a stagecoach. Half an hour later (11:30 A.M.) he captured a train that came in from the east, and murdered 24 unarmed Federal soldiers. His men then robbed the passengers and killed two men who attempted to hide valuables. They set the train on fire and left with $3,000 found in the Express car. About two hours later Maj. A. E. V. Johnson arrived with three companies of the 39th Mo. and was attacked by Anderson. The Federals made a dismounted attack three miles from town. The guerrillas charged and slaughtered the attackers, killing 124 of the 147 (Monaghan; E.&B.).

CENTREVILLE, La. See IRISH BEND AND FORT BISLAND.

CHAFIN'S FARM, Va., 29 Sept. '64. NEW MARKET HEIGHTS, same date.

CHAIN SHOT. Two balls connected by a chain. Designed for use against masts and rigging of ships. Bar shot differed only in that the balls were connected by a bar.

CHALMERS, James Ronald. C.S.A. gen. 1831–98. Va. After S.C. College he became a lawyer and entered politics. He was commissioned Capt. C.S.A. Mar. '61 and Col. 9th Miss. Apr. '61. Appointed B.G. C.S.A. 13 Feb. '62 he fought at Santa Rosa Island and led the 2d Brig., 3d Div., II Corps at Shiloh. He then commanded the 2d Brig., 2d Div. under Polk at Munfordville and Stones River where he was wounded. In Apr. '63 he was put in command of the Dist. of Miss. and eastern Ark. and in 1864 commanded the 1st Cav. Div. He was with Forrest at Ft. Pillow, fought in northern Miss., Tenn., and Ky. and in the Franklin and Nashville campaign. On 18 Feb. '65 he took command of all the cavalry in Miss. and West Tenn. After the war he was a Democratic legislator and was later sent to Congress. In Washington he engaged in three disputes over his right to be seated.

CHAMBERLAIN, Joshua Lawrence. Union gen. 1828–1914. Me. Educated at a Me. military academy, Bowdoin College, and Bangor Theological Seminary, he became a professor at Bowdoin in 1855. Scheduled to study abroad in '62, he went into the army instead, being commissioned Lt. Col. 20th Me. 8 Aug. He fought at Antietam, Fredericksburg, Chancellorsville, Gettysburg, Spotsylvania, and Cold Harbor with his regiment, having been promoted Col. 20

May '63. Given the Medal of Honor (11 Aug. '93) for Little Round Top, he commanded 3, 1, V 26 Aug.–19 Nov. '63 and 10–25 Aug. '65 as well as 1, 1, V 6–18 June '64; 19 Nov. '64–5 Jan. '65; 27 Feb.–11 Apr. '65 (Petersburg where he was W.I.A.). On 18 June '64 he was promoted B.G. USV. He also led 1st Div., V Corps, 25 Apr.–28 June '65. Breveted Maj. Gen. USV 29 Mar. '65, he was mustered out in 1866 and elected Gov. of Me. 1866–71. He was president of Bowdoin until 1883 and then in railroading and industry in Fla. As Maj. Gen. of the Me. State Mil., he kept order during the disputed election of 1878–79. He wrote *The Passing of the Armies* (1915) and others on Me. and the Civil War.

CHAMBERLAIN, Samuel Emery. Union officer. 1829–1908. Mass. Pvt. 1846–49; 1st Lt. 3d Mass. Mil. 23 Apr.–22 July '61; Capt. 1st Mass. Cav. 25 Nov. '61; Maj. 8 Dec. '62; Lt. Col. July '64; mustered out 28 July '65; Col. 5th Mass. Cav. 11 Sept. '65; Bvt. B.G. USV 24 Feb. '65. *My Confession*, the illustrated memoir of his experiences, military and otherwise, in the Mexican War was first published by *Life* magazine in 1956, and the original manuscript given to the West Point Museum. Wounded seven times in Civil War: Poolesville (also captured), Kelly's Ford, Brandy Station, St. Mary's Church, Malvern Hill, Reams's Station, and Boydtown Plank Road.

CHAMBERS, Alexander. Union gen. 1832–88 N.Y. USMA 1853 (43/52); Inf. First on garrison and frontier duty, he fought in the Seminole War and was promoted Capt. 18th US Inf. 14 May '61 and Col. 16th Iowa 15 Mar. '62. He led his regiment at Shiloh where twice wounded, at the siege of Corinth, and at Iuka, where he was severely wounded. He was promoted B.G. USV 11 Aug. '63, but this appointment was revoked 6 Apr. '64; and he returned to the 18th US Inf. He commanded in the Army of the Tenn.: 3, 6, XVII 6 June–30 July '63 (Vicksburg campaign) and 23 Aug.–14 Sept. '63; 6th Div., XVII 30 July–23 Aug. '63 and 3–14 Sept. '63; 3, 1, XVII 10 Oct. '63–20 Apr. '64 (Sherman's raid to Meridian and Canton) and 1st Div., XVII 14–28 Sept. '63. He was breveted for Shiloh, Iuka, Vicksburg, Champion's Hill, and Meridian (B.G. USV). In the R.A. after the war, he died on active duty.

CHAMBERSBURG, Pa., burned, 30 July '64. (EARLY'S WASHINGTON RAID) In reprisal for Hunter's destruction of private property in Va. (Lynchburg campaign) Early sent the cavalry brigades of McCausland and Bradley Johnson to levy an assessment of $100,000 gold or $500,000 in greenbacks on the town of Chambersburg. If the citizens refused to make this payment to indemnify the injured Virginians, Early ordered that McCausland burn the town. About 5:30 A.M. the Confederates arrived and presented their demands. McCausland waited until 9 o'clock, then ordered the town's 3,000 inhabitants evacuated and the place burned. Col. Wm. E. Peters, 21 Va. Cav., refused to comply with the order and was placed (temporarily) under arrest. Other officers and men objected, but the rest started applying the torch. Two thirds of the town was destroyed.

CHAMBLISS, John Randolph, Jr. C.S.A. gen. 1833–64. Va. USMA 1853 (31/52); Arty. Resigning the next year, he became a Virginia planter and served as a militia Maj. and A.D.C. to the Governor 1856–61. He was later Col. and commissioned that same rank in the 13th Va. Cav. in July '61, serving under Stuart. In July '62 he was on duty in southeast Virginia, and the following Oct. served under G. W. Smith along the Rappahannock. In Nov. '62 he was

in W. H. F. Lee's cavalry brigade and commanded his regiment at Fredericksburg. He commanded the 5th Va. Cav. at Chancellorsville and succeeded "Rooney" Lee 9 June '63 as brigade commander. He led these troops at Aldie, Middleburg, Gettysburg, and Bristoe (Oct. '63). Appointed B.G. C.S.A. 19 Dec. '63, he commanded a brigade in the Wilderness campaign and the battles around Petersburg. He was killed 16 Aug. '64 at Deep Bottom.

CHAMPION, Thomas Emmet. Union officer. N.Y. Col. 96th Ill. 6 Sept. '62; Bvt. B.G. USV 20 Feb. '65. Commanded 1, 1, Res. Corps (Cumberland); 2, 1, IV. Died 1873.

CHAMPION'S HILL, Miss. 16 May '63. Battle in VICKSBURG CAMPAIGN.

CHAMPLIN, Stephen Gardner. Union gen. 1827–64. N.Y. A lawyer and politician, he was commissioned Maj. 3d Mich. 10 June '61, fighting at Williamsburg, Fair Oaks (where he was seriously wounded), Groveton, and Antietam. Promoted Col. 22 Oct. and B.G. USV 29 Nov. '62, he was stationed in Grand Rapids (Mich.), his home, dying from his wound 24 Jan. '64.

CHANCELLORSVILLE CAMPAIGN, Apr.–May '63.
After Burnside's bloody repulse at Fredericksburg and his subsequent "mud march" fiasco, Hooker succeeded to the command of the Army of the Potomac. Although extremely unpopular with many officers of the Old Army, "Fighting Joe" immediately demonstrated ability as an administrator and strategic planner. Since Lee's Army of Northern Va. had strengthened their defensive positions overlooking Fredericksburg, Hooker evolved an excellent plan for driving the enemy back on Richmond by making a wide strategic envelopment by way of Kelly's Ford. Hooker was to lead approximately one third of his

134,000-man army in this TURNING MOVEMENT; Sedgwick with another third was to make a diversionary attack across the Rappahannock to hold Lee in his entrenchments above Fredericksburg; the remaining troops were to be in reserve, prepared to reinforce either wing.

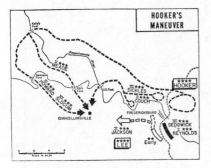

With an underfed and poorly equipped army of 60,000 (Longstreet was absent on a foraging expedition with the divisions of Pickett and Hood), Lee was in the difficult situation of trying to hold his good defensive position on the route to Richmond without being annihilated by Hooker's overwhelming forces, either wing of which almost equaled his entire strength. After waiting calmly until reports from Stuart's cavalry definitely established that Hooker was advancing in force through the Wilderness to strike him in the rear, Lee decided on the bold strategy of splitting his forces in the face of the enemy. Leaving Early with 10,000 to contain Sedgwick, Lee marched against Hooker with the remainder of his forces. Surprised by this unexpected move, Hooker called back his advance elements and organized a defensive position within the restricted and densely wooded Wilderness. Although he later admitted that he had simply lost his nerve, there was some tactical merit to his action: he had picked up false reports that Lee had been reinforced by Hood; he also thought that if Lee was

determined to fight, it would be better to accept battle in prepared defensive positions and let the Confederates bleed themselves white as the Federals had done at Fredericksburg. In making this decision, however, Hooker surrendered the initiative and Lee was quick to profit. While Lee probed the strong Federal defenses, Stuart's cavalry, ranging unhindered through the Wilderness (Hooker had sent his own cavalry off on a fruitless operation known as STONEMAN'S RAID), discovered that the enemy's right flank was "in the air." Meanwhile, Stonewall Jackson's corps had come up in a fast march from southeast of Fredericksburg.

Battle of Chancellorsville, 1–4 May

During the night of 1 May Lee found a guide who could lead Jackson's corps on the 16-mile march through the confusing trails to Wilderness Tavern whence they could strike the exposed Federal flank. So, further splitting his forces, Lee kept 17,000 men to continue holding attacks against Hooker's front while Jackson led 26,000 men in the hazardous daylight movement across the Federal front (not more than two and a half miles away) to get on their west (right) flank. By 6 P.M. Jackson was in position with six of his 15 brigades. Although Howard's troops had detected this maneuver, they were unable to convince Howard or Hooker of the real danger. In the two hours of daylight remaining Jackson drove the Federal flank back with great confusion and heavy losses. He was organizing a night attack to drive on through the Chancellorsville clearing and cut off the Federal retreat route through US Ford when Jackson was mortally wounded by the accidental fire of his own men. Stuart took command of the corps and launched a skillful and vigorous attack at dawn of 3 May. Hooker, now hopelessly confused, was drawing back into

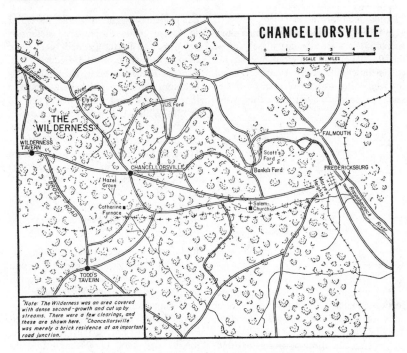

CHANCELLORSVILLE

SCALE IN MILES

Note: The Wilderness was an area covered with dense second-growth and cut up by streams. There were a few clearings, and these are shown here. "Chancellorsville" was merely a brick residence at an important road junction.

a stronger defensive position when he was rendered temporarily out of action by the concussion of a shell that landed near him.

Sedgwick, in the meantime, had finally gotten under way with his belated secondary attack. After four bloody repulses he finally broke through Barksdale's Mississippians on Marye's Heights and started driving to the relief of the beleaguered forces in the Wilderness some 12 miles away.

Seeing this new threat, Lee turned to complete his masterpiece. Leaving Stuart with 25,000 to contain well-dug-in forces of Hooker, now 75,000 strong, Lee marched with about 20,000 to reinforce Early. Attacked on three sides, Sedgwick was driven back across the river by way of Scott's Ford. Hooker, meanwhile, remained inactive.

Although Hooker now occupied an almost impregnable position, he withdrew his forces north of the Rappahannock on 6 May. This saved Lee from the costly error of carrying out an attack planned for that same day against Hooker's elaborate field fortifications.

Known as "Lee's masterpiece," this campaign is studied by military men as the almost perfect battle. Nevertheless, it was a Pyrrhic victory. Stonewall Jackson could not be replaced, and without this brilliant corps commander Lee was never again able to execute the strategy that had heretofore characterized his operations. The Army of Northern Va. never recovered the virility it had formerly possessed.

There is considerable disagreement among the authorities as to the numbers engaged and the losses. Livermore adds 1,575 killed and 9,594 wounded to get a total of 11,116; he estimates

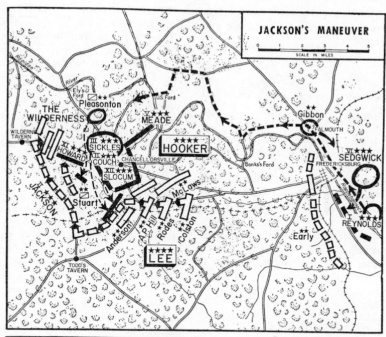

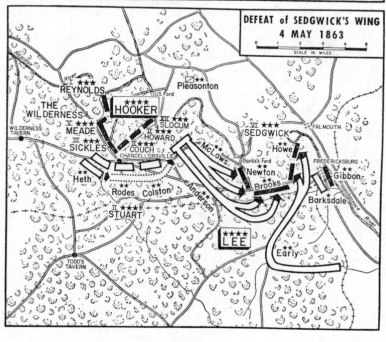

97,382 Union effectives. The figures of Bigelow would appear to be the most reliable:

	Aggregate	Killed, Wounded, and Missing	Per cent
Army of the Potomac	133,868	17,278	13
Army of Northern Virginia	60,892	12,821	22

Special mention should be made of *The Campaign of Chancellorsville*, by Major John Bigelow, Jr., Yale, 1910. Kenneth P. Williams calls this 528-page, large quarto, "a book without a peer in American military literature, as an exhaustive study of a single campaign."

CHANDLER, Zachariah. Radical Republican. 1813–79. N.H. Elected to the Senate from Michigan, he was one of the Radical leaders and was appointed Sec. of the Int. in 1875 by Grant. He died shortly after being re-elected to the Senate. Member of the Committee on the Conduct of the War.

CHAPIN, Edward P. Union gen. c. 1831–63. N.Y. Commissioned Capt. 44th N.Y. 6 Sept. '61, he was promoted Maj. 2 Jan. and Lt. Col. 4 July '62. Resigning on that date, he was named Col. 116th N.Y. 5 Sept. '62 and commanded 1, 1, XIX, Gulf, from 9 Feb. until his death, 27 May '63, at Pt. Hudson. He was promoted B.G. USV on the same day.

CHAPIN'S FARM (BLUFF), Va. "Chapin" is apparently a misspelling of CHAFIN or Chaffin.

CHAPLIN, Daniel. Union officer. Me. Commissioned Capt. 2d Me. 28 May '61, he was promoted Maj. 13 Sept. of that year and Col. 1st Me. Arty. 21 Aug. '62. He died 20 Aug. '64 after having been mortally wounded three days before at Deep Bottom, for which he was breveted B.G. USV 17 Aug. '64.

CHAPLIN HILLS, Ky. 8 Oct. '62. Alternate name for PERRYVILLE.

CHAPMAN, George Henry. Union gen. 1832–82. Mass. A midshipman during the Mexican War, he resigned in 1851 to become a lawyer and Republican politician. He was commissioned Maj. 3d Ind. Cav. 2 Nov. '61, promoted Col. 12 Mar. '63, and led his regiment at Upperville, Gettysburg, Falling Waters, and Brandy Station during the Pennsylvania campaign. He commanded 1, 1, Cav. Corps, Potomac (2 Sept.–12 Nov. '63 and 21 Dec. '63–25 Mar. '64) at Culpeper Courthouse, Morton's Ford, Bealton Station, and Muddy Run. He led 2, 3, Cav. Corps, Potomac (20 Apr.–7 Aug. '64), having been promoted B.G. USV 21 July '64. He was wounded at Winchester commanding 2, 3, Cav. Corps, Shenandoah (6 Aug.–19 Sept. and 1–10 Nov. '64). He also led the 2d Cav. Div., W. Va. (13 Jan.–Feb. '65); 1, 3, Cav. Corps, Shenandoah (10 Nov. '64–5 Jan. '65 and 30 Jan.–25 Feb. '65); and 3d Div., Cav. Corps, Shenandoah (5–30 Jan. '65). He was breveted Maj. Gen. USV for Winchester, served on court-martial boards, and resigned in 1866.

CHARLES CITY CROSSROADS, Va., 30 June '62. Alternate name for WHITE OAK SWAMP.

CHASE. "The conical part of the gun in front of the reinforce," or that part of the cannon generally between the TRUNNIONS and the swell of the muzzle.

CHASE, Kate. See Kate Chase SPRAGUE.

CHASE, Salmon Portland. Union Sec. of the Treas. and statesman. 1808–73. N.H. After graduating from Dartmouth, he practiced law in Ohio and became a leader in the Liberty (later Free-Soil) party. Elected to the Senate in 1849, he was chosen Governor of Ohio, representing the new Republican party, in 1855 and served for two terms. He had an extreme anti-slavery viewpoint, which prevented his getting the presidential nomination in 1860. Resigning his Senate seat, he became Lincoln's Sec. of the Treas., serving until July '64, and was appointed Chief Justice of the United States Supreme Court in Oct. of that year, succeeding Roger B. Taney. Kate Chase Sprague was his daughter and Washington hostess.

CHATTAHOOCHEE RIVER, Ga., 4–9 July '64. (ATLANTA CAMPAIGN) Johnston withdrew from Smyrna on 4 July into his strong bridgehead north of the Chattahoochee. Thomas's army invested this position, while McPherson's army threatened to cross at Turner's Ferry, six miles downstream. About the same distance upstream Schofield's army prepared to make a surprise crossing in ponton boats near the mouth of Soap Creek.

At 3 P.M. on the 8th the 12th Ky.

crossed the river in 20 pontons that had been hidden in Soap Creek. Byrd's brigade covered the operation by fire from the friendly bank, while Cameron's brigade rushed across a fish dam about a mile above the mouth of Soap Creek. A small Confederate cavalry force with one gun attempted to oppose the crossing, but it was quickly silenced by the fire of Byrd's brigade. This unit was then ferried across and a ponton bridge laid. By daylight of the 9th a strong bridgehead was established. Garrard's cavalry crossed farther upstream at Roswell with the support of the XVI Corps and Newton's (2d) division of IV Corps. Johnston abandoned his bridgehead the night of 9 July.

CHATTANOOGA CAMPAIGN, Oct.–Nov. '63.

After the Southern victory at Chickamauga, Rosecrans withdrew into Chatta-

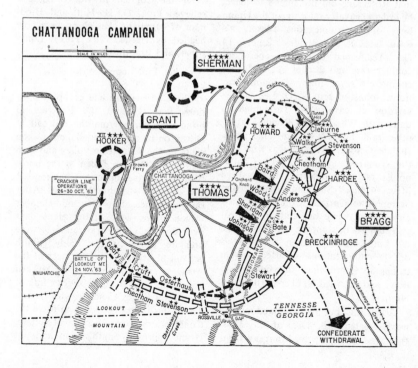

nooga, and Bragg laid siege. After a council meeting to which the President was called in the middle of the night, the authorities in Washington ordered sizable reinforcements to the scene. Hooker left Manassas 25 Sept. with the XI and XII Corps, and his advance elements started arriving five days later (30 Sept.) at Bridgeport. Demonstrating strategic mobility provided by the railroads, 20,000 men and more than 3,000 horses and mules were moved 1,157 miles in less than three weeks. As early as 13 Sept. Halleck had ordered reinforcements sent to Rosecrans from Memphis and Vicksburg. By 15 Nov. 17,000 men had arrived at Bridgeport, having moved 675 miles by boat, rail, and foot.

Bragg expected Rosecrans to evacuate Chattanooga, and undertook no active operations until 1 Oct. Then, convinced that Rosecrans did not intend to leave, he ordered cavalry raids to cut the Union lines of communications. WHEELER'S RAID, 1–9 Oct. and Roddey's Raid, 7–14 Oct., reaffirmed that such operations could harass and disrupt but could not completely sever lines of communications. Johnston sent S. D. Lee with a division of cavalry to Tuscumbia to unite with Wheeler and Roddey in another raid, but this did not take place. In late October Wheeler was sent into the Tennessee Valley above Chattanooga and Lee returned to northern Miss. to check Sherman's march from Memphis to Corinth. Confederate cavalry action, while not cutting off Federal supplies or stopping reinforcements, did put Rosecrans's men and animals on starvation rations, diverted combat troops to guard lines of communications, and detained Hooker's artillery at Nashville.

Grant was put in command of the newly-created Mil. Div. of the Miss. (see MISSISSIPPI, UNION MILITARY DIVI-SION OF THE) in mid-October, and arrived at Chattanooga the 23d to take personal charge of the situation there. Thomas succeeded Rosecrans as C.G., Army of the CUMBERLAND. The Federal force under Grant at Chattanooga ultimately consisted of the following: Army of the Cumberland (IV and XIV Corps, plus W. F. ["Baldy"] Smith's Engineer Troops, Brannan's Artillery Reserve, Eli Long's cavalry brigade, and the three regiments constituting Parkhurst's Post of Chattanooga); Army of the Tennessee (Sherman with three divisions of XV Corps and John E. Smith's 2d Div. of XVII Corps); Hooker's detachment from the Army of the Potomac (Howard with two divisions of XI Corps, and Geary's division of XII Corps). (For more detail, see separate entries for these armies and corps.)

On the Confederate side Bragg had relieved Polk, D. H. Hill, and Hindman of command. His corps were now headed by Hardee (vice Polk), Longstreet, and Breckinridge.

"Cracker Line" operations, 26–30 Oct. '63.

The Confederates had occupied positions that required the Federals to bring in supplies from the railroad at Stevenson by a long, roundabout wagon route up the Sequatchie Valley and then south over Walden Ridge to the north bank of the river opposite Chattanooga. The distance was about 60 miles. After rainy weather started in mid-October wagon trains were taking eight days over this route and draft animals were breaking down. When "Baldy" Smith arrived to become chief engineer of the Army of the Cumberland he worked up a plan for opening a shorter line of supply via Kelley's and Brown's ferries. To do this it was necessary to drive the Confederates from Raccoon Mountain. Grant approved Smith's plan and put him in charge of its execution. Hooker's force at Bridgeport moved secretly across the Tennessee the night of 26 Oct. Howard's XI Corps led the advance along the line of the railroad south of the river toward Wauhatchie. Cruft's Div. (IV) crossed northwest of Whiteside and joined Hooker. At 3 A.M., 27 Oct., about 1,500 picked men under Hazen were silently cast loose at Chattanooga to drift downstream past the enemy sentinels to Brown's Ferry. Here they landed, secured the heights overlooking the site, and fought off a small enemy counterattack. Turchin's brigade then crossed from the north bank at Brown's Ford. A ponton bridge was put over. Hooker's column drove back an outpost from Law's brigade. In withdrawing the Confederates destroyed the railroad bridge across Lookout Creek and occupied high ground. Hooker left Geary at Wauhatchie to guard the road, and the next day linked up with the Federal bridgehead.

The Confederates failed to wipe out Geary's isolated division in the WAUHATCHIE NIGHT ATTACK, 28–29 Oct. '63. The morning of 30 Oct. the steamboat *Chattanooga* arrived at Kelly's Ford with 40,000 rations and tons of forage. The cry went up from the troops: "The Cracker line open. Full rations, boys!" (B.&L., III, 678)

Bragg realized that he had lost his opportunity of retaking Chattanooga, and turned his immediate attention to Burnside in east Tenn. On 4 Nov. he ordered Longstreet and Wheeler to reinforce the West. Va. troops of Samuel Jones and operate against Burnside. Although this was of great concern to Grant and the authorities in Washington, Grant correctly reasoned that the best way to he'p Burnside was not to send him reinforcements, but to destroy the weakened forces of Bragg around Chattanooga as quickly as possible and then mass to destroy Wheeler and Longstreet.

In order to take some positive action to assist Burnside while awaiting Sherman's arrival, Grant ordered Thomas to attack Bragg's north flank. It was hoped that this would force the recall of Longstreet. Grant also had reason to suspect that Bragg might be withdrawing. Due to the weakened condition of his animals, Thomas could not move enough artillery to support such an attack and the operation was not executed.

Lines of communications, particularly the railroad, played a prominent part in the operations around Chattanooga. Both sides had brought in sizable reinforcements from other theaters. Opening the "Cracker line" shaped Grant's initial tactical moves in preparing to defeat Bragg. The Confederate supply line ran up the railroad to their right flank, and Longstreet had used the railroad to Loudon in moving to oppose Burnside; this made Bragg's right his strategic flank, and it was against this point that Grant properly planned his next attack. Repair of railroads over which to supply not only the troops of Thomas, Howard, and Hooker in Chattanooga, but also those of Burnside in east Tenn. and those Sherman was bringing, were logistical problems Grant had to cope with while shaping his strategy.

Sherman had originally been ordered to repair the railroads as he advanced so that he could be supplied over them. Since this requirement was resulting in unacceptable delays, Grant told Sherman to cease this work and march with all speed for Chattanooga. Grant made provisions for Sherman to be supplied by water from St. Louis, up the Tennessee to Bridgeport. Use of water routes had been an integral part of Federal success in the West. The division of G. M. Dodge (8,000) was ordered to halt at Athens, Ala., and repair the considerable damage to the railroads between Decatur and Nashville. These unglamorous provisions for his logistical support have a little-understood or appreciated importance not only in Grant's victory at Chattanooga, but also in the clearing of east Tenn. and in Sherman's subsequent Atlanta campaign.

Sherman reached Bridgeport 15 Nov. (Van Horne) with his leading divisions. He went forward the same day to be briefed by Grant on his part in the coming battle, which Grant planned to start the 21st. The head of Sherman's column reached Brown's Ferry on the 20th, but heavy rains delayed the attack until the 24th.

Orchard Knob—Indian Hill, 23 Nov. '63.

Learning that Bragg had weakened his lines on Missionary Ridge, Grant directed Thomas to conduct reconnaissance in force to see whether the Confederates were withdrawing. Actually, Bragg had ordered the divisions of Buckner and Cleburne to reinforce Longstreet. Wood on the left and Sheridan attacked at 2 P.M. and drove the Confederate outpost line from Orchard Knob, a low ridge halfway between the lines. Howard's (XI) corps protected the left flank and Baird's division (XIV) protected the right. Bragg stopped the reinforcement to Longstreet (Bushrod Johnson had already departed with two brigades), and ordered the divisions of Jackson, Stevenson, and Gist from the extreme left of his line to the extreme right of Missionary Ridge. (Jackson was commanding "Cheatham's" and Gist was commanding "Walker's" division.)

Grant's plan for the battle, in general terms, was this. The main attack was to be made by Sherman's four divisions against the Confederate north flank. The secondary attack was to be made frontally by Grant's center after Sherman had started rolling up the enemy flank. A diversion was to be made by Hooker against the enemy's south flank to draw strength away from the main attack.

Sherman was to cross the ponton bridge at Brown's Ferry, march to the mouth of North Chickamauga Creek where he would find Davis's division (XIV), and the necessary river-crossing equipment (which was hidden in the creek). Weakening of the bridge at Brown's Ferry delayed Sherman. Osterhaus's division was unable to cross in time and Grant attached it to Hooker's polyglot command rather than further delay the main attack; Davis's division was assigned to Sherman in its place. Sherman crossed and by daylight had 8,000 men in the bridgehead; by noon a ponton bridge was completed; at 1 o'clock he moved forward with four divisions, and by 4 P.M. had seized the north end of Missionary Ridge without encountering anything but enemy outposts. Sherman was then surprised to find a wide depression separating him from Tunnel Hill. The latter position had been occupied at 2:30 by Cleburne's division, which had been called back from its previous mission of going to reinforce Longstreet. Sherman dug in for the night.

Lookout Mountain, 24 Nov. '63 (The Battle above the Clouds)

On the other flank, while Sherman was making his initial attack, Hooker had moved out with three divisions. His mission was to get into Chattanooga Valley and occupy Rossville Gap. Grant realized that once the battle started, Hooker's previous mission of protecting the vital line of communication down Lookout Valley had no further importance. Accordingly, Howard's corps had been withdrawn from Hooker's command and moved to Chattanooga before the battle started. Grant originally planned to move Hooker's other two divisions to Chattanooga so they could advance on Rossville Gap without having to fight their way past Lookout Mountain. But difficulties with the ponton bridge made this impossible, and resulted in Hooker's having three divisions instead of two. Grant accordingly, ordered him to attack around Lookout Mountain.

The Confederates were holding Lookout Mountain to guard against an enemy approach from Trenton. Sherman had, in fact, sent Ewing's division toward that place as a diversion; it rejoined his main body for the attack on Missionary Ridge.

Lookout Mountain drops precipitously several hundred feet from a plateau nearly 1,100 feet above the river. The top was occupied by two Confederate brigades. Walthall's brigade (Cheatham) blocked the narrow passage around the northern face of the mountain, and Moore's brigade of the same division was posted up the slope from it.

Geary's division, reinforced by one of Cruft's brigades, crossed Lookout Creek above Wauhatchie at about 8 A.M. Osterhaus and the rest of Cruft's division followed. Contact was made at about 10 o'clock, and a sharp fight took place around Craven's Farm ("the White House"). A heavy fog covered the scene as both sides brought up reinforcements. About noon the defenders were driven from Craven's Farm to a new position about 400 yards away. Here they were reinforced by the two brigades from the plateau, and held this position from 2 o'clock until after midnight, when they were ordered to withdraw. The name "Battle above the Clouds" was given to this engagement after the war. The next morning a party from the 8th Ky. scaled the heights to plant the Stars and Stripes at a point where it was dramatically visible to the rest of Grant's forces in the valley below.

Missionary Ridge, 25 Nov. '63.

Bragg had a strong natural position on Missionary Ridge. His right, or "strategic," flank was held by 14 brigades in Hardee's corps. Breckinridge had nine brigades with which to cover a two-and-a-half-mile front opposite Grant's center. Three parallel lines of entrenchments had been laid out and partially completed. One line was along the base of the ridge; another had been started about half-way up the slope; and a third was along the crest.

Grant established his headquarters on Orchard Knob 24 Nov., and about midnight sent word to Sherman to resume his attack at dawn. Hooker was ordered to continue his advance to Rossville Gap.

Ewing's division (of Sherman's force) attacked south; the brigade of Corse, reinforced by a regiment of Lightburn, spearheaded the advance, while the brigades of Cockerill, Alexander, and Lightburn were initially to hold the hill taken the day before. Morgan Smith's division advanced along the eastern slope, maintaining contact with Corse on his right. Along the western slope the brigade of Loomis was to advance with two brigades from John Smith's division in support.

Corse moved out under heavy fire and took some high ground about 80 yards from the enemy's main position. From this base he launched repeated assaults for over an hour without success. The forces on his left and right gained ground, thereby relieving some pressure, but were not able to achieve any permanent lodgment. Federal batteries (Callender, Wood, and Dillon) did what they could to support the infantry, but the terrain and the close fighting were such that they could not render effective assistance. Corse was severely wounded about 10 A.M. The fighting on this flank continued with varying results until about 3 P.M.

Meanwhile, Hooker's advance had been delayed four or five hours (Steele) in rebuilding the bridge the Confederates had destroyed over the Chattanooga and in removing other obstructions. It was late afternoon before he was in a position to threaten Bragg's left flank. Bragg, in the meantime, had reinforced his right with the divisions of Cheatham and Stevenson.

Showing outstanding generalship, Grant did not make the error of throwing troops from his center into the planned frontal attack before some decisive results had been achieved on the flanks. Sherman's situation, however, was critical, and the original plan had to be modified. At 10 o'clock he made Howard's two divisions (XI) available to reinforce Sherman's left. A new Federal attack gained some ground, but was driven back by a counterattack which routed the brigades of John Smith (on the right). The brigades of Corse and Loomis then drove the Confederates back into their original positions.

Continuing to reinforce the left, Grant at 12 o'clock ordered Baird's division to move from the right of Indian Hill to reinforce Sherman. Baird arrived behind Sherman's position, was told he was not needed, and then moved to a position on Wood's left. He formed in line at 2:30 (Van Horne).

Hooker, in the meantime, had started attacking the Confederate left. The 27th Mo. (1, 1, XV), deployed as skirmishers, rushed into the gap at Rossville. The rest of Wood's brigade headed for high ground on the right of the gap, and Williamson's (2, 1, XV) moved up on the left. The Confederates withdrew, leaving a considerable quantity of supplies. By this time the bridge was completed and the rest of Hooker's forces

reinforced the leading brigades. Hooker sent Cruft's division along the ridge and Geary and Osterhaus on his left and right, respectively. The 9th and 36th Ind. (3, 1, IV) spearheaded an assault that started crushing Bragg's left flank.

Grant now saw that even though Sherman's envelopment had failed he must make a final effort before dark. Between 3 and 4 P.M. (Van Horne) the long-awaited six cannon shots signaled the assault. The divisions of Baird (XIV), Wood, and Sheridan (both IV), and Johnson (XIV) were on line from left to right.

"I felt no fear for the result," wrote a Confederate brigade commander later, "even though the arrangements to repel the attack were not such as I liked. . . . I think, however, that I noticed some nervousness among my men as they beheld this grand military spectacle, and I heard remarks which showed that some uneasiness existed, and that they magnified the host in their view to at least double their number." (Manigault, who commanded a brigade in Hindman's [Anderson's] Division, quoted by Alexander.)

Grant had intended that the troops halt after taking the first line, and reorganize. Much to his consternation, Grant saw the troops capture the first line and then press on immediately for the summit. The attackers had found out that lingering in the initial position would subject them to murderous fire from the crest, and that the safest thing was to charge up the hill. This they did on their own initiative, turning it into a "SOLDIERS' BATTLE." Grant is reported to have asked Thomas and Granger: "Who ordered those men up the hill?" Unable to find the answer he said: "Someone will suffer for it, if it turns out badly." (Alexander; B. & L., III, 725.) The commanders actually tried to stop this advance. Turchin's brigade

(1, 3, XIV) was halted; Wagner's brigade (2, 2, IV) was called back from an advanced position (Van Horne).

Bragg had made several mistakes in his defensive dispositions. He had split his forces, putting half at the bottom of the hill with secret orders to fire a volley when the enemy got to within 200 yards, and then to withdraw up the slopes (Alexander). Many men apparently were not informed of this plan, and defended the first line even when others had pulled back. A Confederate engineer had taken his instructions literally when told to put the final line on the highest ground. This line was along the geographic or topographic crest instead of the "military crest" (the highest place from which you can see and fire on an approaching enemy). The attackers, therefore, found "dead space" through which they could advance under cover, and came forward in about six separate lines of approach. Footholds were established at various places, and enfilade fire from these penetrations destroyed the Confederate strong points that had been able to resist the frontal assault. As for which regiment reached the crest first, it would be difficult to find a regimental historian who recorded that his own unit was the second. ". . . there is no room to doubt that General Wood's division first reached the summit," writes Van Horne. Sheridan was the only division commander who maintained enough cohesion in his unit to pursue; he took a large number of guns and prisoners, and came very close to capturing Bragg, Breckinridge, and a number of other high-ranking officers. The final assault had lasted about an hour; 37 guns and 2,000 prisoners were taken (Steele).

Hooker, meanwhile, was rolling up the left. Many Confederate units panicked, but Grant was unable to pursue effectively. The Confederates rallied on a ridge about 500 yards to the rear. Cleburne continued to hold Sherman after the firing had died out along the rest of the line. Bragg withdrew that night toward Dalton, while Hardee's corps covered the rear.

The loss of Chattanooga was a severe blow to the dying Confederate cause. A vital line of lateral communications was lost, and the stage was set for Sherman's move to split the Confederacy further by his Atlanta campaign and march to the sea.

Numbers and losses at Chattanooga, 23–25 Nov. '63 (Livermore):

	Union	Confederate
Effectives	56,359	64,165
Killed	753	361
Wounded	4,722	2,160
Missing	349	4,146
Total losses	5,824 (10%)	6,667 (14%)

Using Livermore's system of comparing the relative effectiveness of opposing troops, the Federals killed or wounded 44 of the enemy for every 1,000 of their own troops engaged; the Confederates killed or wounded 118 for every 1,000 of their own troops engaged.

CHEATHAM, Benjamin Franklin. C.S.A. gen. 1820–86. Tenn. After fighting in the Mexican War, he farmed, went to Calif. for the Gold Rush, and was promoted Maj. Gen. in the Tenn. militia. He was named B.G. of state forces 9 May '61 and B.G. C.S.A. 9 July '61. For the next three years he commanded his division in first Polk's and then Hardee's corps, having been promoted Maj. Gen. 10 Mar. '62. He was at Belmont, Shiloh, Perryville, Stones River, Chickamauga, Chattanooga, and the Atlanta campaign. During the Franklin and Nashville campaign he succeeded Hardee as corps commander and is incorrectly listed in the B.&L. order of battle as Lt. Gen.

(neither Wright nor Wood accords him this rank). He surrendered with Johnston in N.C. and was a farmer after the war, holding several minor public offices.

CHEATHAM'S CORPS. See I CORPS (Polk's, Hardee's, Cheatham's), Confed. Armies of Miss. and of Tenn.

CHEAT MOUNTAIN (Elkwater), W. Va., 10-15 Sept. '61. (WEST VIRGINIA OPERATIONS IN 1861) Although a minor action, this is of interest because it was R. E. Lee's first campaign of the Civil War. His mission was to recover the portions of western Va. that McClellan had captured from Garnett, and as a result of which McClellan had been elevated to top Federal command.

J. J. Reynolds's (1st) brigade was guarding the Staunton-Parkersburg road along which Lee wished to operate. Col. Nathan Kimball's 14th Ind. held the vital Cheat Summit, while the rest of Reynolds's command was to the west at Elkwater in the Tygart Valley. The distance between these two Federal positions was seven miles by mountain trail along Cheat Mountain, and 18 miles by the wagon road through Huttonsville.

CHEAT MOUNTAIN, W. Va.
10-15 SEPT. 1861

Reconnaissance finally revealed two concealed routes by which Reynolds's strong positions might be attacked. Col. Albert Rust, who had found a way of enveloping the Cheat Summit position from the west, was to lead a column of 2,000 men in a surprise attack against Kimball's right. S. R. Anderson was to lead his brigade in a deeper envelopment and cut the road about two and a half miles behind Kimball. H. R. Jackson's brigade would occupy Cheat Summit when Rust had opened the way. Lee with the three other brigades (J. S. Burks, D. S. Donelson, and Wm. Gilham) would advance down the valley against Elkwater. (W. W. Loring, nominally in command of this operation, led the brigades of Burks and Gilham.)

Lee started advancing on the 10th through rugged mountain terrain. The weather was cold and wet. At Conrad's Mill on the 11th his main body made contact. On the 12th the Federal outposts had been driven back to Elkwater, and Anderson had cut the road behind Kimball. However, Rust's attack, which was to be the signal for a general engagement, had failed to materialize. Since surprise had now been lost, Lee withdrew Anderson, and tried unsuccessfully to get his tired, demoralized troops to attack in the valley.

At 3 A.M. the next day Reynolds sent the 13th Ind. and most of the 3d Ohio and 2d Va. to re-establish contact with Kimball. In the valley Lee ordered reconnaissance to find some way of turning the position at Elkwater. His aide, Col. J. A. Washington, was killed while reconnoitering with Rooney Lee and a few men. Failure of Rush to accomplish his mission made Lee's position untenable, and on the 15th he withdrew.

Rush had gotten into position undetected but had failed to attack. Captured Federals had tricked him into believing that Cheat Summit was held by over

4,000 men, well entrenched. Actually there were only 300.

"His first campaign had ended ingloriously," writes Lee's biographer (*R. E. Lee,* I, 574). Although Lee reported sustaining few casualties, Federals claimed 20 prisoners and estimated 100 Confederate killed and wounded. Reynolds reported 21 killed and wounded, and 60 prisoners (many of whom escaped and rejoined him).

CHESNUT, James, Jr. C.S.A. gen. 1815–85. S.C. A wealthy planter's son, he studied law after graduating from Princeton. In the state legislature and the U.S. Senate he was an ardent secessionist and defender of slavery, resigning his seat 10 Nov. '60 to aid his state. Elected to C.S.A. Congress, he was Beauregard's A.D.C. at Ft. Sumter and 1st Bull Run and then served on the Executive Council of S.C. Appointed Davis's A.D.C. and Col. he held this position under the friend of his Senate days until appointed B.G. C.S.A. 23 Apr. '64. He was given command of the reserve forces in S.C. After the war he was active in overthrowing the Reconstruction politicians. His wife wrote the delightful *Diary from Dixie.*

CHETLAIN, Augustus Louis. Union gen. 1824–1914. Mo. A successful Galena businessman, he had sold out and was traveling in Europe when he returned for the 1860 political campaign. He was commissioned Capt. 12th Ill., 2 May '61, Lt. Col. the next day, and Col. 27 Apr. '62. Fighting at Fts. Henry and Donelson, Shiloh, Iuka, and Corinth, he commanded the post of Corinth after occupation. As B.G. USV (18 Dec. '63), he recruited and organized colored troops in Tenn. and Ky. and then held administrative commands (i. e., Dist. Memphis, Dept. of the Tenn., 20 Jan. '65) in Tenn. and Alabama. He was breveted Maj. Gen. USV

18 June '65 and mustered out in 1866. Settling in Utah for a while, he was Consul at Brussels 1869–72 and then active in Chicago banking circles. He engaged in philanthropic and veterans' activities and published *The Red River Colony* (1893) and *Recollections.*

CHICAGO CONSPIRACY. See SWEET, Benjamin Jeffery.

CHICKAHOMINY, Va., 27 June '62. GAINES'S MILL.

CHICKAMAUGA CAMPAIGN, Aug.–Sept. '63.

Rosecrans' successful TULLAHOMA CAMPAIGN turned Bragg out of his positions in Tenn. north of Chattanooga and opened the way for the capture of that vital communications hub. The town was too well fortified to be taken by frontal assault, so Rosecrans planned another strategic envelopment. He decided to operate west of the town, rather than to the east, so as to make the best use of the rail lines to Stevenson for supplying his forces. Bragg expected his opponent to shift his line of operations to the other side of Chattanooga, where he would be in a better position to secure the assistance of Burnside's forces in east Tenn. The sketch shows the strength and dispositions of the opposing forces at the start.

The Confederate authorities considered another offensive into Tenn., but decided they lacked the means. They then ordered a reorganization of Bragg's forces in order to assure the defense of Chattanooga. Buckner was put under Bragg's command, and Longstreet was ordered from the Army of Northern Va. with the divisions of McLaws and Hood to reinforce Bragg. (For the organization of the opposing armies at this time see: CUMBERLAND, ARMY OF THE; and TENNESSEE, CONFEDERATE ARMY OF.)

After much unsuccessful urging, the

authorities in Washington on 5 Aug. sent Rosecrans and Burnside orders to advance and gain possession of the upper Tennessee Valley. On 15 Aug. Rosecrans issued orders for an advance to the Tennessee River, and Burnside ordered an advance on Knoxville and Kingston. Rosecrans' forces reached their initial objectives 21 Aug. and spent the rest of the month preparing to cross.

Bragg began concentrating his forces around Chattanooga when he learned from Wheeler's cavalry that the Federals were starting to cross the river. About 1 Sept. he was reinforced by two divisions from the Army of the Miss. (Breckinridge and W. H. T. Walker). Bragg reorganized his army into four corps of two divisions each under Polk, D. H. Hill, Buckner, and Walker. Wheeler and Forrest remained in command of the cavalry corps. On the morning of the 18th three brigades of Longstreet's corps arrived, under Hood's command. Longstreet himself arrived the next night with two more brigades. The sixth brigade of the eastern troops and E. P. Alexander's artillery did not arrive in time for the battle.

Rosecrans crossed the river without opposition, completing the operation 4 Sept. Assuming from incorrect reports that Bragg was evacuating Chattanooga, Rosecrans advanced through the mountainous terrain on a 40-mile front to cut off Bragg's retreat. By 6 Sept. his three corps were in the valley of Lookout Creek, with the most advanced division in Steven's Gap. Burnside occupied Knoxville and Kingston this same day. It was also on 6 Sept. that Bragg decided to abandon Chattanooga, concentrate at LaFayette, and defeat the Federals as they emerged from the mountain passes. Hill moved the night of the 7th to LaFayette; Polk started the next morning for Lee and Gordon's Mill; Walker joined Hill near LaFayette; and

Buckner took up a position generally between the two wings.

There followed a complex sequence of maneuvers in which the failures of Bragg's subordinates deprived the Confederates of their opportunity for defeating isolated Federal units in detail. The first failure was on the 10th when faulty coordination between the divisions of Hindman (Polk) and Cleburne (Hill) enabled Negley's isolated division at Dug Gap to be reinforced before the Confederates could attack it. Rosecrans now believed the entire enemy army was around LaFayette and started concentrating his own forces. Crittenden, who had taken Chattanooga and then moved to Ringgold, started westward on 12 Sept. to Lee and Gordon's Mill. Walker was ordered from LaFayette to reinforce Polk and to attack Crittenden. The forces of both commanders now began to shift to the north. Rosecrans ordered McCook (south flank) to withdraw from Alpine and move west of Lookout Mountain to join Thomas (center) at Steven's Gap.

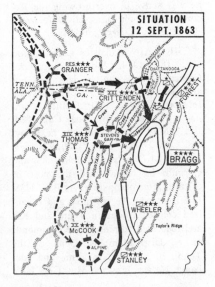

Both commanders shifted troops as bits of enemy information were reported. Bragg, having missed repeated opportunities for destroying isolated Federal forces, now was content to await his reinforcements from Miss. and Va. The night of 17–18 Sept. the forces were disposed as shown in the sketch.

Bragg ordered a dawn attack for 18 Sept. against Crittenden's corps on the Federal north flank. This well-conceived plan was frustrated by Federal mounted brigades. Bushrod Johnson's division finally succeeded in forcing a crossing against Minty's cavalry at Reed's Bridge late in the afternoon. Wilder's cavalry inflicted heavy losses on Liddell's division (Walker's corps), succeeding finally in dismantling Alexander's bridge and forcing the Confederates to cross at Lambert's Ford. Polk was to attack Crittenden frontally at Lee and Gordon's Mill after the enveloping force of Forrest, Buckner, W. H. T. Walker, and Bushrod Johnson crossed the creek; the failure of the envelopment meant that Polk could not attack. As a result, Crittenden's corps was not engaged at all during the day.

The action of the 18th set the stage for the two-day battle of Chickamauga.

Battle of Chickamauga–
First Day (19 Sept. '63)

During the night preceding the battle both sides were shifting troops. "Neither army knew the exact position of the other.... It is probable that division commanders on either side hardly knew where their own commands were, in the thick woods, let alone the other troops of their own army, or the troops of the hostile army. The lines were at this time about six miles long" (Steele, 432).

On the morning of the 19th Thomas ordered Brannan's division, then posted on the road two miles north of the Lee and Gordon's Mill, to reconnoiter toward Chickamauga Creek. Brannan en-

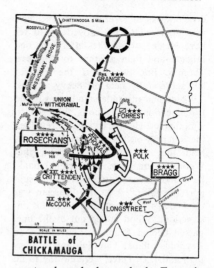

BATTLE of CHICKAMAUGA

countered and drove back Forrest's dismounted cavalry, which called on the nearest Confederate infantry for help. This brought on an all-day battle. Every division of the XIV, XX, and XXI Corps was committed. Of the Confederate forces, only the divisions of Breckinridge and Hindman, on the south flank, were not engaged. Neither side gained any decided advantage.

Battle of Chickamauga–
Second Day (20 Sept. '63)

During the night the two opposing forces further rearranged their dispositions in the difficult terrain. Rosecrans prepared defensive positions, and Bragg planned an attack. Longstreet had arrived during the night; he was given command of the left wing of Bragg's army, and Polk was given command of the other.

Bragg's units were to attack successively from north to south. Breckinridge attacked on the north at 9 o'clock Sunday morning. Thomas, commanding the Federal left wing, called for Negley's division, which was supposed to be in reserve. Due to an error, however, Negley was in the line. Wood, whose division was in reserve where Negley's was supposed to be, moved up to relieve Negley, while the latter sent one brigade and then another to reinforce Thomas. For two hours the Federal left successfully held off heavy attacks. Rosecrans' misunderstanding as to the true location of his units then led to a fatal error. He was trying to strengthen the defenses on his right while Thomas held the other flank. Thinking that Wood was on Reynolds's (right) flank, he ordered Wood "to close up and support Reynolds." Actually, Brannan was on Wood's left, and following his instructions, Wood pulled out of the line, passed behind Brannan, and fell in on Reynolds's flank. The divisions of Sheridan and J. C. Davis were closing to fill this gap at about 11:30 when Longstreet attacked. By a strange coincidence, Longstreet hit the precise point left open by the Federal error. Sheridan's and Davis' divisions were shattered by superior force, and the Federal right was driven back on its left flank.

Rosecrans, McCook, and Crittenden, unable to rally the troops around them, fled to Chattanooga, thinking the entire army was being destroyed. Thomas remained on the field, turning Wood and Brannan to block Longstreet on the south. Bragg had failed to provide for a general reserve, and so was unable to exploit Longstreet's success. Three brigades of Granger's Reserve Corps ("Army of the Kentucky") were near McAffee's Church with orders to remain there and protect the flank. In a splendid example of battlefield initiative Granger violated his orders and "at the moment of greatest need reported to Gen. Thomas with two brigades" (Whittaker and Mitchell from Steedman's division). Van Horne says "the opportune aid of these two brigades saved the army from defeat and rout" (Van Horne, I, 353). Thomas held the field

until dark and then, on orders from Rosecrans, withdrew to Rossville Gap.

Rosecrans withdrew his army into the defenses of Chattanooga. Bragg followed, occupied Missionary Ridge, and laid siege to the town.

Although Bragg had won a decided tactical victory, his piecemeal method of attack and lack of a general reserve deprived him of the success that an outstanding general might have achieved under the circumstances—particularly the rare bit of luck occasioned by Longstreet's attack finding a gap. Failure to pursue the shattered Federals deprived Bragg of the fruits of his victory. The work of Thomas—the "Rock of Chickamauga"—the steadfastness of the troops on his wing, and the initiative of Granger, all helped make this a Pyrrhic victory for the South.

Numbers and losses according to Livermore (19–20 Sept.):

	Union	Confederate
Effectives	58,222	66,326
Killed	1,657	2,312
Wounded	9,756	14,674
Missing	4,757	1,468
Total losses	16,170 (28%)	18,454 (28%)

An evaluation of these statistics shows that the Union had 19.6 per cent killed and wounded and the Confederates 25.9 per cent. Using Livermore's "hit by 1,000" system of comparing the combat effectiveness, Rosecrans' troops killed or wounded 292 Confederates for every 1,000 Federal soldiers engaged; Bragg's forces, on the other hand, killed or wounded only 172 Federals for every 1,000 of their own troops engaged. The battle, fought in a densely wooded area which permitted little or no tactical control of units, was one of the bloodiest of the war.

Chickamauga was a maker and

breaker of reputations. Thomas's performance elevated him to top command, and Granger was also marked for higher responsibility. Rosecrans, Alexander McCook, Crittenden, and Negley were relieved; the last three were charged with misconduct but acquitted. The fractious Bragg, whose personality defects were largely responsible for the poor cooperation of his subordinates, relieved Polk, D. H. Hill, and Hindman for unsatisfactory performance during the campaign.

CHICKASAW BLUFFS (Bayou) (Walnut Hills), Vicksburg, Miss., 27–29 Dec. '62. As one of the preliminary attempts of the VICKSBURG CAMPAIGN, Grant moved overland along the Mississippi Central R.R. against Vicksburg, while Sherman led a force down the river to land on the Yazoo River above the city and attack it from that point. Sherman's 32,000-man expedition was composed of divisions under A. J. Smith (commanding 1st Div., and also the 2d on 29 Dec.), Morgan L. Smith (wounded the 28th, and temporarily succeeded by David Stuart), G. W. Morgan, and Frederick Steele. This force was known as Sherman's right wing, XIII Army Corps, during this operation.

Martin L. Smith commanded the defenses of Vicksburg. At the time of Sherman's landing he had 6,000 troops available to defend the strong line of bluffs that extended from the river north of Vicksburg to Snyder's (or Drumgould's) Bluff 10 miles northeast. These troops were the Provisional Division of S. D. Lee. Since Grant's overland advance was halted by Van Dorn's capture of HOLLY SPRINGS 20 Dec., Pemberton was able to reinforce the defenses of Vicksburg with 6,000 men from Grenada on the 26th. These troops were in the brigades of Seth Barton, J. C. Vaughn, and E. D. Tracy. Additional reinforcements, from Bragg, were also en route, and had swelled the Con-

federate ranks to 25,000 before Sherman withdrew (B.&L., III, 471).

After landing on the Yazoo opposite Steele's Bayou (Johnson's Plantation) on the 26th, the brigades of De Courcy (3, 3), Stuart (4, 2), and Blair (1, 4) moved forward to develop the situation. Sherman formed four columns to advance through the swampy terrain. A. J. Smith's division on the right was to move straight toward Vicksburg. M. L. Smith was to advance on his left. Morgan, reinforced with Blair's brigade, would move up the west bank of Chickasaw Bayou. Steele (less Blair) would be on the Federal left and across the bayou from Morgan. Confederate pickets were driven back until the Federals were stopped the morning of the 28th by Fishing Lake and the bayou. This obstacle was covered by Confederate fire from the bluffs. After several unsuccessful attempts to push across, further reconnaissance revealed two places where dry sandbars made passage possible (see O. R. atlas, XXVII, 2). These points were covered by abatis and by enemy fire. An attack was ordered for noon the next day, 29 Dec.

De Courcy's brigade attacked in the face of murderous fire and advanced to the foot of the bluff, where it was stopped. Blair's brigade crossed a mile to the left, at the junction of Fishing Lake and Chickasaw Bayou, and also reached the base of the bluff. Thayer's brigade (3, 4) was ordered to advance, but it got lost and only the 4th Iowa became engaged. (It sustained 112 casualties.) The 6th Mo. (1, 2), under Lt. Col. J. H. Blood, fought its way across on M. L. Smith's front but was pinned down and had to withdraw after dark. The difficult terrain had deprived the attackers of effective artillery support, while the Confederate gunners were able to fire with great effect. De Courcy and Blair could not be reinforced and were being cut to pieces by fire from their front and flanks; at 3 P.M. they withdrew.

Federal troops remained opposite the strong enemy position, shivering in a driving rain, and expecting to get orders to renew the assault. Sherman and Porter worked out a plan to move up the Yazoo and attack the Confederate right flank at Drumgould's Bluff, a mile below Haines's Bluff, with 10,000 troops (Steele's division, and Burbridge's brigade). After dense fog had delayed the water movement the night of the 31st, and bright moonlight the next night, made a surprise movement unlikely, Sherman abandoned his attempts to take the position. On 2 Jan. he dropped down to the mouth of the Yazoo, where McClernand arrived and assumed command. The Federals then undertook the capture of ARKANSAS POST, 4–12 Jan. '63.

Total Federal losses were 1,776 (208 killed, 1,005 wounded, and 563 missing). Of these De Courcy's brigade had 724 casualties and Blair's had 603.

Pemberton reported a loss of 207 (63, 134, 10), and cited the following regiments for outstanding performance: 40th, 42d, and 52d Ga.; 17th, 26th, and 28th La.; 3d, 30th, and 80th Tenn.

According to Livermore, the numbers engaged were 30,720 Federals and 13,792 Confederates.

CHICKERING, Thomas Edward. Union officer. 1824–71. Mass. Col. 3d Mass. Cav. 1 Nov. '62; Bvt. B.G. USV (war service); mustered out 1 Sept. '64. Son of the founder of the Chickering Piano Company, he succeeded his father as its president.

CHILTON, Robert Hall. C.S.A. gen. c. 1816–79. Va. USMA 1837 (48/50); Dragoons-Q.M.-Paymaster. He served on the frontier in the Mexican War (1 brevet) and in Indian fighting before resigning as a Maj. 29 Apr. '61 to become a Lt. Col. in the Adj. Gen.'s office in Richmond the same month. Soon promoted Col., he relieved Richard S. Ewell at the cavalry camp in Ashland. From Sept. '62 until 1 Apr. '64, he was Lee's Chief of Staff and signed the famous lost order of the ANTIETAM CAMPAIGN. Appointed B.G. C.S.A. (Special) 20 Oct. '62, his nomination was rejected by the Senate 11 Apr. '63. Wright says he was reappointed, but fails to give the date. In Apr. '64 he was put in command of the Adj. and I.G. Dept. From May until Nov. '64 he commanded the 57th Va. at the Wilderness and Spotsylvania. He returned to staff duty in Richmond. After the war he was a manufacturer in Georgia.

CHIPMAN, Henry Laurens. Union officer. N.Y. R.A. Lt. Col. 2d Mich. 25 May '61; resigned 24 June '61; Capt. 11th US Inf. 14 May '61; Col. 102d US Col. Inf. 15 Apr. '64; Bvt. B.G. USV. Brevets for Chancellorsville, Gettysburg, war service.

CHIPMAN, Norton Parker. Union officer. Maj. 2d Iowa 23 Sept. '61; Col. Add. A.D.C. 17 Apr. '62; Bvt. B.G. USV (meritorious service in Bureau of Mil. Justice).

CHRIST, Benjamin C. Union officer. Pa. Lt. Col. 5th Pa. 21 Apr. '61; mustered out 25 July '61; Col. 50th Pa. 20 Sept. '61; Bvt. B.G. USV 1 Aug. '64 (Ny River, Petersburg); mustered out 30 Sept. '64. In IX Corps commanded 2d Brig. 1st Div.; 1st Div.; 1st Brig., 1st Div.; 2d Brig., 1st Div.; 3d Brig., 2d Div. (Ohio); 3d Brig., 2d Div. (Tenn.); 1st Brig., 3d Div.; 2d Brig., 3d Div. Died 1869.

CHRISTENSEN, Christian Thomsen. Union officer. Denmark. 1st Lt. 1st N.Y. 24 Apr. '61; Capt. 5 Nov. '61; Maj. A.D.C. Vols. 13 Sept. '62; Maj. Asst. Adj. Gen. Vols. 11 Mar. '63; Lt. Col. Asst. Adj. Gen. Assigned 11 May '64–

22 July '65; Bvt. B.G. USV (war service).

CHRISTIAN, William Henry. Union officer. N.Y. Pvt., Cpl., Sgt., and 1st Sgt. 1846–48; Col. 26th N.Y. 21 May '61; Bvt. B.G. USV (war service); resigned 19 Sept. '62. Commanded 2, 2, III; 2, 2, I. Died 1887.

CHRYSLER, Morgan Henry. Union gen. 1826–90. N.Y. A farmer, he was commissioned Capt. 30th N.Y. 1 June '61, Maj. 11 Mar. '62, Lt. Col. 30 Aug. '62, mustered out 13 June '63 and named Lt. Col. 2d N.Y. Vet. Cav. 8 Sept. '63. He was promoted Col. 13 Dec. '63 and then commanded 4th Brig., Cav. Div., XIII, Gulf (6 Aug.–22 Sept. '64). He also led 1st Brig., Lucas Div. Cav. W. Fla. (28 Mar.–14 Apr. '65) and 3, 1, Cav. Corps, Gulf (28 Apr.–9 May '65), and was promoted B.G. USV 11 Nov. '65. Breveted B.G. USV 23 Jan. '65 and Maj. Gen. USV for war service. He was mustered out in 1866.

CHURCHILL, Mendal. Union officer. Ohio. Capt. 27th Ohio 7 Aug. '61; Maj. 19 Jan. '63; Lt. Col. 31 Mar. '64; Bvt. B.G. USV (war service); resigned 15 Sept. '64. Died 1902.

CHURCHILL, Sylvester. Union officer. Vt. Joining the R.A. in the War of 1812, he was retired Sept. '61 for ill-health and died 7 Dec. '62, having been breveted B.G. USA retroactive to 1847 for the Mexican War. Phisterer lists him as a Civil War general.

CHURCHILL, Thomas James. C.S.A. gen. 1824–1905. Ky. Appt.-Ark. After college he studied law at Transylvania University and fought in the Mexican War, where he was captured. He then became a planter and was Little Rock's postmaster. Commissioned Col. 1st Ark. Mtd. Rifles, he fought at Wilson's Creek and was named B.G. C.S.A. 4 Mar. '62. He then commanded his brigade in the defense of Arkansas Post and was forced

to surrender to McClernand when, without his knowledge, some of his men raised the white flag. He led a detachment of Price's army, fighting Banks during the Red River campaign of 1864 and against Steele at Jenkins' Ferry. Promoted Maj. Gen. 18 Mar. '65, he then followed Kirby Smith to Tex. and unwillingly surrendered there. After the war he was active in Democratic politics and was Ark. Governor in 1880.

CILLEY, Jonathan Prince. Union officer. 1835–? Me. Capt. 1st Me. Cav. 19 Oct. '61; Maj. 15 May '62; Lt. Col. 1 July '64; Bvt. B.G. USV 12 June '65 (war service). He was wounded and captured at Middletown 24 May '62.

CINCINNATI. See GRANT'S HORSES.

CIST, Henry Martyn. Union officer. 1839–1902. Ohio. Pvt. 6th Ohio 20 Apr. '61; 2d Lt. 52d Ohio 16 Oct. '61; 1st Lt. Adj. 74th Ohio 22 Oct. '61; Capt. Asst. Adj. Gen. Vols. 20 Apr. '64; Maj. Asst. Adj. Gen. Vols. 13 Mar. '65; Bvt. B.G. USV. Brevets for war service, Stones River, Chickamauga. Served on staffs of Rosecrans and Thomas. He wrote *Army of the Cumberland* (1882) and collected one of the best private libraries on the Civil War.

CITY BELLE, capture of transport. 3 May '64. RED RIVER CAMPAIGN incident. See ALEXANDRIA, La., 1–8 May '64.

CLANTON, James Holt. C.S.A. gen. 1827–71. Ga. After fighting in the Mexican War as a young man he was a lawyer and legislator. In 1861 he was the Capt. of an Ala. mounted company that served on the Florida coast until fall. At Shiloh he led the 1st Ala. Cav. as Col. and was Bragg's A.D.C. at Farmington. He led a brigade at Booneville and was appointed B.G. C.S.A. 16 Nov. '63. Next fighting at "Ten Islands" on the Coosa River in 1864, he was ordered then to Dalton and was Polk's A.D.C. at Resaca, Adairsville, and

Cassville. He commanded his brigade in the Dept. of Ala., Miss., and Eastern La. until seriously wounded and captured at Bluff Spring (Fla.) on 25 Mar. '65. After the war he was a lawyer and Democratic leader until killed at Knoxville in a private feud.

CLAPP, Dexter E. Union officer. N.Y. Capt. 148th N.Y. 14 Sept. '62; Lt. Col. 38th US Col. Inf. 7 Mar. '64; Bvt. B.G. USV (war service). Commanded 2, 3, XVIII. Died 1882.

CLARK, Charles. C.S.A. gen. and Governor of Mississippi. 1811–77. Ky. After graduating from college in Kentucky, he moved to Mississippi where he taught school, studied law, and sat in the legislature. He fought in the Mexican War and was named first B.G. and then Maj. Gen. in the state militia when Civil War came. He was appointed B.G. C.S.A. 22 May '61 and was wounded at Shiloh commanding his division. In July '62 he was wounded and captured at Baton Rouge. After being taken to New Orleans, his wife was allowed through the lines to nurse him. Never able to walk without crutches, he resigned upon his exchange 31 Oct. '63 and was elected Governor to succeed Pettus in that year. He practiced law and ran his plantation after the war.

CLARK, George Washington. Union officer. Ind. 1st Lt. 3d Iowa 24 June '61; resigned 17 July '62; Col. 34th Iowa 15 Oct. '62; Bvt. B.G. USV (war service). Commanded 2, 4, XIII. Died 1898.

CLARK, Gideon. Union officer. Pa. Lt. Col. 119th Pa. 1 Sept. '62; Bvt. B.G. USV (Petersburg 1865). Commanded 3, 1, VI.

CLARK, Henry Toole. C.S.A. Gov. of North Carolina. ?–1874. A graduate of the University of North Carolina, he was president of the state senate and succeeded to the governorship upon John W. Ellis's death 7 July '61. He

served in this post until 1 Jan. '63, when Zebulon B. Vance was elected. After the war he again served in the legislature.

CLARK, John Bullock, Jr. C.S.A. gen. 1831–1903. Mo. After attending Missouri University, he graduated from Harvard Law School and practiced until the Civil War, holding the commission of Lt. in the Mo. Inf. He commanded a militia unit at Wilsor's Creek, was commissioned Capt. 6th Mo., and was a major at the battles of Carthage (5 July '61) and Springfield (25 Oct. '61). Promoted Col. by '62, he led a brigade at Pea Ridge and was appointed B.G. C.S.A. 6 Mar. '64, serving under Marmaduke and Shelby. After the war he was a lawyer and US Congressman 1873–83. His father, John B. Clark, Sr., was a prewar Congressman, a B.G. in the Mo. State Guard 1861–62, and a Confederate Congressman.

CLARK, John S. Union officer. N.Y. Col. 19th N.Y. 22 May '61; Col. Add. A.D.C. 18 Nov. '61; Bvt. B.G. USV (war service).

CLARK, Meriwether Lewis. C.S.A. officer. 1809–81. Mo. USMA 1830 (23/42); Inf. He served in garrison and the Black Hawk War, resigning in 1833 to become an architect, civil engineer, and legislator. Volunteering for the Mexican War, he was appointed B.G. Mo. State Guard in Oct. '62 and commissioned Maj. C.S.A. in Mar. '62. Until Apr. of that year he was Price's Chief of Arty. and then served as Col. of Arty. under Bragg from May–Dec. '62. He was on Bragg's staff at Stones River and in Aug. '64 was given inspection duty for the Confederate Ordnance Dept. Heitman incorrectly lists him as a gen.; he appears on none of the authenticated lists, and Cullum gives his highest rank as Col. C.S.A. After the war he was commandant of cadets and professor of mathematics at Ky. Mil. Inst. Son of

William Clark .of the Lewis and Clark exploration team.

CLARK, William Thomas. Union gen. 1831–1905. Conn. A schoolteacher and lawyer, he raised the 13th Iowa "with the assistance of a chaplain, a drummer, and a fifer" (D.A.B.) and was commissioned 1st Lt. Adj. 2 Nov. '61. He was promoted Capt. Asst. A.G. Vols. 6 Mar. '62, fighting at Shiloh, Corinth, Port Gibson, Raymond, Jackson, Champion's Hill, and Vicksburg. As Maj. Asst. A.G. USV 24 Nov. '62 and Lt. Col. Asst. A.G. Assigned 10 Feb. '63–22 Apr. '65, he was McPherson's A.G. and brought Sherman word of his death before Atlanta. He commanded 1, 3, XV, Tenn. (26 Jan.–26 Apr. '65) and 2, 4, XV, Tenn. (26 Apr.–1 May '65), was promoted B.G. USV 31 May '65 and sent to Texas to command 3d Div., XXV, in the fall of '65. There he recommended the purchase of Matamoros in an effort to thwart Maximilian, a scheme endorsed by Sherman and Grant but vetoed by Washington. He was breveted B.G. USV 22 July '64 for Atlanta and Maj. Gen. USV 24 Nov. '65 for war service. After resigning (1866) in Galveston, he helped organize one of the first national banks in Texas. Entering public life as a "carpetbagger" in reconstruction Texas, he had the backing of the Negro faction. Later, in the Bureau of Internal Revenue, he was called "the last of the carpetbaggers" in Texas. His wartime staff work is termed "energetic and efficient," and he is described as wearing "for forty years . . . the same type of slouch hat and the same type of high-top boots." (D.A.B.)

CLARKE, Henry F. Union officer. c. 1821–87. Pa. USMA 1843 (12/39); Arty.-Comsy. He served in the Mexican War (1 brevet), taught artillery and mathematics at West Point, and fought in the Seminole War before being Chief of Commissariat of the Utah Expedition. Promoted Maj. Comsy. of Subsist. 3 Aug. '61 and Col. Add. A.D.C. 28 Sept. '61, he was Chief of Commissariat for the Dept. of Fla. 13 Apr.–31 May '61 and of the Army of the Potomac 2 July '61–8 Jan. '64. He then held similar posts in N.Y. and New England and continued in the R.A., retiring in 1884 as Col. He was breveted B.G. and Maj. Gen. for Gettysburg and war service, respectively.

CLARKE, William Hyde. Union officer. Asst. A.G., USV (Maj.). Bvt. B.G. USV 13 Mar. '65 (Phisterer). Not listed as an officer by Heitman.

CLARY, Robert E. Union officer. Mass. c. 1805–90. USMA 1828 (13/33); Inf.-Q.M. He served on the frontier and in the Seminole War and was Chief Q.M. of the Dept. of W. Va. Nov. '61–July '62. Holding the same position in the Army of Va. until Oct. '62 and in the Dept. of the Northwest until 20 Mar. '63, he was promoted Col. Add. A.D.C. 5 July '62 and Lt. Col. Deputy Q.M. Gen. 15 Apr. '64. He was in the Q.M. Gen.'s office until 24 Aug '64, when he took charge of the Memphis Depot until 1866. Continuing in the R.A., he was retired in 1869 as Col. and breveted B.G. USA.

CLAY, Cassius Marcellus. Politician and Union gen. 1810–1903. Ky. A lawyer and politician who fought in the Mexican War, he was a crusading aboli-tionist and editor in the stormy border-state politics of Kentucky. Appointed Minister to Russia 28 Mar. '61, he delayed his departure to organize troops for the defense of Washington. When appointed Maj. Gen. USV 11 Apr. '62, he returned in June to accept the commission. Soon, however, he announced that he would not fight so long as slavery continued to be protected in the Southern states. Resigning 11 Mar. '63, he returned to Russia where he remained as Minister until 1869. Upon his return he continued to be active in politics as a member of the liberal Republican movement in 1872, supporting Horace Greeley for president and attacking Grant's administration. He was a cousin of Henry Clay.

CLAY, Cecil. Union officer. Pa. 1st Lt. 58th Pa. 1 Sept. '61; Capt. 1 Jan. '62; Maj. 30 Sept. '64; Lt. Col. 19 Nov. '64; Bvt. B.G. USV (war service). Medal of Honor 19 Apr. '92 for Ft. Harrison (Va.) 29 Sept. '64 where he was W.I.A., losing right arm and severely wounded in his left while leading a charge.

CLAY, Clement Claiborne. Confed. statesman. 1816–1882. After serving as US Sen. from Ala., he became Confederate Sen. and was sent by Jefferson Davis in 1864 to Canada to negotiate peace with Lincoln. After a year in Canada Lincoln decided not to receive the delegation and Clay returned to the South. Upon the assassination of Lincoln, a reward was offered for him in the belief that while in Canada he had taken part in the conspiracy. Giving himself up, he was held in prison for a year without trial and then released.

CLAYTON, Henry DeLamar. C.S.A. gen. 1827–89. Ga. Appt.-Ala. Graduating from Emory and Henry College, he was a lawyer and legislator when commissioned Col. 1st Ala. 28 Mar. '61. He commanded a brigade at Pensacola and later organized the 39th Ala., becoming its Col. and leading it at Stones River. Seriously wounded in that battle, he was appointed B.G. C.S.A. upon his recovery (22 Apr. '63) and led the Ala. Brig. at Chickamauga (again wounded), Dalton, New Hope Church, the battles around Atlanta, Jonesboro, and the Tenn. campaign. Promoted Maj. Gen. 7 July '64, he took over the division on this date and also fought in the Caro-

linas. After the war he was a planter, lawyer, and judge.

CLAYTON, Powell. Union gen. 1833–1914. Pa. Educated at a Pa. military academy and Delaware engineering school, he was a civil engineer when commissioned Capt. 1st Kans. 29 May '61. He was named Lt. Col. 5th Kans. Cav. 28 Dec. '61, Col. 7 Mar. '62, and B.G. USV 1 Aug. '64. In the Dept. of the Tenn. he commanded 2d Brig., Cav. Div. East Ark. (Apr.–May '63); Cav. Brig., 13th Div., XVI (28 July–10 Aug. '63) and Cav. Brig., Ark. Exp., XVI (4 Aug. '63–6 Jan. '64). He was in charge of the Post of Pine Bluff when he repulsed Marmaduke and in the Dept. of Ark., VII Corps, also led the Ind. Cav. Brig., and the Separate Brig., Dismounted Cav. Div. (30 May–10 June '65). Settling on a cotton plantation near Pine Bluff after being mustered out 24 Aug. '65, he was Republican Gov. in 1868 and lifelong Republican boss in that state. He was impeached by the House in 1871, but the Senate was friendly, and the charges were dropped. In that same year he was elected US Senator and was indicted for faulty election procedures upon reaching Washington, but these charges were also dropped. He was active in the building of Eureka Springs (Ark.) and in railroading. Served as Ambassador to Mexico 1897–1905.

CLEARY, Robert E. Misspelling by Phisterer for Robert Emmet CLARY.

CLEBURNE, Patrick Ronayne. C.S.A. gen. 1828–64. Ireland. Appt.-Ark. In his native country he failed French, Latin, and Greek in the apothecaries' test and joined the army, finally purchasing his release and coming to America. He was a druggist and lawyer when the war came and he organized the Yell Rifles. With this unit he seized the Little Rock Arsenal and was commissioned Capt. when Ark. seceded. Named Col. 1st Ark. and later with the 15th Ark., he was appointed B.G. C.S.A. 4 Mar. '62 and fought at Shiloh, Richmond (Ky.) (wounded), and Perryville. He was then promoted Maj. Gen. 20 Dec. '62, to rank from the 13th, and commanded the 2d Div. in Hardee's corps at Stones River. At Chickamauga he led his division under Hill and returned to Hardee's corps for Chattanooga. In the Atlanta campaign he led his division and succeeded Hardee as corps commander, receiving the C.S.A. Thanks of Congress for saving Bragg's artillery and wagons at Ringgold Gap. During this campaign he entered the field of politics by signing, with 13 other officers, a statement that slaves should be freed and used as soldiers. Johnston declined to forward it to Richmond on the grounds that it was not really a military subject, but someone else sent it to Davis. Cleburne went with Hood to Tenn., where he was killed 30 Nov. '64 at Franklin. He was called the "Stonewall Jackson of the West."

CLENDENIN, David Ramsay. Union officer. Pa. Capt. 8th Ill. 18 Sept. '61; Maj. 18 Sept. '61; Lt. Col. 5 Dec. '62; Bvt. B.G. USV 11 July '65 (war service). Died 1895.

CLINGMAN, Thomas Lanier. C.S.A. gen. 1812–97. N.C. Standing first in his class at Chapel Hill, he studied law and entered politics, first as a Whig and later as a Democrat. He sat in the state legislature, US Congress, and then in the C.S.A. Congress. Commissioned Col. 25th N.C. in the fall of 1861, he was appointed B.G. C.S.A. 17 May '62 and participated in the defense of Goldsboro, Battery Wagner, and New Bern in Feb. '64. He commanded a brigade under Hoke at the Wilderness and fought at Drewry's Bluff, Cold Harbor (wounded), the Petersburg assaults and siege, and Weldon R.R. (severely wounded). After a

long convalescence he was able to rejoin his command only a few days before the surrender at Greensboro. After the war he was a power in the state Democratic party and, indulging his liking for mountain exploration in the Great Smokies, he developed the mica mines in that area.

CLITZ, Henry B. Union officer. c. 1824–88. N.Y. Appt.-At Large. USMA 1845 (36/41); Inf. He served in the Mexican War (1 brevet) and taught infantry tactics at West Point before going to the frontier. During the Civil War he was in the defense of Ft. Pickens, promoted Maj. 12th U.S. Inf. 14 May '61 and fought in the Peninsular campaign, where he was wounded once at Yorktown and twice at Gaines's Mill. Captured at the latter battle, he was paroled on 17 July '62 after being held in Libby and served as Commandant of Cadets at West Point until 4 July '64. He then served in garrison and continued in the R.A. after the war, retiring in 1885 as Col. 10th U.S. Inf. He was breveted for Gaines's Mill and war service (B.G. USA).

CLOUGH, Joseph Messer. Union officer. N.H. Capt. 4th N.H. 18 Sept. '61; Lt. Col. 18th N.H. 18 Oct. '64; Col. 29 July '65; Bvt B.G. USV (war service).

CLOVER HILL, Va., 9 Apr. '65. Engagement of XXIV Corps and Birney's (2d) Division of XXV Corps more commonly known as APPOMATTOX COURTHOUSE.

CLUSERET, Gustave Paul. Union gen. 1823–1900. France. Educated at St. Cyr, he won the Legion of Honor (Chevalier) five months after being commissioned for suppressing the Insurrection of June 1848. He fought in Algeria and the Crimea, commanded Garibaldi's French Legion, and was breveted for gallantry and wounded at

Capua. Coming to America, he was named Col. Add. A.D.C. to McClellan 10 Mar. '62 and later joined Frémont's advance guard. He fought at Cross Keys during Jackson's Valley campaign and was promoted B.G. USV 14 Oct. '62. Resigning 2 Mar. '63, he advocated Frémont's nomination for president. Returning to France, he became politically involved and went into exile in Geneva.

C. N. An abbreviation in Civil War reports for certain portions of INDIAN TERRITORY. The latter was divided into tribal areas. (See O.R. atlas plates CLIX-CLXI.) C.N. could refer to Cherokee, Creek, Choctaw, or Chickasaw Nation.

COATES, Benjamin Franklin. Union officer. Ohio. Lt. Col. 91st Ohio 10 Aug. '62; Col. 9 Dec. '64; Bvt. B.G. USV (war service). Commanded 2d Brig., 2d Inf. Div. and 2d Brig., 1st Inf. Div., Army of W. Va. Died 1899.

COATES, James Henry. Union officer. Pa. Capt. 11th Ill. 30 July '61; Maj. 4 Sept. '62; Lt. Col. 31 May '63; Col. 8 July '63; Bvt. B.G. USV (war service). Commanded 2, 1, XVII.

COBB, Amasa. Union officer. Ill. Col. 5th Wis. 12 July '61; elected to Congress and resigned 25 Dec. '62; Col. 43d Wis. 29 Sept. '64; commanded Johnsonville (Tenn.) post; Bvt. B.G. USV (Williamsburg, Golding's Farm, Va.; Antietam). Commanded 1, 2, VI; 3d Brig., 1st Sub Dist. Mid. Tenn.

COBB, Howell, C.S.A. gen. 1815–68. Ga. The son of a wealthy and educated planter, and brother of T. R. R. Cobb, he studied at the Univ. of Ga. and became a lawyer. As Whig Congressman, he was an outspoken foe of sectionalism and urged loyalty to the Union and compromise in the slavery situation. He was Governor of his state 1851–54 and Buchanan's first Sec. of the Treasury.

After Lincoln's inauguration, however, he became an advocate of secession and was the chairman of the Montgomery convention. Commissioned Col. 16th Ga. 15 July '61, he was appointed B.G. C.S.A. 13 Feb. '62 and fought at Antietam. Sent to Ga. in 1863 to command the state's reserve forces, he was promoted Maj. Gen. 9 Sept. of that year and took command of the Dist. of Ga. His forces defeated and received the surrender of Stoneman. After the war he returned to the law.

COBB, Thomas Reade Rootes. C.S.A. gen. 1823–62. Ga. After the Univ. of Ga. he practiced law and wrote numerous books on the law, on slavery as an institution, as well as newspaper and magazine articles. He is said to have been one of the most potent forces in taking Ga. out of the Union. After serving in the C.S.A. Congress like his brother Howell, he was commissioned Col. of Cobb's Legion 28 Aug. '61. He led these troops in the Seven Days' Battles, at 2d Bull Run and Antietam before being appointed B.G. C.S.A. 1 Nov. '62. While commanding his brigade under McLaws at Fredericksburg he was killed (13 Dec. '62).

COBHAM, George Ashworth, Jr. Union officer. England. Lt. Col. 111th Pa. 28 Jan. '62; Col. 7 Nov. '62; Bvt. B.G. USV 19 July '64 (Chancellorsville, Gettysburg, Wauhatchie, Lookout Mountain, Missionary Ridge, Ringgold, Mill Creek Gap, Peach Tree Creek). K.I.A. 20 July '64 Peach Tree Creek. Commanded 2, 2, XII (Potomac; Cumberland) and 3, 2, XX.

COBURN, Abner. Gov. of Me. 1803–85. Me. A surveyor and lumberman, he was also engaged in railroading when elected as a Whig to the legislature. Joining the Republican party, he was chosen Governor in 1862, retiring from public life but continuing to be active in Republican councils and state education.

COBURN, John. Union officer. Ind. Col. 33d Ind. 16 Sept. '61; Bvt. B.G. USV (war service); mustered out 20 Sept. '64. Commanded 27th Brig., 7th Div. (Ohio); 1st Brig., 3d Div., Army of Ky. (Ohio); then in the Army of the Cumberland he commanded 1st Brig., Baird's division, Army of Ky. (see KENTUCKY, UNION DEPARTMENT AND ARMY OF); 3, 1, Res. Corps; Unattached Brig.; Coburn's brigade, Murfreesboro Tenn. Div.; 2, 1, XI; 2, 3, XX. (Source: Dyer, pp. 450 and 542; his index has two errors on Coburn's assignments.)

COCHRAN, John. Erroneous listing by Phisterer for COCHRANE, JOHN, B.G. USV.

COCHRANE, John. Union gen. 1813–98. N.Y. He had been a Congressman and Buchanan's appointee to the USMA Board of Visitors when he was commissioned Col. 65th N.Y. 11 June '61 and B.G. USV 17 July '62. He fought at Fair Oaks, Malvern Hill, and Fredericksburg, commanding 3, 1, IV (5 July–26 Sept. '62) at Antietam and Williamsport. Resigning 25 Feb. '63 with a physical disability, he ran for vice-president on the ticket with Frémont in the 1864 election and was later a Tammany Hall leader.

COCKE, Philip St. George. C.S.A. gen. 1809–61. Va. After attending the Univ. of Va., he graduated from USMA in '32 (6/45) and went into the Arty. He served in garrison until resigning '34 to manage his seven plantations in Virginia and Mississippi. Writing extensively on agriculture, he also gave a great deal of time and money to V.M.I. Commissioned B.G. in the state army 21 Apr. '61, he commanded the military district along the Potomac until mustered into the C.S.A. as Col. Mustering troops in the Va. Piedmont, he

began concentrating his forces 9 May '61 at Manassas Junction. He led the 5th Brig. at 1st Bull Run and Blackburn's Ford. He commanded the troops left along Bull Run until appointed B.G. C.S.A. 21 Oct. '61. Returning home shortly thereafter in shattered health, and being, D.A.B. says, "overwrought and naturally impetuous," he killed himself 26 Dec.

COCKERILL, Joseph Randolph. Union officer. Va. Col. 70th Ohio 20 Dec. '61; Bvt. B.G. USV (war service); resigned 13 Apr. '64. Commanded 3, Dist. Memphis, XIII; 2, 1st Dist. Memphis R.W., XIII; 2, 1, XVII; 2, 1, XVI; 3, 1, XVI; 3, 4, XV. Died 1875.

COCKRELL, Francis Marion. C.S.A. gen. 1834–1915. Mo. After college he practiced law. Enlisted when the Civil War came. He fought from Carthage to Vicksburg (where he commanded the 1st Mo. as Col.) and was appointed B.G. C.S.A. 18 July '63. He led a brigade under French in the Atlanta campaign and ended the war at Mobile. He was five times wounded and three times captured. After the war he practiced law with T. T. Crittenden and succeeded Carl Schurz in 1874 as US Senator. In 1905, on the day he left the Senate, Theodore Roosevelt appointed him to the I.C.C., and he held this post until 1910. D.A.B. describes him as an "uncompromising Democrat . . . over six feet tall and weighing 200 pounds. . . ."

COEHORN MORTAR. Originally a small muzzle-loading smoothbore mortar or howitzer, caliber generally 4⅗ inches, named for its Dutch inventor, Baron Menno van Coehoorn (1641–1704). Mounted on a block or platform, it was portable, easily adjusted, took little powder, and was particularly effective in sieges. The US Army had a 24-pounder brass coehorn that weighed 164 pounds (Scott), or 296 pounds when mounted on its oak mortar bed (Wilhelm). Larger siege mortars are sometimes incorrectly referred to as coehorns.

COGGIN'S POINT (James R.), Va. See HAMPTON-ROSSER CATTLE RAID, 16 Sept. '64.

COGSWELL, William. Union officer. 1838–95. Mass. Capt. 2d Mass. 11 May '61; Lt. Col. 23 Oct. '62; Col. 25 June '63; Bvt. B.G. USV 15 Dec. '64. Commanded 3, 3, XX. Went to sea "before the mast" while still in his teens and later became a prominent lawyer and politician.

COIT, James Bolles. Union officer. Conn. Pvt. Co. A and Sgt. Maj. 2d Conn. 16 Apr.–5 Aug. '61; 1st Lt. 14th Conn. 20 Aug. '62; Capt. 1 May '63; Maj. 11 Oct. '63; Bvt. B.G. USV; resigned 6 Sept. '64. Brevets for Antietam, Gettysburg, Wilderness. Died 1894.

COLD HARBOR (FIRST), Va. 27 June '62. GAINES'S MILL.

COLD HARBOR, Va., 31 May–12 June '64. From TOTOPOTOMOY CREEK Grant and Lee started the night of 1 June toward the vital road junction of (Old) Cold Harbor. Fitz Lee's cavalry had been holding this place the morning of the 31st and had just been reinforced by Clingman's brigade when they were attacked and driven back by Torbert's (1st) cavalry division. Clingman lost 65 captured. Having learned that W. F. Smith's XVIII Corps was about to arrive on the battlefield from Butler's immobilized army at Bermuda Hundred, Lee acted quickly to recapture Cold Harbor and, if possible, roll up the Federal left before Grant could attempt a similar operation against his own right. Anderson's corps was moved from the Confederate center to the right flank. Hoke's entire division, which Beauregard had sent from the Bermuda Hundred lines, was in position on Anderson's right before dawn. The Confederates attacked early in the morning and were repulsed. Led by the inexperienced Col. L. M. Keitt, Kershaw's brigade broke and was routed. Anderson's attack was halted, and Hoke's division did nothing. Sheridan's cavalry (Torbert had been reinforced by Gregg), armed with the new Spencer carbines and with artillery support, held until Wright's corps came up at 9 A.M. to relieve them.

Although this mismanaged attack had deprived him of an irretrievable opportunity, Lee ordered strength shifted to his right flank. Three Federal attacks against the left and center of the line were repulsed. Smith's march from White House had been delayed by two erroneous orders. At 6 P.M. the VI and XVIII Corps assaulted the divisions of Kershaw, Pickett, Field, and Hoke. The Confederate brigades of Clingman and Woffert were driven back by Rickett's Division (3, VI), which hit between Hoke and Kershaw. Hunton's brigade (Pickett) reinforced Hoke and recaptured some ground. The Federals withdrew with a loss of 1,200 killed and wounded in VI Corps and 1,000 in XVIII Corps. Col. E. S. Kellogg, commanding the newly-joined 2d Conn. Heavy Arty. (in Upton's brigade, 2, 1, VI), was killed.

This same day (1 June) Wilson's cavalry division with the mission of destroying the railroad at Hanover C. H. was heavily engaged by the divisions of Hampton and W. H. F. Lee. Chapman's brigade was sent to destroy the two railroad bridges across the South Anna, while McIntosh's (1st) brigade went to Ashland to cover the operation and also to destroy the railroad. McIntosh was attacked by Hampton with Rosser's brigade from the east and then by W. H. F. Lee from the south. Although the 1st Maine Cav. was sent from Chapman's brigade to reinforce him, McIntosh was driven back to Hanover C. H. where

Wilson's division encamped for the night. The bridges had been destroyed.

The night of 1 June Hancock's corps moved to Cold Harbor from its previous position on the Totopotomoy and arrived at 6:30 A.M. Its late arrival caused postponement until 5 P.M. of an attack planned for that morning. The same night the Confederate divisions of Breckinridge, Mahone, and Wilcox moved south to fill the gap between Cold Harbor and the Chickahominy on the south.

On Lee's left, Early's corps was reinforced by Heth's division and again attacked toward Bethesda Church, where the IX and V Corps held the Federal right. Rodes advanced during the afternoon with Heth and Gordon on his left and right respectively. Burnside, on the right, was in the midst of his withdrawal and his covering force was driven back by Rodes with the loss of many prisoners. Skirmishers on the exposed right of Warren's V Corps were also surprised and captured. Griffin's division, which had been assembled at Bethesda Church in preparation for the march south, was deployed to counterattack. Rodes was forced back and Doles was killed. Crittenden's division was hit by Heth, but held its ground until Willcox and Potter could be deployed to block the Confederate advance. Early's three divisions intrenched for the night along the Shady Grove Church Road.

Grant's general assault planned for 2 June was postponed from early morning until 5 P.M., and then until 4:30 A.M. on the 3d. A heavy rain started the afternoon of the 2d and continued through the night. Up until this time the weather had been unbearably hot.

Since this is such a complicated action, it might be best to take an over-all look at the battle before going into more detail.

The main Federal assaults of 3 June were made by the II, VI, and XVIII

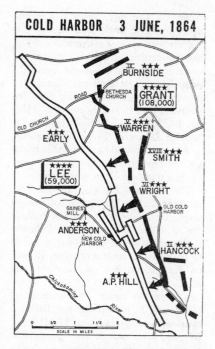

COLD HARBOR   3 JUNE, 1864

SCALE IN MILES

Corps (from left to right) against the corps of A. P. Hill (on the south) and Anderson. The Army of the Potomac had a strength of 108,000 against Lee's 59,000. The attacks were repulsed with a loss of 7,000 Federals to probably less than 1,500 Confederates. "The time of actual advance was not over eight minutes," wrote Martin T. McMahon in *Battles and Leaders* (IV, 217). "In that little period more men fell bleeding as they advanced than in any other like period of time throughout the war. A strange and terrible feature of this battle was that as the three gallant corps moved on, each was enfiladed while receiving the full force of the enemy's direct fire in front. . . . Each corps commander reported and complained to General Meade that the other corps commanders, right or left, as the case might be, failed to protect him from enfilading fire by silencing batteries in their respective fronts: ... The three corps had moved upon diverging lines, each directly facing the enemy in its immediate front, and the farther each had advanced the more its flank had become exposed." Although the facts do not support the popular statement that Grant "lost ten thousand men in twenty minutes" (Miller, III, 87), Cold Harbor represents a horrible failure of Federal generalship.

With this general background in mind, we can now go back and look at some of the other high-lights of the battle. The attack had started at 4:30 A.M. all along the line. The Federals advanced through murderous frontal and enfilade fire to within 30 to 50 yards from the Confederate works before being forced to lie down to take protection. Barlow on the left, Gibbon on the right, and Birney in reserve, had led the II Corps attack on the south. The brigades of Miles and J. R. Brooke led Barlow's division, and Byrnes and MacDougall followed in the second line. The division captured an advanced position after a heavy fight, turned three enemy guns on the Confederates, but was repulsed in an attempt to carry the main works. A counterattack by troops of Breckinridge and A. P. Hill retook the position. Brooke was severely wounded; Byrnes and Col. O. H. Morris of the 66th N.Y. were killed. (Col. L. O. Morris, 7th N. Y. Hv. Arty. was killed in the trenches on 4 June.)

Gibbon's division attacked with the brigades of R. O. Tyler and T. A. Smyth leading and H. B. McKeen and J. T. Owen in the second line. They penetrated through a swampy area held with only light forces but covered from strong Confederate works on an encircling ridge to the rear. The attackers became separated and were counterattacked by a brigade under Finegan. Tyler and McKeen were killed. Col. Frank Haskell succeeded McKeen and was mortally

wounded. Col. James P. McMahon, 164th New York, died after planting the regimental color on the enemy's main works. Instead of pushing forward to exploit the lodgment made by Smyth and McMahon, Owen deployed on Smyth's left and the opportunity for a penetration was lost. Col. Peter A. Porter died at the head of his 8th New York Hv. Arty. a few yards from the enemy's main position. Gibbon reported a loss of 65 officers and 1,032 men killed and wounded.

The attack of Wright's VI Corps had been made with the divisions of Russell, Ricketts, and Neill on line from left to right. The advance works on the right were captured, but fourteen successive assaults on Anderson's main line were repulsed prior to 8 o'clock. (R. E. Lee, III, 389.) Wright's men maintained their advanced positions. They had lost 800 killed and wounded.

Smith's XVIII Corps attacked across an open area swept by frontal and enfilade fire. Devens' division was posted on the right as flank protection. Martindale was to take advantage of a ravine to make the main attack while Brooks advanced on his left and maintained contact with him and with VI Corps on the left. Martindale carried the enemy outpost line, but had to change front somewhat to answer a heavy fire against his right. Being enfiladed from the other flank also, he was ordered to wait until Brooks could advance on his left to neutralize that fire. Martindale mistook firing from the VI Corps front to be that of Brooks's advance and resumed his own attack. Stannard's brigade made three gallant but unsuccessful assaults. The attack column being formed by Brooks came under such heavy fire that he was ordered to keep his men under cover until it ceased. When Smyth reported to Meade that he could not advance until the fire on his flanks was silenced, Meade replied at 8 A.M. that both Smyth and Wright were to press their attacks independently of each other. Burnham's brigade was the only one Smith could use for a continued attack. While it formed, additional artillery was brought up to attempt to neutralize the galling cross fire the Confederates continued to pour into XVIII and VI Corps.

At 1:30 P.M. Meade ordered further frontal assaults suspended. Smith had lost about 1,000 officers and men, including four regimental commanders. (Col. F. F. Wead, Lt. Cols. Edgar Perry, 139th N.Y.; Hiram Anderson, Jr., 58th Pa.; G. E. Marshall, 92d N.Y.); Col. J. C. Drake was killed commanding a brigade (2, 3, XVIII).

On the right (Bethesda Church area) Burnside sent forward the divisions of Potter and Willcox early 3 June and drove back the outposts of the line Early had established late 1 June along Shady Grove Church road (see above). The Confederates held their advanced positions with Heth on the north flank and Rodes and Gordon to his right. Early reported heavy skirmishing during the day, especially against Cook's brigade of Heth. The Federal brigades of Curtin (1, 2, IX) and Hartranft (1, 3, IX) captured some outposts. Griffin's division (1, V) reinforced IX Corps in this operation and repulsed a counterattack by Gordon. D. B. Birney's division (3, II) was sent to reinforce Warren's left. Federal losses were about 800 in IX Corps and 400 in V Corps.

An attack planned by Burnside to start at 1 P.M. was canceled by Meade. Wilson's cavalry, however, which was supposed to attack the Confederate left (north) and rear in conjunction with this operation, skirmished with Barringer's brigade at Haw's Shop. When the Confederate cavalry withdrew, Wilson engaged Heth's left (Fry's brigade) near Via's house; he took and held some rifle pits for an hour before withdrawing to Haw's Shop without having made contact with Burnside's flank units. After making several counterattacks, Early withdrew at night to his previous position.

At 8 P.M. Breckinridge and Finegan were attacked while re-establishing their outposts, and shortly thereafter Hoke was attacked. The Federals were repulsed.

The lines remained stabilized within a hundred yards of each other for ten days. It was not until 7 June that Grant requested a truce to pick up the wounded between the lines and bury the dead.

In his memoirs Grant said "I have always regretted that the last assault at Cold Harbor was ever made." (II, p. 276.) Humphreys says ". . . as early as seven o'clock General Grant had directed General Meade to suspend the offensive the moment it became certain that an assault could not succeed" (p. 188). Freeman has pointed out, however, that Lee "had won his last great battle in the field." (*R. E. Lee,* III, 391.)

In a month of incessant campaigning the North had lost 50,000 and the South 32,000. This represented 41 per cent of Grant's original strength and 46 per cent of Lee's. But whereas the North had replaced its losses within a few weeks, the South was virtually unable to restore Lee's losses.

COLD SPRING FOUNDRY. Located across the Hudson from the US Military Academy and known also as the West Point Foundry, this installation, under Robert P. PARROTT, turned from such peaceful manufacturing as machinery for the Jersey City waterworks to the production of 25 guns and 7,000 projectiles a week. During the Civil War it produced more than 1,700 guns and 3,000,000 projectiles (Benton, 549; Wise says 1,200 guns, having perhaps incorrectly deciphered the broken type of Benton's footnote). Lincoln visited the foundry on 24 June '62.

COLE, George W. Union officer. N.Y. Commissioned Capt. 12th N.Y. 13 May '61, he was named to the same rank in the 3d N.Y. Cav. 20 Sept. '61 and promoted Maj. 31 Dec. '62. As Col. 2d U.S. Col. Cav. 10 Dec. '63, he was breveted B.G. USV and Maj. Gen. USV for war service and mustered out in 1866. He died 1875.

COLFAX, Schuyler. Union politician. 1823–85. N.Y. After a smattering of law and several years as a clerk, he became a newspaper editor and owner in Ind. He ran unsuccessfully for a number of offices as a Whig and joined the new Republican party. Elected to Congress in 1854, he was Speaker of the House from Dec. '63 until 1869, when he was elected vice-president on Grant's ticket. He served for one term and continued to be active in politics but was implicated in the *Crédit Mobilier* scandal in 1873. This shadowed the remainder of his life, although no charges were ever proved against him.

COLGROVE, Silas. Union officer. N.Y. Capt. 8th Ind. 20 Apr. '61; Lt. Col. 27 Apr. '61; mustered out 5 Aug. '61; Col. 27th Ind. 12 Sept. '61; Bvt. B.G. USV 7 Aug. '64 (war service); mustered out 4 Nov. '64.

COLLIER, Frederick H. Union officer. Pa. Col. 139th Pa. 1 Sept. '62; Bvt. B.G. USV (war service). Commanded 3, 3, VI.

COLLIS, Charles Henry Tucky. Union officer. Ireland. Commissioned Capt. of an independent company of Pa. Zouaves 17 Aug. '61, he was named Col. 114th Pa. 1 Sept. '62 and mustered out 20 May '65. He was breveted B.G. USV 28 Oct. '64 and Maj. Gen. USV for war service and given the Medal of Honor 1893 for Fredericksburg. He died 1902.

COLQUITT, Alfred Holt. C.S.A. gen. 1824–94. Ga. After graduating from Princeton, he studied law, fought in the Mexican War, and became a planter before entering politics. An extreme states-rights Democrat, he was in US Congress and the state legislature, and attended the Ga. secession convention. Named Capt. of C.S.A. Inf. and then Col. 27 May '61, he commanded the 6th Ga. at Williamsburg and the other Peninsula battles, and led Colquitt's brigade under Hill at Antietam. Appointed B.G. C.S.A. 1 Sept. '62, he commanded his brigade at Fredericksburg and Chancellorsville and went with D. H. Hill to N. C., fighting at Olustee (Fla.). Back in Va. for the Wilderness and Spotsylvania, he also commanded his brigade during the Petersburg siege. A licensed Methodist preacher and an early and vigorous champion of temperance, he was "an unusually astute politician" (D.A.B.). He was Democratic Governor of Georgia 1876–82. Accused of dishonesty, which was never proved, he sat in the US Senate until his death.

COLSTON, Raleigh Edward. C.S.A. gen. 1825–96. France. He received his early education in Paris and then came home to graduate from V.M.I., remaining to teach French. Commissioned Col. 16th Va. and named B.G. C.S.A. 24 Dec. '61, he led his brigade under Longstreet in the Peninsula and was on sick leave from June until Dec. '62. Given a brigade under Jackson in Apr. '63, he commanded a division at Chancellorsville and served under Beauregard in the defense of Petersburg in 1864. He was in command at Lynchburg at war's end. After establishing a military school in N.C., he later served as Col. in the Egyptian Army. While on an exploration trip in the Sudan he fell from a camel and was paralyzed from the waist down. In this condition he continued his explorations until months later his party connected with another that had come down from the source of the Nile. Sent by litter back to Alexandria, he was discharged in '79 and came home, impoverished and crippled. He held a job as clerk in the War Dept. and spent his last two years in the C.S.A. Soldiers' Home in Richmond.

COLT REPEATING RIFLE, Model 1855. Samuel Colt made an unsuccessful attempt to use the principle of his splendid six-shot pistol in the production of a repeating rifle. The weapon was unpopular because of a gas and flame leakage between the cylinder and the barrel and because there occasionally was an accidental discharge of all six barrels simultaneously.

COLT REVOLVER. In early 1836 the 22-year-old Samuel Colt patented and started producing his revolvers. Despite the antipathy of Army Ordnance experts, and the resulting failure of his first "Patent Arms Manufacturing Company" in 1842, Colt finally gained military acceptance of his revolver when the Mexican War created a demand for revolvers.

The first type manufactured in quantity for the government was the Model 1848, of which about 30,000 were produced. Known as the "Dragoon" or "Holster Pistol"—the word revolver not yet being current—this was a huge cal. .44 rifled pistol that weighed four pounds one ounce.

The Model 1851 "Navy" was a cal. .36 pistol that weighed only two pounds, ten ounces. Over 200,000 of these were made up until 1865. The "Navy" remained more popular in the South and was the prototype of practically all Confederate-made revolvers (Albaugh and Simmons, 9).

The Model 1860 was a streamlined cal. .44 weapon that became the official US Army pistol and was the principal revolver of the war. Between 4 Jan. '61

and 10 Nov. '63 the War Department was furnished 107,156 of them. They became known as the New Model Army Pistol, and the 1848 weapon was then known as the Old Army Model Pistol.

The Model 1861 Navy pistol was not so popular as the Model 1851 Navy, and relatively few were made. The army purchased 2,056, and the navy bought only a few.

See also COLT REPEATING RIFLE.

COLUMBIA, S.C., BURNED. 17 Feb. '65. Sherman's forces reached Columbia on 16 Feb. '65, and Wood's division (1, XV) entered it the next day after the mayor surrendered the city. A fire then broke out and destroyed over half of the city before Federal troops brought it under control. The cause of the fire is still a matter of controversy. Wade Hampton, who commanded the cavalry rear guard, charged in a letter read before the U.S. Senate a year after the war ended that Sherman "burned it to the ground, deliberately, systematically and atrociously." Sherman said that, to the contrary, his troops prevented complete destruction of Columbia by putting out fires started by the Confederates. Bales of cotton had been broken open and set on fire to prevent their falling into Federal hands. A high wind scattered burning cotton throughout the city and set widespread fires.

COLUMBIAD. Large cannon developed by Col. George Bomford, USA (1780–1848), cast as early as 1811, and first used in the War of 1812. In 1860 the type constructed by RODMAN was adopted for all US seacoast cannon. With certain qualities of the gun, howitzer, and mortar, it was a cast-metal homogeneous, smoothbore, bronze cannon that fired a 50-pound shot about 600 yards. After several later modifications, including the use of cast iron to make the gun by Rodman's system, the weapon was

produced in calibers of 8, 10, and 15
inches. Rodman's 15-inch Columbiad
in a barbette mount fired a 320-pound
shell 5,730 yards; the gun weighed
49,100 pounds (Scott's *Mil. Dict.*).
Rifled Columbiads of 6.4-inch and 5.82-
inch caliber were also used in the Civil
War.

COLVILLE, William, Jr. Union offi-
cer. N.Y. Capt. 1st Minn. 29 Apr. '61;
Maj. 28 Aug. '62; Lt. Col. 26 Sept. '62;
Col. 11 June '63; mustered out 5 May
'64; Col. 1st Minn. Arty. 26 Apr. '65;
Bvt. B.G. USV (war service).

COMLY, James Munroe Stuart.
Union officer. 1832–87. Ohio. Maj. 23d
Ohio 24 Oct. '61; Lt. Col. 24 Oct. '62;
Col. 11 Jan. '65; Bvt. B.G. USV (war
service). A journalist, newspaper editor,
and noted historian.

COMMAGER, Henry Steele. Union
officer. c. 1825–67. Pa. 2d Lt. 67th Ohio
8 Oct. '61; Capt. 10 Nov. '61; Maj. 8
Aug. '62; Lt. Col. 4 Sept. '62; Col. 184th
Ohio 22 Feb. '65; Bvt. B.G. USV 27
Feb. '65. A leading Democrat in Toledo
(Ohio), he worked for the Internal
Revenue Service a short time before his
death. Heitman, whose work contains
very few typographical errors, has the
middle name spelled "Steal." The distinguished historian namesake of the
above officer assures me, "It's Steele, all
right. It's that way in the Official Records, too. H.S.C."

COMMITTEE OF FIFTEEN. Group
sent by Republicans to gather information in the South for congressional
guidance in formulating reconstruction
policies. Much resented in South for
"political" approach to investigation, it
reported to Congress 18 June '66.

COMMITTEE ON THE CONDUCT
OF THE WAR, THE. Organized 20
Dec. '61, the joint committee of Congress continued in being until June
'65. Sen. Wade was chairman, and the

members were Chandler and Johnson
for the Senate, and Gooch, Covode,
Julian, and Odell for the House. As the
majority of members were RADICAL RE-
PUBLICANS, they grew more and more
antagonistic to Lincoln's war plans. In
1864 the committee's duties were extended to include investigation into
contracts and expenditures as well as
military affairs. All of the commanding
generals of the Army of the Potomac
except Grant were investigated. Its findings were published in *Reports of the
Joint Committee on the Conduct of the
War*, Senate Documents, 37th Congress,
3d Session, Washington, 1863, and 38th
Congress, 2d Session, 1865. They constitute a rich historical source.

COMPANY. See ORGANIZATION.

COMPANY FUND. A means of introducing variety into the rations, this
practice was adopted on recommendation of the SANITARY COMMISSION. By
Nov. '61 40 per cent of the companies
of 200 regiments had one, and the
money was used to buy milk, butter,
pepper, cooking utensils, cutlery, and
so forth.

COMPROMISE OF 1850. As the
tension between the sections built up,
the question of extending slave territory
brought about, in 1850, the possibility
of secession. Henry Clay returned to
the Senate and proposed compromise
measures largely originated by Stephen
A. Douglas: Calif. as a free state,
N. Mex. and Utah to be territories with
option to choose status when granted
statehood, settlement of the Tex. Republic debts, abolition of slave trade in
the District of Columbia, a more stringent fugitive slave law. Although facing
great opposition, these points were
eventually passed as separate bills.

COMSTOCK, Cyrus Ballou. Union
officer. c. 1831–1910. Mass. USMA 1855
(1/34); Engrs. He served on engineer-

ing duty and taught at West Point before being in the defenses of Washington and as Asst. to the Chief Engr. of the Army of the Potomac until 2 June '62. He was Gen. Sumner's Chief Engr. until 3 July and commanded an engineer battalion in the Peninsular campaign, at South Mountain and Antietam. Named Chief Engr. of the Army of the Potomac, he served there until 30 Mar. '63, served with engineer troops at Chancellorsville, and went to the Dept. of the Tenn. June '63, where he was at the siege of Vicksburg. Named Chief Engr. of the Army of the Tenn. 1 July–16 Oct. '63, he was Asst. I.G. of the Mil. Div. of the Miss. 19 Nov. '63–20 Mar. '64 and became Grant's A.D.C., serving until 1866. During this time he also participated in the Cape Fear River expedition as Chief Engr. and as Canby's senior engr. in the Mobile campaign. He was breveted for Vicksburg, the Wilderness, Ft. Fisher (B.G. USV) and Mobile (B.G. USA and Maj. Gen. USV). Continuing in the R.A., he again served as Grant's A.D.C. and retired in 1895 as Col.

CONCENTRIC ADVANCE, or "concentration on the battlefield," is a maneuver to which amateur strategists are much attracted and that almost always leads to their DEFEAT IN DETAIL. The term is self-explanatory. It may be contrasted with "concentration off the battlefield," which means bringing separated units to within SUPPORTING DISTANCE (i.e., "concentrating") at a point far enough from the enemy to avoid fighting until your forces are concentrated. Napoleon made a fetish of avoiding concentric advances.

CONFEDERATE ARMY. Officially entitled the "Army of the Confederate States of America," it was the regular force established by the act of 6 Mar. '61 (Confederate Provisional Congress). This "regular army" never really existed. The true Confederate army was the volunteer or Provisional Army established in acts of 28 Feb. and 6 Mar. These gave the President control of military operations, accepted state forces and 100,000 volunteers for a year. By Apr. Davis had called for 82,000 men, and on 8 May '61 Congress had voted enlistments for the duration of the war. On 8 Aug., after four more states had joined the Confederacy, Congress authorized 400,000 volunteers for from one to three years. These troops all entered the army through the medium of the state authorities, and it was not until Apr. '62 and the first Confederate conscription act that men entered the Provisional Army directly. One of the most hotly-debated subjects is the total enlistment of the Confederate army. Figures range from 600,000 to 1,500,000, but the best estimate would appear to lie almost midpoint between these extremes (see NUMBERS AND LOSSES). Only 174,223 surrendered in 1865.

The absentee problem was even greater in the Confederate army than in the Union army, particularly as approaching defeat lowered morale. In the Antietam campaign Lee's stragglers totaled an estimated third to half of his entire force. Many Southern soldiers felt that their commitment to the C.S.A. government did not include the invasion of Northern soil. After the twin disasters of Gettysburg and Vicksburg the number of unauthorized absentees was estimated at between 50,000 and 100,000. As Grant's campaign of attrition continued against the A.N.V., the Confederate authorities were unable to check desertion. "President Davis, according to the Richmond *Enquirer* of October 6 [1864], 'emphatically announced the startling fact that two-thirds of the army are absent from the ranks'" (Wiley's *Reb,* 144). Two months before the surrender an estimated 100,000 deserters were at large in the South (*ibid.*).

See also GENERAL OFFICERS, DEPARTMENTS, NEGRO TROOPS, ORGANIZATION.

CONFEDERATE CABINET. *Vice-president:* Alexander H. Stephens; *State:* Robert Toombs (Feb.–July '61), R. M. T. Hunter (July '61–Mar. '62), Judah P. Benjamin (Mar. '62–Apr. '65); *War:* Leroy P. Walker (Feb.–Sept. '61), Benjamin (Sept. '61–Mar. '62), George W. Randolph (Mar.–Nov. '62), Gustavus W. Smith (Nov. '62), James A. Seddon (Nov. '62–Jan. '65), John C. Breckinridge (Jan.–Apr. '65); *Navy:* Stephen R. Mallory (Feb. '61–Apr. '65); *Treasury:* Christopher G. Memminger (Feb. '61–June '64), George A. Trenholm (June '64–Apr. '65); *Attorney General:* Benjamin (Feb. '61–Sept. '61), Thomas Bragg (Sept. '61–Mar. '62), Thomas H. Watts (Mar. '62–Jan. '64), George Davis (Jan. '64–Apr. '65); *Postmaster General:* J. H. Reagan, (Mar. '61–Apr. '65). The provisional organization was in force from 8 Feb. '61 to 22 Feb. '62 when the reorganization and the permanent government went into effect. Biographical sketches of the above are to be found in the proper alphabetical sequence.

CONFEDERATE DEBT. Approximately $2,000,000,000 by the end of the war, the obligations incurred by the C.S.A. were declared invalid by the 14th Amendment. These included loans from the individual states as well as from French and English bankers.

CONFEDERATE GOVERNORS. *Alabama:* Andrew B. Moore (1857–61), John G. Shorter (1861–63), Thomas H. Watts (1863–65); *Arkansas:* Henry M. Rector (1860–62), Thomas Fletcher (1862), Harris Flanagin (1862–64), Isaac Murphy (1864–68); *Florida:* Madison S. Perry (1857–61), John Milton (1861–65); *Georgia:* Joseph E. Brown (1857–65); *Kentucky:* George W. Johnson (1861–62), Richard Hawes (1862–65); *Louisiana:* Thomas Overton Moore (1860–64), Henry W. Allen (1864–65); *Union:* George F. Shepley (1862–64), Michael Hahn (1864–65); *Mississippi:* John J. Pettus (1860–62), Charles Clark (1863), Jacob Thompson (1863–64); *Missouri:* Claiborne F. Jackson (1861), Thomas C. Reynolds (1862–65); *North Carolina:* John W. Ellis (1858–61), Henry T. Clark (1861–63), Zebulon B. Vance (1863–65); *South Carolina:* Francis W. Pickens (1860–62), Milledge L. Bonham (1862–64), Andrew G. Magrath (1864–65); *Tennessee:* Isham G. Harris (1857–63), Robert L. Carruthers (elected 1863 but never inaugurated); *Union:* Andrew Johnson (1862–65); *Texas:* Edward Clark (1861), Francis R. Lubbock (1861–63), Pendleton Murrah (1863–65); *Virginia:* John Letcher (1860–64), William ("Extra Billy") Smith (1864–65); *Arizona Territory:* John R. Baylor (1864–65). Biographical sketches of most of the above are to be found in the proper alphabetical sequence.

CONFEDERATE MONEY. Paper notes in denominations as small as 50 cents and payable six months after the ratification of a peace treaty were printed and distributed by the Confederate government. This money depreciated as the war progressed. Using gold as the standard, the Confederate paper dollar was worth the following at various periods of the war: 1 Dec. '61, 80¢; 15 Dec. '61, 75¢; 1 Feb. '62, 60¢; 1 Feb. '63, 20¢; June '63, 8¢; Nov. '64, 4½¢; Jan. '65, 2½¢; 1 Apr. '65, 1½¢. "After that date it took from $800 to $1,000 in Confederate money, up to the time of the Appomattox surrender, to buy a gold dollar or a $1 greenback bill" (Wood). The expense account of a Confederate officer who left Richmond about a month before the surrender to go to Augusta lists the following expenses: $2,700 for a coat, vest, and pair of trousers; $700 for two weeks' board; $6,000 for the purchase of $60 gold; $1,700 for an ounce of sulphate quinine (*ibid.*).

CONFEDERATE NAVY. See NAVAL PARTICIPATION.

CONFEDERATE STATES OF AMERICA. The government set up by those states who withdrew by ordinance of secession. Formed in Feb. '61, the C.S.A. included Alabama, Arkansas, Florida, Georgia, Louisiana, Mississippi, North Carolina, South Carolina, Tennessee, Texas, and Virginia. There were Confederate governments, also, in Kentucky and Missouri. See also SECESSION SEQUENCE AND DATES.

CONFISCATION ACTS. In order to deprive the Confederacy of the military and economic advantages of slaves, these acts were passed by Congress in 1861 and '62 to provide that all Negroes used in transportation of stores or munitions or in forts and trenches should be freed. They also stated that all slaves in those areas of the South invaded by the Northern armies would be liberated. Acting without authority, Frémont in Mo. and Hunter in S.C. emancipated all slaves in the areas held by them; Lincoln nullified these proclamations, considering them to be politically unsound at that time. See EMANCIPATION PROCLAMATION.

CONGDON, James A. Union officer. N.Y. Maj. 12th Pa. Cav. 28 Apr. '62; Lt. Col. 1 Jan. '65; Bvt. B.G. USV (war service).

CONGRESSIONAL MEDAL OF HONOR. See MEDAL OF HONOR.

CONKLIN, James Tallmadge. Union officer. N.Y. 1st Lt. Regt. Q.M. 14th Wis. 30 Jan. '62; Capt. Asst. Q.M. Vols. 31 July '63; Col. Q.M. Assigned 17 Sept. '64–4 Aug. '65; Bvt. B.G. USV (war service). Died 1893.

CONNER, James. C.S.A. gen. c. 1829–83. S.C. After S.C. College he studied law and became an active seces-

sionist. A Capt. in the local militia company, the "Montgomery Guards," and at Ft. Sumter, he was commissioned with the same rank in May '61 in Hampton's Legion. Promoted Maj. 21 July '61 at 1st Bull Run, he led the Legion as senior captain when Hampton was wounded. He fought at Yorktown, New Stone Point, West Point, Seven Pines, and Mechanicsville (wounded in the leg), having been promoted Col. in June '62. He led the 22d N.C. at Chancellorsville and Gettysburg and then served on court-martial duty. Named B.G. C.S.A. 1 June '64 in command of McGowan's and Lanes's brigades, he fought at Riddle's Shop, Darby's Farm, Fussell's Mill, Petersburg, Jerusalem Plank Road, and Reams's Station. Going to the Valley under Kershaw, he commanded his brigade at Winchester, Pt. Republic (1864), Cedar Creek. He was wounded in the same leg near Fishers Hill in Oct. '64. Although the leg was amputated, he continued to command in the field. C.M.H. says that his Maj. Gen. commission was approved in 1865 but failed to reach him. Wright makes no mention of this. After the war he became Atty. Gen. of S.C. (1876) and helped Wade Hampton eradicate the carpetbaggers.

CONNER, Patrick E. Erroneous listing by Phisterer for CONNOR, Patrick Edward, B.G. USV.

CONNER, Seldon. Erroneous listing by Phisterer for CONNOR, Selden, B.G. USV.

CONNOR, Patrick Edward. Union gen. 1820–91. Ireland. He was in the R.A. during the Florida War, in business in Texas when he joined again for the Mexican War and wounded at Buena Vista. He raised the 3d Calif. and was commissioned its Col. 4 Sept. '61. Ordered to Utah to settle a Mormon revolt and clear the overland route of Indians, he fought the Indians at the Bear River in Washington Territory 29 Jan. '63 and was promoted B.G. USV 30 Mar. '63. He commanded the Utah District and at the end of the war led a large command to pacify the Indians again. Breveted Maj. Gen. USV for war service, he was mustered out in 1866. Settling in Utah, he started the first newspaper, the first silver mine, wrote the first mining laws, founded the town of Stockton, and introduced navigation on the Great Salt Lake.

CONNOR, Selden. Union gen. 1839–? Me. A lawyer, he enlisted as Pvt. 1st Vt. Inf. 2 May '61, was mustered out 15 Aug. '61, was commissioned Lt. Col. 7th Me. 22 Aug. '61, and fought in the Peninsular campaign, at Antietam, Fredericksburg (where he was wounded), and at Gettysburg. He was named Col. 19th Me. 11 Jan. '64 and commanded 1, 2, III, Potomac (27 Feb.–25 Mar. '64). Severely wounded in the thigh at the Wilderness, he was appointed B.G. USV 11 June '64 and, unfit for field service, handled administrative duties until mustered out in 1866. He was Republican Gov. of Me. 1876–79.

CONRAD, Joseph. Union officer. 1830–97. Germany. Capt. 3d Mo. 22 Apr. '61; Maj. 31 July '61; Lt. Col. 15th Mo. 24 May '62; Col. 29 Nov. '62; Bvt. B.G. USV. Brevets for Atlanta (2), Franklin (Tenn.), Nashville. Commanded 2, 2, IV; 3, 2, IV; 2d Div., IV Corps. A graduate of the military academy of Hesse and ex-German officer, he retired as Col. in the US Army in 1882.

CONSCRIPTION, CONFEDERATE. On 16 Apr. '62 Congress conscripted for three years' service all white males between 18 and 35 who were not legally exempt. The age was raised to 45 in Sept., and by Feb. '64 the limits were 17 and 50. Another act at this time legalized the conscription of free Negroes and slaves for auxiliary services,

and on 13 Mar. '65 the recruitment of slaves for field service was authorized.

CONSCRIPTION, UNION. By Nov. '62 the state governors were no longer able to raise enough troops for the Union Army, and the Federal government then passed the Enrollment Act of 3 Mar. '63. This precipitated the DRAFT RIOTS. The state governors finally accepted the authority of the central government to enforce a draft. See also UNION ARMY.

CONTRABANDS. Three slaves of a Virginia owner sought refuge at Ft. Monroe, Va., on 23 May '61, and the Southerner demanded their return under the FUGITIVE SLAVE ACTS. Ben Butler refused, saying that since Va. had seceded, she had no right to the Federal laws. In a report to the Sec. of War 30 July '61, he referred to the slaves as "contraband of war," and the name came into unofficial usage as the slang term for Negro or slave. The idea of contraband as a doctrine disappeared after the passage of the CONFISCATION ACTS (the first on 6 Aug. '61).

CONWAY, William. Ordinary seaman, USN, who refused the order of Lt. F. B. Renshaw to haul down the US flag when Com. Armstrong surrendered Pensacola (see PENSACOLA BAY) on 12 Apr. '61.

CONY, Samuel. Gov. of Me. 1811–70. Me. After graduating from Brown Univ. he was a lawyer and legislator before being elected judge. He was active in the Democratic party and in favor of war to settle the sections' differences, but was rejected by the pacifist element of the party in 1861 and was elected to the legislature in 1862 as a War Democrat. Chosen Governor on this ticket the next year, he was twice re-elected to that office.

COOK, John. Union gen. 1825–? Ill. After college he was a merchant in St.

Louis and Springfield, serving as Mayor of the latter place and as Sheriff of Sangamon County. He was the grandson of Gov. Ninian Edwards (Lincoln's brother-in-law) and the son of the man for whom Cook County was named. Commissioned Col. 7th Ill. 25 Apr. '61, he was mustered out three months later and recommissioned in the same regiment with the same rank the next day (25 July '61). After commanding a brigade at Ft. Donelson, he was appointed B.G. USV 21 Mar. '62 and was breveted Maj. Gen. USV 23 Aug. '65 for war service, being mustered out the same day. After the war he entered politics.

COOK, Philip. C.S.A. gen. 1817–94. Ga. He fought as a boy in the Seminole War, attended Oglethorpe Univ. and studied law at Univ. of Va.; practicing until the Civil War. In May '61 he enlisted as a private in the Macon County Volunteers, which became the 4th Ga., and was stationed at Portsmouth. There he was made Regt. Adj. He fought in the Seven Days' Battles, was wounded at Malvern Hill, and was promoted Lt. Col. before 2d Bull Run. After Antietam he was commissioned Col. 1 Nov. '62 and led his regiment at Fredericksburg and Chancellorsville, where he was wounded in the leg by a Minié bullet. After three months' convalescence, he rejoined his command at Orange Courthouse and later took a leave of absence to sit in the Ga. legislature. Commissioned B.G. 5 Aug. '64, he succeeded Doles as brigade commander and served with Early in the Valley, fighting under Ramseur at Cedar Creek. Wounded several times during the war, he was captured 3 Apr. '65 in the Petersburg hospital after he had been shot in the right elbow at Ft. Stedman 25 Mar. Returning to his law practice, he was in the legislature, the US Congress, and held several other public offices.

COOK, Philip St. George. Misspelling by Phisterer for P. St. G. COOKE.

COOKE, Edwin Francis. Union officer. 1835–67. N.Y. Capt. 2d N.Y. Cav. 11 Aug. '61; Maj. 6 Dec. '62; Bvt. B.G. USV (war service). Served as Chief of Staff of Gen. Kilpatrick's Cav. Div. His horse was killed from under him by same volley that killed Col. Dahlgren in the KILPATRICK-DAHLGREN RAID (1864) from the west. He was taken prisoner in this action and was held in Libby and S.C. and Ga. prisons. Escaping, he was recaptured within two months but was exchanged in 1864. He was offered the post of secretary of the Chilean legation but died from the effects of his imprisonment before he could accept.

COOKE, John Esten. C.S.A. officer. 1830–86. Va. A lawyer and writer, he entered the C.S. army in 1861, enlisting as private in the Cav. and then serving in the Cav. and as ordnance officer for J. E. B. Stuart, husband of Cooke's first cousin. By the end of the war he was Lee's I.G. of the Horse Arty. He wrote many novels and historical sketches as well as magazine articles and poetry, among these *Life of Stonewall Jackson* (1863), *Surry of Eagle's Nest* (1866) about the Confederate cavalry and John PELHAM, *Life of Gen. R. E. Lee* (1871). See also BROTHER AGAINST BROTHER.

COOKE, John R. C.S.A. gen. 1833–91. Mo. Appt.-N.C. After graduating from Harvard as an engineer, he joined the R.A. in '55 and served on the frontier, resigning in '61 to be commissioned 1st Lt. under Holmes and stationed at Fredericksburg. He fought at 1st Bull Run. Promoted Maj. in Feb. '62, he was Chief of Arty. for the Dept. of N.C. until Apr. of that year when he was named Col. 27th N.C. He was wounded at Seven Pines and upon recovery was appointed B.G. C.S.A. 1 Nov. '62, taking over a N.C. brigade. At Fredericksburg his brigade held the famous stone wall where he was wounded again. He was also wounded at Bristoe Station and the Wilderness. After the war he was a Richmond merchant and a power in the Democratic party as well as being active in veterans' organizations. He was the son of Philip St. George Cooke (Maj. Gen. USV) and brother-in-law of J. E. B. Stuart (Maj. Gen. C.S.A.).

See also BROTHER AGAINST BROTHER.

COOKE, Philip St. George. Union gen. c. 1809–95. Va. USMA 1827 (23/38); Inf.-Cav. He served on the frontier and in Indian fighting, in the Mexican War (1 brevet), and on the Utah Expedition in command of the cavalry. Promoted B.G. USA 12 Nov. '61, he did not follow the South with the rest of his family but commanded a brigade of R.A. cavalry in Washington until 10 Mar. '62 and a cavalry division at Yorktown, Williamsburg, Gaines's Mill, and Glendale. He served on court-martial duty until Aug. '63, when he took command of the Baton Rouge Dist. until 2 May '64. For the remainder of the war he was in command of the army's recruiting service. Breveted Maj. Gen. USA, he was retired in 1873. He was the father-in-law of J. E. B. STUART, uncle of John Esten COOKE, and father of John R. COOKE.

See also BROTHER AGAINST BROTHER.

COON, Datus Ensign. Union officer. N.Y. Capt. 2d Iowa Cav. 31 Aug. '61; Maj. 14 Sept. '61; Col. 5 May '64; Bvt. B.G. USV 8 Mar. '65. Commanded 2, 1st Cav. Div. West. Tenn.; 2, 5, Cav. Corps (Mil. Div. Miss.). Died 1893.

COOPER, Douglas H. C.S.A. gen. 1815–79. Appt.-Miss. He was sent by the Confederate government to secure alliances with the Cherokee, Creek, Choctaw, Chickasaw, and Seminole tribes and won portions of these tribes to the Southern cause. Commissioned Col. 1st Choctaw and Chickasaw Mtd. Rifles, he patrolled the Indian Territory in Nov. and Dec. '61, fighting battles at Chusto-Talasah and Chustenahla that drove the Federal Indians into Kansas. He fought under Pike at Pea Ridge and Newtonia 30 Sept. '62 and was appointed B.G. C.S.A. 2 May '63. On duty in the Indian Territory for the rest of the war, his troops cooperated with Price during his 1864 Missouri raid.

COOPER, James. Union gen. 1810–63. Md. A lawyer in Thaddeus Stevens's office in Gettysburg, he was US and state Representative and as US Senator was a member of the Committee of Thirteen that framed the COMPROMISE OF 1850. A member of the Frederick (Md.) home guard, he was commissioned B.G. USV 17 May '61 and commanded 1st Brig., Sigel's division, Shenandoah (4–26 June '62); 1, 2, II Army Va. (26 June–16 July '62) and succeeded to command the division 26 June–7 July '62. He later commanded Camp Wallace near Columbus (O.) and Camp Chase where he died on active duty 28 Mar. '63.

COOPER, Joseph Alexander. Union gen. 1823–1910. Mo. An enlisted man in the Mexican War, he was a farmer and interested in politics when named Col. 1st Tenn. 8 Aug. '61. He fought at Stones River, Chickamauga, and Chattanooga with his regiment and commanded 3, 3, XXIII, Ohio (1–4 June '63). At Chattanooga he argued with Spears and joined with other officers in having him court-martialed for Southern sympathies. He also led 3, 3, XII, Cumberland (7 Mar.–14 Apr. '64) and 1, 2, XXIII, Ohio (25 Apr.–3 May '64; 4 June–11 Oct. '64; 11 Nov. '64–2 Feb. '65), having been promoted B.G. USV 30 July '64. He also commanded 2d Div., XXIII, Ohio (11 Oct.–11 Nov. '64 and 14 Jan.– 2 Feb. '65) at Atlanta; 1, 2, XXIII,

N.C. (9 Feb.-6 Mar. '65; 4-20 Apr. '65 and 26-30 Apr. '65); 2d Div., XXIII, N.C. (20-26 Apr. '65 and 30 Apr.-12 June '65). Breveted Maj. Gen. USV for Franklin and Nashville, he was mustered out in 1866 and became an influential man in his community. D.A.B. says of him: "Before the Civil War, [he] had been little more than a poorly educated, impecunious farmer without any great significance even in his own county, but his war record was brilliant and he rapidly rose to prominence."

COOPER, Samuel. C.S.A. gen. 1798-1876. USMA 1815 (36/40); Arty. The highest ranking officer in the C.S.A. Being appointed a full gen., from Va., 16 May '61, he served throughout the war in Richmond as "adjutant and inspector general." Born in Hackensack, N.J., he was one of the few West Pointers of Northern origin who sided with the Confederacy. After field service in the Seminole War, he had been on staff duty in Washington during the Mexican War. He had known Jeff Davis when the latter was Sec. of War, 1852-56. Cooper's high-level administrative experience before the war was of great use to Davis in organizing the Confederate War Dept. and army. He fled with Davis from Richmond. After being paroled he lived in Alexandria, Va. (Note: Cooper's class standing at West Point, 36/40, is based on the length of time he spent as a cadet, not academic merit. Prior to '18 there was no system of establishing the latter.)

COOPER'S SHOP SALOON. See Anna Maria Ross.

COPELAND, Joseph Tarr. Union gen. 1830-93. Me. Named Lt. Col. 1st Mich. Cav. 22 Aug. '61, he was mustered out 29 Aug. '62 and commissioned Col. 5th Mich. Cav. 30 Aug. and B.G. USV 29 Nov. '62. He fought at 2d Bull Run, commanded Prov. Brig., Casey's Mil. Dist. Washington and 1st Brig., Cav. Div., XXII, Washington, as well as the Annapolis Draft Rendezvous. He later headed the post and military prison at Alton (Ill.) and resigned 8 Nov. '65.

COPPERHEADS. Those Northern Democrats who opposed the Union's war policy and favored a negotiated peace. Lincoln assumed strong executive powers in suppressing them, including arrests, suppression of the press, suspension of *habeas corpus,* and censorship. Their organizations included the KNIGHTS OF THE GOLDEN CIRCLE, Order of American Knights and Sons of Liberty, and their strength lay mainly in Ohio, Ill., and Ind. Among their leaders were Representative Clement L. VALLANDIGHAM who was arrested, Alexander Long, and Fernando Wood. Also known as the Peace Democrats.

CORBIN, Henry Clarke. Union officer. 1842-? Ohio. 2d Lt. 83d Ohio 28 July '62; transferred to 79th Ohio 29 Aug. '62; 1st Lt. 11 May '63; resigned 13 Nov. '63; Maj. 14th US Col. Inf. 14 Nov. '63; Lt. Col. 4 Mar. '64; Col. 23 Sept. '65; Bvt. B.G. USV. Brevets for war service, Decatur (Ala.), Nashville. Joining the R. A. in 1866, he became Maj. Gen. Adj. Gen. 6 June 1900.

CORCORAN, Michael. Union gen. 1827-63. Ireland. The son of a British Army captain, he was commissioned in 1845 in the Irish Constabulary and in 1849 resigned and emigrated to the US. Joining the N.Y. militia, he was appointed Col. in 1859. He had refused to order out the 69th N.Y. to honor the visiting Prince Albert of Wales and was awaiting court-martial when the war began. Commissioned Col. 69th N.Y. Mil. 29 Apr. '61 in Federal service, he led them at 1st Bull Run where he was captured and spent a year in prison

when he refused to sign a parole. (See
ENCHANTRESS AFFAIR.) He was exchanged 15 Aug. '62 and made B.G.
USV retroactive to 21 July '61. Raising
the CORCORAN LEGION, he commanded
them in the Div. at Suffolk, VII, Nov.
'62–9 Apr. '63, succeeding to command
of the Div. 30 Sept. '62–2 Jan. '63. He
also led the 1st Div., VII (9 Apr.–11
July '63); 1, King's Div., XXII (15 July–
Oct. '63) and King's division, XXII
(Oct. '63). On 22 Dec. '63 he was accidentally killed near Fairfax (Va.) while
riding with Gen. Thomas Meagher, when
his horse fell on him.

CORCORAN LEGION. A brigade
composed of the 155th, 164th, 170th,
and 182d N.Y., raised by Michael COR-
CORAN and assigned to VII Corps (Dept.
of Va.) in Nov. '62. The Legion was
in the vicinity of Washington from July
'63 to May '64, when it joined the Army
of the Potomac as part of the 2d Div.,
II Corps.

CORDUROY ROAD. One surfaced
with branches and/or small tree trunks
laid side by side across the road. Commonly used today as in ancient warfare. See also PLANK ROAD.

CORINTH, Miss. (Halleck's advance), 29 Apr.–10 June '62.
After SHILOH Halleck arrived to take
personal command of the forces there
and began preparations to capture Corinth. His force, which started the campaign with 90,000 and reached Corinth
with 110,000, was composed of Grant's
Army of the Tenn., Buell's Army of the
Ohio, and Pope's Army of the Miss.
Halleck moved Grant, in whom he had
little confidence, into the honorary and
useless position of second-in-command
and put Gen. George H. Thomas in his
place. (Grant considered requesting to
be relieved but was talked out of it by
W. T. Sherman.)
Beauregard, who had withdrawn to

Corinth with 30,000 of the 40,000 that
had fought at Shiloh, realized the importance of holding Corinth and called
for reinforcements. He set about fortifying the place, and his force was built up
to 66,000. His command consisted of
Bragg's Army of the Mississippi (corps
of Polk and Ruggles) and Van Dorn's
Army of the West (which came from
its defeat at PRAIRIE GROVE).
Starting 29 Apr., Halleck advanced
cautiously and met some resistance at
Farmington, Seven Mile Creek, and
Russell's House. He entrenched at the
end of each day's march. By 25 May,
having taken almost a month to advance
20 miles, Halleck was about ready to
start a bombardment of Corinth. Beauregard accepted the necessity of abandoning the place to save his army. During
the night of 29–30 May he escaped and
took up a defense along the Tuscumbia
River. Pope's force undertook a pursuit
in which Col. Philip Sheridan's cavalry
distinguished itself. On 11 June the
Federal pursuit was halted, and Halleck
decided to consolidate his gains in
Tenn. rather than to push into Miss.
after the Confederate army.

CORINTH, Miss., 3–4 Oct. '62.
After the action at IUKA, 19 Sept., Van
Dorn moved to join Price at Ripley.
Van Dorn decided to attack Rosecrans
at Corinth, believing that Rosecrans was
weaker than Ord at Bolivar, and much
weaker than himself. Actually, Rosecrans had 23,000 with which to oppose
Van Dorn's 22,000. Other forces under
Grant's command were 12,000 under
Ord and Hurlbut at Bolivar; 7,000 under Sherman at Memphis; and 6,000 in
reserve at Jackson.
When Federal scouts picked up Van
Dorn's movement north from Ripley on
29 Sept., Grant had no way of knowing
which of the above four places was his
objective. Van Dorn turned east when
he reached Pocahontas and on the night

of 2 Oct. was nine miles from Corinth. At 10 A.M. the next day he drove in the Federal outposts and attacked. Rosecrans' force was not entirely concentrated, and the initial attack fell on the divisions of McKean and Davies. The Federals withdrew to an inner line of works where they fought off desperate attacks until early afternoon, when Van Dorn broke off the action and began to retire west along the railroad. Battery Robinett was the scene of particularly heavy fighting on 4 Oct.

Grant had ordered reinforcements to Corinth as soon as he had learned of the attack. McPherson arrived from Jackson with two brigades at 4 P.M., a few hours after the battle ended. On the 5th they joined the divisions of Rosecrans in a pursuit. Another column under Ord, coming down from Bolivar with 6,500 men, reached Pocahontas just as the Confederates were crossing the Hatchie River. This forced Van Dorn to countermarch after a loss of nearly 300 prisoners and to cross the river farther south. Ord, who had relieved Hurlbut while the column was en route to Pocahontas, was wounded, and Hurlbut resumed command. The Federal pursuit ended at Ripley, and Van Dorn escaped with the bulk of his forces to Holly Springs.

Rosecrans lost 2,520 out of 21,147 actually engaged. Out of 22,000 engaged, Van Dorn lost 2,470 killed and wounded and 1,763 missing in the battle and the retreat (Livermore). Among the Federal casualties were Brig. Gen. Hackleman, K.I.A., and Brig. Gen. Oglesby, W.I.A.

CORPS, ARMY. An "army corps," generally referred to simply as a corps, is the military organization that consists of two or more divisions. (See also ORGANIZATION.) Union corps were commanded by major generals, whereas Confederate corps were commanded by lieutenant generals. Corps existed un-

officially in the Union armies from the start of the war, but they did not take on official designations until 17 July '62. These corps were numbered (with the exception of the cavalry corps); the XXV US (infantry) Corps being the highest number to appear during the war. Due to the unofficial nature of their organization prior to 17 July '62, several different organizations held the designations of I through VI Corps, and for identification it was necessary to specify the army to which each belonged. From the summer of 1862 until the end of the war, however, newly organized corps were assigned new numbers—or, in the case of the IV Corps, the number of a corps that had been discontinued was later assigned to a newly organized one. Confederate corps organizations were not authorized until 18 Sept. '62 and were not actually formed until 6 Nov. '62. Prior to this time their divisions were grouped for a given operation into organizations known as "Longstreet's Wing," "Jackson's Command," etc. Although it was not the practice during the Civil War, by modern military convention, Roman numerals are used to designate corps; this style is used in this book for clarity and brevity.

Confederate corps will be listed below in the following sequence: numbered corps in the East, numbered corps in the West, and "named" corps in alphabetical order. Federal corps will be listed numerically.

CORPS, CONFEDERATE

(Note. The following entries, which cover all army corps—US and Confederate—of the war, are written in a style intended to make them of maximum value as references. They should not be looked on as histories of the corps, but rather as basic raw material useful in checking for specific dates, statistics, and names of commanders.)

I CORPS (Longstreet's), Confed. Army of Northern Va. The genesis of this organization can be traced to Beauregard's I Corps, Army of the Potomac, which was announced 20 June '61. Although this was an "unofficial" corps, some of its eight brigades went to make up a division of about 14,000 men, commanded by Longstreet, and designated "Center of Position, Army of Northern Va.," at the start of the Peninsular campaign.

This division of Longstreet was composed of six brigades. The first three were "Manassas Brigades" formerly commanded by Longstreet, Cocke, and D. R. Jones; they were now commanded, respectively, by A. P. Hill, Pickett, and R. H. Anderson. The other three brigades were C. M. Wilcox's (Alabama and Mississippi regiments from G. W. Smith's division), R. E. Colston's (from Huger's division) and R. A. Pryor's (from Magruder's "Army of the Peninsula").

At Seven Pines (Fair Oaks) Longstreet's "Right Wing" consisted of the divisions of Longstreet (under R. H. Anderson and composed of brigades commanded by Kemper, Jenkins, Pickett, Wilcox, Colston, and Pryor); D. H. Hill (brigades commanded by Garland, Rodes, Rains, and G. B. Anderson); and Huger (Armistead, Mahone, and Blanchard).

During the Seven Days' Battles "Longstreet's Command" consisted of six brigades of his own division (under Kemper, R. H. Anderson, Pickett, Wilcox, Pryor, and Featherston); six brigades of A. P. Hill's division (Field, Gregg, J. R. Anderson, Branch, Archer, and Pender); and three brigades of T. T. Holmes's division (Ransom's 2d, Daniel's 3d, and J. G. Walker's 4th).

In the reorganization preceding the 2d Bull Run campaign Longstreet's "Right Wing" was established to consist of the following five divisions: R. H. Anderson (brigades of Armistead, Mahone, and A. R. Wright); D. R. Jones (brigades of Toombs, Drayton, G. T. Anderson); C. M. Wilcox (Wilcox, Pryor, Featherston); Hood (Hood and E. M. Law); and Kemper (M. D. Corse, Jenkins, Hunton, and N. G. Evans).

During the Antietam (Sharpsburg) campaign Longstreet's command comprised the divisions of McLaws (Kershaw, Cobb, P. J. Semmes, and Barksdale); Anderson (Wilcox's brigade, under Cumming; Mahone's brigade, under Parham; Featherston's, under Posey; Armistead's; Pryor's; and Wright's); D. R. Jones (Toombs; Drayton; Pickett's, under Garnett; Kemper's; Jenkins', under J. Walker; and G. T. Anderson's); Walker's division (Manning and Ransom); and Hood (Hood's brigade, under Wofford, and Law's brigade).

When Lee's army was formally organized into corps (6 Nov. '62), Longstreet's command was designated the I Corps and comprised the following divisions: McLaws', Anderson's, Pickett's (Garnett, Armistead, Kemper, Jenkins, and M. D. Corse), Hood's (Law's, Robertson's, Anderson's, and Toombs's, under Benning), and Ransom's (Ransom and J. R. Cooke). This was its composition during the Fredericksburg campaign. During the battle of Chancellorsville Longstreet was absent (in the Suffolk area) with the divisions of Pickett and Hood. His other two divisions, McLaws' and Anderson's, took part in the Chancellorsville campaign.

After the reorganization that followed the death of Jackson and the creation of a III Corps, Longstreet's I Corps was composed of three divisions: McLaws' (with the brigades of Kershaw, Semmes, Barksdale, and Wofford); Pickett's (Garnett, Armistead, and Kemper); and Hood's (Law, G. T. Anderson, J. B. Robertson, and Benning). As such the corps took part in the Gettysburg campaign.

Longstreet's corps, less all but Jenkins's brigade of Pickett's division (which remained in the Richmond-Petersburg area), was in the West during the period Sept. '63–Apr. '64. Longstreet commanded the Left Wing under Bragg at Chickamauga. Hood commanded the corps, which was reinforced to three divisions by the addition of Bushrod Johnson's division. Law, who had succeeded Hood when the latter was wounded at Gettysburg, again took command of "Hood's Division." When Hood was again wounded at Chickamauga, Law remained in command of the division, although Jenkins was in temporary command during the battle of WAUHATCHIE. After the latter preliminary engagement of the battles around Chattanooga, Longstreet's corps was detached from Bragg's main body to operate against Burnside in east Tennessee (Knoxville campaign).

The corps returned to the East to oppose Grant's final campaign against the Army of Northern Va. Pickett's division did not rejoin until 1 June (after the Drewry's Bluff operation against Butler and in time for Cold Harbor). The other two divisions, totaling about 10,000, were now commanded by Kershaw (vice McLaws) (brigades of Henagan [vice Kershaw], Humphreys, Wofford, and Bryan); and C. W. Field (vice Hood and Law) with the brigades of Jenkins (killed in the Wilderness), G. T. Anderson, Law, Gregg (vice Jerome Robertson) and Benning.

R. H. Anderson commanded the I Corps during the period 6 May–19 Oct. '64 when Longstreet was recovering from serious wounds received in the Wilderness. Famous Chief of Arty. of the corps was E. P. Alexander.

II CORPS (Jackson's, Ewell's, Early's), Confed. Army of Northern Va.

An unofficial II Corps, Army of the Potomac, was briefly in existence 25 Sept.–22 Oct. '61 when G. W. Smith was put in command of all troops of the Confederate Army of the Potomac that were not part of Beauregard's I Corps. After 22 Oct. this force, which was composed of five brigades and numbered 20,000, became the 2d Div. These brigades subsequently went to make up D. H. Hill's division, the Reserve, and the 2d Div. of the Army of Northern Va. Most of them eventually ended up in Jackson's corps.

During his Valley campaign Stonewall Jackson commanded his own division, Ewell's division, and a cavalry force. "Jackson's Command" in the Seven Days' Battles was composed of his own division (brigades of Winder, R. H. Cunningham, Fulkerson, and A. R. Lawton); Ewell's division (Elzey, Trimble, Taylor); D. H. Hill's division (Rodes, G. B. Anderson, Garland, Colquitt, and R. S. Ripley); and Whiting's division (Hood and Law). In the reorganization that preceded the 2d Bull Run campaign Jackson's Command included his own division (under Winder initially, then W. B. Taliaferro), A. P. Hill's division (Branch, Pender, E. L. Thomas, Gregg, Archer, and Field), and Ewell's division (Lawton, Trimble, Early, and Hays).

When the A.N.V. was officially organized into I and II Corps after Antietam, Jackson's II Corps was composed of his former division (under W. B. Taliaferro, and consisting of brigades under Paxton, J. R. Jones, E. T. H. Warren, and Edmund Pendleton); and the divisions of D. H. Hill (Rodes, Doles, Colquitt, Iverson, and Grimes); A. P. Hill (Brockenbrough, Gregg, E. L. Thomas, J. H. Lane, J. J. Archer, and W. D. Pender); and Ewell (commanded by Early, with the brigades of Lawton [under Atkinson], Trimble [under Hoke], Early [under Walker] and Hays).

At Chancellorsville his corps was composed of the same divisions, but there had been considerable change in the brigade commanders. The "light division," under A. P. Hill, had the brigades of Heth, Thomas, Lane, McGowan, Archer, and Pender. D. H. Hill's division, commanded by Rodes, was composed of the brigades of Rodes, Colquitt, Ramseur, Doles, and Iverson. Early's division consisted of the brigades of Gordon, Hoke, William Smith, and Hays. Trimble's division, commanded by Colston, had four numbered brigades whose commanders were Paxton, J. R. Jones, E. T. H. Warren and F. T. Nicholls.

The third reorganization of the Army of Northern Va. took place after Chancellorsville during the period 7 May–6 June '63. Ewell succeeded to command of II Corps (after A. P. Hill and Jeb Stuart had temporarily commanded it). Troops were transferred out to make up the new III Corps. At Gettysburg his division and brigade commanders were as follows: Early with the brigades of Hays, Hoke (under Avery), William Smith, and Gordon; Johnson with the brigades of Steuart, Nicholls (under J. M. Williams), J. A. Walker (Stonewall Brigade), and J. M. Jones; Rodes with the brigades of Daniel, Iverson, Doles, Ramseur, and E. A. O'Neal.

During the battles of the Wilderness and Spotsylvania Ewell's II Corps was composed of the divisions of Early, Edward Johnson, and Rodes, with A. L. Long's five battalions of artillery (18 guns). The divisions were composed of three, four, and five brigades each, respectively.

Early took command of the corps on 29 May '64 when Ewell's physical disability became so serious he could no longer serve in that capacity. At Cold

Harbor the divisions of Early's II Corps were commanded by Gordon, Ramseur, and Rodes. The number of brigades remained the same in each, but Long's artillery had been reduced to four battalions and 13 guns.

The II Corps left Richmond 13 June and reached LYNCHBURG, Va., 18 June in time to stop Hunter's advance. Early then undertook his Washington Raid. He organized his force into two corps: the first was commanded by Rodes and composed of the latter's division (led by C. A. Battle) and Ramseur; the second was commanded by Breckinridge and composed of the divisions of Gordon and John Echols.

After his defeat by Sheridan at Winchester, 19 Sept. (where Rodes was killed), and the return of Breckinridge with his troops to the latter's Dept. of Southwest Va., Early was forced to effect another reorganization. Ramseur was transferred to replace Rodes, and John Pegram replaced Ramseur. The latter was killed at Cedar Creek and succeeded by Grimes. Gordon retained command of the third division, to which were transferred the forces previously called Breckinridge's division (but actually commanded by Wharton during the time Breckinridge was commanding his own and Gordon's division [*Lee's Lts.,* III, 582]).

In Dec. '64 Early was left in the Valley with 3,000 men (under Wharton) to oppose Sheridan's farther advances, while the three divisions of II Corps rejoined Lee at Petersburg. Gordon was put in temporary command, but since Early did not rejoin after his humiliating final defeat at WAYNESBORO, 2 Mar. '65, Gordon remained as the actual corps commander.

Gordon's II Corps, the smallest in Lee's army, numbered 8,600 effectives at the end of 1864. The divisions were now commanded by Pegram, Grimes, and C. A. Evans. Pegram was killed at Hatcher's Run, 6 Feb. '65, and James A. Walker took command of his division.

III CORPS (A. P. Hill's), Confed. Army of Northern Va.

In the reorganization following Chancellorsville a new (III) corps was formed of A. P. Hill's division (from Jackson's II Corps), Anderson's division (from I Corps) and Heth's newly-formed division (brigades of Brockenbrough and Archer and the newly-acquired N.C. brigade of Pettigrew and Miss. brigade of J. R. Davis). The new corps was formed 30 May '63, and A. P. Hill was put in command of it 1 June. It fought in all the subsequent campaigns of the Army of Northern Va. until Hill's death at Petersburg, 2 Apr. '65. Its troops were then merged into the I Corps.

IV CORPS (R. H. Anderson's), Confed. Army of Northern Va.

Organized late in 1864, after Longstreet's return to command of I Corps (19 Oct. '64) and in order to give Dick Anderson a command in keeping with his rank. It was composed of only two divisions, Hoke's and Bushrod Johnson's, and after Hoke started for Wilmington on 20 Dec. '64 it contained only the four brigades of Johnson's (Elliott, Gracie, Mat. Ransom, and Wise). Before the detachment of Hoke (whose brigades were Hagood's, Colquitt's, Clingman's, and Kirkland's) Anderson's IV Corps included also the artillery battalion of Col. H. P. Jones and had a strength of about 14,000.

I CORPS (Polk's, Hardee's, Cheatham's), Confed. Armies of Miss. and of Tenn.

Leonidas Polk commanded the 1st Div. in the Western Dept. (No. 2) from June '61 to Mar. '62. This force numbered about 25,000 troops along the Mississippi from Columbus, Ky., to Memphis and in the interior of Tenn. and Miss. Upon formation of the Army of Miss. under Beauregard on 5 Mar. '62 Polk's force became the First Grand Div. When the new Army of Miss. was organized 29 Mar. under A. S. Johnston, Polk's command was designated the I Corps. This was a force of 9,136 men that took part in the battle of Shiloh. It was composed of Charles Clark's division with the brigades of R. M. Russell and A. P. Stewart; B. F. Cheatham's division with the brigades of B. R. Johnson and W. H. Stephens. (Stewart commanded the division after Clark was wounded, and Preston Smith commanded Johnson's brigade after the latter was wounded.)

Another reorganization, effective 15 Aug. '62, gave Polk command of 15,000, designated the Right Wing. With the organization of the Army of Tenn., 7 Nov. '62, Polk's corps comprised: Cheatham's division (with the brigades of D. S. Donelson, A. P. Stewart, George Maney, and A. J. Vaughan, Jr.); and Withers' division (Loomis, J. R. Chalmers, J. P. Anderson, and A. M. Manigault). This was Polk's command during the Stones River campaign.

At Chickamauga Polk commanded the Right Wing. This was composed of D. H. Hill's corps (divisions of Cleburne and Breckinridge) and Cheatham's division of his own corps. His other division, now commanded by Hindman, fought as part of Longstreet's Left Wing. When Polk was relieved after Chickamauga the I Corps, Army of Tenn., was commanded temporarily by Cheatham. Hardee then took command.

Hardee's corps consisted of the divisions of Cheatham, Cleburne, and W. H. T. Walker initially; C. L. Stevenson's division was later added. At Chattanooga it was composed of Cheatham's division (under J. K. Jackson) with Jackson's brigade, under C. J. Wilkinson; Walthall's; J. C. Moore's; and M. J. Wright's brigades. Stevenson's division had brigades commanded by J. C. Brown, E. W. Pettus, Alfred Cumming, and A. W. Reynolds. Pat Cleburne's division had the brigades of M. P. Lowrey, L. E. Polk, Liddell (commanded by D. C. Govan), and Smith (commanded by H. B. Granbury). Walker's division was commanded by S. R. Gist, and composed of the brigades of Gist, C. C. Wilson, and G. E. Maney.

Hardee's corps in the Atlanta campaign was operating without Stevenson's division (assigned to Hood's or Lee's II CORPS), but with the substitution of Bate's division. Commanders were as follows: Cheatham's division, commanded in turn by Cheatham, George Maney, and J. C. Carter; Maney's brigade, commanded by G. C. Porter in Maney's absence; Wright's brigade, commanded by J. C. Carter; O. F. Strahl's brigade; and Vaughan's brigade, commanded by A. J. Vaughan, Jr., M. Magevney, and G. W. Gordon; Cleburne's division was led by M. P. Lowrey during the period Cleburne commanded the corps; L. E. Polk's brigade; Lowrey's brigade was commanded by John Weir in Lowrey's absence; Govan's brigade, commanded by D. C. Govan and P. V. Green; and Granbury's brigade was commanded by Granbury, J. A. Smith, and R. B. Young. Walker's division was commanded by H. W. Mercer in Walker's absence; J. R. Jackson's brigade; Gist's brigade, commanded by S. R. Gist and James McCullough; Stevens' brigade, commanded by C. H. Stevens, H. R. Jackson, and W. D. Mitchell; Mercer's brigade, commanded by H. W. Mercer, W. Barkuloo, M. Rawls, C. S. Guyton, and C. H. Olmstead; Bate's division, commanded by W. B. Bate and J. C. Brown; J. H. Lewis' brigade, T. B. Smith's brigade, and Finley's brigade commanded by J. J. Finley and R. Bullock. Cleburne commanded the corps tem-

porarily in late Aug. '64 when it covered Hood's retreat from Jonesboro, Ga.

Cheatham took command when Hardee left in Oct. '64 for Savannah. And although the numerical designation was not used, the III Corps of Hood's Army of Tenn. during the Franklin and Nashville campaign was essentially the same organization that had been known as "Hardee's Corps" and that was now "Cheatham's Corps." It included the infantry divisions of Brown, Cleburne, and Bate, and the cavalry division of J. R. Chalmers. "Brown's Division" had the brigades of Gist, Maney, Strahl, and Vaughan, which were commanded, respectively, by Z. L. Walters, H. R. Feild, A. J. Kellar, and W. M. Watkins. Cleburne's division was commanded by J. A. Smith, with the brigades of Lowrey, Govan, and Granbury (commanded by Capt. E. T. Broughton). Bate's division had Tyler's brigade, under T. B. Smith; Finley's brigade, under Maj. G. A. Ball; and H. R. Jackson's brigade. J. R. Chalmers' cavalry division had the brigades of E. W. Rucker and J. B. Biffle.

In the Carolinas campaign Hardee again commanded a corps. At Bentonville, 19 Mar. '65, it included the divisions of Hoke, McLaws, and W. B. Taliaferro. After the reorganization of 9 Apr. Hardee's corps consisted of Brown's (formerly Cleburne's) division under J. C. Brown, with the brigades of J. A. Smith and Govan; Hoke's division, with the brigades of Clingman, Colquitt, Hagood, and Kirkland, and the "First Brigade Junior Reserves," under L. S. Baker; Cheatham's division with the brigades of J. B. Palmer and Gist (under W. G. Foster).

II CORPS (Bragg's, Hardee's, D. H. Hill's, Hood's, S. D. Lee's), Confed. Armies of Miss. and of Tenn. When Bragg joined Beauregard with 10,000 men from Pensacola and Mobile in early Mar. '62 he was put in command of a division of Beauregard's recently-created (5 Mar.) Army of Miss. When A. S. Johnston arrived to form a new Army of Miss. (29 Mar.) for the Shiloh campaign, Bragg was put in command of the II Corps of that army. Numbering 13,589, it was composed of the following units: Ruggles' division, with the brigades of Gibson, Patton Anderson, and Preston Pond, Jr.; Withers' division, with the brigades of Gladden, J. R. Chalmers, and J. K. Jackson. Samuel Jones took command of the corps in July '62, and on 15 Aug., when Bragg took command of the army, it was under Hardee. Between 15 Aug. and 7 Nov. the organization was known as the Left Wing; after that it was again designated II ("Hardee's") Corps. Hardee assumed command 13 Nov. D. H. Hill succeeded Hardee 19 July '63, when Hardee took command of the I Corps after Polk's relief. Subsequent commanders were Breckinridge (8 Nov.), Hindman (15 Dec. '63), Hood (28 Feb. '64), C. L. Stevenson, and S. D. Lee.

As Breckinridge's corps at Chattanooga it was composed of Hindman's division (brigades of Anderson, [under W. F. Tucker], Manigault, Deas, and A. J. Vaughan); and Breckinridge's division (under W. B. Bate) with the brigades of Bate (under R. C. Tyler, A. F. Rudler, and J. J. Turner), J. H. Lewis, and J. J. Finley and A. P. Stewart's division (brigades of Stovall, Strahl, Clayton [under Holtzclaw]) and Adams (under R. L. Gibson)

In the Atlanta campaign, as Hood's or Lee's corps, it was commanded successively by Hood, Stevenson, Cheatham, and S. D. Lee. Division and brigade commanders were: Hindman's division, commanded successively by Hindman, J. C. Brown, Patton Anderson, and Edward Johnson; Deas's brigade commanded by Z. C. Deas, J. G. Coltart,

G. D. Johnston, and H. T. Toulmin; Manigault's brigade; W. F. Tucker or J. H. Sharp's brigade; and Walthall's or Brantley's brigade, commanded by Walthall, Samuel Benton, and W. F. Brantley. C. L. Stevenson's division with Brown's brigade, commanded by J. C. Brown, E. C. Cook, J. B. Palmer; Cumming's brigade, commanded by Alfred Cumming, C. M. Shelley; Reynolds' brigade, commanded by W. W. Reynolds, R. C. Trigg, J. B. Palmer; and E. W. Pettus' brigade. Stewart's division, commanded by A. P. Stewart and H. D. Clayton; Stovall's brigade, commanded by M. A. Stovall and Abda Johnson; Clayton's brigade, commanded by H. D. Clayton, Holtzclaw, and Bushrod Jones; Alpheus Baker's brigade; and R. L. Gibson's brigade.

In the Franklin and Nashville campaign S. D. Lee's corps was technically the I Corps. It was composed of Edward Johnson's division with the brigades of Deas, Manigault (under W. L. Butler), J. H. Sharp, and W. F. Brantly; C. L. Stevenson's division with the brigades of Cummings (under E. P. Watkins) and Pettus; H. D. Clayton's division with the brigades of Stovall, R. L. Gibson, and Holtzclaw. (These were the commanders at Nashville, 15–16 Dec. '64.)

In the Carolinas campaign the corps was commanded by D. H. Hill at Bentonville, 19 Mar. '65. He had the following divisions: Stevenson's, Clayton's, and D. H. Hill's (under Col. J. G. Coltart). S. D. Lee resumed command of the corps after the reorganization of 9 Apr. His divisions then were D. H. Hill's, with the brigades of J. H. Sharp and W. F. Brantly; and Stevenson's, with the brigades of R. J. Henderson and E. W. Pettus.

III CORPS (Hardee's, Polk's, A. P. Stewart's), Confed. Armies of Miss. and of Tenn. Hardee's III Corps came into being when A. S. Johnston organized the (second) Army of Miss. on 29 Mar. '62 just prior to the battle of Shiloh. This 6,789-man "corps," having only the three brigades of T. C. Hindman, P. R. Cleburne, and S. A. M. Wood, was actually a division.

After the Army of Miss. merged with the Army of Ky. on 20 Nov. '62 to form the Army of Tenn., there were only two infantry corps. The designation "III Corps" was never used in the latter army, even though it was eventually organized into three infantry corps. Therefore, it is only to facilitate reference that the units known as Polk's and A. P. Stewart's corps are covered here under the heading of III Corps.

When Polk rejoined the Army of Tenn. 12 May '64 for the Atlanta campaign he commanded a force known until his death, 14 June, as "Polk's Corps" or as the "Army of (the) Miss." It had no connection with the previous "Polk's Corps" (See I CORPS, Confed. Armies of Miss. and of Tenn.). W. W. Loring took command when Polk was killed, and was succeeded the same day by A. P. Stewart.

During the Atlanta campaign it was composed of Loring's division, with the brigades of Featherston, John Adams, and T. M. Scott; S. G. French's division, with the brigades of Ector, Cockrell, and Sears; Cantey's (or Walthall's) division, with the brigades of Quarles, D. H. Reynolds, and Cantey (commanded by V. S. Murphy and E. A. O'Neal); and W. H. Jackson's cavalry division, with the brigades of F. C. Armstrong, L. S. Ross, and S. W. Ferguson.

During the Franklin and Nashville campaign it contained the same three infantry divisions, although the cavalry division now operated as part of Forrest's corps. Loring's brigades, still bearing the names of Featherston, Adams, and Scott, were now commanded by

I. B. Palmer, Lowry, and John Snodgrass, respectively. French's brigades of Ector and Cockrell were now commanded by Coleman and Flournoy, while Sears retained command of his brigade. In Walthall's division Quarles's brigade was now commanded by G. D. Johnson; Reynolds remained in command of his own; and Cantey's brigade was led by C. M. Shelley.

In the Carolinas the final organization of Stewart's corps (9 Apr. '65) contained the divisions of Loring, Walthall, and Patton Anderson. Loring still had Featherston and Lowry as brigade commanders; Shelley had joined him from Walthall's old division. Walthall now commanded what had been McLaws's division: Harrison's brigade and Conner's brigade (under J. D. Kennedy). Anderson led the division formerly commanded by W. B. Taliaferro and consisting of Stephen Elliott's brigade and Rhett's brigade (under Col. William Butler). During the period 16 Mar.–9 Apr. the corps was led by Cary Walthall (while Stewart was commanding all the infantry and artillery of the army).

ANDERSON'S CORPS. See IV CORPS, Army of Northern Va.

BEAUREGARD'S CORPS. See I CORPS, Army of Northern Va.

BRAGG'S CORPS (Miss.). See II CORPS, Armies of Miss. and of Tenn.

BRECKINRIDGE'S CORPS (Reserve Corps, Army of Miss.). Organized 5 Mar. '62 under G. B. Crittenden, who was relieved for drunkenness and succeeded 31 Mar. by Breckinridge. Numbering only 6,439, it was composed of three brigades under R. P. Trabue, J. S. Bowen, and W. S. Statham. Jones M. Withers commanded the unit at one time. After fighting at Shiloh (6–7 Apr. '62) and in the siege of Corinth, this "corps" went to Louisiana for the attack on Baton Rouge, 6 Aug. '62. It returned with Breckinridge to form the Army of Middle. Tenn. In Nov. '62 it became the 1st Div. of Hardee's II Corps, Army of Tenn.

BUCKNER'S CORPS, Army of Tenn. A temporary corps commanded at Chickamauga by Simon B. Buckner. It comprised the divisions of A. P. Stewart, Wm. Preston, and B. R. Johnson.

CHEATHAM'S CORPS. See I CORPS, Armies of Miss. and of Tenn.

EARLY'S CORPS. See II CORPS, Army of Northern Va.

EWELL'S CORPS. See II CORPS, Army of Northern Va.

FORREST'S CAVALRY CORPS, Confed. Army of Tenn.

After being promoted B.G. in mid-'62, Forrest took command of a brigade composed of three regiments: Wharton's, Adams', and Scott's. With this force he conducted raids during Bragg's invasion of Ky. In Nov. '63 Forrest was put in command of all cavalry forces in west Tenn. and northern Miss. During the Chickamauga campaign his corps consisted of F. C. Armstrong's division with "Armstrong's" and "Forrest's" brigades commanded, respectively, by J. T. Wheeler and G. G. Dibrell; and John Pegram's division, with the brigades of H. B. Davidson and J. S. Scott.

During the Franklin and Nashville campaign Forrest's cavalry corps had four divisions: J. R. Chalmers', with the brigades of E. W. Rucker, Robert McCulloch, and J. J. Neely; Abraham Buford's, with the brigades of T. H. Bell and Edward Crossland; W. H. Jackson's division, with the brigades of L. S. Ross and F. C. Armstrong; and P. D. Roddey's division.

HAMPTON'S CAVALRY CORPS. See STUART'S CAVALRY CORPS, Army of Northern Va.

HARDEE'S CORPS. See I, II, and III Corps, Armies of Miss. and of Tenn.

A. P. HILL'S CORPS. See III CORPS, Army of Northern Va.

D. H. HILL'S CORPS. See II CORPS, Armies of Miss. and of Tenn.

HOOD'S CORPS. See II CORPS, Armies of Miss. and of Tenn.

JACKSON'S CORPS. See II CORPS, Army of Northern Va.

S. D. LEE'S CAVALRY CORPS, Confed. Dept. of Ala., Miss., and Eastern La. In Aug. '63 S. D. Lee was put in command of all cavalry in this department. He led this corps at Tupelo and in other actions until May '64, when he succeeded Polk as department commander.

S. D. LEE'S CORPS. See II CORPS, Armies of Miss. and of Tenn.

LONGSTREET'S CORPS. See I CORPS, Army of Northern Va.

MARTIN'S CAVALRY CORPS. During part of the Knoxville campaign (Nov.–Dec. '63) William T. Martin moved up from command of his division to lead WHEELER'S (II) CAVALRY CORPS, Confed. Army of Tenn.

PEMBERTON'S CORPS, Confed. Dept. of Miss. and E. La. On 14 Oct. '62 Pemberton assumed command of this department "including the forces intending to operate in Southwestern Tenn." The O.R. index refers to "Pemberton's corps" of this department, meaning, presumably, the force he headed at Chickasaw Bluffs: M. L. Smith's "Defenses of Vicksburg" (brigades of Barton, Vaughn, Gregg, and Tracy), and the Provisional Division commanded by S. D. Lee and D. H. Maury (with Col. Wm. T. Withers and Allen Thomas as provisional brigade commanders). Effective strength was built up to 25,000 before Sherman's withdrawal. (B.&L., III, 471.)

POLK'S CORPS. See I and III CORPS, Armies of Miss. and of Tenn.

RESERVE CORPS (Breckinridge's). See BRECKINRIDGE'S CORPS.

G. W. SMITH'S CORPS. See II CORPS, Army of Northern Va.

KIRBY SMITH'S CORPS, Confed. Army of E. Tenn., Ky., Tenn. The troops that were put under command of E. Kirby Smith in Feb. '62 to constitute the Army of EASTERN TENN. were redesignated the Army of Ky. on 25 Aug. '62. Under Bragg's command for the operations in Kentucky that ended with the battle of Perryville, 8 Oct., the Army of Ky. was also called Kirby Smith's corps (Horn, 188). When the Armies of Kentucky and Mississippi were merged on 20 Nov. '62, to form the Army of Tenn., the former became "Kirby Smith's Corps," Army of Tenn. However, he did not join Bragg's army with his corps, but remained virtually an independent commander in his Dept. of Eastern Tenn. McCown's division was ordered to join Bragg at Murfreesboro and Stevenson's division was sent to join Pemberton at Vicksburg. This left Kirby Smith with only 6,000 troops in his department by the time he was ordered to command the Southwestern Army on 14 Jan. '63.

STEWART'S CORPS. See III CORPS, Armies of Miss. and of Tenn.

STUART'S CAVALRY CORPS, Confed. Army of Northern Va. (Hampton's, Fitzhugh Lee's). After Chancellorsville, when Lee reorganized his army into three infantry corps, he put all his cavalry units under Jeb Stuart. Although frequently called a "corps," this was actually a division. It contained the brigades of Wade Hampton, B. H. Robertson, W. E. ("Grumble") Jones, Fitz Lee, A. G. Jenkins, W. H. F. ("Rooney") Lee, and John D. Imboden; it also included a battalion of artillery under Maj. R. F. Beckham and later James Breathed.

After Gettysburg, Stuart's cavalry was reorganized into a true corps. Wade Hampton and Fitz Lee were promoted to Maj. Gen. and put in command of the two divisions. Hampton's division comprised the following brigades: James B. Gordon's (formerly Lawrence Baker's), P. M. B. Young's (formerly M. C. Butler's), and T. L. Rosser's (formerly W. E. Jones's). (Baker and Butler were wounded; "Grumble" Jones had been tried and found guilty of disrespect to Stuart.) Fitz Lee had the brigades of J. R. Chambliss (formerly "Rooney" Lee's), Lomax's (formerly part of Fitz Lee's and Jones's, with the 15th Va. Cav. added), and Wickham's (the core of Fitz Lee's former brigade). (*Lee's Lts.,* III, 215.) Imboden's brigade remained separate.

When "Rooney" Lee returned, before the start of the Wilderness campaign, the brigades were regrouped to create another division. Hampton's division was left with three brigades: Young's, Rosser's, and Butler's. Fitz Lee retained the brigades of Lomax and Wickham. Lee was given his old brigade, now under Chambliss, and Gordon's (*ibid.,* 411).

After Stuart's death at Yellow Tavern, Wade Hampton succeeded to command of the cavalry corps. Fitz Lee was acting commander upon occasion. After Hampton went to S.C. with his old division (now under M. C. Butler), in mid-Jan. '65, Fitz Lee succeeded him in command of the remaining 5,500 troopers (*ibid.,* 656). Munford moved up to head Fitz Lee's division, which now had the brigades of W. A. Morgan, Wm. Payne, and M. W. Gary. "Rooney" Lee's division had the brigades of Rufus Barringer, Capt. S. H. Burt (Beale's), and W. P. Roberts. Rosser's brigades were led by James Dearing and McCausland (B.&L., IV, 753).

VAN DORN'S (I) CAVALRY CORPS, Confed. Army of Tenn. Earl Van Dorn's cavalry division was reorganized 16 Mar. '63—as was Wheeler's —and redesignated "Van Dorn's" or the I Cavalry Corps, Army of Tenn. (Wheeler's became "Wheeler's" or the II Cav. Corps.) With headquarters at Spring Hill he directed the brigades of Forrest, W. H. Jackson, and F. C. Armstrong in a series of raids. He was killed 7 May '63 in a "private matter." Most of the units went to make up FORREST'S CAVALRY CORPS.

WHEELER'S (II) CAVALRY CORPS, Confed. Army of Tenn. Joseph Wheeler's cavalry division at Stones River (Murfreesboro) comprised his own brigade and brigades of Abraham Buford, John Pegram, and J. A. Wharton. Three weeks later, on 22 Jan. '63, he was put in command of all cavalry units in middle Tenn. as a reward for his outstanding performance in Ky; a Maj. Gen. now at the age of 26, this placed him over Forrest and Morgan (Horn, 193). On 16 Mar. the cavalry divisions of Wheeler and Van Dorn were reorganized and redesignated corps. At Chickamauga Wheeler's corps comprised Wharton's division with the brigades of C. C. Crews and Thomas Harrison; and W. T. Martin's division with the brigades of J. T. Morgan, A. A. Russell, and P. D. Roddey.

Wheeler accompanied Longstreet to Knoxville in Nov. '63 with 5,000 cavalry. His division commanders were W. T. Martin, F. C. Armstrong, and John T. Morgan; brigade commanders were Harrison, Russell, Crews, and Dibrell. Wheeler's corps was joined 27–28 Nov. by the brigades of Wm. E. Jones and H. L. Giltner from Ransom's Dept. of Southwestern Va. (B.&L., III, 752).

In the Atlanta campaign Wheeler's corps included three divisions and Roddey's command: W. T. Martin's division, with the brigades of J. T. Morgan (or W. W. Allen) and Iverson; J. H. Kelly's division with Allen's (or Anderson's) brigade, commanded in turn by Allen, R. H. Anderson, and Edward Bird; G. G. Dibrell's; and M. W. Hannon's brigades; W. Y. C. Humes's division, composed of Humes's brigade, commanded by J. T. Wheeler and H. M. Ashby; Thomas Harrison's brigade; and Grigsby's (or Williams') brigade, commanded by J. W. Grigsby and J. S. Williams.

When Hood led the Army of Tenn. into the Franklin and Nashville campaign, Wheeler's cavalry corps remained in Ga. to oppose Sherman. During Sherman's March to the Sea almost all of the relatively small amount of fighting was between Wheeler's and Judson Kilpatrick's (Fed.) cavalry.

In the Carolinas campaign Wheeler's corps became part of Wade Hampton's cavalry command. "The division and brigade commanders mentioned in General Wheeler's official report of the campaign are W. Y. C. Humes, W. W. Allen, Robert H. Anderson, M. W. Hannon, James Hagan, George G. Dibrell, F. H. Robertson, Thomas Harrison, M. S. Ashby, and C. C. Crews" (B.&L., IV, 700). Wheeler's effective strength during the campaign varied from 4,442 effectives to 5,172 in mid-Feb. '65 and 4,965 on 17 Apr. '65 (ibid).

CORPS, UNION

I CORPS (Potomac), 3 Mar. '62– 4 Apr. '62 and 12 Sept. '62–24 Mar. '64.

The original I Corps (Potomac) under Irvin McDowell is the one that was supposed to join McClellan for the Peninsular campaign but never got there (see KERNSTOWN and SHENANDOAH VALLEY CAMPAIGN OF JACKSON). It was composed of the divisions of W. B.

Franklin, G. A. McCall, and Rufus King; strength was 30,000. It was merged into the Dept. of the Rappahannock 4 Apr. '62, when the latter was created.

The second I Corps was created from III Corps (Va.). This is the I Corps identified with all the battles of the Army of the Potomac until after Mine Run. Since there were not enough replacements to keep all corps at effective strength, the divisions of I and III Corps were transferred to bring II, V, and VI Corps up to strength. Troops from I Corps were formed into the 2d and 4th divisions of V Corps. They were permitted to continue wearing their I Corps badges.

Corps commanders were Joseph Hooker, 12–17 Sept. '62 (South Mountain and Antietam [W.I.A.]); G. G. Meade, 17–29 Sept. '62; J. S. Wadsworth, who was in temporary command for Reynolds 2–4 Jan. '63 and 1–9 Mar. '63; J. F. Reynolds, 29 Sept. '62 to 1 July '63 (Fredericksburg and Gettysburg [K.I.A.]); Abner Doubleday, 1–2 July '63 (Gettysburg); John Newton, 2 July '63 to 24 Mar. '64 (Mine Run). On 28 Nov. '64 I Corps was ordered re-created of veterans but the war ended before the nine regiments raised were ready for combat (Fox, 66). This organization, which had been commanded by Hancock, was discontinued 11 July '66 and its troops mustered out (O.Q.M.G. data).

I Corps badge was a circle or disk.

I CORPS (Va.), 26 June–12 Sept. '62.

Troops of what had been the Mountain Dept. were on 26 June '62 redesignated I Corps, Army of Virginia. When Frémont refused to serve under John Pope, command of the corps passed to Franz Sigel; division commanders were Schenck, Von Steinwehr, and Carl Schurz. When the Army of Va. was merged 12 Sept. '62 into the Army of the Potomac, most of its troops went to make up the new XI ("German") Corps.

II CORPS (Potomac), 3 Mar. '62–28 June '65

"The Second Corps had a record of longer continuous service, a larger organization, hardest fighting, and greatest number of casualties, than any other in the Eastern armies. . . . Of the hundred Union regiments which lost the most men in battle, thirty-five belonged to the Second Corps" (Miller, X, 159). "Until the battle of Spotsylvania, on May 10, 1864, it never lost a gun or a color" (ibid., 188). When organized, the corps consisted of the divisions of I. B. Richardson and Sedgwick; Blenker's division was assigned, but never joined. The 3d Div., French's, was added 10 Sept. '62. In the reorganization of 23 Mar. '64, the 1st and 2d divisions of the discontinued III Corps were transferred intact and numbered the 3d and 4th, under Birney and Mott, respectively. The units of the II Corps were consolidated into two divisions, under Barlow and Gibbon. At this time the corps strength was over 46,000, with 28,854 present for duty (Fox, 69).

Commanders were: E. V. Sumner, 13 Mar.–7 Oct. '62 (Peninsula and Antietam); D. N. Couch, 7 Oct. '62 to 22 May '63 (Fredericksburg and Chancellorsville) [John Sedgwick commanded the corps 26 Dec. '62 to 26 Jan. '63, and O. O. Howard was in command 26 Jan. to 5 Feb. '63]; W. S. Hancock, 22 May to 3 July '63 (Gettysburg) [John Gibbon commanded the corps 1–2 July '63]; William Hays, 3 July– 16 Aug. '63 [Hancock W.I.A. 3 July]; G. K. Warren, 16 Aug. to 24 Mar. '64 (Bristoe and Mine Run) [except for three short periods when J. C. Caldwell was in command: 26 Aug.–2 Sept. '63; 16–29 Dec. '63; 9–15 Jan. '64]; Hancock, 24 Mar.–26 Nov. '64 (Wilderness, Spotsylvania, North Anna, Totopotomoy, Cold Harbor, Petersburg, Deep Bottom) [except when D. B. Birney was in command 18–27 June '64, at Reams's Station and Boydton Road]; A. A. Humphreys, 26 Nov. '64–28 June '65 (capture of Petersburg and pursuit to Appomattox) [except for brief periods when the corps was commanded by Gershom Mott, 15–17 Feb. and 9–20 June '65; N. A. Miles, 17–25 Feb. '65; and F. C. Barlow, 22 Apr.–5 May '65].

Badge: trefoil (three-leaf clover).

II CORPS (Va.), 26 June–12 Sept. '62

Banks's V Corps of the Army of the Potomac had been created 3 Mar. '62 and then abolished a month later to make up Banks's Dept. of the Shenandoah. When the Army of Va. was ordered into existence 26 June, these same troops were designated the II Corps of that army, and Banks became the corps commander. After the campaign of 2d Bull Run, the Army of Va. was merged into the Army of the Potomac and Banks's two divisions were reorganized into the newly-constituted XII Corps under Mansfield. As part of the Army of Va., Banks's II Corps fought at Cedar Mountain; during 2d Battle of Bull Run its mission was to guard supply trains.

III CORPS (Potomac), 3 Mar. '62– 24 Mar. '64

Made up originally from troops that had been in the divisions of Heintzelman, Porter, and Hooker. Porter's men were transferred in May to what was to become V Corps. Troops from VIII and XXII corps later came into III Corps. This organization fought in all the battles of the Army of the Potomac except Antietam (when it was in the defenses of Washington). During 2d Bull Run campaign the corps sent the divisions of Kearny and Hooker to reinforce the Army of Va. In the reorganization of

24 Mar. '64 the corps was discontinued; the 1st and 2d divisions were transferred to II Corps, and the 3d Div. to VI Corps. As in the case of I Corps men similarly transferred, the III Corps veterans were permitted to continue wearing their old corps badges. Principal commanders were S. P. Heintzelman, 13 Mar.–30 Oct. '62 (Peninsula; 2d Bull Run); George Stoneman, to 5 Feb. '63; Daniel Sickles, to 2 July '63 (Fredericksburg; Chancellorsville; Gettysburg, where he was wounded); W. H. French to 24 Mar. '64 (Bristoe and Mine Run). D. B. Birney was temporarily in command 29 May–3 June '63, 2–7 July '63, and 28 Jan.–17 Feb. '64.

Badge: diamond. The idea of corps badges originated when Kearny ordered the men of his division identified by a red-flannel diamond sewed to their caps.

III CORPS (Va.), 26 June–12 Sept. '62

Formed 26 June '62 from troops that had comprised McDowell's Dept. of the Rappahannock, it served under McDowell as III Corps (Va.) during 2d Bull Run campaign. When the Army of Va. was merged into the Army of the Potomac, 12 Sept. '62, the troops of III Corps (Va.) were used to constitute I Corps (Potomac) under Hooker.

IV CORPS (Cumberland), 28 Sept. '63–1 Apr. '65

XX and XXI Corps were consolidated 28 Sept. '63 to form IV Corps (Cumberland). Since the original IV Corps (Potomac) had passed out of existence two months earlier, the same number was reassigned. Of the western regiments that sustained the highest battle losses more were in this corps than in any other (this takes into consideration the fighting they had done while part of XX and XXI Corps also [Fox]). Commanders and operations were: Gordon Granger, 10 Oct. '63–10 Apr. '64 (Chattanooga, Knoxville); O. O. Howard, to

27 July '64 (part of Atlanta campaign); D. S. Stanley, to 1 Dec. '64 (Atlanta, Franklin, and Nashville); T. J. Wood, to 31 Jan. '65 (Franklin and Nashville); D. S. Stanley, to 1 Aug. '65. After fighting its last battle at Nashville, the corps moved into east Tenn. to prevent the possible escape of Lee's or Johnston's forces in that direction. In June the corps moved through New Orleans to Tex., where it was part of Sheridan's Army of Occupation.

Badge: triangle (same as original IV Corps).

IV CORPS (Potomac), 3 Mar. '62–1 Aug. '63

Made up initially of the divisions of D. N. Couch, W. F. Smith, and Silas Casey of the earlier Army of the Potomac plus some new organizations. E. D. Keyes was in command during its entire existence. Smith's division was detached 18 May '62 and assigned to the newly formed VI Corps. Keyes's Corps fought through the Peninsular campaign. At Seven Pines (Fair Oaks) its two divisions bore the brunt of the attack, sustaining 2,597 casualties out of less than 12,000 engaged. Couch's division lost over 600 men at Malvern Hill, while the rest of the corps guarded the trains during McClellan's shift of base. Couch's division accompanied the Army of the Potomac on the Antietam campaign, where it saw little action; this division was then transferred to VI Corps to become the 3d Div. The other division (Peck's) remained on the Peninsula for a few months and then moved to Suffolk. Its troops were gradually transferred to other commands. On 1 Aug. '63 the corps was discontinued. See IV CORPS (Cumberland).

Badge: triangle.

V CORPS (Potomac), 3 Mar.–4 Apr. '62; and 18 May '62–28 June '65

Created 3 Mar. '62 as part of McClellan's Army of the Potomac, this organization consisted of the divisions of A. S. Williams and James Shields under N. P. Banks. On 15 Mar. '62 it was made independent of the Army of the Potomac. When the new Dept. of the Shenandoah was organized 4 Apr. '62, Banks was made its commander and his V Corps transferred to it. The latter department was abolished when Pope's Army of Va. was established 26 June '62. Banks's organization then became II Corps of that short-lived army. A new V Corps was organized provisionally in the Army of the Potomac 18 May '62. It consisted initially of Porter's division of III Corps (Morell commanding this division), and Sykes's R.A. units. McCall's division, formerly of I Corps, was assigned during the period 18 June–26 Aug. '62. The War Department confirmed the organization 22 July and directed that it be officially designated V Corps. Other units were added from time to time. When I Corps was abolished on 26 Mar. '64, it absorbed units of that corps, which became the 4th Div. under J. S. Wadsworth (until the 27th), and then under Lysander Cutler; this 4th Div. was discontinued in Aug. '64 and its troops transferred to the other divisions. Commanders were: Banks, 20 Mar.–4 Apr. '62 (Kernstown); Fitz-John Porter, 18 May–10 Nov. '62 (Peninsula; 2d Bull Run; in reserve at Antietam); Joseph Hooker, until 16 Nov. '62; Daniel Butterfield, until 24 Dec. '62 (Fredericksburg); George G. Meade commanded until 28 June '63 (partially engaged at Chancellorsville), except for short periods when V Corps was commanded by Sykes, 1–5 Feb. and 16–23 Feb. '63, by Griffin, 26 Jan–1 Feb., and Humphreys, 23–28 Feb. '63; Sykes commanded 28 June '63–23 Mar. '64 (Gettysburg, Bristoe, and Mine Run), except for 7–15 Oct. '63, when S. W. Crawford was in command; G. K. Warren commanded 23 Mar. '64–1 Apr.

'65 (Wilderness to Five Forks), except for the period 2–27 Jan. '65, when Crawford was in command; Charles Griffin commanded until 28 June '65 (pursuit to Appomattox). The corps was discontinued on the latter date and its troops designated 3d Div., Prov. Corps. Badge: Maltese cross.

VI CORPS (Potomac; Shenandoah), 18 May '62–28 June '65

Provisionally organized 18 May in the Army of the Potomac and confirmed 22 July '62. It has been called "the most famous corps of the Civil War." Originally made up of Franklin's division under W. W. Slocum) from McDowell's Dept. of the Rappahannock, and W. F. ("Baldy") Smith's division from IV Corps. The division of D. N. Couch joined 13 Sept. '62, was discontinued 10 Jan. '64, leaving only its 2d Brig., which was transferred to the 2d Div.; this 3d Div. was re-created in Mar. '64 from troops of the deactivated III Corps. The corps left the Army of the Potomac 8 July '64 to become part of the Army of the Shenandoah; it rejoined 6 Dec. '64. Commanders were W. B. Franklin, to 16 Nov. '62 (Peninsula; present but not engaged at 2d Bull Run; Antietam); W. F. Smith, to 4 Feb. '63 (Fredericksburg); John Sedgwick, to 9 May '64 (Chancellorsville; one brigade [Shaler's 1, 3] at Gettysburg; Wilderness to Spotsylvania, where Sedgwick was K.I.A.); J. B. Ricketts commanded temporarily 6–13 Apr. '64; H. G. Wright, to 28 June '65 (Spotsylvania to initial assaults of Petersburg; Monocacy and defense of Washington against Early's raid; Sheridan's Valley campaign; Petersburg to Appomattox); G. W. Getty was temporarily in command 16 Jan.–11 Feb. '65. Badge: St. Andrew's cross.

VII CORPS (Ark.), 6 Jan. '64–1 Aug. '65

As happened also in the case of the IV Corps designation, VII Corps was assigned as a designation to another, unrelated, organization after the original VII CORPS (VA.) was discontinued. The second VII Corps was formed by the consolidation of troops in the Dept. of Ark. It was composed of the divisions of Salomon and Thayer, with Carr's cavalry division attached. Its principal fighting was done during Steele's Arkansas expedition, especially at Jenkins' Ferry. At this time the corps comprised 17 infantry regiments, five light artillery batteries, and 10 cavalry regiments. The corps was commanded by Frederick Steele to 22 Dec. '64; and J. J. Reynolds to 1 Aug. '65.

Badge: crescent and star.

VII CORPS (Va:), 22 July '62–1 Aug. '63

Organized from troops under John A. Dix at Fortress Monroe, Camp Hamilton, Norfolk, Suffolk, Portsmouth, and Yorktown. At this time it had about 9,600 effectives. In Apr. '63 it comprised the divisions of Corcoran, Getty, and Gurney, plus two brigades at Yorktown under Keyes and one brigade at Norfolk under Egbert Viele; effective strength was about 24,000. Its troops fought at Deserted House, Va., 30 Jan. '63 (Corcoran's division); and the defense of Suffolk (Corcoran and Getty). Getty's division was composed of veterans from IX Corps. Present for duty strength 31 May '63 was about 32,400. After various units had been detached, the corps was discontinued 1 Aug. '63 and its remaining troops merged into XVIII Corps. Commanders were: Dix until 16 July '63; H. M. Naglee, 16–20 July '63; G. W. Getty until 1 Aug. '63.

Badge: crescent and star.

VIII CORPS (Middle Department), 22 July '62–1 Aug. '65

Troops of the MIDDLE DEPARTMENT were organized into VIII Corps, which was commanded until 22 Dec. '62 by John E. Wool. The mission of the department was such that VIII Corps did no fighting as a unit, and its subordinate units, likewise, did little. Its forces were roughly handled by Ewell at the start of the GETTYSBURG CAMPAIGN. The 1st Separate Brig. under E. B. Tyler took part in the Federal defeat on the Monocacy 9 July '64 (Early's raid). Crook's Army of W. Va. was composed initially of two divisions (Thoburn and Duval) that, under a provisional arrangement, formed part of VIII Corps; for this reason Crook's command is sometimes referred to as VIII Corps (Fox, 80). Strictly speaking, however, it should not be considered as such: Dyer and the O.Q.M.G. records do not. Commanders of VIII Corps after Dix were: R. C. Schenck, 22 Dec. '62–5 Dec. '63 (except when W. W. Morris was in command 12–22 Mar.; 10–31 Aug., and 22–28 Sept. '63; and E. B. Tyler was in command 28 Sept.–10 Oct. '63); H. H. Lockwood, 5 Dec. '63–22 Mar. '64; Lew Wallace, until 1 Aug. '65, except for the period 1 Feb.–19 Apr. '65, when W. W. Morris commanded.

Badge: six-pointed star.

IX CORPS (Potomac; Ohio; Wash.), 22 July '62–1 Aug. '65

"A wandering corps, whose dead lie buried in seven states" (Fox, 81), it was formed from troops of the Dept. of the South and from Burnside's Expeditionary Corps (N.C. operation). The corps consisted initially of the divisions of Stevens, Reno, and Parke. The division of Cox was temporarily attached during the Antietam campaign. Commanders and operations while first with the Army of the Potomac were: Burnside, 22 July–3 Sept. '62 (Reno and Stevens in 2d Bull Run campaign, in which Stevens was K.I.A.); Jesse Reno, 3–14 Sept. '62 (South Mountain, where Reno was K.I.A.); J. D. Cox, to 8 Oct. '62 (Antietam); O. B. Willcox to 16 Jan. '63 (Fredericksburg); Sedg-

wick to 5 Feb. '63; W. F. Smith to 17 Mar.; Burnside to 19 Mar. '63; and then J. G. Parke.

On 19 Mar. '63 the corps was ordered to the Dept. of the Ohio, where it remained a year. Parke was in command until 11 Apr.; Willcox to 5 June; Parke to 25 Aug. '63. After arriving in the West, the corps had had two months of pleasant occupation duty in Ky. until June, when it was ordered to Vicksburg to take part in the siege. After this it participated in the Knoxville campaign. R. B. Potter was in command 25 Aug. '63–17 Jan. '64; Willcox to 26 Jan.; Parke to 16 Mar.; and Willcox until 13 Apr. '64.

Upon returning to the East in Apr. '64, the corps was ordered to Annapolis for reorganization, and Burnside again became its commander. The corps comprised the divisions of Stevenson, Potter, Willcox, and Ferrero (the latter a Negro unit). Since both Burnside and Parke, his C. of S. were senior to Meade, IX Corps was put under the direct command of Grant and not made part of the Army of the Potomac. During the Wilderness campaign this arrangement proved so awkward that on Burnside's suggestion (Fox, 83) the corps was made part of Meade's army on 25 May '64. Burnside remained in command until 14 Aug. '64, when he was relieved for unsatisfactory performance in the PETERSBURG MINE ASSAULT. Parke commanded the corps until 1 Aug. '65 (siege and final capture of Petersburg). In June '65 the corps was transferred to the Dept. of Washington. Willcox commanded 1–12 Jan.; 24 Jan–2 Feb.; and 17 June–2 July '65 in the absence of Parke.

Badge: shield crossed by anchor and cannon.

X CORPS (South), 3 Sept. '62–17 Apr. '64; (James), 17 Apr.–3 Dec. '64; (N.C.), 27 Mar.–1 Aug. '65.

Created 3 Sept. '62 from troops in the Dept. of the South, it participated in operations around Charleston and, 5 Feb. '64, Hawley's division ("US Forces St. Helena Island") went to Fla. where they sustained heavy casualties in the battle of Olustee (Ocean Pond).

When in the Army of the James it fought around Drewry's Bluff. Then, 30 May '64, its 2d and 3d divisions were sent to Cold Harbor to reinforce the XVIII Corps. These two X Corps divisions included 15 infantry regiments, two of which were Negro. They were reorganized into a new division, their units being brigaded with seven regiments from Hinks's Col. Div. and six colored infantry regiments from elsewhere to form the 3d Div. of XVIII Corps for this battle. The X Corps was next engaged at Deep Bottom, Darbytown Road, and Fair Oaks. On 3 Dec. '64 the corps was discontinued; most of its troops, along with the white units of the XVIII Corps, were used to create the XXIV Corps. Ames's (2d) division of the new corps plus Abbott's (2d) Brig. of the 1st Div. were organized on 6 Jan. '65 into Terry's Provisional Corps (N.C.) for the Fort Fisher expedition.

X Corps was re-created 27 Mar. '65 from Terry's Provisional Corps and included "all troops in N.C., not belonging to corps in Gen. W. T. Sherman's command." This organization was discontinued 1 Aug. '65.

While X Corps was part of the Dept. of the South, commanders were: John M. Brannan, 3 Sept.–17 Sept. '62; O. M. Mitchell to 27 Oct.; Brannan to 20 Jan. '63; David Hunter to 12 June; and Q. A. Gillmore to 17 Apr. '64.

In the Army of the James, X Corps commanders were: A. H. Terry, 28 Apr.–3 Dec. '64; (Gillmore, 4 May–14 June; W. T. H. Brooks, 21 June–18 July; D. B. Birney, 23 July–10 Oct.; Adelbert Ames, 4–18 Nov. '64).

In the Dept. of N.C., X Corps commanders were: Terry, 27 Mar.–13 May '65; Ames, to 1 Aug. '65.

Badge: square bastion.

XI CORPS (Potomac), 12 Sept. '62–25 Sept. '63; (Cumberland) 25 Sept. '63–14 Apr. '64

Known as "The German Corps" because of its high percentage of German-speaking units, this was a "hard-luck outfit" throughout its service with the Army of the Potomac. It was originally constituted 12 Sept. '62, mainly from the divisions of Schenck, Von Steinwehr, and Schurz that had been in Franz Sigel's I Corps, Army of Va. Not put into action during the Antietam or Fredericksburg campaigns, it was assigned to what was expected to be an inactive sector in the Chancellorsville campaign, but ended up taking the brunt of Stonewall Jackson's brilliant surprise envelopment. The first day at Gettysburg (1 July '63), two divisions under Schurz were routed with heavy losses. During its service in the East commanders were: Franz Sigel, 12 Sept. '62–22 Feb. '63 (except: J. H. Stahel, 10–19 Jan. '63; Carl Schurz, 19 Jan.–5 Feb. '63); O. O. Howard, 2 Apr.–25 Sept. '63 (Chancellorsville, Gettysburg) (except: Von Steinwehr, 22 Feb.–5 Mar. '63; Schurz, 5 Mar.–2 Apr, and temporarily on 1 July '63).

The 1st Div., (originally Stahel's, finally Gordon's) was tranferred in Aug. '63 to the Dept. of the South (Charleston Harbor) and 3 Sept. '63 became part of X Corps (South), with the designation "US Forces, South End of Folly Island." The other two divisions went to Tenn. with Hooker to support Grant in the Chattanooga campaign and, then, to take part in Sherman's operations in the relief of Knoxville.

This XI Corps (Cumberland) was

officially constituted 25 Sept. '63. In Jan. '64 Ward's and Coburn's brigades, formerly at Nashville and Murfreesboro, respectively, were added to form the corps's 1st Div. (under W. T. Ward). Howard led the corps (except for the period 21 Jan.–25 Feb. '64, when Schurz commanded) while it was in the Army of the Cumberland. The corps was discontinued 14 Apr. '64 and merged into the reorganized XX Corps.

Badge: crescent.

XII CORPS (Potomac), 12 Sept. '62–25 Sept. '63; (Cumberland) 25 Sept. '63–4 Apr. '64

Smallest corps in the Army of the Potomac, it consisted of the two divisions that Banks had commanded successively as V Corps (Potomac) and II Corps (Va.). The 1st Div. had been under A. S. Williams throughout these changes of corps designation; the 2d had been under Shields, Augur, G. S. Greene, and in XII Corps was under J. W. Geary. It is referred to by Fox as "the corps that never lost a color or a gun" (p. 87). Commanders were: J. F. K. Mansfield, 12–17 Sept. '62 (Antietam, Mansfield K.I.A.); A. S. Williams, 17 Sept.–20 Oct. '62, 1–4 July '63 (vice Slocum, who commanded the Right Wing during the battle of Gettysburg), and 31 Aug.–13 Sept. '63; H. W. Slocum, 20 Oct. '62–25 Sept. '63 (Chancellorsville and Gettysburg campaign [see above]). The XII and XI Corps, both under Hooker, were sent to the Army of the Cumberland 25 Sept. '63 to support Grant's operations around Chattanooga. (Slocum continued to command the corps while it was in the West.) Geary's "White Star" division (i.e., 2d) distinguished itself in the battle of WAU-HATCHIE, the "Battle Above the Clouds," and at Missionary Ridge. Slocum with Williams' ("Red Star") division had the mission of guarding the railroad from Murfreesboro to Bridgeport during this campaign. On 14 Apr. '64 XI and XII Corps were discontinued and their troops became part of the reorganized XX Corps.

Badge: five-pointed star.

XIII CORPS (Tenn.; Gulf), 24 Oct. '62–11 June '64; (Gulf), 18 Feb.–20 July '65

The original XIII Corps dates from 24 Oct. '62 when all troops in the Dept. of Tenn. (created 16 Oct. '62) were assigned to it. Although widely scattered (Sherman's District of Memphis; and the districts of Corinth and Jackson), they comprised, technically, the XIII Corps under the command of Grant.

On 18 Dec. '62 there was a reorganization that created four corps out of what had formerly been one; they were: XIII (New), XV, XVI, and XVII Corps. The new XIII and XV Corps were not actually organized as such until Jan. '63; during the period 18 Dec. '62–12 Jan. '63 the troops that were to make up these corps were part of Sherman's YAZOO EXPEDITION.

On 28 July '63, following the capture of Vicksburg, the corps was reorganized and transferred to the Dept. of the Gulf. On 11 June '64 it was abolished and most of its units went to the Reserve Corps (Gulf).

On 18 Feb. '65 a new XIII Corps was constituted, largely from the same units that had been transferred previously into the Reserve Corps (Gulf). The corps was discontinued permanently 20 July '65 at Galveston.

Commanders and operations were: Grant, 24 Oct.–18 Dec. '62; W. T. Sherman and G. W. Morgan, during the period 18 Dec. '62–12 Jan. '63, commanded units that ultimately comprised the XIII Corps (Yazoo and Arkansas Post operations); G. W. Morgan, 4–31 Jan. '63; J. A. McClernand to 19 June '63 (Vicksburg); E. O. C.

Ord, to 28 July '63 (Vicksburg; 13th Div. at Helena). The corps was reorganized 28 July '63 and transferred 7 Aug. '63 to the Dept. of the Gulf. Commanders were: C. C. Washburn, 28 July–25 Oct. '63 (except 15 Sept.–19 Oct., when Ord commanded); N. J. T. Dana, 25 Oct.–9 Jan. '64 (Tex. coast operations); Ord, 9 Jan.–20 Feb.; McClernand to 15 Mar. '64. During the Red River Expedition of 1864, in which the 3d and 4th divisions participated, the corps was commanded by T. E. G. Ransom, 15 Mar.–8 Apr., and R. A. Cameron, 27 Apr. '64. M. K. Lawlor then commanded, 27 Apr.–9 May; W. P. Benton to 11 June '64. The reorganized corps was commanded by Gordon Granger, 18 Feb.–20 July '65 (Mobile).

Badge: none.

XIV CORPS (Cumberland; Ga.), 24 Oct. '62–1 Aug. '65

When the second Army of the Cumberland was created 24 Oct. '62, the troops were officially designated XIV Corps (formerly Buell's Army of the Ohio). Another reorganization 9 Jan. '63 redesignated as XXI, XIV, and XX Corps the formations that had formerly been known, respectively, as the Left, Center, and Right wings, XIV Corps, Army of the Cumberland. The corps was discontinued 1 Aug. '65. Commanders were: W. S. Rosecrans, 24 Oct. '62–9 Jan. '63 (conclusion of Stones River campaign); George H. Thomas to 28 Oct. '63 (Tullahoma operation, Chickamauga); John A. Palmer to 7 Aug. '64 (Chattanooga, Atlanta campaign); R. W. Johnson to 22 Aug. '64 (fighting south of Atlanta); Jefferson C. Davis to 1 Aug. '65 (March to the Sea, final campaign in the Carolinas).

Badge: acorn.

XV CORPS (Tenn.), 18 Dec. '62–1 Aug. '65

Created 18 Dec. '62 by the order that created the XIII (New), XVI, and XVII Corps. As was the case with the XIII Corps also, the troops that were to constitute XV Corps were until 12 Jan. '63 part of Sherman's Yazoo Expedition and McClernand's Army of the Miss. (both of which see for further explanation). Commanders and campaigns were: W. T. Sherman, 18 Dec. '62–29 Oct. '63 (Yazoo Expedition, Arkansas Post, Vicksburg); Frank P. Blair, Jr., to 11 Dec. '63 (Chattanooga); John A. Logan to 23 Sept. '64 (Atlanta); M. L. Smith, 22–27 July '64; P. J. Osterhaus, 23 Sept. '64–8 Jan. '65 (March to the Sea); Logan to 23 May '65 (Carolinas); W. B. Hazen to 1 Aug. '65.

Badge: cartridge box with numeral 40.

XVI CORPS (Tenn.), 18 Dec. '62–7 Nov. '64; (Gulf) 18 Feb. '65–20 July '65

Created 18 Dec. '62 by the same order that established the new XIII Corps and the XV and XVII Corps. Originally it was composed of the following organizations of the old XIII Corps: 6th, 7th, and 8th divisions; and the Districts of Memphis, Jackson, and Columbia. On 20 Jan. '63 the 6th and 7th divisions were transferred to XVII Corps, and the 1st and 4th divisions and the Dist. of Corinth were transferred from the same corps. Considerable additional shifting of troops into and out of the XVI Corps continued to take place throughout its existence; it was never able to operate as a single unit and suffered more than any other by detachment of its divisions.

The four divisions of W. S. Smith, G. M. Dodge, Nathan Kimball, and J. G. Lauman were stationed in the vicinity of Memphis, LaGrange, and Corinth until June '63. All except Dodge were then sent to reinforce Grant in his siege of Vicksburg; they were placed under the command of C. C. Washburn (Fox, 96). These divisions did not do any heavy fighting during the siege operations. At Jackson, 10–16 July '64,

Lauman's division (attached to XIII Corps) and W. S. Smith's (attached to IX Corps) took part in fighting that cost them 700 casualties. Most of the troops of Kimball's (3d) division were transferred to Steele's VII Corps (Ark.) 28 May '63 (Dyer, 509). A new 3d division of XVI Corps was organized 24 Jan. '64 from the Dist. of Columbus (6th division), and headed by A. J. Smith. In Sept. '63 W. S. Smith's (1st) division was transferred to XV Corps and Lauman's to XVII Corps. Tuttle's (later Mower's) division of XV Corps was later transferred to XVI Corps and designated 1st Div. Dodge's (2d) division moved with Sherman to the relief of Chattanooga (Nov. '63) but had a mission of guarding the Nashville and Decatur R.R. during the actual fighting. In Feb. '64 A. J. Smith's and Veatch's divisions accompanied Sherman on his Meridian expedition. During the Atlanta campaign the divisions of Sweeny (formerly Dodge's) and Veatch were designated the XVI Corps (under Dodge) and made up part of the Army of the Tenn. (with XIII and XV Corps). After Atlanta fell, these divisions were transferred to the other two corps.

Meanwhile, the divisions of Mower (1st) and A. J. Smith (2d) remained in the Miss. Valley, where they were known as "the right wing of XVI Corps." Most of Kimball's division had been ordered to Ark. to become part of Steele's VII Corps. In Apr. '64 Mower's and A. J. Smith's divisions (both under A. J. Smith, and known as "Detachment, Army of the Tennessee") took part in Banks's Red River Expedition. In 1864, therefore, the 1st and 3d divisions were fighting under A. J. Smith along the Mississippi, while the 2d and 4th were fighting under Dodge in the operations from Chattanooga to Atlanta.

On 7 Nov. '64 the corps was ordered deactivated, but in Dec. A. J. Smith arrived from the Mississippi to take part in the battle of Nashville (15 Dec. '64). Although still officially designated as "Detachment, Army of the Tennessee," they were generally known simply as XVI Corps.

On 18 Feb. '65 the corps was officially re-created. A. J. Smith was in command; divisions were those of McArthur, Garrard, and E. A. Carr. This organization went to the Army of the Gulf, where it took part in the siege of Mobile. The corps took Fort Blakely, Ala., on 9 Apr. '65, the day of Lee's surrender at Appomattox and in the last infantry battle of the war. The corps was finally discontinued 20 July '65.

The official records show the following corps commanders: S. A. Hurlbut, 22 Dec. '62–17 Apr. '64 (C. S. Hamilton, 10 Jan.–5 Feb. '63); no commander 17 Apr.–15 Oct. '64; N. J. T. Dana, 15 Oct. '63–7 Nov. '64; A. J. Smith, 18 Feb.–20 July '65.

Badge: crossed cannon.

XVII CORPS (Tenn.; Gulf), 18 Dec. '62–1 Aug. '65

Created 18 Dec. '62, at the same time as the XIII (New), XV, and XVI Corps, this corps is best known for its performance under McPherson in the Vicksburg campaign. The corps was subsequently divided in much the same manner as was the XVI Corps: half remained in the Miss. Valley with the Army of the Gulf, while the other half went with Sherman to Atlanta.

Parts of the corps remaining in the Valley took part in Banks's Red River Expedition of Apr. '64. Organized with elements of the XVI Corps into a unit under the command of A. J. Smith (known variously as XVI Corps and as the Detachment, Army of the Tennessee), six regiments of the 2d Div., XVII Corps, were formed into a unit known as the Provisional Div., or as the Red River Div. of XVII Corps. The latter unit was commanded by T. Kilby Smith. Parts of the Red River Div. served also on McArthur's Yazoo City Expedition (4–13 May '64) and on Slocum's expedition to Jackson. A few regiments were engaged also under Sturgis at Brice's Cross Roads and in A. J. Smith's expedition to Tupelo. In November '64 the Red River Div. accompanied A. J. Smith's forces to Nashville.

As for the other part of the corps, on 8 June '64 the 3d and 4th divisions under Frank P. Blair joined Sherman's army for the Battles of Big Shanty and Kenesaw Mountain (9–30 June). As the XVII Corps, Army of the Tenn., it took part in the remainder of the Atlanta campaign and the march through the Carolinas. After the fall of Atlanta, Fuller's Div. of the XVI Corps was transferred in to become the 1st Div. of the XVII Corps. Throughout most of its subsequent actions, marked more by hard marching than by heavy fighting, the three divisions were commanded by Mower, Leggett, and Giles A. Smith.

Commanders and principal campaigns were: J. B. McPherson, 18 Dec. '62–23 Apr. '64 (Vicksburg); F. P. Blair, Jr. to 19 July '65 (Atlanta, Carolinas); (T. E. G. Ransom commanded 22 Sept.– 10 Oct. '64; M. D. Leggett, 10–24 Oct. '64 and on 8 May '65; and J. A. Mower, 24–31 Oct. '64); W. W. Belknap, 19 July '65–1 Aug. '65.

Badge: arrow.

XVIII CORPS (N.C.; James), 24 Dec. '62–3 Dec. '64

On 24 Dec. '62 the troops in the Dept. of N.C. were organized into a corps and designated the XVIII. It included Peck's division (formerly of IV Corps [Potomac]), some of the regiments that had fought under Burnside at Roanoke Island and New Bern, together with troops that had been garrisoning New Bern, Plymouth, and Beaufort. In Feb. '64 the corps lost the divi-

sions of Ferry and Naglee (16 regiments) which were transferred to X Corps in Charleston Harbor. In June it lost 12 regiments whose nine-month term of enlistment had expired. On 1 Aug., however, it acquired units that had formerly belonged to VII Corps; among these were the excellent division of Getty's, formerly of IX Corps, which had been left in the defenses of Suffolk when IX Corps went to the West.

After an uneventful period of service the corps along with X Corps became part of Butler's Army of the James on 15 July '63 when the departments of Va. and N.C. were merged. Under W. F. ("Baldy") Smith, a former VI Corps general, XVIII Corps participated in Butler's unsuccessful operations in the vicinity of Bermuda Hundred, including the bloody failure at Drewry's Bluff.

XVIII Corps then moved to reinforce Grant and took part in the battle of Cold Harbor. Before this operation Hinks's recently organized (20 Apr. '64) division of colored troops was temporarily broken up and its regiments brigaded with units from X Corps and elsewhere to form a provisional second division for the battle. Corps losses at Cold Harbor were over 3,000, almost 450 of whom were killed.

After being withdrawn by water from the Army of the Potomac, the corps arrived 14 June '64 at Bermuda Hundred to take part in the abortive attempts to capture Petersburg before Lee could shift troops from Grant's front to defend that place in strength. Hinks's Col. Div.'s part in this action marked the first time in the war that colored troops in brigade strength had been employed tactically.

The corps then participated in the siege of Petersburg until 26 Aug. when it was relieved by X Corps and ordered back to the defenses of Bermuda Hundred. A month later it moved to the north bank of the James where the 1st Div. (Stannard's) took part in the assault of Fort Harrison at Chafin's Farm. The corps also fought the second battle of Fair Oaks, 27 Oct. '64.

On 3 Dec. '64 the corps was deactivated. Its white troops went with those of X Corps to form the new XXIV Corps; its colored troops went with those of X Corps to form the new XXV Corps. The regiments of the XVIII Corps were organized under Devens to become the 3d Div. of XXIV Corps.

Commanders and campaigns: J. G. Foster, 24 Dec. '62–18 July '63 (in Dept. of N.C.); I. N. Palmer to 18 Aug. '63 (in Dept of Va. and N.C.); Foster to 11 Nov. '63; B. F. Butler to 2 May '64 (Bermuda Hundred); W. F. Smith to 10 July '64 (Cold Harbor, Petersburg); (J. H. Martindale, 10–21 July '64); E. O. C. Ord, 21 July–29 Sept. '64 (operations north of James); (John Gibbon, 4–22 Sept. '64); C. A. Heckman, 29 Sept.–1 Oct. '64 (operations north of James); Godfrey Weitzel to 3 Dec. '64 (operations north of James).

Badge: trefoil cross.

XIX CORPS (Gulf; Shenandoah), 14 Dec. '62–20 Mar. '65

Organized under an order dated 5 Jan. '63, but retroactive to 14 Dec. '62, the corps was to consist immediately of all troops in the Dept. of the Gulf and was to be commanded by Banks. A large number of troops were en route by sea when the order was published. In addition to the regiments in the area and six new regiments of La. Negroes, the following came by sea: 39 New England regiments, 22 N.Y. regiments, and the 47th Pa. Initial operations included engagements at Fort Bisland (12 Apr. '63), Irish Bend (14 Apr.), and Port Hudson, which surrendered 9 July after the XIX Corps had sustained over 4,300 casualties in trying to take it by siege and assault. Until Mar. '64 the corps per-

formed garrison duty. On 15 Mar. the 1st and 2d divisions (Emory and Grover) left on Banks's Red River Expedition under the command of Franklin. The 3d Div. remained in New Orleans.

In July '64 the 1st and 2d divisions went to Va. under Emory's command where their first action was against Jubal Early's raid toward Washington. As part of the Army of the Shenandoah (Sheridan) this force was initially known as "Detachment XIX Corps"; after 7 Nov. '64 it was officially designated XIX Corps and the division that had been left in La. became part of the Gulf Reserve Corps.

In Jan. '65 Grover's 2d Div. went to Savannah and was followed by the 1st Div., which left the Valley in April and participated in the Grand Review in Washington (24 May). In March the 2d Div. (now Birge's) left for N.C. minus the 4th Brig., which was left in Savannah; these three brigades were temporarily designated the 1st Div., X Corps. In May the two divisions that had constituted XIX Corps were back in Savannah; they all remained until Aug. '65, but some regiments stayed as late as 1866. Officially, however, the corps was deactivated 20 Mar. '65.

The element that had stayed in New Orleans (3d Div.) participated in the spring of 1865 in Canby's operations against Fort Blakely, Spanish Fort, and Mobile.

XIX Corps commanders and campaigns were: N. P. Banks, 16 Dec. '62–20 Aug. '63 (Port Hudson); Wm. B. Franklin to 2 May '64 (Red River '64); Wm. H. Emory, to 2 July '64; B. S. Roberts, 2–6 July '64; M. K. Lawlor, 6–7 July '64; J. J. Reynolds, 7 July–7 Nov. '64 (commanding 3d Div. in La.); Wm. H. Emory, 6 Aug. '64–20 Mar. '65 (Sheridan's Valley campaign); (Cuvier Grover, 8–28 Dec. '64).

Badge: a maltese cross-like figure.

XX CORPS (Cumberland), 9 Jan.
'63–28 Sept. '63; and 4 Apr. '64–1 June
'65

What had been the Right Wing, XIV
Corps, Army of the Cumberland, became XX Corps (Cumberland) on 9
Jan. '63. Under McCook this unit took
part in the Stones River and the Chickamauga campaigns. On 28 Sept. '63 its
troops along with those of XXI Corps
were combined to form the newly-desig-
nated IV Corps (Cumberland) under
Gordon Granger.

A new XX Corps was formed 4 Apr.
'64 by taking the XII Corps (consisting
of the two veteran divisions of A. S.
Williams and Geary) and adding Butterfield's new division. On paper, a fourth
division, Rousseau's, was also added,
but it remained on detached duty and
was never physically part of the corps.
The new XX Corps, under Hooker, also
appropriated the badge (star) of the
old XII Corps. Its operations included
the Atlanta campaign, the March to the
Sea and the operations in the Carolinas.
With the XIV Corps it made up Slocum's
Army of Ga.

Commanders were: A. McD. Mc-
Cook, 9 Jan. '63–9 Oct. '63 (Stones
River, Chickamauga); Joseph Hooker,
14 Apr. '64–28 July '64 (Atlanta); A. S.
Williams to 27 Aug. '64; H. W. Slocum
to 11 Nov. '64 (Atlanta); A. S. Williams to 2 Apr. '65 (March to the Sea);
J. A. Mower to 9 June '65 (operations
in Carolinas).

Badge: star.

XXI CORPS (Cumberland), 9 Jan.–
28 Sept. '63

Created 9 Jan. '63 from what had
formerly been known as the Left Wing,
XIV Corps, Army of the Cumberland.
It participated in the Stones River and
Chickamauga campaigns. On 28 Sept.
'63 the corps was merged with the XX
Corps to form the new IV Corps (Cum-
berland).

Commanders were: T. L. Crittenden,
9 Jan.–10 Oct. '63; (T. J. Wood, 19
Feb.–19 Mar. '63); (J. M. Palmer, 15
July–17 Aug. '63).

Badge: none.

XXII CORPS (Department of Washington, D.C.), 2 Feb. '63–11 June '66

Formed 2 Feb. '63 from troops defending Washington, its organization
changed continuously throughout the
war as units were taken away and new
ones added. Its only action was at Fort
Stevens, 12 July '64, when Early's raid
reached the outskirts of the capital.

Commanders were: S. P. Heintzelman, 2 Feb. '63–13 Oct. '63; C. C. Augur,
13 Oct. '63–11 June '66; (J. G. Parke,
7–26 June '65).

Badge: pentagon cross.

XXIII CORPS (Ohio), 27 Apr. '63;
(N.C.) (Cumberland), Jan. '65–1 Aug.
'65

Organized 27 Apr. '63 from regiments
stationed in Ky. and placed under the
command of G. L. Hartsuff. This corps
and the IX Corps (which had arrived
from Va.) made up Burnside's Army
of the Ohio in the operations against
Longstreet (also arrived from Va.) in
East Tenn. that ended in Burnside's capturing and then being besieged in Knoxville during the Chickamauga and Chattanooga campaigns.

Schofield took command of the corps
4 Apr. '64 and led it through the Atlanta campaign, during which period
it was known as the Army of the Ohio.
In the spring of 1864 Hovey's division
of Ind. troops joined the corps and was
designated the 1st Div. The 2d and 3d
divisions were commanded by Henry M.
Judah and Jacob D. Cox, respectively.
On 6 June '64 the 1st Div. was broken
up and its troops assigned to the other
two divisions.

After the fall of Atlanta, the XXIII
Corps was under Thomas' command
for the operations in Tenn. against

Hood. Still under Schofield, the corps was actively engaged in the battle of Franklin, but most of it was held in reserve during the battle of Nashville.

In Jan. '65 Schofield and two divisions of his XXIII Corps were transferred to the East with the contemplated mission of joining the Army of the Potomac besieging Petersburg. However, the success of Terry's expedition in capturing Fort Fisher (Cape Fear), N.C., led Grant to the decision to employ Schofield's troops in that area with a view to establishing a base of supplies for the forces of Sherman advancing north from Savannah. Accordingly, the Dept. of N.C. was re-established 31 Jan. '65 with Schofield in command. Cox's division landed at Cape Fear 9 Feb. and was followed by the divisions of Couch (formerly Ruger's) to Beaufort, and a new one under Ruger. Field forces at the disposal of Schofield were designated the Army of the Ohio; they included, in addition to his own XXIII Corps, TERRY'S PROVISIONAL CORPS and MEAGHER'S PROVISIONAL DIVISION. There were various provisional organizations to which divisions of the XXIII Corps belonged until 31 Mar., when J. D. Cox succeeded Schofield as corps commander. As for the divisions that remained in the West, the 4th Div. was under Jacob Ammen after 10 Apr. '64 and the 5th (or Dist. of Ky.) under S. G. Burbridge, after its organization in Apr. '64.

After making a junction with Sherman's forces at Goldsboro, the corps remained in N.C. until 1 Aug. '65, when it was discontinued.

Commanders and major campaigns were: G. L. Hartsuff, 28 May–24 Sept. '63; M. D. Mason to 20 Dec. (Knoxville); J. D. Cox to 10 Feb. '64, 4–9 Apr. '64, 26–27 May '64, 14 Sept.– 22 Oct. '64; George Stoneman, 10 Feb.– 4 Apr. '64; J. M. Schofield, 9 Apr. '64–

31 Mar. '65 (Atlanta, Franklin-Nashville, N.C.); J. D. Cox, 31 Mar.–17 June '65; T. H. Ruger, 17–27 June '65; S. P. Carter, 27 June–1 Aug. '65.

Badge: shield.

XXIV CORPS (James), 3 Dec. '64–1 Aug. '65

Created 3 Dec. '64 from white troops of the X and XVIII Corps, the former constituting the 1st and 2d divisions and the latter the 3d Div. under Foster, Ames, and Devens, respectively. The corps operated on the north bank of the James until the last month of the war, when it crossed to join the Army of the Potomac in the final assault on Petersburg (2 Apr.) and the pursuit to Appomattox.

In the meantime, however, it underwent several changes in composition. In Dec. '64 Ames's (2d) Div. formed part of Butler's unsuccessful expedition against Fort Fisher, N.C. On 6 Jan. '65 this division and Abbott's brigade of the 1st Div. were transferred into the provisional corps that was organized for Terry's successful expedition against Fort Fisher. Turner's 1st Div., VIII Corps, joined the corps from the Army of the Shenandoah 26 Dec. and was designated the Independent Div. The only significant action while north of the James was a minor one 10 Dec. '64 at Spring Hill when Longstreet launched a limited attack against the Union right.

On 27 Mar. '65 the divisions of Foster and Turner with one division from XXV Corps, all under the command of Ord, joined the Army of the Potomac. In the final operations of the war the corps saw hard fighting in the assault of Petersburg (Forts Gregg and Whitworth) 2 Apr.; at Rice Station 6 Apr.; and at Appomattox Courthouse 9 Apr.

Corps commands were: Ord, 3–6 Dec. '64; A. H. Terry to 2 Jan. '65; Charles Devens, Jr. to 15 Jan.; John Gibbon to

27 Apr.; John W. Turner to 17 May; Gibbon to 8 July; and Turner to 1 Aug. '65.

Badge: heart.

XXV CORPS (James), 3 Dec. '64–8 Jan. '66

Created 3 Dec. '64 from the colored units previously belonging to the X and XVIII Corps. A total of 32 regiments of infantry and one of cavalry were organized into the three divisions commanded by Kautz, Wm. Birney, and C. J. Paine. The latter division was detached from the corps in Jan. '65 to become part of Terry's expedition to Fort Fisher, N.C.; it never rejoined XXV Corps, but was eventually attached to X Corps when the latter was reorganized.

In Mar. '65 Birney's (2d) Div. was part of the force led by Ord to reinforce the Army of the Potomac in front of Petersburg; this unit took part in the final operations resulting in the capture of that place, and in the pursuit to Appomattox. Kautz's (1st) Div. remained in the defenses of Bermuda Hundred and was the first to enter Richmond.

In May the corps accompanied Weitzel to Tex. where it was part of the Army of Occupation until discontinued 8 Jan. '66.

Some of the regiments of colored troops that became part of the XXV Corps in Dec. '64 had previously seen action at the Petersburg assault, the Battle of the Crater, Chafin's Farm, Fort Gilmer, Darbytown Road, and the second battle of Fair Oaks.

Commanders were: Godfrey Weitzel, 3 Dec. '64–1 Jan. '65; C. A. Heckman, 1 Jan. '64–2 Feb. '65; Weitzel, 2 Feb. '65–8 Jan. '66.

Badge: diamond (lozenge) on a square.

CAVALRY CORPS, Union Army of the Potomac. Feb. '63–May '65. Joe ("Who ever saw a dead cavalryman?")

Hooker was the first commander of the Army of the Potomac to prescribe a proper organization for its cavalry. On 12 Feb. '63 Stoneman took command of a corps composed of three cavalry divisions and numbering 11,402 present for duty (Fox, 110). Division commanders initially were Pleasonton, Averell, and D. McM. Gregg, with a reserve brigade under John Buford. Poor performance in the Chancellorsville campaign led Hooker to replace Stoneman with Pleasonton on 22 May, and Buford succeeded to command of the 1st Div. Hooker relieved Averell for unsatisfactory performance and A. N. Duffié took command of the 2d Div. on 16 May.

The battle of BRANDY STATION, Va., 9 June '63, showed that the Federal cavalry was finally a threat to the supremacy that Stuart's troopers had heretofore enjoyed. Division commanders at this time were Buford, Duffié, and David Gregg. On 11 June the latter's 3d Div. was merged into the 2d Div., and Gregg succeeded Duffié. The actions at ALDIE, MIDDLEBURG, and UPPERVILLE, 17–21 June, gave further evidence that the Federal cavalry was now on a par with Stuart's. On 28 June the 3d Div. was reorganized from the cavalry division, XXII Corps, with Kilpatrick as its commander. It was this organization, Pleasonton commanding the divisions of Buford, David Gregg, and Kilpatrick, that took part in the remainder of the Gettysburg campaign. Corps strength was 11,000 men and 27 guns. Buford distinguished himself in the first day at GETTYSBURG. Custer's Michigan brigade (2, 3) sustained the heaviest casualties.

When the Army of the Potomac was reorganized in Apr. '64 Sheridan took command of the cavalry corps (4 Apr. '64). He had a strength of 12,424 in the divisions of Torbert, David Gregg, and James Wilson. (Another body of cavalry, 1,812 men, was attached to the IX

Corps.) Kilpatrick had been requested by Sherman and in Apr. was commanding the 3d Cav. Div., Army of the Cumberland.

The most memorable operation of the cavalry corps during the fighting from the Wilderness to Spotsylvania was SHERIDAN'S RICHMOND RAID, which resulted in the death of Jeb Stuart at YELLOW TAVERN.

In Aug. '64, when Sheridan went to undertake his SHENANDOAH VALLEY CAMPAIGN he took with him the 1st and 3d Cav. divs. When he was reinforced by the cavalry divisions of Averell and Duffié, Torbert was moved up from command of the 1st Div. to head the cavalry corps and Wesley Merritt took over the division. Becoming increasingly dissatisfied with Torbert and Averell, Sheridan relieved the latter on 26 Sept. '64. W. H. Powell succeeded Averell. On 30 Sept. James Wilson left to command Sherman's cavalry in the West, and Custer took command of the 3d Div. On 26 Jan. '65 Merritt took command of the corps and led it until Lee's surrender. Devin succeeded Merritt as commander of the 1st Div.

The cavalry corps rejoined the Army of the Potomac on 25 Mar. '65. Crook's division (formerly Gregg's 2d div.) was back to restore the corps to its original composition. With Merritt at the head of the divisions now led by Devin, Crook, and Custer, the cavalry corps had a strength of 13,820 men, in 37 regiments (Fox, 111). The remnants of STUART'S CAVALRY CORPS now numbered 5,500 (*Lee's Lts.,* III, 656). At FIVE FORKS 1 Apr. '65 Sheridan won the battle that broke open the defenses of Petersburg and led to Lee's surrender on the 9th when his further retreat had been blocked at APPOMATTOX COURTHOUSE (Clover Hill). (Command dates from Dyer, 323, 409.)

CAVALRY CORPS, Union Mil. Div. of the Miss. 29 Oct. '64–26 June '65. In the Federal armies of the West the cavalry was not organized into a corps until James Wilson came from Sheridan's corps (30 Sept. '64) to join Thomas at Nashville and organize one.

On 29 Oct. '64 Wilson took command of a corps of seven divisions (Dyer, 462). In the battle of Nashville, 15–16 Dec. '64 a decisive role was played by the part of the new corps that participated. E. M. McCook was absent with the 2d and 3d Brig. of his 1st Cav. Div. on an expedition into western Ky.; only his 1st Brig. under J. T. Croxton, took part in the battle. The other participating divisions were: Edward Hatch's 5th (brigades of R. S. Stewart and Datus Coon); R. W. Johnson's 6th (with T. J. Harrison and James Biddle); and J. F. Knipe's 7th Div. (J. H. Hammond and G. M. L. Johnson's brigades). In his subsequent operations Wilson led the 1st, 2d, 4th, and 5th divisions under E. M. McCook, Eli Long, Emory Upton, and E. W. Hatch (until 18 Jan. '65, then under R. R. Stewart).

Kilpatrick's 3d Div. operated with Sherman in the March to the Sea and Carolinas operations. The 1st Brig. of this division was commanded by T. J. Jordan during the periods 29 Oct.–10 Nov. '64 and 20 Jan.–26 June '65; E. H. Murray commanded during the intervening time. The 2d Brig. was commanded by Wm. Thayer until 5 Nov. '64 and then by S. D. Atkins. The 3d Brig. was commanded by E. H. Murray until it was discontinued 10 Nov. '64; the brigade was reorganized in Jan. '65, being commanded by G. E. Spencer until Apr. and then by M. Kerwin until 25 Apr. and T. T. Heth from then until 26 June '65.

Prior to the organization of Wilson's corps, the following major forces of

Federal cavalry had operated in the West.

During Sherman's Atlanta campaign the attached cavalry operated in four columns under Stoneman, Kilpatrick, Garrard, and E. M. McCook.

In 1863 the cavalry attached to the Army of the Cumberland operated as a separate command, instead of being piecemealed out to separate brigades as previously (and as had been done in the Army of the Potomac prior to Hooker's assuming command). At Stones River (Murfreesboro) D. S. Stanley commanded a cavalry force consisting of John Kennett's division (brigades of Minty and Lewis Zahm).

At Chickamauga the cavalry corps of R. B. Mitchell was composed of the following: E. M. McCook's 1st Div., with the brigades of A. P. Campbell, D. M. Ray, and L. D. Watkins; the 2d Div. of George Crook with the brigades of Minty and Eli Long.

During Banks's Red River Campaign (1864) the cavalry of the Dept. of the Gulf, accompanying him under A. L. Lee (succeeded by Richard Arnold), was organized into five brigades.

During Grant's Miss. campaigns W. S. Smith and Cyrus Bussey commanded cavalry forces.

RESERVE CORPS, Union Army of the Cumberland (Provisional). This is the official designation of the force popularly known as Gordon's "Army of Ky." It played a decisive part in the battle of CHICKAMAUGA.

TERRY'S PROVISIONAL CORPS, Union. Organized under A. H. TERRY in Jan. '65 for operations against FORT FISHER, N.C., from elements of XXIV and XXV CORPS. Formed nucleus of reorganized X CORPS (N.C.).

CORPS BADGES. See BADGES, Corps.

CORPS D'AFRIQUE. See NEGRO TROOPS.

CORSE, John Murry. Union gen. 1835–93. Pa. He attended USMA (ex-1857) and was a lawyer and politician when, on 13 July '61, he was commissioned Maj. 6th Iowa. On Pope's staff at New Madrid and Island No. 10, he was promoted Lt. Col. 21 May '62 and Col. 29 Mar. '63. Fighting at Corinth and Vicksburg, he was appointed B.G. USV 11 Aug. '63 and commanded 4, 4, XV, Tenn. (27 Aug.–1 Sept. '63) and 2, 4, XV, Tenn. (25 Oct.–25 Nov. '63) at Missionary Ridge where he was severely wounded. During the Atlanta campaign and the March to the Sea and through the Carolinas, he led the 2d Div., XVI (26 July–23 Sept. '64) and 4th Div., XV (1 Sept.–16 Oct. '63 and 23 Sept. '64–24 July '65). He received a great deal of publicity for his actions at ALLATOONA, also being breveted Maj. Gen. USV (5 Oct. '64) for it. Mustered out in 1866, he was in railroad and bridge construction and was active in Mass. Democratic politics.

CORSE, Montgomery D. C.S.A. gen. 1816–95. Va. A businessman in Alexandria, he fought in the Mexican War, went to California for the Gold Rush, and served in a militia unit there and returned to Va. to become a banker. In 1860 he organized the "Old Dominion Rifles" and later that year was commissioned Maj. in command of a battalion formed of several such volunteer companies. He was Asst. Adj. Gen. in Alexandria until that city's evacuation and then was commissioned Col. 17th Va., fighting at Blackburn's Ford, 1st Bull Run, Yorktown, Williamsburg, Seven Pines, and the Seven Days' Battles. During the battle of 2d Bull Run he led a brigade and was slightly wounded, as he was at Boonesboro also. His regiment was down to 56 men at the beginning of the Antietam campaign and was reduced further to seven: one major, one lieutenant, and five privates. Corse was severely wounded and left behind enemy lines before a Confederate advance recovered him. During the battle, however, his regiment captured two battle flags. Appointed B.G. C.S.A. 1 Nov. '62, he took over Pickett's old brigade and was married just before Fredericksburg. He served under Pickett in that battle and during Gettysburg kept his brigade at Hanover Junction on guard. Going to Ga. with Longstreet, he fought at Chickamauga, at Dandridge (Tenn.), and returned for the Wilderness, fighting in Hoke's division. He fought Butler at Drewry's Bluff and was sent to the defense of New Bern. Returning to Petersburg, he fought at Dinwiddie Courthouse and Five Forks before being captured with Ewell at Sayler's Creek. Held in Ft. Warren until Aug. '65, he returned to banking in Alexandria. He was partially blind for some years before his death.

COSBY, George Blake. C.S.A. gen. c.1831–1909. Ky. USMA 1852 (17/43); Mtd. Rifles-Cav. He served on the frontier, was severely wounded in Indian fighting, and taught cavalry tactics at West Point before resigning as a Capt. 10 May '61 to become Capt. of C.S.A. cavalry. In Sept. '61 he was promoted Maj. and served under Buckner in south and central Kentucky and was that general's Chief of Staff at Donelson. He took the famous surrender note from Buckner to Grant. Captured and exchanged, he was promoted Col. of Cav. and then B.G. C.S.A. 20 Jan. '63 (appointed 23 Apr. '63). He led a brigade under Van Dorn at Thompson's Station (Tenn.) 5 Mar. '63 and also fought in the Vicksburg and Meridian campaigns. He continued to serve in the Dept. of Ala., Miss. and Eastern La. until war's end. Later a California farmer, he held

several public offices and sat on the USMA Board of Visitors.

COTTONCLAD SHIP. See RAM.

COUCH, Darius Nash. Union gen. 1822–97. N.Y. USMA 1846 (13/59); Arty. He fought in the Mexican War (1 brevet) and the Seminole War. On leave of absence in 1853 he gained distinction as a naturalist while exploring in Mexico with an expedition from the Smithsonian Institution. Resigning in 1855, he engaged in business and manufacturing. On 15 June '61 he became Col. of the 7th Mass. and in Aug. was commissioned B.G. USV with rank from 17 May. Commanding the 1st Div., IV (Keyes's) Corps (13 Mar.–12 July '62), he took part in the Peninsular campaign. Promoted Maj. Gen. USV 4 July '62, he led his division in the 2d Bull Run and Antietam campaigns. This division was attached to Franklin's VI Corps 13 Sept. and on 26 Sept. '62 became part of that corps, being redesignated the 3d Div. Couch's unit saw action only on 17 Sept. (Crampton's Gap) during these two campaigns. Taking command of II Corps 7 Oct., Couch led this unit with distinction in the battles of Fredericksburg and Chancellorsville. Disgusted with Hooker's blundering in the latter campaign, Couch asked to be relieved and was given command of the Dept. of the Susquehanna. During the Gettysburg campaign he was engaged in organizing Pa. home-guard levies for the defense of the state. Going then to the West, he commanded the 2d Div., XXIII Corps (8 Dec. '64–30 Apr. '65) at Nashville (15–16 Dec. '64) and in N.C. On leave of absence until he resigned 26 May '65. After being an unsuccessful Democratic candidate for Gov. of Mass., he was US Collector for the port of Boston for five months, but his appointment ceased 4 Mar. '67 when the Senate failed to confirm it. He was president of a mining and manufacturing concern in Va. in 1867, then Q.M. Gen. of Conn. (1876–78) and Adj. Gen. (1883–84).

COUGHLIN, John. Union officer. Vt. Lt. Col. 10th N.H. 5 Sept. '62; Bvt. B.G. USV 9 Apr. '65; Medal of Honor 24 Aug. '93 for night attack 9 May '64 at Swifts Creek (Va.) upon Burnham's brigade.

COULTER, Richard. Union officer. Pa. After fighting in the Mexican War, he was commissioned Capt. 11th Pa. 24 Apr. '61 and Lt. Col. two days later. Mustered out 1 Aug. '61, he was commissioned Col. 11th Pa. when it was reorganized 27 Nov. '61 and mustered out in July '65. He was breveted B.G. USV 1 Aug. '64 for the Wilderness and Spotsylvania and Maj. Gen. USV 1 Apr. '65 for Five Forks.

COUNTERRECONNAISSANCE. All measures taken to keep enemy RECONNAISSANCE forces from gaining information.

COUP DE MAIN. "A sudden and vigorous attack, for the purpose of instantaneously capturing a position" (Wilhelm).

COUP D'OEIL. "The gift of rapidly grasping and turning to the best account the contingencies of war, and the features of the country which is its scene" (Wilhelm). Meaning literally "glance," it is an old military term used in evaluating generals and means the ability to size up a situation, particularly with respect to terrain, rapidly and accurately.

COWDEN, Robert. Erroneous listing by Phisterer for COWDIN, Robert, B.G. USV.

COWDIN, Robert. Union gen. 1805–74. Vt. He was commissioned Col. 1st Mass. 25 May '61. At Blackburn's Ford (18 July '61) he is described as standing conspicuously in white shirt sleeves and, when told to sit down, saying, "The bullet is not cast that will kill me today."

He was right, and lived to fight at 1st Bull Run, Williamsburg, Fair Oaks, Glendale, Malvern Hill, and Chantilly. Appointed B.G. USV 26 Sept. '62, he commanded 1st Brig., Abercrombie's military division, Washington, Potomac (Oct. '62–Feb. '63) and 2d Brig., Abercrombie's division, XXII, Washington (2 Feb.–31 Mar. '63) when his commission expired.

COWEN, Benjamin Rush. Union officer. 1831–? Ohio. Maj. Add. paymaster Vols. 1 June '61; Bvt. B.G. USV. Brevets for war service, equipping etc., Ohio Natl. Guards. He was a well-known journalist, legislator, and merchant.

COX, Jacob Dolson. Union gen. and politician. 1828–1900. Born in Canada of US parents. After living in N.Y. he went to Ohio in 1846 and graduated from Oberlin in 1851. He was a lawyer and state Senator (Republican) at outbreak of the war. Fletcher Pratt calls Cox a universal genius, "world-famous as an authority on microscopy and cathedral architecture, literator, politician, artist, soldier—everything" (*Ordeal by Fire,* 302). A B.G. of militia, he entered Federal service and was commissioned B.G. USV 17 May '61. Commanding the "Brigade of the Kanawha" (W.Va.), he later headed the Dept. of the Kanawha until Aug. '62, when he joined Pope's Army of Virginia. Commanding the Kanawha division, IX Corps, he distinguished himself at South Mountain. On the death of Jesse Reno in the latter engagement Cox assumed command of the corps and led it in the Battle of Antietam. He was commissioned Maj. Gen. USV 6 Oct. '62. Returning to W. Va., he cleared that area of Confederate forces and was department commander until 16 Apr. '63. On the latter date he assumed command of the District of Ohio and also of the 3d Div., XXIII Corps (Ohio). He led this division in the Atlanta and the Franklin and

Nashville campaigns. He accompanied the XXIII Corps to N.C. and later commanded the corps. (See XXIII CORPS.) He was Gov. of Ohio 1866–67 and Grant's Sec. of the Int. from Mar. '69 until Dec. '70, when he resigned in disagreement with policies of the administration. He resumed his law practice in Cincinnati, became president of the Wabash R.R. in 1873; and was elected to Congress in 1876. His two-volume *Military Reminiscences of the Civil War* was published in 1900. He is also author of *Atlanta* and *The March to the Sea— Franklin and Nashville* (1882), which are frequently cited in this work.

COX, John Cooke. Union officer. Pa. Capt. Comsy. of Subsist. Vols. 5 Aug. '61; Lt. Col. Comsy. of Subsist. Assigned 1 Jan. '63–27 June '64; Bvt. B.G. USV 4 July '63 (war service); resigned 27 June '64. Died 1872.

COX, Robert Courton. Union officer. Pa. Maj. 171st Pa. 19 Nov. '62; mustered out 8 Aug. '63; Col. 207th Pa. 9 Sept. '64; Bvt. B.G. USV 2 Apr. '65 (Ft. Stedman; Ft. Sedgwick, Va.). Commanded 2, 3, IX.

COX, William Ruffin. C.S.A. gen. 1832–1919. N.C. After Franklin (Tenn.) College and law study at Lebanon College, he was an attorney and planter in N.C. Having organized and equipped a militia company and studied military tactics before the war, he was more than usually well equipped to be commissioned Maj. 2d N.C. He commanded the regiment at Chancellorsville as colonel and was wounded five times during the battle. Named B.G. C.S.A. 31 May '64 and given temporary command of a brigade, he is listed as Col. of his regiment at the Wilderness, although at Cedar Creek he is shown as a B.G. and brigade commander under Ramseur. Wounded 11 times during the war. He was a judge and Congressman

afterward and active in the Democratic party and the Episcopal Church. D.A.B. describes him as having a "striking physical appearance, cultured and courtly; and his political choices indicate wisdom as well as character."

COZZENS, William Cole. Gov. of R.I. 1811–76. R.I. A wealthy merchant and banker, he was Mayor of Newport and in the legislature. In Mar. '62, after the Gov. and Lt. Gov. had both resigned, Cozzens, as president of the state senate, served as Gov. for about three months.

"CRACKER LINE" OPERATIONS. Phase of CHATTANOOGA CAMPAIGN.

CRAIG, Henry Knox. Union officer. Pa. Entering the R.A. in 1812, he commanded several arsenals and armories before becoming the Chief of Ord. of the Army of Occupation in Tex. and N. Mex. in 1847. He received 1 brevet for the Mexican War and was Col. and Chief of Ord. Bureau from 1851 until 23 Apr. '61. Retired 1 June '63, he was breveted B.G. USA and died in 1869.

CRAIG, James. Union gen. 1820–88. Pa. A lawyer, he was in the Mexican War and then Democratic Congressman from Mo. Named B.G. USV 21 Mar. '62, he commanded Dist. of Nebr., Dept. of Kans., June '62–4 June '63, when he resigned. He was later B.G. Enrolled Mo. State Mil. 19 May '64 until 2 Jan. '65.

CRAM, George Henry. Union officer. Pa. R.A. Capt. 9th Ky. 26 Nov. '61; Lt. Col. 10 May '62; Col. 10 Mar. '63; Bvt. B.G. USV (Stones River, Chickamauga, Shiloh, Missionary Ridge, Atlanta); W.I.A. Stones River, Missionary Ridge; mustered out 15 Dec. '64. Died 1872.

CRAM, Thomas Jefferson. Union officer. c. 1807–83. N.H. USMA 1826 (4/41); Topo. Engrs. Maj. Topo. Engrs. 6 Aug. '61; Lt. Col. 9 Sept. '61; tr. to

Engrs. 3 Mar. '63; Col. Add. A.D.C. to Gen. Wool 25 Sept. '61–23 Nov. '65; Col. Engrs. 23 Nov. '65; Bvt. B.G. USV; Bvt. B.G. and Maj. Gen. USA 13 Jan. '66 (war service). After teaching at USMA he served as a railroad engineer in the West and was chief Topo. Engr. of the Dept. of the Pacific. After the war he was in charge of harbor improvement in the Great Lakes.

CRAMER, Francis L. Union officer. Nebr. 2d Lt. 1st Nebr. Cav. 17 July '61; 1st Lt. and Adj. 30 Jan. '62; Maj. 1st Ala. Cav. 24 Oct. '63; Bvt. B.G. USV (war service).

CRAMPTON'S GAP (PASS), Md. 14 Sept. '62. Action during ANTIETAM CAMPAIGN.

CRANBERRY, Hiram B. Misspelling of Confed. Gen. Hiram B. GRANBURY.

CRANDAL, Frederick Mortimer. Union officer. Pa. Appt.-Md. 1st Lt. 33d Ill. 15 Aug. '61–23 Nov. '62; Capt. Add. Adj. Gen. Vols. 2 Oct. '62; Col. 48th US Col. Inf. 8 Aug. '63; Bvt. B.G. USV 24 Oct. '65. Brevets for war service, Ark. Post, Ft. Blakely, Ala. Commanded 1st, 1st USCT Dist. West Fla. Ex-cadet, USMA 1852.

CRANE, Charles Henry. Union officer. R.I. Appt.-Mass. Joining the R.A. as Asst. Surgeon in 1848, he served in the Seminole War, the Mexican War, and on the frontier in Indian fighting. Promoted Maj. 21 May '61, he supervised the medical care of recruits in N.Y.C. until Jan. '62, when he became Med. Dir. of the Dept. of Fla. until June '62. Taking the same post in the Dept. of the South, he was there until June '63, became Med. Insp. of P.O.W.'s until Sept. of that year and finished the war in the Surg. Gen.'s office. Breveted B.G. USA for war service, he died on active duty in 1883 as B.G. USA and Surg. Gen.

CRANE, Nirom M. Union officer. N.Y. Lt. Col. 23d N.Y. 16 May '61; mustered out 23 May '63; Col. 107th N.Y. 24 June '63; Bvt. B.G. USV (Ga. and Carolinas campaign).

CRANOR, Jonathan. Union officer. N.C. Capt. 11th Ohio 20 Apr. '61; Lt. Col. 40th Ohio 21 Aug. '61; Col. 11 Sept. '61; Bvt. B.G. USV (war service); resigned 5 Feb. '63. Commanded 3d, Kanawha Dist., Army of W. Va.; Dist. of Eastern Ky., Army of Ohio. Died 1896.

CRAPO, Henry H. Gov. of Michigan. 1804–69. Mich. A manufacturer and lumberman, he had long held minor political offices and then joined the new Republican party when it was organized in the state. He sat in the legislature and was elected Gov. 1864–68.

CRATER, BATTLE OF THE. See PETERSBURG MINE ASSAULT.

CRAWFORD, Samuel Johnson. Union officer. Ind. Capt. 2d Kans. Cav. 14 May '61; Col. 83d US Col. Inf. 1 Nov. '63; Bvt. B.G. USV (war service); resigned 7 Nov. '64.

CRAWFORD, Samuel Wylie. Union gen. 1829–92. Pa. R.A. A graduate of the U. of Pa. medical school, he was made Asst. Surg. in 1851 and served in the Southwest, being commissioned Maj. 13th US Inf. 14 May '61 after commanding a battery during the bombardment of Ft. Sumter. On 25 Apr. '62 he was promoted B.G. USV and led 1st Brig., 1st Div., Shenandoah, at Winchester (25 May–26 June '62) and 1, 1, II, Army of Va. at Cedar Mountain (26 June–4 Sept. '62). At Antietam he commanded 1, 1, XII and, succeeding Williams at division, was severely wounded. He commanded the PENNSYLVANIA RESERVES (3d Div., V) at Gettysburg (28 June–28 Aug. '63); the 2d Div. V (2–5 June '64) and the V Corps (7–15 Oct. '63 and 2–27 Jan. '65). Breveted for

Gettysburg, Five Forks (B.G. USA), war service (Maj. Gen. USA) and the Wilderness, Spotsylvania Courthouse, Jericho Mills, Bethesda Church, Petersburg, and Globe Tavern (Maj. Gen. USV 1 Aug. '64), he continued in the R.A. until 1873, when he retired as B.G. USA.

"CRAZY BET." See Elizabeth VAN LEW, Union spy in Richmond.

CREWS, Charles C. C.S.A. gen. Commissioned Lt. Col. 2d Ga. Cav. in 1861, he was captured in fall '62 during a raid into Kentucky and soon exchanged. Promoted to Col., he led the regiment in Wheeler's cavalry corps in mid-Tenn. and in the Atlanta campaign. Wounded in the Carolinas, he was named B.G. C.S.A. some time between 15 Apr. '65 and Johnston's surrender 26 Apr. He is listed by Heitman and C.M.H. as a general officer, but not by Wright.

CREW'S FARM, Va., 1 July '62. See MALVERN HILL, same date.

CRITTENDEN, George Bibb. C.S.A. gen. 1812–80. Ky. USMA 1832 (26/45); Inf. After serving in the Black Hawk War and in garrison, he resigned in 1833 to practice law. In 1842 he went to Tex. and was captured in the ill-fated Mier expedition. Sent to prison in Mexico when he drew the white bean (while those who drew the black ones were shot), he was eventually freed and returned to Ky. He was reappointed to the R.A. in 1846 and fought in the Mexican War (1 brevet) before resigning 10 June '61 as Lt. Col. Mtd. Rifles. Commissioned B.G. C.S.A. 15 Aug. '61 from Ky. and promoted Maj. Gen. 9 Nov. '61, he was soundly defeated at LOGAN CROSS ROADS, Ky., 19–20 Jan. '62. He was arrested and censured, and this caused him to resign 23 Oct. '62. During the rest of the war he served without rank on J. S. Williams's staff. Brother of T. L. Crittenden.

CRITTENDEN, John Jordan. Statesman. 1787–1863. Ky. After graduating from William and Mary he became Atty. Gen. in the territory of Ill. and fought in the War of 1812. He held several public posts including Gov. of Ky., US Atty. Gen., and US Senator (1817–19, 1835–41, 1842–48, and 1855–61). He opposed secession and supported Lincoln's administration. The Crittenden Compromise (1860), the proposed extension of the Missouri Compromise line to the Pacific, was unacceptable to both sides. He worked to keep Ky. in the Union. One of his sons, George, became a Confederate general; another, Thomas L., and a nephew, Thomas T., were Union generals.

CRITTENDEN, Thomas Leonidas. Union gen. 1815–93. Ky. Son of Sen. J. J. CRITTENDEN, Thomas had been a lawyer in Ky., served in the Mexican War, was Consul to Liverpool (1849–53), and a Louisville businessman when the Civil War started. He was appointed B.G. USV 27 Oct. '61 and commanded the 5th Div., Ohio, at Shiloh. Appointed Maj. Gen. USV 17 July '62 for the latter action, he took command of a division in the Army of the Tenn. He commanded a corps under Buell and, later, Rosecrans, seeing action at Stones River (where he was breveted for gallantry) and Chickamauga (where his command was routed). Moving to the East, he commanded the 1st Div., IX Corps, until 13 Dec. '64, when he resigned. He entered the R.A. as a Col. of the 32d Inf. 28 July '66, transferred to the 17th Inf. in 1869, and served with that unit until his retirement in 1881. He had a "thin, staring face, and hair hanging to his coat collar—a very wild-appearing major-general, but quite a kindly man in conversation," according to Lyman.

CRITTENDEN, Thomas Theodore. Union gen. 1832–1909. Ala. A lawyer who fought in the Mexican War, he was named Capt. 6th Ind. 19 Apr. '61 and Col. 27 Apr. '61. He fought at Phillippi and was named B.G. USV 28 Apr. '62. Captured at Murfreesboro, he later commanded 3, 1, XX, Cumberland 9 Mar.–5 Apr. '63 and resigned 5 May. First cousin of George B. (CSA) and Thomas L. (USA).

CROCKER, John Simpson. Union officer. N.Y. Col. 93d N.Y. 3 Feb. '62; Bvt. B.G. USV (war service); mustered out 7 Sept. '64. Commanded 2, 3, II. Died 1890.

CROCKER, Marcellus Monroe. Union gen. 1830–65. Ind. First a cadet at USMA (ex-1851), he was a lawyer when he was commissioned Capt. 2d Iowa 27 May '61. He was promoted Maj. 31 May, Lt. Col. 6 Sept., and Col. 13th Iowa 30 Dec. '61. In the Army of the Tenn., he commanded 1st Brig., 1st Div. (23 Feb.–15 Mar. '62 and 6 Apr. '62 at Shiloh); 3d Brig., 6th Div. (8 Apr.–24 July '62) and 3d Brig., 6th Div. Dist. Corinth (24 July–1 Nov. '62). He was promoted B.G. USV 29 Nov. '62 and in the Dept. of the Tenn. led 3, 6, XIII (12 Nov.–18 Dec. '62); 3, 6, XVI (22 Dec. '62–20 Jan. '63); 3, 6, XVII (20 Jan.–30 Apr. '63). He also led the 7th Div., XVII (2–16 May '63); 4th Div., XIII (28 July–17 Aug. '63); and 4th Div., XVII (7 Aug. '63–27 May '64) during the Atlanta campaign where his brigade was called "Crocker's Greyhounds." Suffering from tuberculosis, he was sent to N. Mex. for his health and died in Washington, 26 Aug. '65.

CROOK, George. Union gen. and Indian fighter. 1829–90. Ohio. USMA 1852 (38/43); Inf. Served in Pacific Northwest before war; wounded 1857 by poisoned arrow. Appointed Col. of 36th Ohio 13 Sept. '61, led it in West Va. operations; commanded 3d Prov. Brig. 1 May–15 Aug. '62; wounded at Lewisburg 23 May. Promoted B.G. USV 7 Sept. '62, he commanded the Kanawha division at South Mountain and Antietam. Then engaged in W. Va. operations until Feb. '63, when he was ordered to the West. In command of the Independent Division at Carthage, Tenn., until June '63, he took part in the Tenn. campaign and the advance on Tullahoma. Given command of the 2d Cav. Div. on 1 July, he took part in subsequent operations through Chickamauga. In the pursuit of Wheeler's cavalry (1–10 Oct.) he won a victory at Farmington and drove the enemy across Tenn. Grant ordered him back to the East in Feb. '64 to command the Kanawha District and gave him the mission of interrupting rail communications between Lynchburg and E. Tenn.; he engaged in numerous raids and skirmishes including Cloyd Farm, Dublin Station, and New River Bridge. In Aug. '64 he succeeded David Hunter as commander of the Dept. of West Va. He led the Army of West Va. in Sheridan's Shenandoah campaign, fighting at Winchester, Fishers Hill, and Cedar Creek. On 21 Oct. '64 he became a Maj. Gen. USV. He and B. F. Kelley were captured 21 Feb. '65 at Cumberland, Md., when 70 Confederate cavalrymen under Capt. John H. McNeill entered the town at night in Union uniforms. After spending some time in Libby Prison he was exchanged. On 26 Mar. '65 he took command of the cavalry of the Army of the Potomac and fought from Dinwiddie Courthouse through the pursuit to Appomattox. He was breveted for Lewisburg, Antietam, Farmington, W. Va.; and Fishers Hill. After the war he earned the reputation of being the most successful Indian fighter the army ever produced. Known to his men during the Civil War as "Uncle George," and called "Gray Fox" by the Indians.

CROSMAN, George Hampton. Union officer. c. 1798–1882. Mass. USMA 1823 (30/35); Inf.-Q.M. He served on the frontier, was Chief Q.M. of the Seminole War 1836–37, and fought in the Mexican War (1 brevet). During the Civil War he was Chief Q.M. of the Dept. of Pa. and the Shenandoah 29 Apr.–24 Aug. '61 and in charge of the Q.M. Dept. in Philadelphia until 27 Aug. '64. Promoted Col. 26 Feb. '63 for the remainder of the war, he wrote "Manual for the Quartermaster's Department." Breveted B.G. and Maj. Gen. USA, he continued in the R.A. until 1866, when he retired.

CROSS, Nelson. Union officer. N.H. Commissioned Lt. Col. 67th N.Y. 24 June '61, he was promoted Col. 9 Oct. '62. He was mustered out 4 July '64 as Bvt. B.G. USV and Maj. Gen. USV for war service.

CROSS, Osborne. Union officer. c. 1803–76. Md. USMA 1825 (26/37); Inf.-Q.M. He served on the frontier and as Chief Q.M. of the Army of Mexico and the Pacific Division. Cullum says that he was "awaiting trial, and suspended, 1858–62 . . . Served . . . as Chief Quartermaster of the Army of the Mississippi" 13 Apr.–13 June '62. From 14 Oct. '62 to 5 Mar. '63 he was on inspection duty in N.C., S.C., and Dept. of the Gulf, and was Chief Q.M. of the Pittsburgh Depot for the remainder of the war. In 1866 he was retired as Col. Asst. Q.M. Gen., having been breveted B.G. USA.

CROSS KEYS (UNION CHURCH) AND PORT REPUBLIC, Va., 8–9 June '62. (SHENANDOAH VALLEY CAMPAIGN OF JACKSON) After eluding the Federal trap at Strasburg, 1 June, Jackson retired up the Valley. Frémont was pursuing up North Fork while Shields moved up the South Fork with the mission of cutting off the Confed-

erate retreat. At Port Republic, Jackson turned for a final blow against his adversaries. Since the head of Shields's column was still about a day's march away (Conrad's Store), Jackson planned to defeat Frémont first and then mass against Shields. On the 7th he tried in vain to draw the cautious Frémont into attacking Ewell's division at Cross Keys. Early the next morning scouts from Carroll's brigade (Shields) approached Port Republic and at about 9 A.M. a force penetrated the town, almost capturing Jackson. About the same time Frémont attacked, and Jackson faced the danger of being forced to fight on two fronts. Since Jackson had ordered the destruction of bridges across the South Fork below Port Republic, there was no coordination between the two Federal commanders and this danger did not materialize. After a cannonade, Blenker's division attempted an envelopment of Ewell's right which was held by Trimble's brigade. They approached to within musket range before they were driven back. Trimble pursued about a mile before being ordered at about noon to halt. Frémont took no further action that day.

Jackson gave Trimble the mission of holding Frémont the next day with his brigade, Patton's 42d Va., and the 1st Va. Bn. Ewell was to move the rest of his command across the wooden bridge at Port Republic, over an improvised bridge on the South Branch, and against Shields's force. The latter consisted of about 3,000 men in the brigades of Tyler and Carroll, under the command of the former. Shortly after 7 A.M. Winder led the Stonewall brigade in a frontal assault against the right of a strong defensive position. Scott attacked their left. The situation became critical as this attack was repulsed, and Ewell's arrival was delayed by the partial collapse of the improvised bridge. Taylor's brigade finally came up and was sent on an envelopment through dense laurel thickets against a key battery on the Federal left (Lewiston coaling). Just as Winder's situation had become critical, Taylor's envelopment reached the Federal flank: Two attacks were repulsed and Taylor's decimated force was facing destruction in defending positions taken in their third attack when Ewell led reinforcements up (Scott's 44th and 58th Va.). It was about 11 A.M. when the Confederates started a pursuit that netted about 450 prisoners, a gun, and about 800 muskets.

Frémont, meanwhile, had driven to the river but, since Trimble burned the bridge in his withdrawal, was unable to cross to Shields's assistance.

Federal forces engaged were Frémont's 12,000 at Cross Keys and about 5,000 at Port Republic (D. S. Freeman says "no more than 3,000"). Frémont reported a loss of 114 killed, 443 wounded, and 127 missing. Ewell reported 41 killed, 232 wounded, and 15 missing; Gens. G. H. Stuart and Elzey, C.S.A., were wounded. At Port Republic the Federals lost 1,018 and Jackson lost over 800 (*Lee's Lts.*, I, 462).

CROSSMAN, George H. Misspelling in Phisterer for George Hampton CROSMAN.

CROWNINSHIELD, Casper. Union officer. Mass. Capt. 20th Mass. 18 Aug. '61; transferred to 1st Mass. Cav. 28 Nov. '61; Maj. 2d Mass. Cav. 31 Jan. '63; Lt. Col. 18 Mar. '64; Col. 18 Nov. '64; Bvt. B.G. USV (war service). In the Army of the Shenandoah he commanded 3d Res. Brig., 1, Cav. Corps; 1st Div., Cav. Corps. Died 1897.

CROXTON, John Thomas. Union gen. 1837–74. Ky. A Yale graduate, he was a lawyer and Republican politician. He was commissioned Lt. Col. 4th Ky. Mounted Inf. 9 Oct. '61, Col. 9 May

'62, B.G. USV 30 July '64, and commanded 1, 1, Cav. Corps, Cumberland (20–30 July and 12 Aug.–29 Oct. '64). He also led 1, 1, Cav. Corps, Mil. Div. Miss. (29 Oct. '64–26 June '65) and was breveted Maj. Gen. USV for Franklin and the Atlanta campaign 27 Apr. '65. He resigned 26 Dec. '65. In 1873 he was appointed Minister to Bolivia for his health, dying there the following year.

CRUFT, Charles. Union gen. ?–1883. Ind. He was commissioned Col. 31st Ind. 20 Sept. '61 and commanded 1st Brig., 3d Div. Mil. Dist. Cairo, Tenn. (1–17 Feb. '62) and in the Army of the Ohio 13th Brig.; 13th, 5th (2 Dec. '61–16 Feb. '62). In the Army Tenn. he commanded 3d, 4th (17 Feb.–5 Apr. '62, Apr. '62); 2d Brig., Army of Ky., Ohio; and 22, 4, II, Army of Ohio. He was promoted B.G. USV 16 July '62 and distinguished himself at Richmond (Ky.) 29–30 Aug. '62. In the Army of the Cumberland he led 1, 2d Div. Left Wing, XIV (5 Nov. '62–9 Jan. '63); 1, 2, XXI (9 Jan.–21 Mar. '63, 21 Apr.–15 July '63, 17 Aug.–9 Oct. '63); 2d Div., XXI (15 July–17 Aug. '63); 1, 1, IV (15 Jan.–13 Feb. '64, 14 Mar.–10 June '64); 1st Div., IV (27 Oct.–21 Nov. '63, 13 Feb.–14 Mar. '64); 2d Div., Sep., Etowah; Prov. Dist. Etowah; 1st Brig., Dist. East Tenn. (June '65); 4th Div., Dist. East Tenn. (17 May–June '65). He was breveted Maj. Gen. USV 5 Mar. and mustered out 24 Aug. '65.

CRUMP'S HILL (Piney Woods), La. 2 Apr. '64. Skirmish of RED RIVER CAMPAIGN.

CULLUM, George Washington. Union gen. 1809–92. N.Y. Appt.-Pa. USMA 1833 (3/43); Engrs. He served in harbor and fortification construction on the East Coast as well as teaching and supervising construction at West

Point. A Capt. (1838), he was Lt. Col. and A.D.C. to Scott 9 Apr.–6 Aug. '61, named both Maj. Engrs. and Col. Add. A.D.C. on the latter date, and promoted B.G. USV 1 Nov. '61. He served on the US Sanitary Commission 13 June '61–24 Feb. '64 and was Chief Engr. of the Dept. of Mo. 19 Nov. '61–11 Mar. '62 and of the Dept. of Miss. 11 Mar.–11 July '62. He was Halleck's Chief of Staff in the Dept. of Mo. and the Miss. and when Halleck was Gen. in Chief. He was also Chief Engr. of the armies commanded by Halleck in the Tenn. and Miss. campaigns of Apr.–July '62 and also served on a number of boards. He was Supt. of USMA 8 Sept. '64–28 Aug. '66 and retired in 1874 as Col. His brevets were B.G. USA and Maj. Gen. USA for war service. He wrote numerous books on engineering and military history as well as his monumental *Biographical Register of the Officers and Graduates of the United States Military Academy,* containing the full summary of the careers of every graduate from 1802 to 1889. He also helped organize the USMA Association of Graduates and donated the memorial Cullum Hall at the Military Academy. D.A.B. described him as having ". . . a passionate devotion to West Point, a high idealism and a most fervent patriotism." He married Elizabeth, Gen. Halleck's widow, Schuyler HAMILTON's sister, and Alexander Hamilton's granddaughter.

CULP'S (KULP'S) HOUSE, Ga., 22 June '64, KENESAW MOUNTAIN. (Culp's *Hill* is at Gettysburg.)

CUMBERLAND, Union Department and Army of the. First existed between 15 Aug. and 9 Nov. '61. Commanders were Robert Anderson until 8 Oct. and then W. T. Sherman. It included Tenn. and Ky. except for the portion within 15 miles of Cincinnati (which was in the Dept. of the Ohio after 19 Sept.), and except for the forces operating near

the junction of the Tenn., Cumberland, Ohio, and Mississippi rivers (which were part of the Western Department). The department was merged into the newly-organized departments of the Ohio and the Mo.

A second Dept. of the Cumberland was created 24 Oct. '62 to include that part of Tenn. east of the Tennessee River and the portions of Ala. and Ga. to fall under Federal control. The forces previously known as Buell's Army of the Ohio then became the Army of the Cumberland. W. S. Rosecrans took command 30 Oct. '62. Another reorganization 9 Jan. '63 divided the army into the XIV, XX, and XXI Corps. On his own initiative Rosecrans also organized a reserve corps under Granger which was known as the Army of Kentucky (see KENTUCKY, UNION DEPARTMENT AND ARMY OF).

On 25 Sept. '63 the XI and XII Corps (Potomac) were transferred to the Army of the Cumberland. On 28 Sept. the XX and XXI Corps were merged into the new IV Corps under Granger. Rosecrans was replaced by Thomas on 19 Oct. On 4 Apr. '64 the XX Corps was re-formed by merging the XI and XII Corps. The Army of the Cumberland, now consisting of the IV, XIV, and XX Corps, was commanded by Thomas throughout the Atlanta campaign. In Nov. '64 Sherman regrouped his forces for the operations against Hood (Franklin and Nashville campaign) and for the March to the Sea. The IV Corps participated in the former as part of what is generally referred to as "US Forces" under Thomas. The other two corps, XIV and XX, were put under Slocum's command to form what was officially known as the Left Wing in Sherman's March to the Sea. Although Fox refers to "Slocum's Army of the Cumberland" (p. 104) and also to "Slocum's Army of Georgia" (p. 93), Slocum's command was commonly known by the latter name. (See GEORGIA, UNION ARMY OF.) It can be said that the Army of the Cumberland disappeared after the fall of Atlanta.

CUMBERLAND GAP, Tenn. This critical point was occupied in Sept. '61 by 4,000 Confederates under Zollicoffer, and later by the brigade of James E. Rains. On 11 Apr. '62 G. W. Morgan arrived at Cumberland Ford, with orders to take the gap, 14 miles to the south. His 7th Div., Army of the Ohio, numbered 8,000; Rains had 4,000. Reconnaissances in force on 14 Feb. (detachment of 1st Bn., Ky. Cav.) and 21–23 Mar. (S. P. Carter, commanding 1st E. Tenn., 7th Ky., 16th Ohio, 49th Ind., 1st Bn. Ky. Cav., and a section of the 9th Ohio Btry.) had revealed that the Confederates held the gap in force. On 18 June '62 G. W. Morgan occupied the gap after Rains had destroyed stores there and withdrawn (because of feints Buell had ordered against Chattanooga). On 17 Sept. '62 Morgan had to evacuate the gap when he was cut off by Kirby SMITH'S INVASION OF KENTUCKY. He escaped by way of Booneville northeast to the Ohio River at Greenup with all his equipment and a loss of only 80 men. (See G. W. Morgan's article, B.&L., III, 62ff.) Bragg reoccupied the gap 22 Oct. '62. It was recaptured by Federals under Burnside, 8–10 Sept. '63, with the loss of 36 guns, 3,000 stand of small arms, and its garrison of 2,500 under J. W. Frazer. Loss of the gap, along with Buckner's withdrawal from Knoxville (at the start of the Chickamauga campaign), deprived the Confederates of the lateral rail line between Chattanooga and the East.

CUMMING, Alfred. C.S.A. gen. 1829–1910. Ga. USMA 1849 (35/43); Inf. He served on the frontier, in garrison, as Twiggs's A.D.C. 1851–53, and on the Utah Expedition before resigning 19 Jan. '61 as Capt. Commissioned Lt. Col. Augusta Vol. Bn., he resigned to be Maj. 1st Ga. and Lt. Col. 10th Ga. in June '61. Serving under Lafayette McLaws, he succeeded him as Col. in Oct. '62, having commanded the regiment during the Yorktown siege, Savage's Station, and Malvern Hill where he was wounded. At Antietam, where he was again wounded, he commanded Wilcox's brigade and was appointed B.G. C.S.A. 29 Oct. '62. He commanded the Ala. Brig. at Mobile until ordered to the relief of Vicksburg 15 Apr. '63. During the siege he commanded the 3d Brig. under Stevenson and fought at Champion's Hill and in the final assaults. After being exchanged, he reorganized his brigade in Oct. '63 at Decatur (Ga.) and commanded it at Chattanooga. In Hood's corps during the Atlanta campaign his brigade captured four battle flags at Missionary Ridge and fought at Resaca, New Hope Church, Marietta, and Jonesboro. Cumming was severely wounded in this last battle and invalided home, being on crutches for the rest of the war. He was later a farmer and held minor public offices.

CUMMING, Gilbert W. Union officer. 1817–? N.Y. Col. 51st Ill. 20 Sept. '61; Bvt. B.G. USV (Island No. 10); resigned 30 Sept. '62. Commanded 2d Brig., 4th Div., Army of the Miss. He was apprenticed when still a boy to a carriage maker but studied law in his spare time and became prominent in that profession.

CUMMINGS, Alexander. Union officer. Pa. Col. 19th Pa. Cav. 24 Oct. '63; Bvt. B.G. USV 19 Apr. '65 (war service).

CUMMINS, John E. Union officer. Ohio. Lt. Col. 99th Ohio 26 Aug. '62; transferred to 50th Ohio 31 Dec. '64; Col. 185th Ohio 27 Feb. '65; Bvt. B.G. USV 4 Nov. '65.

CUNNINGHAM, James Adams. Union officer. Mass. 1st Lt. 32d Mass. 2 Dec. '61; Capt. 6 Mar. '62; Maj. 24 July '64; Lt. Col. 10 Nov. '64; Bvt. B.G. USV 1 Apr. '65. Brevets for Five Forks (2), Cox's Cross Roads, Richmond campaign. Died 1892. He has been credited with meeting Lee's first flag of truce on 9 Apr. '65.

CURLY, Thomas. Union officer. Ireland. Maj. 7th Mo. 21 Aug. '61; Lt. Col. 24 May '62; resigned 18 Sept. '62; Col. 27th Mo. 10 Jan. '63; Bvt. B.G. USV (war service).

CURTIN, Andrew Gregg. Gov. of Pa. 1817-94. Pa. A lawyer, he was active in Whig politics before being nominated by the Republicans in 1860 for Gov. in the expectation that he help carry the state for Lincoln. He was an active supporter of the Union, supplying troops and matériel for the Federal government, and taking exceptional care also of the soldiers' dependents. Re-elected in 1863, he served out that term and was considered for vice-president in 1868. When that post went to Schuyler Colfax instead, Grant named him minister to Russia. He returned to the US in 1872 and subsequently became a Democrat, serving three terms in Congress.

CURTIN, John Irwin. Union officer. Pa. Capt. 45th Pa. 9 Sept '61; Maj. 30 July '62; Lt. Col. 4 Sept. '62; Col. 13 Apr. '63; Bvt. B.G. USV 12 Oct. '64 (war service). Commanded 1, 2, IX; 3d Div., IX.

CURTIS, Arthur Russell. Union officer. Mass. 2d Lt. 20th Mass. 25 Nov. '61; 1st Lt. 1 Mar. '62; Capt. 1 May '63; Lt. Col. 14 Aug. '64; Bvt. B.G. USV. Brevets for Fredericksburg, Wilderness, war service.

CURTIS, Greely S. Union officer. N.H. Capt. 2d Mass. 25 May '61; Maj. 1st Mass. Cav. 30 May '61; Lt. Col.

1 Nov. '62. Bvt. B.G. USV (war service); mustered out 4 Mar. '64. Died 1897.

CURTIS, James Freeman. Union officer. Mass. Maj. 2d Cal. 2 Sept. '61; Lt. Col. 4th Cal. 25 June '63; Col. 20 May '64; Bvt. B.G. USV (war service). In the Army of the Cumberland, he commanded 2, Dist. Etowah; 2, 2d Sep. Div., Dist. Etowah.

CURTIS, Newton Martin. Union gen. 1835-1910. N.Y. He was a lawyer and farmer when commissioned Capt. 16th N.Y. 15 May '61. Fighting at 1st Bull Run and West Point (Va.), 7 May '62, he was promoted Lt. Col. 142d N.Y. 22 Oct. '62 and Col. 21 Jan. '63. He fought at Cold Harbor and then commanded 2, 3, XVIII (9-19 June '64) and 1, 2, X (21 June-17 Sept. '64, 4-29 Oct. '64, 14 Nov.-13 Dec. '64) against Petersburg. He continued in this area with 1, 2, XXIV (3 Dec. '64-6 Jan. '65) and went down to N.C. to lead 1, Ames's Div., Terry's Prov. Corps (6-15 Jan. '65) against Ft. Fisher. There he won the Medal of Honor (28 May '91) for his gallantry, having been wounded four times and losing his left eye. His B.G. USV commission was dated from that, and he also won the Thanks of Congress for his deed. Before he was mustered out in 1866, he was Chief of Staff for the Dept. of Va. and commanded the Dist. of Southwest Va. He was breveted B.G. USV 28 Oct. '64 for New Market and Maj. Gen. for Ft. Fisher. After serving as Congressman 1891-97, he was active in scientific farming, insane-asylum reforms, and the abolition of capital punishment. He wrote *From Bull Run to Chancellorsville* (1906). D.A.B. describes him as "... in appearance ... a typical soldier; tall, broad-shouldered, and erect ... a genial, broad-minded man, and a public-spirited citizen."

CURTIS, Samuel Ryan. Union gen. 1817–66. N.Y. Appt.-Ohio. USMA 1831 (27/33); Inf. After a year of frontier duty he resigned to be a civil engineer and lawyer. In the Ohio militia he rose to the rank of Col. and in 1846 was state Adj. Gen. with the task of raising volunteers for the Mexican War. As Col. of the 2d Ohio he successfully accomplished his mission of keeping Taylor's line of communications open. After engaging in engineering in the West, he moved to Iowa in 1855 and practiced law. He was elected to Congress as a Republican and was serving his third term when he resigned in 1861 to become Col. of the 2d Iowa. On 17 May '61 he became B.G. USV. He commanded the large camp of instruction near St. Louis; then the Southwest District of Mo. until Feb. '62; and the Army of the Southwest (Feb.–31 Aug. '62). He led a series of successful operations in southwest Mo. and Ark., winning the Battle of Pea Ridge (6–8 Mar.) (promoted Maj. Gen. USV 21 Mar.) and occupying Helena (14 July–29 Aug. '62) after a 1,000-mile march through difficult terrain. He was on leave of absence for a month to serve as president of the Pacific R.R. convention in Chicago. He then commanded the Dept. of the Mo. until May '63, and the Dept. of Kans. until 7 Feb. '65, and the Dept. of the Northwest until 26 July '65. During this time he checked PRICE'S RAID IN MISSOURI, Sept.–Oct. '64. After the war he served as Indian commissioner and as examiner of the Union Pacific R.R. until Apr. '66. He died at Council Bluffs, Iowa, 26 Dec. '66.

CURTIS, William Baker. Union officer. Md. Capt. 12th W. Va. 25 Aug. '62; Maj. 1 Sept. '63; Col. 28 Jan. '64; Bvt. B.G. USV (Ft. Gregg, Va.; war service). Commanded 2, 1st Inf. Div. (W. Va.); 2, Independent Div., XXIV (Va.).

CURTISS, James Edward. Union officer. N.Y. Capt. 152d N.Y. 14 Oct. '62; Maj. 16 Feb. '65; Lt. Col. 7 June '65; Bvt. B.G. USV (war service). Died 1901.

CUSHING, Alonzo Hersford. Union officer. c. 1841–63. Wis. Appt.-N.Y. USMA June '61 (12/34); Arty. He fought at 1st Bull Run, Yorktown, the Seven Days' Battles, the Maryland campaign, and Fredericksburg. At Gettysburg as 1st Lt. and commander of Battery A, 4th US Arty., he ordered his guns down to the stone wall as Pickett's infantry swarmed forward. Wounded repeatedly, he manned one of his remaining two guns himself and "held his guts in his hand as the charge came to the wall. / And his gun spoke out for him once before he fell to the ground." (S. V. Benet. *John Brown's Body*.) The Confederate general Armistead fell dead over the muzzle of his cannon, marking "The High Tide of the Confederacy." Brother of William B. Cushing.

CUSHING, William B. Union naval officer. 1842–74. Wis. Resigning from the Naval Academy 23 Mar. '61, he was appointed master's mate in May '61 in the Union Navy. He was assigned to the North Atlantic blockading squadron and was commissioned Lt. 16 July '62. After a number of battles in Fla. and the Carolinas, he destroyed the Confederate ram ALBEMARLE 24 Oct. '64 in the Roanoke River with a torpedo-tipped spar. He was promoted Lt. Cmdr. 27 Oct. for this. At Ft. Fisher he marked the channel, working for six hours in a small skiff under heavy fire. In a final assault he led a charge of sailors and marines from the *Monticello*. Continuing in the navy, he died on active duty as Cmdr. Brother of Alonzo H. Cushing.

CUSHMAN, Pauline. Union spy. 1835–93. La. She was born in New Orleans but came to N.Y.C. at 18 to become an actress. She was dismissed from the cast of a road show in Kentucky in 1863 for drinking to the Southern cause on stage and was admitted to the Southern lines as a sympathizer. In reality, she had taken an oath of allegiance to the Federal government and was a commissioned spy who had already performed valuable services. She was captured with compromising papers on her, taken to Bragg's headquarters, court-martialed, and sentenced to be hanged in 10 days. The Confederates had to evacuate Shelbyville before the sentence could be carried out. Her knowledge of the Southern forces was a great help to Rosecrans, but she was too well known to continue espionage work. She then lectured in the North.

CUSTER, George Armstrong. Union gen. 1839–76. Ohio. USMA June '61 (34/34); Cav. An outstanding cavalry leader, he was named B.G. USV 29 June '63 at the age of 23, and Maj. Gen. USV 15 Apr. '65 at the age of 25. From 1st Bull Run campaign to Lee's surrender he took part in every battle of the Army of the Potomac except one. After serving on the staffs of Kearny, W. F. Smith, McClellan, and Pleasonton, he took command of the Mich. Brig. (2d Brig., 3d Cav. Div.) and led them through the Gettysburg campaign. He continued to lead a cavalry brigade through the subsequent operations of the Army of the Potomac until 2 Oct. '64, when he took command of the 3d Cav. Div. He led this division in Sheridan's Shenandoah Valley campaign and in the final, Five Forks to Appomattox operations of the Army of the Potomac.

Although conspicuous in all engagements, he was breveted for gallant and meritorious services at the following specific battles: Gettysburg, Yellow Tavern, Winchester, Fishers Hill, and Five Forks. A fine physical specimen, nearly six feet tall and never exceeding 170 pounds in weight, Custer had the *beau sabreur* temperament of the outstanding cavalry leader. During the war he had 11 horses killed under him, although wounded only once himself. While he excelled as a tactical commander of cavalry, like Napoleon's Marshal Murat (whom Custer admired), he lacked the qualities for higher command of combined infantry, artillery, and cavalry operations. This was revealed tragically at the Little Big Horn, 25 June '76, when Custer led his men into a strategic ambush. Lyman said he "looks like a circus rider gone mad! He wears a huzzar jacket and tight trousers of faded black velvet trimmed with tarnished gold lace ... the General's coiffure [consists of] short, dry, flaxen ringlets! ... he has a very merry blue eye, and a devil-may-care style" (Agassiz).

Thomas Ward Custer, 1845–76, his brother, served as his aide and—despite his youth—was a fine cavalryman. Tom Custer was commissioned in the R.A. after the war, joined his brother's regiment in July '66, and died in the massacre.

CUSTER'S CAVALRY BRIGADE. This unit sustained the highest casualties of any cavalry unit of the Federal army during the war: 525 killed and died of wounds. It was composed of the 1st, 5th, 6th, and 7th Mich. Cav.

CUTCHEON, Byron M. Union officer. N.H. 2d Lt. 20th Mich. 15 July '62; Capt. 16 Aug. '62; Maj. 14 Oct. '62; Lt. Col. 19 Nov. '63; Col. 8 Jan. '64; Col. 27th Mich. 19 Dec. '64; Bvt. B.G. USV. Brevets for Wilderness (2), Spotsylvania (2), Petersburg. Medal of Honor 29 June '91 for Horseshoe Bend (Ky.) 10 May '63. Commanded 2, 1, IX.

CUTLER, Lysander. Union gen. c. 1806–66. He was commissioned Col.

6th Wis. 16 July '61 and commanded 3, 3, I (13 Mar.–4 Apr. '62); 3d, King's Div., I, Rappahannock; and 4, 1, I (5–26 Nov. '62) before being promoted B.G. USV 29 Nov. '62. In the Army of the Potomac he led 2, 1, I (26 Mar.–15 July '63); 1st Div., I (15 July–5 Aug. '63, 23 Sept.–13 Nov. '63, 13 Nov. '63–14 Jan. '64, 10 Feb.–20 Mar. '64); 1, 4, V (25 Mar.–6 May '64) and 4th Div., V (6 May–24 Aug. '64). Breveted Maj. Gen. USV 19 Aug. '64, he resigned 30 June '65, having been wounded twice in action.

CUTTING, William. Union officer. N.Y. Capt. Add. Q.M. Vols. 16 Nov. '61; Maj. A.D.C. Vols. 22 July '62; Bvt. B.G. USV. Brevets for Wilderness, Spotsylvania, Bethesda Church, Petersburg, East. Tenn. campaign, Knoxville, Fredericksburg.

CUTTS, Richard Dominicus. Union officer. D.C. Col. Add. A.D.C. 29 Nov. '61; Bvt. B.G. USV (war service). Died 1883.

CUYLER, John Meck. Union officer. Ga. Joining the R.A. as Asst. Surg. in 1834, he served in the Seminole War, the Mexican War, at West Point, and on the frontier. He was promoted Lt. Col. Med. Insp. 11 June '62 (Maj. since 1847) and retired in 1882 as Col. and Bvt. B.G. USA for war service. He died 1884.

CYNTHIANA, Ky., 11–12 June '64. John MORGAN's capture of E. H. Hobson and about 300 officers and men of the 171st Ohio N.G. near this place (Keller's Bridge) on the 11th, and Morgan's defeat by Burbridge the next day led to an interesting legal question that is covered under PAROLE.

D

DABNEY'S MILLS, Va. (Hatcher's Run; Boydton Road; Armstrong's Mill; Rowanty Creek; Vaughan Road), 5–7 Feb. '65. (PETERSBURG CAMPAIGN) Gregg's cavalry was ordered to move via Reams's Station to Dinwiddie Courthouse and destroy Confederate wagon trains believed to be using the Boydton Plank Road into Petersburg. To support this cavalry action II Corps was to occupy a position on Hatcher's Run near the Vaughan Road crossing and V Corps was to take up a position about two miles to their south (Monks Neck). Gregg advanced to his objective, took a few prisoners, and was ordered back; the morning of the 6th he joined Warren. The II Corps had occupied positions about 1,000 yards from some new

Confederate entrenchments, and about 5 P.M. Smyth's division repulsed a determined attack by Mahone's division.

About 1 P.M. 6 Feb. Warren's force reconnoitered toward Gravelly Run and Dabney's Mills. These forces were attacked by Pegram's division, which was driven back after inflicting over 2,300 casualties. Pegram was killed. The Federals extended their trenches to Hatcher's Run at the Vaughan Road crossing.

DAGGETT, Aaron Simon. Union officer. Me. 1st Lt. 5th Me. 24 June '61; Capt. 15 Aug. '61; Maj. 14 Apr. '63; mustered out 27 July '64; Lt. Col. 5th US Vet. Vol. Inf. 23 Jan. '65; Bvt. B.G. USV. Brevets for war service, Rappahannock Sta. (Va.}, Wilderness. W.I.A. Cold Harbor.

DAGGETT, Rufus. Union officer. N.Y. 1st Lt. 14th N.Y. 17 May '61; mustered out 4 Dec. '61; Maj. 117th N.Y. 20 Aug. '62; Lt. Col. 5 Sept. '63; Col. 12 Aug. '64; Bvt. B.G. USV 15 Jan. '65. Commanded 1, 2, XXIV; 1, Ames's division. Terry's Prov. Corps; 1, 2, X; 2d Div., X Corps.

DAHLGREN, John Adolph. Union admiral. 1809–70. Pa. Son of the Swedish consul at Philadelphia, he was appointed Midshipman in the US Navy in 1826. He served as Ord. officer for 16 years, during which time he invented the DAHLGREN GUN, a rifled cannon, and boat howitzers with iron carriages. Taking command of the Washington Naval Yard 22 Apr. '61, when Buchanan went with the Confederacy, he was appointed Chief of the Ord. Bur. 18 July '62 and promoted Capt. 16 July. He was appointed Rear Admiral 7 Feb. '63 and took command of the South Atlantic Blockading Squadron in July of that year. Continuing in the navy, he died of heart disease while on active duty. Father of Ulric DAHLGREN.

DAHLGREN, Ulric. Union officer. 1842–64. Pa. Son of Admiral DAHLGREN, he studied civil engineering and law before becoming Sigel's A.D.C. He was that general's Chief of Arty. at 2d Bull Run and then served as Burnside's A.D.C. At Chancellorsville he was on Hooker's staff and at Gettysburg on Meade's. On the retreat from Gettysburg he was severely wounded in the foot, and his leg was amputated. Promoted Col., he returned to active service on crutches and was co-commander of the KILPATRICK-DAHLGREN RAID in Jan. '64. See also DAHLGREN PAPERS.

DAHLGREN GUN. Invented by John A. DAHLGREN, this was a type of gun used primarily in the navy. The large ones were "cast metal homogeneous" and cooled from the outside.

"To produce uniformity in the cooling, the piece is cast nearly cylindrical, and then turned down to the required shape, ..." The metal was thicker toward the breech and the gun tapered more rapidly toward the muzzle (i.e., the CHASE), giving the characteristic profile and the nickname "soda-water bottle." The principal Dahlgrens were the 9- and 11-inch. The larger, 15- and 20-inch Dahlgrens were cast by the RODMAN system (Benton).

DAHLGREN PAPERS. Controversial documents allegedly found by 13-year-old William Littlepage on the body of Col. Ulric Dahlgren after the KILPATRICK-DAHLGREN RAID. They consisted of a proposed address to his troops, a set of instructions to part of his command, and a memorandum book. The first two documents contained instructions to kill Jeff Davis and his cabinet. A theory that these papers were forged is supported mainly by the facts that the address was not actually delivered, and that the signature is misspelled and in a form Dahlgren did not normally use ("U. Dalhgren" instead of "Ulric Dahlgren"). This is refuted on the grounds that there was no time for forgery, and that the error in signature could have been made by a clerk in Dahlgren's headquarters. "Whether in someone else's handwriting or however written, the guilt was there," writes V. C. Jones. "The notes in the memorandum book were obviously the basis for the finished address and instructions, yet no one, not even his father, ever denied that these or the name of the owner of the book legibly set down on its cover were in Dahlgren's handwriting" (*Eight Hours before Richmond,* 174).

A letter from Mr. Jones to the author, 28 Apr. 1959, says, "I now, through the use of photography and a combination of lights, have proved *be-*

yond a doubt that the signature was not misspelled. This was done in the laboratory of the National Archives, which now agrees with me." By a rare coincidence, apparently, ink leaked through the paper—both sides of which were used in the message—in such a manner as to give the appearance of a transposition of letters in the name Dahlgren.

DALLAS, Ga. 25 and 27 June '64. (ATLANTA CAMPAIGN) Also known as New Hope Church, Pumpkin Vine Creek, Allatoona Hills, Burned Hickory. After Johnston's retreat from RESACA, 16 May, and his decision not to stand at Cassville, 19 May, he took up a defense in Allatoona Pass. Realizing the natural strength of this position, Sherman decided to abandon the railroad line and attempt an envelopment to the west through Dallas. As soon as Johnston detected this he moved his own army west to block the maneuver.

On 23 May W. H. Jackson's Confederate cavalry formed a screen along Pumpkin Vine Creek while infantry took up positions to cover crossings of that creek toward Dallas and Atlanta. Hardee was on the left, Polk in the center, and Hood on the right. Wheeler's cavalry screened from the right flank at Lost Mountain northeast almost 20 miles to the abandoned position in Allatoona Pass.

McCook's Federal cavalry, skirmishing toward Burned Hickory ahead of Hooker's XX Corps, reached that place on 24 May at 2 P.M. and learned that the Confederate army was moving toward Dallas. Garrard's cavalry also had a skirmish near Dallas and identified Bate's division of Hardee's corps. Sherman thus learned that Johnston had once more maneuvered across his path.

On 25 May at 11 A.M. Geary's (2d) division of Hooker's XX Corps, leading the Federal advance, made contact with the enemy in considerable force. Geary crossed a burning bridge over Pumpkin Vine Creek at Owen's Mill and deployed the 5th Ohio at the head of Candy's (1st) brigade to lead the advance. Four and a half miles from Dallas a strong enemy position was developed. As Candy pushed forward Geary brought up his other two brigades (Bushbeck and Ireland) in support. Hooker, who was with this division in the center, sent for the other two, Williams and Butterfield. Upon arrival late in the afternoon they attacked toward New Hope Church, where they were stopped by artillery. Geary moved from reserve to make another assault and was repulsed by part of Hood's corps. Massed fire of 16 Confederate guns firing canister and short-range fire of 5,000 infantry exacted a toll that led Federal soldiers to call the place "Hell Hole."

The next day was spent massing Federal forces. On 27 May at 5 P.M. Hazen's (2d) brigade of T. J. Wood's 3d Div., IV Corps, assaulted the right flank of the Confederate line held by two regiments of Cleburne's division of Hardee's Corps near Pickett Mill. R. W. Johnson's division (1, XIV) was supposed to move up on the left in support and McLean's brigade on the right was supposed to move forward to draw enemy fire away from the main attack. By the time Scribner's brigade (3, 1, XIV) could come up, Wood had been forced to commit other troops to support Hazen. When Scribner did come up on Hazen's left he was brought under such heavy attack from his left that he had to change direction to protect his flank. McLean, meanwhile, had not appeared to draw the enemy's attention. Cleburne counterattacked and brought such fire against both flanks of the Federal penetration that Howard ordered a withdrawal. Losses in Wood's division were 1,400; R. W. Johnson's losses were lighter, but he himself was wounded.

The brigades of Kimball and Wagner (1 and 2, 2, IV) repulsed a Confederate attack and inflicted heavy casualties. Dan McCook's brigade (3, 2, XIV) captured a pass in the center of the Confederate position and held it against night attacks by Polk's corps.

The night of the 27th Hood was pulled out of the line to make an attack the next day against the Federal left. This operation was canceled, however, when it was found that R. W. Johnson's division was strongly posted to repel it.

Having been frustrated in his attempted turning movement, Sherman started maneuvering back to the east toward the railroad he had temporarily abandoned. Johnson countered with a corresponding shift of position. This brought on a series of actions culminating in the bloody Federal repulse at KENESAW MOUNTAIN, 27 June.

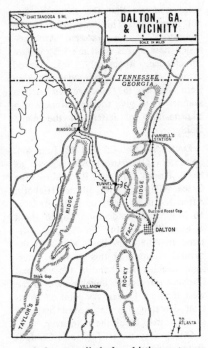

DALTON, Ga., 22–27 Feb. '64. Reconnaissance in force by Palmer's XIV Corps and the 1st Div., IV Corps, temporarily under Cruft, to verify a report that J. E. Johnston had weakened his forces around Dalton to reinforce Polk and Longstreet. On the 22d Confederate cavalry was driven from Varnell's Station, and the next day 12 prisoners were taken within four miles of Dalton. On the 24th the Federals drove enemy outposts from Tunnel Hill to Buzzard Roost Gap. Although strong enemy resistance had now been developed Palmer made a coordinated effort on 25 Feb. to force the pass. While the divisions of R. W. Johnson and J. C. Davis (1 and 2, XIV) attacked frontally, the remainder of his force planned an envelopment by way of Rocky Face Ridge, moving from the north against the gap. Skirmishing started early in the morning. Shortly after 11 o'clock Palmer led the enveloping force for-

ward about a mile before hitting a strong Confederate defense along a wooded ridge. Cruft's brigades of Grose (3d) and Champion (2d) took this position after a brisk fight. About 3 P.M. Champion attacked the right of the next Confederate position but was not able to carry it.

The brigades of J. D. Morgan and Dan McCook (1 and 3, 2, XIV) had been ordered by Davis to push skirmishers toward the front of the Confederate position when firing was first heard from the east. The Federal batteries of Harris and Hotchkiss opened fire. At first the Confederates did not disclose their positions by returning the fire but they were soon forced to do so when the skirmishers approached. Morgan's brigade suffered heavy casualties from frontal and enfilade fires. The brigades of King and Hambright (2 and 3, 1, XIV) moved up from reserve to relieve Davis's brigades late in the day.

Having determined that the enemy still held Dalton in force, Palmer withdrew on the 26th. His total casualties were 345. Confederate losses in two commands were reported as 167, but are not available from all units involved.

DALTON, Ga. For actions of 5–11 May '64 see ROCKY FACE RIDGE.

DALTON, Ga., 14–16 Aug. '64. Wheeler's cavalry approached this place about 4 P.M. on Sunday, 14 Aug., and demanded its surrender. Col. Bernard Laiboldt refused, and with the 2d Mo. and convalescents of the 7th Ky. Cav. successfully defended the place against two attacks. He reported 50 casualties.

"DAMN THE TORPEDOES" [mines]. Attributed to Admiral Farragut when running past FORTS GAINES, MORGAN, Ala., 5 Aug. '64, in the Battle of Mobile Bay, same date.

DANA, Charles Anderson. 1819–97. After serving on the staff and as managing editor of Greeley's N.Y. *Tribune,* he became Asst. Sec. of War in 1863–64 and afterward editor and owner of the influential N.Y. *Sun.*

DANA, Edmund Lovell. Union officer. Pa. Col. 143d Pa. 18 Nov. '62; Bvt. B.G. USV 26 July '65 (war service). Commanded 1, 3, I; 2, 3, II. Died 1889.

DANA, James Jackson. Union officer. Mass. Appt.-N.Y. Entering the R.A. in 1855, he served mainly on the frontier and was promoted Capt. Asst. Q.M. 3 Aug. '61. He was named Lt. Col. Q.M. Assigned 1 Jan–17 July '63 and Col. Q.M. Assigned 2 Aug. '64–1 Jan. '67. During the Civil War he was in charge of transportation in Washington until Feb. '63, when he became Chief Q.M. of the I Corps and fought at Chancellorsville and Gettysburg. Returning to the transportation office until

Aug. '64, he then became a division head in the Q.M. Gen. office. Continuing in the R.A., he retired in 1885 as Lt. Col. and Bvt. B.G. USA. He died 1898.

DANA, Napoleon Jackson Tecumseh. Union gen. 1822–1905. Me. USMA (29/56); Inf. Wounded and breveted in Mexican War, he resigned in 1855 to become banker in St. Paul and militia B.G. He was commissioned Col. 1st Minn. 2 Oct. '61 and appointed B.G. USV 3 Feb. '62. After service in the Shenandoah (Nov. '61–Apr. '62), he commanded the 3d Brig. of Sedgwick's second division, Sumner's II Corps through the Peninsular and Antietam campaigns. He was severely wounded at Antietam and on sick leave until July '63, when he commanded the defenses of Philadelphia during the Gettysburg campaign. He was promoted Maj. Gen. USV to rank from 29 Nov. '62. Going to the Dept. of the Gulf he then took command of a force that landed at the Rio Grande and drove the Confederates to Laredo. He subsequently commanded the XIII Corps (Dec. '63–Jan. '64); Dist. Vicksburg (Aug.–Oct. '64); XVI Corps and districts of West Tenn. and Vicksburg (Nov. '64); and the Dept. of Miss. (to 27 May '65). He resigned 27 May '65 and engaged in various mining, commercial and railroad activities in the West and in Ill. From 1893 until 1897 he held various positions in the Pension Department in Washington. He was the nephew of the famous chemists James F. and Samuel L. Dana; the latter is author of *Muck Manual for Farmers* (1842), one of the country's earliest scientific agricultural works, and of *An Essay on Manures* (1850).

DANA, Richard Henry. Writer. 1815–82. Mass. Author of the classic *Two Years Before the Mast,* he was a founder of the FREE-SOIL PARTY.

DANDY, George Brown. Union officer. Ga. R.A. 1st Lt. 3d US Arty. 3 Mar. '61; Capt. Add. Q.M. 24 Mar. '62; Col. 100th N.Y. 29 Aug. '62; Bvt. B.G. USV and USA. Brevets for Ft. Wagner, S.C., Deep Bottom, Ft. Gregg, Va. (2), war service. Commanded 2, Morris Island, S.C., X (South); 3, 1, X (Va. and N.C.); 3, 1, XXIV (Va.); 2, 1, XXIV (Va.).

DANIEL, Junius. C.S.A. gen. 1828–64. N.C. Appt. At Large. USMA 1851 (33/42); Inf. He served in garrison and on the frontier in Indian scouting and fighting before resigning in 1858 to take over his father's La. plantation. Commissioned Col. 14th N.C. 3 June '61, he fought in the Seven Days' Battles and had his horse shot from under him at Malvern Hill. He was appointed B.G. C.S.A. 1 Sept. '62 and was stationed in the Drewry's Bluff vicinity until sent to N.C. in Dec. '62. Going to Gettysburg from there, he commanded his brigade under Rodes in Pa. and led the same organization at the Wilderness and Spotsylvania. He was mortally wounded 12 May '64 in the "Bloody Angle" and died the next day.

DANIEL WEBSTER. See McCLELLAN'S HORSES.

DARBYTOWN, Va., 27–29 July '64. See DEEP BOTTOM RUN, same dates.

DARBYTOWN AND NEW MARKET ROADS, Va., 7 Oct. '64 (PETERSBURG CAMPAIGN). After NEW MARKET HEIGHTS the Federal cavalry division of Kautz held the captured Confederate intrenchments near the Johnson farm covering the Darbytown Road. Determined to recapture this portion of the line, Lee planned a dawn attack for 7 October. Gary's dismounted cavalry brigade and the remnants of Perry's Fla. brigade were to turn Kautz's north flank, while Gregg's Tex. brigade was to lead Field's division in a frontal as-sault. Kautz was driven back with a loss of eight guns and re-formed behind the well-prepared X Corps positions. An attack on this second line at about 10 A.M. was driven back by Federal artillery (particularly Battery D, 1st US Arty.) and by the failure of Hoke to attack as planned on Field's right. Lee abandoned his efforts to restore these positions and constructed a new line of intrenchments. The Federals reported 399 casualties and put Confederate losses at 1,350. Gregg was killed and Bratton wounded; Col. Spear, USV, was wounded.

DARBYTOWN ROAD, Va., 13 Oct. '64 (PETERSBURG CAMPAIGN). Terry's X Corps, supported by Kautz's cavalry, was repulsed with a loss of 337 men in an attempt to penetrate Lee's new defenses near the Johnson farm. (See DARBYTOWN ROAD, Va., 7 Oct. '64.)

DARR, Francis. Union officer. Ohio. 1st Lt. Regt. Q.M. 10th Ohio 4 June '61; Capt. Comsy. of Subsist. Vols. 3 Aug. '61; Lt. Col. Comsy. of Subsist. Assigned 1 Jan.–27 Oct. '63; Bvt. B.G. USV. Brevets for service as Chief of Comsy. of Subsist. Army of the Ohio and XVIII Corps, service in Subsist. and P.M.G.'s depts. during war. Died 1895.

DAVENPORT, Jean Margaret. See LANDER, Jean Davenport.

DAVID, The. Confederate SUBMARINE.

DAVIDE'S FERRY, La. Scene of action under RED RIVER CAMPAIGN OF 1864.

DAVIDSON, Henry B. C.S.A. gen. c. 1831–99. Tenn. USMA 1853 (33/52); Dragoons. Given his appointment to West Point for gallantry at the battle of Monterey as a Sgt. of Tenn. Vols., he later served on the frontier in Indian scouting and fighting. He was dropped 30 July '61 as Capt. from the US Army for failure to report at the end of his leave of absence. Commissioned Col. C.S.A. in 1862, he commanded the post of Staunton. Appointed B.G. C.S.A. 18 Aug. '63, he fought in Pegram's division at Chickamauga and early in 1864 led his cavalry brigade under Wheeler at Rome (Ga.). Returning to Va., he fought under Early in the Valley. He settled first in New Orleans and then in California, holding minor public offices in each place.

DAVIDSON, John Wynn. Union gen. 1823–81. Va. Appt. At Large. USMA 1845 (27/41); Dragoons-Cav. He served on the frontier, in the Mexican War and fighting Indians, where he was seriously wounded. Offered a commission in the Confederate Army, he declined, choosing to remain with the Union. (See LOYALTY OF REGULAR ARMY OFFICERS.) A Capt. (1855), he was assigned to the 1st US Cav. 3 Aug. '61 and became Maj. 2d US Cav. 14 Nov. '61. He led 2, W. F. Smith's div., Potomac (26 Oct. '61–13 Mar. '62); 3, 2, IV, Potomac (13 Mar.–18 May '62); and 3, 2, VI, Potomac (18 May–July '62). In the Peninsular campaign he fought at Gaines's Mill, Golding's Farm, Lee's Mill, Mechanicsville, Savage's Station, and Glendale. He was named B.G. USV 3 Feb. '62. He also commanded in the Dept. of Mo.: the Dist. St. Louis (6 Aug.–13 Nov. '62); Dist. Southeast Mo. (13 Nov. '62–23 Feb. '63); Army Southeast Mo. (Oct.–Nov. '62). Other commands were 1st Cav. Div. Southeast Mo., Dept. of Mo. (6 June–10 Sept. '63), and 1st Cav. Div., Ark. Expedition, Army of Tenn. (10 Aug.–3 Nov. '63 and Dec. '63–6 Jan. '64) at Brownsville, Bayou Meto, Ashley's Mills and Little Rock (Ark.). He also commanded the Post of Natchez, Dist. of Vicksburg, Miss. (26 Feb.–May '65). Mustered out of USV in 1866, he continued in the R.A. He was a Col. when he died of injuries sus-

tained when his horse fell on him. His brevets were Gaines's Mill, Golding's Farm, Little Rock (B.G. USA), war service (Maj. Gen. USA and USV).

DAVIES, Henry Eugene. Union gen. 1836–94. N.Y. Attended Harvard and Williams, graduated from Columbia, and then practiced law until commissioned Capt. 5th N.Y. 9 May '61. Promoted Maj. in Kilpatrick's 2d N.Y. Cav. 1 Aug. '61, he served under McDowell in the defenses of Washington and fought with his regiment at 2d Bull Run. Named Lt. Col. 6 Dec. '62, Col. 16 June '63, and B.G. USV 16 Sept. '63. In the Cav. Corps of the Potomac, he commanded 1st Brig., 3d Div. (12–25 July; 22 Aug. '63–12 Feb. '64 and 12–30 Apr. '64) and then led the 1st Brig., 2d Div. (17 Apr.–30 July; 13–15 Sept.; 25 Sept.–22 Dec. '64). Succeeding to command of the 2d Div., he led it 12–25 Sept. '64; 22 Dec. '64–19 Jan. '65 and 14–27 Mar. '65. He participated in the Richmond raids in 1864 and in the cavalry activities of the Petersburg and Appomattox campaigns. Was promoted Maj. Gen. USV 4 May '65 and breveted Maj. Gen. USV 1 Oct. '64 for Vaughan Rd. (Va). Resigning in 1866, he returned to his law practice, held several public offices, and wrote a number of books, notably *General Sheridan* (1895).

DAVIES, Thomas Alfred. Union gen. 1809–99. N.Y. USMA 1829 (25/46); Inf. He served on the frontier, resigning in 1831 to become a civil engineer and merchant. Commissioned Col. 16th N.Y. 15 May '61, he commanded the 2d Brig., 5th Div., Army of Northeast Va. in the summer of '61 at 1st Bull Run and was promoted B.G. USV 7 Mar. '62. He then commanded 2d Div., Army West Tenn. (14 Apr.–2 June '62) in the advance and siege of Corinth; 1st Div., Army of West Tenn. (2–10 June '62); 2d Dist., Corinth, Tenn. (5 Aug.–24 Oct. '62) in the battle of Corinth; Dist.

Miss., Tenn. (5–30 Oct. '62); Dist. Columbus, Ky., XIII, Tenn. (1 Nov.– 22 Dec. '62); Dist. Columbus, Ky., XVI, Tenn. (18 Dec. '62–11 Jan. '63); Dist. Rolla, Dept. of Mo. (13 Mar. '63–25 Mar. '64); Dist. North Kansas, Dept. of Kans. (25 June '64–4 Apr. '65). He was breveted Maj. Gen. USV 11 July '65 and mustered out the next month. In his later years he wrote many theological texts.

DAVIS, Benjamin Franklin. ("Grimes"). Union officer. c. 1832–63. Ala. Appt.-Miss. USMA 1854 (32/46); Inf.-Cav. He served on the frontier and in Indian fighting (wounded) before being promoted Capt. 1st U.S. Cav. 30 July '61. In spite of his Southern heritage, he continued in the Union Army and was named Lt. Col. 1st Calif. Cav. 19 Aug.–1 Nov. '61. He was first in Washington and then fought at Yorktown and Williamsburg. Commissioned Col. 8th N.Y. Cav. 25 June '62, he led his regiment in the famous escape from Harpers Ferry 14 Sept. and later in the Rappahannock campaign. Breveted Maj. USA for the Harpers Ferry escape, he was killed 9 June '63 at Beverly Ford (Brandy Station). See DAVIS AND DAVIS ESCAPE FROM HARPERS FERRY.

DAVIS, Charles Henry. Union admiral. 1807–77. Mass. Entering the navy as Midshipman in 1823, he served in the Pacific, the Mediterranean, the South Atlantic, and along the New England coast. Promoted Capt. in Nov. '61, he was Chief of Staff and Fleet Officer in the Port Royal expedition. He was promoted Flag Officer in May '62 of the Mississippi flotilla, fighting at Ft. Pillow, Memphis, around Vicksburg, and up the Yazoo River. As Com. (July '62), Davis was made chief of the Bureau of Navigation and promoted Rear Admiral in Feb. '63. Continuing in the navy, he was superintendent of the Naval Observatory and commander of the South Atlantic Squadron, dying on active duty.

DAVIS, Edmund Jackson. Union gen. 1827–83. A lawyer and jurist in Texas, he turned to the Union when defeated as delegate to the Secessionist Congress. He organized a regiment of Unionists in Mexico and narrowly escaped hanging by Confederate soldiers in Matamoros. Appointed Col. 1st Tex. Cav. 26 Oct. '62, he was promoted B.G. USV 10 Nov. '64. He led an unsuccessful attack on Laredo (Tex.) that same year, but spent the rest of his service in Louisiana where he commanded, in the Dept. of the Gulf, the following: 4, Cav. XIX; Sep. Cav. Brig.; Dist. Morganza (27 Feb.–3 Mar. '65); Cav. Brig., Dist. Baton Rouge (15–27 Feb. '65); and Dist. Baton Rouge (11–18 Mar. '65). He was mustered out 24 Aug. '65 and declined Sheridan's appointment as Chief Justice of the Texas Supreme Court that year. In 1866–69 he was active in the series of constitutional conventions where he advocated radical measures of retribution and punishment for the rebels, and in 1869 he was elected Gov. of Texas in an election sponsored by the military governor. Running an incompetent carpetbag government, he distinguished himself as one of the worst of the Reconstruction governors. After the next election, "the verdict of the people [being] that almost all of [his] appointees were either incapable or dishonest" (D.A.B.), he was beaten but refused to give up the office. He barricaded himself, the incumbent legislature, and a company of Negro troops in the state capitol. When Grant refused his request for aid, he acquiesced and lived out his remaining years in the state, taking an active part in politics.

DAVIS, Edwin Page. Union officer. Pa. 1st Lt. 62d N.Y. 30 June '61; Capt. 1 Oct. '61; mustered out 4 Nov. '62; Maj. 153d N.Y. 14 Nov. '62; Col. 1 May '63; Bvt. B.G. USV 19 Oct. '64 (Opequon, Fishers Hill, Middletown [Va.]). In Dept. of the Shenandoah he commanded 1, 1, XIX; 2, 1, XIX; 2, 1st Div. (Prov.). Died 1890.

DAVIS, George. C.S.A. Atty. Gen. 1820–96. N.C. Descended from an old and aristocratic Carolina family, he graduated from Chapel Hill at 18 with first honors and became a lawyer. He was an active worker against secession and was a N.C. commissioner to the Washington peace conference in the winter of 1860–61. Elected C.S.A. Senator on 18 June '61 and re-elected in 1862, he followed Thomas H. Watts as Atty. Gen. on 4 Jan. '64 and served in this post until the end of the war. He then returned to his law practice and avoided politics the rest of his life.

DAVIS, Hasbrouck. Union officer. 1827–70. Mass. Lt. Col. 12th Ill. Cav. 18 Nov. '61; Col. 5 Jan. '64; Bvt. B.G. USV (war service). Commanded 2, Cav. Div., West. Tenn. Grandson of George Bancroft, the historian. Participated in Stoneman's raid during Chancellorsville campaign, and in escape from Harpers Ferry during Antietam campaign. (See DAVIS AND DAVIS ESCAPE . . .) Lawyer by profession. Lost at sea in 1870.

DAVIS, Henry Greene. Union officer. Vt. 1st Lt. 29th Ind. 27 Aug. '61; Capt. 1 Mar. '62; Lt. Col. 101st US Col. Inf. 2 Sept. '64; Bvt. B.G. USV (war service). Died 1898.

DAVIS, Henry Winter. Radical Republican. 1817–65. Md. After graduating from Kenyon College and studying law at the Univ. of Va., he practiced in Alexandria before moving to Baltimore in 1849. Elected to the House of Representatives on the Know-Nothing ticket in 1854, he remained neutral on the slavery issue until 1860, when he voted with the Republicans on an important issue. He was censured by the Md. legislature and not re-elected. An opponent of Hicks and the other Marylanders with Southern sympathies, he was sent back to Congress in 1863 and stringently opposed Lincoln's policies, substituting a radical and punitive Reconstruction plan of his own for Lincoln's moderate one. This was embodied in the Wade-Davis bill (and, later, the manifesto) of 1864 that was killed by Lincoln's pocket veto. (See RECONSTRUCTION PLAN OF WADE AND DAVIS.) Defeated for re-election in 1864, he retired to private life but continued to dictate the actions of Congress through Thaddeus STEVENS.

DAVIS, Jefferson, C.S.A. pres. 1808–89. Ky. Appt.-Miss. USMA 1828 (23/33); Inf.-Dragoons. Before graduating from Transylvania Univ., he was appointed to West Point and for the first seven years of his army career served on the Northwest frontier. Eloping with Zachary Taylor's daughter (Dick TAYLOR's sister), he resigned as 1st Lt. in 1835 and settled down in Miss. as a planter. His wife died three months after their marriage, and in 1845 he married Varina Howell. Elected the same year to the US Congress, he resigned to fight in the Mexican War, serving under Taylor and being severely wounded at Buena Vista. He declined the appointment of B.G. USA in 1847 and returned to public life as Sen. In 1853 he was appointed Sec. of War by Pierce and re-entered the Senate, serving there until Jan. '61, when Miss. seceded. Appointed Maj. Gen. of the State Militia, he was chosen provisional president of the government set up by the C.S.A. Congress at Montgomery in a compromise between the extremists and the moderates in the Confederacy. Inaugurated provisional president in Feb. '61 at Montgomery, he was elected to a six-year term and was inaugurated president of the permanent government at Richmond on 22 Feb. '62. As the war progressed, the president took over more of the powers and became dictatorial and autocratic, a trend that ran counter to the states-rights philosophy of the seceding states. D.A.B. speaks of his "imperious temper aggravated by ill health." Beauregard succinctly summed up both Davis's and the Confederacy's problem when he said: "We needed for President either a military man of high order, or a politician of the first-class without military pretensions. The South did not fall crushed by the mere weight of the North; but it was nibbled away at all sides and ends, because its executive head never gathered and wielded its great strength under the ready advantages that greatly reduced or neutralized its adversary's naked physical superiority" (B.&L., I, 226). Fleeing from Richmond with his cabinet, he presided over them for the last time 24 Apr. '65 at Charlotte, N.C., and was captured 10 May at Irwinsville, Ga. He was held for two years at Fort Monroe. Never brought to trial, he was finally released on bail, and a *nolle prosequi* was ordered by the Federal government. He wrote *The Rise and Fall of the Confederate Government* (1881).

DAVIS, Jefferson Columbus. Union gen. 1828–79. Ind. A private in the Mexican War, he was commissioned in the R.A. (1848) and was at Ft. Sumter as 1st Lt. 1st US Arty. during the bombardment (12–13 Apr. '61). Promoted Capt. 14 May '61, he was named Col. 22d Ind. 1 Aug. '61, and at Wilson's Creek (10 Aug.) he commanded a brigade in the Army of the Southwest. He led the 3d Div. at Pea Ridge and commanded the 4th Div., Army of Miss. (24 Apr.–12 Aug. '62) at Corinth and Booneville. In May '62 he was named B.G. USV to date from 18 Dec. '61. Brooding over a rebuke given him by his commanding officer, William Nelson, Davis accosted him on 29 Sept. '62 in a Louisville hotel lobby and, after "high words," he crumpled a card and threw it in Nelson's face, whereupon Nelson slapped him.

Davis left to return with a revolver and mortally wounded Nelson as he passed through the hall. He was never punished for this and shortly restored to active duty, partly on his military abilities and partly on the political influence of Gov. Oliver P. Morton, who had accompanied him during the altercation. Assuming command of the 1st Div. Right Wing, XIV, Cumberland, on 5 Nov. '62, he led it at Stones River and relinquished it 9 Jan. '63 to take over the 1st Div., XX, Cumberland, which he commanded at Chickamauga and led until 9 Oct. '63. He also commanded the 2d Div., XIV, Cumberland (10 Oct. '63–22 Aug. '64) and the XIV Corps (22 Aug. '64–1 Aug. '65) during the Atlanta campaign, on the March to the Sea and through the Carolinas. Although recommended for Maj. Gen. by Rosecrans and Grant, he never attained this rank and bitterly resented this slight, although he never regretted killing Nelson (D.A.B.). He was breveted for Pea Ridge, Resaca, Rome (Ga.), Kenesaw Mt., and Jonesboro, the last being Bvt. Maj. Gen. USA. He also was Bvt. Maj. Gen. USV. Continuing in the R.A., he served in Alaska and in the Modoc War. Gen. Fry described him as ". . . brave, quiet, obliging, humorous in disposition and full of ambition, daring, endurance and self-confidence."

DAVIS, Joseph Robert. C.S.A. gen. 1825–96. Miss. Jefferson Davis's nephew, he graduated from Miami Univ. in Oxford (Ohio), became a lawyer, and sat in the legislature. He was commissioned Lt. Col. 10th Miss. and four months later (31 Aug. '61) was named Col. on Davis's staff. Appointed B.G. C.S.A. 15 Sept. '62, he led a brigade of Miss. troops in the Army of Northern Va., fighting at Gettysburg, the Wilderness, Cold Harbor, and the battles around Petersburg. He surrendered at Appomattox and resumed his law practice.

DAVIS, Nelson H. Union officer. c. 1821–90. Mass. USMA 1846 (49/59); Inf.-I.G. He fought in the Mexican War (1 brevet) and served in the West in Indian fighting before, as Capt. 2d U.S. Inf. (since 1855), fighting at 1st Bull Run. Named Col. 7th Mass. 4 Sept. '61, he became Maj. Asst. I.G. 12 Nov. '61 and participated in Yorktown, Williamsburg, Fair Oaks, White Oak Swamp, Glendale, Malvern Hill, and Harrison's Landing. He was also at South Mountain, Antietam, Chancellorsville, and Gettysburg before going to the Dept. of N. Mex. where he remained until June '65. Continuing in the R.A. after the war, he retired in 1885 as B.G. USA I.G. He was breveted for Gettysburg, Indian fighting, and war service (B.G. USA).

DAVIS, William G. M. C.S.A. gen. 1812–98. Va. Appt.-Fla. A lawyer, he raised a regiment and on 1 Jan. '62 was commissioned Col. 1st Fla. Cav. and given command of the provisional forces in the eastern part of the state. Sent to Johnston in Tenn. on 25 Mar. '62, he was appointed B.G. C.S.A. 4 Nov. of that year and commanded the Dept. of Eastern Tenn. until his resignation 6 May '63.

DAVIS, William Watts Hart. Union officer. Pa. Capt. 25th Pa. 18 Apr. '61; mustered out 26 July '61; Col. 104th Pa. 5 Sept. '61; Bvt. B.G. USV (Charleston, S.C.); mustered out 30 Sept. '64. Commanded 2, 2, XVIII (Dept. of N.C.); then in X Corps, Dept. of the South, he headed various forces on St. Helena, Port Royal, Folly, and Morris Islands, finally commanding the Dist. of Hilton Head, S.C.

DAVIS AND DAVIS ESCAPE FROM HARPERS FERRY, 14 Sept. '62. When Federal forces under D. S. Miles were surrounded at Harpers Ferry during the Antietam campaign, a group of about 1,300 Federal cavalry fought their way out. The plan was proposed by the Mississippian Col. B. F. ("Grimes") Davis of the 8th N.Y. Cav. and seconded by Lt. Col. Hasbrouck Davis of the 12th Ill. Cav. "Under the inspiration and immediate direction of the two Davises, who rode together at the head of the column, the escaping force accomplished the brilliant achievement of reaching the Union lines [at Greencastle, Pa.] without the loss of a man, capturing on the way a Confederate ammunition train [Longstreet's reserve] of 97 wagons and its escort of 600 men" (B.&L., II, 613).

DAVIS' BRIDGE, Tenn. 25 Sept. '62. Guerrillas surprised a scouting party under the command of Lt. Col. John McDermott at this point on Hatchie River between Pocahontas and Chewalla. Federal force composed of 200 men of 11th Ill. Cav. and 70 of Ford's Company. They fought their way out with a loss of about 70.

DAVIS' FARM. See WELDON R.R. OPERATIONS, 22–23 June '64.

DAWES, Rufus R. Union officer. Ohio. Capt. 6th Wis. 16 July '61; Maj. 30 June '62; Lt. Col. 24 Mar. '63; Col. 5 July '64; Bvt. B.G. USV (war service); mustered out 10 Aug. '64. Died 1899.

DAWSON, Andrew Rea Zina. Union officer. Ohio. 2d Lt. 15th Ohio 23 Apr. '61; Capt. 9 Sept. '61; Maj. 28 July '64; Col. 187th Ohio 2 Mar. '65; Bvt. B.G. USV 21 Nov. '65 (war service). Died 1896.

DAWSON, Samuel K. Union officer. c. 1817–89. Pa. USMA 1839 (22/31); Arty.-Inf. He served on the frontier, in the Mexican War (1 brevet), and in the Seminole War before being promoted Maj. 19th U.S. Inf. 14 May '61. During the Civil War he was at Ft. Pickens 10 July–3 Dec. '61 and, as Lt. Col. 15th U.S. Inf. (4 July '63), at Chickamauga (severely wounded). On sick leave until

24 May '64, he was on detached service in N.Y. for the remainder of the war and was breveted B.G. USA. Continuing in the R.A., he retired in 1870 as Col.

DAY, Hannibal. Union officer. c. 1804-91. Vt. USMA 1823 (23/35); Inf. He served in garrison, in the Seminole War, in the Mexican War, and on the frontier, before being named Lt. Col. 2d U.S. Inf. 25 Feb. '61. During the Civil War he commanded the 2d Inf. in Washington until 16 Dec. '61, when he went into recruiting service, being promoted Col. 6th Inf. 7 Jan. '62. He fought at Gettysburg and served on boards and commissions until he retired 1 Aug. '63. He was breveted B.G. USA 13 Mar. '65.

DAY, Henry Martyn. Union officer. N.Y. Lt. Col. 1st Ill. Cav. 19 July '61; mustered out 14 June '62; Col. 91st Ill. 8 Sept. '62; Bvt. B.G. USV (Mobile). Commanded 2, 2, XIII; 2, 3, XIII; 2, 3, Res. Corps (Gulf). Died 1900.

DAY, Nicholas Wykoff. Union officer. N.J. Q.M. Sgt. 71st N.Y. 26 Apr.–28 July '61; Capt. 96th N.Y. 22 Feb. '62; Maj. 131st N.Y. 11 Sept. '62; Lt. Col. 31 Dec. '62; Col. 15 Jan. '63; Bvt. B.G. USV (Opequon, Va.). Commanded 2, 2, XIX (Shenandoah); 2, 2d Dist. Savannah. XIX (South); and 3, 1, X (N.C.).

DAYTON, Oscar Veniah. Union officer. N.Y. Maj. 62d N.Y. 3 July '61; Lt. Col. 31 May '62: mustered out 21 Nov. '62; Maj. Vet. Res. Corps 17 June '63; Lt Col. 25 Sept. '63; Col. 4 Dec. '63; Bvt. B.G. USV (war service). Died 1898.

DAYTON, Va. Burning of. Sheridan ordered all houses within five miles of this small town near Harrisonburg burned in retaliation for the death of his staff officer, Lt. John R. MEIGS, whom he believed to have been murdered by guerrillas on 3 Oct. '64. After watching the enthusiastic Custer start to carry out this order, Sheridan revoked it and ordered, instead, that all able-bodied men in the area be seized as prisoners of war.

DEARING, James. C.S.A. gen. 1840-65. Va. A cadet at West Point, he resigned from the class of 1862 when Va. seceded and was commissioned Lt. in New Orleans' "Washington Artillery." He commanded the Va. battery in Pickett's command during the Peninsular campaign and at Fredericksburg as a Capt. and was promoted Maj. after Chancellorsville. Given a battalion of 18 guns in Longstreet's reserve artillery, he fought under Pickett at Gettysburg and commanded Pickett's cavalry in the winter of 1863-64 in the Dist. of N.C. (headquarters at Petersburg) with the temporary rank of Col. Commissioned Lt. Col., he was named 5 Apr. '64 to command the horse artillery in the Army of Northern Va. Later that month (29 Apr. '64), he was given a cavalry brigade in the New Bern expedition and appointed B.G. C.S.A. He fought around Petersburg at Weldon Railroad, Drewry's Bluff, Reservoir Hill, and High Bridge, where he was mortally wounded. He died a few days after the surrender, at Lynchburg.

DEAS, Zachariah Cantey. C.S.A. gen. 1819-82. S.C. Educated in S.C. and France, he was a cotton broker of immense wealth in Ala. and fought in the Mexican War. Enlisting with the Ala. Vols., he was J. E. Johnston's A.D.C. and commissioned Col. 22d Ala. in the fall of '61. He armed his regiment with Enfield rifles at a cost of $28,000 in gold and was reimbursed with C.S.A. bonds. At Shiloh he succeeded to brigade command and was badly wounded himself. He led his regiment under Bragg through Ky. and was appointed B.G. C.S.A. 13 Dec. '62, superseding Franklin Gardner at Murfreesboro (D.A.B.). Leading his brigade at Stones River, Chickamauga, and Missionary Ridge, he fought under Hood in the Atlanta campaign and followed him to Franklin and Nashville. Returning to Georgia, he opposed Sherman there and through the Carolinas. After the war he was in the cotton trade and owned a seat on the stock exchange in New York. Nephew of James Chesnut, Jr.

DEBRAY, Xavier Blanchard. C.S.A. gen. c. 1818–95. France. Appt.-Texas. A graduate of St. Cyr, he was in the French diplomatic service until he emigrated to Tex. in 1852. He raised a cavalry regiment (26th Tex. Cav.) in Bexar County, after serving as the governor's A.D.C., and was commissioned Col. 5 Dec. '61. After fighting under Magruder at Galveston on 1 Jan. '63, he served under Taylor at Mansfield and Pleasant Hill and commanded a cavalry brigade in pursuit of Banks. He was appointed B.G. C.S.A. by Kirby Smith 13 Apr. '64. A Spanish newspaper publisher in San Antonio before the war, he was a translator in the state's general land office later. Wright does not list him as a general officer, but he is mentioned as such by Heitman, Wood, C.M.H., and Lonn.

DECORATIONS. At the start of the Civil War there was no provision for awarding gallantry or merit by individual decorations. The MEDAL OF HONOR was created during the war. Other Federal decorations were the FORT SUMTER AND FORT PICKENS MEDALS, the KEARNY MEDAL AND THE KEARNY CROSS, the BUTLER MEDAL for colored troops, the GILLMORE MEDAL, and the XVII Corps Medal. (John Wike, "Individual Decorations of the Civil War and Earlier," M. C. & H., Sept. 1953.) These decorations are not be confused with the corps BADGES, which were devised merely for unit identification, or the various other badges worn by men of Sheridan's and Wilson's cavalry corps, the Engineer and Signal Corps, and by Hancock's corps of veteran volunteers (See O. R. atlas

plate CLXXV for illustrations of the latter).

The Confederate government intended to award medals and badges for gallantry and meritorious conduct, but was never able to supply the emblems. In lieu thereof the Confederate congress passed an act in Oct. '62 providing that a Roll of Honor be published after each battle (Wiley, *Reb,* 82).

DEEMS, James Munroe. Union officer. Md. Maj. 1st Md. Cav. 20 Dec. '61; Lt. Col. 10 Nov. '62; Breveted B.G. USV (war service); mustered out 10 Nov. '63. Died 1901.

DEEP BOTTOM RUN, Va. (Darbytown; Malvern Hill; New Market Road; Strawberry Plains). 27–29 July '64 (PETERSBURG CAMPAIGN). To aid the PETERSBURG MINE ASSAULT (30 July) Grant ordered a surprise attack north of the James to draw Confederate strength from Petersburg. The plan was for Hancock's II Corps to move secretly across the James the night of 27 July, attack out of the bridgehead held by Foster's division of X Corps, and move toward Chafin's Bluff. Sheridan was to cross the river behind him with the cavalry divisions of Torbert and Gregg, pick up Kautz's cavalry division (Army of the James) and lead a raid that would enter Richmond if possible or, otherwise, destroy the Virginia Central R.R.

Miles's brigade of Barlow's division led the Federal infantry toward the Confederate defenses along Bailey's Creek; they drove back the enemy outposts, capturing a battery of four 20-pounder Parrott guns. However, near the crossing of the New Market Road over the creek the Federals were surprised to find themselves opposed by the divisions of Wilcox and Kershaw. The latter launched a successful counterattack that held the Federals east of the creek.

Meanwhile, according to plan, Sheridan had crossed the James with the divisions of Torbert and Gregg, and was joined by Kautz. Moving across Strawberry Plains to the Darbytown Road, Sheridan found the crossing of the creek blocked by the enemy. Gibbon's division was given the mission of holding Hancock's initial position to the south, while Barlow and Mott moved up the creek to join the cavalry. The Federals were unable to find an assailable flank, as the Confederate line extended to Fussell's Mill and its flank was refused. Sheridan led a charge that took ground near the Darbytown Road, but no further gains could be made. Heth's division arrived during the day to reinforce the Confederate defenses, and on the 28th W. H. F. Lee's cavalry division arrived. The next day the infantry division of Field and the cavalry division of Fitz Lee reinforced from south of the James.

Grant arrived on the scene the afternoon of the first day and realized he had underestimated Confederate strength in the area. An envelopment of the Confederate north flank was planned for the 28th to shake the cavalry loose for its raid. Foster's division was to conduct a demonstration to its front. However, Sheridan was attacked about 10 A.M. (on the 28th) by Kershaw's division and his outposts driven back. Sheridan's dismounted troopers, armed with repeating carbines, then drove Kershaw back, pursued and captured 300 prisoners and two stands of colors. Gibbon was ordered to the scene but arrived after the action was finished; he was then posted to guard the approaches to the Long Bridge Road while the cavalry was withdrawn to the New Market Road. In the latter action Gregg's division was hotly engaged and lost an artillery piece. Hancock disposed his forces to prevent a threat against his line of withdrawal from the direction of Malvern Hill. On the 29th he was ordered back to the

Petersburg trenches. The operation succeeded in drawing Confederate strength from Petersburg, but the prompt Confederate reaction prevented a raid by Sheridan that would have been difficult to oppose (D.S.F.). Union losses were reported as 334 killed and wounded (E.&B.); Confederate figures are not known.

DEEP BOTTOM RUN, Va. (Strawberry Plains), 13–20 Aug. '64 (PETERSBURG CAMPAIGN).

Acting on (erroneous) information that Lee's defenses of the Deep Bottom Run (Bailey's Creek) line north of the James had been reduced to one division (8,500 men) by the detachment of troops to support Early in the Shenandoah, Grant planned another attack in this sector. The troops here (part of X Corps) were to be reinforced by the remainder of X Corps from Bermuda Hundred, and by Hancock's II Corps and Gregg's cavalry division from the Petersburg area. Taking measures to make the Confederates believe Federal troops were being shipped to Washington, Hancock's infantry marched to City Point and boarded transports; his artillery and Gregg's cavalry marched to the ponton bridges over the James opposite Deep Run. The night of 13–14 Aug. D. B. Birney's troops, Gregg's cavalry, and Hancock's artillery crossed over the two bridges; the infantry came up by water. Difficulty in unloading the transports delayed the attack, which was supposed to start at dawn, until after 9 A.M.

The plan was for Birney's X Corps on the left (south) to attack Confederate positions opposite Deep Bottom, penetrate their line along Four Mile Creek, and move toward Chafin's Bluff and Richmond; Mott (3, II), on Birney's right, was to move up the New Market Road; Barlow, with the other two divisions of II Corps, was to attack the enemy positions near the Jennings House (vicinity Fussell's Mill). Gregg, on the extreme right flank, was to make a dash for Richmond after the infantry attacks had loosened the enemy's defenses. The entire operation was directed toward turning the Confederates out of their Chafin's Bluff positions.

Instead of finding the enemy weak, however, Mott ran up against Field's division entrenched along Deep Run, and Wilcox's division was within supporting distance. The defenders were further reinforced by three Confederate divisions: Mahone's infantry and W. H. F. Lee's cavalry from south of the James; and M. C. Butler's cavalry, which had been on its way to join Early.

Birney made some progress due to the weakening of the Confederate south flank to reinforce around Fussell's Mill. Barlow's attack in the latter sector was late and ineffectual. The Federal advance was then stopped all along the line. Gregg's cavalry, however, broke loose and advanced well up the Charles City Road. The night of 14-15 Aug. Hancock massed to his right (north), where he planned an envelopment by Birney's corps the next day. On the 16th Gregg, supported by Miles's brigade (1, II), again attacked up the Charles City Road as a diversion to assist Birney's envelopment; Gregg reached White's Tavern, seven miles from Richmond, and the Confederate General John Chambliss was killed in this action. Birney, however, took so wide a circuit around the enemy north flank that he was not able to attack this day. (The dense woods, flat terrain, and confusing trails of the Peninsula made this operation difficult.) At 10 o'clock the Federals attacked at Fussell's Mill with Terry's division. (1, X), Craig's brigade (2, 3, II), and the colored brigade of William Birney (1, 3, X). Although this attack succeeded in overrunning the Confederate positions

and capturing several hundred prisoners, the Confederates counterattacked later in the day and by nightfall had restored their line. Col. Craig was killed. The fighting in the heavy woods was confused, and Hancock was unaware of the true situation for several hours. At 5 P.M. Gregg was driven back behind Deep Bottom Creek.

The night of 16-17 Aug. a fleet of Federal transports was moved up to Deep Bottom to make the enemy think an evacuation was taking place and to trick them into making an attack. The ruse did not work. There was no further action until 5 P.M. on the 18th, when the Confederates attacked Fussell's Mill. Miles, now in command of the 1st Div., II Corps, counterattacked the Confederate north flank and drove them back with considerable loss. The night of the 20th Hancock's force was withdrawn to the south of the James to take part in the actions at GLOBE TAVERN and REAMS'S STATION.

According to Livermore the forces engaged were 27,974 Federals and 20,008 Confederates. Fox puts Federal losses at 2,899. Confederate losses, considerably lower, since they did most of their fighting from behind breastworks, have been estimated at 1,000. Senior officers killed in addition to Chambliss and Craig were Gen. GIRARDEY, C.S.A., and Col. Daniel Chaplin, C.O. 1st MAINE HEAVY ARTY.

DEFEAT IN DETAIL. In the military sense, this term does not mean annihilation or "complete defeat," but means "the defeat in turn of the separated parts of a force" (M.A.&E., *Notes*). To avoid defeat in detail a commander keeps his units within SUPPORTING DISTANCE.

DE GROAT, Charles Henry. Union officer. N.Y. Capt. 32d Wis. 25 Sept. '62; Maj. 10 May '63; Lt. Col. 8 July '64; Col. 2 Aug. '64; Bvt. B.G. USV

(Ga. and Carolinas). Commanded 3, 1, XVII (Tenn.).

DE HART, Richard P. Union officer. Ohio. 1st Lt. Adj. 46th Ind. 5 Nov. '61; Lt. Col. 99th Ind. 18 Oct. '62; Col. 128th Ind. 18 Mar. '64; Bvt. B.G. USV (war service).

DEITZLER, George Washington. Union gen. 1826–84. Pa. A Kansas farmer and real-estate agent when that territory was becoming a state, he was active as a Free-Soiler and on a trip East procured Sharps rifles, sending them in boxes marked "Books." (See BEECHER, Henry Ward.) He fought in the Kansas wars and was arrested for treason but later released. He held several public offices before being commissioned Col. 1st Kans. 5 June '61. He led his regiment at Wilson's Creek where he was wounded. He commanded 1, 6, XIII, Tenn. (1 Nov.–18 Dec. '62) and was promoted B.G. USV 29 Nov. '62. Also in the Army of the Tenn., he commanded 1, 6, XVI (22 Dec. '62–20 Jan. '63) and 1, 6, XVII (20 Jan.–22 Apr. '63). He resigned his commission 27 Aug. '63 because of poor health, but when Price invaded Mo. and eastern Kans. in Oct. '64 he was put in command of the Kans. State Mil. as Maj. Gen.

DE LACY, William. Union officer. England. 1st Lt. 37th N.Y. 8 July '61; Capt. 10 Sept. '61; Maj. 8 Oct. '62; Lt. Col. 164th N.Y. 3 Nov. '63; Col. 4 July '64; Bvt. B.G. USV (war service). Commanded 2, 2, II (Potomac). Died 1898.

DELAFIELD, Richard. Union gen. 1798–1873. USMA 1818 (1/23); Engrs. He served in engineering duty on rivers and harbors and as Superintendent of West Point twice (1838–45 and 1856–1 Mar. '61) before serving on the Gov.'s staff in outfitting N.Y. troops for the Civil War. As Lt. Col. 6 Aug.

'61 and Col. 1 June '63, he supervised harbor fortifications for New York and took command of the Corps of Engrs. 18 May '64. Continuing in the army, he was retired in 1866 as B.G. USA and Chief of Engrs. and Bvt. Maj. Gen. USA.

DE LAGNEL, Julius Adolphus. C.S.A. gen. 1827–1912. N.J. Appt.-Va. Serving in the 2d US Arty., he joined the R.A. in 1847 and resigned 17 May '61 as 1st Lt. to go with his adopted state, Va. He was commissioned Capt. 16 Mar. '61 and served as Garnett's Chief of Arty. in West Va. where he was wounded at Hart House. Recovering behind the enemy lines, he attempted to rejoin the army but was discovered and captured. Upon his release he was promoted Maj. 20th Bn. of Va. Arty. 3 July '62, having declined on 31 July the appointment of B.G. C.S.A. 18 Apr. '62 to rank from the 15th. For most of the war he was second-in-command to Gorgas in the Ordnance Bureau in Richmond. He is not listed in C.M.H.

DE LAND, Charles Victor. Union officer. Mass. Capt. 9th Mich. 15 Oct. '61; discharged 25 Feb. '63; Col. 1st Mich. Sharpshooters 7 July '63; Bvt. B.G. USV (war service). Captured at Murfreesboro (Tenn.) 12 July '62; W.I.A. Spotsylvania C.H. (twice) 12 May '64 and Petersburg mine 30 July '64; captured a second time at Poplar Spring Church (Va.) 30 Sept. '64.

DEMOCRATIC PARTY. In the Civil War the party split into Northern and Southern factions, and when Lincoln won the 1860 election as a Republican, the Democrats were destroyed as an entity. The PEACE DEMOCRATS ran McClellan unsuccessfully as a presidential candidate in 1864. It was not until 1876 that the party was able to regain its former power and virility. The basic concepts of the Democratic party were opposition to a strong Federal government and insistence upon personal liberty. In this way the Southern faction had more of a claim to the old party standard, and the Northern wing was left with little to rally around when the war began. Most of the Union army officers were Democrats (Hesseltine, 285).

DEMONSTRATION. "A show of force on a front where the decision is not sought, with the object of deceiving the enemy; no advance against the enemy is made by the demonstrating force" (M.A.&E., *Notes*). In this last regard it differs from a FEINT.

DENISON, Andrew Woods, Union officer. 1831–77. Md. Commissioned Col. 8th Md. 12 Sept. '62, he led it throughout the war and commanded the Md. brigade in Robinson's division at Laurel Hill where he lost an arm. Again wounded near Petersburg, he was breveted B.G. USV 19 Aug. '64 (the Wilderness and Spotsylvania) and Maj. Gen. USV 31 Mar. '65 (White Oak Road). Mustered out in May '65, he was the postmaster of Baltimore after the war.

DENNIS, Elias S. Union gen. ?–1894. N.Y. Named Lt. Col. 30th Ill. 28 Aug. '61, he was promoted Col. 1 May '62 and B.G. USV the following 29 Nov. During the Vicksburg campaign he commanded 2, 3, XVII (13 Apr. 11–May '63) and also led Dist. N.E. La. (11 May–19 July '63); 1st Div., XV (28 July–1 Sept. '63); 1st Div., XVII (23 Oct. '63–22 Sept. '64); 2d Div., XIX (18 Aug.–7 Nov. '64); 2d Brig., Res. Div., Gulf; 2, 1, Res. Corps, Gulf; 2, 1, XIII (18 Feb.–25 May '65); and 1st Div., XIII (25 May–20 July '65). He was breveted Maj. Gen. USV 13 Apr. '65 for Mobile and mustered out 24 Aug. '65.

DENNIS, John Benjamin. Union officer. Conn. Pvt. Co. G 6th Mass. Mil. 16 Apr.–2 Aug. '61; Capt. 7th Conn. 5 Sept. '61; Maj. Add. Paymr. Vols. 25 Jan. '65; Bvt. B.G. USV. Brevets for Morris Island (S.C.), Drewry's Bluff (Va.), war service. Died 1894.

DENNISON, A. W. Misspelling in Phisterer for Andrew Woods DENISON.

DENNISON, William. Union Gov. of Ohio and Postmaster Gen. Ohio. 1815–82. After graduating from Miami Univ. in Ohio, he practiced law and served in the legislature before becoming Gov. in 1859. By practically assuming control of the state's transportation and communication facilities, and using public funds without special appropriation, he managed to outfit his state for the war. He was appointed Postmaster Gen. in Lincoln's second term and served also under Johnson.

DENT, Frederick Tracy. Union gen. 1821–92. Mo. USMA 1843 (33/39); Inf. Classmate and brother-in-law of U. S. Grant, he served on the frontier and in the Mexican War, where he was wounded and received two brevets. He was stationed in the West where he went on several expeditions and fought Indians and where he remained until '63 when, as Maj. 4th US Inf. (9 Mar. '63), he returned to the East to command his regiment in the Army of the Potomac (12 Aug.–8 Sept. '63). He went to New York to suppress the Draft Riots that winter and on 29 Mar. '64 was appointed Lt. Col. A.D.C. to Grant, serving until 5 Apr. '65 when he was promoted B.G. USV. He was then military governor of Richmond and commanded the garrison in Washington, D.C. Mustered out of USV in 1866, he was again Lt. Col. A.D.C. to Grant 3 May–25 July '66 and to Sherman until 31 Dec. '72. He remained in the R.A. until retired as Col. in 1883. His brevets were for the Wilderness, Petersburg, and war services (B.G. USA).

DENVER, James William. Union gen. 1817–92. Va. He served in the

Mexican War as a Capt. after being a Midwestern lawyer and newspaper editor. Moving to California for the gold rush, he was elected to the state senate. In an 1852 duel he killed a critic of his methods, but according to D.A.B., the public agreed with Denver, and no action was taken against him. He was also Democratic congressman and Governor of the Kans. Territory (Denver, Colo., was named for him), and Indian Commissioner. Appointed B.G. USV 14 Aug. '61, he commanded the troops in Kans. and fought at Shiloh. He commanded in the Army of the Tenn. the following: 3d Brig., 5th Div. (12 May–21 July '62); 2d Brig., 5th Div. Dist. of Memphis (21 July–26 Oct. '62); 2, 5th Div. Dist. of Memphis, XIII; 2d Div. Dist. of Memphis, XIII; 1st Div., XVII (18 Dec. '62–19 Jan. '63); 1st Div., XVI. He resigned 5 Mar. '63 to practice law, re-entering politics later.

DEPARTMENT. As mentioned in the article on ORGANIZATION, the basic territorial organization was the department, which usually gave its name to the field ARMY operating within its boundaries. Although all the principal departments and territorial "divisions" (the next higher echelon) are covered separately within this book, the following list from a special index of the *Official Records* will be useful:

Alabama, Union Dept. of
Alabama and West Florida, Confed. Dept. of
Alabama, Mississippi, and East Louisiana, Confed. Dept. of
Alexandria, Confed. Dept. of
Annapolis, Union Dept. of
Arkansas, Union Dept. of
Atlantic, Union Military Division of the
California, Union Dept. of
Columbia, Union Dept. of the
Cumberland, Union Dept. of the
Department No. 1 (Confed.)
Department No. 2 (Confed.)
East, Union Dept. of the
East Tennessee, Confed. Dept. of
Florida, Union Dept. of
Fredericksburg, Confed. Dept. of
Georgia, Confed. Dept. of
Georgia, Union Dept. of
Gulf, Confed. Dept. of the
Gulf, Union Dept. of the
Gulf, Confed. District of the
Gulf, Union Military Division of the
Henrico, Confed. Dept. of
James, Union Military Division of the
Kansas, Union Dept. of
Kentucky, Union Dept. of
Key West, Florida, Union Dept. of
Louisiana, Confed. Dept. of
Louisiana and Texas, Union Dept. of
Maryland, Union Dept. of
Middle Department (Union)
Middle Military Division (Union)
Middle and Eastern Florida, Confed. Dept. of
Mississippi, Union Dept. of the (11 Mar. '62)
Mississippi, Union Dept. of (28 Nov. '64)
Mississippi, Union Dept. of (27 June '65)
Mississippi, Union Military Division of the
Mississippi and East Louisiana, Confed. Dept. of
Missouri, Union Dept. of the
Missouri, Union Military Division of the
Monongahela, Union Dept. of the
Mountain Department (Union)
New England, Union Dept. of
New Mexico, Union Dept. of
New York, Union Dept. of
Norfolk, Confed. Dept. of
North Carolina, Confed. Dept. of
North Carolina, Union Dept. of
North Carolina and Southern Virginia, Confed. Dept. of
Northeastern Virginia, Union Dept. of
Northern Department (Union)

Northern Virginia, Confed. Dept. of
Northwest, Union Dept. of the
Ohio, Union Dept. of (3 May '61)
Ohio, Union Dept. of the (19 Aug. '62)
Ohio, Union Dept. of the (27 June '65)
Oregon, Union Dept. of
Pacific, Union Dept. of the
Pacific, Union Military Division of the
Peninsula, Confed. Dept. of the
Pennsylvania, Union Dept. of
Potomac, Union Dept. of the
Potomac, Union Military Division of the
Potomac Department (Confed.)
Rappahannock, Union Dept. of the
Richmond, Confed. Dept. of
Shenandoah, Union Dept. of the
South, Union Dept. of the
South Carolina, Confed. Dept. of
South Carolina, Union Dept. of
South Carolina and Georgia, Confed. Dept. of
South Carolina, Georgia, and Florida, Confed. Dept. of
Southern Mississippi and East Louisiana, Confed. Dept. of
Southern Virginia, Confed. Dept. of
Southwest, Confed. Dept. of the
Southwest, Union Military Division of the
Southwestern Virginia, Confed. Dept. of
Southwestern Virginia and East Tennessee, Confed. Dept. of
Susquehanna, Union Dept. of the
Tennessee, Confed. Dept. of
Tennessee, Union Dept. of the
Tennessee, Union Military Division of the
Tennessee and Georgia, Confed. Dept. of
Texas, Confed. Dept. of
Texas, Union Dept. of
Texas, New Mexico, and Arizona, Confed. District of

Trans-Allegheny Department (Confed.)
Trans-Mississippi Dept. (Confed.)
Trans-Mississippi, Confed. District of
Utah, Union Dept. of
Valley District (Confed.)
Virginia, Union Dept. of
Virginia and North Carolina, Confed. Dept. of
Virginia and North Carolina, Union Dept. of
Washington, Union Defenses of
Washington, Union Dept. of
West, Confed. Dept. of the
West, Union Dept. of the
West, Confed. Military Division of the
Western Department (Confed.)
Western Department (Union)
Western Kentucky, Confed. Dept. of
Western Virginia, Confed. Dept. of
Western Virginia, Union Dept. of
Western Virginia and East Tennessee, Confed. Dept. of
West Florida, Confed. Dept. of
West Mississippi, Union Military Division of
West Tennessee, Union District of
West Virginia, Union Dept. of
Winchester, Confed. Dept. of

DEPARTMENT NO. 1 (Confed.). The state of La. comprised the main part of this department. A portion of the state along the eastern boundary that is formed by the Mississippi River was not in the department originally, but was in Dept. No. 2. East of the Mississippi River the department initially extended to include Mobile Bay and all of Miss. and Ala. south of the 31st parallel. (This parallel is the northern boundary of East La. and of West Fla.)

By the end of 1861 the department comprised all of La., but its southeastern boundary had been moved back to the Pascagoula River. On 25 June '62 —two months after the Federal capture of New Orleans—the department disappeared, the part east of the Mississippi going into Dept. No. 2, and the other part into the Trans-Miss. Dept.

Twiggs commanded the department until he was succeeded 18 Oct. '61 by Lovell (O.R., I, VI, 436; and XVII, 1). Headquarters were at New Orleans. Troop strength at the end of 1861 was 7,000, few of whom were regular troops.

DEPARTMENT NO. 2 (Confed.). At the start of the war this comprised a narrow strip of the Miss. Valley extending north from the 31st parallel to include the part of Ark. east of the White River and Tenn. west of the Tenn. River. It included a portion of Miss. along the Miss. River, and that portion of La. along the river that was not in Dept. No. 1. An appendix extended east to include a thin strip of northeastern Miss. and northern Ala. that was bounded on the north by the Tenn. border and on the south by the Memphis to Chattanooga R.R.

By the end of 1861 its area included all of Ark. and Tenn.; and Miss. west of the Miss. Central R.R.

On 26 May '62 Dept. No. 2 was extended to embrace all of Miss. south of the 33d parallel (which is the northern boundary of La.) and west of the Pascagoula and Chickasawhay rivers, and La. east of the Miss. River (O.R., I, XV, chronology). The order assigning Bragg to temporary command on 17 June (see also below) refers to this as Dept. No. 2 "or Western Department" (O.R., I, XVI). The O.R. atlas, however, does not use the two designations synonymously. On 25 June '62 Dept. No. 1 was merged into Dept. No. 2. On 18 July the department was extended to embrace all of Miss., East La., and West Fla. (west of the Chattahoochie River). According to O.R. atlas, plate CLXV, on 30 June '62 the department included all of Miss. and Ala. Ark. had gone into the Trans-Miss. Dept. All of Tenn. except the

Dept. of EAST TENN. was in Dept. No. 2, as was the northwestern part of Ga. west of the Chattanooga, Atlanta, Montgomery R.R. East Fla., as previously mentioned, was also in the department.

As for commanders of Dept. No. 2, Polk assumed command on 13 July '61, and on 2 Aug. his authority was extended over Ark. and military operations in Mo. (O.R., I, IV, 175). A. S. Johnston superseded Polk on 15 Sept.; and Beauregard took command on Johnston's death at Shiloh, 6 Apr. '62. Bragg temporarily succeeded Beauregard on 17 June '62, was assigned to permanent command on the 20th, and assumed command on the 27th. Polk was announced as Bragg's second-in-command on 2 July, and commanded temporarily, vice Polk, during the period 24 Oct–3 Nov. '62.

On 1 Oct. '62 the Dept. of MISS. AND E. LA. had been constituted under Pemberton. Dept. No. 2 was now reduced in area to Ala., West and Central Tenn., and West Fla. The DEPT. OF THE WEST was created to include these two other departments. Dept. No. 2 disappeared when the Dept. of Tenn. was created 25 July '63 (see TENNESSEE, CONFEDERATE DEPARTMENT OF).

DEPARTMENT OF THE WEST (J. E. Johnston's). See Confed. DIVISION OF THE WEST.

DE RUSSY, Gustavus Adolphus. Union gen. 1818–91. N.Y. Appt.-Va. Resigning as a cadet at USMA (ex-1839), he was appointed 2d Lt. in the R.A. in 1847 and fought in the Mexican War (2 brevets). He served in garrison and frontier duty and as quartermaster and was Capt. 4th US Arty. when the Civil War began. He was with the Arty. Reserve (Potomac) until June '62 when he became Chief of Arty. for Hooker's division and served in the Peninsular campaign. Named Col. 4th

N.Y. Arty. 17 Mar. '63 and B.G. USV 23 May '63, he commanded Defenses South of the Potomac, XXII Corps, Wash. (25 May '63–20 Aug. '65). He was breveted for Fair Oaks, Malvern Hill, and war service (2), once as B.G. USA. He continued in the R.A. until retired as Col. 3d Arty. in 1882. He was the nephew of L. G. De Russy, USMA 1814 and Col. in the C.S.A., and son of R. E. De Russy, Superintendent of West Point.

DE RUSSY, René E. c. 1790–1865. West Indies. Appt.-N.Y. USMA 1812 * (18/18); Engrs. He fought in the War of 1812 (1 brevet), served as Superintendent of West Point, and participated in normal engineering duty until 1858, when he took command of the Corps of Engineers. Holding this post until 2 Jan. '61, he then superintended the San Francisco harbor fortifications until 23 Nov. '65, when he died on active duty as Col. and breveted B.G. USA.

DESERTIONS were high in both armies. See BOUNTY JUMPERS, CONFEDERATE ARMY, and UNION ARMY.

DESHLER, James. C.S.A. gen. 1833–63. Ala. USMA 1854 (7/46); Arty. He served on the frontier in Indian fighting, in garrison, and went on the Utah Expedition before being dropped by the army 15 July '61 for having overstayed his leave of absence. Commissioned Capt. of C.S.A. Arty. (appointed from Ga.), he was H. R. Jackson's Adj. in western Va. on the Greenbrier River on the Cheat Mountain expedition. He was wounded at Allegheny Summit 13 Dec. '61. Promoted Col. of Arty. in N.C., he was with Holmes as Chief of Staff in 1862 when that general was sent to the Trans-Miss. Captured at Arkansas Post in

* There was no class standing prior to 1818, and the cadets are listed in the order in which they were commissioned.

Jan. '63 while leading the Tex. brigade, he was exchanged in June and appointed B.G. C.S.A. 28 July '63. He commanded his brigade under Cleburne at Chickamauga where he was killed 20 Sept. '63.

DETACHMENT, ARMY OF THE TENNESSEE. Designation of a unit under A. J. Smith that participated in Banks's Red River expedition of 1864. The force consisted of two divisions from the XVI Corps, Army of the Tenn.: 1st (Mower's) and 3d (A. J. Smith's). This force, reinforced by the RED RIVER DIVISION, XVII CORPS, took part in the battle of Nashville (15 Dec. '64) under the official designation of "Detachment, Army of the Tennessee," although it was unofficially known as XVI Corps.

DE TROBRIAND, Philip Regis Denis de Keredern. Union gen. 1816–97. France. The son of the Baron de Trobriand, "he engaged in duels, wrote poetry, and published a novel" (D.A.B.) before coming to America on a trip. While in this country he married an heiress and settled down, becoming an American citizen and serving as Col. of the "Guards Lafayette" of the N.Y. State Mil. He was commisioned Col. 55th N.Y. 28 Aug. '61 and transferred to the 38th N.Y. 21 Dec. '62, commanding, in the meantime 3, 1, III, Potomac (Oct.–Nov. '62). Continuing in the Army of the Potomac, he commanded 2, 1, III (26 Jan.–15 Feb.; Mar.–Apr. and 29 May–3 June '63) and 3, 1, III (3 June–22 Nov. '63). Mustered out 22 Nov. '63, he was appointed B.G. USV 5 Jan. '64 and took command of 1, 3, II (21 Oct. '64–2 Jan. '65; 25 Jan.–15 Feb. '65; 2 Mar–6 Apr. '65 and 16 May–28 June '65). He also led the division (3, II) 8–21 Oct. '64; 15 Feb.–2 Mar. '65; 6 Apr.–16 May '65 and 9–20 June '65. Breveted Maj. Gen. USV 9 Apr. '65 for the closing campaigns of the war, he continued in the R.A., retiring in 1879 as Col. 13th U.S. Inf. He succeeded his father to the title in 1874. His *Quatre Ans de Campagnes à l'Armée du Potomac* (1867–68) is one of the better histories of the war.

DEVALL'S BLUFF, Ark., on the White River, was scene of a number of minor actions. On 6 July '62 Col. G. N. Fitch led about 2,000 men (24th Ind.) up the White and routed some 400 Confederate cavalry with the loss of 84 Confederate killed and wounded and 22 Federals. After the fall of Arkansas Post, W. A. Gorman led an expedition of some 10,000 men up the White in transports and gunboats, while over 1,000 cavalry moved west from Helena to cooperate in breaking up Confederate concentrations along the river. During the period 13–19 Jan. '63 Gorman succeeded in capturing prisoners and matériel at Devall's Bluff and Des Arcs without the loss of a single Federal. During the Federal occupation of northern Ark. there were numerous skirmishes with Confederate raiders in this area.

DEVELOP. In the tactical or strategic sense, to find out, by reconnaissance and/or attack, the enemy's location and strength.

DEVENS, Charles. Union gen. 1820–91. Mass. A Harvard graduate, he practiced law and held several public offices. He was a firm opponent of slavery. A B.G. in the Mass. State Militia, he entered the Union Army as Maj. 3d Bn. Mass. Rifle Militia 19 Apr. '61, was mustered out 20 July '61 and named Col. 15th Mass. 24 July. Wounded at Ball's Bluff, he was promoted B.G. USV 15 Apr. '62 and commanded 1, 1, IV, Potomac (1–31 May) when he was wounded at Fair Oaks. Other commands were in the Army of the Potomac: 1, 1, IV (26 July–26 Sept. '62);

1, 3, VI (26 Sept.–Oct. '62); 2, 3, VI (Oct.–Dec. '62 and Feb.–Apr. '63); 3d Div., VI (Dec. '62–Feb. '63). He was leading the 1st Div., XI Corps (20 Apr.–2 May '63) at Chancellorsville when he was wounded a third time. He then commanded in the Dept. of Va. and N.C.: 3, 1, XVIII (26–30 May '64); 3d Div., XVIII (30 May–4 June '64); at Cold Harbor while on stretcher crippled with inflammatory rheumatism; 1st Div., XVIII (29 Oct.–3 Dec. '64) and in the Dept. of Va.: 3d Div., XXIV (3 Dec. '64–10 July '65) and XXIV Corps (2–15 Jan. '65). He was later on the Mass. Supreme Court, then served Pres. Hayes as Attorney Gen., and returned to the bench. Camp Devens (Mass.) is named in his honor, and his statue stands on the State House lawn.

DEVEREUX, Arthur Forrester. Union officer. Mass. Ex-cadet USMA 1857. Capt. 8th Mass. 18 May–1 Aug. '61; Lt. Col. 19th Mass. 3 Aug. '61; Col. 1 May '63; Bvt. B.G. USV (war service); resigned 27 Feb. '64. Commanded 2, 2, II. W.I.A. Antietam and 2d Bull Run. His regiment met "Pickett's charge" head on at Gettysburg, and when the smoke cleared Devereux had four CSA colors draped over his arm.

DEVIN, Thomas Casimer. Union gen. 1822–78. N.Y. A painter by trade, he was Lt. Col. 1st N.Y. State Mil. in 1861 and commissioned Capt. 1st N.Y. Cav. 19 July. Mustered out 19 Oct. '61, he was named Col. 6th N.Y. Cav. 18 Nov. '61 and commanded 2, 1, Cav., Potomac (16 Feb.–6 June '63; 9 June–3 Jan. '64 and 25 Jan.–16 Aug. '64) at Front Royal, where his troops captured two stand of colors, and he was severely wounded. He also commanded 1st Div., Cav., Potomac (6–9 June '63 and 25 Mar.–28 May '65) at Five Forks. Promoted B.G. USV 19 Oct. '64 he was breveted for Fishers Hill, Front Royal (B.G. USV 15 Aug. '64), Sayler's Creek

(B.G. USA), and war service. (Maj. Gen. USV). Continuing in the R.A., he died on active duty as Col. 3d US Cav.

DEVOL, Henry F. Union officer. 1831–? Ohio. Capt. 36th Ohio 24 Aug. '61; Maj. 7 Sept. '62; Lt. Col. 21 Oct. '62; Col. 19 Mar. '64; Bvt. B.G. USV (war service). Commanded 1st Brig., 2d Div., Army of W. Va. during Sheridan's Valley campaign. In the South on business in May 1861 he made his way north with difficulty. W.I.A. in reconnaissance in front of Chattanooga. Note: This officer appears in Phisterer's list as Duval, Hiram F. The above information and name appear in Heitman, Dyer, and Whitelaw Reid's *Ohio in the War*.

DEWALL, Isaac H. Misspelling in Phisterer for Isaac Hardin DUVAL.

DEWEY, George. Union naval officer. 1837–1917. Vt. Graduating from the Naval Academy in 1858, he served under Farragut as executive officer on the *Mississippi* at New Orleans and Port Hudson. He held the same position aboard the *Colorado* at Ft. Fisher and continued in the navy after the war, winning fame in 1898 at the battle of Manila Bay.

DEWEY, Joel Allen. Union gen. 1840–73. Vt. He was commissioned 2d Lt. 58th Ohio 10 Oct. '61 while a student at Oberlin. Promoted Capt. 43d Ohio 12 Jan. '62, he served on Rosecrans's staff and was named Col. 111st US Col. Inf. 14 Feb. '64. He was promoted Col. 29 Apr '65 and B.G. USV 20 Nov. '65, serving mainly in Tenn. and Ala. Mustered out in 1866, he went to law school and served as Tenn.'s Atty. Gen. from 1869 until his death at 33.

DE WITT, David Porter. Union officer. c. 1817–89. N.Y. USMA 1836 (14/49); Arty. Maj. 2d Md. 21 Sept. '61; Col. 3d Md. 29 Mar. '62; resigned 8 Oct. '62; Col. 143d N.Y. 8 Oct. '62; resigned on account of ill-health 30 Apr. '63; Maj. Vet. Res. Corps 9 June '63; Col. Vet. Res. Corps 29 Sept. '63; Bvt. B.G. USV (war service). Commanded ?, 2, II. Resigned from the R.A. in 1836 and worked in US and Canada as a civil engineer and for the US Express Company. He rejoined the company after the war as its Superintendent of Supplies in New York.

DIBRELL, George Gibbs. C.S.A. gen. 1822–88. Tenn. With little education, he farmed for a time and then became a bank and court clerk and merchant. Opposing secession, he nonetheless went with the South and enlisted as a private. He was elected Lt. Col. and served in Tenn. and Ky. under Zollicoffer. Upon reorganization of the army at Corinth, he was not re-elected by his regiment, so he raised the 8th Tenn. Cav. behind Federal lines to operate as independent partisan rangers. Joining Forrest at Stones River, he was commissioned Col. and his regiment was mustered in. On 1 July '63 he succeeded Starnes (K.I.A.) to command Forrest's "old brigade" and led it for the remainder of the war. After Chickamauga he was detached from Forrest and sent to J. E. Johnston at Dalton, fighting under him in the Atlanta campaign, the March to the Sea, and through the Carolinas. From Raleigh, he was sent to Davis at Greensboro and finally disbanded his command at Washington (Ga.), He was appointed B.G. C.S.A. 28 Jan. '65. A highly successful merchant and railroading and mining financier, he was later in Congress.

DICK, George Frederick. Union officer. Germany. Capt. 20th Ind. 22 July '61; Maj. 13 Oct. '62; Lt. Col. 86th Ind. 1 Nov. '62; Col. 14 Jan. '63; Bvt. B.G. USV (war service). In Army of Cumberland he commanded 2, 3, XXI; and 3, 3, IV.

DICKERSON, Christopher J. Union officer. N.Y. Lt. Col. 10th Mich. 20 Nov. '61; Bvt. B.G. USV (war service). W.I.A. and captured at Buzzard Roost (Ga.) 25 Feb. '64. Died 1873.

DICKEY, William Henry. Union officer. Mich. 2d Lt. 6th Mich. 9 Oct. '61; 1st Lt. 1 Sept. '62; Col. 84th US Col. Inf. 16 Dec. '63; Bvt. B.G. (war service). In the Dept. of the Gulf he commanded 1st Brig., Corps d'Afrique USCT; 2d Brig., Dist. of Morganza, La.; Dist. of Morganza.

DICKINSON, Joseph. Union officer. Pa. 1st Lt. Adj. 26th Pa. 1 June '61; Capt. Asst. Adj. Gen. Vols. 22 Aug. '61; Maj. Asst. Adj. Gen. Vols. 22 Aug. '62; Lt. Col. Asst. Adj. Gen. Assigned 10 Nov. '62–1 Nov. '63; Bvt. B.G. USV. Brevets for Williamsburg, Antietam, Gettysburg (2). Resigned 26 Jan. '64.

DICTATOR. A 13-inch seacoast mortar, mounted on a reinforced railroad car, and used by the Federals in the siege of Petersburg. This type of mortar weighed 17,000 pounds and with a 20-pound charge could throw a 200-pound explosive shell 4,325 yards when elevated at 45 degrees (Roberts). Under the direction of H. L. ABBOT, and served by Co. G, 1st Conn. Hv. Arty., the Dictator operated against Petersburg during the period 9–31 July '64 from its railroad mount. It was fired from a curved section of the Petersburg & City Point R.R., an arrangement that facilitated lateral adjustment of fire. During this period it fired 45 rounds, 19 of them during the battle of the Crater. Most of this firing was done with a charge of 14 pounds and a range of 3,600 yards. It was then moved to a permanent emplacement near Battery 4. The gun was also called the "Petersburg Express." (See Miller, III, 186–7; and V, 51.)

DILWORTH, Caleb James. Union officer. Ohio. Lt. Col. 85th Ill. 27 Aug. '62; Col. 26 June '63; Bvt. B.G. USV (Atlanta). In Dept. of the Cumberland commanded 3, 2, XIV; and 2, Dist. Etowah. Died 1900.

DIMICH, Justin. Misspelling by Phisterer for Justin DIMICK.

DIMICK, Justin. Union officer. c. 1800–71. Conn. Appt.-Vt. USMA 1819 (11/29); Arty. He taught infantry tactics at West Point, fought in the Seminole wars (1 brevet), and in the Mexican War (1 wound, 2 brevets) and served on the frontier. Named Col. 1st US Arty. 26 Oct. '61, he was in command of the P.O.W. camp at Ft. Warren, Mass., until 1 Jan. '64. Retired from active service 1 Aug. '63. He was breveted B.G. USA.

DIMMICK projectile. A type of Civil War shell. It is not described in the standard ordnance references.

DIMON, Charles Augustus Ropes. Union officer. Conn. Pvt. 7th Mass. Mil. 19 Apr.–1 Aug. '61; 1st Lt. Adj. 30th Mass. 6 Dec. '61; Maj. 2d La. 14 Oct. '62; mustered out 22 June '63; Maj. 1st USV 18 Mar. '64; Lt. Col. 2 Apr. '64; Col. 7 Aug. '64. Bvt. B.G. USV (war service).

DINWIDDIE C.H., Va., 31 Mar. '65. See FIVE FORKS.

DISPOSITIONS. Manner in which elements of a military force are put in position (i.e., "disposed") for an operation. As an example, "He learned the enemy's dispositions from a captured map."

DIVEN, Alexander Samuel. Union officer. 1809–96. N.Y. Lt. Col. 107th N.Y. 13 Aug. '62; Col. 21 Oct. '62; mustered out 11 May '63; Maj. Asst. Adj. Gen. Vols. 13 May '63; Bvt. B.G. USV 20 Aug. '64 (war service). A railroad promoter and executive, he also practiced law and held public offices.

DIVEN, Charles Worth. Union officer. Pa. Capt. 12th Pa. Cav. 25 June '61; Maj. 19 Apr. '64; mustered out 11 June '64; Col. 200th Pa. 3 Sept. '64; Bvt. B.G. USV 25 Mar. '65; (Petersburg). Commanded 1, 3, IX (Potomac). Died 1889.

DIVERS, Bridget. Union army nurse. When her husband enlisted in the 1st Mich. Cav., she followed him to war and served as VIVIANDIÈRE and agent of the SANITARY COMMISSION, usually for the entire brigade. She used up eight or ten horses, several being shot from under her, and rallied the regiment on numerous occasions. At Fair Oaks she looked up from tending her wounded husband, and yelled, "Arragh, go in, b'ys! Bate the bloody spalpeens and revinge me husband and God be wid yez!" This broke a rout and propelled the men back into a charge. She was called variously Irish Bridget and Michigan Bridget. At Cedar Creek she was surrounded but rode through the enemy and had a similar experience on one of Sheridan's raids. At the end of the war she was heartsick at leaving the army but brightened when the Indian fighting army needed four laundresses per company in the West. These were usually wives of the enlisted men, and Bridget turned happily to "Soapsuds Row," spending the rest of her life in the army.

DIVISION OF THE WEST, Confed. Not to be confused with the Confederate army of the West (Van Dorn-Price) or DEPT. NO. 2 ("Western Department"), the Department of the West was created 24 Nov. '62 under J. E. Johnston as a "super headquarters" to coordinate the operations of Bragg, Kirby Smith, and Pemberton. Although designated a *department* it was actually a territorial *division* made up of Bragg's DEPT. NO. 2; Kirby Smith's Dept. of EAST TENN.; and Pemberton's Dept. of MISS. AND EAST LA.

Johnston's command also included northwestern Ga. and a small part in the northwestern corner of S.C. (O. R. atlas, plate CLXVI.)

After Pemberton's defeat at Vicksburg and Bragg's defeat at Chattanooga, Johnston took command of the Army of Tenn. 27 Dec. '63. The Dept. of the West ceased to exist.

The Military Division of the West was created 17 Oct. '64 under Beauregard with essentially the same boundaries as Johnston's Dept. of the West had had. Its purpose was to coordinate Hood's contemplated invasion of Tenn. (FRANKLIN AND NASHVILLE CAMPAIGN). Beauregard's area comprised Hood's Dept. of TENN. AND GA. and Taylor's Dept. of ALA., MISS., AND EAST LA. (This organization was now called a *division* [O. R. atlas, plates CLXX and CLXXI].) Still in existence when the war ended, its area had been extended when the Dept. of TENN. AND GA. was enlarged. Beauregard became second-in-command to J. E. Johnston in the Army of Tenn. on 16 Mar. '65 (in the Carolinas).

DIX, Dorothea Lynde. Union nurse. 1802–87. An important figure in the reform of prisons, almshouses, and insane asylums, she was the Union's superintendent of women nurses during the Civil War.

DIX, John Adams. Union gen. 1798–1879. N.H. Appt.-N.Y. After an unusual education supervised by his father, he wanted to fight in the War of 1812, so his father, a Maj. of infantry, got him a commission as ensign, and at fourteen fought at Lundy's Lane. Continuing in the R.A., he helped support his widowed mother and eight children. Becoming a good friend of J. C. Calhoun, he studied law and then resigned in 1828 to enter into politics in N.Y. State. Rapidly acquiring power in the Democratic party, he was Sen. 1845–50 and engaged in railroading until asked to be Sec. of the Treasury. He undertook his new duties on 15 Jan. '61, and shortly thereafter issued his famous AMERICAN FLAG DISPATCH. Lincoln appointed him Maj. Gen. USV on 16 May, and he commanded the Dept. of Annapolis 19–25 July '61. From 25 July to 24 Aug. '61 he commanded the Dept. of Pa. and then led the Middle Dept. 22 Mar.–9 June '62. He commanded the Dept. of Va. 17 June '62–15 July '63 and the VII Corps in the Dept. 22 July '62–16 July '63. From 18 July '63 until the end of the war he commanded the Dept. of the East. Resigned 30 Nov. '65. He was later Minister to France and Gov. of N.Y. 1872–74.

DIXIE. Popular name for the South, apparently originating in early La. There, in a predominantly French area, the French word for ten, "dix," was printed on the ten-dollar bills. La. became then to be known as Dix's Land, and changed slightly to Dixie, this took in the entire South. A better theory is that Dixie comes from MASON AND DIXON LINE. Daniel D. Emmett, the famous minstrel, composed the song and first sang it in New York in 1859. The tune was an immediate success and quickly adopted by the South. It was first used by the Confederates on 18 Feb. '61, when a march arrangement was played at Davis' inauguration at Montgomery.

DIXON, William Dunlap. Union officer. Pa. Capt. 6th Pa. Res. 1 June '61; Lt. Col. 15 Sept. '63; Bvt. B.G. USV. Brevets for Wilderness, Spotsylvania C.H. North Anna, Bethesda Church. Mustered out 11 June '64.

D'LAGNEL, Julius A. Erroneous spelling of DE LAGNEL.

DOAN, Azariah Wall. Union officer. Ohio. 1st Lt. 12th Ohio 22 Apr. '61; Capt. 20 June '61; Lt. Col. 79th Ohio 19 Aug. '62; Bvt. B.G. USV (war service).

DOCKERY, Thomas P. C.S.A. gen. 1833–98. Appt.-Ark. As Col. 19th Ark. he fought at Wilson's Creek and Corinth. When Price crossed the Miss., he was given command of the Middle Subdivision of Ark. and later commanded his regiment and the 2d Brig., Bowen's Div., at Vicksburg. He was appointed B.G. C.S.A. 10 Aug. '63 and led his brigade against Steele in '64 at Marks's Mills and Jenkins' Ferry. After the war he was a civil engineer.

DODD, Levi Axtell. Union officer. Pa. Capt. 169th Pa. 16 Nov. '62; mustered out 25 July '63; Lt. Col. 211th Pa. 16 Sept. '64; Col. 4 Apr. '65; Bvt. B.G. USV 2 Apr. '65 (Petersburg). Died 1901.

DODGE, Charles Cleveland. Union gen. 1841–? N.J. Commissioned Capt. 1st N.Y. Mtd. Rifles 10 Dec. '61 and promoted Maj. 3 Jan. '62, he was in command of outposts at Newport News and of a cavalry column in Wool's advance on Norfolk where he received the surrender before his superior officers arrived. He commanded also at Suffolk (Va.) and Hertford Ford (N.C.) and was promoted Lt. Col. 1 July '62, Col. 13 Aug. '62, and B.G. USV 29 Nov. '62 before resigning 12 June '63.

DODGE, George S. Union officer. Vt. Capt. Asst. Q.M. Vols. 12 May '62; Maj. Q.M. Assigned 2 Aug. '64–16 Sept. '64; Col. Q.M. Assigned 17 Sept. '64–28 Apr. '65; Bvt. B.G. USV 15 Jan. '65 (Ft. Fisher, N.C.).

DODGE, Grenville Mellen. Union gen. 1831–1916. Mass. After graduating from Norwich Univ., Vt., he surveyed for railroads and engaged in engineering as far west as the Missouri River. Settling in Iowa, he was active in the home guard and was on Gov. Kirkwood's staff when war came. Commissioned Col. 4th Iowa 6 July '61, he commanded 1st Brig., Army Southwest Mo. (Jan.–Feb.

'62) and 1st Brig., 4th Div., Army Southwest Mo. (Feb.–June '62). Wounded at Pea Ridge in March, he was named B.G. USV 21 Mar. '62, and then commanded Dist. Miss., Army of the Tenn. (29 Sept.–5 Oct. '62). Continuing in the Army of the Tenn., he commanded 4th Div., Dist. Jackson (5–20 Oct. '62); 4th Div. (30 Oct.–11 Nov. '62); Dist. Corinth, XIII (11 Nov.–18 Dec. '62); Dist. Corinth, XVII (18 Dec. '62–20 Jan. '63); Dist. Corinth, XVI (20 Jan.–18 Mar. '63); 2d Div., XVI (18 Mar.–12 Aug. '63); Left Wing, XVI (7 July–7 Aug. and 15 Oct. '63–19 Aug. '64). On the last-named date he was severely wounded in the head in front of Atlanta and was on sick leave of absence until 9 Dec. '64 when he took over the Dept. of Mo., commanding it until 27 June '65. He resigned in 1866, having been named Maj. Gen. USV 7 June '64. He was then Chief Engr. of the Union Pacific R.R. in the Southwest and, after the Spanish-American War, in Cuba. He was also a Congressman, active in Republican politics and veterans' organizations.

DOLES, George Pierce. C.S.A. gen. 1830–64. Ga. A Milledgeville businessman, he had been active in the militia before being commissioned Col. 4th Ga. in May '61. His regiment was sent to the vicinity of Norfolk and later fought at Antietam. He succeeded Ripley in command of the brigade there and was appointed B.G. C.S.A. 1 Nov. '62. Commanding this brigade at Fredericksburg, Chancellorsville, Gettysburg and the Wilderness, he was killed 2 June '64 at Bethesda Church.

DONALDSON, James Lowry. Union officer. 1814–85. Md. USMA 1836 (15/49); Arty.-Q.M. He fought in the Seminole War, on the frontier, and in the Mexican War (2 brevets) before transferring to the Q.M. Dept. He was Chief Q.M. of N. Mex. from 1858 until 30 Sept. '62 when as Maj. 3 Aug. '61

(Capt. since 1847) he became Chief Q.M of the Middle Dept. 18 Mar.–25 Oct. '63. He held the same position with the Dept. of the Cumberland 10 Nov. '63–21 June '65 and retired in 1869 as Col. Asst. Q.M. General after having been breveted for the Atlanta campaign (2, including B.G. USA 17 Sept. '64) and war service (Maj. Gen. USA and USV 20 June '65).

DONELSON, Daniel S. C.S.A. gen. 1801–63. Tenn. USMA 1825 (5/37); Arty. Resigning the next year, he was in the legislature, ran his plantation, and served as B.G. in the state militia. In May '61 he was named to the same rank in the state forces and was appointed B.G. C.S.A. 9 July '61. He chose the site for Ft. Donelson, which was named for him. Also that year he commanded a brigade under Loring in West Va., and was sent to Charleston in early 1862. He joined Bragg at Tupelo to take command of the Tenn. Brig. and led it at STONES RIVER. Promoted Maj. Gen. 22 Apr. '63 (to rank from 17 Jan. '63), he died 17 Apr. '63 at Napoleon (Ark.), according to Cullum. Wright and C.M.H. give the place of death as Knoxville, with only the latter source giving the year. Palmer Bradley says he died at Montvale Springs, Tenn.; he confirms the date given by Cullum.

DONOHOE, Michael Thomas. Union officer. Mass. Capt. 3d ,N.H. 23 Aug. '61; resigned 31 July '62; Col. 10th N.H. 5 Sept. '62; Bvt. B.G. USV (war service). Commanded 2, 1, XVIII: 2, 3, XXIV. Died 1895.

DOOLITTLE, Charles Camp. Union gen. 1832–1903. Vt. Named 1st Lt. 4th Mich. 30 June and Capt. 20 Aug. '61, he was commissioned Col. 18th Mich. 13 Aug. '62 after being wounded at Gaines's Mill. He commanded 3d Brig., 1st Div. Army of Ky. (Oct. '62); 3d Brig., Dist. Central Ky. (Jan.–Apr. '63);

and 3, 2, Reserve Corps, Cumberland (8 June–10 Aug. '63). On 30 Oct. '64 he was in command at Decatur and repulsed Hood in three successive attacks. He then led 1, 3, XXIII (14 Dec. '64–13 Jan. '65) and 1, 3, IV (15 May–2 June '65). Breveted Maj. Gen. USV 13 June '65 for war service, he was mustered out 30 Nov. and was a bank cashier in Toledo.

DORNBLASER, Benjamin. Union officer. Ill. Commissioned 1st Lt. Adj. 46th Ill. 15 Oct. '61, he was promoted Maj. 8 Feb. '62 and Col. 25 Oct. '62. Mustered out in 1866, he was breveted B.G. USV 20 Feb. '65 and Maj. Gen. USV for war service.

DOSTER, William Emile. Union officer. Pa. Maj. 4th Pa. Cav. 18 Oct. '61; Lt. Col. 30 Oct. '62; Bvt. B.G. USV (war service); resigned 7 Dec. '63.

DOUANE, James C. Misspelling by Phisterer for James Chatham DUANE.

DOUBLEDAY, Abner. 1819–93. Union gen. and developer of modern baseball. N.Y. USMA 1842 (24/56); Arty.-Inf. Of a family outstanding in civil and military life, he is credited with inventing and naming baseball in 1835. Before entering West Point he had been a civil engineer two years. Served in Mexican and Seminole wars; aimed first gun fired in defense of Ft. Sumter; served under Patterson in Shenandoah June–Aug. '61. B.G. USV 3 Feb. '62, led a brigade (2, 1, III-Va.) at 2d Bull Run and took command of the division 30 Aug. when Hatch was wounded. Led the division at South Mountain, Antietam, and Fredericksburg. Maj. Gen. USV 29 Nov. '62. Commanded 3d Div., I Corps, at Chancellorsville, and headed that corps when Reynolds was killed at Gettysburg 1 July '63. Had administrative duties the remainder of the war, except when he took command of portion of Washington defenses 12 July '64 against Early's raid. Breveted in USA for war services. Retired in 1873. Author of *Reminiscences of Forts Sumter and Moultrie in 1860–61* (1876) and *Chancellorsville and Gettysburg* (1882). An older brother, Thomas Donnely, became colonel of the 4th N.Y. Arty. in 1862 and was fatally injured on Broadway by a bus; he died 9 May '64. Another brother was Ulysses DOUBLEDAY.

DOUBLEDAY, Ulysses. Union officer. 1824–93. N.Y. Maj. 4th N.Y. Arty. 23 Jan. '62; discharged 7 Mar. '63; Lt. Col. 3d US Col. Inf. 2 Oct. '63; resigned 5 Oct. '64; Col. 45th US Col. Inf. 8 Oct. '64; Bvt. B.G. USV (war service). Commanded 2, 3, X; 2, 2, XXV. Brother of Abner Doubleday, he was a member of the N.Y. Stock Exchange.

DOUBLE SHOTTING. An emergency method of getting more than the prescribed effect out of an artillery piece by doubling the load of canister or grape. "Treble shot" was also known (Wilhelm, 138). Zachary Taylor's "Give me a little more grape, Captain [Braxton] Bragg" at Buena Vista (Mex., 23 Feb. '47) is a refinement of his actual words "Double shot those guns and give 'em hell!" (A.F.M. 21–13, *The Soldier's Guide*, G.P.O. (1952), p. 57.)

DOUGLAS, Stephen Arnold. Statesman and Democrat. 1813–1861. Vt. An outstanding legislator and one of the founders of the DEMOCRATIC PARTY in Ill., he is best known for his part in the Lincoln-Douglas debates in 1858. A supporter of the POPULAR SOVEREIGNTY theory for territorial government, he felt that this would unite the two opposing wings of the Democratic party and at the same time settle the slavery question peaceably. Failure to do so meant the loss of his political supremacy and his chances for the presidency. After narrowly losing to BUCHANAN for the Democratic nomination in 1856 he supported him wholeheartedly for the presidency, only to turn against him when Buchanan in 1857 decided to support the pro-slavery faction in Kans., which represented the minority view. Though a courageous stand, he netted little by it and gained the Democratic nomination in 1860 only after much party bickering, delay, and after the Southern faction had withdrawn from the convention. To the end he worked and hoped for a compromise between the North and the South, but after the firing at Ft. Sumter he came out in strong support of Lincoln's call for troops. He then went into the Northwest to rally the people's support in the crisis only to die from typhoid fever after a brilliant address in Springfield, Ill.

DOUGLASS, Frederick. Anti-slavery leader. 1817–95. Md. Actually named Frederick Augustus Washington Bailey. The son of a slave and a white man, he escaped from slavery in 1838 and went North where he was eventually employed by the Mass. Anti-Slavery Society (1841) as a lecturer. He went to Europe to escape capture as a fugitive slave, made enough money to buy his freedom, and returned to found and edit the *North Star,* an abolitionist paper that favored legal and political methods of freeing the slaves. He recruited Negro regiments during the war and conferred with Lincoln. In 1877 he was appointed US marshal for the District of Columbia; in 1881, recorder of deeds, D.C.; in 1889 US Minister to Haiti.

DOVER. Alternate name, in many accounts, for the action at Fort Donelson, Tenn. See HENRY AND DONELSON CAMPAIGN, Feb. '62.

DOW, Neal. Union gen. 1804–97. Me. Raised in a Quaker family and, carrying those convictions, he was later dismissed from the Society of Friends for his wartime activities. He was suc-cessful in business and turned to a temperance crusade, causing in 1851 the passage of the famed "Maine Law" banning liquor in that state. He was commissioned Col. 13th Me. 23 Nov. '61 and commanded, in the Dept. of the Gulf, Dist. West Fla. (2 Oct. '62–24 Jan. '63) and 1, 2, XIX (26 Feb.–27 May '63) when he was twice wounded at Port Hudson. While recovering, he was captured and sent to Libby, later exchanged for W. H. F. Lee 14 Mar. '64. He resigned 30 Nov. '64 because of health.

D.O.W. Abbreviation for "died of wounds." See CASUALTY, definition of.

DOX, Hamilton Bogart. Union officer. N.Y. Maj. 12th Ill. Cav. 4 Jan. '64; Lt. Col. 29 Oct. '64; Bvt. B.G. USV 29 May '66.

DRAFT RIOTS. On Aug. '62 the President called on the states for 300,000 militia to serve nine months and ordered the governors to draft from the militia if the quota could not be filled by volunteers. This precipitated riots in Wis., Ind., and threats of riots in Pa. Stanton then postponed the draft. The Enrollment Act of 3 Mar. '63 brought about the N.Y.C. Draft Riots (13–16 July '63. Gov. Seymour of N.Y. challenged the constitutional right of the government to enforce a draft. On Saturday, 11 July '63, the provost marshal drew the first names for the draft, and on Sunday these were published in the papers. That afternoon mobs started gathering and the next day, when the drawing was resumed, the rioting started. Gov. Seymour, Mayor George Opdyke, and the police were unable to restore order. The mob, which soon numbered 50,000, burned a Negro church and orphanage, attacked the office of the N.Y. *Tribune,* wrecked the home of the provost marshal, terrorized large parts of the city, started fires, did $1,500,000 worth of property damage, and killed more than a dozen people. Irish working men made up the majority of the mobs; their main victims were Negroes. Federal troops from the Army of the Potomac finally arrived to disperse the rioters, killing or wounding over 1,000. The draft was postponed until 19 Aug.

John Dix took command of the Distr. of the East (Hq. in N.Y.C.) on 18 July, and Seymour finally bowed to Federal authority. In Boston a mob gathered, started stoning the troops, and dispersed after they had been fired on and several would-be rioters were killed (Hesseltine, *Lincoln and the War Governors*). Other minor riots took place at Rutland, Vt.; Portsmouth, N.H.; and Wooster, Ohio.

DRAGOON. A mounted infantryman, that is, a soldier who uses the horse for transportation to the battlefield, or for mobility on the battlefield, but who dismounts to fight. Although a cavalryman theoretically fights from the saddle, the "cavalry" of the American Civil War was used as mounted infantry with a few rare exceptions, such as the battle of BRANDY STATION.

DRAKE, Francis Marion. Union officer. 1830–1903. Ill. Lt. Col. 36th Iowa 4 Oct. '62; Bvt. B.G. USV 22 Feb. '65. Commanded 1, 2, VII. W.I.A. and captured Marks's Mills (Ark.) 25 Apr. '64. A railroad builder and promoter, he gave generously to Drake University at Des Moines and served as Gov. of Iowa 1896–98.

DRAKE, George Bernard. Union officer. Mass. R.A. 2d Lt. 12th Mass. 26 June–26 Aug. '61; 2d Lt. 6th US Inf. 5 Aug. '61; 1st Lt. 20 Sept. '63; Capt. Add. A.D.C. 22 May '62; Maj. Asst. Adj. Gen. Vols. 11 Mar. '63; Lt. Col. Asst. Adj. Gen. Assigned 5 May–1 Nov. '63 and 4 Nov. '64–23 Mar. '65; Bvt. B.G. USV (war service). W.I.A. Antie-

tam. Served in Banks's Red River expedition.

DRAPER, Alonzo Granville. Union officer. 1835–65. Vt. Capt. 1st Mass. Arty. 5 July '61; Maj. 28 Feb. '63; Col. 36th US Col. Inf. 1 Aug. '63; Bvt. B.G. USV 28 Oct. '64 (Spring Hill, Va.). Commanded Dist. St. Mary's, XVIII and XXII; 2, 3, XVIII; 3, XVIII; 1, 3, XXV; 1, 1, XXV (Va. and N.C.); 1, 1, XXV (Tex.); 1, XXV; 3, XXV. A journalist and city official of Lynn (Mass.) before the war, he died in Texas from an accidental gunshot wound.

DRAPER, William Franklin. Union officer. 1842–1910. Mass. Pvt. 25th Mass. 9 Sept. '61; 2d Lt. 7 Oct. '61; 1st Lt. 15 Apr. '62; Capt. 36th Mass. 27 Aug. '62; Maj. 1 Sept. '63; Lt. Col. 9 Aug. '64; Bvt. B.G. USV (war service); mustered out 12 Oct. '64. W.I.A. Wilderness and Pegram's Farm (Va.). He was engaged in the manufacture of textile machinery and served as Ambassador to Rome 1897–1900.

DRAYTON, Thomas Fenwick. C.S.A. gen. 1808–91. S.C. USMA 1828 (28/33); Inf. After serving in garrison and on topographical duty, he resigned in 1836 to run his S.C. plantation and engage in railroad surveying. He was active in the militia, sat in the state legislature, and was a railroad director. Appointed B.G. C.S.A. 25 Sept. '61, he was commanding the military district around Port Royal when his brother, Capt. Percival Drayton, led the attacking Union ship. He was given a brigade in Va. in June '62 under Longstreet, and fought at Thoroughfare Gap, 2d Bull Run, South Mountain, and Antietam. His advanced age (compounding a basic incompetence, according to Palmer Bradley) rendered him unfit for field command, so his brigade was broken up, and he was put on court-martial duty. Returning to the field in Aug. '63, he commanded a brigade in the Dist. of

Ark. and commanded the Sub Dist. of Tex. for a time. He was president of the court of inquiry called for Price's Missouri expedition. After the war he returned to farming and also was in a life insurance company.

DRED SCOTT DECISION. Scott, a Negro slave, was taken by his master, Dr. John Emerson, in 1834 from St. Louis to Rock Island, Ill., where slavery had been forbidden by the Ordinance of 1787, and later to Ft. Snelling, in Wis. Territory, where slavery was forbidden by the Missouri Compromise. In 1846 Scott sued for freedom in the Mo. courts on the grounds that his stay in a free state and free territory had released him from slavery. The case (carried on for him by the abolitionists) involved the following issues: Whether Scott was a citizen of Mo. and thus entitled to sue in the federal courts, whether his temporary stay in free territory had given him freedom upon his return to the slave state of Mo., and the constitutionality of the Missouri Compromise in prohibiting slavery to the Territory of Wis. The Supreme Court ruled that Negro slaves and their dependents were not citizens of the US or of the state of Mo. and hence not entitled to sue in the courts, that Scott's status was determined by his residence at the time the question was raised and not on his stay in free territory, and that the Missouri Compromise was unconstitutional under the 5th Amendment, which states that Congress may not deprive persons of property without due process of law. The decision was the first since Marbury v. Madison in 1803 to declare an act of Congress unconstitutional, was bitterly attacked in the North, and considerably widened the sectional animosity.

DREW, Charles Wilson. Union officer. N.Y. 1st Lt. 75th N.Y. 17 Sept. '61; mustered out 29 Dec. '62; Col. 76th US Col. Inf. 8 Apr. '63; Bvt. B.G. USV 26 Mar. '65 (Mobile). In the Dept. of

the Gulf he commanded 1st Div. USCT; 2d Div. USCT; 3, 1st Div. USCT West Fla. Died 1903.

DREWRY'S BLUFF, Va., 4–16 May '64. (Including Port Walthall Junction; Swift's Creek; Kautz's cavalry raids; Bermuda Hundred line.) As part of Grant's over-all strategy for the final phase of the war, Butler's Army of the James was ordered to operate against Richmond from the south side of the James River. For this purpose Butler was to be reinforced by Gillmore's X Corps from S.C. On 4 May the X and XVIII Corps (W. F. Smith) embarked at Yorktown and the next day moved up the James. The colored division of XVIII Corps (Hinks's 3d) took possession of City Point, and the main body proceeded to Bermuda Hundred where a three-mile line of entrenchments was constructed across the neck of the peninsula. From this point, only two miles east of the Richmond-Petersburg R.R., Butler could threaten either of these cities.

George E. Pickett had been in command in this area since 23 Sept. '63 with headquarters at Petersburg, but in late April Beauregard succeeded him. Pickett was preparing to leave Petersburg when scouts informed him on 5 May of Butler's movement. At his disposal he had only one regiment, the Washington Arty. (21 guns), the City Bn. of Petersburg, and some militia. Beauregard wired that he was sick and could not join Pickett immediately. The morning of 6 May troops started arriving from S.C. (Graham's 21st N.C. of Hagood's Brigade). Richmond was held by four infantry brigades and local artillery.

On 6 May Butler sent Heckman's brigade (1, 2, XVIII) to reconnoiter toward Petersburg. Graham with 600 North Carolinians held off two attacks until reinforced by Bushrod Johnson's brigade of 800 from the Richmond defenses. Hagood arrived after dark (6 May), and before daylight of the 7th there were 2,668 infantrymen at Port Walthall Junction to oppose Butler. D. H. Hill had been sent to advise Hagood and Johnson. Drewry's Bluff (Fort Darling) was, meanwhile, reinforced by Archibald Gracie's brigade from Richmond.

On 7 May the Federals drove back skirmishers that Graham had sent toward their entrenchments, and at 2 P.M. launched another attack. W. H. T. Brooks commanded the brigades of H. M. Plaisted (3, 1, X), W. B. Barton (2, 2, X), J. C. Drake (2, 3, X), and Hiram Burnham (2, 1, XVIII) in an attack led by the 8th Conn. (of Burnham's brigade). They held the railroad long enough to tear up 300 to 500 yards of track and cut the telegraph wires before withdrawing about 4 P.M. with a loss of 289 men. The defenders lost 184. This action is known by the name of Port Walthall Junction.

On 8 May Kautz's cavalry from the Suffolk area had captured and burned the 110-foot Weldon R.R. bridge at Stony Creek, 19 miles south of Petersburg, and the 210-foot Nottoway Bridge, five miles farther south. This seriously slowed the arrival of troops and supplies from the South.

Butler remained inactive the 8th, but moved in strength toward Petersburg on the 9th. When stopped by strongly entrenched positions along Swift's Creek, Butler disapproved of a proposal by Smith and Gillmore to turn this defense by use of a ponton bridge across the Appomattox to the south. Although such a maneuver would have brought overwhelming strength against the defenders of Petersburg, Butler was content to destroy more railroad track and started to withdraw about noon on the 10th and was back in his Bermuda Hundred defenses on 11 May. This

enabled Beauregard to send Hoke with six brigades to defend Drewry's Bluff and to go there himself on the 14th, leaving only a garrison (under Whiting) behind at Petersburg.

On 12 May Butler started advancing toward Drewry's Bluff with Smith's corps on the right and Gillmore's on the left. Hinks's division remained at City Point, and Ames's division (3, X) was posted at Walthall Junction to guard against an advance from Petersburg. Kautz's cavalry left from Chester Station to raid the Richmond and Danville and the Petersburg and Lynchburg railroads. The next morning the Confederates had been driven from their outer works into the main Drewry's Bluff positions. The river was not deep enough to allow the planned movement of Federal monitors up to support Butler, but Admiral Lee did manage to get some gunboats up to a point where they came under the fire of the guns at Chafin's Bluff.

Butler's army was disposed as follows from left (west) to right: Gillmore's divisions of Turner, A. H. Terry; W. F. Smith's divisions of Brooks and Weitzel. Heckman's brigade was on the extreme right. An attack was planned for the 15th, but canceled because Butler was so involved with defensive measures that he had no troops left to form an attacking force. Smith reconnoitered his right and found it vulnerable; accordingly he refused the flank of Heckman's brigade and got authority to use the three regiments of Ames's division that were posted in reserve at the Halfway House. Smith strengthened his line by stringing telegraph wire between stumps along the front of Brooks's division and Stedman's brigade of Weitzel's division. This is probably the first use of wire entanglements in war and proved highly effective (see B.&L., IV, 210, 212). There was, unfortunately, not enough wire to be scavanged from the turnpike telegraph line to extend the obstacle across the front of Heckman.

Beauregard considered the situation as one that would permit the destruction of Butler's army. Although a grandiose plan of having his own command reinforced at the expense of the Richmond garrison and Lee's army was disapproved, Beauregard hastily organized his 10 available brigades into three divisions and prepared to attack. At 4:45 A.M., 16 May, the four brigades of Ransom's division attacked the Federal right. Despite a dense fog, the brigades of Gracie (on the left) and Lewis advanced abreast, followed by Terry and Fry in the second line. Within an hour they had overpowered Heckman's brigade, capturing that general, five stands of colors, and about 400 prisoners. However, Ransom had lost heavily, was low on ammunition, and his troops had become disorganized in the fog. Weitzel and W. H. T. Brooks repulsed frontal attacks in the center. On the opposite (west) flank Hoke's attack was delayed by the fog until about 6:30. Then Hagood (on the left) and Bushrod Johnson advanced and took some ground along Gillmore's front. The Confederate brigades of Clingman and Corse advanced on the extreme right but had to be called back when a gap developed between them and Bushrod Johnson. The latter came under heavy attack on his exposed right flank and had to be reinforced. There followed a period of confused fighting at the end of which Butler withdrew his forces to prevent being cut off by Ransom's envelopment. By 10 A.M. Beauregard had used up all his reserves; Hoke on his right was still under attack; and Ransom did not believe he could continue his advance.

As part of Beauregard's over-all plan, Whiting was to advance from Petersburg with two brigades (Wise and Martin) and Dearing's cavalry to strike Butler's rear while the 10 brigades from Drewry's Bluff hit him frontally and turned his right flank. Whiting, however, displayed a strange lack of aggressiveness and allowed himself to be blocked at Walthall's Station by Ames's division. Butler was able to withdraw in a heavy rainstorm to Bermuda Hundred. Beauregard followed and by the morning of the 17th Butler's Army of the James was "bottled up" (Grant's phrase).

In the operations of 12–16 May '64 Butler lost 4,160 out of 15,800 engaged, whereas Beauregard lost 2,506 out of 18,025 engaged (Livermore).

DRUM, Richard Coulter. Union officer. Pa. He fought in the Mexican War as a private before being commissioned 2d Lt. 9th US Inf. in 1847 (1 brevet). After serving in the West and in Indian fighting, he was promoted Maj. Asst. Adj. Gen. 3 Aug. '61 (1st Lt. since 1850) and spent the war years in the Dept. of the Pacific. He was named Lt. Col. 17 June '62 and retired in 1889 as B.G. USA and the Adj. Gen., having been breveted B.G. USA in 1865.

DUANE, James Chatham. Union officer. 1824–97. N.Y. USMA 1848 (3/38); Engrs. He served two tours at West Point teaching engineering, supervised river and harbor construction, and was on the Utah Expedition. Named Capt. 6 Aug. '61 (1st Lt. since 1855), he was assigned by McClellan to organize engineer and bridge-building equipage. He designed several types of ponton trains and engineering equipment for the construction of fixed bridges and for the siege and fieldworks. Appointed Chief Engr. of the Army of the Potomac, he held this position from Antietam until McClellan was dismissed 7 Nov. '62 and was named to the same position in the Dept. of the South in 1863. He was promoted Maj. 3 Mar. '63 and in July of that year was recalled to be Chief Engr. of the Army of the Potomac again. He was breveted for operations before Petersburg and the Petersburg siege (B.G. USA). He retired in 1888 as B.G. Chief of Engrs., a position he had held since 1886.

DuBOSE, Dudley M. C.S.A. gen. 1834–83. Tenn. Appt.-Ga. He graduated from the Univ. of Miss. and Lebanon Law School before being commissioned Lt. 15th Ga. and fighting in the Va. and Md. campaigns in Toombs's (his father-in-law) brigade. As Col. 15th Ga. in Jan. '63, he led his regiment at Gettysburg, Chickamauga (wounded), and the Wilderness. Appointed B.G. C.S.A. 16 Nov. '64, he commanded Wofford's brigade under Kershaw in the Petersburg and Appomattox campaigns and was captured with Ewell at Sayler's Creek. After the war he was a lawyer and US Congressman.

DUCAT, Arthur Charles. Union officer. Ireland. 2d Lt. 12th Ill. 2 May '61; 1st Lt. and Adj. 11 May '61; Capt. 1 Aug. '61; Maj. 24 Sept. '61; Lt. Col. 1 Apr. '62; Lt. Col. Asst. I.G. Assigned 14 Nov. '62–19 Feb. '64; Bvt. B.G. USV (war service); discharged 19 Feb. '64. Died 1896.

DUDLEY, Nathan Augustus Munroe. Union officer. Mass. R.A. Capt. 10th US Inf. 7 May '61; Col. 30th Mass. 1 Mar. '62; mustered out USV 16 Feb. '65; Maj. 15th US Inf. 13 Sept. '64; Bvt. B.G. USV. Brevets for Baton Rouge, Pt. Hudson (La.) war service. Commanded 3, 1, XIX; 1, 1, XIX; 4, Cav. XIX; 1, Cav. XIX; 3, 1, XIX; 1, 1, XIX; 2d Brig., 1st Sub Dist. Middle Tenn.

DUDLEY, William Wade. Union officer. c. 1840–? Vt. Capt. 19th Ind. 29 July '61; Maj. 18 Sept. '62; Lt. Col. 8 Oct. '62; discharged 30 June '64; Capt. Vet. Res. Corps 25 Mar. '65; Bvt. B.G. USV. Brevets for war service, Gettysburg. W.I.A. Gettysburg, losing right leg.

DUER, John O. Union officer. Md. 2d Lt. 45th Ill. 20 Nov. '61; 1st Lt. 1 Mar. '62; Capt. 30 June '62; Maj. 26 Oct. '63; Lt. Col. 26 Mar. '65; Col. 11 May '65; Bvt. B.G. USV 12 July '65 (war service). Died 1880.

DUFF, William L. Union officer. Scotland. Lt. Col. 2d Ill. Arty. 30 Jan. '62; Bvt. B.G. USV (war service). Died 1897.

DUFFIÉ, Alfred Nattie. Union gen. 1835–80. France. A graduate of St. Cyr, he fought in Algiers, Senegal, and the Crimea as 1st Lt. Cav. and won several medals for valor in the campaign against Austria. Coming to the US for the Civil War, he was commissioned Capt. 2d N.Y. Cav. 9 Aug. '61, Maj. 5 Oct. '61, and Col. 1st R.I. Cav. 6 July '62. Commanding 1, 2, Cav., Potomac (16–26 Feb. '63), he succeeded to command of the division (16 May–11 June '63) and was promoted B.G. USV 23 June '63. He also led, in the Dept. of W. Va.: 3d Brig., 3d Div. (Dec. '63–Apr. '64); 1st Brig., 2d Cav. Div. (26 Apr.–6 June '64); and 1st Cav. Div. (9 June–20 Oct. '64). Mustered out 24 Aug. '65, he was US Consul at Cadiz at the time of his death. Duffié figures prominently in accounts of cavalry actions in the East. He is mentioned frequently in Miller's *Photographic History* and is featured in a full-page picture (IV, 233). (See also KELLY'S FORD, Va., 17 Mar. '63; BRANDY STATION, Va., 9 June '63; and MIDDLEBURG, Va., 17 June '63.)

DUG GAP, GA., 8 May '64. See ROCKY FACE RIDGE.

DUKE, Basil Wilson. C.S.A. gen. 1838–1916. Ky. He graduated from Centre College and law school in Ky. before setting up a practice in St. Louis. Active in the Mo. secessionist movement and a brother-in-law of John H. Morgan, he was nearly hanged as a spy by both sides before he enlisted as a private in Morgan's "Lexington Rifles." Soon elected 1st Lt., he was commissioned Lt. Col. and then Col. when the company became part of the 2d Ky. Cav. He was wounded at Shiloh and captured in the Ohio raid of 1863, being appointed B.G. C.S.A. 15 Sept. '64 upon his release. Commanding a cavalry brigade, he operated in eastern Ky. and western Va. until Lee's surrender. He disbanded his infantry and took his cavalry to join Johnston, escorting Jefferson Davis from Charlotte until his capture. A lawyer and U.S. Rep. after the war, he wrote many books and articles on the Civil War, including *History of Morgan's Cavalry* (1867) and his memoirs (1911). D.A.B. describes him as being "small in stature and slight in frame . . . [with the] moustache and goatee of the traditional Kentucky gentleman."

DUMONT, Ebenezer. Union gen. 1814–71. Inf. A lawyer, legislator, and banker, he fought in the Mexican War, rising to Lt. Col. He was commissioned Col. 7th Ind. 27 Apr. '61, mustered out 2 Aug. '61, and appointed Col. 7th Ind. 13 Sept. '61. Commissioned B.G. USV 3 Sept. '61, he commanded in the Army of the Ohio the 17th Brig. (Dec. '61); 17th Brig., 3d Div. (22 Dec. '61–21 Mar. '62); and 12th Div. (Sept.–Nov. '62). He also commanded 5th Div. Centre, XIV Corps, Cumberland (5 Nov.–11 Dec. '62). He resigned 28 Feb. '63 for his health and served as Unionist Congressman from Ind. 1863–67. He was appointed Gov. of the Idaho Territory shortly before his death.

DUNCAN, Johnson Kelly. C.S.A. gen. 1827–62. Pa. Appt.-Ohio. USMA 1849 (5/43); Arty. After serving in the Seminole War, in garrison and on railroad explorations, he resigned in 1855 to hold government positions in New Orleans. He was also a civil engineer, surveyor, and architect. Commissioned Col. from La. and then B.G. C.S.A.

7 Jan. '62, he commanded the New Orleans coastal defenses. After Farragut by-passed them he surrendered. Upon exchange he served as volunteer A.D.C. to Bragg. He died at Knoxville 18 Dec. '62 of typhoid fever.

DUNCAN, Samuel Augustus. Union officer. N.H. Commissioned Maj. 14th N.H. 23 Sept. '62 and resigned a year later. On 24 Nov. '63 he was commissioned Col. 4th U.S. Col. Inf. and breveted for Spring Hill (B.G. USV 28 Oct. '64) and war service (Maj. Gen. USV) before being mustered out in 1866. He died 1895.

DUNCAN, Thomas. Union officer. Ill. After fighting in the Black Hawk War as a private, he entered the R.A. in 1846 and fought in the Mexican War. Stationed in the West and engaged in Indian fighting, he was promoted Maj. 3d US Cav. 10 June '61 (Capt. since 1848) and continued on the frontier. He was wounded at Albuquerque (N. Mex.) and was retired in 1873 as Lt. Col. 5th US Cav. and Bvt. B.G. USA. He died 1887.

DUNHAM, Thomas Harrison. Union officer. Mass. Cpl. 11th Mass. 9 May '61; Sgt. Maj. 5 Feb. '63; 2d Lt. 6 Feb. '63; 1st Lt. 15 Sept. '63; Capt. 18 June '64; Maj. 10 Jan. '65; Lt. Col. 16 June '65; Col. 11 July '65; Bvt. B.G. USV (war service). W.I.A. Chancellorsville and the Wilderness.

DUNLAP, Henry C. Union officer. Ky. 1st Lt. Adj. 5th Ky. 9 Sept. '61; Capt. 3d Ky. 26 May '62; Col. 27 Apr. '63; Bvt. B.G. USV; mustered out 13 Oct. '64.

DUNLAP, James. Union officer. Ky. Appt.-Ill. Capt. Asst. Q.M. Vols. 8 Aug. '61; Lt. Col. Q.M. Assigned 1 Jan.–15 Sept. '63; Bvt. B.G. USV (war service); resigned 11 June '64. Died 1897.

DUNN, William McK. Union officer. Ind. Entering the army as Maj. and

Judge Advocate USV, he was promoted Col. and Asst. Judge Advocate USA in June '64 and breveted B.G. USA for war service.

DUNN'S BAYOU, La. 5 May '64. Destruction of *Covington, Signal,* and the transport *Warner* during skirmishing around ALEXANDRIA, 1–8 May (RED RIVER CAMPAIGN).

DUNOVANT, John. C.S.A. gen. 1825–64. Appt.-S.C. He served as Maj. in the state troops at Ft. Sumter and was commissioned Col. 1st S.C. in '62. Fighting on Sullivan's Island and at Ft. Moultrie, he became Col. 5th S.C. later that year and served in the state until dispatched to Va. in Mar. '64. He led his regiment at Drewry's Bluff, Cold Harbor, and Trevilian Sta. and was appointed B.G. C.S.A. 22 Aug. '64. He commanded a brigade under Hampton until killed 1 Oct. '64 at Ft. Harrison (Vaughan Road).

DUPEE, Mary E. Union nurse. Me. She began working in the Naval School Hospital in Aug. '63, caring mainly for newly released prisoners from Andersonville, Salisbury, Belle Isle, and Libby. In Jan. '65 she went to City Point where she was an agent for the Me. Camp and Hospital Association in nursing soldiers from that state.

DU PONT, Samuel Francis. Union admiral. 1803–65. N.J. Appt.-Del. Named Midshipman in 1815, he served in European waters, the West Indies, along the South American coast, and in the Mediterranean. In the Mexican War he operated along the Pacific coast and later in the Far East before being put in command of the Philadelphia Navy Yard as Capt. (since 1855) in 1860. He was president of the board convened in Washington in June '61 to plan the war's naval operations and was promoted flag officer in Sept. '61. In Oct. he commanded the fleet that sailed to Port Royal, and received the Thanks of Congress and the rank of Rear Admiral (to rank from 16 July '62) for this victory. He was defeated at Charleston in Apr. '63 following orders with which he did not agree and asked to be relieved, leaving the command 5 July '63. In poor health, he died on active duty in June '65 after having served on boards and commissions for the remainder of the war. Nephew of Éleuthère Irénée Du Pont, founder of the chemical company.

DURYEA, Hiram. Union officer. N.Y. Capt. 5th N.Y. 25 Apr. '61; Maj. 15 Aug. '61; Lt. Col. 3 Sept. '61; Col. 26 Sept. '62; Bvt. B.G. USV (Gaines's Mill); resigned 12 Nov. '62. (See also 5TH NEW YORK.)

DURYÉE, Abram. Union gen. 1815–90. N.Y. Making a fortune as a N.Y. City merchant, he was active in the state militia and twice wounded during the 1849 Astor Place riots. Named Col. 5th N.Y. 25 Apr. '61, he commanded 2d Brig., Ord's Div., Rappahannock (16 May–10 June '62) and led 1st Brig., Ord's Div., Rappahannock (10–26 June '62). He was commissioned B.G. USV 31 Aug. '61 and given a training command. He led 1, 2, III, Va. (26 June–12 Sept. '62) at Cedar Mt., Rappahannock Station, Thoroughfare Gap, Groveton, 2d Bull Run where he was twice wounded, and Chantilly. He commanded 1, 2, I, Potomac (12 Sept.–5 Oct. '62) at South Mountain and at Antietam where he was wounded three times. After a 30-day leave, he returned to find a junior officer had been promoted over him and, unable to rectify this, he resigned 5 Jan. '63. After the war he held several public offices in N.Y.C.

DURYEE, Jacob Eugene. Union officer. N.Y. Pvt. 7th N.Y. Mil. 26 Apr. '61; discharged 4 May '61; 1st Lt. 5th N.Y. 9 May '61; Capt. 8 Sept. '61;

Lt. Col. 2d Md. 21 Sept. '61; Bvt. B.G. USV (war service); resigned 5 Oct. '62.

DUSTIN, Daniel. Union officer. Vt. Capt. 8th Ill. Cav. 18 Sept. '61; Maj. 12 Jan. '62; Col. 105th Ill. 2 Sept. 62; Bvt. B.G. USV 16 Mar. '65 (Ga. and S.C. campaigns). Commanded 2, 3, XX; 3d Div., XX Corps. Died 1892.

DUTCH GAP CANAL. After the failure of Butler's attack on Drewry's Bluff (12–16 May '64) and his subsequently becoming bottled up at Bermuda Hundred, passage of Federal gunboats up the James was blocked at Trent Reach by Confederate batteries as well as by obstructions Butler ordered built in the river. To permit Federal gunboats to go up the river to attack Chafin's and Drewry's Bluffs, Butler conceived of constructing a canal at Dutch Gap. At this point there is a neck of land 174 yards across. Capt. (later Bvt. B.G.) Peter S. Michie was put in charge of the project. Digging started 10 Aug., was completed 30 Dec., and the next day the bulkhead at the northern end was blown out by a 12,000-pound charge of powder. Nearly 67,000 cubic yards were excavated, mostly by colored troops, working under the fire of enemy batteries. The canal was not completed until Apr. '65, too late to be of military value; however, it was subsequently improved and became the usual channel for navigation, cutting off 4¾ miles of the horseshoe bend around Farrar's Island. (See B.&L., IV, 575; Miller, V, 243.)

DUTTON, Arthur Henry. Union officer. 1838–64. Conn. USMA June 1861 (3/34); Corps of Engrs. Bvt. 2d Lt. Engrs. 24 June '61; 2d Lt. 3 Aug. 61; 1st Lt. 3 Mar. '63; Capt. 2 Oct. '63; Col. 21st Conn. 5 Sept. '62; Bvt. B.G. USV 16 May '64; died 5 June '64 from wounds received 26 May '64 at Bermuda Hundred (Va.). Brevets for Fred-

ericksburg, Suffolk, Bermuda Hundred (2). Commanded 3, 3, IX; 3, 3, VII; Heckman's brigade, Dist. Newport News; 3, 1, XVIII. Served on staff of Gen. Mansfield (1861) and was Chief of Staff to Gens. Peck and W. F. Smith.

DUTTON, Everell Fletcher. Union officer. Mass. 1st Lt. 13th Ill. 24 May '61; Capt. 6 Aug. '61; Maj. 105th Ill. 22 Sept. '62; Lt. Col. 31 July '64; Bvt. B.G. USV 16 Mar '65. Brevets for Atlanta–Savannah campaigns, Goldsboro (N.C.), Smith's Farm (N.C.) (2), Ga. and Carolinas campaigns. Died 1900.

DUVAL, Hiram F. Union officer listed by Phisterer as Col. 36th Ohio and Bvt. B.G. USV 13 Mar. '65. See DEVOL, HENRY F.

DUVAL, Isaac Hardin. Union gen. 1824–? Va. A hunter in the Rocky Mountains, he explored the West, Mexico, and Central America. He was commissioned Maj. 1st W. Va. 1 June '61 and mustered out three months later. Given the same rank in the reorganized 1st W. Va. 29 Oct. '61, he was promoted Col. 9th W. Va. 19 Sept. '62. He was appointed B.G. USV 24 Sept. '64 and took command of the 1st Div., VIII Corps. Breveted Maj. Gen. USV for Opequon, he was mustered out in 1866 and entered W. Va. politics and the insurance business after the war. His name is spelled Dewall by Phisterer.

DWIGHT, William. Union gen. 1831–88. Mass. Resigning as a USMA cadet (ex-1853), he went into manufacturing. He was commissioned Lt. Col. 70th N.Y. 29 June '61 and Col. 1 July '61. At Williamsburg he was wounded three times, left on the field for dead, and captured. He was promoted B.G. USV 29 Nov. '62 and commanded in the Dept. of the Gulf the following: 1, 4, XIX (12 Feb.–30 May

'63) at Bayou Teche and Irish Bend and Port Hudson; 2d Div., XIX (30 May–18 July '63); 3d Div., XIX (6 July–15 Aug. '63); 1, 1, XIX (20–25 Feb. and 25 Mar.–18 Apr. '64); 1st Div., XIX (1–5 July '64). He was Banks's Chief of Staff during the Red River campaign. He also commanded 1st Div., XIX, Shenandoah at Winchester, Fishers Hill, and Cedar Mountain (6 Aug.–15 Oct. '64, 24 Oct. '64–25 Jan. '65, 1–20 Mar. '65) and Dwight's division, XXII, Washington. He was mustered out 15 Jan. '66 and later engaged in railroading in Ohio.

DYE, William McEntire. Union officer. 1831–99. Pa. Appt.-Ohio. USMA 1853 (32/52); Inf. Capt. 8th US Inf. 14 May '61; Col. 20th Iowa 25 Aug. '62; mustered out USV 8 July '65; Bvt. B.G. USV 13 Mar. '65; discharged 1870 as Maj. at own request. Brevets for Vicksburg, Red River campaign, Mobile, war service. Commanded 2, 2d Army Frontier; 1, 2, XIII; 2, 2, XIII; 1st Brig., US Forces Tex.; Guppy's brigade, US Forces Mobile Bay; 1, 3, XIX; 4th Brig., Res. Corps. He served as Col. Egyptian Army 1873–78 (wounded in Abyssinia), Supt. of Police in Washington, and military advisor to the King of Korea upon the recommendation of Gen. Sheridan (1888–99). He wrote *Moslem Egypt and Christian Abyssinia* or *Military Service Under the Khedive* (1880) and a treatise in Korean on military tactics.

DYER, Alexander B. Union officer. c. 1815–74. Va. Appt.-Mo. USMA 1837 (6/50); Arty.-Ord. He served in the Seminole War and the Mexican War (1 brevet declined, 1 accepted) before taking command as Capt. (1853) of the Springfield Armory 22 Aug. '61. Promoted Maj. 3 Mar. '63, he served there until 12 Sept. '64 when he was named B.G. USA and Chief of Ordnance. He died on active duty in 1874 after having been breveted Maj. Gen. USA for war service.

DYER, Isaac. Union officer. Me. Lt. Col. 15th Me. 19 Dec. '61; Col. 28 Aug. '62; Bvt. B.G. USV (war service). Commanded Dist. W. Fla. XIX Corps.

DYER projectile. Cast-iron body with a soft metal expanding cup attached to the base. The 3-inch projectile had a corrugated cap at the point to direct that portion of the flame of the charge which escapes over the projectile on to the fuze to ignite it. "This projectile, as improved by Mr. Taylor at the Washington Arsenal, gives good results for even as large a caliber as 12 inches" (Benton, 559).

E

EARLY, Jubal Anderson ("Old Jube" or "Jubilee"). C.S.A. gen. 1816–94. Va. USMA 1837 (18/50); Arty. After fighting in the Seminole War he resigned in 1838 to become a lawyer and Whig legislator. He fought in the Mexican War and voted against Va.'s secession but followed his state and was commissioned Col. 24th Va. After commanding the 6th Brig. at 1st Bull Run, he was appointed B.G. C.S.A. 21 July '61, and led his brigade in the Peninsular campaign until he was wounded at Williamsburg. Back with the 4th Brig. at 2d Bull Run, he succeeded Lawton in command of Ewell's division at Antietam and continued to lead this unit at Fredericksburg. He was promoted Maj. Gen. 23 Apr. '63 and continued to lead his division at Chancellorsville, Gettysburg, the Wilderness, and Spotsylvania. He succeeded Ewell as C. G. II Corps on 29 May '64 and led it at Cold Harbor. Taking the II Corps, he was given in June '64 an independent mission and undertook EARLY'S WASHINGTON RAID. He was then outgeneraled in the SHENANDOAH VALLEY CAMPAIGN OF SHERIDAN. After the final defeat at Waynesboro on 2 Mar. '65, he was relieved by a sympathetic Lee who had to bow to the clamoring press and people. Early then started west in disguise to reach Kirby Smith, but when that general surrendered, he went to Mex. and then Canada. Considering emigration to New Zealand at one time, he eventually returned to practice law at Lynchburg and was employed by the Louisiana Lottery. While still in Canada he wrote *A Memoir of the Last Year of the War for Independence in the C.S.A.* (1866). This was expanded into his better known *Autobiographical Sketch and Narrative* ... (1912). He was president of the Southern Historical Society and, according to Freeman, "a prolific contributor to the Gettysburg controversy" (*R. E. Lee,* IV, 562). A 44-year-old bachelor at the beginning of the war, he was about six feet tall, weighed under 170 pounds, and was stooped by arthritis contracted in Mex. "His long [black] beard, his keen, flashing black eyes, his satirical smile, his avowed irreligion, his incisive but not unmusical voice, and his rasping, mordant wit made him appear almost saturnine to those who did not know how much of loyalty and of generosity he hid behind a forbidding front," Freeman says of him (*Lee's Lts.,* I, 86). Although unduly impetuous in his earlier battles, he developed into a

sound commander whose record "from Cedar Mountain to Salem Church is second only to that of Jackson himself" (*op. cit.,* II, xxviii).

EARLY'S CORPS. See II CORPS, Confed., A.N.V.

EARLY'S Operations in the Shenandoah (1864). See EARLY'S WASHINGTON RAID and SHENANDOAH VALLEY CAMPAIGN OF SHERIDAN.

EARLY'S WASHINGTON RAID, 27 June–7 Aug. '64. To divert Federal strength from Lee's front, Early undertook an offensive in the Shenandoah. On 27 June, following Hunter's repulse at LYNCHBURG, 18 June, Early was at Staunton. Here he reorganized his 10,000 infantry into two corps of two divisions each for an invasion of the North. The first, under Robert Rodes, consisted of divisions under Ramseur and C. A. Battle. The other corps, under Breckinridge, had the divisions of Gordon and Echols. The four cavalry brigades that had been opposing Hunter were organized into a cavalry division under Robert Ransom, with a strength of about 4,000.

On 2 July Early reached Winchester. Federal cavalry warned Sigel at Martinsburg of the Confederate offensive. Imboden's cavalry had gone down the South Branch of the Potomac to cut the B. & O. R.R. By attacks against Federal garrisons 3–4 July, Early forced Sigel to concentrate his forces on Maryland Heights, opposite Harpers Ferry. Finding the latter place too strong, Early crossed the Potomac at Shepherdstown and reached Frederick, Md., on the 9th. McCausland had entered Hagerstown 6 July and levied a requisition of $20,000. Early levied $200,000 in Frederick.

It was not until 5 July, when Early was crossing the Potomac, that either Grant or Halleck believed the Confederates were undertaking a serious offensive. The next day, however, reinforcements were sent from the Army of the Potomac: Ricketts' division (3, VI) of 5,000 men, and 3,000 dismounted cavalry reached Baltimore on the 7th. The dismounted cavalry went to Washington, and Ricketts joined the brigade of infantry and the brigade of cavalry under Lew Wallace near Frederick. The battle of the MONOCACY, Md., 9 July '64, forced Wallace to fall back to Baltimore.

Early threatened Baltimore with a cavalry brigade, left some cavalry on the Monocacy to protect his line of communications, and marched on Washington.

Until this time Grant had been counting on the arrival of Hunter's force (which had retreated into W. Va. after LYNCHBURG) to help oppose Early. Since Hunter's movement had been delayed by low water on the Ohio, Grant sent the rest of Wright's VI Corps north. Wright arrived with the first of his troops at noon of the 11th and moved that night into the fortifications of Washington opposite Early. Administrative troops and civilian volunteers were hastily organized to defend the city. The 1st division of XIX Corps, which had arrived at Fort Monroe from New Orleans, was also diverted to Washington. Lincoln even proposed to Grant that he leave the Army of the Potomac at Petersburg and take personal command of the forces defending the capital.

Early reached the outskirts of Washington (Silver Spring, Md.) on 11 July at about noon and saw that its defenses had been reinforced. (It was about this time that 1,500 of the dismounted cavalry from Meade's army started moving into the works.) Early spent the rest of the day reconnoitering and ordered an assault to take place on the 12th. During the night, however, Early learned of the arrival of VI Corps troops, and postponed his attack. There was some heavy skirmishing around FORT STEVENS. Early then decided he lacked the strength for a successful assault.

The Confederates withdrew the night of the 12th (after burning the house of Montgomery Blair) and crossed the Potomac at Leesburg the morning of the 14th. Here they rested until the 16th before retreating to Berryville. Wright led an inffective pursuit with his two divisions. He reached Poolesville, Md., opposite Leesburg, on the 14th and waited for Ricketts to join him from Baltimore, and for the XIX Corps troops to join him from Washington.

Advancing into Loudoun Valley, where he was joined by Crook (commanding Hunter's field forces), Wright re-established contact 19 July on the Shenandoah River.

Early retreated toward Strasburg from Berryville when he learned that Averell, with a strong mixed brigade, was advancing from Martinsburg and threatening his trains. Ramseur was defeated by Averell at WINCHESTER, Va., 20 July. The next day Averell entered Winchester and was joined on the 22d by Crook.

Inability of the Federals to deal effectively with Early stemmed partly from the fact that four separate military subdivisions were involved (Middle Dept., and Depts. of the Susquehanna, W. Va., and Washington). The night of 20 July Wright started preparations to return to Washington with his command. Grant believed Early would rejoin Lee, or, if not, that Hunter could deal with him. But Halleck convinced Grant that Early was still a threat and received permission to retain the VI Corps. Meanwhile, Wright was on his way back, in response to Grant's earlier orders. On the 23d Wright reached

Washington. That night Grant sent new orders that the VI Corps be sent to Meade if it had reached Washington, but that the division of XIX Corps might be retained. Proposals were then made for setting up a separate command to take care of the threat from the Shenandoah. Grant recommended that W. B. Franklin be put in command. Lincoln disapproved on the grounds that at Fredericksburg (13 Dec. '62) Franklin had failed to carry out Burnside's instructions. Grant then proposed Meade, whom he considered an excellent commander, but who had lost the confidence of his corps commanders in the Army of the Potomac. While Lincoln delayed approval of this last suggestion, Early took advantage of the Federal military inactivity to resume the offensive. Then, much to Grant's displeasure, Halleck was put in command of the operations against Early.

Early defeated Crook at KERNSTOWN, Va., 23–24 July, and wrecked the railroad facilities at Martinsburg. He then captured and burned CHAMBERSBURG, Pa., 13 July (employing two cavalry brigades), while demonstrating along the Potomac with his other forces to cover the operation. His cavalry took Hancock, Md., and threatened Cumberland, Md. At MOOREFIELD, W. Va., 7 Aug. '64, McCausland was surprised and defeated by Averell.

Grant finally accepted the fact that he would have to take positive measures to end the Confederates' use of the Shenandoah for strategic diversions. He then took steps to put Sheridan in command of reorganized Federal forces in the area. The result was the highly-successful SHENANDOAH VALLEY CAMPAIGN OF SHERIDAN.

EAST, UNION DEPARTMENT OF THE. In existence at the start of the war, it comprised all of the US east of the Mississippi River; commanded by Maj. Gen. John E. Wool, with headquarters at Albany, until the department was abolished 17 Aug. '61. Until the latter date, while new departments were being created within its former boundaries, the Department of the East retained theoretical jurisdiction of the remaining portions of its original area (about half of which was Confederate territory). On 3 Jan. '63 the department was re-created and comprised N.Y., N.J., and the New England states. Headquarters were in New York. Wool was again in command (12 Jan.–18 July '63) until succeeded by Maj. Gen. John A. Dix, who took command after the New York Draft Riots and remained until 27 June '65.

EASTERN TENNESSEE, Confed. Army of. Small force of about 1,500 militia organized in 1861 from Wise, Scott, and Lee counties under Humphrey Marshall. With the mission of occupying eastern Ky. it fought its principal action at Pound Gap, Ky., 16 Mar. '62, where it was scattered by Federals under B. G. James A. Garfield. See also EAST TENNESSEE, Confed. Dept. of.

EASTMAN, Seth. Union officer. c. 1807–75. Me. USMA 1829 (22/46); Inf. He served on the frontier, taught drawing at West Point, fought in the Seminole War, and served in the Bureau of Indian Affairs before the Civil War. Named Lt. Col. 1st U.S. Inf. 9 Sept. '61, he was mustering and disbursing officer for Me. and N.H. until Jan. '63, when he became military governor of Cincinnati. He was retired 3 Dec. '63 for ill-health and breveted B.G. USA in 1866 for war service.

EASTON, Langdon C. Union officer. c. 1814–84. Mo. USMA 1838 (22/45); Inf.-Q.M. He fought in the Seminole War and the Mexican War before serving as head of the Q.M. depot at Ft. Leavenworth until 3 Dec. '63. Promoted Maj. 3 Aug. '61 and Col. USV (*ex officio*) 2 Aug. '64. He was Chief Q.M. of the Army of the Cumberland until 4 May '64 when he became Sherman's Chief Q.M. in the Atlanta Campaign and the March to the Sea and through the Carolinas. Continuing in the R.A., he retired in 1881 as Col. and Asst. Q.M. Gen., having been breveted B.G. USA 17 Sept. '64 for the Atlanta campaign and Maj. Gen. USA for war service.

EASTPORT, THE. Federal ironclad destroyed 26 Apr. '64 in RED RIVER CAMPAIGN.

EAST TENNESSEE, Confed. Dept. of (and Army of Kentucky). Established 25 Feb. '62 after the Confed. defeat at LOGAN C.R. (19 Jan.). Kirby Smith came from the A.N.V. to assume command 9 Mar. with headquarters at Knoxville. On 3 June the tip of N.C. west of the Blue Ridge was assigned to the department, which now encompassed an area about 170 miles wide by 100 miles from north to south, and including Chattanooga. On 18 July the area was further extended.

Kirby SMITH'S INVASION OF KENTUCKY started 17 Aug. and on the 24th J. P. McCown was assigned temporarily to command of the department. (He assumed temporary command 1 Sept., and on 27 Sept. was assigned permanent command. O.R., XVI.)

The name Army of Ky. was given 25 Aug. to the force Kirby Smith led into the field. It consisted of the divisions of C. L. Stevenson (which had been left initially to contain G. W. Morgan's Federals in Cumberland Gap), Henry Heth, Cleburne (which Bragg had assigned to Kirby Smith for the operation), T. J. Churchill, and the small cavalry brigades of John Morgan and J. S. Scott.

On 1 Nov. Bragg's command was extended to include the Dept. of East

Tenn., but on 23 Dec. Kirby Smith resumed command of his department. By the end of 1862 Chattanooga had been excluded from the department. After cooperating with BRAGG'S INVASION OF KENTUCKY, culminating in the battle of PERRYVILLE, 8 Oct. '62, Kirby Smith objected to further service under Bragg. He was promoted Lt. Gen. in early Oct., and on 14 Jan. '63 assigned command of the Trans-Miss. Dept.

Heth was temporarily in command of the Dept. of East Tenn. until 17 Jan. '63 when he was ordered to Va. and D. S. Donelson replaced him. At this time the troop strength in the department was 7,000.

On 25 Apr. '63 D. H. Maury assumed command. Two days later Buckner was assigned to command but did not actually assume command until 12 May. By mid-'63 more of Tenn. had been excluded and the western tip of Va. had been added to the department.

On 25 July '63 the Dept. of Tenn. was created under Bragg's command and on Buckner's suggestion. The Dept. of East Tenn., strictly speaking, ceased to exist on that date, being merged into the Dept. of Tenn. Cooper, however, prescribed that Buckner continue to report direct to Richmond. Bragg compounded the organizational confusion on 6 Aug., when he actually assumed command, by ordering that Buckner's *troops* constitute the III or "Buckner's" Corps of his Army of Tenn., but that Buckner retain *administrative* responsibility for the area of East Tenn. The Dept. of Tenn., therefore, continues to show in the O.R. atlas as a separate territorial organization, an anomaly made more monstrous when Federal strategy soon took the form of simultaneous operations against Knoxville and Chattanooga (see KNOXVILLE, and CHICKAMAUGA campaigns). (Horn, 241.)

Longstreet took command of the department in Nov. '63 when he entered the area to oppose Burnside in the KNOXVILLE CAMPAIGN. Buckner was temporarily in command 8–18 Mar. '64 when Longstreet went to Richmond for a conference on strategy. On 12 Apr. Buckner resumed command of the department when Longstreet returned with his corps to the East. On 20 Feb. '65 the area became part of Early's Dept. of WESTERN AND SOUTHWESTERN VIRGINIA.

EATON, Amos B. Union officer. c. 1806–77. N.Y. USMA 1826 (36/41); Inf.-Comsy. He served in garrison, the Seminole War, and as Chief Comsy. of Subsist. under Taylor in the Mexican War (1 brevet). Named Maj. 9 May '61, he was Depot Comsy. at New York, Purchasing Commissioner for the armies in the field 1861–64, and Comsy. Gen. (B.G. USA 29 June '64) of the US Army. He was breveted Maj. Gen. USA for war service and retired in 1874.

EATON, Charles G. Union officer. Mass. Capt. 72d Ohio 11 Jan. '62; Maj. 1 July '62; Lt. Col. 24 Dec. '63; Col. 9 Apr. '64; Bvt. B.G. USV (Nashville, war service). Commanded 1st Brig., 1st Div., Det. Army of Tenn. Died 1875.

EATON, John Jr. Union officer. 1829–? N.H. Chaplain 27th Ohio 15 Aug. '61; Col. 63d US Col. Inf. 10 Oct. '63; Bvt. B.G. USV (war service). Chosen in November 1862 by Grant to look after the increasing numbers of "CONTRABANDS," he was given the colonelcy of a Negro regiment to have the rank necessary for the job, as his jurisdiction included the Dept. of Tenn. and Ark. The Freedman's Bureau was later modeled on his plan, and he was chosen its commissioner for the area including D.C., Md. and parts of Va. He was a member of the USMA Board of Visitors in 1869, US Commissioner of Education in 1870, and later president of the Marietta (Ohio) and Sheldon Jackson (Salt Lake City) colleges.

EATON, Joseph H. Union officer. c. 1816–96. Mass. Appt.-At Large. USMA 1835 (43/56); Inf.-Paymaster. He served on the frontier, taught infantry tactics at West Point, and fought in the Mexican War (2 brevets) after being Taylor's A.D.C. Resigning in 1856, he was reappointed as Add. Paymaster 1 June '61 on Frémont's staff and as Paymaster for the Dist. of Kans. 9 Nov. '61–19 Jan. '63. As Maj. 21 Apr. '64, he was then Asst. to the Paymaster Gen. for the remainder of the war. He was breveted three times for war service, including B.G. USA, and retired in 1881.

ECHOLS, John. C.S.A. gen. 1823–96. Va. He attended V.M.I., Washington and Harvard and practiced law before attending his state's secession convention. Commissioned Lt. Col., he mustered volunteers in the Valley for J. E. Johnston and led the 27th Va. at 1st Bull Run in the Stonewall brigade. Fighting under Jackson in the Valley, he was severely wounded at Kernstown, appointed B.G. C.S.A. 16 Apr. '62 and given, a few months later, command of a brigade in the Army of Western Va. He participated in Loring's occupation of the Kanawha Valley in Sept. '62 and succeeded him as commander of the Army of Southwest Va. on 16 Oct. '62. He was succeeded on 10 Nov. by J. S. Williams and served on the Court of Inquiry called for the surrender of Vicksburg. At Droop Mountain, later that year (1863), he commanded the Confederate forces and in May '64 commanded the Right Wing under Breckinridge at New Market. He then took his brigade to Cold Harbor and on 22 Aug. '64 took over the Dist. of Southwest Va. On 30 Mar. '65 he succeeded Early in the W. Va. Dept. and was on his way to join Lee when told of the surrender.

Changing his course, he linked up with Johnston and went with Davis to Augusta (Ga.), surrendering there. After the war he was a lawyer and legislator with banking and railroad interests. C.M.H. describes him as a "magnificent figure, standing six feet four inches."

ECKERT, Thomas Thompson. Union officer. 1825-? Ohio. Maj. Add. A.D.C. 7 Apr. '62; Capt. Asst. Q.M. Vols. 17 July '62-28 Feb. '67; Bvt. B.G. USV (war service); Asst. Sec. of War 27 July '66-28 Feb. '67; resigned 28 Feb. '67. During Peninsular campaign was McClellan's Supervisor of Military Telegraphs. In September 1862 he was transferred to Washington to establish the military telegraph headquarters in the War Department buildings. Was later president of several telegraph companies and Presiding Judge of Texas Court of Appeals after the war.

ECTOR, Matthew Duncan. C.S.A. gen. ?-1879. Tex. Commissioned Col. 14th Tex. Cav. in 1862, he was appointed B.G. C.S.A. 23 Aug. of that year. He fought at Richmond (Ky.) and Stones River, leading a brigade in McCown's division. He commanded his brigade under Walker at Chickamauga and was sent to Miss. until the spring of 1864, when he returned to Ga. for the Atlanta campaign. Leading his brigade in French's division, he lost a leg in the battles around Atlanta and upon his recovery went with Hood to Tenn. He ended the war in the defense of Mobile.

EDGED WEAPONS. Bayonets, sabers, swords, short swords, cutlasses, Bowie knives, pikes, and lances, classified as "edged weapons," appeared in considerable profusion during the Civil War. Although they served to decorate their original possessors and delight modern collectors, they inflicted few casualties. In *Regimental Losses* Fox points out that of the approximately 250,000 wounded treated in Union hospitals during the war only 922 were the victims of sabers or bayonets. "And a large proportion of these originated in private quarrels, or were inflicted by campguards in the discharge of their duty" (Fox, 24). A few instances of BAYONET ATTACKS are recorded.

Sabers, which are cavalry swords, are a legitimate weapon of the mounted service and dangerous in the hands of a trained trooper. The volunteer horsemen, however, had trouble learning to handle them. There were a good many lop-eared horses in the early months of the war. Gigantic "wrist breakers" with 42-inch scimitar-type blades were soon cut down to 36 inches and were reasonably effective.

Swords until recent years in America were the symbol of an officer's authority, and served this primary function in the Civil War. The short artillery sword—with which the gunners were supposed to disembowel the horse that had overrun their position and then dispatch the rider—was among the most useless of weapons (Albaugh and Simmons, 118).

The lance, another serious weapon in the hands of a trained trooper, also appeared in the war. The 6th Pa. Cav., "Rush's Lancers," was armed with this weapon, in addition to its pistols and a few carbines, until May '63 (see Miller, IV, 56 and 74). The weapons shortage in the South led its leaders to give serious consideration to arming troops with lances and pikes. In early 1862 a set of resolutions provided for 20 regiments of Southern pikemen, and on 10 Apr. '62 an act was passed that two companies in each regiment be armed with pikes. "Strangely enough, such foolishness met with the complete approval of the military leaders, and even Gen. Lee on April 9, 1862, wrote Col. Gorgas (Chief of Confederate Ordnance), 'One thousand pikes should be sent to Gen. Jackson if practicable' " (Albaugh and Simmons, 124). Georgia's gov. spurred the production of weapons that are now known as "JOE BROWN'S PIKES."

Many different forms of military cutlery, known generically as BOWIE KNIVES, were popular among Confederate soldiers until discarded after real campaigning started.

EDGERTON, Alonzo Jay. Union officer. 1827–96. N.Y. Pvt. 10th Minn. 14 Aug. '62; Capt. 21 Aug. '62; Col. 67th US Col. Inf. 15 Feb. '64; transferred to 65th US Col. Inf. 15 Aug. '65; Bvt. B.G. USV (war service). Commanded 2d Brig., 1st Div., C. d'A., USCT. A jurist and politician, he served as US Sen. from Minnesota.

EDMONDS, Joseph Cushing. Union officer. Mass. 1st Sgt. 24th Mass. 9 Oct. '61; Capt. 32d Mass. 13 Aug. '62; Maj. 29 Dec. '62; Lt. Col. 29 July '64; Col. 1 Nov. '64; Bvt. B.G. USV (war service). Commanded 3, 1, V. Captured 16 Dec. '63 and taken to Libby prison. Wounded at Gettysburg 3 July '63, Petersburg 19 July '64, and at Peeble's Farm 30 Sept. '64. Died 1878.

EDWARDS, Clark Swett. Union officer. Me. Capt. 5th Me. 25 June '61; Maj. 1 July '62; Lt. Col. 22 Nov. '62; Col. 8 Jan. '63; Bvt. B.G. USV (war service); mustered out 27 July '64.

EDWARDS, John. Union gen. 1815–94. Ky. He had been a lawyer and legislator in Indiana and Iowa when he was commissioned Lt. Col. and A.D.C. to the Iowa Gov. 21 May '61. On 8 Aug. of that year he was commissioned Col. 18th Iowa. He commanded the 2d. Brig., Dist. Frontier, Mo., and in the Dept. of Ark.: 2d, Dist. Frontier, VII; 1, Dist. Frontier, VII; Dist. Frontier, VII; 1, 3, VII; 2, 2, VII. Dyer lists these as his commands but gives no dates. He was

later US congressman for the Liberal Republican party in his state.

EDWARDS, Oliver. Union gen. 1835–1904. Mass. At the war's beginning he owned an Ill. foundry but returned home to become 1st Lt. Adj. 10th Mass. 21 June '61, also serving as Gen. Couch's A.D.C. Promoted Col. 37th Mass. 4 Sept. '62, he led his regiment in the Peninsula campaign, at Fredericksburg, and at Gettysburg before commanding a special brigade during the New York draft riots in July '63. He commanded 4, 2, VI, Potomac (29 Jan.–26 Mar. '64), was a regimental commander at the Wilderness (5–7 May), and then resumed brigade leadership (9 May–6 July '64) at Spotsylvania where troops under his command held the "bloody angle" for 24 hours (11 hours with his own brigade and 13 hours with 21 other regiments). Commanding 3, 1, VI, Shenandoah (6 Aug.–19 Sept. and 21 Sept.–31 Oct. '64) and 1st Div., VI, Shenandoah (19–21 Sept. '64) during Sheridan's Valley campaign, he was in charge of Winchester. He received the surrender of Petersburg from its mayor as commanding general of 3, 1, VI, Potomac (17 Mar.–21 June '65). This same command at Sayler's Creek captured Dick Ewell and staff, Custis Lee and staff, an entire Rebel brigade, and miscellaneous prisoners. He was promoted B.G. USV 19 May '65 and breveted for Spotsylvania and Winchester (B.G. USV) and Sayler's Creek (Maj. Gen. USV). He was mustered out in 1866 and became a manufacturer, later patenting improvements on the sewing machine and inventing an oil stove and a spring skate.

EGAN, Thomas Washington. Union gen. 1836–87. N.Y. He was commissioned Lt. Col. 40th N.Y. 1 July '61 and promoted Col. 5 June '62. He commanded 1, 1, III, Potomac (4 May '63) at Chancellorsville and 3, 1, III, Poto-

mac (22 Nov.–30 Dec. '63, Feb.–24 Mar.
'64). He led the 1st Brig., 3d Div., II,
Potomac (24 Mar.–20 Apr. and 12 May–
14 June '64) at Spotsylvania Courthouse
and also commanded 1, 2, II, Potomac
(27 Aug.–4 Sept. and 25 Sept.–15 Nov.
'64). He was named B.G. USV 3 Sept.
'64 and commanded 2d Div., II, Potomac (4–25 Sept. and 8–29 Oct. '64) as
well as the 3d Provisional Div., Army
Shenandoah, in the spring of '65. He
was wounded at the siege of Petersburg
in Nov. '64. Named Bvt. Maj. Gen. USV
27 Oct. '64 for the Boydton Plank Road
battle. He was mustered out in 1866.

EGGLESTON, Beroth B. Union officer. N.Y. Capt. 1st Ohio Cav. 29 Aug.
'61; Maj. 20 June '62; Col. 13 Apr. '63;
Bvt. B.G. USV (war service). Commanded 2, 2, Cav. (Cumberland and
Mil. Div. Miss.). Captured 25 July '62;
received surrender of Atlanta under
Gen. Wilson's orders; Chief of Staff,
Dept. of Orangeburg (S.C.). Died 1891.

EGLOFFSTEIN, Baron Fred W. von.
Union officer and Bvt. B.G. USV listed
thusly by Heitman. See VON EGLOFF-
STEIN, BARON FRED W.

EKIN, James Adams. Union officer.
1819–91. Pa. R.A. 1st Lt. 12th Pa. 25
Apr. '61; mustered out 5 Aug. '61; Capt.
Asst. Q.M., Vols. 7 Aug. '61–14 Apr. '63;
Capt. Asst. Q.M. USA 13 Mar. '63;
Lt. Col. Q.M. Assigned 15 Feb.–1 Aug.
'64; Col. Q.M. Assigned 2 Aug. '64–
1 Jan. '65; Bvt. B.G. USV 8 Mar. '65.
Brevets for war service, Q.M. Dept.
service. Served as Q.M. of Cav. Bureau,
Chief Q.M. of Cav. Corps (Potomac)
Feb. '64; retired as Col. Asst. Q.M.
Gen. Before the war he was a ship-
builder.

ELDRIDGE, Hamilton N. Union
officer. 1831–82. Mass. Lt. Col. 127th
Ill. 6 Sept. '62; Col. 1 Mar. '63; Bvt.
B.G. USV (Arkansas Post, Vicksburg
assault); resigned 29 July '63. At the

siege of Vicksburg he carried the regimental colors after several color bearers
had been shot. He was a classmate of
Pres. GARFIELD at Williams (Class of
1856) and later practiced law at Chicago.

ELKHORN TAVERN, Ark. Con-
federate name for battle of PEA RIDGE.

ELKWATER, W. Va. See CHEAT
MOUNTAIN, 10–15 Sept. '61.

ELLET, Alfred Washington, Union
gen. ?–1895. Pa. He was commissioned
Capt. 59th Ill. 20 Aug. '61 and promoted
to Lt. Col. Add. A.D.C. 28 Apr. '62.
He was named B.G. USV 1 Nov. '62.
Appleton's credits him with ordering the
burning 24 May '63 of Austin (Miss.)
in retaliation for the information given
by its citizens to rebel soldiers, enabling
them to fire upon Federal transports in
the river. He resigned 31 Dec. '64. He
was the brother of Charles Ellet, the
engineer and inventor of the steam
RAMS used at Memphis in '62.

ELLET RAM FLEET. See RAM.

ELLIOTT, Isaac Hughes. Union officer. Ill. Capt. 33d Ill. 2 Sept. '61; Maj.
30 May '63; Lt. Col. 13 Sept. '64; Col.
30 Sept. '65; Bvt. B.G. USV. Brevets for
war service, Port Gibson, Champion's
Hill, Black River Bridge, siege of Vicksburg, Spanish Ft.

ELLIOTT, Samuel Mackenzie. Union
officer. 1811–75. Scotland. Lt. Col. 79th
N.Y. 29 May '61; Bvt. B.G. USV (war
service); resigned 10 Aug. '61. Resigned
because of spine injuries sustained when
his horse was shot and fell on him at
1st Bull Run. An oculist, educated at
the College of Surgeons at Glasgow, his
eccentricities caused difficulties with his
professional colleagues in New York,
where he practiced.

ELLIOTT, Stephen, Jr. C.S.A gen.
1832–66. S.C. The son of an Episcopal
bishop, he ran his plantation until Ft.
Sumter, when he took up arms as Capt.
of the Beaufort battery. Standing guard

at Port Royal and Pinckney Island in Aug. '62, he was Chief of Arty. for the 3d Mil. Dist. of S.C. Promoted Maj. and Lt. Col., he occupied Sumter during the bombardment of Charleston and in May '64, as Col. in Holcombe's Legion, was sent to Petersburg. He led his brigade at the Wilderness and was appointed B.G. C.S.A. 24 May '64. Fighting in the siege of Petersburg, he was mortally wounded at the Crater and sent home to Beaufort where he died 21 Mar. '66 (C.M.H.).

ELLIOTT, Washington Lafayette. Union gen. 1825–88. Pa. R.A. He sailed with his naval officer father to the West Indies when he was six and to France in 1835 aboard the *Constitution*. Failing to graduate from West Point (ex-1845), he joined the R.A. (2d Lt. Mounted Rifles) in 1846 and participated in the Mexican War until illness during the siege of Vera Cruz brought him back to the US. He served mainly on the frontier, until the Civil War, when he was named Capt. 3d US Cav. 3 Aug. '61 and fought at Wilson's Creek (Mo.). He was commissioned Col. 2d Iowa Cav. 14 Sept., promoted Maj. 1st US Cav. 5 Nov. '61 and led his regiment at New Madrid (13 Mar. '62), Island No. 10 (7 Apr. '62) and siege of Corinth. He then assumed command of 2, Cav. Div. Army Miss., Mo. (24 Apr.–1 June '62) and the Cav. Div., Miss. (30 July–11 Aug. '62). He was promoted B.G. USV 11 June '62. Wounded at 2d Bull Run, he led the first cavalry raid of the war on the Mobile and Ohio R.R. and served as chief of cavalry for the Army of Va. He also commanded 1, 2, VIII, Miss. (Feb.–26 June '63); Elliott's division, VIII, Middle (June–July '63); 3d Div., III, Potomac (10 July–5 Oct. '63); 1st Div., Cav. Corps, Cumberland (12 Oct.–20 Nov. '63); Cav. Corps, Cumberland (20 Nov. '63–19 Aug. '64) in the pursuit of Hood; 2d Div., IV, Cumber-

land (2 Dec. '64–24 June '65) and the Dept. of the Northwest. He was breveted for Island No. 10, Corinth, Nashville (B.G. USV and Maj. Gen. USV), war service (Maj. Gen. USA). He continued in the R.A. until he retired as Col. in 1879 and was later a banker in California.

ELLIS, Augustus Van Horne. Union officer. N.Y. Col. 124th N.Y. 5 Sept. '62; Bvt. B.G. USV 2 July '63 (Gettysburg); K.I.A. Gettysburg 2 July '63. Commanded 1, 3, III.

ELLIS, John Willis. C.S.A. Gov. of N.C. 1820–61. N.C. After graduating from Chapel Hill and practicing law, he served as a jurist and legislator as an advocate of states rights. Elected Gov. in 1858 and again in 1860, he had the foresight to enlarge the state militia and promptly seized the Federal arsenals and works in the state. He died 7 July '61 of overwork and strain.

ELLIS, Theodore Gunville. Union officer. 1829–83. Mass. 1st Lt. Adj. 14th Conn. 23 Aug. '62; Maj. 4 Apr. '63; Lt. Col. 22 Sept. '63; Col. 11 Oct. '63; Bvt. B.G. USV (war service). Commanded 3, 2, II. His regiment captured five battle flags in a bayonet charge at Gettysburg. A civil engineer in railroads and mining, he published many papers on engineering.

ELLISON'S MILL, Vā., 26 June '62. MECHANICSVILLE, same date.

ELLSWORTH, E(phraim) Elmer. War hero. 1837–61. N.Y. He was famous before the war for organizing the Chicago Zouaves and staging spectacular drill exhibitions throughout the country. In Aug. '60 he had performed on the White House lawn. He accompanied Lincoln to Washington for the inauguration, and after attempting to secure a War Department post, he raised the Fire Zouaves (see 11TH NEW YORK) and returned at their head to Washington in

May '61. He was killed by James T. Jackson, proprietor of the Marshall House Tavern in Alexandria, 24 May '61, after removing a Confederate flag from the roof of that building. Jackson was immediately killed by Private Francis E. BROWNELL. A correspondent of the New York *Tribune* was on the scene, and the episode was an immediate sensation that contributed much to arousing war sentiment in the North. (See also ZOUAVES.)

ELMIRA (N.Y.) PRISON. This Federal PRISON was started in May '64 by enclosing barracks on the Chemung River near Elmira when, after the exchange of prisoners was halted, the Union's facilities were found to be vastly inadequate. The buildings could hold only half of the 10,000 prisoners at Elmira, and the rest lived in tents, even during the hard winter. Death rate here was around 5 per cent a month, and the sick rate was extremely high. Ten per cent of the prisoners had no blankets, and the food was scanty and spoiled. Only enlisted men were held here.

ELSTNER, George Ruter. Union officer. Ohio. 1st Lt. Adj. 50th Ohio 12 July '62; Maj. 5 May '63; Lt. Col. 1 July '63; Bvt. B.G. USV 8 Aug. '64 (Atlanta); K.I.A. 8 Aug. '64 at Atlanta.

ELWELL, John Johnson. Union officer. 1820–1900. Ohio. Capt. Asst. Q.M. Vols. 3 Aug. '61; Lt. Col. Q.M. Assigned and Chief Q.M. Dept. of the South 8 Nov. '62–1 Feb. '64; Bvt. B.G. USV (Q.M. war service). Chief Q.M. for X Corps and Vol. A.D.C. at Secessionville (S.C.) to Gen. Benham. After studying medicine, he took up the law, becoming a contributor to and eventually editor of John Bouvier's *Law Dictionary*. Later he established the *Western Law Monthly*.

ELY, John. Union officer. Pa. Commissioned Maj. 23d Pa. 7 Oct. '61, he was promoted Lt. Col. 20 July '62 and Col. 13 Dec. '62. He resigned 6 Dec. '63 and was commissioned Col. 26th Vet. Res. Corps 14 Dec. of that year. Breveted B.G. and Maj. Gen. USV 15 Apr. '65 for war service, he was mustered out in 1867 and died two years later.

ELY, Ralph. Union officer. N.Y. Capt. 8th Mich. 12 Aug. '61; Maj. 10 Sept. '62; Lt. Col. 1 Feb. '63; Col. 7 May '64; Bvt. B.G. USV 2 Apr. '65; Brevets for Wilderness, Petersburg assault. Commanded 2, 1, IX. W.I.A. Secessionville (S.C.) 16 June '62. Died 1883.

ELY, William Grosvenor. Union officer. c. 1835–? Conn. Lt. Col. 6th Conn. 13 Sept. '61; Col. 18th Conn. 22 Aug. '62; Bvt. B.G. USV (war service); resigned 18 Sept. '64. Commanded 2d Brig., 1st Inf. Div., Army W. Va. Captured 13 June '63 at Front Royal Pike (Va.), he escaped from Libby Prison in Richmond with 108 others through a tunnel under the street. He was one of the 50 recaptured after four days but was then exchanged in time to participate in Piedmont (Va.) where he was W.I.A. 4 June '64 in the throat.

ELZEY, Arnold. C.S.A. gen. 1816–71. Md. USMA 1837 (33/50); Inf. During his West Point years he dropped his last name (Jones) and used his middle name, that of his paternal grandmother. He served in the Seminole wars, on the frontier, in Indian fighting, and in the Mexican War (1 brevet) before resigning 25 Apr. '61 as Capt. After surrendering the US arsenal at Augusta (Ga.) to superior rebel forces, he withdrew his command and brought them intact to Washington before returning to Richmond to be commissioned Lt. Col. 1st Md. At 1st Bull Run he succeeded Kirby Smith in command of the brigade as senior Col. and was appointed B.G. C.S.A. on that date (21 July '61). He then commanded his brigade under Jackson in the Valley, the Seven Days' Battles, Port Republic (where he had his horse shot from under him and was slightly wounded), and Cold Harbor, where he was seriously wounded in the face and head. Upon his return to duty he was promoted Maj. Gen. 4 Dec. '62 and took command of the Dept. of Richmond. In the fall of '64 he organized the "Local Defence Brigade," served briefly at Staunton in organizing the Va. reserves, and was Hood's Chief of Arty. in the Tenn. campaign. After the war he farmed in Md.

EMANCIPATION BEFORE 1863. See John C. FRÉMONT and David HUNTER.

EMANCIPATION PROCLAMATION. Presidential decree issued 22 Sept. '62 to take effect 1 Jan. '63, freeing all slaves in those parts of the nation still in rebellion. In July '62 Lincoln had proposed such a move to his cabinet and read them a preliminary draft of the proclamation. Seward suggested that he wait, believing that such a dynamic change in the war's focus (heretofore fought to preserve the Union and not to disrupt the South's social fabric) would be little more than a plea for support without a military victory. The battle of Antietam, while hardly decisive, gave Lincoln that opportunity.

EMBALMED BEEF. Union soldiers' name for meat canned by Chicago packers and issued in the field.

EMORY, William Hemsley. Union gen. 1811–87. Md. USMA 1831 (14/33); Arty. After garrison duty and Indian fighting he resigned in 1836 to become a civil engineer. Reappointed two years later as 1st Lt. Topo. Engrs. he supervised harbor improvements, was breveted for a border survey, fought during the Mexican War on Kearny's California expedition (2 brevets). He served on the frontier, in "bleeding" Kans. during the border disturbances, and on the Utah Expedition. As Lt. Col. 1st U.S. Cav. 31 Jan. '61 (Maj. since 1855), he concentrated his troops in the Indian territory at Ft. Leavenworth, capturing the advance guard of the Tex. rebel militia in the process. Resigning 9 May, he was reappointed Lt. Col. 6th U.S. Cav. five days later and was promoted B.G. USV 17 Mar. '62. In the defenses of Washington he commanded Emory's brigade, Cav. Div. Reserve, Potomac (13 Mar.–5 July '62) and at Harrison's Landing led 1, 2, IV (6 July–10 Aug. '62). At Port Hudson and Camp Bisland he led the 3d Div., XIX, Gulf (3 Jan.–2 May '63); commanded the defenses of New Orleans (21 May–25 Aug. '63) fighting at LaFourche Crossing; then headed the 4th Div., XIX (30 July–25 Aug. '63). He went back to the 3d Div., XIX (4–17 Sept. '63) and then led the 1st Div. of that corps (13 Dec. '63–2 May '64) in the RED RIVER CAMPAIGN. He led the XIX Corps (2 May–2 July '64) at Marksville, La., and then in the Shenandoah (6 Aug.–8 Dec. and 28 Dec. '64–20 Mar. '65) at Opequon, Fishers Hill, and Cedar Creek. Promoted Maj. Gen. USV 25 Sept. '65, he was breveted for Hanover Courthouse, Fishers Hill (B.G. USA), war service. (Maj. Gen. USV 23 July '64) and Cedar Creek (Maj. Gen. USA). He remained in the R.A., retiring in 1876 as B.G.

ENCHANTRESS **AFFAIR.** Walter W. Smith, prize master of the schooner *Enchantress,* with a prize crew from the CSS *Jeff Davis,* was captured 22d July '61, tried for piracy (22–28 Oct.), and convicted. Judah Benjamin prepared to retaliate, and ordered that a high-ranking Federal prisoner be chosen by lot as a hostage for Smith, and that 13 others be selected as hostages for the crew of the *Savannah,* another privateer captured 3 June. "The names of the six colonels were placed in a can. The first name drawn was that of Col. M. Corcoran,"

J. H. Winder reported 11 Nov. to Benjamin. "In choosing the thirteen from the highest rank, . . . there being only ten field officers, it was necessary to draw by lot three captains. . . . The list of thirteen will therefore stand—Colonels Lee, Cogswell, Wil[l]cox, Woodruff, and Wood; Lieutenant Colonels Bowman and Neff; Majors Potter, Revere, and Vodges; Captains Ricketts, McQuaide, and Rockwood" (O.R., II, III, 738-9). The convictions were not upheld, the Confederates ruled to be prisoners of war and not pirates (Miller, VII, 29 and 34 and 36).

ENFIELD RIFLE MUSKET. Adopted by the British Army in 1855, and its general infantry weapon until adoption of the breech-loader in 1867, this weapon weighed 9 pounds, 3 ounces, with bayonet, and had a bore diameter of .577 inch. It fired a bullet similar to the Minié, was very accurate at 800 yards, and fairly accurate at 1,100 yards (E. B., XXXIII, 326; Wilhelm). Almost half a million were imported by the North before production could meet requirements. Caleb Huse purchased more than 100,000 of these arms. "It was perhaps the most popular gun in the Confederate service [after 1862] and one of the most effective" (Wiley, *Reb,* 291).

ENGELMAN, Adolph. Union officer. Germany. Lt. Col. 43d Ill. 16 Dec. '61; Col. 12 Apr. '62; Bvt. B.G. USV (war service); mustered out 16 Dec. '64. Commanded 1, 3, XVI; 1st, Kimball's Prov. Div., XVI; 1st, Kimball's Dist. East Ark., XVI; 2, 2d Div. Arkansas Exp., XVI; 2d Div. Arkansas Exp., XVI; 2, 2, VII; 3, 3, VII; 2, 1, VII; 1st Div., VII. Died 1890.

ENLISTED MEN, LOYALTY OF REGULAR ARMY. See LOYALTY OF REGULAR ARMY ENLISTED MEN.

ENOCHS, William Henry. Union officer. Ohio. W. Va. Pvt. Co. B 2d Ohio 17 Apr.–9 Aug. '61; 1st Lt. 5th W. Va. 15 Sept. '61; Capt. 19 Apr. '62; Lt. Col. 29 Sept. '63; transferred to 1st W. Va. Vet. Inf. 9 Nov. '64; Col. 23 Dec. '64; Bvt. B.G. USV (war service). Died 1893.

ENON (AENON) CHURCH. Alternate name for HAW'S SHOP, VA. 29 May '64.

ENT, Wellington Harry. Union officer. Pa. Capt. 6th Pa. Res. 28 May '61; Maj. 21 Sept. '62; Lt. Col. 1 May '63; Col. 1 July '63; Bvt. B.G. USV (Wilderness, Spotsylvania C.H., Bethesda Church); mustered out 11 June '64. Commanded 1, 3, V. Died 1871.

ENVELOPMENT. An ATTACK directed toward the enemy's flank(s) or rear. There are single and double envelopments. The TURNING MOVEMENT, although also called a strategic envelopment, is a somewhat different operation.

ENYART, David A. Union officer. Ohio. Lt. Col. 1st Ky. 28 June '61; Col. 22 Jan. '62; Bvt. B.G. USV (war service); mustered out 18 June '64. Commanded 1, 2, XXI; 1, 1, IV. Died 1867.

EPROUVETTE. A small mortar used to prove the strength of gunpowder. Another type of eprouvette, used in the US, was a cannon or musket on a pendulum.

ERICSSON, John. Marine engineer. 1803–89. Sweden. After serving as an engineer officer in the Swedish Army, he resigned and went to England, where he invented and manufactured a number of improvements in locomotives and naval guns. He also invented the screw propeller and designed and built the MONITOR in 1861.

ERSKINE, Albert. Union officer. Me. Pvt. Co. E 13th Ill. Cav. 20 Sept. '61; 1st Lt. 19 Dec. '61; Capt. 25 Feb. '63; Maj. 28 Dec. '63; Col. 1 June '64; Bvt. B.G. USV (war service). Commanded 1, Cav. Div., VII. Died 1875.

ESTE, George Peabody. Union gen. 1830–81. N.H. After Dartmouth he practiced law until commissioned Lt. Col. 14th Ohio 24 Apr. '61. Mustered out 13 Aug., he was named Lt. Col. 14th Ohio three days later and Col. on 20 Nov. '62. He commanded 3d Div., XIV, Cumberland 25 Oct.–25 Nov. '63 and then led 3, 3, XIV (1 Apr.–25 Oct. and 16 Nov. '64–29 Mar. '65) at Snake Creek Gap, Resaca, Kenesaw Mountain, Chattahoochee, where his horse was shot from under him, Peach Tree Creek, and Jonesboro where he was slightly wounded and another horse was shot from under him. He also led this brigade on the March to the Sea and through the Carolinas. Breveted B.G. USV 9 Dec. '64, he was promoted B.G. USV 26 June '65 and resigned the following 4 Dec. After the war he practiced law in Washington.

ESTES, Lewellyn Garrish. Union officer. Me. 1st Sgt. Co. A 1st Me. Cav., 19 Oct. '61; 1st Lt. 24 Mar. '62; Capt. 1 Aug. '63; Capt. Asst. Adj. Gen. Vols. 4 Sept. '63; Maj. Asst. Adj. Gen. Vols. 2 Feb. '65; Bvt. B.G. USV. Brevets for Ga. and Carolinas campaign, war service. Medal of Honor 28 Aug. '94 for Flint River (Ga.) 30 Aug. '64.

ETHERIDGE, Anna. Union Army nurse. Wis. At the outbreak of war she was visiting in Detroit and enlisted as nurse with the 2d Mich. Serving from 1st Bull Run until Lee's surrender, she was under fire bandaging and succoring the wounded until Grant sent her to the City Point Hospital during his Petersburg siege. She was attached variously to the 3d and 5th Mich. and was called "Michigan Annie" and "Gentle Anna" by the soldiers. Kearny had planned to make her regimental Sgt. Maj. but was killed before this could be done, and Birney gave her the Kearny Cross for bravery. Wounded only once, a grazed hand, she acquired many bullet holes through her long dresses. After the war she worked in a government office to support her destitute father.

EUSTIS, Henry Lawrence. Union gen. 1819–85. Mass. After graduating from Harvard in 1838, he entered West Point (USMA 1842 [1/56]; Engrs.). He served on the East Coast and as assistant professor of engineering at USMA, resigning in 1849 to become professor of engineering at Harvard. Commissioned Col. 10th Mass. (21 Aug. '61), he led his regiment at Williamsport, Md., 20 Sept. '62, and commanded 2, 3, VI, Potomac (Dec. '62–Jan. '63) at Fredericksburg and 2d Div., VI, Potomac (21 Feb.–25 Mar. '64) at Marye's Heights, Salem. Gettysburg, Rappahannock Station, and Mine Run. He was promoted B.G. USV 12 Sept. '63 and led 4, 2, VI, Potomac (26 Mar.–9 May '64) at the Wilderness and 3, 1, VI, Potomac (9 May–12 June '64) at Spotsylvania and Cold Harbor. He resigned 27 June '64 because of poor health. He returned to Harvard in the fall, where he taught for the rest of his life. Author of many articles on technical and scientific subjects, he was a fellow of several learned societies.

EVANS, Clement Anselm. C.S.A. gen. 1833–1911. Ga. A lawyer, judge, and legislator, he was commissioned Maj. 31st Ga. 19 Nov. '61 and promoted Col. in Apr. '62. Serving under Jackson, Early, and Gordon, he led his regiment on the Peninsula, at Fredericksburg, where he succeeded to command of Lawton's brig., at Gettysburg and the Wilderness. Appointed B.G. C.S.A. 19 May '64, he took over Gordon's old brigade, commanding it in Early's Washington raid and the subsequent Valley campaign. He was wounded at Monocacy. At Petersburg in Nov. '64 he succeeded Gordon in command of the division and surrendered this group at Appomattox. Much depressed by the carnage he had seen at Fredericksburg, he determined to enter the ministry after the war and was a Methodist preacher for over 25 years. He was active in veterans' organizations and wrote about the war. He published *Military History of Georgia* in 1895 and edited the 12-vol. *Confederate Military History* in 1899.

EVANS, George Spafford. Union officer. Mich. Maj. 2d Calif. Cav. 16 Oct. '61; Lt. Col. 1 Dec. '61; Col. 1 Feb. '63; Bvt. B.G. USV (war service); mustered out 31 May '63. Died 1883.

EVANS, Nathan George ("Shanks"). C.S.A. gen. 1824–68. S.C. He attended Randolph-Macon and graduated from USMA 1848 (36/38); Dragoons. Serving on the frontier and in Indian fighting, he resigned 27 Feb. '61 as Capt. to become Maj. Adj. Gen. in the S.C. army during the bombardment of Sumter. Commissioned Capt. of C.S.A. Cav. in May '61, he led a small brigade at 1ST BULL RUN. Posted on the extreme left, at the Stone Bridge, he played a conspicuous and distinguished part in the Confederate victory. He was promoted Col. a few days later. He next led the Confed. force in the small but famous action at BALLS BLUFF. Given the C.S.A. Thanks of Congress and a Gold Medal from his state for this, he was also appointed B.G. C.S.A. 21 Oct. '61 and took command of an independent brigade. This force was usually in the Carolinas but was so often sent elsewhere on temporary duty that it came to be called the "tramp brigade." He led them at 2d Bull Run, South Mountain, Antietam under Lee, and then under J. E. Johnston at Vicksburg. However, troubles began to plague him from the beginning of 1863. He was tried and acquitted twice: first for drunkenness and second for disobedience. Deprived of his command by Beauregard, who considered him incompetent, he returned to the field in the spring of 1864 but shortly fell from his horse and was painfully injured. He was on duty in spring

1865 for a few months until Davis was captured in Ga. After the war he was a high-school principal in Ala. "He was 37 [when the war started], of medium height, slightly bald, with the fiercest of black mustachios, and small, restless eyes to match. His look was quick, cunning and contentious, as if he were always suspecting a Comanche ambush." As for the origin of his nickname, it was a matter of "his thinnest members receiving stoutest acclaim." (Above description is from *Lee's Lts.,* I, 87.)

EVARTS, William Maxwell. Union statesman. 1818–1901. Sec. of Union defense committee during Civil War and sent on diplomatic missions to England in 1863–64. He was Johnson's chief counsel during impeachment proceedings, and it was largely through his efforts that Johnson was acquitted. He also handled the *Savannah* privateers case. See ENCHANTRESS AFFAIR.

EVERETT, Charles. Union officer. Mass. Appt.-La. Capt. 6th Mass. Btry. 20 Jan. '62; Lt. Col. 2d La. 3 Oct. '62; Col. 1 Apr. '64; Bvt. B.G. USV (war service). Commanded 1, Cav. Div., Dept. of the Gulf. Died 1879.

EVERETT, Edward. Orator and statesman. 1794–1865. Mass. Unitarian clergyman who made many famous speeches in the Union cause, the best known was his two-hour oration preceding Lincoln's five-minute Gettysburg Address. He also served as US Representative, Gov. of Massachusetts, Minister to Great Britain, president of Harvard University, Sec. of State and US Sen.

EWELL, Richard Stoddert ("Dick"). C.S.A. gen. 1817–72. D.C. Appt.-Va. USMA 1840 (13/42); Dragoons. He served on the frontier, in the Mexican War (1 brevet), and in Indian fighting before resigning 7 May '61 as Capt. Commissioned Col. C.S.A., he took over the camp of cavalry instruction at Ashland and on 17 June '61 was appointed B.G. C.S.A. He commanded the 2d Brig. at 1st Bull Run and was promoted Maj. Gen. 23 Jan. '62. In the Shenandoah Valley he commanded his division under Jackson at Winchester and Cross Keys and went with him to the Peninsula where he fought in the Seven Days' Battles. He also fought at Cedar Mountain, 2d Bull Run, and lost his leg at Groveton. Returning to duty 23 May '63 as Lt. Gen., in command of II CORPS, Confed., A.N.V., he was lifted on his horse and strapped in his saddle to lead the advance into Pa. He reached Carlisle before being called back to fight at GETTYSBURG. Wounded again at Kelly's Ford, he led his corps at the Wilderness and Spotsylvania until a fall from his horse at the "bloody angle" left him unfit for further field service. Given command then of the Dept. of Henrico, he took over the defenses of Richmond. On the retreat to Appomattox he was captured at Sayler's Creek 6 Apr. '65 and was not paroled until 19 Aug. of that year. "The character *sui generis* of Lee's Army," Freeman calls him, "bald, pop-eyed and long beaked, with a piping voice that seems to fit his appearance as a strange, unlovely bird; he probably has stomach ulcers and chronically complains of headaches, sleepless nights and indigestion; but he quickly shows that he has a chivalrous, fighting spirit along with a sharp tongue and an odd sense of humor." When he returned from convalescent leave—having acquired a wife in the interim—he soon showed an inability to make the transition from a closely controlled division commander under Stonewall Jackson to a corps commander under Lee's discretionary orders. "After exploits that would have added to the fame of 'Stonewall' himself, Ewell loses the power of decision

[e.g., Gettysburg]" (*Lee's Lts.*, I, xlvi; III, xxix).

EWELL'S CORPS. See II CORPS, Confed., A.N.V.

EWING, Charles. Union gen. 1835–83. Ohio R.A. After the Univ. of Va. he practiced law and was commissioned Capt. 13th US Inf. 14 May '61. As Lt. Col. Asst. I.G. Assigned (22 June '63–1 Apr. '65), he served on (his brother-in-law) W. T. Sherman's staff. At Vicksburg he was severely wounded while planting his battalion flag on the parapet. Promoted B.G. USV 8 Mar. '65 and breveted for Vicksburg, Atlanta, and war service, he resigned in 1867 to practice law in Washington. Brother of Thomas and Hugh Ewing.

EWING, Hugh Boyle. Union gen. 1826–1905. Ohio. After attending USMA (ex-1848), he went to California for the gold rush in 1849 where he participated in a rescue expedition into the High Sierras sent by his father, then Sec. of the Interior. He later practiced law at Ft. Leavenworth (Kans.) with his foster brother W. T. Sherman, his younger brother Thomas Ewing, and Daniel McCook. Returning to Ohio, he was named Brig. Insp. for the Ohio Vols. 6 May '61 and Col. 30th Ohio 20 Aug. '61. He led a charge at South Mt. (14 Sept. '62), dislodging the enemy from the summit and shortly (29 Nov.) was named B.G. USV. D.A.B. says that he commanded a brigade on the left at Antietam 17 Sept. '62, although Dyer gives his first brigade command as 3, 2, XV, Tenn. (9 Jan.–21 July '63) under Sherman at Vicksburg. He then commanded 1st Div., XVI, Tenn. (20–28 July) and 4th Div., XV, Tenn. (28 July–1 Sept. and 6 Oct. '63–8 Feb. '64) in the advance of Sherman's army where they sustained heavy losses taking Missionary Ridge. He also commanded 2d Div. Dist. Ky., XXIII, Ohio and 2d Div., Army of

Ky. Breveted Maj. Gen. USV for war service, he was planning an expedition up the Roanoke River in N.C. when the war ended. He was Minister to Holland in 1866–70 and later a lawyer.

EWING, Thomas, Jr. Union gen. 1829–96. Ohio. At 19 he was one of Pres. Taylor's secretaries while his father was Sec. of the Interior. He then went to college and law school, practicing in Leavenworth with his brother Hugh, his foster brother W. T. Sherman, and Daniel McCook. When the war came, the firm went en masse to join the Union Army, all becoming general officers. An ardent opponent of slavery, he had been largely instrumental in stopping Kansas from being admitted as a slave state in 1858. In 1861 he was appointed first Chief Justice of the Kansas Supreme Court. Named Col. 11th Kans. Cav. 15 Sept. '62, he led his regiment in several engagements in Arkansas and was promoted B.G. USV 13 Mar. '63. He commanded 1st Div., Army of the Frontier, Mo. (26 Apr.–5 June '63) and while leading the Border Dist., Mo. (July '63– Mar. '64), he issued the famous Order No. 11 depopulating the Mo. counties to combat rebel guerrillas. In command of St. Louis (25 Mar.–21 Nov. '64) when Sterling Price invaded in Sept., he checked the Confederates' progress, first retiring to Ft. Davidson and then to St. Louis strenuously pursued by the enemy. He also commanded Rolla, Mo. (21 Nov.–9 Dec. '64), was breveted Maj. Gen. USV for Pilot Knob (Mo.) and resigned 23 Feb. '65. He returned to the law and entered politics as a member of the Greenback party.

EX-CADET. Man who attended West Point but did not graduate.

EXCELSIOR (SICKLES') BRIGADE (2, III. Potomac). Composed of the 70th, 71st, 72d, 73d, 74th, and 120th N.Y., this brigade had the fifth highest number of killed and mortally wounded in the war (876).

EXCHANGE OF PRISONERS. Although numbers of prisoners had been released on PAROLE early in the war, the first discussions on formal exchange did not take place until 23 Feb. '62. One reason for this delay was that the Union did not recognize the Confederacy as a nation and felt that to enter into negotiations would give the South tacit recognition. Gen. Wool met with Gen. Howell Cobb, but no arrangements could be made. Gen. Dix then met with Gen. D. H. Hill in July '62, and an agreement was reached on the 22d of that month. Points of exchange were City Point in the East and Vicksburg in the West. A general officer was to be exchanged for 60 enlisted men, a colonel for 15, a lieutenant for 4, and a sergeant for 2. (O.R., II, IV, 267). Gen. E. A. Hitchcock became Union commissioner in the latter part of July. However, as the year progressed, the commissioners and their agents became estranged over the disposition of Negro troops and other matters, and on 28 Dec. '62 Stanton suspended the exchange of officers. Halleck stopped all exchanges on 25 May '63, but in certain instances, by special agreement, the practice continued. After Grant assumed over-all command, the exchange of prisoners virtually ceased. The normally dispassionate E. P. Alexander has this comment: "Grant decided beforehand not to exchange prisoners. This added much to the suffering to be endured on both sides. It may be condoned as tending to shorten the war, but the way in which it was done savored more of the 'sharp trick' than of Grant's usual dignity and frankness of character. We had, perhaps unwisely, 'outlawed' Butler, and Grant's trick consisted in making him 'Commissioner for exchange of prisoners' in hopes that we would decline to hold communication with him. When we swallowed our pride and offered exchanges, pretenses were found still to refuse." (*op. cit.*, 495-6.) The South found itself so burdened with Union prisoners that by Nov. '64 they were sending prisoners from Andersonville and elsewhere to the North without man-for-man exchange.

EZRA CHAPEL (CHURCH), Ga., 28 July '64. "Hood's Third Sortie." (ATLANTA CAMPAIGN) After the battle of ATLANTA, 22 July '64, Sherman moved to cut Hood's line of communications to the south. STONEMAN'S AND MCCOOK'S RAIDS to Macon and Lovejoy were part of his plan. Howard's army moved from the extreme Federal left to the extreme right and enveloped through Ezra Church toward the railroad. Hood ordered the corps of S. D. Lee from Atlanta to check this maneuver. A meeting engagement took place at Ezra Church. Logan's XV Corps, on the right of Howard's army, was unsuccessfully attacked by the division of J. C. Brown and three brigades of Clayton's. The Federals dug in and then repulsed an attack byWalthall's division of Stewart's Corps, which had been sent out from Atlanta to reinforce S. D. Lee's Corps. There was heavy fighting from 2 P.M. until dark, when Hood withdrew his forces to Atlanta. Logan reported a total loss of 562.

F

FAGAN, James Fleming. C.S.A. gen. 1828-93. Ky. Appt.-Ark. A farmer and Whig legislator, he fought in the Mexican War before being commissioned Col. 1st Ark. 6 May '61. After fighting at Shiloh, he was appointed B.G. C.S.A. 12 Sept. '62 and was transferred to the Trans-Miss. Dept. He was at Prairie Grove and was sent in 1863 to raise troops for the defense of Ark. After defeating Steele in his Camden expedition, he was promoted Maj. Gen. 25 Apr. '64 and went with Price in his last Mo. raid. Fagan finally surrendered 14 June '65 and returned to farming and politics after the war.

FAIRBANKS, Erastus. Gov. of Vt. 1792-1864. Mass. A manufacturer, he was elected to the legislature and was a railroad president. He had been Gov. in 1851 and was chosen again in 1860 by the Republicans, although quite old.

FAIRCHILD, Cassius. Union officer. 1828-68. Ohio. Lt. Col. 16th Wis. 23 Dec. '61; Col. 17 Mar. '64; Bvt. B.G. USV (war service). Commanded 1, 3, XVII. W.I.A. Shiloh 6 Apr. '62. He was US Marshal in Wisconsin until his early death from the effects of his wound.

FAIRCHILD, Harrison Stiles. Union officer. N.Y. Col. 89th N.Y. 4 Dec. '61; Bvt. B.G. USV (war service). Commanded 1, 3, IX; 1, 2, VII; 2, North End Folly Island, X; 4, 1, XXIV; 1, 1, XXIV; 2, 1, XXIV. Died 1901.

FAIRCHILD, Lucius. Union gen. 1831-96. Ohio. After traveling to California as a '49er, he returned to the Midwest and held several public offices as a Democrat before the outbreak of the Civil War brought him into the Republican party. He enlisted as Pvt. 1st Wis. 17 Apr. '61, was promoted Capt. a month later, and mustered out 17 Aug. '61. Commissioned Lt. Col. 2d Wis. 20 Aug. '61, he was promoted Col. 1 Sept. '62 and led his regiment, part of the IRON BRIGADE, at 2d Bull Run and at

Gettysburg where he was wounded and captured on the first day. His health broken by this, he resigned 20 Aug. '63, was named Capt. 16th US Inf. 5 Aug., resigned that commission on 19 Oct. and was promoted B.G. USV the same day. He resigned this last commission 2 Nov. He was Governor of Wisconsin 1866–72, Consul at Liverpool until 1878, Consul Gen. at Paris until 1880 and in Spain until 1882. He returned to Wisconsin hoping for high office but none was proffered so he became active in veterans' organizations. His was the famous malediction: "May God palsy the hand that wrote that order, may God palsy the brain that conceived it, and may God palsy the tongue that dictated it," uttered at a G.A.R. meeting denouncing Cleveland's order in 1887 to return the C.S.A. battle flags. He was the younger brother of Cassius FAIRCHILD.

FAIRFAX (COURTHOUSE), Va., 27 June '63. (Stuart's Gettysburg raid.) At about 8:30 A.M. Hampton's leading regiment sighted Companies B and C, 11th N.Y. Cav., under the command of Maj. Remington. The Confederates pursued, scattered, and captured all but about 18 of the Federals. (Fairfax C.H. was the scene of numerous other skirmishes throughout the war.)

FAIR OAKS, Va. 27–28 Oct. '64. (PETERSBURG CAMPAIGN) To support the HATCHER'S RUN operation, Butler was directed to make a diversionary effort north of the James. While part of Terry's X Corps made a demonstration up the Charles City and Darby roads, part of Weitzel's XVIII Corps, preceded by Spear's cavalry brigade, moved to the Fair Oaks battlefield of the Peninsular campaign. Here Col. Holman's colored brigade (1, 3, XVIII) was detached to probe for the Confederate left flank while the main body (four brigades) moved up the Williams-

burg road toward Richmond. Longstreet correctly deduced that Terry's action was a feint and ordered the divisions of Field and Hoke to move against Weitzel. An attack by the brigades of Cullen and Marston at about 3:30 P.M. on the 27th was repulsed by Hoke. Holman crossed the railroad and attacked a position occupied by Gary's dismounted cavalry along the New Bridge Road. The Federal attack succeeded, but was driven back by a counterattack. Weitzel ordered a withdrawal. Terry, meanwhile, had been repulsed in his sector. At about 10 A.M. on the 28th the entire Federal force was ordered back. Federal losses were 1,103 and Confederate losses 451 (Humphreys and E.&B.).

FAIR OAKS AND SEVEN PINES, Va., 31 May–1 June '62. (PENINSULAR CAMPAIGN) J. E. Johnston determined to take advantage of the isolated position of Keyes's (IV) Corps at Fair Oaks and Seven Pines, south of the Chickahominy, and destroy it. While A. P. Hill

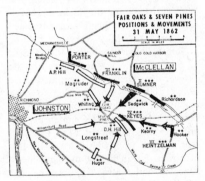

and Magruder screened along the line of the river to the north, Longstreet's corps reinforced by Whiting's division was to envelop Keyes's right via the Nine Mile Road. D. H. Hill was to make a secondary attack along the Williamsburg Road and Huger was to protect the Confederate right flank by an advance southeast along the Charles

City Road.. The plan was spoiled by Longstreet's failure to move along the route that had been orally prescribed for him. In what D. S. Freeman has termed "A Battle of Strange Errors," Longstreet got his troops on the roads assigned to D. H. Hill and Huger; in so doing he delayed the advance of these two divisions as well as Whiting's. The battle which was supposed to start at dawn did not get under way until 1 P.M., when D. H. Hill attacked at Seven Pines alone. In boggy, wooded terrain and heavy fighting, progress was made by the brigades of Garland, G. B. Anderson, Rains, and Rodes. The latter lost 1,094 killed and wounded out of 2,000 taken into action; Gordon's 6th Ala. of this brigade had 60 per cent casualties. R. H. Anderson's brigade (Longstreet) came up late in the day to make an attack that marked the high tide of D. H. Hill's advance. Longstreet also committed the brigades of Wilcox and Kemper on the Williamsburg road, and those of Colston and Pryor on the right.

On the Federal side part of Naglee's brigade (1, 2, IV) made a bayonet attack that enabled Casey to withdraw his artillery from its initial positions and form a new line. Couch himself led an attack of the 7th Mass. and 62d N.Y. to reinforce the 23d and 61st Pa. on the right flank. However, the Confederates crushed this flank and Couch joined Abercrombie (2, 1, IV) at Fair Oaks to avoid being cut off. Peck (1, 1, IV) held on the left for two hours before withdrawing in good order. Kearny's division (3, III) hurried forward over muddy roads from Bottom's Bridge to reinforce the weakening Federal line. When the brigades of Berry and Jameson arrived Casey tried to regain some of his positions, but his attack was repulsed. Late in the afternoon the 10th Mass. was led by

Keyes across half a mile of open ground to a piece of critical terrain whose retention made it possible for the Federals to hold their third line. At 6 P.M. the fighting ceased in this sector. Huger's division and six of Longstreet's brigades had not been engaged.

At about 4 P.M. the division of Whiting was ordered to move down the Nine Mile Road toward Fair Oaks to reinforce D. H. Hill's attack. McClellan had heard the firing south of the river at 2:30 P.M. and immediately sent Sumner's (II) corps to reinforce. The leading division, Sedgwick's, arrived at Fair Oaks just as Whiting's force started attacking Abercrombie there. Whiting turned to meet this unexpected threat to his flank, attacked, was repulsed, and then driven back.

J. E. Johnston was severely wounded and succeeded by G. W. Smith (who had been nominally in command of the Left Wing during the battle). Longstreet was ordered to attack the next day at dawn. The latter failed to act aggressively, being under the impression that the Federals were about to attack him; an advance by two Confederate brigades was stopped by the division of Richardson (1, II), which had reinforced from north of the Chickahominy during the night. R. E. Lee, who arrived at about 2 P.M. to succeed J. E. Johnston, ordered a withdrawal to the original Confederate positions.

Almost exactly the same number were engaged on each side: 41,797 Federals and 41,816 Confederates. Losses were 5,031 Federals and 6,134 Confederates (Livermore).

FALLING WATERS, W. Va., 14 July '64. (GETTYSBURG CAMPAIGN) In his retreat from Gettysburg Lee had reached Williamsport, Md., on 6 July and set up a defensive position while constructing bridges over which to cross the A.N.V. back into Va. Covering this withdrawal on 14 July, Heth's division was attacked by the 1st and 3d US Cav. divisions (Buford's and Kilpatrick's) early in the morning. The Confederates lost two guns and "approximately 500 stragglers from many brigades. Difficulties considered, Heth's performance was wholly creditable, but the Federals would not have it so. Because some of their leaders sensed public disappointment that Lee had escaped, they exaggerated Heth's withdrawal of the rear guard as a serious Confederate disaster" (*Lee's Lts.*, III, 167). Pettigrew was mortally wounded in the action.

FALLOWS, Samuel. Union officer. 1835-1922. England. Chap. 32d Wis. 25 Sept. '62; resigned 29 June '63; Lt. Col. 40th Wis. 20 May '64; mustered out 21 Sept. '64; Col. 49th Wis. 28 Jan. '65; Bvt. B.G. USV 24 Oct. '65 (war service). Becoming a Methodist minister in 1858, he was president of Illinois Wesleyan University after the war and later left that faith to become a Reformed Episcopal minister and bishop.

FARDELLA, Enrico. Union officer. Sicily. Col. 101st N.Y. 7 Mar. '62; mustered out 7 July '62; Col. 85th N.Y. 26 June '63; Bvt. B.G. USV (Plymouth, N.C.).

FAREWELL TO THE ARMY OF NORTHERN VIRGINIA. See LEE'S FAREWELL.

FARMVILLE AND HIGH BRIDGE, Va., 7 Apr. '65. (APPOMATTOX CAMPAIGN) Longstreet halted at Rice Station for the other corps to close up. These, however, were virtually destroyed at SAYLER'S CREEK. Ord made contact but, having only the two divisions of Gibbon (XXIV) available, did not attack. At dark, 6 Apr., Longstreet retreated toward Farmville where he crossed the Appomattox with the divisions of Heth and Wilcox. Mahone and Gordon (commanding the remnants of Ewell's and Anderson's corps) crossed at High Bridge. Fitz Lee covered the rear.

Mahone's division covered Gordon's withdrawal over the wagon bridge that runs under and alongside High Bridge. Mahone, a former railroad construction engineer and later president of the Southside R.R. that owned this bridge, failed to order fire set to the bridges in time. As a result, Barlow's division seized the wagon bridge and started crossing immediately while repelling a cloud of Confederate skirmishers who were trying to rectify the error. Since the river was unfordable, capture of the bridge speeded the Federal pursuit. Col. Thomas L. Livermore, of Humphreys' staff, led a party of pioneers who put out the fires on High Bridge while skirmishers were fighting 60 feet below the open deck on which they worked. Humphreys pursued toward Farmville. He moved with the divisions of Miles and De Trobriand (1st and 3d) northwest while Barlow (2d) pursued Gordon along the railroad bed. Gen T. A. Smyth (3d Brig.) was killed while pressing this pursuit. Lee's army was found entrenched around Farmville, where his starving troops had received rations. The bridges at Farmville had been burned, so the corps of Wright (VI) and Gibbon (XXIV) could not cross from the south. The cavalry brigade of J. I. Gregg, however, was able to ford the stream and was then attacked and defeated by Fitz Lee's cavalry (Munford and Rosser), supported by Heth's infantry. Gregg was captured. Humphreys, north and east of Lee's position, interpreted the sound of this skirmish as evidence of a Federal advance in strength from south of the river. An attack by part of G. W. Scott's brigade

(1, 1, II) on the Confederate left flank was repulsed by Mahone with reinforcements from G. T. Anderson's brigade (Field).

Lee continued his withdrawal during the night, but the enforced delay from noon to nightfall enabled the encircling force (Sheridan, followed by Ord's Army of the James) to capture his next supply point at APPOMATTOX STATION, and to block his retreat at APPOMATTOX COURTHOUSE. II Corps losses during the day were 571 (Humphreys). Other losses were not reported.

FARNSWORTH, Addison. Union officer. N.Y. Lt. Col. 38th N.Y. 8 June '61; Col. 79th N.Y. 28 Dec. '61; mustered out 17 Feb. '63; Maj. Vet. Res. Corps 13 Aug. '63; Col. 29 Sept. '63; Bvt. B.G. USV 27 Sept. '65 (war service); resigned 10 Dec. '64. Commanded 4, 2, Dept. of the South. Died 1877.

FARNSWORTH, Elon John. Union gen. 1837-63. Mich. On Johnston's 1857-58 Utah Expedition he hurried home to join his uncle's (J. F. Farnsworth) regiment, the 8th Ill. Cav., as 1st Lt. Regt. Adj. 18 Sept. '61. Said never to have missed a battle or skirmish with the regiment during the rest of his service, he participated in 41 (D.A.B.). Promoted Capt. 25 Dec. '61, he was Acting Chief Q.M. of the IV Corps and in the spring of 1863 Pleasonton's A.D.C. He was named B.G. USV 29 June '63. During the Gettysburg campaign his command (1, 3, Cav., Potomac 28 June–3 July '63) was sent up after Stuart and then fought at Little Round Top. On the third day of the battle he received orders from Kilpatrick to charge the enemy. Farnsworth protested that conditions were unfavorable for such a cavalry maneuver: uneven ground and the enemy behind walls. Overruled, he led his troops in one of the bravest as well as one of the most disastrous charges of the entire war, receiving five mortal wounds.

FARNSWORTH, John Franklin. Union gen. 1820-97. Canada. A Democratic politician, he became an abolitionist and served as Republican Congressman 1856-60. Raising the 8th Ill. Cav. (Col. 18 Sept. '61) and leading his regiment in the Peninsular and Antietam campaigns, he was severely injured at the end of 1862. He commanded 1st Brig., Pleasonton's cavalry (Nov. '62–Jan. '63) and 2d Brig., Cav. Div. (Sept.–Nov. '63). He resigned 4 Mar. '63 to take the congressional seat he had won the previous fall, and held it until 1873, becoming one of the first Radicals. He was a leader in Johnson's impeachment and enthusiastically championed the Emancipation Proclamation and the Thirteenth Amendment. Uncle of Elon John Farnsworth.

FARNUM, John Egbert. Union officer. 1824-70. N.J. Maj. 70th N.Y. 27 June '61; Lt. Col. 29 June '61; Col. 14 Jan. '63; mustered out 1 July '64; Col. Vet. Res. Corps. 26 July '64; Bvt. B.G. USV 3 Jan. '66 (war service). Commanded 2, 2, III. W.I.A. Williamsburg 5 May '62. Serving in the Mexican War as an enlisted man, he also participated in the Lopez expedition to Cuba and Walker's Nicaraguan expeditions and had been indicted as a slaver in Savannah.

FARRAGUT, David Glasgow. Union admiral. 1801-70. Tenn. He entered the navy as Midshipman in 1810 after having been virtually adopted by Commodore David Porter. The friendship between the two families began when Porter's father was buried on the same day as Farragut's mother in New Orleans two years previous. At 12 years of age he was prize master of a ship captured in the Pacific by Porter during the War of

1812. He was sent back to school for a time, sailed in the Mediterranean, and then returned to his books, this time in Tunis. Serving in the West Indies and the South Atlantic, he fought in the Mexican War, and was awaiting orders at his home in Norfolk during the secession crisis. Told that a person with Union sentiments could not live in Va., he packed up his Virginia-born wife (his second, the first also being a Norfolk girl) and son and moved to the North. He was given command of the NEW ORLEANS expedition in Dec. '61 and sailed from Hampton Roads in Feb. '62. Promoted Rear Admiral 16 July '62 for his success in opening up the Mississippi to Vicksburg, he spent the next year in operations against Port Hudson and returned to N.Y.C. in Aug. '63 to a hero's welcome. He returned to the Gulf in Jan. '64 to prepare for the assault on MOBILE BAY, took the port on 5 Aug., and again returned in Dec. '64 to N.Y.C., this time in failing health. The city gave him a public reception and $50,000 to purchase a home there, and on 23 Dec. '64 he was promoted Vice Admiral, the rank having been established the previous day. He was one of the first Northerners to enter Richmond after it fell. Promoted Admiral on 25 July '66, he was the first in the US Navy to hold this rank.

FARRAR, Bernard Gains. Union officer. Mo. Maj. A.D.C. Mo. State Troops 12 May–27 July '61; Col. A.D.C. Mo. State Troops 4 Dec. '61–6 Sept. '62; Col. 30th Mo. 29 Oct. '62; Col. 6th US Col. Arty. 21 Jan. '64; Bvt. B.G. USV 9 Mar. '65. Commanded 1, 1, XV.

FASCINE. A long cylindrical bundle of brush or stakes bound tightly together and used in constructing REVETMENTS or to fill in ditches and depressions as a hasty bridge.

FAUNTLEROY, Thomas T. Va. State gen. 1795–1883. Va. A Lt. in the War of 1812, he practiced law before returning to the army in 1836. He served in the Mexican War and in Indian fighting before resigning in 1861 as Col. 1st US Dragoons. Offering his services to the Confederacy, he was not accepted, but was named B.G. of Va. state troops (*Lee's Lts.*, I, 722), but had been "found too old for Confederate service or too proud to accept the assignment given him and, at his own request, had been relieved of command as a Virginia Brigadier General" (*ibid.*, 261, citing O.R. I, V, 807).

FEARING, Benjamin Dana. Union officer. 1837–81. Ohio. Pvt. 2d Ohio 17 Apr.–9 Aug. '61; Maj. 77th Ohio 17 Dec. '61; Lt. Col. 92d Ohio 14 Sept. '62; Col. 14 Apr. '63; Bvt. B.G. USV 2 Dec. '64 (Chattanooga-to-Atlanta campaign, Atlanta-to-Savannah campaign). W.I.A. Chickamauga and Bentonville. With a Philadelphia publishing house before the war, he later engaged in manufacturing in Cincinnati.

FEATHERSTON, Winfield Scott. C.S.A. gen. 1819–91. Tenn. A lawyer, he fought in the Creek Indian War, and was Democratic Congressman from Miss. before becoming Col. 17th Miss. He fought on the Peninsula as B.G. C.S.A. (6 Mar. '62 to rank from the 4th) and led Featherston's brigade in the 4th Div. Serving under Anderson at Fredericksburg, he was sent to Vicksburg in 1863 at his own request but was not captured there. In the Atlanta campaign under Johnston he commanded his own brigade, led Loring's division temporarily, and returned to his brigade at Franklin and Nashville. After the war he was a legislator and jurist.

FEINT. A show of force to mislead the enemy. It normally involves a limited objective attack by a small portion of the total force. A demonstration, on the other hand, has the same purpose but differs in that no actual attack is made.

FENTON, Reuben Eaton. Gov. of New York. 1819–85. N.Y. A logger and lumberman as a young man, he entered politics as a Democrat, sitting in the legislature and Congress before his antislavery sentiments made him leave the party. He was one of the N.Y. founders of the Republican party, was elected to Congress again, and chosen Gov. in 1864, defeating Horatio Seymour. Reelected in 1866, he went into the Senate in 1869 and was later a banker.

FERGUSON, Samuel Wragg. C.S.A. gen. c. 1835–1917. S.C. USMA 1857 (19/38); Dragoons. He served on the Utah Expedition and in the Washington Territory before resigning 1 Mar. '61 as 2d Lt. to join the Confederacy. Appointed B.G. C.S.A. 23 July '63 from Miss., he commanded his cavalry brigade in Polk's Corps in the Atlanta campaign. After the war he was a lawyer and public office holder in Miss. He is listed as a general officer by Wright and Wood but not by C.M.H.

FERNANDINA, Fla., 4 Mar. '62. Occupied by US Marines from *Pawnee* on the 4th and by H. G. Wright's brigade on the 5th.

FERRERO, Edward. Union gen. 1831–99. Spain. Continuing the dancing school established by his Italian father in N.Y.C. and teaching the West Point cadets, he was also active in the state militia and was a Lt. Col. by 1861, when he was commissioned Col. 51st N.Y. (14 Oct.). He led his regiment during the winter of 1861–62 at Roanoke Island and New Bern and commanded 2d Brig., 2d Div., N.C. (2 Apr.–6 July '62). He commanded 2, 2, IX, Potomac (22 July '62–Feb. '63 and Mar.–19 Mar. '63) at 2d Bull Run, Chantilly, South Mountain, Antietam,

and Fredericksburg. He was promoted B.G. USV 10 Sept. '62, but his commission expired 4 Mar. '63. Also in the Army of the Potomac, he led 2d Div., IX (7 Feb.–6 Mar. '63). Transferring to the West, he commanded 2, 2, IX, Ohio (18 Mar.–Apr. '63 and 5 June.–22 Aug. '63) and 2, 2, IX, Tenn. (14 June–18 Aug. '63) at Vicksburg, having been reappointed B.G. USV 6 May '63. At Knoxville he commanded 1st Div., IX, Ohio (18 Aug. '63–19 Apr. '64). He is, however, best known for his part in the Petersburg Mine Explosion, 30 July '64. His command, a Negro division (4, IX, Potomac), was selected by Burnside to lead the assault into the Crater. After they had been drilled some weeks for this role, Meade canceled the order, and Grant concurred. In an unbelievable multiplication of errors the division was sent into the breach after the Confederates were able to recover from their surprise and confusion and set up heavy fire between the Union trenches and the Crater. And, as Catton says (*A Stillness at Appomattox*), citing O.R.: "As the men advanced General Ferrero dropped off in the same bombproof that housed General Ledlie and borrowed a swig of his jug of rum, leaving his brigadiers to direct the fight." He was blamed for his part in the debacle, having "exercised little control over his troops and left them to fight practically uncommanded" (D.A.B.). The same criticism was made of him at Knoxville, where his division made a charge without any orders from him. Breveted Maj. Gen. USV 2 Dec. '64 for Petersburg and Richmond campaigns, he also commanded 3, IX, Potomac (13 Sept.–9 Oct. '64, 25 Oct.–15 Dec. '64); 1, IX, Potomac (11 Apr.–18 Aug. '63). He was mustered out 24 Aug. '65 and later managed several large ballrooms in N.Y., including Tammany Hall, although he was not in politics.

FERRY, Orris Sanford. Union gen. 1823-75. Conn. He was judge, state Sen., and US Representative (1858-60) as a Republican before the war. Commissioned Col. 5th Conn. 23 July '61, he served in the Shenandoah Valley campaign and was then promoted B.G. USV 17 Mar. '62. He commanded 2d Div. St. Helena Island, XVIII, South (Jan.-6 Mar. '63); 1st Div. St. Helena Island, XVIII, South (5 Mar.-17 Apr. '63); Seabrook Island, X, South (16 Apr.-11 May '63); and 3d Div., X, James (19 June-27 Aug. '64). He was breveted Maj. Gen. USV 23 May '65 for Peninsular campaign and Army of Potomac service and resigned 15 June '65. Characterized as the worst possible radical, his election to the US Senate in 1866 was, apparently, somewhat less than fair. Once he took office, however, he voted moderately until the impeachment proceedings when he voted for Johnson's conviction and filed an opinion on the case.

FESSENDEN, Francis. Union gen. 1839-1906. Me. Son of Lincoln's Sec. of the Treasury and brother of James Deering Fessenden, he graduated from Bowdoin and Harvard and practiced law. Commissioned Capt. 19th US Inf. 14 May '61 (assigned to the R.A. by Cameron), he spent the first part of the war in routine garrison service, finally fighting with his regiment under Buell at Shiloh, where he was wounded. Promoted Col. 25th Me. 29 Sept. '62, he was quartered (Mar.-July '63) around Centreville, where his younger brother Samuel had been killed the year before. During this time he commanded 1, Casey's division, XXII, Washington (2 Feb.-17 Apr. '63) and 1, Abercrombie's division, XXII, Washington (18 Apr.-28 June '63). He was mustered out 10 July '63 and recommissioned Col. 30th Me. 11 Jan. '64. During the Red River campaign he led an assault at Monett's

Bluff 23 Apr. '64, while commanding 3, 1, XIX (15 Feb.-29 Mar. and 9-22 Apr. '64), and lost his right leg. Appointed B.G. USV 10 May '64, he was engaged in administrative work until May '64, when he commanded 1st Brig., 2d Div. Inf., W. Va., and 1st Div. Inf., W. Va. He was promoted Maj. Gen. USV 9 Nov. '65 and, continuing in the R.A., was breveted for Shiloh, Monett's Bluff, and war service (B.G. and Maj. Gen. USA). Retiring as B.G. USA in 1866, he returned to the law, showing little interest in politics. His biography of his father was published posthumously in 1907.

FESSENDEN, James Deering. Union gen. 1833-82. Me. A lawyer, he was commissioned Capt. 2d US Sharpshooters 2 Nov. '61 and promoted Col. Add. A.D.C. on Gen. Hunter's staff in the Carolinas 16 July '62. D.A.B. credits him with having ". . . organized and disciplined the first regiment of colored soldiers in the national service, although Gen. Hunter's action was afterward disallowed, and the regiment disbanded." He served during the siege of Charleston but was seriously injured by a fall from his horse and transferred to Mustering and Disbursing in the summer of 1863. The following Sept. he rejoined Hunter and served at Lookout Mountain, Missionary Ridge, Resaca, New Hope Church, Kenesaw Mountain and Peach Tree Creek in the Atlanta campaign. Promoted B.G. USV 8 Aug. '64, he joined the Army of the Shenandoah and fought at Winchester 19 Sept. His commands, all in the Shenandoah, were 2, 1, XIX (26 Oct.-1 Nov. '64); 3, 1, XIX (1 Nov. '64-20 Mar. '65); 3, 1st Prov. Div. (Mar.-Apr. '65). He was later a lawyer and legislator. He was the son of W. P. Fessenden, Lincoln's Sec. of Treasury in 1864, and brother of Francis Fessenden, Maj. Gen. USV.

FESSENDEN, William Pitt. Union Sec. of the Treasury. 1806–69. N.H. After graduating from Bowdoin College he practiced law and served in the legislature and US Congress. He left the Whig party to organize the Republicans and was sent to the US Senate by the anti-slavery element. Here he made his reputation as a debater and expert on public finance, and he served as Lincoln's Sec. of the Treasury from June '64 to Mar. '65. Re-elected to the Senate, he was chairman of the joint committee on Reconstruction and authored most of the group's famous report. However, his actions during the impeachment proceedings labeled him a conservative Radical and made him, for a time, unpopular with his constituency. Father of Francis and James D. Fessenden, Union generals.

FIELD, Charles William. C.S.A. gen. 1828–92. Ky. USMA 1849 (27/43); Dragoons. He served on the frontier and instructed cavalry at West Point before resigning 30 May '61 as Capt. Commissioned in the same rank in the C.S.A. cavalry, he served under Jeb Stuart until 9 Mar. '62, when he was appointed B.G. C.S.A. and given an infantry brigade. This he commanded in fighting during McDowell's advance on Fredericksburg and in the Seven Days' Battles, Cedar Mountain, and 2d Bull Run, where he was wounded in the hips. He never entirely recovered. After a long convalescence he was promoted Maj. Gen. 12 Feb. '64 and led Hood's Tex. division under Longstreet at the Wilderness, Cold Harbor, Deep Bottom, and the Petersburg siege. He surrendered at Appomattox. He was in business in Baltimore and Georgia until 1875. In that year he accepted a commission in the Khedive's army and returned to the US to serve as doorkeeper in the US House of Representatives 1878–81. He was also a civil engineer. D.A.B. describes him as being of "vigorous intellect and indomitable will, of superb physique."

FIFTEEN SLAVE ("Nigger") LAW. Exempted from military service one white man for every plantation of 15 or more slaves. Purpose was to assure an adequate number of overseers, but the law caused ill feeling because it favored the wealthier Southerners. Prior to this there had been a Twenty Slave Law.

"FIFTH WHEEL." See SANITARY COMMISSION.

FIGHTING JOE HOOKER. See Joseph HOOKER for origin of nickname.

FIGHTING McCOOKS. See McCOOKS OF OHIO.

"FIGHT IT OUT ON THIS LINE IF IT TAKES ALL SUMMER." Phrase in a communication from Grant to Halleck on 11 May '64, written at Spotsylvania, illustrating Grant's determination to continue to move on Richmond despite tremendous casualties and little apparent success.

FINEGAN, Joseph. C.S.A. gen. 1814–85. Appt.-Fla. A lawyer, he was named to head his state's military affairs by Gov. Milton in early 1861. Appt. B.G. C.S.A. 5 Apr. '62, he commanded the Dept. of Middle and Eastern Fla. He fought at Olustee and remained in the state until sent to Va. with his brigade in May '64. There he led his forces at Cold Harbor and in the Petersburg siege, returning to Fla. 20 Mar. '65. He was a lawyer again after the war.

FINLEY, Clement Alexander. Union officer. Ohio. Joining the R.A. as Surgeon's Mate in 1818, he served in the Mexican War and on the frontier before being promoted Col. and Surgeon Gen. USA in May '61. He was retired in Apr. '62 for disability and was breveted B.G. USA in 1865. He died 1879.

FINLEY, Jesse Johnson. C.S.A. gen. 1812–1904. Tenn. After Lebanon Law School he practiced law, fought in the Seminole War, and sat in the Ark. legislature. Later the Mayor of Memphis, he moved to Fla., taking an active part in Whig politics and serving as legislator and judge. Appointed in 1861 Judge of the C.S.A. courts, he resigned in Mar. '62 to enlist as a private in the 6th Fla. Later elected Capt., he was promoted Col. 14 Apr. '62 and fought in Kirby Smith's Kentucky campaign. Upon his return to Knoxville he was president of the departmental court-martial until ordered to Tullahoma. He commanded his regiment under Trigg at Chickamauga and was appointed B.G. C.S.A. 16 Nov. '63. Taking command of a Fla. brigade in the Army of Tenn., he led it through the Atlanta campaign, fighting at Missionary Ridge, Resaca, where he was wounded, and the battles around Atlanta until Jonesboro, where his horse was shot from under him and he was seriously wounded. Upon his recovery he tried to rejoin his brigade in N.C. but was unable to get past Sherman's forces, so he linked up with Cobb at Columbus instead. After the war he sat in the US Congress and Senate.

FIRE-EATER. A. S. Johnston's horse. A thoroughbred bay of magnificent proportions which the general was riding when he was mortally wounded at Shiloh.

"FIRE-EATERS." Extremist Southern politicians whose violent advocacy of secession and complete animosity to abolition reacted against them after the formation of the Confederacy, and they were not given important governmental positions. Among their leaders were Edmund RUFFIN, William L. YANCEY, and R. B. RHETT.

FIRE ZOUAVES. See Elmer ELLSWORTH and 11TH NEW YORK.

FISER, John C. C.S.A. officer. As Lt. Col. he commanded the 17th Miss. in Barksdale's brigade at Antietam and Fredericksburg. At the latter battle he also had 10 sharpshooters from the 13th Miss. and three companies of the 18th Miss. His command was in rifle pits above the bridge site on the Confederate left. During the assaults he was knocked down and stunned by a falling wall but, regaining consciousness as his men tried to carry him from the field, he held his post doggedly, cheering his troops on. He led them also at Gettysburg and Knoxville, where he lost an arm during the storming of Fort Sanders.

FISHER, Benjamin Franklin. Union officer. Pa. 1st Lt. 3d Pa. Res. 18 June '61; Capt. 8 July '62; Maj. Sig. Corps 3 Mar. '63; Col. Chief Signal Officer 3 Dec. '64; Bvt. B.G. USV (war service).

FISHER, Joseph Washington. Union officer. Pa. Lt. Col. 5th Pa. Res. 21 June '61; Col. 1 July '62; mustered out 11 June '64; Col. 195th Pa. 24 July '64; mustered out 4 Nov. '64; Col. 195th Pa. 12 Mar. '65; Bvt. B.G. USV 4 Nov. '65 (war service). Died 1900.

FISHERS HILL, Va., 22 Sept. '64. (SHENANDOAH VALLEY CAMPAIGN OF SHERIDAN) After his defeat at WINCHESTER, 19 Sept., Early withdrew up the Valley and occupied a strong natural position at Fishers Hill, overlooking Strasburg. He had been considerably weakened by his loss of troops and commanders at Winchester, and was further weakened when Breckinridge was ordered away. To stretch his meager forces along the four-mile front along Tumbling Run between the North Fork of the Shenandoah and Little North Mountain, Early dismounted the cavalry of Lomax, and placed them on his left. Continuing from left to right were the divisions of Ramseur, Pegram, Gordon, and Wharton (O. R. Atlas LXXXII, 11).

To avoid a frontal assault up the steep and heavily wooded ridge, Sheridan's plan was for Crook to work his way secretly into position to attack the flank from Little North Mountain. There has been controversy as to whether this plan originated with Sheridan or Crook. The flank march took the entire day of the 22d, but Crook's attack just before sunset achieved surprise and routed Lomax. Meanwhile the VI and XIX Corps had been advancing frontally to occupy the enemy's attention. They now assaulted frontally. Ricketts (3, VI) soon linked up with Crook's enveloping forces, and the remainder of the VI and the XIX Corps, "taking up the charge, descended into the ravine of Tumbling Run, with a headlong rush over fields, walls, rocks, and felled trees. Making their way across the brook, they were soon scrambling up heights that it had seemed

madness to attack, while Sheridan and his admirable staff were on every part of the line, shouting 'Forward! Forward everything!' and to all inquiries for instructions the reply was still, 'Go on, don't stop, go on!'" (Pond, 177.)

Federal losses at Fishers Hill were 528, of whom only 52 were killed (O'Connor, 210), whereas Early reported a loss of 1,235 in the infantry and artillery. Confederate cavalry losses were not reported, but light. Sheridan reported taking 1,100 prisoners. In attempting to cover the retreat, some of the artillery stayed in position too long and lost 12 guns. "Sandie" Pendleton was mortally wounded while trying to establish a new line, and left to die in Federal hands.

FISK, Clinton Bowen. Union gen. 1828–90. N.Y. A banker in Mich. and a friend of Grant and Lincoln, he had been ruined by the Panic of 1857 and was in St. Louis when the war began. He was named Col. 33d Mo. 5 Sept. and B.G. USV 24 Nov. '62, after having

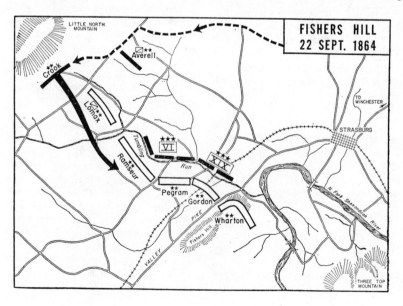

served in the Home Guard and seizing Camp Jackson 9 May '61. He commanded 13th Div., XIII, Tenn. (22 Jan.–8 Feb. '63) and 2, 13, XIII, Tenn. (8 Feb.–10 June '63) as well as the Dists. of Southeast Mo. (20 July–20 Nov. '63), Northern Mo. (10 June '64–24 May '65), and St. Louis (30 Nov. '63–25 Mar. '64). He was breveted Maj. Gen. for war service and appointed to the Freedman's Bureau because, as Johnson said, "Fisk ain't a fool, he won't hang everybody" (D.A.B.). Finding a cause and a purpose there, he opened in 1866, in an abandoned army barrack at Nashville, a Negro school chartered the next year as Fisk University. He was president of the Board of Indian Commissioners 1881–90 and, with an "aversion to drink and profanity" and as "an ardent Methodist" (D.A.B.), Prohibition party presidential candidate in 1888.

FISK, Henry C. Union officer. N.Y. 1st Sgt. 67th N.Y. 24 July '61; 2d Lt. 15 Oct. '61; Capt. 2 June '62; transferred to 65th N.Y. 4 July '64; Lt. Col. 2 Dec. '64; Col. 20 June '65; Bvt. B.G. USV 6 Apr. '65. Brevets for Petersburg (2), Sayler's Creek.

FISKE, Francis Skinner. Union officer. N.H. Lt. Col. 2d N.H. 27 May '61; Bvt. B.G. USV (war service); resigned 23 Oct. '62.

FISKE, William Oscar. Union officer. Mass. Appt.-La. Capt. 31st Mass. 1 Jan. '62; mustered out 8 May '62; Maj. 1st La. 18 Aug. '62; Lt. Col. 6 Feb. '63; Col. 18 Aug. '63; Bvt. B.G. USV (Port Hudson Siege). W.I.A. in leg, Irish Bend (La.) 12 Apr. '63. Died 1886.

FITZHUGH, Charles Lane. Union officer. N.Y. R.A. 1st Lt. 4th US Arty. 24 Oct. '61; Col. 6th N.Y. Cav. 18 Feb. '65; transfered to 2d N.Y. Prov. Cav. 17 June '65; Bvt. B.G. USV.

Brevets for Shiloh, Five Forks (Va.), Smithfield (Va.), war service. Commanded 2, 1, Cav. Corps, Army of the Potomac. Ex-cadet USMA 1863. A.D.C. to Gen. D. C. Buell '61–'63.

FITZ SIMMONS, Charles. Union officer. N.Y. Capt. 3d N.Y. Cav. 1 July '61; Maj. 12 May '62; mustered out 11 June '63; Lt. Col. 21st N.Y. Cav. 18 Sept. 63; Bvt. B.G. USV (war service). Commanded 1st Brig., Cav. Div. (W. Va.).

FIVE FORKS, Va., 30 Mar.–1 Apr. '65. (APPOMATTOX CAMPAIGN)

On 29 March Sheridan, who had just returned to the Army of the Potomac from his successful Shenandoah campaign and his raid in northern Va., led Merritt's three cavalry divisions (13,-000) from an assembly area near Globe Tavern, across Rowanty Creek at Malone Bridge, and toward Dinwiddie Courthouse. Sheridan's maneuver, together with a simultaneous advance of II and V Corps against the Confederate right, was planned to turn the Confederates out of their Petersburg defenses. Having anticipated such an attempt, Lee promptly dispatched Pickett with 19,000 infantry and cavalry toward Five Forks. The Confederates had to hold this place in order to use the Southside R.R. in the contemplated movement to join forces with J. E. Johnston in N.C.

Munford's cavalry located the Federals near Dinwiddie Courthouse on 30 Mar., where they had been halted by heavy rains. The next day the Federal cavalry had moved about three miles toward Five Forks when they were hit on the west flank by Pickett and driven slowly back toward the courthouse. Warren's V Corps, some three miles to the east, was also pushed back by another Confederate counterattack. At about 5 P.M. Warren ordered Bartlett's brigade (3, 1, V) to Sheridan's support. During the afternoon and evening various orders and counter-orders were issued to get reinforcements to Sheridan, who was believed to be in danger of defeat in detail. Sheridan, on the other hand, saw the situation as one favoring the defeat of Pickett's isolated force.

Ranald Mackenzie's small but excellent cavalry brigade joined Sheridan the evening of the 31st, and by 8 A.M. the next day Warren had reported with his three divisions. Learning of these reinforcements, Pickett started withdrawing to Five Forks.

There was a three-mile gap between Pickett and the main Confederate defenses to the east. Pickett screened this gap with the under-strength cavalry brigade of William P. Roberts and a regiment of dismounted cavalry from Munford's division. He covered his other flank with W. H. F. Lee's cavalry division. The Confederate infantry brigades, from east to west, were dug in along White Oak Road as follows: Ransom, Wallace, "Maryland" Steuart, Mayo (Terry's brigade), and Corse. The eastern end of this line of infantry was "refused" so that the last 100 yards formed a hook or "return." (Most Federal accounts [e.g., Humphreys; B.&L.] have the positions of Ransom and Wallace reversed; according to Freeman, Ransom was on the flank.)

Sheridan's cavalry (the divisions of Custer on the west, and Devin, both under Merritt) maintained pressure and drove the Confederates back to their entrenchments. Due to the difficult nature of the terrain, all but Custer's two left brigades were fighting on foot. Mackenzie's cavalry was given the mission of striking the White Oak Road about three miles east of Five Forks and then driving west along this road to rejoin the main body. "Little Phil," meanwhile, was chafing at the delays in forming Warren's corps for the decisive maneuver.

With two divisions abreast and one in reserve Warren's corps was to move northwest from Gravelly Run Church and crush the enemy's east flank while Merritt's cavalry feinted at their opposite flank. About 4 P.M. the long-delayed attack moved out. Since the enemy line did not extend so far to the east as expected, the initial Federal blow landed in the air; they had crossed the White Oak Road against nothing but light musket fire and were continuing on their original axis of advance when the division of Ayres, on the left, was brought under a sudden and heavy enfilade fire. Ayres changed front and answered the fire coming from the Confederates' refused flank, or "return."

Since the Federal attack had hit almost 800 yards too far to the east, there had to be some rapid changes of disposition. Sheridan, who had accompanied Ayres, ordered the other two divisions swung around so that Crawford (who had been on Ayres's right) and Griffin (who had been following to the right rear of Crawford) would form on Ayres's right. A dangerous gap developed, but by the time Crawford and Griffin were turned in the right direction, Ayres had crushed the Confederate left and was forming to roll up their flank. The other two divisions then hit the Confederate rear. Mayo's brigade was pulled back to counter this threat, and he was reinforced by the withdrawing elements of Wallace's and Ransom's brigades from the east flank. Steuart, Corse, and W. H. F. Lee held their positions until the Federal attack began to push back the Confederate forces at their rear. Corse was ordered to form a new line running north and south to his original position in order to cover the Confederate withdrawal.

Federal cavalry had clashed with W. H. F. Lee on the west flank earlier in the afternoon, but the latter had been able to maintain his position. Col. Fitzhugh's brigade (Devin) charged the Five Forks road junction after Mayo had withdrawn past that position, "capturing the three guns, two battle-flags and over a thousand of the enemy" (Humphreys, 351). Mackenzie had reached Hatcher's Run and then taken a position on the Ford road that blocked this direct route of enemy retreat.

Pickett and Fitzhugh Lee were north of Hatcher's Run at a shad bake with Rosser (who was in reserve) when the battle started (see *Lee's Lts.,* III, 665–70). Pickett ran a gantlet of enemy musket fire to reach Five Forks after the battle was under way, but Fitz Lee was forced to remain with Rosser. Although Pickett is generally condemned for making a stand at Five Forks, it was R. E. Lee who ordered him to hold this vital point (*ibid.,* 661–62). Pickett and Fitz Lee, however, failed to understand "the dread immediacy of the crisis" (*ibid.,* 665), and are guilty of tactical errors.

Federal accounts (e.g., Humphreys; B.&L., IV, 708ff) appear to exaggerate Confederate numbers and losses in this action. D. S. Freeman estimates Pickett's force at less than 10,000, and puts his losses in prisoners at about 5,200 (3,244 taken by Warren; up to 2,000 taken by the cavalry). Warren's troops took 11 flags, one gun, and sustained 634 casualties. Among the dead were Frederick Winthrop, Bvt. B.G. USV, and William Johnson Pegram, Col. C.S.A. Warren was relieved by the fiery Sheridan for lack of aggressiveness in the battle. (See WARREN COURT OF INQUIRY.)

FIXED AMMUNITION. When the projectile is fixed so as to form a single unit with the propelling charge,

igniter, and primer, the entire unit is known as a round of fixed ammunition.

FLAGS, Confed. The "Stars and Bars," first of four Confederate flags, consisted of two horizontal red stripes separated by a white one and seven white stars in a circle on a blue field. It was designed by Prof. Nicola Marschall in Feb. '61, adopted 4 Mar., and raised the same day at the Confederate Capitol (then in Montgomery, Ala.) by the granddaughter of Pres. John Tyler. The more familiar Battle Flag, often referred to erroneously as the Stars and Bars, was designed by Beauregard to avoid battlefield confusion between Marschall's flag and the Stars and Stripes; it was adopted after 1st Bull Run. This flag was red with a blue St. Andrew's cross on which 13 white stars were superimposed. The "National Flag" was adopted 1 May '63 to replace the Stars and Bars; it was white with the Battle Flag in the upper right quarter. On 4 Mar. '65 a fourth flag was adopted when a broad vertical red bar was added to the edge of National Flag of 1863 so that, when furled, it would not show only white (C.M.H., XII, plate facing p. 369; and correspondence between the author and O. C. Costlow, a descendant of Marschall).

Captured Confed. battle flags were returned to the South in 1905, during Theodore Roosevelt's administration. A War Department order of 7 June '87 for their return was approved by Cleveland but revoked 15 June as the result of popular opposition led by organized Union veterans' groups. (For an example of the latter hostile sentiment, see FAIRCHILD, Lucius.)

FLANAGIN, Harris. C.S.A. Gov. of Ark. 1817–74. N.J. Moving West as a boy, he was a lawyer and legislator in Ark. before being commissioned Capt. of the 2d Ark. Mtd. Rifles in 1861. Shortly elected Col., he resigned to become Gov. 15 Nov. '62, succeeding Rector, and served until Isaac Murphy was elected to the post in 1864. After the war he was a lawyer and held several minor public offices.

FLANIGAN, Mark. Union officer. Ireland. Lt. Col. 24th Mich. 15 Aug '62; Bvt. B.G. USV (Gettysburg); discharged 21 Nov. '63. W.I.A. Gettysburg, losing a leg. Died 1886.

FLANKING POSITION. A form of defense in which the defender takes up a position so located that the enemy will expose his flanks or line of communications if he continues his advance. A good flanking position must have these characteristics: strong defensive terrain; protection for one's own line of communications; the possibility of sallying forth to attack the enemy if he does try to ignore the position and continue his advance. The defender must have sufficient strength so that the attacker cannot contain him with part of his force while he continues to his original objective. Jackson's position at Swift Run Gap at the start of his SHENANDOAH VALLEY CAMPAIGN was an excellent flanking position.

FLEETWOOD (HILL), Va., 9 June '63. See BRANDY STATION, same date.

FLEMING, Rufus Edward. Union officer. Va. Pvt. Co. G 6th W. Va. 25 June '61; 2d Lt. 1 Aug. '62; Capt. 23 Sept. '62; Lt. Col. 30 Oct. '64; Bvt. B.G. USV (war service).

FLETCHER, Thomas. C.S.A. Gov. of Ark. 1817–74. Tenn. A lawyer and politician, he did not move to Ark. until 1850, and then sat in the legislature when, as president of the Senate, he was interim Gov. from the resignation of Rector on 4 Nov. '62, until Flanagin was chosen in a special election on the 15th of that month. He practiced law and was a legislator after the war.

FLETCHER, Thomas Clement. Union officer. 1827–99. Mo. Col. 31st Mo. 7 Oct. '62; resigned 16 June '64; Col. 47th Mo. 17 Sept. '64; Bvt. B.G. USV (Pilot Knob, Mo.); resigned 18 Nov. '64. W.I.A. and captured Chickasaw Bayou. An early supporter of Lincoln, Fletcher was a lawyer and Gov. of Mo. 1865–69.

FLOOD, Martin. Union officer. Mass. Capt. 3d Wis. 29 June '61; Maj. 4 May '63; Lt. Col. 31 May '63; Maj. Vet. Res. Corps 4 Dec. '63; Lt. Col. 20 Jan. '64; Bvt. B.G. USV (war service).

FLORIDA seceded on 10 Jan. '61. After the operations around PENSACOLA BAY, OLUSTEE (20 Feb. '64) was the only important battle fought in the state. Its ports and coast line were blockaded during the entire conflict. The state re-entered the Union on 25 June '68.

FLORIDA, The. Confederate ship commanded by Commodore Maffitt that was procured from the British in 1862 and outfitted at Nassau. She ran the blockade into Mobile and four months later left on a raid that was to carry her from N.Y. to the Brazilian coast. This continued until Oct. '64, when she was captured, in violation of international law, by the Federal *Wachusett* off Bahía and towed to Hampton Roads where she was sunk. According to Fox, the *Florida* captured or destroyed 37 vessels. See ALABAMA CLAIMS.

FLORIDA EXPEDITION (1864). See OLUSTEE, Fla. 20 Feb. '64.

FLORIDA, Middle and Eastern, Confed. Dept. of. On 11 Mar. '61 Bragg was assigned command of troops in Fla., although this was not designated a department until 21 Aug., when J. B. Grayson was assigned command. The O.R. atlas plates show no line separating this department and the Dept. of S.C., Ga., and Fla. Orders assigning Kirby Smith to command of the department 10 Oct. were revoked and J. H. Trapier assigned 22 Oct. '61. He was again assigned 14 Mar. '62 and succeeded on the 19th by W. S. Dilworth.

On 7 Apr. '62 the department came under the authority of Pemberton's Dept. of S.C. and Ga. It continues to be shown in the O.R. atlas, however, as a separate department. Joseph Finegan was assigned 8 Apr. and took command ten days later (O.R., I, VI; and XIV, 1). On 7 Oct. '62 it became part of the Dept. of S.C. and Ga. (now under Beauregard) (*ibid.*, 2).

FLORIDA, UNION DEPARTMENT OF. Prior to 11 Apr. '61 the entire state was in the Department of the East. Until 11 Jan. '62, the entire state was in the Dept. of Fla. with headquarters near Pensacola (Fort Pickens); after that date the Dept. of Key West was created to include Key West, the Tortugas, and the mainland on the west coast as far as Appalachicola and to Cape Canaveral on the east coast. From 15 Mar.–8 Aug. '62, the entire state was in the Dept. of the South. West Fla. then went to the Dept. of the Gulf; the remainder of the state stayed in the Dept. of the South. From 16 Mar. '63–10 Feb. '65 Key West, the Tortugas, and West Fla. were in the Dept. of the Gulf, the remainder in the Dept. of the South. From 10 Feb.–17 May '65 Key West, the Tortugas, and West Fla. were in the Div. of West. Miss.

FLORIDA WARS. See SEMINOLE WARS.

FLOYD, John Buchanan. C.S.A. gen. 1806–63. Va. After graduating from S.C. College he was a lawyer and cotton planter in Ark. Serving in the legislature and as states-rights Democratic Gov., he was Buchanan's Sec. of War from 1857 until 29 Dec. '60. During this time he had disputed the choice of J. E. John-

ston as Q.M. Gen. with Jefferson Davis, the future president, believing that A. S. Johnston should have been given the post. He was accused in the North of concentrating guns in the Southern arsenals in anticipation of their capture by Confederate forces. Raising a brigade, he was appointed B.G. C.S.A. 23 May '61 and served in W. Va. at Cross Lanes and Carnifex Ferry. Going to the West, he was sent to Ft. Donelson. When loss of this place appeared imminent, he turned command over to Buckner and escaped. Davis relieved him from command for this 11 Mar. '62, and he was appointed Maj. Gen. of the Va. State Line by the legislature 17 May '62. His health was broken down by prolonged exposure, and he died 26 Aug. '63.

FLYING TELEGRAPH TRAIN. A system of battlefield SIGNAL COMMUNICATIONS developed by A. J. MYER and using the BEARDSLEE TELEGRAPH.

FLYNN, John. Union officer. Ireland. 1st Lt. Adj. 28th Pa. 10 July '61; Capt. 12 Nov. '61; Lt. Col. 17 Dec. '61; Col. 9 June '64; Bvt. B.G. USV (war service). Commanded 1, 2, XX. Died 1875.

FOGG, George Gilman. Union statesman. 1813–81. One of the founders of the Republican party, he was Minister to Switzerland during Civil War. He was also interested in the Free-Soil party and was most famous as journalist.

FOGG, Isabella. SANITARY COMMISSION worker. Me. When her son enlisted in the summer of 1861, she became a nurse with a Me. regiment in Annapolis and later in hospitals in Washington. During the Peninsular campaign she worked on the Sanitary Commission hospital boat *Elm City* and during the Seven Days' Battles established a field hospital at Savage's Station. Rejoining the army after a rest in Me., she began after Antietam to work in hospitals again and was at Fredericksburg. She also nursed at Chancellorsville, Gettysburg, the Mine Run operations, and the Wilderness. Her son was seriously wounded at Cedar Run, and she collapsed from overwork after nursing him to health. In Nov. '64 she was sent to the hospital in Louisville (Ky.) and in Jan. '65 was permanently crippled by a fall.

FONDA, John G. Union officer. N.Y. 1st Lt. 2d Ill. Cav. 12 Aug. '61; resigned 27 Dec. '61; Maj. 12th Ill. Cav. 8 Mar. '62; resigned 17 Nov. '62; Lt. Col. 118th Ill. 29 Nov. '62; Col. 15 Dec. '62; Bvt. B.G. USV 28 June '65 (war service). In Dept. of the Gulf, he commanded 1st Brig., Cav. Div.; 2d Brig., Cav. Div.; Cav. Brig., Dist. of Baton Rouge; and Dist. of Baton Rouge.

FOOTE, Andrew Hull. Union admiral. 1806–63. Entering the navy in 1822, he sailed in the West Indies, off Africa, and along the China coast. He was given command of the western flotilla at the beginning of the Civil War, and in Feb. '62, in cooperation with Grant, he moved upon Fort Henry on the Tennessee. Wounded at Fort Donelson, he aided Pope on the Mississippi, but his wound was not healing, and he was obliged to give up his command. Having proved himself to be an outstanding fighter on the rivers, he received the Thanks of Congress and was appointed Rear Admiral 16 June '62. Four days later he was put in charge of the Bureau of Equipment and Recruiting. On 4 June '63 he was chosen to take over the fleet off Charleston from Du Pont but died on the way to this assignment on 26 June.

FOOTE, Henry Stuart. Confed. Congressman. 1804–80. Va. Member of the Confederate Congress who opposed Jefferson Davis's administration, he was constantly engaged in plans for peace. As US Sen. from Miss. in 1847–51, he had supported the Missouri Compromise and defeated Davis for Gov. (1852–54). After the war he supported Reconstruction policies. He wrote *The War of the Rebellion* (1866).

FORBES, Edwin. WAR CORRESPONDENT and artist. 1839–95. N.Y. At the beginning of the war he joined the Army of the Potomac as artist for *Frank Leslie's Illustrated Newspaper* and remained in the field until 1864. His sketches in the form of copper-plate etchings were given a medal at the Centennial Exposition of 1876 and Sherman bought the first proofs for the government.

FORCE, Manning Ferguson. Union gen. 1824–99. D.C. Son of the historian and archivist Peter Force, he prepared for West Point but went to Harvard College and Law School and practiced until named Maj. 26th Ohio 26 Aug. '61. Promoted Lt. Col. 11 Sept. '61, he fought at Fort Donelson and Shiloh and was named Col. 1 May '62, serving with Grant in southwest Tenn. and northern Miss. 1862–63. He was employed to guard the road as far back as Clinton when Sherman marched on Jackson during the Vicksburg siege. He received the XVII Corps Gold Medal after the fall of Vicksburg. Named B.G. USV 11 Aug. '63, he commanded 2, 3, XVII (3 June–17 Nov. '63). In Sherman's Meridian and Atlanta campaigns he commanded in the XVII Corps the 1st Brig., 3d Div., XVII (17 Nov. '63–6 Mar. '64 and 2 May–22 July '64) when he was severely wounded in the upper part of the face by a gunshot while standing on a hill outside Atlanta. He also commanded that brigade Oct. '64–15 Jan. '65 during the March to the Sea and through the Carolinas as well as the 3d Div. (15 Jan.–3 Apr. '65) and 1st Div. (5 Apr.–1 Aug. '65). He was breveted Maj. Gen. for Atlanta, mustered out in 1866, and given the Medal of Honor 31 May '92 for that battle. He later practiced law and sat on the bench. Writing books on history and archaeology, he also published *From Ft. Henry to Corinth* (1881) and *Gen. Sherman* (1899).

FORD, James Hobart. Union officer. Capt. Indpt. Co. Colo. Inf. 21 Dec. '61; Maj. 2d Colo. 1 Nov. '62; Col. 2d Colo. Cav. 5 Nov. '63; Bvt. B.G. USV 10 Dec. '64. Commanded Dist. Upper Ark., Dept. of Kans. Died 1867.

FORNEY, John Horace. C.S.A. gen. 1829–1902. N.C. Appt.-Ala. USMA 1852 (22/43); Inf. He served in garrison and on the frontier in the Utah Expedition before resigning 23 Jan. '61 as 1st Lt. on duty as infantry tactics instructor at West Point. Commissioned Col. of Ala. Arty., he was sent to command at Pensacola and on 16 Mar. '61 was commissioned Capt. C.S.A. and assigned to Bragg's staff. Promoted Col. 10th Ala. 4 June '61, he served under Kirby Smith at 1st Bull Run and led the brigade for three months after the latter was wounded. He commanded the brigade for three months and was leading his regiment at Dranesville when severely wounded in the arm. Appointed B.G. C.S.A. 10 Mar. '62 and Maj. Gen. 27 Oct. of that year, he commanded the Dept. of Southern Ala. and West Florida, serving a year at Mobile before going to Vicksburg where he led his division. He remained in that area for the rest of the war and was a planter afterward.

FORNEY, William Henry. C.S.A. gen. 1823–94. N.C. Graduating from the Univ. of Ala., he became a lawyer and fought in the Mexican War before being commissioned Capt. 10th Ala. Sent to Va., he was wounded in the leg at Dranesville, and was promoted Maj. and Lt. Col. (17 Mar. '62). He was wounded in the shoulder at Williamsburg and captured while in the hospital.

Exchanged four months later and promoted Col. 27 June '62. He led his regiment at Fredericksburg, Chancellorsville, and Salem Church, where he was wounded in the leg again. At Gettysburg, while leading his regiment, he was shot in the arm and leg, left on the battlefield, and was captured. Crippled for life by this, he was exchanged and while on crutches was appointed B.G. C.S.A. 8 Nov. '64 (C.M.H.) and given a brigade. Wright says that he was not appointed until 15 Feb. '65, Palmer Bradley dates the appointment 23 Feb. '65, and the order of battle for Petersburg in B.&L. (IV, 594) lists him as a Col. commanding his regiment in Sanders' Brigade of Mahone's division, III Corps. He fought at Petersburg, Hatcher's Run, High Bridge, Farmville, and Appomattox. After the war he was a lawyer and legislator.

FORREST, Nathan Bedford. C.S.A. gen. 1821–77. Tenn. When he enlisted as a private a month before his 40th birthday, Forrest had risen from poverty to become a wealthy businessman (cotton, real estate, livestock, and slaves) and Memphis alderman. With about six months of formal schooling, he had been helping support his widowed mother and numerous brothers and sisters since he was 15. "There was six feet two of him, lithe and powerful of build, with steady eyes . . . altogether a man of striking and commanding presence" (Henry, *Forrest*, 13).

He raised and mounted a battalion at his own expense and in Oct. '61 was commissioned Lt. Col. to command them. He escaped from Fort Donelson with his own command and several hundred volunteers from other units. He conducted a vigorous rear-guard action to cover the Confederate retreat from SHILOH and was seriously wounded on 8 Apr. '62. On 21 July he was appointed B.G. C.S.A. and started conducting the raids for which he became famous. After having received a near-fatal pistol wound from a disgruntled subordinate (Lt. A. Wills Gould) at Columbia, Tenn., on 14 June '63, he held this officer's pistol hand, used his teeth to pry open his penknife, and with his free hand inflicted a mortal wound in the abdomen of his assailant. After Chickamauga he had a clash with Bragg that resulted in his being transferred. On 4 Dec. '63 he was promoted Maj. Gen. The controversial FORT PILLOW "MASSACRE" took place in Apr. '64.

FORREST'S OPERATIONS DURING THE ATLANTA CAMPAIGN led Sherman to say, in desperation, " 'That devil Forrest' . . . must be 'hunted down and killed if it costs ten thousand lives and bankrupts the Federal treasury' " (Henry, *op. cit.*, paraphrasing O.R., I, XXXIX, 121). Forrest then went on to give reality to Sherman's expressed fears that "there never will be peace in Tennessee till Forrest is dead." He then joined Hood for the Franklin and Nashville campaign. On 28 Feb. '65 he was promoted Lt. Gen. In the closing days of the war he was unable to stop WILSON'S RAID TO SELMA, marking his only failure of the war. He surrendered with Taylor.

"I went into the army worth a million and a half dollars," he said, "and came out a beggar." He became a planter again and was engaged in railroading. He had a connection with the Ku Klux Klan soon after its organization, and there is evidence that he was its Grand Wizard.

When asked to name the war's greatest soldier, J. E. Johnston once answered without hesitation: "Forrest, who, had he had the advantages of a thorough military education and training, would have been the great central figure of the Civil War" (Wyeth, *Forrest*, 635). A born military genius, his "GET THERE FIRST WITH THE MOST MEN" sums up

volumes of Jomini and Clausewitz. Five of his brothers and two half brothers saw military service. John, next in age to Nathan Bedford, was disabled by wounds received in Mexico; Jeffery, the youngest, was a B.G. at 26 and killed leading his brigade at Okolona, Miss.; Aaron, a regimental commander, died of pneumonia; Jesse, a Lt. Col., was disabled by wounds; William, a Capt., led a body of scouts, was seriously wounded, but recovered to finish the war; two half brothers fought, and the third joined the Confederacy in its last days before he had become 16 (Henry, *op. cit.*, 23).

FORREST'S CAVALRY CORPS. See CORPS, Confed.

FORREST'S FIRST RAID, Tenn., July '62. Concurrently with MORGAN'S FIRST RAID in Ky. and with the same general purpose, Forrest (who had just been made a B.G.) undertook a devastating raid. Leaving Chattanooga on 6 July with about 1,000 men, he moved through McMinnville, surprised the brigade of T. L. Crittenden (1,040 men) at Murfreesboro 13 July, and captured the entire command and stores valued at almost a million dollars. Starting again from McMinnville on the 19th, he marched for Lebanon and followed its retreating garrison to Nashville. He destroyed two railroad bridges south of the city, cutting off the Federal force under Wm. ("Bull") Nelson being sent to catch him at Murfreesboro and McMinnville. As a result of the raid Gov. Andrew Johnson felt an attempt was being made to capture Nashville; the Nashville-Stevenson R.R. was out of operation 20–27 July; and two Federal divisions (Nelson's and Wood's) were ordered to protect the railroad; and Buell's offensive was further delayed.

FORREST'S OPERATIONS DURING THE ATLANTA CAMPAIGN,

June–Nov. '64. After the FORT PILLOW "MASSACRE," Forrest remained in Tenn. recruiting new troops and then went to Tupelo. Miss., to rest and reorganize his command. As Sherman was anxious to eliminate the continued threat to his lines of communications in central Tenn., he ordered a force raised to destroy Forrest. S. D. Sturgis took command of 3,000 cavalry, 4,800 infantry, and 18 guns for this purpose. Grierson commanded the cavalry brigades of Waring and Winslow. Col. W. L. McMillen commanded the infantry division, which had one colored and two white brigades.

Sturgis left Memphis on 2 June and marched via Ripley, Miss., toward Fulton. At the battle of Guntown or BRICE'S CROSS ROADS, Miss., 10 June '64, Forrest gave him a humiliating beating. The Federals retreated with a loss of over 2,000 men, 16 guns, and 250 wagons.

In late June A. J. Smith rejoined Sherman with his "Right Wing, XVI Corps" after participating in Banks's Red River Expedition. A new field force of 11,000 infantry, 3,000 cavalry, and 20 guns, all under the command of A. J. Smith, was formed to operate against Forrest. This expedition consisted of Smith's 1st and 3d divisions, XVI, under J. A. Mower and David Moore; Grierson's cavalry division; and Edward Bouton's brigade of colored troops.

To oppose this operation S. D. Lee united the cavalry of Forrest, Chalmers, and Roddey (10,000 total) at Columbus, Miss. The Federals left Grand Junction on 2 July and were attacked at Harrisburg, near TUPELO, Miss., 14 July. Several Confederate assaults were repulsed at a loss of 996. According to an enthusiastic Federal account in *Battles and Leaders*, "Smith had defeated Forrest as he had never been defeated before. But our rations and ammunition were low, and Grierson's cavalry having

destroyed the railroad, Smith could, from a military point of view, do no more, so he decided to return to Memphis" (B.&L., IV, 422). He arrived there on 23 July.

Shortly after this engagement S. D. Lee went to Atlanta to command Hood's corps and Forrest assumed command of northern Miss. Sherman, now around Atlanta, ordered Smith to undertake another expedition to eliminate, if possible, the continued menace of Forrest to his attenuated supply line back to Nashville. With about the same force as before, Smith left Grand Junction on 3 Aug. for Oxford. He planned to repair the railroad and gather supplies at Oxford for a movement on Columbus, Miss. Forrest sent Chalmers to Holly Springs to delay Smith's advance and followed with the rest of his command. When the Federals reached the Tallahatchie River Forrest decided to try a diversion. With 2,000 picked men he moved via Panola and entered Memphis at dawn, 21 Aug., where he almost succeeded in capturing Gens. Hurlbut and Washburn. He withdrew with a loss of 62, having inflicted 196 casualties, including four officers captured. Efforts to cut off Forrest's retreat failed, and Smith's force was called back.

Having not only frustrated attempts to destroy him, but also having disposed of the enemy forces in East Tenn., Forrest now undertook the operations Sherman most feared. He left Chalmers with one brigade in northern Miss. and took his other three to Tuscumbia where he found Wheeler and Roddey, who had just come from raids in Tenn. Wheeler's corps was too exhausted to assist him. but Roddey gave him a brigade, making his force 4,500 strong.

Forrest first attacked Athens, Ala., 23–24 Sept. and captured its 600-man garrison. He then captured a large detachment that was guarding the railroad trestles north of there. Finding Pulaski, Tenn., too well defended, he went toward Fayetteville. He was unable to reach this place (where he had intended to wreck the railroad) and was pursued across the Tennessee to Florence. In two weeks he had captured 1,200 men, 800 horses, 7 guns, and had caused Sherman to send Thomas back to Chattanooga with two divisions.

About 15 Oct. Forrest moved to Jackson, Tenn., where Chalmers joined him and brought his force up to 3,500 men. Moving down the Tennessee, he joined Abraham Buford, who had constructed a trap for Federal boats "by a judicious disposition of the troops and batteries sent for this purpose" (Forrest's report). At Ft. Heiman and Paris Landing, two and six miles upstream from Fort Henry, respectively, they constructed masked (concealed) batteries.

On the 29th the new steamer *Mazeppa* with two barges in tow was captured and burned after her 700-ton cargo had been unloaded. The next day the *Anna* got through the batteries but sank before reaching Paducah. Then the transports *Cheeseman* and *Venus* with two barges and the gunboat *Undine* were engaged, abandoned by their crew, and captured. Burning all the other vessels, Forrest's troops kept the *Venus* and *Undine* for their advance upstream to Johnsonville. Just below the latter town they found a place where Reynoldsburg Island compressed the river into a narrow curved chute with a highly irregular channel. They emplaced 15 rifled guns to cover this defile and ambush Federal boats on their way to Johnsonville. On 2 Nov. the *Venus* was recaptured by the Federals near this place and towed back to Johnsonville (where she was destroyed 4 Nov.). The next day another action forced the Confederates to withdraw downstream with the

Undine to prevent her recapture. On the 4th Federal gunboats moved against the "chute" from north and south. The northern force found the *Undine* and forced the Confederates to burn and abandon her. But Confederate guns then registered 19 hits on the *Key West* and forced her to withdraw. The five gunboats coming from the south were also driven back.

Forrest's next action was at JOHNSONVILLE, 3–5 Nov., where he terrorized the Federals into destroying a fleet of ships and a large quantity of supplies. Thomas ordered the XXIII Corps to defend that place. Forrest reached Corinth, Miss., on the 10th and joined Hood at Tuscumbia on 16 Nov. During this "Raid into West Tennessee" (16 Oct.–10 Nov.) he lost two men killed and nine wounded. He claimed destruction of 4 gunboats, 14 transports, 20 barges, 26 guns, $6,700,000 worth of property, and the capture of 150 prisoners.

FORREST'S SECOND RAID, W. Tenn., 11 Dec. '62–3 Jan. '63. (STONES RIVER) Having organized a brigade of four regiments and several smaller detachments, about 2,500 total, Forrest was directed by Bragg to destroy the railroads between Grant's base at Columbus, Ky., and his army in northern Mississippi. Leaving Columbia 11 Dec., Forrest crossed the Tennessee at Clifton (13th–15th). He defeated a cavalry force at LEXINGTON, Tenn., 18 Dec., struck the railroad between Humboldt and Jackson, and followed it northward into Kentucky, destroying bridges and stations en route. He captured TRENTON, 20 Dec., and Humboldt, but did not take JACKSON, 19 Dec. From near Columbus he retired by way of Dresden. At PARKER CROSS ROADS, 31 Dec., just before reaching Lexington, he was defeated and escaped with the loss of most of his captured property. Although opposed by some of Dodge's troops sent from Corinth, he succeeded in recrossing the Tennessee at Clifton.

Forrest lost about 500 men, one gun, and a number of caissons. Aside from the 382 casualties he inflicted at Lexington and Parker Cross Roads, he had captured and paroled many prisoners and thoroughly wrecked the Mobile & Ohio R.R. Although the latter was his assigned mission, Grant profited from it by changing his base from Columbus, Ky., to Memphis (Fiebeger).

FORSYTH, George Alexander. Union officer. Pa. R.A. Pvt. Chicago Dragoons 19 Apr.–18 Aug. '61; 1st Lt. 8th Ill. Cav. 18 Sept. '61; Capt. 12 Feb. '62; Maj. 1 Sept. '63; Bvt. B.G. USV. Brevets for Opequon and Middletown, Dinwiddie Courthouse, Five Forks. Military Sec. and A.D.C. to Sheridan 1869–73, 1878–81. Bvt. B.G. USV 1868 for Indian fight at Arickaree Fork of Republican River.

FORSYTH, James William. Union gen. 1835–1906. Ohio. USMA 1856 (28/49); Inf.-Cav. Serving on the frontier, he was 1st Lt. (15 Mar. '61) 9th US Inf. when the war started and transferred to the 18th US Inf. 14 May '61. He was promoted Capt. 24 Oct. '61 and commanded the 20th Brig., Army of the Ohio (Jan. '62) and 20th Brig., 6th Div., Army of the Ohio (11 Feb.–5 Apr. '62). From 15 Mar. to 15 Sept. '62, he served on McClellan's staff during the Peninsular and Maryland campaigns. He fought at Chickamauga in Sept. '63 and then served as Asst. I.G. Cav. Corps, Army of the Potomac. Named Maj. Asst. A.G. Vols. 7 Apr. '64, he was Sheridan's Chief of Staff in the Richmond and Shenandoah campaigns. He was named Lt. Col. Asst. I.G. Assigned 19 Apr. '64–19 May '65 and promoted B.G. USV 19 May '65. Mustered out of USV, he was Lt. Col. A.D.C. to Sheridan 1869–73 and his Lt. Col. Military

Secretary 1873–78. He organized the School for Cavalry and Field Artillery at Fort Riley (Kans.) 1887–90 and commanded at Wounded Knee 1890–91. He was promoted B.G. USA in 1894 and Maj. Gen. USA in 1897, retiring that same year. His brevets were for Chickamauga, Cedar Creek, Five Forks, war service (B.G. USA) and Opequon, Fishers Hill, and Middletown (B.G. USV).

FORT BISLAND, La. 13 Apr. '63. See IRISH BEND AND FORT BISLAND.

FORT BLAKELY, Ala. See BLAKELY, Ala., 1–9 Apr. '65.

FORT DARLING, Va. Confederate battery at Drewry's Bluff on the James River seven miles south of Richmond. It was hastily constructed in May '62, and on the 12th blocked the advance of the ironclads *Monitor* and *Galena*. It protected Richmond from naval attack until the end of the war. Butler failed to capture the battery in an action known as DREWRY'S BLUFF, 12–16 May '64.

FORT DE RUSSY, La., 14 Mar. '64. Confederate fort captured at beginning of RED RIVER CAMPAIGN.

FORT DONELSON, Tenn. 15 Feb. '62. See HENRY AND DONELSON CAMPAIGN.

FORT ESPERANZA (Pass Cavallo, entrance to Matagorda Bay), 27–29 Nov. '63. Besieged during TEXAS COAST OPERATIONS OF BANKS IN 1863 and evacuated by the Confederates 30 Nov.

FORT FILLMORE, N. Mex., 27 July '61. See NEW MEXICO AND ARIZONA OPERATIONS IN 1861–62.

FORT FISHER, N.C., 7–27 Dec. '64. (Butler's Expedition) During the Petersburg campaign Grant ordered Butler to organize an expedition to operate with the navy to reduce Fort Fisher and close the port of Wilmington. The latter was "the last gateway between the Confederate States and the outside world" (Wm. Lamb in B.&L., IV, 642). Butler took personal command of the army troops under Weitzel, which consisted of the divisions of Ames (2, XXIV) and Paine (3, XXV). Strength was 6,500 men and two batteries. On 8 Dec. the troops moved down the James on transports to Fortress Monroe, leaving there the 13th. On the 18th they were joined by Porter's fleet. When Lee learned (on the 18th) that a large force had left Hampton Roads, he suspected it was headed for Wilmington and sent Hoke's division (6,155 men) from the Army of Northern Va. to defend the vital port (Lee's Lts., III, 617–8). Gunboats were already bombarding the fort when Weitzel's troops, delayed by bad weather, arrived on the 24th. By noon the next day the Half Moon and Flag Pond Hill batteries, two miles up the coast from the fort, had been silenced and troops landed. Curtis's brigade (1, 2, XXIV) captured the Half Moon battery and pushed skirmishers to within 75 yards of the fort while the gunboats delivered supporting fires. Before dark, however, it was apparent that, despite the naval preparation, the assault on Fort Fisher would be costly. It was also learned that Hoke was only five miles away. (He, too, had been delayed in his train movement via Danville and Greensboro.) "At the time this spread suspicion of deliberate treachery, but it should have been accepted as warning that the long-threatened collapse of transportation now was imminent" Lee's Lts., III, 618). On Weitzel's recommendation the troops were withdrawn and returned to Hampton Roads. Federal casualties were 15 wounded and one drowned. Confederate losses included 300 men and four guns captured.

One curiosity of Butler's attack was the explosion of a "powder ship" (23 Dec.) near the fort in the hope that this would either destroy the fort or its defenders. A charge of 215 tons of powder was used, and the experiment failed to have any effect on the defenders. (See O. R. Atlas, LXVII, 5, for drawing of "powder vessel.")

FORT FISHER, N.C., 6–15 Jan. '65. (Terry's Expedition) Dissatisfied with the failure of Butler's expedition against Fort Fisher (see above), Grant ordered A. H. Terry (C.G., XXIV) to organize another expedition and take the fort by assault or by siege. This 8,000-man force is generally known as Terry's Provisional Corps and became the nucleus of the reorganized X Corps. It was made up from the following units: 1,400 from J. C. Abbott's brigade (2, 1, XXIV); 3,300 from Ames's (2d) division of the same corps, and the same number from C. J. Paine's division of colored troops (3, XXV); four guns of the 16th N.Y. independent battery; Btry. E. 3d US Arty.; and three companies of siege artillery with 24 guns and 20 small mortars.

Terry's troops left Bermuda Landing on the 4th and were joined by Porter's North Atlantic Blockading Squadron 25 miles off Beaufort, N.C. The naval force had nearly 60 vessels and 627 guns. Storms delayed the arrival of this armada off Fort Fisher until late afternoon of the 12th. On learning of the enemy's approach, W. H. C. Whiting, the Confederate district commander, reinforced Colonel Wm. Lamb's Fort Fisher garrison of 1,200 North Carolinians and 47 heavy guns with 600 additional men. Braxton Bragg, the department commander, sent Hoke's division (6,000 infantry and cavalry) to occupy the peninsula north of the fort to oppose any landing. About midnight of the 12th the naval forces started their bombardment and four hours later the transports moved in to start disembarking the assault troops.

By 3 P.M. (13 Jan.) the infantry had landed and during the night had dug in opposite Hoke's line. On the 14th artillery was brought ashore, the Federal beachhead was consolidated, and reconnaissances were made. Curtis's brigade (1, 2, XXIV) captured a small, unfinished work facing the west end of the land front of Fort Fisher.

Terry's plan was to bombard the fort until 3 P.M. on the 15th and then assault down the peninsula in two columns. Ames was to lead his division along the Wilmington road that ran on the west side of the peninsula, while a volunteer force of 2,261 sailors and marines was to attack the northeast salient of the fort.

At 8 A.M. (15 Jan.) the naval bombardment opened at point-blank range. Fire was directed against the front, flank, and rear of the face of the fort that the land columns were going to assault. At 2 P.M. a group of 60 sharpshooters from the 13th Ind., armed with Spencer repeating rifles, and 40 men from Curtis's brigade, rushed forward with shovels and dug themselves in within 175 yards of the fort. When the sharpshooters had gone into action to cover the parapet, Curtis moved his brigade from the work he had captured earlier and took up a position 50 yards to their rear. Pennypacker's brigade (2, 2, XXIV) took over the position vacated by Curtis and Bell's brigade (3, 2, XXIV) went into position 200 yards behind Pennypacker.

At 3:25 P.M. Curtis's brigade led the assault, axmen hacking gaps through the palisades, and the rest of his brigade gaining the parapet. Pennypacker then moved forward on Curtis's right. Bell attacked to Pennypacker's right. The parapet on this side did not extend all the way to the river, but there were pits

from which sand had been taken for the construction of the fort, and desperate hand-to-hand combat took place in this area and in the traverses of the works. Abbott's brigade (2, 1, XXIV) was committed about 9 P.M. and broke the last Confederate resistance. At about 10 P.M. the surviving defenders (400) at Battery (Fort) Buchanan surrendered.

The column of sailors and marines, led by Captain (of the navy) K. R. Breese, was repulsed and forced to retire with a loss of about 300. "The mistake was in expecting a body of sailors, collected hastily from different ships, unknown to each other, armed with swords and pistols to stand against veteran soldiers . . ." (B.&L., IV, 660).

Among the 112 officers and 1,971 men the Federals claimed to have captured were Whiting, the garrison commander, Colonel Wm. Lamb (both wounded). From the prison camp at Ft. Columbus (Governor's Island) Whiting asked that an investigation be made of Bragg's conduct of the defense of Ft. Fisher. The main criticism of Bragg's leadership was that he made no effective effort to use Hoke's division to hit the Federal rear during the land attack on Fisher.

Of 8,000 army troops engaged, 955 were casualties (184 killed, 749 wounded, 22 missing). Naval casualties —in addition to the 300 in the assaulting column—numbered 386 (B.&L., IV, 654). Curtis and Pennypacker received Medals of Honor.

The morning after the surrender two drunken sailors unwittingly entered an ammunition bunker with torches looking for booty. The resulting explosion of 13,000 pounds of powder killed 25 Federals, wounded 66, and resulted in 13 missing (mostly from the 169th N.Y.). Some wounded Confederates were also lost. "The telegraph wires between a bomb proof near this magazine, and

Battery Lamb across the river, gave rise to the impression that the Confederates had caused the explosion, but an official investigation traced it to these drunken sailors," said Lamb (M.H.S.M. papers, IX, 383).

FORT GILMER, Va. See NEW MARKET HEIGHTS, 29 Sept. '64.

FORT GREGG, Va. Strong point in Petersburg defenses where elements of XXIV and XXV Corps saw action during PETERSBURG FINAL ASSAULT, 2 Apr. '65.

FORT HARRISON, Va., 29–30 Sept. '64. See NEW MARKET HEIGHTS, same dates.

FORT HENRY, Tenn. See HENRY AND DONELSON CAMPAIGN.

FORT HINDMAN, Ark. See ARKANSAS POST.

FORT HUGER, Va. 19 Apr. '63. During the siege of SUFFOLK a combined army-navy force of some 270 Federals under Getty and Lt. R. H. Lamson (USN) captured this fort by a brilliantly successful coup de main. Landing about 6 P.M. at a point 400 yards from the fort, the Federals established a foothold without opposition and brought four guns ashore. The garrison of the fort surrendered its seven officers, 130 men, and five guns after a brief fight. The incident led to an altercation between E. M. Law and Col. J. K. Connally, both of whom had troops engaged, and each of whom assumed the other was picketing the river in the area where the Federals landed unopposed. Connally took exception to a report by Captains L. R. Terrell and John Cussons of Law's staff that men of Connally's 55th N.C. had not properly supported Stribling's battery. This resulted in a double duel in which nobody was hurt. (See Lee's Lts., II, 486–90.)

FORT McALLISTER, Ga. Naval bombardments. On 28 Feb. '63 the Federal monitor Montauk (Capt. John L. Worden) attacked and destroyed the Confederate raider Nashville while the latter lay under the protection of the guns of Fort McAllister. On 3 Mar. the ironclads Passaic, Patapsco, and Nahant, with three gunboats and three mortar schooners, attacked the fort to test the effectiveness of Ericsson's monitors. Although little permanent damage was done to the fort, the Passaic sustained 34 hits without serious damage.

FORT McALLISTER, Ga., 13 Dec. '64. In connection with the siege of Savannah, W. B. Hazen's division (2, XV) captured the garrison of 250 Confederates under Maj. G. W. Anderson. The Federals lost 134, some of them to land mines ("torpedoes"). There were 48 Confederates killed and wounded (T.U.A.). In the Official Records is this remarkable communication from Sherman's aide, Dayton, to Slocum: "Dear General: Take a good big drink, a long breath, and then yell like the devil. The fort was carried at 4:30 P.M., the assault lasting but fifteen minutes. The general signaled from this side to the fleet and got answers, and vessels were seen coming up the sound when Colonel Ewing left. I am, general, yours, &c., L.M. DAYTON, Aide de Camp" (O.R., I, LXIV, 704). This action was of great strategic significance in that Sherman now had reached the coast, where the Federal Navy could support him.

FORT PICKENS. See PENSACOLA BAY.

FORT PICKENS MEDAL. See FORT SUMTER AND FORT PICKENS MEDALS.

FORT PILLOW "MASSACRE" (12 Apr. '64). The Confederate cavalry division of Brig. Gen. James R. Chalmers (1,500 men) was sent by Forrest on 10

Apr. '64 from Jackson, Tenn., to "attend to" Ft. Pillow, Tenn. The latter was held by 262 Negroes and 295 whites of the 11th US Col. Troops (6th US Col. Hv. Arty., and the 1st Ala.); Battery F, US Col. Lgt. Arty.; and Bradford's Bn. of the 13th Tenn. Cav. Under the command of Maj. Lionel F. Booth, and reinforced by Capt. James Marshall's gunboat *New Era,* the fort had the mission of protecting Federal navigation along the Mississippi.

Arriving at dawn 12 Apr., the Confederates drove in the pickets and surrounded the place. Forrest arrived at 10 o'clock to take personal command. With an eye for the tactical weaknesses of the defenses, he worked his men into positions from which they could assault the fort without coming under the fire of its guns or those of the *New Era.* At 3:30 P.M., after completing preparations for his attack, he sent in a surrender ultimatum. Maj. William F. Bradford, having taken command when Booth was killed by a sniper, asked for an hour to make his decision. During this period there were movements which both sides interpreted as truce violations. Forrest announced he would not wait the full hour but would have to know the Federals' answer within 20 minutes. Bradford sent the message "I will not surrender."

The Confederates then swarmed into the fort with little difficulty. At this point Southern and Northern accounts diverge. Federal losses were (approximately) 231 killed, 100 seriously wounded, 168 whites and 58 Negroes captured. Forrest's losses were 14 killed and 86 wounded. Southern accounts maintain that Federal losses were incurred in fighting their way back to the river's edge and before they surrendered. Northern accounts maintain that the Federals surrendered as soon as the fort was overrun and were shot down in cold blood by Rebels shouting "No quarter! No quarter! Kill the damned niggers; shoot them down!" The Committee on the Conduct of the War concluded that the Confederates were guilty of atrocities which included murdering most of the garrison after it surrendered, burying Negro soldiers alive, and setting fire to tents containing Federal wounded. Most Northern historians agree. The Southern view is that the House Report (No. 65, 38th Congress, 1864) was sheer propaganda, fabricated to stir up war hatred; that Fort Pillow was simply an overwhelming tactical victory against troops that refused to surrender in the face of inevitable annihilation. (For a scholarly analysis and reference to the basic authorities, see "The Fort Pillow Massacre: A Fresh Examination of the Evidence," by Albert Castel, in *Civil War History,* Vol. 4, No. 1 [March 1958]. He concludes that there was a "massacre.")

FORT PULASKI, Ga., 10–11 Apr. '62. After the Federal capture of the forts at PORT ROYAL SOUND, 7 Nov. '61, which was primarily a naval action (Hilton Head), Fort Pulaski, guarding the sea approach to Savannah, was captured in a "purely military [army] operation" (Mahan, 61). The fort was of enclosed masonry construction with about 40 guns in casemates and in barbette. Q. A. Gillmore established rifled guns on Tybee Island at a range of from one to two miles. After a bombardment that started at 8 A.M. on the 10th and continued without interruption, the Confederates surrendered at 2 P.M. on the 11th. With a loss of one killed, the Federals killed one Confederate, seriously wounded another, and inflicted about a dozen other casualties. About 360 prisoners were taken. Extensive damage was done to the fort. "It was the first combat of rifled guns and masonry forts and led to a revolution in the construction of seacoast defense" (Fiebeger, 85).

FORT ST. PHILIP, La. See New Orleans.

FORT SANDERS (Knoxville), Tenn., 29 Nov. '63. (Knoxville Campaign) The point selected by Longstreet for his assault on Burnside's command in Knoxville was a bastioned earthwork on a hill, forming a sharp salient in the northeast corner of the town's entrenchments. It was covered by a ditch 12 feet wide and an average of eight feet deep. An almost vertical slope rose to the top of the parapet, 15 feet above the bottom of the ditch. The Confederates called the position Ft. Loudon; to the Federals it was known as Fort Sanders, in honor of the cavalry general killed near it on 18 Nov.

Freeman says that the position was held by 250 men under Lt. S. L. Benjamin when the attack started (*Lee's Lts.*, III, 297). The article in *Battles and Leaders* by O. M. Poe, the Federal engineer responsible for organizing the defense of Knoxville, says the position was held by 440 men and 12 guns at the time of the main attack. The units, according to Poe, were these: 29th Mass. (75 men), 2d Mich. (60 men), 20th Mich. (80), 79th N.Y. (120), and the batteries of Benjamin and W. W. Buckley. An additional 40 men of the 2d Mich., under Capt. C. H. Hodskin, had orders to hold a forward position in the counterscarp salient as long as possible and then withdraw; they took no part in the final defense of Ft. Sanders (O. M. Poe in B.&L., III, 742–43).

Longstreet's final plan called for a surprise infantry attack just before dawn on Sunday, 29 Nov. "This was a bitter disappointment to the artillery, after so many days spent in preparation," wrote E. P. Alexander. "We believe that in daylight, with our aid,

the result would have been different" (B.&L., III, 748). The following brigades of McLaws' division, with an average strength of 1,000, were selected to make the assault: Humphreys's Mississippians and the Georgians of Bryan and Col. S. Z. Ruff (Wofford's). Anderson's Georgia brigade (of Jenkins' Div.) was to follow in reserve.

During a bitterly cold night the assault troops moved forward and lay in final assembly positions within 150 yards of the objective. The defenders were alerted by this action. At first light the Confederates assaulted. Despite some difficulty getting through wire entanglements (telegraph wire stretched close to the ground between stakes and stumps) the attackers reached the ditch without heavy losses. Their further advance was made almost impossible by the steep slope of the parapet. Their problem was aggravated by the fact that the ground was frozen and the slope covered with sleet. In the absence of scaling ladders, the men climbed on the shoulders of their comrades and planted the colors of the 16th Ga., and the 13th and 17th Miss. on the parapet (B.&L., III, 743), and maintained them there by a succession of color bearers for some time. Ruff was killed, as were Cols. H. P. Thomas (16th Ga.) and Kennon McElroy (13th Miss.). Lt. Col. Fiser (17th Miss.) lost an arm on the parapet. Adj. T. W. Cumming (16th Ga.) and Lt. Munger (9th Ga.) penetrated through embrasures, the former being captured and the latter fighting his way back out. For 20 minutes other men remained in the ditch, unable to go forward or retreat. When the withdrawal was finally undertaken, about 200 unwounded men were captured in the ditch. Anderson's brigade was not notified of the withdrawal and moved forward to be driven back with a loss of 200 men.

Exaggerated reports of the effectiveness of the wire entanglements and news of Bragg's defeat at Missionary Ridge (25 Nov.) caused Longstreet to cease further efforts to penetrate the defenses of Knoxville. Confederate losses were 813, of whom 216 were missing (Alexander, 492). Total Federal losses were 20 killed and 80 wounded (E.&B.), including those sustained by forces outside of the fort. Casualties within Fort Sanders were eight killed and five wounded (*Lee's Lts.*, III, 297).

FORTS GAINES, MORGAN, and POWELL (Mobile Bay), Ala., 3–23 Aug. '64. These forts, along with a system of pile obstructions and mine fields, covered the entrances to Mobile Bay from the Gulf and (in the case of Fort Powell) from Mississippi Sound. D. H. Maury was in over-all command in Mobile; and Col. R. L. Page commanded Forts Gaines and Morgan. Behind the protection of the forts was the Confederate ironclad *Tennessee* and three wooden gunboats, all under Adm. Franklin Buchanan. The Federals wanted to seize the forts before the enemy could finish the additional ironclads under construction in Mobile. Diversion of land forces to take part in Banks's RED RIVER CAMPAIGN had delayed Farragut's proposed operations against Mobile.

About 5,500 troops in Gordon Granger's XIII Corps were finally made available. On 3 Aug. Granger landed 1,500 men on the western end of Dauphine Island and the next day invested Fort Gaines. After a day's delay Farragut's fleet started running through the main channel, under the guns of Fort Morgan, and about three miles away from those of Fort Gaines. In a fight lasting little more than an hour Farragut defeated Buchanan in the battle of MOBILE BAY, 5 Aug. Fort Powell (140

men) was abandoned that night after having been attacked by the 4-gun monitor *Chickasaw*. Col. C. D. Anderson surrendered his garrison of 600 men at Fort Gaines early 8 Aug. after a faint-hearted show of resistance (according to the official report of his superiors). Granger reported taking 818 prisoners (O.R.). Granger now moved his entire force of about 5,500 to attack the 400-man garrison (R. L. Page in B.&L.) in Fort Morgan. A siege train arrived from New Orleans and was landed on the 17th. On the 22d a heavy bombardment opened from guns of the army and navy, while Granger's forces pushed their trenches to within assaulting distance. At 6 A.M. the next day (23 Aug.) the white flag was shown and at 2:30 P.M. Page surrendered. The killed and wounded on each side were almost negligible. Grant reported the capture of 1,464 prisoners and 104 pieces of artillery at the three forts (B.&L., IV, 411n.).

FORT SMITH and Van Buren, Ark. The post, on the edge of Indian Territory, was important as the terminus of the overland stage to Calif. On 25 Apr. '61 Ark. state troops under Sen. Borland took possession after Capt. S. D. Sturgis escaped with two troops of cavalry. At the end of Dec. '62 J. G. Blunt captured Ft. Smith and Van Buren after the battles of Prairie Grove and Cane Hill. The Federals did not hold Ft. Smith, but reoccupied it 1 Sept. '63.

FORT STEDMAN, Va., 25 Mar. '65. (PETERSBURG CAMPAIGN) Lee was ordered by Davis to make one more offensive effort at Petersburg before the growing Federal strength could capture that strong point and move on to Richmond. Since A. P. Hill was on sick leave, Gordon was given the responsibility of planning and leading this attack. Gordon selected Fort Stedman, a mere 150 yards from the Confederate lines, as being the most promising point. It was hoped that a penetration of the Federal line at this place and a subsequent attack on the Federal lines of communications to City Point would cause Grant to shorten his lines, thereby enabling Lee to release some of his own troops to go to Johnston's support in N.C. The Confederates attacked at 4 A.M. and captured Fort Stedman and a number of surrounding positions. The plan called for the capture of a number of smaller forts behind Stedman from which fire could then be placed on the Federal rear to widen the gap and permit Confederate cavalry to pour through. Three columns of 100 selected men each moved toward these forts, but were unable to find them. It is probable that Gordon was mistaken as to the existence of these works and that they did not exist. About 7:30 Hartranft's division counterattacked and forced Gordon's men back into Fort Stedman and nearby Battery 10. About 8 o'clock Lee sent orders to withdraw. By this time, however, the Confederate line of retreat was being raked by a murderous crossfire and large numbers of Gordon's men chose surrender rather than risking the return to their own lines. The Confederates lost about 3,500, of whom approximately 1,900 were captured (*Lee's Lts.*, III, 651); the defenders lost 1,044 (Fox, 548). Later in the day Meade directed an attack that brought total casualties to between 4,400 and 5,000 Confederates and 2,080 Federals (D.S.F., *op. cit.*).

FORT STEVENS, D.C., 11–12 July '64. A fort in the defenses of Washington which Early's forces probed before deciding to abandon their hopes of entering the capital. It was here that on two occasions Lincoln "exposed his tall form to the gaze and bullets of the enemy in a manner to call forth earnest remonstrance from those near him" (Nicolay).

FORT SUMTER, S.C., 12–14 Apr. '61. Southern-born Maj. Robert Anderson, in command of Federal forts in Charleston harbor, secretly withdrew his garrison from vulnerable Fort Moultrie into Fort Sumter the night of 26 Dec. '60. Confederate batteries were constructed on Morris Island and on 9 Jan. '61 turned back the unarmed *Star of the West*, in which Scott had tried to send supplies and reinforcements. The Confederates continued to erect batteries around Sumter, and Beauregard arrived in early Mar. to take command. On 1 Apr. Beauregard telegraphed the Confederate capital: "Batteries ready to open Wednesday or Thursday [4th or 5th]. What instructions?" On the 10th Beauregard was ordered to demand the evacuation of Sumter, or to reduce it. When Anderson received the ultimatum he answered that he would evacuate the fort by noon of 15 Apr. unless attacked, or unless he received supplies or other instructions from Washington. Beauregard notified Anderson that he would open fire on Sumter at 4:20 on the morning of the 12th.

The bombardment started at 4:30 A.M. with the firing of a 10-inch mortar near old Fort Johnson (James Island) as the signal. Capt. George S. James fired the first gun, after Roger PRYOR had declined his offer of this "honor" (B.&L., I, 76; see also Edmund RUFFIN). The first round landed in the deserted parade ground. Then the 30 guns and 17 mortars took up the fire at ranges varying from 1,800 to 2,500 yards.

Fort Sumter was a pentagonal fort of brick construction on an artificial island in the middle of Charleston's main ship channel. It was about 300 by 350 feet in size, with walls 40 feet high and from eight to 12 feet thick. Although construction had been started in 1829, the fort was incomplete, despite the expenditure of nearly a million dollars. Only 48 of the prescribed 140 guns were ready for use when the attack started. Twenty-one of these were in the upper of the two tiers of casemates, and 27 were on the rampart *en barbette*. The 56-year-old Anderson had eight other officers, 68 noncoms and privates, eight musicians, and 43 noncombatant workmen under his command (Nicolay, *Outbreak,* 63).

Abner Doubleday, then a captain, fired the first answering round at about 7:30 A.M. By this time Anderson had seen from the nature of the enemy fire that he could not man the barbette guns without prohibitive losses. (Sgt. John Carmody did, however, sneak out and fire some of them [B.&L., I, 69]). About 1 P.M. the Federal garrison was cheered by the sight of three ships of the relieving force they had been told to expect. Through an error, however, part of this force, including its commander, had been sent to the relief of Fort Pickens in Pensacola Bay, and bad weather prevented the other ships from reinforcing Anderson. Owing to dwindling ammunition supplies, by the afternoon of the first day only six guns answered the fire of the Confederates. During the night these guns were silent, and the enemy's bombardment was continued with the mortars only.

Although the first day's shelling had inflicted little serious damage, the Confederates noticed that their hot shot had been effective in setting fire to the buildings just inside the walls. On the second day, therefore, they increased their use of this type of missile. By noon there were raging fires of such intensity as to endanger the defenders in the heretofore-safe casemates. About 1:30 the flagstaff of the fort was shot

away. After some initial misunderstanding with former Sen. WIGFALL, who had entered the fort under a flag of truce, Anderson (see B.&L., I, 82) surrendered with the honors of war. During the 34-hour bombardment approximately 4,000 shells had fallen on the fort. At noon on Sunday, 14 Apr., he evacuated his garrison by steamer to New York after ceremoniously lowering the Stars and Stripes from an improvised staff. An accidental explosion of powder behind the salute gun took place when the 50th round of a planned 100-round salute was fired. Private HOUGH became the first Federal soldier of the war to be killed. One other man died of wounds, and a third was seriously wounded. These were Sumter's only casualties.

On 14 Apr. '65, a few hours before Lincoln's assassination, Anderson was present when the original flag was again raised over Fort Sumter.

FT. SUMTER, S.C., 7 Apr. '63. With eight monitors and one ironclad battleship Du Pont made an unsuccessful attempt to force the entrance to Charleston harbor. He was unable to pass the floating obstruction just in rear of Fort Sumter, and his monitors could not silence the batteries either on Sullivan Island or at Fort Sumter. The repulse was a disappointment to the Federal authorities, who had hoped Charleston could be taken by naval action.

FT. SUMTER, S.C., 8 Sept. '63. Federal heavy artillery from Morris Island destroyed the Confederate artillery at Fort Sumter in a week's bombardment that started 17 Aug. Beauregard withdrew the artillery garrison and replaced it with infantry. The night of 8 Sept. Dahlgren sent a boat party of about 400 to capture the fort by surprise. After a loss of 125 the Federals withdrew, and the navy abandoned its hopes of capturing Charleston.

FORT SUMTER AND FORT PICKENS MEDALS.

On 6 June '61 the N.Y. Chamber of Commerce adopted a resolution to present bronze medals to the defenders of FORTS SUMTER and PICKENS. Bearing the profile portraits of Robert ANDERSON and Adam SLEMMER, 168 of these medals were made up and awarded in May '62 to all recipients who could attend the ceremony. The medals were in the shape of disks, varying from six inches in diameter to two and a half inches. They were not designed to be worn on the uniform. See also DECORATIONS.

FORT WAGNER, S.C., Assaults of 10 and 18 July '63.

To capture Charleston, Gillmore, and Dahlgren, who had recently relieved Hunter and Du Pont, planned first to gain a foothold on Morris Island. The principal land defense of Morris Island was Fort Wagner, an isolated redoubt that extended entirely across a narrow part of the island. It was a mile and a half from Fort Sumter.

On 10 July George C. Strong led his brigade (1, 1, X) from Folly Island, about 400 yards away, and secured a foothold on the southern part of Morris Island. The following morning he lost 339 men out of the two and a half regiments he led in a daylight assault against the 1,200 defenders of Fort Wagner. Confederate casualties were 12.

Siege artillery was installed, and on the 18th the Confederate defenders, under Wm. Taliaferro, were bombarded by 26 rifled guns and 10 siege mortars. At dusk Truman Seymour assaulted with the brigades of George Strong and H. S. Putnam (2, 1, X). The action was spearheaded by the 54th Mass. Col. Inf. in a much-lauded attack that cost them 25 per cent casualties including their colonel, R. G. Shaw (killed). The brigade commander, Strong, was mortally wounded, and only one of his six regimental commanders was not killed or wounded. Putnam was killed, and Seymour was wounded.

Although the Federals had secured a foothold, they were driven out of the fort before reinforcements could arrive. Of 5,264 engaged, there were 1,515 casualties. Taliaferro lost 174 out of 1,785 Confederates engaged (Livermore).

Gillmore now undertook formal siege operations. By 6 Sept. his approaches had reached the ditch of Fort Wagner and an assault was ordered for the 7th. The Confederates, however, abandoned Morris Island during the night of the 6th.

FORTY ACRES AND A MULE.

Legend that sprang up among the newly-freed slaves that the Federal government would give them portions of confiscated plantations. It is believed that this came from the division of lands by Sherman's army on the southeast coast in Jan. '65.

FOSTER, George Perkins. Union officer. Vt. Capt. 4th Vt. 21 Sept. '61; Maj. 18 July '62; Lt. Col. 5 Nov. '62; Col. 23 Apr. '64; Bvt. B.G. USV 1 Aug. '64 (Richmond and Shenandoah Valley). Commanded 2, 2, VI. Died 1879.

FOSTER, John A. Union officer. N.Y. Lt. Col. 175th N.Y. 17 Jan. '63; Bvt. B.G. USV 28 Sept. '65 (war service). Died 1890.

FOSTER, John Gray. Union gen. 1823–74. N.H. USMA 1846 (4/59); Engrs. After the Mexican War (1 wound, 2 brevets), he taught engineering at West Point, supervised harbor fortifications, and served under Anderson at Fort Sumter during the bombardment. With the Engineer Bureau in Washington, constructed forts along the New Jersey coast and commanded troops in Annapolis until 20 Dec. '61, having been appointed B.G. USV 23 Oct. (Capt. since 1860). At Roanoke Island, New Bern, and Fort Macon, he commanded 1st Brig., N.C. Exp. (Dec. '61–Apr. '62). Promoted Maj. Gen. USV 18 July '62, he led the XVIII Corps and the Dept. of N.C. (24 Dec. '62–18 July '63), commanding, from Jan. until Feb. of that year the Detachment of XVIII Corps at St. Helena in the Dept. of the South. He then commanded the Dept. of Va. and N.C. (11 July–11 Nov. '63) and the Dept. of Ohio (11 Dec. '63–9 Feb. '64). He asked to be relieved from the latter to recover from injuries received in a fall from his horse and was on sick leave until assigned command of the Dept. of the South (26 May '64–9 Feb. '65). Breveted for Fort Sumter, Roanoke Island, New Bern, Savannah (B.G. USA), and war service (Maj. Gen. USA), he continued in the R.A., dying on active duty as Lt. Col. of Engrs.

FOSTER, Robert Sanford. Union gen. 1834–1903. Ind. Learning the tinner's trade as a boy, he worked in an uncle's store in Indianapolis until commissioned Capt. 11th Ind. 22 Apr. '61 and fighting under Lew Wallace at Romney and Rich Mountain. Named Maj. 13th Ind. 19 June '61, Lt. Col. 28 Oct. '61, and Col. 30 Apr. '62, he led his regiment in the Valley and during the retreat to Harrison's Landing. He commanded Foster's brigade, Division at Suffolk, VII, Va. (23 Sept. '62–9 Apr. '63) and 2, 1, VII, Va. (9 Apr.–7 July '63). In the X Corps, Dept. of the South, he commanded 1st, North End Folly Island (16 Aug.–16 Dec. '63); Forces North End Folly Island (16 Dec. '63–15 Jan. '64); Vodges' Dist. Fla. (15 Jan.–25 Feb. '64); 1st Brig., 2d Dist. Fla. (25–28 Feb. '64); and 2d Dist. Fla. (28 Feb.–25 Apr. '64). He was then Gillmore's (X Corps) Chief of Staff and then led, in the X Corps, Dept.

of Va. and N.C., during the Petersburg siege and the pursuit to Appomattox: 1st Div. (14–21 June '64, and 18–23 July '64); 3, 1st Div. (23 June–18 July '64, and 23 July–23 Aug. '64); 2d Div. (23 Aug.–3 Dec. '64); and 1st Div., XXIV Corps, Va. (6 Dec. '64–1 Jan. '65, 2 Feb.–2 May '65, 8 July–1 Aug. '65). He served on the military commission that tried Lincoln's assassins, and breveted Maj. Gen. USV 31 Mar., and resigned 25 Sept. '65, returning to Indianapolis, where he held several public offices.

FOUGASS. A land mine formed by placing a charge of gunpowder at the base of a pit in such a way as to project stones or shells. It was placed at a point over which the enemy was expected to pass, such as the moat of a fortification.

FOUST, Benezst Forst. Union officer. Pa. c. 1840–? 1st Lt. Adj. 88th Pa. 3 Oct. '61; Capt. 28 July '62; Maj. 31 Dec. '62; Capt. Vet. Res. Corps 30 Oct. '63; Maj. 4 Dec. '63; Lt. Col. 20 June '64; Bvt. B.G. USV (Fredericksburg, Chancellorsville, Gettysburg, Cedar Mountain, Mitchell Station, White Sulphur Springs, Thoroughfare Gap). W.I.A. Gettysburg in right arm.

FOWLE, Elida Rumsey. Philanthropist. c. 1841–? D.C. Small and not pretty, she had been too young for Miss Dix's army nurse group at the beginning of the war, so she organized her own service, visiting hospitals in a forerunner of today's Gray Lady organization. She had a beautiful voice and not only sang in the hospitals but went on a concert tour with her fiancé, John Fowle, as accompanist to raise money for a soldiers' library and a small clubhouse in Washington. After 2d Bull Run they went in the field to nurse the wounded. When, after a two-year engagement, they were married, it was in the House of Representatives before a joint session of Congress and 4,000 spectators. Their national reputation as war workers brought forth an invitation from Lincoln to marry there, and his wife made the bride's bouquet. At the end of the ceremony, Elida was asked to sing "The Star-Spangled Banner," which she did "with never more fervor in her beautiful voice."

FOWLER, Edward Brush. Union officer. N.Y. Lt. Col. 84th N.Y. 23 May '61; Col. 9 Dec. '62; Bvt. B.G. USV (war service); mustered out 6 June '64. Commanded 1, 1, I. Died 1896.

FOX, Gustavus Vasa. Union naval officer. 1821–83. Mass. Appointed Midshipman in 1838, he served on various stations, on the coast survey, and in the Mexican War before resigning in 1856 as Lt., his commission being dated the day previous to his resignation. He went into the manufacturing of woolens and was called by Gen. Scott in Feb. '61 to consult on sending troops and supplies to Anderson at Fort Sumter. This plan was vetoed by Pres. Buchanan, but when Lincoln became president, Fox was sent to see the embattled commander at Fort Sumter and upon his return to Washington put the plan into effect. When the Confederates heard that the expedition was on its way, they opened fire and all that the ships could do was remove the Union troops after they had surrendered. (See also SEWARD-MEIGS-PORTER AFFAIR.) Lincoln named Fox the First Asst. Sec. of the Navy, a post which he held for the remainder of the war, and it was Fox who to a large degree planned the capture of New Orleans, the opening of the Mississippi and the appointment of Farragut to command. Working in close cooperation with Gideon WELLES, the Sec. of the Navy, he was a superb administrator and planner. He went to Russia in

1866, where he negotiated informally for the purchase of Alaska ("Seward's Folly") and then returned to the woolens business.

FOX'S GAP (PASS), Md. Featured in battle of South Mountain in ANTIETAM CAMPAIGN.

FRANCHOT, Richard. Union officer. N.Y. Col. 121st N.Y. 23 Aug. '62; Bvt. B.G. USV (war service); resigned 25 Sept. '62.

FRANCINE, Louis R. Union officer. Pa. Capt. 7th N.Y. 23 Aug. '61; Lt. Col. 8 July '62; Col. 9 Dec. '62; Bvt. B.G. USV 2 July '63 (Gettysburg); W.I.A. 2 July '63 at Gettysburg; died 16 July '63.

FRANK, Paul. Union officer. Germany. Col. 52d N.Y. 25 Oct. '61; Bvt. B.G. USV (war service); mustered out 28 Oct. '64. Commanded 3, 1, II; 1st Div., II. Died 1875.

FRANKLE, Jones. Union officer. Prussia. Maj. 17th Mass. 22 July '61; Col. 2d Mass. Arty. 28 Dec. '63; Bvt. B.G. USV 3 Sept. '65 (Dept. of N.C.).

FRANKLIN, William Buel. Union gen. 1823–1903. Pa. USMA 1843 (1/39); Engrs. On surveying expeditions in Kearny's Rocky Mountain Expedition, in the Mexican War (2 brevets), taught at West Point, supervising harbor improvements, and was on other construction projects. Named Col. 12th U.S. Inf. 14 May '61 (Capt. since 1857) and B.G. three days later, he commanded 1st Brig., 3d Div. (June–Aug. '61) at 1st Bull Run. He then led Franklin's brigade, Division of the Potomac (Aug.–Oct. '61); Franklin's division, Potomac (3 Oct. '61–13 Mar. '62); and 1st Div., I, Potomac (13 Mar.–4 Apr. '62). At the siege of Yorktown and at West Point he commanded 1st Div., Rappahannock (4 Apr.–18 May '62). In the Peninsula campaign he commanded VI Corps, Potomac (18 May–16 Nov.

'62) at Golding's Farm, White Oak Bridge, Savage's Station, Malvern Hill, Harrison's Landing, Crampton's Gap, South Mountain, and Antietam. Named Maj. Gen. USV 4 July '62, he led the Left Grand Division at Fredericksburg after which he was blamed by Burnside and later by the Committee on the Conduct of the War for the Union debacle. In the Red River Expedition he commanded the XIX Corps (20 Aug. '63–2 May '64) at Sabine Cross Roads, where he was wounded, Pleasant Hill, and Cane River. While on sick leave of absence for this wound, his train was captured 11 July '64 by Early's men as they marched toward Washington, but he escaped the next night. He saw no further service in the field, serving on boards and "awaiting orders" until the end of the war. He was breveted for Peninsula (B.G. USA 30 June '62) and war service (Maj. Gen. USA) and continued in the R.A., resigning in 1866. From then until 1888 he was vice-president and general manager of the Colt's Fire Arms Manufacturing Company and held various public offices as well as acting as consulting engineer.

FRANKLIN, Tenn., 30 Nov. '64 (FRANKLIN AND NASHVILLE CAMPAIGN). Turned from his delaying position at Columbia, and successfully getting past Hood at Spring Hill, Schofield reached Franklin early 30 Nov. He decided to hold this place, which was south of the river, long enough to assure the safe withdrawal of his trains across the inadequate fords and bridges. Having 32,000 with which to oppose an attack by Hood's 38,000, Schofield organized his defense as shown in the sketch.

Apparently demoralized by their failure at Spring Hill to close the trap on Schofield's army, the Confederates did not pursue vigorously. Opdycke's (1st) brigade of Wagner's division (2, IV)

conducted the rear-guard action with little difficulty and then went into general reserve at Franklin. In a misguided effort to delay the Confederate attack on the main position as long as possible, Wagner stopped the rest of his division

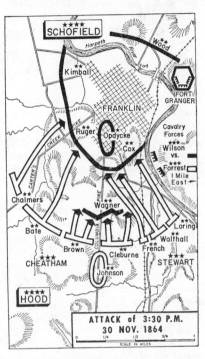

—the brigades of Lane and Conrad— astride the Columbia Pike about a half mile south of the main lines. By 3 P.M. the trains were nearly all over the river, and Schofield had issued orders for a general withdrawal across the river at 6 P.M. if the enemy did not attack before sunset.

About 3:30, however, the Confederates attacked vigorously. Wagner had been ordered to withdraw his two advance brigades at the first indication of a general enemy advance. However, from his observation post near the Carter House Wagner failed to see the

Confederates move forward, and he did not issue the necessary orders. From elsewhere along the Federal line, however, the Confederates were seen to be advancing on a broad front. "It was now four o'clock, and to the amazement of the thousands who were watching them, Wagner's infantry opened fire. There was a rattling fusilade for a few moments, Cleburne and Brown were checked for an instant, but the Confederate forces passed the flanks of Lane and Conrad, to right and left, a rush and a yell followed, and the two hapless brigades came streaming to the rear in a disorganized crowd, running rapidly to reach the parapets behind them" (J. D. Cox's *The March to the Sea— Franklin and Nashville,* 88-89). The Federal units astride the Columbia Pike had to hold their fire as the two brigades retreated for safety. However, this center section of the line was then carried back in confusion along with Wagner's routed brigades. Opdycke rushed into the gap with his reserve brigade, and there was heavy hand-to-hand fighting. The Confederates penetrated this gap and captured eight guns before being repulsed. Other parts of the line came under heavy attack and the Confederates secured footholds at several points. It was 9 P.M. before Hood halted his attacks, and firing continued until 11. That night Schofield withdrew toward Nashville.

"The annals of war may long be searched for a parallel to the desperate charge of the Army of Tennessee at Franklin, a charge which has been called 'the greatest drama in American history,' " writes Horn (*op. cit.,* 402-03). In comparing it with "Pickett's Charge," Horn points out these differences: at Gettysburg the charge was made across a mile of open ground after a tremendous artillery preparation, and against improvised fieldworks; at Franklin the charge was made across two miles of open ground, without any artillery preparation, and against carefully constructed works.

The Confederate cavalry divisions of Abraham Buford and William Jackson had crossed the Harpeth River east of Franklin and attacked Wilson's cavalry at about 3:30 P.M. There was heavy fighting on this flank during the battle of Nashville, but Forrest's troopers were driven back and recrossed to the south bank after dark. The third Confederate cavalry division, Chalmers's, was on the other (west) flank. An attack by Chalmers and Bate was repulsed with little difficulty by the Federal divisions of Kimball (1, IV) and Ruger (2, XXIII).

Of 27,939 Federals engaged, there were 2,326 casualties, of whom 1,104 were missing. Of 26,897 Confederates engaged, 6,252 were lost, of whom 702 were missing. The Confederates lost 22 battle flags to Reilly's division and 10 to Opdycke's brigade (Cox, *op. cit.,* 94). Five Confederate generals were killed: Cleburne, John Adams, Strahl, S. R. Gist, and H. B. Granbury.

FRANKLIN AND LITTLE HARPETH, Tenn. See BRENTWOOD, 25 Mar. '63.

FRANKLIN AND NASHVILLE CAMPAIGN (Hood's Invasion of Tenn.), 18 Sept. '64-10 Jan. '65. After giving up Atlanta on 1 Sept. Hood remained at Lovejoy, 25 miles south of the city, until the 18th. As soon as he realized that Sherman did not intend to continue his advance south, Hood decided to strike at the Federal line of communications and to draw Sherman as far north as possible. On the 18th Hood started moving west to Palmetto on the Atlanta–Montgomery R.R. Here he stayed until the end of the month while supplies were collected at Blue Mountain.

At Hood's request, Hardee was relieved and Cheatham took command of his corps. The other two infantry corps, each numbering about 11,000, continued to be led by S. D. Lee and A. P. Stewart; Wheeler continued to command the cavalry corps, and W. H. Jackson led the separate cavalry division. There was no major change in the organization of Sherman's forces.

FORREST'S OPERATIONS DURING THE ATLANTA CAMPAIGN, and WHEELER'S RAID of 10 Aug.–10 Sept. forced Sherman to send Thomas back to Chattanooga and Nashville to restore order in his department and to prepare for the invasion he had anticipated Hood would launch. Three infantry divisions were also sent back.

On 1 October Hood's Army of Tenn., preceded by Jackson's cavalry division, headed north toward Lost Mountain (west of Marietta). On the 4th Confederate cavalry wrecked the railroad near Acworth and was followed by Stewart's corps. French's division was sent from there to capture Allatoona. In response to a wigwag message from Sherman, Corse rushed from Rome with a brigade to the threatened point. The hotly contested and much-publicized action of ALLATOONA, 5 Oct., ended with the successful defense of that place.

Early 5 Oct. Sherman was near Marietta with all of his corps except the XX, which had been left to hold the intrenched camp of Atlanta. Hood circled westward around Rome (Van Wert–Cedartown and Cave Springs–Coosaville–Villanow), while Sherman continued to move north along the railroad. Wheeler's cavalry joined Hood at Coosaville and thereafter screened his movements. Jackson's cavalry remained south of the Coosa River in the vicinity of Rome. Although Federal troops were able to hold Resaca on the 12th and 13th the corps of S. D. Lee and Cheatham captured the rail-

road from that place north to Tunnel Hill, including the junction at Dalton. Hood then circled southwest, massed his forces at LaFayette, and moved down to Gadsden, Ala., where he arrived 22 Oct.

Hood had drawn Sherman back north, although Atlanta still remained in Federal hands. Now, however, Sherman took up a position just west of Rome which enabled him to retain control of the vital points of Chattanooga and Atlanta. Hood's corps commanders did not believe their troops were capable of offensive action against Sherman. Beauregard visited Hood and approved his plan of moving against Tenn.; Beauregard required, however, that Wheeler's cavalry be left behind to observe Sherman. Forrest was to join Hood from East Tenn. to provide cavalry for Hood's operations.

Whereas Hood hoped to pull Sherman out of Georgia by threatening Nashville, Sherman was not to be deterred from his planned March to the Sea. He recalled the two divisions from Chattanooga. Giving Thomas the mission of checking Hood, and sending him the IV and XXIII Corps as reinforcements, Sherman started his other corps back to Atlanta. He reinforced Kilpatrick's division to 3,500 well-mounted troopers from the other cavalry divisions and sent the rest of his cavalry to Nashville; here they were to be mounted and reorganized by J. H. Wilson, who had come from the East for this task.

Hood reached Decatur on 26 Oct. Although he intended to launch his offensive from here, he found that Forrest's arrival had been delayed. He therefore moved farther west to Tuscumbia and waited there to gather supplies and to be joined by Forrest. Florence was captured from Croxton's cavalry brigade, Corinth was again fortified, and the Meridian–Corinth–Tuscumbia R.R. repaired so as to facilitate the gathering of supplies. Forrest joined on 17 Nov.

While Hood was making this fateful three-week delay Thomas organized the defense of his department. During the period 1–5 Nov., Stanley's IV Corps concentrated at Pulaski on the Nashville and Decatur R.R. After Ruger's division (1, XXIII) reached Nashville (4 Oct.) one brigade was sent south to Columbia and the rest of the unit was sent 65 miles west to the railroad terminus at JOHNSONVILLE on the Tennessee River. On the 15th Cox's division (2, XXIII) arrived in the vicinity of Pulaski to reinforce the IV Corps. To observe the main Confederate force at Florence, two infantry brigades were sent to reinforce Croxton.

On 14 Nov. Schofield established his headquarters at Pulaski. As commander of the field forces opposing Hood, he had 25,000 infantry (IV and XXIII Corps) and 5,000 cavalry. An additional 40,000 Federal troops were between Nashville and Dalton, Ga. Hood had 33,000 present for duty and Forrest about 6,000.

On 19 Nov. Forrest led Hood's forces north, and S. D. Lee followed the next day. On the 21st the three Confederate infantry corps were advancing on parallel routes toward Columbia, 80 miles away. The weather was particularly unfavorable, alternately freezing and thawing, with snow, sleet, and rain. Hood's strategy was to turn Schofield out of his position in Pulaski by taking Columbia. On the 22d Schofield started evacuating Pulaski, and two days later was at Columbia with the IV Corps and all but one brigade of the XXIII Corps. In order to hold the bridges over the Duck River for a possible offensive move, the Federals intrenched south of the river. Hood's infantry reached Columbia

the morning of 26 Nov. Since Schofield was in danger of again being turned, he withdrew the next night to the north bank and destroyed the two bridges. The XXIII Corps guarded the fords near the town, and the IV Corps was held in reserve. The afternoon of the 28th Forrest's cavalry crossed 10 miles upstream at Huey's Mill and drove the Federal cavalry north toward Franklin. That night S. D. Lee's corps, minus Johnson's division, remained at Columbia with the supply trains and all but two batteries of the artillery. The rest of Hood's infantry crossed a ponton bridge at Davis' Ford, a few miles upstream. While S. D. Lee kept up a show of activity at Columbia to hold the Federals in position, Hood was attempting to get behind them at Spring Hill. The morning of the 29th Wilson sent word to Schofield and Thomas that the Confederates were crossing the river; he advised Schofield to withdraw at once to Spring Hill. Schofield, however, believed that Hood intended to move west toward Columbia and unite there with the forces of S. D. Lee before moving north. Wheeler's cavalry captured Thomas's message to Schofield telling the latter to withdraw to Franklin. However, although Schofield initially intended to stay at Columbia an additional day and there to delay Hood, he did take some action as a result of Wilson's suggestion: he sent Stanley with Wagner's division (2, IV), the IV Corps artillery, and the army supply wagons to Spring Hill; he also sent an infantry reconnaissance toward the enemy crossing site. About 3 P.M. he finally realized that he was being turned, and ordered his force to withdraw at dark toward Franklin.

Stanley's force reached Spring Hill before 2 P.M. Forrest's cavalry arrived at the same time from the north, having made a wide envelopment to the east through Hurt's Corner. Forrest's attack made no progress until about dark when Cleburne's division arrived at the head of Cheatham's Corps. Although the Federals were driven back, they held Spring Hill and kept the road open for the withdrawal of the main body. Hood had arrived near Spring Hill with Cheatham's corps about an hour and a half before dark. But due to some mistake the Confederates did not then take advantage of their opportunity to cut off Schofield's retreat by blocking the road. Hood accused Cheatham of failing to carry out instructions to block the road and requested Richmond to replace Cheatham, but the next day withdrew the request. Cheatham claims not to have been given specific orders. (See B.&L., IV, 438, and Horn, 385–89, for this controversy.) In any event, only Cleburne's division attacked. During the night Schofield's forces escaped the trap. The head of the Federal column, Cox's division (3, XXIII), cleared Spring Hill about 11 P.M. and reached Franklin at dawn. The divisions of Ruger (2, XXIII), Kimball, and Wood (1 and 3, IV) followed, while Wagner (2, IV) was rear guard. Wagner left Spring Hill at dawn and reached Franklin about noon.

Forrest's cavalry attacked the Federal supply trains at Thompson's Station (two miles north of Spring Hill) during the night and captured a few wagons. Wilson's cavalry had withdrawn up the Lewisburg and Franklin road expecting to find Schofield at Franklin that night.

When Schofield reached Franklin about dawn of 30 Nov. at the head of his troops he found that he was going to have difficulty getting his forces across the river. While his engineers worked to improve the one ford available and to floor the railroad bridge and a pile bridge which had been burned, his infantry divisions formed a defense south

of the river. In very heavy fighting the Confederates drove in the outer Federal positions, but were unable to break through the main defenses. That night Schofield withdrew, having gained enough delay to evacuate his supply trains from south of the river. (See FRANKLIN, Tenn., 30 Nov. '64.)

Schofield retired into the entrenched position of Nashville, and Thomas took personal command. Having failed at Spring Hill and Franklin to destroy any sizable portion of Thomas's army, Hood was not sufficiently strong to attack his position at Nashville. He took up positions southeast of the town and dug in. Thomas, on the other hand, did not feel he could undertake an immediate counteroffensive. He wanted to give Wilson time to find horses for several thousand of his cavalrymen who were still unmounted. A. J. Smith's three divisions of XVI Corps finally started arriving at Nashville 30 Nov. and were all there the next day. By 2 Dec. Steedman had brought up 5,200 men from Chattanooga; most of whom were "casuals" from Sherman's army. Thomas formed a provisional division of new regiments and other "casuals" in the area; this was put under the command of Cruft. Miscellaneous quartermaster personnel were also organized into another division under Col. J. L. Donaldson. While Thomas was making these preparations not only successfully to attack Hood but also then to pursue and destroy the Confederate army, Washington authorities became impatient. Urged by Stanton, Grant started sending Thomas telegrams to attack. On 6 Dec. Grant ordered Thomas to "attack Hood at once," but Thomas delayed until the 8th to give Wilson more time. On the 8th there was a freezing spell that prompted Thomas to postpone his attack again. Grant decided to relieve Thomas with Schofield, and then with

Logan, and on the 15th was himself at Washington preparatory to going to Nashville.

On the latter date, however, Thomas attacked and "gained such a splendid and decisive victory as to hush censure for all time." (Steele, 583.) (See NASHVILLE, Tenn., 15–16 Dec. '64.)

During the first two weeks of Dec., Forrest's cavalry had taken advantage of the absence of Wilson's cavalry south of the Cumberland River to engage in a number of independent operations. The cavalry division of Chalmers on the west flank captured some Federal transports below Nashville. Forrest, with the other two divisions (Abraham Buford and W. H. Jackson), moved down the Nashville and Chattanooga R.R. toward Murfreesboro, where L. H. Rousseau commanded a force of 10,000 Federals, and captured blockhouses numbers 1 through 4. Near Murfreesboro Forrest found Bate's division of Cheatham's corps, which had been sent there from Franklin to block the rail movement of reinforcements from Chattanooga to Nashville. When Bate reported to Hood that the garrison was much larger than the 5,000 previously estimated, Hood reinforced Forrest with two additional infantry brigades. On 7 Dec. the Confederates were defeated by two provisional brigades under R. H. Milroy. (See MURFREESBORO, Tenn., 7 Dec. '64.) Two days later Bate's division and the brigade from French's division returned to their corps at Nashville, and a brigade from J. A. Smith's division was sent to Forrest. During the battle of Nashville, Forrest was near Murfreesboro with his two cavalry divisions and his two attached infantry brigades. This force rejoined Hood at Columbia (via Eagleville and Berlin) between 18 and 20 Dec.

Hood started his retreat on the night of the 16th to the Duck River. Stewart's and Cheatham's corps led the way while S. D. Lee brought up the rear. Clayton's division was the rear guard to Franklin, and Stevenson's was rear guard to Columbia. Since the disorganized division of Chalmers was the only cavalry available with Hood's main body until Forrest rejoined at Columbia 20 Dec., the rear guard was greatly harassed by Wilson's cavalry. By the 27th Hood's entire force had withdrawn via Pulaski and had crossed the river east of Florence. Hood's destruction of bridges and rivers swollen by rains that had set in shortly after the battle of Nashville made it impossible for Federal infantry to catch up with Hood. The shattered Army of Tenn. reached Tupelo, Miss., on 10 Jan. '64. Here Hood was relieved of command at his own request.

FRANKLIN'S CROSSING (OR DEEP RUN), Va., 5 June '63 (Gettysburg campaign). A reconnaissance in force which Hooker ordered Sedgwick to make to check evidence that the Confederates were withdrawing from Fredericksburg. The 26th N.J., 5th Vt. (2, 2, VI), supported by the 15th and 50th N.Y. Engrs. and other VI Corps troops, attempted to cross at Franklin's Crossing opposite Deep Run. Confederates in rifle pits on the opposite shore could not be driven out by small arms or artillery fire. Infantry then crossed in pontons, drove the enemy riflemen back, taking 35 prisoners and suffering 6 killed and 35 wounded (E.&B.). Sedgwick reported that he thought the main enemy army was still in position. Hooker then ordered a cavalry reconnaissance that resulted in the battle of BRANDY STATION.

FRASER, John. Union officer. Scotland. Lt. Col. 140th Pa. 9 Sept. '62; Col. 4 July '63; Bvt. B.G. USV (war service). Commanded in II Corps, Army of the Potomac: 1st Brig., 1st Div.;

2d Brig., 2d Div.; 3d Brig., 1st Div.; 4th Brig., 1st Div. Died 1878.

FRATERNIZATION and informal truces between front-line troops were common during the Civil War, as in other wars before and since. This was particularly true in stabilized situations, such as the Petersburg trenches, where the opposing pickets would establish a relationship of "I won't shoot at you if you won't shoot at me." Soldiers would meet between the lines to exchange items, the Southerners trading whisky and tobacco for coffee and newspapers. (See Bell I. Wiley, *The Life of Billy Yank*, 352–57.)

FRAYSER'S FARM, Va., 30 June '62. WHITE OAK SWAMP.

FRAZAR, Douglas. Union officer. Mass. Maj. 13th N.Y. Cav. 7 Aug. '63; mustered out 13 Mar. '65; Col. 104th US Col. Inf. 27 Mar. '65; Bvt. B.G. USV (war service). Died 1896.

FRAZER, John W. C.S.A. gen. c. 1827–1906. Tenn. Appt.-Miss. USMA 1849 (34/43); Inf. After serving in garrison and on the frontier, he resigned 15 Mar. '61 as Capt. to be commissioned Capt. of C.S.A. Inf. Promoted Lt. Col. 8th Ala., he resigned to become Col. 28th Ala. and fight with Bragg at Corinth and Munfordville (Ky.). He resigned this commission and was appointed B.G. C.S.A. 19 May '63 and led his brigade in eastern Tenn. In charge of Cumberland Gap in Sept. '63, he surrendered to Burnside on the 9th of that month. His B.G. nomination was rejected by the C.S.A. senate 16 Feb. '64. After the war he was a merchant and planter.

FREDERICK, Calvin Harlowe. Union officer. N.Y. Mo. R.A. Lt. Col. 59th Ill. 17 July '61; resigned 23 Jan. '63; Lt. Col. Vet. Res. Corps 25 Sept. '63; Bvt. B.G. USV. Brevets for war service, Southwest campaigns, Pea Ridge

(2), Stones River. W.I.A. Pea Ridge (Ark.) and disabled by the falling of his horse. Died 1902.

FREDERICKSBURG, Va., Confed. Dept. of. Forces around Fredericksburg at the beginning of the war were commanded by T. H. Holmes. The District of AQUIA was established 22 Oct. '61, still under Holmes's command, to include this area.

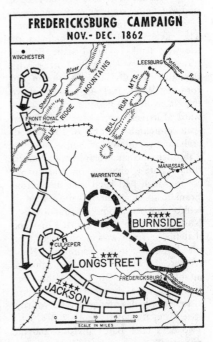

FREDERICKSBURG CAMPAIGN. Nov.–Dec. '62. Burnside replaced McClellan 7 Nov. '62. The Army of the Potomac had been advancing cautiously south and was in a position to strike between the separated wings of Lee's army and defeat them in detail. Burnside, however, abandoned this promising plan and decided to shift his line of operations to the east to attack along the line Fredericksburg–Richmond. Sumner's newly organized Right Grand Divi-

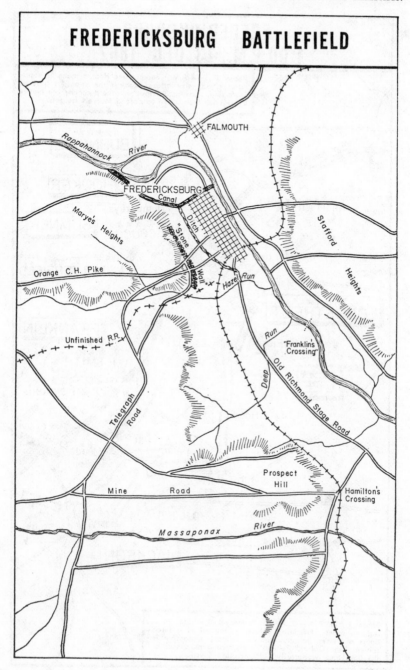

FREDERICKSBURG   BATTLEFIELD

FALMOUTH

Rappahannock   River

FREDERICKSBURG

Canal

Maryes' Heights

Stafford

Ditch

"Stone Wall"

Sunken Road

Orange C.H. Pike

Hazel Run

Heights

Unfinished R.R.

Deep Run

"Franklins' Crossing"

Telegraph Road

Old Richmond Stage Road

Prospect Hill

Mine   Road

Hamilton's Crossing

Massaponax   River

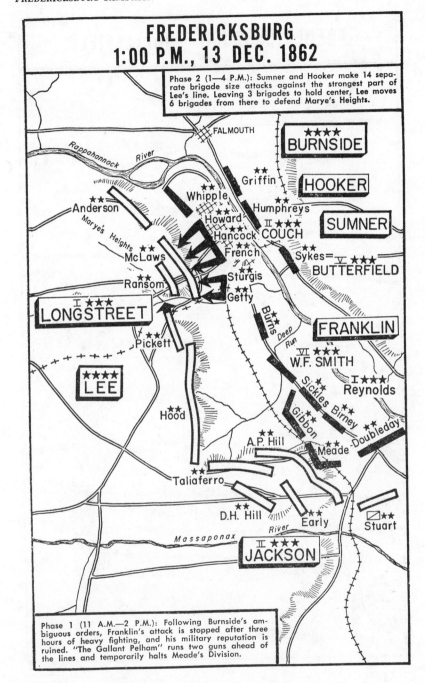

FREDERICKSBURG
1:00 P.M., 13 DEC. 1862

Phase 2 (1—4 P.M.): Sumner and Hooker make 14 separate brigade size attacks against the strongest part of Lee's line. Leaving 3 brigades to hold center, Lee moves 6 brigades from there to defend Marye's Heights.

FALMOUTH

Rappahannock River

★★★★ BURNSIDE

★★ Griffin

★★★★ HOOKER

★★ Whipple

★★ Humphreys

★★ Howard

II ★★★ COUCH

★★ Hancock

★★★★ SUMNER

★★ Anderson

Marye's Heights

★★ McLaws

★★ French

Sykes═ V ★★★ BUTTERFIELD

★★ Ransom

★★ Sturgis

★★ Getty

I ★★★ LONGSTREET

Burns

Deep Run

★★★★ FRANKLIN

★★ Pickett

VI ★★★ W.F. SMITH

★★★★ LEE

Sickles

I ★★★★ Reynolds

★★ Hood

Birney ★★★

Gibbon ★★

Doubleday ★★

★★ A.P. Hill

Meade ★★

★★ Taliaferro

★★ D.H. Hill

★★ Early

☐ ★★ Stuart

Massaponax River

II ★★★ JACKSON

Phase 1 (11 A.M.—2 P.M.): Following Burnside's ambiguous orders, Franklin's attack is stopped after three hours of heavy fighting, and his military reputation is ruined. "The Gallant Pelham" runs two guns ahead of the lines and temporarily halts Meade's Division.

sion (Couch's II Corps and Willcox's IX Corps) arrived opposite Fredericksburg on 17 Nov. before Longstreet's newly organized I Corps (Confederate) could get there (18 Nov.) to oppose a crossing of the Rappahannock at this point. Burnside's next error was not allowing Sumner to try a hasty river crossing. Stonewall Jackson's II Corps was still in the Shenandoah Valley and did not join Lee at Fredericksburg until 30 Nov. Although Lee had originally intended to drop back to the line of the North Anna, he decided to capitalize on Burnside's slowness and use the excellent defensive terrain on the south bank of the Rappahannock to contest the Federal crossing. Burnside's plan depended on the arrival of a large ponton train to bridge the 400-foot stream. This equipment did not arrive until 25 Nov., so Burnside was forced to modify his strategy. Meanwhile, Lee had his entire army of 78,500 in position to oppose the Federal force of 122,000.

The Battle—13 Dec. '62

Although his strategy had been delayed so long as to lose whatever merit it may have originally possessed, Burnside proceeded to try to force a crossing. Issuing tardy and confused orders, he started 11 Dec. to put five bridges across the icy stream at three points along a 10,000-yard front. The battle opened 13 Dec. when Franklin crossed with 50,000 men opposite Prospect Heights and was repulsed despite vigorous attacks by the divisions of Meade and Gibbon against Stonewall Jackson's defenses. To the north, opposite Marye's Heights, Sumner's crossing was initially delayed by sharpshooters in Fredericksburg. A senseless bombardment of the town failed to drive out the latter. Finally, infantry got across in boats, cleared out the Confederate riflemen, and the ponton

bridge was completed. Union troops massed at the base of the hill and started a series of futile, piecemeal frontal assaults against a strong natural position which was valiantly defended by troops under Longstreet's command. As Burnside ordered Sumner and Hooker to keep up their suicidal attacks, Lee shifted strength to this side of his line from his center and south flank, where he was not being pressed. Federal dead piled in front of the stone wall that ran in front of the sunken road at the base of Marye's Heights. Out of an estimated 106,000 Federals who actually participated in the attacks, 12,700 were killed or wounded. Confederate losses were 5,300 out of 72,500 engaged.

Lee has been criticized for not following up his successful defense by a counterattack to destroy the remainder of Burnside's battered forces; less than half of the Confederate brigades had been employed. However, Lee did not realize how much damage the enemy had suffered and was expecting a renewal of the attack the next day. Furthermore, Federal artillery dominated the battlefield from positions on Stafford Heights on the Union side; Antietam (Sharpsburg) was too fresh in Lee's mind for him to entertain the idea of an attack under such similar circumstances. Burnside, in fact, issued orders for the attack to be renewed the next morning, but his commanders talked him into revoking them. Federal forces remained in position astride the river 14–15 Dec. without renewing the battle. They withdrew the night of 15 Dec.

FREDERICKSBURG, Second Battle of. See Chancellorsville Campaign.

FREEDMAN. Generic term applied to all ex-slaves after the adoption of the Thirteenth Amendment (see under Abolition of Slavery). The bitterness and resentment shown by the South against the political importance of the freedmen (estimated at some four million) were responsible for much of the harsh reconstruction policy compounded by the RADICAL REPUBLICANS. See BLACK REPUBLICANS; FREEDMAN'S BUREAU; FREEDMAN'S BUREAU ACT; REPUBLICAN PARTY.

FREEDMAN'S BUREAU. In order to protect the interests of the former slaves, Congress established the Bureau as part of the War Department in 1865 for a period of a year, with Oliver O. HOWARD in command. Charged with obtaining labor contracts for them, helping them find homes, settling their disputes, and obtaining employment for them, it distributed hundreds of its agents throughout the South to facilitate this program and to do additional work in educational facilities, relief, and the administration of justice. During its existence it founded over 100 hospitals, rendered medical aid to 500,000 patients, distributed over 20,000,000 rations to Negroes and white people, settled thousands of freedmen (see FREEDMAN) on abandoned or confiscated lands, and established over 4,000 schools for Negro children, spending $17,000,000 in this program.

FREEDMAN'S BUREAU ACT. Setting up and empowering the FREEDMAN'S BUREAU, the first bill was vetoed by President Johnson in Feb. 1866, and the second was passed by Congress over his veto in July 1866.

FREE-SOIL PARTY. A minor political party organized in the 1840's to combat the extension of SLAVERY into the newly acquired territories, although not principally an ABOLITIONIST party. It was mostly concerned with the status of slavery in the territory obtained from Mexico. Its presidential candidate in the election of 1848, Martin Van Buren, drew enough votes from the Democratic candidate, Lewis Cass, to assure the election of the Whig candidate, Zachary Taylor. Thereafter the expanding strength of the southern DEMOCRATS substantially reduced the Free-Soilers' power, and its following was absorbed into the new REPUBLICAN PARTY after 1854.

FRÉMONT, John Charles. Union gen. 1813–80. Ga. After teaching mathematics in the Navy, he joined the Army Topographical Engineers Corps in 1838 as 2d Lt. For the next seven years, he gained prominence as an explorer and was called "The Pathfinder" for his journeys across the Rockies. In 1846 his appearance saved California for the U.S., and he was elected governor by the settlers. He was subsequently courtmartialed for defying the orders of Stephen W. Kearny (uncle of Phil KEARNY) when that officer arrived with the authority from Washington to set up a government. President Polk approved his conviction for mutiny and disobedience, but let him resign to avoid dismissal. Frémont then served in the Senate from California and made two more explorations of the Far West before being nominated by the new Republican party in 1856 for president. Although defeated by Buchanan, he retained powerful political supporters—the Blairs, the German-American element, and the anti-slavery faction of his party. He was appointed Maj. Gen. USV 3 July '61 and put in command of the newly created Western Dept. He arrived in St. Louis 25 July to find a complex military situation and a burgeoning army to supply—neither of which problems he was able to handle. T. Harry Williams in *Lincoln and His Generals* characterizes Frémont as "weak and unstable" giving "at the same time an impression of wise maturity and of buoyant youth." Saying that "his every action was dramatic," Williams continues: ". . . soon he imagined himself surrounded on all sides by dangers and difficulties . . . Lincoln had sent a boy to do a man's work. Frémont was a sincere and attractive person, but a giddy and fumbling general." He attracted a motley collection of fancily dressed and useless staff officers, mostly Germans and Hungarians, who not only did no work themselves but kept out those who had good reason to confer with the general. He handed out contracts with abandon, and most of them to dishonest contractors, although he himself did not profit. The mounting bills alarmed the government. After quarreling with the Blairs, he angered Lincoln by his emancipation policy. On 30 Aug., he established martial law in Missouri and freed the slaves of all who resisted the government. Asked by the President to modify this, he refused, and Lincoln then revoked Frémont's emancipation proclamation. The President sent Montgomery Blair, Q.M. Gen. Meigs, and David Hunter to advise Frémont. Jessie Benton Frémont, daughter of the redoubtable Thomas Hart Benton and the General's wife, came to Washington to plead his case personally with Lincoln. In a stormy and antagonistic interview, she did her husband's cause much harm.

After the defeat of Frémont's forces at WILSON'S CREEK (Lyon was in command, and Frémont disclaimed responsibility) and continued Federal military reverses in Missouri, Lincoln sent Simon Cameron to St. Louis, with an order for Frémont to turn his command over to Hunter. Frémont begged the Secretary for more time, and another removal order was sent. Lincoln sent this one to Gen. Curtis in St. Louis, but instructed him not to deliver it if Frémont had meanwhile won a battle or was about to do so. On 2 Nov., after the original courier had been replaced by a volunteer captain disguised as a farmer to get through the guards Frémont had posted to stop the order,

the relief order was handed to the General.

On 29 Mar. '62, he took command of the newly-established Mountain Dept. and unsuccessfully opposed the SHENANDOAH VALLEY CAMPAIGN OF JACKSON, culminating in the battle of CROSS KEYS. When his corps became the I Corps, Army of Va., on 26 June '62 under Pope, Frémont refused to serve under him and was relieved 28 June. He spent the rest of the war in N.Y., "awaiting orders."

In May '64, a group of Radical Republicans offered to support him for president. He accepted but withdrew in Sept. when another faction of the party requested it. He was then engaged in railroad financing and building. In 1873 he was convicted, fined, and sentenced in default by the French government for swindles in the proposed transcontinental line from San Francisco to Norfolk. Governor of Arizona in 1878–81, he was named Maj. Gen. on the retired list in 1890.

FRENCH, Samuel Gibbs. C.S.A. gen. 1818–1910. N.J. USMA 1843 (14/39); Arty.-Q.M. He served in garrison and the Mexican War (2 brevets, 1 wound) and was then on quartermaster duty in Washington and the frontier before resigning in 1856. Taking over a plantation near Vicksburg, he was named the Chief of Ord. when Miss. seceded and was commissioned Maj. of C.S.A. Arty. in Apr. '61. Appointed B.G. C.S.A. 23 Oct. '61, he commanded Evansport (Va.), blocking the Potomac 14 Nov. '61–8 Mar. '62 and was then sent to take over New Bern. On 17 July '62 he took command of the Dept. of Southern Va. and N.C. and was promoted Maj. Gen. 22 Oct. '62 to rank from 31 Aug. On 28 May '63 he was sent to join Johnston at Jackson, Miss. (Vicksburg campaign), and led his division in the Atlanta campaign and Hood's Franklin and Nashville campaign. See ALLA-TOONA, 5 Oct. '64.

FRENCH, William Henry. Union gen. 1815–81. Md. Appt.-D.C. USMA 1837 (22/50); Arty. In Seminole and Mexican wars, A.D.C. to Franklin Pierce and winning two brevets in latter. In command at Eagle Pass (Tex.) he refused to follow Twiggs into the Confederacy and marched his garrison down-river to the Gulf and sailed for Key West, remaining in command there until 28 Sept. '61, when he was named B.G. USV (Capt. 1st Arty. since 1848). In the Defenses of Washington he commanded 3d Brig., Sumner's division (25 Nov. '61–13 Mar. '62) and then led 3, 1, II (13 Mar.–20 July '62) at Yorktown, Fair Oaks, Oak Grove, Gaines's Mill, Peach Orchard Station, Savage's Station, Glendale, and Malvern Hill. He also commanded this brigade 10 Aug.–6 Sept. '62 and led 3d Div., II Corps (10 Sept.–20 Dec. '62) at Antietam and Fredericksburg and (10 Jan.–28 June '63) at Chancellorsville. He was appointed Maj. Gen. USV 29 Nov. '62. Leading French's command, VIII, Middle Dept. (June–July '63) in the Harpers Ferry District, he later commanded the III Corps (7 July '63–28 Jan. '64) at Manassas Gap, Auburn, Kelly's Ford, Brandy Station, and in the Mine Run operations. Meade held French principally responsible for the Mine Run failure, and when the Army of the Potomac was reorganized that winter, he was displaced and saw no further field service after commanding the III Corps again from 17 Feb.–24 Mar. '64. He was in garrison at Fort McHenry (Md.) and Chief and Inspector of Arty. for the Middle Dept. Jan.–July '65. Breveted for Fair Oaks, Antietam, Chancellorsville (B.G. USA), and Maj. Gen. USA (war service), he continued in the R.A., retiring as Col. 4th Arty. in 1880. A tall, bulky man, Lyman said he looked

like "one of those plethoric French Colonels, who are so stout, and who look so red in the face, that one would suppose someone had tied a cord tightly around their necks."

FRENCH, Winsor Brown. Union officer. Vt. 1st Lt. Adj. 77th N.Y. 24 Sept. '61; Maj. 1 June '62; Lt. Col. 18 July '62; Bvt. B.G. USV (war service); mustered out 13 Dec. '64. Commanded 3d Brig., 2d Div., Army of Potomac.

FRINK, Henry Alexander. Union officer. Conn. Maj. 11th Pa. 22 Aug. '61; Lt. Col. 1 Sept. '62; Col. 186th Pa. 30 May '64; Bvt. B.G. USV 4 Oct. '65 (war service). Ex-cadet USMA 1850. Died 1892.

FRISBIE, Henry Newton. Union officer. N.Y. Capt. 37th Ill. 18 Sept. '61; Maj. 12 July '62; Lt. Col. 31 Dec. '62; resigned 17 Oct. '63; Col. 92d US Col. Inf. 24 Oct. '63; Bvt. B.G. USV (war service). Commanded 1st Brig., 1st Div., Corps d'Afrique; 1st Brig., USCT Morganza, La. Died 1897.

FRITCHIE, Barbara. Immortalized by Whittier's poem bearing her name for an act of patriotic defiance which she probably did not perform. There is evidence that it was not the 95-year-old Barbara who waved the flag, but Mrs. Mary A. Quantrill, a relative of the notorious bushwhacker. The facts apparently are these: Mrs. Quantrill stood by her gate with a young daughter and waved several Union flags at Jackson's troops as they passed through Frederick on 6 Sept. '62 (Antietam campaign). This performance elicited growls at first and then admiration from the marching Rebs. One passing officer is alleged to have saluted with a chivalrous, "To you, madam, not to your flag." The story somehow got around almost immediately that it was the aged Barbara who had flaunted the Stars and Stripes with a paraphrased version of " 'Shoot if you must, this old gray head, But spare your country's flag,' she said." Burnside's troops had heard the tale when they came through town shortly after Jackson's men had left. A member of the family thoughtfully provided her with a Union flag, and she waved this at the passing Federals. Jesse Reno looked her up, and tried without success to buy the flag. Garbled word of the affair got to the poet Whittier via Mrs. E. D. E. N. Southworth, a lady novelist from Frederick. Whittier in good faith wrote the poem. (See B.&L., II, 618–19; and Connelley's *Quantrill*, 22ff.)

FRITZ, Peter, Jr. Union officer. Pa. Capt. 99th Pa. 25 Feb. '62; Lt. Col. 3 Oct. '64; Bvt. B.G. USV. Brevets for Spotsylvania C.H., Petersburg.

FRIZELL, Joseph Washington. Union officer. Ky. Lt. Col. 11th Ohio 25 Apr. '61; resigned 21 Dec. '61; Col. 94th Ohio 23 Aug. '62; Bvt. B.G. USV (war service); resigned 22 Feb. '63. Died 1874.

FROHOCK, William Thompson. Union officer. Me. Ill. R.A. Pvt. Co. F 3d Bn. D.C. 29 Apr. '61; mustered out 24 July '61; 1st Lt. Adj. 45th Ill. 26 Dec. '61; Capt. 18 May '63; Col. 66th US Col. Inf. 13 Jan. '64; resigned 20 Sept. '64; Maj. 7th US Vet. Vols. 26 Mar. '65; Bvt. B.G. USV. Brevets for war service (2), Shiloh, Vicksburg. W.I.A. Vicksburg assault. Judge Advocate Vicksburg. Died 1878.

FRONTAL ATTACK. Although often used in the literal sense of "an attack against the enemy's front" (as opposed to an ENVELOPMENT), in the strict sense it is "an attack wherein the available forces are equally distributed and strike the enemy all along his front" (M.A.&E., *Notes*). Frontal attacks are generally costly and ineffective except in "secondary attacks" (see ATTACKS for definition), since they violate the

principles of mass and economy of force (see PRINCIPLES OF WAR).

FRONTIER, UNION DISTRICT AND ARMY OF THE. On 12 Oct. '62 the field forces of the departments of Mo. and Kans. were organized into an army under Brig. Gen. John M. Schofield. The latter was nominally in command until 30 Mar. '63, but while he was on sick leave the army was commanded by Maj. Gen. James G. Blunt at Prairie Grove. Maj. Gen. F. J. Herron commanded from Schofield's departure until 5 June '63, when the army was disbanded. The Dist. of the Frontier was constituted 9 June '63 in Ark. (when that state was part of the Dept. of Mo.), and commanded by Blunt until 6 Jan. '64, when the district became part of the newly-created Dept. of Ark. Its designation was changed to Frontier Div. on 3 Dec. '64. The organization was discontinued 1 Feb. '65.

FRONT ROYAL, Va., 23 May '62. (SHENANDOAH VALLEY CAMPAIGN OF JACKSON) After the battle of McDOWELL Jackson moved down the North Fork toward Strasburg where Banks was located with his main body of 7,000 men. Screening in this direction with Ashby's cavalry, Jackson unexpectedly crossed the Massanuttens by the New Market Road and was joined at Luray by Ewell. On the 23d he brought his entire strength of 16,000 against a force of about 1,000 Federals under Col. J. R. KENLY at Front Royal (1st Md., two companies of the 29th Pa., the 5th N.Y. Cav., Knap's 1st Pa. Battery, and Mapes's Pioneers). Dick Taylor, commanding the advance guard (1st Md. and Wheat's La. Tigers), was met on the outskirts of the town by the spy Belle BOYD, who furnished such accurate information of Federal dispositions that Taylor launched an immediate attack. Jackson arrived and directed the employment of the other Confederate units as they came up. Kenly reported being attacked about 2 P.M. and being able to maintain his position until nearly 5 o'clock, when forced to withdraw to avoid being cut off. He made a stand along the river and then dropped back to another delaying position (B.&L., II, 289n). Here he was overwhelmed by a charge of Col. Flournoy's 6th Va. Cav. and most of the Federals captured. Kenly was severely wounded and taken prisoner. A curiosity of this action was the capture of the 1st Md. of the Union Army by the Confederate 1st Md. Of 1,063 Federals in Kenly's force, 904 were killed, wounded, or captured; Jackson lost fewer than 50 (*Lee's Lts.*, I, 382). An estimated $300,000 worth of supplies was captured (but lost 30 May).

FRONT ROYAL, Va., 30 May '62. (SHENANDOAH VALLEY CAMPAIGN OF JACKSON) The 12th Georgia under Col. Z. T. Connor (Edward Johnson's command) had been left to guard prisoners and supplies taken 23 May (see above). Kimball's (1st) brigade, leading Shields's (1st) division back into the Valley, approached Front Royal at 11:30 A.M. after an all-night march. (See Kimball's article, B.&L., II, 311.) Connor "lost his head and...started precipitately for Winchester to report." (*Lee's Lts.*, I, 416.) The Confederates set fire to their supplies and retreated toward Winchester under command of 59-year-old Capt. William F. Brown. Belle Boyd was captured when the Federals entered the town. A pursuit by 30 men of the 1st R.I. Cavalry netted 156 prisoners with the loss of 14 Federals (E.&B.). Of the Federal prisoners taken 23 May, 24 were recovered. (Shields's report in O.R.) When Jackson learned of this action he placed Connor under arrest.

FROST, Daniel Marsh. C.S.A. gen. c. 1823–1900. N.Y. USMA 1844 (4/25); Arty.-Mtd. Rifles. He served in garrison, the Mexican War (1 brevet), on the frontier, and in Indian scouting, and in Europe on "professional duty" for a year before resigning in 1853. Settling in St. Louis, he ran a planing mill, sat in the state legislature, and served on the USMA Board of Visitors as well as being a general in the state militia. He commanded the force that was to be used in Jackson's plan of seizing the St. Louis arsenal and was himself seized by Lyon. Exchanged, he led his Mo. state brigade at Pea Ridge and was then appointed B.G. C.S.A. 10 Oct. to rank from 3 Mar. '62. He was I.G. of the Army of the West 8–26 May '62, and then served under Hindman in Ark. Fighting at Prairie Grove in Dec. '62, he succeeded Hindman in command of the division 2 Mar. '63, and returned to his brigade on the 30th of that month. He was in the Helena and Little Rock campaigns and, according to Wright, was dropped by the C.S.A. 9 Dec. '63. C.M.H. says only that he was on "detached duty" in 1864. After the war he farmed near St. Louis.

FRY, Birkett Davenport. C.S.A. gen. 1822–91. Va. After attending V.M.I. and Washington College (Pa.), he was dismissed from West Point (ex-1846) for failing mathematics. A lawyer, he joined the R.A. during the Mexican War, went to Calif. and was a B.G. on Walker's filibustering expedition to Nicaragua. He was a cotton-mill manager in Ala. when commissioned Col. 13th Ala. In the Peninsular campaign, he was wounded at Seven Pines. His arm was shattered at Antietam, and he was again wounded at Chancellorsville after succeeding to command of Archer's brigade. At Gettysburg he again started out leading his regiment, succeeded to the command of Archer's brigade, and was wounded a fourth time and captured in "Pickett's Charge." Exchanged nine months later, he was appointed B.G. C.S.A. 24 May '64 and commanded both Walker's and Archer's brigades at Cold Harbor. He commanded the Mil. Dist. in Augusta until the end of the war. He returned to cotton milling and manufacturing. Described by D.A.B. as "slight in build and quiet in manner," he was "a man of gunpowder reputation," according to Bragg.

FRY, Cary H. Union officer. c. 1817–73. Ky. USMA 1834 (20/36); Inf. He served briefly on the frontier and resigned after two years to become a doctor in Louisville. Returning to fight in the Mexican War, he again practiced medicine as a civilian and was commissioned Maj. Paymaster in the R.A. in 1853. During the Civil War he was Acting Paymaster Gen. 15 July–10 Dec. '62 and served in Washington until 1863, when he was sent to San Francisco. He died on active duty there as Lt. Col., having been breveted B.G. USA in 1867 for war service.

FRY, James Barnett. Union gen. c. 1827–94. Ill. USMA 1847 (14/38); Arty.-Adj. Gen. He fought in the Mexican War after teaching artillery at West Point and then served in garrison and on the frontier. After a second tour at West Point he was in the expedition to suppress John Brown's Harpers Ferry raid and, 28 May–12 Nov. '61, was McDowell's Chief of Staff at 1st Bull Run. He then became Buell's Chief of Staff until 30 Oct. '62, fighting at Shiloh, the advance upon and siege of Corinth, and Perryville. After serving as Asst. Adj. Gen. in Washington, he was named Col. and Provost Marshal Gen. 17 Mar. '63. Continuing in the R.A., he retired in 1881 as B.G. USA (21 Apr. '64). He was breveted for 1st Bull Run, Shiloh, and Perryville (B.G. USA) and war service (Maj. Gen. USA).

FRY, Speed Smith. Union gen. 1817–92. Ky. After serving in the Mexican War he was a lawyer and judge. Organizing the 4th Ky. Inf. and named Col. 9 Oct. '61, he commanded 2, 1, Army Ohio (22 Mar.–29 Sept. '62); 1, 3, Army Ohio; 2, 1, III, Army Ohio (Sept.–18 Oct. '62); and 1st Div., N. Central Ky., XXIII, Ohio. He was promoted B.G. USV 21 Mar. '62 and mustered out 24 Aug. '65, later holding numerous public offices in his native state. Fry played a conspicuous part in the battle of LOGAN CROSS ROADS, Ky., 19 Jan. '62, where he killed the C.S.A. General Zollicoffer under peculiar circumstances.

FUGITIVE SLAVE ACTS. Two laws passed by Congress in 1793 and 1850 to provide for the return of escaped slaves. The latter, part of the Omnibus Act, was nullified to a certain extent by the Personal Liberty Laws passed by the Northern states and the actions of the UNDERGROUND RAILROAD.

FULLER, Henry William. Union officer. N.H. 1st Lt. 1st N.H. 30 Apr. '61; mustered out 9 Aug. '61; 1st Lt. Adj. 4th N.H. 20 Sept. '61; resigned 29 Oct. '62; Lt. Col. 16th N.H. 29 Oct. '62; mustered out 20 Aug. '63; Col. 75th US Col. Inf. 23 Nov. '63; Bvt. B.G. USV (war service). Commanded Dist. Morganza, La. Died 1885.

FULLER, John Wallace. Union gen. 1827–91. England. A bookseller and politician in Ohio, he was commissioned Col. 27th Ohio 18 Aug. '61 and led his regiment at New Madrid and Island No. 10 He commanded 1st Brig., 2d Div., Army Miss. (10 Sept.–26 Oct. '62) at Iuka and Corinth where his troops checked the C.S.A. charge and broke their lines. In the Army of the Tenn. he led 1st, 8th Div., Left Wing, XIII (1 Nov.–18 Dec. '62); 8th Div., XIII (18 Dec. '62–3 Apr. '63) defeating Forrest at Parker Crossroads; 4, 2d Div., Dist. Corinth, XVI (18 Mar.–2 May '63) at Decatur; 3, 5th Div. Dist. Memphis, XVI (1 May–25 July '63 and 25 Aug.–14 Nov. '63). He also commanded Fuller's brigade, 2d Div., Left Wing, XVI (11 Nov. '63–2 Jan. '64 and 2 Feb.–10 Mar. '64); 1, 4, XVI (10 Mar.–17 July '64 and 4–19 Aug. '64); 4th Div., XVI (19 Aug.–23 Sept. '64, and 17 July–4 Aug. '64) at Atlanta and Chattahoochee; 1, 1, XVII (7 Nov.–24 Dec. '64 and 25 Jan.–24 June '65) and 1st Div., XVI (22 Sept.–23 Oct. '64) on the March to the Sea and through the Carolinas. Breveted Maj. Gen. USV for war service, he resigned 15 Aug. '65 and held numerous public offices after the war.

FULLERTON, Joseph Scott. Union officer. Ohio. 1st Lt. 2d Mo. 14 Oct. '62; Maj. Asst. Adj. Gen. Vols. 11 Mar. '63; Lt. Col. Asst. Adj. Gen. Assigned 10 Nov. '63–1 Aug. '65; Bvt. B.G. USV. Brevets for war service, Atlanta. On Gen. O. O. Howard's staff during Atlanta campaign. Died 1897.

FUNKE, Otto. Union officer. Germany. Capt. 11th Ill. Cav. 26 Nov. '61; Maj. 10 Dec. '62; Lt. Col. 30 June '64; Col. 21 May '65; Bvt. B.G. USV (war service). Commanded 1st Brig., Cav. Dist. West. Tenn. Died 1885.

FURNITURE. The "furniture" of a firearm consists of its mountings and certain decorative features (barrel bands, butt plate, patch box, and trigger guard, for example). "Horse furniture are ornaments and embellishments which are adopted by military men when they are mounted for service or parade, consisting chiefly of housings, saddle cloth, etc." (Wilhelm).

FUZES for artillery projectiles. The three general types were: concussion, which was operated by the shock of discharge or impact and was particularly suited to spherical SHELL; percussion, which was operated when the shock of impact set off a fulminate that exploded the charge in the shell—used effectively with rifled projectiles—and time fuze. The basic type of time fuze was a wooden or paper tube containing a burning composition that would be ignited by the charge of the gun and then burn down until it ignited the bursting charge of the shell. It could be set, theoretically, by cutting the tube to a given length. A more advanced type was the BORMANN FUZE. While the other two types were dependable, time fuzes of the Civil War were notoriously unreliable, particularly in the Confederate artillery. "A shell with a two-second fuze often went further before exploding than one cut for twice that time, if they both went off at all" (Weller, 33).

FYFFE, Edward Pierce. Union officer. Ohio. Col. 26th Ohio 18 June '61; discharged 18 Dec. '63; Col. Vet. Res. Corps 18 June '64; Bvt. B.G. USV (war service). Commanded 1, 1, XXI. Died 1867.

G

GABION. "A cylindrical basket with open ends, made of brush or metal ribbon woven on pickets, and used as a REVETMENT in constructing field works." (G.&B.)

GAGE, Joseph S. Union officer. Me. Capt. 6th Mo. 12 July '61; Maj. 13 Mar. '63; Maj. 29 Mo. 11 June '63; Lt. Col. 27 Aug. '63; Col. 10 Mar. '64; Bvt. B.G. USV 15 June '65 (war service).

GAINES'S MILL, Va., 27 June '62. (Cold Harbor; Chickahominy.) Third of the Seven Days' Battles, PENINSULAR CAMPAIGN. After his failure at MECHANICSVILLE, 26 June, to destroy Porter's isolated corps, Lee pressed toward Gaines's Mill, where the Federals had set up a new defensive position. When A. P. Hill renewed his attack along Beaver Dam Creek early 27 June, he encountered only a delaying force. Gregg's brigade was vigorously opposed by Col. Thomas Cass's 9th Mass. at Gaines's Mill. A. P. Hill was then stopped (about 2 P.M.) by the main Federal line which was located on strong defensive terrain along Boatswain's Swamp. Attacks by the brigades of Gregg, Branch, Pender, J. R. Anderson, Archer, and Field also failed to get through the fire-swept swamp to attack the Federal positions. Longstreet, arriving on A. P. Hill's right, saw that he would face the same difficulties, and Lee ordered him to delay his attack until Jackson could get into position to hit the opposite flank. As had happened at Mechanicsville, Jackson's arrival was delayed. D. H. Hill had hit the Federal right but found it so strong he decided to await Jackson's arrival there. Longstreet was ordered to conduct a diversionary attack to relieve the pressure on the Confederate right until Jackson could attack. Pickett's brigade was stopped with heavy loss. Jackson had left Walnut Grove Church with a guide who was told to lead the column to Old Cold Harbor. The guide had chosen the shortest route. When Jackson found this would take him through Gaines's Mill, a point he wished to avoid, he ordered a countermarch of four miles (*Lee's Lts.*, I, 521 [sketch] and 524). He reached D. H. Hill's position about 3 P.M., but, not understanding that the attack of A. P. Hill and Longstreet had been stopped,

Jackson held his own division and corps and D. H. Hill's inactive, for fear of moving them into the fire of the other Confederate troops.

Meanwhile, Porter had been reinforced by Slocum's division (VI) and the Federal line held fast. About an hour before dark the Confederates finally started an attack all along their front. After severe fighting the Federals were driven back. Meagher's (2d) and French's (3d) brigades of the 1st Div., Slocum's (II) corps, arrived just too late to reinforce Porter's defense, but they did support Sykes's regulars in covering the withdrawal. (A battalion of the 5th US Cav. lost all but one of its officers in a futile charge to cover the retreat.)

South of the Chickahominy during the battles of Mechanicsville and Gaines's Mill, Magruder with 25,000 men had conducted diversionary attacks that fixed 60,000 Federals in position while Porter bore the brunt of Lee's attacks.

Out of 34,214 Federals engaged, there were 6,837 casualties (893 killed, 3,107 wounded, and 2,836 missing). Of 57,018 Confederates engaged there were 8,751 killed and wounded (Livermore, and Fox).

GALLAGHER, Thomas Foster. Union officer. Pa. Col. 11th Pa. Res. 1 July '61; resigned 17 Dec. '62; Col. 54th Pa. Mil. 4 July '63; Bvt. B.G. USV (war service); mustered out 17 Aug. '63. Commanded 3, 3, III; 3, 3, I. Died 1883.

GALLATIN, Tenn., 12–21 Aug. '62. (Kirby SMITH'S INVASION OF KENTUCKY) With the mission of cutting the Louisville & Nashville R.R., and after making forced marches from Sparta, Col. J. H. Morgan surprised and captured the garrison of Gallatin and burned the lining of an 800-foot railroad bridge. Morgan reported 80 Federals killed or wounded and 200 captured, and put his own loss at 24. Federal forces engaged were the 2d Ind., 4th and 5th Ky., and 1st Tenn. Cav. The next day Col. J. F. Miller led the 69th Ohio and 11th Mich. in driving the Confederates from the town. On 21 Aug., R. W. Johnson was captured at Hartsfield with 75 others while attempting to defeat Morgan with a force of 640 cavalry from McMinnville.

GALLUP, George W. Union officer. N.Y. 1st Lt. Regt. Q.M. 14th Ky. 10 Dec. '61; Lt. Col. 12 May '62; Col. 13 Jan. '63; Bvt. B.G. USV (war service). Commanded 1st Dist. Eastern Ky., XXIII; 1, 1, Dist. Ky. 5, XXIII; 1, 2, XXIII. Died 1880.

"GALVANIZED YANKEES." Federal prisoners who had taken an oath of allegiance to the Confederate government and were enlisted in the C.S.A. G. W. Smith speaks of using such a unit at Savannah (B.&L., IV, 669n). A "Galvanized Confederate" would be just the converse. In 1864 Confederate prisoners of war were organized into six infantry regiments of US Volunteers, the 1st through the 6th, and used on the frontier for operations that did not involve fighting against the Confederacy.

GALVESTON, Tex. Shelled 3 Aug. '61 by Federal ships. On 17 May refused a demand to surrender. Captured without resistance 5 Oct. '62 by a naval force under Comdr. W. B. Renshaw and garrisoned by 260 men under Col. I. S. Burrell, 42d Mass. On 1 Jan. '63 Magruder surprised the garrison at dawn and forced their surrender after a four-hour fight. With the support of two cotton-clad steamers, *Neptune* and *Bayou City,* carrying sharpshooters and artillery, he captured the *Harriet Lane.* In this action Comdr. Wainwright was killed and his first lieutenant mortally wounded; eight men were killed, 10 wounded, and 110 captured. Renshaw was killed when his grounded ship, the *Westfield,* blew up prematurely after he had ordered it set afire to avoid capture. The rest of the Federal ships escaped, and the blockade was resumed. Galveston was surrendered 2 June '65.

GAMBLE, Hamilton Rowan. Union gov. of Missouri. 1798–1864. Va. He attended Hampton Sidney, became a lawyer, and later served as Missouri's Sec. of State. Later a judge, he sat in the legislature and was named Provisional Gov. in 1861 when Claiborne F. Jackson joined the Confederacy. Hoping for a compromise of the country's troubles, he labeled Lincoln's first call for troops unconstitutional and commanded the state militia against rebel guerrillas. He served until his death 31 Jan. '64.

GAMBLE, William. Union gen. c. 1819–66. Ireland. R.A. He fought in the Florida War as Sgt. and Sgt. Maj. 1st US Dragoons, was discharged in 1843, and became a civil engineer. Named Lt. Col. 8th Ill. Cav. 18 Sept. '61, he fought in the Peninsula and was severely wounded at Malvern Hill leading a charge. He was promoted Col. 5 Dec. '62 and commanded (in the Army of the Potomac) 1st Brig., Pleasonton's Cav. Div. (Jan.–Feb. '63) and 1, 1, Cav. Corps (27 May–6 June '63, 9 June–2 Sept. '63 and 12 Nov.–21 Dec. '63). Breveted B.G. USV 14 Dec. '64, he was mustered out 17 July '65, named B.G. USV 25 Sept. '65, and mustered out again in 1866. He went into the R.A. four months later and died in Dec. 1866, on active duty as Maj. 8th US Cav.

GANO, Richard M. C.S.A. gen. 1830–1913. Appt.-Texas. In 1861 he commanded two companies of Tex. cavalry under Morgan and went on Kirby Smith's Invasion of Ky. in Aug. '62. First mentioned as Col. in 1863, he commanded the 7th Ky. Cav., was sent to the Trans-Miss. Dept. and given command of a Tex. cavalry brigade in the Indian Territory. After the Red River campaign of 1864 and before Price's Raid in Mo., he skirmished against Fort Smith and Fort Gibson. He was named B.G. C.S.A. on 17 Mar. '65. After the war he was a minister in the Christian Church for 45 years.

GANSEVOORT, Henry Sanford. Union officer. N.Y. R.A. Pvt. 7th N.Y. Natl. Guards 19 Apr. '61; 2d Lt. 5th US Arty. 14 May '61; 1st Lt. 1 Mar. '62; Capt. 13 Aug. '66 *; Lt. Col. 13th N.Y. Cav. 20 June '63; Col. 28 Mar. '64; Bvt. B.G. USV 24 June '65. Brevets for Antietam (W.I.A.), Manassas Gap, war service. Commanded Indpt. Cav. Brig., XXII Corps; 1, 2, Cav. Corps. Graduate of Princeton College and Harvard Law School. Died 1871. * Note: These were R.A. promotions before he went into the USV.

GANTT, Edward W. C.S.A. gen. Appt.-Ark. He is listed as a general officer, appointed in 1862, by Wood and also by Heitman but does not appear on any other list.

GARDINER, Alexander. Union officer. N.H. 1st Lt. Adj. 14th N.H. 20 Sept. '62; Maj. 5 Nov. '63; Col. 18 Sept. '64; Bvt. B.G. USV 19 Sept. '64 (Winchester) (W.I.A.). Died 7 Oct. '64.

GARDNER, Franklin. C.S.A. gen. 1823–73. N.Y. Appt. to USMA from Iowa. USMA 1843 (17/39); Inf. He served in the Mexican War (2 brevets), the Seminole War, on the frontier, and in Indian scouting and on the Utah Expedition before being dropped 7 May '61 "for leaving . . . and abandoning his command" as Capt. Commissioned Lt. Col. of C.S.A. Inf. 16 Mar. '61, he served in Tenn. and Miss. the first year and commanded a cavalry brigade at

Shiloh. He was appointed from La. to be B.G. C.S.A. 11 Apr. '62 and led his brigade in Polk's corps. After the Kentucky campaign he was promoted Maj. Gen. 13 Dec. '62 and took command of Port Hudson early the next year. Captured there, he was soon exchanged and served the remainder of the war in Miss. and under Taylor. He was later a planter.

GARDNER, John Lane. Union officer. Mass. Entering the R.A. in 1813, he was Q.M. at West Point, fought in the Seminole wars, won two brevets in the Mexican War, and commanded Fort Moultrie (S.C.) until 1860. He retired in Nov. '61 as Col. 2d US Arty. and Bvt. B.G. USA. After serving on several commissions in S.C. and Pa., he died in 1869.

GARDNER, William Montgomery. C.S.A. gen. c.1824–1901. Ga. USMA 1846 (55/59); Inf. He fought in the Mexican War (1 wound, 1 brevet) and then served in garrison and on the frontier in Indian scouting before resigning 19 Jan. '61 as a Capt. Commissioned Lt. Col. in Bartow's 8th Ga., he was seriously wounded at 1st Bull Run commanding the regiment. This injury was thought to be fatal, and he was commissioned Col. on the date of the battle, 21 July '61. Upon recovery he was unable to resume field service and was appointed B.G. C.S.A. 14 Nov. '61 and given command of the Dist. of Middle Fla. On 26 July '64 he was named to command all military prisons in the states east of the Mississippi, excluding Ga. and Ala. and by 28 Nov. of that year was in command of the post of Salisbury (N.C.). From Jan. until Apr. '65 he commanded the post of Richmond.

GARFIELD, James Abram. Union gen. and 20th Pres. of US. 1831–81. Ohio. After a hard-working and poverty-stricken childhood on the frontier, he worked his way through Williams College and became active in Republican politics, serving as state Sen. in 1859. Upholding the right of the Federal government to coerce a state, he approved Lincoln's policy toward the South. Commissioned Lt. Col. 42d Ohio 21 Aug. and Col. 27 Nov. '61. Appointed B.G. USV 11 Jan. '62, he commanded the 18th Brig., Army of the Ohio (17 Dec. '61–Mar. '62) at MIDDLE CREEK, Ky., 10 Jan. '62, and POUND GAP, Ky., 16 Mar., '62, against Humphrey Marshall. He commanded the 20th Brig., 6th Div., Army of the Ohio (5 Apr.–10 July '62) at Shiloh, served on Fitz-John Porter's court-martial, and then was Rosecrans' Chief of Staff (beginning Jan. '63) at Chickamauga. He was promoted Maj. Gen. USV 19 Sept. '63. Elected to Congress in Dec., he resigned on the 5th of that month. He was elected President in 1880, took office in 1881, and was shot 2 July of that year by a disappointed office seeker. He died 19 Sept. '81.

GARLAND, John. Union officer. Va. Entering the R.A. in 1813, he fought in the Seminole War and the Mexican War (1 wound, 1 brevet) and died on active duty 5 June '61 as Col. 8th US Inf. He was breveted B.G. USA retroactive to 1847 for the Mexican War, and Phisterer lists him as a Civil War gen.

GARLAND, Samuel, Jr. C.S.A. gen. 1830–62. Va. After graduating from V.M.I., he studied law at the Univ. of Va. After the attack at Harpers Ferry by John Brown in 1859, he organized the Lynchburg Home Guard and was mustered into the Confederate Army on 24 Apr. '61 as Capt. 11th Va. A few days later he was elected Col. and led the regiment at Blackburn's Ford, 1st Bull Run, and Dranesville (Dec. '61). Wounded at Williamsburg, he did not leave the field. He was

appointed B.G. C.S.A. 23 May '62. During the rest of the Peninsular campaign he commanded his brigade under Hill at Seven Pines, Gaines's Mill, and Malvern Hill. During the 2d Bull Run campaign he held McDowell at Fredericksburg. He was mortally wounded leading his brigade 14 Sept. '62 at South Mountain, dying the same day.

GARNETT, Richard Brooke. C.S.A. gen. c.1817–63. Va. USMA 1841 (29/52); Inf. He fought in the Seminole War and then served on the frontier, was Gen. Brooke's A.D.C. in New Orleans during the Mexican War, and went on the Utah Expedition, resigning 17 May '61 as a Capt. to be commissioned Maj. of C.S.A. Arty. On 14 Nov. '61 he was appointed B.G. C.S.A. and took over the STONEWALL BRIGADE. From Jan. until Apr. '62 he fought in the Valley and was arrested by Jackson for withdrawing the brigade at Kernstown. Brought to trial about 6 Aug., he was released when Jackson hurriedly moved to Cedar Mountain. He commanded Pickett's brigade in the Md. campaign and led his own brigade under Pickett at Fredericksburg. In March '63 he went with D. H. Hill to Tarborough (N.C.) and in Apr. went to Suffolk, Va. He led his brigade in the Gettysburg campaign and was killed 3 July '63 in "Pickett's" charge. Cousin of Robert S. Garnett and grandson of the French Gen. DeGouges.

GARNETT, Robert Selden. C.S.A. gen. c.1819–61. Va. USMA 1841 (27/52); Arty. He served on the frontier, as a tactics instructor at West Point, and A.D.C. to Wool and Taylor in the Mexican War (2 brevets). He was then West Point commandant, in Indian fighting, and was on a leave of absence in Europe when the war began. Returning, he resigned as a Maj. 30 Apr. '61 and was assigned to be Adj.

Gen. of the Va. state troops. He was appointed B.G. C.S.A. 6 June '61 and commanded all Confederate troops in northwestern Va. While conducting the retreat from Laurel Hill, he was killed at CARRICK'S FORD (Va.) 13 July '61. Grandson of the French Gen. De-Gouges and cousin of Richard B. Garnett.

GARNETT'S AND GOLDING'S FARMS, Va., 27–28 June '62. Minor action of Seven Days' Battles during PENINSULAR CAMPAIGN. As part of Magruder's holding attacks south of the Chickahominy during GAINES'S MILL, G. T. Anderson was ordered to test the strength of the Federal flank while the brigade of Robert Toombs on his right would move forward to exploit any success. Anderson's advance was promptly checked, but Toombs decided to advance anyway. At about dark (8 P.M.) Col. W. M. McIntosh of the 15th Ga. was killed in an attack repulsed by Hancock's (1st) brigade of W. F. Smith's division (2, VI).

Due to a failure in coordination, Toombs attacked again the next morning, this time using the 7th and 8th Ga. Smith's division was withdrawing to Golding's Farm to escape artillery fire from across the Chickahominy and from a battery the Confederates had moved to Garnett's Farm during the night. The 49th Pa. and 33d N.Y. were covering the retrograde. Col. L. M. Lamar of the 8th Ga. was wounded and among the 50 Confederates captured in this uncoordinated action. Total losses for the two days were 368 Federals and 461 Confederates. Next day Magruder's force fought at Allen's Farm (Peach Orchard) and SAVAGE'S STATION.

GARRARD, Israel. Union officer. Ohio. Col. 7th Ohio Cav. 18 Sept. '62; Bvt. B.G. USV 20 June '65 (war service). In the Dept. of the Ohio he com-manded 1, 2, Cav. Corps; 2d Div., Cav. Corps; 1, 1, Cav. Corps; 1, Cav. Dist. Ky. 5, XXIII; Cav. Div.; and XXIII. He then led 2, 4, Cav. Corps (Mil. Div. Miss.).

GARRARD, Jephtha. Union officer. Ohio. Capt. 3d N.Y. Cav. 18 Sept. '61; Maj. 27 Sept. '62; Col. 1st US Col. Cav. 7 Dec. '63; Bvt. B.G. USV (war service).

GARRARD, Kenner. Union officer. 1828–79. Ky. Appt.-At Large. USMA 1851 (8/42); Arty.-Dragoons-Cav. After attending Harvard and graduating from the Military Academy, he served in garrison and on frontier exploration expeditions and was captured 12 Apr. '61 in San Antonio by Southern sympathizers. On parole until 27 Aug. '62, he was in the Comsy. Gen.'s office and at West Point as cavalry instructor and Commandant of Cadets. He was commissioned Col. 146th N.Y. 23 Sept. '62 and led his regiment at Fredericksburg, Chancellorsville, and Gettysburg, succeeding to the command of 3, 2, V on 3 July and commanding it, during the Rappahannock and Mine Run campaigns, until 7 Dec. Named B.G. USV 23 July '63, he was promoted Maj. 3d US Cav. 2 Nov. He was in charge of the Cavalry Bureau in Washington from Dec. '63 to Jan. '64 and then led 2d Div., Cav. Corps, Cumberland (3 Feb.–29 Oct. '64) at Covington (Ga.) and the same command in the Mil. Div. Miss. (29 Oct.–16 Nov. '64) from Dalton to Rome (Ga.). He then commanded 2d Div. Det. Army Tenn., Cumberland (7 Dec. '64–July '65) at Nashville and Mobile. Breveted for Gettysburg, Covington, Nashville (B.G. USA), war service (Maj. Gen. USA) and Nashville (Maj. Gen. USV 15 Dec. '64), he resigned in 1866. He devoted his time to real estate and historical studies.

GARRARD, Theophilus Toulmin. Union gen. 1812–1902. Ky. He was a politician and had served in the Mexican War as an R.A. Capt. He later went to California for the gold rush. Named Col. 7th Ky. 22 Sept. '61, he was promoted B.G. USV 29 Nov. '62 and commanded 1, 9, XIII, Tenn. (4 Feb.–19 May '63) and Forces at Somerset (Ky.) 1st Div. XXIII, Ohio (Aug. '63–Jan. '64). He was mustered out 4 Apr. '64. He was an uncle of Kenner GARRARD.

GARRETT, Thomas. Abolitionist. 1789–1871. A Quaker and member of the Pennsylvania Abolition Society, he operated a station on the UNDERGROUND RAILROAD and is supposed to have helped over 2,000 slaves escape.

GARRISON, William Lloyd. Abolitionist. 1805–79. Mass. A newspaper publisher, he edited *The Liberator,* a strong and influential voice of abolition begun in 1831 and continued for 35 years. He did not believe in using force to gain his ends but rather relied upon moral persuasion. He opposed the war until after Lincoln issued the Emancipation Proclamation. Although he engaged in numerous other reforms, he is most famous for his stand on slavery.

GARROTT, Isham W. C.S.A. gen. 1816–63. N.C. After graduating from Chapel Hill, he became a lawyer and states-rights Democratic legislator and leader. He was sent as a commissioner from Ala. to urge N.C. to secede and was then commissioned Col. 20th Ala. On guard duty in Mobile and eastern Tenn., he led his regiment in the beginning of the Vicksburg campaign. Appointed B.G. C.S.A. 28 May '63, he led the 2d Brig. until killed at Vicksburg 17 June by a sharpshooter while inspecting an outpost.

GARTRELL, Lucius Jeremiah. C.S.A. gen. 1821–91. Ga. The son of a prominent planter, he attended the Univ. of Ga. and Randolph-Macon. He read law in Robert Toombs's office and was elected to the state legislature and US Congress. An extreme states-rights Whig, he shifted to the Democratic party and resigned his seat in Washington when Ga. seceded. Commissioned Col. 7th Ga., he led his regiment at 1st Bull Run where his 16-year-old son was killed. In Oct. '61 he was elected to the C.S.A. Congress and was appointed B.G. C.S.A. 22 Aug. '64. He commanded his brigade of Ga. Reserves in S.C. and was wounded near the end of the war. Afterward, he was a highly successful criminal lawyer.

GARY, Martin Witherspoon. C.S.A. gen. 1831–81. S.C. After attending S.C. Univ., he went to Harvard and became a criminal lawyer. He was a secession leader in the legislature and was commissioned Capt. of the Watson Guards (which became Co. B of the HAMPTON LEGION). He commanded the Legion temporarily at 1st Bull Run and was promoted Lt. Col. then Col. of C.S.A. Inf. After fighting in the Peninsular campaign he was at 2d Bull Run, Boonsboro, Antietam, Fredericksburg, Suffolk, Chickamauga, Bean's Station, Campbell's Station, and Knoxville. His regiment was then mounted to become cavalry and he commanded on the north side of the James. After Riddle's Shop, he was appointed B.G. C.S.A. 19 May '64 and was the last general officer to leave Richmond when it fell. At Appomattox his forces cut through the lines to join Davis at Greensboro and escorted him to Cokesbury (S.C.), where one of the last cabinet meetings took place in Gary's mother's home.

After the war he was a lawyer and legislator. D.A.B. describes him as "Thin, erect, and baldheaded," and says he was called the Bald Eagle.

GATES, Theodore Burr. Union officer. N.Y. Lt. Col. 80th N.Y. 10 Sept. '61; Col. 22 Sept. '62 Bvt. B.G. USV (war service); mustered out 22 Nov. '64.

GATES, William. Union officer. c. 1788–1868. Mass. USMA 1806 (1/15)*; Arty. He fought in the War of 1812, the Seminole wars, and the Mexican War before taking a leave of absence 1861-63. Upon his return he commanded New England forts as Col. 3d US Arty. (since 1845) before being retired 1 June '63 and breveted B.G. USA 13 Mar. '65.

GATH. Pen name of George Alfred TOWNSEND.

GATLIN, Richard Caswell. 1809–96. N.C. C.S.A. gen. USMA 1832 (35/45); Inf. He went on the Black Hawk expedition, fought in the Seminole wars, and in the Mexican War (1 wound, 1 brevet) and participated in the Utah Expedition. Captured 23 Apr. '61 while on a visit to Fort Smith by the Ark. militia, he was paroled, resigned as a Maj. from the R.A. 20 May '61, and was named Adj. Gen. of the N.C. Mil. Commissioned Col. of C.S.A. Inf., he commanded the coastal defense of the Southern Dept. and was named B.G. C.S.A. 8 July '61. While he was preparing for the defense of New Bern, he became seriously ill and was relieved. Resigning 8 Sept. '62, he served as the N.C. Adj. and I.G. After the war he farmed in Arkansas.

GATLING GUN. Dr. Richard Gatling's multiple-barrel weapon of small-arm caliber (1-, ½-, and .45-inch) with a rapid rate of fire that saw some use near the end of the war. Ben Butler used two around Petersburg and

*There was no class standing prior to 1818, and the cadets are listed in the order in which they were commissioned.

eight on gunboats; Porter acquired one; and Hancock ordered 12 for his I (Veteran) Corps. Although a good weapon, it was not adopted by the US Army until 1866. It is erroneously referred to as a machine gun, but was not strictly speaking in this category since it was powered by an external source: a hand crank in the early models and an electric motor in the improved model. It is also confused with Ager's "Coffee Mill Gun," another hopper-fed rapid-firing gun that was a much inferior weapon but one that was better promoted. (See Bruce, 118ff and 290ff.)

GAY, Sidney Howard. 1814–88. Newspaper editor. Mass. After studying at Harvard, he became an ardent abolitionist with GARRISON and edited an anti-slavery newspaper until 1858 when he joined the New York *Tribune*. He was managing editor from 1862 to 1866 and was credited by many with having kept the *Tribune* "a war paper in spite of Greeley." From 1868 until the Chicago fire in 1871 he edited the *Tribune* of that city and then returned to N.Y.C. where he eventually joined William Cullen Bryant as author of the *Bryant's History of the United States* (1876–81). He also wrote *Life of James Madison* (1884). See WAR CORRESPONDENTS.

GEARY, John White. Union gen. 1819–73. Pa. A surveyor and railroad engineer, he fought in the Mexican War and was chosen by Pres. Polk in 1849 to set up Calif.'s postal system. He was then first *alcalde* of San Francisco and, declining the governorship of Utah, accepted that of Kans. in 1856 where he brought peace out of the anarchy of Bleeding Kansas. Named Col. 28th Pa. 28 June '61, he was wounded at Harpers Ferry 16 Oct. '61 and captured at Leesburg in March '62. As B.G. USV 25 Apr. '62, he commanded Sep. Brig., Rappahannock (May–June '62); 2, 1, II (26 June–16

July '62), and 1, 2, II (16 July–9 Aug.
'62) at Cedar Mountain, where he was
seriously wounded. At Chancellorsville
and Gettysburg he led 2d Div., XII
(15 Oct. '62–25 Sept. '63). In the Army
of the Cumberland he commanded 2d
Div., XII at Wauhatchie, Lookout
Mountain, and Missionary Ridge (25
Sept. '63–27 Jan. '64 and 18 Feb.–14
Apr. '64). His son was killed at Wauhatchie. He also led the 2d Div., XX
(14 Apr. '64–1 June '65) on the March
to the Sea and through the Carolinas.
Breveted Maj. Gen. USV 15 Jan. '65
for "fitness to command and prompt-
ness to execute" (Heitman), he was
Mil. Gov. of Savannah and mustered
out in 1866. From 1867 to 1873 he
was Republican Gov. of Pa.

GEDDES, James Loraine. Union officer. 1827–87. Scotland. Lt. Col. 8th
Iowa 23 Sept. '61; Col. 7 Feb. '62; Bvt.
B.G. USV 5 June '65 (war service).
Commanded 3, 3, XV; 3, 1, XVI; 3,
3, XVI. After emigrating with his parents to Canada, he went to India under
the auspices of an uncle and studied at
the British Military Academy in Cal-
cutta. He spent seven years in the Royal
Horse Guards, serving under Gens.
Gough, Napier, and Campbell, before
returning to Canada where he became
a Col. in the Canadian Army. He was
farming and teaching in Iowa prior
to the Civil War. At Shiloh he was
W.I.A. and captured, although exchanged in time for Vicksburg and
Jackson, and he served as Provost
Marshal of Memphis. He was with
Iowa State College until his death.

GENERAL OFFICERS. In the
Union Army 1,978 generals were appointed during and immediately after
the war. Of this number, 1,700 held
only the BREVET RANK of gen.; they
are, therefore, classified in this book as
"Union officers" and not "Union gens."
With the exclusion of Grant, who was
a Lt. Gen., only two grades of general

officer existed in the Union Army: Maj.
Gen. (two stars) and B.G. (one star).
Within each of these categories, however, there were two subcategories:
USA and USV appointments, and
within these subcategories there were
full and Bvt. Gens. In the USA there
were nine full Maj. Gens., 152 Bvt.
Maj. Gens., two full B.G.'s, and 165
Bvt. B.G.'s. In the USV there were 71
full and 242 Bvt. Maj. Gens., and 195
full and 1,140 Bvt. B.G.'s

There were 427 *bona fide* Confederate gens., according to Marcus
Wright.* He lists an additional nine
who were assigned to duty as B.G. by
E. Kirby SMITH and one (T. T. MUN-
FORD) by Fitz Lee, but who were not
confirmed by the C.S.A. congress. Under Confederate law the President
alone was authorized to appoint general
officers, and Jefferson Davis repudiated
Smith's appointments. Davis did, however, approve four or five of Smith's
appointments in March '65. Heitman lists
464 C.S.A. gens., omitting four listed
by Wright (Goggin, B. J. Hill, Levin
M. Lewis, and Jackman—the last two

* Ezra Warner's *Generals in Gray*
(Louisiana State University Press, 1959)
was not published in time for me to
benefit from his scholarship for the first
printing of this book. Thanks to the
assistance of experts who checked
proofs, particularly E. B. Long and
Palmer Bradley, my errors are more
those of omission than of commission.
A few entries have, however, been corrected on the basis of Warner's material.

As evidence of how hard it is to find
information about many Confederate
generals, Warner states that 200 of the
425 officers he considers to have been
"real" generals are not in D.A.B., and
"at least fifty . . . did not appear in any
published source, however recondite."

Mr. Warner's *Generals in Blue* is now
anxiously awaited.

being Kirby Smith appointments), and giving 33 whom Wright does not consider to be generals.

GENERAL RESERVE. The reserve under the control of the overall commander, as contrasted with the local reserves of his subordinate commanders.

"GENTLE ANNA." See Anna ETHERIDGE.

GEORGE, Mrs. E. E. SANITARY COMMISSION worker. ?–1865. Ind. Described as being "in that period of life which suggests the quiet of the fireside," she became a hospital nurse in Jan. '63 at Memphis. She devoted herself to the Indiana regiments, in particular, and continued to serve with the army, going on Sherman's Atlanta campaign with the XV Corps. After caring for the wounded in the Tenn. campaign, she went to Wilmington (N.C.) to nurse the released prisoners. Here she succumbed to typhoid fever.

GEORGIA. Long a center of states-rights sentiment, the state seceded 19 Jan. '61 and felt little of the war until Sherman took Atlanta and marched on to the sea in '64. Readmitted to the Union in '68 Georgia underwent a second reconstruction when Negro members were expelled from her legislature.

GEORGIA, THE. Confederate cruiser procured by Matthew Fontaine Maury in Scotland in Mar. '63 for the South. In a seven-month cruise she captured or destroyed nine vessels (Fox) and was sold at Liverpool to a British merchant 1 June '64 after eluding the Federals.

GEORGIA, UNION ARMY OF. Name applied to the force composed of the XIV and XX Corps, and Kilpatrick's cavalry, under Maj. Gen. Henry W. Slocum, in the March to the Sea and operations in the Carolinas. Both corps had previously been part of Thomas' Army of the Cumberland (together with the IV Corps). When first placed under Slocum's command after the fall of Atlanta, this force was known as the Left Wing of Sherman's command. However, Slocum's force adopted the name Army of Ga. unofficially; on 28 Mar. '65 it was officially recognized. Some writers have referred to Sherman's entire command as the Army of Ga. (e.g., Fiebeger).

GERHARDT, Joseph. Union officer. Germany. Maj. 46th N.Y. 16 Sept. '61; Lt. Col. 1 June '62; Col. 17 Dec. '62; Bvt. B.G. USV (war service); mustered out 8 Nov. '63. Died 1881.

"GET THERE FIRST WITH THE MOST MEN." Nathan Bedford Forrest, comparing notes with John Hunt Morgan during the war, "explained his success with the impatient exclamation, 'I just . . . got there first with the most men.' The phrase is given in the same form in perhaps the earliest printed reference to it, in Lieutenant General Dick Taylor's informative and delightful memoirs" (R. S. Henry, *Forrest*, 19, citing Basil Duke's *Reminiscences* [1911] as the source of the first quote, and referring to Taylor's *Destruction and Reconstruction* [1879]). As for the popular "git thar fustest with the mostest" distortion, Henry writes: "Forrest would have been totally incapable of so obvious and self-conscious a piece of literary carpentry. What he said, he said simply and directly, . . . although doubtless his pronunciation was 'git thar fust,' that being the idiom of the time and place."

GETTY, George Washington, Union gen. 1819–1901. D.C. USMA 1840 (15/42); Arty. Fighting in the Mexican War (1 brevet) and the Seminole wars and serving on the frontier, he transferred to the 5th US Arty. 14 May '61 as Capt. (since 1853) and was appointed Col. Add. A.D.C. 28 Sept. '62.

He commanded four batteries at Yorktown, Gaines's Mill, Malvern Hill, South Mountain, and Antietam. Named B.G. USV 25 Sept. '62, he led 3d Div., IX (4 Oct. '62–2 Mar. '63) at Fredericksburg and 2d Div., VII (21 Mar.–1 Aug. '63) at Hill's Point in April, when he led a storming column in a successful assault of Battery Huger. He commanded the VII Corps (15 July–1 Aug. '63) and the Army of Va. (15–20 July). He then commanded the forces at Norfolk and Portsmouth (15 July '63–14 Jan. '64) and the 2d Div., VI (25 Mar.–6 May '64) at the Wilderness, where he was severely wounded. He had been Acting I.G. of the Potomac earlier that year. At Winchester, Cedar Creek, and Fishers Hill he commanded the 2d Div., VI (6 Aug.–19 Oct. and 19 Oct.–6 Dec. '64). On 19 Oct. '64 he led VI, Army of the Shenandoah, during the siege of Petersburg; he commanded VI Potomac (16 Jan.–11 Feb. '65). Breveted for Suffolk, the Wilderness, Petersburg (B.G. USA), war service (Maj. Gen. USA) and Winchester and Fishers Hill (Maj. Gen. USV 1 Aug. '64), he continued in the R.A. and was a member of the board that reversed Fitz-John Porter's court-martial in 1878–79. He retired in 1882 as Col. D.A.B. characterizes him as a "dignified, courteous, modest soldier," a "constant reader of military works."

GETTYSBURG, THE OLD HERO OF. See John BURNS.

GETTYSBURG ADDRESS. Delivered 19 Nov. '63 by Lincoln at the dedication of the national cemetery at Gettysburg, the speech was apparently not written hastily on the train as tradition holds, but was completed in Washington, with only a few minor changes made later. After a two-hour oration by Edward EVERETT, the crowd applauded Lincoln's five-minute address without enthusiasm. Lincoln said to the man who had introduced him, "[Ward Hill] Lamon, that speech won't scour. It is a flat failure." Although some recognized its literary quality immediately, Lincoln's political enemies belittled it.

The following version is from the second draft, which Lincoln is believed to have held at the ceremony.

"Four score and seven years ago our fathers brought forth, upon this continent, a new nation, conceived in Liberty, and dedicated to the proposition that all men are created equal.

"Now we are engaged in a great civil war, testing whether that nation, or any nation, so conceived, and so dedicated, can long endure. We are met here on a great battlefield of that war. We have come to dedicate a portion of it as a final resting place for those who here gave their lives that that nation might live. It is altogether fitting and proper that we should do this.

"But in a larger sense we can not dedicate—we can not consecrate—we can not hallow—this ground. The brave men, living and dead, who struggled here, have consecrated it, far above our poor power to add or detract. The world will little note, nor long remember, what we say here, but can never forget what they did here. It is for us, the living, rather to be dedicated here to the unfinished work which they have, thus far, so nobly carried on. It is rather for us to be here dedicated to the great task remaining before us—that from these honored dead we take increased devotion to that cause for which they here gave the last full measure of devotion—that we here highly resolve that these dead shall not have died in vain; that this nation shall have a new birth of freedom; and that this government of the people, by the people, for the people, shall not perish from the earth."

GETTYSBURG CAMPAIGN, June–July '63. After frustrating two Federal attempts to penetrate the strong defensive positions at Fredericksburg and march on Richmond, the Confederates again undertook the strategic offensive. Although some consideration was given to a plan for part of the Army of Northern Va. to go to the West for an offensive under Lee's command against Rosecrans, the decision to invade the North was finally accepted by Richmond authorities. It was believed that a victory on Northern soil would strengthen the growing peace movement in the North, and that it might encourage England's intervention on behalf of the South. The Confederates wanted to shift the

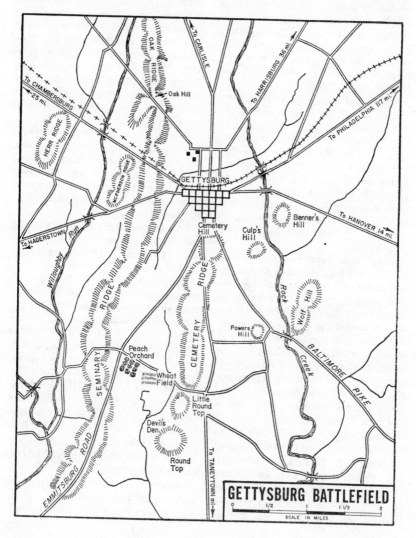

GETTYSBURG BATTLEFIELD

SCALE IN MILES

fighting from Va. into the abundant Cumberland Valley. They also hoped that the invasion would relieve pressure on Vicksburg and Chattanooga by making the Federals withdraw strength from those areas to counter Lee's threat.

The Army of Northern Va. had been reorganized into the I Corps (still under Longstreet), II Corps (Ewell had succeeded Stonewall Jackson), III Corps (A. P. Hill), and Stuart's cavalry (increased to six brigades). The Army of the Potomac retained its organization of seven infantry corps and a cavalry corps. Lee's strength was 89,000 and Hooker had 122,000.

Lee started moving troops north from Fredericksburg on 3 June, and by the 8th had concentrated near Culpeper all corps except A. P. Hill's, which remained in the old positions to deceive Hooker. On 4 June Hooker, who had known for a week that Lee was preparing to undertake some movement, ordered reconnaissance operations that resulted in the battles of FRANKLIN'S CROSSING (5 June) and BRANDY STATION (9 June).

After these engagements Lee knew that Hooker was alerted as to his general intentions and might spoil his invasion plans by an attack toward Richmond. On 10 June, therefore, Ewell was started toward the Shenandoah to destroy the garrison in that area and, thereby, to force the Washington authorities to pull the Army of the Potomac back for defensive operations. Hooker, in fact, had proposed just the plan Lee was worrying about, but it had been disapproved.

Troops of Schenck's US VIII Corps (Middle Department) were guarding the Valley. B. F. Kelley's (1st) division, about 10,000, was concentrated at Harpers Ferry with B. F. Smith's brigade (1,200) at Martinsburg. Milroy's (2d) division, about 9,000, was at Win-

chester, with A. T. McReynolds' (3d) brigade (1,800) at Berryville. Late 11 June Milroy had been ordered to drop back to join Kelley; believing he could hold Winchester, he had not done so.

In moving to join Ewell, Jenkins' cavalry brigade had located and clashed with Milroy's outposts at Middletown, Strasburg, Cedarville, and along the Front Royal Road. When Ewell reached the Valley on 12 June, via Chester Gap, he split his forces. Rodes and Jenkins were ordered to BERRYVILLE and MARTINSBURG to capture the Federal garrisons. With his other two divisions (Early and Johnson), Ewell drove Milroy's outposts toward Winchester in the hope of surrounding and capturing the main Federal force there.

Due to faulty coordination between Rodes's infantry and Jenkins' cavalry, the bag of Federal prisoners at Berryville and Martinsburg was disappointing. WINCHESTER was, however, a complete Southern victory that virtually destroyed Milroy's force.

Jenkins crossed the Potomac 15 June, and Rodes's infantry followed the next day. At Williamsport they waited for Ewell's main body to catch up.

Longstreet and A. P. Hill had remained on the line of the Rappahannock to deceive Hooker. On 11 June, the day after Ewell's departure, Hooker started extending his right toward the line of the Orange and Alexandria R.R. Two days later he ordered the concentration of his army near Centreville. The next day (14 June) Hill left Fredericksburg and followed Ewell's route into the Valley. Longstreet left Culpeper 15 June and moved east of the Blue Ridge to cover the passes and confuse Hooker as to Lee's objective (Washington or Pennsylvania).

Cavalry covered the flanks of both armies; Pleasonton tried to penetrate Stuart's COUNTERRECONNAISSANCE screen to give Hooker information of Lee's movement. This resulted in fine cavalry employment by both sides, and brought on the famous series of engagements at ALDIE, MIDDLEBURG, and UPPERVILLE.

Stuart started 24 June on his controversial Gettysburg raid. Two days before this Lee had written him: "If you find that he [Hooker] is moving northward, and that two brigades can guard the Blue Ridge and take care of your rear, you can move with the other three into Maryland and take position on General Ewell's right, place yourself in communication with him, guard his flank and keep him informed of the enemy's movements." Given the choice, Stuart decided on a route around Hooker's rear and flank, rather than the shorter, more protected one west of the Blue Ridge. He took the brigades of Hampton, Fitzhugh Lee, and W. H. F. Lee. While Stuart has been almost universally accused of poor military judgment in his conduct of this operation, a strong case has also been made in his defense. Cutting across the Army of the Potomac's main supply route, Stuart captured 125 new wagons at Rockville and, in the course of the raid, further encumbered himself with over 400 prisoners. Skirmishes took place at FAIRFAX, WESTMINSTER, HANOVER, and CARLISLE.

Ewell spearheaded the virtually unopposed Confederate movement up the Cumberland Valley. Couch, commanding the newly-created Dept. of the Susquehanna, did what little he could to organize the Federal militia units for defense of the state. W. T. H. Brooks, commanding the Dept. of the Monongahela, played a similar role on Ewell's west flank. Skirmishes took place at GREENCASTLE, McCONNELLSBURG, and SPORTING HILL. Federal troops of Schenck's VIII Corps (Middle Department) were engaged in skirmishes with Stuart's raiding column and Milroy's retreat.

When Hooker learned that the Army of Northern Va. had crossed the Potomac he moved into Md., concentrating his army around Frederick by 28 June. His plan was to stop Lee's invasion by cutting the vulnerable Confederate line of communications. He ordered Slocum's XII Corps to join Federal forces near Harpers Ferry and to operate against Lee's rear. When Halleck counter-

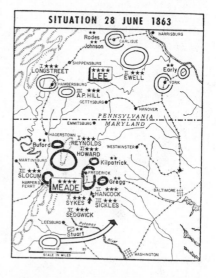

SITUATION 28 JUNE 1863

manded these orders, Hooker, who had come to feel unbearably hampered by interference from Halleck, asked to be relieved. The administration had been looking for an opportunity to replace Hooker with a minimum of political repercussion; Meade moved up from V Corps to succeed him.

Other significant events took place on 28 June. In the morning Lee, still ignorant of the enemy situation and eagerly awaiting news of Stuart, had ordered Ewell to cross the Susquehanna and seize Harrisburg. His other two corps were to move forward from around

Chambersburg and Greenwood to join Ewell. That night he received from Longstreet's mysterious agent, Harrison, a report of the true situation. Lee was forced to begin an immediate concentration around Cashtown and Gettysburg.

Battle of Gettysburg—First Day

Meade's strategy was to maneuver through Frederick toward Harrisburg, thereby menacing Lee's line of communications while keeping between the enemy and Washington. This also kept Federal forces disposed so they could make Lee turn and fight before crossing the Susquehanna.

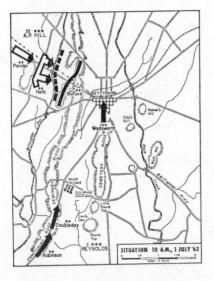

SITUATION 10 A.M., 1 JULY '63

A meeting engagement took place 1 July when Buford's Federal cavalry division, scouting ahead of the main forces near Gettysburg, encountered Pettigrew's brigade (Heth's division of A. P. Hill's corps) moving into Gettysburg to capture a supply of shoes reported there.

Buford recognized the importance of Gettysburg as a communications center and organized his badly outnumbered cavalrymen to defend it. Heavy fighting started at 10. Buford's dismounted troopers, armed with the new Spencer carbines, held off the first infantry attacks of Heth and Pender's divisions (A. P. Hill) while Reynolds' I Corps and Howard's XI ("German") Corps rushed up. Federal infantry started arriving at about 10:30. The Confederates built up superior strength, captured McPherson Ridge, and pushed toward Seminary Ridge. Reynolds was killed by a sharpshooter; the famous Iron Brigade sustained casualties from which it never recovered; Archer became the first Confederate general officer to be captured since Lee had taken command; the 2d and 42d Miss. were captured by the 6th Wis. in a railroad cut on Seminary Ridge. Around noon the fighting died down while the Union forces built up their defenses and the Confederates reorganized for another attack on Seminary Ridge. XI Corps started arriving about 1 o'clock and two divisions under Schurz extended the Federal north flank while the third was posted as a general reserve on Cemetery Hill.

Ewell's corps then arrived from the north to threaten the exposed Federal north flank. Rodes's division moved along Oak Ridge and Early advanced along the line of the Harrisburg road. Union forces were moved around to meet this new threat; the Federal corps of Sickles (III) and Slocum (XII), respectively twelve and five miles away, were ordered up with all speed to strengthen the line. Ewell drove the XI Corps back with heavy losses; despite efforts to reinforce this wing, Union forces were driven back to Cemetery Hill. On Seminary Ridge the troops of I Corps, now commanded by Abner Doubleday, were put in an untenable position by the collapse of XI Corps. They withdrew also to Cemetery Hill where Union forces were being rallied for a new stand.

Meade sent Hancock to organize the troops on Cemetery Hill and to recommend whether Gettysburg was an advantageous place to bring on a general engagement. A defensive position had been reconnoitered farther south along Big Pipe Creek but Meade did not overlook the possibility of fighting farther north. After ordering Federal positions extended to Culp's Hill, Hancock examined the terrain with Howard and Warren and then reported back to Meade that this would be the place to fight. The latter had, however, already started the movement of the army toward that place.

The first day's fighting had been a Southern victory. XI Corps had lost over 4,000 men captured, and had many "stragglers." Lee, however, was still in the dark as to his enemy's true dispositions and ordered his two corps to avoid bringing on a general engagement until Longstreet's corps could arrive.

Whether Lee should have attacked Cemetery Hill the first day is one of the great controversies of the war. Ewell, ordered to do so "if possible," did not make the attempt.

The Second Day, 2 July

Hancock had recognized the natural strength of the Gettysburg position. Further, he had seen the importance of Culp's Hill and had ordered troops to occupy it. A strategic weakness which Hancock reported to Meade was that the Gettysburg position could be "turned" from the northeast; that is, a Confederate attack from that direction would threaten the Federal line of communications along the Baltimore pike. This was foremost in Meade's mind as he made his troop dispositions during the night of 1–2 July. In his concern for this "strategic flank" he did not make ade-

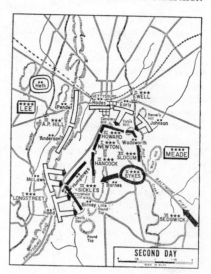

SECOND DAY

quate provisions for the defense of the Round Tops.

Lee was also oriented in his strategic planning toward this north flank. Ewell, however, told him he could not take Cemetery and Culp's hills, and recommended that Longstreet attack the Round Tops. Longstreet was opposed to attacking at all; he advocated a defensive posture. The repeated success in repulsing Federal attacks (1st Bull Run, 2d Bull Run, Antietam, Fredericksburg) had convinced "Old Pete" that the war should be won by a policy of "strategic offense—tactical defense." But Lee was resolved to attack, and ordered Longstreet to make the main effort on 2 July against Meade's south flank.

At dawn 2 July Meade's forces were disposed in the form of a fishhook, with the tip at Culp's Hill, the hook curving around Cemetery Hill, the shank along Cemetery Ridge, and the "eye" at the Round Tops. Lee stretched around the outside of this hook, with Ewell on the north, A. P. Hill in the center, and Longstreet on the south. The Federals had not only the advantage of observation and fields of fire, but their numerical superiority was further strengthened by a central position.

In the absence of Stuart, Lee lacked complete information of the terrain and enemy dispositions on which to base his tactical plan. This led him into the erroneous belief that the main enemy defensive line was along the Emmitsburg pike, with its flank near the Wheat Field. His plan was for Longstreet to hit this flank with two divisions (Hood on the right, and McLaws) then turn north and roll up the enemy line by an attack along the pike. Ewell and A. P. Hill were to make the secondary effort; that is, they were to attack so as to prevent Meade from shifting troops from unthreatened parts of his line to reinforce against Longstreet's main effort.

Although Lee's plan was defective, it was further jeopardized by faulty execution. Since Ewell was reluctant to attack on the north, Lee decided to reduce the overextension of his army. He told Ewell to close in on A. P. Hill's corps unless he could see some way of attacking profitably against the Federal north flank on 2 July. Ewell was reluctant to move west because it would have meant abandoning some of his seriously wounded. Also, during the evening of 1 July he had reports that Culp's Hill was unoccupied; he then decided to attack this position after all. Freeman sums up the Confederate failure at Gettysburg with: "Jackson is not here."

The Round Tops–Sickles' Salient

On moving to his assigned sector on 2 July Sickles went forward, without permission, to occupy some higher ground. This resulted in the formation of "Sickles' salient," which took in the soon-to-be famous spots known as the Peach Orchard, the Wheat Field, and Devil's Den.

After many delays the second day's fighting opened about 4 P.M. with the attack of Hood's division toward the Round Tops. It was about this time that Warren saw this threat and started rushing troops to occupy Little Round Top. The 15th and 47th Ala. (Law's brigade; Hood) drifted to the right in their advance and a gap developed in Law's brigade. Three companies of the 47th Ala. were left at the base of Round Top for flank security and the rest of the Confederates—approximately 500 men, now commanded by Col. Oates of the 15th Ala.—climbed Round Top and paused to catch their breaths before turning north to cross the saddle that separated them from Little Round Top.

Chamberlain's 20th Me., in the meantime, had been moving up as the advance regiment of Vincent's brigade (3, 1, V) and rushed 308 men into position on the southern side of Little Round Top. O'Rorke's 140th N.Y. was in the advance of Weed's brigade (3, 2, V), which Warren, on his own initiative, had ordered up; the lead regiment was accompanied by Lt. Hazlett's battery (D, 5th US). The attack on the Round Tops was repulsed. Vincent, Weed, O'Rorke, and Hazlett were killed. Hood was wounded early in the engagement, permanently losing the use of one arm.

In a poorly managed afternoon of gallant fighting the Confederate brigades continued to assault in sequence from the right. The attackers were enfiladed by fire from their left, and Meade was able to rush reinforcements to stop each individual brigade-size attack. Severe fighting took place in the Wheat Field, the Peach Orchard, and the Apple Orchard as Sickles' III Corps was driven back and divisions from V, VI, I, and XII Corps were rushed forward to plug the gap.

In the Confederate center Hill's failure to attack in time and with sufficient effort had enabled Meade to shift forces from his front to reinforce the Federal left. Anderson's division on Hill's right advanced somewhat on Longstreet's left; Pender's division had remained on Seminary Ridge.

On the other end of the line, Ewell's effort had been limited until 6 P.M. to an artillery barrage that had been finally silenced by counterbattery fire from Cemetery and Culp's Hills. At about 6 P.M. he ordered his three divisions to attack the Federal north flank. These commands of Rodes, Early, and Johnson (from west to east) were separated from each other by the town of Gettysburg and Rock Creek. Early, in the center, attacked Cemetery Hill with his two available brigades (Hays and Avery). They succeeded in getting a foothold on the hill, where Federal strength had been reduced by detachments to Meade's threatened left. Ames's single brigade was driven back, losing several artillery positions; Ames managed to halt the panic and with reinforcements by Carroll's brigade (II), which moved up on his right, drove the Confederates back. Rodes's division did not get into position until the attack of Hays and Avery had been repulsed; he realized that any advance by his single, unsupported force would be futile, and did not attack. On the other end of Ewell's line only three brigades of Johnson's division got across the creek by dark. Culp's Hill, although a strong natural position further improved by earthworks, was held at this time only by Greene's brigade; the rest of XII Corps had gone to support Sickles. "Maryland" Steuart led his brigade into some abandoned trenches up the southeast slopes of Culp's Hill. The other two brigades were stopped at the base of the hill by Greene's thin line. Johnson's attack degenerated into "a random and ineffective musketry fire" (Alexander, 410).

Third Day, 3 July

Despite Longstreet's vehement objections, Lee was determined to attack again the third day. Morale of his troops was still high, he had gained ground favorable for attack, he had been reinforced by the arrival of Pickett's fresh division, and he had unlimited faith in the ability of the Army of Northern Va. With the benefit of 20/20 hindsight it is

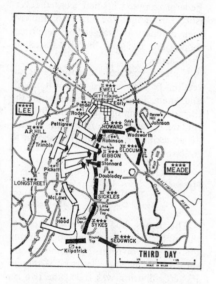

apparent that Lee's judgment was faulty and that Longstreet was right. Meade, however, was so little confident of the outcome of a third day's fighting that it was only after a formal council of war that he made his decision to stay and accept battle.

Lee's plan now was to hit the center of Meade's line with 10 brigades, supported by 159 guns. Meade guessed the point of attack by the simple reasoning that Lee had previously attacked both flanks.

Early 3 July a garbled order sent Mudge's 2d Mass. and Colgrove's 27th Ind. into a gallant but hopeless charge against the three brigades of Johnson around the base of Culp's Hill. The Mass. regiment lost its colonel, four color bearers, and 250 men. The Confederates made one more attempt to take Culp's Hill, but were repulsed by the now-reinforced defenders with heavy losses by 10:30.

The day which had dawned sultry became oppressively hot as the sun burned through the haze at about noon. Federal troops, who had worked feverishly throughout the night to improve their defenses and to get final reinforcements into position, literally rested on their arms.

Under Longstreet's unenthusiastic direction Pickett formed his own troops and then directed the placing of the brigades coming up from other divisions for the attack. The formation of the 10 attacking brigades may be shown as follows.

	PETTIGREW				PICKETT	
Mayo	Davis	Marshall	Fry	Garnett	Kemper	
	TRIMBLE					Wilcox
	Lane	Lowrance		Armistead		

The names shown above are those of the officers actually commanding during the attack; division commanders are shown in capital letters. Although Pickett's division was fresh, the two on his left had been badly disorganized in the fighting of the first two days; only Lane's brigade "was in the keeping of a Brigadier of tested combat experience" (*Lee's Lts.,* III, 150). Trimble took command of his two brigades only as they were actually moving into position. In an error that proved fatal, these two brigades (Lane and Lowrance) were not placed in echelon to the left behind Pettigrew's exposed flank, as had been directed.

There is no good reason why this famous operation has inaccurately been called "Pickett's Charge." Longstreet was in command. Pickett's only over-all responsibility was that of forming the brigades before the attack (which he had accomplished by about noon). Nor did Pickett's troops form the major portion of the total attacking force.

Following a heavy artillery preparation, 15,000 Confederate infantry attacked at about 1:45 P.M. Across a half mile of open field, over the plank fences along the Emmitsburg road, against a Federal force which waited behind breastworks they had improvised along the stone walls, the Southerners moved in tight formation. Although Federal artillery opened up, Union infantrymen did not fire. Lee's men halted a few hundred feet from the enemy and dressed their lines. Then began the final assault.

The "little clump of trees," located near a part of the line known as "the Angle," was the point on which Fry's brigade advanced, and those on either side guided on him.

Even when they got within range of canister, Pickett's men maintained their formations and advanced, as did the right brigades of Pettigrew's division. On the left, however, the brigades of Davis and Mayo began to show hesitation. While Garnett, Kemper, Armistead, Marshall, and Fry converged on the little clump of trees, followed by the brigades of Lowrance and Lane, the Confederate left began to collapse and then to pull back. The 8th Ohio, posted as skirmishers in an advanced position, brought a demoralizing enfilade fire to bear. Hand-to-hand fighting broke out as Armistead led the advance through the angle. Alonzo Cushing, already wounded three times, rolled a gun down to the stone wall and died directing its fire at point-blank range. Armistead was killed. Federal reinforcements rushed into the melee from adjacent parts of the line and the Confederate advance was stopped. The "high tide of the Confederacy" then began to recede, leaving 19 regimental colors in Federal hands.

Stannard led a counterattack with part of his (New) Vt. Brig. against the right of the Confederate penetration and hastened their withdrawal.

There was demoralization but no general panic. Longstreet rallied the retreating Confederates and started reorganizing them for the expected counteroffensive. A few Federal skirmishers did start forward, but were driven back by artillery.

The next day, the Fourth of July, Lee awaited an attack. Early in the afternoon it began to rain, and by evening there was a deluge. Aided by weather that made pursuit difficult, Lee then began his retreat.

It was not until years after the Civil War that historians started pointing to Gettysburg as the turning point. (Antietam is considered by many to deserve this distinction.) As Lee's survivors trudged south they could console themselves with the thought that they had won the first two days and lost the third; as was the case after Antietam, the Army of the Potomac was too badly hurt to administer the knock-out.

Cavalry Actions

Stuart reached Gettysburg the afternoon of 2 July. By noon of the 3d he was on the north flank two and a half miles east of Rock Creek. While the infantry charge took place, Stuart was trying to cut Meade's line of communications along the Baltimore Pike. Opposing him was David McM. Gregg, commanding the cavalry brigades of J. I. Gregg, McIntosh, and Custer. Stuart was repulsed after a heavy encounter in which both sides fought mounted and on foot.

Kilpatrick covered the other flank with the brigades of Farnsworth and Merritt. While the infantry attack was in progress, Kilpatrick ordered a senseless and suicidal attack against Hood. Hood, protected by thick woods and

stone walls, repulsed the gallant but futile attack, killing Farnsworth.

The Retreat

The severe storm that slowed Meade's pursuit also made the Potomac unfordable when Lee's advance guard reached Williamsport 6 July. Buford attacked Imboden here but was repulsed. The rest of Lee's army reached Hagerstown 7 July and entrenched to await replacement of the ponton bridge destroyed by Federal cavalry. Meade decided against attacking this position, and Lee withdrew across the Potomac the night of 13–14 July. Heth commanded a rearguard action at FALLING WATERS, W. Va., the next day, in which he lost two guns, 500 prisoners, and in which Pettigrew was mortally wounded.

Livermore's figures on the three days' fighting are:

	Federal	Confederate
Engaged	88,289	75,000
Killed	3,155	3,903
Wounded *	14,529	18,735
Missing	5,365	5,425
Total losses	23,049	28,063

* Includes mortally wounded and captured.

In the case of Federal losses, Livermore accepts the figures of the *Official Records;* Fox differs only slightly (3,070 killed; 14,497 wounded and died of wounds; 5,434 captured and missing; 23,001 total).

As for Confederate strength and losses, there is considerable disagreement. Fox puts Confederate losses at: 2,592 killed, 12,706 wounded, including mortally wounded, 5,150 captured, and missing: 20,448 total.

Covered separately in alphabetical sequence in the book are a number of battles and skirmishes which are part of the Gettysburg campaign. In the following list these actions are grouped in accordance with particular phases of the campaign. Hooker's reconnaissances in force: FRANKLIN'S CROSSING and BRANDY STATION; Ewell's advance through the Shenandoah: BERRYVILLE, MARTINS-BURG, and WINCHESTER; cavalry flank actions: ALDIE, MIDDLEBURG 17 and 19 June, and UPPERVILLE; Stuart's raid: FAIRFAX, WESTMINSTER, HANOVER, and CARLISLE; Milroy's retreat and militia actions: GREENCASTLE, McCONNELLS-BURG, and SPORTING HILL. Minor actions not included are: Frying Pan, Va., in which a detachment of the 5th Mich. Cav. sustained 17 casualties; Seneca (Mills), Md., 11 June, where Co. I, 6th Mich. Cav. lost five men and the Confederates two men in a skirmish; and Low Creek, W. Va., 21 June, which is not mentioned in the *Official Records*.

After Lee started his invasion, forces from IV and VII Corps in Dix's Dept. of Va. conducted unsuccessful diversionary operations on the Peninsula which resulted in the following engagements: SOUTH ANNA, 26 June '63; and BALTIMORE CROSS ROADS (Va.), 26 June '63.

GHOLSON, Samuel Jameson. C.S.A. gen. 1808–83. Ky. Appt.-Miss. A lawyer, legislator, and Democratic Congressman, he was a federal judge for 22 years and became a strong advocate of secession. He enlisted in the Monroe Volunteers as a private, was soon elected Capt., and was commissioned Col. 14th Miss. Named B.G. of Miss. state troops in 1861, he was wounded in the right lung and captured at Fort Donelson. Exchanged, he was promoted Maj. Gen. of Miss. state troops in 1863 and appointed B.G. C.S.A. 6 May '64. Given command of a cavalry brigade, he lost his left arm at Egypt, Miss., 27 Dec. '64. After the war he returned to the law and the legislature.

GIBBON, John. Union gen. 1827–96. Pa. Appt.-N.C. USMA 1847 (20/38); Arty. After serving in the Seminole War, on the frontier, and as artillery instructor at West Point, he cast his lot with the Union although he had three brothers fighting for the South. At first McDowell's Chief of Arty. (29 Oct. '61–2 May '62), he was named B.G. USV on the latter date and given command of 4, 1, III, Army of Va. (26 June–12 Sept. '62) which he led at Gainesville and 2d Bull Run. (This was the Black Hat Brigade.) He commanded 4, 1, I, Potomac (12 Sept.–6 Nov. '62) at South Mountain (where it won the name IRON BRIGADE) and Antietam, and was seriously wounded at Fredericksburg while commanding 2d Div., I Corps (5 Nov.–13 Dec. '62). Disabled until 23 Mar. '63, he led 2d Div., II Corps (11 Apr.–1 July '63) at the storming of Marye's Heights and took over the II Corps (1–2 July '63) at Gettysburg, where he was again severely wounded. After a sick leave he commanded a draft depot in Cleveland in Nov. '63 and went back to the 2d Div., II Corps (21 Dec. '63–31 July '64) at the Wilderness, Spotsylvania, North Anna, Totopotomoy, Cold Harbor, and Petersburg. As Maj. Gen. USV (7 June '64), he also commanded the XVIII Corps, Va. and N.C. (4–22 Sept. '64) and the XXIV Corps, Va. (15 Jan.–27 Apr. and 17 May–8 July '65) at Petersburg and was one of the surrender commissioners at Appomattox. Breveted for Antietam, Fredericksburg, Spotsylvania (B.G. USA), and Petersburg (Maj. Gen. USA), he continued in the R.A. as Col. 7th U.S. Inf. Stationed mainly on the frontier and active in Indian fighting, he led the relief column to Little Big Horn in 1876 and buried the massacre victims. Named B.G. USA in 1885, he retired in 1891 and was later C. in C. of the Loyal Legion. He wrote *Personal Recollections of the Civil War* (1928) and *The Artil-*

lerist's Manual (1860). Lyman described "steel-cold General Gibbon, [as] the most American of Americans, with his sharp nose and up-and-down manner of telling the truth, no matter whom it hurts."

GIBBS, Alfred. Union gen. 1823–68. N.Y. USMA 1846 (42/59); Mtd. Rifles-Cav. Serving in the Mexican War where he was wounded and received two brevets, he was also wounded in Indian fighting and later was stationed on the frontier. He was the Depot Commissary at Albuquerque (N. Mex.) 1860–61 as Capt. Mtd. Rifles and 3d Cav. (3 Aug. '61). Captured 27 Aug. '62 at San Augustine Springs (N. Mex.). Became Col. 130th N.Y. 6 Sept. '62. He commanded 2d Prov. Brig., Suffolk (Va.) Div., VII, Va. (5 Dec. '62–21 Jan. '63), was transferred to 19th N.Y. Cav. 11 Aug. '63, and led Reserve Brig., 1st Div., Cav. Corps, Potomac (12 Aug.–12 Sept. '63; 21 Nov. '63–10 Apr. '64; 7–25 May '64 at Todd's Tavern and Spotsylvania; 25 Mar.–25 May '65). Promoted B.G. USV 19 Oct. '64, he also commanded 2, 1, Cav. Corps, Shenandoah (13–28 Nov. '64); 1st Div., Cav. Corps, Shenandoah (3–10 Feb. '65) and Reserve Brig., 1st Div., Cav. Corps, Shenandoah (6 Aug.–8 Sept. '64; 13–31 Dec. '64; 15–18 Jan. '65; 10 Feb.–25 Mar. '65) when he was with Sheridan in several cavalry raids. He was at Cold Harbor; in all the battles of Sheridan's Valley campaign; Five Forks and Sayler's Creek. His brevets were for Trevilian Station (Va.), Winchester, Five Forks, war service (B.G. USA, Maj. Gen. USV, Maj. Gen. USA). He continued in the R.A. until his death at 44 as Maj. 7th US Cav.

GIBSON, George. Union officer. Pa. Entering the R.A. in 1808, he was named Col. Comsy. Gen. of Subsist. in 1818, breveted B.G. USA in 1826 for "ten years' faithful service in one grade," and breveted Maj. Gen. USA in 1848 for the Mexican War. He died in Sept. '61 and appears on Phisterer's list of Civil War generals.

GIBSON, Horatio Gates. Union officer. 1828–1924. Md. Appt.-Pa. USMA 1847 (17/38); Arty. Capt. 3d US Arty. 14 May '61; Lt. Col. 2d Ohio Hv. Arty. 1 Aug. '63; Col. 15 Aug. '65; mustered out USV 23 Aug. '65; Maj. 3d US Arty. 5 Feb. '67; retired 1891 as Col.; Bvt. B.G. USV. Brevets for Williamsburg, Antietam, war service. Commanded 2, 4, XXIII. When he died at the age of 96 he was the oldest living graduate of the Military Academy.

GIBSON, Randall Lee. C.S.A. gen. 1832–92. Ky. Graduating from Yale, he studied law at the Univ. of La. and traveled extensively in Europe. Named attaché in Madrid, he returned in a few years to become a lawyer and sugar planter in La. He was A.D.C. to T. O. Moore and in Mar. '61 was commissioned Capt. 1st La. Arty. As Col. 13th La. he fought at Shiloh and commanded the brigade when Daniel W. Adams was wounded. He led his regiment at Perryville, led the 13th and 20th La. regts. at Stones River, and succeeded to command of the 1st Brig. under Hardee. Again in command of the same two regiments, he again succeeded Adams to lead the brigade at Chickamauga and continued to lead it at Chattanooga. Named B.G. C.S.A. 11 Jan. '64, he commanded a brigade under Hood in the Atlanta and Tenn. campaigns and also fought at Spanish Fort (Mobile). After the war he was a lawyer, Democratic Congressman and Senator, and was Paul Tulane's chief agent in the founding of Tulane University.

GIBSON, William Harvey. Union officer. Ohio. Col. 49th Ohio 20 Aug. '61; Bvt. B.G. USV (war service); mustered out 5 Sept. '64. Commanded

6th Brig., 2d Div., Army of Ohio; 6, 2, I; 1, 2d Div. of the Right Wing, XIV; 1, 2, XX; 2d Div., XX; 1, 3, IV. Whitelaw Reid, in *Ohio in the War,* says that Gibson, the Ohio Treasurer, entered the army under a cloud, having shielded his predecessor, a relative, who took nearly $750,000 from the state. Died 1894.

GIDDINGS, Joshua Reed. Abolitionist. 1795–1864. Pa. A radical abolitionist, he served in the House of Representatives from Ohio 1838–42, resigned after criticism of his anti-slavery policies, and was re-elected in 1842–59. He was a bitter opponent of the Compromise of 1850 and served as US Consul Gen. to Canada 1861–64.

GIESY, Henry H. Union officer. Ohio. Capt. 17th Ohio 22 Apr. '61; mustered out 15 Aug. '61; 2d Lt. 46th Ohio 1 Oct. '61; Capt. 16 Oct. '61; Maj. 16 Oct. '62; Bvt. B.G. USV 28 May '64 (Dallas, Ga.); K.I.A. Dallas (Ga.) 28 May '64.

GILBERT, Charles Champion. Union gen. 1822–1903. Ohio. USMA 1846 (21/59); Inf. He served in the Mexican War, on the frontier, at USMA as asst. professor, and in the Indian wars. He was Capt. 1st Inf. (since 1855) when the war began, fought at Dug Springs (Mo.) 2 Aug., and was severely wounded at Wilson's Creek 10 Aug. '61. Serving as Acting I.G. Dept. of the Cumberland and Army of the Ohio until 11 Mar. '62, he fought at Shiloh (7 Apr.) and was promoted B.G. USV 9 Sept. '62. He was acting Maj. Gen. in charge of the Army of Ky. 1–27 Sept. He commanded 10th Div., I Corps, Army of Ohio (8 Oct.–5 Nov. '62) at Perryville and, temporarily, III Corps, Army of Ohio. His B.G. commission expired 4 Mar. '63, not having been confirmed by the Senate, and on 2 July '63 he was commissioned Maj. 19th US Inf. His brevets were for Shiloh, Richmond

(Ky.), and Perryville. He continued in the R.A. until retired in 1886 as Col.

GILBERT, James I. Union gen. c. 1824–84. Ky. A businessman, he was named Col. 27th Iowa 3 Oct. '62 and participated in the Red River campaign of 1864. He was cited for gallantry at Fort De Russy and subsequent engagements and in front of Nashville and Mobile. Promoted B.G. USV 9 Feb. '65, he was breveted Maj. Gen. USV 26 Mar. '65 for Mobile and mustered out 24 Aug. '65.

GILBERT, Samuel Augustus. Union officer. 1828–68. Ohio. Maj. 24th Ohio 10 June '61; Lt. Col. 22 June '61; Col. 44th Ohio 15 Oct. '61; 8th Ohio Cav. Jan. '64; Bvt. B.G. USV (war service); resigned 20 Apr. '64. Commanded 2d Brig., 2d Div., Army of Ky., Army of Ohio; 1st Brig., Dist. Central Ky.; 2, 1, XXIII; 2, 4, XXIII; 1, 3, XXIII. With the US Coast Survey before the war, Gilbert captured a Confederate battery at Lewisburg (Va.) 21 May '62 and in November 1863 was appointed engineer on Gen. J. G. Foster's staff.

GILCHRIST, Charles A. Union officer. Vt. Capt. 10th Mo. 21 Aug. '61; Col. 50th US Col. Inf. 27 July '63; Bvt. B.G. USV 26 Mar. '65 (Mobile).

GILE, George W. Union officer. N.H. c. 1830–96. R.A. 1st Lt. 22d Pa. 23 Apr. '61; mustered out 7 Aug. '61; Maj. 88th Pa. 18 Sept. '61; Lt. Col. 1 Sept. '62; Col. 24 Jan. '63; mustered out 2 Mar. '63; Maj. Vet. Res. Corps 22 May '63; Col. 29 Sept. '63; Bvt. B.G. USV 6 May '65. Brevets for Ft. Slocum (D.C.), 2d Bull Run, South Mountain, Antietam. Commanded 1, Vet. Res. Corps, XXII. W.I.A. Antietam in the leg.

GILGAL CHURCH, Ga., 15–17 June '64. See KENESAW MOUNTAIN.

GILLEM, Alvan Cullem. Union gen. 1830–75. Tenn. USMA 1851 (11/42); Arty. After the Seminole War, frontier

343

and garrison service, he was promoted Capt. Asst. Q.M. 12 July '61 and took part in the defense of Fort Taylor (Fla.) Jan.–Oct. '61. As Brig. Q.M. in Ky. 9 Nov. '61–6 Feb. '62, he fought at Mill Springs and commanded the siege artillery. He was Chief Q.M. of the Army of the Ohio (Feb.–June '62) at Shiloh and the advance upon and siege of Corinth. Commissioned Col. 10th Tenn. 13 May '62, he was Provost Marshal of Nashville from Aug. until Dec. and then commanded a brigade in the Tennessee operations (24 Dec. '62–1 June '63) at Lavergne and Harpeth River. Adj. Gen. of Tenn. 1 June '63–1 Apr. '65 and promoted B.G. USV 17 Aug. '63. While guarding railroads and leading sorties against the rebels in the area he commanded 4th Div., Cav. Corps, Cumberland (1 Apr.–16 Aug. '64) and led an expedition to East Tenn. Aug. '64 to Mar. '65, during which Morgan was killed at Greenville. He also participated in the skirmishes at Carter's Station, Morristown, Bull's Gap, Rogersville, and Kingsport. During Stoneman's raid into Southwest Va., he was in command of the Tenn. Cav. at Wytheville, Marion, and Saltville. He then commanded Cav. Div. Dist. E. Tenn., Cumberland, 17 Mar.–July '65, and was promoted Maj. Gen. USV 3 Nov. '65. Continuing in the R.A., he was breveted for Mill Springs, Marion, war service (Col. and B.G. USA), and Salisbury, N.C. (Maj. Gen. USA) and died on active duty as Col. 1st U.S. Cav. He was active in Reconstruction and the Modoc wars.

GILLMORE, Quincy Adams. Union gen. 1825–88. Ohio. USMA 1849 (1/43); Engrs. He supervised harbor fortification construction and taught engineering and served as Q.M. at West Point before being named Capt. 6 Aug. '61 and acting as Chief Engr. on the Port Royal expedition to S.C. He was promoted B.G. USV 28 Apr. '62 and commanded 2d Div., Army Ky., Ohio (14 Oct. '62–25 Jan. '63) and Dist. Central Ky. (25 Jan.–10 Apr. '63) at Somerset. Appointed Maj. Gen. USV 10 July '63, he commanded the X Corps and the Dept. of the South (12 June '63–1 May '64) at Charleston. He fought at Bermuda Hundred, Swift's Creek, and Drewry's Bluff, as commander of the X Corps, Va. and N.C. (4 May–14 June '64). He was severely injured by a fall from his horse on 14 July '64, while pursuing Jubal Early in the Valley. At this time he was commander of two divisions of the XIX Corps in the Defenses of Washington. Recovering from this, he served on numerous boards and commissions and commanded the Dept. of the South and the X Corps again from 9 Feb. to 28 June '65. Breveted for Ft. Pulaski, Somerset, Fort Wagner (B.G. USA), and Morris Island (Maj. Gen. USA), he continued in the R.A., dying on active duty as Col. He wrote many professional books and treatises and served as president of the Mississippi River Commission.

GILLMORE MEDAL. Quincy Gillmore had 400 medals made for presentation to enlisted men who had distinguished themselves in the operations around Charleston, S.C., in July–Sept. '63. The bronze medals had on one side a facsimile of the Gen.'s autograph with the words "For Gallant and Meritorious Conduct," and a representation of Fort Sumter in ruins and the date "Aug. 23d 1863" on the other. The clasp by which the medal was pinned to the uniform was engraved with the name of the recipient. Known as the Gillmore Medal of Honor, it was accompanied by a certificate. (See also Decorations.)

GILMER, Jeremy Francis. C.S.A. gen. 1818–83. N.C. USMA 1839 (4/31); Engrs. He taught engineering at West

Point, served in the Mexican War, and in harbor fortification construction, was Chief Engr. of the Dept. of the West, and participated in river and harbor work in the South before resigning 29 June '61 as Capt. Commissioned Lt. Col. C.S.A. Engrs., in Sept. '61, he was A. S. Johnston's Chief Engr. in Dept. No. 2, fighting at Fort Henry, Fort Donelson, and Shiloh (wounded). On 4 Aug. '62 he was named Chief Engr. of the Dept. of Northern Va. On 4 Oct. of that year he was named Chief of the Engr. Bur. of the C.S.A. War Dept. Never a B.G., he was promoted Maj. Gen., from Col., on 25 Aug. '63. At this time he was also named second-in-command of the Dept. of S.C., Ga., and Fla., and served during the bombardment of Charleston. After fortifying Atlanta he returned to the Dept. of Northern Va. After the war he was in railroading and engineering.

GILMER, FORT, Va., 29–30 Sept. '64. See NEW MARKET HEIGHTS, same dates.

GILMORE, Joseph Albree. Gov. of New Hampshire. 1811–67. Vt. A merchant and construction agent, he was also a railroad superintendent and active in the Whig party. Joining the new Republican party, he was elected to the legislature and in Mar. '63 chosen Gov. Re-elected the next year, he took over in the darkest period of the war, when patriotism was beginning to wane, but managed to raise additional troops without having to invoke the draft ordered by Lincoln.

GILSON, Helen. SANITARY COMMISSION worker. Mass. The niece of Frank B. Fay, she was a small and gentle girl in her late twenties when she began working on the Peninsula. Her particular forte was working with contrabands and freedmen. She could organize a kitchen force of ignorant and woebe-gone Negroes into a smoothly working team that turned out food and services of the highest quality. In the hospitals with the wounded colored troops she prayed with them, sang for them, and cared for them with tenderness and skill. Contemporary reports of her work invariably start out clinical and end sentimental.

GINGER PANADA. See PANADA.

GINTY, George Clay. Union officer. Canada. Maj. 39th Wis. 3 June '64; mustered out 22 Sept. '64; Col. 47th Wis. 23 Feb. '65; Bvt. B.G. USV 28 Sept. '65 (war service). Died 1890.

GIRARDEY, Victor J. B. C.S.A. gen. ?–1864. Ga. Commissioned Lt. with the 3d Ga. in '61, he was sent to Va. and promoted Capt. and Adj. Gen. for Wright in Jan. '62. He fought in the Peninsular campaign, at Chancellorsville, and at Gettysburg, and took over a brigade during the skirmish at Manassas Gap when the colonel was wounded. Freeman says that he was appointed B.G. C.S.A. on the spot by Lee 30 July '64 for his performance in the Petersburg Mine Assault. This was a direct promotion from Capt. to B.G., the only instance in the war. Leading Wright's brigade, he was killed at Deep Bottom 16 Aug. '64.

GIST, States Rights. C.S.A. gen. 1831–64. S.C. Attended S.C. College and Harvard Law School. Named the Adj. and I.G. of the S.C. state army early in 1861, he served during Fort Sumter and was Bee's volunteer A.D.C. at 1st Bull Run. He succeeded him in command of his brigade and then returned to S.C. as Adj. Gen. Appointed B.G. C.S.A. 20 Mar. '62, he served under Pemberton on the S.C. coast and was sent to Vicksburg in May '63. He commanded Walker's division at Chickamauga and Missionary Ridge and led his own brigade in the Atlanta campaign. He was killed at Franklin 30 Nov. '64 while leading his brigade on foot after his horse had been shot.

GIVEN, Josiah. Union officer. Pa. Capt. 24th Ohio 17 June '61; Lt. Col. 18th Ohio 6 Sept '61; Col. 74th Ohio 5 June '63; Bvt. B.G. USV (war service); resigned 29 Sept. '64. Commanded 3, 1, XIV.

GIVEN, William. Union officer. Ohio. Col. 102d Ohio 18 Aug. '62; Bvt. B.G. USV (war service). Died 1866.

GLADDEN, Adley H. C.S.A. gen. ?-1862. S.C. He was wounded in the Mexican War and commissioned Col. 1st La. early in 1861. Appointed B.G. C.S.A. 30 Sept. '61, he led his brigade at Pensacola and went in Jan. '62 to Mobile. He was mortally wounded 6 Apr. '62 at Shiloh and died the same day.

GLASGOW, Samuel Lyle. Union officer. Ohio. 1st Lt. 4th Iowa 31 Aug. '61; resigned Jan. '62; Maj. 23d Iowa 19 Sept. '62; Lt. Col. 1 Dec. '62; Col. 19 May '63; Bvt. B.G. USV (Vicksburg). Commanded 2, 1, XIII; 1, 3, XIX; 1, 2, Res. Corps; 1, 2, XIII.

GLASGOW, Mo., 15 Oct. '64. Captured with over 400 Federals by Shelby during PRICE'S RAID IN MISSOURI.

GLEASON, John Hasset. Union officer. Ireland. Commissioned 1st Lt. 63d N.Y. 16 Sept. '61, he was mustered out 8 Jan. '62 and given the same rank when the regiment was reorganized 26 Feb. '62. Promoted Capt. 17 Sept. '62, he was mustered out 12 June '63 and again commissioned in the same rank and regiment 5 Apr. '64. He was named Maj. 1 Aug. '64 and Lt. Col. 2 Nov. '64 and breveted B.G. and Maj. Gen. USV for war service. Mustered out in May '65, he died in 1889. His name is spelled Gleeson by Phisterer.

GLEASON, Newell, Union officer. Vt. Lt. Col. 87th Ind. 28 Aug. '62; Col. 22 Mar. '63; Bvt. B.G. USV (war service). Commanded 2, 3, XIV. Died 1886.

GLEESON, John H. Misspelling by Phisterer of John Hasset GLEASON.

GLENDALE, Va., 30 June '62. See WHITE OAK SWAMP.

GLENNY, William. Union officer. N.Y. Capt. 64th N.Y. 10 Dec. '61; Lt. Col. 1 Aug. '64; Bvt. B.G. USV (war service). Commanded 4, 1, II. Died 1900.

GLOBE TAVERN, Va. (Weldon R.R.; Six Mile House), 18-21 Aug. '64 (PETERSBURG CAMPAIGN).

After failure of the Petersburg Mine Assault, and while Hancock was conducting operations north of the James (DEEP BOTTOM RUN), a new attempt was made by the Federals to extend their lines to the west and to further cut Confederate communications into Petersburg. This resulted in operations known by the names of Globe Tavern, Six Mile House, and Weldon R.R.

The night of 14-15 Aug. Warren's V Corps was relieved from its positions in the Petersburg trenches by the IX Corps and assembled behind the Federal left (west) flank. Warren was ordered to move out at 4 A.M. on the 18th to make a lodgment on the Weldon R.R. near Globe Tavern and then destroy track as far south as possible. Spear's cavalry brigade was attached and Warren was told to consider his operation a reconnaissance in force and to take advantage of any enemy weakness he might discover. In addition to cutting vital Confederate communications into Petersburg, Grant also wanted to draw Confederate strength from the Valley, thereby facilitating Sheridan's operations.

Opposed only by Dearing's cavalry brigade, Warren reached the railroad without difficulty. Griffin's division was formed along the west side of the track and started its destruction. Ayres's division moved north along the railroad about a mile, and Crawford's division formed on his right (east). Cutler's division remained to the rear in reserve. The weather was oppressively hot and rainy; the terrain was densely wooded and visibility greatly restricted.

The Confederates reacted promptly. Heth attacked Ayres's left flank at about 2 P.M., surprising and driving back Dushane's Md. brigade. Ayres pulled back his flank to keep from being enveloped, and then counterattacked. Federal losses were 936 in this action (Humphreys, 275). Both Grant and Lee decided to reinforce their troops in this area. Mott's division (II) was withdrawn from north of the James the night of 18-19 Aug. and used to extend the Federal lines toward Warren's newly-won positions.

On the 19th A. P. Hill, with five infantry and one cavalry brigades, moved out of the Petersburg lines for an attack. At about 4:30 they launched a double envelopment that drove back the divisions of Ayres and Crawford. Warren then led a counterattack that took back the ground that had been lost. After the fighting had temporarily ceased, Warren withdrew his line from one to two miles to get better defensive positions. The night of 20–21 Aug. Lee started withdrawing most of his troops from north of the James to reinforce Hill. Grant withdrew the rest of Hancock's (II) corps and posted it so as to be able to reinforce Warren. There was some skirmishing the morning of the 20th. On the 21st Hill made a coordinated attack on Warren's new position but was unable to break through. Lee arrived during the afternoon with additional troops, but he soon realized that further attack would

be futile. By this time the Federal flank had been reinforced by the IX Corps.

In the four days' fighting there were 20,289 Federals engaged, of whom 1,303 were killed and wounded and 3,152 missing. Out of 14,787 Confederates engaged, an estimated 1,200 were killed and wounded, and 419 missing (Livermore, 118).

GOBIN, John Peter Shindel. Union officer. 1837–? Pa. 1st Lt. 11th Pa. 23 Apr. '61; mustered out 31 July '61; Capt. 47th Pa. 2 Sept. '61; Maj. 20 Aug. '64; Lt. Col. 4 Nov. '64; Col. 3 Jan. '65; Bvt. B.G. USV (war service); B.G. USV 9 June '98; discharged 28 Feb. '99. A lawyer, state senator, and Lt. Governor of Pennsylvania, he was a B.G. in the Pa. National Guard (1885) and C. in C. of the G.A.R. (1897).

GODDARD, William. Union officer. R.I. Maj. 1st R.I. 27 June '61; Bvt. B.G. USV; mustered out 2 Aug. '61. Brevets for raising troops, 1st Bull Run, war service.

GODMAN, James Harper. Union officer. Va. Maj. 4th Ohio 4 May '61; Lt. Col. 9 Jan. '62; Col. 22 May '63; Bvt. B.G. USV (war service); resigned 28 July '63. Died 1891.

GODWIN, Archibald C. C.S.A. gen. ?–1864. Va. A businessman, he was appointed to the C.S.A. staff from N.C. and was commissioned Col. 57th N.C. During the Maryland campaign his regiment was guarding Richmond. He fought at Fredericksburg and led Hoke's brigade at Gettysburg. On 7 Nov. '63 he was captured while commanding three regiments of this brigade at Rappahannock Station. He was exchanged in the summer and named B.G. C.S.A. 5 Aug. '64. Given command of his old brigade, he led them in Early's Valley campaign and was killed 19 Sept. '64 at Winchester.

GOFF, Nathan Jr. Union officer. R.I. Capt. 2d R.I. 6 June '61; Maj. 24 July '62; Lt. Col. 12 Dec. '62; Col. 22d US Col. Inf. 31 Dec. '63; Col. 37th US Col. Inf. 25 Oct. '64; Bvt. B.G. USV (war service). Commanded 3, 3, X. Died 1903.

GOGGIN, James M. C.S.A. officer. Appt.-Va. He was a Maj. at Fort Loudon (Knoxville) and, in the same rank, on McLaws' staff in the spring of 1864. Appointed B.G. C.S.A. to rank from 4 Dec. '64, this appointment was canceled. He is listed neither by Wood nor by C.M.H., although he appears on Wright's list.

GOLDING'S FARM, Va., 27 to 28 June '62. See GARNETT'S FARM.

GOLGOTHA, Ga., 16 June '64. See KENESAW MOUNTAIN.

GOODELL, Arthur Augustus. Union officer. 1839–82. N.Y. Capt. 36th Mass. 15 Aug. '62; Maj. 29 Jan. '63; Lt. Col. 1 Sept. '63; Bvt. B.G. USV; mustered out 5 May '64. Brevets for Vicksburg campaign, eastern Tenn. campaign. W.I.A. Blue Springs (Tenn.) 10 Oct. '62.

GOODING, Oliver Paul. Union officer. c. 1839–1909. Ind. USMA 1858 (24/27); Inf. He served in the Utah Expedition and was named 1st Lt. 10th US Inf. 7 May '61. In Washington until 15 Feb. '62, he was promoted Col. 31st Mass. 18 Feb. of that year and went on the New Orleans expedition. He commanded Forts Jackson and St. Philip 20 Sept. '62–19 Jan. '63 and led a brigade in the XIX Corps until 28 July '63, fighting at Camp Bisland and Port Hudson. After a leave of absence he commanded the Dist. of Baton Rouge 1 Sept.–19 Oct. '63 and served on a military commission in Washington until 27 Jan. '64, when he returned to the Gulf to command a brigade (24 Feb.–5 June) and a division (5 June–

11 July '64) in the Red River campaign. He then commanded a cavalry brigade in the Gulf 23 Sept.–11 Nov. '64, was mustered out of volunteer service 26 Nov. '64, and served as Inspecting Officer until he resigned 20 Mar. '65. For his service he was breveted B.G. USV and Maj. Gen. USV (Port Hudson and Red River campaign). After the war he was a lawyer and police commissioner of St. Louis.

GOODWIN, Ichabod. Gov. of New Hampshire. 1796–1882. N.Y. A merchant seaman until 1832, he then went into business ashore and entered politics as a Whig. He served in the legislature and was elected Republican Gov. in 1859. Serving until June '61, he answered Lincoln's first call for troops although the legislature was not in session.

GOODYEAR, Ellsworth D. S. Union officer. Conn. Capt. 10th Conn. 22 Oct. '61; Maj. 1 Dec. '64; Lt. Col. 17 Feb. '65; Bvt. B.G. USV 2 Apr. '65. Brevets for war service, Ft. Gregg (Va.).

GORDON, B. Frank. C.S.A. gen. Listed as Col. 5th Mo. Cav., he was appointed B.G. C.S.A. 16 May '65 by Kirby Smith in the Trans-Miss. Dept. His name appears in the lists of Wright and Heitman but not in C.M.H. and Wood.

GORDON, George Henry. Union gen. 1823–86. Mass. USMA 1846 (43/59); Mtd. Rifles-Inf. He fought in the Mexican War (2 wounds, 1 brevet) and served on the frontier, resigning in 1854 to attend Harvard Law School. Commissioned Col. 2d Mass. 25 May '61, he commanded 1st Brig., Banks's division, Potomac (28 Aug.–18 Oct. '61); 3d Brig., Banks's division (13–14 Mar. '62), and 3, 1, Banks's V (13 Mar–4 Apr. '62). As B.G. USV 9 June '62, he commanded 3d Brig., 1st Div., Shenandoah (4 Apr.–

27 May '62 on Banks's retreat from the Valley and 18–26 June '62). He also led 3, 1, II, Army of Va. (26 June–12 Sept. '62) at Chantilly and Cedar Mountain; 3, 1, XII, Potomac (12–17 Sept. '62) at Antietam and South Mountain, succeeding to division 17 Sept.–20 Oct. In the Army of the Potomac he commanded 2d Div., IV (4 May–15 July '63) at Suffolk and 1st Div., XI (17 July–5 Aug. '63). He commanded South End Folly Island, X (16 Aug.–24 Oct. and 28 Nov. '63–15 Jan. '64); Forces Folly Island, X (15–28 Jan. '64), and Dist. Fla. South (13 May–2 June '64). He also commanded US Forces Mobile Bay, Gulf (1–31 Aug. '64). Breveted Maj. Gen. USV for war service 9 Apr. '65, he was mustered out in Aug., his health ruined by the war. He returned to his Boston law office and wrote a number of books on the Civil War in Va. D.A.B. says of these: "His strong opinions and trenchant criticisms which hindered his promotion in the army are evident . . . [although they have] a sense of humor and a large fund of anecdotes . . . [and the] narrative is vivid and animated, he frequently wrote too much."

GORDON, George Washington. C.S.A. gen. 1836–1911. Tenn. He studied under Bushrod Johnson in Nashville and was a surveyor when the war began. Named drillmaster of the 11th Tenn., he served in eastern Tenn. under Zollicoffer and Kirby Smith. Promoted Capt., Lt. Col., and finally Col. in Dec. '62, he fought under Bragg at Stones River where he was wounded. He commanded his regiment at Chickamauga and Missionary Ridge and started on the Atlanta campaign, but was appointed B.G. C.S.A. 15 Aug. '64 and took over Vaughan's brigade. At Franklin he was wounded and captured. After the war he studied law at Cumberland Univ. and was a planter until 1883, when

he was named to a series of public offices. He was also U.S. Representative and C. in C. of the United Confederate Veterans.

GORDON, James B. C.S.A. gen. 1822–64. N.C. Graduating from Emory and Henry College in Va., he was a merchant and legislator when commissioned Capt. in N.C. state troops. In May he joined the 1st N.C. Cav. and in the spring of '62 was promoted Lt. Col. in Hampton's Legion. The next spring he was named Col. and skirmished at Hagerstown during the retreat from Gettysburg. Appointed B.G. C.S.A. 28 Sept. '63, he took command of the N.C. Cav. Brig. and fought at Bethesda Church, Culpeper Courthouse, Auburn (wounded), Mine Run (where his horse was shot from under him), Spotsylvania, Yellow Tavern, Ground Squirrel Church, and Meadow Bridge, where he was mortally wounded 12 May '64. He died six days later in Richmond.

GORDON, John Brown. C.S.A. gen. 1832–1904. Ga. After graduating from the Univ. of Ga., he was a lawyer and then superintended a coal mine in Alabama. As Capt. of the Raccoon Roughs, a volunteer company of mountaineers, he was sent to Va. Named Col. of the 6th Ala., he fought in the Peninsular campaign, and succeeded Rodes in the command of the brigade at Seven Pines. He was wounded leading his regiment at Antietam and was appointed B.G. C.S.A. 1 Nov. '62. This was not confirmed, and he was reappointed 11 May '63 to rank from the 7th. He commanded his Ga. brigade at Chancellorsville, Gettysburg, the Wilderness, and Spotsylvania, before being named Maj. Gen. 14 May '64. During the siege of Petersburg and in Early's Valley campaign he led his division and returned to Petersburg near the end of

1864. He planned and led the assault on FORT STEDMAN at Petersburg.

D.A.B. incorrectly says he was promoted Lt. Gen. in 1865 and the B.&L. order of battle for Appomattox lists him with that rank. He was never a Lt. Gen.

After the war he served as Democratic U.S. Sen., Gov., and again Sen. A "courtly and impressive" man (D.A.B.), he was C. in C. of the United Confederate Veterans and wrote *Reminiscences of the Civil War* (1903).

His wife, Fanny Haralson Gordon, left their children with Gordon's mother and accompanied him in all his campaigns. She was a prime annoyance to Jubal Early, who was once heard to wish to God that the Federals would capture her.

GORGAS, Josiah. C.S.A. gen. and Chief of Ord. 1818–83. Pa. Appt.-N.Y. USMA 1841 (6/52); Ord. He served in various arsenals, spent time in Europe studying foreign armies, and fought in the Mexican War before resigning 3 Apr. '61 as Capt. Commissioned Maj. C.S.A. Chief of Ord. (appointed from Ala.) on 8 Apr., he was faced with the staggering dearth of matériel and manufacturing in the South. However, by 1863 he had the ordnance bureau operating efficiently and was promoted through the grades, becoming B.G. C.S.A. 10 Nov. '64. After the war he operated a blast furnace, then taught and was chancellor at Sewanee. He was also president and later librarian of the Univ. of Ala. His son was the noted Surg. Gen. William C. Gorgas.

GORMAN, Willis Arnold. Union gen. 1816–76. Ky. A lawyer and legislator, he was seriously wounded in the Mexican War and served as Gov. of Pueblo in 1848. He was a Democratic Congressman, Gov. of the Minn. Ter. in 1853–57, and active in politics until the war. Commissioned Col. 1st Minn.

29 Apr. '61, he fought at 1st Bull Run. He was named B.G. USV 7 Sept. '61 and commanded 1st Brig., Stone's division, Potomac (3 Oct. '61–13 Mar. '62) at Balls Bluff, and 1, 2, II (13 Mar.–29 Oct. '62) at South Mountain and Antietam. In Dec. '62 he commanded Dist. E. Ark., Mo. He also commanded Dist. E. Ark., XIII, Tenn. (22 Dec. '62–8 Feb. '63) and 12th Div., XIII, Tenn. (22 Jan.–8 Feb. '63). He was mustered out 4 May '64 and resumed his law practice.

GOVAN, Daniel Chevilette. C.S.A. gen. 1829–1911. N.C. After attending S.C. College, he joined his kinsman Ben McCulloch in the gold rush. He returned to the South to become a planter in Miss. and Ark. and was commissioned Lt. Col. 2d Ark. when the war began. Fighting in the Ky. and Tenn. campaigns, he was a Col. and led the regiment at Shiloh. He also led the 2d Ark. at Stones River and commanded Liddell's brigade at Chickamauga and the battles around Chattanooga. Appointed B.G. C.S.A. 29 Dec. '63, he commanded his brigade under Hardee in the Atlanta campaign and was captured with his old regiment 1 Sept. '64 in front of Atlanta. Exchanged shortly, he led his brigade at Franklin and Nashville and surrendered with J. E. Johnston. He returned to his plantations and was an Indian Agent for a short time.

GOVERNOR MOORE PLANTATION, La. Scene of skirmishing during the RED RIVER CAMPAIGN of 1864, particularly during the actions around ALEXANDRIA, 1–8 May '64.

GOVERNORS. See BORDER STATE WAR GOVERNORS; CONFEDERATE GOVERNORS; and UNION WAR GOVERNORS.

GOWEN, George Washington. Union officer. Pa. 1st Lt. 48th Pa. 10 Aug. '61; Capt. 21 Sept. '62; Lt. Col. 20

Dec. '64; Col. 1 Mar. '65; Bvt. B.G. USV 2 Apr. '65 (Petersburg assault); K.I.A. Petersburg 2 Apr. '65.

GRACIE, Archibald Jr. C.S.A. gen. 1832–64. N.Y. Appt.-N.J. USMA 1854 (14/46); Inf. He had studied at Heidelberg before going to West Point. He served on the frontier and in Indian fighting before resigning in 1856. Joining his father in Ala., he was a successful merchant in Mobile when the Civil War started. As Capt. of the Washington Light Inf. Co. of that city, he led the troops that seized the US arsenal at Mt. Vernon (on the governor's orders) before the state seceded. This unit became the 3d Ala. and on 12 July '61 Gracie was commissioned Maj. 11th Ala. In the spring of '62 he was named Col. 43d Ala., serving under Kirby Smith in eastern Tenn. He was appointed B.G. C.S.A. 4 Nov. '62 and commanded his brigade under Preston at Chickamauga. Wounded at Bean's Station, he fought in the May '64 campaign around the Wilderness and Spotsylvania and fought in the Petersburg siege June '64 until killed by a sharpshooter 2 Dec.

GRAHAM, Charles Kinnard. Union gen. 1824–89. N.Y. Serving as a Midshipman in the Gulf during the Mexican War, he was a licensed lawyer but never practiced, turning, instead, to engineering. He was the surveyor for Central Park and built the drydocks and landings at the Brooklyn Navy Yard. When war came, he enrolled with 400 navy-yard workmen and was named Col. 74th N.Y. 26 May '61. He led them at Fair Oaks, Malvern Hill, Yorktown, Williamsburg, Oak Grove, Glendale, and during the Seven Days' Battles. Promoted B.G. USV 29 Nov. '62, he commanded 2, 2, III, Potomac (Feb.–Mar. '63), 3d Div., III (3 May–20 June '63) at Chancellorsville, and 1, 1, III (June–2 July '63), where he was wounded in the head and captured in the Peach Orchard at Gettysburg. Exchanged in Sept., he commanded Naval Brig., Va. and N.C. (28 Apr. '64–17 Feb. '65) on expeditions up the James and adjacent waters. Near Fredericksburg he shelled the house of the brother of the C.S.A. Sec. of War, James Alexander Seddon, under orders by Butler in retaliation for Early's having burned Blair's house in Silver Spring (Md.). He later commanded the Defenses of Bermuda Hundred (17 Feb.–19 Mar. '65), was breveted Maj. Gen. USV for war service and was mustered out 24 Aug. '65. Returning to engineering, he was N.Y. State Commissioner of Gettysburg Monuments.

GRAHAM, Harvey. Union officer. Pa. 1st Lt. 1st Iowa 14 May '61; mustered out 21 Aug. '61; Maj. 22d Iowa 9 Sept. '62; Lt. Col. 30 Sept. '62; Col. 5 May 64; Bvt. B.G. USV 25 July '65 (war service). Commanded 2d Brig., Grover's division Savannah; 1, 1, X. Died 1884.

GRAHAM, Lawrence Pike. 1815–? Union gen. Va. R.A. Entering the army in 1837, he served in the Seminole War and Mexican War (1 brevet). Named Maj 2d US Cav. 3 Aug. '61, he raised and commanded Graham's brigade, Army of the Potomac (Aug.–Oct. '61) and was promoted B.G. USV (31 Aug.) and Lt. Col. 5th US Cav. (1 Oct.). He also commanded 2, Buell's division, Potomac (3 Oct. '61–13 Mar. '62) and 2, 1, IV, Potomac (13 Mar.–19 May '62). He was president and member of a court-martial and several retirement boards until the end of the war. He was mustered out of USV 24 Aug. '65 and continued in the R.A. until retired in 1870 as Col. He was breveted B.G. USA for war service.

GRAHAM, Samuel, Union officer. Ireland. Col. 5th N.Y. Hv. Arty. 6 Mar.

'62; Bvt. B.G. USV (Harpers Ferry, 1864). Commanded 2d Brig., 3d Div. and 2d Brig., 2d Div. (W. Va.).

GRAHAM, William Alexander. Political leader. 1804–75. N.C. A member of the Confederate senate although he had opposed secession, he had had a long political career up until that time. He had been state legislator, US Sen., Gov., US Sec. of the Navy (1850–52), and unsuccessful Whig candidate for vice-president in 1852.

GRAHAM, William M. US Officer. c.1798–1847. Va. Appt.-Va. USMA 1817* (4/19); Inf. Although he was killed in 1847 at the battle of Molino del Rey in the Mexican War as Lt. Col. 11th U.S. Inf., he was breveted B.G. USA 13 Mar. '65.

GRANBERRY, Hiram B. Sometime spelling of GRANBURY, Hiram Bronson. Former version is given by Wright and Miller; Granbury is form used by B.&L., C.M.H., Horn, and is the spelling in the Waco, Tex., court records.

GRANBURY, Hiram Bronson. C.S.A. gen. 1831–64. Appt.-Tex. Named Capt. 7th Tex., he was sent to Ky. and promoted Maj. in Nov. '61. Captured at Donelson, he was exchanged and promoted Col. 7th Tex. 29 Aug. '62. His regiment fought in Gregg's brigade in northern Mississippi until Vicksburg fell. He commanded the 7th Tex. at Raymond (Miss.), Chickamauga, and Missionary Ridge, where he succeeded to James A. Smith's brigade. Leading the Tex. Brig. at Ringgold Gap, he was appointed B.G. C.S.A. 29 Feb. '64 and continued to command the brigade throughout the Atlanta campaign. He was killed in a charge at Franklin 30 Nov. '64. See GRANBERRY for comment on spelling of name.

*There was no class standing prior to 1818, and the cadets are listed in the order in which they were commissioned.

GRAND REVIEW. Parade of the Armies of the Potomac, the Tenn., and Ga. 23–24 May '65 in Washington. Miller estimates that 150,000 men marched in review before the President and the commanding generals. The volunteer army was then disbanded.

GRANGER, George Frederick. Union officer. Me. 1st Lt. 9th Me. 22 Sept. '61; Capt. 23 Sept. '61; Maj. 1 July '63; Lt. Col. 25 Sept. '64; Col. 9 Oct. '64; Bvt. B.G. USV 12 June '65 (war service). Commanded 3, 2, XXIV; 3, Ames, Terry's Prov.; 3, 2, X. Died 1883.

GRANGER, Gordon. Union gen. 1822–76. N.Y. USMA 1845 (35/41); Inf.-Mtd. Rifles. After winning two brevets in Mexico, he participated in Indian fighting and served on the frontier. Named Capt. 5 May '61 and transferred to the 3d Cav. 3 Aug., he served on McClellan's staff with an Ohio appointment as Lt. Col. 23 Apr.–31 May of that year. He was on Sturgis' staff at Dug Spring and Wilson's Creek and commanded the St. Louis Arsenal 1 Sept.–31 Dec. Named Col. 2d Mich. Cav. 2 Sept. '61 and B.G. USV 26 Mar. '62, he commanded the Cav. of the Army of Miss. (4 Mar.–30 July '62) at New Madrid, Island No. 10, and the advance upon and siege of Corinth. He led the 5th Div., Army of Miss. (30 July–4 Sept. '62); the "Army of Ky." in the Army of the Ohio (25 Aug.– 7 Oct. '62); and Dist. of Central Ky. (17 Nov. '62–25 Jan. '63), having been appointed Maj. Gen. USV 17 Sept. '62. During the advance on Tullahoma and at Chickamauga, he led the Res. Corps of the Cumberland (8 June–9 Oct. '63), and at Missionary Ridge and Knoxville he commanded the IV Corps (Cumberland). In the Dept. of the Gulf he led the Dist. S. Ala. (Dec. '64–Feb. '65); Res. Corps (3–18 Feb. and 12 Jan.–3

Feb. '65) and XIII Corps (18 Feb.–20 July '65) at Mobile. He was breveted for Wilson's Creek, Chickamauga, Chattanooga, Mobile (B.G. USA) and Forts Gaines and Morgan (Maj. Gen. USA). Continuing in the R.A., he died on active duty as Col. 15th Inf. After having been elevated to command of a corps for his remarkable performance at CHICKAMAUGA, Granger failed in subsequent actions to live up to the promise shown in that battle. D.A.B. says "outspoken and rough in manner, kindly and sympathetic at heart . . . [his] independence occasionally came near to insubordination, and at ordinary times he lacked energy." See also KENTUCKY, ARMY OF.

GRANGER, Robert Seamen. Union gen. 1816–94. Ohio. USMA 1838 (28/45); Inf. He served in the Florida War, as an asst. prof. at West Point, and in the Mexican War, as well as on the frontier. When Capt. 1st Inf. (since 1847), he was captured with Maj. Sibley's command on the Tex. coast 27 Apr. '61. Promoted Maj. 5th Inf. 9 Sept. '61, he commanded the post of Louisville and then took over Ky. State Troops Sept. '62 and led them at Shepherdsville, Lebanon Junction, and Lawrenceburg (Ky.). He was promoted B.G. USV 20 Oct. '62 and commanded the post of Bowling Green (Ky.). In the Army of the Cumberland he led 1st Div., XIV (17 Jan.–29 Mar. '63) in a skirmish near Eaglesville (Tenn.) Feb. '63; 3, 1, XIV (17 Apr.–6 May '63); 3d Div., Reserve Corps (8 June–9 Oct. '63); Dist. of Nashville (28 May '63); post of Nashville (Nov. '63–June '64); 1st Brig., Dist. Nashville (Jan. '64); 1, 3, XII (2 Jan.–14 Apr. '64) and Dist. North Alabama (2 June '64–10 Sept. '65). He was mustered out of USV 24 Aug. '65 and continued in the R.A. until retired in 1873 as Col. His brevets were for Lawrenceburg (Ky.), Decatur (Ala.) as B.G. USA. war service (Maj. Gen. USV and Maj. Gen. USA).

GRANT, Lewis Addison. Union gen. 1829–1918. Vt. A schoolteacher and lawyer, he was commissioned Maj. 5th Vt. 15 Aug. '61, Lt. Col. 25 Sept. '61, and Col. 16 Sept. '62, leading his regiment at Fredericksburg, where he was wounded. He commanded 2, 2, VI (Feb.–Dec. '63) at Salem Heights, where he led his troops over the enemy's breastworks, captured three battle flags, and was wounded again, winning the Medal of Honor for this 11 May '93. Promoted B.G. USV 27 Apr. '64, he commanded 2, 2, VI, Shenandoah (6 Aug.–18 Sept. and 3–19 Oct. '64), succeeding to division on the last-named date at Cedar Creek. He was wounded again at Petersburg in Apr. '65, breveted Maj. Gen. USV 19 Oct. '64 for the Richmond and Shenandoah Valley campaigns, and was mustered out 24 Aug. '65. In 1890–93 he was Asst. Sec. of War.

GRANT, Ulysses Simpson. Union gen. 1822–1885. Ohio. USMA 1843 (21/39); Inf. A man who would probably have been voted at the beginning of the Civil War as "least likely to succeed," Sam Grant emerged as the great military leader of the Union. Undistinguished as a cadet, he finished the Mexican War as a Capt. with two citations for gallantry and one for meritorious conduct. Unable to bear the futility and monotony of postwar military service on the West Coast, lonely for his wife and children, Grant began drinking heavily and neglecting his duty. He resigned in 1854 to avoid court-martial, and went to live in Mo. at the home of his wife (Julia Dent, sister of a classmate). He became increasingly destitute as he failed at a number of undertakings. When Lincoln called for volunteers in 1861, Grant offered his services. He was eventually given command of the 21st Ill., was appointed B.G. at the instigation of Congressman Washburne, and given command of a district with headquarters at Cairo, Ill. After his inauspicious attack on BELMONT, Mo., 7 Nov. '61, he gained national attention with his operations at Forts Henry and Donelson, Shiloh, and Vicksburg. Promoted to Lt. Gen. (9 Mar. '64) after his victories around Chattanooga, he was made Gen. in Chief of the Armies of the United States on 12 Mar. '64, and took over the strategic direction of the war. Accompanying Meade's Army of the Potomac, Grant directed the "relentless pounding" of Lee's army in the costly campaign of attrition through the battles of the Wilderness, Spotsylvania, Cold Harbor, the crossing of the James, the siege of Petersburg, and the pursuit to Appomattox. After the war he remained as head of the army, was named Sec. of War in Stanton's place by President Johnson as part of the latter's test of strength with the Senate. Elected president by a small popular majority on the Republican ticket in 1868, and re-elected for a second term, Grant's political career, although honest and well meaning, resulted in an administration that was corrupt and badly managed. For two years after retiring as president he made a triumphal tour of the world. In 1880 he frustrated the efforts of influential friends to secure his nomination for a third term in the White House. In a financial venture in 1884, with the unprincipled Ferdinand Ward, Grant lost his entire savings and was reduced to a state of poverty. To recoup his fortunes he accepted an offer of the *Century Magazine* to write about his war experiences. This proved so successful that he undertook an autobiography which, honest and straightforward, was completed a few days before his death of throat cancer. The two-

volume *Personal Memoirs of U.S. Grant*, published by the firm of Mark Twain, sold 300,000 copies and earned $450,000 for his widow; it is considered one of the greatest autobiographies in the English language. A man whose stature grows with the passage of time, the military epitaph of this enigmatic American general can best be stated in Lincoln's words: "He fights." Lyman described him as ". . . rather under middle height, of a spare, strong build; light-brown hair, and short, light-brown beard . . . eyes of a clear blue; forehead high; nose aquiline; jaw squarely set, but not sensual. His face has three expressions: deep thought; extreme determination; and great simplicity and calmness."

GRANT'S HORSES. His favorite, Cincinnati, was given to him by an admirer sometime after the battle of Chattanooga and carried him throughout the rest of the war. Standing 17½ hands high, this mount was rarely ridden by anyone other than Grant, Lincoln in his last visit to City Point being one of the few exceptions. Grant had a number of other horses during the course of the war, the first being Jack. He bought this cream-colored horse in Galena at the beginning of the war and rode him as an extra or ceremonial mount until the fall of 1863. During the actions around Donelson and at Shiloh he had a roan named Fox, and his mount during the Vicksburg campaign, Kangaroo, was a raw-boned and ugly horse left on the field at Shiloh by the Confederates. Grant, who was an outstanding horseman, saw that the animal was a thoroughbred, and after a period of rest and care turned him into a magnificent mount. Also during this campaign he had a black pony named Jeff Davis, captured on the plantation of the brother of the Confederate president.

GRAPE SHOT. A number of iron balls (usually nine) put together by means of two iron plates, two rings, and an iron pin passing through the top and bottom plates. Another method was to place the balls in tiers around an iron pin attached to an iron tampion at the bottom, put this into a canvas bag, and "quilt" the balls into place with a strong cord. Effective in field guns at ranges between those for canister and shell (i.e., about 1,000 yards), it was being superseded by canister in 1861, but continued to be used in 8-inch howitzers and Columbiads. Some authorities (e.g. Van Naisawald) maintain that grape was not used in Civil War field pieces.

GRATIOT STREET PRISON. This Federal PRISON in St. Louis, held, in addition to prisoners of war, Union army deserters, bounty jumpers, spies, bushwhackers, and disloyal citizens. Originally a medical college, the building held around 500 with safety but usually 1,000 were confined there. The inmates were a desperate and violent group, and the building was twice set on fire by them. A number tried to escape by attacking the guards or tunneling under the walls.

GRAVELLY RUN, Va., 29–30 Mar. '65. See QUAKER ROAD.

GRAY, Henry. C.S.A. gen. 1816–92. Appt.-La. Entering the 28th La. (presumably) early in the war as an officer, he was Col. by 17 May '62 and fought under Taylor during the Vicksburg siege. He was wounded at Bayou Teche and fought at Camp Bisland. In the Red River campaign he led a brigade in Mouton's division and was named B.G. C.S.A. 18 Mar. '65 to rank from the 17th.

GRAYDON, James ("Paddy"). Union officer. An R.A. soldier, he had been authorized to organize and lead an independent "spy company" of N. Mex. volunteers. Composed almost entirely of local natives of Mexican origin, the force harassed Sibley's retreat during the NEW MEXICO AND ARIZONA OPERATIONS IN 1861–62. See also VALVERDE. Although Graydon is called a Capt., Heitman does not list him as an officer.

GRAYSON, John Breckinridge. C.S.A. gen. 1807–61. Ky. USMA 1826 (22/41); Arty.-Comsy. He served in garrison and the Seminole War before being Scott's Chief of Commissariat in the Mexican War (2 brevets). Holding the same post in the Dept. of N. Mex., he resigned as a Maj. 1 July '61 to become B.G. C.S.A. 15 Aug. '61. He was commanding the Dept. of Middle and Eastern Fla. when he died at Tallahassee 21 Oct. '61.

GREAT LOCOMOTIVE CHASE. See ANDREWS' RAID.

GREELEY, Edwin Seneca. Union officer. N.H. 1st Lt. 10th Conn. 22 Oct. '61; Capt. 25 Apr. '62; Maj. 4 Mar. '63; Lt. Col. 7 Sept. '64; Col. 16 Feb. '65; Bvt. B.G. USV (war service). Commanded 3, 1, XXIV.

GREELEY, Horace, Editor and politician. 1811–72. N.H. One of the first Republican editors, he was a considerable influence during the Civil War era. He founded the N.Y. Tribune in 1841 which became a powerful voice for organized labor and an opponent of the Compromise of 1851, the Kansas-Nebraska Act, and slavery. Greeley supported Lincoln rather belatedly and strongly opposed his conciliatory attitude toward the border states. Greeley also advocated immediate emancipation and after the war was one of the signers of Jefferson Davis' bail, an act which cost his paper almost half its subscribers. Nominated by the liberal Republicans for president in 1872 and endorsed by the Democrats, he was defeated by Grant.

GREEN, Colton. C.S.A. gen. Appt.-Mo. At the beginning of the war he was a Capt. in the Mo. militia when sent to Montgomery to procure arms. He fought at Helena (Ark.) 4 July '63, as Col., leading a brigade of Mo. cavalry in Marmaduke's division. Kirby Smith assigned him B.G. C.S.A. in the Trans-Miss. Dept. His name appears in the lists of Heitman and Wright, who spelled his first name "Cullen," but not of Wood or C.M.H.

GREEN, Martin E. C.S.A. gen. 1825-63. Mo. Serving under Price at Lexington (Mo.), he was a general in the Mo. State Guard and led his militia troops at Pea Ridge. Commissioned B.G. C.S.A. 21 July '62, he led the 3d Brig. of Price's army at Iuka, Corinth, Hatchie Bridge, and Port Gibson. He was wounded 25 June while in command of the 2d Brig. at Vicksburg and killed two days later by a sharpshooter.

GREEN, Thomas. C.S.A. gen. 1814-64. Va. Appt.-Tex. He joined the Tex. army as a young man and later fought Indians in Tex. and defended the border during the Mexican invasion. After fighting under Taylor during the Mexican War he was clerk of the Supreme Court of Tex. until commissioned Col. 5th Tex. Mtd. Rifles in Aug. '61. He served under Sibley in the NEW MEXICO operations in 1861-62 and commanded the line troops at Galveston 1 Jan. '63. In Apr. '63 he fought under Dick Taylor at Camp Bisland and was given Sibley's brigade. Appointed B.G. C.S.A. 20 May '63, he led them at LaFourche, Fordoche, and Bayou Bourbeau. Leading a division of cavalry, he went to Tex. to fight Banks when he invaded near the Rio Grande. He then went back to La. for the Red River campaign of 1864. He was killed 12 Apr. '64 at Blair's Landing

while leading a cavalry attack against Federal gunboats. Taylor, to whom he was related, speaks of him in terms of highest praise. "Upright, modest, and with the simplicity of a child, danger seemed to be his element, and he rejoiced in combat. His men adored him, and would follow wherever he led. . . ." (Taylor, 216). C.M.H. states erroneously that he was appointed Maj. Gen. in early '64. His highest rank was B.G.

GREEN, William N., Jr. Union officer. Mass. Cpl. 25th Mass. 16 Sept. '61; 2d Lt. 102d N.Y. 7 Mar. '62; Capt. 19 Dec. '62; resigned 15 May '63; Lt. Col. 173d N.Y. 8 Aug. '63; Bvt. B.G. USV 9 Apr. '64 (war service, Pleasant Hill, La.). Died 14 May '64 of wounds received 9 Apr. at Pleasant Hill.

GREENCASTLE, Pa., 20 June '63 (Gettysburg campaign; Ewell's advance). 1st N.Y. Cav. (Pierce's brigade, Dept. of the Susquehanna, at this time [Dyer, 1367]), covering Milroy's retreat, inflicted 20 casualties (missing).

GREENE, George Sears. Union gen. 1801-99. R.I. USMA 1823 (2/35); Arty. He taught mathematics and engineering at USMA and served in garrison, resigning in 1836 to engage in railroad engineering and construction. Commissioned Col. 60th N.Y. 18 Jan. '62 and B.G. USV 28 Apr. '62, he fought at Winchester 25 May. He then commanded 3, 1st Div., Shenandoah (27 May-18 June '62); 3, 2, II, Army of Va. (1-19 Aug. '62) at Cedar Mountain and succeeded to division (9 Aug.-12 Sept. '62) at White Sulphur Springs. He led 3, 2, XII, Potomac (18 Sept. '62-25 Sept. '63) at Chancellorsville and Gettysburg, also commanding division (12 Sept.-15 Oct. '62) at Antietam. At Wauhatchie, while commanding 3, 2, XII, Cumberland (25 Sept.-29 Oct. '63), he was shot through the face. Out of action for about a year and a half, he had a difficult operation in May '64 and then served on courts-martial until he took over the 3d Brig., 3d Div., XIV, Cumberland (9 Apr.–6 June '65) during the March through the Carolinas. Breveted Maj. Gen. USV for war service, he was mustered out in 1866 and returned to engineering. He was responsible for the water supply, elevated railroads, and many new streets in N.Y.C.; for the Washington, D.C., sewer system; and for water supplies in Detroit, Troy, and Yonkers. One of the founders and president of the American Society of Civil Engineers, he was interested in genealogy and quite proud of living long enough to be the oldest living graduate of USMA. D.A.B. says: "Harsh in manner and a strict disciplinarian, he was not a man to win immediate affection, but those under him soon learned to appreciate his ability and his rigid sense of justice." Father of Samuel Dana Greene, executive officer of the *Monitor.*

GREENE, James D. Union officer. Mass. Commissioned Lt. Col. 17th US Inf. May '61, he commanded the regiment in Me. until June '63, when he led them at Gettysburg. He was promoted Col. 6th US Inf. Sept. '63 and was stationed at Charleston. Breveted B.G. USA for war service, he resigned in 1867.

GREENE, Oliver Duff. Union officer. c. 1833–1904. N.Y. USMA 1854 (26/46); Arty.-Adj. Gen. He served on the frontier and in the Kans. border disturbances before being promoted 1st Lt. 2d US Arty. 25 Apr. '61. Fighting at 1st Bull Run, he was named Capt. Asst. Adj. Gen. 3 Aug. '61 and served in the Depts. of the Ohio and the Cumberland before being promoted Maj. 17 July '62. As Adj. Gen. of the VI Corps at South Mountain and Antietam, he won the Medal of Honor for the latter battle and served in headquarters in Washington and the Dept. of the South

before being named Capt. 2d US Arty. 1 Oct. '63. Adj. Gen. of the Dept. of the Mo. until 21 Sept. '64, he was on leave of absence for the rest of the war. He continued in the R.A., retiring in 1897 as Col.

GREENHOW, Rose O'Neal. Southern spy. ?–1864. Md. A Washington society leader and aunt of Mrs. Stephen A. Douglas, she knew everyone in the capital who counted and knew him well. She had been given a cipher code by a member of Beauregard's staff and informed the general of McDowell's plans for the 1st Bull Run campaign. After 23 Aug. '61 she was put in house arrest, and her Sixteenth Street home became a women's prison when the Federal authorities turned up more female prisoners than they had room for in the other Washington jails. After a series of security breaches at Fort Greenhow, as the house was called, she was sent in Jan. '62 to the Old Capitol Prison with her small daughter, Rose. Late that spring she was released and sent South, where she was hailed as a heroine. After meeting with high Confederate officials and visiting Beauregard at Charleston, she ran the blockade to France. She had a private audience with Napoleon III, put little Rose in a convent, and headed for England to continue her personal triumph. After being presented to Queen Victoria, she wrote *My Imprisonment* and returned without her daughter to the Confederacy. Her ship ran aground 30 Sept. '64 off Wilmington, N.C., and she asked, with two Confederate agents, to be put ashore. She drowned when their boat was overturned by a wave and was buried with the honors of war. Little Rose later became an actress.

GREER, Elkanah. C.S.A. gen. ?–1877. Miss. Appt.-Tex. Commissioned Col. 3d Tex. Cav. on 1 July '61, he fought at Wilson's Creek and Pea Ridge before resigning 1 June '62. On 8 Oct. of that year he was recalled to be appointed B.G. C.S.A. and named Chief of the Bureau of Conscription in the Trans-Miss. Dept. In 1864 he also commanded the reserves in that department.

GREGG, David McMurtrie. Union gen. 1833–1916. Pa. USMA 1855 (8/34); Cav. During the six years before the war he was in the West on Indian fighting duty and was named Capt. 3d US Cav. 14 May '61. Transferring to the 6th US Cav. 3 Aug. '61 and named Col. 8th Pa. Cav. 24 Jan. '62, he led his regiment at Seven Pines, Fair Oaks, Savage's Station, White Oak Swamp, Glendale, and Malvern Hill. He was promoted B.G. USV 29 Nov. '62, having commanded (7–16 July '62) the 2d Brig., cavalry division, Potomac. He led 2d Brig., Pleasonton's cavalry division, Potomac (Nov. '62–13 Dec. '62) and Gregg's cavalry brigade, Left Grand Div., Potomac (13 Dec. '62–12 Feb. '63). At Rappahannock River Bridge, on Stoneman's Raid, and at Beverly Ford, he commanded 3d Div., cavalry corps, Potomac (12 Feb.–11 June '63). He commanded 2d Div., cavalry corps, Potomac 11 June–24 Aug. '63 at Aldie, Upperville, Gettysburg, Shepherdstown, and Warrenton; 4 Sept.–22 Dec. '63 at Rapidan Station, Beverly Ford, Auburn, and New Hope Church; 5 Jan.–22 Jan. '64; 12 Feb.–25 Mar. '64; 4 Apr.–2 Aug. '64 at Todd's Tavern, Ground Squirrel Church, Meadow Bridge, Haw's Shop, Gaines's House, Trevilian Station, Tunstall Station, St. Mary's Church, Warwick Swamp, Darbytown, and Lee's Mill; 6 Aug.–15 Sept. '64 at Deep Bottom and Reams's Station; 25 Sept.–22 Dec. '64 at Peeble's Farm, Vaughan Road, Boydtown Plank Road, Stony Creek Station, and Bellefield; and 19 Jan.–9 Feb. '65. He commanded the cavalry corps 22 Jan.–12 Feb. '64; 25 Mar.–4 Apr. '64 and 2–6 Aug. '64. Breveted Maj. Gen. USV 1 Aug. '64, he

resigned 3 Feb. '65 and lived quietly in Reading (Pa.) until named Consul at Prague in 1874. He was active in municipal and charitable affairs and wrote a book on the 2d Cav. Div. at Gettysburg. "... A rare combination of modesty, geniality and ability, he was universally liked and respected" (D.A.B.).

GREGG, John. C.S.A. gen. 1828–64. Ala. Appt.-Tex. After graduating from college, he taught school and was later a lawyer and district judge. A member of the Tex. secession convention, he was sent as a state representative to Montgomery and sat in the C.S.A. Congress until commissioned Col. 7th Tex. in Sept. '61. Commanding the regiment at Fort Donelson, he surrendered it and was exchanged to become B.G. C.S.A. 29 Aug. '62 and take command of the Tex. and Tenn. brigade under Johnston during the Vicksburg campaign. Wounded at Chickamauga, he took over Hood's Texans and, serving under Longstreet, went with him to Va. He fought at the Wilderness, Spotsylvania, and at Petersburg and was killed on the Darbytown Road 7 Oct. '64 after almost five months of continuous fighting.

GREGG, John Irvin. Union officer. Pa. After fighting in the Mexican War, he was commissioned Capt. 3d US Cav. 14 May '61 and transferred to the 6th US Cav. three months later. He fought in the Peninsular campaign and was named Col. 16th Pa. Cav. 14 Nov. '62. From Apr. '63 to Apr. '65 he commanded a cavalry brigade at Beverly Ford, Aldie, Middleburg, Upperville, Gettysburg, Culpeper, Bristoe Station, Todd's Tavern, Haw's Shop, Cold Harbor, Trevilian Station, Deep Bottom (wounded), Hatcher's Run (wounded), Dinwiddie Court House, Five Forks, Amelia Court House (wounded), Sayler's Creek, and Farmville. Captured at the latter, he was held for three days and released upon Lee's surrender. Continuing in the R.A., he was breveted for Kelly's Ford, Sulphur Springs, Deep Bottom, Richmond (B.G. USV), and war service (B.G. USA and Maj. Gen. USV). He retired in 1879 as Col. 8th US Cav.

GREGG, Maxcy. C.S.A. gen. 1814–62. S.C. A lawyer and leader of the states-rights faction, he fought in the Mexican War and returned to public life more convinced than ever of the right of secession. Commissioned Col. 1st S.C., he served in the Charleston area from Jan. '61 until Fort Sumter's fall and then went to Va. Returning to S.C., he was appointed B.G. C.S.A. 14 Dec. '61 and commanded his brigade during the Peninsular campaign at Frayser's Farm, Malvern Hill. He then fought under Jackson at Cedar Run, 2d Bull Run (wounded), Antietam (where his horse was shot from under him), and Shepherdstown. At Fredericksburg he was mortally wounded and died in a few hours. D.A.B. describes him as "well versed in the classics, especially in Greek literature and philosophy . . . [a] student of botany and ornithology . . . [with] a well-equipped astronomical observatory at his home."

GREGG, William M. Union officer. N.Y. Maj. 23d N.Y. 16 May '61; mustered out 22 May '63; Col. 179th N.Y. 5 Sept. '64; Bvt. B.G. USV 2 Apr. '65 (Petersburg assault). Died 1881.

GREGORY, Edgar M. Union officer. N.Y. Commissioned Col. 91st Pa. 2 Aug. '61, he served throughout the war in that rank and was mustered out in 1867. He was breveted for Poplar Spring Church (B.G. USV 30 Sept. '64) and Five Forks (Maj. Gen. USV 9 Aug. '66). He died 1871.

GRESHAM, Walter Quintus. Union gen. 1832–95. Ind. As a conservative opponent of slavery, he believed that time alone would be sufficient to end it

and so curtailed the local activities of the Underground Railroad around his home. When Republican legislator, he broke with Gov. Morton over the spoils system and was refused when he asked for a commission. He enlisted and was named Lt. Col. 38th Ind. 18 Sept. '61 and Col. 53d Ind. 10 Mar. '62. He fought at Corinth, through the Mississippi operations, and to the fall of Vicksburg, being named B.G. USV 11 Aug. '63 and commanding 3, 4, XVII, Tenn., 26 Aug. '63–27 May '64. He succeeded to division (27 May–20 July '64) at Kenesaw Mountain and Leggett's Hill where he was wounded by a sharpshooter. Breveted Maj. Gen. for war service, he was mustered out in 1866 and returned to politics. As Postmaster Gen. in 1883, he brought about the end of the Louisiana Lottery by refusing to let it through the mails. He was a Democratic judge in 1892 and Sec. of State from 1893 until his death two years later.

GRIER, David Perkins. Union officer. Pa. Capt. 8th Mo. 20 June '61–11 Sept. '62; Col. 77th Ill. 11 Sept. '62; Bvt. B.G. USV 26 Mar. '65 (Mobile). Commanded 2, 10, XIII; 2, 4, XIII; 1, 4, XIII; 1, 3, Res. Corps; 1, 3, XIII; 3d Div., XIII. Died 1891.

GRIER, William N. Union officer. c. 1813–85. Pa. USMA 1835 (54/56); Dragoons-Cav. He served on the frontier, taught infantry and cavalry tactics at West Point, fought in the Mexican War (1 brevet) and participated for several years in Indian scouting and fighting (1 wound). Promoted Maj. 2d US Cav. 20 Apr. '61, he was acting I.G. of the Army of the Potomac until, as Lt. Col. 1st US Cav., 15 Feb. '62, he commanded his regiment at Yorktown, Williamsburg (wounded), Gaines's Mill, and Seven Days' Battles. For the remainder of the war he served on recruiting and court-martial duty in Iowa,

Ohio, and Mo. Breveted for Williamsburg and war service (B.G. USA), he continued in the R.A. until retired in 1870 as Col.

GRIERSON, Benjamin Henry. Union gen. 1826–1911. Pa. Moving first to Ohio and then to Ill., he taught music for a short time as a young man and then went into the produce business. Volunteer A.D.C. to Gen. Prentiss 8 May '61 until commissioned Maj. 6th Ill. Cav. 24 Oct. Promoted Col. 12 Apr. '62, he participated in several small raids in western Tenn. and northern Miss. Commanding Grierson's cavalry brigade, Right Wing, XIII, Tenn., in Nov. and Dec. '62, he led 1, 1st Div. Cav., XVI, Tenn. (18 Dec. '62–May '63) on GRIERSON'S RAID. As B.G. USV 3 June '63, he commanded 1st Cav. Div., XVI, Tenn. (24 July–23 Sept. '63; 24 Oct. '63–27 Apr. '64 and 11 May–20 June '64) and then commanded the Dist. of West Tenn., Cav. Corps, Tenn. (June–Nov. '64) raiding in Tenn. and Miss. He led 4th Div., Cav. Corps, Mil. Div. Miss. 9 Nov.–13 Dec. '64 and then took over cavalry division West Tenn., Army of the Tenn. Dec. '64–Mar. '65. He led the Cav. Corps, Mil. Div. of West Miss. from Mar. until May '65 in Indian fighting, and was promoted Maj. Gen. USV 27 May '65. Breveted Maj. Gen. USV 10 Feb. '65, B.G. USA for Grierson's Raid, and Maj. Gen. USA for his raids in 1864. Continued in the R.A. as Col. 10th US Cav. in Indian fighting. He retired in 1890 as B.G. USA.

GRIERSON'S RAID. 17 Apr.–2 May '63. (VICKSBURG CAMPAIGN) To divert Pemberton's attention from Grant's crossing of the Mississippi south of Vicksburg, Col. Benjamin H. Grierson led a successful raid that covered 600 miles in 16 days. He had 1,700 men of his own 6th Ill. Cav. (under Col. Reuben Loomis), Col. Edward Prince's 7th Ill. Cav., Col. Edward Hatch's 2d Iowa Cav., and the six two-pounders of Capt. Jason B. Smith's Btry. K, 1st Ill. Arty.

The Federal raiders left La Grange (near Memphis) at dawn of 17 Apr. and made initial contact early the next day near Ripley, Miss., with a company from Col. J. F. Smith's 1st Miss. Cav. (militia). These Confederate troopers were part of the cavalry force under Lt. Col. C. R. Barteau, who was charged with the defense of this portion of Daniel Ruggles's 1st Mil. Dist. of Pemberton's Dept. of Miss. Barteau commanded his own 2d Tenn. Cav. of 400 or 500 men and an equal number of state troops. Maj. Gen. Samuel Gholson was also in the area with three new regiments of state troops that were still being organized and trained. On the 20th Grierson culled out some 175 men who showed signs of not being fit to continue the operation and sent them back toward La Grange with his dozen or so prisoners. Maj. Hiram Love, 2d Iowa, was put in command of this self-styled "Quinine Brigade" and instructed to conduct his hazardous return in such a manner as to deceive the enemy into believing that Grierson's entire force was withdrawing back to the north through Ponottoc.

The next day, 21 Apr., Hatch was also given the mission of circling east toward the vital Mobile & Ohio R.R. and then moving north to decoy the Confederates into pursuing him while the main column continued south. Barteau, meanwhile, had gotten on Grierson's trail and was following. Hatch conducted a successful rearguard action at Palo Alto and withdrew to the east with Barteau in pursuit. Gholson arrived to take command of the Confederate cavalry and another skirmish took place 24 Apr. at Birmingham, near Okolona. Until the afternoon of this day Ruggles was deceived by this gambit. Late in the day he learned that Grierson with his main body had reached the railroad at Newton, due east of Vicksburg.

On the 22d Abraham Buford's infantry brigade, which was en route from Ala. to reinforce Vicksburg, had been halted at Meridian. W. W. Loring was sent to this place to command all available troops and do what Ruggles had failed to accomplish: stop Grierson. On the 24th, when he got word of Grierson's presence at Newton Station, 50 miles from his headquarters at Jackson, Pemberton ordered additional troops sent in that direction. To stop a possible advance west against Jackson, Col. John Adams was sent to Morton (on the railroad about 12 miles west of Newton) to defend that place with three infantry regiments and supporting artillery. To cut off a possible retreat to the north, Chalmers was ordered to Okolona from Panola. Lloyd Tilghman was ordered to send forces from Canton to Carthage so that any attempted escape to the northwest would be checked. Pemberton even considered that Grierson might attempt to reach Banks's troops in the Dept. of the Gulf, and ordered Franklin Gardner at Port Hudson, La., to send cavalry to block this route across the Tangipahoa (i.e., along the Jackson–New Orleans R.R. east of Baton Rouge).

Meanwhile, Capt. Henry Forbes's Co. B, 7th Ill. Cav., had left the main column just south of Starkville on 22 Apr., and had been operating independently to the east of Grierson's force. After raiding Macon and Enterprise on the Mobile & Ohio R.R. Forbes rejoined Grierson five days later at the crossing of the Pearl River.

Moving due south from Newton, Grierson then headed west toward Natchez. Pemberton, still baffled, thought his objective might be Grand Gulf. Accordingly, John Bowen was ordered to send the seven cavalry companies of Col. Wirt Adams from Port Gibson to locate and defeat Grierson.

Adams attempted to establish an ambush near Union Church, but one of the BUTTERNUT GUERRILLAS learned of the trap, and Grierson was able to avoid it by circling back eastward to Brookhaven. Confederate forces were now converging on the tired raiders, who had been riding day and night for two weeks. At Wall's Bridge, just north of the La. line, Grierson had his bloodiest action of the raid. Here he attacked and drove off three cavalry companies under Maj. James De Baum. The Federals then raced for Baton Rouge, covering 76 miles in the last 28 hours.

Grierson's official report gives this summary:

> During the expedition we killed and wounded about one hundred of the enemy, captured and paroled over 500 prisoners ... destroyed between fifty and sixty miles of railroad and telegraph, captured and destroyed over 3,000 stand of arms, and other army stores and Government property to an immense amount; we also captured 1,000 horses and mules.
>
> Our loss during the entire journey was 3 killed, 7 wounded, 5 left on the route sick; the sergeant-major and surgeon of the Seventh Ill. left with Lieutenant-Colonel Blackburn [mortally wounded at Wall's Bridge], and 9 men missing, supposed to have straggled.

Grant said, "It has been one of the most brilliant cavalry exploits of the war, and will be handed down in history as an example to be imitated" (O.R.). (For a definitive history see D. Alexander Brown, *Grierson's Raid*, Univ. of Ill. 1954, on which the above account is based.)

GRIFFIN, Charles. Union gen. 1825–67. Ohio. USMA 1847 (23/38); Arty.

After fighting in the Mexican War, he served on the frontier, in Indian fighting and scouting, and instructed artillery at West Point. Named Capt. 2d U.S. Arty. 25 Apr. '61 (1st Lt. since 1849) and transferred to 5th US Arty. in May, he commanded a battery in Washington, at 1st BULL RUN and on the Peninsula. He was appointed B.G. USV 9 June '62 and commanded 2, 1, V (26 June–30 Oct. '62) at the Yorktown siege, Hanover Court House, Mechanicsville, Gaines's Mill, Malvern Hill, 2d Bull Run, Antietam, and Shepherdstown. He commanded the 1st Div. of that corps 30 Oct.–1 Nov. '62 and 16 Nov.–26 Dec. '62 at Fredericksburg, leading his brigade in the interval. From 26 Jan. to 1 Feb. '63 he commanded the V Corps, and from 1 Feb. to 5 May '63 he commanded the 1st Div. at Chancellorsville. He then returned to command the division, leading them at Gettysburg (3 July–24 Oct. '63) and the Wilderness, Spotsylvania, Jericho Ford, Bethesda Church, siege and assaults of Petersburg, Weldon Railroad, Peeble's Farm, Hatcher's Run, and Five Forks (3 Apr.–21 July; 9 Aug.–24 Dec. '64 and 4 Jan.–1 Apr. '65). Commanding V Corps 1 Apr.–28 June, he was named Maj. Gen. USV 2 Apr. '65 and one of the surrender commissioners at Appomattox. He was breveted for 1st Bull Run, the Wilderness, Weldon Railroad, Five Forks (B.G. USA), and war service (Maj. Gen. USV 1 Aug. '64 and Maj. Gen. USA). Continuing in the R.A., he died of yellow fever in Galveston while carrying out Reconstruction policies as Col. 35th US Inf. He was characterized as bluff, bellicose, outspoken, and quick to take offense.

GRIFFIN, Daniel F. Union officer. Nova Scotia. 1st Lt. Adj. 38th Ind. 18 Sept. '61; Maj. 25 Mar. '62; Lt. Col. 26 Sept. '62; Bvt. B.G. USV (war service); resigned 8 Nov. '64. Died 1865.

GRIFFIN, Simon Goodell. Union gen. 1824–1902. N.H. A lawyer and legislator, he was named Capt. 2d N.H. 1 June '61, fought at 1st Bull Run, and resigned 31 Oct. '61. As Lt. Col. 6th N.H. 28 Nov. '61, he went on Burnside's N.C. expedition in '61–'62 and was promoted Col. 22 Apr. '62. He fought at 2d Bull Run, South Mountain, Antietam, and Fredericksburg. In the 2d Div. of the IX Corps, he commanded 1st Brig., Potomac (Feb.–Mar. '63); 1st Brig., Ohio (21 May–30 Aug. '63); 1st Brig., Tenn. (14 June–18 Aug. '63); Division, Ohio (25 Aug.–Oct. '63); Division, Potomac (2 Apr.–May '64), at the Wilderness; and 2d Brig. Potomac (25 Feb.–2 Apr. '65), at Petersburg. He was promoted B.G. USV 12 May '64, breveted Maj. Gen. USV 2 Apr. '65 for Fort Sedgwick, and mustered out 24 Aug. '65. He was later active in politics, railroading, and manufacturing.

GRIFFITH, Richard. C.S.A. gen. ?–1862. Appt.-Miss. The Miss. state treasurer when the war came, he was commissioned Col. 12th Miss. and sent to Va. He was appointed B.G. C.S.A. 2 Nov. '61 and commanded Charles Clark's brigade under J. E. Johnston at Seven Pines and the Seven Days' Battles. He died 30 June '62 of wounds received the day before at Savage's Station.

GRIMES, Bryan. C.S.A. gen. 1828–80. N.C. Graduating from Chapel Hill, he was a planter and attended the secession convention before being commissioned Maj. 4th N.C. in May '61. After commanding the regiment at Seven Pines where all officers but himself and 462 of the 500 men were killed or wounded, he was promoted Lt. Col. and then Col. (19 June '62) and commanded the unit at Mechanicsville. Stricken with typhoid fever, he was out of action until Antietam. At Fredericksburg he led the 5th Brig. in the II Corps, and returned to the 4th N.C. for Chancellorsville, Gettysburg, where he went in advance of Ewell's corps in the invasion and fought in the rear guard during the retreat, and the Wilderness and Spotsylvania. Taking over Daniel's brigade and being appointed B.G. C.S.A. 19 May '64, he fought in Early's Valley campaign and Washington raid, took over Ramseur's division at Cedar Creek, and was named Maj. Gen. 15 Feb. '65. He fought at Petersburg, Fort Stedman, Sayler's Creek, and Appomattox before the surrender. After the war he returned to his plantation and was killed by an assassin in 1880 (C.M.H.).

GRINDLEY, James Glass. Union officer. N.Y. Capt. 146th N.Y. 7 Oct. '62; Maj. 18 May '64; Lt. Col. 1 Jan. '65; Col. 1 Mar. '65; Bvt. B.G. USV. Brevets for Spotsylvania, North Anna, war service. Commanded 1, 2, V.

GRINNELL, Josiah Bushnell. Abolitionist and politician. 1821–91. Vt. As a founder of the Republican party in Iowa and a leading abolitionist, he served in the House (1863–67) and supported Lincoln. Moving west, he settled in Iowa and with others founded the town of Grinnell and planned Grinnell College of which he was a trustee for 30 years. He lost his position of power in the Republican party when he supported Horace Greeley in 1872.

GRISWOLDVILLE, Ga., 21–22 Nov. '64. (MARCH TO THE SEA) On the 21st some of Kilpatrick's cavalry leading C. C. Walcutt's brigade (2, 1, XV) on a reconnaissance toward Macon entered Griswoldville and captured a train of 13 cars loaded with military supplies. The cavalry burned the station and some factory buildings. The next day Wheeler's cavalry hit the 9th Pa. Cav., inflicting three casualties and capturing 18 before being driven back. Walcutt's infantry then arrived, pushed the Con-

federates out of the town, and took up a strong defensive position around the Duncan Farm. Here the Federals were vigorously attacked by the division of Georgia militia under P. J. Phillips, which had been marching toward Gordon to block the Federal advance toward Savannah. Acting "with more courage than discretion" (Cox, 30) Phillips continued his attacks for several hours before being forced to retreat after dark. The Confederates lost 51 killed and 472 wounded, according to G. W. Smith (B.&L., IV, 667), but other estimates put the loss at over 600 (ibid., 664n; Cox, 30; E.&B.). Walcutt was wounded early in the action and succeeded by Col. R. F. Catterson. Federal casualties were between 62 (E.&B.) and 94 (Cox).

GROSE, William. Union gen. 1812–1900. Ohio. At first Democratic politician, he was an organizer of the Republican party and served in the state legislature and on the bench. Named Col. 36th Ind. 23 Oct. '61, he fought at Shiloh and later commanded in the Army Ohio: 10th Brig., 4th Div. (16 Aug.–29 Sept. '62); 19th Brig., 4th Div. (2 June–10 July '62); and 10th Brig., 4th Div., II. At Stones River he commanded 3, 2 Left Wing, XIV, Cumberland (5 Nov. '62–9 Jan. '63). Also in the Cumberland he led 3, 2, XXI (9 Jan.–12 Mar. and 14 Apr.–9 Oct. '63) at Vicksburg, Chattanooga, and Chickamauga. He commanded 3, 1, IV (10 Oct.–31 Dec. '63) at Lookout Mountain and Missionary Ridge; (31 Jan.–27 July '64) at Dalton; (5 Aug.–5 Sept. '64) in the battles before Atlanta; (29 Nov. '64–16 Feb. '65) at Franklin and Nashville; 16 Feb.; 15–31 Mar.; and 9 May–7 June '65. He succeeded to division 27 July–5 Aug. '64 and 16 Feb.–16 Mar. '65, and commanded 2, 2, IV, Cumberland 10 Oct.–29 Nov. '64. Breveted Maj. Gen. USV 13 Aug. '65, he was president of a court-martial in Nashville before resigning in Dec. He later held many public offices and served in the state senate. "Deliberate and self-possessed" (D.A.B.), he wrote in 1891 *The Story of the Marches, Battles and Incidents of the 36th Regiment, Indiana Volunteer Army.*

GROSSMAN, George H. Misspelling by Phisterer for George Hampton CROSMAN.

GROSVENOR, Charles Henry. Union officer. 1833–1917. Conn. Maj. 18th Ohio 25 Sept. '61; Lt. Col. 9 June '63; Col. 19 Apr. '65; Bvt. B.G. USV (war service). Commanded Post of Chattanooga; 3d Brig., Prov. Div.; Dist. Etowah; 2d Brig., Dist. Etowah. Called "Old Figgers" for his skill in predicting election results, he was an active Republican and served as State Speaker of the House and US Congressman. He was a Chautauqua speaker, a brilliant debater, and spellbinding conversationalist. He wrote *William McKinley, His Life and Work* (1901) and *The Book of the Presidents, with Biographical Sketches* (1902).

GROSVENOR, Thomas W. Union officer. N.Y. Capt. 12th Ill. Cav. 28 Feb. '62; Maj. 7 Nov. '62; Lt. Col. 15 Feb. '64; Bvt. B.G. USV. Brevets for Darksville (Va.), war service. Resigned 3 Aug. '64. Died 1871.

GROUND SQUIRREL BRIDGE (or CHURCH), Va., 11 May '64. See SHERIDAN'S RICHMOND RAID.

GROVER, Cuvier. Union gen. 1828–85. Me. USMA 1850 (4/44); Arty.-Inf.-Cav. In railroad explorations he crossed the Rockies in 1853 and went on the Utah Expedition against the Mormons in 1858–59. He was in command at Fort Union (N. Mex.) in 1861 as Capt. 10th US Inf. (1858), when a force of Confederates demanded his surrender. Instead, he burned the supplies and, making a forced march, got his command

safely across the Missouri River. On 14 Apr. '62 he was named B.G. USV, leading 1, 2, III, Potomac (27 Apr.–16 Sept. '62) at Yorktown, Williamsburg, Fair Oaks, Savage's Station, Glendale, Malvern Hill, Harrison's Landing, Bristoe Station, and 2d Bull Run. In the Gulf he commanded 4th Div., XIX (3 Jan.–30 July '63) at Irish Bend, Vermillion Bayou, Port Hudson, and Mansura. He also led the 3d Div., XIX (2 Oct. '63–12 Jan. '64) and 2d Div., XIX (15 Feb.–18 June and 25 June–5 July '64). In the Army of the Shenandoah he led 2d Div., XIX (6 Aug.–19 Oct.; 10 Nov.–8 Dec. and 28 Dec. '64–6 Jan. '65), at Opequon, Winchester, Fishers Hill, and Cedar Creek where he was W.I.A. He also commanded the XIX Corps 8–28 Dec. '64. He commanded Grover's division, Dist. Savannah, South (6 Jan.–12 Feb. '65) and Dist. Savannah, South (12 Feb.–5 June '65). He was breveted for Williamsburg, Fair Oaks, Cedar Creek, and Shenandoah Valley campaign (B.G. USA); war service (Maj. Gen. USA); and Winchester and Fishers Hill (Maj. Gen. USV 19 Oct. '64). Continuing in the R.A., he died on active duty as Col. 1st US Cav.

GROVER, Ira Glanton. Union officer. Ind. 1st Lt. 7th Ind. 24 Apr. '61; mustered out 2 Aug. '61; Capt. 7th Ind. 13 Sept. '61; Maj. 1 July '62; Lt. Col. 12 Mar. '63; Col. 23 Apr. '63; Bvt. B.G. USV (Carrick's Ford and Wilderness, Va.); mustered out 20 Sept. '64. Died 1876.

GRUBB, Edward Burd. Union officer. N.J. 1841–? 1st Sgt. 3d N.J. 25 May '61; 2d Lt. 13 June '61; 1st Lt. 8 Nov. '61; Maj. 23d N.J. 25 Nov. '62; Lt. Col. 26 Dec. '62; Col. 9 Apr. '63; mustered out 27 June '63; Col. 37th N.J. 23 June '64; Bvt. B.G. USV (war service); mustered out 1 Oct. '64. He was in the mining and coal business in

Virginia after the war and served as Minister to Spain.

GUINEY, Patrick Robert. Union officer. Ireland. Capt. 9th Mass. 11 June '61; Maj. 25 Oct. '61; Lt. Col. 28 Jan. '62; Col. 26 July '62; Bvt. B.G. USV (war service); mustered out 21 June '64. Commanded 2, 1, V. He was wounded in the face at the Wilderness. Died 1877.

GULF, CONFED. DISTRICT OF THE. Constituted 2 July '62 under J. H. Forney, succeeded 14 Dec. by Wm. Mackall and 23 Dec. by Buckner. Strength at the end of the year was 7,500. On 27 Apr. '63 Dabney Maury was ordered to assume command when relieved in East Tenn. by Buckner. In Jan. '65 Maury had 10,000 troops available for the defense of Mobile.

GULF, UNION DEPARTMENT AND ARMY OF THE. Organized 23 Feb. '62 with headquarters at New Orleans to comprise the general areas of the Miss. Gulf states occupied by Federal troops, it was commanded successively by Maj. Gens. B. F. Butler, N. P. Banks, S. A. Hurlbut, and E. R. S. Canby. Its troops took part in operations against Port Hudson (La.), along the Texas coast (26 Oct. '63–4 Jan. '64), and the Red River campaign of 1864. The XIX CORPS is the field force principally associated with this department. The following corps were also assigned to it at one time or another: XIII, XVI, and XVII (all of which see). On 7 May '64 the department was merged in the Mil. Div. of West Miss. (Trans-Miss. Div.), but retained virtual separate existence.

GUN. Although the term is generally, and incorrectly, applied to all firearms, a gun is technically a type of CANNON with a relatively long barrel, high muzzle velocity, and a flat trajectory.

GUNTOWN, Miss. BRICE'S CROSS ROADS, Miss. 10 June. '64.

GUPPEY, Joshua James. Union officer. N.H. Lt. Col. 10th Wis. 29 Oct. '61; resigned 25 July '62; Col. 23d Wis. 30 Aug. '62; Bvt. B.G. USV (war service). Commanded 3d Brig., "Gulf" 2d Div., XIX.

GURNEY, William. 1821–79. Union officer. N.Y. 1st Lt. 7th N.Y. State Mil. 27 Apr. '61; mustered out 3 June '61; Capt. "Fighting Chasseurs" 65th N.Y. 11 July '61; Col. 127th N.Y. 22 Aug. '62; Bvt. B.G. USV 19 May '65 (war service). Commanded 3d Brig., Abercrombie's Mil. Dist., Washington; 3d Brig., Abercrombie's Mil. Dist., XXII; Gurney's division, VII Corps; 1, 2, IV; 1st Brig., South End Folly Island (S.C.), X; North Dist., Morris Island. Asst. I.G. on Gov. Morgan's staff in 1862. W.I.A. Devoe's Neck (S.C.) in the arm. After the war he returned to Charleston where he engaged in business and politics.

GUSS, Henry Ruhl. Union officer. Pa. Commissioned Capt. 9th Pa. 24 Apr. '61, he was mustered out three months later and named Col. 97th Pa. 29 Oct. of that year. He resigned 22 June '64 and was breveted B.G. USV for war service (Heitman). Phisterer lists him as Bvt. Maj. Gen. USV also.

GWYN, James. Union officer. Ireland. Commissioned Capt. 23d Pa. 18 Apr. '61, he was mustered out three months later and given the same commission when the regiment was reorganized 2 Aug. '61. This he resigned 15 July '62 and was named Lt. Col. 118th Pa. 10 days later. He was promoted Col. 5 Dec. '63, mustered out in June '65, and breveted B.G. USV 20 Sept. '64 for battles around Petersburg and Maj. Gen. USV 1 Apr. '65 for Five Forks.

H

HACKLEMAN, Pleasant Adam. Union gen. 1814–62. Ind. A jurist and legislator, he was an early member of the Republican party. Commissioned Col. 16th Ind. 20 May '61, he was promoted B.G. USV 28 Apr. '62 and commanded in Army of Tenn. 1, 2d Div., and 1st Brig., 2d Div. Dist. of Corinth (1 Sept.–3 Oct. '62). He was killed on the latter date at the battle of Corinth.

HAGAN, James. C.S.A. gen. Ireland. Appt.-Ala. Coming to the US as a small boy, he was educated in Pa. and in business in Mobile. He fought in the Mexican War in Hays's Tex. Rangers, entered the R.A., was a Capt. of Inf. 5 Mar. '47, and was mustered out 31 July '48. He was Capt. of the Mobile Cavalry Company when the Civil War started. According to Lonn he was appointed B.G. in Aug. '63 while serving under Wheeler. B.&L., however, shows him as Col. of the 3d Ala. Cav. during the Atlanta campaign. Although Heitman lists him as a B.G., neither Wright nor Wood does. He died in 1901.

HAGNER, Peter Valentine. Union officer. c. 1815–93. D.C. USMA 1836 (25/49); Arty.-Ord. He served in the Florida War and in the Mexican War (2 brevets, 1 wound) before going to Europe on professional duty 1848–49. Named Insp. of Contract Arms and Ordnance Stores 25 Apr. '61–25 Dec. '63 and promoted Lt. Col. 1 June '63, he commanded the Watervliet Arsenal from then until the end of the war. Continuing in the R.A., he was retired in 1881 as Col. and Bvt. B.G. USA.

HAGOOD, Johnson. C.S.A. gen. 1829–98. S.C. After graduating from the Citadel, he was a lawyer and planter and served as deputy Adj. Gen. of the S.C. militia. Commissioned Col. 1st S.C., he was in the Fort Sumter bombardment and fought at 1st Bull Run before returning to the defenses of Charleston. Named B.G. C.S.A. 21 July '62, he led his brigade at the Wilderness and Weldon Railroad. At Petersburg he was in a section of the defenses for 65 days, losing about 1,500 of his 2,300 men (D.A.B.). He returned to his Barnwell plantation after the war to begin rebuilding, taking a leading part in restoring the educational system of the South and preaching the merits of diversified farming. Uniting with Hampton and his party, he helped end Reconstruction politics and served as Gov. in 1880.

HAHN, Michael. Unionist war gov. 1830–86. Bavaria. After graduating from the Univ. of La. in law, he became a strong advocate of abolition and an adherent of Stephen A. Douglas. He was active in trying to stem the movement toward secession, and when Farragut took over New Orleans, Hahn took the oath of allegiance to the United States and represented the state in Congress as a Republican. In Mar. '64 he was inaugurated Gov. of La. and was elected Sen. in 1865 but did not claim his seat. A newspaper editor and sugar planter, he served in the legislature and Congress and as District Judge, running always as a Republican.

HAINES, Thomas J. Union officer. c. 1828–83. N.H. USMA 1849 (4/34); Arty.-Comsy. He served in garrison, taught mathematics at West Point, and fought in the Seminole War. Promoted Capt. 13th US Inf. 14 May '61, he declined the appointment and was Acting

Asst. Adj. Gen. of the Dept. of Va. from June until Aug. '61. He was promoted Capt. Comsy. of Subsist. 3 Aug. '61 and was Chief Comsy. of the Dept. of the Mo. 30 Nov. '61–31 Oct. '62. For the rest of the war he was Chief Purchasing and Supervising Comsy. in the Depts. of the Mo., Tenn., and the Northwest, and was promoted Maj. 9 Feb. '63. Continuing in the R.A., he was breveted B.G. USA for war service and died on active duty.

HAINES'S BLUFF (Snyder's Mill), Miss. 30 Apr.–1 May '65. To divert attention from the landing of Grant's main force at PORT GIBSON on 1 May during the VICKSBURG CAMPAIGN, Sherman with detachments from his XV Corps and gunboats shelled the Confederate batteries on Haines's and Drumgould's bluffs. On the 30th infantry was landed and deployed as if to attack. The next day the troops probed roads behind the Confederate positions, while the gunboats continued their shelling. Sherman's force then withdrew. The only casualties were three Confederates wounded.

HALL, Caldwell K. Union officer. Pa. 1st Lt. Adj. 5th N.J. 28 Aug. '61; Lt. Col. 27 Aug. '62; Bvt. B.G. USV. Brevets for Cold Harbor, Monocacy (Md.). Commanded 1, 3, VI. Resigned 10 Sept. '64. Died 1870.

HALL, Cyrus. Union officer. Ill. Capt. 14th Ill. 25 May '61; Maj. 7th Ill. Cav. 21 Sept. '61; Col. 14th Ill. 1 Feb. '62; mustered out 25 May '64; Col. 144th Ill. 21 Oct. '64; resigned 7 Mar. '65; Col. 14th Ill. 13 Mar. '65; Bvt. B.G. USV (war service). Commanded 2, 4 (Right Wing), XIII; 2, 4, XVII; 2, 4, XVI; 2, 4, XIII; 2, 4, XVII. Died 1878.

HALL, Henry Seymour. Union officer. N.Y. Pvt. Co. G 27th N.Y. 24 Apr. '61; 2d Lt. 7 May '61; Capt. 21 Apr. '62; mustered out 31 May '63; Capt.

121st N.Y. 16 June '63; mustered out 29 Mar. '64; Lt. Col. 43d US Col. Inf. 2 Apr. '64; Bvt. B.G. USV. Brevets for war service, Petersburg Mine Assault. Medal of Honor 17 Aug. '91 for Gaines's Mill 27 June '62 and Rappahannock Sta. 7 Nov. '63.

HALL, Jairus William. Union officer. N.Y. 2d Lt. 4th Mich. 1 May '61; 1st Lt. 1 Sept. '61; Capt. 1 July '62; Maj. 22 May '63; Lt. Col. 13 July '63; Col. 26 July '64; Bvt. B.G. USV (war service).

HALL, James Abram. Union officer. Me. 1st Lt. 2d Me. Btry. 20 Nov. '61; Capt. 22 May '62; Maj. 1st Bn. Me. Arty. 19 July '63; Lt. Col. 9 Sept. '64; mustered out 22 July '65; Col. 2d US Vet. Inf. 15 Aug. '65; Bvt. B.G. USV 7 Mar. '65. Commanded Lgt. Arty. Depot, XX Corps. Died 1893.

HALL, James Frederick. Union officer. N.Y. Maj. 1st N.Y. Engrs. 10 Oct. '61; Lt. Col. 25 Apr. '62; Col. 20 Mar. '65; Bvt. B.G. USV 24 Feb. '65. Died 1884.

HALL, Maria M. C. Union army nurse. D.C. In the summer of 1861 she applied to become one of Dorothea DIX's nurses but was turned down because she was too young and pretty. However, in July '61 she started working in the Indiana Hospital in a wing of the Patent Office for a year until she went to the Peninsula on a hospital transport. Here she met Eliza HARRIS and joined her later at Antietam as a SANITARY COMMISSION worker. She continued working in the field until the summer of 1863, when she was persuaded to take over the administrative duties at the Annapolis hospital for the rest of the war.

HALL, Robert M. Union officer. Scotland. R.A. Sgt. and 1st Sgt. Co. M 1st US Arty. 1853–13 Nov. '61; 2d Lt. 1st US Arty. 24 Oct. '61; 1st Lt. 20 Feb.

'62; Col. 38th US Col. Inf. 31 Dec. '64; mustered out USV 25 Jan. '67; Bvt. B.G. USV. Brevets for Bermuda Hundred, Darbytown Road near Richmond, war service (2), "official conduct." Commanded 1, 1, XXV; 2, 1, XXV. Was Acting Asst. Adj. Gen. to Seymour and Hatch. Died 1874.

HALLECK, Henry Wager. Union gen. 1815-72. N.Y. USMA 1839 (3/31); Engrs. Known in the army before the war as "Old Brains"—he had graduated number three in his West Point class, was the author of *Elements of Military Art and Science* (1846) and had translated Jomini's *Vie de Napoléon*—Halleck spent most of the war as Lincoln's military adviser and Gen. in Chief. He had served in Calif. during the Mexican War in various responsible military government assignments, retiring as a Capt. in 1854 to become head of the leading law firm in that area and to publish two books on mining law. In August 1861 Lincoln appointed him Maj. Gen. and on 19 Nov. he took over as commander of the Mo. Dept. to succeed FRÉMONT. As a field commander in the departments of Mo., Ohio, Kans., Ky., and Tenn., he proved an able organizer and administrator, but an incompetent leader of field armies. (See CORINTH, Miss.) In July 1862 he was ordered to Washington where his administrative aptitude was of great value but his lack of strategic sense handicapped Federal commanders in the field. When Grant was given supreme command in Mar., '64, Halleck's role was reduced to that of Chief of Staff. After the war he commanded various military departments. A man completely lacking in physical attractiveness or charm —pop-eyed, flabby, surly, and crafty— he had the reputation of being the most unpopular man in Washington. While displaying a conspicuous incompetence in matters of strategy and leadership,

Halleck played a major role in the administration of the Civil War. Brother-in-law of Schuyler HAMILTON.

HALLOWELL, Edward Needles. Union officer. 1837-71. Pa. 2d Lt. 20th Mass. 23 Jan. '62; 1st Lt. 30 Jan. '62; Capt. 54th Mass. 30 Mar. '63; Maj. 13 May '63; Lt. Col. 1 July '63; Col. 1 Sept. '63; Bvt. B.G. USV 27 June '65 (war service). Commanded 3, 6, XVII. Served as A.D.C. to Gen. Frémont and at Antietam was on Gen. N. J. T. Dana's staff. W.I.A. Fort Wagner 18 July '63. A brother of Richard Price Hallowell, prominent abolitionist.

HALPINE, Charles Graham. Union officer and author. 1829-68. Ireland. Wrote under name of "Pvt. Miles O'Reilly." Pvt. Co. D 69th N.Y. State Mil. 20 Apr. '61; mustered out 3 Aug. '61; Maj. Asst. Adj. Gen. Vols. 5 Sept. '61; Lt. Col. Asst. Adj. Gen. Assigned 8 Nov. '62-1 July '63; Bvt. B.G. USV. Brevets for Piedmont (Va.), war service (2). Resigned 31 July '64. His poem, "Sambo's Right to Be Kilt," appeared in the N.Y. *Herald* in 1862 when Gen. David Hunter at Hilton Head (S.C.) organized the first troop of Negro soldiers to be mustered into Federal service. Halpine, who was serving on Hunter's staff, prepared the order that implemented this action. When he first came to this country he had worked for a time as P. T. Barnum's private secretary and then wrote advertising copy in verse. Getting into newspaper work, he represented the N.Y. *Times* during Walker's Nicaraguan expedition, as well as being that paper's Washington correspondent and associate editor. He then became Stephen Douglas's private secretary and joined Tammany Hall as an active politician. Resigning from the army because of failing eyesight, he turned against the N.Y. Democrats and led a reform ticket in city government. The D.A.B. describes him as stuttering, adding, "He was versatile, impetuous, and of a tremendous and restless energy." He died from an overdose of chloroform taken to cure insomnia.

HAMBLIN, Joseph Eldridge. Union gen. 1828-70. Mass. An insurance broker active in the militia in N.Y. and St. Louis, he was "nearly six and a half feet in height and well proportioned" (D.A.B.). Named 1st Lt. Adj. 5th N.Y. ("Duryee's Zouaves") 14 May '61, he fought at Big Bethel and was named Capt. 8 Sept. and Maj. 65th N.Y. 4 Nov. '61. He served in the Baltimore fortifications and in the Peninsula at Yorktown, Williamsburg, Fair Oaks, Glendale, and Malvern Hill. Named Lt. Col. 20 July '62, he fought at Antietam, Fredericksburg, and Chancellorsville. He was promoted Col. 26 May '63 and led his regiment at Gettysburg, the Wilderness, Spotsylvania, and Cold Harbor. He commanded 1, 3, VI (30 Dec. '63–10 Jan. '64); 4, 1, VI (20 June–6 July '64); 2, 1, VI (19 Sept.–19 Oct. '64) at Winchester, Fishers Hill, Hatcher's Run, and Cedar Creek, where wounded; 3, 1, VI (31 Jan.–17 Mar. '65); and 2, 1, VI (17 Mar.–28 June '65) at Petersburg and Sayler's Creek. Named B.G. USV 19 May '65, he was breveted for Middletown (B.G. USV 19 May '65) and Sayler's Creek (Maj. Gen. USV 5 Apr. '65) and mustered out in 1866. He returned to the insurance business and militia activities in N.Y.C.

HAMBRIGHT, Henry Augustus. Union officer. Pa. R.A. Capt. 1st Pa. 20 Apr. '61; mustered out 26 July '61; Capt. 11th US Inf. 14 May '61; Col. 79th Pa. 18 Oct. '61; mustered out USV 20 July '65; Bvt. B.G. USV 7 June '65. Brevets for Murfreesboro (Tenn.), Chickamauga, Atlanta campaign, war service. In the Army of the Cumberland (XIV Corps) he commanded 3d Brig., 1st Centre Div.; 3d Brig., 1st Div.; 1st Brig., 1st Div.; 2d Brig., 1st Div. Died 1893.

HAMILTON, Andrew Jackson. Union gen. 1815-75. Ala. Appt.-Tex. A lawyer and Congressman, he remained in Washington after his colleagues had returned to Tex., speaking against secession. He was elected in Mar. '61 to the Tex. legislature as a Unionist, but was unable to persuade the state from its course of rebellion and when war came had to escape through Mexico. Appointed B.G. USV 14 Nov. '62, his appointment expired 4 Mar. '63 but was reissued 18 Sept. '63. He was also appointed provisional Gov. of Tex. and spent most of his time in New Orleans waiting to assume office. He resigned 19 June '65 and, as reconstruction Gov., D.A.B. says that "within a year he had brought something like order out of the chaos which followed the war." He turned the state over to the duly-elected officials in 1866 and went to Washington where, oddly enough, he became enemy of Johnson. He then switched sides again and opposed the Radical plan of Reconstruction. The Tex. conservatives ran him for Gov., but the military authorities set this selection aside to place a more radical candidate in office, thereby bringing on the carpetbagger era in Tex.

HAMILTON, Charles Smith. Union gen. 1822-91. N.Y. USMA 1843 (26/39); Inf. In the Mexican War (1 brevet, 1 wound) and on the frontier before resigning in 1853. A farmer and flour miller, he became Col. 3d Wis. 11 May, and B.G. USV 17 May '61. In the Valley he commanded 3d Brig., Banks's division, Potomac (8 Oct. '61–13 Mar. '62) and then led the 3d Div., III, Potomac (13 Mar.–30 Apr. '62) in the siege of Yorktown. Going to the West, he commanded 3d Div., Army of the Miss. (18 June–26 Oct. '62) at Iuka and Corinth. Promoted Maj. Gen.

USV 19 Sept. '62. In the Army of the Tenn. he commanded Dist. Corinth (20–26 Oct. '62); Dist. Corinth, XIII (24–30 Oct. '62); Left Wing, XIII (1 Nov.–18 Dec. '62); Left Wing, XVI (22 Dec. '62–1 Apr. '63); and the XVI Corps (10 Jan.–5 Feb. '63). He resigned 18 Apr. '63 and returned to Wis., where he manufactured linseed oil and paper, served on the Board of Regents of Wis. Univ., and held several public offices, as well as taking an active part in the Loyal Legion and the G.A.R.

HAMILTON, Schuyler. Union gen. 1822–1903. N.Y. USMA 1841 (24/52); Inf. He had taught tactics at West Point and fought in the Mexican War (2 severe wounds, 2 brevets) and was Scott's A.D.C. for over seven years before resigning in 1855. After farming in Conn., he was associated with his brother-in-law, Henry HALLECK, in quick-silver mining in Almaden, Calif. Enlisting as Pvt. 7th N.Y. State Mil. (19 Apr.–9 May '61), he was Lt. Col. and Mil. Sec. to Scott from 9 May to 7 Aug. and Col. Add. A.D.C. from the latter date until Scott's retirement on 1 Nov. He was Asst. Chief of Staff to Halleck (12 Nov. '61–2 Jan. '62) and was promoted B.G. USV on the former date. At New Madrid and Island No. 10 he commanded 1st Div., Army Miss. (23 Feb.–4 Mar. '62) and is credited with having suggested to Pope the cutting of the canal at the Island to turn the enemy's position. Also in the Army of the Miss., he commanded the 2d Div. (4 Mar.–24 Apr. '62) and the 3d Div. (24 Apr.–29 May '62) during the advance upon and siege of Corinth. He was appointed Maj. Gen. USV 17 Sept. '62 but caught malaria before he could accept. His resignation came 27 Feb. '63, under the rule that no officer unfit for service should be named to Congress for confirmation (D.A.B.). In poor health for years afterward from the fever and from his Mexican War lance wound in the lung, he returned to his New England farm. Grandson of Alexander Hamilton.

HAMILTON, William Douglas. Union officer. 1833–? Scotland. Capt. 32d Ohio 31 Aug. '61; discharged 19 Nov. '62; Maj. 9th Ohio Cav. 6 Dec. '62; Lt. Col. 4 Nov. '63; Col. 16 Dec. '63; Bvt. B.G. USV 9 Apr. '65 ("campaign for C.S.A. surrender"). Commanded Mounted Brig., cavalry division, XXIII Corps. An Ohio lawyer, he raised a 3-year company that was assigned to the 32d Ohio. He was in Ohio recruiting when it was surrendered at Harpers Ferry.

HAMLIN, Charles. Union officer. Me. Maj. 1st Me. Arty. 21 Aug. '62; Maj. Asst. Adj. Gen. Vols. 27 Apr. '63; Bvt. B.G. USV (war service). Commanded 2d Brig., 1st Div. Corps d'Afrique; Dist. Port Hudson; 1st Div. Corps d'Afrique; 3d Div. USCT. Son of Hannibal HAMLIN. Commended by Gen. A. A. Humphreys for his actions at Round Top (D.A.B.). Present at Ford's Theatre when Lincoln was killed, he immediately called out the artillery to quell the rumored uprising. "With leisure and means at his command, less aggressive, more scholarly and painstaking than his distinguished father, he collected rare books and prints, studied Maine genealogies, made after-dinner speeches, and published articles on the Civil War and on the jurists of Maine" (D.A.B.).

HAMLIN, Cyrus. Union gen. 1839–67. Me. A lawyer, he was named Capt. Add. A.D.C. to Gen. Frémont 3 Apr. '62 and fought at Cross Keys 8 June '62. He was named Col. 80th US Col. Inf. 12 Feb. '63 and commanded 2d Brig., 1st Div. Corps d'Afrique, Gulf (22 Sept. '63–23 Apr. '64); 1st Div., Corps d'Afrique, Gulf (23 Apr.–9 June

'64); 3d Div., USCT, Gulf; and Post of Pt. Hudson, Gulf (13 Feb.–July '65). He had been promoted B.G. USV 13 Dec. '64 and was breveted Maj. Gen. USV for war service. Mustered out in 1866, he remained in New Orleans, practicing law and taking an active part in the Reconstruction. He died there the next year of an illness contracted while in the army. Son of Hannibal HAMLIN, Lincoln's first vice-president, and brother of Charles HAMLIN, Bvt. B.G. USV.

HAMLIN, Hannibal. Lincoln's vice-president. 1809–91. Me. A lawyer, he served in the legislature, Congress, and the Senate as a Democrat, but his anti-slavery leanings brought him to the new Republican party in 1856. He was elected Gov. of Me. in the same year and shortly resigned to enter the Senate, where he became increasingly prominent. Chosen as Lincoln's running mate in 1860, he was again elected to the Senate in 1869, supporting the reconstruction policies of his party, and served until 1881, when he was named Minister to Spain. His sons, Cyrus and Charles, were both senior officers during the Civil War.

HAMMELL, John Sweeney. Union officer. Mass. 1st Lt. 66th N.Y. 6 Sept. '61; Regt. Adj. 1 Nov. '61; Capt. 15 Apr. '62; Lt. Col. 11 Jan. '63; Bvt. B.G. USV. Brevets for Richmond campaign, Wilderness, Rapidan to Petersburg. Died 1873.

HAMMOND, John. Union officer. N.Y. Capt. 5th N.Y. Cav. 18 Oct. '61; Maj. 26 Sept. '62; Lt. Col. 24 Mar. '64; Col. 3 July '64; Bvt. B.G. USV (war service); mustered out 3 Sept. '64. Died 1889.

HAMMOND, John Henry. Union officer. N.Y. Pvt. 5th Cav. 5 Oct. '61; 2d Lt. 5 Nov. '61; Capt. Asst. Adj. Gen. Vols. 20 Nov. '61; Maj. Asst. Adj. Gen. Vols. 9 June '62; Lt. Col. Asst.

Adj. Gen. Assigned 10 Feb. '63–29 June '64; Bvt. B.G. USV 31 Oct. '64. Commanded 1, 2d Div. Dist. Ky., XXIII; 1, 7, Cav. Corps; 7th Div., Cav. Corps. Died 1890.

HAMMOND, William A. Union gen. 1828–1900. Md. Graduating with an M.D. degree in N.Y.C. in 1848, he entered the army the next year as Asst. Surgeon. He spent 11 years on the frontier and resigned in 1860 to teach at the Univ. of Md. but re-entered the army in May '61 as Asst. Surgeon. He organized hospitals in Md. and was appointed Surgeon Gen. as B.G. USA in Apr. '62. In Aug. '64 he was tried by court-martial and dismissed for irregularities in the liquor contracts, but this was reviewed in 1879, and he was restored as B.G. and put on the retired list. Prominent in the study of diseases of the nervous system, he later practiced in N.Y.C.

HAMPTON, Wade. C.S.A. gen. 1818–1902. S.C. The son and grandson of wealthy S.C. planters, he inherited not only rich plantations but also an intellectual and aristocratic heritage. "Fabled as a sportsman and adept in all the arts of woodcraft, he was renowned no less for his physical strength. Just under six feet in height, he had the balance of the horseman and the smooth muscles of the athlete. His courage, personal, moral, and political, was in keeping with his physique" (*Lee's Lts.,* I, 93). He ran his plantations in S.C. and the lower Mississippi Valley and held several small public offices before the war, coming to doubt the economic soundness of slavery. "When the demand for secession arose, he admitted the right of withdrawal from the Union but disputed the policy. Once S.C. acted, he put all doubt and argument behind him and placed at the command of the state his wealth and his services" (*ibid.*). He raised the HAMPTON LE-

GION, was commissioned Col., and led this unit at 1st Bull Run, where he was slightly wounded. He commanded his brigade during most of the Peninsular campaign and was appointed B.G. C.S.A. 23 May '62. He was again wounded at Seven Pines. On 28 July '62 he was assigned command of a brigade of cavalry and after 2 Sept. was second-in-command to Stuart. He fought in the Antietam campaign, took part in the Chambersburg raid and the Gettysburg campaign. He became Maj. Gen. on 3 Sept. '63. At Gettysburg he was again wounded. After the battle of the Wilderness he succeeded Stuart in command of the cavalry corps. He led this force at Haw's Shop, blocked Sheridan's TREVILIAN RAID, and fought at Sappony Church, Reams's Station, and Burgess Mill (Petersburg campaign). As remounts became scarce, he trained his cavalry to fight on foot, but in Jan. '65 he left Va. to look for horses in his home state. He was appointed Lt. Gen. on 15 Feb. '65. Ordered to cover Johnston's retreat through S.C., he was considered technically exempt from surrendering with him. He considered joining Davis and crossing the Mississippi to continue resistance in Tex. When this scheme failed, he returned to his ruined lands in S.C. and set about repairing his fortunes. Although he favored Johnson's Reconstruction program, he held aloof because he felt his name might impede it. Nevertheless, he was almost chosen Gov. in 1865. When the Radical program went into effect, he protested vigorously and then submerged himself in his private affairs for the next seven years, returning to public life to end the carpetbag era in the state. Elected Gov. in 1876, he was re-elected in 1878 and shortly chosen US Sen., a post he held until 1891. His public career came to an end when the rising farm and artisan faction swept away his conservative, predominantly "Old South" party.

HAMPTON LEGION. Soon after S.C.'s secession the immensely wealthy Wade HAMPTON started enlisting a legion of six infantry companies, four cavalry companies, and a battery of artillery. More than twice as many men volunteered than he was authorized to accept. At his own expense he bought much of their equipment, including six field guns of the revolutionary BLAKELY type. The inexperienced Hampton led his legion with distinction at 1st Bull Run where he was wounded and his unit suffered 20 per cent casualties among the 600 engaged. On 16 Nov. '61 the Hampton Legion became part of Longstreet's division (*Lee's Lts.,* I, 165n). After the Peninsular campaign the infantry companies, under Col. M. W. Gary, became part of HOOD's TEXAS BRIGADE. The artillery became known as Hart's South Carolina Battery, and the cavalry regiments joined Rosser's cavalry regiment.

HAMPTON ROADS PEACE CONFERENCE. On 3 Feb. '65 a meeting was held on board a steamer in Hampton Roads to attempt to restore peace. Lincoln and Seward represented the Federal government, while Stephens, Robert M. T. Hunter, and J. A. Campbell were the Confederate agents. This was brought about through the efforts of F. P. Blair, who had unofficially discussed the possibility of a meeting with Jefferson Davis. The conference failed because the Confederates insisted on independence and because Lincoln and Seward refused to condone any plan that permitted the continuance of slavery.

HAMPTON-ROSSER CATTLE RAID. 16 Sept. '64. Confederate scouts reported a large number of cattle in a well-guarded camp at Coggin's Point (Va.). Hampton moved out on 11 Sept.

to capture them. Having learned of this advance, the 13th Pa. Cav. (150 men) made a stand at Sycamore Church. They and the 1st D.C. Cav. were driven back to where the cattle were enclosed by a strong abatis. The 7th Va. Cav. made a dismounted attack, while the other regiments enveloped. "The herders then broke down the fence of the corral and tried by firing pistols to stampede the cattle, and thus get them beyond Hampton's reach. But Hampton's cavalry were born cowboys, and, heading off the frightened cattle, soon rounded them up, so that the expedition returned with [2,486] cattle to Lee's starving soldiers" (Miller, IV, 110). Losses were put at 400 Federals and 50 Confederates (E.&B.). (Coggin's Point is on the south bank of the James, six miles below City Point, about opposite Harrison's Landing; Sycamore Church is four miles inland. See O.R. Atlas, plate XCIII.)

HAMPTON'S CAVALRY CORPS. See CORPS, Confed.

HANCOCK, Cornelia. Army nurse. Pa. Taken into the nursing service during the Gettysburg campaign, she was young and pretty, two qualifications that should have automatically ruled her out of Miss Dix's organization. After three hard-working weeks in the field this dedicated Quaker decided to remain as a nurse and worked in this capacity throughout the war.

HANCOCK, Winfield Scott. Union gen. 1824–86. Pa. USMA 1840 (18/25); Inf. After serving on the frontier, in the Mexican War (1 brevet), and the Seminole War, and in Kans. during the border disturbances, he was Chief Q.M. Southern Dist. Calif. (Capt. since 1855) until 3 Aug. '61. Named B.G. USV 23 Sept. '61, he commanded 3d Brig., W. F. Smith's division (3 Oct. '61–13 Mar. '62), in Washington. During the Penin-

sular campaign he led 1, 2, IV (13 Mar.–18 May '62) at Yorktown and Williamsburg and 1, 2, VI (18 May–17 Sept. '62) at Chickahominy, Golding's Farm, Savage's Station, White Oak Swamp, Crampton's Gap, and Antietam. From 17 Sept. '62 until 24 Jan. '63 he led 1st Div., II, at Antietam and Fredericksburg and again (20 Feb.–22 May '63) at Chancellorsville. He was appointed Maj. Gen. USV 29 Nov. '62. Succeeding to command of the II Corps, he led it (22 May–1 July and 2–3 July '63) at Gettysburg where he was wounded severely; at the Wilderness, Spotsylvania, North Anna, Totopotomoy, Cold Harbor, and Petersburg assaults when his Gettysburg wound broke out (24 Mar.–18 June '64) and at Deep Bottom, Reams's Station, Boydton Plank Road, and Petersburg siege (27 June–26 Nov. '64). From 27 Nov. '64 until 27 Feb. '65 he was organizing and was commander of the 1st Corps of Veterans. He then led the Dept. of W. Va. (28 Feb.–1 Mar.; 7–20 Mar.; 22 Mar.–27 June '65) and the Middle Mil. Div. (27 Feb.–27 June '65). Named B.G. USA 12 Aug. '64, he continued in the R.A. and was appointed Maj. Gen. USA in 1866. He was breveted for Spotsylvania (Maj. Gen. USA) and one of fifteen army officers given the Thanks of Congress (for Gettysburg). He was the unsuccessful Democratic candidate for president in 1880, losing to Garfield. Grant described him as "tall, well-formed ... young and fresh-looking," while Lyman had this to say of him: "A tall, soldierly man, with light-brown hair and a military heavy jaw; and has the massive features and the heavy folds around the eye that often mark the man of ability ... who always has a clean *white* shirt (where he gets them nobody knows) ... [a] very great and vehement talker but always says something worth hearing."

HANNA, William. Union officer. Ind. Capt. 50th Ill. 12 Sept. '61; Maj. 12 May '63; Lt. Col. 1 Sept. '64; Bvt. B.G. USV (Allatoona, Ga.)

HANOVER, Pa., 30 June '63. (Stuart's Gettysburg raid) At about 9:45 A.M. the 13th Va. Cav., while approaching this place, saw and attacked a body of Federal cavalry. The Confederate pursuit was carried into the streets of Hanover and a number of prisoners and ambulances captured. Farnsworth (commanding 1st Brig. of Kilpatrick's 3d Cav. Div.) rallied the Federals, organized a spirited counterattack that routed the Confederates. Stuart was almost captured and escaped only by jumping his thoroughbred, Virginia, across a ditch against which he appeared to have been trapped. Losses were 12 Federals killed and 43 wounded; 75 Confederates wounded and 60 missing. (E.&B.; Meade's report.)

Fox gives the following casualties:

	Killed	Wounded Incl. P.O.W.	Missing Incl. P.O.W.	Total
Union	19	73	123	215
Confederate	9	50	58	117

HANOVER C.H., Va., 27 May '62. (PENINSULAR CAMPAIGN) On 25 May McClellan ordered Fitz-John Porter, commanding the Provisional V Corps, to reconnoiter toward Hanover C.H., where a Confederate force was believed to be located. Two days later Porter was ordered to drive off enemy units in this area that could threaten the flank and rear of the Federal army. With Morell's division (Martindale's, Griffin's, and Butterfield's brigades), the small infantry brigade of G. K. Warren (3, 2, V), and W. H. Emory's mixed brigade of cavalry and artillery, Porter left New Bridge at 4 A.M. on the 27th and moved toward Hanover C.H. Branch's N.C. brigade, about 4,500

strong, was located in this vicinity, having recently moved down from Gordonsville with orders to protect the railroad. After contact was made at Peake's Station (near Lebanon Church and about four miles south of Hanover C.H.), Porter threw out the 25th N.Y. and Berdan's Sharpshooters as skirmishers and then brought the rest of his force into action. In an affair that Freeman says was "in no sense discreditable to Branch," the Confederates were driven west to Ashland after putting up a stiff fight. With a loss of 355 Federals, Porter claimed to have buried 200 Confederates and to have taken 730 prisoners. "Branch reported 243 killed and wounded, excluding those in J. H. Lane's Twenty-eighth North Carolina," says Freeman. "If this discrepancy is reconcilable at all, it must be by the inclusion among the prisoners of troops of other Confederate commands, picked up along the railroads" (*Lee's Lts.*, I, 220n.). This battle is also known as Kinney's Farm and Slash Church.

HANOVER TOWN, Va., 27 May '64. See TOTOPOTOMOY CREEK.

HANSON, Roger Weightman. C.S.A. gen. 1827-63. Ky. Fighting in the Mexican War, he was later in a duel that shortened a leg and gave him "a peculiar gait" (D.A.B.). He went to Calif. for the gold rush and returned to Ky. to enter politics. Conservative, but resenting Union domination, he joined the neutrality movement and was Col. in the state guard. Joining the Confederate army, he led his men to Camp Boone in Clarksville (Tenn.), where they formed the nucleus of the 2d, 3d, 4th, and 5th Ky. regiments. As Col., he held the Confederate right at Donelson for part of the siege with his regiment, the 2d Ky., and was captured on 16 Feb. '62. By Oct. of that year he was back with his regiment and then took over the 1st

Brig., fighting under Forrest at Nashville, 5 Nov. On J. H. Morgan's expedition against Hartsville he captured over 2,000 Union prisoners on 7 Dec., losing 68 of his own men. He was appointed B.G. C.S.A. 13 Dec. '62 and led the 4th Brig. under Hardee at Stones River, where he was killed 2 Jan. '63.

HARDEE, William Joseph. C.S.A. gen. 1815–73. Ga. USMA 1838 (26/45); Dragoons. He fought in the Seminole War, studied two years at the French cavalry school at Saumur, served on the frontier, and fought in the Mexican War (2 brevets, captured) before becoming commandant of cadets at West Point and instructing infantry, artillery, and cavalry tactics. On leave in Ga. when his state seceded, he resigned 12 days later (31 Jan. '61) as Lt. Col. and was commissioned Col. C.S.A. Appointed B.G. C.S.A. 17 June '61, he organized the Ark. brigade, and transferring in the fall of 1861 to Ky., was promoted Maj. Gen. 7 Oct. '61. He led his corps at Shiloh, Perryville, Stones River, Missionary Ridge, and the Atlanta campaign, having been named Lt. Gen. 10 Oct. '62. In Sept. '64 he was named to command the Dept. of S.C., Ga., and Fla. Trying to stop Sherman on his March to the Sea, Hardee had an ineffective force that was powerless before the Federal hordes. He evacuated Savannah 18 Dec. '64 and left Charleston in Jan. '65 to join J. E. Johnston in N.C.

HARDEE'S CORPS. See I CORPS, II CORPS, III CORPS, Confed. Armies of Miss. and of Tenn.

HARDEMAN, William P. C.S.A. gen. ?–1898. Appt.-Tex. Commissioned Capt. in the 4th Tex. Mtd. Vols., he fought under Sibley in N. Mex. and was promoted Col. in the latter part of 1862. He succeeded Green as brigade commander for a short time, and led his

regiment in the Red River campaign of 1864. He was appointed B.G. C.S.A. 17 Mar. '65.

HARDENBERGH, Jacob Brodhead. Union officer. N.Y. Maj. 80th N.Y. 24 Sept. '61; Lt. Col. 22 Sept. '62; Col. 19 Dec. '64; Bvt. B.G. USV (war service). Died 1892.

HARDIE, James Allen. Union gen. 1823–76. N.Y. Appt. at Large. USMA 1843 (11/39); Arty. He taught at the Military Academy, served in Calif. during the Mexican War, and in garrisons in the East, and participated in Indian fighting. Named Lt. Col. Add. A.D.C. 28 Sept. '61 (from Capt. 5th Arty. since 1857), he was on McClellan's staff and Asst. A.G. of the Army of the Potomac through the Peninsular campaign, fulfilling similar duties under Burnside during the Maryland campaign and at Fredericksburg. His faithfulness and accuracy were so dependable that Burnside and Wm. B. Franklin agreed to accept his field dispatches as correct records of the failure and responsibility of that battle. He was named B.G. USV 29 Nov. '62, his appointment was revoked 22 Jan. '63, and he was then named Maj. Asst. A.G. 19 Feb. '63. McClellan asked him to prepare the memorial that restored him to command, and Hooker made him Judge Adv. Gen. of the Potomac. When he was in the Sec. of War's office in June 1863 he was entrusted to deliver the secret order transferring command from Hooker to Meade before Gettysburg. He was named Col. I.G. 24 May '64, breveted B.G. and Maj. Gen. USV for war service, and continued in the R.A., dying on active duty.

HARDIN, Martin D. Union gen. 1837–1923. Ill. USMA 1859 (11/22); Arty.-Inf. He served in garrison and on the frontier before becoming (1st Lt. 14 May '61) acting A.D.C. to Col.

H. J. Hunt of the Reserve Arty. during the Peninsular campaign. He fought at Yorktown, Seven Days' Battles, Malvern Hill, and Harrison's Landing, and was named Lt. Col. 12th Pa. Reserves 8 July '62. Leading his regiment at Groveton (28 Aug. '62) and 2d Bull Run, he was wounded twice at the latter. He was named Col. 1 Sept. '62 and commanded 3, 3, I (30 Dec. '62–10 Jan. '63) and 3, 3, V (June–July and 18 Sept.–4 Dec. '63) at Bristoe Station, Rappahannock Station, Mine Run, and Catlett's Station, where he lost his left arm, being shot by guerrillas while inspecting pickets. In the spring of 1863 he had served as P.M. and on courtmartial duty, before returning to lead his regiment at Gettysburg and Falling Waters. He then commanded 1, 3, V at Spotsylvania, North Anna, where wounded, Totopotomoy, and Bethesda Church. Commanding Defenses North of the Potomac, XXII, Washington, he defended against Early's raiders (8 July '64–2 Aug. '65), having been named B.G. USV 2 July '64. He was breveted for Groveton, 2d Bull Run, the guerrilla engagement near Catlett's Station, North Anna, and war service (B.G. USV). He continued in the R.A. until retired in 1870, with the rank of B.G. He was the last surviving member of his class at USMA.

HARDING, Abner Clark. Union gen. 1807–74. Conn. A man of diversified interests, he was in banking and railroad construction and elected to the legislature as an anti-slave Republican. He was named Col. 83d Ill. 21 Aug. '62 and led his regiment at Forts Henry and Donelson. While in command of the post at Fort Donelson 3 Feb. '63, he was attacked by Wheeler, Forrest, and Wharton. He was named B.G. USV 13 Mar. '63, commanded the post of Murfreesboro, and resigned 3 June '63 because of failing eyesight. He served as

Representative 1864–67 and left an estate of about $2 million.

HARDING, Chester, Jr. Union officer. Mass. Lt. Col. Asst. Adj. Gen. 1st Brig. Mo. Vols. 12 May '61; Col. 10th Mo. 15 Aug. '61; resigned 5 Dec. '61; Col. 25th Mo. 14 June '62; resigned 3 Feb. '64; Col. 43d Mo. 22 Sept. '64; Bvt. B.G. USV 27 May '65 (war service). Commanded Dist. Northern Mo.; 1st Brig., 2d Div. Army Southeast Mo.; 2d Div. Army Southeast Mo.; Dist. Central Mo. Son of Chester Harding, noted American portrait painter, young Harding had one brother (Edward Harding, Capt. Comsy. of Subsist. Vols. and Maj. Comsy. of Subsist. Mo. State Militia) in the Union Army and two brothers in the Confederate Army. See BROTHER AGAINST BROTHER.

HARKER, Charles Garrison. Union gen. 1837–64. N.J. USMA 1858 (16/27); Inf. He served on the frontier and a surveying expedition and was promoted 1st Lt. 15th US Inf. 14 May '61. As Capt. (24 Oct.), he drilled Ohio volunteers and participated in Buell's Ky. operations Nov. '61–Mar. '62. Commissioned Col. 65th Ohio 11 Nov. '61, he fought at Shiloh, the siege of Corinth, and Buell's advance on Louisville June–Sept. '62. During this he commanded in the Army of the Ohio 20th Brig., 6th Div. (10 July–29 Sept.) and also 20th, 6th, II (Sept.–Nov. '62). He commanded 3, 1st Div., Left Wing, XIV, Cumberland (5 Nov. '62–9 Jan. '63) at Stones River 31 Dec. '62 and led 3, 1, XXI, Cumberland (9 Jan.–17 Feb. '63 and 17 Mar.–9 Oct. '63) at Chickamauga. He was promoted B.G. USV 20 Sept. '63 and commanded 3, 2, IV, Cumberland (10 Oct. '63–27 June '64) at Missionary Ridge, on the march to the relief of Knoxville, Dalton, Resaca (where he was wounded), Dallas, and Kenesaw Mountain (where he was killed 27 June '64 leading his brigade in a charge).

HARLAN, Emory B. Union officer. Ohio. 2d Lt. 49th Ill. 1 Dec. '61; 1st Lt. 22 Mar. '62; Capt. Asst. Adj. Gen. Vols. 12 Nov. '64; Bvt. B.G. USV (war service). Died 1875.

HARLAND, Edward. Union gen. 1832–? Conn. Graduating from Yale, he was a lawyer until named Col. 8th Conn. 5 Oct. '61. He went on Burnside's N.C. expedition in 1861–62 and then commanded 2, 3, IX (22 July '62– 2 Mar. '63) at South Mountain, Antietam, and Fredericksburg. He also led 2, 2, VII (21 Mar.–31 July '63) at the siege of Suffolk; 2, Getty's division Norfolk and Portsmouth (15 July–29 Dec. '63); Sub Dist. Pamlico (13 Mar.–2 May '64); defenses New Bern (27 July '64– 31 Jan. '65); Sub Dist. New Bern (31 Jan.–9 Feb. '65) and 1st Div. Dist. Beaufort (1 Mar.–18 Mar. '65). Named B.G. USV 29 Nov. '62, he resigned 22 June '65 and was later a state legislator and president of a savings bank.

HARNDEN, Henry. Union officer. Mass. Capt. 1st Wis. Cav. 1 Jan. '62; Maj. 8 June '64; Lt. Col. 6 Jan. '65; Bvt. B.G. USV (war service). W.I.A. Dallas (Ga.) in the shoulder, and at West Point (Ga.) in the thigh. On 6 May '65 he was ordered by Gen. Croxton to lead the search for Jefferson Davis, and although his party did not apprehend the fleeing president, they were instrumental in his capture. Later active as a lumberman and politician. Died 1900.

HARNEY, William A. Union gen. 1800–89. Tenn. Joining the R.A. in 1818, he fought in the Seminole War (1 brevet), the Mexican War (1 brevet), and in the West against the Indians. A Southern sympathizer, he was appointed B.G. USA in 1858 and given command of the Dept. of the West, with headquarters in St. Louis. Married to a wealthy woman from St. Louis, he subscribed to the convictions of his slave-holding friends and was an embarrassment to Blair and Lyons, if not actually a threat to their plans to consolidate the state's Union sympathizers. He was relieved from his command 29 May '61, retired 1 Aug. '63 and breveted Maj. Gen. USA 13 Mar. '65.

HARPERS FERRY, W. Va. 12–15 Sept. '62. See ANTIETAM CAMPAIGN.

HARPERS FERRY ARSENAL AND ARMORY. On 18 Apr. '61 the Federal authorities abandoned this large establishment after setting fire to its shops and the building in which 17,000 finished muskets were stored. The muskets were destroyed, but the shops were saved with their machinery, tools, and large quantities of matériel and musket and pistol parts. By 18 June all of this had been evacuated and it became the core of the Confederate ordnance effort. All machinery for making the US RIFLE MODEL 1841 ("Mississippi Rifle") was sent to the captured arsenal at Fayetteville, N.C. Machinery for making the US RIFLE MUSKET, Model 1855, was kept for the RICHMOND ARMORY AND ARSENAL. The US government abandoned the arsenal at Harpers Ferry after the war.

HARPERS FERRY RAID (1859). See John BROWN.

HARPERS FERRY RIFLE was a popular name for the US RIFLE, Model 1855, which was a shorter version of the RIFLE MUSKET of the same year.

HARRIMAN, Samuel. Union officer. Me. Capt. 30th Wis. 21 Oct. '62; Col. 37th Wis. 26 Apr. '64; Bvt. B.G. USV 2 Apr. '65 (Ft. Sedgwick, Va.). Commanded 1, 1, IX. Died 1897.

HARRIMAN, Walter. Union officer. 1817–84. N.H. Col. 11th N.H. 2 Sept. '62; resigned 26 June '63; Col. 11th N.H. 26 Jan. '64; Bvt. B.G. USV (war service). Commanded 2, 2, IX (Potomac and Ohio). Captured at the Wilderness, he was placed with 49 other officers under the fire of Federal batteries on Morris Island for 52 days until Gen. Foster put 50 C.S.A. officers of equal rank under the fire of the Fort Sumter and Fort Moultrie guns. He was exchanged in time to command his regiment at Petersburg. An able historian, he was also Gov. of N.H. 1867–68.

HARRIS, Andrew Linturn. Union officer. Ohio. 2d Lt. 20th Ohio 17 Apr. '61; Capt. 27 May '61; mustered out 18 Aug. '61; 2d Lt. 75th Ohio 3 Oct. '61; Capt. 9 Nov. '61; Maj. 1 Mar. '63; Col. 22 May '63; Bvt. B.G. USV (war service). Commanded 2, 1, XI.

HARRIS, Benjamin Foster. Union officer. c. 1831–95. Me. Capt. 6th Me. 15 July '61; Maj. 10 Mar. '62; Lt. Col. 9 Mar. '63; resigned 19 July '64; Maj. Vet. Res. Corps 15 Sept. '64; Bvt. B.G. USV. Brevets for war service, Marye's Heights, Rappahannock Station. W.I.A. Gettysburg and lamed for life.

HARRIS, Charles L. Union officer. N.J. Lt. Col. 1st Wis. 17 May '61; mustered out 21 Aug. '61; Col. 11th Wis. 21 Oct. '61; Bvt. B.G. USV (war service). Ex-Cadet USMA 1857. Commanded 1st Brig. 1st Div. Army Southeastern Mo.; 2, 14, XIII (Tenn.); 2, 1, XIII (Gulf); 3, 2, XVI (Gulf).

HARRIS, David Bullock. C.S.A. officer. 1814–64. Va. USMA 1833 (7/43); Arty. He served on the frontier in Indian fighting and taught engineering at West Point before resigning in 1835 to become a civil engineer, tobacco merchant, and planter. Commissioned Capt. Va. Engrs., in July '61, he fought at 1st Bull Run and succeeded Kirby Smith when that officer was wounded. In March and April '62 he served as engineer under Beauregard fortifying Fort Pillow and Island No. 10. In the latter part of April he served in the Vicksburg

defenses under M. L. Smith, and his return was requested in Dec. '62 by Beauregard. From Mar. '63 until Mar. '64, he was variously Maj., Lt. Col., and Col., serving under Beauregard in S.C. On Beauregard's staff, he engineered the defenses at Drewry's Bluff and around Petersburg. Sent in Oct. '64 to Charleston, he died of yellow fever on the 10th. Although Heitman and Cullum list him as a general officer, and although he deserved to be one, he died as a Col.

HARRIS, Eliza. (Mrs. John Harris.) SANITARY COMMISSION worker. Pa. Famous for her hot gruel, PANADA, and her newspaper stories in the Pa. press that brought a constant stream of money for the Commission, she seemed to be wherever the army needed her most in the East. She distributed food, helped with the amputations, nursed the sick and wounded, scrounged and cooked the food, cleaned up the gore, and prayed over the boys, writing fully and vividly of her experiences all the while, from 1st Bull Run to Gettysburg. In the fall of 1863 she went to Tenn., continuing her energetic efforts in hospitals in Chattanooga and Nashville until the beginning of Sherman's Atlanta campaign. In poor health to begin with, she had been seriously ill, and returned to Washington for a time but then went to the Fredericksburg hospital in 1864 and continued her activities in Va. and N.C., ending the war by caring for the released Andersonville prisoners.

HARRIS, Isham Green. C.S.A. Gov. of Tenn. 1818–97. Tenn. A merchant and lawyer in Tenn. and Miss., he served in the former state's legislature and as U.S. Congressman before being elected Gov. in 1857, 1859, and 1861. He was A. S. Johnston's A.D.C. at the beginning of the war and served after Shiloh in the general headquarters of the Army of the West. In 1863 he was succeeded by Robert L. Carruthers, and after the war he fled to Mexico and England before returning to hold his Senate seat for six terms.

HARRIS, Mrs. John. See Eliza HARRIS.

HARRIS, Nathaniel Harrison. C.S.A. gen. 1834–1900. Appt.-Miss. Practicing law with his brother in Vicksburg, he organized the Warren Rifles that were mustered into state service 8 May '61. Entering the 19th Miss. 1 June '61, he joined Johnston in the upper Shenandoah but was not at 1st Bull Run. He was commended for bravery at Williamsburg and promoted Maj. 5 Mar. '62. After the Maryland campaign he was promoted Lt. Col. and made Col. 2 Apr. '63 of the 19th Miss. He led this regiment under Jackson at Chancellorsville, and served in Posey's brigade at Gettysburg. Appointed B.G. C.S.A. 20 Jan. '64, he commanded his brigade at Spotsylvania's "bloody angle" and in all subsequent battles before the Petersburg siege. In the Petersburg line his brigade occupied the river salient until relieved in Nov. '64 to go into reserve. He fought around the Weldon Railroad in the next two months, and in Mar. '65 was in command of the inner defenses of Richmond. After the Federal final assault on Petersburg started he was ordered to throw two regiments each into batteries Gregg and Whitworth. These held until Longstreet arrived to form the inner defense line. At Appomattox he commanded Mahone's division. Returning to Vicksburg, he was a lawyer and railroad president before eventually going West. He died in England.

HARRIS, Thomas Mealey. Union gen. 1817–? Va. A doctor before the war, he was named Lt. Col. 10th W. Va. 17 Mar. '62 and promoted Col. 20 May '62. He commanded 3, Indpt. Div., **XXIV, Va.** (24 Mar.–27 Apr. '64); 1,

3, W. Va. (July '64); 3, 1st Inf. Div., W. Va. (Aug.–19 Oct. '64); 1st Inf. Div., W. Va. (19 Oct.–24 Dec. '64); Indpt. Div., XXIV, Va. (24 Dec. '64–25 Mar. '65 and 25 Apr.–10 July '65); 1st Indpt. Brig. XXIV, Va. (10 July–Aug. '65). He was promoted B.G. USV 29 Mar. '65 and breveted B.G. USV for Middletown (Va.) and Maj. Gen. USA for Petersburg assault. He was later active in politics.

HARRISBURG, Miss. TUPELO, Miss., 13–15 July '64.

HARRIS' FARM, Va., 19 May '64. Attack by Ewell on Federal right that concluded SPOTSYLVANIA.

HARRISON, Benjamin. 23d pres. of US and Union officer. Ohio. 1833–1901. 2d Lt. 70th Ind. 14 July '62; Capt. 22 July '62; Col. 7 Aug. '62; Bvt. B.G. USV (Brig. Comdr.). In the Army of the Cumberland he commanded 2, 3, Res. Corps; 1, 1, IX; 1, 3, XX; 1st Brig., Prov. Div. D.A.B. says, "Harrison soon became unpopular ... because he insisted on turning raw recruits into disciplined soldiers." Great-grandson of Benjamin Harrison, Va. signer of the Declaration of Independence, and grandson of William Henry Harrison, ninth pres. He became leading corporation lawyer after the war, served as Republican US Sen., and in 1888 ran against Grover Cleveland for president. Although Harrison polled fewer popular votes than his opponent, he won the election in the Electoral College. He was defeated after one term by Cleveland.

HARRISON, George P. J. C.S.A. gen. 1841–? Ga. While still a student in a Ga. military academy, he was a member of the force that seized Fort Pulaski (3 Jan. '61). Later that month he was commissioned 2d Lt. 1st Ga. Regulars and was commandant of the academy in the spring. After graduation in May he was named Adj. and sent with the regiment to Va. He fought at Langley's Farm and was commissioned Col. 5th Ga. state troops that winter. This regiment served its six months' enlistment along the Ga. coast. He was then named Col. 32d Ga. and given a brigade in July '63, fighting in the defenses of Charleston, James Island, Morris Island, Fort Wagner, and John's Island. In 1864 he built a prisoner stockade at Florence (S.C.) and fought at Olustee, where he was wounded. C.M.H. says he was appointed B.G. C.S.A. in the winter of 1864 and led a brigade in A. P. Stewart's Corps at Honey Hill, Pocotaligo, Savannah, River's Bridge, Broxton's Bridge, Cheraw, and Bentonville in the Carolinas campaign. Wright says he was appointed B.G. 16 May '65 by Kirby Smith in the Trans-Miss. Dept. After the war he settled in Alabama to become a lawyer.

HARRISON, James E. C.S.A. gen. ?–1875. Appt.-Tex. Commissioned Lt. Col. 15th Tex., he was engaged in scouting and skirmishing until 29 Sept. '63, when he led a brigade under Taylor at Fordoche (La.). He fought at Bayou Bourbon 1 Nov. '63, was named Col. in '64, and later that year (22 Nov.) was appointed B.G. C.S.A.

HARRISON, Marcus La Rue. Union officer. N.Y. Capt. 1st Ark. Cav. 10 July '62; Col. 7 Aug. '62; Bvt. B.G. USV (war service). Died 1890.

HARRISON, Richard. C.S.A. Wood and Heitman list him as B.G. C.S.A., the former saying that he was appointed from Tex. in 1865. Neither Wright nor C.M.H. includes him in their lists of general officers. However, in the B.&L. orders of battle he is listed as Col. 43d Miss. at Vicksburg, the Atlanta campaign, and Franklin and Nashville.

HARRISON, Thomas. C.S.A. gen. ?–1891. Appt.-Tex. Commissioned Capt.

8th Tex. Cav. (the "Texas Rangers"), he was a Maj. at Shiloh and named Col. in Nov. '62. He led his regiment at Stones River, led Wharton's brigade at Chickamauga, and fought under Wheeler to thwart McCook's raid near Atlanta in Aug. '64. After going with Hood to Tenn., he returned to Ga. to be appointed B.G. C.S.A. 14 Jan. '65 after having led his brigade for more than a year. He surrendered with Johnston in N.C.

HARRISON, Thomas Jefferson. Union officer. Ky. Capt. 6th Ind. 22 Apr. '61; mustered out 2 Aug. '61; Col. 8th Ind. Cav. 29 Aug. '61; Bvt. B.G. USV 31 Jan. '65. Died 1871.

HARRISON'S LANDING, Va., 3 July–16 Aug. '62. Position on James River to which McClellan moved his army to end the PENINSULAR CAMPAIGN. On 3 Aug. Halleck ordered his withdrawal (to support Pope in the 2d BULL RUN CAMPAIGN). On 14–16 Aug. the withdrawal was accomplished and all troops except the rear guard were across the Chickahominy. By the 20th the last troops were ready to embark from Yorktown, Fort Monroe, and Newport News.

HARRISON'S LANDING LETTER of McClellan to Lincoln. 7 July '62. When Lincoln visited McClellan at Harrison's Landing upon conclusion of the Peninsular campaign, McClellan handed him a letter in which he volunteered his opinions on the future conduct of the war. (On 20 June he had asked permission to indulge in some suggestions.) Although the letter, which Lincoln read in McClellan's presence without significant comment, was not published until after McClellan's relief from command, it had undoubtedly done much to consolidate hostility of the Cabinet toward him, and probably contributed to his downfall. Here is the letter.

Headquarters, Army of the Potomac, Camp near Harrison's Landing, Va., July 7, 1862.

Mr. President: You have been fully informed that rebel army is in front, with the purpose of overwhelming us by attacking our positions or reducing us by blocking our river communications. I cannot but regard our condition as critical, and I earnestly desire, in view of possible contingencies, to lay before your excellency, for your private consideration, my general views concerning the existing state of the rebellion, although they do not strictly relate to the situation of this army or strictly come within the scope of my official duties. These views amount to convictions, and are deeply impressed upon my mind and heart. Our cause must never be abandoned; it is the cause of free institutions and self-government. The Constitution and the Union must be preserved, whatever may be the cost in time, treasure, and blood. If secession is successful other dissolutions are clearly to be seen in the future. Let neither military disaster, political faction, nor foreign war shake your settled purpose to enforce the equal operation of the laws of the United States upon the people of every state.

The time has come when the government must determine upon a civil and military policy covering the whole ground of our national trouble.

The responsibility of determining, declaring, and supporting such civil and military policy, and of directing the whole course of national affairs in regard to the rebellion, must now be assumed and exercised by you, or our cause will be lost. The Constitution gives you power sufficient even for the present terrible exigency.

This rebellion has assumed the character of war; as such it should be regarded, and it should be conducted upon the highest principles known to Christian civilization. It should not be a war looking to the subjugation of the people of any State in any event. It should not be at all a war upon population, but against armed forces and political organization. Neither confiscation of property, political executions of persons, territorial organization of States, or forcible abolition of slavery should be contemplated for a moment. In prosecuting the war all private property and unarmed persons should be strictly protected, subject only to the necessity of military operations. All private property taken for military use should be paid or receipted for; pillage and waste should be treated as high crimes; all unnecessary trespass sternly prohibited, and offensive demeanor by the military towards citizens promptly rebuked. Military arrests should not be tolerated, except in places where active hostilities exist, and oaths not required by enactments constitutionally made should be neither demanded nor received. Military government should be confined to the preservation of public order and the protection of political rights. Military power·should not be allowed to interfere with the relations of servitude, either by supporting or impairing the authority of the master, except for repressing disorder, as in other cases. Slaves contraband under the act of Congress, seeking military protection, should receive it. The right of the Government to appropriate permanently to its own service claims to slave labor should be asserted, and the right of the owner to compensation therefor should be recognized.

This principle might be extended, upon grounds of military necessity and security, to all the slaves within a particular State, thus working manumission in such State; and in Missouri, perhaps in Western Virginia also, and possibly even in Maryland, the expediency of such a measure is only a question of time.

A system of policy thus constitutional and conservative, and pervaded by the influences of Christianity and freedom, would receive the support of almost all truly loyal men, would deeply impress the rebel masses and all foreign nations, and it might be humbly hoped that it would commend itself to the favor of the Almighty.

Unless the principles governing the future conduct of our struggle shall be made known and approved, the effort to obtain requisite forces will be almost hopeless. A declaration of radical views, especially upon slavery, will rapidly disintegrate our present armies. The policy of the government must be supported by concentrations of military power. The national forces should not be dispersed in expeditions, posts of occupation, and numerous armies, but should be mainly collected into masses and brought to bear upon the armies of the Confederate States. Those armies thoroughly defeated, the political structure which they support would soon cease to exist.

In carrying out any system of policy which you may form you will require a commander-in-chief of the army, one who possesses your confidence, understands your views and who is competent to execute your orders by directing the military forces of the nation to the accomplishment of the objects by you proposed. I do not ask that place for myself. I am willing to serve you in such position as you may assign me, and I will do so as faithfully as ever subordinate served superior.

I may be on the brink of eternity; and as I hope forgiveness from my Maker, I have written this letter with sincerity towards you and from love for my country.

Very respectfully,
your obedient servant,
Geo. B. McClellan,
Maj.-Gen. Commanding.
(*McClellan's Own Story*, 487-89.)

HARROW, William. Union gen. c.1820-72. Ky. He was commissioned Maj. 14th Ind. 7 June '61 and promoted Lt. Col. 14 Feb. '62. He fought at Winchester (23 Mar. '62) and became Col. 26 Apr. Resigning that commission 29 July, he went back to the 14th Ind. as Col. 23 Aug. and became B.G. USV 29 Nov. '62. At Antietam he lost more than half his regiment either killed or wounded. During the Gettysburg campaign, he commanded the following: 1, 3, II (8 June–1 July and 2–4 July '63); 2d Div., II Corps (1–2 July and 4 July–15 Aug. '63). Dyer also lists the 4th Div., V Corps, Potomac, as his command but gives no dates. He resigned 20 Apr. '65.

HARROW'S BRIGADE (2, II, Potomac). Suffered the highest percentage of casualties in any brigade in any one action during the war. Officially reported losses of its four regiments, the 19th Me., 15th Mass., 1st Minn., and 82d N.Y. (2d N.Y. State Militia) was 61 per cent (Gettysburg).

HART, Charlie. Alias of the Confederate bushwhacker, William C. QUANTRILL.

HART, James H. Union officer. Ohio. 1st Lt. 71st Ohio 8 Oct. '61; Maj. 15 Jan. '62; Lt. Col. 7 Apr. '64; Bvt. B.G. USV (war service).

HART, Orson H. Union officer. Conn. Pvt. Co. A 7th N.Y. State Mil. 19 Apr.–4 June '61; 1st Lt. Adj. 70th N.Y. 7 June '61; Capt. Asst. Adj. Gen. Vols. 16 May '62; Lt. Col. Asst. Adj. Gen. assigned 3 Feb. '63–11 June '66; Bvt. B.G. USV (war service). Died 1874.

HARTFORD, The. As Farragut's flagship, she was famous during the capture of New Orleans, the bombardment of Vicksburg and Port Hudson, and at the battle of Mobile Bay. She was a wooden-screw steam vessel of 2,790 tons, 226 feet by 43 feet, and launched at Boston in 1858. Her armament included 22 nine-inch smoothbore guns in broadside and two 20-pounder Parrott rifles.

HARTRANFT, John Frederick. Union gen. 1830–89. Pa. In law and politics, he was named Col. 4th Pa. 20 Apr. '61, mustered out 27 July, appointed Col. 51st Pa. 16 Nov. '61, and named B.G. USV 12 May '64. He commanded in the IX Corps, Potomac: 2d Brig., 2d Div. (Feb.–Mar. '63), succeeding to division (21 May–5 June and 16 Nov. '63–26 Jan. '64). He also led 1st Brig., 3d Div. (20 Apr.–28 Aug. '64); 2, 1st Div. (20 Sept.–9 Oct. '64), and 1st Div. (28 Aug.–1 Sept. '64). He led 1, 1st Div. (25 Oct.–28 Nov. '64), Prov. Brig. (28 Nov.–15 Dec. '64), and 3d Div. (2–13 Sept., 9–25 Oct. and 15 Dec. '64–3 May '65). He also commanded 2, 2, IX, Ohio in Apr. and May '63. Breveted Maj. Gen. USV 25 Mar. '65 for Fort Stedman, he was given the Medal of Honor 21 Aug. '86 for having volunteered his services at 1st Bull Run when the rest of his regiment marched to the rear to be mustered out. He was mustered out in 1866 and served as Republican Gov. of Pa. 1872–78, commanded the Pa. National Guard, and held numerous other public offices.

HARTSHORNE, William Ross. Union officer. Pa. 1st Lt. 13th Pa. Res. 21 June '61; Regt. Adj. 1 Mar. '62; Maj. 22 May '63; mustered out 11 June '64; Col. 190th Pa. 23 July '64; Bvt. B.G. USV (war service). Commanded 3, 3, IX.

HARTSUFF, George Lucas. Union gen. 1830–74. N.Y. Appt.-Mich. USMA 1852 (19/43); Arty. In garrison and on the frontier, he was wounded in the Seminole War and then taught tactics at West Point. Named Bvt. Capt. Asst. Adj. Gen. 22 Mar. and to that full rank on 3 Aug. '61, he was at Fort Pickens (Fla.) until July and then went to the Dept. of W. Va. as Chief of Staff to Rosecrans. Appointed B.G. USV 15 Apr. '62, he commanded 2d Brig., 1st Div., Shenandoah (30 Apr.–10 May '62) and 3d Brig., Ord's division., Rappahannock (May–26 June '62). At Cedar Mountain and 2d Bull Run he commanded 3, 2, III, Army of Va. (26 June–29 Aug. and 2–12 Sept. '62). Taking command of 3, 2, I, Potomac (12–17 Sept. '62), he led this brigade at South Mountain and Antietam, being seriously wounded on the latter date. He was promoted Maj. Gen. USV 29 Nov. '62. On sick leave until 18 Dec. '62, he served on boards and commissions until 28 May '63, when he took command of the XXIII Corps, Army of the Ohio. Leaving this post 24 Sept. '63, he was "awaiting orders," being unfit for field service, from Nov. until 23 July '64 when he served on courts-martial until Mar. '65. During the Petersburg siege he commanded the defenses of Bermuda Hundred, Dept. of Va. and N.C. (19 Mar.–16 Apr. '65). Breveted for Antietam and war service (B.G. USA and Maj. Gen. USA), he continued in the R.A. until 1871, when he was retired with the rank of Maj. Gen.

HARTSUFF, William. Union officer. N.Y. Capt. 10th Mich. 1 Oct. '61; Lt. Col. Asst. I.G. Assigned 13 May '63–1 Aug. '65; Bvt. B.G. USV 24 Jan. '65 (Franklin and Nashville, Tenn).

HARTWELL, Alfred Stedman. Union officer. Mass. 1st Lt. 44th Mass. Mil. 12 Sept. '62; Capt. 54th Mass. 30 Mar.

'63; Lt. Col. 55th Mass. 19 June '63; Col. 1 Dec. '63; Bvt. B.G. USV 30 Dec. '64 (Honey Hill, S.C.). W.I.A. Honey Hill, when his horse was shot from under him, he received two additional wounds while being removed from the field.

HARTWELL, Charles A. Union officer. Mass. R.A. 1st Lt. 11th US Inf. 5 Aug. '61; Col. 77th US Col. Inf. 8 Dec. '63; transferred to 10th US Col. Arty. 1 Oct. '65; Bvt. B.G. USV 2 Dec. '65. Brevets for Gaines's Mill, Port Hudson, war service (2). Commanded 3d Brig., 3d Div. USCT. Died 1876.

HARVEY, Cordelia. SANITARY COMMISSION worker. After the death of her husband, Wis. Gov. Louis P. HARVEY, in the spring of 1862, she began visiting and caring for Wis. soldiers in the field. She worked in the West and after the war started a home for orphans in her state which she superintended for several years.

HARVEY, Louis Powell. Gov. of Wis. 1820–62. Conn. Graduating from the Western Reserve College, he taught school and edited a Whig newspaper before becoming a manufacturer in Wis. He was elected to the legislature and in 1861 was chosen Republican Gov. He was drowned 19 Apr. '62 while on his way to Shiloh with supplies for the wounded.

HASCALL, Milo Smith. Union gen. 1829–1904. N.Y. Appt.-Ind. USMA 1852 (14/43); Arty. Resigning the next year, he was a railroad builder, lawyer, and politician before being named Capt. A.D.C. to Gen. Morris of the Indiana Vols. He commanded a regiment at Phillippi, 3 June '61 and was commissioned Col. 17th Ind. 12 June '61. In the Army of the Ohio he commanded the 15th Brig.; 15th Brig., 4th Div. (2 Dec. '61–9 Mar. '62); 15, 6th Div. (9 Mar– 29 Sept. '62) and, having been pro-

moted B.G. USV 25 Apr. '62, 15, 6, II. At Stones River he led 1, 1 Left Wing, XIV (5 Nov. '62–31 Dec. '62) and succeeded to division (31 Dec. '62–9 Jan. '63). He also led 1, 1, XXI, Cumberland (9 Jan.–19 Feb. '63), as well as in the Army of the Ohio: 3d Div., XXIII (6 Aug. '63–12 Mar. '64); 2d Div. (2 Feb.–16 Apr. '64); 2, 3, XXIII (16–18 May '64); and 2, 2, XXIII (16 Apr.–16 May '64). During the Atlanta campaign he commanded 2d Div., XXIII (18 May–11 Oct. '64). He resigned 27 Oct. '64 and devoted himself to banking and real estate.

HASKELL, Llewellyn Frost. Union officer. 1842–? N.J. Pvt. Co. C 14th N.Y. State Mil. 18 Apr.–14 Aug. '61; 2d Lt. 5th Mo. 25 Aug. '61; transferred to 27th Mo. 18 Dec. '62; Lt. Col. 7th US Col. Inf. 28 Oct. '63; Col. 41st US Col. Inf. 1 Nov. '64; Bvt. B.G. USV (war service). Commanded 2, 2, XXV. On Gen. Asboth's staff at Pea Ridge (Ark.) and on Gen. Prince's staff at Cedar Mountain, where although W.I.A. he was the only officer on Prince's staff not killed or mortally wounded.

HASKIN, Joseph Abel. Union gen. 1817–74. N.Y. USMA 1839 (10/15); Arty. He served in garrison, on the frontier, and in the Mexican War, where he won two brevets and lost his left arm. As Capt., 1st Arty., he surrendered the Baton Rouge Arsenal in 1861. Promoted Maj. 3d US Arty. 20 Feb. '62, he was in the defenses of Washington until 1864, having been promoted Lt. Col. Add. A.D.C. 26 June '62 and B.G. USV 5 Aug. '64. He commanded Def. N. Potomac, Mil. Dist. Wash., Potomac (Aug. '62–Feb. '63); defenses of Washington, Potomac; and Def. N. Potomac, XXII, Washington (2 Feb. '63–8 July '64). He was Chief of Arty., Washington, 26 July '64–10 Apr. '66. He was breveted three times for war service, including B.G. USA. Named Lt. Col.

1st US Arty. in '66, he was retired in 1870 for disabilities.

HASTINGS, Russell. Union officer. 1835–? Mass. 2d Lt. 23d Ohio 11 June '61; 1st Lt. 14 Apr. '62; Capt. 15 Aug. '63; Lt. Col. 30 Apr. '65; Bvt. B.G. USV. Brevets for Valley campaign (1864), Opequon (Va.). W.I.A. Opequon.

HATCH, Edward. Union gen. 1832–89. Me. A sailor and Iowa lumberman, he became Capt. 2d Iowa Cav. 12 Aug. '61, Maj. 5 Sept., and Lt. Col. 11 Dec. '61. He fought at New Madrid and Island No. 10 and was promoted Col. 13 June '62. At Iuka and Corinth he commanded 1st Brig., cavalry division, Army Miss. (11 Aug.–1 Nov. '62) and at Coffeeville (Miss.) 5 Dec. he led 2d Brig., cavalry division Right Wing, XIII, Tenn. (26 Nov.–18 Dec. '62). In the spring of 1863 he went on Grierson's Raid and then commanded 2, 1st Cav. Div., XVI (9 June–20 Aug. and 17 Nov. '63–5 Jan. '64). He also commanded 3, 1st Cav. Div., XVI (20 Aug.–30 Nov. '63); 1st Cav. Div., XVI (24 Sept.–24 Oct. '63); and 1st Div., cavalry West Tenn., Tenn. (June–Nov. '64). He led 5th Div., cavalry corps, military division Miss. (9 Nov. '64–18 Jan. '65) in delaying Hood's Tenn. invasion, culminating in Franklin and Nashville. Breveted for Franklin (B.G. USA 2 Mar. '67) and Nashville (Maj. Gen. USA), he continued in the R.A., participating in the Indian fighting and dying on active duty as Col. 9th US Cav. D.A.B. describes him as "a man of decision, firm of character, and with a well-balanced judgment."

HATCH, John Porter. Union gen. 1822–1901. N.Y. USMA 1845 (17/41); Inf. He fought in the Mexican War (2 brevets), served on the frontier, and participated in Indian fighting and scouting. Named Capt. in 1860, he transferred to the 3d Cav. 3 Aug. '61 and was promoted B.G. USV 28 Sept. Commanding cavalry brigade, Banks's V Corps (28 Mar.–4 Apr. '62) at Annapolis, he led several reconnaissances along the Rappahannock and Rapidan. At Winchester he led cavalry brigade (4 Apr.–26 June '62) and in the Army of Va. he commanded cavalry brigade, II (26 June–27 July); 1, 1, III (27 July–28 Aug.) at Groveton and succeeded to division (28–30 Aug.) at 2d Bull Run and Chantilly. He led 1, 1, I, Potomac (12–14 Sept. '62) and succeeded to division on the latter date at South Mountain, where he was severely wounded. After his convalescence, he served on courts-martial and commanded a draft rendezvous and a cavalry depot. In the Dept. of the South he commanded Dist. of Fla. (24 Mar.–25 Apr. '64); the Dept. (1–26 May '64); Dist. Hilton Head (2 June–1 Aug. '64); Dist. Fla. (4 Aug.–26 Oct. '64); Morris Island (14–30 Nov. '64 at Honey Hill and 23 Jan.–26 Feb. '65); coast division (Nov. '64–Mar. '65) and the 4th Sep. Brig. (26 Oct.–14 Nov. '64). He was breveted for 2d Bull Run, South Mountain, war service and field service (B.G. USA and Maj. Gen. USV), and given the Medal of Honor 28 Oct. '93 for South Mountain. He continued in the R.A., retiring in 1886 as Col. 2d US Cav.

HATCHER'S RUN, Va. (Boydton Road; Vaughan Road; Burgess Farm), 27 Oct. '64 (PETERSBURG CAMPAIGN).

Grant ordered this operation in the hope of cutting the Boydton Road and the Southside R.R. Hancock with two divisions of his II Corps was to cross Hatcher's Run on the Vaughan Road and head north at the first crossroad to the Boydton Plank Road. Parke with 11,000 men of his IX Corps was to attack the enemy entrenchments north of Hatcher's Run. Warren, in the center, was to support IX Corps with 11,000 men of his V Corps; if the IX Corps attack penetrated the Confederate line north of Hatcher's Run, Warren was to advance through the gap with IX Corps; if this attack north of the creek did not succeed, Warren was to attack the Confederate lines south of the creek. The Federal forces in the Petersburg trenches were thinned out to make 43,000 of their total of 57,000 available for this attack. To oppose it, Lee had 28,000 south of the Appomattox.

The movement began at 7:30 on the dark, rainy morning of 27 Oct.; by noon Hancock had reached the Boydton Road with Gregg's cavalry division on his right. On the Federal right, however, IX and V Corps were unable to penetrate the Confederate line north of Hatcher's Run held by Wilcox's division. Crawford's division (V) was then ordered to cross the creek and attack up the south bank; due to the dense undergrowth and difficulty of maintaining direction, this effort did not succeed in penetrating the Confederate position. A. P. Hill, with the vigor that characterized his activities in the defense of Petersburg, sallied forth with the divisions of Mahone, Heth, and Hampton's cavalry to attack Hancock's advanced positions. The fighting lasted from 4 P.M. until dark; the Confederates gained some ground on each flank and were then driven back by counterattacks. Since it was not possible to reinforce or resupply Hancock, the Federal forces were withdrawn and on the 28th occupied the former positions.

Out of an estimated 42,823 Federals engaged, there were 1,194 killed and wounded and 564 missing. An estimated 20,324 Confederates were engaged; there is no record of their losses (Livermore, 130–31).

HATCHER'S RUN, Va., 8–9 Dec. '64. (PETERSBURG CAMPAIGN) As a diversion to assist the WELDON R.R. EXPEDITION, 7–11 Dec., the 1st Div., II Corps and three cavalry regiments (3d and 13th Pa., 6th Ohio) reconnoitered toward Hatcher's Run. Total Federal casualties were 125 (E.&B.).

HATCHER'S RUN, Va., 5–7 Feb. '65. See DABNEY'S MILLS, same date.

HATTERAS INLET (Forts Hatteras and Clark), N.C., 28–29 Aug. '61. In an operation ordered by B. F. Butler, army and naval forces under Admiral Silas H. Stringham (7 naval vessels mounting 143 guns) and Rush Hawkins (880 men of 9th and 20th N.Y.; 2d U.S. Arty.; and Coast Guard) captured and garrisoned Forts Hatteras and Clark. With a loss of only one man in the 319-man landing party (wounded in Fort Clark by own naval fire), the Federals captured 670 prisoners and 35 cannon. The Confederate surrender at about noon on the 29th resulted almost entirely from the effectiveness of Stringham's bombardment. The latter had his ships fire while moving (thereby presenting a much more difficult target to the heavy coastal batteries), an innovation the naval historian Boynton says was not recognized until later employed by Du Pont (B.&L., I, 634n). This combined operation, insignificant as it was, boosted Butler's reputation as a strategist.

HATTON, Robert. C.S.A. gen. 1827–62. Tenn. After Harvard he became a lawyer, legislator, and US Congressman. Commissioned Col. 7th Tenn., he went to Staunton, Va., in June '61. During the Cheat Mountain campaign he was under Loring and fought with Jackson in the Valley. Ordered back to join Johnston, he was appointed B.G. C.S.A. 23 May '62, and killed leading his brigade at Seven Pines (31 May).

HAUGHTON, Nathaniel. Union officer. N.Y. 1st Lt. 25th Ohio 27 June '61; Capt. 30 July '62; Maj. 23 Sept. '63; Lt. Col. 21 July '64; Col. 25 May '66;

Bvt. B.G. USV (war service). Died 1899.

HAUPT, Herman. Union gen. 1817–1905. Pa. USMA 1835 (31/56); Inf. Resigning three months after graduation, he entered railroad engineering and taught civil engineering, architecture, and mathematics at Penn College at Gettysburg. He was later chief of transportation and chief engineer of the Penn Railroad and constructed and financed the Hoosac (Mass.) tunnel despite many difficulties and public criticism. Named Col. Add. A.D.C. to McDowell 27 Apr. '62, he was in charge of transportation and construction on the US military railroads. Named B.G. USV, 5 Sept. '62, he resigned a year later, saying that he was willing to serve without official rank or pay so long as no restrictions were placed on his work but could not tolerate interference. He continued in railroading and pipeline building and developed a superior pneumatic drill. He wrote many important books on engineering and bridges as well as one on his Civil War experiences (*Reminiscences*). He was the last surviving member of his West Point class.

HAWES, James Morrison. C.S.A. gen. c. 1823–89. Ky. USMA 1845 (29/41); Dragoons-Cav. He fought in the Mexican War, winning two brevets and declining one of them. Then on duty at West Point, he taught infantry and cavalry tactics, and mathematics. After two years at the French cavalry school (Saumur), went to the frontier and was in Kans. during the border disturbances. Resigning 9 May '61, he was commissioned Capt. in the Confederate Army and was promoted 16 June '61 to Maj. Ten days later he was elected Col. of the 2d Ky. and resigned later to join the Confederate regular army. He was appointed B.G. C.S.A. 14 Mar. '62 to rank from the 5th, and commanded the cavalry in the Western Dept. under A. S. Johnston until 7 Apr. '62. After Shiloh he asked to be relieved of the entire cavalry command to lead a brigade in Breckinridge's division, and in Oct. '62 was sent to the Trans-Miss. to lead the Tex. Brig. near Little Rock. He commanded his brigade in 1863 at Milliken's Bend during the Vicksburg siege and in 1864 commanded troops and fortifications on Galveston Island. After the war he was a hardware merchant in Ky.

HAWES, Richard. C.S.A. Gov. of Kentucky. 1797–1877. Va. After graduating from Transylvania Univ., he practiced law and served in the state legislature and US Congress. In the fall of 1861 he entered the Confederate Army as Maj. and served as brigade commissary until chosen provisional Gov. in May '62 to succeed Johnson. Inaugurated at Frankfort on 4 Oct. of that year, he held the position throughout the war and was elected a judge in 1866.

HAWKES, George Perkins. Union officer. Mass. Capt. 21st Mass. 19 July '61; Maj. 2 June '62; Lt. Col. 18 Dec. '62; Bvt. B.G. USV (war service); discharged 3 July '64.

HAWKINS, Isaac R. Union officer. Lt. Col. 7th Tenn. Cav. Bvt. B.G. USV 13 Mar. '64 (Phisterer). Not in Heitman.

HAWKINS, John Parker. Union gen. 1830–1914. Ind. USMA 1852 (40/43); Inf. Serving on the frontier and in garrison duty before the war, he was named Brig. Q.M. Defenses of Washington 19 June–3 Aug. '61 and promoted Capt. Comsy. of Subsist. on the latter date. He was then Asst. Comsy. at St. Louis, Chief Comsy. of Dist. of Southwest Mo., Inspecting Comsy. of Dept. of Mo. (16 Dec. '61–7 Mar. '62), and of Dist. of West Tenn. (to 29 Oct. '62). He was named Chief Comsy. of the XIII Corps and Lt. Col. Assigned on

1 Nov. On 23 Dec. he transferred to the same post with the Army of the Tenn., holding this until 13 Apr. '63 when he was promoted B.G. USV. He commanded a brigade of colored troops and the Dist. of Northeast Louisiana (17 Aug. '63–7 Feb. '64); 1st Div. USCT Dist. West Fla., Gulf (9 Feb. '64–Aug. '65) during the Mobile campaign. He held several other positions of command in '65 and '66, being breveted for Mobile and war service 5 times including B.G. and Maj. Gen. USA and Maj. Gen. USV. He continued in the R.A. until retired in 1894 as Brig. Gen. Comsy. Gen.

HAWKINS, Rush Christopher. Union officer. 1831–1920. Vt. Col. 9th N.Y. 4 May '61; Bvt. B.G. USV (war service); mustered out 20 May '63. Commanded 4th Brig., Dept. of N.C.; 1, 3, IX; 1, 2, VII. He served in the Mexican War while still a minor and at the beginning of the Civil War organized "Hawkins' Zouaves," which became the 9th N.Y. He married Annmary Brown, the granddaughter of Nicholas Brown of Brown Univ. in R.I., and after making a fortune in investments and real estate, they collected incunabula. "Of the 238 towns into which printing was introduced during the fifteenth century, the British Museum in 1909 had specimens from 166 of them, and Hawkins, 141. Of the 111 towns in which printing was known between 1450 and 1480, 94 were represented at the Museum and 84 in the Hawkins collection. Although a born fighter and usually involved in some controversy, the General was a very earnest student of his cherished books" (D.A.B.).

HAWLEY, Harriet W. F. (Mrs. Joseph R. HAWLEY) Union Army nurse. Conn. After her husband entered the Union Army, she joined him in 1862 at Beaufort and began nursing. In Jan. '63 she went with him to Fla. and returned to S.C. (St. Helena Island) in Nov. of that year. When in Apr. '64 her husband's brigade in the X Corps joined Butler on the James, she went to a Washington hospital and continued there until Mar. '65, when she went to her husband's new command in Wilmington. There she took care of the Andersonville prisoners and refugees.

HAWLEY, Joseph Roswell. Union gen. 1826–1905. N.C. A lawyer and active Free-Soiler, he was one of the Republican party organizers in Conn. and also a newspaperman. Commissioned Capt. 1st Conn. 22 Apr. '61, he fought at 1st Bull Run, and was mustered out 31 July. He was named Lt. Col. 7th Conn. 17 Sept. '61, participated in the siege of Fort Pulaski, and, as Col. 20 June '62, led his troops at James Island and Pocotaligo and in the Fla. expedition. At Fort Wagner and Charleston he commanded 3, Morris Island, X (19 Sept.–19 Oct. '63) and then led US forces St. Helena, X (Dec. '63–5 Feb. '64). He commanded 2, 1st Dist. Fla., X (16–29 Feb. '64) at Olustee, and 3, 1, X, James (28 Apr.–2 May '64). At New Market, Drewry's Bluff, Deep Run, and Darbytown Road he commanded 2, 1, X (2 May–12 Sept. '64) and at intervals during the siege of Petersburg (12–20 Oct; 29 Oct.–4 Nov.; 18 Nov.–3 Dec. '64). Named B.G. USV 13 Sept. '64, he was sent to N.Y.C. with a picked brigade to keep peace during the November elections and also commanded 3d Div., X (20–29 Oct. '64). He returned to lead 2, 1, XXIV, Va. (3 Dec. '64–1 Jan. '65); 1st Div., XXIV (1 Jan.–2 Feb. '65) and Dist. Wilmington N.C., X, N.C. (1 Mar.–23 June '65). He then served as Gen. Terry's Chief of Staff and was mustered out in 1866, having been breveted Maj. Gen. USV 28 Sept. '65 for war service. In 1866–67 he was Republican Gov. of Conn. and was president of his party's national convention the next year. He was also US Congressman and Sen. for several terms.

HAWLEY, William. Union officer. N.Y. R.A. Capt. 3d Wis. 24 Apr. '61; Lt. Col. 14 Nov. '62; Col. 29 June '64; Bvt. B.G. USV 16 Mar. '65 (Ga. and S.C. campaign). Commanded 2, 1, XX. W.I.A. Cedar Mt. (Va.), Chancellorsville, and Resaca (Ga.). Died 1873.

HAW'S SHOP (ENON CHURCH), Va., 29 May '64. During movement to TOTOPOTOMOY CREEK, Gregg's cavalry made contact about a mile from Haw's Shop with Wickam's and Rosser's cavalry brigades, reinforced by the 5th and half of the 4th S.C. The latter were inexperienced troopers of Calbraith Butler's brigade that had just come up from S.C. Gregg's attacks were repulsed in a seven-hour action, fought mostly on foot in the dense woods. Custer's brigade (1, 1) arrived and the Confederates were driven back after delivering a volume of musket fire that led Federal reports to grossly overestimate their strength. The Federals reported 344 casualties. (This account follows *Lee's Lts.*, III, 499, which varies from Federal versions [e.g., Humphreys, 164] and puts the date at 29 instead of 28 May.) There was action at Haw's Shop, 2 and 3 June, during COLD HARBOR.

HAWTHORN, Alexander T. C.S.A. gen. 1835-99. Appt.-Ark. Commissioned Lt. Col. 6th Ark. in 1861, and promoted Col. the next spring, he led the regiment at Shiloh. During the Vicksburg campaign he fought at Helena under Holmes and was also at Fort Hindman. Appointed B.G. C.S.A. 18 Feb. '64, he led a brigade at Jenkins' Ferry (Ark.). After the war he was a businessman in Atlanta.

HAY, John. Author and statesman. 1838-1905. Ind. Lincoln's assistant private secretary (1860-65), he authored with John Nicolay the outstanding 10-volume *Abraham Lincoln: a History* (1890), after serving in various European legations and as Asst. Sec. of State in 1878. He was Ambassador to Great Britain in 1897 and served as Sec. of State for both McKinley and Roosevelt, being responsible for the Open-Door Policy in China in 1899 and providing for the construction of the Panama Canal by negotiating treaties with Colombia, England, and Panama.

HAYDEN, Julius. Union officer. N.Y. Appt.-Fla. Entering the R.A. in 1839, he served in the Mexican War (1 brevet, 1 wound) and was promoted Maj. 10th US Inf. Feb. '62. He retired in 1870 as Lt. Col. and was breveted for Chancellorsville and war service (B.G. USA).

HAYES, Edwin L. Union officer. N.Y. Capt. 44th Ill. 13 Sept. '61; Maj. 100th Ohio 26 Aug. '62; Lt. Col. 13 May '63; Col. 2 Jan. '65; Bvt. B.G. USV 12 Jan. '65.

HAYES, Joseph. Union gen. 1835-? Me. Graduating from Harvard in 1855, he was in business several years before being commissioned Maj. 18th Mass. 24 Aug. '61. He was promoted Lt. Col. 25 Aug. '62 and Col. 1 Mar. '63. His commands were 1, 2, VIII, Middle; 3, 1, V, Potomac (19 Nov. '63-3 Apr. '64); 1, 2, V, Potomac (3 Apr.-28 June '65). He was named B.G. USV 12 May '64 and breveted Maj. Gen. USV for Weldon R.R. Appleton's states that he was captured and imprisoned in Libby but does not give the date. He declined a R.A. commission and was mustered out 24 Aug. '65, after having served as US Commissioner of Supplies in the seceded states since Jan. of that year. He is credited with introducing the American system of hydraulic mining to Colombia in 1877.

HAYES, Philip Cornelius. Union officer. 1833-? Conn. Capt. 103d Ohio 16

July '62; Lt. Col. 18 Nov. '64; Bvt. B.G. USV (war service). A graduate of Oberlin Univ. and the Theological Sem., he was on the staff of Gen. Schofield. He later served as a Republican Congressman and wrote his regimental history.

HAYES, Rutherford Birchard. Union gen. and 19th president of the United States. 1822–93. Ohio. An early member of the Republican party and not an advocate of abolition, he did not, on the other hand, condone the extension of slavery into the West. Named Maj. 23d Ohio 27 June '61, he participated in the guerrilla fighting in western Va. and was promoted Lt. Col. 24 Oct. '61. He served under Frémont in the Valley, and was wounded in the arm at South Mountain, and was promoted Col. 24 Oct. '62. He commanded 1, 3, VIII, Middle Dept. (17 Mar.–26 June '63); 1st Brig., Scammon's division, W. Va. (28 June–Dec. '63); 1st, 3d Div., W. Va. (Dec. '63–Apr. '64); and 1st Brig., 2d Inf. Div., W. Va. (Apr.–19 Oct. '64), at Winchester and Cedar Creek, succeeding to division (19 Oct.–24 Dec. '64). He went back to 1st Brig., 2d Inf. Div. W. Va. (24 Dec. '64–Jan. '65), and then led 1st Brig., 1st Inf. Div., W. Va. (Jan.–25 Feb. '65) and division (25 Feb.–Apr. '65). He served in garrison until the end of the war and was breveted for Fishers Hill and Cedar Creek (Maj. Gen. USV). Resigning 8 June '65, he was president until 1880 after winning the disputed election in 1876 against Tilden.

"HAY FOOT, STRAW FOOT." Method used by drill sergeants to designate left and right in teaching raw recruits to drill.

HAYMAN, Samuel Brinkle. Union officer. 1820–95. Pa. USMA 1842 (51/56); Inf. Capt. 7th US Inf. 3 Mar. '55; Col. 37th N.Y. 28 Sept. '61; mus-tered out USV 22 June '63; Maj. 10th US Inf. 21 Jan. '63; Bvt. B.G. USV. Brevets for Chancellorsville, Wilderness, Fair Oaks (Va.). W.I.A. Wilderness. Commanded 1, 1, III; 3, 1, III. During the Mexican War he participated in the assault and capture of Mexico City.

HAYNIE, Isham Nicolas. Union gen. 1824–68. Tenn. He practiced law, taking time out to fight in the Mexican War, and then served as state legislator and judge. Named Col. 48th Ill. 10 Nov. '61, he led his regiment at Forts Henry and Donelson, Shiloh, where he was severely wounded, and Corinth. He was promoted B.G. USV 29 Nov. '62 and, although this commission expired 4 Mar. '63, he commanded 1, 3, XVII, Tenn. from 25 Jan. to 23 Apr. '63. He was later Adj. Gen. of Ill.

HAYS, Alexander. Union gen. 1819–64. Pa. USMA 1844 (20/25); Inf. He served on frontier duty and in the Mexican War (1 brevet), resigning in 1848 for the gold rush and then back to Pa. in construction and engineering. He was named Capt. 16th US Inf. 14 May '61, Maj. 12th Pa. 25 Apr., and mustered out 5 Aug. '61. Commissioned Col. 63d Pa. 9 Oct. '61, he fought at Yorktown, Williamsburg, Fair Oaks, Peach Orchard, Glendale, and Malvern Hill. He also led his regiment at Bristoe Station (26 Aug. '62) and 2d Bull Run, where he was severely wounded. Named B.G. USV 29 Sept. '62, he commanded 3d Brig., Abercrombie's division, XXII, Washington (17–26 Apr. and 6 May–26 June '63) and 3d Brig., Casey's division, XXII, Washington (2 Feb.–17 Apr. '63). He led 3d Div., II (28 June–15 Aug. '63) at Gettysburg, Auburn, Bristoe Station (again), and Mine Run (6 Sept.–14 Dec. '63) and later (4 Jan.–10 Feb. '64). He was commanding 2, 3, II (25 Mar.–5 May '64) when K.I.A. at the Wilderness. He was breveted for Fair Oaks, Peach Orchard, Glendale,

Malvern Hill, Gettysburg, and Gettysburg–Peninsula–the Wilderness (Maj. Gen. USV 5 May '64).

HAYS, Harry Thompson. C.S.A. gen. 1820–76. Miss. Appt.-La. A New Orleans lawyer, he fought in the Mexican War and was active in Whig politics before the Civil War. Commissioned Col. 7th La., he fought at 1st Bull Run and served in Taylor's (8th, or Louisiana) brigade during Jackson's Valley campaign. Wounded at Port Republic, he did not return to the field until Antietam, when he was named B.G. C.S.A. 25 July '62 and succeeded Taylor as commander of the LOUISIANA BRIGADE. He led this force at Fredericksburg, Chancellorsville, Gettysburg, the Wilderness, and Spotsylvania, where he was severely wounded. In the fall of that year he had recovered enough to take over duties in La. and was named Maj. Gen. by Kirby Smith on 10 May '65. After the war he and Daniel Adams practiced law together. He also served as sheriff of New Orleans Parish for a year before being removed.

HAYS, William. Union gen. 1819–75. Va. USMA 1840 (18/42); Arty. He fought in the Mexican War (2 brevets, 1 wound), the Seminole War, and later served on the frontier. Named Lt. Col. Add. A.D.C 25 Sept. '61, he commanded a brigade of flying artillery at Antietam and was promoted B.G. USV 29 Nov. '62. He led the right division of artillery reserve at Fredericksburg and 2, 3, II (12 Feb.–3 May '63) at Chancellorsville, where he was wounded and captured. He rejoined the Army of the Potomac for Gettysburg, leading the II Corps (3 July–16 Aug. '63). He was P.M. in N.Y.C. and then commanded 2d Div., II (25 Feb.–6 Apr. '65) at Petersburg and subsequent engagements. Breveted for the Peninsular campaign and war service (B.G., USA), he con-

tinued in the R.A., dying on active duty as Maj. 5th US Arty.

HAZARD, John Gardner. Union officer. R.I. 1st Lt. 1st R.I. Arty. 25 Aug. '61; Capt. 18 Aug. '62; Maj. 19 Apr. '64; mustered out 1 July '65; Col. 5th US Vet. Vols. 14 July '65; Bvt. B.G. USV 3 May '65. Brevets for Cold Harbor, war service. Died 1897.

HAZEN, William Babcock. Union gen. 1830–87. Vt. Appt.-Ohio USMA 1855 (28/34); Inf. After Indian fighting (1 wound, 1 brevet) he taught tactics at West Point 21 Feb.–18 Sept. '61. Commissioned Col. 41st Ohio 29 Oct. '61, after having been promoted 1st Lt. 1 Apr. and Capt. 14 May '61. During the operations in Ky. he commanded his regiment and the 19th Brig., Army of the Ohio (Dec. '61–Jan. '62). At Shiloh and on the advance upon Corinth he led 19th Brig., 4th Div. (3 Jan.–2 June '62) and also commanded these troops (10 July–29 Sept. '62) while supervising repairs on the Nashville & Decatur R.R., and as commanding officer of Murfreesboro. At Perryville he commanded the same brigade, now in the IV Corps (Sept.–Nov. '62) and was promoted B.G. USV 29 Nov. '62. He led 2d Brig., 2d Div., Left Wing, XIV, Cumberland (5 Nov. '62–9 Jan. '63) at Stones River and then commanded 2, 2, XXI (9 Jan.–3 Sept. and 13 Sept.–9 Oct. '63) at Chickamauga. In the battles around Chattanooga and at Missionary Ridge he commanded 2, 3, IV (10 Oct. '63–17 Mar. '64), also leading the brigade at Rocky Face Ridge, Resaca, Adairsville, Cassville, Pickett's Mills, Kenesaw Mountain, Chattahoochee, Peach Tree Creek, and Atlanta (17 Apr.–17 Aug. '64). He next commanded 2d Div., XV, Tenn. (17 Aug. '64–18 May '65) at Jonesboro, East Point, on the March to the Sea, and in the Carolinas. Maj. Gen USV 13 Dec. '64. From 23 May to 1 Aug. '65 he commanded the XV Corps. Continuing in the R.A., he was breveted for Chickamauga, Chattanooga, Atlanta, Fort McAllister (B.G. USA), and war service (Maj. Gen. USA), serving for a time on the frontier in Indian fighting. He was reprimanded by a court-martial for unduly criticizing a superior, but this did not harm his career, and he died on active duty as B.G. Chief Sig. Off. and head of the Weather Bureau (since 1880). He wrote extensively on military and historical subjects.

HEALY, Robert Wallace. Union officer. Ill. Capt. 58th Ill. 24 Dec. '61; Maj. 29 Oct. '64; Lt. Col. 10 Apr. '65; Col. 3 Oct. '65; Bvt. B.G. USV. Brevets for Mobile, war service.

HEATH, Francis Edward. Union officer. Me. 1st Lt. 3d Me. 4 June '61; Capt. 12 Sept. '61; Lt. Col. 19th Me. 26 Aug. '62; Col. 21 Feb. '63; Bvt. B.G. USV (war service); resigned 4 Nov. '63. Died 1897.

HEATH, Herman H. Union officer. N.Y. Commissioned Capt. 1st Iowa Cav. 24 Sept. '61, he was honorably discharged 28 Feb. '63 and named Maj. 7th Iowa Cav. 15 May of that year. Promoted Col. 29 May '65, he was honorably discharged in 1866 as Bvt. B.G. USV (war service) and Maj. Gen. USV (Indian fighting). He died 1874.

HEATH, Thomas Tinsley. Union officer. Ohio. Lt. Col. 5th Ohio Cav. 7 Oct. '61; Col. 11 Aug. '63; Bvt. B.G. USV 15 Dec. '64. Commanded 1st Brig., 1st Cav. Div.; XVI; 3, 3, Cav. Corps (Mil. Div. Miss.).

HÉBERT, Louis. C.S.A. gen. 1820–1901. La. USMA 1845 (3/41); Engrs. Resigning in 1847, he ran his plantation and was Col. in the state militia, state sen. and Chief Engr. of La. Commissioned Col. 3d La. in McCulloch's brigade, he fought at Wilson's Creek and was captured at Pea Ridge. Appointed

B.G. C.S.A. 26 May '62, he was exchanged to lead the 2d Brig. of Little's division in Price's Army in Northern Miss. He fought at Iuka, led Little's division temporarily, distinguished himself at Corinth, and fought at Vicksburg. In N.C. he was in charge of the heavy artillery in the Cape Fear Dept. and was Chief Engr. of the Dept. of N.C. when the war ended. Returning to La., he was an editor and teacher in the postwar period. Cousin of Paul O. Hébert.

HÉBERT, Paul Octave. C.S.A. gen. 1818–80. La. USMA 1840 (1/42); Engrs. He taught engineering at West Point and resigned five years later to become Chief Engr. of La., as was his cousin Louis Hébert some time later. Entering the R.A. for the Mexican War, he was Democratic Gov. of La. in 1852 and was commissioned B.G. C.S.A. 17 Aug. '61. He commanded the troops in La. in 1861 and then took over the Dept. of Tex. and the defenses of Galveston. During the Vicksburg campaign, when he was in command of the Sub-Dist. of Northern La., he fought at Milliken's Bend. After Lee's surrender Kirby Smith turned command of the Trans-Miss. Dept. over to Magruder, who then handed it to Hébert, who surrendered it to Granger. He resumed his business in La. and held several appointive posts as engineer.

HECKMAN, Charles Adam. Union gen. 1822–96. Pa. He served in the Mexican War as a young man and was commissioned Lt. Col. 9th N.J. on 8 Oct. '61. He was promoted Col. 10 Feb. '62 and commanded during Burnside's N.C. Expedition 1, 3, N.C. (2 Apr.–6 July '62), being wounded at New Bern 14 Mar. and Young's Cross Roads 26 July. He was named B.G. USV 29 Nov. '62 and led Heckman's brigade, N.C. (10 Dec. '62–2 Jan. '63); 1, 2, XVIII, N.C. (2 Jan.–6 Mar. and 16 Apr.–10 May '63); 2d Div., XVIII,

N.C. (6 Mar.–16 Apr. '63). Dyer lists another command of his (2d Div. St. Helena Island, XVIII, South) for these same dates. He also commanded Dist. Beaufort (N.C.), XVIII, N.C. (2–25 May and 29 May–21 July '63); Defenses New Bern, Va. and N.C. (to 14 Aug. '63); Sub-Dist. Beaufort (N.C.), XVIII, Va. and N.C. (to 11 Oct. '63); Newport News Va., Va. and N.C. (18 Oct. '63–14 Jan. '64); Getty's division at Norfolk and Portsmouth, Va. and N.C. (14 Jan.–28 Apr. '64). He was wounded at Port Walthall (Va.) 7 May '64 and captured at Drewry's Bluff (Va.) 16 May '64 after his brigade had repulsed five attacks. During his imprisonment he was placed under the Union guns bombarding Charleston. Upon his release he commanded the XVIII Corps (29 Sept.–1 Oct. '64) at New Market Heights; 3d Div., XXV, Va. (3–30 Dec. '64); and XXV Corps, Va. (1 Jan.–2 Feb. '65). He resigned 25 May '65.

HEDRICK, John Morrow. Union officer. Ind. 1st Lt. 15th Iowa 1 Nov. '61; Capt. 14 Mar. '62; Maj. 1 Mar. '63; Lt. Col. 3 June '63; Col. 22 Mar. '65; Bvt. B.G. USV (war service). Died 1886.

HEINE, Wilhelm. Union officer. Germany. N.Y. Capt. 1st Md. 9 Dec. '61; resigned 7 Dec. '62; Col. 103d N.Y. 15 May '63; Bvt. B.G. USV (war service). Commanded 2, Forces Folly Island, X; 3, Defenses South of the Potomac, XXII. In his native Dresden he had been a painter and writer who fled in 1848 after engaging in street fighting during the revolution. He became a sailor and later a capable engineer in America and after the war was US Consul Gen. in Paris. Died 1885.

HEINRICHS, Gustav. Union officer. Germany. 1st Lt. Adj. 3d Mo. 4 May '61; mustered out 22 Aug. '61; Maj. 5th Mo. Cav. 1 Nov. '61; transferred to 4th Mo. Cav. 15 Nov. '62; Lt. Col. 41st

Mo. 1 Nov. '64; Bvt. B.G. USV (war service).

HEINTZELMAN, Samuel Peter. Union gen. 1805–80. Pa. USMA 1826 (17/41); Inf. Serving on the frontier, he won a brevet in the Mexican War and in Indian fighting. Named Col. 17th US Inf. and B.G. USV on 17 May '61. He captured Alexandria (Va.) on 24 May and was wounded at 1st Bull Run, where he commanded 3d Div. (28 May–17 Aug. '61). He commanded Heintzelman's brigade, Div. of the Potomac (Aug.–Oct. '61); and Heintzelman's division, Army Potomac (3 Oct. '61–13 Mar. '62). During the Peninsular campaign he commanded III Corps, Potomac (13 Mar.–30 Oct. '62) at Yorktown, Williamsburg, Fair Oaks, Savage's Station, Glendale, Malvern Hill, 2d Bull Run, and Chantilly. He was named Maj. Gen. USV 5 May '62. In the defenses of Washington he commanded the Mil. Dist. Washington (27 Oct. '62–2 Feb. '63) and the XXII Corps and the Dept. of Washington (D.C.) (2 Feb.–13 Oct. '63). From 12 Jan. until 1 Oct. '64 he commanded the Northern Dept. and then served on courts-martial until the end of the war. He was breveted for Fair Oaks (B.G. USA 31 May '62) and Williamsburg (Maj. Gen. USA), and continued in the R.A., being retired as Maj. Gen. USA in 1869. A man who lacked the essential qualities of leadership as well as one who greatly magnified the difficulties before him, he was personally brave and gallant but without initiative. D.A.B. describes him as "stern, rather unkempt [in] appearance, with full beard and long, thin hair."

HELENA, Ark. Federal troops of Curtis's Army of the Southwest advanced from Jacksonport, Ark., and captured Helena 12 July '62. In June '63 B. M. Prentiss was left at Helena with 4,000 after the other troops had been withdrawn for the Vicksburg campaign. T. H. Holmes, C. G. Confed. Dist. of Ark., had failed to comply with his orders to send reinforcements to Pemberton at Vicksburg. As a diversion to assist Pemberton, he decided to attack Helena with 6,500 men in the infantry division of Sterling Price and the cavalry division of Marmaduke. At 3 A.M. on 4 July (the day Pemberton surrendered), Price started a mismanaged attack that cost him 400 killed and 1,200 captured (Prentiss's report). The Federals, who had repulsed the assault by 10:30 A.M., lost 239 (*ibid.*).

HELM, Benjamin Hardin. C.S.A. gen. 1830–63. Ky. USMA 1851 (9/42); Dragoons. He resigned the next year to be a Ky. lawyer and legislator and in 1856 married Mrs. Lincoln's half sister. Although their politics varied widely, the two men were close friends. In Apr. '61 Lincoln offered Helm the job of army paymaster. Helm declined, organized the 1st Ky. Cav., and was made its Col. on 19 Oct. '61. He was promoted B.G. C.S.A. 14 Mar. '62 and commanded a brigade under Breckinridge at Vicksburg. Remaining there until the summer of 1862, he went to La. and was seriously injured by a fall from his horse just before the battle of Baton Rouge. He continued on duty in the Dept. of the Gulf until Jan. '63, when he took over Hanson's brigade under Breckinridge and led it in the Tullahoma campaign and at Chickamauga. He was mortally wounded there 20 Sept. '63 and died the same day. A statue was erected to him on the spot where he fell.

HENDERSON, Robert Miller. Union officer. 1827–? Pa. Capt. 7th Pa. Res. 21 Apr. '61; Lt. Col. 4 July '62; Bvt. B.G. USV. Brevets for Charles City Cross Roads (Va.), 2d Bull Run. W.I.A. Charles City Cross Roads. Resigned 30 Apr. '63. Later active as a lawyer and jurist.

HENDERSON, Thomas Jefferson. Union officer. 1824–? Tenn. Col. 112th Ill. 22 Sept. '62; Bvt. B.G. USV 30 Nov. '64 (Ga. and Tenn. campaigns; Franklin, Tenn.). Commanded 2, 1, Cav. Corps; 3, 3, XXIII (Ohio and N.C.). After the war he was a Republican Congressman from Illinois.

HENDERSON'S HILL (Bayou Rapides), La., 21 Mar. '64. RED RIVER CAMPAIGN.

HENDERSON'S MILL, Tenn., 11 Oct. '63. Skirmish following J. S. Williams's retreat from BLUE SPRINGS.

HENDRICKSON, John. Union officer. c. 1831–1902. N.J. 1st Lt. 83d N.Y. 27 May '61; Capt. 1 July '61; Maj. 1 Nov. '62; Lt. Col. 1 Jan. '63; Col. 18 Jan. '63; mustered out 1 Aug. '63; Maj. Vet. Res. Corps 28 Aug. '63; Col. 5 Oct. '63; Bvt. B.G. USV (war service). W.I.A. Fredericksburg, losing right leg above the knee.

HENNESSY, John A. Union officer. New Brunswick. 2d Lt. 52d Pa. 2 Dec. '61; Capt. 11 Oct. '62; Maj. 5 Feb. '65; Lt. Col. 3 June '65; Bvt. B.G. USV (war service). Died 1877.

HENRICO, CONFED. DEPT OF. John H. Winder took command in Dec. '61 and continued in this post until May '64. (It is a reasonable assumption that these dates coincide with the creation and discontinuance of the department.) The department encompassed the county of Henrico, in which Richmond is located, and was extended on 26 Mar. '62 to include Petersburg and vicinity. Winder's main responsibility was for the Federal prisoners at Belle Isle and Libby, although he was also P.M.G. of the Confederacy and P.M. of Richmond. See also RICHMOND, Confed. Dept. and Defenses of; and WINDER, John H.

HENRICO, Va., 25 June '62. See OAK GROVE.

HENRY, Guy Vernor. Union officer. c. 1838–99. Indian Territory. N.Y. USMA May 1861 (27/45); Arty. 2d Lt. 1st US Arty. 6 May '61; 1st Lt. 14 May '61; Col. 40th Mass. 9 Nov. '63; Bvt. B.G. USV 28 Oct. '64. Brevets for Pocotaligo River (S.C.), Olustee (Fla.), Petersburg (2), war service. Medal of Honor 5 Dec. '93 for Cold Harbor 1 June '64 where leading brigade in charge he had two horses shot from under him. He was breveted B.G. USA in 1890 for Rosebud Creek (Mont.) against Indians. During the Spanish-American War he commanded a division. At his death in 1899 he was a Maj. Gen. USV and B.G. USA (full rank). He wrote *Military Record of Civilian Appointments in the United States Army* (to supplement Cullum's data on USMA graduates), and other military works.

HENRY, William Wirt. Union officer. Vt. 1st Lt. 2d Vt. 20 June '61; resigned 5 Nov. '61; Maj. 10th Vt. 1 Sept. '62; Lt. Col. 3 Nov. '62; Col. 6 June '64; Bvt. B.G. USV 7 Mar. '65. Medal of Honor 21 Dec. '92 for Cedar Creek (Va.) 19 Oct. '64. Resigned 17 Dec. '64.

HENRY AND DONELSON CAMPAIGN, Feb. '62.

Fort Henry, Tenn., 6 Feb. '62

As the first step in the strategic penetration of the South Grant received permission to attempt the capture of Fort Henry with the aid of naval forces under Flag Officer Foote. Grant and Foote had seen the possibilities of using major rivers as lines of operations, army and naval forces working together. Foote had undertaken the construction of a number of river boats designed specifically for this type of joint operation. Seizure of Forts Henry and Donelson would open routes of invasion along

the Tennessee and Cumberland; furthermore, it would "turn" the Confederates under A. S. Johnston from their position in Kentucky (Bowling Green).

Fort Henry was a closed fieldwork mounting 17 guns, built in low ground near the edge of the Tennessee River. Immediately behind it was an entrenched camp on a high plateau. The works were not completed, and on the day of the attack the river fort was partially flooded. Brig. Gen. Lloyd Tilghman commanded the Confederate garrison of about 100 artillerymen after sending the rest of the garrison to Fort Donelson. Fort Heiman, on the west bank, was on high ground protecting Fort Henry, but had not been finished either.

Grant's force of 15,000 men was organized into a division of three brigades under Brig. Gen. C. F. Smith and a division of two brigades under Brig. Gen. McClernand. Foote's naval force consisted of three unarmed gunboats and four ironclad river gunboats. The latter mounted 12 guns, each of which was more powerful than those of the enemy's shore batteries.

Tilghman surrendered 80 surviving artillerymen of the river fort and 16 patients on a hospital boat after a short bombardment by the gunboats. Grant's force, which had been delayed by weather and muddy roads, was not needed for the intended assault. Foote's losses were 11 killed, 5 missing, and 31 injured; Grant's troops had no casualties. The Federals reported 5 Confederates killed, 11 wounded, and 63 missing (E.&B.).

A portion of the naval forces continued up the Tennessee, destroying the railroad bridge of the Memphis & Ohio and all Confederate gunboats as far as Florence, Ala. The entire gunboat fleet then returned to the Ohio River, en-

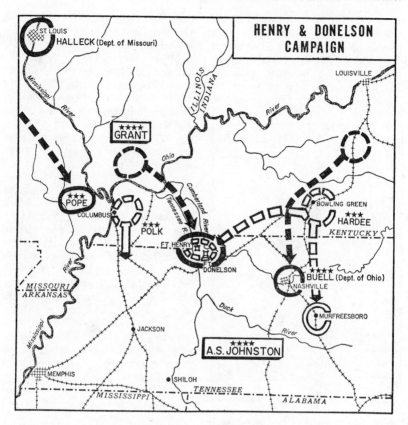

HENRY & DONELSON
CAMPAIGN

tered the Cumberland, and moved to support Grant's attack on Donelson.

Knowing that his plan would be disapproved by the cautious Halleck, Grant, according to popular legend, sent a message that he was proceeding overland toward Fort Donelson and then cut his telegraph communications to the rear. Although this story is entirely credible, it is nonetheless apocryphal.

On 7 Feb., immediately after the fall of Fort Henry, Johnston decided to withdraw the Army of Ky. south of the Cumberland. To protect this movement, Johnston believed it necessary to hold Donelson. Accordingly, the divi-

sions of Buckner and Floyd at Bowling Green were eventually (after considerable indecision on Johnston's part) ordered to Donelson to reinforce the three brigades of Tilghman's division (now commanded by Pillow). The Confederate garrison had orders to try to hold the fort until the Confederate forces in Ky. had crossed the Cumberland.

Fort Donelson (Dover), Tenn., 12–16 Feb. '62.

Grant's force camped at Fort Henry until the night of 11 Feb. It then started overland for Donelson and invested that place on the 12th. A third division, under Lew Wallace, was formed from a brigade sent from Buell's army and a number of separate regiments; it landed the night of 13 Feb. at a point on the Cumberland north of Donelson and joined Grant. That afternoon the weather turned from fair and mild to

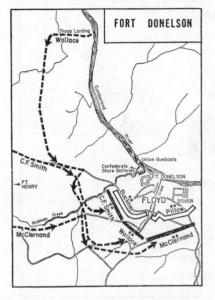

bitter cold. After dark the thermometer plunged to 10° and a roaring blizzard set in.

Foote's gunboats arrived and were repulsed by the shore batteries on 14 Feb. Foote was severely wounded. Surrounded from the land side, Floyd called a council of war in which it was decided to attempt to break through on the south and retire up the river (east). Early 15 Feb. the Confederates attacked and by noon had opened a route of withdrawal toward Clarksville. But the inept Floyd "listened first to Buckner's timid counsel and then to Pillow's rash advice," writes Steele, "and ended by doing nothing that was right. At this crisis either one of two things would

have been right: to have gone ahead with the plan agreed upon and marched to Nashville by the road that was open; or to have thrown every man into the line and completed the victory so well begun," continues Steele. "Floyd did neither. Pillow had just noticed a movement of the enemy toward the breastworks on the right, Buckner's old place, now held by a single regiment. He ordered Buckner to return to the works and defend them. Buckner refused and went to Floyd. Floyd sustained him and went to Pillow. Then Floyd changed his mind and agreed with Pillow. He ended by ordering his whole victorious left wing to return to the trenches" (Steele, 159).

When Buckner tried to reoccupy his former positions opposite C. F. Smith he found that the latter had taken possession of them. Although Buckner was able to halth Smith's further advance, he could not recapture his old positions.

Grant, who had been absent conferring with Foote on the gunboats, returned to take personal command of the field. Late in the afternoon he reinforced his right wing with a brigade of Smith's division and moved forward on this front. Since Pillow had already started a retreat, the Federals advanced without resistance to their original lines.

Now invested by an enemy that outnumbered them almost two to one, the Confederates were in a hopeless situation. Floyd, who had been Buchanan's Sec. of War (1857–60) and feared execution as a traitor, passed command to Pillow. The latter passed the command immediately to Buckner (Horn, 95). Floyd and Pillow then escaped across the river, the former with about 3,000 of his Va. troops. Forrest, meanwhile, had gotten authority to take his cavalry out through the backwaters, and escaped with a considerable number of accompanying infantrymen.

Grant answered Buckner's request for surrender with his famous UNCONDITIONAL SURRENDER message, and on the 16th accepted surrender of the garrison.

Authorities disagree widely as to the numbers and losses at Fort Donelson. Livermore gives these figures:

	Union	Confederate
Engaged	27,000	21,000
Killed	500	
Wounded	2,108	
Killed or wounded		2,000
Missing	224	14,623
Total losses	2,832	16,623

Fox puts Confederate losses during the period 14–16 Feb. at 15,829, with 13,829 of these listed as missing. Horn, on the other hand, says Floyd's strength was "less than 15,000" and estimates that the number captured by the Federals was "probably somewhere near 7,000 or 8,000" (Horn, 97).

This Federal victory with raw troops heralded the rise of Grant to prominence. It also brought Forrest into the public eye for the first time. The strategic importance was considerable. Not only were the Confederates forced to abandon their foothold in Ky. and to give up a large portion of Tenn., but the stage was set for the splitting of the entire Confederacy by a drive down the line of the Mississippi to Vicksburg.

HENRY REPEATING RIFLE. The first magazine rifle used in quantity by the Union Army. The government bought 1,731 Henry rifles and 4,610,400 cartridges between 23 July '63 and 7 Nov. '65. Several states armed their troops with the weapon, bringing the total of the Henry rifles used during the war to an estimated 10,000 (Gluckman, 318). The distinctive feature of the Henry was a tubular magazine under the barrel that held 15 rim-fire copper cartridges of cal. .44 short. When the trigger guard lever was pulled down and pushed back into position again, the hammer was cocked, the empty shell ejected, and a new round loaded. Although the weapon had a number of imperfections, it became famous with the Confederates as "that damn Yankee rifle that can be loaded on Sunday and fired all week" (Gluckman; others credit the SPENCER with this reputation also). The arm and its improved cartridge were invented and patented by B. Tyler Henry, plant superintendent of Oliver Winchester's New Haven Arms Co. in 1860. To this day the Winchester firm stamps an H on all their rim-fire cartridges in Henry's honor.

HENSON, Josiah. Negro leader. 1789–1883. Negro leader thought by many to be the prototype of Uncle Tom in Harriet Beecher Stowe's *Uncle Tom's Cabin*. He escaped to Canada with his family and lectured on the Negro cause in England.

HERNDON, William Henry. Lincoln's junior law partner. 1818–91. His vigorous anti-slavery views influenced the president into taking strong action toward emancipation.

HEROLD, Davy. See LINCOLN'S ASSASSINATION.

HERRICK, Walter F. Union officer. N.Y. 1st Lt. Regt. Q.M. 43d Ohio 3 Sept. '61; Maj. 3 Sept. '61; Lt. Col. 22 Oct., '62; Bvt. B.G. USV (war service); discharged 9 Nov. '64. Died 1887.

HERRING, Charles Paine. Union officer. Pa. Maj. 118th Pa. 22 Aug. '62; Lt. Col. 1 Nov. '63; Bvt. B.G. USV. Brevets for Richmond, Hatcher's Run (Va.). Died 1889.

HERRON, Francis Jay. Union gen. 1837–1902. Pa. After the Univ. of Pittsburgh, he was a banker and active in the militia company, "Governor's Grays," which became the 1st Iowa (Capt. 14 May '61). He fought with them at Wilson's Creek and was commissioned Lt. Col. 9th Iowa 24 Sept. '61. Wounded and captured at Pea Ridge, he was named B.G. USV 16 July '62. At Prairie Grove he commanded 3d Div. Army Frontier, Mo. (12 Oct. '62–Feb. '63) and was appointed Maj. Gen. USV 29 Nov. '62. He then led the Army Frontier (30 Mar.–5 June '63) and Herron's division, XIII, Tenn. (11 June–28 July '63) at Vicksburg. He also commanded the 2d Div., XIII Corps, Tenn. (28 July–7 Aug. '63) and the same division in the Gulf (7 Aug.–28 Sept. '63 and 3 Jan.–11 June '64). Also in the Gulf he commanded U.S. Forces Tex. (1 May–9 June '64) and Dist. Port Hudson (6 Aug.–3 Oct. '64 and 9 Feb.–July '65). In 1893 he was given the Medal of Honor for Pea Ridge. Resigning 7 June '65, he was a lawyer, and active in Reconstruction politics in the South and manufacturing in N.Y.C.

HETH, Henry (heath). C.S.A. gen. 1825–99. Va. USMA 1847 (38/38); Inf. Having refused an appointment to Annapolis, he served in the Mexican War, in the West in Indian fighting, and in garrison, when he resigned 25 Apr. '61 as Capt. Commissioned Capt. C.S.A. shortly after that, he was promoted through the grades to Col. in 1861 and in the fall organized Floyd's command for the W. Va. campaign. Appointed B.G. C.S.A. 6 Jan. '62, he commanded the military district in the vicinity of Lewisburg (Va.) and in May fought Frémont and Crook. Assigned to Kirby Smith by Davis, he was post and division commander in Bragg's army during the Ky. expedition and later commanded the Dept. of Eastern Tenn. Transferring to the Army of Northern Va. in Jan. '63 at Lee's request, he took over a brigade under A. P. Hill and

succeeded him at Chancellorsville. He was promoted Maj. Gen. 24 May '63, and commanded a division in the Gettysburg campaign. His skirmishers unexpectedly engaged the enemy 1 July to precipitate the battle of Gettysburg. Within 23 minutes his division was reduced to half strength and Heth himself was wounded. On 3 July, his division, now under Pettigrew, took part in "Pickett's Charge." He continued to command this unit for the rest of the war, fighting at the Wilderness, Spotsylvania, the Petersburg siege, and on the retreat to Appomattox. After the war he was in the insurance business and later served the government as a surveyor and in the Office of Indian Affairs.

HICKENLOOPER, Andrew. Union officer. 1837–1900. Ohio. Capt. 5th Ohio Btry. 31 Aug. '61; Lt. Col. Asst. I.G. Assigned 14 Sept. '64–13 May '65; Bvt. B.G. USV (war service). Commanded 3, 4, XVII. After Shiloh and Iuka he was Div. Comdr. of Arty., appointed by Gen. McKean. On 26 Oct. '62 he was on McPherson's staff as Chief of Ordnance and Artillery, then he was XVII Corps's Chief Engr., in charge of Vicksburg siege operations. He won a gold medal from the Corps's Board of Honor when that city fell. He was also highly praised for his cotton-bale bridge over the Big Black River for the pursuit of Pemberton. He was Judge Advocate for the Army of the Tenn. and later Chief of Arty. for the Dept. and Army of the Tenn. Howard succeeded McPherson on the latter's death and retained Hickenlooper as his Judge Advocate and Asst. Chief of Arty. He also served as Asst. I.G. for the XVII Corps. His B.G. brevet was awarded on the recommendations of Howard, Sherman, and Grant. Hickenlooper was Lt. Gov. of Ohio in 1879 and was prominent in public utilities.

He wrote *Battle of Shiloh* (1903) and several books on gas and lights.

HICKORY HILL. Wickham family plantation in Hanover County, Va., where their son-in-law Rooney Lee was captured 26 June '63 while convalescing after his wound at Brandy Station. Members of the Lee family stayed there throughout the war.

HICKS, Thomas Holliday. Gov. of Md. 1798–1865. Md. From his election as sheriff at the age of 26 until his death 41 years later, he almost continuously held public office. At first a Democrat, he became a Whig and served as such in the state General Assembly. He was, however, elected Gov. on the American party platform in 1857. Credited with keeping Md. in the Union, he accomplished this by delaying any official action while the state was split on the issue of secession. By the time a session of the legislature was called there were so many Union troops in Md. that any course other than loyalty was impossible. When his term expired in 1862, he was appointed to an unexpired Sen. term, was elected to this in 1864, and died in office. He was offered the rank of B.G. USV 27 July '62 but declined.

HIGGINS, Edward. C.S.A. gen. Appt.-La. Entering the navy in 1836 as a Lt., he commanded an ocean steamer 1844–48, and resigned to enter the merchant marine. When war came, he was commissioned Capt. 1st La. Arty. in Apr. '61 and was A.D.C. to Twiggs at New Orleans. In Feb. '62 he was named Lt. Col. 22d La. and commanded Forts Jackson and St. Philip when Farragut attacked New Orleans. Captured and exchanged, he was named Col., and led the 22d La. Arty. at Snyder's Mill (Dec. '62). In early 1863 he commanded the heavy artillery river batteries at Vicksburg. He was again cap-

tured and exchanged. Appointed B.G. C.S.A., 29 Oct. '63, he was in command of posts and batteries around Mobile. He died in 1875.

HIGH BRIDGE, Va., 6 Apr. '65. (APPOMATTOX CAMPAIGN) While II and VI Corps were engaged in the battles of SAYLER'S CREEK, Ord's Army of the James advanced on a parallel route to the south toward Burke's Junction. In response to Grant's order to burn the bridges on Lee's line of retreat at Farmville and High Bridge, Ord formed a task force of the 54th Pa., 123d Ohio (500 total), and his headquarters cavalry, the 4th Mass. (80 sabers; troops I, L, and M, under Col. Francis Washburn). Theodore Read, Ord's Chief of Staff, commanded the force (Freeman says the force must have exceeded 800 or 900. *Lee's Lts.,* III, 708n.).

After leaving Burkeville at 4 A.M., Read's infantry made contact shortly before noon about two miles from High Bridge with some dismounted troops of Rosser. The latter attacked, but were then driven back by Federal cavalry. Rosser, who had been surprised, rallied his troopers in a wood and launched an attack that overpowered the Federals. The infantry surrendered after little resistance. About 780 Federals were captured, Read was killed, Washburn mortally wounded, and all other Federal cavalry officers killed (Humphreys). Confederate Gen. Dearing, Col. Reuben B. Boston (5th Va. Cav.), and Maj. James W. Thompson (Horse Arty.), were killed, and Rosser was lightly wounded.

High Bridge is so called because it is built on 60-foot piers across the narrow river and the long northern approach over low ground. It was partially destroyed the next day during the action of FARMVILLE. (See photo in Miller, III, 311).

HIGH BRIDGE, Va., 7 Apr. '65. See FARMVILLE AND HIGH BRIDGE, same date.

"HIGH TIDE OF THE CONFEDERACY." Poetic term for the limit of the Confederate advance on the third day at Gettysburg ("Pickett's Charge").

HILL, Adams Sherman. WAR CORRESPONDENT. 1833–1910. Mass. After graduating from Harvard College and Law School, he became the N.Y. *Tribune*'s correspondent. He fled from Blackburns's Ford in a panic. However, he took over the Washington bureau of the paper, succeeding WILKESON, and ran it with precision and energy. He resigned in Dec. '63, unable to cope with Greeley's ever-changing policies, and set up with VILLARD and Horace White of the Chicago *Tribune* the Independent News Room Service in Washington. This venture was not successful, in the face of the powerful A.P., and soon collapsed. However, he continued in newspaper work until 1872 when he joined the faculty of Harvard and in time became chairman of the English department.

HILL, Ambrose Powell. C.S.A. gen. 1825–65. Va. USMA 1847 (15/38); Arty. He served in the Mexican War, in garrison, and in the Seminole wars and on the frontier before resigning 1 Mar. '61 as 1st Lt. Commissioned Col. 13th Va., he served in W. Va. and was in the reserve at 1st Bull Run. Stationed in northern Virginia during the winter of 1861–62, he was appointed B.G. C.S.A. 26 Feb. '62 and given a brigade. He fought at Williamsburg before being promoted Maj. Gen. 26 May and leading his division at Mechanicsville, Gaines's Mill and Frayser's Farm. Called "Hill's Light Division" for its speed in marching, this unit was sent to Jackson after Hill quarreled with Longstreet, and served at Cedar Mountain, 2d Bull Run, Harpers Ferry, ANTIETAM, and Fredericksburg. At Chancellorsville he marched with Jackson and succeeded him until wounded himself. Named Lt. Gen. 23 May '63, he took command of the newly-created III CORPS, leading it through the Gettysburg and Wilderness campaigns. As a corps commander he did not live up to expectations. Freeman puts it this way: "He does not fail beyond excuse or explanation; he does not succeed.... It may be because of ill health or a sense of larger, overburdening responsibility" (*Lee's Lts.*, III, xxix). Absent on sick leave during the period 8–21 May '64, he rejoined his corps for North Anna, Cold Harbor, and the Petersburg campaign. In the latter he rose to his greatest heights as a corps commander. In late Mar. '65 he was again away on sick leave but returned for the final defense of Petersburg, in which he was killed 2 Apr. Freeman in D.A.B. says he was "genial, approachable, and affectionate in private life, he was restless and impetuous in action." His wife was the sister of John H. MORGAN.

HILL, Benjamin Harvey. Statesman. 1823–82. Ga. An opponent of secession he nonetheless signed the Ordinance of Secession for Ga. and served as Sen. in the Confederate Congresses in 1861–65. A member of the Know-Nothing party and a prominent Georgia lawyer, he had favored the Compromise of 1850. After the war he was elected to the US House of Representatives (1875–77) and the US Senate (1877–82).

HILL, Benjamin J. C S A. gen. ?–1880. Appt.-Tenn. Commissioned Col. 35th Tenn. in Sept. '61, he was named to command the 5th Tenn. in the spring of 1862, leading it at Shiloh. He commanded Cleburne's brigade at Richmond (Ky.) and returned to lead his regiment at Stones River. At Chickamauga he commanded the 35th Tenn., and led this regiment and the 48th Tenn. at Missionary Ridge. In 1863–64 he was general Provost-Marshal of the Army of Tenn. and in the Atlanta campaign led the 35th and 48th Tenn. as well. In Hood's dash to Tenn. he commanded a brigade and was appointed B.G. C.S.A. 30 Nov. '64.

HILL, Bennett H. Union officer. c. 1817–86. D.C. USMA 1837 (21/50); Arty. He fought in the Seminole wars and the Mexican War, and served on the frontier where, in Feb. '61, he refused to surrender Fort Brown (Tex.) to a group of Confederates. Sent to Fort Jefferson and put in command of Key West until 1862, he was promoted Maj. 2d US Arty. 28 Aug. '61 and then superintendent W. Va's. volunteer recruiting service until 22 Apr. '63. He took over the same job in Mich. and held it for the remainder of the war. Promoted Lt. Col. 5th US Arty 1 Aug. '63, he continued in the R.A., and retired in 1870 as Bvt. B.G. USA (31 Jan. '65).

HILL, Charles W. Union Officer. Vt. Named B.G. Ohio State Volunteers in 1861, he was commissioned Col. 128th Ohio 25 Dec. '63 and mustered out in July '65. He was breveted B.G. and Maj. Gen. USV for war service and died in 1881.

HILL, Daniel Harvey. C.S.A. gen. 1821–89. S.C. USMA 1842 (28/56); Arty.-Inf. He served on the border, in garrison, and in the Mexican War (2 brevets) before resigning in 1849 to teach mathematics at Washington College (Lexington, Va.). His wife and Jackson's second wife were sisters, and in 1854 he went to Davidson to teach mathematics where his father-in-law had been president. Named superintendent of N.C. Mil. Inst. in 1859, he organized the state's first instruction camp and was commissioned Col. 1st

N.C. Fighting at BIG BETHEL, he was appointed B.G. C.S.A. 10 July '61 and Maj. Gen. 26 Mar. '62. Leading his division in the Peninsular campaign, he fought at Seven Pines, in the Seven Days' Battles, and at South Mountain and Antietam. Sent to N.C., he was recalled to defend Richmond during the Gettysburg campaign. He was promoted Lt. Gen. (from N.C.) 11 July '63. Sent to aid Bragg at Chickamauga, he recommended the latter's removal on grounds of incompetence, and Davis then refused to send his commission to the Senate for approval, relieving Hill instead. Hence, Harvey Hill served as Lt. Gen. from 19 July to 15 Oct. '63, while Congress was not in session, and he was never nominated for confirmation in that grade, reverting to Maj. Gen. in the fall. He was given a remnant of a division at Bentonville and surrendered with Johnston in N.C. After the war he ran a newspaper and magazine in N.C. before becoming president of the Univ. of Ark., 1877–84 and of what became Ga. Mil. Acad. in 1885–89. He wrote an algebra text and several religious tracts as well as two articles in *Battles and Leaders.*

"His individuality may be briefly illustrated by an official indorsement placed upon the application of a soldier to be transferred from the infantry to the band. 'Respectfully forwarded, disapproved. Shooters are more needed than tooters' " (Alexander, 367n.).

HILL, Jonathan Augustus. Union officer. Me. Capt. 11th Me. 2 Nov. '61; Maj. 6 June '64; Lt. Col. 25 June '64; Col. 5 Apr. '65; Bvt. B.G. USV 9 Apr. '65 (for "surrender of R. E. Lee").

HILL, Sylvester G. Union officer. R.I. Col. 35th Iowa 18 Sept. '62; Bvt. B.G. USV 15 Dec. '64 (Nashville, where K.I.A.). Commanded 3d Brig., 1st Div., Detach. Army Tenn.; 3, 1, XVI.

HILLIARD, Henry Washington. C.S.A. officer. 1808–92. N.C. A lawyer and Ala. legislator, he was an opponent of secession while sitting in the House of Representatives. Nonetheless following his state when she seceded, he led Hilliard's Legion under Braxton Bragg. Appleton's says that he was appointed B.G. C.S.A., but Wright does not confirm this. He was Minister to Brazil 1877–81 and had been Chargé d'Affaires in Belgium before the war.

HILLIS, David Burke. Union officer. Ind. Lt. Col. 17th Iowa 14 Mar. '62; Col. 4 Sept. '62; Bvt. B.G. USV (war service); resigned 30 May '63. Died 1900.

HILLSBORO, Ga., 31 July '64. See STONEMAN'S RAID, same date.

HILL'S (A.P.) CORPS. See III CORPS, Confed. A.N.V.

HILL'S (D.H.) CORPS. See II CORPS, Confed., Army of Miss. and of Tenn.

HILLYER, William Silliman. Union officer. 1831–74. Ky. Appt.-Mo. Capt. Vol. A.D.C. to Gen. Grant 8 Sept. '61; Col. Add. A.D.C. 3 May '62; Bvt. B.G. USV (war service); resigned 15 May '63. A friend of Grant in Mo., Hillyer recommended Grant for St. Louis county engineer. When he died, he was the last surviving member of Grant's original staff.

HILTON HEAD, S.C., 7 Nov. '61. Du Pont's naval action at PORT ROYAL SOUND, same date.

HINDMAN, Thomas Carmichael. C.S.A. gen. 1828–68. Tenn. Attended school in N.J., fought in Mexico, became a lawyer, and was elected to Congress. From a family of politicians, he "understood every angle of practical politics" (Monaghan, 251) and was an ardent secessionist. After being commissioned Col. he was appointed B.G. C.S.A. from Ark. on 28 Sept. '61. He commanded a division at Shiloh, and then headed the Trans-Miss. Dept. (31 May–30 July '62) until succeeded by Holmes. He was appointed Maj. Gen. on 18 Apr. '62. At PRAIRIE GROVE, Ark., 7 Dec. '62, he was unsuccessful in checking Curtis's advance. Asking for transfer, he commanded a division in Polk's corps and fought at Chickamauga, Chattanooga, and received an eye wound in the Atlanta campaign that disqualified him for further field service. After the war he was a coffee grower in Mexico before returning to Ark. Becoming involved in Reconstruction politics, he was shot and killed on 28 Sept. '68. "He was a dapper little man, five feet one inch tall, who dressed in tight-fitting clothes, ruffled shirts, and patent-leather boots. Lamed in an accident, he wore one boot heel higher than the other, . . ." (ibid.).

HINKS, Edward Ward. Union gen. 1830–94. Me. R.A. A printer and legislator, he was named 2d Lt. 2d US Cav. 26 Apr. '61, resigning 4 June '61. He was commissioned Lt. Col. 8th Mass. 30 Apr. '61, Col. 16 May, and mustered out 1 Aug., being named Col. 19th Mass. two days later and B.G. USV 29 Nov. '62. During that time he fought in all the engagements from Balls Bluff to Antietam, where he was seriously wounded. He was on court-martial duty and in charge of the Camp Lookout (Md.) P.O.W. compound until Apr. '64. During the Petersburg siege he commanded Hinks's USCT Div. (20 Apr.–19 June '64) and 3d Div., XVIII (16 June–1 July '64). He was then in command of a draft rendezvous in N.Y. from Oct. '64 to Jan. '65 and served as mustering officer in N.Y.C. until the end of the war. Breveted for Antietam, Petersburg (B.G. USA), and war service (Maj. Gen. USV), he resigned 30 June '65, returned to the R.A. in 1866, and was retired as Col. in 1870.

Later he was in charge of soldiers' homes in Wash., Va., and Wis.

HITCHCOCK, Ethan Allen. Union gen. 1798–1870. Vt. USMA 1817. The grandson of Revolutionary hero Ethan Allen, he served in garrison and as tactics instructor and commandant of cadets at West Point before fighting in the Seminole War, serving on the frontier, participating in Indian fighting, and winning two brevets in the Mexican War, one as B.G. Resigning in 1855 as Col. 2d US Inf., he settled in St. Louis and engaged in writing and study. He twice refused the post of Gov. of Liberia. Commissioned Maj. Gen. USV 10 Feb. '62 by Scott, he served mainly on staff duty, although he was commissioner for the Exchange of War Prisoners (15 Nov. '62) and as Comsy. Gen. of Prisoners (3 Nov. '65). He was mustered out in 1867 and returned to his studies and writings on science, philosophy, and religion. In 1907, his manuscript, *Fifty Years in Camp and Field*, was published by his descendants.

HITCHCOCK, George Howard. Union officer. N.Y. Maj. 132d N.Y. 4 Oct. '62; Lt. Col. 12 Dec. '62; Bvt. B.G. USV 28 June '65 (war service).

HITZ, Ann. (Mrs. John Hitz.) Wife of the Swiss Consul. Switzerland. Mother Hitz, as she was called by the soldiers, was particularly active in caring for German-speaking Union soldiers. She and her husband made their Washington home into an aid society, and she was also engaged in visiting the wounded in the hospitals. That she could speak their native language was most important, as many of the soldiers spoke little or no English.

HOAX, 1864 PROCLAMATION. See Joseph HOWARD, Jr.

HOBART, Harrison Carroll. Union officer. Mass. Capt. 4th Wis. 2 July '61; Lt. Col. 21st Wis. 15 Oct. '62; Col. 1

Nov. '64; Bvt. B.G. USV 12 Jan. '65. Commanded 1, 1, XIV. Died 1902.

HOBSON, Edward Henry, Union gen. 1825–1901. Ky. He was in his father's business, fought in the Mexican War (1 brevet), and returned to commerce and banking. Named Col. 13th Ky. 1 Jan. '62, he fought in the center at Shiloh, where he was wounded and was promoted B.G. USV 29 Nov. '62. From 1 to 26 July '63 his command pursued Morgan for 900 miles through Ky., Ohio, and Ind., 25 days of skirmishing that culminated in the defeat of the raiders at BUFFINGTON ISLAND on the 19th and the capture of Morgan and the survivors at New Lisbon on the 26th. He commanded 1, 2, XXIII, Ohio (16–25 Apr. '64), and then again pursuing Morgan at Cynthiana (11 June) he was wounded and captured. There followed an interesting legal problem that is covered under PAROLE. He commanded 2, 2, XXIII, Ohio (18 June–11 Aug. '64) and, appointed Burnside's Chief of Cav. but prevented by ill health from taking it, was commander at Lexington (Ky.). He was mustered out 24 Aug. '65 and engaged in railroading, being also active in Republic politics. He died at a G.A.R. encampment.

HOBSON, William. Union officer. Me. Capt. 17th Me. 18 Aug. '62; Lt. Col. 18 Jan. '65; Bvt. B.G. USV 6 Apr. '65 (Amelia Springs, Va.). Commanded 1, 2, XXIII; 2, 2, XXIII. Died 1897.

HODGE, George B. C.S.A. gen. 1828–c. 77. Ky. USNA 1845. He resigned from the navy in 1851 to become a lawyer, Democratic leader, and legislator. Enlisting as private when the war came, he was elected to the C.S.A. Congress and alternated between the two positions. He was promoted Capt. and Acting Adj. Gen. in Breckinridge's division, and fought at Shiloh before being promoted Maj. 6 May '62. He was named Col. exactly a year later and was I.G. at Cumberland Gap. In eastern Tenn. he led Preston's cavalry and took part in Wheeler's raid in mid-Tenn. after Chickamauga. Appointed B.G. C.S.A. 20 Nov. '63, the Senate refused to confirm this appointment on 17 Feb. '64 and he was reappointed 4 Aug. '64. He commanded the Dist. of Southwest Miss. and Eastern La. for the remainder of the war. He returned to the law, the legislature, and politics.

HOFFMAN, Henry C. Union officer. N.Y. Col. 23d N.Y. 16 May '61; Bvt. B.G. USV (war service); mustered out 22 May '63. Died 1883.

HOFFMAN, William. Union officer. c. 1808–84. N.Y. USMA 1829 (18/46); Inf. He served on the frontier in Indian fighting, the Seminole War, and the Mexican War (2 brevets) before being captured when Twiggs surrendered Tex. to the Confederacy. Exchanged 27 Aug. '62 and promoted Col. 3d US Inf. 25 Apr. of that same year, he was Comsy. Gen. of Prisoners at Washington until 3 Nov. '65, and was breveted B.G. USA 7 Oct. '64 and Maj. Gen. USA 13 Mar. '65. He continued in the R.A. until 1870, when he retired.

HOFMANN, John William. Union officer. Pa. Capt. 23d Pa. 21 Apr. '61; mustered out 31 July '61; Lt. Col. 56th Pa. 1 Oct. '61; Col. 8 Jan. '63; Bvt. B.G. USV 1 Aug. '64 (war service). Commanded 2, 1, III; 2, 1, I; 2, 4, V; 3, 2, V; 3, 3, V. Died 1902.

HOGE, George Blaikie. Union officer. Pa. Capt. 25th Mo. 25 July '61; Col. 113th Ill. 1 Oct. '62; Bvt. B.G. USV (war service). Transferred to R.A. in 1865 and resigned 1874 as Capt. Commanded 2, 5th Dist. Memphis, X Corps; 1st Brig., Dist. Memphis. Captured at Lexington (Mo.) Sept. 1861. W.I.A. Shiloh and Vicksburg. Provost

Marshal XV Corps. Commanded at Corinth Oct. '63–Jan. '64. Died 1898.

HOGE, George Washington. Union officer. 1832–81. Ohio. 1st Lt. 126th Ohio 4 Sept. '62; Capt. 28 June '63; Col. 183d Ohio 18 Nov. '64; Bvt. B.G. USV (war service). W.I.A. 5 times. Commanded 3, 2, XXIII.

HOGE, Jane. (Mrs. A. H. Hoge.) SANITARY COMMISSION founder and administrator. Pa. With her friend Mary A. LIVERMORE, she helped organize and run the Chicago branch of the Commission. She made many lecture tours to raise money and supplies for the soldiers and then went to the front to supervise their distribution. She originated and organized the first Sanitary Fair in Chicago, making $80,000 in that city alone. Her lectures both in the Midwest and the East brought recognition and more funds to the Commission.

HOGG, Joseph Lewis. C.S.A. gen. ?–1862. Appt.-Tex. Commissioned Col. in '61, he was appointed B.G. C.S.A. 14 Feb. '62 and took command of a brigade after Shiloh. He died of fever 16 May '62. His son, James Stephen Hogg, was Gov. of Tex. 1890–94.

HOKE, Robert Frederick. C.S.A. gen. 1837–1912. N.C. After graduating from Ky. Mil. Inst., he entered his family's manufacturing business and was commissioned 2d Lt. 1st N.C. in 1861. As Maj. and Lt. Col. 33d N.C. he fought from Hanover Court House to 2d Bull Run and Antietam. He was promoted Col. 21st N.C. in Aug. '62. He commanded Trimble's brigade at Fredericksburg and was named B.G. C.S.A. 17 Jan. '63, having been actually appointed on 23 Apr. '63. Leading his unit at Chancellorsville, he was wounded and did not return to active duty until fall of 1863, when he was sent to the Piedmont section of the Carolinas to quell the outlawry and arrest deserters.

Early in 1864 he went to the tidewater section of N.C. to check possible Union sentiments by the show of military force and was promoted Maj. Gen. 20 Apr. of that year as a result of his brilliant action in capturing Plymouth and its garrison on that date. He figured prominently in bottling Ben Butler up in Bermuda Hundred, at Cold Harbor, and fought in the battles around Petersburg. Of his actions at this time Freeman says that, in spite of his superb record, as a Maj. Gen. he was unable to cooperate, and this, his only defect apparently, was enough to cancel his military virtues. He fought at Bentonville and surrendered with Johnston in N.C.

HOLABIRD, Samuel Beckley. Union officer. c. 1826–1907. Conn. USMA 1849 (31/43); Inf.-Q.M. He served on the frontier and at West Point as Adj. before being named Capt. Asst. Q.M. 13 May '61. He was Q.M. in Pa., and Md., acting in that position for Banks July–Aug. '62. Promoted first Maj. Add. A.D.C. 2 July and then Col. Add. A.D.C. 11 July '62, he was in Aug.–Sept. '62 Q.M. of the II Corps and of the Army of the Potomac Sept.–Nov. In Dec. '62 he became Chief Q.M. of the Dept. of the Gulf and continued in this job for the rest of the war. He received four brevets for war service, including that of B.G. USA, and continued in the R.A., retiring in 1890 as B.G. USA Q.M. Gen. In 1865 he translated Jomini's *Treatise on Grand Military Operations*.

HOLBROOK, Mellen Taft. Union officer. Mass. Capt. 173d N.Y. 11 Oct. '62; Lt. Col. 7 Jan. '65; Bvt. B.G. USV. Brevets for Pleasant Hill (La.), Cane River Crossing (La.).

"HOLD THE FORT." See ALLATOONA, Ga., 5 Oct. '64.

HOLLAWAY, Ephraim Samuel. Union officer. Ohio. 1st Lt. 41st Ohio 29 Oct. '61; Capt. 31 Oct. '62; Maj.

6 Dec. '64; Lt. Col. 28 Mar. '65; Col. 31 May '65; Bvt. B.G. USV (war service). Died 1895.

HOLLINS, George Nichols. CSN Commodore. 1799–1878. Md. A US naval officer during the War of 1812, he was captured at Bermuda and later served in the bombardment of Nicaragua in 1854. Resigning in 1861 as Capt. (since 1855), he joined the Confederate Navy only after evading Federal troops when his resignation was refused and he was branded an unloyal person. Upon reaching Montgomery he was named Commander and captured the *St. Nicholas* 29 June '61 on the Potomac. On 10 July '61 he was put in command of the defenses of the James and 21 days later took over the naval station at New Orleans. After defeating the Union blockade of the Mississippi in Oct. '61, he took command of the Confederate naval forces on the upper river as Commodore in Dec. '61. He assisted in the defense of the works at Columbus (Ky.) and returned to New Orleans in Apr. '62 when Farragut threatened. Before that city was captured he was assigned to the Court of Inquiry sitting on the *Virginia*'s destruction and continued to serve on boards for the rest of the war.

HOLLY SPRINGS, Miss., 20 Dec. '62. While Forrest's cavalry raided the railroad between Bolivar, Tenn., and Columbus, Ky., Van Dorn left Grenada with 3,500 mounted troops and surprised Grant's secondary base at Holly Springs. Many Federals of Col. R. C. Murphy's 8th Wis. were caught in their beds. Van Dorn paroled 1,500 men, destroyed $1,500,000 worth of supplies, and continued to Bolivar, attacking one small post after another. He then escaped to Grenada. These actions of Forrest and Van Dorn forced Grant to withdraw to La Grange and Grand Junction from Oxford, at which place he had concentrated to support Sherman's Chickasaw

Bluffs operation. Murphy was dismissed from the service.

HOLMAN, John H. Union officer. Me. 2d Lt. 4th Mo. Res. Corps 8 May '61; resigned 25 Jan. '63; Col. 1st US Col. Inf. 22 May '63; Bvt. B.G. USV (war service). Commanded African Brig., Forces Norfolk and Portsmouth; 1, 3, XVIII; 3d Div., XVIII; 3, 3, XXV; 3d Brig., Paine's division, Terry's Provisional Corps; 2, 3, X. Died 1883.

HOLMES, Oliver Wendell. Jurist. 1841–1935. Mass. After graduating from Harvard in 1861, he served with the Union Army at Antietam, Fredericksburg, etc., and returned to graduate from Harvard Law School in 1866.

HOLMES, Theophilus Hunter. C.S.A. gen. 1804–80. N.C. USMA 1829 (44/46); Inf. He served on the frontier, in the Seminole and Mexican wars (1 brevet), and in garrison before resigning 22 Apr. '61 as Maj. Returning to N.C., he helped organize and then commanded the Southern Dept. of Coastal Defense. His West Point classmate Jefferson Davis appointed him B.G. C.S.A. 5 June '61 and he commanded the reserve brigade at 1st Bull Run. Promoted Maj. Gen. 7 Oct. '61, he was sent to the eastern part of N.C., where he took over a division recruited for him and returned to Va., where he fought at Malvern Hill. Named commander of the Trans-Miss. Dept., he was promoted Lt. Gen. 10 Oct. '62. The elderly Holmes had at first declined this command and had accepted only at Davis's urging. He later "asked friend Jeff Davis to relieve him . . . and assign the post to his assistant, E. Kirby-Smith" (Monaghan, 278). After the action at HELENA 3 July '63, he was sent to N.C., taking charge of that state's reserves in 1864.

HOLT, Joseph. Union Judge Advocate Gen. 1807–94. Ky. A renowned lawyer and Democratic orator in Ky.

and Miss., he was Buchanan's Commissioner of Patents (1857), Postmaster Gen. (1859), and Sec. of War (1861). When Lincoln was inaugurated, he returned to Ky. to try to turn that state from a policy of neutrality. He then was named Col. and the first Judge Advocate Gen. 3 Sept. '62, holding the prerogative of certain civil powers of arrest and of holding persons in arrest without writ of *habeas corpus*. Promoted B.G. USV Judge Advocate Gen. 22 June '64 upon the establishment of the Bureau of Military Justice, he tried Fitz-John Porter as well as the assassination conspirators before Hunter's military commission. His popularity with the Radicals grew until a series of developments refuting some of his earlier military decisions brought the conservative element into power and forced him to stop dispensing his brand of justice. In line with this change in the temper of the country, he was severely criticized for obtaining Mrs. SURRATI's death warrant from Pres. Johnson by keeping the military commissioners' plea of clemency for her from him. He was breveted Maj. Gen. USV for faithful service and retired in 1875.

HOLT, Thomas. Union officer. England. Capt. 70th N.Y. 20 Apr. '61; Maj. 18 Oct. '61; Lt. Col. 1 Dec. '62; Bvt. B.G. USV (war service); mustered out 11 July '64. Died 1897.

HOLTEN, Marcellus John Wesley. Union officer. Ohio. 1st Lt. 59th Ohio 17 Oct. '61; mustered out 1 Nov. '64; Lt. Col. 195th Ohio 20 Mar. '65; Bvt. B.G. USV (war service).

HOLTZCLAW, James T. C.S.A. gen. 1833–93. Ga. He was appointed to West Point in the class of 1853 but did not enter on account of his brother's death. A lawyer then, he was commissioned Lt. in the Montgomery True Blues and sent to Pensacola in 1861. By Aug. of that year he was named Maj. in the 18th Ala. and fought at Shiloh, where he was supposedly mortally wounded in the right lung. Back in three months, he went in the fall of 1862 to Mobile in charge of a brigade and was then promoted Col. He led the 18th Ala. at Chickamauga (wounded) and commanded Clayton's brigade at Lookout Mountain and Missionary Ridge. During the Atlanta campaign he led his regiment and succeeded to a brigade in Clayton's division, being appointed B.G. C.S.A. 7 July '64. He also fought at Nashville and then went to Mobile where he was at Spanish Fort. He surrendered with Richard Taylor. After the war he returned to the law and was a Democratic leader.

HOMER, Winslow. Artist and WAR CORRESPONDENT. 1836–1910. Mass. Trained as a lithographer, he worked for a New York publishing house before covering the Civil War, on and off for eight months, for *Harper's Weekly*. He continued to gain mastery of his painting and by 1864, after several exhibits, was elected to the National Academy as an associate and was made an academician the next year. Principally known for his seascapes and his ability with oils and water colors, he soon ceased working for the press.

HONEY HILL (Grahamville), S.C., 30 Nov. '64. J. G. Foster sent J. P. Hatch from Hilton Head to Boyd's Neck with 5,500 men and 10 guns to secure a foothold for Sherman's forces that were approaching Savannah, and to cut off Confederate reinforcements from Savannah. About three miles south of Grahamville Station at Honey Hill, G. W. Smith with about 1,400 effectives of the Ga. militia repulsed Hatch's attacks. At dark Hatch withdrew to his boats, having lost 88 killed, 623 wounded, and 44 missing. Smith reported a loss of 8 killed and 42 wounded.

HOOD, John Bell. C.S.A. gen. 1831–79. Ky. USMA 1853 (44/52); Inf. He served in garrison, on the frontier, and was wounded in Indian fighting before resigning in Apr. '61 as 1st Lt. Commissioned in the same rank in the Confederate Army, he was sent to Yorktown where he commanded Magruder's cavalry force and was appointed B.G. C.S.A. 6 Mar. '62 (to rank from the 3d) from Tex. Given command of the "Texas Brigade," he led it at Gaines's Mill, 2d Bull Run, and Antietam before he was promoted Maj. Gen. 10 Oct. and given a division under Longstreet. He led this unit at Fredericksburg and was badly wounded at Gettysburg, recovering in time to command Longstreet's corps plus three divisions of the Army of Tenn. at Chickamauga, where he lost his right leg. Promoted Lt. Gen. 1 Feb. '64 to rank from the battle (20 Sept. '63), he commanded his corps during the Atlanta campaign. Succeeding Johnston 17 July '64, he was given the temporary rank of full Gen. (18 July '64–23 Jan. '65) and commanded the Army of Tenn. during the rest of the Atlanta campaign. Taking the offensive, he led his army in the FRANKLIN AND NASHVILLE CAMPAIGN. After the bloody failure of this counteroffensive, he was relieved at his own request and reverted to the rank of Lt. Gen. After trying to reach Kirby Smith in the Trans-Miss. Dept., he surrendered 31 May '65 at Natchez. He became a factor and commission merchant in New Orleans. He married in 1868, with Buckner as his best man, and had 11 children in 10 years. In business he was at first prosperous, but was then wiped out in the financial crisis resulting from the yellow-fever epidemic of 1878. He, his wife, and their eldest daughter died of the disease the next summer.

A blond, six-foot two-inch giant, with the sad eyes of a bloodhound and a rather quiet and reserved manner, "the Gallant Hood" was without peer as a combat leader at the brigade and division level. He loved to fight, and he knew how to make men follow him. "Hood's Brigade" retained a standard of combat proficiency throughout the war. The troops of "Hood's Division" were "man for man, perhaps, the best combat troops in the Army [of Northern Virginia]" (*Lee's Lts.*, II, xxviii). A crippled left arm from Gettysburg and nothing but a stump remaining of his right leg after Chickamauga did not dampen his ardor for combat; strapped to the saddle, he led the Army of Tenn. at Atlanta and in Tenn. in a series of disastrous but gallant offensives. As an administrator and strategist, however, he did not measure up to the task of commanding a corps and an army. Evidence that he was not overburdened with brains can be found in places other than his low academic standing at West Point. He had an allegiance to the Confederate cause, to Lee, and to Jeff Davis that was so strong as to obscure the defects of even the latter. On the other hand, he despised Joe Johnston. One ugly feature of an otherwise admirable personal character was the tendency to blame subordinates for his own failures (e.g., Hardee at Atlanta; Cheatham at Spring Hill).

HOOD'S CORPS. See II CORPS, Confed., A. of Miss. and of Tenn.

HOOD'S TEXAS BRIGADE. Although commanded for less than six months by the Ky.-born John B. Hood, the brigade was known throughout the rest of the war as "Hood's Texas Brigade." It was in the Army of Northern Va. from the Seven Days' Battles to Appomattox except for the time it served under Longstreet in the West (Chickamauga, Chattanooga, Knoxville).

Organized 12 Nov. '61 in Va. as the Texas Brigade under Col. Lewis T. Wigfall of the 1st Tex. Inf., it was composed of the 4th Tex., under John B. Hood, the 5th Tex., under J. J. Archer, and the 18th Ga. under W. T. Wofford (later S. Z. Ruff). When Wigfall was elected to the Confederate Senate, Hood was appointed B.G. and assigned command of the brigade on 3 Mar. '62. After the Seven Days' Battles the infantry companies of HAMPTON LEGION, commanded by Col. M. W. Gary, were attached to Hood's Brigade.

When Hood moved up to command the division he was succeeded by Col. Jerome B. Robertson (5th Tex.), who became a B.G. on 1 Nov. '62. The brigade was now composed of the regiments that formed it throughout the remainder of the war: the 1st, 4th, and 5th Tex., and the 3d Ark. (under Col. Van H. Manning). When Robertson received his third wound at Gettysburg he was temporarily succeeded by Col. P. A. Work. When the brigade went to the West to fight at Chickamauga, Chattanooga (Wauhatchie), and Knoxville, Robertson was subsequently relieved of command when Longstreet and Jenkins became increasingly dissatisfied with him. (See ROBERTSON.) The Texan John Gregg was brought in to command the Texas Brigade. Returning to the East, the Texans distinguished themselves under the eyes of Lee in the fighting of 6 May '64 in the Wilderness. When Lee rode forward as if to accompany their attack along the Plank road there occurred the famous "Lee to the rear" scene. (For this, as well as Lee's high opinion of the Texans, see *Lee's Lts.*, III, 357; and *R. E. Lee*, III, 287-88.) The brigade then lost over 400 out of 711 men in an unsupported attack before being ordered back.

Gregg was killed 7 Oct. '64 in the fighting along the Darbytown and New Market roads (Petersburg campaign). Col. C. M. Winkler was in command until F. S. Bass recovered from wounds and succeeded him. Later the brigade's senior colonel, R. M. Powell, was exchanged and commanded the brigade until the end of the war (Henderson, H. McC. *Texas in the Confederacy*, San Antonio: The Naylor Company, 1955).

HOOKER, Ambrose Eugene. Union officer. N.Y. R.A. Lt. Col. 7th Calif. 16 Feb. '63; Lt. Col. 2d Calif. Cav. 1 Nov. '65; Bvt. B.G. USV (war service). Died 1883.

HOOKER, Joseph. Union gen. 1814–79. Mass. USMA 1837 (29/50); Arty. He served in the Seminole War, on the frontier, and as Adj. at West Point before fighting in the Mexican War (3 brevets). In Mexico he served on the staffs of Generals Hamer, P. F. Smith, Butler, and Pillow, and drew Scott's wrath by testifying for Pillow during that general's fracas with Scott. Resigning in 1853, Hooker settled in the far west as a farmer and had a disagreement with Halleck while Col. in the Calif. Mil. When war came he offered his services to the Union and was repeatedly snubbed by the War Dept. Finally, however, he was commissioned B.G. USV 17 May '61 and commanded Hooker's brigade in the defenses of Washington Aug.-Oct. '61. He then led Hooker's division Oct. '61–Mar. '62 and 2d Div., III Corps (13 Mar.–5 Sept. '62) at Yorktown, Williamsburg, Fair Oaks, Glendale, Malvern Hill, Bristoe Station, 2d Bull Run, and Chantilly. Promoted Maj. Gen. USV 5 May '62, he commanded the III Corps in the Army of Va. 6–12 Sept. '62 and then led the I Corps, Army of the Potomac (12–17 Sept.) at South Mountain and Antietam (wounded). He was commissioned B.G. USA 20 Sept. '62, commanded V Corps (10–16 Nov. '62) and led the Centre Grand Division (composed of the III and II Corps) at Fredericksburg 16 Nov. '62–26 Jan. '63. Named commander of

the Army of the Potomac on the latter date, he was defeated at CHANCELLORS-VILLE, and was relieved 28 June '63 by Meade. He was given the Thanks of Congress for defending Baltimore and Washington against Lee, being one of 15 army officers to receive the honor in the war. Going to the West, with the XI and XII Corps, he was given command of the XX Corps 24 Sept. '63 and led them at Lookout Mountain, Missionary Ridge, Ringgold, Mill Creek Gap, Resaca, Cassville, New Hope Church, Pine Mountain, Chattahoochee, Peach Tree Creek, and the siege of Atlanta. When Howard was named to succeed McPherson, Hooker asked to be relieved and left this command 28 July '64. He was then sent to the Northern Dept. (1 Oct. '64–27 June '65) and continued in the R.A., heading other departments, until his retirement as Maj. Gen. USA in 1868 after a paralytic stroke. He had been breveted Maj. Gen. USA for Chattanooga. D.A.B. describes him in his youth as "tall, robust, bronze-haired, sharp-eyed ... [with] frank, affable manners [that] brought him early recognition." Lyman, seeing him in 1864, said that he was "red-faced, very, with a lacklustre eye and an uncertainty of gait and carriage that suggested a used-up man. His mouth, also, is wanting in character and firmness; though, for all that, he must once have been a very handsome man."

The nickname, Fighting Joe, was derived from the tag line of a series of takes sent out by the Associated Press during the Seven Days' Battles. The unknown copyist headed them "Fighting-Joe Hooker," and newspapers all over the country simply removed the hyphen and used "Fighting Joe Hooker" as a subhead. Much to Hooker's disgust the name was forever associated with him He reciprocated by contributing some-thing new to American journalism when, just before Chancellorsville, he ordered that all news dispatches sent from the Army of the Potomac should be signed, thus assuring responsible reporting. Up until this time all dispatches had been anonymous with the exception of those from a few famous reporters, which were signed with initials, and editorials from well-known and influential editors.

HOOKER'S LETTER from Lincoln on being given command of the Army of the Potomac:

EXECUTIVE MANSION
Washington, D.C.
January 26, 1863

Major-General HOOKER.

GENERAL: I have placed you at the head of the Army of the Potomac. Of course I have done this upon what appears to me to be sufficient reasons, and yet I think it best for you to know that there are some things in regard to which I am not quite satisfied with you. I believe you to be a brave and skillful soldier, which, of course, I like. I also believe you do not mix politics with your profession, in which you are right. You have confidence in yourself, which is a valuable, if not an indispensable, quality. You are ambitious, which, within reasonable bounds, does good rather than harm; but I think that during General Burnside's command of the army, you have taken counsel of your ambition, and thwarted him as much as you could, in which you did a great wrong to the country and to a most meritorious and honorable brother officer. I have heard, in such a way as to believe it, of your recently saying that both the Army and the Government needed a dictator. Of course it was not for this, but in spite of it, that I have given you the command. Only those generals who gain success can set up dictators. What I now ask

of you is military success, and I will risk the dictatorship. The Government will support you to the utmost of its ability, which is neither more nor less than it has done and will do for all commanders. I much fear that the spirit which you have aided to infuse into the army, of criticizing their commander and withholding confidence from him, will now turn upon you. I shall assist you as far as I can to put it down. Neither you, nor Napoleon if he were alive again, could get any good out of an army while such a spirit prevails in it. And now beware of rashness. Beware of rashness, but with energy and sleepless vigilance go forward and give us victories.

Yours, very truly,

A. LINCOLN

According to Nicolay and Hay, "A friend to whom Hooker showed this letter immediately upon its reception, says it made a deep impression upon the general. While he was somewhat chagrined by its severe chiding he was touched by its tone of mingled authority and kindness. 'He talks to me like a father,' the general said. 'I shall not answer this letter until I have won him a great victory'" (N.&H., VII, 88). Others discount this story of Hooker's reaction, saying that it is "out of character." (Note. The typographical style of this letter as reproduced above follows that of O.R. I, XXV, Part II, p. 4.)

HORN, John Watts. Union officer. Scotland. Capt. 5th Md. 23 Oct. '61; resigned 23 July '62; Lt. Col. 6th Md. 3 Sept. '62; Col. 27 Mar. '63; Bvt. B.G. USV 19 Oct. '64 (Richmond and Shenandoah Valley). Commanded 2, 3, III. Died 1897.

"HORNET'S NEST." Landmark in the fighting at SHILOH.

HORSES, Famous. Covered elsewhere are GRANT'S HORSES (Cincinnati, Jack, Fox, Kangaroo, and Jeff Davis); TRAVELLER as well as others of LEE'S HORSES (Richmond, The Roan or Brown-Roan, Lucy Long, and Ajax); McCLELLAN'S HORSES (Daniel Webster and Burns); SHERMAN'S HORSES (Sam and Lexington); Stonewall Jackson's OLD SORREL; Sheridan's RIENZI, also named Winchester; A. S. Johnston's FIRE-EATER; Hooker's LOOKOUT; KEARNY'S HORSES (Moscow, Decatur, and Bayard); George H. Thomas' Billy; STUART'S HORSES (Virginia and Highfly); and Meade's BALDY. Other famous war horses not covered in detail were: Fitzhugh Lee's Nellie Gray, who was killed at Opequon; Cleburne's Dixie, killed at Perryville; Adam R. Johnson's Joe Smith; Forrest's King Phillip; and Ben Butler's Almond Eye.

HOTCHKISS, Charles Truman. Union officer. N.Y. Pvt. Co. F 11th Ill. 23 Apr. '61; 1st Lt. Adj. 2 May '61; Capt. 30 July '61; Lt. Col. 89th Ill. 25 Aug. '62; Col. 24 Feb. '63; Bvt. B.G. USV (war service). Commanded 1, 3, IV (Cumberland).

HOTCHKISS, Jedediah. C.S.A. Topo. Engr. 1827?–1899. He had moved to Va. from N.Y., opened an academy, and made maps as a sideline. He had done some topographical work during Garnett's W. Va. operations before being mustered into the service 23 Mar. '62 as acting Adj. of the militia regiment from Augusta County, Va. Three days later Jackson sent for him and ordered him to make a map of the Shenandoah Valley from Harpers Ferry to Lexington, "showing all the points of offense and defense between those points." This was the beginning of an association that made Hotchkiss the foremost mapmaker of the war and that contributed much to Jackson's tactical successes. "His name appears more frequently than that of any other topographer in the pages of the *Official Records,* and no less than half of all the Confederate maps that eventually found their way into the *Atlas* were from his hand," says Commager in the republished *Official Records* atlas. The Hotchkiss Papers, which Freeman used extensively, are a "large and invaluable collection of diaries, war letters, maps, and post-bellum clippings, letters and pamphlets." His highest rank was Maj.

HOTCHKISS PROJECTILE AND GUN. Although Wise mentions the Hotchkiss as one of the foreign *guns* imported in small numbers by the South, apparently it was the Hotchkiss *projectile* that was used on both sides. The latter was composed of three parts: the body, an expanding ring of lead, and a cast-iron cup. The iron cup pushes against the lead ring when the gun is fired, forcing the lead into the rifling of the gun. Various modifications were also developed. The Union purchased a large number of the projectiles from the Hotchkiss factory in New York.

HOT SHOT. Defined in Wilhelm as "shot made red-hot for the purpose of setting fire to buildings, shipping, etc. The charges for hot shot are from one-fourth to one-sixth the weight of the shot. . . . They are heated by means of furnaces erected for the purpose. . . . after the furnace is once heated, a 24-pounder shot is brought to a red heat in twenty-five minutes. Red-hot shot is not in general use." They were effective in the Confederate bombardment of Fort Sumter.

HOUGH (huff), Daniel. A private in Btry. E, 1st US Arty., he was killed 14 Apr. '61 in an accidental explosion that took place while a salute was being fired before the evacuation of FORT SUMTER. If this accident is considered a military action, Hough can be called the first fatality of the Civil War.

HOUGH, John. Union officer. N.H. Pvt. Co. A 17th Ill. 25 May '61; Capt. Asst. Adj. Gen. Vols. 15 May '63; Maj. Asst. Adj. Gen. Vols. 2 July '64; Lt. Col. Asst. Adj. Gen. Assigned 15 Mar.–1 Aug. '65; Bvt. B.G. USV (war service). Died 1891.

HOUGHTALING, Charles. Union officer. N.Y. Capt. 10th Ill. 20 Apr. '61; Capt. 1st Ill. Arty. 30 July '61; Maj. 22 Feb. '63; Col. 20 Aug. '64; Bvt. B.G. USV (war service). Died 1883.

HOUGHTON, Moses Barrett. Union officer. N.Y. Capt. 3d Mich. 13 May '61; Maj. 1 Sept. '62; Lt. Col. 20 Jan. '64; Col. 29 July '64; Bvt. B.G. USV (war service).

HOUSATONIC, The. Federal sloop blockading Charleston, torpedoed and sunk by the Confederate SUBMARINE *Hunley* on 17 Feb. '64.

HOVEY, Alvin Peterson. Union gen. 1821–91. Ind. After the Mexican War, he became a state Supreme Court associate justice as an ardent Democrat. Changing parties when Republicanism was established, he was named Col. 24th Ind. 31 July '61 and promoted B.G. USV 28 Apr. '62 for gallantry at Shiloh. He commanded 2d Dist. East Ark.; 1, 12, XIII, Tenn. (22 Jan.–8 Feb. '63) and succeeded to division (8 Feb.– 26 July '63) for the Vicksburg campaign. Grant credited him with the victory at Champion's Hill, where his brigade lost a third of its strength killed or wounded. He also led 4th Div., XVI, Tenn. (12–23 July '63) and 1st Div., XXIII, Ohio (10 Apr.–9 June '64). In July '64 he was directed to recruit 10,000 men, which he did, taking only unmarried men, and the group was known as "Hovey's Babies." He was breveted for war service (4 July

'64) and resigned 7 Oct. '65. In Dec. he was appointed Minister to Peru, a post he held until 1870, when he returned to law practice. He was in Congress in 1886 and elected Gov. of Ind. in 1888, dying in office. Distant kin of Charles E. HOVEY.

HOVEY, Charles Edward. Union gen. 1827–97. Vt. After Dartmouth, he taught school and was superintendent of public schools in Peoria (Ill.) 1856– 57. He started the first Ill. Normal College in the latter year and recruited the 33d Ill. ("Normal Regiment") from its students and teachers, being commissioned its Col. 15 Aug. '61. He was promoted B.G. USV 5 Sept. '62 and commanded 1st Brig., 2d Div. Dist. East Ark.; 2, 11, XIII, Tenn. (Dec. '62); 2, 4th Div. Yazoo Expedition (Dec. '62– Jan. '63) and 2, 1, XV, Tenn. (3 Jan.– 22 May '63) at Arkansas Post where he was severely wounded. His appointment expired 4 Mar. '63, and he practiced law in Washington, being breveted Maj. Gen. USV 13 Mar. '65 for Arkansas Post. Distant kin of Alvin P. HOVEY.

HOWARD, Charles Henry. Union officer. Me. Pvt. 3d Me. 4 June '61; principal musician 27 June '61; 2d Lt 61st N.Y. 24 Jan. '62; 1st Lt. 8 Oct. '62; Maj. A.D.C. Vols. 25 Aug. '63; Lt. Col. Add. I.G. Assigned 4 May–17 Aug. '64; Vol. 128th US Col. Inf. 6 Apr. '65; Bvt. B.G. USV 15 Aug. '65 (war service).

HOWARD, Joseph, Jr. WAR CORRE-SPONDENT. 1833–1908. He began reporting the war at 1st Bull Run for the N.Y. *Times* and was a confidant of Mrs. Lincoln. Raucous and rosy-faced, he had held open the wires for his paper by telegraphing the genealogy of Jesus and sneaked into Phil Kearny's funeral procession, from which reporters had been banned, by wearing a surplice and carrying a prayer book. His sparkling copy earned him one of the first regular by-lines in the *Times,* but by May '64 he was on the city desk of the Brooklyn *Eagle* and not happy. After trying to regain his positions on various N.Y.C. papers, he and an *Eagle* reporter, Francis A. Mallison, perpetrated one of the most infamous hoaxes in American history. They forged on A.P. "flimsies" a document purportedly from Lincoln announcing that Grant's Va. campaign had come to an unsuccessful end, set aside "a day of fasting, humiliation, and prayer," and called for a draft of 400,000 men. Mallison hoped to make a killing in the gold market with the terrible news, and Howard apparently wanted additional notoriety and revenge on the editors who had refused him jobs. Only the *World* and *Journal of Commerce* actually printed the news, the other papers having discovered in time that the source was suspicious and destroyed those editions that had been printed. The two guilty men were arrested and thrown in Fort Lafayette, where they stayed for several months. But the military arrest and occupation of the *World* and *Journal* offices, ordered by Stanton and signed by Lincoln, brought specters of the police state before the public and the press. This, however, did not interfere with Lincoln's renomination. Howard went on to work for a number of N.Y.C. papers and was president of the N.Y. Press Club for a time. "Howard's Column" was widely syndicated in 1886 and tremendously popular, and he was an extremely successful lecturer.

HOWARD, Oliver Otis. Union gen. 1830–1909. Me. USMA 1854 (4/46); Ord. After serving on the frontier and in arsenals, he taught mathematics at West Point and resigned as 1st Lt. 7 June '61 to become Col. 3d Me. 4 June. At 1st Bull Run he commanded 3d

Brig., 3d Div. (June–Aug. '61) and then led Howard's brigade, Div. Potomac (Aug.–Oct. '61). He was promoted B.G. USV 3 Sept. '61 and led 1st Brig., Sumner's division, Potomac, 25 Nov. '61–13 Mar. '62. On the latter date he assumed command of 1, 1, II, and commanded it at Yorktown and Fair Oaks where he sustained two serious wounds and lost his right arm. He then led 2, 2, II (27 Aug.–17 Sept. '62) at Centreville and Antietam, succeeding to command of the division (17 Sept. '62–26 Jan. '63), leading it at Antietam and Fredericksburg and later (7 Feb.–1 Apr. '63). He was promoted Maj. Gen. 29 Nov. '62 and commanded the II Corps 26 Jan.–5 Feb. '63 and the XI Corps (2 Apr.–25 Sept. '63) at Chancellorsville and Gettysburg. Going to the Army of the Cumberland, he commanded the XI Corps (25 Sept. '63–21 Jan. '64 and 25 Feb.–18 Apr. '64) at Lookout Mountain and Missionary Ridge. In the Atlanta campaign, he commanded the IV Corps (10 Apr.–27 July '64) at Dalton, Resaca, Adairsville, Cassville, Dallas, Pickett's Mill (wounded), Kenesaw Mountain, Smyrna Camp Ground, Peach Tree Creek, and Atlanta. On the latter date he succeeded Logan in command of the Army of the Tenn. and led it at Ezra Church, Jonesboro, before the fall of Atlanta and during the March to the Sea at Griswoldville, Congaree Creek, Cheraw, Fayetteville, Bentonville, and Goldsboro. He was named B.G. USA 21 Dec. '64 and breveted Maj. Gen. USA for Ezra Church and the Atlanta campaign and received the Thanks of Congress (one of 15 army officers) for Gettysburg. In 1893 he was given the Medal of Honor for Fair Oaks. Named a commissioner of the Freedman's Bureau 12 May '65, he did much to help the Negro but lacked the necessary executive ability to keep the bureau from becoming corrupt. After many accusations of dishonesty, he asked for, and was exonerated by, a court of inquiry in 1874. He founded Howard Univ. for Negroes in Washington and served as its president 1869–74. Continuing in the R.A., he was peace commissioner to the Apaches, commanded the Depts. of the Columbia and the Platte, participated in Indian fighting, served as USMA Superintendent, and commanded the Div. of the East before retiring in 1894 as Maj. Gen. USA (since 1886). He was then active in many religious and educational projects and Republican politics. While he wrote on many military and historical subjects, he never published anything on the Civil War.

HOWE, Albion Parris. Union gen. 1818–97. Me. USMA 1841 (8/52); Arty. He taught mathematics at West Point, fought in the Mexican War (1 brevet), served on the frontier and in garrison, and was sent with his battery (Capt. 4th US Arty.) to Harpers Ferry during John Brown's raid. He then served with McClellan in western Va. and commanded 3, 1, IV (Mar.–5 July '62) at Yorktown, Williamsburg, Mechanicsville, and the Seven Days' Battles. Promoted B.G. USV 11 June '62, he also led 2, 1, IV (5 July–26 Sept. '62) at 2d Bull Run, South Mountain, and Antietam and then commanded 2, 3, VI (26 Sept.–Oct. '62). He commanded 3, 3, VI (Oct.–Nov. '62); 2d Div., VI (16 Nov. '62–4 Jan. '63); and Light Arty. Camp, XXII, Washington (3 Mar. '63–9 July '64), at Fredericksburg, Salem, Gettysburg, Rappahannock Station, and Mine Run as well as later (9 Aug.–22 Sept.; 12–20 Oct.; 1 Nov. '64-7 Apr. '65; 7 May-20 July '65). He was a member of the Guard of Honor over Lincoln's body when it lay in state in the White House and on the funeral procession to Springfield, and

was on the military commission that tried the conspirators. Breveted for Malvern Hill, Salem, Rappahannock Station, and war service (B.G. USA, Maj. Gen. USV and Maj. Gen. USA), he continued in the R.A., retiring in 1882 as Col. 4th US Arty.

HOWE, John Homer. Union officer. N.Y. 1st Lt. 124th Ill. 9 Aug. '62; Lt. Col. 2 Sept. '62; Bvt. B.G. USV (war service). Commanded 2, Dist. Memphis 5th Div., XVI; 2, 4, XVI; 3, 4, XVI. Died 1873.

HOWE, Julia Ward. Writer and reformer. 1819–1910. N.Y. A leader with her husband, Samuel Gridley Howe, in the Abolitionist movement, she wrote the BATTLE HYMN OF THE REPUBLIC in spring 1862.

HOWE, Samuel Gridley. SANITARY COMMISSION organizer and worker. 1801–76. Mass. He had been a surgeon in the Greek Army, a friend of Florence Nightingale for many years, and a reformer most of his life, when he became interested in the Commission. Throughout the war he worked in it, becoming one of the superintendents for the New England troops. His wife was Julia Ward Howe.

HOWELL, Joshua B. Union gen. ?–1864. Pa. Commissioned Col. 85th Pa. 12 Nov. '61, he led his regiment at Fair Oaks. Going to the Dept. of N.C., he commanded 2, 3, XVIII (6 Jan.–Feb. '63) and 2, 2, XVIII. In the Dept. of the South he commanded 2, 2d Div. St. Helena Island, X (Jan.-Apr. '63); 2, Forces Folly Island, X (June–July '63); 2, Forces Morris Island, X (19 July–19 Sept. '63) at the siege of Ft. Wagner; 3, South End Folly Island, X (Oct.–Dec. '63); Howell's brigade, Hilton Head Dist., X (28 Dec. '63–6 Feb. '64); Hilton Head Dist., X (5 Feb.–26 Apr. '64). Going with his command to the Army of the James, he led

1, 1, X (2 May–11 June '64; 14 June–28 July; 18 Aug.–1 Sept.) in a charge at Bermuda Hundred 20 May. He also commanded 1st Div., X Corps, 11–14 June '64. He was given command of 3d Div., X, on 1 Sept. but on the 12th was fatally injured in a fall from his horse and died two days later. His commission as B.G. USV was dated from the 12th.

HOWLAND, Horace Newton. Union officer. Ohio. Capt. 3d Ohio Cav. 8 Oct. '61; Maj. 7 Feb. '63; Lt. Col. 14 Feb. '64; Col. 17 May '65; Bvt. B.G. USV (war service). Commanded 2, 2, Cav. Corps, Mil. Div. Miss. Died 1895.

HOWLAND, Joseph. Union officer. N.Y. 1st Lt. Adj. 16th N.Y. 15 May '61; Capt. Add. Adj. Gen. Vols. 16 Sept. '61; Col. 16th N.Y. 12 Mar. '62; Bvt. B.G. USV (Gaines's Mill); resigned 29 Sept. '62.

HOYT, Charles Henry. Union officer. Conn. 1st Lt. 37th N.Y. 8 June '61–8 June '62; Capt. Asst. Q.M. Vols. 12 May '62–12 Apr. '67; Col. Q.M. Assigned 2 Aug. 64–31 Dec. '66; Bvt. B.G. USV (war service); transferred to R.A.; retired Maj. Q.M. 1889. In the summer of 1864, while serving in the office of the Q.M.G., he commanded a provisional company of quartermaster employees organized to defend Washington against Jubal Early's threatened attack. Died 1897.

HOYT, George H. Union officer. Mass. 2d Lt. 7th Kans. Cav. 11 Dec. '61; Capt. 27 May '62; resigned 3 Sept. '62; Lt. Col. 15th Kans. Cav. 17 Oct. '63; Bvt. B.G. USV (Newtonia, Mo.).

HOYT, Henry Martyn. Union officer. 1830–92. Pa. Lt. Col. 52d Pa. 5 Nov. '61; Col. 6 Nov. '63; Bvt. B.G. USV (war service); mustered out 3 Nov. '64. Commanded 2, Forces Morris Island (S.C.), X Corps. Captured during assault on Fort Johnson in the siege of Morris Island, he escaped only to be recaptured and finally exchanged. A lawyer and teacher, he was Governor of Pa. 1878–83.

HUBBARD, James. Union officer. Conn. Capt. 2d Conn. Arty. 11 Sept. '62; Maj. 6 Feb. '64; Lt. Col. 6 June '64; Col. 25 Jan. '65; Bvt. B.G. USV 6 Apr. '65 (Petersburg and Little Sayler's Creek, Va.). Commanded 2d Brig., Defenses S. of Potomac, XXII; 2, 1, VI. Died 1886.

HUBBARD, Lucius Frederick. Union officer. 1836–1913. N.Y. Pvt. Co. A 5th Minn. 19 Dec. '61; Capt. 4 Feb. '62; Lt. Col. 24 Mar. '62; Col. 30 Aug. '62; Bvt. B.G. USV 16 Dec. '64 (Nashville). Commanded 2, 3, XV; 2, 1, XVI; 2, 1st Det. Army of Tenn.; 3, 1st Det. Army of Tenn.; 2, 1, XVI, B.G. USV in Spanish-American War. W.I.A. Corinth. Elected Republican Governor of Minn. 1881–85.

HUBBARD, Thomas Hamlin. Union officer. Me. 1st Lt. Adj. 25th Me. 29 Sept. '62; mustered out 11 July '63; Lt. Col. 30th Me. 19 Dec. '63; Col. 2 July '64; Bvt. B.G. USV (war service). Cited by Joseph BAILEY for dams he built at Alexandria (La.) during Banks's Red River expedition of 1864. Later he was a lawyer and railroad executive.

HUDNUTT, Joseph O. Union officer. N.Y. Lt. Col. 38th Iowa 4 Nov. '62; Bvt. B.G. USV (war service). Commanded 1, 2, XIII (Gulf).

HUDSON, Frederic. Newspaper editor. 1819–75. Mass. Coming to N.Y.C. as a young man, he joined the *Herald* in 1836 and rose to be managing editor. He retired in 1866 after nearly 30 years on the paper, dedicated to implementing James Gordon Bennett's journalistic ideas. He was one of the founders of the Associated Press, its president for 25 years, and certainly one of the foremost journalists of the era. He was offered a number of lucrative positions after his retirement (his salary while with the *Herald* was the highest on any newspaper) but turned them all down. His *Journalism in the United States from 1690 to 1872* (1873) was the first history of journalism in America. See WAR CORRESPONDENTS.

HUDSON, John G. Union officer. N.Y. Capt. 33d Mo. 29 Aug. '62; Col. 60th US Col. Inf. 30 Nov. '63; Bvt. B.G. USV (Helena, Ark.). Commanded 2, 1, VII (Ark.).

HUEY, Pennock. Union officer. Pa. Capt. 8th Pa. Cav. 17 Sept. '61; Maj. 1 Jan. '62; Col. 25 June '63; Bvt. B.G. USV (war service). Commanded 2, 2, Cav. Corps (Potomac).

HUFF, John A. Union private who mortally wounded Jeb Stuart. c. 1816–64. After serving two years in the 1st US Sharpshooters (Berdan's), where he had won a prize for being the best shot in the regiment, the 48-year-old veteran enlisted in Co. E, 5th Mich. Cav. He mortally wounded Stuart at YELLOW TAVERN, and was himself mortally wounded 17 days later at Haw's Shop, Va.

HUGER (pronounced u'-gee, according to Appleton's), Benjamin. C.S.A. gen. 1805–77 S.C. USMA 1825 (8/37); Arty.-Ord. From a French Huguenot family that had produced many soldiers and patriots, he had served on topographical duties and studied in Europe before transferring to the ordnance department. After serving in arsenals and armories, he was Scott's Chief of Ord. in Mexico, winning three brevets. He resigned 22 Apr. '61 as Maj. Appointed B.G. C.S.A., 17 June '61, he was given command of the Dept. of Norfolk 23 May '61 and named Maj. Gen. 7 Oct. '61. In the opening phases of the Peninsular campaign he evacuated Norfolk

(9 May '62) and withdrew to join the army defending Richmond. He led a division without distinction at Seven Pines, Gaines's Mill, Glendale, and Malvern Hill. Subsequently investigated by the C.S.A. Congress and held responsible for the loss of Roanoke Island (8 Feb. '62), he was relieved of command and transferred to the West. Freeman attributes his ineptitude for field command to the "slow, peace-time routine of the ordnance service" and surmises, also, that he was suffering from hardening of the arteries (*Lee Lts.,* I, 612). In the West he was Inspector of Arty. and Ord. until transferred again to the Trans-Miss. After the war he was a farmer in Va. and N.C.

HUGUNIN, James R. Union officer. N.Y. Capt. 12th Ill. 2 May '61; Maj. 27 Apr. '62; Bvt. B.G. USV (war service); resigned 12 July '64. Died 1892.

HUMES, William Y. C. C.S.A. gen. ?–1883. Appt.-Tenn. As Lt. of Arty. when the war began, he was promoted Capt. of C.S.A. Arty. in June '61 and commanded the guns at New Madrid. He was captured at Island No. 10 and went into the cavalry after being exchanged. Appointed B.G. C.S.A. 16 Nov. '63, he led a brigade in Wheeler's corps and commanded his own division during the Atlanta campaign. He fought with Hood in Tenn. and then harassed Sherman in Ga. and the Carolinas.

HUMPHREY, Thomas W. Union officer. Ohio. Lt. Col. 95th Ill. 4 Sept. '62; Col. 3 Apr. '63; Bvt. B.G. USV for action 10 June '64 at Guntown, Miss., where he was killed. Commanded 2, 1, XVII.

HUMPHREY, William. Union officer. N.Y. Capt. 2d Mich. 25 Apr. '61; Col. 16 Feb. '63; Bvt. B.G. USV 1 Aug. '64 (war service); mustered out 30 Sept. '64. W.I.A. Spotsylvania 12 May

'64. Commanded 3, 1, IX; 2, 3, IX; 2, 1, IX. Died 1899.

HUMPHREYS, Andrew Atkinson. Union. gen. 1810–83. Pa. USMA 1831 (13/33); Arty. After fighting in the Seminole War and serving in garrison, he resigned in 1836 to become a civil engineer for the government. Two years later he went back in the army as 1st Lt. Topo. Engrs. and worked on bridges and harbors and coastal and railroad surveys. His *Report upon the Physics and Hydraulics* of the Mississippi River (1861), co-authored with Henry L. ABBOT, formed the basis for subsequent flood control and navigation improvement. Named Maj. 6 Aug. '61 (Capt. since 1848), he was on McClellan's staff from 1 Dec. '61 to 5 Mar. '62, being commissioned on the latter date Col. Add. A.D.C. and named Chief Topo. Engr. of the Army of the Potomac. In this post he was at Yorktown, Williamsburg, the Seven Days' Battles, and Malvern Hill, having been appointed B.G. USV 28 Apr. '62. He commanded 3d Div., V, Potomac (12 Sept. '62–27 Jan. '63) covering Frederick (Md.) and pursuing the enemy after Antietam and (12 Feb.–25 May '63) at Chancellorsville. He led the V Corps 23–28 Feb. '63 and the 2d Div., III (23 May–8 July '63) at Gettysburg. As Maj. Gen. USV, 8 July '63, he was Meade's Chief of Staff from that date until 25 Nov. '64, participating in Bristoe Station, Manassas Gap, the Mine Run Operations, the Wilderness, Spotsylvania, North Anna, Totopotomoy, Cold Harbor, Petersburg assaults and mine, Weldon R.R., Peeble's Farm, and Boydton Plank Road. Then, commanding II Corps (26 Nov. '64–15 Feb. '65; 25 Feb.–22 Apr. '65; 5 May–9 June '65 and 20–28 June '65), he was at the Petersburg siege, Hatcher's Run, Sayler's Creek, High Bridge, and Farmville. Breveted for Fredericksburg,

Gettysburg (B.G. USA) and Sayler's Creek (Maj. Gen. USA), he continued in the R.A. and was named B.G. Chief of Engrs. in 1866, retiring in 1879. He was a member of the American Philosophical Society, the American Academy of Arts and Sciences, an incorporator of the National Academy of Sciences, and honorary member of scientific and philosophical societies in Austria, France, and Italy. Of his war experiences he wrote *From Gettysburg to the Rapidan* (1883) and *The Virginia Campaign of 1864 and 1865* (1885). The latter is a standard work. His father and grandfather were both naval architects, and each had headed the USN Construction Bureau. Lyman describes him as "an extremely neat man ... continually washing himself and putting on paper dickeys ... an extremely gentlemanly man ... there was never a nicer old gentleman [he was 54 at the time], and so boyish and peppery that I continually want to laugh in his face."

HUMPHREYS, Benjamin Grubb. C.S.A. gen. 1808–82. Miss. A cadet at West Point (ex-1829), he was dismissed with many others after a student riot on Christmas Eve, 1826. He was a lawyer, legislator, and planter in Miss. and an opponent of secession. When the war came, however, he raised a company and was commissioned Capt. 21st Miss. 18 May '61. Elected Col. 11 Sept. '61, he led his regiment through all the major battles of the Army of Northern Va. except 2d Bull Run, until Gettysburg, when he succeeded Barksdale as brigade commander. Appointed B.G. C.S.A. 14 Aug. '63, he fought under Longstreet at Chickamauga and elsewhere in Ga. and Tenn. from Sept. '63 until spring '64 and led his brigade in Kershaw's division at the Wilderness. Active in Early's Valley campaign in 1864, he was wounded at Berryville,

Va., 3–4 Sept., and then given command of a military district in Miss. After the war he was elected Gov. of Miss., holding the office from 16 Oct. '65 until June '68, when he was ejected by the Federal military authority. He was then a planter and in the insurance business.

HUNLEY, The. Confederate SUBMARINE. See also HOUSATONIC.

HUNT, Henry Jackson. Union gen. 1819–89. Mich. USMA 1839 (19/31); Arty. After fighting in the Mexican War (2 wounds, 1 brevet), he was on a board in 1856 with W. F. Barry and W. H. French to revise light artillery tactics, their findings being used throughout the Civil War. He prepared Harpers Ferry arsenal early in 1861 for "defense or destruction" and was named Maj. 5th US Arty. 14 May '61. He marched his battery on the extreme left at 1st Bull Run and broke the C.S.A. pursuit 21 July at Blackburn's Ford. He was then named Col. Add. A.D.C. 28 Sept. '61 on McClellan's staff and organized the Arty. Reserve of the Army of the Potomac which he commanded at Gaines's Mill and at Malvern Hill, where he had two horses shot from under him. Promoted B.G. USV 15 Sept. '62, he fought at Antietam and, as Chief of Arty., organized the 147-gun battery which opened the battle of Fredericksburg. His was the suggestion to send the infantry over in boats. Hooker curtailed his authority, but when the artillery was poorly handled at Chancellorsville, his full command was restored, and at Gettysburg his guns mowed down "Pickett's Charge." He took part in the offensive through the Wilderness, and on 27 June '64 Grant put him in charge of all siege operations at Petersburg. Breveted for Gettysburg, Petersburg siege (B.G. USA), Gettysburg and Rapidan to Petersburg campaign (Maj. Gen. USV 6 July '64) and war service (Maj. Gen.

USA), he continued in the R.A., commanding the Frontier Dist. shortly after the war and the Dept. of the South 1880–83, when he retired as Col. 4th US Arty. His first wife was the sister of G. A. DE RUSSY.

HUNT, Lewis Cass. Union gen. 1824–86. Wis. USMA 1847 (33/38); Inf. He served in the Mexican War, on garrison duty, on the frontier, and Indian scouting. During the Civil War he fought in the Peninsular campaign as Capt. 4th US Inf. (1855), at the siege of Yorktown, and Col., 92d N.Y. (25 May '62) at Fair Oaks, where he was severely wounded. He was promoted B.G. USV 29 Nov. '62 and commanded 1st Brig., 1st Div., N.C. (28 Dec. '62–2 Jan. '63) and 1, 4, XVIII, N.C. (2 Jan.–12 Mar '63 and 13 Apr.–3 May '63), fighting at Kinston (15 Dec. '62), Whitehall (17 Dec.), and Goldwater (18 Dec. '62). He was named Maj. 14th US Inf. 8 June '63 and put in charge of the New Haven (Conn.) draft rendezvous. He was then sent on special duty in Kans. and Mo. Mar.–June '64 and commanded the defenses of New York Harbor July '64–Jan. '66. He was breveted for Fair Oaks, Kinston, and war service (twice, once as B.G. USA). Continuing in the R.A., he died on active duty with the rank of Col.

HUNT, Lewis Cass. Union officer. Ohio. Capt. 67th Ohio 1 Sept. '62; Lt. Col. 26 Mar. '65; Bvt. B.G. USV (war service). Died 1868.

HUNTER, David. Union gen. 1802–86. D.C. Appt.-Ill. USMA 1822 (25/40); Inf.-Dragoons. He served on the frontier and resigned in 1836, returning during the Mexican War as Maj. Paymaster. Stationed in Kans. in 1860, he corresponded with Lincoln on secession rumors and was invited to make the inaugural journey with him to Washington. Named Col. 3d US Cav.

i4 May and B.G. USV 17 May '61, he was severely wounded at 1st Bull Run commanding the 2d Div. As Maj. Gen. USV 13 Aug. '61, he led Hunter's brigade Potomac (Aug. '61) and relieved Frémont in Mo. as commander of the Western Dept. and repudiated Frémont's agreement with Sterling Price to force disbandment of unauthorized armed bodies. He commanded Kans. (20 Nov. '61–11 Mar. '62) and sent detachments to Forts Henry and Donelson and to Canby in New Mex. As Commander of the Dept. of the South (31 Mar.–22 Aug. '62), he besieged Fort Pulaski (Ga.), which fell on 11 Apr. The next day he issued an order liberating all slaves then in Union hands, and on 9 May liberated all in the Dept. On 19 May Lincoln annulled these orders on the grounds that Hunter had exceeded his authority. Hunter also sanctioned the first Negro regiment (1st S.C.), and Congress upheld him in this. The C.S.A. labeled him a "felon to be executed if captured." In an attempt to take Charleston he was defeated at Secessionville 16 June and suspended further operations. He then served on the court-martial of Fitz-John Porter and inquired into the loss of Harpers Ferry. Returning to the X Corps, South (20 Jan.–12 June '63), he served on boards and commissions until he took over West Va. (21 May '64) after Sigel's defeat in the Valley. Ordered to disrupt supplies and communications, he was successful until repulsed by Early at Lynchburg. He retreated into West Va., leaving the way open for EARLY'S WASHINGTON RAID. On 8 Aug. he resigned his command in favor of Sheridan and served on courts-martial from 1 Feb. '65 until war's end. He accompanied Lincoln's body to Springfield and returned to Washington to preside over the commission that tried the assassination conspirators. He was breveted

for the battle of Piedmont and the Shenandoah Valley campaign (B.G. USA) and war service (Maj. Gen. USA), and retired in 1866.

HUNTER, Morton Craig. Union officer. 1825–96. Ind. Col. 82d Ind. 20 Sept. '62; Bvt. B.G. USV (war service). Commanded 1, 3, XIV. Active in the Republican party, he was an Indiana Congressman for several years.

HUNTER, Robert Mercer Taliaferro. C.S.A. Sec. of State. 1809–87. Va. After graduating from the Univ. of Va.; he practiced law and entered politics, serving as legislator, US Congressman, and Speaker of the House, and Sen. He was a close friend and political ally of John C. Calhoun and favored not only states rights but also slavery. Resigning as Congressman, he sat in the C.S.A. provisional congress from Va. and succeeded Robert Toombs in July '61 as Sec. of State. He served until the following March, when he became a C.S.A. Sen. In the final days of the war he attended the Hampton Roads Peace Conference and was arrested by Federal authorities after the surrender. He held several public offices later and was a farmer.

HUNTON, Eppa. C.S.A. gen. 1823–1908. Va. A schoolteacher and lawyer, he was a militia general and active in Democratic politics. He attended the secession convention and was commissioned Col. 8th Va., having organized and equipped them. Leading this unit at 1st Bull Run, he became ill and was operated upon; he commanded his regiment at Balls Bluff from a wagon. He rejoined his regiment for the Seven Days' Battles despite his doctor's orders and took over Pickett's brigade at Gaines's Mill. He commanded the 8th Va. at Antietam and Gettysburg, where he was severely wounded in "Pickett's Charge." His B.G. C.S.A. appointment was delayed by his ill-health until 9 Aug. '63. He commanded his brigade at the Wilderness, Cold Harbor, and Petersburg. He was captured at Sayler's Creek 6 Apr. '65, when quite ill, and was held prisoner until July. A lawyer and Congressman, he served on the commission to settle the disputed Hayes-Tilden election and was then US Sen.

HURD, John Ricker. Union officer. Ohio. Capt. 2d Ky. 5 June '61; Maj. 28 Jan. '62; Lt. Col. 3 Feb. '63; mustered out 19 June '64; Col. 173d Ohio 21 Sept. '64; Bvt. B.G. USV (Shiloh, Stones River, Chickamauga, war service).

HURLBUT, Stephen Augustus. Union gen. 1815-82. S.C. Appt.-Ill. A lawyer, he fought in the Seminole War and served in the legislature as a Republican. He was appointed B.G. USV 17 May '61, and at Shiloh led the 4th Div., Army of the Tenn. (17 Feb.– 6 Apr. and 6 Apr.–July '62). He commanded the 4th Div. Dist. Memphis (July–Sept. '62) and was appointed Maj. Gen. USV 17 Sept. '62. At Corinth he led the 4th Div. Dist. Jackson (24 Sept.–5 Oct. '62) and then commanded the Dist. Jackson, XIII (26 Oct.–19 Nov. '62). He next commanded Dist. Memphis, XIII (25 Nov.–22 Dec. '62) and led the XVI Corps (22 Dec. '62–10 Jan. '63; 5 Feb. '63–17 Apr. '64) during the Vicksburg campaign. Commanding the Dept. of the Gulf (23 Sept. '64–22 Apr. '65), he was charged, and apparently rightfully so, with corruption, but was honorably mustered out 20 June '65. He became the Republican leader of Ill. and was then accused of corruption and drunkenness, again apparently with reason. Serving in the legislature, he was the first commander in chief of the G.A.R. (1866–68) and was Minister to Colombia 1869–72. He

was US Congressman for six years and then served as Minister to Peru (1881–82) during the Peru-Chile War, embarrassing the US by his altercation with Judson Kilpatrick, US Minister to Chile.

HURST, Samuel H. Union officer. Ohio. Capt. 73d Ohio 7 Nov. '61; Maj. 21 June '62; Lt. Col. 27 June '64; Col. 10 July '64; Bvt. B.G. USV. Brevets for Ga. and Carolinas campaign (war service).

HUSBAND, Mary Morris. SANITARY COMMISSION worker. Pa. In 1861 she was engaged in hospital visiting in Philadelphia but in July '62 she started nursing on the Commission's hospital boats, removing wounded from the Peninsula. She continued working in hospitals, in the field, and in Washington, until May '65, when she began devoting her energy to the returning soldiers.

HUTCHINS, Rue Pugh. Union officer. Mass. Capt. 94th Ohio 24 Aug. '62; Maj. 23 May '63; Lt. Col. 19 Jan. '64; Bvt. B.G. USV (war service).

HUTCHINSON, Frederick Sharpe. Union officer. Ohio. Sgt. Co. F 15th Mich. 12 Nov. '61; 2d Lt. 1 May '62; 1st Lt. 1 Oct. '62; Maj. 16 Oct. '63; Lt. Col. 17 July '64; Col. 22 May '65; Bvt. B.G. USV 24 May '65 (war service). W.I.A. Shiloh 6 Apr. '62 and Jonesboro (Ga.) 31 Aug. '64. Captured and escaped on the same day at Bolivar (Tenn.) in July, 1861; also captured at Holly Springs (Miss.) in December 1862. Commanded 3, 2, XV.

HUTCHINSON FAMILY SINGERS. Popular singers identified as early as 1841 with the abolitionist and temperance movements. The original singers, the 16 living children (three died in infancy) of Jesse and Mary Hutchinson of N.H., had retired, and their children and grandchildren were carrying on the family tradition during the Civil War. In the summer and fall of 1861 McClellan barred their appearances in the Va. camps when their anti-slavery songs had angered many of the soldiers. After the offending verses were read by Chase to Lincoln at a cabinet meeting, the President said, "It is just the character of song that I desire the soldiers to hear." Thereafter the Hutchinsons were permitted tunefully to do their part for the war effort.

HYDE, Thomas Worcester. Union officer. Italy. Maj. 7th Me. 21 Aug. '61; Lt. Col. 1 Dec. '63; transferred to 1st Me. Vet. Inf. 20 Sept. '64; Col. 22 Oct. '64; Bvt. B.G. USV 2 Apr. '65 (Petersburg); Medal of Honor 8 Apr. '91 for Antietam. Commanded 3, 2, VI (Shenandoah and Potomac). Died 1899.

I

"IF ANY MAN ATTEMPTS TO HAUL DOWN THE AMERICAN FLAG, SHOOT HIM ON THE SPOT." Instructions of John A. Dix, sometimes referred to as the AMERICAN FLAG DISPATCH.

IHRIE, George Percy. Union officer. Pa. Ex-cadet USMA 1849. Appt.-N.J. Lt. Col. 3d Calif. 4 Sept. '61; resigned 11 Dec. '61; Col. Add. A.D.C. 7 May '62; Bvt. B.G. USV (siege and battle of Corinth, Iuka, Tallahatchie, Grenada, Jackson, Humboldt, Vicksburg); discharged 18 Aug. '63; joined R.A. 1866; Bvt. B.G. USA 1867 (for same actions as in USV brevet). Died 1903.

9TH ILLINOIS

Colonels: Eleazer A. Paine (USMA; Brig. Gen.), August Mersy (Bvt. B.G.), Samuel T. Hughes.

Battles: Fort Donelson, Shiloh, Corinth, Lundy's Lane (Ala.), Meed Creek (Miss.), Jackson (Tenn.), Grenada (Miss.), Bear Creek (Tenn.), Salem (Miss.), Montezuma (Tenn.), Wyatt (Miss.), Snake Creek Gap (Ga.), Resaca, Dallas, Rome, Nancy's Creek, Atlanta, Milledgeville, Orangeburg (S.C.). Present also at Saratoga (Tenn.), Cherokee, Florence, Athens, Moulton, Flint River.

The 9th lost more men killed than any other Illinois regiment. Initially a three months' regiment, it enlisted for three years and left Cairo 5 Sept. '61. It went to Paducah, Ky., and stayed there until Feb. '62, when it moved with Grant's army to Fort Donelson as part of McArthur's brigade of C. F. Smith's division. Its loss at Donelson was 210, of whom 55 were killed. At Shiloh in W. H. L. Wallace's division the 9th Ill. had more total losses than any other regiment in the battle, and it sustained more killed and wounded (366) than any other infantry regiment during the war (Fox). It withdrew in good order after sustaining severe attacks; the best testimony of its discipline lies in the casualty figures: out of 578 present for duty, 103 were killed (or died of wounds), 258 were wounded, but only five were listed as missing. The regiment was then assigned to Oglesby's (2d) brigade, Davies' (2d) division, Army of West Tenn. At Corinth, 4 Oct. '62, it lost another 148 out of the 359 engaged.

In March '63 the 9th Ill. was converted to mounted infantry and became part of XVI Corps. It was mustered out 20 Aug. '64. Remaining recruits were consolidated into a seven-company battalion, assigned to XVII Corps, for Sherman's final operations.

36TH ILLINOIS

Colonels: Nicholas Greusel, Silas Miller (K.I.A.), Benjamin F. Campbell.

Battles: Pea Ridge, Chaplin Hills, Stones River, Chickamauga, Missionary Ridge, Resaca, Adairsville, Dallas, Kenesaw Mountain, Atlanta, Franklin, Nashville. Present also at Corinth, Hoover's Gap, Rocky Face Ridge, New Hope Church, Peach Tree Creek, Jonesboro, Lovejoy, Spring Hill. Fought in every important battle in the West.

Mustered in 23 Sept. '61, it moved to Rolla, Mo., where it camped until 14 Jan. '62. Moved into Arkansas with Osterhaus' brigade and fought at Pea Ridge, losing 10 killed, 31 wounded, and 27 missing. It then moved with Asboth's division to Corinth, thence to Rienzi where it spent the summer. In the fall it moved to Louisville, where it was assigned to Sheridan's division and fought at Chaplin Hills; losses here were 23 K.I.A., 50 W.I.A., and 4 missing. At Stones River the 36th Ill. was in Sill's (1st) brigade, Sheridan's (3d) division of McCook's Corps. Losses were 212, of whom 65 were killed; Col. Greusel assumed command of the brigade when Sill was killed. In Lytle's brigade at Chickamauga the regiment lost 141 (35 K.I.A.). In Oct. '63 the regiment was placed in Steedman's (1st) brigade, Sheridan's (2d) division, IV Corps, where it remained. Col. Miller was killed at Kenesaw Mountain. At Franklin the brigade, under Opdycke, played a decisive part and captured 10 flags; Lt. Col. Porter C. Olson was killed in this action. The regiment went to Texas with IV Corps and was mustered out in Oct. '65.

55TH ILLINOIS

Colonels: David Stuart (B.G.), Oscar Malmbourg, Charles A. Andress.

Battles: Shiloh, Russell's House (Tenn.), Chickasaw Bayou, Arkansas Post, Vicksburg assaults of 19 and 22 May '63 and siege, Jackson, Black River, Kenesaw (19 and 27 June '64), Ezra Chapel, Atlanta (22 July and 3 Aug. and siege), Jonesboro, Bentonville. Present also at siege of Corinth, Shelby Depot, Champion's Hill, Missionary Ridge, Lovejoy, March to the Sea, Fort McAllister, Savannah, Columbia, the Carolinas.

Mustered in 31 Oct. '61 at Chicago, it went to St. Louis 9 Dec. where it stayed a month before moving to Paducah. On 8 Mar. '62 the regiment moved to Pittsburg Landing. As part of Sherman's (5th) division, the regiment's casualties at Shiloh were 275 out of 512 in the line. Col. Stuart commanded the brigade here and Malmbourg commanded the regiment. During the Vicksburg campaign the 55th Ill. was in Lightburn's (2d) brigade, Blair's (2d) division, XV Corps. In the attacks on Kenesaw Mountain the regiment lost 14 killed, including Captain Augustine, who was commanding, and 33 wounded. In the entire Atlanta campaign the regiment lost 122, or about 50 per cent. Fox says. "There were 91 pairs of brothers in the regiment; of these men, 43 were killed in battle, and 15 died of disease. The 55th followed closely the fortunes of General Sherman—from Benton Barracks, St. Louis, where he was in charge. to the Grand Review at the close of the war. Its dead lie buried in nine different states; and it traveled, on foot and by transports, 11,965 miles, of which 3,240 were done on foot."

93D ILLINOIS

Colonels: Holden Putnam (K.I.A.), Nicholas C. Buswell.

Battles: Jackson (Miss.), Champion's Hill, Vicksburg (22 May) assault and siege, Missionary Ridge, Allatoona Pass. Ogeechee Canal (Ga.), Carolinas. Also present at Jackson siege, Dalton, Savannah siege, Congaree River (S.C.), and Bentonville.

Organized at Chicago in Sept. '62, ordered to Memphis 9 Nov., where it remained until the opening of the Vicksburg campaign. Engaged in Grant's march through northern Mississippi and on the Yazoo Expedition. During Vicksburg campaign it served in Boomer's (3d) brigade, Quinby's division, XVII Corps. At Champion's Hill, the regiment's heaviest fight, it lost 162. After the Vicksburg campaign the regiment was transferred to XV Corps. Col. Putnam was killed in the assault on Missionary Ridge; regimental losses here were 49. As part of John E. Smith's division during the Atlanta campaign the regiment was guarding the line of communications and was engaged in the defense of Allatoona Pass. In this action the regiment lost 83 out of its 290 effectives. The 93d took part in the XV Corps's march through Ga. and the Carolinas.

IMBODEN, John Daniel. C.S.A. gen. 1823–95. Va. Graduating from Washington College, he was a lawyer and legislator, organizing the Staunton Arty. He commanded this unit when Harpers Ferry was occupied and supported Bee's brigade at 1st Bull Run. Named Col. in 1862, he commanded the 1st Partisan Rangers fighting at Cross Keys and Port Republic. He was given a special appointment as B.G. C.S.A. under the Act of 11 Oct. '62, Sec. 2, on 28 Jan. '63 and led JONES'S AND IMBODEN'S W. VA. RAID in Apr. and May '63. On the advance into Pa., his brigade protected the left flank and covered the retreat, saving wagon trains and the wounded. During the Bristoe campaign he captured Charleston (W. Va.) and fought at Piedmont and New Market during the first phase of Early's Valley campaign. In the fall of 1864 he was felled by typhoid fever and was sent to Aiken (S.C.) on prison duty. After the war he was a lawyer and land developer, writing a great deal about Va.'s natural resources. In B.&L. he wrote five articles, ranging from Harpers Ferry up to Gettysburg and back to New Market. He was married five times.

IMBODEN'S WEST VIRGINIA RAID. Apr. '63. See JONES'S AND IMBODEN'S W. VA. RAID.

19TH INDIANA (IRON BRIGADE)
Colonels: Solomon Meredith (Bvt. Maj. Gen.), Samuel J. Williams (K.I.A.), John M. Lindley (Bvt. B.G.).

Battles: Lewinsville (Va., 11 Sept. '61), Manassas, South Mountain, Antietam, Fredericksburg, Fitz Hugh's Crossing, Gettysburg, Wilderness, Spotsylvania, North Anna, Bethesda Church, Cold Harbor, Petersburg, White River (Ark.; gunboat service). Also at Chancellorsville, Mine Run, Totopotomoy, and Weldon R.R.

Organized 29 July '61 in Indianapolis, it arrived in Washington 5 Aug. At Manassas (2d Bull Run) it lost 259 out of 423 engaged. At South Mountain it lost 53, at Antietam it lost 72 out of 200 engaged, at Gettysburg it lost 210 out of 288 engaged, and in the fighting from the Wilderness to Petersburg (5 May to 30 July '64) it lost 226. Major Isaac M. May was killed at Manassas, Lt. Col. Alois O. Bachman was killed at Antietam, and Col. Williams was killed at the Wilderness. See also IRON BRIGADE.

20TH INDIANA
Colonels: William L. Brown (K.I.A.), John Wheeler (K.I.A.), William C. Taylor, and William Orr.

Battles: Oak Grove, Glendale, Manassas, Chantilly, Fredericksburg, Chancellorsville, Gettysburg, Kelly's Ford, Mine Run, Wilderness, Spotsylvania, North Anna, Totopotomoy, Cold Harbor,

Petersburg siege, Deep Bottom, Boydton Road, Hatcher's Run, and Farmville. Also at White Oak Swamp, Malvern Hill, Poplar Spring Church, Strawberry Plains, and Appomattox.

After leaving the state 2 Aug. '61, its first duty was guarding the railroad near Cockeysville, Md. It went then to Hatteras Inlet, N.C., 24 Sept., and two months later arrived at Fort Monroe where it spent the winter. During the *Monitor-Merrimac* duel the regiment took up positions on shore that prevented the disabled *Congress* from being captured. Joining McClellan's force on the Peninsula, the regiment was assigned to Robinson's (1st) brigade, Kearny's (3d) division, III Corps. As part of the Union left on 25 June '62 the regiment (at Oak Grove or "The Orchards") bore the brunt of the Confederate attack and sustained 125 casualties in its first major action. At Glendale it was again heavily engaged, losing 10 killed. At Manassas the regiment lost 45, and Col. Brown was killed. Due to heavy losses the III Corps did not participate in the Antietam campaign but was assigned to the defenses of Washington for recuperation. At Gettysburg, as part of Ward's brigade, Birney's division, its losses were 156. Colonel Wheeler was killed. In 1864 the regiment became part of II Corps and sustained heavy casualties in the Wilderness (33 killed), Spotsylvania (18 killed), and the siege of Petersburg (22 killed). Lt. Col. Meikel was killed at Petersburg.

27TH INDIANA

Colonel: Silas Colgrove (Bvt. B.G.).

Battles: Winchester, Cedar Mountain, Antietam, Chancellorsville, Gettysburg, Resaca, New Hope Church, Peach Tree Creek, Atlanta siege. Present also at Front Royal, Cassville, Dallas, Lost Mountain, Kenesaw.

After leaving the state 15 Sept. '61 it arrived in Washington and was assigned to Banks's command, in which it saw action in Jackson's Valley campaign (Gordon's [3d] brigade of Williams's [1st] division). It was assigned to the XII Corps when the latter was created 12 Sept. '62, and remained in Williams's division thereafter.

Its casualties were high at Cedar Mountain (50), Antietam (209 killed and wounded, no missing in action), Chancellorsville (150), and Gettysburg (110, only one of whom was M.I.A.). Moving to the West, the regiment at Resaca captured the colors and the colonel of the 38th Ala., and is credited with inflicting five times as many casualties as it itself suffered (68).

INDIAN HILL, Tenn., 23 Oct. '63. See CHATTANOOGA CAMPAIGN.

INDIAN TERRITORY. An area now in the state of Oklahoma, excluding the panhandle (which was known as the Public Land Strip). See also C.N.

INDIAN TERRITORY, CONFED. DEPT. AND DIST. OF. On 13 May '61 Benjamin McCulloch was assigned command in Indian Territory (roughly the present state of Oklahoma). On 22 Nov. '61 it was established as a department under command of Albert Pike. It ceased to be a separate department 26 May '62, when it was embraced in the TRANS-MISSISSIPPI Dept., that was created on that date. Pike resigned 5 Nov. '62 after a controversy with Hindman over use of Indian troops at Pea Ridge. On 11 Dec. '63 S. B. Maxey was "assigned to command of the Indian Territory," and on 9 May '64 he "resumed command" (O.R., I, XXII, I, 9; and XXXIV, I, 6). On 21 Feb. '65 D. H. Cooper was assigned to command of the "District of the Indian Territory"; on 1 Mar. he assumed command of the above "and superintendency of Indian Affairs" (*ibid.*, XLVIII, I, 4).

INDIAN TROUBLES. The threat of an Indian uprising was of considerable concern in the West. In Aug. '62 "The 'farmer' Sioux in Minnesota had joined the 'blanket' Sioux in the massacre of two or three hundred white settlers" (Monaghan, 255). Gov. Ramsey appointed H. H. Sibley a B.G. USV to quell it. In six weeks his brigade captured over 1,000, and 303 of these were sentenced to die. The War Dept. established the Dept. of the Northwest on 6 Sept. '62 to deal with this problem, and put John Pope in command. Lincoln intervened to review the records of the convicted men and authorized the execution of 39 (Hesseltine, 276). On 26 Dec. '62, 38 Indians were hanged from a single gallows. Gov. Solomon in neighboring Wis. wired hysterical reports to Stanton that Confederate emissaries were stirring up the Winnebagos, but—perhaps because of the experience of the Sioux—this threat did not materialize (*ibid.*).

The Navajos had caused trouble ever since the U.S. had occupied New Mexico in 1846. When the regular troops were sent East in the Civil War, Col. "Kit" CARSON moved in with 700 volunteer cavalry with orders to round up and evacuate the Navajos. In Jan. '64 he trapped a large number in the Canyon de Chelly and they were herded on the 300-mile "Long Walk" to Ft. Sumner, N.M.

The *Official Records* refer to a Sioux Expedition in the Dakotas, 16 June–13 Sept. '63. (O.R., I, XXII.)

INFORMAL TRUCES. See FRATERNIZATION.

INGALLS, Rufus. Union gen. 1820–93. Me. USMA 1843 (32/39); Dragoons-Q.M. He fought in the Mexican War (1 brevet), served on the frontier, and was Q.M. on exploration expeditions before being named Lt. Col. Add. A.D.C. 28 Sept. '61 to McClellan. Serving as Chief Q.M. of the Army of the Potomac 10 July '62–16 June '64, he was named B.G. USV 23 May '63. He was present at South Mountain, Antietam, Fredericksburg, Chancellorsville, Gettysburg, and the Mine Run Operations. As Chief Q.M. of the Armies against Richmond (16 June '64–9 May '65), he was present at the Wilderness, Spotsylvania, Cold Harbor, Petersburg. He established and superintended the Army Depot at City Point (Va.) and was breveted Lt. Col. through Maj. Gen. USA and Maj. Gen. USV for war service. Continuing in the R.A., he was retired in 1883 as B.G. Q.M. Gen.

INGRAHAM, Timothy. Union officer. c. 1811–76. Mass. Lt. Col. 18th Mass. 24 Aug. '61; Col. 38th Mass. 21 Aug. '62; Bvt. B.G. USV 2 Oct. '65 (war service). Provost Marshal Washington 1863–65. Commanded 1, 3, XIX.

INNES, William Power. Union officer. N.Y. Col. 1st Mich. Engrs. 12 Sept. '61; Bvt. B.G. USV (war service); mustered out 2 Nov. '64. Died 1893.

INTERIOR LINES. A term used in tactics and strategy to indicate a *situation* in which one commander has an advantage in being able to employ his forces against the enemy faster than the enemy can counter his moves. The correct use of "interior lines" has been the hallmark of successful generals through the ages, and the term has been misunderstood by readers of military history for almost as long a period. A commander may possess "interior lines" by virtue of a *central position* with respect to his opponent. But he may also possess it by virtue of *superior lateral communications*. Thus the South, despite its central position, did not actually possess "interior lines" because the North had a superior railroad network. Evidence of this paradox is that the Federals could move reinforcements from Va. to Chattanooga faster than the Confederates could do so, even though the Confederates had a shorter straight-line distance to cover. Interior lines at Sharpsburg (Antietam) enabled Lee to avoid annihilation. In this instance it was his central position that permitted him to move troops rapidly from unthreatened parts of his line to meet Burnside's PIECEMEAL attacks. Meade's interior lines at Gettysburg played a major role in his defeat of Lee's assaults. Pope lost the 2d Bull Run campaign despite his interior lines. If a commander does not possess interior lines to start with he may get them by a "strategic penetration," which was one of Napoleon's favorite maneuvers.

6TH IOWA (XVI Corps)

Colonels: John A. McDowell, John M. Corse (Bvt. Maj. Gen.), William H. Clune.

Battles: Shiloh, Jackson (14 May '63), Vicksburg, Jones's Ford, Jackson (16 July '63), Missionary Ridge, Resaca, Dallas, New Hope Church, Big Shanty, Kenesaw Mountain, Atlanta, Ezra Chapel, Lovejoy, Griswoldville, Columbia, Bentonville, Goldsboro. Present also at Athens (Mo.), Corinth siege, Chulahoma (Miss.), Holly Springs, Jonesboro, East Point, Coosaw River (S.C.), and Savannah.

Organized 17 July '61 at Burlington, it took part in Oct. in Frémont's Mo. campaign against Price. During the winter of '61–'62 it guarded the railroad between Sedalia and Tipton. In Mar. '62 it moved to Shiloh, where it was assigned to Sherman's division. Col. McDowell took command of the brigade and Capt. John Williams commanded the regiment in the battle; losses were 183 out of less than 650 engaged.

Through the siege of Corinth the regiment remained in Sherman's division, after which McDowell's brigade moved to Memphis. It spent the winter of '62–63 at La Grange, Tenn. Under Corse the regiment won special commendation at Jackson, Miss., 16 July '63. At Missionary Ridge the regiment was in Ewing's division, XV Corps.

IOWA BRIGADE (Belknap's) (XVII Corps). Composed of the 11th, 13th, 15th and 16th Iowa, this unit sustained 443 killed and mortally wounded during the war.

IRISH BEND AND FORT BISLAND, La. 12–14 Apr. '63. (Also known as Bayou Teche, Centreville, and Indian Ridge, Bend, or Village.) As part of his strategy to take PORT HUDSON, Banks decided to advance up the Atchafalaya and Bayou Teche to Alexandria, La., thus clearing the Confederates from the west bank of the Mississippi and "turning" their Port Hudson defenses. (This was Banks's RED RIVER CAMPAIGN OF 1863.)

To oppose this threat Taylor had 2,700 in the vicinity of Fort Bisland. His vulnerable flank on Grand Lake was protected by the *Queen of the West* and his right flank on Bayou Teche was covered by the *Diana*. Alert to the possibility of cutting off and annihilating this force, Banks ordered Grover's division (4, XIX) up Grand Lake to cut Taylor's line of retreat at Irish Bend. Emory's division (3, XIX) and Weitzel's brigade (2, 1, XIX) were to attack Fort Bisland to hold the Confederates in place while Grover enveloped. Banks's total strength was 15,000.

Grover's departure was delayed until the morning of 12 Apr.; his movement up the lake was delayed by the grounding of the *Arizona*, one of his four accompanying gunboats under Lt. Comdr. Cooke; his debarkation was delayed until 4 P.M. of the next day by difficulties in finding a location from which adequate roads led inland to the Teche, and because the boats could get no nearer than 100 yards from shore.

(Grover's report in O.R., I, XV, 358. Madame Porter's plantation, where he first tried to find a landing place, and McWilliams's plantation "about 6 miles farther [north]" are not shown in the O.R. atlas.)

Meanwhile, the main body had marched up the bayou the morning of the 12th and was in contact with the defenders of Fort Bisland at 2 P.M. Attacking the main defenses early the next day, Emory and Weitzel had pushed to within 400 yards of the fort by nightfall. When the attack was resumed the morning of the 14th the Confederates were gone.

Early this same morning Taylor struck the flank of Birge's brigade near Irish Bend and forced Grover to deploy his division. In a skillfully conducted action Taylor extricated himself from the trap. Federal pursuit was "without energy or vigor," according to Taylor's memoirs.

Most accounts give Confederate strength in this operation as about 5,000. In his official report (*ibid.*, 391) Taylor says he had less than 4,000 at the beginning of the operation, and that he was reinforced by Clack's battalion from New Iberia. In *Destruction and Reconstruction* Taylor says he had 2,700 before Clack's arrival (pp. 151–52). Referring to Banks's claim of over 2,500 prisoners taken, Taylor says "At the time my entire force in western Louisiana was under three thousand" (*ibid.*, 161).

The Federals reported 350 casualties. Capt. O. J. Semmes (CSN), son of Adm. Raphael Semmes (of the *Alabama*), was captured while destroying the *Diana*.

(See also RED RIVER CAMPAIGN OF 1863 and SIBLEY AND GRANT COURTS-MARTIAL.)

IRISH BRIDGET. See Bridget DIVERS.

IRISH BRIGADE (1st Div., II Corps, Potomac). As originally organized, the brigade consisted of the 63d, 69th, and 88th N.Y. In the fall of 1862 the 28th Mass. and the 116th Pa. were added. The 29th Mass. served with the brigade during the Peninsular and Antietam campaigns (before the 28th joined). In Sept. '64 the remnant of the 7th N.Y. Hy. Arty. was added. The 116th Pa. was transferred out in July '64. The Irish Brigade distinguished itself in attacks against the Stone Wall at Marye's Heights (Fredericksburg). Commanders were Brig. Gen. Thomas F. Meagher, Col. Patrick Kelly (killed at Petersburg), Bvt. Maj. Gen. Thomas A. Smyth (mortally wounded at Farmville, Va., while commanding another brigade), Col. Richard Byrnes (mortally wounded at Cold Harbor), and Brig. Gen. Robert Nugent. Each regiment of the brigade carried a green flag in addition to the national color.

IRON BRIGADE OF THE WEST. One of the most famous outfits of the war, it was originally composed of the 19th Ind. and the 2d, 6th, and 7th Wis. regiments (total: 2,400 men) under John Gibbon. Known initially as the Black Hat Brigade (because of its own special non-regulation slouch hats), it distinguished itself in its first engagement at Groveton (2d Bull Run) when it suffered 33 per cent casualties while fighting as part of King's division against Stonewall Jackson's corps. In three weeks the brigade fought five battles and lost 58 per cent of its original strength. The 24th Mich. joined the brigade just before Gibbon led them to further distinction in the Antietam campaign. It was here that a war correspondent gave them the name "Iron Brigade." After fighting at Fredericksburg and Chancellorsville, the brigade entered the Gettysburg campaign as the 1st Brig., 1st Div., I Corps; its new commander was politically selected Solomon Meredith, formerly the colonel of the 19th Ind. In the severe fighting for Seminary Ridge, on the first day of the battle, the brigade lost two thirds of its 1,800 effectives. Casualties in the 24th Mich. were 399 out of 496 (80 per cent). Although the Iron Brigade of the West continued to exist as a unit, it never recovered its former punch.

Another "Iron Brigade," less well remembered, although of earlier origin, was that of J. P. Hatch. It was composed of the 2d US Sharpshooters and the 22d, 24th, 30th, and 84th N.Y. When Gibbon's "Black Hat Brigade" was the 4th Brig. of King's division during the 2d Bull Run campaign, Hatch's "Iron Brigade" was the 1st Brig. of that same division. The correspondent who gave Gibbon's brigade its nickname at Antietam was apparently unaware that it had been borne previously by another unit of the same division. Hatch's "Iron Brigade" ceased to exist in May '63 when the 22d, 24th, and 30th N.Y. were mustered out at the expiration of their two years' service.

IRONCLAD OATH. Passed by Congress 2 July '62, it was taken by every civilian or military officeholder (either "for honor or profit"). It stated allegiance to the Constitution, declared that the swearer had never voluntarily borne arms against the Union, or aided in any way such a rebellion. This was the key implementation of the RADICAL REPUBLICAN reconstruction policy after the war.

IRVINE, William. Union officer. N.Y. Lt. Col. 10th N.Y. Cav. 25 Nov. '61; Bvt. B.G. USV (war service); mustered out 6 Dec. '64. Died 1882.

IRWIN, William Howard. Union officer. Pa. Capt. 1847–48; won 1 brevet. Col. 7th Pa. 23 Apr. '61; mustered out 23 July '61: Col. 49th Pa. 28 Feb. '62;

Bvt. B.G. USV (Antietam); resigned 24 Oct. '63. Died 1886. Listed by Phisterer as Irvin, William H.

IRWINSVILLE, Ga. 10 May '65. Jeff Davis captured by 1st Wis. Cav. and 4th Mich. Cav. with loss of two Federals killed and four wounded as a result of pursuers firing into each other.

ISLAND NO. 10. See NEW MADRID and ISLAND NO. 10, Mar. '62.

IUKA, Miss., 19 Sept. '62. Sterling Price, with 17,000 troops at Tupelo, had orders from Bragg to prevent the movement of Rosecrans' two divisions from Corinth to reinforce Buell in middle Tenn. A different plan was proposed by Van Dorn, who had 7,000 troops at Holly Springs: Van Dorn, who was senior to Price, proposed that the two combine forces to attack Grant's extended lines in western Tenn.

Believing Bragg's instructions to be more imperative, Price drove a small force from Iuka on 13 Sept., occupied that place, and waited further developments. Grant decided to attack Price before Van Dorn could reinforce him. The plan was for Ord to advance with three small divisions (8,000) along the railroad to Iuka, while Rosecrans would lead his two divisions (Stanley and Hamilton, 9,000) south through Jacinto to cut off Price's retreat.

Although Ord's column was in position within two miles of Iuka the night of the 18th, Rosecrans was delayed. By late afternoon Rosecrans had pushed to within two miles of Iuka when, about 4:30, his leading brigade (Sanborn's of Hamilton's division) was suddenly attacked by two Confederate brigades under Henry Little. The first two attacks were repulsed in heavy fighting, but a third assault pushed Hamilton's division to the rear. The fight continued until dark (about two hours), at which time Rosecrans' three brigades had stopped the two under Little. The latter was killed.

Ord had not heard the battle and did not participate. Grant had not intended to attack until the 20th. Price, however, was surprised by the strength of Rosecrans' attack, and when he learned that Ord was also in position to attack he retreated southward during the night (19-20 Sept.). The next engagement was at CORINTH, 3-4 Oct.

The Federals lost 782 (144 killed, 598 wounded, 40 missing), and the Confederates 1,516 (263, 692, 561) (E.&B.; Drake).

IVERSON, Alfred. C.S.A. gen. 1829–1911. Ga. He left military school to fight in the Mexican War and then became a lawyer and railroad contractor. Entering the R.A. in 1855, he was a 1st Lt. with the 1st Cav. and served in garrison and on the frontier, in Indian fighting, in the Kansas border disturbances, and in the Utah Expedition. When Ga. seceded, he resigned and was appointed from N.C. as Capt. in the provisional Confederate army. Sent to Holmes at Wilmington (N.C.), he fought along the Cape Fear River and was commissioned Col. 20th N.C. 20 Aug. '61. Wounded in the Seven Days' Battles, he led his regiment at South Mountain and Antietam and when Garland was killed he took over the brigade. He was appointed B.G. C.S.A. 1 Nov. '62 and led the brigade at Fredericksburg, Chancellorsville, and Gettysburg. Sent to Rome (Ga.), he was in charge of organizing the state troops gathered there. He returned to field duty for the Atlanta campaign, leading his brigade in the cavalry corps. He fought Stoneman near Macon, capturing him at Sunshine Church. After the war he was in business in Ga. and owned an orange grove in Fla. Iverson's father was a distinguished and radical secessionist whose birth and death dates (1789–1873) have been confused by Wright with those of his son.

IVES, Brayton. Union officer. 1840–? Conn. 1st Lt. Adj. 5th Conn. 23 July '61; Capt. 25 Sept. '61; Capt. Asst. Adj. Gen. Vols. 28 Apr. '62; resigned 5 Aug. '63; Maj. 1st Conn. Cav. 31 May '64; Lt. Col. 1 Nov. '64; Col. 17 Jan. '65; Bvt. B.G. USV (Reams's Station, Deep Bottom, Five Forks, Sayler's Creek). He was president of the N.Y. Stock Exchange and won renown as a collector of rare, antique books, having at one time a Gutenberg Bible.

IVEY (or Ivy) Farm (or Hills). See WEST POINT, Miss. 21 Feb. '64.

J

JACKMAN, Sidney D. C.S.A. gen. Appt.-Mo. Listed as Col. 7th Mo., he was appointed B.G. C.S.A. 16 May '65 by Kirby Smith in the Trans-Miss. Dept. His name appears in the lists of Wood, Wright, and Heitman, but not in C.M.H.

JACKSON, Miss., 14 May and 9-16 July '63. 5 Feb. and 3-9 July '64.

On 14 May '63, XV and XVII Corps captured Jackson (Vicksburg campaign). After the surrender of Vicksburg (4 July '63), Sherman moved against J. E. Johnston's forces in Jackson. Sherman laid siege during the period 9-16 July, on which latter date Johnston withdrew. Union forces involved were IX, XIII, XV Corps, and two divisions of XVI Corps, which were attached to IX and XIII Corps for this operation. Considered part of this siege are the skirmishes at Rienzi, Bolton Depot, Canton, and Clinton. Although Fox states that XVII Corps (less Logan's division, occupying Vicksburg) took part in this operation, the official records do not credit this corps with participation (Fox, 98).

On 5 Feb. '64 part of XVII Corps and cavalry units fought at Jackson and Clinton during the course of the Meridian campaign.

During the period 3–9 July '64 troops of the 1st ("Red River") Div., XVII Corps, fought around Jackson during Slocum's expedition from Vicksburg to destroy the bridge over the Pearl River (which he accomplished). On the 6th Slocum entered the town and the next day had to fight his way through a Confederate position three miles west of Jackson. After a three-hour action in which he lost about 220 of his 2,800 men, Slocum continued his withdrawal to Vicksburg.

JACKSON, Tenn., 19 Dec. '62. (FORREST'S SECOND RAID; STONES RIVER) After Forrest's success at LEXINGTON, 18 Dec., the commander of the Dist. of Jackson, J. C. Sullivan, hurried infantry reinforcements toward Jackson. Only the 43d and 61st Ill. arrived in time to support the cavalry detachments of the 11th Ill., 5th Ohio, and 2d West Tenn. that guarded the place. The morning of the 19th Col. A. Englemann made contact and dropped back toward the town. At the Salem Cemetery the infantry held their fire and then delivered an effective fire from their concealed position. The Federal cavalry then counterattacked and drove Forrest off, estimating his loss at 73 and reporting their own as one killed, five wounded. Action also known as Salem Church.

JACKSON, Alfred E. C.S.A. gen. ?–1889. Appt.-Tenn. In 1861 he served as Zollicoffer's Q.M. and was under Kirby Smith in the Dept. of Eastern Tenn. in 1862. No rank is given for him in these positions. He was appointed B.G. C.S.A. 29 Oct. '62, but the appointment was canceled, and he was reappointed 22 Apr. '63 to rank from 9 Feb. '63. Assigned on the last-named date to the Dept. of Eastern Tenn. under Donelson, he commanded a brigade against Federal raiders and fought in Oct. '63 at Greenville (Tenn.). He was declared unfit for further field service on 23 Nov. '64—reasons unspecified—and reported to Breckinridge, presumably for staff duty.

JACKSON, Conrad Feger. Union gen. 1813–62. Pa. In railroading, he was appointed Col. 9th Pa. Res. 27 July '61 and commanded his regiment at Dranesville (Va.) 20 Dec. '61. In the Peninsular campaign he took over Seymour's brigade (3, 3, V) 30 June and commanded it until 26 Aug. '62. He was promoted B.G. USV 17 July '62 and led 3, 3, III, Army Va. (26–30 Aug. '62) at 2d Bull Run. While commanding 3, 3, I, Potomac (2 Oct.–13 Dec. '62), he was killed leading the column of attack at Fredericksburg.

JACKSON, Henry Rootes. C.S.A. gen. 1820–98. Ga. An Honor Man at Yale, he was a lawyer and fought in the Mexican War before becoming a judge and later *chargé d'affaires* and Minister Resident in Austria 1853–58. When the war came, he was appointed C.S.A. judge and resigned this post to be appointed B.G. C.S.A. 4 June '61. He served in W. Va. but resigned 2 Dec. '61 to become Maj. Gen. of Ga. state troops and command a division. After Atlanta's fall he was reappointed B.G. C.S.A. 23 Sept. '63 and commanded a brigade at Nashville, where he was captured 16 Dec. '64. He was released in July '65 and then returned to the law, becoming in time Minister to Mexico 1885–86 and a Democratic politician. He was interested in history and wrote poetry.

JACKSON, James Streshly. Union gen. 1823–62. Ky. A lawyer, he provoked a duel with a fellow officer during the Mexican War and resigned to avoid a court-martial. In 1861 he gave up his Unionist congressional seat to become Col. 3d Ky. Cav. 13 Dec. '61. He was promoted B.G. USV 16 July '62 and given command of the 10th Div., Army Ohio, in September. He then commanded 10th Div., I Corps, from Sept. until 8 Oct. '62, when he was killed at Perryville.

JACKSON, James T. Southern sympathizer who killed ELLSWORTH.

JACKSON, John K. C.S.A. gen. 1828–66. Ga. After graduating with honors at S.C. College he became a lawyer and joined the Oglethorpe infantry when war came. Named Lt. Col. in the battalion of the city of Augusta, he was commissioned Col. 5th Ga. in May '61 and commanded the post of Pensacola until Jan. '62, fighting at Santa Rosa Island. He was appointed B.G. C.S.A. 14 Jan. '62 and led his brigade at Pensacola. In Feb. '62 he was sent to Grand Junction (Tenn.) to organize troops sent for the Army of Tenn. He commanded his brigade at Shiloh and Stones River and was then in charge of communications from Chattanooga to Tullahoma. Fighting under Polk at Chickamauga and Hardee at Missionary Ridge, he was in Walker's division during the first part of the Atlanta campaign and was sent to Charleston 1 July '64. He then fought in Fla. during the siege of Savannah and in the Carolinas. After the war he was a lawyer.

JACKSON, Joseph Cooke. Union officer. 1835–? N.J. 2d Lt. 1st N.J. 11 Oct. '61; Capt. A.D.C. Vols. 20 Aug.

'62; appointment revoked 14 Feb. '63; Lt. Col. 26th N.J. 2 Dec. '62; Bvt. B.G. USV. Brevets for war service, Fredericksburg. Resigned 5 Jan. '63. A.D.C. to Gens. Robert Anderson and Philip Kearny. On staff in W. B. Franklin's division and in VI Corps (Potomac).

JACKSON, Nathaniel James. Union gen. c. 1825–92. Mass. He was commissioned Col. 1st Me. 3 May, mustered out 5 Aug., and appointed Col. 5th Me. 3 Sept. '61. Named B.G. USV 24 Sept. '62, he commanded 2, 2, XII, Potomac (28 Oct.–22 Dec. '62 and 3 Jan.–21 Mar. '63); 2, 1, XII, Potomac (21–29 Mar. '63); and 1st Div., XX, Cumberland (11 Nov. '64–2 Apr. '65). He was wounded at Gaines's Mill 27 June '62.

JACKSON, Richard Henry. Union gen. 1830–92. Ireland. R.A. Enlisting as Pvt. during the Seminole War in 1851, he was commissioned eight years later after passing the examining boards. A 1st Lt. 4th US Arty. 4 May '61 at Fort Pickens and Pensacola, he was promoted Capt. 20 Feb. '62; Lt. Col. Asst. I.G. Assigned 15 Apr. '63–23 May '65; and B.G. USV 19 May '65. He was on Folly Island during the Charleston siege and commanded 2d Div., XXV Corps, Va. (10 Apr.–4 Nov. '65). Breveted for Drewry's Bluff 15 May '64, New Market Heights 7 Oct. '64, and war service (B.G. USA, B.G. USV and Maj. Gen. USV 24 Nov. '65), he continued in the R.A., dying on active duty in 1892 as Lt. Col. 4th US Arty.

JACKSON, Samuel McCartney. Union officer. Pa. Capt. 11th Pa. Res. 8 June '61; Maj. 2 July '61; Lt. Col. 28 Oct. '61; Col. 9 Apr. '63; Bvt. B.G. USV (Wilderness, Spotsylvania Court House, Bethesda Church); mustered out 13 June '64. Commanded 1, 3, V.

JACKSON, Thomas Jonathan ("Stonewall"). C.S.A. gen. 1824-63. Va. USMA 1846 (17/59); Arty. Coming to West Point as an awkward, ill-educated boy in homespun clothes, Jackson was not an impressive plebe. After struggling to maintain minimum academic proficiency the first few months, he gradually improved his class standing; "and it was a frequent remark amongst his brother cadets that if the course had been a year longer he would have come out first" (Henderson, *Stonewall Jackson,* 12). He served with distinction in Magruder's battery in the Mexican War and won two brevets. In 1851 he resigned to teach at V.M.I. Jackson's first wife died 14 months after their marriage, and he remarried a few years later. While still in Mexico he had joined the church, and during his 10 years in Lexington he became a zealous and hardworking Presbyterian. In his personal habits he became increasingly austere. "He never smoked, he was a strict teetotaler, and he never touched a card. His diet, for reasons of health, was of a most sparing kind. . . ." (*ibid.*).

As events led up to the Civil War, Jackson commanded a company of V.M.I. cadets at John Brown's hanging in 1859 and on 21 Apr. '61 took the battalion of cadets to Richmond, where they were wanted as drillmasters for the mobilizing troops of Va. Appointed Col. of C.S.A. Inf., he was then ordered to Harpers Ferry where he organized what was shortly to become famous as the STONEWALL BRIGADE. Appointed B.G. C.S.A. 17 June '61, he and his brigade distinguished themselves at 1st Bull Run, where they both won the nickname "Stonewall." He was promoted Maj. Gen. 7th Oct. '61 and sent back to the Valley. Here, after the unsuccessful winter operation against Bath and Romney, the LORING-JACKSON INCIDENT, and his defeat at KERNS-

TOWN, he conducted the campaign that ranks with the most brilliant in history. See SHENANDOAH VALLEY CAMPAIGN OF JACKSON.

Joining Lee on the Peninsula, he then exhibited an amazingly inept leadership, the reasons for which still have the analysts baffled. See JACKSON OF THE CHICKAHOMINY. In the 2d Bull Run campaign his mania for secrecy led to his failure at Cedar Mountain to take advantage of a strategic opportunity. Then, however, his genius showed itself again in his lightning envelopment of Pope's army and the battle of 2D BULL RUN. In the Antietam campaign he continued to excel as a commander of independent operations, while Lee accompanied the slower-moving Longstreet.

He was appointed Lt. Gen. on 10 Oct. '62 and given command of the newly-established II CORPS, A.N.V. He had a prominent part in the battle of FREDERICKSBURG, where he held the right of the line. As Lee's strong right arm, it was Jackson who executed the audacious plan that resulted in the masterpiece of CHANCELLORSVILLE. On 2 May '62 he was mortally wounded by his own men and died eight days later of pneumonia resulting from his wounds. Lee said, "I know not how to replace him." Freeman sums up the defeat at Gettysburg with the statement, "Jackson is not here."

"A man he is of contrasts so complete that he appears one day a Presbyterian deacon who delights in theological discussion and, the next, a reincarnated Joshua. He lives by the New Testament and fights by the Old. Almost 6 feet in height and weighing about 175 pounds, he has blue eyes, a brown beard and a commonplace, somewhat rusty appearance" (*Lee's Lts.,* I, xlii).

Called "Old Jack" at West Point;

"Tom Fool Jackson" by his V.M.I. cadets; "Old Blue Light," "Stonewall," and then "Old Jack" by his soldiers, he is "Stonewall" to posterity.

JACKSON, William A. C.S.A. gen. See JACKSON, William Lowther.

JACKSON, William Hicks. C.S.A. gen. 1835–1903. Tenn. USMA 1856 (38/49); Cav. He served on the frontier and in Indian fighting, resigning 16 May '61 as 2d Lt. Commissioned Capt. of C.S.A. Arty., he was wounded at Belmont (Mo.) and named Col. 7th Tenn. and 1st Miss. upon his recovery. After the battle of Holly Springs, he was appointed B.G. C.S.A. 29 Dec. '62 and then commanded a division in Tenn. the next spring. After Van Dorn's death (8 May '63) Jackson commanded the cavalry in Miss. under Pemberton and Johnston at Vicksburg and in the Meridian campaign. In the Atlanta campaign he covered the left wing of Johnston's army and was in Forrest's corps covering Hood's retreat from Tenn. In Feb. '65 he was put in command of all the Tenn. cavalry and a Tex. brigade and at war's end was a Confederate commissioner for the parole of troops in Ala. and Miss. Called "Red" by his soldiers. He was a cotton planter for a time after the war and then raised thoroughbred horses at Belle Meade near Nashville.

JACKSON, William Lowther. C.S.A. gen. 1825–90. W. Va. Appt.-Va. A lawyer, jurist, and public official, he enlisted early in 1861 as a private and was elected Lt. Col. Va. Vols. in June of that year. In the western Va. operations he was with the 31st Va. and served as volunteer A.D.C. to his cousin, Stonewall Jackson, in the Valley campaign, the 2d Bull Run campaign, and the Maryland campaign at Harpers Ferry and Antietam. He was then authorized to raise a regiment within the enemy lines in W. Va. on 17 Feb. '63 and was commissioned Col. 19th Va. Cav. early in April. During the remainder of that year he participated in several raids and was Adj. Gen. of Jenkins' brigade. The following spring he was given a brigade at Warm Springs and in May '64 opposed Crook's raid. In June he engaged in the defense of Lynchburg and the next month went on Early's raid to Washington. Before being appointed B.G. C.S.A. 19 Dec. '64, he had fought at Winchester, Cedar Creek, Fishers Hill, and Port Republic. Refusing to surrender, he disbanded his brigade 15 Apr. '65. After the war, was a lawyer and judge in Kentucky. C.M.H. gives the above version of his name, although Wright lists his middle initial as A.

JACKSON OF THE CHICKA-HOMINY. A phrase used to distinguish the brilliant "Jackson of the Valley" from the ineffective Stonewall Jackson who failed five times during the Seven Days' Battles (at Mechanicsville, Gaines's Mill, Savage's Station, Glendale, and Malvern Hill). See Henderson's *Stonewall Jackson,* Vandiver's *Mighty Stonewall,* and Freeman's chapter entitled "The Enigma of Jackson's State of Mind" in *Lee's Lts.,* I, 655–69.

JACKSON'S ("Stonewall") CORPS. See II CORPS, Confed., A.N.V.

JACKSONVILLE, Fla., 23–31 Mar. '63. Occupied by 8th Me. and detachments of 6th Conn. and Higginson's colored troops with naval support. Col. Montgomery with 120 men and gunboat *Paul Jones* advanced 75 miles up the river to Palatka, capturing 15 prisoners and taking some cotton, horses, etc. Part of the city was set on fire before the expedition left.

JACKSONVILLE, Fla. Occupied by Federals 7 Feb. '64 prior to battle of OLUSTEE, 20 Feb.

JACOBS, Ferris, Jr. Union officer. 1836–86. N.Y. Capt. 3d N.Y. Cav. 26 Aug. '61; Maj. 13 June '63; Lt. Col. 22 July '64; mustered out 12 Oct. '64; Lt. Col. 26th N.Y. Cav. 15 Mar. '65; Bvt. B.G. USV (war service). He represented his state as a Republican Congressman after the war.

JÄGER RIFLE. Name initially applied to the U.S. RIFLE, Model 1841. Also a foreign type.

JAMES, William Levis. Union officer. Pa. Capt. Asst. Q.M. Vols. 26 Nov. '62; Col. Q.M. Assigned 13 May '65–31 July '66; Bvt. B.G. USV 1 Mar. '66 (war service).

JAMES, UNION ARMY OF THE. Butler's Army of the James (in his Department of VIRGINIA AND NORTH CAROLINA) was organized in Apr. '64 to operate against Richmond from the south of the James River while the Army of the Potomac attacked Lee's forces from the north. It consisted of Gillmore's X Corps, W. F. Smith's XVIII Corps, and A. V. Kautz's cavalry division. After the failure of the initial Petersburg assaults the X and XVIII Corps commanders were relieved by D. B. Birney and Ord, respectively. In Aug. the army had 17,000 infantry and 2,300 cavalry "present for duty, equipped." On 8 Jan. '65 Ord succeeded Butler, and, after a final reorganization 31 Jan. '65, his army consisted of Gibbon's XXIV Corps, Weitzel's XXV (Col.) Corps, and Mackenzie's cavalry division.

JAMES, UNION MILITARY DIVISION OF THE. Created at the end of the war (19 Apr. '65) to consist of the Dept. of Va. and such parts of N.C. as are not occupied by the command of Maj. Gen. W. T. Sherman. Commanded by Maj. Gen. H. W. Halleck.

JAMESON, Charles Davis. Union gen. 1827–62. Me. One of the most extensive lumber shippers and manufacturers in that state, he was commissioned Col. 2d Me. 28 May '61 and B.G. USV 3 Sept. '61. He commanded 3d Brig., Heintzelman's division (3 Oct. '61–13 Mar. '62) and 1, 3, III, Potomac (13 Mar.–12 June '62). Ill with "camp fever" after Fair Oaks, he returned to Me., where he died 6 Nov. '62. Phisterer spells his last name Jamison.

JAMES PROJECTILE AND GUN. Charles T. James of R.I. developed a type of projectile that could be used in any cannon specially rifled for it. It was service tested in 1860, and Gillmore used some James rifles in his reduction of Fort Pulaski in Apr. '62.

JAMES RIVER BRIDGE (PETERSBURG CAMPAIGN). The "longest continuous ponton bridge ever used in war" (Mitchell, 514) was built 14 June '64 (Humphreys, 203) between Windmill Point and Fort Powhatan for the movement of the Army of the Potomac across the James. The river was 2,100 feet wide, up to 15 fathoms deep in mid-channel, had a strong tidal current and a tidal range of four feet (Humphreys). The work was accomplished by 450 engineers under Capt. G. H. Mendell, directed initially by Maj. J. C. Duane and then by Gen. Benham; working from both sides, the bridge was completed in eight hours (exclusive of the time for preparing the approaches). (Planning had been started two months previously.) One hundred and one pontons and three schooners were used. The crossing was completed at 7 P.M., 18 June, at which time the bridge was then broken into three rafts and floated to City Point, where it arrived about dawn. (Source: Humphreys, pp. 9, 203; Miller, Vol. V, pp. 236, 242, states Benham received orders at 11 A.M., 15 June, to start construction of the bridge, and gives 2,200 feet as the width of the water gap.)

JAMISON, Charles D. Erroneous listing by Phisterer for Charles Davis JAMESON.

JARDINE, Edward. Union officer. N.Y. Capt. 9th N.Y. 4 May '61; Maj. 14 Feb. '62; mustered out 20 May '63; Lt. Col. 17th N.Y. 17 Oct. '63; mustered out 10 May '64; Capt. Vet. Res. Corps 3 May '64; Bvt. B.G. USV 2 Nov. '65 (war service). Died 1893.

JARVIS, Dwight, Jr. Union officer. N.Y. Ex-Cadet USMA 1856; Appt.-Ohio. 1st Lt. 13th Ohio 25 Apr. '61; Capt. 25 Oct. '61; Maj. 14 Aug. '62; Lt. Col. 24 Dec. '62; Col. 1 Jan. '63; Bvt. B.G. USV (war service); mustered out 26 June '64.

JEFFERIES, Noah Lemuel. Union officer. Pa. 1st Lt. Adj. 29th N.Y. 14 Oct. '61; Capt. Asst. Adj. Gen. Vols. 26 Mar. '62; Maj. Asst. Adj. Gen. Vols. 12 Aug. '63; resigned 30 Nov. '63; Lt. Col. Vet. Res. Corps 26 Nov. '63; Col. 12 Feb. '64; Bvt. B.G. USV 30 Mar. '65 (recruitment service). Died 1896.

JENKINS, Albert Gallatin. C.S.A. gen. 1830-64. Va. After graduating from Harvard Law School he was a Democratic Congressman who resigned his seat in Apr. '61 to join the Confederacy. He was commissioned Capt. of a cavalry company in Va. Promoted Lt. Col. and then Col. 8th Va., he was engaged in raids throughout the mountain counties until Feb. '62, when he was sent to the C.S.A. Congress. He was appointed B.G. C.S.A. 5 Aug. '62 and led his brigade on a 500-mile raid

through W. Va. and into Ohio later that month and in Sept. In the Gettysburg campaign he was with the advance guard, capturing Chambersburg and reconnoitering to Harrisburg. Wounded at Gettysburg, he was wounded again and captured 9 May '64 at Cloyd's Mountain (Va.), dying shortly thereafter.

JENKINS, Horatio, Jr. Union officer. Mass. 1st Lt. 40th Mass. 5 Sept. '61; Capt. 1 Nov. '62; mustered out 18 Feb. '65; Lt. Col. 4th Mass. Cav. 12 Mar. '65; Col. 29 May '65; Bvt. B.G. USV. Brevets for High Bridge (Va.), war service. W.I.A. High Bridge.

JENKINS, Micah. C.S.A. gen. 1835-64. S.C. A member of the plantation aristocracy for generations, he graduated from the S.C. Mil. Academy at the head of his class and then helped establish other military schools in his state. He was commissioned Col. 5th S.C., leading it at 1st Bull Run and commanded Jenkins' Palmetto Sharpshooters in the Peninsula. After commanding a brigade at Williamsburg, Seven Pines, and Frayser's Farm, he was appointed B.G. C.S.A. 22 July '62 and severely wounded at 2d Bull Run. He commanded his brigade at Fredericksburg, Chickamauga, Knoxville, and the Wilderness, where he was fatally shot 6 May by a Confederate soldier, near the place and in much the same way as Stonewall Jackson.

JENKINS' FERRY (Saline R.), Ark., 30 Apr. '64. (ARKANSAS CAMPAIGN) While retreating from Camden, closely pursued by Kirby Smith, Steele's command was attacked while astride the Saline River. Steele escaped with a loss of 528 (64 killed, 378 wounded, 86 missing) but had to abandon his ponton train (Fiebeger, 395). S. A. Rice, commanding the 1st Brig. of Solomon's division, was mortally wounded. The Confederates lost 443 (86, 356, 1) (Fox, pp. 80, 546, 551).

JENNISON, Samuel Pearce. Union officer. Mass. 2d Lt. 2d Minn. 5 July '61; 1st Lt. Adj. 17 Jan. '62; Lt. Col. 10th Minn. 10 Sept. '62; Bvt. B.G. USV (war service). Commanded 1st Brig., 2d Det., Army of Tenn.

JERICHO BRIDGE, Va., 25 May '64. See NORTH ANNA RIVER.

1ST JERSEY BRIGADE (1st Div., VI Corps, Potomac). Composed of the 1st, 2d, 3d, 4th, 10th, and 15th N.J., this brigade had the fourth highest number of killed and mortally wounded in the war (total 900). At Fredericksburg the brigade was commanded by Col. Alfred T. A. Torbert. At Chancellorsville (Salem Church) it was commanded initially by Col. Henry W. Brown. Col. William H. Penrose, 15th N.J., took Brown's place temporarily until Col. Samuel L. Buck's arrival (Buck commanded 2d N.J.); Penrose resumed command after Buck was wounded. Torbert commanded the brigade at Gettysburg and Brown during the Wilderness campaign. Penrose was in command at Cold Harbor and when the war ended.

JERUSALEM PLANK ROAD. See WELDON R.R. OPERATIONS, 22–23 June '64.

JETERSVILLE, Va., 5 Apr. '65. See AMELIA SPRINGS.

JOE BROWN'S PIKES. With the mistaken idea that the pike would make a suitable infantry weapon, Gov. Joseph E. Brown of Ga. in 1862 spurred production of this implement. Thousands were produced by over a hundred makers and bought at $5.00 each. Most of them consisted of a 12-inch, double-edged blade on a six- or seven-foot pole. Some had a sharp, curved hook known as a "bridle cutter." Although never used in combat, they decorate many a modern museum (Albaugh and Simmons, 125ff.).

JOHNS, Thomas Denton. Union officer. c. 1824–83. Pa. USMA 1848 (32/38); Inf. Col. 7th Mass. 28 Mar. '63; Bvt. B.G. USV (Fredericksburg and war service); mustered out 27 June '64. W.I.A. Fredericksburg. Resigning as a 2d Lt. in 1851, he was a merchant and silver mine superintendent in California before the war.

JOHNSON, Adam R. C.S.A. gen. 1834–1922. Appt.-Ky. Wright lists him as appointed B.G. C.S.A. 6 Sept. '64 to rank from 1 June of that year under the special provision that gave the president power to appoint major and brigadier generals in the public interest whether or not the necessary troops for them to command had been mustered. This same source says that Johnson retired from active service 23 Mar. '65 and "applied for amnesty and took oath of allegiance to United States at Henderson, Ky., July 28, 1865. Died from wounds in Trigg County, Ky." Wood gives the date of his appointment as 4 Aug. '64 and says that he was from Tex. C.M.H. does not mention him.

JOHNSON, Andrew. Lincoln's vicepres. and 17th pres. of the US, 1808–75. N.C. Apprenticed to a tailor, he moved to Tenn. and settled in the non-slaveholding community of Greenville. He was without education and learned to read only after his wife taught him, but he rose to a position of trust and popularity among the small white farmers of the South. From 1830 onward he held a succession of public offices, including mayor, legislator, Congressman, gov. of the state and Sen. When his state seceded, he became an avid opponent of slavery, although a lifelong Democrat, and was appointed military Gov. of Tenn. by Lincoln in 1862.

(B.G. USV 4 Mar. '62; resigned 3 Mar. '65). Two years later he had succeeded in organizing a loyal government in the state and was nominated vice-pres. with Lincoln on the Union-Republican ticket. Upon Lincoln's assassination in Apr. '65 he succeeded to the presidency and resolved to follow Lincoln's plans for reconstruction without bitterness or malice. The RECONSTRUCTION PLAN OF JOHNSON clashed head on with the Radical Republican element in Congress. His term in office was one humiliation after another, culminating on 24 Feb. '68 with a resolution of impeachment against him. This failed by one vote to pass, and he served out his term. In Jan. '75 he was again elected to the Senate but he died that summer.

JOHNSON, Bradley Tyler. C.S.A. gen. 1829–1903. Md. After Princeton he became a lawyer and entered Democratic politics. He was commissioned Maj. 1st Md. and fought with Johnston in the Valley and at 1st Bull Run. Promoted Col. in 1862, he led his regiment at Front Royal, Winchester, Harrisonburg, and Gaines's Mill. His regiment was then disbanded and he led J. R. Jones's brigade at 2d Bull Run, Antietam, and the Wilderness. In Feb. '64 he led the Md. cavalry under Hampton, opposing the Kilpatrick-Dahlgren raid toward Richmond. He was appointed B.G. C.S.A. 28 June '64 and led Wm. E. Jones's cavalry brigade under Early in the Valley and into Md. It was Johnson who executed Early's orders to burn CHAMBERSBURG, Pa. In July '64 he was surprised at MOOREFIELD, W. Va., and narrowly escaped capture. He continued to fight against Sheridan in the Valley. In Nov. of that year he was sent to Salisbury (N.C.) as commandant of prisons. After the war he returned to the law and sat in the state legislature. He wrote extensively on state finances, the law, and history, publishing *A Memoir of the Life and Public Service of Joseph E. Johnston* in 1891 and *General Washington* in 1894.

JOHNSON, Bushrod Rust. C.S.A. gen. 1817–80. Ohio. USMA 1840 (23/42); Inf. He served in the Seminole War, on the frontier, and in the Mexican War, before resigning in 1847 to teach at Western Mil. Inst. in Ky. When this was merged with the Univ. of Nashville, he was named superintendent of the military college and professor of civil engineering. He was also active in the state militia. Commissioned Col. of C.S.A. Engrs., he was appointed B.G. C.S.A. 24 Jan. '62 (from Tenn.). He commanded Fort Donelson 7–9 Feb. until the arrival of Pillow, after which he headed what was, in effect, a division. He himself escaped through the lines at Fort Donelson and commanded his brigade at Shiloh (wounded). He also led his brigade at Perryville and Stones River before succeeding to command of a division under Buckner at Chickamauga and Knoxville. Promoted Maj. Gen. 21 May '64, he led his division in the battles around Petersburg and at Drewry's Bluff as well as at the Wilderness. He commanded the S.C. troops at the Crater, where he captured three stand of colors and 130 prisoners. After the war, served as chancellor of the Univ. of Nashville.

JOHNSON, Charles Adams. Union officer. N.Y. Maj. 17th N.Y. 24 May '61; Lt. Col. 25th N.Y. 4 Oct. '61; Col. 1 Apr. '62; Bvt. B.G. USV (Hanover C.H.); mustered out 10 July '63. Commanded 1, 4, XVI. Died 1891.

JOHNSON, Edward ("Allegheny"). C.S.A. gen. 1816–73. Ky. USMA 1838 (32/45); Inf. He fought in the Seminole War, served on the frontier, and participated in the Mexican War (2 brevets) before resigning 10 June '61 as Capt. Commissioned Col. 12th Va., he was appointed B.G. C.S.A. 13 Dec. '61 and was wounded at McDowell (Va.) 8 May '62 while leading his brigade. He also fought at Winchester and Martinsburg and commanded Jackson's old division at Gettysburg after having been promoted Maj. Gen. 28 Feb. '63. Fighting at Payne's Farm and the Wilderness, he was captured at Spotsylvania's "bloody angle." Exchanged a short time later, he led his division under S. D. Lee in Hood's invasion of Tenn. and was captured at Nashville. After the war he was a farmer.

JOHNSON, George W. C.S.A. Gov. of Ky. 1811–62. Ky. Graduating from Transylvania Univ., he studied law and was a planter in Ky. and Ark. A legislator in the former state, he was an advocate of the Confederacy and joined A. S. Johnston at Bowling Green, setting up the provisional government of the state and becoming its first Gov. He left the state when Johnston withdrew, and served as Breckinridge's A.D.C. at Shiloh. When his horse was shot he fought on foot and enlisted on the night of the first day as Pvt. in 1st Ky. He was mortally wounded the next day and was left on the field, where McCook found him. He died 9 Apr. '62 on a Federal hospital boat.

JOHNSON, Gilbert Marquis La Fayette. Union officer. Ohio. 1st Lt. 2d Ind. Cav. 18 Nov. '61; Capt. 22 Apr. '62; Lt. Col. 11th Ind. Cav. 4 Mar. '64; Col. 13th Ind. Cav. 29 Apr. '64; Bvt. B.G. USV (war service). Commanded 2, 7, Cav. Corps, Mil. Div. Miss.; 2, 1, Cav. Corps, Dept. of Gulf. Died 1871.

JOHNSON, James M. Union officer. Ark. Vol. A.D.C. to Gen. Curtis 15 Apr. '62–Feb. '63; Col. 1st Ark. 25 Mar. '63; Bvt. B.G. USV (war service). Commanded 1, 3, VII.

JOHNSON, Lewis. Union officer. Germany. Pvt. Co. E. 10th Ind. 18 Apr.–6 Aug. '61; 1st Lt. 10th Ind. 18 Sept. '61; Capt. 29 Aug. '62; Col. 44th US Col. Inf. 16 Sept. '64; Bvt. B.G. USV (war service). Brevets for Mill Springs, Corinth, Missionary Ridge. Commanded 1st Col. Brig., Dist. Etowah; 2d Brig., Dist. Eastern Tenn. Transferred to R.A. and retired as Maj. in 1895. Died 1900.

JOHNSON, Reverdy. Union statesman. 1796–1876. A lawyer and legislator, he served in the Senate and as US Atty. Gen. before acting as counsel for the defense in the DRED SCOTT case. He was an important influence in keeping Md. in the Union during the Civil War and as US Sen. (1863–68) supported the RECONSTRUCTION PLAN OF JOHNSON. He was appointed Minister to Great Britain by that president.

JOHNSON, Richard W. Union gen. 1827–97. Ky. USMA 1849 (30/43); Inf. He had served on the frontier and in Indian fighting when, while Capt. 5th US Cav., he was promoted B.G. USV 11 Oct. '61. He commanded in the Army of the Ohio 3d Brig., McCook's division (Oct–Nov. '61); 6th Brig. (Nov–Dec. '61); 6th Brig., 2d Div. (2 Dec. '61–24 July '62) in the advance upon and siege of Corinth; and 2d Div., I Corps (29 Sept.–Nov. '62) in the Tenn. campaign. At Stones River he led 2d Div., Right Wing, Cumberland (5 Nov. '62–9 Jan. '63) and from 9–19 Jan. '63 and 20 Feb.–19 Sept. '63, he commanded 2d Div., XX, Cumberland, at Tullahoma, Liberty Gap, and Chickamauga. He led the 1st Div., XIV, Cumberland (17 Nov. '63–29 May '64) at Missionary Ridge, Dalton, Resaca, and New Hope Church, where he was severely wounded. He also commanded that division 13 July–7 Aug. and 2–8 Nov. '64, serving as Chief of Cav., Mil. Div. Miss., in between. He was C.G.

of the XIV Corps 7–22 Aug. and of the Cav. Corps, Cumberland, 19 Aug.–29 Oct. '64. He commanded the 6th Div., Mil. Div. Miss. (17 Nov. '64–July '65) at the battle of Nashville, for which he was breveted Maj. Gen. USV and B.G. USA. He also commanded the 2d Sub-Dist. Middle Tenn., Cumberland (July–Sept. '65). His other brevets were for Chicakamauga, Chattanooga, and war service (Maj. Gen. USA). He retired as Maj. Gen. USA 1867 and as B.G. USA 1875. He was later professor of military science at the Univs. of Mo. and Minn. and active in Democratic politics. Among his writings were manuals for the Sharps rifle and Colt revolver (which were included in *The Volunteer's Manual* 1861) and *A Memoir of Gen. George H. Thomas* (1881).

JOHNSON, Robert. Union officer. Tenn. Col. 1st Tenn. Cav. 28 Feb. '62; Bvt. B.G. USV (war service); resigned 31 May '64. Commanded 2, 3, II, Army of the Potomac.

JOHNSON FARM, Va., 7–29 Oct. '64. (PETERSBURG CAMPAIGN) Figured in the actions known as NEW MARKET HEIGHTS, 28–30 Sept. '64, and DARBYTOWN AND NEW MARKET ROADS, 7 Oct. '64. On 29 Oct. '64 Col. H. M. Plaisted's brigade (3, 1, X), supported on the right by West's cavalry, succeeded in re-establishing cavalry pickets on the Johnson Farm. Federal infantry then withdrew. Casualties were light.

JOHNSON'S ISLAND. Union PRISON camp in Sandusky Bay of Lake Erie. Around 3,000 Confederate officers were held prisoner on the island at the end of the war.

JOHNSONVILLE, Tenn., 3–5 Nov. '64. (FORREST'S OPERATIONS DURING THE ATLANTA CAMPAIGN) After his destruction of Federal shipping on the Tennessee, 29–30 Oct., Forrest moved up the west bank against Johnsonville. This was an important depot and place where supplies were transferred from river boats for rail shipment to Nashville, 78 miles east. It was covered by a fort, various other works, and three gunboats, under Lt. Comdr. E. M. King. Col. C. R. Thompson commanded a mixed force of about 2,000 men (43d Wis., 700; detachments of 12th, 13th, and 100th US Col. Inf., 400; 11th Tenn. Cav., 20; and 800 "armed quartermaster's employees").

On the 3d Forrest started secretly working his men and approximately 8 guns into position across the river. The next day at 2 P.M. (according to Chalmers) or 3 P.M. (Forrest) he opened fire. The Federals answered with fire from eight guns on their boats and 14 from the fort on the hill. About 15 minutes after the fight opened King ordered his three gunboats run aground and set them on fire along with the seven transports to avoid capture. This set fire to a large quantity of supplies along the wharf and ignited the small warehouse.

Although there had been only eight Federals killed and wounded and "1,200 muskets and 20 guns" were available to defend the place, they seem to have been terrified by the thought that Forrest would cross the river (1,100 feet) to capture the place.

An inspector general sent from Washington to investigate reported that after the fires started "a general system of theft was inaugurated" with the sanction and participation of the gunboat officers (O.R.). He also reported that the stationmaster, C. H. Nabb, "ran off with a train of cars loaded with clothing and some 400 men from the gunboats," continuing to Nashville with only the engine and tender after abandoning the cars at Waverly.

Forrest bombarded the town again

the morning of the 5th, and then withdrew to Corinth, Miss., arriving 10 Nov. The Federal inspector (above) reported that Forrest's damage on the Tennessee 29–30 Oct. and at Johnsonville could be estimated at $2,200,000, including steamboats and barges.

JOHNSTON, Albert Sidney. C.S.A. gen. 1803–62. Ky. Appt.-La. USMA 1826 (8/41); Inf. He served in garrison and the Black Hawk War before resigning because of his wife's health in 1834. After she died, the next year, he tried to farm but was unsuccessful, and enlisted as Pvt. in the Tex. army in 1836. Named senior B.G. in 1837, he was the army commander and was seriously wounded in a duel with a jealous rival. Serving the next year as Sec. of War in the Republic of Tex., he resigned this post in 1840 and settled in Brazoria County, Tex. He fought in the Mexican War and was commissioned Col. 2d U.S. Cav. in 1849. He commanded the Dept. of Tex. in 1856 and led the Utah Expedition as Bvt. B.G. (1858–60) before going to the Dept. of the Pacific in Jan. '61. He resigned the latter post 10 Apr. '61 but remained in command until his successor arrived. The Federal government then offered him a commission as second-in-command to Scott. Although he had not been in communication with the Confederacy, he was named Gen. C.S.A. 30 Aug. '61 to rank from 30 May, appointed from Tex. He was assigned the Western Dept., seized Bowling Green, and started recruiting. Outnumbered two to one, his subordinates were defeated at Logan C.R. 19 Jan. '62 and at HENRY AND DONELSON. He then withdrew from Ky. and massed his forces around Corinth, Miss. At SHILOH he was hit in the leg and bled to death before it was realized that the wound was serious. His body was temporarily entombed at New Orleans and after the war was returned to Tex.,

where Sheridan forbade any public display. This they circumvented by "silently following his body as it was carried through the streets" (D.A.B.). A tall man, standing over six feet in height, he was massively built with broad shoulders and a large, square-jawed head. He was "a man of strong physique, commanding presence and magnetic personality" (Horn, 52).

"If there was any one thing on which everybody seemed agreed in 1861 it was that Albert Sidney Johnston was the Number One soldier of the continent," wries Horn. "There are many Southerners today who agree with [Jeff Davis] that Johnston was 'the greatest soldier, the ablest man, civil or military, Confederate or Federal, then living.' Johnston's outstanding and incomparable military merit has become axiomatic, and to question the legend now is sheer audacity. Through a perspective of eighty years, however, it is hard to find the basis for this almost unchallenged opinion that he was the supremely qualified soldier, that his death was an irremediable catastrophe."

JOHNSTON, George Doherty. C.S.A. gen. 1832–1910. N.C. After college he practiced law and held several public offices and a seat in the state legislature. Commissioned Lt. 4th Ala., he fought at 1st Bull Run, remaining in Va. until Jan. '62, when he became Maj. 25th Ala. He commanded the regiment at Shiloh and was promoted Lt. Col. on that day. Continuing to lead the unit, he fought at Stones River and Chickamauga before being named Col. 27 Oct. '63. He fought at Chattanooga and started on the Atlanta campaign in this grade. He took over Deas's brigade, was appointed B.G. C.S.A. 26 July '64, and was wounded three hours after receiving notification of the promotion on the 28th. On crutches, he led Quarles's brigade into

Tenn. and down the Carolinas. After Johnston's surrender he tried to reach Taylor but was unsuccessful. He returned to his law practice later.

JOHNSTON, Harriet Lane. See Harriet LANE.

JOHNSTON, Joseph Eggleston. C.S.A. gen. 1807–91. Va. USMA 1829 (13/46); Arty. He served in garrison, the Black Hawk expedition, the frontier, and in the Seminole War, where he was Scott's A.D.C., before resigning in 1837 to become a civil engineer in Florida. When his expedition was routed by Indians, he took charge of the rear guard and conducted the retreat with skill and courage, even though wounded twice in the forehead. He was commissioned 1st Lt. Topo. Engrs. in 1838 and breveted Capt. for this exploit. During the Mexican War he was five times wounded, won three brevets, and led the storming column at Chapultepec. In the period between the wars he was Chief of Topo. Engrs. in Tex., and served as Lt. Col. 1st U.S. Cav. 1855–60 on the frontier and in Kans. during the border disturbances. On A. S. Johnston's Utah Expedition, he was acting I.G. and was appointed B.G. and Q.M. USA 28 June '60. Resigning 22 Apr. '61, he joined the Confederacy, was named Maj. Gen. of Va., and B.G. C.S.A. 14 May '61, and assigned to command at Harpers Ferry. He joined Beauregard at Manassas and commanded the combined forces at 1ST BULL RUN. Then assigned to command the DEPT. OF THE POTOMAC, he was appointed Gen. 31 Aug. to rank from 4 July '61. This put him fourth in seniority among the general officers (Cooper, A. S. Johnston, and Lee preceding him), and he protested that he had been the senior USA officer and should retain this status in the Confederacy. This touched off his feud with Davis. After being twice wounded at Seven Pines, he was relieved

by Lee 1 June '62. Returning for duty in Nov. '62, he was put in command of the Dept. of the WEST over both Bragg in Tenn. and Pemberton in Miss. Davis's refusal to approve Johnston's strategy led to the defeat of Bragg and Pemberton at STONES RIVER, VICKSBURG, CHICKAMAUGA, and CHATTANOOGA. He took command of the Army of Tenn. 27 Dec. '63 with orders to reorganize it and assume the offensive. In the ATLANTA CAMPAIGN that followed Johnston dropped back skillfully before Sherman's overwhelming strength. On 17 July '64 he was relieved by Hood. Reassigned 23 Feb. '65 to command the Army of Tenn., he led them through the CAROLINAS CAMPAIGN. On 18 Apr. '65 he signed an armistice with Sherman and surrendered 26 Apr., even though Davis ordered him south to continue the war. After this he was in the insurance business in Savannah and Richmond and served in Congress. Settling in Washington later, he was a railroad commissioner. He wrote a number of books and articles about the war, particularly *Narrative of Military Operations* (1874) and several articles in *Battles and Leaders*. He died of pneumonia contracted by standing hatless in the rain at Sherman's funeral.

"In appearance he is small, soldierly and graying, with a certain gamecock jauntiness," Freeman says of him; he has "unmistakable strategical sense, though doubts concerning his administrative capacity and his attention to detail gradually accumulate. . . . A difficult and touchy subordinate he is, though a generous and kindly superior—in sum, a military contradiction and a temperamental enigma" (*Lee's Lts.*, I, xxxviii).

JOHNSTON, Robert D. C.S.A. gen. Appt.-N.C. Serving in the N.C. state troops, he was commissioned Capt. 23d N.C. 15 July '61 and served on the

Peninsula in 1861 and spring of '62. He fought at Williamsburg and was promoted Lt. Col. 21 May '62, commanding the regiment at Seven Pines (wounded). He also led the force at South Mountain and Antietam, and took over the 12th N.C. at Chancellorsville when the major commanding the regiment was killed. After Gettysburg he was appointed B.G. C.S.A. 1 Sept. '63 and commanded his brigade under Rodes at the Wilderness. He was severely wounded at Spotsylvania and then fought in Early's Valley campaign and at Petersburg and Appomattox. C.M.H. says that he practiced law until 1887 but does not make clear if this is the date of his death.

JOINT COMMITTEE OF FIFTEEN. Popular name for the Joint Congressional Committee on Reconstruction appointed 13 Dec. '65 under the chairmanship of Sen. Fessenden. It was this group, mainly RADICAL REPUBLICANS, that worked out the punitive Reconstruction measures imposed upon the South.

JONES, David Rumph. C.S.A. gen. 1825-63. S.C. USMA 1846 (41/59); Inf.-Adj. Gen. Serving in the Mexican War (1 brevet), he was then stationed on the frontier and in garrison before resigning 15 Feb. '61 as Bvt. Capt. Named Maj. and Beauregard's Chief of Staff during the Fort Sumter bombardment, he was appointed B.G. C.S.A. 17 June '61 and commanded his brigade at 1st Bull Run. In Mar. '62 he was given a division and promoted Maj. Gen. on 5 Apr., but this was not confirmed until the following Nov. In temporary command of Magruder's division, he successfully withdrew from Yorktown and fought during the Seven Days' Battles, 2d Bull Run, where he secured Thoroughfare Gap for Jackson's passage, and then fought at South Mountain and Antietam. Stricken with heart trouble soon after that, he died 15 Jan. '63 in Richmond.

JONES, Edward Franc. Union officer. Mass. Col. 6th Mass. 22 Apr. '61; mustered out 2 Aug. '61; Col. 26th Mass. 28 Aug. '61; Bvt. B.G. USV (war service); discharged 28 July '62.

JONES, Fielder A. Union officer. Pa. Capt. 6th Ind. 24 Apr. '61; mustered out 2 Aug. '61; Lt. Col. 8th Ind. Cav. 29 Aug. '61; Col 1 Mar. '65; Bvt. B.G. USV (war service). Commanded 1, 2, XX; 2, 3, Cav. Corps. Died 1882.

JONES, John Marshall. C.S.A. gen. 1821-64. Va. USMA 1841 (39/52); Inf. He served on the frontier, taught tactics at West Point, and went on the Utah Expedition before resigning 27 May '61 as Capt. As Ewell's Adj. Gen. in 1861, he fought at Front Royal, Winchester, Cross Keys, and Port Republic, and was promoted Lt. Col. of Arty. by June '62. He fought in the Seven Days' Battles, at Cedar Mountain, and Groveton. He was also at 2d Bull Run and was I.G. at Fredericksburg. Appointed B.G. C.S.A. 15 May '63, he fought at Gettysburg and was killed 5 May '64 leading the Stonewall Brigade at the Wilderness.

JONES, John R. C.S.A. gen. ?-1901. Va. A Capt. in the Stonewall Brigade (33d Va.), he fought at 1st Bull Run and in the Valley campaign, attaining the rank of Lt. Col. He was appointed B.G. C.S.A. to rank from 23 June '62, but his appointment was never confirmed (*Lee's Lts.,* I, 588). "Named at the instance of 'Stonewall' himself" (*ibid.*), he commanded the 2d Brig. under Jackson at 1st Cold Harbor and Malvern Hill. Wounded after 2d Bull Run, he rejoined his command at Frederick (Md.) and took command of Jackson's division at Harpers Ferry. When it surrendered to the Confederates, he joined Lee at Antietam. He was disabled early in the battle by a shell burst overhead and turned his brigade over to William E. Starke, who was later killed. He led his brigade at Chancellorsville until the night of 2–3 May, when he left the field claiming an ulcerated leg (*Lee's Lts.*, II, 589n). He was formally charged with cowardice (*ibid.*, 500n) and cashiered (Palmer Bradley). Wright says he was captured at Smithburg, Tenn., 4 July '63 and not released from Fort Warren, Mass., until 24 July '65.

JONES, John Sills. Union officer. 1836–1903. Ohio. 1st Lt. 4th Ohio 4 May '61; Capt. 1 July '62; mustered out 21 June '64; Col. 174th Ohio 21 Sept. '64; Bvt. B.G. USV 27 June '65 (war service). W.I.A. at Winchester while beside Gen. Shields on whose staff he was serving. W.I.A. Mine Run (Va.). President of the Examining Board and post commander of Charlotte (N.C.) after Johnston's surrender. A lawyer and county prosecuting attorney before the war, he was Republican Congressman from Ohio later.

JONES, Joseph Blackburn. Union officer. Ill. Capt. 15th Ill. 24 May '61; resigned 28 July '61; Col. 68th US Col. Inf. 27 June '64; Bvt. B.G. USV (war service). Died 1896.

JONES, Patrick Henry. Union gen. ?–1900. Ireland. Named 2d Lt. 37th N.Y. 7 July and 1st Lt. Adj. 4 Nov. '61, he was promoted Maj. 21 Jan. '62 and fought at Williamsburg and Fair Oaks. As Col. 154th N.Y. 8 Oct. '62, he led his regiment at Fredericksburg, Chancellorsville, and Wauhatchie. On 6 Dec. '64 he was promoted B.G. USV and commanded 1, 2, XI, Cumberland (30 Jan.–25 Feb. '64) and 2, 2, XX, Cumberland (7 June–8 Aug. '64; 17 Sept. '64–19 Jan. '65 and 30 Mar.–1 June '65) during the Atlanta campaign and on the March to the Sea and in the Carolinas.

JONES, Samuel. C.S.A. gen. 1820–87. Va. USMA 1841 (19/52); Arty. He served on the frontier, in garrison, and at West Point as mathematics teacher for two tours and tactical and artillery instructor for one tour each before resigning 27 Apr. '61 as Capt. At 1st Bull Run he was Col. and Chief of Arty. and Ord., being appointed B.G. C.S.A. on the day of the battle (21 July '61). Leading the Va. brigade, he served in W. Va. until Jan. '62, when he was sent to Bragg in Pensacola. In Apr. of that year he relinquished his command at Mobile, forwarded his ammunition to Bragg, and reported to Beauregard. He had been promoted Maj. Gen. 10 Mar. '62. In June he was given command of Hindman's corps in the Army of Miss. and was soon relieved by Van Dorn in the presence of his men. Beauregard then gave him a larger and better organized division. During Nov.–Dec. '62 he was commander of the Western Dept. to succeed J. S. Williams. He spent most of 1863 (Jan. to Nov.) in this area guarding the salt works and was superseded in Mar. '64 by Breckinridge. In turn, he succeeded Beauregard in command of the Dept. of S.C., Ga., and Fla. and in Oct. of '64 was succeeded by Ransom when he was felled by poor health. In May '65 he was paroled and returned home to serve as clerk in Va. and in the Washington office of the Adj. Gen.

JONES, Samuel B. Union officer. N.Y. Capt. 78th N.Y. 2 Jan. '62; Lt. Col. 78th US Col. Inf. 26 Feb. '63; Col. 10 Dec. '63; Bvt. B.G. USV (war service). Commanded Ullman's brigade, Corps d'Afrique, XX; 2d Brig., 2d Div. Corps d'Afrique.

JONES, Theodore. Union officer. D.C. Lt. Col. 30th Ohio 20 Aug. '61; Col. 18 Apr. '63; Bvt. B.G. USV (war service).

JONES, Thomas Marshall. C.S.A. gen. c. 1832–1913. Va. USMA 1853 (47/52); Inf. He served in garrison and on frontier duty, being A.D.C. to Twiggs when he resigned 28 Feb. '61 as 1st Lt. Named Col. 27th Miss. in Mar. '62, he took command of the "Army of Pensacola" on the 8th and evacuated Pensacola two months later. At Perryville he commanded the 4th Brig., II Corps, and at Stones River led the 27th Miss. until succeeded by Lt. Col. James Autry (B.&L. Orders of Battle). He next appears as commander of Fort Caswell on the Cape Fear River, being reported to be with Whiting and Louis Hébert in N.C. from July to Sept. '64. Presumably he surrendered there. Although neither Wright nor Wood lists him as a gen., Cullum and Heitman say he was a B.G. After the war he farmed and was active in public education.

JONES, Wells S. Union officer. Ohio. Capt. 53d Ohio 3 Oct. '61; Col. 21 May '62; Bvt. B.G. USV (war service). Commanded 2, 2, XV; 3, 4, XV.

JONES, William Edmonson ("Grumble"). C.S.A. gen. 1824–64. Va. USMA 1848 (10/38); Mtd. Rifles. After serving in garrison and on the frontier, he resigned in 1857 to farm. In May '61 he was commissioned Maj. and assigned to train the Va. cavalry. Elected Col. in Sept. '61, he commanded the 7th Va. Cav. from Mar. until Oct. '62 at Cedar Mountain, Groveton, 2d Bull Run, and in northern N.C. He was appointed B.G. C.S.A. 19 Sept. '62 and given a brigade in the Valley in Dec. '62. In the Gettysburg campaign he fought with Stuart and went in Feb. '64 with Longstreet to eastern Tenn. Returning to Va. in the spring of '64, he was killed 5 June at Piedmont.

JONES, William Price. Union officer. Conn. Vol. A.D.C. 24 Apr.–10 Sept. '61; Maj. Add. A.D.C. 10 Sept. '61; Bvt. B.G. USV (war service); resigned 29 Dec. '62. Died 1876.

JONESBORO, Ga., 31 Aug.–1 Sept. '64. (ATLANTA CAMPAIGN) The night of 30 Aug. Hood sent Hardee and S. D. Lee from Atlanta to Jonesboro to hit Sherman's forces approaching there from the west. Hardee attacked at 2 P.M., 31 Aug., with his own corps (under Cleburne) on the left and Lee on the right. Cleburne was to envelop the Federal right (south) flank, and Lee would attack frontally when he heard that Cleburne was engaged. Mistaking the sound of skirmishing on his left for Cleburne's attack, Lee moved forward. Hazen's division (2, XV) on the Federal left got the brunt of Cleburne's premature attack. Bryant (1, 3, XVII) was first sent to Hazen's support, and then the rest of C. R. Wood's division (3, XVII). Carlin's division (1, XIV) was also sent to the threatened left flank, but arrived after the Confederates had been repulsed in this sector.

Kilpatrick was at Anthony's bridge, a mile and a half south of Howard, when the battle started. Seeing the threat to the Federal right, he dismounted five cavalry regiments and posted them on the flank of Cleburne's advance. Covered by his artillery, Kilpatrick attacked and forced Cleburne to change front. After repulsing two Confederate attacks, Kilpatrick was then forced back across the bridge with the loss of two guns. G. A. Smith's division (4, XVII) was ordered to the scene and drove back the Confederates, recapturing the two guns. The 92d Ill. Mounted Inf. had distinguished itself in covering Kilpatrick's withdrawal across the bridge.

Lee's Corps left Jonesboro at 2 A.M., 1 Sept., and was halted at Rough and Ready to protect Hood's west flank as the latter moved south from Atlanta.

(Hood evacuated the city and started south at 5 . P.M. toward Lovejoy.) This left Hardee's corps alone at Jonesboro. Although Sherman had been primarily interested in destroying the railroad south of Atlanta, he now saw the opportunity to annihilate Hardee. Thomas and Schofield were ordered to reinforce Howard at Jonesboro. Stanley, whose IV Corps was destroying the railroad near Rough and Ready, was ordered to Jonesboro. Davis' XIV Corps was ordered to move to Howard's left flank. The two divisions of Blair's XVII Corps, with Kilpatrick's cavalry attached, were ordered to cut the railroad south of the town. Schofield was to continue destroying track, but was also to follow Stanley and be prepared to reinforce him.

Hardee had posted his divisions to meet an attack from the west. Cleburne's division was on the right with his brigades as follows: Granbury on the left, Govan holding a salient in the center, and Lewis to the right and rear. About noon, 1 Sept., Davis arrived on Howard's left and pushed forward Edie's brigade (2, 1, XIV) to reconnoiter. Edie drove back some skirmishers, captured a hill from which he could command the salient in Hardee's lines. Prescott's battery (C, 1st Ill., 1, XIV) went into action from this ridge and brought effective enfilade and counterbattery fire against the Confederates. Edie then gained a foothold in Govan's line but was repulsed with heavy losses when reinforcements did not arrive. At about 5 P.M. Estes' brigade (3, 3, XIV) carried the salient. Two Federal divisions, Carlin on the left and Morgan (1 and 2, XIV) on the right, then executed a double envelopment that destroyed Govan's brigade. This Confederate general was captured with most of his men. Lewis and Granbury fell back to a new position, al-

though the Confederate left and center were able to hold their trenches until dark. Stanley arrived on Davis' left about the time of this last attack, but it was dark and the fighting had ended before he could become effectively engaged. During the night Hardee fell back to join Hood at Lovejoy, where forces from Atlanta were retreating via the McDonough Road.

On 31 Aug. the Federals lost 179 out of 14,170 engaged. The Confederates lost about 1,725 out of 23,811. On 1 Sept. the Federals lost 1,274 out of 20,460 engaged. Hardee had 12,661 engaged; Cleburne lost 911 (of whom 659 were missing), but the losses of the other two divisions are not known.

JONES'S AND IMBODEN'S W. VA. RAID, Apr. '63. Wm. E. Jones, who commanded a brigade of Stuart's cavalry as well as the (Confed.) Valley Dist., left the vicinity of Harrisonburg, Va., on 20 Apr. to march via Mount Jackson, Petersburg, and the Northwestern Turnpike to attack the B.&O. R.R. between Oakland, Md. (near the western boundary) and Rowlesburg, W. Va. From the vicinity of Monterey, Va., John Imboden started at the same time with a mixed brigade of 3,500, only 700 of whom were mounted, to capture Beverly, W. Va., and link up with Jones around Grafton or Clarksburg.

Jones accomplished his part of the mission, destroying railroad bridges between Rowlesburg and the Allegheny Mountains. He then moved north to Morgantown, W. Va., and threatened Wheeling and Pittsburgh, Pa. Returning down the Monongahela, he destroyed the railroad bridge at Fairmont and joined Imboden at Weston. The latter had captured Beverly and Buckhannon but had not been able to reach the railroad (Fiebeger, 180).

JORDAN, Thomas. C.S.A. gen. 1819–95. Va. USMA 1840 (41/42); Inf. A roommate of W. T. Sherman at West Point, he fought in the Seminole War and the Mexican War, and served on the frontier in Indian fighting. He resigned 21 May '61 as Capt. and was commissioned Lt. Col. of Va. troops. Serving as Adj. Gen. at 1st Bull Run, he was Beauregard's Chief of Staff at Shiloh, in the Corinth campaign, and the operations around Charleston, remaining in this post until the end of the war. He wrote many articles and books about the war, including a scurrilous attack on Jefferson Davis in the Oct. '65 *Harper's Magazine* and "Notes of a Confederate Staff Officer at Shiloh" in B.&L., I, and *The Campaigns of Lt.-General Nathan B. Forrest* in collaboration with J. B. Pryor in 1868. He was a Memphis newspaper editor and in 1869 headed the insurgent force in Cuba. Highly praised by Beauregard, he is noted chiefly for his organizational ability.

JORDAN, Thomas Jefferson. Union officer. Pa. Maj. 9th Pa. Cav. 22 Oct. '61; Col. 13 Jan. '63; Bvt. B.G. USV 25 Feb. '65. Commanded 1, 3, Cav. Corps (Cumberland); 1, 3, Cav. Corps, Mil. Div. Miss. Died 1895.

JOURDAN, James. Union officer. Ireland. Commissioned Maj. 84th N.Y. 23 May '61, he was promoted Lt. Col. 56th N.Y. 19 Dec. '61 and Col. 158th N.Y. 5 Sept. '62. He resigned 17 Mar.

'65 and was breveted B.G. USV 28 Oct. '64 (Fort Harrison) and Maj. Gen. USV (war service).

JUDAH, Henry Moses. Union gen. 1821–66. Md. USMA 1843 (35/39); Inf. He served in the Mexican War (2 brevets), on the frontier and fighting Indians. He was commissioned Col. 4th Calif. 6 Sept. '61 and B.G. USV 21 May '62 while Acting I.G. of the Army of the Tenn. (12 Apr.–16 July '62). He was promoted Maj. 4th US Inf. 30 June '62. During the advance and siege of Corinth he commanded 1st Div., Army of West Tenn. (3–14 May '62). He then commanded Camp Dennison (Ky.) and Covington (Ky.) and was Acting I.G. Army of the Ohio 10 Oct. '62–25 Feb. '63. He also commanded Dist. Western Ky. and 3d Div., XXIII, Ohio (24 June–6 Aug. '63). He led the 2d Div., XXIII, Ohio (26 Jan.–18 May '64); 1st Brig., 2d Div. Separate Etowah, Cumberland (Mar.–Sept. '65) and 2d Div. Separate Etowah, Cumberland (Mar. '65).

JUDSON, Roscius Winslow. Union officer. N.Y. Col. 142d N.Y. 29 Sept. '62; Bvt. B.G. USV (war service); resigned 21 Jan. '63. Died 1894.

JUDSON, William R. Union officer. N.Y. Maj. 6th Kans. Cav. 27 Jan. '61; Col. 10 Sept. '61; Bvt. B.G. USV (war service). Commanded 1st Brig., 1st Div., Army Frontier; Dist. Frontier, VII; 3, Dist. Frontier, VII; 2, Dist. Frontier, VII. Died 1880.

K

KAEMERLING, Guitar. See KAMMERLING, Gustave.

KAMMERLING, Gustave. Union officer. A "German citizen of Cincinnati" (T.U.A.), he was commissioned

Capt. 9th Ohio and fought at Rich Mountain, Carnifex Ferry, and Mill Springs, where his regiment made the decisive charge. He was promoted Maj. 1 Nov. '61, Lt. Col. 8 Mar. '62, and

Col. 6 Aug. '62. At Chickamauga he led a bayonet charge to recapture a battery lost by the Union artillery. Returning to their lines and finding that Thomas' right was threatened, they charged once more. Thomas, a spare man with praise, mentions only one regiment, the 9th Ohio, in his report on Chickamauga. On 5 Jan. '64 Kammerling was commissioned B.G. USV but declined, preferring to serve with his regiment. He commanded 2, 3, XIV, Cumberland 14 Jan.–16 Feb. '64 and led his troops at Resaca. He was mustered out 7 June '64 and "then engaged in peaceful pursuits in the city of his adoption" (T.U.A.). Kammerling is not listed in Heitman and is erroneously listed in Phisterer as Kaemerling, Guitar.

KANAWHA CAMPAIGN, W. Va., 6–16 Sept. '62. See WEST VIRGINIA OPERATIONS IN 1862.

KANAWHA, CONFED. ARMY OF THE. Southern troops in the Kanawha Valley of western Va. were put under command of Henry Wise on 6 June '61. J. B. Floyd, who had been called on by Pres. Davis to raise troops in this area, took command 11 Aug. Due to personal animosity between Wise and Floyd, both politicians and former governors of Virginia, Wise continued to look upon himself as virtually an independent commander. On 25 Sept. an order arrived from Benjamin instructing Wise to turn over his command to Floyd and report to Richmond for further instructions. In Nov., after the failures of the WEST VIRGINIA OPERATIONS IN 1861, Floyd went to Bowling Green, Ky., with his brigade and that of Mc-Causland to become the 3d Div., Central Army of Kentucky.

KANAWHA DIVISION. In the WEST VIRGINIA OPERATIONS OF 1862 J. D. Cox had been operating with four bri-

gades along the Great Kanawha River. In Aug. Cox took his two best brigades to participate in the 2d Bull Run and Antietam campaigns, and these constituted the "Kanawha Division." The 1st Brig. was commanded by E. P. Scammon and then by Hugh Ewing when Cox took command of Burnside's IX Corps and Scammon moved up to lead the division. The 1st Brig. was composed of the 12th, 23d, 30th Ohio Inf., the 1st Ohio Independent Btry., Gilmore's W. Va. Cav. Co., and Harrison's W. Va. Cav. Co. Colonel of the 23d Ohio was Rutherford B. HAYES (to be 19th president of the US) who was severely wounded at South Mountain. Also with the regiment was 19-year-old Comsy. Sgt. William McKINLEY, who was to be the 24th president. The 2d Brig. was commanded by Augustus MOOR, until he was captured and succeeded by George CROOK. This brigade included the 11th, 28th, 36th Ohio Inf., Simmonds Ky. Btry., Schambeck's Ill. Cav., and the 3d Independent Co. of Ohio Cav. The division had 84 casualties at South Mountain, and 73 at Antietam.

KANE, Thomas Leiper. Union gen. 1822–83. Pa. An ardent Free-Soiler, he wrote many abolition articles for newspapers. Serving as US District Commissioner, he found, upon the passage of the Fugitive Slave Law, that his duties conflicted with his conscience, and resigned. The District Judge (his father) construed his letter of resignation as contempt and had him jailed, an action that was overruled by the Supreme Court. Upon release he became an active agent of the Underground Railroad and also assisted Brigham Young and the US government in moving the Mormons westward. When war came, he organized the 13th Pa. Reserves ("Bucktails") and gave the honor of colonelcy to the Mexican War veteran Charles J. Biddle. He was commissioned Lt. Col. 21 June '61 and fought at Dranesville 20 Dec. '61 (wounded), and at Harrisonburg 6 June '62 (captured). Promoted B.G. USV 7 Sept. '62, he commanded 2, 1, XII (6 Oct. '62–21 Mar. '63) and 2, 2, XII (21 Mar.–7 May '63) at Chancellorsville. He was in a Baltimore hospital suffering from pneumonia just before Gettysburg when given a message that the Confederates had broken the Union cipher. He delivered it with great difficulty to Meade, and resumed command of 2, 2, XII on the second day of the battle although too weak to sit on his horse. He resigned because of ill-health 7 Nov. '63 and was breveted Maj. Gen. USV for Gettysburg. Brother of Elisha Kent Kane (author of *Arctic Expeditions* and *Adrift in the Arctic Ice*).

1ST KANSAS COLORED VOLUNTEERS. See 79TH US COLORED INFANTRY, and NEGRO TROOPS.

KANSAS-NEBRASKA ACT. Passed in 1854 after vigorous support by Sen. Stephen A. Douglas, this bill provided that Kans. and Nebr. be organized as territories on the basis of popular sovereignty toward the slavery question. See "BLEEDING KANSAS."

KANSAS-NEBRASKA WAR. See "BLEEDING KANSAS."

KANSAS, UNION DEPARTMENT AND ARMY OF. Created 9 Nov. '61, to consist of Kans., the Indian Territory west of Ark., and the Territories of Nebr., Colo., and Dakota. Headquarters at Fort Leavenworth. It was merged into the Dept. of the Miss. 11 Mar. '62, re-created 2 May, merged into the Dept. of Mo. 19 Sept. '62, and re-created 1 Jan. '64. It was then merged into the Dept. of Mo. 30 Jan. '65. Commanders were Maj. Gen. David Hunter, 20 Nov. '61–11 Mar. '62; Brig. Gen. James G. Blunt, 5 May–19 Sept. '62; and Maj. Gen. S. R. Curtis from 16 Jan. '64 until

30 Jan. '65. Strength 31 Dec. '64 was 7,000. It included the Districts of North Kans., South Kans., Upper Ark., Nebr., and Colo. Forces from this geographical area were sometimes referred to as "the Army of Kansas," even during periods when the department was not in existence (e.g., in some accounts of the fight at Newtonia, Mo., 30 Sept. '62). (See also FRONTIER, UNION DISTRICT AND ARMY OF THE.)

KARGÉ, Joseph. Union officer. Germany. Lt. Col. 1st N.J. Cav. 18 Oct. '61; resigned 22 Dec. '62; Col. 2d N.J. Cav. 25 Sept. '63; Bvt. B.G. USV (war service). Wounded at Fredericksburg. Commanded 1, 1st Cav. Div., XVI; 1, 2d West Tenn. Div., Cav. Corps (Tenn.); 2, 4, Cav. Corps (Mil. Div. Miss.); 1, 1, Cav. Corps (Gulf); and 2, 1, Cav. Corps (Gulf). Transferred to R.A. and mustered out as 1st Lt. in 1871. In the Prussian Army, he was imprisoned for his part in the 1848 revolution. Escaping, he came to America and by 1851 was running a successful private classical school in N.Y.C. He became a professor of modern languages at Princeton in 1871 and died in 1892.

KAUTZ, August Valentine. Union gen. 1828–95. Germany. Appt.-Ohio. USMA 1852 (35/43); Inf. After serving in the Mexican War he graduated from West Point and served on the frontier, where he was twice wounded in Indian fighting. Named Capt. 3d US Cav. 14 May '61, he transferred to the 6th US Cav. 3 Aug. and fought with them at Mechanicsville, Yorktown, Hanover Court House, and Malvern Hill. Promoted Col. 2d Ohio Cav. 2 Sept. '62, he commanded Camp Chase (Ohio) and then Cav. Brig., Dist. Central Ky., Ohio (Apr.–June '63) at Monticello (Ky.) and 3, 1, XXIII (24 June–6 Aug. '63) at the capture of Morgan and his raiders. In Nov. and Dec. of that year he was Chief of Cav. for the XXIII Corps and then served in the Cav. Bureau in Washington. In the actions around Petersburg and at Reams's Station and Darbytown he commanded Cav. Div., Va. and N.C. (28 Apr.–23 Oct. '64 and 5 Nov. '64–11 Mar. '65) and 1st Div., XXV, Va. (27 Mar.–4 May '65) in the occupation of Richmond. He had been promoted B.G. USV 7 May '64 and was breveted for Monticello (Ky.); Petersburg 9 June '64; Darbytown Road; war service (B.G. and Maj. Gen. USA); and Richmond (Maj. Gen. USV 28 Oct. '64). He was a member of the military commission that tried Lincoln's assassins, and later participated in the Indian fighting. He also commanded the Dept. of Columbia, retiring in 1892 as B.G. USA. He wrote several books on army duties and customs, and the article "The Operations South of the James River" in B.&L. (IV, 533).

KEARNY (car'-nee), Philip. Union gen. 1814–62. N.Y. Coming into the army in 1837 after graduating from Columbia and studying law, he was an observer with the French cavalry in the Algerian war of 1840. He distinguished himself in the Mexican War, losing his left arm in the capture of Mexico City. Resigning in 1851 to travel, he fought with the French in Italy, winning the Legion of Honor at Solferino. He was appointed B.G. USV 17 May '61 and took command of the first N.J. brigade to be formed. During the Peninsular campaign he distinguished himself at Williamsburg and Seven Pines, being appointed Maj. Gen. USV on 4 July '62. After an outstanding performance in the 2d Bull Run campaign, he was killed at Chantilly, 1 Sept. '62. He had ridden accidentally into the enemy lines and, called on to surrender, tried to fight his way out. Phil Kearny was the nephew of the distinguished General Stephen Watts Kearny (1794–1848) and was related to Adm. Lawrence Kearny (1789–1868). Kearny, N.J., is named after Phil Kearny.

KEARNY MEDAL AND KEARNY CROSS. On 29 Nov. '62 officers of the late Phil Kearny's command adopted a gold medal in his honor that was to be awarded to officers who had served honorably in battle under Kearny. The medal was a small Maltese cross superimposed with a circle bearing the words *Dulce et decorum est pro patria mori,* and the word Kearny on a disk in the center, and suspended from a ribbon. Manufactured at $15 each by Ball, Black & Co. of N.Y.C., about 317 were distributed.

D. B. Birney, who succeeded Kearny, directed on 13 Mar. '63 that a "cross of valor" be awarded to enlisted men who had distinguished themselves in battle. This was a bronze cross pattee with "Kearny Cross" on the front and "Birney's Division" on the back. No recipient of the Kearny Medal could be awarded the cross. Among the first to receive the award were two women, Ann ETHERIDGE and Marie TEBE (John Wike, M.C.&H., Sept. 1953). (See also DECORATIONS.)

KEARNY PATCH. See BADGES, Corps.

KEARNY'S HORSES. His most conspicuous mount was Moscow, a high-spirited white horse. Another, Decatur, was a light bay killed at Seven Pines. When Kearny was killed at Chantilly, he was riding Bayard, a light brown horse.

KEARSARGE, THE. Union ship that sunk the Confederate *Alabama* off Cherbourg 19 June '64. Commanded by Capt. John A. Winslow, the Federal vessel was 1,031 tons, 8 guns and carried 162 men. Her crew lost one killed and two wounded in the *Alabama* engagement.

KEENE, Laura. American actress. 1826–73. England. Abraham Lincoln was assassinated while watching her star in her greatest success, OUR AMERICAN COUSIN, at Ford's Theatre in Washington. See John Wilkes BOOTH.

KEIFER, Joseph Warren. Union officer. Ohio. 1836–? Graduating from Antioch College, he practiced law and was commissioned Maj. 3d Ohio 27 Apr. '61. He was promoted Lt. Col. 12 Feb. '62 and Col. 110th Ohio 30 Sept. of that year. Mustered out in June '65, he was breveted for Opequon-Fishers Hill-Middletown (B.G. USV 19 Oct. '64) and Petersburg-to-Appomattox (Maj. Gen. USV 9 Apr. '65). He returned to his practice, sat in the legislature, and was a Congressman and Speaker of the House before returning to the army as Maj. Gen. USV in 1898 for the Spanish-American War.

KEILY, Daniel J. Union officer. Ireland. Appt.-Ireland. Capt. Add. A.D.C. 9 Apr. '62; Col. 2d La. Cav. 6 and 7 Sept. '64; Bvt. B.G. USV (war service). He served in the Papal Brigade just before the Civil War. At one time Shields's Chief of Staff, he distinguished himself at Port Republic. Died 1867.

KEIM, William High. Union gen. 1813–62. Pa. After holding a Democratic congressional seat and several other public offices, he was commissioned Maj. Gen. commanding the 2d Div. of Pa. Vols. 20 Apr. and mustered out 21 July '61. He was then commissioned B.G. USV 20 Dec. '61 and commanded 2d Brig., Casey's division (Dec. '61–Mar. '62) and 2, 3, IV (13 Mar.–7 June '62), both in the Army of the Potomac. He died of "camp fever" 18 May '62.

KELLEY, Benjamin Franklin. Union gen. 1807–91. N.H. He was a merchant and railroad agent when appointed Col. 1st W. Va. 22 May '61. He was promoted B.G. USV 17 May '61 and severely wounded at Philippi (W. Va.) 3 June. He commanded Kelley's brigade, Army of Occupation, W. Va. (May–Aug. '61) and Railroad Dist., W. Va. (11 Oct. '61–11 Mar. '62) when he captured Romney and Blue's Gap. He also commanded the Railroad Dist., Mtn. Dept. (11 Mar.–26 June '62); Railroad Dist., Mid. Dept. (22 July–20 Sept. '62) and Defenses Upper Potomac, VIII, Mid. Dept. (5 Jan.–Feb. '63). He was later in government service.

KELLOGG, John Algor. Union officer. Pa. Capt. 6th Wis. 12 Dec. '61; Lt. Col. 4 Dec. '64; Col. 18 Dec. '64; Bvt. B.G. USV 9 Apr. '65 (war service). Captured at the Wilderness. Commanded 1, 3, V. Died 1883.

KELLY, John Henry. Union officer. Ohio. Ex-cadet USMA June 1861; appt. Calif. Maj. 114th Ohio 10 Sept. '62; Lt. Col. 6 Feb. '63; Col. 27 Nov. '64; Bvt. B.G. USV (Mobile, war service). Died 1881.

KELLY, John Herbert. C.S.A. gen. 1840–64. Ala. A cadet at West Point, he resigned (ex-June '61) when Ala. seceded and was commissioned 2d Lt. C.S.A. and sent to Fort Morgan. He went with Hardee to Mo. and was promoted Capt. and Asst. Adj. Gen. 5 Oct. '61. At Shiloh he led the Ark. Bn. as a Maj. and one month later was named Col. 8th Ark. He led this regiment at Perryville and Stones River (severely wounded), and then commanded a brigade under Buckner at Chickamauga. On 16 Nov. '63 he was appointed B.G. C.S.A., being not yet 24 years old, and during the Atlanta campaign he commanded a cavalry division under Wheeler. He was killed 20 Aug. '64 near Franklin, Tenn.

KELLY'S FORD (Kellysville), Va., 17 Mar. '63. Averell's 2d Div. of the newly-organized cavalry corps (Potomac) was ordered to attack the Confederate cavalry reported to be around Culpeper. His advance guard reached Kelly's Ford at 5 A.M. (according to Confederate reports; Averell puts the time three hours later). Here there was a cavalry outpost of 20 men which had been reinforced by an additional 40. Only a dozen or so of these were effectively engaged, however, since every fourth man was a "horse-holder" and the 40 reinforcements were initially posted too far to the rear. After an hour and a half the 1st R.I. Cav. succeeded in rorcing a crossing, capturing 25 prisoners. Averell then took two hours to move his entire force across the swift stream. (The above, and most of the rest of this account, is based primarily on H. B. McClellan.)

Fitz Lee at Culpeper learned of the Federal crossing at 7:30 A.M. and started his 800 available troopers forward to stop their threatened advance on Brandy Station and the vital O.&A. R.R. Jeb Stuart and John Pelham rode forward to witness the action. Averell was found "about half a mile from the ford, in no great strength, and appeared to be deployed as if he expected to receive, rather than to deliver, an attack" (*Lee's Lts.*, II, 460). Federal skirmishers were in position along a stone fence, with their right flank near an open field at the C. T. Wheatley house. Preceded by one dismounted squadron deployed as skirmishers, the 3d Va. Cav. charged toward the fence in the belief that they would find a gate or low spot that would enable them to scatter the enemy sharpshooters and strike the Federal rear. Finding no passage, they rode down the fence toward the Federal right, firing at the defenders, and expecting to find a gap. "The Gallant Pelham" was

mortally wounded by a shell fragment. The 4th and 16th Pa. Cav. of McIntosh's brigade moved toward the Wheatley house to meet them, and the 5th Va. Cav. joined the 3d in the action that developed in this area. The Virginians were then forced to withdraw, and the Pennsylvanians moved forward in pursuit.

On the opposite flank, meanwhile, an attack was launched by the 1st R.I., 4th Pa., and 6th Ohio Cav. of Duffié's brigade. The 1st, 2d, and 4th Va. moved to meet this threat. Federal accounts speak of the Confederate line's being driven back in confusion (e.g., Miller, IV, 233), whereas Southern accounts point out that only nine of their men were captured and their final and successful stand was only a mile behind their initial position. At 5:30 P.M. Averell withdrew, giving as reasons the exhaustion of his horses, defective artillery ammunition, and what H. B. McClellan calls "the phantom of 'rebel infantry.'" With 2,100 men and six guns against 800 men and four guns Averell had advanced two miles in 12½ hours; he had lost 78 men (41 of whom were in the 1st R.I.), while inflicting 133 casualties. Despite this unimpressive over-all record, the Federal troopers and the regimental and brigade commanders had shown evidence that Stuart's cavalry would soon be in for a contest. This evidence was to be strengthened three months later in the same area at BRANDY STATION.

KELLY'S FORD, Va., 7 Nov. '63. See RAPPAHANNOCK BRIDGE AND KELLY'S FORD, same date (BRISTOE CAMPAIGN).

KELTON, John Cunningham. Union officer. c. 1828–93. Pa. USMA 1851 (26/42); Inf.-Adj. Gen. He served on the frontier and taught at West Point before becoming Chief Purchasing Comsy. at St. Louis 11 May–5 Aug. '61. Named Capt. Asst. Adj. Gen. 3 Aug.

'61, he served in the Depts. of the West and of the Mo. until 11 Mar. '62, when he went to the Dept. of the Miss. As Col. 9th Mo. 19 Sept. '61 (resigned 12 Mar. '62) and Col. Add. A.D.C. 4 Jan. '62, he was at Corinth and served as Halleck's Asst. Adj. Gen. 11 July '62– 1 July '65. Continuing in the R.A., he was breveted four times for war service, including B.G. USA. He retired in 1892 as B.G. USA, the Adj. Gen.

KEMPER, James Lawson. C.S.A. gen. 1823–95. Va. After attending Washington College and V.M.I., he was a lawyer and fought in the Mexican War before becoming an active Va. politician. He was in the Va. House of Delegates and later elected its Speaker. He resigned to fight as Col. 7th Va. 2 May '61. He commanded his regiment from 1st Bull Run to Williamsburg and was appointed B.G. C.S.A. 3 June '62. Leading his brigade, he fought at Seven Pines, Frayser's Farm, 2d Bull Run (temporarily in command of the division), South Mountain, Antietam, and Fredericksburg. Going to New Bern, he returned to lead his brigade under Pickett at Gettysburg. Desperately wounded, he was captured and exchanged three months later in such a serious condition that he was not expected to live. Seeing no more field service, he was promoted Maj. Gen. 19 Sept. '64 and headed the Conscript Bureau and the reserve forces in Va. After the war he was Va.'s Gov. from 1874 to 1877. D.A.B. describes him as a man of "fine bearing, fearlessness, dash ... impassioned eloquence . . . good sense and high conception of duty."

KENESAW MOUNTAIN, Ga., 27 June '64. (ATLANTA CAMPAIGN) After two weeks of almost constant skirmishing around DALLAS (New Hope Church), 25 May–4 June, the capture of Allatoona Pass and Ackworth by the cavalry of Stoneman and Garrard threatened to turn the Confederate right. Johnston, consequently, shifted his entire line east and the night of 4 June took up positions on Lost, Pine, and Brush Mountains. W. H. Jackson's cavalry held the left flank; then, to the right, were the corps of Hardee, Polk, Hood, and Wheeler's cavalry.

Sherman shifted troops to oppose Johnston's new line but was so weakened by detachments to protect his line of communications that he waited until 10 June to make any general advance. During this time he was reinforced by Blair's XVII Corps (10,500), the 3d Brig. of Garrard's cavalry (2,500); J. E. Smith's division of XV Corps came up to guard the railroad at Cartersville; and XXIII Corps received 4,000 additional troops. The Confederates were reinforced by Cantey's 3d Brig. from Mobile.

Contact was established on 10 June and Sherman began to probe Johnston's new position. Almost constant rains for two weeks slowed operations. On 15 June Johnston withdrew the single division from the salient formed by Pine Mountain when this was partially enveloped by the XXIII and IV Corps. Polk was killed here by an artillery round 14 June and W. W. Loring temporarily succeeded to the command of his corps. The night of 17–18 June the Confederates abandoned Lost Mountain and Brush Mountain because of another threatened envelopment. Loring's corps now held Kenesaw Mountain with Wheeler's cavalry protecting its right. Hardee was in the center facing west, Hood was to his left, and Jackson's cavalry protected the extreme right of Johnston's new position.

Although it is the general assault of 27 June with which the name Kenesaw Mountain is generally associated, the following actions took place in the area: Pine Mountain, 14 June; Gilgal Church, 15–17 June; Golgotha, 16 June; Mud

Creek and Noyes's (Nose) Creek, 17 June; Pine Knob, 19 June; and Culp's (Kulp's) House, 22 June. Cavalry of the Army of the Cumberland had skirmishes at McAfee's Cross Road, 12 June; and at Lattermore's Mills and Powder Springs, 20 June. The names Marietta and Big Shanty are also associated with Kenesaw Mountain.

Sherman decided for various reasons not to continue his heretofore successful strategy of maneuvering Johnston's numerically inferior troops out of position. The weather was unfavorable; his troops apparently preferred a real fight to continued marching; he believed Johnston's position weakly held; and he had extended his own lines as far as he believed wise. On 24 June he gave the order for a general assault to be made three days later.

As a diversionary move Schofield, on the extreme Federal right, established a bridgehead near Olley's Creek. Reilly's brigade (1, 3, XXIII) advanced from Cheney's Farm on 26 June and drove back the outposts of Jackson's cavalry. Myers' Ind. battery supported the advance of Byrd's (3d) brigade which crossed the creek, built a bridge, and dug in on a hill to the northeast of Reilly. At dawn of the 27th Cameron's (2d) brigade crossed Byrd's bridge and secured a lodgment on the Confederate left flank. These operations were designed to draw attention from the main attack that started at 9 A.M., 27 June, against the center.

The main effort was made by the divisions of M. L. Smith (2, XV), Newton (2, IV), and J. C. Davis (2, XIV). Smith took the Confederate outpost line in the face of heavy fire and held these after failing to take the second line. Newton's division was repulsed after heavy losses. Harker, on the right, was mortally wounded in leading his brigade in a second assault. Wagner, on his left, was also repulsed. Kimball's brigade tried and also failed. Newton held the captured outposts until relieved by the division of Stanley.

The attack of Davis' division was led by the brigades of Dan McCook and Mitchell. McCook was mortally wounded as was Col. Harmon, who succeeded him. Col. C. J. Dilworth took command and led the brigade in a gallant but unsuccessful continuation of the assault. Mitchell's brigade experienced a similar failure. A combination of heat, rough terrain, strong natural defensive positions, and determined Confederate resistance made Kenesaw Mountain impregnable. A Federal withdrawal in the face of the commanding Confederate positions would have been almost as costly as a continued assault. Davis dug in a few yards from the enemy. Most of the fighting was done by the Confederate divisions of Cleburne, Cheatham, and Featherston, and about half of the divisions of French and Walthall.

The night of the 29th the Confederates failed in an attempt to drive Davis from his positions. The night of 1 July Sherman moved McPherson from the extreme left to the right and started another strategic envelopment of Johnston's position. Johnston withdrew the next night to Smyrna and then to a line along the CHATTAHOOCHEE RIVER.

An estimated 16,225 Federals were engaged 27 June, of whom 1,999 were killed and wounded and 52 were missing. An estimated 17,733 Confederates were engaged, of whom 270 were killed and wounded and 172 missing (Livermore).

KENLY, John Reese. Union gen. 1822–91. Md. A lawyer, he served in the Mexican War and was commissioned Col. 1st Md. 11 June '61. After Front Royal (May '62), where he was severely wounded and captured, he was promoted B.G. USV 22 Aug. '62. He commanded

Harpers Ferry, Md. Div., VIII, Mid. Dept. (17 Sept. '62–5 Jan. '63); Md. Defenses Upper Potomac, VIII, Mid. Dept. (5 Jan.–Feb. '63); 1st Brig., 1st Div., VIII, Mid. Dept. (27 Mar.–26 June '63); and 3d Div., I, Potomac (11–18 June, 11 July '63–24 Mar. '64). He also led in the Mid. Dept.: Dist. Delaware, VIII (2 Apr.–5 May '64); 3d Sep. Brig., VIII (16 May–20 July '64, 18 Nov.–20 Dec. '64 and 5 June–31 July '65); and Dist. Eastern Shore, VIII (13 Dec. '64–1 June '65). He was breveted Maj. Gen. USV for war service and mustered out 25 Aug. '65.

KENNEDY, John Doby. C.S.A. gen. 1840–96. S.C. After graduating from S.C. College he became a lawyer and was commissioned Capt. 2d S.C. in 1861. He succeeded Kershaw as Col. of the regiment in Feb. '62 fought at Savage's Station, and was wounded leading it at Antietam. Continuing under Kershaw, he fought at Fredericksburg, Chancellorsville, Gettysburg (again wounded), Chickamauga, Knoxville, the Wilderness, Spotsylvania, Petersburg, and Cedar Creek. He was appointed B.G. C.S.A. 22 Dec. '64 and took over Kershaw's brigade, leading it against Sherman at Averasboro and Bentonville. After the war he was active in Democratic politics, serving as a legislator, Lt.-Gov. and Consul Gen. in Shanghai, 1885–89. He was also prominent in veterans' organizations.

KENNEDY, Robert Patterson. Union officer. 1840–1918. Ohio. 2d Lt. 23d Ohio 11 June '61; Capt. Asst. Adj. Gen. Vols. 7 Oct. '62; Maj. Asst. Adj. Gen. Vols. 16 Nov. '64; resigned 8 Apr. '65; Col. 196th Ohio 14 Apr. '65; Bvt. B.G. USV. Brevets for W. Va. and Shenandoah campaigns, war service. On staffs of Gens. Scammon, Crook, and Kenner Garrard. At Antietam, D.A.B. says, "... he was in temporary charge of a portion of the left wing of the

army, and upon the review of that army by President Lincoln on the battlefield, he was called to the front and presented as 'the youngest commander of the Army of the Potomac.'" He was Ohio's Lt. Gov. in 1883, resigned in 1887, to be US Representative, and continued to be active in politics for many years.

KENNER, Duncan Farrar. Confed. statesman. 1813–87. La. A delegate to the Confed. Prov. Congress and then a La. representative in the Confed. Congress, he was sent by Benjamin on a secret mission to England and France to offer emancipation in return for diplomatic recognition. He later served as Tariff Commissioner under Arthur.

KENNETT, Henry Gassaway. Union officer. Ohio. Lt. Col. 27th Ohio 18 Aug. '61; Col. 79th Ohio 1 Nov. '62; Bvt. B.G. USV (war service); resigned 1 Aug. '64. Commanded Cav. Div. (Ohio).

KENT, Loren. Union officer. N.H. 1st Lt. Adj. 29th Ill. 1 Dec. '61; Lt. Col. 31 Oct. '62; Col. 14 Nov. '63; Bvt. B.G. USV 22 Mar. '65 (war service). In the Dept. of the Gulf he commanded 3, 1, Res. Corps; and 3, 1, XIII. Died 1866.

5TH KENTUCKY (US)

Colonels: Lovell H. Rousseau (Bvt. Maj. Gen., USA), Harvey M. Buckley, William W. Berry.

Battles: Shiloh, Stones River, Liberty Gap, Chickamauga, Brown's Ferry, Orchard Knob, Missionary Ridge, Rocky Face Ridge, Dalton, Blain's Cross Roads, Resaca, Dallas, Kenesaw, Chattahoochee, Atlanta. Also at Bowling Green, Corinth siege, Adairsville, Peach Tree Creek, Jonesboro, Lovejoy.

Organized at Camp Joe Holt, Ind., 9 Sept. '61, and crossing soon thereafter into Kentucky, this regiment first served in Rousseau's brigade, McCook's division. In Mar. '62 it marched with Buell's army to reinforce Grant at Shiloh at the critical moment and helped turn defeat into a Union victory. During the Stones River campaign it served in Baldwin's (3d) brigade, Johnson's (2d) division of McCook's corps. Its severest losses were at Chickamauga. In Oct. '63 the regiment became part of Hazen's (2d) brigade, Wood's (3d) division of IV Corps (Cumberland). It played a decisive role in the battles of Orchard Knob and Missionary Ridge. On 14 Sept. '64 the regiment was mustered out. The 5th Ky. ranks No. 19 among Federal regiments in per cent killed in combat on the basis of total enrollment.

15TH KENTUCKY (US)

Colonels: Curran Pope (USMA; K.I.A.), James B. Forman (K.I.A.), Marion C. Taylor.

Battles: Chaplin Hills, Stones River, Tullahoma, Hoover's Gap, Chickamauga, Resaca, New Hope Church, Kenesaw Mountain, Atlanta, Shepherdsville, and Lebanon Junction (Ky.) (against guerrillas). Present also at Missionary Ridge, Buzzard Roost, Peach Tree Creek, and Jonesboro.

Mustered in 14 Dec. '61 and ordered to the Army of the Cumberland, O. M. Mitchel's division. In the Stones River campaign the regiment lost the following at Chaplin Hills: 82 killed, 114 wounded, and no missing. In this action all three field officers and two line officers were killed. Colonel Forman, the "Brave Boy Colonel," was killed at Stones River. At Chickamauga the regiment fought as part of Beatty's (1st) brigade, Negley's (2d) division, XIV Corps. In Oct. '63 it became part of Carlin's (1st) brigade, Palmer's (1st) division, XIV Corps. After the fall of Atlanta the regiment was assigned to garrison duty. It was mustered out 14 Jan. '65.

Only 30 other Federal regiments sustained more battle deaths, on the basis of per cent of total enrollment, than the 15th Ky.

KENTUCKY, CONFED. ARMY OF. Designation assigned 25 Aug. '62 to troops in Dept. of EAST TENN. after the start of Kirby SMITH'S INVASION OF KENTUCKY.

KENTUCKY, CONFED. CENTRAL ARMY OF. Initially composed of the forces in central Ky. under Buckner in Sept. '61. The O.R. state that he assumed command of the "Central Division of Kentucky" on 18 Sept. (Vol. IV, p. 175). A. S. Johnston took command 28 Oct., at which time the army consisted of Buckner's 4,000 at Bowling Green, Zollicoffer's 4,000 at Cumberland Gap, and Polk's 11,000 at Columbus, Ky. (Horn, 56). Hardee was ordered from northeastern Ark. with his small force and on 5 Dec. was put in temporary command of the army. On 23 Feb. '62 A. S. Johnston assumed immediate command (O.R., VII, 1 and 2). On 29 Mar. the army, which then numbered about 23,-000, was consolidated with the Army of (the) MISSISSIPPI and the designation Army of Ky. disappeared. See also KANAWHA, Confed. Army of the.

KENTUCKY, KIRBY SMITH'S CONFED. ARMY OF. See EAST TENNESSEE, Confed. Dept. of.

KENTUCKY OPERATIONS IN 1861. On 6 Sept. Grant occupied Paducah, at the mouth of the Tennessee, and shortly thereafter occupied Smithland, at the mouth of the Cumberland. The Confederates took possession of the bluffs at Columbus. Union troops from Cincinnati took Louisville and Covington, and the Confederates advanced from Nashville and Knoxville to Bowling Green and the Cumberland. During the remainder of the year both sides strengthened these positions.

KENTUCKY, UNION DEPARTMENT AND ARMY OF. At the start of the war, while opposing governments tried to win Ky. to their side, Naval Lt. (later Brig. Gen.) William ("Bull") Nelson and Col. (later Maj. Gen.) Lovell H. Rousseau were assembling Federal volunteers at Camp Dick Robinson and Camp Joe Holt, near Danville and Louisville, respectively. On 28 May '61 the Dept. of Ky. was established to comprise all of the state within 100 miles of the Ohio River. Its commander was Brig. Gen. Robert Anderson of Fort Sumter fame. On 15 Aug. the department was merged into the newly-created but short-lived Dept. of the Cumberland. (The state of Ky. was not officially occupied, however, until Sept. '61.) On 10 Feb. '65 the department was re-created. Commander: Maj. Gen. John M. Palmer (Dyer, 540). On 25 Aug. '62 the forces that had been commanded by Nelson were designated the Army of Kentucky and put under Granger. They consisted of only the brigades of M. D. Manson and Charles Cruft; all these troops were captured at Richmond, Ky., 30 Aug. '62 (Dyer, 524). Other sources (e.g., Cullum) call this command of Granger's "the 5th Division and cavalry (Army of the Mississippi)." In Oct. this "army" was reconstituted, mainly from new regiments, into the three divisions initially commanded by Burbridge, G. C. Smith, and Baird. This organization was broken up almost as soon as formed. The next unit known as Granger's Army of Ky. was a force of four brigades (Coburn's and S. D. Atkins' from the former Army of Ky.; W. P. Reed's from the Dist. of Western Ky.; and George Crook's from W. Va.). These four brigades were grouped together as the division of Baird (Dyer, 450). Between 8 June and 9 Oct. '63 Granger commanded the Reserve Corps of Rosecrans' Army of the Cumberland. This force consisted of the divisions of Baird (later Steedman), Morgan, and R. S. Granger (Van Horne, I, 299). Since several regiments of this organization had been in Gran-

ger's original Army of Ky., this designation was often applied to the entire force. The "Army of Ky." which distinguished itself at Chickamauga consisted of Whitaker's and Mitchell's brigades of Steedman's division.

KERNSTOWN, Va. ("First Kernstown"), 23 Mar. '62. (SHENANDOAH VALLEY CAMPAIGN OF JACKSON) Banks's advance caused Jackson to evacuate Winchester 12 Mar. and retire up the Valley to Mount Jackson. Williams' division remained at Winchester and Shields's advanced to Strasburg. On 20 Mar. Williams started for Manassas to reinforce McDowell for the Peninsular campaign and Shields prepared to follow. On 21 Mar. Ashby's cavalry detected this Federal retrograde and notified Jackson. Since it was Jackson's mission to prevent Federal reinforcements from leaving the Valley to reinforce McDowell (who was preparing to march overland from Fredericksburg to reinforce McClellan on the Peninsula), Jackson advanced by forced marches· to attack the retreating Federals. Ashby attacked with his one available cavalry company on the 22d. His sources of information in Winchester led him to believe that Shields had withdrawn and left only a rear guard; he estimated that only four infantry regiments were locally available, whereas Shields had the rest of his division (9,000 total) at hand. Jackson came up with his entire force next day and, despite religious misgivings about fighting on Sunday, attacked to annihilate what he thought to be inferior forces. Fulkerson's and Garnett's (Stonewall) brigades maneuvered to assault the Federal right, while Ashby's small cavalry force held the Valley pike with J. S. Burks's small infantry brigade in support. Jackson's attack hit Tyler's brigade and was pushing it back until Kimball's brigade was moved out of its concealed position north of Kernstown and sent to Tyler's support. The Confederates, low on ammunition and outnumbered, were routed. When Jackson learned that Garnett had ordered a withdrawal of the Stonewall Brigade he relieved him of command. After evacuating his wounded, and his supply wagons, Jackson withdrew four and a half miles to Newtown and Ashby checked the Federal pursuit a mile and a half south of Kernstown.

Of 9,000 Federals engaged 22–23 Mar., there were 590 casualties, including Shields (wounded). Of 4,200 Confederates engaged, there were 700 casualties. Although Jackson had been beaten, the Federals assumed that he would not have attacked unless he had been reinforced and they were led to make strategic errors that greatly benefited the Confederates. (See SHENANDOAH VALLEY CAMPAIGN OF JACKSON.)

KERNSTOWN, Va. ("Second Kernstown"), 23–24 July '64. (EARLY'S WASHINGTON RAID) Crook's VIII Corps was encamped around Winchester when attacked by Early. There were cavalry skirmishes on the 23d and, the next day, a general attack, conducted almost entirely by Echols's division under the leadership of Breckinridge. Crook's cavalry was driven in confusion toward Bunker Hill, where his infantry arrived about 9 P.M. after some units had stampeded. Crook crossed the Potomac to Williamsport, where he rallied his men and repulsed the cavalry pursuit. Federal losses were 1,185, including 479 prisoners. Confederate officers captured at STEVENSON'S DEPOT, 20 July, were recovered (including R. D. Lilley).

KERR RIFLE. An English arm used in small numbers by the Confederates as a sniper's rifle. (See also WHITWORTH RIFLE.) It was 53 inches in total length and had a 37-inch, .44 cal. barrel with an elevated rear sight and a folding front sight (Albaugh and Simmons, 236). A 5-chamber double action, .44 cal. Kerr revolver was also imported into the South (*ibid.*).

KERSHAW, Joseph Brevard. C.S.A. gen. 1822–94. S.C. The son of an old and distinguished family, he was a lawyer, legislator, and fought in the Mexican War. After attending the secession convention in 1860, he was commissioned Col. 2d S.C. in Apr. '61, serving at Morris Island and in Bonham's brigade at 1st Bull Run. He was appointed B.G. C.S.A. 13 Feb. '62 and commanded his brigade under Longstreet at the Peninsula, 2d Bull Run, South Mountain, Fredericksburg, Chancellorsville, and Gettysburg. In the West with Longstreet, he fought at Chickamauga and returned to the A.N.V. to become Maj. Gen. 2 June '64 with rank from 18 May. Taking over McLaws' division, he fought under Longstreet at the Wilderness, Spotsylvania, Cold Harbor, the battles around Petersburg and Sayler's Creek, where he surrendered with Ewell. After several months in a Boston prison he returned to S.C. and was a legislator and jurist. He wrote articles for B.&L. on his brigade's performance at Fredericksburg and Gettysburg.

KETCH, bomb (or mortar). Small boats specially designed for firing mortars and used principally on western waters.

KETCHAM, John Henry. Union gen. 1831–? N.Y. He had held several public offices including a seat in the legislature when he was commissioned Col. 150th N.Y. 11 Oct. '62. He was breveted B.G. USV 6 Dec. '64 and promoted B.G. USV 1 Apr. '65, resigning 2 Dec. '65 to become Republican congressman from N.Y. He was breveted Maj. Gen. USV for war service.

KETCHUM, William Scott. Union gen. 1813–71. Conn. USMA 1834

(32/36); Inf. After serving in garrison duty, on the frontier and in the Seminole War, he was Maj. 4th US Inf. when the war began. He was Acting I.G. for the Dept. of the Mo. in Mar. '61 and commissioned Lt. Col. 10th US Inf. 1 Nov. '61. As B.G. USV (3 Feb. '62), he was in charge of Pa. recruits at Harrisonburg and later served in the War and Q.M. depts. He was mustered out of USV in 1866 and continued in the R.A. until retired in 1870 as Col. He was breveted for war service three times, including once each as B.G. and Maj. Gen. USA.

KETNER, James. Union officer. Ohio. 1st Lt. 1st Kans. 29 May '61; Capt. 1 Sept. '61; Maj. 19 May '63; mustered out 17 June '64; Maj. 16th Kans. Cav. 8 Oct. '64. Bvt. B.G. USV (war service).

KEYES (keeze), Erasmus Darwin. Union gen. 1810–95. Mass. Appt.-Me. USMA 1832 (10/45); Arty. Serving in garrison and on the frontier, he was Winfield Scott's A.D.C. twice, taught cavalry and artillery at West Point, and was a member of the USMA Board of Visitors in 1844. He also participated in Indian fighting and coastal defense. From 1 Jan. '60 until 19 Apr. '61 he was Scott's Mil. Sec. as Lt. Col. and then served on N.Y. Gov. Morgan's staff in dispatching troops until 25 June '61. He was named Col. 11th U.S. Inf. 14 May and B.G. USV three days later. At 1st Bull Run he commanded 1st Brig., 1st Div., and then commanded Keyes's brigade in the Div. Potomac (Aug.–Oct. '61) and in McDowell's division (3 Oct.– 9 Nov. '61). He led Keyes's division (vice Buell), Potomac (9 Nov. '61–13 Mar. '62) when he took command of the IV Corps, Potomac, leading it from its inception until its discontinuation 1 Aug. '63. He participated in the Peninsular campaign at Lee's Mill, Yorktown, Bottom's Bridge, Savage's Station, Fair Oaks, Charles City Cross Roads,

Malvern Hill, and Harrison's Landing. He was named Maj. Gen. USV 5 May '62. Then, still in command of the IV Corps, he commanded Yorktown Dist., VII, Va. and Div. at Suffolk, VII, Va. (6–14 Apr. '63). During this time he led an expedition to West Point 7 May '62, organized a raid on White House 7 Jan. '63, and took part in the diversionary movements against Richmond during the Gettysburg campaign (BALTIMORE C.R.; S. ANNA RIVER). In a controversy with Dix over his participation in these forays, he was refused an official investigation. He then served on various boards and commissions from 15 July '63 until he resigned 6 May '64. He had been breveted for Fair Oaks (B.G. USA 31 May '62). Moving to San Francisco, he engaged in gold mining, banking, and wine growing. He wrote "The Rear Guard at Malvern Hill," B.&L., II, 434.

KEY WEST, UNION DEPARTMENT OF. In existence from 11 Jan. '62 (Phisterer) or 21 Feb. '62 (Dyer) until 15 Mar. '62, when merged into the Dept. of the South. Commanded by Brig. Gen. J. M. Brannan. (See also FLORIDA, UNION DEPARTMENT OF.)

KIDD, James Harvey. Union officer. Mich. Capt. 6th Mich. Cav. 13 Oct. '62; Maj. 9 May '63; Col. 19 May '64; Bvt. B.G. USV (war service). W.I.A. Falling Waters (Md.) 14 July '63 and Winchester (Va.) 19 Sept. '64.

KIDDOO, Joseph Barr. Union officer. Pa. c. 1840–80. Enlisting in Apr. '61 in the 12th Pa., he was discharged in Aug. In the 63d Pa. 1 Nov. '61–24 Aug. '62 at Yorktown, Williamsburg, Fair Oaks, and Malvern Hill, he was commissioned Lt. Col. 137th Pa. on the latter date. He was promoted Col. 15 Mar. '63 and fought at South Mountain, Antietam, Fredericksburg, and Chancellorsville. Mustered out 1 June '63, on 5 Oct. '63

459   KILPATRICK, H. J.

he became Maj. 6th US Col. Inf. Promoted Col. 22d US Col. Inf. 6 Jan.'64 and severely wounded at Petersburg in Oct., he was breveted for Petersburg assault (B.G. USV), war service (Maj. Gen. USV), and Fair Oaks (B.G. USA). Continuing in the R.A., he was retired in 1870 with the rank of B.G. USV.

KIERNAN, James Lawlor. Union gen. 1837–69. N.Y. He was a doctor and editor of N.Y.C.'s *"Medical Press"* when he was commissioned Surg. 6th Mo. Cav. 1 Mar. '62. He resigned 24 May '63 and was appointed B.G. USV 1 Aug. '63. He was wounded, captured, and escaped near Port Gibson (Miss.). On 3 Feb. '64 he resigned and was later Surg. of the Pension Bureau and US Consul at Chin Kiang, China.

KILBURN, Charles Lawrence. Union officer. c. 1819–99. Pa. USMA 1842 (22/56); Arty.-Comsy. He served in garrison and the Mexican War (2 brevets) before being promoted Maj. Comsy. of Subsist. 11 May '61. During the Civil War he served on commissary duty at Washington, Baltimore, and Cincinnati until 1864, and as Chief Comsy. of the Dept. of the South for the rest of the war. Continuing in the R.A., he retired in 1882 as Col. and Bvt. B.G. USA.

KILGOUR, William Mather. Union officer. Pa. 2d Lt. 13th Ill. 24 May '61; resigned 3 Feb. '62; Maj. 75th Ill. 2 Sept. '62; Lt. Col. 3 Feb. '63; Bvt. B.G. USV 20 June '65. Brevets for war service, Missionary Ridge, Atlanta, Nashville. Transferred to R.A. and retired in 1873 as Capt. Died 1885.

KILPATRICK, Hugh Judson ("Kill Cavalry"). Union gen. 1836–81. N.J. USMA 1861 (17/45); Arty.-Cav. Graduating as 2d Lt. 6 May and being commissioned Capt. 5th N.Y. ("Duryee's Zouaves") 9 May '61, he was wounded

at Big Bethel 10 June (the first R.A. officer W.I.A.) and then promoted Lt. Col. 2d N.Y. Cav. 25 Sept. '61. He served with his regiment in the defenses of Washington until 29 Jan. '62 when, as Lt. Col. Add. A.D.C., he went to Kans. to serve as Chief of Arty. on Gen. Lane's Tex. expedition. When this was abandoned 21 Mar. '62, he returned to his regiment at Arlington, Va., and participated in raids and skirmishes at Carmel Church, Brandy Station, Freeman's Ford, Sulphur Springs, Waterloo Bridge, Thoroughfare Gap, and Haymarket and in the battle of 2d Bull Run. Named Col. 2d N.Y. Cav. 6 Dec. '62, he commanded 1, 3, Cav. Corps, Potomac (16 Feb.–13 May '63) on Stoneman's raid toward Richmond and (7–14 June '63) at Beverly Ford. He was appointed B.G. USV 13 June '63 and led 2, 2, Cav. Corps (14–28 June '63) at Aldie, Middleburg, and Upperville. Then commanding the 3d Div., Cav. Corps, Potomac, he fought at Hanover, Hunterstown, Gettysburg (28 June–15 July '63); the expedition to destroy enemy gunboats on the Rappahannock, Culpeper, Somerville Ford, Brandy Station, and Gainesville (4 Aug.–25 Nov. '63) and the KILPATRICK-DAHLGREN RAID to Richmond and Ashland, Va. (20 Dec. '63–13 Apr. '64). He then went to the western theater at the request of Sherman, who is alleged to have said "I know Kilpatrick is a hell of a damned fool, but I want just that sort of man to command my cavalry on this expedition." In the cavalry corps of the Army of the Cumberland he commanded the 3d Div. (26 Apr.–13 May and 23 July–29 Oct. '64) during the Atlanta campaign, fighting at Ringgold and Dalton (severely wounded). When the CAVALRY CORPS, Mil. Div. Miss., was organized, Kilpatrick commanded the 3d Div. (29 Oct. '64–26 June '65), constituting Sherman's cav-

KILPATRICK-DAHLGREN RAID **460**

alry force during the MARCH TO THE SEA and the Carolinas campaign. He was promoted Maj. Gen. USV 18 June '65. Breveted for Aldie, Gettysburg, Resaca, Fayetteville (B.G. USA), and the Carolinas (Maj. Gen. USV and USA), he resigned 1 Dec. '65 and served as Minister to Chile until 1868. As a Republican, he was active in politics, running unsuccessfully for Congress and supporting Democrat Horace Greeley in 1872. He was reappointed to Chile in 1881 and died at Santiago while involved with Stephen A. HURLBUT, US Minister to Peru, in a political controversy during the war between these two South American countries.

A controversial man "whose notorious immoralities and rapacity set so demoralizing an example to his troops that the best disciplinarians among his subordinates could only mitigate its influence," he displayed in combat "a dare-devil recklessness that dismayed his opponents and imparted his own daring to his men" (J. D. Cox, *March,* 40). Described as "young for a brigadier, a wiry, restless, undersized man with black eyes, a lantern jaw ... a member of Meade's staff said it was hard to look at Kilpatrick without laughing." His nickname "Kill Cavalry" came not only from some vigorous and admirable fighting by his command, but also from such poor judgment as ordering the attack of E. J. FARNSWORTH at Gettysburg, and the KILPATRICK-DAHLGREN RAID to Richmond.

KILPATRICK-DAHLGREN RAID TO RICHMOND, VA., 28 Feb.–4 Mar. '64. Reports of crowded conditions in Richmond prisons and a belief that the city was protected by only 3,000 militia led the Federals during the winter of 1863–64 to consider raids to release the prisoners. The first of these, Ben Butler's in early 1864, was prompted by favorable intelligence reports from "Crazy Bet" VAN LEW. The Confederates learned of this operation, however, and blocked the raid.

Judson Kilpatrick then persuaded Lincoln and Stanton to authorize a raid that would not only permit him to seize Richmond by a *coup de main* and free the prisoners, but would also enable him to distribute amnesty proclamations within enemy lines. To support him, Custer undertook a diversionary raid in ALBEMARLE COUNTY, 28 Feb.–1 Mar.

At 11 P.M. on the 28th Kilpatrick drove off enemy outposts and crossed the Rapidan at Ely's Ford. He had 3,584 picked cavalrymen, six guns, eight caissons, three wagons, and four ambulances (Kilpatrick's report, O.R. I, XXXIII, 183). The column separated the next day at Spotsylvania, Kilpatrick leading the main body toward Richmond and Col. Ulric Dahlgren leading 500 men to Goochland, 30 miles above the city.

The night of 29 Feb. the Confederate War Department learned of the raid and emergency measures were put into effect. The next morning Col. W. H. Stevens, commander of the Richmond defenses, had disposed his 500 men and six guns at three points guarding the approaches to the city from the north. G. W. Custis Lee moved his Local Defense Brig. (five battalions of workers from the Armory, Arsenal, Tredegar Works, Navy, and governmental departments) to block any approach from the west. Wade Hampton, through whose pickets Kilpatrick had penetrated at Ely's Ford, took up the pursuit when he was able to ascertain the direction of the Federal raiders. Artillery of Early's corps was also involved, as was a small force known as the North Anna Home Guards.

Kilpatrick reached the Richmond fortifications on 1 Mar. (Tuesday) and found them too strong to assault. Having failed to achieve surprise, and encountering stronger resistance than anticipated, his self-confidence appears to have vanished. He turned east and recrossed the Chickahominy at Mechanicsville. After remaining around Cold Harbor, skirmishing with the enemy and awaiting the arrival of Dahlgren, he withdrew and linked up with Butler's column at New Kent Court House on the 4th. Here Butler's troops—4,000 infantry, Spear's 2,200 cavalry and two guns, all led by I. J. Wistar–had been stopped by strong Confederate resistance.

Meanwhile, Dahlgren had reached the neighborhood of Goochland early 1 Mar. Here he split his force, sending Capt. J. F. Mitchell ·vith 100 men of the 2d N.Y. Cav. down the north bank of the James to destroy property and to dash into Richmond. With the assistance of a Negro boy, Martin Robinson, Dahlgren was to ford the river and enter Richmond from the south.

Either through ignorance or by design the Negro led Dahlgren to a point where there was no ford and the river was too swollen by recent rains to ford. Dahlgren summarily hanged him for suspected treachery. About 3:30 P.M. Dahlgren and Mitchell joined forces at a point (Short Pump) about eight miles from Richmond. At dusk they encountered stiff resistance (Custis Lee's force) and pressed to within two and a half miles of the capital. After losing heavily in this aggressive action, Dahlgren finally ordered a withdrawal. The night was cold, wet, and black, and the Federals became separated. Early 3 Mar. Mitchell rejoined Kilpatrick near Tunstall Station with 260 men.

Dahlgren with about 100 men took a route farther north, crossing the Pamunkey at Hanovertown—where Confederate cavalry took up the pursuit— and crossing the Mattapony at Aylett's.

Lt. James Pollard with Co. H, 9th Va. Cav. (Chambliss's brigade; Fitz Lee's division) maintained contact during the day, and then circled ahead to set up an ambush near King and Queen Court House. Here he was joined by Capt. E. C. Fox, Co. E, 5th Va. (Lomax's brigade, Lee's division) and miscellaneous detachments to make a total of about 150 (Fox's report in O.R.). About 11 P.M. Dahlgren rode into the trap; he was killed and 92 of his men and 38 Negroes were captured (ibid.). Although Fox was in command, by virtue of rank Jeb Stuart made it clear that "To Lieutenant Pollard's skillful dispositions and to his activity it is mainly due that Dahlgren was killed and his party captured" (O.R.).

A 13-year-old boy named William Littlepage found papers on Dahlgren's body that disclosed an intent of the raiders to burn Richmond and kill Jeff Davis and his cabinet. These DAHLGREN PAPERS precipitated a controversy that has never been fully resolved.

Reinforced with infantry and cavalry, Kilpatrick raided the country near the site of Dahlgren's death. He then returned to Yorktown, and then rejoined Meade by water. The operation cost the Federals 340 men and 583 horses; 480 of the animals that returned were unfit for further service. In addition to a large amount of equipment and accouterments, the following weapons were lost: 90 Spencer rifles, 504 carbines, 516 pistols, and 500 sabers.

For a recent and definitive study see V. C. Jones, *Eight Hours before Richmond*, New York, 1957.

KILPATRICK'S RAID TO JONESBORO, 18–22 Aug. '64. (ATLANTA CAMPAIGN) Taking advantage of the absence of most of the Confederate cavalry on WHEELER'S RAID, 10 Aug.– 10 Sept. '64, Sherman ordered a raid on Hood's line of communications south of Atlanta. It was hoped that this would force Hood to withdraw. Kilpatrick was reinforced with two brigades of Garrard's division and ordered to destroy the railroad between Jonesboro and Griffin. Kilpatrick left Sandtown late 18 Aug. and reached Jonesboro the following evening. After destroying about a mile of track he was attacked by Confederate cavalry and moved about midnight to the southeast. W. H. Jackson's cavalry pursued him, and at Lovejoy, 20 Aug., Confederate infantry blocked his attempt to recross the railroad and move west. Kilpatrick then fought his way through Jackson's cavalry and reached Decatur on the 22d. His raid had failed to accomplish its mission.

KIMBALL, John White. Union officer. Mass. Maj. 15th Mass. 1 Aug. '61; Lt. Col. 1 May '62; Col. 53d Mass. 10 Nov. '62; Bvt. B.G. USV (war service); mustered out 2 Sept. '63.

KIMBALL, Nathan. Union gen. 1823–98. Ind. A doctor, he fought in the Mexican War and was named Col. 14th Ind. 7 June '61. Commanded his regiment at Cheat Mountain and Greenbrier, and 1, 2, Banks's V (13 Mar.–4 Apr. '62) in the Valley. On 22 Mar. '62, when Shields was wounded by Ashby's preliminary skirmish, Kimball succeeded him as division commander, defeating Jackson the next day at Kernstown. Promoted B.G. USV 15 Apr. '62 for this, he commanded 1st Brig., 2d Div., Shenandoah (4 Apr.–10 May); 1st Brig., Shields's division, Rappahannock (10 May–26 June) and Kimball's brigade, II, Potomac (July–Sept. '62). At Antietam and Fredericksburg, where he was wounded, he commanded 1, 3, II (10 Sept.–13 Dec. '62). During the siege and assaults of Vicksburg he led 3d Div., XVI (Mar.–28 May '63) and Kimball's Prov. Div., XVI (28 May–10 Aug. '63). He then

commanded Kimball's division, Dist. East Ark., XVI (29 July–4 Aug. '63); 2d Div., Ark. Exp., XVI (13 Sept.–30 Nov. '63); 3d Div., Ark. Exp., XVI (4 Aug.–13 Sept. '63); 2d Div., VII (13 Feb.–25 Apr. '64); and 1, 2, IV Cumberland (22 May–4 Aug. '64). During the Atlanta campaign he led 1st Div., IV, Cumberland (5 Aug.–19 Sept. '64) as well as at Franklin and Nashville (28 Nov. '64–16 Feb. '65) and later (16 Mar.–1 Aug. '65). He was breveted Maj. Gen. USV 1 Feb. '65 and mustered out 24 Aug., returning to politics as a Republican in Ind. and Utah. He wrote "Fighting Jackson at Kernstown" in B.&L., II, 302–13.

KIMBALL, William King. Union officer. Me. Lt. Col. 12th Me. 15 Nov. '61; Col. 31 July '62; mustered out 7 Dec. '64; Col. 2d Me. 10 Apr. '65; Bvt. B.G. USV (war service). Commanded 2, 4, XIX. Died 1875.

KIMBALL'S BRIGADE. See STEEDMAN'S — KIMBALL'S — OPDYCKE'S BRIGADE.

KIMBERLY, Robert Lewis. Union officer. Conn. 2d Lt. 41st Ohio 29 Oct. '61; 1st Lt. 21 Jan. '62; Capt. 17 Mar. '62; Maj. 6 Dec. '62; Lt. Col. 15 Apr. '63; discharged 1 Mar. '65; Col. 191st Ohio 10 Mar. '65; Bvt. B.G. USV (war service). Commanded 2, 3, IV (Cumberland).

KING, Adam Eckfeldt. Union officer. Pa. 2d Lt. 31st N.Y. 2 Jan. '62; 1st Lt. 9 May '62; Capt. Asst. Adj. Gen. Vols. 11 Mar. '63; Maj. Asst. Adj. Gen. Vols. 15 July '64; Lt. Col. Asst. Adj. Gen. Assigned 10 June '65–11 June '66; Bvt. B.G. USV. Brevets for Wilderness, Spotsylvania, Cold Harbor, Monocacy (Md.), war service (2).

KING, John Fields. Union officer. Ill. Lt. Col. 114th Ill. 18 Sept. '62; Bvt. B.G. USV (war service); resigned 7 Dec. '64.

KING, John Haskell. Union gen.
1818–88. Mich. R.A. Entering the army
in 1837, he served in Fla., on the frontier, and during the Mexican War. He
was Maj. 15th US Inf. (14 May '61)
when the Civil War began, and led his
battalion at Shiloh, the advance on
Corinth, and at Murfreesboro, where
he was wounded and then injured by
the fall of his horse. Promoted B.G.
USV 29 Nov. '62, he led a brigade at
Chickamauga and during the Atlanta
campaign and commanded a division
during part of this (1, XIV, Cumberland: 26 July–23 Aug. '63, 29 May–6
June '64, 13 June–13 July '64, 7–17
Aug. '64). His commands were 3, 1,
XIV, Cumberland (6 May–26 July '63,
24 Aug.–10 Oct. '63); 2, 1, XIV, Cumberland (9–13 Oct. '63, 15 Nov. '63–
13 June '64, 13 July–7 Aug. '64); Reg.
Brig., Dist. of Chattanooga, Cumberland, and 1st Sep. Brig., 1st Div. Separate Etowah, Cumberland, in 1864 and
1865. His brevets were for Chickamauga, Ruff's Station (Ga.) as B.G.
USA and war service as Maj. Gen.
USA. He continued in the R.A. until
retired in 1882 as Col.

KING, Rufus. Union gen. 1814–76.
N.Y. USMA 1833 (4/43); Engrs. He
served on survey and construction work
until resigning in 1836 to become a
railroad engineer and newspaper editor.
He served as Atty. Gen. of N.Y. under
Wm. Seward (1839–43) and served on
the USMA Board of Visitors as well as
working for free education in Wis. He
was appointed Minister to the Vatican
but Fort Sumter occurred as he was
about to sail, and he declined the post
to remain and fight. He organized the
"IRON BRIGADE" as a Wis. State B.G.
and was commissioned B.G. USV 17
May '61. He commanded 3d Brig.,
McDowell's division, Potomac (3 Oct.
'61–13 Mar. '62); King's 3d Div., I,
Potomac (13 Mar.–4 Apr. '62) and

King's division, Rappahannock (4 Apr.–
26 June '62). While in command of 1st
Div., III, Army of Va. (26 June–26
Aug. '62) he was surprised at GROVE-
TON (28 Aug. '62) by Stonewall Jackson's entire corps. He also led 1st Div.,
I, Potomac 12–14 Sept. '62, served on
the commission that tried Fitz-John
Porter, and then commanded Ind. Brig.,
VII, Va. (1 Apr.–June '63); Ind. Brig.,
IV, Potomac (May–June '63); 1st Div.,
IV, Potomac (17 June–15 July '63)
and King's division, XXII, Washington
(15 July–Oct. '63). He resigned 20 Oct.
'63 because of ill-health (he suffered
from epilepsy). Reappointed to the
Vatican, he apprehended John H. Surratt who had fled to Italy after Lincoln's
assassination.

KING, William H. C.S.A. gen. Appt.-
Tex. On 15 Oct. '61 he was named
Maj. and Q.M. of H. E. McCulloch's
division, which by Jan. '62 was called
John G. Walker's "Greyhounds." There
is mention of his fighting in Sept. '63
in La. as Col. 18th Tex., and by 11
May '64 he was promoted B.G. C.S.A.
and given a brigade under Walker. He
was temporarily in command of the
division 17 July–2 Sept. '64 when Forney took over, and in Feb. '65 he was
given command of the 4th Brig. of the
division. Wood and Henderson (*Texas
in the Confederacy*) list him as a general officer, although the former's date
is a month previous to the latter's.
Wright does not list him, but Heitman
does.

KING, William Sterling. Union officer. 1818–82. Mass. Capt. 35th Mass.
10 Aug. '62; Maj. 19 Jan. '63; Lt. Col.
1 May '63; mustered out 14 Nov. '64;
Col. 4th Mass. Arty. 22 Nov. '64; Bvt.
B.G. USV (war service). Commanded
3d Brig., Defenses South of Potomac,
XXII. W.I.A. South Mountain, Antietam, in 7 places. Served as Chief of
Staff (1862–63) 2d Div., IX Corps;

Provost Marshal of Ky.; military commander Lexington (Ky.) Dist.

KINGSBURY, Charles P. Union officer. c. 1818–79. N.Y. Appt.-N.C. USMA 1840 (2/42); Ord. He served on armory and arsenal duty until the Mexican War, when he was Wool's Chief of Ord. and Taylor's Add. A.D.C. (1 brevet.) During the Civil War he was in command of the Harpers Ferry Armory when it was destroyed just before the Confederates captured it. He was next Chief of Ord. of the Dept. of the Ohio 7 June–12 Aug. '61 and of the Army of the Potomac 12 Aug. '61–15 July '62, serving from Yorktown through the Seven Days' Battles. Relieved at Harrison's Landing for sickness, he was on special duty with the War Dept. and then served on a number of boards and commissions for the remainder of the war. He was named Col. Add. A.D.C. 28 Sept. '61 and Maj. Ord. 3 Mar. '63 before being breveted B.G. USA for war service. He retired in 1870 as Lt. Col.

KINGSBURY, Henry Denison. Union officer. Ohio. 1st Lt. Regt. Q.M. 14th Ohio 24 Apr. '61; mustered out 13 Aug. '61; Capt. 14th Ohio 14 Aug. '61; Maj. 15 Sept. '62; Lt. Col. 12 Mar. '63; mustered out 8 Nov. '64; Col. 189th Ohio 7 Mar. '65; Bvt. B.G. USV 10 Mar. '65.

KINGSMAN, J. Burnham. Misspelling by Phisterer for Josiah Burnham KINSMAN.

KING'S SCHOOL HOUSE, Va., 25 June '62. See OAK GROVE.

KINNEY, Thomas Jefferson. Union officer. N.Y. Col. 119th Ill. 7 Oct. '62; Bvt. B.G. USV 26 Mar. '65 (Mobile). Commanded 4, Dist. Memphis 5, XVI.

KINNEY'S FARM, Va., 27 May '62. See HANOVER C.H., same date.

KINSEY, William Baker. Union officer. Pa. Pvt., Cpl., Sgt., and 1st Sgt.

Co. A, 23d N.Y. 16 May '61–16 Sept. '62; 1st Lt. Adj. 161st N.Y. 16 Sept. '62; Lt. Col. 14 July '63; Bvt. B.G. USV (Sabine Cross Roads, La.). Commanded 3, 1, XIII (Gulf).

KINSMAN, Josiah Burnham. Union officer. Me. Appt.-Mass. Commissioned Lt. Col. Add. A.D.C. 24 June '62, he was mustered out in 1866 and breveted for service as superintendent of Negro affairs in 1864 in the Dept. of Va. and for war service (B.G. USV and Maj. Gen. USV).

KINSTON, N.C. See CAROLINAS CAMPAIGN.

KIRBY, Byron. Union officer. Ohio. R.A. Pvt. and Sgt. Co. B 6th US Cav. 6 Sept.–29 Nov. '61; 2d Lt. 6th US Inf. 24 Oct. '61; 1st Lt. 23 Feb. '64; Maj. 3d Md. Cav. 26 Sept. '63; Lt. Col. 23 Jan. '64; Bvt. B.G. USV 6 Sept. '65. Brevets for Murfreesboro, war service (2). Died 1881.

KIRBY, Dennis Thomas. Union officer. N.Y. Capt. 8th Mo. 25 June '61; Maj. 15 July '62; mustered out 7 July '64; Lt. Col. 27th Mo. 6 Nov. '64; Bvt. B.G. USV. Brevets for war service, Chickasaw Bayou (Miss.), Vicksburg assault, Chickamauga, Missionary Ridge, Rivers Bridge (S.C.). Transferred to R.A. and cashiered in 1868 as Capt. Medal of Honor 31 Jan. '94 for Vicksburg assault 22 May '63.

KIRBY, Edmund. Union gen. 1840–63. N.Y. Appt.-At Large. USMA May '61 (10/45); Arty. Commissioned 2d Lt. 1st US Arty. 6 May '61 upon graduation, he was promoted to 1st Lt. on 14 May and fought at 1st Bull Run, Balls Bluff, and in the Peninsula where he commanded a battery at Yorktown, Fair Oaks, Savage's Station, Glendale, and Malvern Hill. He also commanded a battery at Fredericksburg and Chancellorsville where he was severely wounded helping rescue guns for a volunteer battery. Infection set in, and although his leg was amputated, he was told, shortly before a visit by Lincoln to his Washington hospital, that the surgeons would be unable to save him. Kirby could face his death serenely, but was worried about his widowed mother and sisters, who would lose their sole source of support. Hearing of this, Lincoln commissioned him B.G. USV at his bedside (23 May '63), thus assuring his family a good-sized pension. Kirby died five days later.

KIRBY, Isaac Minor. Union officer. 1834–? Ohio. Capt. 15th Ohio 12 Sept. '61; resigned 3 May '62; Capt. 101st Ohio 30 Aug. '62; Maj. 1 Dec. '62; Col. 14 Feb. '63; Bvt. B.G. USV 12 Jan. '65. Commanded 1, 1, IV (Cumberland).

KIRBY SMITH, Edmund. See Edmund Kirby SMITH.

"KIRBY-SMITHDOM." Name given to the TRANS-MISS. DEPT. shortly after E. Kirby Smith succeeded Holmes as its commander.

KIRBY SMITH'S CORPS. See under CORPS, Confed.

KIRK, Edward Needles. Union gen. 1828–63. Ohio. He was commissioned Col. 34th Ill. 7 Sept. '61 and commanded the 5th Brig., 2d Div., Army Ohio (8 Jan.–7 Apr. and 20 June–29 Sept. '62) and 5th Brig., 2d Div., I Corps, Army Ohio (Sept.–Nov. '62). He was promoted B.G. USV 29 Nov. '62 and led the 2, 2, XIV Right Wing, Cumberland (5 Nov.–31 Dec. '62) at Stones River where he was severely wounded. He died of this 29 July '63.

KIRKHAM, Ralph Wilson. Union officer. c. 1821–93. Mass. USMA 1842 (37/56); Inf.-Q.M. He served on the frontier and in the Mexican War (1 wound, 2 brevets) before being named Chief Q.M. of the Dept. of the Pacific, where he served throughout the war. Promoted Maj. Q.M. 26 Feb. '63 (Capt.

since 1854), he was breveted B.G. USA and resigned as Lt. Col. in 1870.

KIRKLAND, William W. C.S.A. gen. Appt.-N.C. Commissioned Col. 11th N.C., he fought at 1st Bull Run and served under Ewell in the Valley, leading the 21st N.C. He was wounded at Winchester and returned to his regiment for Gettysburg. Meanwhile, he had been Cleburne's Chief of Staff at Murfreesboro. Appointed B.G. C.S.A. 29 Aug '63, he commanded a brigade in the Bristoe campaign, where he was again wounded and was out of active duty until the Wilderness, where he commanded his brigade under Heth. He fought with Longstreet around Richmond, and going to the Carolinas, fought at Fort Fisher, Wise's Fork and Bentonville. He surrendered at Greensboro, N.C.

KIRKWOOD, Samuel Jordan. Gov. of Iowa. 1813–94. Md. A lawyer and public official in Ohio, he moved to Iowa in 1855, where he was elected to the legislature. He was chosen Gov. in 1860 and 1862, being particularly active in the raising of troops for the Union. Later in the Senate, he was returned as Gov. in 1876 and was Garfield's Sec. of the Int.

KISE, Reuben C. Union officer. Ind. Capt. 10th Ind. 23 Apr. '61; mustered out 6 Aug. '61; 1st Lt. Adj. 10th Ind. 18 Sept. '61; Capt. Asst. Adj. Gen. Vols. 21 June '62; resigned 16 Mar. '64; Maj. 120th Ind. 16 Mar. '64; Lt. Col. 15 Sept. '64; Col. 9 Sept. '65; Bvt. B.G. USV (war service). Died 1872.

KITCHELL, Edward. Union officer. Ill. Lt. Col. 98th Ill. 3 Sept. '62; Bvt. B.G. USV (war service). Died 1869.

KITCHING, John Howard. Union officer. 1840–65. N.Y. Capt. 2d N.Y. Arty. 18 Sept. '61; mustered out 6 July '62; Lt. Col. 6th N.Y. Arty. 6 Sept. '62; Col. 26 Apr. '63; Bvt. B.G. USV 1 Aug. '64 (Richmond); W.I.A. Cedar

Creek (Va.) 19 Oct. '64 and died 10 Jan. '65 from these wounds. Commanded 1, Defenses North of Potomac, XXII.

KNEFFNER, William C. Misspelling by Phisterer for William C. KUEFFNER.

KNEFLER, Frederick. Union officer. Hungary. 1st Lt. 11th Ind. 24 Apr. '61; Capt. 5 June '61; mustered out 10 Aug. '61; Capt. 11th Ind. 31 Aug. '61; Capt. Asst. Adj. Gen. USV 21 Oct. '61; Maj. Asst. Adj. Gen. USV 16 May '62; resigned 8 Sept. '62; Col. 79th Ind. 28 Sept. '62; Bvt. B.G. USV (war service). Commanded 1, 3, XXI; 3, 3, IV (Cumberland). Chosen Chief of Pension Bureau by Pres. Hayes. Died 1901.

KNIGHTS OF THE GOLDEN CIRCLE. A secret order in the North of Southern sympathizers. Originally starting in the South, its purpose was the extension of slavery in the 1850's, and as the movement spread into other parts of the country it became the organization of the PEACE DEMOCRATS, who disapproved of the war. In the latter part of 1863 the name was changed to Order of American Knights, and in 1864 to Sons of Liberty. Vallandigham was supreme commander of this last-named order, having been active in the original organization as well.

KNIPE, Joseph Farmer. Union gen. 1823–1901. Pa. He was an enlisted man in the Mexican War, later becoming a prominent merchant. Commissioned Col. 46th Pa. 31 Oct. '61, he commanded 1, 1, II, Army of Va. (4–12 Sept. '62) and 1, 1, XII, Potomac at Chancellorsville (17 Sept. '62–18 May '63 as well as 26 July–31 Aug. and 13–25 Sept. '63). He was promoted B.G. USV 29 Nov. '62 and led the 1st Div., XII, Potomac, 31 Aug.–13 Sept. '63, and in the Army of the Cumberland he commanded 1, 1, XX, in the Atlanta campaign at Resaca (14 Apr.–3 July

'64), where he was wounded (17–28 July '64, 28 Aug.–21 Sept. '64), and 1st Div., XX, at the siege of Atlanta (28 July–27 Aug. '64). He also commanded 1st Div., XII, Cumberland (22 Dec. '63–30 Jan. '64) and 2, 1, Cav., West Miss. (14–17 Apr. '65). His other commands were the 7th Div., Cav. Corps, Mil. Div. Miss.; 1st Div., Cav. Corps, West Miss.; and 1, 2, Cav., West Miss. He was wounded twice at Winchester and at Cedar Mountain also. After being mustered out 24 Aug. '65, he was a superintendent at the federal penitentiary at Fort Leavenworth (Kans.).

KNOWLES, Oliver Blachly. Union officer. Pa. Pvt., Cpl. and 1st Sgt. Co. C 1st N.Y. Cav. 19 July '61; 2d Lt. 21 July '62; 1st Lt. 16 Aug. '63; Maj. 21st Pa. Cav. 6 Apr. '64; Col. 18 Jan. '65; Bvt. B.G. USV (war service). Commanded 1, 2, Cav. Corps (Potomac). Died 1866.

KNOXVILLE CAMPAIGN, 1863 Although the "Knoxville campaign" is generally considered to start with Longstreet's advance from Chattanooga in early Nov. '63, and to consist primarily of his Knoxville siege, 17 Nov.–5 Dec. '63, certain preliminary operations will be outlined here.

In Mar. '63 Burnside had been ordered to enter Ky. with two divisions of IX Corps, to take command of the Dept. of the Ohio, and to move as soon as practicable against Knoxville. Meanwhile, the government was urging Rosecrans to attack Bragg in Tenn. (following Stones River). About the end of May Burnside had concentrated the IX and XXIII Corps on the upper Cumberland and was ready to advance. However, he was then required to send the IX Corps (under Parke) to reinforce Grant (Vicksburg campaign). To meet Burnside's threat, Buckner was ordered from Mobile to command the Confederate Dept. of East Tenn. and to organize its defense. While awaiting the return of his IX Corps Burnside sent Wm. P. Sanders with a mixed brigade of cavalry and mounted infantry (1,500 total) on a raid toward Knoxville; starting 14 June and returning the 23d, Sanders disrupted Confederate communications and destroyed railroad bridges, including a 1,600-foot one over the Holston River. Rosecrans, meanwhile, had undertaken his Tullahoma campaign, 24–30 June, forcing Bragg back toward Chattanooga.

About 15 Aug. Burnside finally began his advance. Rosecrans' advance had caused Bragg to pull Buckner in closer to Chattanooga; leaving one brigade in Cumberland Gap and another on the railroad east of Knoxville, Buckner retired with Preston's infantry division and the cavalry brigades of Pegram and Scott to Loudon. When Rosecrans began crossing the Tennessee at the start of the Chickamauga campaign, Bragg ordered Buckner to Chattanooga.

Burnside with part of the XXIII Corps occupied Knoxville on 2 Sept. and sent a column to invest Cumberland Gap from the south. The advance brigade of the IX Corps in Ky. was ordered to invest it from the north. On 9 Sept. the Confederate brigade of J. W. Frazer (2,000 men) surrendered. While Bragg was engaged in the Chickamauga campaign the XXIII Corps was moved east to meet Samuel Jones, who had assembled a Confederate infantry division and a cavalry brigade at Abingdon, Va. A Union cavalry brigade was pushed south as far as the Hiwassee River. After the battle of Chickamauga, Burnside moved the main body of the XXIII Corps to Loudon and called up the IX Corps from Ky. The latter reached Knoxville via Cumberland about the end of the month.

In October the Confederate force in western Va. invaded Tenn. and near Greenville, at Blue Springs, Tenn., 10 Oct. '63, was defeated by the IX Corps and forced to withdraw. The IX Corps then returned to Knoxville and toward the end of the month took up a position on the railroad near Loudon at the junction of the Tennessee and Little Tennessee rivers. The XXIII Corps guarded the river between Loudon and Kinston, and the cavalry division of this corps guarded the Little Tennessee between the railroad and the mountains. A division of new troops, under O. B. Willcox, was attached to IX Corps and stationed at Jonesboro, Tenn., to guard against further Confederate advances from western Va. Two small cavalry brigades covered the Rogersville road.

In November Longstreet was sent from the vicinity of Chattanooga to oppose the threat of Burnside in Ky. This dangerous and faulty weakening of Bragg's Army of Tenn. was conceived by Jeff Davis and prompted largely by the fact that Bragg and Longstreet could not get along. Longstreet was detached on 4 Nov. with the divisions of McLaws and Micah Jenkins (Hood's), Alexander's and Leyden's artillery battalions (23 and 12 guns). He reached Loudon by rail on the 12th. Wheeler, who had moved from the Tennessee River in Ala. to Cleveland, Tenn., was directed to cooperate with Longstreet in an attack on Burnside at Knoxville. This gave Longstreet 10,000 infantry and 5,000 cavalry.

Leaving two brigades along the railroad near Athens, on the 13th Wheeler crossed the Little Tennessee with four brigades and drove Federal cavalry out of Marysville the next day. On the 15th he approached Knoxville from the south with the intention of capturing the heights on the south bank of the Holston River overlooking the town. This plan was frustrated by Sanders's cavalry division and by the fortifications on the south bank. Wheeler then crossed to the north bank of the Tennessee and joined Longstreet's infantry.

On the 14th Longstreet threw a bridge over the Tennessee west of Loudon and crossed the divisions of McLaws and Jenkins with two battalions of artillery (10,000 total). At CAMPBELL'S STATION, 16 Nov., the Confederates failed to cut off Burnside's withdrawal to Knoxville. On the 18th Sanders was killed while commanding a delaying action.

Lacking the means of undertaking a regular siege of the town, whose defenses had been planned and supervised by Orlando Poe (see his article in B.&L., III, 731ff), Longstreet planned an assault. He finally selected a salient on the northwest corner of the works, built on a hill, and named Fort Sanders in honor of the Federal cavalryman who had fallen on the 18th. Although his infantry was in position by the 20th, he delayed his attack for over a week to await the arrival of Bushrod Johnson with two brigades (his own and Gracie's, a total of 3,500 men) and to have his plans checked by Bragg's chief engineer, Danville Leadbetter, who arrived with Johnson from Chattanooga. Leadbetter, wrote Alexander, "being the oldest military engineer in the Confederate service, was supposed to be the most efficient" (op. cit., 485). Two cavalry brigades, led by Wm. E. ("Grumble") Jones, joined Longstreet from southwest Va. on 27–28 Nov.

Longstreet's mishandled assault on FORT SANDERS, 29 Nov., was repulsed.

Bragg, meanwhile, had been defeated at Missionary Ridge on the 25th. Before Longstreet could comply with Bragg's order to withdraw toward Chattanooga, Grant sent Sherman with his XV Corps and Gordon Granger's IV Corps to succor Burnside. The latter considered himself to be in desperate straits, and the Washington authorities were worried about his safety. When Longstreet learned of Sherman's approach, he started (night of 3 Dec.) to withdraw his trains toward Va. On 4 Dec., when Sherman was a day's march away, Longstreet moved his infantry toward Rogersville. Being reinforced then by Robert Ransom's infantry division from Va., Longstreet returned to Morristown and finally took up winter quarters at Greenville, Tenn.

Sherman reached Maryville on the 5th and sent his cavalry ahead on a forced march to Knoxville. Then, since Longstreet had lifted his siege, and since Burnside wanted only two divisions, Sherman sent Granger (with the divisions of Sheridan and Wood) to Knoxville, and returned to Chattanooga with the remainder of his force.

Burnside's failure to pursue Longstreet and drive him out of Tenn. forced Grant to keep a large force in this territory until the following April. On 9 Dec. Burnside was relieved at his own request and succeeded by J. G. Foster. Longstreet, long plagued by dissension among his subordinate commanders (see, for example, WAUHATCHIE), relieved and eventually brought charges against McLaws, Law, and Robertson. The Richmond authorities, however, elected to transfer these officers to other commands (see Lee's Lts., III, 299–306).

KOZLAY, Eugene A. Union officer. Germany. Col. 54th N.Y. 16 Oct. '61; resigned 18 Mar. '63; Col. 54th N.Y. 19 Mar. '64; Bvt. B.G. USV (war service). After the war he worked in the N.Y. customs office and was later engineer with the city's waterworks. Died 1883.

KREZ, Conrad. Union officer. Rhenish Bavaria. 1828–97. Col. 27th Wis. 7 Mar. '63; Bvt. B.G. USV 26 Mar. '65 (Mobile). Commanded 3, 3, Res.

Corps and 3, 3, XIII (Gulf). He was a member of Von Tann's 1848 expedition to aid Schleswig-Holstein in the revolt against the Danes and participated in the 1849 uprising in Baden and the Rhenish Palatinate. As a result of the latter, he left Germany and settled for a while in France before emigrating to America. Here he studied and practiced law, as well as continuing to write. He had his first volume of verse published in Germany and his second in France, as well as several in this country. Lonn calls him the most gifted German poet in America.

KRYZANOWSKI, Waldimir ("Kriz"). Union officer. Poland. Col. 58th N.Y. 22 Oct. '61; B.G. Vols. 29 Nov. '62; appointment expd. 4 Mar. '63, and he reverted to Col. 58th N.Y.; Bvt. B.G. USV 2 Mar. '65. Commanded 2, 3, I (Va.); 2, 3, XI (Potomac and Cumberland); 3, Defenses Nashville & Chattanooga R.R. Participated in Polish revolution of 1846 and later civil engineer in US. Lonn says: "Schurz declared that the reason he [Kryzanowski] did not attain the general's rank was that when his promotion was before the Senate for confirmation, none of the Senators could pronounce his name." After the war he held several offices in the Treasury Dept., was customs inspector in Panama, and was in the N.Y.C. customs office.

KUEFFNER, William C. Union officer. Germany. Migrating from Mecklenburg to Tex., he moved north at the beginning of the war, disagreeing with secession. He was named Sgt. 9th Ill. 25 Apr. '61 and commissioned 1st Lt. 25 May '61. Mustered out 25 July, he was commissioned Capt. 9th Ill. 28 July '61 and discharged 23 Nov. '63. He was wounded four times, severely at Shiloh and Corinth. Entering the Veteran Reserve Corps as Capt. 23 Oct. '63, he recovered his health and resigned 14 Feb. '65 to become Col. 149th Ill. the next day. Breveted for war service (B.G. USV), he was mustered out in 1866 with one of the war's longest combat records—participation in 110 engagements. He died 1893. Phisterer spells his name, Kneffner, and Lonn gives it as Küffner.

KÜFFNER, William C. See William C. KUEFFNER.

L

LABORATORY. See ARSENAL.

LAFLIN, Byron. Union officer. Mass. Maj. 34th N.Y. 15 June '61; Lt. Col. 20 Mar. '62; Col. 22 Jan. '63; Bvt. B.G. USV (war service); mustered out 30 June '63. Commanded 1, 2, II (Potomac). Died 1901.

LAGOON. See LAGOW, Clark B.

LAGOW, Clark B. Union officer. Ill. 1st Lt. 21st Ill. 28 June '61; Col. Add. A.D.C. 3 May '62; Bvt. B.G. USV (war service); resigned 12 Dec. '63. Died 1867. Listed by Phisterer as Lagoon, Clark B.

LA GRANGE, Oscar Hugh. Union officer. N.Y. Capt. 4th Wis. 2 July '61; Maj. 1st Wis. Cav. 10 Dec. '61; Lt. Col. 12 June '62; Col. 5 Feb. '63; Bvt. B.G. USV (war service). Commanded 2, 1, Cav. Corps (Cumberland); 2, 1, Cav. Corps, Mil. Div. Miss.

LAMAR, Lucius Quintus Cincinnatus. Confed. statesman. 1825–93. A lawyer and legislator, he served with the

Confederate Army although opposed to secession. As Confederate commissioner in Europe (1862–63), he was a supporter of Davis and his policies. After the war he sat in both houses of Congress, was Cleveland's Sec. of the Int. and was Assoc. Justice of the US Supreme Court (1888–93). Nephew of Mirabeau B. Lamar, president of the Tex. Rep.

LA MOTTE, Charles Eugene. Union officer. Del. Capt. 1st Del. 2 May '61; mustered out 13 Aug. '61; Vol. A.D.C. 12 Sept. '61–10 Mar. '62; 1st Lt. Adj. 4th Del. 25 June '62; Maj. 16 Aug. '62; Lt. Col. 1 Oct. '63; mustered out 3 June '65; Col. 6th US Vet. Vol. Inf. 22 Aug. '65; Bvt. B.G. USV. Brevets for Petersburg, war service. Died 1887.

LANDER, Frederick West. Union gen. 1821–62. Mass. A railroad surveyor for the government, he was on Isaac Steven's staff for the Northern Pacific explorations and made several transcontinental expeditions (1854–60) for the proposed Puget Sound-Mississippi River railroad. In 1861 he was commissioned by the government to make a secret trip to Sam Houston, then Gov. of Tex., to order the US troops stationed there to support Houston if the Gov. thought this advisable. He was named B.G. USV 17 May '61 and A.D.C. to McClellan at Philippi and Rich Mountain. Commanding 2d Brig., Stone's division, he held Edward's Ferry after the Union defeat at Balls Bluff, being severely wounded in the leg. Then, leading Lander's division, W. Va., he fought at Hancock (Md.) 5 Jan. '62, before his wound had healed, and led a charge at Blooming Gap. While preparing to move his division to the Valley to aid Banks, he died suddenly from pneumonia 2 Mar. '62. He had married Jean Margaret Davenport, a noted actress of the era. He wrote a number of patriotic poems.

LANDER, Jean Margaret Davenport. Actress and Union nurse. 1829–1903. Married to Frederick W. LANDER in 1860, she took charge of the Federal hospitals at Port Royal, S.C., upon his death in 1862, and worked there over a year. After the war she resumed her successful stage career.

LAND MINES AND BOOBY TRAPS were first used by American troops in the Civil War. Confederate Gen. G. J. RAINS is credited with the innovation, which made its first appearance at Yorktown in May '62. Ordinary 8- or 10-inch Columbiad shells were buried a few inches below ground level and so arranged with fulminate, or with the ordinary artillery friction primer, that they exploded when stepped on or moved. McClellan mentions that the entry into Yorktown "was much delayed by the caution made necessary by the presence of these torpedoes. I at once ordered that they should be discovered and removed by the Confederate prisoners" (*Own Story,* 326). Both sides considered the innovation unsporting, and Longstreet ordered Rains' to cease his mining activities. These land mines ("torpedoes"), however, were subsequently used by both sides.

LANDRAM, William Jennings. Union officer. Ky. Col. 19th Ky. 2 Jan. '62; Bvt. B.G. USV (war service); mustered out 26 Jan. '65. Commanded 2d Brig., 1st Div. Army of Ky. (Ohio); in the Dept. of the Tenn.; 2d Brig., 10th Div., Left Wing, XIII; 2d Brig., 1st Div., Yazoo expedition; 2, 10, XIII; and in the Dept. of the Gulf: 2, 4, XIII; 1, 4, XIII; 4th Div., XIII; 2d Brig., Cav. Div. Died 1895.

LANE, Harriet. Washington hostess. 1833–? Pa. An orphan, she was raised by her uncle, James Buchanan, and as a young lady was his hostess in London and at the White House. In 1866 she married Henry Elliott Johnston of Maryland.

LANE, James Henry. C.S.A. gen. 1833–1907. Va. Appt.-N.C. After graduating from V.M.I. and the U. of Va., he taught mathematics and tactics at V.M.I. and was commissioned Maj. 1st N.C. in the spring of 1861. His scouting on 10 June '61 brought on the battle of Big Bethel, and his unit was thereafter called "Bethel Regiment." Elected Lt. Col. 1 Sept. '61, he succeeded D. H. Hill as Col. 28th N.C. some two weeks later. He was twice wounded on the Peninsula, led his regiment at 2d Bull Run, and succeeded to the command of Branch's brigade at Antietam. Appointed B.G. C.S.A. 1 Nov. '62, he commanded his brigade at Fredericksburg, Chancellorsville and Gettysburg, the Wilderness, and Petersburg. He surrendered at Appomattox and returned to teaching at Virginia Polytechnic Institute, Missouri School of Mines, and Alabama Polytechnic Institute. During the war he was nicknamed "The Little General."

LANE, James Henry. Kans. political leader. 1814–66. Ind. Moving West, he was the leader of the Free State movement in Kans., was Maj. Gen. of militia during the "bleeding Kansas" era, and became known as the "Liberator of Kansas." As Sen. (1861–66), he supported Lincoln and the emancipation and arming of the slaves.

LANE, John Quincy. Union officer. Ohio. Col. 92d Ohio 2 Sept. '62; Bvt. B.G. USV (war service). Commanded 2, 2, IV (Cumberland).

LANE, Walter Payne. C.S.A. gen. 1817–92. Ireland. Appt.-Tex. Settling in Ohio, he met Stephen F. Austin and Archer in Ky., and they persuaded him to join Sam Houston in the fight for Tex. independence. He fought at San Jacinto and was a privateer in the Gulf. He was then a schoolteacher and farmer until he was nearly killed by marauding Indians. Getting a job as a clerk, he fought Indians as a side line and served with the Tex. Rangers during the Mexican War. D.A.B. said that although he was "ruthless and careless of [Mexican] property . . . [he was nonetheless] so brave and efficient as a scout that he made himself indispensable." Just before the Civil War he was mining gold in South America and the western US. Commissioned Lt. Col. 3d Tex. Cav., he fought at Wilson's Creek, Pea Ridge, Corinth, and in the Red River campaign in 1864 (wounded). On 17 Mar. '65 he was appointed B.G. C.S.A.

LANGDON, Elisha Bassett. Union officer. 1827–67. Ohio. Maj. 1st Ohio 6 Aug. '61; Lt. Col. 2 June '62; Bvt. B.G. USV (Shiloh, Chickamauga, Missionary Ridge); mustered out 24 Sept. '64. A lawyer and legislator before the war. I.G. of McCook's staff after Corinth in 1862. Had horses shot from under him at Perryville and Stones River. Died in 1867 from the effects of wounds at Missionary Ridge.

LANSING, Henry Seymour. Union officer. N.Y. Col. 17th N.Y. 24 May '61; Bvt. B.G. USV (war service); mustered out 2 June '63; Capt. 12th US Inf. 5 Aug. '61; resigned 17 July '63. Commanded 3. 1. V (Potomac). Died 1882.

LASELLE, William Polke. Union officer. Ind. 1st Sgt. Co. K 9th Ind. 24 Apr.–29 July '61; Capt. 9th Ind. 5 Sept. '61; Maj. 27 Sept. '62; Lt. Col. 1 May '63; Bvt. B.G. USV (war service). Died 1896.

LATHAM, George R. Union officer. Va. Capt. 5th W. Va. Cav. 25 May '61; Col. 24 May '62; transferred to 6th W. Va. Cav. 14 Dec. '64; Bvt. B.G. USV (war service).

LATIN FARMERS. Highly educated German refugees from the 1848 revolutions who, although conversant with Latin and Greek, became farmers in the US through necessity. Lonn described them as "a class of Germans who . . . did not disdain to plow their own fields as they meditated on the philosophy of Kant or recalled passages of Goethe, and who sought their recreation in choral societies. . . ." It was they who for many years provided the leadership of the German element in the US. Several became Civil War generals, for example, Carl SCHURZ and VON STEINWEHR.

LATTERMORE'S MILLS, Ga., 20 June. '64. See KENESAW MOUNTAIN.

LAUGHLIN, Rankin G. Union officer. Pa. Maj. 94th Ill. 20 Aug. '62; Lt. Col. 17 Apr. '63; Bvt. B.G. USV. Brevets for Mobile (2). Died 1878.

LAUMAN, Jacob Gartner. Union gen. 1813–67. Md. A merchant, he was named Col. 7th Iowa 11 July '61 and was wounded at Belmont (Mo.) 7 Nov. '61. Promoted B.G. USV 21 Mar. '62, he commanded 4, 2d Div. Mil. Dist. Cairo (1–17 Feb. '62) at Fort Donelson and 1, 2d Div., Army Tenn. (17 Feb.–5 Apr. '62); at Shiloh he led 3, 4th Div., Army Tenn. (5–6 Apr. '62); 1, 4th Div., Army Tenn. (6 Apr.–July '62); and 4th Div., Army Tenn. (6 Apr. '62). He also commanded 1st Brig., 4th Div. Dist. Memphis, Tenn. (July–Sept. '62); Reserve Brig., Dist. Memphis XIII (23 Nov.–9 Dec. '62); 4th Div. Right Wing, XIII (9–18 Dec. '62) and 4th Div., XVI, Tenn. (20 Jan.–16 July '63), being relieved by Sherman after the capture of Jackson (Miss.). He returned to Iowa, was breveted Maj. Gen. USV for war service and mustered out 24 Aug. '65.

LAUREL HILL, Va. See NEW MARKET HEIGHTS, 28–30 Sept. '64.

LAUREL HILL, W. Va., 10 July '61. See WEST VIRGINIA OPERATIONS IN 1861.

LAW, Evander McIvor. C.S.A. gen. 1836–1920. S.C. Appt.-Ala. After studying at the Citadel, he taught in several Southern military schools and was commissioned Capt. of a company taken largely from his students in Tuskegee, Ala. They were at Pensacola and he was first commissioned Capt. C.S.A. and then Lt. Col. 4th Ala. Serving with his regiment at 1st Bull Run, he was severely wounded. He was elected Col. 8 Oct. '61 and led his regiment as well as Whiting's brigade in the Peninsular campaign. At Malvern Hill, 2d Bull Run, and Antietam, he continued to command this unit and was appointed B.G. C.S.A. 3 Oct. '62. He led his brigade in the attack on the Round Tops at Gettysburg and took command of the division when Hood was wounded early in the action. At Chickamauga he succeeded Hood again. He led his brigade at the Wilderness, Spotsylvania, and North Anna and commanded two brigades at Cold Harbor, where he was severely wounded. Sent to the Carolinas, he commanded at Columbia as Sherman approached, and in Feb. '65 took over Butler's cavalry brigade. He was on J. E. Johnston's staff at Bentonville.

LAWLER, Michael K. Union gen. 1814–82. Ireland. After serving in the Mexican War he was commissioned Col. 18th Ill. 20 June '61 and B.G. USV 29 Nov. '62, fighting at Fort Donelson. In the Army of the Tenn. he commanded post of Jackson; 1st Brig., Dist. Jackson Left Wing, XVI (18 Dec. '62–18 Mar. '63); 2, 3, XVI (18 Mar.–22 Apr. '63) and 2, 14, XIII (2 May–28 July '63). In the XIII Corps, Gulf, he led 4th Div. (17 Aug.–30 Sept. '63); 3, 1st Div. (23 Sept.–19 Oct., 26 Oct.–23 Dec. '63, 28 Feb.–10 Mar. '64); 1st Div. (19–26 Oct. '63 and 23 May–11 June '64) and 2, 1st Div. (10 Mar.–27 Apr. and 2–23 May '64). He was breveted Maj. Gen. USV for war service and mustered out in 1866.

LAWRENCE, Albert Gallatin. Union officer. N.Y. 1834–87. 1st Lt. 54th N.Y. 5 Dec. '62; resigned 20 Mar. '63; Capt. 2d US Col. Cav. 12 Feb. '64; Bvt. B.G. USV 25 Mar. '65. Brevets for Fort Fisher (N.C.), war service. Educated in Switzerland and at Harvard, he was US Attaché at Vienna before the war. W.I.A. Fort Fisher (N.C.), losing right arm. He was later US Minister to Costa Rica.

LAWRENCE, William Henry. Union officer. Mass. 1st Lt. Adj. 1st Mass. 25 May '61; Maj. Add. A.D.C. Vols. 10 Nov. '62; Bvt. B.G. USV. Brevets for Antietam, Lookout Mountain, Peach Tree Creek. Died 1874.

LAWRENCE, William Hudson. Union officer. 1834–74. N.J. Pvt. and Wagoner Co. F 7th N.Y. State Militia 29 Apr. '61; mustered out 3 June '61; 1st Lt. 14th US Inf. 14 May '61; Capt. 25 Oct. '61; Col. 34th N.J. 9 Nov. '63; Bvt. B.G. USV (war service). Served as A.D.C. to Hooker and for a time after the war was a member of Ben Butler's staff. W.I.A. at 2d Bull Run, he commanded a flag-of-truce party and remained on the battlefield six days to care for the wounded. He was disabled by a sunstroke on the march to Gettysburg. Commanded Columbus (Ky.) during period of Confederate raids in early 1864. The main action on 11 Apr. '64 was mentioned by Grant in final report. Later active in the commissions and brokerage business and as agent for payment of US pensions in N.Y.C.

LAWRENCE PRIMING SYSTEM. A disk primer magazine invented by R. S. Lawrence and first patented in 1857. It was used extensively on SHARPS rifles and carbines after the MAYNARD TAPE system was abandoned in 1859. The primers were contained in a screw closed magazine, forced upward by a spring, and fed on the cone by a finger. The latter was operated by the cocking of the hammer (Gluckman, 226).

LAWTON, Alexander Robert. C.S.A. gen. 1818–96. S.C. USMA 1839 (13/31); Arty. Resigning in 1840, he graduated from Harvard Law School two years later and practiced in Savannah. He was active in the Ga. militia, served as railroad president, and sat in the legislature as a leading advocate of secession. Before his state had left the Union he seized Fort Pulaski under Gov. Brown's orders, as Col. 1st Ga. He was appointed B.G. 13 Apr. '61 and given command of the Georgia coast before going to the Valley under Jackson in June '62. Fighting in the Seven Days' Battles, he succeeded the wounded Ewell at 2d Bull Run and commanded his division until wounded at Antietam and was succeeded in turn by Jubal Early. Disabled until May '63, he was appointed Q.M. Gen. 17 Feb. '64 over his violent protests. This difficult job he handled well, and after the war he was active in Democratic politics and his law practice. He was president of the American Bar Association 1882 and served as Cleveland's Minister to Austria 1887–89. He married a sister of E. P. ALEXANDER.

LAY'S FERRY, Ga. See RESACA, Ga. 13–16 May '64.

LEADBETTER, Danville. C.S.A. gen. 1811–66. Me. USMA 1836 (3/49); Arty.-Engr. He was engaged in river and harbor improvements, lighthouse and defense construction, and served as the Assistant to the Chief Engr. before resigning in 1857. Appointed Chief of Engrs. for Ala., he continued to improve Mobile Bay, the same job he had held while in the US Army, and was also active in the militia. Commissioned Lt. Col. of Ala. state troops, he was commander of Fort Morgan and appointed B.G. C.S.A. 6 Mar. '62 to rank from 27 Feb. Sent to East Tenn. for a short time, he was back working on the defenses of Mobile Bay and as Chief Engr. for the Army of Tenn. constructed the lines along Missionary Ridge. He advised Longstreet before the attack on FORT SANDERS (Knoxville). He escaped to Mexico and died in Canada.

LEAKE, Joseph Bloomfield. Union officer. N.J. Capt. 20th Iowa 25 Aug. '62; Lt. Col. 26 Aug. '62; Bvt. B.G. USV (war service).

LEBANON, Ky., 5 July '63. Captured in MORGAN'S OHIO RAID.

LEDLIE, James Hewitt. Union gen. 1832–82. N.Y. A civil engineer, he was commissioned Maj. 3d N.Y. Arty. 22 May, Lt. Col. 28 Sept., and Col. 23 Dec. '61. He was promoted B.G. USV 24 Dec. '62 and later that year was Chief of Arty. for J. G. Foster in N.C. (4 Dec. '62–May '63). His commission expired 4 Mar. '63, but he was reappointed 27 Oct. '63 and then commanded 1, 1, IX, Potomac (12 May–9 June '64). He succeeded to division on the latter date, commanding it during the Petersburg mine assault. Of his actions there Catton says: "... General Ledlie, who commanded the Division, was snugly tucked away in a bombproof 400 yards behind the line, plying himself with rum borrowed from a brigade surgeon" (*Stillness,* 246) with Edward FERRERO. Grant described him as ". . . being otherwise inefficient, proved also to possess disqualification

less common among soldiers" (i.e. cowardice) in *Memoirs,* II, 313. Ledlie resigned 23 Jan. '65 and returned to engineering, taking the entire contract for the construction of bridges, trestles, and snow sheds for the Union Pacific R.R. and also building the breakwater for Chicago's harbor. He was later a railroad president and chief engineer.

LE DUC, William Gates. Union officer. 1823–1917. Ohio. Minn. Capt. Asst. Q.M. Vols. 14 Apr. '62; Lt. Col. Q.M. Assigned 7 Nov. '62–19 Nov. '63 and 12 July '64–3 July '65; Bvt. B.G. USV (war service). Attended the Lancaster (Ohio) Academy with W. T. Sherman, John Sherman, and Thomas Ewing. As Lt. Col. Q.M. he served under McClellan, Hooker, Sherman, and Thomas. A railroad promoter and developer, he worked on a number of inventions and aided in perfecting the Remington typewriter. He was US Commissioner of Agriculture (1877–81) under Hayes.

LEE, Albert Lindley. Union gen. 1834–? N.Y. An Associate Justice of the Kans. Supreme Court, he was commissioned Maj. 7th Kans. Cav. 29 Oct. '61 and Col. 17 May '62. He commanded 2, Cav. Div., Army Miss. (4 Sept.–1 Nov. '62) at Corinth and was promoted B.G. USV 29 Nov. '62. He then led 2, Cav., XVI (18 Dec. '62–Mar. '63); 9th Div., XIII, Tenn. (17–19 May '63) at Champion's Hill and Big Black River; and 1, 9, XIII, Tenn. (19 May '63) at the Vicksburg assault, where he was wounded in the face and head. He commanded 12th Div., XIII (26–28 July '63); 3d Div., XIII (28 July–7 Aug. '63); 3d Div., XIII, Gulf (7 Aug.–13 Sept. '63); and 1, 3, XIX, Gulf (27 June–16 Aug. '64). On the Red River expedition he led the cavalry (14 Sept. '63–18 Apr. '64). He resigned 4 May '65, spending a number of years in Europe and in business in N.Y.C.

LEE, Edward M Union officer. N.J. 1st Lt. 5th Mich. Cav. 14 Aug. '62; Capt. 1 Jan. '63; Lt. Col. 13 Apr. '65; Bvt. B.G. USV (war service). Captured at Buckland's Mills (Va.) 19 Oct. '63.

LEE, Edwin G. C.S.A. gen. 1835–70. Va. After graduating from William and Mary he was a lawyer and commissioned 2d Lt. of the 2d Va. when his state seceded. He was elected 1st Lt. and then became Stonewall Jackson's A.D.C. at 1st Bull Run. During the Valley campaign he was in the 33d Va. as Maj. and Lt. Col., fighting with this unit on the Peninsula. As Col. he led the regiment at 2d Bull Run and Antietam. Early in 1863 he retired because of his health but returned to active duty in June '64 to recruit defenses for the Valley. He was appointed B.G. C.S.A. 23 Sept. '64 to rank from the 20th, and sent to Canada on a secret mission. The Senate rejected his nomination or 24 Feb. '65. C.M.H. gives his first name as Edmund.

LEE, Fitzhugh ("Fitz"). C.S.A. gen. 1835–1905. Va. USMA 1856 (45/49); Cav. The nephew of R. E. Lee and also of James M. Mason, he narrowly avoided dismissal for his behavior as a cadet at West Point while his uncle was Superintendent. Serving on the frontier and in Indian fighting (severely wounded), he was a tactical officer at the Military Academy when he resigned 21 May '61 as 1st Lt. Commissioned in the same rank in the C.S. Army, he served on Ewell's and J. E. Johnston's staffs during the Peninsular campaign, after having been promoted Lt. Col. 1st Va. Cav. in Aug. '61. A Col. the following Mar., he went with Stuart on the ride around McClellan and was appointed B.G. C.S.A. 24 July '62. He commanded his cavalry brigade at South Mountain and Antietam and on the Dumfries and Occoquan raids in Dec. '62. Fighting at

Kelly's Ford in Jan. '63, he guarded Jackson's maneuver at Chancellorsville and also fought at Gettysburg. Promoted Maj. Gen. 3 Aug. '63, he led his command at Spotsylvania and took his cavalry division to support Early in the Valley in Aug. '64. Seriously wounded at Winchester 19 Sept. '64, after having three horses shot from under him, he was out of action until Jan. '65 when he returned to command the cavalry on the north side of the James. Although he succeeded Hampton as the senior cavalry commander in the A.N.V., he did not act as chief of the decimated cavalry corps until practically the end of the Petersburg siege. He was absent during the battle of FIVE FORKS, but in command at Appomattox on 9 Apr. Riding through the Federal lines with part of his troops he surrendered two days later at Farmville, Va. After the war, he became a farmer. Elected Democratic governor of Virginia 1885–89, he was Consul Gen. to Havana in 1896–98 and displayed outstanding firmness and tact during the difficult times before the Spanish-American War. Entering the army as Maj. Gen. USV in 1898, he commanded the VII Corps in Cuba and retired in 1901 as B.G. USA after having commanded the Dept. of Mo. for two years. Among other historical works he wrote *General Lee* (1894). Freeman refers to Fitz Lee as a "laughing cavalier" but a serious and competent fighter. The heavy beard protected the youth of a man who was a Maj. Gen. before he was 28.

LEE, George Washington Custis. "Custis," R. E. Lee's eldest son. C.S.A. gen. 1832–1913. Va. USMA 1854 (1/46); Engrs. He was engaged in river and harbor improvements and served in the office of the Chief of Engrs. in Washington until he resigned 2 May '61 to join the Confederacy. Commissioned Capt. of C.S.A. Engrs. 1 July '61, he superintended the fortifications of Richmond and on 31 Aug. '61 was named Col. of Cav. and A.D.C. to Jefferson Davis. His war service was almost entirely in this post and he was appointed B.G. C.S.A. 25 June '64 and Maj. Gen. 21 Oct. '64. He trained the local defense brigade in the Dept. of RICHMOND, and commanded it during the KILPATRICK-DAHLGREN RAID. Under Ewell, he retreated from Richmond toward Appomattox, only to be captured at Sayler's Creek. After the war he was professor of engineering at V.M.I. from 1865 to 1871, when he succeeded his father as president of Washington & Lee, serving until 1897.

LEE, Horace Clark. Union officer. Mass. Col. 27th Mass. 20 Sept. '61; Bvt. B.G. USV (war service); mustered out 25 Sept. '64. Commanded 3, 1st Div., Dept. of N.C.; Lee's Brig., Dept. of N.C.; 2, 1, XVIII; 2, Getty's division, Norfolk, Va. (Va. and N.C.). While city clerk and treasurer, he was an acting B.G. in the Mass. State Militia. Captured at Drewry's Bluff (Va.). Served as Provost Marshal for Depts. of N.C. and Va., and N.C. Died 1884.

LEE, John C. Union officer. Ohio. Maj. 55th Ohio 24 Oct. '61; Col. 28 Nov. '61; resigned 8 May '63; Col. 164th Ohio 3 May '64; Bvt. B.G. USV (war service); mustered out 27 Aug. '64. Commanded 2, 1, XI; 1, Defenses South of Potomac, XXII. He practiced law and was Lt. Gov. of Ohio in 1867. Died 1891.

LEE, Mary W. SANITARY COMMISSION worker. England. When on 23 Apr. '61 Sherman's howitzer battery passed through Philadelphia on its way to Washington, there occurred in a working-class district one of those spontaneous outbreaks of good will during which the people suddenly came pouring out of the houses bearing food and water for the thirsty, tired men. Mrs. Lee, seeing this, then set up a stove and coffeepot in an old boathouse and called it the Union Refreshment Saloon. This grew to include bathing facilities, dormitories, a medical center, serving 4,000,000 during the war. During the Peninsular campaign she became a SANITARY COMMISSION nurse at White House and served almost constantly in field hospitals until Lee's surrender.

LEE, Robert Edward. 1807–1870. Va. USMA 1829 (2/46); Engrs. Great leader of the lost Confederate cause, in which capacity he earned rank with history's most distinguished generals, Lee revealed qualities of intellect and character that made him a legend in his own lifetime. Scion of a prominent Va. family, he graduated second in his class at West Point, went into the Corps of Engrs., and emerged from the Mexican War with one wound, three brevets for gallantry, and a brilliant reputation. He was Superintendent at West Point during the period 1852–55. Being in Washington when John Brown made his raid on Harpers Ferry, he was sent to put down that insurrection. On Scott's recommendation Lincoln offered Lee command of the Federal armies 18 Apr. '61. He declined, and resigned two days later to take command of Va. troops. His first campaign in the field led to failure at CHEAT MOUNTAIN, W. Va., in Sept. He then commanded forces along the South Atlantic coast before being recalled to Richmond. After serving as military advisor to Davis until 1 June '62, he succeeded the wounded J. E. Johnston in the command of the force that then became known as the ARMY OF NORTHERN VIRGINIA. For almost three years, with inferior numbers and material resources, he not only frustrated Federal attempts to capture Richmond but also undertook two invasions of the North.

One of the most aggressive and pugnacious generals in history, his military successes were due primarily to an ability to determine his enemy's strengths and dispositions, predict his movements, and to maintain the initiative. His famous cavalry leader, Jeb Stuart, kept him informed of the enemy's activities; his great corps commanders, Stonewall Jackson and Longstreet, were able to execute his audacious plans with speed and skill. After achieving his military masterpiece at Chancellorsville, Lee's army was too weakened by the death of Jackson and dwindling supplies of man power and matériel ever to recover its former combat effectiveness. Furthermore, the Federal armies were increasing in strength and proficiency and competent military leadership was finally being found. The high tide of the Confederacy was reached when Lee was unable to destroy the Army of the Potomac at Gettysburg and he was forced to retreat into Va. Coming from the simultaneous and equally decisive victory at Vicksburg, Grant assumed command of all Federal armies, formulated an over-all strategic plan, and then proceeded to destroy Lee's Army of Northern Va. in a costly 11-month campaign of attrition. It was not until Feb. of 1865—two months before the surrender—that Lee was given over-all command of all Confederate armies. Accepting the presidency of Washington College, after the war, he served until his death 22 Oct. '70, at the age of 64. (The name was later changed to Washington and Lee University. He is buried there.) D. S. Freeman's four-volume *R. E. Lee* (1934) is a magnificent biography of this great American.

LEE, Stephen Dill. C.S.A. gen. 1833–1908. S.C. No kin to the Virginia Lees, he graduated from USMA 1854 (17/46); Arty. He served on the frontier, in the Seminole War before resigning in Feb. '61 as 1st Lt. Commissioned a Capt. first in the S.C. volunteers and then in the Confederate army, he was Beauregard's A.D.C. during the bombardment of Fort Sumter. He was promoted Maj. of C.S.A. Arty. in Nov. '61 and fought at Seven Pines, Savage's Station, Malvern Hill, 2d Bull Run, and Antietam, having meanwhile been named Col. and having commanded his own battalion at Antietam. Appointed B.G. C.S.A. 6 Nov. '62, he was sent to Vicksburg and fought at Chickasaw Bayou and Champion's Hill. Captured at Vicksburg and exchanged within a few months, he was promoted Maj. Gen. 3 Aug. '63 and put in command of all the cavalry in Miss. In Feb. '64 he was given command of all the cavalry west of Ala. and on 23 June was named Lt. Gen. The government confirmed this appointment on 14 Feb. '65, reconsidered it two days later, and confirmed it as "temporary" on 16 Mar. '65 to rank from the original date of appointment. When Hood took command of the army, Lee succeeded Hood as corps commander, leading it in the battles around Atlanta and at Nashville (wounded). Married on 9 Feb. '65, he reassumed command of the corps after the reorganization 9 Apr. and surrendered on the 26th. After the war he was a planter, legislator, and president of Miss. A. and M. College 1880–99. Active in veterans' activities, he was a commissioner to organize the Vicksburg National park and was C. in C. of the United Confederate Veterans when he died.

LEE, William Henry Fitzhugh ("Rooney"). R. E. Lee's second eldest son. 1837–91. Va. Graduating from Harvard where he was a classmate of Henry Adams and Theodore Lyman, he joined the R.A. as 2d Lt. 6th US Inf. during the Utah Expedition and resigned in 1859 to farm "White House," the Custis plantation on the Pamunkey River left him by his grandfather. Commissioned Capt. and then Maj. of C.S.A. Cav. in May '61, he was Loring's Chief of Cav. during the W. Va. campaign and spent the winter of 1861–62 around Fredericksburg. He was named Lt. Col. and then Col. of the 9th Va. Cav. and served with Stuart in all his campaigns, including the ride around McClellan. During the Antietam campaign he was unhorsed and left unconscious at Turner's Gap, but recovered in time for the Chambersburg raid. He was appointed B.G. C.S.A. to date from 15 Sept. '62. He led the 3d Brig. at Fredericksburg and Chancellorsville and was severely wounded in the leg at Brandy Station. While convalescing at the Wickham family home, "Hickory Hill," he was captured 26 June during a Federal raid (SOUTH ANNA RIVER) and was held until Mar. '64. His wife Charlotte Wickham Lee had died in Dec. '63. He was promoted Maj. Gen. 23 Apr. '64 and opposed Wilson's raid in June. At Globe Tavern he commanded the Confederate cavalry, and at Five Forks and the rest of the retreat from Petersburg to Appomattox he commanded the forces on the right. D.A.B. describes him as "six feet two inches in height and of powerful frame . . . a courteous, genial gentleman . . . not the dashing type of cavalry officer, but he was a scientific fighter." After the war he returned to "White House," where he farmed and later sat in the state legislature and US Congress.

LEE, William Raymond. Union officer. c. 1804–91. Ex-cadet USMA 1829. Mass. Col. 20th Mass. 21 July '61; Bvt. B.G. USV (Antietam, war service); resigned 17 Dec. '62. Commanded 3, 2, II (Potomac). A civil engineer and railroad superintendent before the war. Captured at Balls Bluff 21 Oct.

'61. Selected with Paul Joseph REVERE as hostage for the C.S.A. privateers (see ENCHANTRESS AFFAIR). Severely wounded at Nelson's Farm (Va.) when his horse fell on him.

LEECH, William Albert. Union officer. Pa. Maj. 17th Pa. 25 Apr. '61; mustered out 2 Aug. '61; Lt. Col. 90th Pa. 10 Mar. '62; Bvt. B.G. USV (war service). Ex-cadet USMA 1854. Died 1870.

LEED'S & CO. A New Orleans cannon maker, and with TREDEGAR IRON WORKS one of the two first-class foundries and machine shops in the South. Its loss was one of the most serious consequences of Farragut's capture of New Orleans. It is variously referred to as Leeds Co., Leed's & Co., or Leed's Foundry.

LEE'S (Fitzhugh) CAVALRY CORPS. See under CORPS, Confed., STUART'S CAVALRY CORPS.

LEE'S (S. D.) CAVALRY CORPS and S. D. Lee's (Infantry) Corps. See under CORPS, Confed.

LEE'S FAREWELL TO THE ARMY OF NORTHERN VIRGINIA.

"Headquarters, Army of
Northern Virginia
April 10, 1865

"After four years of arduous service, marked by unsurpassed courage and fortitude, the Army of Northern Virginia has been compelled to yield to overwhelming numbers and resources. I need not tell the survivors of so many hard-fought battles, who have remained steadfast to the last, that I have consented to this result from no distrust of them; but, feeling that valour and devotion could accomplish nothing that could compensate for the loss that would have attended the continuation of the contest, I have determined to avoid the useless sacrifice of those whose past services have endeared them to their countrymen. By the terms of the agreement, officers and men can return to their homes and remain there until exchanged. You will take with you the satisfaction that proceeds from the consciousness of duty faithfully performed; and I earnestly pray that a merciful God will extend to you His blessing and protection. With an increasing admiration of your constancy and devotion to your country, and a grateful remembrance of your kind and generous consideration of myself, I bid you an affectionate farewell.

"R. E. Lee, General."

LEE'S HORSES. In addition to TRAVELLER, R. E. Lee had a number of other mounts throughout the war, although none was so satisfactory as the gray. When Lee came to Richmond in the spring of 1861, he was given a bay stallion named Richmond. This horse was quite nervous and when around strange horses was prone to squeal. Lee took him to W. Va. and bought another horse there, whom he called The Roan or Brown-Roan. During the Seven Days' Battles The Roan began to go blind, and Richmond died after Malvern Hill. Stuart then got him a quiet mare named Lucy Long after 2d Bull Run, and about this same time he was also given a sorrel named Ajax.

LE FAVOUR, Heber. Union officer. R.I. Capt. 5th Mich. 19 June '61; Lt. Col. 22d Mich. 20 Aug. '62; Col. 5 Jan. '63; Bvt. B.G. USV (war service). W.I.A. Williamsburg 5 May '62; captured at Chickamauga 20 Sept. '63. Commanded 3, 2, Res. Corps (Cumberland); Res. Brig. (Cumberland); 3d Brig., 2d Div. Separate Etowah. Died 1878.

LEGION. The military organization known as the "legion" in US military history is one that includes infantry, artillery, and cavalry. (Its modern counterpart is the "combat team.") Among the better-known units of this type in the Civil War were Cobb's Legion, the CORCORAN LEGION, HAMPTON LEGION.

LEGAL TENDER ACTS. Laws enacted by Congress in 1862, 1863, and 1864 to aid in financing the war. The first act authorized the issuance of $150,000,000 in treasury notes as legal tender in payment of taxes and debts; amending legislation provided for an additional $300,000,000. These were popularly called greenbacks and fluctuated in value during and after the war. Their constitutionality was decided in 1871 by the Supreme Court, which ruled that their issuance was a valid exercise of congressional powers.

LE GENDRE, Charles William. Union officer. 1830–99. France. Maj. 51st N.Y. 4 Nov. '61; Lt. Col. 20 Sept. '62; Col. 14 Mar. '63; Bvt. B.G. USV (war service); discharged 4 Oct. '64. Lost part of jaw at New Bern (N.C.), 14 Mar. '62, and was cited for bravery. In the Wilderness, 6 May '64, he lost the bridge of his nose and his left eye. In 1866 as US Consul at Amoy (China) he performed the following service. A naval landing party had landed on Formosa to avenge the massacre of a shipwrecked US crew by warlike tribes. They were ambushed, and Le Gendre in turn led a party that was able to pacify and make agreements with the natives. He was foreign advisor to the Japanese government (1872–75) and was the first person, foreign or native, to receive the Second Class of Merit of the Order of the Rising Sun after its establishment by the Emperor. In 1890 he was first with the Korean Home office and later that year became the advisor to the Household Department of the King of Korea. He died in Seoul of apoplexy.

LEGGETT, Mortimer Dormer. Union gen. 1821–96. N.Y. After Western Reserve College he studied medical jurisprudence and was a school superintendent when the war began. Serving as a volunteer A.D.C. to his friend McClellan in western Va., he was then commissioned Lt. Col. 78th Ohio 18 Dec. '61, promoted Col. 21 Jan. '62, and fought at Fort Donelson, Shiloh, and Corinth. Appointed B.G. USV 29 Nov. '62, he commanded 2d Brig., 3d Div., Right Wing, XIII, Tenn. (1 Nov.– 18 Dec. '62) and 1, 3, XVII (3 June– 17 Nov. '63) at Vicksburg. He then commanded 2, 3, XVII (18 Dec. '62– 13 Apr. '63 and 11 May–3 June '63) and in the Atlanta campaign led the 3d Div., XVII (17 Nov. '63–6 Mar. '64; 6 Apr.–23 Aug. '64) as well as on the March to the Sea and through the Carolinas (22 Sept. '64–15 Jan. '65 and 3 Apr.–1 Aug. '65). At Atlanta (on 21 July) his command captured Bald Hill and held it the next day (Battle of ATLANTA); it is now called Leggett's Hill in his honor. He commanded the XVII Corps 10–24 Oct. '64 and temporarily on 8 May '65. Promoted Maj. Gen. USV 21 Aug. '65, he had been breveted that rank 1 Sept. '64 for the Atlanta and Savannah campaigns. Resigning 28 Sept. '65, he was Grant's Commissioner of Patents 1871–74 and founded the Brush Electric Co. that was later absorbed by General Electric.

LEIB, Herman. Union officer listed erroneously by Phisterer. See LIEB, Herman.

LEIPER, Charles Lewis. Union officer. Pa. Pvt. 1st Troop Phila. City Cav. 29 Apr.–17 Aug. '61; 1st Lt. 6th Pa. Cav. 7 Sept. '61; Capt. 20 Nov. '62; Maj. 1 Sept. '64; Lt. Col. 10 Feb. '65; Col. 27 May '65; transferred to 2d Pa. Prov. Cav. 17 June '65; Bvt. B.G. USV (war service). Died 1899.

LE MAT REVOLVER. A Confederate nine-shot double-barreled pistol developed by the French-born New Orleans physician, Dr. (or Col.) J. A. F. LeMat. An eight-chambered, cal. .44 cylinder fired through the top shotgun barrel, and the lower barrel fired a cal. .60-shot · charge. It was popular with Southern generals, including Stuart and Beauregard. The latter had been in partnership with LeMat in 1856. When he could not get the machinery to manufacture 5,000 of his pistols on contract for the Confederate government he boarded the *Trent* with Mason and Slidell and went to Paris. There he produced approximately 3,000 pistols and carbines (Albaugh and Simmons; Wiley, *Reb.*).

LEONARD, Hiram. Union officer. Vt. Appt.-N.Y. Entering the R.A. in 1846, he was promoted Lt. Col. and Deputy Paymaster Gen. USA in Sept. '62. He retired in 1872 as Bvt. B.G. USA.

LESLIE, Thomas J. Union officer. c. 1797–1874. England. Pa. USMA 1815 * (27/40); Engrs. He was paymaster and treasurer at West Point for 23 years and was Chief of Paymaster's Dept. for the N.Y. Dist. 1861–69. In 1869 he retired as Maj. and Bvt. B.G. USA.

LETCHER, John. C.S.A. Gov. of Va. 1813–84. Va. After attending Washington and Randolph-Macon Colleges, he became a lawyer and ran the Lexington newspaper. He was active in Democratic politics and was in Congress before being elected Gov. in 1860. Serving until 1864, when "Extra Billy" Smith succeeded him, he was imprisoned for several months after the surrender. He

* There was no class standing prior to 1818, and the cadets are listed in the order in which they were commissioned.

was in the state legislature until his death. See also LORING-JACKSON INCIDENT.

LEVENTHORPE, Collett. C.S.A. gen. 1815–89. England. After Winchester College he served as an officer in the British Army and then settled in N.C. Commissioned Col. 34th N.C. in Nov. '61, he commanded a brigade by Dec. He was named Col. 11th N.C. 2 Apr. '62 and commanded the Dist. of Wilmington until Sept. On guard along the Blackwater, he fought in Jan. '63 at White Hall. At Gettysburg he led the regiment, was captured on the retreat, and kept a prisoner for nine months. He was promoted B.G. of N.C. state troops and led them around Petersburg, defending the Weldon railroad, and in Feb. '65 was appointed B.G. C.S.A. He declined the appointment 6 Mar. '65 and surrendered with Johnston. Remaining in the South, he was a businessman after the war. "Notably handsome man, nearly six and one-half feet tall in height, erect and stately in bearing, and gentle as well as brave," (C.M.H.) he was descended from a "knightly family of Yorkshire" (Lonn).

LEWIS, Charles W. Union officer. Calif. Col. 7th Calif. 11 Jan. '65; Bvt. B.G. USV (war service). Commanded 1st Brig., Cav. Div. (Va. and N.C.). Died 1871.

LEWIS, John Randolph. Union officer. c. 1834–1900. Pa. R.A. Sgt. Co. H 1st Vt. 2 May–15 Aug. '61; Capt. 5th Vt. 16 Sept. '61; Maj. 16 July '62; Lt. Col. 6 Oct. '62; Col. 5 June '64; mustered out 11 Sept. '64; Col. Vet. Res. Corps 8 Sept. '64; Bvt. B.G. USV (Wilderness). Other brevets for White Oak Swamp, Wilderness. Commanded 2, 13, XIII; 2d Brig., 3d Div. Ark. Exp.; 2, 3, VII. W.I.A. Wilderness in right leg and lost left arm.

LEWIS, Joseph Horace. C.S.A. gen. 1824–1904. Ky. After Centre College he was a lawyer and a Whig legislator, changing in time to the Democratic party. He recruited for the Confederacy in Ky. and was commissioned Col. 6th Ky. in Sept. '61, fighting at Shiloh, Stones River, and Chickamauga. At the last battle he succeeded to Helm's brigade and was appointed B.G. C.S.A. 30 Sept. '63. He led his brigade under Breckinridge at Chattanooga and under Bate in the Atlanta campaign, opposing Sherman in the March to the Sea and through the Carolinas. His command was shifted to a number of different organizations and was called the "Orphan Brigade." After the war he served in the legislature and Congress and was Chief Justice of the Ky. Supreme Court.

LEWIS, Levin M. C.S.A. gen. Appt.-Mo. Listed as Col. 3d Mo., he was assigned by Kirby Smith as B.G. C.S.A. 16 May '65 in the Trans-Miss. Dept. Wright and Wood include him in their lists, but C.M.H. does not.

LEWIS, William Delaware, Jr. Union officer. Pa. Col. 18th Pa. 24 Apr. '61; mustered out 6 Aug. '61; Col. 110th Pa. 2 Jan. '62; Bvt. B.G. USV (war service); resigned 20 Dec. '62. Died 1872.

LEWIS, William Gaston. C.S.A. gen. 1835–1901. N.C. He went to the Raleigh Military School and the Univ. of N.C., and engaged in teaching, surveying, and engineering. A member of the Edgecombe Guards, a militia company, he was commissioned Ensign and Lt. of the 1st N.C. 21 Apr. '61 and fought at Big Bethel. As Maj. 33d N.C., he fought at New Bern and served under Ewell in the Valley as Lt. Col. 43d N.C. He also fought at Malvern Hill, Gettysburg, Bristoe Station, Mine Run, and Plymouth. Named Col. in

Apr. '64, he fought at Drewry's Bluff and was appointed B.G. C.S.A. 31 May '64. Returning to the Shenandoah, he fought against Sheridan and then around Petersburg. He was severely wounded and captured 7 Apr. '65 at Farmville, Va. After the war he was a civil and railroad engineer.

LEXINGTON. One of SHERMAN'S HORSES.

LEXINGTON, Tenn. 18 Dec. '62. (FORREST'S SECOND RAID; STONES RIVER) In an attempt to interrupt Forrest's raid, Col. Ralph G. Ingersoll with a battery of artillery and 200 men of the 11th Ill. Cav. reached Lexington on the morning of the 17th and was joined by 200 men of the 5th Ohio Cav. and 272 of the 2d West Tenn. Cav. Reconnaissance revealed a large body of Confederate cavalry near Beach Creek. Ingersoll withdrew his main body to within half a mile of Lexington, and ordered detachments to destroy bridges on roads leading toward the town. Next morning (18th) Maj. Funke with a battalion of the 11th Ill. Cav. and two guns checked Forrest's attempt to advance along the Stage (or "upper") road from Beach Creek. But through failure to destroy the bridge on the "lower" road a force led by Col. Hawkins was attacked and routed by Confederate cavalry approaching Lexington from this direction. The 11th Ill. charged and temporarily slowed the pursuit, and the force on the Stage road repulsed two attacks before being overrun. The Federal cavalry was then routed and pursued toward Jackson with the loss of 124 prisoners, including Ingersoll. Forrest's next action was at PARKER CROSS ROADS, 31 Dec.

LIBBY PRISON. Situated on the James River in Richmond, the building was the warehouse of Libby and Sons, ship chandlers, before the Civil War.

Only officers were held there, perhaps the most notorious prison after ANDERSONVILLE. It was a temporary shelter after a series of threatening Union cavalry raids forced the Confederates to send the inmates to a new prison at Macon (Ga.) in May '64.

LIDDELL, St. John R. C.S.A. gen. La. He was a Col. on Hardee's staff at Bowling Green and in Feb. '62 carried reports from A. S. Johnston to Richmond. During the siege of Corinth he commanded the Ark. brigade and was appointed B.G. C.S.A. 12 July '62. He commanded the 1st Brig. in the Ky. campaign, fighting at Perryville, led the 2d Brig. at Stones River and at Chickamauga commanded a division. Going to the Trans-Miss. Dept., he commanded the sub-district of northern La., fought in the Red River campaign of 1864 and in Aug. of that year was put in command of southern Miss. When Mobile was assaulted, he was given command of the Eastern Div. of the Dept. of the Gulf and was captured 9 Apr. '65 at Fort Blakely. He settled in New Orleans after the war.

LIEB, Herman. Switzerland. Pvt. Co. B 8th Ill. 30 Apr. '61; mustered out 25 July '61; Capt. 8th Ill. 25 July '61; Maj. 1 Nov. '62; Col. 5th US Col. Arty. 7 Aug. '63; Bvt. B.G. USV (war service). Led expeditions against Marion (Ark.) in May '63 and Jan. '64. Listed by Phisterer as Leib, Herman.

LIGHTBURN, Joseph Andrew Jackson. Union gen. 1824–1901. Pa. He wanted to go to West Point, but the appointment for his area was given Stonewall Jackson instead. After the Mexican War (Pvt. to Sgt. 1846–51) he engaged in farming and milling, and in 1861 was a member of the convention in Wheeling that formed W. Va. Commissioned Col. 4th W. Va. 14 Aug. '61, he succeeded Cox as commander of the forces

in the Kanawha Valley (15 Aug.–Sept.
'62) and conducted the retreat down to
Point Pleasant before Loring's troops.
He was promoted B.G. USV 14 Mar.
'63 and commanded 2, 2, XV, Tenn.
(2 May–26 July at Gettysburg; and 19
Oct. '63–12 Jan. '64 at Missionary
Ridge and Chickamauga; and 12 Feb.–
22 July at Resaca; 27 July–5 Aug. '64
and 17–24 Aug. '64 during the Atlanta
campaign), succeeding to division (26
July–10 Sept. '63; 22–27 July '64 and
5–17 Aug. '64). He was wounded in
Aug. '64 in the head. He also led 2d
Inf. Div., W. Va. (Jan.–May '65). Resigning 22 July '65, he was in the W. Va.
legislature 1866–67 and ordained a Baptist minister two years later, remaining
active in the ministry until his death.

LILLEY, Robert D. C.S.A. gen.
?–1886. Appt.-Va. In the spring of
'61 he was Capt. of the "Augusta Lee
Rifles," and fought at Rich Mountain,
Greenbrier River, and Allegheny, and
at McDowell (May '62). He then served
in the Valley under Ewell and fought
at Cedar Mountain and 2d Bull Run.
Named Maj. in Jan. '63, he served
under Imboden in Apr. and May in
western Va. and then fought in the
Stonewall Brigade at Gettysburg as Lt.
Col. He participated in the Mine Run
campaign and fought at the Wilderness and Spotsylvania. Appointed B.G.
C.S.A. 31 May '63, he commanded
Early's old brigade during his march on
Washington and was wounded and captured near Winchester 20 July of that
year. Recaptured a few days later, he
commanded the reserve forces in the
Valley Dist. from 28 Nov. '64 until the
end of the war.

LINCOLN, Abraham. 16th US Pres.
1809–65. Ky. Born and raised on the
edge of the frontier, he grew up with
scant formal education and first saw the
world in a flatboat trip to New Orleans
in 1828. His family then settled in Ill.,

and Lincoln held various clerking jobs,
was partner in a grocery store that
failed and left him heavily in debt. He
then studied law. His forceful character and honesty made him a favorite in
the community, and he served in the
state legislature as a Whig. Licensed as
a lawyer in 1836, he settled in Springfield, where he married Mary Todd in
1842. After one term in Congress
(1847–49) he was not returned by his
constituents and retired from public
life. In opposition to Stephen A. Douglas and the Kansas-Nebraska Act, he
entered in the growing debate of sectionalism and joined the Republican
party in 1856. The famous Lincoln-
Douglas debates of 1858 ended in
Douglas' election to the Senate, but
Lincoln emerged as a powerful national
figure, and he was nominated on the Republican ticket for president in 1860.
He was elected on 6 Nov. and determined to save the Union at all costs.
The South saw the end of their political power in the Union. When he ordered the provisioning of Fort Sumter,
the Confederacy objected to what they
considered a course of coercion, and
the Civil War began. Although Lincoln
had war powers that were virtually dictatorial, his wisdom in handling these
for the good of the Union, despite a
Cabinet rent with jealousies and hatred
and a country torn by a civil conflict,
brought forth a nation stronger in the
end than had been possible before the
war. After Antietam he issued his
Emancipation Proclamation, giving
the Northern cause a high moral tone,
but the preservation of the Union was
still his primary purpose. His enemies
mustered strength before the 1864 election, and it looked as though he would
be displaced in the White House. But
the military successes of Grant and
Sherman swung sentiment to him, and
he was re-elected. His view of Recon-

struction was described in the immortal words of his second inaugural address: "With malice toward none; with charity toward all." His assassination by John Wilkes BOOTH on 14 Apr. '65 at Ford's Theatre put the Radical Republicans in control of the nation. When Lincoln died early the next morning, with him died all hope of piecing the Union together without bitterness.

LINCOLN'S ASSASSINATION. On 14 Apr. '65 shortly before 10 P.M., John Wilkes BOOTH shot Lincoln in Ford's Theatre. This was the culmination of a plot begun the year before when Booth conceived the idea that if Lincoln were kidnapped and given to the Confederate government as a hostage, the Union would have to release all their prisoners, returning manpower then so desperately needed by the South. His conspirators were Samuel Arnold, Confederate deserter and clerk; Michael O'Laughlin, also a deserter and clerk; John SURRATT, Confederate spy and agent; George Atzerodt, carriage maker and Confederate agent; and Davy Herold, a boy who knew the Maryland area well. Several attempts at an abduction from Ford's Theatre were planned, none of which were brought to a final stage of plotting. Then the conspirators ceased their efforts for a few months when Booth's theatrical commitments took him away from Washington. In Mar. '65, their plot failed when Lincoln did not attend a theatrical performance outside Washington. Lewis Paine (born Powell), an Alabama deserter, had joined the crew by then, more from hero worship of Booth than from any deep convictions about the plan, and only two of Booth's original conspirators had remained with him. Apparently not until after Appomattox did the idea of assassination occur to Booth. When, on Good Friday following the surrender, the Lincolns

planned an evening at Ford's Theatre, Booth hastily assigned duties. He was to shoot Lincoln himself. (See John W. BOOTH for his actions, escape, and death.) Atzerodt was to kill Johnson, but lacked the courage even to try. Paine was to murder Seward—a mission which he almost accomplished, leaving the Secretary maimed and near-dead. And Herold, the boy, was to help Paine escape through Maryland.

Several hundred people were arrested on suspicion of conspiracy, including all the above-named but Booth, John Surratt, and Herold. The plotters were thrown in Fort Monroe in irons, along with Edward Spangler, a scene-shifter friend of Booth's from Ford's Theatre. Mrs. SURRATT, at whose boardinghouse Booth had conferred with her son, was added to the group, as was Dr. Samuel MUDD, a Maryland doctor whose misfortune it was to have met Booth in church and to have set his broken leg after the assassination. After a military trial, Paine, Atzerodt, Herold, and Mrs. Surratt were hanged 7 July '65. O'Laughlin, Arnold, Spangler, and Mudd were sent to life imprisonment in the Dry Tortugas. They were released from this in 1869; see Dr. Samuel MUDD for details. Surratt escaped to Italy where he joined the Papal Guards. Recognized and finally sent back to the U.S., he was tried, resulting in a hung jury, and the charges against him were nol-prossed.

LINCOLN, Mary Todd. Wife of Abraham Lincoln. 1818–82. Ky. Of an aristocratic Kentucky family, she was living with her sister, wife of Gov. of Ill., Ninian Edwards, when she met and married Lincoln. Much criticized, and apparently with justification, she was an unhappy woman bordering on insanity most of her life. After the death of their son Willie in 1862, the assassination of Lincoln at her side in the theater, and Tad's death in 1871, she was declared insane. She was later certified sane. See BROTHER AGAINST BROTHER.

LINCOLN, Robert Todd. Son of Abraham Lincoln. 1843–1926. Ill. After graduating from Harvard in 1864, he was on Grant's staff for the remainder of the war. He then studied law in Chicago, became an able corporation lawyer there and in Washington, and was also active in railroading and was president of the Pullman Company from 1897 to 1911. He was a retiring man and never entered politcs, although he served as Sec. of War for both Garfield and Arthur. Under Harrison he was Minister to Great Britain.

LINCOLN, William Sever. Union officer. c. 1811–89. Mass. Lt. Col. 34th Mass. 31 July '62; Col. 27 Nov. '64; Bvt. B.G. USV 23 June '65 (Shenandoah Valley). W.I.A. and captured New Market (Va.). Commanded 1st Brig., Independent Div., XXIV.

LINDLEY, John M. Union officer. Pa. Capt. 19th Ind. 29 July '61; Maj. 1 May '63; Lt. Col. 1 July '64; Bvt. B.G. USV. Brevets for Gainesville (Va.), Gettysburg. Mustered out 19 Oct. '64. Died 1874.

LIPPINCOTT, Charles Elliott. Union officer. Ill. Capt. 33d Ill. 2 Sept. '61; Lt. Col. 1 Mar. '62; Col. 17 Sept. '62; Bvt. B.G. USV 17 Feb. '65. Died 1887.

LIPPITT, Francis James. Union officer. R.I. Col. 2d Calif. 2 Sept. '61; Bvt. B.G. USV (war service); mustered out 11 Oct. '64. Died 1902.

LISTER, Frederick William. Union officer. England. 2d Lt. 45th Ohio 10 July '61; 1st Lt. Regt. Adj. 12 July '61; Maj. 31st Ohio 24 Oct. '61; Lt. Col. 5 Mar. '62; Col. 40th US Col. Inf. 12 July '65; Bvt. B.G. USV (war service).

LITCHFIELD, Allyne C. Union officer. Mass. Capt. 5th Mich. Cav. 14 Aug. '62; Lt. Col. 7th Mich. Cav. 14 Nov. '62; Col. 1 Mar. '64; Bvt. B.G. USV (war service). Captured 1 Mar. '64 on Kilpatrick's raid to Richmond.

LITTELL, John Smith. Union officer. Pa. Capt. 76th Pa. 28 Aug. '61; Lt. Col. 21 Aug. '64; Col. 29 Oct. '64; Bvt. B.G. USV 15 Jan. '65. Commanded 2, 2, X; 2d Div., X.

LITTLE, Henry. C.S.A. gen. 1817–62. Md. Appt.-Mo. Entering the Confederate Army as Maj., he served as Col. and Adj. Gen. for Price in Mo. and commanded a brigade in the Right Wing at Pea Ridge. He was appointed B.G. C.S.A. 12 Apr. '62 and joined Beauregard at Corinth, where he took over Price's old 1st Div. in the Army of the West. On 19 Sept. '62 he was killed at Iuka. The above information comes from C.M.H., which says that he was a member of the USMA class of 1839, although Cullum does not confirm this.

LITTLEFIELD, Milton Smith. Union officer. 1832–99. N.Y. Capt. 14th Ill. 25 May '61; mustered out 26 Nov. '62; Col. 21st US Col. Inf. 1 Apr. '63; Bvt. B.G. USV 26 Nov. '64. Commanded 3d African Brig., North End Folly Island, X; 3d Brig., 1st Dist. Fla., X; Dist. of Hilton Head (S.C.). Studied law in Lincoln's Springfield (Ill.) office and practiced law there for several years. In 1862 he was Sherman's Provost Marshal and also served on Gillmore's staff and as I.G. of Colored Troops.

LITTLEJOHN, DeWitt Clinton. Union officer. N.Y. 1818–92. Col. 110th N.Y. 25 Aug. '62; Bvt. B.G. USV (war service); resigned 3 Feb. '63. He held several public offices as a Republican, among them US Congressman.

LITTLE ROCK, Ark. The US arsenal surrendered 8 Feb. '61. Steele reoccupied the city 10 Sept. '63, losing 20 men and driving the Confederates south.

LIVERMORE, Mary Ashton Rice. SANITARY COMMISSION organizer. 1821-? Mass. After teaching school, she married Daniel P. Livermore, a Universalist clergyman. They lived in New England and later Chicago, where she helped her husband publish a paper. When the war started, she became increasingly concerned with the lack of provision made for the soldiers' comfort and health, and joined with others, notably Jane HOGE, in forming the Chicago branch of the Commission in 1862. She then traveled throughout the area, organizing other aid societies, and became in Dec. '62 a national director of the organization. For the rest of the war she made many battlefield inspection trips and lecture tours and was instrumental in putting on the first Sanitary Fair. After the war she turned her energies to other reforms, lectured extensively, and wrote about women.

LIVINGSTON, Robert Ramsey. Union officer. Canada. Capt. 1st Nebr. Cav. 11 June '61; Maj. 1 Jan '62; Lt. Col. 22 Apr. '62; Col. 4 Oct. '62; Bvt. B.G. USV 21 June '65 (war service). Commanded 2, 5, Army Southeast Mo.; Dist. of Northeast Ark., VII. Died 1888.

"LIZZIE, MISS." See Elizabeth VAN LEW.

LOB-SCOUSE. Slang for a dish soldiers concocted for themselves. A naval term derived from "lob's course," it was composed of baked or stewed salt meat with vegetables and hardtack substituting for the ship's biscuit.

LOCKE, Frederick Thomas. Union officer. N.Y. Capt. Asst. Adj. Gen. Vols. 2 Sept. '61; Lt. Col. Asst. Adj. Gen. Assigned 20 Aug. '62-1 Aug. '65; Bvt. B.G. USV 1 Apr. '65 (war service; Five Forks). Died 1893.

LOCKMAN, John Thomas. Union officer. N.Y. 1st Lt. 83d N.Y. 27 May

'61; Capt. 25 Nov. '61; resigned 22 Sept. '62; Lt. Col. 119th N.Y. 16 Oct. '62; Col. 3 May '63; Bvt. B.G. USV (Atlanta campaign). Commanded 2, 3, XI (Cumberland); 2, 2, XX.

LOCKWOOD, Henry Hayes. Union gen. 1814-99. Del. USMA 1836 (22/49); Arty. After the Seminole War he resigned in 1837 and farmed. Then he was appointed mathematics professor by the US Navy and was at the capture of Monterey (Calif.) on the frigate *United States*. He taught at USNA until commissioned Col. 1st Del. 25 May '61 and B.G. USV (Aug. '61). In the VIII Corps Middle Dept., he commanded Dist. Eastern Shore (22 July '62-5 Jan. '63); 1st Separate Brig. (5 Jan.-4 Feb., and 14 Feb.-26 June, 28 June-18 Dec. '63 and 12-24 May '64); and Lockwood's brigade, French's command (June-July '63). At Gettysburg he led 2, 1, XII, Potomac, and then commanded Md. Heights Div., W. Va. as well as 3d Separate Brig., VIII, Middle (24 Mar.-14 May and 20 July '64-31 July '65). He also led 2d Div., V, Potomac (9 May-2 June '64) at Hanover Court House; and VIII Corps and Middle Dept. (5 Dec. '63-Apr. '64). He was mustered out 24 Aug. '65 and returned to Annapolis, later serving with the naval observatory and writing on naval gunnery.

LOCOMOTIVE CHASE IN GEORGIA, THE. See ANDREWS' RAID.

LOGAN, John Alexander. Union gen. 1826-86. Ill. A lawyer, he fought in the Mexican War and then served in the state legislature and US Congress. He was a Democrat and believed by many to be a Southern sympathizer. Although not in the army, he marched to 1st Bull Run with a Mich. regiment and was then commissioned Col. 31st Ill. 18 Sept. '61. He was wounded leading his regiment at Fort Donelson and commissioned B.G. USV 21 Mar. '62. He commanded, in the Army of the Tenn., 1st Brig., 1st Div. (19 Apr.–July '62); 1st Brig., 1st Div., Dist. of Jackson (July–Sept. '62); and Dist. of Jackson (Sept. '62). As Maj. Gen. USV (29 Nov. '62), he commanded 3d Div. Right Wing, XIII, Tenn. (1 Nov.–18 Dec. '62) and 3d Div., XVII (18 Dec. '62–20 July '63) during the Vicksburg campaign as well as Sept.–17 Nov. '63. He commanded the XV Corps 11 Dec. '63–22 July '64, succeeding McPherson as commander of the Army of the Tenn. He was, however, relieved by Lincoln five days later upon Sherman's recommendation. The latter, while feeling that Logan was a first-rate combat soldier, said that he expressed deep contempt for the necessary though tedious logistical preparation of an army. He returned to the XV Corps, leading it 27 July–23 Sept. '64 and 8 Jan.–23 May '65 during the remainder of the Atlanta campaign and on the March to the Sea and through the Carolinas. He again commanded the Army of the Tenn. 19 May–1 Aug. '65. Resigning 17 Aug. '65, he re-entered politics as a Republican, serving as US Congressman and Sen. for many years. He was the unsuccessful vice-presidential candidate on the ticket with Cleveland in 1884. He was one of the organizers of the G.A.R. and was three times its president; helped found the Society of the Army of the Tenn., and began the observance of Memorial Day. Wrote *The Volunteer Soldier of America* (1887).

LOGAN, Thomas Muldrup. C.S.A. gen. 1840–1914. S.C. Standing first in his graduating class at S.C. College in 1860, he was a volunteer at the bombardment of Sumter and was commissioned 1st Lt. in the Hampton Legion. As Capt. he fought at 1st Bull Run, was wounded at Gaines's Mill, and also participated in 2d Bull Run and Antietam campaigns. Named Maj., he served in Micah Jenkins's brigade and was wounded in 1864. He was appointed B.G. C.S.A. 15 Feb. '65 and took over M. C. Butler's brigade, which was transferred to Johnston's command. At Bentonville he led the last charge. At the surrender Sherman had expressed astonishment that this "slight, fair-haired boy," only 25 years of age, had commanded a brigade. Becoming first a lawyer, he started to organize a more efficient railroad system for Richmond and organized what is now called the Southern Railway. When he sold it, he made approximately one and one half million dollars *profit.* D.A.B. describes him as "an old-fashioned Southern host, a lover of good literature, an influential speaker and writer."

LOGAN CROSS ROADS (Mill Springs; Fishing Creek; Somerset; Beech Grove), Ky., 19 Jan. '62. Early in the struggle for Ky., Zollicoffer occupied and fortified Cumberland Gap with 4,000 Confederate troops (Sept. '61). As G. H. Thomas' 1st Div., Army of the Ohio, started advancing to recover eastern Ky., there were several preliminary skirmishes. At Wild Cat Mountain, 21 Oct. '61, Zollicoffer had been driven back into Cumberland Gap by Albin Schoepf's 1st Brig. Schoepf was later forced into a panicky retreat that became known as the "Wild Cat Stampede" (Horn, 67).

In Nov. Zollicoffer moved from his mountain position and advanced about 70 miles northwest to Mill Springs on the Cumberland. Although he could have best accomplished his mission of guarding the approaches to southeast Ky. from this position, Zollicoffer then crossed the river and dug in near Beech Grove. Schoepf had withdrawn to Somerset, about 15 miles northeast. When George B. Crittenden arrived at Knoxville (24 Nov.) to take command of the district, he ordered Zollicoffer to withdraw south of the river. Crittenden arrived to take personal command in early Jan., and found that his order had not been obeyed. Since the enemy was now advancing in force, Crittenden decided to defend in place rather than accept the greater hazard of trying to recross the flooded Cumberland in the face of a strong enemy.

Schoepf had remained near Somerset. Zollicoffer had issued a proclamation on 16 Dec. urging Kentuckians to join him in driving the Federals out of the state. Meanwhile Zollicoffer's cavalry had been active. A reconnaissance in force by Schoepf on the 18th, with the support of S. D. Carter's 12th Brig. of Thomas's division, revealed that the Confederates were strongly intrenched in the angle formed by Fishing Creek and the Cumberland. Buell had refused Thomas permission to take his entire division to support Schoepf because another Confederate force under Hindman (7,000) was threatening Columbia. On the 29th, however, Buell ordered Thomas to join Schoepf and destroy Zollicoffer or drive him across the river (Van Horne, 52ff.).

On 31 Dec. Thomas left Lebanon with Manson's (2d) brigade, two regiments of R. L. McCook's (3d), a battalion of Wolford's 1st Ky. Cav., and Kinney's artillery (C, 1st Ohio). Due to miserable road conditions, which required eight days to cover one stretch of 40 muddy miles, Thomas with the leading elements on 17 Jan. reached Logan Cross Roads. This place was 10 miles from the Confederate beachhead and eight miles from Somerset. Thomas called on Schoepf for three regiments and an artillery battery to support him until the tail of his column could close up.

Crittenden decided to take the initiative. Moving out at midnight in a driving rain, he made contact with Wolford's cavalry pickets at about 5:30 the morning of the 19th. Manson (2d Brig.) ordered up the 10th Ind. to meet the attack and sent Speed S. Fry's 4th Ky. to his support. Zollicoffer led his 1st Brig. in an attack that drove the cavalry and the 10th Ind. back to the edge of a woods. Fry's regiment moved up on the left of the Indianans, and the line was stabilized until reinforcements could form on them. There was a ravine opposite Fry's line which the Confederates used as a covered route of approach to within a short distance. Fry considered this unsporting and, "mounting the fence, in stentorian tones denounced them as dastards, and defied them to stand up on their feet and come forward like men" (B.&L., I, 388). A short time later, during a lull, Fry rode to a flank to reconnoiter and was approached by another officer whose uniform was concealed by a white raincoat. When the latter told Fry that his troops were firing into their own men, Fry was about to have his troops cease fire when a Confederate rode up, shot, and wounded Fry's horse. Fry (and several other Federals who observed the incident) then shot and killed the stranger, who turned out to be Zollicoffer.

Although Zollicoffer's two regiments were thrown into confusion by the loss of their leader, Crittenden rallied them, brought up Carroll's brigade, and ordered a general advance. Thomas arrived on the field and committed Carter's (12th) brigade to stop an attempt to envelop the left of the 4th Ky. McCook came up with two regiments (2d Minn. and 9th Ohio) and relieved the 10th Ind. and 4th Ky., whose ammunition was about exhausted. There was a hot engagement for the next half-hour as Crittenden's renewed assault gathered momentum. By this time the 10th and 4th were back in line, having replenished their ammunition. Carter now advanced on the left (with the 1st and 2d East Tenn.), the 2d Minn. maintained a galling base of fire in the center, and the 9th Ohio attacked with fixed bayonets on the Federal right.

The Confederate left was crushed and then their entire line broke. Thomas pursued to Beech Grove. Crittenden managed to withdraw his troops across the river during the night on a small sternwheeler and two old flatboats, but he had to abandon most of his heavy equipment. The morning of the 20th the Federals moved into the abandoned camp, taking 12 guns and their caissons, small arms, about 150 wagons, over 1,000 horses and mules, and a large quantity of commissary stores. There was no further pursuit, but Crittenden's troops were so demoralized that many of them deserted.

Of the 4,000 troops Thomas had on the field, an estimated 2,500 were engaged. (Schoepf joined Thomas with three regiments after the fighting had ceased on the 19th.) Thomas reported 246 casualties (39 killed, 207 wounded). Crittenden said he had about 4,000 effectives.

LOMAX, Lunsford Lindsay. C.S.A. gen. 1835–1913. R.I. Appt.-At Large. USMA 1856 (21/49); Cav. A classmate and close friend of Fitzhugh Lee, he served on the frontier in Indian fighting before resigning 25 Apr. '61 as 2d Lt. The son of a Virginia-born army officer, he was commissioned Capt. of Va. state troops and named Asst. Adj. Gen. to J. E. Johnston. Then serving as I.G. in the Confederate Army with the same rank on McCulloch's staff, he became Lt. Col. and I.G. until Oct. '62, when he became I.G. for the Army of East Tenn. Coming East in 1863, he was promoted Col. and led the 11th Va. Cav. at Gettysburg before

being appointed B.G. C.S.A. 23 July '63. He led his brigade under Fitzhugh Lee from Culpeper Court House through the Wilderness and in the battles around Petersburg, being promoted Maj. Gen. 10 Aug. '64 and going to join Early in the Shenandoah Valley. Captured at Woodstock 23 Sept. of that year, he escaped in a few hours and was given command of the Valley Dist. on 29 Mar. '65. When Richmond fell, he removed his troops to Lynchburg in a vain effort to link up with Echols, and finally surrendered with Johnston in N.C. After the war he became a farmer and was later president of the college that is now Va. Polytechnic Inst. He moved to Washington later to aid in the compilation of the *Official Records* and was also a commissioner of Gettysburg National Park.

LONG, Armistead Lindsay. C.S.A. gen. 1825–91. Va. USMA 1850 (17/44); Arty. He served in Fla., on the frontier, and in Indian fighting and in garrison before becoming A.D.C. to Edwin V. SUMNER, his father-in-law, on 20 May '61. Resigning 10 June '61 as 1st Lt., he went to western Va. and reported to Lee in the fall of 1861 in S.C. When Lee took command of the A.N.V., Long became his Mil. Sec. with the rank of Col. He held this post until 21 Sept. '63, when he was appointed B.G. C.S.A. of Arty. He fought the rest of the war with Jackson's old corps. After the surrender he was engineer for a canal company until 1870, when he became totally blind from exposure suffered during the war. His wife was named postmistress of Charlottesville (Va.) by Grant after this. Long wrote, on a special slate, the valuable *Memoirs of Robert E. Lee, His Military and Personal History* (1886).

See also BROTHER AGAINST BROTHER.

LONG, Eli. Ky. Union gen. 1837–1903. R.A. Graduating from a Ky. military school, he was appointed 2d Lt. 1st US Cav. in 1856. He participated in Indian fighting and was promoted 1st Lt. 1 Mar., Capt. 24 May '61, and transferred to the 4th US Cav. in Aug. He fought at Stones River 31 Dec. '62 and was named Col. 4th Ohio Cav. 23 Feb. '63. Commanding 2, 2, Cav., Cumberland (Mar. '63-20 Aug. '64), he led his troops at Tullahoma, Murfreesboro, Chickamauga, Farmington (Tenn.) 7 Oct. '63, and Lovejoy. He was named B.G. USV 18 Aug. '64 and commanded 2d Div., Cav., Mil. Div. Miss. (16 Nov. '64-2 Apr. '65) on Wilson's raid through Ga. and Ala., ending at Selma (Ala.) on the latter date where he was wounded. He was breveted for Farmington, Knoxville, Lovejoy, Selma (B.G. USA), and war service (Maj. Gen. USV and USA). He was retired as Maj. Gen. in 1867 and as B.G. in 1875.

LONGSTREET, James ("Pete"). C.S.A. gen., and Lee's "Old War Horse." 1821–1904. S.C. Appt.-Ala. USMA 1842 (54/62); Inf. He served in Fla., the Mexican War (1 wound, 2 brevets), in garrison, and on the frontier against the Indians before resigning 1 June '61. Seeking the post of paymaster, which he had held in the old army, he was instead appointed B.G. C.S.A. 17 June '61. At 1st Bull Run he commanded the 4th Brig. Promoted Maj. Gen. 7 Oct. '61, he led a division at Yorktown and Williamsburg. He led the Right Wing at FAIR OAKS AND SEVEN PINES where his mistakes caused the operation to fail. During the Seven Days' Battles he won Lee's confidence and in the reorganization that followed the Peninsular campaign was given command of a wing containing over half of Lee's infantry. (See I CORPS, A.N.V.) He followed Jackson's strategic envelopment of Pope in the 2d Bull Run campaign, and he again deprived his commander of a great victory by not attacking as soon as he fell in on Jackson's flank (29 Aug.), as Lee wanted him to do. He fought well at Antietam and was promoted Lt. Gen. 9 Oct. '62. Shortly thereafter his command was reorganized and designated the I CORPS, A.N.V. At Fredericksburg he again performed with distinction. During the Chancellorsville campaign he was sent (17 Feb. '63) with the divisions of Pickett and Hood to the Suffolk, Va., area. Here, as commander of the Confed. Dept. of NORTH CAROLINA AND SOUTHERN VIRGINIA, he showed little aptitude for independent command.

Rejoining Lee's A.N.V., he was appalled by the audacity of the plan again to invade the North. He favored a strategic offensive in Va., the reinforcement of Bragg in the Chattanooga area, and an offensive under Lee's direction in the West. Failing to see this plan adopted, he felt that the Gettysburg campaign should be a strategic offensive but a tactical defensive; he had the erroneous impression that his chief subscribed to this theory. His delay in attacking on the second day at GETTYSBURG, and his lethargy in organizing "Pickett's Charge" on the third exposed him to the most vindictive criticism by Southerners after the war. D. S. Freeman points out, however, that "Lee never gave any intimation that he considered Longstreet's failure at Gettysburg more than the error of a good soldier" (*Lee's Lts.*, III, 188).

In Sept. '63 he was sent with two of his divisions—McLaws' and Hood's—and Jenkins' brigade of Pickett's division to support Bragg in the West. After CHICKAMAUGA and WAUHATCHIE Longstreet was sent to oppose Burnside in the KNOXVILLE CAMPAIGN. Again he showed ineptitude for independent command: it was not remarkable that he had not been able to serve with Bragg, but dissension within his own corps led to charges being preferred against Mc-Laws, Law, and Robertson, the general nature of which was lack of cooperation.

He led his command back to join Lee for the WILDERNESS campaign. He was seriously wounded on 6 May '64 by his own men, almost precisely a year after Jackson had been mortally wounded under similar circumstances but a few miles away. "A Minié ball [sic] had entered near the throat and had crashed into the right shoulder. Hemorrhage was severe . . ." (ibid., 365). He was out of action until 19 Oct. He was then put in command of the forces at Bermuda Hundred (Pickett's division) and north of the James (Field's and Hoke's divisions). After the war he became president of an insurance company, was a cotton factor in New Orleans, and joined the Republican party. Southern sentiment turned against him with increasing vehemence as it became more evident that Gettysburg had been the turning point of the war, and that he might be considered largely responsible for the Confederate defeat. As a result, he had to depend on political appointments for a living. He was at one time Minister Resident to Turkey. His *From Manassas to Appomattox* (1896) was written late in life and without reference to his earlier articles. "Because of inaccuracies," writes Freeman, "the book is even more unjust to the wartime Longstreet than to any of those he criticized" (ibid., 815).

Freeman in D.A.B. describes him as "slightly below middle height, broad-shouldered and somewhat heavy in his prime. . . . Essentially a combat officer . . . an almost ideal corps commander . . . [he] did not possess the qualities necessary to successful independent command, and his skill in strategy was not great."

LONGSTREET'S CORPS. See I CORPS, Confed., A.N.V.

"LONG TOM." Name given 30-pounder Parrott gun captured at 1st Bull Run by Confederates, and subsequently used as generic term for that type of piece. It was also the name for a famous gun at Cumberland Gap. The Boers had given this nickname to their big guns in 1899, and US troops in World War II so designated the 155-mm. rifle. (Wise, 370n.).

LOOKOUT. Joe Hooker's horse was a chestnut standing nearly 17 hands high with long, slender legs and a fast trot. He was about seven years old at the battle of Chattanooga, where he acquired his name.

LOOKOUT MOUNTAIN, Tenn. Scene of "The Battle Above the Clouds" in CHATTANOOGA CAMPAIGN

LOOMIS, Cyrus O. Union officer. N.Y. Capt. 1st Mich. Arty. 28 May '61; Col. 8 Oct. '62; Bvt. B.G. USV 20 June '65 (war service). Died 1872.

LOOMIS, Gustavus. Union officer. c. 1789–1872. Vt. USMA 1811 * (10/19); Inf. He fought in the War of 1812, served on the frontier, and fought in the Seminole wars and the Mexican War. As Col. 5th US Inf. (since 1851), he mustered in volunteers in Conn. and R.I. and served on boards and commissions until retired 1 June '63. He was breveted B.G. USA for war service.

LORD, Therndon Ellery. Union officer. N.Y. Ensign 3d N.Y. 14 May '61; 1st Lt. 19 Aug. '61; Capt. 21 Mar. '63; Maj. 1 June '65; Bvt. B.G. USV. Brevets for 1864 campaign, 1865 campaign, war service. Died 1886.

LORING, Charles Greeley. Union officer. Mass. Commissioned Capt. Asst.

* There was no class standing prior to 1818, and the cadets are listed in the order in which they were commissioned.

Q.M. USV 3 Feb. '62, he was named
Lt. Col. Asst. I.G. Assigned from 22
July '62 until 10 Aug. '65 when he was
mustered out. He was breveted for
the Wilderness, Spotsylvania, Bethesda
Church, Petersburg campaign, East
Tenn. campaign (B.G. USV 1 Aug.
'64), and war service (Maj. Gen. USV).
He died 1902.

LORING, William Wing. C.S.A. gen.
1818-86. N.C. Appt.-Fla. Fighting in
the Seminole War as a boy, he graduated from Georgetown College and became a lawyer and legislator before
entering the Mexican War. There he
won two brevets and lost his arm at
Chapultepec. Entering the R.A., he
commanded the Dept. of Ore. 1849-51,
served on the frontier in Indian fighting, went on the Utah Expedition, and
spent a year in Europe studying foreign
armies before taking command of the
Dept. of N. Mex. 1860-61. He resigned
13 May '61 in approval of states rights,
although not in favor of secession.
Commissioned B.G. C.S.A. 20 May '61,
he took part in the WEST VIRGINIA
OPERATIONS IN 1861 and 1862. Put
in command of the army in southwestern Va., he was promoted Maj. Gen.
17 Feb. '62. Soon after the LORING-
JACKSON INCIDENT he was sent to the
West. He fought in the Vicksburg campaign, and Pemberton blamed him for
the defeat at Champion's Hill. During the
Atlanta campaign he was a corps commander, and was Hood's second-in-
command at Franklin and Nashville.
He returned to Johnston's army and
surrendered with him in N.C. After the
war he was a New York banker before
going in 1869 to serve the Khedive of
Egypt as B.G. In command of the defenses of Alexandria and the entire
Egyptian coast, he commanded a division in the Abyssinian campaign, was
decorated, and made a pasha before returning to the US in 1879. He wrote

many newspaper and magazine articles
and a book on his war experiences.

LORING-JACKSON INCIDENT.
Jan. '62. After his unsuccessful attempt
in early Jan. '62 to destroy the isolated
force of 5,000 Federals under B. F.
Kelley at Romney, Jackson did take
possession of that place on the 10th.
Desiring to hold the village, which was
astride the line of communications between Rosecrans' scattered forces in
western Va. and Banks's scattered V
Corps along the Potomac, Jackson assigned the mission to Loring's Army of
the Northwest. "But this officer and his
ill-disciplined command were so dissatisfied ... that Loring appealed directly to
the Confederate Secretary of War and
got his command ordered back to Winchester" (Steele, 220).

On 30 Jan. Benjamin sent Jackson
this message: "Our news indicates that
a movement is making to cut off General Loring's command; order him back
immediately" (Henderson, 151, citing
O.R. V, 1053). The next day Jackson
forwarded a letter to Benjamin through
J. E. Johnston that read: "Your order
... has been received and promptly
complied with. With such interference
in my command I cannot expect to be
of much service in the field, and, accordingly, respectfully request to be
ordered to report for duty to the
Superintendent of the Virginia Military
Institute at Lexington.... Should this
application not be granted, I respectfully
request that the President will accept
my resignation from the army."

Jackson was sufficiently astute to
write also to the Gov. of Va. about the
matter. "Governor Letcher took the Secretary of War to task. Mr. Benjamin,
who had probably acted in ignorance
rather than defiance of the military
necessities, at once gave way," writes
Henderson. The incident, says Steele,

"taught the Confederate war department a lesson in military ethics and usage. . . ."

On 9 Feb. Loring was transferred from Jackson's command.

LOST MOUNTAIN. See KENESAW MOUNTAIN.

LOUDOUN RANGERS. A Federal force recruited among the Germans northwest of Leesburg, Va., and mustered in on 20 June '62. These troops were an independent command that pursued Mosby's PARTISAN RANGERS, although they were no more successful than the regular units of the Federal army.

LOUISIANA seceded 26 Jan. '61 and was the scene of considerable fighting, notably NEW ORLEANS, PORT HUDSON and the RED RIVER CAMPAIGNS OF 1863 and 1864. The state was readmitted to the Union on 29 May '65, but military control was not withdrawn finally until Apr. '77.

LOUISIANA, CONFED. ARMY OF. Designation sometimes applied to the La. State troops under the command first of Bragg and later of Col. P. O. Hébert.

LOUISIANA BRIGADE. There were two La. brigades in the A.N.V. The first, officially designated as the 8th Brig. of Dick Ewell's division during Jackson's Valley campaign, was commanded by Dick Taylor. It was composed of I. G. Seymour's 6th La.; H. T. Hay's 7th La.; H. B. Kelly's 8th La.; L. A. Stafford's 9th La.; and Rob Wheat's La. Bn. ("Tigers"). The brigade adopted the nickname of Wheat's battalion, and called themselves the Louisiana Tigers. Hays succeeded Taylor and led this brigade in the II Corps, A.N.V., until wounded at Spotsylvania. The unit generally known as the 2d La. Brig., in the 2d Bull Run campaign, was composed of the 2d, 9th, 10th, and

15th La., and was commanded by L. A. Stafford. The 1st and 14th La. were added later, and Stafford commanded the brigade until killed 5 May. The two brigades were then consolidated into one, and became part of Gordon's division.

LOVE, George Maltby. Union officer. 1831–87. N.Y. 1st Sgt. Co. D and Sgt. Maj. 21st N.Y. 13 May–23 Aug. '61; 1st Lt. 44th N.Y. 23 Aug. '61; Capt. 2 Jan. '62; Maj. 116th N.Y. 5 Sept. '62; Col. 16 July '63; Bvt. B.G. USV 7 Mar. '65; transferred to R.A. Brevets for Plain's Store (La.), Cedar Creek, war service. Medal of Honor 6 Mar. '65 for Cedar Creek 19 Oct. '64. W.I.A. Port Hudson (La.). Commanded 1, 1, XIX; 3, 1, XIX; 1, 1, XIX.

LOVEJOY (Lovejoy's Station), Ga., 2–6 Sept. '64 (ATLANTA CAMPAIGN) Hardee evacuated his position at JONESBORO the night of 1 Sept. and withdrew six miles south to Lovejoy and dug in. He was pursued the next morning by the IV and XXIII Corps. About noon the Federals attacked, pushed back the outposts, and closed in on the almost completed Confederate earthworks. Part of Stanley's IV Corps gained a foothold in Hardee's lines but were then forced to withdraw. The rest of Hood's army was massed at Lovejoy by 4 Sept., having started evacuating Atlanta at 5 P.M. on the 1st (Hood in B.&L.). Skirmishing continued around this place until the 5th, after which Sherman's forces were withdrawn to Atlanta.

LOVEJOY, Ga. 16 Nov. '64. (MARCH TO THE SEA) Part of the 8th Ind. Cav. (Kilpatrick's division) made a dismounted attack that captured the lines held by two brigades and two guns of Wheeler's cavalry. Murray's entire brigade then charged and routed the Confederates. In a pursuit to Beaver Creek Station (about four miles down the track toward Macon) the Federals (Atkins' brigade) captured 50 prisoners and two Rodman guns. Other casualties were not reported.

LOVELL, Charles Swain. Union officer. Mass. Enlisting in the R.A. in 1831, he was commissioned six years later and served on the frontier in Indian fighting and in the Mexican War. He was promoted Maj. 10th US Inf. 14 May '61 and fought in the Peninsular campaign. Commanding a brigade, he fought at Malvern Hill, Gaines's Mill, 2d Bull Run, Antietam, and Fredericksburg. He was promoted Lt. Col. 18th US Inf. Jan. '63 and served on provost marshal duty in Wis. Apr. '63–Aug. '65. Breveted for Gaines's Mill, Malvern Hill, and Antietam (B.G. USA), he retired in 1870 as Col. 14th US Inf. and died in 1871.

LOVELL, Frederick Solon. Union officer. 1814–78. Vt. Lt. Col. 33d Wis. 18 Oct. '62; Col. 46th Wis. 2 Mar. '65; Bvt. B.G. USV 11 Oct. '65 (war service). He was prominent in his state as a lawyer and politician.

LOVELL, Mansfield, C.S.A. gen. 1822–84. Md. USMA 1842 (9/56); Arty. Son of the Surg. Gen., he served in garrison, on frontier, and in the Mexican War (1 brevet, 2 wounds) before resigning in 1849. He was an iron manufacturer and superintendent of street improvements and deputy street commissioner of N.Y.C. Active in the militia, he instructed the City Guard in the use of the Fort Hamilton guns. Johnston had recommended him as a division commander to Davis one month before Lovell resigned his N.Y.C. job in Sept. '61. Named Maj. Gen. 7 Oct. '61, he was unable to prevent the capture of NEW ORLEANS, 25 Apr. '62. At Corinth, Miss., 3–4 Oct., he led a corps and fought the rear-guard action after Coffeeville, Miss., 5 Dec., so skillfully that his opponent Rosecrans praised him in his official report

(D.A.B.). Meanwhile, mounting political pressure resulted in his being relieved of command in Dec. '62 for the loss of New Orleans. (See NEW ORLEANS for Lovell Court of Inquiry.) He had no further command assignments, but served as J. E. Johnston's volunteer staff officer in the summer of 1864. After the war he was a civil engineer, surveyor, and was assistant engineer to John NEWTON on the Hell Gate project.

LOVELL COURT OF INQUIRY. See NEW ORLEANS, 25 Apr. '62.

LOWE, William Warren. Union officer. 1831–98. Ind. Iowa. USMA 1853 (30/52); Dragoons. 1st Lt. Regt. Adj. 2d US Cav. 31 May '58–'61; Capt. 9 May '61; 5th US Cav. 3 Aug. '61; Col. 5th Iowa Cav. 1 Jan. '62; Bvt. B.G. USV and USA. Brevets for Chickamauga, Huntsville (Ala.), war service. Commanded in the Army of the Cumberland: 3, 2, Cav.; 1, 2, Cav.; 1, 3 Cav.; 3d Div., Cav. Corps. Also 2, 6, Cav. Corps, Mil. Div. Miss. Resigned in 1869 and engaged in mining, railroad building, and oil exploration in the West.

LOWELL, Charles Russell. Union gen. 1835–64. Mass. After graduating from Harvard with First Honors, he traveled extensively in Europe and then engaged in railroading and managing an ironworks in Md. He was commissioned Capt. 3d US Cav. 14 May '61 and was on McClellan's staff until Nov. '62, fighting in the Peninsular campaign and at Antietam. On 10 May '63 he was commissioned Col. 2d Mass. Cav. and commanded Indpt. Cav. Brig., XXII, Washington (1 Aug. '63–Feb. '64 and Apr.–July '64). With Sheridan in the Valley, he commanded 3d Brig., Reserve, 1st Div., Cav. Corps (9 Aug.–8 Sept. '64) and Reserve Brig., 1st Div., Cav. Corps (8 Sept.–19 Oct. '64) at Cedar Creek, where he was wounded but refused to leave his command. He received additional wounds and died the next day. He was commissioned B.G. USV to date from the battle (19 Oct. '64). In three years of service he had 12 horses shot from under him. His younger brother, James Jackson Lowell, was killed at Glendale.

LOWREY, Mark Perrin. C.S.A. gen. 1828–85. Tenn. He received little education, living with his widowed mother in the newly-settled part of Miss. Volunteering for the Mexican War, he saw no action, later became a brickmason, and at 24 entered the Baptist ministry. He was commissioned Col. 4th Miss. in the fall of 1861 and the next year raised and organized the 32d Miss. Wounded in the arm at Perryville, he fought at Chickamauga, leading the 45th Miss. in addition to his own regiment. He was appointed B.G. C.S.A. 4 Oct. '63. In the Atlanta campaign he led his brigade in Hardee's corps. At Franklin and Nashville he fought under Cleburne and resigned 14 Mar. '65. Returning to Miss., he started reorganizing and reviving the churches of the state. Eventually this self-taught man founded a women's college and was a member of the board of trustees of the state university. From 1868 to 1877 he was president of the Miss. Baptist Convention.

LOWRY, Robert. C.S.A. gen. 1830–1910. S.C. Appt.-Miss. A merchant and lawyer, he enlisted as private in the Rankin Grays and was elected Maj. 6th Miss. in Aug. '61. Twice wounded at Shiloh, he was promoted Col. in 1862 and fought at Vicksburg. In the Atlanta campaign he commanded both his regiment and Featherston's brigade and took over John Adams' brigade in Hood's invasion of Tenn. He was appointed B.G. C.S.A. 4 Feb. '65 and surrendered with Johnston. After the war he was a legislator and a member of the commission that requested Andrew Johnson's release of Davis. In 1881–89 he was Democratic Gov. of Miss.

LOYALTY OF REGULAR ARMY ENLISTED MEN. Of the approximately 15,000 enlisted men in the R.A. in 1861, only 26 are known to have deserted to the Confederacy at the outbreak of the Civil War.

LOYALTY OF REGULAR ARMY OFFICERS. In 1861 there were 1,080 R.A. officers in active service; 620 were from Union territory and 460 from seceding states. About 25 per cent of all R.A. officers had been appointed from civil life; the remainder, 821, were West Pointers. They divided as follows:

	Stayed in U.S. Army	Resigned to Join C.S.A.
Northerners		
West Point graduates	491	475	16*
From civil life	129	129	none
Southerners		
West Point graduates	330	162	168
From civil life	130	1**	129
TOTALS	1,080	767	313

* All of whom had married into Southern families.
** Gen. Winfield Scott.

(The above facts and figures are from R. Ernest Dupuy, *The Compact History of the United States Army* (Hawthorn: New York, 1956), pages 122–23. There is a similar summary in Upton's *Military Policy*.

LUBBOCK, Francis Richard. C.S.A. Gov. of Tex. 1815–1905. S.C. A merchant, he moved first to New Orleans and then to Tex. in 1836, serving in minor political positions and as Lt. Gov. in 1857. He represented Tex. at the Charleston convention and was elected Gov. in 1861, serving until 1863, when he declined renomination, and entered the Confederate Army as Lt. Col. As Col. and A.D.C. in 1864, he was on Davis's staff and fled Richmond with the president. He returned to Tex. and became a merchant and state treasurer.

LUCAS, Thomas John. Union gen. 1826–? Ind. The son of a Napoleonic veteran who emigrated after Waterloo, he learned his father's trade of watchmaking and enlisted as a drummer boy with the 4th Ind. during the Mexican War. Mustered out in 1848 as 2d Lt. Adj., he returned to horology until the Civil War, when he was named Lt. Col. 16th Ind. 20 May '61. He covered the Union retreat at Balls Bluff and was named Col. 27 May '62 of his re-enlisted regiment. He was wounded three times during the Vicksburg campaign and commanded 1, 4, XIII, Gulf (20 Sept.–7 Oct. '63) and 1st Brig., Cav. Div., Gulf (3 Nov. '63–9 Apr. '64) during the Red River expedition of 1864. Promoted B.G. USV 10 Nov. '64, he commanded Lucas' cavalry division West Fla. (28 Mar.–Apr. '65); Separate Cav. Brig., Dist. W. Fla. (8 Feb.–28 Mar. '65) and 3, 1, Cav., Gulf. After his command was mustered out, he was sent to New Orleans at Sheridan's request to await settlement of the situation in Mexico. Breveted Maj. Gen. USV 26 Mar. '65 for Mobile, and mustered out in 1866. He entered politics and held several appointive offices.

LUDLINGTON, Marshall Independence. Union officer. 1839–? Pa. Capt. Asst. Q.M. Vols. 20 Oct. '62–14 Mar. '67; Maj. Q.M. Assigned 2 Aug.–23 Oct. '64; Col. Q.M. Assigned 23 Oct. '64–1 Jan. '67; transferred to R.A. in 1867; B.G. Q.M. Gen. 1898; Maj. Gen. 1903; Bvt. B.G. USV 13 Mar. '65 (war service).

LUDLOW, Benjamin Chambers. Union officer. 1831–98. Ohio. Capt. 4th Mo. Cav. 23 Sept. '61; Maj. 14 Oct. '62; Lt. Col. 8 July '65; Bvt. B.G. USV 28 Oct. '64 (Dutch Gap and Spring Hill, Va.). Graduated as M.D. from Univ.

of Pa. W.I.A. Feb. '62, while holding line of communications open at Lebanon (Mo.). A.D.C. to Hooker at Chancellorsville; Meade's Inspector of Arty. (1863–64) at Gettysburg, Williamstown, Mine Run, and Rappahannock Station. In Feb. '64 he was Ben Butler's Chief of Cav. in charge of defending work on the Dutch Gap Canal. Brother-in-law of Salmon Chase.

LUDLOW, William Handy. Union officer. N.Y. Enlisting in the 73d N.Y. 27 July '61, he was commissioned 2d Lt. 29 Sept. of that year and named Maj. Add. A.D.C. 18 Nov. As Lt. Col. Asst. I.G. Assigned 20 Aug. '62–4 Apr. '64, he was breveted B.G. USV for war service (Heitman). Phisterer, on the other hand, gives his highest brevet rank as Maj. Gen. USV. He was mustered out in 1866 and died in 1890.

LUNETTE. In artillery, the eye or ring on the end of a gun trail that drops over the pintle of the limber for towing. In fortification, a type of outwork having two faces and an open or partially closed entrance ("gorge").

LYLE, Peter. Union officer. Pa. Col. 19th Pa. 27 Apr. '61; mustered out 29 Aug. '61; Col. 90th Pa. 10 Mar. '62; Bvt. B.G. USV (war service); mustered out 26 Nov. '64. Commanded in the Army of the Potomac: 2, 2, I; 1, 2, I; 1, 2, V; 4, 4, V; 1, 3, V. Died 1879.

LYMAN, Luke. Union officer. c. 1824–89. Mass. Lt. Col. 27th Mass. 20 Sept. '61; Bvt. B.G. USV; resigned 27 May '63. Brevets for Little Washington, N.C., war service. At the outbreak of the war he requested to be assigned as military instructor at Amherst College. Military commander of Little Washington, N.C.

LYMAN, Theodore. Vol. A.D.C. to Meade. 1833–97. Mass. After graduating from Harvard he became a naturalist and served as volunteer aide to Gen. Meade during the war. His letters to his wife, gathered in book form by George R. Agassiz and entitled *Meade's Headquarters,* are a delightful and highly literate source of vignettes and pen portraits of the Union leaders. After the war he was active in the preservation and development of food fish, sat in Congress, and engaged in civil-service reform.

LYNCH, James Canning. Union officer. Conn. 2d Lt. 106th Pa. 17 Aug. '61; 1st Lt. 31 Jan. '62; Capt. 4 Jan. '63; Lt. Col. 183d Pa. 24 June '64; Col. 19 July '64; Bvt. B.G. USV (Deep Bottom, Va.; war service); mustered out 5 Oct. '64. Commanded 1, 1, II (Potomac). Died 1901.

LYNCH, William Francis. Union officer. N.Y. Sgt. Maj. 23d Ill. 18 June '61; discharged 25 Sept. '61; Col. 58th Ill. 25 Jan. '62; Bvt. B.G. USV 31 Jan. '65; mustered out of USV 1865; joined USA 1866; retired 1870 as B.G. Brevets for Pleasant Hill (La.), Yellow Bayou (La.). Commanded 1, 3, Detachment XVI (Gulf). Died 1876.

LYNCHBURG, Va., 17–18 June '64. After his victory at PIEDMONT, 5 June, David Hunter proceeded with his advance on the vital rail center at Lynchburg, Va. On the 6th he was informed by Grant that Sheridan's TREVILIAN RAID was under way, and Grant suggested that Hunter attempt to link up with Sheridan at Charlottesville, either directly or by way of Lynchburg. This same date Lee, learning of Jones's defeat and death, sent Breckinridge with his two brigades to Rockfish Gap, west of Charlottesville, to reinforce Vaughn and to reassume command of the Dept. of Western Va. On 12 June, in response to Breckinridge's call for more strength with which to oppose Hunter, Lee sent Early's corps to the Valley. Early left

Richmond the 13th, marched to Charlottesville, and entrained for Lynchburg.

On 18 June Hunter attacked Lynchburg and was repulsed by the troops of Breckinridge and part of Early's corps, which had arrived about noon. Informed of Early's advance to the Valley, Hunter retreated west via Salem (21 June), Lewisburg (25th), Charleston, W. Va. (30th), and thence by rail and water and rail to Parkersburg and Martinsburg, Va. EARLY'S WASHINGTON RAID then started.

LYON, Hylan Benton. C.S.A. gen. 1836–1907. Ky. USMA 1856 (19/49); Arty. He fought in the Seminole War and served on the frontier in Indian scouting and fighting. Resigning 30 Apr. '61 as a 1st Lt., he was commissioned in the same rank in the C.S.A. Arty. Promoted Capt. of Cobb's battery, on 3 Feb. '62 he was named Lt. Col. 8th Ky. He commanded the regiment at Donelson, was promoted Col. soon after his exchange, and fought at Coffeyville. Appointed B.G. C.S.A. 14 June '64, he led a brigade under Forrest and fought in Tenn. with Hood. After the war he held several public offices.

LYON, Nathaniel. Union officer. 1818–61. Conn. USMA 1841 (11/52); Inf. He served in the Seminole War, on frontier duty, in the Mexican War (1 brevet, 1 wound), in Indian fighting, and in "Bleeding Kansas." The latter experience shaped the political views of the fiery little redhead, and he became a prolific writer, advocating Lincoln and the Republican party.

Serving as a captain of the 2d US Inf. at the St. Louis arsenal in early 1861, he and F. P. BLAIR, Jr. collaborated to safeguard Union property and interests from the sizable disloyal element in the state. Together they worked out and executed the strategy that saved the weapons in the arsenal, and captured the rebel force that was assembling at nearby CAMP JACKSON under Gen. D. M. Frost. Together they also succeeded in eliminating Lyon's pro-Southern superior, Gen. W. S. Harney, from the scene. With Blair's influence, Lyon was appointed B.G. of Mo. Vol. on 12 May '61, and he became B.G. USV five days later. He then undertook military operations in southwest Mo. that ended with his death at WILSON'S CREEK, 10 Aug. '61. He became the North's first military hero. (See also Mary Whitney PHELPS.)

LYON, William Penn. Union officer. 1822–1913. N.Y. Col. 13th Wis. 26 Sept. '62; Bvt. B.G. USV 26 Oct. '65 (war service). Commanded 1, 3, Res. Corps (Cumberland). From a Quaker family, he practiced law before the war and later was Supreme Court Justice and Chief Justice for Wisconsin.

LYTLE, William Haines. Union gen. 1826–63. Ohio. Wanting to enter USMA but acquiescing to his family's insistence that he become a lawyer, he did fight in the Mexican War and then served in the state legislature as a Democrat. Gov. Chase appointed him Maj. Gen. and commander of the 1st Div. Ohio Mil., and 3 May '61 he was named Col. 10th Ohio. He was wounded at Carnifex Ferry 10 Sept. '61 and at Perryville 8 Oct. '62 while commanding 17, 3, I, Army Ohio (Sept.–8 Oct. '62) when he was left on the field as dead and then captured. Named B.G. USV 29 Nov. '62, he also commanded 17th Brig., 3d Div., Army Ohio (2–22 Dec. '61; 21 Mar.–19 Aug. '62; 23 Aug.–29 Sept. '62) and 1, 3, XX, Cumberland (12 Apr.–19 Sept. '63). On the last date he was severely wounded while leading a charge on the second day at Chickamauga and died the next day. A prolific writer, he is best remembered for his poetry, including "Anthony and Cleopatra."

M

MABRY, Hinchie P. C.S.A. officer. Wood and Heitman list him as B.G. C.S.A., the former saying that he was appointed Mar. '62 from Tex. Neither Wright nor C.M.H. lists him as a general officer. He was Col. of the 3d Tex. Cav. and commanded temporarily the Tex. brigade after Vicksburg.

MACARTHUR, Arthur. Union officer. 1845–1912. Mass. Appt.-Wis. Commissioned 1st Lt. Adj. 24th Wis. 4 Aug. '62, he was promoted Maj. 25 Jan. '64 and Lt. Col. 18 May '65. He was breveted for Perryville–Stones River–Missionary Ridge–Dandridge and Atlanta Campaign–Franklin, winning the Medal of Honor in 1890 for Missionary Ridge. Continuing in the R.A., he served in Cuba and the Philippines during the Spanish-American War and was Mil. Gov. of the latter 1900–01. He was appointed Lt. Gen. in 1906. Father of Gen. Douglas MacArthur.

MACAULEY, Daniel. Union officer. N.Y. 1st Lt. Adj. 11th Ind. 25 Apr. '61; mustered out 4 Aug. '61; 1st Lt. Adj. 11th Ind. 31 Aug. '61; Maj. 21 Apr. '62; Lt. Col. 4 Sept. '62; Col. 10 Mar. '63; Bvt. B.G. USV (Cedar Creek, Va.). Commanded 1, 3, XIII; 3, 2, XIX; 2d Sep. Brig., VIII. Died 1894.

MACKALL, William Whann. C.S.A. gen. c. 1816–91. D.C. Appt.-Md. USMA 1837 (8/50); Arty. He had fought in the Seminole War (ambushed and wounded) and in the Mexican War (1 wound, 2 brevets) as well as on the frontier and in the Eastern Div. and Dept. of the Pacific as Asst. Adj. Gen. Resigning 3 July '61 as Lt. Col., Staff, he was commissioned Lt. Col. C.S.A. and became A. S. Johnston's Adj. Gen. Appointed B.G. C.S.A. 6 Mar. '62 to rank from 27 Feb., he was at New Madrid and Island No. 10, taking command when McCown was relieved. After being exchanged, he commanded his brigade in Tenn. and in Dec. '62 took over the Dist. of the Gulf. Succeeded by Buckner in Feb. '63, he took command of the western part of that district and became Bragg's Chief of Staff until relieved by his own request after Chickamauga. In Nov. '63 he was given command of Hébert's brigades in the Dept. of Miss. and E. La. and in Jan. '64 became J. E. Johnston's Chief of Staff, holding this position throughout the Atlanta campaign. He surrendered at Macon 20 Apr. '65 and farmed in Va. until his death.

MACKAY, Andrew Jackson. Union officer. N.Y. Appt.-Tex. Capt. Asst. Q.M. Vols. 7 Oct. '61; Lt. Col. Q.M. Assigned 28 June '63–9 June '65; Col. Q.M. Assigned 9 June–Dec. '65; Bvt. B.G. USV (war service). Died 1901.

MACKENZIE, Ranald Slidell. Union gen. 1840–89. N.Y. Appt.-N.J. USMA 1862 (1/28); Engrs.-Inf.-Cav. As 2d Lt. (17 June '62) he was assistant engineer for the IX Corps at the battles of Kelly's Ford and 2d Bull Run and was wounded at the latter. During the Md. campaign he was in the engineer battalion responsible for bridges. He was engineer for Sumner's Grand Div. at Fredericksburg, Chancellorsville, and Gettysburg and was promoted 1st Lt. 3 Mar. '63 and Capt. 6 Nov. '63. Then he was with an engineer company in the Rapidan campaign, at the Wilderness, Todd's Tavern, Spotsylvania, and the Petersburg siege, where he was wounded. Named Col.

2d Conn. Arty. 10 July '64, he was pulled back to the defenses of Washington. He was given a brigade in the Army of the Shenandoah (2, 1, VI), leading it 3 Nov.–4 Dec. '64 at Opequon, Fishers Hill, and Cedar Creek, where he was again wounded. Appointed B.G. USV 19 Oct. '64, he led the same brigade in the Army of the Potomac (6 Dec. '64–23 Jan. '65 and 6 Feb.–17 Mar. '65) in the Petersburg siege. Grant, in his *Memoirs*, said, "... I regarded Mackenzie as the most promising young officer in the army. Graduating at West Point, as he did, during the second year of the war, he had won his way up to the command of a corps before its close. This he did upon his own merit and without influence" (p. 541). Cullum says that he commanded a cavalry division at Five Forks and Appomattox and was stationed in Richmond until Aug. '65. He was breveted for 2d Bull Run, Chancellorsville, Gettysburg, Petersburg siege, Cedar Creek, and war service (B.G. USA and Maj. Gen. USA 31 Mar. '65). Continuing in the R.A., he became a prominent Indian fighter. In 1873, on direct orders from Sheridan, he led a raid into Mexico to clean out villages where Indian raiders took refuge after plundering in Tex. His force traveled an estimated 160 miles in 32 hours and accomplished its mission. He and George CROOK revenged the Custer massacre, and Mackenzie continued to subdue Indians in Tex., Colo., Ariz., N. Mex., and the Plains. Wounded seven times in the Civil War and Indian fighting, he was thrown on his head from a wagon in 1875 and remained dazed for several months. In 1882 he was appointed B.G. USA. Named commander of the Dept. of Tex. in 1883, he returned to San Antonio. Here he became engaged to a widow with whom he had been in love 14 years earlier. He made plans for retirement in the area, but almost immediately began to show signs of irrationality. He was sent to an asylum in N.Y.C. about a month after taking command in San Antonio, and the following spring (1884) was retired for disability incurred in the line of duty. He went to live with a sister on Staten Island and died five years later at the age of 48.

His father, Alexander Slidell, was the brother of John SLIDELL, and took his mother's maiden name at the request of a maternal uncle. The elder Mackenzie was a veteran naval officer and commander of the *Somers* in 1842, when he hanged Philip Spencer, Acting Midshipman and son of the Sec. of War, for "mutiny" under strange circumstances. His other son, named for him, was a Union naval officer who fought at New Orleans and the bombardment of Charleston. Ranald's aunt married Commodore Matthew C. Perry.

One of America's most remarkable soldiers, Mackenzie is a forgotten hero. Cullum and Appleton's have information on him, but he is not included in D.A.B. (See "Border Warrior" by Edward S. Wallace in *American Heritage,* June, 1958.) See also BROTHER AGAINST BROTHER.

MACLAY, Robert Plunket. C.S.A. gen. c. 1820–1903. Pa. USMA 1840 (32/42); Inf. He fought in the Seminole and Mexican wars (wounded in the latter) and served on the frontier and in Indian scouting before resigning 31 Dec. '60 to be a Louisiana planter. Entering the Confederate Army, he was Maj. of Arty. and assigned by Kirby Smith as B.G. C.S.A. 30 Apr. '64. He is listed by Wright and Cullum as a general officer, but is not included in Wood or C.M.H.

MACON (Ga.) Confederate PRISON. See also LIBBY PRISON.

MACON, Ga., 30 July '64. Action during STONEMAN'S RAID, 26–31 July '64.

MACY, George Nelson. Union officer. Mass. Commissioned 1st Lt. 20th Mass. 8 Aug. '61, he was promoted Capt. 8 Nov. '61 and Maj. 18 Dec. '62. On 1 May '63 he was named Lt. Col. and a year later Col. Mustered out in July '65, he was breveted for the Wilderness and Deep Bottom (B.G. USV 14 Aug. '64) and the Appomattox campaign (Maj. Gen. USV 9 Apr. '65). He died 1875.

MADILL, Henry John. Union officer. Pa. Commissioned Maj. 6th Pa. Res. 27 July '61, he was promoted Col. 141st Pa. 5 Sept. '62. Mustered out May '65, he was breveted for Petersburg (B.G. USV 2 Dec. '64) and war service (Maj. Gen. USV).

MAFFITT, John Newland. C.S.N. Capt. 1819–86. Born at sea. Entering the navy as a midshipman in 1832, he resigned 2 May '61 as Lt. to join the Confederacy, being appointed from N.C. In the early part of 1862 he took a cargo of cotton to England and assumed command there of a steamer *Oreto* which was rechristened the *Florida*. He then succumbed with all his crew to yellow fever and upon recovery ran the blockade into Mobile Bay where the ship was further outfitted with guns and armaments. Rerunning the blockade, he took the steamer out to the Gulf of Mexico and then up to N.Y. and down to the equator and back, capturing Federal and merchant ships all the time for a total of around 55. He took his ship into Brest for repairs and asked to be relieved, as he was exhausted by the fever and the campaign. He saw no more sea duty, and lived after the war in Wilmington.

MAGEE, David Wood. Union officer. Pa. Lt. Col. 86th Ill. 27 Aug. '62; resigned 25 Mar. '64; Col. 47th Ill. 25 Mar. '65; Bvt. B.G. USV (war service).

MAGOFFIN, Beriah. Union gov. of Ky. 1815–85. Ky. After graduating from Centre College and studying law at Transylvania, he practiced in Miss. and returned to Ky., where he entered politics. Sitting in the legislature, he was active in the Democratic party and was elected Gov. in 1859. He was looking for a compromise solution to the slavery question when the president issued his call for troops, and Magoffin answered, in part, that Ky. would "furnish no troops for the wicked purpose of subduing her sister southern states." In May '61 he issued a proclamation of neutrality for the state and in Aug. sent letters to Davis and Lincoln further stating this policy. However, Federal troops were stationed in the state at that time (unofficially), and Leonidas Polk shortly occupied Columbus. A number of Unionist acts were passed over his veto by the legislature, and he resigned in Aug. '62. He later sat in the legislature.

MAGRATH, Andrew Gordon. C.S.A. Gov. of S.C. 1813–93. S.C. Graduating from South Carolina College and Harvard Law School, he was a state legislator and Democratic politician before being named District Judge. He resigned from the bench upon Lincoln's election to become a delegate to the state secession convention and to serve on Gov. Pickens's staff. Returning to the post of Judge under the Confederacy, he was elected Gov. in Dec. '64 and served throughout the war. After the war he returned to his law practice.

MAGRUDER, John Bankhead. ("Prince John"). C.S.A. gen. 1810–71. Va. USMA 1830 (15/42); Inf. After service in garrison, on the frontier, and in the Seminole War, he fought in Mexico (2 brevets). The nickname came from his courtly manner and reputation for lavish entertainment while stationed at Newport. He resigned 20 Apr. '61

as a Capt., was made Col. C.S.A. on 16 May, and won immediate fame with his victory at BIG BETHEL, 10 June. He was appointed B.G. C.S.A. 17 June and Maj. Gen. 7 Oct. '61. At Yorktown and in holding the bulk of McClellan's forces south of the Chickahominy during the battles of Mechanicsville and Gaines's Mill he showed "a certain aptitude for independent command . . . , and with it ability to bluff an adversary" (*Lee's Lts.*, I, xxxiv). In subsequent action during the Seven Days' Battles, however, he was cautious and bumbling. He was then sent to command the Dist. of Tex. on 10 Oct. '62, and his area was later enlarged to include N. Mex. and Ariz. He captured Galveston 1 Jan. '63. In Mar. '64 he sent most of his troops to oppose Banks's Red River campaign. At the end of the war he refused a parole, became a Maj. Gen. under Maximilian in Mexico, and returned to lecture about his war experiences.

MAGRUDER'S ARMY. Informal designation of the Confed. Army of the PENINSULA.

MAHAN, Dennis Hart. USMA Professor. c. 1802–71. N.Y. Appt.-Va. USMA 1824 (1/31); Engrs. He taught at West Point, was sent to France as an observer and student, and then returned to West Point. In 1832 he was appointed "Professor of Military and Civil Engineering, and of the Science of War." Author of *Advanced-Guard, Out-Post* (1847, '53, '63), Mahan had a great influence on the leaders of the Mexican War and the Civil War. Making a fetish of mobility, surprise, and boldness on the battlefield, he preached that "Celerity is the secret of success." He influenced cadets by his instruction at West Point, helped organize V.M.I. (whose summer encampment until 1860 had been called "Camp Mahan"), and his *Out-Post* had been used by volunteer officers both in the North and the South. His son was Alfred Thayer Mahan (*The Influence of Sea Power upon History*).

MAHONE, William ("Little Billy"). C.S.A. gen. 1826–95. Va. Son of a tavernkeeper, he rode the mail as a boy before graduating from V.M.I. He taught at another military academy and by 1861 was president, chief engineer, and superintendent of a railroad. Appointed Va. quartermaster upon secession, he was promoted Lt. Col. and Col. of the 6th Va. in rapid succession, and participated in the capture of the Norfolk Navy Yard. As B.G. C.S.A. 16 Nov. '61, he commanded the Norfolk Dist. until the evacuation in May '62 and then commanded the Drewry's Bluff defenses on the James. During the Peninsular campaign he led his brigade at Seven Pines and Malvern Hill. He was wounded at 2d Bull Run. He also fought at Fredericksburg, Chancellorsville, Gettysburg, the Wilderness, and Spotsylvania before being named Maj. Gen. 30 July '64 in an on-the-spot promotion by Lee for his performance at the Petersburg crater. He took over Anderson's old division. Freeman says promotion transfigured him from an undistinguished brigade commander into the leader of "the most renowned shock troops of the Army. In the last phase of the war, when he boasts the age of 38, he is the most conspicuous division commander" (*Lee's Lts.*, III, xxxviii). His brigade had unusual *esprit de corps* and held enthusiastic postwar reunions. Returning to the railroad as president, he was US Sen. in 1880–82 and controlled the machine-dominated Republican party in Va., breaking the solid Democratic South for a time. D.A.B. described him as "short, spare, and long-bearded, always in a gray slouch hat and peg-top trousers, eyes blue and restless, voice thin and piping."

17TH MAINE

Colonels: Thomas A. Roberts, George W. West (Bvt. B.G.), and Charles P. Mattocks (Bvt. B.G.).

Battles: Fredericksburg, Chancellorsville, Gettysburg, Wapping Heights, Mine Run, Wilderness, Spotsylvania, North Anna, Cold Harbor, Petersburg assault and siege, Jerusalem Road, Boydton Road, Hatcher's Run, Sayler's Creek, Farmville. Present at Auburn, Po River, Totopotomoy, Strawberry Plains, Deep Bottom, and Appomattox.

Recruited from the counties of York, Cumberland, Oxford, and Androscoggin. It reached Washington 23 Aug. '62, where it remained until Oct. It joined the 3d (Berry's) brigade, 1st (Birney's) division, III Corps. At Gettysburg it lost 133 men in the fight for "Sickles' Salient." When the III Corps was disbanded in Mar. '64 the regiment was transferred to the 2d (Hays's) brigade, 3d (Birney's) division, II Corps. With a strength of 507 men, the regiment under Col. West lost 192 men in the battle of the Wilderness. In June it was transferred to the 1st Brig. (De Trobriand's) and took part in the assaults against Petersburg. Even with the transfer of 129 men from the 3d Me. (whose term of service had expired), the 17th Me. could then muster little over 200 effectives. On 4 June '65 it was mustered out. The regiment ranks 22d among Federal regiments sustaining the highest percentage of killed in action.

20TH MAINE

Colonels: Adelbert Ames (USMA; Bvt. Maj. Gen. USA), Joshua L. Chamberlain (Bvt. Maj. Gen. USV), Charles D. Gilmore, Ellis Spear (Bvt. B.G. USV).

Battles: Fredericksburg, Aldie, Gettysburg, Sharpsburg Pike, Rappahannock Station, Wilderness, Spotsylvania, North Anna, Bethesda Church, Petersburg siege, Jerusalem Road, Peeble's Farm,

Boydton Road, Dabney's Mills, Gravelly Run, Five Forks, Appomattox. Also at Antietam, Chancellorsville, Mine Run, Totopotomoy, Weldon R.R., and Hatcher's Run.

Two of the most capable and famous Federal generals of the war, Ames and Chamberlain, went from the 20th Me. to higher command. The regiment distinguished itself in the fight for Little Round Top under Chamberlain. It lost 125 killed and wounded in this action.

1st MAINE HEAVY ARTILLERY Colonels: Daniel Chaplin (Bvt. Maj. Gen.; K.I.A.), Russell B. Shepherd (Bvt. B.G.).

Battles: Fredericksburg Pike, North Anna, Totopotomoy, Petersburg assaults of 16, 17, and 18 June '64, Jerusalem Road, Petersburg siege, Deep Bottom, Weldon R.R., Boydton Road, Hatcher's Run (25 Mar. '65), Sayler's Creek. Present at Cold Harbor, Vaughan Road, Farmville, Appomattox.

This unit has the distinction of sustaining more battle losses than any other of the 2,047 Federal regiments. Only the 2d Wis. had a higher percentage of killed. This is particularly remarkable since these losses were incurred in the last 10 months of the war. At Petersburg, 18 June, the 1st Me. H.A. sustained the greatest losses of any one regiment in any one action of the war: out of 900 who attacked, 632 were killed or wounded. (These are Fox's figures; he notes that the official figure is 580 casualties, and the State Reports put it at 604.) In this action 13 officers were killed and 12 wounded.

The regiment was organized 21 Aug. '62. Most of its men came from the Penobscot Valley. In Dec. it was converted to a heavy artillery unit and remained in the defenses of the capital until May '64. In mustering all possible combatant strength for his final offensive against Lee, Grant converted many cavalry and artillery units, particularly the "heavies," to infantry. This unit joined the Army of the Potomac near Spotsylvania and lost 476 killed and wounded in its first fight, 19 May, on the Fredericksburg Pike. Initially the regiment was in the 3d Brig. (Mott's), 3d Div. (Birney's), II Corps. In the final phase of the war it was in the 1st (De Trobriand's) Brigade of the same division (now commanded by Mott) and the same corps. The regiment had 12 companies (rather than the usual 10) and its total enrollment was 2,202 men.

MAJOR, James Patrick. C.S.A. gen. 1836–77. Mo. USMA 1856 (23/49); Cav. He served on the frontier and did a great deal of Indian fighting before resigning 21 Mar. '61 as 2d Lt. Appointed from Tex., he became Lt. Col. C.S.A. on Van Dorn's staff and aided him in capturing Tex. outposts. At Wilson's Creek he commanded the 1st Cav. Bn. of the Mo. State Guard and was an engineer during the building of the defenses of Vicksburg in 1862. As Col. he led the Tex. cavalry brigade under Taylor and was appointed B.G. C.S.A. 21 July '63. He fought during the Red River campaign of 1864 at Mansfield and Pleasant Hill, playing a major role in the actions around ALEXANDRIA, 1–8 May. At the end of the war he was in command of a brigade under Wharton in western La. After the war he was a planter in La. and Tex.

MALLISON, Francis A. See Joseph HOWARD, Jr.

MALLORY, Stephen Russell. C.S.A. Sec. of the Navy. 1813–73. West Indies. Appt.-Fla. Born in Trinidad, he grew up in Fla. and became inspector of customs at Key West at 19 years of age. After studying law, he was a judge, fought in the Seminole War, and served in the US Senate until resigning in 1861. He was named Sec. of the Navy from 21

Feb. '61 until the dissolution of the government, and after the war practiced law in Pensacola.

MALLOY, Adam Gale. Union officer. Ireland. Capt. 6th Wis. 16 July '61; mustered out 2 Feb. '62; Lt. Col. 17th Wis. 3 Mar. '62; Col. 1 Dec. '62; Bvt. B.G. USV. Brevets for Vicksburg, Kenesaw Mountain, Atlanta, Nashville, war service. Transferred to R.A. and discharged at own request as 1st Lt. in 1870. The 17th Wis. was almost entirely Irish and carried the Irish colors as well as those of their state. William DeLoss Love in *Wisconsin in the War of the Rebellion* says that in the regiment's bayonet charge at Corinth Malloy led his men "with the impetuous and daring gallantry characteristic of [his] race." While commanding a detachment of the XVII Corps guarding the railroads in Ga., Tenn., and Ala., he led them back to Nashville to meet Hood in battle. Commanded 2, 1, XVII; 3, 3, XVII; 1st Brig., 2d Dist. Beaufort (N.C.).

MALTBY, Jasper Adalmorn. Union gen. 1826–68. Ohio. He was a private in the Mexican War and wounded at Chapultepec. Lt. Col. 45th Ill. 26 Dec. '61; Col. 5 Mar. '63; B.G. USV 4 Aug. '63. He was wounded at Fort Donelson and Vicksburg. He commanded 3, 3, XVII (Tenn.) 8 Sept. '63–1 May '64; 3d Div., XVII (Tenn.) 6 Mar.–6 Apr. '64; Maltby's brigade, Vicksburg Dist. Dept. of the Tenn., Jan. '64–Sept. '65. He was mustered out 15 Jan. '66. On 8 Sept. '67 he was appointed mayor of Vicksburg by the military governor and served in that position until his death the following March.

MALVERN HILL, Va., 1 July '62. Last of the Seven Days' Battles of the PENINSULAR CAMPAIGN. After failing at WHITE OAK SWAMP to hit McClellan's retreating army with a coordinated attack, Lee made his final attempt, and failed again at Malvern Hill. The latter was a strong natural position to which Porter's V Corps had withdrawn and which he had been organizing for defense since 9 o'clock on the morning of the 30th. Gen. Hunt, the Federal artillery commander, had time to post some 250 guns to cover enemy approaches to the position. Although both commanders throughout the Peninsular campaign had operated without adequate maps or knowledge of the terrain, Lee had been warned by Rev. L. W. Allen, a member of D. H. Hill's staff who was familiar with the region, that Malvern Hill could be made almost impregnable if McClellan chose to defend it. Lee nevertheless determined to attack it, apparently overestimating the damage the Army of the Potomac had suffered in its change of base (Ropes).

Stonewall Jackson was to continue on his line of advance from the north and to approach Malvern Hill along the Quaker or Willis Church Road. (His command included his own division as well as those of Whiting, Ewell, and D. H. Hill.) Magruder, whose division was somewhat behind Jackson's, was to advance along this same road and form on Jackson's right (west) for the main assault. Huger would receive orders on arrival. Longstreet and A. P. Hill, who had done most of the fighting at WHITE OAK SWAMP, were to be in reserve. Lee planned to mass his artillery to support the Confederate attack.

Jackson's column reached Western Run, a formidable swamp barrier, and halted to reconnoiter the strong enemy defenses covering this approach. Magruder was misinformed by local guides and took the Long Bridge Road southwest and marched away from the battlefield to an obscure country lane his guides assured him was "Quaker Road."

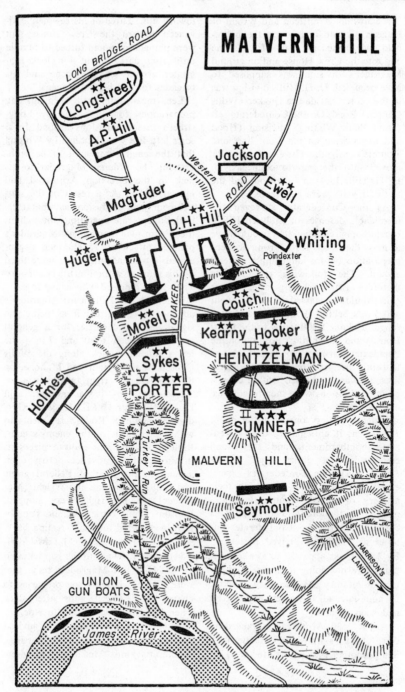

MALVERN HILL

LONG BRIDGE ROAD

Longstreet

A.P. Hill

Jackson

Western

Ewell

ROAD

Magruder

D.H. Hill

Whiting

Huger

Poindexter

Run

Couch

Morell

QUAKER

Kearny   Hooker

III ★★★

HEINTZELMAN

Sykes

V ★★★

PORTER

Holmes

II ★★★

SUMNER

Turkey Run

MALVERN   HILL

Seymour

UNION
GUN BOATS

HARRISON'S

LANDING

James   River

Meanwhile, Armistead and Wright of Huger's division arrived on the battlefield and formed the right of Lee's line opposite the Crew House and on ground Magruder's division was supposed to have occupied. D. H. Hill's division was in the center astride the Quaker (Willis Church) Road. On the Confederate left (east) flank Whiting's division (Hood and Law) were on the front line, and Trimble's brigade (Ewell) was later moved into the gap to connect with D. H. Hill. Jackson's division and the rest of Ewell's were in reserve.

As the Confederates surveyed the formidable defenses of Malvern Hill it became apparent that they would have to mass their guns for a strong artillery preparation before launching a general assault. The following orders were therefore issued shortly after noon: guns would be massed on a hill about 400 yards behind Armistead (and at a range of about 1,200 yards to the Crew House) and in Whiting's position on the Poindexter Farm; when Armistead saw that this fire had broken the Federal lines, he was to advance "with a cheer"; all other divisions were then to advance on this signal.

Federal artillery opened up at about 1 P.M. "as if anticipating the Confederate bombardment, and they soon commanded the entire front" (*Lee's Lts.*, I, 596). The Confederates experienced much difficulty in getting their artillery organized. Completely dominating the situation, the Federal gunners concentrated on the Confederate batteries as the latter arrived piecemeal. By 2:30 it was apparent to Lee that his guns were not going to succeed in giving his infantry the necessary support; an hour later all but a few of his guns had been silenced.

About 3:30 Armistead advanced to drive back skirmishers of Berdan's Sharpshooters who had started working

toward him. Three of his regiments advanced toward the Crew House, but were pinned down and forced to remain until after dark. About 4 o'clock Magruder arrived on the scene and his brigades formed behind Huger's.

Lee, meanwhile, had been making preparations for an attack by Longstreet's reserve divisions around Jackson's left. But when notified by Whiting that the enemy appeared to be withdrawing, he ordered Magruder to attack in the direction Armistead had moved earlier. As a result of the staff and command confusion that characterized Confederate operations throughout the Peninsular campaign, Magruder's planned attack of 15,000 men degenerated into an advance by a mere third of this number without artillery support. They were repulsed with heavy loss.

When D. H. Hill heard Magruder's advance he construed it as being the signal prescribed earlier for a general assault. Between 6:30 and 7 P.M. he led a suicidal attack along the Willis Church Road. Wright and Mahone, on the Confederate right, also advanced. "It was not war—it was murder," said D. H. Hill later (B.&L., II, 394). Gordon led some of Rodes's regiments to within 200 yards of the enemy's guns. Ripley's brigade was shot to pieces as it attempted to advance across open ground in the face of Federal grape and canister. Mahone and Wright (Magruder) on the right were stopped. Ransom, Cobb, Barksdale, and Toombs were committed and sent reeling back. Semmes and Kershaw (McLaws' division) were thrown into the gap between D. H. Hill and Magruder; they, too, were stopped. Trimble was preparing to charge the Federal guns after dark when Jackson ordered him to stop.

Although Porter and Hunt advised holding the position and, possibly, counterattacking, McClellan withdrew that night to his new base at Harrison's Landing and entrenched. His losses had been 3,214, while Lee's had been 5,355 (Fox). In estimating the number of troops engaged, Livermore combines the battles of 29 June–1 July and puts the opposing strengths at 83,345 Federals and 86,784 Confederates.

MALVERN HILL, Va., 27–29 July '64. DEEP BOTTOM RUN, same dates.

MANASSAS. The battles along Bull Run, Va., in July '61 and Aug. '62 are given different names in Federal and Confederate accounts. The action of 18 July '61 that the Federals called "The Affair at Blackburn's Ford" was known to the Confederates as the "First Battle of Bull Run." The major engagement of 21 July '61 that the Federals ultimately designated the "First Battle of Bull Run" was usually referred to by the Confederates as "First Manassas." Pope's defeat of 29–30 Aug. '62 was known to the Federals variously as "Manassas" and "2d Bull Run." It was generally called "Second Manassas" by the Confederates.

MANDERSON, Charles Frederick. Union officer. 1837–1911. Pa. Capt. 19th Ohio 30 May '61; mustered out 31 Aug. '61; Capt. 19th Ohio 26 Sept. '61; Maj. 7 Apr. '62; Lt. Col. 28 Feb. '63; Col. 14 Apr. '63; Bvt. B.G. USV (war service); resigned 17 Mar. '65. Commanded a demi-brigade (19th Ohio and 2 other regiments) in the Atlanta campaign. W.I.A. Lovejoy (Ga.) 2 Sept. '64. US Sen. from Nebr. for 2 terms in 1883 and Pres. Pro Tem of the Senate in 1891. Pres. of the American Bar Association, he was a known orator and after-dinner speaker. He wrote *The Twin Seven-Shooters* (1902), a romance of Civil War times.

MANEY, George Earl. C.S.A. gen. 1826–1901. Tenn. After graduating from the Univ. of Nashville, he fought in the Mexican War and was in the R.A. 1847–48. Becoming a lawyer, he was commissioned Capt. 11th Tenn. and then Col. 1st Tenn. in May '61. He led his regiment at Cheat River, Bath and Romney, and Shiloh, succeeding to command of the 2d Brig. at Shiloh. Appointed B.G. C.S.A. 16 Apr. '62, he commanded his brigade at Perryville, Stones River, Chickamauga, Chattanooga (wounded), and in the Atlanta campaign. He then took over a division and fought in the Carolinas. After the war he was a railroad president, legislator, Minister Resident to Colombia 1881, to Bolivia in 1882, to Paraguay and Uruguay 1889–90, later having the title Envoy Extraordinary and Minister Plenipotentiary in Uruguay.

MANIGAULT, Arthur Middleton. C.S.A. gen. 1824–86. S.C. A Charleston exporter, he was active in the militia, fought in the Mexican War, and owned a rice plantation. He was commissioned Capt. of the North Santee Mtd. Rifles in Dec. '60 and early in Apr. '61 became A.D.C. to Beauregard at Sumter. Being appointed Lt. Col. Adj. and I.G. on Beauregard's staff, he was named Col. 10th S.C. 31 May '61 and commanded the 1st Mil. Dist. of S.C. before being sent to Corinth. He led Polk's 4th Brig. at Stones River and was appointed B.G. C.S.A. 26 Apr. '63. At Chickamauga, Chattanooga, and the Atlanta campaign he led his brigade under Hindman and was slightly wounded at Resaca. Upon recovery he fought in all the battles of the Army of Tenn. until Nashville, when he received a severe head wound. After the war he was a planter and public officeholder. (See also CHATTANOOGA for quote.)

MANK, William G. Union officer. Germany. 1st Lt. 32d Ind. 24 Aug. '61; Capt. 18 May '62; Maj. 26 Nov. '63; mustered out 7 Sept. '64; Lt. Col. 8th US Vet. Vol. Inf. 27 Mar. '65; Bvt.

B.G. USV 8 Dec. '65 (war service). Died 1887.

MANN, Orrin L. Union officer. Ohio. Maj. 39th Ill. 11 Oct. '61; Lt. Col. 1 Dec. '61; Bvt. B.G. USV (Richmond).

MANNING, Stephen Hart. Union officer. Me. Q.M. Sgt. 1st Me. 29 Apr.– 5 Aug. '61; 1st Lt. Regt. Q.M. 5th Me. 3 Sept. '61–24 Jan. '63; Capt. Asst. Q.M. Vols. 26 Nov. '62; Lt. Col. Q.M. Assigned 26 May–1 Aug. '65; Col. Q.M. Assigned 9 Nov. '65–5 Oct. '66; Bvt. B.G. USV. Brevets for Richmond, Shenandoah Valley, war service, Q.M. Dept. service.

MANSFIELD, John. Union officer. c. 1821–96. N.Y. Capt. 2d Wis. 11 June '61; Maj. 26 Jan. '63; Lt. Col. 1 Sept. '63; resigned 26 Aug. '64; Col. Vet. Res. Corps 3 Dec. '64; Bvt. B.G. USV (war service). W.I.A. Wilderness by Minié ball through the thigh.

MANSFIELD, Joseph King Fenno. Union gen. 1803–62. Conn. USMA 1822 (2/40); Engrs. After superintending coastal defenses in the southern coastal states he was Taylor's Chief Engr. in Mexico (3 brevets, 1 wound). He was named Col. and I.G. in 1853 by Jefferson Davis, then Sec. of War. In the Civil War he commanded the Dept. of Washington 28 Apr. '61–15 Mar. '62, having been breveted B.G. USA 6 May '61 and promoted to that full rank eight days later. He was appointed Maj. Gen. USV 18 July '62. Then in a command under Gen. Wool at Fort Monroe he next led the division at Suffolk, VII, Va. (22 July–8 Sept. '62) and the XII Corps, Potomac (12–17 Sept. '62). On the latter date he was mortally wounded at Antietam, leading his men in a charge, and died the same day. Nephew of Jared Mansfield, West Point mathematics professor and US Army Surveyor-Gen.

MANSFIELD, La. Confederate name for SABINE CROSS ROADS, 8 Apr. '64.

MANSON, Mahlon Dickerson. Union gen. 1820–95. Ohio. He had been an officer in the Mexican War and later was in state politics. Capt. 10th Ind. 17 Apr. '61; Maj. 25 Apr. '61; Col. 10 May '61; resigned 21 Dec. '64. At Rich Mountain (W. Va.) he commanded his regiment 11 July '61 and was mustered out 6 Aug. '61. He was named Col. 10th Ind. 18 Sept. '61. From Nov. to Dec. '61 he led the 2d Brig., Army of the Ohio, and commanded 2, 1, Army of the Ohio 2 Dec. '61–22 Mar. '62, fighting at Mill Springs (Ky.) in January. He was promoted B.G. USV 24 Mar. '62 and commanded the 22d Brig., 4th Div., Army of the Ohio, from 30 May until 16 Aug. '62 when he was wounded and captured at Richmond (Ky.). After his exchange, he was given the 1st Brig., Army of Ky., Dept. of the Ohio, 7 Oct. '62–8 June '63. During Morgan's raid in Indiana and Ohio he commanded 1, 3, XXIII (24 June–6 Aug. '63) and then led the 2d Div., XXIII Corps, 6–21 Aug. He next commanded the XXIII Corps, 24 Sept.–20 Dec. and on 24 Dec. took over the 2d Div. of that corps and led them until 26 Jan. '64. He commanded 2, 3, XXIII from 7 Apr. until 14 May '64 when he was wounded at the battle of Resaca (Ga.). After the war he held several public offices, including Democratic congressman.

MANSURA, La., 16 May '64. Skirmish of RED RIVER CAMPAIGN.

MARAIS DES CYGNES, Kans., 25 Oct. '64. About 60 miles south of WESTPORT, Mo., the Confederates retreating from PRICE'S RAID IN MISSOURI turned to fight a delaying action that cost them 1,000 prisoners, including Marmaduke (wounded) and Cabell, and 10 guns. The actions at the Little Osage River, Mine Creek, and Marmiton (or Charlot), which took place the same day between the same forces, are usually considered part of the engagement of Marais des Cygnes ("swan swamp").

MARCH TO THE SEA (Savannah campaign). 15 Nov.–21 Dec. '64. By 1 Nov. Sherman had repaired the railroad between Atlanta and Chattanooga, had reinforced Thomas in Tenn. with the IV and XXIII Corps and all the cavalry except Kilpatrick's division, and had assembled supplies in Atlanta for his proposed advance on Savannah. On the 11th Corse's division (4, XV) destroyed its fortifications and the factories and bridges at Rome, Ga., and started for Atlanta. The next day Thomas wired assurance that Sherman need not worry about the threat of Hood's army to his rear.

On 15 Nov. Sherman destroyed the military resources of Atlanta and started with 20 days' rations for Savannah. His well-equipped force of 55,000 infantry, 5,000 cavalry, and 2,000 artillerymen (64 guns) was organized into two wings. The Right Wing (Army of the Tenn.) was under O. O. Howard, and consisted of Osterhaus's XV Corps (divisions of C. R. Woods, W. B. Hazen, J. E. Smith, and J. M. Corse); and F. P. Blair's XVII Corps (1st Div. of J. A. Mower, 3d Div. of M. D. Leggett, and 4th Div. of G. A. Smith). The Left Wing ("Army of Georgia") under Slocum was composed of J. C. Davis' XIV Corps (W. P. Carlin, J. D. Morgan, and Absalom Baird); and A. S. Williams' XX Corps (N. J. Jackson, J. W. Geary and W. T. Ward). The cavalry, which did most of the limited fighting of the campaign, was composed of two brigades, under E. H. Murray and S. D. Atkins, in Kilpatrick's 3d Cav. Div.; and two unattached regiments: the 1st Ala. Cav. (which served with the Left Wing) and the 9th Ill. Mtd. Inf.

Concentrated around Lovejoy were about 13,000 Confederate troops, the only field forces available to stop Sherman's advance. These consisted of G. W. Smith's Georgia militia and state troops (3,050) and Wheeler's cavalry corps. The latter force had been reinforced by one of W. H. Jackson's brigades, and its strength has been estimated at 10,000. In his official report of the campaign, however, Wheeler says: "My force never exceeded 3,500 men, and was so distributed in front, rear, and on both flanks that I seldom had more than 2,000 under my immediate command, . . ." (O.R., I, XLIV, 411). Troops of Hardee's Dept. of S.C., Ga., and East Fla., and such units as could be spared from the Dept. of N.C. were ordered sent to oppose Sherman's advance. At one time Beauregard, Bragg, Dick Taylor, and McLaws were all in Ga. with G. W. Smith and Hardee, but they brought no troops. In actuality, then, the Federal advance was opposed only by 13,000 troops.

Sherman's two wings marched from Atlanta in such directions as to deceive the Confederates as to the true destination of the main body. Kilpatrick's cavalry led Howard's wing down the Macon railroad toward Lovejoy. Smith and Wheeler withdrew toward Macon, and Kilpatrick's dismounted troopers defeated two cavalry brigades that remained to fight a rear-guard action at LOVEJOY, 16 Nov. While Kilpatrick continued to demonstrate along the Macon railroad nearly to Forsyth, Howard turned southeast at Jonesboro and marched to the rail junction at Gordon, south of Milledgeville.

Slocum on the other wing (which Sherman accompanied) had moved 70 miles along the railroad toward Augusta, destroying track and threatening an attack on the latter place. Beyond Madison, where Sherman's wings reached their point of farthest divergence—50 miles airline—Slocum destroyed the bridge across the Oconee, but then turned south along the right bank of that river. At Milledgeville on 23 Nov. the two wings joined, having deceived the Confederates as to whether their true objective was Macon, Augusta, or Savannah. On the 17th the Richmond authorities had sent Hardee orders to assume over-all command in the area (O.R., I, XLIV, 864). On the 21st he had reached Macon from Savannah and had realized, from the dispersion of the two Federal wings, that the enemy's objective was not Macon but Augusta or Savannah (Cox, 28). He therefore ordered Smith to move rapidly eastward to block this advance, and directed Wheeler to continue to harass the enemy's flank and rear. He himself returned to Savannah to strengthen its defenses and to be in communication with Augusta, Charleston, and Richmond (ibid.).

At GRISWOLDVILLE, 22 Nov. (10 miles east of Macon) the Ga. militia, in compliance with Hardee's orders, vigorously but futilely tried to stop Howard's right wing. Another skirmish took place at Clinton. Kilpatrick, meanwhile, after demonstrating toward Forsyth, had crossed the Ocmulgee with the infantry and then raided almost to Macon on the 20th. Wheeler's cavalry now moved to get in front of the Federal advance. He supported the infantry in rear-guard actions at BALL'S FERRY, 24–25 Nov., and at SANDERSVILLE (Buffalo Creek), 26 Nov. Kilpatrick was then shifted also to the east flank, and there followed a series of cavalry engagements that are covered under the general heading of WAYNESBORO, 27–29 Nov. These resulted in considerable success for Wheeler. Kilpatrick got permission to deliver a return blow, and after resting his men a day or two he marched with the support of Baird's infantry division (3, XIV) from Louisville toward Waynesboro. Wheeler was then pressed hard in a

series of skirmishes at Millen Grove, 1 Dec.; Rocky Creek Church, 2 Dec.; Thomas' Station, 3 Dec.; Waynesboro and Brier Creek, 4 Dec.; and Ebenezer Creek (Cypress Swamp), 7 Dec.

Meanwhile, a force sent by J. G. Foster (C.G. Dept. of South) to assist Sherman's advance by securing a foothold on the Charleston R.R. was forced to withdraw after being defeated at HONEY HILL (Grahamville), S.C., 30 Nov.

As Sherman's forces made their virtually unopposed advance on Savannah they destroyed the railroads and within a band 50 to 60 miles wide they methodically confiscated or destroyed all resources and property that might be of any military value to the Confederates. It is still difficult to discuss unemotionally the morality of Sherman's devastation in Ga., and later in the Carolinas. However, it is appropriate to attempt here to summarize the two conflicting arguments.

In what might be considered representative of the Northern viewpoint, J. D. Cox says this:

"The subsistence of the army upon the country was a necessary part of Sherman's plan, . . . Each regiment organized a foraging party of about one-twentieth of its numbers under command of an officer. These parties set out first of all, in the morning, those of the same brigades and divisions working in concert, keeping near enough together to be a mutual support if attacked by the enemy, and aiming to rejoin the column at the halting place appointed for the end of the day's march. . . .

"The orders given these parties forbade their entering occupied private houses, or meddling with private property of the kinds not included in supplies and munitions of war, and in the best-disciplined divisions these orders were enforced; discipline in armies, however, is apt to be uneven, and among sixty thousand men there are men enough who are willing to become robbers, and officers enough who are willing to wink at irregularities or to share the loot, to make such a march a terrible scourge to any country. A bad eminence in this respect was generally accorded to Kilpatrick, whose notorious immoralities and rapacity set so demoralizing an example to his troops that the best disciplinarians among his subordinates could only mitigate its influence. . . .

"Then, the confirmed and habitual stragglers soon became numerous enough to be a nuisance upon the line of march. . . . It was to these that the name 'bummer' was properly applied. This class was as numerous in the Confederate as in the National Army, in proportion to its strength, and the Southern people cried out for the most summary execution of military justice against them. . . . Their leading newspapers demanded the cashiering and shooting of colonels and other officers, and declared their conduct worse than the enemy's. It is perhaps vain to hope that a great war can ever be conducted without abuses of this kind, and we may congratulate ourselves that the wrongs done were almost without exception to the property, and that murders, rapes and other heinous personal offenses were nearly unknown" (J. D. Cox, *The March to the Sea—Franklin and Nashville* 38–41).

From the Southern viewpoint the "military necessity" of Sherman's policy and the "abuses" of some of his troops are more difficult to accept. Several selections in Commager's *The Blue and the Gray* recount Sherman's passage in the words of Southern victims. Dolly Lunt, a Me. girl who was managing her planta-tion as a widow, speaks of Federal soldiers who confiscated the Sunday clothes of her Negroes on the pretext that these actually belonged to the white folks. She speaks of their "forcing my boys [slaves] from home at the point of the bayonet" (Commager, II, 955ff, quoting Lunt, *A Woman's Wartime Journal*).

Inability of Federal commanders to control their troops may be inferred from the following order issued by O. O. Howard on 22 Nov.:

"It having come to the knowledge of the major-general commanding that the crime of arson and robbery have become frequent throughout the army, notwithstanding positive orders both from these and superior headquarters have been repeatedly issued, and with a view to the prompt punishment of offenses of this kind, it is hereby ordered: That hereafter any officer or man . . . discovered in pillaging a house or burning a building without proper authority, will, upon sufficient proof thereof, be shot" (O.R., I, LXIV, 521).

The British historian and professional soldier, J. F. C. Fuller, in his *Decisive Battles of the U.S.A.* (p. 306), roundly damns Sherman not only for inability to control his troops but also for prescribing policies that fostered "brigandage." "Terror was the basic factor in Sherman's policy; he openly says so," writes Fuller. He then quotes Sherman as follows: "Until we can repopulate Georgia, it is useless to occupy it; but the utter destruction of its roads, houses and people will cripple their military resources. . . . I can make the march, and make Georgia howl" (O.R., I, LXXIX, 162). To Hardee in Savannah: "Should I be forced to assault . . . I shall then feel justified in resorting to the harshest measures, and shall make little effort to restrain my army" (O.R., I, XCII, 737). Elsewhere he wrote: ". . . we can punish

South Carolina as she deserves ... I do sincerely believe that the whole United States, North and South, would rejoice to have this army turned loose on South Carolina to devastate that State, in the manner we have done in Georgia . . ." (*ibid.*, 743). "The truth is the whole army is burning with an insatiable desire to wreck vengeance upon South Carolina. I almost tremble for her fate..." (*ibid.*, 799).

Fuller also gives the following famous quote from Hitchcock: "At one place I am told they killed five or six full grown dogs and as many more pups, and to the woman interceding for the latter as harmless they replied that the pups would soon be dogs if not killed."

By 10 Dec. Sherman had reached Savannah. On the 13th Hazen's division (2, XV) took FORT MCALLISTER, thereby establishing contact with Dahlgren's fleet and, through him, with Foster at Port Royal. This re-established Sherman's line of communications. Since Savannah refused to surrender immediately, and since an assault did not seem advisable, Sherman sent to Port Royal for siege guns. Hardee evacuated the town on 21 Dec. and withdrew across the Savannah River.

In his March to the Sea (Savannah campaign) Sherman had successfully violated military convention by operating deep in a hostile territory without a line of communications. This was the operation he had advised Grant against in the Vicksburg campaign, and an operation both he and Grant had seen Winfield Scott perform successfully in the Mexican War. Sherman has been criticized for his calculated risk in leaving Thomas to cope with Hood's invasion of Tenn. (FRANKLIN AND NASHVILLE CAMPAIGN). However, the results vindicated Sherman's strategy. With fewer than 2,200 casualties he destroyed a large portion of the South's remaining

war potential in Georgia, and he put his armies in position to cooperate effectively with Grant's forces in Va. To achieve the latter purpose, he undertook his CAROLINAS CAMPAIGN.

MARCY, Randolph Barnes. Union gen. 1812–87. Mass. USMA 1832 (29/45); Inf. Serving on frontier duty and exploration, in the Mexican and Seminole wars and on the Utah Expedition, he was Col. I.G. 9 Aug. '61 for McClellan, his son-in-law. Appointed B.G. USV 23 Sept. '61, he was assigned inspection duties in the Depts. of the Northwest, Mo., Ark., Miss., and Gulf. His appointment expired 17 July '62, and he was reappointed 13 Sept. '62, only to have that one expire 4 Mar. '63. Breveted B.G. USA and Maj. Gen. USV for war service, he continued in the R.A., retiring in 1881 as B.G. Insp. Gen. Among his writings were *Prairie Traveler* (1859), a semi-official guidebook sponsored by the army; *Thirty Years of Army Life on the Border* (1860); and *Border Reminiscences* (1871).

MARIETTA, Ga. See KENESAW MOUNTAIN.

MARKHAM. See BARBEE'S CROSS ROADS, 5 Nov. '62.

MARKOE, John. Union officer. Pa. Pvt. Co. A 17th Pa. 18 Apr. '61; discharged 17 May '61; 2d Lt. 71st Pa. 21 May '61; 1st Lt. 23 June '61; Capt. 19 July '61; Capt. Add. A.D.C. 23 May '62; Lt. Col. 71st Pa. 4 Oct. '62; Bvt. B.G. USV; resigned 27 Feb. '63. Brevets for Fair Oaks, Fredericksburg.

MARKS'S MILL, Ark. 25 Apr. '64. (ARKANSAS CAMPAIGN) Fagan's cavalry brigade attacked a Federal wagon train that was escorted by McLean's infantry brigade and some cavalry. In a three-hour fight the Federal force was overwhelmed and 211 wagons captured.

Losses were 450 Federals (100 killed, 250 wounded, 100 captured) and 293 Confederates (41, 108, 144) (Fox, pp. 546 and 551). McLean was wounded.

MARKSVILLE (or AVOYELLES) PRAIRIE, La., 15 May '64. Skirmish near end of RED RIVER CAMPAIGN.

MARMADUKE, John Sappington. C.S.A. gen. 1833–87. Mo. USMA 1857 (30/38); Inf. He had attended Yale and Harvard before going to West Point. Upon graduation he went on the Utah Expedition, and was on the frontier when the secession crisis came. His father, former Gov. of Mo., favored remaining in the Union but counseled his son to go his own way. Marmaduke resigned 17 Apr. '61 as 2d Lt. Commissioned Col. in the State Militia, he fought at Boonville 17 June '61 and was named 1st Lt. C.S.A. He served in Ark. and was promoted Col. 3d Mo., leading his regiment at Shiloh. Appointed B.G. C.S.A. 15 Nov. '62, he returned to Ark. and also fought in raids and skirmishes in Mo. He was promoted Maj. Gen. in Sept. '63 (Eliot) or Mar. '64 (D.A.B.) or 17 Mar. '65 (Wright). In Price's raid in Mo. (1864), he commanded the cavalry and had two horses shot from under him at the Little Blue. Captured at Marais des Cygnes, he was held prisoner until the summer of 1865. He then went into the commission and insurance business in St. Louis. In 1884 he was elected Democratic Gov. of Mo. "Marmaduke looked the beau ideal his name connoted. A handsome six-footer with small hands and feet, he sat his horse with consummate grace. . . . Unmarried, he was the 'catch' of the river towns. A peculiar squint in his eyes was due to nearsightedness" (Monaghan).

MARPLE, William Warren. Union officer. Pa. Capt. 104th Pa. 12 Sept. '61; Lt. Col. 34th US Col. Inf. 3 July '63; Col. 26 Jan. '65; Bvt. B.G. USV (war service).

MARSHALL, Elisha G. Union officer. c. 1828–83. N.Y. USMA 1850 (25/44); Inf. He served on the frontier and in the Utah Expedition and was promoted Capt. 6th US Inf. 14 May '61. Until early 1862 he worked with the N.Y. volunteer troops and was named Col. 13th N.Y. 20 Apr., leading them at Yorktown, Mechanicsville, Gaines's Mill, Malvern Hill, Antietam, and Fredericksburg where he was severely wounded. On sick leave until 23 May '63, he returned to N.Y. and worked with the volunteers for a year before being commissioned Col. 14th N.Y. Hv. Arty. (4 Jan. '64). Leading them in the Wilderness, Spotsylvania, North Anna, Totopotomoy, and Cold Harbor, he was severely wounded in the Petersburg assaults. He fought in the mine assault and was captured at the crater, being held by the Confederates for the rest of the war. Breveted for Gaines's Mill, Fredericksburg, Petersburg mine, and war service (B.G. USV and B.G. USA), he was retired from the R.A. in 1867 as Col. because of disabilities.

MARSHALL, Humphrey. C.S.A. gen. 1812–72. Ky. USMA 1832 (42/45); Mtd. Rangers. Resigning a year after graduation to become a lawyer, he was active in Whig politics, the state militia, and the Mexican War, sitting in the US Congress for his party. After serving as Minister Resident to China in 1853–54, he joined the Know-Nothings and again served in Congress. After trying unsuccessfully to hold the border states on a peaceful course through the secession crisis, he became B.G. C.S.A. 30 Oct. '61. He fought along the Big Sandy River (Ky.–W. Va. border) against the forces under James A. GARFIELD (Middle Creek, Ky., 10 Jan. '62; and Pound Gap. Ky., 16 Mar.) (See B.&L., I, 393–7). He forced J. D. Cox to fall back

from PRINCETON, W. Va., 16–17 May
'62. Resigning 16 June '62, he was reappointed four days later to rank from
his original appointment, and participated in Bragg's invasion of Ky. the
next fall. He resigned on 17 June '63
to sit in the 2d C.S.A. Congress and
fled to Tex. at war's end. Returning to
Louisville, he resumed his law practice.
A portly, democratic man, he was not
enough of a disciplinarian to command
volunteers effectively. "So well known
was his leniency, that an officer of his
staff made a standing offer to eat the
first man the general should shoot for
any crime" (*ibid.*). He was a nephew
of James G. Birney, who was the father
of the Union Gen. William BIRNEY;
also kin to John Marshall. He was an
eloquent speaker and a lawyer of great
distinction.

MARSHALL, William Rainey. Union
officer. 1825–96. Mo. Pvt. 8th Minn.
13 Aug. '62; Lt. Col. 7th Minn. 28 Aug.
'62; Col. 6 Nov. '63; Bvt. B.G. USV
(war service). Served with Gen. Sibley
against the Sioux. W.I.A. at Spanish
Fort in the Mobile campaign. He was
chairman of the convention that founded
the Republican party in Minn. and served
as Gov. of that state 1865–69. He was
a founder and life-long member of the
Swedenborgian Church of St. Paul.

MARSTON, Gilman. Union gen.
1811–90. N.H. As Col. 10th N.H. 10
June '61, he led his regiment at 1st Bull
Run, in the Peninsular campaign, and
at Fredericksburg. Promoted B.G. USV
29 Nov. '62, he commanded in the Dept.
of Va. and N.C.: Dist. of St. Mary's
(1 Dec. '63–28 Apr. '64); 1, 1, XVIII
(1 May–18 June '64); 1, 3, X (19 June–
27 Aug. '64); 1st Div., XVII (18–20
June, 3–15 Sept., 29 Sept.–29 Oct. '64).
He resigned 20 Apr. '65, having been
wounded several times. After the war
he was a lawyer and Republican Congressman.

MARTIN, James Green. C.S.A. gen.
1819–78. N.C. USMA 1840 (14/42);
Arty. He served in garrison, the Mexican War (1 brevet, 1 wound) where he
lost his right arm, and on the frontier
before resigning 14 June '61 as Capt.
(since 1847). Named Adj. Gen. of N.C.
troops 20 Sept. '61, he was appointed
Maj. Gen. of militia 28 Sept. In this
position he prepared all state troops for
Confederate service and supervised the
entire defense of the state. To "Old One
Wing" goes the credit for the superior
training and equipping of N.C. troops.
He was appointed B.G. C.S.A. 2 June
'62, commanding the Dist. of N.C., and
in the fall of 1863 took the field with a
brigade. Going to Petersburg in the summer of 1864 he was conspicuous at the
battle at Howlett's House, but his health
broke, and he was sent to command the
Dist. of Western N.C. He surrendered
at Waynesville 10 May '65. After the
war was a lawyer and Episcopal layman.

MARTIN, James Stewart. Union officer. 1825–? Va. Col. 111th Ill. 18 Sept.
'62; Bvt. B.G. USV 28 Feb. '65. Commanded 1, 2, XV; 2, 2, XV. A leading
Republican, he was active as a judge
and Congressman. He was also a lawyer
and president of a mining company.

MARTIN, John Alexander. Union
officer. 1839–89. Pa. Lt. Col. 8th Kans.
27 Oct. '61; Col. 1 Nov. '62; Bvt. B.G.
USV (war service); mustered out 15
Nov. '64. Served as Provost Marshal of
Nashville and commanded 3, 1, XX
(Cumberland). While not yet 19 he
bought a Kans. paper (variously titled
*Freedom's Champion, Champion, Atchi-
son Champion*) and ran it successfully
for several years. He was Gov. of Kans.
1884–88.

MARTIN, William Henry. Union
officer. Mass. Pvt. Co. C 1st Ohio 19
Apr.–2 Aug. '61; Capt. 93d Ohio 18 July
'62; Lt. Col. 3 Apr. '63; Bvt. B.G. USV

8 June '65 (war service); resigned 2 Dec. '63. Prewar railroad conductor.

MARTIN, William Thompson. C.S.A. gen. 1823–1910. Ky. Appt.-Miss. After graduating from Centre College, he was district attorney and opposed secession, although he had determined to follow his state. He raised the Adams (Miss.) County cavalry troops as Capt. in the spring of 1861 and after the bombardment of Fort Sumter took his men to Richmond. On the Peninsula, during Jeb Stuart's raid around McClellan, and at Antietam he commanded the Jeff Davis Legion as Lt. Col. He was R. E. Lee's A.D.C. at the latter battle. Going to the West, he fought at Chickamauga, after having been appointed B.G. C.S.A. 2 Dec. '62. Promoted Maj. Gen. 10 Nov. '63, he commanded a division of Wheeler's cavalry in the Atlanta campaign and in the latter months of 1864 went to northwestern Miss. After the war he was in railroading, education, and Democratic politics, serving as legislator.

MARTINDALE, John Henry. Union gen. 1815–81. N.Y. USMA 1835 (3/56); Dragoons. Deeply disappointed that he was unable to enter the Corps of Engrs., he resigned in 1836 while on a leave of absence and before ever having served with troops, when offered a job as railroad engineer. Commissioned B.G. USV 9 Aug. '61, after a successful career as lawyer, he was in the defenses of Washington and commanded 2, Fitz-John Porter's division (3 Oct. '61–13 Mar. '62) 1, 1, III (13 Mar.–18 May '62) at Yorktown and 1, 1, V (18 May–10 July '62) at Hanover C.H., Mechanicsville, Gaines's Mill, Malvern Hill, and Harrison's Landing. While recovering from typhoid fever after the Peninsular campaign, he was investigated on charges preferred by Fitz-John Porter that he had influenced his men to surrender at Malvern Hill. He was exonerated and then served as Mil. Gov. Dist. of Columbia, XXII (2 Feb.–16 Sept. '63 and 1 Oct. '63–2 May '64). At Bermuda Hundred and Cold Harbor he commanded 2d Div., XVIII (20 May–10 July '64) and during the Petersburg siege he led the XVIII Corps (10–21 July '64). Resigning because of ill health on 13 Sept. '64, he was breveted Maj. Gen. USV for Malvern Hill. He returned to the practice of law and became one of N.Y.'s most prominent and able lawyers.

MARTINSBURG, W. Va., 14 June '63. (GETTYSBURG CAMPAIGN) The Union garrison was commanded by Col. B. F. Smith's 3d Brig., 1st Div., VIII Corps (126th Ohio, 106th N.Y., Potomac Home Brigade, 1st N.Y. Cav., 13th Pa. Cav., and Maulsby's W. Va. battery). Brig. Gen. Daniel Tyler arrived early 14 June to take command but, since the fighting had already started, assumed the role of advisor; as senior officer present, however, he made the main decisions, and is sometimes shown as being the Federal commander in this engagement. Skirmishers made contact on the Winchester road about 8 A.M. At about 11 A.M. Tyler learned that Confederate forces had cut the road to Winchester at Bunker Hill and that Milroy's retreat was probably blocked. He thereupon ordered evacuation of the baggage train to Williamsport and decided to delay only long enough to secure their withdrawal. About noon Smith refused an ultimatum from Jenkins to surrender the town. During the afternoon the Confederates continued to maintain pressure on the north while working other forces around to attack from the west. About sunset the 106th N.Y., in support of Maulsby's artillery, broke under a sudden enemy shelling. While it was being rallied by its officers, Col. Smith withdrew and the 126th Ohio and the 106th followed. There ensued a confused situation in which the two regiments and the artillery started toward the Potomac on different routes. The main body finally ended up on the road to Shepherdstown, crossing the river at about 1 A.M. and reaching Harpers Ferry about 7 (15 June). Maulsby's guns were separated: one withdrew with the 106th N.Y., leaving a gun that had been disabled; the other four guns took the Williamsport road and were captured. Confederate pursuit was disorganized and, in the darkness, failed to cut off the Federals. Losses were: 200 Federals missing; three Confederates killed and wounded.

MARTINSBURG, W. Va. 31 Aug. '64. Skirmish during SHENANDOAH VALLEY CAMPAIGN OF SHERIDAN. Averell's (2d) Cav. Div. was attacked by Rodes's division and driven back to Falling Waters with a loss of 48 Federals killed and wounded. Rodes's casualties not reported.

MARTIN'S (W.T.) CAVALRY CORPS (Wheeler's). See CORPS, Confed.

MARYLAND CAMPAIGN. See ANTIETAM CAMPAIGN.

MARYLAND, UNION DEPARTMENT OF. See ANNAPOLIS, Union Department of.

MASON, Edwin Cooley. Union officer. Ohio. Capt. 2d Ohio 29 Apr. '61; mustered out 24 June '61; Capt. 17th US Inf. 14 May '61; Col. 7th Me. 22 Aug. '61; mustered out USV 5 Sept. '64; Col. 176th Ohio 23 Sept. '64; mustered out USV 14 June '65; Bvt. B.G. USV 3 June '65. Brevets for Fredericksburg, Wilderness, Spotsylvania, war service. Commanded 3, 2, VI (Potomac); 2, 4, XX (Cumberland); 1st Brig., Dist. of Nashville (Cumberland). Continued in R.A. until retirement in 1895 as Col.; Bvt. B.G. USA for Lava Beds (Calif.) and for Clearwater (Ida.). Died 1898.

MASON, James Murray. Confed. diplomat. 1798–1871. D.C. Descended from the prominent Va. family, he became a lawyer and was elected to the Senate and House. In the former he drafted the FUGITIVE SLAVE ACT in 1850. He sat in the Confederate Congress and was sent to France with John SLIDELL as a diplomatic representative. In 1861 he was seized by the British on the British mail steamer *Trent,* and this almost started another war between the US and Great Britain. This also generated a great deal of sympathy for the Confederacy in England. (See TRENT AFFAIR.)

MASON, John Sanford. Union gen. 1824–97. Ohio. USMA 1847 (9/38); Arty. He served in the Mexican War and on the frontier. As Capt. 11th US Inf. 14 May '61 and Col. 4th Ohio 3 Oct. '61, he fought in western Va. and the Valley at Romney, Blue Gap, and Winchester. He led his regiment at Harrison's Landing and Fredericksburg, where he also commanded 1, 3, II (Potomac) when Kimball was wounded. Named B.G. USV 29 Nov. '62, he commanded troops at Columbus (Ohio) and the draft depot at Camp Chase, served on the staff of the Dept. of Calif. and Nev. and commanded the Dist. of Ariz. He retired in 1888 as Col., having been breveted for Antietam, Fredericksburg, and war service (B.G. USA).

MASON AND DIXON LINE. Symbolic border between the North and South that originated as a line surveyed in 1763 and 1767 to settle boundary differences between the Penn family of Pa. and the Calverts of Md. The line goes along the parallel 39 degrees, 42 minutes, 23.6 seconds. In the antebellum era it was understood to be the dividing line between slave and free territory and was the boundary between Pa. to the north and Del., Md. and W. Va. to the south.

2D MASSACHUSETTS

Colonels: George H. Gordon (USMA, R.A.), George L. Andrews (USMA), Samuel M. Quincy, William Cogswell, Charles F. Morse. (The first two were breveted Maj. Gen., Quincy and Cogswell were breveted Brig. Gen.)

Battles: Winchester, Cedar Mountain, Antietam, Chancellorsville, Beverly Ford, Gettysburg, Elk River, Resaca, Kenesaw Mountain, Atlanta siege, Averasboro. Also present at Front Royal, Manassas, Cassville, New Hope Church, Peach Tree Creek, siege of Savannah, Bentonville, March to the Sea, the Carolinas.

"The best officered regiment in the entire Army," says Fox. "Its colonel and lieutenant-colonel were educated at West Point, the latter graduating at the head of his class; the line officers were selected men, for the most part collegians whose education, supplemented by the year of practical service in the field preliminary to the first battle, left nothing that could be desired to make them equal in every respect to any line of officers, regulars or volunteers. Of the sixteen officers who lost their lives, thirteen were Harvard men, whose names appear on the bronze tablets in the Harvard Memorial Hall. The company officers were not elected by the men, as in other volunteer commands, but were selected by the authorities who raised the regiment. The enlisted men were also above the average in intelligence and soldierly bearing. The Second sustained the heaviest loss in action of any regiment in the corps. At Cedar Mountain its casualties were 40 killed, 93 wounded, and 40 missing. At Chancellorsville, 21 killed, 110 wounded, and 7 missing; and at Gettysburg, 23 killed, 109 wounded, and 4 missing, out of 316 engaged. The latter loss occurred [at Culp's Hill] within a few minutes, in a hopeless assault made by the Second, and Twenty-seventh Indiana, which was ordered by mistake; the blunder was apparent to all, but no one faltered, and each soldier did his duty gallantly; Lieutenant Colonel Mudge, who was in command, remarked: 'It is murder, but it's the order,' and fell dead while waving his sword and cheering on his men."

The regiment was organized in May '61 and re-enlisted.

At Cedar Mountain the 2d Mass. (commanded by Andrews) was in the 3d Brig. (Gordon's), 1st Div. (Williams's), II (Banks's) Corps. Brigaded with it were the 27th Ind., the Pa. Zouaves d'Afrique, and the 3d Wis. (Ruger). This brigade, reinforced by the addition of the 13th N.J. and the 107th N.Y., became part of XII Corps (Mansfield) when the latter was created 12 Sept. '62. It remained in this organization (3d Brig., 1st Div., XII) through the Gettysburg campaign. The regiment went with XI and XII Corps, under Hooker, to join the Army of the Cumberland near Chattanooga in Sept. '63. In Apr. '64, when these two corps were consolidated to form the XX Corps, the 2d Mass. became part of the 2d Brig., 1st Div.

15TH MASSACHUSETTS

Colonels: Charles Devens (Bvt. Maj. Gen.), George H. Ward (Bvt. B.G.; K.I.A.), George C. Joslin.

Battles: Balls Bluff, Fair Oaks, Antietam, Fredericksburg, Gettysburg, Bristoe Station, Mine Run, Wilderness, Spotsylvania, Totopotomoy, Cold Harbor, and Petersburg. Present also at Yorktown, West Point, Peach Orchard, Savage's Station, Glendale, Malvern Hill, Vienna, Fredericksburg ('63), Po River, and North Anna.

In the celebrated BALLS BLUFF affair the regiment (under Devens) had 44 killed of the five companies employed; Ward lost a leg. At Antietam, in Gorman's (1st) brigade of Sedgwick's (2d) division, II Corps, it attacked McLaws' division in the West Woods (Lt. Col. Kimball was in command) and lost 318 out of 606 engaged. At Gettysburg the regiment lost 148 (over 60 per cent) of the 239 engaged; Ward was killed.

Still in the 1st Brig., 2d Div., II Corps, the 15th Mass. entered the final campaign against Richmond with 275 men. From the Wilderness to Petersburg it lost 143, including 47 captured at Petersburg.

The regiment was raised in Worcester County and left the state 8 Aug. '61. After Yorktown a company of the Andrew Sharpshooters was permanently attached, making an 11th company. The 15th Mass. was mustered out in July '64.

22D MASSACHUSETTS

Colonels: Henry Wilson, Jesse A. Gove (R.A.; K.I.A.), Charles E. Griswold, William S. Tilton (Bvt. B.G.).

Battles: Yorktown siege, Mechanicsville, Gaines's Mill, Malvern Hill, Shepherdstown, Fredericksburg, Chancellorsville, Gettysburg, Rappahannock Station, Wilderness, Laurel Hill, Spotsylvania, North Anna, Totopotomoy, Bethesda Church, Petersburg assault and siege. Also present at Hanover Courthouse, Manassas, Antietam, Mine Run, and Cold Harbor.

Organized at Lynnfield by Henry Wilson (later elected vice-president with Grant), the regiment arrived in Virginia in Oct. '61. It continued training there until Mar. '62 when it moved to the Peninsula to serve in Martindale's (1st) brigade, Morell's (1st) division of Fitz-John Porter's (V) corps. Heavily engaged at Gaines's Mill, the regimental commander, Gove, was killed; Major Tilton was wounded and captured; and a total of 283 casualties were sustained (84 killed). At Malvern Hill the 22d

Mass. was again heavily engaged. At Gettysburg the regiment was commanded by Lt. Col. Thomas Sherwin when Tilton moved up to command the 1st Brig.; it was still part of the 1st Div. (now Barnes's), V Corps (now Sykes's). At greatly reduced strength the regiment lost 121 men in the battles of the Wilderness and Spotsylvania, or almost 50 per cent.

28TH MASSACHUSETTS

Colonels: William Montieth, Richard Byrnes (R.A.; K.I.A.), George W. Cartwright, James Fleming.

Battles: James Island (S.C.), Manassas, Chantilly, South Mountain, Antietam, Fredericksburg, Gettysburg, Auburn, Wilderness, Spotsylvania, Totopotomoy, Cold Harbor, Petersburg, Strawberry Plains, Deep Bottom, Reams's Station, Hatcher's Run. Also at Chancellorsville, Bristoe Station, Mine Run, North Anna, Sutherland Station, Sayler's Creek, Farmville, and Appomattox.

Organized at Boston, mostly from men of Irish birth, the regiment left the state 11 Jan. '62 and was in South Carolina until August. It was in Stevens' division, IX Corps, during the 2d Bull Run campaign, in which (under the command of Maj. Cartwright) it lost 234 men. In Willcox's division at Antietam the regiment lost 48 out of its effective strength of less than 200. In Nov. '62 it was transferred to the Irish Brig. of Hancock's (1st) division, II Corps, where it remained. It was heavily engaged at Fredericksburg (losing 158 out of 416), at the Wilderness (losing 115 out of 505), and at Spotsylvania (losing 110, half of whom fell in the 18 May attacks). Maj. Andrew J. Lawler was killed in the latter action. Col. Byrnes was killed at Cold Harbor. The regiment was mustered out 13 Dec. '64; the recruits and re-enlisted men were consolidated into a battalion of five companies which served the rest of the war.

57TH MASSACHUSETTS ("Second Veteran")

Colonels: William F. Bartlett (Bvt. Maj. Gen. USV), N. B. McLaughlin (Bvt. B.G., USA).

Battles: Wilderness, Spotsylvania, North Anna, Bethesda Church, Petersburg assault (17 June '64), Petersburg siege, Petersburg Mine, Weldon R.R., Poplar Spring Church, Fort Stedman. Present at Cold Harbor, Boydton Road, final Petersburg assault.

In its first engagement, at the battle of the Wilderness, the regiment, in the 1st (Stevenson's) Division, 1st Brig. (Carruth's), IX Corps, had its greatest casualties. Of 545 officers and men engaged it lost 245, including Col. Bartlett (seriously wounded). Although in service less than a year, only two other Federal regiments had a higher percentage of killed. It was in the 3d Brig., 1st Div., at end of war.

MATHER, Thomas S. Union officer. Conn. Col. 2d Ill. Arty. 30 Jan. '62; Bvt. B.G. USV 28 Sept. '65 (war service). Died 1890.

MATHEWS, Joseph Ard. Union officer. Pa. Maj. 46th Pa. 27 Sept. '61; Col. 128th Pa. 1 Nov. '62; mustered out 19 May '63; Col. 205th Pa. 2 Sept. '64; Bvt. B.G. USV 2 Apr. '65 (Forts Stedman and Sedgwick, Va.). Commanded 1, 3, IX; 2, 3, IX. Died 1872.

MATHEWS, Salmon S. Union officer. Mich. 1st Lt. 5th Mich. 19 June '61; Capt. 11 Oct. '61; Maj. 3 May '63; Lt. Col. 11 June '64; Bvt. B.G. USV (Glendale and the Wilderness); resigned 21 Dec. '64. Listed by Phisterer as Matthews, Solomon S.

MATTHIES, Charles Leopold. Union gen. 1824–68. Prussia. After Prussian military service he came to Iowa in 1849. As Capt. 1st Iowa 14 May '61,

Lt. Col. 23 July '61, and Col. 23 May '62, he fought with his regiment at Wilson's Creek, Island No. 10, and Corinth. Promoted B.G. USV 29 Nov. '62, he commanded 3, 7, XVI (22 Dec. '62–20 Jan. '63); 3, 7, XVII (20 Jan–12 Feb. '63, 2 June–27 July '63, 28 Aug.–14 Sept. '63); 2, 7, XVII (12 Feb.–24 Apr. '63); 3, 2, XVII (14 Sept.–25 Nov. '63); 3, 3, XV (2 May–1 June '63 and 14 Mar.–15 May '64). He was wounded at Chattanooga, and resigned 16 May '64.

MATTOCKS, Charles Porter. Union officer. 1840–? Vt. 1st Lt. 17th Me. 2 Aug. '62; Capt. 4 Dec. '62; Maj. 22 Dec. '63; Col. 15 May '65; Bvt. B.G. USV. Brevets for Grant's Virginia campaign, war service. Medal of Honor 29 May '99 for Sayler's Creek (Va.), where his regiment captured 200 prisoners and a stand of C.S.A. colors. Full B.G. USV 8 June '98; discharged 30 Oct. '98. He was a lawyer and legislator.

MAURY, Dabney Herndon. C.S.A. gen. 1822–1900. Va. USMA 1846 (37/59); Mtd. Rifles-Cav. After graduating from the Univ. of Va. and studying law, he entered West Point. He fought in the Mexican War (1 brevet), taught at West Point for five years, and served on the frontier before being dismissed for "treasonable designs" 25 June '61 as 1st Lt. Commissioned Capt. of C.S.A. Cav. in 1861, he was named Col. Asst. Adj. Gen. and Chief of Staff to Van Dorn the next year in the Trans-Miss. Dept. After fighting at Pea Ridge, he was appointed B.G. C.S.A. 12 Mar. '62 and then served with the Army of the West at Iuka, Corinth, and Hatchie Bridge. He was promoted Maj. Gen. 4 Nov. '62 and put in command of the Dist. of the Gulf in July '63, remaining in this post until the end of the war. Penniless, he returned to Richmond, where he taught school and in 1868 organized the Southern Historical Society. As chairman for 20 years, he saw that its papers were available to the US War Records Office; the latter reciprocated. Besides writing for the society, he authored a number of other histories. A man of principles and honor, he turned down $30,000 a year to be a supervisor of the Louisiana Lottery and once gave up his business, although he could hardly afford to be without his salary, to be a volunteer nurse in a New Orleans yellow-fever epidemic. D.A.B. describes him as "a small, spare man, socially, and, at least in his younger days, even convivially inclined, but with a sense of duty and honor worthy of the best of the traditional Virginia gentlemen officers." Matthew Fontaine MAURY was an uncle.

MAURY, Matthew Fontaine. Renowned hydrographer and C.S.N. Commander. 1806–73. Va. At 19 he joined the navy as a midshipman and published in 1834 his first book, *Maury's Navigation.* He was injured and lamed for life in 1839 and settled into a life of study and writing, from which came proposals for improving the navy and establishing the naval academy. Also among his projects were the establishment of a river-wide system of information on the Mississippi's condition and the enlargement of the inland canal system. In 1842 he was named head of the hydrographical office of the navy and also took over the naval observatory. He brought out his paper on the Gulf Stream, ocean currents, and great circle sailing in 1844 and books entitled *A Scheme for Rebuilding Southern Commerce, Wind and Current Charts,* and *Sailing Directions.* He called a general maritime conference that standardized the logs kept by captains, and in 1856 published *The Physical Geography of the Sea.* Honored all over the world as the founder of a new science, he was the first man to describe

the Gulf Stream and to mark routes across the Atlantic. He also instituted the system of deep-sea sounding and suggested the laying of transoceanic cables. When Va. seceded, he resigned as Commander and entered the Confederate Navy on 10 June '61 with the same rank. He served on court-martial duty and in Oct. '62 established the naval submarine battery service. Sent to Europe to continue his experiments, he invented a method of arranging and testing torpedo mines which he was about to put into use when Lee surrendered. He also purchased and outfitted armed cruisers abroad for the Confederacy. After the war he went to Mexico and served under Maximilian, returning to Europe, where he was when that government collapsed. Declining a number of posts in Europe, he became physics professor at V.M.I. and wrote a great many other books on the sea and geography. He is the uncle of D. H. Maury and often called the "Pathfinder of the Seas."

MAXEY, Samuel Bell. C.S.A. gen. 1825–95. Ky. USMA 1846 (58/59); Inf. After fighting in the Mexican War (1 brevet) and serving in garrison, he resigned in 1849 to become a lawyer with his father. They both moved to Tex. and were strong advocates of secession. He declined election to the state legislature in 1861 to become Col. 9th Tex. Inf. Appointed B.G. C.S.A. 7 Mar. '62 to rank from the 4th, he fought in Tenn. and Miss. and was named 11 Dec. '63 to command INDIAN TERRITORY. He organized three brigades of Indians and through respect for tribal loyalties, impassioned orations at council fires, and printed propaganda, he gained their confidence as no one had since Sam Houston. Wood says he was promoted Maj. Gen. 18 Apr. '64 and Cullum affirms this but gives no date, while Wright, C.M.H., and D.A.B.

make no mention of any rank higher than B.G. He led a cavalry division in 1865. Returning to his law practice, he was in the Senate 1875–87.

MAXIMILIAN AFFAIR. Taking advantage of the Civil War, Napoleon III established Austrian Archduke Maximilian (1832–67) as emperor of Mexico and sent French troops—including elements of the Foreign Legion—to support him. During the war Napoleon III ignored Seward's demands that French troops be evacuated. In May '65 Sheridan was sent with 50,000 troops along the Rio Grande. Schofield was sent to Europe in June to persuade Napoleon to get out of Mexico. Seward then sent Sherman on a mission to Juárez, the revolutionary leader, as a gesture of recognition. Napoleon withdrew his troops in May '66, leaving Maximilian to be overthrown and executed.

MAXWELL, Norman Jay. Union officer. Pa. Q.M. Sgt. Co. E 100th Pa. 27 Aug. '61; 2d Lt. 16 Feb. '62; 1st Lt. 1 Mar. '63; Capt. 24 Apr. '63; Maj. 12 Dec. '64; Col. 18 Apr. '65; Bvt. B.G. USV 18 Apr. '65 (war service).

MAXWELL, Obediah Craig. Union officer. Ohio. 2d Lt. 1st Ohio 17 Apr. '61; 1st Lt. 11 June '61; mustered out 16 Aug. '61; Capt. 2d Ohio 2 Sept. '61; Lt. Col. 21 Jan. '63; discharged 1 Feb. '64 for wounds; Lt. Col. 194th Ohio 15 Mar. '65; Bvt. B.G. USV (war service). Commanded 1st Div. Dist. Southwest Ky., XXIII; 2, 2d Div. Dist. Ky., XXIII. Died 1872.

MAY, Dwight. Union officer. Mass. Capt. 2d Mich. 25 Apr. '61; resigned 2 Dec. '61; Lt. Col. 12th Mich. 8 Oct. '62; Col. 10 June '65; Bvt. B.G. USV 24 Oct. '65 (war service). Died 1880.

MAYNADIER, Henry E. Union officer. c. 1830–68. Va. Appt.-At Large.

USMA 1851 (17/42); Arty.-Inf. He served on the frontier and in the Utah Expedition before being promoted Capt. 10th US Inf. 19 Jan. '61. In the bombardment of Island No. 10, Fort Pillow, Chickasaw Bluffs, and Vicksburg, he was Ord. officer of the Miss. Mortar Flotilla. He joined the Army of the Potomac in Oct. '62 and commanded a battalion at Fredericksburg. As Maj. 12th US Inf. 4 Nov. '63, he served in Washington in the Provost Marshal Gen.'s office and then went to the West and N.Y. State, seeing no more field service. Continuing in the R.A. and dying on active duty, he was breveted for war service, mortar duty (B.G. USV), and Indian fighting (Maj. Gen. USV).

MAYNADIER, William. Union officer. c. 1806–71. Md. Appt.-D.C. USMA 1827 (3/38); Arty.-Ord. Before the war he had served on ordnance duty and as Scott's A.D.C. in the Black Hawk War and was promoted Maj. 5 May '61 (Capt. since 1838). Promoted Lt. Col. 3 Aug. '61, he was executive asst. in the Ord. Bureau until 17 Sept. '63 and promoted Col. 1 June '63. Inspector of arsenals, armories, and ordnance depots until 25 Aug. '64, he returned to the Ord. Bureau for the rest of the war. Breveted B.G. USA, he died on active duty.

MAYNARD CARBINE. A breechloading percussion carbine by the inventor of the MAYNARD TAPE primer. When the trigger guard was lowered, the breech tipped upward for loading with an unprimed brass cartridge that had a small hole in the center of its base. It was fired by a conventional percussion cap. The carbine weighed about six pounds and was 36 7/8 inches in total length. It saw considerable service in the Civil War, 20,202 being bought by the government (Gluckman, 389). The weapon was the first to use the expansion of the cartridge as a gas check, a feature of all but the largest of modern cannon.

MAYNARD TAPE. A primer device invented by Dr. Edward Maynard, a Washington, D. C., dental surgeon, and patented in 1845. Resembling the caps used in toy cap pistols, the primer was made of two narrow strips of varnished paper between which were glued pellets of fulminate of mercury. The strip was coiled in a magazine, and each time the hammer was cocked a pellet was brought into position to be exploded by the fall of the hammer. The defect was that moisture spoiled the tape. Old arms could be modified for the Maynard system by drilling a circular recess into the lock plate of the weapon.

McAFEE'S CROSSING, Ga., 12 June '64. See KENESAW MOUNTAIN.

McALESTER, Miles Daniel. Union officer. N.Y. c. 1823–69. Appt.-Mich. USMA 1856 (3/49); Engrs. He served in the East on engineering duty and was promoted 1st Lt. 2 May '61. Asst. Engr. in the defenses of Washington (until Mar. '62), he was Chief Engr. of the III Corps at Yorktown, Williamsburg, Fair Oaks, Oak Grove, Malvern Hill, South Mountain, and Antietam. He was then Chief Engr. of the Dept. of the Ohio (30 Oct. '62–Apr. '63), promoted Capt. 3 Mar. '63, served under Grant during the Vicksburg campaign, and taught engineering at West Point until 22 June '64. For the rest of the war he was Chief Engr. of the Mil. Div. of West Miss. Continuing in the R.A., he was breveted for the Peninsular campaign, the Mobile campaign, and the siege of Mobile (B.G. USA 9 Apr. '65) and died on active duty as Maj.

McALLISTER, Miles D. Misspelling by Phisterer for Miles Daniel McALESTER.

McALLISTER, Robert. Union officer. Pa. Commissioned Lt. Col. 1st N.J. 6 June '61, he resigned 25 July '62 and was named Col. 11th N.J. on 18 Aug. '62. Mustered out in June '65, he was breveted for the Boydton Plank Road (B.G. USV 27 Oct. '64) and war service (Maj. Gen. USV). He died 1891.

McARTHUR, John. Union gen. 1826–? Born in Scotland, he was a blacksmith, like his father, until he came to America when 23. Becoming a foundry foreman, he owned his own plant at the beginning of the Civil War. Col. 12th Ill. 3 May '61; mustered out 1 Aug. '61; Col. 12th Ill. 1 Aug. '61; B.G. USV 21 Mar. '62; Bvt. Maj. Gen. USV 15 Dec. '64 (Nashville); mustered out 24 Aug. '65. He commanded a brigade in the Fort Donelson assault (1, 2, Dist. Cairo) and at Shiloh (2, 2d Div., Army Tenn.). There he was wounded in the foot but returned to command a division (2d Div., Army Tenn.) when W. H. L. Wallace was mortally wounded. He commanded a division (6, 17, Tenn.) in McPherson's corps at Vicksburg and in Andrew J. Smith's corps (1, 16, Tenn.) at Nashville, as well as several other brigades and divisions.

McARTHUR, William Miltimore. Union officer. Me. Capt. 8th Me. 7 Sept. '61; Maj. 11 Apr. '64; Lt. Col. 13 Sept. '64; Col. 13 Mar. '65; Bvt. B.G. USV (Drewry's Bluff 14 May '64 and Williamsburg [Va.] 27 Oct. '64).

McBRIDE, James Douglass. Union officer. Ohio. Sgt. Co. I 1st Ohio 16 Apr. '61; mustered out 2 Aug. '61; 2d Lt. 5th W. Va. 10 Apr. '62; resigned 8 Jan. '63; Maj. 8th US Col. Arty. 20 Aug. '64; Lt. Col. 9 Feb. '65; Bvt. B.G. USV (war service).

McCALL, George Archibald. Union gen. 1802–68. Pa. USMA 1822 (26/40); Inf. He served on garrison duty, as

523 MC CAUSLAND, J.

A.D.C. to Gen. Edmund P. Gaines (1831–36), in the Seminole wars, in Indian fighting, and in the Mexican War (2 brevets), where he commanded an infantry battalion. He was Col. and I.G. of the army when he resigned in 1853. B.G. USV 17 May '61; resigned 31 Mar. '63. He commanded the Pa. Res. Corps as Maj. Gen. Pa. Vols. (15 May–23 July '61) and was named B.G. USV on 17 May '61. When that group entered the Army of the Potomac, it was called McCall's Division (30 Oct. '61–13 Mar. '62). He also commanded 2d Div., I Corps (13 Mar.–4 Apr. '62) and 3d Div., V Corps (18–30 June '62). In the summer of 1862 he was captured at New Market Cross Roads and sent to Libby Prison. After the Civil War he farmed in Pa. until his death.

McCALL, William H. H. Union officer. Pa. Sgt. Co. D 5th Pa. Res. 5 June '61; Capt. 5 Mar. '63; mustered out 11 June '64; Lt. Col. 200th Pa. 3 Sept. '64; Bvt. B.G. USV 2 Apr. '65. Brevets for Fort Stedman (Va.), Fort Sedgwick (Va.). Commanded 1, 3, IX (Potomac). Died 1883.

McCALLUM, Daniel Craig. Union officer. 1815–78. Scotland. An architect, builder, and railroad engineer, he was appointed (11 Feb. '62) director of all the military railroads in the country. Commissioned Col. Add. A.D.C. on that same day, he was mustered out in 1866 and breveted B.G. USV 24 Sept. '64 and Maj. Gen. USV, both for war service.

McCALMONT, Alfred Brunson. Union officer. 1825–? Pa. Lt. Col. 142d Pa. 1 Sept. '62; Col. 208th Pa. 12 Sept. '64; Bvt. B.G. USV (war service). Commanded in Army of the Potomac: 1, 3, I; 1, 3, IX. He served as Asst. US Attorney-General during Buchanan's administration.

McCANDLESS, William. Union gen. Pa. Pvt. 31st Pa. (2d Pa. Res.); Maj. 21 June '61; Lt. Col. 22 Oct. '61; Col. 1 Aug. '62; mustered out 16 June '64 when regiment's enlistment expired; B.G. USV 21 July '64 (declined). He fought with his regiment (in the Pa. Res.) at Mechanicsville, Gaines's Mill, Glendale, 2d Bull Run, Chantilly, near Frederick (Md.), South Mountain, and Antietam. Commanded 1, 3, I (Potomac) from 13 Dec. '62 (Fredericsburg) till 17 Feb. '63. He commanded 1, 3, XV, Potomac (28 June–28 Aug.) at Gettysburg, where he captured the 15th Ga. Inf. colors. He also led this brigade 1 Nov.–20 Feb. '64 and 1–8 May '64. His other commands were 1, Pa. Res., XXII (Washington), 6 Feb.–29 May '63 and 29 May–26 June '63 and 3d Div., 5th Corps, 28 Aug.–1 Nov. '63 (Bristoe Station and Mine Run) and 20 Feb.–1 May '64. He was wounded at the Wilderness.

McCAUSLAND, John. C.S.A. gen. 1836–1927. Mo. Appt.-Va. Standing at the top of his V.M.I. class, he studied at the Univ. of Va. and returned to V.M.I. to teach mathematics. He commanded a detachment of cadets at John Brown's execution, and when the state seceded, was sent by Lee to recruit in the Kanawha Valley. Commissioned Col. 36th Va., he served under Floyd in western Va. and joined A. S. Johnston in Ky. in the latter part of 1861. He commanded the Va. brigade at Fort Donelson and escaped capture. From Apr. '62 until June '64 he commanded his brigade in the Dept. of Western Va. Appointed B.G. C.S.A. 18 May '64, he led a cavalry brigade against Hunter in the Shenandoah and delayed the Federal advance upon Lynchburg until Early could reinforce it. He fought at Monocacy, led his troops to the outskirts of Washington, and burned CHAMBERSBURG, Pa. He was defeated at Moorefield, W. Va., and later joined Lee. Refusing to surrender at Appomattox, he led his brigade through the Federal lines. After the war he spent several years in Europe and Mexico before returning to his W. Va. farm.

McCLEARY, James. Union officer. Ohio. Pvt. Co. D 19th Ohio 27 Apr. '61; 2d Lt. 41st Ohio 26 Aug. '61; 1st Lt. 9 Jan. '62; Capt. 26 May. '63; Bvt. B.G. USV. Brevets for war service, Shiloh (2), Stones River (2), Chickamauga, Missionary Ridge (2). Lost right arm at Shiloh and again wounded at Stones River. Died 1871.

McCLELLAN, George Brinton. Union gen. 1826–85. Pa. USMA 1846 (2/59); Engrs. Hailed at the beginning of the war as the "Young Napoleon," McClellan proved to be a brilliant military organizer, administrator, and trainer of men but an officer totally lacking in the essential qualities of successful command of large forces in battle. Son of George McClellan (1796–1847), the distinguished surgeon and teacher, he graduated second from the top in his West Point class, won three brevets in the Mexican War for gallant and meritorious conduct, and gained a further military reputation for an outstanding report submitted after spending a year in Europe observing foreign military methods. He resigned in 1857 as a Capt. and was successful in business, becoming vice-president of the Illinois Central R.R. In the latter capacity he became acquainted with Abraham Lincoln, who was a lawyer for the I.C. He started the war as a Maj. Gen. of Ohio volunteers and was soon made a Maj. Gen. of the R.A. and given command of the Dept. of the Ohio. He was then 35 years old. His success in the minor victory at Rich Mountain, W. Va., just 10 days before the Federal disaster at Bull Run, put him in the public eye

at a critical time. Given command of the armies around Washington (Div. of the Potomac) and later succeeding General Scott as C. in C. of the army, he undertook with marked success the complex task of organizing and training the Union armies. His failure in the Peninsular campaign led Halleck to give Pope command of the next major operation. After the latter's defeat at the 2d Battle of Bull Run, McClellan resumed his former role. The administration became increasingly dissatisfied with his reluctance to march against the enemy. After Antietam, when McClellan delayed in pursuing Lee, Lincoln finally lost patience and ordered Burnside to take command of the Army of the Potomac. McClellan was a presidential candidate in 1864. After the war he was chief engineer of the N.Y.C. Dept. of Docks (1870–72) and Gov. of N.J. (1878–81). His autobiography, *McClellan's Own Story,* (1887) is a convincing defense of his military record. Still a military enigma, a brilliant administrator, and a man possessing much good strategic sense, there is ample evidence to support the theory of his admirers that he was never given a fair chance. But the record shows that he was a commander who consistently overestimated the strength of his adversary and who always demanded more men and supplies before undertaking offensive action. "Sending reinforcements to McClellan is like shoveling flies across a barn," Lincoln is alleged to have said in final despair. To parody Lincoln's reasons for liking Grant, of McClellan Lincoln might have said "I *can* spare this man; he won't fight."

McCLELLAN'S HORSES. Gen. McClellan favored Daniel Webster, a dark bay about 17 hands high. "That devil Dan" carried Little Mac about Washington at breakneck speed. He also had a black horse named Burns, named after an army friend who had given him the animal. Since Burns always bolted for his oats at dinnertime, no matter how important it may have been for McClellan to remain where he was, the Gen. was always careful not to ride him in the afternoon.

McCLENNAN, Matthew Robert. Union officer. Pa. Capt. 138th Pa. 20 Aug. '62; Lt. Col. 2 Sept. '62; Col. 2 May '63; Bvt. B.G. USV 2 Apr. '65 (Petersburg siege). Died 1872.

McCLERNAND, John Alexander. Union gen. 1812–1900. Ky. Appt.-Ill. A lawyer, he fought in the Black Hawk War, traded along the Mississippi River, served in the state legislature and US Congress, and was active in the state militia. He was appointed B.G. USV 17 May '61 and took command of the 1st Brig., Mil. Dist. Cairo (14 Oct. '61–1 Feb. '62). At Forts Henry and Donelson he commanded 1st Div. Mil. Dist. Cairo (Feb.–Mar. '62). Failing to block the retreat after Fort Henry, despite orders, he credited his own troops with the victory. Leading 1st Div., Dist. West Tenn., Army Tenn. (17 Feb.–3 May '62) at Shiloh, he commanded 1st Div., Dist. Jackson (July–Sept. '62) and Dist. Jackson (July–Sept. '62). In Oct. '62 he received authorization from Halleck and Lincoln to raise a force in the Northwest for a river expedition against Vicksburg. For his activities at ARKANSAS POST (FORT HINDMAN) Expedition, see MISSISSIPPI, McCLERNAND'S UNION ARMY OF THE. At Champion's Hill, Grand Gulf, and the assaults on Vicksburg he commanded the XIII Corps, Gulf (31 Jan.–19 June '63). After the 22 May assaults he supplied the press with congratulatory stories of his victory. Grant, already unsympathetic with McClernand's attitude and dubious fighting ability, ordered him to Ill. after this, but he

returned to command the Corps (20 Feb.–15 Mar. '64) during the Red River expedition. Ill-health brought about his resignation 30 Nov. '64. D.A.B. characterizes him as "ambitious and untactful, he resented dictation, disliked West Pointers, and never forgot his political fences in Illinois."

McCLURG, Alexander Caldwell. Union officer. 1832–1901. Pa. Capt. 88th Ill. 27 Aug. '62; Capt. Asst. Adj. Gen. Vols. 29 Feb. '64; Lt. Col. Asst. Adj. Gen. Assigned 3 Oct. '64–1 Aug. '65; Bvt. B.G. USV 18 Sept. '65 (war service). Chief of Staff for Gens. Baird (1864) and J. C. Davis. D.A.B. says, "He served through the Chickamauga and Chattanooga campaigns with great distinction, being frequently mentioned in dispatches and winning recognition as one of the ablest staff officers in the western army." After the war he was a partner in a Chicago publishing and book-selling firm.

McCOMB, William. C.S.A. gen. Pa. A manufacturer in Tenn., he enlisted as private and was soon elected Lt. and Adj. in the 14th Tenn. He was at Cheat Mountain, with Jackson in the Valley, and was promoted Maj. in the winter of 1862. After Seven Pines he was named Lt. Col. and was at Cedar Run and 2d Bull Run. He was promoted Col. 2 Sept. '62 and led the regiment at Antietam, Chancellorsville, (wounded) and the Wilderness. After Archer's death in Oct. '64 he succeeded to command the brigade, was appointed B.G. C.S.A. 20 Jan. '65, and fought at Petersburg.

McCONIHE, John. Union officer. N.Y. Capt. 1st Nebr. 30 June '61; resigned 2 Sept. '62; Lt. Col. 169th N.Y. 6 Oct. '62; Col. 12 Apr. '64; Bvt. B.G. USV 1 June '64 (Cold Harbor), where he was K.I.A.

McCONIHE, Samuel. Union officer. N.H. Capt. 93d N.Y. 9 Jan. '62; Maj. 3 Dec. '63; Bvt. B.G. USV Wilderness. Brevets for Wilderness (2), Spotsylvania (2), war service (2). Died 1897.

McCONNELL, Henry Kumler. Union officer. Ohio. 2d Lt. 71st Ohio 4 Oct. '61; Capt. 14 Nov. '61; Col. 7 June '63; Bvt. B.G. USV (war service). Commanded 2, 3, IV (Cumberland). Died 1889.

McCONNELL, John. Union officer. N.Y. Maj. 3d Ill. Cav. 11 Sept. '61; resigned 13 Mar. '63; Col. 5th Ill. Cav. 27 May '64; Bvt. B.G. USV (war service). Died 1898.

McCONNELLSBURG, Pa., 24 and 29 June '63. (Gettysburg campaign, Milroy's retreat) The 1st N.Y. Cav. and 12th Pa. Cav. (Pierce's brigade) engaged in actions here. The action in which the 12th Pa. Cav. took part 24 June was not reported in detail, and there is no record of casualties. On 25 June a detachment under Maj. Alonzo W. ADAMS drove in the enemy pickets, created confusion in the Confederate ranks "creating a great commotion in a large Confederate force there. No casualties are reported." The action of 29 June by the 1st N.Y. Cav. resulted in one Union wounded and two Confederates killed, 30 missing (E.&B.).

McCOOKS OF OHIO. The table at right shows kinship of Ohio's 17 "Fighting McCooks" of the "tribe of Dan" and the "tribe of John." (There is also a separate article on each.)

McCOOK, Alexander McDowell. Union gen. and one of the McCOOKS OF OHIO. 1831–1903. Ohio. USMA 1852 (30/47); Inf. He served on the frontier and in Indian fighting and as a tactical instructor at West Point before being commissioned Col. 1st Ohio

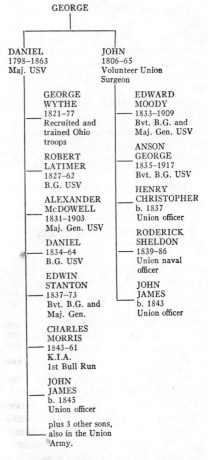

GEORGE

DANIEL	JOHN
1798–1863	1806–65
Maj. USV	Volunteer Union Surgeon

GEORGE WYTHE 1821–77 Recruited and trained Ohio troops

ROBERT LATIMER 1827–62 B.G. USV

ALEXANDER McDOWELL 1831–1903 Maj. Gen. USV

DANIEL 1834–64 B.G. USV

EDWIN STANTON 1837–73 Bvt. B.G. and Maj. Gen.

CHARLES MORRIS 1843–61 K.I.A. 1st Bull Run

JOHN JAMES b. 1845 Union officer

plus 3 other sons, also in the Union Army.

EDWARD MOODY 1833–1909 Bvt. B.G. and Maj. Gen. USV

ANSON GEORGE 1835–1917 Bvt. B.G. USV

HENRY CHRISTOPHER b. 1837 Union officer

RODERICK SHELDON 1839–86 Union naval officer

JOHN JAMES b. 1843 Union officer

16 Apr. '61 (1st Lt. since 1858). He led his regiment at Vienna and 1st Bull Run, was mustered out 16 Aug., and appointed B.G. USV 3 Sept. '61. From Oct. to Dec. '61 he commanded the division at Nolan, Ky., Army of the Ohio, and then commanded the 2d Div. of the army (2 Dec. '61–29 Sept. '62) at Shiloh. He was promoted Maj. Gen. USV 17 July '62. At Corinth, Nashville, and Perryville he commanded the I Corps, Army of the Ohio (29 Sept.–Nov. '62) and the Right Wing, XIV, Cumberland (24 Oct. '62–9 Jan.

'63) at Stones River. At Chickamauga he commanded the XX Corps (9 Jan.– 9 Oct. '63) and was blamed for the Union fiasco, but a court of inquiry exonerated him. He next commanded the Dist. East Ark., VII, Ark. (9 Mar.– 25 May '65). Breveted for 1st Bull Run, Nashville, Shiloh, Perryville (B.G. USA) and war service (Maj. Gen. USA). He continued in the R.A., serving as A.D.C. to Sherman with the rank of Col. from 1875 to 1880. Named B.G. USA in 1890 and Maj. Gen. USA in 1894, he retired the next year.

McCOOK, Anson George. 1835–1917. Union officer. Ohio. Capt. 2d Ohio 17 Apr. '61; mustered out 31 July '61; Maj. 2d Ohio 6 Aug. '61; Lt. Col. 1 Jan. '63; Col. 20 Jan. '63; Bvt. B.G. USV (war service). Commanded 1, 1, XIV. One of the McCOOKS OF OHIO, he was a lawyer, legislator, and editor of the *Daily Register* (later the *N.Y. Law Journal*).

McCOOK, Charles Morris. Union soldier. 1843–61. Ohio. A member of the "tribe of Dan" of the Fighting Mc-COOKS OF OHIO, he volunteered in the Union Army while a freshman at Kenyon College. As Pvt. in the 2d Ohio he was killed at 1st Bull Run in front of his father, Daniel McCOOK, who had volunteered as a nurse.

McCOOK, Daniel. Union officer. 1798–1863. Pa. Father of 10 Fighting McCOOKS OF OHIO ("the tribe of Dan") and uncle of the remaining five ("the tribe of John"), he was commissioned Add. Paymaster USV 24 Mar. '62. He was mortally wounded 19 July '63 trying to intercept the Confederate raider Morgan near Buffington Island, Ohio. He died two days later. His own father, George, was an Irishman of Scottish descent who had fled Ireland in 1780 when the "United Irishmen" movement failed.

McCOOK, Daniel. Union gen. and one of the McCOOKS OF OHIO in the tribe of Dan. 1834–64. Ohio. McCook was the law partner of Thomas Ewing and W. T. Sherman in Leavenworth (Kans.). The firm shut its doors and joined the Union Army, each member becoming a general. As Capt. (1st Kans. 31 May–9 Nov. '61), McCook was with Lyon at Wilson's Creek. He then served as chief of staff (Capt. Asst. Adj. Gen. Vols. 9 Nov. '61) for the 1st Div. (Army of the Ohio) in the Shiloh campaign. He was named Col. 52d Ohio 15 July '62. His brigade (3, 2, XIV) was selected by Sherman to lead the assault on Kenesaw Mountain. Appleton's says that before the assault he recited, to his assembled troops, the stanza of Macaulay's "Horatius" beginning, "And how can man die better than facing fearful odds?" The account continues: ". . . He had reached the top of the enemy's works and was encouraging his men to follow him when he was fatally wounded." He was promoted B.G. USV 16 July '64 and died of his wounds the next day. His other commands in the Army of the Ohio were 36, 11th Div. (Sept. '62); 36, 11, III (Sept.–Nov. '62); and in the Army of the Cumberland: 2, 4th Centre, XIV (5 Nov. '62–9 Jan. '63); 2, 4, XIV 9 Jan.–8 June '64); 2, 2, Res. Corps (8 June–9 Oct. '63); 3, 2, XIV (10 Oct.–16 Dec. '63).

McCOOK, Edward Moody. Union gen. and one of the McCOOKS OF OHIO. 1833–1909. A lawyer and Kans. legislator, he was a volunteer US secret agent at the beginning of the war and given an R.A. appointment (1st Lt. 1st US Cav. 8 May '61) for his services. He was commissioned Maj. 2d Ind. Cav. 29 Sept. '61, promoted Lt. Col. 11 Feb. '62 and Col. 30 Apr. '62. In Sept.–Nov. '62 he commanded 1st Brig., Cav. Div., Army Ohio, and in the Army of the Cumberland he led 2, 1, Cav. Corps (9 Jan.–9 Sept.–2 Oct. and 20 Nov. '63), succeeding to command of the division 9 Sept.–12 Oct. and 20 Nov. '63–29 Oct. '64. Promoted B.G. USV 27 Apr. '64, he also commanded 1st Div., Cav. Corps, Mil. Div. Miss. 29 Oct. '64–26 June '65. Breveted for Shiloh, Perryville, Chickamauga, cavalry operations in East Tenn., Selma, and war service (B.G. USA and Maj. Gen. USV), he resigned in 1866 to serve as Minister to Hawaii (until 1869). He was twice appointed Gov. of Colo. Territory by Grant.

McCOOK, Edwin Stanton. Union officer, and one of the Fighting McCooks OF OHIO. 1837–73. Ohio. Graduating from Annapolis, he served as Midshipman until 1856 and was commissioned Capt. 31st Ill. 18 Sept. '61. After Fort Henry and Fort Donelson, where he was wounded, he was promoted Lt. Col. 16 Feb. '62 and Col. 9 Apr. '63. He was at Vicksburg, Chattanooga, the Atlanta campaign, and the March to the Sea, and resigned 26 Sept. '64. Wounded three times during the war, he was breveted B.G. USV for war service.

McCOOK, George Wythe. Ohio patriot and one of the Fighting McCooks OF OHIO. 1821–77. Pa. After graduating from Ohio Univ., he studied law with Edwin Stanton and was later his law partner. He fought in the Mexican War and was offered a brigadier generalship in the state militia when the Civil War began. Declining it on account of his health, he was active in recruiting and training Ohio regiments. He is the son of Daniel McCook.

McCOOK, Henry Christopher. Union chaplain. 1837–? Ohio. After graduating from college he studied theology and became a Presbyterian minister. During the war he was 1st Lt. and chaplain for nine months, and then took a pastorate in the Midwest. In addition to his theological writings he published several books on ants and was a member of several learned societies. He was a member of the "tribe of John" of the Fighting McCooks OF OHIO.

McCOOK, John. Union surgeon. 1806–65. Pa. Father of five Fighting McCooks OF OHIO ("the tribe of John") and uncle of the other 10 ("the tribe of Dan"), he was an Ohio doctor and volunteered as a surgeon with the Union Army during the Civil War. He died in Oct. '65 while visiting his son Anson G. McCook in the latter's headquarters at Washington. His own father, George, was an Irishman of Scottish descent who had fled Ireland in 1780 when the "United Irishmen" movement failed.

McCOOK, John James. Union soldier. 1843–? Ohio. Graduating from Trinity, Conn., in 1863, he was commissioned Lt. in the (Union) 1st Va., a regiment recruited almost entirely in Ohio. He fought in W. Va. and then entered the Episcopal ministry. Professor of modern languages at Trinity, he edited the *Church Weekly* and wrote several books and articles. He was a member of the "tribe of John" of the Fighting McCooks OF OHIO.

McCOOK, John James. Union officer. 1845–? Ohio. After finishing his freshman year at Kenyon College he volunteered in the 6th Ohio Cav. This member of the "tribe of Dan" of the Fighting McCooks OF OHIO was commissioned Capt. A.D.C. 18 June. '63 and was wounded at Shady Grove, Va. After the war he was a lawyer in N.Y.C.

McCOOK, Robert Latimer. Union gen. and one of the Fighting McCooks OF OHIO. 1827–62. As Col. of the 9th Ohio (8 May '61), he was the adored leader of the German Turner regiment although he spoke little of their language. He commanded McCook's Brig., W. Va. at Carnifex Ferry during Mc-Clellan's campaign there and also led 2, Kanawha, Western Va. (Oct.–Nov. '61); 3d Brig., Army Ohio (Nov.– Dec. '61) and 3, 1, Army Ohio (2 Dec. '61–6 Aug. '62). Promoted B.G. USV 21 Mar. '62, he was wounded in the leg and had a horse shot from under him at Mill Springs (Ky.) 19–20 Jan. '62. He refused to leave his command and later in the day led the charge which routed the Confederates. While this wound was healing, he directed his command from an ambulance. While his escort was reconnoitering, C.S.A. guerrillas overturned the car and killed him in cold blood near Decherd (Tenn.). His regiment (9th Ohio) wrecked a number of homes in the vicinity and hanged several of the culprits in revenge.

McCOOK, Roderick Sheldon. Union naval officer. 1839–86. Ohio USNA 1859. Promoted Lt. 31 Aug. '61, he fought in various battles on the James and along the N.C. coast. At New Bern, 14 Mar. '62, he commanded a battery of naval howitzers. His health was seriously injured in the Fort Fisher engagement and, although not retired until 1885, he spent most of his postwar service on lighthouse duty on the Ohio River. He was a member of "the tribe of John" of the Fighting McCooks of Ohio.

McCOOL HOUSE. Common, but incorrect, spelling of McCoull.

McCORMICK, Charles Comly. Union officer. Pa. Capt. 7th Pa. Cav. 21 Sept. '61; Col. 10 Jan. '65; Bvt. B.G. USV (war service). Died 1884.

McCOULL HOUSE, Va. Landmark of Spotsylvania fighting, located in the "Mule Shoe" or "Bloody Salient" held by Ewell. Usually spelled McCool or McColl. (See Lee's Lts., III, 404n.)

McCOWN, John Porter. C.S.A. gen. 1815–79. Tenn. USMA 1840 (10/42); Arty. He served on the frontier, in the Mexican War (1 brevet), in Indian fighting and scouting, in the Seminole War and the Utah Expedition before resigning 17 May '61 as Capt. He was commissioned Lt. Col. of C.S.A. Arty. and was promoted Col. in May '61. Appointed B.G. C.S.A. 12 Oct. of that year, he served in Tenn. with his brigade and was named Maj. Gen. 10 Mar. '62. Taking command of the Army of the West 20 June '62 while Van Dorn led the department, he went to Chattanooga and there led a division in the Army of Ky. under Kirby Smith. In the fall of 1862 he commanded the Dept. of Eastern Tenn. and fought at Stones River. After the war he was a schoolteacher.

McCOY, Daniel. Union officer. c. 1841–1902. Ohio. Sgt. 24th Ohio 17 June '61; 2d Lt. 16 Feb. '63; 1st Lt. 4 July '63; Capt. 6 May '64; mustered out 23 June '64; Lt. Col. 175th Ohio 19 Sept. '64; Bvt. B.G. USV (war service, Nashville). W.I.A. Stones River (Tenn.) where, as 1st Sgt., he commanded the company. W.I.A. Chickamauga in leg and received 9 bullet holes in his clothing. W.I.A. Franklin (Tenn.) 3 times severely.

McCOY, Robert Abbott. Union officer. Pa. 2d Lt. 11th Pa. Res. 10 June '61; 1st Lt. 1 Nov. '61; Regt. Adj. 21 Apr. '62; Maj. 28 Oct. '63; Lt. Col. 21 Mar. '64; Bvt. B.G. USV; mustered out 13 June '64. Brevets for Wilderness, Spotsylvania C.H., Bethesda Church. Died 1893.

McCOY, Thomas Franklin. Union officer. 1824–99. Pa. Col. 107th Pa. 6 Aug. '62; Bvt. B.G. USV 1 Apr. 65 (war service). Commanded in Army of the Potomac: 1, 2, I; 1, 3, V. As Lt.· in Mexican War, he won a brevet at

Molino del Rey. Served as deputy Q.M. of Pa. and later won renown as a lawyer.

McCRAY, Thomas H. C.S.A. gen. Ark. Although not listed as a general officer by Wright, he served in Bragg's invasion of Ky., commanded a brigade under T. J. Churchill, and fought at Kingston (Tenn.). Wood says he was appointed B.G. C.S.A. in 1863, and Heitman and C.M.H. include him in their lists.

McCREARY, David Berkley. Union officer. Pa. Capt. 145th Pa. 27 Aug. '62; Lt. Col. 5 Sept. '62; Bvt. B.G. USV (war service).

McCRILLIS, Lafayette. Union officer. N.H. Lt. Col. 3d Ill. 30 Aug. '61; Col. 25 July '62; Bvt. B.G. USV 4 Sept. '64 (war service); mustered out 5 Sept. '64. Commanded 1st, 2d, and 3d Brig. in the 1st Cav. Div., XVI. Died 1876.

McCULLAGH, Joseph Burbridge. WAR CORRESPONDENT and editor. 1842–96. Ireland. He reported the war in the West for the Cincinnati *Gazette* and was Commodore Foote's volunteer secretary in the *St. Louis* when Grant went from Henry to capture Fort Donelson. Here he narrowly escaped death when the vessel was hit 65 times, the pilot killed, and Foote's leg shattered. He later worked for the Cincinnati *Commercial* for four years in Washington before becoming managing editor for the Cincinnati *Enquirer* and then the Chicago *Republican*. He founded the St. Louis *Morning Globe* and combined it with the *Democrat* to produce one of the famous papers of that area.

McCULLOCH, Ben. C.S.A. gen. 1811–62. Tenn. He followed his neighbor Davy Crockett to Tex., distinguished himself at San Jacinto, and became a surveyor in the new republic. An Indian fighter, he was a Tex. Ranger and fought with them in the Mexican War, where he began to study the great captains. Going to California for the gold rush, he returned to serve as marshal along the Tex. coast and was a commissioner to the Mormons in Ill. A Col. of Tex. State troops in Feb. '61, he received the surrender of Twiggs and was appointed B.G. C.S.A. 11 May '61. He commanded troops in Ark., was in command of Confed. forces at Wilson's Creek, and led his brigade at Pea Ridge, where he was killed 7 Mar. '62 by sharpshooters. "Of medium height and slender, with quiet manners," he was "one of the most popular figures in Texas" (D.A.B.). Brother of Henry E. McCULLOCH.

McCULLOCH, Henry Eustace. C.S.A. gen. ?–1895. Tenn. A sheriff and legislator in Tex., he served as a Capt. in the Tex. Rangers during the Mexican War. Later US Marshal, he was commissioned Col. 1st Tex. Mtd. Rifles 15 Apr. '61 and commanded the Dept. of Tex. 4–18 Sept. '61. Assigned to command the district of San Antonio and the coast, he was appointed B.G. C.S.A. 14 Mar. '62 (C.M.H. gives this date as 12 June '62). He then took command of the troops in East Tex. and forwarded units to Little Rock, later taking command of a division at Devall's Bluff, Ark. Next in charge of the northern Dist. of Tex., he led a brigade under Walker during the Vicksburg campaign and fought at Millikens Bend. Returning to northern Tex. for a time, he took over a brigade in the Trans-Miss. Dept. in fall 1864 for the rest of the war. His brother was Ben McCULLOCH.

McCULLUCH, Hugh. Union Sec. of the Treasury. 1808–95. Me. After graduating from Bowdoin College and studying law in Boston, he became a banker in Fort Wayne (Ind.). He was named to a post in the Treasury by Chase in 1863 and Lincoln appointed him Sec. in

1865. He remained in this post throughout Johnson's term, was a banker in England for an American firm for a period, and was again Sec. of the Treasury, 1884–85.

McDOUGALL, Charles. Union officer. Ohio. Appt.-Ind. Joining the R.A. as Asst. Surgeon in 1832, he served in the Seminole War, at West Point, and on the frontier. As Maj. and Surgeon (since 1838), he was Medical Director of the Army of the Tenn. Apr.–Sept. '62, and held the same post in N.Y.C. for the remainder of the war. Continuing in the R.A., he retired in 1869 as Lt. Col. and Bvt. B.G. USA, dying in 1885.

McDOUGALL, Clinton Dugald. Union officer. 1839–? Scotland. Capt. 75th N.Y. 16 Sept. '61; Lt. Col. 111th N.Y. 20 Aug. '62; Col. 3 Jan. '63; Bvt. B.G. USV 25 Feb. '65. He was later Republican Congressman and holder of several other public offices.

McDOWELL, Irvin. Union gen. 1818–85. USMA 1838 (23/45); Arty. He attended the Collège de Troyes in France and then graduated from West Point. Serving first on the border and as tactics instructor and adjutant at the Military Academy, he was Gen. Wool's A.D.C. and Adj. in the Mexican War (1 brevet), served on the frontier, and then in army headquarters in Washington. It was then, through Gen. Scott, that he became well acquainted with the officials of Lincoln's administration, particularly S. P. Chase. Named B.G. USA 14 May '61 (from Maj. since 1856), he was given command of the Union troops south of the Potomac (28 May–17 Aug. '61). After his defeat at 1st Bull Run he commanded McDowell's division (3 Oct. '61–13 Mar. '62) and was named Maj. Gen. USV 14 Mar. '62. He then commanded the I Corps, Army of the Potomac (13 Mar.–4 Apr. '62) and led the

Army of the Rappahannock (4 Apr.– 26 June '62). At Cedar Mountain, Rappahannock Station, and 2d Bull Run he commanded the III Corps, Army of Va., and was severely criticized for his performance. Relieved of command, he demanded and was ultimately exonerated by a court of inquiry and then served on boards and commissions in Washington until going to command the Dept. of the Pacific (1 July '64–27 June '65). Continuing in the R.A., he commanded the Depts. of the East and South and retired in 1882 as Maj. Gen. USA (since 1872). He was later Park Commissioner of San Francisco. D.A.B. describes him as "squarely and powerfully built . . . [with a] manner . . . frank and agreeable."

McDOWELL, Va., 8 May '62. (SHENANDOAH VALLEY CAMPAIGN OF JACKSON) The advance of Banks's superior force (15,000) up the Valley forced Jackson to drop back to Swift Run Gap to prevent the isolation and destruction of his 6,000. In late April he was reinforced by Ewell's 8,000 and given command of Edward Johnson's 3,000. The latter had dropped back to West View (seven miles west of Staunton) in the face of Frémont's threatened advance from W. Va. Ordered to create a strategic diversion in the Valley to draw Federal troops away from the campaign against Richmond, Jackson decided to strike first at Frémont. He left Ewell in the flanking position at Swift Run Gap to prevent Banks from moving to Staunton. Ashby was ordered to make feints toward Banks's leading unit at Harrisonburg. On the afternoon of 30 Apr. Jackson with his own brigades started what Freeman has called "one of the muddiest, most difficult marches of the entire war." To deceive the enemy as to his objective, he took the route Port Republic–Brown Gap–Mechum's

River Station–Staunton (by rail)–West View. At the latter place he picked up Johnson's division and marched toward McDowell. During late afternoon of 7 May Johnson's leading elements drove Milroy's outposts back. When the Federals learned of Jackson's approach, Schenck's brigade hurried to Milroy's support—making a 34-mile march in 23 hours. The Confederates had marched 92 miles in four marching days (not including the 25-mile train ride).

The afternoon of 8 May the Confederates took up a position on Sitlington's Hill, overlooking the Federal camp across the Bull Pasture River. While Jackson was scouting for a way to turn the Federal position the Federals took the initiative. Despite the superior numbers and good defensive position of the enemy, Schenck (who took command of the two brigades by virtue of his seniority) ordered an attack. The Federals were repulsed although they sustained fewer casualties (256) than the defenders (498). Jackson was unable to conduct an effective pursuit because of poor roads and effective delaying actions. He reached Franklin, W. Va., on the 12th. Leaving Ashby's cavalry to screen his withdrawal, he then marched back to the Valley to undertake the next phase of his campaign (FRONT ROYAL).

McEWEN, Matthew. Union officer. Pa. Surg. 2d W. Va. Cav. 1 Mar. '63; Bvt. B.G. USV. Brevets for Winchester to Appomattox C.H. campaign, war service. Died 1883.

McFERRAN, John C. Union officer. c. 1821–72. Ky. USMA 1843 (34/39); Inf.-Q.M. He served on the frontier and in the Mexican War before he was named Chief Q.M. of the Dept. of N. Mex., serving there throughout the Civil War. Promoted Maj. 30 Nov. '63, he was breveted B.G. USA for war service and died on active duty as Lt. Col.

McGARRY, Edward. Union officer. N.Y. Maj. 2d Calif. Cav. 17 Oct. '61; Lt. Col. 18 Oct. '64; Col. 29 Nov. '64; Bvt. B.G. USV (war service). Lt. in Mexican War. He became a Lt. Col. in the 32d US Inf. 28 July '66. Died 31 Dec. '67.

McGINNIS, George Francis. Union gen. 1826–? Mass. He served in the Mexican War and enlisted as Pvt. Co. K, 11th Ind., 15 Apr. '61, being named Capt. the next day and Lt. Col. 25 Apr. Mustered out on 4 Aug., he was commissioned Lt. Col. 11th Ind. 31 Aug. and Col. 3 Sept. and B.G. USV 29 Nov. '62, after fighting at Fort Donelson and Shiloh. He commanded 2, 2d Div. E. Ark., Mo. (Dec. '62–Jan. '63) and 1, 12, XIII (Feb.–14 July '63) on the Yazoo Pass expedition and during the Vicksburg campaign. Other commands were 3, 12, XIII (22 Jan.–Feb. '63); 1, 3, XIII (7 Aug.–13 Sept. '63); 3d Div., XIII (13 Sept. '63–3 Mar. '64 and 24 May–11 June '64); 3, 3, XIX (6 Nov.–5 Dec. '64); 3d Div., XIX (25 Aug.–7 Nov. '64); 2d Div., XIX (18–25 June '64); US Forces Mouth White River, Gulf (10 Dec. '64–30 May '65) and 3d Brig., Res. Corps, Gulf (5–10 Dec. '64). He was mustered out 24 Aug. '65 and held public offices after the war.

McGLASHAN, Peter Alexander Selkirk. C.S.A. gen. c. 1831–1900. Scotland. Moving to the US as a boy, he was living in Thomasville, Ga., when the war began, and he enlisted in Aug. '61 in the 29th Ga. Serving on the Ga. coast, he was commissioned 1st Lt. 50th Ga. Mar. '62 and fought in the Seven Days' Battles. He was promoted Col. 28 Feb. '65 and was commanding Bryan's brigade under Kershaw when captured 5 Apr. '65. His B.G. appointment was the last one signed by Davis before he left Richmond, but McGlashan never received it. Held prisoner on Johnson's Island, he was released in late Aug. '65.

The son of a Napoleonic veteran, he had served under Walker in Nicaragua. C.M.H. and Lonn in *Foreigners in the Confederacy* say he was a general, but he is not listed by Wright, Miller, or Wood.

McGOWAN, John Encill. Union officer. Ohio. 2d Lt. 21st Ohio 23 Apr. '61; mustered out 12 Aug. '61; Capt. 111th Ohio 5 Sept. '62; Maj. 1st US Col. Arty. 24 Mar. '64; Lt. Col. 5 Nov. '64; Col. 5 Sept. '65; Bvt. B.G. USV (war service). Died 1903.

McGOWAN, Samuel. C.S.A. gen. 1819–97. S.C. After graduating from S.C. College he was a lawyer and entered politics, sitting in the state legislature. He was a Maj. Gen. in the S.C. militia, fought in the Mexican War, and as B.G. in the S.C. army commanded a state brigade in the bombardment of Fort Sumter. At Blackburn's Ford and 1st Bull Run he was a volunteer A.D.C. to Bonham and was commissioned Lt. Col. in the fall of 1861. As Col. 14th S.C. in 1862, he fought in Maxey Gregg's brigade in the Peninsular campaign (wounded), Cedar Mountain, 2d Bull Run (wounded), Antietam, and Fredericksburg. At Chancellorsville he commanded McGowan's brigade and was again wounded, having been appointed B.G. C.S.A. 23 Apr. '63 to rank from 17 Jan. Leading his own brigade at the Wilderness and Spotsylvania, he was wounded again in the "Bloody Angle." He continued in the Army of Northern Va. until Appomattox. After the war he was a legislator and associate justice of the S.C. supreme court.

McGREGOR, John Dunn. Union officer. N.Y. Lt. Col. 4th N.Y. 15 May '61; Col. 9 July '62; Bvt. B.G. USV (war service); mustered out 25 May '63. Died 1878.

McGROARTY, Stephen Joseph. Union officer. 1830–70. Ireland. Capt. 10th Ohio 13 May '61; resigned 28 Oct. '61; Lt. Col. 61st Ohio 23 Apr. '62; Col. 23 Sept. '62; transferred to 82d Ohio 31 Mar. '65; Bvt. B.G. USV 1 May '65 (war service). Commanded 1, 3, XI; 3, 3, XI; 3d Div., XI. W.I.A. Carnifex Ferry (W. Va.), where he was shot through the right lung, and Peach Tree Creek (Ga.), where he lost his left arm. Received 23 wounds in all during the war. He was a merchant and well-known criminal lawyer.

McINTOSH, James. C.S.A. gen. 1828–62. Fla. USMA 1849 (43/43); Inf. He served mainly on the frontier and was engaged in Indian scouting and fighting and quelling the border disturbances in Kans. Resigning as Capt. 7 May '61, he was commissioned Capt. C.S.A. Cav. that month and stationed at Little Rock on H. M. Rector's staff. He fought at Wilson's Creek and in Oct. '61 was commissioned Col. 2d Ark. Mtd. Rifles. In Dec. he fought at Chustenahlah (Cherokee Nation) and in several skirmishes with the Creeks and Seminoles. Appointed B.G. C.S.A. 24 Jan. '62, he continued to serve in the Indian Territory until killed 7 Mar. at Pea Ridge. Brother of John Baillie McINTOSH.

McINTOSH, John Baillie. Union gen. 1829–88. Fla. A Midshipman during the Mexican War, he was in business when the Civil War began and "considered as a blot on his family honor the resignation from the Federal service of his brother [James McQueen McIntosh, B.G., C.S.A.], who had been educated at West Point" (D.A.B.). He was commissioned 2d Lt. 2d US Cav. 8 June '61, transferred to the 5th US Cav. 3 Aug. '61, and was promoted 1st Lt. 27 June '62. He fought at White Oak Swamp, South Mountain, and Antietam before being named Col. 3d Pa.

Cav. 15 Nov. '62. At Kelly's Ford and Chancellorsville he led 2, 2, Cav. Corps, Potomac (17 Feb.–13 May '63) and commanded 1, 2, Cav. Corps, Potomac (11 June–1 Oct. '63) at Gettysburg. He was severely injured in Sept. by a fall from his horse and was assigned to the Cav. Depot in Washington during his recuperation, commanding cavalry division Camp Stoneman, XXII, Washington (9 Jan.–2 May '64). He then commanded 1, 3, Cav. Corps, Potomac (5 May–6 Aug. '64) and 1, 3, Cav. Corps, Army Shenandoah (6 Aug.–19 Sept. '64) at Winchester on the latter date, where he was severely wounded and had a leg amputated. He was breveted for White Oak Swamp, Gettysburg, Ashland, Winchester (B.G. USA), war service (Maj. Gen. USA) and Opequon (Maj. Gen. USV). Continuing in the R.A., he was retired with the rank of B.G. USA 1870. D.A.B. characterizes him as a "born fighter, a strict disciplinarian, a dashing leader, and a polished gentleman. He represents the highest type of volunteer soldier." Brother of James McINTOSH.

McIVOR, James Patrick. Union officer. Ireland. Commissioned Lt. Col. 170th N.Y. 7 Oct. '62, he was promoted Col. 1 Mar. '63 and mustered out in July '65. He was breveted for the Appomattox campaign (B.G. and Maj. Gen. USV 9 Apr. '65).

McKAY, Charlotte. Union Army nurse. Mass. After the death of her husband and only child, she became on 24 Mar. '62 a nurse in the Frederick, Md., hospital. After Fredericksburg she went to a Washington hospital to take care of the wounded, and in Jan. '63 nursed at the III Corps hospital at Falmouth. She was in the field during Chancellorsville, returned to Washington, and then went to Gettysburg after the battle. By June '64 she had been named dietician of the Cav. Corps hospital and she was awarded the Kearny Cross and, later, a gold badge from the hospital inmates. After May '65 she no longer nursed, but aided the Va. freedmen.

McKEAN, Thomas Jefferson. Union gen. 1810–70. Pa. USMA 1831 (19/33); Inf. He served on garrison duty and resigned in 1834 to be a civil engineer. With the Pa. Vols. during the Seminole War, he was then civil engineer and state constitutional delegate from Iowa. Failing to obtain a commission during the Mexican War, he drilled Iowa troops and enlisted as private. As Sgt. Maj. 15th US Inf., he was severely wounded at Churubusco but declined the brevet of 2d Lt. He then went into railroad engineering and surveying and was commissioned Add. Paymaster USV 1 June '61, with troops at Washington and St. Louis. Named B.G. USV 21 Nov. '61, he commanded Jefferson City Central Dist. Mo. (Dec. '61–Mar. '62) and 6th Div., Army Tenn. (10–30 Apr. and 10–15 June '62). During the advance upon and siege of Corinth he led 6th Div. Dist. Corinth (24 July–21 Sept. and 3–6 Oct. '62). His other commands were 4th Div. Right Wing, XIII, Tenn. (11 Nov.–9 Dec. '62); Dist. North Mo. (29 Jan.–4 June '63); Dist. Nebr. (4 June '63–Jan. '64); Dist. S. Kans. (25 June–1 Sept. '64); Dist. W. Fla. (25 Nov. '64–15 Feb. '65); Dist. Morganza (3–29 Mar. '65); Dist. Southwest Mo. (19 June–10 July '65). He was breveted Maj. Gen. for war service and mustered out 24 Aug. '65. Later a farmer, he held a number of appointed positions as a Republican.

McKEEVER, Chauncey. Union officer. c. 1829–1901. Md. Appt.-At-Large. USMA 1849 (14/43); Arty.-Adj. Gen. He served in the Seminole War, taught mathematics at West Point, fought Indians in the West, and went on the Utah Expedition before being promoted Capt. Asst. Adj. Gen. 3 Aug. '61. From 12 June–31 July '61 he was on Heintzelman's staff, joined McDowell's 31 July–3 Aug. '61, and became Frémont's Asst. Adj. Gen. 28 Aug.–20 Nov. '61. In the Peninsular campaign he was Chief of Staff for the III Corps, fighting at Yorktown, Williamsburg, Oak Grove, Glendale, Malvern Hill, and 2d Bull Run. Promoted Lt. Col. 20 Aug.–31 Dec. '62, he was on special duty in the War Dept. for the remainder of the war. He was breveted B.G. USA for war service and retired in 1893 as Col.

McKENNEY, Thomas Irving. Union officer. Ill. 1st Lt. 2d Iowa 27 May '61; Regt. Adj. 23 Sept. '61; Maj. Add. A.D.C. 17 Apr. '62; Bvt. B.G. USV (war service).

McKIBBIN, David Bell. Union officer. Pa. R.A. 1st Lt. 9th US Inf. 1 Mar. '61; Capt. 14th US Inf. 14 May '61; Col. 158th Pa. 24 Nov. '62; mustered out USV 12 Aug. '63; Col. 214th Pa. 5 Apr. '65; mustered out of USV and continued in USA until retired as Maj. in 1875. Bvt. B.G. USV 13 Mar. '65. Brevets for North Anna, Bethesda Church, war service. Commanded 1st Brig., Dist. Pamlico (N.C.), XVIII. Ex-cadet USMA 1850. Died 1890.

McKIBBIN, Gilbert Hunt. Union officer. N.Y. 2d Lt. 51st N.Y. 9 Oct. '61; 1st Lt. 16 May '62; Capt. Asst. Adj. Gen. Vols. 6 Oct. '62; Bvt. B.G. USV 2 Dec. '64 (war service). Commanded 1st Brig., Defenses Bermuda Hundred (Va.) and N.C.

McKINLEY, William. Union officer; 24th US pres. 1843–1901. Entering the service as Pvt. 23d Ohio on 23 June '61, he was promoted Comsy. Sgt. 15 Apr. '62. After fighting in the KANAWHA DIVISION, with Rutherford B. HAYES as his regimental commander, he was promoted 2d Lt. on 23 Sept. '62. He was made 1st Lt. on 7 Feb. '63, Capt. on 25 July '64, and was breveted Maj., USV, 13 Mar. '65, for "gallant and meritorious service during the campaign in W. Va. and in the Shenandoah Valley." He was mustered out 26 July '65. Elected pres. 4 Mar. '97. He died 14 Sept. 1901 of wounds inflicted by an assassin 6 Sept. at Buffalo (Heitman).

McKINSTRY, Justus. Union gen. c. 1816–97. N.Y. Appt.-Mich. USMA 1838 (40/45); Inf.-Q.M. After serving on garrison duty, in the Fla. war, the Mexican War (1 brevet), and on the frontier, he was (as Maj. Q.M. 3 Aug. '61) Chief Q.M., Dist. of the West and B.G. USV 2 Sept. '61, an appointment which expired 17 July '62. Accused of dishonesty in his transactions as Q.M. and arrested by Hunter, Frémont's successor, he was "... dismissed 28 Jan. '63 for neglect and violation of duty, to the prejudice of good order and military discipline" (Cullum). He was later a stockbroker in N.Y.C. and a land agent in Mo.

McLAREN, Robert Neill. Union officer. 1828–86. N.Y. 2d Lt. 6th Minn. 1 Aug. '62; Capt. 18 Aug. '62; Maj. 22 Aug. '62; Col. 2d Minn. Cav. 14 Jan. '64; Bvt. B.G. USV 14 Dec. '65 (war service). Participated in Gen. H. H. Sibley's campaigns across the northwestern plains in the Sioux War and was Post Commandant at Ft. Snelling (Minn.) when the Indian chiefs Little Six and Medicine Hat were hanged there. He was also a leader in the Republican party.

McLAUGLEN, Napoleon Bonaparte. Union officer. 1823–87. Vt. R.A. Pvt., Cpl., and Sgt. Co. F, 2d US Dragoons, and general service 27 May '50–28 Apr. '59; 2d Lt. 1st US Cav. 27 Mar. '61; 1st Lt. 3 May '61; 4th US Cav. 3 Aug. '61; Capt. 17 July '62; Col. 1st Mass. 1 Oct. '62; mustered out 28 May '64; Col. 57th Mass. 14 Sept. '64; Bvt. B.G. USV 30 Sept. '64; mustered out of USV and continued in R.A. until retired as Maj. in 1882. Brevets for Chancellorsville,

Gettysburg, Fort Stedman (Va.), war service, Poplar Grove Church (Va.). Captured at Fort Stedman and in Libby Prison (Richmond) until end of war. Served as I.G. of Army of Ky. Commanded 3, 1, IX; 1st Div., IX.

McLAWS, Lafayette. C.S.A. gen. 1821–97. Ga. USMA 1842 (48/56); Inf. He had attended the Univ. of Va. before graduating from West Point, and then served on the frontier, in garrison, in the Mexican War, on the Utah Expedition, and in Indian fighting before resigning 10 May '61 as Capt. Commissioned Maj. C.S.A. at first, he was elected Col. 10th Ga. on 17 June '61 and was appointed B.G. C.S.A. 25 Sept. '61. He fought at Yorktown before being promoted Maj. Gen. 23 May '62. As a division commander he went with Jackson to capture Harpers Ferry, fought at Antietam, defended Marye's Heights at Fredericksburg, and served under Longstreet at Chancellorsville. His troops fought in the Peach Orchard and Devil's Den (Gettysburg). Accompanying Longstreet to the West, he was relieved for general lack of cooperation during the Knoxville campaign. After McLaws pressed for a court-martial, Longstreet restricted his charges to improper preparations for the attack on Fort Sanders (Knoxville) 29 Nov. '62. The findings (announced 4 May '64) and their subsequent disapproval by Davis three days later added up to "a vindication of McLaws and a humiliation of Longstreet" (*Lee's Lts.*, III, 373). He was then given command of the Dist. of Ga. and the defense of Savannah. After the Carolinas campaign he surrendered with Johnston's army. After the war he was in the insurance business, then with the Internal Revenue and Post Office departments. His wife was a cousin of Richard TAYLOR.

He was characterized by Freeman as a stout, short Georgian, square and solid from the moral as well as the physical point of view, but who does not develop as the war progresses. He fights well at Fredericksburg when he has ample force and a strong position, but misses his chance at Chancellorsville to deliver a hammerstroke, and "has no lustre in the red glare of Gettysburg, though the fault is scarcely his" (*Lee's Lts.*).

McLEAN, Nathaniel Collins. Union gen. 1815–? Ohio. He was a lawyer and son of the Associate Justice of the US Supreme Court who gave the dissenting opinion in the Dred Scott case. Appointed Col. 75th Ohio 18 Sept. '61, he led his regiment at McDowell (Va.) 8 May '62 and commanded 2, 1, I, Army Va. (26 June–12 Sept. '62); 2, 1, XI, Potomac (12 Sept. '62–10 Jan. '63, 5 Feb.–10 Mar. '63, and 20 Apr.–2 May '63 at Chancellorsville). Here he succeeded to 1st Div., XI, when Devens was wounded (2–24 May '63). He also commanded that division 10 Jan.–5 Feb. '63, 10 Mar.–20 Apr. '63. He took over 3, 3, XXIII, Ohio (4–17 June '63); 1, 2, XXIII, Ohio (3 May–4 June '64); and 1st Div. Dist. of Ky., XXIII, Ohio (6 July–29 Dec. '64). He commanded 3, 2, XXIII, Ohio (2–8 Jan. '65); 3, 2, XXIII, N.C. (9–28 Feb. '65); and 2d Div., XXIII, N.C. (28 Feb.–4 Apr. '65). He resigned 20 Apr. '65.

McLEAN HOUSES. One of the first artillery rounds fired during the war hit the kitchen of Wilbur McLean's house on Bull Run while a meal was being prepared there for Beauregard. Continued military activity in the Centreville area forced McLean to abandon this farm and move to another he owned at a small place known as Appomattox Courthouse. On this farm occurred the last fighting of Lee's army, and on 9 Apr. '65 this second "McLean House" was the scene of the surrender.

McMAHON, John. Union officer. Ireland. Pvt. 105th Pa. 23 Dec. '61; 1st Lt. 8 Jan. '62; Capt. 25 Mar. '62; transferred to 94th N.Y. Mar. '63; Maj. 10 May '64; mustered out 21 Oct. '64; Col. 188th N.Y. 31 Mar. '65; Bvt. B.G. USV 30 June '65 (war service). Died 1891.

McMAHON, Martin Thomas. Union officer. 1838–? Canada. A lawyer and post office and Indian agent in the West, he was commissioned Capt. Add. A.D.C. 25 Oct. '61 to McClellan. He was promoted Maj. A.D.C. (29 Oct. '62–14 Feb. '63) and Lt. Col. Asst. Adj. Gen. Assigned (1 Jan. '63–15 Aug. '65). In the latter rank he served as Adj. Gen. and Chief of Staff for the VI Corps under Franklin, Sedgwick, and Wright. Breveted for Richmond and war service (B.G. and Maj. Gen. USV), he was given the Medal of Honor in 1891 for White Oak Swamp. He was mustered out in 1866 and held several public offices after the war. In 1868–69 he was Minister to Paraguay and was also active in veterans' organizations.

McMILLAN, James Winning. Union gen. 1825–1903. Ky. He enlisted in the Mexican War and in the Union Army was commissioned Col. 1st Ind. Arty. 24 July '61. He was named B.G. USV 29 Nov. '62. His commands were 2, 1, XIX, Army Shenandoah (6 Aug.–15 Oct. '64, 24–26 Oct. '64, and 3 Dec. '64–25 Jan. '65); 1st Div., XIX, Army Shenandoah (15–24 Oct. '64 and 25 Jan.–1 Mar. '65); 1st Ind. Div., W. Va. (Apr.–May '65). He resigned 15 May '65. Listed by Phisterer as McMillen, James W.

McMILLAN, William Linn. Union officer. 1829–1902. Ohio. He was a surgeon with the Russian Army in the Crimean War and with the 1st Ohio 17 Apr.–16 Aug. '61. Commissioned Col. 95th Ohio, 16 Aug. '62, he fought in the West and led a brigade at Nashville. He was mustered out in Aug. '65 and breveted for Nashville (B.G. USV 16 Dec. '64) and war service (Maj. Gen. USV). After the war he was a La. planter and legislator. In 1872 and 1873 he was sent to the US Senate but not admitted, and later was New Orleans' postmaster.

McMILLEN, James W. Erroneous listing by Phisterer for McMILLAN, James Winning.

McNAIR, Evander. C.S.A. gen. ?–1902. Appt.-Ark. As Col. 4th Ark. (17 Aug. '61), he fought at Wilson's Creek and Pea Ridge, where he succeeded Ben McCulloch in command of his brigade after Hébert was captured. He commanded a brigade under Bragg at Richmond (Ky.) and was appointed B.G. C.S.A. 4 Nov. '62. After leading his brigade at Stones River, he was sent in May '63 to join Johnston in the relief of Vicksburg, fighting in that campaign and at Jackson. Wounded at Chickamauga, he went in 1864 to the Trans-Miss. Dept., where he served for the remainder of the war.

McNARY, William H. Union officer. N.Y. Lt. Col. 158th N.Y. 12 Sept. '62; Col. 16 Apr. '65; Bvt. B.G. USV (war service). Commanded 1, 3, XV; 1, 1, XVI; 1st Brig., 1st Div., Detachment Army Tenn. (Cumberland); 1, 1, XVI (Gulf). Died 1890.

McNAUGHT, Thomas Alexander. Union officer. Ind. Capt. 59th Ind. 10 Oct. '61; Maj. 16 Nov. '62; Lt. Col. 10 Apr. '65; Col. 28 June '65; Bvt. B.G. USV 4 Aug. '65 (war service).

McNEIL, John. Union gen. 1813–91. Nova Scotia. A hatter first in Boston then for 20 years in St. Louis, he was also in the state legislature and president of an insurance company. Named Col. 3d Mo. 8 May '61, with 600 men he routed the Confederates at Fulton under Gen. D. B. Harris 17 July '61 and was then mustered out 17 Aug. '61. On 30 June '62 he was commissioned Col. 2d Mo. State Militia Cav. (commanding the Dist. of Northern Mo. until 29 Jan. '63) and cleared that area of C.S.A. guerrillas. Promoted B.G. USV 29 Nov. '62, he next commanded Dist. Southwest Mo. (15 July–15 Oct. '63); Dist. La Fourche (4 May–9 June '64); Dist. Rolla (23 Aug.–5 Sept. '64) during Price's raid; Dist. Port Hudson (9 June– 9 Aug. '64) and Dist. Central Mo. (27 Feb.–2 Apr. '65). Breveted Maj. Gen. USV 12 Apr. '65, he resigned on that date and went back into politics.

McNETT, Andrew James. Union officer. N.Y. Capt. 93d N.Y 11 Oct. '61; mustered out 12 June '63; Lt. Col. 141st N.Y. 13 Feb. '64; Bvt. B.G. USV 28 July '66 (Resaca [2], Dallas, Culp's Farm and Peach Tree Creek [2]); W.I.A. in front of Atlanta, losing right arm; continued in R.A. until retired as Col. in 1870. Died 1895.

McNULTA, John. Union officer. N.Y. Capt. 1st Ill. Cav. 3 July '61; mustered out 14 July '62; Lt. Col. 94th Ill. 20 Aug. '62; Col. 21 June '63; Bvt. B.G. USV (Spanish Fort, Ala.). Commanded 2d Brig., 3d Div. Army of the Frontier (Mo.). Died 1900.

McPHERSON, James Birdseye. Union gen. 1828–64. Ohio. USMA 1853 (1/52); Engrs. After teaching engineering at West Point he was then engaged in river and harbor improvement and seacoast fortifications before being promoted Capt. 6 Aug. '61. He was next Lt. Col. and Add. A.D.C. to Halleck in the Dept. of Mo. (12 Nov. '61) and became Grant's Chief Engr. 1 Feb. '62. He was at Fort Henry, Fort Donelson, Shiloh, and the advance upon and siege of Corinth. Promoted Col. Add. A.D.C. 1 May '62, and B.G. USV 14 days later, he commanded the Engr. Brig., Army Tenn. (4 June–4 Oct. '62) at Iuka and

various skirmishes during Grant's Tenn. campaign. He was then appointed Maj. Gen. USV 8 Oct. '62 and commanded 2d Div., Tenn. 16–24 Oct. and the same division in the XIII Corps 24 Oct.– 2 Nov. '62. He led the Right Wing, XIII (1 Nov.–18 Dec. '62) and the XVII Corps (18 Dec. '62–26 Mar. '64) during the Vicksburg campaign. He then took command of the Army of the Tenn. and led it until his death in the battle of ATLANTA, 22 July '64. He was 35 years old.

McQUADE, James. Union officer. N.Y. 1829–85. Educated in Montreal, he was a lawyer, banker, and politician before being commissioned Col. 14th N.Y. 17 May '61. After Malvern Hill he succeeded to command of the brigade and served for 18 months in this position. He was mustered out 24 May '63 when poor health and exhaustion invalided him at Chancellorsville. Breveted B.G. USV and Maj. Gen. USV for war service, he returned to politics and was active in veterans' organizations.

McQUEEN, Alexander G. Union officer. Ohio. Pvt. Co. A 1st Iowa Cav. 13 June '61; 1st Lt. 23 July '61; Capt. 11 Dec. '61; Maj. 12 Oct. '63; Lt. Col. 31 Dec. '64; Bvt. B.G. USV (war service).

McQUISTON, John Craven. Union officer. Ind. Capt. 16th Ind. 14 May '61; mustered out 14 May '62; Col. 123d Ind. 9 Mar. '64; Bvt. B.G. USV (war service). Commanded 4, 2, XXIII; 2, 1, XXIII; 2, 1, Prov. Corps (N.C.); 2, 1, XXIII (N.C.).

McRAE, Dandridge. C.S.A. gen. Appt.-Ark. Named Col. of the 21st Ark., he fought in McCulloch's brigade at Wilson's Creek and Pea Ridge. Appointed B.G. C.S.A. 5 Nov. '62 he led his brigade at HELENA. At Marks's Mill and Jenkins' Ferry he commanded his unit in Ark. in 1864 and continued to skirmish in northern Ark. and Mo. until he resigned later in 1864.

McRAE, William. C.S.A. gen. 1834–82. N.C. A civil engineer, he was commissioned Capt. 15th N.C. in the spring of 1861 and promoted Lt. Col. in Apr. '62. He fought on the Peninsula and at 2d Bull Run in Howell Cobb's brigade. At Antietam he led the regiment and succeeded Cobb as brigade commander. Only 250 strong to start with, the brigade had 50 men left. He commanded his regiment at Fredericksburg, was promoted Col. in Feb. '63, and served in J. R. Cooke's N.C. brigade in N.C. and southeast Va. until after Gettysburg. After Bristoe Station he took over the brigade as temporary B.G. C.S.A. 22 June '64, when Kirkland was wounded at Cold Harbor. He led this unit in the battles around Petersburg, was appointed B.G. C.S.A. 4 Nov. '64, and surrendered at Appomattox. After the war he was general superintendent of a railroad.

MEADE, George Gordon. 1815–72. Born in Spain of US parents. USMA 1835 (19/56); Arty. Commander of the Army of the Potomac from just before Gettysburg to the end of the war. Appointed to West Point from Pa., he resigned a year after graduation to become a civil engineer. In 1842 he re-entered the army, saw service in Mexico, and then performed the duties of a military engineer. A B.G. of volunteers with practically no experience as a troop leader, he advanced steadily from command of a brigade during the Peninsular campaign (wounded at White Oak Swamp) and the 2d Bull Run campaign to the command of a division at Antietam and Fredericksburg, and command of the V Corps at Chancellorsville. In the search for a successor to Hooker, the more qualified John F. Reynolds was passed over in favor of Meade, whose foreign birth disqualified him as a presidential candidate.

Although Meade showed remarkable courage in accepting battle at Gettysburg, a mere two days after he had assumed command of the army, his failure to pursue and his subsequent conduct of the Bristoe and Mine Run campaigns proved him to be what Napoleon would have called "an ordinary general." In the closing campaigns of the war, from the Wilderness to Appomattox, he was in the anomalous position of commanding the Army of the Potomac while his superior, Grant, remained at his elbow. Grant comments in his memoirs on the commendable manner in which Meade functioned in this difficult situation.

His irascible disposition, the strain of the heavy fighting, and his difficult command situation conspired to make him so unpopular with his subordinates that Grant gave serious consideration to replacing him. Meade quarreled with "Baldy" Smith, Sheridan, Wright, Warren, and James Wilson. "I don't know any thin old [49] gentleman with a hooked nose and cold blue eye, who, when he is wrathy, exercises less of Christian charity than my well-beloved Chief," wrote Lyman.

"General Meade was an officer of great merit, with drawbacks to his usefulness that were beyond his control," says Grant in his memoirs. "He was brave and conscientious, and commanded the respect of all who knew him. He was unfortunately of a temper that would get beyond his control, at times.... No one saw this better than he himself, and no one regretted it more. This made it unpleasant at times, even in battle, for those around him to approach him even with information."

After the war he commanded the Div. of the Atlantic with headquarters at Philadelphia. In early 1867 he took command of the Reconstruction district that comprised Ala., Ga., and Fla. (Mil. Distr. No. 3), with headquarters at Atlanta. Bitterly disappointed when Sheridan and not he was appointed Lt. Gen. when Sherman moved up to succeed Grant, Meade returned to command the Div. of the Atlantic. Three years later he died of pneumonia at 57, his system never having recovered from his wound at White Oak Swamp.

MEADOW BRIDGE, Va., 12 May '64. (SHERIDAN'S RICHMOND RAID) The 5th Mich. Cav., ordered to cross the Chickahominy at this place, found the bridge destroyed. The regiment crossed by the railroad bridge and drove the Confederates into intrenchments on a nearby hill. Merritt's remaining troops and Wilson's 3d Cav. Div. reinforced and, after an hour's fight, established a bridgehead for the withdrawal of Sheridan's cavalry after YELLOW TAVERN.

MEAGHER (marr), **Thomas Francis.** Union gen. 1823–67. Ireland. The Irish-American leader in N.Y.C., he had been banished to Tasmania for sedition and treasonous activity in his native Ireland and had escaped to the US in 1852 and taken out citizenship papers. He had been a lawyer, lecturer, and newspaper editor when commissioned B.G. USV 3 Feb. '62 to command the Irish Brigade (2, Sumner's Div., Potomac; later 2, 1, II, Potomac) that he had raised that winter in N.Y. He led it 13 Mar.–28 June during the Peninsular campaign; 29 June–16 July; 8 Aug.–17 Sept. at 2d Bull Run and Antietam; 18 Sept.–20 Dec. at Fredericksburg and 18 Feb.–8 May '63 at Chancellorsville. He resigned 14 May '63 when his brigade was decimated and ineffective, but his resignation was canceled 23 Dec. '63, and he was given command of Dist. Etowah. He was with Sherman at Atlanta, commanded a provisional division (see below), and resigned 15 May '65, having been given a gold medal by N.Y.C. for

leading the Irish Brigade. He was territorial secretary and temporary Gov. of Mont. when, in 1867, he drowned in the Missouri River, falling from the deck of a steamer while on a reconnaissance near Fort Benton.

MEAGHER'S PROVISIONAL DIVISION. A message from Beauregard to Cooper, dated 4 Feb. '65 from Augusta, said that the XIX Corps was at Savannah "and General [T. F.] Meagher with the stragglers of Sherman's army" (O.R., I, XLVII, I, 1047). In Cox's war journal there is reference to this unit, saying it was "made up of detachments belonging to Sherman's army, waiting for an opportunity to rejoin him . . ." (ibid., 930). Other provisional units were made up of convalescents and garrison troops for the Carolinas campaign and eventually placed under the command of I. N. Palmer and S. P. Carter (Cox, March, 155).

MECHANICSVILLE, Va., 26 June '62. (Ellison's Mill) Second of the Seven Days' Battles (PENINSULAR CAMPAIGN). McClellan had maintained his dangerous position astride the Chick-

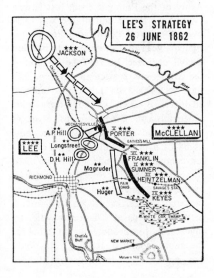

ahominy, with Porter's (V) corps and Stoneman's cavalry on the north side to link up with the expected overland movement of McDowell's corps from Fredericksburg. Lee planned to take advantage of this situation and the fact that Jackson's forces were available after having completed the valley campaign to mass overwhelming combat power against this separated wing and annihilate it. While Magruder with 25,000 conducted a secondary attack against the 60,000 Federals south of the Chickahominy, Lee would hit Porter (30,000) with the remainder of his army (47,000 of Longstreet and the two Hills plus Jackson's 18,500).

McCall's division was disposed along Beaver Dam Creek with the brigades of Seymour, Meade, and J. F. Reynolds from south to north. Sykes's division was to McCall's left rear along the Chickahominy. Morell's division was in reserve, with one brigade opposite New Bridge. The Confederate plan was as follows: Jackson was to leave Ashland at 3 A.M. and make contact at Half Sink with Branch's brigade of A. P. Hill's division. When A. P. Hill learned that Jackson was approaching Mechanicsville, Hill was to force a crossing of the Chickahominy at Meadow Bridge and move southeast against Mechanicsville, where the Federal flank was supposed to be. Longstreet would cross the bridge and support A. P. Hill; D. H. Hill would move across the same bridge and support Jackson, whose prescribed line of advance would bring him into position to hit behind the Federal flank. After overwhelming Porter, the two leading divisions were to move toward Cold Harbor and cut McClellan's line of communications, the railroad to White House.

It was not until 9 A.M., six hours behind schedule, that the head of Jackson's column neared Merry Oaks, on the Virginia Central R.R., and he sent word to A. P. Hill through Branch of his approach. About 3 P.M. Jackson approached Totopotomoy Creek from the north. A. P. Hill, in the meantime, had become impatient at the delays and, without authority, had started his attack. By 5 o'clock he was under heavy fire from McCall's division, and by dark he had been stopped along Beaver Dam Creek. Having detected Jackson's approach, Porter ordered up Griffin's and Martindale's brigades (Morell) from reserve to extend his right flank. They arrived at dark. At about 5 P.M. Jackson reached Pole Green Church, less than three miles northeast of where the battle was raging. Not finding A. P. Hill on his right or D. H. Hill in support for the attack he had been told he would take part in, Jackson was at a loss as to what action to take. At 5 P.M. he went into bivouac. D. H. Hill and Longstreet, meanwhile, had crowded up behind A. P. Hill. Lee arrived on the field and shortly thereafter sent A. P. Hill word not to advance but to hold the ground taken. The latter, apparently thinking this order allowed him the discretion of attacking on his left, sent the brigades of Ripley and Pender into a gallant but suicidal attack against the Federal right. Small-arms fire continued until 9 P.M., and artillery for another hour or more. McCall was ordered to fall back to GAINES'S MILL, where a major action took place the next day.

Out of 15,631 Federal troops engaged there were 361 casualties (49 killed, 207 wounded, and 105 missing). Out of 16,356 Confederates engaged (A. P. Hill's division and Ripley's brigade of D. H. Hill) the total loss was 1,484, according to Livermore, and 1,365, according to Fox.

MEDAL OF HONOR is the highest decoration for valor given by the US Army and Navy. It was first authorized for naval enlisted men in Dec. '61 and for army enlisted men in July '62. On 3 Mar. '63 it was extended to include army officers and made retroactive to the beginning of the Civil War. Naval and marine officers were not included until 1915. Criteria for award were much lower in the beginning, and during the Civil War some 1,200 were given. The first Medals of Honor were given to the six survivors of the ANDREWS' RAID.

MEDALS. See DECORATIONS.

MEETING ENGAGEMENT. An unexpected collision between opposing forces that takes place before either can execute a planned attack or defense. Gettysburg is a classic example.

MEHRINGER, John. Union officer. Germany. Maj. 27th Ind. 12 Sept. '61; resigned 15 Jan. '62; Lt. Col. 91st Ind. 2 Oct. '62; Col. 20 Oct. '63; Bvt. B.G. USV (war service). Commanded 2, 2, XXIII (N.C.).

MEIGS, John Rodgers. Union Lt., son of Gen. Meigs (Q.M.G.) and much-esteemed Topo. Engr. on Sheridan's staff, whose alleged "murder by bushwhackers" (O'Connor, 214) 3 Oct. '64 led Sheridan to order the burning of all houses within a five-mile radius of Dayton, Va. Although Heitman and Cullum say he was "killed by guerrillas," it was learned after the war that he was killed by one of Wickham's scouts while trying to avoid capture (B.&L., IV, 525n; Pond, 199n.). He was 22, had stood at the top of his USMA class of 1863, and had been breveted for Opequon and Fishers Hill. (See also DAYTON, Va.)

MEIGS, Montgomery Cunningham. Union gen. c. 1816–92. Ga. Appt.-Pa. USMA 1836 (5/49); Arty.-Engrs.-Q.M. He served in various peacetime engineering assignments and was promoted Col. 11th US Inf. 14 May '61 (Capt.

since 1853). The next day he was appointed B.G. USA and Q.M.G. Energetic and efficient, he served in that difficult position throughout the war. He retired in 1882, having been breveted Maj. Gen. USA 5 July '64.

MEMMINGER, Christopher Gustavus. C.S.A. Sec. of the Treasury. 1803–88. Germany. Appt.-S.C. Coming to the US as an infant and left an orphan at four in Charleston, he was placed in an asylum until adopted by Thomas Bennett, later Gov. of S.C. He graduated from college, studied law, and then entered politics, taking a stand against the doctrine of nullification and acting as one of the establishers of the public-school system in his state. Against abolition, he served in the legislature and was a member both at the secession convention and the provisional C.S.A. Congress at Montgomery. Named Sec. of the Treasury 21 Feb. '61, he negotiated a European loan on cotton and a number of other revenue-providing measures before resigning in July '64. After the war, he returned to the law and also was active in the industrial and educational development of S.C.

MENDENHALL, Elizabeth. SANITARY COMMISSION worker. Va. A native of Cincinnati, she started working in the hospital there early in 1862. She organized the Great Western Sanitary Fair in that city, that, in Jan. '64, made $250,000.

MERCER, Hugh Weedon. C.S.A. gen. 1808–77. Va. USMA 1828 (3/33); Arty. He served in garrison and as Scott's A.D.C. 1832–34, resigning the next year to become a Savannah banker. Long active in the militia, he was commissioned Col. 1st Ga. when the state seceded and appointed B.G. C.S.A. 29 Oct. '61. He commanded the post of Savannah most of the war, joining the

Army of Tenn. as a brigade commander under Hardee during the Atlanta campaign. He led his troops at Dalton, Kenesaw Mountain, and Marietta, and succeeded W. H. T. Walker as division commander. Relieved because of ill-health, he was sent to Savannah with Hardee. After the war he was a banker and commission merchant.

MERCHANT, Charles S. Union officer. c. 1795–1879. N.Y. USMA 1814* (2/30); Arty. He fought in the War of 1812, the Seminole War, and the Mexican War before being promoted Col. 4th US Arty. 28 Aug. '61. During the Civil War he commanded posts in the East and served on court-martial duty, after being retired from active duty 1 Aug. '63, and breveted B.G. USA.

MEREDITH, Solomon. Union gen. 1810–75. N.C. Commissioned Col. 19th Ind. 29 July '61, he was W.I.A. at Gainesville while leading his regiment. Named B.G. USV 6 Oct. '62, he commanded 26 Nov. to 13 Dec. '62 and 1 Mar. to 16 Jun. '63 the 4, 1, I (Potomac). He took over the IRON BRIGADE 16 June and commanded it until the second day of Gettysburg, when he was wounded. He also commanded 1st Div., I Corps (Potomac) 27 Feb.–1 Mar. '63 and 13 Nov. '63; Dist. Western Ky. (Ohio) 11 Sept. '64–21 May '65; Dist. Western Ky. (Ky.) 1 Feb. '65–24 Aug. '65. Bvt. Maj. Gen. USV 14 Aug. '65 (war service); mustered out 24 May '65. A public office-holder before the war, he was later Surveyor-General of the Mont. Territory and an Ind. farmer. Appleton's describes him as being "... six feet six inches in height, of commanding presence, and a ready speaker." He had three sons in the Union Army, two of whom were killed.

*There was no class standing prior to 1818, and the cadets are listed in the order in which they were commissioned.

MEREDITH, Sullivan Amory. Union gen. 1816–74. Pa. At the beginning of the war he supervised drilling, equipping, and forwarding of over 30,000 Pa. troops (Appleton's). With the 10th Pa. (Col. 26 Apr. '61) in Patterson's Valley campaign, he was mustered out 1 Aug. '61. He later organized the 56th Pa. (Col. 6 Mar. '62) and joined McDowell's corps at 2d Bull Run, where he was severely wounded. When partially recovered, he was commissioner for exchange of prisoners and served under Rosecrans in St. Louis from 1864 until mustered out 24 Aug. '65.

MERIDIAN CAMPAIGN, Miss., 3 Feb.–5 Mar. '64. After the capture of Vicksburg Lincoln expressed a desire that Ark. and La. be recovered. Sherman was ordered to cooperate with Banks's proposed RED RIVER CAMPAIGN OF 1864. But since the rivers would be too low for naval support until March, Sherman decided in the meantime to strengthen the Federal hold on Vicksburg by destroying the railroads and resources of central Mississippi. On 3 Feb. he left Vicksburg to capture Meridian and break up the railroads. His force of about 25,000 was composed of the following units: Veatch's and A. J. Smith's divisions, XVI, under Hurlbut; Leggett's and Crocker's divisions, XVII, under McPherson; plus the 5th and 11th Ill., 4th Iowa, 10th Mo., and Foster's battalion of Ohio cavalry.

In conjunction with Sherman's advance from the west, Wm. Sooy Smith was to advance to Meridian from Memphis with 7,000 cavalry, dispersing Forrest's cavalry en route.

To oppose these Federal operations were Polk's two infantry divisions under Loring and French near Jackson and Meridian, S. D. Lee's cavalry near Jackson, and Forrest's cavalry in northern Miss. Each of these four units numbered about 5,000. Polk withdrew without seriously contesting Sherman's advance; Loring and French moved into Ala., and S. D. Lee went north. Sherman entered Meridian 14 Feb. after having had skirmishes on Big Black River (4 Feb.), Clinton and Jackson (5 Feb.), Morton (8 Feb.), Decatur and Chunky Station (12th), and Tunnel Hill (13th). After spending five days in Meridian destroying its facilities, and waiting the arrival of Sooy Smith, he withdrew into central Miss., concentrated at Canton (27 Feb.–3 Mar.), and then withdrew them to Vicksburg. There were skirmishes at Lauderdale Springs (16 Feb.) and Marion (17 Feb.). In March Sherman sent 10,000 troops under A. J. Smith to reinforce Banks. He himself went to Nashville to prepare for the ATLANTA CAMPAIGN.

The "Sooy Smith Expedition" had meanwhile resulted in a humiliating failure when Forrest routed the larger Federal force at WEST POINT, Miss., 21 Feb. '64 (which see for details of the expedition, the engagements, and the ensuing Smith-Sherman controversy).

Sherman reported a loss of 170 in the Meridian expedition (21 killed, 68 wounded, and 81 missing). He put Confederate losses at 400 killed and wounded and 200 captured.

MERRILL, Lewis. Union officer. c. 1834–96. Pa. USMA 1855 (20/34); Dragoons. 1st Lt. 2d US Dragoons 24 Apr. '61; 2d US Cav. 3 Aug. '61; Col. 2d Mo. Cav. ("Merrill's Horse") 23 Aug. '61; mustered out USV 1865; Bvt. B.G. USV. Brevets for Northern Mo., Little Rock; Northwest Ga., war service. In Aug., '61 he was Col. and Chief of Cav. on Frémont's staff. In pursuit of the rebels at Little Rock, his regiment captured more than 400 prisoners. Continued in R.A., retiring in 1886 as Lt. Col. Bvt. B.G. USA 1890 (Canyon Creek, Mont.)

MERRITT, Wesley. Union gen. 1834–1910. N.Y. Appt.-Ill. USMA 1860 (22/41); Dragoons. Serving on the frontier until Aug. '61, he was promoted Capt. 2d US Cav. 5 Apr. '62 and served as Philip St. George Cooke's A.D.C. (Feb.–Sept. '62) when the latter commanded the Cav. of the Army of the Potomac. Remaining in the headquarters of the Dept. of Washington until Apr. '63, he was Stoneman's A.D.C. (Apr.–May '63). He was appointed B.G. USV 29 June '63 and commanded the Res. Brig., 1st Div., Cav. Corps (28 June–12 Aug. '63) at Gettysburg and Rappahannock Station; (12 Sept.– 21 Nov. '63) at Culpeper C.H.; (10 Apr.–7 May '64) at the Furnaces and Todd's Tavern; and (25 May–6 Aug. '64) at Old Church, Cold Harbor, on Sheridan's raid toward Charlottesville, Trevilian Station, and Darbytown. Commanding 1st Div., Cav. Corps, Potomac (15 Aug.–15 Sept. '63; 21 Nov. '63–10 Apr. '64 and 7–25 May '64), he fought at Barnett's Ford, on Sheridan's raid toward Richmond, Yellow Tavern, and Meadow Bridge. Leading the same division in the Army of the Shenandoah, he fought at Stone Chapel, Newtown, Cedarville, Kearnysville, Bunker Hill, Smithfield, Berryville, Opequon, Millford, Luray, Browns Gap, Mount Crawford, Tom's Run, Cedar Creek, and Middletown (6 Aug.–13 Nov. '64) as well as at Gordonsville (28 Nov.–31 Dec. '64 and 15–26 Jan. '65). Commanding the Cav. Corps of the Shenandoah, he participated in the skirmish at Ashland (26 Jan.–25 Mar. '65) and then commanded the Cav. Corps of the Potomac (25 Mar.–22 May '65) at Dinwiddie C.H., Five Forks, Sayler's Creek, and Appomattox. He was promoted Maj. Gen. USV 1 Apr. '65 and breveted for Gettysburg, Yellow Tavern, Haw's Shop, Winchester–Fishers Hill (Maj. Gen. USV 19 Oct. '64), Five

Forks (B.G. USA), and war service (Maj. Gen. USA). Continuing in the R.A., he was engaged principally in Indian fighting after the war and served as USMA superintendent. Commanding the first Philippine expedition in 1898 (promoted B.G. USA in 1887 and Maj. Gen. USA in 1895), he received the surrender of Manila with Adm. Dewey and was Mil. Gov. for a short while. He was one of the US Representatives to the Peace Commission in France and retired in 1900. One of the "boy wonders" of the war, he was "a fine-looking man of strong will and wide experience . . . highly competent and at the same time modest and agreeable" (D.A.B.).

MERSY, August. Union officer. Germany. Capt. 9th Ill. 25 Apr. '61; Lt. Col. 26 Apr. '61; mustered out 24 July '61; Lt. Col. 9th Ill. 26 July '61; Col. 5 Sept. '61; Bvt. B.G. USV (war service); mustered out 20 Aug. '64. Commanded 2d Brig., 2d Div. (Tenn.); 2d Brig., 2d Div., Dist. Corinth (Tenn.); 2d Brig., Dist. Corinth, XIII; 2, Dist. Corinth, XVII; 2, Dist. Corinth, XVI; Left Wing, XVI; 2, 2, XVI; 2d Div., XVI. Died 1866.

MESSER, John. Union officer. N.H. Capt. 101st Ohio 30 Aug. '62; Lt. Col. 14 Feb. '63; Bvt. B.G. USV (Chickamauga); resigned 7 Jan. '64. Died 1874.

MESSES. At the beginning of the war the men "messed in squads." All took turns cooking, and the first one to complain did the cooking the next time. In Mar. '63 Congress required the food to be prepared by companies, and cooks were hired, but the preparation by squads and individuals continued.

MESS GEAR. Each Union soldier was issued a knife, fork, tin plate, and tin cup. In 1863 a spoon was added.

MEYER, Edward Seraphim. Union officer. Ohio. Pvt. and Sgt. Co. F 4th Ohio and Sgt. Co. A 19th Ohio 20 Apr.–31 Oct. '61; 1st Lt. 19th Ohio 1 Nov. '61; resigned 27 Sept. '62; Capt. 107th Ohio 11 Nov. '62; resigned 1 Jan. '65; Maj. 5th US Vet. Vol. Inf. 16 Feb. '65; Bvt. B.G. USV (war service); transferred to R.A. Brevets for Shiloh and Chancellorsville.

M.I.A. Abbreviation for "missing in action." See CASUALTY, definition of.

MICHIE (my'-key), Peter Smith. Union officer. 1839–1901. Scotland. USMA 1863 (2/20); Engrs. 1st Lt. 11 June '63; Lt. Col. Asst. I.G. Assigned 23 Mar–6 June '65; Bvt. B.G. USV. Brevets for campaign of 1864 against Richmond, campaign ending at Appomattox C.H., meritorious service in 1864. He served as assistant engineer in the construction of the siege batteries at Charleston in 1863, as chief engineer in 1864 of Gen. Seymour's division in Fla., and as chief engineer of the Army of the James. In charge of DUTCH GAP CANAL PROJECT. In 1871 he became the professor of natural and experimental philosophy at USMA. He wrote several texts on mechanics, physics, and astronomy as well as *Life and Letters of Emory Upton* (1885), *Personnel of Sea Coast Defenses* (1887), and *General McClellan* (1901).

"MICHIGAN ANNIE." See Anna ETHERIDGE.

1ST MICHIGAN (1st Division, V Corps)

Colonels: John C. Robinson (R.A.; Bvt. Maj. Gen. USA), Horace S. Roberts (K.I.A.), Franklin W. Whittlesey, Ira C. Abbott (Bvt. B.G.), William A. Throop (Bvt. B.G.).

Battles: Mechanicsville, Gaines's Mill, Malvern Hill, Gainesville and Manassas, Shepherdstown, Fredericksburg, Chancellorsville, Gettysburg, Wilderness, Spotsylvania, North Anna, Bethesda Church, siege of Petersburg, Weldon R.R., Peeble's Farm, Hatcher's Run, Five Forks. Present also at Peach Orchard, Savage's Station, White Oak Swamp, Antietam, Rappahannock, Mine Run, Totopotomoy, White Oak Road, and Appomattox.

Originally a three months' regiment, organized in Apr. '61, it returned to its state after the 1st Bull Run, and reorganized under a three years' enlistment. During the winter of 1861–62 it camped at Annapolis Junction, Md., with the mission of guarding the railroad. At the start of the Peninsular campaign it was assigned to the 1st (then Morell's) Div., V Corps, with which it remained throughout the war. The regiment lost 151 casualties at Gaines's Mill, where Roberts was in command. Losses at Manassas were 178 out of the 20 officers and 220 men engaged. Colonel Roberts was killed, as were four captains and three lieutenants; eight line officers were wounded. Abbott led the regiment at Fredericksburg (Barnes's brigade, Griffin's division); losses were 8 killed and 40 wounded. At the start of the Wilderness campaign the regimental strength was down to 176 muskets. Fighting now in the 3d Brig. (Bartlett's) the regiment lost another 86 casualties in the Wilderness and at Spotsylvania. In Feb. '64, 213 men re-enlisted to continue the regiment's existence to the end of the war.

4TH MICHIGAN (2d Brigade, 1st Division, V Corps)

Colonels: Dwight A. Woodbury (K.I.A.), Jonathan W. Childs, Harrison H. Jeffords (K.I.A.), George W. Lombard (K.I.A.), Jairus W. Hall (Bvt. B.G.).

Battles: Hall's Hill, Yorktown, Newbridge, Mechanicsville, Gaines's Mill, Malvern Hill, Turkey Creek, Shepherdstown Ford, Fredericksburg, Chancel-lorsville, Gettysburg, Wilderness, Spotsylvania, North Anna, Totopotomoy, Bethesda Church, Petersburg. Also at Hanover Courthouse, Manassas, Antietam, Mine Run, and Rappahannock Station.

Organized at Adrian 16 May and leaving the state 25 June '61, the regiment participated in the 1st Bull Run campaign, but was not engaged. It spent the winter at Miner's Hill, Va., and early the next spring moved to the Peninsula. Here it joined the 2d Brig. (Griffin's), 1st Div. (Morell's), V Corps, where it remained the rest of its service. At Gaines's Mill and Malvern Hill, within a space of five days, it lost 252 casualties. Col. Woodbury was killed at the latter place.

At Gettysburg (where Barnes commanded the division and Sweitzer the brigade) the regiment lost 165 in the desperate fighting in "The Wheat Field," of whom 76 were listed as missing. In the hand-to-hand fighting here, Col. Jeffords shot an enemy officer who seized the regimental colors; a Confederate soldier bayonetted Jeffords and was, himself, killed by Maj. Hall's revolver. The next regimental commander, Lombard, was killed at the Wilderness. The regiment was mustered out 20 June '64.

The 4th Mich. ranks No. 34 among the 50 Federal regiments sustaining the highest percentage of total enrollment killed.

5TH MICHIGAN

Colonels: Henry D. Terry (Brig. Gen.), Samuel E. Beach, John Pulford (Bvt. B.G.).

Battles: Pohick Church (9 Jan. '62), Williamsburg, Fair Oaks, Glendale, Malvern Hill, Manassas, Fredericksburg, Chancellorsville, Gettysburg, Mine Run, Wilderness, Spotsylvania, North Anna, Totopotomoy, Cold Harbor, Petersburg assault, Strawberry Plains,

Boydton Road, Hatcher's Run, fall of Petersburg, Sayler's Creek. Also at Yorktown, Chantilly, Wapping Heights, Auburn, Kelly's Ford, Deep Bottom, Farmville, Appomattox.

In Berry's (3d) brigade, Kearny's (3d) division of III Corps, the 5th, 2d, and 3d Mich. (along with the 1st and 37th N.Y.) distinguished themselves at Williamsburg. The 5th Michigan lost 144. At Fair Oaks it lost 155 out of fewer than 330 engaged. In the Seven Days' Battles it lost 59 out of 216 effectives. Maj. John D. Fairbanks, commanding the regiment, was killed at Glendale. Successive commanders were also killed in action: Lt. Col. John Gilluly at Fredericksburg and Lt. Col. Edward T. Sherlock at Chancellorsville. At Gettysburg, in Birney's division, the regiment was on the left flank of "Sickles' Salient"; in this action it lost 109 officers and men. Entering the final offensive against the Army of Northern Va. with 365 men, the regiment lost 97 in the Wilderness and 58 the next week at Spotsylvania. In June the regiment received 325 men from the 3d Mich. which, with subsequent additions, enabled it to continue in existence until the end of the war.

The 5th Mich. ranks 43d in the list of Federal regiments having the highest percentage of battle deaths.

7TH MICHIGAN (3d Brigade, then 1st Brigade, 2d Division, II Corps)

Colonels: Ira A. Grosvenor, Henry Baxter (Bvt. Maj. Gen.), Norman J. Hall (USMA; R.A.), George W. La-Point.

Battles: Fair Oaks, Seven Days, Antietam, Fredericksburg ('62 and '63), Gettysburg, Mine Run, Wilderness, Spotsylvania, North Anna, Totopotomoy, Cold Harbor, Petersburg siege, Strawberry Plains, Deep Bottom, Reams's Station, Boydton Road, Hatcher's Run, Farmville. Also present at Yorktown, West

Point, Peach Orchard, Savage's Station, Glendale, Malvern Hill, Chancellorsville, Bristoe Station, Sayler's Creek, and Appomattox.

Organized in Aug. '61, the 7th reenlisted and served through the war. During the Peninsular campaign the 7th Mich. was in Dana's (3d) brigade, Sedgwick's (2d) division, of Sumner's II Corps. This unit was hurried across Grapevine Bridge to reinforce the hard-pressed IV (Keyes's) corps and break up the Confederate attack at Fair Oaks. It lost 22 K.I.A. During the Seven Days' Battles the regiment had 23 killed and at Antietam 59 killed.

At Fredericksburg the 7th Mich. made a hasty assault crossing of the river to drive out Confederate sharp-shooters who, despite massed artillery fires that destroyed the town, prevented completion of a ponton bridge at this critical point. The 19th and 20th Mass. (who, with the 42d N.Y., had been brigaded with the 7th Mich. since the Peninsular campaign) followed in boats to establish a bridgehead.

At Gettysburg the regiment, Hall's (3d) brigade, Gibbon's (2d) division (II Corps), lost 65 out of 151 who entered the action. Lt. Col. Amos E. Steele Jr., who was in command, was killed.

During Grant's final campaign against Richmond the 7th Mich. became part of the 1st Brigade (Webb's) along with the 19th Me., 15th, 19th, and 20th Mass., 42d, 59th, and 82d (2d Mil.) N.Y. regiments. This brigade remained part of the 2d Division, II Corps, and fought the costly engagements of that organization from the Wilderness to Petersburg.

27TH MICHIGAN (IX Corps)

Colonels: Dorus M. Fox, William B. Wright, Byron M. Cutcheon (Bvt. B.G.), and Charles Waite (Bvt. B.G.).

Battles: Jackson (Miss.), Blue Springs

(Tenn.), Campbell's Station (Tenn.), Fort Sanders (Tenn.), siege of Knoxville, Wilderness, Spotsylvania, North Anna, Bethesda Church, Cold Harbor, Petersburg assault and trenches, Petersburg Mine, Weldon R.R., Peeble's Farm, Petersburg capture. Present also at Jamestown (Ky), Vicksburg, Loudon (Tenn.), Ny River, Hatcher's Run, Fort Stedman.

Ordered to Kentucky, after leaving Michigan 12 Apr. '63 with eight companies only, the regiment was assigned to the 1st Brig., 1st Div. (Welch's), IX Corps. Companies I and K joined the regiment in Mar. '64. The next month, after arriving in Va., two independent companies of sharpshooters were attached and designated L and M. During the Wilderness campaign the regiment was in Hartranft's (1st) brigade, Willcox's (3d) division, but was subsequently placed in the 1st Brig. of the 1st Div. (which Willcox commanded). In the May fighting the regiment lost 283 of the 864 with which it started. During June and July it lost another 318.

It ranks No. 20 among the 50 Federal regiments sustaining the highest percentage of total enrollment killed.

MICHLER, Nathaniel. Union officer. c. 1827–81. Pa. USMA 1848 (7/38); Engrs. He served in the West and was named Capt. 9 Sept. '61. As Chief Topo. Engr. of the Dept. of the Cumberland to 21 Oct. '61, he held the same position with the Dept. of the Ohio until 11 Mar. '62, with the Army of the Ohio until 30 Oct. '62, and with the Army of the Cumberland to 1 June '63. He was captured 28 June '63 at Rockville (Md.) while on his way to join the Army of the Potomac and was paroled, engaging in a survey of the Harpers Ferry area 24 July–18 Sept. '63. From 20 Sept. '63 to 12 Apr. '65 he headed the Topo. Dept. of the Army

of the Potomac and was promoted Maj. 22 Apr. '64. Breveted for Petersburg and war service (B.G. USA 2 Apr. '65), he continued in the R.A., dying on active duty as Lt. Col.

MIDDLEBURG, Va., 17 June '63. (Gettysburg campaign) Duffié's 1st R.I. was virtually annihilated when it followed instructions to move through Thoroughfare Gap to Middleburg 17 June while Gregg's division advanced on ALDIE. After routing Stuart and his staff from the latter place, the 1st R.I. was surrounded by the brigades of Munford, Robertson, and Chambliss. Duffié fought his way out with 31 others. He reported a loss of 268 (many of whom straggled in later). (H. B. McClellan.)

MIDDLEBURG, Va., 19 June '63. (Gettysburg campaign) On 18 June Pleasonton sent J. I. Gregg's brigade to Middleburg to support Duffié (see above). Gregg arrived too late and withdrew to Aldie. On 19 June the brigade again advanced and cleared the town by a charge of the 4th Pa. Cav. The division of D. M. Gregg followed and pressed the attack with mounted and dismounted troopers, supported by artillery. Stuart withdrew about half a mile to a defensive position, which the Federals did not attack. Fox estimates 99 Federal casualties; Confederate loss has been reported as 40 missing (E.&B.).

MIDDLE CREEK, Ky., 10 Jan. '62. Buell ordered GARFIELD to advance up the Big Sandy River against the forces of Humphrey MARSHALL. On the 10th Garfield attacked with about 900 of his available 1,700 and was unable to dislodge Marshall's 1,500 from their strong defensive position. Both sides withdrew, and both claimed the victory. Each lost about 25 killed and wounded (B.&L., I, 396}.

MIDDLE DEPARTMENT (Union). Created 22 Mar. '62, to consist of N.J., Pa., Del., and Eastern Shore of Md. and Va., and the counties of Cecil, Harford, Baltimore, and Ann Arundel, Md. On 22 July '62 its troops were organized into the VIII Army Corps, Middle Department. W. Va. was added in Mar. '63, since Crook's division had left for the West and only Scammon's division remained in the *District* of W. Va. Maj. Gen. John A. Dix commanded the Middle Dept. until 9 June '62; he was relieved by Maj. Gen. John A. Wool. The latter remained in command when the VIII Corps was created, and was succeeded 22 Dec. '62 by Maj. Gen. Robert C. Schenck. He remained in command until 5 Dec. '63, except for three brief periods when Bvt. Brig. Gen. W. W. Morris was in command 12–22 Mar.; 10–31 Aug.; 22–28 Sept. '63; and when Brig. Gen. E. B. Tyler was temporarily in command (28 Sept.–10 Oct. '63). Subsequent commanders were Brig. Gen. H. H. Lockwood, 5 Dec. '63–22 Mar. '64; Maj. Gen. Lew Wallace, 22 Mar. '64–1 Feb. '65, and again 19 Apr.–1 Aug. '65; and W. W. Morris during the interim period 1 Feb.–19 Apr. '65. Among the missions assigned to the Middle Dept. at various times were the defense of Baltimore and Williamsport, Md.; Harpers Ferry; Martinsburg, W. Va.; and Winchester, Va. Present for duty strength 31 Dec. '63 was 7,000.

MIDDLE MILITARY DIVISION, DEPARTMENT AND ARMY OF THE SHENANDOAH (Union). Organized in Aug. '64, under Maj. Gen. Philip Sheridan, with the mission of driving Confederate Gen. Jubal Early from the Valley and removing any further threat from this troublesome region, it consisted of the following troops: H. G. Wright's VI Corps, transferred from the Army of the Potomac;

Emory's detachment (consisting of the 1st and 2d divisions) of XIX Corps from the Army of the Gulf; the 1st (Merritt's) and 3d (J. H. Wilson's) cavalry divisions from the Army of the Potomac; and Crook's Army of W. Va. (or W. Va. Corps). This is the force properly designated the Army of the Shenandoah. (See also PENNSYLVANIA, UNION DEPARTMENT OF.) After the successful conclusion of SHENANDOAH VALLEY CAMPAIGN OF SHERIDAN, Sheridan turned command of the department over 28 Feb. '65 to Maj. Gen. A. T. A. Torbert and, at the head of the cavalry elements, rejoined the Army of the Potomac. (See SHENANDOAH, UNION ARMY OF THE, for composition of "Sheridan's Cavalry.") Maj. Gen. W. S. Hancock succeeded Torbert in command from 7 Mar '65–27 June, when the department was abolished. Strength 31 Dec. '64 was 64,000.

MIDDLE TENNESSEE, CONFED. ARMY OF. On 27 Sept. '62 Samuel Jones was assigned to command of the District of Middle Tenn. (O.R., I, XVI, 4). Forrest was in command of a small cavalry force around Murfreesboro, Tenn., with the mission of threatening Nashville during Bragg's invasion of Ky. When Breckinridge arrived 28 Oct. with his 6,000 men (BRECKINRIDGE'S CORPS), the combined force was called the Army of Middle Tenn. When the Army of Tenn. reached Murfreesboro after the battle of Perryville, Breckinridge's force became Breckinridge's Division of Hardee's Corps.

MILES COURT OF INQUIRY. On 10 Aug. '61 a court was instituted on application of Col. D. S. Miles "to examine into certain allegations made against him" by I. B. Richardson that Miles had been drunk during the 1st Battle of Bull Run. Members of the court were W. B. Franklin, John Sedgwick, and (then Capt.) Truman Seymour. Miles had changed dispositions of two regiments in Richardson's (4th) brigade during the battle. After Mc-Dowell had put Richardson in command of the sector, Richardson had refused to obey Miles's further orders, and Miles had threatened to arrest Richardson. The court made the following "Statement of Facts": "1. That Col. I. B. Richardson was justified in applying the term drunkenness to Col. D. S. Miles's condition about 7 o'clock P.M. on the 21st. 2. That the evidence is clear that Colonel Miles had been ill for several days before July 21 last—was ill on that day; that the surgeon had prescribed medicines for him, and on the day of the battle had prescribed for him small quantities of brandy. The court, however, considers his illness as a very slight extenuation of the guilt attached to his condition. . . . The court is of the opinion that evidence cannot now be found sufficient to convict Colonel Miles of drunkenness before a court-martial; that a proper court could only be organized in this Army with the greatest inconvenience at present, and that it will not be for the interests of the service to convene a court in this case." McClellan confirmed the proceedings on 6 Nov. (O.R., I, II, 375-6; 438-9).

MILES, Nelson Appleton. Union gen. 1839-1925. Mass. A store clerk in Boston, attending night school and also acquiring some military education from a French Army colonel, he was commissioned 1st Lt. 22d Mass. 9 Sept. '61. As Lt. Col. 61st N.Y. 31 May '62, he was on O. O. Howard's staff during the Peninsular campaign, and while leading reinforcements to the 61st N.Y. at Fair Oaks was wounded. He led his regiment at Antietam and was named Col. 30 Sept. '62. Wounded at Fredericksburg, he also fought at Chancellorsville, the Wilderness, and Spotsyl-

vania. He commanded 1, 1, II (4-19 July and 28 July-25 Dec. '63) and was named B.G. USV 12 May '64. At Petersburg, where he was wounded, and Reams's Station, he commanded 1st Div., II, Potomac (29 July '64-15 Feb. '65 and 25 Feb.-20 May '65), commanding the II Corps in the interval (17-25 Feb.). He was promoted Maj. Gen. USV 21 Oct. '65 and continued in the R.A. as Col. 40th, and later 5th, US Inf. Breveted for Reams's Station (Maj. Gen. USV 25 Aug. '64), Chancellorsville (B.G. USA), and Spotsylvania (Maj. Gen. USA), he was given the Medal of Honor in 1892 for Chancellorsville. After the war he was Jefferson Davis's custodian at Fortress Monroe and was criticized unjustly for his treatment of the C.S.A. president. Participating mainly in Indian fighting after the war, he was promoted B.G. USA in 1880, Maj. Gen. USA in 1890, and Lt. Gen. USA in 1900, retiring three years later. From 1895 through the Spanish-American War and the Moro insurrection, he was C. in C. of the army. Described by D.A.B. as a man of "indefatigable industry, sound judgment and personal bravery," he engaged in many civic activities after his retirement in 1903. He married a niece of W. T. Sherman.

MILES, W. R. C.S.A. Wood and Heitman list him as B.G. C.S.A., the former saying that he was appointed in 1864 from Miss. Neither Wright nor C.M.H. lists him as a general officer.

MILITARY TELEGRAPH SYSTEM. See SIGNAL COMMUNICATIONS.

MILL CREEK GAP, Ga. Confederate name for actions of ROCKY FACE RIDGE, 5-11 May '64.

MILLER, Abram O. Union officer. Ohio. 1st Lt. 10th Ind. 25 Apr. '61; Capt. 23 June '61; mustered out 6 Aug. '61; Capt. 10th Ind. 18 Sept. '61; Maj.

18 Sept. '61; Lt. Col. 5 Apr. '62; Col. 72d Ind. 24 Aug. '62; Bvt. B.G. USV (war service). Commanded 40th Brig., 12th Div. (Ohio); 2, 5th Div. Centre, XIV; 1, 4, XIV; 3, 2, Cav. Corps (Cumberland); 1, 2, Cav. Corps (Mil. Div. Miss.); 3, 2, Cav. Corps (Mil. Div. Miss.).

MILLER, John Franklin. Union gen. 1831–86. Ind. A lawyer and Republican politician, he served in the legislature, resigning to be commissioned Col. 29th Ind. 27 Aug. '61. He commanded a brigade at Stones River where he was wounded. Appointed B.G. USV 5 Jan. '64, he was also wounded at Liberty Gap. He commanded a division at Nashville and was breveted Maj. Gen. USV for that battle. Resigning in Sept. '65, he settled in San Francisco. A founder and president of an Alaskan fur company, he became an extremely wealthy man. Continuing in politics, he was a California Senator 1881–86.

MILLER, Madison. Union officer. 1811–96. Pa. Capt. 1st Mo. 20 Apr. '61; transferred to 1st Mo. Arty. 1 Sept. '61; Col. 18th Mo. 31 Jan. '62; resigned 15 Mar. '64; B.G. Enrolled in Mo. State Militia 28 Sept. '64–12 Mar. '65; Bvt. B.G. USV (Shiloh). As a Capt. in the Mexican War he was W.I.A. at Buena Vista. He was captured at Shiloh and a member of the commission sent to Washington to arrange for their own exchange. A jurist and railroad executive before the war, he served in the US Senate afterward.

MILLER, Morris S. Union officer c. 1814–70 N.Y. USMA 1834 (14/36); Arty.-Q.M. He fought in the Seminole War and the Mexican War and was promoted Maj. Q.M. 17 May '61. During the Civil War he was Q.M. at Washington until 1864, and served on boards and commissions for the remainder of the war. He died on active duty as Lt. Col. and Bvt. B.G. USA.

MILLER, Stephen. Union gen. 1816–81. His regiment (Col. 1st Minn. 29 Apr. '61) served with the Army of the Potomac until 1862, when he returned to Minn. (Col. 7th Minn. 24 Aug. '62) to quiet the Indian riots in that state. Named B.G. USV 26 Oct. '63, he resigned 18 Jan. '64 to be Gov. of Minn. He was later a railroad agent.

MILLER, William. C.S.A. gen. Appt.-Fla. After Shiloh he commanded a battalion as Maj. in the 1st Fla. and was named Col. in time to lead the regiment in the Ky. campaign and at Perryville. He succeeded John C. Brown as brigade commander and, leading his regiment and the 3d Fla., was wounded at Stones River. Appointed head of the C.S.A. Conscript Bureau in southern Fla. and Ala., he was promoted B.G. C.S.A. 2 Aug. '64 and about a month later took command of the reserve forces of Fla. From 29 Sept. '64 until the end of the war he commanded the Dist. of Fla.

MILLS, James K. Union officer. Ill. Lt. Col. 24th Mo. 2 Aug. '61; Col. 22 Apr. '63; Bvt. B.G. USV (war service); resigned 26 Nov. '64. Died 1874.

MILLS, Madison. Union officer. N.Y. Joining the R.A. as Asst. Surgeon in 1834, he served on the frontier and in the Mexican War before going to St. Louis on hospital duty Sept. '61–May '62. Named Medical Director of the Dept. of the Mo., he served there until Nov. '63, and was promoted Col. Medical I.G. 1 Dec. '64. He served in that position throughout the war and, continuing in the R.A., died on active duty in 1873. During the Civil War he was breveted for Vicksburg and war service (B.G. USA).

MILL SPRINGS, Ky. 19 Jan. '62. Alternate name for LOGAN CROSS ROADS.

MILROY, Robert Huston. Union gen. 1816–90. Ind. After Norwich (Vt.) Univ. he fought in the Mexican War, won his law degree at Ind. Univ., served as a judge, and became active in politics. Commissioned Capt. 9th Ind. 23 Apr. '61 and Col. four days later, he was mustered out 29 July and recommissioned Col. 9th Ind. 27 Aug. '61. On 3 Sept. he was appointed B.G. USV and commanded Milroy's Brig., Cheat Mountain Dist., Mountain Dept. (19 Apr.–26 June '62). He commanded the Dist. 11 Oct. '61–11 Mar. '62 and 11 Mar.–19 Apr. '62 and then took over 2d Brig., I Corps, Army of Va., 26 June–12 Sept. '62. Promoted Maj. Gen. USV 29 Nov. '62, he commanded Milroy's Upper Potomac Div., VIII, Middle Dept., and the Dist. of Winchester, VIII (Jan.–Feb. '63). Heading the 2d Div. in that department (Feb.–26 June '63), he retreated before the Confederate advance into Pa.; extremely high casualties in this withdrawal brought him before a Board of Investigation which exonerated him of any blame. He later commanded the defenses of the Nashville and Chattanooga R.R. (July '64–Apr. '65). His suppression of guerrillas in W. Va. was so vigorous that the Confederates put a price on his head. Resigning 26 July '65, he was later a canal trustee and Indian agent.

MILTON, John. C.S.A. Gov. of Fla. 1807–65. Ga. A lawyer, he practiced in Georgia, Mobile, and New Orleans, entering politics as a nullification partisan, and fighting in the Seminole War. He moved to Fla. in 1846 to become a planter and Democratic legislator. Elected Gov. in 1860, he served throughout the war, dying 1 Apr. '65 of a stroke.

MINDIL, George Washington. Union officer. Germany. Commissioned 2d Lt. Pa. 15 July '61, and 1st Lt. six weeks later, he was promoted Capt. 5 Oct.

'61 and transferred to the 61st Pa. in Feb. '62. This he resigned 6 Oct. of that year to become Col. 27th N.J. 10 Oct. '62. Mustered out 2 July '63, he was named Col. 33d N.J. 5 Sept. '63 and mustered out of this regiment in July '65. He won two Medals of Honor.

MINE ASSAULT (Battle of the crater; Petersburg mine). PETERSBURG MINE ASSAULT.

MINE RUN CAMPAIGN, Va., 26 Nov.–1 Dec. '63. Following Lee's BRISTOE CAMPAIGN, 9 Oct.–9 Nov. '63, Meade took the initiative and attempted to maneuver Lee out of his position on the Rapidan. He successfully crossed at Germanna Ford with his five corps and then turned west toward Orange Court House. Lee's cavalry detected the movement immediately, and Meade found the Army of Northern Va. strongly posted along Mine Run to contest his further advance.

Finding no assailable point of this line, Meade withdrew without attacking and went into winter quarters around Culpeper. This ended major operations in the east until Grant arrived and launched the WILDERNESS CAMPAIGN in May '64.

MINIE BULLET. Inaccurately pronounced *minnie,* and incorrectly called a *ball,* this was a cylindro-conoidal (i.e., bullet-shaped), lead projectile designed by French Army Captain Minié to be shot from a muzzle-loading rifle. When the piece was fired, expanding gas entered the bullet's hollow base and forced its outer side into the rifling of the barrel. The bullet appeared in 1849 and was quickly adopted by the U.S. It had a revolutionary effect on tactics by greatly improving the accuracy, range, and rate of small arms fire.

MINTY, Robert Horatio George. Union officer. 1831–? Ireland. An ensign in the British Army, he had served in the West Indies, Central America, and Africa before retiring in 1853 and settling in Mich. He was commissioned Maj. 2d Mich. Cav. 2 Sept. '61 and promoted Lt. Col. 3d Mich. Cav. five days later. As Col. 4th Mich. Cav. 31 July '62, he commanded the "Sabre Brigade," capturing Shelbyville (Tenn.) in June '63. He also commanded the cavalry on the left at Chickamauga and covered Thomas's retreat to Chattanooga. Breveted for war service (B.G. and Maj. Gen. USV), he was mustered out Aug. '65.

MINTZER, William Mintzer [sic]. Union officer. Pa. Q.M. Sgt. 4th Pa. 20 Apr.–27 July '61; 1st Lt. 53d Pa. 18 Sept. '61; Capt. 2 June '62; Lt. Col. 29 Sept. '64; Col. 30 Oct. '64; Bvt. B.G. USV (war service). Commanded 3, 1, II; 4, 1, II.

1ST MINNESOTA

Colonels: Willis A. Gorman (Brig. Gen.), Napoleon J. T. Dana (Maj. Gen.), Alfred Sully (Maj. Gen.), George N. Morgan, William Colville, Jr. (Bvt. B.G.), Charles P. Adams (Bvt. B.G.), and Mark W. Downie.

Battles: First Bull Run, Goose Creek (Va.), Fair Oaks, Savage's Station, Glendale, Flint Hill, Vienna, Antietam, Fredericksburg, Gettysburg, Bristoe Station, Petersburg assault and siege, Jerusalem Road, Deep Bottom, Reams's Station and Boydton Road. Also at Yorktown, West Point, Peach Orchard, Malvern Hill, Fredericksburg ('63), Mine Run, Strawberry Plains, Hatcher's Run, Farmville, and Appomattox.

The 1st Minn. has the distinction of sustaining the highest regimental loss in any battle, in proportion to the number engaged, in modern history. The second day of the battle of Gettysburg, when the Confederates had broken through Sickles' position, the 1st Minn. lost 215 out of the 262 with which it counterattacked to restore the Federal line. Col. Colville commanded in this action.

Organized 29 Apr. '61, it was the first in the Union Army to be mustered in for three years. At 1st Bull Run, as part of Franklin's brigade, Heintzelman's division, it lost 180 men, the highest of any regiment engaged. Soon after, the regiment was assigned to the 1st Brig., 2d Div., II Corps, in which it remained the rest of its service.

In percentage of total enrollment killed during the war, the 1st Minn. ranks 23d out of 2,047 Federal regiments.

MISSIONARY RIDGE. Overlooking Chattanooga, Tenn., it was Bragg's main defensive position during the CHATTANOOGA CAMPAIGN and the scene of the decisive battle 25 Nov. '63.

MISSISSIPPI, CONFEDERATE ARMIES OF. The first of these was formed 5 Mar. '62 under Beauregard from troops in the Western Dept. (No. 2). Corps commanders were Polk and Bragg. When A. S. Johnston arrived at Corinth, Miss. (24 Mar. '62), with his Central Army of Ky. for operations that led to the battle of Shiloh the two armies were combined. The new Army of Miss., headed by Johnston with Beauregard as second-in-command, was organized on 29 Mar. into four bodies designated as corps, although they were actually of divisional size. Total strength, including artillery and cavalry, was over 40,000. Polk's I Corps, 9,136 men, had the divisions of Charles Clark (succeeded by A. P. Stewart when Clark was wounded at Shiloh) and B. F. Cheatham. Bragg's II Corps, 13,589 men, had the divisions of Daniel Ruggles and J. M. Withers. Hardee's III Corps, 6,789 men, had the brigades of Hindman, Cleburne, and S. A. M. Wood. The Reserve Corps, 6,439 men, was composed of three brigades under Trabue, J. S. Bowen, and W. S. Statham;

this "corps" was commanded by G. B. Crittenden until 31 Mar., and then by Breckinridge. (See CORPS, Confederate, for further detail as to composition and history of these units.) Army commanders were: A. S. Johnston until 6 Apr. '62 (K.I.A.); Beauregard until 27 June; Bragg until 5 July; Hardee until 15 Aug.; Bragg until 27 Sept.; Polk until 7 Nov. '62. Bragg returned 7 Nov. and resumed command. This Army of Miss. ceased to exist on 20 Nov., when it was merged with the Army of Ky. to become the Army of Tenn., with Bragg as its first commander.

Pemberton's Army of Miss. was created 7 Dec. '62 when Van Dorn's Army of WEST TENNESSEE was redesignated. The organization now consisted of the corps of Price and Van Dorn. Price's corps continued to be called by its former name of Army of the West, however; and the name Army of West Tenn. continued to be used in connection with the combined corps of Price and Van Dorn. In Jan. '63 these two corps were changed into divisions and shortly thereafter the designation "Army of Mississippi" disappeared.

Army of (the) Miss. was the designation which Polk adopted for his corps on 12 May '64 when he joined Johnston's Army of Tenn. for the Atlanta campaign. (In Dec. '63 Polk had succeeded Pemberton as commander of the troops in the Dept. of Ala., Miss., and East La. During the winter of 1863–64 his force of two cavalry divisions [about 20,000] had opposed Sherman's operations in Miss.) After Polk's death, 14 June '64, his corps ceased to be known as the Army of (the) Miss. Thereafter it was generally known as Stewart's Corps, after its commander, A. P. Stewart (14 June '64–16 Mar. '65).

(A note in the general index to the Official Records mentions the existence of these three Confederate Armies of Miss.—Bragg's [Beauregard's], Pemberton's, and Polk's—and says: "As no distinction seems to have been made between these armies in some of the volume indexes [of the O.R.] [especially in the later volumes] none has been made in this index.")

MISSISSIPPI, McCLERNAND'S UNION ARMY OF THE. (Organization) 4–12 Jan. '63. In the capture of Ark. Post (Fort Hindman, Ark.) a force known as McClernand's Army of the Miss. was briefly in existence. I Corps of this "army" was commanded by G. W. Morgan and comprised troops that had formerly been known (18 Dec.–4 Jan. '63) as the 1st (A. J. Smith's) and 3d (Morgan's) divisions of Sherman's Yazoo (Chickasaw Bluffs) Expedition. II Corps of McClernand's force was commanded by Sherman and consisted of the former 2d (M. L. Smith's and, after 28 Dec., D. Stuart's) and 4th (Frederick Steele's) divisions of the Yazoo Expedition. The I and II Corps, McClernand's Army of the Miss., are sometimes referred to also as XIII Corps (New) and XV Corps, Army of the Tenn. The confusion stems from the fact that these latter organizations were ordered into existence 18 Dec. '62 (G.O., 210), but the troops that were to make up these corps were used until 12 Jan. '63 in the task forces existing under the names of Sherman's YAZOO EXPEDITION and McClernand's Army of the Miss. After 12 Jan. '63, however, when McClernand's Army of the Miss. ceased to exist, Morgan's force became XIII Corps (New) and Sherman's became XV Corps, both being part of Grant's Army of the Tenn. as constituted by General Order No. 210, dated 18 Dec. '62.

MISSISSIPPI, POPE'S AND ROSE-CRANS' UNION ARMY OF THE.

Organized by Pope for the New Madrid-Island No. 10 campaign, it was in existence from 23 Feb. until 26 Oct. '62. It was commanded by Maj. Gen. John Pope until 26 June and W. S. Rosecrans. Strength: 19,000, exclusive of fleet. Consisting of five divisions, several cavalry brigades, and a flotilla brigade, it captured Island No. 10, Tenn. (16 Mar.–8 Apr.) and participated in the Corinth campaign and initial phases of the Stones River and Vicksburg campaigns. Most of its troops went into the (original) XIII Corps, which Grant formed under Sherman for the Vicksburg campaign.

MISSISSIPPI, UNION DEPARTMENT OF THE. The Dept. of *the* Miss. was created 11 Mar. '62 to combine under Halleck's command the forces formerly included in the three separate departments of Mo. (Halleck's), of the Ohio (Buell's), and of Kans. (Hunter's). Headquarters were at St. Louis. It lost part of its territory 19 Aug. '62 when the Dept. of the Ohio was revived, and on 6 Sept. when the Dept. of the Northwest was created. On 19 Sept. '62 it was merged into the new Dept. of Mo. Halleck's Dept. of the Miss. was in existence during the Shiloh campaign and the capture of Corinth, Miss. The Dept. of Miss. was established 28 Nov. '64. Its commanders were N. J. T. Dana (8 Dec. '64–14 May '65), G. K. Warren (to 24 June '65), and H. W. Slocum (to 27 June '65). There were two provisional forces known as "the Army of the Mississippi." See MISSISSIPPI, MC-CLERNAND'S UNION ARMY OF THE; and MISSISSIPPI, POPE'S AND ROSECRANS' UNION ARMY OF THE.

MISSISSIPPI, UNION MILITARY DIVISION OF THE. (Grant; Sherman) Finally recognizing the need for unified command in the West, the War Department ordered the Depts. of the Ohio, the Tenn., the Cumberland, and Ark. to be organized into the Mil. Div. of the Miss.

under Grant. The order was dated 16 Oct. '63 and delivered to Grant in Louisville the 17th or 18th by Sec. of War Stanton in person. Sherman replaced Grant 18 Mar. '64 (when the latter became general in chief of all Federal armies) and commanded the Mil. Div. of the Miss. until 27 June '65. Combat forces under Sherman in the Atlanta campaign were: Thomas' Army of the Cumberland: IV, XIV, XX, and cavalry corps; McPherson's Army of the Tenn.: XV, XVI, and XVII Corps; Schofield's Army of the Ohio: XXIII Corps, and cavalry division. After the fall of Atlanta the forces under the personal command of Sherman in his March to the Sea and Carolinas operations were: Howard's Army of the Tenn. (Right Wing): XV, XVII (XVI discontinued); Slocum's Army of Ga. (Left Wing): XIV, XX (IV in East Tenn.).

MISSISSIPPI AND EAST LOUISIANA, CONFEDERATE DEPARTMENT OF. Van Dorn assumed command of the troops in the Dist. of Southern Miss. and East La. (part of Dept. No. 2) on 20 June '62 (O.R., I, XV; and XVII, 1). The Distr. of (the) Miss. was established 2 July '62 (*ibid.;* the second reference includes "the" in the designation); on 5 Sept. Ruggles succeeded Van Dorn as district commander.

The Dept. of Miss. and East La. was constituted 1 Oct. '62 under Pemberton, who assumed command the 14th (*ibid.*) with headquarters at Jackson. (Meanwhile, on the 12th Van Dorn had assumed [temporary] command of all troops in Miss.)

On 7 Dec. '62 a reorganization caused the forces of Van Dorn and Price to drop their former designations as "armies" and to become the I and II Corps of Pemberton's new Army of MISSISSIPPI. A short time later they were redesignated "divisions."

After Pemberton's defeat and capture at Vicksburg Polk was assigned to command of the department on 22 Dec. '63 and pending Johnston's arrival was given temporary command of the Department of TENNESSEE at the same time (O.R., I, XXXI, 4). The next day Polk assumed command of "the 'Department of the Southwest' (Miss. and East La.)" (*ibid.*).

During the winter of 1863–64 Polk had a force of two cavalry divisions with which he opposed Sherman's operations in Mississippi. The Department of ALABAMA, MISSISSIPPI, AND EAST LOUISIANA was created under S. D. Lee in May '64 and Polk rejoined the Army of Tenn. on 12 May for the Atlanta campaign.

On 24 Jan. '65 Forrest assumed command of the *District* of Miss., East La., and West Tenn.; and on the 27th he was assigned command of the *District* of Miss. and East La. (O.R., I, XLIX, 1).

"MISSISSIPPI RIFLE." Name applied after 1847 to the UNITED STATES RIFLE, Model 1841.

MISSOURI, CONFEDERATE ARMY OF (1864). Also called Price's Expeditionary Corps and the "Army in the Field," this was the designation of the 12,000-man force (divisions of Fagan, Marmaduke, and Shelby) that undertook PRICE'S RAID IN MISSOURI, Sept.–Oct. '64. After his return, 2 Dec., the force again was part of the Trans-Miss. Dept. and its special designation disappeared.

MISSOURI, UNION DEPARTMENT OF (THE). Created 9 Nov. '61 to consist of Mo., Iowa, Minn., Wis., Ill., Ark., and that portion of Ky. west of the Cumberland River. Strength 31 Dec. '61 was 91,000. Merged into the new Dept. of the Miss. 11 Mar. '62. On 5 June '62 it became a district and was divided into divisions. Re-created

19 Sept. '62 to meet the threat of Hindman's invasion it consisted of Mo., Ark., Kans., and the bordering Indian Territory. Colo. and the Nebr. territories were added 11 Oct. '62. Strength 31 Dec. '62 was 46,000; 31 Dec. '63: 40,000. The department gradually lost territory by the creation of the departments of Kans. 1 Jan. '64 (re-created), and Ark. 6 Jan. '64, until it included only the state of Mo. itself. On 30 Jan. '65 it was expanded by the addition to its territory of the former Dept. of Kans. Commanded by the following major generals with headquarters at St. Louis: H. W. Halleck, 19 Nov. '61–11 Mar. '62; S. R. Curtis, 24 Sept. '62 to 24 May '63; J. M. Schofield to 30 Jan. '64; W. S. Rosecrans to 9 Dec. '64; G. M. Dodge to 27 June '65.

MISSOURI COMPROMiSE. First legislative compromise between the slavery and "free" factions in a series of crises that led to the Civil War. By 1818 Mo.'s population warranted statehood. As most settlers had come from slaveholding areas, Mo. was expected to follow this pattern. When statehood bill was brought before the House of Representatives, an amendment to stop further importation of slaves and to emancipate those already in the state was proposed by James Tallmadge of N.Y. Although this passed the House, it failed in the Senate, and in the ensuing debates sectional differences and bitterness became apparent for the first time in the legislative chambers. As the danger of conflict became clear, the issue of Mo.'s statehood hung in abeyance. In Jan. '20, a bill to admit Me. was passed in the House, giving the free states an edge in representation. It was seen that by pairing Mo. (as a slave state) with Me. (a free state) the legislative balance would be maintained. The two House bills were combined in the Senate deleting the amendment forbidding slavery in Mo. and adding a clause prohibiting slavery in the remainder of the Louisiana Purchase north of the southern boundary of Mo. The House first rejected this compromise, but then passed it in a slightly different form after a special committee was called. Henry Clay, as Speaker of the House, is credited with achieving the compromise.

MISSOURI OPERATIONS IN 1861. See F. P. BLAIR, Jr., Nathaniel LYON, WILSON'S CREEK CAMPAIGN and the cross references from these entries.

MISSOURI STATE GUARD. Confed. force of 3,000 raised in response to Gov. C. F. Jackson's call on 12 June '61 for 50,000 state militia for active service. Commanded by Sterling Price and M. M. Parsons from 29 Oct. '61 to 17 Mar. '62, when it was merged into the Army of the West. On 9 Apr. Parsons again assumed command (O.R., I, VIII, 3) and on 13 July '62 the organization was relieved of duty east of the Mississippi and ordered to join Hindman in the Trans-Miss. Dept. (*ibid.,* XIII, 3).

MITCHEL, Ormsby McKnight. Union gen. 1810–62. Ky. Appt.-Ohio. USMA 1829 (15/46); Arty. After teaching mathematics at West Point and serving in garrison in Fla., he resigned in 1832 to teach mathematics and astronomy in Cincinnati College. He also practiced law, sat on the Board of Visitors of USMA, lectured, and wrote several books on astronomy, and engaged in railroading. Named B.G. USV 9 Aug. '61, he commanded the Dept. of the Ohio 21 Sept.–15 Nov. '61 and the 3d Div., Army of the Ohio, 2 Dec. '61–2 July '62. Promoted Maj. Gen. USV 11 Apr. '62, he commanded the Dept. of the South and the X Corps (17 Sept.–27 Oct. '62). Died on 30 Oct. at Beaufort of yellow fever.

MITCHELL, Greenville McNeel. Union officer. Ky. Capt. 1st Ill. Cav. 19 July '61; Lt. Col. 54th Ill. 1 Jan. '62; Col. 18 Jan. '63; Bvt. B.G. USV 22 Aug. '65 (war service). Commanded 3, 2, VII (Ark.). Died 1895.

MITCHELL, John Grant. Union gen. 1838–94. Ohio. Commissioned 1st Lt. Adj. 3d Ohio (30 July '61), Capt. (21 Dec. '61), and Lt. Col. 113th Ohio (2 Sept. '62), he fought in W. Va. under Rosecrans and in Tenn. and Ala. with O. M. Mitchel. As Col. (6 May '63), he led his regiment in the Tullahoma campaign. He commanded 2, 1, Res. Corps, Cumberland (9 Sept.–9 Oct. '63) at Chickamauga. During the Atlanta campaign (Rocky Face Ridge, Resaca, Rome, Dallas, and New Hope Church), he led 2, 2, XIV, Cumberland. His troops joined with Daniel McCook's in the assault on Kenesaw Mountain. He commanded his brigade in the rest of the Atlanta campaign; and the 2d Brig., Prov. Div., Cumberland, at Nashville, in pursuit of Hood and in the Carolinas. He was promoted B.G. USV 12 Jan. '65 and Bvt. Maj. Gen. USV (Averasboro, Bentonville, N.C.). He resigned 3 July '65 to resume his law practice.

MITCHELL, Robert Byington. Union gen. 1823–82. Ohio. A lawyer, he had moved to Kansas after serving in the Mexican War. There he took part in the "BLOODY KANSAS" struggle as a "Free-Soiler" and held several political offices for that party. As Col. 2d Kans. (23 May '61), he was wounded at Wilson's Creek. He raised a regiment of cavalry when he recovered and then (8 Apr. '62) received his commission as B.G. USV. His commands were 1st Brig., 4th Div., Army Miss. (24 Apr.–12 Aug. '62); 4th Div., Army Miss. (12 Aug.–26 Sept. '62); 9th Div., Army Ohio (Sept. '62); 9th Div., III Corps, Army Ohio (Sept.–Nov. '62); 1st Div. Right Wing, XIV Corps, Cumberland (14 Oct.–5 Nov.

'62); 4th Div. Centre, XIV, Cumberland (5 Nov. '62–9 Jan. '63); 1st Div., Cav. Corps, Cumberland (Mar.–9 Sept. '63); Cav. Corps, Cumberland (9 Sept.–9 Nov. '63); Dist. North Kans., Kans. (11 Apr.–28 June '65); and Dist. Nebr., Kans. (Jan. '64–11 Apr. '65). He was mustered out 15 June '66.

MITCHELL, William Galbraith. Union officer. Pvt. Co. E 25th Pa. 18 Apr. '61; transferred to 7th Pa. 23 Apr. '61; Sgt. Maj. 23 Apr. '61; 1st Lt. 2 June '61; mustered out 5 Aug. '61; 1st Lt. 49th Pa. 25 Aug. '61; Maj. A.D.C. Vols. 25 June '63; Lt. Col. Asst. I.G. Assigned 18 June '65–11 June '66; Bvt. B.G. USV. Brevets for Wilderness (2); Boydton Plank Road, Va. (2); war service; Spotsylvania. A.D.C. to Gen. Hancock from Lee's Mill (Va.) to Chancellorsville and after the war. Transferred to R.A., he held the rank of Maj. at his death in 1883.

MIX, Elisha. Union officer. Conn. Capt. 8th Mich. Cav. 1 Nov. '62; Maj. 2 Mar. '63; Lt. Col. 16 Apr. '64; Col. 1 Sept. '64; Bvt. B.G. USV (war service). Commanded 1, 6, Cav. Corps (Mil. Div. Miss.). Died 1898.

MIZNER, Henry Rutgeras. Union officer. N.Y. R.A. Capt. 18th US Inf. 14 May '61; Col. 14th Mich. 22 Dec. '62; mustered out USV 1865; Bvt. B.G. USV. Brevets for Murfreesboro, Atlanta campaign, Jonesboro, war service. On recruiting duty June–Sept. '61; Q.M. and Comsy. for Mich. to Jan. '62; recruiting to May '62, when he rejoined his regiment. Continuing in the R.A., he was Col. when he retired in 1891.

MIZNER, John Kemp. Union officer. 1837–98. N.Y. Appt.–Mich. USMA 1856 (33/49); Dragoons. 1st Lt. 2d US Dragoons 9 May '61; 2d US Cav. 3 Aug. '61; Capt. 12 Nov. '61; Col. 3d Mich. Cav. 7 Mar. '62; mustered out USV 1866; Bvt. B.G. USV. Brevets for Cor-

inth (Miss.), Panola (Miss.), war service. He was Gen. Rosecrans' chief of cavalry in the Army of the Miss. and Acting Assistant I.G. on Gen. Merritt's staff in the Dept. of the Gulf. Continuing in the R.A., he retired in 1897 as Col.

MOBILE, CONFEDERATE ARMY OF. In existence from 27 Jan. to 27 June '62. Composed of about 10,000 Ala. troops, its first commander was Jones M. Withers. Col. J. B. Villepigue then commanded temporarily, until succeeded on 15 Mar. by Samuel Jones. Many of its regiments went to fight at Shiloh under Withers as part of Bragg's II Corps. After additional regiments had been sent to the Army of Miss., the Army of Mobile was discontinued.

MOBILE BAY, NAVAL BATTLE OF, 5 Aug. '64. With the cooperation of Granger's XIII Corps (see FORTS GAINES, MORGAN, AND POWELL) Adm. Farragut with four monitors and 14 wooden ships started at about 6 A.M. to run past the forts into Mobile Bay and destroy the ironclad ram *Tennessee* and three wooden gunboats (*Morgan, Gaines,* and *Selma*) under command of Adm. Buchanan. Fort Morgan opened fire at 7:07, the *Brooklyn* opened with bow guns at 7:10; the fleet opened with bow guns at 7:15, and with broadside guns was in action from 7:30 until 7:50. The *Tecumseh* hit a mine ("torpedo") and sank at 7:45, and at 7:52 Farragut's flagship *Hartford* took the lead. At about 8 o'clock the *Tennessee* moved to attack the Federal fleet, which had now passed the forts with little loss. The *Monongahela, Lackawanna,* and *Hartford* in turn rammed the underpowered *Tennessee* at five-minute intervals, starting at 9:25. The Confederate ironclad suffered no significant damage, but due to defective fuzes did not fire another round after about 9:40. As the *Hartford* circled to ram again, the

Lackawanna ran into her at a point near where Farragut was standing. The Adm. narrowly escaped death. (The above timetable is from Mahan, 244.)

Meanwhile the monitors had come up and opened fire. Soon the *Tennessee* was out of control and Buchanan incapacitated by a broken leg. At 10 o'clock, after enduring another 20 minutes of pounding, Capt. J. D. Johnston surrendered the *Tennessee*.

Of the 3,000 Federals engaged, there were 319 casualties, including 93 drowned and four captured when the *Tecumseh* sank. Of 470 Confederate naval personnel engaged there were 312 lost; the *Tennessee* had two killed, nine wounded, and 280 captured (including Buchanan).

During this action the 63-year-old Farragut was twice "lashed in the rigging" by solicitous subordinates so that if wounded he would not fall to his death from the high perch to which he climbed better to view the battle. It was also during this action that, when warned by the *Brooklyn* that the *Tecumseh* had been sunk by a submarine mine ("torpedo"), he is alleged to have said "Damn the torpedoes" (B.&L., IV, 391).

MOBILE CAMPAIGN, Ala., 17 Mar.–12 Apr. '65. On 17 Mar. E. R. S. Canby (C.G. Mil. Div. of West Miss.) undertook operations with 45,000 troops to capture Mobile. The latter place was held by 10,000 troops and 300 guns under D. H. Maury, supported by five gunboats. While Frederick Steele led one column of 13,000 men from Pensacola, Canby led the other column from the captured forts at the mouth of Mobile Bay (Forts Gaines and Morgan). Canby's approach to Mobile was from the east with the support of the navy. This led to his capture of SPANISH FORT, 27 Mar.–8 Apr., and BLAKELY, 1–9 Apr. Having sustained 1,417 casualties (B.&L., IV, 411n), he entered Mobile the morn-

ing of the 12th. Maury had left the night before with his remaining 4,500 troops, 27 guns, and his supply train. The Confederates moved toward Montgomery. On 4 May they were surrendered by Richard Taylor. "I had tried for more than two years to have an expedition sent against Mobile when its possession by us would have been of great advantage," wrote Grant in his *Memoirs* (II, 519). "It finally cost lives to take it when its possession was of no importance. . . ."

MOCCASIN BEND (Point), Tenn. Figured in CHATTANOOGA CAMPAIGN.

MOFFITT, Stephen. Union officer. N.Y. 1st Lt. 96th N.Y. 19 Nov. '61; Capt. 17 June '62; Lt. Col. 19 May '63; Col. 20 June '65; Bvt. B.G. USV (war service).

MOLINEUX, Edward Leslie. Union officer. England. Commissioned Lt. Col. 159th N.Y. 27 Sept. '62, he was promoted Col. 25 Nov. of that year and mustered out in Aug. '65. He was breveted for Opequon–Fishers Hill–Middletown (B.G. USV 19 Oct. '64), and war service (Maj. Gen. USV).

MOLLY MAGUIRES. A secret society of miners, predominantly Irish, in the W. Va. and Pa. anthracite coal fields. The union was well organized and powerful during the Civil War, coming into its strongest era in the 1870's. Strongly opposed to conscription, the Molly Maguires believed in direct action and assaults to gain their ends, and greatly hindered the draft in their areas.

MONETT'S BLUFF (Ferry), La., 23 Apr. '64. Action of RED RIVER CAMPAIGN, known also as Cane River Crossing or Cloutiersville.

MONITOR. Generic term for a shallow-draught warship mounting one or two large guns and especially designed for bombarding. The name was coined by John Ericsson, their inventor, because he said this type of vessel "will admonish the leaders of the Southern Rebellion that the batteries on the banks of their rivers will no longer present barriers to the entrance of the Union forces." (The word is from the Latin *monere,* to warn, advise.) See also RAM.

MONITOR-MERRIMAC (VIRGINIA) DUEL, Hampton Roads, Va., 9 Mar. '62. History's first battle between ironclad ships. When the Federals were forced to abandon the Norfolk Navy Yard, 20–21 Apr. '61, the recently commissioned (1856) screw steamer *Merrimack* (awaiting engine repairs) had to be burned and scuttled. The Confederates raised her and improvised an ironclad ram, renamed the *Virginia.* The *Merrimack's* hull was cut down to the water line and a 170-foot long superstructure with sides sloping at about 35 degrees from the vertical was built. The armor consisted of four inches of wrought-iron bars (and greased with tallow) laid crisscross on 22 inches of oak. Forward and aft of this "citadel" the decks were just awash when the 263-foot ship was in fighting trim, giving it the appearance of a floating barn roof. The armament consisted of six 9-inch smoothbores (Dahlgrens) and four rifled guns of 6- and 7-inch caliber. A cast-iron prow projected four feet. With a draught of 22 feet, the two salvaged 600-horsepower engines of the old *Merrimack* (which had been condemned before she was scuttled) could produce a speed of only four knots. The vessel was difficult to maneuver and took 30 minutes to turn around. The *Virginia* was completed 5 Mar. and on the 8th sailed into Hampton Roads, under Commodore Franklin Buchanan and a crew of about 350 (B.&L., I, 718) to attack the Federal ships there.

(Note. *Merrimack*—with the "k"— was the official name on the US Navy lists, she being named for the Merri-

mack River rather than the town of Merrimac in northeastern Mass. After her conversion into an ironclad, common usage has come to sanction dropping the "k." Also, she continued to be better known by her original name than by her new one, the *Virginia.* Different specifications have been given for the *Merrimack* before her conversion: 3,200 tons, 275 feet, and 4,500 tons, 300 feet. Professors Potter and West of the US Naval Academy explain that this disparity comes probably from the lack of fixed standards until recent times. The length difference was probably the difference between water-line length and over-all length; the tonnage difference is probably the difference between deadweight and displacement tons.)

Whereas the *Virginia* was "an ingenious adaptation of the materials at hand and a tribute to her builders' skill at improvisation" (Potter, 319), the *Monitor* represented a completely new concept of naval design. It has been estimated that the ship contained at least 40 patentable ideas. Although the design had been maturing in the mind of its inventor, John ERICSSON, for many years, its actual construction was accomplished in remarkably short time. Her keel was laid 25 Oct. '61, steam was first applied to her boilers on 30 Dec., she was launched on 30 Jan. '62 (after 101 working days), and commissioned 25 Feb.

"Ericsson's Folly" was 172 feet long, displaced 1,200 tons, and drew 10½ feet. A 140-ton revolving turret housed two 11-inch smoothbores (Dahlgrens) and was powered by an auxiliary steam engine that could rotate it through a full circle. The circular turret was covered by eight layers of one-inch iron plates, and the vertical sides of the raft-like deck had four and a half inches of iron armor. The decks were awash with only the 9-foot-high turret and the 4-foot-high pilothouse showing. This led to her being called the "Yankee cheese box on a raft." On the morning of 6 Mar. she left New York for Hampton Roads under the command of Lt. Lorimer Worden and a partially trained crew of 58.

The *Virginia* had sailed into Hampton Roads at about 1 P.M., 8 Mar., with two small gunboats, and opened the attack an hour later. Engaging the 50-gun *Congress* and the 30-gun *Cumberland,* she rammed the latter and then forced the *Congress* aground. At about 3:30 the *Cumberland* sank. About an hour later the *Congress* surrendered after taking a heavy fire from the *Virginia.* Buchanan was wounded during this action and was succeeded by Lt. Catesby ap Roger Jones (who had superintended the ship's armament). Three Federal steam frigates ran aground while approaching the scene of battle from Old Point Comfort; one of them, the *Minnesota,* was saved from possible destruction because the tide had ebbed, and the *Virginia* could not get to her. About 5 P.M. the Confederate ironclad retired with the intention of returning the next day to destroy the *Minnesota.* Confederate losses so far had been 21.

At dawn the next day (9 Mar.) the Confederates saw the long-expected ironclad lying between the *Virginia* and the *Minnesota.* At 9 A.M. a two-hour battle started in which the *Monitor* was able to outmaneuver her opponent but in which neither vessel inflicted any significant damage. The Federal boat withdrew to resupply ammunition, and the engagement was renewed about 11:30. The *Virginia* now concentrated her fire on the pilothouse. About noon a shot struck the sight hole of the *Monitor* and blinded Worden, causing the Federal ironclad to withdraw. The *Virginia* waited a short time and then returned to Norfolk.

Although the battle was indecisive, the North was relieved of the anxiety that the *Virginia* might destroy the Federal fleet and attack the coastal cities. When Norfolk was evacuated 9 May the Confederates had to destroy their ironclad because she could not go up the James and was not sufficiently seaworthy to sail to a new coastal base. The *Monitor* was lost in a gale off Cape Hatteras on 31 Dec. '62. The duel between the ironclads introduced a new era of naval warfare.

See also NEWPORT NEWS, 8–9 Mar. '62 for casualties and Federal infantry regiments participating.

MONOCACY, Md., 12 Oct. '62. Attempting to intercept Confederate forces withdrawing from STUART'S CHAMBERSBURG RAID, Pleasonton reached the mouth of the Monocacy at about 8 A.M. with 400 troopers. There was a clash in which the Federals were driven back. Elements of the 3d and 4th Me. Inf. were later engaged, but were driven from White's Ford, thereby allowing Stuart to retreat safely (H. B. McClellan, 155–58).

MONOCACY, Md., 9 July '64. (EARLY'S WASHINGTON RAID) At about 8 A.M. Early's advance guard found a Federal force along the Monocacy River just southeast of Frederick. These were an infantry brigade and a cavalry brigade of Lew Wallace's troops, reinforced by the recently arrived division of Ricketts (3, VI). (Wallace was in overall command.) About noon, while Early was still formulating his plan of attack, McCausland led his cavalry brigade across the river and assaulted the Federal left. Gordon's division was then sent across in the same area. Up hill and across open fields obstructed by fences and grain stacks Gordon's men advanced and drove the Federals from two lines.

While Gordon was maneuvering for an assault against the third line, his men saw enemy troops rushing forward to occupy a fence line between the opposing forces. Against Gordon's wishes, an impromptu charge was made and the final Federal line routed. Ramseur's division then attacked across the railroad bridge, while Rodes crossed two miles upstream and advanced along the Baltimore Pike. Early did not pursue vigorously because he did not want to burden himself with more prisoners.

Of the 6,050 Federal troops engaged there were 1,880 casualties, including 1,188 missing. Early lost less than 700 of his 14,000 troops present for the action.

MONONGAHELA, UNION DEPARTMENT OF THE. Created 9 June '63, to consist of that portion of Pa. west of Johnstown and the Laurel Hill range of mountains and the counties of Hancock, Brooke, and Ohio in the state of W. Va., and the counties of Columbiana, Jefferson, and Belmont in Ohio. Created at the same time and for the same reason was the Department of the SUSQUEHANNA with which it was merged 6 Apr. '64. Commanded by Maj. Gen. W. T. H. Brooks, with headquarters at Pittsburgh.

MONROE, George Wood. Union officer. Ky. Lt. Col. 22d Ky. 10 Jan. '62; Col. 12 Dec. '62; transferred to 7th Ky. 10 Dec. '64; Bvt. B.G. USV (war service). Died 1869. Phisterer lists him as Munroe, George W.

MONTGOMERY, Milton. Union officer. Ohio. Col. 25th Wis. 14 Sept. '62; Bvt. B.G. USV (Ga. and Carolinas). Lost an arm, and captured at Decatur (Ga.) 19 July '64. Commanded 3d Brig., Kimball's Prov. Div., XVI; 3d Brig., Kimball's Dist. East Ark., XVI; Dist. East Ark., XVI; 1, 4, XVI; 2, 1, XVII.

MONTGOMERY, William Reading. Union gen. 1801-71. N.J. USMA 1825 (28/37); Inf. He served on the frontier in the 1st Seminole War and the Mexican War (2 brevets and twice wounded). He was dismissed in 1855 for misappropriation of military lands for a town site (Cullum). He organized and was Col. of 1st N.J. 21 May '61 and named B.G. USV to date from 17 May '61. He was military Gov. of Alexandria (Va.), commanded Union troops at Annapolis and Philadelphia, and served as military commissioner at Memphis from 1863 until he resigned 4 Apr. '64.

MONTGOMERY CONVENTION. (4 Feb. '61). See SECESSION, SEQUENCE AND DATES.

MOODY, Granville. Union officer. 1812-87. Me. Col. 74th Ohio 28 Feb. '62; Bvt. B.G. USV (Stones River, Tenn.; war service); resigned 16 May '63. A Methodist minister when asked to be Col. of the 74th Ohio, he consulted with his church members and accepted the commission with their permission. At Stones River, where he received the nickname "Fighting Parson," he was wounded four times and had his horse shot from under him but would not leave the field (Reid). After the war he returned to the ministry.

MOODY, Young Marshall. C.S.A. gen. 1822-66. Va. A schoolteacher and merchant, he was commissioned Capt. 11th Ala. in 1861 and became Lt. Col. of Gracie's 43d Ala. a year later. He fought at Perryville and led the regiment at Chickamauga, Knoxville, and Bean's Station before joining Beauregard at Petersburg. Wounded in the ankle at Drewry's Bluff, he then succeeded to brigade command upon Gracie's death 2 Dec. '64. He was appointed B.G. C.S.A. 4 Mar. '65. He fought in the Petersburg siege and assaults and was captured the day before Appomattox.

Described by C.M.H. as being of "soldierly bearing, six feet in height, slender and erect." He died less than a year after the war of yellow fever while in New Orleans on business.

MOON, John Carter. Union officer. Ohio. Pvt. 85th Ohio 28 May '62; Capt. 9 June '62; Capt. 88th Ohio 28 Sept. '62; Lt. Col. 118th US Col. Inf. 27 Aug. '64; Col. 1 Dec. '64; Bvt. B.G. USV 21 Nov. '65 (war service). Commanded 1, 1, XXV; 2, 1, XXV. Died 1895.

MOONLIGHT, Thomas. Union officer. Scotland. R.A. Pvt., Cpl., Sgt. & 1st Sgt. Co. D 4th US Arty. 17 Mar. '53–17 May '58; Capt. 1st Kans. Btry. 20 July '61; Capt. Asst. Adj. Gen. Vols. 14 Apr. '62; Lt. Col. 11th Kans. Cav. 20 Sept. '62; Col. 25 Apr. '64; Bvt. B.G. USV. Monaghan in *Civil War on the Western Border* says he "distinguished himself as a captain with one cannon at Dry Wood (Mo.) in September 1861." Commanded 2d Kans. Brig. in 1864. Died 1897.

MOOR, Augustus. Union officer. Germany. Col. 28th Ohio 16 July '61; Bvt. B.G. USV (Droop Mountain and Piedmont, Va.); mustered out 23 July '64. Commanded (W. Va.): 2, Dist. Kanawha (captured at South Mountain); 1st Brig., 4th Div.; 1st Brig., 1st Inf. Div. Served as an officer in the Fla. war and the Mexican War. Died 1883. See also KANAWHA DIVISION.

MOORE, Andrew Barry. C.S.A. Gov. of Ala. 1806–73. S.C. Coming to Ala. as a young man, he practiced law and entered politics as a Democrat, sitting in the legislature and acting as Speaker. A judge until 1857, he was elected Gov. then and served for two years, ordering the seizure of Pensacola and the organization of state troops during his term. He was then named special A.D.C. to his successor, John G. Shorter, and

was arrested by the Federals in 1865. After the war he practiced law.

MOORE, David. Union officer. Ohio. Capt. 1st Northeast Mo. Home Guards 14 June '61; mustered out 14 July '61; Col. 1st Northeast Mo. 25 Oct. '61; transferred to 21st Mo. 1 Feb. '62; mustered out 11 Feb. '65; Col. 51st Mo. 1 May '65; Bvt. B.G. USV 21 Feb. '65. Commanded 4, Dist. Memphis 5, XVI; 1, 3, XVI; 1st Brig. 2d Div. Det. Army Tenn. (Cumberland); 2d Div. Det. Army Tenn. (Cumberland).

MOORE, Frederick William. Union officer. Ohio. 2d Lt. 5th Ohio 20 Apr. '61; 1st Lt. 14 Sept. '61; Capt. 9 Jan. '62; mustered out 23 July '62; Col. 83d Ohio 13 Sept. '62; Bvt. B.G. USV 26 Mar. '65 (Mobile and defenses). In Banks's Red River expedition; commanded the post of Galveston. Commanded also 1, 2d Div. Army Ky. (Ohio); 1, 4, XIII; 4th Div. XIII; 3, 3, XIX; 3, 2, XIII. Later in R.A. but resigned shortly to become a lawyer.

MOORE, Jesse Hale. Union officer. 1817–83. Ill. Col. 115th Ill. 13 Sept. '62; Bvt. B.G. USV 15 May '65 (war service). Commanded 2, 1, IV (Cumberland). He resigned his Methodist pastorate in Decatur (Ill.) to raise the 115th, a regiment particularly active in the pursuit of Hood. He returned to the ministry for a while, later becoming a Republican Congressman and US Consul to Callao (Peru), where he died.

MOORE, John Creed. C.S.A. gen. 1824–1910. Tenn. USMA 1849 (17/43); Arty. After fighting in the Seminole War and serving on the frontier, he resigned in 1855 to be a schoolteacher in Tenn. In Apr. '61 he was commissioned Capt. C.S.A. Arty. from Tex. and served until Dec., having been promoted Col. of Arty. around Galveston. From Jan. to Oct. '62 he was Col. of the 2d Tex. Vols. and assigned to Houston. He commanded his regiment at Shiloh and was appointed B.G. C.S.A. 26 May '62. In Sept. '62 he was assigned command of the area south of Booneville, Tenn., with headquarters at Tupelo. He led his brigade at Corinth and Hatchie River. He commanded his brigade at Vicksburg and was exchanged in time to fight at Chattanooga under Hardee. In July '64 he was in Hood's corps in the Atlanta campaign and by Oct. of that year was at Selma, Ala., where he reported that he had no guns or ammunition. After the war Moore returned to Tex. and taught school.

MOORE, Jonathan Baker. Union officer. Ind. Col. 33d Wis. 18 Oct. '62; Bvt. B.G. USV 26 Mar. '65 (Mobile and defenses). Commanded 1, Prov. Div., XVII; 1, 3d Div., Det. Army Tenn. (Cumberland); 3d Div., Det. Army Tenn. (Cumberland); 1, 3, XVI; 3d Div., XVI.

MOORE, Marshall F. Union officer. Ohio. Commissioned Lt. Col. 17th Ohio 4 Oct. '61, he resigned 14 Feb. '63 and was named Col. 69th Ohio 23 Feb. of that year. He resigned that commission 7 Nov. '64 and was breveted for Jonesboro (B.G. USV) and war service (Maj. Gen. USV). He died in 1870.

MOORE, Patrick T. C.S.A. gen. 1821–83. Ireland. He lived in Canada as a boy and moved to this country when his father became Consul at Boston. Moving to Richmond, Moore became a merchant and was active as militia captain. He was commissioned Col. 1st Va. in the spring of '61 and fought under Longstreet at 1st Bull Run, where he was wounded in the head. During the Peninsular campaign, being still unfit for field service, he was on Longstreet's staff, and in May '64 was put temporarily in charge, under Gen. Kemper, of organizing the Va. reserves. Appointed B.G. C.S.A. 30 Sept. '64, he commanded the 1st Brig.

of Va. reserves in the Dept. of Richmond. After the war he headed an insurance agency.

MOORE, Thomas Overton. C.S.A. governor of La. 1803–76. N.C. A cotton planter in Rapide Parish, he sat in the legislature before being elected Democratic Gov. in 1860. He was in favor of secession and called a convention to take the state out of the Union early in 1861. When New Orleans fell, he called the legislature to meet first in Opelousas and then in Shreveport, where it remained for the rest of the war. He was succeeded by Henry W. Allen as military Gov. late in 1864. His grandfather had been a Maj. under Light Horse Harry Lee in 1776.

MOORE, Timothy Cummings. Union officer. N.J. Capt. 6th N.J. 29 Aug. '61; discharged 16 Jan. '63; Lt. Col. 34th N.J. 6 Oct. '63; Col. 14 Jan. '66; Bvt. B.G. USV 11 Nov. '65 (war service).

MOORE, Tredwell. Union officer. c. 1825–76. Ohio. USMA 1847 (26/38); Inf. Q.M. He served in the Mexican War, on the frontier, and on the Utah Expedition before the Civil War. As Capt. Asst. Q.M. (since 1859), he was on duty in Calif., N. Mex., and Ariz. until 1863. He was on Q.M. duty at Wheeling (W. Va.) 20 June '63–June '64 and "awaiting orders" for the remainder of the war. Continuing in the R.A., he died on active duty as Lt. Col. and Bvt. B.G. USA (war service).

MOOREFIELD, W. Va., 7 Aug. '64. (EARLY'S WASHINGTON RAID) After burning CHAMBERSBURG, Pa., the Confederate cavalry brigades of McCausland and Bradley Johnson bivouacked around Moorefield, W. Va. Here they were surprised and routed by Averell in a dawn attack. The Federals reported capturing 420 men, four guns, and 400 horses. Johnson was captured but escaped.

MOREHEAD, Turner Gustavus. Union officer. Md. Col. 22d Pa. 23 Apr. '61; mustered out 5 Aug. '61; Col. 106th Pa. 28 Aug. '61; Bvt. B.G. USV (war service); discharged 4 Apr. '64. Commanded in the 2d Div., II Corps (Potomac): 1st Brig., 3d Brig., 2d Brig. Served as Capt. in the Mexican War. Died 1892.

MORELL, George Webb. Union gen. 1815–83. N.Y. USMA 1835 (1/56); Engrs. His first army duties were on the Great Lakes and Atlantic seacoast harbor projects. Resigning in 1837, he was a railroad engineer and lawyer. He was commissioned in the N.Y. Volunteers during the Mexican War, but his regiment never was in federal service. Named Col. Q.M. on Gen. Sanford's staff N.Y. Vols. 16 May–25 July '61, and B.G. USV 9 Aug. '61, he commanded 1, Fitz-John Porter's division, Army Potomac (3 Oct. '61–13 Mar. '62) in guarding the approaches to Washington. He also led the 2, 1, III, Potomac (13 Mar.–18 May '62) and 1st Div., V, Potomac (18 May–30 Oct. '62). He participated in battles of Howard's Bridge, Yorktown, Hanover C.H., Mechanicsville, Gaines's Mill, Malvern Hill, 2d Bull Run, and Antietam. He was named Maj. Gen. USV 4 July '62, but his appointment expired 4 Mar. '63. He then guarded the upper Potomac and spent 1863 in Washington "awaiting orders." He was commanding the Draft Rendezvous in Indianapolis when he was mustered out 15 Dec. '64.

MORGAN, Charles Hale. Union gen. 1834–75. N.Y. USMA 1857 (12/38); Arty. On garrison and frontier duty prior to the war, he served first as 1st Lt. 4th US Arty. (1 Apr. '61) in western Va. and at Yorktown. Promoted to Capt. 5 Aug. '62 and Lt. Col. Asst. I.G. Assigned 1 Jan. '63–25 May '65, he was Chief of Arty., Asst. I.G. and Chief of Staff for the II Corps and for the I Corps (Potomac). He commanded the II Corps Arty. at Fredericksburg, Chancellorsville, Gettysburg, Auburn, Bristoe Station, Mine Run, the Wilderness, Todd's Tavern, Spotsylvania, North Anna, Totopotomoy, Cold Harbor, Petersburg, Deep Bottom, Reams's Station, Boydton Plank Road, and the Petersburg siege. He was later Asst. I.G. and Chief of Staff for Hancock in the Middle Mil. Div. He was breveted for Gettysburg, Bristoe Station, Spotsylvania (2), and the Wilderness. He was breveted B.G. USV and USA for war service. Remaining in the R.A., he was Maj. 4th US Arty. at his death.

MORGAN, Edwin Denison. Gov. of N.Y. and Union gen. 1811–83. Mass. Appt. N.Y. Wholesale grocer and N.Y.C. merchant; active in banking and brokerage. Serving as Whig state sen., he introduced the bill establishing Central Park. Unable to agree with his party's abolitionist methods, he changed parties and served as the Republican national chairman. While Gov. of N.Y., 1858–62, he was commissioned Maj. Gen. USV 28 Sept. '61. He commanded the Dept. of N.Y. from 26 Oct. '61 until it was merged with the Dept. of the East on 3 Jan. '63, when he resigned to enter the US Senate.

MORGAN, George Nelson. Union officer. 1825–66. N.Y. Capt. 1st Minn. 29 May '61; Maj. 23 Oct. '61; Lt. Col. 2 Oct. '62; Col. 14 Nov. '62; resigned 5 May '63; Maj. Vet. Res. Corps 26 May '63; Col. 25 Sept. '63; Bvt. B.G. USV (war service). Owned a machine and foundry shop in Minn. before the war. He was discharged 30 June '66. Died 24 July.

MORGAN, George Washington. Union gen. 1820–93. Pa. He had left college at 16 to join in the Texas War for Independence where he held the ‑ank of Capt. Entering USMA in 1841, he resigned in his second year and then studied law. At the age of 26 he was Col. 2d Ohio in the Mexican War and was commissioned Col. 15th US Inf. in 1847. He was wounded at Contreras and Churubusco and breveted B.G. for those battles. After practicing law and farming, he was named US Consul at Marseilles (1856) and Minister to Lisbon (1858), the post which he resigned to come home for the Civil War. Named B.G. USV 12 Nov. '61, he commanded 7th Div., Army Ohio (26 Mar.–10 Oct. '62) in driving the Confederates from the Cumberland Gap; Cumberland Dist., Ohio (Oct.–Dec. '62); 9th Div. Left Wing, XIII, Tenn. (Nov.–Dec. '62); 3d Div., Yazoo Expedition, Tenn. (Dec. '62–Jan. '63); and XIII Corps, Tenn. (4 Jan.–31 Jan. '63) in the capture of Ft. Hindman (Ark.). A disagreement with Sherman (see Morgan's account of Chickasaw Bayou in B.&L., III, 468, and Sherman's *Memoirs*) in addition to illness and his dissatisfaction with the use of Negro troops caused his resignation on 8 June '63. After the war, he served as Democratic Congressman and was much opposed to the Radical Republican form of reconstruction.

MORGAN, James Dada. Union gen. 1810–96. Miss. At 16 he went to sea, but the crew mutinied and burned the ship, leaving Morgan and a party adrift for 14 days before landing in South America. He became an Ill. merchant and led a militia unit during that state's Mormon troubles in 1844–45. He was also an officer in the Mexican War. Commissioned Lt. Col. 10th Ill. 29 Apr. '61 and promoted Col. 29 July '61, he commanded 4, 1st Mil. Dist. Cairo, Mo. (to Feb. '62) and 2, 1, Army Miss. (24 Apr.–1 May '62). He was named B.G. USV 17 July '62 and led 1st Div., Army Miss. (15 July–15 Aug. '62); 1st Brig., 4th Div., Army Miss. (4 Mar.–24 Apr.

'62); 2d Brig. 13th Div., Army Ohio (Sept.–Nov. '62). In the Army of the Cumberland he led 1, 4th Centre, XIV (5 Nov. '62–9 Jan. '63); 4th Div., XIV (9 Jan.–5 May '63); 2d Div., Res. Corps (8 June–8 Oct. '63); 1, 2, XIV (12 Nov. '63–12 Aug. '64); 2d Div., XIV (22 Aug. '64–23 June '65). He was breveted Maj. Gen. USV 19 Mar. '65 (Bentonville, N.C.) and mustered out 24 Aug. '65. After the Civil War he was prominent in banking and philanthropy in Ill.

MORGAN, John Hunt. C.S.A. gen. and raider. 1825–64. Ala. After fighting in the Mexican War, he was a businessman in Lexington, Ky., and raised in 1857 the Lexington Rifles, a militia group. He was commissioned Capt. in Sept. '61 and given a squadron of cavalry for scouting. The next year saw the start of the famous MORGAN'S RAIDS. At Shiloh he commanded the Ky. Squadron of Cav., having been promoted Col. 4 Apr. '62, and in June he was given a brigade. Appointed B.G. C.S.A. 11 Dec. '62, he commanded a cavalry division and on 1 May '63 he and his command were given the C.S.A. Thanks of Congress for "varied, heroic and invaluable services in Tennessee and Kentucky immediately preceding the battles before Murfreesboro. . . ." He was captured 26 July '63 near New Lisbon (Ohio) and escaped with others from the Ohio State Penitentiary (Columbus) 26 Nov. In Apr. '64 he commanded the Dept. of Southwest Va. and on 4 Sept. '64 was surprised and killed by Federal troops at Greenville, Tenn. His courtship and marriage to Mattie READY were in the romantic tradition of his military operations.

MORGAN, John Tyler. C.S.A. gen. 1824–1907. Tenn. Appt.–Ala. After a classical education he became a lawyer active in Democratic politics and was a delegate to the Ala. secession convention. Enlisting as a private in the "Cahaba Rifles," he was soon elected Lt. Col. 5th Ala. and then resigned to recruit and become Col. of the 51st Ala. He was under Forrest in the Stones River campaign, fought at Chickamauga and Knoxville, and was appointed B.G. C.S.A. 6 June '63. This he declined 14 July '63 but was reappointed 17 Nov. '63 to rank from the 16th. During the Atlanta campaign he commanded his brigade in the cavalry corps and was raising Negro troops in Miss. when the war ended. After the war he was a long-time member of the US Senate.

MORGAN, Michael Ryan. Union officer. c. 1833–1911. Nova Scotia. Appt.-La. USMA 1854 (16/46); Arty.-Inf.-Comsy. He served on the frontier in Indian fighting and on the expedition to suppress John Brown's Harpers Ferry raid before declining the promotion to Capt. 110th US Inf. 14 May '61. On 3 Aug. '61 he took the same rank in the Comsy. of Subsist. and was Chief of Commissariat to the Port Royal expedition (12 Aug. '61–31 Mar. '62) and of the Dept. of the South until 1 May '64. He held the same position with the X Corps until 16 June '64 when he became Chief of Commissariat for the armies operating against Richmond (until 6 June '65). Continuing in the R.A., he was breveted for the Richmond campaign and war service (B.G. USA 9 Apr. '65). He retired in 1897 as B.G. USA Comsy. Gen.

MORGAN, Thomas Jefferson. Union officer. 1839–1902. Ind. 1st Lt. 70th Ind. 1 Aug. '62; Lt. Col. 14th US Col. Inf. 1 Nov. '63; Col. 1 Jan. '64; Bvt. B.G. USV (war service). Commanded 1st Col. Brig., Dist. Etowah (Cumberland). D.A.B. describes him as being "prominent in the enlistment of Negro troops and eloquent in their defense. . . ." He was also a leader in providing schools for the ex-slaves. After

the war he became a Baptist minister and was president of state normal schools and Commissioner of Indian Affairs (1889–93) under Harrison. The author of many religious and pedagogical books, including two on Negroes, he was secretary for 10 years of the American Baptist Home Mission Society.

MORGAN, William Henry. Union officer. Ohio. Capt. 10th Ind. 22 June '61; mustered out 6 Aug. '61; Lt. Col. 25th Ind. 19 Aug. '61; Col. 1 May '62; resigned 20 May '64; Col. 3d Vet. Vol. Inf. 10 Jan. '65; Bvt. B.G. USV (war service). Commanded in the XVI Corps (Tenn.); 2d Brig., Dist. Memphis 5; 3d Brig., 1st Cav. Died Mar. '78.

MORGAN'S FIRST RAID, Ky., July '62. As Buell moved toward Chattanooga with the mission of capturing that place (following his participation at SHILOH and CORINTH), his operations were thrown into confusion by the raids of Forrest and Morgan. On 4 July Morgan led two regiments (800 men) from Knoxville and on the 9th attacked and captured a cavalry post of four companies at Tomkinsville, Ky. He captured a depot at Glasgow on the 10th and one at Lebanon on the 11th. Moving via Harrodsburg, Lawrenceburg, Versailles, and Georgetown, he had a sharp engagement with militia at Cynthiana on the 17th. He then withdrew through Paris, Richmond, Crab Orchard (where he destroyed a depot on the line of supply to CUMBERLAND GAP), and Somerset. On the 22d he reached Monticello and was back in Tenn. on 1 Aug. In 24 days he had covered over 1,000 miles, had captured and paroled 1,200 prisoners, and had lost fewer than 100 men. The raid did much damage to Federal morale and led to criticism of Buell.

MORGAN'S SECOND RAID, Lexington, Ky., Oct. '62. (STONES RIVER) After accompanying Kirby Smith's retreat from Lexington, when Morgan reached Crab Orchard he received permission to lead his brigade of 1,800 cavalry on a raid. Circling eastward, he captured Lexington, Ky., 18 Oct., with little difficulty. He then went through Versailles and Lawrenceburg to Bardstown. Crossing the railroad near Elizabethtown, he marched through Leitchfield and Morgantown to Hopkinsville, Ky. He then returned via Springfield to Gallatin, Tenn. He captured a number of small posts and destroyed railroad bridges.

MORGAN'S THIRD RAID, 21 Dec. '62–1 Jan. '63. (STONES RIVER) After organizing a division of two brigades (under Basil Duke and A. R. Johnson), about 4,000 total, Morgan left Alexandria (near Carthage), Tenn., 21 Dec., to raid Rosecrans' lines of communications. He struck directly north through Glasgow to Bardstown, hit the Louisville & Nashville R.R. just north of Munfordville and followed it to Rolling Fork, just north of Elizabethtown, which he had captured 27 Dec. Here he turned east and was attacked, while crossing the river, by a Union infantry brigade sent from Gallatin. He reached Bardstown with some loss and marched to Springfield, where he learned that a large enemy force was at Lebanon. Avoiding the latter by a night march, he reached Columbia, Tenn., on 1 Jan. With a loss of two killed and 24 wounded, he had taken 1,887 prisoners and destroyed $2,000,000 worth of property (Horn, 195).

MORGAN'S OHIO RAID, 2–26 July '63. In early June '63 Bragg had authorized Morgan to undertake a raid into Ky. to slow Rosecrans' advance on Chattanooga. Authorizing him to move wherever he chose in Ky., Bragg had disapproved Morgan's proposal to extend his raid north of the Ohio. Morgan's operation was detained by Sanders's raid during the KNOXVILLE CAMPAIGN.

On 2 July, with picked men in the brigades of Basil Duke (1,460) and A. R. Johnson (1,000) and four guns, Morgan crossed the Cumberland near Burkesville. In so doing he eluded 10,000 Federals under Hartsuff and Judah, who were supposed to prevent such a crossing of the river. On the 4th he was repulsed by five companies of Col. O. H. Moore's 25th Mich. when he attempted to force a crossing of the Green River. The next day at Lebanon he defeated Col. C. S. Hanson's 20th Ky. in a hot engagement, taking 400 prisoners and a considerable quantity of supplies, including medical stores. He entered Bardstown on the 6th and Garnettsville the next day. He reached the Ohio at Brandenburg and started crossing on two steamers that had been captured by a force sent ahead for this purpose. Despite some interference from a gunboat and home guards, he had completed his crossing to the Ind. shore by midnight. He captured Croydon on the 9th, inflicting 360 casualties (of whom 345 were missing) on the Ind. Home Guards under Col. Lewis Jordan. By this time the militia of two states were alerted and the troops of Judah and Burnside could be expected to be found around Cincinnati. Morgan continued east through Salem, Vienna, Lexington (where Federal cavalry nearly captured him in his sleep), Paris, Vernon, Dupont, Summansville, and at 1 P.M. on the 13th he entered Harrison, Ohio. With his force now reduced to about 2,000, and forced to change his tired mounts for unshod horses captured en route, Morgan passed through the suburbs of Cincinnati the night of 13–14 July and reached Williamsburg at 4 P.M. In his greatest effort he had marched more than 90 miles in about 35 hours since leaving Summansville,

Ind. (Furse, *The Art of Marching,* 507). He reached Pomeroy on the 18th and began to encounter serious enemy action. At about 1 P.M. he entered Chester. Halting here for an hour and a half for the column to close up and give his troops some rest, he did not reach Buffington until 8 P.M. It was here that Morgan had intended to recross the Ohio. However, he found his passage barred by a redoubt too strong for him to attempt to reduce by a night action. In a fight the next day (19th) Morgan was badly beaten by the forces of Hobson and Shackelford, who were supported by militia and by gunboats that steamed up the river to Buffington. While the Federals lost only 25 (E.&B.), Morgan had about 120 killed and wounded and 700 captured (B.&L., III, 635n.). Morgan himself escaped with 300 men and tried to reach Pa. Hobson pursued relentlessly. On 26 July he was brought to bay near New Lisbon (or Beaver Creek) and forced to surrender his remaining 364 officers and men (B.&L., *ibid.*). E.&B. puts Morgan's casualties in this final action at 23 killed, 44 wounded, and 304 missing.

This raid is remarkable for the endurance exhibited by Morgan's command: an average of 21 hours a day in the saddle from the time he crossed the Ohio. "However, the real object of the raid has remained a mystery," wrote Furse (*op. cit.*). "This reckless adventure . . . deprived him of his well-earned reputation" (*ibid.*). Although he escaped (27 Nov.) and rejoined the Confederates, "his days of usefulness to the Army of Tennessee were over" (Horn, 233).

MORRELL, George Webb. Incorrect spelling for MORELL, G. W.

MORRILL, John. Union officer. N.H. Capt. 64th Ill. 3 Dec. '61; Lt. Col. 12

Sept. '62; Col. 1 Mar. '64; Bvt. B.G. USV (Atlanta). Commanded 1, 4, XVI (Tenn.). Died 1893.

MORRIS, Henry W. Union Commodore. 1806–63. N.Y. Entering the navy in 1819, he served in N.Y.C., the African coastal waters, the South Atlantic, and the Mediterranean. He was promoted Capt. in 1856 and supervised the construction of the *Pensacola* in late 1861, commanding the steam sloop of war in the battle of New Orleans. Remaining there, he guarded the coastal area and held the city until his health broke. He was promoted Commodore 16 July '62 and died on active duty in N.Y.C. 14 Aug. '63. Kin of Mary Morris HUSBAND.

MORRIS, Thomas Armstrong. Union gen. 1811–1904. Ky. Appt.-Ind. USMA 1834 (4/36); Arty. He resigned his commission two years after graduating from USMA and became an engineer and railroad president, occupations he returned to after his Civil War service. Commanding Morris' Indiana brigade, Army of Occupation, W. Va., as B.G. Ind. Vols. (27 Apr. '61), he mustered W. Va. volunteer regiments in the Union Army with McClellan's support. His troops drove the Confederates from Philippi, but later McClellan refused to reinforce him and then criticized him for not pursuing the enemy more energetically at Laurel Hill. After the battle of Carrick's Ford the enlistment term of his brigade expired. Morris then expected a US commission, but when he did not receive one until 20 Sept. '62 (B.G. USV), he declined it, feeling that he was not needed in the Union Army.

MORRIS, William Hopkins. Union gen. 1827–1900. N.Y. USMA 1851 (27/42); Inf. He served on garrison and frontier duty, resigning in 1854 to join his father as asst. editor of the *New*

York Home Journal. In 1859 he invented a conical repeating carbine. Commissioned Capt. Asst. A.G. USV 20 Aug. '61 on the staff of J. J. Peck, he was at Yorktown, Williamsburg, and Fair Oaks, resigning 1 Sept. '62 to become, the next day, Col. 6th N.Y. Arty. and serve in the defenses of Baltimore. He was promoted B.G. USV 29 Nov. and commanded 2, 1, VIII, Middle (27 Mar.–26 June '63) at Maryland Heights overlooking Harpers Ferry. In reserve at Gettysburg, his next command was 1, 3, III, Potomac (10 July '63–24 Mar. '64) at Bristoe Station and during the advance to the Rappahannock. From 25 Mar. until 13 May '64 he led 1, 3, VI, Potomac at the Wilderness and Spotsylvania, where he was wounded. Breveted Maj. Gen. USV for the Wilderness, he was mustered out 24 Aug. '65, having served on military commissions until the end of the war. He returned to publishing and was active in the N.Y. National Guard. In 1864 he had authored a system of infantry tactics.

MORRIS, William W. Union officer. c. 1801–65. N.Y. USMA 1820 (30/30); Inf.-Arty. He served on the frontier fighting Indians and in the Seminole wars and the Mexican War before being named Lt. Col. 4th US Arty. 14 May '61. From 1861 to 1 Feb. '65, he commanded the harbor defenses of Baltimore and then took charge of the VIII Corps until Dec. '65. He died on active duty as Col. 2d US Arty. (1 Nov. '61), Bvt. B.G. USA (9 June '62), and Bvt. Maj. Gen. USA (10 Dec. '65).

MORRISON, David. Union officer. Scotland. Capt. 79th N.Y. 27 May '61; Lt. Col. 19 Dec. '61; Col. 17 Feb. '63; Bvt. B.G. USV (Spotsylvania C.H.); mustered out 31 May '64. Commanded in the IX Corps: 1st Brig., 1st Div.

(Potomac); 1st Brig., 1st Div. (Tenn.). Died 1896.

MORRISON, Joseph Johnson. Union officer. N.Y. Capt. 83d N.Y. 27 May '61; mustered out 29 July '61; Capt. 3d N.Y. Arty. 18 Dec. '61; mustered out 5 May '63; Col. 16th N.Y. Arty. 18 Jan. '64; Bvt. B.G. USV (war service).

MORRISON, Pitcairn. Union officer. N.Y. Entering the R.A. in 1820, he served in the Mexican War (1 brevet) and on the frontier. He was promoted Col. 8th US Inf. June '61 and commanded his regiment until his retirement in Oct. '63 because of ill-health. In Mar. '65 he was breveted B.G. USA.

MORROW, Henry Andrew. Union officer. Va. After fighting in the Mexican War, he was commissioned Col. 24th Mich. 15 Aug. '62 and fought at Fredericksburg, Chancellorsville, Gettysburg (wounded), the Wilderness (wounded), and Dabney's Mills (severely wounded). Transferring to the R.A., he served on the frontier and died on active duty in 1891 as Col. 21st US Inf., Bvt. B.G. USV (1 Aug. '64 for Richmond campaign) and Bvt. Maj. Gen. USV (Petersburg). He was also breveted for Hatcher's Run 6 Feb. '65.

MORSE, Henry Bagg. Union officer. 1836–74. N.Y. Maj. 114th N.Y. 8 Sept. '62; Lt. Col. 26 Aug. '63; Bvt. B.G. USV (war service). W.I.A. Port Hudson. Served on Board of Prison Inspectors in the Dept. of the Gulf at New Orleans and as Acting Chief Q.M. for the XIX Corps. He was later a Republican politician and judge in Arkansas.

MORTON, James St. Clair. Union gen. 1829–64. Pa. USMA 1851 (2/42); Engrs. He was engaged in engineering projects on the East Coast, went on the Chiriqui expedition in 1860, and had taught engineering at West Point. As

Capt. 6 Aug. '61, he was named Chief Engr. Army of the Ohio (9 June–Oct. '62). He was also Chief Engr. of the Army of the Cumberland (27 Oct. '62–22 Aug. '63 and 17 Sept.–14 Nov. '63) as well as commanding the Pioneer Brig., XIV, Cumberland 3 Nov. '62–7 Nov. '63 at Stones River and Chickamauga, where he was wounded. Promoted B.G. USV 20 Nov. '62, he then fortified Chattanooga in the fall of '63 and was superintending Engr. of the defenses of Nashville, Murfreesboro, Clarksville and Fort Donelson (14 Nov. '63–30 Jan. '64); Asst. to the Chief Engr., in Washington until 16 May '64; and Chief Engr. IV Corps until 17 June '64, when he was killed leading an assault at Petersburg. He had also fought at North Anna, Totopotomoy, and Bethesda Church and was breveted for Stones River, Chickamauga, and Petersburg (B.G. USA 17 June '64). He was the author of a number of books on fortifications.

MORTON, Oliver Perry. Gov. of Indiana. 1823–77. Ind. After graduating from Miami (Ohio) Univ., he practiced law and was a circuit judge before being elected Lt. Gov. in 1860 on the Republican ticket. When Henry S. Lane was elected to the Senate, Morton became Gov. (1861) and is considered one of the Union's most sturdy adherents despite a hostile legislature. Resigning in 1867, he became Sen. and a Radical Republican.

MOSBY, John Singleton. Confederate Partisan Ranger. 1833–1916. Va. While at the Univ. of Va., he shot another student in a provoked incident and was finally released. Meanwhile, he had read law with his defense counsel in jail. He practiced law at Bristol and was commissioned into the state forces in early 1861. When Va. seceded, he became a private in "Grumble" JONES's 1st Va. Cav. and fought at 1st Bull Run. He was commissioned 1st Lt. in Feb. '62 and began scouting for J. E. B. Stuart shortly afterward, guiding him on the famous ride around McClellan in June. After having been a prisoner for a few weeks in July, he was given permission in Jan. '63 to organize his PARTISAN RANGERS and engage in guerrilla warfare around the Loudoun Valley of northern Va. In Mar. '63 he captured B. G. Edwin H. STOUGHTON from his bed, uncovering the sleeping general and slapping him on the behind. During the Wilderness campaign a great deal of Union energy was spent trying to track Mosby down. V. C. Jones, in his excellent *Ranger Mosby*, advances the theory that Mosby prolonged the life of the Confederacy by diverting much of Grant's strength to combat the Partisan Rangers. During the last winter of the war the Rangers were supreme in eastern Va., and that area was called "Mosby's Confederacy." Promoted Maj. in Apr. '63 and Lt. Col. 11 Feb. '64, he was named Col. 7 Dec. of that year. The command, numbering 100 at first and around 200 by the end of the war, was mustered into the Confederate Army as the 43d Bn. of Va. Cav. on 10 June '63. In Dec. '64 the troops were split into two battalions. Rather than surrender, Mosby disbanded his Rangers on 20 Apr. '65 and returned to his law practice. He later became involved in Reconstruction politics and was tremendously unpopular in the South for supporting Grant for president. After serving as Consul in Hong Kong and practicing law in Calif., he returned to Va., where he spent the rest of his long life. His *War Reminiscences* was published in 1887. Jones describes him as of medium height with sandy blond hair and a clean-shaven face. He wore a gray cape lined with scarlet that was thrown back over his shoulder, and a curling ostrich plume decorated his hat, the second most famous feather in the Confederacy. Weighing only 125 pounds, he was agile and fearless—his pictures show a man whose determination bordered on ruthlessness but never overlapped into cruelty. Grant said in his memoirs: "Since the close of the war, I have come to know Colonel Mosby personally and somewhat intimately. He is a different man entirely from what I had supposed. . . . He is able and thoroughly honest and truthful."

MOSBY'S CONFEDERACY. See John S. Mosby.

MOSLER, Henry. Artist and War Correspondent. 1841–1920. N.Y. He studied drawing and woodcarving until 1861, residing for several periods in Nashville and Richmond. In 1862 he went to the West as correspondent for *Harper's Weekly* and joined Gen. Nelson's staff, where he painted portraits of a number of generals. The next year he went to Germany and France to study, and settled in Paris in 1877. His genre work won him the cross of the Legion of Honor.

MOTT, Gershom. Union gen. 1822–84. N.J. After serving in the R.A. during the Mexican War, he was active in banking and in a port and canal company. Commissioned Lt. Col. 5th N.J. 17 Aug. '61, he was with his regiment at Williamsburg and named Col. 6th N.J. 7 May '62. This regiment was in support at the Seven Days' Battles and fought at 2d Bull Run, where Mott was wounded. Appointed B.G. USV 7 Sept. '62, he commanded 3, 2, III, Potomac (25 Dec. '62–3 May '63) at Chancellorsville, where he was again wounded and in the Mine Run campaign and later (29 Aug. '63–16 Feb. '64 and Feb.–24 Mar. '64). He commanded 1, 4, II (25 Mar.–2 May '64) at the Wilderness and Spotsylvania and succeeded

to the command of the division 2–13 May. Leading the 3d Div., II Corps, he participated in the Petersburg and Richmond campaigns and was present at the crater assault (18–27 June; 23 July–8 Oct.; 21 Oct. '64–15 Feb. '65; 2 Mar.–6 Apr. '65 and 16 May–9 June '65 and 20–28 June '65). He commanded the II Corps on 16 May–9 June and 20–28 June '65, having been named Maj. Gen. USV 26 May '65. Breveted Maj. Gen. USV 1 Aug. '64 for war service, he resigned in 1866 and was later Maj. Gen. in the N.Y. National Guard as well as holding several public offices and engaging in railroading and iron smelting.

MOTT, Samuel Rolla. Union officer. Ohio. Pvt. 57th Ohio 18 Sept. '61; Capt. 57th Ohio 20 Oct. '61; Lt. Col. 24 May '63; Bvt. B.G. USV (war service). In XXIII Corps he commanded 2, 4; 2, 1; 1, 2; and in XV Corps he commanded 1, 2. Died 1899.

MOUNTAIN DEPARTMENT (Union). Created 11 Mar. '62 from the Dept. of Western Va., its area included W. Va., southwest Va., and eastern Ky. Frémont was put in command, but Rosecrans headed the department until his arrival 29 Mar. The department was abolished 26 June '62, and its troops, which Jackson had defeated at McDowell and Cross Keys (Jackson's Valley campaign), became the I Corps, Army of Va.

MOUTON, Alfred. C.S.A. gen. 1829–64. La. USMA 1850 (38/44); Inf. After graduating in June, he resigned in Sept. to become a railroad and civil engineer and was B.G. of the La. Mil. from 1850 until 1861. He was commissioned Col. 18th La. 5 Oct. '61 and severely wounded at Shiloh. Appointed B.G. C.S.A. 16 Apr. '62, he commanded a brigade in La. at La Fourche, Atchafalaya area, Berwick Bay, and Bayou Teche. He was commanding a division at Mansfield when killed 8 Apr. His oldest son was also killed in the war. Gen. Mouton was christened Jean Jacques Alexandre Alfred.

MOWER, Joseph Anthony. Union gen. 1827–70. Vt. Appt.-Conn. After attending Norwich Univ., he worked as a carpenter, fought in the Mexican War as a private in the Engrs. and in 1855 joined the R.A. as an officer. Promoted Capt. 1st US Inf. 9 Sept. '61 (1st Lt. since 1857), he was commissioned Col. 11th Mo. 3 May '62 and commanded 2, 2d Div., Army of the Miss. (9 Aug.–26 Oct. '62) at Corinth, where he was wounded, captured, and recaptured. He was promoted B.G. USV 29 Nov. '62 and led 2, 8, XVI, Tenn. (18 Dec. '62–3 Apr. '63). During the Vicksburg campaign and later he commanded 2, 3, XV (3 Apr.–4 July and 15 Sept.–20 Dec. '63) and then led 2, 1, XVI (20 Dec. '63–7 Mar. '64). In the Red River campaign of 1864 he commanded 1st Div. Det. Army of the Tenn., Gulf (Mar.–June '64) and commanded the XVII Corps temporarily (24–31 Oct. '64). He led 1st Div., XVII Corps (31 Oct. '64–5 Apr. '65), on the March to the Sea and through the Carolinas and was promoted Maj. Gen. USV 12 Aug. '64. From 2 Apr. to 4 June '65 he commanded the XX Corps, Army of Ga. Continuing in the R.A., he was breveted for Farmington (Miss.), Iuka, Jackson, Fort de Russy (B.G. USA), and Salkehatchie River, Ga. (Maj. Gen. USA). He died on active duty as Col. 25th US Inf.

MUD CREEK, Ga., 17 June '64. See KENESAW MOUNTAIN.

MUDD, Dr. Samuel. 1833–83. Alleged conspirator in LINCOLN'S ASSASSINATION. A Maryland doctor who had met John Wilkes BOOTH in church, he set the actor's broken leg after he had shot Lincoln. Mudd was arrested and tried as a conspirator, although his only involvement was through humane motives. Sent to Fort Jefferson in the Dry Tortugas off Key West, Fla., for life imprisonment, he nursed the garrison and prisoners through yellow fever after the army surgeons died in the epidemic. Michael O'Laughlin, one of the plotters, died in this also. Mudd, Samuel Arnold, and Edward Spangler were pardoned in 1869, and the doctor returned to Maryland.

MUDGETT, William S. Union officer. Me. Pvt. and Sgt. Co. B 2d Me. 28 May '61; 1st Lt. 9 Sept. '61; Capt. 9 July '62; Lt. Col. 80th US Col. Inf. 9 Mar. '63; Col. 7 Mar. '65; Bvt. B.G. USV (war service). Died 1899.

MUD MARCH, Burnside's. 20–23 Jan. '63. After his bloody repulse at Fredericksburg, 13 Dec. '62, and despite his army's low morale and loss of confidence in his generalship, Burnside was determined to make another attempt to cross the Rappahannock. An attempted turning movement downstream from Lee's strong position, the initial movements for which he started on 26 Dec., was vetoed by the president when the latter was told of it by some of Burnside's subordinates. Burnside then undertook an envelopment via Banks's Ford. This got under way on 20 Jan., but that night a two-day rainstorm set in "and every road became a deep quagmire, and even small streams were impassable torrents" (Alexander, 314). Two days later the operation was abandoned. It became known, even in the official reports, as the "Mud March." In justice to the ill-starred Burnside, Alexander points out that "but for the rain-storm—the 'Act of God'— he certainly had reasonable ground to hope for success." But this final exposure to Burnside's leadership so demoralized the Army of the Potomac that he had to be relieved of its command.

MULCAHY, Thomas. Union officer.
Ireland. Capt. 139th N.Y. 9 Sept. '62;
Maj. 9 Oct. '63; Lt. Col. 3 July '64;
Bvt. B.G. USV (war service). Com-
manded 1, 1, XVIII (Va. and N.C.).
Died 1893.

"MULE CHARGE." See WAUHAT-
CHIE NIGHT ATTACK (Chattanooga campaign), and VALVERDE.

MULFORD, John Elmer. Union officer. N.Y. Capt. 3d N.Y. 14 May '61;
Maj. 10 June '63; Lt. Col. 8 Dec. '64;
Col. 9 Apr. '65; Bvt. B.G. USV 4 July
'64 (meritorious conduct).

MULHOLLAND, St. Clair Augustin.
Union officer. Ireland. Commissioned
Lt. Col. 116th Pa. 26 June '62, he was
mustered out 24 Feb. '63 and named
Maj. 116th Pa. 27 Feb. of that year.
Promoted Col. 3 May '64, he was mus-
tered out in June '65 and breveted B.G.
USV (war service) and Maj. Gen. USV
(Boydton Plank Road.) He was given
the Medal of Honor in 1895 for Chan-
cellorsville.

MULLIGAN, James Adelbert. Union
officer. 1830–64. N.Y. Col. 23d Ill.
("Irish Brigade," which he raised) 18
June '61; Bvt. B.G. USV 23 July '64
(Winchester, Va.). Accompanied J. L.
Stephenson on his Panamanian expedition in 1857. Captured at Lexington
(Mo.) 20 Sept. '61 and exchanged the
following Nov. W.I.A. at Winchester.
As his men were removing him from
the field, he saw that the colors were
about to be captured and shouted, "Lay
me down and save the flag!" As they
hesitated, he repeated his cry. They
obeyed, but before they could return
he was captured himself. He died from
his wounds three days later (D.A.B.).
Commanded 5, 1, VIII; Mulligan's
Brig., 1st Div. (W. Va.); 2d Div. (W.
Va.); 3d Div. (W. Va.).

MUMFORD, William B. New Orleans gambler hanged by Ben Butler.
On 27 Apr. '62, after Farragut's capture of New Orleans, a 42-year-old
professional gambler named Mumford
pulled down a US flag that had been
raised, without Farragut's knowledge
or subsequent approval, over the Mint.
On his arrival in New Orleans Butler
arrested Mumford—who had appeared
before Federal headquarters and defied
Butler's authority. Mumford was tried,
convicted of treason, and despite pleas
of his wife and local citizens, hanged
at the scene of his crime on 7 June.

MUNDEE, Charles. Union officer.
Hungary. Appt.-Kans. Capt. Asst. Adj.
Gen. Vols. 24 Aug. '61; Maj. Asst. Adj.
Gen. Vols. 16 Aug. '62; Bvt. B.G. USV
2 Apr. '65. Brevets for Winchester,
Fishers Hill, Cedar Creek, Petersburg.
Died 1871.

MUNFORD, Thomas Taylor. C.S.A.
gen. 1831–? Va. After graduating from
V.M.I., he was a planter and commissioned Lt. Col. 13th Va. Mtd. Inf. 8
May '61. After 1st Bull Run he was
named Col. 2d Va. Cav., and in the
spring of 1862 fought with Ewell along
the Rappahannock. Going to the Shenandoah, he served under Jackson, succeeded Turner Ashby, and fought at
Cross Keys, Harrisonburg, the advance
on the Chickahominy, Frayser's Farm,
White Oak Swamp, 2d Bull Run (twice
wounded), Crampton's Gap, and Antietam. He led his regiment at Fredericksburg and fought in the Pa. campaign
at Beverly Ford, Aldie, and Gettysburg.
After taking part in the Bristoe campaign he went to the Valley to fight
under Early. Appointed B.G. C.S.A.
in Nov. '64 he took command of Fitzhugh Lee's division and fought at Five
Forks, High Bridge, Sayler's Creek,
and Appomattox. After the war he was
a farmer and engaged in various business enterprises. His feud with Rosser
continued until the latter's death in
1910.

MUNFORDVILLE, Ky., 14–17 Sept. '62. (BRAGG'S INVASION OF KENTUCKY) The Confederate brigade of J. R. Chalmers, leading Bragg's force, launched a premature assault that was repulsed with heavy losses early on the 14th. While the rest of Bragg's army moved up, the Federals reinforced the town. On the 16th Bragg had surrounded the 4,133 Federals with his entire force. The next day Col. J. T. Wilder was formally demanded to surrender the garrison. There then followed a most remarkable series of events. "Wilder was an Indiana industrialist with no military experience whatever. He did not like the idea of surrendering —but could see nothing else to do. Finally he adopted the unorthodox (but probably sensible) expedient of going under a flag of truce to General Buckner's headquarters and asking his advice. He explained his ignorance, said he had been told Buckner was not only a trained soldier but a gentleman who would not deceive him. . . . Buckner, taken aback by this naïveté, declined to advise his trusting enemy. . . . Wilder asked politely if he might be permitted to inspect the beleaguering forces and count the cannon. Buckner in his most gentlemanly manner consented to this; and Wilder, convinced by ocular demonstration, said sadly: 'I believe I'll surrender.' So Buckner took him to Bragg, and Wilder gave up the fort and its entire garrison, together with all its artillery and stores and 5,000 stand of small arms" (Horn, 168). The defenders had lost 15 killed, 57 wounded. Chalmers reported a Confederate loss of 35 killed and 253 wounded.

MURFREESBORO, Tenn., 13 July '62. See FORREST'S FIRST RAID.

MURFREESBORO, Tenn., 7 Dec. '64. (FRANKLIN AND NASHVILLE CAMPAIGN) Forrest's cavalry divisions of Buford and W. H. Jackson had conducted a raid down the railroad to Murfreesboro, where they found Rousseau holding the place in strength. Forrest had been joined here by Bate's division of Cheatham's corps and was then reinforced further by Sears's brigade of French's division and Palmer's brigade of Stevenson's division. Forrest had the bulk of his force concentrated around Salem, five miles southwest of Murfreesboro, with skirmishers located within half a mile of the Federal strong point.

Rousseau ordered a reconnaissance in force undertaken by R. H. Milroy. With 3,325 men organized into two brigades under Cols. M. T. Thomas and Edward Anderson, Milroy moved out the Salem pike at 10 A.M., 7 Dec., and soon made contact. The six guns of Capt. Bundy's 13th N.Y. Arty. moved forward and opened up a spirited fire across an open field that separated the two forces. Unable to draw the Confederates into attacking him, Milroy withdrew so as to have Fortress Rosecrans (see O.R. atlas, CXII, 3) to his rear and sent Bundy back to replenish his ammunition. He then organized his force into two lines: Thomas was in the front with the 61st Ill. advanced as skirmishers; Anderson formed a second line. The Confederates had been pushed back to a wooded area when the attack began to waver. Milroy then committed the 178th Ohio on the left and moved the rest of Anderson's brigade forward to restore the momentum of the attack. The Confederates were driven back, and Bundy returned to the field just in time to repulse a cavalry counterattack on Milroy's flank. Milroy was pausing to reorganize when Rousseau ordered him to withdraw to avoid a sizable threat from the north.

The Federals lost 22 killed, 186 wounded, and reported the capture of 197 prisoners, two Napoleon guns, and a battle flag (T.U.A.). Forrest's losses, including both infantry and cavalry, were 19 killed and 73 wounded (Drake).

MURPHY, John Kidd. Union officer. Pa. Col. 29th Pa. 1 July '61; discharged 23 Apr. '63; Capt. Vet. Res. Corps 14 Mar. '64; Bvt. B.G. USV (war service). Commanded 3, 1, XII (Potomac). Died 1876.

MURRAH, Pendleton. C.S.A. Gov. of Tex. ?-1866. S.C. A lawyer, he moved first to Ala. and then Tex., where he sat in the state legislature. He was elected Gov. in 1863 to succeed Lubbock, and served throughout the war, fleeing to Mexico, where he died.

MURRAY, Benjamin Bixby. Union officer. Me. Capt. 15th Me. 6 Dec. '61; Lt. Col. 7 Oct. '62; Bvt. B.G. USV (war service).

MURRAY, Edward. Union officer. N.Y. Lt. Col. 5th N.Y. Arty. 7 Mar. '62; Bvt. B.G. USV (war service). Died 1876.

MURRAY, Eli Huston. Union officer. 1844-96. Ky. Maj. 3d Ky. Cav. 12 Nov. '61; Col. 9 Oct. '62; Bvt. B.G. USV 25 Mar. '65 (war service). Commanded 3, 3, Cav. Corps (Cumberland); 3d Div., Cav. Corps (Cumberland); 1, 3, Cav. Corps (Mil. Div. Miss.). Entering the Union Army at the age of 17, he was a Bvt. B.G. before he was 21. He later had a successful career as a newspaperman. Was appointed Gov. of Utah.

MURRAY, John B. Union officer. Vt. Capt. 50th N.Y. Engrs. 30 Sept. '61; resigned 22 July '62; Maj. 148th N.Y. 14 Sept. '62; Lt. Col. 23 Nov. '63; Col. 14 Dec. '64; Bvt. B.G. USV (war service). Died 1884.

MUSKET. A smoothbore firearm fired from the shoulder. See also SMALL ARMS OF THE CIVIL WAR.

MUSSEY, Reuben Delavan. Union officer. 1833-92. N.H. Appt.-Ohio. R.A. Capt. 19th US Inf. 14 May '61; Col. 100th US Col. Inf. 14 June '64; mustered out Vols. 1865; Bvt. B.G. USV (recruitment and organization of colored troops); resigned R.A. 1866. In Sept. '63 he was sent to Nashville to assist in the organization of colored regiments. Reid credits him with being the first regular officer to ask permission to raise Negro troops. He is also supposed to have been the first to suggest that they be US rather than state regiments. He served as Pres. Johnson's confidential secretary from Lincoln's assassination until Nov. '65.

MYER, Albert James. Union chief signal officer. 1827-80. N.Y. After graduation from Buffalo Medical College in 1851, he entered the army 18 Sept. '54 as an assistant surgeon. In medical school he had become interested in Baine's telegraphic alphabet as the basis for a deaf-and-dumb language. While Morse's alphabet used four elements to form letters, Baine's used only two: a dot and a dash. Working with E. P. ALEXANDER, he developed the "wigwag" signal system. On 27 June '60 he became the army's first signal officer, a post Congress created as a reward for his accomplishments. He was called to Washington from the Southwest on 17 July '61, and during 1st Bull Run spent the day in a frustrating effort to drag an inflated observation balloon to the battlefield. He served as McClellan's signal officer on the Peninsula and through the Antietam campaign. He then served in Washington and was promoted Col. 3 Mar. '63. As the result of what today would be called a conflict of roles and missions between Myer's Signal Corps and Stager's Military Telegraph System, Myer was ordered to the western theater of operations and the activities of the Signal

Corps, now under Major William Nicodemus, were curtailed. (See SIGNAL
COMMUNICATIONS.) Myer became Chief
Signal Officer in Canby's command and
arranged the terms of surrender of
Fort Gaines. Stanton then relieved him
of command when his appointment expired 4 July '64. His appointment was
revoked 21 July '64 and he reverted
to his permanent grade of Maj. On 28
July '66 he again became a Col. and
Chief Signal Officer. On 16 June '80
he was appointed B.G., shortly before
his death on 24 Aug. Meanwhile, he had
done significant work in the field of
meteorology and had earned the nickname "Old Probabilities" for his per-
sistent and scientific approach to technical problems. He was breveted for
Hanover C.H., Malvern Hill, and war
service, being particularly cited for the
work of his signalmen at ALLATOONA,
Ga.

MYERS, Abraham C. C.S.A. Q.M.
Gen. c. 1811–89. S.C. USMA 1833
(32/43); Inf. He served in the Seminole wars, the Mexican War (2 brevets), and as Chief Q.M. in various frontier departments, including Tex., before
resigning 28 Jan. '61 as Bvt. Lt. Col.
Appointed Q.M. Gen. of the Confederacy with the rank of Col., he served
in the position from 15 Mar. '61 to 10
Aug. '63, when he resigned. Son-in-law
of David TWIGGS.

MYERS, Frederick. Union officer.
c. 1822–74. Conn. USMA 1846 (44/59);
Inf.-Q.M. He fought in the Mexican
War and served on the frontier before
organizing the Ohio volunteers (until
Apr. '62). Named Maj. Add. A.D.C.
23 May '62, he was Chief Q.M. of the
Dept. of the Rappahannock and the III
Corps in the Peninsula. He was pro-
moted Lt. Col. 15 July '62 and served
as Deputy Chief Q.M. of the Army of
the Potomac until he became Chief
Q.M., in Apr. '63, of the Dept. of the
Northwest, where he remained for the
rest of the war. Continuing in the
R.A., he died on active duty as Bvt.
B.G. USA.

MYERS, George Ranney. Union officer. N.Y. Maj. 18th N.Y. 17 May
'61; Lt. Col. 11 Nov. '61; Col. 9 Dec.
'62; Bvt. B.G. USV (war service); mustered out 28 May '63. Ex-cadet USMA
1860.

MYERS, William. Union officer.
1830–87. Pa. USMA 1852 (32/43); Inf.
1st Lt. 9th US Inf. 1857; Capt. Asst.
Q.M. 17 May '61; Col. Add. A.D.C.
14 June '62–31 May '66; Bvt. B.G. USV
(war service). In 1861–63 he was Asst.
to the Chief Q.M. Dept. of the Mo.
and 1863–65 he was chief of the St.
Louis Depot and Q.M. of the Dept. of
the Mo. After the war he was Chief
Q.M. of various departments, retiring
in 1883 as Col. Deputy Q.M.G.

N

NAGLE, James. Union gen. 1822–66.
Pa. He served in the Mexican War as
Capt. and was commissioned Col. 6th
Pa. 22 Apr. '61, being mustered out 26
July. Organizing the 48th Pa. and
appointed their Col. 1 Oct. '61, he com-
manded 1st Brig., 2d Div., N.C. (2

Apr.–6 July '62). He led 1, 2, IX
Potomac (22 July '62–Feb. '63), including the battles of Crampton's Gap,
South Mountain, and Antietam where
he helped capture the stone bridge. Appointed B.G. USV 10 Sept. '62, and
having the appointment expire 4 Mar.

'63, he was reappointed on 13 Mar. and resigned 9 May '63 after commanding 1, 2, IX, Ohio (19 Mar.–21 May '63). When Lee invaded Pa. in June '63, Nagle organized the 39th Pa. Mil. (Col. 1 July '63), commanded a brigade protecting the state, and was mustered out 2 Aug. On 24 July '64 he was commissioned Col. in the 100 days' regiment he organized, the 194th Pa., to guard the approaches to Baltimore. He was mustered out 5 Nov. '64.

NAGLEE, Henry Morris. Union gen. 1815–86. Pa. USMA 1835 (23/56); Inf. Resigning six months after graduation, he was a civil engineer until the Mexican War when he served as Capt. with the 1st N.Y. in Calif. and Baja Calif. He remained in San Francisco and engaged in banking. Appointed Lt. Col. 16th US Inf. 14 May '61, he never joined his regiment but resigned 10 Jan. '62 and was named B.G. USV 4 Feb. '62. He commanded 1, Casey's division (Dec. '61–Mar. '62), and 1, 3, IV, Potomac (27 Apr.–7 June '62). Leading 1, 2, IV, Potomac (28 Sept. '62–May '63), he was wounded at Fair Oaks. He also commanded VII Corps (25 July '63–20 Jan. '64) and 2d Div., XVIII Corps (2 Jan.–6 Mar. '63 and Apr. '63). In the Dept. of N.C., he led Naglee's brigade (Dec. '62–2 Jan. '63) and 2d Div., XVIII (2 Jan.–6 Mar., 16 Apr.–10 May '63). He commanded 1st Dist., St. Helena, X, South (Jan.–5 Mar. '63) and St. Helena, X, South (Feb. '63). In the XVIII Corps, he commanded the 2d Div. (2 Jan.–6 Mar. '63 and Apr. '63) and the Dist. of Va. (18 Aug.–23 Sept. '63). He was mustered out 4 Apr. '64 and returned to San Francisco where, in addition to banking, he raised Riesling and Charbonneau grapes for Naglee brandy.

NAMOZINE CHURCH AND WILLICOMACK CREEK, Va., 3 Apr. '65 (Appomattox Campaign) After Five Forks Wells's brigade of Custer's cavalry led the pursuit and overtook Barringer's brigade of Fitz Lee's cavalry along Willicomack Creek. The Federals carried this position by a dismounted action and continued the pursuit to Namozine Church. Here the 8th N.Y. Cav. repulsed a desperate Confederate charge. The Confederates separated, Fitz Lee moving toward Amelia C.H. and "Rooney" Lee toward Bevill's Bridge. At dark Wells's brigade attacked Fitz Lee's position along Deep Creek. By the time Pennington's reserve regiment could come up the Confederates had continued their withdrawal. Custer's command dug in for the night and waited for the II, V, and VI Corps to close up. Federal losses during the day were 95. Barringer and most of his men were captured.

NAPOLEON GUN HOWITZER. The basic artillery piece on both sides was the 12-pounder Napoleon. It was a smoothbore, muzzle-loading fieldpiece with a caliber of 4.62 inches. Developed under the auspices of Napoleon III, it appeared in 1856 and was adopted by the US Army before the Civil War. The Confederates used not only the large number captured on the battlefield, but also copied the design for their own manufacture. Initially made of bronze, when this metal became scarce in the South the Napoleons were cast of iron with a reinforcing jacket at the breech.

Maximum range of the gun was 1,680 yards (solid shot fired at an elevation of 5 degrees), but its maximum effective range was between 800 and 1,000 yards. Although it could fire Grape Shot, Spherical Case Shot, and Shell —in addition to ball or Shot—it was most effectively employed with Canister in close support of the infantry. (See also Cannon.) There was also a 6-pounder Napoleon.

NASE, Adam. Union officer. Pa. Capt. 15th Ill. 24 May '61; Maj. 17 Dec. '62; Bvt. B.G. USV (war service); resigned 7 July '63. Died 1879.

NASHVILLE, Tenn., 15–16 Dec. '64. (FRANKLIN AND NASHVILLE CAMPAIGN) Hood's forces were too weakened by their losses at FRANKLIN, 30 Nov., to attack Thomas's growing strength at Nashville. The Confederate commander, therefore, took up a position close to the Federal defenses with the vague hope of some favorable development (such as reinforcements from Texas or the successful repulse of a Federal attack).

Thomas, after several delays, attacked early 15 Dec. His plan was for A. J. Smith (XVI) and Wood (IV) to hit the Confederate corps of A. P. Stewart on Hood's left. Schofield's corps (XXIII) was in reserve and positioned so as to be able to reinforce this attack. Steedman's provisional division was to attack the other flank to divert Hood's attention. Thomas's tactical plan was masterly: it was a coordinated attack; his main effort—Smith and Wood —was weighted to assure combat superiority at this point; his secondary attack (Steedman) was planned so as to give maximum assistance to the main effort; he had provided for an adequate, properly located reserve (Schofield); and he used his mobile troops (cavalry) to screen his flank and extend the envelopment of the enemy left. The tactical dispositions of Hood, on the other hand, had several defects that contributed to his defeat: his troops were extended over a longer line than their strength warranted; this line was concave to the enemy (thereby depriving Hood of INTERIOR LINES); he did not have a general reserve; his cavalry was absent on a mission of minor importance when it should have been available for the battle to protect

his open left flank. Strategically, he did not have sufficient strength to justify accepting battle at Nashville.

Steedman started advancing along the Murfreesboro road before 6 A.M. under cover of fog. Two hours later he attacked Hood's right between the road and the railroad. While the enemy's attention was drawn in this direction, the main attack moved against the opposite flank. The envelopment by Smith's corps on the extreme right took longer than expected because of the muddy roads. It was 10 A.M. before McArthur's division (1, XVI) had cleared the Harding road sufficiently to enable Hatch's cavalry division to take position on the flank of the enveloping column. (The rest of Wilson's cavalry then screened this exposed southwest flank.) After driving Coleman's brigade (French's division) from the first of Hood's detached works, the Federals soon had possession of the others and were beginning to make contact with the forces of A. P. Stewart on the Confederate left. The dispositions of the attacking Federal divisions may be shown schematically:

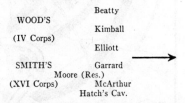

	Beatty
WOOD'S	
	Kimball
(IV Corps)	
	Elliott
SMITH'S	Garrard
	Moore (Res.)
(XVI Corps)	McArthur
	Hatch's Cav.

On Stewart's left and facing generally west was Walthall's division with the brigades of Reynolds, Shelley, and Quarles from south to north. Extending this line north to the tip of the salient was Sears's brigade of French's division. Then, on a line facing generally north, was the division of Loring with the brigades of Adams, Scott, and Featherston from west to east. S. D. Lee's corps was to the right of A. P.

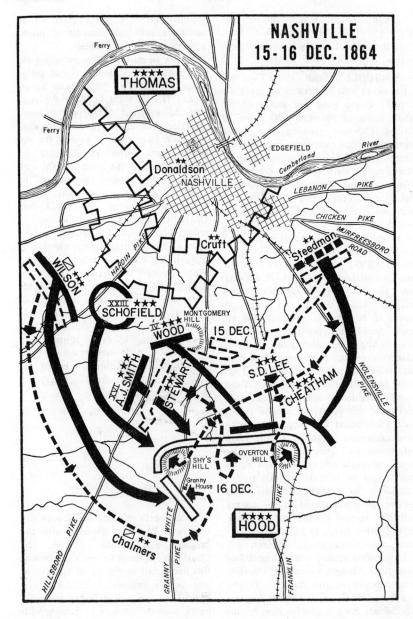

NASHVILLE
15-16 DEC. 1864

Stewart's (O. R. Atlas, LXXIII, 2). Coleman's brigade was attached to Walthall after it had been pushed back and was posted on his left flank.

Although Walthall and Loring held fast against frontal attacks, Smith's corps advanced past Walthall's south flank without meeting any significant resistance. The brigades of Manigault and Deas of Johnson's division had been rushed from S. D. Lee's unthreatened center portion of the line to extend the left against this threatened envelopment. These two brigades went into position behind the stone wall east of the Hillsboro pike, but as the Federals swarmed toward them they broke and ran (Horn, 414).

From Schofield's corps, which, as the general reserve, had been following behind the right wing, Couch's division (2, XXIII) moved past the right of XVI Corps to extend the envelopment. Cooper's brigade captured the portion of the ridge parallel to and west of the Granny (or Craning) White Pike. Couch sent his other brigades up to consolidate and hold this critical terrain. Two brigades of Cox's division (3, XXIII) occupied positions to the south of Couch, while the 3d Div. (Stiles's) stayed west of Richland Creek to protect the flank. It was about dark when these movements were completed. Schofield's advance had cut Coleman's brigade off from Walthall, but Coleman rallied his troops on a hill later named Shy's Hill (see below). This became the left flank of the new Confederate line.

Wood's corps had attacked at 1 o'clock on Smith's left. Col. P. S. Post's brigade (2, 3, IV) had spearheaded this movement by capturing Montgomery Hill, a strong outpost about midway between the two closest points of the opposing lines. Kimball's (1st) division continued the attack and

struck the salient held by G. D. Johnston's and Shelley's brigades of Walthall's division. The Confederate center was then forced steadily back.

As soon as he identified the main Federal attack, Hood had ordered Cheatham to send reinforcements from the right flank to the threatened left. These did not arrive in time to stop Smith and Schofield. Steedman maintained pressure as Cheatham's wing withdrew.

Hood formed a new line in the Brentwood Hills after dark. Extending from Shy's Hill on the west to Overton (or Peach Orchard) Hill on the east, this position covered the two main roads by which he could retreat south.

Thomas could not determine whether Hood would retreat during the night and apparently issued no orders during the night for the continuation of the attack. The Federal corps commanders reorganized their lines somewhat and at dawn started probing the new enemy defenses. Steedman's division came up on the extreme Federal left, northeast of Overton Hill, and made contact with Wood's left near the Franklin pike.

The single Confederate cavalry division of Chalmers having been drawn back to cover Hood's exposed flank to the southwest, Wilson could now mass his entire cavalry force. His dismounted troopers worked their way into a good position on Schofield's right from which they could envelop Hood's left in the direction of Granny House.

On the Federal left an unsuccessful attack was made at 3 P.M. against S. D. Lee's positions around Overton Hill. Post had conducted a reconnaissance that led him to believe the hill could be taken. His brigade (2, 3, IV) led an attack that was supported by Streight. Thompson's 2d Col. Brig. of Steedman's division, supported by Grosvenor's brigade (also of Steedman's), were to attack simultaneously from the east. After an artillery preparation the Federals advanced behind a cloud of skirmishers and succeeded in reaching the main intrenchments in several places before being driven back with heavy losses. Post was among those killed.

The decisive action started about 3:30 against the other flank. Here Wilson's dismounted troopers were driving back the Confederate cavalry division of Chalmers. Hood had to reinforce Chalmers with Govan's brigade from Cheatham's left. Coleman's brigade was moved left from Shy's Hill to take the position vacated by Govan, and Bate's division was stretched to the left to hold the salient of Shy's Hill. Federal artillery was able to bring enfilade fire on Bate's position and make it almost untenable. An attack at about 4 P.M. crushed Hood's left and forced his entire line to retreat. Wilson's wide envelopment had been the decisive action. This was, however, supported by closer-in envelopments by the infantry brigades of Stiles (3, 3 XXIII) and W. L. McMillan (1, 1, XVI). The Confederate divisions of Bate and Lowry were taken from the rear and routed after offering determined resistance. Col. W. M. Shy (20th Tenn.), who was killed in this action, so distinguished himself in its defense that the hill was given his name. (Shy is often erroneously identified as commander of the 37th Ga.)

According to Livermore, the forces engaged in the battle were 49,773 Federals and 23,207 Confederates. This disparity in numbers and Thomas's excellent plan account not only for the decisive Federal victory, but also for the relatively small number of killed and wounded on both sides. Thomas reported a loss of 3,061 (387 killed, 2,562 wounded, and only 112 missing). Confederate losses are not known, but Hood reported them as being "very small." Horn says the Confederate killed and wounded probably did not exceed 1,500 (*op. cit.,* 417). Thomas reported capturing 4,462. Three Confederate generals were captured: Edward Johnson, H. R. Jackson, and T. B. Smith.

NAST, Thomas. Artist and WAR CORRESPONDENT. 1840–1902. Bavaria. As a young man and after very little instruction, he became an artist for an American illustrated newspaper and went in 1860 to England and Italy as correspondent for a weekly. At the latter place he made sketches of Garibaldi's campaigns for the *New York Illustrated News,* the *London Illustrated News,* and *Le Monde Illustré.* In July '62 he started making Civil War sketches for *Harper's Weekly* and soon became known for his devastating political cartoons.

NATIONAL UNION PARTY. Name used by REPUBLICAN PARTY in campaign of 1864. Also used by Johnson's supporters at an independent convention in Aug. '66 to unite the opponents within the party of the RADICAL REPUBLICANS.

NAVAL PARTICIPATION. Both the Federal and the Confederate Navies played a vital part in the war. The early establishment of the BLOCKADE and Farragut's capture of NEW ORLEANS not only brought about the economic strangulation of the South but also killed any hope the Confederates had of French intervention (D.A.H., I, 389). The Navy also had a critical role in the strategy that split the Confederacy by capturing the line of the Mississippi.

In 1861 the US Navy was in a demoralized condition (*ibid.*) with its 1,457 officers and 7,600 men scattered all over the globe. Less than half of its 90 ships were ready for active service. Of its meager officer personnel, the following defected to the South: 16 captains, 34 commanders, 76 lieutenants,.

and 111 regular and acting midshipmen (Miller, VI, 78). Abandonment of the Norfolk Navy Yard, 20–21 Apr. '61, resulted in the loss of 11 ships and 3,000 pieces of ordnance. After Gideon Welles was appointed Sec. of the Navy, he and his assistant Sec., Gustavus V. Fox, built the US Navy in four years from 23 to 641 ships of all types (West, 305). Such outstanding designers as John B. Eads, Charles Ellet, Jr., John Ericsson, and Samuel M. Pook played a vital role in giving the navy revolutionary river- and gunboats. The navy produced commanders with sufficient mental flexibility to handle the radically new ships and tactics.

The Confederate Navy, nonexistent in 1861, showed even more remarkable powers of improvisation. Stephen R. Mallory, Chief of the Confed. Navy Dept., had problems that paled those of his Union counterpart. "Not a single marine engine could be manufactured anywhere in the South. No forge capable of turning out a proper shaft for a major war vessel lay anywhere in the Confederacy.... If the North's command problem was irritating, that of the South was intolerable" (Fahr, C.W.H.).

The unfortunate SEWARD-MEIGS-PORTER AFFAIR prevented assistance being sent to Fort Sumter. The successful defense of Fort Pickens, Fla., in PENSACOLA BAY, was, however, supported by the Federal Navy. Successful naval actions, in cooperation with the Army, were at HATTERAS INLET and Hilton Head in PORT ROYAL SOUND in 1861.

In 1862 BURNSIDE'S EXPEDITION TO N.C. further consolidated Federal control of the Atlantic coast. The MONITOR-MERRIMAC DUEL ushered in a new era of naval warfare. In the West the stage was set for the strategic penetration of the South by the HENRY AND DONELSON CAMPAIGN and the Federal capture of NEW MADRID AND ISLAND

No. 10. The naval forces played a vital part in these. Farragut's capture of NEW ORLEANS was almost exclusively a naval operation, but his VICKSBURG BOMBARDMENT demonstrated the limitations of naval power operating without support of ground forces.

In 1863 the Federal Navy had a vital role in the logistics that made it possible for the Federals to use the Western rivers for lines of operations. The navy also supported the TEXAS COAST OPERATIONS OF BANKS IN 1863. Along the Atlantic coast in 1863, after several unsuccessful attacks on FORT SUMTER, the Federals were forced to abandon the hope of taking Charleston by naval action alone. Attacks against FORT MCALLISTER, Ga., were also unsuccessful, although the Confederates were forced to abandon FORT WAGNER.

In 1864 the KEARSARGE sank the *Alabama* 19 June off Cherbourg, France, but other Confederate raiders continued the successful depredations on Northern commerce that resulted in the ALABAMA CLAIMS. Farragut won his great victory in MOBILE BAY, 5 Aug.

In 1865 the capture of FORT FISHER, N.C., on 15 Jan. deprived the South of her last port, Wilmington.

See also: MONITOR, RAM, STONE FLEETS, and SUBMARINES.

NEAFIE, Alfred. Union officer. N.Y. Capt. 156th N.Y. 13 Sept. '62; Lt. Col. 9 Jan. '64; Bvt. B.G. USV. Brevets for Winchester (2), Fishers Hill (Va.). Commanded 3, 2, XIX (Shenandoah).

NEFF, Andrew Jackson. Union officer. Ohio. 1st Lt. 84th Ind. 3 Sept. '62; Maj. 5 Sept. '62; Lt. Col. 10 Dec. '63; Bvt. B.G. USV (war service). Resigned 7 Sept. '64.

NEFF, George Washington. Union officer. 1833–92. Ohio. Lt. Col. 2d Ky. 28 June '61; Col. 88th Ohio 31 July '63; Bvt. B.G. USV (war service). Captured at Scarry Creek (W. Va.) 17 July '61 and held until Aug. '62. Served on Gen. Wallace's staff during Kirby Smith's raid. Commanded Camp Dennison when John Morgan attacked.

NEGLEY, James Scott. Union gen. 1826–1901. Pa. He fought in the Mexican War and was a B.G. in the Pa. militia when Civil War came. Commissioned B.G. of the Pa. Vols. (19 Apr.–20 July '61), he commanded the post of Philadelphia and served during the summer with Patterson in Pa., Md. and Va. Commissioned B.G. USV 1 Oct. '61, he commanded the 7th Independent Brig., Army of the Ohio (Nov.–Dec. '61) and 8th Div., Army of the Ohio (14 Sept.–Nov. '62). He was promoted Maj. Gen. USV 29 Nov. '62 and commanded 2d Div. Centre, XIV, Cumberland (5 Nov. '62–9 Jan. '63) at Stones River. Leading the 2d Div., XIV (9 Jan.–10 Oct. '63) at Chickamauga, he was swept back by the enemy with all the other commanders on the Union right. Relieved of command, he was cleared by a court of inquiry of charges of cowardice and desertion, but he was given no more field commands and resigned 19 Jan. '65 after serving on boards and commanding draft rendezvous in the North. He bitterly resented this treatment, blaming it on the West Pointer's distrust of "civilian" soldiers. A man of "large physique and fine appearance," he was "affable and urbane, but of an independent spirit" (D.A.B.). After the war he was a Republican Congressman and railroad president.

NEGRO TROOPS. In the American Revolution there were some 1,000 free and slave Negro soldiers enlisted, and in the War of 1812 there were none except from La., where free Negroes fought with Jackson defending New Orleans. No records have disclosed Negro troops in the Mexican War. Free Negroes tried to enlist at the beginning of the Civil War, and in Sept. '62 a temporary "black brigade" was raised in Cincinnati, without weapons and uniforms, to combat Morgan's raiders. The previous month Ben Butler had raised the La. Native Guards (Corps d'Afrique) and mustered the 1st La. N.G. in 27 Sèpt. '62, the first black regiment in the USA. The 2d La. N.G. was mustered in on 12 Oct. '62 and the 3d on 24 Nov. '62. David HUNTER in S.C. had started to do the same in May of that year, and both efforts were vetoed by Lincoln. R.I. issued the first state call for Negro troops, and Kans. and Mass. followed. After the EMANCIPATION PROCLAMATION (1 Jan. '63) was issued, Lincoln called for four Negro regiments. By the end of the war there were some 300,000 colored troops in 166 regiments (145 infantry, 7 cavalry, 12 heavy artillery, 1 field artillery, and 1 engineer regiment). About 60 of these were employed in the field. According to Livermore, 97,598 colored troops were called from the territories and Southern states and "all· but one regiment enrolled after 1862" (Livermore, 50n.).

"Of the regiments brought into action," Fox points out, "only a few were engaged in more than one battle; the war was half over, and so the total of killed does not appear as great as it otherwise would have done. The total number killed or mortally wounded in the colored troops was 143 officers and 2,751 men. The officers were whites."

The first colored regiment to be engaged in combat was the 79th US COLORED INFANTRY (First Kans.) at Island Mounds, Mo., 28 Oct. '62. In the assault on PORT HUDSON, La., 27 May '63, colored troops were used for the first time in a general engagement. On 7 June '63 the colored garrison was attacked by Walker's division at Millikens Bend, La., and retained their position after hand-to-hand fighting. Colored troops next participated in Gillmore's unsuccessful assault on FORT WAGNER, S.C., 18 July '63. The 54th Mass. led the attack and lost 272 out of 650 engaged, including their commander. One of the severest regimental losses of the war occurred in the 8th U.S.C.I. at OLUSTEE, Fla., 20 Feb. '64. This regiment later distinguished itself at Chafin's Farm.

Ferrero's 4th Div., IX Corps, was the first Negro unit to serve with the Union army in Va. It was not committed to action until the ill-fated PETERSBURG MINE ASSAULT, 30 July '64, where the misguided interference of Meade and Grant with Burnside's plans led to their being butchered. Hinks's division, XVIII Corps, made up entirely of Negro regiments, made a successful attack on the Petersburg defenses 15 June '64. Paine's colored division of XVIII Corps and William Birney's Col. Brig. of X Corps, about 10,000 total strength, were actively engaged in the action at Chafin's Farm, 29 Sept. '64. At Darbytown Road, Va., 27 Oct. '64, the 29th Conn. C.I. performed good service. Two colored brigades took part in the battle of Nashville, Tenn., 15 Dec. '64. The 13th U.S.C.I. lost 221 men in its assault on Overton Hill, which was the greatest regimental loss of the battle. At Honey Hill, S.C., 30 Nov. '64, a colored regiment, the 55th Mass., had the highest casualties: 144 men. In the closing battle of the war Fort Blakely, Ala. (Mobile), 9 Apr. '65, the 68th and 76th U.S.C.I. lost 192 men. Fox, from whom the above is paraphrased, lists the following additional battles in which Negro troops were prominently engaged: Morris Island, S.C.; Yazoo City, Miss.; Poison Springs, Ark.; Saline River, Ark.; Morganza, La.; Tupelo, Miss.; Bermuda Hundred, Va.; Darbytown Road, Va.; Saltville, Va.; Cox's Bridge, N.C.; Spanish Fort, Ala.; James Island, S.C.; Pleasant Hill, La.; Camden, Ark.; FORT PILLOW, Tenn.; Jacksonville, Fla.; Athens, Ala.; DUTCH GAP, Va.; Hatcher's Run, Va.; Deveaux Neck, S.C.; Fort Fisher, N.C.; the fall of Richmond; Liverpool Heights, Miss.; Prairie d'Ann, Ark.; Jenkins' Ferry, Ark.; Natural Bridge, Fla.; Brice's Cross Roads, Miss.; Drewry's Bluff, Va.; Deep Bottom, Va.; Fair Oaks, Va. (1864); Boykin's Mills, S.C.; Wilmington, N.C.; and Appomattox, Va.

In the last months of the war the XXV CORPS was organized to consist entirely of Negro troops.

The Confederate Army used many Negro servants and laborers, but did not employ Negro combat troops. A regiment was organized in New Orleans but not accepted into service. In 1863 a proposal to arm slaves was briefly considered. In Jan. '64 a movement by Pat CLEBURNE to use slaves as soldiers, giving them freedom for good service, was suppressed by Davis when he learned of it. In Nov. '64 Davis considered the limited use of Negro troops, and R. E. Lee agreed that the idea had merit. In Mar. '65 the Confederate congress passed a law authorizing that up to 300,000 slaves be called for military service, but there was no mention of their being freed in connection with this duty. The next month a few companies were organized, but the surrender came before any of them were used (Wiley, *Reb*, 328–30).

NEIDE, Horace. Union officer. c. 1837–? Pa. 2d Lt. 2d Pa. Res. 27 May '61; 1st Lt. 12 Dec. '61; Capt. 2 Apr. '62; Maj. 1 Aug. '62; resigned 24 Nov. '62; Capt. Vet. Res. Corps 8 June '63; Maj. 4 Dec. '63; Lt. Col. 20 June '64; Bvt. B.G. USV. Brevets for Mechanicsville (2), Gaines's Mill (3), Charles City Cross Roads (2), war service, Glendale (Va.). Wounded in left arm and captured at Glendale (Va.) in July '62. In R.A. until retired as Capt. in 1893.

NEILL, Thomas Hewson. Union gen. 1826–85. Pa. USMA 1847 (27/38); Inf.-Cav. He served in garrison and on frontier duty, taught drawing at the Military Academy, and participated in the Utah Expedition before serving on Gen. Cadwalader's staff in the summer of 1861 as Capt. 4th US Inf. (since 1857). Fighting his regiment during the Peninsular campaign and at Antietam, he was named B.G. USV 29 Nov. '62. He then commanded 3, 2, VI (13 Dec. '62–28 May '63; 10 June '63–4 Jan. '64; 25 Mar.–6 May '64) at Fredericksburg, Chancellorsville, Gettysburg, Rappahannock Station, and the Wilderness. Succeeding to division (4 Jan.–21 Feb. and 7 May–21 June '64) for Spotsylvania, North Anna, Totopotomoy, Cold Harbor, and the siege of Petersburg, he joined Sheridan in the Valley and as acting I.G., he was at Cedar Creek. Breveted for Malvern Hill, Chancellorsville, Spotsylvania, and war service (B.G. USA and Maj. Gen. USV), he continued in the R.A., serving as Commandant of Cadets at the Military Academy and fighting in the Indian wars. He was retired in 1883 as Col. 8th US Cav.

NELSON, Allison. C.S.A. gen. ?–1862. Tex. Commissioned Col. 10th Tex. in '61, he served under Hindman in 1862 at Devall's Bluff (Ark.) and was given command of a brigade there. Appointed B.G. C.S.A. 12 Sept. '62, he was leading a division when he died sometime in the next few months.

NELSON, William. Union gen. 1824–62. Ky. A midshipman in the navy during the Mexican War, "Bull" Nelson was sent in the spring of 1861 to observe the situation in his home state and report to Lincoln. (He was the brother of Thomas H. Nelson, Lincoln's Minister to Chile, and a long-time friend of the President.) In Apr. Lincoln sent him to arm the loyal Ky. Home Guard and commissioned him B.G. USV 16 Sept.

'61. He commanded the 4th Div., Army of the Ohio (2 Dec. '61–16 Aug. '62), at SHILOH, the advance upon Corinth and at RICHMOND (Ky.), where he was wounded. Promoted Maj. Gen. USV 17 July '62, he was commanding the Army of Ky. and engaged in organizing the defenses of Louisville when he was killed by J. C. DAVIS (USA) on 29 Sept. '62. "Nelson was a huge ox of a man—three hundred muscular pounds on a frame six feet four, and a man who alternately glowed with hail-fellow geniality and stormed with titanic rage. . . . Buell considered him one of the Union's most valuable officers" (Catton, *Glory Road*, 19).

NELSON'S FARM, Va., 30 June '62. See WHITE OAK SWAMP.

NETTLETON, Allured Bayard. Union officer. Ohio. 1st Lt. 2d Ohio Cav. 8 Oct. '61; Capt. 10 Mar. '62; Maj. 18 July '63; Lt. Col. 5 Nov. '64; Col. 22 Apr. '65; Bvt. B.G. USV (war service). Listed by Phisterer as Nettleton, Bayard A.

NEW BERN, N.C., 14 Mar. '62. Captured by Federals during BURNSIDE'S EXPEDITION TO N.C. It remained in Federal hands to the end of the war.

NEWBERRY, Walter Cass. Union officer. 1835–? N.Y. 1st Lt. 81st N.Y. 21 Dec. '61; Capt. 31 May '62; discharged 7 Sept. '63; Maj. 24th N.Y. Cav. 10 Jan. '64; Lt. Col. 8 Feb. '64; Col. 2 Mar. '65; Bvt. B.G. USV 31 Mar. '65 (Dinwiddie C.H., Va.). Commanded in Army of the Potomac: 2, 3, IX; 2, 1, IX; 1, 2, Cav. Corps. W.I.A. Dinwiddie C.H. Settled in Petersburg (Va.) after the war and elected mayor. He later moved to Chicago and represented Ill. in Congress.

NEW ENGLAND, UNION DEPARTMENT OF. Created 1 Oct. '61, with headquarters at Boston, to include the six New England states, it was discontinued 20 Feb. '62. Commander: Maj. Gen. B. F. Butler. Its creation was an administrative device to solve the clash between state and Federal interests in the matter of recruiting troops in Mass.

NEW HOPE CHURCH. See DALLAS, GA.

15TH NEW JERSEY (1st Jersey Brigade, 1st Division, VI Corps)

Colonels: Samuel Fowler, William H. Penrose (R.A.; Bvt. B.G. USA), Edward L. Campbell (Bvt. B.G. USV).

Battles: Fredericksburg, Salem Heights, Gettysburg, Brandy Station, Wilderness, Spotsylvania (8, 10, and 12 May '64), North Anna, Cold Harbor, Winchester, Opequon, Fishers Hill, Cedar Creek, Petersburg capture. Also present at Rappahannock Station, Mine Run, Hanover Courthouse ('64), Weldon R.R., Strasburg, Charlestown, Hatcher's Run, Fort Stedman, Sayler's Creek, and Appomattox.

Left the state 27 Aug. '62 with strength of 947. Fowler resigned because of ill health within a few months and was succeeded by Penrose, who was then a Lt. in the 3d US Infantry. However, Penrose was in command of the brigade much of the time and the 15th N.J. was commanded by Campbell in many of its battles. Its first action was at Fredericksburg, where its losses (8 K.I.A.) were relatively light. Fighting around Fredericksburg in the Chancellorsville campaign, however, the regiment (in Brooks's division) saw heavy action around Salem Church; losses were 154, of whom 41 were killed. In Grant's final offensive the regiment crossed the Rapidan with 15 officers and 429 men. At Spotsylvania they lost nearly 300, of whom 116 were killed. At Cold Harbor 18 were killed. In two weeks the strength of the 15th N.J. was down to six officers and 136 men. Moving with VI Corps for Sheridan's Valley campaign, the

regiment continued to see severe fighting and to take a high percentage of casualties, considering their reduced strength. At Cedar Creek, where Maj. Lambert Boeman was killed, the regiment lost 26 other killed or mortally wounded. Although replacements joined the regiment during the winter of 1864–65, they arrived too late to spare the veterans the heaviest casualties. See also 1ST JERSEY BRIGADE for composition of this unit.

NEW LISBON (or Beaver Creek), Ohio, 26 July '63. Capture of last survivors of MORGAN'S OHIO RAID.

NEW MADRID AND ISLAND NO. 10, Mar. '62.

Confederate forces under Brig. Gen. Pillow started construction of these two

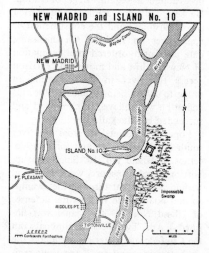

NEW MADRID and ISLAND No. 10

positions in April 1861, to block Federal navigation of the Mississippi. When Polk withdrew from Columbus, Ky., during the period 29 Feb.–2 Mar. '62 in the preliminary moves of the Shiloh campaign, he sent the 5,000-man division of McCown to reinforce the 2,000 then occupying these two river positions. On a peninsula 10 miles long by three miles wide the defenses consisted of a two-regiment redoubt at New Madrid, and land batteries and a floating battery at Island No. 10. The latter was covered by land batteries on the Tenn. shore. Federal forces had to reduce these forts in connection with their general offensive down the Mississippi. (Henry-Donelson and Shiloh campaigns.) Halleck had sent some of Pope's force in central Mo. to reinforce Grant's attack on Donelson; he also told Pope to organize a corps from the remaining troops in Mo. and to capture New Madrid. Pope began organizing his Army of the Miss. on 20 Feb. '62 and on 3 Mar. was in front of New Madrid.

Pope realized that the 50 heavy guns and the small fleet of gunboats the Confederates had in and near the position necessitated a regular siege operation. He sent for siege artillery and started a bombardment and the construction of approaches on 13 Mar. On this same date McCown ordered the evacuation of New Madrid and moved the garrison across the river to the peninsula in order to avoid being isolated. For this action he was relieved of command and succeeded by Mackall.

Pope now decided to cross the river south of New Madrid and turn the defenses of Island No. 10. Since his supporting naval transports were upstream, he had a canal cut through the swamps so that boats could by-pass the defenses of Island No. 10. The canal was finished 4 Apr. Two Federal gunboats ran the Confederate batteries to support the river crossing, and on 7 Apr. four regiments were ferried across the Mississippi to cut the Confederate line of retreat at Tiptonville. Mackall surrendered 3,500 men (over 1,500 of whom were sick) and 500 escaped through the swamps. Pope's victory opened the Mississippi to Fort Pillow, and gave him a reputation which led to his being selected by Lincoln two months later to command the Army of Va. (2d Bull Run campaign).

NEW MARKET, Va., 15 May '64. Gen. Franz Sigel moved up the Shenandoah with about 6,500 men in the divisions of Gens. J. C. Sullivan (Inf.) and Julius Stahel (Cav.). The Confederate cavalry of Gen. Imboden, delaying this advance, was reinforced at New Market by Gen. J. C. Breckinridge with the brigades of Gens. John Echols and Gabriel Wharton, and a battalion of 247 V.M.I. cadets under one of their professors, Lt. Col. Scott Shipp. Breckinridge attacked early in the morning; by 11 o'clock Sigel was forced back about 800 yards. After Shipp was wounded Capt. Henry A. Wise commanded the cadets. The Federal withdrawal was hampered by heavy rain. About 4 P.M., under continued attack, Sigel ordered a general retreat and fell back to Strasburg; on 19 May he was relieved of command. Of 5,150 engaged, the Federals lost 831; the Confederates lost 577 (including 10 V.M.I. cadets killed and 47 wounded) out of 5,000 engaged.

NEW MARKET CROSS ROADS, Va., 30 June '62. See WHITE OAK SWAMP.

NEW MARKET HEIGHTS, Va. (Chafin's Farm; Laurel Hill; Forts Harrison and Gilmer), 28–30 Sept. '64 (PETERSBURG CAMPAIGN).

Grant ordered a surprise attack against Forts Harrison and Gilmer, important redoubts on the outer defenses of Richmond; his purpose was to prevent further reinforcements of Early in the Shenandoah (Fiebeger, 303). The Confederate defenses were manned initially by three infantry brigades of Field (Benning, Law, and Gregg), Fulton's brigade of Johnson's division, two militia brigades, and Gary's cavalry brigade.

Ord, C.G. XVIII Corps, was to cross on a ponton bridge to be constructed the night of 28 Sept. opposite the Varina road, advance up that road, and capture the flank of the enemy defensive works near the river at Chafin's Bluff. His force consisted of 2,000 selected men from Stannard's 1st Div. and the same number from Heckman's 2d Div. The 3d (Negro) Div. under Paine was attached to X Corps for the operation. D. B. Birney, C.G. X Corps, was to lead the other column across the Deep Bottom bridge and move on Richmond by the New Market and Darby roads. His force consisted of the 1st and 2d divisions under Terry and Ames, respectively, William Birney's brigade of colored troops, and Paine's division from Ord's corps. Kautz's cavalry division was to follow Birney across the bridge and operate along the Darby Road.

After driving back Confederate skirmishers (Lee's forces had abandoned the Deep Bottom line), Ord's (west) column hit enemy resistance at Chafin's Farm, near Fort Harrison. Burnham's brigade (2, 1, XVIII) assaulted across 1,400 yards of open, fire-swept ground and captured Fort Harrison from its few defenders (*Lee's Lts.*, III, 590) after a sharp skirmish in which Burnham was killed. (His two successors were seriously wounded.) Heckman's division enveloped the position from the right. Ord attacked down the line of entrenchments toward the positions on Chafin's Bluff that protected the vital Confederate ponton bridge below Drewry's Bluff. This attack was beaten off and Ord was disabled by a leg wound. Fort Gilmer, which commanded the Chafin's Bluff position, had meanwhile been reinforced by the Confederates. An attack by Heckman, who had succeeded Ord in command of the corps, was repulsed with heavy losses.

Meanwhile, Birney, about a mile to the east, drove the Confederate outposts into their main line and established contact with Heckman's column. Grant arrived on the scene and ordered a coordinated attack. Terry's division was sent to support Kautz's cavalry on the north flank. About 3 P.M. an attack by Ames's division and William Birney's colored brigade was repulsed with heavy losses; the latter unit is reported to have particularly distinguished itself on a day when the Federal assaults were marked by great gallantry (Humphreys, 288). The X Corps units withdrew to Laurel Hill and entrenched. During the night of the 29th the Federals worked to prepare Fort Harrison for the expected counterattack. Lee—who had arrived on the scene during the afternoon—ordered reinforcements from south of the James; by dawn there were 10 brigades at Fort Gilmer. At 3 P.M. Anderson (commanding Longstreet's corps) made a desperate attack which failed due to faulty coordination. Two additional assaults were repulsed by the Federal defenders under Stannard, who lost an arm in the second assault. The Federals fortified their positions; the next action was 7 Oct. and is known as DARBYTOWN AND NEW MARKET ROADS.

Of the 19,639 Union and 10,836 Confederate troops engaged (Livermore) there were 3,327 Union casualties (Fox). Southern losses were not reported, but are estimated at 2,000 by Federal reports (E.&B.).

NEW MARKET ROAD, Va., 27 July '64. DEEP BOTTOM RUN, same date.

NEW MARKET ROAD, Va., 7 Oct. '64. DARBYTOWN AND NEW MARKET ROADS, same date.

NEW MEXICO, CONFEDERATE ARMY OF (Sibley's Ariz. Brig.). A force of 3,700 organized 14 Dec. '61 by H. H. Sibley and consisting of all troops on the Rio Grande above Fort Quitman and those in the territories of N. Mex. and Ariz. It included the 4th,

5th, and 7th Tex. Vol. Cav., Baylor's five mounted companies, a six-gun howitzer battery, and three independent companies. Known also as the Arizona Brig., it undertook the NEW MEXICO AND ARIZONA OPERATIONS IN 1861–62. After this, most of its troops went to make up Green's Tex. Brig. and saw action at GALVESTON, 1 Jan. '63, and in the RED RIVER CAMPAIGN OF 1864.

NEW MEXICO, UNION DEPARTMENT OF. In existence at the start of the war, it comprised that part of the N. Mex. Territory which is now in the state of N. Mex. (i.e., east of the 110 degree of longitude) and a part of what is now southwest Colo. Headquarters were at Santa Fe. On 1 Jan. '61 the department consisted of the area now comprising the state of N. Mex. Between 3 July and 9 Nov. '61 it was in the Western Dept. From 9 Nov. '61 to the end of the war the department consisted of the entire Territory of N. Mex. (i.e., the present N. Mex., Ariz. and southern tip of Nev.). Commanders were Col. W. W. Loring until 16 June; Bvt. Lt. Col. E. R. S. Canby to 22 June '61; Brig. Gen. James H. Carleton from 18 Sept. '62 to 27 June '65.

NEW MEXICO AND ARIZONA OPERATIONS IN 1861–62. After the surrender of Twiggs and John BAYLOR's "buffalo hunt," the Confederate Dept. of Tex. had been established. Baylor then raised the 2d Tex. Mtd. Rifles and marched it from San Antonio to occupy Fort Bliss (El Paso) with 300 men the first week in July '61. He had left San Antonio, 700 miles away, with about 700 men; some of these had been dropped off to garrison Forts Clark and Davis en route.

On 23 July '61 Baylor moved with 250 men up the Rio Grande toward the 700-man garrison of the 7th US Inf. under Maj. Isaac Lynde at Fort Fillmore. The Federals came forth 25 July

with 380 men to demand Baylor's surrender, lost nine men in a skirmish, and withdrew. Afraid that he would be cut off, Lynde immediately issued orders for a withdrawal during the night and abandonment of the fort. His ill-disciplined command was intercepted and captured the next day, 27 July, without a fight. Baylor with fewer than 200 had captured 700 regulars, 2 guns, 200 cavalry mounts, and 300 head of cattle. (Lynde was dropped from the army rolls on 25 Nov. '61, but restored and put on the retired list 27 Nov. '66). On 1 Aug. '61 Baylor issued a proclamation stating that the territory south of the 34th parallel would constitute the Confederate Territory of Ariz., with its capital at Mesilla and himself as Gov.

Sibley then organized the 3,700-man Army of NEW MEXICO. By 14 Dec. '61 he had joined forces with Baylor at Fort Bliss. On the 20th he issued a proclamation to the people of Ariz. and N. Mex. that in effect claimed the area for the Confederacy. He then undertook his ill-fated expedition to drive Federal forces from his domain.

The Federal Dept. of N. Mex. had been re-established 9 Nov. '61 under E. R. S. Canby. Early in Jan. '62 Sibley started up the Rio Grande with 2,600 men. On 16 Feb. he made contact with the Federal garrison of Fort Craig and near there defeated the more numerous Federal force in the battle of VALVERDE, 21 Feb. '62. By-passing the fort, Sibley pushed on toward Santa Fe, where he expected to find much-needed supplies. Capt. Herbert M. Enos, Asst. Q.M. in charge of the depot at Albuquerque, evacuated or destroyed his stores on 1 Mar. when he learned that the Confederates were at Belen, 35 miles to the south. On 4 Mar. the Federals evacuated 120 wagonloads of supplies from the more important depot at Santa Fe. Sibley's force took the town on 23 Mar.

When the Confederates pushed on toward Fort Union, about 60 miles east, Federal resistance began to stiffen. Skirmishes in Apache Canyon (Johnson's Ranch and Glorieta) on 26 and 28 Mar., while indecisive, were in favor of the Federals.

Canby, meanwhile, moved north from Fort Craig with 860 regulars and 350 volunteers to join forces with the Fort Union groups against Sibley. Lacking the strength to attack either of these Federal bases, and being unable to re-supply his forces, Sibley decided to withdraw. Although Canby had a force twice the size of Sibley's, the Federal commander was content to let the Confederates withdraw unmolested. When Sibley reached Fort Bliss the first week in May, he learned of the approach of the CALIFORNIA COLUMN under Carleton. He therefore continued his retreat to San Antonio, reaching there with 1,700 fewer men than he had started with. Explaining his severely criticized lack of aggressiveness, Canby said he was not prepared to supply and feed a large number of prisoners.

NEW ORLEANS, La., 25 Apr. '62. Captured by Farragut. Although New Orleans is of immense commercial and strategic importance as the gateway to the Mississippi Valley, it was not until 15 Nov. '61 that the Federal authorities approved a joint army-navy operation to capture it. The operation was conceived by Porter, who then "sold" Welles and McClellan on its feasibility. After some hesitation Farragut (a Tennessean who had lived many years in Norfolk) was selected to lead the joint expedition. The force then being raised in New England by Ben Butler was earmarked as the army element to participate. As a cover plan, a new blockading squadron was established in the western part of the Gulf to indicate that Butler's troops were to be used against Pensacola, Mo-bile, or some port other than New Orleans.

The Crescent City was defended by a small force of militia under Mansfield Lovell dispersed among the small forts that cover the many water approaches to the city. About 90 miles down the river were the permanent masonry forts, Jackson on the west bank and St. Philip about 800 yards north of it on the east bank. The river had been barricaded by a chain, floated on barges and hulks, that extended east from Fort Jackson. High water had partially destroyed this in late Feb. '62 and again on 11 Apr., just a few days before Farragut's attack. The ram *Manassas,* the unpowered *Louisiana,* and the unfinished *Mississippi,* along with an assortment of other ships and fire barges, were part of the Confederate river defenses. The forts were manned by about 500 men and 75 or 80 guns that could bear on the river (Lovell's report).

In a preliminary action the Confederate ram *Manassas* had dropped down the river and routed the steamer *Richmond* and the sailing sloops *Vincennes* and *Preble* in a surprise night attack 11 Oct. '61. On 3 Dec. the Federals had occupied Ship Island, which guards the approach to Lake Pontchartrain, and during Feb. and Mar. '62 Butler used the island as a staging area for his 15,000 army troops. In late Feb. Lovell wrote confidently: "I regard Butler's Ship Island expedition as a harmless menace so far as New Orleans is concerned."

Farragut's force consisted of 24 wooden vessels (about 200 guns total) and Porter's 19 mortar boats, armed with one 13-inch mortar each. On 18 Apr. the mortars started a bombardment that was supposed to silence the forts and permit the wooden ships to pass them safely. J. K. Duncan, the Confederate commander of the coast defenses, reported that the Federals fired 2,997 mortar shells at Fort Jackson between 9 A.M. and 7 P.M. on this day (O.R., I, VI, 525). After a week's bombardment Farragut saw that the mortars, in which he had never had much faith, were doing little damage. At 2 A.M. on the 24th he gave the signal to run past the forts, and by dawn he had accomplished this. He did not lose a ship, although three small gunboats failed to get past the forts. A brief engagement resulted in annihilation of the Confederate river fleet with the loss of only one Federal vessel, the converted merchantman *Varuna*.

Dropping off two small gunboats to support Butler's command, which was approaching "Quarantine" overland from a landing on the Gulf, Farragut continued up the river and captured the undefended city the next day (25 Apr.). Lovell had withdrawn his 4,000 troops about this time and turned the city over to the civil authorities, who surrendered New Orleans on the 29th. Farragut had lost 36 killed and 135 wounded.

With New Orleans captured, the forts flooded, and their only line of retreat cut off by Butler, the demoralized troops in Forts Jackson and St. Philip mutinied and forced their commanders to surrender 28 Apr. (Only the Saint Mary's Cannoneers in Fort Jackson did not mutiny.) Fewer than 50 Confederates in the forts had been killed or wounded. Butler garrisoned the forts with one regiment, occupied New Orleans on 1 May, and started his efficient and controversial military administration of the city.

He had reported on 29 Apr.: "I find the city under the dominion of the mob. They have insulted our flag—torn it down with indignity. This outrage will be punished in such a manner as in my judgment will caution both the perpetrators and abettors of the act, so that they shall fear the stripes if they do not reverence the stars of our banner" (O.R., op. cit., 515). The "judgment" to which he referred was ultimately questioned not only in the South, but also in the North and in Europe. Incidents including the MUMFORD hanging and his "WOMAN ORDER" resulted in his recall.

Lovell called for a court of inquiry, which met 4 Apr. and reported 9 July '63 on his defense of New Orleans. T. C. Hindman was appointed president, and the other voting members were T. F. Drayton and W. M. Gardner; Maj. L. R. PAGE was judge advocate and recorder. The court submitted the opinion that Lovell had defended New Orleans energetically and competently with his green troops, that he had made sufficient provisions to repel a land attack, and was not responsible for the fact that "the so-called river-defense fleet was wholly useless." They found fault only with his failure to issue orders for the withdrawal of M. L. Smith's command (1,000 infantry and five artillery batteries) from the Chalmette line after the Federal fleet had passed this point and the city had been evacuated (O.R., op. cit., 554–654).

NEWPORT, Reece Marshall. Union officer. Pa. Appt.-Ohio. Capt. Asst. Q.M. Vols. 26 Nov. '62; Col. Q.M. Assigned 24 Sept. '64–7 Feb. '66; Bvt. B.G. USV (war service).

NEWPORT NEWS, Va., 8–9 Mar. '62. During the action of the *Virginia* the day before the MONITOR-MERRIMAC duel and on the day of the duel, the 20th Ind. and the 7th and 11th N.Y. fired from the shore in support of the Federal ships. Total Federal casualties were reported 409 in these regiments and on the *Congress, Cumberland, Minnesota,* and *Monitor* (E.&B.).

"NEWS WALKERS." Soldiers who, after the day's fighting, would go from

campfire to campfire, exchanging information and bringing news. Catton says
"they were in fact amateur and self-
appointed reporters, hunting the information by which they could judge how
the battle was going, what army morale
was like, and what the prospects were
for the morrow."

NEWTON, John. Union gen. 1823–
95. Va. USMA 1842 (2/56); Engrs.
He was engaged in the construction of
fortifications, lighthouses, rivers and
harbors before teaching at West Point
and serving as A. S. Johnston's Chief
Engr. on the Utah Expedition. As Capt.
(since 1856), he was Chief Engr. for
the Dept. of Pa. (29 May–23 July '61)
at Falling Waters and for the Dept. of
the Shenandoah (July–Aug.). Promoted
Maj. 6 Aug. '61 and B.G. USV 23 Sept.
'61, he commanded 3d Brig., Franklin's
division, Potomac (3 Oct. '61–13 Mar.
'62) in the defenses of Washington and
3, 1, I, Potomac (13 Mar.–4 Apr. '62).
At West Point he commanded 3d Brig.,
1st Div., Rappahannock (4 Apr.–18
May '62) and at Gaines's Mill, Glendale, South Mountain, and Antietam he
led 3, 1, VI, Potomac (18 May–21 Sept.
'62). He led 1st Div., VI Corps, Potomac (15–18 Oct. '62) and 3d Div. of
that corps (18 Oct.–Dec. '62) at Fredericksburg and (Feb.–1 July '63) at
Chancellorsville and Gettysburg. During
the latter battle he succeeded J. F.
Reynolds in command of the I Corps
2 July, and led it until 24 Mar. '64. He
had been named Maj. Gen. USV 30 Mar.
'63, and when his appointment was revoked 18 Apr. '64 he was reappointed
B.G. USV on the same day. In the
Atlanta campaign he commanded 2d
Div., IV, Cumberland (16 Apr.–30 Sept.
'64) at Rocky Face Ridge, Dalton,
Adairsville, Dallas, Kenesaw Mountain,
Peach Tree Creek, Jonesboro, and Lovejoy. From 15 Oct. '64 to July '65 he
commanded Dist. Key West, Gulf. Bre-

veted for Antietam, Gettysburg, Peach
Tree Creek (B.G. USA) and war service
(Maj. Gen. USA and USV), he continued in the R.A. and was retired in
1886 as B.G. and Chief of Engrs. (since
1884). His greatest achievement was the
blasting of reefs and obstructions at Hell
Gate in N.Y. Harbor with over 250,000
pounds of explosives. He was later Commissioner of Public Works in N.Y. and
a railroad president.

NEWTONIA, Mo., 28 Oct. '64. Delaying action during PRICE'S RAID IN
MISSOURI.

5TH NEW YORK ("Duryee Zouaves")
Colonels: Abram Duryee (Bvt. Maj.
Gen. USV), G. K. Warren (USMA;
R.A.; Bvt. Maj. Gen. USA), Hiram
Duryea (Bvt. B.G. USV), Cleveland
Winslow (K.I.A.).

Battles: Big Bethel, Yorktown siege,
Gaines's Mill, Manassas, Shepherdstown Ford, Fredericksburg, and Chancellorsville. Also at Hanover Court
House, Seven Days, Malvern Hill,
Antietam.

A colorful unit from New York City
that was famous not only for its gay
uniforms and precise parade-ground
drill, but also for its effectiveness in
combat. All its service was with the
Division of Regulars (Sykes's) in V
Corps. Under Hiram Duryea it won
the admiration of the Regulars at
Gaines's Mill where, after having its
ranks torn by several volleys, it coolly
paused under fire to "count off" and
realign its ranks. At Manassas it had
117 killed out of the 490 it took into
action. Although a two-year regiment,
it had a high percentage of three-year
enlistees; the latter were transferred to
the 146th N.Y. when the regiment's
enlistment expired 14 May '63. Colonel
Winslow then organized another regiment bearing the designation 5th N.Y.
This unit rejoined the V Corps to finish
the war. Winslow was mortally wounded

at Bethesda Church, and his successor, Col. Winthrop, was killed at Five Forks while commanding the brigade.

11TH NEW YORK ("1st New York Fire Zouaves," and "Ellsworth's Zouaves")

Organized in Apr. '61 from volunteer firemen in New York City (hence the nickname) by the famous Zouave drillmaster E. Elmer ELLSWORTH. Although enlisted for two years it was disbanded after little more than a year (Fox 481n.). While in Washington 2–23 May the Fire Zouaves became famous for their rowdy conduct, their gaudy uniforms, and their spectacular performance in putting out a fire that threatened to spread to Willard's Hotel. During the occupation of Alexandria the incident took place that resulted in the death of their commander, Ellsworth. At 1st Bull Run the Fire Zouaves distinguished themselves in supporting the batteries of Griffin and Ricketts. They then performed duty in N.Y. (Sept.–Oct. '61) and at Newport News (to May '62). They took part in the *Monitor–Merrimac* action. The regiment was mustered out 2 June '62 (Dyer). The summer of 1863 an unsuccessful attempt was made to reorganize the regiment.

69TH NEW YORK (Irish Brigade)

Colonel: Robert Nugent (R.A., Bvt. B.G.).

Battles: Fair Oaks, Gaines's Mill, Peach Orchard, White Oak Swamp, Malvern Hill, Antietam, Fredericksburg, Chancellorsville Gettysburg (2 companies), Bristoe Station, Wilderness, Spotsylvania, Totopotomoy, Cold Harbor, Petersburg assaults of 16–18 June '64, Petersburg siege, Deep Bottom, Reams's Station, Hatcher's Run, Sayler's Creek, and Farmville. Present also at Yorktown, Savage's Station, Mine Run, Po River, North Anna, Strawberry Plains, White Oak Road, fall of Petersburg, Appomattox.

There were three regiments known as the 69th N.Y. The one whose battle honors are listed above is the regiment generally associated with the designation; it served throughout the war as part of the Irish Brigade. Another 69th N.Y. was a militia unit that served at Bull Run (under Corcoran) and throughout the war during different emergencies. The third unit, 69th Natl. Guard Arty. (Corcoran's Legion), was officially the 182nd N.Y. Volunteers.

The 69th N.Y. (Irish Brigade) was organized in Sept. '61 and re-enlisted at the end of its three years' service. At Bloody Lane (Antietam) eight regimental color bearers were shot down. (Here the regiment was in Richardson's division.) "At Fredericksburg a color sergeant of the Sixty-ninth was found dead, with the flag concealed and wrapped around his body, a bullet having pierced that flag and his heart" (Fox.) Out of 18 officers and 210 men engaged in that battle, the regiment lost 16 officers and 112 men.

79TH NEW YORK ("Highlanders")

Colonels: James Cameron (K.I.A.), Isaac Stevens (USMA; Maj. Gen.; K.I.A.), Addison Farnsworth (Bvt. B.G.), and David Morrison (Bvt. B.G.).

Battles: 1st Bull Run, Lewinsville, James Island (S.C.), Manassas, Chantilly, South Mountain, Antietam, Blue Springs, Fort Sanders, Knoxville siege, Spotsylvania. Present also at Blackburn's Ford, Pocotaligo (S.C.), Kelly's Ford, Fredericksburg, Vicksburg, Jackson (Miss.), Campbell's Station, Wilderness, Hatcher's Run, Petersburg.

A State National Guard unit, composed mostly of Scotsmen, which volunteered at the start of the war. On ceremonial occasions the officers wore kilts and the men wore pantaloons of the Cameron tartan. Colonel Cameron, the regimental commander, was the brother of the Sec. of War.

At First Bull Run, where Cameron was killed, the regiment lost 198. At the battle of James Island its losses were 110 out of 474 engaged. At 2d Bull Run and Chantilly, 105 men. In the latter engagement, Stevens, former regimental commander now commanding the division, was killed after taking the regimental colors from the hands of the sixth color bearer who had fallen. The regiment's enlistment expired 13 May '64.

121ST NEW YORK (2d Brigade, 1st Division, VI Corps)

Colonels: Richard Franchot (Bvt. B.G. USV), Emory Upton (USMA; R.A.; Bvt. Maj. Gen. USA), Egbert Olcott (R.A.).

Battles: Fredericksburg, Salem Heights, Rappahannock Station, Wilderness, Spotsylvania, Cold Harbor, Petersburg, Charlestown, Opequon, Cedar Creek, Petersburg siege, Hatcher's Run, f ll of Petersburg, Sayler's Creek. Also at Crampton's Gap, Gettysburg, Funkstown, Mine Run, Fort Stevens, Fishers Hill, and Appomattox.

From Herkimer and Otsego counties the 121st was mustered into service in Aug. '62 and joined the Army of the Potomac for the Antietam campaign. It was in the 2d Brig., 1st Div., VI Corps throughout the war. At Salem Church the regiment lost 276 out of 453 engaged. The regimental commander, Emory UPTON, was one of the finest soldiers this country has ever produced. The 121st led Upton's assault at Spotsylvania, in which it lost 49 killed, 106 wounded, and had no missing in action. The regiment saw action in the Valley when VI Corps was ordered to join the Army of the Shenandoah. Upon completion of SHENANDOAH VALLEY CAMPAIGN OF SHERIDAN the regiment returned with VI Corps to the Army of the Potomac. The 121st N.Y. captured four flags at Rappahannock Station and two at Sayler's Creek.

126TH NEW YORK

Colonels: Eliakim Sherrill (K.I.A.), James M. Bull, William H. Baird (K.I.A.), and Ira Smith Brown.

Battles: Maryland Heights, Gettysburg, Auburn Ford, and Bristoe Station (13 Oct. '64), Morton's Ford, Wilderness, Po River, Spotsylvania, Totopotomoy, Cold Harbor, Petersburg assault and siege, Weldon R.R., Deep Bottom, Reams's Station, Hatcher's Run, Sutherland Station. Present also at Mine Run, North Anna, Strawberry Plains, Boydton Road, Farmville, and Appomattox.

From Ontario, Seneca, and Yates counties it was organized in Aug. '62. It had a strange baptism of fire, losing 55 men at Maryland Heights and being surrendered a few days later with the rest of the Harpers Ferry garrison. After two months in Camp Parole, Chicago, Ill., it joined the Army of the Potomac in June '63. It was assigned to Willard's brigade, Hays's (3d) division, II Corps. At Gettysburg the 126th captured five stand of colors. In the desperate defense of Cemetery Ridge against the so-called Pickett's Charge, the regimental commander, Sherrill, was killed after taking over command of the brigade after Willard had been killed. The regiment lost 231. At Bristoe Station the 126th had the highest regimental casualties. Transferred to Barlow's (1st) division, the regiment entered the final campaign against Richmond with less than 300 men, of whom 100 were detailed to headquarters as provost guard. It lost 126 at the Wilderness, Po River, and Spotsylvania. Colonel Baird was killed at Petersburg.

NEW YORK, UNION DEPARTMENT OF. Organized 26 Oct. '61, with headquarters at Albany; merged into the Dept. of the East on 3 Jan. '63. Commander: Maj. Gen. E. D. Morgan.

8TH NEW YORK HEAVY ARTILLERY (originally 129th New York Infantry)

Colonels: Peter A. Porter (K.I.A.), Willard W. Bates (K.I.A.), James M. Willet, Joel B. Baker.

Battles: Spotsylvania, North Anna, Cold Harbor, Petersburg assault and siege, Weldon R.R., Deep Bottom, Reams's Station, Boydton Road, Hatcher's Run, Dabney's Mills, White Oak Road. Present also at Totopotomoy, High Bridge, Farmville, Appomattox.

Organized at Lockport in Aug. '62 as the 129th Inf. Its men were from Niagara, Orleans, and Genesee counties. In Dec. '62 the regiment was converted to heavy artillery and in Jan. '64 two additional companies (L and M) were added. After performing garrison duty until May '64, it was reconverted (with other heavy artillery units) to infantry for Grant's final operations against Richmond. It was assigned to Gibbon's (2d) division of II Corps. At Cold Harbor the regiment lost 505; Col. Porter and seven other officers were killed.

Col. Bates and Maj. Blake were killed in the Petersburg assault. During the initial actions against this Confederate strong point, 15–23 June '64, regimental losses were 308. A large regiment with 12 companies of 150 men each, instead of the normal 10 companies of 101 men each, the total enrollment was 2,575. In its 10 months of combat it lost 1,010 in action, of whom 361 (or 14 per cent) were killed.

182D NEW YORK VOLUNTEERS (Corcoran Legion)

Official designation of a unit organized Nov. '62, often referred to as the 69TH NEW YORK. The 182d was known unofficially as the 69th National Guard Arty., whence confusion with other two 69th N.Y. regiments.

NICOLAY, John George. Lincoln's private secretary and biographer. 1832–1901. Bavaria. Coming to America at the age of six, he lived in Ill. and became a close friend of John HAY while working on the Pittsfield *Free Press.* Later editor of the paper (1854–56), he was a dedicated Republican and supporter of Lincoln. He became the future president's private secretary in 1860 and continued through the war in this post, being named Consul in Paris shortly before Lincoln's death. From 1872 to 1887 he was marshal of the US Supreme Court, and in 1890 he and Hay published their 10-volume *Abraham Lincoln: A History,* which they had planned since 1861. Their *Abraham Lincoln: Complete Works* was brought out in 1905.

NICHOLLS, Francis Reddin T. C.S.A. gen. 1834–1912. La. USMA 1855 (12/34); Arty. Resigning the next year, he was a lawyer when commissioned Capt. 8th La. Promoted Lt. Col. 9 June '61, he fought under Jackson in the Shenandoah and was wounded in the elbow near Winchester. On 24 June '62 he was named Col. 15th La. and appointed B.G. C.S.A. 14 Oct. '62. He commanded the Dist. of Lynchburg until 16 Jan. '63, when he took over the 2d La. Brig. in Jackson's corps. Leading them at Chancellorsville, he was wounded and his foot amputated. Unfit for further field service, he was sent to the Trans-Miss. Dept. in 1864, serving there for the rest of the war. Returning to his law practice, he was twice Gov. of his state, served on the USMA Board of Visitors, and was Chief Justice of the Louisiana Supreme Court 1892–1904.

NICHOLS, George F. Union officer. N.Y. Maj. 118th N.Y. 21 Aug. '62; Lt. Col. 12 Aug. '63; Col. 13 Nov. '64; Bvt. B.G. USV (Fort Harrison, Va.). Commanded 1, 3, XXIV (Va.).

NICHOLS, George Sylvester. Union officer. N.Y. 1st Lt. Adj. 9th N.Y. Cav. 19 Nov. '61; Maj. 23 Nov. '61; Lt. Col. 1 May '63; Col. 1 Mar. '65; Bvt. B.G. USV (Sheridan's Valley campaign). Commanded 2, 1, Cav. Corps (Potomac); 2, 1, Cav. Corps (Shenandoah).

NICHOLS, William A. Union officer. c. 1818–69. Pa. USMA 1838 (19/45); Arty. Adj. Gen. He served on the frontier, in the Mexican War (2 brevets) and in the Adj. Gen.'s office. Captured when Twiggs surrendered Tex., he was released and promoted Lt. Col. 3 Aug. '61. Adj. Gen. of the Dept. of the East until Nov. '61 and of the Dept. of N.Y. until Dec. '61, he served in the Adj. Gen.'s office for the rest of the war and later was first Sherman's and then Sheridan's Chief of Staff. As Bvt. B.G. USA 24 Sept. '64 and Bvt. Maj. Gen., he died on active duty as Col.

NICKERSON, Franklin Stebin. Union gen. 1826–? Me. He was commissioned Maj. 4th Me. 15 June '61 and mentioned favorably by O. O. Howard for his conduct at 1st Bull Run. Promoted to Lt. Col. 6 Sept. and to Col. 14th Me. 25 Nov. '61, he was named B.G. USV 29 Nov. '62. In the XIX Corps, Gulf, he commanded 3d Brig., 2d Div. (12 Jan.–10 Aug. '63); 1st Brig., 2d Div. (15 Feb.–29 June '64); 2d Div. (28–30 May '63); 1st Brig., 3d Div. (10 July–15 Aug. '63); 3d Div. (15–29 Aug. '63). He resigned 13 May '65 and returned to the customs office in Boston. Appleton's lists an officer with this identical record as Nickerson, Frank Stillman.

NICKERSON, Frank Stillman. See NICKERSON, above.

NIGHT ATTACKS were rare in the Civil War. For examples, see WAUHATCHIE, Tenn., 28–29 Oct. '63; RAPPAHANNOCK BRIDGE AND KELLY'S FORD, Va., 7 Nov. '63; FORT WAGNER, S.C., 18 July '63.

NILES, Nathaniel. Union officer. N.Y. Col. 130th Ill. 25 Oct. '62; Bvt. B.G. USV (war service); resigned 5 Dec. '63.

NOBLE, John Willock. Union officer. 1831–1912. Ohio. 1st Lt. 3d Iowa Cav. 2 Sept. '61; Regt. Adj. 5 Sept. '61; Maj. 18 Nov. '62; Lt. Col. 1 May '64; Col. 27 June '64; Bvt. B.G. USV (war service); served as J.A.G., Army of the Southwest. Lawyer and conservationist, he moved to Iowa to exercise his Republican and Free-Soil convictions. Appointed Sec. of the Int. (1889) by Pres. Harrison.

NOBLE, William H. Union officer. Conn. Col. 17th Conn. 22 July '62; Bvt. B.G. USV (war service). Commanded 2, 1, XI (Potomac); 2, South End Folly Island, X; 2, Forces Folly Island S.C., X; 1, 1st Dist. Fla., X; 4th Separate Brig., Dist. Fla. Died 1894.

NORTH ANNA RIVER, Va., 23–27 May '64. Also known as Hanover Junction; Jericho Mills, Ford, or Bridge; Taylor's Bridge. Frustrated at SPOTSYLVANIA, Grant planned another turning movement to the south. Hancock's II Corps, which had been heavily reinforced, was to move with a strong cavalry force along the Richmond, Fredericksburg, and Potomac R.R. toward Hanover Junction. Grant hoped Lee would attack this corps and that the rest of the army could then hit Lee before he could intrench. If this stratagem failed, the operation would make Lee abandon his strong positions at Spotsylvania. To support this strategy, Grant shifted his base of supply to Port Royal.

Lee again interpreted Grant's movements correctly and, taking advantage of interior lines, was intrenched across Grant's path at Hanover Junction before Grant could mass his forces against that point. Ewell arrived the morning of the 22d, Anderson arrived at noon, and A. P. Hill was there the next morning. Hancock's and Wright's Corps arrived on the 23d. At Jericho Mills, a few miles above Lee's intrenched position, Wright's V Corps started crossing the river. Bartlett's brigade (3, 1, V) waded over and established a bridgehead after driving back a few outposts. The stream had high banks and a curious series of rocky steps ("shelfing"). A ponton bridge was constructed and by 4:30 P.M. the infantry was across and forming line of battle against positions of A. P. Hill that had been found partly dug in along the Virginia Central R.R. An attack, made principally by Wilcox's division, took place at 6 P.M. It fell with most severity against Cutler's (4th) division, which was just going into position on the right, and against Griffin's (1st) division in the center. The attack failed after heavy fighting and Wilcox's division sustained 642 casualties. Humphreys states that "the loss in killed and wounded was probably equal on both sides" (p. 129). This action is known as Jericho Mills, or Jericho *Bridge,* as it was erroneously shown on Federal maps. Lee was reinforced by Pickett's division, Hoke's brigade, and two brigades under Breckinridge (which had just defeated Sigel at NEW MARKET, 15 May); these new units swelled Lee's numbers by 8,000. Lee's sickness resulted in failure to take advantage of Grant's faulty dispositions astride the river and to defeat Wright and Warren (south of the river) in detail (*Lee's Lts.,* III, 497–98).

Finding the enemy position too strong to assault, Grant withdrew the night of 26–27 May toward Hanover Town. Here he crossed the Pamunkey and moved to TOTOPOTOMOY CREEK where Lee again blocked him. A major engagement was then fought at COLD HARBOR, 31 May–3 June '64.

NORTH CAROLINA. The next to last state to join the Confederacy, it seceded 20 May '61 only after Lincoln's call for troops. Union sentiment was strong, although there were over 300,-000 slaves in the state. N.C. contributed around 125,000 soldiers, led the South in blockade running, sustained about one fourth of the Confederate losses, and fed and clothed its own soldiers. A number of important battles, principally along the seacoast, occurred in the state, and Joseph E. Johnston surrendered there near Durham. The state was readmitted to the Union 25 June '68, after military control had been finally withdrawn the preceding day.

NORTH CAROLINA, UNION DEPARTMENT OF. Created 7 Jan. '62 (in connection with Burnside's expedition) to consist of the state of N.C. Merged 15 July '63 into the Dept. of Va. and N.C. Re-created 31 Jan. '65. Commanders were Maj. Gen. A. E. Burnside, 13 Jan. to 6 July '62; and J. G. Foster, until 15 July '63. XVIII Corps was the designation of the troops in the department. It was created 24 Dec. '62, and transferred 15 July '63 to the Dept. of Va. and N.C. It was commanded by Maj. Gen. J. G. Foster. Terry's Provisional Corps was organized under Maj. Gen. Alfred H. Terry during the period 6 Jan.–27 Mar. '65 for the expedition against Fort Fisher, N.C. It was merged into the reorganized X Corps. XXIII Corps was transferred from the Army and Dept. of the Ohio in Feb. '65; it was disbanded 1 Aug. Its commanders during this period were Maj. Gen. J. M. Schofield, to 31 Mar.; and J. D. Cox to 17 June '65. Bvt. Maj. Gen. T. H. Ruger was in command until 27 June; and Brig. Gen. S. P. Carter was in command until 1 Aug. '65. The S.C. Expeditional [sic] Corps was organized in Sept. and Oct. '61 (Port Royal expedition) and transformed into the Dept. of the South on 15 Mar. '62. It was commanded by Brig. Gen. T. W. Sherman (not W. T. Sherman).

NORTH CAROLINA AND SOUTH-ERN VIRGINIA, CONFEDERATE DEPT. OF. Constituted 19 Sept. '62 under G. W. Smith, this department included territory previously included in other territorial organizations. Huger had taken command of the Dept. of Norfolk on 23 May '61. This originally included only the immediate vicinity of Norfolk, but by the end of the year had been extended to include Albemarle Sound, N.C. (Roanoke Island excluded). On 12 Apr. '62 Huger's department came under the authority of J. E. Johnston, when the latter moved troops from his Dept. of Northern Va. south for the PENINSULAR CAMPAIGN. On 9 May Huger withdrew from Norfolk to Petersburg and the Federals occupied the port; the Albemarle Sound region was lost during BURNSIDE'S EXPEDITION TO N.C., Feb.–July '62.

The "defenses of North Carolina" were put under the command of Richard C. Gatlin on 20 Aug. '61. J. R. Anderson and D. H. Hill were ordered to N.C. on 3 and 29 Sept., respectively. On 22 Jan. '62 Henry Wise was assigned to command forces at Roanoke Island (O.R., I, IV, 566; and IX, 72). The Dept. of N.C. was then headed in turn by Anderson, vice Gatlin, effective 12 Mar. '62; and T. H. Holmes on 24 Mar. On 2 June J. G. Martin was put in command of the Dist. of N.C. On 3 June the portion of the state west of the Blue Ridge was made part of the Dept. of East Tenn. On 21 June the department was extended to the south bank of the James, and D. H. Hill was assigned to its command 17 July. After failing to accomplish his mission of harassing McClellan's with-drawal from Harrison's Landing at the conclusion of the Peninsular campaign, Hill later rejoined Lee's army.

The Dept. of N.C. and Southern Va. was constituted 19 Sept. '62 under G. W. Smith. It was also referred to as the Dept. of Va. and N.C., and often simply as the Dept. of N.C. On 8 Nov. '62 Whiting was assigned command of the defenses of the Cape Fear River (Wilmington area); he actually took command on the 17th. D. H. Hill again took command of the troops in N.C. on 25 Feb. '63. S. G. French took temporary command on 17 Feb.

Longstreet assumed command on 26 Feb. '63 and on 1 Apr. his command was reorganized into three departments: the Dept. of N.C. under D. H. Hill; the Dept. of S. Va. under S. G. French; and the Dept. of Richmond under Arnold Elzey. On 28 May Petersburg was placed under Longstreet's jurisdiction. Actually these three "departments" were in existence at the time Longstreet took command; the order of 1 Apr. "made clear the formal, military relationship" (Lee's Lts., II, 469 and 480). This order also prescribed that Longstreet's entire command would remain under Lee's supervision (ibid., citing O.R., I, XVIII, 953).

The above arrangement put Whiting under D. H. Hill. When the latter was promoted to Lt. Gen. and sent to the West, Whiting took command of the Dept. of N.C. on 14 July '63. On 26 Sept. he was put at the head of the separate "District of the Cape Fear River and the Defenses of Wilmington."

Pickett, meanwhile, was assigned to head the Dept. of N.C. (and South Va.) on 23 Sept. '63. He was succeeded by Beauregard, who was assigned 18 Apr. '64 but did not reach Pickett's head-quarters at Petersburg until 10 May, during Butler's operations against DREWRY'S BLUFF.

Johnston took command of all troops in the department on 6 Mar. '65 during the CAROLINAS CAMPAIGN. (Note: The designation "Dept. of N.C." is often used synonymously with the more complete designation "Dept. of N.C. and South Va.")

NORTHCOTT, Robert Sanders. Union officer. Tenn. Lt. Col. 12th W. Va. 25 Aug. '62; Bvt. B.G. USV (war service); resigned 5 Jan. '65. Commanded 1st Brig., 1st Inf. Div., IV (W. Va.).

NORTHEASTERN VIRGINIA, UNION DEPARTMENT OF. Briefly in existence from 27 May–25 July '61 (when it was merged into the short-lived Mil. Dist. of the Potomac and then on 15 Aug. '61 into the Dept. and Army of the Potomac). It consisted of that part of Va. east of the Allegheny Mountains and north of the James River, with the exclusion of Fortress Monroe and the area within a 60-mile radius of the latter place. It was commanded by Maj. Gen. Irvin McDowell.

NORTHERN DEPARTMENT (Union). Constituted 12 Jan. '64 to consist of Mich., Ohio, Ind., and Ill. Headquarters at Columbus, Ohio. Following major generals commanded: S. P. Heintzelman, 20 Jan. to 1 Oct. '64; Joseph Hooker to 27 June '65.

NORTHERN VIRGINIA, CONFEDERATE ARMY OF. Principal Confederate field force which, under R. E. Lee, opposed the Federal Army of the Potomac (and Pope's short-lived Army of Va.) in the eastern theater of operations throughout the war.

When J. E. Johnston was wounded on 31 May '62 (at Seven Pines) he was temporarily succeeded by G. W. Smith. On 1 June R. E. Lee took command of the Confederate forces that had been opposing McClellan's advance on Richmond. These included the troops of three departments, Northern Va., the Peninsula, and Norfolk, all of which had been under Johnston since 12 Apr. '62. He had usually referred to his command as the Army of the POTOMAC.

The name "Army of Northern Virginia" dates from Lee's assumption of command, according to D. S. Freeman (See *R. E. Lee*, II, 77–78n.). During the Peninsular campaign it was composed of 11 infantry divisions, Stuart's cavalry (a brigade of 11 regiments), and W. N. Pendleton's artillery (six brigades). The infantry divisions were grouped under the command of Jackson, Longstreet, and Magruder for the Seven Days' battles.

Before the 2d Bull Run campaign the Army of Northern Va. was reorganized. Longstreet's Right Wing included the division of Anderson, Jones (D.R.), Wilcox, Hood, and Kemper. Jackson's Left Wing included his former division and those of A. P. Hill and Dick Ewell. The cavalry division, under Jeb Stuart, included the brigades of B. H. Robertson and Fitzhugh Lee. The divisions were regrouped for the Antietam campaign. "Longstreet's Command" had the divisions of McLaws, Anderson, D. R. Jones, Walker, and Hood. "Jackson's Command" comprised the divisions of Ewell (commanded by A. R. Lawton), A. P. Hill, Jackson (under J. R. Jones), and D. H. Hill. Stuart's cavalry had been increased by the addition of Wade Hampton's brigade; T. T. Munford was in command of "Robertson's" brigade.

After Antietam the Army of Northern Va. was officially organized into the I and II Corps under Longstreet and Jackson, respectively. Ewell succeeded Jackson after Chancellorsville. Shortly thereafter, on 30 May '63, A. P. Hill's III Corps was formed. At the same time the (army) reserve artillery was abolished; all guns were assigned to divisions with a few held as corps reserve. After Gettysburg Stuart's cavalry was reorganized to form a true corps (i.e., the brigades were grouped into divisions). A IV Corps was created in late '64 under Dick Anderson.

See CORPS, Confederate, for more detailed treatment.

NORTHERN VIRGINIA, CONFEDERATE DEPARTMENT OF. Constituted 22 Oct. '61 under J. E. Johnston to consist of the following three districts: Potomac, under Beauregard until 26 Jan. '62 when he was ordered to Columbus, Ky., and then under Johnston; AQUIA, under T. H. Holmes; and the Valley, under Stonewall Jackson. On 12 Apr. '62 in the maneuvering that preceded the Peninsular campaign Davis ordered that "the Departments of Norfolk and of the Peninsula were 'embraced for the present within the limits of operations of the Army of Northern Virginia'" (*Lee's Lts.*, I, 147). Despite Davis' reference here to the "Army of Northern Virginia," Johnston's army continued to be generally known as the Army of the POTOMAC until Lee took command on 1 June '62.

NORTHROP, Lucius Bellinger. C.S.A. Comsy. Gen. of Subsist. 1811–94. S.C. USMA 1831 (22/33); Inf.-Dragoons. He served on the frontier and in Indian fighting and was severely wounded in the Seminole War. Retired in 1839 on "permanent sick furlough," he studied medicine and was dropped from the army rolls for practicing on charity patients in Charleston. Reinstated eight months later by Jefferson Davis, he resigned 8 Jan. '61 and was commissioned Col. and Comsy. Gen. of the Confederacy. As the war progressed he was severely criticized and was perhaps, next to Bragg, the most unpopular Davis appointee. He was appointed a special B.G. C.S.A. 26 Nov. '64. The C.S.A. Senate acquitted him in Jan. '65 of the charge that he was inadequately feeding Union prisoners. Davis removed him a month later after the C.S.A. House had passed a bill demanding this step. He was arrested 30 June '65 by the order of US authorities and released 31 Oct. of that year on conditional parole. D.A.B. characterizes him as "peevish, obstinate, condescending, and fault-finding."

NORTHWEST, CONFEDERATE ARMY OF THE. Troops operating in northwestern Va. were put under the command of R. S. Garnett on 8 June '61 and became known as the Army of the Northwest. This unit opposed McClellan and Rosecrans in western Va. and was defeated at RICH MOUNTAIN, 11 July. Henry R. Jackson was temporarily in command from Garnett's death on 13 July until W. W. Loring was put in command 20 July. After the defeat at CHEAT MOUNTAIN, 12–13 Sept., Loring's forces were split up in Nov. He went to Winchester with three brigades, coming under the orders of Stonewall Jackson; his force continued to be known as the Army of the Northwest. After Jackson's unsuccessful winter campaign against Bath and Romney, W. Va., and the LORING-JACKSON INCIDENT, the army was disbanded 9 Feb. '62. Forces under Edward Johnson in the upper Shenandoah then became known as the Army of the Northwest (B.&L., II, 301) and were also known as the Army of the Allegheny. This organization finally became part of Jackson's Valley District, whence it passed into the Army of Northern Va. (See also WEST VIRGINIA OPERATIONS IN 1861.)

NORTHWEST, UNION DEPARTMENT OF THE. Constituted 6 Sept. '62 (after INDIAN TROUBLES of Aug. '62) to include Wis., Iowa, Minn. and the Territories of Nebraska and Dakota

Hq. at Madison, Wis.; then Milwaukee. Commanders: Maj. Gen. John Pope, 16 Sept. '62 to 28 Nov. '62; Brig. Gen. W. L. Elliott to 18 Feb. '63; Maj. Gen. John Pope to 13 Feb. '65; Maj. Gen. S. R. Curtis to 27 June '65.

NORTHWEST CONSPIRACY. See SWEET, Benjamin Jeffery.

NORTON, Charles Benjamin. Union officer. Conn. 1st Lt. Regt. Q.M. 39th N.Y. 6 June '61; discharged 6 Aug. '61; 1st Lt. Regt. Q.M. 50th N.Y. Engrs. 15 Aug. '61; Capt. Asst. Q.M. Vols. 11 June '62; Lt. Col. Q.M. Assigned 20 Aug. '62–6 Jan. '63; Bvt. B.G. USV (war service); resigned 6 Jan. '63. Died 1891.

NOSE CREEK, Ga. Misspelling of NOYES's CREEK.

NOYES, Edward Follansbee. Union officer. 1832–90. Mass. Maj. 39th Ohio 24 July '61; Lt. Col. 8 July '62; Col. 1 Nov. '62; Bvt. B.G. USV (war service); W.I.A. (left foot amputated) Nickajack Creek (Ga.) 4 July '64. Served on Gen. Pope's staff in Mo. and after the war was judge and Republican Gov. of Ohio (1871–75). Appointed Minister to France (1877–81) by Pres. Hayes.

NOYES'S CREEK, Ga. Sometimes spelled Nose's Creek. Scene of several actions on Johnston's left at KENESAW MOUNTAIN, particularly on 17 June. Accounts give no details.

NUGENT, Robert. Union officer. Ireland. Lt. Col. 69th N.Y. 20 Apr. '61; mustered out 3 Aug. '61; Capt. 13th US Inf. 5 Aug. '61; Col. 69th N.Y. 1 Nov. '61; mustered out USV 28 Nov. '63; Col. 69th N.Y. 30 Oct. '64; Bvt. B.G. USV. Brevets for Gaines's Mill, Fredericksburg, Petersburg siege, war service. Mustered out of USV, continuing in R.A. until retired in 1879 as Maj. Acting Provost Marshal Asst. of

N.Y.C. April–Nov. '63. During the N.Y. Draft Riots his house and its belongings were destroyed by the mob. Died 1901.

NULLIFICATION, Theory of. See John C. CALHOUN.

NUMBERS AND LOSSES. In the Union Army a total of 2,128,948 men served and 359,528 are known to have died. Of the troops engaged, 75,215 were regulars, 1,933,779 were volunteers, 46,347 were drafted, and 73,607 were substitutes. Of the total casualties, 67,058 were killed in action, 43,012 died of wounds, 224,586 died of disease, and 24,872 died from accidents or other causes. The above figures are from the Adj. Gen.'s Office as published in the *Army Almanac* of 1950.

The strength of the Confederate Army has been the subject of much controversy, the estimates ranging between 600,000 and 1,500,000. Taking a total of 2,893,304 enlistments in the Union Army during the war, and between 1,227,890 and 1,406,180 enlistments in the Confederate Army during the war, and reducing both figures to the standard of three-year enlistments, Livermore puts Union strength at 1,556,678 and Confederate strength at 1,082,119.

Confederate battle deaths are estimated at 94,000, a figure both Fox and Livermore consider inaccurate but probably the best available. Using Fox's "experience figure" of 2½ wounded for every man killed or who died of wounds, total Confederate killed and wounded would be 329,000 (Livermore, 64). The report of the U.S. Provost Marshal Gen. gives the following figures of Confederate deaths: killed, 52,954; died of wounds, 21,570; died of disease, 59,297. As Fox points out, the returns from nearly all Ala. units were missing when this tabulation was made. This helps account for the figure of only 74,524 battle deaths, instead of the 94,000 cited above. The number of Confederates surrendered in 1865 was 174,223.

NY RIVER, Va., 10 May '64. During the SPOTSYLVANIA CAMPAIGN Burnside, whose IX Corps was located on the north in a relatively quiet sector, was ordered on the morning of 10 May to make a reconnaissance toward the Court House. Although this is listed as an engagement of the war, it is not mentioned in accounts of Spotsylvania other than to say that Gen. T. G. Stevenson was killed by a sharpshooter (Alexander). The corps dug in parallel to and about 1,000 yards northeast of Early's lines.

NYE, George Henry. Union officer. Me. Commissioned 2d Lt. 1st Me. 3 May '61, he was mustered out three months later and commissioned Capt. 10th Me. 3 Oct. '61. He was promoted Maj. 18 Oct. '64 and Col. 20 Dec. '64. Mustered out in 1866, he was breveted for war service (B.G. 29 Oct. '64 and Maj. Gen. USV).

O

OAKES, James. Union officer. 1826–1910. Pa. USMA 1846 (34/59); Dragoons-Cav. He served in the Mexican War (2 brevets), on frontier duty, and in Indian fighting, where he was severely wounded twice. During the Civil War he was promoted Maj. 2d US Cav. 6 Apr. '61 and served until Sept. in Wheeling (W. Va.) on mustering duty. On 17 May '61 he was offered the rank of full B.G. USV but declined the commission. Transferring to the 5th US Cav. 3 Aug. '61 and named Lt. Col. 4th US Cav. 12 Nov. '61, he commanded the regiment in Washington Sept. '61–Jan. '62 and in the move on Nashville, at Shiloh, and at Corinth. From Oct. '62 until Apr. '63 he was engaged in mustering and disbursing at Jackson (Mich.), and until Sept. '66 he was Acting Asst. Provost Marshal Gen. for Illinois. He was named Col. 6th US Cav. 31 July '66 and breveted Col. and B.G. USA 30 Mar. '65 for his recruiting service.

OAK GROVE, Va., 25 June '62. Known also as Henrico, King's School House, or The Orchards. First of the Seven Days' Battles (PENINSULAR CAMPAIGN). McClellan had moved all of his corps except Porter's V south of the Chickahominy and was preparing to move against Richmond. Heintzelman (III), located at Fair Oaks-Seven Pines, was ordered to drive in the outposts opposite him (Huger's division). At 8 A.M. Hooker's division moved forward led by Sickles' brigade on the Williamsburg road, Grover's on the left, and Carr's in reserve. Kearny, on the left, and Richardson were ordered to push forward their pickets to assist. Hooker was stopped by superior forces and D. B. Birney's brigade (Kearny) was ordered to his support. Gen. Marcy, McClellan's Chief of Staff, arrived on the field and ordered Hooker to withdraw. About 1 P.M. McClellan arrived and ordered the attack renewed. Palmer's brigade (Couch) was sent up to reinforce. DeRussy's battery came forward and with canister drove back the enemy pickets. Federal infantry occupied the evacuated positions but, as it was almost dark, operations were halted. The next day the Confederates seized the initiative at MECHANICSVILLE. There were 626 Federal and 441 Confederate casualties (Fox).

O'BEIRNE, James Rowan. Union officer. Ireland. 2d Lt. 37th N.Y. 9 July '61; 1st Lt. 9 Aug. '61; Capt. Vet. Res. Corps 23 July '63; Maj. 12 May '64; Bvt. B.G. USV 26 Sept. '65 (war service). W.I.A. Chancellorsville in lung, right leg, right knee, forehead, and shot through the body. (FR, OVRC) Medal of Honor 20 Jan. '91 for Fair Oaks (Va.) 31 May–1 June '62. Listed by Phisterer as Beirne, Jas. R.O.

OBLIQUE ORDER. Also referred to in Civil War literature as an echelon or progressive type of attack, it involves attacking with one flank refused so that the other flank makes contact with the enemy first. Generally the plan is to reinforce this advanced wing so as to bring overwhelming strength against the point of the enemy line first encountered, thus crushing this segment of his line and then "rolling up his flank" as successive parts of your own line make contact. Epaminondas achieved his classic victory against a superior Spartan force with this maneuver at Leuctra (371 B.C.) and Frederick the Great used it with spectacular results at Leuthen (1757). Although unsuited for use against an enemy who had any battlefield mobility, Confederate generals displayed a curious predilection to try it. Commenting on the failure of the Confederate attacks on the second day at Gettysburg, Alexander writes: "We had used this method [echelon or progressive order of attack] on four occasions—at Seven Pines, Gaines's Mill, Frazier's [Frayser's] Farm or Glendale, and Malvern Hill—and always with poor success" (Alexander, 393). It was used by Bragg at Chickamauga and by Hood at Peach Tree Creek.

A clue as to its popularity with Civil War generals may possibly be found in Jomini's *Treatise on Grand Military Operations,* which first appeared in 1804 and had great influence. In this Jomini rhapsodizes over the oblique order. (See S. B. Holabird's 1865 translation, New York: Van Nostrand, pp. 257–62.)

O'BRIEN, George Morgan. Union officer. Ireland. Maj. 7th Iowa Cav. 13 July '63; Bvt. B.G. USV (war service). Died 1887.

OCEAN POND, Fla., 20 Feb. '64. See OLUSTEE.

O'DOWD, John. Union officer. Ireland. Capt. 10th Ohio 1 May '61; resigned 13 July '62; Capt. 181st Ohio 6 Oct. '64; Col. 17 Oct. '64; Bvt. B.G. USV (Murfreesboro, Tenn.; war service). Commanded 3, 2, XXIII (Ohio). Died 1869.

OFFICERS, LOYALTY OF REGULAR ARMY. See LOYALTY OF REGULAR ARMY OFFICERS.

OGLESBY, Richard James. Union gen. 1824–99. Ky. He fought in the Mexican War, practiced law, went to Calif. for the gold rush, and served as a Republican legislator before being commissioned Col. 8th Ill. 25 Apr. '61. Mustered out 24 July, he was recommissioned the next day and commanded 2d Brig., Mil. Dist. Cairo 14 Oct. '61–1 Feb. '62. At Forts Henry and Donelson, he commanded 1st Brig., 1st Div. Mil. Dist. Cairo (1–21 Feb. '62) and also led 1st Brig., 1st Div., Army of the Tenn. (17–23 Feb. '62). He was promoted B.G. USV 21 Mar. '62 and then commanded 3, 1st Div. (13–15 Apr. '62) and 2, 2d Div. (15 Apr.–July '62). At Corinth, where he was wounded, he commanded 2d Brig., 2d Div. Dist. Corinth (July–Oct. '62) and was promoted Maj. Gen. USV 29

Nov. '62. Returning from sick leave 1 Apr. '63, he commanded the Left Wing of the XVI Corps, until 7 July '63. He resigned 26 May '64, having been elected Gov. of Ill. During the rest of the war he was an admirer of Lincoln and his policies, but denounced Johnson and demanded his impeachment. He was later U.S. Sen. Called "Uncle Dick," he is characterized as having a bluff, friendly manner with wit and good humor.

49TH OHIO (IV Corps—Cumberland).

Colonels: William H. Gibson (Bvt. B.G.) and Joseph R. Bartlett.

Battles: Shiloh, Stones River, Liberty Gap, Chickamauga, Missionary Ridge, Morristown, Rocky Face Ridge, Pickett's Mills, Kenesaw, Atlanta, Jonesboro, Nashville, Columbia. Present also at Munfordville, Corinth siege, Dog Walk (Ky.), Resaca, Cassville, Lovejoy, Franklin.

Raised in Sept. '61 at Tiffin, the 49th Ohio was the first completely organized regiment to arrive in Kentucky. Assigned to Johnson's brigade, Mc-Cook's division, it went into winter quarters until Mar. '62. It arrived at Shiloh in time to take part in the battle. At Stones River the regiment was in Willich's (1st) brigade, Johnson's (2d) division of McCook's corps. After re-enlisting, the 49th Ohio became part of Gibson's (1st) brigade, Wood's (3d) division, IV Corps.

The regiment went to Tex. with the IV Corps after the battle of Nashville and remained there until mustered out in Dec. '65.

OHIO AND CUMBERLAND, ARMIES OF, NAME CHANGING. What was in effect the same army changed names in a confusing way at different times throughout the war. The following tabulation may be illuminating:

The force of . . .	in Department of . . .	during . . .	was known as the "Army of . . .
Robt. Anderson	Ky., then of the Cumberland	28 May–8 Oct. '61	"the Cumberland."
W. T. Sherman	the Cumberland	8 Oct.–9 Nov. '61	"the Cumberland."
D. C. Buell	the Ohio	Shiloh, Corinth, start of Stones River campaign	"the Ohio."
W. S. Rosecrans	the Ohio	End of Stones R., Chickamauga	"the Cumberland."
Geo. H. Thomas	Mil. Div. of the Miss.	Chattanooga, Atlanta, Franklin and Nashville	"the Cumberland."
J. M. Schofield	Mil. Div. of the Miss., then Dept. of North Carolina	Knoxville, Atlanta, to Carolinas Campaign	"the Ohio."

Granger's "Army of Ky." was part of Rosecrans' Army of the Cumberland, which was located in the Dept. of the Ohio. Buell's Army of the Ohio, after disappearing when its troops became Rosecrans' Army of the Cumberland, reappears as a new Army of the Ohio in Aug. '62. Although the latter was officially designated XXIII Corps, this force was commonly known as Schofield's Army of the Ohio in the Knoxville, Atlanta, and Franklin and Nashville campaigns.

OHIO, UNION DEPARTMENT AND ARMY OF THE. First established 3 May '61, to consist of Ill., Ind., and Ohio. On 9 May its area was extended to include the western third of Pa. and a portion of western Va. On 6 June Mo. was added. Ill. was transferred to the Western Department 3 July. McClellan was in command from 13 May until 23 July, when he was succeeded by Rosecrans. Part of this organization at this time was the Army of Occupation of WEST-(ERN) VIRGINIA. On 19 Sept. '61 the department was changed to consist of Ohio, Ind., and "so much of Kentucky as lies within 15 miles of Cincinnati." Brig. Gen. O. M. Mitchel was in command, with headquarters at Cincinnati, until 15 Nov. '61. The same order put Rosecrans in command of the new Department of WESTERN VIRGINIA. On 9 Nov. '61 there was another reorganization: the department now consisted of Ohio, Mich., Ind., and Ky. east of the Cumberland River; headquarters was at Louisville. This is the Army of the Ohio associated with Buell, who commanded it 15 Nov. '61–11 Mar. '62. The department was abolished 11 Mar. '62, when it was merged with the Mountain Dept. and Halleck's Dept. of Miss. Buell's force, however, continued to be called the Army of the Ohio (under which designation it fought at Shiloh,

6–7 Apr.) until 24 Oct. when another reorganization re-created the Dept. of the Cumberland. On this latter date Buell was replaced by Rosecrans and the Army of the Ohio was officially redesignated XIV Corps; however, to add to the confusion, it then started calling itself the "Army of the Cumberland," a name the original portions of it had used under Anderson and Sherman (Van Horne, I, 207). The Dept. of the Ohio was revived 19 Aug. '62 (Stones River campaign). Its area included Ill., Ind., Ohio, Mich., Wis. (until 6 Sept.), and Ky. east of the Tennessee River, including Cumberland Gap. Headquarters were at Cincinnati. Maj. Gen. H. G. Wright was in command from 25 Aug. '62 to 25 Mar. '63. Troops of the department were at this time scattered through many districts. Some of its brigades constituted Granger's so-called Army of Ky. which distinguished itself at Chickamauga. Burnside, who had arrived with his IX Corps from the east, assumed command of the department 25 Mar. '63 and on 27 Apr. the troops therein were organized into the XXIII Corps. It is the latter force that became known as Schofield's Army of the Ohio in the Knoxville, Atlanta, and Franklin and Nashville campaigns. Department commanders after Burnside were the following major generals: J. G. Foster, 11 Dec. '63–9 Feb. '64; J. M. Schofield to 17 Nov. '64; George Stoneman to 17 Jan. '65, when the department was annexed to the Dept. of the Cumberland. The XXIII Corps was transferred to the Dept. of N.C. in Feb. '65, with the exception of the 4th and 5th divisions, which went to the Dept. of the Cumberland. (When sources have conflicted on facts about the Dept. and Army of the Ohio, I have accepted the version of Dyer,

254.) (See also OHIO AND CUMBERLAND, ARMIES OF, NAME CHANGING.)

OKOLONA, Ark., 3 Apr. '64. Skirmish during Steele's Arkansas campaign.

OKOLONA, Miss., 21–22 Feb. '64. Forrest routed forces of Sooy Smith. See WEST POINT, Miss., 21 Feb.

O'LAUGHLIN, Michael. See LINCOLN'S ASSASSINATION and Dr. Samuel MUDD.

OLD ABE. Nickname for Abraham LINCOLN and also for the live eagle mascot of the 8th Wis.

OLD CAPITOL PRISON. Used mainly for prisoners of war, deserters, suspected spies, and persons awaiting trial, the Washington PRISON was housed in a temporary and hastily-built substitute for the US Capitol burned by the British in the War of 1812. It was later used as a hotel but had fallen on evil days and was dilapidated and run down when pressed into use by the Federals.

OLD CHURCH, Va., 30 May '64. Cavalry action at TOTOPOTOMOY CREEK.

OLDEN, Charles Smith. Gov. of N.J. 1799–1876. N.J. A merchant in Philadelphia and New Orleans, he was treasurer of Princeton College before being elected legislator. He was chosen Gov. by the Republicans in 1859 and attended the Washington Peace Conference in the winter of 1861. His term ended in 1863, and he was later a judge.

OLD FORT WAYNE, Indian Territory, 22 Oct. '62. Gen. J. G. Blunt led a pursuit of Gen. Douglas Cooper's (Confederate) Indian brigade into Indian Territory after NEWTONIA. He defeated them, captured their artillery, and scattered them after inflicting 150 casualties with a loss of 14 Federals.

OLD FUSS AND FEATHERS. Nickname for Winfield SCOTT, referring to his love of military pageantry, show uniforms, and meticulousness in military procedure and etiquette.

OLD SACRAMENTO. Mexican War cannon captured by A. W. Doniphan at Sacramento, Calif., and used by the Confederates at Carthage, Wilson's Creek, Lexington, and lost at Pea Ridge (Monaghan).

OLD SORREL. The horse, who was about 11 years old when the war began, was acquired by Jackson in May '61 at Harpers Ferry. He was riding the animal when shot at Chancellorsville, and Old Sorrel was venerated by the South for years after the war.

OLD TOWN CREEK, Miss. TUPELO, Miss., 13–15 July '64.

OLEY, John H. Union officer. N.Y. Maj. 7th W. Va. Cav. 29 Oct. '61; Lt. Col. 2 Oct. '62; Col. 1 Mar. '63; Bvt. B.G. USV (W. Va. and Shenandoah Valley campaigns). Commanded in W. Va.: 3d Brig., 4th Div.; 1st Brig., 2d Cav. Div.; 3d Brig., 2d Cav. Div.; 1st Separate Brig., Dist. Kanawha.

OLIPHANT, Samuel Duncan. Union officer. c. 1826–? Pa. Capt. 8th Pa. Res. 24 Apr. '61; Lt. Col. 28 June '61; discharged 29 Dec. '62; Maj. Vet. Res. Corps 9 June '63; Lt. Col. 28 Sept. '63; Col. 4 Dec. '63; Bvt. B.G. USV 27 June '65. It is stated in FR, OVRC that he was "suffering from paralysis" in 1865 after participating in the battles of Mechanicsville, Gaines's Mill, White Oak Swamp, and Malvern Hill.

OLIVER, John Morrison. Union gen. 1827–72. N.Y. A druggist and court recorder, he joined the Union Army as 1st Lt. 4th Mich. 20 June '61 and was promoted Capt. 25 Sept. '61. He was named Col. 15th Mich. 13 Mar. '62 and won a commendation from Gen. McCook for his "conspicuous bravery and efficient service" at Shiloh. He commanded 1st Brig., 6th Div., Army Tenn., temporarily in Apr. '62 and 2d Brig., 6th Div., Army Tenn., 20 Apr.–24 July '62. In the XV Corps, Army of Tenn., he led: 2, 4 (5 Aug.–25 Oct. '63); 3, 4 (6 May–4 Aug. '64); 1, 4 (4 Aug.–14 Sept. '64); 3, 2 (2 Nov. '64–18 May '65) and 2d Div. (18 May–1 Aug. '65). He was promoted B.G. USV 12 Jan. '65, breveted Maj. Gen. USV (war service) and mustered out 24 Aug. '65. Remaining in Little Rock, the scene of his last command, he practiced law and served as tax assessor before Grant appointed him to the Southwest Postal Service.

OLIVER, Paul Ambrose. Union officer. 1830–1912. Born in the English Channel aboard his father's ship. 2d Lt. 12th N.Y. 29 Oct. '61; 1st Lt. 17 May '62; Capt. 22 Apr. '64; transferred to 5th N.Y. 1 June '64; Bvt. B.G. USV 8 Mar. '65; Medal of Honor 12 Oct. '92 for "while being in charge of a brig[ade] assist[ing] in preventing a disaster caused by Union troops firing into each other at Resaca (Ga.) 15 May '64" (Heitman). (See also TREMAIN, Henry Edwin.) The other brigade was commanded by Benjamin Harrison, and the medal was awarded during his term of office. Oliver had studied German military science when a boy in Altona (Germany) and in his first company perfected a German bayonet drill that favorably impressed his superior officers and led to his being A.D.C. to Gens. Butterfield, Meade, Hooker, and Warren. In the cotton export trade before the war, he later invented explosive formulas and machines for their manufacture. He is generally credited with the invention of dynamite and black powder (D.A.B.). His factory in the Pa. anthracite coal area was purchased by Du Pont, and he retired a wealthy man.

OLMSTED, William Adams. Union officer. N.Y. Capt. 2d N.Y. 14 May '61; Lt. Col. 27 July '61; mustered out 26 May '63; Col. 59th N.Y. 3 Nov. '64; Bvt. B.G. USV 9 Apr. '65 (campaign ending with the surrender of R. E. Lee). Other brevets for Malvern Hill, Fredericksburg, Hatcher's Run (Va.). In R.A. until resignation in 1869 as 1st Lt. Commanded 1, 2, II (Potomac).

OLUSTEE (Ocean Pond), Fla., 20 Feb. '64. On 7 Feb. Truman Seymour's division of X Corps landed at Jacksonville, Fla., to secure it as a base. Meeting no opposition, he marched 20 miles inland to Baldwin where on the 9th he was joined by Gillmore. About 3 P.M. on the 20th the cavalry brigade of Guy V. Henry made contact and, with a loss of 25, drove Confederate outposts back to the main body of troops commanded by Joseph Finegan. The 7th N.H. had just deployed for an attack when it was itself hit and routed. The 8th US Col. Inf., in the same area, also broke and fled when its colonel was killed. The 54th Mass. Col. Inf. occupied this position and held until dark. Seymour then withdrew with heavy losses, including 6 guns and 39 horses. According to Livermore, Seymour had 5,115 effectives, of which he lost 1,861 (203 killed, 1,152 wounded, 506 missing). The Confederates lost 934 killed and wounded out of 5,200 engaged.

O'NEAL, Edward Asbury. C.S.A. gen. 1818–90. Ala. A lawyer and politician, he advocated secession and enlisted in 1861. Elected Maj. 9th Ala. in Oct., he was promoted Lt. Col. 26th Ala. in the spring of 1862. He led his regiment on the Peninsula, being wounded at Seven Pines. He was also wounded at Boonsboro during the Md. campaign and, taking over Rodes's brigade at Chancellorsville, was wounded a third time. At Gettysburg he commanded his own brigade in Rodes's division and was sent to Alabama early in 1864 to recruit and reorganize. He had been appointed B.G. C.S.A. 6 June '63 to rank from the same date, but this was canceled by Davis. Sent to Dalton, he commanded his regiment in the beginning of the Atlanta campaign and took over Cantey's brigade at Marietta and Peach Tree Creek. After this last battle he was relieved from command and served on detached duty. At war's end he was in Ala. arresting deserters from the Army of Tenn. During the Reconstruction era he was a Democratic leader and Gov. of Ala. in 1882-86. His term marked the turning point toward normalcy and prosperity.

OOSTENAULA, Ga. RESACA, 13-16 May '64.

OPDYCKE, Emerson. Union gen. 1830-84. Ohio. Entering the Army as 1st Lt. 41st Ohio 26 Aug. '61, he was Capt. (9 Jan. '62) at Shiloh, when he carried the colors of his regiment and led a charge. Resigning 17 Sept. '62, he was named Lt. Col. 125th Ohio 1 Oct. '62 and Col. 14 Jan. '63. He led a demi-brigade at Chattanooga, and his troops were among the first to reach the crest of Missionary Ridge. He had this same command at Chickamauga, Rocky Face Ridge, Resaca (where he was wounded), and Kenesaw Mountain. Commanding 1, 2, IV, Cumberland (4 Aug. '64-15 Feb. '65 and 15 Mar.-7 June '65), he was credited by Thomas for saving the day at FRANKLIN by leading his brigade without orders from reserve into a gap made by Hood's assault. He also commanded 2d Div., IV Corps, Cumberland (24 June-11 July '65). Later in the wholesale dry-goods business in N.Y.C. He wrote many articles about the Civil War.

OPDYCKE'S BRIGADE. See STEED-MAN's — KIMBALL's — OPDYCKE's BRIGADE.

OPEQUON, Va., 19 Sept. '64. WINCHESTER, same date.

ORCHARD KNOB—INDIAN HILL, 23 Oct. '63. See CHATTANOOGA CAMPAIGN.

ORCHARDS (THE), Va., 25 June '62. OAK GROVE.

ORD, Edward Otho Cresap. Union gen. 1818-83. Md. Appt. D.C. USMA 1839 (17/31); Arty. In the Seminole War, on the frontier in Indian fighting, and in the expedition to suppress John Brown at Harpers Ferry in 1859. Named B.G. USV 14 Sept. '61 (from Capt. 3d U.S. Arty. since 1850), he commanded 3d Brig., McCall's division, Potomac (3 Oct. '61-13 Mar. '62) in the defenses of Washington and at Dranesville (Va.). He then commanded 3, 2, I, Potomac (13 Mar.-4 Apr. '62); 3, 2d Div., Rappahannock (4 Apr.-16 May '62) and Ord's division, Rappahannock (16 May-10 June '62), having been promoted Maj. Gen. USV 2 May '62. In the Army of the Tenn. he commanded 2d Div. (2 June-5 Aug. '62); 2d Div. Dist. Corinth (July-5 Aug. '62) and Dist. Jackson (24 Sept.-5 Oct. '62) at Corinth and Hatchie, where he was severely wounded. During the Vicksburg campaign and at Jackson he led the XIII Corps (19 June-28 July '63) and then commanded that corps in the Dept. of the Gulf (15 Sept.-19 Oct. '63 and 9 Jan.-20 Feb. '64). At Fort Harrison, where he was again wounded, he commanded the XVIII Corps, Va. N.C. (21 July-4 Sept. and 22-29 Sept. '64). During the siege of Petersburg and the Appomattox campaign he commanded the XXIV Corps (3-6 Dec. '64) and the Dept. of Va. (31 Jan.-May '65). Breveted for Dranesville, Iuka, Hatchie (B.G. USA) and Fort Harrison (Maj.

Gen. USA), he continued in the R.A., retiring as B.G. in 1880 and being put on the retired list in 1881 as Maj. Gen.

ORDER OF AMERICAN KNIGHTS. See KNIGHTS OF THE GOLDEN CIRCLE.

ORDER OF BATTLE. Although defined in the official army dictionary as "the manner in which military forces are organized and disposed," the term can have two rather different connotations. 1. It can mean a tabulation of organizations participating in an action; in B.&L. this information appears under the heading of "Opposing Forces," and in the O.R. as "Organization." 2. It can also mean "the general or geometrical disposition of troops for battle" (G.&B.). In Civil War literature the term will always be used in the latter sense, but in modern military writings (including this book) it will usually mean the former.

ORDINANCE OF SECESSION. Meeting at Charleston 20 Dec. '60, a special convention passed the ordinance by unanimous vote of its 169 members. This declared that the ratification of the Constitution of the US in 1788 "is hereby repealed and the Union now subsisting between South Carolina and the other states, under the name of the United States of America, is hereby dissolved." See also SECESSION SEQUENCE AND DATES.

ORDNANCE GUN (3-inch). Sometimes called the Rodman rifle (Weller, 34), this gun was developed by the US Ord. Dept. in 1863. The 10-pounder Parrotts, originally 2.9-inch caliber, were modified to take the same ammunition as the ordnance gun. Both guns were accurate, had an extreme range of over 4,000 yards, and were favored by the horse artillery.

ORDWAY, Albert. Union officer. 1843–97. Mass. Pvt. 4th Bn. Mass. Mil.

19 Apr. '61; 1st Lt. 24th Mass. 2 Sept. '61; Capt. 5 July 64; Maj. 21 Nov. '64; Lt. Col. 6 Apr. '65; Col. 7 May '65; Bvt. B.G. USV (war service). A.D.C. to Henry Prince at New Bern (N.C.). P.M.G. of Va. after the war. Moved to Washington and was commander of the D.C. National Guard at death.

OREGON, UNION DEPARTMENT OF. In existence before the start of the war with headquarters at Vancouver, it had included the area of the present states of Wash., Ida., and all of Ore. except the southwestern corner (which had been in the Dept. of Calif.). Merged 1 Jan. '61 into the newly-created Dept. of the Pacific.

O'REILLY, Private Miles. Pen name of Charles Graham HALPINE.

ORGANIZATION. The land forces of the North and South were divided into "territorial organizations" and "operational organizations."

"Military posts, territorial districts, territorial departments, and territorial divisions belong to the first [category]," writes Fiebeger, "infantry and cavalry divisions, army corps, and field armies belong to the second" (*Army Organization,* 1917).

The *departments* comprised the basic and best-known territorial subdivisions of the Union forces, and they generally gave their names to the field army operating within its boundaries and under the same commander. The subject of Federal territorial organization has been well covered in Thian's *Military Geography of the United States*–1813–1880 (Washington: G.P.O., 1881). It is also covered to some extent in Dyer and Phisterer. These Federal territorial organizations and their field forces, of which there are over 60 indexed in the *Official Records,* are all to be found alphabetically in this book.

Confederate territorial organizations

have not had a Thian, and information as to their limits, commanders, dates of formation, and discontinuance must be patched together from various sources. About 56 of them, including some duplication due to variations in names, are indexed in the O.R. The latter source also gives dates on which their various commanders were assigned and assumed their duties. From this data I have compiled brief sketches of each, although these are not so satisfactory or so accurate as the comparable information on the Union organizations. For an alphabetical list, see DEPARTMENT. The atlas of the O.R. also has a series of plates showing the boundaries and the names of these organizations—Federal and Confederate.

ARMIES were the largest of the "operational organizations." In the case of the Federal forces, these generally took their name from their department. "The Federals followed a general policy of naming their armies for the rivers near which they operated; the Confederates named theirs from the states or regions in which they were active. Thus the Federals had an Army of *the* Tennessee —not to be confused with the Confederate Army of Tennessee" (Horn, 450). Actually, it would appear that the armies took their names from the *departments* in which they operated (or were originally formed), and these departments took their names from *rivers* in the case of the Federals and from *states or regions* in the case of the Confederates. There were no firm rules on this matter of names, however: there was a Confederate Army of the Potomac; and the Confederate Army of (the) Mississippi is referred to in the *Official Records* about as often with "the" as without. These armies, of which there were at least 16 on the Union side and 23 on the Confederate

side, are listed under ARMIES and also will be found in proper alphabetical sequence in this book.

CORPS were composed of two or more divisions. Standard organization on the Union side was 45 infantry regiments and nine batteries of light artillery. There were about five regiments to a brigade, about three brigades to a division, and about three divisions in a corps. The South did not adopt the corps organization until 6 Nov. '62. See CORPS for sketches of Federal and Confederate corps.

Divisions were formed of two or more brigades. At Chancellorsville the Federal divisions averaged 6,200 and the Confederate divisions 8,700 officers and men.

Brigades were made up of two or more regiments and two or more brigades comprised a division. At Chancellorsville, according to Bigelow, Federal brigades averaged 4.7 regiments and about 2,000 men, while on the Confederate side they averaged 4.5 regiments and about 1,850 men. Northern brigades were officially designated by number within their division. In the western armies, however, this convention was not adopted until 1863. Nelson's 4th Div., Army of the Ohio, at Shiloh was composed of the 10th, 19th, and 22d brigades. Sheridan's 11th Div. at Perryville was composed of the 35th, 36th, and 37th brigades. In this book brigades are designated by a series of three numbers to show the division and corps to which they belong: (3, 1, IV), signifies "3d Brig. of the 1st Div. of the IV Corps."

Confederate brigades were known by the names of their commanders or former commanders, a much less prosaic system than that of the Federals, but a very confusing one. For example, the unit of "Pickett's Charge" at Gettysburg shown in Steele's *American*

Campaigns as "McGowan's Brigade" was commanded by Pettigrew until 1 July '62 and then by Marshall. In this attack Pettigrew is commanding "Heth's Division," Trimble is commanding "Pender's Division," Mayo is commanding "Brockenbrough's Brigade," Marshall is commanding "McGowan's" or "Pettigrew's Brigade," Fry is commanding "Archer's Brigade," and Lowrance is commanding "Scales's Brigade."

Infantry regiments were composed of 10 companies, except in the case of the 12-company heavy artillery regiments that had been retrained as infantry. Cavalry regiments also had 12 companies. These companies were lettered in alphabetical order, with the letter "J" omitted. (There has been much erroneous theorizing as to why the US Army has never had a J Company. See Boatner, 88–89.) Battalions did not exist in the infantry regiments, but the "heavies" were composed of three four-company battalions, each commanded by a major.

Confederate regiments were organized in generally the same manner as the Federal, although some had battalions (e.g., the 55th Ala.) and the 7th Ala. had two cavalry companies initially (C.M.H., VII, 78).

In the Union Army an infantry company had a maximum authorized strength of 101 officers and men, and a minimum strength of 83. The company was allowed to recruit a minimum of 64 or a maximum of 82 privates. Other company positions were fixed as follows: one captain, one first lieutenant, one second lieutenant, one first sergeant, four sergeants, eight corporals, two musicians, and one wagoner. Company officers were elected in most volunteer units.

As Schiebert, the Prussian observer, points out, this was the only possible way of getting rapidly the large number of troop leaders needed. By the second year of the war a system of examinations was instituted by both armies, and incompetent officers could be eliminated (Schiebert, 39–40).

Regimental headquarters consisted of a colonel, lieutenant colonel, major, adjutant, quartermaster, surgeon (major), two assistant surgeons, and a chaplain. Regimental headquarters noncommissioned officers were the sergeant major, quartermaster sergeant, commissary sergeant, hospital steward, and two principal musicians. Authorized strength of an infantry regiment was a maximum of 1,025 and a minimum of 845. Since it was the Civil War practice to organize recruits into new regiments rather than to send them to replace losses in veteran units, regimental strengths steadily declined. According to Fiebeger the average company strength at Gettysburg was 32 officers and men per company. Livermore gives these average regimental strengths in the Union army at various periods: Shiloh, 560; Fair Oaks, 650; Chancellorsville, 530; Gettysburg, 375; Chickamauga and the Wilderness, 440; and in Sherman's battles of May '64, 305. According to Bigelow the average strength of Federal regiments at Chancellorsville was 433 and of Confederate regiments 409.

The North raised the equivalent of 2,047 regiments during the war of which 1,696 were infantry, 272 were cavalry, and 78 were artillery. Allowing for the fact that nine infantry regiments of the Regular Army had 24 instead of the normal 10 companies, the total number of regiments would come to about 2,050, not including the Veteran Reserve Corps. (Above figures from Phisterer, 23.) According to the computations of Fox, made before the *Official Records* had all been published, the South raised the equivalent of 764 regiments that served all or most of the war. Using later data, and including militia and other irregular organizations, Col. Henry Stone estimated an equivalent of 1,009½ Confederate regiments. (For exhaustive study of Confederate strengths see Livermore.)

ORME, William Ward. Union gen. 1832–66. D.C. A lawyer and politician, he was appointed Col. 94th Ill. 20 Aug. '62. Commanding 2d Brig., 3d Div., Army of Frontier, Mo. (12 Oct.–Dec. '62), he was promoted B.G. USV 29 Nov. He also led 2d, Herron's division, XIII, Tenn. (11 June–28 July '63) and 2, 2, XIII, Gulf (28 July–7 Aug. '63). Resigning 26 Apr. '64, he was afterward with the Treasury.

OSBAND, Embury D. Union officer. N.Y. Capt. 4th Ill. Cav. 26 Sept. '61; Col. 3d US Col. Cav. 10 Oct. '63; Bvt. B.G. USV 5 Oct. '64 (war service). Commanded in Tenn.: Cav. Brig.; Dist. Vicksburg; 3d Brig., Cav. Div. West Tenn.; Cav. Div. West Tenn. Died 1866.

OSBORN, Francis Augustus. Union officer. Mass. Capt. 4th Bn. Mass. Mil. 20 Apr. '61; Lt. Col. 24th Mass. 31 Aug. '61; Col. 1 Jan. '63; Bvt. B.G. USV (New Market, Va.); mustered out 14 Nov. '64. Commanded 3, 2, X (Va. and N.C.).

OSBORN, Thomas Ogden. Union gen. 1832–1904. Ohio. After Ohio Univ. he read law in Lew Wallace's offices and practiced in Chicago. Commissioned Lt. Col. 39th Ill. 11 Oct. '61 and promoted Col. 1 Jan. '62, he led his regiment at Fort Wagner in July, where he was W.I.A. In the XVIII Corps he commanded 3, 2, Div. St. Helena Island (Jan.–Apr. '63); 2, Morris Island (19 Sept.–12 Oct. '63); and 1, 3 (6 Jan.–Feb. '63). His right elbow was shattered while leading his regiment at Drewry's Bluff 12–16 May '64, and during his convalescence he campaigned for Lincoln's re-election, speaking in Mich., Ill.,

and Ind. He commanded 1, 1, XXIV, Va. (12 Dec. '64–2 May '65 at Fort Gregg and 8–25 July '65) as well as 1st Div., XXIV, Va. from 2 May until 8 July '65. Promoted B.G. USV 1 May '65, he resigned on 28 Sept. '65 after being breveted B.G. USV 10 Mar. '65 and Maj. Gen. USV 2 Apr. '65 for the campaign before Richmond and Petersburg. He held several public offices and was Minister to Argentina 1874–85.

OSTERHAUS, Peter Joseph. Union gen. 1823–1917. Prussia. After graduating from military school in Berlin and serving in the infantry, he emigrated to the US in 1848 and became a merchant and bookkeeper in Mo. Commissioned Maj. Battalion of Mo. Inf. 27 Apr. '61, he was mustered out 27 Aug., having fought at Wilson's Creek, and was commissioned Col. 12th Mo. 19 Dec. of the same year. At Pea Ridge he commanded 2d Brig., Army Southwest Mo. (Jan.–Apr. '62) and also led 1st Brig., 1st Div. Army Southwest Mo. (Feb.–May '62). Appointed B.G. USV 9 June '62, he next commanded 3d Div., Army Southwest Mo. (May–Dec. '62) and 1st Brig., 1st Div. Dist. East Ark. (Dec. '62). During the Vicksburg campaign he commanded 9th Div., XIII, Tenn. (4 Jan.–28 July '63) and was wounded at the Big Black River. At Missionary Ridge he commanded 1st Div., XV, Tenn. (1 Sept. '63–4 Jan. '64) and later (6 Feb.–15 July and 19 Aug.–24 Sept. '64), and was named Maj. Gen. USV 23 July '64. He led the XV Corps, Tenn. (23 Sept. '64–8 Jan. '65), was Chief of Staff of the Mil. Div. West Miss. (8 Jan.–27 May '65), and was mustered out in 1866. From 1866 until 1877 he was Consul to France and then served as vice- and deputy-consul at Mannheim, Germany, 1898–1900.

OTIS, Calvin Nicholas. Union officer. N.Y. Maj. 100th N.Y. 10 Jan. '62; Lt.

Col. 6 Nov. '62; Bvt. B.G. USV (war service); resigned 20 June '63. Died 1883.

OTIS, Elwell Stephen. Union officer. 1838–1909. Md. R.A. Capt. 140th N.Y. 13 Sept. '62; Lt. Col. 23 Dec. '63; W.I.A. Petersburg 1 Oct. '64; Bvt. B.G. USV. Brevets for Spotsylvania (2), Chapel House (Va.) Commanded 1, 2, V (Potomac). As Lt. Col. he took part in several Indian campaigns, including Little Big Horn in 1876 and 1877. Organized and commanded (1880–85) School of Application for Infantry and Cavalry at Fort Leavenworth, forerunner of today's Army Command and General Staff College. Commanded Dept. of the Columbia 1893–97 as B.G. USA; Maj. Gen. USV 1898, when he went to the Philippines and became Mil. Gov.; Maj. Gen. USA 1900, when he was succeeded by Arthur MAC-ARTHUR. Retired 1902.

OTIS, John L. Although listed by Phisterer as Col. 10th Conn. and Bvt. B.G. USV 13 Mar. '65, he does not appear in either Heitman or Dyer.

OUR AMERICAN COUSIN. Play by Tom Taylor, starring Laura Keene, was presented the night Lincoln was shot at Ford's Theater in Washington. See John Wilkes BOOTH.

OWEN, Joshua Thomas. Union gen. 1821–87. Wales. Coming to America as a young man, he established the Chestnut Hill Academy for Boys in Philadelphia with his brother and was later a lawyer and legislator. He was named Col. 24th Pa. 8 May '61 and mustered out 10 Aug. Then he was Col. 69th Pa. 18 Aug. '61 and B.G. USV 29 Nov. '62. His appointment expired 4 Mar. '63 and he was renamed B.G. USV 30 Mar. Fighting in all the battles of the Army of the Potomac from Fair Oaks to Cold Harbor, he commanded in the II Corps: 3d Brig., 3d Div. (15 Aug.–14 Dec. '63 and 4 Jan.–10 Feb. '64); 3d Div. (15 Aug.–6 Sept. '63, 14 Dec. '63–4 Jan. '64 and 10 Feb.–25 Mar. '64); 2d Brig., 2d Div. (10–30 July '62, 17 Sept. '62, 12 Nov. '62–26 Jan. '63, 7 Feb.–1 Apr. '63, 11 Apr.–28 June '63, 25 Apr.–12 June '64); and 2d Div. (1 Apr.–11 Apr. '63). He was mustered out 18 July '64.

OZBURN, Lyndorf. Union officer. Phisterer lists him as being Col. 31st Ill., Bvt. B.G. USV 13 Mar. '65. There is no record of him in Heitman. Dyer lists Ozborn, L., as commander of the 2d Brig., Dist. Jackson, Army of the Tenn.

P

PACIFIC, UNION DEPARTMENT OF THE. Created 1 Jan. '61 by consolidation of the former Dept. of Ore. and Calif. Headquarters at San Francisco. Between 27 July '61 and 17 Feb. '65 it included the area of the former Dept. of Utah. Bvt. Brig. Gen. Albert Sidney Johnston was in command until 25 Apr. '61. Succeeding commanders were Brig. Gen. E. V. Sumner (25 Apr.–30 Oct. '61), Col. George Wright (until 1 July '64), and Maj. Gen. Irvin McDowell (until 27 June '65).

PACKARD, Jasper. Union officer. 1832–99. Ohio. Pvt. 48th Ind. 24 Oct. '61; 1st Lt. 48th Ind. 1 Jan. '62; Capt. 12 Sept. '62; Lt. Col. 128th Ind. 17 Mar. '64; Col. 26 June '65; Bvt. B.G. USV (war service). W.I.A. Vicksburg assault. He was prominent in Ind. as a newspaper editor and legislator.

P. A. C. S. Provisional Army of the Confederate States, corresponding roughly to the USV (United States Volunteers) as distinguished from the Regular Army. Note: The regular Confederate Army, although prescribed on paper, never actually came into existence.

PAGE, Charles Anderson. WAR CORRESPONDENT. 1838-73. Ill. After graduating from college and editing an Iowa weekly, he was working as clerk in Washington when the *Tribune* hired him as a part-time correspondent and sent him to the front during the Seven Days' Battles. His dispatches were so good that he was given a by-line: C.A.P., an honor rarely given by the *Tribune*. When the reporters were banned, he joined Pope's army as a hospital attendant. During the Gettysburg campaign he had had to return to his regular job but was soon put on as a regular correspondent. His reputation for accuracy caused Greeley to say, "If Page says that, it is so." He was appointed Consul in Zurich in 1865 and then went into the evaporated-milk business in Switzerland. Died a few years later in London.

PAGE, Richard Lucian. C.S.A. gen. 1807-1901. Va. A nephew of Robert E. Lee, he served in the navy until the Civil War, when he became Gov. Letcher's A.D.C. and was assigned to naval organization. He supervised fortifications at the mouth of the James and along the Nansemond River and Pagan Creek. On 10 June '61 he was named commander of the C.S.A. Navy and was ordnance officer at Norfolk. Then appointed Capt., he was in charge of the Charlotte, N.C., depot for two years and was listed as B.G. C.S.A. 1 Mar. '64. In that capacity he commanded the outer defenses of Mobile Bay and was captured at Fort Morgan 23 Aug. '64. Settling in Norfolk, he was in business and active in civic work.

PAINE, Charles Jackson. Union gen. 1833-1916. Mass. A lawyer after Harvard, he was commissioned Capt. 22d Mass. 5 Oct. '61, Maj. 30th Mass. 16 Jan. '62, and mustered out 27 Mar. '62. Named Col. 2d La. 23 Oct. '62, he commanded 1, 1, XIX, Gulf (27 May–11 July '63) at Port Hudson and was discharged 8 Mar. '64. He was then promoted B.G. USV 4 July '64 and commanded 3d Div., XVIII, James (3 Aug.–14 Oct. '64 at New Market and 3 Nov.–3 Dec. '64). He also led 1st Div., XXV, James (3–31 Dec. '64); 3d Div., XXV, James (31 Dec. '64–6 Jan. '65); Paine's division, Terry's Prov. Corps, N.C. (6 Jan.–27 Mar. '65) at Fort Fisher and 3d Div., X, N.C. (27 Mar.–6 July '65). He was breveted Maj. Gen. USV 15 Jan. '65 for war service and mustered out the next year, engaging in railroad building and development. A wealthy man, he was a skillful yachtsman who defended the America's Cup several times. D.A.B. says, ". . . an unpretentious man, avoiding any kind of display. The old straw hat and plain garb in which he sailed his cup defenders were often contrasted with the elaborate costumes of less famous and less wealthy owners . . . his unobtrusiveness may have contributed to an underestimation of his ability and achievement."

PAINE, Eleazer A. Union gen. 1815-82. Ohio. USMA 1839 (24/31); Inf. He served in the Fla. war on Gen. Taylor's staff and resigned in 1840, becoming a lawyer and a politician. Active in the Ohio militia, he was B.G. from 1845 until 1848. Commissioned Col. 9th Ill. 26 July '61, he was named B.G. USV on 3 Sept. From Jan. to Feb. '62 he commanded 3d Brig., 1st Div. Mil. Dist. Cairo and then led the 4th Div., Army Miss. (4 Mar.–24 Apr. '62) at New Madrid, Island No. 10, Fort Pillow, and Memphis. He then commanded 1st Div., Army Miss. (24 Apr.–15 July and 15–30 Aug. '62) and the Dist. of West Ky., guarding railroads and commanding the Dist. of West Tenn. during the rest of the war. He resigned 5 Apr. '62 and engaged in business after the war. Cousin of Halbert E. Paine.

PAINE, Halbert Eleazer. Union gen. 1826–1905. Ohio. After Western Reserve College he was Carl Schurz's law partner, but in 1861 "turned the key in his office and joined the army" (D.A.B.). As Col. 4th Wis. 2 July '61 and on his way to the front, he was offered in Harrisburg a stock train for his men. He refused to put them in cattle cars and, arming the regiment with pickaxes, stopped the next suitable train that came down the tracks and ordered his men aboard. Promoted B.G. USV 13 Mar. '63, he commanded 2, 3, XIX, Gulf (3 Jan.–14 June '63) during the siege of Port Hudson, where he lost a leg. Described as an idealist and a crusader, he had his own ideas of how to run a war, refusing to return "contrabands," and declining to obey Butler's orders to burn Baton Rouge He later served on boards and commissions and as commander of the military district of Ill. Resigning 15 May '65 after being breveted Maj. Gen. USV for Port Hudson 27 May '63, he was a Radical Republican in the House. A practical politician, he was chairman of the committee on contested elections and was "sometimes forced to answer Thaddeus Stevens' question 'Which is *our* rascal?' " (D.A.B.) Later commissioner of patents at Schurz's instigation, he instituted a number of beneficial changes, among them the use of typewriters by the office clerks and the use of drawn plans rather than scaled working models.

PAINE, Lewis. See LINCOLN'S ASSASSINATION.

PAINTER, William. Union officer. Pa. Capt. Asst. Q.M. Vols. 31 Oct. '61; Maj. Add. A.D.C. 16 June '62; Lt. Col. Q.M. Assigned 7 July '63–29 Mar. '64; Bvt. B.G. USV (war service); resigned 14 Sept. '64. Died 1884.

PALFREY, Francis Winthrop. Union officer. 1831–89. Mass. 1st Lt. 4th Bn. Mass. Mil. 20 Apr. '61; Lt. Col. 20th Mass. 19 July '61; Col. 24 Jan. '63; Bvt. B.G. USV (Antietam, war service); resigned 13 Apr. '63. W.I.A. Nelson's Farm 30 June '62 and at Antietam severely in the shoulder. The son of an active anti-slave author and emancipation advocate, he was a graduate of Harvard College and Law School. After the war he wrote several books on military subjects.

PALFREY, John Carver. Union officer. c. 1834–1906. Mass. USMA 1857 (1/38); Engrs. After engineering assignments in New England he was in the defenses of Hampton Roads and promoted 1st Lt. 3 Aug. '61. He worked in the Mississippi River fortifications and was A.D.C. to Phelps and Butler. For the remainder of the war he was in charge of the construction and repairs of the defenses around New Orleans and also participated in the siege of Port Hudson, the Red River campaign, and the Mobile campaign. Continuing in the R.A., he was breveted for Forts Gaines and Morgan, Mobile, and war service (B.G. USA 26 Mar. '65) before resigning in 1866. He then engaged in running mill works and was an overseer of the Engineering School at Dartmouth.

PALMER, Innis Newton. Union gen. 1824–1900. N.Y. USMA 1846 (38/59); Mtd. Rifles-Cav. After serving in the Mexican War (2 brevets, 1 wound), on the frontier, and on exploration expeditions, he was promoted Maj. 2d US Cav. 25 Apr. '61 and commanded the

R.A. cavalry at 1st Bull Run. Transferring to the 5th US Cav. 3 Aug. '61, he was named B.G. USV 23 Sept. and commanded 3, Casey's division, Potomac (Dec. '61–Mar. '62). At Yorktown, Williamsburg, and Fair Oaks, he led 3, 3, IV (13 Mar.–7 June '62) and at Glendale and Malvern Hill he led 1, 1, IV (7 June–26 July '62). He commanded the XVIII Corps in N.C. (18 July–18 Aug. '63) and the defenses of New Bern (14 Aug.–7 Oct. '63 and 7 Nov. '63 to 15 Jan. '64). He also led the Dist. of N.C., Va. and N.C. (4 Jan.–5 Feb. '64, 28 Apr. '64–31 Jan. '65); the Sub.-Dist. of New Bern (9 Feb.–27 June '65); the Dept. of N.C. (31 Jan.–9 Feb. '65); Sub-Dist. of Beaufort (25 Feb.–1 Mar. '65); and 1st Div. Beaufort (1–18 Mar. '65). Breveted for 1st Bull Run and war service (B.G. USA and Maj. Gen. USV), he continued in the R.A. until retired in 1879 as Col.

PALMER, John McAuley. Union gen. 1817–1900. Ky. A lawyer and Democratic legislator, he became an early Republican and was a delegate to the Washington Peace Conference in 1861. Commissioned Col. 14th Ill. 25 May '61, he fought at New Madrid, Point Pleasant, and Island No. 10, having been appointed B.G. USV 20 Dec. '61. In the Army of the Miss., he led 2d Div. (23 Feb.–4 Mar. '62); 3d Div. (4 Mar.–24 Apr. '62); 1st Brig., 1st Div. (24 Apr.–10 Aug. '62) and 1st Div. (31 Aug.–29 Sept. '62). He then commanded 13th Div., Army of the Ohio (Sept.–Nov. '62) and was appointed Maj. Gen. USV 29 Nov. '62. At Stones River he led 2d Div. Left Wing, XIV, Cumberland (10 Dec. '62–9 Jan. '63), and at Chickamauga he commanded 2d Div., XXI, Cumberland (9 Jan.–15 July and 17 Aug.–9 Oct. '63). Also in the Army of the Cumberland he commanded the XXI Corps (15 July–17 Aug. '63); 1st Div., IV (10–27 Oct. '63)

and the XIV Corps (28 Oct. '63–7 Aug. '64). He asked to be relieved from the last-named command after an altercation with Sherman, brought on by his refusal to take orders from Schofield whom he considered to be junior. Mustered out in 1866, he was Gov. of Ill. 1868–72 and then, returning to the Democratic party, served as US Sen. In 1896 he was the National (or "Gold") Democratic presidential candidate.

PALMER, Joseph B. C.S.A. gen. ?–1890. Appt.-Tenn. A lawyer in Stones River, he was commissioned Col. 18th Tenn. when the war started and was captured at Fort Donelson. Held in Fort Warren until Aug. '62, he rejoined his regiment at Vicksburg, moved to Jackson, Miss., and was wounded three times at Stones River. At Chickamauga he was wounded in the shoulder and was out of action until the latter part of the Atlanta campaign, when he was assigned to command a brigade. Appointed B.G. C.S.A. 15 Nov. '64, he went with Hood to Tenn. and surrendered with Johnston in N.C.

PALMER, Oliver H. Union officer. N.Y. Col. 108th N.Y. 18 Aug. '62; Bvt. B.G. USV (war service); discharged 2 Mar. '63. Commanded 2, 3, II (Potomac). Died 1884.

PALMER, William Jackson. Union officer. 1836–1909. Del. Capt. 15th Pa. Cav. 28 Sept. '61; Col. 8 Sept. '62; Bvt. B.G. USV 6 Nov. '64 (war service); Medal of Honor 24 Feb. '94 for Red Hill (Ala.) 14 Jan. '65. Commanded 3, 6, Cav. Corps, Mil. Div. Miss. Although raised a Quaker, he followed his own conscience in becoming a soldier. He was a prisoner 1862–63. He became wealthy as a railroad executive in the West and Mexico and was a founder of Colorado Springs and Colorado College. He also aided Hampton Institute. (See ARMSTRONG, Samuel Chapman.)

PALMER'S CREEK, Va. Part of action at DREWRY'S BLUFF, 12–16 May '64.

PALMETTO ARMS. S.C. was the only Southern state that, before the war, attempted to remedy the lack of arms in the South by local manufacture. A contract dated 15 Apr. '51 was awarded to William Glaze and Benjamin Flagg for the manufacture of 1,000 rifles, 6,000 muskets, 1,000 cavalry sabers, 1,000 artillery swords, and 2,000 pistols. Glaze converted his Palmetto Iron Works in Columbia, S.C., into an armory that became known as the Palmetto Armory. Flagg's musket factory at Milbury, Mass., and Water's Armory, Mass., furnished the machinery for construction of muskets and pistols copied from the US models 1842 of each of these arms. The manufacture and converting of arms was done in 1852 and 1853. During the war the Palmetto Armory made no arms, but made bombshell, cannon balls, Minié bullets, and rollers for the powder mills at Raleigh and Columbia. It also made several of the cannon that were patterned after the Colt revolver and which turned out to be unsatisfactory for field service.

Sherman partially destroyed the armory, but it was rebuilt and operated until relatively recently.

Palmetto muskets, pistols, rifles, and cavalry sabers are in existence, but the artillery swords have not been identified. The rarest item is the rifle, which is a MISSISSIPPI RIFLE type. (This article is based on Albaugh and Simmons, 3ff and 251ff.)

PANADA. Hot gruel made of corn meal, army crackers mashed in boiling water, ginger, and wine. Invented by Eliza HARRIS of the SANITARY COMMIS-SION, it was used in both the eastern and western theaters. Also called ginger panada and bully soup.

PARDEE, Ario, Jr. Union officer. Pa. Capt. 28th Pa. 28 June '61; Maj. 1 Nov. '61; Lt. Col. 147th Pa. 10 Oct. '62; Col. 19 Mar. '64; Bvt. B.G. USV 12 Jan. '65 (Peach Tree Creek, Ga). Commanded 1, 2, XII; 1, 2, XX. He was the son of a wealthy philanthropist who equipped and paid the expenses of the 28th Pa. Died 1901.

PARDEE, Don Albert. Union officer. 1837–1919. Ohio. USNA 1854–57. Maj. 42d Ohio 27 Oct. '61; Lt. Col. 14 Mar. '62; Provost Marshal of Baton Rouge, 1863; Bvt. B.G. USV (war service); mustered out 25 Nov. '64. Moving to New Orleans to practice law, he became a federal and state judge. "It is remarkable how quickly Pardee overcame the handicaps attendant upon his going to live in the South at the close of the war. That he was no Carpet-bagger was immediately apparent" (D.A.B.).

PARK, Sidney Wesley. Union officer. N.Y. Capt. 2d N.Y. 14 May '61; Col. 17 Oct. '62; Bvt. USV (war service); mustered out 26 May '63.

PARKE, John Grubb. Union gen. 1827–1900. Pa. USMA 1849 (2/43); Topo. Engrs. Engaged in surveying for railroads and boundary lines and supervisor of harbor and river construction before the war, he was promoted Capt. 9 Sept. '61 (1st Lt. since 1856) and B.G. USV 23 Nov. '61. Commanding 3d Brig. on Burnside's N.C. expedition Dec. '61–Apr. '62, he fought at Roanoke Island, Fort Forrest, New Bern, and Fort Macon. At South Mountain and Antietam he led 3d Div., IX, Potomac (22 July–3 Sept. '62 and 17 Sept.–4 Oct. '62), having been appointed Maj. Gen. USV 18 July '62. He was Burnside's Chief of Staff (7 Nov. '62–25 Jan. '63) at Fredericksburg and then commanded the IX Corps, Ohio (19 Mar.–11 Apr.; 5 June–25 Aug. '63 and 26 Jan.–16 Mar. '64) at Vicksburg. He commanded the IX Corps when it was in the Army of the Tenn. (14 June–18 Aug. '63) and when it was reattached to the Potomac (19 Mar.–4 Apr. '63; 14 Aug.–31 Dec. '64 at Peeble's Farm and Hatcher's Run; 12–24 Jan. '65; 2 Feb.–17 June '65 at Fort Stedman; and 2 July–1 Aug. '65). At the Wilderness, Spotsylvania, the James River campaign, and at Petersburg, he was Chief of Staff of the IX Corps and commanded the Army of the Potomac 30 Dec. '64–11 Jan. '65 during Meade's absence. He then commanded the Dist. Alexandria, XXII, Washington (26 Apr.–5 June '65) and XXII Corps (7–26 June '65) and was breveted for Fort Macon, Jackson, Knoxville, (B.G. USA), and Fort Stedman (Maj. Gen. USA). Continuing in the R.A., he retired as Col. in 1889 after having been Asst. Chief of Engrs. and Superintendent of West Point. Lyman said he was "a very pleasant-looking man and liked apparently by everyone."

PARKER, Ely Samuel. Seneca Indian and Union officer. 1828–95. N.Y. Son of a famous Seneca chief, he became sachem of the tribe in 1852. After reading law, he was refused admission to the bar because he was not a citizen. He then graduated as an engineer from Rensselaer and, in 1857, when working in Galena, Ill., became a close friend of a store clerk named Sam Grant. When the war started he was unable to get a commission from the Gov. of N.Y., "and Seward even went so far as to tell him that the war would be won by the whites without the aid of the Indians" (D.A.B.). He finally became Capt. Asst. Adj. Gen. Vols. 25 May '63, and served as J. E. Smith's (7th) division engineer (XVII, Tenn.). He was then Grant's military secretary, with the rank of Lt. Col., from 30 Aug. '64 to 25 July '66. At Appomattox "it was the Indian, Parker, who at Grant's orders . . . transcribed in a fair hand the official copies of the document that ended the Civil War" (D.A.B.). Bvt. B.G. USV 9 Apr. '65 (Appomattox) and Bvt. B.G. USA 2 Mar. '67 (war service); resigned as Col. in 1869 after serving three years as Grant's A.D.C. Grant appointed him Commissioner of Indian Affairs. After later making and losing several fortunes, he died a relatively poor man. (See also James H. WILSON.)

PARKER, Joel. Gov. of N.J. 1816–88. N.J. After graduating from Princeton, he studied law and was elected to the legislature as a Democrat in 1847. He was named B.G. in the militia in 1857 and Maj. Gen. in 1861. Long opposed to war, he supported the Federal government after Sumter was fired upon, and was elected Gov. in 1862 as a Democrat. Serving until 1866, he was re-elected in 1870 and became a justice of the state Supreme Court later.

PARKER CROSS ROADS, Tenn. 31 Dec. '62. (FORREST'S SECOND RAID; STONES RIVER) At this point, near Lexington, Forrest found his road blocked by skirmishers from Col. Cyrus L. Dunham's brigade (3, 8, XVI). He was successfully driving this force back when hit from the rear by Fuller's brigade (1, 8, XVI). Forrest was routed with a loss of 300 prisoners, six guns, 350 horses, and other matériel he had previously captured. He escaped by crossing the Tennessee at Clifton.

PARKHURST, John Gibson. Union officer. N.Y. Lt. Col. 9th Mich. 10 Sept. '61; Col. 6 Feb. '63; Bvt. B.G. USV 22 May '65 (war service).

PAROLE. In one sense, a parole is a "watch-word differing from the countersign in that it is only communicated to officers of the guard, while the counter-sign is given to all members. The parole is usually the name of a person, gener-ally a distinguished officer, while the countersign is the name of a place, as of a battle-field." (Wilhelm.)

In the other sense it derives from the French *parole d'honneur,* and is a pledge or oath under which a prisoner of war is released with the understanding that he will not again bear arms until ex-changed. The following instructions from Winfield Scott to McClellan at Beverly, W. Va., on 14 July '61 will illustrate the normal wording of such a pledge: "Discharge all your prisoners of war under the grade of commissioned officer who shall willingly take and subscribe a general oath in these terms: 'I swear (or affirm) that I will not take up arms against the United States or serve in any military capacity whatsoever against them until regularly discharged accord-ing to the usages of war from this obli-gation [i.e., until exchanged].' " Officers took a similar oath which included the phrase "we pledge our words of honor as officers and gentlemen."

The capture of Federal general E. H. Hobson and members of his command by John Morgan at Cynthiana, Ky., 11 July '64, illustrates the legal aspects of the parole. Hobson with his staff and J. F. Asper's 171st Ohio N.G. (100-days men) entrained at Covington at 11 P.M. on 10 June and moved toward Cynthiana to reinforce troops in that area opposing Morgan's raiders. The next day after a five-hour defense of a position in which Morgan had trapped them, the Federals surrendered. Their effective strength was about 300 officers and men. Since these would have been a burden to Morgan's continued opera-tions, and since the men were close to the end of their term of service, Hobson, Asper, and six other officers of their

staffs were finally convinced to sign this "agreement":

"[we] do hereby give our parole of honor to place ourselves in immediate communication with the military author-ities of the United States for the purpose of obtaining an exchange for officers of equal rank with ourselves, and should we fail to accomplish said exchange we give our word of honor that we will report direct to Brig. Gen. John H. Mor-gan in the shortest time practicable, and by the most direct route, under charge of three [Confederate] officers and one private selected to escort us."

By the time Hobson and his party reached Falmouth at dusk, 12 June, and entered the Federal camp under a flag of truce, Morgan had been defeated and driven off by Burbridge (Cynthiana, Ky., 12 June '64). On this same day Morgan had paroled the rest of his pris-oners. The legal question was whether Hobson and the seven officers who had signed the agreement were to be con-sidered under parole not to fight again until a like number of Confederates had been exchanged. It was further pointed out that the other prisoners from the 171st Ohio N.G. had not really been paroled, since they had not been cap-tured "within the permanent lines of the rebel army."

In submitting his report to Burbridge (C.G. Dist. of Ky.), Hobson asked a decision as to his status: was he under parole or not? He received word that "the general commanding considers no officers and men prisoners of war except such as Morgan retained and took off with him, and directs that you and your staff report here for duty as soon as practicable, and that the three rebel offi-cers be held as prisoners." (O.R. I, XXXIX, I, 33–62, particularly p. 60.) (See also EXCHANGE OF PRISONERS.)

PARRISH, Charles Sherman. Union officer. Ohio. Capt. 8th Ind. 23 Apr. '61;

mustered out 6 Aug. '61; Maj. 8th Ind. 5 Sept. '61; Lt. Col. 25 May '62; Col. 130th Ind. 12 Mar. '64; Bvt B.G. USV (gallantry in action). Commanded in the XXIII Corps (Ohio): 2d Brig., 1st Div.; 4th Brig., 2d Div. Phisterer lists him as Parish, Charles S.

PARROTT, Robert Parker. Union officer. 1804–77. N.H. USMA 1824 (3/31); Arty.-Ord. Resigned in 1836 as Capt. Inventor of PARROTT GUN and projectile. Superintendent of West Point Iron and Cannon Foundry 1836–67.

PARROTT GUN. Rifled, muzzle-loading cannon, varying in size from 3-inch (10-pound shell) to 10-inch (250-pound projectile), of a design invented by R. P. PARROTT. To make a gun barrel strong enough to withstand the greater pressures required in rifled artillery, Parrott's system was to heat shrink a heavy wrought-iron band around the breech, where the pressures were greatest. This was successful with cast-iron gun tubes. Combining Parrott's technique with a Rodman type of cast-iron barrel, even larger rifled artillery could be made. Due to their characteristic external appearance—a rather ungraceful, thick cylindrical band around the breech—Parrott guns are easy to identify.

Ammunition for the Parrott gun had to solve the problem of being suited to muzzle-loading while still being able to "take" the rifling when fired. The Parrott projectile did this with a brass ring around its base; this ring was grooved so that the gas pressure of the propellant would get into it and force its outside edge into the rifling.

Although the smoothbore Napoleons were the basic field-artillery weapons of both the Union and the Confederates, each side used Parrotts. Being considerably more accurate and having over twice the range of smoothbores, the Parrotts were decisive in many situations. The larger ones were particularly effective in knocking down masonry fortifications.

The 3-inch Parrott was found to be ineffective and was replaced by the 3-inch ordnance gun. The 20-pounder Parrott (3.67-inch) had a maximum range of over two miles (3,500 yards with solid shot and 10-degree elevation) and was the basic rifled fieldpiece in common use. The 30-pounder Parrott (4.20 inch) had a maximum range of 4,400 yards. Maximum effective range for rifled artillery was, however, about 2,500 yards. See also CANNON OF THE CIVIL WAR.

PARRY, Augustus Commodore. Union officer. 1828–66. N.J. Maj. 2d Ohio 29 Apr. '61; mustered out 31 July '61; Maj. 47th Ohio 27 Aug. '61; Lt. Col. 1 Sept. '62; Col. 12 Mar. '63; Bvt. B.G. USV (war service). W.I.A. Kenesaw Mountain. Died in 1866 of consumption.

PARSONS, Lewis Baldwin. Union gen. 1818–1907. N.Y. Appt.-Mo. After Yale he taught school in Miss. and went to Harvard Law School. He was in railroading when he served as A.D.C. to Francis P. Blair, Jr., at the capture of Camp Jackson and, realizing that war was inevitable, offered his services to McClellan. Commissioned Capt. Asst. Q.M. USV 31 Oct. '61, he was put in charge of all river and rail transportation for the Dept. of the Miss. (from Yellowstone to Pittsburgh to New Orleans) in Dec. There he "brought a semblance of order out of the existing chaos, drafting a set of regulations for rail transportation that became the basis of the general rules of army transportation adopted later" (D.A.B.). Named Col. Add. A.D.C. to Halleck 19 Feb. '62, he was sent to Washington 2 Aug. '64 as Col. Q.M. Assigned and headed all rail and river transportation in the country until 12

May '65. On 11 May he was promoted B.G. USV and held in the army until Apr. '66 to see to the transportation of discharged soldiers. D.A.B. says that "One of his most striking achievements . . . was the moving of General Schofield's army and all its equipment from Mississippi to the Potomac within a period of seventeen days." He spent two years in Europe recovering from overwork and then went into banking and railroading. He was also a leader in Democratic politics and the Presbyterian Church.

PARSONS, Mosby Munroe. C.S.A. gen. 1819–65. Va. Appt.-Mo. A lawyer, legislator, and public officeholder, he fought in the Mexican War and raised the MISSOURI STATE GUARD when the Civil War came. Serving in Mo. in 1861, he was appointed B.G. C.S.A. 5 Nov. '62, having led his brigade at Wilson's Creek and Pea Ridge. In the Red River campaign of 1864 he commanded the Mo. brigade under Price at Mansfield and Pleasant Hill and fought against Steele in Ark. at Marks's Mills and Jenkins' Ferry. He went on Price's raid into Mo. and then escaped to Mexico to join the Republicans. On 17 Aug. '65 he was killed in action at Camargo, Mex. Wright says that although no record of appointment or confirmation has been found, Parsons was paroled as Maj. Gen. and that on an order dated 13 May '64, Headquarters Trans-Miss. Dept., he was promoted to Maj. Gen. with rank from 30 Apr. '64.

PARTISAN RANGERS. Organized by John S. MOSBY in Jan. '63, the most famous force was at first nine men detached from Stuart's command in Loudoun County to harass the Federal rear and draw the cavalry away from the main Confederate force. They would meet by prearrangement, dash through the Federals in dizzying fashion, procure the wagon train or other objective, and melt into the countryside, scattering in all directions. The Federals spent a great deal of time, effort, and troops trying to track them down but to no avail, and Mosby disbanded them 21 Apr. '65. See also LOUDOUN RANGERS.

PARTRIDGE, Frederick William. Union officer. Vt. Capt. 13th Ill. 24 May '61; Maj. 25 June '61; Lt. Col. 17 Feb. '63; Bvt. B.G. USV (Lookout Mountain; Chattanooga; Ringgold Gap, Ga.); mustered out 18 June '64. Died 1899.

PATRICK, Marsena Rudolph. Union gen. 1811–88. N.Y. USMA 1835 (48/56); Inf. Running away from the "excessive Puritanism" at home, he became an Erie Canal driver and schoolteacher before entering USMA as the protégé of Gen. Stephen van Rensselaer. He fought in the Florida war, served on garrison duty, and won a brevet in the Mexican War before resigning in 1850. First a railroad president, he was then president of the N.Y. agricultural college that was Cornell's antecedent and resigned this to become B.G. I.G. N.Y. Vols. in the service of the US 16 May '61–9 Feb. '62. He was on McClellan's staff as I.G. of the N.Y. Vols. 16 Nov. '61–17 Mar. '62 when he was commissioned B.G. USV. He commanded 2, McDowell's Div., Potomac (12–13 Mar. '62); 2, 3, I (17 May–4 Apr. '62) in the defenses of Washington and 2, King's, Rappahannock (4 Apr.–26 June '62). At Beverly Ford, Warrenton Springs, Gainesville, 2d Bull Run, and Chantilly, he led 3, 1, III, Army Va. (26 June–12 Sept. '62) and 3, 1, I, Potomac (12 Sept.–6 Oct. '62) at South Mountain and Antietam. He was named Provost Marshal Gen. of the Army of the Potomac and later of all armies against Richmond (12 Sept. '62–12 Apr. '65), being present at all engagements. From 25 May until 9 June '65, he was commander of the Dist. of Henrico (including Richmond), from which post Grant suggested to Halleck that he be relieved lest his kindheartedness "interfere with the proper government of the city." He was relieved, at his own request, and resigned 12 June '65, having been breveted Maj. Gen. USV for war service. He was later president of an agricultural society and governor of a soldiers' home in Ohio where, D.A.B. says, "ever the disciplinarian, he was denounced as a tyrant, but, swayed neither by politics nor by expediency, gradually gained the respect and love of the veterans and townspeople alike." Described as being "of commanding presence, with patriarchal beard and thunderous voice, a self-disciplined Presbyterian fearing God only, he had the air of an Old Testament prophet with a dash of the Pharisee" (D.A.B.).

PARTRIDGE, Benjamin Franklin. Union officer. Mich. 2d Lt. 1st Mich. Lancers 12 Oct. '61; mustered out 20 Mar. '62; 1st Lt. 16th Mich. to rank from 12 Oct. '61; Capt. 16 Apr. '63; Maj. 1 June '64; Lt. Col. 30 Sept. '64; Col. 17 Dec. '64; Bvt. B.G. USV 31 Mar. '65. Brevets for Peeble's Farm (Va.), White Oak Road (Va.). Died 1892.

PATTEE, John. Union officer. Canada. Capt. 7th Iowa Cav. 23 Oct. '61; Maj. 1 Sept. '62; Lt. Col. 3 June '63; Bvt. B.G. USV (war service).

PATTEE, Joseph B. Union officer. Canada. 2d Lt. 10th Pa. Res. 19 June '61; 1st Lt. 21 July '61; Capt. 22 Apr. '63; Lt. Col. 190th Pa. 6 June '64; Bvt. B.G. USV 9 Apr. '65. Brevets for Petersburg siege, Appomattox C.H.

PATTEN, Henry Lyman. Union officer. Mass. 2d Lt. 20th Mass. 25 Nov. '61; 1st Lt. 1 Oct. '62; Capt. 30 Aug. '63; Maj. 7 May '64; Bvt. B.G. USV. Brevets for Gettysburg, Wilderness, Deep Bottom (Va.). W.I.A. Nelson's Farm

30 June '62, Gettysburg twice, and Deep Bottom, where he had a leg amputated 16 Aug. '64. He died 10 Sept. '64 from the latter.

PATTERSON, Francis Engle. Union gen. 1827–62. Pa. R.A. Fighting in the Mexican War with McCulloch's "Texas Rangers," he resigned in 1857 and went into business, returning to the Army 25 Apr. '61 as Col. 17th Pa. He was mustered out 2 Aug. '61 and named B.G. USV 11 Apr. '62. At Williamsburg and Fair Oaks he commanded 3, 2, II (3–31 May and 6 June–22 Nov. '62). On the latter date he was killed in camp near Fairfax C.H. by the accidental discharge of his own pistol.

PATTERSON, Joab Nelson. Union officer. N.H. 1st Lt. 2d N.H. 5 June '61; Capt. 23 May '62; Lt. Col. 4 July '63; Col. 22 June '65; Bvt. B.G. USV (war service). Commanded 3, 1, XVIII (Va. and N.C.); 2, 3, XXIV (Va.).

PATTERSON, Robert. Union (Pa. state) gen. 1792–1881. Ireland. The father of Francis E. Patterson, he had served with the Pa. militia 1812–13 and in the R.A. until 1815. In the Mexican War he was Maj. Gen. USV, and Gov. Curtin assigned him to command the Pa. three-months volunteers as Maj. Gen. (Pa. Vols.) 15 Apr. '61. He was in command of the Mil. Depts. of Pa., Del., Md. and D.C. when ordered, in mid-July, to prevent Johnston from reinforcing Beauregard at Bull Run while McDowell advanced. He failed to engage the enemy in battle, explaining that he had not received *orders to attack*. Much criticized for this, he was mustered out 27 July '61.

PATTERSON, Robert Emmet. Union officer. 1830–1903. Pa. USMA 1851 (29/42); Inf. Resigned 1857 as 1st Lt.; Add. Paymaster USV 1 June '61; Col. 115th Pa. 25 June '62; Bvt. B.G. USV (war service); resigned as Col. 115th

Pa. 2 Dec. '62 and as Add. Paymaster 23 Dec. '62. A Philadelphia cotton commission merchant before and after the war.

PATTERSON, Robert Franklin. Union officer. Me. 2d Lt. 5th Iowa 15 July '61; Regt. Q.M. 15 July '61; Regt. Adj. 27 Jan. '62; Lt. Col. 29th Iowa 1 Dec. '62; Bvt. B.G. USV 26 Mar. '65. Brevets for Mobile (2).

PAUL, Gabriel René. Union gen. c. 1811–86. Mo. USMA 1834 (18/36); Inf. He served in the Indian Territory and on frontier posts and fought in the Seminole and Mexican wars (1 brevet, 1 wound in the latter). Named Maj. 8th US Inf. 22 Apr. '61, he was acting I.G. of N. Mex. until commissioned Col. 4th N. Mex. 9 Dec. '61. He fought at Peralta (N. Mex.) 15 Apr. '62, was named Lt. Col. 8th US Inf. 25 Apr., and mustered out of USV 31 May. As B.G. USV 5 Sept. '62, he commanded 3, 1, I, Potomac (14 Oct. '62–17 Feb. '63) at Fredericksburg (9–29 Mar.), and at Chancellorsville (20 Apr.–16 June '63). He succeeded to division 22–27 Dec. '62 and 1–9 Mar. '63. Commanding 1, 2, I at Gettysburg (17 June–1 July '63), he lost his sight by a rifle wound. His B.G. appointment had expired 4 Mar. and was renewed 18 Apr. '63. Breveted for Gettysburg (B.G. USA 23 Feb. '65), he retired in 1865 as Col. and in 1866 as B.G. "by a resolution of Congress." He had been given a sword by the citizens of St. Louis for his Mexican War service, and the 29th N.J. gave him a jeweled sword for Gettysburg. The son and grandson of Napoleonic officers, he was, "though small in stature ... great in heart and mighty in valor" (Appleton's).

PAXTON, Elisha Franklin. C.S.A. gen. 1828–63. Va. Appt.-Tenn. After Washington College and Yale he stood at the head of his Univ. of Va. law class and practiced in Lexington until failing eyesight made him take up farming in 1860. A secessionist, he was commissioned 1st Lt. Rockbridge Rifles and left Lexington 18 Apr. '61 for Harpers Ferry. He fought with the 4th Va. at 1st Bull Run and was elected Maj. 27th Va. in Oct. '61. In the spring of 1862 he served on Jackson's staff and was later Adj. Gen. and Chief of Staff for Jackson's corps. Appointed B.G. C.S.A. 1 Nov. '62, he led the STONEWALL BRIGADE at Fredericksburg and at Chancellorsville. He was killed there 3 May, at 35 years of age.

PAY. Union privates were paid $13 per month until after the final raise of 20 June '64, when they got $16. In the infantry and artillery, officer pay was as follows at the start of the war: colonels, $212; lieutenant colonels, $181; majors, $169; captains, $115.50; first lieutenants, $105.50; and second lieutenants, $105.50. Other line and staff officers drew an average of about $15 per month more. Pay for one-, two-, and three-star generals was $315, $457, and $758, respectively.

The Confederate pay structure was modeled after that of the US Army. Privates of artillery and infantry continued to be paid at the prewar rate of $11 per month until June '64, when the pay of all enlisted men was raised $7 per month. Confederate officers' pay was a few dollars lower than that of their Union counterparts. A Southern B.G., for example, drew $301 instead of $315 per month; Confederate colonels of infantry received $195, and those of artillery, engineers, and cavalry got $210. While the inflation of CONFEDERATE MONEY reduced the actual value of a Southerner's military pay, this was somewhat counterbalanced by the fact that promotion policies in the South were more liberal.

As for the pay of noncommissioned

officers, when Southern privates were making $11 per month, corporals were making $13, "buck" sergeants $17, first sergeants $20, and engineer sergeants were drawing $34. About the same ratio existed in the Northern army between the pay of privates and noncommissioned officers.

Soldiers were supposed to be paid every two months in the field, but they "were fortunate if they got their pay at four-month intervals [in the Union Army] and authentic instances are recorded where they went six and eight months" (Shannon). Payment in the Confederate Army was even slower and less regular.

PAYNE, Eugene Beuharnais. Union officer. N.Y. 2d Lt. Chicago Zouaves 16 Apr.–20 July '61; Capt. 37th Ill. 1 Aug. '61; Maj. 31 Dec. '62; Lt. Col. 24 Dec. '63; Bvt. B.G. USV (war service); resigned 9 Sept. '64.

PAYNE, Oliver Hazard. Union officer. 1839–1917. Ohio. Lt. Col. 124th Ohio 11 Sept. '62; Col. 1 Jan. '63; Bvt. B.G. USV (war service); resigned 2 Nov. '64. W.I.A. Chickamauga. Commanded 2, 1, XXI; 2, 3, IV. He made a fortune in the iron and oil industries. He was an enthusiastic sailor and crossed the Atlantic many times in his yacht. A bachelor, he left $8 million to found and finance the Cornell Medical School and $1 million apiece to the N.Y. Public Library, Lakeside (Cleveland) Hospital, and Yale Univ., his alma mater.

PAYNE, William Henry Fitzhugh. C.S.A. gen. 1830–1904. Va. Graduating from the Univ. of Va., he was a lawyer and held several public offices before the war. During the occupation of Harpers Ferry he served as a private and was commissioned Capt. of the Black Horse Cav. 26 Apr. '61. On 27 Sept. '61 he was named Maj. 4th Va. Cav. and commanded his regiment at Williamsburg. During this battle he was severely wounded and captured, being exchanged two or three months later. In Sept. '62 he returned to duty as Lt. Col. and in temporary command of the 2d N.C. Cav. The next month he was ordered to the hospital in Lynchburg and in Feb. '63 was temporary commander of the 4th Va. Cav. He led the 2d N.C. Cav. 20 Mar.–8 June '63, fighting at Chancellorsville, but when their colonel was killed the next day (9 June '63) at Brandy Station, he resumed command and led them on Stuart's Pa. raid. At Hanover his horse was shot from under him and, wounded by a saber cut in his side, he was captured again. He was held on Johnson's Island until exchanged and appointed B.G. C.S.A. 1 Nov. '64, taking command of a brigade in the Valley under Early. He led them at Winchester, Fishers Hill, Cedar Creek. During the final operations around Richmond he commanded a brigade under Munford. Wounded at Five Forks, he was captured in Richmond and returned to Johnson's Island. After the war he was a lawyer and legislator. He was descended from the Washington and Mason families.

PEACE DEMOCRATS. A faction of the Democratic party that opposed the war and wrote into the 1864 platform a provision favoring peace. McClellan repudiated the latter before becoming the candidate of what might be called the regular Democrats, who comprised the bulk of the party.

PEACH ORCHARD, Va., 29 June '62. See SAVAGE'S STATION.

PEACH TREE CREEK, Ga. ("Hood's First Sortie"), 20 July '64. (ATLANTA CAMPAIGN) Sherman turned J. E. Johnston's defense of the CHATTAHOOCHEE RIVER, 4–9 July '64. On the 17th Hood succeeded Johnston as commander of the Confederate forces. On the morning of 20 July Thomas' Army of the Cumberland had secured a shallow bridgehead across Peach Tree Creek. Newton's division (2, IV) was on the left across the Buckhead–Atlanta road and less than half a mile south of Collier's Bridge. Geary was to his right (west) and Ward was behind the interval between the other two divisions. Williams' division (1, XX) was to Geary's right rear, and the brigade of Anson McCook (1, 1, XIV) was on the extreme right flank opposite Howell's (or Powell's) Mill. Schofield and McPherson were enveloping Atlanta to the east, and there was a gap of nearly two miles between Thomas and Schofield.

Adopting Johnston's plan of hitting Thomas' unsupported army while it was astride the creek, Hood ordered an attack to start at 1 P.M. While Cheatham and Wheeler screened to the east against Schofield and McPherson, Stewart and Hardee would attack Thomas. Hardee formed his divisions on line in the order Bate, Walker, and Maney from right to left, with Cleburne in reserve. Stewart's divisions of Loring and Walthall, from right to left, extended this line to the west, with French in reserve. The attack was to be executed in oblique order, starting with Bate on the right. Hood charged Hardee with delaying the attack until 4 P.M. by failing to follow his instructions to deploy half a division to his right to assist Cheatham in protecting that flank. Most accounts say the attack started at 3 o'clock.

Bate's advance took him to Newton's exposed east flank where he was repulsed by the brigades of Blake and Bradley (the latter moving up from reserve). Walker's attack then hit between Newton's two front-line brigades, Blake and Kimball, and was stopped. Maney then hit between Newton and Geary, that is between the brigades of

Kimball and Candy. Ward's division led by Bloodgood's 136th N.Y. came up to fill this gap and repulse the attack.

Stewart's divisions then made contact with Geary's right. This flank was exposed because Williams' division was somewhat to the rear. Leaving five regiments on his original front, Geary faced the rest of his division to the right and extended his line to connect with Williams. The latter moved two brigades onto line, Robinson on his left and Knipe on the right, and held Ruger in reserve. Williams was attacked almost immediately by Walthall's division. Stewart pressed his attack vigorously against Geary, Williams, and the brigade of Anson McCook. However, the Confederate oblique order and the refused right flanks of Geary and Williams combined to expose the attackers to a devastating enfilade fire. Loring lost 1,062 men in a few minutes (T.U.A., V, 59). General Thomas again showed the qualities that had made him the "Rock of Chickamauga"; after rushing artillery forward he went up to direct the defense in person. The 27th Ind. hurried up to reinforce Knipe's exposed right flank and, with the 46th Pa., held this position. The Confederates continued their furious assaults until 6 P.M.

Hood had the highest praise for the conduct of Stewart's attack, but says that "the troops of Hardee—as their losses on that day indicate—did nothing more than skirmish with the enemy" (B.&L., IV, 337).

Of the 20,139 Federals engaged, there were about 1,600 killed and wounded. Of the 18,832 Confederates engaged, Livermore estimates 2,500 were killed and wounded. Hood left 600 dead on the field, and Ward captured 246 prisoners and 7 flags (Van Horne, II, 116). Sherman puts Hood's losses at 4,796, but Livermore finds no basis for adopting this figure. (The best battlefield map is O.R. Atlas Plate CI, 7; see also XLVII, 5.)

PEARCE, John Stoneman. Union officer. Ohio. Maj. 98th Ohio 21 Aug. '62; Lt. Col. 13 June '63; Bvt. B.G. USV (Perryville, Resaca, Dallas, Kenesaw Mountain, Jonesboro, Bentonville). Commanded 2, 2, XIV (Cumberland). Died 1903.

PEARCE, Nicholas Bartlett. C.S.A. gen. c. 1816–94. Ky. USMA 1850 (26/44); Inf. He served on the frontier and on the Utah Expedition before resigning in 1858 to be a farmer and merchant. In May '61, as Ark. State B.G., he raised troops and fought at Wilson's Creek. He was named Chief Comsy. of the Indian Territory in Dec. of that year, apparently with the C.S.A. rank of Maj. In June '63 he was Chief Comsy. of Tex. and accused of dealing with speculators. He was assigned B.G. C.S.A. by Kirby Smith in the Trans-Miss. Dept. Listed by Cullum and Wright, he is not included in the lists of Wood and C.M.H.

PEA RIDGE (Elkhorn Tavern), Ark., 7–8 Mar. '62. In Dec. '61 Gen. Sam Curtis took command of the (Union) Army of the Southwest, which had been operating in Mo. under Gens. Lyon and Frémont. On 10 Feb. '62 he advanced toward Springfield, Mo., where Gen. Sterling Price's Confederate force of 8,000 Missourians had wintered. Price offered little resistance as he withdrew into northwest Ark.; he proposed to join forces in this area with Gen. Benjamin McCulloch, who was retreating from Keetsville, Mo. Gen. Earl Van Dorn, who had recently been put in command of the (Confederate) Trans-Miss. Dist. with orders to defeat Curtis, halted Price and McCulloch in the Boston Mountains south of Fayetteville. He then rushed reinforcements up to them and prepared to lead an attack against the overextended Federals.

Curtis' force consisted of Gen. Franz Sigel's two divisions under Asboth and Osterhaus, and the divisions of Jefferson C. Davis and E. A. Carr. With attached artillery and cavalry the Federals numbered about 11,000. Van Dorn's force consisted of Price's Mo. State Guard, McCulloch's division (Louis Hébert's La. infantry brigade, and a cavalry brigade under James McIntosh); and Albert Pike's command of three Indian regiments and Welch's Tex. cavalry squadron as well as miscellaneous other units (see B.&L., I, 337). Total strength was about 17,000.

When Curtis learned from one of his scouts, "Wild Bill" Hickok, that the Confederates were advancing in force, he decided to concentrate and take up a defensive position near Pea Ridge, where Davis and Carr were already located. Sigel's divisions had to fight their way back, but by nightfall of 6 Mar. the Federals were formed in line of battle on the high ground overlooking Little Sugar Creek and facing south.

The weather had turned cold in late Feb. and Van Dorn's troops, short on rations, massed opposite the Federal position after completing a 55-mile march in a wet, driving snow. (Van Dorn himself was sick and directed the battle from an ambulance wagon.) Pike's force of several thousand Indians under Stand Watie, Daniel McIntosh, and John Drew arrived during the night. Van Dorn's plan was to leave his campfires, to deceive the enemy, and to execute a strategic envelopment via the Bentonville and Keetsville Road. The main attack was to be made against Curtis' left rear at Elkhorn Tavern. McCulloch with his division and Pike's Indians was to make a secondary attack from the northwest toward Leetown to draw enemy reserves. Van Dorn then planned to launch a decisive envelopment around the south end of Pea Ridge against Leetown.

The cold, clear dawn of 7 Mar. revealed that the Confederates had left their bivouacs, but their turning movement was soon detected. Between 6 and 7 A.M. skirmishing broke out a mile northeast of Elkhorn Tavern. At 8 o'clock Carr's division was ordered to form a defense near the tavern, where the Confederate advance up a narrow valley would have to emerge. At the same time Curtis ordered Cyrus Bussey with all of the cavalry except the 3d Ill. to move against the threat from the northwest; Osterhaus was to support this movement with his division and to command the Federal west wing. Davis was moved into the Federal center, below Pea Ridge on the right flank of Osterhaus, while Sigel was left along Sugar Creek with Asboth's division.

Carr attacked on the Federal right (about 10:30) and made some progress up the Wire Road before being stopped and driven back. He repulsed a second attack but at about dusk was finally driven back to a new line southwest of the tavern. Asboth's division came up to form a new line through which Carr could withdraw his battered regiments.

On the other flank Bussey and Osterhaus were routed by the Tex. cavalry followed by Stand Watie's dismounted Indians. Drew's regiment followed on horseback. McCulloch exploited this initial success by an attack on Davis, who gave some ground but then held fast. McCulloch and James McIntosh were killed and Louis Hébert captured. Shortly after 3 P.M. Osterhaus drove the disorganized Indians from the ground they had taken. The Federals reported finding more than 30 scalped corpses, although this has never been proved.

During the afternoon Van Dorn drew troops from the west flank to reinforce his main attack. Of the Indians, only Watie's Cherokees and D. N. McIntosh's 200 Creeks were willing to stay with the colors after the day's action; they were posted on top of Pea Ridge to hold the Confederate right flank during the night. Despite the failure of this attack, Van Dorn was determined to renew the battle on the 8th. Curtis, on the other hand, correctly estimated the weakened condition of his opponent, drew in his forces for a more compact defense, and accepted the challenge.

On the second day (8 Mar.) Sigel, who had taken little part in the action so far, was ordered to attack on the left where his two divisions had formed during the night. After a particularly effective artillery action his infantry charged and drove the Confederates from Pea Ridge. An attack was then started from the Federal right and Van Dorn's forces driven in confusion from the field. They retreated to the Arkansas River, where Van Dorn received orders to leave Ark. to assist in the defense of the Mississippi River. He arrived at Memphis after the battle of SHILOH.

Of approximately 11,250 Union troops engaged there were 1,384 casualties; out of about 14,000 Confederates engaged there were approximately 800 casualties (Livermore, 79).

PEARSALL, Uri Balcom. Union officer. N.Y. 1st Sgt. 4th Wis. Cav. 16 May '61; 2d Lt. 1 July '62; Lt. Col. 99th US Col. Inf. 2 Sept. '63; Col. 48th Wis. 12 Apr. '65; Bvt. B.G. USV (war service).

PEARSON, Alfred L. Union officer. 1838–1903. Pa. A lawyer, he was commissioned Capt. 155th Pa. 2 Sept. '62 and Maj. 31 Dec. '62. He was named Lt. Col. 1 Nov. '63 and Col. 1 July '64. Mustered out in June '65. Breveted for Peeble's Farm (Bvt. B.G. USV 30 Sept. '64) and war service (Maj. Gen. USV 1 May '65), he was given the Medal of

Honor in 1897 for Lewis Farm. Returning to his law practice, he held several minor political offices and was active in the militia and veterans' organizations.

PEARSON, Robert Newton. Union officer. Pa. Pvt. Co. A 10th Ill. 20 Apr.–29 July '61; Pvt. Co. K 31st Ill. 18 Sept. '61; 1st Lt. Adj. 31st Ill. 17 May '62; Maj. 24 Feb. '63; Lt. Col. 1 July '63; Col. 3 Apr. '65; Bvt. B.G. USV (war service).

PEASE, Phineas. Union officer. 1826–93. Conn. Lt. Col. 49th Ill. 31 Dec. '61; Col. 6 Mar. '63; Bvt. B.G. USV (war service); mustered out 9 Jan. '65. W.I.A. Shiloh. He was active in railroad development and management.

PEASE, William Russell. Union officer. c. 1831–95. N.Y. USMA 1855 (31/34); Inf. 1st Lt. 7th US Inf. 23 Mar. '61; Capt. 8 June '61; Col. 117th N.Y. 15 Aug. '62; resigned USV 26 Aug. '63; retired 28 Aug. '63; Bvt. B.G. USV. Brevets for Suffolk (Va.), service with Vol. troops, war service. Commanded 3d Brig., 3d Div. Def. North Potomac, Mil. Dist. Wash.

PECK, Frank Henry. Union officer. Conn. Maj. 12th Conn. 12 Feb. '62; Lt. Col. 31 Jan. '63; Bvt. B.G. USV 19 Sept. '64 (Winchester, Va.). W.I.A. and died 19 Sept. '64 at Winchester.

PECK, John James. Union gen. 1821–78. N.Y. USMA 1843 (8/39); Arty. After serving in garrison, the Mexican War (2 brevets), the frontier, and Indian fighting, he resigned in 1853 to engage in railroading and banking and became active in Democratic politics. Appointed B.G. USV 9 Aug. '61, he commanded 3d Brig., Buell's (Keyes's) division, Potomac (3 Oct. '61–13 Mar. '62) in the defenses of Washington. In the beginning of the Peninsular campaign he led 3, 1, IV (13 Mar.–23 June '62) at Yorktown, Williamsburg, and

Fair Oaks. During the Seven Days' Battles he commanded the 2d Div., IV Corps (24 June–26 Sept. '62). Promoted Maj. Gen. USV 4 July '62, he commanded the division at Suffolk, VII, Dept. of Va. (8–30 Sept. '62; 2 Jan.–6 Apr. '63 and 14 Apr.–1 Aug. '63) and was relieved when seriously injured. He next commanded the Dist. of N.C., Dept. of Va. and N.C. (14 Aug. '63–4 Jan. '64 and 5 Feb.–28 Apr. '64) before being mustered out 24 Aug. '65. After the war he was president of an insurance company.

PECK, Lewis Mead. Union officer. Conn. Commissioned Capt. 67th N.Y. 24 June '61, he was promoted Col. 173d N.Y. 11 Oct. '62 and Col. 16 Mar. '63. He was mustered out in Oct. '65 and breveted for war service (B.G. USV) and Cedar Creek (Maj. Gen. USV).

PECK, William R. C.S.A. gen. Wright says he was appointed B.G. C.S.A. from La. to rank from 18 Feb. '65 and that he was paroled at Vicksburg 6 June of that year. Wood and C.M.H. do not list him.

PECULIAR INSTITUTION. Euphemistic Southern term for slavery. After Calhoun had defended the "peculiar labor" of the South in 1828 and the "peculiar domestic institution" in 1830, the term came into general use.

PEEBLE'S FARM, Va., 30 Sept.–2 Oct. '64. POPLAR SPRINGS CHURCH, same dates.

PEGRAM, John. C.S.A. gen. 1832–65. Va. USMA 1854 (10/46); Dragoons. He served on the frontier, as cavalry instructor at West Point, on the Utah Expedition, and then a two-year leave of absence in Europe, returning for Indian scouting and fighting before resigning 10 May '61 as 1st Lt. Commissioned Lt. Col. C.S.A., he surrendered to McClellan after being beaten in the WEST VIRGINIA OPERATIONS IN

1861. From Apr. '62 until Oct. he was Col. and Chief Engr. for Beauregard and Bragg. Appointed B.G. C.S.A. 7 Nov. '62, he served under Kirby Smith, fought at Lexington (Ky.), and led the cavalry at Stones River. From Mar. to May '63 he was on the expedition with Kirby Smith and fought at Gordon's Mills, LaFayette, and Chickamauga. Going to the A.N.V., he fought under Ewell in the Mine Run operations and was wounded at the Wilderness. He returned to active duty in July '64 and fought under Early in the Shenandoah Valley. Married on 19 Jan. '65 to Hetty Cary of Baltimore. He was killed 6 Feb. at Hatcher's Run in the battles around Petersburg. Freeman says that he was only a B.G. at his death and that there is no record of his nomination or confirmation as Maj. Gen. in the records of the C.S.A. Congress, even though he was commanding a division and had for some time carried out the duties of the higher rank. Wood and Cullum say he was a Maj. Gen., Wood giving 26 Nov. '64 as the effective date.

His younger brother, William Johnson Pegram, was mortally wounded two months later at Five Forks, a Col. of Arty. at 23. A "shy, nearsighted young student [when the war began]," he was "one of those rare men who expand in battle" and a favorite of D. S. Freeman in *Lee's Lts.*

PEGRAM'S FARM, Va., 30 Sept.–2 Oct. '64. POPLAR SPRINGS CHURCH, same dates.

PEIRSON, Charles Lawrence. Union officer. Mass. 1st Lt. Adj. 20th Mass. 19 July '61; Lt. Col. 39th Mass. 6 Sept. '62; Col. 19 Aug. '64; Bvt. B.G. USV; resigned 4 Jan. '65. Brevets for Wilderness, Spotsylvania, Weldon R.R. Served on staffs of Dana and Sedgwick. Captured at Balls Bluff 21 Oct. '61; W.I.A. Spotsylvania and Weldon R.R. 18 Aug. '64.

PELHAM, John. C.S.A. officer. "The Gallant Pelham." 1838–63. Ala. Resigning from West Point (ex-May '61), and returning to the South through the Federal lines, he entered the C.S.A. Arty. As Capt. he fought at 1st Bull Run, Williamsburg, Gaines's Mill, and 2d Bull Run, and was promoted Maj. in time for Antietam, Stuart's Oct. '62 raid around McClellan and FREDERICKSBURG. It was at the last-named battle that Lee said of him: "It is glorious to see such courage in one so young!" and described him as "gallant." Blond, blue-eyed, and handsome, his modest manner belied his early fame, and he had begun to develop new artillery tactics with his Stuart Horse Arty., which consisted of two rifles and two 12-pound Napoleons. "As grand a flirt as ever lived" (*Lee's Lts.*), he was the *beau ideal* of the Confederacy, and three girls in the neighborhood put on mourning when he was killed in Mar. '63 at KELLY'S FORD. He was promoted Lt. Col. posthumously.

PELOUZE, Louis H. Union officer. c. 1831–78. Pa. USMA 1853 (17/52); Arty. He fought in the Seminole War and served on the frontier in the Kans. border disturbances before being named Capt 15th US Inf. 14 May. '61. As acting Asst. Adj. Gen., he served under Dix on the Port Royal expedition, in Shields's division, and in the same capacity in the II Corps (Army of Va.). During the last-named service he was severely wounded at Cedar Mountain 9 Aug. '62 and on sick leave until October. In Feb. he was named Asst. Adj. Gen. of the Dept. of Va. and in July '63 took the same post with the Dept. of Va. and N.C. before going, in Aug. '63, to the Adj. Gen. office. He remained in Washington for the rest of the war and died on active duty as Maj. (24 Mar. '64), having been breveted for

Cedar Mountain and war service (B.G. USA).

PEMBERTON, John Clifford. Northern-born C.S.A. gen. 1814–81. Pa. USMA 1837 (27/50); Arty. Of Quaker ancestry, he nonetheless served in the Seminole War, on border duty, in the Mexican War (2 brevets, A.D.C. to William J. Worth), on the frontier in Indian fighting and in the Utah Expedition before resigning 24 Apr. '61 as Capt. Scott tried to give him a Federal colonelcy, but he refused and went to his wife's native Va., where he was commissioned Lt. Col. C.S.A. 28 Apr. '61. Ordered to organize the cavalry and artillery of the state, he was named Col. in the Prov. Army of Va. on 8 May '61 and promoted, in rapid order, Maj. of C.S.A. Arty. 15 June '61; B.G. C.S.A. 17 June '61; and Maj. Gen. C.S.A. 15 Jan. '62. In command of the Dept. of S.C., Ga., and Fla., he counseled the abandonment of Fort Sumter and the building of Fort Wagner and Battery B as the basis of defense. Promoted Lt. Gen. 13 Oct. '62, he was given command of the Dept. of Miss. Tenn., and East La. "Placing Pemberton in command in Mississippi must rank as one of Jefferson Davis' major mistakes" (Horn, 212). During the VICKSBURG CAMPAIGN (which see for evaluation of his generalship and the circumstances surrounding selection of 4 July for the surrender) Pemberton was harassed and bewildered not only by Grant's brilliant strategy but also by conflicting instructions from his superiors, Davis and J. E. Johnston. The South, humiliated by the twin defeats of Gettysburg and Vicksburg, suspected treason. There is no evidence that Pemberton was guilty of any offense other than mediocre generalship. After being exchanged, he resigned 18 May '64 and served the rest of the war as Col. and Insp. of Arty. Then he

farmed near Warrenton, Va., before moving to Philadelphia.

PEMBERTON'S CORPS. See under CORPS, Confed.

PENDER, William Dorsey. C.S.A. gen. 1834–63. N.C. USMA 1854 (19/46); Arty. He served on the frontier in Indian fighting and in garrison before resigning in Mar. '61 as 1st Lt. Commissioned Capt. of C.S.A. Arty., he was in charge of the recruiting in Baltimore and on 16 May '61 was elected Col. 3d N.C. Transferring on 15 Aug. of that year to the 6th N.C., he fought in Whiting's brigade on the Peninsula and was promoted B.G. C.S.A. (3 June '62) for his actions at Seven Pines. He then commanded a N.C. brigade under A. P. Hill during the Seven Days' Battles and fought under Jackson at 2d Bull Run, Antietam, Fredericksburg, and Chancellorsville. At the last-named battle he was wounded three times but did not leave the field. At 29 years of age he was promoted Maj. Gen. 27 May '63 and led his division at Gettysburg, where he was severely wounded on the second day. Evacuated to Staunton, he died 18 July after an amputation.

PENDLETON, William Nelson. C.S.A. gen. 1809–83. Va. USMA 1830 (5/42); Arty. He served in garrison and taught mathematics at West Point before resigning in 1833. He was then at Bristol College, Pa., and Delaware College. Ordained an Episcopal minister in 1838, he was principal of Episcopal High School in Alexandria 1839–44 and then moved to Baltimore to take a parish and run a school. Three years later he became minister of a church in Frederick, Md., and in 1853 moved to Lexington, Va. On 1 May '61 he was elected Capt. of the Rockbridge Arty. and was named Col. and J. E. Johnston's Chief of Arty. 13 July '61. He was appointed B.G. C.S.A. 26 Mar. '62 and Lee's Chief of Arty. In the reorganization of May '63 his general artillery reserve was broken up (and the guns sent down to the divisions and corps), but he retained his title of Chief of Arty. He continued in his ministerial duties during the war, preaching when he wasn't directing the guns. Sorrel characterized him as "a well-meaning man without qualities for the high post he claimed—Chief of Artillery of the Army." Similar to Lee in looks, he was frequently mistaken for him. His daughter was married to C.S.A. B.G. Edwin G. Lee and his son was Col. "Sandie" Pendleton of Jackson's staff.

PENINSULA, CONFEDERATE DEPARTMENT AND ARMY OF THE. Colonel J. B. Magruder on 21 May '61 was sent to command operations on the lower Peninsula with headquarters at Yorktown. On the 26th the Dept. of the Peninsula was ordered into existence and his force, which numbered 13,000 by the end of the year, took the name of the department. At BIG BETHEL, 10 June '61, it fought the first land battle of the war. As the Confederates concentrated to oppose McClellan's Peninsular campaign, J. E. Johnston on 26 Apr. '62 was given jurisdiction over the forces of Magruder (who was now a Maj. Gen.). The Army of the Peninsula disappeared as a unit designation, and Magruder's command (reorganized) became known as the Right Wing of Johnston's army.

PENINSULAR CAMPAIGN, Mar.–July '62. The 1st Battle of Bull Run showed the Federal government that they were in for a long struggle to restore the Union. McClellan was made C. in C. of the Union armies succeeding the superannuated Winfield Scott. The "Young Napoleon" proceeded to accomplish efficiently the gigantic task of organizing the Federal levies into

some semblance of a military formation.

The opposing capitals, Washington and Richmond, continued to be the poles around which both Federals and Confederates shaped their strategy.

Erroneously agreeing on Richmond as the objective, McClellan and the Washington authorities disagreed only on the line of operations to be pursued in capturing it. When J. E. Johnston's army withdrew from Manassas to the line of the Rappahannock, McClellan was permitted to execute his plan of advancing on Richmond by water. He was told, however, to leave adequate forces to protect the capital.

After vague assurances to Lincoln that the defense of Washington was provided for, McClellan started 17 Mar. moving 12 divisions by transport to Fort Monroe. The latter place was held by Wool with 12,000. Huger with 9,000 Confederates held Norfolk. Since the Confederate ironclad *Merrimac* had appeared, the Federal Navy could not protect the transports for a movement up the James. Federal forces in the Shenandoah were to be reduced to provide a corps under McDowell to follow McClellan overland to the Peninsula.

The Federal advance up the Peninsula started 4 April and stopped the next day when it came unexpectedly against a defensive position Magruder had organized along the Warwick River. McClellan, the great military administrator, began to evidence the deficiencies that prevented his becoming a great field commander; after a two-day reconnaissance he decided on a formal siege of a position that could have been carried immediately by assault.

R. E. Lee had recently assumed the peculiar position of military advisor to Pres. Davis. In this capacity he formulated Confederate plans to counter the threat to Richmond. The Confederates knew of McClellan's departure from

Alexandria with a large force as soon as it started but did not know whether he would attack Norfolk or move up the Peninsula. On 4 Apr. Lee was certain the attack would be against Magruder and sent him reinforcements from Johnston's army. When McClellan's forces appeared opposite the Yorktown line the Confederates were holding an eight-mile front with not more than 17,000 men. The leading Union corps of Keyes (IV) and Heintzelman (III) numbered 60,000; Sumner's corps (II) had landed and were moving to reinforce them.

McClellan's delay enabled the Confederates to move most of the troops from the Dept. of Northern Va. to oppose his advance. The only Confederate troops elsewhere were Jackson's 4,200 in the lower Shenandoah, Edward Johnson's 3,000 in the upper valley (at McDowell), Holmes's 6,000 at Fredericksburg, and Huger's 9,000 at Norfolk. During the siege of Yorktown McClellan opposed J. E. Johnston's 60,000 with 112,000 Union troops.

On 3 May Johnston dropped back to better defensive positions the Confederate engineers had been preparing around Richmond. McClellan's elaborately prepared attack landed in midair. An insignificant rear-guard action took place 5 May at Williamsburg.

Huger abandoned Norfolk 9 May, when Johnston withdrew, and occupied Petersburg. Troops from Fort Monroe, under the ancient Wool, occupied Norfolk and advanced to Suffolk. This opened the James to a point seven miles below Richmond, where the Federal fleet was repulsed at DREWRY'S BLUFF, 15 May. Confederate evacuation of Norfolk necessitated destruction of the *Merrimac,* since the ironclad was deprived of its base.

Jackson's operations in the Valley had caused Federal authorities to withhold troops McClellan had wanted to use on the Peninsula. The Union commander was further handicapped by Washington's inability to give him a decision as to whether McDowell's (I) Corps of 40,000 was to be withheld indefinitely or temporarily. As a result McClellan was forced to operate north of the Chickahominy to be in a position to cooperate with McDowell if the latter should move overland from Fredericksburg. At the same time he had to prepare to attack Richmond, which was south of the formidable river-swamp barrier. The result was that the Army of the Potomac was astride the Chickahominy and ripe for the southernmost wing to be defeated in detail.

Fitz-John Porter led an aggressive reconnaissance in force toward HAN-OVER C.H., Va., 27 May, during this period.

Johnston's well-conceived plan for the battle of FAIR OAKS AND SEVEN PINES 31 May failed because of faulty execution (or defective staff work, to be more precise) on the part of his subordinates and the aggressive reaction of the Federals. In a series of frustrating blunders the Confederates lost an opportunity to deal McClellan's army a crippling defeat.

R. E. Lee succeeded Johnston (wounded) 1 June. (It is a widespread misconception that Lee took command of all Confederate field armies at this time; he did not become Gen. in Chief until 1865.)

During June McClellan was reinforced by McCall's division of McDowell's corps; it moved from Fredericksburg by water and was attached to Porter's (V) corps. McClellan now readjusted his dispositions, moving all but one of his corps south of the Chickahominy. Porter's corps, screened by Stoneman's cavalry detachment, was left north of the barrier to provide for a link up with McDowell, who had been directed on 8 June to move overland to join McClellan.

Having completed his successful diversion in the Valley, Stonewall Jackson's command (now consisting of Ewell's and Whiting's divisions and Lawton's brigade, in addition to his own division) took up a position at Swift Run Gap on 10 June. Lee saw that there was no immediate danger of a Federal offensive in northern Va. and conceived a plan for using Jackson's force in conjunction with those around Richmond to destroy Porter's relatively isolated corps.

In preparation for this operation (Mechanicsville) he ordered Stuart to reconnoiter Porter's flank and the routes of approach for Jackson's force. With his unfortunate flair for the spectacular, Stuart exceeded his instructions and rode completely around the Federal army, thereby alerting McClellan and facilitating the latter's subsequent change of base.

On 25 June the Seven Days' Battles started. The battles are covered separately. (See SEVEN DAYS' BATTLES for names, dates, and the numerous alternate names for these engagements.)

Although Lee failed to destroy McClellan's army, he did remove the immediate threat to Richmond. McClellan executed a brilliant change of base from the York to the James, thanks largely to Stuart's having alerted him to the need for such an operation. Federal troops conducted an admirable delaying action, showing the fruits of McClellan's training. Federal artillery exhibited a superiority, particularly at Malvern Hill, that was to increase throughout the war.

Stonewall Jackson's mysterious inertia probably accounts, more than any other single factor, for the failure of Lee's plans. The unwieldy organization of Lee's army—seven separate divisions

without any intermediate corps echelon —and lack of qualified staff assistants also contributed to Lee's failure to gain decisive tactical results.

McClellan's army remained at Harrison's Landing until the authorities disapproved his excellent plan of advancing on Petersburg. On the recommendation of Halleck, who had just come to Washington as Gen. in Chief, McClellan's forces were withdrawn to reinforce Pope for the 2d Bull Run campaign.

PENNINGTON, Alexander Cummings McWhorter. Union officer. 1838–1917. N.J. USMA 1860 (18/41); Arty. Bvt. 2d Lt. 2d Arty. 1 July '60; 2d Lt. 1 Feb. '61; 1st Lt. 14 May '61; Col. 3d N.J. Cav. 1 Oct. '64; Bvt. B.G. USV; mustered out USV 1 Aug. '65; continued in R.A. until retired in 1899 as B.G. USV; also served as B.G. USV during Spanish-American War. Brevets for Beverly Ford, Gettysburg campaign, Cedar Creek, war service (2). Commanded 1, 3, Cav. Corps (Potomac and Shenandoah).

PENNSYLVANIA CAMPAIGN. See GETTYSBURG CAMPAIGN.

PENNSYLVANIA RESERVES. Thirteen infantry regiments of Pa. volunteers were designated as the 1st through the 13th Pa. Reserves. Although the latter was the designation by which these regiments were known, they were also assigned "volunteer numbers" of 30th through 42d Pa. Volunteers.

These 13 regiments were grouped into three brigades to constitute a division commonly known as the Pa. Reserves. Its commanders were, in succession, McCall, Reynolds, Meade, and Crawford. The division was first assigned to McDowell's (I) corps. It was part of Porter's (V) corps during the Peninsular campaign. During the campaigns of 2d Bull Run, Antietam, and Fredericksburg it was in I Corps. After its heavy fighting in 1862 the division was ordered to Washington for rest and recuperation. The brigades of McCandless (1st) and Fisher (3d) volunteered to rejoin the Army of the Potomac for the defense of Pa. Assigned to Meade's (later Sykes's) V Corps, they became Crawford's (3d) division. As such these two brigades fought at Gettysburg and in succeeding campaigns of the Army of the Potomac through Spotsylvania. The last action of the Pa. Reserves as a unit was at Bethesda Church, 1 June '64.

Within the division the brigade organizations did not remain fixed. At Fredericksburg McCandless' (1st) brigade had included the 1st, 2d, 6th, and 13th; Magilton's (2d) brigade had included the 3d, 4th, 7th, and 8th; J. W. Fisher's brigade (3d) had included the 5th, 9th, 10th, 11th and 12th regiments. The composition of the 1st and 3d brigades was the same when they rejoined the army for Gettysburg as it had been when they left it after Fredericksburg. Of the regiments that had been in the 2d Brig., the 3d and 4th fought with the Army of W. Va., distinguishing themselves at Cloyd's Mountain, 9–10 May '64. The 7th and 8th Pa. Reserves were assigned to the 1st and 3d brigades, respectively, in the Wilderness campaign. The 9th was withdrawn from the line 4 May '64, just before the battle of the Wilderness, and sent to Washington for discharge.

When the rest of the division was mustered out the next month a large number re-enlisted. These were organized, along with recruits, into the 190th and 191st Pa. and, as the Veteran Reserve Brig., fought at Cold Harbor. They ultimately became part of the 3d Brig., Ayres's (2d) division, V Corps.

The 1st Pa. Cav. and the 1st Pa. Light Arty. were originally part of the Pa. Reserves division, but were detached during the first few months of the division's service.

The term "Pa. Reserves" came about as follows. In the first calls from Washington for troops, Pa.—like most other states—found more men rushing to the colors than had been asked for or than could be supplied by the Federal government. Cameron, a political foe of Gov. Curtin, refused to take into Federal service the 25 militia regiments in excess of the quota that Curtin had raised. The Gov., therefore, organized them into the Pa. Reserves, training and equipping them at state expense (Hesseltine).

8TH PENNSYLVANIA RESERVES
(37th Pa.)

Colonels: George S. Hays and Silas M. Bailey.

Battles: Mechanicsville, Gaines's Mill, White Oak Swamp, Glendale, Manassas, South Mountain, Antietam, Fredericksburg, Wilderness, Spotsylvania. Present also at Dranesville, Malvern Hill, and Chantilly.

Organized 28 June '61 at Pittsburgh, it performed outpost duty in northern Va. before joining McClellan on the Peninsula. Losses in the Seven Days' Battles amounted to 230, most of them being suffered at Gaines's Mill. Throughout the rest of the year the regiment fought in every major engagement of the Army of the Potomac. At Fredericksburg it lost 131 men (almost half its strength) in the attacks against Prospect Hill. After a respite in Washington the regiment rejoined the army for the battles of the Wilderness and Spotsylvania where it lost 17 killed. On 17 May '64 it was pulled out of the line to be mustered out. (See also PENNSYLVANIA RESERVES.)

9TH PENNSYLVANIA RESERVES

Commanders: Col. Conrad F. Jackson (Bvt. B.G., K.I.A.), Col. Robert Anderson, Maj. Charles Barnes.

Engagements: Dranesville, Mechanicsville, Gaines's Mill, Glendale, Manassas, South Mountain, Antietam, Fredericksburg, Culpeper C.H. Also present at Malvern Hill, Gettysburg, Mine Run, Wilderness.

Captured colors of 10th Ala. in fight for Cooper's Battery at Glendale. (See also PENNSYLVANIA RESERVES.)

10TH PENNSYLVANIA RESERVES

Colonels: John S. McCalmont (USMA), James T. Kirk, Adoniram J. Warner (Bvt. B.G.), Ira Ayer, Jr.

Battles: Mechanicsville, Gaines's Mill, Glendale, Manassas, South Mountain, Antietam, Fredericksburg, Gettysburg, Bristoe Station, Manassas Junction (15 Apr. '64), Wilderness, Spotsylvania, North Anna, Bethesda Church. Also present at Dranesville, Malvern Hill, Mine Run, Totopotomoy.

Recruited in May '61 in western Pa., with rendezvous at Pittsburgh, it contained a high percentage of educated men: Co. D came from Jefferson College and Co. I was recruited from students of Allegheny College. Other companies had similar material, "teachers and pupils serving in the ranks together" (Fox). In June '62, as part of McCall's division, it joined Porter's V Corps in the Peninsula. After Gaines's Mill, where it suffered 134 casualties, the regiment rejoined I Corps. After Fredericksburg the regiment was ordered to Washington to recover from its heavy losses of the year's fighting. The regiment was mustered out of service the summer of '64 at the expiration of its three years' service.

11TH PENNSYLVANIA RESERVES
(40th Pa. Inf.)

Colonels: Thomas F. Gallagher and Samuel M. Jackson (both Bvt. B.G.).

Battles: Mechanicsville, Gaines's Mill, Glendale, Manassas, South Mountain, Antietam, Fredericksburg, Gettysburg, Bristoe Station, Wilderness, Spotsylvania, Bethesda Church. Present also at Dranesville, Malvern Hill, Rappahannock Station, Mine Run, North Anna, and Totopotomoy.

The 11th had the heaviest losses of any regiment in the Pa. Reserves; it had the eighth highest percentage of killed in action (on the basis of total enrollment) among all Federal regiments. Recruited in western Pa., it arrived 26 July '61 at Washington and was assigned to the 2d Brig. (then Meade's) of the Pa. Reserves (division). At Gaines's Mill the regiment was cut off and forced to surrender (with the exception of Co. B, which was absent). Officers and men were exchanged 5 Aug. '62 and rejoined the Army of the Potomac before it left the Peninsula. After their losses at 2d Bull Run and South Mountain the regiment entered the battle of Antietam with less than 200. With the addition of recruits and the return of wounded, the regiment went into action at Fredericksburg with 394 men and lost 211 killed and wounded. When relieved from duty 30 May '64 for muster out, the men not eligible for discharge were transferred into the 190th Pa. (See also PENNSYLVANIA RESERVES.)

13TH PENNSYLVANIA RESERVES
("Bucktails")

Colonels: Thomas L. Kane (Bvt. Maj. Gen.), Charles J. Biddle, Hugh W. McNeil (K.I.A.), Charles F. Taylor (K.I.A.), Major W. R. Hartshorn.

Battles: Dranesville; Cos. G, C, Ч, and I at Harrisonburg and Cross Keys; Cos. A, B, D, E, F, and K at Mechanicsville, Gaines's Mill, Glendale, Catlett's Station, Manassas, South Mountain, Antietam, Fredericksburg, Gettysburg, Wilderness, Spotsylvania, Bethesda Church. Present also at New Creek, Malvern Hill, Williamsport, Mine Run, North Anna, Totopotomoy.

Known also as the 1st Pa. Rifles and

Kane Rifles, the regiment was recruited in Apr. '61 from among Pa. lumbermen who were good shots and who brought their own rifles into the service with them. The regiment's nickname stems from the custom of requiring a prospective recruit to bring with him the tail of a buck he had shot, to demonstrate his skill with a rifle. The men wore a buck tail on their hats as a unit identification. The regiment was subsequently armed with Sharps rifles and later with Spencers. Four companies served under Col. Kane in the Shenandoah Valley (against Stonewall Jackson) when the rest of the regiment went with the division to the Peninsula. The regiment was reunited for the 2d Bull Run campaign. McNeil was killed at Antietam and Taylor was killed in the fight for Little Round Top. The regiment was mustered out 11 June '64. (See also PENNSYLVANIA RESERVES.)

49TH PENNSYLVANIA (3d Brigade, 1st Division, VI Corps)

Colonels: William H. Irwin (Bvt. B.G.); Thomas M. Hulings (R.A.; K.I.A.), Boynton J. Hickman.

Battles: Yorktown, Williamsburg, Garnett's Hill, Golding's Farm, Antietam, Marye's Heights, Rappahannock Station, Wilderness, Spotsylvania, Hanovertown, Cold Harbor, Opequon, Petersburg, Sayler's Creek. Present also at Savage's Station, White Oak Swamp, Malvern Hill, Crampton's Gap, Fredericksburg ('62), Salem Church, Gettysburg, Mine Run, Fort Stevens, Hatcher's Run.

Recruited in Mifflin, Centre, Chester, Huntingdon, and Juniata counties, it reached Washington 22 Sept. '61 and was assigned to Hancock's brigade of Wm. F. Smith's Division. After distinguishing itself in the Peninsular campaign, the regiment was transferred in early '63 to 3d Brig., 1st (Brooks's) division, VI Corps, where it remained the rest of the war. Participated in bayonet attack at Rappahannock Station. At Spotsylvania it was in Upton's assaulting column and lost 260 men and officers; among the killed were the regimental commander (Hulings) and Lt. Col. John B. Miles, the second in command. Two days later the regiment had further losses in the assault of the "bloody angle." Regimental losses during the period 6–13 May '64 (Wilderness and Spotsylvania) were 317 killed or wounded out of the 530 who had crossed the Rapidan.

63D PENNSYLVANIA

Colonels: Alexander Hays (USMA; R.A.; Bvt. Maj. Gen.; K.I.A.), A. S. Morgan, William S. Kirkwood (K.I.A.), John A. Danes.

Battles: Pohick Church, Yorktown, Fair Oaks, Oak Grove, Glendale, Manassas, Fredericksburg, Chancellorsville, Gettysburg, Auburn Mills, Kelly's Ford, Mine Run, Wilderness, Spotsylvania, North Anna, Cold Harbor, Petersburg. Present also at Seven Days' Battles, Chantilly, Totopotomoy.

Organized in Aug. '61, seven companies came from Pittsburgh and the others from western counties. Initially assigned to Heintzelman's division, it performed outpost duty until sent to the Peninsula with Jameson's (1st) brigade, which became part of Kearny's (3d) division, III Corps. Its heaviest fighting was at Fair Oaks and the Wilderness. When III Corps was discontinued (24 Mar. '64), the regiment was put in Hays's brigade, Birney's division, II Corps. Its term of service expired 9 Sept. '64, when those not eligible for discharge were transferred to the 99th Pa.

83D PENNSYLVANIA

Colonels: John W. McLane (K.I.A.), Strong Vincent (Brig. Gen.; K.I.A.), O. S. Woodward (Bvt. B.G.), Chauncey P. Rogers.

Battles: Hanover C.H., Gaines's Mill, Malvern Hill, Manassas, Fredericksburg, Chancellorsville, Gettysburg, guerrilla action in Va. 10 Dec. '63, Wilderness, North Anna, Spotsylvania, Bethesda Church, Cold Harbor, Petersburg siege, Peeble's Farm, Dabney's Mills, Gravelly Run, White Oak Road, Five Forks.

Present also at Yorktown, Mechanicsville, Peach Orchard, Savage's Station, White Oak Swamp, Glendale, Antietam, Shepherdstown Ford, Aldie, Rappahannock Station, Mine Run, Totopotomoy, Weldon R.R., Hatcher's Run, Appomattox.

Only one other Federal regiment had more battle casualties than the 83d Pa. It was brigaded with the 44th N.Y. in Butterfield's brigade, Morell's division, V Corps. Col. McLane was killed at Gaines's Mill and Vincent fell in the decisive attack to secure Little Round Top at Gettysburg.

140TH PENNSYLVANIA (Zook's brigade, Caldwell's division. II Corps) Colonels: Richard P. Roberts (K.I.A.), John Fraser (Bvt. B.G.).

Battles: Chancellorsville, Gettysburg, Mine Run, Bristoe Station, Wilderness, Corbin's Bridge, Po River, Spotsylvania, North Anna, Totopotomoy, Cold Harbor, Petersburg, Deep Bottom, Reams's Station, Hatcher's Run, Sayler's Creek, Farmville. Present also at Strawberry Plains and Appomattox.

With 17.4 per cent of its officers and men killed in action, this unit ranks fourth on the list of regiments having the highest percentage of killed (on basis of total enrollment) of the war. Recruited in the western counties, it left the state 10 Sept. '62. In the Wheat Field (Gettysburg) the regiment lost 241 out of 589 engaged; when its regiment commander, Roberts, took command of the brigade after Zook's death, he, too, was killed in action. Its losses at Spotsylvania were even larger in proportion to strength engaged than they had been at Gettysburg; the regiment took part in Hancock's grand charge of 12 May and in other actions of II Corps. The regiment had 169 casualties, of whom 52 were killed. At Farmville, three days before Lee's surrender, the regiment lost 5 K.I.A., of whom two were officers.

141ST PENNSYLVANIA
Colonel: Henry J. Madill (Bvt. Maj. Gen.).

Battles: Fredericksburg, Chancellorsville, Gettysburg, Auburn, Mine Run, Wilderness, Spotsylvania, North Anna, Petersburg assault, Jerusalem Road, Petersburg siege, Deep Bottom, Poplar Spring Church (2 Oct. '64), Boydton Road, Hatcher's Run, Petersburg (25 Mar. '65). Also present at Kelly's Ford, Totopotomoy, Cold Harbor, Strawberry Plains, Sayler's Creek, Farmville, Appomattox.

After recruiting seven companies in Bradford County, two in Susquehanna, and one in Wayne, it left Harrisburg 30 Aug. '62 for immediate active service. It was first assigned to Robinson's (1st) brigade of Birney's (1st) division, III Corps. Serving mostly as local security for artillery ("battery support") at Fredericksburg, it had only two men killed. At Chancellorsville, however, it was heavily engaged. With the mission of counterattacking to disrupt and delay the advancing Confederates, the regiment lost 235 out of 419 effectives in successfully performing this task. Before the battle of Gettysburg the regimental strength had been reduced to 198. In the fighting in the Peach Orchard ("Sickles' Salient") it lost 149 (75 per cent). In the reorganization of 24 Mar. '64 the regiment went with its division to II Corps. Now greatly reduced in strength the 141st became part of Pierce's (2d) brigade in Mott's (3d) division.

142D PENNSYLVANIA

Colonels: Robert P. Cummings (K.I.A.), Alfred B. McCalmont (Bvt. B.G.), Horatio N. Warren.

Battles: Fredericksburg, Gettysburg, Catlett's Station, Wilderness, Spotsylvania, North Anna, Cold Harbor, Petersburg, Boydton Road, Dabney's Mills, Five Forks. Present also at Fitz Hugh's Crossing, Chancellorsville, Mine Run, Totopotomoy, Weldon R.R., Peeble's Farm, Hatcher's Run, Appomattox.

Taking the field in Sept. '62 it was assigned first to Magilton's (2d) brigade of the Pa. Reserves (Meade's division), I Corps. Its first action was at Fredericksburg where it lost 243 out of the 550 engaged. When the Pa. Reserves were withdrawn for rehabilitation in Feb. '63, the 142d Pa. was assigned to Rowley's (1st) brigade of Doubleday's (3d) division. At Gettysburg the regiment was heavily engaged in the first day's fighting, the division of which it was part being on the extreme left flank of the Federal position on McPherson Ridge and bearing the brunt of A. P. Hill's main attack. Col. Cummings was killed; the regiment lost 211 officers and men, most of them in the first day's fighting. In Apr. '64 the regiment was transferred to V Corps where it remained. It was initially assigned to Stone's (3d) brigade of Wadsworth's (4th) division, a division composed of veterans from the disbanded I Corps. The regiment also served in Chamberlain's (1st) brigade of Griffin's (1st) division, and in Crawford's (3d) division.

145TH PENNSYLVANIA

Colonels: Hiram L. Brown (Bvt. B.G.), David B. McCreary (Bvt. B.G.).

Battles: Fredericksburg, Chancellorsville, Gettysburg, Auburn (Va.), Bristoe Station, Spotsylvania, Totopotomoy, Cold Harbor, Petersburg assault and siege, Deep Bottom, Hatcher's Run, Petersburg capture, Sutherland Station. Present at Antietam, Mine Run, Wilderness, Po River, North Anna, Strawberry Plains, Reams's Station, White Oak Road, Sayler's Creek, Farmville, Appomattox.

Six companies recruited in Erie County, the others in western Pa. Five days after leaving the state (12 Sept. '62) the regiment was at Antietam. While at Harpers Ferry it was assigned to Caldwell's (1st) brigade, Hancock's (1st) division, II Corps. At Fredericksburg it lost 229 out of the 505 men of the eight companies engaged; nine officers were killed and the regimental commander (Brown) seriously wounded. At Chancellorsville 112 men were captured in an outpost when the army retreated. At Gettysburg the regiment, as part of Brooke's (4th) brigade, took part in the fighting around the Wheat Field; in this action it lost 84 out of 200 engaged. During the winter of 1863–64 the regiment trained and assimilated recruits before undertaking the final campaign against Richmond. Although not engaged in the Wilderness, it saw heavy fighting at Spotsylvania, losing 172 men. In the Petersburg assault in June '64 it lost nine killed and a large number captured. The regiment finished the war at greatly reduced strength.

148TH PENNSYLVANIA (1st Division, II Corps, throughout the war)

Colonel: James A. Beaver (Bvt. B.G.).

Battles: Chancellorsville, Gettysburg, Wilderness, Po River, Spotsylvania, Totopotomoy, Cold Harbor, Petersburg assault and siege, Jerusalem Road, Deep Bottom, Reams's Station, Hatcher's Run, White Oak Road, Farmville. Present also at Bristoe Station, Mine Run, North Anna, Strawberry Plains, Sutherland Station, Appomattox. Prison Guard at Salisbury, N.C.

Organized at Harrisburg in Sept. '62, seven companies were recruited in Centre County. At the request of the line officers, James A. Beaver of the 45th Pa. was appointed colonel. Beaver was severely wounded at Chancellorsville, again at Petersburg (16 June '64), and Reams's Station; his third wound required amputation of a leg. The regiment saw heavy fighting and had more losses than any other regiment at Spotsylvania. In Sept. '64, when the War Dept. ordered that one regiment in each division be issued breech-loading rifles, Gen. Hancock designated the 148th for this distinction.

PENNSYLVANIA, UNION DEPARTMENT OF. Constituted 27 Apr. '61, with headquarters at Philadelphia, to consist of Pa., Del., and all of Md. not embraced in the Departments of Annapolis and Washington. Merged into the Dept. of the Potomac 24 Aug. '61. Commander was Maj. Gen. Robert Patterson. Troops from this department which Patterson led into the Shenandoah Valley in July '61 are sometimes referred to (unofficially) as the Army of the Shenandoah (e.g., by Upton, 244). The department was re-created 1 Dec. '64 as part of the Middle Mil. Div.

PENNYPACKER, Galusha. Union gen. 1844–1916. Enlisting as Q.M. Sgt. 9th Pa. 22 Apr.–29 July '61, he was commissioned Capt. 97th Pa. 22 Aug. As Maj. 7 Oct. '61, he fought at Fort Wagner 10–11 July '63 and as Lt. Col. 3 Apr. '64 at Drewry's Bluff and Cold Harbor. He was named Col. 15 Aug. '64 and commanded 2, 2, X, James (14 Sept.–3 Dec. '64) and 2, 2, XXIV, Va. (3 Dec. '64–6 Jan. '65) around Petersburg. While commanded 2, Ames's division, Terry's Prov. Corps, N.C. (6–15 Jan. '65), he led his brigade at Fort Fisher, where he was seriously wounded. For this action he was promoted B.G. USV 15 Feb. '65 and given the Medal

of Honor 17 Aug. '91. In the eight months prior to this engagement he was wounded seven times. In addition to his regular appointments, he was *breveted* B.G. USV 15 Jan. '65 for Fort Fisher, Maj. Gen. USV for war service. B.G. USA for Fort Fisher and Maj. Gen. USA for war service. He continued in the R.A. until retired in 1883 as Col. and, having "never married, he spent the last years of his life in lonely retirement at his home in Philadelphia" (D.A.B.).

PENROSE, William Henry. Union gen. 1832–? N.Y. A civil and mechanical engineer in Mich., he was commissioned 2d Lt. 3d US Inf. 13 Apr. '61 and 1st Lt. 14 May '61, serving as Regt. Adj. from 1 Mar. until 18 Apr. '63, when he was commissioned Col. 15th N.J. He fought with his regiment at Gaines's Mill, White Oak Swamp, Malvern Hill, 2d Bull Run, and Fredericksburg. He succeeded Torbert 3 May '63 at Chancellorsville as commander of 1, 1, VI Potomac, leading it until 27 June. Leading his regiment at Gettysburg and Grant's subsequent campaign against Richmond, in early '64, he again commanded 1, 1, VI 9 May–8 July '64 at Cold Harbor and during the Wilderness campaign and 26 Feb.–28 June '65 at the Petersburg siege, where he was wounded. During Sheridan's Valley campaign he led 1, 1, VI, Army Shenandoah (6 Aug.–18 Sept. and 20 Sept.–19 Oct. '64) at Cedar Creek. Breveted for Marye's Heights, Gettysburg, the Wilderness, Cedar Creek, war service (B.G. USA 9 Apr. '65), and Middletown (B.G. USV 19 Oct. '64), he continued in the R.A., retiring in 1896 as Col. 16th Inf.

PENSACOLA, CONFEDERATE ARMY OF. Created 22 Oct. '61 near Pensacola from Ala., Fla., Ga., La., and Miss. regiments. This force of 8,100 was commanded by Bragg until A. H. Gladden took temporary command in

Dec.; Samuel Jones took command 27 Jan. '62. The latter went to the Army of Mobile and was succeeded by Col. Thomas M. Jones on 8 Mar. '62. About 10,000 troops from this army and from the Army of MOBILE went north with Bragg for the Shiloh campaign. The Army of Pensacola ceased to exist on 13 Mar. '62 and became part of the II CORPS (Bragg's, etc.), Armies of Miss. and of Tenn.

PENSACOLA BAY, Fla. Although the town was of little strategic or commercial importance (because of poor communications with the interior), the bay provided the best harbor in the Gulf (Mahan, 3). The entrance was guarded by Forts McRae and Barrancas on the land side and Pickens on the tip of 40-mile-long Santa Rosa Island. The US Navy Yard was surrendered intact on 12 Apr. '61 by the aged Commodore James Armstrong. (Seaman Wm. CONWAY refused the order to haul down the flag.) On 10 Jan., however, Lt. Adam J. Slemmer, commanding Co. G, 1st US Arty., in the absence of Capt. John H. WINDER, had spiked the guns at Barrancas, blown up the ammunition at McRae, and occupied Fort Pickens. This was the day Fla. seceded. After the surrender of the mainland installations, Slemmer's garrison consisted of 81 men, 30 of whom were seamen sent by Armstrong. Although Slemmer's position was not attacked, on 12, 15, and 18 Apr. the Confederates demanded surrender of his fort. On 12 Apr. he was reinforced to 500 men, and on the 18th Col. Harvey Brown landed to establish headquarters of his newly-created Dept. of FLORIDA. (See also Confederate Army of PENSACOLA.)

The Federals held Fort Pickens until 9 May '62, when the Confederates burned and abandoned their positions on the mainland. The Federals reoccupied these positions, and Pensacola became headquarters for the West Gulf Squadron. Retention of Fort Pickens had "nullified the usefulness to the enemy of the most important navy yard south of Norfolk" (West, 28).

A number of actions took place in the area before the Confederates evacuated it. On 2 Sept. '61 Brown sent a boat's crew of 11 men to destroy the dry dock, which he had reason to suspect that the Confederates were going to sink so as to block the channel opposite Fort McRae. Another night expedition (on the 14th) burned the Confederate cruiser *Judah* at the navy yard after a hand-to-hand fight with her crew (see B.&L., I, 32n.). Bragg retaliated with a raid on SANTA ROSA ISLAND, 8–9 Oct. '61. On 22 and 23 Nov. the *Niagara* and *Richmond* joined Fort Pickens in attacking the Confederate steamer *Time* as she entered the harbor and in delivering a bombardment that almost destroyed Fort McRae, and led Bragg to consider its abandonment. On 1 Jan. '62 Forts McRae and Barrancas were again bombarded from Pickens.

PERCUSSION CAPS. "Small metal covers, inlaid with detonating powder, and placed on the nipple of a rifle or revolver. The hammer, striking on the outer surface of the cap, causes the powder to explode and ignite the charge" (Wilhelm). Although invented by the Scottish clergyman, Rev. Alexander John Forsyth, in 1805 they were not used on military weapons until about 30 years later.

PERKINS, Henry Wells. Union officer. Pa. 1st Lt. 50th N.Y. Engrs. 18 Sept. '61; Capt. Asst. Adj. Gen. Vols. 23 Dec. '62; Lt. Col. Asst. Adj. Gen. Assigned 12 Apr. '64–15 June '65; Bvt. B.G. USV. Brevets for "war service in office and field" during Atlanta and Carolinas campaigns (2). Died 1890.

PERLEE, Samuel R. Union officer. N.Y. Lt. Col. 114th N.Y. 8 Sept. '62; Col. 10 July '63; Bvt. B.G. USV (war service). Died 1890.

PERRIN, Abner M. C.S.A. gen. 1827–64. S.C. Commissioned Capt. 14th S.C., he was at Port Royal 1 Jan. '62. He fought in the Peninsular campaign, at Cedar Run, 2d Bull Run, Harpers Ferry, Antietam, and Fredericksburg. Leading the regiment at Chancellorsville as a Col., he succeeded McGowan as brigade commander. At Gettysburg he led the 1st Brig. under Pender and fought in the rear guard at Falling Waters. Appointed B.G. C.S.A. 10 Sept. '63, he commanded his brigade in the II Corps at the Wilderness and was killed in the "bloody angle" at Spotsylvania 12 May.

PERRY, Alexander James. Union officer. c. 1829–1913. Conn. USMA 1851 (13/42); Arty. He served in the Seminole War, taught mathematics at West Point, and fought Indians in the West before serving at Fort Pickens (Fla.) until 18 July '61. Promoted Capt. Asst. Q.M. 17 May '61, he was in charge of the Bureau of Clothing and Equipage in the Q.M. Gen.'s office in Washington for the remainder of the war. He was named Lt. Col. USV 20 Aug. '62 and Col. USV 2 Aug. '64 and breveted B.G. USA for war service. Continuing in the R.A., he retired in 1892 as Col.

PERRY, Edward Aylesworth. C.S.A. gen. 1831–89. Mass. He attended Yale and practiced law in Fla. before being commissioned Capt. 2d Fla. Named Col. in May '62, he was severely wounded at Frayser's Farm and sent home to recover. He was appointed B.G. C.S.A. 28 Aug. '62, upon his return to the army, and was given command of a demi-brigade (three Fla. regiments). At Fredericksburg and Chancellorsville he led them in Anderson's division, but then fell sick of typhoid and missed Gettysburg. He commanded his demi-brigade at the Wilderness and was wounded. His decimated force was turned into a regiment and put in another brigade, and he served during the rest of the war in the reserve forces in Ala. After the war he was a lawyer and outspoken critic of the carpetbag rule. In 1884 he was elected Democratic Gov. of Fla.

PERRY, William Flake. C.S.A. gen. 1823–1901. Ga. Appt.-Ala. Largely self-educated, as he grew up on the then-primitive frontier in Ala., he taught school and became the state superintendent of education. He was president of a women's college at Tuskegee when he enlisted in 1862 as private in the 44th Ala. A few weeks later he was elected Maj. and promoted Lt. Col. 1 Sept, '62. He fought at Antietam and was then named Col. At Gettysburg he commanded his regiment on the Round Tops and fought at Chickamauga under Longstreet before returning to the A.N.V. for the Wilderness. Appointed B.G. C.S.A. 21 Feb. '65, he had commanded a brigade for about six months at Petersburg. After his parole at Appomattox he was a planter and then an educator in Ky.

PERRYVILLE (CHAPLIN HILLS), Ky., 8 Oct. '62 Following BRAGG'S INVASION OF KENTUCKY, Buell had six of his own divisions (Army of the Ohio) and J. C. Davis' division of the Army of the Miss. concentrated at Louisville with four newly-raised divisions. At Bardstown, 35 miles southeast, was Bragg's Confederate Army of the Tenn. (22,500). Kirby Smith's 10,-000, having routed the Federals at RICHMOND, were located in the area Frankfort–Lexington–Harrodsburg, some 30 to 60 miles to the east and northeast.

(See Kirby SMITH'S INVASION OF KENTUCKY.)

On 1 Oct. Buell advanced from Louisville with 60,000 in four columns. The main body, the corps of Alexander McCook (I), Crittenden (II), and Gilbert (III), marched so as to converge on Bragg's army at Bardstown. Two divisions, Sill and Dumont, marched east toward Frankfort where Cleburne's and Humphreys' divisions of Kirby Smith's army were located. Bragg got the mistaken idea that the latter column under Sill was the main Federal force and ordered Polk to move north to attack it in flank while Kirby Smith attacked it in front. Polk's cavalry informed him of the true nature of the situation, however, and instead of obeying the order he fell back (southeast) to Harrodsburg, and Hardee's corps moved to Perryville, 10 miles southwest.

As the Federals approached Perryville on 7 Oct., Gilbert's corps, led by Phil Sheridan's (11th) division, was ahead of the other two corps. A shortage of water resulted in a dispersion of the three Federal corps. When Bragg reached Harrodsburg he ordered Polk to move to that place with one division (Cheatham) to reinforce Hardee and attack Gilbert's corps. He ordered Polk's other division (Withers) to Kirby Smith, who was being hard pressed near Frankfort. The night of the 7th Buell realized that a major engagement was shaping up at Perryville and ordered McCook and Crittenden (on Gilbert's left and right, respectively) to concentrate there.

Before dawn the Federal brigade of Daniel McCook (36, 11, III) moved out to occupy high ground protecting several pools along Doctor's Creek to secure a water supply for the army. Buell did not want to bring on a general engagement until his other corps had arrived. There was some skirmishing by Wheeler's (Confederate) cavalry and Liddell's infantry brigade (Buckner) in the morning as the divisions of J. S. Jackson and Rousseau of Alexander McCook's corps arrived on the Federal left (north) flank. Cheatham's (Confederate) division was moved to the right, and at about 2 P.M. it hit the Federal north flank. This attack routed the green brigade of Terrill (33, 10, I) but was stopped by Starkweather's (28, 3, I). Jackson and Terrill were killed trying to rally their troops. Buckner's division, reinforced by brigades from Anderson's division, then attacked and penetrated to the Russell House. Buckner's attack had found a weak spot between the corps of Gilbert and McCook; the right flank of Rousseau's division was driven back. The brigades of Gooding (30, 9, III) and Steedman (3, 1, III) came up and plugged this gap. Carlin's brigade (35, 9, III) moved to reinforce Sheridan's division. Crittenden's corps reached the field between 10 and 11 A.M. but occupied a position on the right flank, about three miles from the main fighting, and took no part in the action.

Sheridan repulsed the attack against his well-organized position and then committed Carlin in a counterattack that drove the Confederates back through Perryville. Gooding and Steedman attacked the Confederate spearhead in Doctor's Creek and drove it back.

Although Buell's headquarters was only two and a half miles away he did not know until 4 P.M. of the battle that had reached its peak at about 2:30. The corps commanders, Gilbert and Crittenden, likewise did not realize until late in the day that Alexander McCook and Sheridan were under heavy attack. (This is an instance of ACOUSTIC SHADOW.) The result was that only nine brigades were heavily engaged in the battle, while 15 others were within supporting distance. Buell lost the opportunity of achieving a significant victory. Bragg withdrew into east Tenn., leaving his dead and wounded on the field. Out of 36,940 effectives the Federals lost 4,211 (845 killed, 2,851 wounded, and 515 missing). Of 16,000 effectives the Confederates lost 3,396 (510 killed, 2,635 wounded, and 251 missing). (Fox and Livermore.) Union Gen.'s Jackson and Terrill were killed. Confederate Gen.'s S. A. M. Wood, Cleburne, and J. C. Brown were wounded.

PERSONAL LIBERTY LAWS. In an effort to overcome the fugitive-slave provisions of the COMPROMISE OF 1850, the legislatures of 10 Northern states passed these laws. They forbade state officers from aiding in the arrest of fugitive slaves, denied the use of their jails for holding these slaves, and ordered jury trials for the runaways. These laws are an example of "states' rights" in Northern states.

PETARD. An ordnance item used for blowing open gates, demolishing palisades, walls, etc. "They consist of a half-cone of thick iron, filled with powder and ball; they are usually fastened to a plank, and the latter is provided with hooks to allow of its being attached securely to a gate, etc." (Wilhelm).

PETERSBURG ASSAULT OF 9 JUNE '64. Butler (Army of the James) sent three cavalry regiments (1,300) under Kautz and two infantry brigades (3,200) under Gillmore, with six field-pieces, to capture Petersburg from its 2,500 Confederate defenders under Henry A. Wise. The main armies of Grant and Lee were engaged at Cold Harbor. Although Kautz's dismounted troopers took the first line of Confederate intrenchments, they were then stopped by a large ravine when they attempted to continue their attack on

horseback. Due to a misunderstanding, Gillmore's infantry did not advance to support Kautz, but skirmished with the enemy on the other side of the town. Federal troops withdrew with 87 casualties.

PETERSBURG ASSAULTS OF 15–18 JUNE '64. At about 4 A.M., 15 June, Smith's XVIII Corps and Kautz's cavalry left Broadway Landing (where a ponton bridge crossed the Appomattox) and moved to attack Petersburg with a force of 13,700 infantry and 2,400 cavalry. Hancock's II Corps was to cross the James the same day and move the 16 miles (air line) to support Smith's attack.

Beauregard had 5,400 for the defense of Petersburg and the Bermuda Hundred line. Of these, about 2,200—part of Henry A. Wise's Va. Brig. and local militia—were in the Petersburg trenches the morning of the 15th. (D.S.F.) Kautz's cavalry made contact with the dismounted troopers of Dearing's brigade at Baylor's Farm, about four miles from the town. Hinks's colored division drove the Confederates back into their entrenchments. It was not until 7 P.M., however, that Smith's attack got under way. The Confederate line was penetrated at a weak point between Redans 7 and 8, and the entire Jordan salient then captured. The defenders dropped back to a new line along Harrison's Creek. Hancock's arrival was delayed by several errors beyond his control: his map was defective; he had not been instructed to move rapidly to assist Smith's attack; his troops were held at Windmill Point to await rations (which they did not need). Although senior, Hancock on arrival with two of his divisions reported to Smith that these were available to exploit the latter's success and take advantage of the moonlight night to drive on into Petersburg. Making one of the war's biggest errors of generalship, Smith failed to seize this opportunity; he simply asked Hancock to occupy the captured positions so that he could withdraw his own troops. This relief was completed about 11 P.M. Hancock's 3d Div. arrived about midnight.

Beauregard had sent all available reinforcements to Wise as soon as Dearing reported contact with the enemy. About noon he had ordered Hoke's division to Petersburg. These troops arrived during the night and occupied the new defensive line. Beauregard himself arrived just after Smith's assault and soon made the fateful decision to abandon the Bermuda Hundred line in order to strengthen the Petersburg defenses.

About midnight Grant told Hancock to take command of both corps and, unless Petersburg could be captured during the night, to take up a defensive position until additional troops arrived. At 10 A.M., 16 June, IX Corps started deploying on Hancock's left. At the same time Bushrod Johnson's division arrived from the Bermuda Hundred line and formed opposite them on the Confederate right. Grant and Meade reached the field in the morning and ordered a general assault to be made at 6 P.M. Before that time Egan's brigade of Birney's division captured Redan No. 12. In the general assault Redans 4, 13, and 14 were captured, but at considerable loss.

Lee learned at about 2:30 P.M. on the 16th that Beauregard had abandoned the Bermuda Hundred defenses. He ordered the divisions of Pickett and Field to move south of the James to reoccupy them. Since Beauregard had been able to identify only II and XVIII Corps opposite Petersburg, Lee did not yet have conclusive evidence that Grant's main force was attacking south of the James and not toward Richmond north of the river.

Warren's V Corps arrived and the morning of the 17th was deployed on the Federal left. In a remarkable surprise attack Potter's division (2, IX) caught Confederate defenders around the Shand House asleep on their arms, captured the position and 600 prisoners. As on the previous day, the attackers took more positions but were unable to penetrate the Confederate line. Hartranft's brigade (1, 3, IX) lost 840 out of 1,890 in this assault. At dusk the Confederate brigade of Gracie, which had been sent from the Richmond defenses, launched a counterattack that recaptured positions taken by IX Corps during the day. Up to midnight the Confederates held Redan 3 on their extreme left flank and the line south of the Shand House on their right (Redans 15 to 23). Beauregard then withdrew his forces to a shorter and stronger line.

Attacking at dawn (4 A.M.) on the 18th, the Federals were thrown off balance by Beauregard's unexpected withdrawal and by the reinforcement by the divisions of Field and Pickett. II Corps on the north, now under Birney (Hancock's Gettysburg wound having incapacitated him), hit the new positions at the Hare House, about 300 yards behind the old line. Two attacks made after noon were repulsed with heavy losses. The other two corps had to advance across extremely difficult terrain (ravines and woods that had been prepared by slashing) and were slowed by Confederate delaying actions. The result was that the initial attacks were not coordinated. A major assault at 2 P.M. made some headway, and sustained heavy casualties, but was unable to achieve a break-through. The 1st Me. Hv. Arty. (fighting as infantry) attacked at 4 P.M. from the Prince George C.H. Road and sustained the highest casualties of any Union regiment in any single battle of the war: in less than 30 minutes it lost 632 out of about 900 engaged (Fox, 125).

The fighting ended at dark, and Grant abandoned his attempts to take Petersburg by direct assault. During the period 15–18 June there were 63,797 Federal troops and 41,499 Confederates engaged around Petersburg (Livermore, 141). According to Fox (p. 547) Federal losses during the period 15–19 June were: 1,688 killed, 8,513 wounded and died of wounds, and 1,185 captured and missing; a total of 11,386. Confederate losses are not known.

PETERSBURG CAMPAIGN, June '64–May '65. Having been repeatedly blocked with heavy losses in successive attempts to turn Lee's south flank and capture Richmond, Grant in mid-June '64 shifted his line of operations south of the James. His object was to capture Petersburg, a vital communications center, and then move on Richmond from south of the river. The JAMES RIVER BRIDGE was a triumph of military engineering, and by 16 June Grant's entire army was on the south bank. Warren's V Corps and J. H. Wilson's cavalry division screened this movement on the west flank. There is evidence that Lee was completely deceived by Grant's strategy. D. S. Freeman, on the other hand, presents convincing evidence that Lee "was not outgeneralled nor taken by surprise" (*R. E. Lee*, III, 438–47).

North of the Appomattox Butler's Army of the James in its Bermuda Hundred position was reinforced, starting 13 June, by W. F. ("Baldy") Smith's XVIII Corps. A few days previously Butler's army had bungled an opportunity to take Petersburg while it was defended by only 2,500 Confederates under Henry A. Wise (see PETERSBURG ASSAULT OF 9 JUNE '64). Grant visited Butler on the 14th and made plans for an attack to be made the next day against Wise, who had not yet been reinforced. This operation failed not only because of Smith's lack of aggressiveness but also because Grant failed to inform Meade of the part Hancock's II Corps was to play in the operation. See PETERSBURG ASSAULTS OF 15–18 June '64. The bulk of Smith's force returned to Bermuda Hundred on the 17th and two divisions of Wright's VI Corps arrived there the same day. A planned attack had to be canceled because Lee had moved the divisions of Pickett and Field into the Bermuda Hundred defenses from north of the James.

Lee arrived at Petersburg the morning of the 18th, and A. P. Hill's corps started arriving that afternoon. The tactical failures of his subordinates—particularly Butler and Smith—had deprived Grant of the victory that his brilliant strategy had brought within grasp; he now accepted the necessity of undertaking a siege. There followed a 10-month operation that was marked by: "Lack of Union leadership and resolution; decrease in Union offensive ability; slow extension of the opposing lines to the west; and the brilliance of Lee's defense" (*Campaign Summaries*). Total casualties were approximately 42,000 Union and 28,000 Confederate killed, wounded and captured (N.P.S. pamphlet, *Petersburg*).

A large number of actions took place during the campaign. These are referred to in Civil War literature by a confusing abundance of names. The following compilation will give the name under which the actions are covered alphabetically in this book, and will give in parentheses the other names associated with the actions.

South of the James: the WELDON RAILROAD OPERATIONS (Jerusalem Plank Road, Williams' Farm, and Davis' Farm), 22–23 June '64; the PETERSBURG MINE ASSAULT (Battle of the Crater), 30

July; GLOBE TAVERN (Six-Mile House, Weldon R.R.), 18–21 Aug.; REAMS'S STATION, 25 Aug.; POPLAR SPRINGS CHURCH (Peeble's Farm, Pegram's Farm), 30 Sept.–2 Oct.; HATCHER'S RUN (Boydton Road, Vaughan Road, Burgess Farm), 27 Oct.; DABNEY'S MILLS (Hatcher's Run, Boydton Road, Armstrong's Mill, Rowanty Creek, Vaughan Road), 5–7 Feb. '65; and FORT STEDMAN, 25 Mar. '65.

North of the James: DEEP BOTTOM RUN (Strawberry Plains, Malvern Hill, New Market Road, and Darbytown), 27–29 July and 13–20 Aug. '64; NEW MARKET HEIGHTS (Chafin's Farm, Laurel Hill, Forts Harrison and Gilmer), 28–30 Sept.; DARBYTOWN AND NEW MARKET ROADS (near New Market Heights), 7 Oct. '64.

The following raids took place during the period: Sheridan's TREVILIAN RAID, and WILSON AND KAUTZ'S PETERSBURG RAID in June; the HAMPTON-ROSSER CATTLE RAID in Sept.; ROSSER'S NEW CREEK (W. Va.) RAID in Nov., and STONEMAN'S RAID IN SOUTHWESTERN VIRGINIA in Dec.; SHERIDAN'S RAID IN NORTHERN VIRGINIA in Feb.–Mar. '65. EARLY'S WASHINGTON RAID took place in July '64 and was followed by the SHENANDOAH VALLEY CAMPAIGN OF SHERIDAN. The Petersburg assault of 9 June '64 is not considered part of the Petersburg campaign, nor are the battle of FIVE FORKS, 1 Apr. '65, and the PETERSBURG FINAL ASSAULT, 2 Apr. '65. (The latter two are part of the APPOMATTOX CAMPAIGN.)

"PETERSBURG EXPRESS." Another name for the DICTATOR.

PETERSBURG FINAL ASSAULT, 2 Apr. '65. (APPOMATTOX CAMPAIGN) Sheridan's victory at Five Forks (1 Apr.) put Grant's forces in a position to complete the encirclement of Petersburg. Lee was forced to weaken his main defenses by sending Anderson with three brigades to cover the reorganization of Pickett's forces. Early on the morning of the 2d Lee informed Davis that Petersburg and Richmond would have to be evacuated that night. Grant, learning from deserters that Lee had weakened his main defenses, ordered a general assault for dawn of the 2d.

Attacking at 4:30 A.M., Parke's IX Corps got a foothold in the Confederate lines at the Jerusalem Plank Road but was unable to penetrate. Wright's VI Corps made the decisive break-through opposite Fort Fisher and rolled up the Confederate line to the left (southwest) as far as Hatcher's Run. Gibbon's XXIV Corps (less Devens) broke through near Hatcher's Run, attacked down the Plank Road (across the front of VI Corps), and captured Forts Gregg and Whitworth. Humphreys' II Corps, on the left flank, captured the enemy's positions at the Crow Salient and pursued the withdrawing division of Heth up the Claiborne Road. Grant ordered that only Miles's division continue this pursuit, and the latter defeated Heth at Sutherland Station at about 3 P.M. Longstreet and Gordon held Petersburg until dark and then withdrew the night of 2–3 Apr. toward Amelia C.H.

Forces engaged during the day were 63,299 Federals and 18,579 Confederates (Livermore, 141). Fox puts total Federal casualties at 3,361, whereas Livermore's estimate is 4,140. Confederate losses are not known. Among the dead was A. P. Hill.

PETERSBURG MINE ASSAULT, 30 July '64. The idea for the mine came to Lt. Col. Henry Pleasants, C.O. of the 48th Pa., from a remark made by one of his men. His regiment, composed largely of coal miners, was assigned a section of the trenches opposite Elliott's Salient. Pleasants, a mining engineer before the war, sold Burnside on the idea and it was ultimately approved by Grant. Work started 25 June and was completed 23 July; placing of the powder charge was finished four days later. The main shaft ran 511 feet to a point 20 feet under the Confederate battery in the salient; two lateral galleries, with a total length of 75 feet, were run under the enemy trenches. The tunnel averaged five feet in height, was four and a half feet wide at the bottom and about two feet at the top. It was ventilated by an ingenious system whereby fire in a chimney near the entrance drew stale air out of the tunnel, while the resulting vacuum pulled fresh air through a wooden tube that ran along the floor of the tunnel from under an airtight door at the entrance to the end where the men were digging. The powder charge consisted of 320 kegs of black powder, totaling 8,000 pounds; a 38-foot section of the main tunnel was then filled with dirt to provide the necessary tamping effect and a fuse improvised. With little support from higher headquarters in getting necessary surveying instruments, tools, demolition equipment, or man power, Pleasants and his regiment successfully achieved the technical portion of the project.

Grant had never been enthusiastic about the operation because, although Pleasants had selected a good position for constructing such a mine, the location did not favor tactical exploitation of the explosion. However, plans were made for Burnside's IX Corps to attack through the gap made by the mine. Burnside selected his colored division for the initial attack because this was his largest and freshest division. Accordingly, about 18 July Ferrero's division was brought forward and its colored soldiers given special training for the assault. The day before the battle, however. Meade informed Burnside that his contemplated use of Negro troops for such a hazardous operation was fraught with political repercussions and that one of the white divisions would have to be substituted. Grant concurred. Demoralized by this interference, Burnside had his other three division commanders draw straws to see which one would lead the assault. Ledlie (1st Div.) drew the short straw. To further jeopardize the plan, Burnside failed to follow his instructions and prepare passages through his parapets and abatis to make it easier for his attacking elements to sally forth.

The Confederates knew that the enemy was constructing a mine but they were unsuccessful in their countermining operations. Beauregard then ordered construction of entrenchments across the neck of the salient and also emplaced large mortars to cover the threatened point (Humphreys, 251).

The explosion was set for 3:30 A.M., 30 July, but the fuse failed to work. At 4:15 Lt. Jacob Douty and Sgt. Harry Reese crawled into the tunnel and relit the fuse, which had burned out at the splice. At 4:45 the mine exploded. Pleasants' part of the work was a complete success: the explosion created a crater 170 feet long, 60 to 80 feet wide, and 30 feet deep; at least 278 Confederates were killed or wounded (N.P.S., *Petersburg*, 20); nine companies of the 19th and 22d S.C. were blown into the air (Alexander, 569). The exploitation by Federal infantry failed, however, and the reaction of Confederate troops was exemplary. Ledlie himself cowered in a bombproof shelter behind the lines, and the troops of his division were slow to start their assault. Federal troops then herded into the crater where they were pounded by Confederate artillery. The 17th S.C., commanded by Col. McMaster after Gen. Elliott was severely wounded, was particularly conspicuous in the defense. Confederate artillery was brought effectively into play. Two regiments from Wise's and two from Ransom's brigade were brought up to hold the line until elements of Mahone's division started arriving at about 8 A.M. Lee joined Beauregard at the Gee house, 500 yards from the crater, to direct the defense. By about 8:30 over 15,000 troops were massed in the area of the crater. The divisions of Potter and Willcox had followed Ledlie's. Ferrero's colored troops were then ordered forward, and Ferrero himself joined Ledlie in the bombproof.

Mahone launched a final counterattack shortly after 1 P.M. and cleared the crater of Federal troops. The assault had cost the Federals 3,798 (Fox, 547) out of 20,708 engaged (Livermore, 141). The Confederates had an estimated 11,466 engaged; casualties in Johnston's division and Colquitt's brigade were 1,182; losses in Mahone's division and the 61st N.C. are not recorded, but total Confederate casualties were about 1,500 (N.P.S., *Petersburg*, 22).

"The effort was a stupendous failure," wrote Grant in summation. ". . . and all due to inefficiency on the part of the corps commander and the incompetency of the division commander who was sent to lead the assault." A court of inquiry, headed by Hancock, found the following officers responsible in varying degrees for the failure: Burnside, Ledlie, Ferrero, Col. Z. R. Bliss (C.O. 1, 2, XI), and Willcox.

PETTIGREW, James Johnston. C.S.A. gen. 1828–63. N.C. A graduate of the Univ. of N.C., he was with the Naval Observatory and became a lawyer in the firm of his cousin, James L. Petigru [sic]. He studied Roman law in Germany and served in the state legislature, taking a firm stand against the resumption of slave trade. Active in the militia, he had been Col. of the 1st Regt. of Rifles in Charleston. When Anderson occupied Sumter, Pettigrew took over Castle Pinckney and fortified Morris Island. Enlisting in Hampton's Legion, he was commissioned Col. 12th N.C. in May '61 and as B.G. C.S.A. 26 Feb. '62, served under Johnston in the Peninsula. He was wounded, bayonetted, and captured at Seven Pines. Exchanged two months later, he commanded the defenses of Petersburg, fought at Blount's Creek Spring in 1863, and commanded a brigade under Heth at Gettysburg. When Heth was wounded on the first day of fighting, Pettigrew took command of his division and led them in "Pickett's Charge." Although wounded in the hand, he was one of the last to leave the field. Pettigrew had returned to the command of his brigade and was mortally wounded the night of 13–14 July at Falling Waters in Heth's rearguard action. He died 17 July '63.

PETTUS, Edmund Winston. C.S.A. gen. 1821–1907. Ala. A lawyer and state attorney, he fought in the Mexican War and was then a judge. His brother, John, was Gov. of Miss. during the secession crisis, and Edmund was sent to that state from Ala. to persuade them to join the Confederacy. He was commissioned Maj. 20th Ala. and served under Kirby Smith in Ky. as Lt. Col. At Vicksburg he commanded his regiment as Col. and was captured at Port Gibson, managing to escape soon afterward. When Vicksburg surrendered, he was again captured and exchanged to be appointed B.G. C.S.A. 18 Sept. '63. He commanded his brigade at Lookout Mountain, Missionary Ridge, the Atlanta campaign, and at Nashville under Hood. Joining Johnston, he surrendered with him in the Carolinas. After the war he was a lawyer and Democratic US Sen.

PETTUS, John J. C.S.A. Gov. of Miss. 1813–67. Tenn. A lawyer and legislator, he was elected Democratic Gov. of Miss. in 1859. In 1863 he was forced to move the state offices to

Columbus, and served until Charles
Clark succeeded him on 16 Nov. '63.

PHELPS, Charles Edward. Union
officer. 1833–1908. Vt. One of the organizers (1858) of the Md. Nat'l Guard,
he helped surpress the Know-Nothing
uprising. However, he was so out of
sympathy with the Civil War that he
resigned as a Maj. in 1861 against
orders. He changed his mind in 1862
and became Col. 7th Md.; Col. 13 Apr.
'64; Bvt. B.G. USV (war service); discharged 9 Sept. '64. Had his horse shot
out from under him at the Wilderness
and Laurel Hill 8 May '64 (Spotsylvania) and at the latter engagement he
was W.I.A. while leading a brigade,
captured by the Confederates, and then
recaptured by Custer's cavalry; winning
the Medal of Honor 30 Mar. '98 for
this action. Commanded 2, 3, I; 3, 2, V.
He had a varied career later as Congressman, judge, author, amateur scien-
tist, and professor.

PHELPS, John Elisha. Union officer.
Mo. 2d Lt. 3d US Cav.; 1st Lt. 1 Oct.
'63; Col. 2d Ark. Cav. 18 Mar. '64;
Bvt. B.G. USV. Brevets for campaign
of 1864 in southwest Mo. (2), war
service. A.D.C. to Gen. Carr Sept. '62–
Apr. '64. Commanded 1st Brig., Cav.
Div. West Tenn. (Tenn.).

PHELPS, John Smith. Union gen.
1814–86. Conn. After graduating from
(what is now) Trinity College (Conn.),
he was a Democratic legislator and
Congressman. Commissioned Lt. Col.
in Phelps's regiment Mo. Inf. 2 Oct. '61,
he was promoted Col. 19 Dec. '61 and
led it at Pea Ridge. He was mustered
out 13 May '62, appointed B.G. USV
19 July, and served as military Gov. of
Ark. until his appointment expired 4
Mar. '63. He was Gov. of Mo. 1876–80.
Husband of Mary Whitney PHELPS.

PHELPS, John Wolcott. Union gen.
1813–85. Vt. USMA 1836 (24/49);

Arty. He was in the Seminole War,
Indian fighting, Mexican War (1 brevet;
declined) and the Utah Expedition, and
resigned in 1859. An abolitionist writer,
he was commissioned Col. 1st Vt. 9 May
and B.G. USV 17 May '61. He commanded the Ship Island Expedition
(Dec. '61–Mar. '62) and the 1st Brig.
of Butler's New Orleans expedition
(Mar.–Aug. '62). At New Orleans he
had the idea of recruiting Negroes, but
the authorities ordered him to put them
to work instead, so he resigned (21 Aug.
'62). By an order of the C.S.A. government he was declared an "outlaw, for
having 'organized and armed Negro
slaves for military service against their
masters, citizens of the Confederacy' "
(Cullum). Returning to Vt., he was the
American Party (Anti-Mason) presidential candidate in 1880 and wrote
numerous books and articles on history,
politics, education, and science.

PHELPS, Mary Whitney. Wife of
Brig. Gen. John S. Phelps, she turned
their Springfield (Mo.) home into a
hospital. After the battle of Wilson's
Creek she took care of Nathaniel Lyon's
body and was given $20,000 for this
by Congress. With this sum she established a home in Springfield for orphans
of Confederate and Union veterans. She
was born in Portland, Me.

PHELPS, Walter, Jr. Union officer.
N.Y. Col. 22d N.Y. 6 June '61; Bvt.
B.G. USV (war service); mustered out
19 June '63. Commanded 1, 1, I (Potomac). Died 1878.

PHIFER, Charles W. C.S.A. Wood
and Heitman list him as B.G. C.S.A.,
the former saying that he was appointed
25 May '62 from Tex. Neither Wright
nor C.M.H. includes him in their lists
of general officers.

PHILADELPHIA BRIGADE (2, II,
Potomac). Under Gen. Alexander S.
Webb, this unit withstood the brunt of

"Pickett's Charge" at Gettysburg. It was composed of the following Pa. regiments: 69th, 71st, 72d, and 106th.

PHILIPPI, W. Va., 3 June '61. A minor action at the start of WEST VIRGINIA OPERATIONS IN 1861, that challenges BIG BETHEL, Va., 10 June '61, for the distinction of being the first battle of the Civil War. A force of about 1,500 Confederates under Col. Porterfield, as an advance element of Garnett's force at Beverly, was conducting raids toward Grafton. McClellan directed a concentric night attack that routed the Confederates from their sleep and inflicted 15 casualties. The Federals lost two wounded.

PHILLIPS, Jesse J. Union officer. Ill. Capt. 9th Ill. 25 Apr. '61; Maj. 26 Apr. '61; mustered out 24 July '61; Maj. 9th Ill. 26 July '61; Lt. Col. 5 Sept. '61; Bvt. B.G. USV (war service); discharged 31 Aug. '64. Died 1901.

PHILLIPS, Wendell. ABOLITIONIST. 1811–84. Mass. After graduating from the Boston Latin School and Harvard, the son of the first mayor of Boston studied at the Harvard Law School but did not practice long after becoming a disciple and colleague of William Lloyd GARRISON and Elijah P. Lovejoy. He lectured throughout the North and was active in the AMERICAN ANTI-SLAVERY SOCIETY. After the war he became active in other reforms advocating temperance and prohibition, women's suffrage, labor unions and rights of Indians.

PIATT, Abraham Sanders. Union gen. 1821–? Ohio. A farmer and publisher, he was commissioned Col. 13th Ohio 20 Apr. and mustered out three months later. Raising the 34th Ohio, that state's first Zouave regiment, he was commissioned Col. 2 Sept. '61 and B.G. USV 28 Apr. '62. He commanded Piatt's brigade, Whipple's Div. Mil. Dist. Washington, and 1, 3, III, Potomac (8 Nov.–

14 Dec. '62 and Jan.–Feb. '63). Resigning 17 Feb. '63, he went into politics and later wrote poetry.

PICKENS, FORT, Fla. See PENSACOLA BAY.

PICKENS, Francis. C.S.A. Gov. of S.C. 1805–69. S.C. The son of a governor, he studied law after graduating from college and entered politics as a proponent of nullification. He served in the legislature and the US Congress before being appointed Minister to Russia by Buchanan in 1858. Elected Gov. in Dec. 1860, he served for two years before being succeeded by M. L. Bonham. He had a vital role in the Fort Sumter crisis.

PICKETT, George Edward. C.S.A. gen. 1825–75. Va. A lawyer, he also graduated from West Point, ranking at the very bottom of the 59-man USMA class of 1846. Commissioned in the Inf., he won a brevet in the Mexican War and fought Indians on the frontier. After provoking an incident with the British during the joint occupation of Puget Sound, he was commended by the government. Resigning as a Capt. on 25 June '61, he was commissioned Col., C.S.A., and served on the lower Rappahannock before being appointed B.G. 13 Feb. '62 with rank from 14 Jan. Leading the "Gamecock Brigade" at Williamsburg and Seven Pines, he was severely wounded in the shoulder at Gaines's Mill. He was promoted Maj. Gen. 11 Oct. '62 to rank from the 10th, and commanded the center at Fredericksburg, seeing little action. He was immortalized in "Pickett's Charge" the third day at GETTYSBURG, although he did not command this attack, nor did his troops make up the largest part of it. Longstreet did, however, have him form the brigades for this attack as they came onto the field. He went into this terrible action "as if great military fortune has come to him. . . . when the charge has been repulsed, George Pickett's tale is told. Neither he nor his Division ever is the same again" (*Lee's Lts.*, III, xxxvi).

On 23 Sept. '63 he was sent with his shattered division to recuperate and recruit in the Dept. of VIRGINIA AND NORTH CAROLINA, and he was made department commander. His attack on New Bern in late Jan. '64 failed because of poor planning and poor execution by his subordinate, Seth Barton. Although the attack on Plymouth, N.C. (17–20 Apr.) took place in his department, he was not permitted to supervise it personally. He then had a prominent part in the actions of Ben Butler against DREWRY'S BLUFF, Va., 4–16 May '64. Rejoining the I Corps just in time for Cold Harbor, 1 June, his division took part in the Petersburg and Appomattox campaign. He was in command at FIVE FORKS 1 Apr. '65, rejoined Longstreet's corps, and surrendered with him at Appomattox. Although offered a generalship by the Khedive of Egypt and the position of US Marshal by Grant, he declined both to enter the insurance business in Va. A close personal friend of Longstreet, and his favorite division commander, Pickett was "dapper and alert, . . . wore his dark hair in long, perfumed ringlets that fell to his shoulders."

PICKETT, Josiah. Union officer. Mass. 1st Lt. 3d Bn. 3d Mass. Mil. 19 Apr. '61; mustered out 3 Aug. '61; Capt. 25th Mass. 28 Oct. '61; Maj. 20 Mar. '62; Col. 1 Jan. '63; Bvt. B.G. USV 3 June '64 (Cold Harbor, Va.); mustered out 10 Jan. '65. W.I.A. severely at Cold Harbor. Commanded Sub-Dist. Pamlico (N.C.), Dept. of Va. and N.C.

PIECEMEAL is the military term for committing portions of a unit as they become available. Piecemeal attack is common in a MEETING ENGAGEMENT and is considered good tactics provided you are in a position to build up forces faster than the enemy. This is what enabled Lee to win the first day at Gettysburg. Piecemeal commitment of the reserve is a common and serious error in tactics. The timing of a planned action may break down and enable portions of a force to be defeated piecemeal (e.g., Lee's attack the second day at Gettysburg).

PIEDMONT, Va., 5 June '64.
After NEW MARKET Gen. David Hunter replaced Gen. Franz Sigel as commander of the Dept. of Western Va. He himself was located at Strasburg with Gen. J. C. Sullivan's (1st) infantry division and Gen. Julius Stahel's (1st) cavalry division. Gen. George Crook was at Lewisburg with his own (2d) infantry division and Gen. W. W. Averell's (2d) cavalry division. Hunter's field force totaled 11,000 infantry and 5,000 cavalry. Opposing him was Gen. W. E. ("Grumble") Jones (vice Breckinridge) with 3,500 infantry and 5,000 cavalry. On 26 May Hunter started toward Staunton, and on the 31st Crook's command began to advance on the same place via Covington and Warm Springs. When he reached Harrisonburg Hunter turned east to avoid Jones's defensive position on the direct route to Staunton, crossed the Shenandoah at Port Republic, and turned south toward Staunton. In an effort to prevent a junction of these two Federal columns, Jones detached two brigades of cavalry to delay Crook's column and turned with the bulk of his forces (about 5,000) against Hunter's column. On 5 June, at about 6 A.M. Confederate skirmishers were encountered and driven back to a defensive position at Piedmont (7 miles southwest of Port Republic). Hunter's artillery went to work at 9 o'clock and an hour later Col. Augustus Moor's 1st Inf. brigade gained ground on the Federal right. Col. Joseph Thoburn (2d Brig.) took high ground on the left. By 11:30

the Confederate artillery had been silenced. At 1 P.M. Moor attacked and was repulsed. The Confederates attacked Moor an hour later but were stopped and driven back by a counterattack by Thoburn. Moor then attacked, and Col. John E. Wynkoop's cavalry brigade hit the Confederate right. A rout ensued, and Jones was killed. Hunter entered Staunton unopposed the next day, and Crook's column linked up on the 8th. Confederate losses were about 1,600, of whom about 1,000 were prisoners; Hunter lost 780 (Fox).

PIERCE, Byron Root. Union gen. 1829–? N.Y. Commissioned Capt. 3d Mich. 10 June '61, he was promoted Maj. 28 Oct. '61, Lt. Col. 25 July '62, Col. 1 Jan. '63, and B.G. USV 7 June '64. He commanded 3, 1, III (30 Dec. '63–Jan. '64); 1, 2, II (3–22 June '64) and 2, 3, II (23–29 May; 24 June–22 July; 26 Aug. '64–25 Jan. '65 and 15 Feb.–28 June '65). Breveted for Sayler's Creek (Maj. Gen. USV 6 Apr. '65), he was mustered out 24 Aug. '65 and was later commandant of the Soldiers' Home in Grand Rapids.

PIERCE, Francis Edwin. Union officer. N.Y. Capt. 108th N.Y. 18 Aug. '62; Maj. 17 Sept. '62; Lt. Col. 2 Mar. '63; mustered out 28 May '65; Col. 8th US Vet. Vol. Inf. 15 June '65; Bvt. B.G. USV (war service). W.I.A. Chancellorsville, Gettysburg, Norton's Ford (Va.). Commanded in Army of the Potomac: 2, 3, II; 1, 2, II; 3, 2, II. In R.A. until death while Capt. in 1896.

PIERSON, John Frederick. Union officer. N.Y. Capt. 1st N.Y. 27 May '61; Maj. 20 July '61; Lt. Col. 10 Sept. '61; Col. 9 Oct. '62; Bvt. B.G. USV (war service).

PIERSON, William Seward. Union officer. Conn. Lt. Col. 128th Ohio 25 Aug. '63; Bvt. B.G. USV (war service); resigned 15 July '64.

PIKE, Albert. C.S.A. gen. 1809–91. Mass. Appt.-Ark. Being forced by poverty to leave Harvard, he had taught school before moving West. When the war started, he was a wealthy newspaper man, Mexican War veteran, internationally known writer and poet, and a lawyer who had recently won a $140,000 suit for the Creek Indians. In the summer of 1861 he was sent into Indian Territory to win the Five Nations over to the Confederacy. Commissioned B.G. C.S.A. 15 Aug. '61, he took command of the Dept. of Indian Territory and led a force of Indians to take part in the battle of PEA RIDGE, Ark., 7–8 Mar. '62. Resenting the authority of Hindman, C.G. of the Trans-Miss. Dept., Pike submitted his resignation 12 July '62, but this was not accepted until 11 Nov. Thereafter regarded with suspicion by both sides, he spent the rest of the war in Ark. and Tex., and was finally paroled. A huge man with flowing hair and long beard, he was active after the war in Washington and Memphis as a lawyer, journalist, and Free-Mason (Monaghan).

PILE, William A. Union gen. 1829–89. Ind. A Methodist minister, he joined the Union Army as Chaplain 1st Mo. Arty. 12 June '61 and was discharged 1 Mar. '62. Named Lt. Col. 33d Mo. 5 Sept. '62, he was promoted Col. 23 Dec. '62 and B.G. USV 26 Dec. '63. He commanded post of Port Hudson (26 Dec. '64–13 Feb. '65) and 1, 1st Div. USCT West Fla. (19 Feb.–25 Apr. '65). Breveted Maj. Gen. USV 9 Apr. '65 for Fort Blakely (Ala.), he was mustered out 24 Aug. '65. As a Republican he was in Congress 1867–69, then serving as Gov. of the N. Mex. Territory until 1870 and Minister Resident to Venezuela 1871–74.

PILLOW, Gideon Johnson. C.S.A. gen. 1806–78. Tenn. After graduating from the Univ. of Nashville he was a criminal lawyer, partner of James K. Polk, and a considerable power in Democratic politics. In the Mexican War he was successively B.G. and Maj. Gen. (appointed by Polk), and was twice wounded. He quarreled with Scott over an anonymous letter and was cleared by two courts of inquiry. Becoming a Douglas Democrat, he took a moderate course and hoped to solve the secession problem by compromise. When the war came, however, he was appointed the senior Maj. Gen. of the Tenn. state troops. His militia forces were then transferred to the Confederate Army and he was chagrined not to be in charge of them. Belatedly appointed B.G. C.S.A. 9 July '61, he fought at Belmont (7 Nov. '61) and was second-in-command at Fort Donelson. Floyd passed his command to Pillow, who gave it to Bucker, and the first two escaped, leaving their junior to negotiate with Grant. Pillow was reprimanded, suspended, and never given another important command. He practiced law after the war.

PILOT KNOB (Fort Davidson), Mo. 27 Sept. '64. Confederate attack repulsed in first engagement of PRICE'S RAID IN MISSOURI.

PINCKNEY, Joseph Conselyea. Union officer. N.Y. Col. 6th N.Y. State Militia 21 Apr. '61; mustered out 31 July '61; Col. 66th N.Y. 4 Nov. '61; resigned 3 Dec. '62; Capt. Comsy. of Subsist. Vols. 11 Mar. '63; Bvt. B.G. USV (war service). Died 1881.

PINE KNOB; PINE MOUNTAIN. See KENESAW MOUNTAIN.

PINKERTON, Allan. Detective and McClellan's Secret Service Chief. 1819–84. Scotland. Coming to the US as a young man after political difficulties at home, he settled in Ill. and became a deputy sheriff. He was named the first detective for Chicago in 1850, the same year he opened his own detective agency. His principal work was assisting escaping slaves and protecting mail from robbers. He was also the first special US mail agent for his area and in Apr. '61 was summoned to Washington to set up the Federal secret service. However, the confusion and turbulence of the capital made this fruitless, and he left to become McClellan's Chief Detective of the Dept. of the Ohio. After 1st Bull Run he returned to Washington and set up the Secret Service, being known then and for some years after the war as Maj. E. J. Allen. When McClellan was relieved in Nov. '62, Pinkerton left also, although he continued to investigate claims. It was his information gathered from escaping slaves that had apparently caused McClellan to overestimate his enemy. Continuing to run his agency and branching out into protective services for businesses and homes, he wrote several books about his experiences as a detective.

PINTO, Francis Effingham. Union officer. Conn. Lt. Col. 32d N.Y. 31 May '61; Col. 23 Oct. '62; Bvt. B.G. USV (war service); mustered out 19 June '63.

PIRACY CHARGE AGAINST W. W. SMITH, et al. See ENCHANTRESS AFFAIR.

PITCHER, Thomas Gamble. Union gen. 1824–95. Ind. USMA 1845 (40/41); Inf. Serving on the frontier and in the Mexican War (1 brevet), he was at Harpers Ferry in June '62 and also in that year's Va. campaign, as Capt. 8th US Inf. (since 1858). Named B.G. USV 29 Nov. '62, he was wounded severely at Cedar Mountain and on convalescent leave until 10 Jan. '63. He was assigned Comsy. and Provost Marshal duties until the end of the war, and was breveted for Cedar Mountain and war service (B.G. USV). Continuing in the R.A., he was the Superintendent of West Point 1866–71 and Gov. of the Washington (D.C.) Soldiers' Home until retired in 1878 as Col. 44th US Inf. for "disability contracted in the line of duty."

PITTSBURG LANDING, Tenn., 6–7 Apr. '62. Alternate name for SHILOH.

PLAISTED, Harris Merrill. Union officer. 1828–98. N.H. A lawyer, he was commissioned Lt. Col. 11th Me. 30 Oct. '61 and promoted Col. 12 May '62. He fought on the Peninsula, commanded a brigade before Charleston, and served under Grant at Petersburg. Discharged 25 Mar. '65, he was breveted for war service (B.G. USV 21 Feb. '65 and Maj. Gen. USV). After the war he was active in Republican politics and served in Congress and as Gov. of Me.

PLANK ROAD. One surfaced by heavy planking; used principally in boggy areas and through swamps. A sophisticated CORDUROY ROAD.

PLATNER, John S. Union officer. N.Y. Capt. 33d N.Y. 22 May '61; Maj. 24 Jan. '62; mustered out 2 June '63; Lt. Col. 1st N.Y. Vet. Cav. 18 Sept. '63; Col. 1 Mar. '65; Bvt. B.G. USV (war service). Died 1868.

PLEASANT HILL, La., 9 Apr. '64. (RED RIVER CAMPAIGN OF 1864) After his defeat at SABINE CROSS ROADS on the 8th, Banks withdrew 15 miles southeast to Pleasant Hill where Gen. A. J. Smith's force had been left. Gen. Richard Taylor pursued. The afternoon of the 9th the leading Confederate division, Gen. T. J. Churchill's, with the brigades of M. M. Parsons and J. C. Tappan, came up against the line manned by the divisions of Gens. W. H. Emory and J. A. Mower. At about 5 P.M. Taylor attacked. Parsons on the Confederate right and Tappan drove back the left-flank brigade of Col. Lewis Benedict (3, 1, XIX), crushing this unit and killing its commander. Although W. M. Dwight (1, 1, XIX) on the Federal right flank held fast against the attacks of J. G. Walker and H. P. Bee, the center was threatened by the annihilation of their flank. Before the attack reached the Federal reserve positions, however, a counterattack by the brigade of J. W. McMillan (2, 1, XIX) enveloped Parsons' right and drove him back. The center of the Federal line was then led forward by Mower. Taylor ordered C. J. Polignac's brigade up from the reserve to stop the Federal advance; he was not able to arrive in time, and so covered the Confederate retreat. The Federals withdrew to Grand Ecore (near Natchitoches) the night of the battle, united with the rest of Banks's forces, and entrenched. The Confederates left a cavalry screen and turned against Steele in Ark.

The Federals lost 1,369 out of 12,247 engaged; the Confederates lost about 1,500 out of 14,300 engaged (Livermore).

PLEASANT HILL LANDING, La. 12 Apr. '64. Alternate name for action at Blair's Landing during RED RIVER CAMPAIGN.

PLEASANTS, Henry. Union officer. South America. 2d Lt. 6th Pa. 22 Apr. '61; mustered out 26 July '61; Capt. 48th Pa. 10 Aug. '61; Lt. Col. 21 Sept. '62; Bvt. B.G. USV (war service, Petersburg mine construction); mustered out 18 Dec. '64. Commanded 1, 2, IX (Potomac). Died 1880. Famous for his association with the PETERSBURG MINE ASSAULT.

PLEASONTON, Alfred. Union gen. 1824–97. D.C. USMA 1844 (7/25); Dragoons. After serving on the frontier, he fought in the Mexican War (1 brevet) and the Seminole War, served in Indian fighting, and was in Kans. during the border disturbances. Transferred to the 2d US Cav. 3 Aug. '61 as Capt. (since 1855) and promoted Maj. 15 Feb. '62, he fought in the Peninsula with his regiment and was appointed B.G. USV 16 July '62. He commanded 2d Brig., Cav. Div., Potomac (16 July–Sept. '62) and commanded the cavalry corps (Sept. '62–Feb. '63) at South Mountain, Antietam, and Fredericksburg. At Chancellorsville he led 1st Div., Cav. Corps, Potomac (12 Feb.–22 May '63) and was appointed Maj. Gen. USV 22 June '63. He then led the cavalry corps (22 May '63–22 Jan. '64 and 12 Feb.–25 Mar. '64) at Beverly Ford, Aldie, Middleburg, Upperville, Gettysburg, Culpeper Courthouse, and Brandy Station. Going to the Dept. of the Mo., he commanded Dist. Central Mo. (24 July–3 Sept. '64) and Dist. St. Louis (21 Nov.–9 Dec. '64) at Jefferson City during Price's raid. Continuing in the R.A. and being breveted for Antietam, Gettysburg, Price's raid (B.G. USA) and war service (Maj. Gen. USA). He resigned in 1868 as Maj. when the army was reorganized and he was to serve under former subordinates. He was in the Internal Revenue Service for a time but in a conflict of authority was asked to resign. Later became a railroad president. In 1888 he was put on the retired list as Maj.

PLUMMER, Joseph Bennett. Union gen. 1820–62. Mass. USMA 1841 (22/52); Inf. After serving in Fla., on the frontier, and in the Mexican War, he was with Lyon as Capt. 1st US Inf. (since 1852) at Camp Jackson (Mo.). Severely wounded at Wilson's Creek in Aug. '61, he was named Col. 11th Mo. 25 Sept. and fought at Frederickstown (Mo.) 21 Oct., being promoted B.G. USV the next day. During 1862 he commanded in the Army of the Miss.: 5th Div. (4 Mar.–24 Apr.) at New Madrid and Island No. 10; 2, 1 (23 Feb.–4 Mar.); 2, 2 (26 Apr.–29 Mar. and 18 June–9 Aug.); 1, 3 (24 Apr.–26 Apr.) and 3d Div. (29 May–18 June). On 9 Aug. '62 he died from exposure in camp near Corinth.

PLYMOUTH, N.C., 17–20 Apr. '64. Bragg drew up a plan for the capture of this place by the combined operation of the newly-completed ram *Albemarle* and an infantry force under R. F. Hoke. With three brigades, his own and those of Ransom and Kemper, Hoke started his attack at 4 P.M. on the 17th. The Federal garrison, under H. W. Wessells, was composed of four infantry regiments with artillery and cavalry, but was largely dependent on naval gunfire support. Wessells' requests for reinforcements were not answered. The *Albemarle* appeared on the 19th, sank the *Smithfield*, disabled the *Miami*, and drove off the other Federal ships. Hoke, meanwhile, surrounded the town. Infantry attacks and the skillful employment of his artillery, including that of the ram, forced Wessells to run up a white flag at 10 A.M. on the 20th. The Federals lost 2,834, including prisoners, and a considerable quantity of supplies. Davis promoted Hoke to Maj. Gen. for this victory.

POCAHONTAS, Tenn., 25 Sept. '62. See DAVIS' BRIDGE, same date.

POE, Orlando Metcalfe. Union gen. 1832–95. Ohio. USMA 1856 (6/49); Topo. Engrs.-Engrs. After serving in garrison, on surveying expeditions in W. Va., and on the frontier, he was on McClellan's staff as 1st Lt. (since 1860) in organizing the defenses of Washington. As Col. 2d Mich. from 16 Sept. '61 until 16 Feb. '63 and as B.G. USV 29 Nov. '62, he led his regiment at Williamsburg and Fair Oaks and commanded 3, 1, III (5 Aug.–Sept. '62) at

2d Bull Run. He led 1, 1, IX, Potomac at Fredericksburg (15 Nov.–15 Dec. '62 and 11 Feb.–11 Apr. '63) and was leading the same brigade in the Army of the Ohio (19 Mar.–11 Apr. '63), when his appointment as B.G. expired. Named Capt. Engrs. 3 Mar. '63, he was Chief Engr. of the Army of the Ohio and in Dec. '63 named Asst. Engr. of the Mil. Div. of Miss. In Apr. '64 he was named Sherman's Chief Engr. He was breveted for Knoxville, Atlanta, Savannah, and war service (B.G. USA). Continuing in the R.A., he was an outstanding engineer on the Great Lakes and Col. and A.D.C. to Sherman (1873–94).

POINT D'APPUI. Meaning literally a support or fulcrum, this is an old strategic term for "the different advantageous posts, such as castles, fortified villages, etc., which the general of an army takes possession of in order to secure his natural position" (Wilhelm). It might also be defined as a tactical or strategic base.

POINT LOOKOUT. The large Federal PRISON, it was in Md. where the Potomac runs into Chesapeake Bay. It was established 1 Aug. '63 with no barracks, the prisoners, all enlisted men, living in tents. Water was scarce and had to be imported when the shallow wells became polluted. Nearly 20,000 were imprisoned there at times, and there was sufficient shelter, although the tents were often crowded.

POLIGNAC, Prince Camille Armand Jules Marie de. C.S.A. gen. 1832–1913. France. Appt.-La. The 29-year-old Prince de Polignac came to the Confederacy with a distinguished record in the Crimean War. He was named Lt. Col. of C.S.A. Inf. and Chief of Staff to Beauregard on 16 July '61. After fighting at Corinth, he was named B.G. C.S.A. (from France) on 10 Jan. '63 and served under Taylor in the RED RIVER CAMPAIGN OF 1864. Put in command of a Tex. brigade of disgruntled, dismounted cavalry, he was met with disapproval, hostility, and the nickname "Polecat." He won their respect as a combat leader, moved up to command Mouton's division on 8 Apr. '64, when the latter was killed at Sabine C.R., and on 13 June was appointed Maj. Gen. with rank from 8 Apr. He was the only alien to attain high rank in the C.S.A. (Lonn, who points out that Wm. Browne and Pat Cleburne were naturalized.) He continued to lead his division until sent 16 Mar. '65 to ask for French aid for the state of La. This mission a failure, he retired to his estate. A journalist and civil engineer, he did not fight in the Franco-Prussian War. About 6 feet 4 inches tall, thin, with a grave manner and a Napoleonic beard, he was a gallant and talented soldier (Taylor) as well as being one of the war's most romantic figures. His statue is on the Sabine C.R. battlefield.

"POLIUTE." Pen name of F. B. WILKIE.

POLK, Leonidas. C.S.A. gen. and Episcopal bishop. 1806–64. N.C. USMA 1827 (8/38); Arty. Descended from a wealthy and prominent family, kin to Pres. James Polk, he briefly attended the Univ. of N.C. (his father had been one of its founders) before entering West Point. He was converted while a 1st Classman (senior), after three "lively years," and resigned six months after graduation to study for the Episcopal ministry. Ordained a deacon in 1830, he was named Missionary Bishop of the Southwest in 1838 and Bishop of La. in 1841. He was active in the establishment of the Univ. of the South and laid its cornerstone at Sewanee (Tenn.) in 1860. His friend and classmate Jefferson Davis prevailed upon him to accept a commission, and he was appointed Maj. Gen. 25 June '61, more as a symbol than as a military leader. Given the mission of fortifying and defending the Mississippi River, he occupied Columbus (Ky.) 4 Sept. '61, violating Ky.'s neutrality and hurting the Southern cause in the area. Succeeded on 15 Sept. by his ex-roommate, A. S. Johnston, whom he had urged Davis to commission, he defeated Grant 7 Nov. '61 at Belmont, Mo., and commanded the Confederate right at Shiloh, leading four charges personally. At Perryville he was second-in-command to Bragg, and his Lt. Gen. commission was dated 10 Oct. '62. He fought at Stones River, and two months later urged Davis to replace Bragg with J. E. Johnston, another friend from West Point days. Bragg removed him from command after Chickamauga for not attacking when told to, and ordered him court-martialed, but Davis reinstated him. He was killed by a Parrott gun during the Atlanta campaign on 14 June '64 at Pine Mountain. Not an outstanding combat leader, he was a large man with an impressive military bearing and a commanding manner. Although Jeff Davis said the Confederacy had sustained no heavier blow since Stonewall Jackson was killed, S. G. French expressed the opinion of many when he said, "Thus died a gentleman and a high Church dignitary. As a soldier, he was more theoretical than practical" (Horn, 332).

POLK, Lucius Eugene. C.S.A. gen. 1833–92. N.C. A nephew of Leonidas Polk, he was an Ark. planter and enlisted as private in Cleburne's "Yell Rifles." At Shiloh he commanded a company and was wounded in the face. Elected Col. a few days later, his regiment covered the retreat from Corinth. He was wounded again at Richmond, Ky. He led the regiment at Perryville and was named B.G. C.S.A. 13 Dec. '62. Given Cleburne's brigade, he com-

manded it at Stones River, on the Tullahoma campaign, at Chickamauga, Chattanooga, and in northern Ga. At Kenesaw Mountain he was wounded a fourth time and forced to leave active duty. Returning on crutches to his home near Columbia, Tenn., he was active in Democratic politics after the war and served in the state senate. A "distinguished-looking man, brave but extremely modest," he defied the K.K.K. when he whipped one of his Negro hands and routed them from his part of the county.

POLK'S CORPS. See I and II CORPS, Confed. Army of Miss. and of Tenn.

POLLOCK, Samuel McLean. Union officer. Ohio. Lt. Col. 6th Iowa Cav. 31 Jan. '63; Col. 1 July '64; Bvt. B.G. USV (war service). Died 1895.

POMUTZ, George. Union officer. Hungary. 1st Lt. Adj. 15th Iowa 23 Dec. '61; Maj. 3 June '63; Lt. Col. 23 Mar. '65; Bvt. B.G. USV (war service). Commanded 3, 4, XVII (Tenn.). After the war he was Consul at St. Petersburg (1866) and in 1878 was named Consul General for Russia. Died 1882.

PONTON (pon'-ton). Modern military spelling and pronunciation for the low, flat-bottomed boat or some other floating structure, used as a support of a temporary bridge. Scott's *Military Dictionary* (1862) uses the form "pontoon," as does most Civil War literature; Wilhelm's *Military Dictionary* (1881) uses the form "ponton," which is the correct modern military usage.

POPE, Edmund Mann. Union officer. N.Y. Capt. 8th N.Y. Cav. 16 Sept. '61; Maj. 1 Dec. '62; Lt. Col. 15 Feb. '64; Col. 1 Mar. '65; Bvt. B.G. USV (war service).

POPE, John. Union gen. 1822–92. Ky. Appt.-Ill. USMA 1842 (17/56); Topo. Engrs. After duty with surveying expeditions and fighting in the Mexican

War (1 brevet), he explored in the West and experimented with artesian wells in the Llano Estacado. Named B.G. USV 17 May '61 (Capt. since 1856), he commanded Dist. of North Mo. (17 July–Oct. '61); 2d Div., Army of Southwest Mo. (Oct.–Dec. '61) and Dist. Central Mo. (Dec. '61–18 Feb. '62). He then took command of the Army of the Miss. (23 Feb.–26 June '62), leading it at New Madrid, Island No. 10, and on the advance upon and siege of Corinth. Promoted Maj. Gen. USV 21 Mar. '62, he was Lincoln's unilateral selection to head the new Army of Va. (26 June–2 Sept. '62). He alienated his troops by POPE'S ADDRESS, and aroused R. E. Lee's personal animosity by prescribing harsh treatment of Southern sympathizers in the occupied portions of Va. When asked by a reporter where his headquarters would be, he replied "in the saddle." This prompted the quip that Pope had his headquarters where his hindquarters should have been. However, Pope's initial actions in the 2d Bull Run campaign were generally sound; it was only when faced with the combination of Lee's strategy and Stonewall Jackson's tactics that he lost complete control of the situation and got his short-lived army soundly defeated. He was relieved on 2 Sept. and McClellan again headed the army. The PORTER CASE resulted from the campaign, and there was sentiment that McClellan and his adherents had contributed to Pope's defeat by faulty cooperation.

Pope remained on active duty and commanded the Dept. of the Northwest (16 Sept.–28 Nov. '62 and 13 Feb. '63–13 Feb. '65). In the R.A. after the war, he became Maj. Gen. USA in 1882 and retired four years later. Contemporaries described him as dashing, handsome, soldierly, and a fine horseman.

POPE'S ADDRESS on taking command of the Army of Virginia. (Note that this is not datelined "Headquarters in the Saddle.")

Headquarters, Army of Virginia
Washington, D.C., July 14, 1862.
To the Officers and Soldiers of the Army of Virginia:

By special assignment of the President of the United States, I have assumed the command of this army. I have spent two weeks in learning your whereabouts, your condition, and your wants, in preparing you for active operations, and in placing you in positions from which you can act promptly and to the purpose. These labors are nearly completed, and I am about to join you in the field.

Let us understand each other. I have come to you from the West, where we have always seen the backs of our enemies; from an army whose business it has been to seek the adversary, and to beat him when he was found; whose policy has been attack and not defense. In but one instance has the enemy been able to place our Western armies in defensive attitude. I presume that I have been called here to pursue the same system and to lead you against the enemy. It is my purpose to do so, and that speedily. I am sure you long for an opportunity to win the distinction you are capable of achieving. That opportunity I shall endeavor to give you. Meantime I desire you to dismiss from your minds certain phrases, which I am sorry to find so much in vogue amongst you. I hear constantly of "taking strong positions and holding them," of "lines of retreat," and of "bases of supplies." Let us discard such ideas. The strongest position a soldier should desire to occupy is one from which he can most easily advance against the enemy. Let us study the probable lines of retreat of our opponents, and leave our own to take care of themselves. Let us look before us and not behind. Success and glory are in the advance, disaster and shame lurk in the rear. Let us act on this understanding, and it is safe to predict that your banners shall be inscribed with many a glorious deed and that your names will be dear to your countrymen forever.

John Pope
Major General, Commanding.
(B.&L., II, 530.)

POPLAR SPRINGS CHURCH, Va. (Peeble's Farm; Pegram's Farm), 30 Sept.–2 Oct. '64. (PETERSBURG CAMPAIGN). While the operations were taking place north of the James around NEW MARKET HEIGHTS Lee was forced to weaken his Petersburg defenses to reinforce on the Peninsula. Grant ordered a reconnaissance in force to probe the west flank of Lee's lines to envelop this point if possible and at least to prevent the further detachment of troops to reinforce north of the James. Warren (V) moved with the divisions of Griffin and Ayres toward Poplar Springs Church the morning of the 30th. He was followed by Parke (IX) with the divisions of Willcox and Potter. Gregg's cavalry moved to the left rear as flank protection.

Griffin captured a Confederate redoubt, its supporting trenches, and 100 prisoners at Peeble's Farm. In the afternoon Potter's division, moving on the left, was hit near the Pegram house by the Confederate divisions of Heth and Willcox which were advancing to recapture their lost positions. Understanding that Griffin would support his right flank, Potter attacked and forced the Confederate skirmishers back. When Griffin's forces did not appear, Potter had to go on the defensive to protect his exposed flank. The Confederates attacked before the Federals had organized their defense and Potter's men were driven back with some confusion. The 7th R.I., which had been in reserve, formed a new line near the Pegram house and was told to rally the withdrawing units around them. Curtin's brigade formed on the new line and the initial Confederate assault was checked. Griffin's division then came up on the right in time to repulse the next enemy attack. The Federals consolidated their gains, holding the captured positions around Peeble's Farm and entrenching along the Squirrel Level Road, thereby refusing their left flank. On 2 Oct. Gregg was attacked as he moved along the Vaughan Road on the Federal left, but defended himself successfully. Warren was also able to repulse attacks on his part of the line. In the afternoon Mott's division (3, II) was attached to Parke (IX) and formed to his rear. On 2 Oct. Parke advanced and after some sharp skirmishing established a line of entrenchments about a mile from the enemy. The Federal line was then connected with the works near Globe Tavern and with Hatcher's Run. Fox puts Federal losses on 30 Sept. at 2,889, of whom 1,802 were missing. Confederate losses are not known but were estimated in Federal reports as 900 total (E.&B.).

POPULAR SOVEREIGNTY. The doctrine, advanced by Stephen A. Douglas, that people in a territory have the right to decide for themselves through the territorial legislature whether they want their territory to have slavery or not. This is the interpretation put on the term by American history; in political science, it means that the sovereignty of the state rests with the people who have the right to change a government considered detrimental to the interests of the people.

PORTER, Andrew. Union gen. 1820–72. Pa. After USMA (ex-1839), he entered the R.A. during the Mexican War

(2 brevets) and served in the Southwest. Named Col. 16th US Inf. 14 May and B.G. USV 17 May '61 (promoted from Capt.), he led 1st Brig., 2d Div. at 1st Bull Run and commanded the division when Hunter was wounded. He was then Provost Marshal Gen. of the Army of the Potomac (3 Oct. '61-Mar. '62), until he was relieved after McClellan's retreat from the Chickahominy to the James. Commanding a Pa. draft depot next, he was then with Provost Marshal Gen. in Washington and mustered out 4 Apr. '64 because of health, resigning from the R.A. 16 days later. Traveling in Europe, he died in Paris in 1872. Cousin of Horace PORTER, Bvt. B.G.

PORTER, David Dixon. Union Adm. 1813-91. Pa. Sailing with his father, Commodore David Porter, to the West Indies to suppress piracy in 1824 and being commissioned Midshipman in the Mexican Navy three years later, he joined the US Navy in 1829. He served in the Mediterranean, the South Atlantic, and the Gulf during the Mexican War. On 22 Apr. '61 he was named Commander and with his mortar fleet joined Farragut, his foster brother, in Mar. '62 for the capture of NEW ORLEANS. He took command of the Miss. Squadron in Sept. '62 as acting Rear Admiral. In cooperation with Sherman, he captured ARKANSAS POST in Jan. '63 and was present at the surrender of Vicksburg in July '63. He was on Banks's RED RIVER CAMPAIGN OF 1864 where his ships were saved by the engineering skill of Joseph BAILEY. In Oct. '64 he went to the North Atlantic Squadron and fought at Fort Fisher, for which he received his fourth Thanks of Congress during the war. Promoted Vice Admiral in 1866, he was superintendent of the Naval Academy and appointed Adm. of the Navy in 1870. Brother of William D. PORTER and cousin of Fitz-John PORTER.

PORTER, Fitz-John. Union gen. 1822-1901. N.H. Appt.-N.Y. USMA 1845 (8/41); Arty. He fought in the Mexican War (1 wound; 2 brevets), and served as artillery and cavalry instructor at West Point and on the frontier before going on the Utah Expedition. Named Col. 15th US Inf. 14 May '61 (Bvt. Capt. since 1856 and 1st Lt. since 1847), he was appointed B.G. USV three days later. From 27 Apr. to Aug. of that year he was Chief of Staff of the Dept. of Pa. and to Banks and Patterson in the Valley. He commanded Porter's division, Potomac (3 Oct. '61-13 Mar. '62) and directed the Yorktown siege while leading 1st Div., III, Potomac (13 Mar.-18 May '62). Succeeding on the latter date to the command of the V Corps and named Maj. Gen. USV 4 July '62, he led it at New Bridge, Hanover Court House, Mechanicsville, Gaines's Mill, Turkey Bridge, Malvern Hill, 2d Bull Run, Antietam, and Shepherdstown. Relieved by Pope "for disobedience, disloyalty, and misconduct in the face of the enemy" at 2d Bull Run, he was cashiered 21 Jan. '63. (See PORTER CASE.) In 1886 he was reappointed, although without back pay, as Col. of Inf. to rank from 14 May '61 and put on the retired list. He had been breveted B.G. USA 27 June '62 for Chickahominy. Meanwhile, he had been a mine superintendent in Colorado, merchant, and N.Y.C. commissioner of police, fire, and then public works. He was also in the construction business, and 1869 had turned down the Khedive's offer of the position in the Egyptian Army later accepted by Stone.

PORTER, Horace. Union officer. c. 1837-1921. Penn. USMA 1860 (3/41); Ord. As 1st Lt. (7 June '61), he was Asst. Ordnance officer with the Port Royal Expedition and was Chief of Ordnance in the transfer of the Army of the Potomac from Harrison's Landing to Maryland. Going to the Dept. of the Ohio, he was Chief of Ordnance there until 25 Jan. '63 when he took the same position with the Dept. and Army of the Cumberland (until 1 Nov. '63). He served with the War Dept. until 4 Apr. '64 when he became Grant's A.D.C. (Lt. Col.) for the rest of the war. Continuing in the R.A., he was breveted for Ft. Pulaski, the Wilderness, New Market Hgts., and war service (B.G. USA) and resigned in 1873 as Col. After that, he was a railroad official. He wrote, in B.&L., articles about Five Forks and Appomattox that combine wit and information in an agreeable mixture.

PORTER, Samuel Alfred. Union officer. Ohio. Pvt. Co. B 33d Ill. 20 Aug. '61; discharged 4 Apr. '62; 2d Lt. 104th Ill. 27 Aug. '62; 1st Lt. 8 Mar. '63; Capt. 3 Oct. '63; mustered out 24 Aug. '64; 1st Lt. Vet. Res. Corps 22 Aug. '64; Capt. 29 Aug. '64; mustered out 6 Oct. '64; Col. 123d US Col. Inf. 13 Oct. '64; Bvt. B.G. USV; retired from R.A. with rank of Capt. in 1870. Brevets for war service (2), Chickamauga.

PORTER, William David. Union Commodore 1809–64. La. Appointed Midshipman in 1823, he served on active duty and was in the Pacific when the Civil War began. He was named Foote's assistant in the gunboat flotilla on the Tennessee River and was scalded by a bursting boiler at Fort Henry. Also fighting at Fort Donelson, he took his ship, named *Essex* after his father's vessel, past the batteries along the Mississippi. He was promoted Commodore 16 July '62 and served in the Natchez, Vicksburg, and Port Hudson bombardments. For the rest of the war he was on boards and commissions. Son of Commodore David Porter, brother of Admiral David D. PORTER, half brother of Admiral FARRAGUT, and cousin of

Fitz-John PORTER. He had two sons in the Confederacy.

PORTER CASE. Fitz-John Porter was convicted on 10 Jan. '63 after a trial that lasted 45 days, of "willful failure to obey his orders, [which] prevented the capture or destruction of the rebel army under Jackson on the 29th of August, 1862." (Pope's official report.) For the next 24 years the case remained a subject of controversy, which can be summarized with these dates: he was cashiered 21 Jan. '63; the Schofield board re-examined the evidence in 1878, recommended remission of the sentence, but Congress took no action; Pres. Arthur remitted the sentence on 4 May '82; Porter was reappointed Col. on 5 Aug. '86 with rank from 14 May '61 (but without back pay); two days later he was retired at his own request.

There is controversy to this day as to the military qualifications of Fitz-John Porter. E. P. Alexander wrote: "Porter in the Seven Days had proved himself not only a hard fighter, but a skillful commander. He would have made a good leader of an army; but he had a low opinion of Pope, and, in his correspondence with brother officers [principally McClellan] about this period, did not conceal it" (Alexander, 207). Many subscribe to this view, that Porter's offense was not poor combat leadership at 2d Bull Run, but indiscretion in criticizing a superior.

The Schofield Board (1887) concluded after a year's investigation that Porter was relieved, tried, and professionally ruined for failure to obey an impossible order. The board stated that Porter's attack order—sent to him at 4:30 P.M. and received two hours later—". . . was based upon conditions which were essentially erroneous and upon expectations which could not possibly be realized." It required an attack on Jackson's unassailable flank or rear and that the attacking force keep contact with Reynolds, who was two miles away. Steele says Porter "ought to have done something." The board did not agree. It commended him for not needlessly sacrificing his troops (in order to protect his own reputation). As for Steele's accusation that Porter ". . . ought not to have stood idle with 10,000 men during the whole afternoon, while a battle was raging close at his right hand," the board reported: "The display of troops made by Porter earlier in the afternoon had all the desired and all possible beneficial effect" (Upton, 344; Steele, 252).

Kenneth P. Williams, on the other hand, presents a convincing argument that Porter was guilty as charged. (K. P. Williams, II, 785–89.)

PORT GIBSON (Thompson's Hill; Magnolia Hills; skirmishes at Bayou Pierre), Miss., 1 May '63. VICKSBURG CAMPAIGN.

PORT HUDSON, La. Confederate strong point guarding the Mississippi River approximately 25 miles north of Baton Rouge. The first action here took place 14 Mar. '63, when Admiral Farragut bombarded the place during his passage up the river to Vicksburg. The USS *Mississippi* was lost in this action. During the period 8–10 May Federal gunboats again bombarded the place, and silenced the Confederate batteries. The XIX Corps (Banks's Army of the Gulf) advanced to capture Port Hudson and had its first engagement 26 May on the Bayou Sara Road, four miles away. The position was unsuccessfully assaulted 27 May, 11 June, and 14 June. A siege was conducted 27 May to 9 July '63, when Port Hudson finally surrendered. (Vicksburg had surrendered 4 July.) The deprivation seems to have been even greater at Port Hudson than at Vicksburg, according to Wiley. "One of the besieged stated in his diary that he and his comrades ate 'all the beef—all the mules—all the Dogs—and all the Rats' that could be obtained prior to the capitulation" (Wiley, *Reb,* 94). The siege cost the Federals 3,000 men. Confederate losses were over 7,200, including 5,500 prisoners, two steamers, 60 guns, 5,000 small arms, 150,000 rounds of small arms ammunition, and almost 45,000 pounds of gunpowder.

PORT REPUBLIC, Va., 9 June '62. See CROSS KEYS AND PORT REPUBLIC.

PORT ROYAL SOUND (Forts Beauregard and Walker), S.C., 7 Nov. '61. On 29 Oct. Du Pont left Hampton Roads with 17 wooden cruisers and convoyed a force of about 12,000 under Thomas W. Sherman to Port Royal Sound. After a bombardment on 7 Nov. the Federals took possession of Forts Beauregard and Walker to establish a base for subsequent operations along the coast of S.C., Ga. and Fla. Casualties were 31 in Du Pont's force and 66 in the Confederate forts. (The naval action is known as Hilton Head.)

PORT WALTHALL JUNCTION, Va., 6–7, 19, 20 May '64. See DREWRY'S BLUFF.

POSEY, Carnot. C.S.A. gen. 1813–63. Miss. A Capt. in Jeff Davis' Miss. Rifles in Mexico, he was wounded at Buena Vista. As Col. 16th Miss., he was at 1st Bull Run, Balls Bluff, Jackson's Valley campaign, the Seven Days' Battles, and 2d Bull Run. At Antietam he commanded Featherston's brigade and was appointed B.G. C.S.A. 1 Nov. '62. He led his own brigade at Fredericksburg, Chancellorsville, and Gettysburg. He was severely wounded in the left thigh by a shell fragment at Bristoe Station. Less than a month later (13 Nov.) he died of this wound.

POST, Philip Sidney. Union officer. 1833–95. N.Y. 2d Lt. 59th Ill. 17 July '61; 1st Lt. Adj. 21 July '61; Maj. 17 Jan. '62; Col. 20 Mar. '62; Bvt. B.G. USV 16 Dec. '64 (Nashville). W.I.A. Pea Ridge, Overton Hill (Tenn.) 16 Nov. '64, Nashville. Medal of Honor 8 Mar. '63 for Nashville 15 and 16 Dec. '64. Commanded (Cumberland): 1, 1st Right Wing, XIV; 1, 1, XX; 3, 1, IV; 2, 3, IV; 3d Div., IV. A lawyer and editor, he was US Consul in Vienna in 1866, Consul General in 1874, and Republican Congressman in 1886.

POTOMAC, CONFEDERATE ARMY OF THE. Southern troops on the "Alexandria Line," sometimes called also the Dept. of Alexandria (Va.) or the Potomac Dept., were put under the command of M. L. Bonham on 21 May '61. After Beauregard took command on 2 June, the force became known as the Army of the Potomac. When J. E. Johnston joined on 20 July with his Army of the Shenandoah (for the 1st Battle of Bull Run), the combined force was called the Army of the Potomac.

When the Dept. of Northern Va. was created 22 Oct. under J. E. Johnston's command, Beauregard was assigned to head the Potomac Dist. Troops serving in Beauregard's district were formed into the divisions of Van Dorn, G. W. Smith, Longstreet, and Kirby Smith. Beauregard was ordered to Ky. on 26 Jan. '62. The organization that Johnston took to oppose McClellan on the Peninsula continued to be generally referred to as the Army of the Potomac (R. E. Lee, II, 77n.). The designation Army of the North was used by Davis in referring to troops of Johnston's department that remained in the Valley and along the Rappahannock.

In an order issued the day he succeeded Johnston (1 June '62), Lee unofficially bestowed the name Army of Northern Va. on the force that had been formed on the eve of 1st Bull Run (20 July '61) and that had been known most commonly in the interim as the Army of the Potomac (Lee's Lts., I, 49n.).

POTOMAC, UNION DEPARTMENT AND ARMY OF THE. Created 15 Aug. '61 from the Military Dist. of the Potomac. (The date 25 July is sometimes given, ignoring the brief existence of the Military Dist. of the Potomac.) Although there were various territorial reorganizations that affected the geographical area which the Dept. of the Potomac included, the main fighting force in the Eastern Theater of the Civil War was always the "Army of the Potomac" (except for John Pope's short-lived Army of Va. in 2d Bull Run campaign). Its successive commanders were the following major generals: McClellan, 15 Aug. '61–9 Nov. '62 (Peninsular and Antietam campaigns); Burnside, to 26 Jan. '63 (Fredericksburg campaign); Hooker, to 28 June '63 (Chancellorsville campaign); Meade, to 27 June '65 (Gettysburg to Appomattox). John G. Parke was in command briefly from 30 Dec. '64 to 11 Jan. '65.

POTOMAC, UNION MILITARY DISTRICT OF THE. In existence briefly 25 July–15 Aug. '61. Formed by consolidation of the Dept. of Northeastern Va. and the Dept. of Washington; merged into the Dept. and Army of the Potomac. Commander: Maj. Gen. George B. McClellan.

POTTER, Carroll Hagedorn. Union officer. R.I. Capt. Asst. Adj. Gen. Vols. 21 Oct. '61; Maj. Asst. Adj. Gen. Vols. 25 Feb. '65; Col. 6th US Vol. Inf. 27 Mar. '65; Bvt. B.G. USV (war service). Served as Chief of Staff for Gens. Robinson, Stoneman, and Heintzelman.

665

POTTS, B. F.

In R.A. until retired in 1900 as Lt. Col. Ex-cadet USMA 1860. Died 1901.

POTTER, Edward Elmer. Union gen. 1823–89. N.Y. After studying law, he went to Calif. for the gold rush and, returning to N.Y., he farmed until commissioned Capt. Comsy. of Subsist. Vols. 3 Feb. '62. He was named Lt. Col. 1st N.C. 1 Oct. '62, a colored regiment he had raised, and B.G. USV 29 Nov. '62. He commanded US forces Norfolk and Portsmouth (23 Sept.–1 Oct. '63); 3d Sep. Brig., Dist. Hilton Head (1 Aug.–26 Oct. and 14–28 Nov. '64); 1st Sep. Brig., Morris and Folly Is. (26 Oct.–14 Nov. '64); 1st Brig., Coast Div. (28 Nov. '64–23 Jan. '65); and 2d Sep., Dist. Beaufort (23 Jan.–13 May '65).

POTTER, Joseph Adams. Union officer, N.Y. Appt.-Mich. He was commissioned 1st Lt. 15th US Inf. and Capt. Asst. Q.M. 27 Sept. '61. Named Col. Q.M. Assigned 24 Sept. '64–'67, he was in command of several depots and continued in the R.A., retiring in 1879 as Maj. and Bvt. B.G. USA.

POTTER, Joseph Hayden. Union gen. 1822–92. N.H. USMA 1843 (22/39); Inf. After serving on the frontier, in garrison, and the Mexican War (1 wound, 1 brevet) and on the Utah Expedition, he was captured 27 July '61 at St. Augustine (Tex.) as Capt. 7th US Inf. (since 1856). Exchanged a year later and promoted Col. 12th N.H. 22 Sept. '62, he fought at Fredericksburg and at Chancellorsville, where he was wounded and captured. He commanded 2, 3, III, Potomac (12 Jan.–19 Feb. '63) and, after exchange in Oct. '63, was Provost-Marshal General of Ohio. He fought on 29 Sept. '64 at Fort Harrison and then commanded 2, 3, XXIV, James (3 Dec. '64–17 Jan. '65) at Hatcher's Run. Chief of Staff for the XXIV Corps 16

Jan.–10 July '65, he was at the final assault of Petersburg and the Appomattox campaign. Continuing in the R.A., he was breveted for Fredericksburg, Chancellorsville, and war service (B.G. USA) and retired in 1886 as B.G. USA commanding the Dept. of Mo.

POTTER, Robert Brown. Union gen. 1829–87. Mass. Commissioned Maj. 51st N.Y. 14 Oct. and Lt. Col. 1 Nov. '61, he participated in Burnside's N.C. expedition, fighting at Roanoke Island and New Bern, where he was severely wounded. Promoted Col. 10 Sept. '62, he fought at Cedar Mountain, 2d Bull Run, Chantilly, South Mountain, Antietam, and Fredericksburg, and was appointed B.G. USV 13 Mar. '63. During the Vicksburg campaign he commanded the 2d Div., IX Corps, in the Army of the Ohio (5 June–25 Aug. '63) and in the Army of the Tenn. (14 June–18 Aug. '63). He then led the IX Corps in the Army of the Ohio (25 Aug. '63–17 Jan. '64). When the IX Corps went to the Army of the Potomac, he commanded the 2d Div. (1 May–22 Dec. '64 and Jan.–2 Apr. '65) at Spotsylvania, North Anna, Bethesda Church, and the siege of Petersburg. He was severely wounded in the final assault. Promoted Maj. Gen. USV 29 Sept. '65, he was married on the same day and was mustered out in 1866, having been breveted Maj. Gen. USV 1 Aug. '64 for actions around the Rapidan. Lyman described him as "a grave, pleasant-looking man, known for his coolness and courage." He was in railroading after the war, living abroad and in Newport. His father, two brothers, and uncle were Protestant Episcopal bishops.

POTTS, Benjamin Franklin. Union gen. 1836–87. Ohio. A Douglas Democratic politician, he was commissioned Capt. 32d Ohio 20 Aug. '61, Lt. Col. 21 Nov., and Col. 28 Dec. '62. He was with Grant in Memphis and at the

Vicksburg siege. During the Atlanta campaign and the March to the Sea and through the Carolinas he commanded in the XVII Corps, Army of the Tenn.: 2, 3, (17 Nov. '63–6 Mar. '64); 1, 4 (18 July '64–26 June '65 and 9–23 July '65) and 4th Div. (26 June– 9 Jul. '65). He was promoted B.G. USV 12 Jan. '65, breveted Maj. Gen. USV for war service, and mustered out in 1866. Re-entering politics as a Republican, he was appointed Gov. of Mont. (1870–82) and then elected to the territorial legislature. He was ". . . more than six feet tall, with a huge body and great energy" and "tact and good judgment" (D.A.B.).

POUND GAP, Ky., 16 Mar. '62. Humphrey Marshall's Confed. Army of EASTERN TENNESSEE scattered by forces of B. G. James A. Garfield.

POWDER SPRING(S), 20 June '64. See KENESAW MOUNTAIN.

POWELL, Eugene. Union officer. Ohio. Capt. 4th Ohio 4 May '61; Maj. 66th Ohio 22 Oct. '61; Lt. Col. 24 May '62; resigned 11 Apr. '65; Col. 193d Ohio 13 Apr. '65; Bvt. B.G. USV (war service). Commanded 2, 3, XXV (Va.).

POWELL, Lewis. Alias Lewis Paine. See LINCOLN'S ASSASSINATION.

POWELL, R.M. C.S.A. officer. As Col. 5th Tex. (Hood's Tex. brigade), he was wounded and captured at Gettysburg and mistaken by the Federals for Longstreet. Both men were stout, portly, and full-bearded at that time. Contrary to Evander M. Law (B.&L., III, 326), Powell did not die, but recovered to be exchanged and take command of Hood's Texans in the last winter of the war at Petersburg.

POWELL, William Henry. Union gen. 1822–79. Wales. An Ohio manufacturer, he crossed the river to join 2d W. Va. Cav. 8 Nov. '61 as Capt. In 1862 was promoted Maj. 25 June,

Lt. Col. 25 Oct., and Col. 18 May '63. Leading a charge at Wytheville (Va.) 18 July '63, he was wounded and captured, spending six months in Libby. He commanded the 3d Brig., 2d Cav. Div., W. Va. (10 June–July '64) and the 2d Brig. (Aug.–26 Sept. '64) before being promoted B.G. USV 19 Oct. '64. He also commanded 2d Div., W. Va. (30 Sept. '64–13 Jan. '65), resigning on the latter date. Breveted Maj. Gen. USV for the W. Va. campaign and Front Royal, he was given the Medal of Honor 22 July '90 for leading a raid at Sinking Creek (Va.) 26 Nov. '62, in which his 20 men captured a camp of 500 without losing a man or gun. Returning to manufacturing after the war, he was active in Republican politics.

POWERS, Charles James. Union officer. Canada. Commissioned 1st Lt. Adj. 13th N.Y. 14 May '61, he was promoted Capt. Asst. Adj. Gen. 6 Nov. '61 and Lt. Col. 108th N.Y. 9 Oct. '62. He was named Col. 2 Mar. '63 and was mustered out in May '65. Breveted B.G. and Maj. Gen. USV for war service, he died in 1882.

PRAIRIE GROVE, Ark., 7 Dec. '62. After CANE HILL Blunt's division of Schofield's Army of the Frontier remained in that exposed location about 20 miles southwest of Fayetteville. Herron was near Springfield, Mo., with his two divisions. About 3 Dec. Hindman started advancing north from Van Buren with 11,000 men to destroy Blunt, who had about 7,000. When Blunt reported this threat to Gen. Sam Curtis, C.G. Dept. of Mo., the latter ordered Herron to march 125 miles to Blunt's support.

The evening of 6 Dec. Hindman had driven in Blunt's pickets and was getting ready to attack when he learned Herron was approaching Fayetteville (20 miles northeast of Cane Hill). Hindman decided then to leave Col. J. C.

Monroe with a small cavalry force oppo-site Blunt to screen his movement while his main body, led by Gen. Marma-duke's cavalry, would turn the Federal position to the east, get between the two enemy forces, and defeat first Her-ron and then Blunt. At midnight of the 6th Herron's infantry started entering Fayetteville after a forced march that had covered 25 miles a day; the same night some of his cavalry reached Blunt. The weather had been freezing until 2 Dec. There was rain and then snow the next day, and on the 4th the cold weather had returned.

Marmaduke's cavalry, moving out be-fore dawn, led Hindman's envelopment. Elements of this force, including Quan-trill's bushwhackers, hit leading units of Herron's force and drove them back. Gen. J. O. Shelby (C.S.A.) was cap-tured in this action and then rescued. At this point Hindman forfeited his opportunity: instead of attacking Her-ron's tired force, as originally planned, he took up a defensive position. Blunt, eight miles away, was deceived by Mon-roe's demonstration until he heard the fighting to his rear at Prairie Grove.

Herron advanced against Hindman's position, built up a battle line, attacked, and was repulsed. Hindman ordered a counterattack, but found that an entire regiment of his recently raised Ark. troops had deserted. Herron then made two more unsuccessful attacks. About 11 A.M. Blunt, hearing the battle to his rear, marched to Herron's relief. He arrived on the Confederates' left flank early in the afternoon and opened an enfilade fire. Hindman was again unsuc-cessful in getting his Ark. troops to attack. After an hour's bombardment Blunt attacked, rolled up the enemy's flank, but was then driven back by Shelby's cavalry. The Confederates held their positions until dark and during the night withdrew without Blunt's perceiv-ing it.

Burial parties found unwounded men dead of exposure and wounded who had been burned to death around straw stacks. The Federals found that many of Hindman's conscripts had removed the bullets from their cartridges and fired blanks (Monaghan, 271). Out of an estimated 10,000 engaged on each side, the Federals lost 1,251, and the Confederates 1,317 (Livermore, citing O.R.).

PRATT, Benjamin Franklin. Union officer. Mass. Capt. 35th Mass. 11 Aug. '62; Lt. Col. 36th US Col. Inf. 5 Sept. '63; Bvt. B.G. USV (war service). Died 1890.

PRATT, Calvin Edward. Union gen. 1828–96. Mass. A lawyer and politician, he was commissioned Col. 31st N.Y. 14 Aug. '61 (Heitman) and fought at 1st Bull Run (B.&L.) in the 5th Div. Named B.G. USV 10 Sept. '62, he com-manded 1, 2, VI (25 Sept. '62–26 Jan. '63) and Light Brig., VI (26 Jan.–28 Apr. '63), resigning on the last date. He was afterward in the Bureau of Internal Revenue and an Associate Jus-tice of the N.Y. Supreme Court.

PREBLE'S FARM. "Preble" is a mis-spelling of Peeble. For battle of Peeble's Farm, Va., 30 Sept.–2 Oct. '64, see POPLAR SPRINGS CHURCH, same date.

PRENTISS, Benjamin Mayberry. Union gen. 1819–1901. Va. Educated at a military school, he served in the Ill. militia against the Mormons during the Mexican War, and later practiced law. He was a Col. in the militia when com-missioned Capt. 10th Ill. 29 Apr. '61 and promoted Col. the same day. Ap-pointed B.G. USV 17 May, he com-manded 6th Div., Army of the Tenn. (26 Mar.–6 Apr. '62) at Shiloh where he was captured. Released in Oct., he was promoted Maj. Gen. USV 29 Nov.

'62 and served on Fitz-John Porter's court-martial. He then commanded Dist. East Ark. (8 Feb.–3 Apr. '63) and Dist. East Ark., XIII (July–3 Aug. '63) at Helena, resigning 28 Oct. to return to his practice.

PRESCOTT, George Lincoln. Union officer. Mass. Capt. 32d Mass. 15 Nov. '61; Lt. Col. 13 Aug. '62; Col. 28 Dec. '62; Bvt. B.G. USV 18 June '64 (Petersburg). W.I.A. 18 June '64 at Petersburg leading his regiment in a charge, and died the next day. A fort named in his honor was built on the ground gained by this assault.

PRESIDENTS OF THE US, Civil War service of. In addition to Grant, the following men had Civil War service: GARFIELD, Benjamin HARRISON, HAYES, Andrew JOHNSON, and MC-KINLEY.

PRESTON, John Smith. C.S.A. gen. 1809–81. Va. After Hampton-Sidney, Univ. of Va., and Harvard, he settled in S.C. He was a highly successful planter, invested his fortune in art, and married a sister of Wade Hampton. In the legislature 1849–56 he was known as a "radical champion of states' rights." In Feb. '61 he was sent as a commissioner from his state to urge Va. to leave the Union and was one of Beauregard's volunteer A.D.C.'s at Fort Sumter and 1st Bull Run. Commissioned Asst. Adj. Gen. and Lt. Col. 31 Aug. '61, he was later sent on recruiting duty in S.C. In Dec. '61 Beauregard recommended him for a B.G. appointment, and he was given a brigade but not the rank. On 28 Jan. '62 he took command of the prison camp at Columbia, S.C. Although unhappy with the job, he was so efficient that Seddon named him head of the Bureau of Conscription in July '63. He held this post until it was discontinued in Mar. '65, having been finally appointed B.G. C.S.A. 10 June '64. Going

to England upon the collapse of the Confederacy, he returned in 1868 but remained "... completely unreconstructed" (D.A.B.).

PRESTON, Simon Manley. Union officer. Vt. 1st Lt. Regt. Q.M. 15th Ill. 24 May–15 June '61; Capt. Asst. Adj. Gen. Vols. 5 Aug. '61; dismissed 23 Sept. '62; Col. 58th US Col. Inf. 25 Mar. '64; Bvt. B.G. USV 30 Dec. '65 (war service).

PRESTON, William. C.S.A. gen. 1816–87. Ky. After Harvard Law School he practiced until the Mexican War, in which he served as Lt. Col. Later in the legislature and US Congress as a Whig, he joined the Democrats and was Buchanan's Minister to Spain. When the secession crisis loomed, he came home to aid his state and urged Kentuckians to join the Confederacy. He went to A. S. Johnston in Bowling Green and was commissioned Col. on Breckinridge's staff in Sept. '61. Serving in that post until Johnston's death at Shiloh, he was appointed B.G. C.S.A. 14 Apr. '62 and commanded his brigade at Corinth, Stones River, Vicksburg, and Chickamauga. Named Com. of Southwestern Va., he was appointed a foreign minister 7 Jan. '64. On his way to Europe, however, he was foiled by the blockade and forced to land in Mexico, where he made his way up to Tex. and joined Kirby Smith. Wood and C. M. H. say that he was appointed Maj. Gen. in the Trans-Miss. Dept. 1 Jan. '65, although Wright makes no mention of this higher rank. After the war he returned to Mexico and then traveled to the West Indies, England, and Canada. Returning to the US in 1866, he sat in the state legislature again and was active in Democratic politics.

PREVOST, Charles Mallet. Union officer. 1818–87. Md. Appt.-Pa. Capt. Asst. Adj. Gen. Vols. 1 May '62; resigned 16 Aug. '62; Col. 118th Pa. 28 Aug. '62; Col. 16th Vet. Res. Corps 29 Sept. '63; Bvt. B.G. USV (war service). W.I.A. Antietam in shoulder. Fought at Chancellorsville with arm strapped to body. Adj. Gen. on the staff of Gen. Frank Patterson. Upon his return home in 1866 he was appointed Maj. Gen. 1st Div., Pa. National Guard.

PRICE, Francis. Union officer. N.J. 1st Lt. Adj. 7th N.J. 19 Sept. '61; Maj. 1 Apr. '62; Col. 6 Nov. '64; Bvt. B.G. USV (war service). Commanded 3, 3, II (Potomac). Died 1898.

PRICE, Richard Butler. Union officer. Pa. Col. 2d Pa. Cav. 23 Jan. '62; Bvt. B.G. USV (engagement with the 6th Va. Cav. [C.S.A.] and capture of its Col., Sept. '62); mustered out 1 Feb. '65. Commanded Cav. Brig., Mil. Dist. Wash. (Potomac); Indpt. Cav. XXII (Wash.); 2, Cav. Div., XXII (Wash.). Died 1876.

PRICE, Samuel Woodson. Union officer. Ky. Col. 21st Ky. 26 Feb. '62; Bvt. B.G. USV (Kenesaw Mountain, Ga.). Commanded 3, 3d Left Wing, XIV (Cumberland).

PRICE, Sterling ("Pap"). C.S.A. gen. 1809–67. Va. Appt.-Mo. He had been a legislator, lawyer, Mo. farmer, and Congressman before serving as B.G. in the Mexican War and Gov. of Mo. in 1852. In command of the Mo. state troops in 1860, he joined the Confederacy in disgust with Blair's and Lyon's aggressive policies at St. Louis. After the famous Planter's Hotel conference with them in June '61, he went to Jefferson City and then retreated with a small force to southwestern Mo. Recruiting and training about 5,000 men, he united with Ben McCulloch to fight at Wilson's Creek, where he commanded the Mo. State Guard. He captured Lexington 17–20 Sept. and then retreated before Frémont into Ark., joining the Confed-

eracy officially on 6 Mar. '62, when he was appointed Maj. Gen. C.S.A. He fought at Iuka, Corinth, Helena, and the Red River, where he defeated Steele before going on his unsuccessful Mo. raid in 1864 (see PRICE'S RAID IN MISSOURI). Retreating to the Tex. plains, he escaped to Mexico. His personal plans collapsed with Maximilian's government and he returned to Mo. a broken and impoverished man.

PRICE, William Redwood. Union officer. Ohio. 2d Lt. 3d Pa. Cav. 15 Jan. '62; 1st Lt. 7 Sept. '62; Capt. 1 May '63; Maj. Asst. Adj. Gen. Vols. 5 Aug. '64; Bvt. B.G. USV. Brevets for Richmond campaign, war service (2), Five Forks (Va.). In R.A. until death in 1881 as Lt. Col. (1 brevet for Indian fighting). Listed by Phisterer as Price, W. Radwood.

PRICE'S RAID IN MISSOURI, Sept.–Oct. '64. In July '64, when transfer of A. J. Smith's corps and XIX Corps had weakened Federal strength in La., Kirby Smith directed Taylor to cross with his two divisions to the east side of the Mississippi. After several unsuccessful attempts Kirby Smith accepted the fact that he would have to confine his operations to the area west of the river. He decided to attempt the recovery of Mo. by sending Sterling Price into that state with all available cavalry.

Price left Princeton, Ark., in Aug. with the cavalry divisions of J. F. Fagan and Marmaduke. Crossing the Arkansas River unmolested between the Federal garrisons at Little Rock and Fort Smith, he marched through Batesville to Pocahontas, in the northeast part of the state. Here he was joined by the cavalry division of J. O. Shelby. With a force that now totaled 12,000 men (one third of whom were not armed) and 14 guns, he entered Mo. on 19 Sept. and advanced on a broad front. At Fredericktown he concentrated his forces on the

25th. At Pilot Knob (Fort Davidson), 27 Sept., he was repulsed in a bloody six-hour fight by 1,100 Federals under Thomas Ewing. The losses were approximately 1,500 Confederates and 200 Federals. Ewing secretly evacuated the post during the night, and blew it up.

When Price started his raid A. J. Smith's corps with a cavalry brigade was aboard transports on the Mississippi for movement to Nashville. (They had been operating against Forrest in Miss.) This command was diverted to assist in the defense of Mo. Price advanced toward St. Louis, but the arrival there of A. J. Smith's troops precluded his attacking the city. Ewing, meanwhile, had been conducting a delaying action, while Pleasonton with 7,000 cavalry and eight guns advanced to his support. Price wheeled to the west, along the south bank of the Missouri River. Destroying sections of the Pacific R.R. as they went, the Confederates occupied Hermann, 5 Oct.; by-passed Jefferson City, 7 Oct., and took Boonville, 9 Oct. Shelby captured Glasgow, 15 Oct., having forced the surrender of over 400 Federals under Col. Chester Harding, Jr. The same day Shelby captured Sedalia after stampeding about 700 men under the command of Col. J. D. Crawford.

Although thousands of state militia had been mobilized, Price continued westward, skirmishing daily, but unopposed by any organized resistance. Pleasonton followed to his rear, while A. J. Smith's troops and Col. J. E. Phelps's Mo. militia moved on his south flank. Meanwhile, in the pre-election confusion of Kans. an order had been issued mobilizing 10,000 militia. Some of these regiments refused to cross into Mo., but J. G. Blunt moved eastward with the 2d Colo. and 16th Kans. Twenty miles east of Lexington, at Waverly, Mo. (Shelby's home town), Blunt made contact with Price's leading brigade. (This

was "Shelby's Brigade," under M. Jeff Thompson, who had succeeded David Shanks when the latter was mortally wounded 6 Oct.)

Federal resistance was now stiffening. There were actions at Lexington, 19 Oct.; Little Blue River, 21 Oct.; and Independence, Big Blue (Bryam's Ford) and State Line, 22 Oct.

S. G. Curtis, C.G. Dept. of Kans., had now come forward and had been driven from his initial position along the Big Blue (22 Oct.) when Shelby found an exposed flank. During the night of 22–23 Oct. Curtis organized a new line along Brush Creek, just south of Kansas City and Westport. Price now had Federals to his front and rear. Although he had an open route of retreat to the south, he elected to attempt to use his central position first to defeat the forces of Curtis to his front and then turn and destroy the forces of Pleasonton and A. J. Smith. The next day the Confederates were defeated in the battle of WESTPORT, Mo., which Monaghan calls "the biggest Civil War engagement west of the Missouri."

After retreating for 61 miles Price halted to fight a costly rear-guard action at MARAIS DES CYGNES, Kans., 25 Oct. Gens. Marmaduke and W. L. Cabell were captured along with four colonels, 1,000 men, and 10 guns. Other delaying actions were fought the same day on Little Osage or Mine Creek, Kans., and at the Marmiton, or the battle of Charlot, Mo. (O.R. chronology). Price again turned at bay near Newtonia, Mo., 28 Oct., delaying the pursuit three hours and almost capturing Blunt.

Price made an arduous detour through Indian Territory to avoid Fort Smith. On 2 Dec. he re-entered the Confederate lines at Laynesport, Ark., with 6,000 survivors of the ordeal (Monaghan, 343). In summing up his operation Price said, "I marched 1,434 miles;

fought forty-three battles and skirmishes; captured and paroled over 3,000 Federal officers and men; captured 18 pieces of artillery..." (O.R. I, XLI, Part 1, 640). Although he admitted the loss of only 10 guns, about 1,000 small arms, and fewer than 1,000 prisoners (*ibid.*), Monaghan says "he had lost five thousand stand of arms, all his cannon, and the greater part of his army. 'Governor' Reynolds [of Missouri, who had accompanied Price] released to the press a scathing criticism, accusing Price of 'glaring mismanagement and distressing mental and physical military incapacity' " (*ibid.*).

Organized Confederate military operations in the Trans-Miss. region had ended, although guerrilla operations continued unabated.

(See also BUSHWHACKER and CENTRALIA MASSACRE, 27 Sept. '64.)

PRIME, Frederick Edward. Union officer. 1829–1900. Italy. USMA 1850 (1/44); Engr. He built fortifications on the East, West, and Gulf coasts before the war, and in 1861, as a 1st Lt. (since 1856) on his way from Pensacola to Fort Pickens, was captured by the C.S.A. Promoted Capt. 6 Aug. '61, he fought at 2d Bull Run and was Chief Engr. for the Depts. of Ky., the Cumberland, and the Ohio. Wounded and captured during a reconnaissance near Mill Spring (Ky.) 5 Dec. '61, he was next with Grant during the 1862–63 Miss. campaign and fought at Corinth and Vicksburg. Promoted Maj. 1 June '63, he was appointed B.G. USV 4 Aug. but declined. Continuing in the R.A., he was breveted for Corinth, Vicksburg, and war service (B.G. USA) and retired in 1871 as Maj.

PRINCE, Henry. Union gen. 1811–92. Me. USMA 1835 (30/56); Inf. He served in the Seminole War (1 wound), Indian fighting, the Florida War, the Mexican War (2 brevets, 1 wound) and on the Utah Expedition. As B.G. USV

28 Apr. '62 (Maj. since 1855), he led 2, 2, II Army of Va. (16 July–9 Aug. '62) and succeeded to division (9 Aug. '62) at Cedar Mountain, where he was captured. Released in Dec., he commanded 5th Div., XVIII, N.C. (11 Jan.– 2 Apr. '63) at demonstrations in front of New Bern and Kinston. He commanded Dist. Pamlico (22 Apr.–20 June '63) as well as 2d Div., III, Potomac (10 July '63–24 Mar. '64) at Wapping Heights, the Rapidan campaign, and the Mine Run operations. From 25 Mar. to 4 Apr. '64 he led 3d Div., VI, Potomac, and from 25 Jan.–7 Aug. '64 he commanded Dist. Columbus, XVI, Tenn. Breveted for Cedar Mountain and war service (B.G. USA), he continued in the R.A., retiring in 1879 as Lt. Col. Deputy Paymaster Gen.

PRINCETON, W. Va., 16–17 May '62. During the WEST VIRGINIA OPERATIONS IN 1862 J. D. Cox was attacked here by Humphrey Marshall and, when the latter was reinforced by Heth, was forced to fall back to avoid encirclement. The Federals (primarily Augustus Moor's 2d Prov. Brig.) lost 113; Marshall says he had about 15 casualties (T.U.A.).

PRINCIPLES OF WAR. These may be defined as the fundamental truths governing the prosecution of STRATEGY and TACTICS. The nine that have been adopted by the US Army in modern times are listed and explained below for several reasons. First, many of them are encountered in Civil War literature. Second, they provide in capsule form the fundamentals of strategy and tactics. They are useful, if not essential, in any evaluation of generalship.

The definitions given in quotes below are those used in instructing cadets at West Point. They closely follow the US Army's *Field Service Regulations, Operations.*

The Objective. "Direct all efforts toward a decisive, obtainable goal." The proper objective ("purpose") in battle is the destruction of the enemy's combat forces. To do this, however, subordinate commanders must be given "terrain objectives" toward which they move. Thus, Richmond was not a proper (terrain) objective for McClellan's army in 1862 because capturing it would not necessarily destroy the Confederate army and the loss of Richmond in 1862 would not have meant defeat of the Confederacy. It was a proper (terrain) objective for Grant in 1864–65 because it had become so important by that time that Lee was forced to defend it even if it meant destruction of his army. Although Grant's objective was Lee's Army of Northern Va. (not Richmond, *per se*), by directing his efforts toward Richmond he forced Lee to stand and fight him for its defense.

Simplicity. "Prepare uncomplicated plans and concise orders to insure thorough understanding and execution." McDowell at 1st Bull Run violated the principle of simplicity, since his troops were too green to execute properly the maneuver he prescribed.

Unity of Command. "For every task there should be unity of effort under one responsible commander." The Union flagrantly violated this principle after KERNSTOWN. Stonewall Jackson's Valley campaign taught Lincoln and Stanton their lesson, and Unity of Command was obtained by creating Pope's Army of Va. (The Federals were nevertheless defeated in the next [2d Bull Run] campaign.)

The Offensive. "Seize, retain, and exploit the initiative." Lee's generalship embodies this principle, whereas it was the fatal deficiency in McClellan's. It is the quality most conspicuous in the make-up of most successful commanders, particularly Stonewall Jackson and Grant, Sheridan and Forrest.

Maneuver. "Position your military resources to favor the accomplishment of your mission. Maneuver in itself can produce no decisive results [as Hooker at Chancellorsville failed to realize] but if properly employed it makes decisive results possible through the application of the principles of the offensive, mass, economy of force, and surprise." It is by maneuver that a superior general defeats a stronger adversary (e.g., Jackson's Valley campaign).

Mass. "Achieve military superiority at the decisive place and time." Mass in this sense does not mean "more men." "Military superiority" can be attained against a more numerical enemy if you have superiority in such things as weapons, leadership, morale, and training. "Mass" is generally gained by "maneuver."

Economy of Force. "Allocate to secondary efforts minimum essential combat power." This is a misleading term because it does not mean what it sounds like. It does not mean "do the job with minimum combat power." Note that the principle pertains to "secondary efforts," and it is the means by which a superior general achieves "mass" as defined above. Mass and Economy of Force are on opposite sides of the same coin.

Surprise. "Accomplish your purpose before the enemy can effectively react." Tactical or strategic surprise does not mean open-mouthed amazement. Thus, a corps may be "surprised" by an attack it has seen coming for several hours if this attack is too powerful for it to resist by itself and if no other unit is within SUPPORTING DISTANCE. The fate of the XI Corps at Chancellorsville is an example. The principle of war known as "Security" may be defined as all measures taken to avoid "Surprise."

Security. "Never permit the enemy to acquire an unpredicted advantage." Another definition would be "measures taken to prevent surprise." A unit in bivouac, for example, uses outposts and patrols for security. Lack of security at Shiloh resulted in surprise of the Federals.

PRISONS. Although more than 150 places were used as prisons on both sides during the war, only a handful are important. Generally they fit into certain types: the fortifications, former jails and penitentiaries, altered buildings, enclosures around barracks, enclosures around tents and open stockades. Of the first type, the only important example in the Confederacy is CASTLE PINCKNEY. The Union had Fort Warren in Boston Harbor, Fort Lafayette in N.Y., Fort McHenry in Baltimore and, most dreaded in the South, Fort Delaware in the Delaware River. The Union used the Alton, Ill., and the Columbus, Ohio, penitentiaries for prisoners, and the Confederate cavalryman, John MORGAN, escaped from the latter. The Confederacy's LIBBY PRISON and the Union's OLD CAPITOL and GRATIOT STREET PRISONS were converted buildings. Others, all in the South, where tobacco factories were common and excellent for this purpose, were Ligon's in Richmond and CASTLE THUNDER in Richmond and Petersburg. Buildings were also converted in Danville, Lynchburg, and Shreveport, and CAHABA (Ala.) was one of the more important ones. Union prisons that were enclosures around barracks included JOHNSON'S ISLAND, CAMP MORTON, CAMP DOUGLAS, CAMP CHASE, ELMIRA, and ROCK ISLAND. The Confederate BELLE ISLE and the Union POINT LOOKOUT prisons were enclosures built around tents. Prisons that were open stockades existed only in the South, and the most infamous was ANDERSONVILLE. Others of this type were CAMP LAWTON, CAMP FORD AND CAMP GROCE, and stockades at Salisbury (N.C.), Macon (Ga.), Charleston, Florence (S.C.), and Columbia (S.C.).

PRITCHARD, Benjamin Dudley. Union officer. Ohio. Capt. 4th Mich. Cav. 13 Aug. '62; Lt. Col. 26 Nov. '64; Bvt. B.G. USV 10 Mar. '65 (capture of Jeff Davis).

PRIVATEERING. The act of merchant ships preying upon enemy naval or merchant ships during a war. Historically, such ships were issued letters of marque and reprisal, and this right is given to Congress and specifically denied the states in the Constitution. Privateering was abolished by the 1856 Declaration of Paris, but the US, while observing this declaration, did not sign it and could not protest against the Confederate privateering during the Civil War. (See ENCHANTRESS AFFAIR.)

PROCTOR'S CREEK, Va. Part of action at DREWRY'S BLUFF, 12–16 May '64.

PROLONGE. "A stout rope used to connect the lunette of the carriage and pintle hook of the limber to move the piece short distances without limber" (Wilhelm, 236). The rope was carried coiled around "prolonge hooks" on the top side of the stock or trail.

PROMOTION OF REGULAR ARMY OFFICERS. Of the 1,080 R.A. officers on active duty in 1861, only 142 became Union generals during the war. Only 248 reached the grade of colonel or higher. Of the West Pointers, 161 who started the war as captains were still captains or had been promoted only to major when the war ended. An additional 247 West Pointers who were officers when the war started did not pass beyond the grade of major. The main reason for this was the policy of "freezing" R.A. officers and men in R.A. units rather than spreading them throughout the volunteer units where their military training would have made them valuable in higher grades. In this particular the Union acted like a confederacy, depending upon political generals, while the Confederacy followed the policies of a federal government by taking advantage of and promoting their R.A. personnel. The 102 West Pointers who came back into service from civil life during the war were in a position to "shop around" for an assignment with the volunteer units; 51 of them became generals.

PROUDFIT, James Kerr. Union officer. N.Y. 2d Lt. 1st Wis. 17 May '61; mustered out 21 Aug. '61; 1st Lt. Adj. 12th Wis. 18 Dec. '61; Lt. Col. 12 Aug. '63; Col. 17 Dec. '64; Bvt. B.G. USV (war service).

PRYOR, Roger Atkinson. C.S.A. gen. 1828-1919. Va. He graduated from Hampton-Sidney in 1845 as Valedictorian and studied law at the Univ. of Va. before becoming a newspaper publisher. He was sent to Athens as a special agent. He investigated claims against the Greek government by American citizens, and resigned his seat in Congress to join the Confederate Army 3 Mar. '61. As a visitor in Charleston, he urged the bombardment of FORT SUMTER but declined the opportunity of firing the first shot. Sitting in the C.S.A. Congress, he resigned to be commissioned Col. 3d Va. and was appointed B.G. C.S.A. 16 Apr. '62 by Johnston. He commanded his brigade at Williamsburg and Seven Pines. At Antietam he succeeded Anderson as division commander. Resigning 18 Aug. '63 because he had no brigade to command, he enlisted as private in Fitzhugh

Lee's cavalry. He was captured around Petersburg 27 Nov. '64 while serving as a special courier during an informal truce. Exchanged by Lincoln's personal order shortly before Appomattox, he went to N.Y. in Sept. '65 and became a prominent newspaper writer and lawyer. Largely through Dan Sickles' influence he was appointed judge of a lower court and he was later named Assoc. Justice of the N.Y. Supreme Court. "The most effective secessionist speaker in Virginia," he was "tall and straight, with the elastic step of an Indian" (D.A.B.). His wife, Sara A. Rice Pryor, wrote *Reminiscences of Peace and War* (1904).

PUGH, Isaac C. Union officer. Ill. Capt. 8th Ill. 25 Apr. '61; mustered out 24 July '61; Col. 41st Ill. 5 Aug. '61; Bvt. B.G. USV 10 Mar. '65; mustered out 20 Aug. '64. Commanded 1st Brig., 4th Div. (Tenn.); 1st Brig., 4th Div. Right Wing, XIII; 1, 4, XVII; 1, 4, XVI; 1, 4, XIII; 2, 4, XVII. Died 1874.

PULFORD, John. Union officer. N.Y. 1st Lt. 5th Mich. 28 Aug. '61; Capt. 15 May '62; Maj. 1 Jan. '63; Lt. Col. 3 May '63; Col. 12 July '64; Bvt. B.G. USV (war service). Commanded 2, 3, II (Potomac). W.I.A. Malvern Hill in temple and jaw with collarbone broken; Chancellorsville in abdomen; Wilderness with broken back; Boydton Plank Road (Va.) 27 Oct. '64 in right knee. In R.A. until retired as Col. in 1870. He was active in the Indian campaigns in the West.

PUMPKIN VINE CREEK. See DALLAS, Ga.

Q

QUAKER ROAD (GRAVELLY RUN), Va. 29 Mar. '65. (APPOMATTOX CAMPAIGN) In the advance of the Federal left to envelop the defenses of Petersburg, Griffin's (1st) division of Warren's V Corps drove enemy skirmishers from the crossing of Rowanty Creek at about 5 A.M. Arriving at the

crossing of Quaker Road and Gravelly
Run after noon, Griffin had to fight his
way across. Crawford's division moved
over a ponton bridge, took position
on Griffin's left, and the two advanced
against gradually stiffening resistance
until halted near Arnold's sawmill.
Chamberlain's brigade attacked and was
then driven back by troops of Wise's
and Wallace's brigades (Anderson).
Battery B, 4th US Arty., arrived to assist
Chamberlain; then parts of Gregory's
and Bartlett's brigades also reinforced
toward the end of the action. The Confederate attacks were halted and the
Federals advanced to the Boydton plank
road and entrenched. Warren reported
370 killed and wounded. Chamberlain
and Sickles were both wounded. The
Federals reported taking 200 prisoners
and burying 130 of the enemy.

QUAKERS. A religious, pacifist group
who were among the first ABOLITIONISTS
in American history, attacking the institution of slavery and the slave trade in
the late eighteenth century. (See UNDER-
GROUND RAILROAD.)

QUANTRILL, William Clarke. Confed. BUSHWHACKER. 1837–65. Ohio.
After several years on the frontier as a
gambler, ne'er-do-well, and petty thief,
he became entangled in the border disturbances between Kans. and Mo. and
used the upset conditions for his own
purposes. Known variously as Charley
Hart and Billy Quantrill, he fought at
Wilson's Creek and then undertook
guerrilla operations in Mo. On 11 Aug.
'62 he captured Independence (Mo.)
and four days later was commissioned
Capt. C.S.A. with about 150 men
under him. Later in Nov. he went to
Richmond and was given a colonel's
commission although he had hoped for
more. In the meantime his men had
been fighting in Kans. and Mo., and
Quantrill did not join them until Jan.
or Feb. '63. His command burned and

plundered Lawrence (Kans.) 21 Aug.
'63, where about 150 men and boys
were killed and about a million and a
half dollars' worth of property was destroyed. After Price's retreat in 1864,
Quantrill set out for Washington to
assassinate Lincoln but on 10 May he
was fatally wounded by Federal troops
in Ky. He lived 20 days more and left
his doxy, Kate Clarke, $500 in gold,
which she used to start a bawdy house
in St. Louis.

QUARLES, William A. C.S.A. gen.
?–1893. Appt.-Tenn. Commissioned Col.
42d Tenn. in 1861, he served under A. S.
Johnston. He commanded his regiment
at Fort Donelson and upon exchange
was given a consolidated brigade in
Maxey's division at Port Hudson. Serving then under J. E. Johnston at Jackson, he was appointed B.G. C.S.A. 25
Aug. '63 and fought in the Atlanta
campaign in Cantey's division. He was
severely wounded and captured 30 Nov.
'64 at Franklin, Tenn.

QUINBY, Isaac Ferdinand. Union
gen. 1821–91. N.J. USMA 1843 (6/39);
Arty. He served in the Mexican War
and as instructor at West Point, resigning in 1852 to teach at the Univ. of
Rochester (N.Y.). Raising the 13th N.Y.
and commissioned Col. 14 May '61, his
was the first Federal regiment through
Baltimore since the 6th Mass. had been
attacked there in April, and his "firm
and skillful measures forestalled" further violence. He led them at 1st Bull
Run and resigned 4 Aug. to return to
teaching. Named B.G. USV 17 Mar.
'62, he then commanded 6th Div. and
Dist. Corinth West Tenn. in the Army
of the Tenn. He also led the Dist. Miss.
and West Tenn. (24 July–29 Sept. '62);
3d Div., Army Miss. (26 Oct.–2 Nov.
'62); Dist. Corinth, XIII (30 Oct.–11
Nov. '62); and 7th Div., Left Wing,
XIII (1 Nov.–18 Dec. '62). He commanded 7th Div., XVI (22 Dec. '62–

20 Jan. '63) and 7th Div., XVII (20 Jan.–14 Apr. '63) during the Yazoo Pass expedition and (16 May–3 June '63) at Champion's Hill and the Big Black River. He was severely ill with malaria but recovered in time to rejoin his division 16 May '63 for the initial assaults (19 and 22 May). He resigned 31 Dec. '63 because of failing health, and was a consulting engineer and officeholder.

QUINCY, Samuel Miller. Union officer. 1833–87. Mass. Capt. 2d Mass. 25 May '61; Maj. 22 Oct. '62; Col. 18 Jan. '63; resigned 5 June '63; Lt. Col. 73d US Col. Inf. 29 Nov. '63; Col. 29 May '64; transferred to 96th US Col. Inf. 27 Sept. '65; Bvt. B.G. USV (war service). W.I.A. and captured at Cedar Mountain and held in Libby Prison. Served on staff of Gen. Andrews at Port Hudson and as military mayor of New Orleans. After the war he practiced law and was editor of the *Monthly Law Reporter* in Boston.

R

RACCOON MOUNTAIN, Tenn. Figured in CHATTANOOGA CAMPAIGN.

RADICAL REPUBLICANS. An extremist faction that came into being during the war, advocating immediate emancipation and a punitive policy toward the South after the surrender. They believed Reconstruction to be a legislative rather than an executive function, and opposed the moderate policies of Lincoln and Johnson. The latter was impeached in the House by this group, which counted among its leaders Charles SUMNER, Thaddeus STEVENS, Zachariah CHANDLER, Henry W. DAVIS, and Benjamin WADE. They and their backers wanted the complete destruction of the South's economic and political power, and they rightly believed that the destruction of slavery was the first step in this.

RAINS, Gabriel James. C.S.A. gen. 1803–81. N.C. USMA 1827 (13/38); Inf. He served in garrison and on the frontier and fought in the Seminole wars (1 brevet, 1 wound) and the Mexican War. Resigning 31 July '61 as Lt. Col., he was appointed B.G. C.S.A. 23 Sept. and given a brigade under D. H. Hill on the Peninsula. He commanded the post of Yorktown in the winter of 1861–62 and mined the surrounding waters. In covering the retreat up the Peninsula he is credited with the first use of LAND MINES AND BOOBY TRAPS in warfare, an innovation that caused indignation on both sides. He fought in the Seven Days' Battles and was then ordered to work further on explosives. This had been a hobby throughout his army career, although he had never dealt professionally with ordnance or been stationed at an arsenal. Named head of the Torpedo Bureau in June '64, he finally won permission to use land mines in the approaches to Richmond, Mobile, Charleston, and in the James River. He continued to have many opponents to this practice in the Confederacy on ethical grounds, however. After the war he lived in Atlanta for a while and was a clerk in the US Q.M. Dept. in Charleston, 1877–80. Brother of George W. RAINS.

RAINS, George Washington. C.S.A. officer. 1817–98. N.C. USMA 1842 (3/56); Engrs-Arty. He taught at West Point, fought in the Mexican War (2 brevets), and was Pillow's A.D.C. before serving in the Seminole War. Resigning in 1856, he was president of an iron works and was commissioned Maj.

of C.S.A. Arty. 10 July '61. Assigned to the Ordnance Bureau, he was promoted Lt. Col. 22 May '62 and Col. 12 July '63. His special mission was to find gunpowder for the Confederacy, and he started manufacturing it in Augusta (Ga.). Put in charge of all munitions operations in Augusta 7 Apr. '62, he was its commanding officer until the fall of '64, when additional troops, and their commanding general, were sent to defend Augusta against Sherman. After the war he taught chemistry and was dean of the Medical College of Ga. He wrote on chemistry and steam engines and was author of *History of the Confederate Powder Works* (1882). Brother of Gabriel RAINS.

RAINS, James Edward. C.S.A. gen. 1833–62. Tenn. After graduating from Yale, he practiced law and was an editor and public officeholder before being commissioned Col. 11th Tenn. 10 May '61. Serving mainly in eastern Tenn., he spent the winter of 1861–62 in garrison at Cumberland Gap and was appointed B.G. C.S.A. 4 Nov. '62. He commanded his brigade under C. L. Stevenson in Tenn. when Kirby Smith invaded Ky. and was killed 31 Dec. '62 at Stones River.

RAM. Vessel with a massively built prow carrying an iron ram that revived the tactics of the ancient galleys. An armor-plated casemate was situated amidships to cover the artillery, and the sides were sloped, causing projectiles to ricochet. The *Virginia* was the first and most famous of the type, constructed by the Confederates on the salvaged hull of the US frigate *Merrimack*. (See MONITOR-MERRIMAC DUEL.) The South was using or had under construction some 44 ironclads, 14 with rams, and six cotton-clad ships, including the ALBEMARLE, TENNESSEE, *Louisiana, Mississippi,* ARKANSAS, *Manassas, Lady Davis,* and STONEWALL. Union ironclads,

usually of the shallow-draft MONITOR type, included *Queen of the West, General Sumter,* CARONDELET, *Essex, Chillicothe, De Kalb,* and *Galena.* The Ellet Ram Fleet was composed of river steamers converted into rams by Union naval officer Charles Ellet, Jr., in the spring of 1862. Without guns and relying solely on their speed, they were instrumental in opening the river past Memphis. Ellet was killed 6 June '62 in this engagement. Rams, ironclads, and cotton clads figured at the battles of Charleston ('63, '64), MOBILE BAY, PLYMOUTH, NEW ORLEANS, and GALVESTON.

RAMSEUR. Stephen Dodson. C.S.A. gen. 1837–64. N.C. USMA 1860 (14/41); Arty. He resigned 8 Apr. '61 as 2d Lt. and was commissioned 1st Lt. of C.S.A. Arty. and Capt. of N.C. battery soon after this. In spring 1862 he reported to Magruder at Yorktown and was promoted Maj. In Apr. of that year he was elected Col. 29th N.C. and led it at the Seven Days' Battles and Malvern Hill, where he was seriously wounded. He was appointed B.G. C.S.A. 1 Nov. '62 and given a brigade under D. H. Hill, which he commanded at Chancellorsville (wounded), Gettysburg, the Wilderness, and Spotsylvania. Here, fighting at the "bloody angle," he was again wounded. Named Maj. Gen. 1 June '64, he led his division at Cold Harbor and, taking it to the Valley, during the Washington raid and at Winchester. He was mortally wounded 19 Oct. at Cedar Creek and died the next day at Sheridan's headquarters in Winchester. Married a little over a year, he had learned of the birth of his daughter the day before he was wounded.

RAMSEY, Alexander. Gov. of Minn. 1815–? Pa. After graduating from college, he served in Congress from Pa. as a Whig and was named first territorial Gov. of Minn. in 1849. During this term he made several outstanding treaties with the Indians and then served as Mayor of St. Paul before being re-elected Gov. in 1860–63. In the latter year he became Republican US Sen. and was named Sec. of War by Hayes.

RAMSEY, George D. Union gen. c. 1802–82. Va. Appt.-D.C. USMA 1820 (26/30); Arty. He served in arsenals and fought in the Mexican War as Taylor's Chief of Ord. (1 brevet) before being named Maj. 22 Apr. '61 and Lt. Col. 3 Aug. '61. He commanded the Washington Arsenal until 1863, when (1 June) he was promoted Col. and named Chief of Ord. for the US Arty. Later promoted B.G. USA (15 Sept. '63), he held this post until 12 Sept. '64, when he retired. He was breveted Maj. Gen. USA 13 Mar. '65.

RAMSEY, John. Union officer. N.J. Commissioned Capt. 5th N.J. 17 Aug. '61, he was promoted Maj. 5th N.J. 7 May '62, Lt. Col. 21 Oct. '62, and Col. 8th N.J. 1 Apr. '62. He was breveted for Richmond (B.G. USV 2 Dec. '64) and war service (Maj. Gen. USV). Mustered out in July '65. He died 1901.

RANDAL, Horace. C.S.A. gen. c. 1833–64. Tenn. Appt.-Tex. USMA 1854 (45/46); Inf.-Dragoons. He served on the frontier in Indian scouting and fighting before resigning 27 Feb. '61 as 2d Lt. Offered a C.S.A. commission as 2d Lt., he importuned Davis for higher rank, pointing out that he commanded the cavalry in Lincoln's inaugural parade. Randal then fought as a private in Va. until named Col. 28th Tex. Dismounted Cav. in 1862. He commanded a brigade under McCulloch in the Dist. of Ark. and fought at Millikens Bend during the Vicksburg campaign. During the Red River campaign of 1864 he also commanded his unit at Mansfield and Pleasant Hill and was appointed B.G. C.S.A. 4 Apr. '64. (Wright says "assigned" and gives no date; C.M.H.

says "commissioned" and gives the above.) He died of wounds received 30 Apr. '64 at Jenkins' Ferry, Ark. Taylor makes several references in his memoirs to the "fine brigade" of Randal at Mansfield and Pleasant Hill.

RANDALL, Alexander Williams. Gov. of Wis. 1819–72. N.Y. A lawyer, he was elected to the Wis. legislature and was chosen Gov. in 1857. Re-elected in 1859, he was a stanch supporter of the Union. He later served as Minister to Italy and Postmaster General under Johnson, whom he actively supported.

RANDALL, George W. Union officer. Me. Capt. 25th Me. 29 Sept. '62; mustered out 10 July '63; Capt. 30th Me. 12 Dec. '63; Maj. 1 Sept. '64; Lt. Col. 14 Aug. '65; Bvt. B.G. USV. Brevets for Pleasant Hill (La.), Monett's Bluff (La.), Cane River (La.). Died 1897.

RANDOL, Alanson Merwin. Union officer. c. 1837–87. N.Y. USMA 1860 (9/41); Arty.-Ord. Bvt. 2d Lt. 4th US Arty. 1 July '60; transferred to Ord. 9 Oct. '60; transferred to 3d Arty. 14 Jan. '61; 2d Lt. 1st US Arty. 22 Nov. '60; 1st Lt. 14 May '61; Capt. 11 Oct. '62; Col. 2d N.Y. Cav. 23 Dec. '64; Bvt. B.G. USV 24 June '65; mustered out USV 23 June '65; continued in R.A. until death in 1887 as Maj. Brevets for New Market (Va.), Gettysburg, Five Forks (Va.), war service (2). Chief of Arty. for Humphrey's division in the Rappahannock campaign; commanded artillery for the V Corps at Chancellorsville, and brigade of reserve artillery at the Rapidan. Instructor at USMA 27 Aug.–12 Dec. '64.

RANDOLPH, George Wythe. C.S.A. Sec. of War and gen. 1818–67. Va. Born at Monticello, his grandfather's home, he was the son of a Va. governor and brother of Thomas Jefferson Randolph. He studied at Cambridge (Mass.) and was a midshipman in the navy for six years. Then attending the Univ. of Va. and becoming a lawyer, he sat in the State Assembly and organized the Richmond Howitzers, a militia group, after John Brown's raid. He was a Confederate Peace Commissioner and commanded the howitzers on the Peninsula in 1861. At Big Bethel he was Col. and Magruder's Chief of Arty. and was appointed B.G. C.S.A. 12 Feb. '62, fighting Butler in southeast Va. On 22 Mar. '62 he succeeded Benjamin as Sec. of War and resigned the following 15 Nov. to take a field command again. His health, however, failed, and he resigned 18 Dec. '64, and went to France to recover from tuberculosis. He returned to Va. after the war but did not live much longer.

RANSOM, Matthew Whitaker. C.S.A. gen. 1826–1904. N.C. After graduating from Chapel Hill, he became a lawyer and entered politics. At first a Whig, he was a Democrat when he sat in the state legislature. Chosen to represent his state in the Confederate government before N.C. seceded, he opposed secession, but when Lincoln called for troops, he enlisted as private in the 1st N.C. Soon elected Lt., he fought at Seven Pines and Malvern Hill (twice wounded). He was named Col. 35th N.C. in 1862 and led his regiment at Antietam. Appointed B.G. C.S.A. 13 June '63, he succeeded his brother, Robert, in command of the brigade. He led this unit at Drewry's Bluff (wounded), Fort Stedman, Five Forks, and Appomattox. At first a lawyer and farmer, he re-entered politics in 1870. He was US Sen. 1872–95, and was Minister to Mexico until 1897. Tall and impressive, with a rich, resonant voice, he was a highly effective speaker.

RANSOM, Robert, Jr. C.S.A. gen. 1828–92. N.C. USMA 1850 (18/44); Dragoons-Cav. He served on the frontier in Indian fighting and scouting, taught cavalry tactics at West Point, and kept order in Kans. during the border disturbances before resigning 24 May '61 as Capt. Commissioned in the same rank in the C.S. Army, he was named Col. 1st N.C. around 13 Oct. '61 and commanded the Confederate forces in the skirmish at Vienna (Va.) in Nov. Appointed B.G. C.S.A. 6 Mar. '62 to rank from the 1st, he took command of a N.C. brigade attached to Huger's division in June '62 and fought in the Seven Days' Battles. He was under Walker at the reduction of Harpers Ferry and at Antietam. He commanded both "Ransom's Brigade" and "Ransom's Division" (I Corps) at Fredericksburg. Going to N.C. after that, he was promoted Maj. Gen. 26 May '63, and commanded the district that included the Appomattox and Black Water. He was commanding Gen. of the post of Richmond until July '63, when he became ill. In Oct. of that same year he took command in eastern Tenn. He led the cavalry under Longstreet and Buckner, and in Apr. '64 was ordered to Richmond to fight Butler at Bermuda Hundred and defend the city from Sheridan's and Kautz's raids. After Drewry's Bluff he joined Early in the Shenandoah Valley but was relieved because of health in Aug. '64. He served as president of the court of inquiry on Morgan's operations in Ky. In Nov. '64 he went to command the post of Charleston but soon had to give this up because of bad health. He surrendered to Howard on 2 May '65 at Warrenton. Was a farmer and engineer after the war. He was brother of Matthew RANSOM.

RANSOM, Thomas Edward Greenfield. Union gen. 1834–64. Vt. In civil engineering and real estate, he was named Capt. 11th Ill. 24 Apr. '61 and in charge of the regimental training and discipline, both of which were outstanding for a volunteer unit. He was promoted Maj. 4 June, mustered out 29 July, and named Lt. Col. 11th Ill. the next day. He was wounded at Charleston (Mo.) 19 Aug. '61 and also at Fort Donelson 15 Feb. '62, where his regiment was surrounded and cut their way out, losing more than half their strength in the process. Promoted Col. for bravery, with his commission dating from Fort Donelson, he was wounded a third time at Shiloh but again refused to leave his post of command. He served on McClernand's staff during the Corinth campaign and, as B.G. USV 29 Nov. '62, commanded 2, 6, XVI, Tenn. (22 Dec. '62–20 Jan. '63) and 2, 6, XVII, Tenn. (20 Jan.–14 Sept. '63) during the Vicksburg campaign. In Oct. '63 he went on the Tex. expedition from Aransas Pass to Matagorda Bay and then commanded 4th Div., XIII, Gulf (4 Jan.–15 Mar. '64) until participating in the Red River campaign of 1864. There he commanded the advance guard at Sabine Cross Roads and, when his force was overwhelmed, was wounded again. Only partially recovered, he led the 4th Div., XVI Corps, at the siege of Atlanta (4–19 Aug. '64), and then commanded the Left Wing. XVI (19 Aug.–23 Sept. '64) in the turning movement south of Atlanta, ending at Jonesboro. He next led the 1st Div., XVII (22 Sept. '64) and, going to corps, commanded it from 22 Sept. until 10 Oct. '64 in the pursuit of Hood. Ill at the commencement of the operation, he stayed with his command, riding in an ambulance until Gaylesville (Ala.), where he was taken from the field. He died 29 Oct. '64 on the way to Rome (Ga.). He was brevet Maj. Gen. USV 1 Sept. '64. Of ". . . irreproachable character and Cromwellian religious faith," he showed ". . . exceptional personal courage, power of physical endurance, and coolness in action" (D.A.B.).

RAPPAHANNOCK, UNION DEPARTMENT OF THE. Constituted 4 Apr. '62 from the original I Corps of the Army of the Potomac, the department consisted of that portion of Va. east of the Blue Ridge and west of the Potomac River; the Fredericksburg and Richmond R.R., including the Dist. of Columbia and the country between the Potomac and Patuxent rivers. It was merged 26 June '62 into Pope's Army of VIRGINIA as the III Corps. Maj. Gen. Irwin McDowell was its commander.

RAPPAHANNOCK BRIDGE AND KELLY'S FORD, Va., 7 Nov. '63. (BRISTOE CAMPAIGN) To cover his withdrawal Lee held a bridgehead at Rappahannock Bridge, and posted troops four miles downstream at Kelly's Ford to cover that crossing from the south bank. Early's division was responsible for the former, where the La. brigade (Hays's) under Col. D. B. Penn was intrenched north of the river. Rodes had responsibility for the sector that included Kelly's Ford.

About noon on the 7th elements of the Federal III Corps pushed across near Kelly's Ford. Rodes held his main position, however. The V and VI Corps, both commanded by Sedgwick, moved into position astride the railroad and opposite Early's bridgehead at about noon and opened up on the works with artillery. Early reinforced Penn with part of Hoke's brigade, under command of Col. A. C. Godwin. Lee was on the scene and agreed with Early that the position could be held during the night without further reinforcement. Night attacks were rare in the Civil War. (See WAUHATCHIE NIGHT ATTACK.)

Just at dusk (about 5 o'clock), however, Sedgwick ordered an attack. D. A. Russell (I, VI) advanced with two brigades. Upton's 2d Brig. was already deployed forward as skirmishers. The decisive action was a bayonet attack by the 6th Me. and 5th Wis. (3d Brig.) (Fox, 77) after which Upton's men swarmed into the Confederate works and advanced to the head of the ponton bridge that was the only route of retreat. The Louisianians were overwhelmed almost immediately. Godwin held out a short time before being captured with about 65 survivors.

At Kelly's Ford the 30th N.C. had advanced to support the hard-pressed 2d N.C., and both regiments were captured. Rodes's loss in this sector was 349. "For the two Divisions that made 2,023, a figure that outraged the Second [Ewell's] Corps and shocked the entire Army" (*Lee's Lts.*, III, 267). The Federals lost 419 (B.&L., IV, 87n.).

RATION. By definition, a ration is the amount of food authorized for one soldier (or animal) for one day. The Confederate government adopted the official US Army ration at the start of the war, although by the spring of 1862 they had to reduce it. The original Federal ration was: one 16-ounce biscuit (hardtack, pilot bread, or crackers) or 22 ounces of bread or flour, a pound and a quarter of fresh or salt meat or three quarters of a pound of bacon. In June '64 this was increased by six ounces of flour and four ounces of hard bread and three pounds of potatoes. In addition, for each 100 men there was authorized eight gallons of beans, 10 pounds of rice or hominy, 10 pounds of coffee, 15 pounds of sugar, four gallons of vinegar, and two pounds of salt. Men cooked individually or messed by squads until Mar. '63, when cooking by companies was prescribed. Individual or squad cooking did not, however, disappear. Although the Federal soldier often went for long periods without his authorized rations, the Southern soldier fared much worse. The SANITARY COM-

MISSION did much to improve the standards of food in the Union Army.

The problem in the South was not so much a shortage of food as it was the lack of adequate distribution, particularly by rail. Soldiers of both armies relied to a great extent on food sent from home and on the ubiquitous SUTLER.

RATLIFF, Robert Wilson. Union officer. Ohio. Lt. Col. 2d Ohio Cav. 10 Oct. '61; resigned 24 June '63; Lt. Col. 12th Ohio Cav. 22 Oct. '63; Col. 24 Nov. '63; Bvt. B.G. USV (campaigns under Gens. Burbridge and Stoneman in southwest Va.). Commanded 4, 1 Dist. Ky., XXIII. Died 1887.

RAUM, Green Berry. Union gen. 1829–1909. Ill. As a boy made three trips down the Mississippi on a flatboat. Later, when a lawyer in politics, he was a Douglas Democrat who favored war. Named Maj. 56th Ill. 28 Sept. '61, he fought during the siege of Corinth and was promoted Lt. Col. 26 June and Col. 31 Aug. '62. He commanded 2, 7, XVII (10 June–12 Aug. '63) at Vicksburg; 2, 2, XVII (2 Oct.–25 Nov. '63) at Missionary Ridge, where he was wounded; and 2, 3, XV (10 Feb. '64–29 Jan. '65) at Resaca and during the March to the Sea. He was named B.G. USV 15 Feb. '65, having been breveted that rank 19 Sept. '64, and resigned 6 May '65. A railroad president, he became a Radical Republican Congressman who voted for Johnson's impeachment. In the late 1880's he was investigated for malpractice as the Commissioner of Pensions.

RAWLINS, John Aaron. Union gen. 1831–69. Ill. A politician and Democrat supporting Douglas, he was commissioned Capt. Asst. A.G. USV 30 Aug. '61 and served on Grant's staff. "[Grant's] principal staff officer and most intimate and influential advisor," he was promoted Maj. Asst. A.G. USV 14 May '62 and Lt. Col. Asst. A.G. Assigned 1 Nov. '62–30 Aug. '63; B.G. USV 11 Aug. '63. "As Grant rose in rank and responsibility, Rawlins was promoted accordingly" (D.A.B.). During the last part of the war he suffered from t.b., which had killed his first wife in 1861. Named B.G. Chief of Staff USA 3 Mar. '65, he was breveted Maj. Gen. USV 24 Feb. '65 for war service and Maj. Gen. USA 9 Apr. '65 for the Appomattox campaign. In 1867 he went with Gen. Dodge over a proposed Union Pacific route and Rawlins (Wyo.) grew up at one of their camp sites. He was named Grant's Sec. of War, resigned his commission in 1869, and died five months later.

RAYNOLDS, William Franklin. Union officer. c. 1819–94. Ohio. USMA 1843 (5/39); Inf.-Engrs. He served in the Mexican War and on mapping and surveying duty in the West before serving as Chief Topo. Engr. of the Dept. of Va. (until Oct. '61) and of W. Va. (until Apr. '62). Promoted Col. Add. A.D.C. 31 Mar. '62, he was Chief Topo. Engr. of the Mountain Dept. until June '62 during Jackson's Valley campaign, and on sick leave until Aug. of that year. He was Chief Engr. of the Middle Dept. 27 Jan. '63–12 Apr. '64 (Maj. USA 3 Mar. '63) and served on lighthouse duty in the Northwest until 1866. Breveted B.G. USA for war service, he continued in the R.A. until 1884, when he was retired as Col.

RAYNOR, William Henry. Union officer. Ohio. 1st Lt. 1st Ohio 29 Apr. '61; mustered out 1 Aug. '61; Lt. Col. 56th Ohio 22 Nov. '61; Col. 2 Apr. '63; Bvt. B.G. USV (war service); discharged 27 Oct. '64. Commanded 2, 3, XIII.

READ, Samuel Tyler. Union officer. Mass. Capt. 3d Mass. Cav. 17 Sept. '61; Maj. 13 Nov. '63; Bvt. B.G. USV; mustered out 5 Dec. '64. Bvts. for Red River campaign, Winchester, Cedar Creek (Va.). Died 1880. Listed by Phisterer as Reed, S. Tyler.

READ, Theodore. Union officer. Ohio. Appt.-Ill. Capt. Asst. Adj. Gen. Vols. 24 Oct. '61; Maj. Asst. Adj. Gen. Vols. 25 July '64; Lt. Col. Asst. Adj. Gen. Assigned 17 Feb.–6 Apr. '65; Bvt. B.G. USV 29 Sept. '64 (gallantry before the enemy); K.I.A. 6 Apr. '65 at High Bridge (Va.). Asst. Adj. Gen. to Gen. W. T. H. Brooks in the X, XVIII, and XXIV Corps (Army of the James). W.I.A. several times; lost use of left arm; had horse shot from under him.

READY, Mattie (Mrs. John Hunt MORGAN). When Federal troops occupied Murfreesboro, Tenn., Miss Mattie Ready, a local belle, became famous for her defense of the famous Confederate raider, whom she had never met but much admired. When a Yankee tormentor asked her her name she replied, "It's Mattie Ready now, but by the grace of God one day I hope to call myself the wife of John Morgan." Hearing the story, Morgan made it a point to look her up, found her to be "as pretty as she was patriotic," and married her after a whirlwind courtship. Bishop Gen. Polk performed the ceremony in the winter of 1862 with Bragg and his staff as guests (Horn, 195).

REAGAN, John Henninger. C.S.A. Postmaster Gen. 1818–1905. Tenn. Appt.-Tex. Going to Tex. in 1839, he fought against the Indians and studied law, serving in the militia and the legislature while still a student. As Democratic Congressman, he was elected to the provisional Confederate government and was named Postmaster Gen. 6 Mar. '61. He held this post throughout the war and acted as Sec. of the Treasury during the last months of the Confederacy. Captured with Davis, he was held in Fort Warren until Oct. '65. After the war he practiced law and sat in the Congress and Senate for many years after the Reconstruction period.

REAMS'S STATION, 25 Aug. '64. (PETERSBURG CAMPAIGN) The morning of 21 Aug., after his return from the action at DEEP BOTTOM RUN (13–20 Aug.), Hancock was ordered to move with his 1st and 2d Divisions (Miles and Gibbon), the cavalry division of D. McM. Gregg, and Spear's cavalry brigade (Kautz's) to destroy the Weldon R.R. south of Reams's Station. The purpose was to lengthen the distance by which the Confederates would have to haul their supplies by wagon into Petersburg. By the evening of the 24th the railroad had been destroyed to a point three miles south of Reams's Station. That night Hancock was informed that A. P. Hill with his corps and Hampton's cavalry was moving to attack him. The Confederates attacked the Federal pickets west of the station about noon, 25 Aug., and drove them back. After initial repulses at 2 P.M., the Confederates routed the green regiments of Gibbon's division (7th, 39th, and 52d N.Y.); a small reserve brigade under Lt. Col. Rugg was ordered to fill the gap but "could neither be made to go forward nor fire" (Hancock's report). The divisions of Mott (II) and Willcox (IX) had been ordered to Hancock's support, but did not arrive in time. Although Miles and the cavalry fought well, the poor showing of Gibbon's infantry indicated the extent to which Federal combat effectiveness had been reduced by the previous hard campaigning and the poorer quality of man power coming in as replacements. Federal losses were 2,742, of whom 2,073 were captured or missing (Fox). A. P. Hill reported his total loss at 720, and claimed the capture of 2,150 P.O.W., 9 cannon, 12 colors, and over 3,000 stand of arms.

REBEL YELL. First heard at 1st Bull Run, it was one of the most effective Confederate weapons. Described as a high-pitched shout and supposed by some to be a variation of the Southern fox hunters' cry, it invariably produced an eerie feeling within the enemy lines, although there is no record that the Yankees ever turned tail upon hearing it.

RECONNAISSANCE. Efforts undertaken by an armed force to gather information of the enemy's location, strength, activities, etc. It does not include espionage. Spelled "reconnoissance" during the Civil War.

RECONNAISSANCE IN FORCE. An attack by a sizable unit (as distinguished from a combat patrol) to locate and test the enemy's strength. Examples are FRANKLIN'S CROSSING and BRANDY STATION.

RECONSTRUCTION. Those measures taken to bring the Southern states back into the Union. Various proposals were the RECONSTRUCTION PLANS OF JOHNSON, LINCOLN, WADE AND DAVIS (see below), and those of the RADICAL REPUBLICANS. The moderate Republicans were overridden by the Radical element, leading to what has been called the "Tragic Era." The Reconstruction Act of 2 Mar. '67 divided all of the seceded states except Tenn. into five military districts: No. 1, Va.; No. 2, N. and S.C.; No. 3, Ala., Ga., and Fla.; No. 4 Ark. and Miss.; and No. 5, Tex. and La. Tenn. was under military executive control 1862–65. Reconstruction is generally considered to have ended by 1877, during the administration of Hayes.

RECONSTRUCTION PLAN OF JOHNSON. Based on Lincoln's policies, this involved an amnesty to all formerly in rebellion with the exception of certain prominent former Confederates in the army and government. After military governors were appointed for the Southern states, constitutional conventions were to be held, and after the ratification of the Thirteenth Amendment (see under ABOLITION OF SLAVERY) and the acceptance in Congress of the new legislators, the states were to be readmitted to the Union. This was vigorously opposed by the RADICAL REPUBLICANS, leading ultimately to the impeachment proceedings.

RECONSTRUCTION PLAN OF LINCOLN. Based on his theory that the Southern states had never seceded because they could not constitutionally do so, Lincoln's plan dealt with them as rebellious individuals and not as political bodies. In Dec. '63 he issued a proclamation stating that as soon as any seceded state had formed a government with 10 per cent of the voters in 1860, had accepted the Federal views on slavery, and had taken oaths of allegiance, it would be readmitted. La. and Ark. had by the end of the war fulfilled these requirements, but the RADICAL REPUBLICANS would not admit them. The Radicals opposed Lincoln's plan for its absence of vengeance upon the South and its lack of provision for civil rights for the Negroes. The RECONSTRUCTION PLAN OF WADE AND DAVIS was an outgrowth of this opposition.

RECONSTRUCTION PLAN OF WADE AND DAVIS. The Wade-Davis Bill and Manifesto of 1864 was a Reconstruction bill sponsored by Henry W. DAVIS and Benjamin WADE, both of the RADICAL REPUBLICANS. Their plan was in opposition to the more moderate RECONSTRUCTION PLAN OF LINCOLN. Its points were: provisional governors taking over the Southern states until the end of the war, civil government to be restored when half of the male white citizens took the oath of loyalty, no Confederate officeholders or volunteer soldiers to hold state office, slavery to be forever abolished, Confederate debts to be repudiated, state constitutions to be amended to bar ex-Confederates from any position of power. Passed on 2 July '64, it was "pocket vetoed" by Lincoln. Its backers then issued the Wade-Davis Manifesto denouncing the President and his policies.

RECTOR, Henry M. C.S.A. Gov. of Ark. 1816–? Mo. A lawyer and public officeholder, he was US Marshal and associate justice of the Arkansas Supreme Court (1859–60) when he ran for Gov. as a Union candidate in June '60. Stating that he believed in union so long as the states were not coerced, he urged his state toward secession in 1861 and was active in forwarding troops and organizing the state for war. He resigned 4 Nov. '62, when the Constitution shortened his term, expected to be four years, to two, and retired from public life.

RED RIVER CAMPAIGN OF 1863. Apr.–May '63. Banks relieved Butler as C.G., Dept. of the Gulf, in Nov. '62 and was instructed to assist in opening up the Mississippi. He occupied Baton Rouge with 10,000 men and garrisoned New Orleans with 20,000. Alarmed by this activity, the Confederate authorities in Jan. '63 sent Kirby Smith from Tenn. to command the districts of East La. and Tex. A force of 15,000 Confederates under Franklin Gardner, of Pemberton's department, held Port Hudson.

Unwilling to assault Port Hudson until he had cleared the west bank of the Mississippi, Banks ordered Grover's division (4, XIX) from Baton Rouge to Brashear (now Morgan City), La. Emory's division (3, XIX) and Weitzel's brigade (2, 1, XIX) started concentrating at the same place on 9 Apr., having come from the vicinity of New Orleans.

The Federals then advanced up the

Teche and Atchafalaya, missing their opportunity of destroying Taylor's force in the battles of IRISH BEND AND FORT BISLAND, 12–14 Apr. Covered by the brigade of Col. Thomas Green (who had succeeded Sibley), Taylor retreated through New Iberia and Vermillionville to Opelousas. Banks took Alexandria on 7 May with little opposition.

Grant, meanwhile, had crossed the Mississippi below Vicksburg. Although Grant had instructions to move south and cooperate with Banks in taking Port Hudson, Banks's absence made this impossible. Grant therefore moved against Vicksburg. On Halleck's suggestion, Banks moved toward the Mississippi. On 23 May he crossed the river and began operations against PORT HUDSON.

RED RIVER CAMPAIGN OF 1864. 10 Mar.–22 May '64. Because of the French threat (Maximilian) in Mexico, Lincoln wanted military operations undertaken early in 1864 to raise the Federal flag over some part of Tex. Although Grant, Sherman, and Banks were opposed, a line of operations up the Red River was finally prescribed. (Halleck favored it.) Banks, as senior department commander (Gulf), was directed in Jan. '64 to work out a joint operation with the other two department commanders, Sherman (Miss.) and Frederick Steele (Ark.).

As finally agreed, Banks was to move up Bayou Teche with 17,000 troops and link up at Alexandria on 17 Mar. with 10,000 Sherman would send up the Red River. Steele was to advance south from Little Rock with 15,000 and join Banks at Alexandria, Natchitoches, or Shreveport, as seemed best. (As it turned out, Steele was so late starting that he played no part in the operations.)

To oppose this concentric advance Kirby Smith had 30,000 troops in his Trans-Miss. Dept. that were divided into three equal groups: T. H. Holmes was near Camden, Ark.; Magruder was along the Tex. coast; and Richard Taylor was in La. Taylor's forces were disposed as follows: J. G. Walker's division of three brigades and with three attached cavalry companies was located around Marksville, with covering forces in the direction of Simsport and 200 men detached to reinforce the artillery garrison of Fort De Russy. Mouton's newly-created division of two brigades (Henry Gray and Polignac) was posted below Alexandria when Taylor learned of the Federal advance. Vincent's 2d La. Cav. was on the Teche around Vermillionville, except for the three companies with Walker.

The task force Sherman sent to Banks was composed of the division of J. A. Mower, W. F. Lynch, and T. Kilby Smith. A. J. Smith commanded this 10,000-man provisional organization, which is variously referred to in accounts as the "detachment from the Army of the Tennessee," "XVI and XVII Corps," etc. It will be called A. J. Smith's corps or command in the following narrative. (See also the entries on XVI and XVII CORPS for additional details on A. J. Smith's corps.)

On 10 Mar. A. J. Smith's command embarked at Vicksburg and was escorted into the Red River by Admiral Porter with "the most formidable force that had ever been collected in western waters": 13 ironclads and seven light-draught gunboats (B.&L., IV, 362). After leaving Vicksburg Smith learned that Banks had not departed on schedule, and also that the Red River was obstructed at Fort De Russy. The Federals landed at Simsport and captured the partially-completed Fort De Russy, 14 Mar., from the land side with little difficulty. About 250 prisoners were taken and Walker's three cavalry companies were cut off, temporarily depriving him of their reconnaissance. On 18 Mar. A. J. Smith entered Alexandria (population: 600) without opposition, as Taylor retreated up the Red River. Vincent's 2d La. Cav. joined Taylor on the 19th and was sent toward Alexandria. The next two days Vincent skirmished briskly with the Federal advance guard, and he was reinforced with Edgar's battery of light artillery. The night of 21 Mar., which was cold and rainy, A. J. Mower led the brigades of Hubbard and Hill (2 and 3, 1, XVI) with Lucas' cavalry brigade and the 9th Ind. Btry. in an envelopment that surprised and captured about 250 men and Edgar's four guns (O.R., I, XXXIV, I, 225 [sketch]—all the following O.R. references pertain to this volume). This action is known as Henderson's Hill (or Bayou Rapides), 21 Mar. '64.

At Natchitoches, Taylor halted to await the reinforcements Kirby Smith had ordered from Tex. (a cavalry division) and Ark. (two infantry divisions).

On 24 Mar. Banks arrived at Alexandria in person, and two days later the contingent from the Dept. of the Gulf reached that area. His column was composed of Ransom's XIII Corps (3d Div. of R. A. Cameron, and 4th Div. of W. J. Landram); W. B. Franklin's XIX Corps (1st and 2d divisions of W. W. Emory and Cuvier Grover); Albert Lee's cavalry division; and four infantry regiments of Negro troops (73d, 75th, 84th, and 92d U.S.C.T.). There were 13 batteries of artillery with the Gulf troops, and none with A. J. Smith's corps. All of the infantry divisions had only two brigades, with the exception of Lynch's and Emory's, which had three each.

Banks found his further passage endangered by low water that made it only barely possible for the fleet to pass the double rapids just above Alexandria.

He also learned that A. J. Smith's contingent would have to be returned no later than 15 Apr. to participate in the Atlanta campaign. Despite these restrictions and his slow start, Banks ordered an advance on Shreveport.

Leaving Grover's division at Alexandria, Banks reached Natchitoches 2–3 April. There was a minor cavalry skirmish at Crump's Hill (Piney Woods), 2 Apr. He left this place on the 6th with all but Kilby Smith's division. The latter was to be moved by water—20 transports escorted by Adm. Porter with a force of six naval vessels—and to rendezvous with the land column within three days at Springfield Landing, 110 miles by river below Shreveport.

Taylor continued his retreat to Pleasant Hill, where he was joined by Thomas Green's cavalry from Tex. The latter was put in command of a division formed of the brigades of Bee, Major, and Bagby, and given the rear-guard mission. Taylor then fell back to the vicinity of Mansfield, where he was within 20 miles of the two divisions of Churchill (Parsons and Tappan) that had been sent down from Ark.

At Wilson's Plantation (Farm) on 7 Apr. a spirited cavalry clash resulted in Albert Lee's being reinforced the next morning by Landram's infantry division.

Banks expected his advance guard to clear the way and ordered his other troops into bivouac. Cameron and Emory were camped near Pleasant Hill around noon (8 Apr.). The Confederate cavalry was driven to Sabine Cross Roads, a strategic communications hub within three miles of Mansfield. Here Taylor had organized a defensive position with the infantry divisions of Walker and Mouton, and Bee's cavalry. Although neither commander had all his forces available and neither intended to fight a major action here, a general engagement was brought on by Mouton's division late in the day. This was the battle of SABINE CROSS ROADS, 8 Apr. The Federals were routed with a loss of 2,500 prisoners and much matériel. Mouton was killed (succeeded by Polignac). Ransom was wounded and succeeded by Cameron; Franklin was wounded but retained command.

That night Banks withdrew his forward divisions to a line formed by Emory's division and two divisions of A. J. Smith's. Here was fought the battle of PLEASANT HILL, 9 Apr., in which Taylor's attack was repulsed with heavy loss. Walker (C.S.A.) was wounded.

Kirby Smith reached the battlefield and found Taylor's army so demoralized that he ordered a retreat to Mansfield (Fiebeger, 393). The following morning, however, he found that Banks had withdrawn. He decided, therefore, to leave Taylor with Polignac's division and the cavalry (total 5,200) to harass Banks's withdrawal, and to return to Shreveport with Walker and Churchill and operate against Fredcrick Steele. (See ARKANSAS CAMPAIGN IN 1864.)

Banks abandoned his attempt to capture Shreveport since he could expect no assistance from Steele, and since the return of A. J. Smith's corps was already overdue.

At Grand Ecore, near Natchitoches, Banks was rejoined on 15 Apr. by the Porter-Kilby Smith force. The latter had gotten 30 miles up the river before being stopped on the 10th by an obstruction. At Blair's Landing (also called Pleasant Hill Landing), on the 12th, the naval expedition was attacked by Thomas Green's cavalry (750 horses and two batteries, according to Taylor, p. 215). The Confederates broke off the engagement after inflicting seven casualties on the gunboats and 50 on the transports and suffering "scarcely a casualty except the death of General Green [killed], an irreparable one."

Banks left Grand Ecore the night of 21 Apr. and marched 32 miles to Cloutiersville without a halt. With Wm. Steele's brigade, Wharton drove the Federal rear guard from Natchitoches, took some prisoners, and continued the pursuit beyond Cloutiersville. Bee's cavalry was in a position at Monett's Bluff, about six miles due south of Cloutiersville, to block the Federal retreat while Wharton and Polignac attacked their rear. Bee was, however, driven off by a frontal attack by Emory and an envelopment by Birge from the west (Taylor, 220; O.R., I, XXXIV, I, 233). This latter action is known by the names of Monett's Bluff (or Ferry), Cane River Crossing, and Cloutiersville. (Taylor's spelling is Monette.)

Low water continued to impede Porter's struggles to get his fleet down the river. The *Eastport,* largest of the ironclads, struck a mine ("torpedo") eight miles below Grand Ecore and settled on the bottom. She was raised and gotten another 40 miles downstream before grounding again. After being once more floated free, again she was stopped by obstructions in the river. Adm. Porter had boarded the light draught *Cricket* and gone to Alexandria to bring back two pump boats to aid in saving the *Eastport.* However, when he returned with these, the *Champion 3* and *5,* the leak could not be found. When the ironclad grounded again she had to be destroyed (26 Apr.). Meanwhile, a blocking position had been established farther downstream at the junction of the Cane and Red rivers. Here Col. J. H. Caudle of Polignac's division with Capt. Florian Cornay's four-gun battery attacked this last element of Porter's fleet as it made its way toward Alexandria. "Nineteen shells went crashing through the

Cricket and during the five minutes she
was under fire she was struck thirty-
eight times and lost twelve killed and
nineteen wounded out of a crew of
fifty," says the account in *Battles and
Leaders* (IV, 364). "The *Juliet* was
nearly as badly hurt, with 15 casualties,
but got under a bank and managed to
turn back upstream" (Pratt, *Civil War
on Western Waters*, 196). The *Champion 3* exploded after being hit in the
boiler and an estimated 200 of its
Negro crewmen (runaway slaves)
were scalded to death. The *Fort
Hindman* remained upstream. The
Cricket, aground and on fire, got
free and escaped about dark. The next
day the *Hindman* ran the batteries successfully, but the *Champion 5* was sunk
in the attempt. Taylor, in his memoirs,
quotes Porter's report that he had been
engaged by "a large number of cannon,
eighteen in all, every shot of which
struck this vessel [*Cricket*]." Taylor
observes "This is high testimony to the
fighting capacity of two hundred riflemen and four guns. . . ." (*op. cit.,* 223).

Banks had reached Alexandria on 25
Apr., where he found that the water
had gone down so that the fleet could
not pass the double rapids. "At this
point appeared the *deus ex machina*
in the person of Colonel Joseph Bailey . . ." (Pratt, *op. cit.,* 197). In one of
the most imaginative engineering feats
of military history, BAILEY, using a lumberman's technique, raised the water
level by a series of wing dams, and the
fleet completed its passage of the obstacle on 13 May. (For details, see
B.&L., IV, 358–60, 365; and O. R. Atlas
LIII, 2.)

While this engineering project was
going on, Taylor split his small force
(5,200) to block the Red River below
Alexandria while also maintaining pressure on Banks, who had to remain in
the latter town to protect the fleet.

Major's brigade of about 1,000 cavalry
was sent to Davide's Ferry (Snaggy
Point), about 13 air line miles below
Alexandria (25 miles by the river road)
and three miles above Fort De Russy.
Wm. Steele's cavalry (1,000) covered
the river and Rapides roads to the
north and west of Alexandria; Bagby's
cavalry (1,000) covered the Boeuf road
to the south; Polignac's 1,200 infantry
were on the Boeuf road within supporting distance of Major and Bagby. Taylor says that Liddell's 700 newly-organized troopers and four guns were of
little value. In a series of actions known
collectively as ALEXANDRIA, La., 1–8
May, the Confederates harassed Banks's
force, destroyed five Federal boats by
"cavalry action," and effectively blocked
the Red River during the period 4–13
May.

On 13 May Porter and Banks resumed their retreat from Alexandria.
There were skirmishes at Wilson's Landing and Avoyelles (or Marksville) Prairie
on the 14th and 15th. At Mansura, 16
May, the Federals had to fight their way
through a Confederate position. Meanwhile, Liddell's cavalry was harrying
Porter from the north bank of the river.
At Yellow Bayou (Bayou de Glaize),
18 May, there was a loss of 267 Federals and 452 Confederates (B.&L., IV,
360) in the final action of the campaign,
and in the last battle that took place
in the Trans-Miss. region (Taylor, 233).
(This action is known also as Old Oaks
or Norwood Plantation.)

While this final rear-guard action was
taking place, Joseph Bailey's engineering skills were once more called on to
solve the problem of bridging the 600-
yard-wide Atchafalaya River at Simsport without pontons or the usual engineer field equipment. Using steamers,
he improvised a bridge over which
Banks's wagon trains passed the afternoon of the 19th and the troops the

next day (O.R., Banks's report). On 21-22 May A. J. Smith's corps embarked for Vicksburg, and on the 26th the rest of Banks's command reached Donaldsonville, La.

"On both sides this unhappy campaign of the Red River raised a great and bitter crop of quarrels. Taylor was relieved by Kirby Smith, as the result of an angry correspondence; Banks was overslaughed, and Franklin quit the department in disgust; A. J. Smith departed more in anger than in sorrow; while between the admiral and the general commanding recriminations were exchanged in language well up to the limits of 'parliamentary' privilege," wrote a Federal officer in *Battles and Leaders* (IV, 361). One of the secondary purposes of the expedition was to open rich sugar and cotton country, and there was considerable suspicion of "a great cotton speculation." On 14 Mar. Kirby Smith ordered the burning of an estimated 150,000 bales of cotton, then valued at $60,000,000. Banks was relieved of command in May; his campaign became a subject of a congressional investigation and official censure.

RED RIVER DIVISION, XVII Corps. A force of six regiments and one artillery battery from the XVII Corps, Army of the Tenn., that served under the command of T. Kilby Smith in Banks's Red River campaign of 1864. Parts of this division served also on McArthur's Yazoo City expedition (4–13 May '64) and on Slocum's expedition to Jackson, Miss., 3-9 July '64; a few regiments were engaged also under Sturgis at Brice's Cross Roads and in A. J. Smith's expedition to Tupelo. It joined the force that had been known as (A. J. Smith's) "DETACHMENT, ARMY OF THE TENNESSEE" to participate in the Battle of Nashville (15 Dec. '64).

REED projectile. A Confederate type in which a copper base cup was placed in a mold and the body of the projectile cast on it (Benton, 561). Dr. Reed of Ala. developed in 1856 or 1857 the first projectile used in the PARROTT GUN; both had the same general characteristics, but his Confederate projectile had a ring around the forward portion.

REESE, Chauncey B. Union officer. 1837-70. N.Y. USMA 1859 (4/22); Engrs. He was promoted 1st Lt. 6 Aug. '61, after serving at Fort Pickens, and organized the engineering matériel for the Army of the Potomac. After building a bridge at Harpers Ferry in Feb.–Mar. '62, he served in the Peninsular campaign commanding his company. After sick leave he served in the Engr. Bureau until Mar. '63, when he took command of a battalion, as Capt. (3 Mar. '63), at Chancellorsville and Gettysburg. He was then named Asst. Engr. in the Dept. of the South and Chief Engr. of the Army of the Tenn. 29 Apr. '64–3 June '65. Continuing in the R.A., he was breveted for the March through Georgia (four including B.G. USA) and died of yellow fever while on active duty as Maj.

REEVE, Isaac Van Duzer. Union officer. c. 1813–90. N.Y. USMA 1835 (45/56); Inf. He fought in the Seminole War and the Mexican War (2 brevets) and served in the West in Indian fighting. Named Maj. 1st US Inf. 14 May '61, he was captured when Twiggs surrendered Tex., and exchanged 20 Aug. '62. He was promoted Lt. Col. 13th US Inf. 16 Sept. '62. At first mustering and disbursing officer in N.Y.C., he later commanded the Pittsburgh draft rendezvous. He retired in 1871 as Col. and Bvt. B.G. USA.

REGIMENT. See ORGANIZATION for composition of Civil War regiments. Elsewhere, in alphabetical order, will be found outline histories of the outstanding Federal regiments. It has not been possible to give a similar coverage to famous Confederate regiments, since Southern literature has nothing comparable to Fox's *Regimental Losses* or Dyer's *Compendium*. Information on Southern regiments must be dug out of state histories or unit histories; *Confederate Military History* has historical sketches of regiments.

REGULAR ARMY ENLISTED MEN, LOYALTY TO THE UNION. See LOYALTY OF REGULAR ARMY ENLISTED MEN.

REGULAR ARMY OFFICERS, LOYALTY TO THE UNION. See LOYALTY OF REGULAR ARMY OFFICERS.

REGULAR ARMY OFFICERS, PROMOTION OF. See PROMOTION OF REGULAR ARMY OFFICERS.

REID, Hugh Thompson. Union gen. 1811–74. Ind. A lawyer, public official, and railroad president, he was named Col. 15th Iowa 22 Feb. '62 and led his regiment at Shiloh. During the battle he was shot through the neck and knocked off his horse but, remounting, continued to ride up and down the lines encouraging his men. He was promoted B.G. USV 13 Mar. '63 and commanded 1, 6, XVII, Tenn. (22 Apr.–1 Aug. '63) and Dist. Cairo, XVI, Tenn. (25 Jan.–19 Mar. '64) before resigning 4 Apr. '64.

REID, Whitelaw. Journalist. 1837–1912. Ohio. After graduating from Miami (Ohio) Univ., he became a newspaper editor and was active in Republican politics. When the Civil War came, he was the Cincinnati *Gazette* correspondent in Washington. His dispatches, signed "Agate," were written at the capital and in the field. He was Rosecrans's volunteer A.D.C. in W. Va. in 1861 and was also present at Shiloh and Gettysburg. In 1863 he was elected

librarian of the House of Representatives and served there until 1866, when he became a cotton planter in La. His *Ohio in the War* (1868) is one of the most thorough state histories to come out of the Civil War. When that was published, he joined Horace Greeley on the N.Y. *Tribune* as an editorial writer and succeeded Greeley in 1872 as editor and principal owner.

REILLY, James William. Union gen. 1828–96. Ohio. A legislator, he was commissioned Col. 104th Ohio 30 Aug. '62 and commanded 2, 1, XXIII 24–30 June '63. He led 1, 3, XXIII (21 Oct.–14 Dec. '63) at Knoxville; and later (6–16 Jan. '64, 3 Apr.–26 May '64, 27 May–22 Sept. '64) and during the Atlanta campaign and at Franklin and Nashville (22 Oct.–Dec. '64). At Franklin his command captured 1,000 prisoners and 22 stand of colors. He also commanded 3d Div., XXIII 12 Mar.–3 Apr. '64, 26–27 May '64 and 16 Sept.–21 Oct. '64. Named B.G. USV 30 July '64, he resigned 20 Apr. '65.

REMICK, David. Union officer. Vt. Appt.-Iowa. Capt. Comsy. of Subsist. Vols. 5 Aug. '61; resigned 31 Mar. '62; Capt. Comsy. of Subsist. Vols. 10 Sept. '62; Lt. Col. Comsy. of Subsist. Assigned 1 Nov. '63–14 July '65; Bvt. B.G. USV (war service). Served as Chief Comsy. of Subsist. for the IV Corps and Army of the Tenn.

REMINGTON. During the Civil War the Remington Arms Co. (founded 1816) furnished the US government 10,000 Model 1855 saber bayonet rifles, 39,000 Model 1863 rifle muskets, 125,-314 Remington percussion revolvers, and 2,814 Beals revolvers (Gluckman, 95).

REMINGTON CARBINE. A .50-cal. single-shot cartridge carbine that used the SPENCER cartridge. It was developed in late 1863 and used in the latter part of the war. The government bought a large number after the Civil War (Gluckman, 419).

REMINGTON NEW MODEL REVOLVER. A .44-cal., six-shot, single-action percussion revolver weighing two pounds 14 ounces. Second in popularity only to the COLT, 125,314 were purchased by the US government during the war (Gluckman).

RENO, Jesse Lee. Union gen. 1823–62. Va. Appt.-Pa. USMA 1846 (8/59); Ordnance. After the Mexican War (2 brevets) he taught mathematics at West Point, ran surveys in the West, and served as Chief Ord. officer on the Utah Expedition. As 1st Lt. (since 1853) and later Capt. (since 1860), he commanded the Mt. Vernon Arsenal in Ala. until it was seized by Confederates 4 Jan. '61. He was at the Leavenworth Arsenal until named B.G. USV 12 Nov. '61. In Burnside's N.C. expedition he commanded the 2d Brig. (Dec. '61–Apr. '62) and then led 2d Div., N.C. (2 Apr.–6 July '62). Appointed Maj. Gen. USV 18 July '62, he commanded the 2d Div., IX, Potomac (22 July–3 Sept. '62) at 2d Bull Run and led the IX Corps (3–14 Sept. '62) until he was killed at South Mountain. He is associated with the myth of Barbara FRITCHIE. Reno (Nev.) was named for him.

RENO, Marcus Albert. Union officer. 1835–89. Ill. USMA 1857 (20/38); Dragoons-Cav. 1st Lt. 1st US Dragoons 25 Apr. '61; 1st Cav. 3 Aug. '61; Capt. 12 Nov. '61; Col. 12th Pa. Cav. 1 Jan.–20 July '65; mustered out of USV and continued in R.A. until dismissal in 1880 while holding rank of Maj. W.I.A. Kelly's Ford (Va.) 17 Mar. '63. Assistant instructor of tactics at USMA in the fall of 1865 and head of New Orleans Freedman's Bureau, 1865–66. He served in the West, and in 1876 was the subject of a court of inquiry about Custer's Sioux campaign. His dismissal was for "other causes" (Cullum).

REPUBLICAN PARTY. Born out of opposition to the KANSAS–NEBRASKA ACT OF 1854, it drew strength from the anti-slavery and FREE-SOIL elements that were dissatisfied with the old Whig party and had broken away from the Democrats. After showing a remarkable popularity in the elections of 1856 and 1858, the party put Abraham Lincoln in the White House in 1860, and touched off secession. Hostility to the South was one of the party's cornerstones, and as sectional tensions increased, the moderates gave way within the party to the radicals. Lincoln was re-elected over McClellan in 1864 when the party was called the NATIONAL UNION PARTY. But the Republicans began to divide over the President's conservative approach to rehabilitating the South and the approach of RADICAL REPUBLICANS who dominated Congress. Johnson was impeached by the latter element, which continued to control the country's politics. Grant's election in 1868 added to their power, but the corruption and vice in his administration brought about a liberal faction that undermined the Radicals. By the time of the disputed Hayes-Tilden election of 1876 the Republicans were no longer in control of the country, and the Solid (Democratic) South emerged. See also BLACK REPUBLICANS.

RESACA, Ga., 13–16 May '64. (Sugar Valley; Oostenaula), (ATLANTA CAMPAIGN). After the action at ROCKY FACE RIDGE, 5–11 May, Johnston withdrew from Dalton the night of 12 May. With McPherson's army at Snake Creek Gap the Confederate position had been turned. Johnston established a new defense to the north and west of Resaca. The left flank of Polk's newly-joined corps was due west of that town; Hardee occupied the center of the line, and Hood held the right.

Early 13 May Howard (IV Corps) had discovered Johnston's withdrawal and had started in pursuit along the railroad. At 8 A.M. Hooker's XX Corps, preceded by Kilpatrick's cavalry, moved out to support McPherson's advance on Resaca from the west. At Smith's Cross Roads (two miles west of Resaca) Kilpatrick clashed with Wheeler's cavalry and was wounded. Loring's division opposed the Federal advance from this direction. About two miles northeast Palmer's XIV Corps advanced from Snake Creek Gap, and skirmishers developed a strong enemy line along Camp Creek that was covered by a ridge just west of Resaca. Butterfield's division (3, XX) moved forward to support Palmer's right, while Schofield advanced two divisions on his left.

On 14 May there was heavy fighting all along the line as Sherman tried to break through Johnston's strong position. On the north the division of J. D. Cox (3, XXIII) advanced on the Federal left and took some positions. Judah's division (2, XXIII), to his right, was driven back by heavy enfilade fire from the west, after having advanced some distance across difficult terrain. Palmer advanced down a forward slope under enemy fire, crossed Camp Creek, but his attack became disorganized in the heavy underbrush and was driven back with considerable loss. Hood then counterattacked on the north at about 6 P.M. with the divisions of Stewart and Stevenson against J. D. Cox. Although this attack was stopped by reinforcements, Johnston was sufficiently encouraged by its success to order its continuation the next day. This same day McPherson attacked across Camp Creek due west of Resaca and had secured a lodgment near the railroad.

Meanwhile, Sherman had started other forces to turn the Confederate position from the west and south. He ordered a ponton bridge constructed at Lay's Ferry and sent Sweeney's division (2, XVI) of McPherson's army to threaten Johnston's line of communications at Calhoun on the railroad. He also ordered Garrard's cavalry division to move to Rome and then east toward the railroad on an even wider envelopment. Johnston learned late 14 May of the enemy movement across the river at Lay's Ferry, but at noon the next day he received a report that this information was not correct. Nevertheless, after a day of heavy skirmishing on 15 May, and after receiving confirmation that the enemy was in effect moving against his rear, Johnston withdrew from Resaca. The next major engagement was at DALLAS.

RESERVE. For definition and purpose of the reserve, see ATTACKS. See also GENERAL RESERVE.

RESERVE CORPS, Confederate Army of Miss. See CORPS, Confederate, BRECKINRIDGE'S.

REVERE, Joseph Warren. Union gen. 1812–80. Mass. A grandson of Paul Revere, he was a Midshipman from 1828–50. Ranching in Calif., he traded along the Mexican coast and organized the Mexican artillery in 1851. The next year he was wounded at Morelia during an insurrection. First volunteering for the navy and not immediately accepted, he was then named Col. 7th N.Y. 19 Sept. '61 and fought on Peninsula and at Antietam. Promoted B.G. USV 25 Oct. '62, he commanded 2, 2, III at Fredericksburg and 3, 2, III at Chancellorsville, where on 3 May, after fighting from daybreak until 8 A.M., he found himself to be the senior officer in the division and his men to be low on ammunition and rations. Thus, without orders, he moved them three miles to the rear where they rested and ate until ordered back into action at three that afternoon. Joseph B. Carr censured and relieved him, and he was then court-martialled and dismissed. This severe sentence was revoked in view of his previous (excellent) record by Lincoln 10 Sept. '64 and his resignation accepted to date from 10 Aug. '63. After the war he wrote a number of autobiographical articles and books on soldiering and, in poor health, traveled a great deal. Brother of Paul REVERE.

REVERE, Paul Joseph. Union officer. 1832–63. Mass. Maj. 20th Mass. 19 July '61; Lt. Col. Asst. I.G. Assigned 20 Aug. '62–5 Feb. '63; Col. 20th Mass. 14 Apr. '63; Bvt. B.G. USV 2 July '63 (Gettysburg). The grandson of Paul Revere. W.I.A. and captured at Balls Bluff. Kept in Libby and Henrico City prisons until chosen as one of seven hostage officers for safety of C.S.A. privateers convicted of piracy in US courts (see ENCHANTRESS AFFAIR). Served as Asst. I.G. 4 Sept. '62 for Gen. Edwin V. Sumner, Sr. W.I.A. Antietam. W.I.A. 2 July '63 at Gettysburg, and died two days later. Brother of Joseph REVERE.

REVERE, William H., Jr. Union officer. Mass. Appt.-Md. 1st Lt. 11th N.Y. 7 May '61; resigned 1 June '61; Col. 10th Md. 30 July '63; mustered out 29 Jan. '64; Col. 107th US Col. Inf. 11 July '64; Bvt. B.G. USV 17 Aug. '65 (war service). Commanded 1, 3, X. Died 20 Sept. '65.

REVETMENT. A retaining wall or other form of bracing to hold in place the sides of trenches, gun emplacements, and other forms of field fortifications. Wire mesh, wooden strips held by metal or wooden posts or pickets, heavy cloth, and many other means or expedients are used—depending on permanence desired. Wattling (woven brushwork), GABIONS, and FASCINES were generally

used as late as World War I. Sandbags, used in the Civil War, are now the most common means.

REYNOLDS, Alexander Welch. C.S.A. gen. 1817–76. Va. USMA 1838 (35/45); Inf.-Q.M. Serving in the Seminole War, on the frontier, and as Asst. Q.M. in Fla., he escorted wagon trains through Mexico and the Indian Territory and was dismissed in 1855 for alleged discrepancies in accounts. Reinstated in 1857, he was dropped 4 Oct. '61 for being absent without leave, having joined the Confederacy when the rebels took over Tex. As Col. 50th Va. in July '61, he served in W. Va. that winter and was sent to support Kirby Smith in Knoxville. Given a brigade under Stevenson, he was captured at Vicksburg and appointed B.G. C.S.A. 14 Sept. '63 upon his exchange. He commanded his brigade under Hardee at Chattanooga and under Hood in the Atlanta campaign. In 1869 he, his wife, and their son Frank (also a Confederate officer) went to Egypt, where he joined the Khedive's army as Col. He served in various staff assignments and was Loring's Chief of Staff in 1875 but did not accompany him to Abyssinia. He died in Alexandria, mourning his son, who had also been a Col. in the Egyptian Army.

REYNOLDS, Belle. Mass. Army wife. When her husband, a Lt. in the 17th Ill., went to war in 1861, she went with him and served as nurse and morale builder throughout the winter of 1861–62 in the West. During the Vicksburg campaign the Lt. was McClernand's A.D.C., and Belle stayed with the general's wife and Mrs. Grant in Miss. until the spring of 1864. Lt. Reynolds' enlistment then being up, they returned to Peoria, Ill.

REYNOLDS, Daniel H. C.S.A. gen. 1826–1902. Ohio. After graduating from

Ohio Wesleyan and practicing law, he was commissioned Capt. 1st Ark. Mtd. Rifles 14 June '61. He fought at Wilson's Creek and skirmished in Ark. and Mo. before being promoted Maj. 14 Apr. '62. Named Lt. Col. 1 May of that year, he fought under Kirby Smith in the Ky. campaign and later served there under Bragg. At Chickamauga he was named Col. and promoted B.G. C.S.A. 5 Mar. '64. He commanded his brigade in the Atlanta campaign and under Hood in Tenn. After the war he was a state legislator.

REYNOLDS, John Fulton. Union gen. 1820–63. Pa. USMA 1841 (26/52); Arty. After serving in Fla., on the frontier, in the Mexican War (2 brevets), on exploration, and Indian fighting in the West and on the Utah Expedition, he was commandant of cadets at West Point when the war began. Named Lt. Col. 14th US Inf. 14 May and B.G. USV 20 Aug. '61, he commanded 1st Brig., McCall's division, Potomac (3 Oct. '61–13 Mar. '62) in the Defenses of Washington and 1, 2, I (13 Mar.–4 Apr. '62). He was military Gov. of Fredericksburg (4 Apr.–12 June '62) in command of 1st Brig., McCall's division, Rappahannock, and then led 1, 3, V, Potomac (18–23 June '62) at Mechanicsville, Gaines's Mill, and Glendale, where he was captured. At 2d Bull Run he commanded 3d Div., III, Army of Va. (26 Aug.–12 Sept. '62). As Maj. Gen. USV 29 Nov. '62, he led the I Corps, Potomac (29 Sept. '62–2 Jan. '63) at Fredericksburg; and (4 Jan.–1 Mar. and 9 Mar.–1 July '63) in reserve at Chancellorsville and at Gettysburg, where he was killed by a sharpshooter. A superb horseman, with dark hair and eyes and standing an erect six feet tall, he was characterized as courageous and self-reliant. There is a statue of him at Gettysburg where he fell. He was considered when the administration was looking for a general to succeed Hooker, and probably was better qualified for the post than was Meade. The latter, however, had the desirable political quality of having been born abroad and not being a presidential possibility. Brother of William Reynolds.

REYNOLDS, Joseph Jones. Union gen. 1822–99. Ky. USMA 1843 (10/39); Arty. After serving on the frontier and in garrison and teaching at West Point, he resigned in 1857 to teach mechanics and engineering at Washington Univ., St. Louis. He was in the grocery business with his brother in Ind. when commissioned Col. 10th Ind. 25 Apr. and B.G. USV 17 May '61. Commanding the CHEAT MOUNTAIN Dist. of W. Va. under Rosecrans, he repulsed the Confederates there to secure that part of the state for the Union. Resigning 23 Jan. '62 to look after his business after his brother's death, he was active in recruiting and training Ind. regiments until reappointed B.G. USV 17 Sept. and promoted Maj. Gen. USV 29 Nov. '62. He then commanded 5th Div. Centre, XIV, in the Army of the Cumberland (11 Dec. '62–9 Jan. '63); 5th Div., XIV (9 Jan.–8 June '63) and 4th Div., XIV (8 June–9 Oct. '63) at Hoover's Gap and Chickamauga. At Chattanooga he was serving as Chief of Staff of the Army of the Cumberland. Going to the Dept. of the Gulf, he led 4th Div., XIX (25 Jan.–15 Feb. '64); XIX Corps (7 July–7 Nov. '64); Dist. Morganza (16 June–5 July '64) and Reserve Corps (5 Dec. '64–12 Jan. '65). From 22 Dec. '64 until 1 Aug. '65 he commanded the VII Corps and the Dept. of Ark. Breveted for Chickamauga (B.G. USA) and Missionary Ridge (Maj. Gen. USA), he continued in the R.A. In the winter of 1875–76 he captured Crazy Horse's winter hideout, taking the village and pony herd. However, he then withdrew without destroying the dismounted warriors who were fighting fiercely from the woods, and this contributed the following spring to Custer's massacre at Little Big Horn. Reynolds resigned in 1877 after a court-martial, and no explanation has yet been found for his withdrawal.

REYNOLDS, Joseph Smith. Union officer. 1839–? Ill. 2d Lt. 64th Ill. 31 Dec. '61; 1st Lt. 13 Nov. '62; Capt. 24 Nov. '63; Maj. 9 Apr. '65; Lt. Col. 21 May '65; Bvt. B.G. USV 11 July '65 (war service). Serving in 17 battles, he was W.I.A. three times. After the war he was a lawyer and held many public offices.

REYNOLDS, William. Union naval officer. 1815–79. Pa. Entering the navy as midshipman in 1831, he was placed on the retired list 20 years later because of failing health and then assigned to Hawaii, where he was instrumental in securing the treaty of reciprocity. He returned to active service in 1861 and was made commander in 1862 of the naval forces at Port Royal. Promoted Capt. in 1866 (Lt. since 1841), he was retired in 1877 as Rear Admiral. Brother of J. F. Reynolds.

REYNOLDS, William F. Misspelling by Phisterer for William Franklin RAYNOLDS.

REYNOLDSBURG ISLAND, Tenn. Confederate cavalry devise trap for Federal shipping in Nov. '64. See FOR-REST'S OPERATIONS DURING ATLANTA CAMPAIGN.

REYNOLDS' PLANTATION, Ga. See WAYNESBORO, 26–29 Nov. '64.

RHETT, Robert Barnwell. Confederate politician. 1800–76. S.C. A lawyer, he sat in the legislature and Congress before becoming a Sen. in 1851. He was an ardent advocate of secession, a "FIRE-EATER," and served in the Confederate Congress. His biog-

rapher, Laura A. White, calls him "Father of Secession."

RICE, Americus Vespucius. Union gen. 1835–? Ohio. While studying law after graduating from college in 1860, he was commissioned Capt. 21st Ohio 27 Apr. '61. Mustered out 12 Aug. and commissioned Capt. 57th Ohio 2 Sept. '61, he was named Lt. Col. 8 Feb. '62. He fought at Chickasaw Bayou and Arkansas Post before being named Col. 24 May '63 during the siege of Vicksburg. He later fought at Missionary Ridge and lost his leg at Kenesaw Mountain, having been wounded several times in previous battles. Promoted B.G. USV 31 May '65, he commanded 3, 2, XV, Tenn. 23 June–1 Aug. '65 and mustered out in 1866. Later a US Congressman, he was active in banking and Democratic politics.

RICE, Elliott Warren. Union gen. 1835–87. Pa. A lawyer, he enlisted in the 7th Iowa 24 July '61 and was commissioned Maj. 30 Aug. He fought at Belmont (Mo.) 7 Nov. '61, and was promoted Col. 7 Apr. '62 at Shiloh. He also was at Corinth. He commanded 1, 2, XVI (20 July–17 Aug. '63; 7 Sept.–15 Dec. '63; 4 Mar.–23 Sept. '64) during the Atlanta campaign, succeeding to division 25–26 July '64. On the March to the Sea and through the Carolinas he led 1, 4, XV (14 Oct. '64–1 Aug. '65). He was promoted B.G. USV 20 June '64 and breveted Maj. Gen. USV for war service before being mustered out 24 Aug. '65. Brother of Samuel A. Rice.

RICE, James Clay. Union gen. 1829–64. Mass. After Yale he taught in Natchez and practiced law in N.Y.C. Commissioned 1st Lt. 39th N.Y. 10 May '61, he was promoted Capt. in Aug. and named Lt. Col. 44th N.Y. 13 Sept. '61 and Col. 4 July '62. He fought at Yorktown, Hanover C.H., Gaines's Mill, Malvern Hill, 2d Bull Run, Fredericksburg, and Chancellorsville. Commanding 3, 1, V (2 July–26 Aug. '63) at Gettysburg, he secured Little Round Top against a flanking movement and was promoted B.G. USV 17 Aug. '63 for this action. He also commanded 2, 1, I (23–24 Sept. '63), succeeding to division 14 Jan.–10 Feb. '64. Commanding 2, 4, V (25 Mar.–10 May '64), he fought at the Wilderness and was killed on the latter date at Laurel Hill, near Spotsylvania C.H.

RICE, Samuel Allen. Union gen. 1828–64. N.Y. A lawyer and politician, he was named Col. 33d Iowa 1 Oct. '62 and promoted B.G. USV 4 Aug. '63. He commanded 2, 13, XIII, Tenn. (10 June–28 July '63) at Helena (Ark.); 2, 13, XVI, Tenn. (28 July–10 Aug. '63); 3d Div. Ark. Exp., Tenn. (13 Sept.–8 Oct. '63); 2, 3d Div., Ark. Exp., Tenn. (8 Oct.–12 Nov. '63); 2, 3, VII, Ark. (1 Feb.–12 Mar. '64) and 1, 3, VII, Ark. (12 Mar.–30 Apr. '64). On this last date he was mortally wounded at Jenkins' Ferry (Ark.) and, taken to his home in Oskaloosa (Iowa), died 6 July '64. Brother of Elliott W. Rice.

RICE STATION, Va. Point reached by Longstreet's command 6 Apr. '65 while the rest of Lee's forces were engaged at SAYLER'S CREEK. Although XXIV and XX Corps made contact at this place and Fox lists it as a battle credit for each of these units, there was no significant fighting. Longstreet withdrew to FARMVILLE.

RICHARDSON, Albert Deane. WAR CORRESPONDENT. 1833–69. Mass. After working for a newspaper in Philadelphia, he went to Kans. in 1857 and reported the border struggle for the Boston *Journal*. He later went to Pikes Peak with Greeley, the start of a long and warm friendship, and volunteered during secession winter to go south as a secret correspondent for the *Tribune*. After many escapes, he returned just before the bombardment of Sumter and then returned to the field as a war correspondent in Va. and the West. He was captured with two other newspapermen on 3 May '63 while trying to run the batteries of Vicksburg on two barges lashed to a steam tug. After spending 18 months in Southern prisons, they escaped, walking 400 miles from Salisbury, N.C., to Strawberry Plains, Tenn. He later wrote a book about these experiences as well as *A Personal History of U.S. Grant*. A young widower, his wife having died while he was in prison, he fell in love with the wife of a Tammany politician and announced his intention of marrying her as soon as her divorce became final. He was shot in the *Tribune* office by the former husband and was married to his fiancée on his deathbed by Henry Ward Beecher.

RICHARDSON, Hollon. Union officer. Ohio. 1st Lt. 7th Wis. 16 Aug. '61; Capt. 17 Feb. '62; Maj. 14 Jan. '64; Lt. Col. 17 Dec. '64; Bvt. B.G. USV. Brevets for bravery throughout campaigns from Rapidan to Five Forks (2). Love in *Wisconsin in the War of the Rebellion* quotes the Cincinnati *Gazette:* "Captain Richardson . . . seized the colors of a retreating Pennsylvania regiment and strove to rally the men around their flag. It was in vain; none but troops that have been tried as by fire can be reformed under such a storm of death. But the captain, left alone and almost in rebel hands, held on to the flaunting colors of another regiment, that made him a conspicuous target, and brought them safely off." Love also credits Richardson with going through "withering fire" to report a dangerous position on the right of the Iron Brigade to Brig. headquarters at Petersburg 17 June '64. This same source relates that Richardson led a charge of his regiment with their flag in his own hands at Five Forks 1 Apr. '65.

RICHARDSON, Israel Bush. Union gen. 1815–62. Vt. USMA 1841 (38/52); Inf. After fighting in the Seminole War and serving on the frontier, he was in the Mexican War (2 brevets), where he won the nickname "Fighting Dick" for his bravery at Cerro Gordo. After several years of Indian scouting and fighting he resigned in 1855 to farm in Mich. Commissioned B.G. USV 17 May and Col. 2d Mich. 25 May '61, he commanded 4, 1st Div. (June–Aug. '61) at 1st Bull Run. He then led Richardson's Brigade, Div. Potomac (Aug.–Oct. '61) and 1st Brig., Heintzelman's division, Potomac (3 Oct. '61–13 Mar. '62.) During the Peninsular campaign he commanded 1st Div., II (13 Mar.–17 July '62) at Yorktown, Williamsburg, Fair Oaks, and the Seven Days' Battles and (15 Aug.–17 Sept. '62) at South Mountain and Antietam. Wounded on the latter date, he died at Antietam 3 Nov. '62 after being promoted Maj. Gen. USV 4 July.

RICHARDSON, Robert V. C.S.A. gen. Appt.-Tenn. Wright says that he was appointed 3 Dec. '63 to rank from 1 Dec. but that his nomination was returned by the Senate to the President on 9 Feb. '64. He is not included in Wood or C.M.H.

RICHARDSON, William Alexander. Union politician. 1811–75. Ill. Chosen to fill Douglas' unexpired term in 1863, he was a lawyer and Democratic state legislator and US Congressman. He had fought in the Mexican War and was offered the commission of B.G. USV 3 Sept. '61, which he declined.

RICHARDSON, William Pitt. Union officer. 1824–86. Pa. Maj. 25th Ohio 10 June '61; Lt. Col. 26 July '61; Col. 16 May '62; Bvt. B.G. USV 7 Dec. '64. W.I.A. Chancellorsville 2 May '63 in right shoulder. President of a courtmartial at Camp Chase Jan. '64; commander of the camp 11 Feb. '64–Aug. '65. Served as enlisted man in Mexican War. A lawyer and B.G. in the Ohio Mil.

RICHMOND, Ky., 29–30 Aug. '62 (Kirby SMITH'S INVASION OF KENTUCKY).

The 1st and 2d brigades, Army of KENTUCKY, under Gens. M. D. Manson and Charles D. Cruft, respectively, were sent from Louisville to hold Richmond against an expected Confederate invasion. Most of these troops were recruits hastily raised by Gen. William ("Bull") Nelson. Federal cavalry reported enemy contact on the 29th and by early afternoon were pushed back toward Richmond by a Confederate force they estimated at 5,000. Leaving Cruft to protect Richmond, Manson advanced and made contact with the enemy about a mile and a half south of his bivouac at Rogersville. The Confederate advance guard was driven back and Manson repulsed an enemy attempt to drive him from his position. Manson then sent cavalry in pursuit and withdrew to Rogersville, about two miles south of Richmond.

During the night Gen. Patrick R. Cleburne's division was reinforced by Gen. T. J. Churchill's division and Gen. Kirby Smith (who had been with Cleburne) decided to attack Richmond. At 6 A.M. (30 Aug.) Manson learned of the new advance and ordered Cruft's brigade forward to support him on a defensive position established on a wooded hill about a half mile south of Rogersville. After an hour's skirmishing the Confederates (McCray's brigade of Churchill's division) launched an attack against the Federal left. Cruft's brigade started arriving on the field at a time when the Federal left was under heavy assault (16th and 55th Ind. initially; then the 71st Ind. and seven companies from the 69th Ind. on the right). The 59th Ohio (Cruft) took position behind the weakened right flank and was ordered to charge a gun position opposite this part of the line. The attack was repulsed by severe fire and a Confederate counterattack which drove in the Federal right. At this time the Federal left began to collapse also. The 18th Ky., arriving on the field, reinforced the line but was quickly driven back. Cruft's other regiments (12th and 66th Ind.) formed a new line near White's Farm about a mile to the rear, and remnants of the withdrawing regiments were rallied here. Nelson had sent word to withdraw, but Manson could not disengage. The 95th Ohio and 69th Ind. repulsed the initial assault on the left. The 18th Ky. and 12th Ind. on the right held for some time, but were then driven back. Manson's brigade had already been routed, and Cruft's now withdrew in confusion toward their camps just south of Richmond. Here Gen. Nelson arrived to assist Manson in forming a new defensive position near the town and cemetery. A new assault overwhelmed this position and the Federals retreated toward Louisville. Manson was captured and Nelson wounded.

Out of 6,500 Federals engaged, there were 206 killed, 844 wounded, 4,303 missing, or a total of 5,353. Of 6,000 Confederate infantry and 850 cavalry engaged, there were 78 killed, 372 wounded, 1 missing, or a total of 451 (Livermore and Fox). (The numbers and losses cited by Van Horne, I, 182, are obviously wrong. For example, he accepts Cruft's report of 16,000 Confederates engaged, and gives a figure of only 2,000 Federals captured.)

RICHMOND, Va., CONFEDERATE DEPARTMENT AND DEFENSES OF. The Dept. of HENRICO, the county in which Richmond is located, existed under the command of J. H. Winder from Dec. '61 until May '64. What the O.R. refers to as "the defenses of Richmond, etc.," was commanded by G. W. Smith from 30 Aug. '62 until he left 19 Sept. to command the Dept. of N.C. and Southern Va. Arnold Elzey then took command on 12 Dec. On 1 Apr. '63 the Dept. of Richmond was created as part of Longstreet's Dept. of N.C. and Southern Va. It remained under Elzey until 25 Apr. '64, when Robert Ransom succeeded him. When Ewell left his corps on 29 May '64 because of physical disability he was assigned to head the Dept. of Richmond.

Col. W. H. Stevens commanded an artillery force known as the Richmond Defenses. This was composed of four battalions of Va. Hv. Arty.: (10th and 19th in the 1st Div., Inner Line; and 18th and 20th in the 2d Div., Inner Line); plus the La. Guard Arty., and the Engr. Co. A force reported as "local defenses, special service" (O.R. XXXIII, I, 1301) was organized as a result of STONEMAN'S RAID during the Chancellorsville and other earlier Federal raids. It was composed (on 21 Apr. '64) of about 3,000 men from the War, Treasury, Navy, and Postmaster General's departments who were organized into the following battalions: Departmental, Quartermaster, Arsenal, Armory, Naval, and Tredegar. The first of these was known also as the Richmond City Battalion and had been trained by G. W. Custis Lee, the Gen's. son. During the KILPATRICK-DAHLGREN RAID (28 Feb.–4 Mar. '64) this force successfully defended the city.

RICHMOND, Lewis. Union officer. R.I. Capt. Asst. Adj. Gen. Vols. 13 Sept. '61; Maj. Asst. Adj. Gen. Vols. 28 Apr. '62; Lt. Col. Asst. Adj. Gen. Assigned 22 July '62–21 Apr. '65; Bvt. B.G. USV. Brevets for East Tenn. campaign, Knoxville, campaign from the Rapidan to Petersburg (2). Died 1894.

RICHMOND ARMORY AND ARSENAL. This installation accounted for approximately half of the total issue of ordnance materials to the Confederate armies (Miller, V, 170). Between 1 July '61 and 1 Jan. '65 it issued 341 Columbiads and siege guns, 1,306 fieldpieces of all descriptions, 921,441 rounds of artillery ammunition of all classes, 323,-231 infantry arms, 34,067 cavalry carbines, 6,074 pistols, and nearly 72,500,-000 rounds of small-arms ammunition, besides many thousand articles of other ordnance stores (*ibid.,* 168). These figures include work done by Tredegar and outside contractors.

The arsenal was on Byrd Island, and the laboratory and artillery works were nearby. The armory, separate and distinct from the arsenal, was formerly the Virginia Armory that dated back to 1798. TREDEGAR IRON WORKS was also in the immediate vicinity. Arms were made principally from the machinery taken from the HARPERS FERRY ARMORY. (See Albaugh and Simmons, 256-57.)

RICHMOND, Va., SURRENDER, 3 Apr. '65. The Confederates evacuated Richmond the night of 2-3 Apr. Troops of XVIII, XXIV, and XXV Corps (Fox), all under command of Gen. Weitzel, entered the city, taking 6,000 prisoners, of whom 5,000 were in hospitals. Weitzel accepted the formal surrender at 8:15 A.M., at the City Hall.

RICH MOUNTAIN, W. Va., 11 July '61. (WEST VIRGINIA OPERATIONS IN 1861) Rosecrans led four regiments (8th, 9th, 13th Ind., and 19th Ohio) and Burdsal's cavalry around the left (south) of Pegram's position astride the Buckhannon-Beverly Road. He achieved surprise, routing Capt. de Lagnel's 350 men near Hart house, about a mile and

a half behind Pegram's camp, and cutting off Pegram's route of retreat to Beverly. Part of his force escaped, but Pegram was unable to link up with Garnett (see CARRICK'S FORD, 12 July) and surrendered his remaining 553 officers and men the night of 12-13 July (*Lee's Lts.,* I, 34). The Federals reported a loss of 46 (E.&B.).

RICKETTS, James Brewerton. Union gen. 1817-87. N.Y. USMA 1839 (16/31); Arty. Serving in garrison, the Mexican War, and the Seminole War, he was commanding a battery at 1st Bull Run (Capt. 1st US Arty. since 1852) when wounded and captured. Exchanged six months later, he was promoted B.G. USV 21 July '61, the date of the battle, and commanded in the Army of the Rappahannock 1st Brig., Ord's division (16 May-10 June '62) and succeeded to division (10-26 June '62). At 2d Bull Run and Cedar Mountain he led 2d Div., III, Army of Va. (26 June-12 Sept. '62), commanding the corps 5-6 Sept. He led 2d Div., I, Potomac (12 Sept.-4 Oct. '62) at South Mountain and Antietam, where he was wounded. Serving on commissions and courts-martial until 4 Apr. '64, he then commanded 3d Div., VI, Potomac until 8 July '64 at the Wilderness, Spotsylvania, North Anna, Cold Harbor, and Petersburg; also commanding the corps 6-13 Apr. He then went to Washington to intercept Early's advance up the Valley and then commanded, in the Army of the Shenandoah, 3d Div., VI (6 Aug.-16 Oct. '64). He commanded the VI Corps (16-19 Oct. '64) at Cedar Mountain, where he received his sixth wound of the war. Breveted for 1st Bull Run, Cold Harbor, Cedar Creek (B.G. USA), war service (Maj. Gen. USA), and Monocacy-Opequon-Fishers Hill-Cedar Creek (Maj. Gen. USV 1 Aug. '64), he continued in the R.A.

and was retired with the rank of Maj. Gen. in 1867.

RIENZI. The horse was about three years old when Sheridan acquired him in the spring of 1862 while he was stationed near Rienzi, Miss. He stood over 17 hands high with a deep chest and possessed tremendous strength. After Sheridan made his famous ride in Oct. '64, the horse's name was changed to Winchester. The horse is stuffed and in the Smithsonian Institution.

RIFLE. A firearm whose bore is constructed with spiral grooves to spin its projectile and give it a more accurate flight. A rifle can be either a CANNON or a hand weapon. In popular usage a rifle is a weapon fired from the shoulder, as distinguished from a cannon or pistol. See also RIFLE MUSKET.

RIFLE MUSKET. A term adopted in 1855 to designate those shoulder arms that retained the outside dimensions of the old muskets but that had rifled barrels (Shields, 210). "The rifle differs from the rifle-musket in having a shorter and stouter barrel, a sword-bayonet, in the mountings, which are made of brass instead of iron, and in having its barrel browned," says the West Point text of 1867 (Benton, 317). This distinction between the two types is not precisely observed. The *Official Records* atlas plate on weapons (CLXXIII) shows a weapon that answers the description of the UNITED STATES RIFLE, Model 1855 ("Harpers Ferry"), complete with sword-type bayonet, and labels it "Harper's Ferry Rifled Musket." Immediately above this illustration is a longer weapon, with a "musket bayonet," labeled "Springfield Rifled Musket."

RIFLE PITS. Civil War equivalent of "fox holes."

RIGGIN, John, Jr. Union officer. Mo. Vol. A.D.C. to Gen. Grant 23 Dec. '61;

Col. Add. A.D.C. 3 May '62; Bvt. B.G. USV (war service); resigned 14 Oct. '63. Died 1886.

RIMBASES. Short cylinders uniting the trunnions with the body of the gun (Benton).

RINAKER, John Irving. Union officer. Md. Col. 122d Ill. 4 Sept. '62; Bvt. B.G. USV (war service). Commanded 2, 2, XVI; 1, 2, Det. Army Tenn. (Cumberland); 1, 2, XVI.

RIPLEY, Edward Hastings. Union officer. Vt. Capt. 9th Vt. 9 July '62; Maj. 20 Mar. '63; Lt. Col. 19 May '63; Col. 1 June '63; Bvt. B.G. USV 1 Aug. '64. Commanded 2, 2, XVIII; 1, 3, XXIV.

RIPLEY, James Wolfe. Union gen. 1794–1870. Conn. USMA 1814* (12/30); Arty. He fought in the War of 1812 and the Seminole War before serving as arsenal and armory superintendent. Named B.G. USA and Chief of Ordnance 3 Aug. '61, he was a hottempered and vigorous opponent of many improvements, notably breechloading. Finally forced out by Lincoln and Stanton, he retired 15 Sept. '63 and was breveted Maj. Gen. USA. Uncle of Roswell Ripley, C.S.A.

RIPLEY, Roswell Sabine. C.S.A. gen. 1823–87. Ohio. Appt.-N.Y. USMA 1843 (7/39); Arty. He served in garrison, and on coastal surveys, taught mathematics at West Point, and fought in the Mexican War (2 brevets) and the Seminole War before resigning in 1853. Settling in S.C., he was in business and active in the state militia when named Maj. of S.C. Ord. in 1860. As Lt. Col. C.S.A., he commanded the reconditioned Forts Moultrie and Sumter and on 15 Aug. '61 was appointed B.G. C.S.A. Pemberton succeeded to

*There was no class standing prior to 1818, and the cadets are listed in the order in which they were commissioned.

command of S.C. in 1862, and Ripley asked to be relieved after they had a difference of opinion. Serving under Beauregard, he again argued with his superiors, and Cooper wanted to replace him in Oct. '61. That plan was overruled by Davis, and Lee gave him a brigade under Hill. He led this unit at Antietam and was wounded. After his recovery, he was again sent to S.C. at the request of Beauregard and Pickens and was given command of 1st Arty. Dist. in Charleston. His fractious disposition once more embroiled him in arguments, and Beauregard offered him to J. E. Johnston in June '63 as "an excellent field officer." Ripley retained his S.C. command, however, and in Nov. '64 the citizens of Charleston and Gov. Bonham objected to his possible removal. After the city's capture he joined the Army of the West, meeting Johnston at Bentonville and then returned to S.C. Going to England immediately after the war, he was in manufacturing until the operation failed. He then returned to Charleston and N.Y.C.

RIPLEY, Theodore A. Union officer. N.H. Capt. 14th N.H. 2 Oct. '62; Col. 23 Mar. '65; Bvt. B.G. USV (war service). Died 1866.

RISDON, Orlando Charles. Union officer. Ohio. Pvt. 19th Ohio 22 Apr. '61; mustered out 31 Aug. '61; 1st Lt. 42d Ohio 7 Oct. '61; Lt. Col. 53d US Col. Inf. 19 Mar. '63; Col. 24 Mar. '64; Bvt. B.G. USV (Rich Mountain, W. Va.; Middle Creek, Ky.; Tazewell, Tenn.; Chickasaw; Arkansas Post; Port Gibson, Miss.; Champion's Hill; Big Black Bridge, Miss.; Vicksburg siege).

RITCHIE, John. Union officer. Ohio. Capt. 5th Kans. Cav. 16 July '61; Lt. Col. 11 Sept. '61; Col. 17 Sept. '61; resigned 11 Dec. '61; Maj. Add. A.D.C. 29 Jan. '62; discharged 21 Mar. '62;

Col. 2d Indian Home Guards 22 June '62; Bvt. B.G. USV 21 Feb. '65. Died 1887.

ROANE, John Selden. C.S.A. gen. 1817-67. Tenn. After settling in Ark., he served in the legislature, fought in Mexico, and was Gov. 1849-52. He was an opponent of secession but went with the South, being appointed B.G. C.S.A. 20 Mar. '62, and on 11 May was put in command of all Confed. forces in Ark. Succeeded by Hindman, he then fought at Prairie Grove. During the remainder of the war he fought in the District of ARK. and other parts of the TRANS-MISS. After the war he was a planter.

ROANOKE ISLAND, N.C., 8 Feb. '62. Henry Wise was defeated with a loss of 2,500 prisoners and the island occupied at the start of BURNSIDE'S EXPEDITION TO N.C.

ROBBINS, Walter Raleigh. Union officer. N.J. Pvt. Co. A 14th N.Y. 22 Apr. '61; 2d Lt. 1st N.J. Cav. 19 Feb. '62; 1st Lt. 20 Apr. '62; Capt. 1 Mar. '63; Maj. 1 Nov. '64; Lt. Col. 4 May '65; Bvt. B.G. USV (war service).

ROBERTS, Benjamin Stone. Union gen. 1810-75. Vt. USMA 1835 (53/56); Dragoons. After serving on the frontier, he resigned in 1839 to go into the railroad business. He was the N.Y. State Geologist and an assistant to Geo. W. Whistler on the St. Petersburg-to-Moscow railroad and also practiced law. He rejoined the army for the Mexican War (1 brevet) and as Maj. 13 May '61 commanded the Southern Dist. of N. Mex. under Canby. He was Col. 5th N. Mex. 9 Dec. '61-31 May '62 and was promoted B.G. USV 16 June, serving on Pope's staff at Cedar Mountain, Rappahannock Station, Sulphur Springs, and 2d Bull Run. He led a punitive expedition against the Indians in Minnesota and then commanded in the

Middle Dept.: 3d Div., VIII (11–16 Mar. '63) and 4th Sep. Brig., VIII (11 Mar.–23 May '63). He commanded the Cavalry Division (11 Nov.–28 Dec. '64) as well as the XIX Corps (2–6 July '64). He then led the Dist. West Tenn. (3 Feb.–4 Mar. '65) and the Cavalry Division Dist. West Tenn. (15 May–14 July '65). Breveted for Valverde (N. Mex.), Cedar Mountain (B.G. USA), and Cedar Mountain and 2d Bull Run (Maj. Gen. USV), he continued in the R.A. until 1870, when he retired as Lt. Col. 3d US Cav.

ROBERTS, Charles Wentworth. Union officer. Me. Lt. Col. 2d Me. 28 May '61; Col. 29 Aug. '61; Bvt. B.G. USV (Hanover C.H., Va.); resigned 10 Jan. '63. Commanded 1, 1, V. Died 1898.

ROBERTS, Joseph. Union officer. 1814–98. Del. USMA 1835 (8/56); Arty. Maj. 4th US Arty. 3 Sept. '61; Col. 3d Pa. Hv. Arty. 19 Mar. '63; retired Col. 1877; Bvt. B.G. USV 9 Apr. '65; Bvt. B.G. USA. Brevets for war service (Cullum gives his highest brevet as Maj. Gen.). Served as Chief of Arty. for the VII Corps 19 Sept. '62. Commanded Fort Monroe 1863–65 and Fort McHenry 1865–66. Instructed at USMA. At the Arty. School (Fort Monroe) he was superintendent of theoretical instruction. Wrote *Hand-Book of Artillery.*

ROBERTS, Samuel Henry. Union officer. Conn. Lt. Col. 139th N.Y. 9 Sept. '62; Col. 25 Aug. '63; Bvt. B.G. USV 28 Oct. '64 (Fort Harrison, Va.). Commanded 1st Brig., Getty's Div. Norfolk and Portsmouth; Dist. Currituck (Va. and N.C.); 3, 1, XVIII; 3, 3, XXIV. Died 1890.

ROBERTS, William Paul. C.S.A. gen. 1841–1910. N.C. Enlisting in spring 1861 as Pvt. in the 2d N.C. Cav., he was commissioned 3d Lt. 30 Aug. '61 and 1st Lt. 13 Sept. '62. He served

with his regiment along the Rappahannock in 1862 and fought at Fredericksburg, the Suffolk campaign, and Brandy Station. Promoted Capt. 19 Nov. '63 and Maj. soon after that, he was named Col. and given command of his regiment in spring 1864. He led them at Reams's Station and other battles around Petersburg, was appointed B.G. C.S.A. 21 Feb. '65 and commanded his brigade at Five Forks and Appomattox. After the war he was a legislator and held other public offices.

ROBERTSON, Beverly Holcombe. C.S.A. gen. 1826–1910. Va. USMA 1849 (25/43); Dragoons. He served on the frontier in Indian scouting and fighting for his entire career before being dismissed 8 Aug. '61. Commissioned Col. 4th Va. Cav. 19 Nov. '61, he fought from May to Sept. of the next year in cavalry operations in Va. and was appointed B.G. C.S.A. 9 June '62. He commanded his cavalry brigade at Cedar Mountain, 2d Bull Run, and Antietam, and was sent in Oct. '62 to N. C., returning in Apr. '63 to Va. The next month he served under Jeb Stuart guarding passes in South Mountain and fought at Gettysburg and Upperville. In Oct. '63 he was named to command the 2d Dist. of S.C. under Beauregard and in Nov. of that year went with Longstreet to Knoxville. He was relieved of this command "owing to mutinous remarks to his brigade" (C.M.H.) and in 1864 served in S.C. He joined Johnston in Mar. '65 and surrendered with him. After the war he was in business in Washington.

ROBERTSON, Felix H. C.S.A. gen. Appt.-Tex. Commissioned 2d Lt. C.S.A. Arty. on 9 Mar. '61, he served at the bombardment of Fort Sumter and was at Pensacola as acting Adj. Gen. on Gladden's staff, having been named Capt. in Oct. '61. On 1 Jan. '62 he was given command of a battery and led the Ala. Btry. at Shiloh and the Fla. Btry. at Stones River. He was promoted Maj. of Arty. 1 July '63 and commanded a battalion at Chickamauga. Named Lt. Col. in Jan. '64, he commanded the artillery in Wheeler's corps in the Atlanta campaign and was named B.G. C.S.A. 26 July '64. He commanded a cavalry brigade under Wheeler in Tenn. and on the March to the Sea. Wounded 28 Nov. '64, he saw no more field service. His B.G. nomination was rejected by the Senate 22 Feb. '65, but he surrendered with that rank at Macon (Ga.) 20 Apr. '65.

ROBERTSON, James Madison. Union officer. N.H. Appt. from the army. Enlisting in the R.A. in 1838 and fighting in the Mexican War, he was commissioned 10 years later and served in the Seminole War and on the frontier. He was promoted Capt. 2d US Arty. 14 May '61 and served on Santa Rosa Island and at Fort Pickens. In Feb. '62 he joined his battery for the Peninsular campaign. Fighting at Mechanicsville, Gaines's Mill, and Malvern Hill, he was also at South Mountain and Antietam before taking command of a horse artillery brigade for Stoneman's Raid, Beverly Ford, Gettysburg, Culpeper C.H., Todd's Tavern, Spotsylvania, Yellow Tavern, Haw's Shop, and White House Landing. He inspected government horses in St. Louis from Aug. '64 to Jan. '65 and returned to his command in Va. and Md. for the closing months of the war. Continuing in the R.A., he retired in 1879 as Maj. 3d US Arty., having been breveted for Gaines's Mill, Gettysburg, Cold Harbor and the final campaign from the Wilderness to Trevilian Station (B.G. USA). He died 1891.

ROBERTSON, Jerome Bonaparte. C.S.A. gen. 1815–91. Ky. Apprenticed to a hatter by his parents, he then received a medical education from a doctor, and went to fight in the Tex. revolution. Staying to hang out his shingle, he became one of the republic's leading citizens, serving in the legislature and the seccession convention of 1861. He had also been active in the Indian fighting of early Tex. Commissioned Capt. 5th Tex., he fought in Hood's Texans and was commissioned Lt. Col. in Nov. '61. He was promoted Col. 1 June '62 and commanded his regiment during the Seven Days' Battles and 2d Bull Run (wounded). At the battle of Boonsboro Gap he collapsed from the effects of exhaustion and his wound. Appointed B.G. C.S.A. 1 Nov. '62, he succeeded Hood and led the Tex. brigade at Fredericksburg, Gettysburg (lightly wounded) and Chickamauga. In the demoralization that characterized Longstreet's command after Jenkins had succeeded Hood as division commander, both Longstreet and Jenkins became increasingly dissatisfied with Robertson's performance as commander of the Tex. brigade. Robertson had been relieved of command by Longstreet just before the Knoxville campaign, had been reinstated. On 26 Jan. '64 Longstreet filed court-martial charges, but there is no record of their having been acted on. Robertson was, however, relieved of command and in June was ordered to take command of "reserve forces of the State of Texas" (*Lee's Lts.*, III, 303). After the war he was active in railroading in west Tex. A man of strong sense, genial manners, and personal courage, although of little culture or polish, he was not considered to be an outstanding commander (*ibid.*).

ROBESON, William P. Union officer. N.J. 1st Lt. 3d N.J. 28 May '61; Capt. 13 Aug. '62; resigned 12 Jan. '64; Maj. 3d N.J. Cav. 14 Jan. '64; Lt. Col. 6 Dec. '64; Bvt. B.G. USV (war service). Died 1881.

ROBINSON, Charles. Gov. of Kans. 1818–? Mass. After studying at Amherst College he became a doctor and moved west to Calif., where he edited a daily in Sacramento. Seriously wounded in the riots of 1850, he was elected to the legislature and returned to Mass., where he edited a paper for a time. He moved to Kans. in 1854 as the agent of the New England Emigrants' Aid Society and became the leader of the Free-State party. Elected Gov. under its banner in 1856, he was arrested for treason but acquitted. He was elected again by the Free-State party in 1858 and was again chosen when Kans. came into the Union in Jan. '61. After organizing most of the state's regiments, he left office in 1863 and then served in the legislature.

ROBINSON, George Dorgue. Union officer. N.Y. 2d Lt. 75th N.Y. 17 Sept. '61; 1st Lt. 11 June '62, Maj. 95th US Col. Inf. 30 May '63; Col. 97th US Col. Inf. 12 Sept. '63; Bvt. B.G. USV (Pollard and Mobile, Ala.). Commanded 2, 1, IX; 3, 1, IX (Potomac). Died 1873.

ROBINSON, Henry Lee. Union officer. N.Y. Capt. Asst. Q.M. Vols. 6 May '62; Bvt. B.G. USV. Brevets for war service (2). Died 1901.

ROBINSON, James Sidney. Union gen. 1827–92. Ohio. A printer and newspaper editor, he was an early Republican and enlisted 17 Apr. '61 as Pvt. Co. C 4th Ohio, being commissioned 1st Lt. the next day. As Capt. 4 May '61, he fought at Rich Mountain and as Maj. 82d Ohio 31 Dec. '61, he was with Frémont in the Valley. Named Lt. Col. 9 Apr. '62 and Col. 29 Aug. '62, he fought at Cedar Mountain and 2d Bull Run, Chancellorsville, and Gettysburg, where he was seriously wounded. Taking command of 1, 3, IX, Cumberland (13 Mar.–16 Apr. '64) and 3, 1, XX, Cumberland (2 May–24 July '64 and

27 Sept. '64–7 June '65), he led them on the Atlanta campaign and the March to the Sea and through the Carolinas. He was named B.G. USV 12 Jan. '65 and breveted for war service (B.G. USV 9 Dec. '64 and Maj. Gen. USV). Mustered out 24 Aug. '65, he was later a Congressman and held other public and party offices.

ROBINSON, John Cleveland. Union gen. 1817–97. N.Y. A cadet at West Point (ex-1839), he studied law and then joined the R.A. as 2d Lt. 5th US Inf. in 1839. He fought in the Mexican and Seminole wars and served on the frontier and the Utah Expedition against the Mormons. Of this last service he wrote that it was a plot to "denude the eastern states of troops, so that 'a dissolution of the Union' might be easier" (D.A.B. quoting his article in the *Magazine of American History*, 1884). As Capt. (since 1850) he was commanding Fort McHenry 19 Apr. '61 when the 6th Mass. was attacked in Baltimore. He rearmed and secretly supplied his 60 men to withstand a siege, and the mob, deterred by these efforts, did not attack the garrison. Named Col. 1st Mich. 1 Sept. '61 he was promoted B.G. USV 28 Apr. '62 and commanded 2, 3, III (9–12 June '62) and 1, 3, III (12 June–5 Aug. '62) during the Peninsular campaign. He led 1, 1, III (5 Aug.–30 Dec. '62) at Fredericksburg; 2d Div., I (30 Dec. '62–24 Mar. '64) at Chancellorsville and Gettysburg; and 2d Div., V (Apr.–8 May '64) at the Wilderness and Spotsylvania. He was severely wounded while leading a charge at Spotsylvania and lost his left leg. This ended his field service, and he served on commissions and the Freedman's Bureau later. Breveted for Gettysburg, the Wilderness, Spotsylvania (B.G. USA) and war service (Maj. Gen. USA and USV–24 June '64), he continued in the R.A. until retired in 1869 with rank of Maj. Gen. On 28 Mar. '94 he was given Medal of Honor for Laurel Hill, and on the 100th anniversary of his birth, a statue was dedicated at Gettysburg where he held, with two brigades, five C.S.A. brigades at bay for four hours.

ROBINSON, Milton Stapp. Union officer. Ind. Lt. Col. 47th Ind. 13 Dec. '61; Col. 75th Ind. 29 Oct. '62; Bvt. B.G. USV (war service); resigned 29 Mar. '64. Commanded 2, 4, XIV (Cumberland). Died 1892.

ROBINSON, William Andrew. Union officer. Pa. Sgt. Co. A 9th Pa. Res. 1 May '61; 1st Lt. 77th Pa. 30 Nov. '61; Capt. 22 Apr. '62; mustered out 12 Apr. '65; Lt. Col. 77th Pa. 10 June '65; Bvt. B.G. USV (war service).

ROBISON, John K. Union officer. Pa. Capt. 1st Pa. Cav. 16 Aug. '61; resigned 26 Mar. '62; Capt. 16th Pa. Cav. 10 Oct. '62; Lt. Col. 7 Aug. '63; Bvt. B.G. USV. Brevets for Reams's Station (Va.), war service.

ROCK ISLAND PRISON. This Federal PRISON was on an island in the Mississippi between Rock Island, Ill., and Davenport, Iowa. Eighty-four barracks in six rows of 14 each measured 82 by 22 by 12 feet with a cookhouse apiece. A high fence enclosed these on the island that measured three miles by one and a half mile in size. Water was scarce and for a time nonexistent, and only two stoves were in each barracks. Around 5,000 prisoners were sent there in Dec. '63, although the prison, ordered in July '63, was not yet completed. From then until the end of the war it contained from 5,000 to 8,000 prisoners at all times.

ROCK OF CHICKAMAUGA. THOMAS, George H.

ROCKWELL, Alfred Perkins. Union officer. Conn. Capt. 1st Conn. Btry.

20 Jan. '62; Col. 6th Conn. 18 June '64; Bvt. B.G. USV (campaign of 1864).

ROCKY FACE RIDGE, Ga., 5–11 May '64. (ATLANTA CAMPAIGN) Includes Tunnel Hill, Mill Creek Gap, Buzzard Roost, Snake Creek Gap, Varnell's Station, and "action near Dalton." In this, the opening action of the Atlanta campaign, J. E. Johnston was occupying a position running north and south along Rocky Face Ridge covering Dalton. Since this position was too strong to be assaulted, Sherman's strategy was to *turn* it from the west. While McPherson's Army of the Tenn. (24,000) moved through Ship's Gap and Villanow to Snake Creek Gap, Thomas' Army of the Cumberland (61,000) was to attack the Confederates frontally to hold them in position. Schofield's Army of the Ohio (13,500) was to advance due south along the railroad toward Varnell's Station to threaten Johnston's right (north) flank.

On 7 May Palmer's XIV Corps drove Confederate outposts from Tunnel Hill and pushed them to Buzzard Roost (or Mill Creek Gap). The next day Harker's brigade advanced along Rocky Face Ridge and the divisions of Wood, Davis, and Butterfield advanced until they developed the main Confederate defenses of Buzzard Gap. Geary's division (2, XX) was selected to make a strong feint at Dug Gap (where the LaFayette-Dalton road crosses Rocky Face Ridge). The 119th N.Y., deployed as skirmishers, led the way up the steep ridge toward Hardee's positions in a rock palisade at the top. The brigades of Bushbeck (2d) and Candy (1st), on the right and left, formed the main battle line. Two attacks were repulsed after a few men had gained the crest. In a third attempt a few men of the 33d N.J., supported by McGill's rifled battery, gained the crest at a point a half mile to the right. The Confederates had been reinforced and this final attempt failed about dark. Geary reported a loss of 357.

Feints against the ridge were continued, and Johnston reported repulsing five assaults on 9 May. Buzzard Roost was held by the divisions of Stewart and Bate, supported by Stevenson and Anderson.

At Varnell's Station La Grange's brigade of McCook's cavalry division, reconnoitering ahead of Schofield's army, encountered Wheeler's cavalry screen. The Federals pushed successfully to Poplar Place, but were there repulsed with heavy losses. La Grange was captured with 14 other officers; 136 others were lost.

McPherson found Snake Creek Gap defended only by a cavalry brigade, which he routed. At 2 P.M. on 9 May he reached the vicinity of Resaca. Finding this place strongly held, he withdrew to the gap and entrenched, an action for which he has been criticized. Although his maneuver had failed to cut Johnston's line of retreat, it did force the Confederates to abandon Dalton. Sherman's next movement resulted in the actions around RESACA, Ga., 13–16 May.

RODDEY, Philip Dale. C.S.A. gen. 1820–97. Ala. Engaged variously as a tailor, sheriff, and steamboat crewman on the Tennessee River, he raised a company of cavalry when the war began. Commissioned Capt., he was Bragg's personal escort to Shiloh and in Dec. '62 was promoted Col. of the 4th Ala. Cav. For the rest of the war he fought around the Tennessee River under Bragg, Wheeler, and Forrest. He was appointed B.G. C.S.A. 3 Aug. '63. After the war he was a commission merchant in N.Y.C.

RODENBOUGH, Theophilus Francis. Union officer. 1838–1912. R.A. 2d Lt. 2d US Dragoons 27 Mar. '61; 1st Lt. 14 May '61; 2d US Cav. 3 Aug. '61; staff Cav. School of Practice, Carlisle (Pa.) 1861–62; Capt. 17 July '62; Col. 18th Pa. Cav. 29 Apr. '65; breveted B.G. USV 13 Apr. '65; retired Col. 1870. Brevets for Trevilian Station and Opequon (Va.), war service (2), Cold Harbor, Todd's Tavern (Va.). Medal of Honor 21 Sept. '93 for Trevilian Station (Va.). Captured at 2d Bull Run; participated in Stoneman's raid; W.I.A. and had two horses shot from under him at Beverly Ford (Va.) June '63; W.I.A. Winchester and lost right arm, 19 Sept. '64. He wrote extensively on military and historical subjects and was editor of the *Army-Navy Journal*.

RODES, Robert Emmett. C.S.A. gen. 1829–64. Va. Appt.-Ala. After graduating from V.M.I., he taught there until Jackson was given the post he had wanted. Taking up civil engineering then, he worked for railroads and returned to V.M.I. to teach mechanics and engineering, but the war began before he could take up his duties. Commissioned Col. 5th Ala. in May '61, he fought at 1st Bull Run and was appointed B.G. C.S.A. 21 Oct. of that year. Commanding his brigade at Fair Oaks, he was severely wounded but returned to fight at Gaines's Mill, where his unhealed wound laid him up for a considerable time. Wounded again in the Antietam campaign, he commanded his brigade at Fredericksburg and Chancellorsville, succeeding first to Hill's division and then to Jackson's corps, turning the latter over to Stuart upon Jackson's order with good grace. He was promoted Maj. Gen. 7 May '63 to rank from the 2d and led his division at Gettysburg, the Wilderness, and Spotsylvania before going, in June '64, to the Shenandoah Valley. Serving under Early, he fought at Kernstown, on the Washington raid, at Monocacy, and at Winchester, where he was killed 19 Sept. '64.

RODGERS, Hiram C. Union officer. N.Y. Capt. 27th N.Y. 21 May '61; Capt. Asst. Adj. Gen. Vols. 30 June '62; Maj. Asst. Adj. Gen. Vols. 6 Aug. '62; Lt. Col. Asst. Adj. Gen. Assigned 1 Jan. '63–30 Jan. '65; Bvt. B.G. USV (war service); resigned 30 Jan. '65. Died 1897. Phisterer lists him as Rogers, Hiram C.

RODGERS, Horatio, Jr. Erroneous listing by Phisterer for Rogers, Horatio, Jr.

RODMAN, Isaac Peace. Union gen. 1822–62. R.I. A state legislator and banker, he was commissioned Capt. 2d R.I. 6 June '61, fought at 1st Bull Run, and resigned 25 Oct. '61. Named Col. 4th R.I. 30 Oct., he was with Burnside at Roanoke Island, New Bern, and Fort Macon. Felled by typhoid, he was sent home to recover and was then promoted B.G. USV 28 Apr. '62. Taking over the 3d Div., IX Corps, 3 Sept. at Frederick, he led his troops at South Mountain and was mortally wounded 17 Sept. at Antietam, dying on the 30th.

RODMAN, Thomas Jackson. Union officer. 1815–71. Ind. USMA 1841 (7/52); Ord. Inventor of RODMAN GUN, he also improved the propellent quality of black powder by molding it into large grains that burned more steadily than corned powder and gave the projectile a steady shove out the barrel rather than a sudden impetus. He commanded Watertown Arsenal during the Civil War and the Rock Island Arsenal from 1865 until his death. He had three brevets as B.G.

RODMAN GUN. A method of making cannon by casting in iron around a water or air-chilled core so that the inside of the barrel cooled first and was compressed by the contraction of the outside metal. Crystallization of the metal was so regulated, thereby, that guns made in this manner could stand more internal pressure without breaking. The Rodman system was used primarily in the manufacture of large smoothbores of the COLUMBIAD type, one of which had a bore 20 inches in diameter and fired a projectile weighing more than 1,000 pounds. The method was named after its inventor, T. J. RODMAN.

ROGERS, George. Union officer. Ohio. Enlisted 4th Ohio 4 May '61; mustered out 21 Aug. '61; Capt. 20th Ohio 15 Oct. '61; resigned 16 Feb. '63; Lt. Col. 4th US Col. Inf. 2 Sept. '63; Bvt. B.G. USV (war service).

ROGERS, George Clarke. Union officer. 1838–?. N.H. 1st Lt. 15th Ill. 25 Apr. '61; Capt. 4 Sept. '61; Lt. Col. 7 Apr. '62; Col. 2 Nov. '62; Bvt. B.G. USV (war service). W.I.A. four times at Shiloh and three times at Champion's Hill. Engineered the works at Allatoona (Ga.). Active in Democratic politics, he was an earnest supporter of Stephen A. Douglas. Phisterer lists him as Rodgers, George C.

ROGERS, Hiram C. Erroneous listing by Phisterer for Rodgers, Hiram C.

ROGERS, Horatio, Jr. Union officer. R.I. 1st Lt. 3d R.I. Arty. 27 Aug. '61; Capt. 9 Oct. '61; Maj. 18 Aug. '62; Col. 11th R.I. 27 Dec. '62; Col. 2d R.I. 6 Feb. '63; Bvt. B.G. USV (war service); resigned 15 Jan. '64. Listed in Phisterer as Rodgers, Horatio, Jr.

ROGERS, James Clarence. Union officer. N.Y. Capt. 43d N.Y. 16 Sept. '61; Maj. 123d N.Y. 30 Sept. '62; Lt. Col. 3 June '63; Col. 20 Feb. '65; Bvt. B.G. USV (war service).

ROGERS, William Findlay. Union officer. Pa. Capt. 21st N.Y. 13 May '61; Col. 20 May '61; Bvt. B.G. USV (war service); mustered out 18 May '63. Died 1899.

ROMNEY, W. Va., 10 Jan. '62. See LORING-JACKSON INCIDENT.

ROOME, Charles. Union officer. N.Y. Col. 37th N.Y. State Militia 29 May '62; mustered out 2 Sept. '62; Col. 37th N.Y. State Militia 18 June '63; Bvt. B.G. USV (war service); mustered out 22 July '63. Died 1890.

ROOT, Adrian Rowe. Union officer. N.Y. Commissioned Lt. Col. 21st N.Y. 20 May '61, he was promoted Col. 94th N.Y., 2 May '62, and mustered out in July '65. He was breveted B.G. USV 2 Mar. '65 and Maj. Gen. USV. Died 1899.

ROSE, Thomas Ellwood. Union officer. 1830–? Pa. Pvt. Co. I 12th Pa. 25 Apr.–5 Aug. '61; Capt. 77th Pa. 28 Oct. '61; Col. 1 Feb. '63; Bvt. B.G. USV 22 July '65. Brevets for Liberty Gap (Tenn.), Chickamauga, war service. Commanded 1, 1, IV (Cumberland); 2, 2, XX (Cumberland). Captured at Chickamauga and escaped at Weldon (N.C.) but was recaptured the next day. He was a member of the escaping party from Libby through the Twentieth Street tunnel and was one of the 50 recaptured before they could reach Union lines. In R.A. until retired in 1894 as Maj.

ROSECRANS, William Starke. Union gen. 1819–98. Ohio. USMA 1842 (5/56); Engrs. After construction supervising in New England and teaching at West Point, he resigned in 1854 to become a civil engineer, architect, and coal and oil refiner. In the Dept. of the Ohio, he was Vol. A.D.C. and Col. Engrs. in the Ohio Volunteers on McClellan's staff 23 Apr.–12 June '61 and then named Col. 23d Ohio 12–17 June. On 16 June '61 he was appointed B.G. USA and commanded Rosecrans' brigade, Army of Occupation, W. Va. (May–July '61) at Rich Mountain. He then commanded the Army of Occupa-

tion (23 July–11 Oct. '61) and the Dept. of W. Va. (11 Oct. '61–11 Mar. '62) at Carnifex Ferry before leading the Army of the Miss. (26 June–24 Oct. '62) at Iuka. On 21 Mar. '62 he was named Maj. Gen. USV. During the battle of Corinth he was in command of the Dist. of Corinth (July–20 Oct. '62) and then led the Army of the Cumberland (30 Oct. '62–20 Oct. '63) at Stones River, in the Tullahoma campaign, and at Chickamauga. His defeat cost him the command, and he was "awaiting orders" from the latter date until 30 Jan. '64, when he took command of the Dept. of the Mo. for about a year. He was one of 15 Army officers given the Thanks of Congress (for Stones River) during the Civil War and was breveted Maj. USA for this same battle. He resigned in 1867 and served as Minister to Mexico 1868–89, when he was appointed B.G. USA and retired a month later. He was then a Congressman and rancher in Calif. Described as having a testy disposition and hot temper, he was nonetheless able to do without sleep almost entirely during a campaign. His soldiers called him "Old Rosy." While a cadet at West Point he was converted to Catholicism and in turn converted his brother, who later became a bishop.

ROSS, Anna Maria. Union Philanthropist. c. 1811–63. Pa. She started the Cooper's Shop Saloon, near the Union Refreshment Saloon run by Mary W. LEE in the Philadelphia water-front district in 1861. This was a rest station that provided food, rest, clothing, and medical care for the soldiers. She worked tirelessly until her death in Dec. '63.

ROSS, Lawrence Sullivan. ("Sul.") C.S.A. gen. 1838–98. Iowa. His father was an Indian agent in Tex., and Ross was seriously wounded in Indian fighting before being appointed a Capt. in the Tex. Rangers by Sam Houston. While fighting Comanches along the Mexican border he was offered an R.A. commission by Winfield Scott but refused it. He was later Houston's A.D.C. as a Col. Enlisting in the Confederate Army as a private, he was named Maj. 6th Tex. Cav. in Sept. '61 and named Col. in May '62. He covered Van Dorn's retreat from Corinth and was appointed B.G. C.S.A. 21 Dec. '63 for this. In the Atlanta campaign he commanded his brigade under Wheeler. Returning penniless to Tex.'s Brazos Bottom, he made a small fortune from his plantation and served as sheriff during Reconstruction. He was state sen. in 1881–85 and Gov. in 1887–91 and served as president of Tex. A.&M. College until his death.

ROSS, Leonard Fulton. Union gen. 1823–1901. Ill. A lawyer, he fought in the Mexican War and then became a judge. He raised the 17th Ill. and was commissioned Col. 25 May '61, leading it in Ky. and Mo. He had a horse shot from under him at Fredericktown (Mo.) 20 Oct. '61. At Fort Donelson he commanded 3d Brig., 1st Div., Army Tenn. (15–17 Feb. '62) and succeeded to command of the division. Promoted B.G. USV 25 Apr. '62, he also led 2d Div. Dist. Corinth (24 Oct.–1 Nov. '62); 8th Div. Left Wing, XIII (11 Nov.– 18 Dec. '62) and 13th Div., XIII (8 Feb.–25 May '63). He resigned 22 July '63 and was later active in the Republican party.

ROSS, Samuel. Union officer. N.Y. Appt.-Army. R.A. Enlisted man & Bvt. 2d Lt. from 1837 to 1848. Capt. 14th US Inf. 14 May '61; Col. 20th Conn. 8 Sept. '62; Bvt. B.G. USV 13 Apr. '65. Brevets for Chancellorsville, Savannah, and Atlanta campaigns; gallantry and ability as brigade commander in Savannah campaign; campaign against Atlanta. Commanded 2, 1, XII (Po-

tomac); 1, 1, XII (Potomac); 1, 1, XII (Cumberland), 2, 3, XX (Cumberland); 3, 3, XX (Cumberland). Continued in R.A. until retired with rank of Col. in 1875. Drowned 1880.

ROSS, William Edward Wyatt. Union officer. Md. Lt. Col. 10th Md. 2 July '63; mustered out 29 Jan. '64; Col. 31st US Col. Inf. 22 June '64; Bvt. B.G. USV (war service); discharged 11 Mar. '65. Highest rank listed by Phisterer is Lt. Col. 31st US Col. Inf.

ROSSER, Thomas Lafayette. C.S.A. gen. 1836–1910. Va. Appt.-Tex. Resigning from West Point (ex-May '61) as the war approached, he was named 1st Lt. of the Washington Arty. and fought at 1st Bull Run. A Capt. in the Peninsular campaign, he was wounded but had recovered to be promoted Col. 5th Va. Cav. and took part in the raid that captured Pope's headquarters at Catlett's Station. He commanded his regiment at 2d Bull Run, South Mountain, Chancellorsville, and Gettysburg before being appointed B.G. C.S.A. 28 Sept. '63. Taking command of the Laurel Brig., he led it at Buckland Mills in Oct., defeating his erstwhile good friend and classmate, Custer. The two generals became hard-bitten rivals after this, clashing in the Shenandoah Valley and in the retreat from Petersburg to Appomattox. Rosser also fought at Trevilian Station, commanded Early's cavalry at Woodstock and Cedar Creek, and led many successful independent raids. He held open the Southside R.R. the night after the battle of Five Forks. At Appomattox he led his command in a charge through the Union lines, only to be captured 2 May near Hanover C.H. After the war he was in railroading and was chief engineer in the Indian Territory where Custer's command was deployed to protect his construction. The men became close friends once again. A gentleman farmer near Charlottesville, he was commissioned B.G. USA in 1898 and commanded a brigade of Northern volunteers encamped near the Chickamauga battleground during the Spanish-American War. In his prime, he was six feet two inches tall with extraordinary strength and endurance. The nickname, "Saviour of the Valley," was given to Rosser in the Shenandoah.

ROSSER'S BEVERLY RAID (W. Va.), 11 Jan. '65.

With 300 picked men from his various brigades Rosser took advantage of bitter cold weather and deep snow to surprise elements of the 34th Ohio and 8th Ohio Cav. The Federals lost 25 killed and wounded, 583 prisoners (E.&B.), and 10,000 rations (Miller, IV, 114).

ROSSER'S NEW CREEK (W. Va.) RAID, Nov. '64.

The morning of 28 Nov. '64 W. H. Payne's brigade advanced toward New Creek on the B.&O. R.R. about 22 miles west of Cumberland. About 20 Confederates in blue overcoats surprised pickets along the road, who mistook them initially for Federals returning from a scouting party that had gone out the previous day. Rosser's men continued into the town and surprised the garrison of Fort Kelly, capturing several hundred prisoners and large quantities of supplies. The Confederates destroyed the railroad bridge and withdrew. E.&B., quoting R. E. Lee's report, puts the Federal loss at 700 prisoners with five Confederates killed and wounded. T.U.A., VI, says there were seven guns and "some 443 prisoners, 100 of whom later escaped."

ROSSER'S RAID TO MOOREFIELD, W. Va.

On 29 Jan. '64 Rosser crossed the mountains to Moorefield where he learned of a large supply train en route from New Creek to Petersburg. At Medley, near Williamsport, he found the train guarded by the 23d Ill., 2d

Md. Home Brig., 1st and 14th W. Va., and Ringgold's (Pa.) Cav. By moving one regiment around the rear of this force and others on the flank, and opening fire with an artillery piece from their front, Rosser stampeded the Federal cavalry and then routed the force of about 350 infantry with a dismounted attack. He captured 95 wagons. At Patterson's Creek on 1 Feb. he captured the guard and brought off 1,200 cattle, 500 sheep, and 80 prisoners (Miller, IV, 108; Pond, 204n.).

ROSSVILLE (Gap), Ga. Feature of Missionary Ridge which figured prominently in CHICKAMAUGA and CHATTANOOGA CAMPAIGNS.

ROUND TOPS. Two small, rocky hills that figured prominently in the battle of GETTYSBURG.

ROUSSEAU, Lovell Harrison. Union gen. 1818–69. Ky. An Ind. lawyer and Whig legislator, he fought in the Mexican War and became the leading criminal lawyer in Louisville, also serving in the state senate. Active in keeping Ky. in the Union, he was commissioned Col. 3d Ky. 9 Sept. '61 and B.G. USV 1 Oct. '61. He commanded in the Army of the Ohio: 1st Brig., McCook's division; 4th Brig.; 4th Brig., 2d Div. 2 Dec. '61–11 July '62 at Shiloh; 3d Div., I Corps, at Perryville; and 3d Div. 11 July–29 Sept. '62. Then promoted Maj. Gen. USV 8 Oct. '62, he transferred to the Army of the Cumberland and led 1st Div., Centre, XIV (5 Nov. '62–9 Jan. '63); 1st Div., XIV (9–17 Jan. 29 Mar.–26 July, 21 Sept.–17 Nov. '63 at Chickamauga); Dist. Nashville (10 Nov. '63–3 July '65) when Hood attacked; 3d Div., XII (2 Jan.–14 Apr. '64); 4th, XX; and Dist. Mid. Tenn. He also commanded 2, 3, XXIII, N.C. 12–28 June '65. Resigning 30 Nov. '65, he became US Representative and was involved in the bitterness of Reconstruction. Going into the R.A. as B.G. USA in 1867, he was sent to Alaska to receive it from the Russians and arrived back in Washington too late to testify in the impeachment proceedings. He died on active duty while commanding the Dept. of La.

ROUSSEAU'S RAID TO OPELIKA, Ala., 9–22 July '64. (ATLANTA CAMPAIGN) At Sherman's request, and with troops drawn mainly from Kilpatrick's cavalry brigade near Chattanooga, Rousseau left Decatur, Ala., with 2,500 sabers to destroy the railroad between Montgomery, Ala., and Columbus, Ga. Marching through Blountsville, Ashville, and Talladega, he reached the rail junction near Opelika on the 17th. After spending 36 hours wrecking the railroad, he returned via Carrollton, Ga., to Marietta.

ROWANTY CREEK, Va., 5–7 Feb. '65. See DABNEY'S MILLS, same dates.

ROWETT, Richard. Union officer. England. Capt. 7th Ill. 25 Apr. '61; Maj. 1 Sept. '61; Lt. Col. 28 Apr. '62; Col. 2 July '63; Bvt. B.G. USV (war service). Commanded 3, 4, XV; 3, 2, XVI. Died 1887.

ROWLEY, Thomas Algeo. Union gen. 1808–92. Pa. A minor political officeholder, he had fought in the Mexican War and was commissioned Col. 13th Pa. 25 Apr. '61. Mustered out 6 Aug. '61, he was named Col. 102d Pa. 6 Aug. '61 and led his regiment at Yorktown, Williamsburg, Fair Oaks, Malvern Hill, Centreville, and Chantilly, and was in reserve at Antietam. He was promoted B.G. USV 29 Nov. '62 and commanded 3, 3, VI (Nov.–15 Dec. '62) at Fredericksburg. He succeeded to command of the division 30 June–2 July '63 and took over the 1st Brig. (2–10 July '63) at Gettysburg. He resigned 29 Dec. '64 and was US Marshal and a lawyer after the war.

ROWLEY, William Reuben. Union officer. 1824–86. N.Y. 1st Lt. 45th Ill. 20 Nov. '61; Capt. Add. A.D.C. 26 Feb. '62; Maj. A.D.C. Vols. 1 Nov. '62; Lt. Col. A.D.C. to Lt. Gen. Grant 29 Mar.–30 Aug. '64; Bvt. B.G. USV. Brevets for war service (3). Resigned 30 Aug. '64. Before the war he settled in Galena (Ill.), where he knew Grant. At Shiloh he rode from the Hornet's Nest toward Crump's Landing to alert Lew Wallace to bring his troops to the field. He died the day (9 Feb. '86) that closed the official term of mourning for Grant (Appleton's).

RUCKER, Daniel Henry. Union gen. 1812–? N.J. R.A. Joining the army in 1837 as 2d Lt. 1st US Dragoons, he served on the frontier and fought in the Mexican War (1 brevet). As Maj. Q.M. (3 Aug. '61) he commanded the Q.M. Depot in Washington from Apr. '61 until Jan. '67, being promoted Col. Add. A.D.C. 28 Sept. '61 and B.G. USV 23 May '63. Breveted for war service (Lt. Col., Col. B.G. USA 5 July '64, and Maj. Gen. USA and USV), he continued in the R.A., retiring as B.G. USV Q.M. Gen. of the Army in 1882.

RUFF, Charles F. Union officer. c. 1817–85. Pa. USMA 1838 (44/45); Dragoons-Cav. He served on the frontier and resigned in 1843 to practice law but fought in the Mexican War (1 brevet, 1 wound) as Capt. U.S. Mtd. Rifles. Continuing in the R.A., he served in Indian scouting and fighting and was promoted Lt. Col. 3d US Cav. 10 June '61. He was mustering officer in Philadelphia until 1863, when he became Acting I.G. of the Dept. of the Susquehanna (29 June–29 Sept. '63). On the latter date he was awaiting orders "when the prosecution of the court-martial, before which he was arraigned, was abandoned" until 25 Mar. '64 and then retired for "disability, resulting from disease and exposure in the line of duty" (Cullum). On 13 Mar. '65 he was breveted Col. and B.G. USA.

RUFFIN (ruf'-fin), Edmund. Ancient and ardent secessionist. 1794–1865. Va. Prominent agriculturist and writer. Joined Palmetto Guard of S.C. and accompanied them to FORT SUMTER. Sometimes credited with firing the first shot, although it would probably be more accurate to say that after Capt. James had fired the signal gun (B.&L., I, 76) Ruffin fired the first shot from the Stevens battery on Cummings Point. (Even this is questionable.) He committed suicide (gunshot) 15 June '65 "because he was unwilling to live under the US government" (Appleton's).

RUGER, Thomas Howard. Union gen. 1833–1907. N.Y. Appt.-Wis. USMA 1854 (3/46); Engrs.-Inf. Resigning a year after graduation, he practiced law until commissioned Lt. Col. 3d Wis. 29 June '61 and was promoted Col. 1 Sept. '61. He led his regiment in the Shenandoah campaign the next spring and commanded 3, 1, XII (17 Sept.–30 Oct. '62) at Antietam. Promoted B.G. USV 29 Nov. '62, he next commanded 1, 2, XII (20 Oct.–30 Dec. '62); and succeeded to command of the division (1–4 July '63) for Gettysburg. He was sent to N.Y. during the Draft Riots in Aug. '63, and then in the Army of the Cumberland led 3, 1, XII (25 Sept. '63–14 Apr. '64) and 2, 1, XX (14 Apr.–17 Sept. '64 at Resaca, New Hope Church, Peach Tree Creek, and Atlanta; and 17 Oct.–5 Nov. '64). He then led the 2d Div., XIII, Ohio (11 Nov.–8 Dec. '64) at Franklin and commanded the 1st Div. 29 Dec. '64–2 Feb. '65. Commanding the same division, XXIII, N.C. (18 Mar.–17 June '65) at J. E. Johnston's surrender, he also led 1st Div., Prov. Corps, N.C. 25 Feb.–18 Mar. '65 and the Dept. of N.C. 17–27 June '65. Breveted for Franklin and Gettysburg (B.G. USA), he con-

tinued in the R.A. After serving as Superintendent at USMA (1871–76), he commanded the Dept. of the South until 1878 and then the Dist. of Mont. until 1885, retiring in 1897 as Maj. Gen. USA.

RUGGLES, Daniel. C.S.A. gen. 1810–97. Mass. USMA 1833 (34/43); Inf. He served on the frontier, in the Mexican War (2 brevets), and in Indian scouting before resigning 7 May '61 as Bvt. Lt. Col. Commissioned B.G. of Va. state troops, he served from Apr. to July along the Potomac and was appointed B.G. C.S.A. 9 Aug. '61. Sent in Oct. '61 to New Orleans to join Twiggs, he was ill on arrival but recovered to lead the 1st Div., II Corps, at Shiloh. The following May he was sent by Bragg to command the depots and rear guard and in June '62 was named commander of La. east of the Mississippi, with headquarters at Jackson and with Van Dorn as his immediate superior. Replaced in Jan. '63 by J. Adams, he was assigned in Aug. '63 to J. E. Johnston. However, by the spring of 1864 he was virtually without a command and desperately trying to get one. He ended the war in Richmond. He was later in real estate, farming, and on the USMA Board of Visitors.

RUGGLES, George David. Union officer. c. 1833–1904. N.Y. USMA 1855 (19/34); Inf. He served on the frontier and was promoted 1st Lt. 2d US Inf. 2 May and Capt. Asst. Adj. Gen. 3 Aug. '61. After serving as Pope's Chief of Staff and Adj. Gen., he was Asst. Adj. Gen. of the Army of the Potomac in Md. He served on special duty in the War Dept. until 19 Mar. '63 and in the Provost Marshal Gen.'s office until 16 Aug. '64. Then on inspection duty, he was named Adj. Gen. of the Army of the Potomac 1 Feb.–30 June '65. Continuing in the R.A., he was breveted

B.G. USA and B.G. USV 9 Apr. '65 for war service and retired in 1897 as B.G. USA, the Adj. Gen.

RUGGLES, James M. Union officer. Ohio, 1st Lt. Regt. Q.M. 1st Ill. Cav. 10 July '61; Maj. 3d Ill. Cav. 16 Aug. '61; Lt. Col. 25 July '62; Bvt. B.G. USV (war service); mustered out 5 Sept. '64. Died 1901.

RUMSEY, Elida. See Elida R. FOWLE.

RUNKLE, Benjamin Piatt. Union officer. Ohio. Commissioned Capt. 13th Ohio 22 Apr. '61, he fought at Carnifex Ferry and was promoted Maj. 8 Nov. of that year. Wounded at Shiloh, he was named Col. 45th Ohio 19 Aug. '62 and served in Ky. In June '63 he served on the Ohio governor's staff and later commanded a brigade in Ky. and Tenn. He was mustered out 21 July '64 and commissioned Lt. Col. Vet. Res. Corps 22 Aug. of that year. On duty with the Memphis Freedman's Bureau for the remainder of the war, he continued in the R.A. as Maj. 45th US Inf., Bvt. B.G. USV and Bvt. Maj. Gen. USV. Retired in 1870, he was cashiered three years later, reinstated in 1877, and restored in 1887 "to be borne as never having been legally separated from the army (decision Supreme Court 27 May '87)" (Heitman).

RUSH'S LANCERS. The 6th Pa. Cav., which until May '63 was armed with lances. See also EDGED WEAPONS.

RUSK, Jeremiah McClain. Union officer. 1830–93. Ohio. Maj. 25th Wis. 14 Aug. '62; Lt. Col. 16 Sept. '63; Bvt. B.G. USV (war service). W.I.A. 20 Jan. '65 Salkehatchie River (Ga.). Narrowly escaped capture and had horse shot from under him at Decatur (Ga.) 17 July '64. After working as a farmer, stage driver, railroad construction foreman, and tavernkeeper, he became a prosperous businessman in the postwar era, owning a farm and part of a bank and a stage line. As Gov. of Wis. (1881–88) he ordered the troops to fire into the crowd during the industrial strike riots, justifying his decision in the famous words: "I seen my duty and I done it." Appointed Sec. of Agriculture 1889–93.

RUSLING, James Fowler. Union officer. N.J. 1st Lt. Regt. Q.M. 5th N.J. 24 Aug. '61; Capt. Asst. Q.M. Vols. 11 June '62; Lt. Col. Q.M. Assigned 27 May–7 July '63; Col. Q.M. Assigned 29 Apr. '65–1 Jan. '67; Bvt. B.G. USV 16 Feb. '65 (war service).

RUSSELL, Charles Sawyer. Union officer. Mass. Sgt. 11th Ind. 19 Apr.–30 June '61; Capt. 11th US Inf. 14 May '61; Lt. Col. US Col. Inf. 1 May '64; Col. 28th US Col. Inf. 27 Aug. '64; Bvt. B.G. USV 30 July '64 (Cemetery Hill, Va.). Other brevets for Antietam, Chancellorsville, Petersburg mine assault. Commanded 2, 4, IX (Potomac); 2, 3, IX (Potomac); 1, 2, XXV; 3, 2, XXV; 2, 1, XXV; Attached Brig., 1, XXV; 1, 3, XXV (Tex.). Died 1866.

RUSSELL, David Allen. Union gen. 1820–64. N.Y. USMA 1845 (38/41); Inf. He served on the frontier and in the Mexican War (1 brevet) and participated in Indian fighting when named Col. 7th Mass. 18 Feb. '62. He led his regiment during the Peninsular campaign and at South Mountain and Antietam. Promoted B.G. USV 29 Nov. '62, he commanded 3, 1, VI (10 Dec. '62–23 Feb. '63) at Fredericksburg. Distinguished himself at RAPPAHANNOCK BRIDGE 7 Nov. '63. He was wounded in this action but recovered to take command of 2, 3, VI (25 Mar.–7 Apr. '64). At the Wilderness and Petersburg he again commanded 1st Div., VI Corps (9 May–8 July '64). On 6 Aug. '64 he took over 1st Div., VI, Shenandoah, and led them at Opequon where, on 19

Sept., he was wounded in the chest. Concealing this, he continued giving orders on horseback for the rest of the day until killed by a shell fragment through the heart. He was breveted for the Peninsular campaign, Gettysburg, the Wilderness (B.G. USA 6 May '64), and Opequon (Maj. Gen. USV and USA 19 Sept. '64).

RUSSELL, Henry Sturgis. Union officer. Mass. 1st Lt. 2d Mass. 25 May '61; Capt. 13 Dec. '61; Lt. Col. 2d Mass. Cav. 19 Mar. '63; Lt. Col. 5th Mass. Cav. 7 Mar. '64; Col. 5th Mass. Cav. 7 Mar. '64; Bvt. B.G. USV (war service, Baylor's Farm before Petersburg); resigned 14 Feb. '65. Captured at Cedar Mountain 9 Aug. '62. W.I.A. Petersburg 15 June '64.

RUSSELL, William Howard. English war correspondent. 1820–1907. Famous as a war correspondent before and after the Civil War, he exposed mismanagement in the Crimean War (1855–56) and contributed to the fall of the Aberdeen ministry. He is credited with inspiring the work of Florence Nightingale, and with applying the phrase "thin red line" to the British infantry at Balaklava. In America, 1861–63, as a correspondent for the London *Times*. Referring to McDowell's green troops as a "rabble" army, he earned the nickname "Bull Run" Russell for his panic-stricken flight from that battlefield. Of his American experiences he wrote *My Diary, North and South . . ., 1862*. He was knighted in May 1895.

RUSSIAN THUNDERBOLT. See John Basil TURCHIN.

RUST, Albert. C.S.A. gen. Ark. A lawyer and US Congressman, he was commissioned Col. 3d Ark. 5 July '61 and sent to CHEAT MOUNTAIN, W. Va. Here he had a prominent part in R. E.

Lee's unsuccessful operation of 10–15 Sept. '61. He continued to serve in W. Va. until he went into the Shenandoah with Jackson. Appointed B.G. C.S.A. 6 Mar. '62 to rank from the 4th, he led his brigade at Corinth, joined Price in the Trans-Miss. Dept. in Apr. '63, and served there for the rest of the war.

RUST, Henry. Union officer. Me. Sgt. 1st Me. 3 May '61; 1st Lt. 6 May '61; mustered out 5 Aug. '61; Capt. 10th Me. 5 Oct. '61; Lt. Col. 13th Me. 10 Dec. '61; Col. 20 Oct. '63; Bvt. B.G. USV (war service); mustered out 6 Jan. '65. Commanded 2, 4, XIII; 2, 1, XIX. Died 1881.

RUST, John D. Union officer. Me. Lt. Col. 8th Me. 7 Sept. '61; Col. 1 Jan. '62; Bvt. B.G. USV (war service); resigned 19 Aug. '64. Commanded 2, 3, X (Va. and N.C.). Died 1890.

RUTHERFORD, Allan. Union officer. c. 1836–1900. N.Y. Capt. 83d N.Y. 27 May '61; Maj. 7 Jan. '62; Lt. Col. 1 Oct. '62; resigned 25 Nov. '62; Lt. Col. Vet. Res. Corps 4 Dec. '63; Bvt. Lt. Col. and Col. Vols. 13 Mar. '65 (war service). W.I.A. 2d Bull Run by gunshot in head; also suffering from t.b. Continued in R.A. until resigned in 1870 as Capt. Other brevets for 2d Bull Run. Phisterer lists him as a Bvt. B.G. USV (13 Mar. '65) while Heitman gives his highest rank, brevet or full, as Col. (13 Mar. '65).

RUTHERFORD, Friend Smith. Union gen. 1820–64. N.Y. A lawyer, he was named Capt. Comsy. of Subsist. Vols. 30 June '62. Resigning 2 Sept. '62, he was named Col. 97th Ill. 16 Sept. and was at Chickasaw Bayou, Arkansas Post, Champion's Hill, Big Black River, Vicksburg assault, and Jackson. Resigning 15 June '64 because of his health, he died five days later from exposure and fatigue and was appointed B.G. USV **a** week after that. Brother of Reuben C. and George V. Rutherford.

RUTHERFORD, George Valentine. Union officer. Vt. Capt. Asst. Q.M. Vols. 2 Apr. '63; Col. Q.M. Assigned 2 Aug. '64–10 Nov. '66; Bvt. B.G. USV (war service). Died 1876.

RUTHERFORD, Reuben Clifford. Union officer. N.Y. Pvt. Co. E 10th Ill. 29 Apr. '61; 2d Lt. 18 May '61; Regt. Q.M. 20 May '61; resigned 9 Oct. '61; Capt. Comsy. of Subsist. Vols. 26 Nov. '62; Capt. Asst. Q.M. Vols. 20 Dec. '64; Bvt. B.G. USV (Q.M. Dept. service).

S

SABINE CROSS ROADS (Mansfield), La., 8 Apr. '64. (RED RIVER CAMPAIGN) After withdrawing 200 miles in the face of Banks's superior forces, Taylor organized a defensive position three miles southeast of Mansfield. The latter was a vital road center whose possession would facilitate Banks's advance. In the absence of instructions from his superior, Kirby Smith, in Shreveport, Taylor made preparations to defend Mansfield.

Thomas Green's cavalry was being pushed back by Federal cavalry and infantry under Albert Lee and Landram, respectively. Taylor moved his two available infantry divisions into a defensive position early 8 Apr.: Walker's three brigades were on the right and Mouton's two brigades on the left. As Green's troopers withdrew to this position they were dismounted and posted on Mouton's left. The area was heavily wooded, making artillery employment difficult. Taylor estimates that he had 5,300 infantry, 3,000 cavalrymen, and 500 artillerymen present.

The Federal advance guard probed this position during the morning. Banks visited them and ordered Franklin (C.G. XIX) to move up Cameron's and Emory's divisions to support Landram and Lee. Taylor issued orders for Churchill to bring his two divisions up

to reinforce the Confederate line. Neither commander intended to fight a major engagement until the next day. When Federal infantry was seen to be with their cavalry advance guard, however, Taylor reinforced Mouton with Randal's brigade of Walker's division. Then, at about 4 P.M., Taylor ordered his line forward. A general assault developed. Mouton's troops charged the Federal right, Green's dismounted cavalry enveloped their flank, and Walker crushed the opposite flank. Landram's division was routed just as Cameron arrived. The latter was then driven back from a second position at about 5 P.M. Emory was moving up when the first two positions had been overrun. He deployed about three miles behind the original line of contact and had just gotten into position when the Confederate advance reached him at about 6 P.M. After an hour and a half's fight the battle ended without any further Federal loss of ground. This action is known as Pleasant Grove. During the night Taylor attempted to turn the Federal right, but was stopped. Then Banks withdrew, and the next day repulsed Taylor's attack at PLEASANT HILL, 9 Apr.

The battle of Sabine Cross Roads marked the end of Banks's advance. According to Taylor's book (p. 197), it cost the Federals 2,500 prisoners, 20 guns, and 250 wagons (Albert Lee's entire train). Federal losses as reported in E.&B. are 2,900 (200 killed, 900 wounded, 1,800 missing). The following estimate is computed from those of Fox (who combines losses for Sabine Cross Roads with those for Pleasant Hill), and Livermore (who gives the losses for the latter battle only): 2,148 total (108 killed, 643 wounded, 1,397 missing). The Confederates lost about 1,000 total (Livermore, 110).

SABINE PASS, Tex. On 21 Jan. '63 two Confederate cotton-clad steamers attacked the blockading force composed of the sailing ship *Morning Star* and the schooner *Velocity*. The Federal ships, unable to maneuver, were captured with a loss of 13 guns, 109 prisoners, and $1,000,000 worth of property (Campbell, 212). The blockade was resumed the next day by the *New London* and *Cayuga* (B.&L., III, 571). After Banks's unsuccessful attempt to capture the position 8 Sept. '63 (see below), the Confederates held the place until 25 May '65, when they evacuated it.

SABINE PASS, Tex., 8 Sept. '63. As the initial undertaking of the TEXAS COAST OPERATIONS OF BANKS IN 1863, Franklin left New Orleans on 5 Sept. with 4,000 men of his XIX Corps (Gulf) and a naval escort to capture Sabine Pass. On the 7th his transports arrived off the pass. Later in the day he was joined by four gunboats under Lt. Frederick Crocker, USN. At 3:30 on the afternoon of the 8th the *Clifton*, *Sachem*, and *Arizona* entered the pass and attacked the fort that defended it. Half an hour later the *Sachem* was hit in the boilers, and a few minutes later the *Clifton* ran aground and suffered the same fate. About 4:30 both ships were forced to surrender, after having lost about 70 men. (The fourth vessel, *Granite City*, was not engaged.) The operation was then abandoned, and in

Oct. Banks undertook an expedition to the mouth of the Rio Grande.

SABOT. A block of wood that enables the projectile and the cartridge to be attached to form "fixed ammunition" for a field gun.

SACKET, Delos B. Union officer. c.1821–85. N.Y. USMA 1845 (32/41); Dragoons-I.G. He fought in the Mexican War (1 brevet) and served on the frontier in the Kans. border disturbances before being promoted Maj. 1st US Cav. 31 Jan. '61. As Lt. Col. 2d US Cav. 3 May and Col. I.G. 1 Oct. '61, he was Inspecting Officer of the Army of the Potomac 13 Dec. '61–10 Jan. '63, served on boards and commissions until 1 Apr. '64 and then became I.G. for the Depts. of the Tenn., Cumberland, Ark., and N. Mex. He was breveted B.G. USA and Maj. Gen. USA for war service, continued in the R.A., and died on active duty as B.G. USA I.G.

SACKETT, William. Union officer. N.Y. Maj. 9th N.Y. Cav. 20 Nov. '61; Lt. Col. 27 June '62; Col. 1 May '63; Bvt. B.G. USV (Trevilian Station, Va.). W.I.A. 11 June '64 at Trevilian Station, and died of this 14 June '64.

SAFFORD, Mary J. SANITARY COM· MISSION worker. Young and comely, she had started nursing in Cairo (Ill.) when the first western casualties began to come upriver. Called "The Angel of Cairo" by the soldiers, she worked until exhaustion and a spine injury overtook her after Shiloh, and was sent to Paris for treatment by her wealthy brother.

SAILOR'S CREEK, Va. Misspelling of SAYLER'S CREEK.

ST. AUGUSTINE, Fla., 8 Mar. '61. Surrendered to Capt. C. R. P. Rodgers, USN.

ST. JOHN, Isaac Munroe. C.S.A. comsy. gen. 1827–80. Ga. After graduating from Yale he practiced law in N.Y.C., edited a newspaper in Baltimore, and was also engaged in railroading and engineering. He served as engineer under Magruder in fortifying the Peninsula and was named Maj. and Chief of the Mining and Nitre Bureau in May '62. Promoted Col. later on, he was appointed B.G. C.S.A. and Comsy. Gen. 16 Feb. '65. After the war he was a railroad engineer in Ky.

SALEM CHURCH, Tenn. An action at JACKSON, Tenn., 19 Dec. '62.

SALEM CHURCH, Va. 3–4 May '63. (CHANCELLORSVILLE CAMPAIGN) After finally capturing Marye's Heights, above Fredericksburg, shortly after noon on 3 May, Sedgwick continued west toward Chancellorsville to link up with Hooker's main body. Since Early had withdrawn southwest along the Telegraph Road, only the brigade of Wilcox contested Sedgwick's advance.

Lee learned of this long expected threat just as he was about to complete his victory in the Wilderness. He withdrew four brigades (Kershaw and Mahone, then Wofford and Semmes) and sent them under command of McLaws to counter it. By 4 P.M. Wilcox had been pushed back to Salem Church, where McLaws soon joined him to organize a strong Confederate defense. About an hour later Sedgwick's forces launched a series of attacks that lasted until dark. The Federals, who had lost nearly 5,000 since morning, were unable to break through.

Shortly after daylight on 4 May Lee took advantage of Hooker's inactivity to mass more strength against Sedgwick in an attempt to destroy him. Leaving only the corps of Jackson (now temporarily under Jeb Stuart) to contain the main Federal force in the Wilderness, Lee ordered R. H. Anderson to pull the remainder of his division out of the line and to move against Sedgwick. Anderson, however, was not able to get into position on McLaws' right

(Sedgwick's south) until about 6 P.M. Meanwhile, Early had reoccupied Marye's Heights soon after dawn, and was in position to strike Sedgwick's rear.

Despite the fact that it was almost dark before all Lee's forces were ready to advance, the Confederates launched an assault from three directions and continued to attack during the night. Sedgwick was able not only to keep his lines from being penetrated, but was successful in withdrawing his entire corps northwest across the Rappahannock near BANKS'S FORD and in avoiding annihilation.

SALEM CHURCH, Va., 27 May '64. Incident in Grant's movement to TOTOPOTOMOY CREEK, but not reported. E.&B. list gives it as alternate name for HAW'S SHOP, ¼ mile southeast. (O.R. Atlas, Plate XCII.)

SALIENT, THE, Va., 12 May '64. Part of battle of SPOTSYLVANIA.

SALISBURY (N.C.) PRISON. An abandoned cotton factory was turned into a Confederate PRISON in Nov. '61 and was at first designed for spies, Confederate soldiers being court-martialed and deserters as well as prisoners of war. The first Federals came in Dec. '61, and by Mar. '62 there were around 1,500. Food was abundant, quarters were spacious, the weather was salubrious, and in Mar. only one inmate died. These conditions lasted until early 1864, when the prison's capacity was reached, and by Oct. '64 around 10,000 were being held there. When shelter became inadequate, the prisoners lived in tents, burrowed into the earth, or built mud huts partly above and partly below the ground. From Oct. '64 to Feb. '65, 3,419 prisoners died.

SALM-SALM, Princess Agnes. Army wife extraordinary. 1842–81. Her place of birth is given variously as Md. (Appleton's), or Canada, or Vt. (D.A.B.), but she refused to reveal her antecedents. She married Salm-Salm in 1862 under the name of Agnes Leclerq, after having been a circus rider and actress and living in Cuba. Described as lovely, charming, and intelligent, she followed her husband in the field and influenced his career, persuading important people to give him jobs and commissions. Her good deeds for the Bridgeport (Tenn.) hospital won a captain's commission and pay privileges for her from Ill. Gov. Yates. She went with her husband to Mexico and then Europe and, after his death, raised a hospital brigade for the Franco-Prussian War.

SALM-SALM, Prince Felix. Prussian nobleman and Union officer. 1828–70. Prussia. A.D.C. to Gen. Blenker 1861; Col. 8th N.Y. 21 Oct. '62; mustered out 23 Apr. '63; Col. 68th N.Y. 8 June '64; Bvt. B.G. USV (Nashville). He was the younger son of the reigning Prince zu Salm-Salm. Educated at the Cadet School in Berlin, he served in the Prussian cavalry during the Schleswig-Holstein war and was decorated for bravery at Aarhuis (Appleton's). He then joined the Austrian army but shortly resigned for financial reasons. In 1861 he came to the US to offer his services to the Federal government and was assigned to Blenker. After the war he went to Mexico to help Emperor Maximilian and there served as Col. of the General Staff, Maximilian's A.D.C., and Chief of the Foreign Legion. When the Emperor's government fell, he was captured but soon allowed to return to Europe. Re-entering the Prussian army as a Maj. in the Grenadier Guards, he was killed at the battle of Gravelotte.

SALOMON, Charles Eberhard. Union officer. Prussia. Capt. 5th Mo. May '61; Col. 18 May '61; Mustered out 26 Aug. '61; Col. 9th Wis. 26 Sept. '62; Bvt. B.G. USV (war service); mustered out 3 Dec.

'64. Commanded 1, 1, VII; 1, 3, VII. Fled Germany after serving as an officer in the 1848 revolution. Brother of Brig. Gen. Frederick S. Salomon and Wis. Gov. Edward S. Salomon.

SALOMON, Edward S. Gov. of Wis. 1828–? Prussia. After fighting in the 1848 revolution, he fled when that movement collapsed and finally settled in Wis. He was a lawyer and regent of the state university when elected Lt. Gov. by the Republicans, although he himself was a Democrat in 1861. Serving until 1863, he then practiced law in N.Y. Brother of Carl (Charles) Eberhard and Frederick Sigel Salomon, Union generals.

SALOMON, Edward Selig. Union officer. Germany. 1st Lt. 24th Ill. 8 July '61; mustered out 4 Dec. '61; Lt. Col. 82d Ill. 26 Sept. '62; Bvt. B.G. USV (war service). Lonn says he raised and commanded the wealthiest unit in the entire Union army, a company supported by the Chicago Jewish element. They joined Hecker's regiment in appreciation of his liberal attitude toward the Jews. Salomon commanded the division when Hecker was wounded at Chancellorsville. He was appointed Gov. of the Washington Territory after the war. He is no relation to the Salomons of Wis.

SALOMON, Frederick Sigel. Union gen. 1826–97. Prussia. A surveyor and engineer, he had fled Germany in 1848 with his brothers (Edward S. and Charles E., above) after fighting on the losing side of the revolution. Commissioned Capt. 5th Mo. 19 May '61, he fought with Sigel at Wilson's Creek and was mustered out 14 Aug. Named Col. 9th Wis. 26 Nov. '61, he was promoted B.G. USV 16 June '62 and commanded 1st Brig., Kans. (24 Aug.–12 Oct. '62). He then led 1st Brig., 1st Div. Army Frontier, Mo. and Dist. Eastern Ark.,

XIII, Tenn. (June–July '63). Also in the Army of the Tenn., he led 1, 13, XIII (8 Feb.–25 May '63); 13th Div., XIII (25 May–28 July '63); 13th Div., XVI (28 July–10 Aug. '63); 1st Brig., Dist. Eastern Ark., XVI; 3d Div., Ark. expedition. He also commanded the 3d Div. (6 Jan.–11 May '64) and the 1st Div. (11 May–25 July and 25 Sept. '64–1 Aug. '65) in the VII Corps, Ark. Breveted for war service (Maj. Gen. USV), he was mustered out 24 Aug. '65 and then moved to the Utah territory.

SALOMON GUARDS. 9th Wis., which was raised by one brother, Frederick; commanded by another, Charles Eberhard; and named after a third, Edward S., Gov. of Wis. (All these SALOMONS are covered above.)

SALT BEEF. Standard army ration of pickled beef preserved in brine so strong that it was inedible unless soaked thoroughly in water before cooking. Often the pickling process was not successful. Also called salt horse.

SALT HORSE. See SALT BEEF.

SAM. See SHERMAN'S HORSES.

SANBORN, John Benjamin. Union gen. 1826–? N.H. A lawyer and officeholder, he organized five infantry regiments, one cavalry battalion, and two artillery battalions as A.G. and Q.M. Gen. of Minn. Commissioned Col. 4th Minn. 23 Dec. '61, he commanded 1st Brig., 3d Div., Army Miss. (25 June–30 Sept. '62) at Iuka and 1, 7, XIII, Tenn. (1 Nov.–18 Dec. '62). During the Vicksburg campaign he led the 7th Div., XVII, Tenn. (14 Apr.–2 May '63), having commanded the 1st Brig. of that division from 5 Feb. to 12 Apr. '63. Promoted B.G. USV 4 Aug. '63, he commanded the Dist. of Southwest Mo. (15 Oct. '63–9 Dec. '64 and 9 Jan.–10 June '65) and Dist. Upper Ark. (1 July '65). Breveted Maj. Gen. USV 10 Feb. '65, he was mustered out in 1866.

SANBORN, William. Union officer. Me. Maj. 22 Mich. 8 Aug. '62; Lt. Col. 5 Jan. '63; Bvt. B.G. USV. Brevets for Chickamauga, war service. Discharged 7 June '64. Died 1876.

SANDERS, Addison Hiatt. Union officer. Ohio. Lt. Col. 16th Iowa 24 Mar. '62; Bvt. B.G. USV. Brevets for war service. Listed by Phisterer as Saunders, Addison H.

SANDERS, Horace T. Union officer. N.Y. Col. 19th Wis. 17 Apr. '62; Bvt. B.G. USV 19 Apr. '65 (war service). In 1863 he was president of the Military Commission and Provost Judge of Norfolk (Va.). Commanded 3, 1, XVIII.

SANDERS, John Calhoun. C.S.A. gen. 1840–64. Ala. He left the Univ. of Ala. to become Capt. 11th Ala. He fought at Seven Pines, Gaines's Mill, and Frayser's Farm, where he was wounded in the leg. Rejoining his regiment 11 Aug. '62, he led them at Antietam, where he was wounded slightly. He was promoted Col. shortly after that and led them at Fredericksburg, Chancellorsville, and Gettysburg, where he was wounded in the knee. That winter (1863–64) he was president of the division court-martial, led the regiment at the Wilderness, succeeded to brigade command at Spotsylvania, and was appointed B.G. C.S.A. 31 May '64. During the Petersburg siege he commanded the Ala. brig. and was killed 21 Aug. '64 at Weldon R.R.

SANDERS, William Price. Union gen. 1833–63. Ky. Appt.-Miss. USMA 1856 (41/49); Cav. He served in frontier garrisons and was promoted 1st Lt. 2d US Dragoons 10 May '61. As Capt. 3d US Cav. (four days later) and 6th US Cav. (3 Aug. '61), he fought at Yorktown, Williamsburg, Mechanicsville, and Hanover C.H. He was named Col. 5th Ky. Cav. 4 Mar. '63 and pursued Morgan's raiders July–Aug. of that year before being appointed B.G. USV 18 Oct. '63. As Chief of Cav. Dept. of the Ohio Oct.–Nov. '63, he fought at Blue Lick Springs, Lenore, and Campbell's Station, where he was mortally wounded 16 Nov. '63. He died three days later. FORT SANDERS (Knoxville) was named in his honor.

SANDERSON, Thomas Wakefield. Union officer. Pa. 1st Lt. Adj. 2d Ohio Cav. 12 Sept. '61; Capt. 7 Oct. '61; resigned 14 May '62; Maj. 10th Ohio Cav. 15 Jan. '63; Lt. Col. 2 Aug. '64; Col. 9 Apr. '65; Bvt. B.G. USV (war service). Commanded 2, 3, Cav. Corps (Cumberland).

SANDERSVILLE (Buffalo Creek), Ga. 25–26 Nov. '64. (MARCH TO THE SEA) Wheeler's cavalry attacked the advance guard of the XIV and XX Corps as they approached Sandersville on the 25th. The next day Carman's brigade (2, 1, XX) started skirmishing about two miles from the town with forces under command of Maj. A. L. Hartridge. An attack by Col. T. S. Hughes's 9th Ill. Mtd. Inf. dislodged the road block, and an exploitation by the 13th N.J. drove the enemy back. The Confederates evacuated Sandersville in the face of the two Federal corps converging on that place.

SANFORD, Edward Sewall. Union officer. N.Y. Col. Add. A.D.C. 26 Feb. '62; Bvt. B.G. USV (war service). Died 1882.

SANITARY COMMISSION, United States. Inspired by British Sanitary Commission of Crimean war and an outgrowth of various women's organizations, this was unified into Women's Central Association of Relief (in the N.Y.C. area) by Dr. Henry W. Bellows in Apr. '61. The object was to do for the soldiers what the government did not do, and this included raising the hygienic standards of the camps and diet, caring for the wounded, coordinating the program to send food and supplies to the soldiers, and compiling a directory of the sick and wounded in army hospitals. A home in Washington for discharged soldiers and lodges near railroad stations for transients were also among its projects. Skepticism was expressed when the plan was first proposed that it would be a 'fifth wheel to the coach."

SAN JACINTO, USS. See TRENT AFFAIR.

SANTA ROSA ISLAND (PENSACOLA BAY), 8–9 Oct. '61. The night of 8–9 Oct. R. H. Anderson led an amphibious raid on 1,063 men. His mission was to disrupt Federal preparations to bombard Bragg's positions on the mainland and to retaliate for Harvey Brown's successful raids of 2 and 14 Sept. Anderson's force was divided into three columns under J. R. Chalmers, J. P. Anderson, and J. K. Jackson (all of whom were eventually generals), and a special "demolition team" under Lt. J. H. Hallonquist.

The Confederates landed undetected at 2 A.M. At about 3:30 they surprised and routed about 250 men of William Wilson's 6th N. Y. Zouaves, inflicting 27 casualties and partially burning their deserted camp. From Fort Pickens, about a mile away, Harvey Brown ordered Majs. Israel Vodges and L. G. Arnold (both later generals), with four companies of regulars, to move to the scene of action. Having now lost surprise, the Confederates withdrew to their boats. Their withdrawal was jeopardized when the propeller of one boat (*Neaffie*) was entangled in a hawser.

Total Federal casualties were reported at 67, including Vodges captured. Anderson reported a loss of 87; he himself was temporarily incapacitated by a painful wound in the left elbow. Bragg considered the operation a success. McClellan congratulated Brown for "another instance of skill and good conduct on the part of the beleaguered garrison of Fort Pickens. . . ." Brown considered the conduct of the Wilson Zouaves unsatisfactory, and recommended that they be disbanded and the men transferred into the regular companies at Pickens. "The material of the rank and file is very good, and in the hands of even respectably intelligent officers might be made efficient . . ." he wrote the A.G. in Washington (O.R., I, VI, 442).

SAP ROLLER. Cylindrical object of basketwork rolled ahead of men constructing a sap (trench) toward the enemy to provide cover from the enemy's small-arms fire. (For an illustration, see Miller, V, 209.)

SARGENT, Horace Binney. Union officer. 1821–?. Mass. Lt. Col. 1st Mass. Cav. 19 Nov. '61; Col. 1 Nov. '62; Bvt. B.G. USV 21 Mar. '64 (Bayou Rapides, La.); resigned 29 Sept. '64. Served as senior aide on staff of Mass. Gov. John A. Andrew; also A.D.C. to Gen. Mower. W.I.A. at Henderson Hills (Bayou Rapides) 21 Mar. '64. A cousin of John Singer Sargent, the artist.

SATTERLEE, Richard Smith. Union officer. N.Y. Appt.-Mich. Joining the R.A. in 1822 as Asst. Surgeon, he served on the frontier and in the Mexican War as Worth's Chief Surgeon. As Maj. (since 1832), he was Attending Surgeon and Medical Purveyor in N.Y.C. from 1854 until 1866. He retired in 1869 as Lt. Col. and Bvt. B.G. USA (2 Sept. '64). Died in 1880.

SAUNDERS, Addison H. Erroneous listing by Phisterer for Sanders, Addison Hiatt.

SAVAGE'S STATION AND ALLEN'S FARM (Peach Orchard), Va., 29 June '62. Part of the Seven Days' Battles of the PENINSULAR CAMPAIGN.

The night of 27 June, after GAINES'S MILL, McClellan gave his corps commanders orders for a withdrawal to the James River. Keyes (IV Corps) would cross White Oak Swamp the next day and protect the Federal left (west) flank. Porter (V) would follow. The other corps, Franklin (VI), Sumner (II), and Heintzelman (III), were to pull out the night of 28–29 June and constitute the rear guard. Not until early on the 29th, when he was certain which direction McClellan was moving, did Lee give orders for the pursuit. Jackson was to reconstruct the Grapevine Bridge and then, with the divisions of Ewell, Whiting, and D. H. Hill under his command, to advance between the Chickahominy and White Oak Swamp. Magruder was to advance east and cooperate with Jackson's command in maintaining pressure on the enemy's rear. To encircle the retreating Federals, Huger was to take the Charles City road and on the 30th hit the enemy's flank south of the swamp. Longstreet, commanding his division and A. P. Hill's, was to cross the Chickahominy at New Bridge, and proceed via the Darbytown road to attack McClellan's flank. T. H. Holmes, who had been south of the James at Fort Darling, was ordered to cross the river and operate on Longstreet's right to head off the Federal retreat.

After his abortive attacks of 27–28 June (GARNETT'S AND GOLDING'S FARMS), Magruder was still anticipating an attack when, actually, the enemy had withdrawn behind a small covering force. Early 29 June, when notified that Longstreet's forces had already crossed the Chickahominy and were in the abandoned enemy lines, Magruder started forward. About a mile beyond Fair Oaks he made contact at 9 A.M. near Allen's Farm (Peach Orchard) with Sumner's corps. Sumner delayed the Confederates until 11 A.M. and then withdrew to Savage's Station where Franklin had already started organizing the next position. Heintzelman was supposed to move his corps in on the south flank of this position, blocking the Williamsburg road, but he later decided there were already too many Federal troops in the area to operate effectively; without notifying the other two corps commanders he withdrew south across White Oak Swamp. After much unwarranted delay (and still thinking he was in danger of being attacked), Magruder attacked sometime after 4 P.M. Of six brigades available he used only two and a half. Kershaw, south of the railroad, was stopped by Burns's brigade (2, 2, II) and the 1st Minn. Semmes, on Kershaw's right, and supported by the 17th and 21st Miss. from Barksdale's (formerly Griffin's) brigade, was stopped by Brooks's brigade (2, 2, VI). The 5TH VERMONT particularly distinguished itself in a counterattack. Darkness and a severe thunderstorm halted the battle. Jackson's delay in arriving (3 A.M. the next day) saved the Federal rear guard from a serious defeat; they withdrew during the night, leaving large quantities of supplies and 2,500 men in a field hospital. Losses at Allen's Farm (Peach Orchard) and Savage's Station were 1,590 Federals and 626 Confederates (Fox).

SAVANNAH CAMPAIGN. See MARCH TO THE SEA, 15 Nov.–21 Dec. '64.

"SAVIOUR OF THE VALLEY." See Thomas L. ROSSER.

SAWTELLE, Charles Greene. Union officer. c.1835–1913. Me. USMA 1854 (38/46); Inf. He served on the frontier in the Kans. border disturbances and was promoted Capt. Asst. Q.M. 17 May '61, taking charge of a Md. Q.M. depot until Mar. '62. During the Peninsular campaign he superintended the army's supplies at Fort Monroe and was Acting Chief Q.M. 7 Sept.–12 Nov. '62. He then became Chief Q.M. of the II Corps until 24 Jan. '63, when he was named Chief Q.M. of the Cav. Corps (until 13 June '63). In Washington he was Chief Q.M. of the Cav. Bureau until 15 Feb. '64, when he went to the Gulf during the Red River campaign and later was in charge of the department's steam transportation. From June '64 until the end of the war he was Chief Q.M. of the Mil. Div. of West Miss. Continuing in the R.A., he was retired in 1897 as B.G. USA Q.M. Gen., having been breveted for war service (B.G. USA).

SAWYER, Franklin. Union officer. Ohio. Capt. 8th Ohio 29 Apr. '61; Maj. 9 July '61; Lt. Col. 25 Nov. '61; Bvt. B.G. USV (war service); mustered out 13 July '64. Died 1892.

SAWYER projectile and gun. The projectile had six rectangular flanges or ribs to fit the corresponding grooves of the bore. The projectile was coated with lead and brass foil, this being thicker at the corner of the base in order to expand into the grooves (Benton, 559).

SAXTON, Rufus, Jr. Union gen. 1824–1908. Mass. USMA 1849 (18/43); Arty. Serving in the Seminole War, and on the frontier and coastal surveying (where he improved the self-registering thermometer which now bears his name), he taught at West Point and was commander of the artillery detachment (as 1st Lt. since 1855) that broke up the secessionist assembly at Camp Jackson (Mo.) 10 May '61. Named Capt. Asst. Q.M. 13 May, he was the Chief Q.M. on both Lyon's and McClellan's staffs, and also served on T.W. Sherman's staff during the Port Royal expedition of 1861–62. Named B.G. USV 15 Apr. '62, he commanded Harpers Ferry and repulsed Ewell's attack. He then commanded US Forces Beaufort, X, South (19 Feb.–14 June '63 and 6 July '63–17 Apr. '64); Northern Dist., South (1 Sept.–3 Oct. '64); Dist. Beaufort (25 Apr.–1 Sept. '64); and 2d Sep. Brig., Dist. Beaufort, South (26 Oct. '64–23 Jan. '65). Breveted for war service (Lt. Col., Col., B.G. USA 9 Apr. '65, and Maj. Gen. USV 12 Jan. '65), he was awarded the Medal of Honor in 1893 for Harpers Ferry. He ccntinued in the R.A. until retired in 1888 as Col. Asst. Q.M. Gen.

SAYLER'S CREEK (Harper's Farm; Deatonsville), Va., 6 Apr. '65. (APPOMATTOX CAMPAIGN) By noon of 5 Apr. the exhausted and half-starved forces of R. E. Lee had converged at Amelia C.H. The expected rations, for some still-unknown reason, were not there. Seven miles to the southwest at Jetersville, Sheridan's cavalry and Griffin's (V) corps were in position to block Lee's continued retreat; the corps of Humphreys (II) and Wright (VI) were expected to be there during the night. Since the Confederates lacked the strength to fight their way through this resistance, Lee decided to move southwest to Rice Station. Here he could get supplies by rail from Lynchburg (via Farmville), after which he might be able to continue south to link up with J. E. Johnston. Expecting Lee to move south, however, Grant ordered an attack toward Amelia C.H. to be launched early on the 6th. At about 8:30 A.M. elements of II Corps, on the Federal left (west), made contact with Lee's column moving west. II Corps was wheeled to the left to pursue; V Corps was ordered to continue north through Paineville; and VI Corps was to move into position on the left (south) of II Corps.

Having made a night march, the Confederates were well on the way to their objective. Lee rode at the head of the column with Longstreet's two strong divisions of Field and Mahone. Anderson (III) followed, and then came Ewell with a polyglot force of about 3,000 he had led from Richmond. Then came the wagon train, which was followed by Gordon's II Corps as rear guard. Federal cavalry was active on the flanks, and about 11 A.M. the attacks on the wagon train had become so severe that Ewell and Anderson halted their march to let the wagons get farther toward the head of the column. Mahone, whose division was ahead of Anderson, was not notified of this halt and continued his advance with Longstreet's command. The wagons thus moved into a gap, where they were even more vulnerable to enemy cavalry. The Federals took advantage of this error. Anderson, whose movement had been delayed until about 2 P.M., was also stopped by Federal cavalry action soon after resuming his march. Ewell then ordered the part of the supply train still behind him to turn west off the Jamestown road at J. Hott's house (a little less than three miles on the road from Deatonsville) and proceed by a less vulnerable route. Gordon was not notified of this change and followed the wagons west instead of continuing south behind the main body.

While Ewell and Anderson were trying to decide how to deal with the force threatening their advance (this was Custer's division, supported by Devin and Crook) they learned that two infantry divisions (Wheaton's 1st and Seymour's 3d of VI Corps) had come up against Ewell's rear. Ewell deployed along Little Sayler's Creek. The Federals opened fire with two guns from near Hillsman farm and then attacked. Ewell drove back the Federal center; Col. Stapleton Crutchfield, leading the heavy artillerists of the Richmond garrison, was killed. Federal guns and the arrival of Getty's (2d) division halted this threatened penetration, while the Federal wings made a double envelopment of Ewell's outnumbered command. Sheridan attacked when he heard Wright's guns open up. Stagg's brigade (Devin) hit Ewell's right flank and captured most of Kershaw's division. Crook dismounted the brigades of J. I. Gregg and C. H. Smith and ordered Davies to charge Pickett's position. Anderson, Bushrod Johnson, and Pickett managed to escape, but Ewell stayed and tried to lead his remaining troops out of the trap. Com. Tucker, commanding the naval battalion, led a counterattack that drove some of the VI Corps back across the creek before being captured after hand-to-hand fighting.

Gordon's column, meanwhile, had been pursued by II Corps to Perkinson's Mills on Sayler's Creek. Here the Confederates repulsed one assault, but were overwhelmed when additional forces attacked from the south after overrunning Ewell. Gordon's losses were about 1,700, but he rallied survivors west of the creek and led them to HIGH BRIDGE that night. "The day's casualties, which were between 7,000 and 8,000, represented probably one third of the men of all arms that left Amelia and Jetersville the previous day" (*Lee's Lts.*, III, 711). Captured Confederate generals were Ewell, Kershaw, Custis Lee, Dubose, Hunton, and Corse. (Longstreet was not seriously engaged during the day.) The Federals reported a loss of 1,180, only 166 of whom were killed.

SCALAWAGS. Southern politicians who, during the RECONSTRUCTION era, worked with the Northern CARPETBAGGERS to gain political power and profit. Appealing to the freed Negroes, they made many unfulfillable promises and plunged the states further into debt and political chaos. The resentment built up by their policies reflected on the RADICAL REPUBLICANS whose Reconstruction plans had brought the situation about, and this contributed to the solid South (the Democratic supremacy).

SCALES, Alfred Moore. C.S.A. gen. 1827–92. N.C. After graduating from the Univ. of N.C., Chapel Hill, he was a lawyer, legislator, and Congressman before attending his state's secession convention. Commissioned Capt. in the spring of 1861 with the 13th N.C., he was promoted to Col. in Oct. '61 to succeed Pender. He commanded the regiment at Yorktown, Williamsburg, the Seven Days' Battles, and Fredericksburg, where he succeeded to brigade command. Commanding his regiment at Chancellorsville, he was shot in the leg. He was appointed B.G. C.S.A. 13 June '63 while convalescing at home. Taking over Pender's brigade at Gettysburg, he was severely wounded the first day on Seminary Ridge. He commanded his brigade under Wilcox at the Wilderness and during the Petersburg siege and was at home on sick leave at the time of surrender. After the war he was a lawyer, Congressman, banker, and Gov. of N.C.

SCAMMON, Eliakim Parker. Union gen. 1816–94. Me. USMA 1837 (9/50); Arty.-Engrs. He remained at West Point to teach math, then fought in the Seminole War and returned to USMA. During the Mexican War he was A.D.C. to Winfield Scott and was dismissed in 1856 for "disobedience of orders." He was professor and president at Cincinnati College until the war, when he was commissioned Col. 23d Ohio 27 June '62 and commanded Camp Chase. He then led Scammon's brigade, Army of Occupation, W. Va. in Sept. '61; 3d Brig. Kanawha (Oct. '61–Mar. '62); and 1st Brig., Dist. Kanawha, Mountain Dept. (Mar.–Sept. '62), when he led a bayonet charge at South Mountain. Promoted B.G. USV 15 Oct. '62, he commanded 3d Div., VIII, Middle Dept. (27 Mar.–26 June '63); Scammon's division, W. Va. (June–Dec. '63) and 3d Div., W. Va. (Dec. '63–11 Feb. '64), when he was captured and sent to Libby. Then commanding 1st Sep. Brig., Northern Dist., South 3–26 Oct. '64 during the siege of Charleston, he was again captured but shortly released. He next commanded 3d Sep. Brig., Dist. Hilton Head, South (1–14 Nov. '64) and 4th Sep. Brig., Dist. Fla., South (14 Nov. '64–7 Apr. '65). Mustered out 24 Aug. '65, he was US Consul on Prince Edward Island, US Engr. in New York Harbor, and mathematics professor at Seton Hall College in N.J.

SCATES, Walter Bennett. Union officer. 1808–87. Va. Appt.-Ill. Maj. Asst. Adj. Gen. Vols. 30 June '62; Lt. Col. Asst. Adj. Gen. Assigned 1 Jan. '63–8 Apr. '64; Bvt. B.G. USV (war service). Served on McClernand's staff. He was an associate justice of the Ill. supreme court.

SCHAAK, George W. Misspelling by Phisterer for George VON SCHACK.

SCHENCK, Robert C. Union gen. and politician. 1809–90. Ohio. After graduating from Miami (Ohio) Univ., he taught French and Latin and was later a lawyer and politician. He was US Congressman until sent to Brazil in 1851 as Minister, returning in two years to be a railroad president. Appointed B.G. Ohio state troops, he commanded the state troops in eastern Va. and fought at Vienna 17 June '61. He was with Rosecrans in W. Va. and succeeded Lander in the spring of 1862 in command at Cumberland, Md. During Jackson's Valley campaign he commanded the right flank of Frémont's army at Cross Keys and was in temporary command of the I Corps (Army of Va.) between the departure of Fré-

mont and the arrival of Sigel. He was wounded at 2d Bull Run and appointed Maj. Gen. USV for that battle (30 Aug. '62). While on sick leave he was re-elected to Congress and became chairman of the committee on military affairs. Resigning from the army 5 Dec. '63, he served in Washington until 1870 and was named US Minister to England. He delayed his departure for this post to sit on the joint high commission that brought about the treaty of Washington, the Geneva arbitration, and the settlement of the ALABAMA CLAIMS. Accused of complicity in the Emma Mine Fraud, he returned to the US and was completely exonerated but never again entered public life.

SCHENKLE projectile. Composed of a cast-iron body, the posterior portion of which is a cone. The expanding portion is a *papier-mâché* sabot or ring which is expanded into the rifling of the bore by being forced on to the cone by the action of the charge. Proved unreliable because of difficulty in getting the proper amount of material for the sabot, which was supposed to blow off when the projectile cleared the muzzle. (Benton, 558.)

SCHIMMELFENNIG, Alexander. Union gen. 1824–65. Prussia. A Prussian officer, he fled after the 1848 revolt with Blenker, Hecker, and Von Willich. Commissioned Col. 74th Pa. 30 Sept. '61, he fought with Sigel during Pope's Va. campaign and commanded 1, 3, I, Army Va. (22 Aug.–12 Sept. '62) at 2d Bull Run. He was promoted B.G. USV 29 Nov. '62 and commanded 1, 3, XI, (12 Sept. '62–19 Jan., 5 Feb.–5 Mar., 2 Apr.–1 July '63 at Chancellorsville, and 1–13 July '63 at Gettysburg). During the latter battle he was wounded and cut off from his forces, hiding in a stable for the three days of fighting before he could rejoin his troops. Also in the Army of the

Potomac, XI Corps, he commanded 1st Brig., 1st Div. (17 July–6 Aug. '63); 1st Div. (14–17 July '63) and 3d Div. (19 Jan.–5 Feb., 5 Mar.–2 Apr. and 1 July '63). After the severe criticism of the XI Corps for their actions at Chancellorsville, he requested a transfer to the Carolinas and commanded 1st Brig., South End Folly Island, X (16 Aug.–24 Oct. '63). Also in the South he commanded South End Folly Island (24 Oct.–28 Nov. '63); US Forces Folly Island, X (25 Apr.–1 Sept. '64); Northern Dist., X (Feb.–Mar. '64) and 1st Sep. Brig., Northern Dist. (25 Feb.–25 Apr. '64, 28 Nov. '64–23 Jan. '65 and 26 Feb.–8 Apr. '65). Plagued by malaria and the effects of his wound, he was relieved because of ill-health while in command of the defenses of Charleston and returned to Pa., where he died of tuberculosis in the fall of 1865.

SCHMITT, William Andrew. Union officer. Ill. Capt. 27th Ill. 24 Aug. '61; Maj. 11 June '62; Lt. Col. 10 Feb. '63; Bvt. B.G. USV (Stones River, war service); mustered out 20 Sept. '64.

SCHNEIDER, Edward F. Union officer. Ohio. Maj. 8th Kans. 17 Sept. '61; Lt. Col. 21 Dec. '63; Bvt. B.G. USV (war service); mustered out 1 Mar. '64. Died 1871.

SCHOEPF, Albin Francisco. Union gen. 1822–86. Hungary. Appt.-Md. A graduate of the Vienna military academy and a Prussian officer, he went to Hungary to fight under Kossuth in 1848 and was exiled to Turkey, where he fought with and instructed the Ottoman Army. He emigrated to the US, where he worked with the US Coast Survey and Patent Office and was commissioned B.G. USV 30 Sept. '61. He then commanded in the Army of Ohio 1st Brig. (Nov.–Dec. '61); 1st Brig., 1st Div. (2 Dec. '61–29 Sept. '62) (See

LOGAN CROSS ROADS) and 1st Div., III (Sept.–Nov. '62) at Perryville. Mustered out in 1866.

SCHOFIELD, George Wheeler. Union officer. N.Y. 1st Lt. 1st Mo. Arty. 5 Oct. '61; Capt. 1 Sept. '62; Lt. Col. 2d Mo. Arty. 9 Mar. '64; Bvt. B.G. USV 26 Jan. '65 (Ga. and Tenn. campaigns). Other brevets for Champion's Hill, Vicksburg siege. Served as Gen. Schofield's A.D.C. and Mil. Sec. after the war. Continued in R.A. until he died in 1882, having attained the rank of Lt. Col. His kinship to Gen. Schofield is not revealed in the latter's memoirs nor in the standard genealogical references.

SCHOFIELD, Hiram. Erroneous listing by Phisterer for Scofield, Hiram.

SCHOFIELD, John McAllister. Union gen. 1831–1906. N.Y. Appt.-Ill. USMA 1853 (7/52); Arty. Serving in Fla. and teaching at West Point, he was given a leave of absence in 1860 to teach physics at Washington Univ. in St. Louis. As Capt. 1st US Arty. 14 May '61 and Maj. 1st Mo. Arty. 26 Apr. '61, he was Lyon's Chief of Staff at Dug Spring and Wilson's Creek. He was appointed B.G. USV 21 Nov. '61 and B.G. Mo. Mil. five days later, and commanded the Dist. St. Louis 21 Nov. '61–10 Apr. '62. He then commanded the Mil. Dist. Mo. (5 June–24 Sept. '62); the Dist. Southwest Mo. (24 Sept.–10 Nov. '62 and 30 Mar.–24 May '63) and the Army of the Frontier, Dept. of Mo. (12 Oct. '62–30 May '63). On 29 Nov. '62 he was named Maj. Gen. USV, this appointment expiring 4 Mar. '63. He was reappointed B.G. USV on the latter date and Maj. Gen. USV 12 May '63 to rank from 29 Nov. '62. He then commanded 3d Div., XIV, Cumberland (17 Apr.–10 May '63); the Dept. of Mo. (24 May '63–30 Jan. '64), and the XXIII Corps, Dept. of Ohio

(9 Apr.–26 May '64) at Buzzard Roost, Resaca, and Dallas; (27 May–14 Sept. '64) at Kenesaw Mountain, Chattahoochee, and Atlanta; and (22 Oct. '64–2 Feb. '65) at Franklin and Nashville. He commanded the Army of the Ohio 9 Feb.–17 Nov. '64 and was named B.G. USA 30 Nov. '64. During the march through the Carolinas he commanded the XXIII Corps (9 Feb.–31 Mar. '65) and the Dept. of N.C. (31 Jan.–27 June '65) at Fort Anderson, Wilmington, Kinston, and Goldsboro. He was breveted Maj. Gen. USA for Franklin and given the Medal of Honor in 1892 for Wilson's Creek. Sent to France 1865–66 on a secret mission concerning US interference with Maximilian, he continued in the R.A., serving as Sec. of War during the period of Johnson's impeachment and the ensuing confusion. He was named Maj. Gen. USA in 1869 and was then Superintendent of West Point and president of the board that reviewed the Fitz-John PORTER CASE. He served as C. in C. of the army 1888–95, being named Lt. Gen. Retired the latter year.

SCHRIVER, Edmund. Union officer. c. 1812–99. Pa. USMA 1833 (17/43); Arty. He taught infantry tactics at West Point, and fought in the Seminole War before resigning in 1846 to become a railroad official. A.D.C. to the Gov. of N.Y., he was commissioned Lt. Col. 11th US Inf. 14 May '61 and was Chief of Staff of I Corps (Potomac) 15 Mar. '62–Jan. '63. He had been promoted Col. Add. A.D.C. 18 May '62 and Col. I.G. 13 Mar. '63, serving also as Chief of Staff of the III Corps Aug.–Sept. '62 and as I.G. of the Army of the Potomac for the rest of the war. In 1881 he was retired as Bvt. B.G. USA (1 Aug. '64) and Bvt. Maj. Gen. USA.

SCHURZ, Carl. Union gen. 1829–1906. Germany. He was a doctoral candidate at the Univ. of Bonn when he joined the 1848 revolution. Escaping to Switzerland, he returned at considerable personal risk to rescue one of his teachers who was faced with life imprisonment. He then migrated to England and later the US. A LATIN FARMER in Wis., he soon went into politics and law and was Minister to Spain (July '61–Apr. '62), returning to press for abolition. Appointed B.G. USV 15 Apr. '62 from Wis., he commanded 3d Div., I Corps, Army of Va. (26 June–12 Sept. '62) at 2d Bull Run. He commanded the 3d Div., XI, Potomac (12 Sept. '62–19 Jan. '63; 5 Feb.–5 Mar. '63 and 2 Apr.–25 Sept. '63). After CHANCELLORSVILLE he tried unsuccessfully to have a court of inquiry convened to clear the XI Corps. Schurz commanded the XI Corps, Potomac (19 Jan.–5 Feb.; 5 May–2 Apr., and temporarily on 1 July '63). In the Army of the Cumberland he again commanded 3d Div., XI Corps (25 Sept. '63–21 Jan. '64). In command of the XI Corps (21 Jan.–25 Feb. '64) and having trained them for several months at Nashville, he asked to be relieved when the XI and XII Corps were combined to form the XX Corps. Returning to the North, he made numerous campaign speeches for Lincoln and near the end of the war served as Slocum's Chief of Staff before resigning 6 May '65. He then made a report on the Southern states for Johnson and served as Greeley's *Tribune* correspondent in Washington. He was later active in German-language press and was Republican US Sen. from Mo. and Sec. of the Interior. He is perhaps best remembered today for his crusades and reforms, notably in civil service. He published the three-volume *Reminiscences of Carl Schurz* in 1907–08.

SCHWENK, Samuel Klinger. Union officer. Pa. 1st Lt. 50th Pa. 9 Sept. '61; Capt. 1 Nov. '62; mustered out 12 Oct. '64; Maj. 50th Pa. Vet. Inf. 28 Feb.

'65; Lt. Col. 18 May '65; Bvt. B.G.
USV 24 July '65. Brevets for Fort Stedman (Va.), war service, Spotsylvania,
Ny River (Va.), Cold Harbor. In R.A.
until retired in 1876 as Capt.

SCOFIELD, Hiram. Union officer.
N.Y. Pvt. Co. H 2d Iowa 24 May '61;
2d Lt. 25 May '61; Capt. Asst. Adj.
Gen. Vols. 9 June '62; Col. 47th US
Col. Inf. 5 May '63; Bvt. B.G. USV
(war service). Commanded 2d Brig.,
USCT Dist. Vicksburg (Tenn.); 2, 4,
XVI; 2d Brig., 1st USCT West Fla.
(Gulf). Listed by Phisterer as Schofield,
Hiram.

SCOTT, George Washington. Union
officer. N.Y. 2d Lt. 61st N.Y. 19 Sept.
'61; Capt. 4 Dec. '61; Maj. 18 Feb.
'63; Lt. Col. 31 Oct. '64; Col. 16 Nov.
'64; Bvt. B.G. USV (war service).
Commanded 1, 1, II (Potomac).

SCOTT, Robert Kingston. Union gen.
1826–1900. Pa. He fought in the Mexican War and was commissioned Lt. Col.
68th Ohio 30 Nov. '61. Promoted Col.
12 July '62, he led his regiment during
the Vicksburg campaign at Thompson's
Hill, Raymond, Jackson, and Champion's Hill. During the Atlanta campaign he commanded 2, 3, XVII (6
Mar.–22 July '64) at Kenesaw Mountain, Nickajack, Atlanta, Jonesboro, and
Lovejoy. He also led this brigade
30 Sept.–27 Dec. '64 and 28 Mar.–
1 Apr. '65 during the March to the
Sea and through the Carolinas. Promoted B.G. USV 12 Jan. '65, he was
breveted B.G. USV 26 Jan. and Maj.
Gen. USA 5 Dec. '65 for war service.
Until 1868 he headed the S.C. Freedman's Bureau and resigned when elected
Republican Gov. of that state. Of his
administration D.A.B. says he was
". . . largely responsible for the scandals
and disorders that characterized the introduction of Republican rule in South
Carolina." Staying there after his one

term, he then supported the Democrats
but returned to Ohio when they came
to power to avoid possible prosecution.
He later shot a young man for allegedly
making his young son drunk, but was
acquitted.

SCOTT, Rufus. Union officer. N.Y.
Pvt. Co. B 23d N.Y. 16 May '61; Maj.
19th N.Y. Cav. 27 Aug. '62; Lt. Col. 1
Mar. '65; Bvt. B.G. USV (war service).
Died 1896.

SCOTT, Thomas M. C.S.A. gen.
Appt.-La. Commissioned Col. 12th La.
when the war began, he commanded
his regiment at Island No. 10, New
Madrid, Fort Pillow, Port Hudson,
Baker's Creek, and under Johnston during the Vicksburg siege. In the Atlanta
campaign he commanded his brigade
under Loring and was appointed B.G.
C.S.A. 10 May '64. Distinguishing himself at Peach Tree Creek, he went with
Hood to Tenn. and was mortally
wounded at Franklin.

SCOTT, Winfield. Union gen. 1786–
1866. Va. "A year older than the federal Constitution," the venerable Scott,
hero of the War of 1812 and the war
with Mexico, had become Gen. in
Chief of the army in 1841 and occupied
that position when the Civil War began.
Although too old and sick to be seriously considered for retaining this post
in an active war, the septuagenarian
professional soldier was one of the few
men in the country to foresee the need
to prepare for a major military effort.
His ANACONDA PLAN, although ridiculed
when he proposed it, was proved by
subsequent bloody experience to be
sound. Succeeded in Nov. '61 by Mc-
Clellan, he retired to write his two-
volume memoirs and to make a European trip in '64. He died at West Point
and is buried there. A Virginian, he was
the only non-West Pointer of Southern

origin in the R.A. to remain loyal to the Union.

SCOTT'S DAM (Ford), Va., 4 May '63. Alternate name of operation near BANKS'S FORD during CHANCELLORSVILLE CAMPAIGN.

SCRIBNER, Benjamin Franklin. Union officer. Ind. Col. 38th Ind. 18 Sept. '61; Bvt. B.G. USV 8 Aug. '64 (war service); resigned 21 Aug. '64. Commanded in the Army of the Cumberland: 1, 3 centre, XIV; 1, 1, XIV; 3, 1, XIV. Died 1900.

SCURRY, William R. C.S.A. gen. ?–1864. Tex. Commissioned Lt. Col. 4th Tex. Mtd. Rifles in 1861, he fought under Sibley in N. Mex., being in command at Glorieta, and then served in Tex. and Ark. He was appointed B.G. C.S.A. 12 Sept. '62 and commanded the land forces at Galveston 1 Jan. '63. In the Red River campaign of 1864 he commanded his brigade under Walker at Mansfield and Pleasant Hill and went with Kirby Smith to Ark. against Steele. There he was mortally wounded 30 Apr. '64 at Jenkins' Ferry.

SEARS, Claudius Wistar. C.S.A. gen. c. 1817–91. Mass. Appt.-N.Y, USMA 1841 (41/52); Inf. Resigning the next year, he taught mathematics and engineering at the Univ. of La. until commissioned Col. 46th Miss. 11 Dec. '62. He served in northern Miss. and fought at Chickasaw Bayou, Fort Pemberton on the Yazoo, Port Gibson, and Baker's Creek before being captured at Vicksburg. After his exchange he was given a brigade in the early part of 1864 and on 1 Mar. was appointed B.G. C.S.A. He commanded this unit in French's division in the Atlanta campaign but was ill and out of action in the July battles around Atlanta. Fighting next at Allatoona, he went with Hood to Tenn. He fought at Franklin and lost a leg at Nashville and was captured

there 15 Dec. '64. After the war he was a professor at the Univ. of Miss.

SEAVER, Joel J. Union officer. N.Y. Capt. 16th N.Y. 15 May '61; Maj. 11 Nov. '61; Lt. Col. 4 June '62; Col. 29 Sept. '62; Bvt. B.G. USV (war service); mustered out 22 May '63. Died 1899.

SEAWELL, Thomas D. Union officer. Ill. 1st Lt. 10th Mo. 12 Aug. '61; Capt. 27 Jan. '63; Col. 57th US Col. Inf. 10 Aug. '63; Bvt. B.G. USV (war service); resigned 10 May '64.

SEAWELL, Washington. Union officer. c. 1802–88. Va. USMA 1825 (20/37); Inf. He served in the West, fought in the Seminole War (1 brevet) and the Mexican War before being retired from active duty 20 Feb. '62 for disabilities as Col. 6th US Inf. From Mar. '62 to Sept. '63 he was mustering and disbursing officer in Ky. and held the same post in the Dept. of the Pacific for the remainder of the war. He was breveted B.G. USA.

SECESSION SEQUENCE AND DATES: S.C., 20 Dec. '60; Miss., 9 Jan. '61; Fla., 10 Jan. '61; Ala., 11 Jan. '61; Ga., 19 Jan. '61; La., 26 Jan. '61; Tex., 1 Feb. '61. After the fall of Fort Sumter: Va., 17 Apr. '61; Ark., 6 May '61; N.C., 20 May '61; and Tenn., 8 June '61. Those states seceding before the fall of Fort Sumter, with the exception of Tex., whose delegates were late, met at Montgomery 4 Feb. '61. On the 8th the delegates adopted a provisional constitution and the next day elected a president. On 28 Feb. '61 the president was directed to call as many volunteers as required for not more than 12 months. On 6 Mar. of that year 100,000 men were called for, and by mid-April 35,000 had been equipped for the field. The capital was moved to Richmond on 20 May '61. (Both Union and Confederate governments existed in Ky. and Mo. throughout the war. Western Va.

separated from Va. 20 Aug. '62 and was admitted to the Union 20 June '63.) See also ORDINANCE OF SECESSION, and RECONSTRUCTION.

SECESSIONVILLE (James Island), S.C. 16 June '62. After Gillmore had taken a position on James Island he decided to postpone further operations against Charleston. H. W. Benham was left in command of about 9,000 troops (divisions of H. G. Wright, I. I. Stevens, and Robert Williams) with orders not to undertake any offensive operations. Over the objection of his division commanders, however, Benham ordered an attack against the position around Secessionville, which was defended by N. G. Evans. In three assaults between 4 and 10 A.M. Stevens and Wright lost 683 (B.&L., IV, 21n) while inflicting a loss of only 204 on the Confederates (O.R., I, XIV, 96). The first assault was repulsed by 500 men under Col. T. G. Lamar of S.C. Arty. He was reinforced to 2,000 men in time to defeat the subsequent attacks. For this action Lamar was voted the thanks of the Confederate Congress (approved 8 Feb. '64). Benham, on the other hand, was relieved of command, arrested for disobedience of orders, and his appointment as B.G. USV revoked by Lincoln.

SEDDON, James Alexander. C.S.A. Sec. of War. 1815–80. Va. After graduating from the law school of the Univ. of Va., he was elected to Congress and served until 1851, when his poor health made retirement advisable. Coming back into public life during the secession crisis of 1860, he was a Va. delegate to the Washington peace conference and served in the first C.S.A. Congress. Named Sec. of War 21 Nov. '62 succeeding Smith, he held this post until 16 Feb. '65, when he resigned on account of his health.

SEDGWICK, John. Union gen. 1813–64. Conn. USMA 1837 (24/50); Arty. He served in the Seminole War, on the frontier, in the Mexican War (2 brevets), in the Kans. border disturbances, on the Utah Expedition, and in Indian fighting before the war. Promoted Lt. Col. 2d US Cav. 16 Mar. and Col. 1st Cav. 25 Mar. '61, he was acting I.G. of Washington (3–12 Aug. '61) and then commanded 2d Brig., Heintzelman's division, Potomac (3 Oct. '61–19 Feb. '62) and Sedgwick's division, Potomac (19 Feb.–13 Mar. '62) in the Defenses of Washington and guarding the Potomac. He was appointed B.G. USV 31 Aug. '61. During the Peninsular campaign he commanded 2d Div., II, Potomac (13 Mar.–17 Sept. '62) at Yorktown, Fair Oaks, Peach Orchard, Savage's Station, Glendale, and Antietam, being wounded at the last two battles. He was appointed Maj. Gen. USV 4 July '62 and commanded II Corps (26 Dec. '62–26 Jan. '63) and the IX Corps (16 Jan.–5 Feb. '63). Leading the VI Corps, he participated in Chancellorsville, Gettysburg, Rappahannock Station, and the Mine Run operations (4 Feb. '63–6 Apr. '64). He then commanded it from 13 Apr. until 9 May at the Wilderness and Spotsylvania and was killed by a sharpshooter at the latter while making a reconnaissance and directing the placement of artillery. Characterized as the most deeply loved of all the higher officers in the entire army, Sedgwick was called "Uncle John" by his men. A generous, affable bachelor, much addicted to solitaire, he was nonetheless a disciplinarian and a highly competent corps commander. There are statues to him at Gettysburg and West Point, the latter prominently located in front of the commandant's quarters. (Tradition has it that a cadet in danger of being "found deficient" in academics will pass his final examinations if he sneaks out after taps and twirls the rowels of Sedgwick's spurs.)

SELFRIDGE, James Lercon. Union officer. Pa. Lt. Col. 46th Pa. 8 Aug. '61; Col. 10 May '63; Bvt. B.G. USV 16 Mar. '65 (Ga. and S.C. campaign). Commanded 1, 1, XX (Cumberland). Died 1887.

SEMINOLE WARS. Sometimes called the Florida Wars, they were a series of attacks against the Seminole Indians in Fla. Many of the R.A. officers who rose to prominence in the Civil War participated in them. The first Seminole War ran from 1835 to 1842, and the second from 20 Dec. '55 to 8 May '58.

SEMMES, Paul J. C.S.A. gen. ?–1863. Ga. A prominent businessman, active in the militia, he was commissioned Col. 2d Ga. and appointed B.G. C.S.A. 11 Mar. '62. He fought under Magruder at Williamsburg, Seven Pines, Savage's Station, and Malvern Hill. He then commanded his brigade under McLaws at South Mountain, Crampton's Gap, and Antietam. Leading this same force, he fought at Fredericksburg, Chancellorsville, and Gettysburg, where he was mortally wounded the first day and died 2 July.

SEMMES, Raphael. C.S.A. Rear Adm. 1809–77. Md. Named a Midshipman in 1826, he entered active duty in 1832 after having been admitted to the bar in the meantime. He fought in the Mexican War and later published *The Campaign of General Scott* and *Service Afloat and Ashore During the Mexican War*. Having moved to Ala., he resigned when that state seceded and was given the duty by Davis of purchasing matériel and engaging mechanics to manufacture ordnance. Going to the North, he witnessed Lincoln's inauguration, visited the principal shops in N.Y. and New England, purchased percussion caps, and thousands of pounds of powder. C.M.H. says of this: "With a nice sense of honor he never afterward betrayed the names of the thrifty Northerners who thus contributed to the military needs of the South." He was commissioned Commander, put in charge of the lighthouse bureau, and then fitted out the cruiser *Sumter* in New Orleans. Cutting through the river blockade for a six months' cruise, he took 18 prizes. Abandoning this ship at Gibraltar, he went to England to take over what became the *Alabama*. Setting out in Sept. '62, he cruised until June '64, during which time he captured or destroyed 69 ships. He was defeated by the *Kearsarge* off Cherbourg and rescued by an English yacht when the *Alabama* was sunk. After touring the Continent, he returned to the Confederacy and was promoted Rear Adm. He took command of the James River squadron until Richmond was evacuated and surrendered with Johnston as Rear Adm. C.S.N. and B.G. C.S.A. Later a lawyer and newspaper editor, he wrote *The Cruise of the Alabama and Sumter* and *Memoirs of Service Afloat*.

SERRELL, Edward Wellman. Union officer. England. 1826–? Lt. Col. 1st N.Y. Engrs. 10 Oct. '61; Col. 14 Feb. '62; Bvt. B.G. USV (war service); discharged 13 Feb. '65. A civil engineer before the war, he served as Chief Engr. for the X Corps in 1863 and as Chief Engr. and Chief of Staff for Ben Butler in 1864. He designed and superintended the construction of the SWAMP ANGEL battery that bombarded Charleston.

SEVEN DAYS' BATTLES, Va., 25 June–1 July '62. (PENINSULAR CAMPAIGN.) Consisted of the following battles, each of which is covered separately in its alphabetical place elsewhere under the name given below in capitals. In parentheses are other names by which the battles are known.

OAK GROVE (Henrico; King's School House; The Orchards), 25 June '62.

MECHANICSVILLE (Ellison's Mills; Beaver Dam Creek), 26 June.

GAINES'S MILL (First Cold Harbor; Chickahominy), 27–28 June.

GARNETT'S AND GOLDING'S FARMS, 27–28 June.

SAVAGE'S STATION AND ALLEN'S FARM (Peach Orchard), 29 June.

WHITE OAK SWAMP (Glendale; Charles City or New Market Cross Roads; Nelson's or Frayser's Farm; Turkey Bend), 30 June.

MALVERN HILL (Crew's Farm), 1 July.

XVII CORPS MEDAL. On 2 Oct. '63 James McPHERSON directed that a medal be made up for presentation to members of his XVII Corps for "gallantry in action and other soldier-like qualities." The medal was made by Tiffany's and appears to have been in two classes, gold and silver. One of the former was issued to the man who attempted to rescue the mortally wounded McPherson at the battle of Atlanta. The medal featured a star with the numerals "17th," the shield of the US, and a wreath; unlike most medals of this type, it was pinned so as to hang in front of a tricolored ribbon, rather than being suspended by the ribbon. See also DECORATIONS.

SEWALL, Frederick Dummer. Union officer. c. 1826–?. Me. Capt. Asst. Adj. Gen. Vols. 19 Sept. '61; resigned 24 June '62; Col. 19th Me. 26 Aug. '62; resigned 18 Feb. '63; Maj. Vet. Res. Corps 15 June '63; Col. 25 Sept. '63; Bvt. B.G. USV 21 July '65 (war service). Commanded 1, 2, II (Potomac). Tuberculosis, rendering him unfit for field duty, made him eligible for the Vet. Res. Corps.

SEWARD, William Henry. Union Sec. of State. 1801–72. N.Y. After graduating from Union College he studied law and entered Whig politics, serving as Gov. of N.Y. 1839–42. He served later in the Senate, vigorously opposed slavery there, and joined the Republican party in 1856. Twice passed over for president (1856 and 1860), he became Lincoln's Sec. of State, and started inauspiciously in the matter of FORT SUMTER. However, during the war his actions showed a delicate diplomatic touch, particularly in the TRENT AFFAIR and the ALABAMA CLAIMS. He was savagely attacked by an accomplice of Booth at the time of Lincoln's assassination but recovered to serve in the same post under Johnson. Perhaps his most important act was the purchase of Alaska, "Seward's Folly," in 1867 from Russia.

SEWARD, William Henry, Jr. Union gen. 1839–? N.Y. Son of the Sec. of State and a banker and financier himself, he was commissioned Lt. Col. 9th N.Y. 22 Aug. '62 and sent in 1863 on a special mission to La. He was named Col. 10 June '64 after fighting at Cold Harbor and the Wilderness. First commanding Fort Foote (Md.), he was then wounded slightly at Monocacy and later commanded Martinsburg (W. Va.). Promoted B.G. USV 13 Sept. '64, he commanded 1st Brig., 3d Div., W. Va. (Jan.–Apr. '65) and Harpers Ferry (21–27 Feb. '65). He resigned 1 June '65.

SEWARD-MEIGS-PORTER AFFAIR, Apr. '61. A departmental mix-up led to conflicting instructions as to the use of the USS Powhatan. The battleship had first been ordered to accompany the Fort Sumter relief expedition organized by Sec. Welles (Navy). Another relief expedition was then secretly organized by Secretary Seward (State) to support the forts in the Gulf (Forts

Taylor, Jefferson, and Pickens); it was to be composed of a naval force under Porter and 200 army troops under Meigs. Unknown to Welles, Seward got Lincoln's authority to use the *Powhatan*. Before the conflict came to light and could be resolved, the ship departed for the Gulf and, consequently, the other expedition lacked the heavy guns necessary to assist Anderson at Fort Sumter. The episode helped to "define the province of the different departments of the government under President Lincoln" (R. S. West, Jr., quoting Welles).

SEWELL, William Joyce. Union officer. 1835–1901. Ireland. Variously a clerk and a merchant mariner, he worked in Chicago before being commissioned Capt. 5th N.J. 28 Aug. '61. He was promoted Lt. Col. 7 July '62 and Col. 6 Jan. '63. After commanding a brigade and being seriously wounded at Chancellorsville, he was also wounded at Gettysburg. He resigned 6 July '64 and was commissioned Col. 38th N.J. 1 Oct. '64. Mustered out in June '65, he was breveted for Chancellorsville (B.G. USV) and war service (Maj. Gen. USV) and given the Medal of Honor for Chancellorsville in 1896. Active in Republican politics, he sat in the legislature and the US Senate for many years.

SEYMOUR, Horatio. Gov. of N.Y. 1810–86. N.Y. Although educated as a lawyer, he never practiced, and devoted himself to managing his not-inconsiderable inheritance. He entered politics as a Democrat and served in the legislature. Defeated for Gov. in 1850, he was elected two years later and then retired from politics until the secession movement came up later. He believed that war could be avoided through compromise, but when the fighting began he counseled loyalty to the government. In 1863 he again became Gov., and it was during his term that the N.Y. DRAFT RIOTS occurred. He was nominated for president in 1868 and retired from public life after being defeated by Grant.

SEYMOUR, Truman. Union gen. 1824–91. Vt. USMA 1846 (19/59); Arty. He was twice breveted during the Mexican War, taught drawing at West Point, and fought in the Seminole War. As Capt. 1st US Arty., he was at the bombardment of Fort Sumter and then served as McCall's Chief of Arty. 5 Mar.–28 Apr. '62 (transferring to 5th US Arty. 14 May '61). Promoted B.G. USV 28 Apr. '62, he commanded 3d Brig., 2d Div., Rappahannock (16 May–12 June '62). During the Peninsular campaign he led 3, 3, V (18–30 June) at Mechanicsville and Gaines's Mill, succeeding to command of the division 30 June–26 Aug. '62 for Glendale and Malvern Hill. At 2d Bull Run he led 1, 3, III. He commanded 1, 3, I (12–17 Sept. '62) at South Mountain and later (29 Sept.–14 Nov. '62) succeeded to command of the division for Antietam (17–29 Sept. '62). He then commanded US Forces Beaufort, X, South (26 Dec. '62–9 Feb. '63) and was Chief of Arty. and Chief of Staff (8 Jan.–23 Apr. '63), also leading 2d Div. Morris Island, X, South (6–19 July '63) at Fort Wagner, where he was severely wounded. He commanded US Forces Morris Island, X (18 Oct.–10 Nov. '63); US Forces Hilton Head, X (6 Dec. '63–5 Feb. '64); and Dist. Fla., X (16 Feb.–24 Mar. '64) at Olustee. At the Wilderness he led 2, 3, VI (5–6 May '64), when he was captured and put under the guns during the Charleston bombardment. In the Valley he commanded 3d Div., VI Shenandoah, and led the same division in the Army of the Potomac (6 Dec. '64–16 Apr. '65) during the Petersburg siege and assaults, and at Sayler's Creek. He commanded 1, 3, VI (17 Apr.–28 June '65). Breveted for Fort Sumter, South

Mountain, Antietam, Petersburg (B.G. USA), and war service (Maj. Gen. USV and USA). He continued in the R.A. until 1876, when he retired as Maj. 5th US Arty.

SHACKELFORD, James M. Union gen. 1827–? Ky. Serving in the Mexican War, he was commissioned Col. 8th Ky. Cav. 13 Sept. '61 and Col. 25th Ky. 1 Jan. '62. He led his regiment at Fort Donelson, Shiloh, and Corinth. Named B.G. USV 2 Mar. '63, he commanded 1, 2, XXIII, Ohio (24 June–6 Aug. '63), capturing Morgan at Columbiana City (Ohio) in July. He also led 3, 4, XXIII (6 Aug.–10 Sept. '63) and succeeded to division 10 Sept.–3 Nov. '63. He resigned 18 Jan. '64 and returned to his law practice. Later appointed judge of the US Court for the Indian Territory, he then became attorney for the Choctaw Nation in 1893.

SHAFFER, George Thomas. Union officer. Ohio. 1st Lt. 19th Mich. 28 July '62; Capt. 15 May '64; Maj. 28th Mich. 15 Aug. '64; Lt. Col. 10 Dec. '64; Bvt. B.G. USV (Atlanta, Wise Fork, N.C.).

SHAFFER, John Wilson. Union officer. Pa. Capt. Asst. Q.M. Vols. 3 Aug. '61; Col. Add. A.D.C. 30 Jan. '62; Bvt. B.G. USV (Chief of Staff Army of the James during campaign before Richmond, 1864); resigned 26 Aug. '64. Died 1870.

SHAFTER, William Rufus. Union officer. 1835–1906. Mich. 1st Lt. 7th Mich. 22 Aug. '61; mustered out 22 Aug. '62; Maj. 19th Mich. 5 Sept. '62; Lt. Col. 5 June '63; Col. 17th US Col. Inf. 19 Apr. '64; Bvt. B.G. USV (war service, Fair Oaks). Captured at Thompson's Station (Tenn.) Mar. '63. W.I.A. at Fair Oaks. Medal of Honor 12 June '95 for Fair Oaks 31 May '62.

Continued in R.A. until retired as B.G. in 1899 and placed on retired list as Maj. Gen. in 1901. He commanded the army invading Cuba in June 1898 and, although the US forces were victorious, is given no credit for their success.

SHALER, Alexander. Union gen. 1827–? Conn. In the N.Y. State Militia, he was commissioned Lt. Col. 65th N.Y. 11 June '61 and was promoted Col. 17 June '62. He commanded 1, 3, VI (Mar.–May and June–30 Dec. '63), having been promoted B.G. USV 26 May '63. During 1863–64 he commanded the Johnson's Island (Ohio) military prison and during the Wilderness led 4, 1, VI (18 Apr.–6 May '64), when he was captured and placed under the guns during the bombardment of Charleston. He next commanded 3, 2, XIX, Gulf (3 Nov.–5 Dec. '64) and 2d Div., VII, Ark. (28 Dec. '64–1 Aug. '65) at the post of Devall's Bluff. Mustered out 24 Aug. '65 and breveted Maj. Gen. USV 27 July '65 for war service, he was given the Medal of Honor in 1893 for Marye's Heights (Va.) 3 May '63. He was later N.Y.C. Fire Commissioner and consultant to the Chicago Fire Dept., and continued in the National Guard and the National Rifle Association. He successfully bid for the purchase of armory sites and was twice tried for bribery but each time released by a hung jury. In 1861 he wrote the *Manual for Light Infantry Using the Rifle Musket*.

SHANKS, John Peter Clever. Union officer. Va. Appt.-Ind. He was commissioned Col. A.D.C. to Frémont 20 Sept.–19 Nov. '61 and named Col. Add. A.D.C. 31 Mar. '62–9 Oct. '63. As Col. 7th Ind. Cav. 9 Oct. '63, he served for the remainder of the war and was mustered out in Sept. '65. He was breveted B.G. USV 8 Dec. '64 and Maj. Gen. USV for war service.

SHANKS, John T. See SWEET, Benjamin J.

SHARP, Jacob H. C.S.A. gen. ?–1907. Appt.-Miss. Fighting with his regiment at Shiloh, Perryville, and Stones River, he was promoted Col. 44th Miss. before Chickamauga. At Missionary Ridge he succeeded Tucker as brigade commander. He also commanded a brigade in the Atlanta campaign and was appointed B.G. C.S.A. 26 July '64. Going to Tenn. with Hood, he returned to fight at Bentonville and surrendered with Johnston in N.C.

SHARPE, George Henry. Union officer. 1828–1900. N.Y. After graduating from Rutgers and studying law at Yale, he practiced until commissioned Capt. 20th N.Y. State Militia 11 May '61. He was mustered out three months later and commissioned Col. 120th N.Y. 22 Aug. '62. Breveted B.G. USV 20 Dec. '64 and Maj. Gen. USV for war service, he was mustered out in June '65. Having served with the diplomatic corps before the war, he became a special agent for the state department in Europe and held a number of public offices in N.Y., including that of legislator.

SHARPE, Jacob. Union officer. N.Y. Maj. 56th N.Y. 3 Sept. 61; resigned 5 Aug. '62; Lt. Col. 156th N.Y. 17 Sept. '62; Col. 1 Apr. '63; Bvt. B.G. USV (Winchester). Commanded 1st Div., XIX (Gulf); 2, 1, XIX (Gulf); 3, 1, XIX (Gulf); 3, 2, XIX (Shenandoah). Died 1892.

SHARPSBURG. Confederate name for main engagement of ANTIETAM CAMPAIGN.

SHARPS CARBINE AND RIFLE. One of the first successful breech-loading systems was patented in 1848 by Christian Sharps. Counting those acquired before 1861, an estimated 100,-000 Sharps arms were used during the Civil War (W. O. Smith, *The Sharps Rifle,* 7).

Despite bitter opposition to the breech-loader small arm in general, and despite preferential consideration of the inferior COLT REPEATING RIFLE, the US government bought 9,141 Sharps rifles and 80,512 Sharps carbines during the war. The Confederates bought 1,600 of the rifles in Feb. '61 (Albaugh and Simmons, 261) and also manufactured the weapon in the South (the "Richmond Sharps").

The Sharps rifle and the carbine are often confused. The rifle was eventually issued to the special regiments known as SHARPSHOOTERS. (The latter name, incidentally, does not come from the weapon.) The Sharps carbine, purchased in almost nine times the quantity of the rifle, was a cavalry weapon. Both were generally of .52 caliber, while other common bore sizes were .427 and .373.

In both the rifle and carbine the breech block was lowered by pushing forward a lever that doubled as trigger guard. This gave access to the chamber for loading a paper or linen cartridge. (The metallic cartridge Sharps was introduced after the war.) As the breech block closed it cut open the end of the cartridge with a sharp edge to facilitate ignition. The MAYNARD TAPE was used until 1859, then the LAWRENCE PRIMING SYSTEM. The hammer had to be cocked manually. Five types of Sharps carbine were developed, the last of which was the most successful. Early models had a bad gas leakage at the breech, but this was corrected by 1859.

The weapons were accurate up to 600 yards. At 300 yards a 24-inch pattern could be made with 20 shots. A rate of up to 10 rounds per minute could be achieved, which was three times as fast as the muzzle-loader could be fired.

SHARPSHOOTERS, 1st and 2d US (regiments of). In 1861 Col. Hiram BERDAN conceived the idea of forming special regiments of outstanding marksmen. Two regiments were organized: the 1st, under Berdan, and the 2d, under Col. Henry A. Post. Men at first brought their own rifles, but as this created a problem of ammunition supply, Berdan requested SHARPS RIFLES. Scott and Ripley insisted that he be issued muzzle-loading Springfields. On Lincoln's personal intervention, and after witnessing a spectacular exhibition of marksmanship by Berdan, Sharps were issued to Berdan's and Post's regiments, and later to others.

"The unique regiment of the war, Berdan's Sharpshooters were United States troops, in which respect they were different from other volunteer regiments; each company, however, was furnished entirely by some one State" (Fox, 418). In the 1st US Sharpshooters, Cos. A, B, D, and H were from N.Y.; C, I, and K were from Mich.; E was from N.H., F from Vt., and G from Wis. Col. George C. Hastings succeeded Berdan as regimental commander. Lt. Col. Caspar Trepp was killed commanding the regiment at Mine Run. The regiment fought with V Corps on the Peninsula, rendering valuable service at Yorktown with their target rifles in silencing enemy artillery batteries. During this campaign they were issued Sharps rifles. In 1863 the regiment was transferred to III Corps, and in 1864 to II Corps. It distinguished itself at Chancellorsville, where its skirmishers captured the 23d Ga. At Gettysburg Col. Berdan supported the 3d Me. with a detachment the morning of 2 July in the reconnaissance that brought on the fight at "Sickles' Salient." Of 1,392

enrolled during the war the regiment had 546 killed and wounded.

The 2d US Sharpshooters was commanded initially by Col. Henry A. Post and then by Col. Homer R. Stoughton. During the Peninsular campaign it was in McDowell's corps, which was detained and did not join McClellan. Its first serious action was at Antietam, where as part of Phelps's brigade, Doubleday's division, Hooker's corps (1, 1, I), it was employed in line of battle and lost 66 men. "Both of Berdan's regiments, however, were generally employed as skirmishers, and, consequently, never suffered the heavy losses incidental to heavy columns. They were continually in demand as skirmishers on account of their wonderful proficiency as such, and they undoubtedly killed more men than any other regiment in the Army" (Fox, 419). The 2d Reg. served successively in the I, III, and II Corps, most of the time in Birney's division and alongside of the 1st US Sharpshooters. Their heaviest losses were in the Wilderness (76 total) and Spotsylvania (53 total). Co. A was from Minn., B from Mich., C from Pa., D from Me., E and H from Vt., and F and G from N.H. This regiment had only eight companies, whereas the 1st had the normal 10. Out of 1,178 enrolled during the war, the 2d US Sharpshooters lost 462 killed and wounded (Fox, 419).

SHAURMAN, Nelson. Union officer. N.Y. Capt. 90th N.Y. 2 Dec. '61; Lt. Col. 26 Aug. '63; Col. 8 June '64; Bvt. B.G. USV (war service). Died 1880. Phisterer lists him as Schaurman, Nelson.

SHAW, James. Union officer. R.I. Lt. Col. 10th R.I. 26 May '62; Col. 11 Aug. '62; mustered out 1 Sept. '62; Lt. Col. 12th R.I. 31 Dec. '62; mustered out 23 July '63; Col. 7th US Col. Inf. 18 Nov. '63; Bvt. B.G. USV (war service). Commanded 1, 3, X; 2d Div., XXV; 1, 2, XXV.

SHEADS, Carrie. Union nurse. The principal of Oakridge Seminary, a school for young ladies near Gettysburg, she found herself the inadvertent superintendent of a Union Army hospital as the battle progressed. The building was hit more than sixty times and was once invaded by Confederate soldiers, but the principal and students continued to care for the wounded until some days after the battle, when the general hospitals were organized.

SHEDD, Warren. Union officer. N.H. Capt. 30th Ill. 29 Aug. '61; Maj. 24 Apr. '62; Lt. Col. 24 Jan. '63; Col. 13 June '63; Bvt. B.G. USV (war service). Died 1891.

SHEETS, Benjamin Franklin. N.Y. Union officer. Lt. Col. 92d Ill. 4 Sept. '62; Bvt. B.G. USV (war service); resigned 21 Apr. '64.

SHEETZ, Josiah A. Union officer. Pa. 2d Lt. 8th Ill. 25 Apr. '61; 1st Lt. 25 July '61; Capt. 22 Feb. '62; Maj. 6 June '63; Lt. Col. 28 Aug. '63; Col. 25 Nov. '64; Bvt. B.G. USV 26 Mar. '65 (Mobile). Other brevets for Vicksburg, Mobile. Joined R.A. in 1866 as Pvt. and continuing until cashiered in 1875 with rank of 1st Lt. Died 1883.

SHELBY, Joseph O. ("Jo.") C.S.A. gen. 1830–97. Ky. A wealthy young aristocrat who owned land, slaves, and rope factories in Ky. and Mo., he raised and commanded a Ky. Vol. company during the Mo.-Kans. border disputes. In 1861 he refused a Federal commission and entered the C.S. Army as a Capt. of Cav. under Sterling Price at Carthage. He fought at Wilson's Creek, Lexington, Springfield, Pea Ridge, St. Charles, and Devall's Bluff. In June '62 he joined Rains at Van Buren, Ark., to invade Mo., and as a Col. organized a cavalry brigade at Newtonia. As part of Marmaduke's cavalry division he took part in Hindman's abortive invasion of Mo., fighting Blunt at CANE HILL and PRAIRIE GROVE, Ark., 28 Nov. and 7 Dec. '62. He and Marmaduke raided Springfield, Mo., on 8 Jan. '63, being joined by Quantrill's bushwhackers. He took part in numerous raids as Federal and Confederate forces skirmished in the Trans-Miss. Dept. He was wounded in the mismanaged attack on Helena, Ark., 4 July '63. Appointed B.G. C.S.A. on 15 Dec. '63, he played a prominent part in the actions against Steele during the ARKANSAS CAMPAIGN IN 1864 and on PRICE'S RAID IN MISSOURI, Sept.–Oct. '64. Then, rather than surrender, he led his brigade into Mexico to support Maximilian. When the emperor was shot, Shelby returned to Mo. He was appointed US Marshal in 1893 by Cleveland. "Steeped in the romance of Sir Walter Scott and fond of quoting chivalric passages," according to Monaghan's excellent characterization of this picturesque figure, "he soon learned that his short stature gained magnitude on a big horse, that a black plume decorated his hat admirably, and that great exhilaration came from commanding a troop of light-horse." His unit was sometimes known as the Iron Brigade.

SHELDON, Charles S. Union officer. N.J. R.A. Pvt. Gen. Mtd. Sv. 18 Sept. '60; 1st Sgt. Co. G 1st Mo. 23 Apr. '61; 2d Lt. 11 June '61; 1st Lt. 21 Aug. '61; Capt. 1st Mo. Arty. 27 Mar–31 Aug. '62; Maj. A.A.G. Mo. State Mil. 2 Aug–4 Dec. '62; Lt. Col. 18th Mo. 4 Dec. '62; Col. 24 Dec. '64; Bvt. B.G. USV (Ga. and Carolinas campaign). Commanded 1, 1, XVII (Tenn.). Heitman lists him as serving as Pvt. Co. F US Mtd. Rifles, 31 Aug. '58–27 June '60 (under name of Charles S. Sargeant). Died 1900.

SHELDON, Lionel Allen. Union officer. 1829–?. N.Y. Lt. Col. 42d Ohio 27 Nov. '61; Col. 14 Mar. '62; Bvt. B.G. USV (war service); mustered out 2 Dec. '64. Commanded 1, 9 Right Wing, XIII (Tenn.); 1, 3 Yazoo expedition (Tenn.); 2, 9, XIII (Tenn.); 3, 1, XIII (Gulf); 1, 3, XIX (Gulf). W.I.A. Fort Gibson. A lawyer and jurist, he was commissioned B.G. in the Ohio State Militia in 1860. After the war he settled in New Orleans and was active as a lawyer and Republican Congressman. He was appointed Gov. of N. Mex. in 1881–85.

SHELL. Although loosely used to mean any type of projectile, a shell is an artillery projectile containing a bursting charge of powder. It can be spherical or oblong. This type of projectile was rather ineffective because of poor fuzes (particularly in the Confederate Army) and because the black powder bursting charge did not properly fragment the cast-iron "shell." Metallic cartridge cases are also classed correctly as "shell."

SHELLEY, Charles Miller. C.S.A. gen. 1833–1907. Tenn. A contractor and builder, he was named Lt. with the Ala. Mil. Arty. at Fort Morgan in Feb. '61 and was later commissioned Capt. 5th Ala. He fought at 1st Bull Run and in Feb. '62 he was named Col. 30th Ala. He led his regiment at Stones River, Port Gibson, Baker's Creek, Vicksburg, Lookout Mountain, Missionary Ridge, Rocky Face Ridge, Resaca, New Hope Church, Kenesaw Mountain, Atlanta, and Jonesboro. He succeeded to command of Cumming's brigade then and was appointed B.G. C.S.A. 17 Sept. '64. Taking Cantey's brigade into Tenn., he fought at Franklin and Nashville. After the war he was a Congressman, lawyer, Democratic politician, and public officeholder.

SHELTON, Mrs. Mary E. SANITARY COMMISSION worker. Iowa. Going to the front in the fall of 1863, she began her nursing at Helena, Ark. She then went on to Vicksburg and Jackson, inspecting hospitals and urging the Iowans to greater efforts in helping the commission. This work was done with Mrs. Anne Whittenmeyer, president of the Iowa Ladies' Aid. She was for a time Mrs. Whittenmeyer's secretary and was also in charge of diet kitchens in the various hospitals. She continued her activities for the remainder of the war.

SHENANDOAH, THE. Confederate cruiser purchased in England as the Sea King in Sept. '64, she was equipped in Madeira and, under the command of Capt. James Waddell, started for the Pacific. Going by way of the Cape of Good Hope and Australia, she captured or destroyed 36 vessels valued at about $1,400,000. Waddell did not learn of the collapse of the Confederacy until Aug. '65, whereupon he sailed for Liverpool by way of Cape Horn. The British government took over the cruiser and later transferred it to the United States. See ALABAMA CLAIMS.

SHENANDOAH, CONFEDERATE ARMY OF THE. Composed of Va. state troops that Kenton Harper started collecting in the Valley as early as 2 Apr. '61. On 28 Apr. T. J. Jackson (then Col.) relieved Harper and continued mustering volunteers. (See also STONEWALL BRIGADE.) On 24 May J. E. Johnston took command, and by the end of June had organized four brigades of infantry and a cavalry unit with a total strength of over 10,500. This force opposed Patterson in the battles of Falling Waters (2 July) and the skirmishes near Bunker Hill and Charlestown. Reinforced by eight more regiments, it eluded Patterson to reach Manassas in time to turn the 1st Battle of Bull Run into a Confederate victory. It then became part of the Confederate Army of the Potomac (Miller, X, 240).

SHENANDOAH, UNION ARMY OF THE. See MIDDLE MILITARY DIVISION and PENNSYLVANIA, UNION DEPARTMENT OF. Although Upton (p. 244) refers to the troops under Patterson in the Shenandoah in 1861 as "the Army of the Shenandoah," the organization to whom this designation properly belongs is Sheridan's force in the Valley in 1864. (See MIDDLE MILITARY DIVISION.) The cavalry corps of Wesley Merritt (Devin and Custer) in the Va. campaign of 1865 is called "the cavalry corps of the Army of the Shenandoah" (Fiebeger, 415–16) or simply the Army of the Shenandoah. (B.&L., IV, 750.) Merritt's corps plus Crook's division (2d Div., Army of the Potomac) comprised "Sherman's cavalry" in this final operation (*ibid.*).

SHENANDOAH, UNION DEPARTMENT OF. Constituted 18 July '61 to comprise the Valley of Va., the counties of Washington and Allegheny in Md., and those parts of Va. as would be covered in its operations. Discontinued 17 Aug. '61 and merged into the Dept. of the Potomac. Re-created 4 Apr. '62 from Banks's V Corps of the Army of the Potomac, it disappeared 26 June '62, when assigned to Pope's Army of VIRGINIA as the II Corps. (See also MIDDLE MILITARY DIVISION, DEPARTMENT AND ARMY OF THE SHENANDOAH.)

SHENANDOAH VALLEY CAMPAIGN OF JACKSON, May–June '62

One of the most brilliant operations of military history, Jackson's Valley campaign was a strategic diversion to draw strength from McClellan's advance on Richmond (Peninsular campaign).

The Shenandoah Valley was important to the Confederates as a source of provisions and as a route for invading the North. As far as the Federals were concerned, the Valley was not a suitable invasion route; however, it was important that they deny its use to the enemy.

When Joseph E. Johnston left the Valley for the 1st Battle of Bull Run, the defense of the region was left to the Va. State Mil. They were not disturbed until Oct. '61, when Federal forces occupied Romney and threatened Winchester. Stonewall Jackson was then sent to take command of the Valley district. Unimpressed with the quality of militia troops at his disposal, he requested and was given his old brigade. He was also given three poorly-disciplined brigades from Loring's Army of the Northwest. This brought his strength to about 10,000.

Union forces in the area consisted of Banks's corps (18,000) and Rosecrans' scattered detachments in W. Va.

Jackson conducted an undistinguished winter campaign into the snow-covered mountains of W. Va. He failed to capture the isolated enemy garrisons at Bath and Romney, but he did get a considerable quantity of supplies, and he damaged the canal and railroad near Bath. He then withdrew, leaving Loring with a detachment at Romney to block communications between Banks and Rosecrans. This outpost was soon withdrawn in connection with the LORING-JACKSON INCIDENT.

Early in March Banks moved up the Valley and occupied Winchester, which Jackson evacuated on the 11th. Shields's division (9,000) advanced to Strasburg and Williams' (7,000) remained at Winchester. Sedgwick's division (7,000) was at Harpers Ferry. Banks now prepared to leave for the Peninsula, in accordance with McClellan's plan. Williams started to Manassas on 20 Mar.;

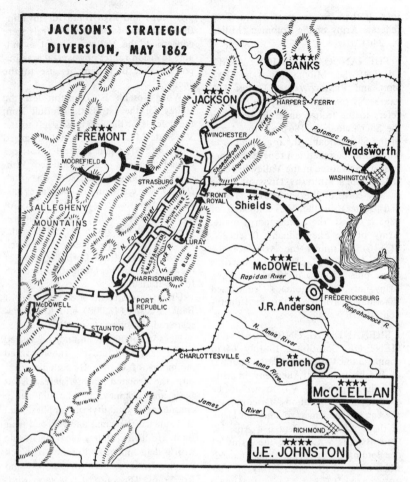

JACKSON'S STRATEGIC
DIVERSION, MAY 1862

Shields dropped back from Strasburg and prepared to follow.

Jackson's mission was to hold Banks's troops in the Valley. When he learned that Federal troops were leaving it, he made a forced march and attacked Shields at KERNSTOWN, 23 Mar. This is a remarkable engagement in that Jackson's tactical defeat led the Washington authorities to make mistakes that benefited the Confederates more than if Kernstown had been a victory: Banks was kept from reinforcing McClellan; Blenker's division was withdrawn from McClellan and sent to oppose Jackson; McDowell's (I) Corps (40,000) was withheld from McClellan; and a hodgepodge of separate commands was established. The latter contributed largely to Jackson's subsequent success. The organizational changes were as follows. Three separate and independent commands were established: McDowell's Dept. of the Rappahannock; Banks's

Dept. of the Shenandoah; and the Mountain Dept. under Frémont, who had succeeded Rosecrans 29 Mar. These separate commands reported direct to Washington, and there was no single general on the scene of action to co-ordinate their operations.

Faced by superior forces, Jackson withdrew slowly up the Valley. Joseph E. Johnston had dropped back from Manassas to Culpeper on 9 Mar., and had then taken the bulk of Confederate forces to oppose McClellan on the Pen-insula, leaving only the division of Ewell (8,000) at Gordonsville. Banks continued his cautious advance; by 26 Apr. his main force was at New Market, and a strong outpost was at Harrison-burg.

Alert to the danger of an advance by Banks through the Massanuttens, Jack-son made a forced march to Swift Run Gap. This put him in a FLANKING POSITION, which not only assured him of continued contact with the rest of the army, but which also made it im-possible for Banks to advance farther up the Valley without first driving him from this position. Ewell's division was put under Jackson's orders and moved to Swift Run Gap. He was also given authority to use Johnson's small division. This brought Jackson's strength to 17,000.

Frémont, meanwhile, had conceived the ambitious plan of invading East Tenn. As an initial step, Milroy's divi-sion was ordered toward Staunton. John-son withdrew from an untenable posi-tion to West View.

A junction of Frémont and Banks would have been disastrous to Jackson. With Lee's authority to formulate his own plan, Jackson decided to strike first at Milroy. Leaving Ewell at Swift Run Gap with orders to prevent Banks's further movement up the Valley, Jack-son moved off with his own division and Ashby's cavalry. Keeping his plans secret from even his own subordinates, Jackson marched up the Shenandoah to Port Republic, crossed the mountains to Mechum's River Station where trains were waiting, rode to Staunton, and marched to join up with Johnson's divi-sion. In the battle of McDOWELL, 8 May the Union attack was repulsed, and their troops pursued to Franklin.

On 13 May Jackson returned to Mc-Dowell, and the next day he started for Harrisonburg. Banks, in the meantime, had been ordered to dig in at Strasburg with Williams' division and to send Shields's division via Fredericksburg to join McDowell. On 12 May Shields was en route, and Banks was left in the Val-ley with only 8,000.

In the second phase of his campaign Jackson screened with Ashby's cavalry to make Banks think he would advance down the North Fork toward Strasburg. Starting his infantry in this direction, Jackson then turned unexpectedly across the Massanuttens, joined forces with Ewell at Luray, and descended with his full 16,000 on the 1,000 Federals at FRONT ROYAL, 23 May. This force was driven toward Strasburg and, despite a gallant fight, largely destroyed.

Jackson had to base his next maneu-ver on four possible Federal courses of action. Banks could stay and defend Strasburg; or he could leave it by any of three directions: west to join Fré-mont, north to Winchester, or east through Front Royal to Manassas, once Jackson was north of the North Fork. Thinking that Banks would most prob-ably remain at Strasburg or head for Manassas, Jackson moved the bulk of his force toward Middletown. Banks had wanted to defend Strasburg, but Gordon had persuaded him that this would be fatal. Gordon conducted a rear-guard action that enabled the bulk of Banks's forces to reach Winchester the night of

24 May. Jackson's pursuit was hampered not only by lack of adequate maps but also because his troops (the crack La. Zouaves and Ashby's troopers) wasted time looting a Union supply train. One column took six hours to march seven miles, and reached Middletown after Banks's column had passed.

Despite these frustrations, Jackson pushed his weary "foot cavalry" throughout the night. He knew the terrain around Winchester and realized that every hour's delay would give the Federals time to fortify the critical high ground that covered this place. In a skillful attack Jackson won the battle of WINCHESTER, 25 May. Banks retreated to Martinsburg and crossed the Potomac at Williamsport 26 May.

The Confederate pursuit was again ineffective. The foot troops were exhausted. Ashby's cavalry was sent toward Berryville to head off a possible Federal retreat through Snickers Gap (which did not materialize). "Maryland" Steuart refused a direct order from Jackson to pursue because the order had not come through his immediate commander, Ewell. An improvised pursuit on artillery horses was ineffective. After a two-day rest near Winchester, Jackson continued toward Harpers Ferry. On 29 May he was concentrated at Halltown, three miles from there.

The Washington authorities were thrown into a turmoil by Jackson's operations. They soon recovered, however, and became obsessed with the idea of trapping Jackson. Despite objections from McDowell and McClellan, who realized that the only purpose of Jackson's operations was to spoil the Peninsular campaign, the civilian authorities—principally Lincoln and Stanton—started directing military operations. McDowell's corps was ordered to converge with Frémont's on Strasburg. Banks and a

hastily-organized force under Saxton were to press Jackson from the rear.

Jackson was interested in maintaining his advanced position to harass the Federals as much as possible and also to give his quartermaster time to accumulate and evacuate his booty, particularly some valuable medical supplies. By 30 May Jackson knew of the movement of Frémont and McDowell. Leaving the Stonewall brigade to check Banks and Saxton, Jackson started 30 May to withdraw. The train on which he was riding ahead of his troops to Winchester was hailed by a courier, who gave him a message that McDowell's advance guard had captured Front Royal. At the time when McDowell and Frémont were closer to Strasburg than Jackson, the head of the Confederate column was 25 miles and the Stonewall brigade 38 miles from Strasburg. Jackson faced this situation with an uncanny calm, not even communicating the details to his subordinates.

Ashby's cavalry checked Frémont's advance, and an infantry brigade halted Shields's division near Front Royal. By noon on 1 June Jackson's entire force— 15,000 troops, 2,000 prisoners, and a double train of wagons seven miles long —had cleared Strasburg. A Federal force of 50,000 had failed to close the trap. McDowell's corps of 40,000 had been withheld from McClellan.

Brilliant as Jackson's operations were, their success was due largely to the blunders into which they led the Federal authorities. Steele says of Stanton, "by his obstinacy and ignorance of the science of war he probably set back the fall of Richmond and the Confederacy just three years" (Steele's *American Campaigns,* 229). The important lesson the Federals learned from their failure to trap Jackson was "unity of command."

The three Federal commanders pursued Jackson up the valley. Frémont followed the Confederates up the North Fork with 15,000 men, including Bayard's cavalry brigade of McDowell's corps. Shields's division moved up the South Fork (Luray Valley) with a view to cutting Jackson off. Jackson had anticipated this maneuver and sent detachments to destroy bridges across the South Fork north of Port Republic so that the two Federal commanders could join forces only by way of Port Republic. He sent a detachment to seize the critical bridge at the latter place to secure his own retreat.

Bayard's cavalry caught up with the retreating Confederates on 2 June between Strasburg and Woodstock and routed their rear guard. Ashby rallied stragglers, hastily organized a defense, and held off the pursuers the next day. Ashby's delaying action and the burning of a bridge across the North Fork delayed the Union pursuit until the morning of the 5th and gave Jackson a 24-hour lead. Contact was regained 6 June, and Ashby was killed in a heated skirmish. Shields, on the east side of the Massanuttens, heard the fighting on Frémont's front, but was unable to go to his assistance because of the bridges Jackson had ordered destroyed. Heavy rains further slowed the Federals and added to their problem of replacing bridges.

At Port Republic Jackson clashed with the advance guard of Shields's division (Carroll's brigade). In a street skirmish Jackson was almost captured. The night of 7 June Jackson was situated between two hostile columns. Rather than withdraw over the Blue Ridge through Browns Gap, Jackson elected to strike a final blow. Since Frémont's force was the larger (15,000), Jackson planned to block this column with Ewell's division (6,500) at Cross Keys, and to overwhelm Shields's two most advanced brigades at Port Republic (5,000; brigades of Tyler and Carroll). After his victory at CROSS KEYS AND PORT REPUBLIC, 8–9 June (the two battles are covered together), Federal forces were ordered withdrawn. Jackson moved to join Lee on the Peninsula for the Seven Days' Battles.

SHENANDOAH VALLEY CAMPAIGN OF SHERIDAN, 7 Aug. '64–2 Mar. '65. As a result of EARLY'S WASHINGTON RAID the Federal authorities established the MIDDLE MILITARY DIVISION under Sheridan. On 7 Aug. '64, when he took command, his troops were disposed as follows: at Harpers Ferry were the VI Corps; the 1st Div., XIX Corps; and the two infantry divisions of Crook's West Va. corps. The cavalry divisions of Torbert and Wilson arrived about two days later from Meade's army. When Averell's cavalry division of Crook's command joined the forces at Harpers Ferry the cavalry was organized into a corps under Torbert, and Merritt moved up to head the latter's division. The second division of XIX Corps later arrived, and by the time the first general engagement took place (Winchester), Sheridan's effectives numbered about 48,000.

Early's four infantry divisions and all of his cavalry except the two brigades at MOOREFIELD, W. Va., 7 Aug., were near Bunker Hill. By mid-August he was reinforced with the infantry division of Kershaw and Fitzhugh Lee's cavalry division; under the over-all command of Richard Anderson this force was to support Early by operations east of the Blue Ridge. When the Federals learned of this reinforcement it was thought that Early might have as many as 40,000 troops, and Sheridan was told to act on the defensive. At this time Early's actual strength was about 23,000 (including Kershaw's 4,500 and Fitz Lee's 2,000). There was a five-week period of maneuvering before the first real battle took place between Sheridan and Early. On 10 Aug. Sheridan advanced from Harpers Ferry toward Berryville; Early fell back to Strasburg to await Anderson's arrival. On the 14th Sheridan started back to Harpers Ferry, destroying military resources as he went. Anderson and Early followed. Anderson with Kershaw's division and one of Lomax's cavalry brigades remained at Charlestown to observe Sheridan, Fitz Lee moved to Williamsport, and Early led the rest of his command to Shepherdstown to threaten another invasion of Md. Lacking the strength for the latter operation, however, Early withdrew on 26 Aug. to Bunker Hill. Anderson withdrew along the railroad to the west side of Opequon Creek. Sheridan started moving south toward Winchester and Berryville.

About 1 Sept. Early was told to return Anderson's force if possible. Since Sheridan's main body appeared to be at Charlestown and did not seem to have any intention of advancing, on 3 Sept. Anderson started east to rejoin Lee. At Berryville he encountered Crook's corps, and Early moved with three infantry divisions to support him. The Confederates then withdrew west behind the Opequon. Since the Federals made no attempt to cross the creek, Anderson started on 14 Sept. for Front Royal to rejoin Lee. Fitz Lee's cavalry remained in the Valley, giving Early a strength of 12,000 infantry and 6,500 cavalry.

In strict compliance with his instructions Sheridan had been waiting for Anderson to rejoin Lee before attacking Early. This lack of aggressiveness had made his opponent overconfident, and on the 17th Early sent two of his divisions north to Bunker Hill.

Grant visited Sheridan and approved his plan of attack. Taking advantage of Early's faulty dispositions, Sheridan intended to feint from the direction of Charlestown (to the northeast) while moving his main force from Berryville against Winchester.

Sheridan defeated Early at WINCHESTER, 19 Sept. '64, and forced him to retreat via Newtown to Fishers Hill, below Strasburg. Although his plan was well conceived, Sheridan's troops were not able to maneuver so fast as Early's veterans and his victory was not so decisive as it could have been. However, his victory did give him confidence in himself, and it gave his troops and the Washington authorities confidence in "Little Phil."

Sheridan took up the pursuit and found Early's new defensive position near Strasburg on 20 Sept. He defeated the Confederates here in the battle of FISHERS HILL, 22 Sept., and pursued Early to Mount Jackson. Confederate resistance had been virtually destroyed.

Sheridan had sent most of his cavalry under Torbert up the Luray Valley after Fitz Lee, and expected him to cut Early off at New Market. Torbert was afraid to attack the two brigades under Wickham whom he found blocking his way at Milford. The poor cavalry leadership of Torbert and Averell enabled Early to reach Browns Gap, where Kershaw's division was again ordered to his support. Sheridan advanced as far as Harrisonburg. Early was ordered not to attack until Kershaw arrived.

After the battle of Fishers Hill James Wilson was sent to command Sherman's cavalry. Averell was relieved for lack of aggressiveness. George Custer and Col. Wm. Powell succeeded them as division commanders. Grant now proposed that Sheridan move on Charlottesville and then destroy the Va. Central R. R. as far as Richmond, but Sheridan believed this would require him to scatter his forces too much. Grant then approved Sheridan's plan to retire to

Winchester and reinforce Grant with troops made available by this operation.

On 6 Oct. Sheridan began his withdrawal, stripping the country as he went. One brigade crossed the mountains and destroyed the railroad bridge over the Rapidan between Gordonsville and Culpeper. The cavalry divisions of Rosser (who had come with his brigade from Lee's army) and Lomax so harried Sheridan's withdrawal that Torbert was told to attack the Confederates and "either whip the enemy or get whipped yourself." Near TOM'S BROOK, 9 Oct., the Confederates were whipped.

Thinking he had finally disposed of the threat from the Shenandoah, Sheridan withdrew to Middletown and started the VI Corps to join Grant by way of Alexandria. When Early appeared at Strasburg on 13 Oct. the VI Corps had reached Front Royal and had to be recalled to Middletown. This same day Sheridan was ordered to Washington to discuss with Stanton and Lincoln the previously considered plan of operating along the railroad to Culpeper and Gordonsville. On the 16th he was proceeding along the Manassas Gap. R.R. with Merritt's cavalry division when an intercepted message informed him that Longstreet was coming to reinforce Early. (The message was a ruse, as Sheridan suspected [O'Connor, 377].) Merritt's division, which he had intended to send to Grant, was therefore sent back to the Valley, where Wright was in command.

Although numerically inferior, Early was confident he could beat the Army of the Shenandoah. The battle of CEDAR CREEK, 19 Oct. '64, drove the Federals back from several successive positions. They had finally rallied when Sheridan arrived after his famous ride from Winchester and organized a counterattack that routed Early.

This final defeat marked the end of major military actions in the Valley. Wright's VI Corps rejoined the Army of the Potomac 6 Dec. '64 and the 2d Div., XIX Corps, was sent to Sherman at Savannah in Jan. Hancock was assigned command of the Middle Mil. Div. late in the same month to free Sheridan for active field operations. The latter now commanded 10,000 first-rate cavalrymen in the divisions of Devin and Custer.

Early now had only two brigades (Wharton's division of 2,000 men) and two artillery battalions. On 27 Feb. Sheridan moved from Winchester and reached Staunton on 2 Mar. Learning that Early was at Rockfish Gap, Sheridan decided to destroy this Confederate force before proceeding with the operation known as SHERIDAN'S RAID IN NORTHERN VIRGINIA (1865). At WAYNESBORO, Va., 2 Mar., Custer annihilated Early's remaining force. Early escaped with Generals Long and Wharton and about 20 others, but this ended his active military career. (See *Lee's Lts.*, III, 636.)

Sheridan's devastation of the Shenandoah Valley has evoked the same emotions as Sherman's March to the Sea. He was acting under the same letter of instructions that Grant had earlier given to Hunter:

In pushing up the Shenandoah Valley . . . it is desirable that nothing should be left to invite the enemy to return. Take all provisions, forage, and stock wanted for the use of your command; such as cannot be consumed, destroy. It is not desirable that buildings should be destroyed— they should rather be protected . . .

After pursuing Early up the Valley Sheridan had concentrated his main force at Harrisonburg, and from there had sent out raiding parties as far south as Staunton to destroy "crops, mills, etc." When he withdrew down the Valley he methodically ravaged it. He sent this report to Grant:

I have destroyed over 2,000 barns filled with wheat, hay, and farming implements; over 70 mills filled with flour and wheat; have driven in front of the army over four herd of stock, and have killed and issued to the troops not less than 3,000 sheep. This destruction embraces the Luray Valley and Little Fort Valley, as well as the main Valley. A large number of horses have been obtained, a proper estimate of which I cannot now make.

Lieutenant John R. Meigs, my engineer officer, was murdered beyond Harrisonburg, near Dayton. For this atrocious act all the houses within an area of five miles were burned.

(Actually, DAYTON was not burned, nor had MEIGS been "murdered.")

Sheridan later sent Merritt with his cavalry division to devastate Loudoun County. Here is the report of what was seized or destroyed:

3,772 horses; 545 mules; 10,918 beef cattle; 12,000 sheep; 15,000 swine; 250 calves; 435,802 bushels of wheat; 77,176 bushels of corn; 20,397 tons of hay; 20,000 bushels of oats; 10,000 pounds of tobacco; 12,000 pounds of bacon; 2,500 bushels of potatoes; 1,665 pounds of cotton yarn; 874 barrels of flour; 500 tons of fodder; 450 tons of straw; 71 flour mills; one woolen mill; eight sawmills; one powder mill; three saltpeter works; 1,200 barns; seven furnaces; four tanneries; one railroad depot; and 947 miles of rail. (O'Connor, citing O. R., I, XLIII, Part I, 37.)

Summing up his devastation, Sheridan said, "A crow would have had to carry its rations if it had flown across the [Shenandoah] valley."

SHENANDOAH VALLEY OPERATIONS OF EARLY (1864). See EARLY'S WASHINGTON RAID. 27 June–7 Aug. '64, and SHENANDOAH VALLEY CAMPAIGN OF SHERIDAN, 7 Aug. '64–2 Mar. '65.

SHEPARD, Isaac Fitzgerald. Union gen. 1816–89. Mass. A school principal and Mass. state legislator, he was named Maj. Asst. A.G. Mo. State Militia 18 June '61 and served as Lyon's A.D.C. He was then commissioned Lt. Col. 19th Mo. 30 Aug. '61 and Col. 18 Jan. '62. On 9 May '63 he was named Col. 51st US Col. Inf., the first and at that time the only colored troops in the Mississippi Valley. He commanded African Brig., Dist. Northeast La. (May–July '63) and Dist. Northeast La. (31 July–Aug. '63) and was promoted B.G. USV 27 Oct. In 1864 he commanded 1st Brig., 1st Div. USCT Dist. Vicksburg, and his appointment expired 4 July '64. In 1874–86 he was US Consul to China and later was active in Republican politics in Mo. and in the G.A.R. He was a newspaper editor and wrote several books of poetry.

SHEPHERD, Oliver Lathrop. Union officer. c.1815–94. N.Y. USMA 1840 (33/42); Inf. He served on the frontier, in the Mexican War, (2 brevets), and in Indian fighting. Promoted Lt. Col. 18th US Inf. 14 May '61, he was in the Defenses of Washington until June '61 and on mustering duty in N.Y.C. until Dec. of that year. He then went on the advance upon and siege of Corinth and with Buell through Ala. and Tenn. (July–Sept. '62). He commanded an R.A. brigade at Stones River and was in charge of recruiting in R.I. for the rest of the war. Breveted for Corinth and Stones River (B.G. USA), he was promoted Col. 15th US Inf. 21 Jan. '63 and retired in 1870.

SHEPHERD, Russell Benjamin. Union officer. Me. 1st Lt. Adj. 1st Me. Arty. 21 Aug. '62; Maj. 1 Jan. '63; Lt. Col. 24 Sept. '64; Col. 21 Oct. '64; Bvt. B.G. USV (war service). Commanded 3, Def. North Potomac, XXII, 1, 3, II (Potomac).

SHEPLEY, George Foster. Union gen. 1819–78. Me. A prominent lawyer, he had worked with Ben Butler in politics, and this led to his being commissioned Col. 12th Me. 16 Nov. '61 and his regiment being sent to Butler in New Orleans. Promoted B.G. USV 18 July '62, he commanded 3d Brig., New Orleans expedition, Gulf, from Mar. to Sept. '62 and was appointed by Butler military commandant of that city 1 May. The next month he was named military Gov. of La. and "must in some measure share with Butler the responsibility for whatever dishonesty there may have been in the army's administration of New Orleans" (D.A.B.). In May '64 he was in command of the Dist. of Eastern Va., Va., and N.C. and in 1865 was Chief of Staff of the XXV Corps for Weitzel, then military Gov. of Richmond. Resigned 1 July '65, he was later a jurist in Me.

SHERIDAN, Philip Henry ("Little Phil"). Union gen. 1831–88. N.Y. Appt.-Ohio. USMA 1853 (34/52); Inf.-Cav. There was little in Sheridan's early military career to indicate that he was to become one of America's top soldiers. At West Point he was involved in a serious breach of discipline—threatening Cadet Sgt. W. R. TERRILL with a bayonet, and then attacking him with his fists after Terrill had reported him for the first offense—and had been graduated a year late. He was a comparatively old Lt. when the war started, and held a number of administrative posts before being given command of troops. After a month as president of a board to audit claims against the government in St. Louis, he became Chief Q.M. and Comsy. of Curtis' Army of the Southwest. When Capt. Sheridan was found to be violating regulations to give vouchers for military supplies taken from Southern sympathizers, Curtis relieved him and preferred court-martial charges. Appealing to Halleck, he was transferred back to St. Louis before the trial could take place. During the battle of Shiloh he was on a roving commission to buy horses at Chicago. He then became Q.M. of Halleck's headquarters during the advance on Corinth and, meanwhile, tried to get himself a command. When Gordon Granger left the 2d Mich. Cav. he apparently recommended that Sheridan succeed him. He was appointed Col. 25 May '62 and "dressed in a coat and trousers of a captain of infantry, but recast as a colonel of cavalry by a pair of well-worn eagles that General Granger had kindly given me," he reported just in time to move out with his new regiment on a raid. Within less than a week (on 2 June) he was in command of the 2d Cav. Brig. (2d Iowa and 2d Mich.), and within 35 days of becoming a Col. he had won his star at BOONEVILLE, Miss., 1 July '62. In Sept. he was given command of the 11th Div., Army of the Ohio, and distinguished himself at PERRYVILLE, Ky., 8 Oct., holding his well-organized position and then launching a successful counterattack. Commanding the 3d Div., Right Wing, XVI (Cumberland) (5 Nov. '62–9 Jan. '63) he played a prominent part at STONES RIVER, Tenn., 31 Dec. '62, winning his second star. He then commanded the 3d Div., XX (9 Jan.–9 Oct. '63) at Winchester, Tenn., and CHICKAMAUGA. Commanding the 2d Div., IV Corps (10 Oct. '63–Apr. '64) he distinguished himself in the CHATTANOOGA CAMPAIGN. Sheridan not only stormed Missionary Ridge, broke through the line, and came close to capturing Bragg and several of his generals, but his division was the only element of the Federal attacking forces that retained enough cohesion to pursue. Grant selected him in Apr. to head the Cavalry CORPS (Potomac). While not conspicuously successful during the battle of the Wilderness, and clashing with Meade over misuse of his cavalry in the advance to SPOTSYLVANIA, he undertook SHERIDAN'S RICHMOND RAID, 9–24 May '64, which resulted in the defeat and death of the legendary Jeb Stuart at YELLOW TAVERN. His TREVILIAN RAID, 7–28 June '64, was blocked by Wade Hampton.

At Grant's insistence, and despite objection that he was too young (33), he was given command of the Middle Mil. Div. (6 Aug. '64–28 Feb. '65) and undertook his brilliant SHENANDOAH VALLEY CAMPAIGN, 7 Aug. '64–2 Mar. '65. Here, after some preliminary maneuvering against Jube Early, Sheridan won a devastating series of victories at WINCHESTER, 19 Sept., FISHERS HILL, 22 Sept., and CEDAR CREEK, 19 Oct. '64. He destroyed the pitiful remnants of Early's army at WAYNESBORO, 2 Mar. '65, and after menacing Lynchburg (see SHERIDAN'S RAID IN NORTHERN VIRGINIA, 27 Feb.–25 Mar. '65) moved to rejoin Grant around Petersburg for the APPOMATTOX CAMPAIGN. His victory over Pickett at FIVE FORKS, 1 Apr., and his vigorous pursuit and blocking of Lee's withdrawal beyond APPOMATTOX, 8 and 9 Apr., concluded his Civil War record on a high note of triumph. He was voted the Thanks of Congress 9 Feb. '65 for his Valley campaign.

In May '65 he moved to the Tex. border with 50,000 veterans in a show of force in connection with the MAXIMILIAN AFFAIR. Then, as military Gov. of Tex. and La. in 1867, his administration was so severe that he was recalled after six months. Made a Lt. Gen. in

1869, during the next two years he was an observer with the German Army, seeing the Franco-Prussian War of 1870. Sent back to La. in 1875 to subdue political disturbances, he was even more severe than before. In 1884 he succeeded Sherman as C. in C. The year of his death, 1888, at the age of 57, he became a full Gen. (four stars) and his two-volume *Personal Memoirs* appeared. In middle age he had married the daughter of D. H. RUCKER (Asst. Q.M. Gen. during the war).

"Little Phil," as his soldiers called him, was described by Lyman as "a small [5 feet 5 inches], broad-shouldered, squat man with black hair and a square head. He is of Irish parents, but looks very like a Piedmontese."

SHERIDAN'S HORSE, Winchester. See RIENZI.

SHERIDAN'S RAID IN NORTHERN VIRGINIA, 27 Feb.–25 Mar. '65. In late Feb. '65 Hancock was put in command of the Middle Mil. Div. so that Sheridan would be free for active operations. In view of the rapidly deteriorating situation of the Confederates, Grant believed Sheridan with his 10,000 well-equipped cavalry could brush past the meager defenders of the Shenandoah and capture Lynchburg. From here he might be able to move on to Danville and join Sherman in N. C., wrecking Southern military resources en route.

On 27 Feb. Sheridan moved up the Shenandoah from Winchester and reached Staunton 2 Mar. At WAYNESBORO, the same day, he defeated the 2,000 Confederates that remained in Early's command, taking 1,600 of them prisoner and capturing 11 guns. He entered Charlottesville, where he rested his troops 4–5 Mar.

Having learned that Lynchburg was strongly held, he decided not to attempt its capture. Custer's division was ordered to wreck the railroad from Charlottesville to a point 16 miles north of Lynchburg and then to move east to the James. Devin's division was to move straight for the James, destroy the canal and mills along its banks. Sheridan planned to unite his two divisions, capture a bridge, and cross the James.

On 10 Mar. Sheridan reached Columbia and learned that all of the James River bridges had been destroyed. Not equipped to bridge the river, he decided to rejoin Grant via the White House. He sent a messenger through the enemy lines to inform Grant of this plan, and moved north on the 12th. Wrecking the railroad as he went, he reached Ashland Station to find that Longstreet was moving against him with the divisions of Fitz Lee and Pickett from Richmond. He escaped northward across the North Anna and followed it down to White House. After resting here a week and being resupplied he was in bivouac south of Petersburg on 28 Mar. His losses were insignificant. Although the atrocious Va. roads of that season had exhausted his horses, within a few days he fought the decisive battle of Five Forks, 1 Apr. '65.

SHERIDAN'S RICHMOND RAID, Va., 9–24 May '64. Believing Meade had misused his cavalry in the Wilderness and the advance to SPOTSYLVANIA, Sheridan got Grant's authority to make a raid toward Richmond and to "whip Stuart." Taking the divisions of Merritt, D. McM. Gregg, and J. H. Wilson (Torbert was ill), he started early 9 May with 10,000 troopers and horse artillery in a column 13 miles long. Stuart learned of this movement almost immediately and started in pursuit with 4,500 sabers. His force consisted of Fitz Lee's division (brigades of Lomax and Wickham) and the separate brigade of James B. Gordon. Wickham made contact at Jarrald's Mill and skirmished with the Federal

rear guard as far as Mitchell's Shop, where his attack was repulsed. Custer's brigade raided BEAVER DAM STATION, 9–10 May, and did much damage. While Gordon continued to maintain direct pressure, Stuart led the rest of his force east and then south in an effort to intercept the Federal column. Davies' brigade (of Gregg) raided Ashland Station 11 May. The same day the rest of Gregg's division repulsed an attack by Gordon at Ground Squirrel Bridge (Church).

At YELLOW TAVERN, 11 May, Sheridan defeated Stuart, mortally wounding the famous Confederate cavalry leader and killing Gordon.

Sheridan realized that a raid into Richmond would be foolhardy, so he decided to move south of the Chickahominy to the James, where he could link up with Butler. The night of 11 May he encountered land mines ("torpedoes") along his route. The next morning his advance toward Fair Oaks was stopped by artillery fire from Mechanicsville and forces moved out from Richmond to trap him against the Chickahominy. He forced a crossing at MEADOW BRIDGE, and on 13 May escaped to Bottom's Bridge. The next day he recrossed the Chickahominy and went into bivouac at Haxall's Landing. Here he established contact with Butler and remained until 17 May, when he undertook the hazardous task of rejoining Grant. Lee's entire force was between him and Grant, and Sheridan did not know the exact location of either army. On 21 May he reached the White House, where he had to improvise a bridge to cross the Pamunkey. The next day he was at Aylett's on the Mattapony. Here he learned the location of the opposing armies, and on the 24th rejoined the Army of the Potomac at Chesterfield Station for the operations along the NORTH ANNA RIVER. In his first independent cavalry action Sheridan had ridden completely around Lee's army, had destroyed vital supplies and communications, had beaten the Confederates in four engagements, and had then extricated himself from a dangerous situation. Federal casualties were 625 men and 300 horses (Miller, IV, 128). The death of Stuart was probably the most significant result.

SHERMAN, Francis Trowbridge. Union gen. Conn. Commissioned Lt. Col. 56th Ill. 31 Oct. '61, he was mustered out 5 Feb. '62 and named Maj. 12th Ill. Cav. 8 Mar. Mustered out of that regiment 26 Aug. '62, he was named Col. 88th Ill. 4 Sept. '62, and fought at Perryville, Chickamauga, and Missionary Ridge. In the Army of the Cumberland he commanded 1, 3, XX (13 Feb.–12 Apr. and 28 Sept.–9 Oct. '63) and 1, 2, IV (18 Oct. '63–4 Mar. '64 and 6 Apr.–22 May '64) at Rocky Face Ridge, Resaca, Adairsville, New Hope Church, Pine Mountain, Mud Creek, Kenesaw Mountain, Smyrna Camp Ground, Atlanta, Jonesboro, Lovejoy, Columbia, Spring Hill, Franklin, and Nashville. He was breveted B.G. USV for war service, promoted B.G. to the full rank 21 July '65, and mustered out in 1866.

SHERMAN, John. Union statesman. 1832–1900. Ohio. A lawyer and brother of William T. Sherman, he was a Whig and helped organize the Republican party in his state. He was a Congressman 1855–61 and Sen. 1861–77 before being named McKinley's Sec. of the Treasury. In the impeachment proceedings he supported Johnson and was a member of the moderate Republican faction. Continuing in public life, he authored the Anti-Trust Act and the Silver Purchase Act, both bearing his name, and was Sec. of State 1897–98.

SHERMAN, Thomas West. Union gen. and "the other General Sherman." 1813–79. R.I. USMA 1836 (18/49); Arty. He served in the Fla. war and won a brevet during the Mexican War. Named Maj. 3d US Arty. 27 Apr. '61, Lt. Col. 5th US Arty. 14 May, and B.G. USV 17 May '61, he commanded the Port Royal expedition (19 Sept. '61–15 Mar. '62). Leading 6th Div., Army Tenn. (30 Apr.–10 June '62) during Halleck's advance upon and siege of Corinth, he was relieved for his "manner of exercising authority." In the Dept. of the Gulf he commanded Sherman's division Carrollton, La. (22 Sept. '62–3 Jan. '63); Defenses New Orleans (9 Jan.–21 May '63 and 18 June '64–9 Feb. '65), and 2d Div., XIX (13 Jan.–27 May '63) where he lost his right leg at Port Hudson. Of his Civil War service D.A.B. says, "He was an officer of unquestioned ability, but his long career in the old regular army of the Indian frontier in some ways unfitted him for handling volunteers not inured to its iron discipline." Breveted for Port Hudson (B.G. USA) and the war service (Maj. Gen. USV and USA), he continued in the R.A. and retired in 1870 with the rank of Maj. Gen.

SHERMAN, William Tecumseh. Union gen. 1820–1891. Ohio. USMA 1840 (6/42); Arty. Stationed in Calif. during the Mexican War, Sherman resigned in 1853 to become a successful banker there. Four years later he decided to practice law with the EWINGS and McCOOKS and had a short, unspectacular career in that field. Disgusted with civilian life, he applied to get back into the army. Friends in the War Dept. instead recommended him as superintendent of a military school being organized at Alexandria, La. He accepted in 1859, and was the successful head of what is now La. State Univ. when La. seceded. Then, despite a genuine affection for the South, where he had lived about 12 years, he resigned his position and volunteered for Federal service. Commissioned Col. 13th Inf., 14 May '61, he took command of the 3d Brig., Tyler's division, in June. In the Bull Run campaign his brigade (13th, 69th, and 79th N.Y. and the 2d Wis.) saw action on 18 and 21 July, losing about 300 killed and wounded and as many missing. Sherman was appointed B.G. USV on 3 Aug. to date from 17 May '61, and on 28 Aug. sent to be second-in-command to Robert ANDERSON in Ky. On 8 Oct. he succeeded Anderson as C.G., Dept. of the Cumberland. His outspoken criticism of the administration's unrealistic strategic policies and his feud with the press almost ended his military career. Accused of insanity by the press, Sherman did show signs of emotional instability at this period. He took command of the Mil. Dist. of Cairo on 14 Feb. '62 and on 1 Mar. took command of the 5th Div., Army of the Tenn. He was wounded early in the battle of SHILOH, but refused to leave the field, and was cited by Grant and Halleck for his part in the battle.

Appointed Maj. Gen. USV on 1 May '62, on 21 July he took command of the Dist. of Memphis. Whereas Sherman had seemed to "find" himself under Grant's leadership in the Shiloh campaign, it was Sherman who convinced Grant to put up with the treatment to which he was being subjected by Halleck during the advance on Corinth and who kept Grant from submitting his resignation. Sherman commanded the CHICKASAW BLUFFS expedition and then participated in McClernand's attack on ARKANSAS POST. He then commanded the XV CORPS (4 Jan.–29 Oct. '63) in the final stages of the VICKSBURG CAMPAIGN, succeeded Grant as C.G. of the

Dept. of the Tenn., and joined Grant for the CHATTANOOGA CAMPAIGN.

When Grant left to take over-all command of the Federal armies, Sherman succeeded him to the command of the Mil. Div. of the Miss., thereby assuming direction of the principal military operations in the West.

After a number of preliminary operations—supporting Banks's Red River campaign of 1864, the MERIDIAN CAMPAIGN—Sherman undertook the ATLANTA CAMPAIGN. In this and his subsequent MARCH TO THE SEA and CAROLINAS CAMPAIGN Sherman demonstrated a military talent that has led some historians to rank him as the top Federal commander of the war.

He became a Lt. Gen. on 25 July '66 and a full Gen. on 4 Mar. '69. Four days later he succeeded Grant as C. in C. of the army and served in that position until 1 Nov. '83—14 years. He retired 8 Feb. '84 and died 14 Feb. '91.

Seeing Sherman during the last weeks of the war, Lyman described him as "the concentrated quintessence of Yankeedom . . . tall, spare, and sinewy, with a very long neck, and a big head . . . all his features express determination, particularly the mouth. . . . He is a very homely man, with a regular nest of wrinkles in his face, which play and twist as he eagerly talks on each subject; but his expression is pleasant and kindly."

SHERMAN'S HORSES. He lost three horses in the battle of Shiloh, two being killed while held by an orderly. Of his other war horses he favored two, Lexington and Sam. He rode Lexington, a Ky. throughbred, when he entered Atlanta, and in the Grand Review. Sam was a large, half-thoroughbred bay with great speed, strength, and endurance, who was wounded several times during the war.

SHERWIN, Thomas. Union officer. Mass. 1st Lt. Adj. 22d Mass. 8 Oct. '61; Maj. 28 June '62; Lt. Col. 17 Oct. '62; Bvt. B.G. USV. Brevets for Peeble's Farm (Va.), Gettysburg, war service. Mustered out 17 Oct. '64. Commanded 1, 1, V (Potomac). W.I.A. and captured at Gaines's Mill. Served as I.G. on Griffin's staff for the 1st Div., V Corps.

SHERWOOD, Isaac Ruth. Union officer. 1835–1925. N.Y. Pvt. 14th Ohio 22 Apr. '61; mustered out 13 Aug. '61; 1st Lt. Adj. 111st Ohio 6 Sept. '62; Maj. 13 Feb. '63; Lt. Col. 12 Feb. '64; Bvt. B.G. USV 27 Feb. '65. An Ohio editor and mayor before the war, he later served as judge and for many years as US Congressman.

SHIELDS, James. Union gen. 1806–79. Born in Ireland, where he "received a good classical education, supplemented by some teaching in tactics and swordsplay" (D.A.B.), he came to America after having been shipwrecked in Scotland. He fought in the Black Hawk War and then practiced law and became active in Democratic politics. As a result of newspaper criticism, he challenged Lincoln to a duel, but upon explanation they resolved their differences and became good friends. He later served in the state legislature and as associate state supreme court justice. Commissioned a B.G. USV in the Mexican War, he was wounded at Cerro Gordo and breveted Maj. Gen. USV. Previously appointed General Land Office Commissioner by Polk, he was next appointed Gov. of the Oregon Territory and then US Sen., first from Ore. and then from Minn. He was mining in Mazatlan (Mexico) when the war came, and was commissioned B.G. USV 19 Aug. '61 from Calif. During the Valley campaign he commanded Lander's division, Potomac; 2d Div., Banks's V Corps, Potomac (13 Mar.–4 Apr. '62); and Shields's division in the Shenandoah (4 Apr.–10 May '62) and the Dept. of the Rappahannock (10 May–26 June '62). He resigned 28 Mar. '63 and was named to a state railroad post in San Francisco. Later he was US Sen. from Ill., Minn., and Mo.

SHILOH CAMPAIGN, Apr. '62. On 11 Mar. Halleck took command of the new Dept. of the Miss., which included what had been Buell's Dept. of the Ohio. Halleck's strategy was to continue up the Tennessee River (i.e., south), destroy enemy railroad centers at Jackson, Humbolt, and Corinth, and destroy the critical railroad bridge across Big Bear Creek east of Iuka. Grant had been temporarily succeeded by C. F. Smith because of Halleck's petulant displeasure with Grant. The new base of operations was to be Savannah, Tenn., where Smith started landing troops 5 Mar. Union troops were organized into the divisions of McClernand (1st), C. F. Smith (2d), Lew Wallace (3d), Hurlbut (4th), and W. T. Sherman (5th). By the middle of Mar. the five divisions were at Savannah.

In order to secure a base for operations against Corinth, Smith had Lew Wallace's division occupy an area on the west bank around Crump Landing. Sherman's division, forced by enemy opposition to abandon its mission of destroying the Big Bear Creek bridge, was put into bivouac around Pittsburg Landing when it returned. Since this was a better bivouac area than Crump Landing it became the main base, and the divisions of Smith (W. H. L. Wallace), McClernand, and Hurlbut were sent there.

On 17 Mar. Grant was given command of the field force and made no change in the dispositions already ordered. Smith had received a leg injury—which was to be fatal—and had turned his division over to W. H. L.

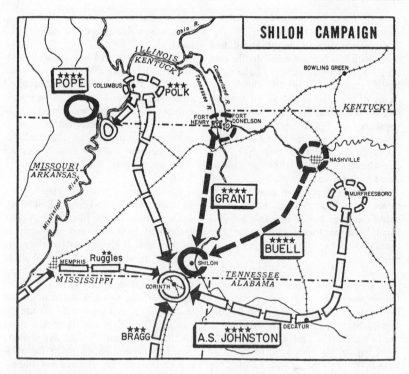

SHILOH CAMPAIGN

Wallace. New Federal troops continued to arrive, and on 26 Mar. the 6th Div., under Prentiss, was formed and sent to Pittsburg Landing.

Buell, in the meantime, had been ordered to march his Army of the Ohio to join Grant's Army of the Miss. at Shiloh. He reached Columbia (Tenn.) 19 Mar., but was then delayed 10 days by the flooded Duck River.

After the battle of LOGAN CROSS ROADS (Ky.) Beauregard was sent to the West, and after the fall of Fort Henry he was placed by Johnston in command of Confederate forces west of the Tennessee River. He established headquarters at Jackson (Tenn.) and started forming his Army of the Miss. Polk continued to hold the line of the Mississippi, with the bulk of his forces at Columbus

(Ky.). By the first week of Mar. 10,000 men under Bragg from Mobile and 5,000 under Ruggles from La. had reinforced Beauregard's army at Corinth.

Expecting a Federal advance along the line of the Tennessee, Beauregard ordered Polk back from Ky. to establish his main force at Humbolt (Tenn.) with an advance post at Union City. The river defenses at Island No. 10 and New Madrid were to be held as strongly as possible, and Fort Pillow was to be reinforced by heavy guns evacuated from Columbus and Pensacola. When Union troops started landing at Shiloh, Polk's forces were withdrawn farther to Jackson and Bethel to cooperate with the corps formed under Bragg around Corinth. The latter corps was made up of six brigades: the three Bragg had brought from Pensacola (via Mobile) and three brigades of Ruggles.

A. S. Johnston, in the meantime, had been withdrawing from Nashville and on 29 Mar. took command of the combined forces at Corinth—called the Army of the Miss.—with Beauregard as second-in-command. This army now consisted of Polk's corps (four brigades), Bragg's corps (six brigades), Hardee's corps (three brigades), and Breckinridge's corps (three brigades). Total strength was 40,000.

The Confederate plan was to attack Grant's force at Shiloh before Buell could reinforce him. Johnston's polyglot force, however, took a day longer than estimated to cover the intervening 25 miles.

Grant was surprised at Shiloh. Not expecting an attack, the five divisions at Shiloh were disposed with a view to favorable camping facilities and not defense. On 5 Apr. Sherman reported a patrol clash that had taken place the night before, but sent word to Grant at Savannah that there was nothing to indicate an enemy attack.

Shiloh—First Day (6 Apr. '62)

After additional delays the Confederates attacked Sunday morning, 6 Apr. A combat patrol of three companies of the 25th Mo. (Prentiss' division) made contact at about 5 o'clock with skirmishers of Hardee's corps. Fighting a delaying action, they were reinforced by four companies of the 16th Wis., five companies of the 21st Mo., and finally by all of Peabody's brigade. About 8 A.M. they were forced back on Prentiss' line.

Hildebrand's brigade (Sherman) received the full impact of the Confederate assault on the left of Sherman's hastily formed line; the 53d Ohio, receiving their baptism of fire, broke, and the other two regiments followed it to the rear. Prentiss' division was then routed. Federal officers rallied survivors

and organized uncommitted divisions to form a new line about two miles to the rear.

The attackers had lost all semblance of brigade organization by this time and their general officers were assigned command of portions of the line without regard to corps organization. The plan of battle was disrupted because of unexpected resistance on the flank toward the river and in a densely wooded area which they named the Hornets' Nest.

Grant hurried from Savannah when he heard the battle begin. "Bull" Nelson's division from Buell's army had arrived at Savannah and was ordered to march to the point on the river opposite Pittsburg Landing. Lew Wallace was ordered to prepare to move from Crump Landing to the battlefield. After giving orders for the defense of the landing area, making provisions for organizing stragglers and returning them to the fight, Grant visited his division commanders and issued orders for holding their lines. He realized the importance of the Hornets' Nest and told Prentiss to hold it at all cost. This second line had held about two hours, but Grant saw that it would soon be driven back. He sent word for Lew Wallace to move to the field.

Johnston was killed about 2:30 in the afternoon while directing the action on the critical east flank. Beauregard took command, and in a hot contest the Federal line was driven back almost to Pittsburg Landing. After 11 unsuccessful attacks Ruggles massed 62 guns on the Hornets' Nest and launched an attack that slowly encircled it. W. H. L. Wallace was mortally wounded leading his division out of the trap through a draw remembered as Hell's Hollow. At 5:30, after a heroic defense, Prentiss surrendered over 2,200 troops remaining in the position.

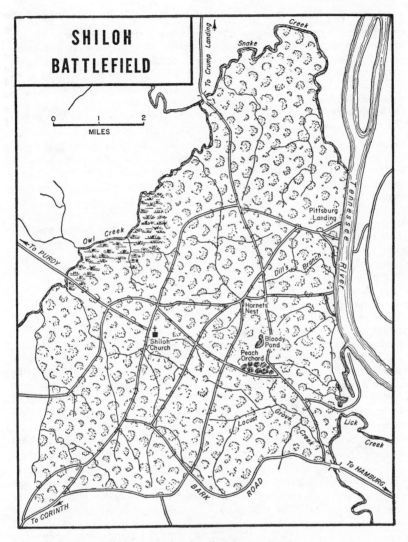

Grant's chief of artillery, Col. Joseph D. Webster, had organized a battery of siege guns in a commanding position near the landing. Their fire was reinforced by two gunboats, and withdrawing fieldpieces were organized to extend the line of heavy guns. Under the protection of this fire the withdrawing Federals organized a line to defend the landing.

Just before a final attack was going to be made on this sector Beauregard suspended operations at about 6 P.M. He had received an erroneous report that led him to believe Buell could not arrive in time to prevent the destruction of Grant's army the next day. Nelson's leading brigade (Ammen) had, however, crossed in time to reinforce the Federal left flank; the rest of the division crossed that night. Lew Wallace misunderstood his instructions and arrived about dark (7:15). All of Buell's divisions, except Thomas', arrived in time for the second day's battle.

Shiloh—7 Apr. '62.

Grant had the fresh divisions of Lew Wallace, Nelson, Crittenden, and one brigade of McCook available at dawn. Prentiss' division had been destroyed. Survivors of W. H. L. Wallace's division had joined Hurlbut's division. Beauregard's forces were disorganized and exhausted; Federal artillery harassed them throughout a miserably wet night.

At 7:30 in the morning Grant attacked. Lew Wallace's division was on his extreme right and Buell's army on his left. The fresh divisions made good progress in retaking most of the area that had been lost the first day. The Confederates then rallied and, taking advantage of the attackers' having outrun their artillery support, drove the Federals back in the vicinity of the Peach Orchard. Federal guns were rushed forward, and the line seesawed back and forth in the broken, heavily overgrown terrain.

Beauregard was anxiously awaiting word of the arrival of 20,000 men under Van Dorn who had been ordered up from Van Buren, Ark. The focal point of the battle became the crossroads at Shiloh Church. Particularly heavy fighting took place around Water Oaks Pond. Beauregard was determined to hold this area, first for use in committing Van Dorn's reinforcements and second as a line of retreat. Union troops were equally determined to capture it.

When Beauregard learned that Van Dorn had not been able to get across the Mississippi from Ark. he ordered a withdrawal. Two hours later he had disengaged his shattered army and started an unmolested retreat to Corinth; the exhausted Federals were content to reoccupy the camps they had occupied before the battle.

On 8 Apr. Wood's and Sherman's divisions, with two brigades of the 4th Ill. Cav., started in pursuit. At Fallen Timbers, about 6 miles from the battlefield, their advance guard was attacked and vigorously driven back by Forrest's cavalry. The Confederates were in turn sharply repulsed when they reached the Federal main body. Forrest was seriously wounded in the side, but his aggressive rear-guard action caused the Federals to give up any further ideas of pursuit.

Beauregard dropped back to Corinth, where he was reinforced by Van Dorn's Army of the West. Halleck undertook his leisurely advance on Corinth, reaching that place 28 May. During the Shiloh campaign Pope's Army of the Miss. was capturing NEW MADRID AND ISLAND NO. 10, the latter falling 7 Apr.

Who won the battle of Shiloh? Although both sides claimed the victory, it was a Northern victory, since it forced the enemy back on Corinth, forced them to evacuate much of Tenn., and opened the way to the final splitting of the Confederacy along the Mississippi. The Confederates failed to destroy the Union army and were forced to withdraw from the battlefield, leaving many of their dead and wounded. The generalship on both sides was defective; "Bloody Shiloh" was a "SOLDIER'S BATTLE."

Using Livermore's interesting system of comparing relative courage and efficiency, the green Confederate troops outfought their equally raw opponents: they hit 252 of the enemy for every

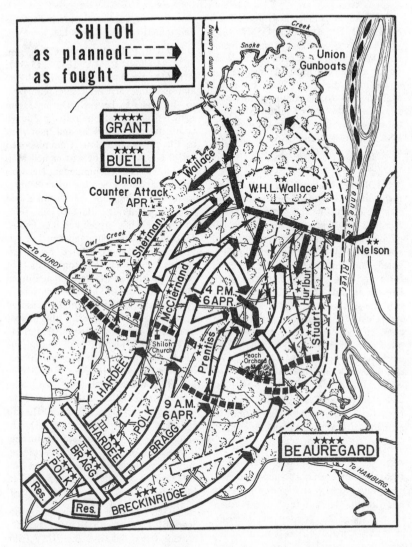

1,000 of their own troops engaged, whereas the Federals hit only 162 of the Confederates for every 1,000 of their own troops engaged.

There is disagreement as to the number of troops engaged at Shiloh but general agreement as to the losses. Livermore's figures are:

	Grant 42,682 Buell 20,000	Confederates
Effectives	62,682	40,335
Killed	1,754	1,723
Wounded	8,408	8,012
Missing	2,885	959
Total losses	13,047	10,694

SHIRAS, Alexander E. Union officer. c. 1812–75. Pa. Appt.-N.J. USMA 1833 (20/43); Arty. He fought in the Seminole War, taught mathematics at West Point, and served in the Comsy. Gen.'s office until the Civil War. Promoted Maj. 11 May '61, he continued in Washington and also served on the SANITARY COMMISSION. After being breveted B.G. USA and Maj. Gen. USA, he died on active duty as B.G. USA Comsy. Gen. of Subsist.

SHODDY. Material for making uniforms at the beginning of the war that was described in a factual article in *Harper's Monthly* at the time as "a villainous compound, the refuse stuff and sweepings of the shop, pounded, rolled, glued, and smoothed to the external form and gloss of cloth, but no more like the genuine article than the shadow is to the substance. . . ." A N.Y. *Tribune* writer called it "poor sleezy stuff, woven open enough for seives [sic], and then filled with shearmen's dust." The magazine article continued: "Soldiers, on the first day's march or in the earliest storm, found their clothes, overcoats, and blankets, scattering to the wind in rags, or dissolving into their primitive elements of dust under the pelting rain."

SHORTER, John Gill. C.S.A. gov. of Ala. 1818–72. Ga. After graduating from the Univ. of Ga., he moved to Ala. and practiced law as a young man. At first in the legislature, he was then elected judge and visited the Georgia secession convention as commissioner from Ala. A member of the C.S.A. provisional Congress, he was elected Gov. in 1861 and served until 1863, when he was succeeded by Thomas H. Watts.

SHOT (an artillery projectile). More precisely known as solid shot, this can be spherical (for smoothbores) or oblong (for rifles), but contains no explosive. It was used against fortifications and matériel. (See also SHELL.)

SHOUP, Francis Asbury. C.S.A. gen. 1834–96. Ind. USMA 1855 (15/34); Arty. He fought in the Seminole War and served in garrison, resigning in 1860 to become a lawyer. During John Brown's raid in 1859 he raised a Zouave company in Indianapolis and then went to Fla. to practice law. Commissioned Lt. of C.S.A. Arty., he was named Maj. in Oct. '61 and commanded Hardee's artillery at Shiloh. Serving under Beauregard and Hindman, he distinguished himself at Prairie Grove and also fought at Mobile. Appointed B.G. C.S.A. 12 Sept. '62, he commanded a La. brigade at Vicksburg. After being exchanged, he was Johnston's Chief of Arty. and on the Atlanta campaign from Dalton to Atlanta he did not lose a gun. In Sept. '64 he was mildly censured by a Court of Inquiry for the loss of stores when Sherman took Atlanta. He was Hood's Chief of Staff during the Tenn. campaign. After the war he became an Episcopal minister, after having joined the Church at Dalton. In 1869 he taught mathematics at the Univ. of the South, also serving as Chaplain. He had churches in Waterford (N.Y.), Nashville, and New Orleans before returning to Sewanee in 1883. Here he wrote on military subjects and mathematics. His wife was the daughter of Bishop Stephen Elliott.

SHOUP, Samuel Newton. Union officer. Ill. Capt. 114th Ill. 18 Sept. '62; Lt. Col. 8 Apr. '65; Bvt. B.G. USV (war service). Died 1885.

SHRAPNEL. A hollow cast-iron projectile filled with lead bullets set in a sulphur matrix and equipped with a time or percussion fuze that would set off a bursting charge and scatter the balls. "It is thus calculated to extend all the advantages of canister shot, to distances far beyond the reach of that projectile," according to Roberts (p. 113). The only practical problem in the way of this theory was the unreliability of Civil War fuzes. Shrapnel is often called CASE SHOT or spherical case shot. (See also CANISTER.)

SHUNK, David. Union officer. Md. Maj. 8th Ind. 27 Apr. '61; mustered out 6 Aug. '61; Lt. Col. 8th Ind. 5 Sept. '61; Col. 25 May '63; Bvt. B.G. USV 9 Feb. '65. Served as Lt. and Capt. in Mexican War. Died 21 Feb. '65.

SHURTLEFF, Giles Waldo. Union officer. Canada. Capt. 7th Ohio 25 Apr. '61; resigned 18 June '63; Lt. Col. 5th US Col. Inf. 29 July '63; Col. 29 Sept. '64; Bvt. USV (war service). Commanded 2, 3, XVIII (Va. and N.C.).

SIBLEY, Caleb C. Union officer. c. 1806-75. Mass. USMA 1829 (28/46); Inf. He had served on the frontier, in the Mexican War, and in Indian fighting and scouting before being captured by Confederates under Van Dorn at Matagorda Bay (Tex.). Promoted Lt. Col. 9th US Inf. 9 Oct. '61, he commanded the regiment at San Francisco until Oct. '64 and then served on detached service in N.Y. for the rest of the war. Retired in 1869, he was breveted B.G. USA 13 Mar. '65.

SIBLEY, Henry Hastings. Union gen. 1811-91. Mich. A fur trader in Minn. and territorial delegate to Congress, he was the first Gov. of Minn. (as a Democrat) in 1858, and was named B.G. USV 29 Sept. '62. During the Sioux outbreak of that year he led a brigade against the Indians, taking about 2,000 prisoners, trying more than 400 of them by court-martial, and executing 38 at one time on 26 Dec. Only direct orders by Lincoln prevented further executions. His commission expired 4 Mar. '63, and he was reappointed 16 days later. Breveted Maj. Gen. USV 29 Nov. '65 for

war service, he was mustered out in 1866 and was active in banking and commerce afterward.

SIBLEY, Henry Hopkins. C.S.A. gen. 1816-86. La. USMA 1838 (31/45); Dragoons. He served in the Seminole War and Mexican War (1 brevet) and on the frontier in Indian scouting, the Kans. border disturbances, and the Utah Expedition. Resigning 13 May '61 as Maj., he was made Col. C.S.A. three days later and appointed B.G. C.S.A. 17 June '61. He commanded the Dept. of N. Mex. and led the NEW MEXICO AND ARIZONA OPERATIONS IN 1861-62. Going to La., he was relieved of command in the early operations of Banks's Red River campaign of 1863. (See SIBLEY AND GRANT COURTS-MARTIAL.) He remained in the Trans-Miss. Dept., and went abroad after the surrender. As Gen. of Arty. in the Khedive's army, he remained in Egypt until 1874. Returning to the US, he lectured on his experiences but died in poverty. Inventor of SIBLEY TENT.

SIBLEY AND GRANT COURTS-MARTIAL. Charges of disobedience and unofficerlike conduct were preferred against Brig. Gen. Henry H. Sibley (C.S.A.) after the action at IRISH BEND AND FORT BISLAND, La., 12-14 Apr. '63. The court, with J. G. Walker as president, acquitted Sibley of the charges, but echoed Taylor's low opinion of his generalship during the action. Although Taylor says in *Destruction and Reconstruction* that "the feeble health of Sibley caused his retirement a few days after he reached the Teche" (p. 149), and mentions in his official report that Sibley had said he was sick, this factor does not appear to have entered into the trial. The same court acquitted Capt. Alexander Grant, of the gunboat *Cotton* or *Mary T.*, of disobedience of orders in abandoning the defenders of Fort Burton on 20 Apr. (Note. The O.R.

gives only the charges, specifications, and findings of the court; there is no record of the trial. I, XV, 1093–96.)

SIBLEY TENT. Invented by Henry Hopkins Sibley before the Civil War, it is described by H. L. Scott (in 1862) as follows: "Conical, light, easily pitched, erected on a tripod holding a single pole, and will comfortably accommodate twelve soldiers with their accouterments. Where means of transportation admit of tents being used, Major Sibley's will probably supersede all others." Wilhelm, writing after the war, adds that "A fire can be made in the center of this tent, and all soldiers sleep with their feet to the fire. This tent is hardly ever used."

SICKEL, Horatio Gates. Union officer. 1817–90. Pa. A coachmaker, he invented in 1848 a method for producing artificial light and became a lamp manufacturer. He had been active in militia organizations before the war and was commissioned Capt. 3d Pa. Res. 27 May '61. Promoted Col. 28 July '61, he was mustered out 17 June '64 and named Col. 198th Pa. 15 Sept. '64. Mustered out again in June '65, he was breveted B.G. USV 21 Oct. '64 and Maj. Gen. USV for war service. He was wounded three times in the war and commanded a brigade in Crook's Kanawha Valley expedition in 1864 and in the V Corps (Potomac) until the surrender. A banker and railroad official, he held several public offices.

SICKLES, Daniel Edgar. Union Gen. 1825–1914. N.Y. A lawyer and legislator, he served as secretary to the US legation in London, state Sen., and US Democratic Sen. 1857–61. In 1859 he was the center of a celebrated trial after shooting and killing Philip Barton Key, son of Francis Scott Key. Young Mr. Key had been having an affair with Mrs. Sickles. Pleading temporary insanity, for the first time in legal history, he was acquitted. He then created a further sensation by taking his wife back to his bed and board. She died eight years later. He raised the Excelsior brigade of N. Y. C. and was commissioned Col. 20th N.Y. 20 June '61, this regiment being one of the five in the brigade. The President nominated him for B.G. USV on 3 Sept. '61 and the Senate rejected this in Mar. '62 but confirmed a second nomination, retroactive to the first. In the meantime, he commanded 2, Hooker's division, Potomac (3 Oct. '61–13 Mar. '62) and 2, 2, III (24 May–16 July '62) at Williamsburg, Fair Oaks, and Malvern Hill. At Antietam and Fredericksburg he commanded the 2d Div., III (5 Sept. '62–12 Jan. '63) and was promoted Maj. Gen. USV 29 Nov. '62. While commanding III Corps (5 Feb.–29 May and 3 June–2 July '63), he fought at Chancellorsville and GETTYSBURG, where he lost his leg. Continuing in active service but not in the field, he was sent in 1865 on a secret mission to South America and was named military Gov. of the Carolinas. He carried out the work of reconstruction so energetically that Pres. Johnson relieved him in 1867, and two years later he retired as Maj. Gen. USA. During the war he had been breveted for Fredericksburg (B.G. USA) and Gettysburg (Maj. Gen. USA) and was given the Medal of Honor for the latter battle. In 1869 he became US Minister to Spain but resigned in 1873 after becoming involved in Cuban interests and the *Virginius* affair. He was named chairman of the N.Y. State Monuments Commission in 1886 but was relieved in 1912 for mishandling funds, and he lived the rest of his long life separated from his family, embittered. It was due largely to his interest and political know-how that the Gettysburg battlefield was preserved as a national park.

SICKLES, Hiram Franklin. Union officer. N.Y. Maj. 9th Ill. Cav. 24 Sept. '61; Lt. Col. 19 Feb. '62; resigned 15 Jan. '63; Col. 147th Ill. 21 Feb. '65; Bvt. B.G. USV (war service). Died 1892.

SIDELL, William H. Union officer. c. 1810–73. N.Y. USMA 1833 (6/43); Inf. He resigned a few months after graduation and was a civil engineer in N. Y. C. and a railroad engineer in the West and Central America. Returning as Maj. 15th US Inf. 14 May '61, he organized the Ky. Volunteers and served as mustering and disbursing officer in the field until July '62. He became acting Asst. Adj. Gen. of the Dept. of the Cumberland until Mar. '63 and returned to Ky. in administrative posts for the rest of the war. Retiring in 1870, he was Lt. Col. 10th US Inf. (6 May '64) and Bvt. B.G. USA.

SIGEL, Franz. Union gen. 1824–1902. Germany. A graduate of the German Military Academy, he resigned from the German Army in 1847 and the next year fought in the ill-fated revolution. Fleeing first to Switzerland and then to England and the US, he taught school in N. Y. C. and served in the militia. He moved to St. Louis, where he was director of the schools when the war began. A leader in the German community, he promptly espoused the Union cause, thus uniting the Northern Germans on the Federal side. He was commissioned Col. 3d Mo. 4 May '61, was B.G. USV 13 days later, and commanded 4th Brig., Army Southwest Mo. Jan.–Feb. '62. He played a prominent but undistinguished part in the battle of WILSON'S CREEK. At PEA RIDGE he commanded 1st Div., Army Southwest Mo. (Feb.–9 May '62) and was appointed Maj. Gen. USV 21 Mar. '62. He led Sigel's division, Shenandoah (4 June–26 June '62) in the Valley campaign against Jackson and then led the I Corps, Army of Va. (30 June–7 July and 12 July–12 Sept. '62) at 2d Bull Run. He commanded the XI ("German") Corps, Potomac (12 Sept. '62–10 Jan. 63 and 5–22 Feb. '63), leaving this post because of poor health. While commanding the Dept. of W. Va. (10 Mar.–21 May '64) he was defeated by Breckinridge at New Market. He then led Res. Div., W. Va. (24 May–8 July '64), during which time he delayed Early at Harpers Ferry but was relieved for "lack of aggression." Although he was an inept general, his ability to rally the German element to the Federal colors had been important. "I fights mit Sigel" had been their slogan. He resigned 4 May '65 and went into journalism in Baltimore. Later moving to N. Y. C., he was active in publishing and politics and popular as a lecturer.

SIGFRIED, Joshua K. Union officer. Pa. Capt. 6th Pa. 22 Apr. '61; mustered out 25 July '61; Maj. 48th Pa. 1 Oct. '61; Col. 20 Sept. '62; Bvt. B.G. USV 1 Aug. '64 ("organizing and disciplining a brig. of colored troops"); mustered out 30 Sept. '64. Commanded 1, 2, IX (Ohio); 2d Div., IX (Ohio); 4th Div., IX (Potomac). Died 1896.

SIGNAL COMMUNICATIONS. The Civil War saw the first use of a field-telegraph system and was the first war in which the electrical telegraph was used extensively. (Morse's system, patented in 1832, saw limited use in the Crimean War, 1854, and the Indian Mutiny, 1857.) The US Signal Corps, established 21 June '60 under A. J. MYER, was the first corps of officers and men in any army whose sole mission was communications. Another "first" was the use of air-to-ground telegraph.

At the start of the war the War Dept. asked the American Telegraph Co. and the Western Union Telegraph Co. to provide military communications in the East. The former company had already established a telegraph system along the eastern seaboard, and Western Union was extending a system through the Allegheny Mountains westward. With the strong backing of Stanton, himself a former director of the Atlantic and Ohio Telegraph Co., the Military Telegraph System with its operators and facilities remained under civilian control throughout the war. It was headed by Anson STAGER, prewar general superintendent of Western Union and a wartime colonel by direct commission.

Myer and Stager got into a conflict of "roles and missions" strongly resembling the interservice rivalries of a later day. Myer felt he should be responsible for "tactical" or battlefield communications, and Stager's organization should operate in the realm of "strategic" communication. The clash became increasingly noisy until Myer was finally relieved of command by Stanton on 10 Nov. '63 and sent to the West. The Signal Corps., now under Maj. William Nicodemus, was ordered to surrender all its telegraph equipment to Stager, and was limited to visual signals. The BEARDSLEE TELEGRAPH which Myer had adopted and used to develop his "Flying Telegraph Train" was discarded, although the insulated field wire continued to be used.

The Federal Military Telegraph System reported direct to the Sec. of War, and the military commanders, including Grant, had no jurisdiction over it. The service employed approximately 12,000 civilian telegraphers, strung approximately 15,000 miles of wire, and during the 12 months starting 1 July '62 it averaged 3,300 messages a day. Its code was never compromised.

Although the Confederates impressed civilian telegraphers and facilities they were never able to develop so extensive or efficient a system as the Federals. The Confederate Signal Corps was established 29 May '62 with a semi-independent status under Samuel Cooper's office. By the end of the war it numbered about 1,500.

SILL, Joshua Woodrow. Union gen. 1831-62. Ohio. USMA 1853 (3/52); Ord. Serving at various arsenals and ordnance depôts, he taught at West Point and resigned in 1861 to teach in a Brooklyn college. Commissioned Col. 33d Ohio 27 Aug. '61, he was in the W. Va. campaign and commanded 9th Brig., Army Ohio Nov.–Dec. '61. Taking over 9th Brig., 3d Div., Army Ohio (2 Dec. '61–10 Aug. '62), he commanded them at Battle Creek (Tenn.) in July and led 1, 3 Right Wing, XIV, Cumberland (5 Nov.–31 Dec. '62) at Stones River, when he was killed on the latter date. He participated in the battle of PERRYVILLE but is not listed either by Dyer or B.&L. as commanding anything larger than a regiment there, although Cullum shows him leading a division in this action.

Fort Sill, Okla., was named for him by his classmate Sheridan in 1869.

SIMMS, James P. C.S.A. gen. ?–1888. Appt.-Ga. A lawyer, he was appointed Maj. 53d Ga. and served in the Peninsular and Maryland campaigns and at Fredericksburg. As Col. he commanded his regiment at Chancellorsville, Gettysburg, the Wilderness, and Petersburg, having gone with Longstreet to Knoxville and led Bryan's brigade under Early in the Shenandoah. Appointed B.G. C.S.A. 8 Dec. '64, he commanded his brigade in Kershaw's division until captured with Ewell at Sayler's Creek 6 Apr. '65. After the war he returned to the law and sat in the legislature.

SIMONSON, John Smith. Pa. Appt.-Ind. He fought in the War of 1812 and the Seminole War as a volunteer before entering the R.A. in 1846. Winning a brevet in the Mexican War, he served on the frontier in Indian fighting and was retired in Sept. '61 as Col. 3d US Cav., for disability. During the Civil War, however, he served on several commissions dealing with the volunteer soldier and was breveted B.G. USA. He died 1881.

SIMPSON, James H. Union officer. c. 1813–83. N.J. USMA 1832 (18/45); Arty.-Engrs. He served in the Seminole War and was Chief Topo. Engr. with the Utah Expedition before being promoted Maj. 6 Aug. '61. In the Dept. of the Shenandoah he was Chief Engr. until 7 Aug. '61, and then fought as Col. 4th N.J. in the Peninsular campaign at West Point and Gaines's Mill, where he was captured. Held prisoner until 12 Aug. '62, he was Chief Engr. of the Dept. of the Ohio for the rest of the war and promoted Lt. Col. 1 June '63. Continuing in the R.A., he retired in 1880 as Col. and Bvt. B.G. USA.

SIMPSON, Marcus [sic] de Lafayette. Union officer. c. 1824–1909. N.Y. USMA 1846 (22/59); Arty. He fought in the Mexican War (2 brevets) and served in the West in Indian fighting. Promoted Maj. Comsy. of Subsist. 1 July '61, he was Asst. to the Comsy. Gen. for the entire war and named Lt. Col. 9 Feb. '63. Continuing in the R.A., he retired in 1888 as Col. and Bvt. B.G. USA and Bvt. Maj. Gen. USA.

SIMPSON, Samuel P. Union officer. Mo. 2d Lt. 3d Mo. Res. Corps 8 May '61; mustered out 18 Aug. '61; Lt. Col. 12th Mo. State Militia Cav. 12 Apr. '62; resigned 13 Sept. '62; Lt. Col. 31st Mo. 17 Sept. '62; Bvt. B.G. USV (war service); resigned 7 Jan. '65.

SIX-MILE HOUSE. Va. See GLOBE TAVERN, Va., 18–21 Aug. '64.

SLACK, James Richard. Union gen. 1818–81. Pa. A lawyer and judge, he was named Col. 47th Ind. 13 Dec. '61 and served under Buell in Ky. and Pope

in Mo. He commanded 1, 2d Div., Army Miss. (23 Feb.–4 Mar. '62); 1, 3d Div., Army Miss. (4 Mar.–24 Apr. '62); 1, 2d Div. Dist. East Ark., Tenn.; 1, 12, XIII, Tenn. (8–20 Feb. '63) and 2, 12, XIII, Tenn. (9 Apr.–28 July '63) during the Vicksburg campaign at Champion's Hill and the final assaults. He led his regiment on the Red River expedition of 1864 and was promoted B.G. USV 10 Nov. '64. Breveted Maj. Gen. USV for war service, he was mustered out in 1866.

SLACK, William Y. C.S.A. gen. ?– 1862. Appt.-Mo. Wright says he was appointed 17 Apr. '62 to rank from the 12th as B.G. C.S.A. and that this was confirmed 17 Apr. He was killed at Pea Ridge on 7 Mar. '62. He is listed by Wood but not by C.M.H.

SLASH CHURCH, Va., 27 May '62. See HANOVER C.H., same date.

SLAUGHTER, James E. C.S.A. gen. ?–1901. Va. He entered the R.A. during the Mexican War in the Voltigeurs in 1847 and transferred the next year to the Arty. Appointed 1st Lt. C.S.A. Arty. in 1861, he served as Beauregard's I.G. in the Dept. of Ala. and West Fla. After participating in the fighting around Pensacola, he was appointed B.G. C.S.A. 8 Mar. '62. In May he was appointed Bragg's I.G. for the Army of Miss. and then commanded troops in Mobile. In Apr. '63 he went to Galveston as Magruder's Chief of Arty. Later that year he commanded the Eastern Sub-Dist. of Tex., the 2d Div., and also served as Chief of Staff. He was included in the Canby-Smith convention for the Trans-Miss. Dept. but went to Mexico before obtaining his personal parole and lived there the rest of his life.

SLAUGHTER MOUNTAIN, Va. Alternate name for battle of Cedar Mountain, 9 Aug. '62, in the 2d BULL RUN CAMPAIGN.

SLAVERY. Negroes were introduced in Va. in 1619 by a Dutch ship. The institution of slavery flourished, particularly in the Southern colonies, until LINCOLN'S EMANCIPATION PROCLAMATION set them free 1 Jan. '63 (but only in the territory in rebellion). The slave trade fostered by the British in the eighteenth century found its principal market in the New World, although not all of the colonies condoned it. (The Germantown Quakers denounced it as early as 1688.) After unsuccessful attempts to subjugate the Indians, the slave labor from Africa became increasingly important to the economics of the country. While more numerous in the South, slaves were also a feature of the North's prosperity. The plantation system of the South pointed up the obvious advantages of a large, unpaid laboring class. Used principally in farm production, slaves and the staggering expenses entailed in their purchase proved unfeasible in the North, where small-scale agricultural ventures were based on a local market. By the Revolution the slave population was 20 per cent of the total, and three fourths of these were in the South, where they constituted 40 per cent of the population. Beginning in R.I. in 1774, abolition swept through Vt., Pa., Mass., N.H., Conn., N.Y. and N.J., so that by 1846 the institution had disappeared in the North. Although moral, religious, intellectual, and economic opposition to slavery had been raised in the South, the Constitution recognized and protected slavery. Until 1818 slavery did not become a political issue. But with Mo.'s request to join the Union and the resultant MISSOURI COMPROMISE (1820), the bitter forces of sectionalism took over to culminate finally in the Civil War. As the abolitionist doctrine gained strength in the North, the cotton economy with the aid of the newly invented cotton gin became the basis for the South's existence, and its widespread cultivation required slave labor. The continued use of land for cotton quickly exhausts the soil, and the need for new land was a constant factor in the Southern economy. These expansionist tendencies brought about the war with Mexico. In the decade prior to the Civil War slavery as an institution brought about the Omnibus Bill, the KANSAS-NEBRASKA ACT, the DRED SCOTT DECISION, the Lincoln-Douglas debates, JOHN BROWN'S raid, the PERSONAL LIBERTY LAWS, and the UNDERGROUND RAILROAD. Lincoln's election in 1860 was taken by the South to mean that their interests were to be disregarded, and secession and the war followed. Supporters of slavery defended it as necessary to the prosperity of the South and pointed out that slaves were fed, sheltered, cared for in bad times, and clothed by their owners, while their religious and moral well-being was of the utmost importance. Opponents attacked it as a violation of humanitarian ideals, drawing on the cruelty shown the field hands, the disruption of families, the violation of personal freedoms, the uneconomic use of the labor, and slave breeding to illustrate the immorality of the system. Plantation slaves were divided into domestic servants, field hands, and mechanics. By 1861 one third of the 12,000,000 population of the South were Negro slaves who were owned by but 384,000 whites, and only about 1,800 of this number owned 100 or more.

SLEMMER, Adam Jacoby. Union gen. 1828–68. Pa. USMA 1850 (12/44); Arty. Serving in the Seminole War and on frontier duty, he taught at West Point and was promoted Maj. 16th US Inf. 14 May '61 (from 1st Lt. since

1854). He was Acting I.G. of Ohio in the fall of 1861 and went on the expedition from Parkersburg to Roane C.H. (Va.) in Sept. Serving with Buell (May–Nov. '62) he distinguished himself in the defense of Fort Pickens in PENSACOLA BAY. He was named B.G. USV 29 Nov. '62 and wounded at Stones River the next Dec. On staff and board duty thereafter, he was breveted for Murfreesboro and war service (B.G. USA) and continued in the R.A., dying on active duty of heart disease at Fort Laramie, Wyoming.

SLEVIN, Patrick Sumerville. Union officer. Ireland. Lt. Col. 100th Ohio 8 Aug. '62; Col. 13 May '63; Bvt. B.G. USV (war service); discharged 30 Nov. '64. Died 1894.

SLIDELL, John. Confed. diplomat. 1793–1871. N.Y. After graduating from Columbia he practiced law in New Orleans and sat in the US House of Representatives. He joined the Confederacy after many years of prominence in the Democratic party and was sent in 1861 on a diplomatic mission with James M. MASON to France. They were captured on the British mail steamer *Trent,* which led to the TRENT AFFAIR, and gained the Confederacy a tremendous amount of public sympathy in Europe. Slidell did not, however, succeed in securing diplomatic recognition from France. He was a paternal uncle of Ranald Slidell MACKENZIE. (See also BROTHER AGAINST BROTHER.)

SLOCUM, Henry Warner. Union gen. 1827–94. N.Y. USMA 1852 (7/43); Arty. One of Sheridan's roommates at West Point, he served in Fla. and resigned in 1856 to practice law. He was in the militia and the legislature. Named Col. 27th N.Y. 21 May '61, he was severely wounded at 1st Bull Run and was on sick leave until Sept. Appointed B.G. USV 9 Aug. '61, he com-

manded, in the Army of the Potomac: 2d Brig., Franklin's division (3 Oct. '61–13 Mar. '62) and 2d Brig., 1st Div., I Corps (13 Mar.–4 Apr. '62). At Yorktown and West Point he led 2d Brig., 1st Div., Rappahannock (4 Apr.–18 May '62). He commanded 1st Div., VI, Potomac (18 May–15 Oct. '62) at Gaines's Mill, Glendale, Malvern Hill, 2d Bull Run, South Mountain, and Antietam. As Maj. Gen. USV 4 July '62, he led the XII Corps (25 Sept. '62–18 Apr. '64) at Fredericksburg (in reserve). Chancellorsville, and the right wing at Gettysburg. When sent with Howard to serve under Hooker in Tenn., Slocum handed in his resignation. Relations between Slocum and Hooker had been strained since Chancellorsville. The problem was solved by giving Slocum command of the post of Vicksburg (20 Apr.–14 Aug. '64). When Howard succeeded McPherson in command of the Army of the Tenn., Hooker asked to be relieved, as Howard had been junior to him. Slocum then succeeded Hooker in command of the XX Corps (a consolidation of the old XI and XII Corps). He commanded this 27 Aug.–11 Nov. '64, when he took over the Army of Ga. for the March to the Sea and through the Carolinas, participating in Savannah, Averasboro, Bentonville, Goldsboro, Raleigh, and J. E. Johnston's surrender. Resigning 28 Sept. '65, he served in Congress for three terms and was active in exonerating Fitz-John Porter. He was later on the Board of the Gettysburg Monument Commissioners.

SLOCUM, Willard. Union officer. Ohio. Capt. 23d Ohio 7 June '61; resigned 18 July '61; 1st Lt. Adj. 120th Ohio 25 Aug. '62; Maj. 17 Apr. '63; Lt. Col. 1 Mar. '64; Bvt. B.G. USV (war service); mustered out 13 Dec. '64. Died 1894. Phisterer lists him as Slocum, William.

SLOUGH (slow), John P. Union gen. 1829–67. Ohio. Expelled from the Ohio legislature for "striking a member," he was active in Democratic politics and was named Capt. 1st Colo. 24 June '61. As Col. (26 Aug. '61), he commanded Fort Garland (Colo.) and fought, against Canby's orders, at Glorieta Pass, defeating Sibley and forcing him to retreat into Tex. Commissioned B.G. USV 25 Aug. '62, he had commanded 2, Sigel's division, Shenandoah (4–26 June '62) and 2, 2, II, Army of Va. (26 June–1 July, '62) and was Mil. Gov. of Alexandria (Oct. '62–Feb. '63; 2 Feb. '63–5 Nov. '64; 5 Dec. '64–26 Apr. '65 and 5 June–20 July '65). Mustered out 24 Aug. '65, he was Chief Justice of the N. Mex. supreme court, but was the target of several resolutions passed by the legislature to remove him. He challenged their author, one William Rynerson, to a duel and was killed.

SMALL, Michael Peter. Union officer. c. 1831–92. Pa. USMA 1855 (11/34); Arty.-Comsy. He served in the Seminole War, the Utah Expedition, and on the expedition to suppress John Brown's raid. Promoted 1st Lt. 2d. US Arty. 27 Apr. '61 and Capt. Comsy. of Subsist. 3 Aug. '61, he served in Q.M. and mustering posts in Mo. and Minn. before becoming Chief Comsy. for the XIII Corps in the Gulf (15 Sept.–9 Nov. '63). He then was named Chief Comsy. of the Dept. of Va. and N.C. for the rest of the war. Continuing in the R.A., he died on active duty as Maj. and Bvt. B.G. USA (9 Apr. '65).

SMALL ARMS OF THE CIVIL WAR. Over 4,000,000 small arms were issued to Federal troops during a five-year period between 1861 and 1866, whereas only 7,892 CANNON were issued to the army during the same span of time (Shannon, I, 126, citing O.R. III, V, 1042).

The term "small arms" is used to designate all firearms smaller than cannon. Swords and other hand weapons are sometimes called small arms, but these will be treated under EDGED WEAPONS.

Although a tremendous variety of small arms appeared during the war, the principal weapon on both sides was the caliber .58 Springfield rifle musket firing the Minié bullet. This was officially designated the UNITED STATES RIFLE MUSKET, MODEL 1861. Several other types of shoulder arms used in the war are covered under their US Model designations. Other types were the unsatisfactory COLT REPEATING RIFLE, the English ENFIELD RIFLE MUSKET, the HENRY REPEATING RIFLE, the KERR RIFLE, the SHARPS CARBINE AND RIFLE, and the WHITWORTH RIFLE. Numerous other species existed, many of which are confused with carbines (see below). The HARPERS FERRY RIFLE, JÄGER RIFLE, and MISSISSIPPI RIFLE were popular names for certain US models. Weapons were also known by the name of the armory that produced them (SPRINGFIELD, RICHMOND, PALMETTO).

What K. P. Williams calls "The Breech-Loader Question" (Vol. II, 782ff) was a major issue during the Civil War. Although several effective breech-loaders had been developed, the military mind opposed their introduction into service. Their increased rate of fire was not looked on as a beneficial improvement of firepower, but as a logistical problem in supplying the additional ammunition on the battlefield. Another problem that bored inventors but plagued ordnance officers was retooling for new weapons when the troops could not be supplied even with the older but satisfactory ones. The Federal cavalry eventually was armed with the highly successful breech-loading SHARPS CARBINE and the SPENCER REPEATING CAR-

BINE. The BURNSIDE CARBINE and the MAYNARD CARBINE saw considerable use by both Federals and Confederates. REMINGTON CARBINE appeared late in the war. Other types were the Starr, Smith, and Merrill. Shotguns were popular with Southern cavalrymen until the end of the war.

About 374,000 revolvers of various makes were purchased by the Federal government during the war at an approximate cost of $6,000,000, according to Gluckman (US. Martial Pistols and Revolvers, 159). This standard reference also says on the same page, however, that according to the Colt Fire Arms Company the Colt Armory furnished the government with 386,417 revolvers during the Civil War. The COLT REVOLVER in its various types, principally the Model 1851 "Navy" and the New Model Army Model 1860, was the most important pistol of the war. The REMINGTON NEW MODEL REVOLVER was second in importance, and the STARR ARMY PERCUSSION REVOLVER was also purchased in large numbers. Other significant types, with government purchases shown in parentheses, were the Savage Navy (11,284), Whitney (11,214), Beal (12,251), Joslyn (1,100).

Foreign weapons were imported in large quantities until US production could get under way. Some of the English revolvers, most of them cal. .44 five-shooters, were: Adams (an English patent, but mostly manufactured by the Mass. Arms Co., although both North and South bought some from England), Bentley, and Tranter. Some revolvers made by the manufacturer of the KERR RIFLE were imported by the South. Other foreign types were the Lefaucheaux, Perrin, Raphael, and the curious LE MAT REVOLVER.

As for manufacture in the South, "practically all Confederate-made re-

volvers are imitations of the .36-caliber Colt navy," according to Albaugh and Simmons in Confederate Arms (p. 9). Fewer than 10,000 revolvers were made by the Confederacy and, although many individuals undertook their manufacture, only four or five "made any real contribution" (ibid. 10). See also PALMETTO ARMS.

At the outbreak of the war the Federals had 300,000 smoothbore muskets and 27,000 rifles in the arsenals still in their possession. The Confederates had confiscated the remainder that had been in Southern arsenals: 260,000 smoothbores and 22,000 rifles (Fiebeger). By the middle of 1862 the North had spent over $10,000,000 for rifles, muskets, and carbines in Europe. "Of these only 116,740 were Enfields, 48,108 were of French official type, and nearly all the rest were a nondescript conglomeration containing 170,255 from Austria, 111,549 from Prussia, 57,194 from Belgium, and 203,831 simply listed as other foreign rifles" (Shannon, I, 118). "The refuse of all Europe passed into the hands of the American volunteers," wrote the Comte de Paris. The Springfield arsenal produced 600,000 of the .58 caliber Model 1861 rifle in the 12 months ending 30 June '64, and by this time the foreign arms were wholly replaced.

Lack of manufacturing facilities, raw materials, and technical skills plagued the South until the end. According to Wiley the South had only about 150,-000 shoulder arms that were fit for use at the start of the war, of which 20,000 were rifles. Raphael Semmes and other agents were having good success buying arms from Northern firms until Federal authorities intervened. Early in Apr. '61 Caleb Huse started buying arms in Europe, but none of these were delivered for several months. He eventually procured more than 100,000 EN-

FIELDS, which were highly regarded by soldiers on both sides. The Confederates captured well over 100,000 Federal small arms in their successful operations of 1862. In 1863 the surplus acquired by capture at Chancellorsville and Chickamauga was canceled out by their losses at Gettysburg, Vicksburg, and Chattanooga. From the beginning of 1864 until the end of the war there was a shortage.

SMALLEY, George Washburn. WAR CORRESPONDENT. 1833–? Mass. After graduating from Yale and Harvard Law School, he practiced law in Boston until the war began. An ardent abolitionist and protégé of Wendell PHILLIPS, in 1861 he became a correspondent for the N.Y. *Tribune* in western Va. and showed considerable ingenuity in the summer of 1862 in circumventing Halleck's ban on reporters with Pope's army. He scored a triumph in his reporting of Antietam when he not only wrote a concise and accurate account but took it to N.Y. himself when he was unable to find a clear telegraph wire. He had delivered orders from Hooker to his subordinates on the battlefield, had been next to the general when he was wounded, and had escaped harm himself only by the greatest luck. Just after Burnside took command of the Army of the Potomac Smalley came down with camp fever and took a desk job in the New York office, where he remained until sent to cover the Prussian-Austrian War in 1866. He organized the European office of the *Tribune* the next year and continued to contribute to the changing face of journalism in the nineteenth century.

SMITH, Alfred Baker. Union officer. 1825–? N.Y. Maj. 150th N.Y. 24 Sept. '62; Lt. Col. 1 Jan. '65; Col. 24 Apr. '65; Bvt. B.G. USV (Ga. and Carolinas campaign). He was prominent in Pough-

keepsie as a lawyer and public office-holder.

SMITH, Andrew Jackson. Union gen. 1815–97. Pa. USMA 1838 (36/45); Dragoons-Cav. After duty on the frontier, in the Mexican War, and Indian fighting, he was Halleck's Chief of Cav. 11 Feb–11 July '62. Appointed B.G. USV 17 Mar. '62, he had been promoted Maj. 13 May '61 (Capt. since 1847) and Col. 2d US Cav. 2 Oct. '61. He then commanded 1st Div. Army Ky., Army of the Ohio (Oct.–13 Nov. '62); 10th Div. Right Wing, XIII, Tenn., (Nov.–Dec. '62) and 1st Div. (Dec. '62) at Chickasaw Bluffs. During the Vicksburg campaign at Arkansas Post, Port Gibson, Champion's Hill, Big Black River, Jackson, and the Vicksburg assaults and siege, he commanded 10th Div., XIII (4 Jan.–7 Aug. '63). Also in the Army of the Tenn. he commanded 6th Div. Dist. of Columbus, XVI (5 Aug. '63–25 Jan. '64); 3d Div., XVI (24 Jan.–7 Mar. '64) and Right Wing, XVI (7 Mar.–5 Dec. '64), repulsing Forrest at TUPELO. In the RED RIVER CAMPAIGN OF 1864 he commanded Det. XVI Corps, Dept. of the Gulf (Mar.–June '64) at Fort DeRussy, Pleasant Hill, and Cane River. Appointed Maj. Gen. USV 12 May '64, he then commanded Det. Army of the Tenn., Cumberland (5 Dec. '64–18 Feb. '65) at Nashville, and then led the XVI Corps, Gulf (18 Feb.–20 July '65) at Mobile. After the battle of Nashville, when Smith's troops had been moved around so often under many commanders, he referred to them as the lost tribes of Israel. Continuing in the R.A., he was breveted for Pleasant Hill, Tupelo (B.G. USA), and Nashville (Maj. Gen. USA), and resigned in 1869 as Col. 7th US Cav. He was put on the retired list in 1889 as Col. of Cav. Small and brusque, he was popular with his men and respected by his superiors.

SMITH, Arthur Arnold. Union officer. Ohio. Lt. Col. 83d Ill. 21 Aug. '62; Col. 4 June '63; Bvt. B.G. USV (war service). Commanded 5th Sub-Dist. Mid. Tenn., Army of the Cumberland. Died 1900.

SMITH, Benjamin Franklin. Union officer. c. 1831–68. N.J. USMA 1853 (39/52); Inf. Capt. 6th US Inf. 14 May '61; Col. 1st Ohio 12 Oct. '61; discharged 2 June '62; Col. 126th Ohio 10 Sept. '62; Bvt. B.G. USV 26 Mar. '65. Brevets for Shiloh, Petersburg siege (2). Served as Provost Marshal Gen. of S.C. in 1865. Continued in R.A. until his death in 1868 at Fort Reno (Dak. Territory) with the rank of Maj. Commanded 3, 3, II (Potomac); 2, 3, VI (Potomac); 2, 1, VIII (Middle Dept.); Martinsburg (Va.), VIII (Middle Dept.).

SMITH, Charles Edward. Union officer. N.Y. Maj. 11th Mich. Cav. 31 Aug. '63; Lt. Col. 4 Oct. '64; Bvt. B.G. USV (war service).

SMITH, Charles Ferguson. Union gen. 1807–62. Pa. USMA 1825 (19/37); Arty. Serving first in garrison, he was at West Point for 13 years as instructor, adjutant to Thayer, and commandant of cadets. In the Mexican War he won three brevets and then participated in explorations and the Utah Expedition, commanding the Dept. of Utah as Lt. Col. 10th US Inf. (since 1855), when the war began. Named B.G. USV 30 Aug. and Col. USA 9 Sept. '61, he commanded Dist. Western Ky., Mo. (8 Sept. '61–31 Jan. '62). Subordinate to Grant, who had been a cadet under Smith, he commanded 2d Div., Army Tenn. (17 Feb.–2 Apr. '62 at Henry and Donelson), leading a charge at the latter place that won him promotion to Maj. Gen. USV 21 Mar. '62. Grant said that he owed his success at Donelson to Smith, and it was he who advised Grant

to ask for UNCONDITIONAL SURRENDER at Donelson. Lew Wallace called him "by all odds the handsomest, stateliest, most commanding figure I had ever seen," and many regulars felt him to be the best all-around soldier in the army. He temporarily succeeded Grant at the start of the SHILOH CAMPAIGN. He died 25 Apr. '62 of a foot infection he got in jumping from one boat to another in the opening stages of that campaign.

SMITH, Charles Henry, Union officer. Me. Commissioned Capt. 1st Me. Cav. 19 Oct. '61, he fought at Cedar Mountain, Raccoon Ford, Rappahannock Station, and 2d Bull Run. He was on provost-marshal duty until Jan. '63 and was promoted Maj. 1st Me. Cav. 16 Feb. '63. As Lt. Col. (1 Mar. '63), he went on Stoneman's raid, and fought at Brandy Station, Aldie, Middleburg, Gettysburg, and Shepherdstown, having been named Col. 18 June '63. He then fought at Bristoe Station and in the Mine Run operations, and joined Sheridan's cavalry (May–June '64) in the battles of Todd's Tavern, South Anna, Haw's Shop, Trevilian Station, and St. Mary's Church, where he was wounded. At Reams's Station and Weldon R.R. he commanded a cavalry brigade and led the 3d Brig. under Gregg in Oct. '64 at Rowanty Creek, Gravelly Run and Boydton Plank Road, Dinwiddie C.H., and the Appomattox campaign. Continuing in the R.A., he retired in 1891 as Col. 19th US Inf., Bvt. B.G. USV (St. Mary's Church 1 Aug. '64), Bvt. B.G. USA (Sayler's Creek), and Bvt. Maj. Gen. USA (war service). He was awarded the Medal of Honor in 1895 for St. Mary's Church. Died 1902.

SMITH, Edmund Kirby. C.S.A. gen. 1824–93. Fla. USMA 1845 (25/41); Inf. He served in the Mexican War (2 brevets), in garrison, and as mathematics professor at West Point before going to the frontier for Indian fighting

(1 wound) and as botanist on a Mexican boundary commission. Resigning 3 Mar. '61 as Maj. 2d US Cav., he was commissioned Col. of C.S.A. Cav. and went to Fla. before serving as J. E. Johnston's Chief of Staff at Harpers Ferry, where he aided in organizing the Army of the Shenandoah. Appointed B.G. C.S.A. 17 June '61, he commanded the 4th Brig. at 1st Bull Run and was severely wounded. While recovering from this, he met and married the girl who had made him a shirt on the joking promise that whoever made the garment would get the handsome colonel who went with it. He was promoted Maj. Gen. C.S.A. 11 Oct. '61 and given command of a division under Beauregard. In Mar. '62 he went to Knoxville to assume command of the Dept. of EAST TENN. and undertake Kirby SMITH'S INVASION OF KENTUCKY. He then joined Bragg for the battle of PERRYVILLE. Named Lt. Gen. 9 Oct. '62 for his operations in Kentucky, he was also given the C.S.A. Thanks of Congress. He was disgusted with Bragg's patent lack of ability and asked to be detached with his own command, which was refused. In Jan. '63 he went to Richmond to aid in the reorganization of the army and the next month was sent to the TRANS-MISSISSIPPI DEPT. When Vicksburg fell in July, this area was cut off from Richmond and became for all purposes a separate command (known as Kirby Smithdom). Promoted to the rank of full Gen. on 19 Feb. '64, he frustrated Banks's RED RIVER CAMPAIGN OF 1864 and then took troops away from Dick Taylor to fight Steele in the ARKANSAS CAMPAIGN. After continued disagreement between the two generals Taylor was then put in a separate command. Smith "appointed" a number of generals, but under Confederate law the president

alone was authorized to make such appointments. Davis repudiated Smith's appointments, but later confirmed a few of them. On 2 June '65 Kirby Smith surrendered the last Confederate force, the Trans-Miss. Dept., at Galveston in the Smith-Canby Convention. On his way about two weeks later to give his personal parole, he heard of Lee's arrest and decided to flee to Mexico and thence to Cuba. Returning to the US in Nov. '65, he was at first the president of an insurance and telegraph company (which was unsuccessful), and was next president of the Univ. of Nashville from 1870 to 1875. Having considered at periods throughout his life becoming an Episcopal minister, he decided that he was too old to embark upon this course, but he did go to the Univ. of the South at Sewanee, where he taught mathematics for 18 years. He and his wife raised 11 children, something that should give pause to any young lady volunteering to make shirts in wartime. The family name has been a subject of much speculation, but perhaps Parks in *General Edmund Kirby Smith, C.S.A.,* is the most authoritative source. Kirby Smith's father gave Edmund and his older brother, Ephraim, their mother's maiden name, Kirby, as a *middle* name. Ephraim, a West Point graduate who was killed as a Capt. in the Mexican War, had been called Kirby. But Edmund, who was more often called "Ted" by his family and "Seminole" by his West Point classmates, took to signing his Civil War reports in the spring of 1861 as E. Kirby Smith to distinguish himself from the other Smiths. The family then became known, as the Gen. became famous, as the Kirby Smiths, hyphenating the two names only after his death. He is most usually indexed alphabetically under Smith, Edmund Kirby; apparently he never considered Kirby as part of his surname.

SMITH, Edward Worthington. Union officer. Vt. R.A. 1st Lt. 15th US Inf. 14 May '61; Maj. Asst. Adj. Gen. Vols. 30 Oct. '62; Lt. Col. Asst. Adj. Gen. Assigned 1 July '63–1 Aug. '65; Bvt. B.G. USV. Brevets for Fort Wagner (S.C.); Petersburg siege, campaigns of 1863 and 1864, war service. A.D.C. to Gen. Hunter in Aug. '61. Continued in R.A. until death in 1883 with rank of Maj.

SMITH, Franklin C. Union officer. N.Y. Lt. Col. 102d Ill. 2 Sept. '62; Col. ?8 Feb. '63; Bvt. B.G. USV (war service). Commanded, 1, 3, XX (Cumberland). Died 1891.

SMITH, George Washington. Union officer. N.Y. Capt. 88th Ill. 27 Aug. '62; Maj. 2 Dec. '63; Lt. Col. 14 Aug. '64; Bvt. B.G. USV. Brevets for Franklin (Tenn.), Nashville, war service. W.I.A. Spotsylvania. Ex-cadet USMA 1838. Died 1898.

SMITH, Giles Alexander. Union gen. 1829–76. N.Y. In the dry-goods and hotel business, he was commissioned Capt. 8th Mo. 14 June '61, serving under his brother Morgan Lewis Smith, and fought at Forts Henry and Donelson, Shiloh, and the siege of Corinth. Promoted Lt. Col. 12 June '62, he succeeded his brother as Col. 30 June '62 and commanded 1st Brig., 2d Div. Dist. Memphis, Right Wing, XIII, Tenn. (12 Nov.–18 Dec. '62). At Chickasaw Bluffs he commanded 1st Brig., 2d Div. (Dec. '62–Jan. '63). In the XV Corps he led the 1st Brig., 2d Div. (4 Jan.–20 July '63) at Arkansas Post, and the Vicksburg campaign (19 Oct.–24 Nov. '63) at Chattanooga and Missionary Ridge, where he was severely wounded; and later (21 Feb.–20 July '64). Promoted B.G. USV 4 Aug. '63, he commanded the 2d Div. of that corps 10 Sept.–6 Oct. '63. Leading the 4th Div., XVII (21

July–20 Sept. and 31 Oct. '64–1 June '65), he distinguished himself at Resaca, Atlanta, on the March to the Sea and through the Carolinas. He commanded 1st Div., XXV, Tex. (29 May–28 Dec. '65) and was promoted Maj. Gen. USV 24 Nov. '65. Breveted Maj. Gen. USV 1 Sept. '64 for the Atlanta and Savannah campaigns, he was mustered out in 1866.

SMITH, Green Clay. Union gen. 1832–95. Ky. In the Mexican War he was later a lawyer and Republican legislator and was named Col. 4th Ky. Cav. 15 Mar. '62. Wounded at Lebanon (Tenn.) 5 May '62, he was promoted B.G. USV 11 June '62, commanded 2d Div., Army of Ky., Ohio (?–14 Oct. '62), and then 1, 2d Div., Army of Ky., Ohio (14 Oct. '62–Jan. '63). Resigning 1 Dec. '63, to become US Congressman, he was breveted Maj. Gen. USV for war service. Later appointed Gov. of Mont. (1866–69), he was ordained a Baptist minister in 1869, became an evangelist, and was the Prohibition party's presidential candidate in 1876.

SMITH, Gustavus A. Union gen. Pa. Col. 35th Ill. 1 Sept. '61; B.G. USV 19 Sept. '62; appointment expired 4 Mar. '63 and reverted to Col. 35th Ill.; dismissed 22 Sept. '63; Col. 155th Ill. 28 Feb. '65; Bvt. B.G. USV (war service). Died 1885.

SMITH, Gustavus Woodson. C.S.A. gen. and Sec. of War. 1822–96. Ky. USMA 1842 (8/56); Engrs. He taught engineering at West Point, supervised harbor construction in New England, won a brevet in the Mexican War, and was again teaching at the Military Academy when he resigned in 1854. Going into construction work, he was in New Orleans and N. Y. before becoming street commissioner (1858–61) for the latter city. Active in the Democratic party, he was also serving on a committee to revise the curriculum at West Point and looking into measures to prevent the approaching war. Going in the late summer of 1861 upon his doctor's orders to Hot Springs for paralysis suffered the previous April, he learned en route that the Federal government had misconstrued his motives and ordered his arrest as a disloyal person. At this he offered his services to the Confederate government and was appointed Maj. Gen. C.S.A. 19 Sept. '61 from Ky. In command at the outset of the Peninsular campaign he suffered another attack of paralysis, on 2 June '62. Feuding with Davis by this time, he was relieved from command by Lee and then sent to command the area from the Rappahannock to Cape Fear with headquarters in Richmond. He was interim Sec. of War 17–20 Nov. '62 and resigned from the army on 17 Feb. '63, when six general officers were promoted over his head to become Lt. Gens. Going to Charleston, he served as Beauregard's volunteer A.D.C., was then superintendent of the Etowah Mining and Manufacturing Company, and in June '64 became Maj. Gen. of the Georgia militia, commanding the 1st Div. attached to the Army of Tenn. He fell back before Sherman's March to the Sea and on 30 Dec. '64 was given command of a sector in the defenses of the Dept. of S.C., Ga., and Fla. He surrendered at Macon in Apr. '65. After the war he ran an iron works and was Insurance Commissioner for Ky. He wrote books on life insurance and the regular army engineers in the Mexican War, as well as *Confederate War Papers* (1884), *Battle of Seven Pines* (1891), and *Generals J. E. Johnston and G. T. Beauregard . . . at Manassas* (1892).

SMITH, Israel Canton. Union officer. Mich. 2d Lt. 3d Mich. 13 May '61; Regt. Adj. 19 July '61; Capt. 1 Jan. '62; Maj. 10th Mich. Cav. 23 Aug. '62; Lt. Col.

18 Feb. '65; Col. 2 Sept. '65; Bvt. B.G. USV (war service). Died 1899.

SMITH, James. Union officer. N.Y. Capt. 80th N.Y. 7 Oct. '61; Lt. Col. 128th N.Y. 5 Sept. '62; Col. 27 May '63; Bvt. B.G. USV (Cane River Crossing, La.); discharged 7 June '64. Commanded 2, 1, XIX (Gulf). Died 1869.

SMITH, James Argyle. C.S.A. gen. c. 1831–1901. Tenn. Appt.-At Large. USMA 1853 (45/52); Inf. He served on the frontier, in Indian fighting, the Kans. border disturbances, and on the Utah Expedition before resigning 9 May '61 as 1st Lt. Appointed Capt. C.S.A. Inf., he was promoted Maj. in Mar. '62 and assigned as acting Adj. Gen. under Polk. At Shiloh he was Lt. Col. 2d Tenn. and at Perryville he was Col. of the 5th Confederate (Regt.). He led this unit at Stones River and Chickamauga, where he also had command of the 3d Confederate. Appointed B.G. C.S.A. 30 Sept. '63, he commanded Granbury's Brigade in the Atlanta campaign and was wounded 22 July near Atlanta. After his recovery he succeeded Cleburne as division commander at Nashville and Bentonville. He was then a farmer and public-school superintendent.

SMITH, James Youngs. Gov. of R. I. 1809–76. Conn. A lumberman and manufacturer, he served in the legislature before being elected Gov. as a Republican in 1863–65. He was an extremely wealthy man and spent much of his own money in support of the war effort.

SMITH, John Coroson. Union officer. Pa. Maj. 96th Ill. 6 Sept. '62; Lt. Col. 1 Nov. '63; Bvt. B.G. USV 20 June '65 (war service).

SMITH, John Eugene. Union gen. 1816–97. Pa. The son of a Napoleonic officer who fought from the Moscow campaign to Waterloo and then came to this country, Smith was a jeweler in Galena (Ill.) when commissioned Col.

45th Ill. 23 July '61. He fought at Forts Henry and Donelson, Shiloh and Corinth. Promoted B. G. USV 29 Nov. '62, he commanded in the Army of the Tenn., 1, 3 Right Wing, XIII (Dec.–18 Dec. '62); 8th Div., XVI (26 Dec. '62–3 Apr. '63) and 1, 3, XVII (23 Apr.–3 June '63) at Port Gibson, Raymond, Jackson, Champion's Hill, and Big Black River. During the final phase of the Vicksburg campaign he led the 7th Div., XVII (3 June–14 Sept. '63) and then led the 2d Div. in that corps (14 Sept.–20 Dec. '63) at Missionary Ridge. He also commanded 3d Div., XVII 20–22 July '63. During the Atlanta campaign and on the March to the Sea and through the Carolinas he led 3d Div., XV (20 Dec. '63–26 Apr. '65). Breveted for Vicksburg (B.G. USA), war service (Maj. Gen. USV) and Savannah (Maj. Gen. USA), he continued in the R.A. and was retired in 1881 as Col. 14th US Inf. after many years of Indian fighting.

SMITH, Joseph R. Union officer. c. 1801–68. N.Y. USMA 1823 (22/35); Inf. He served on the frontier, in the Seminole War, in the Mexican War (2 brevets, 2 wounds) and in garrison, before being retired from active duty 25 Sept. '61 because of ill-health, as Maj. 7th US Inf. In the Civil War he was mustering and disbursing officer and military commander in Mich., being breveted B.G. USA 9 Apr. '65.

SMITH, Joseph Sewall. Union officer. Me. Q.M. Sgt. 3d Me. 4 June '61; 1st Lt. 2 Aug. '61; Capt. Comsy. of Subsist. Vols. 14 Nov. '61; Lt. Col. Comsy. of Subsist. Assigned 1 Jan. '63–11 July '65; Bvt. B.G. USV 11 July '65. Brevets for Reams's Station, Boydton Plank Road (Va.), war service. Medal of Honor 25 May '92 for having led a part of a brigade that saved two pieces of artillery, captured a flag and a number of prisoners at Hatcher's Run (Va.) 27 Oct. '64.

SMITH, Martin Luther. C.S.A. gen. 1819–66. N.Y. USMA 1842 (16/56); Topo. Engrs. His regular army career was spent surveying in Fla., Ga. (where he married), and Tex. before he resigned 1 Apr. '61 as Capt. At this point he was not sure that he would fight with the Confederacy but was positive that he would not fight against it. Commissioned Maj. of C.S.A. Engrs. from Fla. to date from 16 Mar. '61, he planned and built the New Orleans fortifications. He then built those at Vicksburg and commanded troops during their defense. Named Col. 21st La. in Feb. '62 and B.G. C.S.A. 11 Apr. '62, he was promoted Maj. Gen. 4 Nov. of that year and was not exchanged for nearly seven months after the fall of Vicksburg. In Apr.–July '64 he was Chief Engr. for the Army of Northern Va. and held the same position with Hood's Army of Tenn. until Oct. '64, when he became Beauregard's Chief Engr. and constructed the Mobile defenses. After the war he returned to engineering.

SMITH, Morgan Lewis. Union gen. 1821–74. N.Y. Serving under the name of Martin L. Sanford as Sgt. and Drill Instructor 1845–50, he raised the 8th Mo. (composed of "rivermen and recruits from the rougher element of St Louis") and was commissioned Col. 4 July '61. At Fort Donelson he commanded 5, 2d Div., Dist. Cairo, Tenn. (1–17 Feb. '62) and 1, 3d Div., Army Tenn. (17 Feb.–June '62) at Shiloh. Also in the Army of the Tenn., he commanded 1st, 5th Div. (12 May–21 July '62) and 1st, 5th Div. Dist. Memphis (21 July–26 Oct. '62). Promoted B.G. USV 16 July '62, he then led 1, Dist. Memphis, XIII (25 Oct.–25 Nov. '62); 2d Div. Dist. Memphis, XIII (12 Nov.–18 Dec. '62); 2d Div. Yazoo Expedition (18–28 Dec. '62); 2d Div., XV (6 Oct. '63–22 July '64 and 27 July–5 Aug. '64);

XV Corps (22–27 July '64); and Post of Vicksburg (27 Sept. '64–22 June '65). Resigning 12 July '65, he was US Consul Gen. to Hawaii and was in business in Washington, D.C., when he died.

SMITH, Orland. Union officer. Me. Lt. Col. 73d Ohio 26 Nov. '61; Col. 30 Dec. '62; Bvt. B.G. USV (war service). Commanded 2, 2, XII (Potomac and Cumberland). Resigned 17 Feb. '64. He was a railroad executive and builder.

SMITH, Orlow. Union officer. N.Y. 2d Lt. 65th Ohio 5 Oct. '61; Capt. 25 Nov. '61; Maj. 3 Feb. '64; Lt. Col. 1 Nov. '65; Col. 24 Nov. '65; Bvt. B.G. USV (war service). Died 1868.

SMITH, Preston, C.S.A. gen. 1823–63. Tenn. After college and practicing law he was commissioned Col. 154th Tenn. Wounded at Shiloh, he took over the brigade (1, 2, I) at Richmond, Ky. Appointed B.G. C.S.A. 27 Oct. '62, he commanded his brigade in Cheatham's division under Polk at Chickamauga. Here he was killed 19 Sept.

SMITH, Robert Frederick. Union officer. Pa. Col. 16th Ill. 24 May '61; Bvt. B.G. USV (war service). Commanded 2d Brig., 1st Div. (Army Miss.); 1, 4, XIV (Cumberland); 4th Div. XIV (Cumberland); 1, 2, Res. Corps (Cumberland); 1, 2, XIV (Cumberland). Died 1893.

SMITH, Robert Wilson. Union officer. Ohio. Lt. Col. 16th Ill. Cav. 11 June '63; Col. 9 Aug. '64; Bvt. B.G. USV (war service). Died 1890.

SMITH, Thomas Benton. C.S.A. gen. Tenn. Lt. Col. of the 20th Tenn. at Shiloh, he was promoted Col. 5 Aug. '62 and fought at Baton Rouge, Stones River (wounded), and Chickamauga. He commanded Tyler's brigade in the Atlanta campaign and was appointed B.G. C.S.A. 29 July '64. Going with Hood to Tenn., he fought at Franklin and was captured at Nashville.

SMITH, Thomas Church Haskell. Union gen. 1819–97. Mass. A lawyer and telegraph company president, he established the Morse telegraph system in the West and South. He was commissioned Lt. Col. 1st Ohio Cav. 5 Sept. '61–27 Apr. '63 and appointed B.G. USV 29 Nov. '62. In 1863 he was in command of the Wis. Dist., halted the draft riots, and served as I.G., Dept. of the Mo. in 1864. He was mustered out in 1866 and recommissioned in the R.A. in 1878 as Maj., Paymaster, retiring in 1883.

SMITH, Thomas Kilby. Union gen. 1820–87. Mass. He read law in Salmon P. Chase's office and held several public and federal offices. Commissioned Lt. Col. 54th Ohio 9 Sept. '61, and Col. 31 Oct. '61, he commanded his regiment at Shiloh, Corinth, and the Vicksburg siege. From 6 Apr.–12 May '62 he commanded 2, 5th Div., Army Tenn. He next led 2, 2d Div. Yazoo Expedition (28 Dec. '62–4 Jan. '63) and 2, 2, XV (4 Jan.–23 May '63) and was on Grant's staff until he took command of 2, 1, XVII (14 Sept.–29 Oct. '63), having been named B.G. USV 11 Aug. '63. He also commanded 1, 4, XVII (24 Oct. '63–28 Feb. '64); Prov. Div., XVII, Gulf (Mar.–June '64) on the RED RIVER CAMPAIGN; and 3d Div. Det. Army Tenn., Cumberland (4–17 Jan. '65). Breveted for war service (Maj. Gen. USV), he was mustered out in 1866 and was US Consul in Panama and a member of the business staff of the N.Y. *Star.*

SMITH, William. ("Extra Billy.") C.S.A. gen. and Gov. of Va. 1796–1887. Va. A lawyer, he practiced in William H. Winder's office (father of John H. WINDER) and then returned to Va. to set up his office. He started a mail-coach service from Washington to Milledgeville (Ga.), and his nickname came from the numerous extra payments he received from the government as the line rapidly expanded. Active in politics, he was state legislator, US Congressman, and finally Va. Gov. (1846–49) before moving to Calif. to join his two sons. Almost starting another career in the politics of that state, he refused to stand for office, saying that he did not wish to give up his Va. citizenship. Returning in 1852, he was elected the next year to Congress and held his seat until the state seceded in 1861. Gov. Letcher offered him the rank of B.G. but he turned this down to fight at 1st Bull Run as Col. 49th Va. Elected to the C.S.A. Congress, he attended sessions between campaigns. He led his regiment on the Peninsula and at Antietam, succeeding to the command of Early's brigade before being wounded. Given command of the 4th Brig. in Early's division, he was appointed B.G. C.S.A. 23 Apr. '63 to rank from 31 Jan. and was stationed near Fredericksburg. In May of that year he was elected Gov. of Va. and fought at Gettysburg before taking office 1 Jan. '64. He had been promoted Maj. Gen. 12 Aug. '63. Serving in the statehouse until the fall of the Confederacy, he took the state government to Lynchburg and then Danville after Richmond's fall, returning there after Appomattox. He farmed near Warrenton and sat in the state legislature when he was 80.

SMITH, William Duncan. C.S.A. gen. 1826–62. Ga. USMA 1846 (35/59); Dragoons. He fought in the Mexican War (1 wound) and served on the frontier and in garrison before resigning 28 Jan. '61 as Capt. Appointed Capt. C.S.A. Inf. 16 Mar. '61, he was named Col. 20th Ga. 14 July '61 and B.G. C.S.A. 14 Mar. '62 to rank from the 7th. He commanded the Dist. of S.C., at Charleston, and fought at James Island and Secessionville under N. G. Evans. He died 4 Oct. '62 at Charleston of fever.

SMITH, William Farrar ("Baldy"). Union gen. 1824–1903. Vt. USMA 1845 (4/41); Engrs. He was engaged in surveying and teaching mathematics at West Point before going to Fla., where he contracted the malaria that was to bring on periods of weakness and depression the rest of his life. As Col. 3d Vt. 16 July '61 (Capt. since 1859), he fought at 1st Bull Run and then commanded Smith's brigade., Div. Potomac (Aug.–Oct. '61) as B.G. USV 13 Aug. '61. He then led Smith's division, Potomac (3 Oct. '61–13 Mar. '62) and 2d Div., IV (13 Mar.–18 May '62) at the siege of Yorktown, Lee's Mill, and Williamsburg. Commanding 2d Div., VI (18 May–16 Nov. '62) and promoted Maj. Gen. USV 4 July '62, he fought at Fair Oaks, White Oak Swamp, Savage's Station, Glendale, Malvern Hill, South Mountain, and Antietam. Commanding the VI Corps (16 Nov. '62–4 Feb. '63) at Fredericksburg, he and W. B. Franklin wrote to Lincoln after the disaster, objecting to the army's leadership and offering their own plan to get to Richmond. Lincoln, in complete sympathy, was able to head off a plan in Congress to relieve Smith for this criticism, but his appointment as Maj. Gen. was rejected by the Senate and expired 4 Mar. '63. He was transferred from command of the IX Corps (5 Feb.–17 Mar. '63) to that of a division at CARLISLE in the Dept. of the Susquehanna 17 June–3 Aug. '63. He took part in the pursuit after Gettysburg and then led a division in W. Va. 3 Aug.–5 Sept. '63. Transferred to the West, he became Chief Engr. of the Army of the Cumberland and later of Grant's new Mil. Div. of the Miss. He performed conspicuous service in organizing the defenses of Chattanooga and in the "Cracker Line" operations of the CHATTANOOGA CAMPAIGN. He was reappointed Maj. Gen. USV 9 Mar. '64 and commanded XVIII

Corps, Va. and N.C. (2 May–10 July '64). Detached from Butler's Army of the James to reinforce Meade at COLD HARBOR, he returned to take an undistinguished part in the PETERSBURG ASSAULTS OF 15–18 June '64. This fiasco resulted in his again being relieved of field command and placed on "special duty" for the remainder of the war. Breveted for White Oak Swamp, Antietam, Chattanooga (B.G. USA) and war service (Maj. Gen. USA), he continued in the R.A., resigning in 1867 as Maj. in the Corps of Engrs. and being put on the retired list with the same rank in 1889. Lyman described him as being "a short, quite portly man, with a light-brown imperial and shaggy moustache, a round, military head, and the look of a German officer, altogether." A man of great military ability, and several times considered for the command of an army (to relieve Butler or Meade), he had a fatal personality defect. "Smith was a contentious controversialist who spent most of his time criticizing the plans of other generals, particularly those of his superiors" (T. Harry Williams, 293). Although he had more hair than most men his age, he retained his cadet nickname "Baldy," which was given him because at that stage of life his hair was thinner than normal.

SMITH, William Jay. Union officer. England. Pvt. Co. G 6th Tenn. Cav. 18 Sept. '62; 1st Lt. Regt. Q.M. 15 Nov. '62; Maj. 4 Feb. '64; Lt. Col. 26 Apr. '64; Col. 13 Mar. '65; Bvt. B.G. USV 16 July '65 (war service). He was a Pvt. and Capt. in Wheat's Co. Tenn. Vols. in the Mexican War.

SMITH, William Sooy. Union gen. 1830–1916. Ohio. USMA 1856 (6/52); Arty. Resigning the next year, he was an engineer and bridge builder until commissioned Col. 13th Ohio 26 June '61. He was Asst. A.G. at Camp Dennison

and fought at Sutton and Carnifex Ferry in Sept. '61. He commanded 14th Brig., 5th Div., Army Ohio (2 Dec. '61–2 July '62) at Shiloh and on the advance upon and siege of Corinth. Promoted B.G. USV 15 Apr. '62, he commanded in the Army of the Ohio 3d Div. (2–11 July '62); 17, 3d Div. (19–23 Aug. '62); 4th Div. (23 Aug.–28 Sept. '62); and 4th Div., II (Sept.–Nov. '62) at Perryville. He then commanded 2d Div., Left Wing, XIV, Cumberland (5 Nov.–10 Dec. '62) and 1st Div., XVI, Tenn. (Jan.–July '63) during the Vicksburg campaign. He was then Chief of Cav. for the Army of the Tenn. and the Mil. Div. Miss. 20 July '63–15 July '64). As late as 1875 he was involved in a controversy with Sherman over his performance at WEST POINT, Miss., in the MERIDIAN CAMPAIGN of Feb. '64. Resigning 15 July '64, he went back to engineering and improved the pneumatic process of sinking foundations. One of the first bridge builders to use steel in place of wrought iron, he built the first great all-steel bridge across the Missouri River at Glasgow (Mo.).

SMITH'S (G. W.) CORPS. See II CORPS, A.N.V.

SMITH'S (Kirby) CORPS. See CORPS, Confederate, KIRBY SMITH'S CORPS.

SMITH'S INVASION OF KENTUCKY. Aug.–Sept. '62. As the forces under Buell and Bragg shifted toward Chattanooga (following SHILOH and Halleck's advance on CORINTH) east Tenn. and Ky. became a theater of war. While Bragg was massing his forces around Chattanooga for a contemplated offensive against Buell in middle Tenn. he made plans with Kirby Smith for the latter to force the Federal division of G. W. Morgan (8,000) from Cumberland Gap. After this it was Bragg's intention to join with Kirby Smith's forces and drive Buell from middle Tenn.

(Bragg's vagueness as to his strategic aims explains what Fiebeger calls "the lack of definite purpose in the operations of Bragg and [Kirby] Smith in Kentucky.")

In a preliminary operation Col. John H. Morgan raided and occupied GALLATIN, Tenn., 12–21 Aug. Another cavalry brigade, under Col. J. S. Scott, preceded Bragg's main body, leaving Kingston on 13 Aug., capturing London, Ky., on the 17th, and defeating two Federal regiments (7th Ky. Cav. and 3d Tenn.) near Richmond at Big Hill, Ky., 23 Aug.

Kirby Smith left Knoxville on 14 Aug. with the divisions of Heth, Cleburne, and T. J. Churchill (9,000 total). Leaving C. L. Stevenson (9,000) to keep pressure on G. W. Morgan (8,000) in Cumberland Gap, Kirby Smith got behind Morgan at Barboursville on the 18th. He decided that the Federal position was too strong to attack, even from the rear, so started north again on the 24th and decisively defeated and routed 6,500 green Federal troops at RICHMOND, Ky., 30 Aug.

Having dispersed the only organized troops in the area, the Confederate commander entered Lexington on 1 Sept. and was joined there on the 3d by J. H. Morgan's brigade. He then divided his forces to capture Covington and intercept G. W. Morgan, who left CUMBERLAND GAP on 17 Sept. Covington's defenses proved too strong and Morgan succeeded in retreating safely to Greenup (in northeast Ky.).

Kirby Smith was promoted to Lt. Gen. for his invasion of Ky.

Meanwhile, BRAGG'S INVASION OF KENTUCKY had started on 28 Aug. and Bragg joined forces with Kirby Smith for the battle of PERRYVILLE, Ky., 8 Oct. '62.

SMYTH, Thomas Alfred. Union gen. ?–1865. Ireland. A Wilmington coachmaker, he was commissioned Maj. 1st Del. 17 Oct. '61 and promoted Lt. Col. 30 Dec. '62 and Col. 7 Feb. '63. He commanded 2, 3, II, Potomac (16 May–3 July; 4 July–14 Aug.; 3 Sept.–28 Dec. '63; 13 Feb.–25 Mar. '64); 2, 1, II, Potomac (25–17 May '64); 3, 2, II, Potomac (17 May–31 July at Cold Harbor; 23 Aug.–5 Nov.; and 15 Nov.–22 Dec. '64); 2d Div., II, Potomac (31 July–22 Aug. '64 and 23 Dec. '64–25 Feb. '65). Promoted B.G. USV 1 Oct. '64 for his gallantry at Cold Harbor, he was again leading 3, 2, II (28 Feb.–7 Apr. '65) when he was wounded by a sharpshooter near Farmville (Va.) and died two days later. He was breveted for Farmville (Maj. Gen. USV).

SNAGGY POINT (Red River), La. Near Davide's Ferry, three miles above Fort de Russy, this was the scene of cavalry action against Federal ships in RED RIVER CAMPAIGN OF 1864.

SNAKE CREEK GAP, Ga. See ROCKY FACE RIDGE, Ga., 5–11 May '64.

SNIPER, Gustavus. Germany. Capt. 12th N.Y. 15 Dec. '61; mustered out 14 Jan. '62; Maj. 101st N.Y. 1 Feb. '62; Lt. Col. 11 Nov. '62; mustered out 23 Dec. '62; Lt. Col. 185th N.Y. 23 Sept. '64; Col. 1 Mar. '65; Bvt. B.G. USV (Quaker Road and White Oak Road, Va.). Died 1894.

SNYDER'S MILL, Miss., 30 Apr.–1 May '65. See HAINES'S BLUFF, same dates.

SOCIETY OF FRIENDS. See QUAKERS.

"SOLDIER'S BATTLE." One in which the outcome is determined more by the individual courage and initiative of the soldiers and junior officers than by the strategy or leadership of their generals. Shiloh and Missionary Ridge may be cited as examples; also most of the fighting from the Wilderness to Petersburg in May and June '64 (the Wilderness, Spotsylvania, Cold Harbor).

SONS OF LIBERTY. See KNIGHTS OF THE GOLDEN CIRCLE.

SOOY SMITH EXPEDITION IN MISSISSIPPI, Feb. '64. See MERIDIAN CAMPAIGN and WEST POINT, Miss., 21 Feb. '64.

SORREL, Gilbert Moxley (sor-rel'). C.S.A. gen. 1838–1901. Ga. A Capt. on Longstreet's staff, he was at 1st Bull Run as his volunteer A.D.C. and was appointed Acting Adj. Gen. of Longstreet's brigade on 1 Sept. '61. He served in this capacity at Williamsburg, Seven Pines, and the Seven Days' Battles. Then as Maj. and Acting Adj. Gen. of Longstreet's division after 24 July '62, he was at Antietam. When Longstreet was made commander of a permanent corps Sorrel was promoted Lt. Col. and Acting Adj. Gen. 23 June '63 and was at Gettysburg and Chickamauga. In the battle of the Wilderness he had become Adj. Gen. and was in effect corps Chief of Staff. He led four brigades in a successful envelopment of the Federal left at the WILDERNESS. Appointed B.G. C.S.A. on 27 Oct. '64, he was given a brigade of Ga. troops on the 31st and commanded them in Mahone's division at Petersburg. At Hatcher's Run he received an incapacitating chest wound, 7 Feb. '65. After the war he was a merchant and businessman. He is author of what Freeman has called "a famous and delightful memoir," *Recollections of a Confederate Staff Officer* (1905, 1917, and 1958).

SORREL. See OLD SORREL.

SOULÉ, Pierre. C.S.A. gen. 1802–70. France. Educated in Jesuit colleges, he was exiled from France at 15, when he conspired against the Bourbons. After living a year as a shepherd in the Pyrenees he returned to France and was a journalist in Paris until imprisoned in 1825, when his journal attacked the government. He escaped to England and then traveled to Haiti, Baltimore, New Orleans, Tenn. and Ky., where he settled. Working as a gardener until he learned English, he read law on his own and was admitted to the La. bar. He sat in the legislature in 1845 and was US Sen. 1847–53. Named Minister to Spain 1853–55, he was found to be plotting against that country's government and was sent home. He practiced law in New Orleans and was a secret agent of the Confederacy, making several trips to Europe for Davis. Returning to New Orleans, he was arrested in May '62 by Butler and charged with being a member of the Southern Independence Association, a secret society, and of writing "insolent letters" to Farragut that were signed by the mayor. Butler called him the principal supporter of the rebellion in New Orleans and said, in a letter to Halleck, "Mr. Soulé's influence and position, social and political, here render him in my judgment so dangerous..." that he wanted Soulé shot by a firing squad (O.R., II, III, 612). This, however, did not take place, and Soulé again evaded prison, joining Beauregard in Charleston as a member of the Gen.'s staff. He was commissioned B.G. C.S.A. after the defense of Charleston for "special service," a phrase that apparently covered his attempt to recruit a foreign legion for the Confederacy in Europe. After the war he fled to Cuba and returned later to New Orleans and his much-neglected law practice.

SOUTH, UNION DEPARTMENT OF THE. Constituted 15 Mar. '62 with headquarters at Hilton Head, S.C., to include the states of S.C., Ga., and Fla. Dept. of Key West was added the same day. Dist. of West Fla. was detached 8 Aug. '62 and annexed to the Dept. of the Gulf. Commanders were Brig. Gen. T. W. [sic] Sherman, to 31 Mar. '62; and Maj. Gen. David Hunter to 22 Aug. '62. X Corps was created 3 Sept. '62 to consist of troops in this department. Department commanders during this period were Brannan, O. M. Mitchel, David Hunter, and Q. A. Gillmore; for exact dates they were in command, see X Corps (Dept. of the South). When X Corps left the department (17 Apr. '64), Gillmore remained as department commander until 1 May '64; his strength was 26,000 on 31 Dec. '63. Succeeding commanders were: Brig. Gen. J. P. Hatch, until 26 May; Maj. Gen. J. G. Foster, until 9 Feb. '65; and Gillmore, again, until 26 June '65. Effective strength 31 Dec. '64 was 7,000.

SOUTH ANNA RIVER, Va., 23–28 June and 4 July '63. During the Gettysburg campaign the Federals conducted demonstrations in Dix's Dept. of Va. with the object of threatening Richmond from the Peninsula and diverting strength from Lee. Col. S. D. Spear led 1,050 Federal cavalry from White House to Hanover and South Anna Bridge. He succeeded in doing some damage at both places and withdrew before Henry Wise could cut him off. On this raid he captured W. H. F. ("Rooney") Lee.

Getty led a force of 10,000 up the north bank of the Pamunkey with the mission of destroying the railroad bridge across the South Anna and of cutting the railroads north of Richmond. He found the bridge defended by a Confederate brigade and withdrew after destroying smaller bridges between the South Anna and the Chickahominy. Meanwhile, 6,000 men of IV Corps under Keyes had advanced along the Peninsula toward Bottom's Bridge on the Chickahominy to create a diversion that would assist Getty. This column was stopped by two brigades under D. H. Hill. The Confederates pursued and there was some action around BALTIMORE CROSS ROADS, 1–2 July.

SOUTH CAROLINA, with Ga., was the heart of states rights and secessionist sentiments. As early as 1828 the state had advocated nullification in protest to the Tariff of Abominations. (See John C. CALHOUN.) S.C. was the first state to secede (20 Dec. '60; see also ORDINANCE OF SECESSION), and the first shots were fired at Fort Sumter. It was readmitted to the Union 25 June '68, but military control was not withdrawn finally until Apr. '77.

SOUTH CAROLINA, GEORGIA, AND FLORIDA, CONFEDERATE DEPARTMENT OF. The coasts of S.C., Ga., and East Fla. were constituted as a department under R. E. Lee on 5 Nov. '61. Before this there had been a Dept. of S.C., commanded since 21 Aug. by R. S. Ripley; and a Dept. of Ga., commanded since 26 Oct. by A. R. Lawton.

Lee actually assumed command 8 Nov. and when he was called to Richmond 3 Mar. '62 for reassignment was succeeded by J. C. Pemberton. (Pemberton was not *assigned* command until 14 Mar.) On 7 Apr. Pemberton's command was extended over middle and eastern Fla. (O.R., I, VI), but the latter continues to show in the O.R. atlas *plates* as a separate department.

Beauregard superseded Pemberton on 24 Sept. as commander of the Dept. of S.C. and Ga. (*ibid.*, XIV, 2); since Fla. is not mentioned in the department's designation, the order of 7 Apr. was presumably not observed. On 7 Oct. '62 Beauregard's command was extended over middle and eastern Fla. (*ibid.*, XIV, 2) and the Dept. of middle and eastern Fla. disappeared (*ibid.*, atlas plate CLXVI ff.). Although the O.R. atlas shows a Dept. of S.C., Ga., *and* Fla. as existing since 1861, it would appear that Fla. was not really part of the department until 7 Oct. '62.

On 4 Nov. the boundary of the department was extended in Fla. to include the Choctawhatchee River and bay (40 miles west of the Chattahoochie). The northwest corner of the state of Ga. was excluded from the department during the times when the DISTRICT OF THE WEST was in existence. Samuel Jones succeeded Beauregard as department commander on 20 Apr. '64. Hardee took command 5 Oct. '64. J. E. Johnston was given command of all troops in the department on 22 Feb. '65, when he was assigned command of the Army of Tenn.

SOUTH MOUNTAIN, 14 Sept. '62. Engagement of ANTIETAM CAMPAIGN.

SOUTHSIDE R.R. (Sutherland Station), 2 Apr. '65. Action in PETERSBURG FINAL ASSAULT.

SOUTHWEST, CONFEDERATE DEPARTMENT OF THE. Alternate designation of the Department of MISSISSIPPI AND EAST LOUISIANA when Polk assumed command 23 Dec. '63.

SOUTHWEST, UNION MILITARY DIVISION AND ARMY OF THE. Organized 25 Dec. '61 from troops in portions of the Dept. of Mo. (strength, 15,000), and merged 13 Dec. '62 in the Dist. of Eastern Ark., Dept. of Tenn. Commanders were Brig. Gen. S. R. Curtis, Frederick Steele, E. A. Carr, and W. A. Gorman. It fought at Bentonville, Sugar Creek, and Pea Ridge.

SOUTHWESTERN (or SOUTHERN, or TRANS-MISSISSIPPI) ARMY, CONFEDERATE. Constituted 14 Jan. '63 under Kirby Smith from forces in West La. and Tex. On 9 Feb. Kirby Smith was assigned command of the entire TRANS-MISSISSIPPI DEPARTMENT.

SOUTHWESTERN VIRGINIA, CONFEDERATE DEPARTMENT OF. See WESTERN AND SOUTHWESTERN VIRGINIA, Confederate Departments and Armies in.

SOUTHWESTERN VIRGINIA AND EAST TENNESSEE, CONFEDERATE DEPARTMENT OF. See WESTERN AND SOUTHWESTERN VIRGINIA, Confederate Departments and Armies in.

SOUTHWEST MISSOURI, UNION ARMY OF. Another name for Army of the SOUTHWEST. (This is the designation used by Dyer, 540.)

SOWERS, Edgar. Union officer. Ohio. Capt. 118th Ohio 15 Sept. '62; Maj. 31 Oct. '64; Lt. Col. 28 Jan. '65; Bvt. B.G. USV. Brevets for Franklin (Tenn.), Nashville, war service.

SPALDING, George. Union officer. Scotland. Pvt. and Sgt. Co. A 4th Mich. 20 June '61; 1st Lt. 5 Aug. '61; Capt. 13 Jan. '62; Lt. Col. 18th Mich. 18 July '62; Col. 12th Tenn. Cav. 24 Feb. '64; Bvt. B.G. USV 21 Mar. '65 (Tenn. campaign). Commanded 2, 4, Cav. Corps (Cumberland); 4, Cav. Corps (Cumberland); 4, Cav. Corps (Mil. Div. Miss.); Dist. North Mo. (Mo.).

SPANGLER, Edward. See LINCOLN'S ASSASSINATION and Dr. Samuel MUDD.

SPANISH FORT, Ala., 27 Mar.–8 Apr. '65. (MOBILE CAMPAIGN) On 17 Mar. '65 Canby led 32,000 troops to attack Mobile from the east. (Frederick Steele was moving with 13,000 from Pensacola to link up with him.) The XVI Corps moved by water from Fort Gaines and the XIII Corps marched from Fort Morgan; the two forces united at Danley's Ferry and on 27 Mar. laid siege to the Confederate bridgehead at Spanish Fort. Maury reinforced the brigade here and brought its strength to 4,000. Steele closed in on Blakely, five miles north, and on 4 Apr., after a bridge had been put across Bayou Minette, the two Confederate positions were within the same line of investment.

By afternoon of the 8th there were 53 siege guns and 37 field pieces in ac-

781 SPENCER, G. E.

tion against· Spanish Fort. At 5:30 P.M. the 8th Iowa led the rest of Geddes' brigade in an assault that established a foothold in the Confederate works. By midnight the place had been captured with about 500 prisoners and 9 guns. The Confederate commander, R. L. Gibson, reported a loss of 93 killed, 395 wounded, and 250 missing. Most of the defenders escaped over a treadway bridge to Battery Tracy and from there to Mobile. Canby then reinforced Steele in the siege of BLAKELY, Ala., 1–9 Apr. '65.

SPARTA, Tenn., 17 Aug. '63. See CALFKILLER CREEK.

SPAULDING, Andrew. Union officer listed erroneously by Phisterer; see SPURLING, Andrew Barclay.

SPAULDING, Ira. Union officer. N.Y. Capt. 50th N.Y. Engrs. 29 Aug. '61; Maj. 14 Oct. '62; Lt. Col. 1 Jan. '64; Bvt B.G. USV 9 Apr. '65 (fall of Richmond and surrender of R. E. Lee). Died 1875.

SPAULDING, Oliver Lyman. Union officer. 1833–1922. N.H. Capt. 23d Mich. 1 Aug. '62; Maj. 13 Feb. '63; Lt. Col. 6 Apr. '63; Col. 16 Apr. '64; Bvt. B.G. USV 25 June '65 (war service). Commanded 2, 2, XXIII. He was an authority on customs law and administration and served as Congressman, special agent of the Treasury, and Assistant Sec. of the Treasury.

SPEAR, Ellis. Union officer. 1834–?. Me. Capt. 20th Me. 29 Aug. '62; Maj. 28 Aug. '63; Col. 29 May '65; Bvt. B.G. USV 9 Apr. '65. Brevets for Peeble's Farm (Va.), Lewis' Farm (Va.), surrender of R. E. Lee. At Peeble's Farm he commanded a brigade while only a Major. After the war he was a well-known patent lawyer and for a time worked in the US Patent Office.

SPEAR, Samuel Perkins. Union officer. 1815–75. Mass. R.A. Pvt., Cpl., Sgt.

and 1st Sgt. Co. F 2d US Cav. 2 Mar. '60–9 Aug. '61; Lt. Col. 11th Pa. Cav. 5 Oct. '61; Col. 20 Aug. '62; Bvt. B.G. USV (great personal gallantry at Darbytown near Richmond). Commanded cavalry brigade, US forces Yorktown (Va.), Army of Va. and N.C.; 2d Brig., Cav. Div. (Va. and N.C.). Wounded at Five Forks (Va.). Served as enlisted man in Seminole and Mexican wars and against Indians in the West. W.I.A. at Cerro Gordo.

SPEARS, James G. Union gen. ?–1869. Tenn. Commissioned Lt. Col. 1st Tenn. 1 Sept. '61, he was appointed B.G. USV 5 Mar. '62 and fought at Wild Cat, Mill Springs, Cumberland Gap, and on the Kanawha expedition. He was dismissed 30 Aug. '64 (the O.R. gives no reason).

SPEED, James. Union atty. gen. 1812–87. Ky. After college and Transylvania Law School he sat in the state legislature and organized Union troops in his state after effectively opposing Ky.'s secession. He was appointed Atty. Gen. by Lincoln in 1864 to succeed Bates, and resigned in 1866 in protest to Johnson's Reconstruction policies. Later he was professor of law at the Univ. of Louisville.

SPENCER, George Eliphaz. Union officer. 1836–93. N.Y. Appt.-Iowa. Capt. A.A.G. Vols. 24 Oct. '62; Col. 1st Ala. Cav. 11 Sept. '63; Bvt. USV (Ga. and Carolinas campaign). Commanded 3, 3, Cav. Corps (Mil. Div. Miss.). He had practiced law in Iowa and later represented Alabama in the Senate as a Republican. Ranching, mining, and railroading were among his other interests. Appleton's says that his second wife, William Loring Nunez Spencer, was the niece and namesake of Gen. Loring and is nicknamed Major "perhaps because of her masculine name."

SPENCER REPEATING CARBINE. The first successful breech-loading repeating rifled carbine was patented in 1860 by Christopher M. Spencer of Conn. By 1864 it had become the standard arm of the Federal cavalry and by the fall of that year brigades of infantry began to appear with it (Alexander, 53–8). The Confederates were unable to use the ones they captured because they lacked the special cartridges and had no metal for their manufacture.

Up until the end of 1865 the government had purchased 77,181 Spencers and about 60,000,000 cartridges (Gluckman, 439–40).

The carbine was loaded by a tubular magazine that passed through the butt of the stock and held seven copper rimfire .52 caliber cartridges. A spring fed the cartridges toward the breech. The weapon was operated by pulling downward on the trigger guard lever, as with the SHARPS. This dropped the breech block and extracted the fired shell. Closing the lever pushed a live cartridge into the chamber. The hammer was then cocked manually in a separate motion of the thumb. Ten extra magazines could be carried in a special box, giving the soldier 70 rounds for rapid fire. The carbine weighed 8¼ pounds and had a total length of 39 inches.

The Spencer cartridge was the first complete self-contained cartridge. Since it contained only 45 grains of black powder, the arm lacked range and muzzle power. Another limitation was the fact that the copper cartridges tended to stick in the chamber as the weapon became heated.

Alexander says that Spencer carbines "fully doubled the efficiency of the cavalry against ours with only muzzle-loaders." He comments also on the high casualties inflicted by these weapons at Darbytown Road, 7 Oct. '64, and Franklin, Tenn., 30 Nov. '64.

SPHERICAL CASE SHOT. Another term for SHRAPNEL. But see CASE SHOT.

SPICELY, William Thomas. Union officer. N.C. Capt. 24th Ind. 31 July '61; Maj. 5 Apr. '62; Lt. Col. 26 Apr. '62; Col. 14 May '62; Bvt. B.G. USV 26 Mar. '65 (Mobile). Commanded 1, 12, XIII (Tenn.); 1, 3, XIII (Tenn.); 1, 3, XIII (Gulf); 2, 3, XIX (Gulf); 2, 2, Res. Corps (Gulf); 2, 2, XIII (Gulf). In Mexican War as Lt. and Capt. Died 1884.

SPIKING AND UNSPIKING CANNON. The *Confederate Ordnance Manual* gives these directions: "Drive into the vent a jagged and hardened steel spike with a soft point, or a nail without a head; break it off flush with the outer surface, and clinch the point inside by means of the rammer. Wedge a shot in the bottom of the bore by wrapping it with felt, or by means of iron wedges, using the rammer or a bar of iron to drive them in. . . . To unspike a piece . . . if the spike is not screwed in or clinched, and the bore is not impeded, put in a charge of powder of ⅓ the weight of the shot, and ram junk wads over it with a handspike, laying on the bottom of the bore a strip of wood, with a groove on the under side containing a strand of quickmatch by which fire is communicated to the charge; . . .If this method, several times repeated, is not successful, unscrew the vent-piece, if it be a bronze gun, and if an iron one, drill out the spike, or drill a new vent."

SPINOLA, Francis B. Union gen. 1821–91. N.Y. A public officeholder and active in Democratic politics, he raised the Empire Brig. of the N.Y. State Vols. and was commissioned B.G. USV 1 Oct. '62. He commanded Spinola's brigade, division at Suffolk, Va. (1 Oct. '62

-28 Dec. '62); 1, 5, XVIII, N.C. (11
Jan.–22 Apr. '63); 1st Brig., Dist. Pamlico, N.C. (22 Apr.–9 May and 29
May–26 June '63); Beaufort, X, South
(25–29 May '63). Leading Indpt. Brig.,
VII, Va. (June–July '63), he was
wounded while leading in a bayonet
charge at Wapping Heights. Resigning
8 June '65, he was later active in banking and insurance and was US Congressman for a time.

SPOFFORD, John Pembroke. Union
officer. N.Y. Lt. Col. 97th N.Y. 24 Feb.
'62; Col. 18 Feb. '65; Bvt. B.G. USV
(war service). Commanded 1, US Forces
Morris Island, X (South). Died 1884.

SPOILING ATTACK. As the term
indicates, this is an operation used to
disrupt an impending attack while the
enemy is still in the process of forming
or assembling.

SPOONER, Benjamin J. Union officer. 1828–81. Ohio. After fighting in
the Mexican War he was a lawyer. He
was commissioned Capt. 7th Ind. 18
Apr. '61 and promoted Lt. Col. nine
days later. Fighting at Philippi and
Laurel Hill, he was mustered out 25
Aug. '61 and named Lt. Col. 51st Ind.
4 Dec. '61. He resigned this commission 16 June '62 after participating at
Shiloh and the siege of Corinth. Commissioned Col. 83d Ind. 6 Nov. '62, he
fought at Vicksburg, Missionary Ridge,
and the Atlanta campaign, losing his
left arm at Kenesaw Mountain. He
served on military commissions until
May '65, when he resigned after being
breveted for Chattanooga–Resaca–Kenesaw Mountain (B.G. and Maj. Gen.
USV).

SPORTING HILL (near Harrisburg), Pa., 30 June '63. (Gettysburg
campaign.) After the cavalry with the
1st Div., Dept. of the Susquehanna, had
located Confederates occupying this
place, Brig. Gen. John Ewen sent Col.

Roome (37th N.Y.S.M.) with the 22d
and 37th N.Y. Mil., and Landis' battery, to drive them off. In an exchange
of fire starting at 4 P.M. and lasting a
little over an hour, the Confederate fire
was silenced. Union losses are reported
as one wounded and 10 missing. No
Confederate casualties were reported.
(E.&B.; O.R.)

SPOTSYLVANIA CAMPAIGN, Va.,
7–20 May '64. After failing to defeat
Lee in the WILDERNESS, 5–6 May, Grant
issued orders early 7 May for the Army
of the Potomac to continue southward.

He hoped to envelop Lee's flank and
advance toward Richmond. Lee soon
had indications of this move: Stuart
reported contact with Federal cavalry
around Todd's Tavern; at 1 P.M. the
Federal ponton bridge had been removed from Germanna Ford.

At 5 P.M. (7 May) Meade ordered
Warren to start his V Corps at 8:30
P.M. along the Brock Road toward
Spotsylvania. Hancock (II) was to fol-
low the same route. Sheridan's cavalry
was ordered to cover the south flank;
Meade apparently had the mistaken idea
that the Brock Road beyond Todd's
Tavern was open, but it was actually
being patrolled by Fitz Lee's cavalry
division. By 7 P.M. Lee had ordered
Anderson (successor to Longstreet as

C.G. I Corps) to start before 3 A.M., 8 May, with the divisions of Kershaw and Field for Spotsylvania. The latter place was a vital crossroad whose possession by the Federals would threaten Richmond. Fitz Lee's cavalry division was already occupying the road between Todd's Tavern and Spotsylvania, while Merritt's Federal cavalry was along the Brock Road between the flank of II Corps and Todd's Tavern.

Since his men would not be able to get any rest in the burning woods, Anderson started his march at 11 P.M., instead of waiting until 3 A.M. In anticipation of a movement to his right, Lee had ordered Pendleton to cut a road through the woods to shorten the distance to Spotsylvania. At dawn Anderson halted three miles from Spotsylvania to let his men eat and rest after an arduous night march. Firing was heard about two miles away and a courier arrived from Jeb Stuart's cavalry saying that artillery support was urgently needed. Anderson hurried toward the sound of the guns and was able to reinforce Fitz Lee's cavalry along the Brock Road with the brigades of Henagan and Humphreys in time to stop Warren's first assault. Word then came that Rosser's cavalry brigade (of Hampton's division) was holding Spotsylvania C. H. against heavy cavalry attacks and needed prompt support. Some of Fitz Lee's cavalry were sent immediately and were followed by the infantry brigades of Wofford and Bryan. Wilson's division of Federal cavalry took Spotsylvania but was withdrawn when Sheridan realized that Anderson and Fitz Lee were between it and the Federal army. Anderson's early start had won the first battle of the campaign and again frustrated Grant's vigorous attempt to turn Lee's flank.

The morning of 7 May Sheridan's cavalry had skirmished around Todd's Tavern with Stuart and at the end of the day had bivouacked around the tavern. Sheridan had ordered his divisions to move the next morning to seize bridges over the Po River south and west of Spotsylvania; Gregg and Merritt were to advance on their objectives from south of the Po, while Wilson was to advance along the Fredericksburg road south through Spotsylvania.

When Meade reached Todd's Tavern around midnight of the 7th with the head of Warren's V Corps cavalry, he ordered Merritt to move along the Brock Road to clear it for the advance of V Corps to Spotsylvania. Merritt was delayed by obstacles Fitz Lee had thrown across the road; this slowed the infantry.

Meade criticized Sheridan for allowing his cavalry to block the way of the infantry and thereby allowing Lee to win the race to Spotsylvania. Sheridan replied that Meade's orders had caused the improper employment of cavalry. At Grant's suggestion the cavalry corps was then detached to undertake SHERIDAN'S RICHMOND RAID, 9–24 May, which resulted in the death of Jeb Stuart at YELLOW TAVERN.

The morning of 9 May the Confederates had entrenched across Grant's lines of advance. Burnside, whose IX Corps had moved into position on the Spotsylvania–Fredericksburg road, sent Grant the erroneous report that Lee was trying to move toward Fredericksburg. Grant therefore ordered Hancock to attack across the Po River with three divisions to threaten Lee's left flank via Blockhouse Bridge.

On 10 May the division of Mahone (III) guarded the Blockhouse Bridge while Heth's division was sent south via Old Court House to hit Hancock's exposed right flank. Before this attack materialized, however, Hancock had sent Brooke's brigade (4, 1, II) to reconnoiter Mahone's left. Hancock was then

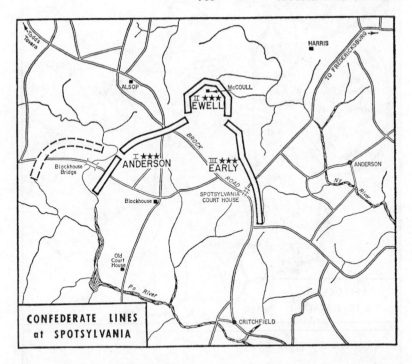

CONFEDERATE LINES
at SPOTSYLVANIA

ordered to withdraw the divisions of Birney and Gibbon from this area and to leave only Barlow south of the Po. (His other division, Mott, had been sent the preceding day to reinforce Wright.) Barlow was attacked by Heth's enveloping force and by Mahone to its front. Brooke and Brown repulsed an initial assault, but were then pushed back in an action known as Waite's Shop. Miles repulsed Heth's attempt to cross the river.

Thinking that the Confederates had weakened their line to make this envelopment, Grant ordered the V and VI Corps to attack. Although Emory Upton led his brigade (2, 1, VI), reinforced by four regiments from Neill's brigade (3, 2, VI) in a successful penetration of Doles's brigade (Rodes's) at 6:10 P.M., he was forced to withdraw with heavy losses because Mott's division (4, II), which was supposed to exploit through the gap he had created, was stopped by artillery fire. He brought back over 1,000 prisoners. An attack at 4 P.M. against Anderson from the neighborhood of the Alsop House had failed after sustaining heavy losses. The latter attack had been made by the divisions of Crawford and Cutler and the brigades of Webb and Carroll of Gibbon's division. Carroll had gained the Confederate parapet but had been driven back by murderous artillery fire.

During a chilly night of heavy rains Grant ordered Hancock to mass his II Corps for an attack at dawn 12 May against the "mule shoe" salient held by Ewell's corps. At 4:30 A.M. a massed attack of 20,000 Federals advanced and 15 minutes later poured through gaps it had made in the line. In 45 minutes, before being halted by a second, and

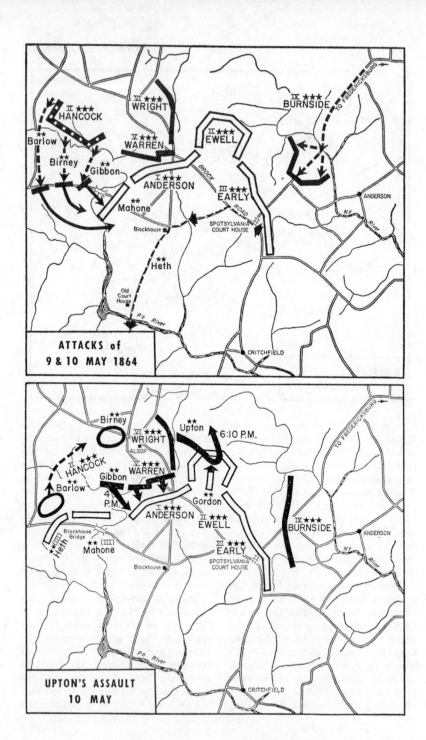

**ATTACKS of
9 & 10 MAY 1864**

**UPTON'S ASSAULT
10 MAY**

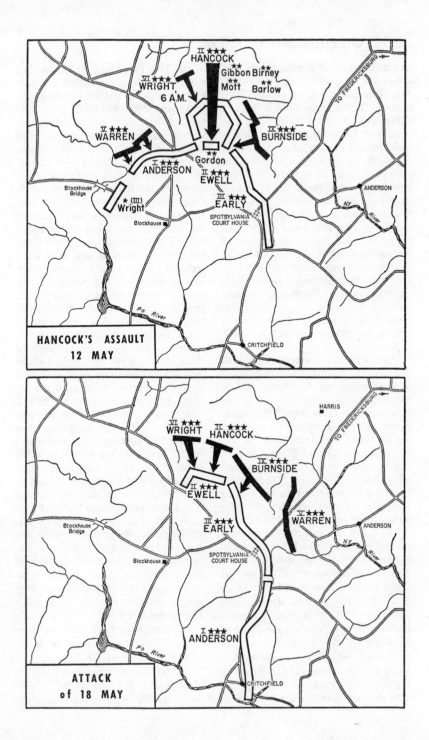

**HANCOCK'S ASSAULT
12 MAY**

**ATTACK
of 18 MAY**

incomplete, line of entrenchments held across the neck of the salient by Gordon, Hancock's men captured 2,000 prisoners (some reports run as high as 4,000) and 20 guns. Among the captured were Gens. Anderson and "Maryland" Steuart. Almost all of the famous Stonewall brigade was cut off and taken prisoner without an opportunity to fire more than a few shots. Gordon counterattacked with the support of several brigades from the divisions of Rodes and Early. At 6 o'clock Wright's VI Corps assaulted the northwest face of the salient which Rodes held. Burnside had attacked the eastern shoulder at 4 o'clock. After extremely bloody fighting Hancock was able to hold the positions he had taken, but the other two corps had no success. This action is known as "Bloody Angle," or "The Salient."

There was no more heavy fighting at Spotsylvania. Sedgwick had been killed by a sniper on the 9th. Emory Upton had demonstrated the ability that was to result in his being made a Brig. Gen. at the age of 24, before he had been out of West Point three years. It was on 11 May that Grant had wired Halleck that he proposed "to fight it out on this line if it takes all summer." The fighting had been so severe that an oak tree 22 inches in diameter was cut down by musket balls (B.&L., IV, 173n.).

The heavy rain that had started early the afternoon of the 11th, and continued during the fight for Bloody Angle, slowed the movement of V and VI Corps from the Federal right for an attack Grant had ordered against Lee's right on 13 May. By the time this operation was ready to start on the 14th Lee had detected the maneuver and had moved Anderson's corps to oppose it.

On 15 May Hancock was shifted to the left of VI Corps and through the 17th the Federals entrenched. The night of the 17th the II and VI Corps were moved back to their original positions to make a daylight attack against Ewell, who now held the Confederate left (north) flank. After a brief attack that started at 4 A.M. the attempt was abandoned as a failure and these two corps moved back to the Federal left. The night of the 18th the IX Corps was moved to the left of VI Corps and II Corps was moved into reserve near Anderson, a little more than a mile to the rear. Kitching's brigade of heavy artillery from Meade's reserve artillery had been retrained to fight as infantry and was assigned to V Corps. Reinforcements arrived also from the Washington defenses: the Irish Legion (a brigade of 2,000), and 7,500 retrained heavy artillerymen who were assigned to the II Corps as its 4th Div.

On 19 May Ewell led his depleted corps (6,000) north against the Federal right flank to determine whether Grant's army was moving. He crossed the Ny River and made contact about 3:30 P.M. with Tyler's "heavies." Ramseur attacked but was repulsed and was then counterattacked. Only the prompt action of Col. John S. Hoffman with Johnson's division and Wade Hampton's horse artillery enabled Ewell to hold until he could withdraw after dark. He had lost 900. Tyler's green troops had held until reinforced by Birney's division (3, II), Kitching's brigade, and Bowerman's Md. brigade. The 1st Md. (regiment), just returning from Fredericksburg after its veteran furlough, attacked without orders and played a prominent part in repulsing the Confederates (Fox, 308). This action is known as Harris' Farm.

Pursuing his policy of "relentless hammering," Grant next faced Lee on the NORTH ANNA RIVER, 23–26 May.

Federal forces engaged 10 and 12 May were 37,822 and 65,785, respectively. Losses were 4,100 and 6,820 killed and wounded on these days. Confederate strengths and losses are not known, although Lee had fewer casualties since he was fighting from entrenchments. Sedgwick, the famous VI Corps commander, and T. G. Stevenson, who commanded the 1st Div., IX, were killed. Wright, Webb, and Carroll were wounded, the last two severely. On the Confederate side, Perrin and Daniel were killed; Walker (who lost a foot), Ramseur, Robert Johnston, and McGowan were wounded; Steuart and Edward Johnson were captured. Jeb Stuart was killed at YELLOW TAVERN.

SPRAGUE, Augustus Brown Reed. Union officer. Mass. Capt. 3d Mass. Rifles 19 Apr. '61; mustered out 3 Aug. '61; Lt. Col. 25th Mass. 9 Sept. '61; Col. 51st Mass. 11 Nov. '62; mustered out 27 July '63; Lt. Col. 2d Mass. Arty. 27 Feb. '64; Col. 18 Sept. '65; Bvt. B.G. USV (war service). Phisterer lists him as Col. 51st Mass. at time of the B.G. brevet.

SPRAGUE, Ezra T. Union officer. Conn. 1st Lt. Adj. 8th Wis. 11 Oct. '61; Col. 42d Wis. 14 Sept. '64; Bvt. B.G. USV 20 June '65 (war service). Commanded Cairo (Ill.) in 1864.

SPRAGUE, John Wilson. Union gen. 1817-93. N.Y. A merchant, he was commissioned Capt. 7th Ohio 25 Apr. '61, Col. 63d Ohio 23 Jan. '62, and B.G. USV 30 July '64. He commanded in the Army of the Tenn.: 3, 5th Div. Dist. Memphis, XVI (25 July-25 Aug. '63); 2, 4, XVI (10 Mar.-18 Sept. '64); 2, 1, XVII (1 Nov. '64-29 Jan. '65 and 28 Mar.-20 May '65) and 1st Div., XVII (23-31 Oct. '64). Mustered out in 1866, he was awarded the Medal of Honor in 1894 for "having with a small command defeated an overwhelming force of the enemy and saved the trains for the movement of the corps at Decatur (Ala.) 22 July '64" (Heitman).

After the war he was in railroading and banking.

SPRAGUE, Kate Chase. Washington belle. 1840-99. Hostess for her widowed father, Salmon P. CHASE, she was the acknowledged beauty of wartime Washington. She and William SPRAGUE were married in the winter of 1863 in a burst of splendor and glory. The couple continued to be the social leaders in Washington, and Kate was active in working for her father's Democratic nomination in the presidential campaign of 1868, which was unsuccessful. However, the marriage was an unhappy one. Sprague drank heavily, and she was said to be too friendly with N. Y. Sen. Roscoe Conkling. In 1873 her father died, a panic took her husband's fortune, and she gave birth to their fourth child, a mentally defective daughter. Six years later her husband attacked Conkling in a drunken rage, and in 1882 Kate won a divorce. She then went to Europe, returning four years later to live at Edgewood, her father's estate outside Washington, where she spent the rest of her life barely earning a living raising chickens and selling milk. Her only son committed suicide in 1890.

SPRAGUE, William. War gov. of R.I. 1830-1915. R.I. From an extremely wealthy and politically influential family, he was Gov. of R.I. from 1859 until 1863, and as Col. of the R.I. State Mil. commanded a regiment and a battery of light horse artillery of the militia at 1st Bull Run, where his horse was shot from under him. Offered the commission of B.G. USV, he declined, though serving during part of the Peninsular campaign at Williamsburg and the Yorktown siege. He was US Sen. 1864-75 and married Kate, the daughter of Salmon P. Chase. Their marriage was an unhappy one, and after the Panic of 1873 swept away his fortune, they were separated, and divorced in 1882.

SPRINGFIELD ARSENAL. After the loss of the HARPERS FERRY ARSENAL the one at Springfield, Mass., was the only important small arms manufactory in the North. From a capacity of 1,200 rifles at the beginning of the war it was capable by 30 June '64 of producing 300,000 "of the finest muskets in the world, annually" (Miller, V, 146). The famous "Springfield" rifle muskets of the Civil War are covered under their official designations of UNITED STATES RIFLE MUSKET, Models 1861 and 1863 (Types 1 and 2). All of these were essentially the same weapon, with minor modifications. The Springfield Armory produced 793,434 of them between 1 Jan. '61 and 31 Dec. '65 (Gluckman).

SPRING HILL, Tenn., 4 Mar. '63. Van Dorn surrounded and captured Coburn's brigade in an action known also as THOMPSON'S STATION (Unionville), 4–5 Mar. '63.

SPRING HILL, Tenn., 29 Nov. '64. (Franklin and Nashville Campaign) Faulty execution by Hood's command enabled Schofield's forces to escape an envelopment that should have cut off their retreat from Columbia to Franklin, Tenn. See FRANKLIN AND NASHVILLE CAMPAIGN.

SPURLING, Andrew Barclay. Union officer. Me. 1st Lt. 1st Me. Cav. 19 Oct. '61; Capt. 16 Feb. '63; Maj. 2d Me. Cav. 12 Jan. '64; Lt. Col. 13 June '64; Bvt. B.G. USV 26 Mar. '65. Brevets for Mobile (2), Pollard (Ala.). Medal of Honor 10 Sept. '97 for Evergreen (Ala.) 23 Mar. '65. Phisterer lists him as Spaulding, Andrew B.

STAFFORD, Joab Arwin. Union officer. N.Y. Capt. 1st Ohio 29 Apr. '61; Maj. 2 June '62; mustered out 17 Aug. '64; Col. 178th Ohio 6 Oct. '64; Bvt. B.G. USV (war service).

STAFFORD, Leroy A. C.S.A. gen. ?–1864. La. As Lt. Col. 9th La. he went with Richard Taylor to Va. and succeeded him as Col. He led the regiment in the Valley campaign under Ewell and in the Seven Days' Battles. After Taylor's illness and Seymour's death he commanded the brigade during the rest of the campaign. In the summer of 1862 he commanded the 2d La. Brig. at Cedar Run and 2d Bull Run; and commanded his regiment at Harpers Ferry, Antietam (where he took over Starke's brigade and was then wounded in the foot), Fredericksburg, Chancellorsville, Winchester, and Gettysburg. Appointed B.G. C.S.A. 8 Oct. '63, he commanded 2d La. Brig. in the Stonewall division in the Mine Run operations and the Wilderness, where he was mortally wounded 5 May.

STAGER, Anson. Union officer. 1825–85. N.Y. Chief of US Mil. Telegraphs Capt. Asst. Q.M. Vols. 11 Nov. '61; Col. Add. A.D.C. to Halleck at War Dept. in Washington 26 Feb. '62; originated and developed the military telegraph cipher system; Bvt. B.G. USV (war service). A telegraph pioneer, "he was the originator of the cunningly devised contract which for many years gave the Western Union an iron-bound monopoly of the privilege of stringing wires along the railroads" (D.A.B.). He was general superintendent of Western Union before the war and was later vice-president. See also SIGNAL COMMUNICATIONS.

STAGG, Peter. Union officer. N.J. 2d Lt. 1st Mich. Cav. 22 Aug. '61; Maj. 12 Nov. '62; Lt. Col. 7 Dec. '62; Col. 17 Aug. '64; Bvt. B.G. USV (war service). Commanded 1, 1, Cav. Corps (Potomac); 1, 1, Cav. Corps (Shenandoah); 1st Div., Cav. Corps (Shenandoah). Died 1884.

STAHEL, Julius. Union gen. 1825–1912. Hungary. Fighting with Kossuth in the 1849 revolution, he fled to Berlin,

London, and finally N. Y., where he became a newspaperman. Commissioned Lt. Col. 8th N.Y. and commanding the regiment in reserve at Centreville during 1st Bull Run, he was promoted Col. 11 Aug. '61 and B.G. USV 12 Nov. '61. He then commanded 1st Brig., Blenker's division, Army of the Potomac (Dec. '61–Mar. '62); in the II Corps, Potomac (Mar.–31 Mar. '62) and in the Mountain Dept. (1 Apr.–26 June '62) at Cross Keys. In the Army of Va. he commanded 1, 1, I (26 June–30 Aug. '62) and 1st Div. of that corps (30 Aug.–12 Sept. '62) at 2d Bull Run. He then led 1st Div., XI, Potomac (12 Sept. '62–10 Jan. '63) and the cavalry division, XXII, Washington (2 Mar.–26 June '63). He was named Maj. Gen. USV 14 Mar. '65. From Apr. until 9 June '64 he commanded the 1st Cav. Div., W. Va., being wounded on 5 June near Piedmont and being awarded (in 1893) the Medal of Honor for this exploit. He then served on court-martial duty and in the Middle Dept. until his resignation 8 Feb. '65. From 1866–69 he was Consul at Yokohama, then engaged in mining, and was Consul at Osaka and Hiogo (1878–84) and at Shanghai (1884–85). He resigned because of his health and went into the insurance business.

STAND OF ARMS. A complete set of equipment for one soldier: the rifle, bayonet, cartridge belt, and box (Webster). Frequently, however, it meant the rifle and belt alone (Wilhelm).

STAND OF COLORS. A *single* color or flag (Wilhelm).

STANLEY, David Sloan. Union gen. 1828–1902. Ohio. USMA 1852 (9/43); Dragoons. After serving on the frontier in the Kans. border disturbances and in Indian fighting, he was offered, and refused, the colonelcy of a C.S.A. regiment at Fort Smith (Ark.) in the spring of 1861. Named Capt. 1st US Cav. 16

Mar. '61 (1st Lt. since 1855), he fought at Forsyth, Dug Spring, and Wilson's Creek before being commissioned B.G. USV 28 Sept. '61. Breaking his leg in Nov., he was disabled until Jan. '62, but assumed command of the 1st Div., Army Miss. (4 Mar.–24 Apr. '62) and led it New Madrid, Island No. 10, and Fo Pillow. He then led 2d Div., Army Mis (24 Apr.–26 Oct. '62) at Iuka an Corinth and commanded 8th Div., Left Wing, XIII, Tenn. 1–11 Nov. '62. As Maj. Gen. USV (29 Nov. '62) and Chief of Cav. of the Army of the Cumberland (5 Nov. '62–9 Jan. '63), he was at Franklin, Nolansville, and Stones River. Then commanding the cavalry corps of the Cumberland (9 Jan.–9 Sept. '63 and 9–20 Nov. '63), he fought at Bradyville, Snow Hill, Franklin, Middleton, Shelbyville, and Elk River. Leading 1st Div., IV, Cumberland (21 Nov. '63–13 Feb. '64 and 14 Mar.–27 July '64), he fought at Dalton, Resaca, Dallas, Kenesaw Mountain, Ruff's Station, Chattahoochee, Peach Tree Creek, the Atlanta assaults, Jonesboro (wounded), and Lovejoy. He succeeded to the command of the IV Corps (27 July–1 Dec. '64) at Spring Hill and Franklin (wounded), and led this corps later (31 Jan.–1 Aug. '65). Breveted for Stones River, Resaca, Ruff's Station (B.G. USA), and Franklin (Maj. Gen. USA), he was given the Medal of Honor in 1893 for the last-named battle. Continuing in the R.A., he was appointed B.G. USA in 1884 and retired in 1892.

STANLEY, Timothy Robbins. Union officer. Conn. Col. 18th Ohio (3 months) 29 May '61; Col. 18th Ohio (3 years) 6 Aug. '61; Bvt. B.G. USV (war service); mustered out 9 Nov. '64. Commanded 2, 2, V (Potomac). Prominent as a lawyer and Republican politician. Died 1874.

STANNARD, George Jerrison. Union gen. 1820–86. Vt. A merchant and in the state militia, he was commissioned Lt. Col. 2d Vt. 20 June '61 and fought at 1st Bull Run. Captured at Harpers Ferry in May, he was promoted Col. the following 9 July and was named B.G. USV 11 Mar. '63. He commanded 2d, Abercrombie's division, XXII, Wash. (17 Apr.–26 June '63); 3, 3, I (25 June–3 July '63) at Gettysburg, where he was severely wounded; 1, 2, XVIII, Va. and N.C. (16 May–20 June '64) at Cold Harbor, where he was wounded; and 1st Div., XVIII, Va. and N.C. (20 June–31 July '64) during the Petersburg siege, where he was again wounded and (15–29 Sept. '64) at Fort Harrison, where he was wounded a fourth time, this time losing his arm. Breveted Maj. Gen. USV 28 Oct. '64 for Fort Harrison, he resigned in 1866 and held public offices later.

STANTON, David Leroy. Union officer. Md. Pvt. and 1st Sgt. Co. A 1st Md. 10 May '61; 2d Lt. 1 Nov. '61; 1st Lt. 12 Dec. '62; Capt. 7 Mar. '64; Maj. 2 Dec. '64; Lt. Col. 21 Feb. '65; Col. 20 Mar. '65; Bvt. B.G. USV 1 Apr. '65 (Five Forks, Va.). Commanded 2, 2, V (Potomac).

STANTON, Edwin McMasters. Union Sec. of War. 1814–69. Ohio. After Kenyon College he practiced law and held various minor public offices before being named Buchanan's Atty. Gen. in 1860. In politics he was a Jacksonian Democrat who deplored slavery but upheld the slaveholders' constitutional rights. In 1862 he succeeded Cameron as Lincoln's Sec. of War and proved to be an able and honorable cabinet member. He remained at the post under Johnson and shortly became a bitter opponent of the president's reconstruction politics. Asked to resign, he refused and was suspended by the president, who appointed Grant as Sec. ad interim. Stanton was restored to his post by the Senate, and Johnson again tried to re-

move him, only to be informed by the Senate that the president did not have the power to do so. After Johnson's impeachment, Stanton resigned and practiced law until appointed Associate Justice of the Supreme Court in 1869. However, he died four days later.

STARBIRD, Isaac Warren. Union officer. Me. Capt. 19th Me. 25 Aug. '62; Maj. 16 Sept. '64; Lt. Col. 8 Nov. '64; Col. 16 Nov. '64; Bvt. B.G. USV 7 Apr. '65 (High Bridge, Va.).

STAR BRIGADE (Heckman's) (XVIII Corps). Composed of the 25th, 27th, and 23d Mass., the 9th N.J., and the 55th Pa., it sustained 686 killed and mortally wounded during the war.

STARKE, Peter B. C.S.A. gen. ?–1888. Appt.-Miss. As Col. 28th Miss. Cav. (commissioned 24 Feb. '62) he fought in the Vicksburg defenses. At Thompson's Station he succeeded W. H. Jackson as brigade commander and opposed Sherman on the Meridian expedition. He commanded his regiment in the Atlanta campaign and was appointed B.G. C.S.A. 4 Nov. '64. After fighting at Franklin and Nashville, he was commanding near Columbus (Miss.) in Feb. '65 and surrendered with Richard Taylor.

STARKE, William E. C.S.A. gen. ?–1862. Va. (?) Appt.-La. Commissioned Col. C.S.A., he was R. S. Garnett's A.D.C. at Cheat River and served under Floyd at Lewisburg as Col. 60th Va. First ordered in Dec. '61 to join Donelson at Bowling Green, he was sent before he could leave for Ky. to Wise at Goldsboro, N.C. He commanded his regiment in Field's brigade during the Seven Days' Battles and was appointed B.G. C.S.A. 6 Aug. '62. In command of the 2d La. Brig., he fought at 2d Bull Run and succeeded Taliaferro in command of the Stonewall division at Harpers Ferry and Antietam. He was killed 17 Sept. at Antietam.

STARKWEATHER, John Converse. Union gen. 1830–90. N.Y. A lawyer, he was named Col. 1st Wis. 17 May '61, fought at Falling Waters (2 July) and Edward's Ferry (29 July) and was mustered out 21 Aug. Named Col. 1st Wis. 8 Oct. '61 and B.G. USV 17 July '63, he commanded in the Army of the Ohio: 28th Brig., 3d Div. (Aug.–Sept. '62), and 28th Brig., 3d Div., I (Sept.–Nov. '62) at Perryville. At Stones River he led 3, 1 Centre, XIV, Cumberland (20 Dec. '62–9 Jan. '63), and then commanded 3, 1, XIV, Cumberland (9 Jan.–9 Mar. '63). He also led 2, 1, XIV, Cumberland (21 Apr.–15 June and 30 July–28 Sept. '63) at Chickamauga, where he was wounded, and Missionary Ridge. After serving on Gen. William A. Hammond's court-martial, he commanded posts in Tenn. and Ala. until 11 May '65, when he resigned.

STAR OF THE WEST. US steamer fired on in Charleston Harbor by S.C. troops 9 Jan. '61 when attempting, unarmed, to take reinforcements and supplies to besieged Fort Sumter. This was the first overt act of the war. She was captured at Indianola, Tex., 17 Apr. '61, by Van Dorn, and on 4 May was made the receiving ship of the C. S. Navy at New Orleans. She was sunk in the Tallahatchie River in front of Fort Pemberton, 13 Mar. '63, to assist in blocking the Federals' Yazoo Pass expedition during the VICKSBURG CAMPAIGN.

STARR ARMY PERCUSSION REVOLVER. A .44 caliber six-shot, double-action revolver, almost 12 inches long and weighing two pounds 15 ounces. It fired a self-consuming, combustible cartridge, and could also be loaded with loose powder and ball. A single-action model was also made, as well as a .36 caliber navy model. The Federal government purchased 47,952 Starr revolvers during the war, most of which were the army type (Gluckman, *Pistols,* 201ff).

STARRING, Frederick Augustus. Union officer. N.Y. Maj. 46th Ill. 12 Sept. '61; transferred to 2d Ill. Arty. 30 Jan. '62; Col. 72d Ill. 21 Aug. '62; Bvt. B.G. USV (war service). Commanded 1, 1, XVII (Tenn.).

STATES RIGHTS. The doctrine of state sovereignty as well as the strict interpretation of the Federal constitution that gives to the states all powers not specifically granted to the central government. The former view was held by CALHOUN and the latter by Thomas Jefferson.

STEDMAN, Edmund Clarence. WAR CORRESPONDENT and poet. 1833–1904. Conn. After studying at Yale he contributed to a number of periodicals, notably *Vanity Fair, Putnam's Monthly,* and *Harper's.* He had begun writing poetry in college and continued to contribute some to the N.Y. *Tribune,* later becoming an editorial writer and correspondent for the *World* in the field 1861–63. In 1864 he purchased a seat on the stock exchange in N.Y.C. and continued to write poetry, being known as "The Bard of Wall Street." Cousin of Griffin Alexander Stedman, Jr., below.

STEDMAN, Griffin Alexander, Jr. Union officer. 1838–64. Conn. Capt. 5th Conn. 22 July '61; Maj. 11th Conn. 27 Nov. '61; Lt. Col. 11 June '62; Col. 17 Sept. '62; Bvt. B.G. USV 5 Aug. '64 (Petersburg). W.I.A. Antietam. Mortally wounded at Petersburg after the mine explosion, he died the same day 5 Aug. '64. Fort Stedman was named in his honor. Commanded 2, 2, XVIII (Va. and N.C.).

STEDMAN, William. Union officer. Ohio. Capt. 7th Ohio 14 May '61; mustered out 18 Aug. '61; 2d Lt. 6th Ohio Cav. 21 Oct. '61; Maj. 27 Oct. '61; Lt.

Col. 6 Aug. '63; Col. 26 Mar. '64; Bvt. USV (war service); mustered out 6 Oct. '64. Commanded 1, 2, Cav. Corps (Potomac). Active as a politician and in the state legislature.

STEEDMAN, James Blair. Union gen. 1817–83. Pa. A printer, he had served in the Tex. army and the Ohio legislature where he was a Douglas Democrat. Commissioned Col. 14th Ohio 27 Apr. and mustered out 13 Aug. '61, he was recommissioned Col. 14th Ohio 1 Sept. '61. Despite his politics, Lincoln nominated him B.G. USV in Mar. '62; Congress, however, refused to confirm the appointment until 17 July '62. He commanded 3, 1, III, Army Ohio (Sept.–Nov. '62) at Perryville. At Stones River he led 3, 3d Div. Centre, XIV, Cumberland (5 Nov. '62–9 Jan. '63) and then commanded 3, 3, XIV (9–28 Jan.) and 3d Div., XIV (9 Jan.–17 Apr. '63). He then led 2, 3, XIV (27 Apr.–15 Aug. '63). At Chickamauga his division (1st, Reserve Corps, Cumberland) lost one fifth its strength in 20 minutes. Steedman had a horse shot from under him and was severely bruised but continued on the field, leading one attack personally while carrying the regimental colors. As he went into this he instructed a staff officer to see that his name was spelled correctly in obituaries—Steedman not Steadman. He had this command from 15 Aug. until 9 Oct. '63 and on 10 Oct. took over 1, 2, IV, Cumberland, for eight days. Named Maj. Gen. USV 20 Apr. '64, he commanded the post of Chattanooga Oct. '63–May '64, and then the Dist. of Etowah (12 Nov. '64–May '65) during the battle of Nashville. Resigning in 1866, he served in the legislature and was active in public affairs and newspapering. A determined man, at his best in emergencies, he was of great size and strength with an aggressive temperament.

STEEDMAN'S — KIMBALL'S — OPDYCKE'S BRIGADE (1, 2, IV, Tenn.). Composed of 36th, 44th, 73d, 74th, Ill., 22d Ind., 21st Mich., 2d and 15th Mo., and 24th Wis. regiments, it had 1,192 killed and died of wounds during war. It distinguished itself at NASHVILLE, where it was Opdycke's brigade (Fox, 73 and 120).

STEELE, Frederick. Union gen. 1819–68. N.Y. USMA 1843 (30/39); Inf. After serving on frontier and garrison duty and fighting in the Mexican War (2 brevets), he was named Maj. 11th US Inf. 14 May '61 and fought at Dug Spring and Wilson's Creek in Aug. '61. Named Col. 8th Iowa 23 Sept. '61 and B.G. USV 29 Jan. '62, he commanded Dist. Southeast Mo. (Jan.–14 May '62). At Round Hill and Helena (Ark.) he commanded 1st Div., Army Southwest Mo. (9 May–29 Aug. '62); 1st Div. Southeast Mo. Dist. Eastern Ark. (May–Dec. '62); and Army Southwest Mo. (29 Aug.–7 Oct. '62). In the Army of the Tenn. he led 1st Div. Dist. East Ark. (Dec. '62) and the 11th Div., XIII (Dec. '62). At Chickasaw Bluffs he led 4th Div. Yazoo Expedition (Dec. '62–Jan. '63). He was named Maj. Gen. USV 29 Nov. '62 and commanded 1st Div., XV (4 Jan.–27 July '63) at Arkansas Post, Jackson, and Vicksburg. Leading the Ark. expedition (10 Aug. '63–6 Jan. '64) at Little Rock, he then commanded the VII Corps, Dept. of Ark. (6 Jan.–22 Dec. '64) and the Dept. of Ark. (30 Jan.–22 Dec. '64) at Jenkins' Ferry, and was ordered to clear the state of Confederate troops that might threaten the flank of operations east of the Mississippi. See ARKANSAS CAMPAIGN IN 1864. In 1865 (3–18 Feb.) he led 1st Div., Res. Corps, Gulf, and then the Dist. W. Fla. (Mar.–June '65) in the Mobile campaign. Breveted for Vicksburg, Little Rock (B.G. USA), and war service (Maj. Gen. USA), he continued in the R.A. as Col. 20th US Inf. His death was the result of an attack of apoplexy that caused him to fall from his carriage.

STEELE, William. C.S.A. gen. 1819–85. N.Y. USMA 1840 (31/42); Dragoons. He served in the Seminole War and the Mexican War (1 brevet) and on the frontier in Indian fighting and was Capt. 2d US Dragoons (since 1851) when he resigned in May '61 to be appointed Col. 7th Tex. Cav. First participating in Sibley's N. Mex. expedition, he was named B.G. C.S.A. 12 Sept. '62 and commanded the Indian Territory in Jan. '63. In Mar. '64 he was given command of the defenses of Galveston and participated in the Red River campaign of that year, succeeding Green in command of the cavalry division. After the war he was a commission merchant and held several public offices.

STEEN, Alexander Early. C.S.A. officer. ?–1862. Appt.-Mo. He served in the R.A. during the Mexican War (1 brevet) and from 1852 until he resigned 10 May '61 as 2d Lt. 3d US Inf. Entering the Confederate army, he was appointed B.G. C.S.A. (according to Wood and Heitman) in Apr. '62, and was killed 27 Nov. '62 at Kane Hill (Ark.). Wright does not list him as a general officer.

STEERE, William Henry Peck. Union officer. R.I. Capt. 2d R.I. 5 June '61; Lt. Col. 22 July '61; Col. 4th R.I. 12 June '62; Bvt. B.G. USV (war service); mustered out 15 Oct. '64. Commanded 1, 2, VII; 3, Getty's division Norfolk and Portsmouth (Va. and N.C.). Died 1882.

STEINER, John Alexander. Union officer. Md. Maj. 1st Potomac Home Brig. Md. Inf. 29 Nov. '61; Lt. Col. 6 Feb. '63; Bvt. B.G. USV (war service); discharged 16 July '63.

STEPHENS, Alexander Hamilton. C.S.A. Vice-pres. 1812–83. Ga. A law-yer, he served in the state legislature and US Congress, believing in personal liberty, local sovereignty, and peace. He formed, with Howell Cobb and Robert Toombs, a triumvirate leading the South away from secession. By 1860 Toombs and Cobb were for secession, but Stephens was still opposed to it. However, when his state seceded anyway, he went with Ga. and became a leader in the Confederacy. Named vice-pres., he was the leader of the moderates and was an early advocate of peace, but after the failure of the HAMPTON ROADS PEACE CONFERENCE in 1864, he had to admit that such a compromise was not possible. Imprisoned for five months in Boston, he returned to Ga., where he was elected almost immediately to the Senate. Unable to take his seat in Washington, he retired from public life to write *A Constitutional View of the Late War Between the States* (1868–70), and later served in Congress and as Gov. of Ga. (1882).

STEPHENSON, Luther, Jr. Union officer. Mass. Capt. 4th Mass. Mil. 22 Apr.–22 July '61; Capt. 32d Mass. 23 Oct. '61; Maj. 13 Aug. '62; Lt. Col. 29 Dec. '62; Bvt. B.G. USV (Richmond campaign); resigned 28 June '64. Shot through the face at Gettysburg and wounded twice slightly at Petersburg.

STEPHENSON'S DEPOT, Va., 20 July '64. (EARLY'S WASHINGTON RAID) Ramseur moved to attack a regiment of Federal infantry and one of cavalry reported to be at this place. In a sudden attack by Averell's cavalry division Godwin's (formerly Hoke's) brigade broke and spread panic in Robert Johnston's brigade. To the mortification of Ramseur, the Federals captured 267 unwounded officers and men and four guns; he also had left 73 dead and 130 wounded, according to Federal reports (*Lee's Lts.*, III, 570).

STERLING, A. M. W. Typographical C.S.A. gen. This name, on the list of Confederate generals in Miller, X, 320, is an inversion of Sterling A. M. Wood.

STEUART, George H. ("Maryland Steuart"). C.S.A. gen. 1828–1903. Md. Appt.-At Large. USMA 1848 (37/38); Dragoons. He served on the frontier, in garrison, in Indian fighting, and on the Utah Expedition before resigning about 19 Apr. '61 as Capt. Commissioned Capt. of C.S.A. Cav., he was named Lt. Col. 1st Md. and fought at 1st Bull Run. Promoted Col. on that day (21 July '61), he succeeded Elzey and was appointed B.G. C.S.A. 6 Mar. '62. He commanded the Va. Cav. Brig. and is the "young pedant" referred to in Steele's *American Campaigns* who refused to obey an order from Jackson to pursue after Winchester because the order had not come "through channels." (See Shenandoah Valley Campaign of Jackson.) After recovering from a wound received at Cross Keys, he commanded an infantry brigade at Gettysburg, the Wilderness, and Spotsylvania, where he was captured in the "bloody angle." Sent to Charleston to be put under the Federal batteries, he was exchanged and commanded his brigade under Pickett at Petersburg. After the war he farmed in Md. and was active in veterans' organizations.

STEVENS, Aaron Fletcher. Union officer. 1819–87. N.H. Maj. 1st N.H. 2 May '61; mustered out 9 Aug. '61; Col. 13th N.H. 23 Sept. '62; Bvt. B.G. USV 8 Dec. '64. W.I.A. Fort Harrison. A lawyer and legislator, he was an early supporter of the Republican party and after the war represented that party in Congress. Commanded 3, 3, IX (Ohio); 1, 1, XVIII (Va. and N.C.).

STEVENS, Ambrose A. Union officer. N.Y. Lt. Col. 3d Mich. 13 May '61; Col. 21st Mich. 25 July '62; resigned 3 Feb. '63; Maj. Vet. Res. Corps 20 July '63; Col. 25 Sept. '63; Bvt. B.G. USV 7 Mar. '65 (war service). Died 1880.

STEVENS, Clement Hoffman. C.S.A. gen. 1821–64. Conn. Appt.-S.C. A banker and businessman, he was cousin and brother-in-law of Barnard E. Bee and served as his volunteer aide in the first part of the war. In early 1861 he invented and built a land battery faced with iron on Morris Island that was used against Sumter. He also invented a portable field oven to insure that his troops had fresh bread on campaign. At 1st Bull Run he was Bee's volunteer A.D.C. and wounded there. Upon recovery he commanded a S.C. militia regiment and then was named Col. 24th S.C., leading this regiment at Secessionville, Vicksburg, and Chickamauga, where he was severely wounded. Appointed B.G. C.S.A. 20 Jan. '64, he commanded the Georgia brigade through the Atlanta campaign. Mortally wounded at Peach Tree Creek 20 July '64, he died five days later. His soldiers in the Atlanta campaign called him "Rock."

STEVENS, Hazard. Union officer. R.I. Appt.-Washington Territory. 1st Lt. Adj. 79th N.Y. Aug. '61; resigned 12 Sept. '61; Capt. Asst. Adj. Gen. Vols. 16 Oct. '61; Maj. Asst. Adj. Gen. Vols. 13 Oct. '64; Bvt. B.G. USV 2 Apr. '65. Brevets for Richmond campaign of 1864, Winchester, Fishers Hill, Cedar Creek, Petersburg siege. Medal of Honor 13 June '94 for Fort Huger (Va.) capture 19 Apr. '63. The son of Isaac Stevens, he accompanied him on several exploration and treaty-making expeditions around the Washington Territory while a boy. He was wounded twice at Chantilly, where his father was killed. During Fredericksburg he was on the staff of Gen. Getty.

STEVENS, Isaac Ingalls. Union gen. 1818–62. Mass. USMA 1839 (1/31); Engrs. In engineering work on the New

England coast and then in the Mexican War (2 brevets, 1 wound). Resigning in 1853, he was Gov. of the Washington Territory until 1857, making many explorations, and then served in the House of Representatives until 1861. He made a number of treaties with the Indians, and was criticized for his Indian policies by Gen. Wool. Commissioned Col. 79th N.Y. 30 July and B.G. USV 28 Sept. '61, he commanded 2, W. F. Smith's division, Potomac (3–26 Oct. '61) in the Defenses of Washington, before going on the S.C. expedition (2, S.C. Div., Exp. Corps, Oct. '61–Apr. '62) and fighting at Port Royal and Coosa River. At Stono River and Secessionville he commanded 2d Div., Dept. of the South (Apr.–July '62) and was appointed Maj. Gen. USV 4 July '62. At 2d Bull Run he commanded 1st Div., IX, Potomac (22 July–1 Sept. '62) and was killed at Chantilly. Short and rather stout, with a massive head, he was dignified and humorless. An officer of great promise, he was being considered as the next commander of the Army of the Potomac.

STEVENS, Thaddeus. Radical Republican. 1792–1868. Vt. After graduating from Dartmouth, he practiced law in Pa. and was elected a Whig legislator. He was later sent to Congress, where he became an uncompromising abolitionist and leader of the RADICAL REPUBLICANS, a group he had helped found. As chairman of the powerful Ways and Means Committee, he exerted a tremendous amount of influence upon the country and the war effort. He was also chairman of the Committee on Reconstruction and was the one to initiate the impeachment proceedings against Johnson, his bitter enemy.

STEVENS, Walter Husted. C.S.A. gen. 1827–67. N.Y. USMA 1848 (4/38); Engrs. He supervised the construction of fortifications and harbors along the Gulf and married a La. girl. When Tex. passed the ordinance of secession, he sent in his resignation 2 Mar. '61 and assisted immediately in that state's preparations for war. The US War Dept. then withheld action on his resignation, and he was dismissed from the army 2 May '61 on a technicality. Meanwhile, he had been commissioned Capt. in C.S.A. Engrs. and was with Beauregard at 1st Bull Run. As Maj. he was the Chief Engr. of Johnston's army during the Peninsular campaign until Lee took command. He then went to the defenses of Richmond as Col. Appointed B.G. C.S.A. 28 Aug. '64, he served as Chief Engr. of the Army Northern Va. until Appomattox, and constructed the Petersburg defenses. Paroled after the surrender, he went to Mexico as a railroad engineer and died there.

STEVENSBURG, Va., 9 June '63. See BRANDY STATION, same date.

STEVENSON, Carter Littlepage. C.S.A. gen. 1817–88. Va. USMA 1838 (42/45); Inf. He served on the frontier and in the Mexican War, where he was Brady's A.D.C., later on duty in railroad explorations, Indian fighting, the Seminole War, and the Utah Expedition. Although he had resigned 6 June '61 as Capt., he was dismissed on the 25th of that month because his commanding officer had neglected to forward the document to the War Dept. Commissioned Lt. Col. of C.S.A. Inf. In July he was named Col. 53d Va. and appointed B.G. C.S.A. 6 Mar. '62 to rank from 27 Feb. on Beauregard's recommendation. He was sent to Tenn. and Ky. and was promoted Maj. Gen. 13 Oct. of that year to rank from the 10th. Given a division in Bragg's command, he was transferred to Pemberton at Vicksburg, fighting at Champion's Hill and the Big Black River and commanding the right during the Vicksburg siege. His division returned to the field in

Sept., an action which the Union claimed was a violation of parole. He fought in Hardee's corps at Missionary Ridge and under Hood during the Atlanta campaign, distinguishing himself particularly at Resaca and Kenesaw Mountain. Going to Tenn., he fought at Nashville and returned to the Carolinas to fight at Bentonville before the surrender. In the meantime he had been in temporary command of the corps between Hood and S.D. Lee and when the latter was wounded at Nashville. After the war he was a civil and mining engineer.

STEVENSON, John Dunlap. Union gen. 1821–97. Va. A lawyer and legislator, he fought in the Mexican War and was commissioned Col. 7th Mo. 1 June '61. During the siege of Corinth he commanded the Dist. of Savannah and then led 4, 3d Div., Right Wing, XIII, Tenn. (1 Nov.–18 Dec. '62), having been promoted B.G. 29 Nov. '62. At Champion's Hill and Vicksburg he led 3, 3, XVII (18 Dec. '62–20 July '63) and then commanded the Dist. of Corinth, XVI, Tenn. (12 Dec. '63–25 Jan. '64). Resigning 22 Apr. '64, he was reappointed B.G. USV on 7 Aug. to date from his original commission and took command of Harpers Ferry (15 Aug. '64–21 Feb. '65 and 27 Feb. '65). He also commanded the 3d Div. of W. Va. (Jan.–Apr. '65) and the Dept. of W. Va. (22–27 Feb. '65). Breveted for Champion's Hill (B.G. USA) and war service (Maj. Gen. USV), he continued in the R.A. until discharged in 1870 at his own request.

STEVENSON, Robert Hooper. Union officer. Mass. Capt. 4th Bn. Mass. Mil. 20 Apr.–3 Aug. '61; Maj. 23d Mass. 2 Sept. '61; Lt. Col. 1 Jan. '63; Bvt. B.G. USV (Roanoke Island and New Bern, war service); resigned 31 May '64.

STEVENSON, Thomas Greeley. Union gen. 1836–64. Mass. Having a reputation as a drill master in the state militia, he was commissioned Col. 24th Mass. 3 Dec. '61 and went on Burnside's N.C. expedition. Appointed B.G. USV 24 Dec. '62, he had commanded 2, 1st Div., N.C. (2 Apr. '62–2 Jan. '63) at Washington (N.C.), Goldsboro, and Kinston. Also in N.C. he led 2, 4, XVIII (2 Jan.–Feb. '63) and 1, 2, XVIII (6 Mar.–17 Apr. '63). His appointment expired 4 Mar. '63, but he was recommissioned 10 days later and commanded 1, 1st Div. St. Helena Island, XVIII (6 Mar.–17 Apr. '63); 1st, 2d Div. St. Helena Island, XVIII (Jan.–6 Mar. '63); Stevenson's brigade, Seabrook Island Dist., X (Apr.–May '63); and succeeded to command of the division 11 May–6 July '63. He also led 1, 1st Div. Morris Island, X (23 Nov. '63–15 Jan. '64); 3d, Morris Island, X (July–19 Sept. '63 at Fort Wagner and Morris Island and 19 Oct.–23 Nov. '63). In the Army of the Potomac he led 1st Div., IX from 19 Apr. until he was killed 10 May '64 at Spotsylvania.

STEWART, Alexander Peter. C.S.A. gen. 1821–1908. Tenn. USMA 1842 (12/56); Arty. After serving in garrison and teaching mathematics at West Point, he resigned in 1845 to teach the same subject at Cumberland Univ. and the Univ. of Nashville. Commissioned Maj. C.S.A., he commanded the heavy artillery at Columbus (Ky.) and Belmont before being appointed B.G. C.S.A. 8 Nov. '61. He led the 2d Brig. at Shiloh, on the Ky. campaign, and at Perryville and at Stones River, and the retreat toward Chattanooga. Promoted Maj. Gen. 5 June '63 to rank from the 2d, he fought in Hardee's corps at Chattanooga, Chickamauga, and in the Atlanta campaign from Dalton to Atlanta. He was named Lt. Gen. 23 June '64 when Polk was killed and was wounded himself at Mount Ezra Church. In N.C. he commanded the Army of Tenn. at the surrender. After the war he returned to teach at Cumberland, was in the insurance business, and served as chancellor of the Univ. of Miss. He was also park commissioner of the Chickamauga and Chattanooga National Parks. His soldiers called him "Old Straight."

STEWART, James Jr. Union officer. N.J. 1st Lt. 9th N.J. 15 Nov. '61; Capt. 10 Feb. '62; Maj. 22 Dec. '62; Lt. Col. 8 Jan. '63; Col. 20 June '64; Bvt. B.G. USV (war service). Commanded 1, 2, XVIII (N.C.); Sub-Dist. Beaufort N.C. (Va. and N.C.); Sub-Dist. Beaufort N.C.; 2, Div. Dist. Beaufort; 3d Div., XXIII (N.C.).

STEWART, William Scott. Union officer. Scotland. Maj. 65th Ill. 15 Mar. '62; Lt. Col. 1 May '62; Col. 29 June '65; Bvt. B.G. USV (war service). Commanded 1, 3, XXIII. Died 1894.

STEWART, William Warren. Union officer. Pa. 1st Sgt. 1st Pa. Res. 4 June '61; 1st Lt. 3 Sept. '61; Capt. 1 Aug. '62; Lt. Col. 1 Mar. '63; mustered out 13 June '64; Col. 192d Pa. 26 Mar. '65; Bvt. B.G. USV. Brevets for Wilderness, Spotsylvania C.H., North Anna (Va.).

STIBBS, John Howard. Union officer. Ohio. Capt. 12th Iowa 25 Nov. '61; Maj. 2 May '63; Lt. Col. 25 Sept. '63; Col. 18 Sept. '65; Bvt. B.G. USV. Brevets for Nashville battles, war service.

STILES, Israel Newton. Union officer. 1833–95. Conn. 1st Lt. Adj. 20th Ind. 22 July '61; Maj. 63d Ind. 11 Sept. '62; Lt. Col. 1 July '63; Col. 19 Mar. '64; Bvt. B.G. USV 31 Jan. '65 (war service). Captured at Malvern Hill and spent six weeks in Libby before being exchanged. Commanded 3, 3, XXIII (Ohio); 1, 1, Prov. Corps. (N.C.); 1, 1, XXIII (N.C.). A lawyer and legislator before the war, he settled in Chicago afterward and practiced law there.

STILLSON, Jerome Bonaparte. War Correspondent. 1841–80. N.Y. After failing miserably during the Wilderness campaign, he became during Early's Valley campaign in the fall of 1864 a first-rate correspondent for the N.Y. *World* and immortalized the battle of Winchester. After the war he was the *World's* managing editor and became a *Herald* reporter in 1876 because he preferred reporting to a desk job. His interview with Sitting Bull after the Custer massacre at Little Big Horn was another journalistic triumph.

STOCKTON, Joseph. Union officer. Pa. Capt. 72d Ill. 21 Aug. '62; Maj. 14 Feb. '63; Lt. Col. 7 July '63; Bvt. B.G. USV. Brevets for war service, Vicksburg siege, Franklin (Tenn.).

STOKES, James Hughes. Union gen. 1814–90. Md. USMA 1835 (17/56); Arty. He served in the Seminole War, in Indian fighting in the West, and on garrison duty, and resigned in 1843 to go into manufacturing and railroading. At the outbreak of war he aided in equipping the Ill. volunteers and then was commissioned Capt. Chicago Board of Trade Battery 31 July '62. He led this at Perryville, Stones River, Chattanooga, Chickamauga, Farmington, and Missionary Ridge, and was named Lt. Col. Q.M. Assigned 10 Feb.–22 Aug. '64 (Inspector of the Q.M. Dept. Mil. Div. Miss.). Then named Capt. Asst. Adj. Gen. USV on the latter date, he was in the Defenses of Washington until mustered out 24 Aug. '65, having been promoted B.G. USV 20 July. He later became blind from a disease contracted during the Fla. war.

STOKES, William B. Union officer. N.C. Col. 5th Tenn. Cav. 15 Nov. '62; Bvt. B.G. USV (war service); resigned 10 Mar. '65. Commanded 3, 3, XXIII (Ohio). Died 1897.

STOLBRAND, Carlos John Mueller. Union gen. 1821–94. Sweden. Graduating from the Swedish Military Academy, he fought in Schleswig-Holstein with the artillery. Coming to this country after that, he was commissioned Capt. 2d Ill. Lgt. Arty. 5 Oct. '61 and named Maj. 3 Dec. '61. He was Logan's Chief of Arty., fought in the siege of Corinth and in the Atlanta campaign and the March to the Sea. Captured during the Atlanta campaign, he escaped twice from Andersonville. Lonn says that he was unhappy about not being promoted, and offered his resignation to Sherman who sent him on an errand to Lincoln. The president read the letter Stolbrand gave him and said, "How do you do, General?" At Stolbrand's look of surprise, he continued, "You are a general, and I need you in the Carolinas." The letter had been one of enthusiastic recommendation from Sherman. His commission was dated 18 Feb. '65, and he returned to command 2, 4, XVII, Tenn. 28 Apr.–15 June '65. Mustered out the next year, he was later in Republican Reconstruction politics in S.C. and a manufacturer.

STONE, Charles Pomeroy. Union gen. and protagonist of the Balls Bluff affair. 1824–87. Mass. USMA 1845 (7/41); Ord.-Inf. After teaching at West Point and serving at various arsenals and in the Mexican War (2 brevets), he resigned in 1856 to pursue commercial explorations in Mexico and was later a San Francisco banker. When war came he was named Col. I.G. and Comdr. D.C. Vols. (16 Apr.–23 July), Col. 14th US Inf. (14 May) and B.G. USV 17 May '61. He led the force that captured Alexandria 24 May '61 and then commanded 7th, 3d Div., Pa.; 3d Brig., Shenandoah (25 July–8 Aug. '61); Stone's brigade, Div. Potomac; and Stone's division, Potomac (3 Oct. '61–9 Feb. '62) at BALLS BLUFF (21 Oct. '61). About three and a half months after the Union fiasco there he was arrested and imprisoned 189 days without trial and

without any charges being presented. Rumor was that he was suspected of treason in connection with Balls Bluff, but no charges were ever presented nor was any official explanation of his arrest ever made. Although he was released 16 Aug. '62, he awaited orders in Washington until the following May. During the siege and the surrender of Port Hudson (27 May–8 July '63) and as Banks's Chief of Staff (25 July–16 Apr. '64), he served in the Dept. of the Gulf, fighting at Bayou Teche, Sabine Cross Roads, and Pleasant Hill. He was mustered out of USV 4 Apr. '64. During the Petersburg siege he commanded 1, 2, V, Potomac (21 Aug.–10 Sept. '64) but was kept under surveillance most of this time. Banks, Hooker, and Grant all requested him for responsible positions, but he was kept in relatively unimportant posts. He finally broke from the strain of the suspicions surrounding him and resigned 13 Sept. '64. In 1865–69 he was superintendent of a Va. mining company and the next year entered the service of the Khedive of Egypt, becoming Chief of the General Staff of the army as Lt. Gen. He was later made a pasha and resigned in 1883. Coming home, he was engineer in chief for the pedestal of the Statue of Liberty.

STONE, George Augustus. Union officer. N.Y. 1st Lt. 1st Iowa 14 May '61; mustered out 20 Aug. '61; Maj. 4th Iowa Cav. 26 Dec. '61; Col. 25th Iowa 27 Sept. '62; Bvt. B.G. USV (war service). Commanded 2, 1, XV (Tenn.); 3, 1, XV (Tenn.). Died 1901.

STONE, Roy. Union officer. N.Y. Maj. 13th Pa. Res. 21 June '61; Col. 149th Pa. 30 Aug. '62; Bvt. B.G. USV 7 Sept. '64 (Gettysburg); resigned 27 June '65. Commanded 2, 3, I (Potomac); 3, 4, V (Potomac). B.G. USV 3 June '98; discharged 31 Dec. '98.

STONE, William Milo. Union officer. N.Y. Capt. 3d Iowa 8 June '61; Maj. 26

June '61; Col. 22d Iowa 9 Sept. '62; Bvt. B.G. USV (war service); resigned 13 Aug. '63. Commanded Dist. Rolla Mo. (Mo.); 2, 1, XIII (Tenn.); 2, 1, XIII (Gulf). Died 1893.

STONE FLEETS, THE. Small sailing ships loaded with stones that were sunk by the Federal Navy at the entrances of Southern harbors. These did not close the channels to blockade runners, as was hoped, for the ships' timbers were soon destroyed by marine worms, and the stones sank in the mud. Three ships were sunk at Ocracoke Inlet, N.C., 18 Nov. '61; 16 in the main entrance to Charleston Harbor 20 Dec. '61; and 20 in a subsidiary entrance to Charleston Harbor, Maffitt's Channel, on 26 Jan. '62.

STONEMAN, George. Union gen. 1822–94. N.Y. USMA 1846 (33/59); Dragoons. After serving in the Mexican War, in Indian fighting, on the frontier, and on a number of Southwestern expeditions, he was in command of Fort Brown, Tex., when Twiggs demanded its surrender to the C.S.A. After escaping with part of his command, he was named Maj. 1st US Cav. 9 May '61. Transferring to the 4th US Cav. 3 Aug., he was appointed B.G. USV ten days later and commanded the cavalry reserve (14 Aug.–Oct. '61) and cavalry command (Oct. '61–Jan. '62) in the Army of the Potomac, making several reconnaissances toward the Rappahannock and Gordonsville in Feb. and Mar. During the Peninsular campaign he commanded the cavalry division (Mar.–Aug. '62) at Yorktown, Williamsburg, on a cavalry advance upon Richmond in May, and during the Seven Days' Battles. He then commanded 1st Div., II Corps (17 July–15 Aug. '62) and 1st Div., III Corps (13 Sept.–30 Oct. '62). Named Maj. Gen. USV 29 Nov. '62, he led the III Corps (30 Oct. '62–5 Feb. '63) at Fredericksburg. Commanding

the newly-established CAVALRY CORPS (Potomac) (see under CORPS, UNION) (12 Feb.–22 May '63), he undertook the operations covered under the heading of STONEMAN'S RAIDS DURING THE CHANCELLORSVILLE CAMPAIGN. He was then relieved of command and, after a sick leave, was Chief of the Cav. Bureau in Washington (18 July '63–29 Jan. '64). He then commanded XXIII Corps (Ohio) (10 Feb.–4 Apr. '64) and then headed the cavalry division of that corps (10 Apr.–31 July '64). During the Atlanta campaign his poor tactical judgment led to his capture with 700 of his men in STONEMAN'S AND McCOOK'S RAIDS to Macon and Lovejoy. Released in a few months, he commanded the Dept. of the Ohio (17 Nov. '64–17 Jan. '65) and led STONEMAN'S RAID IN SOUTHWESTERN VA. 1 Dec. '64–1 Jan. '65. While commanding the Dist. East Tenn., Cumberland (9 Mar.–27 June '65), he led a raid in N.C. and Va. 20 Mar.–23 Apr. '65, to support Sherman's Carolinas campaign. Breveted for Fredericksburg; Salisbury, N.C. (B.G. USA); and war service (Maj. Gen. USA), he continued in the R.A. until retired in 1871 as Col. He lived on his magnificent estate "Los Robles" near Los Angeles and held several public offices in the state, including that of Gov., as a Democrat, in 1883–87. See also STONEMAN'S RAIDS below.

STONEMAN'S AND McCOOK'S RAIDS to Macon and Lovejoy, 26–31 July '64. (ATLANTA CAMPAIGN.) Having wrecked all other railroads leading into Atlanta, Sherman believed that destruction of the one south to Macon would force Hood to evacuate Atlanta. He therefore ordered Stoneman to take his own cavalry division (2,200) and Garrard's (4,500) and move from Decatur to some point on the railroad between Jonesboro and Griffin. McCook with his own division (1,500) and Rousseau's (1,500) was to move on the same point from the Chattahoochee below Sandtown. Since the forces would have less than 40 miles to move, Sherman assumed they could accomplish their mission within three days.

Stoneman requested and was granted permission to raid Macon and liberate the Union prisoners at ANDERSONVILLE after he had accomplished his primary mission. He left on the 27th, but instead of following his orders and moving south with his entire force, he ordered Garrard south to draw the main Confederate cavalry away, while he with his small force of 2,200 headed via Covington for Andersonville. On 28 July Garrard was attacked by Wheeler at Flatshoals (Flatrock bridge) and forced to withdraw to the north. Wheeler ordered one brigade to guard him, and moved with the rest of his Confederate troopers against Stoneman and McCook.

Stoneman reached the outskirts of Macon on 30 July and found it held by state militia. While he was attempting to circle south of the city across the Ocmulgee River to Andersonville, he was cut off and surrounded by three brigades of Wheeler's cavalry under Iverson. Stoneman was captured with 700 men after trying to fight his way out. This action is known by the name of Hillsboro or Sunshine Creek.

Adams cut his way out and was joined the next day (1 Aug.) by part of the 8th Mich., a portion of Biddle's brigade, and Capron with the remnant of his brigade. Heading toward Athens, Capron was separated and near Jug Tavern, 3 Aug., was surprised and scattered; some of his men were drowned when a bridge by which they were trying to escape collapsed (Mulberry Creek). Adams arrived too late to save Capron, but killed 40 Confederates in a pursuit.

McCook reached the railroad between Jonesboro and Griffin on 29 July and spent four hours demolishing track, rolling stock, and supplies. Retracing his route west, he was driven by enemy cavalry to Newman and surrounded here on 30 July. Five Confederate brigades under Wheeler and W. H. Jackson were opposing him. McCook ordered his brigades to cut their way out independently, and they rejoined north of the Chattahoochee. He lost about 500 men, his pack train, two guns, and a large number of horses. Although he had done little permanent damage to the railroad, he had destroyed a large number of Hood's supply wagons.

STONEMAN'S RAID IN NORTH CAROLINA AND VIRGINIA, 20 Mar.–23 Apr. '65. Thomas was ordered to assist Sherman's Carolinas campaign by sending Stoneman's cavalry into the Carolinas from Tenn. as a diversion. Grant suggested that Columbia, S. C., be the initial objective, but by the time Stoneman got started Sherman had reached Goldsboro, N.C. Stoneman finally left Jonesboro, Tenn., 20 Mar., with 4,000 cavalry and a battery of artillery. From Wilkesboro, N. C., he moved north to raid the Tenn.-Lynchburg R.R. between Salem (Va.) and Wytheville (3 Apr.). He returned to N.C. the day Lee surrendered and wrecked part of the railroad between Danville and Greensboro. He then marched through Asheville, N. C., to Hendersonville, where he learned of Johnston's surrender. The only troops available to oppose him had been remnants of Early's command (under Echols) and some small detachments of regular troops and militia. He captured most of these, taking 2,000 prisoners and 14 guns. But his raid had been so late in getting started that it was of little if any value to Sherman and Meade (Grant, II, 518).

STONEMAN'S RAIDS DURING THE CHANCELLORSVILLE CAMPAIGN, 29 Apr.–8 May '63. As part of his strategy for the Chancellorsville campaign, Hooker ordered Stoneman's recently created cavalry corps to precede the main turning movement by two weeks and raid Lee's lines of communications. Only one small brigade of cavalry under Pleasonton was to remain with Hooker's main body.

On 13 Apr. Stoneman left Falmouth on schedule with six brigades and four horse batteries (10,000 total strength). He did not cross the Rappahannock on the 14th as planned; that night a severe storm set in and for two weeks the river was unfordable. The result was that the cavalry did not cross until the 29th, the same day as the infantry.

Hooker then ordered the cavalry to advance in two columns: one, under Averell, toward Gordonsville; and the other, under Buford, to break up the Richmond and Fredericksburg railroad. W. H. F. Lee's brigade, the only Confederate cavalry available to oppose this diversion, fell back before Averell's division and was pursued to Rapidan Station. Averell was then recalled and joined Hooker at Ely's Ford the night of 2 May. The next day he was ordered to reconnoiter Hooker's right. When he returned to report the country impracticable for cavalry work he was relieved by Hooker and replaced by Pleasonton.

Buford and Gregg crossed at Kelly's Ford and proceeded to Louisa C.H. One detachment under Col. Percy Wyndham moved to Columbia and destroyed a portion of the James Canal. Another, under Col. B. F. Davis, destroyed the Va. Central R.R. from the South Anna to Richmond. Col. Judson Kilpatrick led a third to Hungary, where it destroyed a section of the Fredericksburg R.R., rode to within two miles of Richmond, crossed the Chickahominy, and reached Federal lines at Gloucester (on the York River opposite Yorktown).

As the cavalryman Steele wrote in *American Campaigns,* "On the whole the Cavalry Corps exerted no practical influence upon the campaign after the main operations had actually begun; while, if it had been kept with the main army, it would have been of great service. [It was Stuart's cavalry, with Lee's army in the Wilderness, that found Hooker's exposed flank and set the stage for Stonewall Jackson's envelopment.] . . . The corps lost only seventeen killed and seventy-five wounded during all its operations!"

STONEMAN'S RAID IN SOUTHWESTERN VIRGINIA, 1 Dec. '64–1 Jan. '65. At Schofield's suggestion the recently exchanged Stoneman was sent to operate in East Tenn. During Hood's advance into central Tenn. Breckinridge had menaced Knoxville from his Dept. of W. Va. and East Tenn. With Gillem's brigade and a cavalry brigade from Ky., Stoneman drove the Confederates out of East Tenn., captured Saltville and Wytheville in Va., and destroyed the salt works and lead mines. Skirmishes took place also at Kingsport, Bristol, and Marion. He then returned to Ky. and Tenn.

STONES RIVER (or Murfreesboro), Tenn., 31 Dec. '62 and 2 Jan. '63. (The Stones River *campaign* is sometimes considered to include four other operations that are treated separately in this book: Halleck's advance on CORINTH, Miss.; BRAGG'S INVASION OF KENTUCKY; Kirby SMITH'S INVASION OF KENTUCKY; PERRYVILLE (or Chaplin Hills).

After his retreat from PERRYVILLE, Ky., Bragg ordered a concentration at Murfreesboro, Tenn. Both the North and the South were dissatisfied with the performance of their top commanders at Perryville, and both sides made changes in organization. The Federal

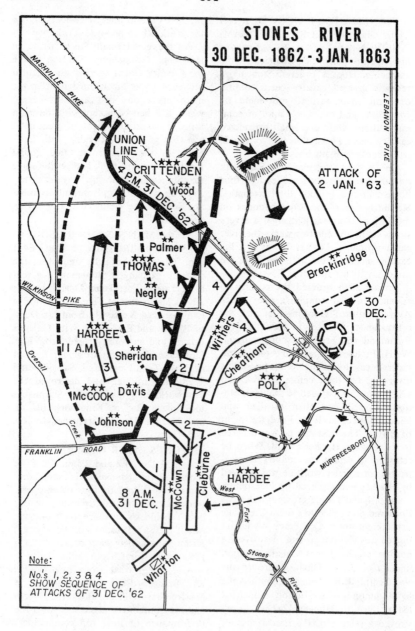

STONES RIVER
30 DEC. 1862 - 3 JAN. 1863

NASHVILLE PIKE

LEBANON PIKE

UNION LINE

CRITTENDEN
★★★
4 P.M. 31 DEC. '62
★★
Wood

ATTACK OF 2 JAN. '63

★★
Palmer

THOMAS
★★★
Negley

WILKINSON PIKE

★★
Breckinridge

★★★
HARDEE
11 A.M.
3

★★
Sheridan

Overall

4

Withers
★★★
4

Cheatham
★★

30 DEC.

★★★
McCOOK Davis

2

★★★
POLK

★★
Johnson

Creek

2

MURFREESBORO

FRANKLIN ROAD

1

8 A.M.
31 DEC.

McCown Cleburne

HARDEE
★★★
West

Fork

Stones

River

Note:
No.'s 1, 2, 3 & 4
SHOW SEQUENCE OF
ATTACKS OF 31 DEC. '62

Wharton

Dept. (and Army) of the CUMBER-LAND was created under Rosecrans. The Confederate Army of TENNESSEE was created under Bragg. J. E. Johnston was sent to command all Confederate armies in the West (DIVISION OF THE WEST).

Three Confederate cavalry operations took place before the armies of Bragg and Rosecrans clashed: MORGAN'S SEC-OND (Lexington) RAID, Oct. '62; FOR-REST'S SECOND RAID (in West Tenn.), 11 Dec. '62–3 Jan. '63; and MORGAN'S THIRD (Christmas) RAID, 21 Dec. '62–1 Jan. '63. Although these raids on the Federal lines of communications did little significant damage, Rosecrans took advantage of this detachment of Confederate cavalry to move out of Nashville and attack Bragg (Fiebeger, 135).

Crittenden's corps advanced southeast along the line of the Nashville and Chattanooga R.R., while the other two corps—McCook and Thomas (less two divisions)—advanced to his right. Bragg was known to be deployed between Triune and Murfreesboro, and Rosecrans' plan was to turn the Confederate left while refusing Crittenden's corps.

Bragg's intelligence sources informed him immediately of Rosecrans' movement. Wheeler's cavalry successfully delayed the Federal advance while Bragg concentrated his forces at Murfreesboro. On 31 Dec. the two armies faced each other just west of Stones River. Strangely, each was planning to attack the other's right.

The Confederate division of Breckinridge (8,000) was left across the river, northwest of Murfreesboro, while Hardee's other two divisions—McCown (4,500) and Cleburne (7,000)—moved into position opposite the Federal right. The Confederate center was held by Polk's two divisions; Withers (8,500) in front, and Cheatham (5,500) to his rear. McCown's division was to attack at dawn.

The Federal right, where the initial Confederate blow was about to fall, was held by Alexander McCook's corps; Johnson's division (6,300) was on the extreme right flank, on the Franklin Road, with the divisions of J. C. Davis (4,600) and Sheridan (5,000) extending left to the Wilkinson Pike. Negley's division (4,700) of Thomas' corps was in the center of the line. Crittenden's divisions of Palmer (4,400) and Wood (5,100) extended the line to the river. In conformity to the Federal plan of attacking with their own left, two divisions were in assembly areas behind this flank: Rousseau's (6,200) of Thomas' corps, and Van Cleve's (3,800) of Crittenden's. (Two of Thomas' divisions were absent: Mitchel's was garrisoning Nashville; Reynolds' was pursuing Morgan's raiders. Only one brigade of Fry's division took part in the battle; one arrived 2 Jan. and the other was pursuing Morgan.) Rosecrans had ordered his attack to start at 7 A.M., after his troops had eaten.

The Federal brigades of Kirk and Willich were driven back by the brigades of Rains, Ector, and McNair as the battle opened at dawn. Although Kirk's outposts detected the enemy advance, Willich's brigade was caught by surprise (Horn, 200). As Cleburne's division kept up the momentum of the attack by moving up on McCown's right, the Federal division of Davis and Sheridan held off the attacks of Hardee's three divisions. A second assault, reinforced by Cheatham's division (Polk's corps), was also repulsed. A third effort enveloped Davis' right, forcing him to retreat and thereby exposing Sheridan's right. About 9:30 Sheridan counterattacked with Roberts' brigade and gained sufficient time to withdraw to a new position behind the Nashville Pike and at a right angle to Negley's division. Rousseau's division was brought up to form on

Sheridan's right. Davis followed Johnson's routed division to the rear, while Wharton's cavalry brigade (2,000 men) harried his flank from the west.

A renewed attack, all along the Federal front, finally forced Sheridan, whose ammunition was exhausted, to withdraw. This left a gap between Negley and Rousseau which the Confederates exploited. Shepherd's brigade of regulars lost 20 officers and 518 killed and wounded in covering a general withdrawal of the Federal right half of the line to a new position. The right of Palmer's division also had to withdraw to avoid being enveloped; but his left—Hazen's brigade—held its strong position on a wooded ridge astride the railroad. This was a four-acre oak grove which reports of the battle call the Round Forest, but which the troops dubbed "Hell's Half Acre." By noon the Federals had been forced back to what turned out to be their final defensive line.

The Federal divisions of Van Cleve and Wood, which were scheduled to move north of the river and make Rosecrans' main attack, had been called back to bolster the Federal defense. Van Cleve had crossed, and Wood was ready to follow, when the Confederate attack started. Wood was held back and put into position on the Federal left. Van Cleve was ordered back and arrived about 11 A.M., just in time to reinforce the final defensive line.

In preparation for what he could hope to be the knockout blow, Bragg called on Breckinridge to send two of his five brigades to reinforce Hardee. Only one was sent in time to be of assistance, however; Pegram's Confederate cavalry had reported the arrival of Van Cleve's division opposite Breckinridge, but had not detected its withdrawal. Breckinridge therefore believed he was in danger of being overwhelmed and

could not spare more than one brigade (Horn, 202).

The final Confederate assaults were vigorously pressed and effectively repulsed by a well-organized Federal defense. Chalmers' brigade which had been waiting 48 hours in shallow trenches and without fires on the extreme right of Withers' division attacked shortly after noon against the Round Forest. Having to charge across an open field against a strongly entrenched position, they were cut to pieces by enemy musket and artillery fire. After desperate fighting, in which some regiments lost six to eight color bearers, Chalmers was wounded, and his brigade fell back. Donelson's brigade (Cheatham's division) made the next effort. After some initial confusion in reaching the field, and in the face of heavy fire, it penetrated the Federal line just west of the Round Forest and took 1,000 prisoners and 11 guns. However, continued possession of the critical Round Forest position by the Federals forced Donelson to retreat. In this action the 8th Tenn. lost 306, including its commander, Col. W. L. Moore, out of 425 engaged. The 16th lost 207 out of its 402 engaged.

Late in the afternoon the four other brigades of Breckinridge were brought south of the river and committed to action against "Hell's Half Acre." First Adams and Jackson, then Preston and Pillow were repulsed with heavy losses.

Special mention should be made of the units that held Round Forest against these attacks. Cruft's brigade had initially been posted in advance of Hazen's. When Sheridan and Negley were driven back at about 11 A.M., Palmer's right had been exposed. The attacks of Chalmers and Donelson had finally driven back Cruft's brigade. The brigade of Grose, in reserve, had to face to the rear and attack in that direction to enable Cruft to withdraw (Van Horne, 239). This left Hazen alone at the tip of the salient against which Bragg now directed his subsequent attacks. Grose was forced again to change front to enable Hazen to adjust his dispositions while Cruft withdrew.

To repulse the attacks of Breckinridge's last four brigades (see above) Hazen had the 41st Ohio, 9th Ind., and 110th Ill. In direct support of Hazen, or on his flanks, the following regiments moved up during the last Confederate attacks of Preston and Pillow: 3d Ky., 24th Ohio, 58th Ind., 100th Ill., 6th Ky., 2d Mo., 40th and 97th Ohio, and the 6th and 26th Ohio. (The units are mentioned in the approximate order of arrival.) Along the riverbank Wagner led two regiments, the 15th and 57th Ind., in a counterattack that drove back the Confederate infantry on its front before being forced by enemy artillery to withdraw.

After some hesitation Rosecrans decided to remain on the field during the night and to resume the offensive if Bragg did not attack. The battlefield was quiet on 1 Jan., but Confederate cavalry under Wheeler and Wharton were active along Rosecrans' line of communications to Nashville. Wheeler attacked a wagon train near LaVergne, dispersed the guard, and destroyed about 30 wagons. Col. Innes, commanding the 1st Mich. Engrs. and Mechanics, held the stockade near the town against several attacks and refused Wheeler's demand to surrender.

When Polk observed that the Federals had abandoned the Round Forest during the night he took possession of this position. Bragg then determined to have Breckinridge recross the river and take high ground from which enfilade fire might drive the Federals from their position. Breckinridge went on record as considering this task impossible, and

Polk told Bragg he considered the operation would accomplish no worthwhile purpose. Bragg insisted, however, and at 4 P.M., 2 Jan., Breckinridge attacked with 4,500 men.

Rosecrans had realized the importance of this high ground and had occupied it with Van Cleve's division (commanded by Beatty, since Van Cleve had been wounded). Beatty was reinforced by the brigades of Grose and Hazen.

The Federals were driven from the hill. However, as the Confederates pursued down the forward slope they were slaughtered by the massed fire of 58 guns that Crittenden's Chief of Arty., Maj. John Mendenhall, had posted across the river. Reinforcements hurried across the river; Beatty rallied his troops for a counterattack; and Breckinridge was driven back to his line of departure. He had lost 1,700 men.

On 3 Jan. Rosecrans held his defensive perimeter west of the river with the corps of Thomas and McCook (less Palmer's division). Crittenden, reinforced with Palmer's division of McCook's corps, was posted north of the river. The night of 3–4 Jan. Bragg withdrew through Murfreesboro toward Shelbyville. Rosecrans did not pursue. It was not until June that Rosecrans renewed operations in this area when his TULLAHOMA CAMPAIGN set the stage for the CHICKAMAUGA and CHATTANOOGA CAMPAIGNS.

Stones River was a tactical victory for the Confederates, but Bragg lacked the strength to destroy Rosecrans' larger army or drive it from the field. The historian Ropes says, "Few battles have been fought which have better exhibited the soldierly virtues than the battle of Murfreesboro or Stones River. The Confederate assaults were conducted with the utmost gallantry and with untiring energy. They were met with great coolness and resolution...." From a strategic viewpoint, however, the campaign was a Confederate failure (*Campaign Summaries*).

According to Livermore, the Federals had 41,400 troops engaged, of which they lost 12,906. The Confederates lost 11,739 out of 34,739 engaged.

"STONE WALL." One, at the base of Marye's Hill at Fredericksburg, figured in the battle of FREDERICKSBURG and also on 3 May '63 during Sedgwick's attack in the CHANCELLORSVILLE campaign. Another "stone wall" marked the main Federal defensive position against "Pickett's Charge" on the third day of GETTYSBURG.

STONEWALL, THE. Confederate ironclad ram built in France and purchased in Denmark by Confederate agents. Commanded by Capt. T. J. Page, she sailed from there 6 Jan. '65 but failed to accomplish her mission before the war ended.

STONEWALL BRIGADE. Famous Confederate organization trained and first led by Jackson. When Jackson moved to higher command, he soon had his old brigade transferred to his army, where it stayed until his death at Chancellorsville. The organization is remarkable for remaining a potent fighting force until late in the war, despite severe attrition. It played a decisive part in both battles of Bull Run, throughout Jackson's Valley campaign, at Gaines's Mill, Cedar Mountain, Antietam, Fredericksburg, Chancellorsville, the Wilderness, and Spotsylvania. At Gettysburg it saw two days of desperate fighting but was not committed in a decisive sector. Of the six commanders who followed Jackson (and before the brigade was reduced to a single regiment) Winder, Baylor, and Paxton were killed, Garnett was killed after leaving the brigade, and Walker was captured after being seriously wounded.

The brigade was composed of the 2d, 4th, 5th, 27th and 33d Va. regiments, formed from the 18 counties in the Shenandoah Valley. Col. Thomas J. Jackson took command of these 4,500 raw but enthusiastic recruits in Apr. '61. His severe training program and ascetic standards of military discipline turned them into an effective military organization.

In their baptism of fire at 1st Bull Run (Manassas), both Jackson and the brigade got their famous nickname. Brig. Gen. Barnard E. Bee's brigade was driven from its advanced position back toward Henry House Hill where Jackson's newly arrived brigade had formed. In rallying his routed troops Bee shouted: "Look at Jackson's brigade; it stands like a stone wall! Rally behind the Virginians" (D.S.F.). While elements of three other brigades rallied, Jackson not only held but counterattacked.

"Stonewall Brigade" was approved as an official designation 30 May '63. The Confederate War Dept. did not honor any other unit during the war by such recognition of a nickname.

Richard S. (Dick) Garnett followed Jackson as brigade commander. At Kernstown (25 Mar. '62) the brigade, out of ammunition, broke under overwhelming enemy pressure and Garnett ordered a withdrawal to a new position. Although this order saved the brigade from complete destruction, Jackson relieved Garnett. Charles S. Winder, the next commander, was greeted with open hostility by the brigade, which believed Garnett had been relieved unjustly. In the brilliant Valley campaign that followed Winder led his men 400 miles in four weeks, fought six engagements, and won their respect as a commander. Moving swiftly to the Peninsula, the brigade's attack at Gaines's Mill (27 June '62) helped break the

Federal right and give Lee one of his hardest-fought victories. At Cedar Mountain (9 Aug. '62) the brigade was badly shot up and Winder killed. Jackson arrived in person to rally his old outfit and win the battle. In the 2d Battle of Bull Run the unit further distinguished itself in a series of costly actions, from which it never fully recovered. On 30 Aug. the Virginians repulsed the attacks of their Federal counterpart, the IRON BRIGADE, and rallied for a counterattack. Its acting commander, Col. W. H. S. Baylor (5th Va.) was killed and the brigade reduced to regimental strength. Temporarily under Lt. Col. Andrew J. Grigsby, the Stonewall Brigade defended Lee's left at Antietam (Sharpsburg). The fighting around the West Woods was so severe that Grigsby was commanding the division at the end of the day. (The brigade was in "Jackson's division," which was commanded by J. R. Jones.)

Col. Elisha F. Paxton, formerly of the 27th Va., moved from Jackson's staff to head the brigade after Antietam. His welcome was the same as Winder's had been; the brigade favored the fighting, cursing, outspoken Grigsby whom, for unknown reasons, Jackson would not give the command. After Fredericksburg, however, Paxton was "accepted." Although the brigade's losses during 1862 had amounted to more than 1,200, their morale was still high. At Chancellorsville the brigade (now in "Trimble's Division," which was commanded by Colston) took part in Jackson's envelopment. Posted as a separate brigade behind Stuart's cavalry on the Confederate right (south) flank, the unit attacked along the Orange Plank Road the evening of 2 May '63. Paxton was killed and more than 600 men out of the brigade's 2,000 were killed or wounded. It was this same night that Jackson was mortally wounded. The ex-

hausted brigade responded the next morning to Jeb Stuart's exhortation: "Remember Stonewall Jackson!" and resumed the attack. Hearing of this action, the wounded Jackson said, "The men of the Brigade will be, some day, proud to say to their children, 'I was one of the Stonewall Brigade.'" Then he added, "The name 'Stonewall' ought to be attached wholly to the men of the Brigade, and not to me; for it was their steadfast heroism which earned it at First Manassas."

James A. Walker, Col. of the 4th Va., was promoted to command the brigade. The veterans greeted this new commander with animosity also, and considered his stern disciplinary methods to be unnecessary. At Stephenson's Depot (15 June '63) the brigade foiled Hooker's attempt to turn Lee's left flank; in a spirited counterattack it captured six Federal regiments. In the Gettysburg campaign, as part of Johnson's division, the brigade arrived with Ewell's corps at the end of the first day's fighting (1 July). The next two days it took part in the hard but unsuccessful frontal assaults against Culp's Hill. In the Wilderness the brigade fought along the Orange Courthouse Turnpike for two bloody days. A week later, at Spotsylvania, it was on the left of the critical salient remembered as the "Bloody Angle." In the attack of Hancock's II (US) Corps all but 200 men of the brigade were killed or were among the 6,080 captured. Johnson, the division commander, and Walker, who was seriously wounded, were among the prisoners. This ended the existence of the brigade as a unit. Its surviving members were consolidated into one regiment.

In Terry's brigade of Gordon's division the regiment fought under Early in what they termed the "Second Valley Campaign." They were prominent in the battle of the Monocacy (9 July '64), routing Lew Wallace's meager defenders and opening the road to Washington. When capture of the capital proved beyond Early's resources the survivors of the old Stonewall Brigade finally gave up their hopes of ultimate Southern victory. Discouragement deepened as Sheridan proceeded to destroy Early's army. They rejoined Lee for the final futile efforts around Petersburg and fought the Army of Northern Va.'s rear-guard action to Appomattox.

(From "The Right Arm of Lee and Jackson," by James I. Robertson, Jr., in *Civil War History,* Vol. III, No. 4, Dec. 1957.)

STOUGH, William. Union officer. Pa. Capt. 38th Ohio 10 Sept. '61; resigned 19 July '62; Capt. 9th Ohio Cav. 7 June '64; Maj. 1 Oct. '64; Lt. Col. 1 Nov. '64; Bvt. B.G. USV (Fayetteville, N.C.).

STOUGHTON (sto'-ton), **Charles Bradey.** Union officer. Vt. 1st Lt. Adj. 4th Vt. 21 Sept. '61; Maj. 5 Feb. '62; Lt. Col. 17 July '62; Col. 5 Nov. '62; Bvt. B.G. USV (war service); resigned 2 Feb. '64. Died 1898.

STOUGHTON, Edwin Henry. Union gen. 1838–68. Vt. USMA 1859 (17/22); Inf. After garrison duty he resigned from the R.A. 4 Mar. '61 and scouted in the Western Territories before being commissioned Col. 4th Vt. 21 Sept. '61 in the USV. During the Peninsular campaign he led his regiment at Yorktown, Lee's Mill, Williamsburg, and Savage's Station and was promoted B.G. USV 5 Nov. '62. He commanded 3, 1, VI (Oct.–Nov. '62); 2, Casey's division, Potomac; and 2, Casey's division, XXII, Washington from 2 Feb. until 9 Mar. '63, when he was captured at Fairfax C.H. by Mosby's raiders. His commission as B.G. USV expired while he was a prisoner in Libby, and when released he practiced law. (For the story of his capture, see MOSBY, John Singleton.)

STOUGHTON, William Lewis. Union officer. 1827–88. N.Y. A lawyer, he was commissioned Lt. Col. 11th Mich. 11 Oct. '61 and promoted Col. 1 Apr. '62. He fought at Stones River and commanded a brigade at Chickamauga, Missionary Ridge, Resaca, New Hope Church, Ruff's Station (wounded), and Atlanta. Mustered out 30 Sept. '64, he was breveted B.G. and Maj. Gen. USV for war service. He was later a Republican Congressman.

STOUT, Alexander Miller. Union officer. Ky. Lt. Col. 17th Ky. 8 Oct. '61; Col. 23 Dec. '62; Bvt. B.G. USV (war service); mustered out 23 Jan. '65. Commanded 3, 3, IV (Cumberland). Died 1895.

STOVALL, Marcellus A. C.S.A. gen. 1818–95. Ga. He fought in the Seminole War and the next year (1836) entered West Point but was invalided out for rheumatism (ex-1840). A merchant in Ga., he was in a volunteer military company, the Cherokee Arty. Named Col. of Ga. Arty. when the war began, he was commissioned Lt. Col. 3d Ga. Bn. 8 Oct '61 and served in garrison at Lynchburg and Goldsboro (N.C.). He fought at Waldron's Ridge and Stones River and was named B.G. C.S.A. 25 Apr. '63 (according to Wright; C.M.H. gives 20 Jan. '63 as the date). At Chickamauga, Chattanooga, and the Atlanta campaign he commanded his brigade. He went with Hood to Tenn. and fought at Bentonville before surrendering with Johnston in N.C. After the war he was in cotton and chemical manufacturing.

STOWE, Harriet Beecher. Abolitionist author. 1811–96. Conn. The ardently anti-slavery author of the novel, *Uncle Tom's Cabin,* which had sold over a million copies by the beginning of the Civil War and has continued to be read. She was the sister of Henry Ward BEECHER.

STRAHL, Otho French. C.S.A. gen. ?-1864. Ohio. A lawyer in Tenn., he was commissioned Capt. 4th Tenn. in May '61 and promoted Lt. Col. early in 1862. He fought at Shiloh, Stones River, and Perryville, and was promoted Col. the first part of 1863. Appointed B.G. C.S.A. 28 July '63, he led his brigade at Chickamauga, Chattanooga, and the Atlanta campaign. He was baptized with Hardee, Shoup, and Govan by Bishop Quintard as an Episcopalian 20 Apr. '64 at Dalton. Going with Hood to Tenn., he was killed 30 Nov. '64 at Franklin.

STRATEGY is the "art of the general." Webster defines it as "the science and art of military command, exercised to meet the enemy in combat under advantageous conditions." It is distinguished from TACTICS primarily in scope. The PRINCIPLES OF WAR are the fundamental truths governing the prosecution of war. For certain other terms and concepts of strategy and tactics see: ATTACKS, CONCENTRIC ADVANCE, COUNTERRECONNAISSANCE, COUP DE MAIN, COUP D'OEIL, DEFEAT IN DETAIL, DEMONSTRATION, ENVELOPMENTS, FEINT, FRONTAL ATTACK, GENERAL RESERVE, INTERIOR LINES, MEETING ENGAGEMENT, OBLIQUE ORDER, PIECEMEAL, POINT D'APPUI, RECONNAISSANCE, RECONNAISSANCE IN FORCE, RESERVE, SPOILING ATTACK, SUPPORTING DISTANCE, TURNING MOVEMENT.

STRATTON, Franklin Asa. Union officer. Mass. Capt. 11th Pa. Cav. 29 Oct. '61; Maj. 1 Sept. '62; Lt. Col. 1 Oct '64; Col. 25 May '65; Bvt. B.G. USV (war service). Died 1879.

STRAWBERRY PLAINS, Va. See DEEP BOTTOM RUN, 27-29 July and 13-20 Aug. '64.

STREIGHT, Abel D. Union officer. N.Y. Col. 51st Ind. 12 Dec. '61; Bvt. B.G. USV (war service); resigned 16 Mar. '65. Commanded Prov. Brig. XIV (Cumberland); 1, 3, IV (Cumberland). Died 1892.

STRICKLAND, Silas A. Union officer. N.Y. Lt. Col. 50th Ohio 17 Aug. '62; Col. 27 Oct. '62; Bvt. B.G. USV 27 May '65 (war service). Commanded 34, 10, I (Ohio); 3, 4, XXIII (Ohio); 3, 2, XXIII (Ohio); 3, 2, XXIII (N.C.). Died 1878.

STRINGHAM, Silas Horton. Union admiral. 1798-1876. N.Y. Entering the navy as midshipman in 1809, he fought in the War of 1812 and the Algerine War. He later served in the West Indies, the Mexican War, and the Mediterranean, and was named commander of the North Atlantic blockading fleet. He commanded the successful expedition to HATTERAS INLET in which he innovated a bombardment technique. However, he declined further promotion on account of his age and was retired as Commodore 21 Dec. '61. He was later promoted Rear Admiral on the retired list (16 July '62) and was commandant of the Boston Navy Yard for the remainder of the war.

STRONG, George Crockett. Union gen. 1833-63. Vt. Appt.-Mass. USMA 1857 (5/38); Ord. Serving in arsenals before the war, he was McDowell's Ord. Officer at 1st Bull Run as 1st Lt. 25 Jan. '61 (2d Lt. since 1859). He was McClellan's Asst. Ord. Officer until 25 Sept. and was named Maj. Asst. Adj. Gen. USV 1 Oct. '61-17 July '62. Butler's Chief of Staff (as B.G. USV 29 Nov. '62) until 16 Dec. of that year, he was on sick leave of absence until June '63, when he took over Forces, St. Helena Island, X, South (13 June-5 July '63). Named Maj. Gen. 18 July '63, he fought at Morris Island and was mortally wounded leading a charge against Fort Wagner while commanding

2, 2d Div. Morris Island, X, South (6–18 July '63). He died 12 days later.

STRONG, James Clark. Union officer. c. 1826–?. N.Y. Capt. 21st N.Y. 20 May '61; Lt. Col. 38th N.Y. 18 Jan. '62; discharged 29 Nov. '62; Col. Vet. Res. Corps Sept. '63; Bvt. B.G. USV (war service). W.I.A. Williamsburg in hip and lamed.

STRONG, Thomas J. Union officer. Vt. Capt. 22d N.Y. 6 June '61; Maj. 23 Mar. '63; Lt. Col. 7 May '63; mustered out 19 June '63; Maj. 16th N.Y. Arty. 5 Jan. '64; Lt. Col. 13 Nov. '64; Bvt. B.G. USV (war service). Died 1885.

STRONG, William Emerson. Union officer. N.Y. Capt. 2d Wis. 11 June '61; Maj. 12th Wis. 4 Oct. '61; Lt. Col. 19 Dec. '64; Lt. Col. Asst. I.G. Assigned 10 Feb. '63–1 Aug. '65; Bvt. B.G. USV 21 Mar. '65. Brevets for Atlanta campaign, S.C. campaign. Died 1891.

STRONG, William Kerly. Union gen. 1805–68. N.Y. A merchant and Democratic politician, he was in Egypt when the war broke. Hastening to France, he helped Frémont and others who were purchasing guns for the Union. He was commissioned B.G. USV 28 Sept. '61 and served briefly under Frémont. For a time (July–12 Aug. '62) he commanded Dist. Cairo and then Dist. St. Louis (6 June–30 Nov. '63) until he resigned. Returning to N.Y.C., he was thrown from his carriage in Central Park and paralyzed for the rest of his life.

STROTHER, David Hunter. Union officer. 1816–88. Va. Capt. Asst. Adj. Gen. Vols. 6 Mar. '62; Lt. Col. 3d W.Va. Cav. 1 June '62; Col. 18 July '63; Bvt. B.G. USV 23 Aug. '65 (war service); resigned 10 Sept. '64. On staffs of Gens. McClellan, Banks, Pope, and Hunter. After studying art in Philadelphia and Europe he began doing magazine illustrations. As "Porte Crayon," he was one of Harper's highest-paid contributors and famous for his written sketches, usually about the South, decorated with pen drawings. Consul Gen. to Mexico City, 1879–85.

STUART, David. Union gen. 1816–68. N.Y. A lawyer and Congressman, he was named Lt. Col. 42d Ill. 22 July '61 and Col. 55th Ill. 31 Oct '61. At Shiloh he was wounded in the shoulder while commanding 2, 5th Div., Army Tenn. (1 Mar.–6 Apr. '62). With his regiment at Corinth he led 4, Dist. Memphis, XIII, Tenn. (26 Oct.–12 Nov. '62). Promoted B.G. USV 29 Nov. '62, he led 2, 2d Div. Dist. Memphis Right Wing XIII, Tenn. (12 Nov.–18 Dec. '62); 2, 2d Div. Yazoo Exp., Tenn. (Dec.–28 Dec. '62); 2d Div. Yazoo Expedition (28 Dec. '62–4 Jan. '63) at Chickasaw Bluffs; and 2d Div., XV, Tenn. (4 Jan.– 4 Apr. '63) at Arkansas Post. His commission as B.G. was negated by the Senate 11 Mar. '63.

STUART, James Ewell Brown. ("Jeb") C.S.A. gen. and cavalry leader. 1833–64. Va. USMA 1854 (13/46); Mtd. Rifles-Cav. He served on the frontier in Indian fighting (seriously wounded) and in Kans. during the border disturbances. While on a leave of absence he was Lee's volunteer A.D.C. during John Brown's raid to Harpers Ferry. Resigning 3 May '61 as Capt., he determined to follow his state, although his Va.-born and West Point-educated father-in-law, Philip St. George COOKE, stayed with the Union. (See BROTHER AGAINST BROTHER.) He was commissioned Lt. Col. of the Va. Inf. on 10 May '61 and 14 days later was named Capt. of C.S.A. Cav. During that first summer he was at Harpers Ferry and 1st Bull Run and, appointed B.G. C.S.A. 24 Sept. '61, fought at Dranesville 20 Dec. '61. In the beginning of the Peninsular campaign he commanded the cavalry at Williamsburg and in June '62 led his troops in his first "ride around McClellan." He then fought in the Seven Days' Battles and at Harrison's Landing and as Maj. Gen. 25 July '62 took command of all the cavalry in the Army of Northern Va. before 2d Bull Run. In that campaign he fought at Catlett's Station (see STUART'S CATLETT'S STATION RAID), Groveton and 2d Bull Run, as well as participating in the Antietam campaign and making his second "ride around McClellan" (STUART'S CHAMBERSBURG RAID). He led his cavalry division in the II Corps at Fredericksburg and succeeded A. P. Hill temporarily as commander of Jackson's Corps 3 May at CHANCELLORSVILLE. In the Gettysburg campaign STUART'S CAVALRY CORPS (see under CORPS, CONFEDERATE) fought the important battle of BRANDY STATION and a number of famous cavalry skirmishes before undertaking the fateful Gettysburg raid (see GETTYSBURG CAMPAIGN). He then fought at the Wilderness and Spotsylvania and was mortally wounded 11 May '64 at YELLOW TAVERN. He died the next day. Satirically called "Beauty" by his West Point classmates, he wore a massive and flowing beard, purportedly to cover a receding chin and certainly to camouflage his youth. His personal bravery, endurance, panache, and high good humor made him a magnificent cavalry leader. Stuart's staff was excellent, and he trained his subordinates with a sober professionalism. Deeply religious and not unlike his good friend Jackson in his sincerity and piety, he also had a wide streak of vanity and exhibitionism in his make-up that contrasted strangely with the other qualities. He was about five feet nine inches tall, "massive and nearly square" (*Lee's Lts.,* I, xlix).

STUART'S CATLETT'S STATION RAID, Va., 22–23 Aug. '62. (2D BULL RUN CAMPAIGN) Pope learned of Lee's proposed turning movement when he captured Stuart's A.A.G. the night of 17–18 Aug., and withdrew to a position along the Rappahannock. Still chagrined about the loss of his hat and cloak—in addition to his adjutant—in the above operation, Stuart got permission to raid the railroad behind Pope's lines. The morning of the 22d he crossed the Rappahannock at Waterloo Bridge and Hart's Ford with two guns and 1,500 men (the brigades of B. H. Robertson and Fitz Lee, less the 3d and 7th Va. Cav.) Without meeting a single enemy scout, he entered Warrenton and then reached Auburn, near Catlett's Station, after dark. Here he overran the Federal camp, but darkness and a sudden storm made further operations appear impossible. At this point a captured Negro, who had known Stuart before, volunteered to lead him to Pope's baggage trains. "Under the guidance of this man, the 9th Virginia Cavalry attacked the camp and captured a number of officers belonging to General Pope's staff, together with a large sum of money, the despatch-book and other papers of General Pope's office, his personal baggage and horses, and other property" (H. B. McClellan). The 1st and 5th Va. Cav., meanwhile, attacked another part of the camp and W. W. Blackford, Stuart's engineer officer, made a determined but unsuccessful attempt to burn the bridge over Cedar Run. Stuart withdrew, taking over 300 prisoners (from the Purnell Legion of Md. and the 1st Pa. Rifles). "For many days thereafter General Pope's uniform was on exhibition in the window of one of the stores on Main Street, in Richmond, and Stuart felt that he had been fully repaid for the loss of his own hat and cloak at Verdiersville" (H. B. McClellan, 95). He had covered 60 miles in 26 hours. The captured papers gave Lee vital information that brought on the decisive maneuver of the 2D BULL RUN CAMPAIGN.

STUART'S CHAMBERSBURG RAID, 9–12 Oct. '64.

In his second ride around McClellan Stuart crossed the Potomac near the mouth of Black Creek (20 miles west of Williamsport) at daylight, 9 Oct. His force consisted of 1,800 selected men of the brigades of Fitzhugh Lee, Wade Hampton and W. E. Jones, and four guns under John Pelham. Avoiding Hagerstown, which was strongly defended, he reached Chambersburg that night. Here he destroyed a machine shop, many public stores, and then bivouacked in the streets of the town. At daybreak he was off with 500 captured horses, passing Emmitsburg the afternoon of the 11th, crossing the B.&O. R.R. east of Frederick, and recrossing the Potomac near the mouth of the MONOCACY, Md., 12 Oct. He had covered 126 miles, and the 80 miles after leaving Chambersburg had been made without a halt.

STUART'S DUMFRIES RAID, 26–31 Dec. '62.

While Lee occupied a defensive position above Fredericksburg, Va., Stuart's cavalry made four raids against Burnside's lines of communications, the last of which is known as the Dumfries Raid. On 28 Nov. '62 Wade Hampton with 158 Carolina and Ga. cavalrymen had captured about 100 horses and 92 officers and men of the 3d Pa. Cav. at Hartwood Church, about seven miles northwest of Falmouth. On 10 Dec. Hampton moved on Dumfries with 520 men and in a three-day operation, without a casualty, captured a wagon train and its 50 guards. In a third raid, 17–18 Dec., Hampton failed in an attempt to reach Occoquan, but got away with 150 prisoners and 20 wagons. Then Stuart himself led the fourth or "Dumfries Raid." With 1,800 men and four guns, the brigades of Wade Hampton, Fitz Lee, and W. H. F. ("Rooney") Lee,

he crossed the Rappahannock at Kelly's Ford the afternoon of 26 Dec. and camped at Morrisville. "Stuart's plan was to strike the Telegraph Road at three points between Aquia Creek and the Occoquan; then, sweeping northward, to reunite his forces wherever the events of the day might determine. Fitz Lee was accordingly directed to strike the Telegraph Road north of the Chopawamsic [Chopowamsic] and move northward to Dumfries, while W. H. F. Lee was sent directly to the latter place. Hampton was directed upon Occoquan" (H. B. McClellan, 197). Stuart rode with Rooney Lee. All three brigades reached their objectives on the 27th. After capturing some prisoners, Fitz and Rooney Lee converged on Dumfries but found the place too well defended to capture. A limited attack cost the life of Capt. J. W. Bullock, 5th Va. Cav., and inflicted 83 casualties on the Federals (68 missing). Hampton attacked the 17th Pa. Cav. at Occoquan and after taking a few prisoners withdrew about nine miles northwest to join the other brigades at Cole's Store. During the night Stuart evacuated the captured wagons and prisoners along with two guns whose ammunition was exhausted. The raid so far had been relatively unprofitable.

Stuart decided to continue his operations north of the Rappahannock in the hope that he might strike a blow at any Federals sent out to meet him, and that he might still be able to have an opportunity for operations north of the Occoquan. On the 28th, in a series of skirmishes with the 2d and 17th Pa. Cav. between Bacon Race Church and Selectman's Ford (near the village of Occoquan), the Confederates inflicted 120 casualties, of whom 100 were captured. In a vigorous pursuit through the icy waters of Selectman's Ford, led by Rosser's 5th Va. Cav. and which

Pelham managed to accompany with his guns, the Confederates overran the Federal camps at Occoquan. Here Stuart was joined by the other brigades. After burning everything that could not be taken with them, Stuart's cavalry moved west. Reaching Burke's Station on the Orange and Alexandria R.R. after dark, Stuart captured the telegraph station operator before he could tap out an alarm. "Stuart always carried with him an accomplished telegraph operator and now had the satisfaction of receiving official information from General Heintzleman's [Heintzelman's] headquarters in Washington concerning the dispositions which were being made to intercept him. After gaining the information he needed,

he caused his operator to send a message to General M. C. Meigs, Quartermaster-General, at Washington, in which he complained that the quality of the mules recently furnished to the army was so inferior as greatly to embarrass him in moving his captured wagons" (H. B. McClellan, 201). Freeman points out that "the text, unfortunately, is lost. In 2 Von Borcke, 168–69, the incident is stated in reverse: Stuart is represented as thanking General Meigs for the mules" (*Lee's Lts.*, II, 405n). After a feint toward Fairfax C.H. Stuart reached Culpeper C.H. 31 Dec. and rode into Lee's lines at Fredericksburg the next day.

Confederate losses had been one

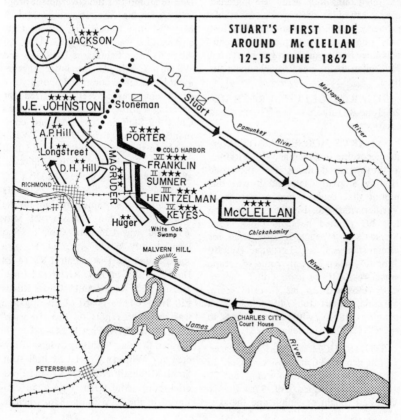

killed, 13 wounded, and 13 missing. Aside from considerable booty, Stuart had killed or wounded about 30 men (E.&B.), taken about 200 prisoners, and an equal number of horses, 20 wagons and sutlers' teams, and 100 or more weapons.

STUART'S FIRST RIDE AROUND McCLELLAN, 12–15 June '62. (PENIN-SULAR CAMPAIGN) In preparation for the battle of MECHANICSVILLE Lee ordered Stuart to reconnoiter the right flank and rear of McClellan's position astride the Chickahominy. Leaving Hanover C.H. on 12 June with 1,000 troopers (including John Mosby) Stuart went beyond his instructions and completely encircled the Union army. He marched nearly 150 miles, destroyed considerable property, captured prisoners, and lost only one man. By turning this reconnaissance into a raid, however, he alerted McClellan to the need for changing his base.

STUART'S GETTYSBURG RAID. 24 June–3 July '63. See GETTYSBURG CAMPAIGN.

STUART'S HORSES. Stuart's favorite, according to Freeman, was Virginia, a thoroughbred mare. He also rode Highfly a great deal, and it was this mount that enabled him to escape at Verdiersville, Va., 18 Aug '62, when he lost his plumed hat and cloak. (See STUART'S CATLETT'S STATION RAID for circumstances.) At HANOVER, Pa., 30 June '63, when his only route of escape was across a 10- to 15-foot ditch, "splendidly mounted on his favorite mare, Virginia, Stuart took the ditch at a running leap . . . with several feet to spare" (H. B. McClellan, 328).

STUMBAUGH, Frederick Shearer. Union gen. Pa. Commissioned Col. 2d Pa. 20 Apr. '61 and mustered out 27 July, he was named Col. 77th Pa. 26 Oct. and fought at Shiloh and the skir-

mishes immediately following it. He was promoted B.G. USV 29 Nov. '62, but his appointment was revoked 22 Jan. '63, and he resigned 15 May '63. He commanded 5th Brig., 2d Div., Army Ohio 7 Apr.–20 June '62.

STURGIS, Samuel Davis. Union gen. 1822–89. Pa. USMA 1846 (32/59); Dragoons-Cav. He was captured in the Mexican War and later served on the frontier in Indian scouting and fighting. In Apr. '61, as Capt. 1st US Cav., he was in command of Fort Smith (Ark.) when his officers resigned to join the C.S.A. Although the fort was surrounded by rebel militia, Sturgis marched his troops out to Fort Leavenworth, taking with them most of the government property under his care. Promoted Maj. 3 May '61 and transferring to 4th Cav. 3 Aug., he was named B.G. USV 10 Aug. '61 after fighting at Dug Gap and Wilson's Creek. At the latter engagement he assumed command upon Lyon's death and was severely criticized for ordering a withdrawal. He was Hunter's Chief of Staff in Nov. '61 and commanded Sturgis's Brig., Mil. Dist. Washington in the summer of '62 at 2d Bull Run. At South Mountain, Antietam, and Fredericksburg, he led 2d Div., IX, Potomac (3 Sept. '62–7 Feb. '63). He commanded the same division in the Army of the Ohio (19 Mar.–21 May '63) and was Chief of Cav. of that Dept. 8 July '63–15 Apr. '64. He also commanded the Dist. Central Ky (4–24 June '63) and 1st Div. XXIII (24 June–10 July '63). After BRICE'S CROSS ROADS (10 June '64), a board of investigation was called to report on this "disaster" (O.R. I, XXXIX, Part I, 147–220). He finished the war "awaiting orders." Breveted for Wilson's Creek, 2d Bull Run, South Mountain (B.G. USA), and Fredericksburg (Maj. Gen. USA), he continued in the R.A. until 1886, when he retired as Col. 6th US Cav. after many years of Indian fighting.

SUBMARINES. The first practical underwater boat was invented in 1775–76 by David Bushnell of Conn. Robert Fulton developed it further, and during the Civil War the Confederates turned to submarines as a means of breaking the blockade at Charleston and Norfolk. The *David* class were steam-propelled semi-submersibles, cylindrical in form with conical ends. Armed with a spar torpedo carrying a charge of 24 to 132 pounds, the *David* damaged the *Iron-sides* 5 Oct. '63 at Charleston, and the *Hunley,* which was hand propelled, sunk the *Housatonic* 17 Feb. '64. Both were lost in these operations, however. The Union navy's one submarine, the *Alligator,* sunk under tow off Cape Hatteras in Apr. '63 after an unsuccessful career since her launching in Nov. '61.

SUFFOLK, Va., 11 Apr.–4 May '63. When the IX Corps was sent in Feb. '63 from Fredericksburg to Fortress Monroe, Lee sent Longstreet with the divisions of Hood and Pickett to block a possible advance on Richmond from Yorktown or Suffolk. Lincoln decided to change Burnside's orders and send him to Ky. instead of to N.C. Getty's (3d) division of IX Corps was then left at Suffolk and the other two sent to the West (Knoxville campaign). After an unsuccessful expedition against NEW BERN, N.C., 13–15 Mar., Longstreet undertook an operation against J. J. Peck at Suffolk. After probing the strong position, which was reinforced from 15,000 to nearly 25,000 during Apr., Longstreet abandoned his attempts to capture Suffolk. In the words of Dix's report, "he sat down before it and commenced an investment according to the most improved principles of military science" (B.&L., IV, 533n). Longstreet reported that the place could be captured in a few days but that he did not

think "we can afford to spend the powder and ball." While investing the place Longstreet foraged in the rich farming area that surrounds it. Freeman points out that his original mission was strategic, and that "Operations for the commissariat developed later . . ." (*Lee's Lts.,* II, 477n). Principal engagements during the siege were an attack on 14 Apr. by land batteries on Federal gunboats in the Nansemond River and the Federal surprise and capture of FORT HUGER, 19 Apr., by combined army and naval forces. US casualties during the period 11 Apr.–4 May were 260 Federals and 900 Confederates, of whom 400 were missing, according to E.&B.

SUGAR CREEK, Ga. Feature of battle of ATLANTA, 22 July '64.

SUGAR VALLEY, Ga. See RESACA, Ga. 13–16 May '64.

SULLIVAN, Jeremiah Cutler. Union gen. 1830–90. Ind. He served in the navy for a short time as a young man and was commissioned Capt. 6th Ind. 18 Apr. '61. Promoted Col. 3d Ind. 19 June '61 after fighting at Philippi 3 June, he also fought at Rich Mountain, Cheat Mountain, and Winchester and commanded 2d Brig., Lander's division, W. Va. (Jan.–Mar. '62) and 2, 2, Banks's V, Potomac (13 Mar.–4 Apr. '62). Promoted B.G. USV 28 Apr. '62, he commanded 2, 2d Div., Shenandoah (4 Apr.–1 May '62); 2, 3d Div., Army Miss. (20 June–3 Oct. '62); Dist. Jackson, XIII, Tenn. (19 Nov.–22 Dec. '62); Maryland Heights, W. Va. (18 Sept.–Dec. '63); 1st Div., W. Va.; 1st Div. Inf., W. Va. (Apr.–3 July '64); and 1st Sept. Brig., Dist. Kanawha, W. Va. (6 Aug.–9 Oct. '64). He resigned 11 May '65. Brother of Algernon Sidney Sullivan, noted philanthropist of the postwar era.

SULLIVAN, Peter John. Union officer. 1821–83. Ireland. Lt. Col. 48th Ohio 23 Nov. '61; Col. 23 Jan. '62; Bvt. B.G. USV (war service); resigned 7 Aug. '63. Served during Mexican War as draughtsman for the Topo. Corps. In 1855 he was elected Col. of a German state militia regiment in Ohio and suppressed the "Know Nothing" riots that year. He raised four regiments at his own expense for the Civil War. He was wounded three times at Shiloh and captured a Confederate flag. From 1865 to 1869 he was US Minister to Colombia.

SULLY, Alfred. Union gen. 1821–79. Pa. USMA 1841 (34/52); Inf. Serving in the Seminole and Mexican wars and in the West in garrison duty and Indian fighting, he was commissioned Col. 1st Minn. 4 Mar. '62 (also Maj. 8th US Inf. 15 Mar. from Capt. since 1852). During the Peninsular campaign he led his regiment at Yorktown, West Point, Fair Oaks, Peach Orchard, Savage's Station, Glendale, Malvern Hill and Harrison's Landing. He also fought at Chantilly, Vienna, South Mountain, and Antietam. Promoted B.G. USV 26 Sept. '62, he commanded 1, 2, II, Potomac (29 Oct.–19 Dec. '62) at Fredericksburg and (10 Mar.–3 May '63) at Chancellorsville. From 20 Dec. '62 to 10 Jan. '63 he led the 3d Div. of that corps. Going to the West, he commanded the Dist. of Dak. from May '63 until Apr. '66, continuing in the R.A. and dying on active duty as Col. 21st US Inf. He was breveted for Fair Oaks, Malvern Hill, Indian campaigns, and battle of White Stone Hill (B.G. USA) and war service (Maj. Gen. USV 8 Mar. '65). Son of Thomas Sully, the artist.

SUMNER, Charles. Radical Republican. 1811–74. Mass. After graduating from Harvard he became a lawyer and taught at the law school before spending three years in Europe. He became an abolitionist, was violently opposed to the extension of slave territory, and was elected Sen. in 1851 on this ticket. In 1856 he delivered an invective-laden speech called "The Crime against Kansas" in which he insulted a S.C. senator who was not present. Two days later Representative Preston Brooks, of S.C., a relative of the reviled man, attacked Sumner viciously with a cane. Sumner did not recover for three years, although he continued to hold his Senate seat. After secession he refused to let the Senate consider a compromise between the sections and constantly urged emancipation and equal rights for Negroes. Although he had nominally supported Lincoln, he was one of the leaders in the impeachment proceedings against Johnson. He left the party to support Greeley in 1872 but later returned to the Republicans.

SUMNER, Edwin Vose. Union gen. 1797–1863. Mass. Appt.-N.Y. R.A. Commissioned 2d Lt. 2d US Inf. in 1819, he served in the Black Hawk and Mexican wars (1 wound; 2 brevets in the latter), the Kans. disturbances and Indian fighting. He commanded the Dept. of the Pacific (25 Apr.–20 Oct. '61), succeeding A. S. Johnston, and was named B.G. USV 16 Mar. '61. Going to the East, he commanded Sumner's division, Potomac (25 Nov. '61–13 Mar. '62) and the II Corps (13 Mar.–7 Oct. '62) on the Peninsula, and at South Mountain and Antietam. He was named Maj. Gen. USV 4 July '62. After commanding the Right Grand Division at Fredericksburg, he was relieved at his own request and died 21 Mar. '63 in N.Y. State on the way to his new command in Mo. He was breveted for Fair Oaks (Maj. Gen. USA 31 May '62). Two sons were Union officers, see below. His son-in-law was Armistead Long, C.S.A. Gen. See also Brother Against Brother.

SUMNER, Edwin Vose, Jr. Union officer. Pa. Son of Gen. Sumner and brother of Samuel Storrow Sumner, B.G. USV. R.A. 2d Lt. 1st US Cav. 5 Aug. '61; 1st Lt. 12 Nov. '61; Maj. A.D.C. Vols. 19 May '63; mustered out USV 15 Aug. '63; Capt. 1st US Cav. 23 Sept. '63; Col. 1st N.Y. Mtd. Rifles 8 Sept. '64; Bvt. B.G. USV; B.G. USA and retired 1899. Brevets for Todd's Tavern (Va.), war service (2). Commanded 3d Brig., Cav. Div., Va. and N.C.

SUMNER, Samuel Storrow. Union officer. Penn. Appt.-N.Y. Commissioned 2d Lt. 2d U.S. Cav. 11 June '61, he transferred to the 5th U.S. Cav. 3 Aug. '61. He served as Capt. and A.D.C. USV to his father, Gen. Edwin V. Sumner, Nov. '61–Aug. '63 and to Gen. Wool until Nov. '63. Commanding a company until Dec. '63, he was detached on mustering and disbursing duty in Illinois until Apr. '65, having been

promoted Capt. USA 30 Mar. '64. He continued in the R.A., and was named B.G. and Maj. Gen. USV in 1898. In 1901 he was promoted B.G. USA. He was breveted for Fair Oaks, Antietam, Vicksburg, and Indian fighting in 1869.

SUNRISE, SUNSET, AND DAYLIGHT. When Civil War accounts refer to sunrise, sunset, dawn, dusk, daylight, etc., it is sometimes useful to be able to convert these into specific times of the day. While sunrise and sunset are subject to precise mathematical determination, "twilight"—the time between total darkness and sunrise or sunset—cannot be accurately translated into terms of visibility. Sky conditions and weather will also affect visibility. Another limitation is the inaccuracy of reports; even if a soldier should be carrying an accurate timepiece, the sun's movements are not the subject of precise scientific observation. Nevertheless, the table on page 820 should permit computation to

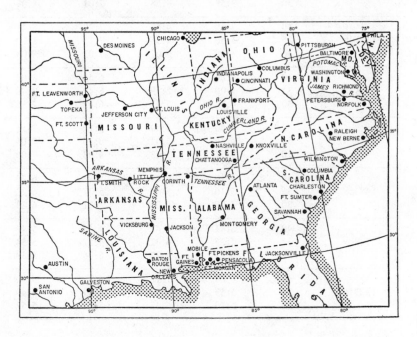

	Lat.	B.M.N.T.	SUN Rise	Set	E.E.N.T.
14 Jan.	40	6:17	7:21	4:57	6:01
	35	6:09	7:08	5:10	6:09
	30	6:02	6:57	5:21	6:16
13 Feb.	40	5:57	6:56	5:33	6:32
	35	5:53	6:49	5:40	6:36
	30	5:50	6:42	5:47	6:39
15 Mar.	40	5:15	6:13	6:06	7:04
	35	5:17	6:12	6:07	7:02
	30	5:19	6:11	6:08	6:59
14 Apr.	40	4:24	5:25	6:37	7:38
	35	4:34	5:30	6:31	7:28
	30	4:42	5:35	6:26	7:20
14 May	40	3:38	4:46	7:07	8:15
	35	3:56	4:58	6:55	7:57
	30	4:10	5:08	6:45	7:43
13 June	40	3:16	4:30	7:29	8:44
	35	3:39	4:45	7:14	8:21
	30	3:58	4:58	7:01	8:02
13 July	40	3:29	4:42	7:29	8:41
	35	3:50	4:55	7:15	8:20
	30	4:08	5:07	7:03	8:03
15 Aug.	40	4:06	5:11	6:58	8:02
	35	4:20	5:19	6:49	7:48
	30	4:32	5:27	6:42	7:37
14 Sept.	40	4:40	5:39	6:12	7:11
	35	4:46	5:41	6:10	7:05
	30	4:51	5:43	6:08	7:00
14 Oct.	40	5:10	6:09	5:23	6:22
	35	5:10	6:04	5:27	6:22
	30	5:09	6:01	5:31	6:23
13 Nov.	40	5:41	6:42	4:46	5:47
	35	5:35	6:32	4:57	5:54
	30	5:29	6:23	5:06	5:59
13 Dec.	40	6:08	7:12	4:35	5:40
	35	5:59	6:59	4:49	5:49
	30	5:50	6:47	5:01	5:57

within about 15 minutes, unless the skies were exceptionally overcast or unless it was raining.

The times given for twilight are those for the beginning of morning nautical twilight ("B.M.N.T.") and the end of evening nautical twilight ("E.E.N.T."). Nautical twilight, which is between astronomical and civil twilight, permits observation of objects on the ground at 400 yards. For all practical purposes, we can consider that at B.M.N.T. and E.E.N.T. a Civil War soldier could see sufficiently well to conduct military operations. To use the table you must first know the date for which you want to determine sunrise, sunset, or twilight. You must then know the latitude with which you are dealing. Somewhat more accurate estimates may be obtained by interpolating both for dates and latitudes. The times given in the table are local mean times, which we can consider to be those used in Civil War accounts. Morning and afternoon times are not indicated in the table by A.M. and P.M., since these can be determined by inspection. Figures are from the *American Nautical Almanac* for 1959, and are within a minute or two of what they were a century ago. Acknowledgement is hereby made to the U.S. Naval Observatory for supplying these figures and for other assistance in preparing this article.

SUNSHINE CREEK (or CHURCH), 31 July '64. Alternate name for Hillsboro, during STONEMAN'S AND MCCOOK'S RAIDS, 26–31 July '64.

SUPPLY TRAINS. See TRAINS.

SUPPORTING DISTANCE. "Distance between two units that can be traveled in time for one to come to the aid of the other" (S.R. 320-5-1). This distance varies in accordance with the size of the units involved. Two regiments, for example, might have to be within a mile or so of each other, whereas two divisions might be within a day's march. The commander who keeps all his units within supporting distance has his force "concentrated," thereby avoiding DEFEAT IN DETAIL. One of Napoleon's strategic principles was to keep his own force always "concentrated," which involved detailed time and space computations on his part. He would then attempt to maneuver so as to gain INTERIOR LINES and DEFEAT IN DETAIL an enemy whose units were not within supporting distance of each other.

SUPPORTS. Artillery supports were infantry troops assigned the mission of close-in protection of artillery units from sharpshooters, infiltrators, etc. "Support," in general, means for one unit to assist another. "A regiment of Zouaves [the FIRE ZOUAVES], following in support of the Federal Batteries [Griffin's and Ricketts's], were charged by a company of cavalry under Col. Stuart" (Alexander, 39).

SURRATT, Mrs. Assassination conspirator. A Md. widow, she moved to Washington around the beginning of the war and ran a boardinghouse. Her eldest son was in the Confederate Army and John (1844–1916), the younger boy, was a Confederate spy and dispatch carrier. His younger sister Anna also lived with them. Although the plot was made in her boardinghouse, Mrs. Surratt was devout and respectable with a blameless character, and her arrest after Lincoln's assassination was brought on by John's escape and by hearsay. Ill and weak, she suffered intensely throughout the public trial and was sentenced to be hanged. This was done with three others (Paine, Atzerodt, and Herold) 7 July '65. See also LINCOLN'S ASSASSINATION.

SURRATT, John H. Alleged conspirator in LINCOLN'S ASSASSINATION. Md. 1844–1916. He had been a Confederate spy and dispatch carrier in the early part of the war and had an older brother in the Southern Army. His mother, Mrs. SURRATT, ran a Washington boardinghouse that became the center of John Wilkes BOOTH's plotting. Surratt was, apparently, not in Washington when Lincoln was shot, but escaped to Canada when suspects were being arrested. Going to England and Rome, he joined the Papal Zouaves. There he was recognized by a fellow-soldier, a Maryland schoolmate, and after a series of adventures was finally returned to the U.S. to stand trial in 1867. This resulted in a hung jury, and the charge against him was nolle-prossed in Sept. '68. Settling in Maryland, he lived an uneventful life as a clerk.

SURRENDER DATES. Lee asked for an armistice on 9 Apr. '65 and surrendered to Grant the same day. J. E. Johnston asked for an armistice on 14 Apr. and surrendered to Sherman on the 26th. Richard Taylor surrendered on 4 May to E. R. S. Canby, thus ending Confederate resistance east of the Mississippi. (See ALABAMA, MISSISSIPPI, AND EAST LOUISIANA, CONFEDERATE DEPARTMENT OF, for further data on actual surrender date.) E. Kirby Smith surrendered his Trans-Miss. Dept. to Canby on 26 May '65.

SUSQUEHANNA, UNION DEPARTMENT OF THE. Created 9 June '63, to organize the improvised forces rushing from adjoining states for the defense of Pa. against Lee's invasion. With headquarters at Chambersburg, the department was headed by Maj. Gen. D. N. Couch. His area consisted of that portion of Pa. east of Johnstown and the Laurel Hill range of mountains. On 6 Apr. '64 the part of Pa. west of this line was made part of the department. On 1 Dec. '64 the state of Pa. was in the re-created Dept. of Pa.

SUTHERLAND STATION (Southside R.R.), 2 Apr. '65. Action in PETERSBURG FINAL ASSAULT.

SUTLER. A person who accompanies troops in the field or in garrison and sells food, drink, and supplies. The articles of war prescribed that "persons permitted to sutle shall supply the soldiers with good and wholesome provisions or other articles at a reasonable price" (Scott).

SWAMP ANGEL. A 200-pounder (8-inch) PARROTT GUN with which Federal forces ineffectively shelled Charleston, S.C., from Morris Island on 22–23 Aug. '63. The gun blew up when firing the 36th round. The range was 7,900 yards, using incendiary shells. Although a few fires were set, "the fiery missiles turned out to have been more destructive to Union gun crews than to rebel property" (Bruce, 244). The Swamp Angel was set as a monument at Perry and Clinton streets, Trenton, N.J., where it still stands (B.&L., IV, 72).

SWAYNE, Wager. Union gen. 1834–1902. Ohio. After Yale and the Cincinnati Law School he practiced in Ohio and was commissioned Maj. 43d Ohio 31 Aug. and Lt. Col. 14 Dec. '61. He fought with his regiment at New Madrid, Island No. 10, and Corinth, and was promoted Col. 18 Oct. '62. In the Atlanta campaign he commanded 2, 4, XVI, Tenn. (18–23 Sept. '64), and on the March to the Sea he led 2, 1, XVII, Tenn. (22 Sept.–1 Nov. '64). He distinguished himself at Resaca, Dallas, Kenesaw Mountain, and Atlanta, and lost his right leg at River's Bridge (S.C.) 2 Feb. '65. Then promoted B.G. USV 8 Mar. and Maj. Gen. USV 20 June '65, he continued in the R.A., serving in the Freedman's Bureau under O. O. Howard. Retiring in 1870 as Col. 45th US Inf., he had been breveted B.G. USV 5 Feb. '65, B.G. USA for River's Bridge, and Maj. Gen. USA for war service and was given the Medal of Honor in 1893 for Corinth. He later practiced law and was active in educational activities and church work.

SWEENY, Thomas William. Union gen. 1820–92. Ireland. Fighting in the Mexican War (losing his right arm, winning 1 brevet and a silver medal from N.Y.C.), he continued in the R.A. in Indian fighting until promoted Capt. 2d US Inf. 19 Jan. '61. Named B.G. Mo. Vols. 20 May '61, he was at Camp Jackson when Lyon took over, and fought at Wilson's Creek where he was severely wounded. Mustered out 14 Aug. '61, he was named Col. 52d Ill. 21 Jan. '62 and led his regiment at Fort Donelson and Shiloh. He commanded 2d Brig., 2d Div., Dist. Corinth; 1st Brig., 2d Div. Dist. Corinth (12 Aug.–1 Sept. and 3 Oct.–1 Nov. '62) and 1st Brig., Dist. Corinth, XIII (24 Oct.–18 Dec. '62). Promoted B.G. USV 29 Nov. '62, he commanded 1st Brig., Dist. Corinth, XVI (18 Dec. '62–20 Jan. '63); 1, 2, XVI (18 Mar.–20 July '63) and succeeded to command of the division (12 Sept. '63–25 July '64) for Snake Creek Gap, Resaca, Kenesaw Mountain, and the battles before Atlanta. He continued in the R.A. and was dismissed in Dec. '65, going on the Fenian raiding party into Canada the next year. Reinstated in the fall of 1866, he retired with the rank of B.G. USA in 1870.

SWEET, Benjamin Jeffery. Union officer. 1832–74. N.Y. Maj. 6th Wis. 16 July '61; Lt. Col. 17 Sept. '61; Col. 21st Wis. 5 Sept. '62; resigned 8 Sept. '63; Col. Vet. Res. Corps 25 Sept. '63; Bvt. B.G. USV 20 Dec. '64. The son of a poor and ill minister, he went to work in the cotton mills at 9. He was able to attend college for a year, studied law at night, and was elected to the Wis. state senate at 27. He was commissioned a Maj. at the war's beginning and raised several other Wis. regiments. Confined

to an ambulance with malaria at Perryville, he left and mounted his horse to command his regiment. Here he was wounded most seriously, and this permanently impaired his health. Entering the Vet. Res. Corps, he took command of Camp Douglas (Ill.) where 10,000 Confederate prisoners were held. In June '64 he received word that an outbreak would occur 4 July to liberate the prisoners and arm them to sack and destroy Chicago. By quickly strengthening his garrison, he discouraged this attempt. However, the following Nov. he again received word that another attack was planned for election night, then only three days away. Allegedly, there were 5,000 armed men and their leaders in Chicago and muskets for 9,000 prisoners. Appleton's says, "Chicago was to be burned, and its flames were to be the signal for a general uprising of 500,000 well-armed men throughout the western country." Sweet had only 796 men in his Vet. Res. Corps garrison, most of whom were not fit for active duty. Realizing that the only plan feasible was the arrest of the Chicago leaders, he called one of the prisoners, a Texas Ranger named John T. Shanks, to locate the rebel conspirators. Sweet arranged for Shanks's escape from the camp to allay the Confederates' suspicions and then had him trailed by detectives under orders to kill him at the first sign of treachery. Shanks, however, served him well, and the leaders were under arrest within 36 hours. The citizens of Chicago held a mass meeting to thank the man who saved their city. He was breveted B.G. USV for this. After the war he practiced law and held several offices in the federal pension and internal-revenue offices.

SWEITZER, Jacob Bowman. Union officer. Pa. Maj. 62d Pa. 4 July '61; Lt. Col. 17 Nov. '61; Col. 27 June '62; Bvt. B.G. USV (war service); mustered out 13 July '64. Commanded 2, 1, V (Potomac); 1st Div., V (Potomac). Died 1888.

SWEITZER, Nelson Bowman. Union officer. c. 1829–98. Pa. USMA 1853 (24/52); Dragoons-Cav. Capt. 1st US Dragoons 7 May '61; 1st Cav. 3 Aug. '61; Lt. Col. Add. A.D.C. 28 Sept. '61; mustered out as A.D.C. 31 Mar. '63; Col. 16th N.Y. Cav. 12 Nov. '64; transferred to 3d N.Y. Prov. Cav. 23 June '65; Bvt. B.G. USV and USA. Brevets for Peninsular campaign, Winchester, Yellow Tavern (Va.), Meadow Bridge (Va.), war service (2). A.D.C. to McClellan July '61–Mar. '63. Participated in Sheridan's raids to Haxall's Landing and toward Gordonsville in May and June '64. The following year he commanded the regiment that tracked down and killed John Wilkes Booth, and captured Dr. Mudd. Continued in R.A. until retired as Col. in 1888.

SWIFT, Frederick William. Union officer. Conn. Capt. 17th Mich. 17 June '62; Lt. Col. 26 Nov. '63; Col. 4 Dec. '64; Bvt. B.G. USV. Brevets for Spotsylvania, war service. Medal of Honor 15 Feb. '97 for Lenoir Station (Tenn.). Captured at Spotsylvania 12 May '64.

SWIFT CREEK, Va., 9 May '64. See DREWRY'S BLUFF, 12–16 May '64.

SWINTON, John. Newspaper editor. 1830–1901. Scotland. Learning the printer's trade in Canada as a boy, he left S.C. to go to Kans. to take part in the free-soil argument there and returned to N.Y.C. in 1857, where he studied medicine. However, he soon joined the N.Y. Times, as had his brother William, and shortly became the managing editor. He resigned this responsible post at the end of the war but continued to write editorials and then became managing editor of the N.Y. Sun. Engaged in labor reforms, he was a prominent Socialist editor and leader. See WAR CORRESPONDENTS.

SWINTON, William. WAR CORRESPONDENT and author. 1833–92. Scotland. After graduating from Amherst he studied to become a Presbyterian minister but soon switched to teaching, and by 1858 had joined the N.Y. Times staff. Sent to the front in 1862 as war correspondent for that paper, he knew a great deal about tactics and strategy but made himself highly unpopular with first Grant and then Burnside. On the night of 5 May '64, during the Wilderness campaign, Meade and his staff were having a conference with Grant when Swinton was caught eavesdropping behind a stump. Some days later he enraged Burnside with an uncomplimentary report, and the general was understood by Grant to want to order the reporter shot. Grant then expelled him from the field. Swinton's Campaigns of the Army of the Potomac (1866) is still a good reference, as he was not only thorough in his research but also sent proofs to Meade, Hooker, Franklin, Couch, Hancock, Lee, and J. E. Johnston. He did not send them to Burnside and Grant, and the book suffers for it. He was professor of English at the Univ. of Calif. for a time and wrote many school texts. Brother of John Swinton.

SWITZLER, Theodore A. Union officer. Mo. Capt. 6th Mo. Cav. 5 July '61; Lt. Col. 13 Aug. '62; Bvt. B.G. USV (war service). Died 1879.

SWORDS, Thomas. Union officer. c. 1807–86. N.Y. USMA 1829 (23/46); Inf.-Q.M. He served on the frontier and in the Mexican War (1 brevet) before being named Col. Asst. Q.M. Gen. 3 Aug. '61. During the Civil War he was Chief Q.M. of the Dept. of the Cumberland (to 15 Nov. '61) and of the Dept. of the Ohio (to 30 May '63), and was supervising Q.M. of the Dept. of the

Cumberland (to 10 Nov. '63) and of the Dept. of the Ohio (to 17 Jan. '65). He retired in 1869 as Bvt. B.G. USA.

SYKES, George. Union gen. 1822–80. Md. USMA 1842 (39/56); Inf. His early service was mainly on the frontier, and he participated in the Seminole War, Mexican War (1 brevet), and Indian fighting and scouting. As Maj. 14th US Inf. 14 May '61 (Capt. since 1855), he led "Sykes's Regulars" at 1st Bull Run and was appointed B.G. USV 28 Sept. '61. He commanded the Reg. Inf. Brig. in Washington (Aug. '61–Mar. '62) and then led the Reg. Inf. Res. Div. (Mar.–May '62) at the siege of Yorktown. He commanded the 2d Div., V Corps (18 May–Dec. '62) at Gaines's Mill, Malvern Hill, 2d Bull Run, Antietam, Shepherdstown, Snicker's Gap, and Fredericksburg and (Jan.–28 June '63) at Chancellorsville. Named Maj. Gen. USV 29 Nov. '62, he also commanded the V Corps 1–5 Feb. and 16–23 Feb. '63; led it at Gettysburg (28

June–7 Oct. '63) and at Centreville, Rappahannock Station, and during the Mine Run operations (15 Oct. '63–23 Mar. '64). Upon reorganization of the army he was relieved and sent to the relatively unimportant Dept. of Kans. (20 Apr. '64–7 June '65), commanding in that time the Dist. South Kans. (1 Sept.–10 Oct. '64). Breveted for Gaines's Mill, Gettysburg (B.G. USA), and war service (Maj. Gen. USA), he continued in the R.A., dying on active duty as Col. 20th US Inf. His nickname was "Tardy George," but D.A.B. says his tardiness was mental, not physical. Lyman comments on an occasion when Sykes, "usually exceedingly stern, became very gracious and deigned to laugh."

SYLVAN GROVE, Ga. See WAYNESBORO, 26–29 Nov. '64.

SYPHER, Jay Hale. Union officer. Pa. 1st Lt. 1st Ohio Arty. 8 Oct. '61; resigned 3 Feb. '64; Col. 11th US Col. Arty. 11 Aug. '64; Bvt. B.G. USV (war service).

T

TABB HOUSE. Misspelling in Alexander and elsewhere of TAPP HOUSE.

TACTICS is the employment of troops in combat. It differs from STRATEGY primarily in scope. The distinction between the two words is important in any discussion of military operations, and many definitions have been contrived. "Tactics is the art of handling troops on the battlefield; strategy is the art of bringing forces to the battlefield in a favorable position," according to Sir Archibald Wavell. Obviously there can be no sharp dividing line where strategy ends and tactics begins, since there is no line around the edge of the battlefield. Clausewitz has provided this famous

definition: "Tactics is the art of using troops in battle; strategy is the art of using battles to win the war." See also STRATEGY.

TALBOT, Thomas Hammond. Union officer. Me. Lt. Col. 1st Me. Arty. 21 Aug. '62; Bvt. B.G. USV (war service); resigned 13 Sept. '64.

TALIAFERRO (pronounced tah'-liver), William Booth. 1822–98. Va. A graduate of William and Mary, he studied law at Harvard, fought in the Mexican War, sat in the legislature, and commanded a militia company at Harpers Ferry after John Brown's raid. He was commissioned Col. C.S.A. and served under Jackson in the Valley in early 1862. Although he signed the petition that caused the LORING-JACKSON INCIDENT, he was appointed B.G. C.S.A. 6 Mar. '62 to rank from the 4th and commanded a brigade in the Valley campaign. Fighting at McDowell, Winchester, and Port Republic, he succeeded Winder at Cedar Mountain in command of the Stonewall division (despite Jackson's objection) and commanded this in 2d Bull Run campaign. He was wounded at Groveton. He also led Jackson's division at Fredericksburg. In Feb. '63 he was sent to Savannah. Then called to Charleston, he defended Fort Wagner (18 July '63) and served on James Island for over a year. Because Taliaferro was a kinsman, Seddon hesitated to advocate his promotion, and he was not named Maj. Gen. until 1 Jan. '65. Meanwhile, he served briefly in Fla. and Savannah. After fighting at Bentonville, he surrendered with Johnston. After the war he was a legislator, judge, and member of the Board of Visitors for several Va. institutions. D.A.B. describes him as "six feet tall and full-bearded . . . by tradition and character, a Virginia gentleman and leader."

TAPPAN, James C. C.S.A. gen. Tenn. Commissioned Col. 13th Ark. in May '61, he fought at Belmont (Ky.) 7 Nov. '61, at Shiloh in the "hornets' nest," and at Richmond and Perryville. Appointed B.G. C.S.A. 5 Nov. '62, he led his brigade under Price in Ark. in 1863 and in the Red River campaign of 1864 at Pleasant Hill. Going to Ark. after that, he fought Steele and went with Price into Mo.

TAPP HOUSE, Va. Landmark in battle of WILDERNESS.

TARBELL, Jonathan. Union officer. N.Y. Maj. 24th N.Y. 17 May '61; Lt. Col. 91st N.Y. 16 Dec. '61; dismissed 23 Aug. '62; reinstated 16 June '63; Col.

11 Feb. '65; Bvt. B.G. USV (war service). Died 1888.

TATTNALL, Josiah. 1795-1871. C.S.N. Commodore. Ga. Educated in England, he joined the navy in 1812 as a midshipman and fought also in the Algerine War with Porter against the pirates in the West Indies, and in the Mexican War (wounded). On 20 Feb. '61 he resigned as Capt. and was commissioned senior flag officer in the Ga. navy 28 Feb. In Mar. he was named Capt. C.S.N. Taking command of the naval defenses of Ga. and S.C., he led a force at Fort Royal in Nov. '61, and the following Mar. he was ordered to relieve the wounded BUCHANAN in command of the *Merrimac* after the battle. When the Confederates abandoned the Peninsula, he destroyed the *Merrimac* to prevent her capture and was sent back to the naval defenses of Ga. At his own request a court of inquiry was called about the destruction of the ironclad ram, and he was censured for it. He then demanded a court-martial, which acquitted him 5 July '62. For the remainder of the war he attacked the blockading fleet, defended the Savannah River, and surrendered with Johnston. He moved to Nova Scotia at first and then returned penniless to Ga., where the city created the post of inspector of the port of Savannah for him.

TAYLOR, Benjamin Franklin. WAR CORRESPONDENT. 1819-87. Mass. A schoolteacher in New England and Mich., he had been literary editor of the Chicago *Evening Journal* for 10 years before going to the field in the fall of 1863. More of an essayist than a factual reporter, he turned in remarkable accounts of the battles around Chattanooga and the first part of the Atlanta campaign. In May '64, however, he gave too much information for Sherman to tolerate, and the general ordered him arrested as a spy. Taylor left hurriedly and went to the Shenandoah Valley, where he covered Early's Washington Raid. After the war he quit journalism to free lance, lecture, and write travel books.

TAYLOR, Ezra. Union officer. Ireland. Maj. 1st Ill. Arty. 23 Oct. '61; Col. 27 Oct. '63; Bvt. B.G. USV (war service); resigned 20 Aug. '64. Died 1885.

TAYLOR, George William. Union gen. 1808–62. N.J. An officer in the navy as a young man, he was in the army during the Mexican War and then active in mining and manufacturing. Commissioned Col. 3d N.J. 4 June '61, he was in reserve at 1st Bull Run. During the Peninsular campaign he succeeded Kearny as commander of 1, 1, VI, 18 May '62 after the battles of West Point, and was commissioned B.G. USV 9 May '62. He led this brigade until 31 Aug. '62 when he died of wounds received at 2d Bull Run.

TAYLOR, Jacob E. Union officer. Ohio. 1st Lt. 2d Ohio 17 Apr. '61; mustered out 31 July '61; Capt. 30th Ohio 29 Aug. '61; resigned 29 Oct. '61; Maj. 40th Ohio 11 Dec. '61; Col. 5 Mar. '63; mustered out 7 Oct. '64; Col. 188th Ohio 5 Mar. '65; Bvt. B.G. USV (war service). Commanded 2, 1, IV (Cumberland). Died 1896.

TAYLOR, John P. Union officer. Pa. Capt. 1st Pa. Cav. 10 Aug. '61; Lt. Col. 5 Sept. '62; Col. 2 Mar. '63; Bvt. B.G. USV 4 Aug. '65; mustered out 9 Sept. '64. Commanded in the Army of the Potomac: 1, 2, Cav. Corps; 2d Div., Cav. Corps.

TAYLOR, Joseph Pannel. Union gen. Ky. Entering the R.A. in 1813, he served on Comsy. of Subsist. duty and was breveted for the Mexican War. He was named Col. and Comsy. Gen. of Subsist. 29 Sept. '61, appointed B.G. USV 9 Feb. '63, and died 29 June '64.

TAYLOR, Nelson. Union gen. 1821–94. Conn. In the Mexican War, he then settled in Calif. and held several public offices before being commissioned Col. 72d N.Y. 23 July '61. During the Peninsular campaign he led 2, 2, III (13 Mar.–11 May '62) and was promoted B.G. USV 7 Sept. '62. He also led 3, 2, I (4 Oct.–13 Dec. '62) and succeeded to division 4 Oct.–5 Nov. '62. The following 19 Jan. he resigned and was Democratic Congressman from N.Y. 1865–67.

TAYLOR, Richard ("Dick"). C.S.A. gen. 1826–79. Ky. Appt.-La. The son of Zachary Taylor, he studied at Edinburgh, in France, and at Harvard and Yale before becoming a La. plantation owner. At first a Whig, he joined the Democratic party and voted for secession at the La. convention. Commissioned Col. 9th La., he arrived too late for 1st Bull Run. Appointed B.G. C.S.A. 21 Oct. '61, he commanded the La. brigade under Jackson in the Valley campaign and during the Seven Days' Battles. Although ill during this last campaign, he directed his troops from an ambulance. As Maj. Gen. (28 July '62) he commanded the Dist. of Western La., stopping Banks in the RED RIVER CAMPAIGN OF 1864. Clashing with Kirby Smith, his superior officer, he asked to be relieved after a sprightly exchange of letters. He was promoted Lt. Gen. 16 May '64 to rank from his victory at Sabine C.R. (Mansfield), 8 Apr. On 15 Aug. he took command of the Dept. of East La., Miss., and Ala. Three months later the command of Hood's shattered Army of Tenn. devolved briefly on him before it moved to the Carolinas. After the defeats in the Mobile campaign (17 Mar.–12 Apr. '65) Wilson's raid to Selma (22 Mar.–20 Apr.), and the surrender of Lee (9 Apr.) and J. E. Johnston (26 Apr.), Taylor realized that further resistance in his department would lead only to its devastation. On 2 May he accepted Canby's terms, on 4 May he met Canby at Citronelle (Ala.) to make the surrender official, and on 8 May the paroles of his men were accepted. Although 4 May is generally accepted as the surrender date, Taylor considered 8 May as the date.

After the war he returned to New Orleans to find himself penniless. Taking advantage of his family background and personal friendship with Presidents Johnson and Grant, he did what he could to plead the case of the South during reconstruction. His *Destruction and Reconstruction,* which was first published the year of his death and was republished in 1955, has been characterized by D. S. Freeman as "among the most fascinating of military memoirs" by "the one Confederate general who possessed literary art that approached first rank."

TAYLOR, Thomas H. Wright says he was appointed B.G. C.S.A. 4 Nov. '62 from Ky., but that the president declined to nominate. He died in 1901.

TAYLOR, Thomas Thompson. Union officer. N.J. 2d Lt. 12th Ohio 16 Apr. '61; 1st Lt. 4 May '61; mustered out 25 July '61; Capt. 47th Ohio 7 Aug. '61; Maj. 1 May '63; Bvt. B.G. USV (war service).

TEBE, Marie. VIVANDIÈRE. Going with the 114th Pa. ("Collis's Zouaves"), she served throughout the war with them. Frank Rauscher in his regimental history, *Music on the March, 1862-65, with the Army of the Potomac,* says "even Marie, the vivandière, received . . . [a medal], but she would not wear it, remarking that General Birney could keep it, as she did not want the present. Had it been made of gold, instead of copper, Marie would have set a higher value upon the souvenir. She was a courageous woman, and often got with-

in range of the enemy's fire whilst parting with the contents of her canteen among our wounded men. Her skirts were riddled by bullets during the battle of Chancellorsville. After that admonition she kept well out of danger" (p. 68).

TENNESSEE, THE. Confederate ram outfitted and commissioned at Mobile on 16 Feb. '64. It was 209 feet long, 48 feet in beam, and armed with six heavy Brooke rifles in an inclined casemate with six inches of armor forward and four inches aft. She served as Buchanan's flagship in the battle of MOBILE BAY, 5 Aug. '64, and was captured.

TENNESSEE, CONFEDERATE ARMY OF. This, the principal Confederate army of the West, was formed on 20 Nov. '62 under Bragg by the merger of Kirby Smith's Army of Ky. and Bragg's Army of Miss. Kirby Smith had been under Bragg's orders in the previous operations that culminated in the battle of Perryville, 8 Oct., and his command had been referred to as "Kirby Smith's Corps" (Horn, 188). In the reorganization of 20 Nov. his force was technically "Kirby Smith's Corps, Army of Tenn." (Miller, X, 258), but it did not actually exist as such. (See Kirby SMITH'S CORPS.) In mid-Dec. Bragg's army was critically weakened by the detachment of Stevenson's division (10,000 men) to reinforce Pemberton at Vicksburg.

In its first engagement, at Stones River (Murfreesboro), Bragg's army numbered 38,000 effectives. It contained the infantry corps of Polk and Hardee and Wheeler's cavalry division. When it dropped back to block the approaches to Chattanooga from Murfreesboro it was reinforced to 44,000 effectives. Turned out of these defensive positions by Rosecrans's skillfully conducted Tullahoma campaign, June '63, Bragg's army withdrew behind the Tennessee

River. On 25 July the Department of TENNESSEE was created.

In Sept. '63 Bragg was reinforced by Longstreet's corps (less Pickett's division) from Va., and by the brigades of W. H. T. Walker, Gregg, and McNair from Miss. Forrest's cavalry also joined him. The army now numbered 47,500 infantry and 14,500 cavalry. The infantry corps were commanded by Polk, D. H. Hill (vice Hardee), Buckner, Longstreet, and W. H. T. Walker. A reserve division, 3,500 men under Bushrod Johnson, was also designated. (In some accounts Walker's command is called the reserve corps, and Bushrod Johnson's force is shown as part of Buckner's corps.) Wheeler and Forrest each led a cavalry corps.

After the battle of Chickamauga there was another reorganization. Polk was relieved of command (for alleged disobedience of orders); on 23 Oct. '63 he was ordered to the Army of Miss. and Hardee was ordered to rejoin Bragg from the latter army. D. H. Hill and Buckner also left. The Army of Tenn. was then reorganized into three corps: Longstreet's, Hardee's, and Breckinridge's. In early Nov. '63 Longstreet's corps was detached to operate against Burnside at Knoxville.

Bragg was relieved on 2 Dec. '63. Before J. E. Johnston assumed command on 27 Dec., the army was headed temporarily by Hardee (2–22 Dec.) and Polk (23–26 Dec.).

Johnston's Army of Tenn. was reorganized into the corps of Hardee, Hood, Polk, and Wheeler's cavalry for the Atlanta campaign. Hardee had taken over Polk's original (I) corps. Polk was absent from late Dec. '63 until he rejoined the Army of Tenn. on 12 May '64 with his Army of Miss. to form the third corps.

Hood relieved Johnston 18 July '64. After the unsuccessful Franklin and Nashville campaign Hood was relieved at his own request and succeeded by Dick Taylor 23 Jan. '65. Johnston resumed command of the greatly weakened army on 25 Feb., together with all troops in the Confederate Dept. of S.C., Ga., and Fla. On 16 Mar. Beauregard was announced as second-in-command, and A. P. Stewart took command of the infantry and artillery of the Army of Tenn. At this time Johnston's enlarged command included the troops of Hardee in the far South and those of Bragg in N.C. The Army of Tenn. numbered about 20,000. On 9 Apr. there was another reorganization, after which the army comprised the infantry corps of Hardee, A. P. Stewart, S. D. Lee, and Hampton's cavalry (including Wheeler's corps and M. C. Butler's division).

Hostilities were suspended 18 Apr. and Johnston surrendered 26 Apr. '65 at Bennett's House, near Durham Station, N.C.

TENNESSEE, CONFEDERATE DEPARTMENT OF. Created 25 July '63 under Bragg on the suggestion of Buckner (Horn, 241), whose troops of the Dept. of EAST TENNESSEE became the III or "Buckner's" corps of Bragg's Army of TENNESSEE. Note that the latter was in existence before the department of the same name was created.

The new department encompassed the following area: central Tenn. and northern Ala. as bounded by the Tennessee River; northern Ga. above the line of the railroad West Point–Atlanta (inclusive)–Augusta; the western tips of S.C., N.C., and Va. (on a line running generally north from Augusta); and bounded on the north by the Ky. border. Note that this includes the Department of EAST TENNESSEE, although the latter actually continued to be a separate department (O.R. atlas, CLXVIII).

Area encompassed by the Dept. of

Tenn. by mid-'64 had been reorganized to include eastern Ala., a portion of west Fla.; a portion of northeast Ga. was excluded (see O.R. atlas, plate CLXIX).

TENNESSEE, UNION DEPARTMENT AND ARMY OF THE. Created 16 Oct. '62 to include Cairo, Forts Henry and Donelson, northern Miss., and portions of Ky. and Tenn. west of the Tennessee River. Maj. Gen. U. S. Grant was in command. Until 18 Dec. the troops of this department were designated the XIII Army Corps; after that date they were organized into the XIII, XV, XVI, and XVII Corps, and were commonly referred to as the Army of the Tenn. Maj. Gen. W. T. Sherman commanded this army from 24 Oct. '63–26 Mar. '64. Maj. Gen. James B. Mc-Pherson then commanded the army until his death at Atlanta, 22 July '64. Subsequent commanders were Maj. Gens. John A. Logan, 22–27 July; Otis O. Howard until 19 May '65; and John A. Logan until 1 Aug. '65.

TENNESSEE AND GEORGIA, CONFEDERATE DEPARTMENT OF. Under Hood this was presumably created 17 Oct. '64 when the Military DIVISION OF THE WEST was organized. It covered the same general area as the former Dept. of Tenn., but with the exclusion of Ala. and the addition of western Tenn. The portion of Tenn. generally north of the line Paris–Nashville was excluded (and was in the Dept. of Western Ky.); northwestern Ga., bounded generally by a line northeast to southwest through Atlanta, was in the new department. In early 1865 the boundaries had been extended to include all of Ga. west of the line Augusta–Macon–Jacksonville (Ga.)–Cedar Keys, Fla. (exclusive). Eastern Fla. between the latter line and the Chattahoochee River were also in the department.

TENNESSEE RIVER. Capture of Federal transports, 29 and 30 Oct. '64. See FORREST'S OPERATIONS DURING ATLANTA CAMPAIGN.

TEPE, Marie. See Marie TEBE.

TERRELL, Alex W. C.S.A. gen. Appt.-Tex. Commissioned Maj. 1st Tex. Cav. at the beginning of the war, he served as Lt. Col. of Terrell's Tex. Cavalry Battalion. This group became Terrell's Tex. Cav. Regt. and then the 34th Tex. Cav. when he was promoted Col. He fought mainly in Tex. and La. and was assigned as B.G. C.S.A. 16 May '65 by Kirby Smith in the Trans-Miss. Dept. Wood confirms Wright in the above information, but C. M. H. does not list him.

TERRILL, James Barbour. C.S.A. gen. 1838–64. Va. After graduating from V. M. I. he was a lawyer. He was commissioned Maj. in May '61 in A. P. Hill's 13th Va. As Col. he led the regiment at 1st Bull Run, Cross Keys, Port Republic, Cedar Run, 2d Bull Run, Fredericksburg, the Wilderness and Spotsylvania. Killed 30 May '64 at Bethesda Church, he was buried by the Union forces. The Senate confirmed his appointment as B.G. C.S.A. the day after his death. His brother, William R. Terrill, Union B.G., was killed at Perryville.

TERRILL, William Rufus. Union gen. 1834–62. Va. USMA 1853 (16/52); Arty. He taught at West Point, fought in the Seminole War, and served on the frontier during the Kans. disturbances. As Capt. 5th US Arty. 14 May '61, he served as acting I.G. of the Dept. of Washington and was then Chief of Arty. for the 2d Div., Army of the Ohio, during Buell's campaign of Jan.–June '62. He commanded a battery that was singled out for special mention at Shiloh and also participated in the advance upon and siege of Corinth. Promoted

B.G. USV 9 Sept. '62, he commanded 33d Brig., 10th Div., Army Ohio in Sept. and 33d Brig., 10th Div., I, Army Ohio from Sept. until 8 Oct. '62, when he was killed at Perryville. Brother of James, above. See also SHERIDAN, Philip Henry.

TERRY, Alfred Howe. Union gen. 1827-90. Conn. After Yale, he practiced law until commissioned Col. 2d Conn. 7 May '61 in a three-months regiment. He led them at 1st Bull Run, was mustered out 7 Aug., and commissioned Col. 7th Conn. 17 Sept. '61. In S.C. he led this regiment in the Port Royal expedition, fighting at Fort Pulaski 10-11 Apr. '62 and then at Secessionville 16 June. He had been commissioned B.G. USV 25 Apr. '62 and commanded the forces at Hilton Head, X, South (20 Oct. '62-12 May '63) at Pocotaligo Bridge. During the siege of Battery Wagner he commanded 1st Div., Morris Island, X, South (6-19 July '63) and then commanded Morris Island (19 July -18 Oct. and 10 Nov. '63-15 Jan. '64). He commanded the Northern Dist., X, South (17 Jan.-Feb. '64 and Mar.-Apr. '64) and led 1st Div., X, Va. and N.C. (4 May-11 June; 21 June-18 July and 23 July-10 Oct. '64). He succeeded to the command of the X Corps, Va. and N.C. (28 Apr.-4 May; 14-21 July; 18-23 July; 10 Oct.-4 Nov. and 18 Nov.-3 Dec. '64) around Richmond and Petersburg. He commanded the 1st Div., XXIV, Va. 3-6 Dec. '64 and led the corps 6 Dec. '64-2 Jan. '65. During the period 6 Jan.-27 Mar. '65 he commanded TERRY'S PROVISIONAL CORPS, N.C. (see CORPS) and then commanded the X Corps, N.C. (27 Mar.-13 May '65) under Schofield in the Carolinas. He commanded the Dept. of Va. May-27 June '65. Continuing in the R.A., he was breveted for war service (Maj. Gen. USV 26 Aug. '64) and Wilmington (Maj. Gen. USA), and was one of 15

in the army to receive the THANKS OF CONGRESS, winning it for Fort Fisher. He was appointed B.G. USA 15 Jan. '65 and retired in 1888 as Maj. Gen. USA. Holding departmental commands in the West and participating mainly in Indian fighting, he was Custer's superior during the Little Big Horn incident. He was later on several Indian treaty boards and also a member of the commission that reviewed the Fitz-John Porter case in 1878. D.A.B. describes him as "about six feet in height, straight, vigorous and active ... [with the supreme] ability to cooperate with superiors, equals, or subordinates."

TERRY, Henry Dwight. Union gen. 1812-69. Conn. A lawyer, he was commissioned Col. 5th Mich. 10 June '61 and was promoted B.G. USV 17 July '62. In the Army of Va., VII Corps, he led Terry's brigade, Division at Suffolk (21 Jan.-9 Apr. '63) and 1st Brig., 1st Div. (9 Apr.-11 July '63). He also commanded 3d Div., VI, Potomac (4 Aug. '63-10 Jan. '64) and resigned 7 Feb. '65.

TERRY, William. C.S.A. gen. 1824-88. Va. After graduating from the Univ. of Va. he practiced law and edited a newspaper as well as serving as Lt. in a militia company. With it he went to Harpers Ferry when John Brown invaded in 1859. Commissioned 1st Lt. 4th Va. in Apr. '61, he served at Harpers Ferry under Jackson and fought at 1st Bull Run. He was named Maj. in the spring of 1862 and fought at Gaines's Mill, Malvern Hill, Cedar Mountain, and 2d Bull Run (wounded). Still a Maj., he commanded the regiment at Fredericksburg, Chancellorsville, Gettysburg, and Paine's Farm, and was named Col. in Sept. '63. After fighting in the Wilderness and Spotsylvania, he was appointed B.G. C.S.A. 19 May '64 and commanded his brigade at Cold Harbor, Petersburg, Shepherdstown, Winchester (wounded), and the final battles around Petersburg. He was again wounded, 25 Mar. '65, at Fort Stedman. After the war he was a lawyer and Congressman.

TERRY, William Richard. C.S.A. gen 1817–97. Va. After graduating from V. M. I. he was a farmer and business-man before being commissioned Capt. of C.S.A. Cav. He fought at 1st Bull Run and was named Col. 24th Va. in Sept. '61. Severely wounded leading a charge at Williamsburg, he returned to his regiment for 2d Bull Run and suc-ceeded Corse in command of Kemper's brigade. At Gettysburg he was wounded in "Pickett's Charge" and again com-manded Kemper's brigade at the Wilder-ness. He went to the Dept. of N.C. and Southern Va. with Pickett, fought at New Bern, and returned to the Army of Northern Va. to fight at Drewry's Bluff and command a brigade in the defenses of Richmond. Appointed B.G. C.S.A. 31 May '64, he fought with Early in the Shenandoah, returned to Petersburg. He was severely wounded 31 Mar. '65 near Dinwiddie C.H. and surrendered at Appomattox. In the legislature after the war, he held other public offices also.

TERRY'S TEXAS RANGERS. See TEXAS RANGERS.

TEVIS, C. Carroll. *Nom de guerre* of Washington Carroll Tevis. See below.

TEVIS, Washington Carroll. Union officer. c. 1828–1900. Pa. USMA 1849 (24/43); Inf. Resigned 1850 as Bvt. 2d Lt.; entered the Turkish Army under the name of Nessim Bey. He served as Bim-bachi (Maj.) 4 Feb. '54 and Quaimaquam (Lt. Col.) 19 June '54. He lived in Paris from 1854 to 1861 and returned for the Civil War. Lt. Col. 4th Del. 18 Aug. '62; mustered out 25 Sept. '63; Lt. Col. 3d Md. Cav. 26 Sept. '63; Col. 23 Dec. '63; Bvt. B.G. USV (war service); discharged 20 July '64. Served

in volunteers under the name of and listed by Phisterer as C. Carroll Tevis. Cullum characterizes him as "soldier of fortune, France, Egypt, Turkey." He died in Paris.

TEW, George Washington. Union offi-cer. R.I. Maj. 4th R.I. 30 Oct. '61; Lt. Col. 20 Nov. '61; resigned 11 Aug. '62; Capt. 5th R.I. Arty. 24 Sept. '62; Maj. 1 Oct. '62; Lt. Col. 2 Mar. '63; Bvt. B.G. USV (war service). Died 1884.

TEXAS. Although a great number of the population opposed it, the state se-ceded on 1 Feb. '61, the 25th anni-versary of Texas' Declaration of Inde-pendence from Mexico. Gov. Sam Houston had fought this move and was forced from office, Lt. Gov. Edward L. Clark succeeding him. Tex. furnished between 50,000 and 65,000 troops to the Confederate Army. Little damaged by the war, the state rejoined the Union in 1869.

According to the census of 1850, Tex. had four times as many cattle and horses as all other Southern states put together.

TEXAS, CONFEDERATE DE-PARTMENT AND DISTRICT OF. See TRANS-MISSISSIPPI, CONFEDERATE DISTRICT, DEPARTMENT, AND ARMY OF.

TEXAS, UNION DEPARTMENT OF. In existence at the start of the war, comprising the entire state, with headquarters at San Antonio and com-manded by Brig. Gen. David E. Twiggs. The latter, on 18 Jan. '61, surrendered all Federal posts and property to state authorities before resigning his Federal commission and joining the Confederate cause. (Twiggs was the only R.A. officer who committed such treason; others of Southern sympathies had first turned over their Federal troops and property to proper Federal authorities before sub-mitting their resignations.) The state be-came part of the Dept. of the Gulf when the latter was organized 23 Feb. '62; and part of the Mil. Div. of W. Miss. 7 May '64.

TEXAS COAST OPERATIONS OF BANKS IN 1863.

After the Federal capture of Vicksburg and Port Hudson had opened the Mississippi, Banks's Dept. of the Gulf was reinforced by Ord's XIII Corps, and on 24 July '63 he was ordered to "raise the flag in Texas." Federal authorities thought this necessary to discourage any idea the French might have of invading the state from Mexico. Although Halleck advocated a movement up the Red River, Banks was allowed to select his own line of operations. He chose Sabine Pass as his objective, with a view toward advancing from there to Beaumont and Houston. This led to failure at SABINE PASS, 8 Sept. '63.

Banks then decided to land near the mouth of the Rio Grande and work his way eastward. On 26 Oct. 3,500 men of the XIII Corps, under N. J. T. Dana, left New Orleans with an escort of three warships (*Monongahela, Owasco,* and *Virginia*). Com. J. H. Strong headed the naval element and Banks accompanied the expedition as over-all commander. After weathering a severe storm on the 30th, on 2 Nov. Dana made a successful landing against light opposition on Brazos Island at the mouth of the Rio Grande. The next day a landing was made on the mainland and Brownsville, 30 miles away, was occupied on the 6th. Dana was left to hold the Rio Grande, while a strong force under T. E. G. Ransom re-embarked on the 16th and landed at Corpus Christi. After marching 22 miles to the upper end of Mustang Island, Ransom's troops with the support of the *Monongahela* captured a small three-gun fort. The Federals then crossed Aransas Pass and laid siege to Fort Esperanza at Pass Cavallo at the entrance to Matagorda Bay (27–29 Nov.). On the 30th the Confederates withdrew, and the light gunboats *Granite City* and *Estrella* entered the bay.

Although Banks had achieved his purpose of raising the Federal flag in Tex., he found his further advance stopped by powerful fortifications at the mouth of the Brazos and at GALVESTON. He felt these could be taken only from the land side, and for such an operation he needed reinforcements. Halleck refused to send additional troops and again advanced his idea of operating up the Red River. Banks therefore started planning his RED RIVER CAMPAIGN OF 1864. Federal garrisons of McClernand's XIII Corps were left at Brownsville and Matagorda Island.

TEXAS, NEW MEXICO, AND ARIZONA, CONFEDERATE DISTRICT OF. See TRANS-MISSISSIPPI, CONFEDERATE DISTRICT, DEPARTMENT, AND ARMY OF.

TEXAS RANGERS. An element of the Confederate Army that was begun in 1836 as a semi-military mounted police force to protect the settlers from Indians. During the Tex. War for Independence they were reorganized by Sam Houston and numbered about 1,600 at that time. B. F. Terry and Thomas S. Lubbock raised a regiment that became the 8th Tex. Cav. and was usually called Terry's Texas Rangers. Fighting in the West, the unit had a fine war record. There were also so-called Texas Ranger companies in the state during the war on militia duty. In the 1870's the Rangers were reorganized again as a police force to patrol the frontier and protect against Indians, bandits, and rustlers. Their great moral influence and exceptional bravery made them a potent force in the era, and they continue in the present time to perform as a state law-enforcement agency separate from the state police.

THANKS OF CONGRESS. Only 15 army officers were given the Thanks of Congress for their actions during the Civil War. They are listed below in the order the joint resolutions were approved and with a brief reference to the reason.

Nathaniel Lyon, 24 Dec. '61, for Wilson's Creek.

W. S. Rosecrans, 3 Mar. '63, for Stones River.

U. S. Grant, 17 Dec. '63, for the gallantry and good conduct of his officers, men, and himself. Grant was at this time also voted a gold medal, the only one awarded in the war.

N. P. Banks, 28 Jan. '64, for Port Hudson.

A. E. Burnside, 28 Jan. '64, for the "gallantry, good conduct, and soldier-like endurance" of himself and his command.

Joseph Hooker, 28 Jan. '64, for defense of Baltimore and Washington.

George Meade } 28 Jan. '64, for
O. O. Howard } Gettysburg.

W. T. Sherman, 19 Feb. '64, for Chattanooga campaign.

Joseph Bailey, 11 June '64, for saving Porter's gunboat flotilla.

W. T. Sherman, 10 Jan. '65, for operations in Ga.

A. H. Terry, 24 Jan. '65, for Fort Fisher.

P. H. Sheridan, 9 Feb. '65, for his Shenandoah Valley campaign.

G. H. Thomas, 3 Mar. '65, for Franklin and Nashville.

W. S. Hancock, 21 Apr. '66, for "services with the Army of the Potomac in 1863" (Gettysburg).

Curtis, Newton Martin, for Fort Fisher.

THAYER, John Milton. Union gen. 1820–1906. Mass. A lawyer, he was the first B.G. of the Nebr. Terr. Mil. and after Indian fighting was then elected Maj. Gen. by the legislature. Upon outbreak of war he was commissioned Col. 1st Nebr. 21 July '61 and commanded 2, 2d Div. Mil. Dist. Cairo, Army Tenn. (1–17 Feb. '62) at Fort Donelson. At Shiloh he led 2, 3, Div., Army Tenn. (17 Feb.–June '62) and was promoted B.G. USV 4 Oct. '62. Also in the Army of the Tenn., he commanded 3, 11, XIII (Dec. '62); 3, 4th Div. Yazoo Expedition (Dec. '62–Jan. '63); 3, 1, XV (3 Jan.–1 Aug. '63) during the Vicksburg campaign, and 1st Div., XV (27–28 July '63). He then went to the VII Corps, Ark., and led Dist. Frontier (23 Feb.–24 Mar.; 19 May–3 Dec. '64 and 5 Jan.–1 Feb. '65) and Dist. Eastern Ark. (25 May–12 June '65). Breveted Maj. Gen. USV for war service, he resigned 19 July '65 and was a Republican US Sen. 1867–71 ("ardent and active radical"). He was appointed Gov. of the Wyo. Territory 1875–79 and elected Gov. of Nebr. 1886–92. A relative of Sylvanus THAYER.

THAYER, Sylvanus. Union officer and "Father of the Military Academy." 1785–1872 Mass. USMA 1808 * (3/15); Engrs. He served on engineering projects in the East and fought in the War of 1812 before going to West Point in 1817 as Superintendent. He organized the course of instruction and established academic procedures that remained basically the same for 150 years. In 1833 he returned to engineering posts. He was retired 1 June '63 as Col. (3 Mar. '63) and Bvt. B.G. USA (31 May '63). Aside from his identification with West Point, Thayer had a tremendous influence on the development of engineering schools in the US and has been called the "Father of American Technology."

* There was no class standing prior to 1818, and cadets are listed in the order in which they were commissioned.

THEORY OF NULLIFICATION. See John C. CALHOUN.

THIRTEENTH AMENDMENT. See ABOLITION OF SLAVERY.

THOM, George. Union officer. c. 1819–91. N.H. USMA 1839 (7/31); Engrs. He served on engineering duty on the frontier, in the Mexican War, and road-building in the West. Named Maj. 9 Sept. '61 (Capt. since 1853), he was Chief Topo. Engr. for the Dept. of the Mo. until 11 Mar. '62, and for the Dept. of the Miss. to 11 July '62. He was Halleck's Chief Topo. Engr. in the advance upon siege of Corinth 15 Apr.–30 May '62 and on his staff 11 July '62–20 Aug. '65. Promoted Col. Add. A.D.C. 16 Nov. '61, he continued in the R.A., retiring in 1883 as Col. and Bvt. B.G. USA.

THOMAS, Allen. C.S.A. gen. 1830–1907. Md. He graduated from Princeton and was practicing law when he moved to La., the home of his wife, a sister-in-law of Richard Taylor. When the war came he was commissioned Maj. in a unit that became the 28th La. and was promoted Col. in Oct. '62 to rank from the previous 3 May. He fought at Chickasaw Bluffs and Vicksburg, where he temporarily commanded a brigade and carried Pemberton's report to Davis. Named B.G. C.S.A. 4 Feb. '64, he took over H. W. Allen's La. brig. and succeeded Polignac in command of the division when the French general returned home. After the war he was a planter, agricultural professor at La. State Univ. and active in Democratic politics. Going into the diplomatic corps, he was consul at La Guaira and then Envoy Extraordinary and Minister Plenipotentiary to Venezuela.

THOMAS, Bryan Morel. C.S.A. gen. c. 1836–1905. Ga. USMA 1858 (22/27); Inf. He served in garrison and on the frontier, participating in Indian fighting and the Utah Expedition, before resigning 6 Apr. '61 as 2d Lt. Commissione' Lt. on Jones M. Withers' staff, he served at Shiloh, in the Ky. campaign and at Stones River. He was promoted Maj. and served under Withers in Ala before being made Col. of a reserv regiment. Named B.G. C.S.A. 4 Aug. '64, he commanded the Ala. reserve brigade and fought at Spanish Fort and Blakely. After the war he was a planter and teacher.

THOMAS, Charles. Union officer. Pa. Commissioned 3d Lt. in 1819, he served on the frontier, in the Mexican War (1 brevet), and in the Q.M. Gen.'s office before the war. As Col. Asst. Q.M. Gen. (since 1856), he was in England purchasing army clothing from Oct. '61 to May '62 and spent the rest of the war on inspection duty and in Washington. Retired in 1866, he was breveted B.G. USA 5 July '64 and Maj. Gen. USA. Died 1878.

THOMAS, De Witt Clinton. Union officer. Ind. Maj. 18th Ind. 16 Aug. '61; Lt. Col. 10 June '62; Col. 93d Ind. 21 Oct. '62; Bvt. B.G. USV (war service). Died 1882.

THOMAS, Edward Lloyd. C.S.A. gen. ?–1898. Ga. After graduating from Emory College, he fought in the Mexican War and returned to run his plantation. He was a wealthy and prominent man when commissioned Col. 35th Ga., 15 Oct. '61. At Seven Pines he succeeded Pettigrew in command of his brigade and during the Seven Days' Battles he succeeded Anderson when the latter returned to the Tredegar Iron Works. Although wounded in that campaign, he did not relinquish command. He led his brigade at 2d Bull Run and Antietam before being appointed B.G. C.S.A. 1 Nov. '62. For the remainder of the war he led this unit, fighting at Fredericksburg, Chancellorsville, Gettysburg, the Wilderness, Spotsylvania, Petersburg, and Appomattox. Returning to his plantation, he was appointed by Cleveland to several offices in the Land and Indian Depts.

THOMAS, George Henry. "The Rock of Chickamauga" and Union gen. 1816-70. Va. USMA 1840 (12/42); Arty. He fought in the Seminole War, served on garrison and frontier duty, and won two brevets in the Mexican War. After teaching artillery and cavalry at West Point, he served as Maj. in the newly-formed 2d US Cav. under A. S. Johnston and R. E. Lee and with Hardee, Stoneman, Hood, Fitz Lee, and Van Dorn. Severely wounded in the face by an arrow, he was given on 1 Nov. '60 a 12-month leave of absence. Although a Virginian, he remained loyal to the Union. Named Lt. Col. 25 Apr. and Col. 3 May '61 in the 2d US Cav., he was transferred to the 5th US Cav. 5 Aug. and appointed B.G. USV 3 Aug. '61. In the Dept. of Pa., he led 1st Brig., 1st Div. (June–25 July '61) and 1st Brig., Shenandoah (July–Aug. '61). He then commanded 1st Brig., Banks's division, Potomac (17 Aug.–27 Aug. '61) and was engaged in organizing and recruiting at Camp Dick Robinson that fall. At Mill Springs (Ky.), Shiloh, and on the advance upon Corinth, he commanded 1st Div., Army of the Ohio (2 Dec. '61–29 Sept. '62) and was second-in-command of the Army of the Ohio (29 Sept.–Nov. '62) at Perryville. When Buell retreated to Louisville, the powers in Washington directed Thomas to supersede him in command, but Thomas declined, saying that Buell had already issued orders for the offensive. He was promoted Maj. Gen. USV 25 Apr. '62 and commanded the Centre Div., XIV, Cumberland (5 Nov. '62–9 Jan. '63) at Stones River. In the Tullahoma campaign and at Chickamauga he commanded the XIV Corps

(9 Jan.–28 Oct. '63) and was promoted B.G. USA 27 Oct. '63. He then took command of the Army and Dept. of the Cumberland (20 Oct. '63–27 June '65), leading it at Lookout Mountain, Missionary Ridge, in the Atlanta campaign, and at Franklin and Nashville. He was then promoted Maj. Gen. USA 15 Dec. '64 for Nashville. Described by D.A.B. as "six feet in height and weighing about 200 pounds . . . [he was] studious in his habits, deliberate but decided in action, and fastidious to the point of exasperation." He acquired, by his eccentricities, one of the most formidable lists of nicknames in the US Army, being called "Old Tom" as a cadet, "Slow Trot" as an instructor at the Military Academy, "Pap Thomas" by the soldiers of the Army of the Cumberland and, his most famous, "The Rock of Chickamauga" for his glorious feat in holding the left wing against tremendous odds. Continuing in the R.A., he died on active duty while commanding the Mil. Div. of the Pacific. He was given the Thanks of Congress for Franklin and Nashville, one of the 15 army officers so honored during the entire war.

THOMAS, Henry Goddard. Union gen. 1837–97. Me. A lawyer, he was commissioned Capt. 5th Me. (24 June–26 Aug. '61), entering the R.A. on 5 Aug. as Capt. 11th US Inf. He had fought at 1st Bull Run and, in Oct. '62, at Snickers Gap. Commissioned Col. 79th US Col. Inf. 20 Mar. '63, he was said to be the first regular officer to accept a colonelcy of colored troops. He became Col. 19th US Col. Inf. 16 Jan. '64 and commanded 2, 4, IX, Potomac (4 May–7 Sept. '64) at the Wilderness, Spotsylvania, and the Petersburg mine, and 2, 3, IX (Oct.–26 Nov. '64) at Hatcher's Run. Promoted B.G. USV 30 Nov. '64, he led the 3, 3, XXV, Va. (15–31 Dec. '64) and 3, 1, XXV, Va.

(31 Dec. '64–27 Apr. '65) during the siege of Petersburg. Breveted for Spotsylvania, Petersburg siege, and war service (B.G. USA and Maj. Gen. USV), he continued in the R.A. until 1891, when he retired as Maj. and Paymaster.

THOMAS, Lorenzo. Union gen. c. 1805–75. Del. USMA 1823 (17/35); Inf. He fought in the Seminole War, was Butler's Chief of Staff in the Mexican War (1 brevet), and served as Scott's Chief of Staff until 7 Mar. '61. Named Col. Asst. Adj. Gen. on the latter date and B.G. USA, the Adj. Gen., 7 May '61, he continued in that post until 23 Mar. '63, when he took over the organization of colored troops. Retired in 1869, he was breveted Maj. Gen. USA for war service.

THOMAS, Minor T. Union officer. Ind. 2d Lt. 1st Minn. 29 Apr '61; 1st Lt. 16 July '61; Lt. Col. 4th Minn. 23 Dec. '61; Col. 8th Minn. 24 Aug. '62; Bvt. B.G. USV. Commanded 3, 1, XXIII (Ohio); 3, 1, Prov. Corps (N.C.); 3, 1, XXIII (N.C.); 1st Div., XXIII (N.C.).

THOMAS, Samuel. Union officer. Ohio. 1st Lt. 27th Ohio 7 Aug. '61; Capt. 31 Mar. '62; Lt. Col. 63d US Col. Inf. 10 Oct. '63; Col. 64th US Col. Inf. 1 Jan. '64; Bvt. B.G. USV (war service). Died 1903.

THOMAS, Stephen. Union gen. 1809–? Vt. A legislator and judge, he was commissioned Col. 8th Vt. 18 Feb. '62 and led his regiment on Butler's New Orleans expedition the next month. Wounded 12 Apr. '63 at Port Hudson, he commanded 2, 1, XIX, Gulf 14 May–11 July '63 and went on the Red River campaign of 1864. Transferring to the Army of the Shenandoah, he led his regiment at Winchester and Fishers Hill and commanded 2, 1, XIX (15 Oct.–24 Oct. '64) at Cedar Creek and later (1 Nov.–3 Dec. '64). Mustered out 24 Aug. '65, he was Lt. Gov. of Vt. 1867–

68 and in 1892 was awarded the Medal of Honor for Cedar Creek.

THOMPSON, Charles Robinson. Union officer. Me. Appt.-Mo. 1st Lt. Engr. Regt. of the West 1 Nov. '61; Capt. A.D.C. Vols. 14 Nov. '62; Col. 12th US Col. Inf. 17 Aug. '63; Bvt. B.G. USV 13 Apr. '65 (war service). Commanded 2d Brig. Col. Dist. Etowah (Cumberland); 3d Sub-dist. East Tenn. (Cumberland). Died 1894.

THOMPSON, David. Incorrect listing by Phisterer for Thomson, David.

THOMPSON, Henry Elmer. Union officer. N.Y. Capt. 6th Mich. Cav. 13 Oct. '62; Lt. Col. 10 June '63; Bvt. B.G. USV (war service); discharged 6 June '64. W.I.A. at Hunterstown (Pa.) 2 July '63.

THOMPSON, James M. Although listed by Phisterer as Lt. Col. 107th Pa. and Bvt. B.G. USV 13 Mar. '65, he does not appear in Heitman or Dyer.

THOMPSON, John Leverett. Union officer. N.H. Pvt. Co. A 1st Ill. Arty. 17 Apr. '61; mustered out 16 July '61; 1st Lt. 1st R.I. Cav. 19 Oct. '61; Capt. 3 Dec. '61; Maj. 4 Aug. '62; Lt. Col. 15 Aug. '62; resigned 24 Mar. '64; Col. 1st N.H. Cav. 29 July '64; Bvt. B.G. USV (war service). Commanded 2, 3, Cav. Corps (Shenandoah). Died 1888.

THOMPSON, M. Jeff. C.S.A. partisan fighter. The mayor of St. Joseph, Mo., in 1860, he was a "lank and colorful Virginian with Yankee mechanical ingenuity and a love of deadly weapons" (Monaghan). After the bombardment of Sumter he organized a battalion and offered it to Gov. Jackson. When refused, he took his troops south, saying that he wanted to protect his state from Blair. He marched with 5,000 men on Giradeau, Mo., when Frémont took over the department. Davis then ordered Pillow to send a detachment of troops to join Thompson's "Swamp Rats," as they

were called, at New Madrid. When
Frémont issued his emancipation proclamation in Aug. '61 Thompson issued
a counter-proclamation and started a
series of raids along the border to give
it emphasis. He directed the rams at
Fort Pillow and in Mar. '62 joined Van
Dorn's command in the Trans-Miss. In
1864 he succeeded Shanks in Price's expedition and surrendered finally on 9
May '65.

THOMPSON, Robert. Union officer.
Pa. Lt. Col. 115th Pa. 16 Apr. '62;
Bvt. B.G. USV (war service); resigned
15 Jan. '63. Died 1880.

THOMPSON, William. Union officer.
Pa. Capt. 1st Iowa Cav. 31 July '61;
Maj. 18 May '63; Col. 20 June '64; Bvt.
B.G. USV (war service). Commanded
2, Cav. Div., VII (Ark.). Other brevets
for Prairie Grove (Ark.), Bayou Meto
(Ark.). Continued in R.A. until retired
in 1875 as Capt. Died 1897.

THOMPSON'S STATION (Spring
Hill, Unionville), Tenn., 4–5 Mar. '63.
In the period of inactivity following the
battle of Stones River a strong Federal
force of one infantry and one cavalry
brigade was sent from Franklin to reconnoiter toward Columbia. At Spring Hill
they were surrounded by Van Dorn with
the cavalry divisions of W. H. Jackson
and Forrest. The Federal cavalry under
T. J. Jordan escaped, but the infantry
under John Coburn (3, 1, Res. Corps,
Army of the Cumberland) with a battery of artillery was forced to surrender.
Of 2,837 Federals engaged in the two
days' fighting they reported 100 killed,
300 wounded, and 1,306 missing, and
put enemy losses at 150 killed, 450
wounded (E.&B.). The Confederates put
the Federal casualties at 100 killed, 300
wounded, 2,000 missing, and their own
total loss at 300 (Drake).

THOMSON, David. Union officer.
Ohio. 2d Lt. 82d Ohio 4 Oct. '61; Capt.

14 Nov. '61; Maj. 9 Apr. '62; Lt. Col.
29 Aug. '62; Bvt. B.G. USV (war service). Died 1893. Listed by Phisterer as
Thompson, David.

THORN, George. Misspelling by Phisterer for George THOM.

THORNTON, William A. Union officer c. 1803–66. N.Y. USMA 1825
(12/37); Arty.-Ord. He taught at West
Point, served on arsenal and ordnance
duty, and was promoted Maj. 28 May
'61. During the Civil War he commanded the Watervliet Arsenal until 17
Dec. '63, and was promoted Lt. Col.
3 Mar. and Col. 15 Sept. '63. For the
rest of the war he was Inspector of
Contract Arms and Ord. and died on
active duty as Bvt. B.G. USA.

THORP, Thomas Jones. Union offi-
cer. N.Y. Lt. Col. 19th N.Y. Cav. 3
Sept. '62; Col. 1 Mar. '65; Bvt. B.G.
USV (war service).

"THOSE PEOPLE." Term habitually
used by Robert E. Lee in referring to
the enemy.

THROOP, William A. Union officer.
N.Y. 2d Lt. 1st Mich. 1 May '61; mustered out 1 Aug. '61; Capt. 1st Mich. 16
Sept. '61; Maj. 30 Aug. '62; Lt. Col.
18 Mar. '63; Col. 22 Dec. '64; Bvt. B.G.
USV. Brevets for "battles in the campaign" through 1864; duty and discipline. Wounded at Gaines's Mill (Va.)
27 June '62; Gettysburg 2 July '63; Cold
Harbor (Va.) 30 May '64; Petersburg
30 June '64. Died 1884.

THRUSTON, Charles Mynn. Union
gen. 1789–1873. Ky. Appt.-D.C. USMA
1814 *-Arty. Fighting in the War of

* As there was no established class
rank at USMA prior to 1818, graduates
are arranged in Cullum according to
date of commission. Thruston was thus
commissioned 15th in a class of 30.
There was also no established length of
the course, and he was a cadet for 13
months.

1812–15 and in the Fla. War, he resigned in 1836 to engage in farming and banking around Cumberland (Md.). Commissioned B.G. USV 7 Sept. '61, he commanded troops guarding the B.&O. R.R. and resigned 17 Apr. '62 to return to farming.

THRUSTON, Gates Phillips. Union officer. 1835–? Ohio. Capt. 1st Ohio 24 Aug. '61; Maj. Asst. Adj. Gen. Vols. 4 Sept. '63; Lt. Col. Asst. Adj. Gen. Assigned 16 Feb.–1 Nov. '63; Bvt. B.G. USV. Brevets for war service, Stones River (Tenn.), Chickamauga. Settling in Nashville after the war, he was known as a lawyer and historian.

THURSTON, William Henry. Union officer. N.H. Capt. 52d Ind. 1 Feb. '62; Lt. Col. Asst. I.G. Assigned 28 Feb. '63–1 Aug. '65; Bvt. B.G. USV (war service). Died 1877.

TIBBITS, William Badger. Union gen. 1837–80. N.Y. A lawyer and manufacturer, he was commissioned Capt. 2d N.Y. 14 May '61, fighting at Big Bethel, Fair Oaks, Malvern Hill, Bristoe Station, and 2d Bull Run. Named Maj. 13 Oct. '62, he fought at Fredericksburg and Chancellorsville before being mustered out 26 May '63. Named Col. 21st N.Y. Cav. 5 Feb. '64, he commanded in W. Va.: 1st Brig., 1st Cav. Div. (Apr.–June and July–Aug. '64); 1st Brig., 2d Cav. Div. (10 Nov. '64–Feb. '65); 2d Brig., 2d Cav. Div. (28 Dec. '64–13 Jan. '65); and 2d Div. Cav. (Feb.–Apr. '65). He was promoted B.G. USV 21 Oct. '65, having been breveted B.G. USV almost one full year previously and was also breveted Maj. Gen. USV for war service. He was mustered out in 1866.

TIDBALL, John Caldwell. Union officer. c. 1825–1906. Va. Appt.-Ohio. USMA 1848 (11/36); Arty. He served in the Seminole War and in the expedition to suppress John Brown's Harpers Ferry raid before being promoted Capt.

2d US Arty. 14 May '61. First at Fort Pickens, he fought in the Peninsular campaign at Yorktown, Williamsburg, New Bridge, Mechanicsville, Gaines's Mill, Malvern Hill, Harrison's Landing, and Antietam. He went on Stoneman's raid and fought at Chancellorsville, Gettysburg, Aldie, and Upperville before being named Col. 4th N.Y. Arty. 28 Aug. '63 and taking command of the II Corps Arty. After fighting in the Wilderness, Spotsylvania, North Anna, Totopotomoy, Cold Harbor, and the Petersburg siege, he was Commandant of Cadets at West Point 10 July–22 Sept. '64. Returning to the field, he commanded the IX Corps Arty. for the remainder of the war. Continuing in the R.A., he retired in 1889 as Col. 1st US Arty., having been breveted for Gaines's Mill, Antietam, the Richmond campaign (B.G. USV 1 Aug. '64), Fort Stedman, war service (B.G. USA) and Forts Stedman and Sedgwick (Maj. Gen. USV 2 Apr. '65).

TILDEN, Charles William. Union officer. Me. 1st Lt. 2d Me. 28 May '61; Capt. 1 July '61; Lt. Col. 16th Me. 9 July '62; Col. 8 Jan. '63; Bvt. USV (war service).

TILGHMAN, Benjamin Chew. Union officer. Pa. Capt. 26th Pa. 31 May '61; Lt. Col. 1 Sept. '62; Col. 1 Mar. '63; Col. 3d US Col. Inf. 28 July '63; Bvt. B.G. USV 13 Apr. '65 (war service). Commanded 2, 2d Dist. Fla., X (South); 4th Sep. Brig., Dist. Fla. (South). Died 1901.

TILGHMAN, Lloyd. C.S.A. gen. 1816–63. Md. USMA 1836 (46/49); Dragoons. Resigning after graduation, he was in civil and railroad engineering until the Mexican War, when he was Twiggs's volunteer A.D.C. He worked with the Panamanian R.R. until the Civil War, when he was appointed B.G. C.S.A. 18

Oct. '61 from Ky. In Feb. '62, he was inspector of Forts Henry and Donelson. He commanded these for a time and surrendered the former. Exchanged in the fall of 1862, he commanded the 1st Brig. under Loring in the Army of the West. He led the unit at Corinth, in the rear guard after Holly Springs, and in the Vicksburg campaign. He was killed 16 May '63 at Champion's Hill.

TILLSON, Davis. Union gen. 1830–95. Me. Resigning from West Point (ex-1853) after two years because of an injured foot that later was amputated, he had been in the state legislature when commissioned Capt. 2d Me. Btry. 30 Nov. '61. As Maj. 1st Me. Arty. 22 May '62, he was McDowell's Chief of Arty. during 2d Bull Run and Rappahannock Station. Promoted Lt. Col. 24 Dec. '62, he was then appointed B.G. USV to date from 29 Nov. '62, and served as Inspector of Arty. until Apr. '63. Sent to the Dept. of Ohio as Chief of Arty., he was in charge of the defenses of Cincinnati and Knoxville. Breveted Maj. Gen. USV for war service, he was mustered out in 1866 and went into the granite business in New England.

TILLSON, John. Union officer. Ill. Capt. 10th Ill. 29 Apr. '61; Maj. 27 May '61; mustered out 29 July '61; Lt. Col. 10th Ill. 9 Sept. '61; Col. 17 July '62; Bvt. B.G. USV 10 Mar. '65. Commanded 1, 2, Res. Corps (Cumberland); 3, 4, XVI (Tenn.); 3, 1, XVII (Tenn.). In R.A. until resigned as Capt. in 1866. Died 1892.

TILTON, William Stowell. Union officer. Mass. 1st Lt. Adj. 22d Mass. 12 Sept. '61; Maj. 2 Oct. '61; Lt. Col. 28 June '62; Col. 17 Oct. '62; Bvt. B.G. USV 9 Sept. '64 (war service); mustered out 17 Oct. '64. W.I.A. and captured at Gaines's Mill 27 June '62. Commanded 1, 1, V (Potomac). Died 1889.

TISHOMINGO CREEK, Miss. BRICE'S CROSS ROADS, Miss., 10 June '64.

TITUS, Herbert Bradwell. Union officer. N.H. 2d Lt. 2d N.H. 31 May '62; 1st Lt. 17 Sept. '61; resigned 1 July '62; Maj. 9th N.H. 7 Aug. '62; Lt. Col. 20 Aug. '62; Col. 25 Nov. '65; Bvt. B.G. USV (war service). Commanded in the Army of the Potomac: 1, 2, IX; 2, 2, IX.

TOD, David. Gov. of Ohio. 1805–68. Ohio. A lawyer, he entered politics as a Democrat and served in the legislature before being Minister to Brazil 1847–52. He advocated compromise to solve the country's differences but believed in the Federal government and was elected Gov. in 1861 by the Republicans, serving one term of two years.

TODD, John Blair Smith. Union gen. 1814–72. Ky. Serving in the Florida and Mexican wars, and in garrison duty and Indian fighting, he resigned in 1856 and was sutler at Fort Randall (Dak.) until 1861. Commissioned B.G. USV 19 Sept. of that year, he commanded N. Mo. Dist. (15 Oct.–1 Dec. '61) and then took a leave of absence to attend the session of Congress from 1 Dec. '61 until May '62 as delegate (Democratic) from the Dak. Territory. Returning to the army, he then commanded 6th Div., Army Tenn. (15 June–16 July '62), when his appointment expired. In Congress until 1865, he was later in the Dak. House of Representatives and Gov. of the Territory 1869–71.

TODD'S TAVERN, Va., 5–9 May '64. Located a mile from the southern edge of the Wilderness at the intersection of the' Brock and Orange C.H. roads, this was the scene of cavalry action during the battle of the WILDERNESS and the SPOTSYLVANIA CAMPAIGN. Sheridan ordered the divisions of Wilson and Gregg to rendezvous here 5 May. Rosser's (Confed.) Cav. brigade was first encountered in this vicinity and then reinforced by more of Stuart's cavalry, which had been near Fredericksburg at the beginning of the campaign. Firing from Todd's Tavern was misinterpreted by Hancock to mean the arrival of Longstreet from this area on 6 May. In a skirmish here 8 May Gregg reported 250 casualties in his 2d Cav. Div. and estimated an equal number on the enemy side (E.&B.). See SPOTSYLVANIA for additional mention of action here 7 May.

TOMPKINS, Charles H. Union officer. 1830–? Va. Appt.-N.Y. After studying at West Point (ex-1851), he was an enlisted man from 1856 until commissioned 2d Lt. 2d US Cav. 23 Mar. '61. Promoted 1st Lt. 30 Apr. '61, he transferred to the 5th US Cav. 3 Aug. and served as regimental Q.M. 28 Aug.–13 Nov. '61. He was named Capt. Asst. Q.M. on the latter date and Col. 1st Vt. Cav. 24 Apr. '62. Resigning that in Sept., he returned to the rank of Capt. for the rest of the war. Continuing in the R.A., he was retired in 1894 as Col. He was breveted for Fairfax C.H., Banks's and McDowell's campaigns in 1862, and war service (B.G. USA). In 1893 he won the Medal of Honor for his reconnaissance 31 May '61 to Fairfax C.H.

TOMPKINS, Sally L. Confederate nurse. A Richmond resident, she established a hospital on her own after 1st Bull Run. When the government took over all medical services, she was commissioned Capt. by Davis and became the only woman to receive a regular commission in the Confederacy. She continued her nursing throughout the war.

TOM'S BROOK, Va., 9 Oct. '64. (SHENANDOAH VALLEY CAMPAIGN OF SHERIDAN) Dissatisfied with the performance of his cavalry, Sheridan told Torbert to turn on the Confederate divisions of Rosser and Lomax and "either whip the enemy or get whipped yourself" (Pond, 203). In a spirited two-hour fight near Fishers Hill (which Sheridan watched from Round Top Mountain) the Confederates were routed. Merritt pursued Lomax 20 miles to Mount Jackson, capturing five guns; Custer drove Rosser to Columbia Furnace on the Back Road, taking six guns. At a loss of nine killed and 48 wounded, the Federals claimed to have inflicted 400 casualties and to have captured "everything else . . . carried on wheels." Jubilant Federals referred to the action as the "Woodstock Races."

TOOMBS, Robert Augustus. C.S.A. gen. and Sec. of State. 1810–85. Ga. After attending the Univ. of Ga. and Union (N.Y.) College, he practiced law, served in the legislature, and in the US Congress and Senate. At first a Whig, he then became a reluctant Democrat and finally a secessionist. He was associated with Howell Cobb and Alexander Stephens in much of his legislative career and was one of the wealthiest planters in Ga. in 1860. Sent as a delegate to the convention at Montgomery, he accepted the position of Sec. of State with some hesitation, as he had wanted to be president. He found, however, that his office was not only a subordinate but also an idle one. He resigned to become B.G. C.S.A. 19 July '61 and take over the Ga. brigade in Va., retaining his seat in the C.S.A. Congress. A fiery volunteer, he wanted to engage the Union forces immediately and reviled the caution of the professional soldiers. He said upon several occasions that the Confederacy would be "died of West Point." After Malvern Hill D. H. Hill reprimanded him for allowing his troops to break ranks and not rallying them, and Toombs demanded satisfaction. This brought forth another reprimand. At Antietam he was severely wounded, but his brigade held the stone bridge in a valiant performance. When no promotion was forthcoming, he resigned on 4 Mar. '63. He spent most of the rest of the war carping at the government's errors and oppressions, and was defeated in a bid for the C.S.A. Senate. But when Sherman advanced on Atlanta he was named Div. Adj. and I.G. in the Ga. militia. Barely escaping arrest in May '65, he fled to Cuba and England, returning to build a large law practice. He never asked for pardon under Reconstruction laws. Then, when he seemed to have repaired the damages to his fortune, his private life became a series of tragedies: his wife died insane and he became blind and began to drink to excess.

TOON, Thomas F. C.S.A. gen. ?–1902. Appt.-N.C. As Col. 20th N.C. he was appointed Temp. B.G. C.S.A. 31 May '64 and reverted to his former rank the following Aug. After the war he was a legislator, educator, and railroad official. He is listed as a general by Wright and D. S. Freeman (in *Lee's Lts.*), but not by Wood or C. M. H.

TORBERT, Alfred Thomas Archimedes. Union gen. 1833–80. Del. USMA 1855 (21/34); Inf.-Cav. He had been stationed on the frontier, scouted against the Indians, fought in the Seminole War, and marched on the Utah Expedition before being promoted 1st Lt. 5th US Inf. 25 Feb. and Col. 1st N.J. 16 Sept. '61. During the Peninsular campaign he led his regiment at Yorktown, West Point, Gaines's Mill, and Charles City C.R. He commanded 1, 1, VI, Potomac (29 Aug.–24 Dec. '62) at 2d Bull Run, South Mountain, where he was wounded, and Antietam. Promoted B.G. USV 29 Nov. '62, he also commanded this brigade (8 Feb.–10 Apr. and 27 June '63–25 Mar. '64) at Gettysburg, Fairfield, Rappahannock Station, and Mine Run.

He led 1st Div., VI (25 Mar.–23 Apr. '64) and 1st Div., Cav. Corps, Potomac (10 Apr.–7 May and May–6 Aug. '64) at Milford Station, North Anna, Hanovertown, Haw's Shop, Matadequin Creek, Cold Harbor, Trevilian Station, Mallory's Ford Cross Roads, Tunstall's Station, and Darby Town. Commanding the cavalry corps of the Middle Mil. Dist. (6 Aug. '64–1 June '65) and Army of the Shenandoah (28 Feb.–27 June '65), he fought at Winchester, Kearnysville, Opequon, Milford, Luray, Waynesboro, Mount Crawford, Tom's Brook, Cedar Creek, Middletown, Liberty Mills, and Gordonsville. From 28 Feb. to 7 Mar. '65 he commanded the Army of the Shenandoah. Breveted for Gettysburg, Haw's Shop, Winchester, Cedar Creek (B.G. USA), and war service (Maj. Gen. USA and USV 9 Sept. '64), he resigned in 1866. He was US Minister Resident to Central America 1869–71 and Consul Gen. at Havana 1871–73 and at Paris 1873–78. In business in Mexico, he was drowned in a shipwreck on his way to N.Y.C.

TORPEDO. The Civil War "torpedo" is what is now called a LAND MINE or marine mine. The latter were of two general types: those detonated by contact with a ship, and those set off by an electric current from the shore.

TOTOPOTOMOY CREEK, Va., 26–30 May '64. In maneuvering from positions along the NORTH ANNA RIVER to COLD HARBOR, Lee and Grant faced each other briefly along the Totopotomoy. Although there was no general engagement, a number of skirmishes took place with the maneuver.

The movement south for another attempt at enveloping Lee was led by Sheridan with the cavalry divisions of Torbert and Gregg (1st and 2d) and the infantry division of Russell (1, VI). This force started the afternoon of the 26th and early the next day had put two ponton bridges across the Pamunkey and occupied Hanovertown. The rest of the army followed the night of 26–27 May. Wilson's (3d) cavalry division formed the rear guard. In a cavalry action at Hanovertown, 27 May, Custer's cavalry brigade (1, 1) drove the Confederate cavalry brigade of Barringer to Crump's Creek and then toward Hanover C. H.

As the rest of Meade's army moved south to cross the Pamunkey the V and IX Corps in the eastern column were ordered to cross at Hanovertown; the VI and II Corps crossed four miles upstream at Huntley's. On 30 May they were in position along the Totopotomoy. Lee, however, by 28 May had already taken up a defense on the opposite side.

In screening the army's advance, Sheridan's cavalry had had a sharp engagement at HAW'S SHOP (Enon Church), 29 May. Wilson's (3d) cavalry division had skirmished at Hanover C. H. and Ashland on 30 May, and on 31 May he had taken possession of Hanover C. H. after a clash with P. M. B. Young's cavalry brigade. Torbert's (1st) cavalry division had been attacked at Old Church on 30 May and had maintained possession of this place. At Bethesda Church on 30 May Pegram's brigade (commanded by Col. Edward Willis) had attacked Crawford's division (3, V) and was repulsed with the loss of Willis, J. B. TERRILL of the 13th Va., and Lt. Col. Watkins of the 52d Va. (all killed).

Hancock (II) probed Lee's positions with the brigades of Brooke (4, 1, II) and Owen (2, 2, II). At 11 A.M., 31 May, D. B. Birney's division (3, II) gained some ground and Barlow and Gibbon pushed up to the Confederate main positions while Wright (VI) moved to within supporting distance. However, the positions were considered too strong to assault, so the night of 31 May both

Grant and Lee maneuvered south to COLD HARBOR.

TOTTEN, James. Union officer. c. 1818–71. Pa. Appt.-Va. USMA 1841 (25/52); Arty. He served in the Mexican War, the Seminole War, and on the frontier in the Kans. border disturbances. He surrendered the Little Rock arsenal in Feb. '61. In the spring of that year he was at the St. Louis Arsenal and fought at Boonville, Dug Spring, and Wilson's Creek. Promoted Maj. 1st Mo. Arty. 19 Aug. and Lt. Col. 1 Sept. '61, he was Frémont's Chief of Arty. until 2 Nov. '61, when he took the same post in the Dept. of the Mo. on Halleck's staff until 19 Feb. '62. He had been promoted Maj. Asst. I.G. 12 Nov. '61 and was also named B.G. Mo. Mil. in the service of the US 20 Feb. '62, when he commanded a division in the Army of the Frontier Oct. '62–21 Mar. '63. He was I.G. of the Dept. of the Mo. until 6 Aug. '64, when in the Mil. Div. of Western Miss. he was named Chief of Arty. and Chief of Ord. for the rest of the war. Breveted for Boonville, Wilson's Creek, Mobile, and war service (B.G. USA), he was promoted Lt. Col. Asst. I.G. in 1867. While I.G. of the Mil. Div. of the South he was dismissed in 1870 for "disobedience of orders," "neglect of duty," and "conduct to the prejudice of good order and military discipline."

TOTTEN, Joseph G. Union gen. 1788–1864. Conn. USMA 1805 * (3/3); Engrs. He fought in the War of 1812, served on various engineering details, and was Scott's Chief Engr. in the Mexican War (Bvt. B.G. USA, 1847), having been named Chief Engr. and Col. in 1838. He continued in command of the Corps of Engrs. and was pro-

* There was no class standing prior to 1818, and the cadets are listed in the order in which they were commissioned.

moted B.G. USA 3 Mar. '63 and breveted Maj. Gen. USA 21 Apr. '64, dying on active duty 22 Apr. '64.

TOURTELLOTTE, John Eaton. Union officer. Conn. Pvt. Co. H 4th Minn. 30 Sept.–12 Dec. '61; Capt. 4th Minn. 13 Dec. '61; Lt. Col. 1 Sept. '62; Col. 5 Oct. '64; Bvt. B.G. USV (war service). Wounded at Allatoona (Ga.) while brigade commander. Other brevets for Vicksburg siege, Allatoona (Ga.), Bentonville (N.C.). Commanded 2, 3, XV (Tenn.). In R.A. after the war; served as Col. A.D.C. to Sherman 1871–84. Retired in 1885 as Maj. Died 1891.

TOWER, Zealous Bates. Union gen. 1819–1900. Mass. USMA 1841 (1/52); Engr. After teaching engineering at West Point, fighting in the Mexican War (3 brevets, 1 wound), and constructing East and West coastal defenses, he was Chief Engr. at Fort Pickens (Fla.) from 20 Feb. '61 until 10 May '62. Named Maj. 6 Aug. and B.G. USV 23 Nov. '61, he commanded 2d Brig., Ord's division, Rappahannock (16 May–10 June '62). At Cedar Mountain, Rappahannock Station and Thoroughfare Gap and 2d Bull Run, he led 2, 3, III, Army of Va. (26 June–30 Aug. '62). Severely wounded at Bull Run, he was on a lengthy sick leave and then served as USMA Superintendent 8 July–8 Sept. '64 before going to the Mil. Div. Miss. as I.G. of Fortifications (20 Oct. '64–July '65). He was Chief Engr. of the defenses of Nashville and fought there against Hood. Breveted for Fort Pickens, Cedar Mountain, Groveton (B.G. USA) and war service (Maj. Gen. USA and USV), he continued in the R.A. until 1883, when he retired as Col.

TOWNSEND, Edward D. Union officer. c. 1817–93. Mass. USMA 1837 (16/50); Arty.-Adj. Gen. He served in the Florida War and in the Adj. Gen.'s office when, as Lt. Col. 7 Mar. '61, he was named Scott's Chief of Staff. From 1 Nov. '61 to 23 Mar. '62 he was in the Adj. Gen.'s office and from the latter date until the end of the war he served as Acting Adj. Gen. of the Army, having been promoted Col. 3 Aug. '61. He retired in 1880 as B.G. USA, the Adj. Gen., and Bvt. B.G. USA and Maj. Gen. USA.

TOWNSEND, Frederick. Union officer. N.Y. Commissioned Col. 3d N.Y. 10 May–12 June '61, he was named Maj. 18th US Inf. 14 May of that year and commanded the N.Y. regiment at Big Bethel 10 June. Going to the West, he was in reserve during Shiloh but fought at Corinth and Perryville and commanded the left wing of the R.A. brigade at Stones River. He was Acting Asst. Provost Marshal of N.Y. State from May '63 until 1866 and was promoted Lt. Col. 9th US Inf. 20 Apr. '64. Breveted for Stones River and war service (B.G. USA), he resigned in 1868 and died in 1897.

TOWNSEND, George Alfred ("Gath"). WAR CORRESPONDENT. 1841–1914. Del. The son of an itinerant Methodist preacher, he won a job with the Philadelphia *Inquirer* on the day he graduated from high school in 1860, and a year later was named city editor of the *Press.* In early 1862 he was accredited as a correspondent and was sent by the New York *Herald* to cover the Seven Days' Battles and Cedar Mountain. His dispatches at this point were signed "By a Correspondent" and "Correspondent's Account." In the fall of that year he went to England, where he lectured and wrote, earning enough money to spend a year in Europe. He returned in time for Five Forks and was one of the first correspondents to enter Richmond. After returning to Europe he wrote features and satire for the Chicago *Tribune* and Cincinnati *Enquirer,* among others. His pen name,

Gath, was a monogram of his initials with an added "h." Of this he said, " 'Hello,' I said, 'that's a Philistine city Hello again,' I said, 'It's written in the scriptures, Tell it not in Gath. So I wrote Gath below the [dispatch].' " In 1896 he headed a fund-raising campaign to build the 60-foot stone arch near his home on the South Mountain battle-field in memory of the Civil War cor-respondents. The names of 157 artists and writers appear on it.

TRACY, Benjamin Franklin. Union officer. 1830-1915. N.Y. Col. 109th N.Y. 28 Aug. '62; discharged 17 May '64; Col. 127th US Col. Inf. 10 Sept. '64; commander of military prison and recruiting camp in Elmira (N.Y.); Bvt. B.G. USV (war service). Medal of Honor 21 June '95 for Wilderness 6 May '64. He organized in 1854 the Re-publican party in Tioga County (N.Y.). As a prominent lawyer of his day he de-fended Henry Ward BEECHER against charges of adultery by Theodore Tilton with Tilton's wife, Elizabeth. The dam-age suit ended in a hung jury. He was appointed Sec. of the Navy (1889) by Harrison and is credited with building up that service. He later was counsel for Venezuela in that country's boundary dispute with Great Britain.

TRACY, Edward Dorr. C.S.A. gen. Ga. 1833-63. A lawyer and politician, he was commissioned Capt. 4th Ala. and fought at 1st Bull Run four days after becoming a Maj. He was named Lt. Col. 12 Oct. '61 in Joseph Wheeler's 19th Ala. At Shiloh his horse was shot from under him. He was appointed B.G. C.S.A. 16 Aug. '62 and commanded an Ala. brigade in eastern Tenn. before entering into the Vicksburg campaign. He was killed at Port Gibson 1 May '63.

TRAGIC ERA. Southern term for RECONSTRUCTION.

TRAINS or SUPPLY TRAINS. In Civil War usage these were wagons (rather than railroad cars).

TRANS-ALLEGHENY or WEST-ERN DEPARTMENT OF VIRGINIA, CONFEDERATE. See WESTERN and SOUTHWESTERN VIRGINIA, Confederate Departments and Armies in.

TRANS-MISSISSIPPI, CONFEDER-ATE DISTRICT, DEPARTMENT, AND ARMY. Friction between Price, commanding the MISSOURI STATE GUARD, and McCulloch, commanding a body of Ark. and La. troops, was solved by creating the Trans-Miss. *Dist.* of Dept. No. 2. on 10 Jan. '62. Van Dorn arrived on the 29th from the A.N.V. to assume command. He organized the Army of the WEST and was defeated by Curtis at PEA RIDGE, 7-8 Mar.

On 26 May '62 the Trans-Miss. *Dept.* was created to encompass Tex., Indian Territory, Ark., Mo. and West La. (O.R., I, XIII, 2). T. C. Hindman be-came department commander on 31 May. On 16 July T. H. Holmes was or-dered from N.C. to succeed Hindman; he actually assumed command on 30 July.

On 9 Feb. '63 Kirby Smith's com-mand in West La. and Tex., to which he had been assigned on 14 Jan. and which had been designated the South-western Army (O.R., I, XV, 3; and XXII, 2), was expanded to include the entire Trans-Miss. Dept. On 7 Mar. he assumed command of all Confederate forces west of the Mississippi (*ibid.,* XII, 3).

Kirby Smith's 30,000 troops were scattered from Fort Smith, Ark., to the Rio Grande. Part of the army, under T. H. Holmes, was defeated at HELENA, Ark., 4 July '63. Other forces, including Taylor's troops of the Dist. of W. La., captured Brashear City, threatened New Orleans, and took part in the RED RIVER CAMPAIGN OF 1863, the RED RIVER

CAMPAIGN OF 1864, and the ARKANSAS CAMPAIGN IN 1864. With a final strength of about 43,000 it was the last Confederate force to surrender (to E. R. S. Canby, 26 May '65).

Prior to creation of the Trans-Miss. Dept. a number of other departments had existed in the area; these later became districts.

The Dept. of Tex. had been created 21 Apr. '61 when Van Dorn was assigned to command in Tex. On 14 Aug. '61 P. O. Hébert was ordered to relieve Van Dorn; on 4 Sept. Van Dorn transferred command to Col. H. E. McCulloch; and on 18 Sept. Hébert actually assumed command. The Dist. of West La. and Tex. was created 28 May '62 under Hébert's command. This was later split into two separate districts. According to conflicting data in the O.R. chronologies, on 18 June '62 Hébert assumed command of the Dept. of West La. and Tex. (XV, 1) or of the Dept. of Tex. (IX, 481). Magruder was assigned to command the Dist. of Tex. on 10 Oct. '62, and on 29 Nov. assumed command of the Dist. of Tex., N. Mex., and Ariz. (XV, 2 and 3). Magruder captured Galveston 1 Jan. '63, and in Mar. '64 sent most of his troops to oppose Banks on the Red River in La.

On 10 June '64 J. G. Walker succeeded Richard Taylor as C. G., Dist. of West La. Magruder assumed command of the Dist. of Ark. on 1 Feb. '65, and on the 15th Parsons was assigned to temporary command. J. G. Walker, meanwhile, had been in command in Tex.; on 31 Mar. '65 Magruder was ordered to succeed him, and on 4 Apr. he assumed command (XLVIII, 6).

Western Louisiana (i.e., that part of the state west of the Mississippi) was included in various territorial organizations. As already mentioned, the Dist. of West La. and Tex. was constituted 28 May '62 under P. O. Hébert. This later became two separate districts (see above), and on 20 Aug. '62 Richard Taylor was assigned to command the Dist. of West La. (XV, 2). J. G. Walker relieved Taylor as district commander on 10 June '64 (XXXIV, 7). On 19 Apr. '65 the Dist. of Ark. and West La. was formed under Buckner (XLVIII, 7).

For other parts of the Trans-Miss. Dept., see ARKANSAS, DISTRICT OF; INDIAN TERRITORY, DEPARTMENT AND DISTRICT OF; MISSOURI STATE GUARD; NEW MEXICO, ARMY OF; and WEST, CONFEDERATE ARMY OF THE.

TRANS-MISSISSIPPI DIVISION (Union). Another name for Union Military Division of WEST MISSISSIPPI.

TRAPIER, James Heyward. C.S.A. gen. c. 1815–66. S.C. USMA 1838 (3/45); Arty.-Engrs. He supervised river and harbor construction and improvements before resigning in 1848. A planter, he was active in the S.C. militia, serving as Chief of Ord. and A.D.C. to the governor before being commissioned Capt. of S.C. Engrs. He constructed batteries for the attack on Fort Sumter and was named Engr.-in-Chief of Morris Island. Promoted Maj., he was soon appointed B.G. C.S.A. 21 Oct. '61 and given command of the Dept. of Eastern and Middle Fla. In March '62, he asked to join Johnston in Ala. and led the 1st Div. under Polk at Corinth and Farmington. In Nov. '62 he was named commander of the 4th Dist. of S.C. and the following spring he commanded Sullivan's Island. He returned to the 4th Dist. for the rest of the war.

TRAUERNICHT, Theodore. Union officer. Germany. Capt. 2d Mo. 23 Apr. '61; mustered out 30 July '61; Capt. 2d Mo. 10 Sept. '61; Lt. Col. 13th US Col. Inf. 19 Nov. '63; Bvt. USV (war service). Died 1887.

TRAVELLER. R. E. Lee's iron-gray horse is one of the most famous in American history. Raised in Greenbrier County (Va.), he was originally called Jeff Davis and later Greenbrier, and Lee first saw him during the W. Va. campaign of 1864. Much taken by "my colt," as he called him, he bought him in the spring of 1862 for $200 in currency. To an artist who proposed painting the animal, Lee wrote: "If I were an artist like you, I would draw a true picture of Traveller; representing his fine proportions, muscular figure, deep chest, short back, strong haunches, flat legs, small head, broad forehead, delicate ears, quick eye, small feet and black mane and tail. Such a picture would inspire a poet, whose genius could then depict his worth and describe his endurance of toil, hunger, thirst, heat and cold, and the dangers and sufferings through which he has passed. He could dilate upon his sagacity and affection, and his invariable response to every wish of his rider. . . . But I am no artist Markie, and can therefore only say that he is a Confederate grey . . ." Traveller died of lockjaw after Lee's death, and his skeleton stands in the Washington and Lee Museum. See LEE's HORSES.

TREATY OF WASHINGTON. See ALABAMA CLAIMS.

TREDEGAR IRON WORKS. Identified with J. R. ANDERSON, this was the only major rolling mill in the South when the war started and the more important of its two first-class foundries and machine shops. (The other was LEED's.) Until the beginning of hostilities it furnished revolvers and gun carriages. During the war Tredegar made cannon and machinery and the armor for the *Virginia*. No carbines, rifles, or revolvers were made here officially (see Albaugh and Simmons, 87). Located in Richmond on the old Kanawha canal, it was just west of the RICHMOND ARMORY AND ARSENAL, with which it may be confused.

TREMAIN, Henry Edwin. Union officer. 1840–1910. N.Y. 1st Lt. 73d N.Y. 14 Aug. '61; Capt. 1 Nov. '62; Maj. A.D.C. Vols. 25 Apr. '63; Bvt. B.G. USV 30 Nov. '65 (war service). Captured at 2d Bull Run and detained in Libby Prison; A.D.C. to SICKLES and on HOOKER's staff. Medal of Honor 30 June '92 for "having at Resaca Ga. 15 May 1864 voluntarily rode [sic] between the lines while two brigades of Union troops were firing into each other and stopped the firing" (Heitman). (See Oliver, Paul Ambrose.) He was active in Republican politics as a lawyer and Federal attorney.

TRENHOLM, George A. C.S.A. Sec. of the Treasury. 1806–76. S.C. A merchant who dealt mainly in foreign trade in cotton, he was active in blockade running and supply trips to Nassau during the first part of the war. Named Sec. of the Treasury 18 July '64, he succeeded Memminger and held the post until Apr. '65, when he was captured and held by the Federals until Oct. of that year.

TRENT AFFAIR. Dispute between the US and Britain over the stopping of the British mail steamer *Trent* by the Union warship *San Jacinto* on 8 Nov. '61. The Confederate commissioners, MASON and SLIDELL, who were on their way to England, were removed and held in Boston until 1 Jan. '62. This provoked war fever and a great sympathy for the Confederacy in England, but hostilities were averted when SEWARD ordered the two men released on the grounds that they were "personal contraband" and that, therefore, WILKES, the captain of the *San Jacinto,* had made a mistake in not bringing in the *Trent* also.

TRENTON, Tenn., 20 Dec. '62. (FORREST'S SECOND RAID; STONES RIVER) Forrest captured a post held by detachments of the 7th Tenn. Cav., 122d Ill. and convalescents. Most of the garrison had been sent to defend JACKSON, Tenn., 18 Dec. The 130 convalescents defended from behind a barricade of cotton bales until forced by the arrival of enemy artillery to surrender. Forrest remained here until the next day.

TREVILIAN RAID, Va., 7–28 June '64. On 6 June, when Grant decided to abandon his operations around COLD HARBOR and cross the James to attack Petersburg, he ordered Sheridan to undertake another cavalry diversion. With the divisions of Torbert and D. McM. Gregg, Sheridan was to join forces with Hunter at Charlottesville and then wreck the Va. Central R.R. from that place to Hanover Junction. (Hunter's advance from the Valley was stopped at LYNCHBURG, 17–18 June.)

Sheridan crossed the Pamunkey at New Castle (above White House), moved westward between the North Anna and the Mattapony. On the 10th he crossed the North Anna at Carpenter's Ford and encamped a few miles northeast of Louisa C.H.

When Lee learned of Sheridan's departure he sent Wade Hampton with his own cavalry division and Fitz Lee's to check it. Hampton left Atlee (about eight miles north of Richmond) early the 9th. The morning of the 11th he was with his own division just west of Trevilian Station and Fitz Lee's was four miles east at Louisa. Having learned from people of the area of Sheridan's general location, Hampton ordered his two divisions to converge on Clayton's Store, a crossroad four miles north of Louisa, where he could logically expect to encounter the advancing Federals.

The brigades of Butler and Young, leading Hampton's division, soon made contact with two of Torbert's brigades. Just as this action was developing satisfactorily Hampton received the disconcerting news that a Federal force was behind him. Custer's brigade of Torbert's division had hit the leading brigade (Wickham's) of Fitz Lee's advancing column. Having momentarily checked Lee's advance, Custer pressed boldly between the two Confederate divisions and got among Hampton's wagons and led horses.

Hampton was forced to break off the action to his front and turn against Custer. In a confused engagement he finally closed in on Custer with his three brigades. He recaptured his 800 horses and vehicles, and also took several hundred Federals and some of their vehicles, including Custer's headquarters wagon. Custer managed to hold Trevilian Station; Fitz Lee was driven toward Louisa and unable to rejoin Hampton until noon the next day.

On 12 June Sheridan's attack against the entrenched troopers of Hampton's division was repulsed with heavy loss. Having been frustrated by Hampton's swift movement across his line of advance, Sheridan was forced to abandon his mission. He rejoined Grant on 28 June after withdrawing through Spotsylvania and Bowling Green to Light House Point on the James.

Federal casualties in the two-day action, 11–12 June, were 735 (E.&B.); for the entire raid they amounted to 1,000, of whom 840 were in Torbert's division (Fiebeger, 284). Total Confederate casualties are not known; Hampton reported a loss of 612 in his own division, and Freeman estimates that Fitz Lee's losses would bring the total to almost 1,000 (*Lee's Lts.*, III, 522n.). Rosser was wounded.

TREVILIAN STATION, Va., 11–12 June '64. Engagement of Sheridan's TREVILIAN'S RAID.

TRIMBLE, Isaac Ridgeway. C.S.A. gen. 1802–88. Pa. Appt.-Ky. USMA 1822 (17/40); Arty. He served on ordnance and topographical duty before resigning in 1832 to become chief engr. and general superintendent of several East Coast railroads. When the war came he burned bridges north of Baltimore to slow the movement of Union troops to Washington and was named Col. of C.S.A. Engrs. in May '61. Appointed from Va., he served in that state until he was named B.G. C.S.A. 9 Aug. '61 and began constructing batteries along the Potomac. In 1862 he commanded a brigade that was assigned to remove stores from Manassas Junction when the army went to the Peninsula. He then served under Ewell along the Rappahannock and fought at Winchester and Cross Keys during Jackson's Valley campaign. During the Seven Days' Battles and at Cedar Mountain and Hazel Run he led his forces, participating in the capture of Federal supplies at Manassas Station, 27 Aug. '62. He was severely wounded at 2d Bull Run. Appointed Maj. Gen. 23 Apr. '63 to rank from 17 Jan., he returned to the field in time for the Gettysburg campaign, and led his troops through the Shenandoah and up the Cumberland Valley as far as Carlisle, Pa. He succeeded Pender on the second day at Gettysburg, taking command of his division while it was forming for "Pickett's Charge." Wounded, captured, and losing a leg in this action, he was not exchanged until Feb. '65. After the war he lived in Baltimore and became a consulting engineer.

TRIPLER, Charles S. Union surgeon. N.Y. Entering the R.A. in 1830, he served in the frontier, the Seminole War, and the Mexican War, where he was medical director for Twiggs's division. During the Civil War he was medical director for Patterson's command until Aug. '61, for the Army of the Potomac until July '62, and for the Northern Dept. Mar. '64–Oct. '66. From 1862 until 1864 he served on medical boards and commissions. He died on active duty in 1866 as Maj. and Bvt. B.G. USA.

TRIPPLER, Charles S. Misspelling by Phisterer for Charles S. TRIPLER.

TROTTER, Frederick Eugene. Union officer. c. 1838–92. N.Y. Pvt. Co. G 7th N.Y. State Militia 26 Apr.–3 June '61; Capt. 102d N.Y. 18 Dec. '61; Maj. 16 July '62; mustered out 18 Mar. '63; Capt. Vet. Res. Corps 18 June '63; Maj. 15 Oct. '63; Lt. Col. 30 Mar. '64; Bvt. B.G. USV (war service). Wounded at Cedar Mountain in the left arm and right foot. Before the war he had been a merchant. In R.A. until his death with the rank of Maj.

TROWBRIDGE, Luther Stephen. Union officer. Mich. Commissioned Maj. 5th Mich. Cav. 2 Sept. '62, he was promoted Lt. Col. 10th Mich. Cav. 25 Aug. '63 and Col. 25 July '64. He was mustered out Sept. '65 and breveted B.G. and Maj. Gen. USV 15 June '65 for war service.

TRUE, James Milton. Union officer. Ky. Capt. 38th Ill. 21 Aug. '61; resigned 26 Dec. '61; Col. 62d Ill. 10 Apr. '62; Bvt. B.G. USV 6 Mar. '65. Commanded 3, 3, XVI (Tenn.); True's brigade, 3d Div. Ark. Exp. (Tenn.); 3, 2, VII (Ark.); 2, 2, VII (Ark.).

TRUEX, William Snyder. Union officer. N.J. Maj. 5th N.J. 24 Aug. '61; Lt. Col. 10th N.J. 7 Mar. '62; Col. 14th N.J. 23 Aug. '62; Bvt. B.G. USV 2 Apr. '65 (Petersburg siege). Commanded 1, 3, VI (Shenandoah). Ex-cadet USMA 1841. Served as enlisted man in the Mexican War. Died 1889.

TRUMBULL, Matthew Mark. Union officer. England. Capt. 3d Iowa 8 June '61; Lt. Col. 22 Aug. '62; resigned 20 Nov. '62; Col. 9th Iowa Cav. 19 Nov.

'63; Bvt. B.G. USV (war service). Commanded cavalry brigade, Post of Little Rock, VII (Ark.). Died 1894.

TRUNNIONS. Two cylinders near the center of gravity of a cannon by which it is supported on its carriage.

TUCKER, John Randolph. Confederate naval comdr. 1812–83. Va. In Mar. '62 he commanded the *Patrick Henry* during the battle between the *Merrimac* and *Monitor* off Hampton Roads and later commanded the wooden fleet during the engagement off Drewry's Bluff. He also commanded the ironclad *Chicora* off Charleston in 1862. After the war he became a Rear Admiral in the Peruvian Navy during the war against Spain and led an expedition along the upper Amazon River in 1873.

TUCKER, William F. C.S.A. gen. ?–1881. Appt.-Miss. He was commissioned Capt. 11th Miss. and mustered in at Lynchburg in May '61. He served in the Shenandoah, fought at 1st Bull Run under Bee, and was promoted Col.

41st Miss. 8 May '62. At Stones River he commanded his regiment and led Anderson's brigade at Missionary Ridge and the Atlanta campaign. Appointed B.G. C.S.A. 1 Mar. '64, he was severely wounded at Resaca and saw no more field service.

TULLAHOMA CAMPAIGN, Tenn., 23–30 June '63. After the battle of Stones River (Murfreesboro), Rosecrans concentrated around Murfreesboro. Bragg withdrew and took up positions to block a Federal advance southeast toward Chattanooga. When the Washington authorities learned that Grant had crossed the Mississippi below Vicksburg on 1 May they were afraid that Bragg would detach troops to reinforce Pemberton for the defense of Vicksburg. Rosecrans, therefore, was urged to undertake an offensive against Bragg to hold Confederate strength in Tenn.

Although it was mid-June before Rosecrans decided on a plan and was prepared to start moving, he then exe-

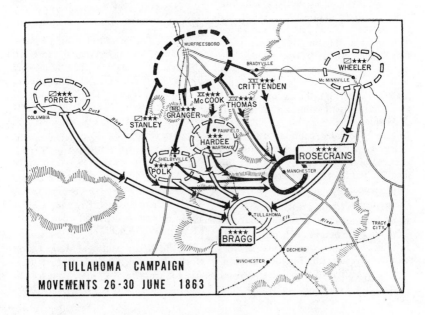

TULLAHOMA CAMPAIGN MOVEMENTS 26-30 JUNE 1863

cuted a skillful maneuver that forced Bragg to withdraw south of the Tennessee River.

Threatening a main attack with Stanley's cavalry corps and Granger's reserve corps against Polk's corps in Shelbyville, Rosecrans sent the corps of Thomas (XIV) and Crittenden (XXI) through Wheeler's cavalry screen and to Manchester, behind Bragg's right flank. McCook's (XX) corps moved a short distance along the Murfreesboro-Shelbyville Pike, to deceive Bragg; it then moved toward Hardee's position around Wartrace. As these five separate Federal columns moved through the watershed north of the Duck River there were skirmishes with Wheeler's cavalry corps (divisions of J. A. Wharton, Wm. T. Martin, and Forrest; Morgan was away on his Ohio raid). These skirmishes were: Middleton-Shelbyville Pike, 24 June (Stanley's cavalry); Hoover's Gap, 24 June (XIV Corps); Liberty Gap or Beech Grove, 25 June (XX Corps); Guy's Gap and Shelbyville, 27 June (Stanley and Granger). Rosecrans reported a total of 560 casualties in these engagements, and put Bragg's losses at 1,634.

Bragg was completely deceived by Rosecrans' strategy (Horn, 235). On the morning of the 26th he ordered Polk to move through Guy's Gap and the next day attack the west flank of the Federal force that was pushing back Hardee's outposts at Liberty Gap. Later the same day Bragg learned of enemy appearing in strength around Manchester. Bragg then ordered his troops to fall back to Tullahoma. "The entire campaign was carried out under conditions extremely difficult for both sides, as extraordinarily heavy rains fell day after day for more than two weeks..." (Horn, 236).

Wilder's mounted infantry was sent to destroy the bridge by which Bragg would have to retreat across the Elk River from Tullahoma to Decherd. Wilder reached the latter place, but was blocked by Forrest's cavalry from destroying the bridge. On 30 June Bragg decided to retreat behind the Tennessee River. He destroyed the bridges over the flooded Elk River and was able to retreat without much further loss. The stage was set for the Chickamauga campaign.

Forces engaged were 56,000 Federal infantry and 9,000 cavalry; 30,000 Confederate infantry and 14,000 cavalry (M.A.&E. atlas, 108).

TULLEY, William C. Although listed by Phisterer as Col. 1st Pa. Reserves and Bvt. B.G. USV 13 Mar. '65, he does not appear in either Heitman or Dyer.

TUNNEL HILL, Ga., 23–24 Feb. '64. See DALTON, Ga., 22–27 Feb. '64.

TUNNEL HILL, Ga., 7 May '64. See ROCKY FACE RIDGE.

TUNNEL HILL, Miss., 13 Feb. '64. Skirmish in MERIDIAN CAMPAIGN.

TUNNEL HILL, Tenn. Terrain feature on east end of Missionary Ridge. See CHATTANOOGA CAMPAIGN.

TUPELO (Harrisburg), Miss., 13–15 July '64. (FORREST'S OPERATIONS DURING THE ATLANTA CAMPAIGN) The cavalry of A. J. Smith's command occupied Tupelo on the 13th, and the Confederate force under S. D. Lee moved to attack him. Although Forrest's cavalry, particularly Buford's division, did most of the fighting in the subsequent engagement, S. D. Lee was on the ground and in command.

On the Federal left (south) was Moore's 3d Div. with Bouton's colored brigade to its rear to assist Grierson's cavalry in protecting that flank and the trains. Mower's 1st Div. was on the right. Each of these infantry divisions had two brigades on line and two in reserve.

Roddey's division was on the right (south), where Lee intended to make his main attack, to cut the Verona-Tupelo road. Buford's division was on the left, with the brigades of Mabry and Crossland (formerly Lyon) from left to right and Bell initially in reserve. In reserve was Chalmers' division with a force of 700 infantry under Gen. Lyon.

The Confederates attacked at about 7 A.M. Crossland's Ky. brigade obliqued to the right to connect with Roddey, and Mabry drifted to the left. Bell's Tenn. brigade was ordered up to fill this gap between Crossland and Mabry. Crossland drove in the enemy skirmishers and charged. The Federals (3d Div.) held their fire until Crossland was within 100 yards of the main line and then delivered a devastating volley and counterattacked. Forrest returned from Roddey's wing, to find that the "Kentucky brigade had been rashly precipitated forward, and were retiring under the murderous fire concentrated on them. I seized their colors, and after a short appeal ordered them to form a new line, when they held their position. The terrific fire poured upon the gallant Kentucky brigade showed that the enemy were supported by overwhelming numbers in an impregnable position, and . . . I did not push forward General Roddey's command when it arrived. . . . Meanwhile the troops on my left were hotly engaged. Mabry's, Bell's, and Rucker's brigades were steadily advancing. They drove a heavy line of skirmishers back to their fortifications, where they were halted by a combination of enemy fire and exhaustion in the oppressive heat" (Forrest's report, O.R.).

About 1 P.M. Lee ordered Forrest to withdraw to a new line near the Sample house. The Federals did not move out of their works. Forrest ordered Rucker's brigade to be mounted and after dark he led it in an attempted envelopment of the enemy left. After getting close without being detected, the Confederates attacked and drove in the outposts. A stand was then made by the 2d and 3d brigades of the 3d Div. and Bouton's colored brigade. Forrest reported that the enemy then subjected his force to "one of the heaviest fires I have heard during the war." The fire was long, however, and he sustained no casualties.

The morning of the 15th Buford moved up the Verona road against Smith's left and drove the outposts back to the main line. "But few men were killed or wounded in this engagement, but I found the road strewn with men fainting under the oppressive heat, hard labor, and want of water." Chalmers, advancing on the other flank, found the enemy retreating. Later in the day, at Old Town Creek, the Federals fought a heated rear-guard action. Bell and Crossland drove the Federal line to the rear but were then repulsed themselves. While organizing another attack on this position Forrest was wounded. Chalmers assumed command and continued the pursuit with the brigades of Roddey and Rucker.

A. J. Smith had 14,000 under his command but the number of "effectives" is unknown. He lost 674 (77 killed, 559 wounded, and 38 missing). Forrest reported having not more than 5,000, but Livermore points out that he is apparently referring only to his own cavalry troops. Counting the 700 infantry and an estimated 900 artillerymen and officers, Livermore puts S. D. Lee's command at about 6,600 effectives and accepts Forrest's estimate of 1,326 (210 killed, 1,116 wounded). Buford's division accounted for 996 of this total, and Chalmers' for 312. Rucker, Mc-

Culloch, Crossland, and Forrest were among the wounded.

TURCHIN, John Basil. Union gen. sometimes called the "Russian Thunderbolt." 1822–1901. Russia. As Ivan Vasilevitch Turchininoff, he graduated from the St. Petersburg Arty. School and, after the Hungarian campaign of 1849, attended the academy for general staff officers. He was on the staff of the Imperial Guards and fought in the Crimean War before taking a trip to America in 1856. Settling in Chicago (apparently without the formality of resigning from the Russian Army), he was in railroading when commissioned Col. 19th Ill. (a Zouave unit) 17 June '61. He commanded the 8th Brig. of the Army of the Ohio (Nov.–Dec. '61) and when it was put in the 3d Div. (2 Dec. '61–2 July '62). He led this command at Huntsville and commanded them to burn Athens (Ala.) in retribution for the townspeople's resistance when his brigade marched into the town. Buell court-martialed and dismissed him for this action, but Turchin's wife hurried to Washington and got Lincoln not only to pardon him but to promote him B.G. USV (17 July '62). Returning to command in the Cumberland: 2d Div. Cav., Cumberland (Mar.–28 July '63); 3, 4, XIV (8 July–9 Oct. '63) at Chickamauga; and 1, 3, XIV (9 Oct. '63–15 July '64) at Missionary Ridge, he resigned 4 Oct. of that year to practice law and civil engineering. He later established a Polish colony in Ill. and wrote a number of scientific and military articles as well as *The Campaign and Battle of Chickamauga* (1888). See Mme. TURCHIN, below.

TURCHIN, Madame John Basil. Army wife. Born and raised in the Russian Army and idol of her father's regiment, she married one of his subalterns and followed him on campaign. After the Hungarian and Crimean wars and a tour in the Imperial Guard and General Staff the Turchins came to America. And when the Civil War came and Col. Turchin left for the field, Madame Turchin went along, serving as nurse and mother confessor to the regiment, and in at least one instance as temporary commander. In Tenn. in 1862 the Col. became ill, and Madame took over, issuing orders and leading the regiment into battle with poise. After Buell put her husband under arrest for the Athens (Ga.) affair and court-martialed him, she rushed to Washington and won from Lincoln not only mercy, but a B.G. commission for her husband. "With all the refinements of a lady, she had the energy and self-reliance of a man."

TURKEY BRIDGE (Bend, Run), Va., 30 June '62. Sykes's division (2, V) with the assistance of Federal gunboats defeated an attempt by Holmes and Wise to envelop the south flank during the battle of WHITE OAK SWAMP. Other minor actions took place in this area 28–29 June and 2 July before and after the battle of MALVERN HILL, 1 July '62.

TURLEY, John Alexander. Union officer. Va. Lt. Col. 22d Ohio 23 May '61; mustered out 19 Aug. '61; Lt. Col. 81st Ohio 19 Aug. '61; resigned 1 Dec. '61; Col. 91st Ohio 22 Aug. '62; Bvt. B.G. USV (Cloyd's Mountain, Va.); discharged 4 Nov. '64. W.I.A. near Lynchburg (Va.) 17 June '64. Died 1900.

TURNER, Charles. Union officer. Mass. Lt. Col. 108th Ill. 28 Aug. '62; Col. 9 July '63; Bvt. B.G. USV 26 Mar. '65 (Mobile). Commanded 3, 3, XVI (Gulf). Died 1880.

TURNER, John Wesley. Union gen. 1833–99. N.Y. Appt.-Ill. USMA 1855 (14/34); Arty. He served in garrison, on the frontier, and in the Seminole War, and was (Capt. Staff Comsy. of

Subsist. 3 Aug. '61) Chief of Commissariat of the Army in Western Mo. (Oct.-Nov. '61); of the Dept. of Kans. (Dec. '61-Mar. '62); and of the Dept. of the South (31 Mar.-19 Apr. '62), when he also fought at Fort Pulaski; and of the Dept. of the Gulf (22 May-23 Dec. '62). Named Col. Add. A.D.C. 3 May '62 and B.G. USV 7 Sept. '63, he was Chief of Staff for the Dept. of the South (13 June '63-4 May '64) and commanded the artillery during the siege of Fort Wagner and Fort Sumter. Commanding 2d Div., X, Va. and N.C. (2-22 May '64 and 22 June-23 Aug. '64), at Bermuda Hundred, Drewry's Bluff, and the Petersburg siege, he was Chief of Staff of that Department and of the James 20 Nov. '64-20 Mar. '65. From 25 Mar. to 27 Apr. '65 he led Indpt. Div. XXIV, Va. at the fall of Petersburg and the pursuit of Lee to Appomattox. He commanded the XXIV Corps 27 Apr.-17 May and 8 July-1 Aug. '65. Breveted for Fort Wagner, Petersburg mine, Fort Gregg, war service (B.G. USA and Maj. Gen. USA and the campaign of 1864) (Maj. Gen. USV 1 Oct. '64), he continued in the R.A. until 1871, when he resigned.

TURNER'S GAP (Pass), Md. Featured in battle of South Mountain in ANTIETAM CAMPAIGN.

TURNING MOVEMENT. A wide (strategic) envelopment that avoids the enemy's main position and by threatening some vital point to the rear forces him to leave his original position and fight elsewhere. It derives its name from its *effect* of turning the enemy out of his position, not because it is executed by turning around (enveloping) the enemy. It differs from an ENVELOPMENT in that it does not involve fighting the enemy on his original position. Although the two terms are often used synonymously by writers, "turning movement" is used in its precise sense in

military memoirs of the Civil War and by such good modern historians as D. S. Freeman and K. P. Williams. Good illustrations of turning movements are Rosecrans' maneuver in the TULLAHOMA CAMPAIGN and Hooker's maneuver at the start of the CHANCELLORSVILLE CAMPAIGN.

TUTTLE, James Madison. Union gen. 1823-92. Ohio. A merchant and politician, he was commissioned Lt. Col. 2d Iowa 31 May '61 and Col. 6 Sept. '61. Leading his regiment in a charge at Fort Donelson, he was wounded but remained on the field. At Shiloh he commanded 1st Brig., 2d Div., Army Tenn., in the "Hornets' Nest" and succeeded to division when W. H. L. Wallace was mortally wounded. Promoted B.G. USV 9 June '62, he led 3d Div., XV (3 Apr.-9 Aug. '63 at Vicksburg and 21 Sept.-20 Dec. '63); 1st Div., XVI (20 Dec. '63-7 Mar. '64) and post of Natchez (Aug. '63-July '64). Resigning 14 June '64, he was later in the legislature and in business.

TWIGGS, David Emanuel. C.S.A. gen. 1790-1862. Ga. Called variously "Old Davy," "The Bengal Tiger," and "The Horse," he began his military career as a Capt. in the War of 1812, entering the R.A. and fighting in the Black Hawk, Seminole, and Mexican wars. A B.G. and Bvt. Maj. Gen. in the latter, he became involved in a dispute with William J. Worth over prestige and rank. He was presented the Sword of Congress for Monterrey. Holding various departmental commands in the South, in Feb. '61 he surrendered Tex. and all the Union forces and supplies to Ben McCulloch and his Texas Rangers. This is the only such dishonorable incident among those R.A. officers who resigned to go with the South. Twiggs was dismissed 1 Mar. '61 and 21 days later was named Maj. Gen. C.S.A. in command of the district of La. In broken health, he died 15 July '62. His daughter married Abraham C. Myers, the Confederacy's first Q.M. Gen. D.A.B. describes him as "a robust, powerfully built man, nearly six feet tall, with thick red face, heavy white hair, and an abundant beard."

TYLER, Daniel. Union gen. 1799–1882. Conn. USMA 1819 (14/29); Arty. Serving in garrison and on ordnance duty, he was sent to France on professional duty and translated *Manoeuvres of Artillery*. Resigning in 1834, he was variously a civil engineer, president of railroads, and on the USMA Board of Visitors. He was commissioned Col. 1st Conn. 23 Apr. '61 and B.G. Conn. Vols. 10 May '61, commanding 1st Div. at Blackburn's Ford and 1st Bull Run. Mustered out 11 Aug. '61, he was named B.G. USV 13 Mar. '62 and commanded 2d Brig., 1st Div., Army Miss. (1 May–27 July '62) at the siege of Corinth, and then commanded Dist. Del., VIII, Middle Dept. (3 July '63–19 Jan. '64). Resigning 6 Apr. '64, he traveled for several years before resuming his business activities. Engaging in iron smelting, he built, and named after his daughter-in-law, Anniston, Ala.

TYLER, Erastus Barnard. Union gen. 1822–91. N.Y. A businessman, he was commissioned Col. 7th Ohio 25 Apr. '61 and led his regiment at Cross Lanes (W. Va.) in Aug. He was promoted B.G. USV 14 May '62 after having commanded 3d, Lander's division, W. Va. (Jan.–Mar.); 3, 2, Banks's V, Potomac (13 Mar.–4 Apr.); and 3, 2d Div., Shenandoah (4 Apr.–10 May). At Winchester and Port Republic he led 3, Shields's division, Rappahannock (10 May–26 June '62) and, at Fredericksburg where he was wounded, the 1st Brig., 3d Div., V, Potomac. He also commanded this brigade 28 Mar.–25 May '63. In the VIII Corps, Middle

Dept., he commanded the defenses of Baltimore (29 June–Oct. '63); the corps and department (28 Sept.–10 Oct. '63); 3d Sep. Brig. (1 Oct.–18 Dec. '63) and 1st Sep. Brig. (18 Dec. '63–12 Mar. '64; 24 Mar.–18 Nov.; and 20 Dec.–5 June '64). Mustered out 24 Aug. '65, he was breveted for war service (Maj. Gen. USV).

TYLER, Robert C. C.S.A. gen. ?–1865. Md. Appt.-Tenn. He went with Walker to Nicaragua in 1859 and moving to Memphis later was named Q.M. of the 15th Tenn. in 1861. In the fall he was promoted Maj. and served on Cheatham's staff. A few months later he was promoted Lt. Col. 15th Tenn. and led it at Shiloh (wounded) before being named Col. He commanded his regiment at Perryville and Chickamauga, where he also commanded the 37th Tenn., and was wounded. At Missionary Ridge he led Bate's brigade and was wounded again. He was appointed B.G. C.S.A. 23 Feb. '64. He was still on crutches near West Point, Ga., when he organized the convalescents and militia in the area to oppose Wilson's raid. On 16 Apr. '65 he was killed at West Point.

TYLER, Robert Ogden. Union gen. 1831–74. N.Y. Appt.-Conn. USMA 1853 (22/52); Arty.-Q.M. Serving on the frontier in Indian fighting, in garrison, and on exploration expeditions, he was Capt. Asst. Q.M. (17 May '61), Depot Q.M. for the Army of the Potomac from May until Aug., '61, and then commissioned Col. 1st Conn. Arty. 29 Aug. In charge of the siege batteries at Yorktown, he also fought at Hanover C.H., Gaines's Mill, and Malvern Hill. Promoted B.G. USV 29 Nov. '62, he was in charge of the Arty. of the Center Grand Division at Fredericksburg. He commanded Arty., Dist. Alexandria, Mil. Dist. Washington; Arty., Def.

Alexandria, XXII (2 Feb.–15 Apr. '63) and Defenses South Potomac, XXII (15–26 Apr. '63). He fought at Chancellorsville and Gettysburg, commanding the Arty. Reserve of the Army of the Potomac May '63–Jan. '64. From then until the following May he commanded King's Div., XXII and also led the heavy artillery division of that corps. He commanded 4, 2, II, Potomac (May–7 June '64) at Spotsylvania, North Anna, Totopotomoy, and Cold Harbor, where he was severely wounded through the ankle, an injury from which he never recovered. On sick leave and commissions for the rest of the war, he was breveted for Fredericksburg, Gettysburg, Spotsylvania, Cold Harbor (B.G. USA and Maj. Gen. USV 1 Aug. '64) and war service (Maj. Gen. USA). He continued in the R.A. and died on active duty.

TYNDALE, Hector. Union gen. 1821–80. Pa. Offered an appointment to West Point, he yielded to his Quaker mother's wishes and went into the glass importing and ceramic business instead. Although not sympathetic to John Brown's raid, he escorted Mrs. Brown in 1859 when she went to see her husband and to bring his body back for burial, because he felt she needed protection. He was in Paris when the war began and returned to be commissioned Maj. 28th Pa. 28 June '61 and Lt. Col. 25 Apr. '62. Commanding 1, 2, XII, Potomac (17 Sept. '62) at Antietam, he had three horses shot from under him and was wounded twice, being left for dead on the field. He next commanded 1, 3, XI, Potomac (13 July–19 Sept. '63); 1, 3, XI, Cumberland at Wauhatchie; 3d Div., XI, Cumberland (15 Feb.–16 Apr. '64); 3, 1, XX, Cumberland (14 Apr.–2 May '64) and 1, 1, IV, Cumberland. Resigning 26 Aug. '64 because of ill health, he returned to his business in Philadelphia.

U

ULLMANN, Daniel. Union gen. 1810–92. Del. A lawyer and master in chancery, he was the Know-Nothing party's unsuccessful gubernatorial candidate in N.Y. in 1854. Commissioned Col. 78th N.Y. 28 Apr. '62, he commanded 2, 2, II, Army Va. (10–16 July '62) and in Aug., after Cedar Mountain, was ill with typhoid and left behind during the retreat. Captured and sent to Libby, he was promoted B.G. USV 13 Jan. '63 and sent to La. to raise colored troops. He then commanded, in the Dept. of the Gulf: Ullmann's brigade, USCT Port Hudson (July–Sept. '63) during siege and capture of Port Hudson; 1st Div., Corps d'Afrique (22 Sept. '63–23 Apr. '64); Dist. Port Hudson and Corps d'Afrique USCT (23 Apr.–9 June '64) and Dist. Morganza (23 Nov. '64–26 Feb. '65). Breveted Maj. Gen. USV for war service, he was mustered out 24 Aug. '65 and spent the rest of his life in scientific and literary studies and travel.

UNCLE TOM'S CABIN. A powerful agent in rousing anti-slavery sentiment, this novel by Harriet Beecher Stowe was first published serially in the Washington *National Era* (1851–52). G. L. Aiken dramatized the story, and the play reached uncounted millions. Despite many inaccuracies the book was credited as being one of the most cogent single reasons for bringing public opinion on the side of the North. Lincoln is alleged to have referred to its author as the "little lady" who caused the Civil War. Many of our familiar folk figures and expressions come from the book, among them Simon Legree, the cruel overseer; Topsy who "jes' growed"; Little Eva of the long golden curls whose soul was gathered to the angels in what must be one of the most famous scenes in American drama; Uncle Tom himself, the prototype of the faithful, lovable "darkie"; and the runaway Eliza who, clutching her baby, was chased across the ice floes by the bloodhounds.

UNCONDITIONAL SURRENDER. After being surrounded at Fort Donelson and abandoned by his two superiors, Buckner requested terms. When Grant asked the crusty old C. F. SMITH for suggestions, Smith said, "No terms to the damned rebels." Grant then penned his famous note: "Headquarters, Army in the Field, Camp Near Donelson, Feb'y. 16th, 1862. Gen. S. B. Buckner, Confed. Army. Sir: Yours of this date proposing Armistice, and appointment of Commissioners, to settle terms of Capitulation is just received. No terms except unconditional and immediate surrender can be accepted. I propose to move immediately upon your works. I am sir, very respectfully, Your obt. svt. U. S. Grant, Brig. Gen."

UNDERGROUND RAILROAD. The loosely organized system of transporting runaway slaves to freedom in the North and Canada. The "stations" of the Railroad were homes of Abolitionists and opponents of slavery, and the "conductors" took the fugitives at night to the next station along the established routes. This activity was particularly prevalent from the borders of Md., Mo., Del., Va., and Ky. into Canada. Ohio had many lines, and Philadelphia, with many members of the Society of Friends, was an important center in the East. There were a few stations in the South itself, but the danger was so much greater in slave territory that this phase of the activity was spasmodic and without much effect. Stringent anti-slave laws were passed, but the Railroad was run by idealists and dedicated Abolitionists who felt that no man should be held in bondage, although their actions actually deprived the slave owner of legally held and often quite valuable property.

UNDERWOOD, Adin Ballou. Union gen. 1828–88. Mass. A Harvard Law School graduate, he practiced until commissioned Capt. 2d Mass. 25 May '61. Promoted Lt. Col. 33d Mass. 13 Aug. '62, he fought at Fredericksburg and, as Col. (3 Apr. '63), led his regiment at Chancellorsville and Gettysburg. Named B.G. USV 6 Nov. '63, he fought under Hooker at Lookout Mountain and was severely wounded. He was breveted Maj. Gen. USV 13 Aug. '65 for war service, mustered out 24 Aug. '65, and was later surveyor of the Port of Boston.

UNIFORMS. At the start of the war uniforms in a staggering variety of cuts and colors appeared on both sides. Many were the dress uniforms of swank militia outfits—for example, the numerous ZOUAVE regiments of the North and South—which not only were unsuited for field service but also failed to distinguish friend from foe. The Federal government took steps early in 1862 to standardize the blue uniform, and by the winter of 1863 had achieved this (Shannon). Although the Confederates had prescribed uniform regulations early in the war, the Southern soldier presented an increasingly ragged and nondescript appearance as the conflict progressed and supplies became more critical. The shortage of shoes was particularly hard on him. The prescribed uniforms, insignia and buttons of both armies are shown in plate CLXXVII of the O.R. atlas.

UNION ARMY. At the beginning of the war the R.A. totaled 16,000 officers and men, and this number was reduced by 313 officers who went with the South. From this meager organization the Union Army numbered over 1,000,000 on 1 May '65, and there were over 2,300,000 three-year enlistments during the war. In a frenzy of patriotic fervor the Northern governors offered about 300,000 troops by Apr. '61, but Lincoln would not call Congress before 4 July, and without new legislation there was no authority to increase the army. On 15 Apr. Lincoln called for 75,000 three-month militia, and beginning on 22 July '61 Congress authorized a volunteer army of 500,000 men. They also legalized Lincoln's call on 3 May for 42,000 three-year volunteers and 22,700 regulars. Most of the R.A., at an authorized strength of 42,000, was sent to guard the border against Indians. On 2 July '62, there was another call for 300,000 volunteers, with the governors still responsible for equipping and outfitting the soldiers. On 4 Aug., after this call produced sparse results, a draft of 300,-000 nine-month militia (act of 17 July '62) was issued. This draft failed, but Federal, state, and local BOUNTIES provided a necessary number. Continued decimation of the army through casualties, desertions, expiration of enlistments, and few enlistments brought about the Enrollment Act of 3 Mar. '63, the first instance of conscription or compulsory military service in US history. A payment of $300, or the hiring of a substitute, could excuse a man from this, and this inequality brought about the DRAFT RIOTS. As Fox points out, "the Union Army was essentially a volunteer army.... the number of drafted men actually held to service was only 52,068" (Fox, 532). By the payment of $300 in commutation, 86,724 drafted men received exemption. Another 42,-581 men enlisted as substitutes for men who, although not drafted, were enrolled under the Conscription Act and liable to future drafts, and who secured exemptions therefrom by sending men to the field in their place. Another 75,429 conscripts sent substitutes into the Union Army (ibid.). All of this gives support to the popular complaint that the Civil War was a rich man's war and a poor man's fight.

A tremendous number of absentees lowered the actual effective strength of the army. Over 250,000 men were honorably discharged for physical disability arising from wounds, accidents, or disease in the service. Although 268,530 desertions were reported during the war, the Provost Marshal Gen. estimated that 25 per cent of these were unintentionally or unavoidably absent. The P.M.G. put the actual number of desertions at 201,397, of which 76,526 were arrested and returned to their regiments. The R.A. had the highest desertion rate, over 24 per cent, while the average rate in the volunteer service was 6 per cent. Kans. troops had the highest desertion rate among the volunteers, losing more than 11 per cent of their enrollment. "In addition to the deserters, there were thousands of other absentees. In March 1863 the returns of the Army of the Potomac showed that 2,922 officers and 81,964 enlisted men were absent, the majority of whom were absent without any known cause; and in December 1862 a return of the Army of the Cumberland showed that with 76,725 present there were 46,677 absent" (ibid.). See also NUMBERS AND LOSSES, ORGANIZATION.

UNION CABINET. Vice-president: Hannibal Hamlin (1861), Andrew Johnson (1865); State: W. H. Seward (1861); Treasury: Salmon P. Chase (1861), W. P. Fessenden (1864), Hugh McCulluch (1865); War: Simon Cameron (1861), E. M. Stanton (1862); *Navy:* Gideon Welles (1861); *Interior:* Caleb B. Smith (1861), John P. Usher (1863); *Postmaster General:* Horatio King (1861), Montgomery Blair (1861), William Dennison (1864); *Attorney General:* Edward Bates (1861), Titian J. Coffey (1863), James Speed (1864). Biographical sketches of most of the above are to be found in the proper alphabetical sequence.

UNION NAVY. See NAVAL PARTICIPATION.

UNION REFRESHMENT SALOON. See Mary W. LEE.

UNION WAR GOVERNORS. *California:* John G. Downey (1860–61), Leland Stanford (1861–63), Frederick F. Low (1863–68); *Connecticut:* William A. Buckingham (1858–66); *Delaware:* William Burton (1859–63), William Cannon (1863–67); *Illinois:* Richard Yates (1861–65); *Indiana:* Oliver P. Morton (1861–67); *Iowa:* Samuel J. Kirkwood (1860–64), William M. Stone (1864–68); *Kansas:* Charles Robinson (1861–63), Thomas Carney (1863–65); *Maine:* Israel Washburn, Jr. (1861–63), Abner Coburn (1863–64), Samuel Cony (1864–67); *Massachusetts:* John Albion Andrew (1861–66); *Michigan:* Austin Blair (1861–64), Henry H. Crapo (1865–69); *Minnesota:* Alexander Ramsey (1859–63), Stephen Miller (1863–66); *Nevada:* (state not admitted until 1864) Henry G. Blasdell (1864–71); *New Hampshire:* Ichabod Goodwin (1859–61), Nathaniel S. Berry (1861–63), Joseph A. Gilmore (1863–65); *New Jersey:* Charles S. Olden (1860–63), Joel Parker (1863–66); *New York:* Edwin D. Morgan (1859–63), Horatio Seymour (1863–65), Reuben E. Fenton (1865–69); *Ohio:* William Dennison (1860–62), David Tod (1862–64), John Brough (1864–65); *Oregon:* John Whit-

taker (1859–62), Addison C. Gibbs (1862–66); *Pennsylvania:* Andrew G. Curtin (1861–67); *Rhode Island:* William Sprague (1860–61), John R. Bartlett (1861–62), William C. Cozzens (1863), James Y. Smith (1863–65); *Vermont:* Erastus Fairbanks (1860–61), Frederic Holbrook (1861–63), J. Gregory Smith (1863–65); *West Virginia:* (admitted 1863) Francis H. Pierpoint (1861–63), Arthur I. Boreman (1863–69); *Wisconsin:* Alexander W. Randall (1857–61), Louis P. Harvey (1861–62), Edward S. Salomon (1862–63), James T. Lewis (1863–66). See also BORDER STATE WAR GOVERNORS.

USCI. United States Colored Infantry. See NEGRO TROOPS.

79TH UNITED STATES COLORED INFANTRY (1st Kans. Col. Volunteers). Commander: Colonel James M. Williams. Battles: Island Mounds, Mo., Sherwood, Mo., Cabin Creek (C.N.), Honey Springs (C.N.), Fort Gibson (C.N.), Lawrence (Kans.), Baxter Springs (C.N.), Horse Head Creek (Ark.), Poison Springs (Ark.), Flat Rock (C.N.), Ivy Ford (Ark.), Roseville (Ark.). Present also at Bush Creek, Prairie d'Ann, Jenkins' Ferry, and Joy's Ford. Originally organized as the 1st Kans. Col. Volunteers, its designation was changed 13 Dec. '64. This regiment had the distinction of being the first colored unit to fight in the Civil War (Island Mounds). Recruiting started in Aug. '62, but a regimental organization was not established until Jan. '63, when six companies were mustered in. The other four companies were organized by May '63. In May '64 Williams was given command of the 2d Brig., Frontier Div., VII Corps, with the 79th Inf. as part of that brigade. Mustered out 1 Oct. '65 (Fox, 422). This regiment ranks 21st among Federal regiments in highest percentage of total enrollment killed in action.

USCT. United States Colored Troops. See NEGRO TROOPS.

UNITED STATES [FLINTLOCK] MUSKET, Model 1822. Due to a shortage of weapons, this Revolutionary War-type weapon was used to some extent at the beginning of the Civil War. It was a smoothbore, muzzle-loading flintlock musket, caliber .69, that used a paper cartridge. A powder flask was used to fill the primer pan. Effective at about 100 yards, it could be fired at a rate of two shots per minute and misfired about one out of six times. The Confederates used this weapon as late as the end of 1862 in the East (Alexander, 53); several Confederate regiments were armed with muskets at Mill Springs, Ky. (19 Jan. '62), where the rainy weather made them virtually useless.

UNITED STATES PERCUSSION MUSKET, Model 1842. About 150,000 of these were available in the Civil War. It "falls into an odd category, chiefly because it was our first regulation percussion shoulder weapon and also our last smoothbore shoulder weapon" (Shields, 62). An improvement over the Model 1822 by the substitution of a percussion cap for the flintlock, it had the same caliber and range, a slightly better rate of fire, but only one misfire in 166. This weapon "made up the bulk of the Confederate armament at the beginning, some of the guns, even all through 1862, being old flintlocks [Model 1822]. . . . Not until after the battle of Gettysburg was the whole army in Virginia equipped with the rifled musket" (Alexander, 53-4).

UNITED STATES RIFLE, Model 1841 ("Mississippi," or "Jäger" [or "Yager"] rifle). The first general issue US Army rifle designed and manufactured for the percussion cap system, this was a .54 caliber rifle, 48¾ inches in over-all length and weighing about 9¾ pounds. The barrel had seven grooves, was coated with brown lacquer, and had a fixed rear sight and a brass-blade front sight. All FURNITURE except the iron swivels was brass. Originally made to use a paper cartridge and spherical lead ball, after introduction of the Minié bullet in 1850 most of the rifles were modified to .58 caliber.

There was no provision on the original model for a bayonet. The altered weapons were equipped with an adjustable rear sight and various mounts for a 22½-inch saber bayonet. A number of variations of this rifle are to be found. The Harpers Ferry Armory made 25,296 of these rifles between 1846 and 1855, after having prepared the pattern weapons in 1841. The Springfield Armory made 3,200 in 1849. Remington made 12,500 before the Civil War and the same number during the war. Other contractors were Robbins, Kendall & Lawrence; Robbins & Lawrence; Tyron; and E. Whitney. Total production of the Model 1841 was 101,096 from all the above sources.

The rifle was so effective that it was honored with the name Jäger, after the German huntsmen or light infantry units. It was called also the "Mississippi Rifle" after being issued in 1847 to Jefferson Davis' 1st Miss. Regt.

UNITED STATES RIFLE MUSKET, Model 1855. Adoption of the Minié bullet by the US in 1855 marked a big advance in the effectiveness of military rifles. The above model was a .58 caliber muzzle-loading, rifled-bore weapon that used the new MAYNARD TAPE primer system. It was five feet in length. Without the bayonet it weighed about nine pounds two ounces. About 47,000 were produced at the Springfield Armory between 1 Jan. '57 and 31 Dec. '61 (Gluckman, 228-9).

UNITED STATES RIFLE, Model 1855 ("Harpers Ferry"). Differed from the United States RIFLE MUSKET, Model 1855, mainly in that its barrel was 33 instead of 40 inches long. It can be distinguished from the former weapon also by the fact that the "Harpers Ferry" had only two iron bands holding the stock to the barrel, whereas the longer "Springfield" had three. See RIFLE MUSKET.

UNITED STATES RIFLE MUSKET, Model 1861. With the slightly modified 1863 models (see below), this was the principal infantry weapon on both sides. The Springfield Armory manufactured about 800,000 during the war, and other sources furnished almost 900,000 more. The Confederates captured approximately 150,000 (Fuller and Steuart, 43). (These figures include the 1861 and the two 1863 models.)

The Model 1861 was fundamentally the same as the Model 1855 except that the percussion cap had replaced the unsatisfactory MAYNARD TAPE. Its over-all length was 56 inches, 3⅞ inches shorter than the 1855. The .58 Minié bullet continued to be used in the Model 1861, and the barrel length remained 40 inches. It weighed about 9¾ pounds with its 18-inch triangular bayonet. At its maximum effective range of 500 yards, under ideal conditions, 10 shots would make a 27-inch pattern. Extreme range was about 1,000 yards. It could be fired about six times per minute. The Springfield Armory made 265,129 of these Model 1861 rifle muskets between 1 Jan. '61 and 31 Dec. '63. Three contractors, Colt, Amoskeag, and Lamson, Goodnow & Yale, made special models patterned after the Springfield.

The Model 1861 rifle was also made for artillery use. It was shorter, the usual barrel length being 33 inches.

UNITED STATES RIFLE MUSKET, Model 1863. Essentially the same weapon as the Model 1861, but slightly simplified to make manufacture easier. The Springfield Armory produced 273,-265 between 1 Jan. '63 and 31 Dec. '64 (Gluckman, 232).

UNITED STATES RIFLE MUSKET, Model 1863, Type 2. Modification of the Model 1863 (above) brought the weapon back to approximately the same design as the Model 1861 (Shields, 75). The arm is of interest as the last US muzzle-loader. The Springfield Armory produced 255,040 between 1 Jan. '64 and 31 Dec. '65 (Gluckman, 232).

UPPERVILLE, Va., 21 June '63. (Gettysburg campaign.) After Aldie and Middleburg continued Federal pressure drove Stuart relentlessly toward the main Confederate force in the Shenandoah. He was forced back from a position about three miles west of Middleburg, and then to a second line along Goose Creek. Attacked by Vincent's infantry brigade (3, 1, V), Gregg's cavalry division, with an additional brigade from Buford's cavalry, the brigades of Hampton and Robertson withdrew toward Upperville. The brigades of Chambliss and Jones, to the north, resisted Buford's attempts to turn Stuart's left flank, and withdrew toward Upperville also. On approaching Upperville, Buford moved down to reinforce D. M. Gregg's division. Kilpatrick charged but was repulsed. After J. I. Gregg's brigade came up on his left and artillery went into position to support him, Kilpatrick's next charge was successful. As Robertson's brigade was withdrawing through Upperville, P. G. Evans' N.C. regiment broke. (He was killed leading his regiment in the last charge of the day.) Wade Hampton led a series of charges against Gregg's division and relieved the pressure from the other brigades. Stuart withdrew his troops in good order and took up a strong defensive position in Ashby's

Gap. Union losses were 209 (Fox); Stuart's losses were 180 (E.&B.). Losses for the battles of Aldie, Middleburg, and Upperville are put at 613 Federals and 510 Confederates (Fox and H. B. McClellan).

UPTON, Emory. Union gen. 1839–81. N.Y. USMA May 1861 (8/45); Arty. Graduated on 6 May '61, he was commissioned 2d Lt. 4th US Arty. on that date and promoted 1st Lt. 5th US Arty. eight days later. He was Gen. Tyler's A.D.C. at Blackburn's Ford and 1st Bull Run (wounded). He took command of a battery after recovering, fighting at Yorktown, West Point, Gaines's Mill, and Glendale. In the Maryland campaign he led the Arty. Brig., 1, VI, at South Mt. and Antietam before being named Col. 121st N.Y. 23 Oct. '62. He fought at Fredericksburg and took command of 2, 1, VI (1–2 July and 4 July–5 Aug. '63) for the battle of Gettysburg and pursuit to Warrenton. Returning to that brigade, he led it at Rappahannock Station, Mine Run operations, the Wilderness, and Spotsylvania (6 Nov. '63–8 July '64). Wounded at the last-named battle, he recovered in time for Cold Harbor and the battles about Petersburg. He was appointed B.G. USV 12 May '64. Going to the defense of Washington when Early threatened, he then commanded his brigade in the Army of the Shenandoah (6 Aug.–19 Sept. '64). He fought at Opequon on the latter date, having succeeded to command of the division, and was wounded there, going on sick leave until 13 Dec. '64. Then going to Ala., he took command of the 4th Cav. Div. under J. H. Wilson, fighting there and in Ga. at Montevallo, Plantersville, Selma, and Columbus. He was breveted for Rappahannock Station, Spotsylvania, Winchester, Selma (B.G. USA), war service (Maj. Gen. USA) and Winchester 19 Oct. '64 (Maj. Gen. USV). Continuing in the R.A., he

served as commandant at West Point and sat on several boards that reviewed and changed the combat arms' tactics in the postwar era, as well as spending two years abroad. He wrote of his findings on this tour in "Armies of Asia and Europe," published in 1878. He also wrote *A New System of Infantry Tactics* (1867–74), *Tactics for Non-Military Bodies* (1870), and his monumental *Military Policy of the United States,* published posthumously in 1904 by Sec. of War Elihu Root. Discovering himself to be the victim of a fatal disease, he committed suicide 15 Mar. '81, at the age of 42, as Col. 4th US Arty. at the Presidio of San Francisco.

UTAH, UNION DEPARTMENT OF. In existence at the start of the war with headquarters at Fort Crittenden (40 miles southwest Salt Lake City) and merged 27 July '61 into the Dept. of the Pacific. From 17 Feb. '65 to the end of the war it was part of the Dept. of the Mo.

UTAH EXPEDITION. The Mormons living around Salt Lake City declared themselves, in 1857, immune from US laws and refused to let California-bound wagon trains pass through their territory, massacring several groups. In the early summer of that year the 5th and 10th US Inf. and two batteries of artillery set out from Fort Leavenworth to pacify them. The 2d US Dragoons were to follow. They were, however, harassed by Mormon guerrillas, and, unable to find supplies in the hostile countryside, finally unable to continue for a lack of food and the cold weather. A. S. Johnston took command in Nov. '57 and by the following spring had enlarged his command to number 5,500 troops—almost half of the entire standing army at that time. The Mormons, when faced with this force, agreed to peace, law, and westward expansion. Many Civil War leaders were veterans

of the Utah Expedition. (See also ROB-
INSON, J. C.)

UTOY CREEK, Ga., 5–6 Aug. '64.
(ATLANTA CAMPAIGN) After being
blocked at EZRA CHAPEL (CHURCH), 28
July, Sherman kept trying to envelop
Hood's left flank. On 2 Aug. Schofield
moved to the right of Howard and, the
next day the XIV Corps was attached
to him for the contemplated offensive.
Schofield planned to force a crossing of
the north fork of Utoy Creek at a bend
near Herring's (or Heron's) Mill with
two divisions initially and to follow with
the rest of his force. The morning of 3
Aug. Hascall's (2d) division of XXIII
Corps crossed near the mill against light
opposition and occupied a hill to the
north and east. Baird's (3d) division of
XIV Corps was supposed to follow and
take up a position on Hascall's right to
secure the bridgehead. It was not until
Sherman arrived and personally ordered
Baird to move that this division crossed
the creek (Cox's *Atlanta*, 190).

The following morning (4 Aug.)
Cox's division of XXIII Corps crossed
and took up a position behind Baird
with orders to support the latter's advance. Palmer (C.G. XIV Corps) was
ordered to have Baird attack to expand
the bridgehead to the south and east,
and to move his other two divisions,
Morgan (2d) and R. W. Johnson (1st),
to reinforce this operation. However,
due to delays later characterized by
Sherman as unpardonable, there was no
offensive action this day except for a
reconnaissance by Gleason's (2d) brigade of Baird's division. Gleason took
25 prisoners but had 26 men killed and
wounded. Later in the day Palmer's
other two divisions crossed the creek
and formed on Baird's right.

Orders to Palmer for 5 Aug. were for
Baird to attack with Morgan and Johnson echeloned to his left and right, re-

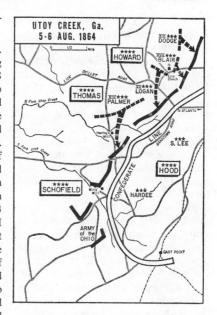

UTOY CREEK, Ga.
5-6 AUG. 1864

spectively. Hascall was to advance his
right flank to support this operation, and
Cox was to support the advance of
Johnson on Baird's right. Although there
was Confederate strength in front of
the Federal divisions, Schofield erroneously believed that this was only an
outpost line.

Baird's advance was supposed to start
at 6 A.M., but he delayed it until 8
o'clock because he did not recognize
Schofield's authority. When his orders
were confirmed by his own corps commander, Palmer, he moved aggressively
forward. Although these Federal delays
had given the enemy time to strengthen
his defenses, Baird drove in the Confederate skirmish line. He lost 83 men,
but captured 140 prisoners. The other
divisions moved up about as called for
in the plan, but did not close with the
enemy.

Schofield reported to Sherman that
he had "totally failed to make any aggressive movement with the Fourteenth

Corps." He then regrouped his forces to get his own XXIII Corps divisions into position to attack. Cox took Johnson's position, the latter relieved Hascall on the left flank, and Hascall formed to the right rear of Cox. These movements were not completed until the morning of the 6th. Hood, meanwhile, had reinforced the threatened wing with elements of Hardee's corps, and the Confederates had spent the night strengthening their defenses with abatis. Their line had also been extended to the left.

The morning of the 6th Cox was ordered to send one brigade forward to probe the Confederate line and to exploit any success with the rest of his division. Reilly (1, 3, XXIII) was reinforced by 200 skirmishers. His skirmish line made good progress and he supported it with the 104th Ohio and then with the rest of his brigade. However, the Federals were stopped with heavy losses in the abatis and subjected to an effective crossfire. Reilly was able to hold until Casement's brigade (2, 3, XXIII) could come forward to cover his retreat.

Hascall, on the right, sent two brigades, Cooper and Swayne, across the creek against Confederate cavalry. This gave the Federals possession of a position that had been enfilading Reilly's lines, and enabled Hascall to bring to bear a fire on the Confederate lines that drove them back to their main fortifications. Bate's division of Hardee's corps was the unit principally engaged in the Confederate defense.

Meanwhile, there had been advances by the other corps to the north of Schofield. On 7 Aug. the extreme Federal right flank was held by Cox, near Willis' Mill. Having failed to achieve any success along Utoy Creek, Sherman maintained his positions here until 25 Aug. He then undertook the decisive action that resulted in the battle of JONESBORO, 31 Aug.–1 Sept. '64.

V

VAIL, Jacob Garetson. Union officer. Ind. Capt. 17th Ind. 12 June '61; Maj. 9 Apr. '64; Lt. Col. 11 Aug. '64; Col. 18 Nov. '64; Bvt. B.G. USV (war service). Commanded 1, 2, Cav. Corps (Mil. Div. Miss.). Died 1884.

VAIL, Nicholas J. Although listed by Phisterer as Lt. Col. 14th US Col. Inf. and Bvt. B.G. USV 13 Mar. '65, he does not appear in Heitman or Dyer.

VALLANDIGHAM, Clement Laird. Politician. 1820–71. Ohio. A lawyer, he entered politics as a Democrat and sat in the state legislature and US Congress before running for Gov. of Ohio in 1863. He was a vicious opponent of Lincoln and was active in the KNIGHTS OF THE GOLDEN CIRCLE. Imprisoned by Burnside for his speeches, he was banished to the Confederacy by Lincoln. He objected also to Davis' handling of the war and was summarily ejected from the South. After going through the blockade to Nassau, he lived in Canada until June '64 when he returned to the US and delivered the keynote speech at the Democratic convention. He was then elected Supreme Commander of the Sons of Liberty (see KNIGHTS OF THE GOLDEN CIRCLE) and after the war was defeated in several attempts for office. He may have been the model for Edward Everett Hale's *Man Without a Country* (Pratt, *Ordeal*, 235) although others have been named for this "distinction."

VALLEY DISTRICT AND ARMY, CONFEDÉRATE.

The Shenandoah Valley was designated as the Valley District of the Dept. of Northern Va. when the latter was established 22 Oct. '61. T. J. Jackson was assigned as its first commander. W. E. ("Grumble") Jones succeeded Jackson on 29 Dec. '62. Trimble followed Jones in May '63. J. D. Imboden was assigned command on 21 July and Early on 15 Dec. '63. Lomax took command on 29 Mar. '65.

VALVERDE, N.M. 21 Feb. '62.

During the NEW MEXICO AND ARIZONA OPERATIONS IN 1861-62, Sibley with his Army of New Mexico advanced up the Rio Grande and made contact with the Federal garrison under Canby at Fort Craig. Sibley then moved north about seven miles and got astride the Federal line of communications to Santa Fe to bring on a battle. Skirmishing started at 8 A.M., and by 11:30 both sides had built up their forces. A two-hour engagement then took place. The Federals, first under Col. B. S. Roberts and then under Canby, failed in an attempt to envelop the Confederates' left flank. They then repulsed a counterattack in which the Texans charged with the lance. Shortly before sunset, the Confederates, under T. J. Green (Sibley was "sick"), made a frontal attack, routed the Federals, and captured a battery. The Federals lost 68 K.I.A., 160 W.I.A., and 35 missing out of 3,810 engaged. The Confederates lost 36 K.I.A. and 160 W.I.A., out of 2,600 engaged. (B.&L., II, 106.) The night before this action Capt. James ("Paddy") Graydon, commanding the Spy Company, packed six 24-pounder howitzer shells on the backs of two mules and led them close to the Confederate picket lines. The mules refused to cooperate by continuing into the Confederate camp and were blown up without damage to the enemy. Col. "Kit" Carson commanded part of the Federal force and was breveted for the battle.

VAN ALEN, James H. Union gen. ?-1886. N.Y. Commissioned Col. 3d N.Y. Cav. 28 Aug. '61, he served under Banks and Stone in the Army of the Potomac. He was promoted B.G. USV 15 Apr. '62 and resigned 14 July '63.

VAN ANTWERP, Verplanck. Union officer. N.Y. Appt.-Iowa. Maj. Add. A.D.C. 29 Jan. '62; discharged 21 Mar. '62; Maj. Add. A.D.C. 19 Apr. '62; Bvt. B.G. USV 13 Feb. '65. I.G. for the Dept. of Kans. in May-Oct. '62. In the field with Gen. Blunt in Ark. and Indian Territory to Jan. '63. Disabled for field service by an accident, Mar. '63. In R.A. as Capt. Mil. Storekeeper Q.M. Dept. until his death in 1875.

VAN BUREN, Daniel Tompkins. Union officer. c. 1826-90. N.Y. USMA 1847 (6/38); Arty. Capt. 20th N.Y. State Militia 4 May '61; Maj. Asst. Adj. Gen. Vols. 3 Aug. '61; Col. Add. A.D.C. 1 June '62; Bvt. B.G. USV (war service). Served as Chief of Staff for Gen. Dix when the latter commanded: Dept. of Pa., Div. of the Army of the Potomac, Middle Dept., Baltimore (Md.), VII Corps, Fort Monroe (Va.), and Dept. of the East. Asst. Adj. Gen. for Gen. Hooker in the Dept. of the East. Van Buren had participated in the Mexican War and served on garrison duty and as assistant professor of natural and experimental philosophy at USMA when he resigned in 1855 as 1st Lt. He then was an attorney and civil engineer in N.Y., also being Col. in the N.Y. Mil. and school commissioner. After the war he became a surveyor and civil engineer.

VAN BUREN, James Lyman. Union officer. N.Y. 2d Lt. 53d N.Y. 26 Oct. '61; Maj. Add. A.D.C. 7 July '62; Bvt.

B.G. USV 2 Apr. '65. Brevets for Wil-
derness, Spotsylvania, Bethesda Church,
Petersburg siege, East Tenn. campaign,
Knoxville siege, Forts Stedman and
Sedgwick (Va.).

VAN BUREN, Thomas Brodhead.
Union officer. N.Y. Col. 102d N.Y. 8
Feb. '62; Bvt. B.G. USV (war service);
resigned 13 Dec. '62. Commanded 2, 2,
II (Va.); 2, 2, XII (Potomac). Died
1889.

VANCE, Robert B. C.S.A. gen. 1828–
99. N.C. A court clerk and merchant,
he organized and was Capt. of the Bun-
combe Life Guards which became part
of the 29th N.C. He was commissioned
Col. in Oct. '61 and was sent to eastern
Tenn. the next month to guard the railroad. In Feb. '62 the regiment was stationed in Cumberland Gap, remaining
there until the retreat in June of that
year. He commanded the regiment at
Shiloh and Stones River, where he took
over the 2d Brig. when J. E. Rains
was killed. While ill with typhoid, he
was appointed B.G. C.S.A. 23 Apr. '63
to rank from 4 Mar. He was captured
at Cosby Creek, Tenn., 14 Jan. '65 and
paroled 14 Mar. After the war he was
a Democratic Congressman.

VANCE, Zebulon Baird. C.S.A. gov.
of N.C. 1830–94. After a year at the
Univ. of N. C. he studied law and
entered politics as a Whig, sitting in
the legislature and the US Congress.
An opponent of secession, he volunteered for the Confederate Army when
his state left the Union and was commissioned Capt. and then Col. 26th
N.C. in Aug. '61, fighting at New Bern
and in the Seven Days' Battles. Elected
Gov., he succeeded Clark on 1 Jan. '63
and was re-elected in 1865. After imprisonment he ran for the US Senate
and was defeated, but in 1877 was
elected Gov. for a third term. Two years
later he was sent to the Senate.

VAN CLEVE, Horatio Phillips. Union
gen. 1809–91. N.J. USMA 1831 (24/33);
Inf. He served on the frontier before
resigning in 1836 to become a farmer,
civil engineer, and surveyor in Mich.
and Minn. Commissioned Col. 2d Minn.
22 July '61 and B.G. USV 21 Mar. '62,
he was at Mill Springs and on the advance upon and siege of Corinth. Commanding 14th Brig., 5th Div., Army
Ohio (2 July–29 Sept. '62) and succeeding to division (Sept.–Nov. '62), he
was wounded at Stones River while
leading 2d Div., Left Wing, XIV Cumberland (5 Nov.–31 Dec. '62). At Ringgold, Lee and Gordon's Mills, and
Chickamauga, he commanded 3d Div.,
XXI, Cumberland (13 Mar.–9 Oct. '63),
and later he led 2, Dist. Nashville; 2, 3,
XII; and post of Murfreesboro (27 Nov.
'63–21 Aug. '65). Breveted Maj. Gen.
USV, he was mustered out 24 Aug. '65
and later held several public offices in
Minn.

VAN DERVEER, Ferdinand. Union
gen. 1823–92. Ohio. Fighting in the
Mexican War, he was later a lawyer
and judge. He was commissioned Col.
35th Ohio 24 Sept. '61 and led his
regiment at Corinth, Perryville, Murfreesboro, and Missionary Ridge. He
commanded 3d Brig., 1st Div., Army
Ohio (6 Aug.–29 Sept. '62); 3, 3, XIV,
Cumberland (28 Jan.–10 Oct. '63) at
Chickamauga; and 2, 3, XIV, Cumberland (30 Nov. '63–14 Jan. '64 and 16
Feb.–27 July '64) at Buzzard Roost,
Dalton, Resaca, Pine Mountain, Kenesaw Mountain, and Peach Tree Creek.
Promoted B.G. USV 4 Oct. '64, he also
commanded 1, 2, XIV (18 Jan.–23 June
'65), succeeded to command of the
division (23 June–18 July '65), after
which he resigned.

VANDEVER, William. Union gen.
1817–93. Md. A Republican Congressman from Iowa, he was commissioned
Col. 9th Iowa 24 Sept. '61 and B.G.

USV 29 Nov. '62. He commanded 2d Brig., 4th Div. Army Southwest Mo. (Feb.–May '62) at Pea Ridge; 1, 9, XIII (4 Jan.–4 Feb. '63) at Arkansas Post; 2d Div., Army Frontier (24 May–5 June '63) at the Vicksburg siege; 1, Herron's division, XIII (11 June–28 July '63) at Vicksburg; 1, 2, XIII (28 July–7 Aug. '63); 1, 2, XIII (7–25 Aug. and 6 Oct.–11 Nov. '63); 3, 2, XVI (20 June–2 Aug. '64) at ALLATOONA; 1, 2, XIV (18 Jan.–23 June '65) at Bentonville and 2d Div., XIV (23 June–18 July '65). He was breveted Maj. Gen. USV 7 June '65 for war service, mustered out 24 Aug. '65, and sent to Congress as a Republican from Calif. after the war.

VAN DORN, Earl. C.S.A. gen. 1820–63. Miss. USMA 1842 (52/56); Inf. He served in garrison and on the frontier, participating in a great deal of Indian scouting and fighting, and in one skirmish with the Comanches was seriously wounded four times. He also fought in the Mexican War (1 wound, 2 brevets) and the Seminole War before resigning 31 Jan. '61 as Maj. Named B.G. of the Miss. troops, he was appointed by the legislature and succeeded Davis as state Maj. Gen. Commissioned Col. of C.S.A. Cav. 16 Mar. '61, he was put in command of the forts below New Orleans. On 11 Apr. '61 he was given command of the Dept. of Tex. Nine days later he captured the STAR OF THE WEST at Galveston. Appointed B.G. C.S.A. 5 June '61, he became Maj. Gen. 19 Sept. of that same year and then led the 1st Div. in the Confederate Army of the Potomac in the latter part of 1861. In Jan. '62 he took command of the Trans-Miss. Dept. and fought at Pea Ridge. Joining Beauregard at Corinth just after the battle of Shiloh, he then commanded the Army of the West until the latter part of May '62. That summer he commanded the Dist. of Miss. with headquarters at Vicksburg and headed the Army of West Tenn. as well as Price's Army of the West. He fought Rosecrans at Corinth, and an investigation vindicated him of any blame for the battle or the retreat. However, he was transferred to command the cavalry and led it at Holly Springs in Dec. '62 and Thompson's Station in Mar. '63. He was "of small, elegant figure, elegant person" (C.M.H.). On 8 May '63 he was killed at Spring Hill by "a resident of the neighborhood, Dr. Peters, who stated in justification of his act that Van Dorn had 'violated the sanctity of his home.' Van Dorn's friends, on the other hand, indignantly deny there was any such reason. They say Van Dorn was shot in the back, in cold blood, and for political reasons" (Horn, 453).

VAN DORN'S CAVALRY CORPS. See CORPS, CONFEDERATE.

VAN LEW, Elizabeth. Union spy. Although from a prominent Richmond family, she was intensely loyal to the Union and became one of the most dependable and highly praised spies in the war. She acted eccentric and sometimes even insane to conceal her real work and was called "Crazy Bet" or "Miss Lizzie" by her neighbors.

VAN PETTEN, John Bullock. Union officer. N.Y. Lt. Col. 160th N.Y. 6 Sept. '62; resigned 27 Jan. '65; Col. 193d N.Y. 10 Apr. '65; Bvt. B.G. USV (war service).

VAN VLIET, Stewart. Union gen. 1815–1901. N.Y. USMA 1840 (9/42); Arty.-Q.M. Serving in the Seminole wars and the Mexican War and on garrison duty, he was Indian fighting when commissioned Maj. Q.M. 3 Aug. '61 (from Capt. since 1847) and B.G. USV 23 Sept. '61. He was Chief Q.M. of the Army of the Potomac for McClellan during the Peninsular campaign (20

Aug. '61–10 July '62), and his B.G. appointment expired a week later. Stationed in N.Y. until the end of the war, he was engaged in supplying and transporting the armies in the field and was again commissioned B.G. USV 13 Mar. '65. Breveted Lt. Col., Col., and B.G. USA (28 Oct. '64) and Maj. Gen. USA and USV (later) for war service, he continued in the R.A. until 1881, when he retired as Col. Asst. Q.M. Gen.

VAN WYCK, Charles Henry. Union gen. 1824–95. N.Y. At first a "Barnburner" (Democrat), he was an early Republican and sat in Congress 1859–63. Commissioned Col. 56th N.Y. 4 Sept. '61, he was promoted B.G. USV 27 Sept. '65, and breveted B.G. USV for war service. Mustered out in 1866, he was re-elected to Congress and served until 1872. He then moved to Nebr., where he was active in the Populist and Farmers' Alliance movements and was state sen. 1877–81.

VARNELL'S STATION, Ga. See ROCKY FACE RIDGE, Ga., 5–11 May '64.

VARNEY, George. Union officer. Me. Maj. 2d Me. 28 May '61; Lt. Col. 29 Aug. '61; Col. 10 Jan. '63; Bvt. B.G. USV (Fredericksburg); mustered out 9 June '63.

VAUGHAN, Alfred J., Jr. C.S.A. gen. 1830–99. Va. Appt.-Tenn. After graduating from V.M.I. he was an engineer in Mo. and Calif. Returning to Miss. before the war, he raised a company, but as the state was not arming and equipping soldiers at that point he took them to Tenn. to be mustered in. Commissioned Capt. 13th Tenn., he was promoted Lt. Col. in June '61 and fought at Belmont, Shiloh, Richmond (Ky.) (where he commanded a brigade), Perryville, Stones River (where he led the 4th Brig.), and Chickamauga (where he was appointed B.G. C.S.A. on the field

and took over a brigade). Wright, however, gives 18 Nov. '63 as the date of his appointment. He led his brigade at Missionary Ridge, and the Atlanta campaign until Vining's Station (4 July '64), where he lost his leg and was disabled for further field service. After the war he was a farmer, merchant, and was active in veterans' organizations.

VAUGHAN, Samuel K. Union officer. Mass. 2d Lt. 2d Wis. 11 June '61; resigned 16 Sept. '61; Capt. 19th Wis. 31 May '62; Maj. 22 Jan. '64; Lt. Col. 3 May '65; Bvt. B.G. USV 9 Aug. '65 (war service).

VAUGHAN ROAD, Va., 27 Oct. '64. HATCHER'S RUN, same date.

VAUGHAN ROAD, Va., 5–7 Feb. '65. DABNEY'S MILLS, same dates.

VAUGHN, John C. C.S.A. gen. 1824–75. Va. Appt.-Tenn. A merchant, he had held several public offices and fought in the Mexican War before going to S.C. for the bombardment of Fort Sumter. He was commissioned Col. 3d Tenn. 6 June '61 and served under Johnston at Harpers Ferry and 1st Bull Run. In the spring of 1862 he was sent to eastern Tenn. and was appointed B.G. C.S.A. 22 Sept. '62. At Vicksburg he commanded his brigade and the upper defenses. After exchange, he was given command of a mounted brigade in eastern Tenn. and southwestern Va. and opposed Hunter in the Valley in 1864. He also served under Early in that area and was wounded near Martinsburg. After Morgan's death he commanded the forces in eastern Tenn. and joined Johnston after Lee's surrender. After the war he was a legislator in Tenn. and a merchant and planter in Ga.

VEATCH, James Clifford. Union gen. 1819–95. Ind. A lawyer and public official, he was commissioned Col.

25th Ind. 19 Aug. '61. He commanded 2, 4th Div., Army Tenn. (17 Feb.–July '62) at Fort Donelson and Shiloh and was promoted B.G. USV 28 Apr. '62. In the Army of the Tenn. he commanded 2, 4th Div. Dist. Jackson (24 Sept.–26 Oct. '62); 5th Div., Dist. Memphis, XVI (5–25 Jan. and 31 Mar. '63–25 Jan. '64) and 4th Div., XVI (24 Jan.–17 July '64). He led the 1st Div., Res. Corps, Gulf (8–18 Feb. '65) and 1st Div., XIII (18 Feb–25 May '65) at Mobile, for which he was breveted Maj. Gen. USV. He was mustered out 24 Aug. '65.

VELAQUES, Loreta Janeta. Confederate officer and spy. 1840–? Cuba. Of an aristocratic Spanish family, she was educated in a New Orleans convent and secretly married in 1856 to an American army officer. They were stationed at Fort Leavenworth when the war began and her husband joined the Confederacy. She then organized and marched a volunteer battalion to his camp, passing herself off as Lt. Harry Buford. The deception was successful, and her husband said that she might go to war as his A.D.C. After he was killed in a firearms accident, she continued the deception, serving first as a temporary company commander under Bee at 1st Bull Run. Discovered in 1863, she then became a secret agent. After the war she remarried, traveled widely, and wrote a book of her adventures.

5th VERMONT (Vermont Brigade [2d], 2d Division, VI Corps)

Colonels: Henry A. Smalley (USMA; R.A.), Lewis A. Grant (Bvt. Maj. Gen.), John A. Lewis (Bvt. B.G.), Ronald A. Kennedy.

Battles: Lee's Mill, Golding's Farm, Savage's Station, Fredericksburg (1862 and 1863), Gettysburg, Funkstown, Wilderness, Spotsylvania, Cold Harbor, Petersburg ('64), Charlestown, Opequon, Cedar Creek, Petersburg (25 Mar. '65 and capture). Present also at Williamsburg, White Oak Swamp, Crampton's Gap, Antietam, Marye's Heights, Salem Heights, Rappahannock Station, Fishers Hill, and Sayler's Creek.

At Savage's Station the Vt. brigade (2d, 3d, 4th, 5th, and 6th Vt.) under Brooks (in Smith's [2d] division, Franklin's [VI] Corps) counterattacked to relieve a serious threat by Magruder to the army's change of base to the James. The 5th Vt. advanced through another regiment that had thrown themselves on the ground and refused to advance. The 5th Vt. advanced so far into the enemy lines that they had to deploy some companies to meet threats to their flanks. After maintaining an advanced position long enough to permit withdrawal of the rest of the army, the regiment withdrew. Casualties were 188 out of 428 committed; Co. E lost 44 out of 59 in line, 25 of whom were killed. Col. Lewis was severely wounded in the Wilderness, where the regiment lost 246. Maj. Charles P. Dudley was killed leading the regiment at Spotsylvania. Capt. Kennedy of the 3d Vt. was made regimental commander of the 5th in Feb. '65.

See also VERMONT BRIGADE.

VERMONT BRIGADE (2d Division, VI Corps, Potomac). Famous on several counts, this was the only one out of more than 200 Civil War brigades that maintained its original organization throughout the war; it was one of the few brigades composed of units all from the same state; it sustained the highest brigade losses during the war.

Composed of the 2d, 3d, 4th, 5th, and 6th Vt. at the start of the war, these regiments all re-enlisted in 1864; the 11th Vt. (1st Hvy. Arty.), which had been serving in the defenses of Washington, joined the brigade at this time (15 May '64).

Its hardest fighting was at the Wilderness and Spotsylvania; within a week it lost 1,645 out of its 2,800 effectives. Commanders were Wm. F. ("Baldy") Smith, W. T. Brooks, Henry Whiting, and Lewis A. Grant.

Another Vt. brigade, that of Stannard which figured so prominently at Gettysburg (counterattacking against "Pickett's Charge"), was composed of nine-month troops that fought only at Gettysburg. They had been dubbed the "Paper Collar Brigade" during their stay near Washington because some of their men had been seen wearing paper collars. After Gettysburg the nickname disappeared.

VETERAN RESERVE CORPS. In Apr. '63 the Union Army established the "Invalid Corps" to consist of officers and men unfit for full combat duty but who could perform limited infantry service. Those who could handle a weapon were put in the 1st Bn. and used for guard duty. The worst crippled formed the 2d Bn. and were used as nurses and cooks around hospitals. Six companies of the 1st Bn. and four from the 2d Bn. made up a regiment in the corps after Sept. '63. In December the corps numbered over 20,000. A total of 24 regiments and 188 separate companies were eventually raised, freeing many able-bodied soldiers for combat duty. Since the initials of the Invalid Corps coincided unfortunately with the "Inspected—Condemned" stamped on worn-out government equipment and animals, the name was changed in Mar. '64 to Veteran Reserve Corps. A small pamphlet entitled *Field Record of Officers of the Veteran Reserve Corps* (Washington: Scrivner & Swing, n.d.) (copy in West Point Library; shelf No. UA37, F45) gives the following information on many officers of the corps: name, age, battles, nature of disability, date he entered the corps, and rank.

"The officers of this Corps were sent to the rear, wounded and mutilated, from every battle-field of the war," says a note in the pamphlet, "and after passing an examination which fully tested their capacity for a proper performance of military duties, were placed in their present positions, not only upon the recommendation of their regimental and brigade commanders, but, also, by the distinct approval of the following distinguished officers: . . ." There follows a roster of 74 Maj. Gens. and Lt. Gens. Scott and Grant.

VETERAN VOLUNTEER ACT, passed early in 1864, provided that any man who re-enlisted would have free transportation home, a month's furlough, and a bounty of $400.

VICKERS, David. Union officer. N.J. 1st Lt. 3d N.J. 25 May '61; Capt. 31 May '61; Maj. 4th N.J. 18 Oct. '63; Col. 21 Mar. '65; Bvt. B.G. USV 31 May '65 (war service). During the Spanish-American War he was Maj. I.G. Vols. 3 June '98; discharged 30 Nov. '98.

VICKSBURG BOMBARDMENT, 18 May–26 July '62. After capturing New Orleans Farragut proceeded virtually unopposed to Vicksburg. Although only a brigade defended the partially completed works, the Confederates refused to surrender. Farragut began a bombardment with his cruisers and gunboats. His mortars arrived and bombarded the place during the period 20–27 June. On 12 July the gunboats and rams from Memphis joined in a shelling that continued until 26 July. Confederate losses were only 22 killed and wounded; two guns were temporarily disabled (Fiebeger, 143).

On 25 June an infantry brigade under Thomas Williams undertook construction of a canal through the peninsula opposite Vicksburg. This project was abandoned 26 July, and the brigade joined the garrison at Baton Rouge. Farragut returned to New Orleans and the Gulf.

VICKSBURG CAMPAIGN, Oct. '62–July '63. The strategic penetration of the South down the Mississippi, which started with Grant's capture of Forts Henry and Donelson and continued through the Shiloh campaign was temporarily slowed down when Halleck arrived to take personal command of the advance on Corinth, Miss. On 25 Oct. '62 Grant was given command of the Dept. of the Tenn., and a week later he started his campaign against Vicksburg. Other forces under Adm. Farragut had captured New Orleans and secured the river as far north as Baton Rouge. To prevent the link-up of the two Union forces the Pa.-born Confederate Gen. John C. Pemberton was put in command of Southern forces in western Miss. Although the term "Vicksburg campaign" is normally restricted to Grant's final operations, 29 Apr.–4 July '63, the unsuccessful preliminary operations will be covered here within this heading.

First Move Against Vicksburg—Dec. '62

Grant's first plan for an all-out military action against Vicksburg envisioned an advance of 40,000 troops due south along the Miss. Central R.R., combined with a movement by water of 32,000 under Sherman against Chickasaw Bluffs, just a few miles north of Vicksburg. The overland advance was stopped by 3,500 cavalrymen under Van Dorn, who struck behind Grant 20–25 Dec., capturing his advance base at Holly Springs, while Forrest's cavalry broke up 60 miles. of railroad north of Jackson, Tenn. Sherman also met with failure at Chickasaw Bluffs, 27–29 Dec. Sherman reported: "I reached Vicks-

burg at the time appointed, landed, assaulted and failed."

The Four Unsuccessful Bayou Expeditions, Feb.–Apr. '63

Although the unusually high water of the winter of 1862–63 made military operations extremely difficult, Grant was determined to maintain the offensive. First, he tried to construct a mile-long canal across the peninsula opposite Vicksburg to get his troop transports past the city's batteries for an attack from the south. (This strategy had succeeded at Island No. 10; see NEW MADRID AND ISLAND NO. 10.) Sherman's corps started the project in Jan. but was forced by high water to abandon it in Mar.

Duckport Canal

A more ambitious project was undertaken to cut a canal at Duckport to connect with a winding route through bayous that would enter the Mississippi 20 miles below Vicksburg. One small steamer was finally gotten through, but low water forced abandonment of this project.

Lake Providence Expedition

While the two canal attempts were being made McPherson's corps was ordered to open a 400-mile route from Lake Providence through the swamps, lakes, and bayous of La. to a point on the Mississippi below Vicksburg. Although this arduous task was being successfully accomplished, it was abandoned the end of Mar. because another, more promising, plan had been devised.

Yazoo Pass Expedition

Blasting a hole in the levee to open the Yazoo Pass, 325 miles north of Vicksburg, the Federals were able to get troop transports into the Tallahatchie River; Grant had hopes of using

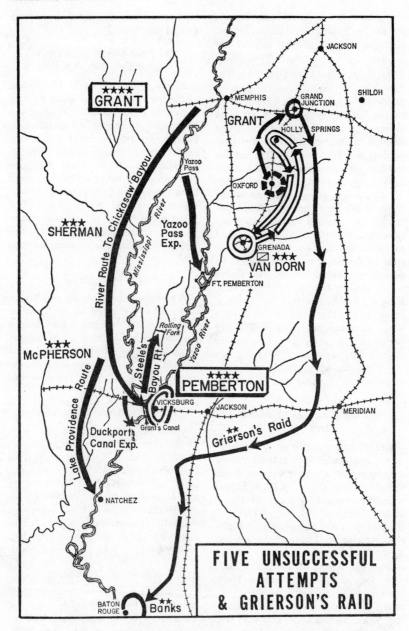

FIVE UNSUCCESSFUL
ATTEMPTS
& GRIERSON'S RAID

this route to send 30,000 men against Vicksburg. Although it involved a 700-mile route to move the 30 miles that separated Vicksburg from Millikens Bend, this approach had these advantages: it permitted use of the Union naval forces; the water routes provided a line of communications which, unlike the railroads and roads, was not subject to destruction by cavalry raids. Pemberton sent Maj. Gen. W. W. Loring with his division to stop this threat. Quickly building Fort Pemberton to block the Yazoo Pass route 90 miles north of Vicksburg, Loring stopped the Federal gunboats on 11 Mar. Six days later this Federal expedition withdrew.

Steele's Bayou Expedition

A 200-mile route up Steele's Bayou had been scouted with a view to supporting the Yazoo Pass operation. However, as the route was further explored it proved to be the most promising yet; an all-out effort was ordered to exploit it. Adm. Porter with 11 vessels pushed his way through the heavily obstructed waterways while Sherman followed with foot troops. The Confederates, however, stopped the boats at Rolling Fork and almost succeeded in bottling up and destroying Porter's fleet. Word of Porter's danger reached Sherman late in the day (19 Mar.). Undertaking a daring night march, lighted by candles stuck in their rifle barrels, Sherman's men arrived in time to save Porter.

Although Grant had been prepared to capitalize on any success, he did not have any real hopes for any of these preliminary attempts. Their purpose was to keep the spirit of the offensive alive in his troops, to satisfy public demand for action, to keep the enemy guessing, until the weather would permit the wide envelopment he had been planning to make from the south of Vicksburg.

Grant's Successful Operation, 29 Mar.–4 July '63

McClernand, who had been planning a separate expedition against Vicksburg, was put under Grant's command and on 29 Mar. was ordered to open a road for the army from Millikens Bend to a point on the river south of Vicksburg. Porter was ordered to run the Vicksburg batteries and rendezvous with the army south of the city; this naval support was vital not only for bringing supplies but also for ferrying the troops across the river. The night of 16 Apr. Porter got 11 boats safely past the river batteries, although every one was hit repeatedly and a twelfth was sunk; they joined Grant at the village of Hard Times. A few nights later six transports and 12 barges ran the batteries to bring supplies; one transport and six barges were lost.

Since the movement of Porter and McClernand toward the south would indicate his line of operations, Grant executed two diversions. Sherman made a successful feint toward Haines's Bluff. Col. R. H. Grierson with 1,000 cavalry moved out from southwestern Tenn. on 16 Apr. to start his highly successful diversionary raid. (See also: GRIERSON'S RAID.) After a six-hour bombardment from the Union gunboats had failed to neutralize the enemy strong point at Grand Gulf—where Grant had intended to cross—the landing was made unopposed the next day (30 Apr.) at Bruinsburg.

Port Gibson, 1 May '63

The Confederate brigades of Tracy and Green, sent from Grand Gulf to dispute the Union advance, were defeated after an all-day fight in which Tracy was killed. McPherson pursued north to Hankinson's Ferry. The Confederates evacuated Grand Gulf, which

Sherman occupied. McClernand moved to Rocky Springs. Pemberton was confused by Sherman's feint at Haines's Bluff, GRIERSON'S RAID, and the crossing below Grand Gulf. His decision was to pull his forces into the vicinity of Vicksburg instead of attacking Grant's bridgehead.

Grant's Bold Decision

Grant's orders had called for a move south after crossing the river and a joint operation with Banks against Port Hudson, La. After this a combined operation would be undertaken against Vicksburg. But the day after making his crossing Grant learned from Banks that the latter was engaged in his RED RIVER CAMPAIGN and would not return to Baton Rouge until 10 May; at that time he would have only 15,000 men to support Grant in any operation against Port Hudson. Against the advice of his subordinates, in violation of orders, and with the full knowledge that his action would meet with disapproval from Washington, Grant made the decision that elevated him to the ranks of the great captains. Knowing that Confederate reinforcements were being assembled at Jackson, 45 miles east of Vicksburg, he undertook the sort of strategic penetration so favored by Napoleon: he would move to get between the separated wings of the enemy's force and defeat first one and then the other by the use of interior lines. Grant also avoided the error of moving straight on Vicksburg without first defeating the forces in the field that could come to Pemberton's assistance. On 12 May the Federal army of 44,000 started forward.

Skirmish at Raymond, 12 May '63

The Confederate brigade of John Gregg formed a line of battle two miles

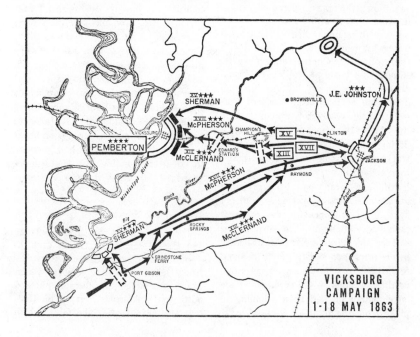

south of Raymond and held off Mc-Pherson's corps from 11 A.M. until late afternoon. This resistance, together with reports from McClernand and Sherman on his left, confirmed Grant's estimate that considerable enemy strength was located at Jackson (15 miles northeast) as well as at Edward's Station, approximately the same distance to his northwest.

Battle of Jackson, 14 May '63

Turning first against the forces in Jackson with the corps of McPherson and Sherman, Grant proceeded to reap the rewards of his bold strategy. J. E. Johnston had gotten orders 9 May to go to Miss. and take command of all Confederate forces. He reached Jackson the evening of the 13th and found the brigades of John Gregg and W. H. T. Walker, a force of 6,000. Two additional brigades were expected the next day, but when Johnston learned of Grant's dispositions between him and Pemberton he wired Richmond, "I am too late." The Confederates occupied previously prepared positions across the two main roads into Jackson from the west; they hoped to hold until vital supplies could be evacuated. Approaching about 10 A.M., in a driving rainstorm, the Federals made contact. Sherman attacked immediately from the southwest and routed Gregg. Worried about getting his ammunition wet, Mc-Pherson, approaching from the west, delayed his attack an hour. From good defensive positions Walker put up more of a fight than Gregg; however, his men at last broke and ran from their trenches at McPherson's final assault. Although Confederate guns delayed McPherson's pursuit, Federal forces finally entered Jackson about 4 P.M. The Confederates escaped to the north.

Champion's Hill—16 May

Despite orders from J. E. Johnston to strike Grant's rear, Pemberton did nothing until 15 May. Then he moved out through the rain and high water with a view to striking Grant's (nonexistent) line of communications. On 16 May he changed his mind and decided to countermarch through Edward's Station to unite with Johnston at Brownsville. By this time Grant had finished his business in Jackson and his skirmishers were in contact with Pemberton's forces.

Champion's Hill is a prominent knoll, about 75 feet high, which provides a good position for blocking the roads to Vicksburg from the east. Pemberton mustered almost 22,000 men with which to oppose the 29,000 under McPherson and McClernand. (Sherman, left in Jackson with two divisions, did not arrive until the battle was over.) McClernand forfeited an opportunity to destroy this entire enemy force by his lack of aggressiveness: instead of attacking the Confederate south flank as soon as he made contact (9:30 A.M.), he waited four and a half hours for orders and then did not attack vigorously. Mc-Pherson, however, hit from the north as soon as he made contact (11 A.M.) McClernand's delay permitted the Confederates to shift reinforcements to oppose McPherson. The hill changed hands several times in severe fighting. The Confederate Gen. W. W. Loring, by failing to obey Pemberton's orders first to attack McClernand on the south flank and then to move to support Stephenson's defense of the north flank, was blamed by Pemberton for the failure. In covering the retreat, Loring was separated from Pemberton's force and lost to the further defense of Vicksburg.

The battle of Champion's Hill (or Baker's Creek) was the most severe of the campaign. Livermore's figures are:

	Union	Confederate (approx.)
Effectives	29,373	20,000
Killed	410	381
Wounded	1,844	c 1,800
Missing	187	1,670
Total losses	2,441	3,851

Battle of the Big Black River— 17 May '63

Sending Sherman's corps—which had reached Bolton by the night of the 16th—north to cross at Bridgeport, Grant moved west along the railroad. Pemberton tried to defend the crossing of the Big Black by digging a trench across the mile-wide neck of the horseshoe bend in Grant's path. In a one-hour fight 10,000 Federals routed Bowen's 4,000, capturing over 1,700 men and 18 guns. Pemberton's forces did manage to slow the pursuit by destroying the bridges. Both wings of Grant's army started crossing the river on their own bridges the morning of the 18th.

Initial Vicksburg Assaults

By noon of the 19th all Grant's forces had closed in around Vicksburg and he ordered a general assault for 2 P.M. However, Pemberton's forces were stronger than expected and they repulsed the attacks all along the line. On 22 May Grant ordered another attempt to take the city by frontal assault. He wanted to avoid a long, deliberate siege for which he would have to draw troops from Memphis. He also wanted to take the city before Johnston could gather sufficient force to come to its relief. However, he underestimated the Confederate strength and will to resist; his attacks were repulsed after heavy fighting. After an hour and a half he was ready to call a halt, but on the basis of McClernand's misleading reports of

success he ordered a final assault. Of Pemberton's 20,000 in Vicksburg, no more than 13,000 had been used in the actual defense; these held against 35,000 Union infantry and inflicted 3,200 casualties. In his memoirs Grant says this attack of 22 May and the final assault at Cold Harbor (3 June '64) were ones he regretted having ordered. (*Personal Memoirs*, II, 276.)

Siege of Vicksburg

Confederate engineers had been working for seven months on the nine-mile line to protect Vicksburg from attack from the rear. Nine forts comprised the strong points covering the principal avenues of approach. Starting on the north they were: Fort Hill, Stockade Redan, Third Louisiana Redan, Great Redoubt, Second Texas Lunette, Railroad Redoubt, Fort Garrott (or Square Fort), Salient Works, and South Fort. Manning these works, from north to south, were the divisions of M. L. Smith, John H. Forney, and Stevenson. The division of Bowen constituted the reserve most of the time and was used to reinforce threatened parts of the line. On 18 May Johnston had warned Pemberton of the danger of becoming besieged in Vicksburg and had advised the city be abandoned so that the army might be saved. After a council of war, however, Pemberton elected to defend Vicksburg. Johnston succeeded in raising the strength of his force to 30,000, but most of these were green troops for whom sufficient supplies and equipment were not available. Other Confederate forces were too occupied with the CHICKAMAUGA CAMPAIGN to assist in relieving Vicksburg. On 15 June Johnston notified Richmond that he considered saving Vicksburg hopeless.

Grant made no further attempt to take the city by assault, but settled down to starve the Confederates into submission. By the time the siege ended he had 71,000 troops available for this purpose, half of which he used to hold off Johnston.

The Vicksburg Mines

Although not so famous as the Petersburg mine, several attempts were made at Vicksburg to penetrate the Confederate defenses by the ancient technique of mining. On 25 June 2,200 pounds of powder were exploded in a tunnel that had been run under the Third Louisiana Redan on the Jackson road. Two regiments attempted to exploit the gap blown in the enemy defenses, but were stopped by a second line that had been prepared to the rear for just such a contingency. On 1 July another mine was exploded, but no attempt made to push troops through the breach. A third mine was set for explosion as part of the attack planned for 6 July.

The Capitulation—4 July '63

Constant shelling and the growing shortage of rations made Pemberton's plight more hopeless each day. Sickness and wounds had rendered 10,000 (about 50 per cent) of the Confederates unfit for active service. Civilians were suffering from the unceasing bombardment and the shortage of food. Opposing commanders met 3 July to discuss terms. Pemberton has been criticized for agreeing to the date of Independence Day for the surrender—at the time there was even some suspicion of treachery on his part. Grant, however, had originally demanded unconditional surrender; Pemberton believed that by giving the Federals the satisfaction of a surrender on the Fourth of July he could get better terms for his army. Grant, in turn, was criticized for giving parole to Pemberton's force; his reason for this was to avoid the use of transportation and loss of time that would

have been involved in evacuating a large number of prisoners of war.

Significance of the Vicksburg Campaign

Coming the day after the Federal victory at Gettysburg, the fall of Vicksburg sounded the death knell of the Confederate cause. Not only was the South cut in half (Port Hudson surrendered to Banks 9 July), but Grant's large forces were free for further operations. Of great importance also was the fact that the Mississippi was now open for resumption of trade between the Midwest and the outside world.

Ulysses Grant had achieved one of the most brilliant military successes in history.

VIELE, Egbert Ludovickus. Union gen. 1825–1902. N.Y. USMA 1847 (30/38); Inf. Fighting in the Mexican War and serving on the frontier, he resigned in 1853 to become a civil engineer. He was chief engineer for Central Park but his plan was later discarded in a change of administration. He wrote several studies of N.Y.C. topography and *The Hand-book for Active Service* (1861). Commissioned Capt. Engrs. 7th N.Y. State Militia (19–30 Apr. '61), he was appointed B.G. USV Aug. '61 and commanded 1st Brig. S.C. Div., Expeditionary Corps (Apr.–May '62). He then commanded Viele's brigade, Va. (8 May–1 June '62) on the march upon Norfolk and was military governor of that city (22 July '62–1 Aug. '63). Going to northern Ohio, he superintended the draft until 20 Oct. '63, when he resigned. In 1868 he suggested a plan for an antecedent of the present subway system of N.Y.C., was Commissioner of Parks in 1883–84, and US (Democratic) Congressman (1885–87).

VIFQUAIN, Victor. Union officer. Pa. 1st Lt. Adj. 97th Ill. 26 Aug. '62; Maj. 7 Feb. '63; Lt. Col. 26 Dec. '64; Bvt.

B.G. USV. Brevets for Mobile, war service. Medal of Honor 8 June '65 for Blakely (Ala.) 9 Apr. '65. Col. 3d Nebr. 27 May '98; mustered out 11 May '99.

VILLARD, Henry. WAR CORRESPONDENT and financier. 1835–1900. Bavaria. After studying at Munich and Würzburg, he came to Ill. and studied law before becoming a correspondent for a Chicago paper. He then took up headquarters at Washington after covering the Lincoln-Douglas debates for a German-American paper and was shortly hired by the N.Y. *Herald*. By the fall of 1861, he was representing the Cincinnati *Commercial* and dispatched the famous report that Cameron considered Sherman insane. He then began contributing also to the N.Y. *Tribune* and was soon taken on as a full-time reporter. Although Greeley never forgave him for having been among the last to send in a report of Shiloh, the mails were to blame. Villard was one of the most outstanding correspondents in the war, and his resignation in Dec. '63, after more criticism from Greeley, left the *Tribune* in a weakened position. He rejoined the paper within a few months and continued to be a newspaperman until 1868. After returning to Germany, he entered the field of finance and became, after losing a fortune or two, a very wealthy man. He had married the daughter of William Lloyd GARRISON.

VILLEPIGUE, John Bordenave. C.S.A. gen. 1830–62. S.C. USMA 1854 (22/46); Dragoons. He served in garrison, on the frontier, and in the Utah Expedition before resigning 31 Mar. '61 as 1st Lt. Commissioned Capt. of C.S.A. Arty., he was named Col. 36th Ga. and served at Pensacola, where he was seriously wounded. Named Bragg's Chief of Engrs. and of Arty., he took command of Pensacola and then Mobile. Joining Bragg, he was appointed B.G. C.S.A. 13 Mar. '62 and took command

of Fort Pillow. He led his brigade at Corinth and died 9 Nov. '62 at Port Hudson of a long and serious illness. Wright spells his named Villepique, but Cullum and B.&L. spell it with a "g."

VINCENT, Strong. Union gen. 1837–63. Pa. Briefly a lawyer, he was commissioned 1st Lt. Adj. Erie Regt. Pa. Vols. (21 Apr.–25 July '61) and then Lt. Col. 83d Pa. 14 Sept. '61. He was in the siege of Yorktown and was ill from swamp fever after Hanover C.H. Named Col. 27 June '62, he fought at Fredericksburg and at Gettysburg, where he commanded 3, 1, V (20 May–3 July '63). In the absence of the division commander he put his brigade on Little Round Top to stop the threatening envelopment. He was mortally wounded, cheering his men on as they hesitated before the enemy, and died four days later. His appointment as B.G. USV was dated 3 July '63.

VINCENT, Thomas McCurdy. Union officer. c. 1832–1909. Ohio. USMA 1853 (11/52); Arty.-Adj. Gen. He served in the Seminole War and taught science at West Point before serving as Asst. Adj. Gen. for McDowell at 1st Bull Run. Promoted Capt. Asst. Adj. Gen. 3 Aug. '61, he served in the Adj. Gen.'s office for the rest of the war, in charge of the organization, muster out, and other details of the volunteer troops. Continuing in the R.A., he retired in 1896 as Col. and Bvt. B.G. USA.

VINTON, David H. Union officer. c. 1803–73. R.I. USMA 1822 (14/40); Arty.-Inf.-Q.M. He served in the Seminole War, was Wool's Chief Q.M. in the Mexican War, and captured by the Confederates when Twiggs surrendered Tex. Promoted Lt. Col. Deputy Q.M. Gen. 3 Aug. '61, he served as Q.M. of N.Y.C. for the Civil War and was breveted B.G. USA. He retired in 1866 as Col.

VINTON, Francis Laurens. Union gen. 1835–79. Me. USMA 1856 (10/49); Cav.-Inf. He resigned from the R.A. in 1856 to attend the École des Mines in France and then taught at Cooper Union. In 1861 he headed the mineral exploration expedition to Honduras but returned to be commissioned Capt. 16th US Inf. 5 Aug. '61 and Col. 43d N.Y. 31 Oct. '61. Fighting in the Peninsular campaign. he commanded 3, 2, VI (25 Sept.–13 Dec. '62) at Fredericksburg, where he was severely wounded. He was on sick leave when his appointment expired (4 Mar. '63) and was renewed (13 Mar. '63), but he resigned 5 May '63. Teaching mining engineering at Columbia, he was later a consulting mining engineer in Denver and wrote many engineering articles.

VIRGINIA left the Union on 17 Apr. '61 and was the principal battleground for the war in the East. Richmond was the capital of the Confederacy, Big Bethel the scene of the first battle, and Appomattox the place of surrender. The state was not readmitted to the Union until 27 Jan. '70.

VIRGINIA, THE. See MONITOR-MERRIMAC DUEL.

VIRGINIA, UNION ARMY OF. This short-lived army was formed 26 June '62, under Maj. Gen. John Pope and merged into the Army of the Potomac under McClellan 12 Sept., after being defeated at the 2d Battle of Bull Run. It was formed to provide the unity of command that had been lacking since 11 Mar. '62 when Pres. Lincoln in a desperate effort to counter Jackson's Valley campaign had divided the Dept. of the Potomac into four independent commands. Pope's army was composed of Frémont's Mountain Dept., Banks's Dept. of the Shenandoah, McDowell's Dept. of the Rappahan-

nock, and Sturgis' brigade from the Mil. Dist. of Wash.

VIRGINIA, UNION DEPARTMENT OF. Created 22 May '61 with headquarters at Ft. Monroe; merged into the Dept. of Va. and N.C. 15 July '63; re-created 31 Jan. '65 (at which time it was also known as the Army of the James). Commanders were Maj. Gen. B. F. Butler 22 May–17 Aug. '61; John E. Wool to 2 June '62; John A. Dix to 15 July '63; Brig. Gen. George W. Getty to 20 July '63. Maj. Gen. E. O. C. Ord was in command from 31 Jan. until 16 Apr. '65. Halleck then commanded the department until 28 June '65. Until 22 July '62 the 10,000 troops were organized into the garrisons of Fortress Monroe, Camp Hamilton, and Newport News, and the brigades of E. L. Viele, Max Weber, J. C. Robinson. After 22 July '62 the troops were organized into the VII Corps.

VIRGINIA AND NORTH CAROLINA, UNION DEPARTMENT OF (Army of the James). Created 15 July '63 by consolidation of the departments of Va. and N.C. with headquarters at Fortress Monroe. Troops of the old IV and VII Corps, Dept. of Va., merged into the XVIII Corps 1 Aug. '63; the latter corps was reorganized in Apr. '64 and, with the X Corps from the Dept. of the South, designated the Army of the James. On 31 Jan. '65 the department was separated back into the original two departments. Maj. Gen. J. G. Foster was in command from 18 July– 11 Nov. '63. Strength 31 Dec. '63 was 29,000 present for duty. Maj. Gen. B. F. Butler then commanded until 8 Jan. '65 except for short periods when Maj. Gen. E. O. C. Ord was in command (27 Aug. '63–7 Sept. '64; 14–24 Dec.). Strength 31 Dec. '64 was 50,000. Ord was in command 31 Jan. '65 when the department was reorganized. (See also JAMES, UNION ARMY OF THE.)

VIRGINIA CAMPAIGN OF 1864 AND 1865. Grant's final operations with Meade's Army of the Potomac against Lee, lasting from May '64 to 9 Apr. '65, are sometimes called the Overland Campaign, Richmond Campaign, or the Virginia Campaign of 1864 and 1865 (the latter being the title of Humphreys' book). There is, however, no commonly accepted designation of these operations. This book covers the operations as a series of separate campaigns under the following names: WILDERNESS; SPOTSYLVANIA CAMPAIGN; NORTH ANNA RIVER; TOTOPOTOMOY CREEK; COLD HARBOR; PETERSBURG CAMPAIGN; APPOMATTOX CAMPAIGN. Concurrent operations of Butler's Army of the James are covered under DREWRY'S BLUFF.

VIVANDIÈRE. A female attendant in the regiment, found in European armies, particularly the French, since the Thirty Years' War. This woman, often a soldier's wife, acted as sutler and nurse, respectable, and respected. In the Civil War there were only a dozen or so vivandières on both sides—all of these serving with the foreign-born, particularly the French, regiments.

VODGES, Israel. Union gen. 1816–73. Pa. USMA 1837 (11/50); Arty. Teaching mathematics at West Point, fighting in the Seminole wars, and serving on the frontier and in garrison before the war, he was Maj. 1st US Arty. 14 May '61 (Capt. since 1847). At Fort Pickens (Fla.) he was captured at Santa Rosa Island 9 Oct. '61 and held until Aug. '62. Serving on J. F. Reynolds' staff in Sept., he was promoted B.G. USV 29 Nov. '62 and then commanded Forces North End Folly Island (16 Aug.–16 Dec. '63) 1st Brig., 2d Div., Folly Island (19 July–1 Aug. '63); Forces North End Folly Island (16 Aug.–16 Dec. '63) and Forces Folly Island (Jan.–July '64); as well as 2d Div. Dist. Fla.

(25–28 Feb. '64)—all in the X Corps, South. From May '64 to Apr. '65 he commanded the defenses of Norfolk and Portsmouth, Va., and N.C. and, from Apr. to Sept. '65, 4th Sep. Brig., Dist. Fla. Continuing in the R.A., he was breveted B.G. USA 9 Apr. '65 for war service and retired in 1881 as Col. 1st US Arty.

VOLTIGEURS. A form of French light infantry or elite troops. The name and reputation, like those of the ZOUAVES, appealed to Americans, and a number of Voltigeur units appeared before and during the Civil War.

VON BLESSINGH, Louis. Union officer. Germany. Capt. 14th Ohio 20 Apr. '61; mustered out 13 Aug. '61; Capt. 37th Ohio 9 Sept. '61; Lt. Col. 2 Oct. '61; Bvt. B.G. USV (war service). He had been an officer in the Prussian Army before coming to America.

VON BORCKE, Heros. C.S.A. officer. Prussia. He was serving on the staff of the Prince of Prussia in 1861 when he requested leave of absence to fight the Civil War. Running the blockade, he joined the A.N.V. and in May '62 became J. E. B. Stuart's Chief of Staff as Maj. He was seriously wounded at Middleburg (June '63) and retired from the field, returning to Europe in Dec. '64 as Col. on a special diplomatic mission to the Court of St. James's. In 1866 he fought in the Austro-Prussian War and then went to his country home, where he farmed in quiet retirement, visiting the South in 1884. Lonn describes him as being six feet four inches tall with a muscular and massive frame, and blond hair and mustache. It was said that he carried the largest sword and rode the largest horse in the Confederacy. His *Memoirs of the Confederate War for Independence* (1866) is characterized by Freeman as overly dramatic and self-glorifying but "useful for the correct interpretation of many incidents in the history of Stuart's cavalry." He collaborated with Justus Scheibert on *Die grosse Reiterschlacht bei Brandy Station* (1893), which Freeman calls "the most comprehensive narrative" of that battle.

VON EGLOFFSTEIN, Baron Fred W. Union officer. Germany. Col. 103d N.Y. 20 Feb. '62; Bvt. B.G. USV (war service); mustered out 12 Nov. '63. He had military training and experience in the German Army before coming to America for the Civil War.

VON SCHACK, George. Union officer. Germany. Maj. 7th N.Y. ("Steuben Rifles") 31 July '61; Col. 8 Feb. '62; mustered out 8 May '63; Lt. Col. 7th N.Y. 15 July '64; Col. 2 Nov. '64; Bvt. B.G. USV (Richmond campaign in 1862). Commanded in the Army of the Potomac: 1, 1, II; 3, 1, II. He came to the country on a 3-year leave of absence from the Prussian Army, where he served as Capt. of Cav. After Lee's surrender he resigned his Prussian commission and took out papers to become a US citizen. Died 1887. Listed by Phisterer as George W. Schaak.

VON SCHRADER, Alexander. Union officer. 1821–67. Germany. Col. 74th Ohio 10 Dec. '61; resigned 10 Apr. '65; Lt. Col. Asst. I.G. Assigned 28 Jan. '63–1 Aug. '65; Maj. Asst. Adj. Gen. Vols. 1 Feb. '65; Bvt. B.G. USV. Brevets for war service, Stones River, Tenn. (2); Chickamauga; Atlanta campaign; Jonesboro, Ga. (2). His father had come up through the ranks to be a Lt. Gen. in the Duke of Brunswick's army and a member of the Prussian nobility. Alexander was a cadet in the Prussian Army at 14 and by 1841 attained the rank of 2d Lt. in the bodyguard of the duke. Coming to America in 1852, he had seen years of abject poverty and miscellaneous jobs when the Civil War began. After serving as drillmaster for the

18th Ohio and then for the 73d Ohio, he was commissioned in the 74th Ohio. Asst. I.G. for Gen. George H. Thomas. In the Wilderness he lost his left arm. Lonn says he was probably one of the most able engineer officers of the army. Entering the R.A. as a 2d Lt. in 1866, he became a Maj. immediately and was breveted Col. USA the next year.

VON STEINWEHR, Adolph Wilhelm August Frederick. Union gen. 1822–77. Germany. The son and grandson of high-ranking Prussian officers, he was educated in the Brunswick Military Academy and served under the Duke of Brunswick. He came to America for the Mexican War and was engaged in surveying Mobile Bay when he married an Ala. girl. Becoming a US citizen, he took his family back to Prussia to resign his commission there and then returned to be a LATIN FARMER in Conn. Commissioned Col. 29th N.Y. ("The Astor Rifles," a completely German regiment) 6 June '61, he was in reserve at 1st Bull Run and promoted B.G. USV 12 Oct. '61. In the Potomac he commanded 2d Brig., Blenker's division (Dec. '61–Mar. '62) and 2, Blenker's division, II. He then led 2d Brig., Blenker's division, Mtn. (1 Apr.–26 June '62) and 2d Div., I, Army Va. (26 June–12 Sept. '62) at 2d Bull Run. Again in the Potomac he commanded 2d Div., XI (12 Sept. '62–22 Feb. '63; 5 Mar.–28 Mar. and 12 Apr.–25 Sept. '63) at Chancellorsville and Gettysburg. He commanded the corps 22 Feb.–5 Mar. '63. In the Army of the Cumberland he led the 2d Div., XI (25 Sept.–28 Nov. '63 and 3 Mar.–16 Apr. '64) at Wauhatchie and commanded the corps there for a time. Resigning 3 July '65, he was later professor of military science at Yale and a US government engineer.

VON VEGESACK, Baron Ernest Mattais Peter. Union officer. Sweden. Appt.-N.Y. A Capt. in the Swedish

Army, he had fought for Denmark in the Schleswig-Holstein War. He came to Washington on a special furlough and a recommendation from the king's brother. With Wool as Maj. Add. A.D.C. 28 Oct. '61–29 Apr. '62 and 8 May '62–3 Aug. '63. According to Lonn he fought at Yorktown and Williamsburg as a private, although Heitman does not mention this service. After Hanover C.H., he joined McClellan's staff and on 19 July '63 became Col. of the 20th N.Y. ("United Turner Rifles"). At 2d Bull Run he commanded the 3d Brig., 2d Div., VI Corps. He was breveted B.G. USV for his war service and awarded the Medal of Honor 23 Apr. '63 for "having while serving as A.D.C. successfully and advantageously changed the position of troops under fire at Gaines's Mill, Va. 27 June '62" (Heitman), thus covering Fitz-John Porter's retreat. The Swedish king allowed him to wear this foreign decoration when he returned to his fatherland in Aug. '63, after having been mustered out of the Union Army on 1 June '63. He retired as a Maj. Gen. in the Swedish Army. Died 1903.

VORIS, Alvin Coe. Union officer. Ohio. Commissioned 2d Lt. 29th Ohio 2 Oct. '61, he was promoted Lt. Col. 67th Ohio 11 Oct. '61 and Col. 1 Sept. '65. Mustered out in Dec. '65, he was breveted B.G. USV 8 Dec. '64 and Maj. Gen. USV 15 Nov. '65.

VREELAND, Michael James. Union officer. Mich. Sgt. Co. I 4th Mich. 20 June '61; 2d Lt. 1 Sept. '62; 1st Lt. 16 Oct. '62; mustered out 30 June '64; Lt. Col. 4th Mich. 26 July '64; Bvt. B.G. USV (war service). W.I.A. at Gettysburg 2 July '63. Died 1875.

W

WADE, Benjamin Franklin. Radical Republican, 1800–78. Mass. Moving to Ohio where he practiced law, he was elected Sen. as a Whig, joined the Republican party, and was stanchly antislavery. He joined Henry W. DAVIS in the RECONSTRUCTION PLAN OF WADE AND DAVIS and Manifesto of 1864 in bitter opposition to Lincoln's Reconstruction and war policies. After Lincoln's death he continued his fight against Johnson's moderate policies.

WADE, James Franklin. Union officer. Ohio. R.A. 1st Lt. 3d US Cav. 14 May '61; 6th US Cav. 3 Aug. '61; Lt. Col. 6th US Col. Cav. 1 May '64; Col. 19 Sept. '64; Bvt. B.G. USV 13 Feb. '65 (war service). Other brevets for Beverly Ford (Va.), Marion (East Tenn.), campaign in southwest Va. Continued in R.A. and named B.G. USA in 1897 and Maj. Gen. Vols. in 1898; Maj. Gen. USA and retired 1903.

WADE, Melancthon Smith. Union gen. 1802–68. Ohio. A retired dry-goods merchant active in the Ohio militia, he was named B.G. USV 1 Oct. '61. The first commander of Camp Dennison (Ohio), he resigned 18 Mar. '62 because of ill health.

WADSWORTH, James Samuel. Union gen. 1807–64. N.Y. After Yale and Harvard he read law in Daniel Webster's office but devoted his time later to managing his large estate. At first a Free-Soiler, he became a Republican and was a delegate to the Peace Convention in Washington during Secession Winter. He was a Volunteer A.D.C. to McDowell at 1st Bull Run and commissioned B.G. USV 9 Aug. '61. In the Army of the Potomac he commanded 2d Brig., McDowell's division (3 Oct. '61–12 Mar. '62); and 2d Brig., 3d Div., I Corps (13–17 Mar. '62); before serving as Military Gov. of Washington (12 Mar.–7 Sept. '62). He was an unsuccessful gubernatorial candidate in N.Y. that fall and returned to command 1st Div., I (4 Jan.–July '63) at Chancellorsville and Gettysburg. He commanded the I Corps 2–4 Jan. '63 and was leading 4th Div., V Corps (25 Mar.–6 May '64) when he was mortally wounded at the Wilderness. Dying two days later on 8 May, he was breveted Maj. Gen. USV 6 May '64 for Gettysburg and the Wilderness.

WAGNER, George Day. Union gen. ?–1869. Ohio. Commissioned Col. 15th Ind. 14 June '61, he fought at Rich Mountain. Greenbrier, Shiloh, the siege of Corinth. and Perryville. He was promoted B.G. USV 29 Nov. '62 and, in the Army of the Ohio, commanded 21, 6th Div. (11 Feb.–29 Sept. '62) and 21, 6, II (Sept.–Nov. '62). In the Army of the Cumberland he led 2, 1st Div. Left Wing, XIV (5 Nov. '62–9 Jan. '63); 2, 1, XXI (9–20 Jan. and 13 Apr.–9 Oct. '63); 1st Div., XXI (19 Feb.–13 Apr. '63); 2, 2, IV (10 Oct. '63–12 Jan. '64, 21 Apr.–10 July '64, and 25 July–30 Sept. '64); 2d Div., IV (17–27 Feb. and 30 Sept.–2 Dec. '64). He commanded Dist. St. Louis, Mo. (8 Apr.–20 June '65) and was mustered out 24 Aug. '65.

WAGNER, Louis. Union officer. Germany. Capt. 88th Pa. 13 Sept. '61; Lt. Col. 24 Feb. '63; Col. 16 June '65; Bvt. B.G. USV (war service). W.I.A. at 2d Bull Run and captured there. After the battle of Chancellorsville the wound broke out again. While invalided at Williams (Pa.), he trained 14,000 colored soldiers. He was breveted B.G. when 27 years of age.

WAINWRIGHT, Charles Sheils. Union officer. N.Y. Maj. 1st N.Y. Arty. 17 Oct. '61; Lt. Col. 30 Apr. '62; Col. 1 June '62; Bvt. B.G. USV 1 Aug. '64 (war service).

WAINWRIGHT, William P. Although listed by Phisterer as Col. 76th N.Y. and breveted B.G. USV 13 Mar. '65, he does not appear in Heitman. Dyer lists his sole command as 2, 1, I, Potomac.

WAITE, Carlos Adolphus. Union officer. N.Y. Entering the R.A. in 1820, he fought in the Mexican War (2 brevets, 1 wound) and was retired in Feb. '64 as Col. 1st US Inf. He was breveted B.G. USA and died in 1866.

WAITE, Charles. Union officer. Vt. 1st Lt. 27th Mich. 10 Oct. '62; Capt. 1 May '63; Maj. 12 May '64; Lt. Col. 18 Nov. '64; Col. 6 Mar. '65; Bvt. B.G. USV 2 Apr. '65 (Petersburg assault). Wounded at Spotsylvania 12 May '64. Died 1898.

WAITE, John M. Union officer. N.Y. 2d Lt. 8th Ill. Cav. 18 Sept. '61; 1st Lt. 8 Jan. '62; Capt. 17 July '62; Maj. 7 Dec. '63; Bvt. B.G. USV (war service).

WALCOTT, Charles Folsom. Union officer. Mass. Capt. 21st Mass. 5 Aug. '61; resigned 25 Apr. '63; Capt. 12th Co. Inf. [sic] Mass. State Militia 16 May–15 Aug. '64; Lt. Col. 61st Mass. 24 Sept. '64; Col. 28 Feb. '65; Bvt. B.G. USV 9 Apr. '65 (Richmond's fall, Lee's surrender). Died 1887.

WALCUTT, Charles Carroll. Union gen. 1838–98. Ohio. A graduate of the military institute near Franklin and a surveyor and civil engineer, he was commissioned Maj. 46th Ohio 1 Oct. '61 and was Asst. I.G. in W. Va. on Gen. Hill's staff. He was promoted Lt. Col. 30 Jan. and Col. 16 Oct. '62. He was wounded in the left shoulder at Shiloh and fought at Jackson. He commanded

1, 1, XVI (20 Jan.–22 Mar. '63). During the Atlanta campaign he commanded 2, 4, XV (25 Nov. '63–12 Mar. '65 and 15 Apr.–14 Sept. '64) at Missionary Ridge, Kenesaw Mountain, Dallas, Burnt Hickory, Noonday Creek, Ezra Church, and Lovejoy. He led 2, 1, XV (25 Sept.–22 Nov. '64) when he was wounded at Griswoldville (Ga.). Hit early in the engagement, Walcutt followed his command through the rest of the battle in a captured carriage. He returned to this brigade 28 Mar.–4 Apr. '65 and succeeded to division 4 Apr.– 17 June and 27 June–18 July '65. Breveted Maj. Gen. USV for Griswoldville, he was mustered out in 1866 and returned to the army briefly in that year. He later held several public offices and was active in public school work in Columbus (Ohio).

WALDEN'S RIDGE, Tenn. Terrain feature between Sequatchie and Tennessee rivers which figured in CHATTANOOGA CAMPAIGN, notably in the action against Rosecrans' supply line conducted during WHEELER'S RAID, 1–9 Oct. '63.

WALKER, Duncan Stephen. Union officer. D.C. Capt. Asst. Adj. Gen. Vols. 27 Feb. '63; Maj. Asst. Adj. Gen. Vols. 27 July '64; Lt. Col. Asst. Adj. Gen. Assigned 7 Nov. '64–12 May '65; Bvt. B.G. USV (war service).

WALKER, Francis Amasa. Union officer. 1840–97. Pvt. and Sgt. Maj. 15th Mass. 1 Aug. '61; Capt. Asst. Adj. Gen. Vols. 14 Sept. '61; Maj. Asst. Adj. Gen. Vols. 11 Aug. '62; Lt. Col. Asst. Adj. Gen. Assigned 1 Jan. '63–9 Jan. '65; Bvt. B.G. USV (Chancellorsville and war service). He was wounded at Chancellorsville, captured and held in Libby Prison for a time. "He became a foremost figure in the new inductive and historical school of economics" (D.A.B.). As an economic theorist, professor (Yale, 1873–81) and president of M.I.T. (1881–97), he won recognition for the idea of a technical education. He was Chief of the Bureau of Statistics in 1869 and when, in 1871, the funds were not available to continue, Grant appointed him Commissioner of Indian Affairs while he continued to work on the census of 1870, for which results he received international recognition as a statistician. He was an adherent of international bimetalism and worked to offset the free-coinage movement of 1896. Wrote *History of the Second Army Corps in the Army of the Potomac* and many books on economics.

WALKER, Henry Harrison. C.S.A. gen. c. 1833–1912. Va. USMA 1853 (41/52); Inf. He served in garrison, on the frontier, in Indian scouting, and as A.D.C. to the Kans. governor during the border disturbances before resigning 3 May '61 as 1st Lt. Promoted Col. 40th Va. in June '62, he was wounded during the Seven Days' Battles and in Sept. '62 was in the defenses of Richmond. In Jan. '63 he took command of Heth's division under A. P. Hill and was appointed B.G. C.S.A. 1 July '63. He led his brigade at Bristoe, Verdiersville, New Market, Harrisonburg, the Wilderness, and Spotsylvania, where he was wounded. In Nov. '64 he was assigned court-martial duty under Early and in Feb. '65 was guarding the railroads outside Richmond. He announced the surrender of the Army Northern Va. to Davis on 13 Apr. in Danville (Va.)

WALKER, James A. C.S.A. gen. 1832–? Va. As Col. 13th Va. he led his regiment at 2d Bull Run, leading Trimble's brigade at Antietam, where he was wounded. At Fredericksburg he led Early's brigade and was appointed B.G. C.S.A. 15 May '63 (according to Wright; Wood says 15 Jan. '63). He commanded the Stonewall brigade at Gettysburg, the Wilderness, and Spotsylvania, and in the battles around Petersburg. Although listed by Wright and Wood as a general, he is not included in the C.M.H. list.

WALKER, John G. C.S.A. gen. 1822–93. Mo. After college he fought in the Mexican War and joined the R.A., resigning in 1861 to be commissioned Maj. of C.S.A. Cav. 16 Mar. Soon promoted Lt. Col. and Col., he led his brigade in Va. in Sept. of that year and was named B.G. C.S.A. 9 Jan. '62. He served under Holmes in the Aquia Dist. and the Dept. of N.C. and was division commander in Southside, Va., during the 2d Bull Run campaign. Joining the Army of Northern Va. for the Antietam campaign, he led his division at Harpers Ferry, seizing Loudoun Heights, and at Antietam. Promoted Maj. Gen. 8 Nov. '62, he led the Tex. infantry division in the Trans-Miss. Dept. and fought in the Red River campaign of 1864. In June '64, he was given command of the Dist. of Tex., N. Mex., and Ariz., staying there until 31 Mar. '65. After the war he was Consul Gen. at Bogota.

WALKER, Leroy Pope. C.S.A. gen. and Sec. of War. Ala. After graduating from the Univ. of Ala., he studied law at the Univ. of Va. and became active in Democratic politics, serving as legislator and jurist. He was an active secessionist and was named first Sec. of War for the Confederate government on 21 Feb. '61. His appointment was dictated by political expediency, and the tremendous and (sometimes) impossible requirements of the office broke his health. He resigned 16 Sept. '61, and Davis appointed him B.G. C.S.A. the next day. He served in the Dept. of Ala. and West Fla. and tried to get an assignment in the field. Failing this, he resigned 31 Mar. '62 and the next year was appointed judge of a military court, a post he held until the end of the war. He was a political power in Ala., exerting influence all out of proportion to his public service.

WALKER, Lucius March. C.S.A. gen. 1829–63. Tenn. Appt. At Large. USMA 1850 (15/44); Dragoons. He resigned in 1852 to become a commission merchant and was made Col. 40th Tenn. 11 Nov. '61. Taking command of the post of Memphis, he was appointed B.G. C.S.A. 11 Apr. '62 (C.M.H. gives the date as 11 Mar. '62) and fought at New Madrid and Farmington (9 May '62), having been sick during the battle of Shiloh. A paper in the O.R. said that in Nov. '62 "imputations now rest on Walker, which will cause his case to be placed before an examining board." No further information is given but Bragg wrote to Cooper that "Carroll and Walker were not safe men to be entrusted with any command. . . ." His application for transfer to the Trans-Miss. Dept. was approved and he reported to Kirby Smith in Alexandria in Mar. '63. He led a cavalry brigade under Marmaduke in the attack on Helena, Ark., 4 July '63. On 6 Sept. '63 he was mortally wounded in a duel with Marmaduke, dying in Little Rock on the 19th at the age of 34. The cause of the duel was not reported in the O.R., and does not appear to be known (Eliot).

WALKER, Mary Edwards. Union surgeon. 1831–1919. N.Y. After graduating from Syracuse she was commissioned Asst. Surgeon in the US Army, the first woman to hold such a post. She served with the Union throughout the Civil War. In fighting for equal rights and suffrage for women she first wore the Bloomer costume and then male attire.

WALKER, Moses B. Union officer. 1819–95. Ohio. Capt. 12th US Inf. 23 Aug. '61; Col. 31st Ohio 23 Sept. '61; Bvt. B.G. USV 27 Mar. '65. Brevets for war service (2). W.I.A. Chickamauga in the spine and left shoulder, inflicting permanent injury. Commanded 1, 1, III

(Ohio); 1, 3d Div. Centre, XIV (Cumberland); 1, 3, XIV (Cumberland). Continued in R.A. until retired with rank of Capt. in 1866 and with rank of Col. 6 months later (Heitman).

WALKER, Reuben Lindsay. C.S.A. gen. 1827–90. Va. Graduating from V. M. I., he was a civil engineer and farmer before being commissioned Capt. of the Purcell Btry. in 1861. He fought at Aquia Creek and 1st Bull Run, and was promoted Maj. in Mar. '62 and named A. P. Hill's Chief of Arty. During the Seven Days' Battles he was ill in Richmond but returned shortly to serve with Hill for the rest of the war. As Lt. Col. he commanded the Arty. at 2d Bull Run, Antietam, and Fredericksburg, and as Col. he fought at Chancellorsville and Gettysburg where he commanded 63 guns. He took no leave other than for illness, and fought in every battle of the Army of Northern Va. with Hill. He was appointed B.G. C.S.A. of Arty. 18 Feb. '65. D.A.B. describes him as "six feet four inches in height and of massive frame, with long dark hair, sweeping moustache and imperial beard ... a superb horseman." After the war he was a farmer and engineer. With his war record of 63 battles and engagements he was sensitive to the question often put to him in later years: "Why, General, not wounded in the war?" His reply was, "No, sir, and it was not my fault."

WALKER, Samuel. Union officer. Pa. Capt. 1st Kans. 1 June '61; Maj. 5th Kans. Cav. 24 May '62; Lt. Col. 16th Kans. Cav. 8 Oct. '64; Bvt. B.G. USV (war service). Died 1893.

WALKER, Thomas McCormick. Union officer. Pa. Maj. 111th Pa. 23 Dec. '61; Lt. Col. 7 Nov. '62; Col. 23 Apr. '65; Bvt. B.G. USV 5 July '65 (war service).

WALKER, William Henry Talbot. C.S.A. gen. 1816–64. Ga. USMA 1837 (46/50); Inf. He fought in the Seminole War (3 wounds, 1 brevet) and resigned the next year only to be reappointed in 1840 and serve in the Mexican War (2 brevets, severely wounded, and not expected to live), as commandant of cadets at West Point, and on the frontier. In poor health all this time, he resigned 20 Dec. '60. On 25 Apr. '61 he was appointed Maj. Gen. of Ga. Vols. and on 25 May B.G. C.S.A. He commanded his brigade at Pensacola and in Va. before resigning 29 Oct. '61, ostensibly because of his health. However, he was immediately reappointed Maj. Gen. of the Ga. troops and joined Gov. Brown in the anti-Davis faction. Reappointed B.G. C.S.A. 9 Feb. '63, he conducted his brigade so well that J. E. Johnston wrote Davis on 18 May that he was the only officer in the western command competent to command a division. He was promoted Maj. Gen. C.S.A. 23 May '63 and commanded the reserve corps at Chickamauga after having led his division in Miss. He was killed in the battle of Atlanta 22 July '64.

WALKER, William S. C.S.A. gen. ?–1899. Appt.-Fla. He fought in the Mexican War as a Midshipman and later resigned to be commissioned Capt. of C.S.A. Inf. Promoted Col. in 1862, he commanded the Confederate forces at the battle of Pocotaligo, S.C., and was promoted B.G. C.S.A. 30 Oct. '62. Taking command of the 3d Mil. Dist. of S.C., he went on 29 Apr. '64 to command the post at Kinston, N.C. He joined Beauregard at Petersburg shortly before Butler advanced. On 20 May he accidentally rode into the Federal lines and, refusing to surrender, was shot in the ankle, had his horse killed from under him, and was captured. His foot was later amputated, and he was exchanged in the fall of that year. On 29 Oct. '64 he was put in command at Weldon.

WALLACE, Lewis. Union gen. and author of *Ben Hur.* 1827–1905. Ind. A precocious boy who hated school and read anything he could find, he was a newspaper reporter and lawyer before fighting in the Mexican War. Then serving in the legislature and active in the militia, he was named the Adj. Gen. of Ind. after Fort Sumter and named Col. 11th Ind. 25 Apr. '61. Leading his regiment at Romney and Harpers Ferry, and being recommissioned 25 Aug. '61, he was named B.G. USV 3 Sept. '61 and Maj. Gen. USV 21 Mar. '62. At Fort Donelson he commanded 3d Div. Mil. Dist. Cairo (1–17 Feb. '62), and at Shiloh he led 3d Div. (17 Feb.–June '62). That fall he was president of the commission investigating Buell's military operations. He held posts on other commissions and boards and next took the field as commander of the VIII Corps (22 Mar. '64–1 Feb. '65 and 19 Apr.–1 Aug. '65) at Monocacy and the Middle Dept. (19 Apr.–27 June '65). Incurring the wrath of Halleck, he was twice removed from command, being restored the first time by Lincoln and the second by Grant. After the war he served on the court-martial of Lincoln's assassins and was president of the court-martial that convicted Henry WIRZ, commandant of ANDERSONVILLE. Resigning 30 Nov. '65, he raised a corps of veterans to help the Mexican liberals and upon the collapse of Maximilian returned to Ind. Appointed Gov. of N. Mex. 1878–81, he was Minister to Turkey 1881–85. He is best remembered for *Ben Hur; A Tale of the Christ* (1880), written while he was living in the Governor's Palace in Santa Fe.

WALLACE, Martin Reuben Merritt. Union officer. Ohio. Maj. 4th Ill. Cav. 12 Oct. '61; Lt. Col. 5 Jan. '63; Col. 3 June '63; Bvt. B.G. USV (war service); mustered out 3 Nov. '64. Died 1902.

WALLACE, William Harvey Lamb. Union gen. 1821–62. Ohio. After the Mexican War he practiced law and was named Col. 11th Ill. 1 May '61. Mustered out 30 July and recommissioned on that date as Col. of the same regiment, he commanded 2d and 3d divisions in the Mil. Dist. Cairo. In the Army of Tenn. he commanded 3d Div. (14 Oct. '61–1 Feb. '62); 2d Brig., 1st Div. (1 Feb.–29 Mar. '62) at Forts Henry and Donelson; and 2d Div. (2–6 Apr. '62) at SHILOH, where he was mortally wounded. Named B.G. USV 21 Mar. '62, he died 10 Apr. '62.

WALLACE, William Henry. C.S.A. gen. 1827–1905. S.C. Graduating from S.C. College, he was a planter, journalist, and lawyer before sitting in the state legislature and becoming an advocate of secession. He enlisted as a private and was almost immediately named Adj. of the 18th S.C. Promoted Lt. Col. in May '61, he fought at Malvern Hill and 2d Bull Run before being named Col. He commanded his regiment at South Mountain, Antietam, and then served in the defenses of Charleston. Sent to Petersburg in the spring of 1864, he was at the Crater and was appointed B.G. C.S.A. 20 Sept. '64. He led Johnson's division at Appomattox. After the war he returned to his plantation and law practice, again serving in the legislature and sitting on the bench as a Democrat.

WALLEN, Henry D. Union officer. c. 1818–86. Ga. Appt.-Fla. USMA 1840 (34/42); Arty.-Inf. He served in the Seminole War and the Mexican War, where he was wounded, before going to the frontier. Promoted Maj. 7th US Inf. 25 Nov. '61, he was on duty in the Dept. of N. Mex. until 1864, and then commanded troops at Fort Schuyler

(N.Y.) for the remainder of the war. He retired in 1871 as Col. 2d US Inf. and Bvt. B.G. USA.

WALTHALL, Edward Cary. C.S.A. gen. 1831–98. Va. Appt.-Miss. A lawyer, he had held several political offices before being commissioned 1st Lt. in the Yalobusha Rifles and, in the summer of 1861, Lt. Col. 15th Miss. He fought at Mill Springs (Ky.) in Jan. '62 and was promoted Col. 29th Miss. 11 Apr. '62. After leading his regiment at Corinth, he was named B.G. C.S.A. 13 Dec. '62 and commanded his brigade at Chickamauga. His unit was reduced to 1,500 men in the defenses of Lookout Mountain, and the next day 600 were left to fight at Missionary Ridge. He was painfully wounded there, but would not leave the field until his men, covering the C.S.A. retreat, were withdrawn. During the Atlanta campaign he was promoted Maj. Gen. 6 June '64 and then went with Hood to fight at Franklin, where he had two horses shot from under him, and at Nashville. After the war he was a power in the Democratic party and sat in the US Senate.

WANGELIN, Hugo. Union officer. Germany. Of a noble Mecklenburg family, his brothers were in the Prussian Army and his father had been with Napoleon in Russia. He himself attended cadet schools, but his widowed mother brought him to America before he could serve in the army. After living as a "LATIN FARMER" he returned to Germany and served a year as a Lt. to protect an inheritance. In the American Civil War he was Maj. 12 Mo. 19 Dec. '61; Col. 20 July '62; Bvt. B.G. USV (war service); mustered out 17 Oct. '64. He lost his left arm at Ringgold and was again wounded at Atlanta. In the Army of the Tenn. he commanded 2, 1, XV; 3, 1, XV. Lincoln named him postmaster at Bellevue, Ill.

WAR CORRESPONDENTS. The "Bohemian Brigade," as the Northern reporters called themselves, were the first large group to cover an American war. A handful had been in Mexico, but it was not until 1861 and the secession crisis that newspaper reporters functioned in the modern sense as informers and molders of public opinion. Newspapers themselves were undergoing a revolution in their purpose at this time and were changing from political sheets consisting mainly of editorials to newspapers, literally, from which their readers could form their own opinions. In the South, on the other hand, the lack of newsprint and the dearth of man power combined to do away with war correspondents almost entirely. Most of the dispatches were written by army staff officers, and a great deal of information was copied from the Northern papers. Louis M. Starr in his excellent *Bohemian Brigade* writes of the following outstanding correspondents, editors, and artists: Charles A. DANA, Sidney Howard GAY, Adams Sherman HILL, Joseph HOWARD Jr., Frederic HUDSON, Joseph Burbridge McCULLAGH, Charles A. PAGE, Whitelaw REID, Albert Deane RICHARDSON, Edmund Clarence STEDMAN, Jerome Bonaparte STILLSON, John SWINTON, William SWINTON, Benjamin Franklin TAYLOR, George Alfred TOWNSEND, Henry VILLARD, Samuel WILKESON, Franc Bangs WILKIE, John Russell YOUNG, Winslow HOMER, Thomas NAST, Henry MOSLER, Eugene BENSON, Edwin FORBES, George W. SMALLEY and Alfred R. Waud. See also Mathew BRADY and William H. ("Bull Run") RUSSELL.

WARD, Durbin. Union officer. 1819–96. Ky. Pvt. 12th Ohio 25 Apr. '61; mustered out 18 Aug. '61; Maj. 17th Ohio 25 Sept. '61; Lt. Col. 3 Mar. '63; Col. 1 Mar. '64; Bvt. B.G. USV 18 Oct. '65 (Chickamauga); resigned 8 Nov. '64. W.I.A. Chickamauga and crippled in the arm. He was active as a lawyer and Democratic legislator.

WARD, George Hull. Union officer. Mass. Lt. Col. 15th Mass. 24 July '61; Col. 29 Apr. '62; Bvt. B.G. USV 2 July '63 (Balls Bluff, Va.; Gettysburg). W.I.A. at Balls Bluff 21 Oct. '61 and lost a leg. K.I.A. at Gettysburg 2 July '63. He had been a B.G. in the Mass. State Mil. Commanded 1, 2, II (Potomac).

WARD, Henry Clark. Union officer. Conn. 1st Sgt. Co. A 25th Conn. 11 Nov. '62; 1st Lt. Adj. 20 Jan. '63; mustered out 26 Aug. '63; Capt. 29th Conn. 16 Jan. '64; Maj. 24 Mar. '64; Lt. Col. 21 July '64; Col. 31st US Col. Inf. 6 Nov. '64; Bvt. B.G. USV 29 Nov. '65 (war service). Commanded 3, 2, XXV (Va.); 3, 2, XXV (Tex.).

WARD, John Henry Hobart. Union gen. 1823-? N.Y. In the R.A. in the Mexican War (1 wound), he was commissioned Col. 38th N.Y. 8 June '61 and commanded 2d Brig., 3d Div. (21 July–Aug. '61) at 1st Bull Run. During the Peninsular campaign, he led his regiment at Yorktown, Williamsburg, Fair Oaks, Glendale, and Malvern Hill, and also at Groveton and Chantilly. He was promoted B.G. USV 4 Oct. '62. In the Army of the Potomac he commanded 2, 1, II (1–13 Sept. '62; 30 Oct. '62–26 Jan. '63 at Fredericksburg; 15 Feb.–Mar. '63; Apr.–29 May '63 at Chancellorsville; 3 June–2 July '63 at Gettysburg, where he also succeeded to command of the division until 7 July; 7 July–Aug. '63; Sept.–29 Dec. '63 at Mine Run; 17–28 Jan. '64; and 17 Feb.–24 Mar. '64). He had commanded the division 29 May–3 June '63 and 17 Feb.–24. Mar. '64 as well as Gettysburg. During the Wilderness and Spotsylvania he led 1, 3, II (20 Apr.–12 May '64). He was wounded at Gettysburg, Wapping Heights, Kelly's Ford, and Spotsylvania, and mustered out 18 July '64.

WARD, Lyman Munson. Union officer. N.Y. Capt. 14th Wis. 30 Jan. '62; Maj. 19 Apr. '62; Lt. Col. 1 July '62; Col. 13 Mar. '63; Bvt. B.G. USV (war service). Commanded the 2d Brig., Prov. Div., XVII (Gulf) during Banks's Red River expedition; 1st Brig., 3d Div. Det. Army of Tenn. (Cumberland); 1, 3, XVI (Gulf); 2, 3, XVI (Gulf). Also commanded the post of Montgomery (Ala.).

WARD, William Thomas. Union gen. 1808-78. Ky. Fighting in the Mexican War, he was a lawyer and legislator when he raised a brigade in 1861 and was commissioned B.G. USV 18 Sept. '61. In the Army of the Ohio he commanded 16th Brig. (Nov. '61–Mar. '62) and Ward's brigade, 12th Div. (Sept.–Nov. '62). In the Army of the Cumberland he led Ward's brigade, Dist. Gallatin; 2, 3, Res. Corps (8 June '62–5 Aug. '63); Ward's brigade, Dist. Nashville; and 1st Div., XI (12 Jan.–16 Apr. '64). During the Atlanta campaign and the March to the Sea and through the Carolinas he led 1, 3, XX (14 Apr.–15 May '64 and 15 May–29 June '64 at Resaca, where he was severely wounded) and the division (29 June–23 Sept. '64 and 25 Oct. '64–1 June '65). Breveted Maj. Gen. USV 24 Feb. '65, he was mustered out 24 Aug.

WAR DEMOCRATS. Northern faction of the Democratic party that supported Lincoln and the Union policies during the Civil War. Led by Stephen A. Douglas and Andrew Johnson, they were opposed by the regular Democrats and the "Peace Democrats."

WARE BOTTOM CHURCH, Va., 9–20 May '64. Location in front of Butler's Bermuda Hundred Line. The 85th Pa. and 39th Ill. had a skirmish here 9 May with enemy pickets; no casualties. On 20 May, after Butler had withdrawn from DREWRY'S BLUFF, the advance rifle pits in front of Ames and Terry were captured. Ames was unable to re-establish his line, but Howell's brigade (Terry), reinforced by the 6th Conn. and 142d N.Y. of Turner's division, recaptured the positions with a loss of 702. Confederate losses were probably as high; W. S. Walker was severely wounded and captured (Humphreys, 158).

WAR GOVERNORS. See UNION, BORDER STATE and CONFEDERATE WAR GOVERNORS.

WARNER, Adoniram Judson. Union officer. 1834–1910. N.Y. Organized the Mercer Rifles and became Capt. of them in the 10th Pa. Res. 21 July '61; Lt. Col. 14 May '62; Col. 25 Apr. '63; Col. Vet. Res. Corps 15 Nov. '63; Bvt. B.G. USV (war service); W.I.A. Antietam. A schoolteacher and superintendent before the war, he became a promoter of Pa. oil and coal fields and railroads. As a leading figure in the silver movement, he was an ardent bimetalist and tried, as Congressman, to pass his free-coinage bill.

WARNER, Darius B. Union officer. Ohio. Maj. 113th Ohio 8 Sept. '62; Lt. Col. 6 May '63; Col. 23 Feb. '65; Bvt. B.G. USV (Kenesaw Mountain).

WARNER, Edward Raynsford. Union officer. c. 1835–1905. Pa. USMA 1857 (21/38); Arty. 1st Lt. 3d US Arty. 14 May '61; Regt. Q.M. 27 Sept. '61–27 Oct. '62; Lt. Col. 1st N.Y. Arty. 1 Nov. '62; Bvt. B.G. USV 9 Apr. '65 (Lee's surrender). Other brevets for Gettysburg (2), Petersburg siege (2), war service. Served as Inspector of Arty. for the Army of the Potomac 1 Nov. '62–1 Dec. '63 and 30 Apr. '64–21 June '65. In R.A. until retired in 1887 as Maj.

WARNER, James Meech. Union gen. c. 1836–97. Vt. USMA 1860 (40/41);

Inf. He served at Fort Wise (Colo.) until 1862, being commissioned 1st Lt. 8th US Inf. May '61 and Col. 11th Vt. 1 Sept. '62. In the Defenses of Washington until 12 May '64, he fought and was wounded at Spotsylvania, commanding 1st, Defenses North of Potomac, XXII (26 Mar.–18 May '64). He then commanded 1, 2, VI, Army Shenandoah (21 Sept.–6 Dec. '64) at Flint Hill, Fishers Hill, and Cedar Creek, and was with the Army of the Potomac at the Petersburg siege and the final assaults. Named B.G. USV 8 May '65, he commanded 1, 2, VI Potomac (2 May–28 June '65). Breveted for Spotsylvania C.H.—Winchester—Fishers Hill—Cedar Creek (B.G. USV 1 Aug. '64) and war service (B.G. USA 9 Apr. '65), he resigned in 1866 and went into manufacturing.

WARNER, Willard. Union officer. 1826–? Ohio. After college he went to Calif. in 1849 and returned to the East where he managed an ironworks and was active in Republican politics. He was commissioned Maj. 76th Ohio 3 Dec. '61 and served at Fort Donelson, Corinth, and Vicksburg before being promoted Lt. Col. 15 Dec. '63. Commanding the regiment, he fought from Vicksburg to Chattanooga, and at the battles of Lookout Mountain, Missionary Ridge, and Ringgold. During the Atlanta campaign he was Sherman's I.G. He was promoted Col. 180th Ohio 27 Oct. '64 and breveted B.G. USV for the Atlanta and Carolinas campaigns. Mustered out in July '65, he sat in the Ohio legislature before moving to Ala. where he planted cotton and entered Reconstruction politics as a Republican. He later went into the iron, steel, and charcoal manufacturing business in Tenn. and Ala.

WARREN, Fitz-Henry. Union gen. 1816–78. Mass. A journalist and politician, he was commissioned Col. 1st

Iowa 13 June '61 and B.G. USV 16 July '62. He commanded 2, 2d Div. Army Southeast Mo., Mo. (Feb.–Mar. '63) and then went to the Gulf, where he led 1, 1, XIII (12 Dec. '63–28 Jan. '64; 30 Jan.–8 Feb. '64; 11 Mar.–3 Apr. '64) and the division (8 Feb.–11 Mar. and 3 Apr.–23 May '64). He also commanded Dist. Baton Rouge (31 May–13 June '64) and US forces Tex. (9 June–1 Aug. '64). Breveted Maj. Gen. USV 24 Aug. '65 for war service, he was mustered out the same day. He was state Sen. and Minister to Guatemala after the war.

WARREN, Gouverneur Kemble. Union gen. 1830–82. N.Y. USMA 1850 (2/44); Topo. Engrs. Before the war he participated in a Mississippi Delta survey, supervised rapids and canal improvements, went with A. A. HUM-PHREYS on the Pacific R.R. expedition, taught mathematics at West Point, and fought Indians. Named Lt. Col. 5th N.Y. 14 May '61, he fought at Big Bethel and was promoted Col. 11 Sept., having been promoted Capt. in the R.A. two days previous. He led the regiment at the Yorktown siege and then commanded 3, 2, V (18 May–Dec. '62) at Gaines's Mill, where he was wounded, Malvern Hill, Harrison's Landing, 2d Bull Run, Antietam, Centreville, and Fredericksburg. Appointed B.G. USV 26 Sept. '62, he also commanded the brigade Jan.–5 Feb. '63 and was then named Chief Topo. Engr. for the Army of the Potomac, becoming (8 June–12 Aug. '63) Chief Engr. and being wounded at Gettysburg. There is a monument to him on Little Round Top, where he distinguished himself on the second day of the battle. As Maj. Gen. 3 May '63, he then commanded the II Corps (2 Sept.–16 Dec. '63) at Auburn, Bristoe Station, Kelly's Ford, and Mine Run; and later (29 Dec. '63–9 Jan. '64 and 15 Jan.–24 Mar. '64).

For the rest of the war he commanded the V Corps (23 Mar. '64–2 Jan. '65 and 27 Jan.–1 Apr. '65), participating at the Wilderness, Spotsylvania, North Anna, Totopotomoy, Bethesda Church, Cold Harbor, Petersburg (assaults, siege, and crater), Weldon R.R., Peeble's Farm, Chapel House, Hatcher's Run. Dabney's Mills, and Five Forks. During this last battle he was summarily relieved by Sheridan (with prior authority from Grant) and put in command of the defenses of Petersburg and the Southside R.R. He commanded the Dept. of the Miss. 14–30 May '64 (Cullum), and resigned his volunteer commission on 27 May. Breveted for Gaines's Mill, Gettysburg, Bristoe Station (B.G. USA), and for war service (Maj. Gen. USA), he remained in the service and was a Lt. Col. of Engrs. when he died 8 Aug. '82. After repeated requests he was granted the WARREN COURT OF INQUIRY which, 14 years after the war, exonerated him of Sheridan's imputations. Meanwhile, however, he had been professionally ruined and he "died of a broken heart" (Cullum).

WARREN, Lucius Henry. Union officer. Mass. 2d Lt. 32d Mass. 11 Aug. '62; 1st Lt. 14 Dec. '62; Maj. 38th US Col. Inf. 9 Apr. '64; Lt. Col. 12 Apr. '66; Bvt. B.G. USV (war service). Brevets for war service, Petersburg siege. W.I.A. at Chancellorsville and siege of Petersburg. A graduate of Princeton (1860) and Harvard Law School (1862), he practiced law after being discharged from the R.A. (at his own request) in 1870 as Capt.

WARREN COURT OF INQUIRY. During the battle of Five Forks Warren was relieved of the command of V Corps by Sheridan, under whose orders he had been for the action. In his 16 May '65 report of the battle Sheridan said, "General Warren did not exert himself to get up his corps as rapidly as he might have done, and his manner gave me the impression that he wished the sun to go down before dispositions for the attack could be completed. . . . During the engagement portions of his lines gave way when not exposed to a heavy fire, and simply for want of confidence on the part of the troops, which General Warren did not exert himself to inspire. I therefore relieved him from the command of the Fifth Corps, authority for the action having been sent to me, before the battle, unsolicited." On 9 Dec. '79, after repeated requests, G. K. Warren was granted a court of inquiry by Pres. Hayes. As finally constituted, the court was composed of Bvt. Maj. Gens. C. C. Augur and John Newton, with Bvt. Lt. Col. Loomis L. Langdon as recorder. After they had conducted "an extended and minute investigation [before which] many Confederate as well as United States officers engaged in that battle appeared" (Humphreys, 357), Warren was exonerated of the principal charges of dilatory personal leadership. Although the court found that Warren had been slow in some specific instances, the general tenor of their opinion was that he had been done an injustice by Sheridan. On 21 Nov. '81, less than 9 months before Warren's death, Pres. Arthur " 'directed that the findings and opinion of the court be published.' No other action was taken" (B.&L., IV, 724).

WASHBURN, Cadwallader Colder. Union gen. 1818–82. Me. A schoolteacher, he surveyed and practiced law before going into banking and public-land speculation in Wis. An early Republican, he served in Congress with his brothers Elihu and Israel and was a delegate to the Washington Peace Conference in 1861. Raising the 2d Wis. Cav., he was commissioned Col. 6 Feb. '62 and commanded the Dist. Eastern Ark., Tenn. (3 Apr.–June '63), after

having been appointed B.G. USV 16 July and Maj. Gen. USV 29 Nov. '62. He also led the 3d Cav. Dist. Eastern Ark. (May–June '63), as well as 2d Cav. Div., XIII (8 Feb.–3 Apr. '63) and 1st Cav. Div., XIII (31 Mar.– 9 June '63). He commanded the XIII Corps 28 July–7 Aug. '63 and the same corps in the Dept. of the Gulf 15 Sept.– 19 Oct. and 26 Oct.–25 Nov. '63. He commanded 1st Div., XIII, Gulf (15 Sept.–19 Oct. and 26 Oct.–25 Nov. '63) and the Dist. Western Tenn., Tenn. (17 Apr. '64–3 Feb. '65 and 4 Mar.–29 May '65). Resigning 25 May '65, he was Congressman and Gov. of Wis. 1872– 73 and was then active in operating and expanding his industrial enterprises. A pioneer in flour-milling processes, he was also active in railroading and philanthropy.

WASHBURN, Francis. Union officer. Mass. 2d Lt. 1st Mass. Cav. 26 Dec. '61; 1st Lt. 7 Mar. '62; Capt. 2d Mass. Cav. 26 Jan. '63; Lt. Col. 4th Mass. Cav. 4 Feb. '64; Col. 25 Feb. '65; Bvt. B.G. USV 6 Apr. '65 (High Bridge, Va.). Wounded at High Bridge by a shot in the head, then falling from his horse and being struck in the head with a saber, and captured. Died from his wounds 22 Apr. '65. He had left his studies in Germany to come home and fight.

WASHBURN, Henry D. Union officer. Vt. Commissioned Lt. Col. 18th Ind. 16 Aug. '61, he was promoted Col. 15 July '62 and mustered out in July '65. He was breveted B.G. USV 15 Dec. '64 and Maj. Gen. USV 26 July '65 for war service. Died 1871.

WASHBURN, Israel. Gov. of Me. 1813–83. Me. A lawyer, he entered politics as a Whig and sat in the legislature and US Congress before being elected Gov. in 1861. Declining renomination, he was appointed in 1863

893   WASHINGTON ARTILLERY

collector of customs at Portland (Me.)
by Lincoln. He was later president of
the board of trustees of Tufts College.
Brother of C. C. WASHBURN.

WASHBURNE, George Abiel. Union
officer. Mass. Maj. 16th Conn. 24 Aug.
'62; resigned 18 Jan. '63; 1st Lt. Vet.
Res. Corps 18 June '63; Capt. 27 June
'63; Maj. 28 Oct. '63; Lt. Col. 30 Mar.
'64; Bvt. B.G. USV (war service, Antietam). Died 1891.

WASHINGTON, D.C., DEFENSES
OF. Created 2 Sept. '62 (when the Mil.
Dist. of Washington was abolished) and
done away with 2 Feb. '63 (when the
Dept. of Washington was established).

WASHINGTON, D. C., TERRITO-
RIAL ORGANIZATIONS IN WHICH
INCLUDED. Dept. of the East from
1 Jan. to 9 Apr. '61; Dept. of Washington to 25 July '61; Mil. Dist. of the
Potomac to 15 Aug. '61; Dept. and
Army of the Potomac to 4 Apr. '62;
Dept. of the Rappahannock to 26 June
'62; Mil. Dist. of Washington to 2 Sept.
'62; Defenses of Washington to 2 Feb.
'63; Dept. of Washington to 11 June '66.
(See entry on each of the above for
commanders and area included.)

WASHINGTON, D.C., UNION DE-
PARTMENT OF. Constituted 9 Apr.
'61 to consist of the Dist. of Columbia
to its original boundaries (i.e., including
Alexandria County, Va.) and the state
of Md. as far as Bladensburg. During
this period it was commanded by Lt.
Col. C. F. Smith from 10–28 Apr., and
by Col. J. K. F. Mansfield. The department was merged into the Mil. Dist. of
the Potomac 25 July '61. Re-created
2 Feb. '63 and designated also as the
XXII Army Corps, it was again discontinued 11 June '66. The following
Maj. Gens. commanded: S. P. Heintzelman to 13 Oct. '63; C. C. Augur to 7
June '65; J. G. Parke to 26 June '65;
and C. C. Augur to 11 June '66. Present

for duty strength 31 Dec. '63 was
24,000. (See also WASHINGTON, D.C.,
TERRITORIAL ORGANIZATIONS IN WHICH
INCLUDED.)

WASHINGTON, D.C., UNION MIL-
ITARY DISTRICT OF. Existed from
26 June '62 (prior to which time Washington had been part of the Dept. of
the Rappahannock) until 2 Sept. '62
(when merged into the Defenses of
Washington, and, four months later,
into the Dept. of Washington). Commander: Brig. Gen. J. S. Wadsworth.

WASHINGTON ARTILLERY of
New Orleans. Composed of wealthy and
prominent men of the city, this was
the most famous of the Confederate
volunteer artillery organizations (Miller,
V, 58). Wise, who mentions it more
frequently in The Long Arm of Lee
than any other Confederate artillery battalion, says: "At the outbreak of the
Civil War there was not a finer organization of citizen soldiery in America."
Organized in 1838, it had fought in
the Mexican War as Co. A of Persifal
Smith's regiment. It had then been
known as the "Native American" Btry.
until reorganized in 1852 as the Washington Arty. Col. J. B. Walton became
its captain in 1857. In the seizure of
the Baton Rouge Arsenal, 11 Apr. '61,
it got much of its equipment for the
Civil War, including six 6-pounder guns
and ammunition. Through Judah Benjamin it offered its services to the Confederacy and was mustered in 26 May
'61. Four batteries served with the
A.N.V., arriving in time for 1st Bull
Run, and another battery fought with
the Army of Tenn. It particularly distinguished itself in the defense of
Marye's Heights during the Fredericksburg and Chancellorsville campaign.

Commanded successively by Walton,
Benjamin F. Eshleman, and William
Miller Owen (who wrote "A Hot Day
on Marye's Heights," B.&L., III. 97–

99), the battalion fought every battle of the A.N.V. After the war they got permission to form the "Washington Artillery Veterans Charitable & Benevolent Association, Inc." They then held secret infantry drills, assembled weapons, and in 1870, when "carpetbag" rule had become intolerable, appeared with two miniature brass cannon to drive Longstreet's Metropolitan Police off the streets.

In the regular service the Washington Artillery sent a battery to fight in Cuba, and distinguished themselves in World Wars I and II.

WASHINGTON PEACE CONFERENCE. Held 4–27 Feb. '61 in the capital, it was called by the Va. legislature in an attempt to satisfy the states in the deep South on slavery. Twenty-one states in all participated, and the BORDER STATES were most active. The seven states that had already seceded did not send delegates, and neither did Ark., Wis., Minn., Calif., or Ore. The Crittenden Compromise (see John J. CRITTENDEN), the basis of discussion, was modified out of existence, and the final recommendations of the conference, presided over by former Pres. Tyler of Va., satisfied no one. They were, however, submitted to Congress on 27 Feb. '61 and are the last attempt at conciliation on the slavery question in the territories.

WASS, Ansel Dyer. Union officer. Me. Capt. 19th Mass. 28 Aug. '61; Maj. 1 July '62; Lt. Col. 41st Mass. 10 Oct. '62; resigned 31 Jan. '63; Lt. Col. 19th Mass. 25 May '63; mustered out 28 July '64; Col. 60th Mass. 6 Aug. '64; Bvt. B.G. USV (war service); mustered out 29 Dec. '64. Commanded 3, 2, II (Potomac). W.I.A. at Gettysburg and Bristoe Station (Va.) 14 Oct. '63. Died 1889.

WATERHOUSE, Richard. C.S.A. gen. ?–1876. Appt.-Tex. Commissioned Col. 19th Tex. 13 May '62, he served in Ark. under Hindman and Holmes. Going to La., he fought under Taylor at Millikens Bend and the other skirmishes of the Vicksburg campaign. He fought in the Red River campaign of 1864. According to C.M.H. he was assigned B.G. C.S.A. 13 May '64 by Kirby Smith to rank from 30 Apr. Wright does not list him as a Kirby Smith appointee but gives the date of his appointment as 17 Mar. '65 and says this was approved by the Senate.

WATERS, Louis Henry. Union officer. Pa. Lt. Col. 28th Ill. 22 Aug. '61; resigned 10 Jan. '62; Col. 84th Ill. 1 Sept. '62; Bvt. B.G. USV 18 June '65 (war service). Commanded in the Army of the Cumberland: 3, 2, XXI; 3, 1, IV.

WATIE, Stand. C.S.A. gen. 1806–71. Ga. Appt.-Indian Territory. The son of a full-blooded Cherokee father and half-blood mother, he attended the mission school and then became a planter. With his brother he ran a Cherokee newspaper. With three others of his tribe he signed the treaty whereby the Ga. Cherokees gave up their lands in that state and moved to Okla. This was against the wishes of the others, and the other three were all killed on the same day. Watie was marked for death but escaped. When the Civil War came, the Cherokees tried to maintain their neutrality but finally signed an alliance with the Confederacy. Watie raised a company of home guard and was commissioned Capt. early in 1861. Sometime later that year he was named Col. of the Cherokee Mtd. Rifles and mustered into the C.S. Army. Active as a cavalry raider, he commanded his troops at Wilson's Creek, PEA RIDGE, and in many skirmishes in Indian Territory and Ark. In 1863 the majority party of the Cherokees had repudiated the Confederate treaty and had thrown in with the Union, but Watie remained loyal to the rebels and led the Southern wing of the tribe as principal chief. He was appointed B.G. C.S.A. 10 May '64 to rank from 6 May. On 23 June '65 he finally surrendered to the Federals. After the war he engaged in planting and tobacco manufacturing.

WATKINS, Louis Douglas. Union gen. 1835–68. Fla. R.A. Enlisting in the 3d Bn. D.C. Inf. 12 Apr. '61, he was commissioned 1st Lt. 14th US Inf. one month later and transferred to the 2d Cav. 22 June and 5th US Cav. 3 Aug. '61. He fought with his regiment in the Peninsula and was severely wounded at Gaines's Mill. Named Capt. 17 July '62, he was A.D.C. to A. J. Smith and then Chief of Cav., Army of Ky. Dec. '62–Jan. '63. Promoted Col. 6th Ky. Cav. 1 Feb. '63, he served on Gen. Granger's staff and commanded 3, 1, Cav. Corps, Cumberland (8 July '63– 5 July '64 and 10 Aug.–29 Oct. '64) guarding the railroads during the Atlanta campaign and fighting at Resaca. He also led 3, 1, Cav. Corps, Mil. Div. Miss. (29 Oct. '64–23 Jan. '65). Breveted for war service, Thompson's Station (Tenn.); LaFayette (Ga.); Resaca (B.G. USA); and LaFayette (B.G. USV 23 June '64), he was promoted B.G. USV 25 Sept. '65 and continued in the R.A., commanding the posts of Baton Rouge and New Orleans. He died on active duty at the latter place.

WATTS, Thomas Hill. C.S.A. Atty. gen. and gov. of Ala. 1819–92. Ala. After graduating from the Univ. of Va., he became a lawyer and served in the legislature as a Whig. He was an opponent of secession until Lincoln's election and the president's use of force on the Southern states. Taking a seat on Alabama's secession convention in 1861, he raised and became Col. of the 17th Ala., serving at Pensacola and Corinth.

In Mar. '62, he followed Thomas Bragg as Davis' Atty. Gen. and held the post until he became Ala.'s Gov. on 1 Dec. '63, George Davis succeeding him in Richmond. After the war he returned to his law practice.

WAUHATCHIE NIGHT ATTACK, 28–29 Oct. '63 (Chattanooga campaign). Although Bragg reacted too slowly to prevent establishment of the bridgehead at Brown's Ferry, he ordered Jenkins'

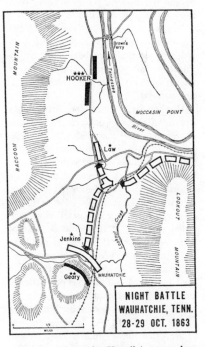

NIGHT BATTLE WAUHATCHIE, TENN. 28-29 OCT. 1863

division (formerly Hood's) to make a night attack against Geary's isolated division at Wauhatchie, about three miles south of Hooker's main body. Since Law had been operating in this area and was familiar with the terrain, he was ordered to move his brigade across the creek after dark and set up a blocking position to cover the Brown's Ferry–Wauhatchie road. Law went into position about 10 P.M. on high ground just east of the road. He was reinforced by the brigades of Benning and Robertson, bringing his command up to about 2,100 men (Alexander). Bratton's brigade (formerly Jenkins'), about 1,800, crossed the creek, moved south, and at about midnight made contact with sentinels of Geary's command. Bratton had been accompanied by a force of sharpshooters under Lt. Col. T. M. Logan. These were ordered to work around behind the Federal position while Bratton's six regiments got into position.

There was heavy and confused fighting around Wauhatchie. Repeated Confederate attacks were beaten off by the brigades of Greene and Cobham. Knaps's battery gave the Federals effective support.

Hooker had heard the firing from Brown's Ferry and ordered the divisions of Schurz and Steinwehr to "double-quick" to Geary's assistance. Tyndale's brigade, leading Schurz's division, was fired on by Law's command and turned to attack. The two following brigades, Hecker and Kryzanowski, were halted as a result of bungled staff work and failed to reach Wauhatchie in time to help Geary. Orland Smith, at the head of Steinwehr's division, was also ordered to attack Law. In a moonlit night, darkened by occasional clouds, the Federals launched several attacks and were repulsed with heavy losses on both sides. Finally, the 136th N.Y. got around the Confederate flank and a final assault drove the Confederates back. Smith's brigade is credited with making one of the most brilliant charges of the war.

Bratton, unable to penetrate Geary's defenses and threatened from the rear, withdrew. Federal losses were reported as 76 killed, 339 wounded, and 22 missing. Bratton sustained 408 casualties, while Law's command lost only 52 (Alexander).

This was one of the rare night attacks of the war and, according to Alexander, one of its "most foolhardy adventures." The fighting was so confused that an accurate account cannot be reconstructed. (The *Official Records*, Serial No. 54, pages 138 ff., clears up the mismanaged movement to reinforce Geary from Brown's Ferry. The accounts of the opposing commanders at Wauhatchie are at variance mainly because neither knew, even after the battle, exactly where the other's troops were located. Jenkins' report is missing.)

Several misconceptions can, however, be corrected. The Federal estimate of 1,600 enemy casualties is obviously over-enthusiastic, particularly since there was no pursuit. Many accounts state that Geary was attacked by Longstreet's entire corps, whereas only Bratton's 1,800 were engaged. Grant perpetuates the "mule charge" myth. Some Federal mules were apparently abandoned by their frightened "skinners" and, terrified by the sounds of battle, charged blindly into Law's lines. The Confederates, taking this for a cavalry charge (so Grant's account in B. & L. goes) "stampeded in turn." Law's command was driven back by Tyndale and Orland Smith before the "mule charge" took place. There is a picturesque story of a recommendation that the mules be breveted as horses.

Schurz called for a court of inquiry in which he and Hecker were cleared of Hooker's implied charges of inefficiency. Longstreet attributes the Confederate failure to "a strong feeling of jealousy among the brigadier generals," and ordered charges preferred against Law. These were dropped because of impending military operations (Longstreet, *From Manassas to Appomattox*, 447; O.R. *op cit.*).

WAUL, Thomas N. C.S.A. gen. 1815–1903. S.C. Appt.-Tex. A graduate of S.C. College, he practiced law and was named Judge before sitting in the 1st C.S.A. Congress. In Feb. '62, when the permanent Confederate government was set up, he raised Waul's Tex. Legion, was named Col. 17 May '62, and served under Van Dorn and Pemberton. He fought in the Vicksburg campaign and, upon his exchange, was appointed B.G. C.S.A. 18 Sept. '63. In Feb. '64 he joined Magruder in Tex. and then led his brigade under Walker in the Red River campaign of 1864. Going to Ark., he fought against Steele at Jenkins' Ferry.

WAUTAUGA BRIDGE AND CARTER'S STATION, Tenn., 30 Dec. '62. See CARTER'S RAID INTO E. TENN.

WAYNE, Henry Constantine. C.S.A. officer. 1815–83. Ga. USMA 1838 (14/45) Arty.-Q.M. He served on the frontier, taught artillery, cavalry, and infantry tactics at West Point, and won a brevet in the Mexican War. In 1855 he was engaged in the War Dept.'s camel experiment in Tex. He resigned 31 Dec. '60 as a Capt. Joining the Confederacy, he was appointed B.G. C.S.A. 16 Dec. '61 and declined this 11 Jan. '62, although Cullum lists him in that rank. He is listed by Wright and Wood, but not by C.M.H.

WAYNESBORO, Ga., 26–29 Nov. '64. (MARCH TO THE SEA) When Sherman left Milledgeville he ordered Kilpatrick to detour north, feint toward Augusta, try to destroy the important railroad bridge at Brier Creek near Waynesboro, and then to move to Millen and release Federal prisoners near there. Wheeler learned of the movement toward Augusta and concentrated his forces to oppose the Federals near Brier Creek. Kilpatrick eluded Wheeler, but the Confederates took up a pursuit. The 8th Ind. and 2d (US) Ky. Cav. of Murray's brigade were performing rear-guard duty and were attacked at Sylvan Grove the night of 26 Nov. Although surprised and driven from their camps, these regiments rejoined the rest of their brigade in good order. Wheeler's continued pressure forced Kilpatrick to abandon his mission of burning the bridge at Brier Creek. Learning that the prisoners had been evacuated from Millen, Kilpatrick moved to rejoin the army at Louisville. Early the morning of the 28th Wheeler came close to capturing Kilpatrick when the latter was surprised some distance from his main body with only the 9th Mich. Cav. Kilpatrick had difficulty fighting his way through Wheeler's entire corps (Dibrell, Hume, and Anderson) to rejoin his main body. Wheeler's pursuit was checked at Buckhead Creek by Col. T. T. Heath and the 5th Ohio, with two guns. At Reynolds' Plantation Kilpatrick decisively checked an attack by Wheeler and then rejoined the infantry column. The names Thomas' Station, Jones's Plantation, and Brown's Cross Road are also associated with these actions.

"During the night Kilpatrick sought the protection of his infantry, which he did not venture to forsake again during the campaign," wrote Wheeler in his official report (O.R., I, XLIV, 409). Kilpatrick then undertook a series of skirmishes that put Wheeler's horsemen on the defensive. (See MARCH TO THE SEA for names and dates.)

WAYNESBORO, Va., 2 Mar. '65. (SHENANDOAH VALLEY CAMPAIGN OF SHERIDAN) Sheridan's destruction of Early's last forces in the Shenandoah occurred here when Custer's cavalry division (4,840 effectives) attacked a small and demoralized Confederate force on a ridge west of the town. According to Freeman, Early had little more than 1,000 infantry and only six guns that could be moved. Federal accounts say Early had 2,000 troops.

Custer enveloped the enemy left with three regiments and made a frontal attack with his other two brigades. Early escaped with generals Long, Wharton, and about 20 others. Federal accounts claimed capture of 1,600 men, 17 flags, 11 guns, and all of Early's supplies (Pond, 253).

WEAPONS of the Civil War are covered first under the general headings of CANNON, SMALL ARMS, and EDGED WEAPONS. These covering articles will make cross reference to entries on individual weapons, their ammunition, and associated terms and definitions.

WEAVER, James Baird. Union officer. 1833-1912. Ohio. 1st Lt. 2d Iowa 27 May '61; Maj. 25 July '62; Col. 10 Nov. '62; Bvt. B.G. USV (war service); mustered out 27 May '64. At the battle of Corinth the Col. and Lt. Col. of his regiment were killed, and Weaver, as Maj., took command. Commanded 1, 2, XVI (Tenn.). Early active in the Republican party, he became interested in the Greenback movement, serving as Congressman and presidential candidate and also running for chief executive under the Populist banner.

WEBB, Alexander Stewart. Union gen. 1835-1911. N.Y. USMA 1855 (13/34); Arty. Serving in the Seminole War, on frontier garrison duty, and at West Point as mathematics professor, he was promoted 1st Lt. 2d US Arty. 28 Apr., Capt. 11th Inf. 14 May, and Maj. 1st R.I. Light Arty. 14 Sept. '61. At 1st Bull Run he was assistant to Chief of Arty. and held this post until 1 Apr. '62, fighting at Yorktown, Mechanicsville, Hanover C.H., Gaines's Mill, Savage's Station, and Malvern Hill. He was Asst. I.G. and Chief of Staff of the V Corps (Sept.-Nov. '62) at Antietam, Snickers Gap, and Shepherdstown, and Inspector of Arty. at Camp Barry (D.C.) Nov. '62-Jan. '63. At Chancellorsville he was

Asst. I.G. of the V Corps (7 Jan.-23 June '63) and commanded 2, 2, II (28 June-15 Aug. '63) at Gettysburg, where he was wounded. Succeeding to division (15 Aug.-10 Dec. '63), he led that at Bristoe Station, Robertson's Tavern, and Morton's Ford. He next commanded 1, 2, II (25 Mar.-12 May '64) at the Wilderness and Spotsylvania, where he was severely wounded. Disabled until 11 Jan. '65, he was Meade's Chief of Staff during the remainder of the Petersburg siege and at Hatcher's Run. Breveted for Gettysburg, Bristoe Station, Spotsylvania, war service (B.G. USA and Maj. Gen. USA) and Gettysburg–Bristoe Station–the Wilderness–Spotsylvania (Maj. Gen. USV 1 Aug. '64), he continued in the R.A. until discharged at his own request in 1870 as Lt. Col. In 1891 he was awarded the Medal of Honor for Gettysburg and there is a statue of him in the Bloody Angle at Spotsylvania. He was president of the City College of N.Y. 1869-1902. In 1881 he wrote *The Peninsula: McClellan's Campaign of 1862.*

WEBBER, Alonzo Watson. Union officer. N.Y. 1st Lt. 1st Mo. 18 May '61; transferred to 5th Mo. July '61; mustered out 12 Aug. '61; 1st Lt. Adj. 3d Mo. 11 Oct. '61; Lt. Col. 51st US Col. Inf. 28 July '63; Col. 15 Mar. '64; Bvt. B.G. USV 26 Mar. '65 (Mobile). Died 1876.

WEBBER, Jules C. Union officer. N.Y. 1st Sgt. Co. I 18th Ill. 28 May '61; 1st Lt. Regt. Q.M. 15 Sept. '61; Capt. A.D.C. Vols. 7 June '64; Lt. Col. 18th Ill. 24 Mar. '65; Bvt. B.G. USV (war service). Died 1872.

WEBER, Max. Union gen. 1824-1901. Germany. A graduate of the German military academy, he was in the army until the 1849 revolution, when he fought under Sigel. He ran a German hotel in N.Y.C. until commissioned Col.

20th N.Y. ("United Turner Rifles") 9 May '61. He commanded Camp Hamilton and then led Weber's brigade, division at Suffolk, VII (22 July–8 Sept. '62). Promoted B.G. USV 28 Apr. '62 he commanded 3, 3, II, Potomac (12–17 Sept. '62) at Antietam, holding his position when Sedgwick's left collapsed. He was severely wounded in the right arm, permanently crippling it. In the Valley in 1864 he served under Hunter and Sigel and was commanding Harpers Ferry when Jubal Early was repulsed there in July. He commanded reserve division, W. Va. (6–15 Aug. '64) and resigned 13 May '65. After the war he was in the Internal Revenue Dept. and US Consul at Nantes.

WEBSTER, Joseph Dana. Union gen. 1811–76. N.H. A civil engineer, he then joined the R.A. as a topographical engineer and fought in the Mexican War. He resigned to become a Chicago manufacturer and was commissioned Maj. Add. Paymaster Vols. 1 June '61. As Col. 1st Ill. Light Arty., 1 Feb. '62, he fought at Forts Henry and Donelson and commanded the artillery at SHILOH. He was promoted B.G. USV 29 Nov. '62 and was Chief of Staff to Grant and later Sherman. Breveted Maj. Gen. USV for war service, he resigned in Nov. '65 and returned to Chicago.

WEED, Stephen Hinsdale. Union gen. 1834–63. N.Y. USMA 1854 (27/46); Arty. He fought in the Seminole wars and served on frontier duty, in Indian fighting, and on the Utah Expedition before being promoted Capt. 5th US Arty. 14 May '61. At Yorktown, Gaines's Mill, Malvern Hill, 2d Bull Run, and Antietam, he commanded a battery. He fought at Chancellorsville, was named B.G. USV 6 June '63 and was killed at GETTYSBURG 2 July '63 holding Little Round Top. This place is marked "Weed's Hill" today.

WEISIGER, Davis Adams. C.S.A. gen. ?–1899. Appt.-Va. A merchant, he fought in the Mexican War and was active in the Va. militia. Named Col. of the 39th Va. in 1853, he held this position until 1860 when it became a battalion of volunteers ready for active service. He was given command of this as Col. and on 20 Apr. '61 went to Norfolk when the Navy Yard was evacuated. Commissioned Col. 12th Va. on 9 May '61, he fought at Seven Pines, Charles City Cross Roads, and the Seven Days' Battles. At 2d Bull Run he succeeded Mahone as brigade commander and was seriously wounded. At the Wilderness he again succeeded Mahone, leading the brigade through Cold Harbor and in the battles around Petersburg. He was given an on-the-spot promotion to B.G. C.S.A. 30 July '64 by Lee for his actions in the Petersburg mine action (appointed 1 Nov. '64 to rank from that date). Wright says he had been appointed B.G. 13 May '64, that this was confirmed 7 June but was canceled, as there was no vacancy. He surrendered at Appomattox after being wounded three times and having two horses shot from under him.

WEITZEL, Godfrey. Union gen. 1835–84. Ohio. USMA 1855 (2/34); Engrs. Engaged in constructing harbor defenses at first, he taught engineering at West Point and was stationed at Fort Pickens (Fla.) 19 Apr.–17 Sept. '61 as 1st Lt. (since 1860). He was Chief Engr. of the fortifications of Cincinnati (Oct.–9 Dec. '61), in the Defenses of Washington until 22 Feb. '62 and then Butler's Chief Engr. in the Gulf until 29 Aug. '62, when he was promoted B.G. USV. He commanded 2, 1, XIX (12 Jan.–14 May '63). Leading Res. Brig., XIX (22 Sept. '63–3 Jan. '64), he commanded 1st Div., XIX (1 Sept.–13 Dec. '63) at Port Hudson, LaFourche, and on the expedition to

Sabine Pass. In the Dept. of Va. and N.C. he commanded the 2d Div., XVIII (7–20 May '64) in the operations before Richmond at Swift's Creek and Drewry's Bluff and was Chief Engr. of the Army of the James until 30 Sept. '64. Promoted Maj. Gen. USV 17 Nov. '64, he commanded the XVIII Corps, Va. and N.C. (1 Oct.–3 Dec. '64) in the Petersburg siege and commanded the XXV, Va. (3 Dec. '64–1 Jan. '65 and 2 Feb. '65–8 Jan. '66) in the capture of Petersburg and the Appomattox campaign. Breveted for Thibodaux (La.), Port Hudson, Fort Harrison and war service (B.G. USA, Maj. Gen. USV 26 Aug. '64 and Maj. Gen. USA), he continued in the R.A., dying on active duty as Lt. Col. Engrs.

WELD, Stephen Minot, Jr. Union officer. c. 1842–? Mass. 2d Lt. 18th Mass. 27 June '62; 1st Lt. 1 Nov. '62; Capt. 1 June '63; discharged 25 Dec. '63; Lt. Col. 56th Mass. 2 Jan. '64; Col. 31 May '64; Bvt. B.G. USV (war service). Commanded 1, 1, IX (Potomac); 2, 2, IX (Potomac). Served as A.D.C. to Gen. Horatio G. Wright and on staff of Fitz-John Porter. Captured at Gaines's Mill on 27 June '62 and held in Libby Prison for six weeks. Served on the staffs of Gens. Benham, Reynolds, and John Newton. Captured at Petersburg crater 30 July '64.

WELDON R.R., Va., 18–21 Aug. '64. See GLOBE TAVERN, same dates.

WELDON R.R. EXPEDITION, Va., 7–11 Dec. '64. (PETERSBURG CAMPAIGN) Gen. Warren's V Corps, reinforced by Gregg's (2d) cavalry division and Mott's division (3, II) destroyed the railroad to Hicksford, 40 miles south of Petersburg. The Federals sustained 100 casualties but completed their work before A. P. Hill could arrive with a force to stop them.

WELDON R.R. OPERATIONS, 22–23 June '64 (Jerusalem Plank Road, William's and Davis' Farms.) (PETERSBURG CAMPAIGN) To extend Federal lines to the west and to cut Confederate supply routes to the south and west Birney's II Corps was ordered to seize the Weldon R.R. while Wright's VI Corps was to advance on its left and cut the Lynchburg road. Due to the wooded nature of the terrain, each corps was to protect its own flanks. A body of Wilson's cavalry reached the railroad 23 June and started destroying track. A. P. Hill, moving to counter this threat, discovered the gap between the Federal corps. Sending Wilcox' division to block Wright's corps, he attacked the exposed flank of Birney's corps with the divisions of Mahone (on the left) and Johnson. Gibbon's (2d) division bore the brunt of the counterattack, and Barlow's (1st) division was hard hit. Perry's Fla. brigade particularly distinguished itself in the attack. Mahone's division took 1,600 prisoners (D.S.F.). Total Union losses were 2,962 (Fox, 547). Wright's corps was also forced back. Although the attack failed to accomplish its mission, Federal forces did retain positions across the Jerusalem Plank Road. The action at GLOBE TAVERN, 18–21 Aug. '64, is sometimes referred to as Weldon R.R.

WELLES, George E. Union officer. Ohio. 1st Lt. Adj. 68th Ohio 30 Oct. '61; Maj. 1 Dec. '62; Lt. Col. 28 Jan. '64; Col. 16 Jan. '65; Bvt. B.G. USV (war service).

WELLES, Gideon. Union Sec. of the Navy. 1802–78. Conn. A newspaper editor and a Democrat, he held various minor political offices and had been in the Navy Dept. before joining the Republican party in 1855. Named Sec. of the Navy by Lincoln, he served with great efficiency, although untrained in naval matters. Completely loyal to Lincoln, his support of Johnson as well made him a steadying influence in the Cabinet. Resigning in 1869, he later wrote *Lincoln and Seward* (1874) and *Diary*.

WELLS, George Duncan. Union officer. Mass. Lt. Col. 1st Mass. 25 May '61; Col. 34th Mass. 31 July '62; Bvt. B.G. USV 12 Oct. '64 (Cedar Creek). Wounded and captured at Cedar Creek 13 Oct. '64, dying on the field. His body was sent through the lines the next day under a flag of truce.

WELLS, Henry Horatio. Union officer. N.Y. Maj. 26th Mich. 4 Oct. '62; Lt. Col. 9 Oct. '62; Col. 30 Mar. '64; Bvt. B.G. USV 3 June '65 (war service). Commanded Dist. of Alexandria (Va.), XXII. Died 1900.

WELLS, Milton. Union officer. Va. Capt. 27th Ohio 15 Aug. '61; resigned 26 Mar. '62; Maj. 15th W. Va. 17 Oct. '62; Lt. Col. 20 Aug. '64; Col. 4 Oct. '64; Bvt. B.G. USV (war service); resigned 6 Apr. '65. Commanded 3d Brig., 1st Inf. Div. (W. Va.).

WELLS, William. Union gen. 1837–92. Vt. A merchant, he enlisted as Pvt. 1st Vt. Cav. 9 Sept. and was promoted 1st Lt. 14 Oct. '61. Promoted Capt. 19 Nov. '61, Maj. 30 Dec. '62, and Col. 2 July '64, he commanded 2, 3, Cav. Corps, Shenandoah (19 Sept.–22 Oct. and 10 Nov. '64–25 Mar. '65). He also commanded 2, 3, Cav. Corps, Potomac (25 Mar.–22 May '65); 3d Div., Cav. Corps (22 May–1 June '65) and the corps (1–24 June '65). Promoted B.G. USV 19 May '65, he had been breveted B.G. USV 22 Feb. '65 and Maj. Gen. USV for war service. He was mustered out in 1866 and held several public offices, including that of state sen.

WELSH, Thomas. Union gen. 1824–63. Pa. After the Mexican War (1 wound), he was in the lumber business when commissioned Capt. and Lt. Col. 2d Pa. on the same day: 20 Apr. '61.

Mustered out 26 July, he was named Col. 45th Pa. 21 Oct. '61 and commanded 2d Brig., 1st Div., South (Apr.–July '62). Promoted B.G. USV 29 Nov. '62, he commanded 2, 1, IX, Potomac (3 Aug.–24 Sept. '62) at South Mountain and Antietam and led the 3d Brig. of that division 26 Sept.–22 Oct. '62 and 27 Jan.–7 Feb. '63. His appointment expired 4 Mar., and he was reappointed 13 Mar. '63. Going to the West, he commanded 1st Div., IX (13 Apr.–18 Aug. '63) during the Vicksburg campaign, dying on the latter date of malaria.

WELSH, William. Union officer. Ohio. Pvt., Cpl. and 1st Sgt. Co. A 4th Ohio 15 Apr. '61–5 June '62; 2d Lt. 5 June '62; 1st Lt. 14 Dec. '62; Capt. 19th US Col. Inf. 19 Mar. '64; Maj. 13 May '65; Lt. Col. 11 July '66; Bvt. B.G. USV. Brevets for war service, Bermuda Hundred, Fredericksburg, Gettysburg. In R.A. until mustered out in 1871 with rank of Capt.

WENTWORTH, Mark Fernald. Union officer. Me. Lt. Col. 27th Me. 30 Sept. '62; Col. 30 Jan. '63; mustered out 17 July '63; Col. 32d Me. 6 May '64; Bvt. B.G. USV (war service); discharged 18 Oct. '64. Medal of Honor 24 Jan. '65 for "volunteering to remain at Arlington Heights, Va., until the result of the battle of Gettysburg, Pa., was known, the term of the regiment having expired before that time" (Heitman). Died 1897.

WESSELLS, Henry Walton. Union gen. 1809–89. Conn. USMA 1833 (29/43); Inf. Serving in the Seminole and Mexican wars (1 wound, 1 brevet) on frontier duty, and in Indian fighting, he was promoted Maj. 6th US Inf. 6 June '61 (Capt. since 1847). Named Col. 8th Kans. 29 Sept. '61, he led his regiment on the Mo. border until Feb. '62, when he came east to fight at Yorktown, Fair Oaks, where he was wounded and in the rear guard at Harrison's Landing. As B.G. USV 25 Apr. '62, he commanded 2, 1, IV (19–24 May '62) and 2, 2, IV (7 June–26 Sept. '62). He also led Wessells' brigade division at Suffolk, VII (26 Sept.–9 Dec. '62) and 1st Div., N.C. (Dec. '62–2 Jan. '63) at Kinston, Goldsboro, and New Bern. From 3 May to 1 Aug. '63 he led 4th Div., XVIII and Dist. Albemarle, N.C., and while commanding Sub-Dist. Albemarle, N.C., he surrendered at Plymouth 20 Apr. '64. He was then placed under the siege guns at Charleston. He was later Comsy. of Prisons and commanded the Draft Rendezvous at Hart's Island (N.Y.). Breveted for Fair Oaks, Plymouth, and war service (B.G. USA), he continued in the R.A., serving in the West, until retired in 1871 as Lt. Col.

WEST, Edward Walter. Union officer. Mass. Pvt. Co. F 7th N.Y. State Militia 26 Apr. '61; mustered out 28 May '61; 2d Lt. 4th R.I. 30 Oct. '61; 1st Lt. 20 Nov. '61; resigned 11 Aug. '63 ("he was appd. lt. col. 33 N.J. inf. but was not must in" Heitman); Bvt. B.G. USV (war service); Pvt. and Sgt. Co. F 14th US Inf. 29 Aug. '63–7 Oct. '63; 2d Lt. 1st US Arty. 3 Oct. '63; resigned 18 Mar. '64. A graduate of Columbia College, he was later a lawyer. Serving as A.D.C. to Hooker, he was also Asst. Judge Advocate on Heintzelman's staff in 1863. Phisterer lists him as Lt. Col. 33d N.J.

WEST, Francis Henry. Union officer. N.H. Lt. Col. 31st Wis. 9 Oct. '62; Col. 1 Feb. '64; Bvt. B.G. USV (war service). At the battle of Bentonville (N.C.), he rallied his regiment as it faltered and later commanded the Union forces during the last part of the fighting (Love). Died 1896.

WEST, George Warren. Union officer. Mass. Capt. 10th Me. 26 Oct. '61; Maj. 17th Me. 31 July '62; Col. 22 Oct. '63;

Bvt. B.G. USV 2 Dec. '64 (war service, Wilderness). Commanded in the Army of the Potomac: 3, 1, III; 2, 3, II; 1, 3, II; 1, 2, II. Died 1899.

WEST, Henry Rienza. Union officer. Ohio. 2d Lt. 62d Ohio 3 Oct. '61; 1st Lt. 18 Dec. '61; Capt. 18 Sept. '62; Lt. Col. 13 Dec. '64; transferred to .67th Ohio 1 Sept. '65; Bvt. B.G. USV 13 July '65. Brevets for Fort Gregg (Va.), war service. Commanded 1, 1, XXIV (Va.). W.I.A. at Fort Wagner, Deep Run, and Rice Station.

WEST, Joseph Rodman. Union gen. 1822–98. La. After fighting in the Mexican War he was in business in Calif. and was named Lt. Col. 1st Calif. 5 Aug. '61 and Col. 1 June '62. That summer he was in the Calif. column that marched from San Pedro to the Rio Grande to recapture N. Mex. Promoted B.G. USV 25 Oct. '62, he commanded 2d Div., VII (25 Apr.–16 June '64); Cav. Div., VII (15 Sept. '64–18 Mar. '65) in the Dept. of Ark. and 1, 1, Cav. (14 Apr.–15 May '65) and 2d Div., Cav. Corps (15 May–12 June '65) in the Gulf. Breveted Maj. Gen. USV in 1866 for war service, he was mustered out that year to become a public official and US (Republican) Sen. from La. He then went to Washington, where he held public offices.

WEST, Robert Mayhew. Union officer. N.J. R.A. Pvt. Co. F US Mtd. Rifles 12 Apr. '56; discharged 5 Feb. '61; Capt. 1st Pa. Arty. 25 July '61; Maj. 13 Sept. '61; Col. 28 July '62; transferred to 5th Pa. Cav. 29 Apr. '64; Bvt. B.G. USV 1 Apr. '65 (Five Forks). Commanded Advance Brig., IV Corps (Potomac); Advance Brig., VII Corps (Va.); 1st Brig., Yorktown, Va. (Va. and N.C.); US forces Yorktown, Va. (Va. and N.C.); 1st Brig., Cav. Div. (Va. and N.C.); cavalry division (Va. and N.C.). Other brevets for Charles City C.H., New Market Heights, Five

Forks. In R.A. until resigned as Capt. in May '69; died four months later.

WEST, CONFEDERATE ARMY OF THE. Designation used after 4 Mar. '62 for forces in the Trans-Miss. Dist. of Dept. No. 2 which Van Dorn had commanded since 29 Jan. '62. Its largest component was Price's MISSOURI STATE GUARD. This army was defeated by Curtis at Pea Ridge, Ark., 7–8 Mar., after which it moved across the Mississippi and took part in the siege of Corinth. After 22 Mar. it consisted of the 1st Div. under Sterling Price and the 2d under Samuel Jones. In May a third division, under John P. McCown, joined to raise the strength to over 20,000. McCown succeeded Van Dorn as commander 20 June. Price assumed command 3 July. Transfer of the Army of Miss. to Chattanooga the end of July left Price in charge of Confederate operations in western Tenn. and northern Miss. Little's division fought at Iuka, Miss., 19–20 Sept. On 28 Sept. Price joined forces with Van Dorn for the battle of Corinth, Miss. (3–4 Oct. '62). Van Dorn assumed command of the new organization, which was designated the Army of West Tenn. Price commanded a corps of this unit and his corps was sometimes referred to still as the Army of the West. (Note: There is no connection between this army and the Confed. Department (or, later, DIVISION) OF THE WEST, which did not include the Trans-Miss. Dept.).

WEST, CONFEDERATE DEPARTMENT AND DIVISION OF. See DIVISION OF THE WEST.

WEST, CONFEDERATE DIVISION OF THE. See DIVISION OF THE WEST.

WEST, UNION DEPARTMENT OF THE. In existence at the start of the war with headquarters at Fort Leavenworth, Kans., it consisted generally of the portion of the US from the Mississippi River to the Rocky Mountains, and south to include Ark. and La., but not to include Tex. It lost Ark. and La. when the latter seceded, and lost Mo. when the latter went into the Dept. of the Ohio (3 May '61). Commanders were Brig. Gen. W. S. Harney, 17 Nov. '60–31 May '61; Brig. Gen. Nathaniel Lyon until 3 July '61. Merged into the Western Dept. 3 July '61.

WESTERN DEPARTMENT (Confederate). Alternate designation for Confederate DEPARTMENT NO. 2. Not to be confused with J. E. Johnston's Dept. of the West or its successor, Beauregard's DIVISION OF THE WEST.

WESTERN DEPARTMENT (Union). Constituted 3 July '61 to consist of Ill. and the states and territories west of the Mississippi River as far as the Rocky Mountains, including N. Mex. Headquarters were at Fort Leavenworth, Kans. It was merged into the Dept. of Mo. and Kans. on 9 Nov. '61. Commanders: Maj. Gen. John C. Frémont until 2 Nov.; Maj. Gen. David Hunter until 9 Nov. '61.

WESTERN AND SOUTHWESTERN VIRGINIA, CONFEDERATE DEPARTMENTS AND ARMIES IN. (Including Trans-Allegheny or Western Dept.; Southwestern Va., and East Tenn.; and Western Va. and East Tenn. departments.)

Western Va. in 1861 had included the Confederate Army of the KANAWHA (Wise-Floyd) and the Army of the NORTHWEST (Garnett-Loring). The latter in 1862 was also known as the Army of the Allegheny.

The Army and Dept. of Southwest-(ern) Va. was constituted 8 May '62 under Loring, who was succeeded 16 Oct. by John Echols. On 10 Nov. J. S. Williams was assigned to command. On 25 Nov. this became the Trans-Allegheny or Western Dept. of Va. Samuel

Jones was assigned command on this date and actually took command on 10 Dec. As originally organized its area was to extend "west to the eastern boundary of Kentucky and as far west of that boundary as circumstances may allow" (O.R., General Index volume, p. xlvi).

Breckinridge was assigned command 25 Feb. '64, (vice Samuel Jones), but did not assume command until 5 Mar. John Morgan "was virtually placed in command in Apr." (B.&L., IV, 422); he assumed command on 22 June (O.R., I, XXXIX, 2). On his death 4 Sept. Breckinridge again headed the department. On 27 Sept. his jurisdiction was extended over "the reserve forces of East Tennessee" (ibid).

On 20 Feb. '65 Early's command in the Valley was extended to include this territory and was designated the department of Western Va. and East Tenn. "This command has been variously indexed in the several volumes [of the O.R.] as the Departments of Southwestern Virginia; Southwestern Virginia and East Tennessee; Western Virginia; and Western Virginia and East Tennessee. ..." (ibid.).

John Echols succeeded Early as department commander when the latter was relieved 30 Mar. '65 after his defeat at Waynesboro, 2 Mar.

WESTERN VIRGINIA, CONFEDERATE DEPARTMENT OF. See WESTERN AND SOUTHWESTERN VIRGINIA, CONFEDERATE DEPARTMENTS AND ARMIES IN.

WESTERN VIRGINIA, UNION DEPARTMENT OF. Created 19 Sept. '61 from Rosecrans' Army of Occupation of Western Va. (in the Department of the OHIO). The order creating this organization prescribed: "So much of Virginia as lies west of the Blue Ridge Mountains will constitute in future a separate command, to be called

the Department of Western Virginia, under Brig. Gen. Rosecrans. Headquarters in the field" (O.R. I, V, 604). It was composed of 20,000 men organized into eight brigades; four, under J. D. Cox, on the Kanawha; one, Milroy's, between Huntsville and Monterey; Schenck's, at Romney, and two on the border between W. Va. and Ky. On 11 Mar. '62 it was merged into the newly-created Mountain Dept. There is no connection between this organization and the later Dept. of W. Va. (28 June '63).

WESTERN VIRGINIA AND EAST TENNESSEE, CONFEDERATE DEPARTMENT OF. See WESTERN AND SOUTHWESTERN VIRGINIA, CONFEDERATE DEPARTMENTS AND ARMIES IN.

WEST LOUISIANA AND TEXAS, CONFEDERATE DISTRICT OF. See TRANS-MISSISSIPPI, CONFEDERATE DISTRICT, DEPARTMENT, AND ARMY.

WESTMINSTER, Md., 29 June '63 (Stuart's Gettysburg raid.) Approaching the town from the south, Stuart was surprised at about 5 P.M. by a charge of Federal cavalry (2 companies of 1st Del. Cav.; part of VIII Corps). A courageous attack led by Maj. N. B. Knight was repulsed by the stronger Confederate force. E.&B. shows nine Union killed and wounded and 18 Confederate killed and wounded (citing O.R.). T.U.A. puts total Federal losses at 67. Freeman, citing H. B. McClellan, speaks of Union prisoners from this engagement; these, not reported in E.&B., presumably account for the discrepancy.

WEST MISSISSIPPI, UNION MILITARY DIVISION OF. Created 7 May '64 to consist of the Depts. of the Gulf and Ark. Sometimes called Trans-Miss. Div. Abolished 17 May '65. Commanded by Maj. Gen. Edward R. S. Canby. The Dept. of Mo. was also included as of 30 June '64 (O.R. Atlas plates CLXIX–CLXX) and as late as 31 Dec. '64.

WEST POINT, Miss., 21 Feb. '64. ("Sooy Smith Expedition"; MERIDIAN CAMPAIGN) In connection with Sherman's advance on Meridian from Vicksburg, Wm. Sooy Smith was given command of all the cavalry in the department and ordered to advance on Meridian from Memphis. His force was composed of three brigades under Waring, Hepburn, and McCrillis; and Capt. Bowman's battalion of the 4th US Cav. It had a strength of 7,000 men and 20 guns. Smith's specific instructions were to leave Memphis on 1 Feb., destroy the Mobile & Ohio R. R. from Okolona south, to attack enemy cavalry en route, and to join Sherman at Meridian as close to 10 Feb. as possible.

Although the rest of his troops were ready in time, Smith waited until the 8th for Waring's brigade, which was delayed by bad weather, to arrive from Union City, Tenn. He then wasted three more days organizing his pack train. Leaving Collierville (near Memphis) on the 11th, he encountered no significant enemy resistance until the afternoon of the 20th. At West Point, Miss., he made contact with Forrest's cavalry. Sherman, meanwhile, had stayed at Meridian until this day, and had then gone to Canton, where he waited until the 28th for news of Smith.

After an insignificant skirmish the next day (21 Feb.) Smith ordered a withdrawal. Apparently he was alarmed by the knowledge that S. D. Lee's cavalry was also in the area. Actually, his 7,000 were opposed only by Forrest with his escort and Faulkner's regiment.

At Okolona on 22 Feb. a six-hour skirmish started at 5 A.M. The 4th US Cav. charged the pursuing Confederates and checked their advance through the town. The 7th Ind. was committed to support the regulars. As McCrillis' (3d) brigade retreated past the town it was diverted to join in the fight. For some inexplicable reason this brigade broke and stampeded to the rear with the loss of five guns abandoned. Smith's entire command then retreated precipitously north. At 5 P.M., after covering nine miles, portions of the brigades of Waring and McCrillis halted, on their own initiative, to check the pursuit. Smith then arrived and sanctioned the decision. On open, gently sloping ground known as Ivey Hills the Federal cavalry deployed to fight on foot. Forrest's onrushing troopers threatened to overwhelm both flanks of this position, so the 4th Mo. Cav. was mounted and formed for a charge. Perhaps the highest tribute paid to these 600 troopers of the 4th Mo. is Forrest's official report that the whole Federal force charged him (B.&L., IV, 417). Forrest's 2d and 7th Tenn. Cav. repulsed the counterattack, but the Confederate pursuit ended. The final Federal line was formed near Ivey's Farm; the action is known variously as Okolona, Mount Ivey, and Ivey Hills. Smith lost 319. Forrest reported that he had no more than 2,500 engaged, and claimed capture of six guns and 33 stand of colors.

The "Battles and Leaders" article by Waring, one of Smith's brigade commanders, says: "The expedition filled every man connected with it with burning shame. It gave Forrest the most glorious achievement of his career." Three pages later an article on Forrest's defeat of Sturgis (10 June '64), written by Waring's A.D.C., says: "... in its immediate results there was no success among the many won by Forrest comparable to that of Guntown [Brice's Cross Roads]" (B.&L., IV, 418 and 421).

Sherman censured Smith for his performance in the operation. The latter considered he had been wronged, and asked Sherman to "amend" his report and *Memoirs*. An appendix to Sherman's *Memoirs* sums up this gentlemanly controversy with correspondence between the principals and Sherman's (unaccepted) offer to have it mediated in 1875 by J. D. WEBSTER (Vol. I, 452–55).

WEST POINT FOUNDRY. Another name for Parrott's COLD SPRING FOUNDRY.

WESTPORT, Mo., 23 Oct. '64. Decisive engagement and Confederate defeat during PRICE'S RAID IN MISSOURI. After being forced back from an initial position along the Little Blue (21 Oct.), through the streets of Independence, and from another position along the Big Blue (Bryam's Ford) (22 Oct.), S. G. Curtis' Army of the Border made a stand along Brush Creek. Price decided to attack on the 23d, although Pleasonton's cavalry was to his rear; at Shelby's suggestion, Price intended to attack Curtis first, defeat him, and then turn against Pleasonton. Although Curtis was driven back initially by Shelby and Fagan, his troops rallied and counterattacked successfully. At the same time Pleasonton drove Marmaduke back. Price was forced to retreat to escape annihilation. There were 20,000 Federals and 9,000 Confederates engaged, to make this "the biggest Civil War engagement west of the Missouri" (Monaghan). Casualties are not known, but were not heavy.

WEST TENNESSEE, CONFEDERATE ARMY OF. Formed 28 Sept. '62 by the merger of Sterling Price's Army of the West and Earl Van Dorn's troops from the Dept. of Southern Miss. and East La. (Van Dorn had left the command of the Army of the West 20 June; his troops occupied Vicksburg and the division of Breckinridge had fought the battle of Baton Rouge 6 Aug.) This new Army of West Tenn. fought the battle of Corinth, Miss., 3–4 Oct. Van Dorn was designated commanding general and Price commanded one of its corps. The name was changed 7 Dec. '62 to the ARMY OF MISSISSIPPI.

WEST TENNESSEE, UNION DISTRICT AND ARMY OF. Organized 17 Feb. '62, and merged into the Dept. of the Tenn. 16 Oct. Grant took command 21 Feb. Although, strictly speaking, this was "the Army of the District of Western Tennessee," Grant speaks of it in his memoirs as "the army on the Tennessee River" and as "the Army of the Tennessee." However, it was the organization created 18 Dec. '62 that has the first valid claim to the latter designation. (See TENNESSEE, ARMY OF.)

7th WEST VIRGINIA (US)

Colonels: James Evans and Joseph Snider.

Battles: Romney, Harrison's Landing, Antietam, Fredericksburg, Chancellorsville, Gettysburg, Mine Run, Morton's Ford, Wilderness, Po River, Spotsylvania, North Anna, Totopotomoy, Cold Harbor, Petersburg, Deep Bottom, Reams's Station, Boydton Road. Also present at Front Royal, Strawberry Plains, Hatcher's Run, Sayler's Creek, Farmville, and Appomattox.

The 7th W.Va. was organized Aug. '61 and served in the Shenandoah Valley until May '62, when it joined Kimball's brigade, French's division, II Corps, at Harrison's Landing. At Antietam Col. Snider and Lt. Col. Lockwood had their horses killed under them, three color bearers were killed, and the regiment lost 145 men (no missing). At Gettysburg occurred one of the strange coincidences of the war: the 7th W.Va. charged the Confederate 7th Va. and captured the nephew of the officer commanding the attack (Lockwood).

WEST VIRGINIA, UNION ARMY OF OCCUPATION OF. Organized 13 May '61, and designated Dept. of Western Va. 11 Oct. '61. Merged into the Mountain Dept. 11 Mar. '62. Commanded by Maj. Gen. George B. McClellan from 13 May until 23 July '61; Brig. Gen. W. S. Rosecrans until 11 Oct. '61.

WEST VIRGINIA, UNION DEPARTMENT AND ARMY OF. Created 28 June '63 from troops of VIII Corps when the Middle Dept. was subdivided at the start of the Gettysburg campaign. It comprised all of Md. west of the Alleghenies and the state of W.Va.; troop strength was 23,000. Commanders were Brig. Gen. B. F. Kelley to 10 Mar. '64; Maj. Gen. Franz Sigel to 21 May; Maj. Gen. David Hunter to 8 Aug.; Bvt. Maj. Gen. George Crook to 22 Feb. '65 (when he was captured); Brig. Gen. J. D. Stevenson to 27 Feb.; Bvt. Maj. Gen. S. S. Carroll to 7 Mar.; Maj. Gen. W. S. Hancock to 27 June '65, except for the period 21–22 Mar. when Crook, having been exchanged, was restored temporarily to command. Maj. Gen. W. H. Emory was temporarily in command during Apr. '65. "The Army of West Virginia" was a 7,500-man force which Crook commanded during Sheridan's Valley campaign. The latter is also called the "W.Va. Corps."

WEST VIRGINIA OPERATIONS IN 1861. (Campaigns of McClellan and R. E. Lee.) At the beginning of the war both the North and the South undertook military operations to secure the region now known as W.Va. (Admitted as a state 20 June '63. The transfer of Berkley and Jefferson counties from Va. to W.Va. was not recognized by Congress until 10 Mar. '66.) On 14 May '61 McClellan was assigned to command the Dept. of the Ohio, which included "Western Virginia." In June, with 20,-000 men from Ohio and Ind., he occupied the Baltimore & Ohio R.R. as far east as Cumberland. There were 5,000 Confederate troops in the area under Robert S. Garnett. Garnett himself was at Laurel Hill with four and a half regiments, while John Pegram was at Rich Mountain with two. At Beverly there was a reserve regiment. An action sometimes called the first battle of the Civil War took place at Philippi, 3 Jun.

On 6 July McClellan had concentrated three brigades at Buckhannon and one at Philippi for an offensive. His strategy was to threaten Garnett with the smaller force, attack Pegram with the three brigades from Buckhannon (under Rosecrans), capture Beverly, and cut off Garnett's retreat. Rosecrans turned Pegram's position and defeated him in the action known as RICH MOUNTAIN, 11 July. Pegram retreated across difficult mountain terrain toward Laurel Hill to find Garnett. The latter position, had, however, been evacuated when Garnett learned of Pegram's defeat. Pegram was hemmed in and his force almost famished, so he surrendered to McClellan at Beverly. At CARRICK'S FORD, 13 July, Garnett was killed while commanding his rear guard.

The Federals occupied a strong position covering Huttonsville. Five Confederate regiments escaped into Va., were reinforced by 12 new ones, and put under W. W. Loring. This force was assembled at Monterey and Huntersville.

While McClellan was operating in northern W.Va., J. D. Cox led his brigade up the Kanawha and occupied Charleston on 25 July. He pursued a small force under Henry Wise to Gauley Bridge and there established a fortified position. Wise fell back to Lewisburg, where he was reinforced by two new brigades under John Floyd and John McCausland.

McClellan's success led to his being named to command all the Federal armies.

In Aug. R. E. Lee took command and attempted to regain the lost territory. Loring was to move on Huttonsville, and Floyd to advance with Wise and McCausland toward Gauley Bridge. Rosecrans had succeeded McClellan. He had 3,000 at Gauley Bridge, 10,000 near Huttonsville, and 7,000 at Sutton. Rosecrans moved from Sutton and attacked Floyd at CARNIFEX FERRY, 10 Sept. Although the Confederates were able to hold their positions during the day, they withdrew after dark. Lee failed at CHEAT MOUNTAIN, 10–15 Sept., to destroy the brigade of J. J. Reynolds and open the way for a Confederate offensive toward Beverly.

This ended operations for 1861. Lee went with one brigade to Charleston to command the defense of S.C. Loring's command was broken up, and he went with three brigades to Winchester. Floyd and McCausland went to Bowling Green, Ky., and Wise went with his brigade to Norfolk. When the year ended Edward Johnson was at Monterey with five regiments and Henry Heth at Lewisburg with two.

WEST VIRGINIA OPERATIONS IN 1862. The area that is now W.Va. became the Mountain Dept. on 11 Mar. '62 with Frémont as commander. Troops of the department under Milroy, Schenck, and Blenker were involved in the SHENANDOAH VALLEY CAMPAIGN OF JACKSON. (See also LORING-JACKSON INCIDENT.)

Meanwhile, J. D. Cox undertook an offensive with the four Federal brigades that were located around Charleston and Gauley. Crook was to lead one of these east through Lewisburg, while Cox was to lead two others (Scammon's and Moor's) to cut the railroad near Newbern, Va. W. W. Loring had two small brigades (Henry Heth and Humphrey Marshall) near Lewisburg and Tazewell with which to oppose this advance.

In April Cox moved one brigade to Flat Top Mountains and the other to Raleigh. Heth moved to Pearisburg. The next month Cox advanced toward Pearisburg by way of Princeton but was compelled to retreat to Flat Top Mountains when Marshall advanced on Princeton from Tazewell. Crook's column got as far as Lewisburg and on 23 May successfully repulsed an attack at that place by Heth after Cox's retreat.

In Aug. Cox took his two best brigades, Scammon's and Moor's, to reinforce Pope and to participate later in the Antietam campaign. (This is the force known as the Kanawha Div.) The other two brigades remained on the Kanawha between Gauley and Charleston. Lee learned of this movement when Stuart captured Pope's dispatch book at Catlett's Station 22 Aug. and ordered Loring to take advantage of this situation to invade W.Va.

In what is sometimes called the Kanawha campaign, 6–16 Sept., Loring captured Charleston (13 Sept.) A. G. Jenkins entered the state via Huttonsville with a small mounted force and captured the supply depots at Buckhannon and Weston. The two Federal brigades (Cols. Edward Siber and S. A. Gilbert) withdrew to the mouth of the Kanawha. After the Antietam campaign Cox returned to the area with the Kanawha Div. (now under Crook) and was put in command of what was now designated the Dist. of Western Va. (Dept. of the Ohio). Cox launched a three-pronged offensive. Milroy, whose division was put under his command, advanced from Clarksburg on Beverly; Crook advanced from Sutton on Gauley Bridge; and Cox led a force up the

Kanawha on Charleston. The Confederates were again driven from the state.

Loring was relieved at his own request and assigned to Pemberton at Vicksburg. The Confederate Dept. of Western Va. was formed and put under the command of Samuel Jones, who came from Bragg's army in Tenn. This ended W.Va. operations for the year.

WEST VIRGINIA OPERATIONS IN 1863. See JONES'S AND IMBODEN'S W. VA. RAID; AVERELL'S RAID TO LEWISBURG; AND KNOXVILLE CAMPAIGN.

WEVER, Clark Russell. Union officer. N.Y. Capt. 17th Iowa 26 Mar. '62; Lt. Col. 15 Nov. '62; Col. 3 June '63; Bvt. B.G. USV 9 Feb. '65 (war service). Commanded in the Army of the Tenn.: 2, 7, XVII; 2, 3, XV. Died 1874.

WHARTON, Gabriel C. C.S.A. gen. ?–1906. Appt.-Va. Commissioned Maj. 45th Va., he served in July '61 in southwestern Va. The next month he was appointed Col. 51st Va. and served in Floyd's western Va. campaign. He commanded the 1st Brig. at Fort Donelson and returned to southwestern Va., where he commanded the 3d Brig. during Loring's occupation of the Kanawha Valley. In July '63 he was sent to Lee's army and given temporary command of the Valley Dist., with headquarters at Winchester. Appointed B.G. C.S.A. 25 Sept. '63 to date from 8 July, he commanded a brigade engaged in guarding railroads in southwestern Va. He joined Longstreet in eastern Tenn. In Apr. '64 he was sent to Breckinridge. He fought at New Market, Cold Harbor, on Early's Washington expedition, and in the Valley campaign, where he commanded a division.

WHARTON, John A. C.S.A. gen. ?–1865. Texas. A lawyer, he went to Va. to fight at 1st Bull Run but fell ill before the battle. He was commissioned Capt. in B. F. Terry's Texas Ranger regiment and fought at Woodsonville (Ky.) 17 Dec. '61 and was named Col. soon after that. At Shiloh he commanded the regiment and was wounded. Recovering to go on the Ky. campaign, he was asked in the meantime to run for the C.S.A. Congress. His mother refused for him, saying that she knew her son would rather fight. Appointed B.G. C.S.A. 18 Nov. '62, he led his brigade under Hardee at Stones River and Chickamauga and was named Maj. Gen. 10 Nov. '63. Going to the Trans-Miss. Dept., he commanded the cavalry in the Red River campaign of 1864. He was killed 6 Apr. '65 in a private feud.

WHEAT, Chatham Roberdeau ("Rob" or "Bob"). C.S.A. officer. 1826–'62. Va. Son of an Episcopal minister and descendant of a distinguished family, he was barely 20 and studying law after graduating from college when he fought in the Mexican War. He settled then in New Orleans and entered politics. Well on his way to prominence as a criminal lawyer, he went to Latin America to fight with Lopez, Caravajal, Walker, and Alvarez, and was commissioned an officer of the Mexican Army when the last named became president. However, he then joined the English Volunteers to fight with Garibaldi in Italy and hurried home to fight in the Civil War. As Maj. and commander of the tough and unruly Louisiana Tigers, he led them effectively at 1st Bull Run but was shot through both lungs. Told that he was mortally wounded, he replied, "I don't feel like dying yet," and lived to lead his Tigers in the Valley campaign. He was wounded at Gaines's Mill, dying that same day, and his troops were never again an effective fighting unit without his discipline and leadership.

"WHEAT FIELD." About a half mile southeast of the Peach Orchard, halfway between that place and Little Round Top, this was the scene of bloody fighting on the second day of the battle of GETTYSBURG.

WHEATON, Frank. Union gen. 1833–1903. R.I. In the R.A., he served on the US-Mexican border survey in 1855 and then was a 1st Lt. with the 1st US Cav. in Indian fighting and on the Utah Expedition. Promoted Capt. 1 Mar. '61 and Lt. Col. 2d R.I. (Burnside's regiment) 10 July '61, he fought at 1st Bull Run and was named Col. 21 July '61. Commanding the regiment in the Peninsular campaign, he was promoted B.G. USV 29 Nov. '62. At Chancellorsville and Gettysburg he led 3, 3, VI (Feb.–1 July '63), succeeding to division 1–4 July '63. He returned to brigade 4 July '63–Jan. '64 and then led 1, 2, VI (24 Mar.–6 May '64) at the Wilderness, again going up to division 6–7 May. He returned to brigade for Spotsylvania and Cold Harbor (7 May–21 June '64) and took over division for another week (21–28 June '64). In the Shenandoah he commanded 1, 2, VI (6 Aug.–21 Sept. '64) and 1st Div., VI (21 Sept.–6 Dec. '64); returning to 1st Div., VI, Potomac (6 Dec. '64–28 June '65) during the Petersburg siege. He was breveted for the Wilderness, Cedar Creek, Petersburg (B.G. USA), war service. (Maj. Gen. USA), and Opequon-Fishers Hill-Middletown (Maj. Gen. USV 19 Oct. '64). Continuing in the R.A., he fought in the Modoc wars and commanded the Dept. of Texas before retiring in 1897 as Maj. Gen. USA.

WHEELER, Joseph ("Fightin' Joe"). C.S.A. gen. 1836–1906. Ga. Appt.-N.Y. USMA 1859 (19/22); Dragoons-Mtd. Rifles. He served on the frontier in Indian fighting before resigning 22 Apr. '61 as 2d Lt. Commissioned 1st Lt. C.S.A. at first, he was then named Col. 19th Ala. and fought at Shiloh. He was appointed B.G. C.S.A. 30 Oct. '62 and led his brigade at Stones River before being named Maj. Gen. 20 Jan. '63. On 18 July of that year he was given command of all the cavalry of the Army of Miss. and started a series of raids against Federal communications (see below). He fought during the Knoxville siege, the Atlanta campaign, the March to the Sea—and through the Carolinas, before being captured near Atlanta after Johnston's surrender. His "dogged aggressiveness" (D.A.B.) and hard-hitting tactics made him a valuable adjunct to the western Confederate defenses. After the war, in which he was three times wounded, he was a commission merchant and Congressman. Wheeler (Ala.), where he lived, was named after him. In the Spanish-American War he became Maj. Gen. USV and fought at San Juan Hill as well as in the Philippines, retiring in 1900 as B.G. USA. He wrote on military subjects, including *Cavalry Tactics* (1863), and "Bragg's Invasion of Kentucky" in B.&L.

WHEELER'S CAVALRY CORPS. See CORPS, Confederate.

WHEELER'S RAID, 1–9 Oct. '63 (Chattanooga campaign)

With the mission of disrupting Rosecrans' extended communications, Wheeler crossed the Tennessee near Decatur, pushed through Brig. Gen. George Crook's (2d Cav. Div.) scattered forces, and at Anderson's Cross Roads early 2 Oct. captured a large wagon train. He sent Wharton's division to destroy the depot at McMinnville, while moving with the rest of his Confederate troopers in the direction of Murfreesboro. Col. E. M. McCook (1st Cav. Div.) moved up the Sequatchie Valley from the vicinity of Bridgeport, attacked Wheeler near Anderson's, and in a series of vigorous actions recaptured 800 mules and some of the wagons. Losses 2 Oct. were 70 Federals, 270 Confederates, according to Federal sources (E. & B.). Crook's division, which had gone after Wharton, was not able to save McMinnville, which surrendered 3 Oct. with a loss of 388 Federals and 23 Confederates (E. & B.); however, he was able to turn Wheeler south before he could attack Murfreesboro. Gen. Mitchell arrived to take command of his two divisions, and the night of 7 Oct. had concentrated the forces of McCook and Crook near Shelbyville. Wheeler withdrew toward the southwest in three columns. In heavy rains Crook pursued a column that had sacked Shelbyville and on the Duck River near Farmington 7 Oct. defeated the more numerous force of Davidson; Federal losses were 75, Confederate losses, 310. Federal cavalry made movements of up to 57 miles despite unfavorable weather and severe fighting. Wheeler was able to withdraw across the Tennessee 9 Oct. near Rogersville, but his rear guard lost 95 men at Sugar Creek (near Pulaski).

Wheeler had destroyed wagons and animals whose loss was nearly fatal to Rosecrans' army (Van Horne). Confederate accounts claim about 500 wagons and over 1000 mules destroyed, some estimates running to twice that number; Rosecrans estimated a loss of 500 wagons; most Union accounts say 300 (Van Horne). Wheeler's cavalry was so roughly handled after he had achieved his initial successes, however, that a hasty withdrawal prevented more extensive operations that had been planned in conjunction with Roddey and S. D. Lee. Crook estimated that Wheeler lost 2,000 men and six guns.

WHEELER'S RAID, 10 Aug.–10 Sept. '64. (ATLANTA CAMPAIGN.) With the mission of destroying the railroads connecting Sherman's armies around Atlanta with their base at Nashville, Wheeler assembled eight Confederate cavalry brigades at Covington, Ga., and on 10 Aug. moved north. He struck the railroad north of Marietta, then near Cassville, and then at Calhoun. He tore up track at each place. From Calhoun he detached one brigade to escort prisoners and captured cattle to Hood. He next destroyed the railroad south of Dalton and threatened Dalton 14–16 Aug. (Sherman ordered KILPATRICK'S RAID TO JONESBORO.) Continuing north, he destroyed track at various points between Dalton and Loudon, Tenn. Blocked there by high water on the Tennessee, he circled Knoxville and crossed above that place. He detached two brigades to wreck the railroad bridge over the Holston, and led the rest of his command to destroy the Nashville–Chattanooga R.R. west of McMinnville. He tore up more track on the Nashville–Decatur R.R. near Franklin. On 10 Sept. he crossed the Tennessee near Tuscumbia. Two brigades he had left in east Tenn. were unable to rejoin him and with part of a third brigade remained in east Tenn. The raid had no significant effect on Sherman's operations other than to remove the Confederate cavalry from his front and facilitate his maneuvering to turn Hood.

WHEELOCK, Charles. Union officer. N.H. Col. 97th N.Y. 7 Feb. '62; Bvt. B.G. USV 19 Aug. '64 (Globe Tavern). Commanded in the Army of the Potomac: 3, 2, I; 2, 2, I; 2, 3, V. Died 21 Jan. '65.

WHERRY, William Macky. Union officer. Mo. 1st Lt. 3d Mo. 8 May '61; mustered out 17 Aug. '61; 1st Lt. 13th US Inf. 26 Oct. '61; Maj. A.D.C. Vols. 12 May '64; Bvt. B.G. USV. Brevets for Atlanta, Franklin (Tenn.), Nashville, war service (2), Ga. and Tenn. campaigns. Medal of Honor 30 Oct. '95 for Wilson's Creek (Mo.) 10 Aug. '61.

Served as A.D.C. to Gen. Lyon in 1861 and Gen. Schofield Sept. '62. He was also the bearer of rolls and terms of surrender of Johnston's army to Washington. He was a St. Louis merchant before the war and joined the R.A. afterward. Served as Lt. Col. and Mil. Sec to Gen. Schofield 11 Feb.–1 May '95. Promoted to B.G. Vols. during the Spanish-American War and retired in 1899 as B.G. USA.

WHIPPLE, Amiel Weeks. Union gen. 1816–63. Mass. USMA 1841 (5/52); Arty.-Topo. Engrs. Engaged in a survey of rivers and boundaries and railroad explorations, he also served on the frontier before the war. As Capt. (since 1855), he was Chief Topo. Engrs. at 1st Bull Run and served on McDowell's staff until 2 Apr. '62, having been promoted Maj. 9 Sept. '61 and B.G. USV 14 Apr. '62. In the Defenses of Washington he commanded Whipple's brigade, Mil. Dist. Washington (May–Aug.) and Whipple's division Mil. Dist. Washington (Aug.–Nov. '62). He then commanded the 3d Div., III Corps (8 Nov. '62–3 May '63) at Fredericksburg and Chancellorsville, where he was mortally wounded. Removed to Washington, he was promoted Maj. Gen. USV 6 May and died the next day. Breveted for 1st Bull Run, Fredericksburg, Chancellorsville (B.G. USA 4 May '63), and war service (Maj. Gen. USA 7 May '63).

WHIPPLE, William Denison. Union gen. 1826–1902. N.Y. USMA 1851 (31/42); Inf. After serving on the frontier and in Indian fighting, he was in Tex. when Twiggs surrendered the department and had to escape through the lines. Named Bvt. Capt. Asst. Adj. Gen. 11 May '61 and Capt. (full rank) Asst. Adj. Gen. 3 Aug. '61, he was Asst. Adj. Gen. to Hunter at 1st Bull Run and later when Hunter commanded the Depts. of Pa. and Va. In 10 Feb. '62 he was promoted Lt. Col. Add. A.D.C., and served as Chief of Staff to Cadwalader during the Peninsular campaign. Named B.G. USV 17 July '63, he was Chief of Staff for Thomas at Chattanooga, Missionary Ridge, Buzzard Roost Gap, Resaca, New Hope Church, Kenesaw Mountain, Peach Tree Creek, Atlanta, Jonesboro, Lovejoy, Nashville, and on the pursuit of Hood. His appointment expired 4 July '64 and was renewed 6 Sept. '64. Breveted for Atlanta and Nashville (Lt. Col., Col., and B.G. USA) and war service (Maj. Gen. USA), he continued in the R.A., serving as Sherman's A.D.C. 1873–81. He retired in 1890 as Col.

WHISTLER, Joseph Nelson Garlan. Union officer. 1822–99. Wis. Appt.-Fla. (Cullum says "At Large.") USMA 1846 (47/59); Inf. Capt. 8th US Inf. 14 May '61; Col. 2d N.Y. Arty. 6 May '63; Maj. 13th US Inf. 31 Dec. '64; Bvt. B.G. USV. Brevets for North Anna, Petersburg siege, war service. Commanded 1st Brig., Def. South Potomac, XXII. W.I.A. Petersburg siege. Served in the Mexican War and breveted for Contreras and Churubusco. Taught at USMA 1861–63. In R.A. until retired in 1886 as Col.

"WHISTLING DICK." Perhaps the most famous single gun of the war (Weller), this was a rifled and banded Confederate 18-pounder in the river defenses of Vicksburg. Made at Tredegar as a smoothbore, it was subsequently rifled in such a manner that its conical projectiles had an erratic spin and, consequently, a distinctive sound while in flight. Among the achievements of this gun, which was centrally located so as to cover the river, was the sinking of the Federal gunboat *Cincinnati* (27 May '63). Considerable mystery surrounds the gun. A cannon captured at Vicksburg and identified as "Whistling Dick" and so captioned in several contemporary photographs, has been on display at

West Point since the Civil War. The latter is a 7.44-inch BLAKELY rifle which has been shortened by the removal of about two feet from the muzzle end. As late as 1957 some of the country's most eminent authorities accepted that this was "Whistling Dick." It has since been established, however, that the West Point gun is actually the "Widow Blakely," another well-known Vicksburg cannon. The authorities have also discredited the pretty story that the emaciated gunners of Vicksburg took "Whistling Dick" out into the Mississippi and "buried" it the eve of the surrender. The romantics can counter with the question, "Then why has the gun never been found?" A photograph of what is apparently the true "Whistling Dick" is in Miller, II, 187, and the same picture is in the N.P.S. *Vicksburg* pamphlet. (This article is based on the West Point Museum file of correspondence with the historian of the Vicksburg National Military Park, Mr. Jac Weller of Princeton, N.J., and Mr. Torbert Slack of Lake Charles, La.)

WHITAKER, Edward Washburn. Union officer. Conn. Sgt. Co. D 2d N.Y. Cav. 21 Aug. '61; Capt. 1st Conn. Cav. 23 Apr. '64; Maj. 1 Oct. '64; Lt. Col. 17 Jan. '65; Bvt. B.G. USV (war service). Medal of Honor 2 Apr. '98 for Reams's Station (Va.) 29 June '64.

WHITAKER, Walter C. Union gen. 1823–87. Ky. In the Mexican War. He was later an outstanding criminal lawyer. Serving in the state senate when the Confederates invaded Ky., he proposed the resolution putting the state with the Union. He was commissioned Col. 6th Ky. 24 Dec. '61 and fought at Muldraugh's Hill against Buckner, at Shiloh, and Stones River. Promoted B.G. USV 25 June '63, he commanded in the Cumberland: 1, 1, Reserve Corps (15 Aug.–9 Oct. '63), going up to division 11–15 Aug.; and 2, 1, IV (10 Oct.–8

Dec. '63; 15 Mar.–30 June '64 and 28 Nov.–23 Dec. '64 at Lookout Mountain, Chattanooga, Atlanta campaign, and Nashville), going up to division 19 Sept.–28 Nov. '64. Breveted Maj. Gen. USV for Atlanta, he was mustered out 24 Aug. '65 and returned to his practice. His ". . . marked individuality of manner and character, and . . . impetuous temper, . . . involved him in numerous personal difficulties, and led to his becoming for a time an inmate of an insane asylum. But in his later years he fully recovered his health, and had his share of legal practice" (Appleton's).

WHITBECK, Horatio Nelson. Union officer. N.Y. 2d Lt. 65th Ohio 2 Oct. '61; Capt. 6 Dec. '61; Maj. 2 Dec. '62; Lt. Col. 3 Apr. '63; Bvt. B.G. USV (war service).

WHITE, Carr Bailey. Union officer. Ky. Maj. 12th Ohio 3 May '61; Lt. Col. 28 June '61; Col. 1 Oct. '61; Bvt. B.G. USV (Cloyd's Mountain, Va.); mustered out 11 July '64. Commanded 2, 3, VIII (Middle Dept.); 2, Scammon's division (W. Va.); 2, 3, (W. Va.); 2, 2d Inf. Div. (W. Va.). Served as enlisted man and officer in Mexican War. Died 1871.

WHITE, Daniel. Union officer. Me. Capt. 2d Me. 16 Dec. '61; mustered out 9 June '63; Capt. 31st Me. 31 Mar. '64; Col. 8 July '64; Bvt. B.G. USV (Wilderness, Petersburg siege). Died 1895.

WHITE, David B. Union officer. N.Y. Capt. 81st N.Y. 21 Feb. '62; Maj. 24 Oct. '62; Lt. Col. 29 Apr. '65; Bvt. B.G. USV (war service). Died 1886.

WHITE, Frank. Union officer. Ohio. Capt. 15th Ind. 14 June '61; Maj. 1 May '63; Lt. Col. 17th Ind. 6 Dec. '64; Bvt. B.G. USV (war service). Commanded 1, 2, Cav. Corps (Mil. Div. Miss.). Died 1879.

WHITE, Frank J. Union officer. N.Y. Capt. 10th N.Y. 27 Apr. '61; resigned 11 Oct. '61; Maj. Asst. Adj. Gen. Mo.

State Militia 13 Feb. '62; Maj. 2d Bn. Mo. State Militia Cav. 1 June '62; resigned 31 Jan. '63; Maj. Asst. Adj. Gen. Vols. 15 Mar. '63; Lt. Col. 2d US Col. Cav. 30 June '65; Bvt. B.G. USV (war service). Died 1875.

WHITE, Harry. Union officer. 1834–?. Pa. Maj. 67th Pa. 13 Dec. '61; Bvt. B.G. USV 2 Mar. '65; mustered out 22 Feb. '65. Served in the Pa. State Sen. 1862–63 and later was a Republican Congressman.

WHITE, Julius. Union gen. 1816–90. N.Y. A lawyer and legislator, he was commissioned Col. 37th Ill. ("Frémont Rifles") 18 Sept. '61 and led his regiment during Frémont's southwest Mo. expedition. Commanding 2, 3d Div., Army Southwest Mo. at Pea Ridge, he was promoted B.G. USV 9 June '62 and commanded White's brigade, Harpers Ferry, Army Va., that summer. When Harpers Ferry surrendered to A. P. Hill, he was captured and paroled. Arrested by the US, a court of inquiry found that he acted with capability and courage, and released him. In the Army of the Ohio he commanded 1, 3, XXIII (6–21 Aug. '63); 4th Div., XXIII (24 June–6 Aug. '63) and 2d Div., XXIII (21 Aug.–24 Dec. '63) at Loudon and Knoxville. Breveted Maj. Gen. USV for war service, he resigned 19 Nov. '64 and was later US Minister to Argentina.

WHITELEY, Robert H. Kirkwood. Union officer. c. 1809–96. Md. Appt.–Del. USMA 1830 (13/44); Arty.-Ord. He served in the Seminole War and on arsenal and ordnance duty until promoted Maj. 3 Aug. '61 at the beginning of the war. Commanding the N.Y. Arsenal until 23 Oct. '62, he was promoted Lt. Col. 1 June '63 and took charge of the Allegheny Arsenal until 1875, when he retired as Col. and Bvt. B.G. USA.

WHITE OAK ROAD, Va., 31 Mar. '65. Engagement of V Corps during operation covered under FIVE FORKS, 30 Mar.–1 Apr. '65.

WHITE OAK SWAMP, Va., 30 June '62. (Glendale, Charles City or New Market Crossroads, Nelson's or Frayser's Farm, or Turkey Bend.) One of the Seven Days' Battles of the PENINSULAR CAMPAIGN. After SAVAGE'S STATION the Army of the Potomac withdrew the night of 29–30 June in a heavy rain. McClellan concentrated behind White Oak Swamp and on a line through Malvern Hill to block Lee's pursuit while his supply trains continued their movement to Harrison's Landing. Jackson's column (his division and D. H. Hill's) reached White Oak Swamp Creek shortly before 11 A.M. to find the bridge destroyed and the divisions of W. F. Smith (2, VI) and Richardson (1, II) in defensive positions. Although he could have forced a crossing by way of several fords in the vicinity, Jackson contented himself with shelling the Federals across the creek. Huger's division, advancing down the Charles City Road (Mahone's brigade leading), encountered abatis in front of Slocum's position (1, VI) and spent the day chopping through these obstructions and shelling the enemy. In the Malvern Hill area, where Porter's (V) corps was in position along Turkey Run, 6,000 unseasoned troops under Holmes were unable to advance through Federal artillery fires. Magruder, moving down the Darbytown Road, was ordered to send reinforcements to Holmes, and his division took no significant part in the day's action. Poor staff work had again prevented Lee's seven divisions from making a coordinated effort to stop McClellan's movements. He nevertheless ordered Longstreet and A. P. Hill to attack even though this could not get under way until 4:30 P.M. and there

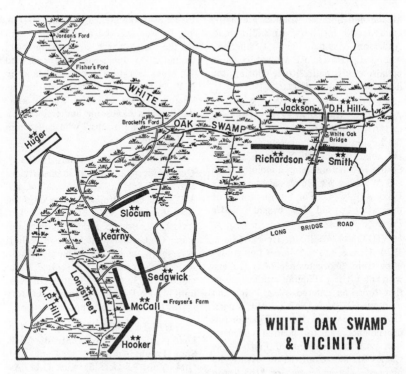

WHITE OAK SWAMP & VICINITY

was little promise of success. McCall's division (3, V) bore the brunt of the attack; it was astride the road to Frayser's Farm with the brigades of Seymour (3), Reynolds (later Simmons) (1), and Meade (2) from south to north. The divisions of Hooker (2, III) and Kearny (3, III) were on his left (south) and right, respectively. Jenkins' brigade opened the engagement, followed by Kemper and then Longstreet's four other brigades. Six companies of the 12th Pa. had to withdraw precipitously to avoid encirclement; when rallied by their colonel, Taggart, they joined Hooker. It was not until the German batteries of Diedrich and Knierim were also forced back with heavy loss that the threatened penetration was stopped by artillery fire. A successful counter-attack by the 1st Mass., 2d N.H., and

26th and 69th Pa. finally secured this portion of the line. The attack then hit McCall's other flank (Meade) and Kearny's front. An assault by the 55th and 60th Va. against Randol's battery resulted in heavy hand-to-hand fighting. Company B, 4th Pa., stood fast while the rest of the regiment gave way, but was then driven back also. A. P. Hill's division was committed to exploit Longstreet's success. McCall right was routed and he himself captured when, in the dusk, he rode into the enemy's lines (B.&L., II, 401-2). J. F. Reynolds took command of the division and also was captured. Taylor's (1st) brigade was moved south from Slocum's division and succeeded in plugging the gap. Darkness had fallen and the battle ended at about 9 P.M.

The Federals lost 2,853 (including

Meade and Sumner wounded) and the Confederates lost 3,615 (including J. R. Anderson, Pender, and Featherston wounded) (Fox and E.&B.). McClellan withdrew his entire force during the night to MALVERN HILL.

WHITFIELD, John W. C.S.A. gen. Appt.-Tex. Made Col. 27th Tex. Cav. in 1861, he fought at Pea Ridge and led the Legion at Iuka (severely wounded). He then fought at Yazoo City and Spring Hill before being appointed B.G. C.S.A. 9 May '63. He was at Messinger's Ferry 4 July '63. For the remainder of the war he led his brigade under Forrest.

WHITING, William Henry Chase. 1824–65. C.S.A. gen. Miss. After graduating from Georgetown (D.C.) College with the highest standing attained up to that time, he entered West Point and graduated USMA 1845 (1/41); Engrs. He was engaged in river and harbor improvements and fortification construction until he resigned 20 Feb. '61 as Capt. In the Confederate Army he planned new defenses for Charleston Harbor and Morris Island and served as J. E. Johnston's Chief Engr. for the Army of the Shenandoah. He fought at 1st Bull Run and temporarily led G. W. Smith's division at Seven Pines, after having been appointed B.G. C.S.A. 28 Aug. '61. Receiving command of the division permanently, he went to reinforce Jackson in the Valley in early June '62 and returned to the Peninsula to fight at Gaines's Mill and Malvern Hill. In Nov. '62 he was named commander of the Mil. Dist. of Wilmington, remaining there until May '64 when he took command of Petersburg. He had been promoted Maj. Gen. 28 Feb. '63 in the meantime. However, as he was unfamiliar with the situation, he failed to back up Beauregard and was sent back to N.C. at his own request. When Fort Fisher was threatened in Dec. '64–Jan. '65, he was relieved by Bragg and sent to the fort. There he was mortally wounded 15 Jan., captured, and died 10 Mar. '65 on Governors Island in N.Y. Harbor. D.A.B. describes him as "Below average height . . . [with] martial bearing, handsome and sinewy . . . idolized by his troops," who called him "Little Billy."

WHITTELSEY, Charles Henry. Union officer. 2d Lt. 1st Conn. Arty. 12 Mar. '62; 1st Lt. 18 June '62; Capt. Asst. Adj. Gen. Vols. 15 May '63; Maj. Asst. Adj. Gen. Vols. 26 May '65; Bvt. B.G. USV. Brevets for Richmond campaign (Peninsula), Shenandoah Valley, Petersburg siege, Petersburg assault, R. E. Lee's surrender, war service. Commanded 3, 3, (Army Tenn.). In R.A. until his death in the Wyoming Territory in 1871 with rank of Capt.

WHITTELSEY, Henry Martyn. Union officer. Conn. Q.M. of Mich. State Troops Apr.–July '61; Capt. Asst. Q.M. Vols. 31 Oct. '61; Col. Q.M. Assigned 26 May–3 July '65; Bvt. B.G. USV (war service). Died 1873. Phisterer lists him as Whittlesey, Henry H.

WHITTIER, Charles Albert. Union officer. Me. 2d Lt. 20th Mass. 8 Aug. '61; 1st Lt. 1 Jan. '62; Capt. 1 Apr. '63; Maj. A.D.C. Vols. 25 Apr. '63; Maj. Asst. Adj. Gen. 7 Mar. '65; Lt. Col. Asst. Adj. Gen. Assigned 21 Jan.–1 Aug. '65; Bvt. B.G. USV 9 Apr. '65. Brevets for Richmond, R. E. Lee's surrender. Served on Sedgwick's staff and was beside him when he was killed. Also on Gen. H. G. Wright's staff. In R.A. until discharged at his own request in 1870 as a Capt. Served with Gen. Halleck in the Dept. of the Pacific 1865–69. In 1898 went back in as Lt. Col. I.G. Vols.; B.G. USV 13 Aug. '98; discharged in 1899.

WHITTIER, Francis Henry. Union officer. Mass. 2d Lt. 30th Mass. 6 Dec. '61; 1st Lt. 10 Dec. '61; Capt. 6 Aug. '62; Lt. Col. 6 July '64; Bvt. B.G. USV. Brevets for Shenandoah Valley, war service. Died 1867.

WHITTLESEY, Eliphalet. Union officer. Conn. Chaplain 19th Me. 25 Aug. '62; Capt. Asst. Adj. Gen. Vols. 25 Aug. '62; Maj. Asst. Adj. Gen. Vols. 11 Mar. '63; resigned 3 June '63; Maj. Judge Advocate Vols. 1 Sept. '64; Col. 46th US Col. Inf. 14 June '65; Bvt. B.G. USV. Brevets for Atlanta and Carolina campaigns, war service.

WHITWORTH GUN. An English rifled cannon of various calibers that was used in small—but well publicized —numbers by the Confederates. The smaller cannon were forged solid, the larger ones were BUILT UP. The bore was hexagonal in cross section, and the projectile was a long bolt (3½ diameters) with twisting surfaces that conformed to the rifling. The two common types were of caliber 2.75 inches (measured across the flats), and were breechloaders. Although explosive shell was made for the Whitworth, the shape of the projectile did not permit a sufficiently large powder cavity for this type to be effective. Solid shot, therefore, was its principal ammunition. The pieces imported after 1863 were muzzleloaders,

The 6-pounder Whitworth (2.15 inches) and the 12-pounder (2.75 inches) were the field pieces employed. A 70-pounder (5 inch) Whitworth was used effectively by the Confederates at Belmont. "The finest guns to be found in either army" (Albaugh and Simmons, 274), "satisfactory from a functional standpoint" (Weller, 66), with "remarkable accuracy" and superior penetrating power (Scott, 525). The A.N.V. had four 3-inch breechloaders in 1863 that had a range of five miles (A.&S.,

above) and in May of the same year started making the ammunition successfully at Tredegar (ibid.). Lee used four of the 6-inch model in the Gettysburg campaign (Wise, 571).

The Federals imported a battery which was taken on the Peninsular campaign but not used. It spent the rest of the war in the Washington defenses (Downey, Gettysburg, 252n.).

WHITWORTH RIFLE (small arm). An English muzzle-loading rifle, particularly effective as a sniper's rifle, imported and used by the Confederates. With a 14½-inch telescope sight on the left side of its stock, the rifle had an effective range of 1,800 yards. Gens. Sedgwick and W. H. Lytle were killed with this rifle (Albaugh and Simmons, 274).

The Whitworth shoulder arm had the same hexagonal bore as the cannon and the bore measured 0.451 in. across the flats. It had a short (33-inch), heavy barrel, and an over-all length of 49 inches. The Confederates imported 12 in early 1863 and sent six to the A.N.V., where two were given to the best marksmen in each corps. The other six went to the West and were used with good effect at Chickamauga. In July '63, 18 Whitworth rifles were sent to the Charleston Arsenal, and in Feb. '64 Cleburne's Sharpshooters were armed with 20 of them and 10 KERR RIFLES. Twenty more of the arms were in the hands of Co. F, 8th N.C., at Morris Island, and two were used by Gordon's brigade at Fort Stedman (ibid.).

WICKHAM, Williams Carter. C.S.A. gen. 1820–88. Va. He graduated from the U. of Va., practiced law, ran his plantation in addition to being a legislator, jurist, and militiaman. Although he had opposed the ordinance of secession, he volunteered and fought at 1st Bull Run as Capt. of the Hanover Dragoons. Named Lt. Col. 4th Va. Cav. in Sept.

'61, he was severely wounded at Williamsburg by a saber and missed the rest of the Peninsular campaign. He was captured at his home by McClellan's advance and exchanged for Thomas Kane of the Pa. Bucktails, a kinsman of his wife. Promoted Col. 4th Va. Cav. in Aug. '62, he fought at 2d Bull Run, Boonsboro, Antietam, and on Stuart's raid into Md. He was wounded while in temporary command of Fitzhugh Lee's brigade at Upperville. Recovering in time for Fredericksburg, he also fought at Chancellorsville and Gettysburg. He was also a C.S.A. Congressman but rarely served in this capacity, preferring to fight. Appointed B.G. C.S.A. 1 Sept. '63, he commanded Wickham's brigade under Fitzhugh Lee in the Mine Run operations, Brandy Station, and Buckland Mills before repelling Kilpatrick's raid to Richmond in Feb. '64. He then commanded his unit at the Wilderness, Spotsylvania, Yellow Tavern, Totopotomoy, Cold Harbor, Trevilian Station, and Reams's Station. On 10 Aug. '64 he joined Early in the Valley to fight. Fought at Winchester, Fishers Hill, and New Market before resigning 9 Nov. '64. Transferring his command to Rosser, he took his long-neglected congressional seat and participated in the unsuccessful Hampton Roads Peace Conference. He joined the Republican party 23 Apr. '65 and was much criticized for this step. Active in politics and serving in the legislature, he was also a railroad president. There is a statue of him on the state capitol grounds.

WIERBOTTOM Church, Va. Alternate spelling of WARE BOTTOM CHURCH.

WIGFALL, Louis Trezevant. C.S.A. gen. 1816–74. S.C. Appt.-Tex. A graduate of the Univ. of Va. and S.C. College, he practiced law in S.C. After a bitter political feud he killed one man and received and inflicted a wound in a duel with Preston Brooks. Going to Tex. in 1848, he sat in the legislature and the US Senate. He resigned his seat there 23 Mar. '61 and went to Charleston to play a conspicuous role in the capture of Fort Sumter (see B.&L.). Commissioned B.G. C.S.A. 21 Oct. '61, he led the Tex. Brig. in Va. before resigning 20 Feb. '62 to become C.S.A. Congressman. Early becoming disillusioned by Davis' conduct of the war, he felt that he was the military genius the South needed for victory. After escaping from Galveston to England he later returned to Tex.

"WIGWAG." A method of SIGNAL COMMUNICATION developed by A. J. MYER and E. P. ALEXANDER.

WILCOX, Cadmus Marcellus. C.S.A. gen. 1824–90. N.C. Appt.-Tenn. After attending the Univ. of Nashville, he graduated from West Point: USMA 1846 (54/59); Arty. Serving as Quitman's A.D.C. in the Mexican War, he won a brevet and then served in garrison and the Seminole War before instructing in tactics at West Point. He was a groomsman in Grant's wedding (1848). Stationed on the frontier until he resigned 8 June '61 as Capt., he was commissioned Col. 9th Ala. and led his regiment at 1st Bull Run. Appointed B.G. C.S.A. 21 Oct. '61 he led a brigade on the Peninsula, 2d Bull Run, Fredericksburg, Chancellorsville, and Gettysburg. He was promoted Maj. Gen. C.S.A. 13 Aug. '63 to rank from 3 Aug., and commanded his division at the Wilderness, Spotsylvania, and the battles around Petersburg before surrendering at Appomattox. After the war he lived in Washington, where he held various government posts. He declined commissions in the armies of Egypt and Korea to remain with his only family, his widowed sister-in-law and several nieces and nephews. He wrote and translated a number of military tactics books. J. E.

Johnston was the chief mourner at his funeral; four C.S.A. and four Union officers were pallbearers. D. S. Freeman used to say that Cadmus Marcellus Wilcox was a name that delighted his tongue. In his lectures to US Army service schools Dr. Freeman cites Wilcox' actions at Banks's Ford on 3 May '63 as a lesson to all soldiers on the importance of skilled observation in war. (See *Lee's Lts.*, II, 621.)

WILCOX, James Andrew. Union officer. 1828–91. Col. 113th Ohio 28 Dec. '62; resigned 29 Apr. '63; Col. 113th Ohio 1 July '65; Bvt. B.G. USV 18 Oct. '65 (recruitment of armies).

WILCOX, John Schuler. Union officer. N.Y. Lt. Col. 52d Ill. 19 Nov. '61; Col. 4 May '63; Bvt. B.G. USV (war service); resigned 20 Feb. '64.

WILD, Edward Augustus. Union gen. 1825–91. Mass. After Harvard medical school and medical lectures in Paris he was a medical officer in the Turkish Army during the Crimean War. Commissioned Capt. 1st Mass. 23 May '61, he fought at 1st Bull Run and during the Peninsular campaign, being wounded at Fair Oaks. Mustered out 23 July '62, he assisted Gov. Andrews in raising colored troops and was named B.G. USV 24 Apr. '63. He commanded African Brig., Northeast Folly Island, X, South (11 Aug.–2 Oct. '63); 2d African Brig., Norfolk, XVIII, Va. and N.C. (2 Nov. '63–19 Jan. '64 leading an expedition through eastern N.C.); US forces Norfolk, XVIII, Va. and N.C. (8 Jan.–28 Apr. '64) and 1, Hinks's division USCT, Va. and N.C. at Wilson's Wharf and the Petersburg siege. It was during this time that he was arrested (June '64) for refusing to obey orders to replace his brigade Q.M. The finding of the courtmartial was set aside by the commanding general, and this was confirmed by the Judge Advocate Gen. He then com-

manded the 3d Div. (30–31 Dec. '64) and the 1st Div. (31 Dec. '64–27 Mar. '65) and 2, 1, XXV, Va. (28 Mar.–18 Apr. '65) before Richmond. With the Georgia Freedman's Bureau, he was mustered out in 1866 and was later in silver mining in Nev. and South America.

WILDER, John Thomas. Union officer. 1830–1917. N.Y. Lt. Col. 17th Ind. 4 June '61; Col. 25 Apr. '62; Bvt. B.G. USV 7 Aug. '64 (war service); resigned 4 Oct. '64. At his insistence his regiment was mounted and armed with Spencer repeaters. Commanded 1, 5, XIV; Wilder's Mounted Brig.; 1, 4, XIV; 3, 2, Cav. Corps (Cumberland). After the war he settled in Tenn., where he became an industrialist and developer of that state's railroads and coal fields.

WILDERNESS, Va. 5–7 May '64. The Army of the Potomac crossed the Rappahannock on 4 May but was forced to stop in the Wilderness to wait for the supply train to catch up. That afternoon Hancock's II Corps bivouacked at Chancellorsville, Warren's V Corps was at Old Wilderness Tavern, and the cavalry divisions of Gregg and J. H. Wilson were forward at Piney Branch Church and Parker's Store, respectively. The Federals had detected some enemy activity along the road from Orange C.H. Lee, who had anticipated Grant's movement and had resolved to hit the Federals while they were in the difficult Wilderness terrain, had Ewell's corps on the Orange Turnpike, and A. P. Hill (minus R. H. Anderson's division) on the Plank Road. The head of Ewell's column was at Locust Grove, little more than three miles from Warren, while A. P. Hill was but slightly more distant from J. H. Wilson. Yet neither army seemed aware of the other's proximity. Longstreet's corps had been at Mechanicsville, and Stuart's cavalry at Fredericksburg; both were moving in to join the rest of the

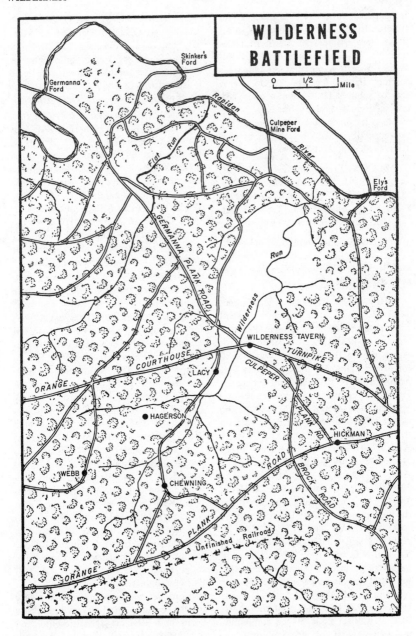

WILDERNESS
BATTLEFIELD

0   1/2   Mile

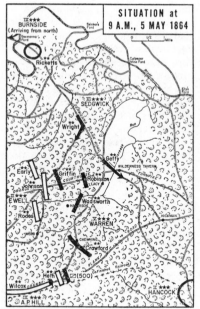

SITUATION at
9 A.M., 5 MAY 1864

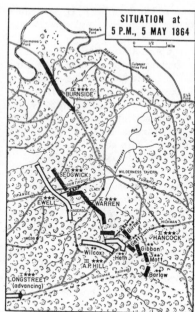

SITUATION at
5 P.M., 5 MAY 1864

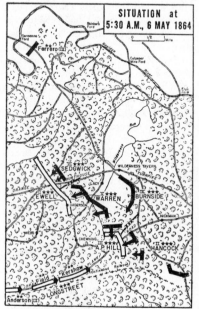

SITUATION at
5:30 A.M., 6 MAY 1864

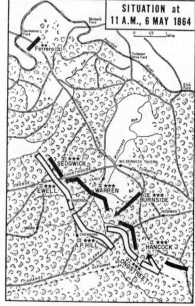

SITUATION at
11 A.M., 6 MAY 1864

Army of Northern Va. R. H. Anderson's division (A. P. Hill) was near Orange C. H.

At 6 P.M. 4 May Grant issued orders to continue the march at 5 o'clock the next morning through the Wilderness to the southeast. Burnside's IX Corps had also been ordered up from its previous mission of guarding the Orange and Alexandria R. R. Sedgwick's VI Corps was just across the Rappahannock. The stage was set.

At 7:15 A.M. 5 May Warren reported a considerable enemy force on the turnpike about two miles from Wilderness Tavern. He was ordered to attack what Grant and Meade believed to be no more than a division.

Crawford, whose division (3, V) had advanced to the Chewning farm, was ordered to hold his position, but to be prepared to send one brigade to support Warren. About noon Griffin (1, V) attacked, routed John M. Jones's brigade of Johnson's division, and then advanced against Battle's and Doles's brigades of Rodes's division (south of the turnpike). Jones was killed. In this advance, however, his right flank became exposed and was attacked by Gordon and Daniel. The Federal brigade of Ayres (1, 1, V) was driven back and Griffin had to pull back his entire line. Stafford was mortally wounded and Pegram wounded. Wright's division (1, VI) had been ordered to move from Spotswood to fall in on Griffin's right for this attack and protect his flank, but had not been able to get up in time. He arrived about 3 P.M. and then repulsed an attack by two brigades of Edward Johnson's division. On the other flank Wadsworth's division (4, V) had been ordered to reinforce Griffin's south flank, but it got lost and was driven back in disorder when its right flank was hit by the advancing brigades of Gordon and Daniel. This created a gap

through which the Confederates advanced and overpowered Denison's brigade of Robinson's division (3, 2, V). McCandless' brigade (1, 3, V) had also been ordered to form on Wadsworth's left, but Wadsworth had moved out before McCandless could make contact with him. McCandless collided with the forces of Gordon that had just defeated Denison and was also defeated with considerable loss after a heavy engagement. Ewell then dug in along the line where contact had first been made. Opposite him Warren formed (south of the pike) and Sedgwick (minus Getty) extended the line north of the pike.

To the south, along the Plank Road, the 5th N.Y. and 3d Pa. Cav. were left to outpost Parker's Store while Wilson moved with the rest of his division southwest toward Craig's Meeting House. Kirkland's brigade of Heth's division led A. P. Hill's advance along the Plank Road and drove the Federals toward Wilderness Tavern. Getty's division (2, VI), which had been marching southeast through the latter crossroads at 9 A.M., was sent to stop this enemy advance. At the same time Hancock's corps was ordered to halt in the vicinity of Todd's Tavern. However, in accordance with his earlier orders, Hancock was already two miles beyond the tavern toward Shady Grove Church, and had to countermarch. Getty reached the intersection of the Brock and Plank roads just in time to stop Heth's advance. Both sides then dug in. D. B. Birney's division (3, II) arrived at 2 P.M. and formed to Getty's south; Mott, Gibbon, and Barlow followed and extended the line to the south. Baxter's brigade (2, 2, V) arrived late in the afternoon. A. P. Hill, meanwhile, had been building up his own line and extending north to link up with Ewell; at the same time he was anxiously

awaiting the expected arrival of Longstreet behind him. Longstreet, however,
had delayed his advance while getting
permission to move via the Catharpin
Road instead of the Plank Road as Lee
had ordered; the result was that he did
not arrive in time for the first day's
fighting.

Hancock had also wasted time digging
a defensive position before attacking
A. P. Hill. Getty attacked at 4:15, after
delaying an hour to shift position to
make room for Hancock. Although he
gained ground with the assistance of
Ricketts' battery against the center of
Heth's position, he was repulsed on both
flanks. The brigade of Col. Lewis A.
Grant (2, 2, VI) lost almost 50 per
cent. Hancock reinforced with the divisions of D. B. Birney (along the road)
and Mott (against the enemy's right);
later he committed Carroll's brigade of
Gibbon's division (3, 2, II) to the right
of the Plank Road in support of Eustis'
brigade of Getty's division (4, 2, VI).
"There was never more desperate fighting than now ensued," wrote E. P.
Alexander. During the action Wilcox'
division reinforced Heth. About 5:30
P.M. the Confederates attacked and
gained about 50 yards. Two of Barlow's
brigades charged and drove back
Hill's right. At 8 P.M., after dark, the
fighting stopped. Five Federal divisions
(38,000 men) had failed to dislodge
A. P. Hill's two divisions (14,000).

Wadsworth's division (4, V) had
been ordered from the north to reinforce Hancock by attacking Hill's exposed left. It was unable to find its way
through the difficult underbrush in time
to be effective.

Along the turnpike there had been
heavy skirmishing. About 5 P.M. the brigades of Seymour (2, 3, VI), Neill (3,
2, VI), and part of Wright's 1st brig.
(under W. H. Penrose) attacked the
strongly-entrenched brigades of Hays

and Pegram south of Flat Run. Neill
and Penrose were repulsed with heavy
loss by guns Pegram had located so as
to enfilade their lines. Seymour attacked
until darkness without being able to
break through.

Since he expected Longstreet to arrive soon to relieve his tired troops on
the Orange Plank Road, A. P. Hill made
the mistake of disapproving the urgent
recommendation of Heth that earthworks be constructed in this sector in
preparation for the anticipated continuation of Federal attacks.

Not having identified either Longstreet's corps or R. H. Anderson's division during the day's fighting, Grant
ordered a general attack to start at
dawn of 6 May. During the night Burnside's IX corps hurried up to reinforce
Hancock, while Longstreet and Anderson moved to reinforce A. P. Hill.

At 5 A.M. Birney attacked with the
support of Getty and two of Gibbon's
brigades. Mott advanced toward Hill's
right. Wadsworth, who had made contact with Hill's left about dark of the
preceding day, was to attack in that
area. Birney was stopped when he came
up against Hill's line, but then succeeded
in enveloping it from the south while
Wadsworth made progress against the
other flank. The Confederates were
about to be routed when Field's and
Kershaw's divisions of Longstreet's
corps arrived and formed a new defensive line.

Gibbon was in command of a force
on the Federal south flank along the
Brock Road to guard against an expected advance by Longstreet from this
direction. In compliance with an order
to attack the Confederate south flank
with Barlow's division, Gibbon had
sent forward only Frank's brigade (3, 1,
II). After hard fighting this unit made
contact with Mott's left. Due to the
difficult terrain Burnside's two divisions

were late. At about 8 o'clock Stevenson's division of this corps reported to Hancock and Hancock was informed at about the same time that Burnside with the two other divisions was in position to attack on his right. Actually Burnside did not get into position until 2 P.M.

Shortly before 9 A.M. Hancock resumed his attack along the Plank Road with Birney, Mott, Wadsworth, part of Stevenson's division, and three brigades of Gibbon's division. Having heard firing to his south, Hancock sent Brooke's brigade (4, 1, II) to guard the Brock Road against a possible approach of Longstreet. Actually, the latter was at this moment on Hancock's front; the firing to the south was a skirmish between Sheridan's and Stuart's cavalry at TODD'S TAVERN. The concern over an attack from this area was further heightened when a column was reported advancing on the Brock Road. This turned out to be a group of Federal convalescents who were trying to rejoin their units. While Hancock diverted strength to guard his left, Burnside's attack failed to materialize on his right. By about 9:45 A.M. Longstreet had pushed Hancock back to his line of departure.

Looking for a way to take the offensive, Longstreet learned of an unfinished railroad cut that would provide a covered approach for attacking the Federal south flank. He put his adjutant, Lt. Col. G. Moxley SORREL, in command of four brigades to make this attempt. The brigades were those of Wofford, G. T. Anderson, Davis, and Mahone. (Many accounts, e. g., Steele, state that Mahone was in command.) Sorrel attacked at 11 A.M., and overwhelmed the Federal flank. Frank's brigade, almost out of ammunition when the attack started, withdrew under heavy pressure; the left of Mott's division then was forced back. Wadsworth was killed while trying to rally his troops. On Birney's suggestion the line was withdrawn to the Brock Road. When Longstreet learned of Sorrel's success, he ordered forward the brigades of Benning, Law, and Gregg. Mahone's men fired by mistake on their own troops, killing Micah Jenkins and seriously wounding Longstreet. (This occurred within five miles of where Stonewall Jackson had been mortally wounded under similar circumstances almost exactly a year before.) Longstreet ordered Field to assume command and press the attack. Lee, however, arrived and ordered this advance delayed until the lines could be straightened out.

There was little fighting in this area between 11 o'clock and 4 P.M. Burnside finally arrived, attacked near the Tapp House, took some ground, but was driven back by reinforcements from Heth's division and Wofford's brigade of Kershaw's division. Before Burnside and Hancock could comply with their orders to attack at 6 P.M., Lee took the initiative. At 4:15 the Confederates advanced to the abatis 100 yards from the Federals' first line of defense and brought it under heavy musket fire. The Federal line held for half an hour; then Ward's brigade (1, 3, II) and part of Mott's division broke. Brush fires had started and Hancock reported that portions of the breastworks were burning so that they could not be defended. Although the Confederates planted their flags over the captured works they were then driven back by Carroll's brigade, supported by Dow's battery. Burnside attacked again but accomplished no more than keeping Heth and Wilcox from moving to Lee's support.

To the north Sedgwick and Warren had attacked repeatedly and failed to penetrate Ewell's lines. Gordon had found the exposed Federal right flank, but Ewell had refused him permission to attack it. When Lee visited this portion of the front at 5:30 P.M. he ordered the attack made. Gordon's brigade, supported by part of Robert Johnston's, attacked Sedgwick's exposed right flank just before dark, while Pegram's brigade attacked frontally. Shaler's brigade (4, 1, VI) was driven back on Seymour's (2, 3, VI) and both of these Federal generals were captured with several hundred men. Johnston reached Wright's rear and captured some prisoners before being ejected from the Federal position. Both sides then entrenched. Brush fires had become such a problem that the fighting stopped at several points throughout the day by mutual consent while soldiers of both sides cooperated in trying to save the wounded. During the night of 7–8 May about 200 men were suffocated or burned to death.

After dark Grant's forces withdrew and both armies maneuvered toward their next encounter at SPOTSYLVANIA, 7–20 May '64.

The Federals lost an estimated 17,666 out of 101,895 (exclusive of cavalry) engaged; of these, 2,246 were killed and 12,073 wounded. Generals Wadsworth and Alexander Hays were killed, Getty and Carroll wounded, and Shaler and Seymour captured. Confederate effective strength is estimated at 61,025. Although there are no complete casualty reports, Livermore estimates that the Confederates lost a total of 7,750. Gens. Jenkins and J. M. Jones were killed, Stafford mortally wounded, Longstreet, Pegram, Hunter, and Jennings were wounded.

WILDES, Thomas Francis. Union officer. 1834–83. Canada. Lt. Col. 116th Ohio 18 Aug. '62; Col. 186th Ohio 28 Feb. '65; Bvt. B.G. USV 11 Mar. '65. Commanded 1, 1st Inf. Div. (W. Va.); 1, Independent Div., XXIV (Va.). Wounded at Piedmont by concussion from shell and at Winchester when thrown from horse. A teacher and editor before the war, he practiced law later.

WILDRICK, Abram Calvin. Union officer. c. 1836–94. N.J. USMA 1857 (14/38); Arty. 1st Lt. 3d US Arty. 27 Apr. '61; Capt. 8 Feb. '64; Col. 39th N.J. 11 Oct. '64; Bvt. B.G. USV 2 Apr. '65 (Petersburg siege). Other brevets for Petersburg siege, war service. In R.A. until retired in Oct. '94, as Lt. Col. Died the next month.

WILES, Greenberry F. Union officer. Ohio. 2d Lt. 78th Ohio 26 Oct. '61; 1st Lt. 13 Dec. '61; Capt. 16 Apr. '62; Lt. Col. 16 May '63; Col. 8 Nov. '64; Bvt. B.G. USV (war service). Died 1899.

WILEY, Aquila. Union officer. Pa. 1st Lt. 16th Ohio 20 Apr. '61; Capt. 4 May '61; mustered out 18 Aug. '61; Capt. 41st Ohio 19 Sept. '61; Maj. 22 June '62; Lt. Col. 6 Dec. '62; Col. 15 Apr. '63; discharged 7 June '64; Capt. Vet. Res. Corps 25 Mar. '65; Maj. 27 Apr. '65; Bvt. B.G. USV (Missionary Ridge, Stones River, Chickamauga, Chattanooga).

WILEY, Daniel Day. Union officer. Vt. Appt.-Mass. Capt. Comsy. of Subsist. Vols. 28 Aug. '62; Bvt. B.G. USV. Received four brevets for war service in Comsy. of Subsist. Dept. Died 1893.

WILKES, Charles. Union naval officer. 1798–1877. N.Y. After a distinguished career in the navy (entered in 1818 as Midshipman), he was prominent in the department of charts and instruments and in 1838 commanded a squadron of six ships and scientists to Antarctica, where an area is named Wilkes Land. His arrest of Mason and Slidell brought about the TRENT AFFAIR and made him a national hero. In 1862 he was promoted Commodore, and in 1866 he was named Adm. on the retired list.

WILKESON, Samuel. WAR CORRESPONDENT. 1817–89. N.Y. After studying at Williams and Union College he was first a staff writer and then correspondent for the N.Y. *Tribune.* His eldest son, Bayard, was killed at Gettysburg commanding his Union artillery battery. After the war Wilkeson became a publicist for Jay Cooke and Company and promoted Northern Pacific stock. He was named secretary of the railroad and continued to hold this job after his old enemy, Henry VILLARD, succeeded Cooke as president.

WILKIE, Franc Bangs. WAR CORRESPONDENT. 1832–92. N.Y. After graduating from Union College he worked for an Iowa paper until in 1861, when he became correspondent for the N.Y. *Times.* He was in charge of reporting all the military movements west of the Allegheny Mountains. In 1863 he became an editorial writer for the Chicago *Times,* later covering the Russo-Turkish War and heading the European bureau of the paper. He wrote a number of travel and historical books, notably *Pen and Powder* (1888), about the war correspondents. He signed his articles "Poliute."

WILLCOX, Orlando Bolivar. Union gen. 1823–1907. Mich. USMA 1847 (8/38); Arty. Serving in the Mexican and Seminole wars and on frontier garrison duty, he resigned in 1857 to practice law. Commissioned Col. 1st Mich. 1 May '61, he was wounded and captured at 1st Bull Run, commanding 2d Brig., 3d Div. (June–21 July '61), and was held as hostage for C.S.A. privateers. (See ENCHANTRESS AFFAIR.) Promoted B.G. USV 21 July '61, he commanded 1st Div., IX Potomac (8 Sept. –8 Oct. '62) at South Mountain and Antietam, led the Corps at Warrenton and Fredericksburg (8 Oct. '62–16 Jan. '63), and went back to command the division 7 Feb.–4 Apr. '63. In the Army of the Ohio he commanded the IX Corps (11 Apr.–5 June '63; 17–26 Jan. '64 and

16 Mar.–13 Apr. '64). From 10 Apr.–4 June '63 he commanded Dist. Central Ky. and then commanded Left Wing Forces, Ohio (11 Sept. '63–11 Jan. '64) at Blue Springs, Walker's Ford, Clinch River, and Strawberry Plains. Commanding 2d Div., IX, Ohio (26 Jan.– 16 Mar. '64), he returned to the Army of the Potomac to lead the 3d Div., IX (19 Apr.–2 Sept. '64) at the Wilderness, Ny River, Spotsylvania, Bethesda Church, Petersburg, and Weldon R.R. At Pegram's Farm, Hatcher's Run, and the Petersburg siege, he commanded 1st Div., IX (13 Sept.–30 Dec. '64; 2–25 Feb. '65 and 7 Mar.–17 June '65) and commanded the IX Corps 31 Dec. '64– 12 Jan.; 23 Jan.–2 Feb. and 17 June–2 July '65. From 25 Apr.–2 Aug. '65 he was Military Gov. of Washington. Breveted for Spotsylvania (B.G. U.S.A.) and Petersburg (Maj. Gen. USA), he was given the Medal of Honor in 1895 for 1st Bull Run. Continuing in the R.A., he was retired in 1887 as B.G. USA.

WILLIAM, John. Col. 12th N.J. Erroneous listing by Phisterer for Willian, John.

WILLIAMS, Adolphus Wesley. Union officer. N.Y. Maj. 2d Mich. 25 Apr. '61; Lt. Col. 6 Mar. '62; Col. 20th Mich. 26 July '62; Bvt. B.G. USV (war service); discharged 21 Nov. '63. W.I.A. at Yorktown in Apr. '62, Williamsburg 5 May '62, Fair Oaks 31 May '62. Died 1879.

WILLIAMS, Alpheus Starkey. Union gen. 1810–78. Conn. After Yale he traveled widely in US and Europe and was then a lawyer, judge, and newspaper publisher. In the Mexican War he was appointed B.G. Mich. Vols. 24 Apr. '61 and B.G. USV 17 May '61. Commanding 3d Brig., 1st Div., Pa. to 25 July '61, he led 1st Brig., Banks's division, Potomac (18 Oct. '61–13 Mar. '62); 1st Div., Banks's V, Potomac (13 Mar.–4 Apr. '62) and 1st Div., Shenandoah (4 Apr.–

26 June '62) at Winchester. In the Army of Va. he commanded 1st Div., II (26 June–4 Sept. '62) and II Corps (4–12 Sept. '62). In the Potomac he commanded 1st Div., XII (12–17 Sept. '62) at South Mountain and Antietam; (20 Oct. '62–1 July '63) at Chancellorsville and Gettysburg; and later (4 July–31 Aug. and 13–25 Sept. '63). He commanded the XII Corps at Antietam (17 Sept.–20 Oct. '62); Gettysburg (1–4 July '63) and later (31 Aug.–13 Sept. '63). In the Army of the Cumberland he led 1st Div., XII (25 Sept.–22 Dec. '63 and 30 Jan.–14 Apr. '64) and succeeded to XII Corps briefly. During the Atlanta campaign, the March to the Sea and through the Carolinas, he commanded 1st Div., XX (14 Apr.–28 July '64; 27 Aug.–11 Nov. '64 and 2 Apr.–4 June '65) and XX Corps (28 July–27 Aug. '64 and 11 Nov. '64–2 Apr. '65). Breveted Maj. Gen. USV 12 Jan. '65 for war service, he was mustered out in 1866. Called "Old Pap," he wore "a beard even more luxuriant than was customary in those days" (D.A.B.). He was Minister to Salvador 1866–69 and a Democratic Congressman, dying in office.

WILLIAMS, David H. Union gen. Pa. Commissioned Col. 82d Pa. 23 July '61, he fought at Fair Oaks, Charles City Crossroads, and Malvern Hill. His regiment was in reserve at Chantilly and fought at Antietam. Promoted B.G. USV 29 Nov. '62, his commission expired 4 Mar. '63.

WILLIAMS, James Monroe. Union officer. N.Y. Capt. 5th Kans. Cav. 12 July '61; Lt. Col. 79th US Col. Inf. 13 Jan. '63; Col. 2 May '63; Bvt. B.G. USV 13 Feb. '65. Commanded Col. Brig., VII (Ark.); 2, Frontier Dist., VII (Ark.); 2, 1, VII (Ark.). On 28 Oct. '62 a detachment of the 79th, before its organization as a regiment, was attacked by a larger Confederate force but drove

them off at Island Mounds, near Butler (Mo.). This is generally credited as the first fight for colored troops (Fox). At Poison Springs (Ark.) in Apr. '64 a foraging expedition commanded by Williams was surrounded and cut their way out. Williams continued in the R.A. until his resignation in 1873 as Capt., having been breveted for Indian fighting in Ariz. Heitman then states: "Capt. cav. 7 Jan. '91 (act 17 Sept. 1890); retired 12 Jan. 1891."

WILLIAMS, John. Union officer. Pa. Capt. 2d Iowa 18 July '61; Maj. 21 May '66; resigned 22 Oct. '62; Pvt. 47th Iowa 7 May '64; Capt. 18 May '64; Lt. Col. 4 June '64; Bvt. B.G. USV (Shiloh, war service); mustered out 28 Sept. '64. Commanded 2, 3, II (Potomac).

WILLIAMS, John Stuart. C.S.A. gen. 1820–98. Ky. After graduation from Miami (Ohio) Univ. he was a lawyer, fought in the Mexican War, raised cattle, and participated in Whig politics. Commissioned Col. 5th Ky. on 16 Nov. '61, he was appointed B.G. C.S.A. on 16 Apr. '62. He commanded a brigade under Humphrey Marshall in the Big Sandy River region and then operated in East Tenn. In Sept. '63 he opposed Burnside's advance to Knoxville. In Nov. he was relieved at his own request and commanded Grigsby's brigade in the Atlanta campaign. In Sept. '64 he was present at an attack on the Abingdon, Va., salt works. After surrendering with Johnston, he was a legislator, senator, railroad promoter, and farmer.

WILLIAMS, Reuben. Union officer. Ohio. 2d Lt. 12th Ind. 6 May '61; Capt. 7 Aug. '61; mustered out 19 May '62; Lt. Col. 12th Ind. 17 Aug. '62; Col. 17 Nov. '62; Bvt. B.G. USV (war service).

WILLIAMS, Robert. Union officer. c. 1825–1901. Va. USMA 1851 (19/42); Dragoons-Adj. Gen.-Cav. He served on the frontier and taught cavalry tactics at West Point before the war. Promoted Capt. Asst. Adj. Gen. 3 Aug. '61, he was with the Dept. of Annapolis and of the Shenandoah until 5 Oct. of that year. He was commissioned Col. 1st Mass. Cav. 7 Oct. '61 and commanded his regiment at Secessionville, James Island, and Hilton before joining the Army of the Potomac Aug.–Oct. '62. As Maj. 17 July '62 he was Asst. in the Adj. Gen. office for the rest of the war, resigning from volunteer service 1 Oct. '62. He continued in the R.A., retiring in 1893 as B.G., the Adj. Gen., having been breveted B.G. USA for war service.

WILLIAMS, Seth. Union gen. 1822–66. Me. USMA 1842 (23/56); Arty.-Adj. Gen. Serving on garrison duty, he was A.D.C. to Robert Patterson during the Mexican War (1 brevet) and was then Adj. at West Point. As Bvt. Maj., (11 May), Maj. (full rank 3 Aug.), and B.G. USV (23 Sept. '61), he was Adj. Gen. of the Army of the Potomac under McClellan, Burnside, Hooker, and Meade. In 1864–66 he was Grant's I.G. and then Adj. Gen. for the Mil. Div. of Atlanta. Breveted for Gettysburg, R. E. Lee's surrender (B.G. USA), war service (Maj. Gen. USA) and the campaign from Gettysburg to Petersburg (Maj. Gen. USV 1 Aug. '64), he continued in the R.A., dying on active duty.

WILLIAMS, Thomas. Union gen. 1815–62. N.Y. Appt.-Mich. USMA 1837 (12/50); Inf. Serving in garrison on the frontier, as mathematics professor at West Point, in the Seminole wars, in Indian fighting, and as A.D.C. to Scott (1844–50) during the Mexican War (2 brevets), he was Maj. 5th US Arty. (14 May '61) when appointed I.G. of the Dept. of Va. in June '61. With his regiment on Butler's N.C. expedition, he was named B.G. USV 28 Sept. '61 and commanded 4th Brig., N.C. expeditionary corps, in Dec. '61–Apr. '62. He commanded the 2d Brig. of the Ship Island expedition and was killed 5 Aug. '62 at Baton Rouge.

WILLIAMS, Thomas J. Union officer. N.J. Capt. 23d Ky. 16 Dec. '61; discharged 1 Jan. '65; Maj. 55th Ky. 1 Mar. '65; Lt. Col. 23 Mar. '65; Bvt. B.G. USV 22 Sept. '65 (war service). Died 1866.

WILLIAMS RAPID-FIRE GUN. The first true machine gun to be successfully used in battle (G.M. Chinn, *The Machine Gun,* 3 vols., Washington, 1951) was invented by Capt. R. S. Williams, C.S.A. It was a 1-pounder steel breechloader with a barrel about four feet long and a 2-inch bore. "It was operated by a lever attached to a revolving cam shaft which rotated a cylinder above which was an ammunition hopper. The cartridges were fired by a sliding hammer which automatically struck the percussion caps at each revolution of the cylinder. The gun had a range of about 2,000 yards. Its first test in action was on May 31, 1862, at the battle of Seven Pines under the direction of the inventor himself, who accompanied Pickett's Brigade. The results obtained were so satisfactory that the Confederate Government had six of the guns made which comprised the material of Williams', later Schoolfield's Battery, of the Western Army" (Wise, 32). One limitation of the gun was that its rapid rate of fire (18 to 20 shots per minute) caused the breech to expand and fail to relock. Tredegar got a contract on 21 Aug. '62 to make 20 of these guns with a caliber of 1.25 inches (Albaugh and Simmons, 275). According to Chinn, two batteries of six guns each were made at Lynchburg, four batteries at Tredegar, and one battery at Mobile. The latter guns were used by Buckner. One, captured at the end of the war, is in the West Point Museum.

WILLIAMSBURG, Va., 4–5 May '62. (PENINSULAR CAMPAIGN) Stuart's cavalry covered Magruder's withdrawal from YORKTOWN, while Stoneman led all available Federal cavalry in pursuit. Stoneman was supported by four horse batteries and the infantry divisions of Hooker (1, III) and W. F. Smith (2, IV). Contact was made near the Half-way House. The division of Longstreet, conducting the rear guard, took up a position in a line of defenses Magruder had constructed earlier (between Half-way House and Williamsburg). On 5 May the Federals, slowed by deep mud and rain, closed up on this line and started attacking. Hooker made an un-successful attack in the center against Fort Magruder, the strongest part of the line. Hooker was being pressed hard by a counterattack when Kearny's divi-sion, delayed by bad roads, came up to reinforce late in the afternoon. D. H. Hill, meanwhile, had reinforced Long-street's left. Opposite Hill, W. F. Smith's division attacked about noon. Hancock's brigade enveloped the enemy left, seized several unoccupied redoubts and held them against determined counterattacks. During the night the Confederates con-tinued their withdrawal up the Peninsula.

Of 40,768 Federal troops engaged, there were 2,239 casualties, of whom 456 were killed and 373 missing. The Confederate strength was 31,823, of whom 1,603 were lost (133 missing) (Livermore).

WILLIAMS' FARM. See WELDON R.R. OPERATIONS, 22–23 June '64.

WILLIAMSON, James Alexander. Union gen. 1829–1902. Ky. Named 1st Lt. Adj. 4th Iowa 8 Aug. '62, he was wounded at Pea Ridge and promoted Lt. Col. 4 Apr. and Col. 21 July '62. He was seriously wounded leading the as-sault on Chickasaw Bluffs 29 Dec. '62, and he then fought at Vicksburg, Green-ville, and Jackson. In the Army of the Tenn. he commanded 3, 1, XV (1 Aug.–15 Sept. '63; 1 Nov.–28 Dec. '64; and

31 Dec. '64–15 Jan. '65) and 2, 1, XV (1 Sept.–28 Dec. '63 at Chattanooga, Lookout Mountain, and Ringgold and 5 May–25 Sept. '64). Promoted B.G. USV 13 Jan. '65, he commanded the Dist. of St. Louis 20 June–21 July '65 and was breveted for Vicksburg, Chattanooga, and Atlanta (B.G. USV 19 Dec. '64) and war service (Maj. Gen. USV). He was mustered out 24 Aug. '65 and was active in Republican politics after the war.

WILLIAN, John. Union officer. Eng-land. 1st Lt. 6th N.J. 26 Aug. '61; Capt. 11 July '62; Maj. 27 Apr. '64; transferred to 8th N.J. 7 Sept. '64; Lt. Col. 5 Jan. '65; Col. 12th N.J. 19 Apr. '65; Bvt. B.G. USV 9 Apr. '65 (R. E. Lee's sur-render). Listed by Phisterer as William, John.

WILLICH, August. Union gen. 1810–78. Germany. Son of a Napoleonic veteran, he was given a military educa-tion and was an officer in the Prussian Army. In 1846 he joined a group of young officers in writing letters of resignation so inflammatory that they were tried by court-martial. He managed to be acquitted and then resigned, join-ing Sigel, Schurz, Hecker, and Blenker two years later in the Baden revolt. Coming through Switzerland and Eng-land, he settled in the US and was em-ployed in the Brooklyn Navy Yard as a carpenter. Later in coastal survey and newspaper work, he was commissioned 1st Lt. Adj. 9th Ohio 8 May '61 and Maj. 13 June '61. Part of his regiment routed Terry's Texas Rangers in Nov. '61 to gain great popular acclaim. He was named Col. 32d Ind. 24 Aug. '61 and B.G. USV 17 July '62. From 10 Aug.–29 Sept. '62 he commanded 6th Brig., 2d Div., Army Ohio; and in the Army of the Cumberland he led 1, 2 Right Wing, XIV (5 Nov.–31 Dec. '62); 1, 2, XX (28 May–19 Sept. '63); 2d Div., XX (19 Sept.–9 Oct. '63); 3d Div.,

IV (8 Jan.–12 Feb. '64) and 1, 3, IV
(10 Oct. '63–8 Jan. '64; 3–15 May '64
and 2 June–1 Aug. '65). Breveted Maj.
Gen. USV 21 Oct. '65 for war service,
he was mustered out in 1866. Returning
to Germany during the Franco-Prussian
War, he offered his services to the king
he had tried once to overthrow, but was
not accepted because of his advanced
age. An adherent of Karl Marx, he was
called sarcastically by the Father of
Communism "a spiritual communist and
Knight of a noble conviction."

WILLOUGHBY, Babcock. Union officer. Lt. Col. 75th N.Y. (Grover's division, XIX), he died 6 Oct. '64 of
wounds received at Winchester, Va., 19
Sept., and was posthumously breveted
B.G. USV as of the latter date (Phisterer).
He is not listed as an officer by Heitman.

WILLOUGHBY RUN. Creek run-
ning from north to south, dividing Herr
Ridge and McPherson Ridge, and figur-
ing in the first day's fighting at GETTYS-
BURG.

WILLSON, Lester Sebastian. Union
officer. N.Y. Sgt. 60th N.Y. 9 Sept. '61;
2d Lt. 6 Aug. '62; 1st. Lt. Adj. 8 Oct.
'62; Capt. 28 Sept. '64; Lt. Col. 4 Apr.
'65; Bvt. B.G. USV (Atlanta). Listed by
Phisterer as Wilson. Lester S.

WILSON Claudius C. C.S.A. gen.
?–1863. Appt.-Ga. Appointed Col. 25th
Ga. 2 Sept. '61, he served along the Ga.
and S.C. coasts and in the Dept. of Ga.,
S.C., and Fla. After going to northern
Miss. in 1863, he was sent to Ga. after
the fall of Vicksburg. He commanded a
brigade at Chickamauga before being
appointed B.G. C.S.A. 16 Nov. '63. He
died 24 Nov. while commanding his
brigade around Chattanooga.

WILSON, James. Union officer.
Azores. 1st Lt. 13th Iowa 21 Oct. '61;
Regt. Adj. 24 Mar. '62; Maj. 9 Mar. '63;
Lt. Col. 18 Apr. '63; Col. 19 Jan. '65;
Bvt. B.G. USV (war service).

WILSON, James Grant, Union officer. 1833–1914. Scotland. Maj. 15th Ill
Cav. 25 Dec. '62; Col. 4th US Col. Cav.
14 Sept. '63; Bvt. B.G. USV (war service). The son and partner of a Pough-
keepsie (N.Y.) publisher, he edited
periodicals and was the coeditor of
*Appleton's Cyclopedia of American
Biography*, one of the first collections
of that type. He also authored many
other historical and biographical works.

WILSON, James Harrison. Union
gen. 1837–1925. Ill. USMA. 1860
(6/41); Topo. Engrs. One of the war's
"boy wonders," he was a Maj. Gen. five
years after graduating from West Point.
He was first stationed on the frontier
and then served under T. W. Sherman
as Chief Topo. Engr. on the Port Royal
expedition as 1st Lt. 9 Sept. '61. Next
on Hunter's staff in the Dept. of the
South (15 Mar.–19 Aug. '62) at Fort
Pulaski, he was volunteer A.D.C. to
McClellan at South Mountain and
Antietam and Chief Topo. Engr. of the
Army of the Tenn. (17 Oct. '62–3 Mar.
'63). Promoted Lt. Col. Asst. I.G. Assigned (8 Nov. '62–17 Nov. '63), he
was Asst. Engr. and I.G. (3 Mar.–31
Oct. '63) at Yazoo Pass, Port Gibson,
Jackson, Champion's Hill, Big Black
River, and the Vicksburg siege. Named
B.G. USV 30 Oct. '63, he was at Missionary Ridge and Knoxville. Although
without previous cavalry experience, he
was selected to head the newly-established Cavalry Bureau in Washington
(17 Feb.–7 Apr. '64), when efforts were
being made to vitalize that arm. He
contributed tremendously to their effectiveness by seeing that they were
armed with the Spencer carbine. Taking
command of the 3d Div., Cav. Corps,
Potomac on 13 Apr., he led these troops
at Spotsylvania, Sheridan's raid to
Haxall's Landing, Beaver Dam, Yellow
Tavern, Meadow Bridge, Mechum's
Creek, Ashland, Haw's Shop, Toto-

potomoy, Long Bridge, White Oak Swamp, Stones Creek, and in the cavalry operations around Petersburg. On 6 Aug. '64 the 3d Div. was transferred to the Army of the Shenandoah, and he led it (until 30 Sept. '64) at Summit Point and Opequon. He then commanded the Cav. Corps of the Mil. Div. Miss. 29 Oct. '64–26 June '66) at Franklin, Nashville, Ebenezer Church, Selma, Montgomery, Columbus, and Macon. Summarizing WILSON'S RAID TO SELMA, Cullum says "in this brief Campaign of 28 days, [he] captured 5 fortified cities, 23 stand of colors, 288 guns and 6,820 prisoners, and finally on May 10, 1865, adding Jefferson Davis, the Rebel President, to the captures made by a detachment of his forces . . ." Grant, in sending Wilson to Sherman, said, "I believe Wilson will add 50 per cent to the effectiveness of your cavalry." "About five feet, ten inches in height, though his erect, military bearing made him appear a trifle taller," (D.A.B.) he was described by Lyman as "a slight person of a light complexion and with rather a pinched face." He was breveted for Fort Pulaski, Chattanooga, Wilderness, Nashville (B.G. USA) and Selma (Maj. Gen. USA), and war service (Maj. Gen. USV 5 Oct. '64). He continued in the R.A. until discharged in 1870 at his own request as Lt. Col. In railroad construction and management, he volunteered during the Spanish-American War, being the senior Maj. Gen. in civil life under retirement age. He was appointed Maj. Gen. USV in 1898, B.G. USV (1899–1901), and B.G. USA in 1901, retiring a month later. During this tour of duty he was active in suppressing the Boxer rebellion and by presidential order represented the US Army at the coronation of Edward VII in 1902. Among many articles and books he wrote *The Life of Ulysses S. Grant* (1868), "The Union Cavalry in the Hood Campaign" (B.&L., IV, 465), and *Under the Old Flag* (1912): He wrote *A Critical Review of the Campaign of Chancellorsville by John Bigelow* which was of such value that it was republished in booklet form in 1910. He was the last survivor of his West Point class.

WILSON, Lester S. Erroneous listing by Phisterer for WILLSON, Lester Sebastian.

WILSON, Thomas. Union officer. c. 1832–1901. D.C. USMA 1853 (29/52); Inf.-Comsy. of Subsist. 1st Lt. 5th US Inf. 1857; Capt. Comsy. of Subsist. 25 Oct. '61; Lt. Col. Comsy. of Subsist. Assigned 26 Dec. '63–1 Aug. '65; Bvt. B.G. USV (war service). Served with headquarters guard to the Gen. in Chief, Washington, Apr.–July '61. Then Acting Asst. Adj. Gen. defense of Washington. Comsy. of Subsist. to supply Burnside's N.C. expedition in 1861 and Grant's Chief of Commissariat (Potomac) for Richmond campaign, 1863–65. In R.A. until retired in 1896 as Col. Asst. Comsy. Gen. of Subsist.

WILSON, William. Union officer. N.Y. Col. 6th N.Y. 25 May '61; Bvt. B.G. USV (war service); mustered out 25 June '63. Commanded 1, 4, XIX (Gulf). Died 1874.

WILSON, William Tecumseh. Union officer. Pa. Capt. 15th Ohio 23 Apr. '61; mustered out 27 Aug. '61; Lt. Col. 15th Ohio 12 Sept. '61; resigned 10 Aug. '62; Lt. Col. 123d Ohio 9 Sept. '62; Col. 26 Sept. '62; Bvt. B.G. USV (war service).

WILSON AND KAUTZ'S PETERS-BURG RAID, 22 June–1 July '64. (PETERSBURG CAMPAIGN) The Federal cavalry division of James Wilson had been operating with Warren's V Corps north of the James River to screen Grant's crossing of that river against Petersburg. On 17 June Wilson himself crossed and his division remained near City Point until the 22d. To support the WELDON R.R. OPERATIONS of II and VI Corps, Wilson received orders on 21 June to lead his own division and that of Kautz (total of 5,000 men) around the Union army, across the Weldon R.R., and to strike the Southside (Lynchburg) R.R. as close to Petersburg as possible. He was then to destroy this railroad as far as Burkeville and thence south along the Danville R.R. to the Roanoke River. Sheridan with two cavalry divisions at White House was expected to contain the divisions of Hampton and Fitz Lee north of the James, leaving only the cavalry division of W. H. F. ("Rooney") Lee to oppose Wilson.

The Federal cavalry started at dawn on the 22d and moved through Dinwiddie C.H. to the Southside R.R. While Wilson remained to the rear destroying the railroad, Kautz was sent ahead to Burkeville. Rooney Lee made contact with the rear of Wilson's division, and then circled ahead to separate the two Federal divisions by occupying Nottoway Station. Here Wilson attacked to protect Kautz, who was destroying the railroad at Burkeville, and an indecisive action took place. Wilson and Kautz then moved south, uniting 24 June on the Danville R.R. While Wilson contained Lee, Kautz moved ahead to destroy the railroad bridge over the Staunton River. Strong Confederate defenses at that point, including six guns, stopped Kautz's attempt, and Wilson decided to return east and link up with friendly forces which he believed to have reached their objectives along the Weldon R.R. He did not know that this operation had failed, nor did he know that Sheridan had crossed the James starting 25 June and that Hampton had begun crossing at Drewry's Bluff the next day. When Wilson reached Stony Creek Station, 10 miles south of Reams's Station, on the 28th he found his path blocked by Hampton's four brigades. He ordered Kautz to move west of the railroad and cross it at Reams's Station while he contained Hampton with his own division. Instead of the expected Union infantry at Reams's Station, Kautz found Fitz Lee's cavalry division. Wilson broke contact with Hampton after the latter had attacked vigorously on the 29th. He joined Kautz the next day to find Reams's Station held by all three Confederate cavalry divisions and an infantry division. Knowing that escape lay only in rapid movement, Wilson burned his trains and ordered a retreat south to the Nottoway River. Before this could be executed, the Confederates separated Wilson and Kautz. The latter escaped with a large part of his command, crossed the Weldon R.R., and reached the security of Federal infantry. Wilson moved with the remainder of his command and was followed by Fitz Lee. Wilson crossed the Nottoway near the railroad on the 30th, marched due east, recrossed the Nottoway, and headed for the James. When his route was ascertained by the enemy, Hampton moved down the Jerusalem Plank Road to intercept his retreat before he reached the Blackwater. By rapid marches Wilson crossed that stream 1 July, before Hampton could catch him.

The raid cost Wilson 1,500 men, his trains, and his 12 guns. He had, however, succeeded in putting out of commission for several weeks a vital link in Lee's communications.

WILSON'S CREEK CAMPAIGN, Mo., Aug.–Nov. '61. Respecting the neutrality of Ky., the Confederates undertook to gain control of Mo. The beginning of Aug. there was a Confederate force of about 10,000 militia and volunteers from Mo., Ark., and La. advancing from southwest Mo. At Pocahontas, in northeast Ark., Wm. J. Hardee was

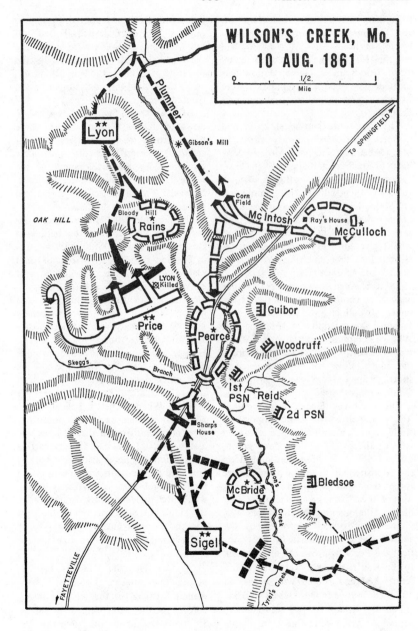

WILSON'S CREEK, Mo.
10 AUG. 1861

organizing 5,000 Ark. volunteers. M. Jeff Thompson's "Mushrats" were nearby in southeast Mo. At New Madrid on the Mississippi a force of 6,000 Tenn. troops under Gideon Pillow was located. The separate commands were expected to cooperate in an advance on St. Louis.

The fiery little Nathaniel Lyon had assumed control of military affairs in Mo. (See CAMP JACKSON, MO., 10 May '61.) Franz Sigel had clashed with Gov. Jackson's forces at Carthage, Mo., 5 July, and then withdrawn to join Lyon at Springfield. Since his department commander, Frémont, showed no concern for the safety of his force and would give him no support, Lyon determined to take the offensive against the advancing enemy.

Lyon planned a concentric advance against the combined Confederate forces under McCulloch that were camped at Wilson's Creek, southwest of Springfield. While he himself led the main attack from the north, Sigel was to attack from the south. Both forces bivouacked a short distance from the unsuspecting Confederates the night of 9 Aug.

The northern column moved out at 4 A.M. and drove back the outposts of Rains. Lyon's main body then advanced west of the creek, while a flank guard, under Capt. J. B. Plummer, moved on the opposite side against a Confederate force that had been seen advancing toward the "Corn Field" from the Ray house. Plummer's battalion of Mo. Home Guards was reinforced by the 1st US Inf. (300 men). In an hour's fight the Federals drove the enemy back to the Ray house, but were then counterattacked and routed with a loss of 80 killed and wounded. Hébert's 3d La. ("Pelican Rifles") and McIntosh's Mounted Ark. were the Confederate troops involved.

By about 6:30 A.M. the Confederate line under Price had been drawn up to oppose Lyon on Oak Hill. Totten's 2d US Arty. and DuBois's were supporting the Federals with 16 guns, while the batteries of Guibor, Bledsoe, Woodruff, and Reid (total, 15 guns) supported the Confederates.

After an hour's fight Price was driven down the hill to Wilson's Creek where he re-formed to counterattack. Greer's cavalry attempted to aid the latter movement by an envelopment of the Federal left by way of Skegg's Branch. However, Totten spotted this threat and repulsed it with his guns.

Sigel, meanwhile, had advanced according to plan toward the battlefield from the south. At 5:30 A.M. he was in position near Tyrel's Creek and had placed a battery on high ground east of Wilson's Creek to fire into the cavalry camps of Greer, Churchill, and Major. When he heard Lyon's opening guns, Sigel routed the Confederate cavalry and then advanced toward Sharp's House, taking up an intermediate position on the way. At Sharp's House he was attacked and routed by McCulloch with Hébert's 3d La. and Churchill's cavalry. When Hébert's Pelican Rifles advanced in their natty gray uniforms, Sigel mistook them for the 1st Iowa and assumed that Lyon had already carried his portion of the field. Reid's battery enfiladed the Federals from positions on high ground east of Wilson's Creek while McCulloch's attack routed them. By 11 o'clock Sigel was out of the fight and the Confederates could mass their entire strength of two to one against Lyon.

On Oak Hill the Federals had repulsed two attacks. Lyon had been wounded twice (in the leg and head) before finally being killed at about 10:30. It was about this time that the third Confederate charge was under way. The 1st Iowa was brought up from reserve but when ordered by Schofield to charge refused to go forward. At 11:30 the Confederates broke off the action and retired down the hill for the fourth time. Maj. Sturgis, who had succeeded Lyon, then ordered a withdrawal. This controversial decision was apparently prompted by Sturgis' lack of confidence in the ability of his tired troops, who were almost out of ammunition, to withstand another attack. "Had the fortunes of battle spared Lyon, Wilson's Creek might have been the most brilliant victory of the Civil War," writes Monaghan. "General Sherman blamed the next four years of strife and pillage in Missouri on Lyon's death" (*op. cit.*, 181).

Although a minor engagement, this was one of the most fiercely-contested of the war. The Federals were outnumbered 11,600 to 5,400. They lost 1,235 (223 killed, 721 wounded, 291 missing) while inflicting on the Confederates a loss of 1,184 (257 killed, 900 wounded, 27 missing). They killed or wounded 214 Confederates for every 1,000 of their own troops engaged, whereas the Confederates inflicted only 81 casualties on the same basis. Considering Sigel's poor performance, this over-all record is particularly remarkable.

McCulloch did not pursue the Federals as they retreated to Rolla. Price occupied Springfield and then captured a Federal brigade at Lexington, Mo., 20 Sept. There were unimportant minor engagements in southern Mo. during Nov. In early Sept. Pillow and Hardee crossed the Mississippi and occupied Columbus, Ky. Opposite this place Grant fought the action at BELMONT, Mo., 7 Nov. '61.

WILSON'S PLANTATION (Farm), La., 7 Apr. '64. Cavalry skirmish of RED RIVER CAMPAIGN.

WILSON'S RAID TO SELMA, Ala., 22 Mar.–20 Apr. '65. With Confederate resistance collapsing on all fronts, James H. Wilson led three cavalry divisions (McCook, Long, and Upton) from the extreme northwest corner of Ala. to raid Selma. The latter was the most important military center in the area, having a large armory, gun factories, foundries, and warehouses.

Moving in three columns to deceive the enemy as to his destination, Wilson concentrated at Jasper on 27 Mar. He reached Montevallo on the 31st, having encountered no resistance other than small detachments of Roddey's brigade. Croxton's brigade was sent from Elyton (now Birmingham) to capture Tuscaloosa and destroy the bridge.

Meanwhile the Confederates had been moving to counter Wilson's threat to Selma. From around Columbus, Miss., two brigades of Chalmers' division started for Selma by way of Marion, and two brigades of Jackson's division moved via Tuscaloosa. Jackson's force crossed the Black Warrior at Tuscaloosa and had just cleared Trion when Croxton appeared to his rear between his main force and the supply trains. Jackson turned and drove Croxton up the river, and then recrossed due west of Elyton.

On the 31st Wilson routed Forrest's smaller force (his bodyguard and Crossland's brigade) south of Montevallo, where Forrest was attempting to delay until Chalmers' arrival. The next day Wilson captured documents that informed him of Forrest's dispositions and intentions. He sent McCook with his other brigade to reinforce Croxton near Trion, and moved on Selma with the other two divisions. Near Plantersville a scratch force of 2,000 cavalry under Forrest (Crossland, Roddey, and Daniel Adam's militia) was routed and driven toward Selma. Here he was joined by one of Chalmers' brigades.

Selma was covered by a strong line

of works about five miles long that
formed a bridgehead on the north bank
of the Alabama River. To defend this
position Forrest had about 2,500 cavalry in three small brigades and about
the same number of militia. The divisions of Long and Upton carried the
works the afternoon of 2 Apr.; Forrest's cavalry resisted strongly, but the
militia abandoned their posts (Fiebeger,
430). The Confederate cavalry escaped
during the night and at Marion were
joined by Chalmers' second brigade.

Wilson remained at Selma until the
9th, and then marched to Montgomery,
which he captured on the 12th. He took
Columbus, Ga., on the 16th and Macon
on the 20th. Here he learned that the
war was over.

Croxton's brigade, separated from
Wilson's main body after the action at
Montevallo, was driven north by Jackson. When the latter moved south, Croxton also moved in that direction and
captured Tuscaloosa on 4 Apr. Chalmers' third brigade blocked his further
attempts to join Wilson. After retiring
to Elyton (Birmingham) he finally rejoined Wilson at Macon on the 20th.
Federal losses for the month's operations were reported at 725; Wilson
claimed 6,820 prisoners and estimated
1,200 Confederates killed and wounded
(E.&B.). (His troops captured Jeff Davis
at IRWINSVILLE 10 May.)

Forrest, who for the first time had
been outmarched and outmaneuvered by
the enemy's cavalry (Fiebeger), moved
his command to Livingston, where they
were surrendered 4 May by Richard
Taylor.

WINCHESTER. See RIENZI, Sheridan's horse.

WINCHESTER, Va., 25 May '62.
(SHENANDOAH VALLEY CAMPAIGN OF
JACKSON) Banks in Strasburg believed
from initial reports that the FRONT
ROYAL action of 23 May was noth-

ing more than a raid and that Jackson's
main body was still at Harrisonburg.
On the advice of Col. G. H. GORDON,
however, he withdrew toward Winchester, starting at 3 A.M., 24 May, thus
saving his army from annihilation. Gordon's effective rear-guard action and
Jackson's inability to coordinate his tired
troops in an effective pursuit kept
Banks's force from being intercepted at
Middletown. Ashby's cavalry and the
La. Tigers wasted valuable time looting

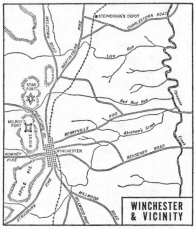

WINCHESTER
& VICINITY

a captured wagon train. After this frustration Jackson pushed his troops relentlessly down the Valley Pike during
the night while Ewell's corps moved ⍳n
Winchester via the Front Royal Road.
There were critical heights southwest
of Winchester that the Confederates had
to take before Banks had time to fortify
them. When sure he was close enough
for an attack at dawn, Jackson (at about
1 A.M.) halted the column on the Valley
Pike and sent an officer to locate Ewell's
column.

Banks, determined to make a stand
at Winchester, posted Gordon's (3d)
brigade on his right and Col. Dudley
Donnelly's on his left. At dawn (Sunday, 25 May) Jackson's old division
crossed Abraham's Creek and drove in

the pickets on the Federal left. Federal cavalry (Hatch) and artillery prevented the Confederates from achieving significant gains. Jackson, now able to determine the enemy's dispositions, brought his artillery into action and sent Taylor and his La. brigade by a covered route to take position on the Federal right flank. Ewell, meanwhile, on his own initiative (Freeman), was maneuvering into a comparable position on the opposite flank. At about 7:30 A.M. Taylor's column attacked successfully through heavy fire. Jackson's center and right advanced simultaneously. The Federals maintained good order for the first few hundred yards, but then broke and stampeded. Again Jackson was unable to organize a pursuit. Ashby could not be reached. Two hours were lost when "Maryland" Steuart insisted on the approval of Ewell (to whom he was attached) before obeying an order from Jackson (through a staff officer) to pursue.

Banks's effectives during the period 23-25 May were probably 8,500, of whom he lost between 2,769 and 3,030 (*Lee's Lts.,* I, 407). (Of these, 1,063 were under Kenly at FRONT ROYAL, 23 May.) During the same period Jackson lost 400 (*ibid.*).

WINCHESTER, Va., 13–15 June '63. (Gettysburg campaign) After driving in Milroy's outposts and isolating Winchester (see BERRYVILLE; MARTINSBURG), Ewell made preparations to attack 14 June. Winchester's defenses were west of the town: the Main (or Flag) Fort and the Star Fort astride the Pughtown Road, and two smaller, unfinished outpost positions about a mile to the northwest. The latter were occupied by Col. Keifer with the 110th and part of the 116th Ohio. While Johnson's and Gordon's brigades made demonstrations to attract the Federals' attention to the east and south, Ewell worked the rest of his infantry and some artillery around to the west by a covered route. About 6 P.M. the Confederates opened fire with 20 guns on the enemy troops working on the southernmost outpost. Federal artillery immediately replied but was silenced after a 45-minute exchange. Hays's La. brigade then took the position and repulsed feeble attempts to retake it. Loss of this critical terrain caused Milroy's other troops to withdraw into the Main Fort. Afraid that the Federals would withdraw during the night, ·Ewell ordered the brigades of Johnson, Steuart, and Nicholls to block the Martinsburg road. Milroy held a counsel of war at 9 P.M. and decided to destroy his wagons and artillery and retreat; at 1 A.M. he started to withdraw along the route Ewell had anticipated. At Stephenson's Depot, four miles to the northeast of Winchester, a hot skirmish started at about 3:30 A.M. Milroy's 1st Brig., under W. L. Elliott, got into a fire fight with the Confederate brigades of Johnson and Nicholls. Walker, delayed because of faulty orders, was a mile to the rear when the fighting started. He arrived on the right of the line just as Milroy was attempting an envelopment, and the Confederate reserve was thrown into the battle at the same time. The Federals tried to escape in several columns. Their total loss was 4,443 (Fox), of whom 3,358 were captured (D.S.F.); Ewell lost about 269. A court of inquiry absolved Milroy of responsibility for the disaster.

WINCHESTER, Va., 23–24 July '64. See KERNSTOWN, same date.

WINCHESTER, Va. ("Third Battle of . . .," or Opequon), 19 Sept. '64. (SHENANDOAH VALLEY CAMPAIGN OF SHERIDAN) On 16 Sept. Sheridan learned from Rebecca West, a Quaker schoolteacher in Winchester who was spying for him, that Kershaw's division and 12 guns had been detached from Early's

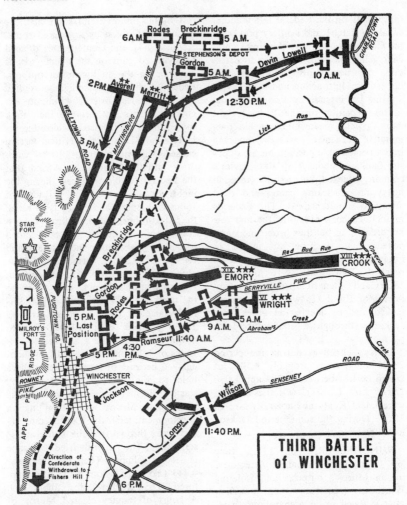

THIRD BATTLE of WINCHESTER

command. Grant arrived the next day (at Charlestown) to present a proposed plan of operation, but instead approved one enthusiastically presented by Sheridan. "After listening to the flood of words from his volatile junior, Grant gave him a two-word instruction which has become a model of soldierly brevity: 'Go in' " (O'Connor, 200).

Not knowing that Sheridan had been under instructions to act on the defensive until Early's reinforcements were sent back to Lee, the Confederate commander made an error in the evaluation of his opponent that, in retrospect, has a certain grim humor. "The events of the last month had satisfied me that the commander opposed to me was without enterprise, and possessed an excessive caution which amounted to timidity," wrote Early after the war (B.&L., IV, 522).

After a reconnaissance in force toward Martinsburg (17–18 Sept.) Early's forces were disposed as follows the night before Sheridan's attack: Gordon had been left at Bunker Hill, 13 miles north of Winchester, with orders to be at Stephenson's Depot at dawn. At the latter place, about five miles north-northeast of Winchester, were the two divisions of Breckinridge (Wharton) and Rodes. Astride the Berryville Pike and on slightly elevated ground between two creeks was the division of Ramseur, about a mile east of the town. The cavalry divisions of Lomax and Fitzhugh Lee covered the left and right, respectively.

Early had 8,500 infantry and 2,900 cavalry with which to oppose Sheridan's 33,600 infantry and 6,400 cavalry (*Lee's Lts.*, III, 577; see also below).

Sheridan planned a concentric advance with his greatly superior force. While Torbert led the cavalry divisions of Merritt and Averell against Early's left along the Martinsburg Pike, Wilson's cavalry division would lead the main body west along the Berryville Pike. The VI and XIX Corps (25,000 total) would then attack along this axis, while Wilson and Crook's command (VIII Corps) would move against the enemy's right (south) flank and cut off their retreat along the Valley Pike.

Early identified the main attack almost immediately and took steps to reinforce Ramseur. The latter withdrew slowly and skillfully until, about 10 o'clock, Gordon and Rodes came up on his left. The Federals had moved out at 2 A.M. and Wright's VI Corps veterans deployed on schedule south of the Berryville Pike. But, in violation of Sheridan's specific instructions, Wright had brought along his entire wagon train and had thereby blocked the advance of Emory's XIX Corps. As a result, the XIX Corps divisions were

slow taking their positions on the right of VI Corps. Gordon and Rodes saw their opportunity and shortly after 11 A.M. attacked in the gap between the Federal corps.

Rodes was killed at the beginning of this attack, and Evans' brigade, on Gordon's left, was hard hit and driven back. Braxton's artillery, without supports, stood its ground and checked the Federal advance. Battle's brigade, of Rodes's division, then arrived on the field and spearheaded a renewed Confederate counterattack that hit between the divisions of Ricketts (3, VI), south of the Berryville Pike, and Grover (2, XIX). Col. J. W. Keifer (2, 3, VI) had noticed this gap developing and, on his own initiative, had moved three of his regiments to the right to fill it. Col. Jacob Sharpe (3, 2, XIX) had ordered his 156th N.Y. to move south to make contact with the VI Corps flank (i.e., Keifer). Battery E, 5th Me. Light Arty. figures prominently in accounts of the action, while the Confederate guns of Braxton continued their close support.

At this critical moment Russell's division (1, VI) hit the shoulder of the Confederate penetration and drove the enemy back. Russell was killed in this action; Sheridan was particularly saddened by this loss, as Russell had at one time been his company commander and was a personal friend.

The slowness of his troops in deploying and Early's counterstroke deprived Sheridan of the results his superior numbers should have made possible. Crook's corps now had to be used to bolster his weakened right, instead of joining Wilson's cavalry on the left to make the decisive envelopment of Early's southern flank.

At the beginning of the battle Breckinridge had moved from Stephenson's Depot due east to oppose the Federal cavalry (brigades of Lowell and Devin) crossing the Opequon on the Charlestown road. After considerable difficulty he had broken contact and joined Early's main body about 2 P.M. He then formed the left of the new defensive line.

By 5 P.M. Sheridan's superior forces had driven Early back to a final position just east of Winchester. While the VI and XIX Corps maintained pressure from the east, Crook advanced with one division (Thoburn) to the right of XIX Corps and with the other (Duval) moved north across Red Bud Run and then came down against Breckinridge from the north. At this time Merritt's and Averell's cavalry divisions were moving down the Martinsburg Pike on Crook's right. On the other flank Wilson had pushed Lomax back to the Millwood Pike.

Early delayed the inevitable order to retreat until late in the day. He then ordered a general withdrawal up the Valley Pike past Strasburg. Here the battle of FISHERS HILL, 22 Sept., took place.

Of 37,711 engaged, Sheridan lost 5,018 (697 killed, 3,983 wounded, 338 missing). Freeman estimates Early's strength at 12,150 (including 1,000 cavalrymen) (*Lee's Lts.*, III, 577 and 581). Among his casualties were 1,818 missing, which Freeman considers to have been captured, whereas Livermore states that some of these were probably killed or wounded. Livermore puts Early's strength at 18,131 present for duty and 16,377 engaged. He estimates Confederate losses as being 3,921 (276 killed, 1,827 wounded, 1,818 missing).

In addition to Rodes, the Confederates had lost A. C. Godwin and Col. George S. Patton, 22d Va., both brigade commanders. Fitz Lee was taken out of action by a bullet wound in the thigh, and Zebulon York lost an arm. On the Federal side D. A. Russell and J. A. Mulligan were killed; McIntosh lost a leg; Upton, Chapman, Duval, and Sharpe were also wounded.

WINDER, Charles Sidney (wine' der). C.S.A. gen. 1829–62. Md. USMA 1850 (22/44); Inf. He served in garrison and on the frontier in Indian fighting before resigning 1 Apr. '61 as Capt. Commissioned Maj. of C.S.A. Arty. 16 Mar. '61, he was at the bombardment of Fort Sumter and commanded the S.C. Arsenal until named Col. 6th S.C. 8 July '61. He arrived too late for 1st Bull Run and was appointed B.G. C.S.A. 7 Mar. '62 to rank from the 1st. In command of the STONEWALL BRIGADE during the Valley campaign, he fought on the Peninsula, and commanded Jackson's old division in the advance against Pope. He was killed by artillery at Cedar Mountain on 9 Aug. Winder had been sick when the battle started but was carried into action in an ambulance. Both Jackson and Lee considered him an officer of great promise.

WINDER, John Henry (wine' der). C.S.A. provost marshal gen. 1800–65. Md. USMA 1820 (11/30); Arty. He served in garrison and on the frontier before resigning 1823. Four years later he returned to the army to be a tactical officer at West Point and fought in the Seminole and Mexican wars (2 brevets in the latter) before resigning 27 Apr. '61 as Maj. He was appointed B.G. C.S.A. 21 June '61 and named Provost Marshal and commander of the Federal prisons, Libby and Belle Isle, in Richmond. In Dec. '61 he was given command of the Dept. of Henrico. From May '62 until Feb. '64 he commanded at Richmond and was also in charge of the prisoners at Danville. In May '64 he was assigned to the 2d Dist. of N.C. and Southern Va., with headquarters at Goldsboro. He was put in charge of Andersonville Prison in June '64 and the next month of all prisoners in Ala.

and Ga. On 21 Nov. '64 he was named Comsy. Gen. of all prisoners east of the Mississippi. He died of fatigue and strain 7 Feb. '65. Repeatedly criticized for his strictness and even cruelty to prisoners, he was defended not only by Davis, Cooper, and Seddon, but also by many of his Northern charges, while other prisoners and Southerners reviled him as a brute and a monster. Eliot says that had he lived, he rather than WIRZ would have been hanged by the Union.

WINKLER, Frederick Charles. Union officer. Germany. Capt. 26th Wis. 17 Sept. '62; Maj. 1 Dec. '63; Lt. Col. 8 July '64; Bvt. B.G. USV 15 June '65 (war service). While a Capt. he commanded the regiment 29 Nov. '63 on the march to Knoxville for the relief of Burnside. W.I.A. Gettysburg 1 July '63 at Cemetery Hill. Received bullet through hat at Kenesaw Mountain but unhurt.

WINSLOW, Bradley. Union officer. N.Y. Capt. 35th N.Y. 11 June '61; Lt. Col. 31 Aug. '61; resigned 31 Oct. '62; Col. 186th N.Y. 22 Sept. '64; Bvt. B.G. USV 2 Apr. '65 (Petersburg assault).

WINSLOW, Edward Francis. Union officer. 1837–1914. Me. Capt. 4th Iowa Cav. 23 Nov. '61; Maj. 6 Feb. '63; Col. 4 July '63; Bvt. B.G. USV 12 Dec. '64. In Apr. '63 his was the only cavalry regiment in Grant's army. W.I.A. 12 May '63 at 14-Mile Creek (Miss.). Commanded cavalry brigade, 3d Div., XV Corps; cavalry brigade, XVII; 2, 1st Cav. Div., XVI; 2, Cav. Div. Western Tenn., Army of Tenn.; 2, 2d Div. Western Tenn., cavalry corps, Army of Tenn.; 1, 4, Cav., Mil. Dist. Miss. He achieved postwar prominence as a railroad builder and executive.

WINSLOW, Robert Emmet. Union officer. Pa. Capt. 68th Pa. 4 Aug. '62;

Maj. 10 Jan. '63; Lt. Col. 13 Nov. '63; Bvt. B.G. USV (war service).

WINTHROP, Frederick. Union officer. N.Y. Enlisting in the N.Y. State Militia 20 Apr. '61, he was commissioned Capt. 12th US Inf. 26 Oct. of that year. He fought at Yorktown, Gaines's Mill, Malvern Hill, 2d Bull Run, Fredericksburg, and Gettysburg, before being named Acting Asst. Adj. Gen. of the 1st R.A. Brig. In this position he fought at Rappahannock Station, the Mine Run operations, and the Wilderness. Commanding a regiment, he led the troops at Spotsylvania and North Anna before serving as Acting Asst. Adj. Gen. of a division at Bethesda Church. He was promoted Col. 5th N.Y. in Aug. '64 and fought in the Petersburg siege and the Appomattox campaign. Killed at Five Forks 1 Apr. '65, he was breveted B.G. USV 1 Aug. '64 and Maj. Gen. USV for Five Forks.

WIRE ENTANGLEMENTS. One of the tactical innovations of the Civil War, apparently first used by the Federals at FORT SANDERS (Knoxville), 29 Nov. '63. Alexander says the obstacle "threw down the leading files and caused a little delay" but was then removed "with very little loss" (p. 488). The best publicized use of wire entanglements took place six months later at DREWRY'S BLUFF, Va. Here, as at Fort Sanders, it consisted of smooth wire stretched between stumps and trees, but this time the attacking Confederates were trapped and "slaughtered like partridges" in what they called "a devilish contrivance which none but a Yankee could devise." Both "Baldy" Smith and Ben Butler claimed credit for the idea (B.&L., IV, 211–12).

WIRZ, Henry. C.S.A. officer. Switzerland. He practiced medicine in La. and was a clerk in Libby Prison early in the war. Wounded at Seven Pines, upon recovery he was promoted Capt., and sent by Davis, at Winder's instigation, to Europe. Promoted Maj., he was a Confederate agent and dispatch bearer in the summer of 1863. He returned in Jan. '64 to become commandant of ANDERSONVILLE for the rest of the war. In Nov. '65 he was executed by the Federal government for his part in permitting Andersonville's intolerable conditions—the "sole execution because of the war" (Lonn, 275).

2d WISCONSIN (Iron Brigade). Colonels: S. P. Coon, Edgar O'Connor (USMA; K.I.A.), Lucius Fairchild (R.A.), John Mansfield.

Battles: Blackburn's Ford, 1st Bull Run, Catlett's Station, Gainesville (Groveton), Manassas, South Mountain, Antietam, Fredericksburg, Gettysburg, Wilderness, Spotsylvania (10 and 21 May '64), North Anna, Petersburg, Hatcher's Run. Present also at Cedar Mountain, Fitz Hugh's Crossing, Chancellorsville, Mine Run, Bethesda Church, Cold Harbor, Weldon R.R.

As part of the famous "Iron Brigade of the West" this regiment had the highest percentage of losses in the Union Army (19.7 per cent killed). Of a total enrollment of 1,203, the regiment lost 753 killed and wounded, 132 missing or captured (of which 17 died in prison), and 60 non-battle casualties (disease, accident). Organized at Madison, mustered in 11 June '61, and leaving the state 20 June '61, it fought in W. T. Sherman's brigade at 1st Bull Run. In August it joined John Gibbon's "Black Hat Brigade" (later called the Iron Brigade of the West). At Groveton the 2d Wis. as part of the Iron Brigade fought a costly drawn battle with the Stonewall Brigade. Col. O'Connor was killed, and the regiment lost 298 men (86 killed). In subsequent fighting with the Iron Brigade the regimental strength after Spotsylvania had been reduced to

less than 100 men present for duty. On 11 June '64 it was ordered home for muster out, after recruits and re-enlisted men were consolidated into a two-company battalion which served as Provost Guard at headquarters, 4th Div., V Corps, until Sept. On 30 Nov. these two companies (A and B) were transferred to the 6th Wis., where they were redesignated G and H.

7th WISCONSIN (Iron Brigade). Colonels: Joseph Van Dor, William W. Robinson, Mark Finnicum, and Hollon Richardson.

Battles: Gainesville, Manassas, South Mountain, Antietam, Fredericksburg, Fitz Hugh's Crossing, Gettysburg, Wilderness, Spotsylvania (9, 10, and 12 May '64), North Anna, Bethesda Church, Petersburg (assault of 18 June and subsequent siege), Hatcher's Run, Gravelly Run, Five Forks. Present also at Cedar Mountain, Catlett's Station, Rappahannock, Chancellorsville, Haymarket, Mine Run, Totopotomoy, Cold Harbor, Weldon R.R., Boydton Road, Appomattox.

Only two other Union regiments had more casualties than the 7th Wis. Part of the famous Iron Brigade, its hardest fights were 2d Bull Run, Antietam campaign, Gettysburg, Wilderness, Spotsylvania, Petersburg, and Gravelly Run.

26th WISCONSIN. Colonels: William H. Jacobs and Fred C. Winkler (Bvt. B.G.)

Battles: Chancellorsville, Gettysburg, Resaca, New Hope Church, Pine Mountain, Culp's Farm, Kenesaw Mountain, Peach Tree Creek, siege of Atlanta, Averasboro, Bentonville. Also present at Lookout Mountain, Missionary Ridge, Rocky Face Ridge, March to the Sea, siege of Savannah.

A German regiment that served initially in the XI ("German") Corps in the East, and subsequently with the XX Corps in the West, organized at Milwaukee, mustered in 17 Sept. '62, it left for Washington 6 Oct. At Chancellorsville (in Kryzanowski's [2d] brigade, Schurz's [3d] division, XI Corps) the regiment lost 198 men in a gallant but unsuccessful effort to halt Jackson's attack down the Turnpike. In a similar situation at Gettysburg the regiment lost 217 men while covering the retreat of the corps toward Cemetery Hill on the first day of the battle. Two divisions of XI Corps were ordered to Tenn. in Sept. '63, and in Apr. '64 merged into Hooker's XX Corps. The regiment became part of the 3d Brig., 3d (Ward's) Div. It was commended for its action at Peach Tree Creek, where it captured the colors of the 33d Miss.

36th WISCONSIN (1st Brigade, 2d Division, II Corps)

Colonels: Frank A. Haskell (K.I.A.), John A. Savage, Jr. (K.I.A.), Harvey M. Brown, Clement E. Warner.

Battles: North Anna, Totopotomoy, Bethesda Church, Cold Harbor (3 June '64 and trenches), Chickahominy, Petersburg assault and siege, Jerusalem Road, Deep Bottom, Reams's Station, Boydton Road, Farmville. Present at Strawberry Plains, Hatcher's Run, Sayler's Creek, High Bridge, Appomattox.

The regiment was organized at Madison, mustered in 23 Mar. '64, and left the state 10 May. Its commander was Col. Frank A. Haskell, Adj. of the 6th Wis., who is now famous for his classic account of the battle of Gettysburg. The regiment was assigned to the 1st Brig. (Webb's), 2d Div. (Gibbon's), II Corps. At Bethesda Church four companies (B, E, F, and G) lost 128 out of 240 men. At Cold Harbor Haskell took command of the brigade and was killed a few minutes later. Col. Savage, the next regimental commander, was killed two weeks later in the 18 June assault on Petersburg. Reduced by battle casualties and disease, regimental strength at Reams's Station was 11 officers and 175

men; of this number 134 were captured Although 35 other Wis. regiments had come into the war ahead of it, only six of these had more men killed. On the basis of percentage of enrollment, the 36th Wis. ranks number 17 in the list of Federal regiments having the most killed in action.

37th WISCONSIN

Colonels: Samuel Harriman (Bvt. B.G.), Anson O. Doolittle (R.A.), John Green.

Battles: Petersburg assaults of 17 and 18 June '64, Petersburg Mine (30 July), Weldon R.R., Poplar Spring Church, Boydton Road, trenches and final assault of Petersburg. Also at Pegram Farm, Hatcher's Run, Fort Stedman.

This regiment, raised in 1864, was intimately identified with the major actions around Petersburg, where it saw all of its combat service. They joined the Army of the Potomac in June and was assigned to the 1st (Hartranft's) brig., 3d (Willcox') Div., IX Corps. In the 17–18 June assaults on Petersburg the green regiment was repulsed only after it had sustained 157 casualties. In the Battle of the Crater the regiment played a prominent part and lost 145 out of the 250 men. Soon after this action the 37th Wis. was transferred to the 1st Brig. of the 1st Div. In the final assault of Petersburg three companies of the regiment were the first troops to enter Fort Mahone. After taking part in the Grand Review it was mustered out 26 July '65. Although this regiment, like the 36th Wis., entered the war in the last year, it ranks 42d out of 2,047 Federal regiments in terms of its percentage of total enrollment killed in battle.

WISE, George D. Union officer. N.Y. Appt.-Mo. Capt. Asst. Q.M. Vols. 28 Sept. '61; Col. Q.M. Assigned 2 Aug. '64–1 Jan. '67; Bvt. B.G. USV (war service). Died 1881.

WISE, Henry Alexander. C.S.A. gen. 1806–76. Va. A graduate of Washington College (Pa.), he studied law under St. George Tucker and practiced first in Memphis and then on his native Eastern Shore. He sat in Congress as a Jacksonian Democrat and then broke with Jackson. For a time a close friend and advisor of Tyler, he soon alienated him and was then sent to Brazil as US Minister 1844–47. He returned to become a power in the Democratic party and served as Va. Gov. (1856–60) during John Brown's raid. He was appointed B.G. C.S.A. 5 June '61 and raised a legion in western Va., serving in that area and at Roanoke Island, where his son was mortally wounded. For the remainder of the war he was in the coastal defenses of S.C., served in the battles around Richmond and Petersburg and on the retreat to Appomattox. Lee promoted him Maj. Gen. at Sayler's Creek 6 Apr. '65, according to D.A.B., although Freeman, Wright, and Wood make no mention of this higher rank. After the war he practiced law in Richmond with a son. A brother-in-law of Meade, he came forward to meet him at Appomattox after the surrender, and Lyman describes him as being "an old man, with an angular, much-wrinkled face, and long, thick, white hair . . . [wearing] a pair of silver spectacles and a high felt hat . . . while the legs kept up their claim of eccentricity by encasing themselves in grey blankets, tied somewhat in a bandit fashion." D.A.B. further characterized him as "lacking in moderation and judgment . . . one of the last great individualists in Virginia history."

WISEWELL, Moses N. Union officer. Vt. Col. 28th N.J. 22 Sept. '62; mustered out 6 July '63; Col. Vet. Res. Corps 25 Sept. '63; Bvt. B.G. USV (Fredericksburg). Died 1888.

WISTAR, Isaac Jones. Union gen. 1827–? Pa. A lawyer with interests in a canal and several coal companies, he was named Lt. Col. 71st Pa. (Baker's "California Regiment") 28 June '61 and Col. 11 Nov. '61 after Balls Bluff. He led his regiment at Fair Oaks, Savage's Station, Charles City Crossroads, and Malvern Hill. They were in the rear guard in the retreat after 2d Bull Run and fought at Antietam where he was wounded. Named B.G. USV 29 Nov. '62, he commanded Res. Brig., Div. at Suffolk, VII, Va. (13 May–June '63); Indpt. Brig., VII, Va. (June–July, '63); US Forces at Yorktown, Va., and N.C. (1 Aug.–22 Dec. '63; 22 Jan.–16 Feb. '64; 8 Mar.–28 Apr. '64); 2, 2, XVIII, Va. and N.C. (7–18 May '64) and 2d Div., XVIII, Va. and N.C. (22 Apr.–7 May '64). He resigned 15 Sept. '64.

WISTER, Langhorne. Union officer. Pa. Capt. 13th Pa. Res. 31 May '61; Col. 150th Pa. 4 Sept. '62; Bvt. B.G. USV (Gettysburg, Fredericksburg, Chancellorsville, war service); resigned 22 Feb. '64. Commanded 1, 3, I (Potomac). Died 1891.

WITCHER, John Sheshol. Union officer. Va. 1st Lt. 3d W. Va. Cav. 13 Dec. '62; Capt. 8 Sept. '63; Maj. 23 May '64; Lt. Col. 6 May '65; Bvt. B.G. USV. Brevets for Shenandoah campaign of 1864 (2), Richmond and Petersburg in 1865 (2), Ford's Station (Va.). In R.A. as Maj. Paymaster in 1880 and retired in 1899.

WITHERS, Jones Mitchell. C.S.A. gen. 1814–90. Ala. USMA 1835 (44/56); Dragoons. After serving briefly on the frontier, he resigned six months after graduation and served on Patterson's and Jessup's staffs during the Creek War the next year. A lawyer and commission merchant, he fought in the R.A. during the Mexican War and was a state legislator and mayor of Mobile in the prewar era. Commissioned Col. 3d Ala..

he went to Norfolk early in 1861 and was given a brigade. In May of that year he was given command of the Eastern Div. of the Dept. of Norfolk and was appointed B.G. C.S.A. 10 July '61. He commanded the defenses of Mobile, led a division at Shiloh, and, as Maj. Gen. 16 Aug. '62 to rank from 6 Apr., commanded Polk's reserve division. He fought at Stones River, in the Tullahoma campaign, and was relieved 13 Aug. '63 by Hindman. He took over the Dist. of Montgomery in early 1864, and by July was commanding the reserves of the state. After the war he was again mayor and a newspaper editor.

WITHINGTON, William Herbert. Union officer. Mass. Capt. 1st Mich. 1 May '61; mustered out 31 Jan. '62; Col. 17th Mich. 11 Aug. '62; Bvt. B.G. USV (South Mountain); resigned 21 Mar. '63. Captured at 1st Bull Run 21 July '61. Medal of Honor 7 Jan. '95 for 1st Bull Run. Commanded 1, 1, IX (Potomac).

WOFFORD, William Tatum. C.S.A. gen. 1823–84. Ga. A lawyer, he fought in the Mexican War, ran his plantation, published a newspaper, and sat in the state legislature as a firm anti-secessionist. But when his state left the Union he volunteered as Col. 18th Ga., serving first in N.C. and then as commander of the only non-Tex. regiment of HOOD'S TEXAS BRIGADE. After the Seven Days' Battles he led Hood's brigade at 2d Bull Run, South Mountain, and Antietam, and was appointed B.G. C.S.A. 23 Apr. '63 to rank from 17 Jan. At Chancellorsville and Gettysburg he succeeded to command of Cobb's brigade and went with Longstreet to the West. He fought under Kershaw around Richmond and Petersburg and the Shenandoah and was wounded at the Wilderness and Spotsylvania. On 20 Jan. '65 he was put in command of the Dept. of Northern Ga. and surrendered at Resaca 2 May.

Elected to Congress in 1865, he was refused a seat by the radical Republicans. He was then active in railroading and public education.

WOLFE, Edward H. Union officer. Ind. Maj. 52d Ind. 25 Oct. '61; Lt. Col. 26 Apr. '62; Col. 19 Sept. '62; Bvt. B.G. USV (Nashville); mustered out 31 Jan. '65. Commanded 3, 3, XVI (Tenn.); 3, 2d Det. Army Tenn. (Cumberland).

"WOMAN ORDER" of Butler. After continued provocation, Ben Butler on 15 May '62 issued General Order No. 28, subsequently known as the Woman Order. "As the officers and soldiers of the United States have been subjected to repeated insults from the women (calling themselves ladies) of New Orleans, in return for the most scrupulous non-interference and courtesy on our part, it is ordered, that hereafter, when any female shall, by word, gesture, or movement, insult or show contempt for any officer or soldier of the United States, she shall be regarded and held liable to be treated as a woman of the town plying her avocation." When Mayor John T. Monroe protested on the part of New Orleans's citizens, Butler put him under arrest. Butler then offered this amplification: "There can be, there has been, no room for misunderstanding of General Order No. 28. No lady will take any notice of a strange gentleman in such a form as to attract attention. Common women do. Therefore, whatever woman, lady, or mistress, gentle or simple, who by gesture, look, or word insults, shows contempt for, thus attracting to herself the notice of my officers or soldiers, will be deemed to act as becomes the vocation of a common woman, and will be liable to be treated accordingly. I shall not, as I have not abated, a single word of that order; it was well considered. If obeyed, it will protect the true and modest woman from all possible insult: the others will take care of themselves."

Butler's order was greeted by disapproval in the North and abroad as well as locally. In the British House of Commons Prime Minister Palmerston said, "An Englishman must blush to think that such an act has been committed by one belonging to the Anglo-Saxon race." The London *Times* demanded intervention by England to stop this "tyranny of victor over vanquished." Although the US government did not revoke Butler's order it was one of the instances of bad judgment that led to his removal from New Orleans on 16 Dec. '62 (Holzman, *Stormy Ben Butler*, 84–88).

WOOD, James, Jr. Union officer. N.Y. Commissioned Col. 136th N.Y. 17 Sept. '62, he was breveted B.G. USV 8 Mar. '65 and Maj. Gen. USV for war service and mustered out in June of that year.

WOOD, Oliver. Union officer. N.Y. 1st Lt. 22d Ohio 17 Apr. '61; mustered out 19 Aug. '61; Capt. 22d Ohio 1 Nov. '61; Maj. 10 May '62; Col. 16 Sept. '62; mustered out 18 Nov. '64; Col. 4th US Vet. Vols. 29 Dec. '64; Bvt. B.G. USV (war service). Commanded 4, Dist. Jackson, Left Wing, XVI (Tenn.); 2, 2 Ark. Exp., XVI (Tenn.); 2, 2, VII (Ark.).

WOOD, Robert Crooke, Union officer. R.I. Joining the R.A. as Asst. Surgeon in 1825, he served on the frontier and in New Orleans before the war. Promoted Col. Asst. Surgeon Gen. 14 June '62, he was in charge of Medical Affairs of the Dept. of the West. In Oct. '63 he was sent to Louisville for the rest of the war. In 1869 he died on active duty with the rank of Bvt. B.G. USA (war service). Robert Crooke Wood, Jr., resigned his R.A. commission in 1858 and fought with the Confederacy as Lt. Col. Miss. Cav. (Heitman).

WOOD, Sterling Alexander Martin. C.S.A. gen. 1823–? Ala. A lawyer and legislator, he was commissioned Col. 7th Ala. and served in Pensacola until Feb. '62. Appointed B.G. C.S.A. 7 Jan. '62, he went to Bowling Green and commanded his brigade at Shiloh (injured when thrown from his horse), Perryville (wounded), Stones River, Liberty Gap, and Chickamauga. He resigned 17 Oct. '63 and returned to his law practice. See also STERLING, A. M. W.

WOOD, Thomas John. Union gen. 1823–1906. Ky. USMA 1845 (5/41); Topo. Engrs.-Dragoons. Serving on Taylor's staff during the Mexican War (1 brevet), he then was on the frontier, in Indian fighting, in Kans. during the border disturbances, and on the Utah Expedition. As Maj. 1st US Cav. (16 Mar. '61) and Lt. Col. 9 May '61, he was mustering troops in Ind. until 11 Oct. '61, when he was named B.G. USV. He led 2d Brig., McCook's Command, Army Ohio (Oct.–Nov. '61) and 5th Brig., 2d Div., Army Ohio (Nov. '61–8 Jan. '62). At Shiloh and on the advance upon the siege of Corinth he commanded the 6th Div., Army Ohio (11 Feb.–29 Sept. '62) and commanded that division in the II Corps (Sept.–Nov. '62) at Perryville. At Stones River, where he was wounded, he led 1st Div., Left Wing, XIV, Cumberland (5 Nov.– 31 Dec. '62) and then led the 1st Div., XXI, Cumberland (10 May–9 Oct. '63) in the Tullahoma campaign and at Chickamauga. He commanded the XXI Corps 19 Feb.–19 Mar. '63. During the Atlanta campaign he led 3d Div., IV Corps, Cumberland (10 Oct. '63–8 Jan. '64) at Missionary Ridge and Knoxville; (12 Feb.–2 Sept. '64) at Dalton, Resaca, Adairsville, New Hope Church, Pickett's Mill, Pine and Kenesaw Mountains, Chattahoochee, Peach Tree Creek, Atlanta siege, Jonesboro, Lovejoy, where he was severely wounded; and later (6 Sept.–2 Dec. '64) at Franklin; and later (31 Ján.–7 Feb. '65 and 20 Mar.–1 Aug. '65). At Nashville he commanded the IV Corps (1 Dec. '64–31 Jan. '65). Breveted for Chickamauga (B.G. USA) and Nashville (Maj. Gen. USA), he was retired as a Maj. Gen. USA in 1868 and as B.G. USA in 1875. The last survivor of his West Point class and the first roommate of U. S. Grant, he was active in veterans' organizations and a member of the USMA Board of Visitors.

WOOD, William D. Union officer. Ohio. Col. 11th Mo. Cav. 14 Dec. '63; Bvt. B.G. USV (war service); resigned 8 Apr. '65. Died 1867.

WOODALL, Daniel. Union officer. Del. Capt. 1st Del. 28 Sept. '61; Maj. 30 Dec. '62; Lt. Col. 5 Nov. '63; Col. 23 Dec. '64; Bvt. B.G. USV 15 June '65 (war service). Commanded 3, 2, II (Potomac). Died 1880.

WOODBURY, Daniel Phineas. Union gen. 1812–64. N.H. USMA 1836 (6/39); Arty.-Engrs. Serving in the construction of roads and fortifications on the East Coast and on the frontier, he was Capt. (since 1853) when he helped build the Washington defenses and made the reconnaissance on which McDowell's orders for 1st Bull Run were based. He fought at Bull Run and was promoted Maj. 6 Aug. '61 and Lt. Col. Add. A.D.C. 28 Sept. '61. As B.G. USV 19 Mar. '62, he commanded the engineer brigade that constructed the Yorktown siege works and the road network over the Chickahominy and White Oak Swamp. His command also built the ponton bridges over the Rappahannock at Fredericksburg. In the Dept. of the Gulf he was commanding the Dist. of Key West and the Tortugas when he died, 15 Aug. '64, of yellow fever. He was breveted for the Peninsular campaigns, Fredericksburg (B.G. USA 13 Dec. '62), and war service (Maj. Gen. USA 15 Aug. '64).

WOODFORD, Stewart Lyndon. Union officer. 1835–1913. Lt. Col. 127th N.Y. 8 Sept. '62; Col. 103d US Col. Inf. 6 Mar. '65; Bvt. B.G. USV 12 May '65 (war service); Mil. Gov. of Charleston. A Republican, he was Lt. Gov. of N.Y. 1867–69, Congressman 1873–74, and Minister to Spain (1897).

WOODHULL, Maxwell Van Zandt. Union officer. D.C. Appt.-N.Y. Capt. A.D.C. Vols. 11 Mar. '63; Maj. Asst. Adj. Gen. Vols. 30 June '64; Lt. Col. Asst. Adj. Gen. Assigned (XV Corps) 17 Feb.–1 Aug. '65; Bvt. B.G. USV (war service).

WOODRUFF, Israel Carle. Union officer. c. 1815–78. N.J. USMA 1836 (30/48); Arty.-Engrs. He taught engineering at West Point and served on engineering duty in the South and West. Promoted Maj. 3 Aug. '61, he was Asst. to the Chief Engr. in Washington until 1866. Named Lt. Col. 15 Aug. '64 and Bvt. B.G. USA for war service. He died on active duty as Col.

WOODS, Charles Robert. Union gen. 1827–85. Ohio. USMA 1852 (20/43); Inf. After serving on the frontier and in garrison, he commanded (as Capt. 9th US Inf. 1 Apr. '61) the futile effort of the *Star of the West* to relieve Fort Sumter. As Col. 76th Ohio 13 Oct. '61 he commanded the land forces in the expedition down the Mississippi, fighting at Millikens Bend, Chickasaw Bluffs, and Arkansas Post. He was in the Vicksburg siege and assaults and was promoted B.G. USV 4 Aug. '63. In the Army of the Tenn. he commanded 1, 1, XV (13 Sept.–14 Dec. '63 at Chattanooga and Ringgold; 6 Feb.–15 July and 19-22 Aug. '64); 2, 1, XV (22 May–30 July at Vicksburg and 24 Aug.–1 Sept. '63); 1st Div., XV (13 Jan.–6 Feb., 6 Feb.–15 July '64 at Resaca, New

Hope Church, Kenesaw Mountain, and the Chattahoochee; 23 Sept. '64–2 Apr. '65 on the March to the Sea, Griswoldville, and Bentonville; and 5 Apr.–1 Aug. '65); 3d Div., XVII (23 Aug.–22 Sept. '64 at Jonesboro). Breveted for Vicksburg, Chattanooga, Atlanta (B.G. USA), Griswoldville (Maj. Gen. USV 22 Nov. '64), and Bentonville (Maj. Gen. USA), he continued in the R.A., serving in the West and in Indian fighting. He retired in 1874 as Col. 2d US Inf. Brother of William Burnam Woods.

WOODS, William Burnam. Union gen. 1824–87. Ohio. After Yale he practiced law, was the leader of the Ohio Democrats, and sat in the state legislature. Named Lt. Col. 76th Ohio 6 Feb. '62, he fought at Fort Donelson and Shiloh, Arkansas Post, where he was slightly wounded, Chickasaw Bluffs, Vicksburg, and Jackson, before being promoted Col. 10 Sept. '63. He was also at Resaca, Dallas, Atlanta, Jonesboro, Lovejoy, and Bentonville, and was promoted B.G. USV 31 May '65 after having commanded 1, 1, XV, Tenn. (21 Jan.–16 June '65). Breveted for Atlanta and Savannah campaigns (B.G. USV 12 Jan. '65) and war service (Maj. Gen. USV), he was mustered out in 1866 and remained in Ala. An ardent Republican and active in Reconstruction, he was a judge and Associate Justice of the US Supreme Court as a representative of the South. Brother of Charles Robert Woods.

"WOODSTOCK RACES." See Tom's Brook, Va., 9 Oct. '64.

WOODWARD, Orpheus Saeger. Union officer. Pa. Capt. 83d Pa. 13 Sept. '61; Col. 28 Mar. '64; Bvt. B.G. USV (war service); mustered out 20 Sept. '64.

WOOL, John Ellis. Union gen. 1789–1869. N.Y. Septuagenarian veteran of the War of 1812, Wool had raised a company at Troy, N.Y., and distin-

guished himself at Queenstown Heights (1812) and Plattsburg (1814). He remained in the army and became a Brig. Gen. in 1841. In the Mexican War he again distinguished himself, leading a body of men 900 miles from San Antonio, Tex., to join Gen. Zachary Taylor for the battle of Buena Vista. He commanded the Dept. of the East when the Civil War broke out. In Aug. '61 he was transferred to Va. and succeeded in keeping Fort Monroe from falling into Confederate hands. In May '62 he occupied Norfolk and Portsmouth, Va., after the Confederate evacuation, and was promoted to the full rank of Maj. Gen., USA, 16 May. This made him the fourth ranking general in the Federal service (junior only to McClellan, Frémont, and Halleck). In June he was given command of the Middle Dept. and headed the VIII Corps when it was created the next month. In Jan. '63 he commanded the re-created Dept. of the East, and remained until retired in July.

WOOLLEY, John. Union officer. N.Y. 1st Lt. Adj. 2d Ind. Cav. 3 Oct. '61; Maj. 5th Ind. Cav. 27 Mar. '63; Lt. Col. 8 Mar. '64; Bvt. B.G. USV (war service). Died 1873.

WORDEN, John Lorimer. Union naval officer. 1818–97. N.Y. Entering the navy as midshipman in 1835, he served at sea and in the naval observatory until the Civil War. Captured after he had delivered special orders to Fort Pickens and attempted to return North by train, he was held for seven months and released in Oct. '61. He then supervised John Ericsson's *Monitor* and was appointed to command, fighting the *Merrimac* in Mar. '62. Worden was blinded by an explosion and Lt. Greene, the second-in-command, took over. He was given a vote of thanks by Congress twice and promoted Comdr. 12 July '62 and Capt. 3 Feb. '63, commanding the *Montauk* in the South Atlantic blockading squadron Jan.–June '63. For the remainder of the war he was on duty with the ironclads in N.Y. Continuing in the navy, he retired in 1886 as Rear Adm.

WORMER, Grover Salman. Union officer. N.Y. Capt. Stanton Guards Mich. Vols. 1 May '62; mustered out 25 Sept. '62; Lt. Col. 8th Mich. Cav. 3 Oct. '62; Col. 30th Mich. 21 Nov. '64; Bvt. B.G. USV (war service).

WRIGHT, Ambrose Ransom. C.S.A. gen. 1826–72. Ga. A lawyer and Democratic politician, he had held a neutral course until Lincoln was elected president, coming out then for secession. He was sent as a state commissioner to persuade Md. to secede, and was named Col. 3d Ga. 8 May '61. Serving on Roanoke Island at first, he was at South Mills in Apr. '62 and named B.G. C.S.A. 3 June '62. He led his brigade in A. P. Hill's command at Malvern Hill, 2d Bull Run, and Antietam (wounded). His A.D.C. son lost a leg at Bull Run. He led his brigade at Fredericksburg, Chancellorsville, Gettysburg, and the Wilderness. Promoted Maj. Gen. 26 Nov. '64, he was sent to Ga. A newspaper editor after the war, he died soon after being elected to Congress.

WRIGHT, Edward. Union officer. Ohio. Maj. 24th Iowa 17 Sept. '62; Lt. Col. 19 Nov. '64; Bvt. B.G. USV (war service).

WRIGHT, Elias. Union officer. N.Y. 2d Lt. 4th N.J. 17 Aug. '61; 1st Lt. 3 Jan. '62; Capt. 29 Dec. '62; Maj. 1st US Col. Inf. 25 June '63; Lt. Col. 29 Apr. '64; Col. 10th US Col. Inf. 15 Aug. '64; Bvt. B.G. USV 15 Jan. '65. Commanded in Va. and N.C.: 2, 3, X; 1, 3, XVIII; 2, 3, XVIII; in Va.: 3, 1, XXV; 3, 3, XXV; in N.C.: 3, Paine's division, Terry's Prov. Corps. Died 1901.

WRIGHT, George. Union gen. 1803–65. Vt. USMA 1822 (24/40); Inf. Serving on frontier duty, Fla. War (1 bvt.) and the Mexican War (2 brevets and 1 wound), he was then in Indian fighting

in the Pacific Northwest and commander of the Dept. of Ore. (5 July '60–13 Sept. '61) as Col. 9th US Inf. Named B.G. USV 28 Sept. '61, he commanded the Dept. of Pacific (20 Oct. '61–1 July '64) and the Dist. of Calif. (1 July '64–27 July '65). Breveted for war service (B.G. USA 19 Dec. '64), he was drowned 30 July '65 in a shipwreck on his way to assume command of the Dept. of the Columbia.

WRIGHT, Horatio Gouverneur. Union gen. 1820–99. Conn. USMA 1841 (2/52); Engr. He taught French and engineering at West Point and supervised harbor and fortification improvements before being named Maj. 6 Aug. '61 (Capt. since 1855). The previous April he had been Chief Engr. on the expedition to destroy the Norfolk Navy Yard, was captured, and shortly released. He was volunteer A.D.C. to Heintzelman when he crossed the Potomac and took possession of Arlington Heights opposite Washington 25 May–15 July '61 and was his Chief Engr. at 1st Bull Run. He held the same post in the organization of the Port Royal expedition and, as B.G. USV 14 Sept. '61, commanded 3d Brig., S.C. expedition (Oct. '61–Apr. '62) at Hilton Head. Leading 1st Div., South (Apr.–July '62) during fighting in Fla. and Secessionville, he was promoted Maj. Gen. USV 18 July '62 and then commanded Dist. W. Ky. (17 Nov. '62–4 Apr. '63) and the Dept. of the Ohio (25 Aug. '62–25 Mar. '63). His appointment was revoked 24 Mar. '63, but he was reappointed B.G. USV the same day. He led 1st Div., VI, Potomac (23 May–16 Dec. '63) at Gettysburg, Rappahannock Station, and during the Mine Run operations, and then served on a board to revise the seacoast fortifications until 23 Apr. '64, when he took over the VI Corps. He led it at the Wilderness, Spotsylvania (wounded), North Anna,

Totopotomoy, Cold Harbor, the Petersburg siege and assaults, and at Snickers Gap (until 9 May '64), when he was named Maj. Gen. USV 12 May '64. Then leading the VI Corps (6 Aug.–16 Oct. and 19 Oct.–6 Dec. '64) at Charlestown, Fishers Hill, and Opequon, he commanded the Dept. of the Shenandoah 16–19 Oct. He then led the VI Corps in the final Petersburg assaults, Sayler's Creek, at Appomattox, and in S.C., opposing Johnston. Continuing in the R.A., he was breveted for Rappahannock Station, Spotsylvania, Cold Harbor (B.G. USA), and Petersburg (Maj. Gen. USA). He retired in 1884 as B.G. Chief of Engrs. (since 1879).

WRIGHT, John Gibson. Union officer. N.Y. Pvt. Co. C 7th N.Y. State Mil. 26 Apr. '61; mustered out 3 June '61; Capt. 51st N.Y. 8 Oct. '61; Maj. 14 Mar. '63; Lt. Col. 20 Apr. '65; Col. 18 May '65; Bvt. B.G. USV (war service). Commanded 3, 1, XVII (Tenn.). Died 1890.

WRIGHT, Joseph Jefferson Burr. Union officer. Pa. Joining the R.A. in 1833 as Asst. Surgeon, he served on the frontier, in the Seminole and Mexican wars, at West Point, and on the Utah Expedition before becoming Medical Director of the Dept. of the Ohio in 1861. He took the same post with the Dept. of the Mo. until 1862, when he was stationed at Carlisle Barracks for the remainder of the war. Retired in 1876 as Col. Surgeon and Bvt. B.G. USA, he died two years later.

WRIGHT, Marcus Joseph. C.S.A. gen. 1831–1922. Tenn. A lawyer and court clerk, he was active in the state militia and was commissioned Lt. Col. 154th Tenn. in Apr. '61 and led his regiment at Belmont. The next year he was named Mil. Gov. of Columbus (Ky.) and led his regiment at Shiloh (wounded). He commanded a brigade at Chickamauga and the battles around Chattanooga after having been appointed B.G. C.S.A. 20 Dec. '62 to rank from the 13th. In the defense of Atlanta he commanded the post of Macon and in Dec. '64 organized the forces in western Tenn. Early in 1865 he was put in command of the Dist. of Northern Miss. and Western Tenn., and surrendered at Grenada, Miss. Returning to his law practice, he became agent for the collection of C.S.A. archives (1878–1917) and was one of the main compilers of the *Official Records.* He wrote many articles in historical magazines as well as *Tennessee in the War, 1861–65* (1908), and *General Officers of the Confederate Army* (1911). See authorities cited, at end of book, for evaluation of latter work.

WRIGHT, Thomas Forster. Union officer. Mo. 1st Lt. Regt. Q.M. 2d Calif. Cav. 2 Oct. '61; resigned 31 Jan. '63; Maj. 6th Calif. 1 Feb. '63; Maj. 2d Calif. 3 Oct. '64; Lt. Col. 23 Nov. '64; Col. 6 Jan. '65; Bvt. B.G. USV (war service). In R.A. until K.I.A. at Lava Beds during Modoc wars 1873 while 1st Lt.

Y

YANCEY, William Lowndes. Confederate politician. 1814–63. Ga. A lawyer in Ala., he sat in Congress where he became a leader of the Southern "FIRE-EATERS" and advocated secession. He was in the Confederate Senate until his death.

YATES, Henry Jr. Union officer. Ky. Capt. 106th Ill. 17 Sept. '62; Lt. Col. 1 July '63; Col. 28 Apr. '64; Bvt. B.G. USV (war service); resigned 8 Sept. '64. Commanded 3, 2, VII (Ark.). Died 1871.

YATES, Richard. 1818–73. Gov. of Ill. Ky. A lawyer, he served in the legislature and Congress as a Whig before joining the new Republican party. He was elected Gov. of Ill. in 1860, serving throughout the war, and was active not only in raising troops but also in suppressing the Southern sympathizers in the state. Later he was in the Senate.

YAZOO EXPEDITION. A 32,000 man force was organized in Dec. '62 for the expedition that ended in Sherman's failure at CHICKASAW BLUFFS, Miss. (Vicksburg), 27–29 Dec. '62. "Yazoo Expedition" is the term applied to the organization Sherman commanded. Since this then went to make up McClernand's Army of the MISSISSIPPI and then the XIII CORPS, its exact composition is of interest. Sherman's Yazoo Expedition consisted of four divisions: 1st (A. J. Smith), which had formerly been the 10th Div., Right Wing, XIII Corps, except for the 48th Ohio, which was from the Dist. of Memphis; 2d (M. L. Smith until 28 Dec.; D. Stuart to 4 Jan. '64), which had formerly been the 2d Div., Dist. of Memphis, XIII Corps; 3d (G. W. Morgan), which had formerly been the 9th Div., Right Wing, XIII Corps; and 4th (Frederick Steele), which had been the 11th Div., Right Wing, XIII Corps. An order (G.O. 210, 18 Dec. '62) had prescribed that the troops in the Dept. of Tenn. be reorganized in the XIII (New), XV, XVI, and XVII Corps, but this was not carried out until Jan. '64. Although that order had named McClernand commander of XIII Corps and Sherman commander of XV Corps, the four divisions making up Sherman's Yazoo Expedition during the period 18 Dec. '62–4 Jan. '63 were "styled the right wing of (General Grant's) Thirteenth Army Corps. . . ." (Sherman's Memoirs, I, 322). During the period 4–12 Jan. '64 the units that had made up the Yazoo Expedition were in McClernand's Army of the Miss.

YELLOW BAYOU (Bayou de Glaize, Norwood Plantation, Old Oaks), La. 18 May '64. Final action of RED RIVER CAMPAIGN.

YELLOW TAVERN, Va., 11 May '64. (SHERIDAN'S RICHMOND RAID) Stuart reached Yellow Tavern at 8 A.M. and took up a position to block Sheridan's approach on Richmond. According to D. S. Freeman he established his two brigades east of the Telegraph Road in a sort of flanking position with Wickham on the north and Lomax to his left. A small force with two guns was just west of the road on Lomax' left.

The Federals made contact at about 11 o'clock, Devin's brigade quickly occupied the unguarded road junction near Yellow Tavern, and the divisions of Wilson and Merritt started forming for an attack. Two probes were beaten off by the 5th Va. Cav., after hand-to-hand fighting in which their commander, Col. H. C. Pate, was killed. Confederate casualties mounted as the Federals continued to feel out other parts of the line.

At 4 P.M. a heavy attack was launched against Wickham. Although this was serious, Stuart realized that his extreme left was the vulnerable point, and rode alone to that exposed flank. Within a short time Custer attacked here. The 1st Mich. Cav. took a covered approach Custer had detected on the extreme Confederate left; led by Lt. Col. Peter Stagg they charged and captured the two guns. The 5th and 6th Mich. Cav., attacking to the left of the 1st, drove back the Confederate line and pursued. Stuart moved to a point near the Telegraph Road where about 80 of his men had rallied, and fired his pistol at the 5th Mich. troopers as they rode past. The Confederates rallied in a ravine some 400 yards to the rear and checked the Federal advance. They were then driven back by the 1st Va. Cav., again passing Stuart. Astride his horse near a fence, he had emptied his pistol at the withdrawing cavalry when he was mortally wounded. A shot fired by Pvt. J. A. HUFF at a range of 10 or 15 yards from a .44-caliber cavalry pistol entered the right abdomen (See *Lee's Lts.*, III, 761–63, for medical details). Stuart died at 7:38 P.M., 12 May '64, at the home of his brother-in-law, Dr. Charles Brewer, in Richmond.

Gregg had attacked Gordon's brigade to the Federal rear, routing the Confederates and killing Gordon. Most of Stuart's cavalry withdrew north toward Ashland, while some went south toward Richmond (Sheridan, II, 379).

YELL RIFLES. See Lucius E. POLK and Patrick R. CLEBURNE.

YEOMAN, Stephen B. Union officer. Ohio. Sgt. Co. F 22d Ohio 22 Apr. '61; mustered out 19 Aug. '61; Capt. 54th Ohio 15 Sept. '61; resigned 8 June '63; Capt. Vet. Res. Corps 5 Sept. '63; Col. 43d US Col. Inf. 8 July '64; Bvt. B.G. USV (war service). Commanded 3, 1, XXV (Va.). Wounded at Shiloh in chest and left arm; at Russell's House (Miss.) 17 May '62 in left leg; during a picket-line fracas in the arm and abdomen; and at Arkansas Post, where his right arm was amputated. He had run away from home and shipped as a sailor when 15.

YORK, Zebulon. C.S.A. gen. ?–1900. Appt.-La. He was commissioned Lt. Col. 14th La. and sent in 1861 to Va., where he fought at Williamsburg and in the Seven Days' Battles before being promoted Col. He led the regiment at 2d Bull Run, Antietam, and Fredericksburg before going to La. to serve under Richard Taylor in the organizing and drilling of conscripts for the La. brigades in the Army of Northern Va. Returning to the East, he led his regiment at Gettysburg and was named B.G. C.S.A. 31 May '64 and given command

of all La. troops in Lee's army. He fought with Early at Lynchburg, Monocacy, and in the Washington raid. He was wounded severely at Winchester, losing him arm, and saw no more field service.

YORKE, Louis Eugene. Union officer. N.J. R.A. Capt. 13th US Inf. 5 Aug. '61; Lt. Col. Asst. I.G. Assigned 20 Sept. '64–1 Aug. '65; Bvt. B.G. USV. Brevets for Vicksburg siege, war service. Died 1873.

YORKTOWN, Va., 5 Apr.–4 May '62. (PENINSULAR CAMPAIGN) Two divisions of Heintzelman's III Corps reached Fortress Monroe 23 Mar. but, due to transportation shortage, waited almost two weeks before starting the advance up the Peninsula. McClellan's first step in the campaign, capture of Yorktown, was delayed by several things that upset his planning: McDowell's corps was withheld and, therefore, could not be used in his contemplated envelopment of Yorktown by way of the York River; his maps were incorrect and he was surprised to find the Warwick River an obstacle; the navy did not feel it within their capabilities to silence the water batteries of Yorktown and Gloucester to permit an amphibious envelopment up the York to West Point. W. F. Smith (2, IV) reported a soft spot in the Confederate defenses of the Warwick River at Lee's Mill but failed 16 Apr. in an attempt to penetrate it. McClellan then decided to undertake a formal siege. Fitz John Porter was put in charge of the operation and was assisted by W. F. Barry and J. G. Barnard, chiefs of artillery and engineers, respectively. About 100 heavy Parrotts, howitzers, and mortars were emplaced, and on 1 May the first battery opened fire with good effect. Magruder's mission was to delay the Federals as long as possible to give Richmond time to be sure that this was where the enemy's main effort was to be made, and to re-

953

YOUNG, W. H.

inforce; in this he succeeded admirably. The night of 3 May, three days before McClellan intended to open his assault, Magruder withdrew. When the Federals entered the abandoned works they encountered LAND MINES, a new weapon in warfare. On 4 May a rear-guard action took place at WILLIAMSBURG.

YOUNG, John Russell. WAR CORRESPONDENT. 1840–99. Pa. Beginning as a copy boy with the Philadelphia *Press* in 1857, he was named correspondent and sent to Va., reporting on the Army of the Potomac from 1st Bull Run until the end of the Chickahominy campaign. He went with Banks on the Red River campaign of 1864 and returned to Philadelphia to take editorial charge of the *Press*. After being associated with several unsuccessful papers, he succeeded GAY as managing editor of the N.Y. *Tribune* until 1871, when he became a European correspondent for the N.Y. *Herald*, later accompanying Grant around the world. He next served as Minister to China and Librarian of Congress.

YOUNG, Pierce Manning Butler. C.S.A. gen. 1836–96. S.C. Appt.-Ga. He attended the Ga. Mil. Acad. and was to graduate with the class of June '61 at West Point when, in Mar. of that year he resigned with misgivings to go with his state. Commissioned 2d Lt. of C.S.A. Arty., he served at Pensacola and was then named 1st Lt. and A.D.C. to W. H. T. Walker. In Cobb's Ga. Legion he served as Adj. and was sent to Va. with them in May '62. As Lt. Col. he commanded the Legion at South Mountain, where he was wounded, and Fredericksburg. He was promoted Col. before Brandy Station and fought at Gettysburg before being named B.G. C.S.A. 28 Sept. '63. In command of Hampton's Legion he was wounded at Ashland and temporarily was in command of Hampton's division. Sent to defend Augusta (Ga.) from Sherman,

he was promoted Maj. Gen. 30 Dec. '64, in spite of Wheeler's opposition, and served in Ga. and S.C. After the war he was a planter, Congressman, and member of the West Point Board of Visitors. He was Consul Gen. at St. Petersburg 1885–87 and Minister to Guatemala and Honduras 1893–96.

YOUNG, Samuel Baldwin Marks. Union officer. Pa. Pvt. Co. K 12th Pa. 25 Apr.–5 Aug. '61; Capt. 4th Pa. Cav. 6 Sept. '61; Maj. 20 Sept. '62; Lt. Col. 1 May '64; Col. 25 June '64; Bvt. B.G. USV 9 Apr. '65 (R. E. Lee's surrender). Other brevets for Sulphur Springs (Va.); Amelia Spring (Va.); Sayler's Creek (Va.). Commanded 2, 2, Cav. Corps (Potomac). W.I.A. at Sulphur Springs, Kernstown, Hatcher's Run, Sayler's Creek. In R.A. and Maj. Gen. USA in 1901.

YOUNG, Thomas Lowry. Union officer. 1832–88. Ireland. In R.A. as enlisted man for 10 years from 1848. Capt. Benton Cadets Mo. Vols. 6 Sept. '61; resigned 10 Dec. '61; Maj. 118th Ohio 17 Sept. '62; Lt. Col. 17 Apr. '63; Col. 11 Apr. '64; Bvt. B.G. USV (Resaca); resigned 14 Sept. '64. He held many public offices, culminating in the Republican governorship of Ohio in 1877.

YOUNG, William Hugh. C.S.A. gen. 1838–1901. Mo. Appt.-Tex. Graduating from the Univ. of Va. in June '61, he remained to study military tactics there and was commissioned Capt. 9th Tex. in Sept. Named Col. after Shiloh, he led his regiment at Perryville, Stones River (wounded in the shoulder and had two horses shot from under him), and at Jackson (shot in the thigh). At Chickamauga he was wounded in the right side of the chest. Commanding first his regiment and then Ector's brigade in the Atlanta campaign, he was shot in the neck and jaw at Kenesaw Mountain and was appointed B.G. C.S.A.

15 Aug. '64. Sent to Allatoona when Hood went to Tenn., he was shot in the ankle and had his horse killed under him and was captured 5 Oct. '64. Released in July '65, he was a lawyer and in the real-estate business after the war.

Z

ZAHM, Louis. Union officer. Germany. Col. 3d Ohio Cav. 27 Sept. '61; Bvt. B.G. USV (war service); resigned 5 Jan. '63. Commanded 2d Brig., Cav. Div. (Ohio). Listed by Phisterer as Zahn, Louis.

ZIEGLER, George Milton. Union officer. Pvt. Co. B 12th Ohio 22 Apr. '61; 1st Sgt. 47th Ohio 15 June '61; 2d Lt. 28 Aug. '61; 1st Lt. 6 Dec. '61; Capt. 28 Dec. '62; Col. 32d US Col. Inf. 2 Aug. '63; Bvt. B.G. USV (war service).

ZIEGLER'S GROVE. The name of the "little clump of trees" on Cemetery Ridge which marked the "High Tide of the Confederacy" in the final Confederate charge on 3 July '63 at GETTYSBURG.

ZINN, George. Union officer. Pa. 2d Lt. 84th Pa. 1 Oct. '61; Capt. 2 Oct. '62; Lt. Col. 1 Aug. '64; transferred to 57th Pa. 13 Jan. '65; Col. 19 Mar. '65; Bvt. B.G. USV 6 Apr. '65 (war service).

ZOLLICOFFER, Felix Kirk. C.S.A. gen. 1812–62. Tenn. A journeyman printer, he was later a newspaper editor and fought in the Seminole War. A Whig political power in his state, he suffered from poor health but managed to sit in the state legislature, hold several public offices, win an election as Congressman, and fight a duel before attending the Washington Peace Conference during Secession Winter. He declined the rank of state Maj. Gen. in command of all Tenn. troops but was appointed B.G. C.S.A. 9 July '61. In command of a brigade in eastern Tenn., he was killed under peculiar circumstances at LOGAN CROSS ROADS 19 Jan. '62 by Speed S. Fry.

ZOOK, Samuel Kosciuzko. Union gen. 1823–63. Pa. Entering the telegraph business as a young man, he made several important discoveries about the nature of electricity. He was active in the N. Y. State Militia before being commissioned Lt. Col. 6th N.Y. State Militia 7 July '61. Mustered out on the 31st of that month, he was named Col. 57th N.Y. 19 Oct. '61 and commanded this regiment in the Peninsula. He led the 3, 1, II, Potomac, and later succeeded to command of the division, being appointed B.G. USV 29 Nov. '62. Wounded mortally 2 July '63 at Gettysburg, he died the next day. He was breveted Maj. Gen. USV posthumously.

ZOUAVE. (Rhymes with suave.) There were many regiments of both the Union and Confederate armies that had modeled themselves on the original Zouaves of the French colonial armies. The latter were Algerian light infantry troops famous for their drill and characteristic, gaudy uniform featuring bright colors, baggy trousers, gaiters, short and open jacket, and a turban or fez. The original Zouaves were also famous for their ability to fire and reload the musket from the prone position. American militia units were attracted to the Zouave drill and uniform and copied them, often down to the detail of shaving their heads like the North Africans. Largely responsible for the wide spread of the Zouave motif among American militia units was Elmer ELLSWORTH.

ZULICK, Samuel Morton. Union officer. Pa. Capt. 29th Pa. 8 July '61; Maj. 3 Mar. '63; Col. 25 Mar. '65; Bvt. B.G. USV (war service). Died 1876.

ATLAS OF SECTIONAL MAPS
COVERING THE CIVIL WAR AREA

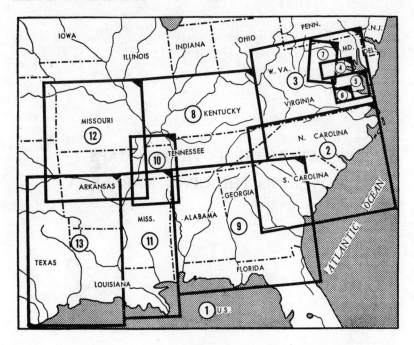

INDEX

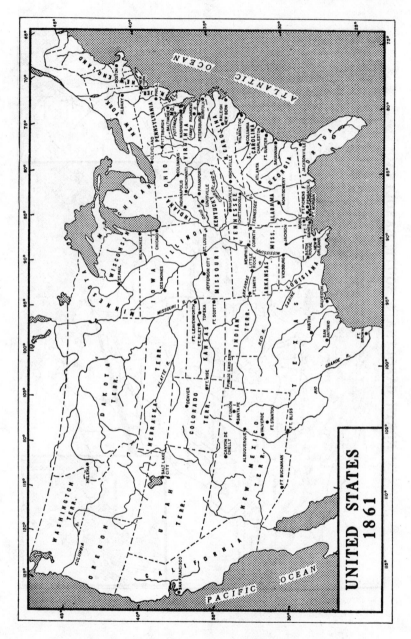

UNITED STATES
1861

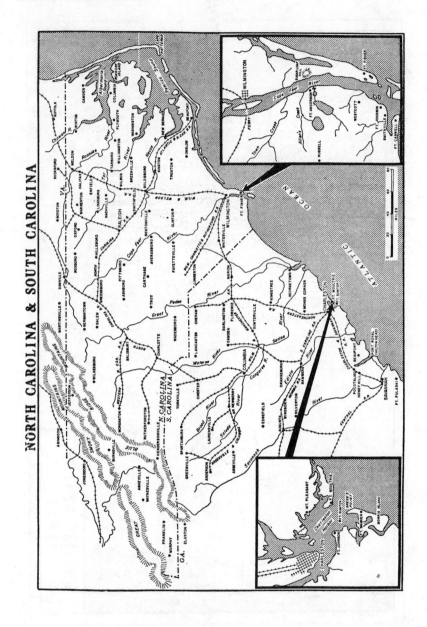

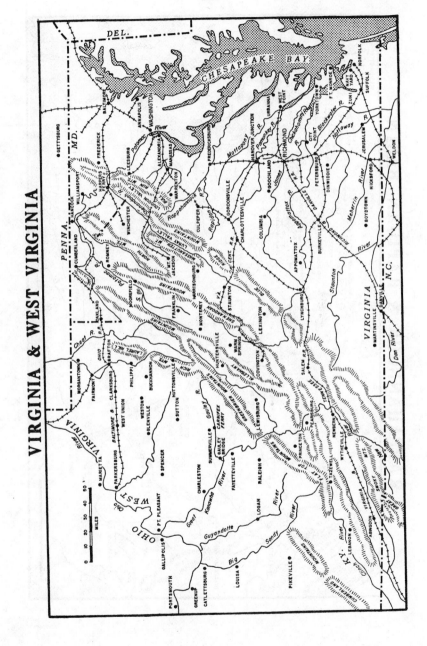

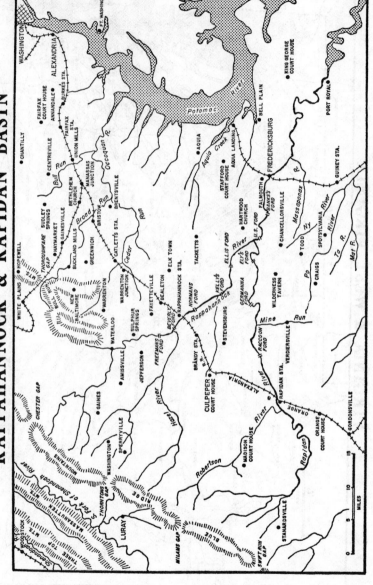

RAPPAHANNOCK & RAPIDAN BASIN

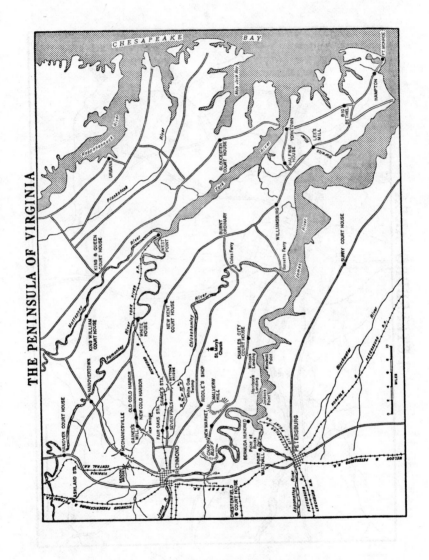

THE PENINSULA OF VIRGINIA

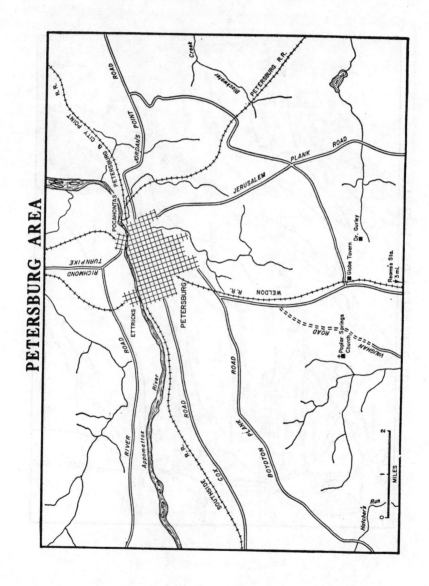

PETERSBURG AREA

SHENANDOAH VALLEY

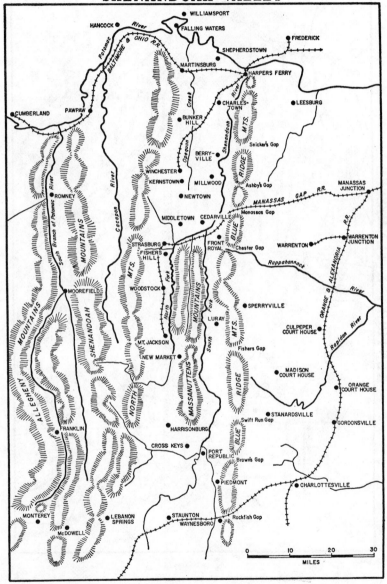

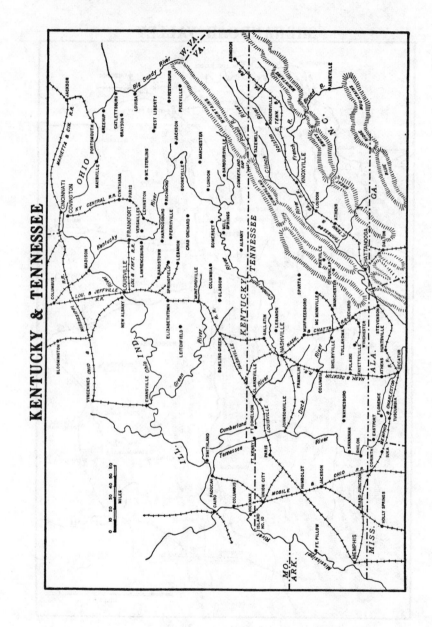

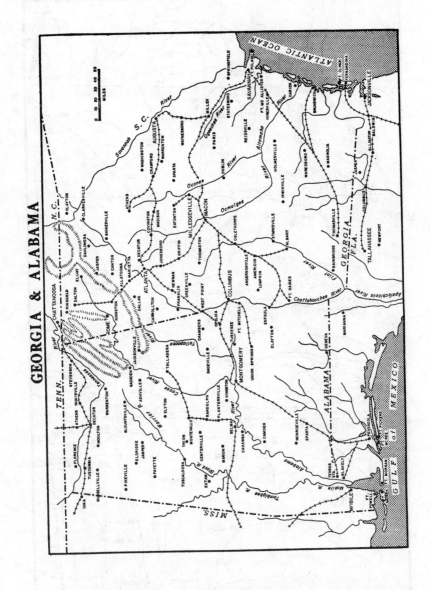

W. TENNESSEE & N. MISSISSIPPI

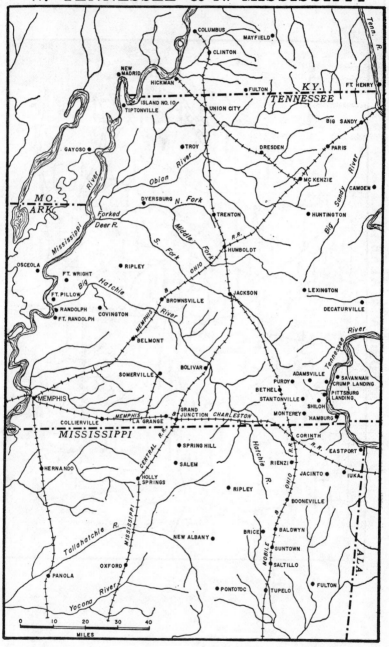

MISSISSIPPI

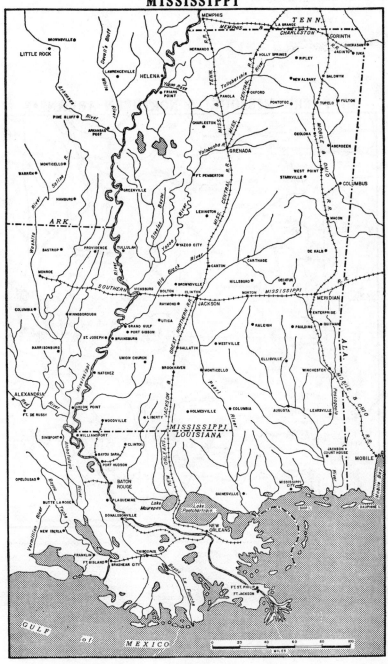

SOUTHERN MISSOURI & NORTHERN ARKANSAS

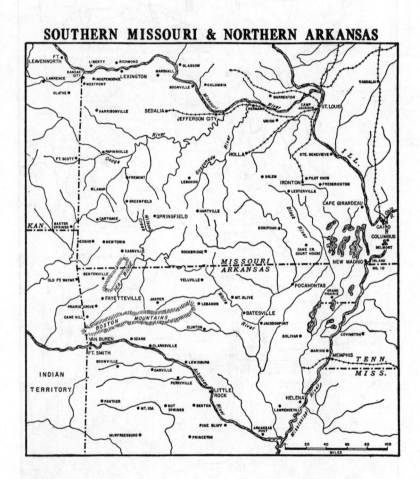

LOUISIANA, SO. ARKANSAS & E. TEXAS

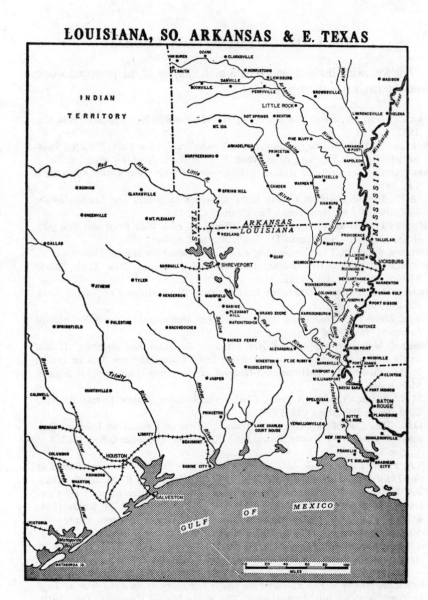

LIST OF AUTHORITIES CITED

The following list is intended as a bibliography of the principal works consulted and as a short-title index.

ALBAUGH and SIMMONS. *Confederate Arms.* Harrisburg, Pa.: The Stackpole Co., 1957.

ALEXANDER, E. P. *Military Memoirs of a Confederate.* New York: Charles Scribner's Sons, 1912. (See also ALEXANDER, E. P., in the body of this work.)

APPLETON'S *Cyclopedia of American Biography.* 7 vols. New York: Appleton & Co., 1891.

B. & L.: JOHNSON, Robert U. AND BUEL, Clarence C. *Battles and Leaders of the Civil War.* 4 vols. New York: The Century Co., 1887.

BENTON, J. G. *Ordnance and Gunnery.* (Third ed. of a West Point text first published in 1867.) New York: D. Van Nostrand Co., Inc., 1883.

BIGELOW, JOHN, JR. *The Campaign of Chancellorsville.* New Haven, 1910.

BOATNER, MARK M., III. *Military Customs and Traditions.* New York: David McKay Company, Inc., 1956.

BROWN, D. ALEXANDER. *Grierson's Raid.* Urbana, Ill.: University of Illinois Press, 1954.

BRUCE, ROBERT V. *Lincoln and the Tools of War.* Indianapolis: The Bobbs-Merrill Company, Inc., 1956.

Cmdrs.-Q.M.G. *Commanders of Army Corps, Divisions and Brigades, United States Army, During the War of 1861 to 1865.* Compiled from data on record in the office of the Quartermaster-General of the Army. Philadelphia: Burk & McFetridge, 1887.

C.M.H.: EVANS, CLEMENT A. (ed.). *Confederate Military History.* 12 vols. Atlanta: Confederate Publishing Co., 1899.

C.O.M.: The Confederate *Ordnance Manual.* (First ed.) Based on Laidley, *Ordnance Manual of the United States,* 1861. Richmond: Ordnance Office, 1863.

C.S. (See M.A.&E.)

C.S.A. Public Laws. *Public Laws of the Confederate States of America Passed at the Third Session of the First Congress; 1863.* Richmond: R. M. Smith, 1863.

C.S.A. Statutes: *The Statutes at Large of the Provisional Government of the Confederate States of America* (through 18 Feb. '62). Richmond: R. M. Smith, 1864.

C.W.H.: *Civil War History.* Quarterly. Iowa City: University of Iowa Press.

CAMPBELL, ROBERT A. *The Rebellion Register.* Kalamazoo, Mich., 1866.

CATTON, BRUCE. *Mr. Lincoln's Army* (1951); *Glory Road* (1952); *A Stillness at Appomattox* (1953). A trilogy. New York: Doubleday & Company, Inc.

———. *This Hallowed Ground.* New York: Doubleday & Company, Inc., 1956.

COMMAGER, HENRY S. *The Blue and the Gray: The Story of the Civil War as Told by Participants.* 2 vols. Indianapolis: The Bobbs-Merrill Company, Inc., 1950.

Confederate Veteran. 40 vols. Nashville, Tenn .:1893–1932.

CONNELLEY, WILLIAM E. *Quantrill and the Border Wars.* Cedar Rapids, Iowa: The Torch Press, 1910.

Cox, J. D. *Atlanta* and *The March to the Sea—Franklin and Nashville.* New York: Charles Scribner's Sons, 1882. (Vols. IX and X of Scribner's splendid "Campaigns of the Civil War" series.)

Cullum, George W. *Biographical Register of the Officers and Graduates of the United States Military Academy.* 2 vols. Boston: Houghton Mifflin Co., 1891.

D.A.B.: *Dictionary of American Biography.* 20 vols. plus index and supplement. New York: Charles Scribner's Sons, 1928.

D.A.H.: *Dictionary of American History.* 5 vols. New York: Charles Scribner's Sons, 1940.

D.S.F.: Douglas Southall Freeman is sometimes cited in this manner when reference to volume and page is not necessary. (See also Freeman, D. S.)

de Chanal, F. V. (See Scheibert.)

Downey, Fairfax. *The Guns at Gettysburg.* New York: David McKay Company, Inc., 1958.

Drake, E. L. *Chronological Summary of Battles and Engagements of the Western Armies of the Confederate States, Including Summary of Lt. Gen. Joseph Wheeler's Cavalry Engagements.* Nashville, 1879.

Dyer, Frederick H. *A Compendium of the War of the Rebellion.* Des Moines, Iowa: Dyer Publishing Co., 1908. 1796 pp.

E.&B.: *Chronological Summary of Engagements and Battles.* No author, publisher, or date given. Copy in USMA library, apparently donated by J. B. Fry, appears to be the list that the Surgeon General of the Army ordered prepared. It lists over 2000 actions, giving the locality, Union troops engaged, Union and Confederate losses and "remarks" (sources of information; general officers of both sides killed and wounded; alternate names of action).

E.B.: *Encyclopaedia Britannica.* 32 vols. (11th & 12th eds.) New York: Cambridge University Press, 1910, 1922.

Fiebeger, G. J. *Campaigns of the American Civil War.* This West Point text and its accompanying atlas were my basic references for military operations and maps. West Point: U.S.M.A. Printing Office, 1914.

Fox, William F. *Regimental Losses in the . . . Civil War.* Albany: Albany Publishing Co., 1898.

Freeman, D. S. *Lee's Lieutenants—A Study in Command.* 3 vols. New York: Charles Scribner's Sons, 1942–46.

———. *R. E. Lee, a Biography.* 4 vols. New York: Charles Scribner's Sons, 1934–35.

———. *The South to Posterity.* New York: Charles Scribner's Sons, 1939.

FR., OVRC: *Field Record of Officers of the Veteran Reserve Corps.* (See article on Veteran Reserve Corps.)

Fuller and Steuart. *Firearms of the Confederacy.* Huntingdon, W. Va.: Standard Publications, 1944.

G.&B.: Garber, M. B., and Bond, P. S. *Modern Military Dictionary.* Washington: P. S. Bond Publishing Co., 1942.

Ganoe, W. A. *The History of the United States Army.* (Revised ed.) New York: Appleton-Century Co., 1942.

Gibbon, Brig. Gen. John. *The Artillerist's Manual.* Washington: D. Van Nostrand Co., Inc., 1860.

GLUCKMAN, COL. ARCADI. *United States Muskets, Rifles and Carbines.* Buffalo: Otto Ulbrich, 1948.

———. *United States Martial Pistols and Revolvers.* Buffalo: Otto Ulbrich, 1939.

H.B.M.: MCCLELLAN, H. B. *The Life and Campaigns of . . . J.E.B. Stuart.* Boston: Houghton Mifflin Co., 1885.

HEITMAN, FRANCIS BERNARD. *Historical Register and Dictionary of the United States Army, from Its Organization . . . to 1903.* 2 vols. Washington: Government Printing Office, 1903.

HENDERSON, G. F. R. *Stonewall Jackson and the American Civil War.* First published in 1898 and reprinted many times; reference in this work is to the American 1-vol. ed. New York: Longmans, Green & Co., Inc., 1936.

HENDERSON, HARRY MCCORRY. *Texas in the Confederacy.* San Antonio: Naylor Co., 1955.

HENRY, GUY V. *Military Record of Civilian Appointments in the United States Army.* 2 vols. New York: Carleton, 1869.

HENRY, ROBERT SELPH. *The Story of the Confederacy.* New York: Grosset and Dunlap, Inc., 1931.

HESSELTINE, WILLIAM B. *Lincoln and the War Governors.* New York: Alfred A. Knopf, Inc., 1955.

HORN, STANLEY F. *The Army of Tennessee.* Indianapolis: The Bobbs-Merrill Company, 1941.

HUMPHREYS, A. A. *The Virginia Campaign of '64 and '65.* New York: Charles Scribner's Sons, 1937.

JONES, VIRGIL C. *Eight Hours before Richmond.* New York: Henry Holt & Co., Inc., 1957.

———. *Ranger Mosby.* Chapel Hill: University of North Carolina Press, 1944.

KREIDBERG and HENRY: KREIDBERG, MARVIN A. and HENRY, MERTON G. *History of Military Mobilization in the United States Army 1775–1945.* Washington: Department of the Army, 1955.

LEECH, MARGARET. *Reveille in Washington 1860–1865.* New York: Harper & Brothers, 1941.

Lee's Lts. (See FREEMAN, D. S.)

LIVERMORE, THOMAS L. *Numbers and Losses in the Civil War in America 1861–65.* Boston: Houghton Mifflin Co., 1901.

LONN, ELLA. *Foreigners in the Confederacy.* Chapel Hill: University of North Carolina Press, 1940.

———. *Foreigners in the Union Army and Navy.* Baton Rouge: Louisiana State University Press, 1951.

LYMAN, THEODORE. *Meade's Headquarters, 1863–65: Letters of Colonel Theodore Lyman from the Wilderness to Appomattox,* ed. George R. Agassiz. Boston, 1922.

M.A.&E.: The Department of Military Art and Engineering at the USMA, which includes instruction in what most people would call "military history," has published a number of texts and atlases. Several of these have been used extensively in this work and are cited as follows: M.A.&E. *Notes* is a pamphlet entitled *Notes for the Course in the History of Military Art;* C.S. is a book entitled *Campaign Summaries;* and M.A.&E. Atlas is the *Atlas to Accompany Steele's American Campaigns,* edited by Col. V. J. Esposito. The latter, long unavailable except for cadet instruction, is being published by Frederick A. Praeger, Inc., in 1959.

M.C.&H.: *Military Collector and Historian Journal.*

M.H.S.M. Papers.: *Papers.* 14 vols. Boston: Military Historical Society of Massachusetts, 1881–1918.

MAXWELL, WILLIAM Q. *Lincoln's Fifth Wheel.* New York: Longmans, Green & Co., Inc., 1956.

MILLER. *Photographic History of the Civil War in Ten Volumes.* 10 vols. New York: The Review of Reviews Co., 1911.

MONAGHAN, JAMES. *Civil War on the Western Border 1854–1865.* Boston: Little, Brown & Co., 1955.

N.P.S.: National Park Service, Historical Handbook Series. An excellent series of inexpensive, well written and illustrated pamphlets including Chickamauga and Chattanooga, Fort Pulaski, Fort Sumter, Gettysburg, Manassas, Petersburg, Shiloh, and Vicksburg.

O.R. *The War of the Rebellion: A Compilation of the Official Records of the Union and Confederate Armies* and the *Official Records of the Union and Confederate Navies.* Begun in 1864 and completed in 1927, the series devoted to the armies comprises 128 vols., 138,579 pp. plus 1,006 maps and sketches in a separate 3-vol. atlas of 175 plates. Only the army volumes are cited in this book, and references are given in the following manner: series, volume, part, and page. The citation O.R. I, XVI, II, 500, for example, refers to Series I, Vol. XVI, Part II, page 500.

O'CONNOR, RICHARD. *Sheridan the Inevitable.* Indianapolis: The Bobbs-Merrill Co., 1953.

PARKS, JOSEPH HOWARD. *General Edmund Kirby Smith, C.S.A.* Baton Rouge: Louisiana State University Press, 1954.

PHISTERER, FREDERICK. *Statistical Record of the Armies of The United States.* New York: Charles Scribner's Sons, 1883.

POND, GEORGE E. *The Shenandoah Valley in 1864.* New York: Charles Scribner's Sons, 1889.

POTTER, E. B. (ed.). *The United States and World Sea Power.* Englewood Cliffs, N. J.: Prentice-Hall, Inc., 1955.

PRATT, FLETCHER. *Civil War on Western Waters.* New York: Henry Holt & Co., Inc., 1956.

———. *Ordeal by Fire: An Informal History of the Civil War.* (Revised ed.) New York: William Sloane Associates, Inc., 1948.

PRESSLY, THOMAS J. *Americans Interpret their Civil War.* Princeton: Princeton University Press, 1954.

REID, WHITELAW. *Ohio in the War: Her Statesmen, Her Generals, and Soldiers.* 2 vols. New York and Cincinnati, 1868.

R. E. Lee. (See FREEMAN, D. S.)

ROBERTS, JOSEPH. *The Hand-Book of Artillery.* (10th ed.) New York: D. Van Nostrand Co., Inc., 1875.

S.B.N. *The South in the Building of the Nation.* 12 vols. Richmond: Southern Historical Publication Society, 1909.

S.H.S.P. *Southern Historical Society Papers.* 47 vols. Richmond: 1876–1930.

SCHEIBERT, J. *La Guerre civile aux Etats-Unis d'Amérique.* French translation of

Der Burger Krieg in den Nordamerikanischen Staaten, published in 1874 "for officers of the German Army." Paris: Dumaine, 1876. A similar book, and equally useful, is *L'Armée américaine pendant la guerre de la sécession,* by Général de Brigade François Victor de Chanal. Paris: Dumaine, 1872.

SCOTT, HENRY L., COL. *Military Dictionary.* New York: D. Van Nostrand Co., Inc., 1862.

SCOTT, ROBERT N. *An Analytical Digest of the Military Laws of the United States* Philadelphia: J. B. Lippincott & Co., 1873.

Scribner's atlas: ADAMS, JAMES TRUSLOW. *Atlas of American History.* New York: Charles Scribner's Sons, 1943.

SHANNON, FRED ALBERT. *The Organization and Administration of the Union Army 1861–1865.* 2 vols. Cleveland: Arthur H. Clark Co., 1928.

SHIELDS, JOSEPH W., JR. *From Flintlock to M 1.* New York: Coward-McCann, Inc., 1954.

SORREL, G. MOXLEY. *Recollections of a Confederate Staff Officer.* Modern edition, ed. Bell I. Wiley. (See SORREL in the body of this work.) Jackson, Tenn.: McCowat-Mercer, 1958.

STEELE, MATHEW F. *American Campaigns.* Washington: U. S. Infantry Assn., 1935.

T.U.A. *The Union Army.* 8 vols. Madison, Wis.: Federal Publishing Co., 1908.

TAYLOR, RICHARD. *Destruction and Reconstruction.* New York: Longmans, Green & Co., Inc., 1955. (See also article on TAYLOR, Richard.)

UPTON, EMORY. *The Military Policy of the United States.* Washington: Government Printing Office, 1917. (See also article on UPTON, Emory.)

VAN HORNE, THOMAS B. *History of the Army of the Cumberland.* 2 vols. and atlas. Cincinnati: Robert Clarke & Co., 1875.

WARNER, EZRA J. See WRIGHT, MARCUS J., below.

WELLER, JAC. "The Field Artillery of the Civil War," M. C. & H., V (1953).

WEST, RICHARD S., JR. *Mr. Lincoln's Navy.* New York: Longmans, Green & Co., Inc., 1957.

WILEY, *Reb.* WILEY, BELL I. *The Life of Johnny Reb.* Indianapolis: The Bobbs-Merrill Co., 1943.

WILEY, *Yank.* ———. *The Life of Billy Yank.* Indianapolis: The Bobbs-Merrill Co., 1952.

WILHELM, THOMAS. *Military Dictionary.* Revised ed. Philadelphia: L. R. Hammersly & Co., 1881.

WILLIAMS, K. P. *Lincoln Finds a General.* 4 vols. New York: The Macmillan Co., 1949–1956. Mr. Williams was working on the fifth of his projected seven-volume set when he died in 1958.

WISE, JENNINGS CROPPER. *The Long Arm of Lee, or The History of the Artillery of the Army of Northern Virginia.* Lynchburg, Va.: J. P. Bell Co., Inc., 1915.

WOOD, ROBERT C. *Confederate Hand-Book.* New Orleans: Graham Press, 1900.

WRIGHT, MARCUS J. *General Officers of the Confederate Army.* New York: Neale Publishing Co., 1911. This has long been the basic authority on the military records of Confederate generals. However, see footnote to article on GENERAL OFFICERS for reference to Ezra Warner's *Generals in Gray.*

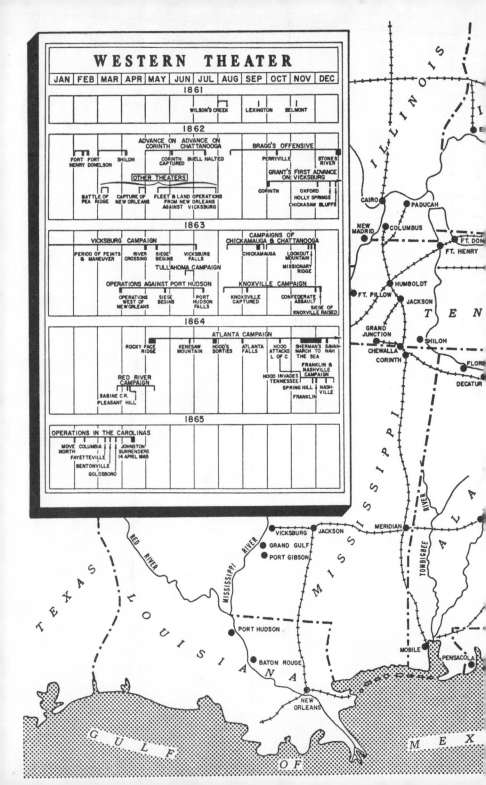